W9-CTW-125

The Contemporary Novel

*A Checklist of Critical Literature on the
English Language Novel Since 1945*

Irving Adelman and Rita Dworkin

Second Edition

The Scarecrow Press, Inc.
Lanham, Md., & London
1997

SCARECROW PRESS, INC.

Published in the United States of America
by Scarecrow Press, Inc.
4720 Boston Way
Lanham, Maryland 20706

4 Pleydell Gardens, Folkestone
Kent CT20 2DN, England

Copyright © 1997 by Irving Adelman and Rita Dworkin

British Cataloguing-in-Publication Information Available

Library of Congress Cataloging-in-Publication Data

Adelman, Irving.
    The contemporary novel : a checklist of critical literature on the
English language novel since 1945 / by Irving Adelman and Rita
Dworkin. — 2nd ed.
        p. cm.
    Includes bibliographical references.
    ISBN 0-8108-3103-1 (alk. paper)
    1. American fiction—20th century—History and criticism—
Bibliography. 2. English fiction—20th century—History and
criticism—Bibliography. 3. English fiction—Foreign countries—
History and criticism—Bibliography. I. Dworkin, Rita. II. Title.
Z1231.F4A34   1996
[PS379]
016.823'91409—dc20   96-17577

ISBN 0-8108-3103-1 (cloth: alk. paper)

Printed in the United States of America

The paper used in this publication meets the minimum requirements
of American National Standard for Information Sciences—Permanence of Paper for Printed Library Materials, ANSI Z39.48-1984.

In Memoriam

Tom Dutelle
and
Paul Dworkin

Contents

Preface to First Edition

We have attempted to survey, selectively, the critical literature on contemporary British and American novels. Generally, selections are from journals and books representing literary scholarship rather than from book reviews. There are exceptions, however, because of our own judgment of the unusual quality of a review, the similar judgment of an authority on an individual writer, or, simply, a lack of other critical material.

Novelists are included if they wrote after 1945 (such as Joseph Heller), if they wrote before 1945 but achieved their most significant recognition after 1945 (such as Henry Roth and William Faulkner), or if they wrote before 1945 but continued with major publications after 1945. This last criterion included writers such as Hemingway and excludes such as Maugham. Once a writer qualified, all his or her work (before and after 1945) for which critiques could be found was included. Some anthologies analyzed included essays or articles originally written before 1945. These have been accepted when the book fell within our period of concern.

The cut-off date on material examined is 1968 for periodicals and 1969 for books. The time lag to publication is accounted for by the fact that every article was examined, except those obviously discussing a specific novel or those few cited as "Not seen." Those pages of articles or books dealing with a specific novel were then listed under that novel. For this reason page references herein are often to a portion of a book chapter or to part of an article rather than to the chapter or article in its entirety.

Preface to Second Edition

We have enlarged the scope of selections, as indicated by the new subtitle, to works by writers in English anywhere in the world, for example, Ghana, Nigeria, West Indies, the Caribbean, India, etc.

Critical literature has been collected through 1982. Once again, all articles listed in GENERAL have been examined for reference to specific novels and specific pages noted.

At the back of this work is a list of Sources Consulted. This provides complete bibliographical data to works cited only briefly here and there throughout the book.

We would like to acknowledge the valued assistance of Maureen Dwyer, East Meadow Public Library, and Arthur Ebbin, Nassau Library System. Also, the State University of New York at Stony Brook, Columbia University and the New York Public Library were their usual treasure troves.

Abbreviations

AAAPSS American Academy of Political and Social Science. Annals

A&S Anglistik & Englischunterricht

A&S Arts and Sciences (New York Un.)

AAus Americana-Austriaca: Beiträge zur Amerika kunde

Abbia (Cameroun)

ABC American Book Collector (Chicago)

ABR American Benedictine Review (Atchison, KS)

Acadiensis: Journal of the History of the Atlantic Region (Un. of New Brunswick)

Accent

ACLALSB ACLALS Bulletin (Mysore, India)

Acme

Adena (Louisville, KY)

ADI Anuario del Departamento de Inglés (Barcelona, Spain)

AdUA Annales de l'Université d'Abidjan

Aegis: A Periodical in Literature & Language (Moorehead [MN] State College)

AF Alternative Futures (Troy, NY)

AForum African Forum: A Quarterly Journal of Contemporary Affairs

AfrCurrents

African Perspectives (Leiden)

AfricaQ Africa Quarterly (New Delhi)

AfricaR Africa Report

Afrika (Munich)

Afriscope (Yaba, Nigeria)

AfrLJ Africana Library Journal: A Quarterly Bibliography and News Bulletin

AfrSAWIB African Studies Association of the West Indies. Bulletin

AfrSR African Studies Review

AFS Asian Folklore Studies

Agenda

Agora: A Journal in the Humanities and Social Studies

AH American Heritage (New York)

AHumor American Humor: An Interdisciplinary Newsletter

AI American Imago (New York)

Aion Aion, a Journal of Cogitation

AION-SG Annali Instituto Universitario Orientale, Napoli, Sezione Germanica

AIQ American Indian Quarterly: A Journal of Anthropology, History and Literature

AIR Adam International Review (Un. of Rochester)

AJES The Aligarh Journal of English Studies

AJFS Australian Journal of French Studies (Monash Un., Clayton, Victoria)

AJP American Journal of Psychoanalysis (New York)

Akzente: Zeitschrift für Literatur

AL American Literature (Duke Un. Pr.)

AlaR Alabama Review (Auburn Un.)

AlitASH Acta Litteraria Academiae Scientiarum Hungaricae (Budapest)

ALS Australian Literary Studies (Un. of Tasmania)

ALT African Literature Today

AmD American Dialog

American Review

Americana-Austriaca: Beiträge zur Amerikakunde (Vienna)

AmerS American Studies

AmEx The American Examiner: A Forum of Ideas (Michigan State Un.)

Amistad: Writings on Black History and Culture

AmMerc American Mercury

AmOx American Oxonian (Philadelphia)

AmSS American Studies in Scandinavia (Oslo)

Amst Amerikastudien/American Studies

AN&Q American Notes and Queries (New Haven, CT)

Anglican Theological Review

Anglo-Irish Studies (Chalfont St. Giles)

Anonymous: A Journal for the Women Writer

AntigR Antigonish Review

AnUBLG Analele Universittii Bucresti. Limbe germanice

Aphra: The Feminist Literary Magazine (New York)
AppalJ Appalachian Journal: A Regional Studies Review
APR American Poetry Review
APSR American Political Science Review
AQ American Quarterly (Un. of Pennsylvania)
AR Antioch Review
ArAA Arbeiten aus Anglistik und Amerikanistik
Arcadia
Archiv Archiv für das Studium der Neuren Sprachen und Lituraturen
ARCS The American Review of Canadian Studies
Arena (Macquarie Un., Sydney)
ArielE Ariel: A Review of International English Literature
Arizona English Bulletin
ArlQ Arlington Quarterly
ArmD Armchair Detective
ArO Archiv Orientální
ArQ Arizona Quarterly (Un. of Arizona)
ArtI Art International
Aryan Path
AS American Speech (Columbia Un. Pr.)
ASch American Scholar (Washington, D.C.)
ASEAB Australian Society for Education Through the Arts. Bulletin (Sydney)
Asemka: A Literary Journal of the University of Cape Coast
ASInt American Studies International
ASIS American Studies in Scandinavia (Oslo)
ASLHM American Society of Legion of Honor Magazine
ASoc Arts in Society (Un. of Wisconsin)
AsSt Asian Student
AT Africa Today
Atlantic Atlantic Monthly
Atlantis: A Women's Studies Journal
AtlantisA (Acadia Un.)
ATQ American Transcendental Quarterly
AUB-LG Analele Universittii, Bucaresti, Limbi, Germanice
AUCP Acta Universitatis Carolinae Philologica (Un. Karlova)
AUMLA Australasian Universities Language and Literature Association. Journal (Christ Church, N.Z.)
AusL Australian Letters (Adelaide)
AUS-PEAS Acta Universitatis Szegediensis de Attila József Nominatae: Papers in English and American Studies
AusQ Australian Quarterly (Sydney)
Australian Left Review
AWest American West
AWR The Anglo-Welsh Review (Pembroke Dock, Wales)

BA Books Abroad (Un. of Oklahoma Pr.)
BAALE Bulletin of the Association of African Literature in English
BAASB British Association for American Studies. Bulletin (now called: Journal of Amer. Studies: also JAMS)
BACLLS Bulletin of the Association for Commonwealth Literature and Language Studies
BakSJ Baker Street Journal
Balcony: The Sydney Review (Un. of Sydney)
BALF Black American Literature Forum (Formerly NALF)
BaratR Barat Review (Barat College)
BARev Black Academy Review: Quarterly of the Black World
Ba Shiru (Un. of Wisconsin)
BB Bulletin of Bibliography and Magazine Notes (Westwood, MA)
BBB Black Books Bulletin (Chicago)

BBr Books at Brown (Brown Un.)
BC Book Collector (London)
BCLQ British Columbia Library Quarterly (Victoria)
BDEC Bulletin of the Department of English (Calcutta)
BeninR Benin Review (Ibadan)
BForum Book Forum: An International Transdisciplinary Quarterly
BHist R Business History Review
BI Books at Iowa (Un. of Iowa)
Bibliotheck The Bibliotheck (Glasgow)
BILEUG Bollettino dell'Instituto de Lingue Estere (Genoa, Italy)
Bim (Barbados, W. Indies)
Biography: An Interdisciplinary Quarterly
BJA British Journal of Aesthetics (London)
BJRL Bulletin of the John Rylands Un. Library of Manchester
BlackI Black Images: A Critical Quarterly on Black Arts and Culture
BlackR Black Review
BlackW Black World
BLR Bodleian Library Record
BLRev The Bluegrass Literary Review
BlSch Black Scholar
BNYPL Bulletin of the New York Public Library
BO Black Orpheus
Boundary Boundary 2: A Journal of Postmodern Literature
BP Banaasthali Patrika
BR Bilingual Review/Revista bilingue (City College, NY)
BRH Bulletin of Research in the Humanities
BRMMLA Bulletin of the Rocky Mountain Modern Language Association (Un. of Colorado)
Brushfire (Un. of Nevada, Reno)
BS Blake Studies
BSE Brno Studies in English
BSJ The Baker Street Journal: An Irregular Quarterly of Sherlockiana
BSM British Studies Monitor (Bowdoin College, ME)
BSTCF Ball State Teachers College Forum (now Ball State University Forum; also BSUF)
BSUF Ball State University Forum (also BSTCF)
BT Black Times (Palo Alto, CA)
BUJ Boston University Journal
BuR Bucknell Review
Busara (Nairobi)
BUSE Boston University. Studies in English
BWVACET The Bulletin of the West Virginia Association of College English Teachers (Marshall Un.)
BYUS Brigham Young University Studies (Provo, UT)

Cabellian The Cabellian: A Journal of the Second American Renaissance
CahiersI Cahiers Irlandais (Lille)
Caliban (Toulouse)
Callaloo: A Black South Journal of Arts and Letters
CalR Calcutta Review
CamQ Cambridge Quarterly (Cambridge, England)
CamR Cambridge Review (London)
CanA&B Canadian Author and Bookman
C&L Christianity and Literature
CanF The Canadian Forum (Toronto)
CanL Canadian Literature/Littérature Canadienne (Vancouver)
CanM Canadian Mennonite

CaQ   California Quarterly (Un. of California, Davis)
Caribbean Quarterly (Un. of the West Indies, Kingston, Jamaica)
CaribS   Caribbean Studies
CarlM   The Carleton Miscellany
CarQ   Carolina Quarterly (Chapel Hill, NC)
Carrell   The Carrell (Friends of Un. of Miami, FL, Library)
CaSE   Carnegie Series in English (Carnegie Inst. of Tech.)
CathW   Catholic World (New York)
CC   Cross Currents (West Nyack, NY)
CCC   College Composition and Communication
CCL   Canadian Children's Literature
CCR   Claflin College Review
CCrit   Comparative Criticism: A Yearbook
CCTE   Proceedings of Conference of College Teachers of English of Texas
CE   College English (Champaign, IL)
CEA   CEA Critic (College English Association)
CEAF   CEA Forum (Centenary College of Louisiana, Shreveport)
CEAfr   Cahiers d'etudes africaines
CE&S   Commonwealth Essays and Studies (Formerly Commonwealth Miscellanies)
CEJ   California English Journal (Auburn, CA)
CEMF   Collected Essays by the Members of the Faculty (Kyoritsu Women's Junior College)
CEMW   Columbia Essays on Modern Writers (Pamphlet Series. Columbia Un.)
Cencrastus (Edinburgh)
CenR   Centennial Review (Mich. St. Un.; also CentR)
Centerpoint: A Journal of Interdisciplinary Studies
CentR   Centennial Review (Mich. St. Un.; also CenR)
CFM   Canadian Fiction Magazine
CH   California History (San Francisco)
CHA   Cuadernos Hispanoamericanos (Madrid)
Chandrabhágá: A Magazine of World Writing (Orissa, India)
Chasqui: Revista de Literatura Latinoamericano
Chauntecleer (Victoria, Australia)
ChC   Christian Century (Chicago)
Chelsea
ChildL   Children's Literature: An International Journal, Inc. Annual of the Modern Language Association Seminar on Children's Literature and the Children's Literature Association
Chim (Quebec)
ChiR   Chicago Review (Un. of Chicago)
Chr&Cr   Christianity and Crisis (New York)
ChronC   Chronicles of Culture (Rockford College Institute, Rockford, IL)
ChrPer   Christian Perspectives (Toronto)
ChrT   Christianity Today
ChrysJ   Chrysallis Journal (Saginaw Valley St. Coll., University Center, MI)
ChS   Christian Scholar (New Haven, CT; now Soundings)
CHum   Computers and the Humanities
CI   Critical Inquiry (Un. of Chicago)
CIEFLB   CIEFL Bulletin
CIL   Contemporary Indian Literature
CimR   Cimarron Review (Oklahoma State Un.)
Cithara (St. Bonaventure Un.)
CJ   Classical Journal
CJAS   Canadian Journal of African Studies/Revue Canadienne des Etudes Africaines
CJF   Chicago Jewish Forum

CJIS   Canadian Journal of Irish Studies (Vancouver)
CL   Comparative Literature (Un. of Oregon)
CLAJ   College Language Association Journal (Morgan State College, Baltimore)
CLAQ   Children's Literature Association Quarterly
ClareQ   Claremont Quarterly (Claremont, CA)
ClassB   Classical Bulletin
CLC   Columbia Library Columns
CLEd   Children's Literature in Education (NY)
Cleo (Sydney)
Clifton: Magazine of the University of Cincinnati
Cliol   CLIO: A Journal of Literature, History, and the Philosophy of History
ClioW   Clio: An Interdisciplinary Journal of Literature, History, and the Philosophy of History (Un. of Wisconsin)
CLQ   Colby Library Quarterly (Waterville, ME)
CLS   Comparative Literature Studies (Un. of Illinois)
Clues: A Journal of Detection (Bowling Green State Un., OH)
CM   Cornhill Magazine (London)
CMC   Crosscurrents/Modern Critiques
CMisc   Commonwealth Miscellanies (Pau)
CML   Classical and Modern Literature: A Quarterly (Terre Haute, IN)
CN&Q   Canadian Notes & Queries
CNIE   Commonwealth Novel in English
ColF   Columbia Forum
ColL   College Literature
Colloquiem: The Australian and New Zealand Theological Review (Auckland)
ColQ   Colorado Quarterly (Un. of Colorado)
ComM   Communication Monographs
Comment   Wayne State University Graduate Comment
Commonwealth Newsl. (Aarhus)
Communiqué (Un. of the North, Pietersburg)
ComN   Commonwealth Newsletter
Comparatist   The Comparatist: Journal of the Southern Comparative Literature Association
Compass   The Compass: A Provincial Review
CompD   Comparative Drama
ComQ   Commonwealth Quarterly
Conch   The Conch: A Biafran Journal of Literary and Cultural Analysis
Confrontation (Long Island Un.)
ConL   Contemporary Literature
ConnR   Connecticut Review (Hartford)
ConR   Contemporary Review (London)
A Journal of Joseph Conrad
Contempora (Atlanta, GA)
ContempR   Contemporary Review (London)
Contrast (Cape Town)
ConvLit   Convorbiri literare (Jassy)
Cornhill
Costerus: Essays in English and American Language and Literature (Amsterdam, The Netherlands)
Courier (Syracuse Un. Library)
CQ   Classical Quarterly (London)
CR   The Critical Review (Melbourne; Sydney)
CRAS   Centennial Review of Arts and Sciences (Michigan State Un.)
Crawdaddy
CRCL   Canadian Review of Comparative Literature/Revue Canadienne de Litterature Comparée

CREL   Cahiers Roumains d'Etudes Littéraires: Revue Trimestrielle de Critique, d'Esthétique et d'Histoire Littéraires
Cresset (Valparaiso Un.)
CRev   The Chesterton Review: The Journal of the Chesterton Society
CRevAS   Canadian Review of American Studies
Crit   Critique: Studies in Modern Fiction (Minneapolis)
CritI   Critical Inquiry: A Voice for Reasoned Inquiry into Significant Creations of the Human Spirit
Critic: Journal of Catholic Christian Culture (Chicago)
Criticism: A Quarterly for Literature and the Arts (Detroit, MI)
CritQ   Critical Quarterly (Manchester)
CritR   Critical Review (Un. of Melbourne)
CritS   Critical Studies
CritSurvey   Critical Survey
CrossCountry
Crosscurrents
CRUX: A Journal on the Teaching of English
CruxP: Crux: A Guide to Teaching English Language and Literature (Pretoria)
Crysalis   Crysallis Journal
CS   Cahiers du Sud (Marseilles)
CSLBull   Bulletin of the New York C. S. Lewis Society
CSR   Christian Scholar's Review
Ctary   Commentary (New York)
CUF   Columbia University Forum
CUlEA   Cultural Events in Africa
Culture
CW   Classical World (Pennsylvania State Un., University Park)
CWCP   Contemporary Writers in Christian Perspective (Grand Rapids, MI)
Cweal   Commonweal (New York)
CWTW   Canadian Writers and Their Works

DA   Dissertation Abstracts International (Ann Arbor, MI)
DAI   Dissertation Abstracts International (Ann Arbor, MI)
Deccan Geographer
Degrés: Revue de Synthèse à Orientation Sémiologique
DelLR   Delaware Literary Review (Un. of Delaware)
Delos: A Journal on and of Translation
Delta: A Literary Review (Sheffield: later at Bristol)
DeltaES   Delta: Revue du Centre d'Etudes et de Cecherche sur les Ecrivains du Sud aux Etats-Unis (Montpellier)
DenverQ   Denver Quarterly (Un. of Denver)
DESB   Delta Epsilon Sigma Bulletin (Loras College, Dubuque)
Descant (Texas Christian Un.)
Dana (Uganda)
DHLR   The D. H. Lawrence Review (Un. of Arkansas)
Diacritics: A Review of Contemporary Criticism
Dialogue (Un. of Pittsburgh at Bradford, PA)
Dickensian (London)
DiderotS   Diderot Studies
DilimanR   Diliman Review (Un. of the Philippines)
DilR   Diliman Review (Un. of the Philippines)
Discourse (Concordia College)
Dismisura: Rivista Bimestrale di Produzione & Crit. Culturale (Alatri, Italy)
DL   Deus Loci: The Lawrence Durrell Newsletter
DLN   Doris Lessing Newsletter
DM   The Dublin Magazine
Dolphin (Un. of Aarhus)
DownR   Downside Review (Bath, England)
DQ   Denver Quarterly

DQR   Dutch Quarterly Review of Anglo-American Letters
DR   Dalhousie Review (Halifax, N.S.)
Drum (Amherst, MA)
DSec   Segre Second: Studies in French Literature
DStudies   Dostoevsky Studies: Journal of the International Dostoevsky Society
DubR   Dublin Review (London; now called Wiseman Review [WiseR])
DUJ   Durham University Journal (England)
DWB   Dietsche Warande en Belfort (Antwerp)

EA   Etudes Anglaises (Vanves, France, and Philadelphia)
EAA   Estudos Anglo-Americanos (São Paulo, Brazil)
EAJ   East Africa Journal (Nairobi)
EAL   Early American Literature
E&S   Essays and Studies by Members of the English Association (Oxford Un.)
EAS   Essays in Arts and Sciences
EB   English Bulletin (Colombo)
ECanW   Essays on Canadian Writing (Downsview, Ontario)
ECLife   Eighteenth-Century Life
Eco-Logos (Denver, CO)
ECr   L'Esprit Créateur (Lawrence, KS)
ECW   Essays on Canadian Writing
Edda: Nordisk Tidsskrift for Litteraturforskning
EDH   Essays by Divers Hands (Royal Society of Literature, London)
EdL   Educational Leadership (Washington, DC)
EDS   Essays by Divers Hands (Royal Society of Literature, London)
EducF   Educational Forum
EEELS   English Literature and Language (Tokyo)
EESB   Expression: Journal of the English Society, UBLS
EFL   Essays in French Literature (Un. of Western Australia)
EFT   English Fiction in Transition (1880-1920) (Purdue Un.)
EI   Etudes Irlandaises (Villeneuve d'Ascq, France)
EIC   Essays in Criticism (Bucks, England)
EigoS   Eigo Seinen [The Rising Generation] (Tokyo)
EIL   Essays in Literature
EinA   English in Africa
Éire   Éire-Ireland: A Journal of Irish Studies (St. Paul)
EJ   English Journal (Nat. Council of Teachers of English)
EL   Educational Leader (Pittsburg, Kansas St. College)
EL   Essays in Literature (Un. of Denver)
ELH   ELH: Journal of English Literary History (Johns Hopkins)
ELLS   English Literature and Language (Tokyo)
ELN   English Language Notes (Un. of Colorado)
ELR   English Literary Renaissance
ELUD   Essays in Literature (Un. of Denver)
ELWIU   Essays in Literature (Western Illinois Un.)
EM   English Miscellany (Rome)
EMD   An English Miscellany (St. Stephen's College, Eelhi)
enclitic
Encounter (London)
Encyclia: The Journal of the Utah Academy of Sciences, Arts, and Letters
English   English (English Association, London)
English Bulletin (Colombo)
EngQ   English Quarterly
EngR   English Record (N.Y. State English Council)
EngRev   English Review
EngS   English Studies (Amsterdam)
Envoy

EON   The Eugene O'Neill Newsletter
ES   English Studies (Amsterdam)
ESA   English Studies in Africa (Johannesburg)
ESC   English Studies in Canada (Toronto)
ESCan   English Studies in Canada (Un. of New Brunswick, Fredericton)
ESELL   Essays and Studies in English Language and Literature (Sendai, Japan)
ESQ   Emerson Society Quarterly (Hartford)
ESRS   Emporia State Research Studies (Kansas State Teachers College of Emporia)
ET   Expository Times (Edinburgh)
Etc   Etc: A Review of General Semantics
Ethics (Chicago Un. Press)
Études de lettres (Lausanne)
Études irlandaises (Université de Lille III, Villneuve d'Asq, France)
EUQ   Emory University Quarterly
EvR   Evergreen Review (New York)
EWN   Evelyn Waugh Newsletter (Naussau Community College, Garden City, NY)
EWR   East-West Review (Doshisha Un., Kyoto, Japan)
Expl   Explicator (Virginia Commonwealth Un.)
Explor   Exploration: Journal of the MLA Special Session on the Literature of Exploration and Travel
Explor   Explorations (Un. of Toronto)
Explorations (Government College, Lahore)
Extracts: An Occasional Newsletter
Extrapolation

Fabula
Falcon
FAR   The French-American Review
FaSt   Faulkner Studies: An Annual of Research, Criticism, and Reviews (Coral Gables, FL)
FHA   Fitzgerald-Hemingway Annual
FictionI   Fiction International
Fiddlehead
Filologija (Sofia)
FitzN   Fitzgerald Newsletter (Charlottesville, VA)
FJS   Fu Jen Studies (Republic of China)
F10B   Flannery O'Connor Bulletin
FloQ   Florida Quarterly (Un. of Florida)
FMLS   Forum for Modern Language Studies (Un. of St. Andrews, Scotland)
FMod   Filologia Moderna (Madrid)
Folio: Papers on Foreign Languages and Literature
Folklore
FolkloreC   Folklore: India's Only English Monthly on the Subject
ForumH   Forum (Un. of Houston; now called Forum of Texas)
Foundation: Review of Science Fiction
FourQ   Four Quartets
FP   Filoloski Pregled (Belgrade)
FQ   Four Quarters (La Salle College)
FR   French Review (American Assoc. of Teachers of French)
Freedomways
Frontiers: Journal of Women Studies
FSt   Feminist Studies
FurmanM   Furman Magazine
FurmS   Furman Studies (Furman Un.)
FW   First World

FWF   Far Western Forum: A Review of Ancient and Modern Letters

GA   Germanistische Abhandlungen
GaR   Georgia Review (Un. of Georgia)
Genre (Un. of Illinois at Chicago Circle)
GHQ   Georgia Historical Quarterly (Savannah)
GissingN   The Gissing Newsletter
GLRev   Great Lakes Review
GothSE   Gothenburg Studies in English
GPQ   Great Plains Quarterly (Omaha, NE)
Gradiva: A Journal of Contemporary Theory and Practice
Greenfield Review
Greyfriar: Siena Studies in Literature
GRLH   Garland Reference Library of the Humanities
GrLR   Great Lakes Review: A Journal of Midwest Culture
GrossR   Grosseteste Review
GSlav   Germano-Slavica
GSUFNF   Godišnik na Sofijskija Universitet: Fakultet po Klasieski i Novi Filologi (Sofia) Formerly GSUFZF
GSUFZF   Godišnikna Sofijskija universitet. Fakulted po zapadni filologii (Sofia)
Gulliver: German-English Yearbook (W. Germany)
Gypsy
GyS   Gypsy Scholar: A Graduate Forum for Literary Criticism

HAB   Humanities Association Bulletin (Canada)
HarvardA   Harvard Advocate (Cambridge, MA)
HC   The Hollins Critic (Hollins College, VA)
Hecate: a Women's Interdisciplinary Journal (Brisbane)
Hekima (Nairobi)
Hemisphere
HemR   Hemingway Review (Ada, OH)
Heresies: A Feminist Publication on Art and Politics
HeythropJ   Heythrop Journal
HGP   Heritage of the Great Plains (Emporia State College, KS)
HINL   History of Ideas Newsletter (New York)
HIS   Humanities in Society
HisJ   Hispanic Journal (Indiana, PA)
Hispania: A Journal Devoted to the Interests of the Teaching of Spanish and Portuguese (Cincinnati, OH)
HJ   Hibbert Journal (London)
HJAS   Hitotsubashi Journal of Arts and Sciences (Tokyo)
HJR   The Henry James Review (Baton Rouge, LA)
HLQ   Huntington Library Quarterly (San Marino, CA)
HMPEC   Historical Magazine of the Protestant Episcopal Church (Austin, TX)
HN   Hemingway Notes
HOK   Heritage of Kansas: A Journal of the Great Plains
HorizonI   Horizon (Ibadan)
HPEN   The Hungarian P.E.N./Le P.E.N. Hongrois
HPR   The Homiletic and Pastoral Review (New York)
HQ   Haltwhistle Quarterly (Polytechnic of Newcastle-Upon-Tyne)
HSE   Hungarian Studies in English (L. Kossuth Un., Debrecen)
HSELL   Hiroshima Studies in English Language and Literature
HSL   Hartford Studies in Literature
HudR   Hudson Review (New York)
Humanist (State Un. of New York at Buffalo)
HUSL   Hebrew University Studies in Literature
HussR   Husson Review
HuW   The Human World

IARB   Inter-American Review of Bibliography (Washington, DC)
Ibadan
ICarbS (Carbondale, IL)
Idol (Union College, Schenectady, NY)
IE   Indiana English (Indiana State Un., Terre Haute)
IEJ   Indiana English Journal (Indiana State Un.)
IEY   Iowa English Yearbook (Iowa State Un.)
IfeAS   Ife African Studies
IFR   International Fiction Review
IHML   International Henry Miller Letter (Njimegen, Netherlands)
IJAS   Indian Journal of American Studies
IJES   Indian Journal of English Studies (Calcutta)
IJWS   International Journal of Women's Studies
ILA   International Literary Annual (London)
ILLQ   Illinois Quarterly
ILR   Indian Literary Review
IndH   Indian Horizons
Indigo (Lagos)
IndL   Indian Literature
IndLing   Indian Linguistics
IndMH   Indiana Magazine of History
Innisfree (Southeastern La. Un.)
Inquiry Magazine
Intellect (Society for the Advancement of Education, NY)
IntellectualD   Intellectual Digest
Intercollegiate Rev: Intercollegiate Review (Bryn Mawr)
Interpretations: Studies in Language and Literature
IntEssays   Interdisciplinary Essays (Mt. St. Mary's College, Emmitsburg, MD)
IowaR   Iowa Review
IPEN   Indian P.E.N.
IPQ   International Philosophical Quarterly (Fordham Un.)
IQ   Italian Quarterly
IR   Iliff Review (Denver)
IrEccRec   Irish Ecclesiastical Record (Dublin)
Irish Renaissance Annual
IrM   Irish Monthly (Dublin)
ISB   Independent School Bulletin (National Assoc. of Independent Schools, Boston)
Islands: A New Zealand Quarterly of Arts and Letters (Christchurch)
ISLL   Illinois Studies in Language and Literature
ISSQ   Indiana Social Studies Quarterly
Issue (Un. of Adelaide)
Ital   Italica (Amer. Assoc. of Teachers of Italian)
ItalAm   Italian Americana
IUR   Irish University Review: A Journal of Irish Studies
IWT   Indian Writing Today

JA   Jahrbuch für Amerikastudien (West Berlin)
JAAC   Journal of Aesthetics and Art Criticism (Wayne State Un.)
JAAR   Journal of the American Academy of Religion
JAC   Journal of American Culture (Bowling Green State Un., Bowling Green, OH)
JAE   Journal of Aesthetic Education (Un. of Illinois at Urbana-Champaign)
JAF   Journal of American Folklore (Un. of Texas Pr.)
JAH   Journal of American History

JAms   Journal of American Studies (London; also BAASB)
JASAT   Journal of the American Studies Association of Texas (Wayland College, Plainview)
JBeckS   Journal of Beckett Studies
JBrS   Journal of British Studies (Trinity College, Hartford, CT)
JBS   Journal of Black Studies (Los Angeles)
JCanStud   Journal of Canadian Studies (Trent Un.)
JCF   Journal of Canadian Fiction
JCL   Journal of Commonwealth Literature (Un. of Leeds)
JCMVASA   Central Mississippi Valley American Studies Association Journal (Lawrence, KS)
JCS   Journal of Caribbean Studies (Coral Gables, FL)
JCSt   Journal of Caribbean Studies (Coral Gables, FL)
JCT   Joseph Conrad Today (State Un. of New York, Oswego)
JEGP   Journal of English and Germanic Philology (Un. of Illinois)
JEI   Journal of the English Institute
JEn   Journal of English (Sana's Un.)
JEngL   Journal of English Linguistics
JEnS   Journal of English Studies (India)
JES   Journal of European Studies
JEthS   Journal of Ethnic Studies
Jewish Affairs (Johannesburg)
JewishQ   Jewish Quarterly
JGE   Journal of General Education (Penn. St. Un.)
JHD   Journal of the Hellenic Diaspora (San Francisco)
JHS   Journal of Historical Studies
JIAS   Journal of Inter-American Studies (Un. of Miami, FL)
JIL   Journal of Irish Literature
JIWE   The Journal of Indian Writing in English
JJCL   Jadavpur Journal of Comparative Literature
JJQ   James Joyce Quarterly (Un. of Tulsa)
JKUH   Journal of the Karnatak University: Humanities
JLN   Jack London Newsletter
JLoN   Jack London Newsletter
JLS   Journal of Literary Studies
JMissH   Journal of Mississippi History (Jackson)
JML   Journal of Modern Literature
JMU   Journal of the Mysore University
JNALA   Journal of the New African Literature and the Arts
JNH   Journal of Negro History (Washington, DC)
JNigESA   Journal of the Nigeria English Studies Association
Jnl. of the Great Plains
JNT   Journal of Narrative Technique (Eastern Michigan Un.)
JOHJ   John O'Hara Journal (Pottsville, PA)
JOJ   John O'Hara Journal (Pottsville, PA)
Joliso: East African Journal of Literature and Society
JourEAfrRD   Journal of Eastern African Research and Development (Nairobi)
Jour. of Afr. Studies
Jour. of Black Studies
JP   Journal of Philosophy (Columbia Un.)
JPC   Journal of Popular Culture (Bowling Green, Ohio, Un.)
JQ   Journalism Quarterly
JR   Journal of Religion
JSL   Journal of the School of Languages
JSoAL   Journal of South Asian Literature
Judaism
Junction (Brooklyn College)
JWest   Journal of the West (Los Angeles, CA)
JWS   Journal of Western Speech

JWSL   Journal of Women's Studies in Literature

KAL   Kyushu American Literature (Fukuoka, Japan)
Kalki: Studies in Branch Cabell
Kalyani: Journal of the University of Kelaniya (Sri Lanka)
KanQ   Kansas Quarterly
Karamu (Eastern Illinois Un., Charleston, IL)
Karnatak Un. Jnl.
KCN   Kate Chopin Newsletter
KFQ   Keystone Folklore Quarterly (Point Park College, Pittsburgh)
KFR   Kentucky Folklore Record
Kiabàrà: Journal of the Humanities
Kingfisher (Un. of Sheffield)
KJES   Kakatiya Journal of English Studies
KM   Kansas Magazine (Kansas St. Un.; now called Kansas Quarterly)
KN   Kwartalnik Neofilologiczny (Warsaw)
KompH   Komparatistische Hefte
KPAB   Kentucky Philological Association Bulletin
KR   Kenyon Review
KRev   The Kentucky Review
Kritikon Litterarum
KRQ   Kentucky Romance Quarterly
KSJ   Keats-Shelley Journal (Harvard Un., Cambridge)
KUJH   Karnatak University Journal, Humanities
Kuka: Journal of Creative and Critical Writing (Zaria, Nigeria)
Kunapipi (Un. of Aarhus, Denmark)
KyR   The Kentucky Review (Un. of Kentucky)

LA   Linguistica Antverpiensia
LAAW   Lotus: Afro-Asian Writings
LaH   Louisiana History (Baton Rouge)
LALR   Latin American Literary Review
L&B   Literature and Belief
Landfall
L&H   Literature and History: A New Journal for the Humanities
L&I   Literature and Ideology (Montreal)
L&L   Linguistica et Litteraria
L&P   Literature and Psychology (Un. of Hartford)
L&U   The Lion and the Unicorn: A Critical Journal of Children's Literature (Brooklyn, NY)
Lang&L   Language and Literature
Lang&S   Language and Style
LanM   Les Langues Modernes
LaS   Louisiana Studies
LauR   Laurel Review (W. Va., Wesleyan College)
LBR   Luso-Brazilian Review
LC   Library Chronicle (Un. of Pennsylvania)
LCrit   Literary Criterion (Un. of Mysore, India)
LCUT   Library Chronicle (Un. of Texas)
LE&W   Literature East and West (Modern Lang. Assoc. of America)
LetN   Lettres Nouvelles (Paris)
Lex et Scientia: International Journal of Law and Science
L'Express
LFQ   Literature/Film Quarterly
LGJ   Lost Generation Journal
LHR   Lock Haven Review (Lock Haven St. College, PA)
LHY   Literary Half-Yearly (Mysore, India)

Library   The Library: A Quarterly Journal of Bibliography
Library Review (Glasgow)
LingI   Linguistic Inquiry
LiNQ: (Literature in North Queensland)
LiNq: (Literature in North Queensland)
Listener (London)
Listening
LitE   The Literary Endeavour: A Quarterly Journal Devoted to English Studies
LitR   Literary Review (Fairleigh Dickinson Un.)
Littcrit (Trivandrum India)
Lituanus: Lithuanian Quarterly (Chicago)
LJGG   Literaturwissenschaftliches Jahrbuch im Auftrage der Görres-Cesellschaft
LJH   Legon Journal of the Humanities (Legon, Ghana)
LJHum   Lamar Journal of the Humanities
LNL   Linguistics in Literature
LonM   London Magazine
Lore&L   Lore and Language
LOS   Literary Onomastics Studies
LPer   Literature in Performance: A Journal of Literary and Performing Art (Chapel Hill, NC)
LR   Literaturnaya rossiya (Moscow)
LRN   Literary Research Newsletter
LS   Spectator (London)
LSUSHS   Louisiana State University Studies. Humanities Series
LugR   Lugano Review
Luna (Kew, Vic., Australia)
The Lutheran
LWU   Literatur in Wissenschaft und Unterrich (Kiel, Germany)

Maatstaf
Macleans
Mahfil: A Quarterly of South Asian Literature (Un. of Chicago)
Maledicta: The International Journal of Verbal Aggression
Mallorn: The Journal of the Tolkien Society
Mambo   Mambo Review of Contemporary African Literature (Salisbury)
M&M   Masses and Mainstream (New York)
MAQR   Michigan Alumnus Quarterly Review (Ann Arbor: now called Michigan Quarterly Review)
MarkhamR   Markham Review
MarxQ   Marxist Quarterly
MAsianS   Modern Asian Studies
MASJ   Midcontinent American Studies Journal
Mawazo (Kampala)
MBL   Modern British Literature
McNR   McNeese Review (McNeese College, LA)
MCR   Melbourne Critical Review
MD   Modern Drama
MDAC   Mystery and Detection Annual (Beverly Hills, CA)
Meanjin   Meanjin Quarterly (Un. of Melbourne)
MEB   Missouri English Bulletin
Melbourne Chronicle (Melbourne, Vic., Australia)
MelbSS   Melbourne Slavonic Studies
MELUS
Menckeniana
Mennonite Life
Merkur: Deutsche Zeitschrift für Europäisches Denken

Mester
MF   Midwest Folklore (Indiana Un.)
MFS   Modern Fiction Studies (Purdue Un.)
MGW   Manchester Guardian Weekly
MHLS   Mid-Hudson Language Studies
MHRev   Malahat Review
MichA   Michigan Acadamecian
Midamerica   Midamerica: The Yearbook of the Society for the Study of Midwestern Literature
Mid-America: Historical Review
MidR   Midwest Review (Nebraska St. Teachers College, Wayne)
Midstream
Midway (Chicago)
MinnR   Minnesota Review (St. Paul)
Miscellany
MissFR   Mississippi Folklore Register
MissQ   Mississippi Quarterly (Miss. St. Un.)
MissR   The Missouri Review
MJ   Midwest Journal (Lincoln Un., Jefferson City, MO)
MLN   Modern Language Notes (Johns Hopkins Press)
MLNew   Malcolm Lowry Newsletter
MLQ   Modern Language Quarterly (Un. of Washington)
MLS   Modern Language Studies
MM   Maclean's Magazine (Toronto)
MMtR   Mill Mountain Review
MMisc   Midwestern Miscellany
ModA   Modern Age (Chicago)
ModSp   Moderne Sprachen: Organ des Verbandes des Oster-reichischen Neupphilologen fur Moderne Sprachen, Literatur, und Pädagogik
ModSt   Modernist Studies: Literature and Culture 1920-1940 (Un. of Alberta, Edmonton)
Monatshefte: A Journal Devoted to the Study of German Language and Literature/für Deutschen Unterricht, Deutsche Sprache and Literatur
Month   The Month
MoOc   Modern Occasions
Moreana (Angers)
Mosaic   Mosaic: A Journal for the Comparative Study of Literature and Ideas
MP   Modern Philology: A Journal Devoted to Research in Medieval and Modern Literature (Un. of Chicago)
MPR   The Mervyn Peeke Review
MQ   Midwest Quarterly (Kansas St. College of Pittsburg)
MQR   Michigan Quarterly Review
MR   Massachusetts Review (Un. of Massachusetts)
MRev   Mediterranean Review
MRR   Mad River Review (Dayton, OH)
MS   Moderna Sprak (Stockholm) (also MSpr)
MSCS   Mankato State College Studies (Minnesota)
MSE   Massachusetts Studies in English (Amherst)
MSEx   Melville Society Extracts
MSI   Moody Street Irregulars: A Jack Kerouac Newsletter
MSLC   Modern Studies: Literature and Culture 1920-1940 (Un. of Alberta, Edmonton)
MsM   Ms. Magazine (New York)
MSpr   Moderna Sprak (Stockholm; also MS)
MTJ   Mark Twain Journal (Kirkwood, MO)
Muse: Literary Journal of the English Association at Nsukka

MV   Minority Voices: An Interdisciplinary Journal of Literature and the Arts
MWoN   Mary Wollstonecraft Newsleter
Mythlore (Maywood, CA)

NA   Nuova Antologia
NALF   Negro American Literature Forum (!ndiana St. Un.)
NAmerR   North American Review
Names: Journal of the American Name Society
NAmR   New American Review
N&Q   Notes and Queries (London)
NAS   Norwegian-American Studies (Northfield, MN)
NassauR   Nassau Review (Nassau Community College)
Nassau Rev   Nassau Review (Naussau Community College)
NatR   National Review (New York)
NCampR   New Campus Review (Metropolitan State College, Denver)
NCarF   North Carolina Folklore
NConL   Notes on Contemporary Literature
NDEJ   Notre Dame English Journal
NDQ   North Dakota Quarterly (Un. of N. Dakota)
Nebraska History
NegroD
NEMLA Newsletter: A Publication of the Northeast Modern Language Association
Neohelicon: Acta Comparationis Litterarum Universarum
Neophil   Neophilologus (Groningen)
NEQ   New England Quarterly (Bowdoin College)
NER   New England Review
New Beacon Reviews: Collection One
New Blackfriars
New Boston Rev
New Edinburgh Review (Edinburgh Un.)
NewL   New Letters
New Quest (Poona, India)
New Rev   The New Review
New St   New Statesman
New World Quarterly
New Worlds
New Zealand Listener
NF   Nigerian Field
NFS   Nottingham French Studies (Un. of Nottingham, England)
NHQ   New Hungarian Quarterly
Nieman Reports (Harvard Un., Cambridge, MA)
NigM   Nigeria Magazine
Nimrod (Un. of Tulsa, OK)
NLauR   New Laurel Review (The Pennington School, Pennington, NJ)
NLH   New Literary History (Un. of Virginia)
NLRev   New Literature Review
NM   Neuphilologische Mitteilungen (Helsinki)
NMAL   Notes on Modern American Literature
NMHR   New Mexico Humanities Review
NMQ   New Mexico Quarterly (Un. of New Mexico)
NMQR   New Mexico Quarterly Review (Un. of New Mexico)
NMW   Notes on Mississippi Writers (Un. of So. Mississippi)
NOQ   Northwest Ohio Quarterly (Maumee, OH)
NoR   Northern Review (Montreal)
NOR   New Orleans Review
Novel: A Forum on Fiction (Brown Un.)

NR   The Nassau Review: The Journal of Nassau Community College Devoted to Arts, Letters, and Sciences
NRep   New Republic (Washington, DC)
NRF   Nouvelle Revue Française (Paris)
NS   Die Neuren Sprachen (Frankfurt)
Nsammlung   Neue Sammlung (Göttingen, W. Germany)
NS&N   New Statesman and Nation (London)
NS&Nation   New Statesman and Nation (London)
NsM   Neusprachliche Mittelungen aus Wissenschaft und Praxis
NStat   New Statesman (London)
NVT   Nieuw Vlaams Tijdschrift
NWQ   New World Quarterly
NWR   Northwest Review (Un. of Oregon)
NY   New Yorker
NyA   Nya Argus (Helsinki)
NYFQ   New York Folklore Quarterly
NYHTBR   New York Herald Tribune Book Review
NYHTBW   New York Herald Tribune Book Review
NYLF   New York Literary Forum
NYQ   New York Quarterly
NYRB   New York Review of Books
NYTBR   New York Times Book Review
NYTM   New York Times Magazine
NZListener   New Zealand Listener
NZMR   New Zealand Monthly Review
NZSJ   New Zealand Slavonic Journal

Obsidian: Black Literature In Review (Fredonia, NY)
OccasionalR   Occasional Review (San Diego, CA)
Odù
Ody   Odyssey: A Journal of the Humanities
OhioanaQ   Ohioana Quarterly
OhR   Ohio Review
OJES   Osmania Journal of English Studies (Osmania Un., Hyderabad)
Okike: An African Journal of New Writing
OL   Orbis Litterarum (Copenhagen)
OldN   Old Northwest: A Journal of Regional Life and Letters (Miami Un., Oxford, OH)
OLR   The Oxford Literary Review
ON   The Old Northwest
OntarioR   Ontario Review: A North American Journal of the Arts
Open Letter (Toronto)
Opinion
Opus (Un. of Rhodesia, Salisbury)
OR   Oxford Review (Cleveland)
Orcrist
ORev   The Occasional Review: A Journal of Contemporary Thought in the Humanities, Arts and Social Sciences
Orion
Oui (Chicago)
OUR   Ohio University Review
Overland (Melbourne)
OW   Orient/West (Tokyo)

PA   Présence Africaine
PacSp   Pacific Spectator (Stanford, CA)
Paintbrush: A Journal of Poetry, Translations, and Letters (Laramie, WY)

PAJ   Pan-African Journal
PanA   Pan-Africanist
P&L   Philosophy and Literature
P&L   Politics and Letters (London)
P&PR   Psychoanalysis and the Psychoanalytic Review (New York)
Panjab   Panjab Un. Research Bulletin (Arts)
PAPA   Publications of the Arkansas Philological Association
Par   Paragone (Florence, Italy)
Parabola: Myth and the Quest for Meaning
ParisR   Paris Review (Flushing, NY)
ParmaE   Parma Eldalamberon (Buena Vista, CA)
Parnassus: Poetry in Review
par rapport: A Journal of the Humanities
Paunch
PBSA   Papers of the Bibliographic Society of America
PCL   Perspectives on Contemporary Literature
PCLS   Proceedings of the Comparative Literature Symposium (Texas Tech Un.)
PCP   Pacific Coast Philology
PCTEB   Pennsylvania Council of Teachers of English Bulletin
PE   Pennsylvania English: Essays in Film and the Humanities
PELL   Papers on English Language and Literature (Southern Illinois Un.)
Pembroke
Per   Perspective (Washington Un.)
Person   Personalist (Un. of So. California)
Perspective (Pakistan)
Philobiblon
PhilP   Philological Papers (West Virginia Un., Morgantown)
PhoenixC   Phoenix (College of Charleston, SC)
PhoenixK   Phoenix (Korea Un.)
Phylon
Planet (Llangeitho, Tregaron, Dyfed)
PLL   Papers on Language and Literature (Southern Illinois Un.)
Ploughshares
PMASAL   Michigan Academy of Science, Arts, and Letters. Papers
PMLA   Publications of the Modern Language Association of America (New York)
PMPA   Publications of the Missouri Philological Association
PN   Poe Newsletter (Washington State Un.)
PNotes   Pynchon Notes
PNR   PN Review
PoeN   Poe Newsletter (Washington State Un.)
PoeS   Poe Studies
Poetics: International Review for the Theory of Literature
Poetry Nation   See PNR
Pol (Sydney)
PolP   Polish Perspectives
PolQ   Political Quarterly (London)
PolR   Polish Review (New York)
POMPA   Publications of the Mississippi Philological Association
PostS   Post Script: Essays in Film and the Humanities
PoT   Poetics Today: Theory and Analysis of Literature and Communication (Tel Aviv, Israel)
PowysN   The Powys Newsletter
PP   Philologica Pragensia
PQ   Philological Quarterly (Un. of Iowa)

PQM   Pacific Quarterly (Moana): An International Review of Arts and Ideas

PR   Partisan Review (New Brunswick, NJ)

Prague Studies in English

Praxis   Praxis: A Journal of Radical Perspectives on the Arts

PRev   The Powys Review

PRom   Papers in Romance (Seattle, WA)

Proof: Yearbook of American Bibliographical and Textual Studies

Prosery   The Prosery

Prospects: Annual of American Cultural Studies

Prov   Provincial (Indianapolis)

PRR   The Journal of Pre-Raphaelite Studies (Supersedes The Pre-Raphaelite Review)

PrS   Prairie Schooner (Un. of Nebraska)

PSciQ   Political Science Quarterly (Columbia Un.)

PSQ   Political Science Quarterly (Columbia Un.)

PsyculR   Psychocultural Review: Interpretations in the Psychology of Art, Literature and Society

PsyR   Psychoanalytic Review (New York)

PTL: A Journal for Descriptive Poetics and Theory

PUASAL   Proceedings of the Utah Academy of Sciences, Arts, and Letters (Salt Lake City)

PULC   Princeton University Library Chronicle

Pulp

PURBA   Panjab University Research Bulletin (Arts)

PUSA   Perspectives U.S.A. (New York)

PVR   Platte Valley Review

PW   Publisher's Weekly

QJLC   Quarterly Journal of the Library of Congress

QJS   Quarterly Journal of Speech (New York)

QQ   Queen's Quarterly (Kingston, Ontario)

QRL   Quarterly Review of Literature (Princeton, NJ)

Quadrant (Sydney, Australia)

Quarto (London)

Quill and Quire

RAL   Research in African Literatures

RALS   Resources for American Literary Study

RANAM   Recherches Anglaises et Américaines

Raritan: A Quarterly Review

RBPH   Revue Belge de Philologie et d'Histoire (Brussels)

RCF   The Review of Contemporary Fiction

RDM   Revue des Deux Monde (Now Nouvelle Revue des Deux Mondes)

RdP   Revue de Paris (Paris)

ReAL   Re: Arts and Letters

Re: Artes Liberales (Stephen F. Austin State Un., Nacoqdoches, TX)

RecL   Recovering Literature

REH   Revista de Estudios Hispánicas

REL   Review of English Literature (Leeds)

Ren   Renascence (Viterbo College, La Crosse, WI)

Renaissance 2

Rendezvous: Journal of Arts and Letters (Idaho State Un.)

Response

Restant: Tijdsohrift voor Recente Semiotische Teorievorming en de Analyse van eksten/Review for Semiotic Theories and the Analysis of Texts

Rev   Review (Blacksburg, VA)

RevI   Revista/Review Interamericana

Review

Revista Canaria de Estudios Ingleses (La Laguna Un., Tenerife)

RevL   Revista de Letras

RevLo   Revue de Louisiane/Louisiana Review (Lafayette)

RevN   La Revue Nouvelle (Paris)

RFEA   Revue Française d'Etudes Américaines

RFI   Regionalism and the Female Imagination (Formerly The Kate Chopin Newsletter)

RGB   Revue générale Belge (Brussels)

Rhodesian History (Un. of Rhodesia, Salisbury)

RIB   Revista Interamericana de Bibliograffa/Inter-American Review of Bibliography (OAS, Washington, DC)

RIP   Rice Institute Pamphlets (Houston; now called Rice University Studies)

RITL   Revista de Istorie i Theorie Literar

RLA   Revista de Letras da Falculdade de Filosofia, Ciencias e Letras de Assis

RLC   Revue de Littérature Comparée (Paris)

RLet   Revista Letras (Paraná, Brazil)

RLJ   Russian Language Journal (Michigan State Un., East Lansing)

RLLR   Revue de Louisiane/Louisiana Review

RLM   La Revue des Lettres Modernes (Paris)

RLMC   Riv. Letterature Moderne e Comparate (Firenze)

RLT   Russian Literature Triquarterly

RLV   Revue des Langues Vivantes (Brussels)

RMRLL   Rocky Mountain Review of Language and Literature (Un. of Utah, Salt Lake City)

RMS   Renaissance and Modern Studies (Un. of Nottingham)

RNL   Review of National Literatures

RO   Revista de Occidente

RomN   Romance Notes (Un. of North Carolina)

ROO   Room of One's Own

Roots (Houston, Texas)

RoR   Romanian Revue

RPol   Review of Politics (Notre Dame, IN)

RQ   Riverside Quarterly (Un. of Saskatchewan)

RS   Research Studies (Washington St. Un.)

RSSCW   Washington State (Un.) . Research Studies

RUCR   Revista de la Universidad de Costa Rica

RUO   Revue de L'Université d'Ottawa (Canada)

RUS   Rice University Studies

RUSEng   Rajasthan University Studies in English

RusR   Russian Review (Hoover Inst., Stanford, CA)

SA   Studi Americani (Rome)

SAB   South Atlantic Bulletin (Chapel Hill, NC)

SAF   Studies in American Fiction

SAfrL   Studies in African Literature: An Introduction to the African Novel

SAfrO   South African Outlook

SAH   Studies in American Humor (Southwest Texas State Un., San Marcos)

SAJL   Studies in American Jewish Literature

SALit   Chu-Shikoku Studies in American Literature, Hiroshima City, Japan

Salmagundi (Skidmore College)

SAmL   Studies in American Literature (The Hague)

S&M   Sun & Moon: A Quarterly of Literature and Art

S&S   Science and Society (New York)

S&W   South & West

SAP   Studia Anglica Posnaniensia: An International Review of English Studies

SAQ   South Atlantic Quarterly (Duke Un.)

SARev   South Asian Review

SatR   Saturday Review (New York)

SatRA   Saturday Review: The Arts

Saturday Night

Savacou (Jamaica)

SB   Studies in Bibliography (Un. of Virginia Bibliographical Society)

SBHC   Studies in Browning and His Circle: A Journal of Criticism, History, and Bibliography

SBL   Studies in Black Literature

SBN   Saul Bellow Journal (Formerly Saul Bellow Newsletter)

Scan   Scandinavica

SCB   South Central Bulletin (South Central Modern Language Association, Houston)

ScholS   Scholia Satyrica

SchP   Scholarly Publishing: A Journal for Authors and Publishers

Sci&Soc   Science and Society (New York)

SCL   Studies in Canadian Literature

ScotLJ   Scottish Literary Journal (Aberdeen Un.)

SCR   South Carolina Review

SCS   Studies in Contemporary Satire: A Creative and Critical Journal (Alliance College)

SDD-UW   Summaries of Doctoral Dissertations, Un. of Wisconsin

SDR   South Dakota Review (South Dakota Un.)

SEA   Studies in English and American (Budapest, Hungary)

Seahorse: The Anaïs Nin/Henry Miller Journal (Formerly Under the Sign of Pisces: Anaïs Nin and Her Circle)

SEAP   Studies in English and American Philology

SECOLB   The SECOL Review: Southeastern Conference on Linguistics (Formerly SECOL Bulletin)

Secolul

SEEJ   Slavic and East European Journal (Un. of Wisconsin)

SEER   Slavonic and East European Review (Cambridge Un.)

SEL   Studies in English Literature/Sibungaku Kinku (English Literary Society of Japan, Tokyo)

SELit   Studies in English Literature (also SE1)

SELL   Studies in English Language and Literature (Tokyo)

Semiotica: Revue Publiée par l'Association Internationale de Semiotique

Semper Floreat (Un. of Queensland, St. Luicia)

Serif   The Serif (Kent, OH)

SES   Sophia English Studies

Seven: An Anglo-American Literary Review

SFic   Science Fiction: A Review of Speculative Literature

SFQ   Southern Folklore Quarterly (Un. of FL)

SFS   Science-Fiction Studies

SFW   Studies in Frank Waters

SG   Studium Generale (W. Berlin)

SGG   Studia Germanica Gandensia (Ghent)

Shanith (Brooklyn)

ShawR   Shaw Review (Penn. St. Un. Press)

Shen   Shenandoah (Washington and Lee Un.)

SHR   Southern Humanities Review (Auburn Un.)

SHum   Studies in the Humanities (Indiana Un. of Pennsylvania)

Signs: Journal of Women in Culture and Society

SinN   Sin Nombre

SJS   San Jose Studies

Skylark

SlavR   Slavic Review (Seattle)

SLeN   Sinclair Lewis Newsletter (St. Cloud State Un.)

SLitI   Studies in the Literary Imagination (Georgia St. Un.)

SLJ   Southern Literary Journal

SLM   Southern Literary Messenger: A Quarterly

SLRJ   Saint Louis University Research Journal of the Graduate School of Arts and Sciences

SMy   Studia Mystica

SN   Studia Neophilologica: A Journal of Germanic and Romance Languages and Literature

SNL   Satire Newsletter (State Un., College, Oneonta, NY)

SNNTS   Studies in the Novel (North Texas State Un.)

Snowy Egret

SoCB   South Central Bulletin (South Central Modern Lang. Association, Houston)

Soc. for Fine Arts Rev.

SocRM   Sociological Review Monographs (Un. of Keele)

SoQ   The Southern Quarterly (Un. of Southern Mississippi)

SoR   Southern Review (Louisiana St. Un.)

SoRA   Southern Review: An Australian Journal of Literary Studies (Un. of Adelaide)

SORev   The Sean O'Casey Review (Holbrook, NY)

SoSt   Southern Studies: An Interdisciplinary Journal of the South

Soundings: A Journal of Interdisciplinary Studies

Southeastern Europe (Arizona State Un.)

Southerly (Sydney)

Soviet Lit   Soviet Literature (Moscow)

SovietR   Soviet Review (White Plains, NY)

SovL   Soviet Literature (Moscow)

Spec   Speculum

Spectator

Sphinx   The Sphinx: A Magazine of Literature and Society

SPL&S   Sheffield Papers on Literature and Society

SQ   Shakespeare Quarterly

SR   Sewanee Review (Un. of the South)

SRA   Studia Romanica et Anglica-Zagrebiensia (Zagreb, Yugoslavia)

SRAZ   Studia Romanica et Angica Zagrebiensia (Zagreb, Yugoslavia)

SRC   Studies in Religion. A Canadian Journal

SRL   Saturday Review of Literature (New York)

SS   Scandinavian Studies (Lawrence, KS)

SSCRev   SSC Review (Shippensburg [PA] State College)

SSEng   Sydney Studies in English

SSF   Studies in Short Fiction (Newberry College, SC)

SSI   Scando-Slavica (Copenhagen)

SSJ   Southern Speech Journal (Un. of Georgia)

SSL   Studies in Scottish Literature (Un. of SC Press)

SSML   Society for the Study of Midwestern Literature

SSMLN   Society for the Study of Midwestern Literature Newsletter

Staffrider

StAH   Studies in American Humor

Stand

Standpunte

StAR   St. Andrews Review

Starship: The Magazine about Science Fiction
StBR Stony Brook
StCS Studies in Contemporary Satire: A Creative and Critical Journal
StHum Studies in the Humanities (Indiana Un. of Pennsylvania)
StIL Studi dell'Instituto Linguistico
StL Studies on the Left (New York)
St. Mark's Review (Canberra)
StMS Steinbeck Monograph Series
StN Steinbeck Newsletter
StQ Steinbeck Quarterly
Streven (Amsterdam)
StTCL Studies in Twentieth Century Literature
Studia Africana
Studies Studies: An Irish Quarterly (Dublin)
STwC Studies in the Twentieth Century
Style (Un. of Arkansas)
SUBBP Studia Universitatis Babes-Bolyai: Philologia
Sub-stance: A Review of Theory and Literary Criticism
SUS Susquehanna University Studies (Selingsgrove, PA)
SVEC Studies on Voltaire and the Eighteenth Century
SwAL Southwestern American Literature
SWR Southwest Review (Southern Methodist Un. Pr.)
SWS Southwest Writers Series (Steck-Vaughn, Austin)
SXX Secolul XX
Sym Symposium (Syracuse Un. Pr.)
Synthesis: Bulletin du Comité National de Littérature Comparée de la République Socialiste de Roumanie (Bucharest, Romania)

TAH The American Hispanist
TAIUS (Texas A&I)
TamR Tamarack Review (Toronto)
T&T Time and Tide (London)
TC Twentieth Century (London)
TCI Twentieth Century Interpretations
TCL Twentieth Century Literature
TCM Twentieth Century (Melbourne)
TCV Twentieth Century Views
Teaching of English (Newtown, NSW)
TEAS Twayne's English Author Series
TFSB Tennessee Folklore Society Bulletin (Middle Tenn. State Un.)
Thalia: Studies in Literary Humor (Ottawa)
Theoria: A Journal of Studies in the Arts, Humanities and Social Sciences
Third Way (London)
Thoth Thoth (Syracuse Un.)
Thought: A Review of Culture and Idea
ThQ Theatre Quarterly
THQ Tennessee Historical Quarterly (Nashville)
Tirade (Antwerp)
TJ Tolkien Journal (Belknap College, NH)
TJQ Thoreau Journal Quarterly
TkJ Tamkang Journal (Taipei City, Taiwan)
TkR Tamkang Review: A Quarterly of Comparative Studies between Chinese and Foreign Literatures
TLS Times Literary Supplement (London)
TolJ Tolkien Journal (Belknap College, NH)

Topic: A Journal of the Liberal Arts (Washington and Jefferson College)
TP Terzo Programma (Rome)
TPRSL Royal Society of Literature. Transactions and Proceedings (London)
TQ Texas Quarterly (Un. of Texas)
Tract (Lewes, Sussex)
Tradition: A Journal of Orthodox Jewish Thought
Tréma (Paris)
TriQ Tri-Quarterly (Northwestern Un.)
Triveni: Journal of Indian Renaissance
TSB Thoreau Society Bulletin: Devoted to the Life and Writings of Henry David Thoreau
TSE Tulane Studies in English
TSFB Tennessee Folklore Society Bulletin
TSL Tennessee Studies in Literature (Knoxville)
TSLL Texas Studies in Literature and Language (Un. of Texas)
TsudaR The Tsuda Review
TSWL Tulsa Studies in Women's Literature
TUSAS Twayne's United States Authors Series
TWA Transactions of the Wisconsin Academy of Sciences, Arts, and Letters
TWAS Twayne's World Authors Series
TwenCS Twentieth Century Studies
TWN The Thomas Wolfe Newsletter (Akron, OH)
Twórczo
TWP Trondheim Workingpapers
TxSE Texas Studies in English (Un. of Texas)

UA United Asia (Bombay)
UCQ University College Quarterly (Mich. St. Un.)
UCSSLL University of Colorado Studies. Series in Language and Literature
UCT Studies in English (Un. of Cape Town)
UDQ University of Denver Quarterly
UDR University of Dayton Review
UES Unisa English Studies (Un. of South Africa)
Ufahamu: Journal of the African Activist Association
UHQ Utah Historical Quarterly (Salt Lake City)
UKCR University of Kansas City Review
ULR University of Leeds Review
Umanesimo (Un. of Maryland)
Umma [Formerly Darlite]
Umoja
UMPAL University of Minnesota Pamphlets on American Literature
UMPAW University of Minnesota Pamphlets on American Writers
UMPEAL University of Miami Publications in English and American Literature
UMPWS University of Michigan Papers in Women's Studies (Ann Arbor)
UMSE University of Mississippi Studies in English
Unicorn
Univ Universitas (Stuttgart)
UPortR University of Portland Review
UPR University of Portland Review
UR University Review (Kansas City)
URajSE University of Rajasthan Studies in English
USCAD University of Southern California Abstracts of Dissertations

USFLQ USF Language Quarterly (Un. of South Florida)
USP Under the Sign of Pisces: Anais Nïn and Her Circle
UTQ University of Toronto Quarterly
UTSH University of Tennessee (Nashville). Studies in the Humanities
UVM University of Virginia Magazine
UVMag University of Virginia Magazine
UWR University of Windsor Review (Ontario)

Venture (Un. of Karachi)
Village Voice
Vinduet (Oslo)
VN Victorian Newsletter (New York Un.)
VNRN The Vladimir Nabokov Research Newsletter
Vort
Voyages (Washington, DC)
VQ Visvabharati Quarterly
VQR Virginia Quarterly Review (Un. of Virginia)
VR Viaa româneasc (Bucharest)
VS Victorian Studies (Indiana Un.)
Vuelta
VWQ Virginia Woolf Quarterly

WA West Africa
WAL Western American Literature (Colorado State Un.)
Walkabout
W&L Women and Literature
WascanR Wascana Review (Regina, Sask.)
Waves (York Un., Ontario)
WB Weimarer Beiträge
WBEP Wiener Beitrage zur englischen Philologie (Vienna)
WCR West Coast Review (Simon Fraser Un., B.C.)
WD Writer's Digest (Cincinnati, OH)
WebR Webster Review
Westerly (Un. of W. Ausralia)
WF Western Folklore (Un. of California)
WGCR West Georgia College Review
WHR Western Humanities Review (Un. of Utah)
WiF William Faulkner: Materials, Studies, and Criticism
WIP Work in Progress (Zaria, Nigeria)
WiseR Wiseman Review (London)

WisSL Wisconsin Studies in Literature (Wisconsin Council of Teachers, Oshkosh)
WLT World Literature Today: A Literary Quarterly of the University of Oklahoma
WLWE World Literature Written in English
WN A Wake Newsletter: Studies in James Joyce's Finnegan's Wake
WoR World Review (Un. of Queensland, Australia)
WP Work in Progress (Zaria, Nigeria)
WR Western Review (Western New Mexico Un.)
WS Women's Studies
WSCL Wisconsin Studies in Contemporary Literature (Un. of Wisconsin)
WSIA Wiener Slawistischer Almanach
WSUB Wichita State University Bulletin
WTW Writers and Their Work (British Council, London)
WVUPP West Virginia University Philological Papers
WWR Walt Whitman Review (Wayne St. Un.)
WWS Western Writers Series (Boise State Un.)
WZUG Wissenschafliche Zeitschrift der Ernst Moritz Arndt-Universität Freifswald

XR X, A Quarterly Review (London)
XUS Xavier University Studies

Yardbird Reader
YCC Yearbook of Comparative Criticism
YCGL Yearbook of Comparative and General Literature (Un. of N. Carolina Studies in Comparative Literature)
YER Yeats Eliot Review
YES Yearbook of English Studies
YFS Yale French Studies
Yiddish
YLM Yale Literary Magazine
YR Yale Review
YULG Yale University Library Gazette

ZAA Zeitschrift für Anglistik und Amerikanistik (Leipzig)
Zambesia: A Journal of the University of Rhodesia
ZRL Zagadnienia Rodzajów Literackich

The Contemporary Novel

A Checklist of Critical Literature
in the English Language Novel Since 1945

ABBEY, EDWARD, 1927-1989

GENERAL

The Westering Experience in American Literature: Bicentennial Essays, Bellingham, WA: Western Washington Un., 1977, 172-6.

McCann, G., *Edward Abbey.*

Pilkington, Tom, "Edward Abbey: Southwestern Anarchist," *WR* 3 (Winter, 1966): 58-62. [Not seen.]

_____, "Edward Abbey: Western Philosopher, or How to be a 'Happy Hopi Hippie'," *WAL* 9, i (May, 1974): 17-31. Also in Pilkington, W. T., ed., *Critical Essays on the Western American Novel*, 210-22.

Ronald, A., *New West of Edward Abbey.*

Twining, Edward S., "Edward Abbey, American: Another Radical Conservative," *UDQ*, 12, iv (Winter, 1978): 3-15.

Wylder, Delbert E., "Edward Abbey and the 'Power Elite'," *WR* 6, ii (Winter, 1969): 18-22. [Not seen.]

BLACK SUN

McCann, G., *Edward Abbey*, 35-7.

Pilkington, Tom, "Edward Abbey: Western Philosopher, or How to be a 'Happy Hopi Hippie'," *WAL* 9, i (May, 1974): 17-31 *passim*. Also in Pilkington, W. T., ed., *Critical Essays on the Western American Novel*, 213-20 *passim*.

Ronald, A., *New West of Edward Abbey*, 155-80.

THE BRAVE COWBOY: AN OLD TALE IN A NEW TIME

Clayton, Lawrence, "The End of the West Motif in the Work of Edward Abbey, Jane Kramer, and Elmer Kelton," *ReAL* 6, i (1979): 11-13.

Ljungquist, Kent, "Shadows Striking Eldorado: Poe's Presence in Abbey's THE BRAVE COWBOY," *SwAL* 7, ii (1982): 24-7.

McCann, G., *Edward Abbey*, 13-17.

Ronald, A., *New West of Edward Abbey*, 16-42.

DESERT SOLITAIRE

Benoit, Raymond, "Again with Fair Creation: Holy Places in American Literature," *Prospects* 5 (1980): 327-9.

Herndon, Jerry A.," 'Moderate Extremism': Edward Abbey and 'The Moon-Eyed Horse'," *WAL* 16, ii (Summer, 1981): 97-103.

McCann, G., *Edward Abbey*, 20-9.

Pilkington, Tom, "Edward Abbey: Western Philosopher, or How to be a 'Happy Hopi Hippie'," *WAL* 9, i (May, 1974): 17-31 *passim*. Also in Pilkington, W.T., ed., *Critical Essays on the Western American Novel*, 213-20 *passim*.

Ronald, A., *New West of Edward Abbey*, 65-91.

FIRE ON THE MOUNTAIN

McCann, G., *Edward Abbey*, 17-20.

Ronald, A., *New West of Edward Abbey*, 43-59.

GOOD NEWS

Ronald, A., *New West of Edward Abbey*, 210-38.

JONATHAN TROY

McCann, G., *Edward Abbey*, 10-13.
Ronald, A., *New West of Edward Abbey*, 5-15.

THE MONKEY WRENCH GANG

Erisman, Fred, "A Variant Text of THE MONKEY WRENCH GANG," *WAL* 14, iii (Fall, 1979): 227-8.
McCann, G., *Edward Abbey*, 37-41.
Ronald, A., *New West of Edward Abbey*, 181-209.

ABISH, WALTER, 1931-

GENERAL

Abish, Walter, "The Writer-to-Be: An Impression of Living," *Sub-stance* 27 (1980): 101-14.
_____, "Walter Abish: An Interview," *FictionI* 4/5 (1975): 93-100.

ALPHABETICAL AFRICA

Caramello, Charles, "On the Guideless Guidebooks of Postmodernism: Reading THE VOLCANOES FROM PUEBLA in Context," *S&M* 9-10 (Summer, 1980): 70-5.

HOW GERMAN IS IT

Klinkowitz, Jerome, "Walter Abish and the Surface of Life," *GaR* 35, ii (Summer, 1981): 416-20.

ABRAHAMS, PETER (HENRY), 1919-

GENERAL

Abah, Andrew A., "' A Mastery over Experience' (A Perspective of Peter Abrahams' Novels)," *HorizonI* 8 (1972): 71-7, [Not seen.]
Essa, Ahmed, "Postwar South African Fiction in English: Abrahams, Paton, and Gordimer," *DA* 30 (1969): 2020A.
Gakwandi, Shatto A., "Nationalism," *SAfrL* 6 (1977): 43-65. [Not seen.]
Gerard, Albert, "Peter Abrahams, *BO* 2, v-vi (1971): 15-19. [Not seen.]
Heywood, Christopher, "The Novels of Peter Abrahams," *SAfrL* 7 (1971): 157-72. Also in Heywood, C., ed., *Perspectives on African Literature*, 157-72.
Leeman, Clive P., "Art and Politics in the Novels of Peter Abrahams: A Study of His Three Political Novels," *DAI* 39 (1978): 3600A.
Maes-Jelinek, Hena, "Race Relationship and Identity in Peter Abrahams's 'Pluralia'," *ES* 50, i (Feb., 1969): 106-12.
Ogungbesan, Kolawole, "A Long Way from Vrededorp: The Reception of Peter Abrahams's Ideas," *RAL* 11, ii (1980): 187-205.
_____, "The Political Novels of Peter Abrahams," *Phylon* 34, iv (Dec., 1973): 419-32. Also in *PA* 83 (Summer, 1972): 33-50.
_____, *Writing Of Peter Abrahams*.
Wannenburgh, A., "Peter Abrahams in Context," *SAfrO* 101 (1971) 181-3.

MINE BOY

Larson, Charles R., "Characters and Modes of Characterization," *Emergence of African Fiction*, 162-6.
MINE BOY. (Study Guide-African Novels, D1 & E2.) Tabora, Tanzania: TMP Book Dept., 1975.
Ogungbesan, K., Writing of Peter Abrahams, 38-52.
Parasuram, A. N., *Guide to Peter Abrahams: MINE BOY*, Madras, Minerva, 1977.
Wade, M., *Peter Abrahams*, 26-48.
Wade, Michael, "South Africa's First Proletarian Writer," in Parker, K., ed., *South African Novel in English*, 95-113.

A NIGHT OF THEIR OWN

Ogungbesan, Kolawole, "The Political Novels of Peter Abrahams," *Phylon* 34, iv (Dec., 1973): 422-6. Also in *PA* 83 (Summer, 1972): 37-42.
_____, *Writing of Peter Abrahams*, 117-30.
Wade, M., *Peter Abrahams*, 153-73.

THE PATH OF THUNDER

Heywood, Christopher, "The Novels of Peter Abrahams," in Heywood, C., ed., *Perspectives on African Literature*, 165-7. From Heywood, Christopher, "The Novels of Peter Abrahams," *SAfrL* 7 (1971): 165-7.
Ogunbesan, Kolawole, "Peter Abrahams's THE PATH OF THUNDER: The Hope Next Time," *ReAL* 6, ii (Fall, 1972): 15-26.
_____, *Writing of Peter Abrahams*, 53-67.
Wade, M., *Peter Abrahams*, 49-73.

SONG OF THE CITY

Heywood, Christopher, "The Novels of Peter Abrahams," *SAfrL* 7 (1971): 160-2. Also in Heywood, Christopher, "The Novels of Peter Abrahams," in Heywood, C., ed., *Perspectives on African Literature*, 160-2.
Ogungbesan, K., *Writing of Peter Abrahams*, 24-37.
Wade, M., *Peter Abrahams*, 14-25.

THIS ISLAND NOW

Ogungbesan, Kolawole, "The Political Novels of Peter Abrahams," *Phylon* 34, iv (Dec., 1973): 426-31. Also in *PA* 83 (Summer, 1972): 42-8.
_____, "The Politics of THIS ISLAND NOW," *JCL* 8, i (June, 1973): 33-41.
_____, *Writing of Peter Abrahams*, 131-46.
Wade, M., *Peter Abrahams*, 174-96.

WILD CONQUEST

Ogungbesan, Kolawole, "Peter Abrahams's WILD CONQUEST," 113-69 in Dept. of English. Ahmadu Bello Univ., Zaria, Nigeria, *Work in Progress: I*, Zaria, Nigeria: Ahmadu Bello Univ., 1972.
_____, "Peter Abrahams's WILD CONQUEST: In the Beginning Was Conflict," *LAAW* 29 (1976): 19-21. Also in *SBL* 4, ii (Summer, 1973): 11-20.
_____, *Writing of Peter Abrahams*, 68-84.
Wade, M., *Peter Abrahams*, 74-97, 201-22.

A WREATH FOR UDOMO

Farid, Maher S., "A WREATH FOR UDOMO," *LAAW* 14 (1972): 180-3.

Gakwandi, S. A., *Novel and Contemporary Experience in Africa*, 43-56.

Gecau, James, "The Various Levels of Betrayal in A WREATH FOR UDOMO," *Busara* 2, i (1969): 4-10. Also in Wanjala, C., ed., *Standpoints on African Literature*, 344-60.

Griffiths, Gareth, "The Language of Disillusion in the African Novel," in Rutherford, A., ed., *Common Wealth*, 62-5.

Lintono-Umeh, Marie, "The African Heroine," in Bell, R. P., et al., eds., *Sturdy Black Bridges*, 40-2.

Maduka, Chukwudi T., "Colonialism, Nation-Building and the Revolutionary Intellectual in Peter Abrahams's A WREATH FOR UDOMO," *Jour. of So. African Affairs* 2, ii (1977): 254-7.

————, "Humanism and the South African Writer: Peter Abrahams' A WREATH FOR UDOMO," *Umoja* 2, i (1977): 17-31.

————, "Limitation and Possibility: The Intellectual as a Hero-Type in Peter Abrahams' A WREATH FOR UDOMO," *ZRL* 24, ii (1981): 51-60.

Ogungbesan, Kolawole, "The Political Novels of Peter Abrahams," *Phylon* 34, iv (Dec., 1973): 420-2.

————, *Writing of Peter Abrahams*, 99-116.

Scanlon, Paul A., "Dream and Reality in Abraham's A WREATH FOR UDOMO," *Obsidian* 6, i-2 (1980): 25-32.

Wade, M., *Peter Abrahams*, 132-52.

BIBLIOGRAPHY

Ogungbesan, Kolawole, "Peter Abrahams: A Selected Bibliography," *WLWE* 13, ii (Nov., 1974): 184-90.

ACHEBE, CHINUA, 1930-

GENERAL

Abanime, Emeka P., "Warfare in the Novels of Chinua Achebe," *PA* 111 (Summer, 1979): 90-100.

Abrahams, Cecil A., "Achebe, Ngugi and La Guma: Commitment and the Traditional Storyteller," *Mana Rev.* (Sura) 2, i (1977): 11-24. [Not seen.]

Adebayo, 'Tunji, "The Past and the Present in Chinua Achebe's Novels," *IfoAS* 1, i (1974): 66-84.

————, "The Writer and the West African Present: Achebe's Crusade Against Cynicism and Apathy," *AfrSAWIB* 7 (1974): 3-16. [Not seen.]

Agetua, J., ed., *Critics on Chinua Achebe*.

Agetua, John, "Interview with Professor Chinua Achebe August 16, 1976, in Agetua, J., ed., *Critics on Chinua Achebe*, 29-45.

Anagbogu, P.W.N., "Titans in Achebe's Trilogy," *Abraka Quart.* 1, ii (1976): 77-81. [Not seen.]

Angogo, R., "Achebe and the English Language," *Busara* 7, ii (1975): 1-14.

Bashier, Mubarak, "Cinua Achebe: An Individual," *Sudanow* 2, x (1977): 56.

Baugh, Lawrence E., "An Interview with Chinua Achebe," *Drum* 5, iii (1974): 1822.

Bottacher, Karl H., "Narrative Technique in Achebe's Novels," *JNALA* 13/14 (1972): 1-12. [Not seen.]

Brown, Lloyd W., "Cultural Norms and Modes of Perception in Achebe's Fiction," *RAL* 3, i (Spring, 1972): 21-35. Also in Innes, C. L., and B. Lindfors, eds., *Critical Perspectives on Chinua Achebe*, 22-36. Also in Lindfors, B., ed., *Critical Perspectives on Nigerian Literatures*, 131-45.

————, "The Historical Sense: T. S. Eliot and Two African Writers," *Conch*, 3, i (Mar., 1971): 59-70.

Carroll, D., *Chinua Achebe*. (1970)

————, *Chinua Achebe*. (1980)

Chargois, Josephine A., "Two Views of Black Alienation: A Comparative Study of Chinua Achebe and Ralph Ellison," *DAI* 34 (1974): 7742A (Ind.).

Chinweizu, "An Interview with Chinua Achebe," *Okike* 20 (Dec., 1981): 19-32.

Chukwukere, B. I., "The Problem of Language in African Creative Writing," *ALT* 3 (1969): 15-26.

Colmer, Rosemary, "The Critical Generation," *Ash Mag.* (Adelaide)

Cott, Jonathan, "Chinua Achebe: At the Crossroads," *Parabola* 6, ii (May, 1981): 30-9. [Interview.]

Davidson, Jim, "Interview: Chinua Achebe," *Meanjin* 39, i (1980): 35-47.

Echeruo, M. J. C., "Chinua Achebe" in King, B., and K. Ogungbesan, eds., *Celebration of Black and African Writing*, 150-63.

Egblewogbe, E. Y., *Folklore in the Novels of Chinua Achebe: An Ethnolinguistic Approach*, Bloomington, IN: Folklore Pubns. Group, 1979.

Egudu, R. N., "Achebe and the Igbo Narrative Tradition," *RAL* 12, i (Spring, 1981): 43-54.

Eko, Ebele, "Chinua Achebe and His Critics: Reception of His Novels in English and American Reviews," *SBL* 6, iii (Fall, 1975): 14-20.

Emenyonu, Ernest and Pat, "Achebe: Accountable to Our Society," *AfricaR* 17, v (May, 1972): 21, 23, 25-7. [Interview.]

Enekwe, Ossie O., "Dialogue with Chinua Achebe," *New Culture* (Ibadan).

Evalds, Victoria K., "An Interview with Chinua Achebe," *SBL* 8, i (1977): 16-20.

Ferris, William R., Jr., "Folklore and the African Novelist: Achebe and Tutuola," *JAF* 86 (Jan.-Mar., 1973): 25-36.

Firebaugh, Joseph J., "Chinua Achebe and the Plural Society," *Jour. of African-Afro-American Affairs* 1, i (1977): 66-87. [Not seen.]

Gachukia, Eddah W., "Chinua Achebe and Tradition," in Wanjala, C. L., ed., *Standpoints on African Literature*, 172-87.

Gere, Anne R., "West African Oratory and the Fiction of Chinua Achebe and T. M. Aluko," *DAI* 35 (1975): 4519A.

Gillard, G. M., "Center and Periphery in Achebe's Novels," *LHY* 21, i (Jan., 1980): 146-54.

Gowda, H. H. Anniah, "The Novels of Chinua Achebe," *LHY* 14, ii (July, 1973): 3-9.

Griffiths, Gareth, "Language and Action in the Novels of Chinua Achebe," *ALT* 5 (1971): 88-105. Also in Innes, C. L., and B. Lindfors, eds., *Critical Perspectives on Chinua Achebe*, 67-83.

Harlech-Jones, Brian, "The Owner Has Noticed: Achebe and the Roots of Corruption," *Communique* (Pietersburg) 6, i (1981): 35-48. [Not seen.]

Hayes, Suzanne, "An Interview with Chinua Achebe: Adelaide, 1980," *NLRev* 11 (Nov., 1982): 43-52.

Innes, C. L., and B. Lindfors, eds., *Critical Perspectives on Chinua Achebe.*

Innes, Catherine L., "Through the Looking Glass: Achebe, Synge Cultural Nationalism," *DAI* 34 (1974): 7234A. (Cornell.)

"An Interview," *Pan African Book World* (Enugu) 1, i (Aug., 1981): 1-3, 5-7.

"An Interview with Chinua Achebe," *TLS* 4117 (Feb. 26, 1982): 209.

Irele, Abiola, "The Tragic Conflict in the Novels of Chinua Achebe," *BO* 17 (June, 1965): 24-32. Also in Beier, Ulli, ed., *Introduction to African Literature: An Anthology of Critical Writing from "Black Orpheus,"* London: Longmans; Evanston: Northwestern Un. Pr., 1967, 167-78. Also in Innes, C. L., and B. Lindfors, eds., *Critical Perspectives on Chinua Achebe*, 10-21.

Jervis, Steven, "Tradition and Change in Hardy and Achebe," *BO* 2, v-vi (1971): 31-8. [Not seen.]

Johnson, John W., "Folklore in Achebe's Novels," *NewL* 40, iii (Spring, 1974): 95-107.

Jones, Rhonda, "Art and Social Responsibility: Two Paths to Commitment," *Ufahamu* 6, ii (1976): 119-31.

Kemoli, A[rthur] M., "The Novels of Chinua Achebe: A Prophecy of Violence," *Joliso* 2, i (1974): 47-66.

Killam, G. D., "Chinua Achebe's Novels," *SR* 79, iv (Autumn, 1971): 514-41.

_____, *Novels of Chinua Achebe.*

King, B., *New English Literatures*, 65-77.

Kjangonè-Bi, N., "Cultural Changes in Achebe's Novels," *LHY* 21, i (Jan., 1980): 156-66.

Klima, Vladimir, "Chinua Achebe, Novels," *PP* 12 (1969): 32-4.

Larson, Charles B., "Characters and Modes of Characterization," *Emergence of African Fiction*, 147-55.

Laurence, Margaret, "The Thickets of Our Separateness," *Long Drums and Cannons*, 97-125.

Lawson, William, "Chinua Achebe in New England: An Interview," *Yardbird Reader* 4 (1975): 99-110.

L. B., "Giving Writers a Voice," *WA* 3334 (June 22, 1981): 1405-7. [Interview.]

Lee, Mary H., "Ethnographic Statement in the Nigerian Novel, with Special Reference to Pidgin," 295-302 in Hancock, Ian F., Edgar Palome, Morris Goodman, and Bernd Heine, eds., *Readings in Creole Studies*, Ghent: Story-Scientia, 1979.

Leslie, Omolara, "Chinua Achebe: His Vision and His Craft," *BO* 2, vii (1972): 34-41. [Not seen.]

_____, "Nigeria, Alienation and the Novels of Achebe," *PA* 84 (1972): 99-108. Also in *BlackW* 22, viii (June, 1973): 34-43.

Lindfors, Bernth, "Achebe on Commitment and African Writers," *AfricaR* 15, iii (1970): 16-18. [Interview.]

_____, "Achebe's African Parable," *PA* 66 (1968): 130-6.

_____, "Achebe's Followers," *RLC* 48 (1974): 569-89.

_____, "Chinua Achebe: An Interview," *SBL* 2, i (Spring, 1971): 1-5.

_____, "Chinua Achebe and the Nigerian Novel," *LAAW* 15 (Jan., 1973): 34-51.

_____, "Chinua Achebe's Proverbs, Part I," *NF* 35 (1970): 180-5. [Not seen.]

_____, "Chinua Achebe's Proverbs," *NF* 36 (1971): 45-8; 90-6. [Not seen.]

_____, "Maxims, Proverbial Phrases, and Other Sententious Sayings in Achebe's Novels," *NF* 36 (1971): 139-43. [Not seen.]

_____, "The Palm Oil with Which Achebe's Words are Eaten," *ALT* 1 (1968): 318. Also in *Folklore in Nigerian Literature*, N.Y.: Africana, 1973, 73-93. Also in Innes, C. L., and B. Lindfors, eds., *Critical Perspectives on Chinua Achebe*, 47-66.

_____, "Styles of Radicalism in Modern African Literature," *Umoja* 2, ii (1975): 48-63. [Not seen.]

Madubuike, Ihechukwu, "Achebe's Ideas on African Literature," *NewL* 40, iv (1974): 79-91. Also in *BlackW* 24, ii (Dec., 1974): 60-70.

_____, "Chinua Achebe: His Ideas on African Literature." *PA* 93 (1975): 140-52. Also in *Renaissance* 2 4 (1975): 14-19.

McCartney, Barney C., "The Traditional Satiric Method and Matter of Wole Soyinka and Chinua Achebe," *DAI* 37 (1976): 2862A-63A.

McDowell, Robert, "Of What is Past, or Passing, or to Come," *SBL* 2, i (Spring, 1971): 9-13.

Middlemann, Michael, "Comments on the Insight Given by Chinua Achebe's Creative Writing into the Last Century of His Society's History," *Janus* (Cape Town) (1979): 37-44. [Not seen.]

Morrell, Karen L., ed., *In Person: Achebe, Awoonar, and Soyinka at the Univ. of Washington,* Seattle: Univ. of Washington African Studies Program, 1975, 33-58.

Nance, Carolyn, "Cosmology in the Novels of Chinua Achebe," *Conch* 3, ii (Sept., 1971): 121-36.

Nandakumar, Prema, "The Theme of Religion in the Fiction of Chinua Achebe," *Jour. of the Karnatak Univ.: Humanities* 20 (1976): 257-64.

Nasser, Merun, "Achebe and His Women: A Social Science Perspective," *AT* 27, iii (1980): 21-8.

Ngugi wa Thiong'o, "Chinua Achebe: A Man of the People," *SAfrL* 4 (1972): 51-4.

Nkosi, Lewis, Donatus Nwoga, Dennis Duerden, and Robert Servmaga, "Chinua Achebe," *SAfrL* 1 (1972): 2-17. [Interviews.]

"The Novelist Chinua Achebe," *LAAW* 30 (Oct.-Dec., 1976): 114-19.

Obilade, Tony, "The Stylistic Function of Pidgin English in African Literature: Achebe and Soyinka," *RAL* 9, iii (1978): 433-44.

Ogbaa, Kalu, "Folkways in Chinua Achebe's Novels," *DAI* 43, iii (Sept., 1982): 799A.

_____, "An Interview with Chinua Achebe," *RAL* 12, i (Spring, 1981): 1-13.

_____, "Names and Naming in Chinua Achebe's Novels," *Names* 28, iv (Dec., 1980): 267-89.

Ogundpipe, Abiodun, "Some Aspects of the Technique of Chinua Achebe," *JNigESA* (1969): 150-2. [Not seen.]

Ogungbesan, Kolawole, "Politics and the African Writer: The Example of Chinua Achebe," *WIP* 2 (1973): 75-93; *AfrSR* 17, i (April, 1974): 43-54. Also in Innes, C. L., and B. Lindfors, eds., *Critical Perspectives on Chinua Achebe*, 37-46.

Okafor, Clement A., "A Sense of History in the Novels of Chinua Achebe," *Jour. of Afr. Studies* 8, ii (Summer, 1981): 50-63.

Okafor, Raymond N., "Alienation in the Novels of Chinua Achebe," *AdUA* 60 (1973): 329-41.

_____, "Individual and Society in Chinua Achebe's Novels," *AdUA* 50 (1972): 219-43.

Okoye, Chukwuma, "Achebe: The Literary Function of Proverbs and Proverbial Sayings in Two Novels," *Lore&L* 2, x (Jan., 1979): 45-63.

Ola, V. U., "Aspects of Development in Chinua Achebe's Treatment of Women," *JEn* 7 (1980): 92-119. [Not seen.]

Olafioye, Tayo, "Chinua Achebe: The African Writer as 'Traditional' Social Critic," *Pacific Coast Africanist Assn. Occasional Paper* 3 (Apr., 1981): 5-6.

Olney, James, "The African Novel in Transition: Chinua Achebe," *SAQ* 70, iii (Summer, 1971): 299-316.

Palangyo, Peter K., "The African Sense of Self with Special Reference to Chinua Achebe," *DAI* 41 (1980): 1589A-90A.

Palmer, Eustace, "Chinua Achebe," *SAfrL* 3 (1979): 63-101. Also in Palmer, E., *Growth of the African Novel*, 63-101.

Peters, J. A., *Dance of Masks*.

Ponnuthurai, Charles S., "The Pessimism of Chinua Achebe," *Crit* 15, iii (1974): 95-109.

Povey, John, "Achebe and Baldwin in C. B. Land—10-4 Good Buddy!!! A Dialogue at the African Literature Association Meeting, Gainesville, Florida, March, 1980," *Pacific Coast Africanist Assn. Occasional Paper*, 3 (Apr., 1981): 7-9.

_____, "The Novels of Chinua Achebe," in King, B., ed., *Introduction to Nigerian Literature*, 97-112.

Ravenscroft, A., *Chinua Achebe*. Also 2nd ed.

Rensburg, A. P. J. van, "Seeking a Better Place," *Donga* 3 (1976): 3-4. [Not seen.]

Rhodes, H. Winston, "Chinua Achebe and Witi Ihimaera," *LHY* 21, i (Jan., 1980): 104-11.

Roscoe, A. A., *Mother is Gold*, 121-31.

Sale, James, "Chinua Achebe, Nigerian Novelist," *QQ* 75, iii (Autumn, 1968): 460-75.

Shelton, Austin J., "Failures and Individualism in Achebe's Stories," *SBL* 2, i (Spring, 1971): 5-9.

_____, "The 'Palm-Oil' of Language: Proverbs in Chinua Achebe's Novels," *MLQ* 30, i (Mar., 1969): 86-111.

Sibley, Francis M., "Tragedy in the Novels of Chinua Achebe," *SHR* 9, iv (Fall, 1975): 359-73.

Soile, 'Sola, "The Myth of the Archetypal Hero in Two African Novelists: Chinua Achebe and James Ngugi," *DAI* 34 (1973): 1296A (Duke).

Subrahmanian, K., "Chinua Achebe on African English," *JES* 10, i (1978): 617-19.

Swados, Harvey, "Chinua Achebe and the Writers of Biafra," *Sarah Lawrence Jnl.* (Spring, 1970): 55-62. Also in *NewL* 40, i (Autumn, 1973): 5-13.

Taiwo, O., *Culture and the Nigerian Novel*, 111-14.

Turkington, Kate, "'This no be them country': Chinua Achebe's Novels," *ESA* 14, ii (Sept., 1971): 205-14.

Umezinwa, Willy A., "The Idiom of Plastic Figures in Chinua Achebe's Novels," *Cahiers des Religions Afr.* 12 (1978): 125-34. [Not seen.]

Vavilov, V. N., "The Books of Nigerian Author Chinua Achebe," in *Africa in Soviet Studies; Annual 1969*, 145-61.

Vincent, Theo, "Register in Achebe," *JNiqESA* 6, i (1974): 95-106. [Not seen.]

Wanjala, Chris L., "Achebe: Teacher and Satirist," in Wanjala, C. L., ed., *Standpoints on African Literature*, 161-71.

Williams, Phillip G., "A Comparative Approach to Afro-American and Neo-African Novels: Ellison and Achebe," *SBL* 7, i (1976): 15-18.

Winters, Marjorie, "Morning Yet on Judgment Day: The Critics of Chinua Achebe," in Parker, C. A., and S. H. Arnold, eds., *When the Drumbeat Changes*, 169-85.

_____, "An Objective Approach to Achebe's Style," *RAL* 12, i (Spring, 1981): 55-68.

Wren, R. M., *Achebe's World*.

Wren, Robert M., "*Ozo* in Chinua Achebe's Novels: The View from the Past," *Nsukka Studies in Afr. Lit.* 3 (1980): 71-80.

_____, "Anticipations of Civil Conflict in Nigerian Novels: Aluko and Achebe," *SBL* 1, ii (Summer, 1970): 21-32.

Wright, Robin, "Chinua Achebe," *BT* 5, ix (1974): 11.

ARROW OF GOD

Anderson, Martha G., and Mary Jo Arnoldi, *Art in Achebe's THINGS FALL APART and ARROW OF GOD*, Bloomington, IN: African Studies Program, 1978.

Arele, Abiola, "Chinua Achebe: The Tragic Conflict in Achebe's Novels, " *BO* 17 (June, 1965): 30-2.

Biani, Sonia, "Three Circles of Reality in Chinua Achebe's ARROW OF GOD," *SRAZ* 33-36 (1972-73): 251-64.

Boafo, Y. S., "ARROW OF GOD: A Case Study of Megalomania," *Asemka* 1, ii (1974): 16-24.

Bonneau, Danielle, "Approaches to Achebe's Language in ARROW OF GOD," *Echos du Commonwealth* (Mont Saint-Aignan, France) 5 (1979-80): 68-88.

Brown, Hugh R., "Africanized Dialogue and Experience in Chinua Achebe's ARROW OF GOD," *DAI* 38 (1978): 5430A-31A.

_____, "Igbo Words for the Non-Igbo: Achebe's Artistry in ARROW OF GOD," *RAL* 12, i (Spring, 1981): 69-85.

Carroll, D., *Chinua Achebe* (1970), 89-118.

_____, *Chinua Achebe* (1980), 88-123.

David, H. Krupa, "The Ibo Society in Achebe's ARROW OF GOD," *JES* 9, ii (1978): 582-5.

Emenyonu, Ernest N., "Ezeulu: The Night Mask Caught Abroad by Day," *PAJ* 4, iv (Fall, 1971): 407-19.

Fabre, Michel, "Chinua Achebe on ARROW OF GOD," *LHY* 21, i (1980): 1-10.

Fido, Elaine, "Time and Colonial History in THINGS FALL APART and ARROW OF GOD," *LHY* 21, i (1980): 64-76.

Gere, Anne R., "An Approach to Achebe's Fiction," *AfricaQ* 16, ii (Oct., 1976): 27-35.

Githae-Mugo, M., *Visions of Africa*, 87-92.

Griffiths, G., *Double Exile*, 20-6.

Griffiths, Gareth, "Language and Action in the Novels of Chinua Achebe," *ALT* 5 (1971): 95-7.

Innes, C. L., "A Source for ARROW OF GOD," *RAL* 9, i (1977): 16-18. Also as Innes, C. L., "A Source for ARROW OF GOD: A Response," in Innes, C. L., and B. Lindfors, eds., *Critical Perspectives on Chinua Achebe*, 244-5.

Iyamabo, Peter, "The Problem of Tragic Responsibility in ARROW OF GOD," *Shuttle* (Lagos) 8 (1980): 40-3.

Jabbi, Bu-Buakei, "Myth and Ritual in ARROW OF GOD," *ALT* 11 (1980): 130-48.

Jones, Eldred D., "Achebe's Third Novel," *JCL* 1 (Sept., 1965): 176-8.

Jordan, John O., "Culture Conflict and Social Change in Achebe's ARROW OF GOD," *Crit* 13, i (1971): 66-82.

Kemoli, A[rthur] M., "The Novels of Chinua Achebe: A Prophecy of Violence," *Joliso* 2, i (1974): 47-66.

Killam, G. D., "Achebe's Aim in ARROW OF GOD," *Echos du Commonwealth* (Mont Saint-Aignan, France) 5 (1979-80): 18-28.

————, "Chinua Achebe's Novels," *SR* 79, iv (Autumn, 1971): 534-9.

————, "Notions of Religion, Alienation, and Archetype in ARROW OF GOD," 152-65 in Smith, Rowland, ed., *Exile and Tradition: Studies in African and Caribbean Literature*, Halifax, Nova Scotia: Dalhousie Un. Pr.; N.Y.: Africana; London: Longmans, 1976.

————, *Novels of Chinua Achebe*, 59-83.

King, Bruce, "The Revised Edition of ARROW OF GOD," *Echos du Commonwealth* (Mont Saint-Aignan, France) 5 (1979-80): 89-98.

Kothandaraman, Bala, "'Where This Rain Began to Fall...': A Reading of ARROW OF GOD," *OJES* 17 (1981): 73-81.

Laurence, Margaret, "The Thickets of Our Separateness," *Long Drums and Cannons*, 111-17.

Lewis, Mary E. B., "Beyond Content in the Analysis of Folklore in Literature: Chinua Achebe's ARROW OF GOD," *RAL* 7 (1976): 44-52.

Lewis, Maureen W., "Priest of a Dead God," *AfrSAWLB* 7 (1974): 39-53.

Lindfors, Bernth, "Ambiguity and Intention in ARROW OF GOD," *Ba Shiru* 5, i (Fall, 1973): 43-8.

————, "The Folktale as Paradigm in Chinua Achebe's ARROW OF GOD," *SBL* 1, i (Spring, 1970): 1-15. Also in Lindfors, B., *Folklore in Nigerian Literature*, 94-102.

————, "The Palm-Oil with which Achebe's Words Are Eaten," *Folkore in Nigerian Literature*, 84-8.

Machila, Blaise N., "Ambiguity in Achebe's ARROW OF GOD," *Kunapipi* 3, i (1981): 119-33.

Mahood, M. M., "Idols of the Den: Achebe's ARROW OF GOD," *Colonial Encounter*, 37-64. Also in Innes, C. L., and B. Lindfors, eds., *Critical Perspectives on Chinua Achebe*, 180-206.

McDaniel, Richard B., "The Python Episodes in Achebe's Novels," *IFR* 3, ii (July, 1976): 100-6.

Melamu, M. J., "The Quest for Power in Achebe's ARROW OF GOD," *ESA* 14, ii (Sept., 1971): 225-40.

Nance, Carolyn, "Cosmology in the Novels of Chinua Achebe," *Conch* 3, ii (Sept., 1971): 128-32.

Nandakumar, Prema, "The Theme of Religion in the Fiction of Chinua Achebe," *Journal of the Karnatak Univ.: Humanities* 20 (1976): 261-2.

Niven, Alastair, "Another Look at ARROW OF GOD," *LHY* 16, ii (1975): 53-68.

Nnolim, Charles E., "A Source for ARROW OF GOD," *RAL* 8 (1977): 1-26. Also in Innes, C. L., and B. Lindfors, eds., *Critical Perspectives on Chinua Achebe*, 219-43.

Nwoga, D. Ibe, "The Igbo World of Achebe's ARROW OF GOD," *RAL* 12, i (Spring, 1981): 14-42.

Obiechina, Emmanuel, "The Human Dimension of History in ARROW OF GOD," in Innes, C. L., and B. Lindfors, eds., *Critical Perspectives on Chinua Achebe*, 170-9.

Ogbaa, Kalu, "Death in African Literature: The Example of Chinua Achebe," *WLWE* 20, ii (Autumn, 1981): 201-13.

Okafor, Clement A., "A Sense of History in the Novels of Chinua Achebe," *Jour. of Afr. Studies* 8, ii (Summer, 1981): 58-60.

Okafor, Raymond N., "Individual and Society in Chinua Achebe's Novels," *AdUA* 5D (1972): 233-7.

Oko, Emelia A., "The Historical Novel of Africa: A Sociological Approach to Achebe's THINGS FALL APART and ARROW OF GOD," *Conch* 6, i-ii (1974): 15-46.

Okoye, Chukwoma, "Achebe: The Literary Function of Proverbs and Proverbial Sayings in Two Novels," *Lore&L* 2, x (Jan., 1979): 45-63.

Palmer, E., *Growth of the African Novel*, 76-101.

Patterson, Ruth, "ARROW OF GOD: C. Achebe's Novel," *EJ* 66 (March, 1977): 64-5.

Peters, J. A., *Dance of Masks*, 115-28.

Ponnuthurai, Charles S., "The Pessimism of Chinua Achebe," *Crit* 15, iii (1974): 98-100.

Povey, John, "The Novels of Chinua Achebe," in King, B., ed., *Introduction to Nigerian Literature*, 106-9.

Ravenscroft, A., *Chinua Achebe*, 24-31. 2nd ed., 23-9.

Sabor, Peter, "'Structural Weaknesses' and Stylistic Revisions in Achebe's ARROW OF GOD," *RAL* 10, iii (1979): 375-9.

Séverac, A., "An Ibo Glossary (of Ibo Words and Phrases Found in Achebe's ARROW OF GOD)," 51-61 in J. P. Petit, ed., *Discourse and Style, II.* (Pubs. de l'Univ. Jean Moulin.) Lyon: L'Hermès, 1980.

Shelton, Austin J., "The 'Palm-Oil' of Language: Proverbs in Chinua Achebe's Novels," *MLQ* 30, i (Mar., 1969): 99-106.

Sibley, Francis M., "Tragedy in the Novels of Chinua Achebe," *SHR* 9, iv (Fall, 1975): 367-70.

Soile, 'Sola, "Tragic Paradox in Achebe's ARROW OF GOD," *Phylon* 37, iii (1976): 283-95.

Taiwo, O., *Culture and the Nigerian Novel*, 132-40.

Tibble, Anne, *African/English Literature*, 108-11. Also in Cooke, M. G., ed., *Modern Black Novelists*, 128-31.

Traore, Ousseynov B., "Aesthetic Ideology and Oral Narrative Paradigms in THINGS FALL APART and ARROW OF GOD," *DAI* 42, x (Apr., 1982): 4448A.

Vargo, Edward P., S.B.D., "Struggling with a Bugaboo: The Priest-Character in Achebe and Greene and Keneally," *FJS* 9 (1976): 1-13 *passim*. Also in Narasimhaiah, C. D., ed., *Awakened Conscience: Studies in Commonwealth Literature*, New Delhi: Sterling Publishers, 1978, 284-94 *passim*.

Vavilov, V. N., in *Africa in Soviet Studies: Annual 1969*, 154-7.

Walsh, W., *Manifold Voice*, 55-61.

Wren, Robert M., "Achebe's Revisions of ARROW OF GOD," *RAL* 7 (1976): 53-8.

————, *Achebe's World*, 105-26.

————, "ARROW OF GOD," in Agetua, J., ed., *Critics on Chinua Achebe*, 5-7. Also in *Afriscope* 5, ix (1975): 43-4. [Concerns revisions in 2nd ed.]

————, "From Ulu to Christ: The Transfer of Faith in Chinua Achebe's ARROW OF GOD," *C&L* 27, ii (Winter, 1978): 28-40.

————, "MISTER JOHNSON and the Complexity of ARROW OF GOD," in Innes, C. L., and B. Lindfors, eds., *Critical Perspectives on Chinua Achebe*, 207-17. Also in Narasimhaiah, C. D., ed., *Awakened Conscience*, 50-62.

A MAN OF THE PEOPLE

Adebayo, Tunji, "The Past and the Present in Chinua Achebe's Novels," *IfeAS* 1, i (1974): 73-9.

Amuzu, Koku, "The Theme of Corruption in A MAN OF THE PEOPLE and THE BEAUTYFUL ONES ARE NOT YET BORN," *Legacy* (Legon) 3, ii (1977): 18-23.

Anozie, Sunday O., "The Problem of Communication in Two West African Novels," *Conch* 2, i (Mar., 1970): 12-20.

Carroll, D., *Chinua Achebe* (1970): 119-45. Also in Innes, C. L., and B. Lindfors, eds., *Critical Perspectives on Chinua Achebe*, 255-78.

_____, *Chinua Achebe* (1980), 124-53.

Ekaney, Nkwelle, "Corruption and Politics in Chinua Achebe's A MAN OF THE PEOPLE: An Assessment," *PA* 104 (1977): 114-26.

Gakwandi, Shatto A., "Disenchantment," *SAfrL* 6 (1977): 66-86. Also in Gakwandi, S. A., *Novel and Contemporary Experience in Africa*, 66-86.

Galparina, Y. L., in *Africa in Soviet Studies: Annual 1969*, 162-6.

Githae-Mugo, M., *Visions of Africa*, 162-71.

Griffiths, G., *Double Exile*, 43-7.

Griffiths, Gareth, "Language and Action in the Novels of Chinua Achebe," *ALT* (1971): 98-104.

Killam, G. D., "Chinua Achebe's Novels," *SR* 79, iv (Autumn, 1971): 539-41.

_____, *Novels of Chinua Achebe*, 84-96.

Laurence, Margaret, "The Thickets of Our Separateness," *Long Drums and Cannons*, 117-22.

Lindfors, Bernth, "Achebe's African Parable," *PA* 66 (1968): 130-6. Also in Innes, C. L., and B. Lindfors, eds., *Critical Perspectives on Chinua Achebe*, 248-54.

_____, "The Palm-Oil with which Achebe's Words Are Eaten," *Folklore in Nigerian Literature*, 88-92.

Maduka, Chukwudi, "Irony and Vision in Achebe's A MAN OF THE PEOPLE," *Ba Shiru* 8, i (1977): 19-30.

Nance, Carolyn, "Cosmology in the Novels of Chinua Achebe," *Conch* 3, ii (Sept., 1971): 133-5.

Nandakumar, Prema, "The Theme of Religion in the Fiction of Chinua Achebe," *Journal of the Karnatak Univ.: Humanities* 20 (1976): 262.

Ngugi wa Thiong'o, "Chinua Achebe: A MAN OF THE PEOPLE," in *Homecoming: Essays on African and Caribbean Literature, Culture and Politics*, London: Heinemann, 1972; N. Y. and Westport, CT: Lawrence Hill, 1973, 51-4. Also in Innes, C. L., and B. Lindfors, eds., *Critical Perspectives on Chinua Achebe*, 279-82.

Obiechina, E. N., "Post-Independence Disillusionment in Three African Novels," *Nsukka Studies in Afr. Lit.*, 1, i (1978): 54-78 *passim*. Also in Lindfors, B., and U. Schild, eds., *Neo-African Literature and Culture*, 119-46 *passim*.

Obumselu, B., "Chinua Achebe's African Aesthetic: A Reconsideration of A MAN OF THE PEOPLE," *Eng. Teachers' Jour.* (Lusaka): 1, ii (1977): 13-20.

Okafor, Clement A., "A Sense of History in the Novels of Chinua Achebe," *Jour. of Afr. Studies* 8, ii (Summer, 1981): 60-2.

Okafor, Raymond N., "Individual and Society in Chinua Achebe's Novels," *AdUA* (1972): 237-42.

Olney, James, "The African Novel in Transition: Chinua Achebe," *SAQ* 70, iii (Summer, 1971): 313-16.

_____, *Tell Me Africa*, 1987-203.

Palmer, E., *Introduction to the African Novel*, 72-84.

Peters, J. A., *Dance of Masks*, 143-58.

Ponnuthurai, Charles S., "The Pessimism of Chinua Achebe," *Crit* 15, iii (1974): 101-5.

Povey, John, "The Novels of Chinua Achebe," in King, B., ed., *Introduction to Nigerian Literature*, 109-12.

Ravenscroft, A., *Chinua Achebe*, 31-6. 2nd ed., 29-34.

Shelton, Austin J., "The 'Palm-Oil' of Language: Proverbs in Chinua Achebe's Novels," *MLQ* 30, i (Mar., 1969): 107-11.

Sibley, Francis M., "Tragedy in the Novels of Chinua Achebe," *SHR* 9, iv (Fall, 1975): 370-2.

Taiwo, O., *Culture and the Nigerian Novel*, 140-7.

Vavilov, V. N., *Africa in Soviet Studies: Annual 1969*, 157-60.

Webb, Hugh, "Drawing the Lines of Battle: A MAN OF THE PEOPLE," *LHY* 21, i (1980): 136-45.

Wren, Robert M., "Achebe's Odili: Hero and Clown," *LHY* 21, i (Jan., 1980): 30-9.

_____, *Achebe's World*, 127-47.

Yankson, Kofi, "The Use of Pidgin in NO LONGER AT EASE and A MAN OF THE PEOPLE," *Asemka* 1, ii (1974): 68-80.

NO LONGER AT EASE

Adebayo, 'Tunji, "The Past and the Present in Chinua Achebe's Novels," *IfeAS* 1, i (1974): 69-73.

Asnani, Skyam M., "Quest for Identity Theme in Three Commonwealth Novels," in Srivatava, A. K., ed., *Alien Voice*, 129-32.

Barthold, B. J., *Black Time*, 139-49.

Beckmann, Susan, "Language as Cultural Identity in Achebe, Ihimaera, Laurence and Atwood," *WLWE* 20, i (Spring, 1981): 121-4.

Carroll, D., *Chinua Achebe* (1970), 65-88.

_____, *Chinua Achebe* (1980), 62-87.

Colmer, Rosemary, " 'The Start of Weeping Is Always Hard': The Ironic Structure of NO LONGER AT EASE," *LHY* 21, i (1980): 121-35.

Cook, David, "Men Fall Apart. A Study of Achebe's NO LONGER AT EASE," *African Literature*, 82-94.

Gakwandi, Shatto A., "The Illusion of Progress," *SAfrL* 6 (1977): 27-42. Also in Gakwandi, S. A., *Novel and Contemporary Experience in Africa*, 27-36.

Gale, Steven H., "The Theme of Emasculation in Chinua Achebe's NO LONGER AT EASE," *PQM* 6, iii-iv (July-Oct., 1981): 146-50.

Griffiths, Gareth, "Language and Action in the Novels of Chinua Achebe," *ALT* 5 (1971): 92-5.

Irele, Abiola, "Chinua Achebe: The Tragic Conflict in Achebe's Novels," *BO* 17 (June, 1965): 28-30.

Killam, G. D., "Chinua Achebe's Novels," *SR* 79, iv (Autumn, 1971): 531-4.

_____, *Novels of Chinua Achebe*, 35-58.

Laurence, Margaret, "The Thickets of Our Separateness," *Long Drums and Cannons*, 107-11.

Lindfors, B., "The Palm-Oil with which Achebe's Words Are Eaten," *Folklore in Nigerian Literature*, 81-4.

Mills, P., *Notes on Chinua Achebe's NO LONGER AT EASE*, Nairobi: Heinemann Educ. Books, 1974.

Moore, G., "Chinua Achebe: Nostalgia and Realism," *Seven African Writers*, 66-71.

Mugo-Githae, M., *Visions of Africa*, 154-61.

Nance, Carolyn, "Cosmology in the Novels of Chinua Achebe," *Conch* 3, ii (Sept., 1971): 132-3.

Nandakumar, Prema, "The Theme of Religion in the Fiction of Chinua Achebe," *Journal of the Karnatak Univ.: Humanities* 20 (1976): 260-1.

Nyborg, Aina, "'Whenever Something Stands, Something Else Will Stand Beside It': Some Aspects of the Concept of Duality as Expressed in Chinua Achebe's Novels THINGS FALL APART and NO LONGER AT EASE" in Grantqvist, R., ed., *Report of Workshop on World Literatures Written in English ...*, 24-37.

Obiechina, Emmanuel, "Chinua Achebe's NO LONGER AT EASE," *Okike* 13 (1979): 124-44.

Okafor, Clement A., "A Sense of History in the Novels of Chinua Achebe," *Jour. of Afr. Studies* 8, ii (Summer, 1981): 56-8.

Okafor, Raymond N., "Individual and Society in Chinua Achebe's Novels," *AdUA* 5D (1972): 221-32.

Olney, James, "The African Novel in Transition: Chinua Achebe," *SAQ* 70, iii (Summer, 1971): 309-13.

_____, *Tell Me Africa*, 181-97.

Palmer, E., *Growth of the African Novel*, 76-82.

_____, *Introduction to the African Novel*, 63-72.

Peek, Andrew, "Betrayal and the Question of Affirmation in Chinua Achebe's NO LONGER AT EASE," *LHY* 21, i (1980): 112-20.

Peters, J. A. *Dance of Masks*, 129-42.

Ponnuthurai, Charles S. "The Pessimism of Chinua Achebe," *Crit* 15, iii (1974): 100-1.

Povey, John, "The Novels of Chinua Achebe," in King, B., ed., *Introduction to Nigerian Literature*, 103-6.

Ravenscroft, A., *Chinua Achebe*, 18-24. 2nd ed. 17-23.

Riddy, Felicity, "Language as a Theme in NO LONGER AT EASE," *JCL* 9 (July, 1970): 38-47. Also in Innes, C. L., and B. Lindfors, eds., *Critical Perspectives on Chinua Achebe*, 150-9.

Shelton, Austin J., "The 'Palm-Oil' of Language: Proverbs in Chinua Achebe's Novels," *MLQ* 30, i (Mar., 1969): 92-9.

Sibley, Francis M., "Tragedy in the Novels of Chinua Achebe," *SHR* 9, iv (Fall, 1975): 365-7.

Taiwo, O., *Culture and the Nigerian Novel*, 124-31.

_____, *Introduction to West African Literature*, 134-51.

Tibble, Anne, *African/English Literature*, 106-8. Also in Cooke, M. G., ed., *Modern Black Novelists*, 126-8.

Vavilov, V. N., in *Africa in Soviet Studies: Annual 1969*, 150-4.

Walsh, W., *Manifold Voice*, 53-5.

Wilson, Roderick, "Eliot and Achebe: An Analysis of Some Formal and Philosophical Qualities of NO LONGER AT EASE," *ESA* 14, ii (Sept., 1971): 215-23. Also in Innes, C. L., and B. Lindfors, eds., *Critical Perspectives on Chinua Achebe*, 160-8.

Wren, R. M., *Achebe's World*, 61-76.

Yankson, Kofi, "The Use of Pidgin in NO LONGER AT EASE and A MAN OF THE PEOPLE," *Asemka* 1, ii (1974): 68-80.

THINGS FALL APART

Abrahams, Cecil A., "George Lamming and Chinua Achebe: Tradition and the Literary Chroniclers," in Narasimhaiah, C. D., ed., *Awakened Conscience*, 294-306.

_____, "Margaret Laurence and Chinua Achebe: Commonwealth Storytellers," *ACLALSB* 5, iii (1980): 74-85.

Ackley, Donald G., "The Male-Female Motif in THINGS FALL APART," *SBL* 5, i (Spring, 1974): 1-6.

Adelusi, Oladapo, and S. Adejumo, *THINGS FALL APART: Notes and Essays*, Ibadan: Onibonoje P., 1972.

Anderson, Martha G., and Mary Jo Arnoldi, *Art in Achebe's THINGS FALL APART and ARROW OF GOD*, Bloomington, IN: African Studies Program, 1978.

Barthold, B. J., *Black Time*, 56-62.

Beckmann, Susan, "Language as Cultural Identity in Achebe, Ihimaera, Laurence and Atwood," *WLW* 20, i (August, 1981): 117-21.

Brown, Lloyd W., "Cultural Norms and Modes of Perception in Achebe's Fiction," *RAL* 3 (1972): 21-35. Also in Lindfors, B., ed., *Critical Perspectives on Nigerian Literatures*, 131-45.

Brown, Raymond, "Aspects of THINGS FALL APART," *Mambo* 1 (Nov., 1974): 11-13.

Carroll, D., *Chinua Achebe* (1970), 36-64.

_____, *Chinua Achebe* (1980), 30-61.

Carter, D., "Probing Identities: UNTOUCHABLE, THINGS FALL APART and THIS EARTH, MY BROTHER..." *LCrit* 14, iii (1979): 14-29.

Champion, Ernest A., "The Story of a Man and His People: Chinua Achebe's THINGS FALL APART," *NALF* 8 (1974): 272-7.

Chukwukere, B. I., "The Problem of Language in African Creative Writing," *ALT* 3 (1969): 18-22.

Cook, David, "The Centre Holds. A Study of Chinua Achebe's THINGS FALL APART," *African Literature*, 65-81.

Coulibaly, Yedieti E., "Weeping Gods: A Study of Cultural Disintegration in James Baldwin's GO TELL IT ON THE MOUNTAIN and Chinua Achebe's THINGS FALL APART," *AdUA* 90 (1976): 531-42.

Dedenuola, J., "The Structure of Achebe's THINGS FALL APART," *NigM* 103 (1969-70): 638-9.

Ezuma, Ben, *Questions and Answers on THINGS FALL APART with a List of Suggested Questions, Phrases and Difficult Words Fully Explained*, Onitsha: Tabansi Printing Enterprises, n.d.

Fido, Elaine, "Time and Colonial History in THINGS FALL APART and ARROW OF GOD," *LHY* 21, i (180): 64-76.

Fraser, Robert, "A Note on Okonkwo's Suicide," *Kunapipi* 1, i (1979): 108-13.

Gillard, G. M., "Centre and Periphery in Achebe's Novels," *LHY* 21, i (Jan., 1980): 146-51.

Githae-Mugo, M., *Visions of Africa*, 28-39.

Gowda, H. H. Anniah, "Ahmed Ali's TWILIGHT IN DELHI (1940) and Achebe's THINGS FALL APART (1958)," *LHY* 21, i (1980): 11-18. Also in Srivastava, A. K., ed., *Alien Voice*, 53-60.

Griffiths, G., *Double Exile*, 12-19.

_____, "Language and Action in the Novels of Chinua Achebe," *ALT* 5 (1971): 88-92.

Guha, Naresh, "The Design of a Novel from Africa," *JJCL* 16/17 (1978/79): 26-37.

Heywood, Christopher, "Surface and Symbol in THINGS FALL APART," *JNigESA* 2 (Nov., 1967): 41-6.

Innes, C. L., "Language, Poetry and Doctrine in THINGS FALL APART," in Innes, C. L., and B. Lindfors, eds., *Critical Perspectives on Chinua Achebe*, 111-25.

Irele, Abiola, "Chinua Achebe: The Tragic Conflict in Achebe's Novels," *BO* 17 (June, 1965): 24-8.

Iyasere, Solomon O., "Narrative Techniques in THINGS FALL APART," *NewL* 40, iii (Spring, 1974): 73-93. Also in Innes, C. L., and B. Lindfors, eds., *Critical Perspectives on Chinua Achebe*, 92-110.

Jabbi, Bu-Buakei, "Fire and Transition in THINGS FALL APART," *Obsidian* 1, iii (1975): 22-36; *SPL&S* 1 (1976): 64-84. Also in Innes, C. L., and B. Lindfors, eds., *Critical Perspectives on Chinua Achebe*, 135-47.

John, Elerius E., "Chinua Achebe: THINGS FALL APART," *Recherche, Pédagogie et Culture* 33 (1978): 50-2. [Not seen.]

Jones, Eldred, "A Comment on THINGS FALL APART," in Moore, Gerald, ed., *African Literature and the Universities*, Ibadan: Ibadan Univ. Pr., 1965, 91-5.

_____, "Language and Theme in THINGS FALL APART," *REL* 5, iv (Oct., 1964): 39-43.

Kanaganayakam, C., "Woolf and Achebe: A Comparative Note on Some of the Themes of THE VILLAGE IN THE JUNGLE and THINGS FALL APART," *English Bulletin* 4 (1980): 21-7.

Kemoli, A[rthur] M., "The Novels of Chinua Achebe: A Prophecy of Violence," *Joliso* 2, i (1974): 47-66.

Killam, G. D., "Chinua Achebe's Novels," *SR* 79, iv (Autumn, 1971): 514-30.

_____, *Novels of Chinua Achebe*, 13-34.

King, B., *New English Literatures*, 65-70.

Kronenfeld, J. Z., "The 'Communalistic' African and the 'Individualistic' Westerner: Some Comments on Misleading Generalizations in Western Criticism of Soyinka and Achebe," *KAL* 6, ii (Fall, 1975): 199-225. Also in Lindfors, B., ed., *Critical Perspectives on Nigerian Literatures*, 260-9.

Landrum, Roger L., "Chinua Achebe and the Aristotelian Concept of Tragedy," *BARev* 1, i (Spring, 1970): 22-30.

Larson, Charles R., "Chinua Achebe's THINGS FALL APART: The Archetypal African Novel," *Emergence of African Fiction*, 27-65.

Laurence, Margaret, "The Thickets of our Separateness," *Long Drums and Cannons*, 99-107.

Leach, Josephine, "A Study of Chinua Achebe's THINGS FALL APART in Mid-America," *EJ* 60, viii (Nov., 1971): 1052-6.

Lindfors, Bernth, "Chinua Achebe and the Nigerian Novel," *LAAW* 15 (Jan., 1973): 38-46. Also in Páricsy, P., ed., *Studies in Modern Black African Literature*, 33-41.

_____, "The Palm-Oil with which Achebe's Words Are Eaten," *Folklore in Nigerian Literature*, 77-81.

Macdonald, Bruce F., "Chinua Achebe and the Structure of Colonial Tragedy," *LHY* 21, i (Jan., 1980): 50-63.

McDaniel, Richard B., "The Python Episodes in Achebe's Novels," *IFR* 3, ii (July, 1976): 100-6.

Meyers, Jeffrey, "Culture and History in THINGS FALL APART," *Crit* 11, i (1968): 25-32.

Moore, G., "Chinua Achebe: Nostalgia and Realism," *Seven African Writers*, 58-66.

Moore, Gerald, *THINGS FALL APART*, London: Heinemann Educational Books for British Broadcasting Corp. and British Council on Behalf of the British Ministry of Overseas Development, 1974.

Nance, Carolyn, "Cosmology in the Novels of Chinua Achebe," *Conch* 3, ii (Sept., 1971): 124-8.

Nandakumar, Prema, "The Theme of Religion in the Fiction of Chinua Achebe," *Journal of the Karnatak Univ.: Humanities* 20 (1976): 258-60.

Nnolim, Charles E., "Achebe's THINGS FALL APART: An Igbo National Epic," *BARev* 2, i-88 (Spring-Summer, 1971): 55-60.

Nwoga, D. Ibe, "The Igbo World of Achebe's ARROW OF GOD," *RAL* 12, i (Spring, 1981): 14-42.

Nyborg, Aina, "'Whenever Something Stands, Something Else Will Stand Beside It': Some Aspects of the Concept of Duality as Expressed in Chinua Achebe's Novels THINGS FALL APART and NO LONGER AT EASE," in Grantqvist, R., ed., *Report of Workshop on World Literatures Written in English ...*, 24-37.

Obiechina, Emmanuel, "Structure and Significance in Achebe's THINGS FALL APART," *EinA* 2, ii (1975): 39-44.

Ogunmola, M. O., *Study Notes on Chinua Achebe's THINGS FALL APART*, Ibadan: Onibonoje Pr., 1969; Oyo: Alliance W. Afr. Pub., n.d.

Okafor, Clement A., "A Sense of History in the Novels of Chinua Achebe," *Jour. of Afr. Studies* 8, ii (Summer, 1981): 54-6.

Okafor, Raymond N., "Individual and Society in Chinua Achebe's Novels," *AdUA* 5D (1972): 221-32.

Oko, Emelia A., "The Historical Novel of Africa: A Sociological Approach to Achebe's THINGS FALL APART and ARROW OF GOD," *Conch* 6, i-ii (1974): 15-46.

Okoye, Chukwuma, "Achebe: The Literary Functions of Proverbs and Proverbial Sayings in Two Novels," *Lore&L* 2, x (Jan., 1979): 45-63.

Olney, James, "The African Novel in Transition: Chinua Achebe," *SAQ* 70, iii (Summer, 1971): 302-9.

_____, *Tell Me Africa*, 166-81.

Palmer, E., *Growth of the African Novel*, 48-63.

Patullo, Patrick J., "Chinua Achebe's THINGS FALL APART," in K. L. Goodwin, ed., *Commonwealth Literature in the Curriculum*, St. Lucia: So. Pacific Assn. for Commonwealth Lit. and Lang. Studies, 1980, 29-35.

Peters, J. A., *Dance of Masks*, 93-114.

Ponnuthurai, Charles S., "The Pessimism of Chinua Achebe," *Crit* 15, iii (1974): 96-8.

Povey, John, "The Novels of Chinua Achebe," in King, B., ed., *Introduction to Nigerian Literature*, 99-103.

Priebe, Richard, "Fate and Divine Justice in THINGS FALL APART," in Lindfors, B., and U. Schild, eds., *Neo-African Literature and Culture*, 159-66.

Ravenscroft, A., *Chinua Achebe*, 8-18. 2nd ed., 8-17.

Rice, Michael, "THINGS FALL APART: A Critical Appreciation," *CRUX* 10, ii (1976): 33-40.

Robertson, P. J. M., "THINGS FALL APART and HEART OF DARKNESS: A Creative Dialogue," *IFR* 7 (1980): 106-11.

Scheub, Harold, "'When a Man Fails Alone'," *PA* 74 (Summer, 1970): 61-89.

Shelton, Austin J., "The Offended *Chi* in Achebe's Novels," *Transition* 3, xiii (Mar.-Apr., 1964): 36-7.

_____, "The 'Palm-Oil' of Language: Proverbs in Chinua Achebe's Novels," *MLQ* 30, i (Mar., 1969): 88-92.

Sibley, Francis M., "Tragedy in the Novels of Chinua Achebe," *SHR* 9, iv (Fall, 1975): 360-5.

Simms, Norman, "Noetics and Poetics: Studying and Appreciating Chinua Achebe's THINGS FALL APART in New Zealand," *Chandrabhg* 5 (Summer, 1981): 57-66.

Stock, A. G., "Yeats and Achebe," *JCL* No. 5 (1968): 105-11. Also in Innes, C. L., and B. Lindfors, eds., *Critical Perspectives on Chinua Achebe*, 86-91.

Taiwo, O , *Culture and the Nigerian Novel*, 114-24.

Taylor, Richard, "Japanese Noh Drama in European and African Dress," *KompH* 4 (1981): 81-101. [Not seen.]

Tibble, Anne, *African/English Literature*, 102-7. Also in Cooke, M. G., ed., *Modern Black Novelists*, 122-6.

Traore, Ousseynou B., "Aesthetic Ideology and Oral Narrative Paradigms in THINGS FALL APART and ARROW OF GOD," *DAI* 42, x (Apr., 1982): 4448A.

Turkington, Kate, *Chinua Achebe: THINGS FALL APART*. (Studies in Eng. Lit. 66.) London: Arnold, 1977.

Urs, S. N. Vikramraj, "THINGS FALL APART: A Novel from the 'Dark' Continent," *Commonwealth Quart.* (New Delhi) 1, i (1976): 28-34.

Uwajeh, P. N., "Chinua Achebe's *Okonkwo*: Individual Stasis versus Social Dynamics," *Neohelicon* 6, ii (1978): 141-52.

Vavilov, V. N., in *Africa in Soviet Studies: Annual, 1969*, 145-50.

Walsh, W., *Manifold Voice*, 50-5.

Wattie, Nelson, "The Community as Protagonist in the Novels of Chinua Achebe and Witi Ihmaere," in Massa, D., ed., *Individual and Community in Commonwealth Literature*, 69-74.

Weinstock, Donald J., "Achebe's Christ-Figure," *JNALA* 5/6/ (1968): 20-6. Also in Okpaku, J. O., ed., *New African Literature and the Arts*, v. 2., 56-65.

_____, and Cathy Ramadan, "Symbolic Structure in THINGS FALL APART," *Crit* 11, i (1969): 33-41. Also in Innes, C. L., and B. Lindfors, eds., *Critical Perspectives on Chinua Achebe*, 126-34.

_____, "The Two Swarms of Locusts: Judgement by Indirection in THINGS FALL APART," *SBL* 2, i (Spring, 1971): 14-19.

Winters, Marjorie, "An Objective Approach to Achebe's Style," *RAL* 12, i (Spring, 1981): 55-68.

Wren, R. M., *Achebe's World*, 23-59.

Wren, Robert M., *Chinua Achebe, THINGS FALL APART*, London: Longman, 1980.

Wynter, Sylvia, "History, Ideology, and the Reinvention of the Past in Achebe's THINGS FALL APART and Laye's THE DARK CHILD," *MV* 2, i (1978): 43-61.

BIBLIOGRAPHY

Anafulu, Joseph C., comp., "Chinua Achebe: A Preliminary Checklist," *Nsukka Library Notes* 3 (1978): 1-52. [Not seen.]

Evalds, Victoria K., "Chinua Achebe: Bio-Bibliography and Selected Criticism, 1970-1975," *AfrLJ* 8, ii (1977): 101-30.

Hanna, S. J., "Achebe: A Bibliography," *SBL* 2, i (Spring, 1971): 20-1.

Innes, C. L., and B. Lindfors, eds., *Critical Perspectives on Chinua Achebe*, 294-310.

Lindfors, Bernth, "A Checklist of Works by and about Chinua Achebe," *Obsidian* 4, i (Spring, 1978): 103-17.

_____, "Recent Scholarship on Achebe," *LHY* 21, i (Jan., 1980): 181-6.

McDaniel, Richard B., "An Achebe Bibliography," *WLWE* No. 20 (Nov., 1971): 15-24.

ADAMS, RICHARD, 1920-

SHARDIK

Chapman, Edgar L., "The Shaman as Hero and Spiritual Leader: Richard Adams' Mythmaking in WATERSHIP DOWN and SHARDIK," *Mythlore* 5, ii (Aug., 1978): 7-11.

Hammond, Graham, "Trouble with Rabbits," *CLEd* 12 (1973): 48-63.

Nelson, Marie, "Non-Human Speech in the Fantasy of C. S. Lewis, J. R. R. Tolkien and Richard Adams," *Mythlore* 5, i (May, 1978): 38-9.

Pawling, Chris, "WATERSHIP DOWN, or Rolling Back the Sixties' Youth-Culture," *Kingfisher* 1, i (1978): 27-35.

Sell, Roger D., "WATERSHIP DOWN and the Rehabilitation of Pleasure," *NM* 82, i (1981): 28-35.

AGEE, JAMES, 1909-1955

GENERAL

Barson, Alfred T., "James Agee: A Study of Artistic Consciousness," *DAI* 30 (1970): 5438A (Mass.)

Behar, Jack, "James Agee: The World of His Work," *DA* 24 (1964): 4690 (Ohio State).

Broughton, George, and R. Panthea, "Agee and Autonomy," *SHR* 4, ii (Spring, 1970): 101-11.

Burger, Nash K., "A Story to Tell: Agee, Wolfe, Faulkner," *SAQ* 63 (196): 32-43.

Concannon, Jeanne M., "The Poetry and Fiction of James Agee: A Critical Analysis," *DAI* 30 (1979): 2962A-63A (Minn.)

Doty, Mark A., "'Tell Me Who I Am': James Agee's Search for Selfhood," *DAI* 39 (1978): 883A.

Eyster, Warren, "Conversations with James Agee," *SoR* 17, ii (April, 1981): 346-57.

Fitzgerald, Robert, "James Agee: A Memoir," *KR* 30 (1968): 587-624. Also (expanded) in Fitzgerald, R., "Introduction," *Collected Short Prose of James Agee*, Boston: Houghton, 1969.

Frohock, W. M., "James Agee: The Question of Unkept Promise," *SWR* 42 (Summer, 1957): 221-9. Also in Frohock, W. M., "James Agee: The Question of Wasted Talent," in *Novel of Violence in America*, 212-30.

Gatlin, Rochelle, "The Personal and Religious Realism of James Agee," *DAI* 39 (1978); 1679A-80A.

Hayes, Richard, "Rhetoric of Splendor," *Cweal* 68 (Sept. 12, 1959): 591-2.

Humphreys, David M., "The Aesthetics of Failure: James Agee's Tragic Sensibility," *DAI* 40 (1979): 2681A.

Kramer, Victor A., "Agee: A Study of the Poetry, Prose and Unpublished Manuscript," *DAI* 30 (1969): 2533A (Texas, Austin).

Kramer, V. A., *James Agee*.

Larsen, E., *James Agee*.

Lawbaugh, William M., "'Remembrance of Things Past': An Analysis of James Agee's Prose Style," *DAI* 34 (1973): 1919A (Mo., Columbia).

Little, Michael V., "Sacramental Realism in James Agee's Major Prose," *DAI* 35 (1974): 2996A-97A (Del.).

Lum, Albert W. H., "James Agee: The Child as Synthesis," *DAI* 38 (1978): 6727A.

MacDonald, Dwight, "James Agee," *Encounter* 19 (Dec., 1962): 73-84.

Mayo, Charles W., "James Agee: His Literary Life and Work," *DAI* 30 (1970): 4993A (Geo. Peabody Coll. for Teachers.).

Newton, Scott, "David McDowell on James Agee," *WHR* 34, ii (Spring, 1980): 117-30.

Ohlin, P. H., *Agee.*

Perry, J. Douglas, Jr., "James Agee and the American Romantic Tradition," *DA* 29 (1968): 1233A (Temple).

da Ponte, Durant, "James Agee: The Quest for Identity," *TSL* 8 (Winter, 1963): 25-37.

Rewak, William J., "The Shadow and the Butterfly: James Agee's Treatment of Death," *DAI* 31 (1970): 2398A (Minn.).

Samway, Patrick, "James Agee: A Family Man," *Thought* 47 (Spring, 1972): 29-39.

Schramm, Richard R., "James Agee and the South," *DAI* 40 (1979): 860A.

Seib, K., *James Agee.*

Silberberg, Elliot D., "The Celluloid Muse: A Critical Study of James Agee," *DAI* 34 (1974): 6662A (Wis., Madison).

A DEATH IN THE FAMILY

Coles, Robert, *Irony in the Mind's Eye*, 56-106.

Culp, Mildred L., "Nobody ... Is Specially Privileged," *Death Education* 2, iv (Winter, 1979): 369-80.

Curry, Kenneth, "The Knoxville of James Agee's A DEATH IN THE FAMILY," *TSL* 14 (1969): 1-14.

_____, "Notes on the Text of James Agee's A DEATH IN THE FAMILY, *PBSA* 64, i (1970): 84-99.

Dietrichson, Jan W., "Theme and Technique in James Agee's A DEATH IN THE FAMILY," *ASIS* 6 (1973-74): 1-20.

Dupee, F. W., "The Prodigious James Agee," *New Leader* 40 (Dec. 9, 1957): 20-1. Also in Dupee, F. W., *King of the Cats*, 80-4.

Fiedler, Leslie, "Encounter With Death," *NRep* 137 (Dec. 9, 1957): 25.

Frohock, W. M., *Novel of Violence in America*, 225-9.

Hayes, Richard, "Rhetoric of Splendor," *Cweal* 68 (Sept. 12, 1958): 591-2.

Hittier, Gayle, "Belief and Unbelief in A DEATH IN THE FAMILY," *Ren* 31 (Spring, 1979): 177-92.

Hoffman, F. J., *Art of Southern Fiction*, 75-7.

Kazin, A., *Contemporaries*, 185-7. Also in Kostelanez, R., ed., *On Contemporary Literature*, 223-4.

Kramer, Victor A., "Agee's Use of Regional Material in A DEATH IN THE FAMILY," *AppalJ* 1, i (Autumn, 1972): 72-80.

_____, "A DEATH IN THE FAMILY and Agee's Projected Novel," *Proof* 3 (1973): 139-54.

_____, *James Agee*, 142-55.

_____, "The Manuscript and the Text of James Agee's A DEATH IN THE FAMILY," *PBSA* 65, iii (1971): 257-66.

_____, "Premonition of Disaster: An Unpublished Section for Agee's A DEATH IN THE FAMILY," *Costerus* n.s. 1 (1974): 83-93.

Larsen, E., *James Agee*, 37-45.

MacDonald, Dwight, "Death of a Poet," *NY* 33 (Nov. 16, 1957): 224-41.

McClary, Ben H., "Sarah Barnwell Elliott's Jerry: An Adolescent Reading Experience Reflected in James Agee's A DEATH IN THE FAMILY," *AN&Q* 20, vii-viii (Mar.-Apr., 1982): 113-15.

Milner, Joseph O., "Autonomy and Communism in A DEATH IN THE FAMILY," *TSL* 21 (1976): 105-13.

Ohlin, P. H., *Agee*, 194-214.

Perry, J. Douglas, Jr., "Thematic Counterpoint in a DEATH IN THE FAMILY: The Function of the Six Extra Scenes," *Novel* 5 (Spring, 1972): 234-41.

Roe, Michael M., Jr., "A Point of Focus in James Agee's A DEATH IN THE FAMILY," *TCL* 12 (Oct., 1966): 149-53.

Ruhe, Edward, *Epoch* 8 (Winter, 1958): 247-51.

Ruoff, Gene W., "A DEATH IN THE FAMILY: Agee's 'Unfinished' Novel," in French, W., ed., *Fifties*, 121-32.

Rupp, Richard H., "James Agee: The Elegies of Innocence," *Celebration in Postwar American Fiction*, 107-10.

Samway, Patrick, "James Agee: A Family Man," *Thought* 47 (Spring, 1972): 29-39.

Seib, K., *James Agee*, 73-96.

Shepherd, Allen, "'A Sort of Monstrous Grinding Beauty': Reflections on Character and Theme in James Agee's A DEATH IN THE FAMILY," *IEY* 14 (Fall, 1969): 17-24.

Sosnoski, James J., "Craft and Intention in James Agee's A DEATH IN THE FAMILY," *JGE* 20 (1968): 170-83.

Stuckey, W. J., *Pulitzer Prize Novels*, 181-4.

Sullivan, Walter, in Rubin, L. D., Jr., and R. D. Jacobs, eds., *South*, 387-8.

Trilling, Lionel, "The Story and the Novel," *The Griffin*, 7 (Jan., 1958): 4-12.

Ward, J. A., "A DEATH IN THE FAMILY: The Importance of Wordlessness," *MFS* 26 (Winter, 1980-81): 597-611.

Whittier, Gayle, "Belief and Unbelief in A DEATH IN THE FAMILY," *Ren* 31, iii (Spring, 1979): 177-92.

THE MORNING WATCH

Barson, A. T., *Way of Seeing*, 155-61.

Chase, Richard, "Sense and Sensibility," *KR* 13 (Autumn, 1951): 688-91.

Frohock, W. M., "James Agee: The Question of Unkept Promise," *SWR* 42 (1957): 228. Also in Frohock, W. M., *Novel of Violence in America*, 224-5.

Hoffman, F. J., *Art of Southern Fiction*, 77-81.

Kramer, V. A., *James Agee*, 131-41.

Kramer, Victor A., "James Agee's Unpublished Manuscript and His Emphasis on Religious Emotion in THE MORNING WATCH," *TSL* 17 (1972): 159-64.

_____, " 'Religion at Its Deepest Intensity': The Stasis of Agee's THE MORNING WATCH," *Ren* 27, iv (Summer, 1975): 221-30.

Larsen, E., *James Agee*, 32-6.

Ohlin, P. H., *Agee*, 182-94.

Phillipson, John S., "Character, Theme, and Symbol in THE MORNING WATCH," *WHR* 15 (Autumn, 1961): 359-67.

Pryce-Jones, Alan, "Preface" to THE MORNING WATCH, N.Y.: Ballantine Books, 1966.

Ramsey, Roger, "The Double Structure of THE MORNING WATCH," *SNNTS* 4, iii (1972): 494-503.

Rewak, William J., S. J., "James Agee's THE MORNING WATCH: Through Darkness to Light," *TQ* 16, iii (1973): 21-37.

Rupp, Richard H., "James Agee: The Elegies of Innocence," *Celebration in Postwar American Fiction*, 103-7.

Seib, K., *James Agee*, 69-73.

BIBLIOGRAPHY

Huse, Nancy, *John Hersey and James Agee: A Reference Guide,* London: Prior: Boston: G. K. Hall, 1978.
Ohlin, P. H., *Agee,* 239-47.
Seib, K., *James Agee,* 153-72.

ALDRIDGE, (HAROLD EDWARD) JAMES, 1918-

GENERAL

Partridge, Eric, "Man of Action, Words in Action: The Novels of James Aldridge," *Meanjin* 20 (1961): 256-63. [Not seen.]

ALGREN, NELSON, 1909-1981

GENERAL

Allen, W., *Modern Novel,* 154-5.
Anderson, Alston, and Terry Southern, "Nelson Algren," in *Writers at Work,* 1st Series, 231-49.
Baxter, David T., "Social Allegory in the Novels of Nelson Algren," *DAI* 31 (1971): 3539A (Un. of Wash.).
Bluestone, George, "Nelson Algren," *WR* 22 (Autumn, 1957): 27-44.
Cox, M. H., and W. Chatterton, *Nelson Algren.*
Donohue, H. E. F., *Conversations with Nelson Algren,* N.Y.: Hill and Wang, 1964.
Eisinger, C. E., *Fiction of the Forties,* 73-85.
Geismar, Maxwell, "Nelson Algren: The Iron Sanctuary," *CE* 14 (Mar., 1953): 311-15. Also in *EJ* 42 (Mar., 1953): 121-5. Also (expanded) in *American Moderns,* 187-94.
Grebstein, Sheldon N., "Nelson Algren and the Whole Truth," in French, W., ed., *Forties,* 298-309.
Laukaitis, William E., "Nelson Algren: A Critical Study," *DA* 29 (1969): 4495A-96A (Md.).
Lid, R. W., "A World Imagined: The Art of Nelson Algren," in Hakutani, Y., and L. Fried, eds., *American Literary Naturalism,* 176-96.
Lipton, Lawrence, "A Voyeur's View of the Wild Side: Nelson Algren and His Critics," *ChiR* 10 (Winter, 1957): 4-14. Also in Ray, David, ed., *Chicago Review Anthology,* Chicago: Un. of Chicago Pr., 1951, 31-41.
Miyamoto, Youkichi, "Chicago Naturalism-Nelson Algren," *SEL* 36 (1959): 177-8. [Not seen.]
O'Connor, W. V., *Grotesque,* 9-11.
Omick, Robert E., "Compassion in the Novels of Nelson Algren," *DA* 28 (1968): 3194A (Iowa).
Perlongo, Robert A., "Interview with Nelson Algren," *ChiR* 11 (Autumn, 1957): 92-8.
Raymer, John, "A Changing Sense of Chicago in the Works of Saul Bellow and Nelson Algren," *ON* 4, iv (Dec., 1978): 371-83.
Robinson, James A., "Nelson Algren's Spiritual Victims," *GyS* 3 (1975): 3-12.
Walcutt, C. C., *American Literary Naturalism,* 299-300.

THE MAN WITH THE GOLDEN ARM

Bluestone, George, "Nelson Algren," *WR* 22 (1957): 35-9.

Cox, M. H., and W. Chatterton, *Nelson Algren,* 111-33.
Eisinger, C. E., *Fiction of the Forties,* 81-5.
Geismar, Maxwell, "Nelson Algren: The Iron Sanctuary," *CE* 14 (1953); 311-15. Also in *EJ* 42 (1953): 123-4. Also in Geismar, M., *American Moderns,* 191-2.
Gelfant, B., *American City Novel,* 252-7.
Grebstein, Sheldon N., in French, W., ed., *Forties,* 305-9.
Lid, R. W., "A World Imagined: The Art of Nelson Algren," in Hakutani, Y., & L. Fried, eds., *American Literary Naturalism,* 188-94.
Robinson, James A., "Nelson Algren's Spiritual Victims," *GyS* 3 (1975): 8-10.
Rosen, Robert C., "Anatomy of a Junkie Movie," in Peary, G., & Shatzkin, R., eds., *Modern American Novel and the Movies,* 189-98.
Veler, Richard P., "THE MAN WITH THE GOLDEN ARM: A Genetic Study," *DA* 25 (1965): 7281 (Ohio State.).

NEVER SOME MORNING

Bluestone, George, "Nelson Algren," *WR* 22 (1947): 30-3.
Cox, M. H., and W. Chatterton, *Nelson Algren,* 93-110.
Eisinger, C. E., *Fiction of the Forties,* 77-80.
Geismar, Maxwell, "Nelson Algren: The Iron Sanctuary," *CE* 14 (1953): 312-13. Also in *EJ* 42 (1953): 122-3. Also in Geismar, M., *American Moderns,* 189-90.
Grebstein, Sheldon N., in French, W., ed., *Forties,* 302-5.
Lid, R. W., "A World Imagined: The Art of Nelson Algren," in Hakutani, Y., & L. Fried, eds., *American Literary Naturalism,* 180-8.

SOMEBODY IN BOOTS

Bluestone, George, "Nelson Algren," *WR* 22 (1957): 27-30.
Cox, M. H., and W. Chatterton, *Nelson Algren,* 59-73.
Eisinger, C. E., *Fiction of the Forties,* 76-7.
Grebstein, Sheldon N., in French, W., ed., *Forties,* 301-2.
Green, Gerald, in Madden, D., ed., *Proletarian Writers of the Thirties,* 27-8.

A WALK ON THE WILD SIDE

Bluestone, George, "Nelson Algren," *WR* 22 (1957): 40-3.
Cox, M. H., and W. Chatterton, *Nelson Algren,* 73-92.
Widmer, L., "Contemporary American Outcasts," in *Literary Rebel,* 130-1

BIBLIOGRAPHY

Cox, M. H., and W. Chatterton, *Nelson Algren,* 149-57.
Studing, Richard, "A Nelson Algren Checklist," *TCL* 19, i (Jan., 1973): 27-39.

ALLEN, PAUL, 1948-

APELAND

Holubetz, Margarete, "Of Apes and Men: Themes and Narrative Patterns in APELAND," *KN* 27, iv (1980): 467-74.

ALTHER, LISA, 1944-

KINFLICKS

Braendlin, Bonnie H., "Alther, Atwood, Ballantyne, and Gray: Secular Salvation in the Contemporary Feminist Bildungsroman," *Frontiers* 4, i (Spring, 1979): 18-22.

_____, "New Directions in the Contemporary Bildungsroman: Lisa Alther's KINFLICK," *W&L* 1 (1980): 160-71.

Hall, Joan L., "Symbiosis and Separation in Lisa Alther's KINFLICKS," *ArQ* 38, iv (Winter, 1982): 336-46.

Waage, Frederick G., "Alther and Dillard: The Appalachian Universe," 200-8 in Somerville, Wilson, ed., *Appalachia/America: Proceedings of the 1980 Appalachian Studies Conference,* [Johnson City, TN]: Appalachian Consortium, 1981.

ALUKO, T(IMOTHY) M (OFOLORUNSO), 1918-

GENERAL

Adamolekun, 'Ladipo, "T. M. Aluko," *Afriscope* 5, ii (1975): 57, 59.

Banjo, Ayo, "Language in Aluko: The Use of Colloquialisms, Nigerianisms," *Ba Shiru* 5, i (Fall, 1973): 59-69.

Dziagu, S. A., "T. M. Aluko as a Social Critic," *LJH* 2 (1976): 28-41.

Gere, Anne R., "West African Oratory and the Fiction of Chinua Achebe and T. M. Aluko," *DAI* 35 (1975): 4519A.

Lindfors, Bernth, "T. M. Aluko: Nigerian Satirist," *ALT* 5 (1971): 41-53.

Ngugi wa Thiong'o, "Wole Soyinka, T. M. Aluko and the Satiric Voice," *SAfrL* 4 (1972): 55-66.

Ngwaba, Francis E., "T. M. Aluko and the Theme of the Crisis of Acculturation," *Nsukka Studies in African Lit.* 2, i (1979): 3-11. [Not seen.]

Omotoso, Kole, "Interview with T. M. Aluko," *Afriscope* 3, iv (1973): 51-2.

Osundare, Olunwaniyi, "Speech Narrative in Aluko: An Evaluative Stylistic Investigation," *JNigESA* 8, i (1976): 33-9. [Not seen.]

Palmer Eustace T., "Development and Change in the Novels of T. M. Aluko," *WLWE* 15, ii (1976): 279-96.

_____, "T. M. Aluko," *SAfrL* 3 (1979): 102-23.

Scott, Patrick G., *A Biographical Approach to the Novels of T. M. Aluko,* University Park, PA: African Lit. Assn., French Dept., Pennsylvania State Univ., 1978. Also in Parker, C. A., & S. H. Arnold, eds., *When the Drumbeat Changes,* 215-39.

_____, "The Cultural Significance of T. M. Aluko's Novels," *Bull. of So. Assn. of Africanists* 7, i (1979): 1-10. [Not seen.]

Taiwo, O., *Culture and the Nigerian Novel,* 149-54.

_____, "T. M. Aluko: The Novelist and His Imagination," *PA* 90 (1974): 225-46.

Wren, Robert M., "Anticipation of Civil Conflict in Nigerian Novels: Aluko and Achebe," *SBL* 1, ii (Summer, 1970): 21-32.

CHIEF THE HONOURABLE MINISTER

Dzeagu, S. A., "T. M. Aluko as a Social Critic," *LJH* 2 (1976): 38-41.

Lindfors, Bernth, "T. M. Aluko: Nigerian Satirist," *ALT* 5 (1971): 47-52.

Taiwo, O., *Culture and the Nigerian Novel,* 172-7.

HIS WORSHIPFUL MAJESTY

Taiwo, O., *Culture and the Nigerian Novel,* 177-9.

KINSMAN AND FOREMAN

Dzeagu, S. A., "T. M. Aluko as a Social Critic," *LJH* 2 (1976): 35-8.

Laurence, M., *Long Drums and Cannons,* 176-7.

Lindfors, Bernth, "T. M. Aluko: Nigerian Satirist," *ALT* 5 (1971): 47-9.

Stegeman, Beatrice, "The Courtroom Clash in T. M. Aluko's KINSMAN AND FOREMAN," *Crit* 17, ii (1975): 26-35.

Taiwo, O., *Culture and the Nigerian Novel,* 167-71.

ONE MAN, ONE MATCHET

Gakwandi, Shatto A., "Nationalism," *SAfrL* 6 (1977): 56-65. Also in Gakwandi, S. A., *Novel and Contemporary Experience in Africa,* 56-65.

Laurence, M., *Long Drums and Cannons,* 170-6.

Lindfors, Bernth, "T. M. Aluko: Nigerian Satirist," *ALT* 5 (1971): 45-7.

Ngugi, J., *Homecoming,* 57-9.

Taiwo, O., *Culture and the Nigerian Novel,* 160-7.

ONE MAN, ONE WIFE

Dzeagu, S. A., "T. M. Aluko as a Social Critic," *LJH* 2 (1976): 29-30, and *passim.*

Laurence, M., *Long Drums and Cannons,* 170-1.

Lindfors, Bernth, "T. M. Aluko: Nigerian Satirist," *ALT* (1971): 42-5.

Stegeman, Beatrice, "The Divorce Dilemma: The New Woman in Contemporary African Novels," *Crit* 15, iii (1974): 85-6.

Taiwo, O., *Culture and the Nigerian Novel,* 154-60.

AMADI, ELECHI, 1934-

GENERAL

Finch, Geoffrey J., "Tragic Design in the Novels of Elechi Amadi," *Crit* 17, ii (1975): 5-16.

Ivker, Barry, "Elechi Amadi: An African Writer Between Two Worlds," *Phylon* 33, iii (Fall, 1972): 290-3.

Osundare, Niyi, "'As Grasshoppers to Wanton Boys': The Role of the Gods in the Novels of Elechi Amadi," *ALT* 11 (1980): 97-109.

Taiwo, O., *Culture and the Nigerian Novel,* 181-5.

THE CONCUBINE

Chandar, K. M., "Elechi Amadi's THE CONCUBINE," *LHY* 21, ii (1980): 123-33.

Finch, Geoffrey J., "Tragic Design in the Novels of Elechi Amadi," *Crit* 17, ii (1975): 5-16.

Griffiths, G., *Double Exile,* 28-31.

Ivker, Barry, "Elechi Amadi: An African Writer Between Two Worlds," *Phylon* 33, iii (Fall, 1972): 290-2.

Jones, Eldred, *JCL* 3 (July, 1967): 127-31.

Laurence, M., *Long Drums and Cannons,* 177-84.

Moore, G., *Chosen Tongue,* 159-61.

Moore, Gerald, "Dirges of the Delta," *Afriscope* 10, xi (Nov., 1980): 24.

Nandakumar, Prema, "Another Image of African Womanhood: (An Appreciation of Elechi Amadi's THE CONCUBINE)," *AfricaQ* 13, i (1973): 38-44.

Nesbitt, Rodney, *Notes on Elechi Amadi's THE CONCUBINE* (H. E. B. Student's Guide), Nairobi: Heinemann, 1975.

Niven, Alastair, "The Achievement of Elechi Amadi," in Rutherford, A., ed., *Common Wealth,* 92-9.

Taiwo, O., *Culture and the Nigerian Novel,* 204-9.

THE SLAVE

Moore, Gerald, "Dirges of the Delta," *Afriscope* 10, xi (Nov., 1980): 24-5.

AMIS, KINGSLEY, 1922-

GENERAL

Amis, Kinglsey, "My Kind of Comedy," *TC* 170 (July, 1961): 46-50.

Barber, Michael, "The Art of Fiction, 59: Kingsley Amis," *ParisR* 64 (Winter, 1975): 39-72.

Bergonzi, Bernard, "Kingsley Amis," *LonM* n.s. 3 (Jan., 19694): 50-65.

————, *Situation of the Novel,* 161-74.

Billington, Michael, "Writing and Warning: An Interview with Kingsley Amis," *Listener* 101 (1979): 262-3.

Bragg, Melvyn, "Kingsley Amis Looks Back: An Interview with Melvyn Bragg," *Listener* 93 (Feb. 20, 1975): 240-1.

Caplan, Ralph, in Shapiro, C., ed., *Contemporary British Novelists,* 3-15.

Chase, Richard, "Middlebrow England. The Novels of Kingsley Amis," *Ctary* 22 (Sept., 1956): 263-9.

Colville, Derek, "The Sane New World of Kinglsey Amis," *BuR* 9 (Mar., 1960): 46-57.

Gardner, P., *Kingsley Amis.*

Gindin, J., "Kingsley Amis' Funny Novels," in *Postwar British Fiction,* 34-50.

Gohn, Jack B., "The Novels of Kingsley Amis: A Reading," *DAI* 39 (1978): 2928A-29A.

Green, Martin, "Amis and Mailer: The Faustian Contract," *Month* 3, ii (Feb., 1971): 45-8, 52.

————, "Amis and Salinger: The Latitude of Private Conscience," *ChiR* 11, iv (Winter, 1958): 20-5.

Hamillton, Kenneth, "Kinglsey Amis, Moralist," *DR* 44 (Autumn, 1964): 339-47.

Harkness, Bruce, "The Lucky Crowd—Contemporary British Fiction," *EJ* 47 (Oct., 1958): 392-4.

Heppenstall, R., *Fourfold Tradition,* 213-25.

Hilty, Peter, "Kingsley Amis and Mid-Century Humor," *Discourse* 3 (Jan., 1960): 26-8.

Hurrell, John D., "Class and Consciousness in John Braine and Kingsley Amis," *Crit* 2, i (1958): 39-53.

Hutchings, W., "Kingsley Amis's Counterfeit World," *CritQ* 19, ii (Summer, 1977): 71-7.

James, Clive, "Profile 4: Kingsley Amis," *NewRev* 1, iv (July, 1974): 21-8.

Kelly, Thomas L., "The Quest for Self in the Early Novels of Kinglsey Amis," *DAI* 36 (1975): 2219A-20A. (Oklahoma.).

Lebowitz, Naomi, "Kinglsey Amis: The Penitent Hero," *Per* 10 (Summer-Autumn, 1958): 129-36.

Lodge, David, "The Modern, the Contemporary, and the Importance of Being Amis," *CritQ* 5, iv (Winter, 1963): 335-54. Also in *Language of Fiction: Essays in Criticism and Verbal Analysis of the English Novel,* London: Routledge and Kegan Paul, N.Y.: Columbia Un. Pr., 1966, 249-67.

MacKillop, I.D., "Armageddon Pier Staff: Second Decade Amis," *CQ* 7, iv (1977): 324-34.

Macleod, Norman, "This Familiar Regressive Series: Aspects of Style in the Novels of Kingsley Amis," in Aitken, A. J., & others, eds., *Edinburgh Studies in English and Scots,* London: longman Group, Ltd., 1971, 121-43.

Mellors, John, "A Piano-Tuner's Ear: The Novels of Kingsley Amis," *LonM* n.s. 14, iii (Aug.-Sept., 1974): 102-6.

Moberg, George, "Structure and Theme in Amis's Novels," *CEA* 25, vi (Mar., 1963): 7, 10.

O'Connor, W. V., "Kingsley Amis: That Uncertain Feeling," in *New University Wits,* 75-102.

Orel, Harold, "The Decline and Fall of a Comic Novelist: Kingsley Amis," *KanQ* 1, iii (Summer, 1969): 17-22.

Pazeroskis, John, "Kingsley Amis: The Dark Side," *StCS* 4 (1977): 28-33. [Not seen.]

Rabinovitz, R., *Reaction Against Experiment in the English Novel,* 38-63.

Ross, T. J., "Manners, Morals, and Pop: On the Fiction of Kingsley Amis," *STwC* No. 4 (Fall, 1969): 61-73.

Salwak, Dale [F.], "An Interview with Kingsley Amis," *ConL* 16 (Winter, 1975): 1-18.

————, "Kingsley Amis: Writer as Moralist," *DAI* 35 (1974): 3007A (So. Calif.).

Sarran, Alain G. de, "The Amis Country: A Critical Survey of the Novelist's Work," *DAI* 37 (1977): 5138A.

Smith, Robert B., "An Analysis of the Novels of Kingsley Amis," *DA* 26 (1965): 2762 (Un. of Washington).

Vorhees, Richard J., "Kingsley Amis: Three Hurrahs and a Reservation," *QQ* 79, i (Spring, 1972): 38-46.

Wilmes, D. R., "When the Curse Begins to Hurt: Kingsley Amis and Satiric Confrontation," *StCS* 5 (1978): 9-22.

THE ALTERATION

Gardner, P., *Kingsley Amis,* 83-91.

Hutchings, W., "Kingsley Amis's Counterfeit World," *CritiQ* 19, ii (Summer, 1977): 71-7.

THE ANTI-DEATH LEAGUE

Anon., in *TLS* (Mar., 17, 1966). Also Anon., "Novels of 1966. Kingsley Amis: The ANTI-DEATH LEAGUE," in *T.L.S. Essays and Reviews, 1966,* 29-31.

Bergonzi, B., *Situation of the Novel,* 171-4.

Biani, Sonia, "Cats, Birds and Freedom," *SRAZ* 29-32 (1970-71): 515-22.

Byatt, A. S., "Mess and Mystery," *Encounter,* 27 (July, 1966): 59-62.

Gardner, P., *Kingsley Amis,* 63-71.

McCabe, Bernard, "Looking for the Simple Life: Kingsley Amis's THE ANTI-DEATH LEAGUE," in Morris, R. K., ed., *Old Lines, New Forces,* 67-80.

Roberts, G. O., "Love and Death in an English Novel: THE ANTI-DEATH LEAGUE Investigated," in Macdonald, A. A., P.A. Flaherty, and G. M. Story, eds., *A Festschrift for Ronald Seary*, St. Johns: Memorial Univ. of Newfoundland, 1975, 201-14.

ENDING UP

Gardner, P., *Kingsley Amis*, 99-105.
McCort, Dennis, "The Dreadful Weight of Days: The Hilarious Heroism of Old Age in Kingsley Amis's ENDING UP," *Sphinx* 4, ii (1982): 101-8.

GIRL

Gardner, P., *Kingsley Amis*, 92-9.

THE GREEN MAN

Gardner, P., *Kingsley Amis*, 71-6.

I LIKE IT HERE

Allsop, K., *Angry Decade*, 55-7.
Gardner, P., *Kingsley Amis*, 50-3.
Hopkins, Robert H., "The Satire of Kingsley Amis's I LIKE IT HERE," *Crit* 8, ii (1966): 62-70.
Hurrell, John D., "Class and Consciousness in John Braine and Kingsley Amis," *Crit* 2, i (1958): 50-2.
Lodge, David, "The Modern, the Contemporary, and the Importance of Being Amis," *CritQ* 5, iv (Winter, 1963): 349-54. Also in *Language of Fiction: Essays in Criticism and Verbal Analysis of the English Novel*, London: Routledge and Kegan Paul: N.Y.: Columbia Un. Pr., 1966, 261-7.
O'Connor, W. V., *New University Wits*, 94-6.
Smith, Robert B., "An Analysis of the Novels of Kingsley Amis," *DA* 26 (1965): 2762 (Un. of Washington.).

I WANT IT NOW

Anon., in *TLS* (Oct. 10, 1968). Also Anon., "Fiction of 1968. Kingsley Amis: I WANT IT NOW," in *T.L.S. Essays and Reviews from the Times Literary Supplement, 1968*, 186-8.
Bradbury, Malcolm, "Delayed Orgasm," *NStat* (Oct., 11, 1968): 464, 466.
Gardner, P., *Kingsley Amis*, 58-62.

JAKE'S THING

Gardner, P., *Kingsley Amis*, 105-12.
Jones, D. A. N., "Don't Want It Now," *Listener* 100 (1978): 379.
Wilson, Keith, "Jim, Jake and the Years Between: The Will to Stasis in the Contemporary British Novel," *ArielE* 13, i (Jan., 1982): 55-69.

LUCKY JIM

Allen, Walter, *Modern Novel*, 279-81.
_____, *Reading a Novel*, 58-61.
_____, in *NStat & Nation* 47 (Jan. 30, 1954): Also in Feldman, Gene, and Max Gartenberg, eds., *The Beat Generation and the Angry Young Men*, N.Y.: Citadel, 1958, 339-41.
Allsop, K., *Angry Decade*, 43-52.
Bell, Robert H., "'True Comic Edge' in LUCKY JIM," *AHumor* 8, ii (Fall, 1981): 1-7.

Boyle, Ted E., and Terence Brown, "The Serious Side of Kingsley Amis's LUCKY JIM," *Crit* 9, i (1967): 100-7.
Brophy, B., in *Sunday Times Magazine Colour Supplement* (London) (Jan., 26, 1964): 11, 13. Also in *Don't Never Forget*, 217-22.
Conquest, Robert, "Christian Symbolism in LUCKY JIM," *CritQ* 7 (Spring, 1965): 87-92.
Dixon, Terrell F., "Chance and Choice in LUCKY JIM," *BSUF* 17, iv (1976): 75-80.
Duek, Jack, "Uses of the Picaresque: A Study of Five Modern British Novels," *DA* 34 (1974): 4255A.
Fallis, Richard, "LUCKY JIM and Academic Wishful Thinking," *SNNTS* 9, i (Spring, 1977): 65-72.
Gardner, P., *Kingsley Amis*, 22-36.
Hurrell, John D., "Class and Consciousness in John Braine and Kingsley Amis," *Crit* 2, i (1958): 43-8.
Karl, F. R., "The Angries: Is There a Protestant in the House?" in *Contemporary English Novel*, 220-9.
Kennedy, A., *Protean Self*, 269-72.
Kenyon, J. P., "LUCKY JIM and After: The Business of University Novels," *Encounter* (June, 1980): 81-4.
Lodge, David, "The Modern, the Contemporary, and the Importance of Being Amis," *CritQ* 5, iv (Winter, 1963): 341-5. Also in *Language of Fiction: Essays in Criticism and Verbal Analysis of the English Novel*, London: Routledge and Kegan Paul: N.Y.: Columbia Un. Pr., 1966, 250-5.
Mehoke, James S., "Sartre's Theory of Emotion and Three English Novelists: Waugh, Green, and Amis," *Wisconsin Studies in Literature*, No. 3 (1966): 110-11.
Noon, William T., S. J., "Satire: Poison and the Professor," *EngR* 11 (Fall, 1960): 56.
O'Connor, W.V., *New University Wits*, 85-90 *passim*.
Proctor, Mortimer R., *English University Novel*, Berkeley and Los Angeles: Un. of California, 1957, 175-6.
Rippier, J. S., *Some Postwar English Novelists*, 140-9.
Smith, Robert B., "An Analysis of the Novels of Kingsley Amis," *DA* 26 (1965): 2762 (Un. of Washington.).
Stovel, Bruce, "Traditional Comedy and the Comic Mask in Kingsley Amis's LUCKY JIM," *ESC* 4 (Spring, 1978): 69-80.
Strauch, Gerard, "Calendar, Construction, and Character in Kingsley Amis's LUCKY JIM," *RANAM* 3 (1974): 57-66.
Wilson, Keith, "Jim, Jake and the Years Between: The Will to Stasis in the Contemporary British Novel," *ArielE* 13, i (Jan., 1982): 55-69.

ONE FAT ENGLISHMAN

Anon., in *TLS* (nov., 14, 1963). Also, Anon., "Novels of 1963. Kinglsey Amis: ONE FAT ENGLISHMAN," in *T.L.S.: Essays and Reviews from the Time Literary Supplement, 1963*, 107-9.
Furbank, P. N., *Encounter*, 22 (Jan., 1964): 76-7.
Gardner, P., *Kingsley Amis*, 53-7.
Hamilton, Kenneth, "Kingsley Amis, Moralist," *DR* 44 (Autumn, 1964): 345-7.
Kelly, Edward, "Satire and Word Games in Amis's ENGLISHMAN," *SNL* 9, ii (Spring, 1972): 132-8.
Kuehn, Robert E., "Fiction Chronicle," *WSCL* 6 (1965): 138-9.
Smith, Robert B., "An Analysis of the Novels of Kingsley Amis," *DA* 26 (1965): 2762 (Un. of Washington).
Soule, George, "The High Cost of Plunging," *Carleton Miscellany* 5 (Fall, 1964): 106-11.

THE RIVERSIDE VILLAS MURDER

Gardner, P., *Kingsley Amis,* 78-82.

TAKE A GIRL LIKE YOU

Bergonzi, B., *Situation of the Novel,* 165-8.

Chinneswararao, G. J., "Amis's TAKE A GIRL LIKE YOU," *IJES* 12 (Dec., 1971): 110-14.

Coleman, John, "King of Shaft," *Spectator* No. 6900 (Sept. 23, 1960): 445-6.

Gardner, P., *Kinglsey Amis,* 42-8.

Lodge, David, "The Modern, the Contemporary, and the Importance of Being Amis," *CritQ* 5, iv (Winter, 1963): 346-9. Also in *Language of Fiction: Essays in Criticism and Verbal Analysis of the English Novel,* London: Routledge and Kegan Paul; N.Y.: Columbia Un. Pr., 1966, 257-9.

O'Connor, W. V., *New University Wits,* 96-8.

Parker, R. B., "Farce and Society: The Range of Kingsley Amis," *WSCL* 2, iii (Fall, 1961): 27-38.

Rippier, J. S., *Some Postwar English Novelists,* 154-8.

Ross, T. J., "Lucky Jenny, or Affluent Times," *NRep* 144 (Mar. 27, 1961): 21-2.

Smith, Robert B., "An Analysis of the Novels of Kingsley Amis," *DA* 26 (1965): 2762 (Un. of Washington.).

Urwin, G. G., ed., *Taste for Living,* 145-8.

THAT UNCERTAIN FEELING

Allsop, K., *Angry Decade,* 52-5.

Chase, Richard, "Middlebrow England: The Novels of Kingsley Amis," *Ctary* 22 (Sept., 1956): 264-7.

Gardner, P., *Kingsley Amis,* 37-42.

Hurrell, John D., "Class and Consciousness in John Braine and Kingsley Amis," *Crit* 2, i (1958): 49-50.

O'Connor, W. V., *New University Wits,* 90-4.

Rees, David, "That Petrine Cock," *Spectator* (Aug. 27, 1965): 268-9.

Rippier, J. S., *Some Postwar English Novelists,* 149-53.

Smith, Robert B., "An Analysis of the Novels of Kingsley Amis," *DA* 26 (1965): 2762 (Un. of Washington.).

Stovel, Bruce, "A Comedy of Conscience: Kingsley Amis's THAT UNCERTAIN FEELING," *IFR* 4 (1977): 162-6.

Wilson, Edmund, "Is It Possible to Pat Kingsley Amis?" *NY* (Mar. 24, 1956, 140-2. Also in Wilson, E., *The Bit Between My Teeth,* N.Y.: Farrar, Straus & Giroux, 1965, 274-81.

BIBLIOGRAPHY

Gohn, Jack B., comp., *Kingsley Amis: A Checklist,* Kent, OH: Kent St. Un. Pr., 1976.

Salwak, Dale, *Kingsley Amis: A Reference Guide,* London: Prior; Boston: Hall, 1978.

Vann, J. Donn, and James T. F. Tanner, "Kingsley Amis: A Checklist of Recent Criticism," *BB* 26, iv (Oct.-Dec., 1969): 105, 111, 115-17.

AMIS, MARTIN, 1949-

GENERAL

Padhi, Shanti, "Bed and Bedlam: The Hard-Core Extravaganzas of Martin Amis," *LHY* 23, i (Jan., 1982): 36-42.

Powell, Neil, "What Life Is: The Novels of Martin Amis," *PNR* 7, vi (1981): 42-5.

DEAD BABIES

Padhi, Shanti, "Bed and Bedlam: The Hard-Core Extravaganzas of Martin Amis," *LHY* 23, i (Jan., 1982): 36-42.

THE RACHEL PAPERS

Padhi, Shanti, "Bed and Bedlam: The Hard-Core Extravaganzas of Martin Amis," *LHY* 23, i (Jan., 1982): 36-42.

ANAND, MULK RAJ, 1905-

GENERAL

Anand, Mulk Raj, "The Changeling," *WLWE* 15, i (April, 1976): 111-20.

_____, "The Taste of the Pudding,"*LCrit* 17, ii (1982): 100-11. [Not seen.]

_____, "Why I Write?" in Sharma, K. K., ed., *Perspectives on Mulk Raj Anand,* 1-8. Also in Sharma, K. K., ed., *Indo-English Literature,* 9-17.

Asnani, Shyam M., "A Critique of Mulk Raj Anand's Literary Creed," *ComQ* 4, xv (Sept., 1980): 64-85.

_____, "Socio-Political Concerns in the Novels of Dr. Mulk Raj Anand," *Triveni* 45, i (Apr.-June, 1976): 38-50.

_____, "The Socio-Political Scene of the 1930's: Its Impact on the Indo-English Novel," *ComQ* 6, xxi (Dec., 1981): 14-23. [Not seen.]

_____, "The Theme of East-West Encounter in the Novels of Mulk Raj Anand," *Littcrit* 7 (1978): 11-19. [Not seen.]

Bald, Suresh R., "Politics of a Revolutionary Elite: A Study of Mulk Raj Anand's Novels," *MAsianS* 8, iv (1974): 473-89.

Berry, M., *Mulk Raj Anand.*

Chatterjee, Debjani, "Gandhi's Influence on Anand and His Fiction," *KJES* 2, i (1977): [Not seen.]

Cowasjee, Saros, "Anand's Princes and Proletarians," *LHY* 9, ii (1968): 83-104.

_____, "Mulk Raj Anand: The Early Struggles of a Novelist," *JCL* 7, i (June, 1972): 49-56.

_____, "Mulk Raj Anand and His Critics," *BP* 4, xii (Jan., 1969): 57-63.

_____, *So Many Freedoms.*

Fisher, Marlene, "Interview with Mulk Raj Anand," *WLWE* 13, i (Apr., 1974): 109-22.

_____, "Mulk Raj Anand: The Novelist as Novelist," *Occasional Papers Series,* Mich. St. Un., 1 (Winter, 1974): 257-69. [Not seen.]

Gowda, H. H. Anniah, "Mulk Raj Anand," *LHY* 6, i (Jan., 1965); 51-60.

Gupta, G. S. Balarama, "The Humanism of Mulk Raj Anand," *CIL* 7, iii (Aug., 1967): 6-8.

_____, *Mulk Raj Anand.*

_____, "Towards a Closer Understanding of Anand," in Sharma, K. K., ed., *Perspectives on Mulk Raj Anand,* 9-15. Also in Sharma, K. K., ed., *Indo-English Literature,* 113-20.

Gupta, Rameshwar, "The Gandhi in Anand," in Sharma, K. K., ed., *Perspectives on Mulk Raj Anand,* 77-83.

Harrex, S. C., "Quest for Structures: Form, Fable and echnique in the Fiction of Mulk Raj Anand," in Sharma, K. K., ed., *Perspectives on Mulk Raj Anand,* 153-68.

_____, "Western Ideology and Eastern Forms of Fiction: The Case of Mulk Raj Anand," in Amirthanayagam, G., ed., *Asian and Western Writers in Dialogue,* 142-58.

Iyengar, K. R. S., *Indian Writing in English,* 331-57.

Joshi, K. and B. S. Rao, "Mulk Raj Anand as a Novelist," *Studies in Indo-Anglian Literature,* 90-9.

Kaushik, R. K., "From Potter's Wheel to Dragon's Teeth: Character Delineation in Mulk Raj Anand's Novels," *Mahfil* 6, iv (Winter, 1970): 17-31.

_____, "Red, Brown and Grey—Ideological Commitment in Mulkk Raj Anand's," in Sharma, K. K., ed., *Perspectives on Mulk Raj Anand,* 16-26. Also in Sharma, K. K., ed., *Indo-English Literature,* 101-12.

Kurmanadham, K., "The Novels of Dr. Mulk Raj Anand," *Triveni* 36, iii (Oct., 1967): 50-7.

_____, "Women Characters in Dr. Anand's Novels," *CIL* 6 (1966): 11-12, 26-7.

Lindsay, J., *Elephant and the Lotus.*

Mathur, O. P., "An Approach to the Problem of National Integration in the Novels of Mulk Raj Anand," in Sharma, K. K., ed., *Perspectives on Mulk Raj Anand,* 64-76.

Mukherjee, Meenaksh, "The Tractor and the Plough: :The Contrasted Visions of Sudhin Ghose and Mulk Raj Anand," *IndL* 13, i (Mar., 1970): 88-101. Also in Mukherjee, M., ed., *Considerations,* 111-21. Also in Narasimhaiah, C. D., ed., *Indian Literture of the Past Fifty Years, 1917-1967,* 121-32.

Murti, K. V. Suryanarayana, "The 'Motif of Virtue' in Dr. Mulk Raj Anand's Novels," *CIL* 6, i (Jan., 1966): 12, 26.

_____, "Nautchization: Mulk Raj Anand's Novel Technique," *Triveni* 45, iii (July-Sept., 1976): 25-31.

_____, "The Theme of Salvation: Mulk Raj Anand and R. K. Narayan," *Triveni* 34, iii (Jan., 1965): 50-9.

Naik, M. K., *Mulk Raj Anand.*

Narasimhaiah, C. D., *Swan and the Eagle,* 106-34.

Nath, Suresh, "The Element of Protest in Anand's Fiction," in Sharma, K. K., ed., *Perspectives on Mulk Raj Anand,* 129-38.

Niven, Alastair, "Mulk Raj Anand: The Poetry of Protest," *Planet* 8 (Oct.-Nov., 1971): 21-5.

_____, *Yoke of Pity.*

Packham, Gillian, "Mulk Raj Anand and the Thirties Movement in England," in Sharma, K. K., ed., *Perspectives on Mulk Raj Anand,* 52-63.

_____, "Mulk Raj Anand's New Myth," *NLRev* 8 (1980): 45-53.

Raizada, Harish, "Ethics and Aesthetics of Mulk Raj Anand," in Sharma, K. K., ed., *Perspectives on Mulk Raj Anand,* 115-28.

Ram, Atma, "Anand's Prose-Style: An Analysis," in Sharma, K. K., ed., *Perspectives on Mulk Raj Anand,* 169-76.

Riemenschneider, Dieter, "'Alienation' in the Novels of Mulk Raj Anand," in Sharma, K. K., ed., *Perspectives on Mulk Raj Anand,* 94-114.

_____, "The Function of Labour in Mulk Raj Anand's Novels," *JSL* 4, i (1976): 1-20.

_____, "An Ideal of Man in Mulk Raj Anand's Fiction," *IndL* 10, i (Jan.-Mar., 1967): 29-51. Also in Riemenscneider, Dieter, *An Ideal of Man in Mulk Raj Anand's Novels,* Bombay: Kutub-Popular, 1967. [Not seen.]

Sharma, Atma R., "Folk Elements in Anand's Novels," *KJES* 2, i (1977): [Not seen.]

Sharma, Govind N., "Anand's Englishmen: The British Presence in the Novels of Mulk Raj Anand," *WLWE* 21, ii (Summer, 1982): 336-41.

Sharma, K. K., ed., *Perspectives on Mulk Raj Anand.*

Shepherd, R., "Alienated Being: A Reappraisal of Anand's Alienated Hero," in Sharma, K. K., ed., *Perspectives on Mulk Raj Anand,* 139-52.

Shivpuri, Jagdish, "Tagore and Anand," in Sharma, K. K., ed., *Perspectives on Mulk Raj Anand,* 84-93.

Singh, Amarjit, "Why Are Anand's Later Novels Unsuccessful?" *ComQ* 4, xii (Dec., 1979): 60-7.

Singh, R. S., *Indian Novel in English,* 38-54.

Singh, Satyanarain, "'Yoke of Pity': The Poet in Anand's Novels," *KJES* 2, i (1977). [Not seen.]

Singh, Sunaina, "Protest in the Novels of Mulk Raj Anand," *OJES* 17 (1981): 123-33.

Sinha, K. N., *Mulk Raj Anand.*

Tharu, Susie, "Decoding Anand's Humanism," *Kunapipi* 4 (1982): 30-42. [Not seen.]

Walsh, William, "The Big Three," in Mohan, R., ed., *Indian Writing in English,* 27-30.

_____, "Some Observations on Mulk Raj Anand's Fiction," in Sharma, K. K., ed., *Perspectives on Mulk Raj Anand,* 177-80.

Williams, H. M., "Mulk Raj Anand: Realism and Politics," *The Miscellany* 55 (Feb., 1973): 9-42.

ACROSS THE BLACK WATERS (See also TRILOGY)

Cowasjee, S., *So Many Freedoms,* 106-12.

Gupta, G. S. B., *Mulk Raj Anand,* 58-63.

Naik, M. K., *Mulk Raj Anand,* 62-70.

Niven, A., *Yoke of Pity,* 68-74.

Sinha, K. N., *Mulk Raj Anand,* 48-50.

THE BIG HEART

Berry, Margaret, "India: A Double Key," *JIWE* 6, i (Jan., 1978): 30-6.

Cowasjee, Saros, "Mulk Raj Anand's THE BIG HEART: A New Perspective," *ACLALSB* 4, ii (1975): 83-6.

_____, *So Many Freedoms,* 125-32.

Gupta, G. S. B., "Anand's BIG HEART: A Study," *BP* [Supp.] 5, xiii (July, 1969): 37-43.

_____, *Mulk Raj Anand,* 69-76.

Lindsay, J., *Elephant and the Lotus,* 18-21.

Naik, M. K., *Mulk Raj Anand,* 77-86.

Narasimhaiah, C. D., *Swan and the Eagle,* 128-33.

Niven, A., *Yoke of Pity,* 81-6.

Riemenschneider, Dieter, "'Alienation' in the Novels of Mulk Raj Anand," in Sharma, K. K., ed., *Perspectives on Mulk Raj Anand,* 109-11.

_____, "The Function of Labour in Mulk Raj Anand's Novel," *JSL* 4, i (1976): 15-17.

Sinha, K. N., *Mulk Raj Anand,* 54-8.

Singh, R. S., *Indian Novel in English,* 46-7.

Singh, Sunaina, "Protest in the Novels of Mulk Raj Anand," *OJES* 17 (1981): 126-9.

CONFESSION OF A LOVER

Cowasjee, Saros, "Mulk Raj Anand's CONFESSION OF A LOVER," *IFR* 4 (1977): 18-22.
_____, *So Many Freedoms*, 183-90.
Fisher, Marlene, "CONFESSION OF A LOVER," *KJES* 2, i (1977): [Not seen.]
Niven, A., *Yoke of Pity*, 41-5.
Riemenschneider, D., "Mulk Raj Anand, CONFESSION OF A LOVER," *WLWE* 16 (1977): 105-9.

COOLIE

Abidi, S. Z. H., *Mulk Raj Anand's COOLIE: A Critical Study*, Bareilly: Prakash Book Depot, 1976.
Asnani, Shyam, "Socio-Political Concerns in the Novels of Dr. Mulk Raj Anand," *Triveni* 45, 1 (April-June, 1976): 43-5.
Cowasjee, Saros, *Mulk Raj Anand, COOLIE: An Assessment*, Delhi: Oxford Un. Pr., 1976.
_____, "Mulk Raj Anand's COOLIE: An Appraisal," *BP* 19 (1972; pub. 1974): 8-19.
_____, *So Many Freedoms*, 60-82.
Gupta, G. S. Balarama, "COOLIE—A Prose Epic of Modern India," *KUJH* 12 (1968): 92-9.
_____, *Mulk Raj Anand*, 37-43.
Iyengar, K. R. S., *Indian Writing in English*, 339-43.
Naik, M. K., *Mulk Raj Anand*, 39-46.
Narasimhaiah, C. D., *Swan and the Eagle*, 118-28.
Niven, A., *Yoke of Pity*, 56-63.
Riemenschneider, Dieter, "'Alienation' in the Novels of Mulk Raj Anand," in Sharma, K. K., ed., *Perspectives on Mulk Raj Anand*, 103-9.
_____, "The Function of Labour in Mulk Raj Anand's Novels," *JSL* 4, i (1976): 10-15.
Singh, R. S., *Indian Novel in English*, 43-6.
Sinha, K. N., *Mulk Raj Anand*, 31-5.
Williams, H. M., "Mulk Raj Anand: Realism and Politics," *The Miscellany* 55 (Feb., 1978): 14-20.

DEATH OF A HERO

Cowasjee, S., *So Many Freedoms*, 163-5.
Gupta, G. S. B., *Mulk Raj Anand*, 76-81.
Naik, M. K., *Mulk Raj Anand*, 105-10.
Niven, A., *Yoke of Pity*, 116-17.
Sinha, K. N., *Mulk Raj Anand*, 76-80.

LAMENT ON THE DEATH OF A MASTER OF ARTS

Berry, Margaret, "'Purpose' in Mulk Raj Anand's Fiction," *Mahfil* 5, i-ii (1968-69): 85-90.
Gupta, G. S. B., *Mulk Raj Anand*, 97-103.
Paul, Premila, "Anand's LAMENT ON THE DEATH OF A MASTER OF ARTS: A Thematic Analysis," *JIWE* 6, ii (1978): 70-7.
Reddy, K. Vankata, "Mulk Raj Anand's LAMENT ON THE DEATH OF A MASTER OF ARTS: A Study," *JIWE* 5, ii (1977): 28-36.
Sinha, K. N., *Mulk Raj Anand*, 39-45.
Varalakshmi, P., "Anand's LAMENT ON THE DEATH OF A MASTER OF ARTS: An Analysis, *JIWE* 7, ii (1979): 82-7.

MORNING FACE

Cowasjee, S., *So Many Freedoms*, 175-83.
Gupta, G. S. B., *Mulk Raj Anand*, 111-18.
Naik, M. K., *Mulk Raj Anand*, 111-15.
Niven, A., *Yoke of Pity*, 26-41 *passim*.
Sinha, K. N., *Mulk Raj Anand*, 137-8.

THE OLD WOMAN AND THE COW (GOWRI)

Cowasjee, S., *So Many Freedoms*, 154-60.
Gupta, G. S. B., *Mulk Raj Anand*, 89-96.
Naik, M. K., *Mulk Raj Anand*, 86-95.
Niven, Alastair, "Myth into Moral: Mulk Raj Anand's THE OLD WOMAN AND THE COW," *ACLALSB* 4, iii (1975): 30-6.
_____, *Yoke of Pity*, 105-13.
Riemenschneider, Dieter, "'Alienation' in the Novels of Mulk Raj Anand," in Sharma, K. K., ed., *Perspectives on Mulk Raj Anand*, 102-3.
_____, "The Function of Labour in Mulk Raj Anand's Novels," *JSL* 4, i (1976): 9-10.
Singh, Sunaina, "Protest in the Novels of Mulk Raj Anand," *OJES* 17 (1981): 129-31.
Sinha, K. N., *Mulk Raj Anand*, 67-73.

PRIVATE LIFE OF AN INDIAN PRINCE

Anand, Shahla, "Images of Indian Princesses and Courtly Concubines in Four Contemporary Works," *SARev* (July, 1979): 27-35.
Chinneswararao, G. J., "Anand's PRIVATE LIFE OF AN INDIAN PRINCE and Malgonkar's THE PRINCES: A Comparison," *JIWE* 4, i (1976): [Not seen.]
Cowasjee, Saros, "Mulk Raj Anand: Princes and Proletarians," *JCL* No. 5 (July, 1968): 52-64.
_____, "Princes and Politics," *LCrit* 8, iv (Summer, 1969): 14-18.
_____, *So Many Freedoms*, 132-51.
Davies, M. Bryn, "British and Indian Images of India," *ArielE* 1, iv (Oct., 1970): 52-5.
Gupta, G. S. B. *Mulk Raj Anand*, 82-8.
Naik, M. K., *Mulk Raj Anand*, 97-105.
Niven, A., *Yoke of Pity*, 96-104.
Sinha, K. N., *Mulk Raj Anand*, 62-6.
Steinvorth, K., "Mulk Raj Anand's PRIVATE LIFE OF AN INDIAN PRINCE and Manohar Malgonkar's THE PRINCES," *LHY* 14, i (1973): 76-91.

THE ROAD

Cowasjee, S., *So Many Freedoms*, 160-3.
Gupta, G. S. B., *Mulk Raj Anand*, 33-6.
Naik, M. K., *Mulk Raj Anand*, 35-8.
Niven, A., *Yoke of Pity*, 115-16.
Riemenschneider, Dieter, "The Function of Labour in Mulk Raj Anand's Novels," *JSL* 5, i (1976): 18-19.
Sinha, K. N., *Mulk Raj Anand*, 73-6.

SEVEN SUMMERS

Cowasjee, S., *So Many Freedoms*, 165-75.
Gupta, G. S. B., *Mulk Raj Anand*, 104-11.
Lindsay, J., *Elephant and the Lotus*, 24-7.

Murthi, K. V., Suryanarayana, "SEVEN SUMMERS: Anand's Fictional Matrix," *KJES* 2, i (1977): [Not seen.]

Naik, M. K., *Mulk Raj Anand*, 115-18.

Niven, A., *Yoke of Pity*, 25-41 *passim*.

Sinha, K. N., *Mulk Raj Anand*, 58-62.

THE SWORD AND THE SICKLE (See also TRILOGY)

Cowasjee, Saros, "Mulk Raj Anand's THE SWORD AND THE SICKLE," *WLWE* 14 (1975): 267-77.

_____, *So Many Freedoms*, 112-24.

Gupta, G. S. B., *Mulk Raj Anand*, 63-8.

Naik, M. K., *Mulk Raj Anand*, 70-6.

Niranjan, Shiva, "The Nature and Extent of Gandhi's Impact on the Early Novels of Mulk Raj Anand and Raja Rao," *ComQ* 3, xi (June, 1979): 40-1.

Niven, A., *Yoke of Pity*, 74-80.

Shepherd, R., "Alienated Being: A Reappraisal of Anand's Alienated Hero," in Sharma, K. K., ed., *Perspectives of Mulk Raj Anand*, 139-52.

Sinha, K. N., *Mulk Raj Anand*, 50-3.

TRILOGY

Iyengar, K. R. S., *Indian Writing in English*, 347-50.

Mukherjee, Meenaksi, "Beyond the Village: An Aspect of Mulk Raj Anand," in Naik, M. K., et al., eds., *Critical Essays on Indian Writing in English*, 223-30.

Niven, Alastair, "The 'Lalu' Trilogy of Mulk Raj Anand," *LHY* 13, i (1972): 31-49. Also in Walsh, W., ed., *Readings in Commonwealth Literature*, 11-26.

TWO LEAVES AND A BUD

Asnani, Shyam, "Socio-Political Concerns in the Novels of Dr. Mulk Raj Anand," *Triveni* 45, i (April-June, 1976): 45-9.

Bhattacharya, B. K., "TWO LEAVES AND A BUD: Truth and Fiction," *KJES* 2, i (1977): [Not seen.]

Cowasjee, Saros, "Anand's TWO LEAVES AND A BUD," *IndL* 16, iii-iv (July-Dec., 1973): 134-47.

_____, *So Many Freedoms*, 82-97.

Gupta, G. S. B., *Mulk Raj Anand*, 44-51.

Iyengar, K. R. S., *Indian Writing in English*, 343-7.

Naik, M. K., *Mulk Raj Anand*, 46-55.

Niven, A., *Yoke of Pity*, 86-90.

Sinha, K. N., *Mulk Raj Anand*, 35-8.

Williams, H. M., "Mulk Raj Anand: Realism and Politics," *The Miscellany* 55 (Feb., 1973): 26-30.

UNTOUCHABLE

Abidi, S. Z. H., *Mulk Raj Anand's UNTOUCHABLE: A Critical Study*, Bareilly: Prakash Book Depot, 1976.

Asnani, Shyam, "Socio-Political Concerns in the Novels of Dr. Mulk Raj Anand," *Triveni* 45, i (April-June, 1976): 41-3.

_____, "Untouchability and Mulk Raj Anand's UNTOUCHABLE," *BP* 16 (1971): 31-6.

Carter, D., "Probing Identities: UNTOUCHABLE, THINGS FALL APART and THIS EARTH MY BROTHER...," *LCrit* 14, iii (1979): 14-29.

Cowasjee, Saros, "Mulk Raj Anand's UNTOUCHABLE: An Appraisal," *LE&W* 17 (Dec., 1973): 199-211. Also in Sharma, K. K., ed., *Indo-English Literature*, 87-99. Also in Sharma, K. K., ed., *Perspectives on Mulk Raj Anand*, 27-38.

_____, *So Many Freedoms*, 41-60.

Gupta, G. S. B., *Mulk Raj Anand*, 24-32.

Harrex, S. C., in Amirthanayagam, G., ed., *Asian and Western Writers in Dialogue*, 151-4.

Iyengar, K. R. S., *Indian Writing in English*, 336-9.

Kulshrestha, Chirantan, "The Hero as Survivor: Reflections on Anand's UNTOUCHABLE," *WLWE* 19, i (1980): 84-91.

Mathur, O. P., "Mulk Raj Anand's UNTOUCHABLE and Richard Wright's Bigger Thomas: A Comparative Study in Social Protest and Affirmation," *LHY* 19, ii (1978): 115-28.

Naik, M. K., *Mulk Raj Anand*, 27-35.

Narasimhaiah, C. D., *Swan and the Eagle*, 111-18.

Niranjan, Shiva, "The Nature and Extent of Gandhi's Impact on the Early Novels of Mulk Raj Anand and Raja Rao," *ComQ* 3, xi (June, 1979): 38-40.

Niven, A., *Yoke of Pity*, 46-55.

Rao, E. Nageswara, "The Dialogue is the Thing: A Contrastive Analysis of Fictional Speech in Forster and Anand," in Shahane, V. A., ed., *Approaches to E. M. Forster*, 138-47.

Riemenschneider, Dieter, "The Function of Labour in Mulk Raj Anand's Novels," *JSL* 4, i (1976): 17-18.

Robertson, R. T., "UNTOUCHABLE as an Archetypal Novel," *WLWE* 14, ii (Nov., 1975): 339-46. Also in *KJES* 2, i 1977): [Not seen.]

Singh, R. S., *Indian Novel in English*, 40-3.

Singh, Sunaina, "Protest in the Novels of Mulk Raj Anand," *OJES* 17 (1981): 125-6.

Singh, Veena, "The Slave Rebel: A Closer Look at Untouchability," *IndL* 25, v (Sept.-Oct., 1982): 123-3.

Sinha, K. N., *Mulk Raj Anand*, 27-31.

Tarinayya, M., "Mulk Raj Anand's UNTOUCHABLE: An Analysis," *JMU* (Sect. A-Arts) 26 (Mar., 1969): [Not seen.]

Williams, H. M., "Mulk Raj Anand: Realism and Politics," *The Miscellany* 55 (Feb., 1973): 20-6.

THE VILLAGE (See also TRILOGY)

Cowasjee, S., *So Many Freedoms*, 99-106.

Gupta, G. S. B., *Mulk Raj Anand*, 52-8.

Niven, A., *Yoke of Pity*, 65-7.

Riemenschneider, Dieter, "Alienation' in the Novels of Mulk Raj Anand," in Sharma, K. K., ed., *Perspectives on Mulk Raj Anand*, 99-102.

_____, "The Function of Labour in Mulk Raj Anand's Novels," *JSL* 4, i (1976): 6-9.

Sinha, K. N., *Mulk Raj Anand*, 46-8.

BIBLIOGRAPHY

Cowasjee, S., *So Many Freedoms*, 191-200.

Naik, M. K., *Mulk Raj Anand*, 187-92.

Sharma, K. K., ed., *Perspectives on Mulk Raj Anand*, 181-6.

Sinha, K. N., *Mulk Raj Anand*, 145-8.

ANAYA, RUDOLFO A(LFONSO), 1937-

GENERAL

Anaya, Rudolfo A., "The Writer's Landscape: Epiphany in Landscape," *LALR* 5, x (Spring-Summer, 1977): 98-102.

Gish, Robert F., "Curanderismo and Witchery in the Fiction of Rudolfo A. Anaya: The Novel as Magic," *NMHR* 2, ii (Summer, 1979): 5-12.

Lattin, Vernon E., "The Quest for Mythic Vision in Contemporary Native American and Chicano Fiction," *AL* 50, iv (Jan., 1979): 625-40.

Márquez, Antonio, "The Achievement of Rudolfo A. Anaya," in Vassallo, P., ed., *Magic of Words*, 33-52.

Vassallo, P., ed., *Magic of Words*.

BLESS ME, ULTIMA

Clements, William M., "The Way to Individuation in Anaya's BLESS ME, ULTIMA," *MQ* 23, ii (1982): 131-43.

Donnelly, Dyan, "Finding a Home in the World," *BR* 1, i (Jan.-Apr., 1974): 113-18.

Gish, Robert F., "Curanderismo and Witchery in the Fiction of Rudolfo A. Anaya: The Novel as Magic," *NMHR* 2, ii (Summer, 1979): 6-11.

Johnson, Elaine D., "A Thematic Study of Three Chicano Narratives: ESTAMPAS DEL ALLE Y OTRAS OBRAS, BLESS ME, ULTIMA, and PEREGRINOS DE AZTLAN," *DAI* 39 (1978): 3614A.

Karen, Ray J., "Cultural and Mythical Archetypes in Rudolfo Anaya's BLESS ME, ULTIMA," *NMHR* 1, iii (Sept., 1978): 23-8.

Lattin, Vernon E., "The Horror Darkness: Meaning and Structure in Anaya's BLESS ME, ULTIMA," *Revista Chicano-Riqueña* 6, ii (Spring, 1978): 51-7.

_____, "The Quest for Mythic Vision in Contemporary Native American and Chicano Fiction," *AL* 50, iv (Jan., 1979): 628-32.

Malpezzi, Frances, "A Study of the Female Protagonist in Frank Waters' PEOPLE OF THE VALLEY and Rudolfo Anaya's BLESS ME, ULTIMA," *SDR* 14, ii (1976): 102-10.

Mitchell, Carol, "Rudolfo Anaya's BLESS ME, ULTIMA: Folk Culture in Literature," *Crit* 22, i (1980): 55-64.

Rogers, Jane, "The Function of the *la llorona* Motif in Rudolfo Anaya's BLESS ME, ULTIMA," *LALR* 5, x (Spring-Summer, 1977): 64-9.

Testa, Daniel, "Extensive, Intensive Dimensionality in [Rudolfo] Anaya's BLESS ME, ULTIMA," *LALR* 5, x (Spring-Summer, 1977): 70-8. Also in Pilkington, W. T., ed., *Critical Essays on the Western American Novel*, 262-70.

Waggoner, Amy, "Tony's Dreams—an Important Dimension in BLESS ME, ULTIMA," *SwAL* 4 (1974): 74-9.

Wilson, Carter, "'Magical Strength in the Human Heart': The Framing of Mortal Confusion in Rudolfo A. Anaya's BLESS ME, ULTIMA," *Ploughshares* 4, iii (1978): 190-7.

HEART OF AZTLAN

Gish, Robert F., "Curanderismo and Witchery in the Fiction of Rudolfo A. Anaya: The Novel as Magic," *NMHR* 2, ii (Summer, 1979): 11-13.

BIBLIOGRAPHY

Márquez, Teresa, "Works by and about Rudolfo A. Anaya," in Vassallo, P., ed., *Magic of Words*, 55-81.

ANTHONY, MICHAEL, 1932-

GENERAL

Barratt, Harold, "Michael Anthony and Earl Lovelace: The Search for Selfhood," *ACLALSB* 5, iii (1980): 62-73. [Not seen.]

Niven, Alastair, "'My Sympathies Enlarged': The Novels of Michael Anthony," *CE&S* 2 (1976): 45-62. [Not seen.]

Sander, Reinhard, "The Homesickness of Michael Anthony: The Predicament of a West Indian Exile," *LHY* 16, i (Jan., 1975): 95-124.

Smyer, Richard I., "Enchantment and Violence in the Fiction of Michael Anthony," *WLWE* 21, i (Spring, 1982): 148-59.

THE GAMES WERE COMING

Sander, Reinhard, "The Homesickness of Michael Anthony: The Predicament of a West Indian Exile," *LHY* 16, i (Jan., 1975): 113-19.

THE YEAR IN SAN FERNANDO

Edwards, Paul, and Kenneth Ramshand, "The Art of Memory: Michael Anthony's THE YEAR IN SAN FERNANDO," *JCL* 7 (July, 1969): 59-72. Also in Walsh, W., ed., *Readings in Commonwealth Literature*, 298-313.

Griffiths, G., *Double Exile*, 87-91.

Luengo, Anthony, "Growing Up in San Fernando: Change and Growth in Michael Anthony's THE YEAR IN SAN FERNANDO," *ArielE* 6, ii (1975): 81-95.

Moore, Gerald, "Discovery," *Chosen Tongue*, 17-20. Also in Cooke, M. G., ed., *Modern Black Novelists*, 159-61.

Ramchand, K., *West Indian Novel and its Background*, 205-22.

Sander, Reinhard, "The Homesickness of Michael Anthony: The Predicament of a West Indian Exile," *LHY* 16, i (Jan., 1975): 105-13.

ARMAH, AYI KWEI, 1938-

GENERAL

Amuta, Chidi, "Ayi Kwei Armah and the Mythopoesis of Mental Decolonization," *Ufahamu* 10, iii (Spring, 1981): 44-56.

_____, "Portraits of the Contemporary African Artist in Armah's Novels," *WLWE* 21, iii (Autumn, 1982): 467-76.

Bishop, Rand, "The Beautyful Ones are Born: Armah's First Five Novels," *WLWE* 21, iii (Autumn, 1982): 531-7.

Britwum, Atta, "Hero-Worshipping in the African Novel: The Case of Ayi Kwei Armah and Others," *Asemka* 3 (1975): 1-18. [Not seen.]

Fraser, R., *Novels of Ayi Kwei Armah*.

Johnson, Lemuel A., "The Middle Passage in African Literature: Wole Soyinka, Yambo Ouologuem, Ayi Kwei Arma," *ALT* 11 (1980): 62-84 *passim*.

Lindfors, Bernth, "Armah's Histories," *ALT* 11 (1980): 85-96.

Nnolim, Charles E., "Dialectic as Form: Pejorism in the Novels of Armah," *ALT* 10 (1979): 207-23.

Povey, John, "The Political Vision of the West African Writer," *EinA* 5, ii (1978): 51-6. [Not seen.]

Priebe, Richard, "Demonic Imagery and the Apocalyptic Vision in the Novels of Ayi Kwei Arma," *YFS* 53 (1976): 102-36.

Sole, Kelwyn, "Criticism, Activism and Rhetoric; or, Armah and the White Pumpkin," *Inspan* 1, i (1978): 129-41.

Steele, Shelby, "Existentialism in the Novels of Ayi Kwei Armah," *Obsidian* 3, 1 (Spring, 1977): 5-13.

Walker, William A., Jr., "Major Ghanaian Fiction in English: A Study of the Novels of Ayi Kwei Armah and Kofi Awoonor," *DAI* 36 (1975): 2816A.

THE BEAUTYFUL ONES ARE NOT YET BORN

Adeyemi, N. A., "The Major Artistic Achievements of Armah in THE BEAUTYFUL ONES ARE NOT YET BORN," *Shuttle* (Lagos) 8 (1980): 46-8.

Aidoo, Ama Atu, "No Saviours," *New African* 52 (1969): Also in Killam, G. D., ed., *African Writers on African Writers*, Evanston: Northwestern Un. Pr., 1973, 14-18.

Amuzu, Koku, "The Theme of Corruption in A MAN OF THE PEOPLE and THE BEAUTYFUL ONES ARE NOT YET BORN," *Legacy* (Legon) 3, ii (1977): 18-23.

Barthold, B. J., *Black Time*, 53-6.

Chakava, Henry, "Ayi Kwei Armah and a Commonwealth of Souls," in Wanjala, C. L., ed., *Standpoints on African Literature*, 197-208.

Collins, Harold R., "The Ironic Imagery of Armah's THE BEAUTYFUL ONES ARE NOT YET BORN: The Putrescent Vision," *WLWE* 20 (Nov., 1971): 37-50.

Folarin, Margaret, "An Additional Comment on Ayi Kwei Armah's THE BEAUTYFUL ONES ARE NOT YET BORN," *ALT* (1971): 116-29.

Fraser, R., *Novels of Ayi Kwei Armah*, 15-29.

Gakwandi, Shatto A., "Freedom as Nightmare," *SAfrL* 6 (1977): 87-99. Also in Gakwandi, S. A., *Novel and Contemporary Experience in Africa*, 87-99.

Goldie, Terry, "A Connection of Images: The Structure of Symbols in THE BEAUTYFUL ONES ARE NOT YET BORN," *Kunapipi* 1, i (1979): 94-107.

Griffiths, Gareth, "The Language of Disillusion in the African Novel," in Rutherford, A., ed., *CommonWealth*, 67-71.

_____, "Structure and Image in Kwei Armah's THE BEAUTYFUL ONES ARE NOT YET BORN," *SBL* 2, ii (Summer, 1971): 1-9.

Hagher, Iorwuese, "The Place of the Home in THE BEAUTYFUL ONES ARE NOT YET BORN," *The Morror* (Zaria) (1973-1974): 17-20.

Izevbaye, D. S., "Ayi Kwei Armah and 'I' of the Beholder," in King, B., and K. Ogungbesan, eds., *Celebration of Black and African Writing*, 232-40.

Kibera, Leonard, "Pessimism and the African Novelist: Ayi Kwei Armah's THE BEAUTYFUL ONES ARE NOT YET BORN," *JCL* 14, i (1979): 64-72.

Larson, C. R., *Emergence of African Fiction*, 258-68.

Moore, Gerald, "Action and Freedom in Two African Novels," *Conch* 2, i (Mar., 1970): 21-8.

Nicholson, Mary, "The Organisation of Symbols in Ayi Kwei Armah's THE BEAUTYFUL ONES ARE NOT YET BORN," *Asemka* 1, ii (1974): 7-15.

Niemi, Richard, "Will the Beautiful Ones Ever Be Born?" *PanA* 3 (Dec., 1971): 18-23.

Obiechina, Emmanuel, "THE BEAUTYFUL ONES ARE NOT YET BORN," *Okike* 1, ii (1971): 49-53.

_____, "Post-Independence Disillusionment in Three African Novels," *Nsukka Studies in Afr. Lit.*, 1, i (1978): 54-78. Also in Lindfors, B., and U. Schild, eds., *Neo-African Literature and Culture*, 119-46 *passim*.

Ogungbesan, Kilawole, "Symbol and Meaning in THE BEAUTYFUL ONES ARE NOT YET BORN," *WLWE* 12 (1973): 4-25. Also in *BeninR* 1 (1974): 59-63. Also in *ALT* 7 (1975): 93-110.

Palmer, E., *Introduction to the African Novel*, 129-42.

Priebe, Richard, "Demonic Imagery and the Apocalyptic Vision in the Novels of Ayi Kwei Armah," *YFS* 53 (1976): 108-22.

Solomon, Jean. "A Commentary on Ayi Kwei Armah's THE BEAUTYFUL ONES ARE NOT YET BORN," *EinA* 1, ii (1974): 25-31.

Walker, William A., Jr., "Major Ghanian Fiction in English: A Study of the Novels of Ayi Kwei Armah and Kofi Awoonor," *DAI* 36 (1975): 2816A.

FRAGMENTS

Colmer, Rosemary, "The Human and the Divine: FRAGMENTS and WHY ARE WE SO BLEST?" *Kunapipi* 2, ii (1980): 77-90.

Fraser, R., *Novels of Ayi Kwei Armah*, 30-47.

Griffiths, G., *Double Exile*, 62-7.

Izevbaye, D. S., "Ayi Kwei Armah and the 'I' of the Beholder," in King, B., and K. Ogungbesan, eds., *Celebration of Black and African Writing*, 232-40.

Johnson, Joyce, "The Promethean 'Factor' in Ayi Kwei Armah's FRAGMENTS and WHY ARE WE SO BLEST?" *WLWE* 21, iii (Autumn, 1982): 487-510.

Kamolo, Ejiet, "Ayi Kwei Armah's Cargo Mentality: A Critical Review of FRAGMENTS," *Dhana* 4, kk (1974): 88-90.

Larson, C. R., *Emergence of African Fiction*, 268-76.

Lobb, Edward, "Armah's FRAGMENTS and the Vision of the Whole," *ArielE* 10, i (1979): 25-38.

Lurie, Joe, "FRAGMENTS Between the Loved Ones and the Community," *Ba Shiru* 5, i (Fall, 1973): 31-41.

Massa, Daniel, "The Postcolonial Dream," *WLWE* 20, i (Spring, 1981): 135-49.

Moore, Gerald, "Armah's Second Novel," *JCL* 9 (1974): 69-71.

_____, "The Writer and the Cargo Cult," in Rutherford, A., ed., *CommonWealth*, 73-8.

Petersen, Kirsten H., "Loss and Frustration: An Analysis of A. K. Armah's FRAGMENTS," *Kunapipi* 1, i (1979): 53-65.

Priebe, Richard, "Demonic Imagery and the Apocalyptic Vision in the Novels of Ayi Kwei Armah," *YFS* (1976): 122-30.

Rassner, Ron, "FRAGMENTS: The Cargo Mentality," *Ba Shiru* 5, ii (1974): 55-64.

Steele, Shelby, "Existentialism in the Novels of Ayi Kwei Aramah," *Obsidian* 3, i (Spring, 1977): 9-12.

Thieme, John, "Myth, Society and the African Artist in Ayi Kwei Armah's FRAGMENTS," *Gulliver* 8 (1980): 53-67.

Yankson, Kofi, "FRAGMENTS: The Eagle That Refused to Soar," *Asemka* 1, i (1974): 53-9.

THE HEALERS

Fraser, R., *Novels of Ayi Kwei Armah*, 82-100.

Lazarus, Neil, "Implications of Technique in Ayi Kwei Armah's THE HEALERS," *RAL* 13, iv (Winter, 1982): 483-98.

Lindfors, Bernth, "Armah's Histories, " *ALT* 11 (1980): 91-5.

TWO THOUSAND SEASONS

Amuta, Chidi, "Ayi Kwei Armah, History, and 'The Way': The Importance of TWO THOUSAND SEASONS," *KompH* 3 (1981): 79-86.

Barthold, B. J., *Black Time*, 71-3.

Evans, Jenny, "Women of 'The Way': TWO THOUSAND SEASONS, Female Images and Black Identity," *ACLALSB* 6, i (Nov., 1982): 17-26.

Fraser, R., *Novels of Ayi Kwei Armah*, 63-81.

Izevbaye, D. S., "Ayi Kwei Armah and the 'I' of the Beholder," in King, B., and K. Ogungbesan, eds., *Celebration of Black and African Writing*, 240-3.

Larson, Charles R., "Ayi Kwei Armah's Vision of African Reciprocity," *AT* 21, ii (1974): 117-19.

Lindfors, Bernth, "Armah's Histories," *ALT* 11 (1980): 87-91.

Palmer, Eustace, "Ayi Kwei Armah," *SafrL* 3 (1979): 221-39. Also in Palmer, E., *Growth of the African Novel*, 221-39.

———, "Negritude Rediscovered: A Reading of the Recent Novels of Armah, Ngugi, and Soyinka," *IFR* 8, i (Winter, 1981): 3-7.

Petersen, Kirsten H., "The New Way: Ayi Kwei Armah's TWO THOUSAND SEASONS," *WLWE* 15, ii (1976): 330-5.

Thomas, McKinley, "'Griotature' in a Book," *Tanzania N&R* 77-78 (1976): 109-11.

Washington, Clifton, "TWO THOUSAND SEASONS: Essay Review," *Black Books Bull.* 7, i (1980): 20-4.

Webb, Hugh, "The African Historical Novel and the Way Forward," *ALT* 11 (1980): 32-7.

WHY ARE WE SO BLEST?

Barthold, B. J., *Black Time*, 169-73.

Booth, James, "WHY ARE WE SO BLEST? and the Limits of Metaphor," *JCL* 15, i (1980): 50-64.

Cheatwood, Kiarri T. -H., "WHY ARE WE SO BLEST? *BlackW* 23, v (1974): 85-90.

Colmer, Rosemary, "The Human and the Divine: FRAGMENTS and WHY ARE WE SO BLEST?" *Kunapipi* 2, ii (1980): 77-90.

Fraser, Robert, "The American Background in WHY ARE WE SO BLEST?" *ALT* 9 (1978): 39-46.

———, *Novels of Ayi Kwei Armah*, 48-62.

Johnson, Joyce, "The Promethean 'Factor' in Ayi Kwei Armah's FRAGMENTS and WHY ARE WE SO BLEST?" *WLWE* 21, iii (Autumn, 1982): 497-510.

Lobb, Edward, "Personal and Political Fate in Armah's WHY ARE WE SO BLEST?" *WLWE* 19, i (1980): 5-19.

Priebe, Richard, "Demonic Imagery and the Apocalyptic Vision in the Novels of Ayi Kwei Armah," *YFS* 53 (1976): 130-6.

Steele, Shelby, "Existentialism in the Novels of Ayi Kwei Armah," *Obsidian* 3, i (Spring, 1977): 6-9.

ARNOW, HARRIETTE (SIMPSON), 1908-1986

GENERAL

Eckley, W., *Harriette Arnow*.

Hobbs, Glenda, "Harriette Arnow's Kentucky Novels: Beyond Local Color," *KCN* 2, ii (1976): 27-32. [Not seen.]

———, "Starting Out in the Thirties: Harriette Arnow's Literary Genesis," in Bogardus, R. F., and F. Hobson, eds., *Literature at the Barricades*, 144-61.

Lucas, Cora, "'A dream ... that's what I came out for': a Recollection and Appreciation of Harriette Arnow, " *Adena* 1, ii (1976): 126-36.

Miller, Danny, "A MELUS Interview: Harriette Arnow," *MELUS* 9, ii (1982): 83-97.

Thorn, Arline R., "Harriette Arnow's Mountain Women," *BWVACET* 4, i (1977): 1-9. [Not seen.]

Wagner, Linda W., "Harriette Arnow and the 1980s," *GrLR* 8, i (Spring, 1982): 1-10.

THE DOLLMAKER

Adams, Pauline, "A Sense of Place: One Aspect of Harriette Arnow's THE DOLLMAKER," *MMisc* 3 (1975): 1-5.

Eckley, W., *Harriette Arnow*, 85-100.

Goodman, Charlotte, "Portraits of the *Artiste Manqué* by Three Women Novelists," *Frontiers* 5, iii (Fall, 1980): 58-9.

Griffin, Joan R., "Fiddle Tunes, Foxes, and a Piece of Land: Region and Character in Harriette Arnow's Kentucky Trilogy," *DAI* 43, iii (Sept., 1982): 802A.

Hobbs, Glenda, "A Portrait of the Artist as Mother: Harriette Arnow and THE DOLLMAKER," *GaR* 33, iv (1979): 851-66.

Lee, Dorothy H., "Harriette Arnow's THE DOLLMAKER: A Journey to Awareness," *Crit* 20, ii (1978): 92-8.

Malpezzi, Frances M., "Silence and Captivity in Babylon: Harriette Arnow's THE DOLLMAKER," *SoSt* 20, i (Spring, 1981): 84-90.

Oates, Joyce Carol, "Harriette Arnow's THE DOLLMAKER," in Madden, D., ed., *Rediscoveries*, 57-66.

Wagner, Linda W., "Harriette Arnow and the 1980s," *GrLR* 8, i (Spring, 1982): 5-10.

HUNTER'S HORN

Eckley, W., *Harriette Arnow*, 63-84.

Griffin, Joan R., "Fiddle Tunes, Foxes, and a Piece of Land: Region and Character in Harriette Arnow's Kentucky Trilogy," *DAI* 43, iii (Sept., 1982): 802A.

Wagner, Linda W., "Harriette Arnow and the 1980s," *GrLR* 8, i (Spring, 1982): 1-5.

MOUNTAIN PATH

Eckley, W., *Harriette Arnow*, 45-55.

Griffin, Joan R., "Fiddle Tunes, Foxes, and a Piece of Land: Region and Character in Harriette Arnow's Kentucky Trilogy," *DAI* 43, iii (Sept., 1982): 802A.

Hobbs, Glenda, "Starting Out in the Thirties: Harriette Arnow's Literary Genesis," in Bogardus, R. F., and F. Hobson, *Literature at the Barricades*, 148-54.

THE WEEDKILLER'S DAUGHTER

Eckley, W., *Harriette Arnow*, 110-21.

ASHTON-WARNER, SYLVIA, 1905-

GENERAL

Durix, Carole, "The Maori in Sylvia Ashton-Warner's Fiction," *LHY* 20, i (Jan., 1979): 13-26.

_____, "Sylvia Ashton-Warner: Portrait of an Artist as a Woman," *WLWE* 19, i (1980): 104-9.

McEldowney, Dennis, "Sylvia Ashton-Warner: A Problem of Grounding," *Landfall* 23 (1969): 230-45.

BELL CALL

McEldowney, Dennis, "Sylvia Ashton-Warner: A Problem of Grounding," *Landfall* 23 (1969): 241-4.

GREENSTONE

Durix, Carole, "The Maori in Sylvia Ashton-Warner's Fiction," *LHY* 20, i (Jan., 1979): 13-26.

_____, "Natural Patterns and Rhythms in GREENSTONE by Sylvia Ashton-Warner," *CE&S* 3 (1977-78): 29-37.

INCENSE TO IDOLS

McEldowney, Dennis, "Sylvia Ashton-Warner: A Problem of Grounding," *Landfall* 23 (1969): 238-41.

Stevens, J., *New Zealand Novel*, 106-8.

SPINSTER

Bettelheim, Bruno, "Violence: A Neglected Mode of Behavior," *AAAPSS* 364 (Mar., 1966): 57-9.

Durix, Carole, "The Maori in Sylvia Ashton-Warner's Fiction," *LHY* 20, i (Jan., 1979): 13-26.

McEldowney, Dennis, "Sylvia Ashton-Warner: A Problem of Grounding," *Landfall* 23 (1969): 236-8.

Stevens, J., *New Zealand Novel*, 103-6; 127-8.

ASTLEY, THEA (BEATRICE MAY), 1925-

GENERAL

Astley, Thea, "The Idiot Question," *Southerly* 30, i (1970): 3-8.

_____, "Writing in North Queensland," *LiNQ* 9, i (1981): 2-10.

Couper, J. M., "The Novels of Thea Astley," *Meanjin* 26, iii (Sept., 1967): 332-7.

Matthews, Brian, "Life in the Eye of the Hurricane: The Novels of Thea Astley," *SoRA* 6, ii (June, 1973): 148-73.

Nash, Ellen, "Thea Astley the Novelist Next Door," *Cleo* 44 (June, 1976): 24-7. [Not seen.]

Tolchard, Clifford, and Lance Nelson, "Thea Astley: Novelist and Teacher," *Walkabout* 35 (June, 1969): 12-14. [Not seen.]

THE ACOLYTE

Matthews, Brian, "Life in the Eye of the Hurricane: The Novels of Thea Astley," *SoRA* 6, ii (June, 1973): 159-68.

BIBLIOGRAPHY

Houghton, Greg, "A Critical Checklist of Two Contemporary Australian Women Writers: Thea Astley and Elizabeth Harrower," *WLWE* 21, iii (Autumn, 1982): 557-70.

ATWOOD, MARGARET (ELEANOR), 1939-

GENERAL

Allen, Carolyn, "Failures of Word, Uses of Silence: Djuna Barnes, Adrienne Rich and Margaret Atwood," *RFI* 4, i (1978): 1-7. [Not seen.]

Anon., "Interview with Margaret Atwood," *Cencrastus* 1 (1979): 2-6.

"An *Atlantis* Interview with Margaret Atwood," *Atlantis* 5, ii (1980): 202-11.

Atwood, Margaret, "An End to Audience?" *DR* 60, iii (Autumn, 1980): 415-33.

Ayre, J., "Margaret Atwood and the End of Colonialism," *Saturday Night* 87 (Nov., 1972): 23-6.

Broege, Valerie, "Margaret Atwood's Americans and Canadians," *ECW* 22 (Summer, 1981): 111-35.

Brown, Russell M., "Atwood's Sacred Wells," *ECW* 17 (Spring, 1980): 5-43.

Cameron, Elspet, "Margaret Atwood: A Patchwork Self," *BForum* 4, i (1978): 35-45.

Davey, Frank, in Heath, J., ed., *Profiles in Canadian Literature* 2, 57-64.

Davidson, A. E., and C. N. Davidson, eds., *Art of Margaret Atwood*.

Davidson, Cathy N., "Chopin and Atwood: Woman Drowning, Woman Surfacing," *KCN* 1, iii (1975-76): 6-10. [Not seen.]

Davidson, Jim, "Margaret Atwood," *Meanjin* 37, ii (July, 1978): 189-205. [Interview.]

Fishburn, Katherine, "Perceptual Violence in Margaret Atwood's Novels," *JAC* 2, iv (Winter, 1980): 719-38.

Fulford, Robert, "The Images of Atwood," *MHRev* 41 (Jan., 1977): 95-8.

Gibson, Mary E., "A Conversation with Margaret Atwood," *ChiR* 27, iv (Spring, 1976): 105-13.

Glicksohn, Susan W., "The Martian Point of View," *Extrapolation* 15 (May, 1974): 161-73.

Grace, S., *Violent Duality*.

Grace, Sherrill E., "Moodie and Atwood: Notes on a Literary Reincarnation," 73-9 in Moss, John, ed., *Beginnings: A Critical Anthology*, Toronto: NC Press, 1980.

Griffith, Margaret, "Verbal Terrain in the Novels of Margaret Atwood," *Crit* 21, iii (1980): 85-93.

Jones, Anne G., "Margaret Atwood: Songs of the Transformer, Songs of the Transformed," *HC* 16, iii (June, 1979): 1-15.

Mansbridge, Francis, "Search for Self in the Novels of Margaret Atwood," *JCF* 22 (1978): 106-17.

McCombs, Judith, "Atwood's Nature Concepts: An Overview," *Waves* (Toronto) 7, i (Fall, 1978): 68-77.

Mitchell, Leila G., "The External World in the Novels of Margaret Atwood," *JCanStud* 15, i (Spring, 1980): 45-55.

Norris, Ken, "Survival in the Writings of Margaret Atwood," *CrossCountry* 1 (Winter, 1975): 18-29.

Oates, Joyce Carol, "A Conversation with Margaret Atwood," *OntarioR* 9 (1978-79): 5-18.

Piercy, Marge, "Margaret Atwood: Beyond Victimhood," *APR* 2, vi (Nov.-Dec., 1973): 41-4.

Rogers, Linda, "Margaret the Magician," *CanL* 60 (Spring, 1974): 83-5.

Rule, Jane, "Life, Liberty and the Pursuit of Normalcy: The Novels of Margaret Atwood," *MHRev* 41 (Jan., 1977): 42-9.

Sandler, Linda, "Interview with Margaret Atwood," *MHRev* 41 (Jan., 1977): 7-27.

Smith, Rowland, "Margaret Atwood: The Stoic Comedian," *MHRev* 41 (Jan., 1977): 134-44.

Struthers, J. R. (Tim), "An Interview with Margaret Atwood," *ECW* 6 (Spring, 1977): 18-27.

Woodcock, George, "Surfacing to Survive: Notes of the Recent Atwood," *ArielE* 4, iii (July, 1973): 16-28.

_____, "Transformation Mask for Margaret Atwood," *MHRev* 41 (Jan., 1977): 52-6.

BODILY HARM

Brydon, Diana, "Carribean Revolution and Literary Convention," *CanL* 95 (Winter, 1982): 181-5.

THE EDIBLE WOMAN

Brady, Elizabeth, "Towards a Happier History: Women and Domination," in Kontos, Akis, ed., *Domination*, Toronto: Un. of Toronto Pr., 1975, 27-30.

Carrington, Iliko de Papp, "'I'm Stuck': The Secret Sharers in THE EDIBLE WOMAN," *ECW* 23 (Spring, 1982): 68-87.

Dawe, A., Introduction to THE EDIBLE WOMAN, Toronto: McClelland & Stewart, 1973, 2-7.

Fishburn, Katherine, "Perceptual Violence in Margaret Atwood's Novels," *JAC* 2, iv (Winter, 1980): 721-6.

Grace, S., *Violent Duality*, 86-96.

Hutcheon, Linda, "Atwood and Laurence: Poet and Novelist," *SCL* 3, ii (Summer, 1978): 255-63.

Lauber, John, "Alice in Consumer-Land: The Self Discovery of Marian MacAlpine," in Moss, J., ed., *Canadian Novel: Here and Now*, 19-31.

Lecker, Robert, "Janus through the Looking Glass: Atwood's First Three Novels," in Davidson, A. E., and C. N. Davidson, eds., *Art of Margaret Atwood*, 177-203.

Lyons, Bonnie, "'Neither Victims Nor Executioners' in Magaret Atwood's Fiction," *WLWE* 17, i (April, 1978): 181-7.

MacLulich, T. D., "Atwood's Adult Fairy Tale: Levi-Strauss, Bettelheim, and THE EDIBLE WOMAN," *ECW* 11 (Summer, 1978): 111-29.

Page, Sheila, "Supermarket Survival: A Critical Analysis of Margaret Atwood's THE EDIBLE WOMAN," *Sphinx* 1 (Winter, 1974): 9-19.

Patterson, Jayne, "The Taming of Externals: A Linguistic Study of Character Transformation in Margaret Atwood's THE EDIBLE WOMAN," *SCL* 7, ii (1982): 151-67.

Woodcock, George, "Margaret Atwood," *LHY* 13, ii (July, 1972): 236-9.

LADY ORACLE

Belkin, Roslyn, "The Worth of the Shadow: Margaret Atwood's LADY ORACLE," *Thalia* 1, ii (1978-79): 3-8.

Cameron, Elspeth, "Margaret Atwood: A Patchwork Self," *BForum* 4, i (1978): 35-45.

Cude, Wilfred, "Bravo Mothball! An Essay on LADY ORACLE," in Moss, J., ed., *Canadian Novel: Here and Now*, 45-50.

_____, "Nobody Dunit: The Loose End as Structural Element in LADY ORACLE," *JCanStud* 15, i (1980): 30-44.

Davey, Frank, "LADY ORACLE's Secret: Atwood's Comic Novels," *SCL* 5 (1980): 209-21.

Davidson, Arnold E., and Cathy N. Davidson, "Margaret Atwood's LADY ORACLE: The Artist as Escapist and Seer," *SCL* 3 (1978): 166-77.

Davidson, Cathy N., "Canadian Wry: Comic Vision in Atwood's LADY ORACLE and Laurence's THE DIVINERS," *RFI* 3, ii-iii (1977-78): 50-5.

Fishburn, Katherine, "Perceptual Violence in Margaret Atwood's Novels," *JAC* 2, iv (Winter, 1980): 731-7.

Freibert, Lucy M., "The Artist as Picaro: The Revelation of Margaret Atwood's LADY ORACLE," *CanL* 92 (Spring, 1982): 23-3.

Grace, S., *Violent Duality*, 111-28.

Irvine, Lorna, "A Psychological Journey: Mothers and Daughters in English-Canadian Fiction," in Davidson, C. N., & E. M. Broner, eds., *Lost Tradition*, 244-5.

Jeannette, M. Sharon, "An Emotional Divide," *Sphinx* 7 (1977): 81-5.

Lecker, Robert, "Janus through the Looking Glass: Atwood's First Three Novels," in Davidson, A. E., and C. N. Davidson, eds., *Art of Margaret Atwood*, 177-203.

MacLean, Susan, "LADY ORACLE: The Art of Reality and the Reality of Art," *JCF* 28-29 (1980): 179-97.

Mansbridge, Francis, "Search for Self in the Novels of Margaret Atwood," *JCF* 22 (1978): 113-17.

Rosowski, Susan J., "Margaret Atwood's LADY ORACLE: Social Mythology and the Gothic Novel," *RS* 49, ii (June, 1981): 87-98.

Ross, Catherine S., "'Banished to This Other Place': Atwood's LADY ORACLE," *ESC* 6 (1980): 460-74.

Stewart, G., *New Mythos*, 93-5, 170-4.

Thomas, Clara, "LADY ORACLE: The Narrative of a Fool-Heroine," in Davidson, A. E., and C. N. Davidson, eds., *Art of Margaret Atwood*, 159-75.

Wilson, Sharon R., "The Fragmented Self in LADY ORACLE," *CNIE* 1, i (Jan., 1982): 50-85.

LIFE BEFORE MAN

Davidson, Cathy N., and Arnold E., "Prospects and Retrospect in LIFE BEFORE MAN," in Davidson, A. E., and C. N. Davidson, eds., *Art of Margaret Atwood*, 205-21.

Grace, Sherrill E., "'Time Present and Time Past': LIFE BEFORE MAN," *ECW* 20 (Winter, 1980-81): 165-70.

Grace, S., *Violent Duality*, 135-8.

Jeannote, M. Sharon, "Tension between the Mundane and the Cosmic," *Sphinx* 3, iv (1981): 74-82.

Tanner, Stephen L., "Those Tedious Extremist Victories," *ChronC* 4, iv (July-Aug., 1980): 13-14.

SURFACING

Bjerring, Nancy E., "The Problem of Language in Margaret Atwood's SURFACING," *QQ* 83, iv (Winter, 1976): 597-612.

Brown, Russell M., "In Search of Lost Causes: The Canadian Novelist as Mystery Writer," *Mosaic* 11, iii (Spring, 1978): 1-15.

Campbell, Josie P. "The Woman as Hero in Margaret Atwood's SURFACING," *Mosaic* 11, iii (Spring, 1978): 17-28.

Cederstrom, Lofelei, "The Regeneration of Time in Atwood's SURFACING," *Atlantis* 6, ii (Spring, 1981): 24-37.

Christ, Carol P., "Margaret Atwood: The Surfacing of Women's Spiritual Quest and Vision," *Signs* 2, ii (1976): 316-30.

_____, "Refusing to be Victim," *Diving Deep and Surfacing*, 41-53.

Colman, S. J., "Margaret Atwood, Lucien Goldmann's Pascal, and the Meaning of 'Canada,'" *UTQ* 48, iii (1979): 245-62.

Davey, Frank, "Atwood Walking Backwards," *Open Letter*, 2nd Ser. 5 (Summer, 1973): 74-84.

Davidson, Arnold E., and Cathy N., "The Anatomy of Margaret Atwood's SURFACING," *ArielE* 10, iii (July, 1979): 38-54.

Ewell, Barbara C., "The Language of Alienation in Margaret Atwood's SURFACING," *CentR* 25, ii (Spring, 1981): 185-202.

Fishburn, Katherine, "Perceptual Violence in Margaret Atwood's Novels," *JAC* 2, iv (Winter, 1980): 726-31.

Garebian, Keith, "SURFACING: Apocalyptic Ghost Story," *Mosaic* 9, iii (Spring, 1976): 1-9.

Gerson, Carole, "Margaret Atwood and Quebec: A Footnote on SURFACING," *SCL* 1, i (Winter, 1976): 115-19.

Gerstenberger, Donna, "Conceptions Literary and Otherwise: Women Writers and the Modern Imagination," *Novel* 9, ii (Winter, 1976): 141-50.

Gottlieb, Lois C., and Wendy Keitner, "Colonialism as Metaphor and Experience in THE GRASS IS SINGING and SURFACING," in Narasimhaiah, C. D., ed., *Awakened Conscience*, 307-14.

Grace, S., *Violent Quality*, 97-110.

Harcourt, Joan, "Atwood Country," *QQ* 80, ii (Summer, 1973): 278-81.

Harrison, James, "The 20,000,000 Solitudes of SURFACING," *DR* 59 (1979): 74-81.

Hinz, Evelyn J., "The Masculine/Feminine Psychology of American/Canadian Primitivism: DELIVERANCE and SURFACING," in Winks, R. W., ed., *Other Voices, Other Views*, 75-96.

_____, and John J. Teunissen, "SURFACING: Margaret Atwood's 'Nymph Complaining'," *CanL* 20 (Spring, 1979): 221-36.

James, William C., "Atwood's SURFACING," *CanL* 91 (Winter, 1981): 174-81.

King, Bruce, "Margaret Atwood's SURFACING," *JCL* 12, i (Aug., 1977): 23-32.

Lecker, Robert, "Janus through the Looking Glass: Atwood's First Three Novels," in Davidson, A. E., and C. N. Davidson, eds., *Art of Margaret Atwood*, 177-203.

Lyons, Bonnie, "'Neither Victims Nor Executioners' in Margaret Atwood's Fiction," *WLWE* 17, i (April, 1978): 181-7.

Mansbridge, Francis, "Search for Self in the Novels of Margaret Atwood," *JCF* 22 (1978): 110-13.

McLay, Catherine, "The Divided Self: Theme and Pattern in Margaret Atwood's SURFACING," *JCF* 4, i (1975): 82-95: Also in Moss, J., ed., *Canadian Novel: Here and Now*, 32-44.

Miller, Hugh, "Surfacing to No Purpose: Margaret Atwood's Apparent Survival," *AntigR* No. 24 (Winter, 1975): 59-61.

Morley, Patricia, "Multiple Surfaces," *JCF* 1, iv (Fall, 1972): 99-100.

Moss, J., *Sex and Violence in the Canadian Novel*, 126-31, 139-44.

Northey, Margot, "Sociological Gothic: WILD GEESE and SURFACING," *Haunted Wilderness*, 62-9.

Onley, Gloria, "Margaret Atwood: Surfacing in the Interests of Survival," *WCR* 7, iii (Jan., 1973): 51-4.

Plaskow, Judith, "On Carol Christ on Margaret Atwood: Some Theological Reflections," *Signs* 2, iii (1976): 331-9.

Pratt, Annis, "SURFACING and the Rebirth Journey," in Davidson, A. E., and C. N. Davidson, eds., *Art of Margaret Atwood*, 139-57.

Quigley, Theresia, "SURFACING: A Critical Study," *AntigR* 34 (1978): 177-87.

Rigney, Barbara H., "'After the Failure of Logic': Descent and Return in SURFACING," in *Madness and Sexual Politics in the Feminist Novel*, 91-115.

Rocard, Mercienne, "Margaret Atwood's SURFACING: A Pilgrimage to the Sources," *Caliban* 14 (1977): 39-46.

Rosenberg, Jerome H., "Woman as Everyman in Atwood's SURFACING: Some Observations on the End of the Novel," *SCL* 3, i (Winter, 1978): 127-32.

Ross, Catherine S., "Nancy Drew as Shaman: Atwood's SURFACING," *CanL* 84 (1980): 7-17.

_____, "'A Singing Spirit': Female Rites of Passage in KLEEWYCK, SURFACING, and THE DIVINERS," *Atlantis* 4, i (1978): 86-94.

Rubinstein, Roberta, "SURFACING: Margaret Atwood's Journey to the Interior," *MFS* 22, iii (Autumn, 1976): 387-99.

Schaeffer, Susan F., "'It Is Time That Separates Us': Margaret Atwood's SURFACING," *CentR* 18, iv (Fall, 1974): 319-37.

Stein, Karen F., "Reflections in a Jagged Mirror: Some Metaphors of Madness," *Aphra* 6, ii (Spring, 1975): 6-10.

Stewart, G., *New Mythos*, 95-7, 157-61.

Sullivan, Rosemary, "SURFACING and DELIVERANCE," *CanL* 67 (Winter, 1976): 6-20.

Sweetapple, Rosemary, "Margaret Atwood: Victims and Survivors," *SoRA* 9, i (Mar., 1976): 50-69.

Woodcock, George, "Surfacing to Survive: Notes of the Recent Atwood," *ArielE* 4, iii (July, 1973): 16-28.

BIBLIOGRAPHY

Fairbanks, Carol, "Margaret Atwood: A Bibliography of Criticism," *BB* 36, ii (Apr.-June, 1979): 85-90, 98.

Horne, Alan J., "Margaret Atwood: An Annotated Bibliography (Prose)," 13-46 in Lecker, Robert, and Jack David, eds., *The Annotated Bibliography of Canada's Major Authors, Volume One*, Downsview: ECW, 1979.

_____, "Margaret Atwood: A Checklist of Writings by and about Margaret Atwood," in Davidson, A. E., and C. N. Davidson, eds., *Art of Margaret Atwood*, 243-85.

_____, comp., "A Preliminary Checklist of Writings by and about Margaret Atwood," *MHRev* 41 (Jan., 1977): 195-222.

AUCHINCLOSS, LOUIS, 1917-

GENERAL

Kane, Patricia, "Lawyers at the Top: The Fiction of Louis Auchincloss," *Crit* 7, ii (Winter, 1964-65): 36-46.

Milne, W. Gordon, "Auchincloss and the Novel of Manners," *UKCR* 29 (Mar., 1963): 177-85.

Tuttleton, James W., "Louis Auchincloss: The Image of Lost Elegance and Virtue," *AL* 43, iv (Jan., 1972): 616-32. Also in Tuttleton, J. W., *Novel of Manners in America*, 245-61.

THE EMBEZZLERS

Westbrook, Wayne W., "Louis Auchincloss' Vision of Wall Street," *Crit* 15, ii (1973): 57-66.

THE HOUSE OF FIVE TALENTS

Macauley, Robie, "Let Me Tell You About the Rich…," *KR* 27 (Autumn, 1965): 653-5.

Tuttleton, James W., "Louis Auchincloss: The Image of Lost Elegance and Virtue," *AL* 43, iv (Jan., 1972): 623-8. Also in Tuttleton, J. W., *Novel of Manners in America*, 253-7.

THE HOUSE OF THE PROPHET

Tanner, Stephen L., "Direct Clarity and Elliptical Subtlelty," *ChronC* 4, v (Sept.-Oct., 1980): 14-15.

THE RECTOR OF JUSTIN

Auchincloss, L., "Writing THE RECTOR OF JUSTIN," in McCormack, T., ed., *Afterwords*, 3-9.

Spender, Stephen, "Traditional vs. Underground Novels," in Encyclopedia Britannica, *Great Ideas Today*, 1965, 186-7.

VENUS IN SPARTA

Allen, W., *Modern Novel*, 313-14.

A WORLD OF PROFIT

Long, Robert E., "The Image of Gatsby in the Fiction of Louis Auchincloss and C. D. B. Bryan," *FHA* (1972): 325-6.

AYRTON, MICHAEL, 1921-1975

THE MAZE MAKER

Davie, Donald, "Michael Ayrton's THE MAZE MAKER," *SoR* 5 (Summer, 1969): 640-54.

BACH, RICHARD, 1936-

JONATHAN LIVINGSTON SEAGULL

Bolen, James G., "Interview: Richard Bach," *Psychic* 5, vi (Sept.-Oct., 1974): 6-11.

Merry, Bruce, "Spiritual Uplift and the Best-Seller: Some Notes on Richard Bach's JONATHAN LIVINGSTON SEAGULL and Erich Segal's LOVE STORY," *LonM* 14, iii (1974): 80-95.

Misra, B. K., "JONATHAN LIVINGSTON SEAGULL: A Critique of Flight," *LCrit* 16, i (1981): 1-10.

Turovskaya, M., "JONATHAN LIVINGSTON SEAGULL," in Vroon, R., tr., *20th Century American Literature: A Soviet View*, 478-83.

BAIL, MURRAY, 1941-

GENERAL

Legasse, Jim, "The Voice of the Form and the Form of the Voice," *Westerly* 25 (Mar., 1980): 97-101. [Not seen.]

HOMESICKNESS

Anderson, Fon, "Murray Bail: HOMESICKNESS," *Westerly* 25, iv (Dec., 1980): 94-6.

BAINBRIDGE, BERYL (MARGARET), 1933-

GENERAL

May, Yolanta, "Interview with Beryl Bainbridge," *New Rev* 3, xxxiii (1976): 48-52.

BAKER, ELLIOTT, 1922-

A FINE MADNESS

Noland, Richard W., "Lunacy and Poetry: Elliott Baker's A FINE MADNESS," *Crit* 8, iii (Spring-Summer, 1966): 71-8.

BALDWIN, JAMES, 1924-1987

GENERAL

Alexander, Charlotte, "The 'Stink' of Reality: Mothers and Whores in James Baldwin's Fiction," *L&P* 18, i (1968): 9-26. Also in Kinnamon, K., ed., *James Baldwin*, 77-95.

Anon., in *TLS* (Sept. 6, 1963). Also, Anon., "Black Man's Burden: James Baldwin as Man and Writer," in *T.L.S.: Essays and Reviews from The Times Literary Supplement, 1963*, 16-21.

Arana, Gregorio, "The Baffling Creator—A Study of the Writing of James Baldwin," *Caribbean Qtly* 12 (1966): 3-23. [Not seen.]

Bachrach, Judy, "James Baldwin: Still Grounded in Despair," *Pacific Coast Africanist Assn. Occasional Paper* 3 (April, 1981): 1-4.

Baker, Houston A., Jr., "The Embattled Craftsman: An Essay on James Baldwin," *Jour of African-Afro-Amer. Affairs* 1, i (1977): 28-51. [Not seen.]

Banta, Thomas J., "James Baldwin's Discovery of Identity," *Mawazo* 2, i (1969): 33-41. [Not seen.]

Bennett, Joanne S., "James Baldwin: A Contemporary Novelist of Manners," *DAI* 35 (1974): 2212A (Ind.).

Berghahn, M., *Images of Africa in Black American Literature*, 171-87.

Bhattacharya, Lokenath, "James Baldwin," *Quest* (India), No. 44 (Winter, 1965): 78-83.

Bigsb, C. W. E., "The Divided Mind of James Baldwin," *JAmS* 13, iii (Dec., 1979): 325-42.

Binder, Wolfgang, "James Baldwin: An Interview," *RevI* 10, iii (Fall, 1980): 326-41.

"The Black Scholar Interviews: James Baldwin," *BSch* 5, iv (1973-74): 33-42.

Bone, R. A., *Negro Novel in America,* 215-39. Also in Kinnamon, K., ed., *James Baldwin,* 28-51.

_____, "The Novels of James Baldwin," *TriQ* No. 2 (Winter, 1965): 3-20. Also in Gross, S. L., and J. E. Hardy, eds., *Images of the Negro in American Literature,* 265-88.

Boyle, Kay, "Introducing James Baldwin," in Moore, H. T., ed., *Contemporary American Novelists,* 155-7.

Bradford, Melvin E., "Faulkner, James Baldwin and the South," *GaR* 20 (Winter, 1966): 431-43.

Breit, Harvey, in Balakian, N., and C. Simmons, eds., *Creative Present,* 5-18.

Britt, David D., "The Image of the White Man in the Fiction of Langston Hughes, Richard Wright, James Baldwin and Ralph Ellison," *DA* 19 (1968): 1532A (Emory).

Champion, Ernest A., "James Baldwin and the Challenge of Ethnic Literature in the Eighties," *MELUS* 8, ii (Summer, 1981): 61-4.

Charney, Maurice, "James Baldwin's Quarrel with Richard Wright," *AQ* 15 (Spring, 1963): 65-75. Also in Gibson, D. B., ed., *Five Black Writers,* 243-53.

Cleaver, Eldridge, "Notes on a Native Son," *Ramparts* 5 (June, 1966): 51-6. Also in Cleaver, E., *Soul on Ice,* N.Y.: McGraw-Hill, 1968, 97-111. Also in Kinnamon, K., ed., *James Baldwin,* 66-76.

Coles, Robert, "Baldwin's Burden," *PR* 31 (Summer, 1964): 409-16.

Dance, Daryl C., "You Can't Go Home Again: James Baldwin and the South," *CLAJ* 18, i (Sept., 1974): 81-90.

Daniels, Mark R., "Estrangement, Betrayal & Atonement: The Political Theory of James Baldwin," *SBL* 7, iii (1976): 10-13.

Dickstein, Morris, "Wright, Baldwin, Cleaver," *NewL* 38, iii (Dec., 1971): 117-24. Also in Ray, D., and R. M. Farnsworth, eds., *Richard Wright,* 183-90.

Elkoff, Marvin, "Everybody Knows His Name," *Esquire* 62, ii (Aug., 1964): 59-64+.

English, Charles, "Another Viewpoint," *Jubilee* 11 (Aug., 1963): 43-6.

Finkelstein, S., *Existentialism and Alienation in American Literature,* 276-84.

Finn, James, "The Identity of James Baldwin," *Cweal* 77 (Oct. 26, 1962): 113-16.

Fisher, Lester A., "The Uses and Effects of Violence in the Fiction and Drama of James Baldwin," *DAI* 38 (1977): 261A.

Foote, Dorothy, "James Baldwin's 'Holler Books,'" *CEA* 25, viii (May, 1963): 8, 11.

Foster, David E., "'Cause my house fell down': The Theme of the Fall in James Baldwin's Novels," *Crit* 13, ii (1971): 50-62.

Gayle, Addison, Jr., "A Defense of James Baldwin," *CLAJ* x (Mar., 1967): 201-8.

Gérard, Albert, "The Sons of Ham," *SNNTS* 3, ii (Summer, 1971): 148-64.

Gibson, Donald B., "James Baldwin: The Political Anatomy of Space," in O'Daniel, T. B., ed., *James Baldwin,* 3-18.

Gray, Simon, "Whose Little Boy?" *Delta* (Cambridge, England) No. 35 (Spring, 1965): 2-8.

Gross, G. L., *Heroic Ideal in American Literature,* 166-79.

Gross, Theodore, "The World of James Baldwin," *Crit* 7, ii (Winter, 1964-65): 139-49.

Harper, H. M., Jr., "James Baldwin—Art or Propaganda?" in *Desperate Faith,* 137-61.

Hernton, Calvin C., "Blood of the Lamb and a Fiery Baptism: The Ordeal of James Baldwin," *Amistad* 1 (1970): 183-217.

Holloway, Clayton G., "James Baldwin as a Writer of Short Fiction: An Evaluation," *DAI* 36 (1976): 7409A.

Howe, Irving, "Black Boys and Native Sons," *Dissent* 10 (Autumn, 1963): 353-68. Also in Howe, I., *World More Attractive,* 98-122. Also in Howe, I., *Decline of the New,* N.Y.: Harcourt, Brace, World, 1970, 167-87. Reprinted in Gibson, D. B., ed., *Five Black Writers,* 254-70.

Hughes, Joanne C., "Elements of the Confessional Mode in the Novels of James Baldwin: 1954-1979," *DAI* 41, vii (Jan., 1981): 3107A.

Isaacs, Harold R., "Five Writers and their African Ancestors," *Phylon* 21 (1960): 322-9.

Jackson, Edward M., "Fathers and Sons: An Analysis of the Writings of James Baldwin," *DAI* 37 (1976): 2181A.

Jackson, Jocelyn E. W., "The Problem of Identity in the Essays and Selected Novels of James Baldwin," *DAI* 34 (1973): 2629A (Emory).

Jones, B. F., "James Baldwin: The Struggle for Identity," *Brit Jnl of Soc* 17 (June, 1966): 107-21.

Kent, George E., "Baldwin and the Problem of Being," *CLAJ* 7, iii (Mar., 1964): 202-14. Also in Kinnamon, K., ed., *James Baldwin,* 16-27. Also in O'Daniel, T. B., ed., *James Baldwin,* 19-29. Also in Gibson, D. B., ed., *Five Black Writers,* 148-58. Also in Kent, G., *Blackness and Adventure of Western Culture,* 139-50.

Kim, Kichung, "Wright, the Protest Novel, and Baldwin's Faith," *CLAJ* 17, iii (Mar., 1974): 387-96.

Kinnamon, K., ed., *James Baldwin.*

Korzus, Margret G. C., "James Baldwin's Concept of the Artist and the Rebel: An Interpretation Based on Albert Camus and Otto Rank," *DAI* 37 (1977): 4354A.

Langer, Lawrence, "To Make Freedom Real: James Baldwin and the Conscience of America," in Lanzinger, Klaus, ed., *Americana-Austriaca,* 217-28.

Lash, John, "Baldwin Beside Himself: A Study in Modern Phallicism," *CLAJ* 8 (Dec., 1964): 132-40. Also in O'Daniel, T. B., ed., *James Baldwin,* 47-55.

Lee, Brian, "James Baldwin: Caliban to Prospero," in Bigsby, C. W. E., ed., *Black American Writer,* Vol. I, 169-79.

Lee, Robert A., "James Baldwin and Matthew Arnold: Thoughts on 'Relevance'," *CLAJ* 14, iii (Mar., 1971): 324-30.

Long, Robert E., "Love and Wrath in the Fiction of James Baldwin," *EngR* 19, iii (Feb., 1969): 50-7.

Lottman, Herbert R., "It's Hard to Be James Baldwin: An Interview," *IntellectualD* (July, 1967): 67-8.

Macebuh, S., *James Baldwin.*

MacInnes, Colin, "Dark Angel: The Writings of James Baldwin," *Encounter* 21, (Aug., 1963): 22-33. Also in Gibson, D. B., ed., *Five Black Writers,* 119-42.

Margolies, E., "The Negro Church: James Baldwin and the Christian Vision," in *Native Sons,* 102-26.

Matatu, Godwin, "James Baldwin, the Renowned Black-American Novelist, Talks to Godwin Matatu," *Africa: Internat. Bus. Econ. & Pol. Monthly,* 37 (1974): 68-9.

McCarthy, H. T., *Expatriate Perspective,* 197-213.

Mergen, Bernard, "James Baldwin and the American Conundrum," *MSpr* 57 (1963): 397-406.

Moller, Karin, "James Baldwin's Theme of 'Identity' and His 'Fall' Metaphor," *EL* 2, ii (Mar., 1974): 34-50.

Mosher, Marlene, "James Baldwin's Blues," *CLAJ* 26, i (Sept., 1982): 112-24.

Mowe, Gregory, and W. Scott Nobles, "James Baldwin's Message for White America," *QJS* 58, ii (April, 1972): 142-51.

Noble, D. W., *Eternal Adam and the New World Garden*, 215-16.

O'Brien, C. C., "White Gods and Black Americans," *NStat* (May, 1964). Also in *Writers and Politics*, N. Y.: Pantheon, 1964, 17-22.

O'Daniel, Therman B., "James Baldwin: An Interpretive Study," *CLAJ* 7 (Sept., 1963): 37-47.

_____, ed., *James Baldwin*.

Ogutu, Martin, "James Baldwin on Christianity," *Kucha* (Nairobi) 1, i (1977): 25-8. [Not seen.]

Orsagh, Jacqueline E., "Baldwin's Female Characters—A Step Forward?" in O'Daniel, T. B., ed., *James Baldwin*, 56-68.

Paliwal, G. D., "African Consciousness in Modern American Fiction: A Note on Novels by Wright, Ellison and Baldwin," *RUSEng* 10 (1977): 62-70. [Not seen.]

Porter, Horace A., "James Baldwin and the Problem of Vocation," *DAI* 42 (1981): 2679A.

Povey, John, "Achebe and Baldwin in C. B. Land—10-4 Good Buddy!!! A Dialogue at the African Literature Assn. Meeting, Gainesville, Florida, March, 1980," *Pacific Coast Africanist Assn. Occasional Paper* 3 (April, 1981): 7-9. [Not seen.]

Pratt, Louis H., "James Bladwin and 'the Literary Ghetto,'"*CLAJ* 20 (1976): 262-72.

_____, "The Mystery of the Human Being: A Critical Study of the Writings of James Baldwin," *DAI* 35 (1975): 6154A.

Reid, Kenneth R., "James Baldwin's Fiction: Literary Artistry in Special Pleading," *DAI* 33 (1972): 2392A (Kan. State).

Rive, Richard, "Writing and the New Society," *Contrast* 12, iii (June, 1979): 60-7.

Roberts, John W., "The Uses and Functions of Afro-American Folk and Popular Music in the Fiction of James Baldwin," *DAI* 37 (1977): 5126A.

Sayre, Robert F., "James Baldwin's Other Country," in Moore, H. T., ed., *Contemporary American Novelists*, 158-69.

Schroth, Raymond A., S. J., "James Baldwin's Search," *CathW* 198 (Feb., 1964): 288-94.

Sen, Sunil K., "The Dilemma of James Baldwin: A Note," *VisvaBharatiQ* 37, iii-iv (Nov., 1971-Apr., 1972): 259-63.

Spillers, Hortense, "The Politics of Intimacy: A Discussion," in Bell, R. P., et al., eds., *Sturdy Black Bridges*, 87-92.

Standley, Fred L., "'...Farther and Farther Apart': Richard Wright and James Baldwin," in Hakutani, Y., ed., *Critical Essays on Richard Wright*, 91-103.

_____, "James Baldwin: The Artist as Incorrigible Disturber of the Peace," *SHR* 4, i (Winter, 1970): 18-30.

_____, "James Baldwin: The Crucial Situation," *SAQ* 65 (Summer, 1966): 371-81.

Sylvander, C. W., *James Baldwin*.

Thornton, Jerome E., "James Baldwin and the Christian Tradition," *DAI* 37 (1977): 5130A-31A.

Van Heusen, Lawrence L., "The Embodiment of Religious Meaning in the Works of James Baldwin," *DAI* 41 (1980): 675A.

Van Sickle, Milton, "James Baldwin in Black and White," *Trace* No. 54 (Autumn, 1964): 222-5.

Virágos, Zsolt, "James Baldwin: Stereotype versus Counter-Stereotype," *HSE* 11 (1977): 131-41.

Vopat, James B., "Beyond Sociology? Urban Experience in the Novels of James Baldwin," in Carter, G. E., J. R. Parker, and S. Bentley, eds., *Minority Literature and the Urban Experience*, 51-8.

Wasserstrom, William, "James Baldwin: Stepping Out on the Promise," in Les, A. R., ed., *Black Fiction*, 74-96.

Watson, Edward A., "The Novels of James Baldwin: Case-Book of a 'Lover's War' with the United States," *QQ* 72 (1965): 385-402.

Werner, Craig, "The Economic Evolution of James Baldwin," *CLAJ* 23, i (Sept., 1979): 12-31.

Zietlow, Edward R., "Wright to Hansberry: The Evolution of Outlook in Four Negro Writers," *DA* 28 (1967): 701A (Un. of Washington).

ANOTHER COUNTRY

Alexander, Charlotte, "The 'Stink' of Reality: Mothers and Whores in James Baldwin's Fiction," *L&P* 18, i (1968): 15-21. Also in Kinnamon, K., ed., *James Baldwin*, 83-90.

Auchincloss, Eve, and Nancy Lynch, "Disburber of the Peace: James Baldwin, An Interview," in Bigsby, C. W. E., ed., *Black American Writer*, Vol. I, 199-215.

Ayman, S. E., "No Country of Young Men," in *Standards*, 78-82.

Beje, Morris, "It Must Be Important: Negroes in Contemporary American Fiction," *AR* 24 (Fall, 1964): 333-6.

Berry, Boyd M., "Another Man Done Gone: Self Pity in Baldwin's ANOTHER COUNTRY," *Mich Qtly Rev* 5 (Fall, 1966): 285-90.

Blount, Trevor, "A Slight Error in Continuity in James Baldwin's ANOTHER COUNTRY," *N&Q* 13 (March, 1966): 102-3.

Bone, R. A., *Negro Novel in America*, 228-39. Also in Kinnamon, K., ed., *James Baldwin*, 41-51.

_____, "The Novels of James Baldwin," *TriQ* No. 2 (Winter, 1965): 12-20. Also in Kinnamon, K., ed., *James Baldwin*, 41-51. Also in Gross, S. L., and J. E. Hardy, eds., *Images of the Negro in American Literature*, 278-88.

Britt, David D., "America: ANOTHER COUNTRY, *Ba Shiru* 4 (1972): 47-51.

Collier, Eugenie W., "The Phrase Unbearably Repeated," *Phylon* 25 (Fall, 1964): 288-96. Also in O'Daniel, T. B., ed., *James Baldwin*, 38-46.

Cox, C. B., and A. R. Jones, "After the Tranquilized Fifties: Notes on Sylvia Plath and James Baldwin," *CritQ* 6 (Summer, 1964): 115-19.

Dane, Peter, "Baldwin's Other Country," *Transition*, 5 (1966): 38-40.

Ferguson, Alfred R., "Black Men, White Cities: The Quest for Humanity by Black Protagonists in James Baldwin's ANOTHER COUNTRY and Richard Wright's THE OUTSIDER," *BSUF* 18, ii (1977): 51-8.

Finkelstein, S., *Existentialism and Alienation in American Literature*, 280-4.

Finn, James, "The Identity of James Baldwin," *Cweal* 77 (Oct. 26, 1962): 114-16.

Foster, David E., "'Cause my house fell down': The Theme of the 'Fall' in Baldwin's Novels," *Crit* 13, ii (1971): 59-62.

Gayle, A., Jr., *Way of the New World*, 214-20.

Gérard, Albert, "The Sons of Ham," *SNNTS* 3, ii (Summer, 1971): 157-64.

Glazier, Lyle, "Suffering Doesn't have a Color," *Litera* 8 (1965): 91-8.

Gross, Barry, "The 'Uninhabitable Darkness' of Baldwin's ANOTHER COUNTRY: Image and Theme," *NALF* 6 (1972): 113-21.

Gross, T. L., *Heroic Ideal in American Literature,* 170-4.

Gross, Theodore, "The World of James Baldwin," *Crit* 7, ii (1965): 142-6.

Harper, H. M., Jr., in *Desperate Faith,* 151-9.

Hentoff, Nat, in *Midstream* 8 (Dec., 1962): 103-6.

Klein, M., in *After Alienation,* 188-95.

Lee, Brian, "James Baldwin: Caliban to Prospero," in Bigsby, C. W. E., ed., *Black American Writer,* Vol. I, 173-6.

Littlejohn, D., *Black on White,* 125-33.

Long, Robert E., "Love and Wrath in the Fiction of James Baldwin," *EngR* 19, iii (Feb., 1969): 51-4.

Macebuh, S., *James Baldwin,* 84-101.

MacInnes, Colin, "Dark Angel: The Writings of James Baldwin," *Encounter* 21, ii (Aug., 1963): 28-31. Also in Gibson, D. B., ed., *Five Black Writers,* 132-6.

Margolies, E., "The Negro Church: James Baldwin and the Christian Vision," in *Native Sons,* 118-22.

Newman, Charles, "The Lesson of the Master: Henry James and James Baldwin," *YR* 56, i (Oct., 1966): 45-59. Also in Kinnamon, K., ed., *James Baldwin,* 52-65.

Podhoretz, Norman, "In Defense of a Maltreated Best Seller," *Show* 2 (Oct., 1962): 91-2. Also in Kostelanetz, R., ed., *On Contemporary Literature,* 232-7. Also in Podhoretz, N., *Doings and Undoings,* 244-50. Also in Gibson, D. B., ed., *Five Black Writers,* 143-7.

Prasad, Thakur G., "ANOTHER COUNTRY: The Tensions of Dream and Nightmare in the American Psyche," Naik, M. K. et al., eds., *Indian Studies in American Fiction,* 296-310.

Rosenblatt, R., *Black Fiction,* 151-8.

Rupp, Richard H., "James Baldwin: The Search for Celebration," *Celebration in Postwar American Fiction,* 144-8.

Sayre, Robert F., in Moore, H. T., ed., *Contemporary American Novelists,* 165-9.

Schraufnagel, N., *From Apology to Protest,* 151-3.

Schrero, Elliott M., "ANOTHER COUNTRY and the Sense of Self," *BARev* 2, i-i (Spring-Summer, 1971): 91-100.

Scott, Robert, "Rhetoric, Black Power, and Baldwin's ANOTHER COUNTRY," *JBS* 1, i (Sept., 1970): 21-34.

Standley, Fred L., "ANOTHER COUNTRY, Another Time," *SNNTS* 4, iii (Fall, 1972): 504-12.

Sylvander, C. W., *James Baldwin,* 52-66.

Thelwell, Mike, "ANOTHER COUNTRY: Baldwin's New York Novel," in Bigsby, C. W. E., ed., *Black American Writer,* Vol. I, 181-98.

Watson, Edward A., "The Novels and Essays of James Baldwin," *QQ* 72 (Summer, 1965): 305-7.

Werner, Craig, "The Economic Evolution of James Baldwin," *CLAJ* 23, i (Sept., 1979): 23-5.

GIOVANNI'S ROOM

Alexander, Charlotte, "The 'Stink' of Reality: Mothers and Whores in James Baldwin's Fiction," *L&P* 18, i (1968): 9-15. Also in Kinnamon, K., ed., *James Baldwin,* 77-83.

Bell, George E., "The Dilemma of Love in GO TELL IT ON THE MOUNTAIN and GIOVANNI'S ROOM," *CLAJ* 17 (1974): 397-406.

Bigsby, C. W. E., "From Protest to Paradox: The Black Writer at Mid Century," in French, W., ed., *Fifties,* 237-40.

Bone, R. A., *Negro Novel in America,* 226-8. Also in Kinnamon, K., ed., *James Baldwin,* 38-40.

_____, "The Novels of James Baldwin," *TriQ* No. 2 (Winter, 1965): 10-12. Also in Gross, S. L., and J. E. Hardy, eds., *Images of the Negro in American Literature,* 275-8.

Foster, David E., "'Cause my house fell down': The Theme of the Fall in Baldwin's Novels," *Crit* 13, ii (1971): 55-9.

Harper, H. M., Jr., *Desperate Faith,* 147-51.

Hoffman, Stanton, "The Cities of Night: John Rechy's CITY OF NIGHT and the American Literature of Homosexuality," *ChiR* 17, ii-iii (1964-65): 198-200.

Klein, M., *After Alienation,* 184-8.

Littlejohn, D., *Black on White,* 124-5.

Macebuh, S., *James Baldwin,* 70-82.

MacInnes, Colin, "Dark Angel: The Writings of James Baldwin," *Encounter* 21, ii (Aug., 1963): 25-8. Also in Gibson, D. B., ed., *Five Black Writers,* 126-31.

Margolies, E., "The Negro Church: James Baldwin and the Christian Vision," in *Native Sons,* 114-18.

Noble, D. W., *Eternal Adam and the New World Garden,* 212-15.

Rupp, Richard H., "James Baldwin: The Search for Celebration," *Celebration in Postwar American Fiction,* 140-4.

Sayre, Robert F., in Moore, H. T., ed., *Contemporary American Novelists,* 163-5.

Straumann, H., *American Literature in the Twentieth Century,* 40-1.

Sylvander, C. W., *James Baldwin,* 45-52.

Watson, Edward, "The Novels and Essays of James Baldwin," *QQ* 72 (Summer, 1965): 391-2.

Werner, Craig, "The Economic Evolution of James Baldwin," *CLAJ* 23, i (Sept., 1979): 21-3.

GO TELL IT ON THE MOUNTAIN

Alexander, Charlotte, "The 'Stink' of Reality: Mothers and Whores in James Baldwin's Fiction," *L&P* 18, i (1968): 21-3. Also in Kinnamon, K, ed., *James Baldwin,* 90-2.

Allen, Shirley S., "The Ironic Voice in Baldwin's GO TELL IT ON THE MOUTAIN," in O'Daniel, T. B., ed., *James Baldwin,* 30-7.

_____, "Religious Symbolism and Psychic Reality in Baldwin's GO TELL IT ON THE MOUNTAIN," *CLAJ* 19 (1975): 173-99.

Allen, W., *Modern Novel,* 320-1.

Barthold, B. J., *Black Time,* 51-3.

Bell, George E., "The Dilemma of Love in GO TELL IT ON THE MOUNTAIN and GIOVANNI'S ROOM," *CLAJ* 19 (1974): 397-406.

Bigsby, C. W. E., "From Protest to Paradox: The Black Writer at Mid Century," in French, W., ed., *Fifties,* 235-7.

Bloomfield, Caroline, "Religion and Alienation in James Baldwin, Bernard Malamud, and James F. Powers," *Religious Education* 57 (Mar.-April, 1962): 100-1.

Bone, R. A., *Negro Novel in America,* 218-25. Also in Kinnamon, K., ed., *James Baldwin,* 31-8.

_____, "The Novels of James Baldwin," *TriQ* No. 2 (Winter, 1965): 5-10. Also in Gross, S. L., and J. E. Hardy, eds., *Images of the Negro in American Literature*, 268-75.

Bryant, Jerry H., "Wright, Ellison, Baldwin: Exorcising the Demon," *Phylon* 37, ii (June, 1976): 174-88.

Cartey, Wilfred, "The Realities of Four Negro Writers," *CUF* 9 (Summer, 1966): 34-42.

Cosgrove, William, "Strategies of Survival: The Gimmick Motif in Black Literature," *STwC* No. 15 (Spring, 1975): 118-23.

Coulibaly, Yedieti E., "Weeping Gods: A Study of Cultural Disintegration in James Baldwin's GO TELL IT ON THE MOUNTAIN and Chinua Achebe's THINGS FALL APART," *AdUA* 90 (1976): 531-42.

Davis, Charles T., "The Heavenly Voice of the Black American," in Strelka, J. P., ed., *Anagogic Qualities of Literature*, 114-18.

Fabre, Michel, "Fathers and Sons in James Baldwin's GO TELL IT ON THE MOUNTAIN," in Kannamon, K., ed., *James Baldwin*, 120-38. Also in Goode, M. G., ed., *Modern Black Novelists*, 88-104.

Foster, David E., "'Cause my house fell down': The Theme of the Fall in Baldwin's Novels," *Crit* 13, ii (1971): 50-5.

Gérard, Albert, "Humanism and Negritude: Notes on the Contemporary Afro-American Novel," *Diogenes* No. 37 (Spring, 1962): 127-32.

_____, "The Sons of Ham," *SNNTS* 3, ii (Summer, 1971): 149-57.

Giles, James R., "Religious Alienation and 'Homosexual Consciousness' in CITY OF NIGHT and GO TELL IT ON THE MOUNTAIN," *CE* 36, iii (Nov., 1974): 369-80.

Graves, Wallace, "The Question of Moral Energy in James Baldwin's GO TELL IT ON THE MOUNTAIN," *CLAJ* 7 (Mar., 1964): 215-23.

Gross, John, "Day of Wrath," *NStat* (July 19, 1963): 79-80.

Harper, H. M., Jr., *Desperate Faith*, 142-7.

Hassan, L., *Radical Innocence*, 81-3.

Kent, George E., "Baldwin and Problem of Being," *CLAJ* 7, iii (Mar., 1964): 204-7. Also in O'Daniel, T. B., ed., *James Baldwin*, 20-3. Also in Kinnamon, K., ed., *James Baldwin*, 18-21. Also in Gibson, D. B., ed., *Five Black Writers*, 149-53. Also in Kent, G., *Blackness and the Adventure of Western Culture*, 141-5.

Klein, M., *After Alienation*, 178-84.

Littlejohn, D., *Black on White*, 121-4.

Lundén, Rolf, "The Progress of a Pilgrim: James Baldwin's GO TELL IT ON THE MOUNTAIN," *SN* 53, i (1981): 113-26.

Macebuh, S., *James Baldwin*, 49-68.

MacInnes, Colin, "Dark Angel: The Writings of James Baldwin," *Encounter* 21, ii (Aug., 1963): 23-5. Also in Gibson, D. B., ed., *Five Black Writers*, 121-6.

Marcus, Steven, "The American Negro in Search of Identity," *Ctary* 16 (Nov., 1953): 459-63.

Margolies, E., "The Negro Church: James Baldwin and the Christian Vision," in *Native Sons*, 109-14.

May, J. R., *Toward a New Earth*, 156-61.

Noble, D. W., *Eternal Adam and the New World Garden*, 209-12.

Rosenblatt, R., *Black Fiction*, 36-54.

Rupp, Richard H., "James Baldwin: The Search for Celebration," in *Celebration in Postwar American Fiction*, 137-40.

Saito, Tadatoshi, "Ralph Ellison and James Baldwin in the 1950's" in *American Literature in the 1950's*, 37-40.

Schraufnagel, N., *From Apology to Protest*, 87-90.

Sayre, Robert F., in Moore, H. T., ed., *Contemporary American Novelists*, 161-3.

Scott, Nathan, Jr., "Judgment Marked by a Cellar: The American Negro Writer and the Dialectic of Despair," *UDQ* 2, ii (1967): 26-9. Also in Mooney, H. J., and T. F. Staley, eds., *Shapeless God*, 159-61.

Scruggs, Charles, "THE TALE OF TWO CITIES in James Baldwin's GO TELL IT ON THE MOUNTAIN," *AL* 52, i (Mar., 1980): 1-17.

Singh, Amritjit, "Self-Definition as a Moral Concern in the Twentieth-Century Afro-American Novel," *IJAS* 8, ii (July, 1978): 29-32.

Sylvander, C. W., *James Baldwin*, 27-44.

Watson, Edward, "The Novels and Essays of James Baldwin," *QQ* 72 (Summer, 1965): 386-8.

Werner, C. H., *Paradoxical Resolutions*, 60-8.

Werner, Craig, "The Economic Evolution of James Baldwin," *CLAJ* 23, i (Sept., 1979): 19-21.

IF BEALE STREET COULD TALK

Anastasyev, N., "Awakening," in Vroon, R., tr., *20th Century American Literature: A Soviet View*, 487-91.

Barthold, B. J., *Black Time*, 118-21.

Burks, Mary F., "James Baldwin's Protest Novel: IF BEALE STREET COULD TALK," *NALF* 10 (1976): 83-7, 95.

Harris, Trudier, "The Eye as Weapon in IF BEALE STREET COULD TALK," *MELUS* 5, iii (1978): 54-66.

McCluskey, John, "IF BEALE STREET COULD TALK," *BlackW* 24, ii (1974): 51-2, 88-91.

Miura, Mitsuyo, "Fanny's Inner Change," *KAL* 17 (1976): 25-8.

Spillers, Hortense, "The Politics of Intimacy: A Discussion," in Bell, R. P., et al., eds., *Sturdy Black Bridges*, 91-104.

Sylvander, C. W., *James Baldwin*, 83-8.

Werner, Craig, "The Economic Evolution of James Baldwin," *CLAJ* 23, i (Sept., 1979): 28-30.

JUST ABOVE MY HEAD

Sylvander, C. W., *James Baldwin*, 125-41.

Traylor, Eleanor, "James Baldwin's JUST ABOVE MY HEAD," *First World* 2, ii (1979): 40-3.

TELL ME HOW LONG THE TRAIN'S BEEN GONE

Farrison, William E., "If Baldwin's Train Has Not Gone," in O'Daniel, T. B., ed., *James Baldwin*, 69-81.

Howe, Irving, "James Baldwin: At Ease in Apocalypse," *Harper's* 237 (Sept., 1968): 92-5. Also in Kinnamon, K., ed., *James Baldwin*, 96-108.

Küster, Dieter, "James Baldwin: TELL ME HOW LONG THE TRAIN'S BEEN GONE," in Busch, F., and Schmidt-von Bardeleben, R., *Amerikanische Erzählliteratur*, 142-54.

Lee, Brian, "James Baldwin: Caliban to Prospero," in Bigsby, C. W. E., ed., *Black American Writer*, Vol. 1, 177-9.

Long, Robert E., "Love and Wrath in the Fiction of James Baldwin," *EngR* 19, iii (Feb., 1969): 54-7.

Macebuh, S., *James Baldwin*, 147-64.

Schraufnagel, N., *From Apology to Protest*, 185-7.

Sylvander, C. W., *James Baldwin*, 67-83.

Thompson, John, "Baldwin: The Prophet as Artist," *Ctary* 45 (June, 1968): 67-9.

Werner, Craig, "The Economic Evolution of James Baldwin," *CLAJ* 23, i (Sept., 1979): 25-8.

BIBLIOGRAPHY

Fischer, Russell, "James Baldwin: a bibliography, 1947-1962," *BB* 24 (Jan.-April, 1965): 127-30.

Gross, S. L., and J. E. Hardy, eds., *Images of the Negro in American Literature*, 301-2.

Kindt, Kathleen A., "James Baldwin, A Checklist: 1947-1962," *BB* 24 (Jan.-April, 1965): 123-6.

O'Daniel, T. B., ed., *James Baldwin*, 243-61.

Standley, F. L., "James Baldwin: a Checklist, 1963-1967," *BB* 25 (May-Aug., 1968): 135-7, 160.

_____, and Nancy V. Standley, *James Baldwin: A Reference Guide*, Boston, MA: G. K. Hall, 1980.

BAMBARA, TONI CADE, 1931-

GENERAL

Salaam, Kalamu ya, "An Interview: Searching for the Mother Tongue," *First World* 2, iv (1980): 48-53.

THE SALT EATERS

Traylor, Eleanor, "THE SALT EATERS: My Soul Looks Back in Wonder," *First World* 2, iv (1980): 44-7, 64.

BANVILLE, JOHN, 1945-

GENERAL

Deane, Seamus, "'Be Assured I Am Inventing': The Fiction of John Banville," *CahiersI* 4-5 (1976): 329-39. Also in Rafroidi, P., and M. Harmon, eds., *Irish Novel in Our Time*, 329-39.

Imhof, Rüdiger, "John Banville's Supreme Fiction," *IUR* 11, i (Spring, 1981): 52-86.

_____, "'My Readers, That Small Band, Deserve a Rest': An Interview with John Banville," *IUR* 11, i (Spring, 1981): 5-12. Also 13-17.

Molloy, Francis C., "The Search for Truth: The Fiction of John Banville," *IUR* 11, i (Spring, 1981): 29-51.

BIRCHWOOD

Imhof, Rüdiger, "John Banville's Supreme Fiction," *IUR* 11, i (Spring, 1981): 63-9.

Molloy, Francis C., "The Search for Truth: The Fiction of John Banville,"_*IUR* 11, i (Spring, 1981): 37-45.

DOCTOR COPERNICUS

Imhof, Rüdiger, "John Banville's Supreme Fiction, *IUR* 11, i (Spring, 1981): 69-73.

Molloy, Francis C., "The Search for Truth: The Fiction of John Banville," *IUR* 11, i (Spring, 1981): 45-50.

KEPLER

Imhof, Rüdiger, "John Banville's Supreme Fiction," *IUR* 11, i (Spring, 1981): 73-84.

NIGHTSPAWN

Imhof, Rüdiger, "John Banville's Supreme Fiction," *IUR* 11, i (Spring, 1981): 59-63.

Malloy, Francis C., "The Search for Truth: The Fiction of John Banville," *IUR* 11, i (Spring, 1981): 32-7.

BIBLIOGRAPHY

Imhof, Rüdiger, "John Banville: A Checklist," *IUR* 11, i (Spring, 1981): 87-95.

BARRIO, RAYMOND, 1921-

THE PLUM PLUM PICKERS

Lattin, Vernon E., "Paradise and Plums: Appearance and Reality in Barrio's THE PLUM PLUM PICKERS," *Crit* 19, i (1977): 49-57. Also in Carter, G. E., and J. R. Parker, eds., *Essays on Minority Cultures*, 165-71.

Lewis, Maravin A., "PEREGRINOS DE AZATLAN and the Emergence of the Chicano Novel," in Carter, G. E., and J. R. Parker, eds., *Essays on Minority Cultures*, 144-6.

Miller, Yvette E., "The Social Message in Chicano Fiction: Tomás Rivera's…AND THE EARTH DID NOT PART and Raymond Barrio's THE PLUM PLUM PICKERS," in Carter, G. E., and J. R. Parker, eds., *Essays on Minority Cultures*, 161-4.

BARTH, JOHN, 1930-

GENERAL

Abádi Nagy, Zoltan, "The Principle of Metamorphic Means in John Barth's Novels (Part One)," *HSE* 9 (1975): 5-31.

_____, "The Principle of Metaphoric Means in John Barth's Novels (Part Two)," *HSE* 10 (1976): 73-94.

Aklonis, Judith L., "'A Broken Bundle of Mirrors': Identity in the Work of John Barth," *DAI* 38 (1978): 4803A-04A.

Allen, M., *Necessary Blankness*, 14-37.

Ayres, Michael S., "Between the Streetlamps and the Stars: A Study of John Barth's Fiction," *DAI* 41, xi (May, 1981): 4711A.

Baird, Louise, "A Metaphysical Emotion: The Art of John Barth," *DAI* 37 (1976): 304A.

Banner, Howard D., "Myth and the Search for Structure in the Fiction of John Barth," *DAI* 41, xi (May, 1981): 4709A.

Begnal, Mary Kate, "Self-Mimesis in the Fiction of John Barth," *DAI* 35 (1975): 7293A.

Bellamy, Joe D., "Having It Both Ways (A Conversation)," *NAmR* 15, 134-50. [Interview.] Also in Bellamy, J. D., ed., *New Fiction*, 1-18.

Bellei, Sergio L. P., "The Dynamics of Incomplete Consistency in the Novels of John Barth," *DAI* 39 (1978): 880A.

Bluestone, George, "John Wain and John Barth: The Angry and the Accurate," *MR* 1 (May, 1960): 582-9.

Bradbury, John M., "Absurd Insurrection: The Barth-Percy Affair," *SAQ* 68, iii (Summer, 1969): 319-29.

Brunette, Peter C., Jr., "Narrators and Narration in the Fiction of John Barth," *DAI* 36 (1976): 6096A.

Bryant, J. H., *Open Decision*, 286-303.

Cantrill, Dante K., "Told by an Idiot: Toward an Understanding of Modern Fiction through an Analysis of the Works of William Faulkner and John Barth," *DAI* 35 (1975): 4505A.

Cosenza, Joseph A., "Paradox as Fictional Design in the Novels of John Barth," *DAI* 39 (1979): 4238A.

Curtler, Hugh M., "Does Philosophy Need Literature?" *P&L* 2, i (Spring, 1978): 110-16.

Dahiya, Bhim, "Structural Patterns in the Novels of Barth, Vonnegut, and Pynchon," *IJAS* 5, i-ii (1976): 53-68. [Not seen.]

Davis, Cynthia, "Heroes, Earth Mothers and Muses: Gender Identity in Barth's Fiction," *CentR* 24, iii (Summer, 1980): 309-21.

Decker, Sharon D., "Passionate Virtuosity: The Fiction of John Barth," *DAI* 33 (1973): 3639A (Va.).

Eberly, Ralph, "John Barth, Patternmaster," in *The Here and Now: Distinguished Professor Lecture Series.* (Monog. Ser.) Little Rock: Univ. of Arkansas at Little Rock, 1980, 34-53.

Enck, John, "John Barth: An Interview," *WSCL* 6 (Winter-Spring, 1965): 3-14.

Farwell, Harold, "John Barth's Tenuous Affirmation: 'The Absurd, Unending Possibility of Love'," *GAR* 28, ii (Summer, 1974): 290-306. Also in Waldmeir, J. J., ed., *Critical Essays on John Barth*, 55-67.

Foeller, Elzbieta, "The Mythical Heroes of John Barth and John Gardner," *KN* 27, ii (1980): 183-97.

Gado, Frank, ed., "An Interview with John Barth," *Idol* (1972): 201-36. Also in Gado, F., ed., *First Person*, 110-41.

Garis, Robert, "What Happened to John Barth?" *Ctary* 42 (October, 1966): 89-95.

Glaser-Wöhrer, E. *Analysis of John Barth's Weltanschauung.*

Gray, Joy M., "The Roles of the Author in the Works of John Barth," *DAI* 38 (1977): 2775A.

Gresham, James T., "John Barth as Minippean Satirist," *DAI* 33 (1973): 5176A-77A (Mich. State).

Gross, Beverly, "The Anti-Novels of John Barth," *ChiR* 20 (Nov., 1968): 95-109. Also in Waldmeir, J. J., ed., *Critical Essays on John Barth*, 30-42.

Harris, Charles B., "John Barth and the Critics: An Overview," *MisQ* 32 (1979): 269-83. Also in Waldmeir, J. J., ed., *Critical Essays on John Barth*, 3-13.

_____, "Paradigms of Absurdity: The Absurdist Novels of John Barth," *Contemporary American Novelists of the Absurd*, 100-20.

Hauck, R. B., "These Fruitful Fruitless Odysseys: John Barth," *Cheerful Nihilism*, 201-36.

Holmes, Frederick M., "Fictional Self-Consciousness in the Works of John Barth and John Fowles," *DAI* 42, viii (Feb., 1982): 3595A.

Hughes, Elaine W., "Development of a Mythic Consciousness in John Barth, the Novelist," *DAI* 41 (1980): 251A.

Hunt, George W., S. J., "John Updike: The Dialectical Vision: The Influence of Kierkegaard and Barth," *DAI* 36 (1976): 6674A.

Janoff, Bruce L., "Beyond Satire: Black Humor in the Novels of John Barth and Joseph Heller," *DAI* 33 (1972): 1728A (Ohio).

Johnstone, Douglas B., "Myth and Psychology in the Novels of John Barth," *DAI* 34 (1974): 5973A (Ore.).

Josenhans, Elinor L., "Form in the Fiction of John Barth," *DAI* 35 (1974): 2993A (Fordham).

Joseph, G., *John Barth.*

Kalin, Jesse, "How Wide the Gulf?" *P&L* 2, i (Spring, 1978): 116-23.

_____, "Philosophy Needs Literature: John Barth and Moral Nihilism," *P&L* 1, ii (Spring, 1977): 170-82.

Kenedy, R. C., "John Barth," *ArtI* 15, vii (Sept. 20, 1971): 26-30.

Kennard, Jean E., "John Barth: Imitations of Imitations," *Mosaic* 3, ii (Winter, 1970): 116-31. Also in Kennard, J. E., *Number and Nightmare*, 57-81.

Klein, James R., "The Tower and the Maze: A Study of the Novels of John Barth," *DAI* 32 (1972): 5794A. (Ill., Urbana-Champaign).

Klinkowitz, Jerome, "John Barth Reconsidered," *PR* 49, iii (1982) 407-11.

Kostelanetz, Richard, "The New American Fiction," *Ramparts* 3 (Jan.-Feb., 1965): 57-60. Also in *New American Arts*, 203-10.

Le Rebeller, Annie, "A Spectatorial Skeptic: An Interview with John Barth," *Caliban* 12 (1975): 93-110.

Loughman, Celeste M., "Mirrors and Masks in the Novels of John Barth," *DAI* 32 (1971): 1519A (Mass.).

Mazurek, Raymond A., "The Fiction of History: The Presentation of History in Recent American Literature," *DAI* 41, viii (Feb., 1981): 3582A-83A.

McConnell, F. D., *Four Postwar American Novelists*, 108-19.

McKenzie, James, ed., "Pole-Vaulting in Top Hats: A Public Conversation with John Barth, William Gass, and Ishmael Reed," *MFS* 22, ii (Summer, 1976): 131-51.

McNall, Sally A., "Order as Surprise: A Stylistic Comparison of Experimental Fiction," *DAI* 36 (1976): 6117A.

Morrell, David B., "John Barth: An Introduction," *DAI* 31 (1971): 4784A (Penn. State).

_____, *John Barth.*

Noland, Richard W., "John Barth and the Novel of Comic Nihilism," *WSCL* 7 (Autumn, 1966): 239-57. Also in Waldmeir, J. J., ed., *Critical Essays on John Barth*, 14-29.

Oshins, Joseph H., "Novel Theory in Practice: A Study of John Barth's Development of a 'New' Fiction," *DAI* 38 (1978): 6717A-18A.

Pinsker, Sanford, "John Barth: Comic Novelist in Search of a Subject," *SJS* 6, ii (May, 1980): 77-82.

_____, "John Barth: The Teller Who Swallowed His Tale," *STwC* 10 (Fall, 1972): 55-68. Also in Pinsker, S., *Between Two Worlds*, 75-84.

Ramage, John D., "The Janus Face of Contemporary American Fiction: Norman Mailer and John Barth," *DAI* 38 (1977): 1394A-95A.

Rice, Elaine E., "The Satire of John Barth and Kurt Vonnegut, Jr.: The Menippean Tradition in the 1960's in America," *DAI* 35 (1975): 7876A-77A.

Robinson, Douglas, "Visions of 'No' End: The Anti-Apocalyptic Novels of Ellison, Barth, and Coover," *AmSS* 13, i (1981): 1-16.

Samuels, Charles T., "John Barth: A Buoyant Denial of Relevance," *Cweal* 85 (Oct. 21, 1966): 80-2.

Schaeffer, Daniel G., "Monomyth and Motif in the Novels of John Barth," *DAI* 36 (1975): 3718A-19A.

Scofield, James D., "Absurd Man and the Esthetics of the Absurd: The Fiction of John Barth," *DAI* 34 (1974): 4285A (Kent State).

Sherman, Marilyn R., "'Point of View' and the Creative Process in the Novels of John Barth," *DAI* 35 (1974): 1123A (Florida).

Shimura, Masao, "Faulkner, De Assis, Barth: Resemblances and Differences," *WiF* 2, ii (1979): 67-79. [Not seen.]

Slethaug, Gordon E., "Barth's Refutation of the Idea of Progress," *Crit* 13, iii (1972): 11-29.

Stark, J. O., *Literature of Exhaustion,* 118-75.

Storms, Charles G., III, "Satire in the Fiction of John Barth," *DAI* 35 (1974): 480A-81A (Rutgers).

Stubbs, John C., "John Barth as a Novelist of Ideas: The Themes of Values and Identity," *Crit* 8, ii (Winter, 1965-66): 101-16.

Tanner, Tony, "The Hoax That Joke Bilked," *PR* 34 (Winter, 1967): 102-9.

Tatham, Campbell, "John Barth and the Aesthetics of Artifice," *ConL* 12, i (Winter, 1971): 60-73. Also in Waldmeir, J. J., ed., *Critical Essays on John Barth,* 43-54.

_____, "Message (Concerning the FELT Ultimacies of One John Barth)," *Boundary* 3, ii (Winter, 1975): 259-87.

_____, "The Novels of John Barth: An Introduction," *DA* 29 (1969): 4471A (Wis.).

Tharpe, Jac, "Beauty as Good: A Platonic Imperative in John Barth?" *SoQ* 15, iv (July, 1977): 335-44.

_____, *John Barth.*

Townsend, Dan. "John Barth: An Interview," *Maryland English Journal* 14, ii (1976): 20-6, 64.

Trachtenberg, Alan, "Barth and Hawkes: Two Fabulists," *Crit* 6, ii (1963): 4-18.

Underwood, Jerry L., "The Fictional Universe of John Barth," *DAI* 36 (1975): 895A.

Urbanski, Kenneth J., "The Forming Artifice in John Barth's Fictions," *DAI* 34 (1974): 7789A (Kan.).

Vickery, John B., "Myths and Fiction in the Contemporary American Novel: The Case of John Barth," *HSE* 12 (1979): 89-106.

Waldmeir, J. J., ed., *Critical Essays on John Barth.*

Weixlmann, Joseph N., "Counter-Types and Anti-Myths: Black and Indian Characters in the Fiction of John Barth," *DAI* 34 (1973): 3439A-40A (Kan. State).

Zamora, Lois P., "The Structural Games in the Fiction of John Barth and Julio Cortazar," *PCL* 6 (1980): 28-36.

THE END OF THE ROAD

Billings, Philip A., "John Barth's Initial Trilogy: A Study of the Themes of Value and Identity in THE FLOATING OPERA, THE END OF THE ROAD and THE SOT-WEED FACTOR," *DAI* 35 (1975): 6129A-30A.

Boyers, Robert, "Attitudes Toward Sex in American 'High Culture'," *AAAPS* 376 (Mar., 1968): 47-9.

Bryant, J. H., *Open Decision,* 289-94.

David, Jack, "The Trojan Horse at the End of the Road," *CollL* 4, ii (1977): 159-64.

Fraustino, Daniel V., "THE COUNTRY WIFE Comes to THE END OF THE ROAD: Wycherley Bewitches Barth," *ArQ* 33 (1977): 76-86.

Glaser-Wöhrer, E., *Analysis of John Barth's Weltanschauung,* 33-50.

Glicksberg, C. I., *Sexual Revolution in Modern American Literature,* 209-13.

Hauck, Richard B., "These Fruitful Fruitless Odysseys: John Barth," *Cheerful Nihilism,* 217-22.

Hirsh, David, "John Barth's Freedom Road," *MRev* 2, iii (1972): 38-47.

Hoskins, Robert V., III, "Swift, Dickens, and the Horses in THE END OF THE ROAD," *James Madison Jour.* 37 (1979): 18-32.

Joseph, G., *John Barth,* 15-22.

Kennard, Jean E., "John Barth: Imitations of Imitations," *Mosaic* 3, ii (Winter, 1970): 122-4. Also in Kennard, J. E., *Number and Nightmare,* 65-7.

Kerner, David, "Psychodrama in Eden," *ChiR* 13 (Winter-Spring, 1959): 59-67. Also in Waldmeir, J. J., ed., *Critical Essays on John Barth,* 91-5.

Lehan, R., *Dangerous Crossing,* 175-7.

Majdiak, Daniel, "Barth and the Representation of Life," *Criticism* 12, i (Winter, 1970): 51-67. Also in Waldmeir, J. J., ed., *Critical Essays on John Barth,* 96-109.

May, J. R., *Toward a New Earth,* 174-80.

McConnell, F. D., *Four Postwar American Novelists,* 126-32.

Morrell, D., *John Barth,* 13-26.

Noland, Richard W., "John Barth and the Novel of Comic Nihilism," *WSCL* 7 (Autumn, 1964): 244-7. Also in Waldmeir, J. J., ed., *Critical Essays on John Barth,* 18-20.

Pütz, Manfred, "John Barth: The Pitfalls of Mythopoesis," *Story of Identity,* 63-6.

Raban, J., "Narrative: Cause and Contingency," in *Technique of Modern Fiction,* 76-8.

Schwartz, Richard A., "Some Formal Devices in John Barth's Early Novels," *NConL* 10, iii (May, 1980): 6-8.

Shimura, Masao, "John Barth, THE END OF THE ROAD, and the Tradition of American Fiction," *SELit* 48 (Eng. No.) (Oct., 1971): 73-87.

Smith, Herbert F., "Barth's Endless Road," *Crit* 6 (Fall, 1963): 68-76.

Stubbs, John C., "John Barth as a Novelist of Ideas: The Themes of Value and Identity," *Crit* 8, ii (Winter, 1965-66): 105-8.

Tanner, T., *City of Words,* 235-41.

Tharpe, J., *John Barth,* 24-33.

Trachtenberg, Alan, "Barth and Hawkes: Two Fabulists," *Crit* 6 (Fall, 1963): 11-15.

Vanderbilt, Kermit, "From Passion to Impasse: The Structure of a Dark Romantic Theme in Hawthorne, Howells, and Barth," *SNNTS* 8, iv (Winter, 1976): 425-9.

Verzosa, Guillermina L., "The Unsayable and Its Expression in John Barth's THE END OF THE ROAD," *SLRJ* 5, ii (June, 1974): 131-87.

THE FLOATING OPERA

Aarseth, Inger, "Absence of Absolutes: The Reconciled Artist in John Barth's THE FLOATING OPERA," *SN* 47, i (1975): 53-68.

Billings, Philip A., "John Barth's Initial Trilogy: A Study of the Themes of Values and Identity in THE FLOATING OPERA, THE END OF THE ROAD and THE SOT-WEED FACTOR," *DAI* 35 (1975): 6129A-30A.

Bryant, J. H., *Open Decision,* 286-9.

Glaser-Wöhrer, E., *Analysis of John Barth's Weltanschauung,* 15-33.

Guetti, J., *Word-Music,* 89-92.

Guzlowski, John Z., "No More Sea Changes: Hawkes, Pynchon, Gaddis, and Barth," *Crit* 23, ii (Winter, 1981-82): 57-9.

Harris, Charles B., "Todd Andrews and Ontological Insecurity: A Laingian Approach to THE FLOATING OPERA," in Marsden, Michael T., comp., *Proceedings of the Sixth National*

Convention of the Popular Culture Association, Chicago, Illinois, April 22-24, 1976, Bowling Green: Bowling Green State Univ. Popular Pr., 1976, 1053-70. Also in *Crit* 18, ii (1976): 34-50.

Hauck, Richard B., "These Fruitful Fruitless Odysseys: John Barth," *Cheerful Nihilism,* 210-16.

Hawkes, John. "THE FLOATING OPERA and SECOND SKIN," *Mosiac* 8, i (1974): 17-28.

Hyman, Stanley E., "John Barth's First Novel," *New Leader* 48 (April 12, 1965): 20-1.

Jordan, Enoch P., "THE FLOATING OPERA Restored," *Crit* 18, ii (Winter, 1976): 5-16. Also in Waldmeir, J. J., ed., *Critical Essays on John Barth,* 79-89.

Joseph, G., *John Barth,* 9-15.

Kennard, Jean E., "John Barth: Imitations of Imitations," *Mosiac* 3, ii (Winter, 1970): 119-22. Also in Kennard, J. E., *Number and Nightmare,* 60-5.

Korkowski, Eugene, "The Excremental Vision of Barth's Todd Andrews," *Crit* 18, ii (1976): 51-8.

Kostelanetz, Richard, "The New American Fiction," *Ramparts* 3 (Jan.-Feb., 1965): 58-9. Also in *New American Arts,* 209-10.

Le Clair, Thomas, "John Barth's THE FLOATING OPERA: Death and the Craft of Fiction," *TSLL* 14 (Winter, 1973): 711-30.

Lehan, R., *Dangerous Crossing,* 172-5.

Martin, Dennis M., "Desire and Disease: The Psychological Pattern of THE FLOATING OPERA," *Crit* 18, ii (1976): 17-33.

McConnell, F. D., *Four Postwar American Novelists,* 119-26.

Morrell, D., *John Barth,* 1-15.

Nathanson, Stephen, "Nihilism, Reason, and Death: Reflections on John Barth's FLOATING OPERA," 137-51 in Tymieniecka, Anna-Teresa, ed., *The Philosophical Reflection of Man in Literature: Selected Papers from Several Conferences Held by the International Society for Phenomenlogy and Literature in Cambridge, Massachusetts,* Dordrecht: Reiel, 1982.

Noland, Richard W., "John Barth and the Novel of Comic Nihilism," *WSCL* 7 (Autumn, 1966): 239-44. Also in Waldmeir, J. J., ed., *Critical Essays on John Barth,* 15-18.

Oggel, L. Terry, "Twin Tongues of Flame: Hawthorne's Pearl and Barth's Jeannine as the Morally Redemptive Child," *NR* 4, i (1980): 41-9.

Putz, Manfred, "John Barth: The Pitfalls of Mythopoesis," *Story of Identity,* 61-3.

Rideout, Phyllis M., "Narrator/Narratee/Reader Relationships in First Person Narrative: John Barth's THE FLOATING OPERA, Albert Camus' THE FALL and Gunter Grass' CAT AND MOUSE," *DAI* 42, i (July, 1981): 205A.

Ryan, Marjorie, "Four Contemporary Satires and the Problem of Norms," *SNL* 6, ii (1969): 44-6.

Schickel, Richard, "THE FLOATING OPERA," *Crit* 6 (Fall, 1963): 53-67.

Schwartz, Richard A., "Some Formal Devices in John Barth's Early Novels," *NConL* 10, iii (May, 1980): 6-8.

Stubbs, John C., "John Barth as Novelist of Ideas: The Themes of Value and Identity," *Crit* 8, ii (Winter, 1965-66): 102-5.

Tanner, Stephen L., "John Barth's Hamlet," *SWR* 56, iv (Autumn, 1971): 347-54.

Tanner, T., *City of Words,* 231-5.

Tharpe, J., *John Barth,* 14-23.

Voelker, Joseph C., "The Drama of Digression: Narrative Technique in John Barth's THE FLOATING OPERA," *CimR* 29 (1974): 34-44.

Wallace, Ronald, "Dwarfed Into Dignity: John Barth's THE FLOATING OPERA," *Last Laugh,* 26-44.

Zivley, Sherry L., "A Collation of John Barth's FLOATING OPERA," *PBSA* 72 (1978): 201-12.

GILES GOAT-BOY

Allen, M., *Necessary Blankness,* 29-36.

Bryant, J. H., *Open Decision,* 299-303.

Byrd, Scott, "GILES GOAT-BOY Visited," *Crit* 9, i (1967): 108-12.

Chaffee, Patricia, "The Whale and the Rocket: Technology as Sacred Symbol," *Ren* 32, iii (Spring, 1980): 146-51.

Christensen, Inger, "John Barth's Metaphysical Redemption," *Meaning of Metafiction,* 79-96.

Cosenza, Joseph A., "GILES GOAT-BOY and Zeno's Paradox," *NMAL* 3 (1979): Item 13.

Glaser-Wöhrer, E., *Analysis of John Barth's Weltanschauung,* 101-41.

Gresham, James T., "GILES GOAT-BOY: Satyr, Satire, and Tragedy Twined," *Genre* 7 (1974): 148-63. Also in Waldmeir, J. J., ed., *Critical Essays on John Barth,* 157-71.

Harris, Charles B., "George's Illumination: Unity in GILES GOAT-BOY," *SNNTS* 8, ii (Summer, 1976): 172-84.

_____, "Paradigms of Absurdity: The Absurdist Novels of John Barth," *Contemporary American Novelists of the Absurd,* 107-15.

Hauck, Richard B., "The Comic Christ and the Modern Reader," *CE* 31 (1970): 498-506. Also in Waldmeir, J. J., ed., *Critical Essays on John Barth,* 147-9.

_____, "These Fruitful Fruitless Odysseys: John Barth," *Cheerful Nihilism,* 230-6.

Joseph, G., *John Barth,* 31-8.

Katz, Bruce L., "This Ruinous Garden: Readable Signs in Pynchon's GRAVITY'S RAINBOW with Remarks on Barth's GILES GOAT-BOY," *DAI* 40 (1980): 4027A.

Kennard, Jean E., "John Barth: Imitations of Imitations," *Mosiac* 3, ii (Winter, 1970): 129-31. Also in Kennard, J. E., *Number and Nightmare,* 73-8.

Kiely, Benedict, "Ripeness Was Not All: John Barth's GILES GOAT-BOY," *HC* 3 (Dec., 1966): 1-12. Also in Dillard, R. H. W., et al., eds., *Sounder Few,* 195-206.

McColm, Pearlmarie, "The Revised New Syllabus and the Unrevised Old," *DenverQ* 1 (Autumn, 1966): 136-8.

McConnell, F. D., *Four Postwar American Novelists,* 140-51.

McDonald, James L., "Barth's Syllabus: The Frame of GILES GOAT-BOY," *Crit* 13, iii (1972): 5-10.

Mercer, Peter, "The Rhetoric of GILES GOAT-BOY," *Novel* 4, ii (Winter, 1971): 147-58.

Morrell, D., *John Barth,* 59-79.

Olderman, R. M., "The Grail Knight Goes to College," *Beyond the Waste Land,* 72-93.

Robinson, Douglas, *John Barth's GILES GOAT-BOY: A Study,* Jyväskylä, Finland: Univ. of Jyväskylä, 1980.

_____, "Visions of 'No' End: The Anti-Apocalyptic Novels of Ellison, Barth, and Coover," *AmSS* 13, i (1981): 9-11.

Rodrigues, Wusebio L., "The Living Sakhyan in Barth's GILES GOATBOY," *NConL* 2, iv (Sept., 1972): 7-8.

Safer, Elaine B., "The Allusive Mode and Black Humor in Barth's GILES GOAT-BOY and Pynchon's GRAVITY'S RAINBOW," *Ren* 32, ii (1980): 89-104.

Samuels, Charles T., "John Barth: A Buoyant Denial of Relevance," *Cweal* 85 (Oct., 21, 1966): 80-2.

Scholes, R., *Fabulators*, 135-73.

_____, "John Barth's GOAT-BOY," *Fabulation and Metafiction*, 75-102.

Sherman, Marilyn R., "GILES GOAT-BOY: or 'Reality' is No Place for a Hero," in Waldmeir, J. J., ed., *Critical Essays on John Barth*, 172-7.

Slethaug, Gordon E., "Barth's Refutation of the Idea of Progress," *Crit* 13, iii (1972): 20-5.

Stuart, Dabney, "A Service to the University," *Shen* 18, i (1966): 96-9. Also in Waldmeir, J. J., ed., *Critical Essays on John Barth*, 150-3.

Tanner, T., *City of Words*, 246-53.

_____, "The Hoax That Joke Bilked," *PR* 34 (Winter, 1967): 102-9.

Tatham, Campbell, "The Gilesian Monomyth: Some Remarks on the Structure of GILES GOAT-BOY," *Genre* 3, iv (Dec., 1970): 364-75.

Tharpe, J., *John Barth*, 52-90.

Tilton, John W., "GILES GOAT-BOY: An Interpretation," *BuR* 18, i (Spring, 1970): 93-119.

_____, "GILES GOAT-BOY: Man's Precarious Purchase on Reality," *Comic Satire in the Contemporary American Novel*, 43-68.

Waldmeir, Joseph J., "GILES GOAT-BOY," in Waldmeir, J. J., ed., *Critical Essays on John Barth*, 154-6.

Walter, James F., "A Psychronology of Lust in the Menippean Tradition: GILES GOAT-BOY," *TCL* 21, iv (1975): 394-410.

Weixlmann, Joseph, "GILES GOAT-BOY and J. B., " *NConL* 7, iii (1977): 6.

Werner, C. H., *Paradoxical Resolutions*, 146-50.

LETTERS

Domini, John, "LETTERS and Ethics: The Moral Fiction of John Barth," *FictionI* 12 (1980): 247-58.

Graff, Gerald, "Under Our Be It and off Our Back: Barth's LETTERS and Postmodern Fiction," *TriQ* 52 (Fall, 1981): 150-64.

Hilton, Earl, "Conventional Unconventionality & Obedient Rebellion," *ChronC* 4, i (Jan.-Feb., 1980): 10-12.

McCaffery, Larry, "Barth's LETTERS and the Literature of Replenishment," *ChiR* 31, iv (1980): 75-82.

Mills, John, "Return of the Dazed Steer," *QQ* 88, i (Spring, 1981): 145-54.

Reilly, Charlie, "An Interview with John Barth," *ConL* 22, i (Winter, 1981): 1-23.

Schulz, Max F., "Barth, LETTERS, and the Great Tradition," *Genre* 14, i (Spring, 1981): 95-115.

Shipe, Timothy, "A Note in LETTERS: POLTROONS AND PATRIOTS and the 'Posthumous' Letters of A. B. Cook IV." *NConL* 10, iv (Sept., 1980): 11.

Stonehill, Brian, "A Trestle of LETTERS," *FictionI* 12 (1980): 259-68.

Thompson, Gary, "Barth's Letters and Hawkes' Passion," *MQR* 19 (1980): 270-8.

THE SOT-WEED FACTOR

Allen, M., *Necessary Blankness*, 21-9.

Anderson, Don, "Comic Modes in American Fiction," *SoRA* 8, ii (1975): 158-60.

Antush, John V., "Allotropic Doubles in Barth's SOT-WEED FACTOR," *CollL* 4, i (1977): 71-9.

Bean, John C., "John Barth and Festive Comedy: The Failure of Imagination in THE SOT-WEED FACTOR," *XUS* 10, i (Spring, 1971): 3-15.

Billings, Philip A., "John Barth's Initial Trilogy: A Study of the Themes of Value and Identity in THE FLOATING OPERA, THE END OF THE ROAD, and THE SOT-WEED FACTOR," *DAI* 35 (1975): 6129A-30A.

Bottorff, William K., "Thoreau and Walden, Ebenezer Cooke and Malden: Barth's Ribald Allusion," *TSB* 152 (1980): 8.

Bryant, J. H., *Open Decision*, 294-9.

Calhoun, John C., "A Groatsworth of Wit: Parallels in John Barth's THE SOT-WEED FACTOR and Thomas Pynchon's V," *DAI* 37 (1976): 2857A-58A.

Christensen, Inger, "John Barth's Metaphysical Redemption," *Meaning of Metafiction*, 59-77.

Conlee, John W., "John Barth's Version of THE REEVES TALE," *AN&Q* 12, ix-x (May/June, 1974): 137-8.

Dippie, Brian W., "'His Visage Wild, His Form Exotick': Indian Themes and Cultural Guilt in John Barth's THE SOT-WEED FACTOR," *AQ* 21 (Spring, 1969): 113-21.

Diser, Philip E., "The Historical Ebenezer Cooke," *Crit* 10, iii (1968): 48-59.

Ewell, Barbara C., S.S.N.D., "John Barth: The Artist of History," *SLJ* 5, ii (Spring, 1973): 32-46.

Ferres, John H., "The Indian Maiden in Leonard Cohen's BEAUTIFUL LOSERS and John Barth's THE SOT-WEED FACTOR," *JAC* 2, iv (Winter, 1980): 690-8.

Fiedler, Leslie A., "John Barth: An Eccentric Genius," *New Leader* 44 (Feb. 13, 1961): 21. Also in Kostelanetz, R., ed., *Contemporary Literature*, 238-43. Also in Fiedler, L., *Collected Essays of Leslie Fiedler*, v. 2, 325-30.

Fort, Deborah C., "Contract Epic: A Study of Joseph Heller's CATCH-22 (1961), Gunter Grass's THE TIN DRUM (DIE BLECHTROMMEL) (1959), John Barth's THE SOT-WEED FACTOR (1960, Revised 1967), and Vladimir Nabokov's PALE FIRE (1962)," *DAI* 35 (1974): 3677A-78A.

Gillespie, Gerald, "Rogues, Fools, and Satyrs: Ironic Ghosts in American Literature," *PCLS* 5 (1972): 89-106. Also in Zyla, W. T., and W. M. Aycock, eds., *Modern American Fiction*, 99-106.

Gladsky, Thomas S., "The SOT-WEED FACTOR as Historiography," *PAPA* 7, ii (Fall, 1981): 37-47.

Glaser-Wöhrer, E., *Analysis of John Barth's Weltanschauung*, 54-100.

Hauck, Richard B., "These Fruitful Fruitless Odysseys: John Barth," *Cheerful Nihilism*, 222-30.

Henderson, H. B., III, *Versions of the Past*, 277-85.

Holder, Alan, "What Marvelous Plot ... Was Afoot? History in Barth's THE SOT-WEED FACTOR," *AQ* 20 (1968): 596-604. Also in Waldmeir, J. J., ed., *Critical Essays on John Barth*, 123-33.

Hyman, S. E., "The American Adam," in *Standards*, 204-8.

Jones, D. Allen, "The Game of the Name in Barth's THE SOT-WEED FACTOR," *RS* 40 (1972): 219-21.

Jordan, Enoch P., "'A quantum swifter and more graceful': John Barth's Revisions of THE SOT-WEED FACTOR," *Proof* 5 (1976): 171-82.

Joseph, G., *John Barth*, 22-31.

Kennard, Jean E., "John Barth: Imitations of Imitations," *Mosaic* 3, ii (Winter, 1970): 124-9. Also in Kennard, J. E., *Number and Nightmare*, 67-73.

Kostelanetz, Richard, "The New American Fiction," *Ramparts* 3 (Jan.-Feb., 1965): 57-8. Also in *New American Arts*, 203-9.

Lee, L. L., "Some Uses of FINNEGANS WAKE in John Barth's the Sot-Weed," *JJQ* 5 (Winter, 1968): 177-8.

Lehan, R., *Dangerous Crossing*, 177-9.

Lewis, R. W. B., "Days of Wrath and Laughter," in *Trials of the Word*, 220-6.

Madden, David W., "THE SOT-WEED FACTOR'S Ironic Narrator," *AN&Q* 19, vii-viii (Mar.-Apr., 1981): 117-19.

McConnell, F. D., *Four Postwar American Novelists*, 132-40.

Miller, Russell H., "THE SOT-WEED FACTOR: A Contemporary Mock-Epic," *Crit* 8, ii (Winter, 1965-66): 88-100.

Morrell, D., *John Barth*, 27-58.

Noland, Richard W., "John Barth and the Novel of Comic Nihililsm," *WSCL* 7 (Autumn, 1966): 247-56. Also in Waldmeir, J. J., ed., *Critical Essays on John Barth*, 21-7.

Puetz, Manfred, "John Barth's THE SOT-WEED FACTOR: The Pitfalls of Mythopoesis," *TCL* 22, iv (Dec., 1976): 454-66. Also in Waldmeir, J. J., ed., *Critical Essays on John Barth*, 134-45. Also in Puetz, M., *Story of Identity*, 66-89.

Richer, Carol F., "The Fabliau: Chaucer to Barth and Back Again," *BSUF* 23, ii (Spring, 1982): 46-52.

Rovit, Earl, "The Novel as Parody: John Barth," *Crit* 6, ii (Fall, 1963): 77-85. Also in Waldmeir, J. J., ed., *Critical Essays on John Barth*, 116-22.

Slethaug, Gordon E., "Barth's Refutation of the Idea of Progress," *Crit* 13, ii (1972): 15-20.

Stubbs, John C., "John Barth as a Novelist of Ideas: The Themes of Value and Identity," *Crit* 8, ii (Winter, 1965-66): 108-13.

Sutcliffe, Denham, "Worth a Guilty Conscience," *KR* 23 (Winter, 1961): 181-6. Also in Waldmeir, J. J., ed., *Critical Essays on John Barth*, 113-15.

Tanner, T., *City of Words*, 241-6.

Tharpe, J., *John Barth*, 34-51.

Thigpen, Kenneth A., "Folkloristic Concerns in Barth's THE SOT-WEED FACTOR," *SFQ* 41 (1977): 225-37.

Trachtenberg, Alan, "Barth and Hawkes: Two Fabulists," *Crit* 6 (Fall, 1963): 15-18.

Vernon, J., *Garden and the Map*, 63-5, 67-8.

Weixlmann, Joseph, "The Use and Abuse of Smith's GENERALL HISTORIE in John Barth's THE SOT-WEED FACTOR," *StAH* 2, ii (1975): 105-15.

Ziegler, Heide, "John Barth's SOT-WEED FACTOR Revisited: The Meaning of Form," *Amst* 25, ii (1980): 199-206.

Zurlo, John, "'A tale well wrought is the gossip o' the gods': Storytelling in John Barth's THE SOT-WEED FACTOR," *BRMMLA* 36, ii (1982): 103-10.

BIBLIOGRAPHY

Bryer, Jackson R., "John Barth," *Crit* 6 (Fall, 1963): 86-9.

Morrell, D., *John Barth*, 176-89.

Vine, Richard A., *John Barth: An Annotated Bibliography*, Metuchen, NJ: Scarecrow Pr., 1977.

Walsh, Thomas P., and Cameron Northouse, *John Barth, Jerzy Kosinski, and Thomas Pynchon: A Reference Guide*, Boston: G. K. Hall, 1977.

Weixlmann, Joseph N., "John Barth: A Bibliography," *Crit* 13, iii (1972): 45-55.

_____, *John Barth: A Descriptive Primary and Annotated Secondary Bibliography, including a Descriptive Catalog of Manuscript Holdings in United States Libraries* (Garland Ref. Libs. in Humanities 25), N.Y.: Garland, 1976.

BARTHELME, DONALD, 1931-1989

GENERAL

Brans, Jo, "Embracing the World: An Interview with Donald Barthelme," *SWR* 67, ii (Spring, 1982): 121-37.

Couturier, M., and R. Durand, *Donald Barthelme*.

Costello, Thomas L., "Parody and Social Satire in the Fiction of Donald Barthelme," *DAI* 37 (1977): 5823A-24A.

Ditsky, John M., "'With Ingenuity and Hard Work Distracted': The Narrative Style of Donald Barthelme," *Style* 9 (1975): 388-400.

Durand, Régis, "Donald Barthelme and the Art of Displacement," 137-44 in Sienicka, Marta, ed., *Proceedings of a Symposium on American Literature*, Pozna: Uniw. Im. Adama Mickicwicza, 1979.

Gordon, L., *Donald Barthelme*.

Johnson, R. E., Jr., "'Bees Barking in the Night': The End and Beginning of Donald Barthelme's Narrative," *Boundary* 5 (1976): 71-92.

Klinkowitz, Jerome, "Donald Barthelme," in Bellamy, J. D., ed., *New Fiction*, 45-54.

Legasse, Jim, "The Voice of the Form and the Form of the Voice," *Westerly* 25 (Mar., 1980): 97-101. [Not seen.]

Leland, John, "Remarks Re-marked: Barthelme, What Curios of Signs!" *Boundary* 5, iii (Spring 1977): 795-811.

McCaffery, Larry, "An Interview with Donald Barthelme," *PR* 49, ii (1982): 184-93.

_____, "Meaning and Non-Meaning in Barthelme's Fictions," *JAE* 13, i (Jan., 1979): 69-79.

Molesworth, C., *Donald Barthelme's Fiction*.

Moran, Charles, "Barthelme the Trash-Man: The Uses of Junk in the Classroom," *CEA* 36, iv (May, 1974): 32-3.

O'Hara, J. D., "Donald Barthelme: The Art of Fiction LXVI," *ParisR* 80 (1981): 180-210.

Robinson, Fred M., "Nonsense and Sadness in Donald Barthelme and Edward Lear," *SAQ* 80, ii (Spring, 1981): 164-76.

Roe, Barbara L., "The Short Works of Donald Barthelme," *DAI* 43, ii (Aug., 1982): 447A.

Schmitz, Neil, "Donald Barthelme and the Emergence of Modern Satire," *MinnR* 1 (Fall, 1971): 109-18.

Stanley, Donald H., "The Self-Conscious Narrator in Donald Barthelme and Vladimir Nabokov," *DAI* 40 (1979): 2057A.

"A Symposium on Fiction," *Shenandoah* 27, ii (1976): 3-31. [Not seen.]

Taylor, David M., "Donald Barthelme: An Approach to Contemporary Fiction," *DAI* 38 (1978): 4832A-33A.

Wilde, Alan, "Barthelme Unfair to Kierkegaard: Some Thoughts on Modern and Postmodern Irony," *Boundary* 5 (1976): 45-70.

THE DEAD FATHER

Davis, Robert., "Post-Modern Paternity: Donald Barthelme's THE DEAD FATHER," *DeltaES* 8 (1979): 107-40.

Farmer, Betty C. D., "Mythological, Biblical, and Literary Allusions in Donald Barthelme's THE DEAD FATHER," *IFR* 6 (1979): 40-8.

Gordon, L., *Donald Barthelme*, 161-78.

Kramer, Hilton, "Barthelme's Comedy of Patricide," *Ctary* 62, ii (Aug., 1976): 56-9.

Maloy, Barbara, "Barthelme's THE DEAD FATHER: Analysis of an Allegory," *LNL* 2, ii (1972): 43-119.

Werner, C. H., *Paradoxical Resolutions*, 98-102.

SNOW WHITE

Flowers, Betty, "Barthelme's SNOW WHITE: The Reader-Patient Relationship," *Crit* 16, iii (1975): 33-43.

Gilman, R., *Confusion of Realms*, 42-52.

Gordon, L., *Donald Barthelme*, 62-83.

Harris, Charles B., *Contemporary American Novelists of the Absurd*, 124-7.

Klinkowitz, J., *Literary Disruptions*, 66-9.

Leland, John, "Remarks Re-marked: Barthelme, What Curios of Signs!" *Boundary* 5, iii (Spring, 1977): 800-10.

Longleigh, Peter J., Jr., "Donald Barthelme's SNOW WHITE," *Crit* 11, iii (1969): 30-4.

McCafferey, Larry, "Barthelme's SNOW WHITE: The Aesthetics of Trash," *Crit* 16, iii (1975): 19-32.

_____, *Metaphysical Muse*, 136-50.

McNall, Sally A., "'But why am I troubling myself about cans?' Style, Reaction, and Lack of Reaction in Barthelme's SNOW WHITE," *Lang&S* 8 (1975): 81-94.

Rother, James, "Parafiction: The Adjacent Universe of Barth, Barthelme, Pynchon, and Nabokov," *Boundary* 5, i (Fall, 1976): 34-7.

Semrau, Janusz, "A Questionnaire: Some Remarks Towards a Study of Novelistic Self-Consciousness," *KN* 29, iii-iv (1982): 285-8.

Shadoian, Jack, "Notes on Donald Barthelme's SNOW WHITE," *WHR* 24 (Winter, 1970): 73-5.

Stott, William, "Donald Barthelme and the Death of Fiction," *Prospects* 1 (1975): 374-81.

Tanner, T., *City of Words*, 401-4.

BIBLIOGRAPHY

Klinkowitz, Jerome, "Donald Barthelme: A Checklist, 1957-1974," *Crit* 16, iii (1975): 49-58.

_____, Asa Pieratt, and Robert M. Davis, *Donald Barthelme: A Comprehensive Bibliography and Annotated Secondary Checklist*, Hamden, CT: Shoe String (Archon), 1977.

McCaffery, Larry, "A Donald Barthelme Checklist," *BB* 31, iii (July-Sept., 1974): 101-2, 106.

BASSO, HAMILTON, 1904-1964

GENERAL

Cowley, Malcolm, "The Writer as Craftsman: The Literary Heroism of Hamilton Basso," *SatR* 47 (June 27, 1964): 17-18.

Ikerd, Clarence F., "Hamilton Basso: A Critical Biography," *DAI* 36 (1976): 6684A.

Millichap, J. R., *Hamilton Basso*.

Rocks, James E., "Hamilton Basso and the World View from Pompey's Head," *SAQ* 71, iii (Sumer, 1972): 326-41.

CINNAMON SEED

Millichap, J. R., *Hamilton Basso*, 39-49.

COURTHOUSE SQUARE

Millichap, J. R., *Hamilton Basso*, 56-66.

DAYS BEFORE LENT

Green, R. B., *Italian-American Novel*, 117-21.

Millichap, J. R., *Hamilton Basso*, 67-76.

THE GREENROOM

Millichap, J. R., *Hamilton Basso*, 91-9.

IN THEIR OWN IMAGE

Bishop, J. P., "Vanity Fair," *NRep* (May 29, 1938). Also in *Collected Essays*, 254-5.

THE LIGHT INFANTRY BALL

Millichap, J. R., *Hamilton Basso*, 114-22.

RELICS AND ANGELS

Millichap, J. R., *Hamilton Basso*, 27-38.

SUN IN CAPRICORN

Millichap, J. R., *Hamilton Basso*, 83-90.

Milne, G., *American Political Novel*, 132-4.

Rubin, Louis D., Jr., "All the King's Meanings," *GaR* 7 (1954): 422-3. Also in Rubin E., "The Concept of Demagoguery: Huey Long and His Literary Critics," *LaS* 15, i (Spring, 1976): 61-83.

A TOUCH OF THE DRAGON

Millichap, J. R., *Hamilton Basso*, 99-105.

THE VIEW FROM POMPEY'S HEAD

Green, R. B., *Italian-American Novel*, 121-5, 127.

Hoffman, F. J., *Art of Southern Fiction*, 25-6.

Millichap, J. R., *Hamilton Basso*, 107-14.

WINE OF THE COUNTRY

Millichap, J. R., *Hamilton Basso*, 76-83.

BIBLIOGRAPHY

Millichap, J. R., *Hamilton Basso*, 159-62.

BAUMBACH, JONATHAN, 1933-

GENERAL

Graham, John, "Jonathan Baumbach," in Garrett, G., ed., *Writer's Voice*, 214-20. [Interview.]

Klinkowitz, Jerome, "Jonathan Baumbach's Superfiction," *ChiR* 26, iv (1975): 178-88.

A MAN TO CONJURE WITH

Klinkowitz, Jerome, "Jonathan Baumbach's Superfiction," *ChiR* 26, iv 1975): 179-82.

WHAT COMES NEXT

Klinkowitz, Jerome, "Jonathan Baumbach's Superfiction," *ChiR* 26, iv (1975): 182-4.

BEAGLE, PETER S(OYER), 1939-

GENERAL

Van Becker, David, "Time, Space & Consciousness in the Fantasy of Peter S. Beagle," *SJS* 1, i (Feb., 1975): 52-61.

THE LAST UNICORN

Foust, R. E., "Fabulous Paradigm: Fantasy, Meta-Fantasy, and Peter S. Beagle's THE LAST UNICORN," *Extrapolation* 21, i (1980): 5-20.

Norford, Don P., "Reality and Illusion in Peter Beagle's THE LAST UNICORN," *Crit* 19, ii (1977): 93-104.

Olderman, R. M., "Out of the Waste Land," *Beyond the Waste Land*, 220-42.

Olsen, Alexandra H., "The Anti-*Consolatio*: Boethius and THE LAST UNICORN," *Mosaic* 13, iii-iv (1980): 133-44.

Stevens, David, "Incongruity in a World of Illusion: Patterns of Humor in Peter Beagle's THE LAST UNICORN," *Extrapolation* 20, iii (1979): 230-7.

BECKETT, SAMUEL, 1906-1989

GENERAL

Abbott, H. P., *Fiction of Samuel Beckett.*

————, "The Fiction of Samuel Beckett: A Study of Imitative Form," *DA* 29 (1969): 3996A.

————, "King Laugh: Beckett's Early Fiction," in Cohn, R., ed., *Samuel Beckett*, 51-62.

————, "A Poetics of Radical Displacement: Samuel Beckett Coming up to Seventy," *TSLL* 17, i (Spring, 1975): 219-38.

Albright, D., *Representation and the Imagination*, 150-208.

Allsop, K., *Angry Decade*, 37-40.

Alvarez, A., *Beckett.*

Andonian, Cathleen C., "After the Trilogy: A Study of Samuel Beckett's Novels and Short Stories from 1955 to the Present," *DAI* 41 (1980): 1585A.

Anon., "Paradise of Indignity," *TLS* (Mar. 28, 1958): 168.

Atlas, James, "The Prose of Samuel Beckett: Notes from the Terminal Ward," *Poetry Nation* 2 (1974): 106-17. Also in Dunn, D., ed., *Two Decades of Irish Writing*, 186-96.

Baalman, Raymond W., Jr., "Samuel Beckett's Fiction and the Language of Music," *DAI* 35 (1975): 4496A.

Baldwin, H. L., *Samuel Beckett's Silence.*

Baldwin, Helen L., "The Theme of the Pilgrim in the Works of Samuel Beckett," *CSR* 8, iii (1978): 217-28.

Barge, Laura, "The Beckett Hero," *PMLA* 92, v (Oct., 1977): 1007-8.

————, " 'Coloured Images' in the 'Black Dark': Samuel Beckett's Later Fiction," *PMLA* 92, ii (Mar., 1977): 273-84.

————, "The Empty Heaven of Samuel Beckett," *Cithara* 15, ii (May, 1976): 3-19.

Barnard, G. C., *Samuel Beckett.*

Beckett at 60: A Festschrift, London: Calder and Boyars, 1967.

Beckmeier, Fiorella S., "The Fiction of Samuel Beckett in the Light of Sartrean Existentialism," *DAI* 40 (1980): 4618A-19A.

Beebe, Maurice, "Reflective and Reflexive Trends in Modern Fiction," *BuR* 22, ii (1976): 13-26. [Not seen.]

Bello, Gerald A., "A Dictionary of Proper Names in Samuel Beckett's Works, Volume I (A-G)," *DAI* 40 (1980): 5448A.

Ben-Zvi, Linda, "Samuel Beckett, Fritz Mauthner, and the Limits of Language," *PMLA* 95, ii (Mar., 1980): 183-200.

Bernheimer, Charles, "Grammacentricity and Modernism," *Mosaic* 11, i (Fall, 1977): 103-16.

Bersani, Leo, "No Exit for Beckett," *PR* 33 (Spring, 1966): 261-8.

Binns, Ronald, in *Contemporary English Novel*, 89-102.

Bishop, Tom, "Camus and Beckett: Variations on an Absurd Landscape," *PCLS* 8 (1975): 53-69. [Not seen.]

————, "Samuel Beckett: Working Multi-Lingually," *Centerpoint* 4, ii (Fall, 1980): 140-2. [Not seen.]

Bové, Paul A., "The Image of the Creator in Beckett's Postmodern Writing," *P&L* 4, i (Spring, 1980): 47-65.

Brée, Germaine, "The Strange World of Beckett's 'grands articulés,'" in Friedman, M. J., ed., *Samuel Beckett Now*, 73-87.

Breuer, Horst, "Disintegration of Time in Macbeth's Soliloquy 'Tomorrow, and tomorrow, and tomorrow'," *MLR* 71, ii (April, 1976): 256-71.

Brienza, Susan D., and Peggy A. Knapp, "Imagination Lost and Found: Beckett's Fiction and Frye's *Anatomy*," *MLN* 95, iv (May, 1980): 980-94.

————, "A Stylistic Analysis of Samuel Beckett's Recent Fiction," *DAI* 37 (1977): 7138A.

Brooke-Rose, Christine, "Samuel Beckett and the Anti-Novel," *LonM* 5, xii (Dec., 1958): 38-46.

Bruns, Gerald L., "The Storyteller and the Problem of Language in Samuel Beckett's Fiction," *MLQ* 30, ii (June, 1969): 265-81.

Castillo, Debra A., "Beckett's Metaphorical Towns," *MFS* 28, ii (Summer, 1982): 189-200.

Chambers, Ross, "Beckett's Brinkmanship," *AUMLA* No. 19 (May, 1963): 57-75.

Chanan, Gabriel, "The Plight of the Novelist," *CamR* 89A (April 26, 1968): 399-401. [Not seen.]

Cismaru, Alfred, and Theodore Klein, "The Concept of Suicide in Camus and Beckett," *Ren* 28, ii (Winter, 1976): 105-10.

Clements, John O., "Samuel Beckett as Self-Translator: A Comparative Study of His French-English Novels," *DAI* 34 (1974): 7224A-25A.

Coe, Richard N., *Beckett.*

_____, "God and Samuel Beckett," *Meanjin* (Mar., 1965): 66-85. Also in O'Hara, J. D., ed., *Twentieth Century Interpretations of MOLLOY, MALONE DIES, THE UNNAMABLE*, 91-113.

Coetzee, John M., "The English Fiction of Samuel Beckett: An Essay in Stylistic Analysis," *DA* 30 (1969): 1555A.

_____, "Samuel Beckett and the Temptations of Style," *Theoria* 41 (1973): 45-50.

Cohn, Ruby, "The Comedy of Samuel Beckett: 'Something old, something new—'," *YFS* No. 23 (Summer, 1959): 11-17.

_____, "Joyce and Beckett, Irish Cosmopolitans," *JJQ* 8, iv (Summer, 1971): 385-91.

_____, "Philosophical Fragments in the Works of Samuel Beckett," *Criticism* 6 (1964): 33-43. Also in Esslin, M., ed., *Samuel Beckett*, 169-77.

_____, "Preliminary Observations," *Per* 11 (Autumn, 1959): 119-31.

_____, *Samuel Beckett*.

_____, ed., *Samuel Beckett*.

_____, "Samuel Beckett Self-Translater," *PMLA* 76 (1961): 613-21.

_____, "Still Novel," *YFS* No. 24 (1959): 48-53.

Conley, Tom, "Crutches," *ChiR* 33, ii (1982): 84-92.

Coonin, Stuart L., "Samuel Beckett: The Eastern Influence," *DAI* 36 (1975): 307A.

Copeland, Hannah C., "Art and Artist in the Works of Samuel Beckett," *DAI* 32 (1971): 3299A.

_____, *Art and the Artist in the Works of Samuel Beckett*.

Cornwell, Ethel F., and Laura Barge, "The Beckett Hero," *PMLA* 92, v (Oct., 1977): 1006-8.

_____, "Samuel Beckett: The Flight from Self," *PMLA* 88, i (Jan., 1973): 41-51.

Cousineau, Thomas J., "Imagination Dead Imagination: A Commentary on the Novels of Samuel Beckett," *DA* 32 (1972): 5224A.

Cronin, Anthony, "Molloy Becomes Unnamable," *Question of Modernity*, London: Secker & Waarburg, 1966, 97-110.

Culotta-Andonian, Cathleen, "Conceptions of Inner Landscapes: The Beckettian Narrator in the Sixties and Seventies," *Symposium* 36, i (Spring, 1982): 3-13.

Currie, R., "Beckett's Transcendental Nihilism," *Genius*, 171-93.

Dearlove, J. E., "Composing in the Face of Choas: Paul Hindemith and Samuel Beckett," *Mosaic* 15, iii (Sept., 1982): 43-53.

_____, "'Last Images': Samuel Beckett's Residual Fiction," *JML* 6, i (Feb., 1971): 104-26.

_____, "To Find a Form: Samuel Beckett's Eccentric Fiction," *DAI* 36 (1976): 4503A-04A.

Dobrez, Livio, "Beckett and Heidegger: Existence, Being and Nothingness," *SoRA* 7, ii (July, 1974): 140-53.

_____, "Beckett, Sartre and Camus: The Darkness and the Light," *SoRA* 7, i (Feb., 1974): 51-64.

_____, "Samuel Beckett's Irreducible," *SoRA* 6, iii (Sept., 1973): 205-22.

Doherty, F., *Samuel Beckett*.

Doll, Mary A., "Samuel Beckett and Archetypal Consciousness," *DAI* 41 (1980): 2598A.

Elovaara, R., *Problem of Identity in Samuel Beckett's Prose*.

Engelborghs, Maurits, "Wat na Joyce?" *DWB* 125 (1980): 364-7. [Not seen.]

Erickson, John D., "Alienation in Samuel Beckett: The Protagonist as Eiron," *PCL* 1, ii (Nov., 1975): 62-73.

_____, "Objects and Systems in the Novels of Samuel Beckett," *ECr* 7 (Summer, 1967): 113-22.

Esslin, Martin, ed., *Samuel Beckett*.

_____, "Samuel Beckett," in Cruickshank, J., ed., *Novelist as Philosopher*, 128-46.

Estess, Ted L., "Dimensions of Play in the Literature of Samuel Beckett," *ArQ* 33, i (Spring, 1977): 5-25.

_____, "The Inenarrable Contraption: Reflections on the Metaphor of Story," *JAAR* 42 (1974): 415-34.

_____, "Nothing-Doing: A Study of Game-Play Motifs in the Literature of Samuel Beckett," *DA* 33 (1972): 307A-08A.

Evers, Francis, "Samuel Beckett: The Incurious Seeker," *DM* 7, i (Spring, 1968): 84-8.

Fallacy, Paulo, "S. Beckett's Symbolism: A Key to the Understanding of Present-Day Society," *BILEUG* 11 (1978): 102-19. [Not seen.]

Federman, Raymond, "Beckettian Paradox: Who is Telling the Truth?" in Friedman, M. J., ed., *Samuel Beckett Now*, 103-17.

_____, "The Impossibility of Saying the Same Old Thing: Beckett's Fiction Since COMMENT C'EST," *Ecr* 11, iii (Fall, 1971): 21-43.

_____, *Journey to Chaos*.

_____, "Samuel Beckett: The Liar's Paradox," in Morot-Sir, E., et al., eds., *Samuel Beckett*, 119-41.

Finch, Roy, "The Reality of the Nothing: The Importance of Samuel Beckett," *Lugano Rev*, iii-iv (Summer, 1965): 211-22.

Fletcher, John, "Beckett and the Fictional Tradition," *Caliban*, n.s., 1, i (1965): 147-58.

_____, "Beckett's Debt to Dante," *NFS* 4 (May, 1965): 41-52.

_____, *Novels of Samuel Beckett*.

_____, "'A Place in the Series': Beckett's Literary Development," *CollL* 8, ii (Fall, 1981): 271-82.

_____, "Reading Beckett with Iris Murdoch's Eyes," *AUMLA* 55 (May, 1981): 7-14.

_____, "Samuel Beckett and the Philosophers," *CL* 17 (Winter, 1965): 43-56.

_____, "Samuel Beckett; or, the Morbid Dread of Sphinxes," *New Durham* (June, 1965): 5-9. [Not seen.]

_____, *Samuel Beckett's Art*, N.Y.: Barnes & Noble, 1967.

Friedman, Melvin J., "The Creative Writer as Polyglot: Valery Larbaud and Samuel Beckett," *TWA* 49 (1960): 229-36.

_____, "A Note on Leibniz and Samuel Beckett," *RomN* 4 (Spring, 1963): 93-6.

_____, "The Novels of Samuel Beckett: An Amalgam of Joyce and Proust," *CL* 12 (Winter, 1960): 47-58.

_____, "Samuel Beckett and the *Nouveau Roman*," *WSCL* 1, ii (Spring-Summer, 1960): 22-36.

_____, ed., *Samuel Beckett Now*.

Furbank, P. N., "Beckett's Purgatory," *Encounter* 22, vi (June, 1964): 69-72.

Gardiner, Alan, "The Human Couple and the Theme of Decay in Beckett's Work," *SEAP* 1 (1971): 270-94. [Not seen.]

Garzilli, E., *Circles Without Center*, 34-8.

Giguere, Nancy J., "Crisis of Confidence: The Image of the Writer in Selected Works of Jorge Luis Borges and Samuel Beckett," *DAI* 42, ii (Aug., 1981): 697A.

Glicksberg, Charles I., "Samuel Beckett's World of Fiction," *ArQ* 18 (Spring, 1962): 32-47.

Gluck, B. R., *Beckett and Joyce*.

Gluck, Barbara G. R., "Beckett and Joyce: Friendship and Fiction," *DAI* 35 (1975): 6710A-11A.

Grauer, Lawrence, and Raymond Federman, eds., *Samuel Beckett: The Critical Heritage* (Critical Heritage Ser.), London: Routledge, 1979.

Gray, Stanley E., "Beckett and Queneau as Formalists," *JJQ* 8, iv (Summer, 1971): 392-404.

Greenberg, Alvin, "The Novel of Disintegration: Paradoxical Impossibility in Contemporary Literature," *WSCL* 7 (Winter-Spring, 1966): 109-12.

Greene, Naomi, "Creation and the Self: Artaud, Beckett, Michaud," *Criticism* 13, iii (Summer, 1971): 265-78.

Hallford, Ruth L., "The English Novels of Samuel Beckett," *DAI* 31 (1970): 2917A.

Hamilton, A., and K. Hamilton, *Condemned to Life*.

_____, "The Guffaw of the Abderite: Samuel Beckett's Use of Democritus," *Mosaic* 9, ii (Winter, 1976): 1-13.

_____, "Samuel Beckett and the Gnostic Vision of the Created World," *SRC* 8, iii (Summer, 1979): 293-301.

Hamilton, Kenneth, "Negative Salvation in Samuel Beckett," *QQ* 69 (Spring, 1962): 102-11.

Hardy, Barbara, "The Dubious Consolations in Beckett's Fiction: Art, Love and Nature," in Worth, K., ed., *Beckett the Shape Changer*, 107-38.

Harrington, John P., "The Irish Beckett: A Study of the Irish Contexts of His Work through the Second World War and the Development of His Prose Style," *DAI* 40 (1980): 6290A.

_____, "Pynchon, Beckett, and Entropy: Uses of Metaphor," *MissR* 5, iii (Summer, 1982): 129-38.

Harvey, Lawrence E., "Samuel Beckett on Life, Art and Criticism," *MLN* 80 (Dec., 1965): 545-62.

Hassan, Ihab, "Beckett: Imagination Ending," *Dismemberment of Orpheus*, 210-46.

_____, "Joyce, Beckett, and the Postmodern Imagination," *TriQ* 34 (Fall, 1975): 179-200.

_____, *Literature of Silence*.

_____, "The Literature of Silence: From Henry Miller to Beckett and Burroughs," *Encounter* 28 (Jan., 1967): 74-82.

Heppenstall, R., *Fourfold Tradition*, 254-66.

Hesla, David H., "Being, Thinking, Telling, and Loving: The Couple in Beckett's Fiction," in Morot-Sir, E., et al., eds., *Samuel Beckett*, 11-23.

_____, *Shape of Chaos*.

Hicks, Granville, "Beckett's World," *SatR* 41 (Oct. 4, 1958): 14.

Hoffman, F. J., *Samuel Beckett*.

Hvistendahl, Marion, "Samuel Beckett: From Bitches to Beatification," *Cresset* 40, ix-x (Sept.-Oct., 1977): 15-18. [Not seen.]

Irvin, Helen D., "Problems of Knowing in the Work of Samuel Beckett," *DAI* 32 (1970): 967A-68A.

Iser, Wolfgang, "The Pattern of Negativity in Beckett's Prose," *GaR* 29, iii (1975): 706-19.

Jacobsen, Josephine, and William R. Mueller, "Beckett as Poet," *PrS* 37 (Fall, 1963): 196-216. Also in Jacobsen, J., and W. R. Mueller, *Testament of Samuel Beckett*.

Janvier, Ludovic, "Place of Narration/Narration of Place," in Cohn, R., ed., *Samuel Beckett*, 96-110.

Johnson, Gerald J., "The Playful Style: Sterne and Beckett," *DAI* 36 (1976): 5271A-72A.

Jones, Christopher J., "The Fool's Progress: Beckett's Clowns in Their Traditional and Popular Contexts," *DAI* 39 (1978): 279A.

Kalaga, Wojciech, "Disintegration of the Body in the Novels of Samuel Beckett," in Lobzowska, Marie, ed., *Aspects of Tragedy in the Twentieth Century English and American Literature*, Katowice, Poland: Uniwersytet Slaski, 1980, 17-35.

_____, *Mental Landscape: The Development of the Novel of Samuel Beckett*, Katowice, Poland: Uniwersytet Slaski, 1982.

Karl, Frederick R., "Waiting for Beckett: Quest and Request," *SR* 69 (Autumn, 1961): 661-76. Also in Karl, F. R., *Contemporary English Novel*, 19-39.

Kay, Wallace G., "Blake, Baudelaire, Beckett: The Romantics of Nihilism," *SoQ* 9, iii (April, 1971): 253-9.

Kennedy, Sighle, "Samuel Beckett's Language: 'Danger: Explosive Materials,'" *Centerpoint* 4, ii (Fall, 1980): 135-7. [Not seen.]

_____, "Spirals of Need: Irish Prototypes in Samuel Beckett's Fiction," in McGrory, K., and J. Unterecker, eds., *Yeats, Joyce, and Beckett*, 153-66.

Kenner, Hugh, "The Beckett Landscape," *Spectrum* 2 (Winter, 1958): 8-24.

_____, "Beckett: The Rational Domain," *ForumH* 3, iv (Summer, 1960): 39-47.

_____, "The Cartesian Centaur," *Per* 11 (Autumn, 1959): 132-41.

_____, *Reader's Guide to Samuel Beckett*.

_____, "Samuel Beckett: Comedian of the Impasse," *Flaubert, Joyce and Beckett: The Stoic Comedians*, Boston: Beacon Pr., 1962, 67-107.

_____, *Samuel Beckett: A Critical Study*, N.Y.: Grove, 1961; London: Calder, 1962.

_____, "Shades of Syntax," in Cohn, R., ed., *Samuel Beckett*, 21-31.

_____, "Voices in the Night," *Spectrum* 5 (Spring, 1961): 3-20. Also in Kenner, H., *Samuel Beckett: A Critical Study*, 1961.

Kermode, Frank, "Beckett, Snow, and Pure Poverty," *Encounter* 15 (July, 1960): 73-7. Also in Kermode, F., *Puzzles and Epiphanies*, 155-61.

Kern, E. G., *Existential Thought and Fictional Technique*, 167-240.

Kern, Edith, "Ironic Structure in Beckett's Fiction," *ECr* 11, iii (Fall, 1971): 3-13.

Klawitter, Robert L., "Being and Time in Samuel Beckett's Novels," *DA* 26 (1966): 7320 (Yale).

Klein, Theodore M., "Classical Myth and Symbolism in Camus and Beckett," *PCLS* 8 (1975): 187-200.

Knapp, Robert S., "Samuel Beckett's Allegory of the Uncreating Word," *Mosaic* 6, ii (Winter, 1973): 71-83.

Knowlson, J., and J. Pilling, *Frescoes of the Skull*.

Kreuter, Katherine E., "The Void as Protagonist: A Study of the Entropic Hero in the Novels of Samuel Beckett," *DAI* 40 (1979): 2091A-92A.

Kroll, Jeri L., "Fair to Middling Heroes: A Study of Samuel Beckett's Early Fiction," *DAI* 35 (1975): 6720A-21A.

_____, "'I Create, Therefore I Am': The Artist's Mind in Samuel Beckett's Fiction," *AUMLA* 55 (May, 1981): 36-53.

Lee, Robin, "The Fictional Topography of Samuel Beckett," in Josipovici, G., ed., *Modern English Novel*, 206-24.

Lemert, Phyllis B., "Undoing the Creation: An Interpretation of Samuel Beckett's Fiction," *DAI* 36 (1975): 2220A.

Leventhal, A. J., "The Beckett Hero," *Crit* 7, ii (Winter, 1965): 18-35. Also in Esslin, M., ed., *Samuel Beckett*, 37-51.

Levin, Karen J. K., "The Search for Lost Selves in Some Major Works of Samuel Beckett and Max Frisch," *DAI* 40 (1979): 2047A.

Levy, E. P., *Beckett and the Voice of Species.*

Libera, Antoni, "Beckett: Five Questions," *Centerpoint* 4, ii (Fall, 1980): 146-7. [Not seen.]

Matthews, H., *Hard Journey*, 139-68.

Mauriac, Claude, *The New Literature*, N.Y.: Braziller, 1959, 75-90.

Mayoux, Jean-Jacques, *Samuel Beckett.*

————, "Samuel Beckett and Universal Parody," in Esslin, M., ed., *Samuel Beckett*, 77-91.

Mays, James, "*Pons Asinorum*: Form and Value in Beckett's Writing, with Some Comments on Kafka and De Sade," *IUR* 4, ii (Autumn, 1974): 268-82.

McMillan, Dougald, "Samuel Beckett and the Visual Arts: The Embarrassment of Allegory," in Cohn, R., ed., *Samuel Beckett*, 121-35.

Meares, Russel, "Beckett, Sarraute, and the Perceptual Experience of Schizophrenia," *Psychiatry* 26 (1973): 61-9.

Megged, Matti, "Beckett and Giacometti," *PR* 49, iii (1982): 400-6.

Menzies, Janet, "Beckett's Bicycles," *JBeckS* 6 (Autumn, 1980): 97-105.

Mercier, V., *Beckett/Beckett.*

————, "Ireland/The World: Beckett's Irishness," in McGrory, K., and J. Unterecker, eds., *Yeats, Joyce, and Beckett*, 147-52.

————, "Samuel Beckett, Bible Reader," *Cweal* (Apr. 28, 1978): 266-8.

Montgomery, Niall, "No Symbols Where None Intended," *New World Writing*, Fifth Mentor Selection, N.Y.: New American Library, 1954.

Mood, John J., "The Descent into the Self: An Interpretation of the Prose Fiction of Samuel Beckett," *DA* 30 (1969): 2033A.

Moorjani, A. B., *Abysmal Games in the Novels of Samuel Beckett.*

————, "A Study of Samuel Beckett: The Intersubjective Dimension of His Work," *DA* 32 (1972): 6992A.

Morot-Sir, Edouard, "Pascal versus Wittgenstein, with Samuel Beckett as the Anti-Witness," *RomN* 15, ii (Winter, 1973): 201-16.

————, et al., eds., *Samuel Beckett.*

————, "Samuel Beckett and Cartesian Emblems," in Morot-Sir, E., et al., eds., *Samuel Beckett*, 25-104.

Morse, J. Mitchell, "The Contemplative Life According to Samuel Beckett," *HudR* 15 (Winter, 1962-63): 512-24.

Motycka, Ronda N., "Beckett's Fiction: The Hero and the Quest," *DAI* 40 (1979): 844A-45A.

Mundhenk, Michael, "Samuel Beckett: The Dialectics of Hope and Despair," *CollL* 8, iii (Fall, 1981): 227-48.

Murphy, Vincent J., "The Beckettian Equation: Formative Ideas in the Works of Samuel Beckett Based on His Early Analysis of Marcel Proust," *DAI* 35 (1974): 1117A.

Murray, Patrick, "The Shandean Mode: Beckett and Sterne Compared," *Studies* 60, ccxxxvii (Spring, 1971): 55-67.

Neill, Mary T., "'Images of Being' in the Works of Samuel Beckett," *DAI* 37 (1977): 6505A-06A.

O'Hara, J. D., ed., *Twentieth Century Interpretations of MOLLOY, MALONE DIES, THE UNNAMABLE.*

————, "Where There's a Will There's a Way Out: Beckett and Schopenhauer," *CollL* 8, iii (Fall, 1981): 249-70.

O'Neill, Joseph P., "The Absurd in Samuel Beckett," *Person* 48 (Winter, 1967): 56-76.

Paine, S., *Beckett, Nabokov, Nin*, 12-47.

Peake, Charles, "The Labours of Poetical Excavation," in Worth, K., ed., *Beckett the Shape Changer*, 41-59.

Pearce, Richard, "Enter the Frame," *TriQ* 30 (Spring, 1974): 71-82.

Persson, Susan A. R., "Samuel Beckett's Outcast and the Irish Tradition," *DAI* 34 (1974): 4278A.

Pilling, J., *Samuel Beckett.*

Rabinovitz, Rubin, "The Deterioration of Outside Reality in Samuel Beckett's Fiction," in McGrory, K., and J. Unterecker, eds., *Yeats, Joyce, and Beckett*, 167-71.

————, "Style and Obscurity in Samuel Beckett's Early Fiction," *MFS* 20, iii (Autumn, 1974): 399-406.

Radke, Judith J., "Doubt and the Disintegration of Form in the French Novels and Drama of Samuel Beckett," *DA* 22 (1962): 3205-6 (Colorado).

Rexroth, Kenneth, "The Point is Irrelevance," *Nation* 182 (Apr. 14, 1956): 325-8. Also in Kostelanetz, R., ed., *On Contemporary Literature*, 244-8.

————, "Samuel Beckett and the Importance of Waiting," *Bird in the Bush: Obvious Essays*, N.Y.: New Directions, 1954, 75-85.

Ricks, Christopher, "The Roots of Samuel Beckett," *Listener* 72 (Dec. 17, 1964): 963-4.

Riva, Raymond T., "Beckett and Freud," *Criticism* 12, ii (Spring, 1970): 354-69.

Robinson, C. J. B., "A Way with Words: Paradox, Silence and Samuel Beckett," *CQ* 5, iii (1971): 249-64.

Robinson, M., *Long Sonata of the Dead.*

Rockmore, Sylvie M., "Proust, Beckett and the 'New Novelists': A Comparative Analysis," *DAI* 35 (1975): 7921A.

Romano, John, "Beckett without Angst," *ASch* 47, i (Winter, 1977-78): 95-102.

Rose, Marilyn G., "The Irish Memories of Beckett's Voice," *JML* 2, i (Sept., 1971): 127-32.

————, "Solitary Companions in Beckett and Jack B. Yeats," *Eire* 4, ii (Summer, 1969): 66-80.

Rosen, Steven J., "Samuel Beckett: A Study of His Thought," *DAI* 34 (1973): 2651A-52A.

Rothenberg, John, "A Form of Tension in Beckett's Fiction," *DSec* 6 (July, 1982): 157-76.

Salgado, Ralph H., Jr., "Monorealism: Form in Samuel Beckett's Post-War Writings," *DAI* 37 (1976): 1874A-75A.

Sawdey, Michael R., "The Incurious Seeker: A Study of the Anti-Quest in Samuel Beckett's Novels," *DAI* 35 (1974): 472A-73A.

Schulz, Hans-Joachim K., "A Hegelian Approach to the Novels of Samuel Beckett," *DA* 29 (1969): 3154A-55A.

————, *This Hell of Stories.*

Scott, Nathan A., Jr., "The Recent Journey into the Zone of Zero: The Example of Beckett and His Despair of Literature," *CRAS* 6 (Spring, 1962): 144-81. Also (slightly revised) in Scott, N. A., Jr., *Craters of the Spirit*, 157-200.

————, *Samuel Beckett.*

Segrè, Elisabeth B., "Style in Beckett's Prose: Repetition and the Transformation of the Functions of Language," *DAI* 36 (1976): 6677A-78A.

Sen, Supti, *Samuel Beckett.*

Sharratt, Bernard, "Samuel Beckett: Language and Being-There," *Anglo-Irish Studies* 1 (1975): 1-35.

Skerl, Jennie, "The Form of Absurdity: The Novels of Samuel Beckett," *DAI* 35 (1974): 3771A.

Sobosan, Jeffrey G., "Time and Absurdity in Beckett," *Thought* 49 (Mar., 1974): 187-95.

Stamirowska, Krystyna, "The Conception of a Character in the Works of Joyce and Beckett," *KN* 14 (1967): 443-7.

Steiner, George, "Of Nuance and Scruple," *NY* 44 (Apr. 27, 1968): 164-74.

Sternlicht, Sanford, "Samuel Beckett," in Kidd, Walter E., ed., *British Winners of the Nobel Literary Prize*, Norman: Univ. of Oklahoma Pr., 1973, 237-65.

Strauss, Walter, "Dante's Belacqua and Beckett's Tramps," *CL* 11 (Summer, 1959): 250-61.

Sypher, Wylie, "The Anonymous Self: A Defensive Humanism," *Loss of the Self in Modern Literature and Art*, N.Y.: Random House, 1962, 147-54.

Szanto, G. H., *Narrative Consciousness*, 71-103, 104-20.

Takahashi, Yasunari, "Fool's Progress," in Cohn, R., ed., *Samuel Beckett*, 33-40.

Theroux, Alexander L., "The Language of Samuel Beckett," *DA* 29 (1969): 2726A.

Tindall, William Y., "Beckett's Bums," *Crit* 2, i (Spring-Summer, 1958): 3-15.

_____, *Samuel Beckett*.

Toyama, Jean M. Y., "Voice, Language and Self in Beckett's *Game*," *DAI* 36 (1976): 8053A.

Trivisonno, Ann M., "Samuel Beckett; Experimental Novelist," *DAI* 34 (1974): 7249A-50A.

Webb, E., *Samuel Beckett*.

Webb, Eugene, "The Spiritual Crisis of Modernity: Keynes, Beckett, Baudelaire," *Soundings* 62, ii (Summer, 1979): 130-43.

Wellershoff, Dieter, "Failure of an Attempt at De-Mythologization: Samuel Beckett's Novels," in Esslin, M., ed., *Samuel Beckett*, 92-107.

Wells, Charles M., "The Transcendence of Life: The Positive Dimension in Samuel Beckett," *DA* 29 (1968): 619A (New Mexico).

Wellwarth, G. E., "Life in the Void: Samuel Beckett," *UKCR* 28 (Oct., 1961): 25-33.

Wendler, Herbert W., "Graveyard Humanism," *SWR* 49 (Winter, 1964): 44-52.

White, Patricia O., "Existential Man in Beckett's Fiction," *Crit* 12, ii (1970): 39-49.

Wicker, Brian, "Samuel Beckett and the Death of the God-Narrator," *JNT* 4, i (Jan., 1974): 62-74. Also in Wicker, B., *Story-Shaped World*, 169-83.

Worth, K., ed., *Beckett the Shape Changer*.

Zeller, Patricia K., "Beckett's Cartesian Dilemma," *DAI* 40 (1979): 2672A.

Zurbrugg, Nicholas, "From 'Gleam' to 'Gloom': The Volte Face between the Criticism and Fiction of Samuel Beckett," *AUMLA* 55 (May, 1981): 23-35.

COMPANY

Bair, Deirdre, " 'Back the Way He Came...or in Some Quite Different Direction': COMPANY in the Canon of Samuel Beckett's Writing," *PE* 9, i (Fall, 1982): 12-19.

Burgin, Richard, "COMPANY," *Parabola* 6, iv (Oct., 1981): 116-18.

Henry, Parrish D., "Got It at Last, My Legend: Homage to Samuel Beckett," *GaR* 36, ii (Summer, 1982): 429-34.

Pilling, John, "COMPANY by Samuel Beckett," *JBeckS* 7 (Spring, 1982): 127-31.

Zurbrugg, Nicholas, "Samuel Beckett, Deirdre Bair, COMPANY and the Art of Bad Biography," 1-9 in Walter, James, ed., *Reading Life Histories: Griffith Papers on Biography*, Nathan, Queensland: Griffith Univ., Inst. for Mod. Biog., 1981.

DREAM OF FAIR TO MIDDLING WOMEN

Knowlson, J., and J. Pilling, *Frescoes of the Skull*, 3-22.

Kroll, Jeri L., "'I Create, Therefore I Am': The Artist's Mind in Samuel Beckett's Fiction," *AUMLA* 55 (May, 1981): 36-53.

Zurbrugg, Nicholas, "From 'Gleam' to 'Gloom': The Volte Face between the Criticism and Fiction of Samuel Beckett," *AUMLA* 55 (May, 1981): 23-35.

HOW IT IS (COMMENT C'EST)

Abbott, H. Porter, "Farewell to Incompetence: Beckett's HOW IT IS and IMAGINATION DEAD IMAGINE," *ConL* 11, i (Winter, 1970): 36-47.

_____, *Fiction of Samuel Beckett*, 138-48.

Alvarez, A., *Beckett*, 66-74.

Barnard, G. C., *Samuel Beckett*, 68-79.

Bruns, Gerald L., "Samuel Beckett's HOW IT IS," *JJQ* 8, iv (Summer, 1971): 318-31.

_____, "The Storyteller and Language in Samuel Beckett's Fiction," *MLQ* 30, ii (June, 1969): 278-81. Also in Bruns, G. L., *Modern Poetry and the Idea of Language*, 177-82.

Cohn, R., *Back to Beckett*, 226-40.

Copeland, Hannah C., "The Couples in COMMENT C'EST," in Morot-Sir, E., et al., eds., *Samuel Beckett*, 237-47.

Cornwell, Ethel F., "Samuel Beckett: The Flight from Self," *PMLA* 88, i (Jan., 1973): 48-50.

Doherty, F., *Samuel Beckett*, 119-31.

Elovaara, R., *Problem of Identity in Samuel Beckett's Prose*, 267-75.

Esslin, Martin, "Samuel Beckett," in Cruickshank, J., ed., *Novelist as Philosopher*, 143-4.

Federman, Raymond, "Beckett and the Fiction of Mud," in Kostelanetz, R., ed., *On Contemporary Literature*, 255-61.

_____, "HOW IT IS: With Beckett's Fiction," *FR* 38 (Feb., 1965): 459-68.

Furbank, P. N., "Beckett's Purgatory," *Encounter* 22, vi (June, 1964): 69-72.

Hamilton, A., and K. Hamilton, *Condemned to Life*, 178-88.

_____, "The Process of Imaginative Creation in Samuel Beckett's HOW IT IS, *Mosaic* 10, iv (Summer, 1977): 1-12.

Harper, Howard, "HOW IT IS," in Morot-Sir, E., et al., eds., *Samuel Beckett*, 249-70.

Hassan, I., *Literature of Silence*, 168-73.

Jones, Anthony, "Samuel Beckett Is Only Human," *ASLHM* 43, ii (1972): 73-88.

Kenner, Hugh, "Beckett Translating Beckett: COMMENT C'EST," *Delos* 5 (1970): 194-211.

_____, *Reader's Guide to Samuel Beckett*, 136-46.

Kermode, Frank, *NYRB* 11 (Mar. 19, 1964): 9-11. Also in Kermode, F., *Continuities*, 169-72.

Kern, E., *Existential Thought and Fictional Technique*, 233-8.

Knowlson, J., and J. Pilling, *Frescoes of the Skull*, 61-78.

Krance, Charles, "Alienation and Form in Beckett's HOW IT IS," *PCL* 1, ii (Nov., 1975): 85-103.

Kuhn, Reinhard, "The Knife and Wound: From Baudelaire to Beckett," *JJQ* 8, iv (Summer, 1971): 411-12.

Levy, E. P., *Beckett and the Voice of Species*, 83-94.

_____, "The Metaphysics of Ignorance: Time and Personal Identity in HOW IT IS," *Ren* 28 (Autumn, 1975): 27-38.

"Novels of 1964. Samuel Beckett: HOW IT IS," *TLS* (May 21, 1964). Also in *T.L.S.: Essays and Reviews from The Times Literary Supplement, 1964*, 45-7.

Robinson, M., *Long Sonata of the Dead*, 213-25.

Sage, Victor, "Innovation and Continuity in HOW IT IS," in Worth, K., ed., *Beckett the Shape Changer*, 87-103.

Schwartz, Paul J., "Life and Death in the Mud: A Study of Beckett's COMMENT C'EST," *IFR* 2, i (Jan., 1975): 43-8.

Scott, N. A., Jr., "Beckett's Journey into the Zone of Zero," *Craters of the Spirit*, 193-4.

Shadoian, Jack, "The Achievement of COMMENT C'EST," *Crit* 12, ii (1970): 5-18.

Tindall, William Y., *Samuel Beckett*, 37-9.

Unterecker, John, "Fiction at the Edge of Poetry," in Friedman, A. W., *Forms of Modern British Fiction*, 185-92.

Van Petten, Carol, "Modulations of Monologue in Beckett's COMMENT C'EST," *Symposium* 31, iii (Fall, 1977): 243-55.

Webb, E., *Samuel Beckett*, 154-69.

MALONE DIES (See also TRILOGY)

Abbott, H. P., *Fiction of Samuel Beckett*, 110-23.

Albright, D., *Representation and the Imagination*, 183-90.

Alvarez, A., *Beckett*, 52-7.

Baldwin, H. L., *Samuel Beckett's Real Silence*, 56-67.

Barnard, G. C., *Samuel Beckett*, 45-56.

Christensen, Inger, *Meaning of Metafiction*, 121-35.

Cmarada, Geraldine, "MALONE DIES: A Round of Consciousness," *Sym* 14 (Fall, 1960): 199-212.

Coe, R. N., *Beckett*, 62-8.

Cohn, R., *Back to Beckett*, 91-100.

Cornwell, Ethel F., "Samuel Beckett: The Flight from Self," *PMLA* 88, i (Jan., 1973): 45.

Doherty, F., *Samuel Beckett*, 60-71.

Elovaara, R., *Problem of Identity in Samuel Beckett's Prose*, 166-85.

Fletcher, John, "Malone 'Given Birth To Into Death'," in O'Hara, J. D., ed., *Twentieth Century Interpretations of MOLLOY, MALONE DIES, THE UNNAMABLE*, 58-61.

_____, *Novels of Samuel Beckett*, 151-76.

Glicksberg, Charles I., "Samuel Beckett's World of Fiction," *ArQ* 18 (Spring, 1962): 39-41.

_____, *Self in Modern Literature*, 127-9.

Gluck, B. R., *Beckett and Joyce*, 126-40, *passim*.

Hamilton, A., and K. Hamilton, *Condemned to Life*, 147-51.

Hardy, Barbara, "The Dubious Consolations in Beckett's Fiction: Art, Love and Nature," in Worth, K., ed., *Beckett the Shape Changer*, 111-38, *passim*.

Hassan, I., *Literature of Silence*, 158-62.

Henkle, Roger B., "Beckett and the Comedy of Bourgeois Experience," *Thalia* 3, i (Spring-Summer, 1980): 35-9.

Hoffman, F. J., *Samuel Beckett*, 127-32. Also in Friedman, M. J., ed., *Samuel Beckett Now*, 50-4.

Hokenson, Jan, "A Stuttering LOGOS: Biblical Paradigms in Beckett's Trilogy," *JJQ* 8, iv (Summer, 1971): 229-304.

Iser, W., *Implied Reader*, 167-70, 266-7.

Karl, F. R., "Waiting for Beckett: Quest and Re-Quest," *Contemporary English Novel*, 35-7.

Kenner, H., *Reader's Guide to Samuel Beckett*, 100-8.

Kern, F. G., *Existential Thought and Fictional Technique*, 208-21.

Lee, Robin, "The Fictional Topography of Samuel Beckett," in Josipovici, G., ed., *Modern English Novel*, 218-19.

Levy, E. P., *Beckett and the Voice of Species*, 54-71.

MacNeice, Louis, *Varieties of Parable*, London: Cambridge Un. Pr., 1965, 141-6.

Nuttall, F. D., "Samuel Beckett: MALONE DIES," *JEn* 2 (1976): 81-94.

O'Hara, J. D., "About Structure in MALONE DIES," in O'Hara, J. D., ed., *Twentieth Century Interpretations of MOLLOY, MALONE DIES, THE UNNAMABLE*, 62-70.

Peake, Charles, " 'The Labours of Poetical Excavation,' " in Worth, K., ed., *Beckett the Shape Changer*, 50-8, *passim*.

Pearce, R., *Stages of the Clown*, 130-4.

Renner, Charlotte, "The Self-Multiplying Narrators of MOLLOY, MALONE DIES, and THE UNNAMABLE," *JNT* 11, i (Winter, 1981): 12-32.

Robinson, M., *Long Sonata of the Dead*, 170-90.

Roudiez, L. S., *French Fiction Today*, 98-101.

Silver, Sally T., "Satire in Beckett: A Study of MOLLOY, MALONE DIES and THE UNNAMABLE," *EFL* 10 (Nov., 1973): 82-99.

Silverman, Hugh J., "Beckett, Philosophy, and the Self," 153-60 in Tymieniecka, Anna-Teresa, ed., *The Philosophical Reflection of Man in Literature: Selected Papers from Several Conferences Held by the International Society for Phenomenology and Literature in Cambridge, Massachusetts*, Dordrecht: Reidel, 1982.

Szanto, G. H., *Narrative Consciousness*, 90-2.

Tindall, William Y., "Beckett's Bums," *Crit* 2, i (Spring-Summer, 1958): 11-13.

_____, *Samuel Beckett*, 26-9.

Walcutt, C. C., *Man's Changing Mask*, 339-42.

Webb, E., *Samuel Beckett*, 118-23, 143-6.

MOLLOY (See also TRILOGY)

Abbott, H. P., *Fiction of Samuel Beckett*, 92-114.

Albright, D., *Representation and the Imagination*, 174-83.

Alvarez, A., *Beckett*, 46-52.

Baldwin, H. L., *Samuel Beckett's Real Silence*, 28-55.

Barnard, G. C., *Samuel Beckett*, 32-44.

Berengo, Adriano, "Samuel Beckett: 'The Mania for Symmetry'." *Gradiva* 1, i (Summer, 1976): 21-37.

Bové, Paul A., "Beckett's Dreadful Postmodern: The Deconstruction of Form in MOLLOY," in Orr, Leonard, ed., *Destructing the Novel: Essays in Applied Postmodern Hermeneutics*, Troy, N.Y.: Whitson Pub. Co., 1982, 185-221.

_____, "The Image of the Creator in Beckett's Postmodern Writing," *P&L* 4, i (Spring, 1980): 53-60.

Bowles, Patrick, "How Beckett Sees the Universe: MOLLOY," *Listener* 59, No. 1525 (June 19, 1958): 1011-12.

Boyle, Kevin, "Molloy: Icon of the Negative," *Westwind* 5, No. 1 (Fall, 1961).

Christensen, Inger, *Meaning of Metafiction*, 109-20.

Coe, R. N., *Beckett*, 54-62.

Cohn, R., *Back to Beckett*, 79-91.

Culik, Hugh, "Samuel Beckett's MOLLOY: Transformation and Loss," *AI* 39, i (Spring, 1982): 21-9.

Cushman, Keith, "MOLLOY: Beckett's 'Nourishing and Economical Irish Stew'," *UDR* 15, iii (Spring, 1982): 75-82.

Davies, R., *Voice from the Attic*, 232-4.

Doherty, F., *Samuel Beckett*, 49-60.

Elovaara, R., *Problem of Identity in Samuel Beckett's Prose*, 80-165.

Esslin, Martin, "Samuel Beckett," in Cruickshank, J., ed., *Novelist as Philosopher*, 135-8.

Fletcher, John, "Interpreting MOLLOY," in Friedman, M. J., ed., *Samuel Beckett Now*, 157-70.

_____, *Novels of Samuel Beckett*, 119-50.

Friedman, Melvin J., "Molloy's 'Sacred' Stones," *RomN* 9 (Autumn, 1967): 8-11.

Gebhardt, Richard C., "Technique of Alienation in MOLLOY," *PCL* 1, ii (Nov., 1975): 74-84.

Glicksberg, Charles I., "Samuel Beckett's World of Fiction," *ArQ* 18 (Spring, 1962): 35-9.

_____, *Self in Modern Literature*, 124-7.

Gluck, B. R., *Beckett and Joyce*, 126-40, *passim*.

Goodrich, Norma L., "Molloy's Musa Mater," in Zyla, Wolodymyr T., ed., *From Surrealism to the Absurd*. Proceedings of the Comparative Literature Symposium, Vol. III, Lubbock: Texas Tech Univ., 1970, 31-53.

Hamilton, A., and K. Hamilton, *Condemned to Life*, 141-7.

Hardy, Barbara, "The Dubious Consolations in Beckett's Fiction: Art, Love and Nature," in Worth, K., ed., *Beckett the Shape Changer*, 111-38.

Hassan, L., *Literature of Silence*, 151-8.

Hayman, David, "Joyce Beckett/Joyce," 37-43 in Benstock, Bernard, ed., *The Seventh of Joyce*, Bloomington: Indiana Un. Pr., 1982. Also in *JBeckS* 7 (Spring, 1982): 101-7.

_____, "MOLLOY or the Quest for Meaninglessness: A Global Interpretation," in Friedman, M. J., ed., *Samuel Beckett Now*, 129-56.

_____, "Quest for Meaninglessness: The Boundless Poverty of MOLLOY," in Sutherland, W. O. S., ed., *Six Contemporary Novels*, 90-112.

Hayward, Susan, "Two Anti Novels: MOLLOY and JACQUES LE FATALISTE," in Fox, J. H., H. Waddier, and D. A. Watts, eds., *Studies in Eighteenth-Century French Literature*. Presented to Robert Niklaus. Exeter: Univ. of Exeter, 1975, 97-107.

Henkle, Roger B., "Beckett and the Comedy of Bourgeois Experience," *Thalia* 3, i (Spring-Summer, 1980): 35-9.

Hesla, D. H., *Shape of Chaos*, 90-103.

Hoffman, F. J., *Samuel Beckett*, 120-7. Also in Friedman, M. J., ed., *Samuel Beckett Now*, 44-50.

Hokenson, Jan, "A Stuttering LOGOS: Biblical Paradigms in Beckett's Trilogy," *JJQ* 8, iv (Summer, 1971): 295-9.

Honoré, Lionel P., "Metaphysical Anguish and Futility in MOLLOY," *KRQ* 27, iv (1980): 435-44.

Iser, W., *Implied Reader*, 164-7, 264-6.

Janvier, Ludovic, "Molloy," in O'Hara, J. D., ed., *Twentieth Century Interpretations of MOLLOY, MALONE DIES, THE UNNAMABLE*, 46-57.

Jones, Christopher J., "Bergman's PERSONA and the Artistic Dilemma of the Modern Narrative," *LFQ* 5, i (Winter, 1977): 85-6.

Karl, F. R., "Waiting for Beckett: Quest and Re-Quest," *Contemporary English Novel*, 31-5.

Kenner, H., *Reader's Guide to Samuel Beckett*, 92-100.

Kern, E. G., *Existential Thought and Fictional Technique*, 194-204.

_____, "Moran-Molloy: The Hero as Author," *Perspective* 11 (Autumn, 1959): 183-93. Also in O'Hara, J. D., ed., *Twentieth Century Interpretations of MOLLOY, MALONE DIES, THE UNNAMABLE*, 35-45.

_____, "Samuel Beckett—Dionysian Poet," *Descant* 3 (Fall, 1958): 33-6.

Kutty, Kannangath N., "The Quest for Being in Samuel Beckett's Trilogy with an In-Depth Analysis of the Quest in MOLLOY," *DAI* 35 (1974): 1107A-08A.

Lee, Robin, "The Fictional Topography of Samuel Beckett," in Josipovici, G., ed., *Modern English Novel*, 215-19.

Lee, Warren, "The Bitter Pill of Samuel Beckett," *ChiR* 10 (Winter, 1957): 84-7.

Levy, E. P., *Beckett and the Voice of Species*, 54-71.

Matthews, H., *Hard Journey*, 151-66.

Moorjani, Angela B., "A Mythic Reading of MOLLOY," in Morot-Sir, E., et al., eds., *Samuel Beckett*, 225-35.

Nadeau, Maurice, "Samuel Beckett: Humor and the Void," in Esslin, M., ed., *Samuel Beckett*, 33-6.

O'Hara, J. D., "Jung and the Narratives of MOLLOY," *JBeckS* 7 (Spring, 1982): 19-47.

Peake, Charles, "'The Labours of Poetical Excavation'," in Worth, K., ed., *Beckett the Shape Changer*, 50-8 *passim*.

Pearce, Richard, "From Joyce to Beckett: The Tale That Wags the Telling," 44-9 in Benstock, Bernard, ed., *The Seventh of Joyce*, Bloomington: Indiana Un. Pr., 1982; Brighton: Harvester, 1982. Also in *JBeckS* 7 (Spring, 1982): 109-14.

_____, *Stages of the Clown*, 128-34.

Rabkin, Eric S., "The Mythic Coherence of MOLLOY," *SCR* 12, i (Fall, 1979): 12-20.

Renner, Charlotte, "The Self-Multiplying Narrators of MOLLOY, MALONE DIES, and THE UNNAMABLE," *JNT* 11, i (Winter, 1981): 12-32.

Robinson, M., *Long Sonata of the Dead*, 140-69.

Rose, Gilbert J., "On the Shores of Self: Samuel Beckett's MOLLOY—Irredentism and the Creative Impulse," *PsyR* 60, iv (Winter, 1973-74): 587-604.

Roudiez, L. S., *French Fiction Today*, 90-8.

Shapiro, Barbara, "Toward a Psychoanalytic Reading of Beckett's MOLLOY, Part I," *L&P* 19, ii (1969): 71-86. Part II *L&P* 19, iii-iv (1969): 15-30.

Sherzer, Dina, "Saying Is Inventing: Gnomic Expressions in MOLLOY," 163-71 in Kirshenblatt-Gimblett, Barbara, ed., *Speech Play: Research and Resources for Studying Linguistic Creativity*, Philadelphia: Un. of Pennsylvania Pr., 1976.

Silver, Sally T., "Satire in Beckett: A Study of MOLLOY, MALONE DIES and THE UNNAMABLE," *EFL* 10 (Nov., 1973): 82-99.

Silverman, Hugh J., "Beckett, Philosophy, and the Self," 153-60 in Tymieniecks, Anna-Teresa, ed., *The Philosophical Reflection of Man in Literature: Selected Papers from Several Conferences Held by the International Society for Phenomenology and Literature in Cambridge, Massachusetts*, Dordrecht: Reidel, 1982.

Solomon, Philip H., "The Imagery of MOLLOY and Its Extension into Beckett's Other Fiction," *DA* 28 (1968): 3198A-99A (Wisc.).

_____, "Lousse and Molloy: Beckett's Bower of Bliss," *AJFS* 6, i (1969): 65-81.

_____, "Samuel Beckett's MOLLOY: A Dog's Life," *FR* 41 (1967): 84-91.

Spraggins, Mary, "Beckett's MOLLOY as Detective Novel," *EL* 2, ii (1974): 11-33.

Tamir, Nomi, "Why I?—A Redefinition and Description of the So-Called 'First-Person Novel'," *DAI* 37 (1976): 1536A.

Tindall, William Y., "Beckett's Bums," *Crit* 2, i (Spring-Summer, 1958): 7-11.

_____, *Samuel Beckett*, 21-6.

Webb, E., *Samuel Beckett*, 140-3.

Wellershoff, Dieter, "Failure of an Attempt at De-Mythologization: Samuel Beckett's Novels," in Esslin, M., ed., *Samuel Beckett*, 93-104.

MURPHY

Abbott, H. P., *Fiction of Samuel Beckett*, 37-55, 57-9.

Ackerley, C. J., "'In the Beginning Was the Pun': Samuel Beckett's MURPHY," *AUMLA* 55 (May, 1981): 15-22.

Alvarez, A., *Beckett*, 25-32.

Arthur, Kateryna, "MURPHY, GERONTION, and Dante," *AUMLA* 55 (May, 1981): 54-67.

Barnard, G. C., *Samuel Beckett*, 9-15.

Chambers, Ross, "Samuel Beckett and the Padded Cell," *Meanjin* 21 (1962): 451-62.

Coe, R. N., *Beckett*, 20-34.

Coetzee, J. M., "The Comedy of Point of View of Beckett's MURPHY," *Crit* 12, ii (1970): 19-27.

Cohn, R., *Back to Beckett*, 29-41.

_____, *Samuel Beckett*, 45-64.

Cooney, Séamus, "Beckett's MURPHY," *Expl* 25 (Sept., 1966): item 3.

Cornwell, Ethel F., "Samuel Beckett: The Flight from Self," *PMLA* 88, i (Jan., 1973): 41-3.

Culik, Hugh, "Mindful of the Body: Medical Allusions in Beckett's MURPHY," *Éire* 14, i (1979): 84-101.

Doherty, F., *Samuel Beckett*, 25-34.

Eade, J. C., "The Seventh Scarf: A Note on MURPHY," *JBeckS* 7 (Spring, 1982): 115-17.

Elovaara, R., *Problems of Identity in Samuel Beckett's Prose*, 29-48.

Ericksen, John D., "Alienation in Samuel Beckett: The Protagonist as Eiron," *PCL* 1, ii (Nov., 1975): 65-72.

Esslin, Martin, "Samuel Beckett," in Cruickshank, J., ed., *Novelist as Philosopher*, 131-3.

Federman, R., *Journey to Chaos*, 56-93.

Fletcher, J., *Novels of Samuel Beckett*, 38-55.

Freese, Wolfgang, and Angela B. Moorjani, "The Esoteric and the Trivial: Chess and Go in the Novels of Beckett and Kawabata," *PCL* 6 (1980): 37-48.

Garzilli, E., *Circles Without Center*, 20-7.

Glicksberg, Charles I., "Samuel Beckett's World of Fiction," *ArQ* 18 (Spring, 1962): 33-5.

_____, *Self in Modern Literature*, 122-4.

Hamilton, A., and K. Hamilton, *Condemned to Life*, 70-5, 123-8.

Harrington, John P., "'That Red Branch Bum Was the Camel's Back': Beckett's Use of Yeats in MURPHY," *Éire* 15, iii (1980): 86-96.

Harrison, Robert, *Samuel Beckett's MURPHY: A Critical Excursion*, Athens: Un. of Georgia Pr., 1968.

Hassan, I., *Literature of Silence*, 140-5.

Hesla, D. H., *Shape of Chaos*, 30-58.

Hoffman, F. J., *Samuel Beckett*, 105-14. Also in Friedman, M. J., ed., *Samuel Beckett Now*, 31-8.

Jacobsen, J., and W. R. Bueller, *Testament of Samuel Beckett*, 25-30, 67-72.

Jacobson, Jerry L., "Experiments in Form: A Study of Samuel Beckett's MURPHY and WATT," *DAI* 34 (1973): 1281A-82A.

Jones, Anthony, "The French Murphy: From 'Rare Bird' to 'Cancre'," *JBeckS* 6 (Autumn, 1980): 37-50.

Karl, F. R., "Waiting for Beckett: Quest and Re-Quest," *Contemporary English Novel*, 20-1, 27-9.

Kennedy, Sighle, "'The Devil and Holy Water': Samuel Beckett's MURPHY and Flann O'Brien's AT SWIM-TWO-BIRDS," in Porter, R. J., and J. D. Brophy, eds., *Modern Irish Literature*, 251-60.

_____, "Murphy's Bed: A Study of Real Sources and Sur-real Associations in Samuel Beckett's First Novel," *DAI* 33 (1972): 315A.

Kenner, H., *Reader's Guide to Samuel Beckett*, 57-71.

Kern, E. G., *Existential Thought and Fictional Technique*, 173-7.

Leisure, Maryse J., "MURPHY, or the Beginning of an Esthetic of Monstrosity," in Morot-Sir, E., et al., eds., *Samuel Beckett*, 189-200.

Levy, E. P., *Beckett and the Voice of Species*, 16-25.

Mays, J. C. C., "Mythologized Presences: MURPHY in Its Time," in Ronsley, J., ed., *Myth and Reality in Irish Literature*, 197-218.

Mintz, Samuel, "Beckett's MURPHY: A 'Cartesian' Novel," *Per* 11 (Autumn, 1959): 156-65.

Mooney, Michael E., "Presocratic Scepticism: Samuel Beckett's MURPHY Reconsidered," *ELH* 49, i (Spring, 1982): 214-34.

Park, Eric [B.], "Fundamental Sounds: Music in Samuel Beckett's MURPHY and WATT," *MFS* 21, ii (Summer, 1975): 157-71.

Peake, Charles, "'The Labours of Poetical Excavation'," in Worth, K., ed., *Beckett the Shape Changer*, 42-58 *passim*.

Robinson, M., *Long Sonata of the Dead*, 82-99.

Roudiez, L. S., *French Fiction Today*, 81-90.

Scott, N. A., Jr., "Beckett's Journey into the Zone of Zero," *Craters of the Spirit*, 178-80. Also in *CRAS* 6 (1962): 162-4.

_____, *Samuel Beckett*, 41-6.

Sebba, Gregor, "Time and the Modern Self: Descartes, Rousseau, Beckett," *SG* 24, iii (1971): 316-18.

Steinberg, S. C., "The External and Internal in MURPHY," *TCL* 18, ii (April, 1972): 93-110.

Stuart, Malcolm, "Notes on Place and Place Names in MURPHY," *RANAM* 14 (1981): 237-35.

Tindall, William Y., "Beckett's Bums," *Crit* 2, i (Spring-Summer, 1958): 5-6.

_____, *Samuel Beckekt*, 13-17.

Tritt, William, "Statistics on Proper Names in MURPHY," in Morot-Sir, E., et al., eds., *Samuel Beckett*, 201-10.

Webb, E., *Samuel Beckett*, 43-55.

Wells, Charles M., "The Transcendence of Life: The Positive Dimension in Samuel Beckett," *DA* 29 (1968): 619A (New Mexico).

TRILOGY

Barrett, William, "How I understand less and less every year...," *CUF* 2 (Winter, 1959): 44-8.

Bersani, Leo, *Balzac to Beckett; Center and Circumference in French Fiction*, N.Y.: Oxford Un. Pr., 1970, 309-28.

Blanchot, Maurice, "Where Now? Who Now?" *EvR* 2 (Winter, 1959): 222-9.

Bruns, Gerald L., "The Storyteller and the Problem of Language in Samuel Beckett's Fiction," *MLQ* 30, ii (June, 1969): 272-7. Also in Bruns, G. L., *Modern Poetry and the Idea of Language*, 171-7.

Chambers, Ross, "Samuel Beckett and the Padded Cell," *Meanjin* 21 (1962): 451-62.

Christensen, Inger, "Samuel Beckett's Trilogy: Circling Disintegration," *Meaning of Metafiction*, 97-150.

Cohn, R., *Back to Beckett*, 112-21.

_____, *Samuel Beckett*, 114-68.

_____, "Still Novel," *YFS* No. 24 (Summer, 1959): 48-53.

Combs, Eugene, "Impotency and Ignorance: A Parody of Prerogatives in Samuel Beckett," *SRC* 2, ii (1972): 114-30.

Conely, James H., Jr., "An Analysis of Form in ARCANA of Edgar Varèse and the Trilogy of Samuel Beckett," *DA* 29 (1969): 3606A-07A.

_____, "ARCANA, MOLLOY, MALONE DIES, THE UNNAMABLE: A Brief Comparison of Forms," *HSL* 4, iii (1972): 187-96.

Friedman, Melvin J., "The Novels of Samuel Beckett: An Amalgam of Joyce and Proust," *CL* 12 (1960): 53-6.

Frye, Northrop, "The Nightmare Life in Death," *HudR* 13 (Autumn, 1960): 442-9.

Gerard, Martin, "Molloy Becomes Unnamable," *XR* 1 (Oct., 1960): 314-19.

Gluck, B. R., *Beckett and Joyce*, 105-22 passim, 126-40.

Goldberg, Gerald J., "The Search for the Artist in Some Recent British Fiction," *SAQ* 62 (Summer, 1963): 396-401.

Greene, Naomi, "Creation and the Self: Artaud, Beckett, Michaux," *JJQ* 8, iv (Summer, 1971): 265-78.

Gurewitch, Morton, "Beckett and the Comedy of Decomposition," *ChiR* 33, ii (1982): 93-9.

Hamilton, Carol, "Portrait in Old Age: The Image of Man in Beckett's Trilogy," *WHR* 16 (Spring, 1962): 157-65.

Hamilton, Kenneth, "Boon or Thorn? Joyce Cary and Samuel Beckett on Human Life," *DR* 38 (1959): 433-42.

Hesla, D. H., *Shape of Chaos*, 86-128, 178-83.

Hill, Leslie, "Fiction, Myth, and Identity in Samuel Beckett's Novel Trilogy," *FM1S* 13, iii (July, 1977): 230-9.

Hokenson, Jan, "A Stuttering LOGOS: Biblical Paradigms in Beckett's Trilogy," *JJQ* 8, iv (Summer, 1971): 293-310.

_____, "Three Novels in Large Black Pauses," in Cohn, R., ed., *Samuel Beckett*, 73-84.

Iser, W., *Implied Reader*, 164-78, 264-9.

Janvier, Ludovic, "Style in the Trilogy," in O'Hara, J. D., ed., *Twentieth Century Interpretations of MOLLOY, MALONE DIES, THE UNNAMABLE*, 82-90.

Jones, Anthony, "Samuel Beckett Is only Human," *ASLHM* 43, ii (1972): 73-88.

Jones, Edwin W., "Beckett's TRILOGY: An Exercise in Phenomenological Structuralism," *DAI* 35 (1975): 7908A-09A.

Kellman, Steven G., "Beckett's Fatal Dual," *RomN* 16, ii (Winter, 1975): 268-73.

Kenner, Hugh, "The Absurdity of Fiction," *Griffin* 8 (Nov., 1959): 13-16.

_____, *Reader's Guide to Samuel Beckett*, 92-115.

Kutty, Kannangath N., "The Quest for Being in Samuel Becket's Trilogy with an In-Depth Analysis of the Quest in MOLLOY," *DAI* 35 (1975): 1107A-08A.

Levy, Eric P., "Voices of Species: The Narrator and Beckettian Man in THREE NOVELS," *ELH* 45, ii (Summer, 1978): 343-58.

Lorich, Bruce, "The Accommodating Form of Samuel Beckett," *SWR* 55, iv (Autumn, 1970): 354-60.

Lyons, Charles R., "Beckett's Major Plays and the Trilogy," *CompD* 5, iv (Winter, 1970): 254-68.

Nudd, Rosemary, S. P., "The Perception of Other as Burden in the Trilogy of Samuel Beckett," *NLauR* 6, ii (1976): 45-51.

Oates, J. C., "The Trilogy of Samuel Beckett," *Ren* 14 (Spring, 1962): 160-5.

Pearce, R., *Stages of the Clown*, 128-35.

Pritchett, V. S., "An Irish Oblomov," *NS&Nation* 59 (April 2, 1960): 489. Also in *Working Novelist*, 25-9.

Roudiez, L. S., *French Fiction Today*, 81-103.

Sachner, Mark J., "The Artist as Fiction: An Aesthetics of Failure in Samuel Beckett's Trilogy," *MQ* 18, ii (Winter, 1977): 144-55.

Scott, N. A., Jr., "Beckett's Journey into the Zone of Zero," *CRAS* 6 (1962): 169-75. Also in *Craters of the Spirit*, 185-92.

_____, *Samuel Beckett*, 60-74.

Silverman, Hugh J., "Beckett, Philosophy, and the Self," in Tymieniecka, Anna-Theresa, ed., *The Philosophical Reflection of Man in Literature: Selected Papers from Several Conferences Held by the International Society for Phenomenology and Literature in Cambridge, Mass.*, Dordrecht: Reidel, 1982, 153-60.

Solomon, Philip H., *The Life After Birth: Imagery in Samuel Beckett's TRILOGY*, University, MS: Romance Monographs, 1975.

Toyama, Jean Y., "Beckett's Trilogy: Problematics of the Origin, Problem of Language," *DSec* 6 (July, 1982): 135-55.

Unterecker, John, "Samuel Beckett's No-Man's Land," *New Leader* 42 (May 18, 1959): 24-5.

Webb, E., *Samuel Beckett*, 72-87.

_____, "Samuel Beckett, Novelist: A Study of His Trilogy," *DA* 28 (1968): 4191A.

Webner, Helene L., "The Real Silence: Intimations of Mysticism in Samuel Beckett's Trilogy MOLLOY, MALONE DIES and THE UNNAMABLE," *DAI* 34 (1974): 5212A.

THE UNNAMABLE (See also TRILOGY)

Abbott, H. P., *Fiction of Samuel Beckett*, 110-12, 124-37.

_____, "A Grammar for Being Elsewhere," *JML* 6, i (Feb., 1977): 39-46.

Albright, D., *Representation and the Imagination*, 190-8.

Alvarez, A., *Beckett*, 57-65.

Baldwin, H. L., *Samuel Beckett's Real Silence*, 68-85.

Barnard, G. C., *Samuel Beckett*, 57-66.

Blanchot, Maurice, "Where Now? Who Now?" *EvR* 2 (Winter, 1959): 224-9. Also (abridged) in Kostelanetz, R., ed., *On Contemporary Literature*, 249-54.

Champigny, Robert, "Adventures of the First Person," in Friedman, M. J., ed., *Samuel Beckett Now*, 119-28 passim.

Christensen, Inger, *Meaning of Metafiction*, 135-50.

Coe, R. N., *Beckett*, 69-79.

Cohn, R., *Back to Beckett*, 100-12.

Cornwell, Ethel F., "Samuel Beckett: The Flight from Self," *PMLA* 88, i (Jan., 1973): 45-8.

Doherty, F., *Samuel Beckett*, 71-85.

Elovaara, R., *Problem of Identity in Samuel Beckett's Prose*, 186-256.

Esslin, Martin, in Cruickshank, J., ed., *Novelist as Philosopher*, 139-43.

Fanizza, Franco, "The Word and Silence in Samuel Beckett's THE UNNAMABLE," in O'Hara, J. D., ed., *Twentieth Century Interpretations of MOLLOY, MALONE DIES, THE UNNAMABLE*, 71-81.

Fitch, Brian T., "L'INNOMMABLE and the Hermeneutic Paradigm," *ChiR* 33, ii (1982): 101-6.

Fletcher, J., *Novels of Samuel Beckett*, 179-94.

Garzilli, E., *Circles Without Center*, 47-52.

Glicksberg, Charles I., "Samuel Beckett's World of Fiction," *ArQ* 18 (Spring, 1962): 41-7.

_____, *Self in Modern Literature*, 129-33.

Gluck, B. R., *Beckett and Joyce*, 126-40 *passim*.

Hamilton, A., and K. Hamilton, *Condemned to Life*, 151-5.

Hardy, Barbara, "The Dubious Consolations in Beckett's Fiction: Art, Love and Nature," in Worth, K., ed., *Beckett the Shape Changer*, 107-38 *passim*.

Hassan, I., *Literature of Silence*, 162-8.

Hesla, D. H., *Shape of Chaos*, 111-25.

Hoffman, F. J., *Samuel Beckett*, 132-7. Also in Friedman, M. J., ed., *Samuel Beckett Now*, 54-8.

Hokenson, Jan, "A Stuttering LOGOS: Biblical Paradigms in Beckett's Trilogy," *JJQ* 8, iv (Summer, 1971): 304-10.

Hutchings, William, "'The Unintelligible Terms of an Incomprehensible Damnation': Samuel Beckett's THE UNNAMABLE, Sheol, and ST. ERKENWALD," *TCL* 27, ii (Summer, 1981): 97-112.

Iser, W., *Implied Reader*, 170-4, 267-8.

Karl, F. R., "Waiting for Beckett: Quest and Re-Quest," *Contemporary English Novel*, 37-9.

Kenner, H., *Reader's Guide to Samuel Beckett*, 108-15.

Kern, E. G., *Existential Thought and Fictional Technique*, 221-32.

Lee, Robert, "The Fictional Topography of Samuel Beckett," in Josipovici, G., ed., *Modern English Novel*, 218-23.

Levy, E. P., *Beckett and the Voice of Species*, 54-71.

_____, "Existence Searching Essence: The Plight of the Unnamable," *Mosaic* 10, i (Fall, 1976): 103-13.

Peake, Charles, "'The Labours of Poetical Excavation'," in Worth, K., ed., *Beckett the Shape Changer*, 50-8 *passim*.

Pearce, R., *Stages of the Clown*, 132-4.

Renner, Charlotte, "The Self-Multiplying Narrators of MOLLOY, MALONE DIES, and THE UNNAMABLE," *JNT* 11, i (Winter, 1981): 12-32.

Rickels, Milton, "Existential Themes in Beckett's UNNAMABLE," *Criticism* 4 (Spring, 1962): 134-47.

Robinson, M., *Long Sonata of the Dead*, 191-207.

Sebba, Gregor, "Time and the Modern Self: Descartes, Rousseau, Beckett," *SG* 24, iii (1971): 318-21.

Silver, Sally T., "Satire in Beckett: A Study of MOLLOY, MALONE DIES and THE UNNAMABLE," *EFL* 10 (Nov., 1973): 82-99.

Silverman, Hugh J., "Beckett, Philosophy, and the Self," 153-60 in Tymieniecka, Anna-Teresa, ed., *The Philosophical Reflection of Man in Literature: Selected Papers from Several Conferences Held by the International Society for Phenomenology and Literature in Cambridge, Massachusetts*, Dordrecht: Reidel, 1982.

Solomon, Philip, "Samuel Beckett's L'INNOMABLE: The Space of Fiction," *FMLS* 7, i (1971): 83-91.

Subrahmanian, K., "THE UNNAMABLE: An Indian Interpretation," *LCrit* 13, i (1978): 62-4.

Szanto, G. H., *Narrative Consciousness*, 92-6.

Teays, Wanda J., "Naming THE UNNAMABLE: Language and Silence in Beckett's Novel," *DAI* 42, iv (Oct., 1981): 1651A-52A.

Tindall, William Y., "Beckett's Bums," *Crit* 2 (Spring-Summer, 1958): 13-14.

_____, *Samuel Beckett*, 29-32.

Webb, E., *Samuel Beckett*, 123-9.

Wehringer, Helen M., "Beckett and His Bilingualism: The Word as Mask and Mirror," *DAI* 40 (1979): 2654A.

WATT

Abbey, Edward, *NMQ* 29 (1959): 381-3.

Abbott, H. P., *Fiction of Samuel Beckett*, 56-74.

Alvarez, A., *Beckett*, 32-8.

Baldwin, H. L., *Samuel Beckett's Real Silence*, 86-106.

Barnard, G. C., *Samuel Beckett*, 16-27.

Brater, Enoch, "Privilege, Perspective, and Point of View in WATT," *CollL* 8, iii (Fall, 1981): 209-26.

Brée, Germaine, "Beckett's Abstractors of Quintessence," *FR* 36 (May, 1963): 567-76.

Brick, Alla, "The Madman in His Cell: Joyce, Beckett, Nabokov, and the Stereotypes," *MR* 1 (1959): 45-9.

Brooke-Rose, Christine, "Samuel Beckett and the Anti-Novel," *LonM* 5, xii (Dec., 1958): 38-43.

Bruns, Gerald L., "The Storyteller and the Problem of Language in Samuel Beckett's Fiction," *MLQ* 30, ii (June, 1969): 267-72. Also in Bruns, G. L., *Modern Poetry and the Idea of Language*, 166-71.

Chalker, John, "The Satiric Shape of WATT," in Worth, K., ed., *Beckett the Shape Changer*, 21-37.

Coe, R. N., *Beckett*, 36-53.

Cohn, R., *Back to Beckett*, 41-56.

_____, *Samuel Beckett*, 65-94.

_____, "WATT in the Light of THE CASTLE," *CL* 13 (Spring, 1961): 154-66.

DiPierro, John C., "Structures in Beckett's WATT," *DAI* 39 (1979): 4302A-03A.

Doherty, F., *Samuel Beckett*, 34-48.

Dreysse, Ursula, "Beckett's WATT: 'A Series of Hypotheses'," in Schuhmann, Kuno, Wilhelm Hartmann and Armin P. Frank, eds., *Miscellanea Anglo-Americana: Festschrift für Helmut Viebrock*, München: Pressler, 1974, 137-47.

Elovaara, R., *Problem of Identity in Samuel Beckett's Prose*, 48-73.

Esslin, Martin, "Samuel Beckett," in Cruickshank, J., ed., *Novelist as Philosopher*, 133-5.

Federman, R., *Journey to Chaos*, 94-132.

Fletcher, J., *Novels of Samuel Beckett*, 59-89.

Gluck, B. R., *Beckett and Joyce*, 86-100.

Greenberg, Alvin, "The Death of the Psyche: A Way to the Self in the Contemporary Novel," *Criticism* 8 (Winter, 1966): 1-18.

Hamilton, A., and K. Hamilton, *Condemned to Life*, 128-35.

Harrington, John P., "The Irish Landscape in Samuel Beckett's WATT," *JNT* 11, i (Winter, 1981): 1-11.

Hassan, I., *Literature of Silence*, 145-51.

Henkels, Robert M., Jr., "Novel Quarters for an Odd Couple: Apollo and Dionysus in Beckett's WATT and Pinget's THE INQUISITION," *StTCL* 2 (Spring, 1978): 141-57.

Hesla, David H., "The Shape of Chaos: A Reading of Beckett's WATT," *Crit* 6, i (Spring, 1969): 85-105.

_____, *Shape of Chaos*, 59-85.

Hoefer, Jacqueline, "Watt," *Per* 11, No. 3 (Autumn, 1959): 166-82.

Jacobsen, Jerry L., "Experiments in Form: A Study of Samuel Beckett's MURPHY and WATT," *DAI* 34 (1973): 1281A-82A.

Jacobsen, J., and W. R. Mueller, *Testament of Samuel Beckett*, 73-7.

Karl, F. R., "Waiting for Beckett: Quest and Re-Quest," *Contemporary English Novel*, 27-9.

Kennedy, Sighle, "'The Simple Games That Time Plays with Space—': An Introduction to Samuel Beckett's Manuscripts of WATT," *Centerpoint* 2, iii (1977): 55-61.

Kenner, H., *Reader's Guide to Samuel Beckett*, 72-82.

Kern, E. G., *Existential Thought and Fictional Technique*, 177-94.

Kern, Edith, "Reflections on the Castle and Mr. Knott's House: Kafka and Beckett," in Zyla, Wolodymyr T., ed, *Proceedings of the Comparative Literature Symposium*. Vol. IV: *Franz Kafka: His Place in World Literature*, Lubbock: Texas Tech. Un., 1971, 97-111.

Law, Richard A., "Mock Evangelism in Beckett's WATT," *MLS* 2, ii (1972): 68-82.

Lee, Robin, "The Fictional Topography of Samuel Beckett," in Josipovici, G., ed., *Modern English Novel*, 210-15.

Levy, E. P., *Beckett and the Voice of Species*, 27-38.

Lombardi, Thomas W., "Who Tells Who WATT?" *Chelsea* 22/23 (June, 1968): 170-9.

Lorich, Bruce, "The Accommodating Form of Samuel Beckett," *SWR* 55, iv (Autumn, 1970): 360-9.

Mood, John J., "'The Personal System—Samuel Beckett's WATT," *PMLA* 86, ii (Mar., 1971): 255-65.

Moorjani, Angela B., "Narrative Game Strategies in Beckett's WATT," *ECr* 17, iii (Fall, 1977): 235-44.

Murphy, Vincent J., "La Peinture de l'empêchement: Samuel Beckett's WATT," *Criticism* 18, iv (Fall, 1976): 353-66.

Nielsen, Erland, "WATT: Beckett's Theory of Knowledge or 'Nihil est in intellectu'," *L&L* 1, iv (1973): 57-82.

Ohmann, Richard, "Speech, Action, Style," in Chatman, S., ed., *Literary Style: A Symposium*, 241-54.

Park, Eric [B.], "Fundamental Sounds: Music in Samuel Beckett's MURPHY and WATT," *MFS* 21, ii (Summer, 1975): 157-71.

_____, "John J. Mood and the Personal System—A Further Note on Samuel Beckett's WATT," *PMLA* 88, iii (May, 1973): 529-30.

Pearce, Richard, "From Joyce to Beckett: The Tale That Wags the Telling," 44-9 in Benstock, Bernard, ed., *The Seventh of Joyce*, Bloomington: Indiana Un. Pr., 1982; Brighton: Harvester, 1982. Also in *JBeckS* 7 (Spring, 1982): 109-14.

Posnock, Ross, "Beckett, Valéry and WATT," *JBeckS* 6 (Autumn, 1980): 51-62.

Rabinovitz, Rubin, "The Addenda to Samuel Beckett's WATT," in Morot-Sir, E., et al., eds., *Samuel Beckett*, 211-23.

_____, "WATT from Descartes to Schopenhauer," in Porter, R. J., and J. D. Brophy, eds., *Modern Irish Literature*, 261-87.

Robinson, Fred M., *Comedy of Language*, 127-74.

Robinson, M., *Long Sonata of the Dead*, 100-31.

Scott, N. A., Jr., "Beckett's Journey into the Zone of Zero," *CRAS* 6 (1962): 164-9. Also in *Craters of the Spirit*, 180-5.

_____, *Samuel Beckett*, 48-58.

Senneff, Susan F., "Song and Music in Samuel Beckett's WATT," *MFS* 10 (Summer, 1974): 137-49.

Skerl, Jennie, "Fritz Mauthner's 'Critique of Language' in Samuel Beckett's WATT," *ConL* 15, iv (Autumn, 1974): 474-87.

Smith, Frederik N., "Beckett and the Seventeenth-Century Port-Royal Logic," *JML* 5, i (Feb., 1976): 99-108.

_____, "The Epistemology of Fictional Failure: Swift's TALE OF A TUB and Beckett's WATT," *TSLL* 15, iv (Winter, 1974): 649-72.

Solomon, Philip H., "A Ladder Image in WATT: Samuel Beckett and Fritz Mauther," *PLL* 7, iv (Fall, 1971): 422-7.

Swanson, Eleanor, "Samuel Beckett's WATT: A Coming and a Going," *MFS* 17, ii (Summer, 1971): 264-8.

Szanto, G. H., *Narrative Consciousness*, 81-5.

Tatham, Campbell, "WATT-Knots Enhance Endogenous Entropy," *Boundary* 5, ii (Winter, 1977): 351-62.

Tindall, William Y., "Beckett's Bums," *Crit* 2, i (Spring-Summer, 1958): 6-7.

_____, *Samuel Beckett*, 17-21.

Trivisonno, Ann M., "Meaning and Function of the Quest in Beckett's WATT," *Crit* 12, ii (1970): 28-38.

Warhaft, Sidney, "Threne and Theme in WATT," *WSCL* 4, iii (Autumn, 1963): 261-78.

Wasserman, Jerry, "Watt's World of Words," *BuR* 22, ii (Fall, 1976): 123-38.

Webb, E., *Samuel Beckett*, 56-69.

Weringer, Helen M., "Beckett and His Bilingualism: The Word as Mask and Mirror," *DAI* 40 (1979): 2654A.

Winston, Mathew, "WATT's First Footnote," *JML* 6, i (Feb., 1977): 69-82.

BIBLIOGRAPHY

Browne, Joseph, "The 'Critic' and Samuel Beckett: A Bibliographic Essay," *CollL* 8, iii (Fall, 1981): 292-309.

Bryer, Jackson R., "Samuel Beckett: A Checklist of Criticism," in Friedman, M. J., ed., *Samuel Beckett Now*, 219-59.

Cohn, R., *Samuel Beckett*, 328-40.

Federman, R., *Journey to Chaos*, 224-35.

Federman, Raymond, and John Fletcher, *Samuel Beckett: His Works and His Critics*, Berkeley: Un. of California, 1970.

Mays, James, "Samuel Beckett Bibliography: Comments and Corrections," *IUR* 2, ii (Autumn, 1972): 189-208.

Tanner, James F. F., and J. Don Vann, *Samuel Beckett: A Checklist of Criticism*, Kent, Ohio: Kent St. Un. Pr., 1969.

BECKHAM, BARRY (EARL), 1944-

GENERAL

Pinsker, Sanford, "A Conversation with Barry Beckham," *SBL* 5, iii (Winter, 1974): 17-20.

MY MAIN MOTHER

Harris, Trudier, "The Barber shop in Black Literature," *BALF* 13, iii (Fall, 1979): 112-18 *passim*.

RUNNER MACK

Pinsker, Sanford, "About RUNNER MACK: An Interview with Barry Beckham," *BlackI* 3, iii (1974): 35-41.

Weixlmann, Joe, "The Dream Turned 'Daymare': Barry Beckham's RUNNER MACK," *MELUS* 8, iv (1981): 93-103.

BIBLIOGRAPHY

Weixlmann, Joe, "Barry Beckham: A Bibliography," *CLAJ* 24, iv (June, 1982): 522-8.

BEDFORD, SYBILLE, 1911-

GENERAL

Evans, Robert O., "Sybille Bedford: Most Reticent, Most Modest, 'O Most Best'," *SLitI* 11, ii (Fall, 1978): 67-78.

A COMPASS ERROR

Evans, Robert O., "Sybille Bedford: Most Reticent, Most Modest, 'O Most Best'," *SLitI* 11, ii (Fall, 1978): 77-8.

A FAVOURITE OF THE GODS

Evans, Robert O., "Sybille Bedford: Most Reticent, Most Modest, 'O Most Best'," *SLitI* 11, ii (Fall, 1978): 75-7.

A LEGACY

Evans, Robert O., "Sybille Bedford: Most Reticent, Most Modest, 'O Most Best'," *SLitI* 11, ii (Fall, 1978): 69-75.

BELLOW, SAUL, 1915-

GENERAL

Abbott, H. Porter, "Saul Bellow and the 'Lost Cause' of Character," *Novel* 13, iii (Spring, 1980): 264-83.

Aharoni, Ada, "The Cornerstone of Saul Bellow's Art," *SBN* 2, i (Fall-Winter, 1982): 1-12.

Allen, Mary L., "The Flower and the Chalk: The Comic Sense of Saul Bellow," *DA* 29 (1967): 3997A. (Stanford).

Allen, Michael, "Idiomatic Language in Two Novels by Saul Bellow," *JAmS* 1 (Oct., 1967): 275-80.

Alter, Robert, "The Stature of Saul Bellow," *Midstream* 10 (Dec., 1964): 3-15. Also (revised) as "Saul Bellow: A Dissent from Modernism," *After the Tradition*, 95-115.

Anders, Jaroslaw, "Saul Bellow's Treatment of Ideas in Three Major Works," *KN* 27, iv (1980): 455-66.

Andres, Richard J., "Self-Consciousness and the 'Heart's Ultimate Need': A Reading of Saul Bellow's Novels," *DAI* 38 (1977): 258A.

Atlas, Marilyn J., "The 'Figurine' in the China Cabinet: Saul Bellow and the Nobel Prize," *Midamerica* 8 (1981): 36-49.

Bailey, Jennifer M., "The Qualified Affirmation of Saul Bellow's Recent Work," *JAmS* 7, i (April, 1973): 67-76.

Baker, Sheridan, "Saul Bellow's Bout with Chivalry," *Criticism* 9 (Spring, 1967): 109-22.

Bakker, J., "In Search of Reality: Two American Heroes Compared," *DQR* 4 (1972): 145-61. [Bellow and Hemingway.]

Balbert, Peter, "Perceptions of Exile: Nabokov, Bellow, and the Province of Art," *SNNTS* 14, i (1982): 95-104.

Bellitt, Ben, "Saul Bellow: The Depth Factor," *Salmagundi* 30 (1975): 57-65.

Bellow, Saul, and Robert Robinson, "Saul Bellow at 60," *Listener* 93 (Feb. 13, 1975): 218-19.

Berets, Ralph, "Saul Bellow's Fiction," *CentR* 20, i (Winter, 1976): 75-101.

Bezanker, Abraham, "The Odyssey of Saul Bellow," *YR* 58 (Spring, 1969): 359-71.

Bigsby, C. W., "Saul Bellow and the Liberal Tradition in American Literature," *ForumH* 14, i (1976): 56-62.

Borrus, Bruce J., "Bellow's Critique of the Intellect," *MFS* 25, i (Spring, 1979): 29-45.

_____, "Thoughts Informed Against Me: The Fiction of Saul Bellow," *DAI* 40 (1979): 848A.

Bosha, Francis J., "The Critical Reception of Saul Bellow in Japan," *SBN* 1, ii (Spring-Summer, 1982): 34-46.

Boyers, Robert, et al., "Literature and Culture: An Interview with Saul Bellow," *Salmagundi* 30 (1975): 6-23.

Bradbury, Malcolm, "'The Nightmare in Which I'm Trying to Get a Good Night's Rest': Saul Bellow and Changing History," in Schraepen, E., ed., *Saul Bellow and His Work*, 11-29.

_____, *Saul Bellow.*

_____, "Saul Bellow and the Naturalist Tradition," *REL* 4, iv (Oct., 1963): 80-92.

_____, "Saul Bellow and the Nobel Prize," *JAmS* 11, i (April, 1977): 3-12.

Braham, E. Jeanne, "The Struggle at the Center: Dostoevsky and Bellow," *SBN* 2, i (Fall-Winter, 1982): 13-18.

Brans, Jo, "Common Needs, Common Preoccupations: An Interview with Saul Bellow," *SWR* 62 (1977): 1-19. Also in Trachtenberg, S., ed., *Critical Essays on Saul Bellow*, 57-72.

Bryant, J. H., *Open Decision*, 341-69.

Buitenhuis, Peter, "A Corresponding Fabric: The Urban World of Saul Bellow," *Costerus* 8 (1973): 13-36.

Bullock, C. J., "On the Marxist Criticism of the Contemporary Novel in the United States: A Re-Evaluation of Saul Bellow," *Praxis* 1, ii (1976): 189-98.

Burgess, Anthony, "The Jew as American," *Spectator* (Oct. 7, 1966): 455-6.

Burns, Robert, "The Urban Experience: The Novels of Saul Bellow," *Dissent* 24 (1969): 18-24.

Chapman, Abraham, "The Image of Man as Portrayed by Saul Bellow," *CLAJ* 10 (June, 1967): 285-98.

Chase, Richard, "The Adventures of Saul Bellow: Progress of a Novelist," *Ctary* 27 (April, 1959): 322-30. Also in Malin, I., ed., *Saul Bellow and the Critics*, 25-38.

Chavkin, Allan, "'The Comic Bellow': A Review Article of Malcolm Bradbury's *Saul Bellow*," *SBN* 2, i (Fall-Winter, 1982): 44-60.

Christhilf, Mark M., "Death and Deliverance in Saul Bellow's Symbolic City," *BSUF* 18, ii (1977): 9-23.

Clayton, J. J., *Saul Bellow.*

_____, *Saul Bellow*, 2nd ed.

Cohen, Sarah B., "The Comic Elements in the Novels of Saul Bellow," *DAI* 30 (1970): 3000A-01A. (Northwestern).

_____, "Saul Bellow's Chicago," *MFS* 24, i (Spring, 1978): 139-46.

_____, *Saul Bellow's Enigmatic Laughter.*

_____, "Saul Bellow's Jerusalem," *SAJL* 5, ii (1979): 16-23.

_____, "Sex: Saul Bellow's Hedonistic Joke," *SAF* 2, ii (Autumn, 1974): 223-9. Also in Trachtenberg, S., ed., *Critical Essays on Saul Bellow*, 175-80.

Crabtree, Ursula M., "Facing the Bogeyman: A Comparative Study of the Motif of the Double in the Novels of Saul Bellow and Günter Grass," *DAI* 39 (1978): 1532A-33A.

Craig, Harry E., "The Affirmation of the Heroes in the Novels of Saul Bellow," *DA* 28 (1968): 5012A (Pittsburgh).

Cronin, Gloria L., "Saul Bellow's Rejection of Modernism," *DAI* 41 (1980): 2603A.

Detweiler, Robert, *Saul Bellow: A Critical Essay* (CWCP), Grand Rapids, Mich.: Eerdmans, 1967.

Dickstein, Morris, "For Art's Sake," *PR* 33 (Fall, 1966): 617-21.

Digennara, Michael W., "The Primitive and the Civilized: The Dialectical Nature of Saul Bellow's Art," *DAI* 39 (1978): 1564A.

Donoghue, Denis, "Commitment and the Dangling Man," *Studies* 53 (Summer, 1964): 174-87.

_____, *The Ordinary Universe: Soundings in Modern Literature*, N.Y.: Macmillan, 1968, 194-203.

Dutton, R. R., *Saul Bellow*.

_____, "The Subangelic Vision of Saul Bellow: A Study of His First Six Novels, 1944-1964," *DA* 27 (1966): 1363A (Un. of the Pacific).

Eiland, Howard, "Bellow's Crankiness," *ChiR* 32, iv (Spring, 1981): 92-107.

Eisinger, Chester E., *Fiction of the Forties*, 341-62.

_____, "Saul Bellow: Love and Identity," *Accent* 18 (Summer, 1958): 179-203.

Feuer, Diana M., "The Rehumanization of Art: Secondary Characterization in the Novels of Saul Bellow," *DAI* 35 (1975): 7903A.

Fiedler, Leslie, "Saul Bellow," *PrS* 31 (Summer, 1957): 103-10. Also in Goldberg, Gerald J., and Nancy M. Goldberg, eds., *The Modern Critical Spectrum*, N.Y.: Prentice-Hall, 1962, 155-61. Also in Kostelanetz, R., ed., *On Contemporary Literature*, 286-95. Also in Malin, I., ed., *Saul Bellow and the Critics*, 1-11. Also in Fiedler, L., *Collected Essays of Leslie Fiedler*, vol. 2, 56-64.

Field, Leslie, "Saul Bellow and the Critics: After the Nobel Award," *MFS* 25, i (Spring, 1979): 3-13.

_____, "Saul Bellow: From Montreal to Jerusalem," *SAJL* 4, ii (1978): 51-9.

Fossum, Robert H., "The Devil and Saul Bellow," *CLS* 3 (1966): 197-206. Also in Panichas, G. A., ed., *Mansions of the Spirit*, 345-55.

Frank, Rueben, "Saul Bellow: The Evolution of a Contemporary Novelist," *WR* 18 (Winter, 1954): 101-12.

Freedman, Ralph, "Saul Bellow: The Illusion of Environment," *WSCL* 1, i (Winter, 1960): 50-65.

Fuchs, Daniel, "Saul Bellow and the Example of Dostoevsky," in MacMillan, D. J., ed., *Stoic Strain in American Literature*, 157-76.

_____, "Saul Bellow and the Modern Tradition," *ConL* 15, i (Winter, 1974): 67-89.

Gallagher, Michael P., "Bellow's Clowns and Contemplatives," *Month* 10 (April, 1977): 131-4.

Galloway, David D., "The Absurd Man as Picaro: The Novels of Saul Bellow," *TSLL* 6 (Summer, 1964): 226-54. Also in *Absurd Hero*, 82-139.

_____, "Culture-Making: The Recent Works of Saul Bellow," in Schraepen, E., ed., *Saul Bellow and His Work*, 49-60.

Geismar, M., "Saul Bellow: Novelist of the Intellectuals," *American Moderns*, 210-24. Also in Malin, I., ed., *Saul Bellow and the Critics*, 10-24.

Gerson, Steven M., "Paradise Sought: Adamic Imagery in Selected Novels by Saul Bellow and Kurt Vonnegut, Jr.," *DAI* 39 (1978): 285A.

Gitenstein, Barbara, "Saul Bellow and the Yiddish Literary tradition," *SAJL* 5, ii (1979): 24-46.

_____, "Saul Bellow of the 1970's and the Contemporary Use of History in Jewish-American Literature," *SBN* 1, ii (Spring-Summer, 1982): 7-17.

Gold, R. Michael, "The Influence of Emerson, Thoreau, and Whitman on the Novels of Saul Bellow," *DAI* 40 (1980): 5055A-56A.

Golden, Daniel, "Mystical Musings and Comic Confrontations: The Fiction of Saul Bellow and Mordecai Richler," *ECW* 22 (Summer, 1981): 62-85.

Golden, Susan L., "The Novels of Saul Bellow: A Study in Development," *DAI* 36 (1976): 4489A-90A.

Goldman, Liela, "Affirmation and Equivocation: Judaism in the Novels of Saul Bellow," *DAI* 41 (1980): 2109A.

Gross, G. L., *Heroic Ideal in American Literature*, 243-61.

Hall, J., *Lunatic Giant in the Drawing Room*, 127-80.

Halperin, Irving, "Saul Bellow and the Moral Imagination," *NER* 1 (1979): 475-88. Also in *Jewish Affairs* 33, ii (1978): 33-6.

Harper, Gordon L., "The Art of Fiction: Saul Bellow, an Interview," *ParisR* No. 36 (Winter, 1966): 48-73. Also in *Writers at Work*, 3rd Series, 175-96. Also in Rovit, E., ed., *Saul Bellow*, 5-18.

Harper, H. M., Jr., "Saul Bellow: The Heart's Ultimate Need," *Desperate Faith*, 7-64.

Harris, Mark, *Saul Bellow: Drumlin Woodchuck*, Athens: Un. of Georgia Pr., 1980.

Hartman, Hugh C., "Character, Theme and Tradition in the Novels of Saul Bellow," *DA* 29 (1968): 898A-9A. (Un. of Washington).

Hassan, Ihab H., *Radical Innocence*, 290-4.

_____, "Saul Bellow," *AR* 40, iii (Summer, 1982): 266-73.

_____, "Saul Bellow: Five Faces of a Hero," *Crit* 3, iii (Summer, 1960): 28-36.

Henry, Jim D., "Mystic Trade: The American Novelist Saul Bellow Talks to Jim Douglas Henry," *Listener* 81 (May 22, 1969): 705-7. [Interview.]

Hoffman, Frederick J., "The Fool of Experience: Saul Bellow's Fiction," in Moore, H. T., ed., *Contemporary American Novelist*, 80-94.

Hollahan, Eugene, "Bellow's Affirmation of Individual Value via Classical Plot Structure," *SBN* 2, i (Fall-Winter, 1982): 23-31.

Hux, Samuel H., "American Myth and Existentialism of Mailer, Bellow, Styron, and Ellison," *DA* 26 (1966): 5437 (Conn.).

_____, "Character and Form in Bellow," *ForumH* 12, i (1974): 34-8.

Jacobs, Rita D., "'Truths on the Side of Life': Saul Bellow, Nobel Prize 1976," *WLT* 51 (1977): 194-7.

Johnson, Gregory A., "'Creatures and More': Codes of Nonverbal Dialogue in the Canon of Bellow," *DAI* 42, iv (Oct., 1981): 1635A-36A.

Johnson, Lee R., "The Novels of Saul Bellow and Norman Mailer: A Study of Their Polar Perceptions of American Reality," *DAI* 40 (1979): 1028A-29A.

Kannan, Lakshmi, "The 'Infected' Area in Saul Bellow's Fiction," *LHY* 18, ii (1978): 103-19.

————, "That Small Voice in Saul Bellow's Fiction," *VQ* 42 (1977): 191-206.

Kar, Prafulla, "Saul Bellow: A Defense of the Self," *DAI* 34 (1973): 778A (Utah).

Karl, Frederick R., "Bellow's Comic 'Last Men'," *Thalia* 1, ii (1978): 19-26.

Kathe, Barbara A., "Self Realization: The Jungian Process of Individuation in the Novels of Saul Bellow," *DAI* 40 (1980): 6279A.

Kauffmann, Stanley, "Saul Bellow: A Closing Note," *Salmagundi* 30 (1975): 90-1.

Kazin, Alfred, "Bellow's Purgatory," *NYRB* (Mar. 28, 1968): 32-6.

————, "My Friend Saul Bellow," *Atlantic* 215 (Jan., 1965): 51-4.

————, "The World of Saul Bellow," *Contemporaries*, 217-25.

————, "The World of Saul Bellow," *Griffin* 8 (June, 1959): 4-9.

Kirstein, Ruth G., "The Dual Vision: Reality and Transcendence in Saul Bellow's Fiction," *DAI* 41 (1980): 252A.

Klein, Marcus, "Saul Bellow: A Discipline of Nobility," *KR* 24 (Spring, 1962): 203-26. Also, expanded, in Klein, M., *After Alienation*, 33-70. Also in Malin, I., ed., *Saul Bellow and the Critics*, 92-113. Also in Waldmeir, J. J., ed., *Recent American Fiction*, 121-38. Also in Rovit, E., ed., *Saul Bellow*, 135-52, including "Postscript 1973," 153-60.

Klug, M. A., "Saul Bellow: The Hero in the Middle," *DR* 56, iii (1976): 462-78.

Kramer, Maurice, "The Secular Mode of Jewishness," *Works* 1 (Autumn, 1967): 110-16.

Kreiger, Barbara S., "The Fiction of Saul Bellow," *DAI* 39 (1978): 2940A.

Kremer, S. Lillian, "Bellow and the Inherited Tradition: A Study of Judaic Influence on Form and Context in Saul Bellow's Fiction," *DAI* 40 (1979): 3301A-02A.

Kulshrestha, Chirantan, "A Conversation with Saul Bellow," *ChiR* 23-24 (1972): 7-15.

————, *Saul Bellow*.

————, "The Making of Saul Bellow's Fiction: Notes from the Underground," *ASInt* 19, ii (1981): 48-56.

Kumar, P. Shiv, "Saul Bellow and the Hebraic Prophetic Tradition," *JEnS* 11, ii (1980): 756-65.

Leese, David A., "Laughter in the Ghetto: A Study of Form in Saul Bellow's Comedy," *DAI* 36 (1975): 321A.

Lehan, R., *Dangerous Crossing*, 108-33.

Le Master, J. R., "Saul Bellow: On Looking for a Way Through the Cracks," in Collmer, R. G., and J. W. Herring, eds., *American Bypaths*, 109-44.

Levenson, J. C., "Bellow's Dangling Men," *Crit* 3, iii (Summer, 1960): 3-14. Also in Malin, I., ed., *Saul Bellow and the Critics*, 39-50.

Levine, Paul, "Saul Bellow: The Affirmation of the Philosophical Fool," *Per* 10 (Winter, 1959): 163-76.

Lewin, Lois S., "The Theme of Suffering in the Work of Bernard Malamud and Saul Bellow," *DA* 28 (1968): 5021A. (Pittsburgh).

Ludwig, Jack, *Recent American Novelists* (UMPAW, No. 22), 1962, 7-18.

Lycette, Ronald L., "Saul Bellow and the American Naturalists," *Discourse* 13, iv (Autumn, 1970): 435-49.

Lyons, Bonnie, "Bellowmalamudroth and the American Jewish Genre—Alive and Well," *SAJL* 5, ii (1979): 8-10.

Mackintosh, Esther M., "The Women Characters in the Novels of Saul Bellow," *DAI* 41 (1980): 253A.

Malin, Irving, in *Jewish Heritage Reader*, 257-63.

————, *Jews and Americans*.

————, "Reputations—XIV: Saul Bellow," *LonM* 4 (Jan., 1965): 43-54.

————, ed., *Saul Bellow and the Critics*.

————, *Saul Bellow's Fiction*.

————, "Seven Images," in Malin, I., ed., *Saul Bellow and the Critics*, 142-76.

Mândra, Mihail, "Saul Bellow's Novel in the Context of European Thought: A Greek World," *Synthesis* 7 (1980): 191-205.

Manning, James B., "Craters of the Spirit: Saul Bellow's Novels of Entrapment," *DAI* 39 (1978): 2276A.

Marin, Daniel B., "Voice and Structure in Saul Bellow's Novels," *DAI* 35 (1973): 6920A-21A. (Iowa).

Markos, Donald W., "The Humanism of Saul Bellow," *DA* 27 (1966): 3875A (Illinois).

Marney, Elizabeth A. B., "Six Patterns of Imagery in Three of Saul Bellow's Novels," *DAI* 38 (1978): 4169A.

Marovitz, Sanford E., "A Jew Is a Jew Is a Jew: The Dilemma of Identity in American Jewish Fiction," *SALit* 14 (1978): 1-18. [Not seen.]

McCadden, J. F., *Flight from Women in the Fiction of Saul Bellow*.

————, "The Hero's Flight from Women in the Novels of Saul Bellow," *DAI* 40 (1979): 855A.

McCormick, John, "Historical Event in the Prose Fiction of Henry de Montherlant and Saul Bellow," *EigoS* 125, iii (1979): 118-21.

McDonnell, F. D., *Four Postwar American Novelists*, 1-11.

McSweeney, Kerry, "Saul Bellow and the Life to Come," *CritQ* 18, i (1976): 67-72.

Michael, Bessie, "What's the Best Way to Live? A Study of the Novels of Saul Bellow," *DAI* 30 (1970): 5451A-52A (Lehigh).

Morahg, Gilead, "Ideas as a Thematic Element in Saul Bellow's 'Victim' Novels," *DAI* 34 (1974): 6599A-600A (Wis., Madison).

Morrow, Patrick, "Threat and Accommodation: The Novels of Saul Bellow," *MQ* 8 (Summer, 1967): 389-411.

Mudrick, M., "Malamud, Bellow and Roth," *On Culture and Literature*, 200-33.

————, "Who Killed Herzog? Or, Three American Novelists," *UDQ* 1, i (Spring, 1966). Also in Mudrick, M., *On Culture and Literature*, 200-33.

Mukerji, Nirmal, "The Bellow Hero," *IJES* 9 (1968): 74-86. [Not seen.]

————, "Bellow's Measure of Man," in Naik, M. K., et al., eds., *Indian Studies in American Fiction*, 286-95.

Nevius, Blake, "Saul Bellow and the Theater of the Soul," *NM* 73, i-ii (1972): 248-60.

Newman, Judie, "Saul Bellow's Sixth Sense: The Sense of History," *CRevAS* 13, i (Spring, 1982); 39-51.

Nilsen, Helge N., "Saul Bellow and Wilhelm Reich," *Amer. Studies in Scandinavia* 10 (1978): 81-91.

Noble, D. W., *Eternal Adam and the New World Garden*, 216-33.

O'Connell, Shaun, "Bellow: Logic's Limits," *MR* 10 (Winter, 1969): 182-7.

Offutt, John C., "A Study of Adult Developmental Stages of Behavior in Saul Bellow's Literary Characters," *DAI* 41, ix (Mar., 1981): 4034A-35A.

Opdahl, Keith, "The Discussion: Refining the Issues," *SAJL* 5, ii (1979): 15.

_____, "God's Braille: Concrete Detail in Saul Bellow's Fiction," *SAJL* 4, ii (1978): 60-71.

_____, *Novels of Saul Bellow*.

_____, "'Stillness in the Midst of Chaos': Plot in the Novels of Saul Bellow," *MFS* 25, i (Spring, 1979): 15-28.

_____, "'Strange Things, Savage Things': Saul Bellow's Hidden Theme," *IowaR* 10, iv (1979): 1-15.

_____, "'True Impressions': Saul Bellow's Realistic Style," in Schraepen, E., ed., *Saul Bellow and His Work*, 61-71.

Orr, John, "Offstage Tragedy: The New Narrative Strategies of John Fowles, Saul Bellow and William Styron," *New Edinburgh Review* 59 (1982): 21-3.

O'Sheel, Patrick, "Laughter from the Styx," *Eco-Logos* 23, lxxxiv (1977): 11-14.

O'Sullivan, Liam, "Saul Bellow's 'Man Thinking'," *DAI* 39 (1979): 4259A-60A.

Peontek, Louana L., "Images of Women in Saul Bellow's Novels," *DAI* 41, vii (Jan., 1981): 3110A.

Pinsker, Sanford, "Meditations Interruptus; Saul Bellow's Ambivalent Novel of Ideas," *SAJL* 4, ii (1978): 22-32.

_____, "Psychological Schlemiels of Saul Bellow," *Schlemiel as Metaphor*, 125-60.

_____, "Saul Bellow and the Special Comedy of Urban Life," *OntarioR* 8 (1978): 82-94.

_____, "Saul Bellow, Soren Kierkegaard and the Question of Boredom," *CentR* 24, i (1980): 118-25.

_____, "The *Schlemiel* as Metaphor: Studies in the Yiddish and American Jewish Novel," *DA* 28 (1968): 3679A-80A. (Un. of Washington).

Podhoretz, N., "The Adventures of Saul Bellow," *Doings and Undoings*, 205-27.

Porter, M. Gilbert, "Hitch Your Agony to a Star: Bellow's Transcendental Vision," in Schraepen, E., ed., *Saul Bellow and His Work*, 73-88.

_____, "The Novels of Saul Bellow: A Formalist Reading," *DAI* 31 (1970): 1287A (Ore.).

_____, *Whence the Power?*

Prabhakar, T., and R. Palanivel, "In Defense of Humanity—Saul Bellow's Novels," *JEnS* 12, i (1980): 820-7.

Radeljkovi, Zvonimir, "Bellow's Search for Meaning," in Thorson, James L., ed., *Yugoslav Perspectives on American Literature: An Anthology*, Ann Arbor: Ardis, 1980, 181-4.

Raider, Ruth, "Saul Bellow," *CamQ* 2 (Spring, 1967): 172-83.

Rans, Geoffrey, "The Novels of Saul Bellow," *REL* 4, iv (Oct., 1963): 18-30.

Raymer, John, "A Changing Sense of Chicago in the Works of Saul Bellow and Nelson Algren," *ON* 4, iv (Dec., 1978): 371-83.

Reiner, Sherry L., "'It's Love That Makes Reality Reality': Women through the Eyes of Saul Bellow's Protagonists," *DAI* 41 (1980): 1058A-59A.

Riehl, Betty Ann J., "Narrative Structures in Saul Bellow's Novels," *DAI* 36 (1975): 2827A.

Rodrigues, Eusebia L., "Quest for the Human: Theme and Structure in the Novels of Saul Bellow," *DAI* 31 (1970): 2936A-37A. (Pa.).

Ross, Theodore J., "Notes on Saul Bellow," *CJF* 18 (Fall, 1959): 21-7.

Roth, Henry, "Segments," *SAJL* 5, i (1979): 58-62.

Rovit, E., *Saul Bellow*.

_____, ed., *Saul Bellow*.

_____, "Saul Bellow and Norman Mailer: The Secret Sharers," in Rovit, E., ed., *Saul Bellow*, 161-70.

_____, "Saul Bellow and the Concept of the Survivor," in Schraepen, E., ed., *Saul Bellow and His Work*, 89-101.

Saposnik, Irving S., "Bellow, Malamud, Roth...and Styron?" *Judaism* 31 (1982): 322-32.

Scheer-Schäzler, Brigitte, "Epistemology as Narrative Device in the Work of Saul Bellow," in Schraepen, E., ed., *Saul Bellow and His Work*, 103-18.

_____, *Saul Bellow*.

Scheffler, Judith, "Two-Dimensional Dynamo: The Female Character in Saul Bellow's Novels," *WascanaR* 16, ii (Fall, 1981): 3-19.

Schraepen, Edmond, "The Rhetoric of Saul Bellow's Novels," 277-84 in *Rhétorique et communication*, Paris: Didier, 1979.

_____, ed., *Saul Bellow and His Work*.

Schroeter, James, "Saul Bellow and Individualism," *Études de lettres* 11, i (1978): 3-28.

Schulz, M. F., "Saul Bellow and the Burden of Selfhood," *Radical Sophistication*, 110-52.

Scott, Nathan A., Jr., "Sola Gratia- The Principle of Saul Bellow's Fiction," in Scott, N. A., Jr., ed., *Adversity and Grace*, 27-57. Also in Scott, N. A., Jr., *Craters of the Spirit*, 233-65.

_____, ed., *Three American Moralists*, 101-49.

Sewell, William J., "Literary Structure and Value Judgment in the Novels of Saul Bellow," *DAI* 35 (1975): 6159A.

Shaw, Peter, "The Tough Guy Intellectual," *CritQ* 8 (Spring, 1966): 23-7.

Shechner, Mark, "Saul Bellow and Ghetto Cosmopolitanism," *SAJL* 4, ii (1978): 33-44.

Shibuya, Yazaburo, "Saul Bellow: Politics and the Sense of Reality," in Ohashi, Kenzaburo, ed., *The Traditional and the Anti-Traditional: Studies in Contemporary American Literature*, Tokyo: American Literary Soc. of Japan, 1980, 43-56.

Singh, Yashoda N., "The City as Metaphor in Selected Novels of James Purdy and Saul Bellow," *DAI* 40 (1979): 2049A.

_____, "Saul Bellow and the Modern American City," *OJES* 17 (1981): 39-47.

"Some Questions and Answers," *OntarioR* 3 (1975): 51-60. [Interview.]

Steinke, Russell, "The Monologic Temper of Bellow's Fiction," *Junction* (Brooklyn Coll.) 1, iii (1973): 178-84.

Stock, Irvin, "The Novels of Saul Bellow," *SoR* 3 (Winter, 1967): 13-42.

Sullivan, Victoria, "The Battle of the Sexes in Three Bellow Novels," in Rovit, E., ed., *Saul Bellow*, 101-14.

Surdaram, T. Soma, "Search for Salvation in Saul Bellow," *BP* 21 (1976): 37-40.

Swados, H., "Certain Jewish Writers," *A Radical's America*, 164-76.

Tajima, Junko, "The Role of Intellection in Saul Bellow's Fiction," *DAI* 42 (1981); 1154A.

Tajuddin, Mohammad, "The Tragicomic Novel: Camus, Malamud, Hawkes, Bellow," *DA* 28 (1968): 2698A-99A (Indiana).

Takizawa, Juzo, "Schopenhauer and Nietzsche in Bellow's Work," in *American Literature in the 1950's*, 50-8.

Tanner, Tony, "Afterword," in Schraepen, E., ed., *Saul Bellow and His Work*, 131-8.

————, *Saul Bellow*.

————, "Saul Bellow: The Flight from Monologue," *Encounter* 24 (Feb., 1965): 58-70.

————, "Saul Bellow: An Introductory Note," *Salmagundi* 30 (1975): 3-5.

Teodorescu, Anda, "Saul Bellow: An Ironical Humanist," *CREL* 4 (1979): 107-12.

Trachtenberg, S., ed., *Critical Essays on Saul Bellow*.

————, "Saul Bellow's *Luftmenschen*: The Compromise with Reality," *Crit* 9, iii (1967): 37-61.

Tudish, Catherine L., "The Schlemiel and the Reality Instructor: Moral Tension in the Novels of Saul Bellow," *DAI* 40 (1979): 2066A.

Vinoda, Mrs., "The Comic Mode in Saul Bellow's Fiction," *JEnS* 10, ii (1979): 662-7.

————, "The Dialectic of Sex in Bellow's Fiction," *IJAS* 7, i (Jan., 1982): 81-7.

————, "Saul Bellow and Gustave Flaubert," *SBN* 1, i (Fall, 1981): 1-5.

————, "The Theme of Death in the Novels of Saul Bellow," *JEnS* 12, 1 (1980): 812-19.

Walden, Daniel, "Bellow, Malamud, and Roth: Part of the Continuum," *SAJL* 5, ii (1979): 5-7.

————, "The Resonance of Twoness: The Urban Vision of Saul Bellow," *SAJL* 4, ii (1978): 9-21.

Walker, Kent W., "The Balancing Perspective: The Paradox of Alienation and Accommodation in the 'Victim' Novels of Saul Bellow," *DAI* 42 (1982): 3144A.

Wallach, Judith D. L., "The Quest for Selfhood in Saul Bellow's Novels: A Jungian Interpretation," *DAI* 36 (1975): 2829A.

Waterman, Andrew, "Saul Bellow's Ineffectual Angels," in Benedikz, B. S., ed., *On the Novel*, 218-38.

Weber, Ronald, "Bellow's Thinkers," *WHR* 22, iv (Autumn, 1968): 305-13.

Weinberg, H., "Kafka and Bellow: Comparisons and Further Definitions," *New Novel in America*, 29-54.

Weinstein, Mark, "Bellow's Imagination-Instructors," *SBN* 2, i (Fall-Winter, 1982): 19-21.

Weissman, Maryjo K., "Saul Bellow: A Reputation Study," *DAI* 40 (1979): 1474A.

White, Harry, "Saul Bellow's Enigmatic Laughter," *GLRev* 1, ii (Winter, 1975): 81-8.

Wieting, Molly S., "A Quest for Order: The Novels of Saul Bellow," *DAI* 30 (1970): 3030A-31A. (Texas, Austin).

————, "The Symbolic Function of the Pastoral in Saul Bellow's Novels," *SoQ* 16, iv (1978): 359-74.

Williams, Patricia W., "Saul Bellow's Fiction: A Critical Question," *DAI* 33 (1973): 6379A-80A (Texas A&M).

Zietlow, E. R., "Saul Bellow: The Theater of the Soul," *Ariel* 4, iv (1973): 44-59.

THE ADVENTURES OF AUGIE MARCH

Alam, Fakrul, "A Possible Source of Augie's Axial Lines," *NConL* 10, ii (1980): 6-7.

Aldridge, J. W., "The Society of Augie March," *In Search of Heresy*, 131-9. Also in *Devil in the Fire*, 224-30.

Allen, Michael, "Idiomatic Language in Two Novels by Saul Bellow," *JAmS* 1 (Oct., 1967): 275-80.

Allen, W., *Modern Novel*, 325-7.

Alter, Robert, *Rogue's Progress*, 121-5.

————, "The Stature of Saul Bellow," *Midstream* 10 (Dec., 1964): 8-9.

Bellamy, Michael O., "Bellow's More-Or-Less Human Bestiaries: AUGIE MARCH and HENDERSON THE RAIN KING," *BSUF* 23, i (1982): 12-22.

Bellow, Saul, "How I Wrote Augie March's Story," *NYTBR* (Jan. 31, 1954): 3+.

Bergler, Edmund, M. D., "Writers of Half-Talent," *AI* (Summer, 1957): 156-9.

Bradbury, M., *Saul Bellow*, 48-52.

Bryant, J. H., *Open Decision*, 350-3.

Buranarom, Nantana Y., "Saul Bellow's Anatomy of Love: A Study of the Theme of Love in THE ADVENTURES OF AUGIE MARCH, HERZOG, and HUMBOLDT'S GIFT," *DAI* 40 (1980): 5863A-64A.

Chapman, Sara S., "Melville and Bellow in the Real World: PIERRE and AUGIE MARCH," *WVUPP* 18 (Sept., 1971): 51-7.

Chase, Richard, *Ctary* 27 (April, 1959). Also in Malin, I., ed., *Saul Bellow and the Critics*, 27-30.

Clayton, J. J., *Saul Bellow*, 26-8, 60-1, 74-6, 83-92, 106-12, 122-8, 241-7.

————, *Saul Bellow*, 2nd ed., 26-8, 60-1, 74-6, 83-92, 106-12, 122-8, 295-302.

Cohen, S. B., *Saul Bellow's Enigmatic Laughter*, 64-89.

Cowley, Malcolm, "Naturalism: No Teacup Tragedies," *The Literary Situation*, N.Y.: Viking, 1954, 91-3.

Crozier, Robert D., "Theme in AUGIE MARCH," *Crit* 7 (Spring-Summer, 1965): 18-32.

Davis, Robert G., in Balakian, N., and C. Simmons, eds., *Creative Present*, 120-4.

————, *NYTBR* (Sept. 20, 1953): 1+.

Dutton, R. R., *Saul Bellow*, rev. ed., 42-74, 1982. 1971 ed., 52-82.

Eisinger, Chester E., *Fiction of the Forties*, 354-62.

————, "Saul Bellow: Love and Identity," *Accent* 18 (Summer, 1958): 192-9.

Finn, James, *ChiR* 8 (Spring-Summer, 1954): 104-11.

Frank, Reuben, "Saul Bellow: The Evolution of a Contemporary Novelist," *WR* 18 (Winter, 1954): 108-12.

Freedman, Ralph, "Saul Bellow: The Illusion of Environment," *WSCL* 1, i (Winter, 1960): 57-61. Also in Malin, I., ed., *Saul Bellow and the Critics*, 59-64.

Frohock, W. M., "Saul Bellow and His Penitent Hero," *SWR* 53 (Winter, 1968): 36-44.

Fuchs, Daniel, "THE ADVENTURES OF AUGIE MARCH: The Making of a Novel," *AAus* 5 (1980): 27-50.

Galloway, David D., *Absurd Hero*, 94-104.

————, "The Absurd Man as Picaro: The Novels of Saul Bellow," *TSLL* 6 (Summer, 1964): 234-41.

Geismar, Maxwell, *Nation* 177 (Nov. 14, 1953): 404.

————, "Saul Bellow: Novelist of the Intellectuals," *American Moderns*, 216-18. Also in Malin, I., ed., *Saul Bellow and the Critics*, 16-19.

Gerson, Steven M., "The New American Adam in THE ADVENTURES OF AUGIE MARCH," *MFS* 25, i (Spring, 1979): 117-28.

Gindin, J., *Harvest of a Quiet Eye*, 314-19.

Goldberg, Gerald J., "Life's Customer: Augie March," *Crit* 3, iii (Summer, 1960): 15-27.

Guerard, Albert J., "Saul Bellow and the Activists: On THE ADVENTURES OF AUGIE MARCH," *SoR* 3 (July, 1967): 582-96.

Guttmann, A., *Jewish Writer in America*, 189-98. Revised in Cohen, S. B., ed., *Comic Relief*, 129-35.

Hall, James, *Lunatic Giant in the Drawing Room*, 149-60.

_____, "Play, the Training Camp, and American Angry Comedy," *HAB* 15 (Spring, 1964): 11-16.

Harper, H. M., Jr., *Desperate Faith*, 23-32.

Harwell, Meade, *SWR* 39 (Summer, 1954): 273-6.

Hassan, I., *Radical Innocence*, 303-11.

Helbling, Mark, "Isaac Bashevis Singer in America," *PolR* 26, iii (1981): 20-5.

Hoffman, Frederick J., in Moore, H. T., ed., *Contemporary American Novelists*, 88-93.

Jones, David R., "The Disappointments of Maturity: Bellow's THE ADVENTURES OF AUGIE MARCH," in French, W., ed., *Fifties*, 83-92.

Kegan, R., *Sweeter Welcome*, 75-98.

Kulshrestha, C., *Saul Bellow*, 97-107.

Lehan, R., *Dangerous Crossing*, 115-18.

LeMaster, J. R., "Saul Bellow: On Looking for a Way Through the Cracks," in Collmer, R. G., and J. W. Herring, eds., *American Bypaths*, 120-4.

Levine, Paul, "Saul Bellow: The Affirmation of the Philosophical Fool," *Per* 10 (Winter, 1959): 167-72.

Ludwig, J., *Recent American Novelists*, 10-15.

Malin, Irving, in *Jewish Heritage Reader*, 260-1.

McCadden, J. F., *Flight from Women in the Fiction of Saul Bellow*, 61-88.

McConnell, F. D., *Four Postwar American Novelists*, 20-9.

Merkowitz, David R., "Bellow's Early Phase: Self and Society in DANGLING MAN, THE VICTIM and THE ADVENTURES OF AUGIE MARCH," *DAI* 32 (1972): 6439A-40A (Mich.).

Meyers, Jeffrey, "Brueghel and Augie March," *AL* 49, i (1977): 113-19. Also in Trachtenberg, S., ed., *Critical Essays on Saul Bellow*, 83-8.

Mizener, Arthur, *NYHTBR* (Sept. 20, 1953): 2.

Morrow, Patrick, "Threat and Accommodation: The Novels of Saul Bellow," *MQ* 8 (Summer, 1967): 401-3.

Nakajima, Kenji, "Freedom in THE ADVENTURES OF AUGIE MARCH," *KAL* 23 (May, 1982): 11-24.

Opdahl, K. M., *Novels of Saul Bellow*, 70-95.

Overbeck, Pat T., "The Women in 'Augie March'," *TSLL* 10 (Fall, 1968): 471-84.

Podhoretz, N., "The Adventures of Saul Bellow," *Doings and Undoings*, 215-19.

Porter, M. G., *Whence the Power?* 61-101.

Priestley, J. B., *Sunday Times* (London) (May 9, 1954): 5.

Pritchett, V. S., *NS&Nation*, n.s., 47 (June 19, 1954): 803.

Rans, Geoffrey, "The Novels of Saul Bellow," *REL* 4, iv (Oct., 1963): 22-6.

Rodrigues, Eusebio L., "Augie March's Mexican Adventures," *IJAS* 8, ii (1978): 39-43.

Rosu, Anca, "The Picaresque Technique in Saul Bellow's THE ADVENTURES OF AUGIE MARCH," *AUB-LG* 22 (1973): 191-7.

Rovit, E., *Saul Bellow*, 20-2.

Rupp, Richard H., "Saul Bellow: Belonging to the World in General," *Celebration in Postwar American Fiction*, 195-9.

Scheer-Schäzler, B., *Saul Bellow*, 32-56.

Schorer, Mark, "A Book of Yes and No," *HudR* 7 (Spring, 1954): 134-41.

Schroeter, James, "Saul Bellow and Individualism," *Études de lettres* 11, i (1978): 7-17.

Scott, Nathan A., Jr., "Sole Gratia—The Principle of Saul Bellow's Fiction," in Scott, N. A., Jr., ed., *Adversity and Grace*, 43-5. Also in Scott, N. A., Jr., *Craters of the Spirit*, 250-2.

_____, *Three American Moralists*, 119-22.

Sherman, B., *Invention of the Jew*, 132-45.

Shulman, Robert, "The Style of Bellow's Comedy," *PMLA* 83 (Mar., 1968): 109-17.

Singh, Yashoda, "Saul Bellow and the Modern American City," *OJES* 17 (1981): 39-47.

Stock, Irvin, "The Novels of Saul Bellow," *SoR* 3 (Winter, 1967): 23-7.

Tanner, T., *City of Words*, 64-73.

_____, *Saul Bellow*, 41-56.

Trachtenberg, Stanley, "Saul Bellow's *Luftmenschen*: The Compromise with Reality," *Crit* 9, iii (1967): 43-9.

Warner, Stephen D., "Representative Studies in the American Picaresque: Investigation of MODERN CHIVALRY, ADVENTURES OF HUCKLEBERRY FINN, and THE ADVENTURES OF AUGIE MARCH," *DA* 32 (1972): 4582A.

Warren, Robert Penn, "Man with no Commitments," *NRep* 129 (Nov. 2, 1953): 22-3.

Way, Brian, "Character and Society in THE ADVENTURES OF AUGIE MARCH," *BAASB* No. 8 (June, 1964): 36-44.

Webster, Harvey C., *SatR* 36 (Sept. 19, 1953): 13-14.

Weinberg, H., "The Heroes of Bellow's Novels," *New Novel in America*, 70-85.

West, Anthony, *NY* 29 (Sept. 26, 1953): 140+.

West, Ray B., *Shen* 5 (Winter, 1953): 85-90.

DANGLING MAN

Abbott, H. Porter, "Saul Bellow and the 'Lost Cause' of Character," *Novel* 13, iii (Spring, 1980): 265-83 *passim*.

Allen, W., *Modern Novel*, 322-5.

Alter, Robert, "The Stature of Saul Bellow," *Midstream* 10 (Dec., 1964): 5-7.

Baim, Joseph, "Escape From Intellection: Saul Bellow's DANGLING MAN," *UR* 33, i (Oct., 1970): 28-34.

Bakker, J., "In Search of Reality: Two American Heroes Compared," *DQR* 4 (1972): 145-61.

Baumbach, J., *Landscape of Nightmare*, 35-9.

Bradbury, M., *Saul Bellow*, 36-40.

Bryant, J. H., *Open Decision*, 342-4.

Clayton, J. J., *Saul Bellow*, 24-6, 56-9, 61-9, 77-83, 97-105, 114-22, 238-40.

_____, *Saul Bellow*, 2nd ed., 24-6, 56-9, 61-9, 77-83, 97-105, 114-22, 293-4.

Cohen, S. B., *Saul Bellow's Enigmatic Laughter*, 22-39.

Davis, Robert G., in Balakian, N., and C. Simmons, eds., *Creative Present*, 112-16.

Donoghue, Denis, "Commitment and the Dangling Man," *Studies* 53 (Summer, 1964): 174-87. Also in Donoghue, D., *The Ordinary Universe*, N.Y.: Macmillan, 1968, 194-203. Also in Rovit, E., ed., *Saul Bellow*, 19-30.

Dutton, R. R., *Saul Bellow*, 1971 ed., 18-32. Rev. ed., 1982, 11-20.

Eisinger, Chester E., *Fiction of the Forties*, 345-9.

_____, "Saul Bellow: Love and Identity," *Accent* 18 (Summer, 1968): 183-8.

Frank, Reuben, "Saul Bellow: The Evolution of a Contemporary Novelist," *WR* 18 (Winter, 1954): 102-5.

Galloway, David D., *Absurd Hero*, 82-9.

_____, "The Absurd Man as Picaro: The Novels of Saul Bellow," *TSLL* 6 (Summer, 1964): 226-31.

Geismar, M., "Saul Bellow: Novelist of the Intellectuals," *American Moderns*, 210-13. Also in Malin, I., ed., *Saul Bellow and the Critics*, 10-13.

Gindin, J., *Harvest of a Quiet Eye*, 305-9.

Glenday, Michael K., "'The Consummating Glimpse': DANGLING MAN's Treacherous Reality," *MFS* 25, i (Spring, 1979): 139-48.

Gross, T. L., *Heroic Ideal in American Literature*, 244-6.

Guttmann, A., *Jewish Writer in America*, 178-83.

Hall, J., *Lunatic Giant in the Drawing Room*, 134-8.

Harper, H. M., Jr., *Desperate Faith*, 8-16.

Hassan, I., *Radical Innocence*, 294-9.

Hoffman, Frederick J., in Moore, H. T., ed., *Contemporary American Novelists*, 83-5.

Kondo, Kyoko, "Pursuit of One Theme: Saul Bellow's Early Novels, DANGLING MAN, THE VICTIM, SEIZE THE DAY," *SES* 3 (1978): 86-98.

Kulshrestha, Chirantan, "Affirmation in Saul Bellow's DANGLING MAN," *IJAS* 5, i-ii (1975): 21-36.

_____, *Saul Bellow*, 64-77.

Lehan, R., *Dangerous Crossing*, 109-11.

_____, "Existentialism in Recent American Fiction: The Demonic Quest," *TSLL* 1 (Summer, 1959): 187-92.

Le Master, J. R., "Saul Bellow: On Looking for a Way Through the Cracks," in Collmer, R. G., and J. W. Herring, eds., *American Bypaths*, 115-18.

Levenson, J. C., "Bellow's Dangling Men," *Crit* 3, iii (1960): 4-7.

Levine, Paul, "Saul Bellow: The Affirmation of the Philosophical Fool," *Per* 10 (Winter, 1959): 164-5.

Lyons, Bonnie, "From DANGLING MAN to 'Colonies of the Spirit'," *SAJL* 4, ii (1978): 45-50.

Malin, Irving, in *Jewish Heritage Reader*, 258-60.

_____, *Saul Bellow's Fiction*, 71-6, 139-40.

McCadden, J. F., *Flight from Women in the Fiction of Saul Bellow*, 13-35.

McConnell, F. D., *Four Postwar American Novelists*, 11-14.

Mellard, James, "DANGLING MAN: Saul Bellow's Lyrical Experiment," *BSUF* 15, ii (Spring, 1974): 67-74.

Merkowitz, David R., "Bellow's Early Phase: Self and Society in DANGLING MAN, THE VICTIM, and THE ADVENTURES OF AUGIE MARCH," *DAI* 32 (1972): 6439A-40A (Mich.).

Morrow, Patrick, "Threat and Accommodation: The Novels of Saul Bellow," *MQ* 8 (Summer, 1967): 397-401.

Narasaki, Hiroshi, "Saul Bellow and the Early 1940's: A Critical Heritage," in *American Literature in the 1940's*, 43-6.

O'Brien, Kate, *Spectator* (Jan. 3, 1947): 26.

Opdahl, K. M., *Novels of Saul Bellow*, 28-50.

Pinsker, Sanford, "RAMEAU'S NEPHEW and Saul Bellow's DANGLING MAN," *NMAL* 4 (1980): Item 22.

_____, *Schlemiel as Metaphor*, 130-40.

Podhoretz, N., "The Adventures of Saul Bellow," *Doings and Undoings*, 206-11.

Rans, Geoffrey, "The Novels of Saul Bellow," *REL* 4, iv (Oct., 1963): 18-20.

Rao, R. M. V. R., "Chaos and the Self: An Approach to Saul Bellow's DANGLING MAN," *OJES* 8, ii (1971): 89-103.

Rovit, E., *Saul Bellow*, 17-18.

Rupp, Richard H., "Saul Bellow: Belonging to the World in General," *Celebration in Postwar American Fiction*, 189-92.

Saposnik, Irving S., "DANGLING MAN: A Partisan Review," *CentR* 26, iv (Fall, 1982): 388-95.

Scheer-Schäzler, B., *Saul Bellow*, 8-17.

Scott, Nathan A., Jr., "Solia Gratia- The Principle of Bellow's Fiction," in Scott, N. A., Jr., ed., *Adversity and Grace*, 37-40. Also in Scott, N. A., Jr., *Craters of the Spirit*, 245-6.

Singh, Yashoda, "Saul Bellow and the Modern American City," *OJES* 17 (1981): 39-47.

Stock, Irvin, "The Novels of Saul Bellow," *SoR* 3 (Winter, 1967): 17-19.

Tanner, T., *Saul Bellow*, 18-25.

Trachtenberg, Stanley, "Saul Bellow's *Luftmenschen*: The Compromise with Reality," *Crit* 9, iii (1967): 39-41.

Weinberg, H., *New Novel in America*, 55-60.

Wisse, R. R., *Schlemiel as Modern Hero*, 79-82.

THE DEAN'S DECEMBER

Bradbury, M., *Saul Bellow*, 91-6.

Chavkin, Allan, "Recovering 'The World That Is Buried Under the Debris of False Description'," *SBN* 1, ii (Spring-Summer, 1982): 47-57.

Wilson, Jonathan, "Bellow's Dangling Dean," *LitR* 26, i (1982): 165-75.

HENDERSON THE RAIN KING

Allen, Michael, "Idiomatic Language in Two Novels by Saul Bellow," *JAmS* 1 (Oct., 1967): 275-80.

Allen, W., *Modern Novel*, 327-8.

Alter, Robert, "The Stature of Saul Bellow," *Midstream* 10 (Dec., 1964): 10-11.

Anon., *TLS* (June 12, 1959): 352.

Axelrod, Steven G., "The Jewishness of Bellow's Henderson," *AL* 47, iii (Nov., 1975): 439-43.

Baim, Joseph, and David Demarest, Jr., "Henderson the Rain King: A Major Theme and a Technical Problem," in *A Modern Miscellany*, 53-63.

Baker, Carlos, *NYTBR* (Feb. 22, 1959): 4-5.

Baumbach, J., *Landscape of Nightmare*, 52-4.

Bellamy, Michael O., "Bellow's More-Or-Less Human Bestiaries: AUGIE MARCH and HENDERSON THE RAIN KING," *BSUF* 23, i (1982): 12-22.

Bradbury, M., *Saul Bellow*, 56-66.

_____, "Saul Bellow's HENDERSON THE RAIN KING," *Listener* 71 (Jan. 30, 1964): 187-8.

Brophy, Robert J., "Biblical Parallels in Bellow's HENDERSON THE RAIN KING," *C&L* 23, iv (Summer, 1974): 27-30.

Bryant, J. H., *Open Decision*, 353-7.

Campbell, Jeff H., "Bellow's Intimations of Immortality: HENDERSON THE RAIN KING," *SNNTS* 1, iii (Fall, 1969): 323-33.

Cecil, L. Moffitt, "Bellow's Henderson as American Imago of the 1950's," *RS* 40, iv (1972): 296-300.

Chase, Richard, "The Adventures of Saul Bellow: Progress of a Novelist," *Ctary* 27 (April, 1959): 323-30. Also in Malin, I., ed., *Saul Bellow and the Critics*, 25-6, 33-8.

Clayton, J. J., *Saul Bellow*, 166-85, 251-2.

_____, *Saul Bellow*, 2nd ed., 166-85, 305-6.

Cohen, S. B., *Saul Bellow's Enigmatic Laughter*, 115-42.

Davis, Robert G., in Balakian, N., and C. Simmons, eds., *Creative Present*, 127-30+.

_____, "Salvation in Lions?" *Midstream* 5 (Spring, 1959): 101-4.

Detweiler, Robert, "Patterns of Rebirth in HENDERSON THE RAIN KING," *MFS* 12 (Winter, 1966-67): 405-14.

Dougherty, David C., "Finding before Seeking: Theme in HENDERSON THE RAIN KING and HUMBOLDT'S GIFT," *MFS* 25, i (Spring, 1979): 232-47.

Dutton, R. R., *Saul Bellow*, 1971 ed., 98-118, rev. ed., 1982, 91-113.

Edwards, Duane, "The Quest for Reality in HENDERSON THE RAIN KING," *DR* 53 (1973): 246-55.

Freedman, Ralph, "Saul Bellow: The Illusion of Environment," *WSCL* 1, i (Winter, 1960): 61-5. Also in Malin, I., ed., *Saul Bellow and the Critics*, 64-8.

Friedman, Alan W., "The Jew's Complaint in Recent American Fiction: Beyond Exodus and Still in the Wilderness," *SoR* 8, i (1972): 49.

Galloway, David D., *Absurd Hero*, 110-23.

_____, "The Absurd Man as Picaro: The Novels of Saul Bellow," *TSLL* 6 (Summer, 1964): 244-53.

_____, "Clown and Saint: The Hero in Current American Fiction," *Crit* 7 (Spring-Summer, 1965): 52-3.

Gindin, J., *Harvest of a Quiet Eye*, 322-6.

Gold, Herbert, *Nation* 188 (Feb. 21, 1959): 169-70.

Goldfinch, Michael A., "A Journey to the Interior," *ES* 43 (Oct., 1962): 439-43.

Greenberg, Alvin, "The Death of the Psyche: A Way to the Self in the Contemporary Novel," *Criticism* 8 (Winter, 1966): 11-14.

Gross, T. L., *Heroic Ideal in American Literature*, 257-61.

Guttmann, Allen, "Bellow's HENDERSON," *Crit* 7, iii (Spring-Summer, 1965): 33-42. Also in Guttmann, A., *Jewish Writer in America*, 201-10. Also, revised, in Cohen, S. B., ed., *Comic Relief*, 135-42.

Hainer, Ralph C., "The Octopus in HENDERSON THE RAIN KING," *DR* 55 (1975): 712-19.

Harper, H. M., Jr., *Desperate Faith*, 39-50.

Hassan, I., *Radical Innocence*, 316-21. Also in Westbrook, M., ed., *Modern American Fiction*, 223-9.

Heiney, Donald, "Bellow as European," *PC1S* 5 (1972): 77-88. Also in Zyla, W. T. and W. A. Aycock, eds., *Modern American Fiction*, 77-88.

Hicks, Granville, *SatR* 42 (Feb. 21, 1959): 20.

Hoffman, Frederick J., in Moore, H. T., ed., *Contemporary American Novelists*, 92-3.

Holm, Astrid, "Existentialism and Saul Bellow's HENDERSON THE RAIN KING," *ASIS* 10, ii (1978): 93-109.

Hruska, Thomas, "Henderson's Riches," *JEnS* 12, i (1980): 779-84.

Hughes, Daniel J., "Reality and the Hero: LOLITA and HENDERSON THE RAIN KING," *MFS* 6 (Winter, 1960-61): 345-64. Also in Malin, I., ed., *Saul Bellow and the Critics*, 69-91.

Hull, Byron D., "HENDERSON THE RAIN KING and William James," *Criticism* 13, iv (Fall, 1971): 402-14.

Jacobson, Dan, "The Solitariness of Saul Bellow," *Spectator* (May 22, 1959): 735.

Kegan, R., *Sweeter Welcome*, 105-24.

Kehler, Joel R., "Henderson's Sacred Science," *CentR* 24, ii (1980): 232-47.

Knipp, Thomas R., "The Cost of Henderson's Quest," *BSUF* 10, ii (Spring, 1969): 37-9.

Leach, Elsie, "From Ritual To Romance Again: HENDERSON THE RAIN KING," *WHR* 14 (Spring, 1961): 223-4.

Lehan, R., *Dangerous Crossing*, 121-5.

LeMaster, J. R., "Saul Bellow: On Looking for a Way Through the Cracks," in Collmer, R. G., and J. W. Herring, eds., *American Bypaths*, 127-31.

Ludwig, J., *Recent American Novelists*, 16-18. Also in Kostelanetz, R., ed., *On Contemporary Literature*, 297-9.

Lutwack, L., *Heroic Fiction*, 100-17.

Majdiak, Daniel, "The Romantic Self and HENDERSON THE RAIN KING," *BuR* 19, ii (Fall, 1971): 125-46.

Markos, Donald W., "Life Against Death in HENDERSON THE RAIN KING," *MFS* 17, ii (Summer, 1971): 193-205.

McCadden, J. F., *Flight from Women in the Fiction of Saul Bellow*, 109-29.

McConnell, F. D., *Four Postwar American Novelists*, 30-6.

Michelson, Bruce, "The Idea of HENDERSON," *TCL* 27, iv (Winter, 1981): 309-24.

Morrow, Patrick, "Threat and Accommodation: The Novels of Saul Bellow," *MQ* 8 (Summer, 1967): 403-6.

Moss, Judith P., "The Body as Symbol in Saul Bellow's HENDERSON THE RAIN KING," *L&P* 20, ii (1970): 51-61.

Noble, D. W., *Eternal Adam and the New World Garden*, 219-21.

Okeke-Ezigbo, Emeka, "The Frogs Incident in HENDERSON THE RAIN KING," *NConL* 12, i (Jan., 1982): 7-8.

Opdahl, K. M., *Novels of Saul Bellow*, 118-39.

Pearce, Richard, "The Ambiguous Assault of Henderson and Herzog," in Rovit, E., ed., *Saul Bellow*, 72-5.

_____, *Stages of the Clown*, 102-16.

Pearson, Carol, "Bellow's HENDERSON THE RAIN KING and the Myth of the King, the Fool, and the Hero," *NConL* 5, v (1975): 8-11.

Podhoretz, N., "The Adventures of Saul Bellow," *Doings and Undoings*, 224-7.

_____, *NYHTBR* (Feb. 22, 1959): 3.

Porter, M. G., *Whence the Power?* 127-45.

Pribanic, Victor, "The Monomyth and Its Function in HENDERSON THE RAIN KING," in Baldanza, F., ed., *Itinerary 3: Criticism*, 25-30.

Price, Martin, *YR*, n.s. 48 (Mar., 1959): 453-6.

Price, Nancy L., "'Certain Flowers Persist': Bellow's Image of Hope in HENDERSON, HERZOG, and HUMBOLDT," *CCTE* 46 (1981): 50-7.

Quinton, Anthony, "The Adventures of Saul Bellow," *LonM* 6, xii (Dec., 1959): 55-9.

Rans, Geoffrey, "The Novels of Saul Bellow," *REL* 4, iv (Oct., 1963): 27-30.

Rodrigues, Eusebio L., "Bellow's Africa," *AL* 43, ii (May, 1971): 242-56.

_____, "The Reference to 'Joxi' in HENDERSON THE RAIN KING," *NConL* 8, iv (1978): 9-10.

_____, "Reichianism in HENDERSON THE RAIN KING," *Criticism* 15, iii (Summer, 1973): 212-33.

_____, "Saul Bellow's Henderson as America," *CentR* 20, ii (Spring, 1976): 189-95.

Rupp, Richard H., "Saul Bellow: Belonging to the World in General," *Celebration in Postwar American Fiction*, 201-4.

Sastri, P. S., "Bellow's HENDERSON THE RAIN KING: A Quest for Being," *PURBA* 3, i (1972): 9-18.

Scheer-Schäzler, B., *Saul Bellow*, 78-89.

Schroeter, James, "Saul Bellow and Individualism" *Études de Lettres* 11, i (1978): 18-21.

Scott, Nathan A., Jr., "Sola Gratia- The Principle of Saul Bellow's Fiction," in Scott, N. A., Jr., ed., *Adversity and Grace*, 50-2. Also in Scott, N. A., Jr., *Craters of the Spirit*, 257-60.

_____, *Three American Moralists*, 125-30.

Seiburth, Renee, "HENDERSON THE RAIN KING: A 20th Century Don Quixote?" *CRCL* 5, i (1978): 86-94.

Smelstor, Marjorie, "The Schlemiel as Father: A Study of Yakov Bok and Eugene Henderson," *SAJL* 4, i (1978): 50-7.

Steig, Michael, "Bellow's HENDERSON and the Limits of Freudian Criticism," *Paunch* 36-37 (April, 1973): 39-46.

Stern, Richard G., "Henderson's Bellow," *KR* 21 (Autumn, 1959): 658-61.

Stock, Irvin, "The Novels of Saul Bellow," *SoR* 3 (Winter, 1967): 31-6.

Stout, Janis, "Biblical Allusion in HENDERSON THE RAIN KING," *SCB* 40, iv (1980): 165-7.

_____, "The Possibility of Affirmation in HEART OF DARKNESS and HENDERSON THE RAIN KING," *PQ* 57, i (1978): 115-31.

Sullivan, Victoria, "The Battle of the Sexes in Three Bellow Novels," in Rovit, E., ed., *Saul Bellow*, 107-11.

Svore, Judy L., "An Ontological Perspective Applied to the Interpretation of Saul Bellow's HENDERSON THE RAIN KING," *DAI* 38 (1978): 5127A.

Swados, Harvey, "Bellow's Adventures in Africa," *New Leader* (Mar. 23, 1959): 23-4.

Symons, J., "Bellow Before Herzog," *Critical Occasions*, 112-18.

Tanner, T., *Saul Bellow*, 71-86.

Toliver, Harold E., "Bellow's Idyll of the Tribe," *Pastoral Forms and Attitudes*, Berkeley: Un. of Calif. Pr., 1971, 523-33.

Toth, Susan A., "HENDERSON THE RAIN KING, Eliot, and Browning," *NConL* 1, v (Nov., 1971): 6-8.

Towner, Daniel, "Brill's Ruins and Henderson's Rain," *Crit* 17, iii (1976): 96-104.

Trachtenberg, Stanley, "Saul Bellow's *Luftmenschen*: The Compromise with Reality," *Crit* 9, iii (1967): 52-5.

Waterhouse, Keith, *NS& Nation* n.s. 57 (June 6, 1959): 805-6.

Weinberg, H., *New Novel in America*, 85-102.

Whittemore, Reed, "Safari Among the Wariri," *NRep* 140 (Mar. 16, 1959): 17-18. Also in Harrison, G. A., ed., *Critic as Artist*, 382-7.

Winchell, Mark R., "Bellow's Hero with a Thousand Faces: The Use of Folk Myth in HENDERSON THE RAIN KING," *MissFR* 14, ii (Fall, 1980): 115-26.

HERZOG

Adams, Timothy D., "La Petite Madeleine: Proust and HERZOG," *NConL* 8, i (1978): 11.

Aldridge, J. W., "The Complacency of Herzog," *Time To Murder and Create*, 133-8. Also in Aldridge, J. W., *Devil in the Fire*, 231-4. Also in Malin, I., ed., *Saul Bellow and the Critics*, 207-10.

Alter, Robert, "The Stature of Saul Bellow," *Midstream* 10 (Dec., 1964): 11-15. Also (revised) in Alter, R., *After the Tradition*, 95-114.

Anders, Jaroslaw, "Saul Bellow's Treatment of Ideas in Three Major Works," *KN* 27, iv (1980): 455-66.

Anon., *TLS* (Feb. 4, 1965). Also as "Novels of 1965. Saul Bellow: HERZOG," in T. L. S., *Essays and Reviews from The Times Literary Review*, 1965, 31-4.

Atkins, Anselm, "The Moderate Optimism of Saul Bellow's HERZOG," *Person* 50, i (Spring, 1969): 117-29.

Axthelm, P. M., *Modern Confessional Novel*, 128-77.

Bailey, Jennifer M., "The Qualified Affirmation of Saul Bellow's Recent Work," *JAmS* 7, i (April, 1973): 67-76.

Baruch, Franklin R., "Bellow and Milton: Professor Herzog in His Garden," *Crit* 9, iii (1967): 74-83.

Bluefarb, Sam, "The Middle-Aged Man in Contemporary Literature: Bloom to Herzog," *CLAJ* 20, i (1976): 1-13.

Bothwell, E. K., *Alienation in the Jewish American Novel of the Sixties*, 130-53, 171-5.

Boulger, James D., "Puritan Allegory in Four Modern Novels," *Thought* 44 (Autumn, 1969): 413-32.

Bradbury, M., *Saul Bellow*, 69-77.

_____, "Saul Bellow's HERZOG," *CritQ* 7 (Autumn, 1965): 269-78.

Brans, Jo, "The Balance Sheet of Love: Money and Meaning in Bellow's HERZOG," *NMAL* 2, iv (1978): Item 29.

Bryant, J. H., *Open Decision*, 357-62.

Buranarom, Nantana Y., "Saul Bellow's Anatomy of Love: A Study of the Theme of Love in THE ADVENTURES OF AUGIE MARCH, HERZOG, and HUMBOLDT'S GIFT," *DAI* 40 (1980): 5863A-64A.

Chavkin, Allan, "Bellow's Alternative to the Wasteland: Romantic Theme and Form in HERZOG," *SNNTS* 11, iii (1979): 326-37.

_____, "The Unsuccessful Search for 'Pure Love' in Saul Bellow's HERZOG," *NMAL* 2, iv (1978): Item 27.

Clayton, J. J., *Saul Bellow*, 186-229, 252-3.

_____, *Saul Bellow*, 2nd ed., 186-229.

Colbert, Robert E., "Satiric Vision in HERZOG," *StCS* 5 (1978): 22-33.

Contraire, A. U., "Herzog and Prufrock: Eyes that Fix You in a Formulated Phrase," *Windless Orchard* 38 (Spring-Summer, 1981): 46-8.

Coonley, Donald E., "To Cultivate, to Dread: The Concept of Death in THE GINGER MAN and HERZOG," *NCampR* 2 (Spring, 1969): 7-12.

Davis, William V., "Bellow's HERZOG," *Orion* 118 (1969): 73.

Donoghue, Denis, *The Ordinary Universe: Soundings in Modern Literature*, N.Y.: Macmillan, 1968, 199-203.

Dutton, R. R., *Saul Bellow*, 1971 ed., 119-38; rev. ed., 1982, 114-34.

Egmond, Peter V., "Herzog's Quotation of Walt Whitman," *WWR* 13, ii (June, 1967): 54-6.

Finkelstein, S., *Existentialism and Alienation in American Literature*, 264-6.

Fisch, Harold, "The Hero as Jew: Reflections on HERZOG," *Judaism* 17 (1968): 42-54.

Flamm, Dudley, "Herzog—Victim or Hero?" *ZAA* 17, ii (1969): 174-88.

Fortson, Kay K., "Saul Bellow's Use of Imagery as Metaphor in HERZOG, MR. SAMMLER'S PLANET, and HUMBOLDT'S GIFT," *DAI* 40 (1979): 3288A-89A.

Fuchs, Daniel, "HERZOG: The Making of a Novel," in Trachtenberg, S., ed., *Critical Essays on Saul Bellow*, 101-21.

Galloway, David D., "Moses-Bloom-Herzog: Bellow's Every-man," *SoR* 2 (Winter, 1966): 61-76. Also in Galloway, D. D., *Absurd Hero*, 123-39.

Gard, Roger, "Saul Bellow," *Delta* (Cambridge, Eng.), No. 36 (Summer, 1965): 27-30.

Garrett, George, "To Do Right in a Bad World: Saul Bellow's HERZOG," *HC* 2, ii (April, 1965): 1-12.

Gerson, Steven M., "Paradise Sought: The Modern American Adam in Bellow's HERZOG," *McNR* 24 (1977-78): 50-7.

Gill, Brendan, "Surprised by Joy," *NY* 40 (Oct. 3, 1964): 218-22.

Gindin, J., *Harvest of a Quiet Eye*, 326-36.

Goldman, Liela, "Bellow's Moses Herzog," *Expl* 37, iv (Summer, 1979): Item 26.

_____, "On the Character of Ravitch in Saul Bellow's HER-ZOG," *AN&Q* 19, vii-viii (1981): 115-16.

Gross, Beverly, "Bellow's Herzog," *ChiR* 17, ii-iii (1964-65): 217-21.

Guttmann, A., *Jewish Writer in America*, 210-17.

_____, "Saul Bellow's Humane Comedy," in Cohen, S. B., ed., *Comic Relief*, 142-7.

Hall, J., *Lunatic Giant in the Drawing Room*, 163-79.

Harper, H. M., Jr., *Desperate Faith*, 51-62.

Hermans, Rob, "The Mystical Element in Saul Bellow's HER-ZOG," *DQR* 11, ii (1981): 104-17.

Hill, Johns S., "The Letters of Moses Herzog: A Symbolic Mir-ror," *SHum* 2, ii (Summer, 1971): 40-5.

Hoffman, Michael J., "From Cohen to Herzog," *YR* 58, iii (Spring, 1969): 348-58.

Howe, Irving, "Odysseus, Flat on His Back," *NRep* (Sept. 19, 1964): 21-4, 26. Also in Harrison, G. A., ed., *Critic as Artist*, 181-91. Also as "Down and Out in New York and Chicago," in Howe, I., *Critical Point*, 121-9.

Hulley, Kathleen, "Disintegration as Symbol of Communitiy: A Study of THE RAINBOW, WOMEN IN LOVE, LIGHT IN AUGUST, PRISONER OF GRACE, EXCEPT THE LORD, NOT HONOUR MORE and HERZOG," *DAI* 34 (1974): 6643A-44A.

Josipovici, Gabriel, "Bellow and Herzog," *Encounter* 37, v (Nov., 1971): 49-55.

_____, "HERZOG: Freedom and Wit," *World and the Book*, 221-35.

Kannan, Lakshmi, "Professor Herzog's Academy," *JEnS* 12, i (1980): 785-9.

Kaplan, Harold, "The Second Fall of Man," *Salmagundi* 30 (Sum-mer, 1975): 66-89.

Kazin, Alfred, "My Friend Saul Bellow," *Atlantic* 215 (Jan., 1965): 53-4.

Kemnitz, Charles, "Narration and Consciousness in HER-ZOG," *SBN* 1, ii (Spring-Summer, 1982): 1-6.

Kermode, F., *NStat* 69 (Feb. 5, 1965): 200-1. Also in Kermode, F., *Continuities*, 221-7.

Knopp, Josephine Z., "Jewish America: Saul Bellow," *Trial of Judaism in Contemporary Jewish Writing*, 129-38.

Kuehn, Robert E., "Fiction Chronicle," *WSCL* 6 (1965): 132-3.

Kulshrestha, C., *Saul Bellow*, 114-32.

Kumar, P. Shiv, "From *Kavanah* to *Mitzvah*: A Perspective on HERZOG and MR. SAMMLER'S PLANET," *IJAS* 10, ii (July, 1980): 30-9.

Lehan, R., *Dangerous Crossing*, 125-30.

Le Master, J. R., "Saul Bellow: On Looking for a Way Through the Cracks," in Collmer, R. G., and J. W. Herring, eds., *American Bypaths*, 131-4.

Löfroth, Erik, "Herzog's Predicament: Saul Bellow's View of Modern Man," *SN* 44, ii (1972): 315-25.

Ludwig, Jack, "The Wayward Reader," *Holiday* 37 (Feb., 1965): 16-19.

Lutwack, L., *Heroic Fiction*, 91-100.

Malin, I., *Saul Bellow's Fiction*, 145-62.

McCadden, J. F., *Flight from Women in the Fiction of Saul Bellow*, 131-61.

McConnell, F. D., *Four Postwar American Novelists*, 36-42.

Mellard, James M., "Consciousness Fills the Void: Herzog, His-tory, and the Hero in the Modern World," *MFS* 25, i (Spring, 1979): 75-91.

Morrow, Patrick, "Threat and Accommodation: The Novels of Saul Bellow," *MQ* 8 (Summer, 1967): 406-10.

Mosher, Harold F., Jr., "Herzog's Quest," in *Le Voyage dans la littérature anglo-saxonne*, Actes du Congrès de Nice (1971): Soc. des Anglicistes de l' Enseignement Superieur, Paris: Didier, 1972, 169-79.

_____, "The Synthesis of Past and Present in Saul Bellow's HERZOG," *WascanaR* 6, i (1971): 28-38.

Noble, D. W., *Eternal Adam and the New World Garden*, 221-3.

Opdahl, K. M., *Novels of Saul Bellow*, 140-66.

Park, Sue S., "The Keystone and the Arch: Another Look at Structure in HERZOG," *MNAL* 2, iv (1978): Item 30.

Pearce, Richard, "The Ambiguous Assault of Henderson and Herzog," in Rovit, E., ed., *Saul Bellow*, 75-80.

Pinsker, Sanford, "Moses Herzog's Fall into the Quotidian," *STwC* 14 (Fall, 1974): 105-15.

_____, "Saul Bellow in the Classroom," *CE* 34, vii (April, 1973): 975-82.

_____, *Schlemiel as Metaphor*, 151-7.

Poirier, Richard, "Bellows to Herzog," *PR* 32 (Spring, 1965): 264-71. Also, revised, as "Herzog, or, Bellow in Trouble," in Rovit, E., ed., *Saul Bellow*, 81-9.

Porter, Gilbert, "HERZOG: A Transcendental Solution to an Existential Problem," *ForumH* 7, ii (Spring, 1969): 32-6.

Porter, M. G., *Whence the Power?* 146-59.

Price, Nancy L., "'Certain Flowers Persist': Bellow's Image of Hope in HENDERSON, HERZOG, and HUMBOLDT," *CCTE* 46 (1981): 50-7.

Raban, J., "Narrative: Dramatized Consciousness," *Technique of Modern Fiction*, 53-5.

Rahv, P., "Saul Bellow's Progress," *Myth and the Powerhouse*, 218-24. Also in Rahv, P., *Literature and the Sixth Sense*, 392-7.

Read, Forrest, "HERZOG: A Review," *Epoch* 14 (Fall, 1964): 81-96. Also in Malin, I., ed., *Saul Bellow and the Critics*, 184-206.

Richter, D., *Fable's End*, 185-92.

Rodrigues, Eusebio L., "Herzog and Hegel," *NMAL* 2, ii (1978): Item 16.

_____, "The Two Manifestations of Jeremiah: Bellow's Crea-tive Use of a Morsel of Experience," *NMAL* 5, i (1980): Item 6.

Rovit, Earl, "Bellow in Occupancy," *ASch* 34 (Spring, 1965): 292-8. Also in Malin, I., ed., *Saul Bellow and the Critics*, 177-83.

Rubin, Louis D., "Southerners and Jews," *SoR* 2 (1966): 705-8. Also in Rubin, L. D., Jr., *Curious Death of the Novel*, 271-5.

Rupp, Richard H., "Saul Bellow: Belonging to the World in General," *Celebration in Postwar American Fiction*, 204-8.

Samuel, Maurice, "My Friend, the Late Moses Herzog," *Midstream* 12 (April, 1966): 3-25.

Scheer-Schäzler, B., *Saul Bellow*, 92-111.

_____, "Short Story and Modern Novel: A Comparative Analysis of Two Texts," *OL* 25, iv (1970): 338-51.

Schraepen, Edmond, "HERZOG: Disconnection and Connection," in Schraepen, E., ed., *Saul Bellow and His Work*, 119-29.

Schueler, Mary D., "The Figure of Madeleine in HERZOG," *NConL* 1, iii (May, 1971): 5-7.

Schulz, M. F., "Saul Bellow and the Burden of Selfhood," *Radical Sophistication*, 131-44.

Scott, Nathan A., Jr., "Sola Gratia—The Principle of Saul Bellow's Fiction," in Scott, N. A., Jr., ed., *Adversity and Grace*, 52-6. Also in Scott, N. A., Jr., *Craters of the Spirit*, 2600-3.

_____, *Three American Moralists*, 130-4.

Solotaroff, Theodore, "Napoleon Street," *Red Hot Vacuum*, 94-102.

Spender, Stephen, "Bellow in Search of Himself," in Encyclopaedia Britannica, *Great Ideas Today*, 1965, 170-3.

Stock, Irvin, "The Novels of Saul Bellow," *SoR* 3 (Winter, 1967): 36-42.

Sullivan, Quentin M., "The Downward Transcendence of Moses Herzog," *GyS* 3, i (1975): 44-50.

Sullivan, Victoria, "The Battle of the Sexes in Three Bellow Novels," in Rovit, E., ed., *Saul Bellow*, 102-5.

Tanner, T., *City of Words*, 299-305.

_____, *Saul Bellow*, 87-102.

_____, "Saul Bellow: The Flight from Monologue," *Encounter* 24 (Feb., 1965): 61-6.

Trachtenberg, Stanley, "Saul Bellow's *Luftmenschen*: The Compromise with Reality," *Crit* 9, iii (1967): 55-8.

Uphaus, Suzanne H., "From Innocence to Experience: A Study of HERZOG," *DR* 46 (Spring, 1966): 67-78.

Van Egmond, Peter, "Herzog's Quotation of Walt Whitman," *WWR* 13 (June, 1967): 54-6.

Vardaman, James M., Jr., "Herzog's Letters," *JEI* 9-10 (1979): 129-49.

Walcutt, C. C., *Man's Changing Mask*, 352-5.

Walker, Marshall, "Herzog: The Professor as Drop-Out?, *ESA* 15, i (Mar., 1972): 39-51.

Waterman, Andrew, "Saul Bellow's Ineffectual Angels," in Benedikz, B. S., ed., *On the Novel*, 229-33.

Weber, Ronald, "Bellow's Thinkers," *WHR* 22, iv (Autumn, 1968): 305-13.

Weinberg, H., *New Novel in America*, 103-7.

Weinstein, Norman, "HERZOG, Order and Entropy," *ES* 54, iv (1973): 336-46.

Werner, C. H., *Paradoxical Resolutions*, 124-32.

Wisse, Ruth R., "The Schlemiel as Liberal Humanist," in Rovit, E., ed., *Saul Bellow*, 90-100. From Wisse, R. R., *Schlemiel as Modern Hero*, 92-107.

Young, James D., "Bellow's View of the Heart," *Crit* 7, iii (1965): 5-17.

HUMBOLDT'S GIFT

Anders, Jaroslaw, "Saul Bellow's Treatment of Ideas in Three Major Works," *KN* 27, iv (1980): 455-66.

Bartz, Fredrica K., "HUMBOLDT'S GIFT and the Myth of the Artist in America," *SCR* 15, i (Fall, 1982): 79-83.

Bradbury, Malcolm, "The It and the We: Saul Bellow's New Novel," *Encounter* 45, v (Nov., 1975): 61-7.

_____, *Saul Bellow*, 85-91.

Bragg, Melvyn, "Off the Couch by Christmas," *Listener* 94 (Nov. 20, 1975): 674-6. [Interview.]

Buranarom, Nantana Y., "Saul Bellow's Anatomy of Love: A Study of the Theme of Love in THE ADVENTURES OF AUGIE MARCH, HERZOG, and HUMBOLDT'S GIFT," *DAI* 40 (1980): 5863A-64A.

Busby, Mark, "Castaways, Cannibals, and the Function of Art in Saul Bellow's HUMBOLDT'S GIFT," *SCB* 41, iv (Winter, 1981): 91-4.

Campbell, Jeff H., "The Artist as American Dreamer: HUMBOLDT'S GIFT," *JASAT* 9 (1978): 3-10.

Chavkin, Allan, "Baron Humboldt and Bellow's Von Humboldt Fleisher: Success and Failure in HUMBOLDT'S GIFT," *NConL* 10, ii (1980): 11-12.

Clayton, John, "'HUMBOLDT'S GIFT': Transcendence and the Flight from Death," in Schraepen, E., ed., *Saul Bellow and His Work*, 31-48.

_____, *Saul Bellow*, 2nd ed., 262-84.

Cohen, Sarah B., "Comedy and Guilt in HUMBOLDT'S GIFT," *MFS* 25, i (Spring, 1979): 47-57.

Dougherty, David C., "Finding before Seeking: Theme in HENDERSON THE RAIN KING and HUMBOLDT'S GIFT," *MFS* 25, i (Spring, 1979): 93-101.

Dutton, R. R., *Saul Bellow*, 147-66.

Epstein, Seymour, "Bellow's Gift," *UDQ* 10, iv (1975): 35-50.

Estrin, Barbara L., "Recomposing Time: HUMBOLDT'S GIFT and RAGTIME," *DQ* 17, i (Spring, 1982): 16-31.

Fortson, Kay K., "Saul Bellow's Use of Imagery as Metaphor in HERZOG, MR. SAMMLER'S PLANET and HUMBOLDT'S GIFT," *DAI* 40 (1979): 3288A-89A.

Gitenstein, R. Barbara, "Saul Bellow of the 1970's and the Contemporary Use of History in Jewish-American Literature," *SBN* 1, ii (Spring-Summer, 1982): 7-17.

Goldman, Mark, "HUMBOLDT'S GIFT and the Case of the Split Protagonist," *MLS* 11, ii (1981): 3-16.

Guttman, Allen, "Saul Bellow's Humane Comedy," in Cohen, S. B., ed., *Comic Relief*, 148-51.

Kerner, David, "The Incomplete Dialectic of HUMBOLDT'S GIFT," *DR* 62, i (Spring, 1982): 14-35.

Kistler, Suzanne F., "Bellow's Man-Eating Comedy: Cannibal Imagery in HUMBOLDT'S GIFT," *NMAL* 2, i (1977): Item 8.

LeMaster, J. R., "Saul Bellow: On Looking for a Way Through the Cracks," in Collmer, R. G., and J. W. Herring, eds., *American Bypaths*, 138-44.

McCadden, J. F., *Flight from Women in the Fiction of Saul Bellow*, 187-212.

McConnell, F. D., *Four Postwar American Novelists*, 47-57.

Mowat, John, "HUMBOLDT'S GIFT: Bellow's 'Dejection Ode'," *DQR* 8, iii (1978): 184-201.

Nault, Marianne, "Humboldt the First," *AN&Q* 15, vi (1976/77): 88-9.

Newman, Judie, "Bellow's 'Indian Givers': HUMBOLDT'S GIFT," *JAmS* 15, ii (Aug., 1981): 231-8.

_____, "Saul Bellow: HUMBOLDT'S GIFT—the Comedy of History," *DUJ* 72 (Dec., 1979): 79-87.

Possler, K. E., "Cannibalism in HUMBOLDT'S GIFT," GyS 5, i (1978): 18-21.

Price, Nancy L., "'Certain Flowers Persist': Bellow's Image of Hope in HENDERSON, HERZOG, and HUMBOLDT," CCTE 46 (1981): 50-7.

Radner, Sanford, "The Woman Savior in HUMBOLDT'S GIFT," SBN 1, i (Fall, 1981): 22-5.

Rodgers, Bernard F., Jr., "Apologia pro Vita Sua: Biography and Autobiography in HUMBOLDT'S GIFT," KN 27, iv (1980): 439-53.

Rodrigues, Eusebio L., "The Two Manifestations of Jeremiah: Bellow's Creative Use of a Morsel of Experience," NMA1 5, i (1980): Item 6.

Rosenberg, Ruth, "Three Jewish Narrative Strategies in HUMBOLDT'S GIFT," MELUS 6, iv (1979): 59-66.

Rosenfeld, Alvin H., "Poet, Magician, and Anthroposophist: Saul Bellow's Latest Fiction," Midstream 21, x (Dec., 1975): 62-7.

Ryan, Steven T., "The Soul's Husband: Money in HUMBOLDT'S GIFT," Genre 13, i (1980): 111-21. Also in Male, R. R., ed., Money Talks, 111-21.

Schraepen, Edmond, "HUMBOLDT'S GIFT: A New Bellow?" ES 62, ii (April, 1981): 164-70.

Siegel, Ben, "Artists and Opportunists in Saul Bellow's HUMBOLDT'S GIFT," ConL 19, ii (Spring, 1978): 143-64. Also in Trachtenberg, S., ed., Critical Essays on Saul Bellow, 158-74.

Singh, Yashoda, "Saul Bellow and the Modern American City," OJES 17 (1981): 39-47.

Smith, Herbert J., "HUMBOLDT'S GIFT and Rudolf Steiner," CentR 22, iv (1978): 479-89.

Vinoda, Mrs., "Renewing Universal Connections: A Study of HUMBOLDT'S GIFT," JEnS 13, i (1981): 876-80.

Yetman, Michael G., "Who Would Not Sing for Humboldt?" ELH 48, iv (Winter, 1981): 935-51.

MR. SAMMLER'S PLANET

Alexander, Edward, "Imagining the Holocaust: MR. SAMMLER'S PLANET and Others," Judaism 22, iii (1973): 288-300.

Anders, Jaroslaw, "Saul Bellow's Treatment of Ideas in Three Major Works," KN 27, iv (1980): 455-66.

Atchity, Kenneth J., "Bellow's Mr. Sammler: 'The Last Man Given for Epitome'," RS 38, i (1970): 46-54.

Bailey, Jennifer M., "The Qualified Affirmation of Saul Bellow's Recent Work," JAmS 7, i (April, 1973): 67-76.

Bayley, John, "By Way of Mr. Sammler," Salmagundi 30 (Summer, 1975): 24-33.

Bolling, Douglass, "Intellectual and Aesthetic Dimensions of MR. SAMMLER'S PLANET," JNT 4, iii (1974): 188-203.

Bothwell, E. K., Alienation in the Jewish Amerian Novel of the Sixties, 153-70, 171-5. [Comparative review of HERZOG and MR. SAMMLER'S PLANET.]

Boyers, Robert, "Nature and Social Reality in Bellow's SAMMLER," Salmagundi 30 (Summer, 1975): 34-56. Also in CritQ 15, iii (Autumn, 1973): 251-71. Also in Trachtenberg, S., ed., Critical Essays on Saul Bellow, 122-40.

Bradbury, M., Saul Bellow, 78-82.

Bryant, J. H., Open Decision, 363-9.

Clayton, J. J., Saul Bellow, 2nd ed., 230-50.

Cohen, S. B., Saul Bellow's Enigmatic Laughter, 176-210.

Cushman, Keith, "Mr. Bellow's SAMMLER: The Evolution of a Contemporary Text," SNNTS 7, iii (Fall, 1975): 425-44. Also in Trachtenberg, S., ed., Critical Essays on Saul Bellow, 141-57.

Dutton, R. R., Saul Bellow, rev. ed., 1982, 135-46; 1971 ed., 155-64.

Finkelstein, Sidney, "The Anti-Hero of Updike, Bellow and Malamud," AmD 7, ii (1972): 12-14, 30.

Fortson, Kay K., "Saul Bellow's Use of Imagery as Metaphor in HERZOG, MR. SAMMLER'S PLANET, and HUMBOLDT'S GIFT," DAI 40 (1979): 3288A-89A.

Galloway, David, "MR. SAMMLER'S PLANET: Bellow's Failure of Nerve," MFS 19, i (Spring, 1973): 17-28.

Gelfant, Blanche, "In 'Terror of the Sublime': Mr. Sammler and Odin," NMAL 2, iv (1978): Item 25.

Gindin, J., Harvest of a Quiet Eye, 334-6.

Gittleman, Sol, "MR. SAMMLER'S PLANET Ten Years Later: Looking Back on the Crisis of 'Mishpocha'," Judaism 30 (Fall, 1981): 480-3.

Glickman, Susan, "THE WORLD AS WILL AND IDEA: A Comparative Study of AN AMERICAN DREAM and MR. SAMMLER'S PLANET," MFS 28, iv (Winter, 1982-83): 569-82.

Goldman, Liela, "The Source for Saul Bellow's MR. SAMMLER'S PLANET," AN&Q 20, vii-viii (1982): 117-19.

Grossman, Edward, "The Bitterness of Saul Bellow," Midstream 16, vii (Aug.-Sept., 1970): 3-15.

Grubb, Daniel S., "Another Gulliver?" StHum 4, i (Mar., 1974): 3-9.

Guthridge, George, "The Structure of Twentieth-Century Society: The Concept of the Intellectual in Bellow's Mr. SAMMLER'S PLANET," SBN 1, i (Fall, 1981): 6-10.

Guttmann, A., Jewish Writer in America, 217-21.

_____, "Saul Bellow's Mr. Sammler," ConL 14, ii (Apr., 1973): 157-68.

Harris, James N., "One Critical Approach to MR. SAMMLER'S PLANET," TCL 18, iv (Oct., 1972): 235-50.

Held, George, "Men on the Moon: American Novelists Explore Lunar Space," MQR 18, ii (1979): 328-33.

Howe, Irving, "Odysseus Flat on His Back," NRep (Sept. 19, 1964): 21-4, 26. Also as "Down and Out in New York and Chicago," Critical Point, 130-6.

Jones, Roger, "Artistry and the Depth of Life: Aspects of Attitude and Technique in MR. SAMMLER'S PLANET," AWR 25, lvi (1975): 138-53.

Kar, Prafulla C., "What It Means to Be Exactly Human: A Study of Bellow's MR. SAMMLER'S PLANET," in Chander, J., and N. S. Pradhan, eds., Studies in American Literature, 97-109.

Kistler, Suzanne F., "Epic Structure and Statement in MR. SAMMLER'S PLANET," NMAL 2, iv (1978): Item 28.

Klein, Jeffrey, "Armies of the Planet: A Comparative Analysis of Norman Mailer's and Saul Bellow's Political Visions," Soundings 58, i (Spring, 1975): 69-83.

Knopp, Josephine Z., "Jewish America: Saul Bellow," Trial of Judaism in Contemporary Jewish Writing, 138-56.

Kulshrestha, C., Saul Bellow, 132-49.

Kumar, P. Shiv, "From Kavanah to Mitzvah: A Perspective on HERZOG and MR. SAMMLER'S PLANET," IJAS l0, iii (July, 1980): 30-9.

_____, "Yahudim and Ostjude: Social Stratification in MR. SAMMLER'S PLANET," LHY 21, ii (1980): 53-67.

Kuna, F. M., "The European Culture Game: Mr. Bellow's Planet," ES 53, vi (Dec., 1972): 531-44.

Lehan, R., *Dangerous Crossing*, 130-3.

Le Master, J. R., "Saul Bellow: On Looking for a Way Through the Cracks," in Collmer, R. G., and J. W. Herring, eds., *American Bypaths*, 134-8.

Levidova, I., "MR. SAMMLER'S PLANET," in Vroon, R., tr., *20th Century American Literature: A Soviet View*, 449-52.

Loris, Michelle C., "MR. SAMMLER'S PLANET: The Terms of the Covenant," *Ren* 30, iv (1978): 217-23.

Maloney, Stephen R., "Half-Way to Byzantium: MR. SAMMLER'S PLANET and the Modern Tradition," *SCR* 6, i (Nov., 1973): 31-40.

Manning, Gerald F., "The Humanizing Imagination: A Theme in MR. SAMMLER'S PLANET," *ESC* 3, ii (1977): 216-22.

May, John R., "Myth and Parable in American Fiction," *Thought* 57, ccxxiv (Mar., 1982): 51-61.

McCadden, J. F., *Flight from Women in the Fiction of Saul Bellow*, 163-85.

McConnell, F. D., *Four Postwar American Novelists*, 42-7.

Mesher, David R., "Three Men on the Moon: Friedman, Updike, Bellow, and Apollo Eleven," *RS* 47, ii (June, 1979): 72-5.

O'Brien, Maureen, S. N. D., "Seeing and Knowing in MR. SAMMLER'S PLANET," *SALit* 12 (1976): 1-8.

Overton, Harvey, "Sharing Mr. Sammler's Planet: Intellect and Conscience in Science and Technology," *JGE* 32, iv (Winter, 1981): 309-19.

Pinsker, Sanford, "Saul Bellow in the Classroom," *CE* 34, vii (April, 1973): 975-82.

Porter, M. G., *Whence the Power?* 160-80.

Rama Murty, M. S., "The Creative Intransigent: A Study of MR. SAMMLER'S PLANET," *JEnS* 12, i (1980): 800-11.

Russell, Mariann, "White Man's Black Man: Three Views," *CLAJ* 17 (1973): 93-100.

Salter, D. P. M., "Optimism and Reaction in Saul Bellow's Recent Work," *CritQ* 14, i (Spring, 1972): 57-66.

Satyanarayana, M. R., "The Reality Teacher as Hero: A Study of Saul Bellow's MR. SAMMLER'S PLANET," *OJES* 8, ii (1971): 55-68.

Scheer-Schäzler, B., *Saul Bellow*, 118-26.

Scheick, William J., "Circle Sailing in Bellow's MR. SAMMLER'S PLANET," *ELWIU* 5, i (1978): 95-101.

Schneider, Joseph L., "The Immigrant Experience in PNIN and MR. SAMMLER'S PLANET," in *On Poets and Poetry: Second Series*, 33-5, 41-8.

Schroeter, James, "Saul Bellow and Individualism," *Études de lettres* 11, i (1978): 22-8.

Schulz, Max F., "Mr. Bellow's Perigee, Or, The Lowered Horizon of MR. SAMMLER'S PLANET," in Malin, I., ed., *Contemporary American Jewish Literature*, 117-32.

Scott, N. A., Jr., *Three American Moralists*, 136-46.

Sharma, D. K., "MR. SAMMLER'S PLANET: Another 'Passage' to India," *PURB* 4, i (April, 1973): 97-104.

Siegel, Ben, "Saul Bellow and Mr. Sammler: Absurd Seekers of High Qualities," in Rovit, E., ed., *Saul Bellow*, 122-34.

Sloss, Henry, "Europe's Last Gasp," *Shen* 22, i (Fall, 1970): 82-6.

Stafford, W. T., *Books Speaking to Books*, 73-4, 76-84.

Vernier, Jean-Pierre, "Mr. Sammler's Lesson," in Johnson, I. D., and C. Johnston, eds., *Les Américanistes*, 16-36.

Waterman, Andrew, "Saul Bellow's Ineffectual Angels," in Benedikz, B. S., ed., *On the Novel*, 233-8.

Weinstein, Mark, "The Fundamental Elements in MR. SAMMLER'S PLANET," *SBN* 1, ii (Spring-Summer, 1982): 18-26.

Wirth-Nesher, Hana, and Andrea C. Malamut, "Jewish and Human Survival on Bellow's Planet," *MFS* 25, i (Spring, 1979): 59-74.

SEIZE THE DAY

Alter, Robert, "The Stature of Saul Bellow," *Midstream* 10 (Dec., 1964): 107-10.

Baker, Robert, *ChiR* 2 (Spring, 1957): 107-10.

Bordewyk, Gordon, "Saul Bellow's DEATH OF A SALESMAN," *SBN* 1, i (Fall, 1981): 18-21.

Bowen, Robert O., *NWR* 1 (Spring, 1957): 52-6.

Bradbury, M., *Saul Bellow*, 52-6.

Bryant, J. H., *Open Decision*, 348-50.

Chase, Richard, *Ctary* 27 (April, 1959). Also in Malin, I., ed., *Saul Bellow and the Critics*, 30-2.

Chavkin, Allan, "'The Hollywood Thread' and the First Draft of Saul Bellow's SEIZE THE DAY," *SNNTS* 14, i (1982): 82-94.

_____, "Suffering and Wilhelm Reich's Theory of Character-Armoring in Saul Bellow's SEIZE THE DAY," *EIL* 9, i (1982): 133-7.

Ciancio, Ralph, "The Achievement of Saul Bellow's SEIZE THE DAY," in Staley, Thomas F., and L. F. Zimmerman, eds., *Literature and Theology*, Tulsa, Okla.: Un. of Tulsa, 1969, 49-80.

Clayton, J. J., *Saul Bellow*, 28-9, 59-60, 69-74,, 92-6, 105-6, 128-34, 247-51.

_____, *Saul Bellow*, 2nd ed., 28-9, 59-60, 69-74, 92-6, 105-6, 128-34, 235-6, 302-4.

Cohen, S. B., *Saul Bellow's Enigmatic Laughter*, 90-114.

Cronin, Gloria L., "Saul Bellow's Quarrel with Modernism in SEIZE THE DAY," *Encyclia* 57 (1980): 95-102.

Davis, Robert G., in Balakian, N., and C. Simmons, eds., *Creative Present*, 124-7.

Dutton, R. R., *Saul Bellow*, 1971 ed., 83-97. Rev. ed., 1982, 75-90.

Eisinger, Chester E., "Saul Bellow: Love and Identity," *Accent* 18 (Summer, 1958): 199-203.

Fossum, Robert R., "The Devil and Saul Bellow," *CLS* 3 (1966): 200-4. Also in Panichas, G. A., ed., *Mansions of the Spirit*, 349-53.

Freedman, Ralph, "Saul Bellow: The Illusion of Environment," *WSCL* 1, i (Winter, 1960): 55-7. Also in Malin, I., ed., *Saul Bellow and the Critics*, 57-9.

Galloway, David D., *Absurd Hero*, 104-10.

_____, "The Absurd Man as Picaro: The Novels of Saul Bellow," *TSLL* 6 (Summer, 1964): 241-4.

Geismar, M., "Saul Bellow: Novelist of the Intellectuals," *American Moderns*, 218-24. Also in Malin, I., ed., *Saul Bellow and the Critics*, 19-24.

Giannone, Richard, "Saul Bellow's Idea of Self: A Reading of SEIZE THE DAY," *Ren* 27, iv (Summer, 1975): 193-205.

Gill, Brendan, *NY* 32 (Jan. 5, 1957): 69-70.

Gindin, G., *Harvest of a Quiet Eye*, 319-22.

Gold, Herbert, "The Discovered Self," *Nation* 183 (Nov. 17, 1957): 435-6.

Guttmann, A., *Jewish Writer in America*, 198-201.

Hall, J., *Lunatic Giant in the Drawing Room*, 159-62.

Handy, W. J., *Modern Fiction*, 119-30.

_____, "Saul Bellow and the Naturalistic Hero," *TSLL* 5 (Winter, 1964): 538-45.

Harper, H. M., Jr., *Desperate Faith*, 32-9.

Hassan, I., *Radical Innocence*, 311-16.

Hoffman, Frederick J., in Moore, H. T., ed., *Contemporary American Novelists*, 93-4.

Jefchak, Andrew, "Family Struggles in SEIZE THE DAY," *SSF* 11, iii (1974): 297-302.

Kazin, Alfred, *NYTBR* (Nov. 18, 1956): 5+.

_____, "Bellow's Purgatory," *NYRB* (Mar. 28, 1968): 34-6.

Kondo, Kyoko, "Pursuit of One Theme: Saul Bellow's Early Novels, DANGLING MAN, THE VICTIM, SEIZE THE DAY," *SES* 3 (1978): 86-98.

Kulshrestha, C., *Saul Bellow*, 77-94.

_____, "SEIZE THE DAY and the Bellow Chronology," *LCrit* 13, iii (1978): 29-33.

Lehan, R., *Dangerous Crossing*, 118-21.

Le Master, J. L., "Saul Bellow: On Looking for a Way Through the Cracks," in Collmer, R. G., and J. W. Herring, eds., *American Bypaths*, 124-7.

Levine, Paul, "Saul Bellow: The Affirmation of the Philosophical Fool," *Per* 10 (Winter, 1959): 172-6.

Ludwig, J., *Recent American Novelists*, 15-16. Also in Kostelanetz, R., ed., *On Contemporary Literature*, 296-7.

Lutwack, L., *Heroic Fiction*, 89-91.

Malin, Irving, in *Jewish Heritage Reader*, 261-3.

_____, *Saul Bellow's Fiction*, 66-8.

Mathis, James C., "The Theme of SEIZE THE DAY," *Crit* 7 (Spring-Summer, 1965): 43-5.

McCadden, J. F., *Flight from Women in the Fiction of Saul Bellow*, 89-108.

McConnell, F. D., *Four Postwar American Novelists*, 28-30.

Morahg, Gilead, "The Art of Dr. Tamkin: Matter and Manner in SEIZE THE DAY," *MFS* 25, i (Spring, 1979): 103-16.

Morrow, Patrick, "Threat and Accommodation: The Novels of Saul Bellow," *MQ* 8 (Summer, 1967): 391-4.

Mukerji, Nirmal, "A Reading of Saul Bellow's SEIZE THE DAY," *LCrit* 9, i (Winter, 1969): 48-53.

Nelson, G. B., *Ten Versions of America*, 129-45.

Opdahl, K. M., *Novels of Saul Bellow*, 96-117.

Pinsker, S., *Schlemiel as Metaphor*, 148-51.

Podhoretz, N., "The Adventures of Saul Bellow," *Doings and Undoings*, 219-24.

Porter, M. Gilbert, "The Scene as Image: A Reading of SEIZE THE DAY," in Rovit, E., ed., *Saul Bellow*, 52-71.

_____, *Whence the Power?* 102-26.

Rans, Geoffrey, "The Novels of Saul Bellow," *REL* 4, iv (Oct., 1963): 26-7.

Raper, J. R., "Running Contrary Ways: Saul Bellow's SEIZE THE DAY," *SHR* 10, ii (1976): 157-68.

Richmond, Lee J., "The Maladroit, the Medico, and the Magician: Saul Bellow's SEIZE THE DAY," *TCL* 19, i (Jan., 1973): 15-26.

Rodrigues, Eusebio R., "Bellow's Confidence Man," *NConL* 3, i (Jan., 1973): 6-8.

_____, "Reichianism in SEIZE THE DAY," in Trachtenberg, S., ed., *Critical Essays on Saul Bellow*, 89-100.

Rugoff, Milton, *MYTBR* (Nov. 18, 1956): 3.

Rupp, Richard H., "Saul Bellow: Belonging to the World in General," *Celebration in Postwar American Fiction*, 199-201.

Scheer-Schäzler, B., *Saul Bellow*, 62-71.

Schwartz, Edward, "Chronicles of the City," *NRep* 135 (Dec. 3, 1956): 20-1.

Scott, Nathan A., Jr., "Sola Gratia—The Principle of Saul Bellow's Fiction," in Scott, N. A., Jr., ed., *Adversity and Grace*, 48-50. Also in Scott, N. A., Jr., *Craters of the Spirit*, 255-7.

Shear, Walter, "STEPPENWOLF and SEIZE THE DAY," *SBN* 1, i (Fall, 1981): 32-4.

Sicherman, Carol M., "Bellow's SEIZE THE DAY: Reverberations and Hollow Sounds," *STwC* 15 (Spring, 1975): 1-31.

Stern, Richard G., *KR* 21 (Autumn, 1959): 655-61.

Stock, Irvin, "The Novels of Saul Bellow," *SoR* 3 (Winter, 1967): 27-31.

Sullivan, Victoria, "The Battle of the Sexes in Three Bellow Novels," in Rovit, E., ed., *Saul Bellow*, 105-7.

Swados, Harvey, *NY Post Week-End Mag* (Nov. 18, 1957): 11.

Tanner, T., *Saul Bellow*, 58-70.

Trachtenberg, Stanley, "Saul Bellow's *Luftmenschen*: The Compromise with Reality," *Crit* 9, iii (1967): 49-52.

Trowbridge, Clinton W., "Water Imagery in SEIZE THE DAY," *Crit* 9, iii (1967): 62-73.

Tuerck, Richard, "Tommy Wilhelm-Wilhelm Adler: Names in SEIZE THE DAY," in Tarpley, Fred, ed., *Naughty Names*, Commerce, TX: Names Institute Pr., 1975, 27-33.

Weiss, Daniel, "Caliban on Prospero: A Psychoanalytic Study on the Novel SEIZE THE DAY, by Saul Bellow," *AI* 19 (Fall, 1962): 277-306. Also in Malin, I., ed., *Psychoanalysis and American Fiction*, 279-307. Also in Malin, I., ed., *Saul Bellow and the Critics*, 114-41.

West, Ray B., Jr., *SR* 64 (Summer, 1957): 498-508.

THE VICTIM

Allen, W., *Modern Novel*, 324-5.

Baumbach, J., "The Double Vision: THE VICTIM," *Landscape of Nightmare*, 35-54.

Bradbury, M., *Saul Bellow*, 40-7.

_____, "Saul Bellow's THE VICTIM," *CritQ* 5 (Summer, 1963): 119-28.

Bryant, J. H., *Open Decision*, 344-8.

Chavkin, Allan, "Ivan Karamazov's Rebellion and Bellow's THE VICTIM," *PLL* 16, iii (1980): 316-20.

Clayton, J. J., *Saul Bellow*, 139-65, 240-1. Also in Rovit, E., ed., *Saul Bellow*, 31-51.

_____, *Saul Bellow*, 2nd ed., 139-65, 294-5.

Cohen, S. B., *Saul Bellow's Enigmatic Laughter*, 40-68.

Davis, Robert G., in Balakian, N., and C. Simmons, eds., *Creative Present*, 116-20.

Dutton, R. R., *Saul Bellow*, 1971 ed., 33-51. Rev. ed., 1982, 20-41.

Eisinger, Chester E., *Fiction of the Forties*, 340-54.

_____, "Saul Bellow: Love and Identity," *Accent* 18 (Summer, 1958): 188-92.

Farrelly, John, *NRep* 117 (Dec. 8, 1947): 27-8.

Fiedler, L., *Love and Death in the American Novel*, 360-1.

Frank, Reuben, "Saul Bellow: The Evolution of a Contemporary Novelist," *WR* 18 (Winter, 1954): 105-8.

Freedman, Ralph, "Saul Bellow: The Illusion of Environment," *WSCL* 1, i (Winter, 1960): 52-5. Also in Malin, I., ed., *Saul Bellow and the Critics*, 53-7.

Galloway, David D., *Absurd Hero*, 89-94.

_____, "The Absurd Man as Picaro: The Novels of Saul Bellow," *TSLL* 6 (Summer, 1964): 231-4.

Geismar, M., "Saul Bellow: Novelist of the Intellectuals," *American Moderns*, 213-16. Also in Malin, I., ed., *Saul Bellow and the Critics*, 13-16.

Gilmore, Thomas B., "Allbee's Drinking," *TCL* 28, iv (Winter, 1982): 381-96.

Gindin, J., *Harvest of a Quiet Eye*, 309-16.

Gordon, Andrew, "'Pushy Jew': Leventhal in THE VICTIM," *MFS* 25, i (Spring, 1979): 129-38.

Guttmann, A., *Jewish Writer in America*, 183-9.

Hall, J., *Lunatic Giant in the Drawing Room*, 138-49.

Harper, H. M., Jr., *Desperate Faith*, 16-23.

Hassan, I., *Radical Innocence*, 299-303.

Hoffman, Frederick J., in Moore, H. T., ed., *Contemporary American Novelists*, 85-8.

Jensen, Emily, "Saul Bellow's THE VICTIM: A View of Modern Man," *Literature* No. 4 (1963): 38-44.

Knopp, Josephine Z., "Jewish America: Saul Bellow," *Trial of Judaism in Contemporary Jewish Writing*, 127-9.

Kondo, Kyoko, "Pursuit of One Theme: Saul Bellow's Early Novels, DANGLING MAN, THE VICTIM, SEIZE THE DAY," *SES* 3 (1978): 86-98.

Kremer, S. Lillian, "Acquiescence to Anti-Semitism in THE VICTIM: An Alternate Reading of Bellow's Daniel Harkavy," *SBN* 1, ii (Spring-Summer, 1982): 27-30.

Lehan, R., *Dangerous Crossing*, 111-15.

Le Master, J. L., "Saul Bellow: On Looking for a Way Through the Cracks," in Collmer, R. G., and J. W. Herring, eds., *American Bypaths*, 118-20.

Le Pellec, Yves, "New York in Summer: Its Symbolical Function in THE VICTIM," *Caliban* 8 (1971): 101-10.

Levine, Paul, "Saul Bellow: The Affirmation of the Philosophical Fool," *Per* 10 (Winter, 1959): 165-7.

Malin, Irving, in *Jewish Heritage Reader*, 259-60.

_____, *Saul Bellow's Fiction*, 59-63.

McCadden, J. F., *Flight from Women in the Fiction of Saul Bellow*, 37-59.

McConnell, F. D., *Four Postwar American Novelists*, 15-20.

Merkowitz, David R., "Bellow's Early Phase: Self and Society in DANGLING MAN, THE VICTIM, and THE ADVENTURES OF AUGIE MARCH," *DAI* 32 (1972): 6439A-40A (Mich.).

Miller, Karl, "Leventhal," *NStat* (Sept. 10, 1965): 360-1.

Morrow, Patrick, "Threat and Accommodation: The Novels of Saul Bellow," *MQ* 8 (Summer, 1967): 395-7.

Murai, Mami, "A Study of THE VICTIM by Saul Bellow: Human Mortality and Chain of Life," *KAL* 23 (May, 1982):85-8.

Nilsen, Helge N., "Anti-Semitism and Persecution Complex: A Comment on Saul Bellow's THE VICTIM," *ES* 60, ii (1979): 183-91.

Opdahl, K. M., *Novels of Saul Bellow*, 51-69.

Pinsker, S., *Schlemiel as Metaphor*, 140-7.

Podhoretz, N., "The Adventures of Saul Bellow," *Doings and Undoings*, 211-15.

Porter, M. G., *Whence the Power?* 29-60.

Rans, Geoffrey, "The Novels of Saul Bellow," *REL* 4, iv (Oct., 1963): 20-2.

Rupp, Richard A., "Saul Bellow: Belonging to the World in General," *Celebration in Postwar American Fiction*, 192-5.

Scheer-Schäzler, B., *Saul Bellow*, 17-28.

Scott, Nathan A., Jr., "Sola Gratia—The Principle of Saul Bellow's Fiction," in Scott, N. A., Jr., ed., *Adversity and Grace*, 40-3. Also in Scott, N. A., Jr., *Craters of the Spirit*, 246-9.

_____, *Three American Moralists*, 116-19.

Shastri, N. R., "Self and Society in Saul Bellow's THE VICTIM," *OJES* 8, ii (1971): 105-12.

Stock, Irvin, "The Novels of Saul Bellow," *SoR* 3 (Winter, 1967): 19-23.

Tanner, T., *Saul Bellow*, 26-37.

Trachtenberg, Stanley, "Saul Bellow's *Luftmenschen*: The Compromise with Reality," *Crit* 9, iii (1967): 41-3.

Trilling, Diana, *Nation* 166 (Jan. 3, 1948): 24-5.

BIBLIOGRAPHY

Field, Leslie, and John Z. Guzlowski, "Criticism of Saul Bellow: A Selected Checklist," *MFS* 25, i (Spring, 1979): 149-71.

Galloway, D. D., *Absurd Hero*, 220-6.

Lercangee, Francine, *Saul Bellow: A Bibliography of Secondary Sources*, Brussels: Center for American Studies, 1977.

Nault, Marianne, *Saul Bellow: His World and His Critics: An Annotated International Bibliography* (GRLH 59), N.Y.: Garland, 1977.

Noreen, Robert G., *Saul Bellow: A Reference Guide*, Boston: G. K. Hall, 1978.

Opdahl, K. M., *Novels of Saul Bellow*, 181-93.

Schneider, Harold W., "Two Bibliographies: Saul Bellow, William Styron," *Crit* 3, iii (1960): 71-91.

BENNETT, HAL (GEORGE HAROLD), 1930-

GENERAL

Walcott, Ronald, "The Novels of Hal Bennett," *BlackW* 23, viii (June, 1974): 36-48, 89-97; ix (July, 1974): 78-96.

THE BLACK WINE

Walcott, Ronald, "The Novels of Hal Bennett," *BlackW* 23, viii (June, 1974): 89-97.

LORD OF DARK PLACES

Walcott, Ronald, "The Novels of Hal Bennett," *BlackW* 23, ix (July, 1974): 79-96.

A WILDERNESS OF VINES

Walcott, Ronald, "The Novels of Hal Bennett," *BlackW* 23, viii (June, 1974): 39-48.

BERGER, JOHN, 1926-

GENERAL

McMahon, Joseph H., "Marxist Fictions: The Novels of John Berger," *ConL* 23, ii (Spring, 1982): 202-24.

Ryan, Kiernan, in Klaus, G. H., ed., *Socialist Novel in Britain*, 179-84.

Selden, R., "Commitment and Dialectic in Novels by David Caute and John Berger," *FMLS* 11, ii (April, 1975): 106-21.

Szanto, George, "Oppositional Way-Signs: Some Passages within John Berger's History-Making, History-Unravelling Experiment," *CE* 40, iv (Dec., 1978): 364-78.

G.

Bergonzi, Bernard, in *Contemporary English Novel*, 50-1.

Caute, David, "What We Might Be and What We Are: The Art of John Berger," *TLS* (June 9, 1972): 645-6. Also in Caute, David, *Collisions: Essays and Reviews*, London: Quartet Books, 1974, 135-46.

Selden, R., "Commitment and Dialectic in Novels by David Caute and John Berger," *FMLS* 11, ii (April, 1975): 106-21.

BERGER, THOMAS, 1924-

GENERAL

Hassan, Ihab, "Conscience and Incongruity: The Fiction of Thomas Berger," *Crit* 5, ii (Fall, 1962): 4-15.

Hughes, Douglas, "Thomas Berger's Elan: An Interview," *Confrontation* 12 (1976): 23-39.

Janssen, Ronald R., "Taking on Reality: Themes and Structures in the Works of Thomas Berger," *DAI* 39 (1978): 1570A-71A.

Landon, Richard B., "Extremes of Parataxis: Nonrationalism in the Writing of Gertrude Stein and Thomas Berger," *DAI* 39 (1978): 2275A.

Moore, Jean P., "The Creative Function of the Popular Arts in the Novels of Thomas Berger," *DAI* 42, iv (Oct., 1981): 1636A-37A.

CRAZY IN BERLIN

Hassan, Ihab, "Conscience and Incongruity: The Fiction of Thomas Berger," *Crit* 5, ii (Fall, 1962): 5-10.

Hughes, Douglas A., "The Schlemiel as Humanist: Thomas Berger's Carlo Reinhart," *Cithara* 15, i (Nov., 1975): 5-10.

LITTLE BIG MAN

Betts, Richard A., "Thomas Berger's LITTLE BIG MAN: Contemporary Picaresque," *Crit* 23, ii (Winter, 1981-82): 85-96.

Bezanson, Mark, "Berger and Penn's West: Visions and Revisions," in Peary, G., and Shatzkin, R., eds., *Modern American Novel and the Movies*, 272-81.

Chapman, Edgar L., "Sacred Circle Imagery and the Unity of LITTLE BIG MAN," *HGP* 15, iv (1982): 21-32.

Cleary, Michael, "Finding the Center of the Earth: Satire, History, and Myth in LITTLE BIG MAN," *WAL* 15 (1980): 195-211.

Dippie, Brian W., "Jack Crabbe and the Sole Survivors of Custer's Last Stand," *WAL* 4, iii (Fall, 1969): 189-202.

Fetrow, Fred M., "The Function of the External Narrator in Thomas Berger's LITTLE BIG MAN," *JNT* 5 (1975): 57-65.

Gurian, Jay, "Style in the Literary Desert: LITTLE BIG MAN," *WAL* 3, iv (Winter, 1969): 255-96.

Harris, Charles B., *Contemporary American Novelists of the Absurd*, 129-31.

Oliva, Leo E., "Thomas Berger's LITTLE BIG MAN as History," *WAL* 8 (1973): 33-54.

Royat, Daniel, "Aspects of the American Picaresque in LITTLE BIG MAN," in Johnston, I. D., and Johnston, C., eds., *Les Americanistes*, 37-52.

Schulz, M. F., *Black Humor Fiction of the Sixties*, 72-7, 130-1.

Trachtenberg, Stanley, "Berger and Barth: The Comedy of Decomposition," in Cohen, S. B., ed., *Comic Relief*, 48-51.

Turner, Frederick W., III, "Melville and Thomas Berger: The Novelist as Cultural Anthropologist," *CentR* 13, i (Winter, 1969): 101-21.

Turner, John W., "LITTLE BIG MAN, the Novel and the Film: A Study of Narrative Structure," *LFQ* 5 (1977): 154-63.

Wylder, Delbert E., "Thomas Berger's LITTLE BIG MAN as Literature," *WAL* 3, iv (Winter, 1969): 273-84.

REGIMENT OF WOMEN

"Thomas Berger's REGIMENT OF WOMAN: Beyond LYSISTRATA," *StCS* 1, ii (1975): 1-3.

REINHART IN LOVE

Hassan, Ihab, "Conscience and Incongruity: The Fiction of Thomas Berger," *Crit* 5, ii (Fall, 1962): 11-14.

Hughes, Douglas A., "The Schlemiel as Humanist: Thomas Berger's Carlo Reinhart," *Cithara* 15, i (Nov., 1975): 10-16.

Ryan, Marjorie, "Four Contemporary Satires and the Problem of Norms," *SNL* 6, ii (Spring, 1969): 44-6.

VITAL PARTS

Hughes, Douglas A., "The Schlemiel as Humanist: Thomas Berger's Carlo Reinhart," *Cithara* 15, i (Nov., 1975): 10-16.

Ryan, Marjorie, "Four Contemporary Satires and the Problem of Norms," *SNL* 6, ii (Spring, 1969): 44-6.

WHO IS TEDDY VILLANOVA?

Madden, David, "Thomas Berger's Comic-Absurd Vision in WHO IS TEDDY VILLANOVA?" *ArmD* 14, i (Winter, 1981): 37-43.

BERGSTEIN, ELEANOR, 1938-

GENERAL

Martin, Wendy, "Eleanor Bergstein, Novelist—An Interview," *WS* 2 (1974): 91-7.

BERRY, WENDELL, 1934-

GENERAL

Dietrich, Mary, "Our Commitment to the Land," *BLRev* 2, i (Fall-Winter, 1980): 39-44.

Tolliver, Gary W., "Beyond Pastoral: Wendell Berry and a Literature of Commitment," *DAI* 39 (1979): 6767A-68A.

A PLACE ON EARTH

Hicks, Jack, "Wendell Berry's Husband to the World: A PLACE ON EARTH," *AL* 51, ii (May, 1979): 238-54.

BIBLIOGRAPHY

Hicks, Jack, "A Wendell Berry Checklist," *BB* 37, iii (July-Sept., 1980): 127-31.

BETTS, DORIS (WAUGH), 1932-

Evans, Elizabeth, "Negro Characters in the Fiction of Doris Betts," *Crit* 17, ii (1975): 59-76.
Holman, David M., "Faith and the Unanswerable Questions: The Fiction of Doris Betts," *SLJ* 15, i (Fall, 1982): 15-22.
Wolfe, George, "The Unique Voice: Doris Betts," [Interview.] *Red Clay Reader* (1970). Also in Carr, J., ed., *Kite-Flying and Other Irrational Acts*, 149-73.

THE RIVER TO PICKLE BEACH

Evans, Elizabeth, "Negro Characters in the Fiction of Doris Betts," *Crit* 17, ii (1975): 69-72.
Moose, Ruth, "Superstition in Doris Betts's New Novel," *NCarF* 21, ii (May, 1973): 61-2.

THE SCARLET THREAD

Evans, Elizabeth, "Negro Characters in the Fiction of Doris Betts," *Crit* 17, ii (1975): 67-9.

TALL HOUSES IN WINTER

Evans, Elizabeth, "Negro Characters in the Fiction of Doris Betts," *Crit* 17, ii (1975): 60-4.

BHATTACHARYA, BHABANI, 1906-

GENERAL

Ameruddin, Syed, "Social Commitment in Bhattacharya's Novels," *Littcrit* 7 (1978): 20-30. [Not seen.]
Arulandram, H. G. S., "Bhabani Bhattacharya's Novels," *Triveni* 46, iii (Oct.-Dec., 1977): 68-73.
_____, "Bhabani Bhattacharya's Novels: A Note on Theory and Practice," *BP* 21 (July, 1976): 10-15.
Asnani, Shyam M., "Form, Technique and Style in Bhabani Bhattacharya's Novels," *Littcrit* 8 (1979): 29-37. [Not seen.]
Badal, R. K., "Bhabani Bhattacharya and His Novels," *LHY* 12, ii (July, 1971): 77-85.
Bhattacharya, Bhabani, "Women in My Stories," *JSoAL* 12, iii-iv (Spring-Summer, 1977): 115-19.
Chandrasekharan, K. R., *Bhabani Bhattacharya*.
Fisher, Marlene, "Personal and Social Change in Bhattacharya's Novels," *WLWE* 12, ii (Nov., 1973): 288-96.
_____, "The Women in Bhattacharya's Novels," *WLWE* 11, i (April, 1972): 95-108.
Gemmill, Janet P., "An Interview with Bhabani Bhattacharya," *WLWE* 14 (1975): 300-9.

Iyengar, K. R. S., *Indian Writing in English*, 412-23.
Joshi, K., and B. S. Rao, "Bhabani Bhattacharya as a Novelist," *Studies in Indo-Anglian Literature*, 118-24.
"*Mahfil* Interviews Bhabani Bhattacharya, Defence Colony, New Delhi, India, January 27, 1968," *Mahfil* 5, i-ii (1968-69): 43-8.
Rao, B. Syamala, "Dr. Bhabani Bhattacharya as a Novelist," *Triveni* 40, i (April, 1971): 35-40.
Shimer, D. B., *Bhabani Bhattacharya*.
Singh, Ram Sewak, "Bhabani Bhattacharya: A Novelist of Dreamy Wisdom," *BP* [Supp.] 5, xiii (1969): 60-75. [Not seen.]

A GODDESS NAMED GOLD

Chandrasekharan, K. R., *Bhabani Bhattacharya*, 86-106.
Shimer, D. B., *Bhabani Bhattacharya*, 58-62.
_____, "Gandhian Influence on the Writing of Bhabani Bhattacharya," *SARev* 5, ii (July, 1981): 74-81.
Singh, R. S., *Indian Novel in English*, 108-10.

HE WHO RIDES A TIGER

Chandrasekharan, K. R., *Bhabani Bhattacharya*, 58-85.
Mukherjee, M., *Twice Born Fiction*, 118-23.
Shimer, D. B., *Bhabani Bhattacharya*, 47-57.
Singh, R. S., *Indian Novel in English*, 105-8.

MUSIC FOR MOHINI

Chandrasekharan, K. R., *Bhabani Bhattacharya*, 36-57.
Shimer, D. B., *Bhabani Bhattacharya*, 35-46.
Singh, R. S., *Indian Novel in English*, 101-5.
Tamilarasan, C., "Bhattacharya's MUSIC FOR MOHINI: A Study," *LitE* 2, iv (1982): 35-43.

SHADOW FROM LADAKH

Chandrasekharan, K. R., *Bhabani Bhattacharya*, 107-27.
Sharpe, Patricia L., "Bhabani Bhattacharya, SHADOW FROM LADAKH," *Mahfil* 5, i-88 (1968-69): 134-9.
Shimer, D. B., *Bhabani Bhattacharya*, 68-84.
Singh, R. S., *Indian Novel in English*, 110-16.

SO MANY HUNGERS!

Chandrasekharan, K. R., *Bhabani Bhattacharya*, 10-35.
Sharma, K. K., "Bhabani Bhattacharya's SO MANY HUNGERS: An Affirmative Vision of Life," in Sharma, K. K., ed., *Indo-English Literature*, 201-14.
Shimer, D. B., *Bhabani Bhattacharya*, 22-34.
Singh, R. S., *Indian Novel in English*, 97-101.
Tarinayya, M., "Two Novels," *IndL* 13, i (1970): 113-21. Also in Narasimhaiah, C. D., ed., *Indian Literature of the Past Fifty Years, 1917-1967*, 178-89.

BIBLIOGRAPHY

Shimer, D. B., *Bhabani Bhattarcharya*, 137-46.

BIRNEY, EARLE, 1904-

GENERAL

Achigner, P., *Earle Birney*.

Davey, F., *Earle Birney.*
MacKendrick, Louis K., "Gleewords and Old Discretions: Birney's Benefictions," *ECanW* 21 (Spring, 1981): 158-73.
Nesbitt, B., ed., *Earle Birney.*

DOWN THE LONG TABLE

Aichinger, P., *Earle Birney*, 30-2, 59-60, 157-8.
Davey, F., *Earle Birney*, 38-43.
Dooley, D. J., "The Satiric Novel in Canada Today: DOWN THE LONG TABLE," *QQ* 64, iv (Winter, 1957-58): 584-5. Also in Nesbitt, B., ed., *Earle Birney*, 95-6.
MacKendrick, Louis K., "Gleewords and Old Discretions: Birney's Benefictions," *ECW* 21 (Spring, 1981): 158-73.
Nesbitt, Bruce, "Introduction," DOWN THE LONG TABLE, Toronto: McClelland and Stewart, 1975, vii-xv. Also in *WCR* 9, iii (Jan., 1975): 35-9.

TURVEY: A MILITARY PICARESQUE

Aichinger, P., *Earle Birney*, 24-6, 60-7.
Davey, F., *Earle Birney*, 28-38.
Dooley, D. J., "The Satiric Novel in Canada Today: TURVEY," *QQ* 64, iv (Winter, 1957-58): 580-4. Also in Nesbitt, B., ed., *Earle Birney*, 76-9.
MacKendrick, Louis K., "Gleewords and Old Discretions: Birney's Benefictions, *ECW* 21 (Spring, 1981): 158-73.
Woodcock, George, "Introduction," TURVEY, Toronto: McClelland and Stewart, 1963, ix-xv. Also in *Odysseus Ever Returning: Essays on Canadian Writers and Writing*, Toronto: McClelland and Stewart, 1963, ix-xv. Also in *Odysseus Ever Returning: Essays on Canadian Writers and Writing*, Toronto: McClelland and Stewart, 1970, 123-9. Also in Nesbitt, B., ed., *Earle Birney*, 85-9.

BISSELL, RICHARD (PIKE), 1913-1977

GENERAL

Anderson, Frank J., "The View from the River: Richard Bissell's Satirical Humor," *MQ* 5, iv (July, 1964): 311-22.

BLATTY, WILLIAM PETER, 1928-

THE EXORCIST

Beit-Hallamhi, Benjamin, "THE TURN OF THE SCREW and THE EXORCIST," *AI* 33, iii (Winter, 1976): 296-303.
Frentz, Thomas S., and Thomas B. Farrell, "Conversion of America's Consciousness: The Rhetoric of THE EXORCIST," *QJS* 61 (1975): 40-7.
Mendeloff, Henry, "Exorcism in Blatty and Berceo," *CLS* 11, iii (Sept., 1974): 218-25.
Merry, Bruce, "The Exorcist Dies So That We Can All Enjoy the Sunset Again," *UWR* 11, i (1975): 5-24.
Scheutz, Janice, "THE EXORCIST: Images of Good and Evil," *WS* 39 (1975): 92-101.

BLECHMAN, BURT, 1927-

GENERAL

Guttmann, A., *Jewish Writer in America*, 76-8.

BOURJAILY, VANCE, 1922-

GENERAL

Bruccoli, Matthew J., "Vance Bourjaily," in *Conversations with Writers, I*, 3-23.
Dienstfrey, Harris, "The Novels of Vance Bourjaily," *Ctary* 31 (April, 1961): 360-3.
Francis, William A. C., "The Novels of Vance Bourjaily: A Critical Analysis," *DAI* 36 (1976): 4487A-88A.
Galligan, Edward L., "Hemingway's Staying Power," *MR* 8 (Summer, 1967): 435-7.
Muste, John M., "The Second Major Subwar: Four Novels by Vance Bourjaily," in Friedman, M. J., and J. B. Vickery, eds., *Shaken Realist*, 311-26.

BRILL AMONG THE RUINS

Towner, Daniel, "Brill's Ruins and Henderson's Rain," *Crit* 17, iii (1976): 96-104.

CONFESSIONS OF A SPENT YOUTH

Bourjaily, Vance, "A Certain Kind of Work," in McCormack, T., ed., *Afterwords*, 177-91.
Dienstfrey, Harris, "The Novels of Vance Bourjaily," *Ctary* 31 (April, 1961): 360-3.
Muste, John M., "The Fractional Man as Hero: Bourjaily's CONFESSIONS OF A SPENT YOUTH," *Crit* 17, iii (1976): 73-85.
_____, "The Second Major Subwar: Four Novels by Vance Bourjaily," in Friedman, M. J., and Vickery, J. B., eds., *Shaken Realist*, 323-5.

THE END OF MY LIFE

Aldridge, J. W., *After the Lost Generation*, 121-32.
Bourjaily, Vance, in Madden, F. F., ed., *Talks with Authors*, 201-14.
DeLancey, Robert W., "Man and Mankind in the Novels of Vance Bourjaily," *EngR* 10 (Winter, 1959): 3-4.
Muste, John M., "The Second Major Subwar: Four Novels by Vance Bourjaily," in Friedman, M. J., and J. B. Vickery, eds., *Shaken Realist*, 313-15.
Waldmeir, J. J., *American Novels of the Second World War*, 20-3.

THE HOUND OF EARTH

DeLancey, Robert W., "Man and Mankind in the Novels of Vance Bourjaily," *EngR* 10 (Winter, 1959): 5-6.
Francis, William A., "The Motif of Names of Bourjaily's THE HOUND OF EARTH," *Crit* 17, iii (1976): 64-72.
Muste, John M., "The Second Major Subwar: Four Novels by Vance Bourjaily," in Friedman, M. J., and J. B. Vickery, eds., *Shaken Realist*, 315-19.

THE MAN WHO KNEW KENNEDY

McMillen, William, "The Public Man and the Private Novel: Bourjaily's THE MAN WHO KNEW KENNEDY," *Crit* 17, iii (1976): 86-95.

THE VIOLATED

Hicks, Granville, "The Maturity of Vance Bourjaily," *SatR* (Aug. 23, 1958): 13.

Muste, John M., "The Second Major Subwar: Four Novels by Vance Bourjaily," in Friedman, M. J., and J. B. Vickery, eds., *Shaken Realist*, 319-23.

BIBLIOGRAPHY

McMillen, William, and John M. Muste, "A Vance Bourjaily Checklist," *Crit* 17, iii (1976): 105-10.

BOWEN, ELIZABETH, 1899-1973

GENERAL

Austin, A. E., *Elizabeth Bowen*.

Blodgett, Harriet H., "Circles of Reality: A Reading of the Novels of Elizabeth Bowen," *DA* 29 (1969): 2250A-51A. (Calif.-Davis).

_____, *Patterns of Reality*.

Brooke, J., *Elizabeth Bowen*.

Church, Margaret, "The Irish Writer, Elizabeth Bowen, 'Her Table Spread': Allusion and 'Anti-Roman'," *Folio* 11 (1978): 17-20. [Not seen.]

Daiches, David, "The Novels of Elizabeth Bowen," *EJ* 38 (June, 1949): 305-13.

Davenport, Gary T., "Elizabeth Bowen and the Big House," *SHR* 8, i (Winter, 1974): 27-34.

Dostal, Sister Rose Margaret, O.S.U., "Innocence and Knowledge in the Novels of Elizabeth Bowen," *DA* 25 (1964): 2509-10. (Notre Dame).

Gindin, James, "Ethical Structures in John Galsworthy, Elizabeth Bowen, and Iris Murdoch," in Friedman, A. W., ed., *Forms of Modern British Fiction*, 29-33.

Greene, George, "Elizabeth Bowen: Imagination as Therapy," *Per* 14 (Spring, 1965): 42-52.

Hall, J., *Lunatic Giant in the Drawing Room*, 17-55.

Hanna, John G., "Elizabeth Bowen and the Art of Fiction: A Study of Her Theory and Practice," *DA* 22 (1961): 1175-6. (Boston Un.).

Hardwick, Elizabeth, "Elizabeth Bowen's Fiction," *PR* 16 (Nov., 1949): 1114-21.

Harkness, Bruce, "The Fiction of Elizabeth Bowen," *EJ* 44 (Dec., 1955): 499-506.

Heath, W., *Elizabeth Bowen*.

Karl, F. R., "The World of Elizabeth Bowen," *Contemporary English Novel*, 107-30.

Kendris, Thomas, "The Novels of Elizabeth Bowen," *DA* 26 (1965): 1648. (Columbia).

Kenney, E. J., *Elizabeth Bowen*.

Kirkpatrick, Larry J., "Elizabeth Bowen and Company: A Comparative Essay in Literary Judgment," *DA* 26 (1966): 6044. (Duke).

Lawson, Judith A., "Professionalized Susceptibilities: Imagination in the Early Novels of Elizabeth Bowen," *DAI* 40 (1979): 2697A.

Lee, H., *Elizabeth Bowen*.

McDowell, Alfred B., "Identity and the Past: Major Themes in the Fiction of Elizabeth Bowen," *DAI* 32 (1972): 4621A. (Bowling Green).

McGowan, Martha J., "Lyric Design in the Novels of Elizabeth Bowen," *DA* 28 (1967): 637A-8A. (Columbia).

Nardella, Anna G. R., "Feminism, Art, and Aesthetics: A Study of Elizabeth Bowen," *DAI* 36 (1975): 2851A-52A.

Noble, Linda R. W., "A Critical Study of Elizabeth Bowen's Novels," *DAI* 36 (1976): 4516A.

O'Faolain, S., *Vanishing Hero*, 146-69.

Parrish, Paul A., "The Loss of Eden: Four Novels of Elizabeth Bowen," *Crit* 15, i (1973): 86-100.

Pendry, E. D., *New Feminism of English Fiction*, 120-52.

Rossen, Janice A., "The Early Novels of Elizabeth Bowen: An Existential Reading," *DAI* 43 (1982): 1155A.

Rupp, Richard H., "The Achievement of Elizabeth Bowen: A Study of Her Fiction and Criticism," *DA* 25 (1965): 5286 (Ind.).

_____, "The Post-War Fiction of Elizabeth Bowen," *XUS* 4 (1965): 55-67.

Sackville-West, Edward, "Ladies whose bright Pens...," *Inclinations*, London: Secker and Warburg, 1949, 78-103; Port Washington, N.Y.: Kennikat Pr., 1967, 78-103.

Seward, Barbara, "Elizabeth Bowen's World of Impoverished Love," *CE* 18 (Oct., 1956): 30-7.

Sharp, Sister M. Corona, O.S.U., "The House as Setting and Symbol in Three Novels by Elizabeth Bowen," *XUS* 2 (Dec., 1963): 93-103.

Snow, Lotus, "The Uncertain 'I': A Study of Elizabeth Bowen's Fiction," *WHR* 4 (Autumn, 1950): 299-310.

Stern, Joan O., "A Study of Problems in Values and the Means by Which They Are Presented in the Novels of Elizabeth Bowen," *DAI* 35 (1974): 3012A-13A. (N.Y.U.).

Stokes, Edward, "Elizabeth Bowen—Pre-Assumptions or Moral Angle?" *AUMLA* No. 11 (Sept., 1959): 35-47.

Strong, Leonard A. G., *Personal Remarks*, N.Y.: Liveright, 1953, 132-45.

Sullivan, Walter, "A Sense of Place: Elizabeth Bowen and the Landscape of the Heart," *SR* 84, i (Winter, 1976): 142-9.

Wagner, Geoffrey, "Elizabeth Bowen and the Artificial Novel," *EIC* 13 (April, 1963): 155-63.

THE DEATH OF THE HEART

Allen, W., *Modern Novel*, 192-4.

Austin, A. E., *Elizabeth Bowen*, 59-66.

Blodgett, H., *Patterns of Reality*, 114-53.

Bogan, Louise, "The Pure in Heart," *Nation* 148 (Jan. 28, 1939): 123+. Also in *Selected Criticism: Prose, Poetry*, N.Y.: Noonday Pr., 1955, 125-8.

Brooke, J., *Elizabeth Bowen*, 21-4.

Coles, Robert, *Irony in the Mind's Life*, 107-53.

Daiches, David, "The Novels of Elizabeth Bowen," *EJ* 38 (June, 1949): 310-11.

Fraser, C. S., "Muffled Poetry," *NS&Nation* (Oct. 13, 1961): 520-1.

Hall, J., *Lunatic Giant in the Drawing Room*, 32-50.

Harkness, Bruce, "The Fiction of Elizabeth Bowen," *EJ* 44 (Dec., 1955): 501-4.

Heath, W., *Elizabeth Bowen*, 83-102.

Heinemann, Alison, "The Indoor Landscape in Bowen's THE DEATH OF THE HEART," *Crit* 10, iii (1968): 5-12.

Karl, F. R., "The World of Elizabeth Bowen," *Contemporary English Novel*, 118-26.

Kenney, E. J., *Elizabeth Bowen*, 53-64.

Lee, H., *Elizabeth Bowen*, 104-28.

McDowell, Alfred, "THE DEATH OF THE HEART and the Human Dilemma," *MLS* 8, ii (1978): 5-16.

Miller, Donald W., "Scene and Image in Three Novels by Elizabeth Bowen," *DA* 28 (1967): 637A-8A. (Columbia).

O'Faolain, S., *Vanishing Hero*, 161-4.

Parrish, Paul A., "The Loss of Eden: Four Novels of Elizabeth Bowen," *Crit* 15, i (1973): 93-6.

Sharp, Sister M. Corona, O.S.U., "The House as Setting and Symbol in Three Novels by Elizabeth Bowen," *XUS* 2 (Dec., 1963): 99-102.

Snow, Lotus, "The Uncertain 'I': A Study of Elizabeth Bowen's Fiction," *WHR* 4 (1950): 306-8.

Strong, Leonard A. G., *Personal Remarks*, N.Y.: Liveright, 1963, 140-4.

Van Duyn, Mona, "Pattern and Pilgrimage: A Reading of THE DEATH OF THE HEART," *Crit* 4, ii (1961): 52-66.

EVA TROUT

Austin, A. E., *Elizabeth Bowen*, 87-91.

Blodgett, H., *Patterns of Reality*, 74-83.

Kenney, E. J., *Elizabeth Bowen*, 95-104.

Lee, H., *Elizabeth Bowen*, 206-11.

Moss, H., "The Heiress Is an Outsider," *NYTBR* (Oct. 13, 1968): 1, 28, 30. Also as "Elizabeth Bowen: Intelligence at War," *Writing Against Time*, 214-19.

Parrish, Paul A., "The Loss of Eden: Four Novels of Elizabeth Bowen," *Crit* 15, i (1973): 96-100.

FRIENDS AND RELATIONS

Austin, A. E., *Elizabeth Bowen*, 49-53.

Blodgett, H., *Patterns of Reality*, 52-5.

Brooke, J., *Elizabeth Bowen*, 14-17.

Daiches, David, "The Novels of Elizabeth Bowen," *EJ* 38 (June, 1949): 306-7.

Heath, W., *Elizabeth Bowen*, 51-8.

Lee, H., *Elizabeth Bowen*, 62-6.

Pendry, E. D., *New Feminism of English Fiction*, 125-8.

THE HEAT OF THE DAY

Allen, W., *Modern Novel*, 194-5.

Austin, A. E., *Elizabeth Bowen*, 69-75.

Blodgett, H., *Patterns of Reality*, 154-89.

Brooke, J., *Elizabeth Bowen*, 24-8.

Brothers, Barbara, "Pattern and Void: Bowen's Irish Landscapes and THE HEAT OF THE DAY," *Mosaic* 12, iii (1979): 129-38.

Daiches, David, "The Novels of Elizabeth Bowen," *EJ* 38 (June, 1949): 311-12.

Dorenkamp, Angela G., "'Fall or Leap': Bowen's THE HEAT OF THE DAY," *Crit* 10, iii (1968): 13-21.

Hall, J., *Lunatic Giant in the Drawing Room*, 50-5.

Hardwick, Elizabeth, "Elizabeth Bowen's Fiction," *PR* 16 (1949): 1116-18.

Heath, W., *Elizabeth Bowen*, 108-24.

Karl, F. R., "The World of Elizabeth Bowen," *Contemporary English Novel*, 126-9.

Kenney, E. J., *Elizabeth Bowen*, 67-76.

Lee, H., *Elizabeth Bowen*, 164-8.

Markovi, V. E., *Changing Face*, 112-22.

Prescott, O., *In My Opinion*, 102-4.

Rupp, Richard H., "The Post-War Fiction of Elizabeth Bowen," *XUS* 4 (1965): 56-9.

Watson, Barbara B., "Variations on an Enigma: Elizabeth Bowen's War Novel," *SHR* 15, ii (Spring, 1981): 131-51.

THE HOTEL

Austin, A. E., *Elizabeth Bowen*, 29-37.

Blodgett, H., *Patterns of Reality*, 31-8.

Heath, W., *Elizabeth Bowen*, 21-33.

Karl, F. R., "The World of Elizabeth Bowen," *Contemporary English Novel*, 111-12.

THE HOUSE IN PARIS

Adams, Timothy D., "'Bend Sinister': Duration in Elizabeth Bowen's THE HOUSE IN PARIS," *IFR* 7 (1980): 49-52.

Austin, A. E., *Elizabeth Bowen*, 53-9.

Blodgett, H., *Patterns of Reality*, 84-113.

Brooke, J., *Elizabeth Bowen*, 20-1.

Daiches, David, "The Novels of Elizabeth Bowen," *EJ* 38 (June, 1949): 308-10.

Hall, J., *Lunatic Giant in the Drawing Room*, 20-32.

Hardwick, Elizabeth, "Elizabeth Bowen's Fiction," *PR* 16 (1949): 1118-19.

Heath, W., *Elizabeth Bowen*, 72-83.

Karl, F. R., "The World of Elizabeth Bowen," *Contemporary English Novel*, 114-18.

Kenney, E. J., *Elizabeth Bowen*, 47-53.

Lee, H., *Elizabeth Bowen*, 80-103.

Miller, Donald W., "Scene and Image in Three Novels by Elizabeth Bowen," *DA* 28 (1967): 637A-8A. (Columbia).

Parrish, Paul A., "The Loss of Eden: Four Novels of Elizabeth Bowen," *Crit* 15, i (1973): 89-93.

Sharp, Sister M. Corona, O.S.U., "The House as Setting and Symbol in Three Novels by Elizabeth Bowen," *XUS* 2 (Dec., 1963): 95-8.

THE LAST SEPTEMBER

Austin, A. E., *Elizabeth Bowen*, 37-41.

Blodgett, H., *Patterns of Reality*, 38-45.

Bowen, E., Preface to THE LAST SEPTEMBER, N.Y.: Knopf, 1952. Also in Bowen, E., *Seven Winters and Afterthoughts*, 197-204.

Brooke, J., *Elizabeth Bowen*, 13-14.

Heath, W., *Elizabeth Bowen*, 32-46.

Kenney, E. J., *Elizabeth Bowen*, 31-7.

Lee, H., *Elizabeth Bowen*, 42-53.

O'Faolain, S., *Vanishing Hero*, 151-6.

Parrish, Paul, "The Loss of Eden: Four Novels of Elizabeth Bowen," *Crit* 15, i (1973): 87-9.

Sharp, Sister M. Corona, O.S.U., "The House as Setting and Symbol in Three Novels by Elizabeth Bowen," *XUS* 2 (Dec., 1963): 93-5.

THE LITTLE GIRLS

Austin, A. E., *Elizabeth Bowen*, 82-7.
Blodgett, H., *Patterns of Reality*, 57-9, 68-74.
Burgess, A., *Urgent Copy*, 149-53.
Greene, George, "Elizabeth Bowen: Imagination as Therapy," *Per* 14 (Spring, 1965): 48-52.
Kenney, E. J., *Elizabeth Bowen*, 86-95.
Lee, H., *Elizabeth Bowen*, 199-206.
McDowell, Frederick P. W., "Elizabeth Bowen's THE LITTLE GIRLS," *Crit* 7 (Spring, 1964): 139-43.
Rupp, Richard H., "The Post-War Fiction of Elizabeth Bowen," *XUS* 4 (1965): 64-6.

TO THE NORTH

Austin, A. E., *Elizabeth Bowen*, 41-6.
Blodgett, H., *Patterns of Reality*, 55-7, 61-8.
Brooke, J., *Elizabeth Bowen*, 17-18.
Heath, W., *Elizabeth Bowen*, 58-70.
Karl, F. R., "The World of Elizabeth Bowen," *Contemporary English Novel*, 113-14.
Kenney, E. J., *Elizabeth Bowen*, 41-6.
Lee, H., *Elizabeth Bowen*, 66-79.
_____, "The Placing of Loss: Elizabeth Bowen's TO THE NORTH," *EIC* 28 (1978): 129-42.

A WORLD OF LOVE

Austin, A. E., *Elizabeth Bowen*, 75-82.
Baker, Carlos, "Death of a Ghost," *Nation* 170 (Feb. 21, 1955): 123.
Blodgett, H., *Patterns of Reality*, 45-52.
Heath, W., *Elizabeth Bowen*, 130-44.
Kenney, E. J., *Elizabeth Bowen*, 77-86.
Lee, H., *Elizabeth Bowen*, 189-98.
McGowan, Martha, "The Enclosed Garden in Elizabeth Bowen's A WORLD OF LOVE," *Éire* 16, i (Spring, 1981): 55-70.
Miller, Donald W., "Scene and Image in Three Novels by Elizabeth Bowen," *DA* 28 (1967): 637A-8A. (Columbia).
Rupp, Richard H., "The Post-War Fiction of Elizabeth Bowen," *XUS* 4 (1965): 59-64.
Wagner, Geoffrey, "Elizabeth Bowen and the Artificial Novel," *EIC* 13 (April, 1963): 156-63.
Wyndham, Francis, *LonM* 2 (June, 1955): 86-9.

BIBLIOGRAPHY

Heath, W., *Elizabeth Bowen*, 170-6.
Sellery, J'nan, "Elizabeth Bowen: A Checklist," *BNYPL* 74, iv (April, 1970): 219-74.

BOWEN, JOHN, 1924-

GENERAL

Gindin, J., "Creeping Americanism," *Postwar British Fiction*, 114-27.

STORYBOARD

Urwin, G. G., ed., *Taste for Living*, 186-9.

A WORLD ELSEWHERE

White, J. J., *Mythology in the Modern Novel*, 175-82.

BOWLES, PAUL, 1910-

GENERAL

Bailey, Jeffrey, "The Art of Fiction LXVII: Paul Bowles," *ParisR* 81 (1981): 62-98.
Bertens, J. W., *Fiction of Paul Bowles*.
Collins, Jack, "Approaching Paul Bowles," *RCF* 2, iii (Fall, 1982): 55-63.
Davis, Stephen, "Paul Bowles in Tangier: Interview," *Zero* 4 (1980): 98-113.
Eisinger, C. E., *Fiction of the Forties*, 283-8.
Evans, Oliver, "An Interview with Paul Bowles," *MRev* 1, ii (Winter, 1971): 3-15.
_____, "Paul Bowles and the 'Natural' Man," *Crit* 3, i (1959): 43-59. Also in Waldmeir, J. J., ed., *Recent American Fiction*, 139-52.
Fytton, Francis, "The Pipe Dreams of Paul Bowles," *LonM* n.s. 6 (Feb., 1967): 102-9.
Haberstroh, Charles, "Paul Bowles' Fiction: Lost Directions," *Explor* 1 (Dec., 1973): 36-41.
Halpern, Daniel, "An Interview with Paul Bowles," *TriQ* 33 (1975): 159-77.
Hassan, Ihab H., "The Pilgrim as Prey: A Note on Paul Bowles," *WR* 19 (Autumn, 1954): 23-36.
Hauptman, Robert, "Paul Bowles and the Perception of Evil," *RCF* 2, iii (Fall, 1982): 71-3.
Metcalf, Paul, "A Journey in Search of Bowles," *RCF* 2, iii (Fall, 1982): 32-41.
Mottram, Eric, "Paul Bowles: Staticity & Terror," *RCF* 2, iii (Fall, 1982): 6-30.
O'Connor, W. V., *Grotesque*, 11-12.
Pounds, Wayne E., "Paul Bowles and the Geography of the Inner Nature: Some Psychological Correlatives of Landscape," *DAI* 37 (1977): 5125A.
Stewart, L. D., *Paul Bowles*.

LET IT COME DOWN

Bertens, J. W., *Fiction of Paul Bowles*, 59-114.
Evans, Oliver, "Paul Bowles and the 'Natural' Man," *Crit* 3, i (1959): 50-3. Also in Waldmeir, J. J., ed., *Recent American Fiction*, 145-8.
Glicksberg, Charles I., "The Literary Struggle for Selfhood," *Person* 42 (Jan., 1961): 62-3.
_____, "Literature and the Meaning of Life," *SAQ* 55 (April, 1956): 157-8.
Hassan, Ihab H., "The Pilgrim as Prey: A Note on Paul Bowles," *WR* 19 (Autumn, 1954): 28-30.
_____, *Radical Innocence*, 87-8.
Lehan, Richard, "Existentialism in Recent American Fiction: The Demonic Quest," *TSLL* 1 (Summer, 1959): 185-6.
Pounds, Wayne, "LET IT COME DOWN and Inner Geography," *RCF* 2, iii (Fall, 1982): 42-50.
Rochat, Joyce H., "The Naturalistic-Existential Rapprochement in Albert Camus' L'ETRANGER and Paul Bowles' LET IT

COME DOWN: A Comparative Study in Absurdism," *DAI* 32 (1971): 3327A-28A. (Mich. State).

Shir, Jay, "Truth and Verisimilitude," *BJA* 20, iii (Summer, 1980): 254-5.

Stewart, L. D., *Paul Bowles*, 87-98.

THE SHELTERING SKY

Aldridge, J. W., *After the Lost Generation*, 186-93.

Allen, W., *Modern Novel*, 300-1.

Bertens, J. W., *Fiction of Paul Bowles*, 17-58.

Cecil, L. Moffitt, "Paul Bowles' Sheltering Sky and Arabia," *RS* 42, i (Mar., 1974): 44-9.

Eisinger, C. E., *Fiction of the Forties*, 285-7.

Emerson, Stephen, "Endings and THE SHELTERING SKY," *RCF* 2, iii (Fall, 1982): 73-5.

Evans, Oliver, "Paul Bowles and the 'Natural' Man," *Crit* 3, i (1959): 45-8. Also in Waldmeir, J. J., ed., *Recent American Fiction*, 141-3.

Glicksberg, Charles I., *Literature and Religion: A Study in Conflict*, Dallas: Southern Methodist Un. Pr., 1960, 183-4.

Hassan, Ihab H., "The Pilgrim as Prey: A Note on Paul Bowles," *WR* 19 (Autumn, 1954): 25-7.

_____, *Radical Innocence*, 86-7.

Hunt, Tim, "Paul Bowles: Past and Present," *RCF* 2, iii (Fall, 1982): 52-5.

Joost, Nicholas, in Gardiner, H. C., *Fifty Years of the American Novel*, 286-7.

Lehan, Richard, "Existentialism in Recent American Fiction: The Demonic Quest," *TSLL* 1 (Summer, 1959): 184-5.

Prescott, O., *In My Opinion*, 116-17.

Stewart, L. D., *Paul Bowles*, 47-74.

Straumann, H., *American Literature in the Twentieth Century*, 79-80.

THE SPIDER'S HOUSE

Bertens, J. W., *Fiction of Paul Bowles*, 115-67.

Evans, Oliver, "Paul Bowles and the 'Natural' Man," *Crit* 3, i (1959): 53-7. Also in Waldmeir, J. J., ed., *Recent American Fiction*, 148-51.

Lehan, Richard, "Existentialism in Recent American Fiction: The Demonic Quest," *TSLL* 1 (Summer, 1959): 186-7.

Stewart, L. D., *Paul Bowles*, 100-10.

UP ABOVE THE WORLD

Bertens, J. W., *Fiction of Paul Bowles*, 169-88.

Stewart, Lawrence D., "Paul Bowles: UP ABOVE THE WORLD So High," *MDAC* (1973): 245-70.

BOYD, MARTIN, 1893-1972

GENERAL

Boyd, Martin, "Dubious Cartography," *Meanjin* 23, i (Mar., 1964): 5-13.

Bradley, Anthony, "The Structure of Ideas Underlying Martin Boyd's Fiction," *Meanjin* 28, ii (June, 1969): 177-83.

Brydon, Diana, "Tradition and Post-Colonialism: Hugh Hood and Martin Boyd," *Mosaic* 15, iii (Sept., 1982): 1-15.

Elliott, Bryan, "Martin Boyd: An Appreciation," *Meanjin* 16, i (Mar., 1957): 15-22. [Not seen.]

Fitzpatrick, K., *Martin Boyd*.

French, A. L., "Martin Boyd: An Appraisal," *Southerly* 26, iv (1966): 219-34.

Gould, Warwick, "The Family Face: Martin Boyd's Art of Memoir," *ALS* 7, iii (May, 1976): 269-78.

Green, Dorothy, "From Yorra Glen to Rome: Martin Boyd, 1893-1972," *Meanjin* 31, iii (Sept., 1972): 245-58.

Herring, Thelma, "Martin Boyd and the Critics: A Rejoinder to A. L. French," *Southerly* 28, ii (1968): 127-40.

Kramer, Leonie, "Martin Boyd," *AusQ* 35, ii (June, 1963): 32-8.

McKernan, Susan, "Much Else in Boyd: The Relationship between Martin Boyd's Non-fiction Work and his Later Novels," *Southerly* 39, iii (Sept., 1978): 309-30.

McLaren, John, "Gentlefolk Errant: The Family Writings of Martin Boyd," *ALS* 5, iv (Oct., 1972): 339-51.

Mitchell, Adrian, "Martin Boyd: The True Amateur of Life," *Issue* 3 (Sept., 1973): 23-5. [Not seen.]

Niall, Brenda, "The Double Alienation of Martin Boyd," *TCM* 17, iii (Autumn, 1963): 197-206.

_____, *Martin Boyd*.

_____, "Martin Boyd as 'Walter Beckett'," *ALS* 8, iii (May, 1978): 369-71.

O'Neill, Terence, "Martin Boyd's Missing Novels: A Partial Solution," *ALS* 8, iii (May, 1978): 366-8.

Smith, David K., "Martin Boyd," *Westerly* 2 (June, 1975): 33-7.

Wallace, F., "The Craft of Martin Boyd," *TCM* 24 (Winter, 1970): 336-42.

Wilkes, G. A., "The Achievement of Martin Boyd," *Southerly* 19, ii (1958): 90-8. Also in Johnston, G., ed., *Australian Literary Criticism*, 158-68.

THE CARDBOARD CROWN (See also LANGTON Tetralogy)

Brydon, Diana, "Tradition and Post-Colonialism: Hugh Hood and Martin Boyd," *Mosaic* 15, iii (Sept., 1982): 1-15.

Fitzpatrick, K., *Martin Boyd*, 20-2.

McFarlane, B., *Martin Boyd's LANGTON Novels*, 8-18.

McKernan, Susan, "Much Else in Boyd: The Relationship between Martin Boyd's Non-fiction Work and his Later Novels," *Southerly* 39, iii (Sept., 1978): 316-20.

Niall, B., *Martin Boyd*, 27-30.

Wallace-Crabbe, Chris, "Martin Boyd and THE CARDBOARD CROWN," *MCR* No. 3 (1960): 23-30.

DEAREST IDOL

Niall, Brenda, "Martin Boyd as 'Walter Beckett'," *ALS* 8, iii (May, 1978): 369-71.

A DIFFICULT YOUNG MAN (See also LANGTON Tetralogy)

Hamilton, K. G., "Two Difficult Young Men," in Hamilton, K. G., ed., *Studies in the Recent Australian Novel*, 145-55.

Kramer, Leonie, "The Seriousness of Martin Boyd," *Southerly* 28, ii (1968): 91-109.

McFarlane, B., *Martin Boyd's LANGTON Novels*, 19-28.

McKernan, Susan, "Much Else in Boyd: The Relationship between Martin Boyd's Non-fiction Work and his Later Novels," *Southerly* 39, iii (Sept., 1978): 320-2.

Niall, B., *Martin Boyd*, 30-3.

LANGTON Tetralogy

Lodge, L. W. McD., "Aspects of the Religious Theme in the Langton Novels of Martin Boyd," *Teaching of English* 34 (May, 1978): 28-34.

McFarlane, B., *Martin Boyd's LANGTON Novels.*

_____, "Martin Boyd's LANGTON Sequence," *Southerly* 35, i (Mar., 1975): 69-87.

Nase, Pamela, "Martin Boyd's LANGTON Novels," in Ramson, W. S., ed., *Australian Experience*, 229-48.

Niall, Brenda, "Second Thoughts on the LANGTON Novels: Martin Boyd's Revisions," *ALS* 7, iii (May, 1976): 321-4.

LUCINDA BRAYFORD

Fitzpatrick, K., *Martin Boyd*, 17-20.

Green, Dorothy, "'The Fragrance of Souls': A Study of LU-CINDA BRAYFORD," *Southerly* 28, ii (1968): 110-26.

Hope, A. D., "Knowing Where to Stop: Martin Boyd's LU-CINDA BRAYFORD," *Native Companions*, 204-15.

McKernan, Susan, "Much Else in Boyd: The Relationship between Martin Boyd's Non-fiction Work and his Later Novels," *Southerly* 39, iii (Sept., 1978): 311-15.

Moon, Kenneth, "Pulp Writing and Coincidence in Martin Boyd's LUCINDA BRAYFORD," *Southerly* 38 (1978): 183-93.

Niall, B., *Martin Boyd*, 19-24.

Ramson, W. S., "LUCINDA BRAYFORD: A Form of Music," in Ramson, W. S., ed., *Australian Experience*, 209-28.

THE MONTFORTS

Eldershaw, M. Barnard, "The MONTFORTS," in *Essays in Australian Fiction*, Melbourne: Melbourne Un. Pr., 1938, 138-57.

NUNS IN JEOPARDY

Niall, B., *Martin Boyd*, 18-19.

O'Neill, Terence, "Literary Cousins: NUNS IN JEOPARDY and PICNIC AT HANGING ROCK," *ALS* 10 (1982): 375-8.

OUTBREAK OF LOVE (See also LANGTON Tetralogy)

French, A. L., "Martin Boyd: An Appraisal," *Southerly* 26, iv (1966): 219-34.

McFarlane, B., *Martin Boyd's LANGTON Novels*, 29-40.

McKernan, Susan, "Much Else in Boyd: The Relationship between Martin Boyd's Non-fiction Work and his Later Novels," *Southerly* 39, ii (Sept., 1978): 322-5.

Niall, B., *Martin Boyd*, 33-6.

SUCH PLEASURE (BRIDGET MALWYN)

Niall, B., *Martin Boyd*, 25-6.

WHEN BLACKBIRDS SING (See also LANGTON Tetralogy)

McFarlane, B., *Martin Boyd's LANGTON Novels*, 41-9.

McKernan, Susan, "Much Else in Boyd: The Relationship between Martin Boyd's Non-fiction Work and his Later Novels," *Southerly* 39, iii (Sept., 1978): 325-7.

BIBLIOGRAPHY

Nase, Pamela, "Martin Boyd: A Checklist," *ALS* 5, iv (Oct., 1972): 404-14.

Niall, Brenda M., *Martin Boyd*, Melbourne: Oxford Un. Pr., 1977. [Bibliography.]

BOYLE, KAY, 1903-1992

GENERAL

Bell, Elizabeth S., "Henry Miller and Kay Boyle: The Divided Stream in American Expatriate Literature, 1930-1940," *DAI* 40 (1980): 5862A.

Carpenter, Richard, "Kay Boyle," *CE* 15 (1953): 81-7. Also in *EJ* 42 (1953): 425-30.

Gado, Frank, "Kay Boyle: From the Aesthetics of Exile to the Polemics of Return," *DA* 29: 4485A-86A (Duke).

Holt, Patricia, "PW Interviews: Kay Boyle," *PW* (Oct. 17, 1980): 8-9.

Jackson, Byron K., "The Achievement of Kay Boyle," *DA* 29 (1968): 899A (Florida).

Spanier, Sandra W., "Kay Boyle and the Failures of Love," *DAI* 42 (1981): 1153A-54A.

Van Gelder, Robert, *Writers on Writing*, 193-6.

AVALANCHE

Wilson, E., *NY* (Jan. 15, 1944): 66-70. Also in *Classics and Commercials*, 128-32.

PLAGUED BY THE NIGHTINGALE

Porter, Katherine Anne, "Example to the Young," *NRep* (April, 22, 1931): 279-80. Also in Harrison, G. A., ed., *Critic as Artist*, 277-81.

BIBLIOGRAPHY

Sharp, Roberta, "A Bibliography of Works by and about Kay Boyle," *BB* 35, iv (Oct.-Dec., 1978): 180-9, 191.

BRACE, GERALD WARNER, 1901-1978

GENERAL

Harris, Arthur S., Jr., "Gerald Warner Brace: Teacher-Novelist," *CE* 18, iii (Dec., 1956): 157-60.

Wagenknecht, E., *Cavalcade of the American Novel*, 458-60.

THE SPIRE

Lyons, J. O., *College Novel in America*, 127-9.

BRADBURY, MALCOLM (STANLEY), 1932-

GENERAL

Todd, Richard, "An Interview with Malcolm Bradbury," *DQR* 11, iii (1981): 183-96.

EATING PEOPLE IS WRONG

Todd, Richard, "Malcolm Bradbury's THE HISTORY MAN: The Novelist as Reluctant Impresario," *DQR* 11, ii (1981): 162-82.

THE HISTORY MAN

Craig, George, "Party Hack," *New Rev* 2, xxii (1976): 66-7.
Todd, Richard, "Malcolm Bradbury's THE HISTORY MAN: The Novelist as Reluctant Impresario," *DQR* 11, iii (1981): 162-82.

STEPPING WESTWARD

Todd, Richard, "Malcolm Bradbury's THE HISTORY MAN: The Novelist as Reluctant Impresario," *DQR* 11, ii (1981): 162-82.

BRADFORD, RICHARD (ROARK), 1932-

RED SKY AT MORNING

Etulain, Richard W., "Richard Bradford's RED SKY AT MORNING: New Novel of the Southwest," *WR* 8, i (1971): 57-62.

BRAGG, MELVYN, 1939-

GENERAL

Fiddick, Peter, "Melvyn Bragg: All His Own Work," *Listener* 94 (Sept. 4, 1975): 299.

A PLACE IN ENGLAND

Bolling, Douglass T., "Melvyn Bragg's A PLACE IN ENGLAND," *QQ* 78, iv (Winter, 1971): 619-23.

BRAINE, JOHN, 1922-1986

GENERAL

Alayrac, Claude, "Inside John Braine's Outsider," *Caliban* 8 (1971): 111-38.
Jain, Jasbir, "The New Philistines: A Study of the Novels of John Braine," *RUSEng* 9 (1976): 58-69. [Not seen.]
Lee, J. W., *John Braine*.
Lockwood, Bernard, "Four Contemporary British Working-Class Novelists: A Thematic and Critical Approach to the Fiction of Raymond Williams, John Braine, David Storey and Alan Sillitoe," *DA* 28 (1967): 1081A (Wisconsin).
Shestakov, Dmitri, "John Braine Facing His Fourth Novel," *Soviet Lit* No. 8 (1964): 178-81.

THE CRYING GAME

Anon., "Fiction of 1968. John Braine: THE CRYING GAME," *TLS* (Aug. 29, 1968). Also in *T.L.S. Essays and Reviews from The Times Literary Supplement, 1968*, 73-5.

THE JEALOUS GOD

Lee, J. W., *John Braine*, 95-107.
Spender, Stephen, "Must There Always be a Red Brick England?" in Encyclopaedia Britannica, *Great Ideas Today, 1965*, 181-3.

LIFE AT THE TOP

Lee, J. W., *John Braine*, 82-94.
McDowell, Frederick P. W., "'The Devious Involutions of Human Character and Emotions': Reflections on Some Recent British Novels," *WSCL* 4, iii (Autumn, 1963): 344-6.
Rippier, J. S., *Some Postwar English Novelists*, 188-92.

ROOM AT THE TOP

Allsop, K., *Angry Decade*, 78-85.
Fraser, G. S., *Modern Writer and His World*, 181-2.
Hurrell, John, "Class and Consciousness in John Braine and Kingsley Amis," *Crit* 2, i (1958): 39-53.
Karl, F. R., "The Angries: Is There a Protestant in the House?" *Contemporary English Novel*, 229-30.
Lee, J. W., *John Braine*, 52-68.
Rippier, J. S., *Some Postwar English Novelists*, 178-85.

THE VODI (FROM THE HAND OF THE HUNTER)

Jelly, Oliver, "Fiction and Illness," *REL* 3 (Jan., 1962): 80-9.
Karl, F. R., "The Angries: Is There a Protestant in the House?" *Contemporary English Novel*, 230-1.
Lee, J. W., *John Braine*, 69-81.
Rippier, J. S., *Some Postwar English Novelists*, 185-8.
Urwin, G. G., ed., *Taste for Living*, 44-7.

BRALY, MALCOLM, 1925-1980

GENERAL

Franklin, H. Bruce, "Malcolm Braly: Novelist of the American Prison," *ConL* 18, ii (Spring, 1977): 217-40. Also in Franklin, H. B., *Victim as Criminal and Artist*, 181-206.

IT'S COLD OUT THERE

Franklin, H. Bruce, "Malcolm Braly: Novelist of the American Prison," *ConL* 18, ii (Spring, 1977): 227-33. Also in Franklin, H. B., *Victim as Criminal and Artist*, 193-8.

ON THE YARD

Franklin, H. Bruce, "Malcolm Braly: Novelist of the American Prison," *ConL* 18, ii (Spring, 1977): 233-40. Also in Franklin, H. B., *Victim as Criminal and Artist*, 198-205.

SHAKE HIM TILL HE RATTLES

Franklin, H. Bruce, "Malcolm Braly: Novelist of the American Prison," *ConL* 18, ii (Spring, 1977): 222-6. Also in Franklin, H. B., *Victim as Criminal and Artist*, 187-91.

BRAUTIGAN, RICHARD GARY, 1935-1984

GENERAL

Pütz, Manfred, "Richard Brautigan: Pastorals of and for the Self," *Story of Identity*, 105-29.
Robbins, Gwen A., "A Magic Box and Richard Brautigan," *DAI* 40 (1980): 4592A.

Schmitz, Neil, "Richard Brautigan and the Modern Pastoral," *MFS* 19, i (Spring, 1973): 109-25.

Walker, Cheryl, "Youth Fishing in America," *MoOc* 2, iii (Spring, 1972): 308-13.

THE ABORTION: AN HISTORICAL ROMANCE 1966

Hackenberry, Charles, "Romance and Parody in Brautigan's THE ABORTION," *Crit* 23, ii (Winter, 1981-82): 24-36.

Schmitz, Neil, "Richard Brautigan and the Modern Pastoral," *CE* 19, i (Spring, 1973): 112-16.

A CONFEDERATE GENERAL FROM BIG SUR

Locklin, Gerald, and Charles Stetler, "Some Observations on A CONFEDERATE GENERAL FROM BIG SUR," *Crit* 13, ii (1971): 72-82.

Tanner, T., *City of Words*, 406-8.

THE HAWKLINE MONSTER: A GOTHIC WESTERN

Willis, Lonnie L., "Brautigan's THE HAWKLINE MONSTER: As Big as the Ritz," *Crit* 23, ii (Winter, 1981-82): 37-47.

IN WATERMELON SUGAR

Hernlund, Patricia, "Author's Intent: IN WATERMELON SUGAR," *Crit* 16, i (1975): 5-17.

Leavitt, Harvey, "The Regained Paradise of Brautigan's IN WATERMELON SUGAR," *Crit* 16, i (1975): 18-24.

Rohrberger, Mary, and Peggy C. Gardner, "Multicolored Loin Cloths, Glass Trinkets of Words: Surrealism in IN WATER-MELON SUGAR," *BSUF* 23, i (1982): 61-7.

Schmitz, Neil, "Richard Brautigan and the Modern Pastoral," *CE* 19, i (Spring, 1973): 116-20.

Tanner, T., *City of Words*, 412-13.

Thomson, George H., "Objective Reporting as a Technique in the Experimental Novel: A Note on Brautigan and Robbe-Grillet," *NConL* 8, iv (Sept., 1978): 2.

TROUT FISHING IN AMERICA

Bales, Kent, "Fishing the Ambivalence, or, A Reading of TROUT FISHING IN AMERICA," *WHR* 29 (1975): 29-42.

Cooley, John, "The Garden in the Machine: Three Postmodern Pastorals," *MichA* 13, iv (Spring, 1981): 405-20.

Hayden, Brad, "Echoes of WALDEN in TROUT FISHING IN AMERICA," *TJQ* 8, iii (1976): 21-6.

Hearron, Thomas, "Escape Through Imagination in TROUT FISHING IN AMERICA," *Crit* 16, i (1975): 25-31.

Kolin, Philip C., "Food for Thought in Richard Brautigan's TROUT FISHING IN AMERICA," *StCS* 8 (Spring, 1981): 9-20.

Schmitz, Neil, "Richard Brautigan and the Modern Pastoral," *CE* 19, i (Spring, 1973): 120-5.

Seib, Kenneth, "TROUT FISHING IN AMERICA: Brautigan's Funky Fishing Yarn," *Crit* 13, ii (1971): 63-71.

Tanner, T., *City of Words*, 408-15.

Vanderwerken, David L., "TROUT FISHING IN AMERICA and the American Tradition," *Crit* 16, i (1975): 32-40.

WILLARD AND HIS BOWLING TROPHIES: A PERVERSE MYSTERY

Gordon, Andrew, "Richard Brautigan's Parody of Arthur Miller," *NMAL* 6, i (Spring-Summer, 1982): Item 8.

BIBLIOGRAPHY

Jones, Stephen R., "Richard Brautigan: A Bibliography," *BB* 33, i (1976): 53-9.

Wanless, James, and Christine Kolodziej, "Richard Brautigan: A Working Checklist," *Crit* 16, i (1975): 41-52.

BRESLIN, JIMMY (JAMES), 1930-

GENERAL

Eckley, Grace, "Two Irish-American Novelists: J. P. Donleavy and Jimmy Breslin," *Illinois School Journal* 55 (1975): 28-33. [Not seen.]

Kennedy, Eugene, "A Day With Jimmy Breslin," *Critic* 33, i (Oct.-Nov.-Dec., 1974): 18-29.

WORLD WITHOUT END, AMEN

Casey, Daniel J., "Heresy in the Diocese of Brooklyn: An Unholy Trinity," in Casey, D. J., and R. E. Rhodes, eds., *Irish-American Fiction*, 156-62. Also (edited version) in *JEthS* (1978).

Rabinowitz, Dorothy, "A Certain Politics," *Ctary* 56, vi (Dec., 1973): 380.

BRODERICK, JOHN, 1927-

GENERAL

Gallagher, Michael P., S. J., "The Novels of John Broderick," *CahiersI* 4-5 (1976): 235-43. Also in Rafroidi, P., and M. Harmon, eds., *Irish Novel in Our Time*, 235-43.

McMahon, Seán, "Town and Country," *Éire* 6, i (Spring, 1971): 120-31.

DON JUANEEN

McMahon, Seán, "Town and Country," *Éire* 6, i (Spring, 1971): 128-9.

THE FUGITIVES

McMahon, Seán, "Town and Country," *Éire* 6, i (Spring, 1971): 126-8.

THE PILGRIMAGE

McMahon, Seán, "Town and Country," *Éire* 6, i (Spring, 1971): 123-6.

THE WAKING OF WILLIE RYAN

McMahon, Seán, "Town and Country," *Éire* 6, i (Spring, 1971): 129-30.

BROOKE-ROSE, CHRISTINE, 1926-

GENERAL

Hayman, David, and Keith Cohne, "An Interview with Christine Brooke-Rose," *ConL* 17 (Winter, 1976): 1-23.

THRU

Kafalenos, Emma, "Textasy: Christine Brooke-Rose's THRU," *IFR* 7 (1980): 43-6.

BROPHY, BRIGID (ANTONIA), 1929-

GENERAL

Dock, Leslie, "Brigid Brophy: Artist in the Baroque," *DAI* 37 (1977): 5844A-45A.
————, "An Interview with Brigid Brophy," *ConL* 17 (1976): 151-70.

BROWN, CECIL M., 1943-

THE LIFE AND LOVES OF MR. JIVEASS NIGGER

Schraufnagel, N., *From Apology to Protest*, 132-3.
Wiggins, William H., Jr., "The Trickster as Literary Hero: Cecil Brown's THE LIFE AND LOVES OF MR. JIVEASS NIGGER," *NYFQ* 29 (1973): 269-86.

BROWN, CHRISTY, 1932-1981

GENERAL

Borel, Françoise, "'I Am Without a Name': The Fiction of Christy Brown," *CahiersI* 4-5 (1976): 287-95.

DOWN ALL THE DAYS

Borel, Françoise, "'I Am Without a Name': The Fiction of Christy Brown," in Rafroide, P., and M. Harmon, eds., *Irish Novel in Our Time*, 287-91. Also in *CahiersI* 4-5 (1976): 287-91.

A SHADOW OF SUMMER

Borel, Françoise, "'I Am Without a Name': The Fiction of Christy Brown," in Rafroidei, P., and M. Harmon, eds., *Irish Novel in Our Time*, 291-3. Also in *CahiersI* 4-5 (1976): 291-3.

BROWN, GEORGE MACKAY, 1921-

GENERAL

Bold, A., *George Mackay Brown*.

GREENVOE

Bold, A., *George Mackay Brown*, 90-9.
Huberman, Elizabeth, "Mackay Brown's GREENVOE: Rediscovering a Novel of the Orkneys," *Crit* 19, ii (1977): 33-43.

MAGNUS

Bold, A., *George Mackay Brown*, 99-110.
Huberman, Elizabeth, "George Mackay Brown's MAGNUS," *SSL* 16 (1981): 122-34.

BROWN, WESLEY, 1945-

TRAGIC MAGIC

Coleman, James W., "Language, Reality, and Self in Wesley Brown's TRAGIC MAGIC," *BALF* 15, ii (Summer, 1981): 48-50.

BRYAN, C(OURTLANDT) D(IXON) B(ARNES), 1936-

THE GREAT DETHRIFFE

Long, Robert E., "The Image of Gatsby in the Fiction of Louis Auchincloss and C.D.B. Bryan," *FHA* (1972): 326-8.

BUCK, PEARL S., 1892-1973

GENERAL

Buck, Pearl S., *My Several Worlds: A Personal Record*, N.Y.: Day, 1954.
Cevasco, George A., "Pearl Buck and the Chinese Novel," *Asian Studies* 5 (Dec., 1967): 437-50.
————, "Pearl Buck's Best Books," *NMAL* 5, iii (Summer, 1981): Item 19.
Doàn-Cao-L, *Image of the Chinese Family in Pearl Buck's Novels*.
Doyle, P. A., *Pearl S. Buck*.
————, *Pearl S. Buck*, Rev. ed.
Gray, J., *On Second Thought*, 28-35.
Thompson, Dody W., in French, W. G., and Kidd, W. E., eds., *American Winners of the Nobel Literary Prize*, 85-110.
Van Gelder, R., *Writers on Writing*, 26-8.
Venne, Peter S. V. D., "Pearl Buck's Literary Portrait of China and the Chinese," *FJS* 1 (1968): 71-86. [Not seen.]
Yü, Yüh-chao, "Chinese Influences on Pearl S. Buck," *TkR* 11, i (Fall, 1980): 23-41.

COMMAND THE MORNING

Doyle, P. A., *Pearl S. Buck*, 137-40. Rev. ed., 124-7.

DRAGON SEED

Doàn-Cao-L, *Image of the Chinese Family in Pearl Buck's Novels*, 109-22.
Doyle, P. A., *Pearl S. Buck*, 117-21. Rev. ed., 106-10.

EAST WIND: WEST WIND

Doàn-Cao-L, *Image of the Chinese Family in Pearl Buck's Novels*, 31-66.
Doyle, P. A., *Pearl S. Buck*, 29-35. Rev. ed., 23-8

THE GOOD EARTH (See also HOUSE OF EARTH Trilogy)

Cevasco, George A., "Pearl Buck and the Chinese Novel," *Asian Studies* 5 (Dec., 1967): 444-9.

Doyle, P. A., *Pearl S. Buck*, 36-54. Rev. ed., 29-46.

Gray, J., *On Second Thought*, 30-2.

Hsu, Pei-Tzu, "The Love of the Land in Pearl Buck's THE GOOD EARTH and Willa Cather's O PIONEERS!" *FJS* 12 (1979): 71-82.

Langlois, Walter G., "THE DREAM OF THE RED CHAMBER, THE GOOD EARTH, and MAN'S FATE: Chronicles of Social Change in China," *LE&W* 11 (Mar., 1967): 1-10.

Shimizu, Mamoru, "On Some Stylistic Features, Chiefly Biblical, of THE GOOD EARTH," *SELit* Engl. (1964): 117-34.

Stuckey, W. J., *Pulitzer Prize Novels*, 90-3.

A HOUSE DIVIDED (See also HOUSE OF EARTH Trilogy)

Cowley, M., "The Good Earthling," *NRep* (Jan. 23, 1935). Also in *Think Back on Us*, 251-4.

Doyle, P. A., *Pearl S. Buck*, 64-70. Rev. ed., 56-61.

HOUSE OF EARTH Trilogy

Doàn-Cao-L, *Image of the Chinese Family in Pearl Buck's Novels*, 67-94.

Doyle, P. A., *Pearl S. Buck*, 57-70. Rev. ed., 50-61.

KINFOLK

Doyle, P. A., *Pearl S. Buck*, 134-7. Rev. ed., 121-4.

THE LIVING REED

Doyle, P. A., *Pearl S. Buck*, rev. ed., 137-9.

THE MOTHER

Doàn-Cao-L, *Image of the Chinese Family in Pearl Buck's Novels*, 128-31.

Doyle, P. A., *Pearl S. Buck*, 70-5. Rev. ed., 62-6.

THE NEW YEAR

Doyle, P. A., *Pearl S. Buck*, rev. ed., 142-3.

OTHER GODS

Doyle, P. A. *Pearl S. Buck*, 108-12. Rev. ed., 98-105.

THE PATRIOT

Doàn-Cao-L, *Image of the Chinese Family in Pearl Buck's Novels*, 95-108.

Doyle, P. A., *Pearl S. Buck*, 104-8. Rev. ed., 94-8.

PAVILION OF WOMEN

Doàn-Cao-L, *Image of the Chinese Family in Pearl Buck's Novels*, 131-40.

Doyle, P. A., *Pearl S. Buck*, 130-4. Rev. ed., 117-21.

Vollmershausen, Joseph, "PAVILION OF WOMEN. A Psychoanalytic Interpretation," *AJP* 10 (1950): 53-60.

THE PROMISE

Doyle, P. A., *Pearl S. Buck*, 121-4. Rev. ed., 110-12.

SONS (See also HOUSE OF EARTH Trilogy)

Doyle, P. A., *Pearl S. Buck*, 58-64. Rev. ed., 50-6.

THIS PROUD HEART

Doyle, P. A., *Pearl S. Buck*, 87-91. Rev. ed., 77-80.

THE THREE DAUGHTERS OF MADAME LIANG

Doyle, P. A., *Pearl S. Buck*, rev. ed., 143-4.

THE TIME IS NOON

Doyle, P. A., *Pearl S. Buck*, rev. ed., 139-42.

THE TOWNSMAN (Under pseudonym, John Sedges)

Doyle, P. A., *Pearl S. Buck*, 125-30. Rev. ed., 113-17.

BIBLIOGRAPHY

Brenni, Vito, "Pearl Buck: A Selected Bibliography," *BB* 22 (May-Aug., 1957): 65-9; (Sept.-Dec., 1957): 94-6.

Zinn, Lucille S., "The Works of Pearl S. Buck: A Bibliography," *BB* 36, iv (1979): 194-208.

BUCKLER, ERNEST, 1908-1984

GENERAL

Cameron, Donald, "Letter from Halifax," *CanL* 40 (Spring, 1969): 55-60.

Cook, G. M., ed., *Ernest Buckler*.

Orange, John, in Heath, J. M., ed., *Profiles in Canadian Literature* 2, 17-24.

Spettigue, Douglas O., "The Way It Was: Ernest Buckler," *CanL* 32 (Spring, 1967): 40-56.

Tallman, Warren, "Wolf in the Snow," *CanL* 5 (Sept., 1960): 7-20; 6 (Autumn, 1960): 41-8. Also in Woodcock, George, ed., *A Choice of Critics: Selections from Canadian Literature 1964-74*, Toronto: Oxford Un. Pr., 1966, 53-76. Also in Mandel, Eli, *Patterns of Literary Criticism*, No. 9, Chicago: Un. of Chicago Pr., 1971, 232-53. Also in Cook, G. M., ed., *Ernest Buckler*, 55-79. Also in *Open Letter*, 3rd Series, No. 6 (Fall, 1977): 131-49.

Young, A. R., *Ernest Buckler*.

THE CRUELEST MONTH

Chambers, R. D., *Sinclair Ross and Ernest Buckler*, 84-98.

Cook, G. M., ed., *Ernest Buckler*, 95-115.

Spettigue, D. O., "The Way It Was: Ernest Buckler," *CanL* 32 (Spring, 1967): 40-56. Also in Woodcock, G., ed., *Canadian Novel in the Twentieth Century*, 155-60.

Young, A. R., *Ernest Buckler*, 37-44.

THE MOUNTAIN AND THE VALLEY

Atkinson, Ian A., "Imagery and Symbolism," in Cook, G. M., ed., *Ernest Buckler*, 132-6.

Barbour, Douglas, "The Critic Criticized: A Reply to Bruce MacDonald," *SCL* 2 (Winter, 1977): 127-8.

_____, "David Canaan: The Failing Heart," *SCL* 1, i (Winter, 1976): 64-75.

Bissell, Claude, T., *Introduction to THE MOUNTAIN AND THE VALLEY*, Toronto: McClelland and Stewart, 1961, vii-xii.

Chambers, R. D., *Sinclair Ross and Ernest Buckler*, 66-83.

Chapman, Marilyn, "The Progress of David's Imagination," *SCL* 3 (Summer, 1978): 186-98.

Doerksen, L. M., "THE MOUNTAIN AND THE VALLEY: An Evaluation," *WLWE* 19, i (Spring, 1980): 45-56.

Dooley, D. J., "Style and Communication in THE MOUNTAIN AND THE VALLEY," *DR* 57 (Winter, 1977-78): 671-83. Also, revised, in Dooley, D. J., *Moral Vision in the Canadian Novel*, Toronto: Clarke, Irwin, 1979, 49-59.

Dyck, Sarah, "In Search of a Poet: Buckler and Pasternak," *GSlav* 2 (Spring, 1978): 325-36.

Kertzer, J. M., "The Past Recaptured," *CanL* 65 (Summer, 1975): 74-85.

MacDonald, Bruce F., "Word-Shapes, Time and the Theme of Isolation in THE MOUNTAIN AND THE VALLEY," *SCL* 1, ii (Summer, 1976): 194-209. [Comments on article by Douglas Barbour: Barbour's reply, *SCL* 2, i (1977): 127-8.]

Moss, J., *Patterns of Isolation*, 232-5.

_____, *Sex and Violence in the Canadian Novel*, 90-4.

Noonan, Gerald, "Egoism and Style in THE MOUNTAIN AND THE VALLEY," in MacKinnon, Kenneth, ed., *Atlantic Provinces Literature Colloquium Papers/Communications du colloque sur la litteratures des provinces atlantiques*, Saint John: Atlantic Canada Inst., 1977, 68-78.

Ricou, Laurence, "David Canaan and Buckler's Style in THE MOUNTAIN AND THE VALLEY," *DR* 57 (Winter, 1977-78): 684-96.

Sarkar, Eilen, "THE MOUNTAIN AND THE VALLEY: The Infinite Language of Human Relations," *RUO* 44 (July-Sept., 1974): 354-61.

Spettigue, D. O., "The Way It Was: Ernest Buckler," *CanL* 32 (Spring, 1967): 40-56. Also in Woodcock, G., ed., *Canadian Novel in the Twentieth Century*, 149-54. Also in Cook, G. M., ed., *Ernest Buckler*, 95-115.

Stewart, Robert J., "Buckler's David Canaan and Joyce's Stephen Dedalus," *CN&Q* 23 (June, 1979): 5-6.

Thomas, Clara, "New England Romanticism and Canadian Fiction," *JCF* 2, iv (Fall, 1973): 80-6.

Wainwright, J. A., "Fern Hill Revisited: Isolation and Death in THE MOUNTAIN AND THE VALLEY," *SCL* 7, i (1982): 63-89.

Watters, R. E., "THE MOUNTAIN AND THE VALLEY," in Cook, G. M., ed., *Ernest Buckler*, 41-8.

Westwater, A. M., "Teufelsdrockh is Alive and Doing Well in Nova Scotia: Carlylean Strains in THE MOUNTAIN AND THE VALLEY," *DR* 56, ii (Summer, 1976): 291-8.

Young, A. R., *Ernest Buckler*, 29-37.

_____, "The Genesis of Ernest Buckler's THE MOUNTAIN AND THE VALLEY," *JCF* 16 (1976): 89-96. Also in Moss, J., ed., *Canadian Novel, Vol. III*, 195-205.

_____, "A Note on Douglas Barbour's 'David Canaan: The Failing Heart'," *SCl* 1, ii (Summer, 1976): 244-6.

_____, "The Pastoral Vision of Ernest Buckler in THE MOUNTAIN AND THE VALLEY," *DR* 53 (Summer, 1973): 219-26.

BIBLIOGRAPHY

Orange, John, "Ernest Buckler: An Annotated Bibliography," 14-56 in Lecker, Robert, and Jack David, eds., *The Annotated Bibliography of Canada's Major Authors, Volume Three*, Downsview: ECW, 1981.

BUECHNER, FREDERICK, 1926-

GENERAL

Myers, Nancy B., "Sanctifying the Profane: Religious Themes in the Fiction of Frederick Buechner," *DAI* 37 (1976): 3628A-29A.

Nelson, Shirley, and Rudy Nelson, "Frederick Buechner," *C&L* 32, i (1982): 9-14. [Interview.]

Thompson, Stacy W., "The Rediscovery of Wonder: A Critical Introduction to the Novels of Frederick Buechner," *DAI* 40 (1980): 5059A-60A.

A LONG DAY'S DYING

Aldridge, J. W., *After the Lost Generation*, 219-30.

Allen, W., *Modern Novel*, 303-5.

Hassan, I., *Radical Innocence*, 153-61.

THE RETURN OF ANSEL GIBBS

Blotner, J., *Modern American Political Novel*, 331-3.

Podhoretz, N., "The New Nihilism and the Novel," *PR* 25 (Fall, 1958): 580-1. Also in Podhoretz, N., *Doings and Undoings*, 164-6.

BURDICK, EUGENE (LEONARD), 1918-1965

GENERAL

Wilkinson, Rupert, "Connections with Toughness: The Novels of Eugene Burdick," *JAmS* 11, ii (Aug., 1977): 223-39.

THE NINTH WAVE

Brown, Steven R., "Political Literature and the Response of the Reader: Experimental Studies of Interpretation, Imagery, and Criticism," *Amer. Political Science Rev.* 71 (1977): 567-84.

BURGESS, ANTHONY, 1917-1993

GENERAL

Aggeler, G., *Anthony Burgess*.

_____, "The Comic Art of Anthony Burgess," *ArQ* 25, iii (Autumn, 1969): 234-51.

Bergonzi, B., *Situation of the Novel*, 178-87.

Brown, Rexford G., "Conflict and Confluence: The Art of Anthony Burgess," *DAI* 32 (1972): 5220A-21A. (Iowa).

Bunting, Charles T., "An Interview in New York with Anthony Burgess," *SNNTS* 5, iv (Winter, 1973): 504-29.

Churchill, Thomas, "An Interview with Anthony Burgess," *MHRev* 17 (Jan., 1971): 103-27.

Coale, S., *Anthony Burgess*.

_____, "An Interview with Anthony Burgess," *MFS* 27, iii (Autumn, 1981): 429-52.

_____, "The Ludic Loves of Anthony Burgess," *MFS* 27, iii (Autumn, 1981): 453-63.

Cullinan, John T., "Anthony Burgess' Novels: A Critical Introduction," *DAI* 35 (1975): 7900A.

_____, "The Art of Fiction XLVIII: Anthony Burgess," *ParisR* 56 (Spring, 1973): 119-63. [Interview.]

Davis, Earle, "'Laugh Now—Think Later': The Genius of Anthony Burgess," *KM* (1968): 7-12.

DeVitis, A. A., *Anthony Burgess*.

Friedman, Melvin J., "Anthony Burgess and James Joyce: A Literary Confrontation," *LCrit* 9, iv (Summer, 1971): 71-83.

Hemesath, James B., "Anthony Burgess," *Transatlantic Rev.* (May, 1976): 44-6, 96-102.

Holte, Carlton T., "Taming the Rock: Myth, Model, and Metaphor in the Novels of Anthony Burgess," *DAI* 38 (1978): 6143A.

Hyman, Stanley E., Afterword to Burgess, A., A CLOCKWORK ORANGE, N.Y.: Norton, 1963. Also in Kostelanetz, R., ed., *Contemporary Literature*, 300-5.

Jennings, C. Robert, "Playboy Interview: A Candid Conversation with the Visionary Author of A CLOCKWORK ORANGE," *Playboy* 21, ix (Sept., 1974): 69-86.

Kennard, Jean E., "Anthony Burgess: Double Vision," in Kennard, J. E., *Number and Nightmare*, 131-54.

LeClair, Thomas, "Essential Opposition: The Novels of Anthony Burgess," *Crit* 12, iii (1971): 77-94.

Levin, Bernard, "Man Must Be Free," *Listener* 105 (1981): 675. [Not seen.]

Lucas, Timothy R., "The Old Shelley Game: Prometheus and Predestination in Burgess' Works," *MFS* 27, iii (Autumn, 1981): 465-78.

Mathews, R., *Clockwork Universe of Anthony Burgess*.

Mitchell, Julian, "Anthony Burgess," *LonM* n.s. 3 (Feb., 1964): 48-54.

Moran, Kathryn L., "Utopias, Subtopias, Dystopias in the Novels of Anthony Burgess," *DAI* 35 (1974): 2286A-87A. (Notre Dame).

Morris, R. K., *Consolations of Ambiguity*.

Murray, William M., "Anthony Burgess on 'Apocalypse'," *IowaR* 8, iii (Summer, 1977): 37-45.

Page, Malcolm, "Anthony Burgess: The Author as Performer," *WCR* 4, iii (Jan., 1970): 21-4.

Parrinder, Patrick, "Updating Orwell? Burgess's Future Fictions," *Encounter* 56, i (Jan., 1981): 45-53.

Pritchard, William H., "The Novels of Anthony Burgess," *MR* 7 (Summer, 1966): 525-39.

Reilly, Lemuel, "An Interview with Anthony Burgess," *DelLR* 2 (1973): 48-55.

Robinson, Robert, "Anthony Burgess: On Being a Lancashire Catholic," *Listener* 96 (Sept. 30, 1976): 397-9.

Steffen, Nancy L., "Burgess' World of Words," *DAI* 38 (1977): 2781A-82A.

Stinson, John J., "Anthony Burgess: Novelist on the Margin," *JPC* 7, i (Summer, 1973): 136-51.

_____, "The Manichee World of Anthony Burgess," *Ren* 26, i (Autumn, 1973): 37-47.

_____, "Waugh and Anthony Burgess: Some Notes toward an Assessment of Influence and Affinities," *EWN* 10, iii (Winter, 1976): 11-12.

Sullivan, Walter, "Death Without Tears: Anthony Burgess and the Dissolution of the West," *HC* 6, ii (April, 1969): 1-11.

Thaddeus, Janice, "Anthony Burgess and the Novel of Game," *PCL* 6 (1980): 49-58.

Wagner, Kenyon L., "Anthony Burgess' Mythopoetic Imagination: A Study of Selected Novels (1956-1968)" *DAI* 35 (1975): 7926A.

ABBA, ABBA

Coale, S., *Anthony Burgess*, 149-53.

BEARD'S ROMAN WOMEN

Aggeler, Geoffrey, "A Ghostly Entertainment: BEARD'S ROMAN WOMEN," *MBL* 2 (1977): 169-75.

Coale, S., *Anthony Burgess*, 110-16.

BEDS IN THE EAST (See also THE LONG DAY WANES Trilogy)

Aggeler, G., *Anthony Burgess*, 45-53.

Coale, S., *Anthony Burgess*, 29-32, 36-8.

DeVitis, A. A., *Anthony Burgess*, 57-64.

Mathews, R., *Clockwork Universe of Anthony Burgess*, 26-33.

A CLOCKWORK ORANGE

Aggeler, G., *Anthony Burgess*, 169-82.

_____, "Pelagius and Augustine in the Novels of Anthony Burgess," *ES* 55, i (Feb., 1974): 43-55.

Anderson, Ken, "A Note on A CLOCKWORK ORANGE," *NConL* 2, v (Nov., 1972): 5-7.

Bergonzi, B., *Situation of the Novel*, 182-5.

Bly, James I., "Structure and Theme in Burgess's HONEY FOR THE BEARS, A CLOCKWORK ORANGE, and TREMOR OF INTENT," *DAI* 39 (1979): 4954A.

Bowie, Robert, "Freedom and Art in A CLOCKWORK ORANGE: Anthony Burgess and the Christian Premises of Dostoevsky," *Thought* 56, ccxxiii (Dec., 1981): 402-16.

Brigham, Jerry C., L. Brooks Hill, and William J. Wallisch, Jr., "A CLOCKWORK ORANGE: Socio-cultural Juices," *Thought* 49 (Mar., 1974): 5-20.

Brophy, Elizabeth, "A CLOCKWORK ORANGE: English and Nadstat," *NConL* 2, ii (Mar., 1972): 4-6.

Carson, Julie, "Pronominalization in A CLOCKWORK ORANGE," *PLL* 12, ii (Spring, 1976): 200-5.

Coale, S., *Anthony Burgess*, 84-98.

Connelly, Wayne C., "Optimism in Burgess's A CLOCKWORK ORANGE," *Extrapolation* 14, i (Dec., 1972): 25-9.

Cullinan, John, "Anthony Burgess' A CLOCKWORK ORANGE: Two Versions," *ELN* 9, iv (June, 1972): 287-92.

DeVitis, A. A., *Anthony Burgess*, 103-12.

Evans, Robert O., "Nadsat: The Argot and Its Implications in Anthony Burgess' A CLOCKWORK ORANGE," *JML* 1, iii (Mar., 1971): 406-10.

_____, "The Nouveau Roman, Russian Dystopias, and Anthony Burgess," *SLitI* 6, ii (Fall, 1973): 27-37.

Fiore, Peter A., "Milton and Kubrick: Eden's Apple or A CLOCKWORK ORANGE," *CEA* 35, ii (Jan., 1973): 14-17.

Fitzpatrick, William P., "Anthony Burgess' Brave New World: the Ethos of Neutrality," *StHum* 3, i (Oct., 1972): 31-6.

Fulkerson, Richard P., "Teaching A CLOCKWORK ORANGE," *CEA* 37, i (Nov., 1974): 8-10.

Gilbert, Basil, "Kubrick's Marmalade: The Art of Violence," *Meanjin* 33, ii (Winter, 1974): 157-62.

Guetti, James, "Voiced Narrative: A CLOCKWORK ORANGE," *Word-Music*, 54-76.

Isaacs, Neil D., "Unstuck in Time: CLOCKWORK ORANGE and SLAUGHTERHOUSE-FIVE," *LFQ* 1, ii (April, 1973): 122-31.

Kennard, J. E., *Number and Nightmare*, 133-7.

Mathews, R., *Clockwork Universe of Anthony Burgess*, 36-43.

McCracken, Samuel, "Novel into Film: Novelist into Critics: A CLOCKWORK ORANGE Again," *AR* 32, iii (1973): 426-36.

Mentzer, Thomas L., "The Ethics of Behavior Modification: A CLOCKWORK ORANGE Revisited," *EAS* 9, i (May, 1980): 93-105.

Morris, R. K., *Consolations of Ambiguity*, 55-75.

Petix, Esther, "Linguistics, Mechanics, and Metaphysics: Anthony Burgess's A CLOCKWORK ORANGE," in Morris, R. K., ed., *Old Lines, New Forces*, 38-52.

Plank, Robert, "The Place of Evil in Science Fiction," *Extrapolation* 14, ii (May, 1973): 100-11.

Pritchard, William H., "The Novels of Anthony Burgess," *MR* 7 (Summer, 1966): 532-4.

Rabinovitz, Rubin, "Ethical Values in Anthony Burgess's CLOCKWORK ORANGE," *SNNTS* 11, i (Spring, 1979): 43-50.

_____, "Mechanism vs. Organism: Anthony Burgess' A CLOCKWORK ORANGE," *MFS* 24, iv (Winter, 1978-79): 538-41.

Ray, Philip E., "Alex Before and After: A New Approach to Burgess' A CLOCKWORK ORANGE," *MFS* 27, iii (Autumn, 1981): 479-87.

Roth, Ellen S., "The Rhetoric of First Person Point of View in the Novel and Forms: A Study of Anthony Burgess' A CLOCKWORK ORANGE and Henry James' A TURN OF THE SCREW and Their Film Adaptations," *DAI* 39 (1979): 4558A.

Samuels, Charles T., "The Context of A CLOCKWORK ORANGE," *ASch* 41, iii (Summer, 1972): 439-43.

Saunders, Trevor J., "Plato's Clockwork Orange," *DUJ* 37, ii (June, 1976): 113-17.

Severin-Lounsberry, Barbara, "Holden and Alex: A Clockwork from the Rye?" *FQ* 22, iv (Summer, 1973): 27-38.

Sheldon, Leslie, E., "Newspeak and Nadsat: The Disintegration of Language in 1984 and A CLOCKWORK ORANGE," *StCS* 6 (1979): 7-13.

Siciliano, Sam J., "The Fictional Universe in Four Science Fiction Novels: Anthony Burgess's A CLOCKWORK ORANGE, Ursula Le Guin's THE WORD FOR WORLD IS FOREST, Walter Miller's A CANTICLE FOR LEIBOWITZ, and Roger Zelazny's CREATURES OF LIGHT AND DARKNESS," *DAI* 36 (1976): 8053A.

Sobchack, Vivian C., "Decor as Theme: A CLOCKWORK ORANGE," *LFQ* 9, ii (1981): 92-102.

Tilton, John W., "A CLOCKWORK ORANGE: Awareness Is All," *Comic Satire in the Contemporary Novel*, 21-42.

THE CLOCKWORK TESTAMENT; OR, ENDERBY'S END (See also ENDERBY Trilogy)

Aggeler, Geoffrey, *Anthony Burgess*, 94-109.

_____, "Enderby Immolatus: Burgess' THE CLOCKWORK TESTAMENT," *MHRev* 44 (Oct., 1977): 22-4, 29-46.

Coale, S., *Anthony Burgess*, 174-8.

Hedberg, Johannes, "Three Contemporary Novelists—Three Novels of 1974," *MSpr* 69, ii (1975): 108-12.

Raban, Joanathan, "What Shall We Do About Anthony Burgess?" *Encounter* 43 (Nov., 1974): 83-5.

DEVIL OF A STATE

Aggeler, G., *Anthony Burgess*, 53-8.

Coale, S., *Anthony Burgess*, 40-7.

DeVitis, A. A., *Anthony Burgess*, 86-95.

Morris, R. K., *Consolations of Ambiguity*, 33-42.

THE DOCTOR IS SICK

Aggeler, G., *Anthony Burgess*, 119-31.

Coale, S., *Anthony Burgess*, 105-10.

DeVitis, A. A., *Anthony Burgess*, 79-86.

Mathews, R., *Clockwork Universe of Anthony Burgess*, 33-6.

EARTHLY POWERS (INSTRUMENTS OF DARKNESS)

Aggeler, Geoffrey, "Faust in the Labyrinth: Burgess' EARTHLY POWERS," *MFS* 27, iii (Autumn, 1981): 517-31.

Coale, S., *Anthony Burgess*, 183-94.

ENDERBY Trilogy

Coale, S., *Anthony Burgess*, 163-6.

Fitzpatrick, William P., "The Sworn Enemy of Pop: Burgess' Mr. Enderby," *BWVACET* 1, i (1974): 28-37.

Hoffmann, Charles G., and A. C. Hoffman, "Mr. Kell and Mr. Burgess: Inside and Outside Mr. Enderby," in Friedman, M. J., and J. B. Vickery, eds., *Shaken Realist*, 304-10.

Kennard, J. E., *Number and Nightmare*, 143-6.

Morris, R. K., *Consolations of Ambiguity*, 75-89.

Solotaroff, Theodore, "The Busy Hand of Burgess," *Red Hot Vacuum*, 269-75.

ENDERBY OUTSIDE (See also ENDERBY Trilogy)

Aggeler, G., *Anthony Burgess*, 86-93.

_____, "Mr. Enderby and Mr. Burgess," *MHRev* 10 (April, 1969): 104-10.

Coale, S., *Anthony Burgess*, 170-4.

DeVitis, A. A., *Anthony Burgess*, 130-3.

Hoffmann, Charles G., and A. C. Hoffmann, "Mr. Kell and Mr. Burgess: Inside and Outside Mr. Enderby," in Friedman, M. J., and J. B. Vickery, eds., *Shaken Realist*, 300-10.

THE ENEMY IN THE BLANKET (See also THE LONG DAY WANES Trilogy)

Aggeler, G., *Anthony Burgess*, 41-5.

Coale, S., *Anthony Burgess*, 35-6.

DeVitis, A. A., *Anthony Burgess*, 49-57.

Mathews, R., *Clockwork Universe of Anthony Burgess*, 21-6.

THE EVE OF ST. VENUS

Aggeler, G., *Anthony Burgess*, 149-57.

Coale, S., *Anthony Burgess*, 145-9.

DeVitis, A. A., *Anthony Burgess*, 148-53.

HONEY FOR THE BEARS

Aggeler, G., *Anthony Burgess*, 131-44.

Bly, James I., "Structure and Theme in Burgess's HONEY FOR THE BEARS, A CLOCKWORK ORANGE, and TREMOR OF INTENT," *DAI* 39 (1979): 4954A.

Coale, S., *Anthony Burgess*, 59-67.

DeVitis, A. A., *Anthony Burgess*, 134-41.

Fitzpatrick, William P., "Black Marketeers and Manichees: Anthony Burgess' Cold War Novels," *WVUPP* 21 (Dec., 1974): 78-91.

Morris, R. K., *Consolations of Ambiguity*, 49-55.

Pritchard, William H., "The Novels of Anthony Burgess," *MR* 7 (Summer, 1966): 536-9.

INSIDE MR. ENDERBY (See also ENDERBY Trilogy)

Aggeler, G., *Anthony Burgess*, 80-6.

Coale, S., *Anthony Burgess*, 166-70.

DeVitis, A. A., *Anthony Burgess*, 124-30.

Hoffmann, Charles G., and A. C. Hoffmann, "Mr. Kell and Mr. Burgess: Inside and Outside Mr. Enderby," in Friedman, M. J., and J. B. Vickery, eds., *Shaken Realist*, 300-10.

THE LONG DAY WANES Trilogy

Aggeler, G., *Anthony Burgess*, 37-53.

Banner, Howard, "Use of Word Play and Malay in Locales of Anthony Burgess' THE LONG DAY WANES," *AN&Q* 20, ix-x (1982): 146-9.

Coale, S., *Anthony Burgess*, 28-40.

DeVitis, A. A., *Anthony Burgess*, 39-68.

Morris, R. K., *Consolations of Ambiguity*, 21-31.

_____, *Continuance and Change*, 71-91.

Pritchard, William H., "The Novels of Anthony Burgess," *MR* 7 (Summer, 1966): 526-9.

A MALAYAN TRILOGY (See THE LONG DAY WANES Trilogy)

MAN OF NAZARETH

Coale, S., *Anthony Burgess*, 180-3.

MF

Aggeler, G., *Anthony Burgess*, 195-207.

_____, "Incest and the Artist: Anthony Burgess's MF as Summation," *MFS* 18, iv (Winter, 1972-73): 529-43.

Coale, S., *Anthony Burgess*, 116-24.

Kennard, Jean, "MF: A Separable Meaning," *RQ* 6, iii (Aug., 1975): 200-6.

_____, *Number and Nightmare*, 146-54.

Lucas, Timothy R., "The Old Shelley Game: Prometheus & Predestination in Burgess' Works," *MFS* 27, iii (Autumn, 1981): 465-78.

Reeve, N. H., in *Contemporary English Novel*, 127-30.

NAPOLEON SYMPHONY: A NOVEL IN FOUR MOVEMENTS

Aggeler, G., *Anthony Burgess*, 208-32.

Coale, S., *Anthony Burgess*, 125-34.

Merrill, Reed, "The Role and Image of the Artist: Burgess's Poetics and the NAPOLEON SYMPHONY," *Explorations* 7, ii (1980): 61-72.

Mowat, John, "Joyce's Contemporary: A Study of Anthony Burgess' NAPOLEON SYMPHONY," *ConL* 19, ii (Spring, 1978): 180-95.

Raban, Jonathan, "What Shall We Do About Anthony Burgess?" *Encounter* 43 (Nov., 1974): 83-6.

1985

Coale, S., *Anthony Burgess*, 75-7.

Parrinder, Patrick, "Updating Orwell? Burgess' Future Fictions," *Encounter* 56, i (Jan., 1981): 45-53.

Stinson, John J., "Better to Be Hot or Cold: 1985 and the Dynamic of the Michaean Duoverse," *MFS* 27, iii (Autumn, 1981): 505-16.

Whellens, Arthur, "Anthony Burgess's 1985," *StIL* 5 (1982): 223-44.

NOTHING LIKE THE SUN

Aggeler, G., *Anthony Burgess*, 68-80.

_____, "A Prophetic Acrostic in Anthony Burgess's NOTHING LIKE THE SUN," *N&Q* 21, iv (April, 1974): 136.

Burgess, Anthony, "Genesis and Headache," in McCormack, T., ed., *Afterwords*, 29-47.

Burke, Maxine E., "James Joyce and His Influences: William Faulkner and Anthony Burgess," *DAI* 42, xi (May, 1982): 4818A-19A.

Coale, S., *Anthony Burgess*, 153-62.

DeVitis, A. A., *Anthony Burgess*, 141-8.

Enright, E. J., "A Modern Disease: Anthony Burgess's Shakespeare," *Man is an Onion*, 39-43. From *NStat* 67 (April 24, 1964): 642-4.

Firestone, Bruce M., "Love's Labor's Lost: Sex and Art in Two Novels by Anthony Burgess," *IowaR* 8, iii (1977): 46-52.

Stinson, John J., "NOTHING LIKE THE SUN: The Faces in Bella Cohen's Mirror," *JML* 5, i (Feb., 1976): 131-47.

ONE HAND CLAPPING

Aggeler, G., *Anthony Burgess*, 145-9.

Coale, S., *Anthony Burgess*, 139-45.

DeVitis, A. A., *Anthony Burgess*, 119-24.

Hoffmann, Charles G., and A. C. Hoffmann, "Mr. Kell and Mr. Burgess: Inside and Outside Mr. Enderby," in Friedman, M. J., and J. B. Vickery, eds., *Shaken Realist*, 302-4.

Mathews, R., *Clockwork Universe of Anthony Burgess*, 51-60.

THE RIGHT TO AN ANSWER

Aggeler, G., *Anthony Burgess*, 110-19.

Coale, S., *Anthony Burgess*, 48-54.

DeVitis, A. A., *Anthony Burgess*, 69-79.

Morris, R. K., *Consolations of Ambiguity*, 42-9.

Pritchard, William H., "The Novels of Anthony Burgess," *MR* 7 (Summer, 1966): 529-32.

TIME FOR A TIGER (See also THE LONG DAY WANES Trilogy)

Aggeler, G., *Anthony Burgess*, 37-41.

Coale, S., *Anthony Burgess*, 32-5.

DeVitis, A. A., *Anthony Burgess*, 39-49.

Mathews, R., *Clockwork Universe of Anthony Burgess*, 16-21.

TREMOR OF INTENT

Aggeler, G., *Anthony Burgess*, 185-94.

_____, "Between God and Notgod: Anthony Burgess' TREMOR OF INTENT," *MHRev* 17 (Jan., 1971): 90-102. Also, revised, in Aggeler, G., *Anthony Burgess*, 185-94.

Bly, James I., "Sonata Form in TREMOR OF INTENT," *MFS* 27, iii (Autumn, 1981): 489-504.

_____, "Structure and Theme in Burgess's HONEY FOR THE BEARS, A CLOCKWORK ORANGE, and TREMOR OF INTENT," *DAI* 39 (1979): 4954A.

Coale, S., *Anthony Burgess*, 67-75.

DeVitis, A. A., *Anthony Burgess*, 153-63.

Duffy, Charles F., "From Espionage to Eschatology: Anthony Burgess's TREMOR OF INTENT," *Ren* 32, ii (1980): 79-88.

Fitzpatrick, William P., "Black Marketeers and Manichees: Anthony Burgess' Cold War Novels," *WVUPP* 21 (Dec., 1974): 78-91.

Kennard, J. E., *Number and Nightmare*, 140-3.

Morris, R. K., *Consolations of Ambiguity*, 15-21.

Palumbo, Ronald J., "Names and Games in TREMOR OF INTENT," *ELN* 18 (Sept., 1980): 48-51.

A VISION OF BATTLEMENTS

Aggeler, G., *Anthony Burgess*, 30-7.

Coale, S., *Anthony Burgess*, 19-28.

DeVitis, A. A., *Anthony Burgess*, 29-39.

Firestone, Bruce M., "Love's Labor's Lost: Sex and Art in Two Novels by Anthony Burgess," *IowaR* 8, iii (1977): 46-52.

Mathews, R., *Clockwork Universe of Anthony Burgess*, 5-16.

Morris, R. K., *Consolations of Ambiguity*, 9-15.

THE WANTING SEED

Aggeler, G., *Anthony Burgess*, 162-9.

_____, "Pelagius and Augustine in the Novels of Anthony Burgess," *ES* 55, i (Feb., 1974); 43-55.

Bergonzi, B., *Situation of the Novel*, 185-7.

Chalpin, Lila, "Anthony Burgess's Gallows Humor in Dystopia," *TQ* 16, iii (Autumn, 1973): 73-84.

Coale, S., *Anthony Burgess*, 77-84.

Cullinan, John, "Burgess' THE WANTING SEED," *Expl* 31, vi (Mar., 1973): Item 51.

DeVitis, A. A., *Anthony Burgess*, 112-18.

Dorenkamp, John H., "Anthony Burgess and the Future of Man: THE WANTING SEED," *UDR* 15, i (Spring, 1981): 107-11.

Evans, Robert O., "The Nouveau Roman, Russian Dystopias, and Anthony Burgess," *SLitI* 6, ii (Fall, 1973): 27-37.

Fitzpatrick, William P., "Anthony Burgess' Brave New World: The Ethos of Neutrality," *StHum* 3, i (Oct., 1972): 31-6.

Kateb, George, "Politics and Modernity: The Strategies of Desperation," *NLH* 3, i (Autumn, 1971): 93-111.

Kennard, J. E., *Number and Nightmare*, 137-40.

Mathews, R., *Clockwork Universe of Anthony Burgess*, 43-51.

Morris, R. K., *Consolations of Ambiguity*, 55-75.

Murdoch, B., "The Overpopulated Wasteland: Myth in Anthony Burgess' THE WANTING SEED," *RLV* 39, iii (1973): 203-17.

Pritchard, William H., "The Novels of Anthony Burgess," *MR* 7 (Summer, 1966): 534-6.

THE WORM AND THE RING

Aggeler, G., *Anthony Burgess*, 58-67.

_____, "A Wagnerian Affirmation: Anthony Burgess's THE WORM AND THE RING," *WHR* 27, iv (Autumn, 1973): 401-10.

DeVitis, A. A., *Anthony Burgess*, 96-103.

BIBLIOGRAPHY

Brewer, Jeutonne, *Anthony Burgess: A Bibliography*. (Scarecrow Author Bibliographies 47), Metuchen, NJ: Scarecrow, 1980.

Coale, Samuel, "Criticism of Anthony Burgess: A Selected Checklist," *MFS* 27, iii (Autumn, 1981): 533-6.

David, Beverly R., "Anthony Burgess: A Checklist (1956-1971)," *TCL* 19, iii (July, 1973): 181-8.

Holte, Carlton, "Additions to 'Anthony Burgess: A Checklist (1956-1971)'" *TCL* 20, i (Jan., 1974): 44-52.

BURNS, ALAN, 1929-

GENERAL

Reeve, N. H., in *Contemporary English Novel*, 114-23.

THE ANGRY BRIGADE

Reeve, N. H., in *Contemporary English Novel*, 121-3.

DREAMERIKA

Reeve, N. H., in *Contemporary English Novel*, 118-21.

BURNS, JOHN HORNE, 1916-1953

GENERAL

Brophy, Brigid, in (London) *Sunday Times Magazine* (Oct., 1964). Also in Brophy, B., *Don't Never Forget*, 192-202.

A CRY OF CHILDREN

Brophy, B., *Don't Never Forget*, 198-9.

THE GALLERY

Aldridge, J. W., *After the Lost Generation*, 140-6.

Allen, W., *Modern Novel*, 294-6.

Brophy, B., *Don't Never Forget*, 192-8.

Eisenger, C. E., *Fiction of the Forties*, 40-1.

French, Warren, in French, W., ed., *Forties*, 27-32.

Healey, Robert C., in Gardiner, H. C., ed., *Fifty Years of the American Novel*, 265-6.

Valk, E. M., "Baraka: A Reminiscence in Memory of John Horne Burns," *LitR* 3 (1959): 280-6.

Vidal, Gore, "John Horne Burns," *NYTBR* (May 30, 1965): 1, 22. Also in Vidal, G., *Homage to Daniel Shays*, 181-5.

Waldmeir, J. J., *American Novels of the Second World War*, 81, 103-7.

BURROUGHS, WILLIAM S., 1914-

GENERAL

Anon., "The Novels of William Burroughs," *TLS* (Nov. 14, 1963). Also in *T.L.S.: Essays and Reviews from The Times Literary Supplement*, 1963, 221-5.

Ansen, Alan, "Anyone Who Can Pick Up a Frying Pan Owns Death," *Big Table* #21 (Summer, 1959): 32-41. Also in Parkinson, T., ed., *Casebook on the Beat*, 107-13.

Bockris, Victor, "Information About the Operation: A Portrait of William Burroughs," *New Rev* 3, xxv (April, 1976): 37-46.

Bryant, J. H., *Open Decision*, 202-8.

Coley, Lemuel B., "Three Essays on William S. Burroughs," *DAI* 40 (1979): 3287A.

Cordesse, Gérard, "The Science-Fiction of William Burroughs," *Caliban* 12 (1975): 33-43.

Fiedler, L. A., *Waiting for the End*, 163-71.

Goodman, Richard, Jr., "An Evening with William Burroughs," *MQR* 13, i (Winter, 1974): 18-24.

Hassan, Ihab, "The Literature of Silence: From Henry Miller to Beckett and Burroughs," *Encounter* 28 (Jan., 1967): 74-82.

————, "The Subtracting Machine: The Work of William Burroughs," *Crit* 6, i (Spring, 1963): 4-23.

Knickerbocker, Conrad, "William Burroughs," *Paris Rev* No. 35 (Fall, 1965): 13-49. Also in *Writers at Work*, 3rd ser., 141-74.

Lee, A. Robert, "William Burroughs and the Sexuality of Power," *TwenCS* 1, ii (Nov., 1969): 74-88.

Mertz, Robert, "The Virus Visions of William Burroughs," in Baldanza, F., ed., *Itinerary 3: Criticism*, 11-18.

Mottram, E., *William Burroughs*.

Odier, Daniel, *The Job: Interviews with William S. Burroughs*, rev. and enl. ed., N.Y.: Grove Pr., 1970.

————, "Journey Through Time-Space: An Interview with William S. Burroughs," *EvR* 13 (June, 1969): 38-41, 78-89.

Oxenhandler, Neal, "Listening to Burrough's Voice," in Federman, R., ed., *Surfiction*, 181-201.

Palumbo, Donald, "Science Fiction as Allegorical Social Satire: William Burroughs and Jonathan Swift," *StCS* 9 (Spring, 1982): 1-8.

————, "William Burroughs' Quartet of Science Fiction Novels as Dystopian Social Satire," *Extrapolation* 20, iv (Winter, 1979): 321-9.

Polkinhorn, Harry G., "William Burroughs: In the Radical Tradition," *DAI* 36 (1976): 7424A-25A.

Rivers, J. E., "An Interview with William S. Burroughs," *RALS* 10, ii (Autumn, 1980): 154-66.

Skerl, Jennie, "Interview with William S. Burroughs," *MSI* 9 (Winter-Spring, 1981): 18-20.

————, "An Interview with William S. Burroughs (April 4, 1980, New York City)," *MLS* 12, iii (Summer, 1982): 3-17.

————, "William S. Burroughs: Pop Artist," *Sphinx* 11 (1980): 1-15.

Solotaroff, Theodore, "William Burroughs: The Algebra of Need," *Red Hot Vacuum*, 247-53.

Stimpson, Catharine R., "The Beat Generation and the Trials of Homosexual Liberation," *Salmagundi* 58-59 (Fall-Winter, 1982-83): 373-92.

Stull, William L., "The Quest and the Question: Cosmology and Myth in the Work of William S. Burroughs, 1953-1960," *TCL* 24, ii (Summer, 1978): 225-42.

Tanner, James E., Jr., "Experimental Styles Compared: E. E. Cummings and William Burroughs," *Style* 10 (1976): 1-27.

————, "The New Demonology," *PR* 33 (Fall, 1966): 547-72.

————, "Rub Out the Word," *City of Words*, 109-40.

Tytell, J., *Naked Angels*, 36-51, 111-39.

Vernon, J., *Garden and the Map*, 85-109.

————, "William S. Burroughs," *IowaR* 3, ii (Spring, 1972): 107-23.

Weston, Donald, "William Burroughs, High Priest of Hipsterism," *Fact* 2 (Nov.-Dec., 1965): 11-17.

Whitelaw, Robert M., "Themes in the Work of William Burroughs," *DAI* 31 (1971): 5434A (Mass.).

JUNKIE: CONFESSIONS OF AN UNREDEEMED DRUG ADDICT

Skerl, Jennie, "William S. Burroughs: Pop Artist," *Sphinx* 11 (1980): 2-5.

Stull, William L., "The Quest and the Question: Cosmology and Myth in the Work of William S. Burroughs, 1953-1960," *TCL* 24, ii (Summer, 1978): 232-4. Also in Bartlett, L., ed., *Beats*, 20-2.

Tytell, J., *Naked Images*, 123-8.

THE NAKED LUNCH

Abel, Lionel, "Beyond the Fringe," *PR* 30 (Spring, 1963): 109-12.

Adam, Ian W., "Society as Novelist," *JAAC* 25 (Summer, 1967): 375-86.

Bliss, Michael J., "The Orchestration of Chaos: Verbal Technique in William S. Burroughs' NAKED LUNCH," *DAI* 40 (1980): 5863A.

————, "The Orchestration of Chaos: Verbal Technique in William Burroughs' NAKED LUNCH," *Enclitic* 1, i (1977): 59-69.

"The Boston Trial of NAKED LUNCH," *EvR* 9 (June, 1965): 40-9, 87-8.

Bradbury, Malcolm, "Saul Bellow's HERZOG," *CritQ* 7 (1965): 269-78.

Goodman, Michael B., *Contemporary Literary Censorship: The Case History of Burroughs' NAKED LUNCH*, Metuchen, NJ: Scarecrow, 1981.

————, "The Customs' Censorship of William Burroughs' NAKED LUNCH," *Crit* 22, i (1980): 92-104.

————, "A Study in Contemporary Literary Censorship: The Case History of NAKED LUNCH by William S. Burroughs," *DAI* 40 (1979): 851A-52A.

Hassan, Ihab, "The Subtracting Machine: The Work of William Burroughs," *Crit* 6, i (Spring, 1963): 11-14.

Hilfer, Anthony C., "Mariner and Wedding Guest in William Burroughs' NAKED LUNCH," *Criticism* 22 (1980): 252-65.

Hoffman, F. J., *Mortal No*, 486-8.

Kostelanetz, Richard, "From Nightmare to Seredipity (sic); A Retrospective Look at William Burroughs," *TCL* 11 (Oct., 1965): 123-30. Also (much abridged) as "The New New American Fiction," in Kostelanetz, R., ed., *New American Arts*, 229-31.

Lodge, David, "Objections to William Burroughs," *CritQ* 8 (Autumn, 1966): 203-12. Also in *Novelist at the Crossroads*, 161-70.

Lydenberg, Robin, "Cut-Up: Negative Poetics in William Burroughs and Roland Barthes," *CLS* 15, iv (Dec., 1978): 414-30.

MacLean, Robert M., "Watch Your Language: Narcissus as Addict in NAKED LUNCH," *Narcissus and the Voyeur*, The Hague: Mouton, 1979, 189-225.

Main, Thomas J., "On NAKED LUNCH and Just Desserts," *ChiR* 33, iii (1982): 81-3.

Malcolm, Donald, "The Heroin of Our Times," *NY* 38 (Feb. 2, 1963): 114-21.

McCarthy, Mary, "Burroughs' NAKED LUNCH," *Encounter* 20 (April, 1963): 92-8. Also in *Writing on the Wall*, 42-53.

_____, "Dejeuner sur l'Herbe," *NYRB* 1, i (1963): 4-5.

McConnell, Frank, "William Burroughs and the Literature of Addiction," *MR* 8 (Autumn, 1967): 665-80. Also in Plimpton, George, and Peter Ardery, eds., *The American Literary Anthology/2*, N.Y.: Random House, 1969, 367-81.

Michelson, Peter, "Beardsley, Burroughs, Decadence, and the Poetics of Obscenity," *TriQ* 12 (Spring, 1968): 148-55. Also in Newman, C., and W. A. Henkin, Jr., eds., *Under 30*, 247-54.

Palumbo, Donald, "William Burroughs' Quartet of Science Fiction Novels as Dystopian Social Satire," *Extrapolation* 20, iv (Winter, 1979): 321-9 *passim*.

Pearce, R., *Stages of the Clown*, 88-94.

Peterson, R. G., "A Picture is a Fact: Wittgenstein and THE NAKED LUNCH," *TCl* 12 (July, 1966): 78-86. Also in Bartlett, L., ed., *Beats*, 30-9.

Selden, E. S., "On NAKED LUNCH," *EvR* No. 22 (Jan.-Feb., 1962): 110-13. Also in Seaver, Richard, Terry Southern, and Alexander Trocchi, eds., *Writers in Revolt: An Anthology*, N.Y.: Frederick Fell, 1963, 323-7.

Skerl, Jennie, "William S. Burroughs: Pop Artist," *Sphinx* 11 (1980): 5-9.

Stull, William L., "The Quest and the Question: Cosmology and Myth in the Work of William S. Burroughs, 1953-1960," *TCL* 24, ii (Summer, 1978): 235-41. Also in Bartlett, L., ed., *Beats*, 23-8.

Tanner, T., *City of Words*, 114-23.

Tytell, J., *Naked Images*, 132-9.

Vernon, J., *Garden and the Map*, 85-109 *passim*.

Wain, John, "The Great Burroughs Affair," *NRep* 147 (Dec. 1, 1962): 21-3. Also in Harrison, G. A., ed., *Critic as Artist*, 351-7.

Widmer, L., "Rebellion Against Rebellion?" *Literary Rebel*, 155-8.

Wilt, Koos van der, "The Author's Recreation of Himself as Narrator and Protagonist in Fragmented Prose: A New Look at Some Beat Novels," *DQR* 12, ii (1982): 119-23.

NOVA EXPRESS

Bernard, Sidney, "Literati: William Burroughs," *Ramparts* 5 (Aug., 1966): 51-2.

Lodge, David, "Objections to William Burroughs," *CritQ* 8 (Autumn, 1966): 203-12. Also in *Novelist at the Crossroads*, 161-70.

Phillips, William, "The New Immoralists," *Ctary* 39 (April, 1965): 66-9.

Skerl, Jennie, "William S. Burroughs: Pop Artist," *Sphinx* 11 (1980): 12-13.

Vernon, J., *Garden and the Map*, 85-109 *passim*.

THE SOFT MACHINE

Hassan, Ihab, "The Subtracting Machine: The Work of William Burroughs," *Crit* 6, i (Spring, 1963): 15-18.

Skerl, Jennie, "William S. Burroughs: Pop Artist," *Sphinx* 11 (1980): 11-12.

Vernon, J., *Garden and the Map*, 85-109 *passim*.

THE TICKET THAT EXPLODED

Hassan, Ihab, "The Subtracting Machine: The Work of William Burroughs," *Crit* 6, i (Spring, 1963): 18-21.

Solotaroff, Theodore, "The Algebra Need," *NRep* (Aug. 5, 1967): 29-34.

BIBLIOGRAPHY

Goodman, Michael B., *William S. Burroughs: An Annotated Bibliography of His Works and Criticism* (Garland Ref. Libs. of Humanities 24), N.Y.: Garland, 1975.

Rushing, Lynda Lee, "William S. Burroughs: A Bibliography," *BB* 29 (1972): 87-92.

Skerl, Jennie, "A William S. Burroughs Bibliography," *Serif* 11, ii (Summer, 1974): 12-20.

BUSCH, FREDERICK, 1941-

GENERAL

Greiner, Donald J., "After Great Pain: The Fiction of Frederick Busch," *Crit* 19, i (1977): 101-11.

DOMESTIC PARTICULARS

Greiner, Donald J., "After Great Pain: The Fiction of Frederick Busch," *Crit* 19, i (1977): 106-11.

MANUAL LABOR

Greiner, Donald J., "After Great Pain: The Fiction of Frederick Busch," *Crit* 19, i (1977): 102-6.

BYATT, A(NTONIA) S(USAN), 1936-

THE VIRGIN IN THE GARDEN

Dusinberre, Juliet, "Forms of Reality in A. S. Byatt's THE VIRGIN IN THE GARDEN," *Crit* 24, i (Fall, 1982): 55-62.

CAIN, JAMES M., 1892-1977

GENERAL

Durham, Philip, "James M. Cain's Struggle with Style," *NM* 57 (1956): 133-48.

Fine, David M., "James M. Cain and the Los Angeles Novel," *AmerS* 20, i (Spring, 1979): 25-34.

Frohock, W. M., *Novel of Violence in America*, 13-18.

_____, "The Tabloid Tragedy of James M. Cain," *SWR* 34, iv (Autumn, 1949): 380-6.

Madden, D., *James M. Cain*.

_____, "James M. Cain and the Pure Novel," *UR* 30, ii (Dec., 1963): 143-8; 30, iii (Mar., 1964): 235-9.

_____, "James M. Cain and the Tough Guy Novelists of the 30's," in French, W., ed., *Thirties*, 63-71.

_____, "James M. Cain: Twenty-Minute Egg of the Hard-Boiled School," *JPC* 1, iii (Winter, 1967): 178-92.

Oates, Joyce Carol, "Man Under Sentence of Death: The Novels of James M. Cain," in Madden, D., ed., *Tough Guy Writers of the Thirties*, 110-28.

Reck, Tom S., "J. M. Cain's Los Angeles Novels," *ColQ* 22, iii (Winter, 1974): 375-87.

Wilson, Edmund, "The Boys in the Back Room," *Classics and Commercials*, 19-22. From *NRep* 103 (Nov. 11, 1940): 665-6.

Zinsser, David, "James M. Cain: The Art of Fiction LXIX," *ParisR* 73 (1978) 117-38.

DOUBLE IDEMNITY

Fine, David M., "James M. Cain and the Los Angeles Novel," *AmerS* 20, i (Spring, 1979): 32-3.

Johnston, Claire, "DOUBLE INDEMNITY," 1000-11 in Kaplan, E. Ann, ed., *Women in Film Noir*, London: BFI, 1980.

MILDRED PIERCE

Fine, David M., "James M. Cain and the Los Angeles Novel," *AmerS* 20, i (Spring, 1979): 31-2.

Madden, D., *James M. Cain*, 72-80 *passim*.

THE POSTMAN ALWAYS RINGS TWICE

Fine, David M., "James M. Cain and the Los Angeles Novel," *AmerS* 20, i (Spring, 1979): 29-31.

Frohock, W. M., "The Tabloid Tragedy of James M. Cain," *SWR* 34, iv (Autumn, 1949): 380-6.

Lehan, Richard, "Camus's L'ETRANGER and American Neo-Realism," *BA* 38 (Summer, 1964): 233-8. Also in Lehan, R., *Dangerous Crossing*, 62-6.

Madden, D., *James M. Cain*, 75-80 *passim*, 12-38 *passim*.

_____, "James M. Cain's THE POSTMAN ALWAYS RINGS TWICE and Albert Camus's THE STRANGER," *PLL* 6, iv (Fall, 1970): 407-19.

Oates, Joyce Carol, "Man Under Sentence of Death: The Novels of James M. Cain," in Madden, D., ed., *Tough Guy Writers of the Thirties*, 118-24.

Wells, W., "The Postman and the Marathon," *Tycoons and Locusts*, 14-35.

SERENADE

Madden, D., *James M. Cain*, 121-30 *passim*.

_____, "Morris' CANNIBALS, Cain's SERENADE: The Dynamics of Style and Technique," *JPC* 8, i (Summer, 1974): 59-70.

Oates, Joyce Carol, "Man Under Sentence of Death: The Novels of James M. Cain," in Madden, D., ed., *Tough Guy Writers of the Thirties*, 124-7.

BIBLIOGRAPHY

Madden, D., *James M. Cain*, 185-92.

CALDWELL, ERSKINE, 1903-1987

GENERAL

Bandry, Michel, "An Interview with Erskine Caldwell," 125-36 in *Etudes Anglo-Américaines*, Paris: Belles Lettres, 1982.

Beach, J. W., *American Fiction*, 219-49. Also in MacDonald, S., ed., *Critical Essays on Erskine Caldwell*, 180-97.

Benedict, Stewart H., "Gallic Light on Erskine Caldwell," *SAQ* 60 (Autumn, 1961): 390-7. Also in MacDonald, S., ed., *Critical Essays on Erskine Caldwell*, 255-61.

Bode, Carl, "Erskine Caldwell: A Note for the Negative," *CE* 17 (Oct., 1955): 357-9. Also in Bode, Carl, *The Half-World of American Culture; A Miscellany*, Carbondale: So. Ill. Un. Pr., 1965, 170-4.

Broadwell, Elizabeth P., and Ronald W. Hoag, "The Art of Fiction LXII: Erskine Caldwell," *ParisR* 86 (Winter, 1982): 126-57.

_____, "'A Writer First': An Interview with Erskine Caldwell," *GaR* 36, i (Spring, 1982): 82-101.

Burke, Kenneth, "Caldwell: Maker of Grotesques," *NRep* 82 (April 10, 1935); 232-5. Also in Burke, K., *The Philosophy of Literary Form*, 2nd ed., Baton Rouge: La. St. Un. Pr., 1967, 350-60. Also in Howe, I., ed., *Modern Literary Criticism: An Anthology*, N.Y.: Grove, 1961 (c. 1958, Beacon Pr.), 291-8. Also in Malin, I., ed., *Psychoanalysis and American Fiction*, 245-54. Also in MacDonald, S., ed., *Critical Essays on Erskine Caldwell*, 167-73.

Caldwell, Erskine, "The Art, Craft, and Personality of Writing," *TQ* 7, i (Spring, 1964): 37-43.

Cantwell, Robert, "Caldwell's Characters: Why Don't They Leave," *GaR* 11 (Fall, 1957): 252-64.

Collins, Carvel, "Erskine Caldwell at Work," *Atlantic* 202 (July, 1958): 21-7.

Cook, Sylvia J., "Caldwell's Politics of the Grotesque," *From Tobacco Road to Route 66*, 64-84.

_____, "Erskine Caldwell and the Literary Left Wing," *Pembroke* 11 (1979): 132-9. Also in MacDonald, S., ed., *Critical Essays on Erskine Caldwell*, 361-9.

Cowley, Malcolm, "Georgia Boy: A Retrospect of Erskine Caldwell," in Bruccoli, Matthew J., and C. E. Frazer Clark, Jr., eds., *Pages*, 62-73.

_____, "The Two Erskine Caldwells," *NRep* 111 (Nov. 6, 1944): 599-600. Also in MacDonald, S., ed., *Critical Essays on Erskine Caldwell*, 198-200.

Cross, Carlyle, "Erskine Caldwell as a Southern Writer," *DA* 24 (1964): 4696-7 (Georgia).

Devlin, James E., "The Fiction of Erskine Caldwell," *DAI* 37 (1976): 1546A.

_____, "Fitzgerald's Discovery of Erskine Caldwell," *FHA* (1978): 101-3.

Frohock, W. M., "Erskine Caldwell: Sentimental Gentleman from Georgia," *SWR* 31 (Autumn, 1946): 351-9. Also as "Erskine Caldwell: The Dangers of Ambiguity," in Frohock, W. M., *Novel of Violence in America*, 106-23. Also in MacDonald, S., ed., *Critical Essays on Erskine Caldwell*, 201-13.

Gossett, L. Y., *Violence in Recent Southern Fiction*, 16-29.

Gray, R. J., "Southwestern Humor, Erskine Caldwell, and the Comedy of Frustration," *SLJ* 8, i (Fall, 1975): 3-26. Also in MacDonald, S., ed., *Critical Essays on Erskine Calwell*, 298-314.

Gurko, L., *Angry Decade*, 137-9.

Hazel, Robert, in Rubin, L. D., Jr., and R. D. Jacobs, eds., *Southern Renascence*, 316-24. Also in Rubin, L. D., Jr., and R. D. Jacobs, eds., *South*, 323-33.

Holman, C. Hugh, "Detached Laughter in the South," in Cohen, S. B., ed., *Comic Relief*, 95-8.

Klevar, Harvey L., "The Sacredly Profane and Profanely Sacred: Flannery O'Connor and Erskine Caldwell as Interpreters of Southern Cultural and Religious Traditions," *DAI* 31 (1971): 5407A-08A (Minn.).

Korges, J., *Erskine Caldwell*.

Landor, Mikhail, "Erskine Caldwell in the Soviet Union," *SovL* 3 (1969): 181-6.

Lelchuk, Alan, and Robin White, "Erskine Caldwell," *Per/Se* 2, i (Spring, 1967): 11-20.

MacDonald, S., ed., *Critical Essays on Erskine Caldwell*.

Maclachlan, John M., "Folk and Culture in the Novels of Erskine Caldwell," *SFQ* 9 (June, 1945): 93-101.

Owen, Guy, "Erskine Caldwell's Other Women," *NLauR* 10, i (Spring, 1980): 7-14.

Sale, Richard B., "An Interview in Florida with Erskine Caldwell," *SNNTS* 3, ii (Fall, 1971): 316-31. Also in MacDonald, S., ed., *Critical Essays on Erskine Caldwell*, 279-93.

Seelye, John, "Georgia Boys: The Redclay Satyrs of Erskine Caldwell and Harry Crews," *VQR* 56, iv (Autumn, 1980): 612-26.

Smith, C. Michael, "The Surprising Popularity of Erskine Caldwell's South," *JPC* 16, iii (Winter, 1982): 42-6.

Snell, G., *Shapers of American Fiction*, 263-76.

Tharpe, Jac, "Interview with Erskine Caldwell," *SoQ* 20, i (Fall, 1981): 64-74.

Thompson, James J., "Erskine Caldwell and Southern Religion," *SHR* 5, i (Winter, 1971): 33-44. Also in MacDonald, S., ed., *Critical Essays on Erskine Caldwell*, 268-78.

Thorp, W., *American Writing in the Twentieth Century*, 261-2.

Van Doren, Carl, "Made in America: Erskine Caldwell," *Nation* 137 (Oct. 18, 1933): 443-4. Also in MacDonald, S., ed., *Critical Essays on Erskine Caldwell*, 155-8.

Van Gelder, Robert, *Writers on Writing*, 34-7.

Wagenknecht, E., *Cavalcade of the American Novel*, 415-17.

Whipple, Anne, "Dos Passos and Caldwell Credited Journalism's Contribution," *LGJ* 5, i (1977): 6-8.

THE BASTARD

Korges, J., *Erskine Caldwell*, 12-13.

Owen, Guy, "The Apprenticeship of Erskine Caldwell: An Examination of THE BASTARD and POOR FOOL," in Durant, J. M., and M. T. Hester, eds., *Fair Day in the Affections*, 197-204.

THE BOGUS ONES

Owen, Guy, "The BOGUS ONES: A Lost Erskine Caldwell Novel," *SLJ* 11, i (Fall, 1978): 32-9.

EPISODE IN PALMETTO

Korges, J., *Erskine Caldwell*, 40-1.

GEORGIA BOY

Frohock, W. M., "Erskine Caldwell: Sentimental Gentleman from Georgia," *SWR* 31 (Autumn, 1946): 351-2. Also in Frohock, W. M., *Novel of Violence in America*, 106-8. Also in MacDonald, S., ed., *Critical Essays on Erskine Caldwell*, 201-2.

Korges, J., *Erskine Caldwell*, 37-9.

GOD'S LITTLE ACRE

Allen, W., *Modern Novel*, 119-20.

Beach, J. W., *American Fiction*, 240-5. Also in MacDonald, S., ed., *Critical Essays on Erskine Caldwell*, 191-4.

Cook, Sylvia J., "Caldwell's Politics of the Grotesque," *From Tobacco Road to Route 66*, 71-6.

Devlin, James E., "GOD'S LITTLE ACRE: Forty-Five Years Later," *ArAA* 4 (1979): 79-93.

Gray, R., *Literature of Memory*, 118-28.

Itofuji, Horomi, "An Aspect of Erskine Caldwell in GOD'S LITTLE ACRE," *KAL* No. 2 (May, 1959): 17-22.

Korges, J., *Erskine Caldwell*, 25-32.

Kubie, Lawrence S., M.D., "GOD'S LITTLE ACRE: An Analysis," *SatR* (Nov. 24, 1934): 305-6, 312. Also in Saturday Review, *The Saturday Review Treasury*, N.Y.: Simon & Schuster, 1957, 89-97. Also in MacDonald, S., ed., *Critical Essays on Erskine Caldwell*, 159-66.

GRETTA

Korges, J., *Erskine Caldwell*, 30-2.

JOURNEYMAN

Beach, J. W., *American Fiction*, 235-8. Also in MacDonald, S., ed., *Critical Essays on Erskine Caldwell*, 188-90.

Frohock, W. M., "Erskine Caldwell: Sentimental Gentleman from Georgia," *SWR* 31 (Autumn, 1946): 356-7. Also in Frohock, W. M., *Novel of Violence in America*, 118-19. Also in MacDonald, S., ed., *Critical Essays on Erskine Caldwell*, 209-10.

Korges, J., *Erskine Caldwell*, 32-5.

MISS MAMA AIMEE

Korges, J., *Erskine Caldwell*, 43-4.

POOR FOOL

Owen, Guy, "The Apprenticeship of Erskine Caldwell: An Examination of THE BASTARD and POOR FOOL," in Durant, J. M., and M. T. Hester, eds., *Fair Day in the Affections*, 197-204.

The SACRILEGE OF ALAN KENT

Korges, J ., *Erskine Caldwell*, 10-12.

Owen, Guy, "THE SACRILEGE OF ALAN KENT and the Apprenticeship of Erskine Caldwell," *SLJ* 12, i (1979): 36-46.

SUMMERTIME ISLAND

Korges, J., *Erskine Caldwell*, 42-3.

TOBACCO ROAD

Beach, J. W., *American Fiction*, 225-31. Also in MacDonald, S., ed., *Critical Essays on Erskine Caldwell*, 184-8.

Brinkmeyer, Robert H., Jr., "Is That You in the Mirror, Jeeter?: The Reader and TOBACCO ROAD," *Pembroke* 11 (1979): 47-50. Also in MacDonald, S., ed., *Critical Essays on Erskine Caldwell*, 3700-4.

Cook, Sylvia J., "Caldwell's Politics of the Grotesque," *From Tobacco Road to Route 66*, 65-71.

Gomery, Douglas, "Three Roads Taken: The Novel, the Play, and the Film," in Peary, G., and R. Shatzkin, eds., *Modern American Novel and the Movies*, 9-18.

Gray, J., *On Second Thought*, 119-23.

Gray, R., *Literature of Memory*, 118-28.

Hoag, Ronald, "Irony in the Final Chapter of TOBACCO ROAD," *NConL* 9, v (1979): 8-10.

Jacobs, Robert D., "The Humor of TOBACCO ROAD," in Rubin, L. D., Jr., *Comic Imagination in American Literature*, 285-94.

_____, "TOBACCO ROAD: Lowlife and the Comic Tradition," in Rubin, L. D., ed., *American South*, 206-24.

Korges, J., *Erskine Caldwell*, 22-4.

Marion, J. H., Jr., "Star-Dust Above TOBACCO ROAD," *ChrC* 55 (Feb. 16, 1938): 204-6. Also in MacDonald, S., ed., *Critical Essays on Erskine Caldwell*, 174-9.

Rubin, Louis D., Jr., "Trouble on the Land: Southern Literature and the Great Depression," 969-113 in Bogardus, Ralph F., and Fred Hobson, eds., *Literature at the Barricades: The American Writer in the 1930's*, Tuscaloosa: Un. of Alabama Pr., 1982.

Snell, G., *Shapers of American Fiction*, 272-4.

TRAGIC GROUND

Frohock, W. M., "Erskine Caldwell: Sentimental Gentleman from Georgia," *SWR* 31 (Autumn, 1946): 354-6. Also in Frohock, W. M., *Novel of Violence in America*, 112-16. Also in MacDonald, S., ed., *Critical Essays on Erskine Caldwell*, 205-8.

Gray, J., *On Second Thought*, 125-6.

TROUBLE IN JULY

Beach, J. W., *American Fiction*, 238-40. Also in MacDonald, S., ed., *Critical Essays on Erskine Caldwell*, 190-1.

Frohock, W. M., "Erskine Caldwell: Sentimental Gentleman from Georgia," *SWR* 31 (Autumn, 1946): 352-4. Also in Frohock, W. M., *Novel of Violence in America*, 108-10. Also in MacDonald, S., ed., *Critical Essays on Erskine Caldwell*, 203-4.

BIBLIOGRAPHY

Korges, J., *Erskine Caldwell*, 47-8.

White, William, "About Erskine Caldwell: A Checklist, 1933-1980 and Addenda," *BB* 39, i (Mar., 1982): 9-16; 39, iv (Dec., 1982): 224-6.

CALDWELL, (JANET MIRIAM) TAYLOR (HOLLAND), 1900-1985

GENERAL

Lund, Mary G., "Love and Sex and Taylor Caldwell's Novels," *Cresset* 32, v (1969): 12-15. [Not seen.]

CALISHER, HORTENSE, 1911-

GENERAL

Hahn, Emily, "In Appreciation of Hortense Calisher," *WSCL* 6 (Summer, 1965): 243-9.

Islas, Arturo, Jr., "The Work of Hortense Calisher: On Middle Ground," *DAI* 32 (1972): 4613A-14A (Stanford).

TEXTURES OF LIFE

Brophy, Brigid, in *NStat* (Sept. 13, 1963): 326. Also in Brophy, B., *Don't Never Forget*, 160-2.

CALLAGHAN, MORLEY, 1903-1990

GENERAL

Aaron, Daniel, "Morley Callaghan and the Great Depression," in Staines, D., *Callaghan Symposium*, 23-35.

"The Achievement of Morley Callaghan (A Panel Discussion)" in Staines, D., *Callaghan Symposium*, 95-107.

Bartlett, Donald R., "Callaghan's 'Troubled (and Troubling)' Heroines," *UWR* 16, i (Fall-Winter, 1981): 60-72.

Boire, Gary A., "The Parable and the Priest," *CanL* 81 (Summer, 1979): 154-62.

Cameron, Barry, "Rhetorical Tradition and the Ambiguity of Callaghan's Narrative Rhetoric," in Staines, D., *Callaghan Symposium*, 67-76.

Conron, B., *Morley Callaghan*.

_____, ed., *Morley Callaghan*.

_____, "Morley Callaghan and His Audience," *JCanStud* 15, i (Spring, 1980): 3-7.

Cude, Wilf, "Morley Callaghan's Practical Monsters: Downhill from Where and When," in Moss, J., ed., *Canadian Novel. Vol. III*, 69-78.

Dahlie, Hallvard, "Destructive Innocence in the Novels of Morley Callaghan," *JCF* 1, iii (Summer, 1972): 39-42.

Darte, M. Madeleine, "Moral Vision and Naturalistic Technique: The Conflict in the Novels of Morley Callaghan," *DAI* 39 (1978): 1546A.

Edel, Leon, "Literature and Journalism: The Visible Boundaries," in Staines, D., *Callaghan Symposium*, 7-22.

Ellenwood, Ray, "Morley Callaghan, Jacques Ferron, and the Dialectic of Good and Evil," in Staines, D., *Callaghan Symposium*, 37-46.

Fajardo, Salvador, "Morley Callaghan's Novels and Short Stories," Dissertation, Un. of Montreal, 1962.

Ferris, Ina, "Morley Callaghan and the Exultant Self," *JCanStud* 15, i (Spring, 1980): 13-17.

Heaton, Cherrill P., "The Great Sin: A Critical Study of Morley Callaghan's Novels," *DA* 27 (1966): 1056A57A (Florida St. Un.).

Hoar, V., *Morley Callaghan*.

Kendle, Judith, "Callaghan and the Church," *CanL* 80 (Spring, 1979): 13-22.

_____, "Callahan as Columnist, 1940-48," *CanL* 82 (1979): 6-20.

_____, "Spiritual Tiredness and Dryness of the Imagination: Social Criticism in the Novels of Morley Callaghan," *JCF* 16 (1976): 115-30.

Klinck, C. F., ed., *Literary History of Canada*, Toronto: Un. of Toronto Pr., 1965, 688-93.

Marshall, Tom, "Tragic Ambivalence: The Novels of Morley Callaghan," *UWR* 12, i (Fall-Winter, 1976): 33-48.

Mathews, Robin, "Morley Callaghan and the New Colonialism: The Supreme Individual in Traditionless Society," *SCL* 3, i (Winter, 1978): 78-92.

McDonald, Larry, "The Civilized Ego and Its Discontents: A New Approach to Callaghan," in Staines, D., *Callaghan Symposium*, 77-94.

McPherson, Hugo, "The Two Worlds of Morley Callaghan: Man's Earthly Quest," *QQ* 64 (Autumn, 1957): 350-65. Also in Conron, B., ed., *Morley Callaghan*, 60-73.

Moon, Barbara, "The Second Coming of Morley Callaghan," *MM* 73 (Dec. 3, 1960): 62-4.

Morley, Patricia, "Callaghan's Vision: Wholeness and the Individual," *JCanStud* 15, i (Spring, 1980): 8-12.

_____, *Morley Callaghan*.

_____, "Morley Callaghan: Magician and Illusionist," in Staines, D., *Callaghan Symposium*, 59-65.

Moss, J., *Patterns of Isolation*, 218-22.

O'Connor, John J., "Fraternal Twins: The Impact of Jacques Maritain on Callaghan and Charbonneau," *Mosaic* 14, ii (Spring, 1981): 145-63.

Ozbalt, Marija A. I., "Social Misfits in Morley Callaghan's Fiction and Ivan Cankar's Fiction," *DAI* 39 (1978): 2260A.

Pacey, D., *Creative Writing in Canada*, 209-14.

Ripley, J. D., "A Critical Study of Morley Callaghan," Unpublished M.A. Thesis, Un. of New Brunswick, 1959.

Staines, D., *Callaghan Symposium*.

Sutherland, Fraser, "Hemingway and Callaghan: Friends and Writers," *CanL* 53 (Summer, 1972): 8-17.

_____, *The Style of Innocence: A Study of Hemingway and Callaghan*, Toronto: Clarke, Irwin, 1972.

Walsh, W., *Manifold Voice*, 185-212. Also in Conron, B., ed., *Morley Callaghan*, 129-54.

_____, "Streets of Life: Novels of Morley Callaghan," *ArielE* 1, i (Jan., 1970): 31-42.

Ward, Margaret J., "The Gift of Grace," *CanL* 58 (Autumn, 1973): 19-25.

Watt, F. W., "Morley Callaghan as Thinker," *DR* 39 (Autumn, 1959): 305-13. Also in Smith, A. J. M., ed., *Masks of Fiction*, 116-27.

Weaver, Robert L., "A Talk with Morley Callaghan," *TamR* 7 (Spring, 1958): 3-29.

Wilson, Edmund, "Morley Callaghan of Toronto," *NY* 36 (Nov. 26, 1960): 224-37. Also in Wilson, E., *O Canada*, 9-31. Also in Conron, B., ed., *Morley Callaghan*, 106-19.

_____, "That Summer in Paris," *NY* 39 (Feb. 23, 1963): 139-48.

Woodcock, George, "Lost Eurydice: The Novels of Morley Callaghan," *CanL* No. 21 (Summer, 1964): 21-35. Also in Canadian Literature, *Choice of Critics*, 185-202. Also in Conron, B., ed., *Morley Callaghan*, 88-103. Also in Woodcock, G., *Odysseus Ever Returning*, 24-39. Also in Woodcock, G., ed., *Canadian Novel in the Twentieth Century*, 72-86.

A BROKEN JOURNEY

Conron, B., *Morley Callaghan*, 70-8.
Morley, P., *Morley Callaghan*, 22-5.

CLOSE TO THE SUN AGAIN

Cude, Wilf, "Morley Callaghan's Practical Monsters: Downhill from Where and When?" in Moss, J., ed., *Canadian Novel. Vol. III*, 69-78.

Morley, P., *Morley Callaghan*, 59-60.

A FINE AND PRIVATE PLACE

Morley, P., *Morley Callaghan*, 55-8.

IT'S NEVER OVER

Conron, B., *Morley Callaghan*, 59-65.
Morley, P., *Morley Callaghan*, 17-20.

Wilson, E., *O Canada*, 24-6. Also in Conron, B., ed., *Morley Callaghan*, 115-16.

THE LOVED AND THE LOST

Conron, B., *Morley Callaghan*, 128-35.

Dooley, D. J., *Moral Vision in the Canadian Novel*, Toronto: Clarke, Irwin, 1979, 61-77.

Gouri, C. R., "Society and Solitude in THE LOVED AND THE LOST," in Sarma, S. Krishna, ed., *English Writing in the Twentieth Century*, Guntar, India: The English Assoc., 1974, 97-103.

Jones, D. G., *Butterfly on Rock*, 52-5.

Kendle, Judith, "Spiritual Tiredness and Dryness of the Imagination: Social Criticism in the Novels of Morley Callaghan," *JCF* 16 (1976): 115-30.

Marshall, Tom, "Tragic Ambivalence: The Novels of Morley Callaghan," *UWR* 12, i (Fall-Winter, 1976): 40-4.

McPherson, Hugo, "The Two Worlds of Morley Callaghan: Man's Earthly Quest," *QQ* 64 (Autumn, 1957): 362-5. Also in Conron, B., ed., *Morley Callaghan*, 70-3.

Morley, P., *Morley Callaghan*, 41-3.

Phelps, Arthur L., *Canadian Writers*, 10-18.

Walsh, W., *Manifold Voice*, 203-6. Also in Conron, B., ed., *Morley Callaghan*, 145-8.

_____, "Streets of Life: Novels of Morley Callaghan," *ArielE* 1, i (Jan., 1970): 36-9.

Wilson, Edmund, "Morley Callaghan of Toronto," *NY* 36 (Nov. 26, 1960): 226-30. Also in Wilson, E., *O Canada*, 12-15. Also in Conron, B., ed., *Morley Callaghan*, 108-9.

THE MANY COLORED COAT

Conron, B., *Morley Callaghan*, 135-47.

McPherson, Hugo, "A Tale Retold," *CanL* No. 7 (Winter, 1961): 59-61.

Morley, P., *Morley Callaghan*, 43-6.

Walsh, W., *Manifold Voice*, 206-12. Also in Conron, B., ed., *Morley Callaghan*, 148-54.

_____, "Streets of Life: Novels of Morley Callaghan," *ArielE* 1, i (Jan., 1970): 402-4.

Watt, F. W., "Fiction," in "Letters in Canada: 1960," *UTQ* 30 (July, 1961): 402-4.

Wilson, Edmund, "Morley Callaghan of Toronto," *NY* 36 (Nov. 26, 1960): 230-3. Also in Wilson, E., *O Canada*, 15-18. Also in Conron, B., ed., *Morley Callaghan*, 109-12.

MORE JOY IN HEAVEN

Clever, Glenn, "Callaghan's MORE JOY IN HEAVEN as a Tragedy," *CFM* 2-3 (1971): 88-93.

Conron, B., *Morley Callaghan*, 108-18.

Marshall, Tom, "Tragic Ambivalence: The Novels of Morley Callaghan," *UWR* 12, i (Fall-Winter, 1975): 38-40.

McPherson, Hugo, "The Two Worlds of Morley Callaghan: Man's Earthly Quest," *QQ* 64 (Autumn, 1957): 360-2. Also in Conron, B., ed., *Morley Callaghan*, 69-70.

Morley, P., *Morley Callaghan*, 34-8.

Walsh, W., *Manifold Voice*, 198-202. Also in Conron, B., ed., *Morley Callaghan*, 141-5.

_____, "Streets of Life: Novels of Morley Callaghan," *ArielE* 1, i (Jan., 1970): 35-6.

NO MAN'S MEAT

Conron, B., *Morley Callaghan*, 65-9.
Morley, P., *Morley Callaghan*, 20-2.

A PASSION IN ROME

Conron, B., *Morley Callaghan*, 155-67.
Morley, P., *Morley Callaghan*, 46-7.
Watt, Frank, "Morley Callaghan's A PASSION IN ROME," Un. of Toronto *Varsity Graduate* 9, v (Mar., 1962): 6, 8, 10, 12. Also in Conron B., ed., *Morley Callaghan*, 84-7.
Wilson, Milton, "Callaghan's Caviare," *TamR* 22 (Winter, 1962): 88-93. Also in Conron, B., ed., *Morley Callaghan*, 79-83.
Woodcock, George, "The Callaghan Case," *CanL* No. 12 (Spring, 1962): 60-4.

STRANGE FUGITIVE

Conron, B., *Morley Callaghan*, 23-8.
Mathews, Robin, "Morley Callaghan and the New Colonialism: The Supreme Individual in Traditionless Society," *SCL* 3, i (Winter, 1978): 82-5.
McPherson, Hugo, "The Two Worlds of Morley Callaghan: Man's Earthly Quest," *QQ* 64 (Autumn, 1957): 352-6. Also in Conron, B., ed., *Morley Callaghan*, 62-5.
Morley, P., *Morley Callaghan*, 13-17.
Wilson, E., *O Canada*, 22-3. Also in Conron, B., ed., *Morley Callaghan*, 114-15.

SUCH IS MY BELOVED

Aaron, Daniel, "Morley Callaghan and the Great Depression," in Staines, D., *Callaghan Symposium*, 27-35.
Conron, B., *Morley Callaghan*, 78-86.
Marshall, Tom, "Tragic Ambivalence: The Novels of Morley Callaghan," *UWR* 12, i (Fall-Winter, 1976): 33-7.
Mathews, Robin, "Callaghan, Joyce, and the Doctrine of Infallibility," *SCL* 6, ii (1981): 286-93.
McPherson, Hugo, "The Two Worlds of Morley Callaghan: Man's Earthly Quest," *QQ* 64 (Autumn, 1957): 357-9. Also in Conron, B., ed., *Morley Callaghan*, 66-8.
Morley, P., *Morley Callaghan*, 27-30.
Walsh, W., *Manifold Voice*, 191-8. Also in Conron, B., ed., *Morley Callaghan*, 134-40.
_____, "Streets of Life: Novels of Morley Callaghan," *ArielE* 1, i (Jan., 1970): 31-5.

THEY SHALL INHERIT THE EARTH

Conron, B., *Morley Callaghan*, 86-96.
Marshall, Tom, "Tragic Ambivalence: The Novels of Morley Callaghan," *UWR* 12, i (Fall-Winter, 1976): 37-8.
Mathews, Robin, "Morley Callaghan and the New Colonialism: The Supreme Individual in Traditionless Society," *SCL* 3, i (Winter, 1978): 85-92.
Morley, P., *Morley Callaghan*, 30-3.
O'Connor, John J., "Fraternal Twins: The Impact of Jacques Maritain on Callaghan and Charbonneau," *Mosaic* 14, ii (Spring, 1981): 145-63.

THE VARSITY STORY

Conron, B., *Morley Callaghan*, 124-6.
Wilson, E., *O Canada*, 26-8. Also in Conron, B., ed., *Morley Callaghan*, 116-18.

BIBLIOGRAPHY

Conron, B., *Morley Callaghan*, 181-4.

CAPOTE, TRUMAN, 1924-1984

GENERAL

Aldridge, J. W., *After the Lost Generation*, 196-219.
Allen, W., *Modern Novel*, 301-3.
Baldanza, Frank, "Plato in Dixie," *GaR* 12 (Summer, 1958): 162-5.
Bogh, Jens, in Bogh, J., and S. Skovmand, eds., *Six American Novels*, 289-302.
Bucco, Martin, "Truman Capote and the Country Below the Surface," *Four Quarters* 7, i (Nov., 1957): 22-5.
Friedman, Melvin J., in Malin, I., ed., *Truman Capote's IN COLD BLOOD*, 163-76.
Garson, H. S., *Truman Capote*.
Goad, Craig M., "Daylight and Darkness, Dream and Delusion: The Works of Truman Capote," *ESRS* 16 (Sept., 1967): 5-57.
Gossett, L. Y., "Violence in a Private World: Truman Capote," *Violence in Recent Southern Fiction*, 145-58.
Hassan, Ihab H., "The Daydream and Nightmare of Narcissus," *WSCL* 1, ii (Spring-Summer, 1960): 5-21. Also, slightly altered, in *Radical Innocence*, 230-5.
Hellmann, John, "The Nature and Modes of the New Journalism: A Theory," *Genre* 13, iv (Winter, 1980): 517-29.
Hienbaugh, Nan S., "The Study of Psychopathology in the Works of Truman Capote," *DAI* 36 (1975): 3043B-44B.
Hill, Pati, "Truman Capote Interview," in Cowley, M., ed., *Writers at Work*, 1st ser., 283-9. Also in Malin, I., ed., *Truman Capote's IN COLD BLOOD*, 131-41.
Johnson, Thomas S., "The Horror in the Mansion: Gothic Fiction in the Works of Truman Capote and Carson McCullers," *DAI* 34 (1973): 2630A. (Texas, Austin).
Keith, Don Lee, "An Interview with Truman Capote," *Contempora* 1, iv (1970): 36-40.
Kempton, Beverly G., "Interview with Truman Capote," *Playboy* 23, xii (Dec., 1976): 47, 50.
Larsen, Michael J., "Capote's 'Miriam' and the Literature of the Double," *IFR* 7 (1980): 53-4.
Levine, Paul, "Truman Capote: The Revelation of the Broken Image," *VQR* 34 (Autumn, 1958): 600-17. Also in Malin, I., ed., *Truman Capote's IN COLD BLOOD*, 141-53. Also in Waldmeir, J. J., ed., *Recent American Fiction*, 153-66.
Littlejohn, David, "Capote Collected," *Cweal* 78 (May 10, 1963): 187-8.
Ludwig, J., *Recent American Novelists*, 33-6.
McKenzie, James, "In Cold Print: An Interview with Truman Capote," *Confrontation* 16 (1978): 25-36.
Meeker, Richard K., in Simonini, R. C., Jr., ed., *Southern Writers*, 181-4.

Moravia, Alberto, "Two American Writers (1949)," *SR* 68 (Summer, 1960): 477-81.

Nance, William L., "Variations on a Dream: Katherine Anne Porter and Truman Capote," *SHR* 3, iv (Fall, 1969): 338-45.

_____, *Worlds of Truman Capote.*

Norden, Eric, "*Playboy* Interview: Truman Capote," *Playboy* (March, 1968): 51-3, 56, 58-62, 160-2, 164-70.

Rabaté, Jean-Michel, "'Being Read to By a Boy Waiting for Rain'," *DeltaES* 11 (1980): 25-30. [Not seen.]

Reed, K. T., *Truman Capote.*

Schorer, Mark, Introduction to *Selected Writings of Truman Capote*, N.Y.: Random House, 1963, vii-xii.

_____, "McCullers and Capote: Basic Patterns," in Balakian, N., and C. Simmons, eds., *Creative Present*, 96-107. Also in Schorer, M., *World We Imagine*, 285-96.

Woodward, Robert H., "Thomas Wolfe: Truman Capote's 'Textbook'," *TWN* 2, i (Spring, 1978): 21.

BREAKFAST AT TIFFANY'S

Clark, Leslie, "Brunch on Moon River," in Peary, G., and R. Shatzkin, eds., *Modern American Novel and the Movies*, 236-46.

Garson, H. S., *Truman Capote*, 79-89.

Goad, Craig M., "Daylight and Darkness, Dream and Delusion: The Works of Truman Capote," *ESRS* 16 (Sept., 1967): 39-41.

Hassan, Ihab H., "Birth of a Heroine," *PrS* 34 (Spring, 1960): 78-83.

_____, "The Daydream and Nightmare of Narcissus," *WSCL* 1, ii (Spring-Summer, 1960): 16-21. Also, slightly altered, in Hassan, I., *Radical Innocence*, 250-5.

Hyman, S. E., "Fruitcake at Tiffany's," *Standards*, 149-50.

Kazin, Alfred, "Truman Capote and the Army of Wrongness," *Reporter* 19 (Nov. 13, 1958): 40-1. Also in Kazin, A., *Contemporaries*, 250-4.

Levine, Paul, *GaR* 13 (Fall, 1959): 350-2.

Ludwig, J., *Recent American Novelists*, 34-6.

Mayhew, Alice E., "Familiar Phantoms in the Country of Capote," *Cweal* 69 (Nov. 28, 1958): 236-7.

Merrick, Gordon, "How to Write Lying Down," *NRep* 139 (Dec. 8, 1958): 23-4.

Nance, W. L., *Worlds of Truman Capote*, 107-24.

Reed, K. T., *Truman Capote*, 88-93.

THE GRASS HARP

Eisinger, C. E., *Fiction of the Forties*, 241-2.

Garson, H. S., *Truman Capote*, 63-77.

Goad, Craig M., "Daylight and Darkness, Dream and Delusion: The Works of Truman Capote," *ESRS* 16 (Sept., 1967): 33-5.

Hassan, Ihab H., "The Daydream and Nightmare of Narcissus," *WSCL* 1, ii (Spring-Summer, 1960): 13-16. Also, slightly altered, in *Radical Innocence*, 245-50.

Hoffman, F. J., *Art of Southern Fiction*, 123-44.

Levine, Paul, "Truman Capote: The Revelation of the Broken Image," *VQR* 34 (Autumn, 1958): 615-17. Also in Malin, I., ed., *Truman Capote's IN COLD BLOOD*, 152-3. Also in Waldmeir, J. J., ed., *Recent American Fiction*, 164-6.

Nance, H. S., *Truman Capote*, 81-8, 122-8.

IN COLD BLOOD

Anon., "A Machine and Sympathy," *TLS* (Mar. 17, 1966): 223.

Bogh, Jens, in Bogh, J., and S. Skoumand, eds., *Six American Novels*, 303-16.

Creeger, George R., "Animals in Exile: Criminal and Community in Capote's IN COLD BLOOD," *JA* 14 (1969): 94-106.

_____, "Animals in Exile: Imagery and Theme in Capote's IN COLD BLOOD," in Weber, Alfred, and Dietmar Haack, eds., *Amerikanische Literatur im 20. Jahrhundert/American Literature in the 20th Century*, Gottlingen: Vandenhoeck & Ruprecht, 1971, 107-26.

DeBellis, Jack, "Visions and Revisions: Truman Capote's IN COLD BLOOD," *JML* 7, iii (Sept., 1979): 519-36.

Dupee, F. W., "Truman Capote's Score," *NYRB* 6 (Feb. 3, 1966): 3-5.

Eckstein, George, *Dissent* (July-Aug., 1966): 433-5.

Enright, D. J., "Account Rendered," *Man is an Onion*, 44-51. Orig. in *NStat* 71 (Mar. 18, 1966): 377-8.

Friedman, Melvin J., in Malin, I., ed., *Truman Capote's IN COLD BLOOD*, 163-76.

Galloway, David, in Malin, I., ed., *Truman Capote's IN COLD BLOOD*, 154-63.

Garrett, George, "Crime and Punishment in Kansas: Truman Capote's IN COLD BLOOD," *HC* 3 (Feb., 1966): 1-12. Also in Malin, I., ed., *Truman Capote's IN COLD BLOOD*, 81-91.

Garson, H. S., *Truman Capote*, 141-64.

Goad, Craig M., "Daylight and Darkness, Dream and Delusion: The Works of Truman Capote," *ESRS* 16 (Sept., 1967): 42-55.

Hellmann, John, "Death and Design in IN COLD BLOOD: Capote's 'Nonfiction Novel' as Allegory," *BSUF* 21, ii (1980): 65-78.

Hollowell, J., *Fact and Fiction: The New Journalism and the Nonfiction Novel*, Chapel Hill: Un. of No. Carolina Pr., 1977, 69-86.

Jacobs, J. V. "IN COLD BLOOD: The Non-Fiction Novel," *UES* 9 (Sept., 1971): 17-22.

Kauffmann, Stanley, "Capote in Kansas," *NRep* 154 (Jan. 22, 1966): 19-21+. Also in Malin, I., ed., *Truman Capote's IN COLD BLOOD*, 60-4.

King, James, "Turning New Leaves," *CanF* 45 (Mar., 1966): 281-2.

Kramer, Hilton, "Real Gardens with Real Toads," *New Leader* (Jan. 31, 1966): 18-19. Also in Malin, I., *Truman Capote's IN COLD BLOOD*, 65-8.

Langbaum, Robert, "Capote's Nonfiction Novel," *ASch* 35 (Summer, 1966): 570-80. Also in Malin, I., ed., *Truman Capote's IN COLD BLOOD*, 114-20.

Levine, Paul, "Reality and Fiction," *HudR* 19 (Spring, 1966): 135-8.

McAleer, John J., "AN AMERICAN TRAGEDY and IN COLD BLOOD," *Thought* 47 (Winter, 1972): 569-86.

Meacham, William S., "A Non-Fiction Study in Scarlet," *VQR* 42 (Spring, 1966): 316-19.

Morris, Robert K., "Capote's Imagery," in Malin, I., ed., *Truman Capote's IN COLD BLOOD*, 176-86.

Murray, Edward, "IN COLD BLOOD: The Filmic Novel and the Problem of Adaptation," *LFQ* 1, ii (April, 1973): 132-7.

Nance, W. L., *Worlds of Truman Capote*, 155-215.

Phillips, William, "But Is It Good for Literature?" *Ctary* 41 (May, 1966): 77-80. Also in Malin, I., ed., *Truman Capote's IN COLD BLOOD*, 102-6.

Pizer, Donald, "Documentary Narrative as Art: William Manchester and Truman Capote," *JML* 2, i (Sept., 1971): 111-18.

Plimpton, George, "The Story Behind a Nonfiction Novel," *NYTBR* (Jan. 16, 1966): 2-3, 38-43. Also in Malin, I., ed., *Truman Capote's IN COLD BLOOD*, 25-43.

Reed, K. T., *Truman Capote*, 101-18.

Tanner, Tony, "Death in Kansas," *Spectator* 208 (Mar. 18, 1966): 331-2. Also in Malin, I., ed., *Truman Capote's IN COLD BLOOD*, 98-102.

Tompkins, Phillip K., "In Cold Fact," *Esquire* 65 (June, 1966): 125+. Also in Malin, I., ed., *Truman Capote's IN COLD BLOOD*, 44-58.

Trilling, Diana, "Capote's Crime and Punishment," *PR* 33 (Spring, 1966): 252-9. Also in Malin, I., ed., *Truman Capote's IN COLD BLOOD*, 107-13.

Walcutt, C. C., *Man's Changing Mask*, 344-6.

West, Rebecca, "A Grave and Reverend Book," *Harper's* 232 (Feb., 1966): 108+. Also in Malin, I., ed., *Truman Capote's IN COLD BLOOD*, 91-8.

Wiegand, William, "The 'Non-Fiction' Novel," *NMQ* 37 (Autumn, 1967): 243-57.

Yurick, Sol, "Sob-Sister Gothic," *Nation* 202 (Feb. 7, 1966): 158-60.

Zaslove, Jerald, "IN COLD BLOOD: More Cultural Cool-Aid," *Paunch* No. 26 (April, 1966): 79-84.

OTHER VOICES, OTHER ROOMS

Aldridge, John W., *After the Lost Generation*, 202-18.

_____, "The Metaphorical World of Truman Capote," *WR* 15 (Summer, 1951): 250-60.

Baumbach, J., *Landscape of Nightmare*, 7-8.

Blake, Nancy, "OTHER VOICES, OTHER ROOMS: Southern Gothic or Medieval Quest?" *DeltaES* 11 (1980): 31-47.

Capote, Truman, "Voice From a Cloud," in McCormack, T., ed., *Afterwords*, 139-45. Also in Capote, T., OTHER VOICES, OTHER ROOMS (Twentieth Anniversary ed.), N.Y.: Random House, 1967.

Coindreau, M. E., *Time of William Faulkner*, 123-31.

Collins, Carvel, "Other Voices," *ASch* 25 (Winter, 1955-56): 108-16.

Davis, Robert C., "OTHER VOICES, OTHER ROOMS and the Ocularity of American Fiction," *DeltaES* 11 (1980): 1-14.

Eisinger, C. E., *Fiction of the Forties*, 237-40.

Garson, H. S., *Truman Capote*, 4-7, 13-25.

Goad, Craig M., "Daylight and Darkness, Dream and Delusion: The Works of Truman Capote," *ESRS* 16 (Sept., 1967): 26-32.

Hassan, Ihab H., "The Daydream and Nightmare of Narcissus," *WSCL* 1, ii (Spring-Summer, 1960): 9-13. Also in Hassan, I. H., *Radical Innocence*, 239-45.

Hoffman, F. J., *Art of Southern Fiction*, 118-22.

Levine, Paul, "Truman Capote: The Revelation of the Broken Image," *VQR* 34 (Autumn, 1958): 610-15. Also in Malin, I., ed., *Truman Capote's IN COLD BLOOD*, 149-52. Also in Waldmeir, J. J., ed., *Recent American Fiction*, 161-4.

Malin, Irving, "The Gothic Family," *Psychoanalysis and American Fiction*, 255-6. Also in Malin, I., *New American Gothic*, 50-2.

Mengeling, Marvin E., "OTHER VOICES, OTHER ROOMS: Oedipus Between the Covers," *AI* 19 (Winter, 1962): 361-74.

Naka, Michiko, "Truman Capote: Negation of Differentiation," in *American Literature in the 1940's*, 75-91 *passim*.

Nance, W. L., *Worlds of Truman Capote*, 40-64.

Perry, J. Douglas, Jr., "Gothic as Vortex: The Form of Horror in Capote, Faulkner, and Styron," *MFS* 19, ii (Summer, 1973): 156-9.

Prescott, O., *In My Opinion*, 114-15.

Reed, K. T., *Truman Capote*, 71-81, 121-8.

Ruoff, Gene W., "Truman Capote: The Novelist as a Commodity," in French, W., ed., *Forties*, 261-9.

Shrike, J. S., "Recent Phenomena, " *HudR* 1 (Spring, 1948): 136-44.

Trilling, Diana, "Fiction in Review," *Nation* 166 (Jan. 31, 1948): 133-4.

Trimmier, Dianne B., "The Critical Reception of Capote's OTHER VOICES, OTHER ROOMS," *WVUPP* 17 (June, 1970): 94-101.

Woodward, Robert H., "Thomas Wolfe: Truman Capote's 'Textbook'," *TWN* 2, i (Spring, 1978): 21.

Young, Marguerite, "Tiger Lilies," *KR* 10 (Summer, 1948): 516-18.

BIBLIOGRAPHY

Bonnet, Jean-Marie, comp., "Truman Capote: A Selected Bibliography," *DeltaES* 11 (1980): 89-104. [Not seen.]

Bryer, Jackson R., "Truman Capote: A Bibliography," in Malin, I., ed., *Truman Capote's IN COLD BLOOD*, 239-69.

Stanton, Robert J., *Truman Capote: A Primary and Secondary Bibliography*, Boston: Hall, 1980.

Vanderwerken, David L., "Truman Capote: 1943-1968: A Critical Bibliography," *BB* 27, iii (July-Sept., 1970): 57-60, 71.

Wilson, Robert A., comp., "Truman Capote: A Bibliographical Checklist," *ABC* 1, iv (1980): 8-15.

CAPPS, BENJAMIN (FRANKLIN), 1922-

THE WHITE MAN'S ROAD

Etulain, Richard W., "THE WHITE MAN'S ROAD: An Appreciation," *SwAL* 1 (1971): 85-92.

CARTER, ANGELA, 1940-

GENERAL

Bedford, William, "Interview with Angela Carter," *New Yorkshire Writing* 3 (1978): 1-2.

Sage, Lorna, "The Savage Sideshow: A Profile of Angela Carter," *NewRev* 4 39/40 (June-July, 1977): 51-7.

CARY, JOYCE, 1888-1957

GENERAL

Adam International Review 18 (Nov.-Dec., 1950): Cary Issue.

Adams, Hazard, "Introduction" to Joyce Cary's POWER IN MEN, Seattle: Un. of Wash. Pr., 1963, vii-xlvi.

_____, "Joyce Cary: Posthumous Volumes and Criticism to Date," *TSLL* 1 (1959): 289-99.

_____, "Joyce Cary's Swimming Swan," *ASch* 29 (Spring, 1960): 235-9.

Allen, W., *Joyce Cary*.

_____, *Modern Novel*, 242-8.

Barba, Harry, "Image of the African in Transition," *UKCR* 29 (Mar., 1963): 215-21.

Bettman, Elizabeth R., "Joyce Cary and the Problem of Political Morality," *AR* 17 (Summer, 1957): 266-72.

Bloom, R., *Indeterminate World*.

Brown, Patricia S., "Creative Losers: Blacks, Children, and Women in the Novels of Joyce Cary," *DAI* 34 (1974): 6627A (Mass.).

Burrows, John, and Alex Hamilton, "The Art of Fiction, Joyce Cary," *ParisR* No. 7 (Winter, 1954-55): 62-78. Also in *Writers at Work*, 1st ser., 51-67.

Cary, Joyce, "The Novelist at Work: A Conversation Between Joyce Cary and Lord David Cecil," *AiR* 18 (Nov.-Dec., 1950): 15-25.

_____, "The Way a Novel Gets Written," *AIR* 18 (Nov.-Dec., 1950): 3-11.

Case, Edward, "The Free World of Joyce Cary," *ModA* 3 (Spring, 1959): 115-24.

Cohen, Nathan, "A Conversation with Joyce Cary," *TamR* No. 3 (Spring, 1957): 5-15.

Collins, Harold R., "Joyce Cary's Troublesome Africans," *AR* 13 (Sept., 1953): 397-406.

Cook, C., *Joyce Cary*.

Cosman, Max, "The Protean Joyce Cary," *Cweal* 69 (Mar. 6, 1959): 596-8.

Craig, David, "Idea and Imagination: A Study of Joyce Cary," *Fox* (Aberdeen Un. Classical, Literary and Philosophical Societies), n.d. (c. 1954): 3-10. [Not seen.]

Creelman, Melba J.A.C., "Joyce Cary: The Art of the Trilogy," *DAI* 38 (1978): 5457A.

Dwyer, John T., "Joyce Cary's Critical Theory and Its Relationship to the Development of His Fiction," *DA* 29 (1968): 258A (Un. of Pa.).

Eberly, Ralph S., "Joyce Cary's Theme of Freedom and a Comparison with James Joyce and Graham Greene," *DAI* 31 (1971): 6601A (Mich.).

Echeruo, Michael J. K., "The Dimensions of Order: A Study of Joyce Cary," *DA* 26 (1966): 5431 (Cornell).

_____, *Joyce Cary and the Dimensions of Order*.

_____, *Joyce Cary and the Novel of Africa*.

Fisher, B., *Joyce Cary*.

_____, "Two Joycean Novelists," *CJIS* 4, ii (1978): 5-22. [Not seen.]

Foster, Malcolm, "Fell of the Lion, Fleece of the Sheep," *MFS* 9, iii (Autumn, 1963): 257-62.

_____, *Joyce Cary*.

Friedman, Alan W., "Joyce Cary's Cubistic Morality," *ConL* 14, i (Winter, 1973): 78-96.

Friedson, Anthony M., "The Novels of Joyce Cary," *DA* 21 (1961): 3781 (Iowa).

Galligan, Edward L., "Intuition and Concept: Joyce Cary and the Critics," *TSLL* (Winter, 1967): 581-7.

Gardner, Helen, "The Novels of Joyce Cary," *E&S* 28 (1975): 76-93.

Geering, R. G., "Joyce Cary: The Man and His Work," *Quadrant* 2 (Winter, 1959): 45-51.

Gindin, J., *Harvest of a Quiet Eye*, 258-76.

Goonetilleke, D.C.R.A., "Africa Through European Eyes: Joseph Conrad and Joyce Cary," *English Bulletin* 2 (1978): 27-35. [Not seen.]

_____, "Joyce Cary: The Clash of Cultures in Nigeria," *Developing Countries in British Fiction*, 199-244.

Hansen, Janis T., "The Novels of Joyce Cary: Uses of the Picaresque," *DA* 26 (1966): 5435 (Oregon).

Hardy, Barbara, "Form in Joyce Cary's Novels," *EIC* 4 (April, 1954): 180-90.

Hatfield, Glenn W., Jr., "Form and Character in the Sequence Novels of Joyce Cary," Thesis (unpublished), Ohio St. Un., 1956.

Heldt, Lucia H., "Triptych-Trilogies: A Study of Joyce Cary's Religious Comedy," *DAI* 39 (1978): 3597A.

Hoffmann, Charles G., *Joyce Cary*.

_____, "Joyce Cary: Art and Reality. The Interaction of Form and Narrator," *UKCR* 26 (June, 1960): 273-82.

_____, "Joyce Cary's African Novels: There's a War On," *SAQ* 62 (Spring, 1963): 229-43.

Holloway, John, "Joyce Cary's Fiction: Modernity and 'Sustaining Power'," *TLS* (Aug. 7, 1959): 14-15.

Hurry, Michael J., "Structure and Creative Imagination: Joyce Cary's Novels," *DAI* 40 (1980): 4591A.

JanMohamed, Abdul R., *Joyce Cary's African Romances*.

Johnson, Pamela H., "Three Novelists and the Drawing of Character: C.P. Snow, Joyce Cary and Ivy Compton-Burnett," in English Association, *Essays and Studies, 1950*, 82-4, 89-94.

Jones, Malcolm V., "Dostoevsky and Europe: Travels in the Mind," *RMS* 24 (1980): 38-57.

Kalechofsky, Roberta, "Joyce Cary—His Political World and Ours," *DAI* 31 (1971): 6614A (N.Y.U.).

Kanu, S. H., *World of Everlasting Conflict*.

Karl, Frederick R., "Joyce Cary: The Moralist as Novelist," *TCL* 5 (Jan., 1960): 183-96. Also in *Contemporary English Novel*, 131-47.

Kelleher, John J., "The Theme of Freedom in the Novels of Joyce Cary," *DA* 26 (1965): 369-70 (Pittsburgh).

Kennedy, Richard S., "Joyce Cary's Comic Affirmation of Life," *PCTEB* No. 13 (May, 1966): 3-14. [Not seen.]

King, Carlyle, "Joyce Cary," *CanF* 33 (Mar., 1954): 273-4.

_____, "Joyce Cary and the Creative Imagination," *TamR* No. 10 (Winter, 1959): 39-51.

Kraus, Richard, "Archetypes and the Trilogy Structure—A Study of Joyce Cary's Fiction," *DA* 27 (1967): 3430A (Stanford).

Larsen, G. L., *Dark Descent*.

Lucchesi, Peter G., "The Charismatic as Center of Irony in the Novels of James (sic) Joyce Cary," *DA* 28 (1967): 683-84A (Wisconsin).

Mahood, M. M., *Joyce Cary's Africa*.

Majumdar, Bimalendu, "Joyce Cary's African Novels: Vision of an Artist," in Chakrabarti, Dipendu, ed., *Essays Presented to Prof. Amalendu Bose*, Bulletin of the Dept. of English 8, ii (1972-1973), Calcutta: Calcutta Un., 91-7.

McDorman, Kathryne S., "Two Views of Empire: Margary Perham and Joyce Cary Analyze the Dual Mandate Policy," *RS* 50, iii-iv (Sept.-Dec., 1982): 153-60.

Moody, P. R., "Road and Bridge in Joyce Cary's African Novels," *BRMMLA* 21 (Dec., 1967): 145-9. [Not seen.]

Noble, R. W., *Joyce Cary*.

Nyce, Benjamin M., "Joyce Cary as a Political Novelist," *DA* 29 (1968): 574A-75A. (Claremont).

O'Connor, W. V., *Joyce Cary*.

O'Grady, Walter A., "Political Contexts in the Novels of Graham Greene and Joyce Cary," *DAI* 32 (1972): 6995A (Toronto).

Ola, Virginia U., "The Vision of Power: Joyce Cary and African Women," *ArielE* 9, i (Jan., 1978): 85-97.

Owen, B. Evan, "The Supremacy of the Individual in the Novels of Joyce Cary," *AIR* 18 (Nov.-Dec., 1950): 25-9.

Prescott, O., *In My Opinion*, 191-9.

Raskin, Jonah, "Forster and Cary: Old and New," *Mythology of Imperialism*, 222-41.

Ready, William B., "Joyce Cary," *Critic* 18 (June-July, 1960): 9-10, 59-60.

Rosenthal, Michael, "Comedy and Despair in Joyce Cary's Fiction," *DA* 28 (1967): 693A (Columbia).

————, "Joyce Cary's Comic Sense," *TSLL* 13, ii (Summer, 1971): 337-46.

Salz, Paulina J., "The Novels of Joyce Cary in Relation to His Critical Writings," *DA* 22 (1962): 3208-9 (So. Calif.).

————, "The Philosophical Principles in Joyce Cary's Work," *WHR* 20 (Spring, 1966): 159-65.

Sharma, K. K., *Joyce Cary*.

Starkie, Enid, "Joyce Cary: A Personal Portrait," *VQR* 37 (Winter, 1961): 110-34. Also in *EDH* 32 (1963): 125-44.

Steinbrecher, George, Jr., "Joyce Cary: Master Novelist," *CE* 18 (May, 1957): 387-95.

Stewart, Douglas, *Ark of God*, 129-58.

Teeling, John, "Joyce Cary's Moral World," *MFS* 9, iii (Autumn, 1963): 276-83.

Thompson, Edwin J., "Innocence, Experience, and Value: A Study of Joyce Cary," *DAI* 35 (1975): 7331A-32A.

Van Horn, Ruth G., "Freedom and Imagination in the Novels of Joyce Cary," *Midwest Jnl* 5 (Winter, 1952-53): 19-30.

Wager, Walter J., "Joyce Cary and the Modern Novel," *DAI* 32 (1972): 7014A (U.C.L.A.).

Webster, Harvey C., "Joyce Cary: Christian Unclassified," *After the Trauma*, 124-51.

Wells, Glenn L., Jr., "The Role of the Female in Relation to the Artist in the Works of Joyce Cary," *DAI* 36 (1976): 4521A.

Wolkenfeld, J., *Joyce Cary*.

————, "Joyce Cary: The Developing Style," *DAI* 30 (1970): 1187A (Columbia).

Wright, Andrew, *Joyce Cary*.

————, "A Note on Joyce Cary's Reputation," *MFS* 9, iii (Autumn, 1963): 207-9.

THE AFRICAN WITCH

Barba, Harry, "Cary's Image of the African in Transition," *UKCR* 29 (June, 1963): 291-3.

Bloom, R., *Indeterminate World*, 52-4.

Echeruo, M. J. C., *Joyce Cary and the Novel of Africa*, 74-113.

Fisher, B., *Joyce Cary*, 168-74.

Foster, M., *Joyce Cary*, 321-4.

Goonetilleke, D. C. R. A., "Joyce Cary: The Clash of Cultures in Nigeria," *Developing Countries in British Fiction*, 212-21.

Hall, Alan, "The African Novels of Joyce Cary," *Standpunte* 12 (Mar.-April, 1958): 47-50.

Hoffmann, Charles G., *Joyce Cary*, 25-34.

————, "Joyce Cary's African Novels: There's a War On," *SAQ* 62 (Spring, 1963): 236-40.

Kanu, S. H., *World of Everlasting Conflict*, 16-39.

Larsen, G. L., *Dark Descent*, 36-45.

Mahood, M. M., *Joyce Cary's Africa*, 145-66.

Meyers, Jeffrey, "Joyce Cary: Authority and Freedom," *Fiction and the Colonial Experience*, 82-8.

Noble, R. W., *Joyce Cary*, 18-24.

O'Connor, W. V., *Joyce Cary*, 19-21.

Ola, Virginia U., "The Vision of Power: Joyce Cary and African Women," *ArielE* 9, i (Jan., 1978): 93-7.

Taiwo, O., *Culture and the Nigerian Novel*, 13-18.

Tucker, M., *Africa in Modern Literature*, 40-2.

Wiley, Paul, *WSCL* 4, ii (Spring-Summer, 1963): 230-2.

Wolkenfeld, J., *Joyce Cary*, 3-20, 78-87, 116-20.

Wright, A., *Joyce Cary*, 60-2, 80-2, 101-3.

AISSA SAVED

Bloom, R., *Indeterminate World*, 46-8.

Cary, Joyce, "My First Novel," *Listener* 49 (April 16, 1953): 637.

Downes, Brian, "'Almost a Fabulous Treatment': A Reading of Joyce Cary's AISSA SAVED," *WP* 3 (1980): 52-62.

Echeruo, M. J. C., *Joyce Cary and the Novel of Africa*, 28-43.

Fisher, B., *Joyce Cary*, 150-8.

Foster, M., *Joyce Cary*, 315-18.

Goonetilleke, D. C. R. A., "Joyce Cary: The Clash of Cultures in Nigeria," *Developing Countries in British Fiction*, 200-8.

Hall, A. D., "The African Novels of Joyce Cary," *Standpunte* 10 (June-July, 1956): 14-23.

Hoffmann, Charles G., *Joyce Cary*, 8-18.

————, "Joyce Cary's African Novels: There's a War On." *SAQ* 62 (Spring, 1963): 229-33.

Kanu, S. H., *World of Everlasting Conflict*, 1-16.

Larsen, G. L., *Dark Descent*, 22-7.

Mahood, M. M., *Joyce Cary's Africa*, 105-24.

Noble, R. W., *Joyce Cary*, 10-13.

O'Connor, W. V., *Joyce Cary*, 17-18.

Ola, Virginia U., "The Vision of Power: Joyce Cary and African Women," *ArielE* 9, i (Jan., 1978): 88-93.

Wolkenfeld, J., *Joyce Cary*, 56-69, 172-4.

Wright, A., *Joyce Cary*, 58-59, 77-9.

AN AMERICAN VISITOR

Bloom, R., *Indeterminate World*, 48-52.

Echeruo, M. J. C., *Joyce Cary and the Novels of Africa*, 44-73.

Fisher, B., *Joyce Cary*, 158-67.

Foster, M., *Joyce Cary*, 318-21.

French, Warren G., "Joyce Cary's American Rover Girl," *TSLL* 2 (Autumn, 1960): 281-91.

Goonetilleke, D.C.R.A., "Joyce Cary: The Clash of Culture in Nigeria," *Developing Countries in British Fiction*, 208-12.

Hall, Alan, "The African Novels of Joyce Cary," *Standpunte* 12 (Mar.-April, 1958): 43-7.

Hoffmann, Charles G., *Joyce Cary*, 18-25.

————, "Joyce Cary's African Novels: There's a War On," *SAQ* 62 (Spring, 1963): 233-6.

Kanu, S. H., *World of Everlasting Conflict*, 40-64.

Larsen, G. L., *Dark Descent*, 27-36.
Mahood, M. M., *Joyce Cary's Africa*, 125-44.
Noble, R. W., *Joyce Cary*, 13-18.
O'Connor, W. V., *Joyce Cary*, 18-19.
Tucker, M., *Africa in Modern Literature*, 39-40.
Wolkenfeld, J., *Joyce Cary*, 69-78, 111-13.
Wright, A., *Joyce Cary*, 59-60, 99-101.

ARABELLA (Unpublished)

Wright, A., *Joyce Cary*, 51-2.

THE CAPTIVE AND THE FREE

Adams, Hazard, "Joyce Cary; Posthumous Volumes and Criticism to Date," *TSLL* 1 (1959): 290-4.
Cecil, David, "Introduction," THE CAPTIVE AND THE FREE, N.Y.: Harper, 1959.
Fisher, B., *Joyce Cary*, 304-29.
Foster, M., *Joyce Cary*, 506-11.
Hoffmann, Charles G., *Joyce Cary*, 99-107, 157-69.
_____, "THE CAPTIVE AND THE FREE: Joyce Cary's Unfinished Trilogy," *TSLL* 5 (1963): 17-24.
Miller, Richard H., "Faith Healing and God's Love in Joyce Cary's THE CAPTIVE AND THE FREE," *AntigR* 21 (Spring, 1975): 71-3.
O'Connor, W. V., *Joyce Cary*, 41-2.
Watson, Kenneth, "THE CAPTIVE AND THE FREE: Artist, Child, and Society in the World of Joyce Cary," *English* 16 (Summer, 1966): 49-54.

CASTLE CORNER

Bloom, R., *Indeterminate World*, 66-72.
Cook, C., *Joyce Cary*, 40-5, 49-56.
Echeruo, M. J. C., *Joyce Cary and the Dimensions of Order*, 26-8.
Fisher, B., *Joyce Cary*, 175-96.
_____, "Joyce Cary as an Anglo-Irish Writer," in Kosok, H., ed., *Studies in Anglo-Irish Literature*, 299-302.
Foster, M., *Joyce Cary*, 352-7.
Groonetilleke, D.C.R.A., "Joyce Cary: The Clash of Cultures in Nigeria," *Developing Countries in British Fiction*, 222-3.
Hoffman, Charles G., *Joyce Cary*, 44-53.
_____, "'They Want To Be Happy': Joyce Cary's Unfinished CASTLE CORNER Series," *MFS* 9, iii (Autumn, 1963): 217-25.
Larsen, G. L., *Dark Descent*, 45-8.
Noble, R. W., *Joyce Cary*, 24-8.
O'Connor, W. V., *Joyce Cary*, 30-1.
Simmons, James, "Joyce Cary in Ireland," in Benedikz, B. S., ed., *On the Novel*, 140-55.
Stevenson, Lionel, "Joyce Cary and the Anglo-Irish Tradition," *MFS* 9, iii (Autumn, 1963): 210-16.
Weintraub, Stanley, "CASTLE CORNER: Joyce Cary's BUDDENBROOKS," *WSCL* 5, i (Winter-Spring, 1964): 54-63.
Wolkenfeld, J., *Joyce Cary*, 87-9.
Woodcock, George, "Citizens of Babel: A Study of Joyce Cary," *QQ* 63 (Summer, 1956): 237-40.
Wright, A., *Joyce Cary*, 66-7, 82-4, 94-6.

CHARLEY IS MY DARLING

Bloom, R., *Indeterminate World*, 59-63.

Cook, C., *Joyce Cary*, 70-9.
Echeruo, M. J. C., *Joyce Cary and the Dimensions of Order*, 30-42.
Fisher, B., *Joyce Cary*, 199-201.
Foster, M., *Joyce Cary*, 346-51.
Hoffmann, C. G., *Joyce Cary*, 54-66.
Kanu, S. H., *World of Everlasting Conflict*, 95-118.
Kerr, Elizabeth M., *WSCL* 2, i (Winter, 1961): 102-6.
Larsen, G. L., *Dark Descent*, 79-82.
Noble, R. W., *Joyce Cary*, 37-42.
O'Connor, W. V., *Joyce Cary*, 23-4.
Webb, Bernice L., "Animal Imagery and Juvenile Delinquents in Joyce Cary's CHARLEY IS MY DARLING," *SCB* 32, iv (Winter, 1972): 240-2.
_____, "Joyce Cary's Redefinition of Car Theft, Illicit Sex, and Porno-graphy in CHARLEY IS MY DARLING," *NLauR* 2, i (1972): 19-22.
Wright, A., *Joyce Cary*, 62-5.

COCK JARVIS (Unpublished)

Foster, M., *Joyce Cary*, 246-58.
Mahood, M. M., *Joyce Cary's Africa*, 96-105.
Wright, A., *Joyce Cary*, 50-1.

DAVENTRY (Unpublished)

Mahood, M. M., *Joyce Cary's Africa*, 89-96.

EXCEPT THE LORD (See also SECOND TRILOGY)

Bellow, Saul, "A Personal Record," *NRep* (Feb. 22, 1954): 20-1.
Bettman, Elizabeth R., "Joyce Cary and the Problem of Political Morality," *AR* 17 (Summer, 1957): 270-1.
Bloom, R., *Indeterminate World*, 139-69.
Cook, C., *Joyce Cary*, 206-17.
Echeruo, M. J. C., *Joyce Cary and the Dimensions of Order*, 107-26.
Fisher, B., *Joyce Cary*, 281-94.
Foster, M., *Joyce Cary*, 483-7.
Hoffmann, C. G., *Joyce Cary*, 139-47.
Hulley, Kathleen, "Disintegration as Symbol of Communication: A Study of THE RAINBOW, WOMEN IN LOVE, LIGHT IN AUGUST, PRISONER OF GRACE, EXCEPT THE LORD, NOT HONOUR MORE, and HERZOG," *DAI* 34 (1974): 6643A-44A.
Mitchell, Giles, "Joyce Cary's EXCEPT THE LORD," *ArlQ* 2, ii (Autumn, 1969): 71-82.
Noble, R. W., *Joyce Cary*, 88-93.
Nyce, Benjamin, "Joyce Cary's Political Trilogy," *MLQ* 32, i (Mar., 1971): 97-103.
Wright, A., *Joyce Cary*, 142-8.

A FEARFUL JOY

Allen, W., *Joyce Cary*, 16-19.
Bloom, R., *Indeterminate World*, 77-83.
Cook, C., *Joyce Cary*, 168-73.
Eastman, Richard M., "Historical Grace in Cary's A FEARFUL JOY," *Novel* 1 (Winter, 1968): 150-7.
Fisher, B., *Joyce Cary*, 251-65.
Foster, M., *Joyce Cary*, 428-34.
Hall, J., *Tragic Comedians*, 84-5.
Hoffmann, C. G., *Joyce Cary*, 118-26.
McCormick, J., *Catastrophe and Imagination*, 151-4.

Noble, R. W., *Joyce Cary*, 76-80.

O'Connor, W. V., *Joyce Cary*, 33-6.

Pittock, Malcolm, "Joyce Cary: A FEARFUL JOY," *EIC* 13 (Oct., 1963): 428-32.

Wolkenfeld, J., *Joyce Cary*, 135-9.

Wright, A., *Joyce Cary*, 69-70.

FIRST TRILOGY

Adams, Hazard, "Blake and Gulley Jimson: English Symbolists," *Crit* 3, i (Spring-Fall, 1959): 3-14.

————, "Joyce Cary's Three Speakers," *MFS* 5 (Summer, 1959): 108-20.

Allen, W., *Joyce Cary*, 19-27.

Averitt, Margie N. T., "And Three's a Crowd: A Study of Joyce Cary's FIRST TRILOGY," *DA* 24 (1964): 5404 (Texas).

Bloom, R., *Indeterminate World*, 83-4.

Brawer, Judith, "The Triumph of Defeat: A Study of Joyce Cary's FIRST TRILOGY," *TSLL* 10, iv (Winter, 1969): 629-34.

Cook, C., *Joyce Cary*, 94-152.

Faber, Kathleen R., and M. D., "An Important Theme of Joyce Cary's Trilogy," *Discourse* 11 (Winter, 1968): 26-31.

Friedman, Alan W., "Joyce Cary's Cubistic Morality," *ConL* 14, i (Winter, 1973): 78-96.

Hall, J., *Tragic Comedians*, 82-98.

Hamilton, Kenneth, "Boon or Thorn? Joyce Cary and Samuel Beckett on Human Life," *DR* 38 (Winter, 1959): 433-42.

Hoffmann, Charles G., "The Genesis and Development of Joyce Cary's FIRST TRILOGY," *PMLA* 78 (Sept., 1963): 43-9.

————, *Joyce Cary*, 67-70.

————, "Joyce Cary and the Comic Mask," *WHR* 13 (Spring, 1959): 135-42.

————, "Joyce Cary: Art and the Reality," *UKCR* 26 (June, 1960): 275-7.

Howell, Gwendolyn A., "Time and Place in Joyce Cary's FIRST TRILOGY," *DAI* 31 (1971): 3550A (Texas, Austin).

Kanu, S. H., *World of Everlasting Conflict*, 133-7.

Lanza, Robert M., "Ourselves Surprised: A Pastoral Approach to Joyce Cary's FIRST TRILOGY," *DAI* 40 (1980): 5439A-40A.

Larsen, G. L., *Dark Descent*, 89-179.

McCrea, Brian, "The Murder of Sara Monday: Art and Morality in Joyce Cary's FIRST TRILOGY," *ELWIU* 7 (1980): 45-54.

McQuaid, Catherine F., "The Multiple Realities of Artistic Creation: Joyce Cary's 'Art and Reality' and His FIRST TRILOGY," *DA* 28 (1967): 2154A-55A (Ohio).

Mitchell, Giles, *The Art Theme in Joyce Cary's FIRST TRILOGY* (De Proprietatibus Litterarum, Ser. pract. 13), The Hague: Mouton, 1971.

Monas, Sidney, "What to Do with a Drunken Sailor," *HudR* 3 (Autumn, 1950): 466-74.

O'Connor, W. V., *Joyce Cary*, 26-9.

Reed, Peter J., "'The Better the Heart': Joyce Cary's Sara Monday," *TSLL* 15 (1973): 357-70.

————, "Trial by Discard: Joyce Cary's FIRST TRILOGY," *DA* 26 (1966): 4672 (Un. of Washington).

Robertson, D., *Voice From the Attic*, 246-9.

Stockholder, Fred, "The Triple Vision in Joyce Cary's FIRST TRILOGY," *MFS* 9, iii (Autumn, 1963): 231-44.

Wolkenfeld, J., *Joyce Cary*, 21-2, 38-45.

HERSELF SURPRISED (See also FIRST TRILOGY)

Bloom, R., *Indeterminate World*, 84-90.

Cary, Joyce, "Three New Prefaces," *AIR* 18 (Nov.-Dec., 1950): 11-12.

Cook, C., *Joyce Cary*, 99-107.

Dueck, Jack, "Uses of the Picaresque: A Study of Five British Novels," *DAI* 34 (1974): 4255A.

Echeruo, M. J. C., *Joyce Cary and the Dimensions of Order*, 61-70.

Fisher, B., *Joyce Cary*, 211-17.

Foster, M., *Joyce Cary*, 381-4.

Hall, J., *Tragic Comedians*, 86-7.

Hoffmann, C. G., *Joyce Cary*, 70-7.

Kanu, S. H., *World of Everlasting Conflict*, 137-53.

Larsen, G. L., *Dark Descent*, 102-25.

Noble, R. W., *Joyce Cary*, 48-52.

Wolkenfeld, J., *Joyce Cary*, 22-3.

Wright, A., *Joyce Cary*, 110-19.

THE HORSE'S MOUTH (See also FIRST TRILOGY)

Adams, Hazard, "Blake and Gulley Jimson: English Symbolists," *Crit* 3, i (Spring-Fall, 1959): 3-14.

Adams, Robert H., "Freedom in THE HORSE'S MOUTH," *CE* 26 (Mar., 1965): 451-4, 459-60.

Allen, W., *Reading a Novel*, 50-4.

Alter, R., *Rogue's Progress*, 129-32.

Barr, Donald, "A Careful and Profound Thinker," *AIR* 18 (Nov.-Dec., 1950): 30-1.

Bloom, R., *Indeterminate World*, 96-105.

Cary, Joyce, "Three New Prefaces," *AIR* 18 (Nov.-Dec., 1950): 13-14.

Cook, C., *Joyce Cary*, 131-49.

Echeruo, M. J. C., *Joyce Cary and the Dimensions of Order*, 70-91.

Fisher, B., *Joyce Cary*, 223-38.

Foster, M., *Joyce Cary*, 389-93.

Fredrickson, Robert S., "Gulley Jimson's Painterly Prose," *BuR* 24, ii (1978): 75-85.

Garant, Jeanne, "Joyce Cary's Portrait of the Artist," *RLV* No. 6 (1958): 476-86.

Hall, J., *Tragic Comedians*, 87-97 *passim*.

Heffernan, James A. W., "Politics and Freedom: Refractions of Blake in Joyce Cary and Alan Ginsberg," in Bornstein, G., ed., *Romantic and Modern*, 178-86.

Hoffmann, C. G., *Joyce Cary*, 85-98.

Kanu, S. H., *World of Everlasting Conflict*, 187-221.

Kelly, Edward H., "The Meaning of THE HORSE'S MOUTH," *MLS* 1, ii (1971): 9-11.

Larsen, G. L., *Dark Descent*, 156-79.

Levitt, Annette S., "'The Mental Traveller' in THE HORSE'S MOUTH: New Light on the Old Cycle," 186-211 in Bertholf, Robert J., and Annette S. Levitt, eds., *William Blake and the Moderns*, Albany, NY: State Un. of New York, 1982.

————, "The *Miltonic* Progression of Gulley Jimson," *Mosaic* 11, i (1977): 77-91.

————, "The Poetry and Thought of William Blake in Joyce Cary's THE HORSE'S MOUTH," *DAI* 31 (1971): 4778A-79A (Penn. State).

Markovi, V. E., *The Changing Face*, 123-37.

Messenger, Ann P., "A Painter's Prose: Similes in Joyce Cary's THE HORSE'S MOUTH," *ReAL* 3, ii (Spring, 1970): 16-28.

Miller, Hugh, "Blake and Gulley Jimson in Joyce Cary's THE HORSE'S MOUTH," *AntigR* 33 (1978): 79-81.

Mustanoja, Tauno F., "Two Painters: Joyce Cary and Gulley Jimson," *NM* 61 (1960): 221-44.

Noble, R. W., *Joyce Cary*, 60-9.

Pearse, James A., "Montage in Modern Fiction: A Cinematographic Approach to the Analysis of Ironic Tone in Joyce Cary's THE HORSE'S MOUTH," *DAI* 34 (1973): 3596A-97A (Aris.).

Petri, Lucretia, "A Tentative Analysis of 'Bourgeois' Substitutes and '...Colour' Compounds in Joyce Cary's THE HORSE'S MOUTH," *AUB-LG* 21 (1972): 35-44.

Raskin, Jonah, "Works of Passion and Imagination," *Mythology of Imperialism*, 319-31.

Reed, Peter J., "Getting Stuck: Joyce Cary's Gulley Jimson," *TCl* 16 (Oct., 1970): 241-52.

Ryan, Marjorie, "An Interpretation of Joyce Cary's THE HORSE'S MOUTH," *Crit* 2, i (Spring-Summer, 1958): 29-38.

Salz, Paulina J., "The Philosophical Principles in Joyce Cary's Work," *WHR* 20 (Spring, 1966): 164-5.

Seltzer, Alvin J., "Speaking Out of Both Sides of THE HORSE'S MOUTH: Joyce Cary vs. Gulley Jimson," *ConL* 15 (1974): 488-502.

Shapiro, Stephen A., "Leopold Bloom and Gulley Jimson: The Economics of Survival," *TCL* 10 (April, 1964): 3-11.

Wolkenfeld, J., *Joyce Cary*, 23-41.

Woodcock, George, "Citizens of Babel: A Study of Joyce Cary," *QQ* 63 (Summer, 1956): 242-4.

Wright, Andrew, "An Authoritative Text of THE HORSE'S MOUTH," *PBSA* 61 (1967): 100-9.

_____, *Joyce Cary*, 124-37, 156-73.

Yeager, D. M., "Love and Mirth in THE HORSE'S MOUTH," *Ren* 33, iii (1981): 131-42.

A HOUSE OF CHILDREN

Bloom, R., *Indeterminate World*, 63-6.

Cook, C., *Joyce Cary*, 81-93.

Echeruo, Michael J. C., "Mood and Meaning in Joyce Cary's A HOUSE OF CHILDREN," *PURBA* 6, i (1975): 3-8.

Fisher, B., *Joyce Cary*, 17-25, 201-10.

_____, "Joyce Cary as an Anglo-Irish Writer," in Kosok, H., ed., *Studies in Anglo-Irish Literature*, 302-4.

Foster, J. W., *Forces and Themes in Ulster Fiction*, 191-7.

Foster, M., *Joyce Cary*, 357-61.

Hoffmann, C. G., *Joyce Cary*, 54-66.

Kanu, S. H., *World of Everlasting Conflict*, 118-30.

Larsen, G. L., *Dark Descent*, 82-8.

Noble, R. W., *Joyce Cary*, 42-7.

O'Connor, W. V., *Joyce Cary*, 24-6.

Simmons, James, "Joyce Cary in Ireland," in Benedikz, B. S., ed., *On the Novel*, 155-60.

Stevenson, Lionel, "Joyce Cary and the Anglo-Irish Tradition," *MFS* 9, iii (Autumn, 1963): 210-16.

Wright, A., *Joyce Cary*, 17-19, 62-5, 88-90.

MISTER JOHNSON

Barba, Harry, "Cary's Image of the African in Transition," *UKCR* 29 (June, 1963): 293-6.

Bloom, R., *Indeterminate World*, 54-9.

Cook, C., *Joyce Cary*, 59-60.

Echeruo, M. J. C., *Joyce Cary and the Novel of Africa*, 121-39.

Fisher, B., *Joyce Cary*, 197-9.

Foster, M., *Joyce Cary*, 324-9.

Fyfe, Christopher, "The Colonial Situation in MISTER JOHNSON," *MFS* 9, iii (Autumn, 1963): 226-30.

Goonetilleke, D. C. R. A., "Joyce Cary: The Clash of Cultures in Nigeria," *Developing Countries in British Fiction*, 223-32.

Hall, Alan, "The African Novels of Joyce Cary," *Standpunte* 12 (Mar.-April, 1958): 50-5.

Hoffmann, Charles G., *Joyce Cary*, 34-43.

_____, "Joyce Cary's African Novels: There's a War On," *SAQ* 62 (Spring, 1963): 240-3.

Kanu, S. H., *World of Everlasting Conflict*, 64-92.

Kemali, Arthur, and David K. Mulwa, "The European Image of Africa and the African," *Busara* 2, ii (1968): 51-3.

Kettle, A., *Introduction to the English Novel*, 177-84.

Kronenfeld, J. Z., "In Search of Mister Johnson: Creation, Politics, and Culture in Cary's Africa," *ArielE* 7, iv (Oct., 1976): 69-97.

Larsen, G. L., *Dark Descent*, 49-79.

Larson, Charles R., "Mr. Johnson—Faithful African Portrait?" *AT* 16, i (Mar., 1969): 19-20.

Mahood, M. M., *Joyce Cary's Africa*, 169-86.

Meyers, Jeffrey, "Joyce Cary: Authority and Freedom," *Fiction and the Colonial Experience*, 88-95.

Moore, Gerald, "MISTER JOHNSON Reconsidered," *Black Orpheus* No. 4 (Oct., 1958): 16-23.

Noble, R. W., *Joyce Cary*, 29-36.

O'Connor, W. V., *Joyce Cary*, 21-3.

Okonkwo, Juliet I., "Joyce Cary, MISTER JOHNSON," *Okike* 13 (1979): 111-23.

Prescott, O., *In My Opinion*, 192-4.

Raskin, Jonah, "MISTER JOHNSON: On the Road," *Mythology of Imperialism*, 294-309.

Sandison, Alan G., "Living Out the Lyric: MR. JOHNSON and the Present Day," *English* 20 (Spring, 1971): 11-16.

Smith, B. R., "Moral Evaluation in MISTER JOHNSON," *Crit* 11, ii (1969): 101-10.

Taiwo, O., *Culture and the Nigerian Novel*, 18-24.

Tucker, M., *Africa in Modern Literature*, 43-7.

Wolkenfeld, J., *Joyce Cary*, 94-103, 121-5.

Woodcock, George, "Citizens of Babel: A Study of Joyce Cary," *QQ* 63 (Summer, 1956): 240-2.

Wren, Robert M., "MISTER JOHNSON and the Complexity of ARROW OF GOD," in Innes, C. L., and B. Lindfors, eds., *Critical Perspectives on Chinua Achebe*, 207-17. Also in Narasimhaiah, C. D., ed., *Awakened Conscience*, 50-61.

Wright, A., *Joyce Cary*, 84-7.

THE MOONLIGHT

Bloom, R., *Indeterminate World*, 72-7.

Cook, C., *Joyce Cary*, 153-68.

Fisher, B., *Joyce Cary*, 239-51.

Foster, M., *Joyce Cary*, 425-8.

Hoffmann, C. G., *Joyce Cary*, 107-18.

Jones, M. V., "An Aspect of Tolstoy's Impact on Modern English Fiction: THE KREUTZER SONATA and Joyce Cary's THE MOONLIGHT," *SEER* 56 (1978): 97-105.

Larsen, G. L., *Dark Descent*, 183-5.

Noble, R. W., *Joyce Cary*, 70-6.

O'Connor, W. V., *Joyce Cary*, 31-3.

Wolkenfeld, J., *Joyce Cary*, 129-35.

Wright, A., *Joyce Cary*, 67-9.

NOT HONOUR MORE (See also SECOND TRILOGY)

Battaglia, Francis J., "Spurious Armageddon: Joyce Cary's NOT HONOUR MORE," *MFS* 13 (Winter, 1967-68): 479-91.

Bettman, Elizabeth R., "Joyce Cary and the Problem of Political Morality," *AR* 17 (Summer, 1957): 271-2.

Bloom, R., *Indeterminate World*, 170-200.

Cook, C., *Joyce Cary*, 217-27.

Echeruo, M. J. C., *Joyce Cary and the Dimensions of Order*, 126-37.

Fisher, B., *Joyce Cary*, 294-303.

Foster, M., *Joyce Cary*, 487-92.

Hoffmann, C. G., *Joyce Cary*, 148-56.

Hulley, Kathleen, "Disintegration as Symbol of Community: A Study of THE RAINBOW, WOMEN IN LOVE, LIGHT IN AUGUST, PRISONER OF GRACE, EXCEPT THE LORD, NOT HONOUR MORE, and HERZOG," *DAI* 34 (1974): 6643A-44A.

Kanu, S. H., *World of Everlasting Confict*, 273-88.

Noble, R. W., *Joyce Cary*, 93-100.

Nyce, Benjamin, "Joyce Cary's Political Trilogy," *MLQ* 32, i (Mar., 1971): 93-7.

Wolkenfeld, J., *Joyce Cary*, 178-81.

Wright, A., *Joyce Cary*, 148-53.

PRISONER OF GRACE (See also SECOND TRILOGY)

Bettman, Elizabeth R., "Joyce Cary and the Problem of Political Morality," *AR* 17 (Summer, 1957): 267-70.

Bloom, R., *Indeterminate World*, 108-38.

Cook, C., *Joyce Cary*, 183-206.

Echeruo, M. J. C., *Joyce Cary and the Dimensions of Order*, 92-107.

Fisher, B., *Joyce Cary*, 266-81.

Foster, M., *Joyce Cary*, 479-82.

Friedman, Alan W., "Joyce Cary's Cubistic Morality," *ConL* 14, i (Winter, 1973): 82-9.

Hoffmann, C. G., *Joyce Cary*, 133-9.

Hulley, Kathleen, "Disintegration as Symbol of Community: A Study of THE RAINBOW, WOMEN IN LOVE, LIGHT IN AUGUST, PRISONER OF GRACE, EXCEPT THE LORD, NOT HONOUR MORE, and HERZOG," *DAI* 34 (1974): 6643A-44A.

Kanu, S. H., *World of Everlasting Conflict*, 249-73.

Mitchell, Giles, "Joyce Cary's PRISONER OF GRACE," *MFS* 9, iii (Autumn, 1963): 263-75.

Noble, R. W., *Joyce Cary*, 81-8.

Nyce, Benjamin, "Joyce Cary's Political Trilogy," *MLQ* 32, i (Mar., 1971): 91-3.

Rosenthal, Michael, "Joyce Cary's Ambiguous Chester Nimmo," *SAQ* 70, iii (Summer, 1971): 332-40.

Wolkenfeld, J., *Joyce Cary*, 183-7.

Woodcock, George, "Citizens of Babel: A Study of Joyce Cary," *QQ* 63 (Summer, 1956): 244-6.

Wright, A., *Joyce Cary*, 137-42.

SECOND TRILOGY

Battaglia, Francis J., "The Problem of Reliability in Joyce Cary's Political Trilogy," *DA* 27 (1967): 2522A-23A (Calif.-Davis).

Cook, C., *Joyce Cary*, 175-233.

Echeruo, M. J. C., *Joyce Cary and the Dimensions of Order*, 92-137.

Friedman, Alan W., "Joyce Cary's Cubistic Morality," *ConL* 14, i (Winter, 1973): 78-96.

Hoffmann, Charles G., *Joyce Cary*, 127-33.

———, "Joyce Cary: Art and Reality," *UKCR* 26 (June, 1960): 277-82.

Hopwood, Alison L., "Separate Worlds: Joyce Cary's Nimmo Trilogy," *TSLL* 13, iii (Fall, 1971): 523-35.

Kanu, S. H., *World of Everlasting Confilct*, 225-9.

Kennedy, A., "Language, Mimesis and the Numinous in Joyce Cary's SECOND TRILOGY," *Protean Self*, 99-149.

Kerr, Elizabeth M., "Joyce Cary's SECOND TRILOGY," *UTQ* 29 (April, 1960): 310-25.

Larsen, G. L., *Dark Descent*, 187-92.

Nyce, Benjamin, "Joyce Cary's Political Trilogy," *MLQ* 32, i (Mar., 1971): 89-106.

Nyce, James M., "Joyce Cary as Political Novelist," *DA* 29 (1968): 574A-5A (Claremont).

O'Connor, W. V., *Joyce Cary*, 36-41.

Rosenthal, Michael, "Joyce Cary's Ambiguous Chester Nimmo," *SAQ* 70, iii (Summer, 1971): 332-40.

Teeling, John P., S. J., "British History in Joyce Cary's SECOND TRILOGY," *DA* 26 (1965): 1655-56 (No. Carolina).

———, "Joyce Cary's Moral World," *MFS* 9, iii (Autumn, 1963): 279-83.

Wolkenfeld, J., *Joyce Cary*, 46-7, 90-4, 178-87.

TO BE A PILGRIM (See also FIRST TRILOGY)

Bloom, R., *Indeterminate World*, 90-6.

Cary, Joyce, "Three New Prefaces," *AIR* 18 (Nov.-Dec., 1950): 12.

Cook, C., *Joyce Cary*, 107-31.

Echeruo, M. J. C., *Joyce Cary and the Dimensions of Order*, 48-60.

Fisher, B., *Joyce Cary*, 217-23.

Foster, M., *Joyce Cary*, 384-9.

Hoffmann, C. G., *Joyce Cary*, 77-85.

Kanu, S. H., *World of Everlasting Conflict*, 154-87.

Larsen, G. L., *Dark Descent*, 125-56.

Lyons, Richard S., "Narrative Method in Cary's TO BE A PILGRIM," *TSLL* 6 (1964): 269-79.

Noble, R. W., *Joyce Cary*, 53-60.

Reed, Peter J., "Holding Back: Joyce Cary's TO BE A PILGRIM," *ConL* 10, i (Winter, 1969): 103-16.

Shapiro, Stephen A., "Joyce Cary's TO BE A PILGRIM: Mr. Facing-Both-Ways," *TSLL* 8 (Spring, 1966): 81-91.

Söderskog, Ingvar, "Joyce Cary's 'Hard Conceptual Labor': A Structural Analysis of TO BE A PILGRIM," Göteborg: Göteborg Un., 1976. [Dissertation]. Also Gothenberg: Acta Univ. Gothaburgensis, 1977. Also *DAI* 38 (1968): 4630C.

Stewart, Robert, "Understanding English Conservatism with Apologies to Joyce Cary," *CJH* 6, ii (Sept., 1971): 153-69.

Wolkenfeld, J., *Joyce Cary*, 139-42.

Wright, A., *Joyce Cary*, 119-24.

BIBLIOGRAPHY

Beebe, Maurice, J. W. Lee, and S. Henderson, "Criticism of Joyce Cary: A Selected Checklist," *MFS* 9, iii (Autumn, 1963): 284-8.

Bloom, R., *Indeterminate World*, 201-8.

Hoffmann, C. G., *Joyce Cary*, 199-202.

Larsen, G. L., *Dark Descent*, 194-8.

Reed, Peter J., "Joyce Cary: A Selected Checklist of Criticism," *BB* 25 (May-Aug., 1968): 133-4, 151.

Wolkenfeld, J., *Joyce Cary*, 193-6.

CASSILL, R(ONALD) V(ERLIN), 1919-

GENERAL

Graham, John, "R. V. Cassill," in Garrett, G., ed., *Writer's Voice*, 1-12. [Interview.]

CAUTE, DAVID, 1936-

GENERAL

Atlas, James, "On David Caute: A Polemic," *MinnR* n.s. 1 (Fall, 1973): 123-31.

Bergonzi, Bernard, in *Contemporary English Novel*, 46-9.

Selden, R., "Commitment and Dialectic in Novels by David Caute and John Berger," *FMLS* 11, ii (April, 1975): 106-21.

CHAPPELL, FRED, 1936-

GENERAL

Dillard, R. H. W., "Letters From a Distant Lover: The Novels of Fred Chappell," *HC* 10, ii (April, 1973): 1-15.

Graham, John, "Fred Chappell," in Garrett, G., ed., *Writer's Voice*, 31-50. [Interview.]

Sopko, John, and John Carr, "Dealing with the Grotesque," [Interview] in Carr, J., ed., *Kite-Flying and Other Irrational Acts*, 216-35.

DAGON

Dillard, R. H. W., "Letters From a Distant Lover: The Novels of Fred Chappell," *HC* 10, ii (April, 1973): 10-12.

THE GAUDY PLACE

Dillard, R. H. W., "Letters From a Distant Lover: The Novels of Fred Chappell," *HC* 10, ii (April, 1973): 12-15.

THE INKLING

Dillard, R. H. W., "Letters From a Distant Lover: The Novels of Fred Chappell," *HC* 10, ii (April, 1973): 7-10.

IT IS TIME, LORD

Dillard, R. H. W., "Letters From a Distant Lover: The Novels of Fred Chappell," *HC* 10, ii (April, 1973): 4-7.

CHEEVER, JOHN, 1912-1982

GENERAL

Aldridge, J. W., "John Cheever and the Soft Sell of Disaster," *Devil in the Fire*, 235-40. Also in *Time to Murder and Create*, 171-7.

Bracher, Frederick, "John Cheever: A Vision of the World," *ClareQ* 11, ii (Winter, 1964): 47-57. Also in Collins, R. G., ed., *Critical Essays on John Cheever*, 168-80.

_____, "John Cheever and Comedy," *Crit* 6, i (Spring, 1963): 66-77.

Brans, Jo, "Stories to Comprehend Life: An Interview with John Cheever," *SWR* 65 (Autumn, 1980): 337-45.

Burhans, Clinton S., Jr., "John Cheever and the Grave of Social Coherence," *TCL* 14, iv (Jan., 1969): 187-209.

Chesnick, Eugene, "The Domesticated Stroke of John Cheever," *NEQ* 44, iv (Dec., 1971): 531-52.

Coale, Samuel, "Cheever and Hawthorne: The American Romancer's Art," in Collins, R. G., ed., *Critical Essays on John Cheever*, 193-209.

_____, *John Cheever*.

Coates, Dennis E., "The Novels of John Cheever," *DAI* 39 (1978): 1563A-64A.

Collins, R. G., ed., *Critical Essays on John Cheever*.

_____, "From Subject to Object and Back Again: Individual Identity in John Cheever's Fiction," *TCL* 28, i (Spring, 1982): 1-13.

D'haen, Theo, "John Cheever and the Development of the American Novel," in Collins, R. G., ed., *Critical Essays on John Cheever*, 272-8.

Donaldson, Scott, "The Machines in Cheever's Garden," in Schwartz, Barry, ed., *The Changing Face of the Suburbs*, Chicago: Un. of Chicago Pr., 1976, 309-22.

Gaunt, Marcia E., "Imagination and Reality in the Fiction of Katherine Anne Porter and John Cheever: Implications for Curriculum," *DAI* 33 (1972): 2933A (Purdue).

Grant, Annette, "John Cheever: The Art of Fiction LXII," in Plimpton, George, ed., *Writers at Work: The Paris Review Interviews*, Fifth Series, Viking, 1981, 113-35. Also in Collins, R. G., ed., *Critical Essays on John Cheever*, 87-100.

Healy, Marsha B., "Cheever the Fabulator: Experimental Technique in His Novels and Short Stories," *DAI* 37 (1977): 7129A.

Karl, Frederick R., "John Cheever and the Promise of Pastoral," in Collins, R. G., ed., *Critical Essays on John Cheever*, 209-19.

Lehman-Haupt, Christopher, "Talk with John Cheever," *NYTBR* (April 27, 1969): 42-4.

Nash, Charles C., "The Brothers Cheever at War and Peace," *PMPA* 6 (1981): 48-53. [Not seen.]

Tavernier-Courbin, Jacqueline, and R. G. Collins, "An Interview with John Cheever," *Thalia* 1, ii (Spring, 1978): 3-9.

Valhouli, James N., "John Cheever: The Dual Vision of His Art," *DAI* 34 (1974): 6667A (Wis., Madison).

Waldeland, L., *John Cheever*.

Wilson, Phillip G., "John Cheever and the Struggle to Affirm Life," *DAI* 43, iii (Sept., 1982): 304A.

Wink, John H., "John Cheever and the Broken World," *DAI* 35 (1974): 3778A (Ark.).

BULLET PARK

Chesnick, Eugene, "The Domesticated Stroke of John Cheever," *NEQ* 44, iv (Dec., 1971): 547-51.

Coale, S., *John Cheever*, 95-105.

Detweiler, Robert, "John Cheever's BULLET PARK: A World Beyond Madness," 6-32 in Stürzl, Edwin A., ed., *Essays in Honour of Professor Tyrus Hillway*, Un. of Salzburg: Inst. für eng. Sprache & Lit., 1977.

Waldeland, L., *John Cheever*, 104-16.
_____, "John Cheever's BULLET PARK: A Key to His Thought and Art," in Collins, R. G., ed., *Critical Essays on John Cheever*, 261-72.

FALCONER

Coale, S., *John Cheever*, 107-13.
Gilbert, Susan, "Children of the Seventies: The American Family in Recent Fiction," *Soundings* 62, ii (Summer, 1980): 200-3.
Iyer, Pico, "A Nice Reliable Chevrolet: Aspects of John Cheever," *LonM* 17 (Nov., 1977): 41-8.
Johnson, Glen M., "The Moral Structure of Cheever's FALCONER," *SAF* 9, i (Spring, 1981): 21-31.
Morace, Robert A., "The Religious Experience and the 'Mystery of Imprisonment' in John Cheever's FALCONER," *Cithara* 20, i (1980): 44-53.
Sahlin, Nicki, "Manners in the Contemporary American Novel: Studies in John Cheever, John Updike, and Joan Didion," *DAI* 41, xii (June, 1981): 5102A.
Sevick, Marly A., "Romantic Ministers and Phallic Knights: A Study of A MONTH OF SUNDAYS, LANCELOT, and FALCONER," *DAI* 40 (1979): 860A.
Waldeland, L., *John Cheever*, 127-40.

THE WAPSHOT CHRONICLE

Bracher, Frederick, "John Cheever and Comedy," *Crit* 6, i (Spring, 1963): 66-77.
Chesnick, Eugene, "The Domesticated Stroke of John Cheever," *NEQ* 44, iv (Dec., 1971): 535-8.
Coale, S., *John Cheever*, 65-80.
Greene, Beatrice, "Icarus at St. Botolphs: A Descent to 'Unwanted Otherness'," *Style* 5 (1971): 119-37. Also in Collins, R. G., ed., *Critical Essays on John Cheever*, 153-68.
Hassan, I., *Radical Innocence*, 187-94.
Karl, Frederick R., "John Cheever and the Promise of Pastoral," in Collins, R. G., ed., *Critical Essays on John Cheever*, 213-16.
O'Hara, James, "Cheever's THE WAPSHOT CHRONICLE: A Narrative of Exploration," *Crit* 22, ii (1980): 20-30.
_____, " 'Independence Day at St. Botolph's': The Wapshot Saga Begins," *MSE* 7, iii (1980): 20-5.
Rupp, Richard H., "John Cheever: The Upshot of Wapshot," *Celebration in Postwar American Fiction*, 28-33.
Waldeland, L., *John Cheever*, 37-48.

THE WAPSHOT SCANDAL

Chesnick, Eugene, "The Domesticated Stroke of John Cheever," *NEQ* 44, iv (Dec., 1971): 543-5.
Coale, S., *John Cheever*, 81-94.
Corke, Hilary, "Sugary Days in Saint Botolphs," *NRep* 150 (Jan. 25, 1964): 19-21. Also in Harrison, G.A., ed., *Critic as Artist*, 71-6.
Garrett, George, "John Cheever and the Charms of Innocence: The Craft of THE WAPSHOT SCANDAL," *HC* 1, ii (April, 1964): 1-4, 6-12. Also in Dillard, R.W.H., & Others, eds., *Sounder Few*, 19-32.
Greene, Beatrice, "Icarus at St. Botolphs: A Descent to 'Unwanted Otherness'," *Style* 5 (1971): 119-37. Also in Collins, R.G., ed., *Critical Essays on John Cheever*, 153-68.
Hyman, S.E., "John Cheever's Golden Egg," *Standards*, 199-203.

Karl, Frederick R., "John Cheever and the Promise of Pastoral," in Collins, R.G., ed., *Critical Essays on John Cheever*, 213-16.
Ozick, Cynthia, "Cheever's Yankee Heritage," *AR* 24 (Summer, 1964): 263-7. Also in Collins, R. G., ed., *Critical Essays on John Cheever*, 62-6.
Rupp, Richard A., "John Cheever: The Upshot of Wapshot," *Celebration in Postwar American Fiction*, 33-9.
Waldeland, L., *John Cheever*, 48-62.

BIBLIOGRAPHY

Bosha, Francis J., *John Cheever: A Reference Guide*, Boston: Hall, 1981.
Coates, Dennis, comp., "A Cheever Bibliography Supplement, 1978-1981," in Collins, R. G., ed., *Critical Essays on John Cheever*, 279-85.
_____, "John Cheever: A Checklist, 1930-1978," *BB* 36, i (Jan.-Mar., 1979): 1-13, 49.
Trakos, Deno, "John Cheever: An Annotated Secondary Bibliography (1943-1978)," *RALS* 9 (1979): 181-99.

CLARK, ELEANOR, 1913-

GENERAL

"Interview with Eleanor Clark and Robert Penn Warren," *NER* 1 (1978): 49-70.

BALDUR'S GATE

Sullivan, Walter, "The Unbuilt Gate: Eleanor Clark's View of the Human Condition," *SR* 79, iv (Autumn, 1971): 634-7.

THE BITTER BOX

Pitchford, Kenneth, "Of Time and THE BITTER BOX," *NER* 2 (1979): 260-7.

CLARKE, AUSTIN C(HESTERFIELD), 1934-

GENERAL

Brown, Lloyd W., "The West Indian Novel in North America: A Study of Austin Clarke," *JCL* 9 (July, 1970): 89-103.
Lacovia, R. M., "Migration and Transmutation in the Novels of McKay, Marshall, and Clarke," *JBS* 7, iv (June, 1977): 437-54 *passim*.
Sanders, Leslie, "Austin Clarke," 93-100 in Heath, Jeffrey M., ed., *Profiles in Canadian Literature 4*, Toronto: Dundurn, 1982.

THE BIGGER LIGHT

Baugh, Edward, "Friday in Crusoe's City: The Question of Language in Two West Indian Novels of Exile," *ACLALSB* 5, iii (1980): 1-12.

THE PRIME MINISTER

Brydon, Diana, "Carribean Revolution & Literary Convention," *CanL* 95 (Winter, 1982): 181-5.

CLEARY, JON (STEPHEN), 1917-

THE SUNDOWNERS

Crawford, John W., "A Novel to Teach: THE SUNDOWNERS," *EngR* 29, iii (1978): 2-5.

COATES, ROBERT M(YRON), 1897-1973

YESTERDAY'S BURDENS

Cowley, Malcolm, "Reconsideration," *NRep* (Nov. 30, 1974): 40-2.

Pierce, Constance, "'Divinest Sense': Narrative Technique in Robert Coates's YESTERDAY'S BURDENS," *Crit* 19, ii (1977): 44-52.

COCHRAN, LOUIS, 1899-

GENERAL

Simms, L. Moody, Jr., "Louis Cochran: Mississippi Writer," *NMW* 9, ii (Fall, 1976): 114-19.

COETZEE, J(OHN) M., 1940-

DUSKLANDS

Wood, W. J. B., "DUSKLANDS and 'The Impregnable Stronghold of the Intellect,' *Theoria* 54 (1980): 13-23.

IN THE HEART OF THE COUNTRY (FROM THE HEART OF THE COUNTRY)

Roberts, Sheila, "Character and Meaning in Four Contemporary South African Novels," *WLWE* 19, i (Spring, 1980): 19-36.

COHEN, ARTHUR A(LLEN), 1928-

IN THE DAYS OF SIMON STERM

Rosenfeld, Alvin H., "Arthur A. Cohen's Messiah," *Midstream* 19, vii (Aug.-Sept., 1973): 72-5.

COHEN, LEONARD NORMAN, 1934-

GENERAL

Almansi, G., "An Erotic Writer: The 'Minestrone' Novels of Leonard Cohen," *LonM* n.s. 15, iii (Aug.-Sept., 1975): 20-39.

Arn, Robert, "Obscenity and Pornography," *CamR* 89A (Dec. 2, 1967): 60-3.

Djwa, Sandra, "Leonard Cohen: Black Romantic," *CanL* No. 34 (Autumn, 1967): 32-42. Also in Gnarowski, M., ed., *Leonard Cohen*, 94-105.

Gnarowski, M., ed., *Leonard Cohen*.

Ondaatje, M., *Leonard Cohen*.

Pacey, Desmond, "The Phenomenon of Leonard Cohen," *CanL* No. 34 (Autumn, 1967): 5-23. Also in Gnarowski, M., ed., *Leonard Cohen*, 74-93.

Scobie, S., *Leonard Cohen*.

Snider, Burr, "Zooey Glass in Europe," *Gypsy* 1 (1971): 10-13. [Not seen.]

BEAUTIFUL LOSERS

Barbour, Douglas, "Down with History: Some Notes Towards an Understanding of BEAUTIFUL LOSERS," *Open Letter* 2, iii (Summer, 1974): 48-60. Also in Gnarowski, M., ed., *Leonard Cohen*, 136-49.

Boyers, Robert, "Attitudes Toward Sex in American 'High Culture'," *AAAPSS* 376 (Mar., 1968): 51-2.

Buitenhuis, Peter, "Two Solitudes Revisited: Hugh MacLennan and Leonard Cohen," *LHY* 13, ii (July, 1972): 19-32.

Ferres, John H., "The Indian Maiden in Leonard Cohen's BEAUTIFUL LOSERS and John Barth's THE SOT-WEED FACTOR," *JAC* 2, iv (Winter, 1980): 690-8.

Gose, E. B., "Of Beauty and Unmeaning," *CanL* No. 29 (Summer, 1966): 61-3.

Hutcheon, Linda, "BEAUTIFUL LOSERS: All the Polarities," *CanL* 59 (Winter, 1974): 42-56. Also in Woodcock, G., ed., *Canadian Novel in the Twentieth Century*, 298-311.

_____, "The Poet as Novelist," *CanL* 86 (Autumn, 1980): 6-14.

Jones, D. G., *Butterfly on Rock*, 77-82.

Lee, Dennis, *Savage Fields: An Essay in Literature and Cosmology*, Toronto: Anansi, 1977, 63-103.

Macri, F. M., "BEAUTIFUL LOSERS and the Canadian Experience," *JCL* 8, i (June, 1973): 88-96.

Monkman, Leslie, "BEAUTIFUL LOSERS: Mohawk Myth and Jesuit Legend," *JCF* 3, iii (1974): 57-9.

Morley, Patricia A., *Immoral Moralists*, 85-97.

Moss, John, "Forgive Us Our Saints: The Sacred and the Mundane in BEAUTIFUL LOSERS," *Sex and Violence in the Canadian Novel*, 169-84.

Northey, Margot, "Towards the Mystical Grotesque: BEAUTIFUL LOSERS," *Haunted Wilderness*, 101-7.

Ondaatje, M., *Leonard Cohen*, 44-56.

Pacey, Desmond, "The Phenomenon of Leonard Cohen," *CanL* No. 34 (Autumn, 1967): 5-23. Also in Gnarowski, M., ed., *Leonard Cohen*, 74-93.

Schulz, M. F., *Black Humor Fiction of the Sixties*, 26-7, 136-7.

Scobie, S., *Leonard Cohen*, 96-125.

_____, "Magic, Not Magicians: BEAUTIFUL LOSERS and STORY OF O," *CanL* No. 45 (Summer, 1970): 56-60. Also in Gnarowski, M., ed., *Leonard Cohen*, 106-10.

Sutherland, Ronald, "Twin Solitudes," *CanL* No. 31 (Winter, 1967): 5-24.

Woodcock, George, "The Song of Sirens: Reflections on Leonard Cohen," *Odysseus Ever Returning*, 107-9.

THE FAVOURITE GAME

Garebian, Keith, "Desire as Art: Leonard Cohen's THE FAVOURITE GAME," *Le Chien d'Or/The Golden Dog*, 4 (Nov., 1974): 29-34.

Morley, P. A., *Immoral Moralists*, 73-84.

_____, "'The Knowledge of Strangerhood'; 'The Monuments Were Made of Worms'," *JCF* 1, iii (Summer, 1972): 56-60. Also in Gnarowski, M., ed., *Leonard Cohen*, 125-35.

Ondaatje, M., *Leoanrd Cohen*, 23-35.

Pacey, Desmond, "The Phenomenon of Leonard Cohen," *CanL* No. 34 (Autumn, 1967): 9-15. Also in Gnarowski, M., ed., *Leonard Cohen*, 78-84.

Scobie, S., *Leonard Cohen*, 74-96.

Woodcock, George, "The Song of Sirens: Reflections on Leonard Cohen," *Odysseus Ever Returning*, 104-7.

BIBLIOGRAPHY

MacDonald, Ruth, "Leonard Cohen, a Bibliography, 1956-1973," *BB* 31, iii (July-Sept., 1974): 107-10.

Whiteman, Bruce, "Leonard Cohen: An Annotated Bibliography," 55-95 in Lecker, Robert, and Jack David, eds., *The Annotated Bibliography of Canada's Major Authors, Volume Two*, Downsview: ECW, 1980.

COHEN, MATT(HEW), 1942-

GENERAL

Kertzer, Jan, "Matt Cohen," 125-32 in Heath, Jeffrey M., ed., *Profiles in Canadian Literature 4*, Toronto: Dundurn, 1982.

_____, "Time and Its Victims: The Writing of Matt Cohen," *ECW* 17 (Spring, 1980): 9-101.

Woodcock, George, "Armies Moving in the Night: The Fictions of Matt Cohen," *IFR* 6, i (Winter, 1979): 17-30.

THE COLOURS OF WAR

Woodcock, George, "Armies Moving in the Night: The Fictions of Matt Cohen," *IFR* 6, i (Winter, 1979): 26-30.

_____, "To the Past via the Future," *CanL* 75 (1977): 74-7.

THE DISINHERITED

Lecker, Robert, "Past the Grinning Masks: Temporal Form and Structure in THE DISINHERITED," *JCanStud* 16, ii (1981): 94-108.

Moss, John, "Canadian Gothic: THE DISINHERITED by Matt Cohen," *Sex and Violence in the Canadian Novel*, 185-98.

Woodcock, George, "Armies Moving in the Night: The Fictions of Matt Cohen," *IFR* 6, i (Winter, 1979): 20-4.

JOHNNY CRACKLE SINGS

Ewing, Betty M., "Matt Cohen's Monologue in Morality," *CanL* 72 (Spring, 1977): 41-4.

KORSONILOFF

Ewing, Betty M., "Matt Cohen's Monologue in Morality," *CanL* 72 (Spring, 1977): 41-4.

WOODEN HUNTERS

Woodcock, George, "Armies Moving in the Night: The Fictions of Matt Cohen," *IFR* 6, i (Winter, 1979): 24-6.

COLTER, CYRUS J., 1910-

GENERAL

Bender, Robert M., "The Fiction of Cyrus Colter," *NewL* 48, i (Fall, 1981): 93-103.

Farnsworth, Robert M., "An Interview with Cyrus Colter," *NewL* 39, iii (Spring, 1973): 17-39.

O'Brien, John, "Forms of Determinism in the Fiction of Cyrus Colter," *SBL* 4, ii (Summer, 1973): 24-8.

_____, ed., *Interviews with Black Writers*, 17-3.

"Work: Beginning to Write at Fifty: A Conversation with Cyrus Colter," *AR* 36, iv (Fall, 1978): 422-36.

THE HIPPODROME

Bender, Robert M., "The Fiction of Cyrus Colter," *NewL* 48, i (Fall, 1981): 93-103.

NIGHT STUDIES

Bender, Robert M., "The Fiction of Cyrus Colter," *NewL* 48, i (Fall, 1981): 93-103.

Grosch, Anthony R., "NIGHT STUDIES: A NOVEL," *ON* 6, iv (Winter, 1980-81): 398-400.

THE RIVERS OF EROS

Bender, Robert M., "The Fiction of Cyrus Colter," *NewL* 48, i (Fall, 1981): 93-103.

O'Brien, John, "Forms of Determinism in the Fiction of Cyrus Colter," *SBL* 4, ii (Summer, 1973): 26-7.

COMFORT, ALEX(ANDER), 1920-

GENERAL

Callahan, Robert D., "Alexander Comfort and British New Romanticism, a Study of THE SILVER RIVER (1938), NO SUCH LIBERTY (1941), THE ALMOND TREE (1942), and THE POWER HOUSE (1944)," *DAI* 32 (1972): 6416A (Un. of Wash.).

Krafft, John M., "Anarcho-Romanticism and the Metaphysics of Counterforce: Alex Comfort and Thomas Pynchon," *Paunch* 40-41 (April, 1975): 78-107.

Salmon, Arthur E., "Against Death and Power: A Study of the Art and Thought of Alex Comfort," *DAI* 35 (1975): 7327A.

BIBLIOGRAPHY

Callahan, Robert D., "Alexander Comfort: A Bibliography in Progress," *WCR* 3, iii (Winter, 1969): 48-67.

COMPTON-BURNETT, IVY, 1892-1969

GENERAL

Allen, W., *Modern Novel*, 188-91.

Amis, Kingsley, "One World and Its Way," *TC* 158 (Aug., 1955): 168-75. Also in *What Became of Jane Austen?* 41-50.

Anon., "Interview with Miss Compton-Burnett," *REL* 3, iv (Oct., 1962): 96-112.

Baldanza, F., *Ivy Compton-Burnett*.

Balutowa, Bronislawa, "Type Versus Character in the Novels of Ivy Compton-Burnett," *KN* 17 (1970): 377-98.

Bland, D. S., "T. S. Eliot's Case-Book," *MLN* 75 (Jan., 1960): 23-6.

Bowen, John, "An Interview with Ivy Compton-Burnett (BBC Home Programme, Sept. 17, 1960)," *TCL* 25, ii (Summer, 1979): 165-72.

Bullock, Alan, "Natalia Ginzburg and Ivy Compton-Burnett: Creative Composition and Domestic Regression in LE VOCI DELLA SERA," *RLMC* 30 (1977): 203-26.

Burkhart, C., ed., *Art of I. Compton-Burnett*.

————, *I. Compton-Burnett*.

————, "I. Compton-Burnett: The Shape of a Career," in Burkhart, C., ed., *Art of I. Compton-Burnett*, 158-71.

"A Conversation Between I. Compton-Burnett and Margaret Jourdain," *Orion, A Miscellany*, Vol. I, London: Nicholson and Watson, 1945, 20-8.

Cottrell, Beekman W., "Conversation Piece: Four Twentieth Century English Dialogue Novelists," *DA* 16 (1956): 2159 (Columbia).

Curtis, Mary M., "The Moral Comedy of Miss Compton-Burnett," *WSCL* 5, iii (Autumn, 1964): 213-21.

Ginger, John, "Ivy Compton-Burnett," *LonM* 9, x (Jan., 1970): 58-71. Also in Burkhart, C., ed., *Art of I. Compton-Burnett*, 172-84.

Gold, Joseph, "Exit Everybody: The Novels of Ivy Compton-Burnett," *DR* 42 (Summer, 1962): 227-38.

Grylls, R. G., *I. Compton-Burnett*.

Horn, Larry V., "Vision and Form in the Novels of I. Compton-Burnett," *DAI* 38 (1977): 2776A.

Hutchinson, Joanne, "Appearances Are All We Have," *TCL* 25, ii (Summer, 1979): 183-93.

Jefferson, D. W., "A Note on Ivy Compton-Burnett," *REL* 1, ii (April, 1960): 19-24.

Johnson, Pamela H., *I. Compton-Burnett*.

————, "Three Novelists and the Drawing of Character: C. P. Snow, Joyce Cary and Ivy Compton-Burnett," in English Association, *Essays and Studies, 1950*, 82-4, 94-9.

Karl, F. R., "The Intimate World of Ivy Compton-Burnett," *Contemporary English Novel*, 201-19.

Kermode, Frank, "The House of Fiction: Interviews with Seven English Novelists," *PR* 30 (Spring, 1963): 71-4.

King, Francis, Rosalie G. Grylls, Michael Mullgate, Violet Powell, Lettice Cooper, Robert Liddell, and James Lees-Milne, "Major/Minor: A Symposium," *TCl* 25, ii (Summer, 1979): 127-34.

Levinsky, Ruth, "Literary Trends and Two Novelists: Natalie Sarraute and Ivy Compton-Burnett," *Proc. of Conf. of College Teachers of English of Texas* 37 (1972): 25-8.

Liddell, Robert, "Notes on Ivy Compton-Burnett," *TCL* 25, ii (Summer, 1979): 135-52.

————, *The Novels of I. Compton-Burnett*, London: Victor Gollancz, 1955.

————, *A Treatise on the Novel*, London: Jonathan Cape, 1947; paperback ed., 1965, 146-63.

MacSween, R. J., "Ivy Compton-Burnett," *AntigR* 24 (1976): 25-30.

————, "Ivy Compton-Burnett: Merciless Understanding," *AntigR* 7 (Autumn, 1971): 38-46.

Marsden-Smedley, Hester, "Ivy ... Friend of the Family," *TCL* 25, ii (Summer, 1979): 173-82.

McCarthy, Mary, "The Inventions of I. Compton-Burnett," *Encounter* 27, v (Nov., 1966): 19-31. Also in *Writing on the Wall*, 112-44.

Nevius, B., *Ivy Compton-Burnett*.

O'Reilly, William M., Jr., "Nature and Convention in the Novels of Ivy Compton-Burnett," *DAI* 3 (1972): 2946A (Conn.).

Pendry, E. D., *New Feminism of English Fiction*, 90-119.

Perry, Sandra J., "Disclosure and Ivy Compton-Burnett: A Guide to Reading Her Dialogue Novels," *DAI* 38 (1977): 1415A.

Powell, Anthony, "Ivy Compton-Burnett," *Spectator* 223 (Sept. 6, 1969): 304-5.

Praz, Mario, "The Novels of Ivy Compton-Burnett," *RAI Radio* (Televisione Italiana), April 1, 1955. Also in Burkhart, C., ed., *Art of I. Compton-Burnett*, 123-8.

Preston, John, "'The Matter in a Word'," *EIC* 10 (July, 1960): 348-56.

Rao, V. Ramakrishna, *Ivy Compton-Burnett*.

Ruff, Lillian M., "Ivy Compton-Burnett—An Old Hollowegian," *N&Q* 19, ix (Sept., 1972): 337-8.

Sackville-West, Edward, "Ladies whose bright Pens...," in *Inclinations*, London: Secker and Warburg, 1949, 78-103. Port Washington, N.Y.: Kennikat Pr., 1967, 78-103.

Shaw, Elizabeth B., "The Comic Novels of Ivy Compton-Burnett and Nathalie Sarraute," *DAI* 35 (1975): 7923A-24A.

Snow, Lotus, " 'Good is Bad Condensed' ": Ivy Compton-Burnett's View of Human Nature," *WHR* 10 (Summer, 1956): 271-6.

Spurling, Hilary, "I. Compton-Burnett: Not One of Those Modern People," *TCL* 25, ii (Summer, 1979): 153-64.

Sykes, Christopher, "The Reign of Terror," *Listener* 85 (Feb. 11, 1971): 183-4.

Tripathy, Biyot, K., "Ivy Compton-Burnett: A Perspective," *BDEC* 5, ii (1969-70): 56-60.

Tristram, Philippa, "Ivy Compton-Burnett: An Enbalmer's Art," *SLitI* 11, ii (Fall, 1978): 27-42.

Webster, Harvey C., "Ivy Compton-Burnett: Factualist," *After the Trauma*, 51-71.

Wilson, Angus, "Ivy Compton-Burnett," *LonM* 2 (July, 1955): 64-70.

BROTHERS AND SISTERS

Baldanza, F., *Ivy Compton-Burnett*, 43-6.

Burkhart, C., *I. Compton-Burnett*, 101-3.

Johnson, P. H., *I. Compton-Burnett*, 27.

May, James B., "Towards Print (Ivy Compton-Burnett: A Time Exposure)," *Trace*, No. 49 (Summer, 1963): 92-9.

Nevius, B., *Ivy Compton-Burnett*, 9-10.

Rowsell, Mary D., "BROTHERS AND SISTERS: A Most Complex Relation," *TCL* 25, ii (Summer, 1979): 207-23.

BULLIVANT AND THE LAMBS (See MANSERVANT AND MAIDSERVANT)

DARKNESS AND DAY

Baldanza, F., *Ivy Compton-Burnett*, 83-6.

Bogan, Louise, *Selected Criticism: Prose, Poetry*, N.Y.: Noonday, 1955, 189-90.

Burkhart, C., *I. Compton-Burnett*, 54-5, 119-21.

Curtis, Mary M., "The Moral Comedy of Miss Compton-Burnett," *WSCL* 5, iii (Autumn, 1964): 216-18.

Johnson, P. H., *I. Compton-Burnett*, 34-5.

DAUGHTERS AND SONS

Baldanza, F., *Ivy Compton-Burnett*, 58-61.
Burkhart, C., *I. Compton-Burnett*, 108-10.
Johnson, P. H., *I. Compton-Burnett*, 30-1.
Nevius, B., *Ivy Compton-Burnett*, 29-31.

DOLORES

Baldanza, F., *Ivy Compton-Burnett*, 39-41.
Johnson, P. H., *I. Compton-Burnett*, 24-5.
Nevius, B., *Ivy Compton-Burnett*, 4-6.
Ruff, Lillian M., "Ivy Compton-Burnett—An Old Hollowegian," *N&Q* 19, ix (Sept., 1972): 337-8.
Sykes, Christopher, "The Reign of Tyranny," *Listener* 85 (Feb. 11, 1971): 183-4.

ELDERS AND BETTERS

Baldanza, F., *Ivy Compton-Burnett*, 69-72.
Balutowa, Bronislawa, "The Group Dynamics in the Plots of Ivy Compton-Burnett," *ZRL* 13, i (1970): 83-92.
Bowen, E., *Collected Impressions*, N.Y.: Knopf, 1950, 85-91.
Burkhart, C., *I. Compton-Burnett*, 113-15.
Johnson, P. H., *I. Compton-Burnett*, 11-13.
Nevius, B., *Ivy Compton-Burnett*, 34-7.
Pittock, Malcolm, "Ivy Compton-Burnett's Use of Dialogue," *ES* 51 (1970): 43-6.

A FAMILY AND A FORTUNE

Baldanza, F., *Ivy Compton-Burnett*, 61-5.
Burkhart, C., *I. Compton-Burnett*, 110-11.
Johnson, P. H., *I. Compton-Burnett*, 14-17.
Kettle, A., *Introduction to the English Novel*, 184-90.
Nevius, B., *Ivy Compton-Burnett*, 31-3.
Potter, Lois, "Show and Dumb Show in A FAMILY AND A FORTUNE," *TCL* 25, ii (Summer, 1979): 194-206.

A FATHER AND HIS FATE

Baldanza, F., *Ivy Compton-Burnett*, 93-6.
Burkhart, C., *I. Compton-Burnett*, 124-5.

A GOD AND HIS GIFTS

Baldanza, F., *Ivy Compton-Burnett*, 102-5.
Brophy, Brigid, in *NStat* (Dec. 6, 1963): 865. Also in Brophy, B., *Don't Never Forget*, 167-70.
Burkhart, C., *I. Compton-Burnett*, 56-7, 128-9.
"Novels of 1963. I. Compton-Burnett: A GOD AND HIS GIFTS," in *T.L.S.: Essays and Reviews from The Times Literary Supplement, 1963*, 178-80. Also in *TLS* (Nov. 21, 1963).
Prescott, O., *In My Opinion*, 98-100.

A HERITAGE AND ITS HISTORY

Baldanza, F., *Ivy Compton-Burnett*, 96-9.
Burkhart, C., *I. Compton-Burnett*, 125-7.
Iser, W., *Implied Reader*, 152-63, 234-56.
Preston, John, "'The Matter in a Word'," *EIC* 10 (July, 1960): 348-56.

A HOUSE AND ITS HEAD

Burkhart, C., *I. Compton-Burnett*, 107-8.
Johnson, P. H., *I. Compton-Burnett*, 30.
McFarlane, Brian, "Ivy Compton-Burnett's A HOUSE AND ITS HEAD: Truth and Wit," *SoRA* 11 (1978): 154-64.
Nevius, B., *Ivy Compton-Burnett*, 28-9.

THE LAST AND THE FIRST

Sykes, Christopher, "The Reign of Tyranny," *Listener* 85 (Feb. 11, 1971): 183-4.

MANSERVANT AND MAIDSERVANT (BULLIVANT AND THE LAMBS)

Baldanza, F., *Ivy Compton-Burnett*, 72-6.
Burkhart, C., *I. Compton-Burnett*, 115-17.
Johnson, P. H., *I. Compton-Burnett*, 32-3.
Karl, F. R., "The Intimate World of Ivy Compton-Burnett," *Contemporary English Novel*, 212-15.
Lewis, Constance, "MANSERVANT AND MAIDSERVANT: A Pivotal Novel," *TCL* 25, ii (Summer, 1979): 224-34.
Nevius, B., *Ivy Compton-Burnett*, 37-8.
Wilde, Alan, "Surfacings: Reflections on the Epistemology of Late Modernism," *Boundary* 8, ii (Winter, 1980): 209-27.

MEN AND WIVES

Baldanza, F., *Ivy Compton-Burnett*, 46-9.
Burkhart, C., *I. Compton-Burnett*, 103-4.
Johnson, P. H., *I. Compton-Burnett*, 27-8.
Nevius, B., *Ivy Compton-Burnett*, 23-5.
Reaney, James, "Novels of Ivy Compton-Burnett," *CanF* 29 (April, 1949): 11-12.

THE MIGHTY AND THEIR FALL

Baldanza, F., *Ivy Compton-Burnett*, 99-102.
Burkhart, C., *I. Compton-Burnett*, 127-8.
Curtis, Mary M., "The Moral Comedy of Miss Compton-Burnett," *WSCL* 5, iii (Autumn, 1964): 214-16, 217-18.
Wiley, Paul, *WSCL* 5, ii (Spring-Summer, 1963): 232-4.

MORE WOMEN THAN MEN

Baldanza, F., *Ivy Compton-Burnett*, 49-53.
Burkhart, C., *I. Compton-Burnett*, 104-6.
Johnson, P. H., *I. Compton-Burnett*, 28-9.
Nevius, B., *Ivy Compton-Burnett*, 27-8.

MOTHER AND SON

Amis, Kingsley, "One World and Its Way," *TC* 158 (Aug., 1955): 168-75.
Baldanza, F., *Ivy Compton-Burnett*, 89-92.
Burkhart, C., *I. Compton-Burnett*, 122-4.
Nevius, B., *Ivy Compton-Burnett*, 42-3.
West, A., *Principles and Persuasions*, 225-32.

PARENTS AND CHILDREN

Baldanza, F., *Ivy Compton-Burnett*, 65-9.
Bowen, E., *Collected Impressions*, N.Y.: Knopf, 1950, 82-5.
Burkhart, C., *I. Compton-Burnett*, 111-13.

Johnson, P. H., *I. Compton-Burnett*, 31-2.
Nevius, B., *Ivy Compton-Burnett*, 33-4.

PASTORS AND MASTERS

Baldanza, F., *Ivy Compton-Burnett*, 41-3.
Burkhart, C., *I. Compton-Burnett*, 100-1.
Greenfield, Stanley B., "PASTORS AND MASTERS: The Spoils of Genius," *Criticism* 2 (Winter, 1960): 66-80.
Johnson, P. H., *I. Compton-Burnett*, 26.
Nevius, B., *Ivy Compton-Burnett*, 7-9.

THE PRESENT AND THE PAST

Baldanza, F., *Ivy Compton-Burnett*, 86-9.
Burkhart, C., *I. Compton-Burnett*, 121-2.
Nevius B., *Ivy Compton-Burnett*, 40-2.

TWO WORLDS AND THEIR WAYS

Baldanza, F., *Ivy Compton-Burnett*, 76-9.
Bellringer, Alan W., "The Impersonal Affirmation of Ivy Compton-Burnett's TWO WORLDS AND THEIR WAYS," *UCT Studies in English* 10 (1980): 49-67.
Burkhart, C., *I. Compton-Burnett*, 118-19.
Johnson, P. H., *I. Compton-Burnett*, 33-4.
Karl, F. R., "The Intimate World of Ivy Compton-Burnett," *Contemporary English Novel*, 215-18.

BIBLIOGRAPHY

Baldanza, F., *Ivy Compton-Burnett*, 135-8.
Burkhart, C., *I. Compton-Burnett*, 135-7.
Huff, Kathy M., "Ivy Compton-Burnett: A Bibliography," *BB* 35, iii (July-Sept., 1978): 132-42.

CONDON, RICHARD (THOMAS), 1915-1996

GENERAL

Smith, Julian, "The Infernal Comedy of Richard Condon," *TCL* 14, iv (Jan., 1969): 221-9.

A TALENT FOR LOVING; OR, THE GREAT COWBOY RACE

Cleary, Michael, "Ever is Heard a Discouraging Word: Richard Condon's A TALENT FOR LOVING," *SwAL* 7, i (1981): 22-33.

CONNELL, EVAN S., JR., 1924-

GENERAL

Blaisdell, Gus, "After Ground Zero: The Writings of Evan S. Connell, Jr.," *NMQR* 36 (Summer, 1966): 181-207.

THE DIARY OF A RAPIST

Blaisdell, Gus, "After Ground Zero: The Writings of Evan S. Connell, Jr.," *NMQR* 36 (Summer, 1966): 200-6.

MRS. BRIDGE

Blaisdell, Gus, "After Ground Zero: The Writings of Evan S. Connell, Jr.," *NMQR* 36 (Summer, 1966): 186-8.
Shepherd, Allen, "Mr. Bridge in MRS. BRIDGE," *NConL* 3, iii (1973): 7-11.
Van Bark, Bella S., "The Alienated Person in Literature," *AJP* 21 (1961): 189-91.

THE PATRIOT

Blaisdell, Gus, "After Ground Zero: The Writings of Evan S. Connell, Jr.," *NMQR* 36 (Summer, 1966): 188-92.

BIBLIOGRAPHY

White, Ray L., "Evan S. Connell Jr.'s MRS. BRIDGE and MR. BRIDGE: A Critical Documentary," *Midamerica* 6 (1979): 141-59.

CONROY, JACK, 1899-1990

GENERAL

Adams, Jimmie R., "Jack Conroy and the Disinherited," *DAI* 42 (1981): 1147A.
Anderson, David D., "Jack Conroy's Return," *SSMLN* 4, ii (1974): 6-8. [Not seen.]
Fried, Lewis, "Conversation with Jack Conroy," *NewL* 39, i (Fall, 1972): 41-60.
Sharma, D. R., "Jack Conroy: An Analysis of His Moral Vision," *PURBA* 3, ii (Oct., 1972): 97-106.
Wixson, Douglas, "From Conroy to Steinbeck: The Quest for an Idiom of the People in the 1930's," *Midamerica* 8 (1981): 135-50. [Not seen.]
————, "Jack Conroy, the Sage of Moberly," *BForum* 6, ii (1982): 201-6.
————, "Literature from the Crucible of Experience: Jack Conroy in Ohio, 1927-30," *MMisc* 8 (1980): 44-60. [Not seen.]

THE DISINHERITED

Anderson, David D., "Three Generations of Missouri Fiction," *MMisc* 9 (1981): 7-20. [Not seen.]
Fried, Lewis, "THE DISINHERITED: The Worker as Writer," *NewL* 39, i (Oct., 1972): 29-40.
Larsen, Erling, "Jack Conroy's THE DISINHERITED or, The Way It Was," in Madden, D., ed., *Proletarian Writers of the Thirties*, 85-95.
Reilly, John M., "Two Novels of Working Class Consciousness," *MQ* 14, ii (Jan., 1973): 183-93.
Wixson, Douglas, "FromConroy to Steinbeck: The Quest for an Idiom of the People in the 1930's," *Midamerica* 8 (1981): 135-50. [Not seen.]

CONROY, PAT, 1945-

THE GREAT SANTINI

Burkholder, Robert E., "The Uses of Myth in Pat Conroy's THE GREAT SANTINI," *Crit* 21, i (1979): 31-7.

COOPER, WILLIAM, Pseud. (Hoff, Harry Summerfield), 1910-

GENERAL

Kéry, Lászlo, "The Novels of William Cooper," *SEAP* 1 (1971): 242-63. [Not seen.]

SCENES FROM MARRIED LIFE

Deakin, Nicholas, "An Appraisal of William Cooper: In Search of Banality," *T&T* 42 (Jan. 27, 1961): 140-1.
Enright, D. J., "The New Pastoral-Comical," *Spectator* No. 919 (Feb. 3, 1961): 154-5.
Johnson, Pamela H., "Smart Chap Grows Up," *Reporter* 24 (Mar. 16, 1961): 55-6.

SCENES FROM PROVINCIAL LIFE

Allen, W., *Modern Novel*, 251-2.
Bradbury, Malcolm, Introduction to SCENES FROM PROVINCIAL LIFE, London: Macmillan, 1969. Also in Bradbury, M., *Possibilities*, 192-200.
Deakin, Nicholas, "An Appraisal of William Cooper: In Search of Banality," *T&T* 42 (Jan. 27, 1961): 140-1.
Enright, D. J., "The New Pastoral-Comical," *Spectator* No. 6919 (Feb. 3, 1961): 154-5.
Fraser, G. S., *Modern Writer and His World*, 164-5.
Johnson, Pamela H., "Smart Chap Grows Up," *Reporter* 24 (Mar. 16, 1961): 55-6.

YOUNG PEOPLE

Allen, W., *Modern Novel*, 252-3.
Fraser, G. S., *Modern Writer and His World*, 165-6.

COOVER, ROBERT, 1932-

GENERAL

Andersen, R., *Robert Coover*.
Balitas, Vincent D., "Historical Consciousness in the Novels of Robert Coover," *KN* 28, iii-iv (1981): 369-79.
Bass, Thomas A., "An Encounter with Robert Coover," *AR* 40, iii (Summer, 1982): 287-302.
Cope, Jackson I., "Robert Coover's Fictions," *Iowa* 2, iv (Fall, 1971): 94-110.
Dillard, R. H. W., "The Wisdom of The Beast: The Fictions of Robert Coover," *HC* 7, ii (April, 1970): 1-11.
Durand, Régis, "The Exemplary Fictions of Robert Coover," in Johnson, I. D., and C. Johnson, eds., *Les Américanistes*, 130-7.
Heckard, Margaret, "Robert Coover, Metafiction, and Freedom," *TCL* 22, ii (May, 1976): 210-27.
Hertzel, Leo J., "An Interview with Robert Coover," *Crit* 11, iii (1969): 25-9.
_____, "What's Wrong with the Christians?" *Crit* 11, iii (1969): 11-24.
Hume, Kathryn, "Robert Coover's Fiction: The Naked and the Mythic," *Novel* 12, ii (Winter, 1979): 127-48.
Kadragic, Alma, "An Interview with Robert Coover," *Shanti* 2 (Summer, 1972): 57-60.

Kentta, William P., "Ironic Dissonance in Robert Coover's Fictions," *DAI* 42, viii (Feb., 1982): 3601A.
Major, Pamela J., "Robert Coover and the Literature of Dream Time," *DAI* 42, viii (Feb., 1982): 3602A.
Mazurek, Raymond A., "The Fiction of History: The Presentation of History in Recent American Literature," *DAI* 41, viii (Feb., 1981): 3582A-83A.
McCafferey, Larry, "The Magic of Fiction Making," *FictionI* 4-5 (Winter, 1975): 147-53.
_____, "The Reliance of Man on Fiction-Making: A Study of the Works of Robert Coover," *DAI* 36 (1975): 2810A.
_____, "Robert Coover on His Own and Other Fictions: An Interview," *Genre* 14, i (Spring, 1981): 45-63.
_____, "Robert Coover's Cubist Fictions," *par rapport* 1 (1978): 33-40.
Robinson, Douglas, "Visions of 'No' End: the Anti-Apocalyptic Novels of Ellison, Barth, and Coover," *AmSS* 13, i (1981): 1-16.
Schmitz, Neil, "Robert Coover and the Hazards of Metafiction," *Novel* 7, iii (Spring, 1974): 210-19.
Wineapple, Brenda, "Robert Coover's Playing Fields," *IowaR* 10, iii (1979): 66-74.
Woodward, Robert H., "An Ancestor of Robert Coover's Mrs. Grundy," *NConL* 3, i (1973): 11-12. [Not seen.]

THE ORIGIN OF THE BRUNISTS

Andersen, R., *Robert Coover*, 40-57.
Balitas, Vincent D., "Historical Consciousness in the Novels of Robert Coover," *KN* 28, iii-iv (1981): 371-3.
Dillard, R. H. W., "The Wisdom of The Beast: The Fictions of Robert Coover," *HC* 7, ii (April, 1970): 3-6.
Heckard, Margaret, "Robert Coover, Metafiction, and Freedom," *TCL* 22, ii (May, 1976): 222-4.
Hertzel, Leo J., "What's Wrong With the Christians?" *Crit* 11, iii (1969): 13-19.
McCaffery, L., *Metafictional Muse*, 29-41.

THE PUBLIC BURNING

Aaron, Daniel, "Fictionalizing the Past," *PR* 47, ii (1980): 235-8.
Andersen, R., *Robert Coover*, 117-33.
Balitas, Vincent D., "Historical Consciousness in the Novels of Robert Coover," *KN* 28, iii-iv (1981): 376-8.
Fogel, Stan, "Richard Nixon by Robert Coover, Roland Barthes by Roland Barthes," *ESC* 8, ii (June, 1982): 187-202.
Gallo, Louis, "Nixon and the 'House of Wax': An Emblematic Episode in Coover's THE PUBLIC BURNING," *Crit* 23, iii (Spring, 1982): 43-51.
LeClair, Thomas, "Robert Coover, THE PUBLIC BURNING, and the Art of Excess," *Crit* 23, iii (Spring, 1982): 5-28.
Martin, Richard, "Clio Bemused: The Uses of History in Contemporary American Fiction," *Sub-stance* 27 (1980): 21-4.
Mazurek, Raymond A., "Metafiction, the Historical Novel, and Coover's THE PUBLIC BURNING," *Crit* 23, iii (Spring, 1982): 29-42.
McCaffery, L., *Metaphysical Muse*, 83-97.
Ramage, John, "Myth and Monomyth in Coover's THE PUBLIC BURNING," *Crit* 23, iii (Spring, 1982): 52-68.
Robinson, Douglas, "Visions of 'No' End: The Anti-Apocalyptic Novels of Ellison, Barth, and Coover," *AmSS* 13, i (1981): 12-13.

Schwartz, Richard A., "Coover's 'Word Golf'," *NConL* 9, i (Jan., 1979): 8.

Werner, C. H., *Paradoxical Resolutions*, 82-8.

THE UNIVERSAL BASEBALL ASSOCIATION, INC., J. HENRY WAUGH, PROP.

Andersen, R., *Robert Coover*, 57-74.

Angelius, Judith W., "The Man Behind the Catcher's Mask: A Closer Look at Robert Coover's UNIVERSAL BASEBALL ASSN.," *DQ* 12, i (Spring, 1977): 165-74.

Balitas, Vincent D., "Historical Consciousness in the Novels of Robert Coover," *KN* 28, iii-iv (1981): 373-6.

Berman, Neil, "Coover's UNIVERSAL BASEBALL ASSOCIATION: Play as Personalized Myth," *MFS* 24, ii (1978): 209-22.

Cope, Jackson I., "Robert Coover's Fictions," *IowaR* 2, iv (Fall, 1971): 100-10.

Dillard, R. H. W., "The Wisdom of The Beast: The Fictions of Robert Coover," *HC* 7, ii (April, 1970): 6-9.

Friedman, Alan J., "Robert Coover's UNIVERSAL BASEBALL ASSOCIATION and Modern Physics," *Tréma* 1 (1975): 147-57.

Hansen, Arlen J., "The Dice of God: Einstein, Heisenberg, and Robert Coover," *Novel* 10, i (Fall, 1976): 48-58.

Harris, Charles B., *Contemporary American Novelists of the Absurd*, 131-4.

Heckard, Margaret, "Robert Coover, Metafiction, and Freedom," *TCL* 22, ii (May, 1976): 224-6.

Hertzel, Leo J., "What's Wrong With the Christians?" *Crit* 11, iii (1969): 11-13, 19-22.

Johnson, R. E., "Structuralism and the Reading of Contemporary Fiction," *Soundings* 58, ii (Summer, 1975): 298-303.

McCaffery, L., *Metaphysical Muse*, 41-59.

Perkins, James A., "Robert Coover and John Gardner: What Can We Do With the Poets?" *NConL* 6, ii (Mar., 1976): 2-4.

Schulz, Max F., *Black Humor Fiction of the Sixties*, 82-6, 137-8.

Shelton, Frank W., "Humor and Balance in Coover's THE UNIVERSAL BASEBALL ASSOCIATION, INC.," *Crit* 17, i (1975): 78-90.

Taylor, Mark, "Baseball as Myth," *Cweal* (May 12, 1972): 237-9.

Wallace, Ronald, "The Great American Game: Robert Coover's BASEBALL," *ELWIU* 5, i (1978): 103-18. Also in *Last Laugh*, 115-35.

BIBLIOGRAPHY

Blachhowicz, Camille, "Robert Coover," *GrLR* 3, i (Summer, 1976): 69-73.

McCaffery, Larry, "A Robert Coover Checklist," *BB* 31, iii (July-Sept., 1974): 103-4.

COPE, JACK, 1913-

THE DAWN COMES TWICE

Rudolph, Harold, "The Dawn Has Gone—Forever," *Standpunte* 30, vi (Dec., 1977): 20-7. [Court censorship decision.]

MY SON MAX

Roberts, Sheila, "Character and Meaning in Four Contemporary South African Novels," *WLWE* 19, i (Spring, 1980): 19-36.

COZZENS, JAMES GOULD, 1903-1978

GENERAL

Adams, R. P., "James Gould Cozzens: A Cultural Dilemma," in Langford, R. E., ed., *Essays in Modern American Literature*, 103-11.

Allen, W., *Modern Novel*, 185-7.

Anon., "The Hermit of Lambertville," *Time* 70 (Sept. 2, 1957): 72-8.

Bracher, Frederick, "James Gould Cozzens: Humanist," *Crit* 1, iii (Winter, 1958): 10-29.

_____, *Novels of James Gould Cozzens*.

_____, "Of Youth and Age: James Gould Cozzens," *PacSp* 5 (Winter, 1951): 48-62.

_____, "Style and Techniques," in Bruccoli, M. J., ed., *Just Representations*, 379-88.

Bruccoli, M. J., ed., *James Gould Cozzens*.

_____, ed., *Just Representations*.

Cass, Colin S., "Heroism in the Apprentice Novels of James Gould Cozzens," *DAI* 37 (1977): 7128A.

Coxe, Louis O., "Comments on Cozzens: A High Place," *Crit* 1, iii (1958): 48-51.

_____, "The Complex World of James Gould Cozzens," *AL* 27 (May, 1955): 157-71. Also in Bruccoli, M. J., ed., *James Gould Cozzens*, 1-14.

Duggan, Francis X, "Facts and All Man's Fictions," *Thought* 33 (Winter, 1958-59): 604-16.

Eisinger, Chester E., "The Voice of Aggressive Aristocracy," *Midway* No. 18 (Spring, 1964): 100-28. Also in Eisinger, C. E., *Fiction of the Forties*, 146-71.

Finn, James, "Cozzens Dispossessed," *Cweal* 68 (April 4, 1958): 11-13.

Frederick, John T., "Love By Adverse Possession: The Case of Mr. Cozzens," *CE* 19 (April, 1958): 313-16.

Frohock, W. M., *Strangers to this Ground*, 63-83.

Galligan, Edward L., "Within Limits: The Novels of James Gould Cozzens," *DA* 19 (1959): 2951-52 (Penn.).

Garrett, George, "Whatever Wishful Thinking May Wish: The Example of James Gould Cozzens," in Bruccoli, M. J., ed., *Just Representations*, 197-203.

Geismar, Maxwell, "Comments on Cozzens: By Cozzens Possessed," *Crit* 1, iii (Winter, 1958): 51-3.

Hamblen, Abigail A.,"The Paradox of James Gould Cozzens," *WHR* 19 (Autumn, 1965): 355-61.

Harlan, Earl, "Somewhat by Love Possessed," *English Record* 10 (Fall, 1959): 35-40.

Hein, Mark W., "Christian Cozzens: The Religious Framework of James Gould Cozzen's Novels," *DAI* 42 (1981): 1149A.

Hicks, Granville, *James Gould Cozzens*.

_____, "The Reputation of James Gould Cozzens," *EJ* 39 (Jan., 1950): 1-7. Also in *CE* 11 (Jan., 1950): 177-83.

Howe, Irving, "James Gould Cozzens: Novelist of the Republic," *NRep* 138 (Jan. 20, 1958): 15-19.

Hyman, Stanley E., "James Gould Cozzens and the Art of the Possible," *NMQ* 19 (Winter, 1949): 476-98.

Janeway, Elizabeth, "Guardian of Middle-Class Honor," *NYTBR* (Aug. 2, 1959): 1, 18.

Keefe, Joseph C., "Social Behaviorism in the Novels of James Gould Cozzens," *DAI* 30 (1970): 3463A (Syracuse).

Kilgo, James P., "Five American Novels of World War II: A Critical Study," *DA* 32 (1972): 6380A.

Krickel, Edward, "Cozzens and Saroyan: A Look at Two Reputations," *GaR* 24, iii (Fall, 1970): 281-96.

Long, Richard A., "The Image of Man in James Gould Cozzens," *CLAJ* 10 (June, 1967): 299-307.

Ludwig, Richard M., "A Reading of the James Gould Cozzens Manuscripts," *PULC* 19 (Autumn, 1957): 1-14.

Lydenberg, John, "Cozzens and the Conservatives," *Crit* 1, iii (Winter, 1958): 3-9.

————, "Cozzens and the Critics," *CE* 19 (Dec., 1957): 99-104.

————, "Cozzens' Man of Responsibility," *Shen* 10, ii (Winter, 1959): 11-18.

Marx, Leo, "Controversy," *ASch* 27 (Spring, 1958): 228-9.

Maxwell, D. E. S., *Cozzens*.

Michel, Pierre, "Cozzens and the Conservative Spirit," in Bruccoli, M. J., ed., *James Gould Cozzens*, 29-43.

————, *James Gould Cozzens*.

————, "A Note on James Gould Cozzens," *RLV* No. 3 (1960): 192-210.

Millgate, M., *American Social Fiction*, 181-94.

————, "The Judgements of James Gould Cozzens," *CritQ* 4 (Spring, 1962): 87-91.

Mizener, A., "... Anthony Powell and James Gould Cozzens," *Sense of Life in the Modern Novel*, 85-9.

————, *Twelve Great American Novels*, 160-4.

————, "The Undistorting Mirror," *KR* 28 (Nov., 1966): 595-611.

Mooney, H. J., Jr., *James Gould Cozzens*.

O'Connor, William V., "Comments on Cozzens: A Muted Violence," *Crit* 1, iii (1958): 54-5.

Parrish, James, "James Gould Cozzens: A Critical Analysis," *DA* 15 (1955): 1856-57 (Florida State).

————, "James Gould Cozzens Fights a War," *ArQ* 18 (Winter, 1962): 335-40.

Perrin, Noel, "The Good Dukes," in Bruccoli, M. J., ed., *Just Representations*, 278-94.

Prescott, O., *In My Opinion*, 182-91.

Rees, David, "Ministers of Fate," *Spectator* (May 21, 1965): 666-7.

Rideout, Walter B., "Comments on Cozzens: James Gould Cozzens," *Crit* 1, iii (Winter, 1958): 55-6.

Rodewald, Frederick A., "Moral Ambiguity as a Theme in the Novels of James Gould Gozzens," *DA* 29 (1969): 2723A (Okla.).

Scholes, Robert E., "The Commitment of James Gould Cozzens," *ArQ* 16 (Summer, 1960): 129-44. Also, in a different form, in Bruccoli, M. J., ed., *James Gould Cozzens*, 44-62.

Updike, John, "Indifference," *NY* 44 (Nov. 2, 1968): 197-201.

Ward, John W., "James Gould Cozzens and the Condition of Modern Man," *ASch* 27 (Winter, 1957-58): 92-9. Also in Bruccoli, M. J., ed., *James Gould Cozzens*, 15-28. Also in *Red, White & Blue: Men, Books, and Ideas in American Culture*, N.Y.: Oxford Un. Pr., 1969, 106-22.

Watts, Harold H., "James Gould Cozzens and the Genteel Tradition," *ColQ* 6 (Winter, 1958): 257-73.

Weaver, Robert, "The World of the Just and the Unjust," *TamR* 5 (Autumn, 1957): 61-7.

Whitehorn, Michael A., "Jones and Cozzens: Divergent Views of Military Leadership," *DAI* 38 (1977): 1398A.

Wiegand, William G., "James Gould Cozzens and the Professional Man in American Fiction," *DA* 22 (1960): 266 (Stanford).

ASK ME TOMORROW

Cass, Colin S., "Cozzens' Debt to Thomas Dekker in ASK ME TOMORROW," *MarkhamR* 11 (Fall, 1981): 11-16.

Eisinger, Chester E., "The Voice of Aggressive Aristocracy," *Midway* No. 18 (Spring, 1964): 111-14. Also in Eisinger, C. E., *Fiction of the Forties*, 158-60.

Hicks, G., *James Gould Cozzens*, 19-23.

Malin, Irving, "The Education of Francis Ellery," *JOHJ* 4, ii (Winter, 1981): 32-8.

Maxwell, D. E. S., *Cozzens*, 27-33, 69-71.

Michel, P., *James Gould Cozzens*, 49-58.

Mooney, H. J., Jr., *James Gould Cozzens*, 63-73.

BY LOVE POSSESSED

Adams, R. P., "James Gould Cozzens: A Cultural Dilemma," in Langford, R. E., ed., *Essays in Modern American Literature*, 106-9.

Anon., "The Hermit of Lambertville," *Time* 70 (Sept. 2, 1957): 72-3.

Boulger, James D., "Puritan Allegory in Four Modern Novels," *Thought* 44 (Autumn, 1969): 413-32.

Bracher, F., *Novels of James Gould Cozzens*, 49-51, 106-8, 155-8.

Burns, Wayne, "Cozzens vs. Life and Art," *NWR* 1 (Summer, 1958): 7-18.

————, "Reiterations," *NWR* 2 (Fall-Winter, 1958): 38-43.

Cass, Colin S., "Two Stylistic Analyses of the Narrative Prose in Cozzens' BY LOVE POSSESSED," *Style* 4 (1970): 213-38.

Davies, H., *A Mirror of the Ministry in Modern Novels*, 162-4.

De Mott, Benjamin, "Cozzens and Others," *HudR* 10 (Winter, 1957-58): 622-6.

Ellmann, Richard, *Reporter* 17 (Oct. 3, 1957): 42-3, 44.

Finn, James, "Cozzens Dispossessed," *Cweal* 68 (April 4, 1958): 11-13.

Frederick, John T., "Love By Adverse Possession: The Case of Mr. Cozzens," *CE* 19 (April, 1958): 313-16.

Frost, William, "Cozzens: Some Reservations about BLP," *CE* 19 (April, 1958): 317-18.

Gardiner, H. C., "Monument to Hollow Men," *In All Conscience*, 143-4. Also in *America* 98 (Oct. 5, 1957): 20.

Garrett, George, "BY LOVE POSSESSED: The Pattern and the Hero," *Crit* 1, iii (Winter, 1958): 41-7.

Geismar, Maxwell, "Comments on Cozzens: By Cozzens Possessed," *Crit* 1, iii (1958): 51-3.

Gould, Edward J., "BY LOVE POSSESSED: A Review from the Legal Point of View," *Am Bar Assn Jnl* 44 (Aug., 1958): 731-4, 799-800.

Harding, D. W., "The Limits of Conscience," *LS* (April 18, 1959): 451.

Hermann, John, "Cozzens and a Critic," *CE* 19 (April, 1958): 316-17.

Hicks, G., *James Gould Cozzens*, 31-5.

Howe, Irving, "BY LOVE POSSESSED," *NRep* (Jan. 20, 1958): 17-19. Also in Harrison, G., ed., *Critic as Artist*, 167-80.

Leopold, Robert E., "The Contemporary Novel and Its Condensation," *DA* 25 (1965): 1211-12 (Columbia).

Macdonald, Dwight, "By Cozzens Possessed: A Review of Reviews," *Ctary* 25 (Jan., 1958): 36-47. Also in Commentary, *Commentary Reader*, 567-85.

McKernan, Louis, "Profile of an Aristocrat: James Gould Cozzens," *CathW* 186 (Nov., 1957): 114-19.

Maxwell, D. E. S., *Cozzens*, 102-6.

Mazzara, Richard A., "'Misère et grandeur de l'homme': Pascal's PENSÉES and Cozzens' BY LOVE POSSESSED," *BSTCF* 5, i (Winter, 1964): 17-20.

Michel, P., *James Gould Cozzens*, 105-27.

————, "A Note on James Gould Cozzens," *RLV* No. 3 (1960): 205-8.

Millgate, Michael, "By Cozzens Unpossessed," *NRep* 138 (June 9, 1958): 21.

Mizener, Arthur, *Twelve Great American Novels*, 164-6.

————, "The Undistorting Mirror," *KR* 28 (Nov., 1966): 595-601.

Mooney, H. J., Jr., *James Gould Cozzens*, 125-56.

Nemerov, Howard, "The Discovery of Cozzens," *Nation* 185 (Nov. 2, 1957): 306-8. Also in Nemerov, H., *Poetry and Fiction*, 270-6.

Noble, D. W., *Eternal Adam and the New World Garden*, 186-93.

Perrin, Noel, "The Good Dukes," in Bruccoli, M. J., ed., *Just Representations*, 289-92.

Powers, Richard S., "Praise the Mighty: Cozzens and the Critics," *SWR* 43 (Summer, 1958): 263-70.

Price, Martin, *YaleR* 47 (Autumn, 1957): 153-5.

Scholes, Robert E., "The Commitment of James Gould Cozzens," *ArQ* 16 (Summer, 1960): 141-4.

Sherwood, John C., "Burns vs. Cozzens: The Defense," *NWR* 2 (Fall-Winter, 1958): 33-7.

Stern, Richard G., "A Perverse Fiction," *KR* 1 (Winter, 1958): 140-4.

Straumann, Heinrich, *American Literature in the Twentieth Century*, 28-9.

————, "The Quarrel About Cozzens or the Vagaries of Book Reviewing," *English Studies* 40 (Aug., 1959): 251-69.

Tuttleton, J. W., *Novel of Manners in America*, 237-45.

Walcutt, C. C., *Man's Changing Mask*, 281-6.

Watts, Harold H., "James Gould Cozzens and the Genteel Tradition," *ColQ* 6 (Winter, 1958): 263-73.

CASTAWAY

Bracher, F., *Novels of James Gould Cozzens*, 38-46.

Fiedler, Leslie, in Madden, D., ed., *Proletarian Writers of the Thirties*, 19-20.

Fowler, Alastair, "Isolation and Its Discontents," *TCL* 6 (July, 1960): 51-64.

Hyman, Stanley E., "My Favorite Forgotten Book," *Tomorrow* 7 (May, 1957): 58-9.

Maxwell, D. E. S., *American Fiction*, 278-80.

————, *Cozzens*, 58-61.

Michel, P., *James Gould Cozzens*, 44-9.

Mooney, H. J., Jr., *James Gould Cozzens*, 17-26.

COCK PIT

Maxwell, D. E. S., *Cozzens*, 35-8.

Michel, P., *James Gould Cozzens*, 26-8.

CONFUSION

Michel, P., *James Goul Cozzens*, 24-5.

GUARD OF HONOR

Bracher, F., *Novels of James Gould Cozzens*, 69-76, 87-8, 130-5, 165-8.

Cassill, R. V., "The Particularity of GUARD OF HONOR," in Bruccoli, M. J., ed., *James Gould Cozzens*, 92-8.

Dillard, R. H. W., "GUARD OF HONOR: Providential Luck in a Hard-Luck World," in Bruccoli, M. J., ed., *James Gould Cozzens*, 81-91.

Eisinger, Chester E., *Fiction of the Forties*, 164-70.

————, "The Voice of Aggressive Aristocracy," *Midway* No. 18 (Spring, 1964): 119-27.

Fergusson, Francis, "Three Novels," *Perspectives USA* No. 6 (Winter, 1954): 30-44.

French, Warren, in French, W., ed., *Forties*, 9-15.

Healey, Robert C., in Gardiner, H. C., ed., *Fifty Years of the American Novel*, 268-9.

Hicks, G., *James Gould Cozzens*, 28-31.

Jones, P., *War and the Novelists*, 79-84.

Maxwell, D. E. S., *American Fiction*, 284-7.

————, *Cozzens*, 92-102.

Michel, P., *James Gould Cozzens*, 86-104.

————, "A Note on James Gould Cozzens," *RLV* No. 3 (1960): 203-5.

Millgate, M., *American Social Fiction*, 188-94.

Mizener, Arthur, *Twelve Great American Novels*, 166-76.

————, "The Undistorting Mirror," *KR* 28 (Nov., 1966): 601-11.

Mooney, H. J., Jr., *James Gould Cozzens*, 99-124.

Parrish, James A., Jr., "James Gould Cozzens Fights a War." *ArQ* 18 (Winter, 1962): 335-40.

Perrin, Noel, "The Good Dukes," in Bruccoli, M. J., ed., *Just Representations*, 286-9.

Scholes, Robert E., "The Commitment of James Gould Cozzens," *ArQ* 16 (Summer, 1960): 138-41.

Stuckey, W. J., *Pulitzer Prize Novels*, 143-51.

Waldmeir, J. J., *American Novels of the Second World War*, 130-7.

Walsh, J., *American War Literature*, 138-41.

Wilson, Raymond J., III, "Cozzens' GUARD OF HONOR and Pynchon's GRAVITY'S RAINBOW," *NConL* 9, v (1979): 6-8.

THE JUST AND THE UNJUST

Eisinger, Chester E., *Fiction of the Forties*, 160-4.

————, "The Voice of Aggressive Aristocracy," *Midway* No. 18 (Spring, 1964): 114-19.

Hicks, G., *James Gould Cozzens*, 23-8.

Maxwell, D. E. S., *American Fiction*, 280-4.

————, *Cozzens*, 81-92.

Michel, P., *James Gould Cozzens*, 70-85.

————, "A Note on James Gould Cozzens," *RLV* No. 3 (1960): 200-3.

Mooney, H. J., Jr., *James Gould Cozzens*, 75-97.

Perrin, Noel, "The Good Dukes," in Bruccoli, M. J., ed., *Just Representations*, 284-6.

Prescott, O., *In My Opinion*, 186-8.

Watts, Harold H., "James Gould Cozzens and the Genteel Tradition," *ColQ* 6 (Winter, 1958): 263-73.

Weimer, David R., "The Breath of Chaos in THE JUST AND THE UNJUST," *Crit* 1, iii (Winter, 1958): 30-40.

Wolff, Morris H., "The Legal Background of Cozzens' THE JUST AND THE UNJUST," *JML* 7 (1979): 505-18.

THE LAST ADAM (A CURE OF FLESH)

Bracaher, F., *Novels of James Gould Cozzens*, 37-8.

Cass, Colin S., "The Title of THE LAST ADAM," in Bruccoli, M. J., ed., *James Gould Cozzens*, 63-80.

Eisinger, Chester E., "Class and American Fiction: The Aristocracy in Some Novels of the Thirties," in Lanzinger, K., ed., *Americana-Austriaca*, 141-3.

_____, *Fiction of the Forties*, 154-8.

_____, "The Voice of Aggressive Aristocracy," *Midway* No. 18 (Spring, 1964): 106-11.

Hicks, G., *James Gould Cozzens*, 12-14.

Lewis, R. W., "The Conflicts of Reality: Cozzens' THE LAST ADAM," in Whitbread, T. B., ed., *Seven Contemporary Authors*, 3-22.

Michel, P., *James Gould Cozzens*, 36-44.

Mooney, H. J., Jr., *James Gould Cozzens*, 27-46.

Ober, William B., M. D., *Carleton Misc.* 4 (Fall, 1963): 101-6.

Perrin, Noel, "The Good Dukes," in Bruccoli, M. J., ed., *Just Representations*, 279-82.

MEN AND BRETHREN

Bracher, F., *Novels of James Gould Cozzens*, 90-1, 99-100, 184-93, 198-9.

Davies, H., *A Mirror of the Ministry in Modern Novels*, 153-62.

Hicks, G., *James Gould Cozzens*, 15-19.

Maxwell, D. E. S., *Cozzens*, 61-9.

Michel, P., *James Gould Cozzens*, 59-70.

Mooney, H. J., Jr., *James Gould Cozzens*, 47-61.

Perrin, Noel, "The Good Dukes," in Bruccoli, M. J., ed., *Just Representations*, 282-4.

Scholes, Robert E., "The Commitment of James Gould Cozzens," *ArQ* 16 (Summer, 1960): 135-7.

Swanson, William J., "Ernest Cudlipp and the Law of Love," *CimR* 15 (April, 1971): 16-23.

Whelan, Bill, "The Hardest-Shelled Protestant Episcopalian," *BForum* 6, ii (1982): 245-7.

MICHAEL SCARLETT

Michel, P., *James Gould Cozzens*, 25-6.

MORNING, NOON AND NIGHT

Cox, Leland H., Jr., "Henry Dodd Worthington: The 'I' in MORNING, NOON AND NIGHT," in Brucolli, M. J., ed., *James Gould Cozzens*, 111-26.

Krickel, Edward, "Cozzens and Saroyan: A Look at Two Reputations," *GaR* 24, iii (Fall, 1970): 283-5.

McNally, James, "Browning Traits in Cozzens' MORNING, NOON AND NIGHT," *SBHC* 8, i (1980): 20-31.

Michel, P., *James Gould Cozzens*, 128-36.

Perrin, Noel, "The Good Dukes," in Bruccoli, M. J., ed., *Just Representations*, 292-4.

Shepherd, Allen, "The Conservative Spirit in Decline: James Gould Cozzens' MORNING, NOON AND NIGHT," *McNR* 21 (1974-75): 80-8.

THE SON OF PERDITION

Bracher, F., *Novels of James Gould Cozzens*, 31-4, 200-2.

Levenson, J. C., "Comments on Cozzens: Prudence and Perdition," *Crit* 1, iii (1958): 53-4.

Maxwell, D. E. S., *Cozzens*, 34-5.

Michel, P., *James Gould Cozzens*, 28-30.

S. S. SAN PEDRO

Bracher, F., *Novels of James Gould Cozzens*, 97-9.

Hicks, G., *James Gould Cozzens*, 9-12.

Maxwell, D. E. S., *Cozzens*, 38-43.

Michel, P., *James Gould Cozzens*, 31-6.

Mooney, H. J., Jr., *James Gould Cozzens*, 5-17.

BIBLIOGRAPHY

Ludwig, Richard M., "James Gould Cozzens: A Review of Research and Criticism," *TSLL* 1 (Spring, 1959): 123-36.

Maxwell, D. E. S., *Cozzens*, 118-19.

Meriwether, James B., comp., *James Gould Cozzens: A Checklist*, Detroit, MI: Gale Research, 1973.

_____, "A James Gould Cozzens Checklist," *Crit* 1 (Winter, 1958): 57-63.

Michel, Pierre, *James Gould Cozzens: An Annotated Checklist* (Serif Ser. in Bibliog., 22.) Kent, OH: Kent St. Un. Pr., 1971.

CREEKMORE, HUBERT, 1907-

GENERAL

Simms, L. Moody, Jr., "Hubert Creekmore: Mississippi Novelist and Poet," *NMW* 4, i (Spring, 1971): 15-21.

CREWS, HARRY, 1935-

GENERAL

Bellamy, Joe D., "Harry Crews: An Interview," *FictionI* 6/7 (1976): 83-93.

Carter, Nancy C., "1970 Images of the Machine and the Garden: Kosinski, Crews, and Pirsig," *Soundings* 61, i (Spring, 1978): 105-22.

DeBord, Larry W., and Gary L. Long, "Harry Crews on the American Dream," *SoQ* 20, iii (Spring, 1982): 35-53.

Foata, Anne, "Interview with Harry Crews, May 1972," *RANAM* 5 (1972): 207-25.

Jeffrey, David K., and Donald R. Boble, "Harry Crews: An Interview," *SoQ* 19, ii (Winter, 1981): 65-79.

Seelye, John, "Georgia Boys: The Redclay Satyrs of Erskine Caldwell and Harry Crews," *VQR* 56, iv (Autumn, 1980): 612-26.

Shelton, Frank W., "Harry Crews: Man's Search for Perfection," *SLJ* 12, ii (Spring, 1980): 97-113.

Shepherd, Allen, "Matters of Life and Death: The Novels of Harry Crews," *Crit* 20, i (1978): 53-62.

Smith, Dave, "That Appetite for Life So Ravenous," *Shen* 25, iv (Summer, 1974): 49-55.

Watson, V. Sterling, "Arguments Over an Open Wound: An Interview with Harry Crews," *PrS* 48, i (Spring, 1974): 60-74.

CAR

Carter, Nancy C., "1970 Images of the Machine and the Garden: Kosinski, Crews, and Pirsig," *Soundings* 61, i (Spring, 1978): 107-12.

DeBord, Larry W., and Gary L. Long, "Harry Crews on the American Dream," *SoQ* 20, iii (Spring, 1982): 42-4.

Shepherd, Allen, "Cars in Harry Crews' CAR," *NConL* 8, i (1978): 8-9.

Willis, Lonnie J., "Harry Crews' CAR: A Possible Source," *NConL* 12, v (Nov., 1982): 9-10.

A FEAST OF SNAKES

DeBord, Larry W., and Gary L. Long, "Harry Crews on the American Dream," *SoQ* 20, iii (Spring, 1982): 44-7.

The GOSPEL SINGER

DeBord, Larry W., and Gary L. Long, "Harry Crews on the American Dream," *SoQ* 20, iii (Spring, 1982): 35-8.

THE GYPSY'S CURSE

Beatty, Patricia V., "Body Language in Harry Crews's THE GYPSY'S CURSE," *Crit* 23, ii (Winter, 1982-82): 61-6.

DeBord, Larry W., and Gary L. Long, "Harry Crews on the American Dream," *SoQ* 20, iii (Spring, 1982): 38-40.

Smith, Dave, "That Appetite for Life So Ravenous," *Shen* 25, iv (Summer, 1974): 53-5.

THE HAWK IS DYING

DeBord, Larry W., and Gary L. Long, "Harry Crews on the American Dream," *SoQ* 20, iii (Spring, 1982): 35-8.

KARATE IS A THING OF THE SPIRIT

DeBord, Larry W., and Gary L. Long, "Harry Crews on the American Dream," *SoQ* 20, iii (Spring, 1982): 40-1.

NAKED IN GARDEN HILLS

DeBord, Larry W., and Gary L. Long, "Harry Crews on the American Dream," *SoQ* 20, iii (Spring, 1982): 47-51.

THIS THING DON'T LEAD TO HEAVEN

DeBord, Larry W., and Gary L. Long, "Harry Crews on the American Dream," *SoQ* 20, iii (Spring, 1982): 51-2.

BIBLIOGRAPHY

Gann, Daniel H., "Harry Crews: A Bibliography," *BB* 39, iii (Sept., 1982): 139-45.

CRONIN, A(RCHIBALD) J(OSEPH), 1896-1981

GENERAL

Frederick, John T., "A. J. Cronin," *CE* 3 (Nov., 1941): 121-9.

GRAND CANARY

Davies, H., *Mirror of the Ministry in Modern Fiction*, 123-4.

THE KEYS OF THE KINGDOM

Davies, H., *Mirror of the Ministry in Modern Fiction*, 124-8.

BIBLIOGRAPHY

Salwak, Dale, *A. J. Cronin: A Reference Guide*, Boston: G. K. Hall, 1982.

CULLINAN, ELIZABETH, 1933-

GENERAL

Kennedy, Eileen, "Bequeathing Tokens: Elizabeth Cullinan's Irish-Americans," *Éire* 16, iv (Winter, 1981): 94-102.

HOUSE OF GOLD

Fanning, Charles, "Elizabeth Culllinan's HOUSE OF GOLD: Culmination of an Irish-American Dream," *MELUS* 7, iv (1980): 31-48.

Kennedy, Eileen, "Bequeathing Tokens: Elizabeth Cullinan's Irish-Americans," *Éire* 16, iv (Winter, 1981): 94-102.

Murphy, Maureen, "Elizabeth Cullinan: Yellow and Gold," in Casey, D. J. and R. E. Rhodes, eds., *Irish-American Fiction*, 144-8.

CUOMO, GEORGE (MICHAEL), 1929-

GENERAL

Bryant, Jerry H., "The Fiction of George Cuomo," *ArQ* 30, iii (Autumn, 1974): 253-72.

AMONG THIEVES

Bryant, Jerry H., "The Fiction of George Cuomo," *ArQ* 30, iii (Autumn, 1974): 259-62.

Green, R. B., *Italian-American Novel*, 301-6.

BRIGHT DAY, DARK RUNNER

Bryant, Jerry H., "The Fiction of George Cuomo," *ArQ* 30, iii (Autumn, 1974): 256-9.

THE HERO'S GREAT GREAT GREAT GREAT GRANDSON

Bryant, Jerry H., "The Fiction of George Cuomo," *ArQ* 30, iii (Autumn, 1974): 268-72.

DAVIES, RHYS, 1903-1978

GENERAL

Rees, D., *Rhys Davies*.

THE BLACK VENUS

Rees, D., *Rhys Davies*, 23-8.

THE PAINTED KING

Rees, D., *Rhys Davies*, 55-6.

THE PERISHABLE QUALITY

Rees, D., *Rhys Davies*, 57-8.

A TIME TO LAUGH

Rees, D., *Rhys Davies*, 17-20.

THE WITHERED ROOT

Rees, D., *Rhys Davies*, 12-14.

DAVIES, ROBERTSON, 1913-1995

GENERAL

Baltensperger, Peter, "Battles with the Trolls," *CanL* 71 (Winter, 1977): 59-67.

Bowen, Gail, "Guides to the Treasure of Self: The Function of Women in the Fiction of Robertson Davies," *Waves* 5, i (Fall, 1976): 64-77.

Brown, Russell, and Donna A. Bennett, "Magnus Eisengrim: The Shadow of the Trickster in the Novels of Robertson Davies," *MFS* 22, iii (Autumn, 1976): 347-63.

Buitenhuis, E., *Robertson Davies*.

Callwood, June, "The Beard," *Maclean's* (Mar. 15, 1952): 16-17, 30-3.

Davies, Robertson, "A Rake at Reading," *Mosaic* 14, ii (Spring, 1981): 1-19.

Dawson, Anthony B., "Davies, His Critics, and the Canadian Canon," *CanL* 92 (Spring, 1982): 154-9.

Dombrowski, Theo, and Eileen Dombrowski, "'Every Man's Judgement': Robertson Davies' Courtroom," *SCL* 3, i (Winter, 1978): 476-61.

Dyment, Margaret, "Romantic Ore," *JCF* 2, i (Winter, 1973): 83-4.

Goldie, Terry, "Folklore in the Canadian Novel," *Canadian Folklore Canadien* 3, ii (1981): 93-101. [Not seen.]

Grant, J. S., *Robertson Davies*.

————, "Robertson Davies, God and the Devil," *BForum* 4 (1978): 56-63.

————, in Heath, J. M., ed., *Profiles in Canadian Literature 2*, 1-8.

Heintzman, Ralph H., "The Virtues of Reverence," *JCanStud* 12, i (Feb., 1977): 1-2, 92-5.

Hoy, Helen, "Poetry in the Dunghill: The Romance of the Ordinary in Robertson Davies' Fiction," *ArielE* 10, iii (July, 1979): 69-98.

King, B., *New English Literatures*, 200-10.

Lawrence, Robert G., "A Survey of the Three Novels of Robertson Davies," *BCLQ* 32, iv (April, 1969): 3-9.

Lewis, Gertrud J., "Vitzliputzli Revisited," *CanL* 76 (Spring, 1978): 132-4.

McPherson, Hugo, "The Mask of Satire: Character and Symbolic Pattern in Robertson Davies' Fiction," *CanL* No. 4 (Spring, 1960): 18-30. Also in Smith, A. J. M., ed., *Masks of Fiction: Canadian Critics on Canadian Prose*, Toronto: McClelland and Stewart, 1961, 162-75.

Monk, P., *Smaller Infinity*.

Moore, Mavor, "Robertson Davies," *EngQ* 5, iii (Fall, 1972): 15-20.

Sutherland, Ronald, "The Relevance of Robertson Davies," *JCanStud* 12, i (Feb., 1977): 75-81. Also, revised, in Sutherland, Ronald, *The New Hero: Essays in Comparative Quebec/Canadian Literature*, Toronto: Macmillan, 1977, 73-83.

White, Douglas P., "The Saviour of Salterton and the Deptford Lives: Narrative Strategies in the Novels of Robertson Davies," *DAI* 40 (1979): 1488A.

DEPTFORD Trilogy

Bonnycastle, Stephen, "Robertson Davies and the Ethics of Monologue," *JCanStud* 12, i (Feb., 1977): 20-40.

Davies, Robertson, "The DEPTFORD Trilogy in Retrospect," in Lawrence, R. G., and S. L. Macey, eds., *Studies in Robertson Davies' DEPTFORD Trilogy*, 7-12.

Davy, Paul, "The Structure of Davies' DEPTFORD Trilogy," *ECW* 9 (Winter, 1977-78): 123-33.

Dawson, Anthony B., "Davies, His Critics, & the Canadian Canon," *CanL* 92 (Spring, 1982): 154-9.

Dean, John, "Magic and Mystery in Robertson Davies' DEPTFORD Trilogy," *Waves* 7, i (Fall, 1978): 63-8.

Goldie, Terry, "The Folkloric Background of Robertson Davies' DEPTFORD Trilogy," in Lawrence, R. G., and S. L. Macey, eds., *Studies in Robertson Davies' DEPTFORD Trilogy*, 22-31.

Grant, J. S., *Robertson Davies*, 35-49.

Lawrence, R. G., and S. L. Macey, eds., *Studies in Robertson Davies' DEPTFORD Trilogy*.

Macey, Samuel L., "Time, Clockwork, and the Devil in Robertson Davies' DEPTFORD Trilogy," in Lawrence, R. G., and S. L. Macey, eds., *Studies in Robertson Davies' DEPTFORD Trilogy*, 32-44.

Monaghan, David, "'People in Prominent Positions': A Study of the Public Figure in the DEPTFORD Trilogy," in Lawrence, R. G., and S. L. Macey, eds., *Studies in Robertson Davies' DEPTFORD Trilogy*, 45-56.

Monk, Patricia, "Confessions of a Sorcerer's Apprentice: WORLD OF WONDERS and the DEPTFORD Trilogy of Robertson Davies," *DR* 56 (Summer, 1976): 366-72.

Moss, John, "The Double Vision of Robertson Davies or, The Deptford Rapes," *Sex and Violence in the Canadian Novel*, 107-22.

Neufeld, James, "Structural Unity in the DEPTFORD Trilogy: Robertson Davies as Egoist," *JCanStud* 12, i (Feb., 1977): 68-74.

Warwick, Ellen B., "The Transformation of Robertson Davies," *JCF* 3, iii (1974): 46-51. Also, expanded, in Moss, J., ed., *Canadian Novel: Here and Now*, 67-78.

FIFTH BUSINESS (See also DEPTFORD Trilogy)

Bjerring, Nancy E., "Deep in the Old Man's Puzzle," *CanL* 62 (Autumn, 1974): 49-60. Also in Woodcock, G., ed., *Canadian Literature in the Twentieth Century*, 161-73.

Bligh, John, "The Spiritual Climacteric of Dunstan Ramsay," *WLWE* 21, iii (Autumn, 1982): 575-93.

Brown, Russell, and Donna A. Bennett, "Magnus Eisengrim: The Shadow of the Trickster in the Novels of Robertson Davies," *MFS* 22, iii (Autumn, 1976): 350-6.

Buitenhuis, E., *Robertson Davies*, 57-66.

Chapman, Marilyn, "Female Archetypes in FIFTH BUSINESS," *CanL* 80 (Spring, 1979): 131-8.

Cude, Wilfred, " 'False as Harlots' Oats': Dunny Ramsay Looks at Huck Finn," *SCL* 2, ii (Summer, 1977): 164-87.

————, "Historiography and Those Damned Saints: Shadow and Light in FIFTH BUSINESS," *JCanStud* 12, i (Feb., 1977): 47-67.

————, "Miracle and Art in FIFTH BUSINESS or Who the Devil is Liselotte Vitzlipützli," *JCanStud* 9, iv (Nov., 1974): 3-16.

Gerson, Carole, "Dunstan Ramsay's Personal Mythology," *ECW* 6 (Spring, 1977): 100-8.

Hoy, Helen, "Poetry in the Dunghill: The Romance of the Ordinary in Robertson Davies' Fiction," *ArielE* 10, iii (July, 1979): 83-90.

Hutcheon, Linda, "The Poet as Novelist," *CanL* 86 (Autumn, 1980): 6-14.

Lennox, John W., "Manawaka and Deptford: Place and Voice," *JCanStud* 13, iii (Fall, 1978): 23-30.

Merivale, Patricia, "The (Auto)-Biographical Compulsion of Dunstan Ramsay," in Lawrence, R. G., and S. L. Macey, eds., *Studies in Robertson Davies' DEPTFORD Trilogy*, 57-65.

Monaghan, David M., "Metaphors and Confusion," *CanL* 76 (Winter, 1976): 64-73.

Monk, Patricia, "Beating the Bush: The Mandala and National Psychic Unity in RIDERS IN THE CHARIOT and FIFTH BUSINESS," *ESC* 5 (Fall, 1979): 344-54.

————, *Smaller Infinity*, 74-104.

Moss, John, "The Double Vision of Robertson Davies or The Deptford Rapes," *Sex and Violence in the Canadian Novel*, 115-22.

Murray, Glenn, "Who Killed Boy Stauntin: An Astrological Witness Reports," *SCL* 2, i (Winter, 1977): 117-23.

Radford, F. L., "The Great Mother and the Boy: Jung, Davies, and FIFTH BUSINESS," in Lawrence, R. G., and S. L. Macey, eds., *Studies in Robertson Davies' DEPTFORD Trilogy*, 66-81.

————, "Heinrich Heine, the Virgin, and the Hummingbird: FIFTH BUSINESS: A Novel and Its Subconscious," *ESC* 4 (1978): 95-110.

Roper, Gordon, "Robertson Davies' FIFTH BUSINESS and 'That Old Fantastical Duke of Dark Corners, C. G., Jung'," *JCF* 1, i (Winter, 1972): 33-9. Also in Moss, J., ed., *Canadian Novel: Here and Now*, 53-66.

Sait, J. E., "Thomas Keneally's BLOOD RED, SISTER ROSE and Robertson Davies' FIFTH BUSINESS: Two Modern Literary Hagiographies," *JCL* 16, i (1981): 96-108.

St. Pierre, Paul M., "Rounding the Ovoid," *Mosaic* 11, iii (Spring, 1978): 127-35.

Warwick, Ellen D., "The Transformation of Robertson Davies," *JCF* 3, iii (1974): 46-51. Also, expanded, in Moss, J., ed., *Canadian Novel: Here and Now*, 68-71.

Webster, David, "Uncanny Correspondences: Synchronicity in FIFTH BUSINESS and THE MANTICORE," *JCF* 3, iii (Summer, 1974): 52-6.

Wood, Barry, "In Search of Sainthood: Magic, Myth, and Metaphor in Robertson Davies' FIFTH BUSINESS," *Crit* 19, ii (1977): 23-32.

LEAVEN OF MALICE (See also SALTERTON Trilogy)

Buitenhuis, E., *Robertson Davies*, 41-8.

Hoy, Helen, "Poetry in the Dunghill: The Romance of the Ordinary in Robertson Davies' Fiction," *ArielE* 10, iii (July, 1979): 76-8.

Lawrence, Robert G., "A Survey of the Three Novels of Robertson Davies," *BCLQ* 32, iv (April, 1969): 3-9 *passim*.

Monk, P., *Smaller Infinity*, 52-9.

THE MANTICORE (See also DEPTFORD Trilogy)

Brigg, Peter, "THE MANTICORE and the Law," in Lawrence, R. G., and S. L. Macey, eds., *Studies in Robertson Davies' DEPTFORD Trilogy*, 82-99.

Edinger, Harry G., "Bear in Three Contemporary Fictions," *HAB* 28 (1977): 144-7.

Hoy, Helen, "Poetry in the Dunghill: The Romance of the Ordinary in Robertson Davies' Fiction," *ArielE* 10, iii (July, 1979): 90-7.

Keith, W. J., "THE MANTICORE: Psychology and Fictional Technique," *SCL* 3 (Winter, 1978): 133-6.

La Bossière, Camille R., "Justice Staunton in Toronto, London, and Zürich: The Case of THE MANTICORE," *SCL* 5 (1980): 290-301.

Monk, Patricia, "Davies and the Drachenloch: A Study of the Archaeological Background of THE MANTICORE," in Lawrence, R. G., and S. L. Macey, eds., *Studies in Robertson Davies' DEPTFORD Trilogy*, 100-13.

————, "Psychology and Myth in THE MANTICORE," *SCL* 2, i (Winter, 1977): 69-81.

————, *Smaller Infinity*, 105-46.

Warwick, Ellen D., "The Transformation of Robertson Davies," in Moss, J., ed., *Canadian Novel: Here and Now*, 71-5.

Webster, David, "Uncanny Correspondences: Synchronicity in FIFTH BUSINESS and THE MANTICORE," *JCF* 3, iii (Summer, 1974): 52-6.

A MIXTURE OF FRAILTIES (See also SALTERTON Trilogy)

Buitenhuis, E., *Robertson Davies*, 49-56.

Hoy, Helen, "Poetry in the Dunghill: The Romance of the Ordinary in Robertson Davies' Fiction," *ArielE* 10, iii (July, 1979): 78-85.

Lawrence, Robert G., "A Survey of the Three Novels of Robertson Davies," *BCLQ* 32, iv (April, 1969): 3-9 *passim*.

Monk, P., *Smaller Infinity*, 59-72.

Thomas, Clara, "The Two Voices of A MIXTURE OF FRAILTIES," *JCanStud* 12, i (Feb., 1977): 82-91.

THE REBEL ANGELS

Cude, Wilfred, "The College Occasion as Rebelaisian Feast: Academe's Dark Side in THE REBEL ANGELS," *SCL* 7, ii (1982): 184-99.

Harris, John, "A Voice from the Priggery: Exorcising Davies' Rebel Angel," *JCF* 33 (1981-82): 112-17.

SALTERTON Trilogy

Grant, J. C., *Robertson Davies*, 26-34.

Morley, Patricia, "Davies' SALTERTON Trilogy: Where the Myth Touches Us," *SCL* 1 (Winter, 1976): 96-104.

Owen, Ivon, "The SALTERTON Novels," *TamR* 9 (Aug., 1958): 56-63.

Radford, F. L., "The Apprentice Sorcerer: Davies' SALTERTON Trilogy," in Lawrence, R. G., and S. L. Macey, eds., *Studies in Robertson Davies' DEPTFORD Trilogy*, 13-21.

TEMPEST-TOST (See also SALTERTON Trilogy)

Buitenhuis, E., *Robertson Davies*, 35-40.

Hoy, Helen, "Poetry in the Dunghill: The Romance of the Ordinary in Robertson Davies' Fiction," *ArielE* 10, iii (July, 1979): 72-6.

Lawrence, Robert G., "A Survey of the Three Novels of Robertson Davies," *BCLQ* 32, iv (April, 1969): 3-9 *passim*.

Monk, P., *Smaller Infinity*, 44-52.

WORLD OF WONDERS (See also DEPTFORD Trilogy)

Brennan, Anthony, "Robertson Davies: Illusionist," *IFR* 3, i (Jan., 1976): 70-2.

Lawrence, Robert G., "Canadian Theatre in Robertson Davies' WORLD OF WONDERS," in Lawrence, R. G., and S. L. Macey, eds., *Studies in Robertson Davies' DEPTFORD Trilogy*, 114-23.

Monk, P., *Smaller Infinity*, 147-81.

Moss, John, "The Double Vision of Robertson Davies or, The Deptford Rapes," *Sex and Violence in the Canadian Novel*, 108-13.

Warwick, Ellen B., "The Transformation of Robertson Davies," in Moss, J., ed., *Canadian Novel: Here and Now*, 75-7.

BIBLIOGRAPHY

Ryrie, John, and Judith S. Grant, "Robertson Davies: An Annotated Bibliography," 57-279 in Lecker, Robert, and Jack David, eds., *The Annotated Bibliography of Canada's Major Authors, Volume Three*, Downsview: ECW, 1981.

DAVIN, DAN(IEL MARCUS), 1913-1990

GENERAL

Bertram, James, "Dan Davin: Novelist of Exile," *Meanjin* 32, ii (June, 1973): 148-56.

ROADS FROM HOME

Rhodes, H. Winston, "Dan Davin's ROADS FROM HOME," in Hankin, C., ed., *Critical Essays on the New Zealand Novel*, 73-87.

DAVISON, FRANK DALBY, 1893-1970

GENERAL

Barnes, John, "Frank Dalby Davison," *Westerly* 3 (1967): 16-20. [Interview.]

_____, "Frank Dalby Davison's Last Book," *Westerly* 1 (1971): 62-4. [Not seen.]

Dow, H., *Frank Dalby Davison*.

Eldershaw, M. Barnard, *Essays in Australian Fiction*, Melbourne: Melbourne Un. Pr., 1938, 41-80.

Heseltine, H. P., "The Fellowship of All Flesh: The Fiction of Frank Dalby Davison," *Meanjin* 27, iii (Spring, 1968): 275-90.

Phillips, Arthur, "Frank Dalby Davison, M.B.E.: 1893-1970," *Meanjin* 29, ii (Winter, 1970): 251-2.

Rorabacher, L. E., *Frank Dalby Davison*.

DUSTY: THE STORY OF A SHEEP DOG

Dow, H., *Frank Dalby Davison*, 16-20.

Rorabacher, L. E., *Frank Dalby Davison*, 139-45.

FOREVER MORNING

Dow, H., *Frank Dalby Davison*, 8-10.

Rorabacher, L. E., *Frank Dalby Davison*, 56-61.

MAN-SHY

Dow, H., *Frank Dalby Davison*, 10-13.

Rorabacher, L. E., *Frank Dalby Davison*, 42-55.

THE WELLS OF BEERSHEBA

Rorabacher, L. E., *Frank Dalby Davison*, 62-8.

THE WHITE THORNTREE

Barnes, John, "Frank Dalby Davison's Last Book," *Westerly* 1 (Mar., 1971): 62-4. [Not seen.]

Davison, Frank D., "Testimony of a Veteran," *Southerly* 29 (1969): 83-92.

Dow, H., *Frank Dalby Davison*, 33-44.

Hadgrafat, Cecil, "Indulgence," in Hamilton, K. G., ed., *Studies in the Recent Australian Novel*, 200-7.

Heseltine, H. P., "The Fellowship of All Flesh: The Fiction of Frank Dalby Davison," *Meanjin* 27, iii (Spring, 1968): 275-6, 284-90.

BIBLIOGRAPHY

Rorabachaer, L. E., *Frank Dalby Davison*, 210-15.

DEAL, BORDEN, 1922-

GENERAL

Calhoun, John C., "Borden Deal: Mississippi Novelist," *NMW* 9, ii (Fall, 1976): 63-76.

DEBOISSIÈRE, RALPH (ANTHONY), 1907-

GENERAL

Birbalsingh, F. M., "The Novels of Ralph DeBoissière," *JCL* No. 9 (July, 1970): 104-8.

DELILLO, DON, 1936-

GENERAL

LeClair, Thomas, "An Interview with Don DeLillo," *ConL* 23, i (Winter, 1982): 19-31.

Oriard, Michael, "Don DeLillo's Search for Walden Pond," *Crit* 20, i (1978): 5-24.

AMERICANA

Green, R. B., *Italian-American Novel*, 379-80.

END ZONE

Burke, William, "Football, Literature, Culture," *SWR* 60, iv (Autumn, 1975): 391-8.

Taylor, Anya, "Words, War, and Meditation in Don DeLillo's END ZONE," *IFR* 4 (1977): 68-70.

DEMBY, WILLIAM, 1922-

GENERAL

Connelly, Joseph F., "William Demby's Fiction: The Pursuit of Muse," *NALF* 10, iii (Fall, 1976): 100, 102-3.

O'Brien, John, "Interview with William Demby," *SBL* 3, ii (Autumn, 1972): 1-6. Also in O'Brien, John, ed., *Interviews with Black Writers*, 35-53.

BEETLECREEK

Bayliss, John F., "BEETLECREEK: Existential or Human Document," *NegroD* 19, i (1968): 70-4.

Bigsby, C. W. F., "From Protest to Paradox: The Black Writer at Mid Century," in French, W., ed., *Fifties*, 224-6.

Hansen, Klaus P., "William Demby's THE CATACOMBS (1965): A Latecomer to Modernism," in Bruck, P., and W. Karrer, eds., *Afro-American Novel Since 1960*, 124-9.

Harris, Trudier, "The Barbershop in Black Literature," *BALF* 13, iii (Fall, 1979): 112-18 *passim*.

Hill, Herbert, "Afterword," in Demby, William, *Beetlecreek*, N.Y.: Avon Books, 1969.

Margolies, E., *Native Sons*, 176-9.

Schraufnagel, N., *From Apology to Protest*, 74-6.

Whitlow, R., *Black American Literature*, 122-5.

THE CATACOMBS

Bone, Robert, "William Demby's Dance of Life," *TriQ* 15 (Spring, 1969): 127-41. Also as "Introduction," in Demby, William, *The Catacombs*, N.Y.: Perennial Library, 1970.

Connelly, Joseph F., "William Demby's Fiction: The Pursuit of Muse," *NALF* 10, iii (Fall, 1976): 100, 102-3.

Hansen, Klaus P., "William Demby's THE CATACOMBS (1965): A Latecomer to Modernism," in Bruck, P., and W. Karrer, eds., *Afro-American Novel Since 1960*, 129-44.

Hoffman, Nancy Y., "The Annunciation of William Demby," *SBL* 3, i (Spring, 1972): 8-13.

_____, "Technique in Demby's THE CATACOMBS," *SBL* 2, ii (Summer, 1971): 10-13.

Margolies, E., *Native Sons*, 179-89.

Schraufnagel, N., *From Apology to Protest*, 128-9.

DENNIS, NIGEL FORBES, 1912-1989

GENERAL

Dooley, D. J., "The Satirist and the Contemporary Non-Entity," *SNL* 10, i (1973): 1-9.

BOYS AND GIRLS COME OUT TO PLAY

Ewart, Gavin, "Nigel Dennis—Identity Man," *LonM* n.s., 3 (Nov., 1963): 35-8.

CARDS OF IDENTITY

Allen, W., *Modern Novel*, 274-6.

Allsop, K., *Angry Decade*, 140-3.

Bergonzi, B., *Situation of the Novel*, 71-4.

Dooley, D. J., "The Satirist and the Contemporary Non-Entity," *SNL* 10, i (1973): 1-2.

Ewart, Gavin, "Nigel Dennis—Identity Man," *LonM* n.s., 3 (Nov., 1963): 39-46.

Gindin, J., "Identity and the Existential," *Postwar British Fiction*, 227-9.

Karl, F. R., "Nigel Dennis's CARDS OF IDENTITY," *Contemporary English Novel*, 249-53.

Olney, James, "CARDS OF IDENTITY and the Satiric Mode," *SNNTS* 3, iv (Winter, 1971): 374-89.

Peake, Charles, "CARDS OF IDENTITY: An Intellectual Satire," *LHY* 1 (July, 1960): 49-57.

Saltzman, Arthur, "CARDS OF IDENTITY and the Case of the Sundered Self," *StCS* 9 (Spring, 1982): 9-16.

A HOUSE IN ORDER

Dooley, D. J., in *Crit* 10, i (1967): 95-9.

_____, "The Satirist and the Contemporary Non-Entity," *SNL* 10, i (1973): 7-8.

Phillips, Robert, "The Artist and the Introvert: Nigel Dennis's A HOUSE IN ORDER," in Morris, R. K., ed., *Old Lines, New Forces*, 109-19.

DESAI, ANITA, 1937-

GENERAL

Alcock, Peter, "Rope, Serpent, Fire: Recent Fiction of Anita Desai," *JIWE* 9, i (Jan., 1981): 15-34.

Belliappa, M., *Anita Desai*.

Iyengar, K. R. S., "A Note on Anita Desai's Novels," *BP* 4, xii (Jan., 1969): 64-9. [Not seen.]

Maini, Darshan S., "The Achievement of Anita Desai," in Sharma, K. K., ed., *Indo-English Literature*, 215-30.

Ram, Atma, "Anita Desai: Exploration of Inner Sensibility," *Perspective* (July, 1978): 54-5. [Not seen.]

———, "Anita Desai: The Novelist Who Writes for Herself," *JIWE* 5, ii (July, 1977): 39-42.

———, "An Interview with Anita Desai," *WLWE* 16, i (Nov., 1977): 95-103.

Rao, B. R., *Novels of Mrs. Anita Desai*.

Sharma, R. S., *Anita Desai*.

Sivaramakrishna, "From Alienation to Mythic Acceptance: The Ordeal of Consciousness in Anita Desai's Fiction," *KJES* 3, i (1978): 7-24. [Not seen.]

BYE-BYE, BLACKBIRD

Aithal, S. Kirshnamoorthy, and Rashmi Aithal, "East-West Encounter in Four Indo-English Novels," *ACLALSB* 6, i (Nov., 1982): 1-16.

Maini, Darshan S., "The Achievement of Anita Desai," in Sharma, K. K., ed., *Indo-English Literature*, 223-7.

Mukherjee, Meenakshi, "The Theme of Displacement in Anita Desai and Kamala Markandaya," *WLWE* 17, i (April, 1978): 225-33.

Prasad, Hari M., "Sound or Sense: A Study of Anita Desai's BYE-BYE, BLACKBIRD," *JIWE* 9, i (Jan., 1981): 58-66.

Rao, B. R., *Novels of Mrs. Anita Desai*, 47-50.

Sharma, R. S., "Alienation, Accommodation and the Locale in Anita Desai's BYE-BYE, BLACKBIRD," *LCrit* 14, iv (1979): 31-49. Also in Sharma, R. S., *Anita Desai*, 69-93.

CLEAR LIGHT OF DAY

Hashmi, Alamgir, "A Reading of Anita Desai's CLEAR LIGHT OF DAY," *Explorations* 8/9 (1981/2): 72-9.

Sharma, R. S., *Anita Desai*, 129-48.

CRY, THE PEACOCK

Belliappa, M., *Anita Desai*, 6-26.

Iyengar, K. R. S., *Indian Writing in English*, 464-8.

Jamkhandi, Sudhakar, R., "The Artistic Effects of the Shifts in Points of View in Anita Desai's CRY, THE PEACOCK," *JIWE* 9, i (Jan., 1981): 35-46.

Maini, Darshan S., "The Achievement of Anita Desai," in Sharma, K. K., ed., *Indo-English Literature*, 217-20.

———, "CRY, THE PEACOCK as a Poetic Novel," in Narasimaiah, C. D., ed., *Indian Literature of the Past Fifty Years, 1917-1967*, 225-34.

Malhotra, M. L., "A Writer of Promise: Anita Desai," *Bridges of Literature*, 207-9.

Rao, B. R., *Novels of Mrs. Anita Desai*, 9-29.

Sharma, R. S., *Anita Desai*, 24-47.

Shastri, N. R., "WHERE SHALL WE GO THIS SUMMER?: A Critical Study," *OJES* 17 (1981): 83-103.

Singh, R. S., *Indian Novel in English*, 169-71.

Weir, Ann L., "The Illusions of Maya: Feminine Consciousness in CRY, THE PEACOCK," *IFR* 6 (1979): 149-52.

FIRE ON THE MOUNTAIN

Alcock, Peter, "Rope, Serpent, Fire: Recent Fiction of Anita Desai," *JIWE* 9, i (Jan., 1981): 26-8.

Asnani, Shyam M., "The Theme of Withdrawal and Loneliness in Anita Desai's FIRE ON THE MOUNTAIN," *JIWE* 9, i (Jan., 1981): 81-92.

Ganguli, Chandra, "FIRE ON THE MOUNTAIN: An Analysis," *ComQ* 6, xxi (Dec., 1981): 40-4.

Krishna, Francine E., "Anita Desai: FIRE ON THE MOUNTAIN," *IndL* 25, v (Sept.-Oct., 1982): 158-69.

Parasuram, Laxmi, "FIRE ON THE MOUNTAIN: A New Dimension of Feminine Self-Perception," *LCrit* 16, iii (1981): 58-64.

Sharma, R. S., "Movement and Stillness in Anita Desai's FIRE ON THE MOUNTAIN," *Littcrit* 4, ii (Dec., 1978): 1-6. Also in Sharma, R. S., *Anita Desai*, 118-28.

VOICES IN THE CITY

Belliappa, M., *Anita Desai*, 26-51.

Iyengar, K. R. S., *Indian Writing in English*, 468-70.

Maini, Darshan S., "The Achievement of Anita Desai," in Sharma, K. K., ed., *Indo-English Literature*, 221-3.

Malhotra, M. L., "Writer of Promise: Anita Desai," *Bridges of Literature*, 209-11.

Rao, B. R., *Novels of Mrs. Anita Desai*, 30-46.

Sharma, R. S., "The Mother and the City: Archtypes in VOICES IN THE CITY," *JLS* 2, ii (Dec., 1979): 57-77. Also in Sharma, R. S., *Anita Desai*, 48-68.

Singh, R. H., *Indian Novel in English*, 171-5.

Srivastava, Ramesh K., "Voices of Artists in the City," *JIWE* 9, i (Jan., 1981): 47-57.

WHERE SHALL WE GO THIS SUMMER?

Alcock, Peter, "Rope, Serpent, Fire: Recent Fiction of Anita Desai," *JIWE* 9, i (Jan., 1981): 20-5.

Asnani, Shyam M., "Anita Desai's Fiction: A New Dimension," *IndL* 24, ii (Mar.-April, 1981): 44-54.

Dudt, Charmazel, "Past and Present: A Journey to Confrontation," *JIWE* 9, i (Jan., 1981): 67-73.

Maini, Darshan S., "The Achievement of Anita Desai," in Sharma, K. K., ed., *Indo-English Literature*, 227-9.

Ram, Atma, "Island on the Island: Anita Desai's WHERE SHALL WE GO THIS SUMMER," *WLWE* 15, ii (Nov., 1976): 381-3.

———, "A View of WHERE SHALL WE GO THIS SUMMER?" *JIWE* 9, i (Jan., 1981): 74-80.

Rao, B. R., *Novels of Mrs. Anita Desai*, 51-60.

Rao, Vimala, "Anita Desai's WHERE SHALL WE GO THIS SUMMER?: An Analysis," *CamQ* 3, ix (Dec., 1978): 144-50.

Sharma, R. S., *Anita Desai*, 94-117.

———, "Anita Desai's WHERE SHALL WE GO THIS SUMMER?: An Analysis," *CamQ* 3, x (Mar., 1979): 50-69.

Shastri, N. R., "WHERE SHALL WE GO THIS SUMMER?: A Critical Study," *OJES* 17 (1981): 83-103.

BIBLIOGRAPHY

Ram, Atma, comp., "Anita Desai: A Bibliography," *JIWE* 9, i (Jan., 1981): 93-8.

Sharma, R. S., *Anita Desai*, 169-72.

DESANI, G(OVINDAS) V(ISHNOODAS), 1909-

ALL ABOUT MR. HATTERR: A GESTURE (ALL ABOUT H. HATTERR: A GESTURE)

Burjorjee, D. M., "The Dialogue in G. V. Desani's ALL ABOUT H. HATTERR," *WLWE* 13 (1974): 191-224.

Goers, Peter, "Kink's English: Whole Language and G. V. Desani's ALL ABOUT H. HATTERR," *NLRev* 4 (1978): 30-40.

Harrex, S. C., "G. V. Desani: Mad Hatterr Sage," *Fire and the Offering*, 201-38.

―――――, "The Novel as Gesture," in Narasimhaiah, C. D., ed., *Awakened Conscience*, 73-85.

Iyengar, K. R. S., *Indian Writing in English*, 489-92.

Moorthy, P. Rama, "G. V. Desani: First Impressions," in Narasimhaiah, C. D., ed., *Indian Literature of the Past Fifty Years, 1917-1967*, 203-12.

Naik, M. K., "Colonial Experience in ALL ABOUT HATTERR," *CNIE* 1, i (1982): 37-49.

Narasimhan, Raji, *Sensibility Under Stress*, 92-9. Also, adapted, in Mukherjee, M., ed., *Considerations*, 102-10.

Srinath, C. N., "G. V. Desani: ALL ABOUT H. HATTERR," *LCrit* 9, iii (Winter, 1970): 40-56.

DE VRIES, PETER, 1910-1993

GENERAL

Boyd, Jack K., "The Novels of Peter De Vries: A Critical Introduction," *DAI* 32 (1971): 2675A (Ark.)

Challenger, Craig, "Peter De Vries: The Case for Comic Seriousness," *StAH* 1, i (April, 1974): 40-51.

Davis, Douglas M., "An Interview with Peter De Vries," *CE* 28 (April, 1967): 524-8.

DeRoller, Joseph M., "The Lower-Case Absurd: A Study of the Novels of Peter De Vries," *DAI* 38 (1977): 786A.

Evans, T. Jeff, "The Apprentice Fiction of Peter De Vries," *Crit* 21, iii (1980): 28-42.

―――――, "Peter De Vries: A Retrospective," *AHumor* 7, ii (Fall, 1980): 13-16.

Hamblen, Abigail A., "Peter De Vries: Calvinist Gone Underground," *Trace* No. 48 (Spring, 1963): 20-4.

Hasley, Louis, "The Hamlet of Peter De Vries: To Wit or Not to Wit," *SAQ* 70, iv (Autumn, 1971): 467-76.

Jellema, Roderick, *Peter De Vries*.

―――――, "Peter De Vries: The Decline and Fall of Moot Point," *The Reformed Journal* 13 (April, 1963): 9-15. [Not seen.]

Rodewald, Fred, "The Comic *Eiron* in the Later Novels of Peter De Vries," *Quartet* (Texas A&M) 6, xli (Winter, 1973): 34-9.

Rome, Joy, "Peter De Vries: Compassionate Satirist," *UES* 9, iii (Sept., 1971): 23-9.

Sale, Richard B., "A *Studies in the Novel* Interview: An Interview in New York with Peter De Vries," *SNNTS* 1, iii (Fall, 1969): 364-69.

Ter Maat, Cornelius J., "Three Novelists and a Community: A Study of American Novelists with Dutch Calvinist Origins," *DA* 24 (1963): 751 (Michigan).

Walsh, William, "The Combination in the Safe. On Peter De Vries," *Encounter* 40, i (Jan., 1973): 74-80.

ANGELS CAN'T DO BETTER

Evans, T. Jeff, "The Apprentice Fiction of Peter De Vries," *Crit* 21, iii (1980): 36-40.

THE BLOOD OF THE LAMB

Challenger, Craig, "Peter De Vries: The Case for Comic Seriousness," *StAH* 1, i (April, 1974): 40-5.

Jellema, R., *Peter De Vries*, 36-40.

Kort, Wesley A., "THE BLOOD OF THE LAMB and the Sense of Transcendent Power," *Shriven Selves*, 36-63.

BUT WHO WAKES THE BUGLER?

Evans, T. Jeff, "The Apprentice Fiction of Peter De Vries," *Crit* 21, iii (1980): 30-4.

COMFORT ME WITH APPLES

Jellema, R., *Peter De Vries*, 18-20.

THE HANDSOME HEART

Evans, T. Jeff, "The Apprentice Fiction of Peter De Vries," *Crit* 21, iii (1980): 34-6.

LET ME COUNT THE WAYS

Jellema, R., *Peter De Vries*, 40-3.

THE MACKEREL PLAZA

Byrd, Max, "The MACKEREL PLAZA by Peter De Vries," *NRep* 175 (Oct. 23, 1976): 29-31.

Davies, H., *A Mirror of the Ministry in Modern Novels*, 164-72.

Jellema, R., *Peter De Vries*, 32-5.

MADDER MUSIC

Evans, T. Jeff, "The Madder Music of Peter De Vries," *StCS* 8 (Spring, 1981): 21-9.

REUBEN, REUBEN

Jellema, R., *Peter De Vries*, 27-31.

THE TENTS OF WICKEDNESS

Jellema, R., *Peter De Vries*, 20-3.

Walcutt, C. C., *Man's Changing Mask*, 247-51.

THROUGH THE FIELDS OF CLOVER

Jellema, R., *Peter De Vries*, 15-18.

THE VALE OF LAUGHTER

Challenger, Craig, "Peter De Vries: The Case for Comic Seriousness," *StAH* 1, i (April, 1974): 45-50.

"Fiction of 1968. Peter De Vries: THE VALE OF LAUGHTER," in *T.L.S. Essays and Reviews from The Time Literary Supplement, 1968*, 188-90. Also in *TLS* (Mar. 7, 1968).

BIBLIOGRAPHY

Straayer, T. A., "Peter De Vries: A Bibliography of Secondary Sources, 1940-1981," *BB* 39, iii (Sept., 1982): 146-69.

DEWLEN, AL, 1921-

GENERAL

Merren, John, "Character and Theme in the Amorillo Novels of Al Dewlen," *WR* 6, i (Summer, 1969): 3-9.

DICKENS, MONICA (ENID), 1915-1992

GENERAL

Hamblen, Abigail A., "Another Dickens Come to Judgment," *Cresset* 33, iii (Jan., 1970): 12-15.

DICKEY, JAMES, 1923-

GENERAL

Arnett, David L., "James Dickey: Poetry and Fiction," *DAI* 34 (1973): 1889A (Tulane).

Bruccoli, Matthew J., "James Dickey," in *Conversations with Writers, I*, 25-45.

Calhoun, R. J., ed., *James Dickey.*

Schwenger, Peter, "The Masculine Mode," *CritI* 5, iv (Summer, 1979): 621-33. [Not seen.]

DELIVERANCE

Armour, Robert, "DELIVERANCE: Four Variations of the American Adam," *LFQ* 1 (July, 1973): 280-5.

Barshay, Robert, "Machismo in DELIVERANCE," *Teaching Eng. in the Two-Year Coll.* (Grenville, NC) 1, iii (1975): 169-73.

Beaton, James F., "Dickey Down the River," in Peary, G., and R. Shatzkin, eds., *Modern American Novel and the Movies*, 293-306.

Beidler, Peter G., " 'The Pride of Thine Heart Hath Deceived Thee': Narrative Distortion in Dickey's DELIVERANCE," *SCR* 5, i (Dec., 1972): 29-40.

Carnes, Bruce, "Deliverance in James Dickey's 'On the Coosawattee' and DELIVERANCE," *NConL* 7, ii (1977): 2-4.

Coulthard, Ron, "From Manuscript to Movie Script: James Dickey's DELIVERANCE," *NConL* 3, v (Nov., 1973): 11-12.

_____, "Reflections upon a Golden Eye: A Note on James Dickey's DELIVERANCE," *NConL* 3, ii (Sept., 1973): 13-15.

Curran, Ronald T., "Biology and Culture: Hollywood and the Deliverance of Dickey's Weekend Backwoodsmen," *SoQ* 18, iv (1980): 81-90.

Davis, Charles E., "The Wilderness Revisited: Irony in James Dickey's DELIVERANCE," *SAF* 4, ii (Autumn, 1976): 223-30.

Doughtie, Edward, "Art and Nature in DELIVERANCE," *SWR* 64 (1979): 167-80.

Edwards, C. Hines, Jr., "Dickey's DELIVERANCE: The Owl and the Eye," *Crit* 15, ii (1973): 95-101.

_____, "A Foggy Scene in DELIVERANCE," *NConL* 2, v (Nov., 1972): 7-9.

Eisiminger, Sterling, "James Dickey's DELIVERANCE: A Source Note," *AN&Q* 19, iii-iv (1980): 53-4.

Eyster, Warren, "Two Regional Novels," *SR* 79, iii (Summer, 1971): 469-72.

Finholt, Richard D., "The Murder of Moby Dick: Mad Metaphysics and Salvation Psychology in American Fiction," *DAI* 36 (1976): 7420A.

Foust, R. E., "*Tacitus Eruditus*: Phenomenology as Method and Meaning of James Dickey's DELIVERANCE," *SAF* 9, ii (Autumn, 1981): 199-216.

Graham, John, "James Dickey," in Garrett, G., ed., *Writer's Voice*, 242-7. [Interview].

Greiner, Donald J., "The Harmony of Bestiality in James Dickey's DELIVERANCE," *SCR* 5, i (Dec., 1972): 43-9.

Guillory, Daniel L., "Myth and Meaning in James Dickey's DELIVERANCE," *CollL* 3, i (Winter, 1976): 56-62.

Guttenberg, Barnett, "The Pattern of Redemption in Dickey's DELIVERANCE," *Crit* 18, iii (1977): 83-91.

Hamilton, James W., "James Dickey's DELIVERANCE: Mid-Life and the Creative Process," *AI* 38, iv (Winter, 1981): 389-405.

Heyen, William, "A Conversation with James Dickey," *SoR* 9 (Jan., 1973): 149-51.

Hinz, Evelyn J., "Contemporary North American Literary Primitivism: DELIVERANCE and SURFACING," in Tulchin, Joseph S., ed., *Hemispheric Perspectives on the United States: Papers from the New World Conference* (Contribs. in American Studies 36), Westport, CT: Greenwood, 1978, 150-71.

_____, "The Masculine/Feminine Psychology of American/Canadian Primitivism: DELIVERANCE and SURFACING," in Winks, R. W., ed., *Other Voices, Other Views*, 75-96.

Holley, Linda T., "Design and Focus in James Dickey's DELIVERANCE," *SCR* 10, ii (1978): 90-8.

Italia, Paul G., "Love and Lust in James Dickey's DELIVERANCE," *MFS* 21, ii (1975): 203-13.

Jameson, Frederic, "The Great American Hunter, or, Ideological Content in the Novel," *CE* 34, ii (Nov., 1972): 181-6, 187-99 *passim.* Comment by Sol Yurick, 198-9.

Kunz, Don, "Learning the Hard Way in James Dickey's DELIVERANCE," *WAL* 12 (1978): 289-301.

Lennox, John, "Dark Journey's KAMOURASKA and DELIVERANCE," *ECW* 12 (1978): 84-104.

Lindborg, Henry J., "James Dickey's DELIVERANCE: The Ritual of Art," *SLJ* 6, ii (Spring, 1974): 83-90.

Longen, Eugene M., "Dickey's DELIVERANCE: Sex and the Great Outdoors," *SLJ* 9, ii (Spring, 1977): 137-49.

Love, Glen A., "Ecology in Arcadia," *ColQ* 21 (Autumn, 1972): 179-82.

Marin, Daniel B., "James Dickey's DELIVERANCE: Darkness Visible," *SCR* 3, i (Nov., 1970): 49-59. Also in Calhoun, R. J., ed., *James Dickey*, 105-17.

Markos, Donald W., "Art and Immediacy: James Dickey's DELIVERANCE," *SoR* 7 (July, 1971): 947-53.

Mitgutsch, Waltraud, "Salvation or Annihilation? The Theme of Regression in Contemporary Literature (Susan Sontag, James Dickey, Theodore Roethke)," *RLV* 45, i (1979): 64-77.

Monk, Donald, "Colour Symbolism in James Dickey's DELIVERANCE," *JAmS* 11, ii (Aug., 1977): 261-79.

Patrick, Richard, "Heroic Deliverance," *Novel* 4 (Winter, 1971): 190-2.

Rothfork, John, "DELIVERANCE as a Western Movie," *SwAL* 7, i (1981): 38-43.

Samuels, Charles T., "How Not to Film a Novel," *ASch* 42 (Winter, 1972-73): 148-50, 152, 154.

Schechter, Harold, "The Eye and the Nerve: A Psychological Reading of James Dickey's DELIVERANCE," in Filler, L., ed., *Seasoned Authors for a New Season*, 4-19.

_____, *New Gods*, 46-60, 91-4.

Shepherd, Allen, "Counter-Monster Comes Home: The Last Chapter of James Dickey's DELIVERANCE," *NConL* 3, ii (Mar., 1973): 8-12.

Stephenson, William, "DELIVERANCE from What? *GaR* 28 (Spring, 1974): 114-20.

Strong, Paul, "James Dickey's Arrow of Deliverance," *SCR* 11, i (1978): 108-16.

Sulllivan, Rosemary, "SURFACING and DELIVERANCE," *CanL* 67 (Winter, 1976): 6-20.

Taylor, Chet, "A Look into the Heart of Darkness: A View of DELIVERANCE," in De La Fuente, P., et al., *James Dickey*, 59-64.

Verburg, T. Larry, "Water Imagery in James Dickey's DELIVERANCE," *NConL* 4, v (Nov., 1974): 11-13.

Wagner, Linda, "DELIVERANCE: Initiation and Possibility," *SCR* 10, ii (1978): 49-55. Also in *American Fiction*, 76-84.

Willig, Charles L., "Ed's Transformation: A Note on DELIVERANCE," *NConL* 3, ii (Mar., 1973): 4-5.

Willson, Robert F., Jr., "DELIVERANCE from Novel to Film," *LFQ* 2 (1974): 52-8.

Winchell, Mark R., "The River Within: Primitivism in James Dickey's DELIVERANCE," *WVUPP* 23 (Jan., 1977): 106-14.

BIBLIOGRAPHY

Elledge, Jim, *James Dickey: A Bibliography, 1947-1974*, Metuchen, NJ: Scarecrow, 1979.

_____, "James Dickey: A Supplementary Bibliography, 1975-1980," *BB* 38, ii (April-June, 1981): 92-100, 104. 38; iii (July-Sept., 1981): 150-5.

DIDION, JOAN, 1934-

GENERAL

Brady, H. Jennifer, "Points West, Then and Now: The Fiction of Joan Didion," *ConL* 20, iv (Autumn, 1979): 452-70.

Henderson, K. U., *Joan Didion*.

Kuehl, Linda, "Joan Didion: The Art of Fiction LXXI," *ParisR* 74 (1978): 143-63.

Mallon, Thomas, "The Limits of History in the Novels of Joan Didion," *Crit* 21, iii (1980): 43-52.

Mickelson, Anne Z., "Joan Didion: The Hurting Woman," *Reaching Out*, 87-111.

Morton, Brian J. W., "The Princess in the Consulate: Joan Didion's Fiction," *Edda* 2 (1982): 73-87.

Stineback, David C., "On the Limits of Fiction," *MQ* 14, iv (July, 1973): 339-48.

Winchell, M. R., *Joan Didion*.

A BOOK OF COMMON PRAYER

Brady, H. Jennifer, "Points West, Then and Now: The Fiction of Joan Didion," *ConL* 20, iv (Autumn, 1979): 465-70.

Gilbert, Susan, "Children of the Seventies: The American Family in Recent Fiction," *Soundings* 62, ii (Summer, 1980): 206-10.

Henderson, K. U., *Joan Didion*, 65-89.

Lohrey, Amanda, "A BOOK OF COMMON PRAYER. The Liberated Heroine: New Varieties of Defeat?" *Meanjin* 38 (1979): 294-304.

Merivale, Patricia, "Through Greene-Land in Drag: Joan Didion's A BOOK OF COMMON PRAYER," *PCP* 15, i (1980): 45-52.

Mickelson, Anne Z., "Joan Didion: The Hurting Woman," *Reaching Out*, 98-111.

Morton, Brian J. W., "The Princess in the Consulate: Joan Didion's Fiction," *Edda* 2 (1982): 84-7.

Strandberg, Victor, "Passion and Delusion in A BOOK OF COMMON PRAYER," *MFS* 27, ii (Summer, 1981): 225-42.

Winchell, M. R., *Joan Didion*, 138-52.

PLAY IT AS IT LAYS

Anderson, Patricia D., "Self-Definition in MANSFIELD PARK and Joan Didion's PLAY IT AS IT LAYS," *James Madison Jour.* (Harrisonburg, VA) 35, iii (1977): 58-66.

Brady, H. Jennifer, "Points West, Then and Now: The Fiction of Joan Didion," *ConL* 20, iv (Autumn, 1979): 463-5.

Chabot, C. Barry, "Joan Didion's PLAY IT AS IT LAYS and the Vacuity of the 'Here and Now'," *Crit* 21, iii (1980): 53-60.

Geherin, David J., "Nothingness and Beyond: Joan Didion's PLAY IT AS IT LAYS," *Crit* 16, i (1975): 64-78.

Goodhart, Lynne H., "Joan Didion's PLAY IT AS IT LAYS: Alienation and Games of Chance," *SJS* 3, i (1977): 64-8.

Henderson, K. U., *Joan Didion*, 19-41.

Mickelson, Anne Z., "Joan Didion: The Hurting Woman," *Reaching Out*, 92-8.

Morton, Brian J. W., "The Princess in the Consulate: Joan Didion's Fiction," *Edda* 2 (1982): 81-3.

Stineback, David C., "On the Limits of Fiction," *MQ* 14, iv (July, 1973): 343-6.

Vincent, Sybil K., "In the Crucible: The Forging of an Identity as Demonstrated in Didion's PLAY IT AS IT LAYS," *PCL* 3, ii (1977): 58-64.

Winchell, M. R., *Joan Didion*, 127-37.

RUN RIVER

Brady, H. Jennifer, "Points West, Then and Now: The Fiction of Joan Didion," *ConL* 20, iv (Autumn, 1979): 456-63.

Henderson, K. U., *Joan Didion*, 42-64.

Morton, Brian J. W., "The Princess in the Consulate: Joan Didion's Fiction," *Edda* 2 (1982): 78-81.

Randisi, Jennifer L., "The Journey Nowhere: Didion's RUN RIVER," *MarkhamR* 11 (1982): 41-3.

Winchell, M. R., *Joan Didion*, 101-11.

BIBLIOGRAPHY

Jacobs, Fred R., *Joan Didion: Bibliography*, Keene, CA: Loop Pr., 1977.

Olendorf, Donna, "Joan Didion: A Checklist, 1955-1980," *BB* 38, i (Jan.-Mar., 1981): 32-44.

Winchell, M. R., *Joan Didion*, 172-5.

DOCTOROW, E(DGAR) L(AWRENCE), 1931-

GENERAL

Cooper, Barbara, "The Artist as Historian in the Novels of E. L. Doctorow," *ESRS* 29, ii (Fall, 1980): 5-44.

Emblidge, David, "Marching Backward into the Future: Progress as Illusion in Doctorow's Novels," *SWR* 62, iv (Autumn, 1977): 397-409.

Gross, David S., "Tales of Obscene Power, Money, Culture, and the Historical Fictions of E. L. Doctorow," *Genre* 13, i (Spring, 1980): 71-92. Also in Male, R. R., ed., *Money Talks*, 71-92.

Lubarsky, Jared, "History and the Forms of Fiction: An Interview with E. L. Doctorow," *EigoS* 124 (1978): 150-2.

Zins, Daniel L., "E. L. Doctorow: The Novelist as Historian," *HC* 16, v (Dec., 1979): 1-14.

BIG AS LIFE

Cooper, Barbara, "The Artist as Historian in the Novels of E. L. Doctorow," *ESRS* 29, ii (Fall, 1980): 14-19.

THE BOOK OF DANIEL

Cooper, Barbara, "The Artist as Historian in the Novels of E. L. Doctorow," *ESRS* 29, ii (Fall, 1980): 19-27.

Culp, Mildred, "Women and Tragic Destiny in Doctorow's THE BOOK OF DANIEL," *SAJL* 2 (1982): 155-66.

Emblidge, David, "Marching Backward Into the Future: Progress as Illusion in Doctorow's Novels," *SWR* 62, iv (Autumn, 1977): 400-4.

Estrin, Barbara L., "Surviving McCarthyism: E. L. Doctorow's THE BOOK OF DANIEL," *MR* 16, iii (Summer, 1975): 577-87.

Forrey, Robert, "Doctorow's THE BOOK OF DANIEL: All in the Family," *SAJL* 2 (1982): 167-73.

Gross, David, "Tales of Obscene Power: Money, Culture, and the Historical Fictions of E. L. Doctorow," *Genre* 13, i (Spring, 1980): 88-91. Also in Male, R. R., ed., *Money Talks*, 88-91.

Hamner, Eugénie, "The Burden of the Past: Doctorow's THE BOOK OF DANIEL," *RS* 49, i (Mar., 1981): 55-61.

Knapp, Peggy, "Hamlet and Daniel (and Freud and Marx)," *MR* 21, iii (Fall, 1980): 487-501.

Levine, Paul, "The Conspiracy of History: E. L. Doctorow's THE BOOK OF DANIEL," *DQR* 11, ii (1981): 82-96.

Lorsch, Susan E., "Doctorow's THE BOOK OF DANIEL as *Künstlerroman*: The Politics of Art," *PLL* 18, iv (Winter, 1982): 384-97.

Stark, John, "Alienation and Analysis in Doctorow's THE BOOK OF DANIEL," *Crit* 16, iii (1975): 101-10.

Strout, Cushing, "Historicizing Fiction and Fictionalizing History: The Case of E. L. Doctorow," *Prospects* 5 (1980):424-9.

Turner, Joseph W., "The Kinds of Historical Fiction: An Essay in Definition and Methodology," *Genre* 12, iii (Fall, 1979): 347-9.

Zins, Daniel L., "Daniel's 'Teacher' in Doctorow's THE BOOK OF DANIEL," *NMAL* 3 (1979): Item 16.

————, "E. L. Doctorow: The Novelist as Historian," *HC* 16, v (Dec., 1979): 6-9.

LOON LAKE

Cooper, Barbara, "The Artist as Historian in the Novels of E. L. Doctorow," *ESRS* 29, ii (Fall, 1980): 40-2.

RAGTIME

Berryman, Charles, "RAGTIME in Retrospect," *SAQ* 81, i (1982): 30-42.

Brienza, Susan, "Doctorow's RAGTIME: Narrative as Silhouettes and Syncopation," *DQR* 11, ii (1981): 97-103.

Campbell, Josie P., "Coalhouse Walker and the Model T. Ford: Legerdemain in RAGTIME," *JPC* 13 (1979): 302-9.

Cooper, Barbara, "The Artist as Historian in the Novels of E. L. Doctorow," *ESRS* 29, ii (Fall, 1980): 28-38.

Ditsky, John, "The German Source of RAGTIME: A Note," *OntarioR* 4 (1976): 84-6.

Emblidge, David, "Marching Backward Into the Future: Progress as Illusion in Doctorow's Novels," *SWR* 62, iv (Autumn, 1977): 404-9.

Estrin, Barbara L., "Recomposing Time: HUMBOLDT'S GIFT and RAGTIME," *DQ* 17, i (Spring, 1982): 16-31.

Faber, Marion, "Michael Kohlhaas in New York: Kleist and E. L. Doctorow's RAGTIME," in Ugrinsky, A., and others, eds., *Heinrich von Kleist Studies*, 147-56.

Foley, Barbara, "From U.S.A. to RAGTIME: Notes on the Forms of Historical Consciousness in Modern Fiction," *AL* 50, i (1978): 85-105.

Gelus, Marjorie, and Ruth Crowley, "Kleist in RAGTIME: Doctorow's Novel, Its German Source and Its Reviewers," *JPC* 14 (1980): 20-6.

Gross, David, "Tales of Obscene Power: Money, Culture, and the Historical Fictions of E. L. Doctorow," *Genre* 13, i (Spring, 1980): 79-83. Also in Male, R. R., ed., *Money Talks*, 79-83.

Hague, Angela, "RAGTIME and the Movies," *NDQ* 50, iii (1982): 101-12.

Helbling, Robert E., "E. L. Doctorow's RAGTIME: Kleist Revisited," in Ugrinsky, A., and others, eds., *Heinrich von Kleist Studies*, 157-67.

Jones, Phyllis, "RAGTIME: Feminist, Socialist and Black Perspectives on the Self-Made Man," *JAC* 2 (1979): 17-28.

Knorr, Walter L., "Doctorow and Kleist: 'Kohlhass' in RAGTIME," *MFS* 22, ii (1976): 224-7.

Kurth-Voight, Lieselotte E., "Kleistian Overtones in E. L. Doctorow's RAGTIME," *Monatshefte* 69 (1977): 404-14.

Neumeyer, Peter F., "E. L. Doctorow, Kleist, and the Ascendancy of Things," *CEA* 39, iv (May, 1977): 17-21.

Piehl, Kathy, "E. L. Doctorow and Random House: The RAGTIME Rhythm of Cash," *JPC* 13 (1980): 404-11.

Pierce, Constance, "The Syncopated Voices of Doctorow's RAGTIME," *NMAL* 3 (1979): Item 26.

Quart, Leonard, and Barbara Quart, "RAGTIME Without a Melody," *LFQ* 10 (1982): 71-4.

Rodgers, Bernard F., Jr., "RAGTIME," *ChiR* 27, iii (1976): 138-44.

Steinberg, Cobbett, "History and the Novel: Doctorow's RAGTIME," *UDQ* 10, iv (1976): 125-30.

Strout, Cushing, "Historicizing Fiction and Fictionalizing History: The Case of E. L. Doctorow," *Prospects* 5 (1980): 429-36.

Thomson, James C., "RAGTIME Revisited: A Seminar with E. L. Doctorow and Joseph Papalco," *Nieman Reports* 31, ii-iii (1977): 3-8, 43-9. [Interview.]

Zins, Daniel L., "E. L. Doctorow: The Novelist as Historian," *HC* 16, v (Dec., 1979): 9-14.

WELCOME TO HARD TIMES

Arnold, Marilyn, "History as Fate in E. L. Doctorow's Tale of a Western Town," *SDR* 18, i (Spring, 1980): 53-63.

Cooper, Barbara, "The Artist as Historian in the Novels of E. L. Doctorow," *ESRS* 29, ii (Fall, 1980): 8-14.

Emblidge, David, "Marching Backward Into the Future: Progress as Illusion in Doctorow's Novels," *SWR* 62, iv (Autumn, 1977): 398-400.

Gross, David S., "Tales of Obscene Power: Money, Culture, and the Historical Fictions of E. L. Doctorow," *Genre* 13, i (Spring, 1980): 83-8. Also in Male, R. R., ed., *Money Talks*, 83-8.

Zins, Daniel L., "E. L. Doctorow: The Novelist as Historian," *HC* 16, v (Dec., 1979): 4-6.

DONLEAVY, J(AMES) P(ATRICK), 1926-

GENERAL

Bakewell, Joan, "The Novelist J. P. Donleavy Talks to Joan Bakewell," *Listener* 81 (Mar. 13, 1969): 340-1.

Croak, Thomas L., "The Hero in the Novels of J. P. Donleavy," *DAI* 36 (1976): 6081A.

Dudding, Griffith, "Between Two Worlds: An Analysis of J. P. Donleavy's Use of 'The Outsider' as Protagonist in His Novels," *DAI* 39 (1979): 6128A-29A.

Eckley, Grace, "Two Irish-American Novelists: J. P. Donleavy and Jimmy Breslin," *Illinois School Journal* 55 (1975): 28-33. [Not seen.]

Jacobson, Kurt, "An Interview with J. P. Donleavy," *JIL* 8, i (1979): 39-48.

Johnson, John, "Tears and Laughter: The Tragic Comic Novels of J. P. Donleavy," *MichA* 9, i (Summer, 1976): 15-24.

Le Clair, Thomas, "A Case of Death: The Fiction of J. P. Donleavy," *ConL* 12, iii (Summer, 1971): 329-44.

Massinton, C. G., *J. P. Donleavy*.

McKaughan, Molly, "The Art of Fiction 53: J. P. Donleavy," *ParisR* 16 (Fall, 1975): 122-66. [Interview.]

Norstedt, Johann A., "Irishmen and Irish-Americans in the Fiction of J. P. Donleavy," in Casey, D. J., and R. E. Rhodes, eds., *Irish-American Fiction*, 115-25.

Sherman, William D., "J. P. Donleavy: Anarchic Man as Dying Dionysian," *TCL* 13 (Jan., 1968): 216-28.

Vintner, Maurice, "The Novelist as Clown: The Fiction of J. P. Donleavy," *Meanjin* 29, i (Autumn, 1970): 108-14.

THE BEASTLY BEATITUDES OF BALTHAZAR B

Masinton, C. G., *J. P. Donleavy*, 54-9.

A FAIRY TALE OF NEW YORK

Masinton, C. G., *J. P. Donleavy*, 63-7.

THE GINGER MAN

Allsop, K., *Angry Decade*, 73-5.
Bryant, J. H ., *Open Decision*, 209-10.

Cohen, Dean, "The Evolution of Donleavy's Hero," *Crit* 12, iii (1971): 95-109.

Coonley, Donald E., "To Cultivate, To Dread: The Concept of Death in THE GINGER MAN and HERZOG," *NCampR* 2 (Spring, 1969): 7-12.

Corrigan, Robert A., "The Artist as Censor: J. P. Donleavy and THE GINGER MAN," *MASJ* 8, i (Spring, 1967): 60-72.

Hassan, I., *Radical Innocence*, 194-200.

Kubal, David L., "Our Last Literary Gentlemen: The Bourgeois Imagination," *BuR* 22, ii (1976): 43-5.

Le Clair, Thomas, "A Case of Death: The Fiction of J. P. Donleavy," *ConL* 12, iii (Summer, 1971): 329-37.

Masinton, C. G., *J. P. Donalevy*, 5-25.

Morris, William E., "J. P. Donleavy's Wild Gingerbread Man: Antichrist and Crazy Cookie," *USFLQ* 6 (Spring-Summer, 1968): 41-2.

Morse, Donald E., "'The Skull Beneath the Skin': J. P. Donleavy's THE GINGER MAN," *MichA* 6 (1974): 273-80.

Norstedt, Johann A., "Irishmen and Irish-Americans in the Fiction of J. P. Donleavy," in Casey, D. J., and R. E. Rhodes, eds., *Irish-American Fiction*, 116-2.

"Novels of 1963. J. P. Donleavy: THE GINGER MAN," in *T. L. S. Essays and Reviews from The Times Literary Supplement, 1963*, 185-7. Also in *TLS* (July 26, 1963).

Podhoretz, N., "The New Nihilism and the Novel," *Doings and Undoings*, 168-70.

Rollins, Ronald, "Desire versus Damnation in O'Casey's WITHIN THE GATES and Donleavy's THE GINGER MAN," *SORev* 1, ii (1975): 41-7.

Shaw, Patrick W., "The Satire of J. P. Donleavy's GINGER MAN," *StCS* 1, ii-2 (1975): 9-16.

Sherman, William D., "J. P. Donleavy: Anarchic Man as Dying Dionysian," *TCL* 13 (Jan., 1968): 216-21.

Ussher, Arland, "Introduction," THE GINGER MAN, Rev. ed., N.Y.: McDowell, Obolensky, 1958.

Weales, Gerald, in Moore, H. T., ed., *Contemporary American Novelists*, 149-53.

Widmer, L., "Contemporary American Outcasts," *Literary Rebel*, 136-9.

THE ONION EATERS

Le Clair, Thomas, "THE ONION EATERS and the Rhetoric of Donleavy's Comedy," *TCL* 18, iii (July, 1972): 167-74.

Masinton, C. G., *J P. Donleavy*, 59-62.

THE SADDEST SUMMER OF SAMUEL S

Cohen, Dean, "The Evolution of Donleavy's Hero," *Crit* 12, iii (1971): 106-9.

Masinton, C. G., *J. P. Donleavy*, 45-51.

Moore, John R., "J. P. Donleavy's Season Discontent," *Crit* 9, ii (1967): 95-9.

Sherman, William D., "J. P. Donleavy: Anarchic Man as Dying Dionysian," *TCL* 13 (Jan., 1968): 226-8.

A SINGULAR MAN

Cohen, Dean, "The Evolution of Donleavy's Hero," *Crit* 12, iii (1971): 101-9.

Le Clair, Thomas, "A Case of Death: the Fiction of J. P. Donleavy," *ConL* 12, iii (Summer, 1971): 337-40.

Masinton, C. G., *J. P. Donleavy*, 26-44.

Moore, John R., "Hard Times and the Noble Savage: J. P. Donleavy's A SINGULAR MAN," *HC* 1, i (Feb., 1964): 1-4, 6-11. Also in Dillard, R. H. W., & others, eds., *Sounder Few*, 3-13.

Sherman, William D., "J. P. Donleavy: Anarchic Man as Dying Dionysian," *TCL* 13 (Jan., 1968): 221-4.

Weales, Gerald, in Moore, H. T., ed., *Contemporary American Novelists*, 153-4.

BIBLIOGRAPHY

Madden, David W., "A Bibliography of J. P. Donleavy," *BB* 39, iii (Sept., 1982): 170-8.

DOS PASSOS, JOHN RODERIGO, 1896-1970

GENERAL

Aaron, Daniel, "The Adventures of John Dos Passos," *Writers on the Left: Episodes in American Literary Communism*, N.Y.: Harcourt, World & Brace, 1961, 343-53.

————, "The Riddle of John Dos Passos," *Harpers* 224 (Mar., 1962): 55-60.

Aldridge, J. W., *After the Lost Generation*, 59-81. Also in *Devil in the Fire*, 106-23.

Babcock, Daryl B., "The Historical Novels of John Dos Passos," *DAI* 39 (1979): 4252A.

Baker, John D., "John Dos Passos, Chronicler of the American Left," *DA* 32 (1971): 3191A.

————, "Whitman and Dos Passos: A Sense of Communion," *WWR* 20 (Mar., 1974): 30-3.

Beach, Joseph W., "Dos Passos, 1947," *SR* 55 (July-Sept., 1947): 406-18.

————, "John Dos Passos: The Artist in Uniform," *American Fiction*, 25-35.

Becker, G. J., *John Dos Passos*.

Belkind, A., ed., *Dos Passos, the Critics, and the Writer's Intention*.

————, "Satirical Social Criticism in the Novels of John Dos Passos," *DA* 27 (1966): 1049A-50A (Un. of So. Calif.).

Bernardin, Charles W., "The Development of John Dos Passos," Unpub. Diss. (Un. of Wisconsin), 1949.

Blake, N. M., *Novelist's America*, 163-8.

Blankenship, R., *American Literature*, 759-61.

Borenstein, Walter, "The Failure of Nerve: The Impact of Pío Baroja's Spain on John Dos Passos," in Stanford, D. E., ed., *Nine Essays in Modern Literature*, 63-87.

Brantley, John D., "Dos Passos' Conversion from Class Struggle to Moral Middle-Class Mobility," *LGJ* 5, i (Spring, 1977): 20-1.
————, *Fiction of John Dos Passos*.

Brown, Deming, "Dos Passos in Soviet Criticism," *CL* 5 (1953): 332-50.

Canario, John W., "A Study of the Artistic Development of John Dos Passos in His Novels from ONE MAN'S INITIATION-1917 Through U.S.A.," *DA* 24 (1964): 4693-4 (Un. of Wash.).

Chalupová, Eva, "The Thirties and the Artistry of Lewis, Farrell, Dos Passos and Steinbeck: Some Remarks on the Influence of the Social and Ideological Developments of the Time," *BSE* 14 (1981): 107-16 *passim*.

Chase, Richard, "The Chronicles of Dos Passos," *Ctary* 31 (May, 1961): 395-400. Also in Hook, A., ed., *Dos Passos*, 171-80.

Clark, Michael, "John Dos Passos, from Nature to Naturalism: The Influence of Walt Whitman and William James on the Early Fiction, 1913-1938," *DAI* 42 (1981): 1147A-48A.

Colley, I., *Dos Passos and the Fiction of Despair*.

Cowley, Malcolm, "Dos Passos and His Critics," *NRep* 120 (Feb. 25, 1949): 21-3.

————, "Dos Passos: The Learned Poggius," *SoR* 9 (Winter, 1973): 3-17.

————, "John Dos Passos: The Poet and the World," in Hook, A., ed., *Dos Passos*, 76-86. From *NRep* 70 (April 27, 1932): 303-5; and 78 (Sept. 9, 1936): 34.

Davis, R. G., *John Dos Passos*.

Diggins, John P., "Dos Passos and Veblen's Villains," *AR* 23 (Winter, 1963-64): 485-500.

————, "Visions of Chaos and Visions of Order: Dos Passos as Historian," *AL* 46, iii (Nov., 1974): 329-46.

Dommerques, Pierre, "John Dos Passos: An Old Dream Behind the Mask of Rebellion," *StAR* 2, i (Fall/Winter, 1972): 56-9.

Donnell, Richard S., "John Dos Passos: Satirical Historian of American Morality," Unpub. Doct. Diss., Harvard Un., 1960.

Dos Passos, John, in Madden, C. F., ed., *Talks with Authors*, 3-11.

Eisinger, C. E., *Fiction of the Forties*, 119-25.

Epstein, Jason, "The Riddle of Dos Passos," *Ctary* 61, i (Jan., 1976): 63-6.

Evans, William A., "Influences on and Development of John Dos Passos' Collectivist Technique," *DA* 27 (1966): 745A-6A (Un. of New Mexico).

Ezell, Marcel D., "John Dos Passos: Conservative Republican," *MFS* 26, iii (Autumn, 1980): 503-17.

Fergusson, Diane S., "John Dos Passos: The Novelist as Satirical Chronicler," *DAI* 36 (1975): 887A.

Fitelson, David, "The Art of John Dos Passos: A Study of the Novels Through U.S.A.," *DA* 25 (1964): 2510 (Emory).

Flynn, Thomas F., "John Dos Passos: Artist and Moralist," *MHLS* 5 (1982): 107-14.

Frohock, W. M., "John Dos Passos: Of Time and Frustration," *SWR* 33 (Winter, 1948): 71-80; 33 (Spring, 1948): 170-9. Also in Frohock, W. M., *Novel of Violence in America*, 23-51.

Gado, Frank, ed., "An Interview with John Dos Passos," *Idol* 45 (1969): 5-25. Also in Gado, F., ed., *First Person*, 31-55.

Geismar, M., *Writers in Crisis*, 89-139.

Gelfant, B. H., "The Novelist as Architect of History," *American City Novel*, 133-8.

————, "The Search for Identity in the Novels of John Dos Passos," *PMLA* 76 (Mar., 1961): 133-49.

Golson, Emily B., "Pio Baroja and John Dos Passos: The Evolution of Two Political Novelists," *DAI* 43 (1982): 1138A.

Gorman, Thomas R., "Words and Deeds: A Study of the Political Attitudes of John Dos Passos," *DA* 21 (1960): 893-4 (Pennsylvania).

Gray, J., *On Second Thought*, 67-9.

Hicks, Granville, "The Politics of John Dos Passos," *AR* 10, i (Mar., 1950): 85-98. Also in Hook, A., ed., *Dos Passos*, 15-30.

Holditch, William K., "Literary Technique in the Novels of John Dos Passos," *DA* 22 (1961): 3184-5 (Miss.).

Hook, A., ed., *Dos Passos*.

Horchler, Richard, "Prophet Without Hope," *Cweal* 75 (Sept. 29, 1961): 13-16.

Howe, Irving, "John Dos Passos: The Loss of Passion," *Tomorrow* 8 (Mar., 1949): 54-7.

Hughson, Lois, "Dos Passos's World War: Narrative Technique and History," *SNNTS* 12, i (Spring, 1980): 46-61.

Isernhagen, Haratwig, "The Boyg: A Note on Dos Passos and Ibsen," *Arcadia* 15 (1980): 44-8.

Joyner, Charles W., "John Dos Passos and World War I," *DA* 29 (1969): 3952A.

Kallich, Martin, "John Dos Passos Fellow Traveller: A Dossier with Commentary," *TCL* 1 (Jan., 1956): 173-90.

————, "John Dos Passos: Liberty and the Father-Image," *AR* 10 (Mar., 1950): 99-106.

Kazin, Alfred, "Dos Passos, Society, and the Individual," in Hook, A., ed., *Dos Passos*, 101-19. From "All the Lost Generations," in Kazin, Alfred, *On Native Grounds*, N.Y.: Harcourt, 1942, 1970, 341-59.

Knox, George, "Dos Passos and Painting," *TSLL* 6 (Spring, 1964): 22-38.

Korth, Philip A., "John Dos Passos, Ralph Chaplin and *The Centralia* Conspiracy," *SSMLN* 9, i (1979): 12-16.

Landsberg, Melvin, "John R. Dos Passos: His Influence on the Novelist's Early Political Development," *AQ* 16 (Fall, 1964): 473-85.

————, "A Study of the Political Development of John Dos Passos from 1912 to 1936—with Emphasis on the Origins of U.S.A.," *DAI* 32 (1971): 1517A (Columbia).

Ledbetter, Kenneth, "The Journey of John Dos Passos," *HAB* 18, ii (Fall, 1967): 36-48.

Lee, Brian, "History and John Dos Passos," in Bradbury, M., and D. Palmer, eds., *American Novel and the Nineteen Twenties*, 197-213.

Lowry, Edward D., "'The Writer As Technician': The Method of John Dos Passos, 1925-1936," *DA* 27 (1966): 1374A (N.Y.U.).

Ludington, Charles T., Jr., "An Individual's Focus on Existence: The Novels of John Dos Passos," *DAI* 31 (1970): 393A (Duke).

————, "The Neglected Satires of John Dos Passos," *SNL* 7, ii (Spring, 1970): 127-36.

Ludington, Townsend, "Dos Passos' School Days: Life Among the American Rover Boys," *LGJ* 5, i (Spring, 1977): 12-16.

————, "Friendship Won't Stand That: John Howard Lawson and John Dos Passos's Struggle for an Ideological Ground to Stand On," in Bogardus, R. F., and F. Hobson, eds., *Literature at the Barricades*, 46-66.

————, "The Hotel Childhood of John Dos Passos," *VQR* 54, ii (Spring, 1978): 297-313.

————, "The Many Autobiographies of John Dos Passos," *RFEA* 7, xiv (May, 1982): 237-43.

————, "The Portuguese Heritage: First and Second Generation Born: The Example of the Two Dos Passos," *Gávea-Brown* 1, ii (July-Dec., 1980): 5-16. [Not seen.]

Lydenberg, John, "Dos Passos and the Ruined Words," *PacSp* 5 (Summer, 1951): 316-27.

Lynde, Lowell F., "John Dos Passos: The Theme is Freedom," *DA* 28 (1967): 235A (La. State).

Lynn, Kenneth, "Dos Passos' Chosen Country," *NRep* (Oct 15, 1966): 15-20.

————, *Introduction to World in a Glass: A View of Our Century. Selected from the Novels of John Dos Passos*, Boston: Houghton-Mifflin, 1966, v-xv. Reprinted in Lynn, Kenneth S., *Visions of America; Eleven Historical Essays* (Contributions in American Studies, N. 6), Westport: Greenwood Pr., 1973, 177-88.

Magny, Claude-Edmonde, "Time in Dos Passos," *Age of the American Novel*, 124-43.

Marz, Charles H., "John Dos Passos: The Performing Voice," *DAI* 37 (1977): 7752A-53A.

McHugh, Vincent, "Dos Passos and the Thirty Thousand Souls," in Fiskin, A. M. I., ed., *Writers of Our Years*, Denver, Colo.: Un. of Denver Pr., 1950, 79-100.

McLuhan, Marshall, "John Dos Passos: Technique vs. Sensibility," in Gardner, H., ed., *Fifty Years of the American Novel*, 151-64. Also in Litz, A. W., ed., *Modern American Fiction*, 138-49. Also in McLuhan, Marshall, *The Interior Landscape: The Literary Criticism of Marshall McLuhan, 1943-1962*, Sel., comp., and edited by Eugene McNamara, N.Y.: McGraw-Hill, 1969, 49-62. Also in Hook, A., ed., *Dos Passos*, 148-61.

Menton, Seymour, "Érico Veríssimo and John Dos Passos: Two Interpretations of the National Novel," *RIB* 14 (Jan.-Mar., 1964): 54-9.

Millgate, M., *American Social Fiction*, 128-41.

Mizener, Arthur, "The Gullivers of Dos Passos," *SatR* (June 30, 1951): 6, 7, 34-6. Also in Hook, A., ed., *Dos Passos*, 162-70.

————, *Sense of Life in the Modern Novel*, 148-60.

Morse, Jonathan I., "Forms of Disillusion in Fitzgerald and Dos Passos," *DAI* 36 (1975): 2826A.

Muste, John M., "Norman Mailer and John Dos Passos: The Question of Influence," *MFS* 17, ii (Autumn, 1971): 361-74.

Orth, William J., "The Later Novels of John Dos Passos," *DAI* 36 (1975): 3698A.

Palmer, Michael H., "The Dramatic, Literary, and Historical Significance of John Dos Passos' Three Plays and Their Relationship to the Major Works," *DAI* 36 (1976): 5300A-01A.

Poster, William, "The Progress of John Dos Passos," *AmMerc* 74 (Mar., 1952): 115-18.

Rao, B. R., *American Fictional Hero*, 46-53.

Reilly, John M., "Dos Passos *Et Al*: An Experiment in Radical Fiction," *MQ* 12, iv (Summer, 1971): 413-24.

Rideout, W. B., *Radical Novel in the U.S.*, 154-64.

Rosen, R. C., *John Dos Passos*.

————, "John Dos Passos: The Writer in History," *DAI* 39 (1979): 6766A-67A.

Sanders, David, "The 'Anarchism' of John Dos Passos," *SAQ* 60 (Winter, 1961): 44-55.

————, "The Art of Fiction XLIV [Interview] with John Dos Passos," *ParisR* 46 (Spring, 1969): 147-72.

————, "Interview with John Dos Passos," *ClareQ* 11, iii (Spring, 1964): 89-100.

Scholl, Peter A., "Dos Passos, Mailer, and Sloan: Young Men's Initiations," *LGJ* 5, i (Spring, 1977): 2-5, 23.

Smith, Ian E., Jr., "John Dos Passos: Historian of Twentieth-Century American Culture," *DAI* 33 (1972): 2953A (Minn.).

Smith, James S., "The Novelist of Discomfort: A Reconsideration of John Dos Passos," *CE* 19 (May, 1958): 332-8.

Snell, G., *Shapers of American Fiction*, 249-63.

Sokoloff, Naomi B., "Spatial Form in the Social Novel: John Dos Passos, Alejo Carpentier, and S. Y. Agnon," *DAI* 41 (1980): 2593A.

Sorenson, Dale A., "The Pastoral Art of John Dos Passos," *DAI* 36 (1976): 5305A.

Spiller, Robert E., *The Third Dimension: Studies in Literary History*, N.Y.: Macmillan, 1965, 163-6.

Stoltzfus, Ben, "John Dos Passos and the French," *CL* 15 (Spring, 1963): 146-63.

Straumann, H., *American Literature in the Twentieth Century*, 22-8.

Thorp, W., "Class and Caste in the Novel, 1920-1950," *American Writing in the Twentieth Century*, 136-42.

Trivedi, A. P., "John Dos Passos: The Writer's Commitment," *JEnS* 13, ii (1982): 913-22.

Vanderwerken, David L., "Dos Passos and the 'Old Words'," *DAI* 34 (1973): 1298A (Rice).

_____, "Dos Passos' Civil Religion," *RS* 48, iv (Dec., 1980): 218-28.

Van Gelder, R., *Writers on Writing*, 237-40.

Wagenknecht, E., "John Dos Passos: The Collectivist Novel," *Cavalcade of the American Novel*, 382-9.

Wagner, L. W., *Dos Passos*.

_____, "John Dos Passos: Reaching Past Poetry," in Waldmeir, Joseph J., ed., *Essays in Honor of Russell B. Nye*, East Lansing: Michigan State Un. Pr., 1979, 226-46.

Wakefield, Dan, "Dos, Which Side Are You On?" *Esquire* 59, iv (April, 1963): 112-18.

Weber, Daniel, "The Passion of John Dos Passos," *DilimanR* 14, iii (July, 1966): 261-72.

Weeks, Robert P., "Dos Passos' Debt to Whitman," in Lanzinger, K., ed., *Americana-Austriaca*, 121-38.

West, T. R., *Flesh of Steel*, 54-70.

Whipple, Anne, "Dos Passos and Caldwell Credited Journalism's Contribution," *LGJ* 5, ii (Spring, 1977): 6-8.

Wilson, Edmund, "Dos Passos and the Social Revolution," *The Shores of Light: A Literary Chronicle of the Twenties and Thirties*, N.Y.: Farrar, Straus & Young, 1952, 432-4. Also in Rubin, L. D., and J. R. Moore, eds., *Idea of an American Novel*, 331-2.

Winner, Anthony, "The Characters of John Dos Passos," *LWU* 2, i (1969): 1-19.

_____, "The Needs of a Man: A Study of the Formation of Themes, Characters and Style in the Work of John Dos Passos," Unpub. Doct. Diss., Harvard Un., 1962.

Wrenn, J. H., *John Dos Passos*.

Zasursky, Y., "Dos Passos' Experimental Novel," in Vroon, R., tr., *20th Century American Literature: A Soviet View*, 331-50.

ADVENTURES OF A YOUNG MAN (See also DISTRICT OF COLUMBIA)

Aldridge, J. W., *After the Lost Generation*, 77-8. Also in Aldridge, J. W., *Devil in the Fire*, 120-21.

Beach, J. W., *American Fiction*, 62-4.

Becker, G. J., *John Dos Passos*, 83-7.

Blake, N. M., *Novelist's America*, 183-93.

Blotner, J., *Modern American Political Novel*, 312-15.

Brantley, J. D., *Fiction of John Dos Passos*, 79-85.

Colley, I., *Dos Passos and the Fiction of Despair*, 120-7.

Davis. R. G., *John Dos Passos*, 31-3.

Eisinger, C. E., *Fiction of the Forties*, 121-2.

Geismar, M., *Writers in Crisis*, 130-5.

Milne, G., *American Political Novel*, 137-8.

Rosen, R. C., *John Dos Passos*, 96-8.

Slochower, H., *No Voice is Wholly Lost*, 74-5.

Snell, G., *Shapers of American Fiction*, 260-1.

Wagner, L. W., *Dos Passos*, 117-20.

THE BIG MONEY (See also U.S.A.)

Bernheim, Mark, "Florida: The Permanence of America's Idyll," *MSLC* 4 (1982): 127-32.

Blake, N. M., *Novelist's America*, 174-5, 177-83.

Colley, I., *Dos Passos and the Fiction of Despair*, 101-19.

Foley, Barbara. "The Treatment of Time in THE BIG MONEY: An Examination of Ideology and Literary Form," *MFS* 26, iii (Autumn, 1980): 447-67.

Geismar, Maxwell, Introduction to THE BIG MONEY, N.Y.: Pocket Books, 1955. Also in Geismar, M., *American Moderns*, 72-6.

_____, *Writers in Crisis*, 123-7.

Magny, Claude-Edmonde, "Time in Dos Passos," in *The Age of the American Novel: The Film Aesthetic of Fiction Between the Two Wars*, N.Y.: Ungar, 1972, 124-43. Also in Hook, A., ed., *Dos Passos*, 128-44.

Mizener, A., *Twelve Great American Novels*, 92-103.

CHOSEN COUNTRY

Brantley, J. D., *Fiction of John Dos Passos*, 102-8.

Colley, I., *Dos Passos and the Fiction of Despair*, 135-7.

Eisinger, C. E., *Fiction of the Forties*, 124-5.

Poster, WIlliam, "The Progress of John Dos Passos," *AmMerc* 74 (Mar., 1952): 115-18.

Rosen, R. C., *John Dos Passos*, 118-21.

DISTRICT OF COLUMBIA

Brantley, J. D., *Fiction of John Dos Passos*, 99-101.

Colley, I., *Dos Passos and the Fiction of Despair*, 120-35.

Davis, R. G., *John Dos Passos*, 34-6.

Lydenberg, John, "Dos Passos and the Ruined Words," *PacSp* 5 (Summer, 1951): 316-27.

Rosen, Robert C., "Dos Passos' Other Trilogy," *MFS* 26, iii (Autumn, 1980): 483-502.

Wagner, L. W., *Dos Passos*, 111-33.

FIRST ENCOUNTER (See ONE MAN'S INITIATION-1917)

THE 42ND PARALLEL (See also U.S.A.)

Colley, I., *Dos Passos and the Fiction of Despair*, 66-84.

England, Donald G., "The Newsreels of John Dos Passos' THE 42nd PARALLEL: Sources and Techniques," *DAI* 31 (1970): 1794A-95A (Texas, Austin).

Geismar, M., Introduction to THE 42nd PARALLEL, N.Y.: Pocket Books, 1952. Also in Geismar, M., *American Moderns*, 65-8.

_____, Introduction, in Dos Passos, John, THE 42nd PARALLEL, N.Y.: Wash. Sq. Pr., 1961.

_____, *Writers in Crisis*, 109-14.

Gray, J., *On Second Thought*, 69-72.

Gurko, L., *Angry Decade*, 50-2.

Wagner, L. W., *Dos Passos*, 85-101.

Wilson, E., *Shores of Light*, 446-50.

THE GRAND DESIGN (See also DISTRICT OF COLUMBIA)

Aldridge, J. W. *After the Lost Generation*, 79-80. Also in Aldridge, J. W., *Devil in the Fire*, 120, 122-3.

Becker, G. J., *John Dos Passos*, 90-4.

Blotner, J., *Modern American Political Novel*, 312-15.

Brantley, J. D., *Fiction of John Dos Passos*, 89-98.

Colley, I., *Dos Passos and the Fiction of Despair*, 130-5.

Davis, R. G., *John Dos Passos*, 34-5.

Diggins, John P., "Dos Passos and Veblen's Villains," *AR* 23 (Winter, 1963-64): 490-2.

Eisinger, C. E., *Fiction of the Forties*, 123-4.

Geismar, Maxwell, in *NYTBR* (Jan. 2, 1949): 4. Also in Geismar, M., *American Moderns*, 76-9.

Hicks, Granville, "Dos Passos and His Critics," *AmMerc* 68 (May, 1949): 623-30.

Howe, Irving, "John Dos Passos: The Loss of Passion," *Tomorrow* 8 (Mar. 1949): 56-7.

Rosen, R. C., *John Dos Passos*, 110-16.

Wagner, L. W., *Dos Passos*, 123-30.

THE GREAT DAYS

Aaron, Daniel, "Dos Passos Obsessed," *New Leader* 41 (June 2, 1958): 24.

Brantley, J. D., *Fiction of John Dos Passos*, 114-22.

Colley, I., *Dos Passos and the Fiction of Despair*, 140-2.

Farrell, James T., "How Should We Rate Dos Passos?" *NRep* 138 (April 28, 1958): 17-18.

Geismar, M., *American Moderns*, 84-90.

Rosen, R. C., *John Dos Passos*, 129-30.

MANHATTAN TRANSFER

Aldridge, J. W., *After the Lost Generation*, 69-72. Also in Aldridge, J. W., *Devil in the Fire*, 114-15.

Arakelian, Paul G., "Feature Analysis of Metaphor in THE WAVES and MANHATTAN TRANSFER," *Style* 12 (Summer, 1978): 274-85.

Arden, Eugene, "MANHATTAN TRANSFER: An Experiment in Technique," *UKCR* 22 (Winter, 1955): 153-8.

Arrington, Phillip, "The Sense of an Ending in MANHATTAN TRANSFER," *AL* 54, iii (Oct., 1982): 438-43.

Beach, J. W., *American Fiction*, 35-44, 47-52. Also, condensed, in Belkind, A., ed., *Dos Passos, the Critics, and the Writer's Intention*, 54-69.

Becker, G. J., *John Dos Passos*, 38-55.

Carver, Craig, "The Newspaper and Other Sources of MANHATTAN TRANSFER," *SAF* 3, ii (Autumn, 1975): 167-79.

Clark, Michael, "John Dos Passos's MANHATTAN TRANSFER: The Woman as City," *NConL* 12, ii (Mar., 1982): 5-6.

Colley, I., *Dos Passos and the Fiction of Despair*, 47-65.

Cowan, Michael, "Walkers in the Street: American Writers and the Modern City," *Prospects* 6 (1981): 298-303.

Davis, R. G., *John Dos Passos*, 18-20.

Friedman, M., *Stream of Consciousness*, 245-6.

Frohock, W. H., "John Dos Passos: Of Time and Frustration," *SWR* 33 (Spring, 1948): 170-4.

————, *Novel of Violence in America*, 36-43.

Geismar, M., *Writers in Crisis*, 102-4.

Gelfant, B. H., "Technique as Social Commentary in MANHATTAN TRANSFER," *American City Novel*, 138-66. Also, as "John Dos Passos: The Synoptic Novel," in Hook, A., ed., *Dos Passos*, 36-52.

Green, Paul, "The Crossing Pathways of MANHATTAN TRANSFER," *RecL* 4, i (1975): 19-42.

Gremla, Josef, "On the Place of MANHATTAN TRANSFER in the Development of John Dos Passos," *HSE* 14 (1981): 37-46.

Hughson, Lois, "Narration in the Making of MANHATTAN TRANSFER," *SNNTS* 8, ii (Summer, 1976): 185-98.

Knowles, A. S., Jr., "Dos Passos in the Twenties," in French, W., ed., *Twenties*, 132-7.

Lane, James B., "MANHATTAN TRANSFER as a Gateway to the 1920's," *CentR* 16, iii (Summer, 1972): 293-311.

Lee, Brian, "History and John Dos Passos," in Bradbury, M., and D. Palmer, eds., *American Novel in the Nineteen Twenties*, 206-9.

Le Page, Raymond, and Claire Le Page, "The Use of Expressive French in Dos Passos' MANHATTAN TRANSFER," *Interpretations* 12 (1980): 14-21.

Lowry, E. D., "The Lively Art of MANHATTAN TRANSFER," *PMLA* 84, vi (Oct., 1969): 1628-38.

————, "MANHATTAN TRANSFER: Dos Passos' Wasteland," *UR* 30 (Oct., 1963): 47-52. Also in Hook, A., ed., *Dos Passos*, 53-60.

————, "'The Writer as Technician': The Method of John Dos Passos, 1925-1936," *DA* 27 (1966): 1374A (N.Y.U.).

Magee, John D., "An Analytical Study of John Dos Passos' MANHATTAN TRANSFER," *DAI* 32 (1971): 2696A-97A (Ball State).

McCormick, Diana F., "A Pessimistic Vision of New York in Literature: MANHATTAN TRANSFER," *Centerpoint* 1, iii (1975): 9-13.

Mizener, A., *Twelve Great American Novels*, 91-2.

Mizener, S. F., *Manhattan Transients*.

Morrow, Patrick, "The Dada World of MANHATTAN TRANSFER," *RS* 38 (1970): 258-65.

Rosen, R. C., *John Dos Passos*, 41-9.

Ruoff, Gene W., "Social Mobility and the Artist in MANHATTAN TRANSFER and the MUSIC OF TIME," *WSCL* 5, i (Winter-Spring, 1964): 64-76.

Snell, G., *Shapers of American Fiction*, 252-5.

Spindler, Michael, "John Dos Passos and the Visual Arts," *JAmS* 15, iii (Dec., 1981): 391-405.

Titche, Leon L., "Döblin and Dos Passos: Aspects of the City Novel," *MFS* 17, i (Spring, 1971): 125-35.

Vanderwerken, David L., "MANHATTAN TRANSFER: Dos Passos' Babel Story," *AL* 49, ii (1977): 253-67.

Wagner, L. W., *Dos Passos*, 47-64.

Walcutt, C. C., *American Literary Naturalism*, 280-3.

Wrenn, J. H., *John Dos Passos*, 121-31.

MIDCENTURY

Becker, G. J., *John Dos Passos*, 94-8.

Brantley, J. D., *Fiction of John Dos Passos*, 122-6.

Chase, Richard, "The Chronicles of Dos Passos," *Ctary* 31 (May, 1961): 396-8. Also in Hook, A., ed., *Dos Passos*, 173-5.

Colley, I., *Dos Passos and the Fiction of Despair*, 342-4.

Davis, R. G., *John Dos Passos*, 39-44.

Diggins, John P., "Dos Passos and Veblen's Villains," *AR* 23 (Winter, 1963-64): 492-6.

Dos Passos, John, in Madden, C. F., ed., *Talks with Authors*, 3-11.

Kilpatrick, James J., "Midnight at Midcentury," *National Rev* 10 (April 22, 1961): 252-3.

Rosen, R. C., *John Dos Passos*, 135-42.

Sanders, David, *WSCL* 2, iii (Fall, 1961): 47-50.

Vidal, Gore, "Comment," *Esquire* (May, 1961): 57-9. Also as "John Dos Passos at Midcentury," *Homage to Daniel Shays*, 96-102.
Wagner, L. W., *Dos Passos*, 151-9.

MOST LIKELY TO SUCCEED

Brantley, J. D., *Fiction of John Dos Passos*, 108-14.
Colley, I., *Dos Passos and the Fiction of Despair*, 137-40.
Rosen, R. C., *John Dos Passos*, 123-5.

1919 (See also U.S.A.)

Blake, N. M., *Novelist's America*, 168-4, 176-7.
Cooperman, S., *World War I and the American Novel*, 141-5.
Cowley, Malcolm, "The Poet and the World," *NRep* 70 (April 27, 1932): 305-3. Also in Harrison, G. A., ed., *Critic as Artist*, 77-85. Also in Zabel, M. D., ed., *Literary Opinion in America*, 488-90. Also in Cowley, M., ed., *After the Genteel Tradition*, 134-46. Also in Cowley, M., *Think Back On Us*, 215-19.
Foley, Barbara, "History, Fiction, and Satirical Form: The Example of Dos Passos' 1919," *Genre* 12 (1979): 357-78.
Geismar, Maxwell, Introduction to 1919, N.Y.: Pocket Books, 1954. Also in Geismar, M., *American Moderns*, 68-72.
_____, Introduction to 1919, N.Y.: Wash. Sq. Pr., 1961.
Katopes, Peter J., "Wesley Everest in John Dos Passos's NINE-TEEN NINETEEN," *N&Q* 23, i (Jan., 1976): 22.
Sartre, J. P., *Literary and Philosophical Essays*, 88-96. Also in Belkind, A., ed., *Dos Passos, the Critics, and the Writer's Intention*, 70-80. Also in Hook, A., ed., *Dos Passos*, 61-9. Also in Sanders, D., comp., *Studies in U.S.A.*, 30-7.

NUMBER ONE (See also DISTRICT OF COLUMBIA)

Aldridge, J. W., *After the Lost Generation*, 78-9. Also in Aldridge, J. W., *Devil in the Fire*, 120-1.
Becker, G. J., *John Dos Passos*, 87-90.
Blotner, J., *Modern American Political Novel*, 215-17.
Brantley, J. D., *Fiction of John Dos Passos*, 85-9.
Colley, I., *Dos Passos and the Fiction of Despair*, 126-9.
Davis, R. G., *John Dos Passos*, 33-4.
Eisinger, C. E., *Fiction of the Forties*, 122-3.
Gray, J., *On Second Thought*, 73-4.
Rosen, R. C., *John Dos Passos*, 101-4.
Wagner, L. W., *Dos Passos*, 120-3.

ONE MAN'S INITIATION- 1917

Aldridge, J. W., *After the Lost Generation*, 59-66. Also in Aldridge, J. W., *Devil in the Fire*, 106-12.
Brantley, J. D., *Fiction of John Dos Passos*, 13-21.
Colley, I., *Dos Passos and the Fiction of Despair*, 27-33.
Davis, R. G., *John Dos Passos*, 8-10.
Geismar, M., *Writers in Crisis*, 92-3.
Holditch, Kenneth, "ONE MAN'S INITIATION: The Origin of Techniques in the Novels of John Dos Passos," in Reck, Rima D., ed., *Explorations of Literature* (LSUSHS, 18), Baton Rouge: La. St. Un. Pr., 1966, 115-23.
Rosen, R. C., *John Dos Passos*, 10-13.
Sanders, David, "'Lies' and the System: Enduring Themes from Dos Passos' Early Novels," *SAQ* 65 (Spring, 1966): 215-26.
Wagner, L. W., *Dos Passos*, 12-15.

STREETS OF NIGHT

Beach, J. W., *American Fiction*, 26-9.
Becker, G. J., *John Dos Passos*, 31-3.
Brantley, J. D., *Fiction of John Dos Passos*, 38-45.
Clark, Michael, "Whitman's Influence on Dos Passos' STREETS OF NIGHT," *WWR* 28 (June-Dec., 1982): 66-72.
Colley, I., *Dos Passos and the Fiction of Despair*, 17-26.
Davis, R. G., *John Dos Passos*, 16-17.
Rosen, R. C., *John Dos Passos*, 38-41.
Sanders, David, "'Lies' and the System: Enduring Themes from Dos Passos' Early Novels," *SAQ* 65 (Spring, 1966): 226-8.
Vanderwerken, David L., "Dos Passos' STREETS OF NIGHT: A Reconsideration," *MarkhamR* 4 (Oct., 1974): 61-5.
Wagner, L. W., *Dos Passos* 23-7.
Wrenn, J. H., *John Dos Passos*, 116-21.

THREE SOLDIERS

Aldridge, J. W., *After the Lost Generation*, 66-8. Also in Aldridge, J. W., *Devil in the Fire*, 112-14.
Allen, W., *Modern Novel*, 136.
Becker, G. J., *John Dos Passos*, 24-31.
Bishop, J. P., "Three Brilliant Young Novelists," *Collected Essays*, 232-3. Also in *Vanity Fair* (Oct., 1921).
Bluefarb, S., "John Andrews: Flight from the Machine," *Escape Motif in the American Novel*, 61-72.
Brantley, J. D., *Fiction of John Dos Passos*, 21-36.
Colley, I., *Dos Passos and the Fiction of Despair*, 33-46.
Cooperman, Stanley, "John Dos Passos' THREE SOLDIERS: Aesthetics and the Doom of Individualism," in Klein, H., ed., *First World War in Fiction*, 23-31.
_____, *World War I and the American Novel*, 152-5, 175-81 *passim*.
Davis, R. G., *John Dos Passos*, 10-12.
Frohock, W. M., "John Dos Passos: Of Time and Frustration," *SWR* 33 (Winter, 1948): 77-80. Also in Frohock, W. M., *Novel of Violence in America*, 31-6.
Geismar, M., *Writers in Crisis*, 93-6.
Gilman, Owen W., Jr., "John Dos Passos: THREE SOLDIERS and Thoreau," *MFS* 26, iii (Autumn, 1980): 470-81.
Hoffman, F. J., "I Had Seen Nothing Sacred," *Twenties*, 57-61.
Johnson, Ellwood, "The Anarchist Theme of John Dos Passos's THREE SOLDIERS," *MarkhamR* 10 (Summer, 1981): 68-71.
Knowles, A. S., Jr., "Dos Passos in the Twenties," in French, W., ed., *Twenties*, 127-31.
Lawrence, Floyd B., "Two Novelists of the Great War: Dos Passos and Cummings," *UR* 36, i (Oct., 1969): 35-41.
Lee, Brian, "History and John Dos Passos," in Bradford, M., and D. Palmer, eds., *American Novel in the Nineteen Twenties*, 202-5.
McIlvaine, Robert, "Dos Passos' THREE SOLDIERS," *Expl* 31, vii (Mar., 1973): Item 50.
Mizener, A., *Twelve Great American Novels*, 89-90.
Rosen, R. C., *John Dos Passos*, 15-23.
Ross, Frank, "The Assailant-Victim in Three War Protest Novels," *Paunch* 32 (Aug., 1968): 46-57.
Sanders, David, "'Lies' and the System: Enduring Themes from Dos Passos' Early Novels," *SAQ* 65 (Spring, 1966): 215-26.
Snell, G., *Shapers of American Fiction*, 250-2.
Wagner, L. W., *Dos Passos*, 15-22.
Walsh, J., *American War Literature*, 69-78.

Wrenn, J. H., *John Dos Passos*, 108-17.

U.S.A.

Aldridge, J. W., *After the Lost Generation*, 71-7. Also in Sanders, D., comp., *Studies in U.S.A.*, 44-8. Also in Aldridge, J. W., *Devil in the Fire*, 116-20.

Allen, W., *Modern Novel*, 144-8.

_____, *Urgent West*, 208-10.

Anon., "Two American Novelists," *TLS* No. 2543 (Oct. 27, 1950): 669-70.

Beach, Joseph W., *American Fiction*, 52-66.

_____, "Dos Passos, 1947," *SR* 55 (July-Sept., 1947): 411-15.

Becker, G. J., *John Dos Passos*, 58-79.

Blake, N. M., *Novelist's America*, 168-83.

Bradbury, Malcolm, "The Denuded Place: War and Form in PARADE'S END and U.S.A.," in Klein, H., ed., *First World War in Fiction*, 193-209.

Brantley, J. D., *Fiction of John Dos Passos*, 55-78.

Chametzky, Jules, "Reflections on U.S.A. as a Novel and Play," *MR* 1 (Feb., 1960): 391-9. Also in Sanders, D., comp., *Studies in U.S.A.*, 60-7.

Christensen, Peter G., "Dos Passos' Use of Biography in U.S.A.," *FMLS* 18, iii (July, 1982): 201-11.

Clark, Michael, "The Structure of John Dos Passos's U.S.A. Trilogy," *ArQ* 38, iii (Autumn, 1982): 229-34.

Colley, I., *Dos Passos and the Fiction of Despair*, 66-119.

Cowley, Malcolm, "John Dos Passos: The Poet and the World," *NRep* 70 (April 27, 1932): 303-5; 87 (Sept. 9, 1936), 34. Also in Zabel, M.D., ed., *Literary Opinion in America*, 485-93. Also in Cowley, M., ed., *Think Back On Us*, 212-19. Also, revised, as "The Poet Against the World," in Cowley, M., ed., *After the Genteel Tradition*, 134-46.

Davis, R. G., *John Dos Passos*, 21-31.

Diggins, John P., "Dos Passos and Veblen's Villains," *AR* 23 (Winter, 1963-64): 487-90.

_____, "Visions of Chaos and Visions of Order: Dos Passos as Historian," *AL* 46, iii (Nov., 1974): 330-6.

Donald, Miles, and Geoffrey Jones, *John Dos Passos' U.S.A.: The Politics of Ambivalence*, Winchester: King Alfred's College, 1980.

Feied, F., *No Pie in the Sky*, 41-56.

Finkelstein, S., *Existentialism and Alienation in American Literature*, 198-203.

Foley, Barbara, "From U.S.A. to RAGTIME: Notes on the Forms of Historical Consciousness in Modern Fiction," *AL* 50, i (Mar., 1978): 85-105.

Geismar, M., *Writers in Crisis*, 109-20, 123-30.

Geist, Stanley, "Fictitious Americans," *HudR* 5 (Summer, 1952): 206-11.

Gelfanat, B. H., "The Fulfillment of Form in U.S.A.," in Gelfant, B. H., *American City Novel*, 166-74. Also in Sanders, D., comp., *Studies in U.S.A.*, 48-54.

Goldman, Arnold, "Dos Passos and His U.S.A.," *NLH* 1 (Spring, 1970): 471-83.

Gurko, Leo, "John Dos Passos' U.S.A.: A 1930's Spectacular," in Madden, D., ed., *Proletarian Writers of the Thirties*, 46-63.

Henderson, H. B., Jr., *Versions of the Past*, 242-6.

Hoffman, Arnold R., "An Element of Structure in U.S.A.," *CEA* 31 (Oct., 1968): 12-13.

Hughson, Lois, "In Search of the True America: Dos Passos' Debt to Whitman in U.S.A.," *MFS* 19, ii (Summer, 1973): 179-92.

Irwin, William R., "Dos Passos and Fitzgerald as Reviewers of the American Social Scene," *NS* (Sept., 1960): 417-22.

Kazin, Alfred, "John Dos Passos: Inventor in Isolation," *SatR* (Mar. 15, 1969): 16-19, 44-5.

_____, *On Native Grounds*, N.Y.: Reynal and Hitchcock, 1942, 353-9. Also in Sanders, D., comp., *Studies in U.S.A.*, 38-43.

Knox, George, "Voice in the U.S.A. Biographies," *TSLL* 4 (Spring, 1962): 109-16. Also in Sanders, D., comp., *Studies in U.S.A.*, 78-86.

Larsson, Donald F., "The Camera Eye: 'Cinematic' Narrative in U.S.A. and GRAVITY'S RAINBOW," 94-106 in Ruppert, Peter, Eugene Crook, and Walter Forehand, eds., *Ideas of Order in Literature and Film*, Tallahassee: Un. Pr. of Florida, 1980.

Leavis, F. R., "A Serious Artist," *Scrutiny* 1 (Sept., 1932): 173-9. Also in Hook, A., ed., *Dos Passos*, 70-5.

Lee, Brian, "History and John Dos Passos," in Bradbury, M., and D. Palmer, eds., *American Novel in the Nineteen Twenties*, 209-13.

Lehan, Richard, "The Trilogies of Jean-Paul Sartre and John Dos Passos," *IEY* 9 (Fall, 1964): 60-4. Also in Lehan, R., *Dangerous Crossing*, 39-46.

Levin, Harry, "Revisiting Dos Passos' U.S.A.," *MR* 20, iii (1979): 401-15.

Lowry, Edward D., "'The Writer as Technician': The Method of John Dos Passos, 1925-1936," *DA* 27 (1966): 1374A (N.Y.U.).

Ludington, Townsend, "The Ordering of the Camera Eye in U.S.A.," *AL* 49, iii (Nov., 1977): 443-6.

Lydenberg, John, "Dos Passos's U.S.A.: The Words of the Hollow Men," in Krause, S. J., *Essays on Determinism in American Literature*, 97-107. Also in Belkind, A., ed., *Dos Passos, the Critics, and the Writer's Intention*, 93-105.

Magny, Claude-Edmonde, "Dos Passos's U.S.A., or The Impersonal Novel," *Age of the American Novel*, 105-23.

Marz, Charles, "Dos Passos' Newsreels: The Noise of History," *SNNTS* 11, ii (1979): 194-200.

_____, "U.S.A.: Chronicle and Performance," *MFS* 26, iii (Autumn, 1980): 398-415.

Maxwell, D. E. S., *American Fiction*, 269-72.

Maynard, Reid, "John Dos Passos' One-Sided Panorama," *Discourse* 11 (Autumn, 1968): 468-74.

McHale, Brian, "Free Indirect Discourse: A Survey of Recent Accounts," *PTL* 3 (1978): 254-71.

_____, "Talking U.S.A.: Interpreting Free Indirect Discourse in Dos Passos' U.S.A. Trilogy, Part One," *Degrés* 16 (1978): 6-67; Part Two, *Degrés* 16 (1978): d-d20.

Millgate, M., *American Social Fiction*, 130-5.

Morse, Jonathan, "Dos Passos' U.S.A. and the Illusions of Memory," *MFS* 23, iv (Winter, 1977-78): 543-55.

Murray, Edward, "John Dos Passos and the Camera-Eye—MANHATTAN TRANSFER and U.S.A.," *Cinematic Imagination*, 168-78.

Nelson, F. William, "An Analysis of John Dos Passos' U.S.A.," *DA* 17 (1957): 1767 (Oklahoma).

Pizer, Donald, "The Camera Eye in U.S.A.: The Sexual Center," *MFS* 26, iii (Autumn, 1980): 417-30.

Rideout, W. B., *Radical Novel in the United States*, 162-4. Also as "The Radicalism of U.S.A.," in Hook, A., ed., *Dos Passos*, 145-7.

Rosen, R. C., *John Dos Passos*, 78-91.

Sanders, D., comp., *Studies in U.S.A.*

Schwartz, Delmore, "John Dos Passos and the Whole Truth," *SoR* 4 (Autumn, 1938): 351-65. Also in Rubin, L. D., Jr., and J. R. Moore, eds., *Idea of an American Novel*, 332-9. Also in Aldridge, J. W., ed., *Critiques and Essays on Modern Fiction*, 176-89.

Sloane, David E., "The Black Experience in Dos Passos' U.S.A.," *CEA* 36, iii (Mar., 1974): 22-3.

Slochower, H., *No Voice is Wholly Lost*, 70-4.

Smith, James S., "The Novelist of Discomfort: A Reconsideration of John Dos Passos," *CE* 19 (May, 1958): 332-8.

Snell, G., *Shapers of American Fiction*, 255-60.

Sokoloff, Naomi, "Spatial Form in the Social Novel: John Dos Passos' U.S.A. and Alejo Carpentier's *El reine de este munde*," *PRom* 2, supp. 1 (1980): 111-19.

Trilling, Lionel, "The America of John Dos Passos," *PR* 4, v (April, 1938): 26-32. Also in Hook, A., ed., *Dos Passos*, 93-100. Also in Sanders, D., comp., *Studies in U.S.A.*, 21-8.

Vanderwerken, David L., "U.S.A.: Dos Passos and the 'Old Words'," *TCL* 23 (May, 1977): 195-228.

Wagner, L. W., *Dos Passos*, 85-108.

_____, "The Poetry in American Fiction," *Prospects* 2 (1976): 522-4.

Ward, John W., "Lindbergh, Dos Passos and History," *Carleton Miscellany* 6 (Summer, 1965): 20-41.

_____, *Red, White, and Blue: Men, Books, and Ideas in American Culture*, N.Y.: Oxford, 1969, 38-47. Also in Hook, A., ed., *Dos Passos*, 120-7.

Weeks, Robert P., "The Novel as Poem: Whitman's Legacy to Dos Passos," *MFS* 26, iii (Autumn, 1980): 431-46.

Westerhoven, James N., "Autobiographical Elements in the Camera Eye," *AL* 48, iii (1976): 340-64.

Whipple, T. K., "Dos Passos and the U.S.A.," *Nation* (Feb. 19, 1938): 210-12. Also in Hook, A., ed., *Dos Passos*, 87-92. Also in Sanders, D., comp., *Studies in U.S.A.*, 17-21.

Widmer, Eleanor, "The Lost Girls of U.S.A.: Dos Passos' 30's Movie," in French, Warren, ed., *The Thirties: Fiction, Poetry, Drama*, De Land, Fl.: Everett Edwards, Inc., 11-19.

Wrenn, J. H., *John Dos Passos*, 154-66. Also in Sanders, D., comp., *Studies in U.S.A.*, 67-78.

Zasursky, Y., "Dos Passos' Experimental Novel," in Vroon, R., tr., *20th Century American Literature: A Soviet View*, 237-46.

BIBLIOGRAPHY

Potter, Jack, *A Bibliography of John Dos Passos*, Chicago: Normandie House, 1950.

Reinhart, Virginia S., "John Dos Passos Bibliography: 1950-1966," *TCL* 13 (Oct., 1967): 167-78.

Rohrkemper, John, "Criticism of John Dos Passos: A Selected Checklist," *MFS* 26, iii (Autumn, 1980): 525-38.

_____, *John Dos Passos: A Reference Guide*, Boston: Hall, 1980.

_____, "John Dos Passos: An Annotated Secondary Bibliography," *DAI* 41 (1980): 1059A.

White, William, "More Dos Passos: Bibliographical Addenda," *PBSA* 45 (1951): 156-8.

Wrenn, J. H., *John Dos Passos*, 198-205.

DOWELL, COLEMAN, 1925-

GENERAL

O'Brien, John, "Interview with Coleman Dowell," *RCF* 2, iii (Fall, 1982): 85-99.

ISLAND PEOPLE

Gunn, Thom, "Pushy Jews and Aging Queens: Imaginary People in Two Novels by Coleman Dowell," *RCF* 2, iii (Fall, 1982): 135-45.

Martin, Stephen-Paul, "Exorcism and Grace: A Study of Androgyny in ISLAND PEOPLE," *RCF* 2, iii (Fall, 1982): 124-8.

Sorrentino, Gilbert, "Some Remarks on ISLAND PEOPLE," *RCF* 2, iii (Fall, 1982): 122-3.

MRS. OCTOBER WAS HERE

Gunn, Thom, "Pushy Jews and Aging Queens: Imaginary People in Two Novels by Coleman Dowell," *RCF* 2, iii (Fall, 1982): 135-45.

TOO MUCH FLESH AND JABEZ

Byrne, Jack, "Coleman Dowell's Frame-Up: What Miss Ethel Did Last Winter," *RCF* 2, iii (Fall, 1982): 145-8.

Kuehl, John, and Linda K. Kuehl, "Miss Ethel and Mr. Dowell," *RCF* 2, iii (Fall, 1982): 129-34.

WHITE ON BLACK ON WHITE

White, Edmund, "Thoughts on WHITE ON BLACK ON WHITE," *RCF* 2, iii (Fall, 1982): 113-17.

DRABBLE, MARGARET, 1939-

GENERAL

Amodio, Bonnie A. S., "The Novels of Margaret Drabble: Contradictory, Hallucinatory Lights," *DAI* 41 (1980): 2116A.

Apter, T. E., "Margaret Drabble: The Glamour of Seriousness," *HuW* 12 (Aug., 1973): 18-28.

Beards, Virginia K., "Margaret Drabble: Novels of a Cautious Feminist," *Crit* 15, i (1973): 35-47. Also in Spacks, P. M., ed., *Contemporary Women Novelists*, 18-29.

Bonfond, Francois, "Margaret Drabble: How to Express Subjective Truth Through Fiction," *RLV* 40 (1974): 41-55.

Burkhardt, Charles, "Arnold Bennett and Margaret Drabble," in Schmidt, D., and J. Seale, eds., *Margaret Drabble*, 91-103.

Campbell, Jane, "Margaret Drabble and the Search for Analogy," in Campbell, J., and J. Doyle, eds., *Practical Vision*, 132-50.

Creighton, Joanne V., "An Interview with Margaret Drabble," in Schmidt, D., and J. Seale, eds., *Margaret Drabble*, 18-31.

Cunningham, Gail, "Women and Children First: The Novels of Margaret Drabble," in Staley, T. F., ed., *Twentieth-Century Women Novelists*, 130-52.

Fox-Genovese, Elizabeth, "The Ambiguities of Female Identity: A Reading of the Novels of Margaret Drabble," *PR* 46, ii (1979): 234-48.

Hardin, Nancy S., "An Interview with Margaret Drabble," *ConL* 14 (Autumn, 1973): 273-95.

Harper, Michael F., "Margaret Drabble and the Resurrection of the English Novel," *ConL* 23, ii (Spring, 1982): 45-68.

Korenman, Joan S., "The 'Liberation' of Margaret Drabble," *Crit* 21, iii (1980): 61-72.

Lambert, Ellen Z., "Margaret Drabble and the Sense of Possibility," *UTQ* 49, iii (1980): 228-51.

Lay, Mary M., "Temporal Ordering in the Fiction of Margaret Drabble," *Crit* 21, iii (1980): 73-84.

Levitt, Morton P., "The New Victorians: Margaret Drabble as Trollope," in Schmidt, D., and J. Seale, eds., *Margaret Drabble*, 168-77.

Libby, Marion V., "Fate and Feminism in the Novels of Margaret Drabble," *ConL* 16, ii (Spring, 1975): 175-92.

Manheimer, Joan, "Margaret Drabble and the Journey to the Self," *SLitI* 11, ii (Fall, 1978): 127-43.

Milton, Barbara, "Margaret Drabble: The Art of Fiction LXX," *ParisR* 74 (1978): 41-65.

Moran, Mary H., "Existing within Structures: Margaret Drabble's View of the Individual," *DAI* 42, v (Nov., 1981): 2144A-45A.

_____, "Spots of Joy in the Midst of Darkness: The Universe of Margaret Drabble," in Schmidt, D., and J. Seale, eds., *Margaret Drabble*, 32-47.

Myer, V. G., *Margaret Drabble*.

Preussner, Dee, "Talking with Margaret Drabble," *MFS* 25 (1979-80): 563-77.

Rayson, Ann, "Motherhood in the Novels of Margaret Drabble," *Frontiers* 3, ii (1978): 43-6.

Rose, Ellen C., "Margaret Drabble: Surviving the Future," *Crit* 15, i (1973): 5-21.

_____, *Novels of Margaret Drabble*.

_____, "Twenty Questions," *DLN* 4, ii (1980): 5. [Not seen.]

Rozencwajg, Iris, "Interview with Margaret Drabble," *WS* 6, iii (1979): 335-47.

Ruderman, Judith, "An Invitation to a Dinner Party: Margaret Drabble on Women and Food," in Schmidt, D., and J. Seale, eds., *Margaret Drabble*, 104-16.

Saylors, Rita D., "Moral Development and Fictional Technique in the Novels of Margaret Drabble," *DAI* 43, iii (Aug., 1982): 454A-55A.

Schmidt, D., and J. Seale, eds., *Margaret Drabble*.

Stovel, Nora F., "Margaret Drabble's Golden Vision," in Schmidt, D., and J. Seale, eds., *Margaret Drabble*, 3-17.

Whittier, Gayle, "Mistresses and Madonnas in the Novels of Margaret Drabble," *W&L* 1 (1980): 197-213.

THE GARRICK YEAR

Beards, Virginia K., "Margaret Drabble: Novels of a Cautious Feminist," *Crit* 15, i (1973): 38-9, 41-2. Also in Spacks, P. M., ed., *Contemporary Women Novelists*, 21-2, 24-5.

Preussner, Dee, "Patterns in THE GARRICK YEAR," in Schmidt, D., and J. Seale, eds., *Margaret Drabble*, 7-14.

THE ICE AGE

Gindin, James, "Three Recent British Novels and an American Response," *MQR* 17 (Spring, 1978): 223-46.

Joseph, Gerhard, "The ANTIGONE as Cultural Touchstone: Matthew Arnold, Hegel, George Eliot, Virginia Woolf, and Margaret Drabble," *PMLA* 96, i (Jan., 1981): 29-30.

Korenman, Joan S., "The 'Liberation' of Margaret Drabble," *Crit* 21, iii (1980): 69-71.

Lay, Mary M., "Temporal Ordering in the Fiction of Margaret Drabble," *Crit* 21, iii (1980): 81-3.

Rose, E. C., *Novels of Margaret Drabble*, 112-29.

JERUSALEM THE GOLDEN

Edwards, Lee R., "JERUSALEM THE GOLDEN: A Fable for Our Times," *WS* 6, iii (1979): 321-34.

Hatvary, Laurel T., "Carrie Meeber and Clara Maugham: Sisters under the Skin," *NMAL* 5, iv (Fall, 1981): Item 26.

Rose, E. C., *Novels of Margaret Drabble*, 28-48.

Seiler, Franklin C., *Boulder-Pushers*, 24-30.

THE MIDDLE GROUND

Efrig, Gail, "THE MIDDLE GROUND," in Schmidt, D., and J. Seale, eds., *Margaret Drabble*, 178-85.

Rose, Ellen C., "Drabble's THE MIDDLE GROUND: 'Mid-Life' Narrative Strategies," *Crit* 23, iii (Spring, 1982): 69-82.

Sadler, Lynn V., "'The Society We Have': The Search for Meaning in Drabble's THE MIDDLE GROUND," *Crit* 23, iii (Spring, 1982): 83-94.

THE MILLSTONE (THANK YOU ALL VERY MUCH)

Butler, Colin, "Margaret Drabble: THE MILLSTONE and WORDSWORTH," *ES* 59 (June, 1978): 353-60.

Cunningham, Gail, "Women and Children First: The Novels of Margaret Drabble," in Staley, T. F., ed., *Twentieth-Century Women Novelists*, 133-6, 139-45.

Firchow, Peter E., "Rosamund's Complaint: Margaret Drabble's THE MILLSTONE," in Morris, R. K., ed., *Old Lines, New Forces*, 93-108.

Hardin, Nancy S., "Drabble's THE MILLSTONE: A Fable for Our Times," *Crit* 15, i (1973): 22-34.

Manheimer, Joan, "Margaret Drabble and the Journey to the Self," *SLitI* 11, ii (Fall, 1978): 131-4.

Korenman, Joan S., "The 'Liberation' of Margaret Drabble," *Crit* 21, iii (1980): 65-9.

Lay, Mary M., "Temporal Ordering in the Fiction of Margaret Drabble," *Crit* 21, iii (1980): 79-81.

THE REALMS OF GOLD

Campbell, Jane, "Margaret Drabble and the Search for Analogy," in Campbell, J., and J. Doyle, eds., *Practical Vision*, 144-50.

Davis, Cynthia A., "Unfolding Form: Narrative Approach and Theme in THE REALMS OF GOLD," *MLQ* 40 (Dec., 1979): 390-402.

Kaplan, Carey, "A Vision of Power in Margaret Drabble's THE REALMS OF GOLD," *JWSL* 1 (1979): 233-42.

Korenman, Joan S., "The 'Liberation' of Margaret Drabble," *Crit* 21, iii (1980): 65-9.

Lay, Mary M., "Temporal Ordering in the Fiction of Margaret Drabble," *Crit* 21, iii (1980): 79-81.

Little, Judy, "Humor and the Female Quest: Margaret Drabble's THE REALMS OF GOLD," *RFI* 4, ii (1978): 44-52.

_____, "Margaret Drabble and the Romantic Imagination: THE REALMS OF GOLD," *PrS* 55, i-ii (Spring-Summer, 1981): 241-52.

Rose, E. C., *Novels of Margaret Drabble*, 94-111.

Rowe, Margaret M., "The Uses of the Past in Margaret Drabble's THE REALMS OF GOLD," in Schmidt, D., and J. Seale, eds., *Margaret Drabble*, 158-67.

Sage, Lorna, In *Contemporary English Novel*, 76-7.

Seiler-Franklin, C., *Boulder-Pushers*, 85-94.

Sharpe, Patricia, "On First Looking into THE REALMS OF GOLD," *MQR* 16 (Spring, 1977): 225-31.

A SUMMER BIRD-CAGE

Beards, Virginia K., "Margaret Drabble: Novels of a Cautious Feminist," *Crit* 15, i (1973): 36-8, 41. Also in Spacks, P. M., ed., *Contemporary Women Novelists*, 19-21, 23-4.

Davidson, Arnold E., "Pride and Prejudice in Margaret Drabble's A SUMMER BIRD-CAGE," *ArQ* 38, iv (Winter, 1982): 303-10.

Myer, V. G., *Margaret Drabble*, 31-4, 127-8.

Rose, E., *Novels of Margaret Drabble*, 1-7.

THE WATERFALL

Beards, Virginia K., "Margaret Drabble: Novels of a Cautious Feminist," *Crit* 15, i (1973): 43-6. Also in Spacks, P. M., ed. *Contemporary Women Novelists*, 26-9.

Campbell, Jane, "Margaret Drabble and the Search for Analogy," in Campbell, J., and J. Doyle, eds., *Practical Vision*, 140-4.

Creighton, Joanne V., "The Reader and Modern and Post-Modern Fiction," *CollL* 9, iii (Fall, 1982): 216-30.

Fuoroli, Caryn, "Sophistry or Simply Truth? Narrative Technique in Margaret Drabble's THE WATERFALL," *JNT* 11, ii (Spring, 1981): 110-24.

Korenman, Joan S., "The 'Liberation' of Margaret Drabble," *Crit* 21, iii (1980): 62-4.

Manheimer, Joan, "Margaret Drabble and the Journey to the Self," *SLitI* 11, ii (Fall, 1978): 135-9.

Myer, V. G., *Margaret Drabble*, 61-4, 122-6, 135-49.

Rose, Ellen C., "Feminine Endings—and Beginnings: Margaret Drabble's THE WATERFALL," *ConL* 21 (Winter, 1980): 81-99.

Rose, E. C., *Novels of Margaret Drabble*, 49-70.

Rubenstein, Roberta, "THE WATERFALL: The Myth of Psyche, Romantic Tradition, and the Female Quest," in Schmidt, D., and J. Seale, eds., *Margaret Drabble*, 139-57.

Seiler-Franklin, C. *Boulder-Pushers*, 116-27.

Walker, Nancy, "Women Drifting: Drabble's THE WATERFALL and Chopin's THE AWAKENING," *DQ* 17 (Winter, 1982): 88-96.

BIBLIOGRAPHY

Schmidt, Dorey, "A Bibliography Update: 1977-1981," in Schmidt, D., and J. Seale, eds., *Margaret Drabble*, 186-93.

DRIVER, C(HARLES) J(ONATHAN), 1939-

GENERAL

Smith, Roland, "The Plot Beneath the Skin: The Novels of C. J. Driver," *JCL* 10, i (Aug., 1975): 58-68. Also in Heywood, C., ed., *Aspects of South African Literature*, 145-54.

ELEGY FOR A REVOLUTIONARY

Smith, Roland, "The Plot Beneath the Skin: The Novels of C. J. Driver," *JCL* 10, i (Aug., 1975): 59-66. Also in Heywood, C., ed., *Aspects of South African Literature*, 146-52.

DURRELL, LAWRENCE, 1912-1990

GENERAL

Alyn, Marc, *The Big Supposer: Lawrence Durrell. A Dialogue*, tr. from the French by Francine Barker, London: Abelard-Schumann, 1973; N.Y.: Grove Pr., 1973.

Arthos, John, "Lawrence Durrell's Gnosticism," *Person* 43 (Summer, 1962): 360-73.

Dasenbrock, Reed W., "Death and the Counterlife of Heresy in Wyndham Lewis and Lawrence Durrell," *DL* 4, i (Sept., 1980): 3-16.

Diehl, Digby, "Lawrence Durrell at Caltech: An Interview," *USP* 6, ii (1975): 13-19.

Flint, R. W., "A Major Novelist," *Ctary* 27 (April, 1959): 353-6.

Fraser, G. S., *Lawrence Durrell*, 1968.

_____, *Lawrence Durrell*, 1970.

_____, *Lawrence Durrell*, rev. ed., 1973.

Friedman, Alan W., "A 'Key' to Lawrence Durrell," *WSCL* 8 (Winter, 1967): 31-42.

Glicksberg, Charles I., "The Fictional World of Lawrence Durrell," *BuR* 11, ii (Mar., 1963), 118-33.

Goldberg, Frederick, "The Movement toward Survival: Remystification in the Works of Lawrence Durrell," *DAI* 36 (1975): 2808A.

Goulianos, Joan, "A Conversation with Lawrence Durrell About Art, Analysis, and Politics," *MFS* 17, ii (Summer, 1971): 159-66.

_____, "Lawrence Durrell's Greek Landscape," *DAI* 31 (1971): 4770A-71A (Columbia).

Green, Martin, "Lawrence Durrell, II: A Minority Report," *YR* 49 (Summer, 1960): 496-508.

Hamard, Jean, "Lawrence Durrell: A European Writer," *DUJ* 60, ii (1968): 171-81.

Henig, Susanne, "Interview with Lawrence Durrell," *VWQ* 2, i-ii (1975): 4-12.

_____, "Lawrence Durrell: The Greatest of Them All," *VWQ* 2, i-ii (1975): 4-12. [Interview.]

Howarth, Herbert, "Lawrence Durrell and Some Early Masters," *BA* 37 (Winter, 1963): 5-11.

Kameyama, Masako, "Lawrence Durrell: A Sketch," in *Collected Essays by the Members of the Faculty*, No. 11, Kyoritsu, Japan: Kyoritsu Womens Junior College, 1968, 32-49.

Kelly, John, "Lawrence Durrell's Style," *Studies* 52 (Summer, 1963): 199-204.

Leslie, Ann, "This Infuriating Man—Lawrence Durrell," *Irish Digest* 82 (Feb., 1965): 67-70. [Not seen.]

Lund, Mary G., "Durrell: Soft Focus on Crime," *PrS* 35 (Winter, 1969): 339-44.

Lyons, Eugene, and Harry Antrim, "An Interview with Lawrence Durrell," *Shen* 22, ii (Winter, 1971): 42-58.

MacNiven, Ian S., "A Room in the House of Art: The Friendship of Anaïs Nin and Lawrence Durrell's 'Science Fiction in the True Sense'," *BRMMLA* 30 (1976): 61-70. [Not seen.]

Mitchell, Julian, and Gene Andrewski, "Lawrence Durrell," *ParisR* No. 22 (Autumn-Winter, 1960): 32-61. Also in *Writers at Work*, 2nd ser., 257-82.

Moore, H. T. ed., *World of Lawrence Durrell*.

Morrison, James R., "Time Structure in the Works of Lawrence Durrell," *DAI* 35 (1974): 116A-17A (Toronto).

Nittis, Dion W., "The Heraldic Universe of Lawrence Durrell," *DAI* 32 (1972): 4012A-13A (U.C.L.A.).

Sajavaara, K., *Imagery in Lawrence Durrell's Prose*.

Stoneback, Harry R., "Et in Alexandria Ego: Lawrence Durrell and the Spirit of Place," *MHLS* 5 (1982): 115-28.

Sullivan, Nancy, "Lawrence Durrell's Epitaph for the Novel," *Person* 44 (Winter, 1963): 79-88.

Unterecker, J., *Lawrence Durrell*. Also in Stade, G., ed., *Six Contemporary British Novelists*, 219-69.

Weigel, J. A., *Lawrence Durrell*.

Whiting, Brooke, comp., "[Special Issue on Lawrence Durrell,]" *Under the Sign of Pisces: Anais Nin & Her Circle* (Columbus, OH) 6, i (Spring, 1975).

Wickes, George, ed., *Lawrence Durrell, Henry Miller: A Private Correspondence*, N.Y.: Dutton, 1962.

Young, Kenneth, "A Dialogue with Durrell," *Encounter* 13 (Dec., 1959): 61-2, 64-8.

THE ALEXANDRIA QUARTET

Adam, Peter, "Alexandria and After: Lawrence Durrell in Egypt," *Listener* 99 (April 20, 1978): 497-500.

Aldington, Richard, in Moore, H. T., ed., *World of Lawrence Durrell*, 3-12.

Anderson, Barbara, "The Cinematic Qualities of Lawrence Durrell's ALEXANDRIA QUARTET," *DL* 2, ii (1978): 3-16.

Anderson, Roger K., "A LA RECHERCHE DU TEMPS PERDU and the ALEXANDRIA QUARTET: Searches for Reality," *DAI* 37 (1976): 291A.

Baldanza, Frank, "Lawrence Durrell's 'Word Continuum'," *Crit* 4, ii (Spring-Summer, 1961): 3-17.

Barrett, John W., "Lawrence Durrell's THE BLACK BOOK and THE ALEXANDRIA QUARTET: Some Existential and Jungian Correspondences," *DAI* 39 (1979): 4952A-53A.

Beja, Morris, *Epiphany in the Modern Novel*, 216-20.

Bliven, Naomi, "Books: Alexandrine in Tetrameter," *NY* 36 (Aug. 13, 1960): 97-103.

Bode, Carl, "Durrell's Way to Alexandria," *CE* 22 (May, 1961): 531-8. Also in Moore, H. T., ed., *World of Lawrence Durrell*, 205-21.

_____, "Lawrence Durrell," *John O'London's* 4 (Feb. 16, 1961): 169.

Bork, Alfred M., "Durrell and Relativity," *CRAS* 7 (Spring, 1963): 191-203.

Brewer, Jennifer L., "Character and Psychological Place: The Justine/Sophia Relation," *DL* 5, i (Fall, 1981): 236-9.

_____, "Lawrence Durrell's ALEXANDRIA QUARTET and the Hermetic Tradition," *DAI* 34 (1974): 5092A-93A (Tufts).

Brown, Sharon Lee, "Lawrence Durrell and Relativity," *DA* 26 (1966): 7310 (Oregon).

Burns, J. Christopher, "Durrell's Heraldic Universe," *MFS* 13 (Autumn, 1967): 375-88.

Card, James V. D., "'Tell Me, Tell Me': The Writer as Spellbinder in Lawrence Durrell's ALEXANDRIA QUARTET," *MBL* 1, i (1976): 74-83.

Cartwright, Michael P., "The ALEXANDRIA QUARTET: A Comedy for the Twentieth Century or Lawrence Durrell, the Pardoner, and His Miraculous Pig's Knuckle," *DAI* 31 (1971): 5391A (Neb.).

Cate, Curtis, "Lawrence Durrell," *Atlantic Monthly* 208 (Dec., 1961): 63-9.

Chaffin, Glenda L., "Musical Structure in Lawrence Durrell's THE ALEXANDRIA QUARTET," *DAI* 40 (1980): 5062A.

Chapman, R. T., "Dead or Just Pretending? Reality in THE ALEXANDRIA QUARTET," *CentR* 16, iv (Fall, 1972): 408-18.

Coffery, Osa D., "The QUARTET and the It: A Study of Lawrence Durrell's ALEXANDRIA QUARTET in Relation to the Theories of Georg Groddeck," *DA* 31 (1970): 1265A.

Coleman, John, "Mr. Durrell's Dimensions," *Spectator* (Feb. 19, 1960): 256-7.

Corke, Hilary, "Lawrence Durrell," *LHY* 2 (Jan., 1961): 43-9.

_____, "Mr. Durrell and Brother Criticus," *Encounter* 14 (May, 1960): 65-70.

Cortland, Peter, "Durrell's Sentimentalism," *EngR* 14 (April, 1964): 15-19.

Cox, W. D. G., in Moore, H. T., ed., *World of Lawrence Durrell*, 112-16.

Creed, Walter G., "Contemporary Scientific Concepts and the Structure of Lawrence Durrell's ALEXANDRIA QUARTET," *DAI* 30 (1969): 1165A (Pa.).

_____, *The Muse of Science and THE ALEXANDRIA QUARTET*, Norwood, PA: Academic-Monographs, Norwood Eds., 1977.

_____, "Pieces of the Puzzle: The Multiple Narrative Structure of THE ALEXANDRIA QUARTET," *Mosaic* 6, ii (Winter, 1973): 19-35.

_____, "'The Whole Pointless Joke'? Darley's Search for Truth in THE ALEXANDRIA QUARTET," *EA* 28, ii (April-June, 1975): 165-73.

Decancq, Roland, "What Lies Beyond? An Analysis of Darley's 'Quest' in Lawrence Durrell's ALEXANDRIA QUARTET," *RLV* 34 (1968): 134-50.

De Mott, Benjamin, "Grading the Emanglons," *HudR* 13 (Autumn, 1960): 457-64.

Dobrée, Bonamy, "Durrell's Alexandrian Series," *SR* 69 (Winter, 1961): 61-79. Also in Moore, H. T., ed., *World of Lawrence Durrell*, 184-204. Also in Dobrée, B., *The Lamp and the Lute*, London: Frank Cass & Co., 1964, 150-68.

Doulis, Thomas, "Stratis Tsirkas, the Voice from the Cellar," *JHD* 3 (July, 1975): 21-36.

Edel, Leon, *The Modern Psychological Novel*, N.Y.: Grosset & Dunlop, 1964, 185-91.

Elliott, George P., In Moore, H. T., ed., *World of Lawrence Durrell*, 87-94.

Enright, D. J., "Alexandrian Nights' Entertainments: Lawrence Durrell's QUARTET," *ILA* 3 (1961): 30-9.

Eskin, Stanley G., "Durrell's Themes in THE ALEXANDRIA QUARTET," *TQ* 5, iv (Winter, 1962): 43-60.

Fordham, Glenn W., Jr. "The Psychological Orientation Towards Growth in Lawrence Durrell's THE ALEXANDRIA QUARTET," *DAI* 42 (1981): 1159A.

Fraiberg, Louis, "Durrell's Dissonant Quartet," in Shapiro, C., ed., *Contemporary British Novelists*, 16-35.

Franklin, Steve, "Space-Time and Creativity in Lawrence Durrell's ALEXANDRIA QUARTET," *PCL* 5 (1979): 55-61.

Fraser, G. S., *Lawrence Durrell*, 129-62.

————, *Lawrence Durrell*, rev. ed., 114-48.

————, *Lawrence Durrell*, 1970, 33-9.

Friedman, Alan W., "Art for Love's Sake: Lawrence Durrell and THE ALEXANDRIA QUARTET," *DA* 27 (1966): 1365A-66A (Rochester).

————, "A 'Key' to Lawrence Durrell," *WSCL* 8 (Winter, 1967): 36-42.

————, *Lawrence Durrell and THE ALEXANDRIA QUARTET*.

Fruin, Jennifer L., "The Importance of Narouz in Durrell's Hermetic Paradigm," *DL* 2, iv (1979): 3-10.

Gindin, J., *Postwar British Fiction*, 215-22.

Glicksberg, Charles I., "The Fictional World of Lawrence Durrell," *BuR* 11, ii (Mar., 1963): 122-33.

————, *Self in Modern Literature*, 90-4.

Godshalk, William L., "Some Sources of Durrell's ALEXANDRIA QUARTET," *MFS* 13 (Autumn, 1967): 361-74.

Goldberg, Gerald J., "The Search for the Artist in Some Recent British Fiction," *SAQ* 62 (Summer, 1963): 387-92.

Gordon, Ambrose, Jr., "Time, Space and Eros: THE ALEXANDRIA QUARTET Rehearsed," in Sutherland, W. O. S., ed., *Six Contemporary Novels*, 6-21.

Gossman, Ann, "Love's Alchemy in the ALEXANDRIA QUARTET," *Crit* 13, ii (1971): 83-96.

————, "Some Characters in Search of a Mirror," *Crit* 8, iii (Spring-Summer, 1966): 179-84.

Goulianos, Joan, "Lawrence Durrell and Alexandria," *VQR* 45, iv (Autumn, 1969): 664-73.

Green, Martin, "Lawrence Durrell, II: A Minority Report," *YR* 49 (Summer, 1960): 498-500. Also in Moore, H. T., ed., *World of Lawrence Durrell*, 132-8.

Hagopian, John V., "The Resolution of the ALEXANDRIA QUARTET," *Crit* 7 (Spring, 1964): 96-106.

Hamard, Jean, "Lawrence Durrell: A European Writer," *DUJ* 60, ii (1968): 171-81.

Hartt, J. N., *Lost Image of Man*, 63-7.

Hawkins, Joanna L., "A Study of the Relationship of Point of View to the Structure of THE ALEXANDRIA QUARTET," *DA* 26 (1965): 3338-39 (Northwestern).

Highet, Gilbert, "The Alexandrians of Lawrence Durrell," *Horizon* 2 (Mar., 1960): 113-18.

Howarth, Herbert, "Durrell Snapped in a Library," *LonM* 12, i (April-May, 1972): 71-84.

————, "A Segment of Durrell's QUARTET," *UTQ* 32 (April, 1963): 282-93.

Hutchens, Eleanor H., "The Heraldic Universe in THE ALEXANDRIA QUARTET," *CE* 24 (Oct., 1962): 56-61.

Ionescu, Mihai C., "Alexandria: Eros, Agape, Agon," *Secolul* 20, ix (1968): 12-18.

Johnson, Ann S., "Lawrence Durrell's 'Prism-Sightedness': The Structure of THE ALEXANDRIA QUARTET," *DA* 29 (1968): 264A (Un. of Pennsylvania).

Jones, Leslie W., "'Selected Fictions': The Intersection of Life and Art in THE ALEXANDRIA QUARTET," *DL* 2, i (1978): 11-23.

Karl, F. R., "Lawrence Durrell: Physical and Metaphysical Love," *Contemporary English Novel*, 40-61.

Katope, Christopher G., "Cavafy and Durrell's THE ALEXANDRIA QUARTET," *CL* 21, ii (Spring, 1969): 125-38.

Kazin, A., *Contemporaries*, 188-92.

Kelly, John C., "Lawrence Durrell: THE ALEXANDRIA QUARTET," *Studies* 52 (Spring, 1963): 52-68.

————, "Lawrence Durrell's Style," *Studies* 52 (Summer, 1963): 199-204.

Kermode, Frank, "Fourth Dimension," *REL* 1, ii (April, 1960): 73-7.

————, *Puzzles and Epiphanies*, 218-27.

"The Kneller Tape (Hamburg)," in Moore, H. T., ed., *World of Lawrence Durrell*, 161-8.

Kolek, Leszek, "Elements of the Novel of Ideas in THE ALEXANDRIA QUARTET," 121-30 in Zins, Henryk, ed., *Studia Anglistyczne Lubelskiego Orodka Naukowego*, Warsaw: PWN, 1975.

Kopper, Edward A., Jr., "A Note on the Religious Imagery in THE ALEXANDRIA QUARTET," *STwC* 10 (Fall, 1972): 115-20.

Kothandaraman, Bala, "The Comic Dimension in THE ALEXANDRIA QUARTET," *OJES* 9, i (1972): 27-37.

Kruppa, Joseph E., "Durrell's ALEXANDRIA QUARTET and the 'Implosion' of the Modern Consciousness," *MFS* 13 (Autumn, 1967): 401-16.

"Lawrence Durrell Answers a Few Questions," in Moore, H. T., ed., *World of Lawrence Durrell*, 156-60.

Lebas, Gérard, "The Fabric of Durrell's ALEXANDRIA QUARTET," *Caliban* 8 (1971): 139-50.

————, "The Mechanisms of Space-Time in THE ALEXANDRIA QUARTET," *Caliban* 7 (1970): 80-97.

Lemon, Lee T., "THE ALEXANDRIA QUARTET: Form and Fiction," *WSCL* 4, iii (Autumn, 1963): 327-32.

Lennon, John M., "Pursewarden's Death: 'A Stray Brick from Another Region'," *MLS* 6, i (1976): 22-8.

Levidova, I., "A 'Four-Decker' in Stagnant Waters," *Anglo-Soviet Jnl.* 23 (Summer, 1962): 39-41.

Levitt, Morton P., "Art and Correspondences: Durrell, Miller, and THE ALEXANDRIA QUARTET," *MFS* 13 (Autumn, 1967): 299-313.

Lewis, Nancy W., "Lawrence Durrell's ALEXANDRIA QUARTET and the Rendering of Post-Einsteinian Space," *DAI* 37 (1977): 7143A-44A.

————, "Two Thematic Applications of Einsteinian Field Structure in THE ALEXANDRIA QUARTET," *DL* 5, i (Fall, 1981): 242-3.

Littlejohn, David, "Lawrence Durrell: The Novelist as Entertainer," *Motive* 23 (Nov., 1962): 14-16.

————, "The Permanence of Lawrence Durrell," *ColQ* 14 (Summer, 1965): 63-71. Also in *Interruptions*, 82-90.

Lund, Mary G., "The Alexandrian Projection," *AR* 21 (Summer, 1961): 193-204.

————, "The Big Rock Crystal Mountain," *FQ* 11 (May, 1962): 15-18.

_____, "Eight Aspects of Melissa," *ForumH* 3, ix (Winter, 1962): 18-22.

_____, "Submerge for Reality: The New Novel Form of Lawrence Durrell," *SWR* 64 (Summer, 1959): 229-35.

Lyons, Eugene, "Thematic Problems in Lawrence Durrell's THE ALEXANDRIA QUARTET," *DA* 31 (1970): 393A-4A.

Mackworth, Cecily, "Lawrence Durrell and the New Romanticism," *TC* 167 (Mar., 1960): 203-13. Also in Moore, H. T., ed., *World of Lawrence Durrell*, 24-37.

Maclay, Joanna H., "The Interpreter and Modern Fiction: Problems of Point of View and Structural Tensiveness," in Doyle, Esther M., and Virginia H. Floyd, eds., *Studies in Interpretation*, v. 1, 155-69.

Manzalaoui, Mahmoud, "Curate's Egg: An Alexandrian Opinion of Durrell's QUARTET," *EA* 15 (July, 1962): 248-60.

Mellard, Joan, "The Unity of Lawrence Durrell's ALEXANDRIA QUARTET," *LNL* 1, i (1975): 77-143.

Michot, Paulette, "Lawrence Durrell's ALEXANDRIA QUARTET," *RLV* No. 5 (1960): 361-7.

Morcos, Mona L., "Elements of the Autobiographical in THE ALEXANDRIA QUARTET," *MFS* 13 (Autumn, 1967): 343-59.

Morris, R. K., *Continuance and Change*, 51-70.

Morrison, Ray, "'A Mirror Reference to Reality': Justine as a Schopenhauerian Woman in THE ALEXANDRIA QUARTET," *DL* 5, i (Fall, 1981): 42-50. Goulianos, Joan R., response, 52-62.

Neifer, Leo J., "Durrell's Method and Purpose of Art," *WisSL* No. 3 (1966): 99-103.

Nichols, James R., "Lawrence Durrell's ALEXANDRIA QUARTET: The Paradise of Bitter Fruit," *DL* 3, ii (1979): 11-28.

_____, "The Paradise of Bitter Fruit: Lawrence Durrell's ALEXANDRIA QUARTET," *DL* 5, i (Fall, 1981): 224-34.

O'Brien, R. A., "Time, Space and Language in Lawrence Durrell's ALEXANDRIA QUARTET," *DL* 5, i (Fall, 1981): 224-34.

_____, "Time, Space and Language in Lawrence Durrell," *Waterloo Rev* 6 (Winter, 1961): 16-24.

Peirce, Carol M., "Pynchon's V. and Lawrence Durrell's ALEXANDRIA QUARTET: A Seminar in the Modern Tradition," *PNotes* 8 (Feb., 1982): 23-7.

_____, "'Wrinkled Deep in Time': THE ALEXANDRIA QUARTET as Many-Layered Palimpsest," *DL* 2, iv (1979): 11-28.

Petrulian, Catrinel P., "Lawrence Durrell's Quartet," *RITL* 25 (1976): 397-401.

Pinchin, Jane L., "Durrell and a Masterpiece of Size," in Pinchin, J. L., *Alexandria Still*, 159-207.

_____, "Durrell's Fatal Cleopatra," *MFS* 28, ii (Summer, 1982): 222-36. Also in *DL* 5, i (Fall, 1981): 24-39. Goulianos, Joan R., response, 52-62.

Ping, Chan Soo, "Lawrence Durrell: Time in THE ALEXANDRIA QUARTET," Unpublished master's thesis, Un. of Malaya, 1969.

Pleu-Petrulian, Catrinel, "Lawrence Durrell's QUARTET," *RITL* 25, iii (1976): 397-401.

Pritchett, V. S., "Alexandrian Hothouse," *Working Novelist*, 30-5.

Proser, Matthew N., "Darley's Dilemma: The Problem of Structure in Durrell's ALEXANDRIA QUARTET," *Crit* 4, ii (Spring-Summer, 1961): 18-28.

Read, Phyllis J., "The Illusion of Personality: Cyclical Time in Durrell's ALEXANDRIA QUARTET," *MFS* 13 (Autumn, 1967): 389-99.

Rieger-Pratt, Anna, "Lawrence Durrell's ALEXANDRIA QUARTET: A 'Novelist's Novel'?" *KN* 28, iii-iv (1981): 357-67.

Rippier, J. S., *Some Postwar English Novelists*, 106-33.

Robillard, Douglas, Jr., "In the Capital of Memory: The Alexandria of Durrell and Cavafy," *DL* 5, i (Fall, 1981): 78-87.

Robinson, W. R., "Intellect and Imagination in THE ALEXANDRIA QUARTET," *Shen* 18 (Summer, 1967): 55-68.

Russo, John P., "Love in Lawrence Durrell," *PrS* 43, iv (Winter, 1969-70): 396-407.

Sajavaara, K., *Imagery in Lawrence Durrell's Prose*, 178-97.

Scholes, Robert, "Return to Alexandria: Lawrence Durrell and the Western Narrative Tradition," *VQR* 40 (Summer, 1964): 411-20. Also in Scholes, R., *Fabulators*, 17-31. Also in *Fabulation and Metafiction*, 29-36.

Schwerdt, Lisa, "Coming of Age in Alexandria: The Narrator," *DL* 5, i (Fall, 1981): 210-21.

Steiner, George, "Lawrence Durrell, I: The Baroque Novel," *YR* 49 (Summer, 1960): 488-95. Also in Steiner, G., *Language and Silence; Essays on Language, Literature and the Inhuman*, N.Y.: Atheneum, 1967, 280-7. Also in Moore, H. T., ed., *World of Lawrence Durrell*, 13-23.

Stoneback, Harry R., "*Et in Alexandria Ego: Lawrence Durrell and the Spirit of Place*," *MHLS* 5 (1982): 115-28.

Stromberg, Robert L., "The Contribution of Relativity to the Inconsistency of Form in THE ALEXANDRIA QUARTET," *DL* 5, i (Fall, 1981): 246-56.

Sullivan, Nancy, "Lawrence Durrell's Epitaph for the Novel," *Person* 44 (Winter, 1963): 79-88.

Sykes, Gerald, in Moore, H. T., ed., *World of Lawrence Durrell*, 146-55.

Tanner, William E., "Charactonyms in THE ALEXANDRIA QUARTET," *South-Central Names Institute Publications* 1 (1971): 123-6. Also in Tarpley, Fred, and Ann Moseley, eds., *Of Edsels and Marauders*, Commerce, TX: Names Institute Pr., 1971, 123-6.

Taylor, Chet, "Dissonance and Digression: The Ill-Fitting Fusion of Philosophy and Form in Lawrence Durrell's ALEXANDRIA QUARTET," *MFS* 17, ii (Summer, 1971): 167-79.

Thornton, Lawrence, "Narcissism and Selflessness in THE ALEXANDRIA QUARTET," *DL* 1, iv (1978): 3-23.

Trilling, Lionel, in Moore, H. T., ed., *World of Lawrence Durrell*, 49-65.

Unterecker, J., *Lawrence Durrell*, 36-46. Also in Stade G., ed., *Six Contemporary British Novelists*, 257-69.

_____, "The Protean World of Lawrence Durrell," in Kostelanetz, R., ed., *On Contemporary Literature*, 322-9.

Vipond, Dianne L., "Art, Artist, and Aesthetics in Lawrence Durrell's ALEXANDRIA QUARTET," *DAI* 41 (1981): 4396A.

Waelti-Walters, Jennifer, "Coincidental Perceptions (Michel Butor and Lawrence Durrell)," *DL* 3, iv (1980): 13-20.

Weatherhead, A. K., "Romantic Anachronism in THE ALEXANDRIA QUARTET," *MFS* 10 (Summer, 1964): 128-36.

Wedin, Warren, "The Artist as Narrator in THE ALEXANDRIA QUARTET," *TCL* 18, iii (July, 1972): 175-80.

_____, "The Unity of a Continuum: Relativity and THE ALEXANDRIA QUARTET," *DAI* 32 (1971): 1535A-36A (Ariz.).

Weigel, J. A., *Lawrence Durrell*, 56-112.

Wotton, G. E., in Moore, H. T., ed., *World of Lawrence Durrell*, 103-11.

Young, Thomas B., "Thematic Emphasis and Psychological Realism in Lawrence Durrell's ALEXANDRIA QUARTET," *DAI* 34 (1974): 5214A-15A (Ohio State).

Zivley, Sherry A. L., "The Unity of Lawrence Durrell's ALEXANDRIA QUARTET," *DAI* 34 (1973): 2667A (Tulane).

THE BLACK BOOK

Allen, W., *Modern Novel*, 284-8.

Barrett, John W., "Lawrence Durrell's THE BLACK BOOK and THE ALEXANDRIA QUARTET: Some Existential and Jungian Correspondences," *DAI* 39 (1979): 4952A-53A.

Brigham, James A., "An Unacknowledged Trilogy," *DL* 2, iii (1979): 3-12.

Brown, Sharon L., "THE BLACK BOOK: A Search for Method," *MFS* 13 (Autumn, 1967): 319-28.

_____, "Lawrence Durrell and Relativity," *DA* 26 (1966): 7310 (Oregon).

Fraser, G. S., *Lawrence Durrell*, 61-83.

_____, *Lawrence Durrell*, rev. ed., 46-68.

_____, *Lawrence Durrell*, 1970, 27-33.

Glicksberg, Charles I., "The Fictional World of Lawrence Durrell," *BuR* 11, ii (Mar., 1963): 118-22.

_____, *Self in Modern Literature*, 89-90.

Moore, Harry T., In Moore, H. T., ed., *World of Lawrence Durrell*, 100-2.

Pollock, John J., "Eliot's 'Little Gidding' and Lawrence Durrell," *CLAJ* 24, ii (Dec., 1980): 190-3.

Pritchett, V. S., "Alexandrian Hothouse," *Living Novel*, 303-9.

Rexroth, Kenneth, "The Artifice of Convincing Immodesty," *The Griffin* 9 (Sept., 1960): 3-9. Also in *Assays*, N.Y.: New Directions, 1962, 125-30.

Richtofen, Patrick von, "Lawrence Durrell, Prince of Denmark," *DL* 4, ii (Dec., 1980): 3-14.

Sajavaara, K., *Imagery in Lawrence Durrell's Prose*, 171-5.

Unterecker, J., *Lawrence Durrell*, 11-12, 24-31. Also in Stade, G., ed., *Six Contemporary British Novelists*, 230-1, 242-8.

Weigel, J. A., *Lawrence Durrell*, 43-8.

CLEA (See also THE ALEXANDRIA QUARTET)

Hagopian, John V., in Hagopian, J. W., and Dolch, M., eds., *Insight II*, 95-103.

Weyergans, Franz, "CLEA, by Lawrence Durrell," *Revue Nouvelle* 32 (July 15, 1960): 94-8.

THE DARK LABYRINTH (CEFALU)

Fraser, G. S., *Lawrence Durrell*, 96-100. Rev. ed., 81-5.

Goldberg, Frederick, "THE DARK LABYRINTH: Journeys beneath the Landscape," *DL* 2, iii (1979): 13-22.

Sajavaara, K., *Imagery in Lawrence Durrell's Prose*, 175-8.

Weigel, J. A., *Lawrence Durrell*, 48-54.

LIVIA

Carley, James P., "Lawrence Durrell's Avignon Quinicunx and Gnostic Heresy," *DL* 5, i (Fall, 1981): 284-304. Also in *Malahat Rev* 61 (Feb., 1982): 156-67.

MacNiven, Ian S., "Steps to LIVIA: The State of Durrell's Fiction," *DL* 5, i (Fall, 1981): 330-47.

MONSIEUR

Carley, James P., "An Interview with Lawrence Durrell on the Background to MONSIEUR and Its Sequels," *MHRev* 51 (1979): 42-6.

_____, "Lawrence Durrell and the Gnostics," *DL* 2, i (1978): 3-10.

_____, "Lawrence Durrell's Avignon Quincunx and Gnostic Heresy," *DL* 5, i (Fall, 1981): 284-304. Also in *Malahat Rev* 61 (Feb., 1982): 156-67.

Dasenbrock, Reed W., "Death and the Counterlife of Heresy in Wyndham Lewis and Lawrence Durrell," *DL* 5, i (Fall, 1981): 306-27.

MacNiven, Ian S., "Steps to LIVIA: The State of Durrell's Fiction," *DL* 5, i (Fall, 1981): 330-47.

MOUNTOLIVE (See also THE ALEXANDRIA QUARTET)

Mullins, Edward, "On MOUNTOLIVE," *Two Cities* 1 (April 15, 1959): 21-4.

NUNQUAM

Dasenbrock, Reed W., "Death and the Counterlife of Heresy in Wyndham Lewis and Lawrence Durrell," *DL* 5, i (Fall, 1981): 306-27.

Fraser, G. S, *Lawrence Durrell*, 1970, 40-3.

_____, *Lawrence Durrell*, rev. ed., 149-68.

Kenedy, R. C., "Lawrence Durrell: TUNC-NUNQUAM," *ArtI* 14, vii (1970): 23-9, 80.

Mablekos, Carole, "Lawrence Durrell's TUNC and NUNQUAM: Rebirth Now or Never," *Sphinx* 4, i (1981): 48-54.

Trail, George Y., "Durrell's Io: A Note on TUNC and NUNQUAM," *NConL* 5, ii (1975): 9-12.

Unterecker, John, "Fiction at the Edge of Poetry," in Friedman, N. W., ed., *Forms of Modern British Fiction*, 181-5.

PANIC SPRING

Brigham, James A., "An Unacknowledged Trilogy," *DL* 2, iii (1979): 3-12.

Weigel, J. A., *Lawrence Durrell*, 41-3.

PIED PIPER OF LOVERS

Brigham, James A., "An Unacknowledged Trilogy," *DL* 2, ii (1979): 3-12.

Weigel, John A., "Lawrence Durrell's First Novel," *TCL* 14 (July, 1968): 75-83.

TUNC

Dasenbrock, Reed W., "Death and the Counterlife of Heresy in Wyndham Lewis and Lawrence Durrell," *DL* 5, i (Fall, 1981): 306-27.

Dickson, Gregory, "Spengler's Theory of Architecture in Durrell's TUNC and NUNQUAM," *DL* 5, i (Fall, 1981): 272-80.

"Fiction of 1968. Lawrence Durrell: TUNC," in *T. L. S. Essays and Reviews from The Times Literary Supplement, 1968*, 63-8. Also in *TLS* (April 25, 1968).

Fraser, G. S., *Lawrence Durrell*, 164-91. Rev. ed., 149-68.

_____, *Lawrence Durrell*, 1970, 40-3.
Kenedy, R. C.,"Lawrence Durrell: TUNC-NUNQUAM," *ArtI* 14, vii (1970): 23-9, 80.
Mablekos, Carole, "Lawrence Durrell's TUNC and NUN-QUAM: Rebirth Now or Never," *Sphinx* 4, i (1981): 48-54.
Sajavaara, K., *Imagery in Lawrence Durrell's Prose*, 197-202.
Trail, George Y., "Durrell's Io: A Note on TUNC and NUN-QUAM," *NConL* 5, iii (1975): 9-12.
Unterecker, John, "Fiction at the Edge of Poetry," in Friedman, A. W., *Forms of Modern British Fiction*, 181-5.

WHITE EAGLES OVER SERBIA

Fraser, G. S., *Lawrence Durrell*, 127-8.
Weigel, J. A., *Lawrence Durrell*, 54-5.

BIBLIOGRAPHY

Beebe, Maurice, "Criticism of Lawrence Durrell: A Selected Checklist," *MFS* 13 (Autumn, 1967): 417-21.
Friedman, A. W., *Lawrence Durrell and THE ALEXANDRIA QUARTET*, 191-213.
Lebas, Gérard, "Lawrence Durrell's ALEXANDRIA QUARTET and the Critics: A Survey of Published Criticism," *Caliban* 6 (1969): 91-114.
Thomas, Alan G., in Fraser, G. S., *Lawrence Durrell*, 200-50.
Weigel, J. A., *Lawrence Durrell*, 163-70.

EARLY, ROBERT, 1940-

POWERS AND DOMINATIONS

Jeffrey, Susu, "Voice as Protaganist: An Interpretation of Robert Early's POWERS AND DOMINATIONS," in Baldanza, F., ed., *Itinerary 3: Criticism*, 63-6.

EASTLAKE, WILLIAM (DERRY), 1917-

GENERAL

Clough, David, "William Eastlake and the Human Beings," *Planet* 49/50 (Jan., 1980): 102-11.
Haslam, Gerry,"William Eastlake: Portrait of the Artist as Shaman," *WR* 8, i (1971): 3-13. [Not seen.]
McCaffery, Larry, "Absurdity and Oppostions in William Eastlake's Southwestern Novels," *Crit* 19, ii (1977): 62-76.
Milton, John R., "The Land as Form in Frank Waters and William Eastlake," *KanQ* 2, ii (Spring, 1970): 104-9.
Phelps, Donald, "The Land of Grace and Isolation," *Nation* 199 (Oct. 12, 1964): 225-7.
Wylder, Delbert E., "The Novels of William Eastlake," *NMQ* 34 (Summer, 1964): 188-203. Also in Pilkington, W. T., ed., *Critical Essays on the Western American Novel*, 197-209.

THE BAMBOO BED

Beidler, Philip D., "Truth-Telling and Literary Values in the Vietnam Novel," *SAQ* 78, ii (Spring, 1979): 146-9.

THE BRONC PEOPLE

Gold, Herbert, "Wit and Truth," *Nation* 187 (Sept. 20, 1968): 158-9.
Woolf, Douglas, "One of the Truly Good Men," *EvR* 2, No. 8 (Spring, 1959): 194-6.
Wylder, Delbert E., "The Novels of William Eastlake," *NMQ* 34 (Summer, 1964): 190-7. Also in Pilkington, W. T., ed., *Critical Essays on the Western American Novel*, 199-205.

GO IN BEAUTY

Graham, Don, "William Eastlake's First Novel: An Account of the Making of GO IN BEAUTY," *WAL* 16, i (Spring, 1981): 27-37.
Wylder, Delbert E., "The Novels of William Eastlake," *NMQ* 34 (Summer, 1964): 189-90. Also in Pilkington, W. T., ed., *Critical Essays on the Western American Novel*, 198-9.

PORTRAIT OF AN ARTIST WITH TWENTY-SIX HORSES

Smith, William J., "An Original, Thus Disturbing, Talent," *Cweal* 78 (June 21, 1963): 357.
Wylder, Delbert E., "The Novels of William Eastlake," *NMQ* 34 (Summer, 1964): 197-200. Also in Pilkington, W. T., ed. *Critical Essays on the Western American Novel*, 205-7.

EKWENSI, CYPRIAN (ODIATU DUAKE), 1921-

Bede, Jacques L. J. B., "African Town Environment in Contemporary Literature," *CM* 1 (1975): 18-32 *passim*.
Emenyonu, E., *Cyprian Ekwensi*.
Granqvist, Raoul, "Interview: Cyprian Ekwensi," *Kunapipi* 4, i (1981): 124-9.
Greenstein, Susan M., "Cyprian Ekwensi and Onitshe Market Literature," in Ballard, W. L., ed., *Esays on African Literature*, 175-90.
Killam, Douglas, in King, B., *Introduction to Nigerian Literature*, 77-95.
Lindfors, Bernth, "Cyprian Ekwensi: An African Popular Novelist," *ALT* 3 (1969): 2-14. Also in Lindfors, B., *Folklore in Nigerian Literature*, 116-28.
_____, "Interview with Cyprian Ekwensi," *Dem-Say*, 24-34.
_____, "Interview with Cyprian Ekwensi," *WLWE* 13 (1974): 142-54.
McClusky, John, "The City as a Force: Three Novels by Cyprian Ekwensi," *JBS* 7, ii (Dec., 1976): 211-24.
Nkosi, Lewis, and Dennis Duerden, "Cyprian Ekwensi," *SAfrL* 1 (1972): 76-83. [Interviews.]
Obiechina, Emmanuel N., "Ekwensi as Novelist," *PA* 86 (Summer, 1973): 152-64.
Okonkwo, Juliet I., "Ekwensi and Modern Nigerian Culture," *ArielE* 7, ii (April, 1976): 32-45.
_____, "Ekwensi and The 'Something New and Unstable' In Modern Nigerian Culture," in Nwoga, D. I., ed. *Literature and Modern West Indian Culture*, Benin City: Ethiope, 1978, 130-42.
Osofisan, Femi, "Domestication of an Opiate: Western Paraesthetics and the Growth of the Ekwensi Tradition," *Positive Rev* 1, iv (Jan.-Feb., 1981): 1-12.
Palmer, Eustace, "Cyprian Ekwensi," *SAfrL* 3 (1979): 36-62.

_____, *Growth of the African Novel*, 36-61.

Passmore, Dennis R.,"Camp Style in the Novels of Cyprian O. D. Ekwensi," *JPC* 4, ii (Winter, 1971): 705-16.

Povey, John, "Cyprian Ekwensi: The Novelist and the Pressure of the City," in Wright, E., ed., *Critical Evaluation of African Literature*, 73-94.

BEAUTIFUL FEATHERS

Emenyonu, E., *Cyprian Ekwensi*, 101-15.

Killam, Douglas, in King, B., ed., *Introduction to Nigerian Literature*, 91-2.

Laurence, M.,"Masks of the City," *Long Drums and Cannons*, 158-61.

McClusky, John, "The City as a Force; Three Novels by Cyprian Ekwensi," *JBS* 7, ii (Dec., 1976): 211-24.

Povey, John, "Cyprian Ekwensi and BEAUTIFUL FEATHERS," *Crit* 8, i (Autumn, 1965): 63-9.

_____, "Cyprian Ekwensi: The Novelist and the Pressure of the City," in Wright, E., ed., *Critical Evaluation of African Literature*, 85-9.

BURNING GRASS

Emenyonu, E., *Cyprian Ekwensi*, 95-100.

Laurence, Margaret, "Masks of the City," *Long Drums and Cannons*, 157-8.

Palmer, E., *Growth of the African Novel*, 54-6.

ISKA

Emenyonu, E., *Cyprian Ekwensi*, 116-23.

Killam, Douglas, in King, B., ed., *Introduction to Nigerian Literature*, 92-3.

Laurence, Margaret, "Masks of the City," *Long Drums and Cannons*, 162-8.

Povey, John, "Cyprian Ekwensi: The Novelist and the Pressure of the City," in Wright, E., ed., *Critical Evaluation of African Literature*, 89-92.

JAGUA NANA

Abraham, Cecil, "No Longer at Ease," *CJAS* 14 (1980): 529-31.

Cook, David, "A Good Bad Heroine. A Study of Cyprian Ekwensi's JAGUA NANA," *African Literature*, 144-57.

Cosentino, Donald, "Jagua Nana: Culture Heroine," *Ba Shiru* 8, i (1977): 11-17.

Emenyonu, E., *Cyprian Ekwensi*, 9-11, 78-95, 105-15.

Hawkins, Loretta A., "The Free Spirit of Ekwensi's Jagua Nana," *ALT* 10 (1979): 202-6.

Killam, Douglas, in King, B., ed., *Introduction to Nigerian Literature*, 86-91.

Larson, C. R., *Emergence of African Fiction*, 87-91.

Laurence, Margaret, "Masks of the City," *Long Drums and Cannons*, 152-7.

Linnemann, Russell J., "Structural Weakness in Ekwensi's JAGUA NANA," *EinA* 4, i (1977): 32-9.

McClusky, John, "The City as a Force: Three Novels by Cyprian Ekwensi," *JBS* 7, ii (Dec., 1976): 211-24.

Palmer, E., *Growth of the African Novel*, 45-53.

Povey, John, "Cyprian Ekwensi: The Novelist and the Pressure of the City," in Wright, E., ed., *Critical Evaluation of African Literature*, 81-5.

Roscoe, A. A., *Mother is Gold*, 90-2.

Shelton, Austin, "'Rebushing' on Ontological Recession to Africanism: Jagua's Return to the Village," *PA* 18 (1963): 49-58.

PEOPLE OF THE CITY

Emenyonu, E., *Cyprian Ekwensi*, 27-46.

Killam, Douglas, in King, B., ed., *Introduction to Nigerian Literature*, 80-7.

Laurence, Margaret, "Masks of the City," *Long Drums and Cannons*, 149-52.

McClusky, John, "The City as a Force: Three Novels by Cyprian Ekwensi," *JBS* 7, ii (Dec., 1976): 211-24.

Melamu, John, "The Plight of the City Man in Ekwensi's PEOPLE OF THE CITY," *EESB* 2, ii (Feb., 1971): 36-8.

Palmer, E., *Growth of the African Novel*, 39-45.

Povey, John, "Cyprian Ekwensi: The Novelist and the Pressure of the City," in Wright, E., ed., *Critical Evaluation of African Literature*, 76-81.

Roscoe, A. A., *Mother is Gold*, 88-90.

Taiwo, O., *Introduction to West African Literature*, 152-62.

WHEN LOVE WHISPERS

Emenyonu, E., *Cyprian Ekwensi*, 23-8.

ELKIN, STANLEY L(AWRENCE), 1930-

GENERAL

Bailey, Peter J., "Pattern and Perception in the Fiction of Stanley Elkin," *DAI* 41 (1980): 1585A.

Bargen, D. G., *Fiction of Stanley Elkin*.

Bernt, Phyllis, and Joseph Bernt, eds. "Stanley Elkin on Fiction: An Interview," *PrS* 50, i (1976): 14-25.

Colbert, Robert E., "The American Salesman as Pitchman and Poet in the Fiction of Stanley Elkin," *Crit* 21, ii (1979): 52-8.

Ditsky, John, "'Death Grotesque as Life': The Fiction of Stanley Elkin," *HC* 19, iii (June, 1982): 1-11.

Duncan, Jeffrey L., "A Conversation with Stanley Elkin and William H. Gass," *IowaR* 7, i (1976): 48-77.

Hardaway, Francine O., "The Power of the Guest: Stanley Elkin's Fiction," *BRMMLA* 32 (1978): 234-45. [Not seen.]

LeClair, Thomas, "The Obsessional Fiction of Stanley Elkin," *ConL* 16, ii (Spring, 1975): 146-62.

_____, "Stanley Elkin: The Art of Fiction LXI," *ParisR* 66 (Summer, 1976): 54-86.

Sanders, Scott [R.]., "An Interview with Stanley Elkin," *ConL* 16, ii (Spring, 1975): 131-45.

A BAD MAN

Bargen, D. G., *Fiction of Stanley Elkin*, 102-17.

Guttmann, A., *Jewish Writer in America*, 84-5.

LeClair, Thomas, "The Obsessional Fiction of Stanley Elkin," *ConL* 16, ii (Spring, 1975): 150-3.

THE BAILBONDSMAN

Bargen, D. G., *Fiction of Stanley Elkin*, 169-76.

BOSWELL: A MODERN COMEDY

Guttmann, Allen, "Stanley Elkin's Orphans," *MR* 7 (Summer, 1966): 598-600. Also in Guttmann, A., *Jewish Writer in America*, 81-3.

LeClair, Thomas, "The Obsessional Fiction of Stanley Elkin," *ConL* 16, ii (Spring, 1975): 148-50.

THE CONDOMINIUM

Bargen, D. G., *Fiction of Stanley Elkin*, 185-94.

THE DICK GIBSON SHOW

Bargen, D. G., *Fiction of Stanley Elkin*, 135-66.

LeClair, Thomas, "The Obsessional Fiction of Stanley Elkin," *ConL* 16, ii (Spring, 1975): 153-6.

Olderman, Raymond M., "The Six Crises of Dick Gibson," *IowaR* 7, i (1976): 127-40.

THE FRANCHISER

Bargen, D. G., *Fiction of Stanley Elkin*, 118-32, 248-52.

_____, "Stanley Elkin's THE FRANCHISER," *SAJL* 2 (1982): 132-43.

McCaffery, Larry, "Stanley Elkin's Recovery of the Ordinary," *Crit* 21, ii (1979): 39-51.

THE LIVING END

Raff, Malvin, "Wyndham Lewis and Stanley Elkin: Salvation, Satire, and Hell," *StCS* 8 (Spring, 1981): 1-8.

THE MAKING OF ASHENDEN

Bargen, D. G., *Fiction of Stanley Elkin*, 177-84, 236-9.

Wilde, Alan, "'Strange Displacement of the Ordinary': Apple, Elkin, Barthelme, and the Problems of the Excluded Middle," *Boundary* 10, ii (Winter, 1982): 188-92.

BIBLIOGRAPHY

Bargen, D. G., *Fiction of Stanley Elkin*, 313-18.

McCaffery, Larry, "Stanley Elkin: A Bibliography, 1957-1977," *BB* 34, ii (April-June, 1977): 73-6.

ELLIOTT, GEORGE P(AUL), 1918-1980

GENERAL

Brustein, Robert, "George P. Elliott," *Asch* 50, iii (Summer, 1981): 355-8.

Gelfant, Blanche H., "Beyond Nihilism: The Fiction of George P. Elliott," *HC* 5 (Dec., 1968): 1-12.

DAVID KNUDSEN

Greensberg, Alvin, "The Novel of Disintegration: Paradoxical Impossibility in Contemporary Fiction," *WSCL* 7 (Winter-Spring, 1966):108-9.

Slatoff, Walter, "George P. Elliott," *Epoch* 12 (Spring, 1962): 60-2.

Solotaroff, Theodore, "The Fallout of the Age," *Red Hot Vacuum*, 37-43.

IN THE WORLD

Kramer, Hilton, "Liberal Verities," *New Leader* 48 (Oct. 11, 1965): 22-3.

Slatoff, Walter, *Epoch* 15 (Winter, 1966): 190-1.

THE KISSING MAN

Duffy, Denis, "George Elliott: THE KISSING MAN," *ConL* 63 (Winter, 1975): 52-63.

ELLISON, RALPH, 1914-1994

GENERAL

Anderson, Jervis, "Profiles: Going to the Territory," *NY* (Nov. 22, 1976): 55-108.

Blake, Susan L., "Ritual and Rationalizaton: Black Folklore in the Works of Ralph Ellison," *PMLA* 94, i (Jan., 1979): 121-36.

Bone, Robert, "Ralph Ellison and the Uses of Imagination," *TriQ* No. 6 (1966): 39-54. Also in Hill, Herbert, ed., *Anger and Beyond: the Negro Writer in the United States*, N.Y.: Harper, 1966, 86-111. Also in Hersey, J., ed., *Ralph Ellison*, 95-114. Also in Reilly, J. M., ed., *Twentieth Century Interpretations of INVISIBLE MAN*, 22-31. Also in Cooke, M. G., ed., *Modern Black Novelists*, 45-63.

Britt, David D., "The Image of the White Man in the Fiction of Langston Hughes, Richard Wright, James Baldwin and Ralph Ellison," *DA* 19 (1968): 1532A (Emory).

Bucco, Martin, "Ellison's Invisible West," *WAL* 10 (Nov., 1975): 237-8.

Callahan, John F., "Chaos, Complexity and Possibility: The Historical Frequencies of Ralph Waldo Ellison," *BALF* 11, iv (1977): 130-8.

Carson, David L., "Ralph Ellison: His Fiction and Its Backgrounds," *DAI* 37 (1977): 5823A.

_____, "Ralph Ellison: Twenty Years After," *SAF* 1, i (1973): 1-23. [Interview.]

Chargois, Josephine A., "Two Views of Black Alienation: A Comparative Study of Chinua Achebe and Ralph Ellison," *DAI* 34 (1974): 7742A (Ind.).

Chester, Alfred, and Vilma Howard, "The Art of Fiction VIII: Ralph Ellison," *ParisR* No. 8 (Spring, 1955). Also in *Writers at Work*, 2nd ser., 317-34. Also in Ellison, Ralph, *Shadow and Act*, N.Y.: Random House, 1964, 167-83.

Chisolm, Lawrence W., "Signifying Everything," *YR* 54, iii (Spring, 1965): 450-4. Also in Hersey, J., ed., *Ralph Ellison*, 31-5.

Corry, John, "Profile of an American Novelist: A White View of Ralph Ellison," *BlackW* 20, ii (1970): 116-25.

Daniel, Therman B., "The Image of Man as Portrayed by Ralph Ellison," *CLAJ* 10, iv (June, 1967): 277-84.

Deutsch, Leonard J., "Affirmation in the Work of Ralph [Waldo] Ellison," *DAI* 33 (1972): 2928A (Kent State).

Dietze, R. F., *Ralph Ellison*.

Ellison, Ralph, "A Dialogue with His Audience," *BaratR* 3 (1968): 51-3.

_____, "That Same Pain, That Same Pleasure: An Interview," *Shadow and Act*, N.Y.: Random House, 1964, 3-23. Also in *December* 3 (Winter, 1961).

Feuser, Willfried F., "The Men Who Lived Underground: Richard Wright and Ralph Ellison," in King, B., and K. Ogungbesan, eds., *Celebration of Black and African Writing*, 87-101.

Geller, Allen, "An Interview with Ralph Ellison," *TamR* No. 32 (Summer, 1964): 3-24. Also in Bigsby, C. W. E., ed., *Black American Writer*, Vol. I, 153-68.

Gibson, Donald B., "Ralph Ellison (1914-) and James Baldwin (1924-)," in Panichas, G. A., ed., *Politics of Twentieth-Century Novelists*, 307-20.

Graham, John, "Ralph Ellison," in Garrett, G., ed., *Writer's Voice*, 221-27. [Interview.]

Hersey, John, "Introduction: A Completion of Personality: A Talk with Ralph Ellison," in Hersey, J., ed., *Ralph Ellison*, 1-19.
_____, ed. *Ralph Elllison*.

Hyman, Stanley E., "Ralph Ellison in Our Time," *New Leader* 47, xxii (Oct. 26, 1964): 21-2. Also in Hersey, J., ed., *Ralph Ellison*, 39-42.

Isaacs, Harold R., "Five Writers and Their African Ancestors," *Phylon* 21 (1960): 317-22.

Kaiser, Ernest, "A Critical Look at Ellison's Fiction and at Social and Literary Criticism by and about the Author," *BlackW* 20, ii (Dec., 1970): 53-9, 81-97.

Kent, George E., "Ralph Ellison and Afro-American Folk and Cultural Tradition," *CLAJ* 13, iii (Mar., 1970): 265-76.

Klein, M., *After Alienation*, 71-107.

Kostelanetz, Richard, "The Negro Genius," *TC* 1033 (1967): 49-50.
_____, "Ralph Ellison: Novelist as Brown Skinned Aristocrat," *Shen* 20, iv (Summer, 1969): 56-77.

Lehan, Richard, "The Strange Silence of Ralph Ellison," *CEJ* 1 (1965): 63-8. [Not seen.]

Maxwell, Joan L. B., "Themes of Redemption in Two Major American Writers, Ralph Ellison and Richard Wright," *DAI* 37 (1976): 1549A.

McPherson, James A., "Indivisible Man," *Atlantic* 226, vi (Dec., 1970): 45-60. Also in Hersey, J., ed., *Ralph Ellison*, 43-57.

Nadel, Alan M., "Invisible Criticism: A Study in Allusion," *DAI* 42 (1981): 1637A-38A.

Neal, Larry, "Ellison's Zoot Suit," *BlackW* 20, ii (Dec., 1970): 31-50. Also in Hersey, J., ed., *Ralph Ellison*, 58-79.

O'Brien, John, ed., *Interviews with Black Writers*, 63-77.

O'Daniel, Therman B., "The Image of Man as Portrayed by Ralph Ellison," *CLAJ* 10 (June, 1967): 277-84.

O'Meally, R. G., *Craft of Ralph Ellison*.
_____, "Riffs and Rituals: Folklore in the Work of Ralph Ellison," in Fisher, Dexter, and Robert B. Stepto, eds., *Afro-American Literature: The Reconstruction of Instruction*, N.Y.: MLA, 1979, 153-69.

Paliwal, G. D., "African Consciousness in Modern American Fiction: A Note on Novels by Wright, Ellison and Baldwin," *RUSEng* 10 (1977): 62-70. [Not seen.]

Pugh, Griffith T., and Others, "Three Negro Novelists: A Symposium," *SHR* 4 (1970): 17-50.

Robinson, Douglas, "Visions of 'No' End: The Anti-Apocalyptic Novels of Ellison, Barth, and Coover," *AmSS* 13, i (1981): 1-16.

Rodnon, Stewart, "Henry Adams and Ralph Ellison: Transcending Tragedy," *SHum* 3, ii (June, 1973): 1-7.

Rubin, Steven J., "Richard Wright and Ralph Ellison: Black Existential Attitudes," *DAI* 30 (1969): 2041A (Mich.).

Sage, Howard, "An Interview with Ralph Ellison: Visible Man," *Pulp* (Flushing, N.Y.) 2, ii (1976): 10-11, 12.

Schultz, Elizabeth A., "The Heirs of Ralph Ellison: Patterns of Individualism in the Contemporary Afro-American Novel," *CLAJ* 22, ii (Dec., 1978): 101-22.

Skerrett, Joseph T., "The Wright Interpretation: Ralph Ellison and the Anxiety of Influence," *MR* 21, i (1980): 196-212.

Stepto, Robert B., and Michael S. Harper, "Study and Experience: An Interview with Ralph Ellison," in Harper, M. S., and R. B. Stepto, eds., *Chant of Saints*, 451-69.

"'Study and Experience': An Interview with Ralph Ellison," *MR* 18 (1977): 417-35.

Thompson, James, Lennox Raphael, and Steve Cannon," 'A Very Stern Discipline": An Interview with Ralph Ellison," *Harpers* 234 (Mar., 1967): 76-95.

Warren, Robert Penn, "The Unity of Experience," *Ctary* 39, v (May, 1965): 91-6. Also in Hersey, J., ed., *Ralph Ellison*, 21-6.

Williams, Philip G., "A Comparative Approach to Afro-American and Neo-African Novels: Ellison and Achebe," *SBL* 7, i (1976): 15-18.

Zietlow, Edward R., "Wright to Hansberry: The Evolution of Outlook in Four Negro Writers," *DA* 28 (1967): 701A (Un. of Wash.).

INVISIBLE MAN

Abrams, Robert E., "The Ambiguities of Dreaming in Ellison's INVISIBLE MAN," *AL* 49, iv (1978): 592-603.

Alexander, Sandra C., "The Scapegoat Archetype in Ralph Ellison's INVISIBLE MAN," in Carter, G. E., and J. R. Parker, eds., *Afro-American Folklore*, 31-8.

Allen, Michael, "Some Examples of Faulknerian Rhetoric in Ellison's INVISIBLE MAN," in Bigsby, C. W. E., ed., *Black American Writer*, Vol. I, 143-51.

Allen, W., *Modern Novel*, 317-20.

Baker, Houston A., Jr., "A Forgotten Prototype: THE AUTOBIOGRAPHY OF AN EX-COLORED MAN and INVISIBLE MAN," *VQR* 49, iii (Summer, 1973): 433-49. Also in Baker, Houston A., Jr., *Singers of Daybreak: Studies in Black American Literature*, Washington, D.C.: Howard Un. Pr., 1974, 17-31.

Balet, S., "The Problem of Characterization in Ralph Ellison's INVISIBLE MAN," *FMod* 15 (1975): 277-81.

Bataille, Robert, "Ellison's INVISIBLE MAN: The Old Rhetoric and the New," *BALF* 12, ii (1978): 43-5.

Baumbach, Jonathan, "Nightmare of a Native Son: Ralph Ellison's INVISIBLE MAN," *Crit* 6, i (Spring, 1963): 48-65. Also in Baumbach, J., *Landscape of Nightmare*, 68-86. Also in Cooke, M. G., *Modern Black Novelists*, 64-78. Also in Gibson, D. B., ed., *Five Black Writers*, 73-87.

Bell, J. D., "Ellison's INVISIBLE MAN," *Expl* 29 (1970): Item 19.

Bellow, Saul, "Man Underground," *Ctary* 13, vi (June, 1952): 608-10. Also in Hersey, J., ed., *Ralph Ellison*, 27-30.

Bennett, John Z., "The Race and the Runner: Ellison's INVISIBLE MAN," *XUS* 5 (Mar., 1966): 12-26.

Bennett, Stephen B., and Willliam W. Nichols, "Violence in Afro-American Fiction: An Hypothesis," *MFS* 17, ii (Summer, 1971): 221-8. Also in Hersey, J., ed., *Ralph Ellison*, 171-5.

Bentson, Kimberly W., "Ellison, Baraka, and the Faces of Tradition," *Boundary* 6, ii (Winter, 1978): 333-54.

Berghahn, M., *Images of Africa in Black American Literature*, 167-71.

Bigsby, C. W. E., "From Protest to Paradox: The Black Writer at Mid Century," in French, W., ed., *Fifties*, 229-34.

Blake, Susan L., "Ritual and Rationalization: Black Folklore in the Works of Ralph Ellison," *PMLA* 94, i (Jan., 1979): 126-30.

Bloch, Alice, "Sight Imagery in INVISIBLE MAN," *EJ* 55 (Nov., 1966): 1019-21, 1024.

Bluestein, Gene, "The Blues as a Literary Theme," *MR* 8 (Autumn, 1967): 600-17. Also in *Voice of the Folk: Folklore and American Literary Theory*, Amherst: Un. of Mass. Pr., 1972, 124-40.

Bone, R. A. *Negro Novel in America*, 197-212.

Bontemps, Arna, in Griffin, W., ed. *Literature in the Modern World*, 119-22.

Boulger, James D., "Puritan Allegory in Four Modern Novels," *Thought* 44 (Autumn, 1969): 413-32 *passim*.

Breit, Harve, in Balakian, N., and C. Simmons, eds. *Creative Present*, 18-21.

Brennan, Timothy, "Ellison and Ellison: The Solipsism of INVISIBLE MAN," *CLAJ* 25, ii (Dec., 1981): 162-81.

Brown, Lloyd W., "Ralph Ellison's Exhorters: The Role of Rhetoric in INVISIBLE MAN," *CLAJ* 13, iii (Mar., 1970): 289-303.

Bryant, J. H., *Open Decision*, 277-81.

_____, "Wright, Ellison, Baldwin: Exorcising the Demon," *Phylon* 37, ii (June, 1976): 174-88.

Butler, Robert J., "Patterns of Movement in Ellison's INVISIBLE MAN," *AmerS* 21, i (1980): 5-21.

Callahan, John F., "The Historical Frequencies of Ralph Waldo Ellison," in Harper, M. S., and R. B. Stepto, eds., *Chant of Saints*, 40-51.

Cash, Earl A., "The Narrators in INVISIBLE MAN and NOTES FROM THE UNDERGROUND: Brothers in the Spirit," *CLAJ* 16 (1973): 505-7.

Cheshire, Ardner R., Jr., "INVISIBLE MAN and the Life of Dialogue" *CLAJ* 20, i (Sept., 1976): 19-34.

Clarke, John H., "The Visible Dimensions of INVISIBLE MAN," *BlackW* 20, ii (1970): 27-30.

Clipper, Lawrence J., "Folkloric and Mythic Elements in INVISIBLE MAN," *CLAJ* 13, iii (Mar., 1970): 229-41.

Collier, Eugenia, "Dimensions of Alienation in Two Black American and Caribbean Novels," *Phylon* 43, i (Mar., 1982): 46-56.

Cowan, Michael, "Walkers in the Street: American Writers and the Modern City," *Prospects* 6 (1981): 303-8.

Deutsch, Leonard J., "Ralph Waldo Ellison and Ralph Waldo Emerson: A Shared Moral Vision," *CLAJ* 16, iii (Dec., 1972): 159-78.

_____, "THE WASTE LAND in Ellison's INVISIBLE MAN," *NConL* 7, vi (1977): 5-6.

Dietze, R. F., *Ralph Ellison*.

Ehlers, Leigh A., "'Give Me the Ocular Proof': OTHELLO and Ralph Ellison's INVISIBLE MAN," *NConL* 6, v (1976): 10-11.

Ellison, Ralph, "Light on INVISIBLE MAN," *Crisis* 60 (Mar., 1953): 157-8.

Fass, Barbara, "Rejection and Paternalism: Hawthorne's MY KINSMAN MAJOR MOLINEAUX and Ellison's INVISIBLE MAN," *CLAJ* 14, iii (Mar., 1971): 317-23.

Fenel, Howard D., "Foxtrot: A Creative Interpolation of the Smoker Scene in INVISIBLE MAN by Ralph Ellison," *NALF* 10 (1976): 106-7.

Fischer, Russell G., "INVISIBLE MAN as History," *CLAJ* 17 (1974): 338-67.

Ford, Nick A., "The Ambivalence of Ralph Ellison," *BlackW* 20, ii (Dec., 1970): 5-9.

_____, "Four Popular Negro Novelists," *Phylon* 15 (1954): 34-7.

Foster, Frances S., "The Black and White Masks of Franz Fanton and Ralph Ellison," *BARev* 1, iv (Winter, 1970): 46-58.

Fraiberg, Selma, "Two Modern Incest Heroes," *PR* 28, v-vi (Fall/Winter, 1961): 655-61. Also in Reilly, J. M., ed., *Twentieth Century Interpretations of INVISIBLE MAN*, 73-9.

Gayle, A., Jr., *Way of the New World*, 204-13.

Geller, Allen. "An Interview with Ralph Ellison," *TamR* No. 32 (Summer, 1964): 3-24.

Gérard, Allbert, "Humanism and Negritude: Notes on the Contemporary Afro-American Novel," *Diogenes* No. 37 (Spring, 1962): 121-4.

Girson, Rochell, "Sidelights on Invisibility," *SatR* 36 (Mar. 14, 1953): 20+.

Glicksberg, Charles I., "The Symbolism of Vision," *SWR* 39 (Summer, 1954): 259-65. Also in Reilly, J. M., ed., *Twentieth Century Interpretations of INVISIBLE MAN*, 48-55.

Godson, Stewart, "THE ADVENTURES OF HUCKLEBERRY FINN and INVISIBLE MAN: Thematic and Structural Comparisons," *NALF* 4 (1970): 45-51.

Goede, William, "On Lower Frequencies: The Buried Men in Wright and Ellison," *MFS* 15, iv (Winter, 1969-1970): 483-501. [Wright's "The Man Who Lived Underground" as a Source for INVISIBLE MAN.]

Gottschalk, Jane, "Sophisticated Jokes: The Use of American Authors in INVISIBLE MAN," *Ren* 30, ii (1978): 69-77.

Gray, Valerie B., "INVISIBLE MAN's Literary Heritage: BENITO CERENO and MOBY-DICK," *DAI* 37 (1977): 7129A.

Gretlund, Jan, in Bogh, J., and S. Skovmand, eds., *Six American Novels*, 185-212.

Griffin, Edward M., "Notes from a Clean, Well-Lighted Place: Ralph Ellison's INVISIBLE MAN," *TCL* 15, ii (Oct., 1969): 129-44.

Griffin, Wilford, "Ellison's INVISIBLE MAN," *Expl* 36, ii (1978): 28-9.

Griffith, Patricia A. T., "The Technoscape in the Modern Novel: Aleksandr Solzhenitsyn's THE FIRST CIRCLE and Ralph Ellison's INVISIBLE MAN," *DAI* 36 (1976): 7403A-04A.

Gross, T. L., *Heroic Ideal in American Literature*, 161-4.

Grow, Lynn M., "The Dream Scenes of INVISIBLE MAN," *WSUB* 50, iii (Aug., 1974): 3-12.

Gunod, Roberta Z., "An Anomaly of 'and'," *LNL* 2, ii (Summer, 1977): 19-42 *passim*.

Guttmann, Alan, "Focus on Ralph Ellison's INVISIBLE MAN American Nightmare," in Madden, D., ed., *American Dreams, American Nightmares*, 188-96.

Gysin, F., *Grotesque in American Negro Fiction*, 165-279.

Hansen, J. T., "A Holistic Approach to INVISIBLE MAN," *MELUS* 6, i (1979): 41-54.

Harris, Trudier, "Ellison's 'Peter Wheatstraw': His Basis in Black Folk Tradition," *MissFR* 9 (1975): 117-26.

Hassan, I., *Radical Innocence*, 169-78.

Haupt, Garry, "The Tragi-Comedy of the Unreal in Ralph Ellison's INVISIBLE MAN and Mark Twain's ADVENTURES OF HUCKLEBERRY FINN," *Interpretations* 4 (1972): 1-12.

Havemann, Carol Sue P., "The Fool as Mentor in Modern American Parables of Entrapment: Ken Kesey's ONE FLEW OVER THE CUCKOO'S NEST, Joseph Heller's CATCH-22 and Ralph Ellison's INVISIBLE MAN," *DA* 32 (1971): 2091A-92A.

Hays, Peter L., "The Incest Theme in INVISIBLE MAN," *WHR* 23, iv (Autumn, 1969): 335-9.

Henderson, H. B., III, *Versions of the Past*, 285-99.

Holland, Laurence B., "Ellison in Black and White: Confession, Violence and Rhetoric in INVISIBLE MAN," in Lee, A. R., ed., *Black Fiction*, 54-73.

Hori, Keiko, "Symbols in INVISIBLE MAN," 538-46 in *Yamakawa Kozo Kyoju Taikan Kinen Ronbunshu*, Toyonaka: n.p., 1981.

Horowitz, Ellin, "The Rebirth of the Artist," in Kostelanetz, R., ed., *On Contemporary Literature*, 330-46. Also in Reilly, J. M., ed., *Twentieth Century Interpretations of INVISIBLE MAN*, 80-8.

Horowitz, Floyd R., "The Enigma of Ellison's Intellectual Man," *CLAJ* 7 (Dec., 1963): 126-32.

_____, "An Experimental Confession from a Reader of INVISIBLE MAN," *CLAJ* 13, iii (Mar., 1970): 304-14.

_____, "Ralph Ellison's Modern Version of Brer Bear and Brer Rabbit in INVISIBLE MAN," *MASJ* 4, ii (Fall, 1963): 21-7. Also in Reilly, J. M., ed., *Twentieth Century Interpretations of INVISIBLE MAN*, 32-8.

Howard, David C., "Points in Defense of Ellison's INVISIBLE MAN," *NConL* 1, i (Jan., 1971): 13-14.

Howe, Irving, "Black Boys and Native Sons," in Howe, I., *World More Attractive*, 112-15. Also in Hersey, J., ed., *Ralph Ellison*, 35-8. Also in Gibson, D. E., ed., *Five Black Writers*, 264-6. Also in *Dissent* 10, iv (Autumn, 1963): 362-4.

Hutchinson, James D., "The INVISIBLE MAN as Anti-hero," *DQ* 6 (Spring, 1971): 86-92.

Hux, Samuel H., "American Myth and Existential Vision: The Indigenous Existentialism of Mailer, Bellow, Styron, and Ellison," *DA* 26 (1966): 5437 (Conn.).

Inness, Jeanne, "Ralph Ellison's INVISIBLE MAN: Five Major Intellectual Ancestors," *DAI* 38 (1977): 263A.

Jackson, Esther M., "The American Negro and the Image of the Absurd," *Phylon* 23 (Winter, 1962): 368-71. Also in Reilly, J. M., ed., *Twentieth Century Interpretations of INVISIBLE MAN*, 64-72.

Johnson, Abby A., "Birds of Passage: Flight Imagery in INVISIBLE MAN," *STwC* 14 (Fall, 1974): 91-104.

_____, "From Ranter to Writer: Ralph Ellison's INVISIBLE MAN," *SAB* 42, ii (1977): 35-44.

Kaiser, Ernest, "A Critical Look at Ellison's Fiction and at Social and Literary Criticism by and about the Author," *BlackW* 20, ii (Dec., 1970): 53-9, 81-97.

Kent, George E., "Ralph Ellison and Afro-American Folk and Cultural Tradition," *CLAJ* 13, iii (Mar., 1970): 265-76. Also in Hersey, J., ed., *Ralph Ellison*, 160-70. Also in Kent, G., *Blackness and the Adventure of Western Culture*, 154-62.

Kist, E. M., "A Laingian Analysis of Blackness in Ralph Ellison's INVISIBLE MAN," *SBL* 7, ii (1976): 19-23.

Klein, M., *After Alienation*, 107-46. Also in Gross, S. L., and J. E. Hardy, eds., *Images of the Negro in American Literature*, 249-64. Also in Gibson, D. B., ed., *Five Black Writers*, 88-101.

Klinzing, John, "The INVISIBLE MAN and Today's Education," *EducF* 35, iv (May, 1971): 431-8.

Klotman, Phyllis R., "The Running Man as Metaphor in Ellison's INVISIBLE MAN," *CLAJ* 13, iii (Mar., 1970): 277-88.

Knox, George, "The Negro Novelist's Sensibility and the Outsider Theme," *WHR* 11 (Spring, 1957): 137-48.

_____, "The ToTenTanz in Ellison's INVISIBLE MAN," *Fabula* 12 (1971): 168-78.

Kostelanetz, Richard, "The Politics of Ellison's Booker: INVISIBLE MAN as Symbolic History," *ChiR* 19, ii (1967): 5-26.

Lane, James B., "Underground to Manhood: Ralph Ellison's INVISIBLE MAN," *NALF* 7 (1973): 64-72.

Langman, F. H., "Reconsidering INVISIBLE MAN," *CR* 18 (1976): 114-27.

Le Clair, Thomas, "The Blind Leading the Blind: Wright's NATIVE SON and a Brief Reference to Ellison's INVISIBLE MAN," *CLAJ* 13, iii (Mar., 1970): 315-20.

Lee, A. Robert, "Sight and Mask: Ralph Ellison's INVISIBLE MAN," *NALF* 4 (1970): 22-33.

Lee, L. L., "The Proper Self: Ralph Ellison's INVISIBLE MAN," *Descant* 10 (Spring, 1966): 38-48.

Lehan, R., *Dangerous Crossing*, 150-7.

_____, "Existentialism in Recent American Fiction: The Demonic Quest," *TSLL* 1 (Summer, 1959): 195-6, 199-200.

_____, "The Strange Silence of Ralph Ellison," *CEJ* 1, ii (1965): 63-8.

Lewis, R. W. B. "Days of Wrath and Laughter," *Trials of the Word*, 218-20.

Lieber, Todd M., "Ralph Ellison and the Metaphor of Invisibility in Black Literary Tradition," *AQ* 24 (1972): 86-100.

Lieberman, Marcia R., "Moral Innocents: Ellison's INVISIBLE MAN and CANDIDE," *CLAJ* 15, i (Sept., 1971): 64-79.

Lillard, Stewart, "Ellison's Ambitious Scope in INVISIBLE MAN," *EJ* 58, vi (Sept., 1969): 833-9.

Littlejohn, D., *Black on White*, 110-19.

Loheyde, Katherine M. J., "Freedom and Identity in INVISIBLE MAN," *EngR* 32, i (1981): 6-8.

Ludington, Charles T., Jr., " Protest and Anti-Protest: Ralph Ellison," *SHR* 4, i (Winter, 1970): 31-9.

Ludwig, J., *Recent American Novelists*, 19-24.

Lutwack, L., *Heroic Fiction*, 122-41.

Marcus, Steven, "The American Negro in Search of Identity," *Ctary* 16 (Nov., 1953): 458-9.

Margolies, E., "History as Blues: Ralph Ellison's INVISIBLE MAN," *Native Sons*, 127-48.

Martin, Mike W., "INVISIBLE MAN and the Indictment of Innocence," *CLAJ* 25, iii (Mar., 1982): 288-302.

Mason, Clifford, "Ralph Ellison and the Underground Man," *BlackW* 20, ii (Dec., 1970): 20-6.

Maxwell, Richard D., "A New Viewpoint: the Invisible Narrator," *CCR* 2, i (1977): 24-9.

May, J. R., *Toward a New Earth*, 146-55.

McDaniel, Barbara A., "John Steinbeck: Ralph Ellison's Invisible Source," *PCP* 8 (1973): 28-33.

Mengeling, Marvin E., "Whitman and Ellison: Older Symbols in a Modern Mainstream," *WWR* 12 (Sept., 1966): 67-70.

Miller, Stuart, *The Picaresque Novel*, Cleveland: Case Western Reserve Un., 1967, 134-5.

Mills, Nicolaus, "Class and Crowd in American Fiction," *CentR* 24, ii (Spring, 1980): 212-17.

Mitchell, Louis D., and Henry J. Stauffenberg, "Ellison's B. P. Rinehart: 'Spiritual Technologist'," *NALF* 9 (1975): 51-2.

_____, Invisibility—Permanent or Resurrective," *CLAJ* 17, iii (Mar., 1974): 379-86.

Mueller, William R.,"A Portrait of the Negro as a Young Man," *Celebration of Life*, 50-68.

Nadel, Alan M.,"The 'Oh Oh Oh' in INVISIBLE MAN," *AN&Q* (Supp. 1) (1978): 320-1.

Nagpal, B. R., "Quest Motif: Ellison's INVISIBLE MAN," *JSL* 5, i-ii (1977-78): 162-5.

Nash, R. W., "Stereotypes and Social Types in Ellison's INVISIBLE MAN," *Sociological Qtly* 6 (1965): 349-60.

Naylor, Carolyn A., "Cross-Gender Significance of the Journey Motif in Selected Afro-American Fiction," *CLQ* 18, i (Mar., 1982): 36-8.

Neal, Larry, "Ellison's Zoot Suit," *BlackW* 20, ii (Dec., 1970): 31-52.

Nettlebeck, C. W., "From Inside Destitution: Céline's Berdamu and Ellison's Invisible Man," *SoRA* 7, iii (Nov., 1974): 246-53.

Nichols, Charles H., "Comic Modes in Black America (A Ramble through Afro-American Humor,)" in Cohen, S. B., ed., *Comic Relief*, 110-16.

Nichols, William W., "Ralph Ellison's Black American Scholar," *Phylon* 31 (Spring, 1970): 70-5.

O'Daniel, Therman B., "The Image of Man as Portrayed by Ralph Ellison," *CLAJ* 10 (June, 1967): 277-84. Also in Gibson, D. B., ed., *Five Black Writers*, 102-7. Also in Reilly, J. M., ed., *Twentieth Century Interpretations of INVISIBLE MAN*, 89-95.

Okeke-Ezigbo, Emeka, "Ellison's INVISIBLE MAN," *Expl* 39, iii (Spring, 1981): 33-4.

Olderman, Raymond M., "Ralph Ellison's Blues and INVISIBLE MAN," *WSCL* 7 (Summer, 1976): 142-59.

Oliver, M. Celeste, "INVISIBLE MAN and the Numbers Game," *CLAJ* 22 (1978): 123-33.

Omans, Stuart E., "The Variations on a Masked Leader: A Study on the Literary Relationship of Ralph Ellison and Herman Melville," *SAB* 40, ii (May, 1975): 15-23.

O'Meall, R. G., *Craft of Ralph Ellison*, 76-104.

————, "INVISIBLE MAN: 'Black and Blue'," *MV* 3, i (1979): 21-35.

Overmyer, Janet, "The INVISIBLE MAN and White Women," *NConL* 6, iii (May, 1976): 13-15.

Palms, Rosemary H. G., "The Double Motif in Literature: From Origins to an Examination of Three Modern American Novels," *DA* 33 (1972): 321A.

Parrish, Paul A., "Writing as Celebration: The Epilogue of INVISIBLE MAN," *Ren* 26, iii (Spring, 1974): 152-7.

Pearce, R., *Stages of the Clown*, 118-23.

Powell, Grosvenor E., "Role and Identity in Ralph Ellison's INVISIBLE MAN, in Burrows, D., and others, *Private Dealings*, 99-105.

Pryse, Marjorie, "Ralph Ellison's Heroic Fugitive," *AL* 46, i (Mar., 1974): 1-15.

————, "INVISIBLE MAN: the World in a Man-of-War," *The Mark and the Knowledge*, 143-67.

Przemecka, Irena, "Search for Identity in the American Negro Novel," *KN* 22, ii (1975): 188-90.

Radford, Frederick L., "The Journey Towards Castration: Interracial Stereotypes in Ellison's INVISIBLE MAN," *JAmS* 4, ii (Feb., 1971): 227-31.

Randall, John H., III,"Ralph Ellison: INVISIBLE MAN," *RLV* 31 (1965): 24-45.

Rao, B. Ramachandra, "INVISIBLE MAN: A Study," in Maini, D. S., ed., *Variations on American Literature*, 93-8.

Reilly, J. M., ed., *Twentieth Century Interpretations of INVISIBLE MAN*.

Robinson, Douglas, "Visions of 'No' End: The Anti-Apocalyptic Novels of Ellison, Barth, and Coover," *AmSS* 13, i (1981): 7-9.

Rodnon, Stewart,"THE ADVENTURES OF HUCKLEBERRY FINN and the INVISIBLE MAN," *NALF* 4 (1970): 45-51.

————, "Henry Adams and Ralph Ellison: Transcending Tragedy," *SHum* 3, ii (June, 1973): 1-7.

————,"Ralph Ellison's INVISIBLE MAN: Six Tentative Approaches," *CLAJ* 12, iii (Mar., 1969): 244-58.

Rollins, Ronald G., "Ellison's INVISIBLE MAN," *Expl* 30, ii (Nov., 1971): Item 22.

Rosenblatt, R., *Black Fiction*, 184-99.

Rovit, Earl H., "Ralph Ellison and the American Comic Tradition," *WSCL* 1, iii (Fall, 1960): 34-42. Also in Waldmeir, J. J., ed., *Recent American Fiction*, 167-74. Also in Hersey, J., ed., *Ralph Ellison*, 151-9. Also in Reilly, J. M., ed., *Twentieth Century Interpretations of INVISIBLE MAN*, 56-63. Also in Gibson, D. B., ed., *Five Black Writers*, 108-115.

Ruotolo, L. P., *Six Existential Heroes*, 81-98.

Rupp, Richard H., "Ralph Ellison: A Riotous Feast of the Self," *Celebration in Postwar American Fiction*, 151-63.

Ruzicka, Dolores A., "Ralph Ellison's INVISIBLE MAN as a Repository of Major Elements from Principal Western Literary Traditions," *DAI* 34 (1974): 4283A-84A (So. Calif.).

Sadler, Lynn V., "Ralph Ellison and the Bird-Artist," *SAB* 44, iv (Nov., 1979): 20-30.

Saito, Tadatoshi, "Ralph Ellison and James Baldwin in the 1950's," in *American Literature in the 1950's*, 32-7.

Sanders, Archie D., "Odysseus in Black: An Analysis of the Structure of INVISIBLE MAN," *CLAJ* 13, iii (Mar., 1970): 217-28.

Sandiford, Keith A., "Ralph Ellison and George Lamming: Two Episodes, One Myth," *MV* 3, ii (Fall, 1979): 19-25.

Savory, Jerold J., "Descent and Baptism in NATIVE SON, INVISIBLE MAN, and DUTCHMAN," *CSR* 3, i (1973): 33-7.

Schafer, William J., "Irony From Underground—Satiric Elements in INVISIBLE MAN," *SNL* 7 (Fall, 1969): 22-8. Also in Reilly, J. M., ed., *Twentieth Century Interpretations of INVISIBLE MAN*, 39-47.

————, "Ralph Ellison and the Birth of the Anti-Hero," *Crit* 10, ii (1968): 81-93. Also in Hersey, J., ed., *Ralph Ellison*, 115-26.

Schor, Edith, "The Early Fiction of Ralph Ellison: The Genesis of INVISIBLE MAN," *DAI* 34 (1973): 2654A-55A (Columbia).

Schraufnagel, N., *From Apology to Protest*, 77-87.

Scott, Nathan A., Jr.,"Judgment Marked by a Cellar: The American Negro Writer and the Dialectic of Despair," *UDQ* 2, ii (1967): 30-4. Also in Mooney, H. J., and T. F. Staley, eds., *Shapeless God*, 164-8.

Scruggs, Charles W., "Ralph Ellison's Use of the AENEID in INVISIBLE MAN," *CLAJ* 17 (1974): 368-78.

Selke, Harmut K., "An Allusion to Sartre's THE FLIES in Ralph Ellison's INVISIBLE MAN," *NConL* 4, iii (May, 1974): 3-4.

————, "'The Education at College of Fools': References to Emerson's 'Self-Reliance' in INVISIBLE MAN," *NConL* 4, i (1974): 13-15.

Sequeira, Isaac, "Notes from the Illuminated Underground: The Initiation of the INVISIBLE MAN," *OJES* 11 (1974-75): 47-60.

————, "The Uncompleted Initiation of the Invisible Man," *SBL* 6, i (Spring, 1975): 9-13.

Singh, V. D. "INVISIBLE MAN: The Rhetoric of Colour, Chaos, and Blindness," *RUSEng* 8 (1975): 54-61.

Singleton, M. K, "Leadership Mirages as Antagonists in INVIS-IBLE MAN," *ArQ* 22 (Summer, 1966): 157-71. Also in Reilly, J. M., ed., *Twentieth Century Interpretations of INVISIBLE MAN*, 11-21.

Spillers, Hortense, "Ellison's 'Usable Past': Toward a Theory of Myth," *Interpretations* 9, i (1977): 53-69.

Stark, John, "INVISIBLE MAN: Ellison's Black Odyssey," *NALF* 7 (1973): 60-3.

Steele, Shelby, "Ralph Ellison's Blues," *JBS* 7, ii (Dec., 1976): 151-68.

Steinbrink, Jeffrey, "Toward a Vision of Infinite Possibility: A Reading of INVISIBLE MAN," *SBL* 7, iii (1976): 1-15.

Stepto, Robert B., "Literacy and Hibernation: Ralph Ellison's INVISIBLE MAN," *From Behind the Veil: A Study of Afro-American Narrative*, Urbana: Un. of Illinois Pr., 1979, 163-94.

Sylvander, Carolyn W., "Ralph Ellison's INVISIBLE MAN and Female Stereotypes," *NALF* 9 (1975): 77-9.

Tanner, Tony, "The Music of Invisibility," in Tanner, T., *City of Words*, 50-64. Also in Hersey, J., ed., *Ralph Ellison*, 80-94.

Thomas, Gillian, and Michael Larsen, "Ralph Ellison's Conjure Doctors," *ELN* 17, iv (June, 1980): 281-8.

Thomas, Gwendolyn A., "The Craft and Ralph Ellison: An Analysis of INVISIBLE MAN," *DAI* 35 (1974): 3773A-74A (Denver).

Tischler, Nancy M., "Negro Literature and Classic Form," *ConL* 10, iii (Summer, 1969): 358-65.

Trimmer, Joseph F., "The Grandfather's Riddle in Ralph Ellison's INVISIBLE MAN," *BALF* 12, ii (1978): 46-50.

Turner, Darwin, "Sight in Invisible Man," *CLAJ* 13, iii (Mar., 1970): 258-64.

Varisco, Raymond, "The Narrator and the Narrative: Didacticism and Artistic Vision in Ralph Ellison's INVISIBLE MAN," *RevI* 9, ii (1979): 232-9.

Vassilowitch, John, Jr., "Ellison's Dr. Bledsoe: Two Literary Sources," *ELWIU* 8, i (Spring, 1981): 109-13.

Virágos, Zsolt, "Ralph Ellison and the Dilemma of Artistic Synthesis," *ALitASH* 20 (1978): 155-64.

Vogler, Thomas A., "INVISIBLE MAN: Somebody's Protest Novel," *IowaR* 1 (Spring, 1970): 64-82. Also in Hersey, J., ed., *Ralph Ellison*, 127-50.

Waghmare, J. M., "Invisibility of the American Negro: Ralph Ellison's INVISIBLE MAN," *Quest* 59 (1968): 23-30.

Walcott, Ronald, "Some Notes on the Blues, Style and Space: Ellison, Gordone, and Tolson," *BlackW* 22, ii (Dec., 1972): 7-14.

Walling, William, "'Art'and'Protest': Ralph Ellison's INVIS-IBLE MAN Twenty Years After," *Phylon* 34, ii (June, 1973): 120-34.

————, "Ralph Ellison's INVISIBLE MAN: 'It Goes a Long Way Back, Some Twenty Years'," *Phylon* 34, i (Mar., 1973): 4-16.

Wasserman, Jerry, "Embracing the Negative: NATIVE SON and INVISIBLE MAN," *SAF* 4, i (Spring, 1976): 93-104.

Wehner, James V., "The Function of a Negative Myth in Ellison's INVISIBLE MAN and Grass's HUNDEJAHRE," *DAI* 35 (1975): 4568A-69A.

Weinstein, Sharon R., "Comedy and the Absurd in Ralph Ellison's INVISIBLE MAN," *SBL* 3, iii (Autumn, 1972): 12-16.

Werner, C. H., *Paradoxical Resolutions*, 134-42.

West, A., *Principles and Persuasions*, 212-18.

Wicks, Ulrich, "Onlyman," *Mosaic* 8, iii (1975): 40-5.

Wiggins, William H., Jr., "The Folklore Elements in Ralph Ellison's INVISIBLE MAN," in Carter, G. E., and J. R. Parker, eds., *Afro-American Folklore*, 39-44.

Williams, John A., "Ralph Ellison and INVISIBLE MAN: Their Place in American Letters," *BlackW* 20, ii (1970): 10-11.

Williams, S. A., *Give Birth to Brightness*, 86-96.

Wilner, Eleanor R., "The Invisible Black Thread: Identity and Nonentity in INVISIBLE MAN," *CLAJ* 13, iii (Mar., 1970): 242-57.

Winther, Per, "The Ending of Ralph Ellison's INVISIBLE MAN," *CLAJ* 25, iii (Mar., 1982): 267-87.

Yarborough, Richard, "The Quest for the American Dream in Three Afro-American Novels: IF HE HOLLERS LET HIM GO, THE STREET, and INVISIBLE MAN," *MELUS* 8, iv (Winter, 1981): 47-57.

BIBLIOGRAPHY

Covo, Jacqueline, *The Blinking Eye: Ralph Waldo Ellison and His American, French, German and Italian Critics, 1952-1971: Bibliographic Essays and a Checklist*, Metuchen, NJ: Scarecrow, 1974.

————, "Ralph Waldo Ellison: Bibliographic Essays and Finding List of American Criticism, 1952-1964," *CLAJ* 15, ii (Dec., 1971): 171-96.

Gross, S. L., and J. E. Hardy, eds., *Images of the Negro in American Literature*, 305.

Moorer, Frank E., and Lugene Baily, "A Selected Checklist of Materials By and About Ralph Ellison," *BlackW* 20, ii (1970): 126-30.

Weixlmann, Joe, and John O'Banion, "A Checklist of Ellison Criticism, 1972-1978," *BALF* 12, ii (1978): 51-5.

ENGEL, MARIAN (RUTH), 1933-1985

GENERAL

Hutchinson, Ann, "Marian Engel, Equilibriste," *BForum* 4, i (1978): 46-55.

Woodcock, George, "Casting Down Their Golden Crowns: The Novels of Marian Engel," in Helwig, D., *Human Elements 2*, 10-37.

BEAR

Cameron, Elspeth, "Midsummer Madness: Marian Engel's BEAR," *JCF* 21 (1977-78): 83-94.

Cowan, S. A., "Return to HEART OF DARKNESS: Echoes of Conrad in Marian Engel's BEAR," *ArielE* 12, iv (Oct., 1981): 73-91.

Gadpaille, Michelle, "A Note on BEAR," *CanL* 92 (Spring, 1982): 151-4.

Hair, Donald S., "Marian Engel's BEAR," *CanL* 92 (Spring, 1982): 34-45.

Morley, Patricia, "Engel, Wiseman, Laurence: Women Writers, Women's Lives," *WLWE* 17, i (April, 1978): 154-6.

Osachoff, Margaret G., "The Bearness of BEAR," *UWR* 15, i-ii (1979-80): 13-21.

Woodcock, George, "Casting Down Their Golden Crowns: The Novels of Marian Engel," in Helwig, D., ed., *Human Elements* 2, 29-33.

THE GLASSY SEA

Woodcock, George, "Casting Down Their Golden Crowns: The Novels of Marian Engel," in *Human Elements* 2, 33-7.

THE HONEYMOON FESTIVAL

Gottlieb, Lois, and Wendy Keitner, "Mothers and Daughters in Four Recent Canadian Novelists," *Sphinx* No. 4 (Summer, 1975): 21-34.

Parker, Douglas H., "'Memories of My Own Patterns': Levels of Reality in THE HONEYMOON FESTIVAL," *JCF* 4, iii (1975): 111-16.

Woodcock, George, "Casting Down Their Golden Crowns: The Novels of Marian Engel," in Helwig, D., ed., *Human Elements* 2, 19-22.

JOANNE

Woodcock, George, "Casting Down Their Golden Crowns: The Novels of Marian Engel," in Helwig, D., ed., *Human Elements* 2, 25-8.

MONODROMOS

Woodcock, George, "Casting Down Their Golden Crowns: The Novels of Marian Engel," in Helwig, D., ed., *Human Elements* 2, 23-5.

NO CLOUDS OF GLORY

Woodcock, George, "Casting Down Their Golden Crowns: The Novels of Marian Engel," in Helwig, D., ed., *Human Elements* 2, 16-18.

EXLEY, FREDERICK (EARL), 1929-

A FAN'S NOTES

Burke, William, "Football, Literature, Culture," *SWR* 60, iv (Autumn, 1975): 391-8.

Chabot, C. Barry, "The Alternative Vision of Frederick Exley's A FAN'S NOTES," *Crit* 19, i (1977): 87-100.

Johnson, Donald R., "The Hero in Sports Literature and Exley's A FAN'S NOTES," *SHR* 13 (1979): 233-44.

Sterling, Phillip, "Frederick Exley's A FAN'S NOTES: Football as Metaphor," *Crit* 22, i (1980): 39-46.

FAIR, RONALD L., 1932-

GENERAL

Fleming, Robert E., "The Novels of Ronald L. Fair," *CLAJ* 15, iv (June, 1972): 477-87.

HOG BUTCHER

Fleming, Robert E., "The Novels of Ronald L. Fair," *CLAJ* 15, iv (June, 1972): 479-83.

MANY THOUSAND GONE

Fleming, Robert E., "The Novels of Ronald L. Fair," *CLAJ* 15, iv (June, 1972): 477-9.

Klotman, Phyllis R., "The Passive Resistant in A DIFFERENT DRUMMER, DAY OF ABSENCE AND MANY THOUSAND GONE," *SEL* 3, iii (Autumn, 1972): 7-12.

FANTE, JOHN, 1909-1983

GENERAL

Green, R. B., *Italian-American Novel*, 157-63.

THE BROTHERHOOD OF THE GRAPE

Brown, Carole, "John Fante's THE BROTHERHOOD OF THE GRAPE and Robert Canzoneri's A HIGHLY RAMIFIED TREE: A Review Essay," *ItalAm* 3 (1977): 256-64.

FULL OF LIFE

Green, R. B., *Italian-American Novel*, 161-3.

FARINA, RICHARD, 1936 (?)-1966

BEEN DOWN SO LONG IT LOOKS LIKE UP TO ME

Bluestein, Gene, "'Laughin Just to Keep from Cryin': Farina's Blues Novel," *JPC* 9 (Spring, 1976): 926-34.

Seed, David, "Richard Farina's Protest Novel," *JAC* 5, ii (Summer, 1982): 104-14.

FARRELL, J(AMES) G(ORDON), 1935-1979

GENERAL

Binns, Ronald, "The Fiction of J. G. Farrell," *MLNew* 5 (1979): 22-4. [Not seen.]

————, "J. G. Farrell: A Note," *MLNew* 7 (1980): 19. [Not seen.]

Mahon, Derek, "J. G. Farrell, 1935-1979," *NStat* (Aug. 31, 1979): 313.

THE SIEGE OF KRISHNAPUR

Bergonzi, Bernard, in *Contemporary English Novel*, 61-4.

Singh, Frances B., "Progress and History in J. G. Farrell's THE SIEGE OF KRISHNAPUR," *Chandrabhágá* 2 (1979): 23-39.

THE SINGAPORE GRIP

Bergonzi, Bernard, in *Contemporary English Novel*, 64-5.

Binns, Ronald, "The Novelist as Historian," *CritQ* 21, ii (Summer, 1979): 70-2.

TROUBLES

Bergonzi, Bernard, in *Contemporary English Novel*, 59-61.

FARRELL, JAMES T(HOMAS), 1904-1979

GENERAL

Aldridge, John W., "The Education of James Farrell," *In Search of Heresy*, 186-91.

Alexis, Gerhard T., "Farrell Since Our Days of Anger," *CE* 27 (Dec., 1965): 221-6.

Anderson, David D., "James T. Farrell: A Memoir," *SSMLN* 9, iii (1979): 5-6. [Not seen.]

Berkow, Ira, "Farrell and Sports," *TCl* 22, i (Feb., 1976): 105-10.

Blake, N. M., "The World of Fifty-eighth Street," *Novelist's America*, 195-225.

Blankenship, R., *American Literature*, 755-8.

Branch, Edgar M., "American Writer in the Twenties: James T. Farrell and the University of Chicago," *ABC* 11, x (Summer, 1961): 25-32.

_____, *James T. Farrell*.

_____, "James T. Farrell: Four Decades after STUDS LONI-GAN," in Marsden, M. T., comp., *Proceedings of the Fifth National Convention of the Popular Culture Association*, 767-77. Also in *TCL* 22, i (Feb., 1976): 28-35.

_____, "The 1930's in James T. Farrell's Fiction," *ABC* 21, vi (Mar.-April, 1971): 9-12.

Butler, Robert J., "The Christian Roots of Farrell's O'Neill and Carr Novels," *Ren* 34, ii (Winter, 1982): 81-98.

_____, "Time and Narrative Design in the Major Novels of James T. Farrell," *DAI* 38 (1978): 6721A.

Callaghan, Morley, "James T. Farrell: A Tribute," *TCL* 22, 1 (Feb., 1976): 26-7.

Chalupová, Eva, "The Thirties and the Artistry of Lewis, Farrell, Dos Passos and Steinbeck," *BSE* 14 (1981): 107-16 *passim*.

Cox, Don R., "A World He Never Made: The Decline of James T. Farrell," *CLAJ* 23, i (Sept., 1979): 32-48.

Curle, Thomas F., "Catholic Novels and the American Culture," *Ctary* 36 (July, 1963): 34-8.

Douglas, Wallace, "The Case of James T. Farrell," *TriQ* No. 2 (Winter, 1965): 105-23.

Eisinger, C. E., *Fiction of the Forties*, 64-6.

Farrell, James T., "C'est Droll," *ABC* 11, x (Summer, 1961): 33.

_____, "Farrell Looks at His Writing," *TCl* 22, i (Feb., 1976): 11-18.

_____, "Farrell Revisits Studs Lonigan's Neighborhood," *NYTBR* (June 20, 1954): 4-5+.

_____, "James Farrell," *NYHTBR* 29 (Oct. 12, 1952): 14.

_____, "James T. Farrell and MOBY DICK: A Reflection," *Extracts* 25 (1976): 7.

_____, *Reflections at Fifty*, N.Y.: Vanguard, 1954.

Flynn, Dennis, and Jack Salzman, "An Interview with James T. Farrell," *TCl* 22, i (Feb., 1976): 1-10.

Fried, Lewis, "James T. Farrell: Shadow and Act.," *JA* 17 (1972): 140-55.

_____, "The Naturalism of James Farrell: A Study of His Major Novels," *DAI* 30 (1970): 4985A (Mass.).

Frohock, W. H., "James Farrell: The Precise Content," *SWR* 25 (Winter, 1950): 39-48. Also in *Novel of Violence in America*, 69-85.

Gelfant, B. H., "James T. Farrell: The Ecological Novel," *American City Novel*, 175-227.

Grattan, C. Hartley, "James T. Farrell: Moralist," *Harpers* 209 (Oct. 8, 1954): 93-4, 96-8.

Gregory, Horace, "James T. Farrell: Beyond the Provinces of Art," in *New World Writing*, No. 5, N.Y.: New American Library, 1954, 52-65.

Hobsbaum, Philip, "The Great American Novel: A Study of James T. Farrell," *Gemini* 2 (Summer, 1959): 39-42.

Lynch, William J., "James T. Farrell and the Irish-American Urban Experience," *PCLS* 9 (1978): 243-54. [Not seen.]

Morris, L., "Thunder on the Left," *Postscript to Yesterday*, 162-6.

O'Malley, Frank, "James T. Farrell: Two Twilight Images," in Gardiner, H. C., ed., *Fifty Years of the American Novel*, 237-56.

Penha, James W., "The Drama of Mind and Spirit: A Study of the Later Fiction of James T. Farrell," *DAI* 39 (1978): 2277A-78A.

Rao, B. R., *American Fictional Hero*, 38-45.

Reiter, Irene M., "A Study of James T. Farrell's Short Stories and Their Relation to His Longer Fiction," *DA* 25 (1965): 5285 (Penn.).

Shannon, W. V., *American Irish*, 249-58.

Snell, G., *Shapers of American Fiction*, 288-300.

Starr, Alvin, "Richard Wright and the Communist Party: The James T. Farrell Factor," *CLAJ* 21, i (Sept., 1977): 41-50.

Stock, Irvin, "Farrell and His Critics," *ArQ* 6 (Winter, 1950): 328-38.

Thorp, W., *American Writing in the Twentieth Century*, 123-6, 170-3.

Van Gelder, Robert, *Writers on Writing*, 278-82.

Walcutt, Charles C., "James T. Farrell and the Reversible Top-coat," *ArQ* 7 (Winter, 1951): 293-310.

Wald, A. M., *James T. Farrell*.

Wallenstein, Barry, "James T. Farrell: Critic of Naturalism," in Hakutani, Y., and L. Fried, eds., *American Literary Naturalism*, 154-75.

Willingham, Calder, "Note on James T. Farrell," *QRL* 2 (1945): 120-4.

BERNARD CARR Trilogy

Branch, E. M., *James T. Farrell* (1963), 29-35.

_____, *James T. Farrell* (1971), 105-16.

Butler, Robert J., "The Christian Roots of Farrell's O'Neill and Carr Novels," *Ren* 34, ii (Winter, 1982): 81-98.

Fried, Lewis, "Bernard Carr and *His* Trials of the Mind," *TCL* 22, i (Feb., 1976): 52-67.

Kligerman, Jack, "The Quest for Self: James T. Farrell's Character Bernard Carr," *UKCR* 29 (Oct., 1962): 9-16.

BERNARD CLARE (See also BERNARD CARR Trilogy)

Branch, E. M., *James T. Farrell* (1971): 105-16 *passim*.

Snell, G., *Shapers of American Fiction*, 298-300.

Walcutt, Charles C., "James T. Farrell and the Reversible Top-coat," *ArQ* 7 (Winter, 1951): 302-6.

_____, "Naturalism in 1946," *Accent* 6 (Summer, 1946): 266-8. Also in Walcutt, C. C., *American Literary Naturalism*, 250-6.

BOARDING HOUSE BLUES

Branch, E. M., *James T. Farrell* (1971), 124-6.

A BRAND NEW LIFE (See also A UNIVERSE OF TIME Series)

Branch, E. M., *James T. Farrell* (1971), 151-3.

DANNY O'NEILL Pentalogy

Beach, J. W., *American Fiction*, 295-305. Also in Aldridge, J. W.,
ed., *Critiques and Essays on Modern Fiction*, 407-14.
Branch, E. M., *James T. Farrell* (1963), 22-9.
_____, *James T. Farrell* (1971), 74-104.
Butler, Robert J., "The Christian Roots of Farrell's O'Neill and
Carr Novels," *Ren* 34, ii (Winter, 1982): 81-98.
Douglas, Wallace, "The Case of James T. Farrell," *TriQ* No. 2
(Winter, 1965): 117-19.
Dyer, Henry H., "James T. Farrell's STUDS LONIGAN and
DANNY O'NEILL Novels," *DA* 26 (1965): 3332 (Un. of
Penn.).
Hobsbaum, Philip, "The Great American Novel: A Study of
James T. Farrell," *Gemini* 2 (Summer, 1959): 39-40.
Snell, G., *Shapers of American Fiction*, 294-6.
Walcutt, Charles C., *American Literary Naturalism*, 245-9.
_____, "James T. Farrell and the Reversible Topcoat," *ArQ* 7
(Winter, 1951): 297-301.

THE DUNNE FAMILY (See also A UNIVERSE OF TIME Series)

Wald, Alan, "A Socially-Committed Writer to the End," *MQR*
17 (178): 263-9.

ELLEN ROGERS

Branch, E. M., *James T. Farrell* (1971), 122-4.
Snell, G., *Shapers of American Fiction*, 297-8.

THE FACE OF TIME (See also DANNY O'NEILL Pentalogy)

Allen, W., *Urgent West*, 102-3.
Branch, E. M., *James T. Farrell* (1971), 74-104 *passim*.
Douglas, Wallace, "The Case of James T. Farrell," *TriQ* No. 2
(Winter, 1965): 119-20.

FATHER AND SON (See Also DANNY O'NEILL Pentalogy)

Branch, E. M., *James T. Farrell* (1971), 74-104 *passim*.

GAS-HOUSE MCGINTY

Beach, J. W., *American Fiction*, 287-94. Also in Aldridge, J. W.,
ed., *Critiques and Essays on Modern Fiction*, 402-7.
Branch, E. M., *James T. Farrell* (1971), 118-21.

INVISIBLE SWORDS

Branch, E. M., *James T. Farrell* (1971), 156-9.

JUDGMENT DAY (See also STUDS LONIGAN Trilogy)

Berry, Newton, "A Preface to the Death Fantasy Sequence of
JUDGMENT DAY," *TriQ* No. 2 (1965): 124-6.
Branch, E. M., *James T. Farrell* (1971), 36-73 *passim*.
Farrell, James T., in Madden, F. F., ed., *Talks with Authors*, 89-102.

JUDITH (See also A UNIVERSE OF TIME Series)

Branch, E. M., *James T. Farrell* (1971), 144-7.

MY DAYS OF ANGER (See also DANNY O'NEILL Pentalogy)

Branch, E. M., *James T. Farrell* (1971), 74-104 *passim*.
Lyons, J. O., *College Novel in America*, 92-3.
Rosenfeld, Isaac, "The Anger of James T. Farrell," *NRep* 109
(Nov. 8, 1943): 657-8. Also in Rosenfeld, I., *Age of Enormity*,
81-5.

NEW YEAR'S EVE/1929

Branch, E. M., *James T. Farrell* (1971), 126-7.

NO STAR IS LOST (See also DANNY O'NEILL Pentalogy)

Branch, E. M., *James T. Farrell* (1971), 74-104 *passim*.

THE ROAD BETWEEN (See also BERNARD CARR Trilogy)

Branch, E. M., *James T. Farrell* (1971), 105-15 *passim*.
Stock, Irvin, "Farrell and His Critics," *ArQ* 6 (Winter, 1950):
335-8.

THE SILENCE OF HISTORY (See also A UNIVERSE OF TIME Series)

Branch, E. M., *James T. Farrell* (1971), 142-4.

STUDS LONIGAN Trilogy

Allen, W., *Modern Novel*, 148-53.
Beach, J. W., *American Fiction*, 273-83. Also (excerpted) in Rubin,
L. D., Jr., and J. R. Moore, eds., *Idea of an American Novel*,
340-3.
Branch, Edgar M., "Destiny, Culture, and Technique: STUDS
LONIGAN," *UKCR* 29 (Dec., 1962): 103-13.
_____, *James T. Farrell* (1963), 16-22.
_____, *James T. Farrell* (1971), 36-73.
_____, "James T. Farrell's STUDS LONIGAN," *ABC* 11, x
(Summer, 1961): 9-19.
_____, in Krause, S. J., ed., *Essays in Determinism*, 29-93.
_____, "STUDS LONIGAN Symbolism and Theme," *CE* 23
(Dec., 1961): 191-6.
Butler, Robert J., "Christian and Pragmatic Visions of Time in
the LONIGAN Trilogy," *Thought* 55 (1980): 461-75.
Douglas, Ann, "STUDS LONIGAN and the Failure of History
in Mass Society: A Study," *AQ* 29 (1977): 487-505.
Douglas, Wallace, "The Case of James T. Farrell," *TriQ* No. 2
(Winter, 1965): 108-15.
Dyer, Henry H., "James T. Farrell's STUDS LONIGAN and
DANNY O'NEILL Novels," *DA* 26 (1965): 3332 (Un. of
Penn.).
Farrell, James T., "The Author as Plaintiff: Testimony in a
Censorship Case," *Reflections at Fifty and Other Essays*, N.Y:
Vanguard, 1954, 188-233. Also in Downs, Robert B., ed., *First
Freedom: Liberty and Justice in the World of Books*, Chicago:
American Library Assn., 1960, 286-301.
_____, "How STUDS LONIGAN Was Written," in Targ,
William, ed., *A Reader for Writers*, N.Y.: Hermitage House,
1951, 148-54.
Gurko, L., *Angry Decade*, 119-25.
Halperin, Irving, "STUDS LONIGAN Revisited," *ABC* 19, iv
(Dec., 1968): 10-12.
Hobsbaum, Philip, "The Great American Novel: A Study of
James T. Farrell," *Gemini* 2 (Summer, 1959): 40-2.

Lee, Hermione, "La Bête Humaine," *NStat* (Sept. 7, 1979): 379-80.

McElroy, Davis D., *Existentialism and Modern Literature: An Essay in Existential Criticism*, N.Y.: Citadel, 1963, 25-6.

Mitchell, Richard, "James T. Farrell's Scientific Novel," *DA* 24 (1964): 5413 (Syracuse).

_____, "STUDS LONIGAN: Research in Morality," *CRAS* 6 (Spring, 1962): 202-14.

Newcomer, James, "Longinus in a Modern Instance," *CJ* 53 (1957): 113-18.

Nunes, Cassiano, "James T. Farrell and Studs Lonigan," *ABC* 23, vi (1973): 7-8.

Pizer, Donald, "James T. Farrell and the 1930's," in Bogardus, R. F., and F. Hobson, eds., *Literature at the Barricades*, 71-81.

Rao, B. R., *American Fictional Hero*, 39-42.

Rosenthal, T. G., "STUDS LONIGAN and the Search for an American Tragedy," *BAASB* No. 7 (Dec., 1963): 46-54.

Shaughnessy, Edward L., "Oliver Alden and Studs Lonigan: Heirs to Spiritual Poverty," *MarkhamR* (May, 1974): 48-52.

Snell, G., *Shapers of American Fiction*, 289-94.

Walcutt, Charles C., *American Literary Naturalism*, 240-5.

_____, "James T. Farrell and the Reversible Topcoat," *ArQ* 7 (Winter, 1951): 293-7.

Wald, Alan, "James T. Farrell's STUDS LONIGAN and American Radicalism," *Internat. Socialist Rev.* 39, iv (1978): 18-20.

THIS MAN AND THIS WOMAN

Branch, E. M., *James T. Farrell* (1971), 121-2.

A UNIVERSE OF TIME Series

Branch, E. M., *James T. Farrell* (1971), 139-59.

Slade, Joseph W., "'Bare-Assed and Alone': Time and Banality in Farrell's A UNIVERSE OF TIME," *TCL* 22, i (Feb., 1976): 68-79.

WHAT TIME COLLECTS (See also A UNIVERSE OF TIME Series)

Branch, E. M., *James T. Farrell* (1971), 147-50.

Douglas, Wallace, "The Case of James T. Farrell," *TriQ* No. 2 (Winter, 1965): 120-3.

A WORLD I NEVER MADE (See also DANNY O'NEILL Pentalogy)

Branch, E. M., *James T. Farrell* (1971), 74-104 *passim*.

Cowley, M., "A Portrait of James T. Farrell as a Young Man," *Look Back on Us*, 304-7. Also in *NRep* (Nov. 18, 1936).

YET OTHER WATERS (See also BERNARD CARR Trilogy)

Branch, E. M., *James T. Farrell* (1971), 105-15 *passim*.

YOUNG LONIGAN (See also STUDS LONIGAN Trilogy)

Beach, J. W., *American Fiction*, 276-80.

Branch, E. M., *James T. Farrell* (1971), 36-73 *passim*.

Woodbridge, Hensley C., "Slang in Farrell's YOUNG LONIGAN," *AS* 36 (Oct., 1961): 225-9.

Woolf, H. B., "Bede, the Sparrow, and Farrell," *N&Q* 198 (1953): 263-4.

THE YOUNG MANHOOD OF STUDS LONIGAN (See also STUDS LONIGAN Trilogy)

Branch, E. M., *James T. Farrell* (1971), 36-73 *passim*.

BIBLIOGRAPHY

Branch, E. M., in Krause, S. J., ed., *Essays in Determinism*, 93-4.

Salzman, Jack, "James T. Farrell: An Essay in Bibliography," *RALS* 6 (1976): 131-64.

FAST, HOWARD MELVIN, 1914-

GENERAL

Campenni, Frank, "Citizen Howard Fast: A Critical Biography," *DAI* 32 (1971): 3296A (Wis.).

Eisinger, C. E., *Fiction of the Forties*, 90-3.

Hicks, Granville, "Howard Fast's One-Man Reformation," *CE* 7 (Oct., 1945): 1-6.

Lifka, Marion, "Howard Fast: Wool Puller?" *CathW* 177 (Sept., 1953): 446-51.

Meisler, Stanley, "The Lost Dreams of Howard Fast," *Nation* 188 (May 30, 1959): 498-500. Also in Nation (Periodical), *View of the Nation*, 40-6.

Rideout, W., *Radical Novel in the United States*, 275-85.

THE AMERICAN

Rideout, W., *Radical Novel in the United States*, 278-9.

CONCEIVED IN LIBERTY

Hicks, Granville, "Howard Fast's One-Man Reformation," *CE* 7 (Oct., 1945): 1-6 *passim*.

THE LAST FRONTIER

Hicks, Granville, "Howard Fast's One-Man Reformation," *CE* 7 (Oct., 1945): 1-6 *passim*.

Rideout, W., *Radical Novel in the United States*, 279-80.

THE PROUD AND THE FREE

Fast, Howard, "Reply to the Critics," *M&M* 3 (Dec., 1950): 53-64.

Rideout, W., *Radical Novel in the United States*, 281-3.

SPARTACUS

Rideout, W., *Radical Novel in the United States*, 283-5.

THE UNVANQUISHED

Eisinger, C. E., *Fiction of the Forties*, 92-3.

FAULKNER, WILLIAM, 1897-1962

GENERAL

Aaron, Daniel, *The Unwritten War: American Writers and the Civil War*, N.Y.: Knopf, 1973, 310-26.

Adamowski, Thomas H., "The Dickens World and Yoknapatawpha County: A Study of Character and Society in Dickens and Faulkner," *DAI* 30 (1970): 2995A-96A (Ind.).

Adams, Percy G., "Faulkner, French Literature and 'Eternal Verities'," in Zyla, W. T., and W. M. Aycock, eds., *William Faulkner*, 7-24.

_____, "The Franco-American Faulkner," *TSL* 5 (1960): 1-13.

Adams, Richard P., "The Apprenticeship of William Faulkner," *TSE* 12 (1962): 113-56. Also in Cox, L. H., ed., *William Faulkner*, 83-134. Also in Wagner, L. W., ed., *William Faulkner*, 7-44.

_____, *Faulkner*.

_____, "Faulkner and the Myth of the South," *MissQ* 14 (Summer, 1961): 131-7.

_____, "Faulkner: The European Roots," in Wolfe, G. H., ed., *Faulkner*, 21-41.

_____, "Some Key Words in Faulkner," *TSE* 16 (1968): 135-48.

Addison, Bill K., "The Past in the Works of William Faulkner," *DAI* 32 (1971): 2669A-70A (Minn.).

Aiken, Charles S., "Yoknapatawpha County: A Place in the American South," *Geographical Rev.* 69 (July, 1979): 331-48.

Aiken, Conrad, "William Faulkner: The Novel as Form," *Atlantic* 164 (Nov., 1939): 650-4. Also in Aiken, Conrad, *ABC: Collected Criticism from 1916 to the Present*, N.Y.: Meridian, 1958, 200-7. Also in Aiken, C., *Reviewer's ABC*, 200-7. Also in *HarvardA* 135 (Nov., 1951): 13, 24-6. Also in Hoffman, F. J., and O. W. Vickery, eds., *William Faulkner*, 135-42. Also in Hoffman, F. J., and O. W. Vickery, eds., *William Faulkner: Two Decades of Criticism*, 139-47. Also in Rubin, L. D., Jr., and J. R. Moore, eds., *Idea of an American Novel*, 354-9. Also in Warren, R. P., ed., *Faulkner*, 46-52. Also in Schmitter, D. M., ed., *William Faulkner*, 45-52. Also in Wagner, L. W., ed., *William Faulkner*, 134-40.

Ait Daraou, Ahmed, "The German Reception of William Faulkner: Books and Dissertations," *DAI* 41 (1980): 1050A.

Akai, Yasumitsu, "A Study on the Negro English in W. Faulkner's Works," *Anglica* 4 (Jan., 1961): 72-90; 4 (Sept., 1961): 44-56.

Alexander, Margaret W., "Faulkner & Race," in Harrington, E., and A. J. Abadie, eds., *Maker and the Myth*, 105-21.

Alexandrescu, Sorin, "A Project in the Semantic Analysis of the Characters in William Faulkner's Work," *Semiotica* 4 (1971): 37-51.

_____, "William Faulkner and the Greek Tragedy," *RoR* 24, iii (1970): 102-10.

Allen, Charles A., "William Faulkner: Comedy and the Purpose of Humor," *ArQ* 16 (Spring, 1960): 59-69.

_____, "William Faulkner's Vision of Good and Evil," *PacSp* 10 (Summer, 1956): 236-41.

Alter, Jean V., "Faulkner, Sartre, and 'nouveau roman'," *Sym* 20 (Summer, 1966): 101-12.

Anastasyev, Nikolai, "The Necessity of Faulkner," *SovL* No. 8 (1977): 180-3.

Anderson, Charles, "Faulkner's Moral Center," *EA* 7 (Jan., 1954): 48-58.

Anderson, Don[ald], "Comic Modes in Modern American Fiction," *SoRA* 8 (1975): 152-65.

Anderson, Helen S., "The Isolated Intellectual in the Fiction of William Faulkner and Marcel Proust: An Analysis of Failure and Success in Transcendence of Time," *DAI* 43, iii (Sept., 1982): 805A-06A.

Antoniadis, Roxandra I., "The Dream as Design in Balzac and Faulkner," *ZRL* 17, ii (1974): 45-58.

_____, "Faulkner and Balzac: The Poetic Web," *CLS* 9, iii (Sept., 1972): 303-25.

_____, "The Human Comedies of Honoré de Balzac and William Faulkner: Similarities and Differences," *DAI* 31 (1971): 4753A (Colo.).

Antrim, Harry D., "Faulkner's Suspended Style," *UR* 32 (Dec., 1965): 122-8.

Archer, Lewis F., "Coleridge's Definition of the Poet and the Works of Herman Melville and William Faulkner," *DA* 28 (1967): 1810A-11A (Drew).

Athos, John, "Ritual and Humor in the Writing of William Faulkner," *Accent* 9 (Autumn, 1948): 17-30. Also in Hoffman, F. J., and O. W. Vickery, eds., *William Faulkner: Two Decades of Criticism*, 101-18.

Arthur, Christopher E., "Possibilities of Place: The Fiction of William Faulkner," *DAI* 38 (1977): 1383A-84A.

Asselineau, Roger, "The French Face of William Faulkner," *TSE* 23 (1978): 157-73.

Aytür, Nocla, "Faulkner in Turkish," in Zyla, W. T., and W. M. Aycock, eds., *William Faulkner*, 25-39.

Backman, M., *Faulkner*.

_____, "Sickness and Primitivism: A Dominant Pattern in William Faulkner's Work," *Accent* 14 (Winter, 1954): 61-73.

Backvis, Claude, "Faulkner Versus Dostoevsky," *Revue de l'Université Libre de Bruxelles* (1970-1973): 205-32.

Bailey, Dennis L., "The Modern Novel in the Presence of Myth," *DAI* 35 (1975): 7292A-93A.

Baker, Carlos, "William Faulkner: The Doomed and the Damned," in Bode, C., ed., *Young Rebel in American Literature*, 145-69.

Baker, James R., "The Symbolic Extension of Yoknapatawpha County," *ArQ* 8 (Autumn, 1952): 223-8.

Baldanza, Frank, "Faulkner's '1699-1945: The Compsons'," *Expl* 19 (May, 1961): Item 59.

Baldwin, James, "Faulkner and Desegregation," *PR* 23 (Summer, 1956): 568-73.

Barbour, Brian M., "Faulkner's Decline," *DAI* 30 (1970): 5436A-37A (Kent State).

Barricklow, Gary E., "Kenneth Burke's Structuralism: A Structural Description of Narrative and Technique in Faulkner's Fiction of the Southern Aristocracy," *DAI* 37 (1976): 2856A.

Barth, J. Robert, S. J., "Faulkner and the Calvinist Tradition," *Thought* 39 (Spring, 1964): 100-20. Also in Barth, J. R., S. J., ed., *Religious Perspectives in Faulkner's Fiction*, 11-31.

_____, ed., *Religious Perspectives in Faulkner's Fiction*.

Bassett, John E., "Faulkner's Readers: Crosscurrents in American Reviews and Criticism, 1926-1962," *DAI* 32 (1971): 1502A (Rochester).

_____, ed., *William Faulkner: The Critical Heritage*. London: Routledge, 1975.

Beach, J. W., *American Fiction*, 123-69.

Beards, Richard, "Parody as Tribute: William Melvin Kelley's A DIFFERENT DRUMMER and Faulkner," *SBL* 5, iii (Winter, 1974): 25-8.

Beauchamp, Fay E., "William Faulkner's Use of the Tragic Mulatto Myth," *DAI* 36 (1975): 297A-98A.

Beck, Warren, *Faulkner*.

_____, "Faulkner After 1940," in Beck, W., *Faulkner*, 55-102.

_____, "Faulkner and the South," *AR* 1 (Spring, 1941): 82-94. Also in Beck, W., *Faulkner*, 18-33.

_____, "Faulkner's Point of View," *CE* 2 (May, 1941): 736-49. Also in Beck, W., *Faulkner*, 3-17. Also in Cox, L. H., ed., *William Faulkner*, 425-39.

_____, "Fictional Entities and the Artist's *Oeuvre*," in Beck, W. *Faulkner*, 103-21.

_____, "Good and Evil," in Beck, W., *Faulkner*, 122-43.

_____, "Realist and Regionalist," in Beck, W., *Faulkner*, 144-274.

_____, "Short Stories into Novels," in Beck, W., *Faulkner*, 275-333.

_____, "William Faulkner's Style," *American Prefaces* 6 (Spring, 1941): 195-211. Also in Hoffman, F. J., and O. W. Vickery, eds., *William Faulkner*, 142-56. Also in Hoffman, F. J., and O. W. Vickery, eds., *William Faulkner: Two Decades of Criticism*, 147-64. Also in Warren, R. P., ed., *Faulkner*, 53-65. Also in Beck, W., *Faulkner*, 34-51. Also in Wagner, L. W., ed., *William Faulkner*, 141-54.

Bedell, George C., "Kierkegaard and Faulkner: Modalities of Existence," *DAI* 30 (1970): 5056A-57A (Duke).

_____, *Kierkegaard and Faulkner*.

Beja, Morris, "A Flash, a Glare: Faulkner and Time," *Ren* 16 (Spring, 1964): 133-41, 145.

_____, "William Faulkner: A Flash, a Glare," *Epiphany in the Modern Novel*, 182-210.

Bellue, John V., "William Faulkner as a Literary Naturalist," *DAI* 36 (1976): 7417A.

Beringause, A. F., "Faulkner's Yoknapatawpha Register," *BuR* 11, iii (May, 1963): 71-82.

Berk, Lynn M. L., "The Barrier of Words: A Study of William Faulkner's Distrust of Language," *DAI* 33 (1973): 5163A-64A (Purdue).

Berner, Robert L., "The Theme of Responsibility in the Later Fiction of William Faulkner," *DA* 21 (1960): 1561 (Wash.).

Bertman, Martin A., "On Faulkner's Thucydidean Aesthetics," *JAC* 7, iii (1973): 99-101.

Black, Victoria, Christine Drake, Evans Harrington, Lucy Howorth, Mary McClain, and Dean Faulkner Wells, "William Faulkner of Oxford: Panel Discussion," *UMSE* 15 (1978): 187-203.

Blackburn, Alexander, "Faulkner and Continuance of the Southern Renaissance," in Fowler, D., and A. J. Abadie, eds., *Faulkner and the Southern Renaissance*, 158-81.

Blackley, Charles, "William Faulkner's Country: A Chronological Guide to Yoknapatawpha," *TAIUS* 4 (1971): 73-86.

Blackwell, Louise, "Faulkner and the Womenfolk," *KM* (1967): 73-7.

Blair, Arthur H., "Faulkner's Military World," *DAI* 36 (1976): 6679A.

Blake, N. M., "The Decay of Yoknapatawpha County," *Novelist's America*, 75-109.

Bleikasten, André, "Fathers in Faulkner," 115-46 in Davis, Robert C., ed., *The Fictional Father: Lacanian Readings of the Text*, Amherst: Un. of Massachusetts Pr., 1981.

Blöcker, Günter, "William Faulkner," in Warren, R. P., ed., *Faulkner*, 122-6.

Blotner, Joseph, "Did You See Him Plain?" in Fowler, D., and A. J. Abadie, eds., *Fifty Years of Yoknapatawpha*, 3-22.

_____, "The Falkners and the Fictional Families," *GaR* 30 (Fall, 1976): 572-92.

_____, "William Faulkner Seminar," *UMSE* 14 (1976): 63-78.

_____, "Romantic Elements in Faulkner," in Bernstein, G., ed., *Romantic and Modern*, 207-220.

_____, "The Sole Owner and Proprietor," in Wolfe, G. H., ed., *Faulkner*, 1-20.

_____, "The Sources of Faulkner's Genius," in Fowler, D., and A. J. Abadie, eds., *Fifty Years of Yoknapatawpha*, 248-70.

_____, "William Faulkner and the Eisenhower Administration," *JMissH* 42 (1980): 49-54.

_____, and Malcolm Cowley, Evans Harrington, Elizabeth Kerr, Gerald Walton, and James Webb, "The Riches of Yoknapatawpha," *UMSE* 14 (1976): 141-61.

Boozer, William, "William Faulkner: Transcending the Place Mississippi," in Wells, D. F., and H. Cole, eds., *Mississippi Heroes*, 191-214.

Boring, Phyllis Z., "Faulkner in Spain: The Case of Elena Quiroga," *CLS* 14 (June, 1977): 166-76.

Boswell, George W., "Epic, Drama, and Faulkner's Fiction," *KFR* 25 (Jan.-June, 1979): 16-27.

_____, "The Legendary Background of Faulkner's Work," *TFSB* 36 (Sept., 1970): 53-63.

_____, "Notes on the Surnames of Faulkner's Characters," *TFSB* 36 (Sept., 1970): 64-6.

_____, "Picturesque Faulknerisms," *UMSE* 9 (1968): 47-56.

_____, "Superstition and Belief in Faulkner," *Costerus* 6 (1972): 1-26.

_____, "Traditional Verse and Music Influence in Faulkner," *NMW* 1 (Spring, 1968): 23-31.

Bouvard, Loic, "Conversation with William Faulkner," *MFS* 5 (Winter, 1959-60): 361-4.

Bowling, Lawrence E., "William Faulkner: The Importance of Love," *DR* 43 (Winter, 1963-64): 474-82. Also in Wagner, L. W., ed., *William Faulkner*, 109-17.

Bradford, Melvin E., "Faulkner, James Baldwin and the South," *GaR* 20 (Winter, 1966): 431-43.

_____, "Faulkner's Doctrine of Nature: A Study of the 'Endurance' Theme in the Yoknapatawpha Fiction," *DA* 29 (1969): 3999A (Vanderbilt).

_____, "On the Importance of Discovering God: Faulkner and Hemingway's THE OLD MAN AND THE SEA," *MissQ* 20 (Summer, 1967): 158-62.

_____, "Spring Paradigm: Faulkner's Living Legacy," *ForumH* 6, ii (1968): 4-7.

Brady, Emily K., "The Literary Faulkner: His Indebtedness to Conrad, Lawrence, Hemingway, and Other Modern Novelists," *DA* 23 (1962): 2131-32 (Brown).

Brady, Ruth A.H.H., "The Reality of Gothic Terror in Faulkner," *DAI* 32 (1972): 5774A-75A (Texas, Austin).

Breaden, Dale G., "William Faulkner and the Land," *AQ* 10 (Fall, 1958): 344-57.

Breit, Harvey, "William Faulkner," *Atlantic* 188 (Oct., 1951): 53-6.

Brennan, Joseph X., and S. L. Gross, "The Problem of Moral Values in Conrad and Faulkner," *Person* 41 (Jan., 1960): 60-70.

Bricker, Emil S., "Duality in the Novels of William Faulkner and Fyodor Dostoevsky," *DAI* 32 (1972): 6413A-14A (Mich.).

Brien, Dolores E., "William Faulkner and the Myth of Woman," *RS* 35 (June, 1967): 132-40.

Brogunier, Joseph E., "The Jefferson Urn: Faulkner's Literary Sources and Influences," *DAI* 31 (1970): 2375A (Minn.).

Brooks, Cleanth, "The British Reception of Faulkner's Work," in Zyla, W. T., and W. M. Aycock, eds., *William Faulkner*, 41-55.

_____, "Faulkner and History," *MissQ* 25 (Supp.) (Spring, 1972): 3-14.

_____, "Faulkner and the Fugitive-Agrarians," in Fowler, D., and A. J. Abadie, eds., *Faulkner and the Southern Renaissance*, 22-39.

_____, "Faulkner and the Muse of History," *MissQ* 28 (Summer, 1975): 265-79.

_____, "Faulkner the Provincial," in Schmitter, D. M., ed., *William Faulkner*, 20-7. From Brooks, C., *William Faulkner*, 1-9.

_____, "Faulkner's Criticism of Modern America," *VQR* 51 (Spring, 1975): 294-308.

_____, "Faulkner's Treatment of the Racial Problem: Typical Examples," in Brooks, Cleanth, *A Shaping Joy: Studies in the Writer's Craft*, N.Y.: Harcourt, 1971, 230-46. Also in Cox, L. H., ed., *William Faulkner*, 440-58.

_____, "Faulkner's Ultimate Values," in Fowler, D., and A. J. Abadie, eds., *Faulkner and the Southern Renaissance*, 266-81.

_____, "Faulkner's Vision of Good and Evil," *MR* 3 (Summer, 1962): 692-712. Also in Brooks, C., *Hidden God*, 22-43. Also in Barth, J. R., S. J., ed., *Religious Perspectives in Faulkner's Fiction*, 57-78. Also in Wagner, L. W., ed., *William Faulkner*, 117-33.

_____, "The Image of Helen Baird in Faulkner's Early Poetry and Fiction," *SR* 85 (Spring, 1977): 218-34.

_____, "The Sense of Community in Yoknapatawpha Fiction," *UMSE* 15 (1978): 3-18.

_____, *William Faulkner*.

_____, *William Faulkner: Toward Yoknapatawpha and Beyond*.

_____, "William Faulkner and William Butler Yeats: Parallels and Affinities," in Wolfe, G. H., ed., *Faulkner*, 139-58.

Broughton, Panthea R., "Abstraction and Insularity in the Fiction of William Faulklner," *DAI* 32 (1972): 5220A (N.C., Chapel Hill).

_____, "The Cubist Novel: Toward Defining the Genre," in Fowler, D., and A. J. Abadie, eds., *"A Cosmos of My Own,"* 36-58.

_____, "Faulkner's Cubist Novels," in Fowler, D., and A. J. Abadie, eds., *"A Cosmos of My Own,"* 59-94.

_____, "An Interview with Meta Carpenter Wilde," *SoR* 18, iv (1982): 776-81.

_____, *William Faulkner*.

Brown, Calvin S., "Faulkner as Aphorist," *RLC* 53 (July-Sept., 1979): 277-98.

_____, "Faulkner's Geography and Topography," *PMLA* 77 (Dec., 1962): 652-9.

_____, "Faulkner's Localism," in Harrington, E., and A. J. Abadie, eds., *Maker and the Myth*, 3-24.

_____, "Faulkner's Manhunts: Fact into Fiction," *GaR* 20 (Winter, 1966): 388-95.

_____, "Faulkner's Universality," in Harrington, E., and A. J. Abadie, eds., *Maker and the Myth*, 146-66.

_____, "Faulkner's Use of the Oral Tradition," *GaR* 22 (1968): 160-9. Also in Banaseric, Nikola, ed., *Actes du V Congrès de l'Assaiation Internationale de Littérature Comparée, Belgrade 1967*, Un. of Belgrade: Amsterdam: Swets & Zeitlinger, 1969, 519-26.

_____, *A Glossary of Faulkner's South*, New Haven, Conn.: London: Yale Un. Pr., 1976.

Brown, May C., "Quentin Compson as Narrative Voice in the Works of William Faulkner," *DAI* 36 (1976): 5291A-92A.

Brown, William R., "William Faulkner's Use of the Material of Abnormal Psychology in Characterization," *DA* 26 (1965): 1036-37 (Arkansas).

Brumm, Ursula, "Forms and Functions of History in the Novels of William Faulkner," *Archiv* 209 (Aug., 1972): 43-56.

_____, "Wilderness and Civilization: A Note on William Faulkner," *PR* 22 (Summer, 1955): 340-50. Also in Hoffman, F. J., and O. W. Vickery, eds., *William Faulkner*, 125-34.

Brylowski, W., *Faulkner's Olympian Laugh*.

Buck, Lynn D., "The Demonic Paradox: Studies in Faulkner's Imagery," *DAI* 37 (1976): 3620A.

Buckley, G. T., "Is Oxford the Original of Jefferson in William Faulkner's Novels?" *PMLA* 76 (Sept., 1961): 447-54.

Buice, Joe C., "The Rise and Decline of Aristocratic Families in Yoknapatawpha County," *DAI* 31 (1970): 2375A-76A (E. Texas State).

Bunselmeyer, J. E., "Faulkner's Narrative Styles," *AL* 53, iii (Nov., 1981): 424-42.

Burns, Mattie Ann, "The Development of Women Characters in the Works of William Faulkner," *DAI* 35 (1975): 4502A-03A.

Burrows, Robert N., "Institutional Christianity as Reflected in the Works of William Faulkner," *MissQ* 14 (Summer, 1961): 138-47.

Byrne, Mary E., "An Exploration of the Literary Relationship Between Sherwood Anderson and William Faulkner," *DAI* 36 (1976): 8055A.

Byrne, Sister Mary Enda, "From Tradition to Technique: Development of Character in Joyce and Faulkner," *DA* 29 (1969): 3091A.

Cain, Kathleen S., "Beyond the Meaning of History: The Quest for a Southern Myth in Faulkner's Characters," *DAI* 39 (1979): 5509A-10A.

Callen, Shirley P., "Bergsonian Dynamism in the Writings of William Faulkner," *DA* 23 (1963): 2521 (Tulane).

Campbell, Harry M., "Faulkner's Philosophy Again: A Reply to Michael Gresset," *MissQ* 23 (Winter, 1970): 64-6.

_____, "Structural Devices in the Works of Faulkner," *Per* 3 (Autumn, 1950): 209-26.

_____, and R. E. Foster, *William Faulkner*.

Campbell, Leslie J., "Exercises in Doom: Yoknapatawpha County Weddings," *PAPA* 4, ii (Spring, 1978): 2-7.

Cantrill, Dante K., "Told by an Idiot: Toward an Understanding of Modern Fiction through an Analysis of the Works of William Faulkner and John Barth," *DAI* 35 (1975): 4505A.

Carey, G. O., ed., *Faulkner*.

_____, "Faulkner and His Carpenter's Hammer," *ArQ* 32 (Spring, 1976): 5-15. Also in Carey, G. O., ed., *Faulkner*, 259-69.

_____, "William Faulkner as a Critic of Society," *ArQ* 21 (Summer, 1965): 101-8.

_____, "William Faulkner: Critic of Society," *DA* 23 (1963): 2522 (Illinois).

_____, "William Faulkner: Man's Fatal Vice," *ArQ* 28 (Winter, 1972): 293-300.

Carlock, Mary S., "Kaleidoscopic Views of Motion," in Zyla, W. T., and W. M. Aycock, eds., *William Faulkner*, 95-113.

Carnes, Frank F., "On the Aesthetics of Faulkner's Fiction," *DA* 29 (1968): 894A-5A (Vanderbilt).

Carothers, James B., "The Myriad Heart: The Evolution of the Faulkner Hero," in Fowler, D., and A. J. Abadie, eds., "A Cosmos of My Own," 252-83.

_____, "The Road to THE REIVERS," in Fowler, D., and A. J. Abadie, eds., "A Cosmos of My Own," 95-124.

Carpenter, Robert A., "Faulkner 'Discovered'," Delta Rev 2 (July-Aug., 1965): 27-9.

Castille, Philip D., "Faulkner's Early Heroines," DAI 38 (1977): 2121A.

Cavanaugh, Hilayne E., "Faulkner, Stasis, and Keats's ODE ON A GRECIAN URN," DAI 38 (1977): 2783A-84A.

Chabot, C. Barry, "Faulkner's Rescued Patrimony," Rev. of Existential Psych. & Psychiatry 13, iii (1974): 274-86.

Chung, Hae-Ja Kim, "Point of View as a Mode of Thematic Definition in Conrad and Faulkner," DAI 35 (1974): 442A-43A (Mich.).

Church, Margaret, "Two Views of Time: James Joyce and William Faulkner," UDR 14, ii (Spring, 1980): 65-9.

_____, "William Faulkner: Myth and Duration," Time and Reality, 227-50.

Ciancio, Ralph A., "Faulkner's Existentialist Affinities," in Woodruff, N., Jr., and Others, eds., Studies in Faulkner, 69-91.

Clark, Anderson A., "Courtly Love in the Writings of William Faulkner," DAI 36 (1976): 4482A-83A.

Clark, Edward D., Sr., "Six Grotesques in Three Faulkner Novels," DAI 32 (1972): 302A (Syracuse).

Clark, Winifred, "The Religious Symbolism in Faulkner's Novels," DAI 32 (1971): 1506A (Tulsa).

Cobley, Evelyn M., "Repetition and Structure: A Study of William Faulkner and Claude Simon," DAI 40 (1980): 5851A-52A.

Coffee, Jessie A., "Empty Steeples: Theme, Symbol, and Irony in Faulkner's Novels," ArQ 23 (Autumn, 1967): 197-206.

_____, "Faulkner's Un-Christlike Christians: Biblical Allusions in the Novels," DAI 32 (1971): 1506A (Nev.).

Cole, Hunter M., "Welty on Faulkner," NMW 9, i (Spring, 1976): 28-49.

Collins, Carvel, in Griffin, William, ed., Literature in the Modern World, 65-71.

_____, in Stegner, W., ed., America Novel, 219-28.

_____, Evans Harrington, Blyden Jackson, Elizabeth Kerr, and Carl Petersen, "Faulkner's Mississippi: Land into Legend: Panel Discussion," UMSE 15 (1978): 205-15.

Collins, R. G., and K. McRobbie, eds., Novels of William Faulkner.

Colson, Theodore L., "The Characters of Hawthorne and Faulkner: A Typology of Sinners," DA 28 (1967): 2204A-05A (Michigan).

Conley, Timothy K., "Beardsley and Faulkner," JML 5 (Sept., 1976): 339-56.

_____, "Shakespeare and Faulkner: A Study in Influence," DAI 39 (1979): 4945A-46A.

Cook, Albert, "Plot as Discovery," The Meaning of Fiction, Detroit: Wayne State Un. Pr., 1960, 232-41.

Cook, Richard M., "Popeye, Flem, and Sutpen: The Faulknerian Villain as Grotesque," SAF 3, i (Spring, 1975): 3-14.

Cook, Sylvia J., "Faulkner's Celebration of the Poor White Paradox," From Tobacco Road to Route 66, 39-63.

Cooley, Thomas W., Jr., "Faulkner Draws the Long Bow," TCL 16 (Oct., 1970): 268-77.

Cooper, Gerald H., "Furious Motion: Metamorphosis and Change in the Works of William Faulkner," DAI 39 (1979): 4946A.

Corridori, Edward L., "The Quest for Sacred Space: Setting in the Novels of William Faulkner," DAI 32 (1972): 5224A (Kent State).

Corwin, Ronald L., "The Development of Narrative Technique in the Apprenticeship Fiction of William Faulkner," DAI 37 (1976): 2869A.

Couch, John P., "Camus and Faulkner: The Search for the Language of Modern Tragedy," YFS No. 25 (1960): 120-5.

Coughlan, Robert, The Private World of William Faulkner, N.Y.: Harper, 1954. Also (excerpted) as "The Private World of William Faulkner," Life 35 (Sept. 28, 1953): 118-36. Also in Life (Periodical), Great Reading from Life: A Treasury of the Best Stories and Articles Chosen by the Editors, N.Y.: Harper, 1960, 204-16. Also in Prize Articles, 1954: The Benjamin Franklin Magazine Awards, administered by the Un. of Illinois, ed. by Llewellyn Miller, N.Y.: Ballantine, 1954, 121-56.

Cowley, Malcolm, "The Etiology of Faulkner's Art," SoR 13, i (Jan., 1977): 83-95.

_____, The Faulkner-Cowley File; Letters and Memories, 1944-1962, N.Y.: Viking, 1966.

_____, Evans Harrington, Elizabeth Kerr, and Robert Oesterling, "Faulkner's Mississippi: Land into Legend," UMSE 14 (1974): 119-61.

_____, "A Fresh Look at Faulkner," SatR 49 (June 11, 1966): 22-6.

_____, "An Introduction to William Faulkner," in Aldridge, J. W., ed., Critiques and Essays on Modern Fiction, 427-46. Also (in part) as "Introduction," in The Portable Faulkner, N.Y.: Viking, 1946, 1-24. Also in Hoffman, F. J., and O. W. Vickery, eds., William Faulkner, 94-109. Also in Hoffman, F. J., and O. W. Vickery, eds., William Faulkner: Two Decades of Criticism, 63-82. Also (condensed) in Warren, R. P., ed., Faulkner, 34-45. Also (in part) as "William Faulkner's Legend of the South," SR 53 (Summer, 1945): 343-61. Also in Tate, Allen, ed., A Southern Vanguard, N.Y.: Prentice-Hall, 1947, 13-27. Also in West, Ray B., ed., Essays in Modern Literary Criticism, N.Y.: Holt, 1952, 513-26. Also, in part, in Schmitter, D. M., ed., William Faulkner, 15-19.

_____, "Magic in Faulkner," in Harrington, E., and A. J. Abadie, eds., Faulkner, Modernism, and Film, 3-19.

Cox, L. H., ed., William Faulkner.

Crane, John K., "The Jefferson Courthouse: An AXIS EXSE-CRABILIS MUNDI," TCL 15, i (April, 1969): 19-23.

Creighton, J. V., William Faulkner's Craft of Revision.

Crow, Peter G., "Faulkner's Vitalistic Vision: A Close Study of Eight Novels," DAI 34 (1973): 764A-65A (Duke).

Cullen, John B., and F. C. Watkins, Old Times in the Faulkner Country, Chapel Hill: Un. of No. Carolina Pr., 1961.

Culley, Margaret M. M., "Eschatological Thought in Faulkner's Yoknapatawpha Novels," DAI 33 (1973): 5167A (Mich.).

_____, "Judgment in Yoknapatawpha Fiction," Ren 23, ii (Winter, 1976): 59-70.

Dabney, L. M., Indians of Yoknapatawpha.

Dahl, James, "William Faulkner on Individualism," WGCR 6 (May, 1973): 3-9.

Darnell, Donald G., "Cooper and Faulkner: Land, Legacy, and the Tragic Vision," SAB 34, ii (Mar., 1969): 3-5.

Dasher, Thomas E., "An Index to the Characters in the Published and Unpublished Fiction of William Faulkner," *DAI* 40 (1979): 1466A.

_____, *William Faulkner's Characters: An Index to the Published and Unpublished Fiction*, N.Y.: Garland, 1981.

Davenport, F. G., *Myth of Southern History*, 82-130.

Davis, Mary E., "William Faulkner and Marie Vargas Llosa: The Election of Failure," *CLS* 16 (Dec., 1979): 332-43.

Dean, Charles W., Jr., "William Faulkner's Romantic Heritage: Beyond America," *DAI* 36 (1975): 885A-86A.

Dean, Elizabeth M. L., "The Contours of Eros: Landscape in Twentieth Century Art and Literature," *DAI* 38 (1977): 3455A-56A.

Degenfelder, E. Pauline, "Essays on Faulkner: Style, Use of History, Film Adaptations of His Fiction," *DAI* 33 (1973): 5169A (Case Western Reserve).

Desmond, John F., "Christian Historical Analogues in the Fiction of William Faulkner and Flannery O'Connor," *DAI* 32 (1972): 3994A-95A (Okla.).

Despain, Norma L., "Stream of Consciousness Narration in Faulkner: A Redefinition," *DAI* 37 (1976): 306A-7A.

Devlin, Albert, "Parent-Child Relationships in the Works of William Faulkner," *DAI* 31 (1970): 2910A (Kan.).

Dickerson, Mary J., "Faulkner's Golden Steed," *MissQ* 31 (Summer, 1978): 369-80.

Dike, Donald, "The World of Faulkner's Imagination," *DA* 15 (1955): 365 (Syracuse).

Dillingham, William B., "William Faulkner and the 'Tragic Condition'," *Edda* 66 (1966): 322-35.

Dillon, Richard T., "Some Sources for Faulkner's Version of the First Air War," *AL* 44 (Jan., 1973): 629-37.

Ditsky, John, "Faulkner Land and Steinbeck Country," in Astro, R., and T. Hayashi, eds., *Steinbeck*, 11-23. Also in Hayashi, T., ed., *Steinbeck's Literary Dimension*, 28-45.

_____, "Faulkner's Harrykin Creek: A Note," *UWR* 12, i (Fall-Winter, 1976): 88-9.

_____, "From Oxford to Salinas: Comparing Faulkner and Steinbeck," *StN* 2, iii (Fall, 1969): 51-5.

_____, "Land-Nostalgia in the Novels of Faulkner, Cather, and Steinbeck," *DA* 28 (1967): 1072A (N.Y.U.).

_____, "Uprooted Trees: Dynasty and the Land in Faulkner's Novels," *TSL* 17 (1972): 151-8.

Di Virgilio, Paul S., "Study of Voice in the Modern Novel," *DAI* 41 (1980): 2592A.

Dodds, John L., "The Fatal Arc: The Evolution of Tragic Image and Idea in Three Novels by William Faulkner," *DAI* 38 (1978): 6722A-23A.

Donnelly, William and Doris, "William Faulkner: In Search of Peace," *Person* 44 (Autumn, 1963): 490-8.

Doran, Leonard, "Form and the Story Teller," *HarvardA* 135 (Nov., 1951): 12+.

Dorsch, Robert L., "An Interpretation of the Central Themes in the Work of William Faulkner," *ESRS* 11, i (Sept., 1962): 5-42.

Doster, William, "The Several Faces of Gavin Stevens," *MissQ* 11 (Fall, 1958): 191-5.

_____, "William Faulkner and the Negro," *DA* 20 (1959): 1094 (Florida).

Douglas, Ellen, "Faulkner in Time," in Fowler, D., and A. J. Abadie, eds., *"A Cosmos of My Own,"* 284-301.

_____, "Faulkner's Women," in Fowler, D., and A. J. Abadie, eds., *"A Cosmos of My Own,"* 149-67.

Douglas, Harold J., and Robert Daniel, "Faulkner and the Puritanism of the South," *TSL* 2 (1957): 1-13. Also in Barth, J. R., S. J., ed., *Religious Perspectives in Faulkner's Fiction*, 37-51.

Douglass, Scott, "Possible Sources for Faulkner's General Compson," *RALS* 11 (1981): 112-14.

Dowell, Bobby R., "Faulkner's Comic Spirit," *DA* 23 (1963): 4355 (Denver).

Doyle, Charles, "The Moral World of Faulkner," *Ren* 19 (Fall, 1966): 3-12.

Duncan, Alastair B., "Claude Simon and William Faulkner," *FMLS* 9 (1973): 235-52.

Duvall, Howard, Robert J. Farley, Phil Mullen, James W. Webb, William M. Reed, William Stone, and William Roane, "Faulkner in Oxford: Panel Discussion," *UMSE* 15 (1978): 161-86.

Eby, Cecil D., "Faulkner and the Southwestern Humorists," *Shen* 11, i (Autumn, 1959): 13-21.

Edmonds, Irene C., "Faulkner and the Black Shadow," in Rubin, L., and R. D. Jacobs, eds., *Southern Renascence*, 192-206.

Egolf, Robert H., "Faulkner's Men and Women: A Critical Study of Male-Female Relationships in His Early Yoknapatawpha County Novels," *DAI* 39 (1979): 4946A-47A.

Eigner, Edwin M., "Faulkner's Isaac and the American Ishmael," *JA* 14 (1969): 107-15.

Eisinger, C. E., *Fiction of the Forties*, 178-86.

Elkin, Stanley L., "Religious Themes and Symbolism in the Novels of William Faulkner," *DA* 22 (1962): 3659-60 (Illinois).

Emerson, O. B., "Prophet Next Door," in Walker, W. E., and Welker, R. E., eds., *Reality and Myth*, 237-74.

Emmanuel, Pierre, "Faulkner and the Sense of Sin," *HarvardA* 135 (Nov., 1951): 20.

Eschliman, Herbert R., "Francis Christensen in Yoknapatawpha County," *UR* 37, iii (Spring, 1971): 232-9.

Everett, W. K., *Faulkner's Art and Characters*.

Fadiman, C., *Party of One*, 98-125.

Falkner, Murry C., *The Falkners of Mississippi: A Memoir*, Baton Rouge: La. St. Un. Pr., 1967.

Fant, Joseph L., III, and Robert Ashley, eds., *Faulkner at West Point*, N.Y.: Random House, 1964.

Farnham, James F., "A Note on One Aspect of Faulkner's Style," *Lang&S* 2 (Spring, 1969): 190-2.

_____, "They Who Endure and Prevail: Characters of William Faulkner," Unpub. Doct. Diss., Western Reserve Un., 1962.

Faulkner, John, *My Brother Bill: An Affectionate Reminiscence*, N.Y.: Trident, 1963.

Faulkner, William, "The Stockholm Address," (Nobel Prize) in Hoffman, F. J., and O. W. Vickery, eds., *William Faulkner*, 347-8.

Fazio, Rocco R., "The Fury and the Design: Realms of Being and Knowing in Four Novels of William Faulkner," *DA* 25 (1964): 1910 (Rochester).

Feldstein, Richard, "The Dispossession of Personae Non Gratae: A Study of Faulkner's Relation to the 'Other'," *DAI* 43 (1982): 1970A-7A.

Ferguson, Robert C., "The Grotesque in the Fiction of William Faulkner," *DAI* 32 (1971): 1508A (Case Western Reserve).

Fiedler, Leslie, "An American Dickens," *Ctary* 10 (Oct., 1950): 384-7. Also in Fiedler, L., *No! In Thunder* 111-18.

_____, "The Death of the Old Men," *A&S* (Winter, 1963-64): 1-5. Also in Fiedler, L. A., *Waiting For the End*, 9-19.

_____, *Love and Death in the American Novel*, 309-15 *passim*.

Finkelstein, S., *Existentialism and Alienation in American Literature*, 184-97.

_____, "William Faulkner," *Mainstream* 15, viii (Aug., 1962): 3-6.

Fitzgerald, James R., "William Faulkner's Literary Reputation in Britain, with a Checklist of Criticism, 1929-1972," *DAI* 34 (1974): 5965A-66A (Ga.).

Flanagan, John T., "Faulkner's Favorite Word," *GaR* 17 (Winter, 1963): 429-34.

_____, "Folklore in Faulkner's Fiction," *PLL* 5 (Summer Supp., 1969): 119-44.

_____, "The Mythic Background of Faulkner's Horse Imagery," *NCarF* 13, i-ii (1965): 135-46. Also in *Folklore Studies in Honor of Arthur Palmer Hudson*, Chapel Hill: No. Car. Folklore Soc., 1965, 135-45.

Fletcher, Mary D., "Jason Compson: Contemporary Villain," *LaS* 15 (Fall, 1976): 253-61.

_____, "William Faulkner: The Calvinistic Sensibility," *DAI* 35 (1975): 5400A.

Flint, R. W., "Faulkner as Elegist," *HudR* 7 (Summer, 1954): 246-57. Also in Cox, L. H., ed., *William Faulkner*, 475-88.

Flynn, Peggy, "The Sister Figure and 'Little Sister Death' in the Fiction of William Faulkner," *UMSE* 14 (1976): 99-117.

Folks, Jeffrey J., "The Influence of Poetry on the Narrative Technique of Faulkner's Early Fiction," *JNT* 9 (Fall, 1979): 184-90.

_____, "Plot Materials and Narrative Form in Faulkner's Early Fiction," *DAI* 38 (1978): 6724A.

_____, "William Faulkner and the Silent Film," *SoQ* 19, iii-iv (Spring-Summer, 1981): 171-82.

Foote, Shelby, Darwin T. Turner, and Evans Harrington, "Faulkner and Race," in Harrington, E., and A. J. Abadie, eds., *South and Faulkner's Yoknapatawpha*, 86-103.

_____, "Faulkner and War," in Harrington, E., and A. J. Abadie, eds., *South and Faulkner's Yoknapatawpha*, 152-67.

_____, "Faulkner's Depiction of the Planter Aristocracy," in Harrington, E., and A. J. Abadie, eds., *South and Faulkner's Yoknapatawpha*, 40-61.

Ford, Dan, "Maybe Happen Is Never Once: Some Critical Thought on Faulkner's Use of Time," *PAPA* 5, ii-iii (Spring-Fall, 1979): 9-15.

_____, "Uses of Time in Four Novels by William Faulkner," *DAI* 35 (1974): 1654A.

Ford, Margaret P., and Suzanne Kincaid, *Who's Who in Faulkner*, Baton Rouge: La. State Un. Pr., 1963.

Foster, Ruel, "Dream as Symbolic Act in Faulkner," *Per* 2 (Summer, 1949): 179-94.

_____, "Social Order and Disorder in Faulkner's Fiction," *Approach* No. 55 (Spring, 1965): 20-8.

Fowler, D., and A. J. Abadie, eds., *"A Cosmos of My Own."*

_____, *Faulkner and the Southern Renaissance*.

Fowler, Doreen F., "Faulkner's Changing Vision: Narrative Progress toward Affirmation," *DAI* 35 (1975): 7302A-03A.

Fowler, D., and A. J. Abadie, eds., *Fifty Years of Yoknapatawpha*.

Franklin, Rosemary F., "Clairvoyance, Vision, and Imagination in the Fiction of William Faulkner," *DA* 29 (1969): 3135A (Emory).

Freedman, Morris, "Sound and Sense in Faulkner's Prose," *CEA* 19, vi (1957): 1, 4-5. [Not seen.]

French, Warren, "The Background of Snopesism in Mississippi Politics," *MASJ* 5 (Fall, 1964): 3-17.

_____, "William Faulkner and the Art of the Detective Story," in French, W., ed., *Thirties*, 55-62.

Friend, George L., "Levels of Maturity: The Theme of Striving in the Novels of William Faulkner," *DA* 25 (1965): 6622-23 (Illinois).

Frohock, W. M., "Faulkner and the *Roman Nouveau*: An Interim Report," *BuR* 10 (Mar., 1962): 186-93.

_____, "Faulkner in France: The Final Phase," *Mosaic* 4, iii (1971): 125-34.

_____, "William Faulkner: The Private View versus the Public Vision," *SWR* 34 (Summer, 1949): 281-94.

_____, "William Faulkner: The Private Vision,'' *Novel of Violence in America*, 144-65.

Gallagher, Susan, "To Love and To Honor: Brothers and Sisters in Faulkner's Yoknapatawpha County," *ELWIU* 7 (Fall, 1980): 213-24.

Garrett, George, "The Influence of William Faulkner," *GaR* 18 (1964): 419-27.

Gegerias, Mary, "Michel Butor and William Faulkner: Some Structures and Techniques," *DA* 30 (1969): 721A.

Géher, István, "A Child's Eye View of Tragedy: Faulkner's Mixed Metaphor," *ALitASH* 23, iii-iv (1981): 281-96.

_____, "Olé, Grandfather: The Presence of a Missing Link in William Faulkner's Life and Work," in Perény, Erzsébet, and Tibor Frank, eds., *Studies in English and American*, Vol. II, Budapest: Dept. of Eng., L. Eotuos Un., 1975, 215-75.

Geismar, M., *Writers in Crisis*, 143-83.

Gerard, Albert, "Justice in Yoknapatawpha County: Some Symbolic Motifs in Faulkner's Later Writing," *Faulkner Studies* 2 (Winter, 1953): 49-57.

Gidley, Mark, "Elements of the Detective Story in William Faulkner's Fiction," *JPC* 7, i (Summer, 1973): 97-123. Also in Landrum, L. N., P. Browne, and R. B. Browne, eds., *Dimensions of Detective Fiction*, 228-46.

_____, "One Continuous Force: Notes on Faulkner's Extra-Literary Reading," *MissQ* 23, iii (Summer, 1970): 299-314.

_____, "Some Notes on Faulkner's Reading," *JAmS* 4, i (July, 1970): 91-102.

_____, "William Faulkner and Some Designs of Naturalism," *SAF* 7 (Spring, 1979): 75-82.

_____, "William Faulkner and Willard Huntington Wright's THE CREATIVE WILL," *CRevAS* 9 (Fall, 1978): 169-77.

Gidley, Mick, "Another Psychologist, a Physiologist and William Faulkner," *ArielE* 2, iv (Oct., 1971): 78-86.

Giorgini, J., "Faulkner and Camus," *Delta Rev* 2, iii (1965): 31+.

Gissendanner, John M., "The 'Nether Channel': A Study of Faulkner's Black Characters," *DAI* 43, iii (Sept., 1982): 802A.

Glicksberg, Charles I., "The Art of Faulkner's Fiction," *Meanjin* 12 (Autumn, 1953): 69-78.

_____, "Faulkner's World of Love and Sex," *Sexual Revolution in American Literature*, 96-120.

_____, "William Faulkner and the Negro Problem," *Phylon* 10 (June, 1949): 153-60.

_____, "The World of William Faulkner," *ArQ* 5 (Spring, 1949): 46-57.

Going, W. T., "Faulkner's Other State: His Fictional View of Alabama," *BSUF* 20, ii (Spring, 1979): 49-52.

Gold, Joseph, "Dickens and Faulkner: The Uses of Influence," *Dr* 49, i (Spring, 1969): 69-79.

_____, "The Humanism of William Faulkner," *Humanist* 20 (Jan.-Feb., 1960): 113-17.

_____, *William Faulkner.*

Goldman, Arnold, "Faulkner and the Revision of Yoknapatawpha History," in Bradford, M., and D. Palmer, eds., *American Novel in the Nineteen Twenties*, 165-95.

_____, "Faulkner's Images of the Past: From SARTORIS to THE UNVANQUISHED," *YES* 8 (1978): 109-24.

Goodenberger, Mary E. M., "William Faulkner's Compleat Woman," *DAI* 38 (1978): 4827A.

Gossett, L. Y., *Violence in Recent Southern Fiction*, 29-47.

Gray, R., "The Individual Talent: William Faulkner and the Yoknapatawpha Novels," *Literature of Memory*, 197-256.

Green, A. Wigfall, "William Faulkner at Home," *SR* 40 (Summer, 1932): 294-36. Also in Hoffman, F. J., and O. W. Vickery, eds., *William Faulkner: Two Decades of Criticism*, 33-47.

Green, M., "Faulkner: the Triumph of Rhetoric," *Re-Appraisals*, 167-94.

Greene, Robert I., "Innocence and Experience in Selected Major Fiction of William Faulkner," *DAI* 40 (1979): 852A-53A.

Greer, Dorothy D., "Dilsey and Lucas: Faulkner's Use of the Negro as a Gauge of Moral Character," *ESRS* 11, i (Sept., 1962): 43-61.

Gregory, Charles T., "Darkness to Appall: Destructive Designs and Patterns in Some Characters of William Faulkner," *DA* 30 (1969): 1565A-66A (Columbia).

Grenier, Cynthia, "The Art of Fiction: An Interview with William Faulkner—September, 1955," *Accent* 16 (Summer, 1956): 167-77.

Gresham, Jewell H., "The Fatal Illusions: Self, Sex, Race, and Religion in William Faulkner's World," *DAI* 31 (1971): 5402A (Columbia).

_____, "Narrative Techniques of William Faulkner's Form," *Nassau Rev* (Nassau Community College) 1, iii (1966): 103-19.

Gresset, Michel, "Epithese," *DeltaES* 3 (Nov., 1976): 173-91.

_____, "Faulkner, 1935," *EA* 29 (July-Sept., 1976): 448-55.

Gretlund, Jan N., "The Wild Old Green Man of the Woods: Katherine Anne Porter's Faulkner," *NMW* 12 (1980): 67-79.

Gribbin, Daniel V., "Men of Thought, Men of Action: A Pattern of Contrasts in Faulkner's Major Novels," *DAI* 34 (1974): 5969A (N.C., Chapel Hill).

Griffin, William C., "How to Misread Faulkner: A Powerful Plea for Ignorance," *TSL* No. 1 (1956): 27-34.

Griffith, Benjamin W., "Faulkner's Archaic Titles and the SECOND SHEPHERD'S PLAY," *NMW* 4, ii (Fall, 1971): 62-3.

Grimwood, James M., "Pastoral and Parody: The Making of Faulkner's Anthology Novels," *DAI* 37 (1977): 5828A.

Guerard, Albert J., "Faulkner the Innovator," in Harrington, E., and A. J. Abadie, eds., *Maker and the Myth*, 71-88.

_____, "Forbidden Games III: Faulkner's Misogyny," *Triumph of the Novel*, 109-35.

_____, "Faulkner: Problems of Technique," *Triumph of the Novel*, 204-34.

_____, "The Faulknerian Voice," in Harrington, E., and A. J. Abadie, eds., *Maker and the Myth*, 25-42.

_____, *The Triumph of the Novel: Dickens, Dostoevsky, Faulkner*, N.Y.: Oxford Un. Pr., 1976.

Gurko, L., *Angry Decade*, 128-36.

Guttmann, Allen, "Collisions and Confrontations," *ArQ* 16 (Spring, 1960): 46-52.

Gwynn, F. L., and J. L. Blotner, eds., *Faulkner in the University.*

_____, "Faulkner in the University," *CE* 19 (Oct., 1957): 1-6.

_____, "William Faulkner on Dialect," *UVMag* 2, i (1958): 7-13; 2, ii (1958): 32-7.

Hafner, John H., "William Faulkner's Narrators," *DAI* 30 (1970): 5445A (Wis.).

Hagopian, John V., "Style and Meaning in Hemingway and Faulkner," *JA* Band 4 (1959): 170-9.

Hall, J., *Lunatic Giant in the Drawing Room*, 56-77.

Hamblin, Robert W., "'Saying No to Death': Toward William Faulkner's Theory of Fiction," in Fowler, D., and A. J. Abadie, eds., "*A Cosmos of My Own*," 3-35.

Hamblin, Bobby W., "William Faulkner's Theory of Fiction," *DAI* 37 (1976): 1546A-47A.

Hamilton, Edith, "Faulkner: Sorcerer or Slave?" *SatR* 25 (July 12, 1952): 8-10, 39. Also in Saturday Review (Periodical), *Saturday Review Gallery*, N.Y.: Simon and Schuster, 1959, 419-29. Also as "William Faulkner," *The Ever-Present Past*, N.Y.: Norton, 1964, 159-73.

Hammond, Donald, "Faulkner's Levels of Awareness," *FloQ* 1, ii (1967): 73-81.

Hanaka, Hisao, "Hawthorne and Faulkner," *SALit* 15 (1979): 17-35.

Hancock, Maxine, "Fire: Symbolic Motif in Faulkner," *EngQ* 3, iii (Fall, 1970): 19-23.

Harder, Kelsie B., "Charactonyms in Faulkner's Novels," *BuR* 8, iii (May, 1959): 189-201.

Hardy, J. E., "William Faulkner: The Legend Behind the Legend," *Man in the Modern Novel*, 137-48.

Harkness, Bruce, "Faulkner and Scott," *MissQ* 20 (Summer, 1967): 164.

Harold, Brent, "The Values and Limitations of Faulkner's Fictional Method," *AL* 47, ii (May, 1975): 212-29.

Harrington, E., and A. J. Abadie, eds., *Faulkner, Modernism, and Film.*

_____, *Maker and the Myth.*

_____, *South and Faulkner's Yoknapatawpha.*

Haselswerdt, Marjorie B., "On Their Hind Legs Casting Shadows: A Psychological Approach to Character in Faulkner," *DAI* 42 (1981): 1149A.

Hauck, Richard B., "The Prime Maniacal Risibility: William Faulkner," *Cheerful Nihilism*, 167-78.

Hawkins, E. O., Jr., "A Handbook of Yoknapatawpha," *DA* 21 (1961): 3457-8 (Arkansas).

Hayakawa, Hiroshi, "Negation in William Faulkner," in Araki, Kazuo, and others, *Studies in English Grammar and Linguistics. A Miscellany in Honour of Takanobu Otsuka*, Tokyo: Kenkyusha, 1958, 103-16.

Hayes, Elizabeth T., "Comedy in Faulkner's Fiction," *DAI* 40 (1979): 256A-57A.

Heller, Terry, "Notes on Technique in Black Humor," *Thalia* 2, iii (1979): 15-21.

Hepburn, Kenneth W., "SOLDIER'S PAY to THE SOUND AND THE FURY: Development of the Poetic in the Early Novels of William Faulkner," *DA* 29 (1959): 2263A (Un. of Wash.).

Hernandez, Joan L., "The Influence of William Faulkner in Four Latin American Novelists (Yánez, Garcia Márquez, Cepeda Asmudio, Donoso)," *DAI* 39 (1979): 6756A.

Herndon, Jerry A., "Faulkner's Nobel Prize Address: A Reading," *SAQ* 81, i (1982): 94-104.

Hirano, Nobuyuki, "Reconsideration of Moral Order and Disorder in Faulkner's Works," *HJAS* 8, i (Sept., 1967): 7-32.

Hoadley, Frank M., "Folk Humor in the Novels of William Faulkner," *TFSB* 23 (1957): 75-82.

————, "The Theme of Atonement in the Novels of William Faulkner," *NWR* 10, iii (Summer, 1970): 30-43.

————, "The World View of William Faulkner," *DA* 16 (1956): 338 (Oklahoma).

Hoffer, Bates, "The Sociolinguistics of Literature: Faulkner's Styles and Dialects," in Robert N. St. Clair, ed., *Perspectives on Applied Sociolinguistics: From the Language Medium of Education to the Semiotic Language of the Media*, Lawrence, KS: Coronado, 1979, 212-23.

Hoffman, Frederick J., in French, W. G., and W. E. Kidd, *American Winners of the Nobel Literary Prize*, 138-57.

————, *William Faulkner*.

————, and O. W. Vickery, eds., *William Faulkner*.

————, "William Faulkner: A Review of Recent Criticism," *Ren* 13 (Autumn, 1960): 3-9+.

————, and O. W. Vickery, eds., *William Faulkner: Three Decades of Criticism*.

Hogan, Patrick G., Jr., "Critical Misconceptions of Southern Thought: Faulkner's Optimism," *MissQ* 10 (Jan., 1957): 19-28.

Hollowell, Dorothy M., "A Study of Conrad and Faulkner: Links to Imperialism," *DAI* 41 (1980): 1054A.

Holman, C. H., "William Faulkner: The Anguished Dream of Time," *Three Modes of Modern Southern Fiction*, 27-47.

Holmes, Edward M., *Faulkner's Twice-Told Tales: His Re-Use of His Material*, The Hague, The Netherlands: Mouton, 1966.

Hopper, Vincent, "Faulkner's Paradise Lost," *VQR* 23 (Summer, 1947): 405-20.

Hornback, Vernon T., Jr., "William Faulkner and the Terror of History: Myth, History, and Moral Freedom in the Yoknapatawpha Cycle," *DA* 25 (1964): 476 (St. Louis).

Horsch, Janice, "Faulkner on Man's Struggle with Communication," *KM* (1964): 77-83.

Hovde, Carl F., "Faulkner's Democratic Rhetoric," *SAQ* 63 (Autumn, 1964): 530-41.

Howe, Irving, "Faulkner and the Negroes," in Gross, S. L., and J. E. Hardy, eds., *Images of the Negro in American Literature*, 204-20.

————, "Faulkner and the Southern Tradition," in Rahv, P., ed., *Literature in America*, 409-14. Also in Howe, I., *William Faulkner*, 22-9.

————, "The Quest for a Moral Style," *A World More Attractive*, 73-6.

————, "The Southern Myth and William Faulkner," *AQ* 3 (Winter, 1951): 357-62. Also in Cohen, Hennig, ed., *The American Culture: Approaches to the Study of the United States*, Boston: Houghton Mifflin, 1968, 43-8.

————, "A Talent of Wild Abundance," in Brown, F., ed., *Opinions and Perspectives*, 194-8.

————, *William Faulkner*.

————, *William Faulkner*, 3rd ed.

————, "William Faulkner and the Negroes," *Ctary* 12 (Oct., 1951): 359-67.

————, "William Faulkner's Enduring Power," *NYTBR* (April 4, 1954): 1+.

Howell, Elmo, "Mark Twain, William Faulkner and the First Families of Virginia," *MTJ* 13, ii (1966): 1-3+.

————, "A Name for Faulkner's City," *Names* 16 (Dec., 1968): 415-21.

————, "A Note on Faulkner's Negro Characters," *MissQ* 11 (Fall, 1958): 201-3.

————, "William Faulkner and Tennessee," *THQ* 21 (Sept., 1962): 251-62.

————, "William Faulkner and the New Deal," *MQ* 5 (July, 1964): 323-32.

————, "William Faulkner and the Plain People of Yoknapatawpha County," *Jnl of Miss Hist* 24 (April, 1962): 73-87.

————, "William Faulkner: The Substance of Faith," *BYUS* 9, iv (Summer, 1969): 453-62.

————, "William Faulkner's Mule: A Symbol of the Post-War South," *KFR* 15 (Oct.-Dec., 1969): 81-6.

————, "William Faulkner's General Forrest and the Uses of History," *THQ* 29, iii (Fall, 1970): 287-94.

————, "William Faulkner's Graveyard," *NMW* 4, iii (Winter, 1972): 115-18.

————, "William Faulkner's New Orleans," *LaH* 7 (Summer, 1966): 229-39.

————, "William Faulkner's Southern Baptists," *ArQ* 23 (Autumn, 1967): 220-6.

Howell, John M, "Faulkner, Prufrock and Agamemnon: Horses, Hell, and High Water," in Carey, Glenn O., ed., *Faulkner*, 213-29.

Hubank, Roger, "William Faulkner: A Perspective View," *Delta* No. 10 (Autumn, 1956): 13-21.

Hudson, Tommy, "William Faulkner: Mystic and Traditionalist," *Per* 3 (Autumn, 1950): 227-35.

Hughes, Richard, "Faulkner and Bennett," *Encounter* 21 No. 120 (Sept., 1963): 59-61.

Hunt, John W., "The Theological Complexity of Faulkner's Fiction," in Hunt, J. W., *William Faulkner*, 25-33. Also in Barth, R., Jr., S.J., ed., *Religious Perspectives in Faulkner's Fiction*, 81-7.

————, *William Faulkner*.

Hunter, E. R., *William Faulkner*.

Hutcheon, Philip L., "Affirming the Void: Futilitarianism in the Fiction of Conrad and Faulkner," *DAI* 35 (1974): 2271A (Rice).

Hutchinson, James D., "TIME: The Fourth Dimension in Faulkner," *SDR* 6 (Autumn, 1968): 91-103.

Hyde, Monique R., "William Faulkner and Claude Simon: A Stylistic Study," *DAI* 32 (1972): 5740A-41A (Ind.).

Ilacqua, Alma A., "Faulkner and the Concept of Excellence," *DAI* 36 (1975): 314A.

————, "From Purveyor of Perversion to Defender of the Faithful: A Summary of Critical Studies of Faulkner's Theological Vision," *LangQ* 20, i-ii (Fall-Winter, 1981): 35-8.

Imbleau, Henry R., "Failed Manhood: Sexual Cowardice in William Faulkner," *DAI* 42, vii (Feb., 1982): 3600A.

Inge, M. Thomas, ed., with an introd. by "Donald Davidson on Faulkner: An Early Recognition," *GaR* 20 (Winter, 1966): 454-62.

————, "William Faulkner and George Washington Harris: In the Tradition of Southwestern Humor," *TSL* 7 (1962): 47-59.

Irvine, Peter L., "Faulkner and Hardy," *ArQ* 26, iv (Winter, 1970): 357-65.

Irwin, J. T., *Doubling and Incest/Repetition and Revenge*.

Izubuchi, Hirochi, "Faulkner and Yeats: An Essay," *WiF* 4, i (Dec., 1981): 1-14.

Jackson, Blyden, "Faulkner's Deception of the Negro," *UMSE* 15 (1978): 33-47.

_____, "Two Mississippi Writers: Wright and Faulkner," *UMSE* 15 (1978): 49-59.

Jackson, Naomi, "Faulkner's Woman: 'Demon-Nun and Angel-Witch'," *BSUF* 8, i (Winter, 1967): 12-20.

Jacobs, Robert D., "Faulkner's Tragedy of Isolation," *Hopkins Rev* 6 (Spring-Summer, 1953): 162-83. Also in Rubin, L. D., and R. D. Jacobs, eds., *Southern Renascence*, 170-91.

_____, "How Do *You* Read Faulkner?" *Prov* 1, iv (April, 1957): 3-5.

_____, "William Faulkner: The Passion and the Pretense," in Rubin, L. D., Jr., and R. D. Jacobs, eds., *South*, 141-76.

Jaffe, Evelyn, "Endure and Prevail: Faulkner's Social Outcasts," *DAI* 38 (1977): 2789A-90A.

James, Stuart, "Faulkner's Shadowed Land," *DQ* 6, iii (Autumn, 1971): 45-61.

Jarrett-Kerr, Fr. Martin, *William Faulkner*.

Jehlen, M., *Class and Character in Faulkner's South*.

Jenkins, L., *Faulkner and Black-White Relations*.

_____, "Faulkner, the Mythic Mind, and the Blacks," *L&P* 27, ii (1977): 74-91.

_____, "Images of the Negro in the Novels of William Faulkner," *DAI* 34 (1973): 3403A (Columbia).

Jordan, Peter W., "Faulkner's Crime Fiction: His Use of the Detective Story and the Thriller," *DAI* 34 (1973): 2630A-31A (Conn.).

Jordan, Robert M., "The Limits of Illusion: Faulkner, Fielding, and Chaucer," *Criticism* 2 (Summer, 1960): 278-89.

Josephs, Mary J., "The Hunting Metaphor in Hemingway and Faulkner," *DAI* 34 (1973): 1282A-83A (Mich. State).

Kaluza, I., "William Faulkner's Subjective Style," *KN* 11, i (1964): 13-29.

Kane, Patricia, "Adaptable and Free: Faulkner's Ratliff," *NConL* 1, iii (May, 1971): 9-11.

Kantak, V. Y., "Faulkner's Technique," in Chander, J., and N. S. Pradhan, eds., *Studies in American Literature*, 77-96.

Kartiganer, D. M., *Fragile Thread*.

_____, "The Individual and the Community: Values in the Novels of William Faulkner," *DA* 25 (1965): 4701-02 (Brown).

_____, "Process and Product: A Study of Modern Literary Form," *MR* 12 (Autumn, 1971): 297-328, 789-816.

Kauffman, Linda S., "Psychic Displacement and Adaptation in the Novels of Dickens and Faulkner," *DAI* 39 (1978): 3573A-74A.

Kawin, Bruce, "The Montage Element in Faulkner's Fiction," in Harrington, E., and A J. Abadie, eds., *Faulkner, Modernism, and Film*, 103-26.

Kay, Wallace G., "Faulkner's Mississippi: The Myth and the Microcosm," *SoQ* 6 (Oct., 1967): 13-24.

Kazin, Alfred, "Faulkner in His Fury," *The Inmost Leaf*, N.Y.: Noonday Pr., 1959, 257-73. Also in Litz, A. W., ed., *Modern American Fiction*, 166-78.

_____, "Faulkner's Vision of Human Integrity," *HarvardA* 135 (Nov., 1951): 8-9+.

Kenner, Hugh, "Faulkner and Joyce," in Harrington, E., and A. J. Abadie, eds., *Faulkner, Modernism, and Film*, 20-33.

_____, 'Faulkner and the Avant-Garde," in Harrington, E., and A. J. Abadie, eds., *Faulkner, Modernism, and Film*, 182-96.

Kent, George E., "The Black Woman in Faulkner's Works, with the Exclusion of Dilsey: Parts I and II," *Phylon* 35 (Dec., 1974): 430-41; 36 (Mar., 1975): 55-67.

_____, "Faulkner and the Heritage of White Racial Consciousness: Notes on White Nationalism in Literature," *Blackness and the Adventure of Western Culture*, 164-82.

Kerlin, Charles M., Jr., "Life in Motion: Genteel and Vernacular Attitudes in the Works of Southwestern American Humorists, Mark Twain, and William Faulkner," *DA* 29 (1969): 4492A (Colo.).

Kerr, Elizabeth, "The Evolution of Yoknapatawph," *UMSE* 14 (1976): 23-62.

_____, "William Faulkner and the Southern Concept of Woman," *MissQ* 15 (Winter, 1961-62): 1-16.

_____, *William Faulkner's Gothic Domain*.

_____, "The Women of Yoknapatawpha," *UMSE* 15 (1978): 83-100.

_____, "Yoknapatawpha and the Myth of the South," *WisSL* No. 1 (1964): 85-93.

_____, *Yoknapatawpha: Faulkner's "Little Postage Stamp of Native Soil,"* N.Y.: Fordham Un. Pr., 1969.

Kilgo, James, "Southern Literature," 17-24 in *The American South*, Athens: Un. of Georgia Center for Continuing Ed., 1979.

Kim, Wook-dong, "The Edge of Nothing: An Existential Reading of William Faulkner," *DAI* 42, xii (June, 1982): 5117A.

King, Richard H., "Framework of a Renaissance," in Fowler, D., and A. J. Abadie, eds., *Faulkner and the Southern Renaissance*, 3-21.

Kinney, Arthur F., "Faulkner and Flaubert," *JML* 6, ii (April, 1977): 222-47.

_____, "Faulkner's Fourteenth Image," *Paintbrush* 2, ii (Autumn, 1974): 36-43.

_____, *Faulkner's Narrative Poetics*.

Kirk, Robert W., and Marvin Klotz, *Faulkner's People: A Complete Guide and Index to Characters in the Fiction of William Faulkner*, Berkeley: Un. of Calif. Pr., 1963.

Klotz, Marvin, "The Triumph Over Time: Narrative Form in William Faulkner and William Styron," *MissQ* 17 (Winter, 1963-64): 9-20.

Kohler, Dayton, "William Faulkner and the Social Conscience," *EJ* 38 (Dec., 1949): 545-52. Also in *CE* 11 (Dec., 1949): 119-27.

Kondravy, Connie R., "Faulkner's Study of Youth," *DAI* 36 (1976): 6100A-01A.

Korenman, Joan S., "Faulkner and 'That Undying Mark'," *SAF* 4, i (Spring, 1976): 81-91.

_____, "Faulkner's Grecian Urn," *SLJ* 7, i (Fall, 1974): 3-23.

Kort, Wesley A., "Social Time in Faulkner's Fiction," *ArQ* 37, ii (Summer, 1981): 101-15.

Kowalczyk, Richard L., "From Addie Bundren to Gavin Stevens: The Direction from Reality," *CEJ* 2, i (1966): 45-52.

Krefft, James H., "The Yoknapatawpha Indians: Fact and Fiction," *DAI* 37 (1976): 1549A.

Kreiswirth, Martin L., "The Making of a Novelist: William Faulkner's Career to the Writing of THE SOUND AND THE FURY," *DAI* 40 (1979): 6208A.

_____, "The Will to Create: Faulkner's Apprenticeship and Willard Huntington Wright," *ArQ* 37, ii (Summer, 1981): 149-65.

Kulin, Katalin, "Reasons and Characteristics of Faulkner's Influence on Modern Latin-American Fiction," *ALitASH* 13 (1971): 349-63.

Labatt, Blair P., Jr., "Faulkner the Storyteller," *DAI* 34 (1974): 7761A (Va.).

Landor, M., "Faulkner's Creative Method in the Making," in Vroon, R., tr., *20th Century American Literature: A Soviet View*, 306-30.

Lang, Eleanor M., "Hawthorne and Faulkner: The Continuity of a Dark American Tradition," *DAI* 31 (1971): 5410A (Lehigh).

Langford, Gerald, "Insights Into the Creative Process: The Faulkner Collection at The University of Texas," in Zyla, W. T., and W. M. Aycock, eds., *William Faulkner*, 115-33.

Lannon, John M., "William Faulkner: A Study in Spatial Form," *DAI* 33 (1973): 5184A.

Larsen, Eric, "The Barrier of Language: The Irony of Language in Faulkner," *MFS* 13, i (Spring, 1967): 19-31.

Lawson, Lewis A., "William Faulkner (1897-1962)," in Panichas, G. A., ed., *Politics of Twentieth-Century Novelists*, 278-95.

Leach, George B., Jr., "Faulkner's Comic Optimism: Structure, Form, and Theme in Four Novels," *DAI* 40 (1980): 5443A.

Leary, L., *William Faulkner of Yoknapatawpha County*.

Leaska, Mitchell A., "The Rhetoric of Multiple Points of View in Selected Contemporary Novels," *DA* 29 (1969): 3145A-46A (N.Y.U.).

Leaver, Florence, "Faulkner: The Word as Principle and Power," *SAQ* 57 (Autumn, 1958): 464-76. Also in Hoffman, F. J., and O. W. Vickery, eds., *William Faulkner*, 199-209. Also in *ICTE Yearbook* (Fall, 1958): 14-19.

Lehan, R., *Dangerous Crossing*, 68-79.

Lennox, Sara Jane K., "The Fiction of William Faulkner and Uwe Johnson: A Comparative Study," *DAI* 34 (1974): 6647A (Wis., Madison).

————, "Yoknapatawpha to Jerichow, Uwe Johnson's Appropriation of William Faulkner," *Arcadia* 14 (1979): 160-76.

Leonard, Diane R., "Simon's L'HERBE: Beyond Sound and Fury," *FAR* 1 (Winter, 1976): 13-30.

Levins, L. G., *Faulkner's Heroic Design*.

————, "William Faulkner: The Heroic Design of Yoknapatawpha," *DAI* 34 (1973): 2635A (N.C., Chapel Hill).

Lilly, Paul R., Jr., "Silence and the Impeccable Language: A Study of William Faulkner's Philosophy of Language," *DAI* 32 (1971): 973A (Fordham).

Lincoln, Ruth T., "Ontological Implications in Faulkner's Major Novels," *DAI* 34 (1973): 1286A (Ind.).

Lind, Ilse D., "The Effect of Painting on Faulkner's Poetic Form," in Harrington, E., and A. J. Abadie, eds., *Faulkner, Modernism, and Film*, 127-48.

————, "Faulkner and Nature," *FaST* 1 (1980): 112-21.

————, "Faulkner's Uses of Poetic Drama," in Harrington, E., and A. J. Abadie, eds., *Faulkner, Modernism, and Film*, 66-81.

————, "Faulkner's Women," in Harrington, E., and A. J. Abadie, eds., *Maker and the Myth*, 89-104.

Linneman, William R., "Faulkner's Ten-Dollar Words," *AS* 38 (May, 1963): 158-9.

Linscott, Robert N., "Faulkner Without Fanfare," *Esquire* 60, i (July, 1963): 36, 38.

Lisk, Thomas D., "Love, Law and the Nature of Character," *DAI* 36 (1975): 2198A.

Litz, Walton, "William Faulkner's Moral Vision," *SWR* 37 (Summer, 1952): 200-9.

Longley, J. L., Jr., *Tragic Mask*.

Loughrey, Thomas F., "Values and Love in the Fiction of William Faulkner," *DA* 23 (1963): 2915 (Notre Dame).

Lubarsky, Jared, "The Highest Freedom: A Reconsideration of Faulkner on Race," *WiF* 3, ii (April, 1981): 9-17.

Lundin, Roger W., "Present Past: Hawthorne, Faulkner, and the Problem of History," *DAI* 40 (1979): 1469A-70A.

Maclachlan, John M., "William Faulkner and the Southern Folk," *SFQ* 9 (Sept., 1945): 153-67.

MacLeish, Archibald, "Faulkner and the Responsibility of the Artist," *HarvardA* 135 (Nov., 1951): 18+.

MacLure, Millar, "William Faulkner: Soothsayer of the South," *QQ* 63 (Autumn, 1956): 334-43.

MacMillan, Kenneth D., "The Bystander in Faulkner's Fiction," *DAI* 34 (1973): 783A (Brit. Columbia).

Magny, Claude-Edmonde, "Faulkner, or Theological Inversion," *Age of the American Novel*, 178-223. Also in Warren, R. P., ed., *Faulkner*, 66-78.

Makuck, Peter L., "Faulkner Studies in France: 1953-1969," *DAI* 32 (1971): 3314A (Kent State).

Malin, Irving, *William Faulkner: An Interpretation*, Stanford: Stanford Un. Pr., 1957.

Mallonee, Helen H., "Land-Character Relationships in Selected Works of Faulkner's Yoknapatawpha Saga," *DAI* 36 (1975): 890A.

Manley, Justine M., "The Function of Stock Humor and Grotesque Humor in Faulkner's Major Novels," *DAI* 35 (1974): 1111A (Loyola, Chicago).

Mansfield, Luther S., "The Nature of Faulkner's Christianity," *Descant* 22, iii (Spring, 1978): 40-8.

Marcovi, Vida, "Interview with Faulkner," *TSLL* 5 (1964): 463-6.

Marshall, Emma J. G., "Scenes from Yoknapatawpha: A Study of People and Places in the Real and Imaginary Worlds of William Faulkner," *DAI* 39 (1978): 2276A.

Martin, Jay, "The Whole Burden of Man's History of His Impossible Heart's Desire: The Early Life of William Faulkner," *AL* 53, iv (Jan., 1982): 607-29.

Mascitelli, David W., "Faulkner's Characters of Sensibility," *DA* 29 (1968): 608A-9A (Duke).

Massey, Tom M., "Faulkner's Females: The Thematic Function of Women in the Yoknapatawpha Cycle," *DAI* 30 (1970): 3468A (Nev.).

Materassi, Mario, "Faulkner Criticism in Italy," *IQ* 15 (Summer, 1971): 47-85.

Matthews, John T., "Creative Responses to Time in the Novels of William Faulkner," *DAI* 37 (1977): 6486A-87A.

————, *Play of Faulkner's Language*.

Matton, Collin G., "The Role of Women in Three Faulkner Families," *DAI* 35 (1974): 2283A (Marquette).

Mayoux, Jean-Jacques, "The Creation of the Real in William Faulkner," in Hoffman, F. J., and O. W. Vickery, eds., *William Faulkner*, 156-73.

McAlexander, Hubert H., Jr., "History as Perception, History as Obsession: Faulkner's Development of a Theme," *DAI* 34 (1974): 6596A-97A (Wis., Madison).

McClelland, Benjamin W., "Not Only to Survive But to Prevail: A Study of William Faulkner's Search for a Redeemer of Modern Man," *DAI* 32 (1972): 6438A-39A (Ind.).

McClennen, Joshua, "William Faulkner and Christian Complacency," *PMASAL* 41 (1956): 315-22.

McColgan, Kristin P., "The World's Slow Stain: The Theme of Initiation in Selected American Novels," *DAI* 36 (1975): 279A.

McCormick, John, "William Faulkner, the Past, and History," *Fiction as Knowledge*, 88-108.

McCorquodale, Marjorie K., "Alienation in Yoknapatawpha County," *ForumH* 1, ii (Jan., 1957): 4-8.

_____, "William Faulkner and Existentialism," Unpub. Doct. Diss., Un. of Texas, 1956.

McDonald, William J., "The Image of Adolescence in William Faulkner's Yoknapatawpha Fiction," *DAI* 40 (1980): 5050A.

McGinnis, Wayne D., "Faulkner's Use of the Mule: Symbol of Endurance and Derision," *NMW* 10, i (Spring, 1977): 19-26.

McGrew, Julia, "Faulkner and the Icelanders," *SS* 31 (Feb., 1959): 1-14.

McHaney, Thomas L., "The Falkners and the Origin of Yoknapatawpha County: Some Corrections," *MissQ* 25 (Summer, 1972): 249-64.

_____, "The Elmer Papers: Faulkner's Comic Portraits of the Artist," *MissQ* 26 (Summer, 1973): 281-311.

_____, "Faulkner's Curious Tools," in Fowler, D., and A. J. Abadie, eds., *Fifty Years of Yoknapatawpha*, 179-201.

_____, "Watching for the Dixie Limited: Faulkner's Impact upon the Creative Writer," in Fowler, D., and A. J. Abadie, eds., *Fifty Years of Yoknapatawpha*, 226-47.

McLaughlin, Carrol D., "Religion in Yoknapatawpha County," *DA* 23 (1963): 2915-16 (Denver).

McWilliams, David D., "The Influence of William Faulkner on Michel Butor," *DAI* 31 (1970): 1282A-83A (Ore.).

Meeks, Elizabeth, "Reflections of the Milieu in Names of William Faulkner's Characters," *SoSt* 20, i (Spring, 1981): 91-6.

Mellard, James M., "Humor in Faulkner's Novels: Its Development, Forms, and Functions," *DA* 25 (1964): 480-1 (Texas).

Memmott, Albert J., "The Theme of Revenge in the Fiction of William Faulkner," *DAI* 34 (1974): 4273A-74A (Minn.).

Meriwether, James B., "A. E. Housman and Faulkner's Nobel Prize Speech: A Note," *JAmS* 4, ii (Feb., 1971): 247-8.

_____, "The Books of William Faulkner: A Guide for Students and Scholars," *MissQ* 30 (Summer, 1977): 417-28.

_____, "Faulkner and the New Criticism," *BA* 37 (Summer, 1963): 265-8.

_____, and Michael Millgate, eds., *Lion in the Garden: Interviews with William Faulkner*, 1926-1962, N.Y.: Random House, 1968.

_____, "Sartoris and Snopes: An Early Notice," *LCUT* 7, ii (1962): 36-9.

_____, "The Text of Faulkner's Books: An Introduction and Some Notes," *MFS* 9 (Summer, 1963): 159-70.

_____, "William Faulkner," *Shen* 10 (Winter, 1959): 18-24.

Meyer, Norma L., "Syntactic Features of William Faulkner's Narrative Style," *DAI* 32 (1972): 6406A (Neb.).

Michel, Laurence, "Faulkner: Saying No to Death," *The Thing Contained: Theory of the Tragic*, Bloomington: Indiana Un. Pr., 1971, 107-30.

Mickelson, Joel C., "Faulkner's Military Figures of Speech," *WisSL* No. 4 (1967): 46-55. [Not seen.]

Miller, Bernice B., "William Faulkner's Thomas Sutpen, Quentin Compson, Joe Christmas: A Study of the Hero-Archetype," *DAI* 38 (1978): 6728A.

Miller, David M., "Faulkner's Women," *MFS* 13, i (Spring, 1967): 3-17.

Miller, Douglas T., "Faulkner and the Civil War: Myth and Reality," *AQ* 15 (Summer, 1963): 200-9.

Miller, James, "William Faulkner: Descent into the Vortex," *Quests Surd and Absurd*, 41-75.

Millgate, M., *Achievement of William Faulkner*.

_____, "'A Cosmos of My Own': The Evolution of Yoknapatawpha," in Fowler, D., and A. J. Abadie, eds., *Fifty Years of Yoknapatawph*, 23-43.

_____, "'The Firmament of Man's History': Faulkner's Treatment of the Past," *MissQ* 25 (Supp.) (Spring, 1972): 25-35.

_____, "Faulkner and History," in Harrington, E., and A. J. Abadie, eds., *South and Faulkner's Yoknapatawpha*, 22-39.

_____, "Faulkner and the South: Some Reflections," in Harrington, E., and A. J. Abadie, eds., *South and Faulkner's Yoknapatawpha*, 195-210.

_____, "Faulkner on the Literature of the First World War," *MissQ* 26 (Summer, 1973): 387-93.

_____, "Faulkner's Masters," *TSE* 23 (1978): 143-55. Also in Cox, L. H., ed., *William Faulkner*, 459-74.

_____, *William Faulkner*.

_____, "William Faulkner: The Problem of Point of View," in La France, Marston, ed., *Patterns of Commitment in American Literature*, Toronto: Un. of Toronto Pr., 1967, 181-92. Also in Wagner, L. W., ed., *William Faulkner*, 179-91.

Millichap, Joseph R., "Distorted Matter and Disjunctive Forms: The Grotesque as Modernist Genre," *ArQ* 33 (Winter, 1977): 339-47.

Milliner, Gladys W., "Faulkner's Young Protagonists: The Innocent and the Damned," *DAI* 31 (1970): 2928A (Tulane).

Millis, Ralph E., "Humanistic and Legal Values in Some Works of Faulkner," *DAI* 38 (1978): 4170A.

Milloy, Sandra D., "The Development of the Black Character in the Fiction of William Faulkner," *DAI* 40 (1979): 856A.

Milum, Richard A., "The Cavalier Spirit in Faulkner's Fiction," *DAI* 33 (1973): 5737A (Ind.).

_____, "Cavaliers, Calvinists, and the Wheel of Fortune: The Gambling Instinct in Faulkner's Fiction," *NMW* 11, i (1978): 3-14.

_____, "Continuity and Change: The Horse, the Automobile, and the Airplane in Faulkner's Fiction," in Carey, Glenn O., ed., *Faulkner*, 157-74.

_____, "Faulkner and the Cavalier Tradition: The French Bequest," *AL* 45 (Jan., 1974): 580-9.

Miner, Ward L., "Faulkner and Christ's Crucifixion," *NM* 57 (1956): 260-9.

_____, *The World of William Faulkner*, Durham, No. Carolina: Duke Un. Pr., 1952.

Minter, David, "Family, Region, and Myth in Faulkner's Fiction," in Fowler, D., and A. J. Abadie, eds., *Faulkner and the Southern Renaissance*, 182-203.

_____, "'Truths More Intense than Knowledge': Notes on Faulkner and Creativity," in Fowler, D., and A. J. Abadie, eds., *Faulkner and the Southern Renaissance*, 245-65.

Mizener, A., *Twelve Great American Novels*, 142-6.

Moloney, Michael, "The Enigma of Time: Proust, Virginia Woolf, and Faulkner," *Thought* 32 (1957): 69-85.

Monteiro, George, "'Between Grief and Nothing': Hemingway and Faulkner," *HN* 1, i (Spring, 1971): 13-15.

_____, "Fugitive Comments on Early Faulkner," *NMW* 10 (Winter, 1977): 95-6.

Moore, Robert H., "Perspectives on William Faulkner: The Author and His Work as Reflected in Surveys of American History. Works on Southern Life and History, and Works and Comments by Mississippians," *DAI* 32 (1972): 5798A-99A (Wis.).

Moreland, Agnes L., "A Study of Faulkner's Presentation of Some Problems That Relate to Negroes," *DA* 21 (1960): 1192-3 (Columbia).

Morimoto, Shin'ichi, "Freedom from Burden: Two Phases in William Faulkner's Novels," *SES* 1 (1976): 71-88.

Morris, L., "Sphinx in the South," *Postscript to Yesterday*, 160-2.

Morris, W., "The Function of Rage: William Faulkner," *Territory Ahead*, 171-84.

_____, "The Violent Land: Some Observations on the Faulkner Country," *Magazine of Art* 45 (Mar., 1952): 99-103.

Mortimer, Gail L., "Rhetoric of Loss: An Analysis of Faulkner's Perceptual Style," *DAI* 37 (1976): 971A-72A.

_____, "Significant Absences: Faulkner's Rhetoric of Loss," *Novel* 14, iii (Spring, 1981): 232-50.

Moses, Edwin P., "Faulknerian Comedy," *DAI* 36 (1975): 1507A.

Müller, Christopher, "On William Faulkner's Manner of Narration," *KN* 25, ii (1978): 201-12.

Murphree, John W., Jr., "A Study of William Faulkner's Informed Dialect Theory and His Use of Dialect Markers in Eight Novels," *DAI* 36 (1975): 177A-78A.

Murray, Edward, "The Stream-of-Consciousness Novel and Film, III—William Faulkner," *Cinematic Imagination*, 154-67.

Musil, Robert K., "The Visual Imagination of William Faulkner," *DAI* 31 (1971): 3558A (Northwestern).

Newhall, Eric L., "Prisons and Prisoners in the Works of William Faulkner," *DAI* 36 (1976): 5300A.

Nicholson, Norman, "William Faulkner," in Martin, E. W., ed., *The New Spirit*, London: Dennis Dobson, 1946, 32-41.

Nigliazzo, Marc A., "Faulkner's Indians," *DAI* 34 (1974): 6650A-51A (New Mexico).

Nilon, Charles H., "Blacks in Motion," in Fowler, D., and A. J. Abadie, eds., *"A Cosmos of My Own,"* 227-51.

_____, "Cooper, Faulkner, and the American Venture," in Fowler, D., and A. J. Abadie, eds., *"A Cosmos of My Own,"* 168-98.

_____, "Faulkner and the Negro," *UCSSLL* No. 8 (Sept., 1962): 1-111. Also in Nilon, C. H., *Faulkner and the Negro*.

Noble, D. W., *Eternal Adam and the New World Garden*, 163-6.

Nochimson, Martha, "Against the Limitations of Rationalism: Undercurrents in the Works of William Faulkner," *DAI* 37 (1976): 1551A.

Nolte, William H., "Mencken, Faulkner, and Southern Moralism," *SCR* 4, i (Dec., 1971): 45-61. Also in *FurmS* 4, i (1971): 45-61.

Nonaka, Ryo, "Faulkner's 'Stream of Consciousness'," *SEL* 36 (1959): 179-80. [Not seen.]

Oberhelman, Harley D., "Faulknerian Techniques in Gabriel García Márquez's Portrait of a Dictator," *PCLS* 10 (1978): 171-81.

_____, "Gabriel García Márquez and the American South," *Chasqui* 5, i (1975): 29-38.

_____, *The Presence of Faulkner in the Writings of García Márquez* (Texas Tech Graduate Studies 22), Lubbock: Texas Tech Pr., 1980.

_____, "William Faulkner's Reception in Spanish America," *TAH* 3, xxvi (1978): 13-17.

O'Brien, Frances B., "Faulkner and Wright, Alias S. S. Van Dine," *MissQ* 14 (Spring, 1961): 101-7.

O'Brien, Matthew C., "William Faulkner and the Civil War in Oxford, Mississippi," *JMissH* 35 (May, 1973): 167-74.

O'Connor, William Van, "Faulkner's Legend of the Old South," *WHR* 7 (Autumn, 1953): 293-301.

_____, "Faulkner's One-Sided 'Dialogue' with Hemingway," *CE* 24 (Dec., 1962): 208-15.

_____, "Hawthorne and Faulkner: Some Common Ground," *VQR* 33 (Winter, 1957): 105-23. Also in O'Connor, W. V., *Grotesque*, 59-77.

_____, "Protestantism in Yoknapatawpha County," *Hopkins Rev* 5 (Spring, 1952): 26-42. Also in Rubin, L., and R. D. Jacobs, eds., *Southern Renascence*, 153-91.

_____, "Rhetoric in Southern Writing: Faulkner," *GaR* 12 (Spring, 1958): 83-6. Also in Schmitter, D. M., ed., *William Faulkner*, 53-7.

_____, *Tangled Fire of William Faulkner*.

_____, *William Faulkner*. Also in O'Connor, W. V., ed., *Seven Modern American Novelists*, 118-52.

_____, "William Faulkner's Apprenticeship," *SWR* 38 (Winter, 1953): 1-14.

O'Dea, Richard J., "Faulkner's Vestigial Christianity," *Ren* 21 (Autumn, 1968): 44-54.

O'Donnell, George M., "Faulkner's Mythology," *KR* 1 (Summer, 1939): 285-99. Also in Hoffman, F. J., and O. W. Vickery, eds., *William Faulkner*, 82-93. Also in Hoffman, F. J., and O. W. Vickery, eds., *William Faulkner: Two Decades of Criticism*, 49-62. Also in Warren, R. P., ed., *Faulkner*, 82-93. Also in Hoffman, F. J., and O. W. Vickery, eds., *William Faulkner: Two Decades of Criticism*, 49-62. Also in Warren, R. P., ed., *Faulkner*, 23-33. Also in Wagner, L. W., ed., *William Faulkner*, 83-93.

Odum, Howard W., "On Southern Literature and Southern Culture," *Hopkins Rev* 7 (Winter, 1953): 60-76. Also in Odum, H. W., *Folk Religion and Society: Selected Papers of Howard W. Odum*, arr. and ed. by Katherine Jocher (and others), Chapel Hill: Un. of No. Carolina, 1964, 202-18. Also in Rubin, L. D., Jr., and R. D. Jacobs, eds., *Southern Renascence*, 84-100.

O'Faolain, S., *Vanishing Hero*, 73-111.

Ohashi, Kinzaburo, "Creation through Repetition or Self-Parody: Some Notes on Faulkner's Imaginative Process," *WiF* 2, ii (1979): 34-47.

Oldenburg, Egbert W., "William Faulkner's Early Experiments With Narrative Techniques," *DA* 27 (1967): 2158A (Michigan).

Ono, Kiyoyuki, "'Life is Motion': An Aspect of William Faulkner's Style," *WiF* 2, ii (1979): 48-66.

Onoe, Masaji, "Some T. S. Eliot Echoes in Faulkner," *WiF* 3, i (1980): 1-15.

Oriard, Michael, "The Ludic Vision of William Faulkner," *MFS* 28, ii (Summer, 1982): 169-87.

Otten, Terry, "Faulkner's Use of the Past: A Comment," *Ren* 20 (Summer, 1968): 198-207, 214.

Page, Sally P., "Faulkner's Sense of the Sacred," in Wolfe, G. H., ed., *Faulkner*, 101-21.

_____, *Faulkner's Women*.

_____, "Woman in the Works of William Faulkner," *DAI* 31 (1970): 2395A (Mass.).

Paliyevsky, Pyotr, "Faulkner's America," *SovL* No. 8 (1977): 177-80.

Parker, Robert D., "Faulkner and the Novelistic Imagination," *DAI* 42, ii (Aug., 1981): 698A.

Parks, Edd W., "Faulkner and Hemingway: Their Thought," *SAB* 22, iv (1957): 1-2.

Parks, Kae I., "Faulkner's Women: Archetype and Metaphor," *DAI* 41 (1980): 1054A.

Pate, Frances W., "Names of Characters in Faulkner's Mississippi," *DAI* 30 (1969): 2036A-37A (Emory).

Patil, Vimala, "William Faulkner—America's Literary Giant," *UA* 14 (Sept., 1962): 523-5.

Patton, Oscar, Jr., "The Dynamistic Vision: An Examination of Faulkner's Sense of Motion," *DAI* 40 (1980): 5058A.

Peabody, Henry W., "Faulkner's Initiation Stories: An Approach to the Major Works," *DAI* 33 (1973): 3663A (Denver).

Pearce, Richard, "Reeling through Faulkner: Pictures of Motion, Pictures in Motion," *MFS* 24, iv (Winter, 1978-79): 483-95.

Peavy, Charles D., *So Slow Now: Faulkner and the Race Question*, Eugene: Un. of Oregon Books, 1971.

_____, "Jason Compson's Paranoid Pseudocommunity," *HSL* 2, ii (1970): 151-6.

Penick, Edwin A., Jr., "The Testimony of William Faulkner," *ChS* 38 (June, 1955): 121-33.

Perry, Thomas E., "Knowing in the Novels of William Faulkner," *DAI* 35 (1974): 2289A (Rochester).

Peters, Erskine A., "The Yoknapatawpha World and Black Being," *DAI* 37 (1977): 5831A.

Peterson, Richard F., "Time As Character in the Fiction of James Joyce and William Faulkner," *DA* 31 (1970): 1285A-86A.

Petesch, Donald A., "Faulkner on Negroes: The Conflict Between the Public Man and the Private Art," *SHR* 10 (Winter, 1976): 55-64.

_____, "Some Notes on the Family in Faulkner's Fiction," *NMW* 10, i (Spring, 1977): 11-18.

Phillips, William L., "Sherwood Anderson's Two Prize Pupils," *Un. of Chicago Mag.* 47 (Jan., 1955): 9-12. Also in White, Ray L., ed., *The Achievement of Sherwood Anderson*, Chapel Hill: Un. of No. Carolina Pr., 1966, 202-10.

Piacentino, Edward J., "No More 'Treachy Sentimentalities': The Legacy of T. S. Stribling to the Southern Literary Renascence," *SoSt* 20, i (Spring, 1981): 67-83.

Pieper, Janet L. S., "Black Characters in Faulkner's Fiction," *DAI* 37 (1976): 2877A.

Pierce, Constance M., "Earth, Air, Fire, and Water: The Elements in Faulkner's Fiction," *DAI* 33 (1973): 6927A (Penn. State).

Pikoulis, J., *Art of William Faulkner*.

Pilkington, J., *Heart of Yoknapatawpha*.

Pindell, Richard P., "The Ritual of Survival: Landscape in Conrad and Faulkner," *DAI* 32 (1971): 3324A (Yale).

Pladott, Dinah, "Absurd and Romantic Elements in the Writing of William Faulkner," Tel-Aviv, 1973. (Diss.).

Player, Raleigh P., Jr., "The Negro Character in the Fiction of William Faulkner," *DA* 27 (1966): 483A-4A (Un. of Michigan).

Plummer, William, "The Faulkner Relation," *Fiction* 6/7 (1976): 130-41.

Polek, Fran, "Tick-tocks, Whirs, and Broken Gears: Time and Identity in Faulkner," *Ren* 29 (Summer, 1977): 193-200.

_____, "Time and Identity in the Novels of William Faulkner," *DA* 29 (1969): 3151A (So. Calif.).

Polk, Noel, "Faulkner and Respectability," in Fowler, D., and A. J. Abadie, eds., *Fifty Years of Yoknapatawpha*, 110-33.

_____, "'I Taken an Oath of Office Too': Faulkner and the Law," in Fowler, D., and A. J. Abadie, eds., *Fifty Years of Yoknapatawpha*, 159-78.

Pollack, Agnes S., "The Current of Time in the Novels of William Faulkner," *DA* 25 (1965): 7276-7 (U.C.L.A.).

Porter, Carolyn, "Faulkner and His Reader," in Carey, Glenn O., ed., *Faulkner*, 231-58.

_____, *Seeing and Being*, 207-76.

Pouillon, Jean, "Time and Destiny in Faulkner," in Warren, R. P., ed., *Faulkner*, 79-87.

Powers, L. H., *Faulkner's Yoknapatawpha Comedy*.

_____, "Hawthorne and Faulkner and the Pearl of Great Price," *PMASAL* 52 (1967): 391-401.

Prasad, V. R. N., "William Faulkner and the Southern Syndrome," in Naik, M. K., et al., eds., *Indian Studies in American Fiction*, 185-202.

Prescott, O., *In My Opinion*, 85-91.

Price-Stephens, Gordon, "Faulkner and the Royal Air Force," *MissQ* 17 (Summer, 1964): 123-8.

Pritchett, V. S., "Books in General," *NS&Nation* 41 (June 2, 1951): 624-6. Also in Pritchett, V. S., *Books in General*, 242-7.

Pruit, Thomas B., "The Economy of Memory in Faulkner's Yoknapatawpha," *DAI* 40 (1979): 2647A.

Putzel, Max, "Evolution of Two Characters in Faulkner's Early and Unpublished Fiction," *SLJ* 5, ii (Spring, 1973): 47-63.

Rabi, "Faulkner and the Exiled Generation," in Hoffman, F. J., and O. W. Vickery, eds., *William Faulkner: Two Decades of Criticism*, 118-38.

Radomski, James, and Yoshinobu Hakutani, "Faulkner's Major Syntactic Features," *HSELL* 23 (1978): 1-13.

_____, "Faulkner's Style: A Syntactic Analysis," *DAI* 36 (1975): 6154A.

Ramos Escobar, José L., "From Yoknapatawpha to Macondo: A Comparative Study of William Faulkner and Gabriel García Márquez," *DAI* 41, xii (June, 1981): 5092A-93A.

Ranald, Ralph A., "William Faulkner's South: Three Degrees of Myth," *Landfall* 18 (Dec., 1964): 329-38.

Randolph, Linda S., "A Question of Responsibility: The Villain in the Yoknapatawpha Fiction of William Faulkner," *DAI* 36 (1976): 7425A-26A.

Ransom, John Crowe, "William Faulkner: An Impression," *HarvardA* 135 (Nov., 1951): 17.

Reed, J. W., Jr., *Faulkner's Narrative*.

Reed, Joseph, "Faulkner, Ford, Ives, and the Senses of the Canon," *FaSt* 1 (1980): 136-42.

Reed, Richard A., "A Chronology of William Faulkner's Yoknapatawpha County," *DAI* 32 (1971): 2101A (Emory).

_____, "The Role of Chronology in Faulkner's Yoknapatawpha Fiction," *SLJ* 7, i (Fall, 1974): 24-48.

Reirdon, Suzanne R., "An Application of Script Analysis to Four of William Faulkner's Women Characters," *DAI* 35 (1975): 4549A.

Rhode, Robert H., "William Faulkner and the Gods of Yoknapatawpha: An Essay in Comparative Mythopoesis," *DAI* 36 (1976): 6761A-62A.

Richards, Lewis A., "The Literary Styles of Jean-Paul Sartre and William Faulkner: An Analysis, Comparison, and Contrast," *DA* 4 (1964): 3755-6 (So. Calif.).

Richardson, H. Edward, "Anderson and Faulkner," *AL* 36 (Nov., 1964): 298-314.

————, *William Faulkner*.

Richardson, K. E., *Force and Faith in the Novels of William Faulkner*.

Richter, Barbara, "*Per Arcdua ad Astra*: Perversity in the Moralilty Puzzle of William Faulkner," *RUCR* 39 (1974): 139-47.

Riedel, F. C., "Faulkner as Stylist," *SAQ* 56 (Autumn, 1957): 462-79.

Riese, Utz, "The Dilemma of the Third Way (William Faulkner's Contradictory Humanism), I," *ZAA* 16, ii (1968): 138-55; II *ZAA* 16, iii (1968): 257-73.

Rigsby, Carol Anne R., "The Vanishing Community: Studies in Some Late Novels by William Faulkner," *DAI* 36 (1975): 1509A-10A.

Rinaldi, Nicholas M., "Game-Consciousness and Game-Metaphor in the Work of William Faulkner," *DA* 24 (1964): 4196-7 (Fordham).

————, "Game Imagery and Game-Consciousness in Faulkner's Fiction,"*TCL* 10 (Oct., 1964): 108-18.

Riskin, Myra J., "Faulkner's South: Myth and History in the Novel," *DAI* 30 (1969): 1148A-49A (Calif., Berkeley).

Robb, Mary C., *William Faulkner: An Estimate of His Contribution to the Modern Novel* (Critical Essays in English and American Literature, No. 1), Pittsburgh: Un. of Pittsburgh Pr., 1957.

Robbins, Deborah L., "Characters in Crisis: Communication and the Idea of Self in Faulkner," *DAI* 37 (1977): 7132A.

Roberts, James A., "William Faulkner: A Thematic Study," *DA* 17 (1958): 3023 (Iowa).

Roberts, James L., "Experimental Exercises—Faulkner's Early Writings," *Discourse* 6 (Summer, 1963): 183-97.

Robinson, Clayton, "Faulkner and Welty and the Mississippi Baptists," *Interpretations* 5, I (1973): 51-4.

Robinson, Evalyne C., "The Role of the Negro in William Faulkner's Public and Private Worlds, *DAI* 32 (1971): 2704A (Ohio State).

Rollyson, Carl E., Jr., "The Uses of the Past in the Novels of William Faulkner," *DAI* 37 (1977): 6488A.

Romig, Evelyn M., "Women as Victims in the Novels of Charles Dickens and William Faulkner," *DAI* 39 (1978): 1600A.

Roscoe, Lavon, "An Interview with William Faulkner," *WR* 15 (Summer, 1951): 300-4.

Rosenman, John B., "A Matter of Choice: The Locked Door Theme in Faulkner," *SAB* 41, ii (May, 1976): 8-12.

Ross, Stephen M., "A World of Voices: 'Talking' in the Novels of William Faulkner," *DAI* 32 (1972): 7002A (Stanford).

Roth, Richard A., "From Gap to Gain: Outrage and Renewal in Faulkner and Mailer," *DAI* 37 (1976): 1554A-55A.

Roth, Russell, "William Faulkner: The Pattern of Pilgrimage," *Per* 2 (1949): 246-54.

Rothford, John, "The Concept of Time in Faulkner's Nobel Speech," *NMW* 11 (Winter, 1979): 73-83.

Rovit, Earl, "Faulkner, Hemingway, and the American Family," *MissQ* 29 (Fall, 1976): 483-97.

Rubel, Warren G., "The Structural Function of the Christ Figure in the Fiction of William Faulkner," *DA* 25 (1965): 5941-2 (Ark.).

Rubin, Louis D., Jr., "Chronicles of Yoknapatawpha: The Dynasties of William Faulkner," *Faraway Country*, 43-71.

————, "The Dixie Special: William Faulkner and the Southern Literary Renascence," in Fowler, D., and A. J. Abadie, eds., *Faulkner and the Southern Renaissance*, 63-92.

————, "William Faulkner: The Discovery of a Man's Vocation," in Wolfe, G. H., ed., *Faulkner*, 43-68. Also in Rubin, L. D., Jr., *Gallery of Southerners*, 3-25.

Runyan, Harry, *A Faulkner Glossary*, N.Y.: Citadel, 1964.

Ruppersburg, Hugh M., "Narrative Mode in the Novels of William Faulkner," *DAI* 39 (1978): 1576A.

Ryan, Steven T., "Faulkner and Quantum Mechanics," *WHR* 33 (Autumn, 1979): 329-39.

Saito, Kazue, "Ethics in Faulkner's Works," *Ushione* 10 (1957): 1-12. [Not seen.]

Sandeen, Ernest, "William Faulkner: Tragedian of Yoknapatawpha," in Gardiner, H. C., ed., *Fifty Years of the American Novel*, 165-82.

Sasiki, Midori, "Southern Appalachian English: The Language of Faulkner's Country People," *SALit* 15 (1979): 37-46.

Savarese, Sister Paul C., C.S.J., "Cinematic Techniques in the Novels of William Faulkner," *DAI* 33 (1972): 1179A (St. Louis).

Scanlan, Margaret C. T., "William Faulkner and THE SEARCH FOR LOST TIME: Three Aspects of Literary Deformation," *DAI* 33 (1972): 1741A-42A (Iowa).

Schermbrucker, William G., "Strange Textures of Vision: A Study of the Significance of Mannered Fictional Techniques in Six Selected Novels of D. H. Lawrence, William Faulkner, and Patrick White, together with a Theoretical Introduction on 'The Novel of Vision'," *DAI* 35 (1974): 473A.

Schlumpf, Otto N., "William Faulkner: Myth-Maker and Morals-Monger: Esthetics and Ethics in Yoknapatawpha County," *DAI* 35 (1975): 7327A.

Schmitter, D. M., ed., *William Faulkner*.

Schultz, William J., "Motion in Yoknapatawpha County: Theme and Point of View in the Novels of William Faulkner," *DA* 29 (1969): 3154A (Kan. State).

Scott, Arthur L., "The Faulknerian Sentence," *PrS* 27 (Spring, 1953): 91-8.

Serafin, Sister Joan M., "Faulkner's Uses of the Classics," *DA* 29 (1969): 3155A-56A (Notre Dame).

Seyppel, J., *William Faulkner*.

Sharma, P. P., "Faulkner's South and the Other South," in Carey, Glenn O., ed., *Faulkner*, 123-37.

Shaw, Joe C., "Sociological Aspects of Faulkner's Writing," *MissQ* 14 (Summer, 1961): 148-52.

Sherwood, J. C., "The Traditional Element in Faulkner," *Faulkner Studies* 3 (1954): 17-23.

Shimura, Masao, "Faulkner, De Assis, Barth: Resemblances and Differences," *WiF* 2, ii (Dec., 1979): 67-79.

Sidney, George, "William Faulkner and Hollywood," *ColQ* 9 (Spring, 1969): 367-77.

Siegel, Roslyn, "Faulkner's Black Characters: A Comparative Study," *DAI* 35 (1974): 3009A-10A (C.U.N.Y.).

Simon, John K., "Faulkner and Sartre: Metamorphosis and the Obscene," *CL* 15 (Summer, 1963): 216-25.

————, "The Glance of the Idiot: A Thematic Study of Faulkner and Modern French Fiction," *DA* 25 (1964): 1220 (Yale).

Simpson, Lewis P., "Faulkner and the Legend of the Artist," in Wolfe, G., ed., *Faulkner*, 69-100.

————, "Faulkner and the Southern Symbolism of Pastoral," *MissQ* 28 (Fall, 1975): 4010-15.

_____, "Sex & History: Origins of Faulkner's Apocrypha," in Harrington, E., and A. J. Abadie, eds., *Maker and the Myth*, 43-70.

_____, "William Faulkner of Yoknapatawpha," in Rubin, L. D., Jr., ed., *American South*, 227-44.

_____, "Yoknapatawpha & Faulkner's Fable of Civilization," in Harrington, E., and A. J. Abadie, eds., *Maker and the Myth*, 122-45.

Singleton, Carl S., "Gavin Stevens: Faulkner's 'Good Man'," *DAI* 43, iii (Sept., 1982): 804A.

Slabey, Robert M., "William Faulkner: 'The Waste Land' Phase (1926-1936)," *DA* 22 (1961): 1632 (Notre Dame).

Slatoff, Walter J., "The Edge of Order: The Pattern of Faulkner's Rhetoric," *TCL* 3 (Oct., 1957): 107-27. Also in Hoffman, F. J., and O. W. Vickery, eds., *William Faulkner*, 173-98. Also in Wagner, L. W., ed., *William Faulkner*, 155-79.

_____, *Quest for Failure*.

Smith, Gary, "William Faulkner and the Adamic Myth," *DAI* 42, viii (Feb., 1982): 3603A-04A.

Smith, Kearney I., "Some Romantic Elements in the Works of William Faulkner," *DAI* 34 (1974): 4286A (Ga.).

Smith, Lewis A., "William Faulkner and the Racist Virus," in Doshisha Women's College of Liberal Arts, *Annual Reports of Studies*, Vol. 21, Kyoto: Doshisha Women's College, 1970, 388-98. [Not seen.]

Smith, Stella P., "The Evolution of Patterns of Characterization from Faulkner's SOLDIERS' PAY (1926) through ABSALOM, ABSALOM! (1936)," *DAI* 37 (1976): 2881A.

Snell, George, "The Fury of William Faulkner," *WR* 11 (Autumn, 1946): 29-40. Also in Snell, G., ed., *Shapers of American Fiction*, 87-104.

Snell, Susan, "Phil Stone of Yoknapatawpha," *DAI* 40 (1979): 259A-60A.

Solomon, Robert H., "Classical Myth in the Novels of William Faulkner," *DAI* 36 (1976): 7428A-29A.

Spiller, R. E., *Cycle of American Literature*, 291-303.

Spivey, Herman E., "Faulkner and the Adamic Myth: Faulkner's Moral Vision," *MFS* 19, iv (Winter, 1973-74): 497-505.

Stanford, Raney, "Of Mules and Men: Faulkner and Silone," *Discourse* 6 (Winter, 1962-63): 73-8.

Stavrou, C. N., "Ambiguity in Faulkner's Affirmation," *Person* 40 (April, 1959): 169-77.

Steene, Birgitta, "William Faulkner and the Myth of the American South," *MS* 54 (1960): 271-9.

Stein, Jean, "William Faulkner," *Paris Rev* 4 (Spring, 1956): 28-52. Also in Cowley, Malcolm, ed., *Writers at Work*, N.Y.: Viking, 1958, 119-41.

Steinberg, Aaron, "Faulkner and the Negro," *DA* 27 (1966): 1385A (N.Y.U.).

Stewart, David H., "Faulkner, Sholokhov, and Regional Dissent in Modern Literature," in Zyla, W. T., and W. M. Aycock, eds., *William Faulkner*, 135-50.

_____, "William Faulkner and Mikhail Sholokhov: A Comparative Study of Two Representatives of the Regional Conscience, Their Affinities and Meanings," *DA* 19 (1959): 3309-10 (Mich.).

Stewart, Randall, "Hawthorne and Faulkner," *CE* 17 (Feb., 1956): 258-62.

_____, "Poetically the Most Accurate Man Alive," *ModA* 6 (Winter, 1961-62): 81-90.

Stock, Jerold H., "Suggestions of Death-Anxiety in the Life of William Faulkner," *DAI* 38 (1977): 2130A-31A.

Stoneback, H. R., "Conrad and Faulkner," *JCT* 1, ii (1976): 5-6.

_____, "*Et in Arcadia Ego*: The Triumph of Place in Lawrence Durrell and William Faulkner," *DL* 5, i (Fall, 1981): 104-19.

Stonum, G. L., *Faulkner's Career*.

_____, "William Faulkner: The Dynamics of Form," *DAI* 34 (1973): 3433A (Johns Hopkins).

Strandberg, Victor, "Between Truth and Fact: Faulkner's Symbols of Identity," *MFS* 21 (Autumn, 1975): 445-57. Also, revised, in Strandberg, V., *Faulkner Overview*, 43-55.

Strandberg, V., *Faulkner Overview*.

_____, "Faulkner's God: A Jamesian Perspective," *FaSt* 1 (1980): 122-35. Also, revised, in Strandberg, V., *Faulkner Overview*, 89-116.

_____, "Faulkner's Poor Parson and the Technique of Inversion (or William Faulkner: An Epitaph)," *SR* 73 (Spring, 1965): 181-90. Also, revised, in Strandberg, V., *Faulkner Overview*, 3-13.

Straumann, Heinrich, "Black and White in Faulkner's Fiction," *ES* 60 (Aug., 1979): 452-70.

Stroble, Woodrow L., "They Prevail: A Study of Faulkner's Passive Suicides," *DAI* 41 (1980): 255A-56A.

Sullivan, William P., "William Faulkner and the Community," *DA* 22 (1962): 4355 (Columbia).

Sutton, George W., "Primitivism in the Fiction of William Faulkner," *DA* 28 (1967): 695A-6A (Miss.).

Swiggart, P., *Art of Faulkner's Novels*.

_____, "The Snopes Trilogy," *SR* 68 (Spring, 1960): 319-25.

_____, "Time in Faulkner's Novels," *MFS* 1 (May, 1955): 25-9.

Swink, Helen M., "The Oral Tradition in Yoknapatawpha County," *DAI* 30 (1970): 3920A (Va.).

_____, "William Faulkner: The Novelist as Oral Narrator," *GaR* 26, ii (Summer, 1972): 183-209.

Tallack, Douglas G., "William Faulkner and the Tradition of Tough-Guy Fiction," in Landrum, L. N., P. Browne, and R. B. Browne, eds., *Dimensions of Detective Fiction*, 247-64.

Tanimura, Junjiro, "Yeoman Farmers and Their Role in Faulkner's Literature," *WiF* 4, i (Dec., 1981): 17-31.

Tate, Allan, "William Faulkner 1897-1962," *SR* 71 (Winter, 1963): 160-4.

Taylor, Nancy D., "The River of Faulkner and Mark Twain," *MissQ* 16 (Fall, 1963): 191-9.

Taylor, Walter, "Faulkner: Nineteenth-Century Imagination," *SCR* 10, i (1977): 57-68.

_____, "Faulkner: Social Commitment and the Artistic Temperament," *SoR* 6, iv (Oct., 1970): 1075-92.

_____, "Faulkner's Curse," *ArQ* 28 (Winter, 1972): 333-8.

_____, "The Roles of the Negro in William Faulkner's Fiction," *DA* 25 (1964): 2990 (Emory).

Thomas, Frank H., III, "The Search for Identity of Faulkner's Black Characters," *DAI* 33 (1973): 6935A (Pittsburgh).

Thompson, Deborah A., "In Celebration of Outrage: William Faulkner and the Tragic Vision," *DAI* 41, viii (Feb., 1981): 3586A.

Thompson, Evelyn J., "William Faulkner's Yoknapatawpha: The Land of Broken Dreams," *DAI* 33 (1973): 4435A-36A (Texas Tech.).

Thompson, L., *William Faulkner*.

Thorp, W., "Southern Renaissance," *American Writing in the Twentieth Century*, 263-74.

Tischler, Nancy P., "William Faulkner and the Southern Negro," *SUS* 7, iv (1965): 261-5.

Tolliver, Kenneth R., "Truth and the Poet," *Delta Rev* 2, iii (1965): 48+.

Tomlinson, T. B., "Faulkner and American Sophistication," *MCR* No. 7 (1964): 92-103.

Tran, Qui-Phiet, "The French and Faulkner: The Reception of William Faulkner's Writing in France and Its Influence on Modern French Literature," *DAI* 38 (1978): 4162A.

————, *William Faulkner and the French New Novelists*, Arlington: Carrollton, 1978.

Trimmer, Joseph F., "A Portrait of the Artist in Motion: A Study of the Artist-Surrogates in the Novels of William Faulkner," *DA* 29 (1969): 3623A (Purdue).

Tritschler, Donald, "The Unity of Faulkner's Shaping Vision," *MFS* 5 (Winter, 1959-60): 337-43.

Trovard, Dawn, "A Morbidity of the Mind: A Study of Psychopathological Rhetoric in William Faulkner's Fiction," *DAI* 42, ii (Aug., 1981): 707A.

Trowbridge, William L., "Myth and Dream in the Novels of William Faulkner," *DAI* 36 (1976): 4498A-99A.

Tuck, D., *Crowell's Handbook of Faulkner*.

Tumulty, Michael J., C. M., "Youth and Innocence in the Novels of William Faulkner," *DAI* 34 (1974): 4292A (St. John's).

Turner, Arlin, "William Faulkner and the Literary Flowering in the American South," *DUJ* 29 (Mar., 1968): 109-18.

————, "William Faulkner, Southern Novelist," *MissQ* 14 (Summer, 1961): 117-30.

Turner, Darwin T., "Faulkner and Slavery," in Harrington, E., and A. J. Abadie, eds., *South and Faulkner's Yoknapatawpha*, 62-85.

Twigg, Carol A., "The Social Role of Faulkner's Women: A Materialist's Interpretation," *DAI* 39 (1978): 1578A.

Urie, Margaret A., "The Problem of Evil: The Myth of Man's Fall and Redemption in the Works of William Faulkner," *DAI* 39 (1979): 4943A.

Van Nostrand, A. D., "The Poetic Dialogues of William Faulkner," *Everyman His Own Poet*, 175-96.

Versluys, Kristiaan, "A Look at Faulkner's Characters," *SGG* 16 (1975): 159-68.

Vickery, Olga W., "Faulkner and the Contours of Time," *GaR* 12 (Summer, 1958): 192-201.

————, "Language as Theme and Technique," *Novels of William Faulkner*, 266-81. Also in Litz, A. W., ed., *Modern American Fiction*, 179-93.

————, *Novels of William Faulkner*.

————, "William Faulkner and the Figure in the Carpet," *SAQ* 63 (Summer, 1964): 318-35. Also in Vickery, O. W., *Novels of William Faulkner*, 294-310. Also in Schmitter, D. M., ed., *William Faulkner*, 28-44.

Vincent, Sybil K., "Sweet and Bitter Sweat: William Faulkner's Work Ethic," *MarkhamR* 8 (1979): 66-9.

Vorpahl, Ben M., "Such Stuff as Dreams Are Made On: History, Myth and the Comic Vision of Mark Twain and William Faulkner," *DA* 28 (1967): 698A (Wisconsin).

Wad, Soren, in Bogh, J., and S. Skormand, eds., *Six American Novels*, 84-95.

Wagenknecht, E., *Cavalcade of the American Novel*, 417-25.

Waggoner, H. H., *William Faulkner*.

————, "William Faulkner: The Definition of Man," *BBr* 18 (Mar., 1958): 116-22.

————, "William Faulkner's Passion Week of the Heart," in Scott, Nathan A., ed., *The Tragic Vision and The Christian Faith*, N.Y.: Association Pr., 1957, 306-23.

Wagner, Linda, "Codes and Codicils: Faulkner's Last Novels," in Baldanza, F., ed., *Itinerary 3: Criticism*, 1-9.

————, "The Early Writing," *Hemingway and Faulkner*, 145-67.

————, "Faulkner and (Southern) Women," in Harrington, E., and A. J. Abadie, eds., *South and Faulkner's Yoknapatawpha*, 128-46. Also in Wagner, L. W., *American Modern*, 42-55.

————, Victoria F. Black, and Evans Harrington, "Faulkner and Women," in Harrington, E., and A. J. Abadie, eds., *South and Faulkner's Yoknapatawpha*, 147-51.

————, "Faulkner: The Craft of Fiction," *Hemingway and Faulkner*, 168-96.

————, "Faulkner: On Facts and Truth," *Hemingway and Faulkner*, 125-44.

————, "Faulkner's Fiction: Studies in Organic Form," *JNT* 1, i (Jan., 1971): 1-14.

————, "Faulkner's Largest Vision—and the Route to It," *Hemingway and Faulkner*, 197-210.

————, ed., *William Faulkner*.

Walhout, Clarence P., "The Earth is the Lord's: Religion in Faulkner," *CSR* 4, i (1974): 26-35.

Wall, Carey G., "Faulkner's Rhetoric," *DA* 25 (1965): 5947 (Stanford).

Walsh, J., *American War Literature*, 87-94.

Warren, Robert Penn, "Cowley's Faulkner," *NRep* 115 (Aug. 12, 1946): 176-80; (Aug. 26, 1946): 234-7. Also in Hoffman, F. J., and O. W. Vickery, eds., *William Faulkner*, 109-24. Also in Hoffman, F. J., and O. W. Vickery, eds., *William Faulkner: Two Decades of Criticism*, 82-101. Also in O'Connor, William Van, ed., *Forms of Modern Fiction*, 125-43. Also in Gibson, William M., and George Arms, eds., *Twelve American Writers*, N.Y.: Macmillan, 1962, 786-95. Also in Rahv, P., ed., *Literature in America*, 464-77. Also, rev. and expanded, in Beaver, Harold, ed., *American Critical Essays*, London: Oxford Un. Pr., 1959, 211-33. Also in Litz, A. W., ed., *Modern American Fiction*, 150-65. Also, in part, in Rubin, L. D., Jr., and J. R. Moore, eds., *Idea of an American Novel*, 359-63. Also in Warren, R. P., *Selected Essays*, 59-79. Also in Wagner, L. W., ed., *William Faulkner*, 94-109.

————, ed., *Faulkner*.

————, "Faulkner: The South, the Negro, and Time," *SoR* n.s. 1 (Summer, 1965): 501-29. Also in Warren, R. P., ed., *Faulkner*, 251-71.

————, "Introduction: Faulkner: Past and Future," in Warren, R. P., ed., *Faulkner*, 1-22. Also in Schmitter, D. M., ed., *William Faulkner*, 58-76.

Washburn, Delores C., "The 'Feeder' Motif in Selected Fiction of William Faulkner and Flannery O'Connor," *DAI* 40 (1979): 861A.

Wasiolek, Edward, "Dostoevsky, Camus, and Faulkner: Transcendence and Mutilation," *P&L* 1, ii (1977): 131-46.

Waters, Maureen A., "The Role of Women in Faulkner's Yoknapatawpha," *DAI* 36 (1975): 332A-33A.

Watkins, Floyd, "Faulkner and His Critics," *TSLL* 10 (Summer, 1968): 317-29.

————, "The Gentle Reader and Mr. Faulkner's Morals," *GaR* 13 (Spring, 1959): 68-75.

_____, "Habet: Faulkner and the Ownership of Property," in Wolfe, G. H., ed., *Faulkner*, 123-37.

_____, "The Hound Under the Wagon: Faulkner and the Southern Literati," in Fowler, D., and A. J. Abadie, eds., *Faulkner and the Southern Renaissance*, 93-119.

_____, "What Stand Did Faulkner Take?" in Fowler, D., and A. J. Abadie, eds., *Faulkner and the Southern Renaissance*, 40-62.

_____, "William Faulkner, the Individual, and the World," *GaR* 14 (Fall, 1960): 238-47.

Watson, James G., "Faulkner: The House of Fiction," in Fowler, D., and A. J. Abadie, eds., *Fifty Years of Yoknapatwpha*, 134-58.

_____, "Literary Self-Criticism: Faulkner in Fiction on Fiction," *SoQ* 20, i (Fall, 1981): 46-63.

Way, Brian, "William Faulkner," *CritQ* 3 (Spring, 1961): 42-53.

Webb, Gerald F., "Jeffersonian Agrarianism in Faulkner's Yoknapatawpha: The Evolution of Social and Economic Standard," *DAI* 33 (1973): 5754A (Fla. State).

Webb, James W., and A. Wigfall Green, eds., *William Faulkner of Oxford*, Baton Rouge: Louisiana St. Un. Pr., 1965.

Weeks, Willis E., "Faulkner's Young Males: From Futility to Responsibility," *DAI* 34 (1973): 2663A (Ariz. State).

Wegelin, Christof, ""Endure' and 'Prevail': Faulkner's Modification of Conrad," *N&Q* 21 (Oct., 1974): 375-6.

Weisgerber, J., *Faulkner and Dostoevsky*.

_____, "Faulkner's Monomaniacs: Their Indebtedness to Raskolnikov," *CLS* 5 (1968): 181-93.

Werner, Craig, "Beyond Realism and Romanticism: Joyce, Faulkner, and the Tradition of the American Novel," *CentR* 23 (Summer, 1979): 242-62.

West, Anthony, et al., "William Faulkner: A Critical Concensus," *Study of Current English* (Tokyo) 10 (Sept., 1955): 28-9. [Not seen.]

Weston, Robert V., "Faulkner and Lytle: Two Modes of Southern Fiction," *SoR* 15 (Jan., 1979): 34-51.

Whatley, John T., "A Topological Study of Thomas Hardy and William Faulkner," *DAI* 39 (1978): 2266A-67A.

Wheeler, Otis B., "Faulkner's Wilderness," *AL* 31 (May, 1959): 127-36.

_____, "Some Uses of Folk Humor by Faulkner," *MissQ* 17 (Spring, 1964): 107-22. Also in Wagner, L. W., ed., *William Faulkner*, 68-82.

Whitaker, Charles F., "Psychological Approaches to Narrative Personality in the Novels of William Faulkner," *DAI* 35 (1975): 7276A-77A.

Widmer, Kingsley, "The Protestant American Fate: Hemingway and Faulkner," in Widmer, K., *Edges of Extremity*, 42-57.

Williams, D., *Faulkner's Women*.

_____, "William Faulkner and the Mythology of Woman," *DAI* 34 (1974): 6610A (Mass.).

Williams, Philip, "William Faulkner's Haunted Stage of History," *JEI* 5 (1973): 1-38. [Not seen.]

Wilson, C., *Strength to Dream*, 36-40.

Wilson, G. Jennifer, "Faulkner's 'Riposte in Tertio'," *AN&Q* 16 (Feb., 1978): 88.

_____, "The Uncreating Word: Creators of Fiction in William Faulkner's Major Novels," *DAI* 38 (1978): 6719A.

Winn, James A., "Faulkner's Revisions: Stylist at Work," *AL* 41, ii (May, 1969): 231-40.

Winslow, William, "Modernity and the Novel: Twain, Faulkner, and Percy," *GyS* 8, i (Winter, 1981): 19-40.

Wittenberg, J. B., *Faulkner*.

_____, "Faulkner and Eugene O'Neill," *MissQ* 33 (Summer, 1980): 327-41.

_____, "William Faulkner: A Feminist Consideration," in Fleischmann, F., ed., *American Novelists Revisited*, 325-38.

Wolfe, Don M., "Faulkner and Hemingway: Image of Man's Desolation," *Image of Man in America*, 344-54.

Wolfe, G. H., ed., *Faulkner*.

Wyld, Lionel D., "Faulkner and Yoknapatawpha: Out of the 'Waste Land'," *Amer Lit Rev* (Japan) 30 (Dec., 1959): 4-12.

Wynn, Lelia C., "A Bookman's Faulkner," *Delta Rev* 2 (July-Aug., 1965): 35-5+.

Wynne, Carolyn, "Aspects of Space: John Marin and William Faulkner," *AQ* 16 (Spring, 1964): 59-71.

Yamada, Agnes A., "The Endless Jar: 'Contraries' in William Faulkner," *DAI* 32 (1972): 5249A (Ore.).

Yep, Lawrence M., "Self-Communion: The Early Novels of William Faulkner," *DAI* 36 (1975): 1513A.

Yonke, Jean M., "William Faulkner as a Moralist and Cultural Critic: A Comparison of His Views With Those of Historians and Social Scientists," *DAI* 42 (1982): 3160A-61A.

Yorks, Samuel A., "Faulkner's Woman: The Peril of Mankind," *ArQ* 17 (Summer, 1961): 119-29.

Young, T. D., and Floyd C. Watkins, "Faulkner's Snopeses," *MissQ* 11 (Fall, 1958): 196-200.

Zender, Karl, "Faulkner at Forty: The Artist at Home," *SoR* 17, ii (1981): 288-302.

_____, "Jason Compson and Death by Water," *MissQ* 31 (Summer, 1978): 421-2.

Ziegfeld, Richard E., "A Methodology for the Study of Philosophy in Literature: Philosophy and Symbol in Selected Works of William Faulkner and Thomas Mann," *DAI* 37 (1977): 5105A.

Zink, Karl E., "Faulkner's Garden: Woman and the Immemorial Earth," *MFS* 2 (Autumn, 1956): 139-49.

_____, "Flux and the Frozen Moment: The Imagery of Stasis in Faulkner's Prose," *PMLA* 71 (June, 1956): 285-301.

_____, "William Faulkner: Form as Experience," *SAQ* 53 (July, 1954): 384-403.

ABSALOM, ABSALOM!

Adamowski, T. H., "Children of the Idea: Heroes and Family Romances in ABSALOM, ABSALOM!" *Mosaic* 10, i (Fall, 1976): 115-31.

_____, "Dombey and Son and Sutpen and Son," *SNNTS* 4, iii (Fall, 1972): 378-89.

Adams, R. P., *Faulkner*, 172-214.

Allen, W., *Modern Novel*, 121-4.

_____, *Urgent West*, 88-90.

Angell, Leslie E., "The Umbilical Cord Symbol as Unifying Theme and Pattern in ABSALOM, ABSALOM!" *MSE* 1 (Fall, 1968): 106-10.

Aswell, Duncan, "The Puzzling Design of ABSALOM, ABSALOM!" *KR* 30 (Winter, 1968): 67-84.

Atkins, Anselm, "The Matched Halves of ABSALOM, ABSALOM! *MFS* 15, ii (Summer, 1969): 264-5.

Backman, M., *Faulkner*, 88-112.

_____, "Sutpen and the South: A Study of ABSALOM, ABSALOM!" *PMLA* 80 (Dec., 1965): 596-604.

Baldanza, Frank, "Faulkner and Stein: A Study in Stylistic Intransigence," *GaR* 13 (Fall, 1959): 274-86.

Bashiruddin, Zeba. "The Lost Individual in ABSALOM, ABSALOM!" *Newsletter Number 11*, American Studies Research Centre, Hyderabad, 1967, 49-52.

Beach, J. W., *American Fiction*, 138-42, 164-9.

Behrens, Ralph, "Collapse of Dynasty: The Thematic Center of ABSALOM, ABSALOM!" *PMLA* 89, i (Jan., 1974): 24-33.

Beja, Morris, "A Flash, A Glare: Faulkner and Time," *Ren* 16 (Spring, 1964): 137-41. Also in Beja, M., *Epiphany in the Modern Novel*, 201-8.

Bell, Arthur H., "ABSALOM, ABSALOM! For Long-hairs: Avoiding the Tangles," *IEJ* 6, ii (1972): 22-6.

Bennett, J. A. W., "Faulkner and A. E. Housman," *N&Q* 27, iii (1980): 234.

Berrone, Louis C., Jr., "Faulkner's ABSALOM, ABSALOM! and Dickens: A Study of Time and Change Correspondences," *DAI* 34 (1974): 5158A (Fordham).

Berzon, J. R., *Neither White Nor Black*, 91-4.

Bilingslea, Oliver L., "The Monument and the Plain: The Art of Mythic Consciousness in William Faulkner's ABSALOM, ABSALOM!," *DAI* 32 (1971): 3293A (Wis.).

Bjork, Lennart, "Ancient Myths and the Moral Framework of Faulkner's ABSALOM, ABSAOM!" *AL* 35 (May, 1963): 196-204.

Bosha, Francis J., "A Source for the Names Charles and Wash in ABSALOM, ABSALOM!" *NMAL* 4 (Spring, 1980): Item 13.

Bradford, M. E., "Brother, Son and Heir: The Structural Focus of Faulkner's ABSALOM, ABSALOM!" *SR* 78, i (Jan.-Mar., 1970): 76-98.

————, "'New Men' in Mississippi: ABSALOM, ABSALOM! and DOLLAR COTTON," *NMW* 2, ii (Fall, 1969): 55-66. [Parallels between Faulkner's Novel and that by his brother, John.]

Brodsky, Claudia, "The Working of Narrative in ABSALOM, ABSALOM!: A Textual Analysis," *Amst* 23, ii (1978): 240-59.

Brooks, Cleanth, "ABSALOM, ABSALOM!: The Definition of Innocence," *SR* 59 (Autumn, 1951): 543-8.

————, "The American 'Innocence,' " in James, Fitzgerald, and Faulkner," *Shen* 16 (Autumn, 1964): 21-37. Also in Brooks, C., *Shaping Joy*, 182-9, 191-4.

————, "History, Tragedy, and the Imagination in ABSALOM, ABSALOM!" *YR* 52 (Spring, 1963): 340-51.

————, "The Narrative Structure of ABSALOM, ABSALOM!" *GaR* 29, ii (1975): 366-94.

————, "On ABSALOM, ABSALOM!" *Mosaic* 7, i (Fall, 1973): 159-83. Also in Collins, R. G., and K. McRobbie, eds., *Novels of William Faulkner*, 159-83.

————, "The Poetry of Miss Rosa Canfield," *Shen* 21, iii (Spring, 1970): 199-206.

————, *William Faulkner: Toward Yoknapatawpha and Beyond*, 301-28, 354-61, 423-6.

————, *William Faulkner*, 295-324, 424-43. Also (condensed) in Warren, R. P., ed., *Faulkner*, 186-203.

Brooks, Peter, "Incredulous Narration: ABSALOM, ABSALOM!" *CL* 34, iii (Summer, 1982): 247-68.

Brown, May C., and Esta Seaton, "William Faulkner's Unlikely Detective: Quentin Compson in ABSALOM, ABSALOM!" *EAS* 8 (May, 1979): 27-33.

Brown, William R., "Mr. Stark on Mr. Strawson on Referring," *Lang&S* 7 (Summer, 1974): 219-24.

Brylowski, W., *Faulkner's Olympian Laugh*, 17-42.

Burgum, E. B., *Novel and the World's Dilemma*, 221-2.

Burns, Stuart L., "Sutpen's 'Incidental' Wives and the Question of Respectability," *MissQ* 30 (Summer, 1977): 445-7.

Callen, Shirley, "Planter and Poor White in ABSALOM, ABSALOM!, 'Wash', and *The Mind of the South*," *SCB* 23, iv (Winter, 1963): 24-36.

Cambon, Clauco, "My Faulkner: The Untranslatable Demon," in Zyla, W. T., and W. M. Aycock, eds., *William Faulkner*, 77-93.

Campbell, Harry M., "Faulkner's ABSALOM, ABSALOM!" *Explicator* 7 (Dec., 1948): Item 24.

Canellas, Maria I. J. C., "Time in Faulkner's ABSALOM, ABSALOM! as Related to Film Technique," *EAA* 2 (1978): 33-44.

Canine, Karen M., "The Case Hierarchy and Faulkner's Relatives in ABSALOM, ABSALOM!" *SECOLB* 3, ii (Summer, 1979): 63-80.

————, "Faulkner's Theory of Relativity: Non-Restrictives in ABSALOM, ABSALOM!" *SECOLB* 5, iii (Fall, 1981): 118-34.

Chavkin, Allan, "The Imagination as the Alternative to Sutpen's Design," *ArQ* 37, ii (Summer, 1981): 116-26.

Church, M., "William Faulkner: Myth and Duration," *Time and Reality*, 241-3.

Clark, Eulalyn, "Ironic Effects of Multiple Perspective in AS I LAY DYING," *NMW* 5, i (Spring, 1972): 15-28.

Clark, William G., "Is King David a Racist?" *UR* 34 (Dec., 1967): 121-6.

Cleopatra, Sr., "ABSALOM, ABSALOM! The Failure of the Sutpen Design," *LHY* 16, i (Jan., 1975): 74-93.

Coanda, Richard, "ABSALOM, ABSALOM!: The Edge of Infinity," *Ren* 11 (Autumn, 1958): 3-9.

Connolly, Thomas E., "Point of View in Faulkner's ABSALOM, ABSALOM!" *MFS* 27, ii (Summer, 1981): 255-72.

————, "A Skeletal Outline of ABSALOM, ABSALOM!" *CE* 25 (Nov., 1963): 110-14.

————, in Krause, S. J., ed., *Essays in Determinism*, 45-7.

Davenport, F. G., *Myth of Southern History*, 88-92, 115-27.

Davis, Thadeous M., "'Be Sutpen's Hundred': Imaginative Projection of Landscape in ABSALOM, ABSALOM!" *SLJ* 13, ii (Spring, 1981): 3-14.

————, "The Yoking of 'Abstract Contradictions': Clytie's Meaning in ABSALOM, ABSALOM!" *SAF* 7, ii (1979): 209-19.

Dickerson, Lynn, "A Possible Source for the Title ABSALOM, ABSALOM!" *MissQ* 31, ii (Summer, 1978): 423-4.

Dillingham, William B., "William Faulkner and 'Tragic Condition'," *Edda* 66 (1966): 327-30.

Dimino, Andrea, "Creating Human Time: Faulkner's Temporal Strategies in THE HAMLET, ABSALOM, ABSALOM! and 'The Bear'," *DAI* 41, xii (June, 1981): 5100A-01A.

Doxey, W. S., "Father Time and the Grim Reaper in ABSALOM, ABSALOM!" *NConL* 8, iii (May, 1978): 6-7.

Donaldson, Laura E., "The Perpetual Conversation: The Process of Traditioning in ABSALOM, ABSALOM!" *MSLC* 4 (1982): 176-94.

Donohoe, Eileen M., "Psychic Transformation through Memory: Work and Negation in William Faulkner's ABSALOM, ABSALOM!" *DAI* 39 (1978): 1546A-47A.

Doody, Terence, "Shreve McCannon and the Confessions of ABSALOM, ABSALOM!" *SNNTS* 6, iv (Winter, 1974): 454-69.

Douglass, Scott, "Possible Sources for Faulkner's General Compson," *RALS* 11, i (Spring, 1981): 112-14.

Edwards, Duane, "Flem Snopes and Thomas Sutpen: Two Versions of Respectability," *DR* 51, iv (Winter, 1971-72): 559-70.

Everett, W. K., *Faulkner's Art and Characters*, 1-6.

Ewell, Barbara N., "To Move in Time: A Study of the Structure of Faulkner's AS I LAY DYING, LIGHT IN AUGUST, and ABSALOM, ABSALOM!" *DAI* 30 (1970): 3940A (Florida St.).

Fazio, Rocco R., "The Fury and the Design: Realms of Being and Knowing in Four Novels of William Faulkner," *DA* 25 (1964): 1910 (Rochester).

Fiedler, L., *Love and Death in the American Novel*, 394-8, 443-6.

Foran, Donald J., S. J., "William Faulkner's ABSALOM, ABSALOM!: An Exercise in Affirmation," *DAI* 34 (1974): 4259A (So. Calif.).

Ford, Daniel G., "Comments on William Faulkner's Temporal Vision in SANCTUARY, THE SOUND AND THE FURY, LIGHT IN AUGUST, ABSALOM, ABSALOM!" *SoQ* 15, iii (1977): 283-90.

_____, "Uses of Time in Four Novels by William Faulkner," *DAI* 35 (1974): 1654A (Auburn).

Forrer, Richard, "ABSALOM, ABSALOM!: Story-Telling as a Mode of Transcendence," *SLJ* 9, i (Fall, 1976): 22-46.

Garzilli, E., *Circles Without Center*, 52-60.

Geismar, M., *Writers in Crisis*, 170-6.

Giordano, Frank R., Jr., "ABSALOM, ABSALOM! as a Portrait of the Artist," in Deakin, Motley, and Peter Lisca, eds., *From Irving to Steinbeck*, 97-107.

Glicksberg, Charles I., "Faulkner's World of Love and Sex," *Sexual Revolution in American Literature*, 109-11.

_____, "William Faulkner and the Negro Problem," *Phylon* 10 (1949): 153-6.

Gold, J., *William Faulkner*, 30-8.

Gossett, L. Y., *Violence in Recent Southern Fiction*, 35-8.

Gowda, H. H. Anniah, "Visions of Decadence: William Faulkner's ABSALOM, ABSALOM! and V. S. Naipul's THE MIMIC MEN," *LHY* 23, i (1982): 71-80.

Gray, R., *Literature of Memory*, 238-54.

_____, "The Meanings of History: William Faulkner's ABSALOM, ABSALOM!" *DQR* 3, iii (1973): 97-110.

Guerard, A. J., "ABSALOM, ABSALOM! The Novel as Impressionist Art," *Triumph of the Novel*, 302-39.

Guetti, James, "The Failure of the Imagination: A Study of Melville, Conrad, and Faulkner," *DA* 25 (1965): 4145-6 (Cornell).

_____, *Limits of Metaphor*, N.Y.: Ithaca: Cornell Un. Pr., 1967, 69-108.

Gwynn, F. L., and J. L. Blotner, eds., *Faulkner in the University*.

Hagan, John, "*Déjà vu* and the Effect of Timelessness in Faulkner's ABSALOM, ABSALOM!" *BuR* 11, ii (Mar., 1963): 31-52.

_____, "Fact and Fancy in ABSALOM, ABSALOM! and the Negro Question," *MFS* 19 (Summer, 1973): 207-11.

_____, "The Biblical Background of Faulkner's ABSALOM, ABSALOM!" *CEA* 36, ii (Jan., 1974): 22-4.

_____, "Black Insight in ABSALOM, ABSALOM!" *FaSt* 1 (1980): 29-37.

Hammond, Donald, "Faulkner's Levels of Awareness," *FloQ* 1, ii (1967): 75-8.

Hartt, J. N., *Lost Image of Man*, 39-45.

Haury, Beth B., "The Influence of Robinson Jeffers' 'Tamar' on ABSALOM, ABSALOM!" *MissQ* 25 (Summer, 1972): 356-8.

Hawkins, E. O., "Faulkner's 'Duke, John of Lorraine'," *AN&Q* 4 (Sept., 1965): 22.

Henderson, H. B., Jr., *Versions of the Past*, 254-69.

Herndon, Jerry A., "Faulkner: Meteor, Earthquake, and Sword," in Carey, Glenn O., ed., *Faulkner*, 175-93.

Hlavsa, Virginia V., "The Vision of the Advocate in ABSALOM, ABSALOM!" *Novel* 8, i (Fall, 1974): 51-70.

Hodgson, John A., "'Logical Sequence and Continuity': Some Observations on the Typographical and Structural Consistency of ABSALOM, ABSALOM!" *AL* 43, i (Mar., 1971): 97-107.

Hoffman, A. C., "Faulkner's ABSALOM, ABSALOM!" *Expl* 10 (Nov., 1951): Item 12.

_____, "Point of View in ABSALOM, ABSALOM!" *UKCR* 19 (Summer, 1953): 233-9.

Hoffman, F. J., *William Faulkner*, 74-9.

_____, in French, W. G., and W. E. Kidd, eds., *American Winners of the Nobel Literary Prize*, 150-2.

Holman, C. Hugh, "'ABSALOM, ABSALOM!' The Historian as Detective," *SR* 79, iv (Autumn, 1971): 542-53. Also in Holman, C. H., *Roots of Southern Writing*, 168-76.

_____, *Three Modes of Modern Southern Fiction*, 27-44+.

Howe, I., *William Faulkner*, 71-8, 221-32.

Hunt, John W., "Keeping the Hoop Skirts Out: Historiography in Faulkner's ABSALOM, ABSALOM!" *FaSt* 1 (1980): 38-47.

_____, *William Faulkner*, 101-36. Also in Barth, J. R., S. J., ed., *Religious Perspectives in Faulkner's Fiction*, 141-69.

Ilacqua, Alma A., "Faulkner's ABSALOM, ABSALOM!: An Aesthetic Projection of the Religious Sense of Beauty," *BSUF* 21, ii (Spring, 1980): 34-41.

Jacobs, Robert D., "Faulkner's Tragedy of Isolation," in Rubin, L. D., and R. D. Jacobs, eds., *Southern Renascence*, 184-91.

_____, "William Faulkner: The Passion and the Penance," in Rubin, L. D., Jr., and R. D. Jacaobs, eds., *South*, 163-9.

Jehlen, M., *Class and Character in Faulkner's South*, 51-73.

Jenkins, L., *Faulkner and Black-White Relations*, 177-219.

Justus, James H., "The Epic Design of ABSALOM, ABSALOM!" *TSLL* 4 (Summer, 1962): 157-76.

Kantak, V. Y., "Faulkner's Technique," in Chander, J., and N. S. Pradhan, eds., *Studies in American Literature*, 77-96 *passim*.

Kartiganer, Donald M., "Faulkner's ABSALOM, ABSALOM!: The Discovery of Values," *AL* 37 (Nov., 1965): 291-306.

_____, *Fragile Thread*, 69-106.

_____, "Process and Product: A Study of Modern Literary Form," *MR* 12 (Autumn, 1971): 297-328, 789-816.

_____, "The Role of Myth in ABSALOM, ABSALOM!" *MFS* 9 (Winter, 1963-64): 357-69.

Kellner, R. Scott, "A Reconsideration of Character: Relationships in ABSALOM, ABSALOM!" *NMW* 7, ii (Fall, 1974): 39-43.

Kerr, Elizabeth M., "ABSALOM, ABSALOM! Faust in Mississippi, or, The Fall of the House of Sutpen," *UMSE* 15 (1978): 61-82.

_____, *William Faulkner's Gothic Domain*.

King, R. H., *Southern Renaissance*, 119-29.

Kinney, A. F., *Faulkner's Narrative Poetics*, 194-215.

_____, "Form and Function in ABSALOM, ABSALOM!" *SoR* 14 (Oct., 1978): 677-91.

Knutsen, Marla T., "The Power of Mr. Compson in ABSALOM, ABSALOM!: Heroism/Homoeroticism/Approach-Avoidance toward Women," *DAI* 41 (1980): 668A-69A.

Landor, Mikhail, "ABSALOM, ABSALOM! in Russian," *SovL* 7 [400] (1981): 164-72.

LaRocque, Geraldine E., "A TALE OF TWO CITIES and ABSALOM, ABSALOM!" *MissQ* 35, iii (1982): 301-4.

Leary, L., *William Faulkner of Yoknapatawpha County*, 96-113.

Lensing, George S., "The Metaphor of Family in ABSALOM, ABSALOM!" *SoR* 11, i (Jan., 1975): 99-117.

Leroy, Gaylord C., "Mythopoeic Materials in ABSALOM, ABSALOM!: What Approach for the Marxist Critic?" *MinnR* 17 (Fall, 1981): 79-95.

Levins, L. G., *Faulkner's Heroic Design*, 7-54.

_____, "The Four Narrative Perspectives in ABSALOM, ABSALOM!" *PMLA* 85, i (Jan., 1970): 35-4.

Lind, Ilse D., "The Design and Meaning of ABSALOM, ABSALOM!" *PMLA* 70 (Dec., 1955): 887-912. Also in Hoffman, F. J., and O. W. Vickery, eds., *William Faulkner*, 278-304. Also in Wagner, L. W., ed., *William Faulkner*, 272-97.

Longley, J. L., Jr., *Tragic Mask*, 206-18. Also in Schmitter, B. M., ed., *William Faulkner*, 110-21.

Lorch, Thomas M., "Thomas Sutpen and the Female Principle," *MissQ* 20 (Winter, 1966-67): 38-42.

Loughry, Thomas F., "Aborted Sacrament in ABSALOM, ABSALOM!" *FQ* 14 (Nov., 1964): 13-21.

MacLure, Millar, "Allegories of Innocence," *DR* 40 (Summer, 1960): 146-9.

Major, Sylvia B. B., "ABSALOM, ABSALOM!: A Study of Structure," *DAI* 34 (1974): 5188A (No. Texas State).

Markowitz, Norman, "William Faulkner's 'Tragic Legend': Southern History and ABSALOM, ABSALOM!" *MinnR* 17 (Fall, 1981): 104-17.

Marshall, Sarah L., "Fathers and Sons in ABSALOM, ABSALOM!" *UMSE* 8 (1967): 19-29.

Mascitelli, David W., "Faulkner's Characters of Sensibility," *DA* 29 (1968): 608A-9A (Duke).

Mathews, James W., "The Civil War of 1936: GONE WITH THE WIND and ABSALOM, ABSALOM!" *GaR* 21 (Winter, 1967): 462-9.

Matlack, James H., "The Voices of Time: Narrative Structure in ABSALOM, ABSALOM!" *SoR* 15, iii (April, 1979): 333-54.

Matthews, John T., "The Marriage of Speaking and Hearing in ABSALOM, ABSALOM!" *ELH* 47 (Fall, 1980): 575-94.

_____, *Play of Faulkner's Language*, 115-61.

McClennen, Joshua, "ABSALOM, ABSALOM! and the Meaning of History," *PMASAL* 42 (1956): 357-69.

McClure, John, "The Syntax of Decadence in ABSALOM, ABSALOM!" *MinnR* 17 (Fall, 1981): 96-103.

Middleton, John, "Shreve McCannon and Sutpen's Legacy," *SoR* 10, i (Jan., 1974): 115-24.

Millgate, M., *Achievement of William Faulkner*, 150-64.

_____, *William Faulkner*, 52-9.

Milum, Richard A., "Faulkner and the Cavalier Tradition: The French Bequest," *AL* 45, iv (Jan., 1974): 580-9.

Minter, David L., "Apotheosis of the Form: Faulkner's ABSALOM, ABSALOM!" *The Interpreted Design as a Structural Principle in American Prose*, New Haven and London: Yale Un. Pr., 1969, 191-219.

_____, "Family, Region, and Myth in Faulkner's Fiction," in Fowler, D., and A. J. Abadie, eds., *Faulkner and the Southern Renaissance*, 191-201.

Monaghan, David M., "Faulkner's ABSALOM, ABSALOM!" *Expl* 31, iv (Dec., 1972): Item 28.

Muehl, Lois, "Faulkner's Humor in Three Novels and One 'Play'," *LC* 34 (Spring, 1968): 78-93.

Muhlenfeld, Elisabeth S., "Shadows With Substance and Ghosts Exhumed: The Women in ABSALOM, ABSALOM!" *MissQ* 25 (Summer, 1972): 289-304. Also in Cox, L. H., ed., *William Faulkner*, 249-66.

_____, "'We have waited long enough': Judith Sutpen and Charles Bon," *SoR* 14, i (Jan., 1978): 66-80.

Nelson, David W., "Two Novels of Speculation: William Faulkner's ABSALOM, ABALOM! and Uwe Johnson's MUTMASSUNGEN UBER JAKOB," *Prom* 2, supp. 1 (1980): 51-7.

Newby, Richard L., "Matthew Arnold, the North, and ABSALOM, ABSALOM!" *AN&Q* 16, vii (1977/1978): 105.

Nilon, Charles H., "Faulkner and the Negro," *UCSSLL* No. 8 (Sept., 1962): 93-6. Also in Nilon, C. H., *Faulkner and the Negro*, 93-6.

Nishiyama, Tamotsu, "The Structure of ABSALOM, ABSALOM!" *KAL* No. 1 (June, 1958): 9-13.

O'Connor, William Van, "Faulkner's Legend of the Old South," *WHR* 7 (Autumn, 1953): 294-9.

_____, "Protestantism in Yoknapatawpha County," in Rubin, L. D., and R. D. Jacobs, *Southern Renascence*, 156-8.

_____, *Tangled Fire of William Faulkner*, 94-100.

_____, *William Faulkner*, 25-8. Also in O'Connor, W. V., ed., *Seven Modern American Novelists*, 138-40.

Ohki, Masako, "The Technique of Handling Time in ABSALOM, ABSALOM!" *KAL* 15 (May, 1974): 89-94.

Page, S. R., *Faulkner's Women*, 102-9.

Parker, Hershel, "What Quentin Saw 'Out There'," *MissQ* 27, iii (Summer, 1974): 323-6.

Parkinson-Zamora, Lois, "The End of Innocence: Myth and Narrative Structure in Faulkner's ABSALOM, ABSALOM! and García Márquez' CIEN ANOS DE SOLEDAD," *HisJ* 4, i (Fall, 1982): 23-40.

Parr, Susan D. R., "'And by Bergson, Obviously': Faulkner's THE SOUND AND THE FURY, AS I LAY DYING and ABSALOM, ABSALOM! from a Bergsonian Perspective," *DAI* 32 (1972): 6996A (Wis.).

_____, "The Fourteenth Image of the Blackbird: Another Look at Truth in ABSALOM, ABSALOM!" *ArQ* 35 (Summer, 1979): 153-64.

Peterson, John, "Hardy, Faulkner, and the Prosaics of Tragedy," *CRAS* 5 (Spring, 1961): 156-75.

Pearce, Richard, "Enter the Frame," *TriQ* 30 (1974): 71-82. Also in Federman, R., ed., *Surfiction: Fiction Now ... and Tomorrow*, Chicago: Swallow, 1981, 47-57.

Placentino, Edward J., "Another Possible Source for ABSALOM, ABSALOM!" *NMW* 10, ii (Winter, 1977): 87-94.

Pikoulis, J., *Art of William Faulkner*, 66-111.

Pilkington, J., *Heart of Yoknapatawpha*, 157-88.

Pinsker, Sanford, "Thomas Sutpen and Milly Jones: A Note on Paternal Design in ABSALOM, ABSALOM!" *NMAL* 1 (1976): Item 6.

Pires, Sister M. Dolorine, S.S.C.C., "Plot Manipulation and Kaleidoscoping of Time as Sources of Tragic Perception in William Faulkner's ABSALOM, ABSALOM!" *DAI* 31 (1971): 4176A (St. Louis).

Pitavy, Francois L., "The Gothicism of ABSALOM, ABSALOM!: Rosa Coldfield Revisited," in Fowler, D., and A. J. Abadie, eds., *A Cosmos of My Own*, 199-226.

Poirier, William R., "'Strange Gods' in Jefferson, Mississippi: Analysis of ABSALOM, ABSALOM!" in Hoffman, F. J., and O. W. Vickery, eds., *William Faulkner: Two Decades of Criticism*, 217-43.

Polek, Fran J., "The Fourteenth Blackbird: Refractive Deflection in ABSALOM, ABSALOM!" *UPR* 28, i (Spring, 1976): 23-34.

————, "From Renegade to Solid Citizen: The Extraordinary Individual and the Community," *SDR* 15, i (Spring, 1977): 61-72.

Porter, C., *Seeing and Being*, 234-40, 259-76.

Powers, L. H., *Faulkner's Yoknapatawpha Comedy*, 106-24.

Putzel, Max, "What Is Gothic About ABSALOM, ABSALOM!" *SLJ* 4, i (Fall, 1971): 3-19.

Randel, Fred V., "Parentheses in Faulkner's ABSALOM, ABSALOM!" *Style* 5 (1971): 70-87.

Raper, J. R., "Meaning Called to Life: Alogical Structure in ABSALOM, ABSALOM!" *SHR* 5, i (Winter, 1971): 9-23.

Richardson, K. E., *Force and Faith in the Novels of William Faulkner*, 29-35.

Rifkin, Ellen R., "ABSALOM, ABSALOM! and the Curse of Inherited Fictions: Wherein a Student of Faulkner Reclaims Her Education and Requests Title to the Deed," *DAI* 41 (1980): 2113A.

Rimmon-Kenan, Shlomith, "From Reproduction to Production: The Status of Narration in Faulkner's ABSALOM, ABSALOM!" *Degrés* 16 (1978): f-f19.

Rinaldi, Nicholas M., "Game-Consciousness and Game-Metaphor in the Work of William Faulkner," *DA* 24 (1964): 4196-7 (Fordham).

————, "Game Imagery in Faulkner's ABSALOM, ABSALOM!" *ConnR* 4, i (Oct., 1970): 73-9.

Rio-Jelliffe, R., "ABSALOM, ABSALOM!" *MissQ* 34, iii (Summer, 1981): 315-24.

Rodewald, F. A., "Faulkner's Possible Use of THE GREAT GATSBY," *FHA* (1975): 97-101.

Rodnon, Stewart, "THE HOUSE OF SEVEN GABLES and ABSALOM, ABSALOM!: Time, Tradition and Guilt," *SHum* 1, ii (Winter, 1969-70): 42-6.

Rollyson, Carl E., Jr., "ABSALOM, ABSALOM! The Novel as Historiography," *L&H* 5 (1977): 42-54.

————, "Faulkner and Historical Fiction: RED GAUNTLET and ABSALOM, ABSALOM!" *DR* 56 (Winter, 1976-77): 671-81.

————, "The Re-Creation of the Past in ABSALOM, ABSALOM!" *MissQ* 29, iii (Summer, 1976): 361-74.

Rome, Joy J., "Love and Wealth in ABSALOM, ABSALOM!" *UES* 9, i (Mar., 1971): 3-10.

Rose, Maxine, "Echoes of the King James Bible in the Prose Style of ABSALOM, ABSALOM!" *ArQ* 37, ii (Summer, 1981): 137-48.

————, "From Genesis to Revelation: The Grand Design of Faulkner's ABSALOM, ABSALOM!" *DAI* 34 (1974): 6656A (Ala.).

————, "From Genesis to Revelation: The Grand Design of William Faulkner's ABSALOM, ABSALOM!" *SAF* 8, ii (1980): 219-28.

Rosenman, John B., "Anderson's POOR WHITE and Faulkner's ABSALOM, ABSALOM!" *MissQ* 29, iii (Summer, 1976): 437-8.

Rosenzweig, Paul, "The Narrative Frames in ABSALOM, ABSALOM! Faulkner's Involuted Commentary on Art," *ArQ* 35 (Summer, 1979): 135-52.

Ross, Stephen M., "Conrad's Influences on Faulkner's ABSALOM, ABSALOM!" *SAF* 2, ii (Autumn, 1974): 199-209.

————, "The Evocation of Voice in ABSALOM, ABSALOM!" *ELWIU* 8, iii (Fall, 1981): 135-49.

————, "Faulkner's ABSALOM, ABSALOM! and the David Story: A Speculative Contemplation," in Frontain, Raymond-Jean, and Jan Wojcik, eds., *The David Myth in Western Literature*, West Lafayette: Purdue Un. Pr., 1980, 136-53.

Roudiez, Leon S., "ABSALOM, ABSALOM! The Significance of Contradictions," *MinnR* 17 (Fall, 1981): 58-78.

Rubin, Louis D., Jr., *Faraway Country*, 50-4.

————, "Scarlett O'Hara and the Two Quentin Compsons," in Harrington, E., and A. J. Abadie, eds., *South and Faulkner's Yoknapatawpha*, 168-94. Also in Rubin, L. D., Jr., *Gallery of Southerners*, 26-48.

————, *The Writer in the South: Studies in a Literary Community*, Athens: Un. of Ga. Pr., 1972, 107-14.

Rudich, Norman, and Carol Remes, "Faulkner and Marxist Criticism," *MinnR* 17 (Fall, 1981): 53-4.

————, "Faulkner and the Sin of Private Property," *MinnR* 17 (Fall, 1981): 55-7.

Rukas, Nijole M., "A Comparison of Faulkner's and Rulfo's Treatment of the Interplay between Reality and Illusion in ABSALOM, ABSALOM! and PEDRO PARAMO," *DAI* 43 (1982): 818A.

Sabiston, Elizabeth, "Women, Blacks, and Thomas Sutpen's Mythopoetic Drive in ABSALOM, ABSALOM!" *MSLC* 1, iii (1974-75): 15-26.

Sachs, V., *Myth of America*, 103-24.

Samway, Patrick, S. J., "Storytelling and the Library Scene in Faulkner's ABSALOM, ABSALOM!" *WiF* 2, ii (Dec., 1979): 1-20.

Schmidtberger, Loren F., "ABSALOM, ABSALOM!: What Clytie Knew," *MissQ* 35, iii (1982): 255-64.

Schoenberg, E., *Old Tales and Talking*.

Schoenberg, Estella E. I., "Quentin Compson and the Fictive Process: A Four-Dimensional Study of ABSALOM, ABSALOM!" *DAI* 35 (1975): 6732A-33A.

Schrank, Bernice, "Patterns of Reversal in ABSALOM, ABSALOM!" *DR* 54, iv (1974-75): 648-66.

Schrero, Elliott M., "ANOTHER COUNTRY and the Sense of Self," *BARev* 2, i-ii (Spring-Summer, 1971): 91-100.

Schultz, William J., "Just Like Father: Mr. Compson as Cavalier Romancer in ABSALOM, ABSALOM!" *KanQ* 14, ii (1982): 115-23.

Scott, Arthur L., "The Faulknerian Sentence," *PrS* 27 (1953): 91-8.

————, "The Myriad Perspectives of ABSALOM, ABSALOM!" *AQ* 7 (Fall, 1954): 210-20.

Sederberg, Peter C., "Faulkner, Naipaul and Zola: Violence and the Novel," in Barber, B. R., and M. J. McGrath, eds., *Artist and Political Vision*, 299-313.

Seiden, Melvin, "Faulkner's Ambiguous Negro," *MR* 4 (Summer, 1963): 675-90.

Sewall, Richard B., *The Vision of Tragedy*, New Haven: Yale Un. Pr., 1959, 133-47.

Seyppel, J., *William Faulkner*, 62-6.

Shirley, William, "The Question of Sutpen's Innocence," *SLM* 1, i (Spring, 1975): 31-7.

Singleton, Marvin K., "Personae at Law and Equity: The Unity of Faulkner's ABSALOM, ABSALOM!" *PLL* 3 (Fall, 1967): 354-70.

Slabey, Robert M., "Faulkner's 'Waste Land': Vision in ABSALOM, ABSALOM!" *MissQ* 14 (Summer, 1961): 153-61.

_____, "Quentin Compson's 'Lost Childhood'," *SSF* 1 (Spring, 1964): 173-83.

Slatoff, W. J., *Quest for Failure*, 13-14, 71-2, 118-19, 198-202, 256.

Sowder, William J., "Colonel Thomas Sutpen as Existentialist Hero," *AL* 33 (Jan., 1962): 485-99.

Stafford, William T., "A Whale, an Heiress, and a Southern Demigod: Three Symbolic Americas," *CollL* 1, ii (Spring, 1974): 100-12. Also in Stafford, W. T., *Books Speaking to Books*, 11-26.

Stark, John, "The Implications for Stylistics of Strawson's 'On Referring', with ABSALOM, ABSALOM! as an Example," *Lang&S* 6 (Fall, 1973): 273-80.

Steinberg, Aaron, "ABSALOM, ABSALOM!: The Irretrievable Bon," *CLAJ* 9 (Sept., 1965): 61-7.

_____, "Faulkner and the Negro," *DA* 27 (1966): 1385A (N.Y.U.).

Stewart, David H., "ABSALOM Reconsidered," *UTQ* 30 (Oct., 1960): 31-44.

Stonum, G. L., *Faulkner's Career*, 123-56.

Suda, Minoru, "The Development of William Faulkner's Literature: With Special Emphasis on THE SOUND AND THE FURY and ABSALOM, ABSALOM!" *ESELL* 70 (1979): 23-40.

Sugiura, Ginsaku, "Nature, History, and Entropy: A Reading of Faulkner's ABSALOM, ABSALOM! in Comparison with MOBY-DICK and V.," *WiF* 2, ii (Dec., 1979): 21-33.

Sullivan, W., *Requiem for the Renascence*, 9-11.

Sullivan, Walter, "The Tragic Design of ABSALOM, ABSALOM!" *SAQ* 50 (Oct., 1951): 552-66.

Sullivan, William P., "William Faulkner and the Community," *DA* 22 (1962): 4355 (Columbia).

Swiggart, P., *Art of Faulkner's Novels*, 149-70.

Sykes, S. W., "The Novel as Conjuration: ABSALOM, ABSALOM! and LA ROUTE DES FLANDRES," *RLC* 53 (July-Sept., 1979): 348-57.

Thomas, Douglas M., "Memory-Narrative in ABSALOM, ABSALOM!" *Faulkner Studies* 2 (Summer, 1953): 19-22.

Thompson, Lawrance, "A Defense of Difficulties in William Faulkner's Art," *Carrell* 4, (Dec., 1963): 7-16.

_____, *William Faulkner*, 53-65, 191-3.

Tindall, W. Y., *Literary Symbol*, 264-7.

Tobin, Patricia, "The Time of Myth and History in ABSALOM, ABSALOM!" *AL* 45, ii (May, 1973): 252-70.

Tritschler, Donald H., "Whorls of Form in Faulkner's Fiction," *DA* 17 (1957): 3025 (Northwestern).

Tuck, D., *Crowell's Handbook of Faulkner*, 56-66.

Uroff, Margaret D., "The Fictions of ABSALOM, ABSALOM!" *SNNTS* 11, iv (1979): 431-45.

Van Nostrand, A. D., "The Poetic Dialogues of William Faulkner," *Everyman His Own Poet*, 184-9.

Vande Kieft, Ruth M., "Faulkner's Defeat of Time in ABSALOM, ABSALOM!" *SoR* 6, iv (Oct., 1970): 1100-09.

Vickery, O. W., *Novels of William Faulkner*, 84-102.

Vidan, Ivo, "ABSALOM, ABSALOM! and WUTHERING HEIGHTS," *SRAZ* 41/42 (1976): 395-411.

Volpe, E. L., *Reader's Guide to William Faulkner*, 184-212.

Wad, Soren, in Bogh, J., and Skovmand, eds., *Six American Novels*, 96-115.

Waggoner, Hyatt H., "The Historical Novel and the Southern Past: The Case of ABSALOM, ABSALOM!" *SLJ* 2, ii (Spring, 1970): 69-85.

_____, *William Faulkner*, 148-69. Also (condensed) in Warren, R. P., ed., *Faulkner*, 175-85.

Walters, P. S., "Hallowed Ground: Group Areas in the Structure and Theme of ABSALOM, ABSALOM!" *Theoria* 47 (1976): 35-55.

Watkins, Evan, "The Fiction of Interpretation: Faulkner's ABSALOM, ABSALOM!" *The Critical Act: Criticism and Commentary*, New Haven and London: Yale Un. Pr., 1978, 188-212.

Watkins, Floyd C., "Thirteen Ways of Talking About a Blackbird," *Flesh and the World*, 216-33.

_____, "What Happens in ABSALOM, ABSALOM!" *MFS* 13, i (Spring, 1967): 79-87.

Watson, James G., "'If Was Existed': Faulkner's Prophets and the Patterns of History," *MFS* 21 (Winter, 1975): 499-507.

Weatherby, L., "Sutpen's Garden," *GaR* 21 (Fall, 1967): 354-69.

Wee, Morris O., "Confronting the Ghost: Quentin Compson's Struggle with His Heritage in Faulkner's ABSALOM, ABSALOM!" *DAI* 35 (1975): 6166A.

Weinstein, A. L., *Vision and Response in Modern Fiction*, 136-53.

Weisgerber, J., *Faulkner and Dostoevsky*, 236-48.

Whan, Edgar, "ABSALOM, ABSALOM! as Gothic Myth," *Per* 3 (Autumn, 1950): 192-201.

Wigley, Joseph A., "An Analysis of the Imagery of William Faulkner's ABSALOM, ABSALOM!" *DA* 16 (1956): 2464-65 (Northwestern).

_____, "Imagery and the Interpreter," in Doyle, Esther M., and Virginia H. Floyd, eds., *Studies in Interpretation*, v. 1, 171-89.

Wijesinghe, Rajiva, "A Basis of Confusion: ABSALOM, ABSALOM! with Some Light from Conrad," *EB* 3 (1981): 1-7.

William, J. Gary, "Quentin Finally Sees Miss Rosa," *Criticism* 21 (Fall, 1979): 331-46.

Williams, Philip E., "The Biblical View of History: Hawthorne, Mark Twain, Faulkner, and Eliot," *DA* 25 (1965): 4159-60 (Pennsylvania).

_____, "Faulkner's Satan Sutpen and the Tragedy of ABSALOM, ABSALOM!" *ESELL* Nos. 45-46 (Dec., 1964): 179-99.

Wilson, Mary Ann, "Search for an Eternal Present: ABSALOM, ABSALOM! and ALL THE KING'S MEN," *ConnR* 8, i (Oct., 1974): 95-100.

Wittenberg, J. B., *Faulkner*, 140-55.

Woodward, Robert H., " Poe's Raven, Faulkner's Sparrow, and Another Window," *PoeN* 2, i-ii (April, 1969): 37-8. [Parallels between Poe's THE RAVEN and a paragraph in ABSALOM, ABSALOM!]

Young, Thomas D., "Narration as Creative Act: The Role of Quentin Compson in ABSALOM, ABSALOM!" in Harrington, E., and A. J. Abadie, eds., *Faulkner, Modernism, and Film*, 82-102.

Zamora, Lois P., "The Myth of Apocalypse and the American Literary Imagination," in Zamora, L. P., ed., *Apocalyptic Vision in America*, 119-22.

Zoellner, Robert H., "Faulkner's Prose Style in ABSALOM, ABSALOM!" *AL* 30 (Jan., 1959): 486-502.

AS I LAY DYING

Adamowski, T. H., " 'Meet Mrs. Bundren': AS I LAY DYING—Gentility, Tact, and Psychoanalysis," *UTQ* 49, iii (1980): 205-27.

Adams, R. P., *Faulkner*, 71-84.

Alldredge, Betty, "Spatial Form in Faulkner's AS I LAY DYING," *SLJ* 11, i (Fall, 1978): 3-19.

Allen, Charles A., "William Faulkner: Comedy and the Purpose of Humor," *ArQ* 16 (Spring, 1960): 61-4.

Allen, William R., "The Imagist and Symbolist Views of the Function of Language: Addie and Darl Bundren in AS I LAY DYING," *SAF* 10, ii (Autumn, 1982): 185-96.

Annas, Pamela J., "The Carpenter of AS I LAY DYING," *NMW* 8, iii (Winter, 1976): 84-99.

Backman, Melvin, "Addie Bundren and William Faulkner," in Carey, Glenn O., ed., *Faulkner*, 7-23.

_____, *Faulkner*, 50-66.

Baker, Carlos, "William Faulkner: The Doomed and the Damned," in Bode, C., ed., *Young Rebel in American Literature*, 150-4.

Bakker, J., "Faulkner's World as the Extension of Reality: AS I LAY DYING Reconsidered," in Bakker, J., and D. R. M. Wilson, eds., *From Cooper to Philip Roth*, 57-68.

Bassett, John E., "AS I LAY DYING: Family Conflict and Verbal Fiction," *JNT* 11, ii (1981): 125-34.

Beach, J. W., *American Fiction*, 132-5.

Bedient, Calvin, "Pride and Nakedness: AS I LAY DYING," *MLQ* 29 (Mar., 1968): 61-76. Also in Cox, L. H., ed., *William Faulkner*, 202-21.

Beidler, Peter G., "Faulkner's Techniques of Characterization: Jewel in AS I LAY DYING," *EA* 21 (1968): 236-42.

Benstock, Shari, " 'Voice' in AS I LAY DYING," *PMLA* 90 (Oct., 1979): 957-8.

Bleikasten, André, *Faulkner's AS I LAY DYING*, rev. and enl., ed., tr., Roger Little with the collab. of the author. Bloomington and London: Indiana Un. Pr., 1973.

Blotner, Joseph L., "AS I LAY DYING: Christian Lore and Irony," *TCL* 3 (April, 1957): 14-19.

Bradford, M. E., "Addie Bundren and the Design of AS I LAY DYING," *SoR* 6, iv (Oct., 1970): 1093-9.

Brady, Ruth H., "Faulkner's AS I LAY DYING," *Expl* 33, vii (Mar., 1975): Item 60.

Branch, Watson G., "Darl Bundren's 'Cubistic Vision'," *TSLL* 19 (Spring, 1977): 42-59.

Bridgman, Richard, "As Hester Prynne Lay Dying," *ELN* 2 (June, 1965): 294-6.

Brooks, C., *William Faulkner*, 141-66, 398-401.

Brumm, Anne-Marie, "The World as Madhouse: Motifs of Absurdity in Virginia Woolf's MRS. DALLOWAY, William Faulkner's AS I LAY DYING, and Jean-Paul Sartre's LE MUR," *Neohelicon* 4, iii-iv (1976): 295-330.

Brylowski, W., *Faulkner's Olympian Laugh*, 86-96.

Burgum, E. B., *Novel and the World's Dilemma*, 215-17.

Chase, R., *American Novel and Its Tradition*, 207-10.

Church, M., "William Faulkner: Myth and Duration," *Time and Reality*, 235-7.

Clark, Eulalyn W., "Ironic Effects of Multiple Perspective in AS I LAY DYING," *NMW* 5, i (Spring, 1972): 15-28.

Collins, Carvel, "Faulkner and Mississippi," *UMSE* 15 (1978): 139-59.

_____, "The Pairing of THE SOUND AND THE FURY and AS I LAY DYING," *PULC* 18 (Spring, 1957): 115-19.

Cook, Sylvia A., "Faulkner's Celebration of the Poor White Paradox," *From Tocacco Road to Route 66*, 41-6.

Cox, Dianne L., "William Faulkner's AS I LAY DYING: A Critical and Textual Study," *DAI* 42 (1981): 1148A.

Cross, Barbara M., "Apocalypse and Comedy in AS I LAY DYING," *TSLL* 3 (Summer, 1961): 251-8.

D'Avanzo, Mario L., "Reason and Madness: Darl's Farewell Scene in AS I LAY DYING," *NConL* 9, i (Jan., 1979): 9-10.

Degenfelder, E. Pauline, "Yoknapatawphan Baroque: A Stylistic Analysis of AS I LAY DYING," *Style* 7 (1973): 121-56.

Despain, LaRene, "The Shape and Echo of Their Word: Narration and Character in AS I LAY DYING," *MSE* 6, i-ii (1979): 49-59.

_____, and Roderick A. Jacobs, "Syntax and Characterization in Faulkner's AS I LAY DYING," *JEngL* 11 (Mar., 1977): 1-8.

Despain, Norma L., "Stream of Consciousness Narration in Faulkner: A Redefinition," *DAI* 37 (1976): 306A-07A.

Devlin, Albert J., "The Complex Pastoralism of AS I LAY DYING," *PMPA* 2 (1977): 46-52.

Dickerson, Mary J., "AS I LAY DYING and THE WASTE LAND: Some Relationships," *MissQ* 17 (Summer, 1964): 129-35.

_____, "Some Sources of Faulkner's Myth in AS I LAY DYING," *MissQ* 19 (Summer, 1966): 132-42.

Ditsky, John M., "'Dark, Darker Than Fire': Thematic Parallels in Lawrence and Faulkner," *SHR* 8 (Fall, 1974): 497-505.

_____, "Faulkner's Carousel: Point of View in AS I LAY DYING," *LauR* 10, i (1970): 74-85.

Everett, W. K., *Faulkner's Art and Characters*, 7-15.

Ewell, Barbara N., "To Move In Time: A Study of the Structure of Faulkner's AS I LAY DYING, LIGHT IN AUGUST, and ABSALOM, ABSALOM!" *DAI* 30 (1970): 3940A (Fla. State).

Fazio, Rocco R., "The Fury and the Design: Realms of Being and Knowing in Four Novels of William Faulkner," *DA* 25 (1964): 1910 (Rochester).

Franklin, Rosemary, "Animal Magnetism in AS I LAY DYING," *AQ* 18 (Spring, 1966): 24-34.

_____, "Narrative Management in AS I LAY DYING," *MFS* 13, i (Spring, 1967): 57-65.

Garrett, George P., "Some Revisions in AS I LAY DYING," *MLN* 73 (June, 1958): 414-19.

Garrison, Joseph M., Jr., "Perception, Language, and Reality in AS I LAY DYING," *ArQ* 32 (Spring, 1976): 16-30.

Garzilli, E., *Circles Without Center*, 60-5.

Geismar, M., *Writers in Crisis*, 161-2.

Godden, Richard, "William Faulkner, Addie Bundren, and Language," *UMSE* 15 (1978): 101-23.

Goellner, Jack G., "A Closer Look at AS I LAY DYING," *Per* 7 (Spring, 1954): 42-54.

Gold, Joseph, "'Sin, Salvation and Bananas': AS I LAY DYING," *Mosaic* 7, i (Fall, 1973): 55-73. Also in Collins, R. G., and K. McRobbie, eds., *Novels of William Faulkner*, 55-73.

Goodman, Charlotte, "The Bundren Wagon: Narrative Strategy in Faulkner's AS I LAY DYING," *SAF* 7, ii (1979): 234-42.

Gossett, L. Y., *Violence in Recent Southern Fiction*, 32-4.

Gray, R., *Literature of Memory*, 221-30.

Guetti, J., *Word-Music*, 149-56.

Gwynn, F. L., and J. L. Blotner, eds., *Faulkner in the University*.

Hammond, Donald, "Faulkner's Levels of Awareness," *FloQ* 1, ii (1967): 78-81.

Handy, William J., "AS I LAY DYING: Faulkner's Inner Reporter," *KR* 21 (Summer, 1959): 437-51. Also in Westbrook, M., ed., *Modern American Novel*, 153-69. Also in Handy, W. J., *Modern Fiction*, 75-93.

Harwick, Robert D., "Humor in the Novels of William Faulkner," *DA* 26 (1965): 1646 (Nebraska).

Hauck, Richard B., "The Prime Maniacal Risibility: William Faulkner," *Cheerful Nihilism*, 195-200.

Hemenway, Robert, "Enigmas of Being in AS I LAY DYING," *MFS* 16, ii (Summer, 1970): 133-46.

Hirano, Nobuyuki, "Reconsideration of Moral Order and Disorder in Faulkner's Works," *HJAS* 8, i (Sept., 1967): 19-25.

Hoffman, F. J., *William Faulkner*, 60-5.

Howe, I., *William Faulkner*, 52-6, 175-91.

Howell, Elmo, "Faulkner's Jumblies: The Nonsense World of AS I LAY DYING," *ArQ* 16 (Spring, 1960): 70-8.

Humphrey, R., *Stream of Consciousness in the Modern Novel*.

Hunter, E. R., *William Faulkner*, 49-60.

Idei, Yasuko, "A Quest for Identity and the Meaning of the *Be-Verb* in AS I LAY DYING," *KAL* 19 (May, 1978): 32-44.

Jacobs, Robert D., "William Faulkner: The Passion and the Penance," in Rubin, L. D., Jr., and R. D. Jacobs, eds., *South*, 153-5.

Kartiganer, D. M., *Fragile Thread*, 23-33.

Kehler, Joel R., "Faulkner, Melville, and a Tale of Two Carpenters," *NMAL* 1 (Summer, 1977): Item 22.

Kerr, Elizabeth M., "AS I LAY DYING as Ironic Quest," *WSCL* 3, i (Winter, 1962): 5-19. Also in Wagner, L. W., ed., *William Faulkner*, 230-43.

King, Roma, Jr., "The Janus Symbol in AS I LAY DYING," *UKCR* 21 (Summer, 1955): 287-90.

Kinney, A. F., *Faulkner's Narrative Poetics*, 161-77.

Kirk, Robert W., "Faulkner's Anse Bundren," *GaR* 19 (Winter, 1965): 446-52.

Kloss, Robert J., "Addie Bundren's Eyes and the Difference They Make," *SCR* 13, i (Fall, 1981): 85-95.

————, "Faulkner's AS I LAY DYING," *AI* 38, iv (Winter, 1981): 429-44.

Komar, Kathleen, "A Structural Study of AS I LAY DYING," *FaSt* 1 (1980): 48-57.

Leary, L., *William Faulkner of Yoknapatawpha County*, 63-77.

Leath, Helen L., " 'Will the Circle Be Unbroken'?: An Analysis of Structure in AS I LAY DYING," *SwAL* 3 (1973): 61-8.

Levins, L. G., *Faulkner's Heroic Design*, 94-114.

Lewis, R. W. B., *Picaresque Saint*, 218-19.

Lilly, Paul R., Jr., "Caddie and Addie: Speakers of Faulkner's Impeccable Language," *JNT* 3 (Sept., 1973): 170-82.

Little, Matthew, "AS I LAY DYING and 'Dementia Praecox' Humor," *StAH* 2, i (1975): 61-70.

Lyday, Charles L., "Faulkner's *Commedia*: An Interpretation of THE SOUND AND THE FURY, SANCTUARY, AS I LAY DYING, and LIGHT IN AUGUST," *DAI* 39 (1978): 886A-87A.

Lyday, Lance, "Jewel Bundren: Faulkner's Achilles," *NConL* 10, ii (Mar., 1980): 2.

May, J. R., *Toward a New Earth*, 93-114.

McCarthy, Paul, "Several Words, Shapes, and Attitudes in AS I LAY DYING," *NMW* 14, i (1981): 27-38.

Mellard, James M., "Faulkner's Philosophical Novel: Ontological Themes in AS I LAY DYING," *Person* 48 (Autumn, 1967): 509-23.

Middleton, David, "Faulkner's Folklore in AS I LAY DYING: An Old Motif in a New Manner," *SNNTS* 9, i (1977): 46-53.

Millgate, M., *Achievement of William Faulkner*, 104-12. Also in Schmiter, D. M., ed., *William Faulkner*, 91-101.

————, *William Faulkner*, 34-9.

Monaghan, David M., "The Single Narrator of AS I LAY DYING," *MFS* 18, ii (Summer, 1972): 213-20.

Murray, Trudy K., "Tricked by Words: Syntax and Style in Faulkner's AS I LAY DYING," *DAI* 36 (1975): 3660A.

Nadeau, Robert L., "The Morality of Act; A Study of Faulkner's AS I LAY DYING," *Mosaic* 6, iii (Spring, 1973): 23-5.

O'Connor, W. V. *Tangled Fire of William Faulkner*, 45-53.

————, *William Faulkner*, 14-17. Also in O'Connor, W. V., ed., *Seven Modern American Novelists*, 128-31.

Page, S. R., *Faulkner's Women*, 111-22.

Palliser, Charles, "Fate and Madness: The Determinist Vision of Darl Bundren," *AL* 49, iv (1978): 619-33.

Palumbo, Donald, "The Concept of God in Faulkner's LIGHT IN AUGUST, THE SOUND AND THE FURY, AS I LAY DYING, and ABSALOM, ABSALOM!" *SCB* 39, iv (1979): 142-6.

Parr, Susan D. R., " 'And by Bergson, Obviously,' Faulkner's THE SOUND AND THE FURY, AS I LAY DYING, and ABSALOM, ABSALOM! from a Bergsonian Perspective," *DAI* 32 (1972): 6996A (Wisconsin).

Parsons, Thornton H., "Doing the Best They Can," *CaR* 23 (Fall, 1969): 292-306.

Patten, Catherine M., R.S.H.M., "A Study of William Faulkner's AS I LAY DYING. Based on the Manuscript and Text," *DAI* 34 (1973): 331A-32A (N.Y.U.).

Peek, Charles A., "The Signboard for New Hope: Faulkner's AS I LAY DYING," *DAI* 32 (1972): 4015A (Neb.).

Perlis, Alan D., "AS I LAY DYING as a Study of Time," *SDR* 10, i (Spring, 1972): 103-10.

Pierce, Constance, "Being, Knowing, and Saying in the 'Addie' Section of Faulkner's AS I LAY DYING," *TCL* 26, iii (1980): 294-305.

Pilkington, J., *Heart of Yoknapatawpha*, 87-110.

Pitavy, François L., "Through Darl's Eyes Darkly: The Vision of the Poet in AS I LAY DYING," *WiF* 4, ii (July, 1982): 37-62.

————, *William Faulkner: AS I LAY DYING and LIGHT IN AUGUST*, Paris: Librarie Armand Colin, 1970; rev. and enlarged, Gillian E. Cook, ed. and transl., Bloomington: Indiana Un. Pr., 1973.

Powers, L. H., *Faulkner's Yoknapatawpha Comedy*, 50-72.

Presley, Delma E., "Is Reverend Whitefield a Hypocrite?" *RS* 36, i (Mar., 1968): 57-61.

Randall, Julia, "Some Notes on AS I LAY DYING," *Hopkins Rev* 4 (Summer, 1951): 47-51.

Reaver, J. Russell, "This Vessel of Clay: A Thematic Comparison of Faulkner's AS I LAY DYING and Latorre's THE OLD WOMAN OF PERALILLO," *Fla. St. Un. Studies* No. 14 (1954): 131-40.

Reed, J. W., Jr., *Faulkner's Narrative*, 84-111.

Richardson, K. E., *Force and Faith in the Novels of William Faulkner*, 73-6.

Richmond, Lee J., "The Education of Vardaman Bundren in Faulkner's AS I LAY DYING," in Levith, M. J., ed., *Renaissance and Modern*, 133-42.

Roberts, James L., "The Individual and the Family: Faulkner's AS I LAY DYING," *ArQ* 16 (Spring, 1960): 26-38.

Robinson, Fred M., *Comedy of Language*, 51-88.

Rooks, George, "Vardaman's Journey in AS I LAY DYING," *ArQ* 35 (Summer, 1979): 114-28.

Rosenman, John B., "Another OTHELLO Echo in AS I LAY DYING," *NMW* 8, i (Spring, 1975): 19-21.

_____, "AS I LAY DYING: A Study of the Poor White in Faulkner," *DAI* 31 (1971): 6069A-70A (Kent State).

_____, "A Note on William Faulkner's AS I LAY DYING," *SAF* 1 (Spring, 1973): 104-5.

_____, "Physical-Spatial Symbolism in AS I LAY DYING," *CollL* 4 (Spring, 1977): 176-7.

Ross, Stephen M., "Shapes of Time and Consciousness in AS I LAY DYING," *TSLL* 16 (Winter, 1975): 723-37.

_____, "'Voice' in AS I LAY DYING," *PMLA* 94, ii (Oct., 1979): 958-9.

_____, "'Voice' in Narrative Texts: The Example of AS I LAY DYING," *PMLA* 94, ii (Mar., 1979): 300-10.

Rossky, William, "AS I LAY DYING: The Insane World," *TSLL* 4 (Spring, 1962): 87-95.

Rubin, L. D., Jr., *Faraway Country*, 62-3.

Rule, Philip C., S. J., "The Old Testament Vision in AS I LAY DYING," in Barth, J. R., S. J., ed., *Religious Perspectives in Faulkner's Fiction*, 107-18.

Sadler, David F., "The Second Mrs. Bundren: Another Look at the Ending of AS I LAY DYING," *AL* 37 (Mar., 1965): 65-9.

Sanderlin, Robert R., "AS I LAY DYING: Christian Symbols and Thematic Implications," *SoQ* 7, ii (Jan., 1969): 155-66.

Sawyer, K. B., "Hero in AS I LAY DYING," *Faulkner Studies* 3 (Autumn, 1954): 30-3.

Seib, Kenneth, "Midrashic Legend in Faulkner's AS I LAY DYING," *NMAL* 2 (1977): Item 5.

Seltzer, Leon F., "Narrative Function vs. Psychopathology: The Problem of Darl in AS I LAY DYING," *L&P* 25, ii (1975): 49-64.

_____, and Jan Viscomi, "Natural Rhythms and Rebellion: Anse's Role in AS I LAY DYING," *MFS* 24, iv (Winter, 1978-79): 556-64.

Seyppel, J., *William Faulkner*, 47-9.

Shoemaker, Alice, "A Wheel within a Wheel: Fusion of Form and Content in Faulkner's AS I LAY DYING," *ArQ* 35 (Summer, 1979): 101-13.

Simon, John K., "The Glance of the Idiot: A Thematic Study of Faulkner and Modern French Fiction," *DA* 25 (1964): 1220 (Yale).

_____, "The Scene and the Imagery of Metamorphosis in AS I LAY DYING," *Criticism* 7 (Winter, 1965): 1-22.

_____, "What Are You Laughing At, Darl?" *CE* 25 (Nov., 1963): 104-10.

Sitter, Deborah A., "Self and Object Representations in AS I LAY DYING," *HSL* 12, i (1980): 143-55.

Slabey, Robert M., "AS I LAY DYING as an Existential Novel," *BuR* 11, iv (Dec., 1963): 12-23.

Slatoff, W. J., *Quest for Failure*, 9-11, 104-6, 158-73.

Stallman, Robert W., "A Cryptogram: AS I LAY DYING," *The Houses that James Built and Other Literary Studies*, Lansing: Mich. St. Un. Pr., 1961, 200-11.

Stitch, K. P., "A Note on Ironic Word Formation in AS I LAY DYING," *NMW* 8, iii (Winter, 1976): 100-3.

Stonesifer, Richard J., "In Defense of Dewey Dell," *EL* 22 (July, 1958): 27-33.

Stonum, Gary L., "Dilemma in AS I LAY DYING," *Ren* 28, ii (1976): 71-81.

_____, *Faulkner's Career*, 94-123, 128-41.

Sutherland, Ronald, "AS I LAY DYING: A Faulkner Microcosm," *QQ* 73 (Winter, 1966): 541-9.

Swiggart, P., *Art of Faulkner's Novels*, 57-9, 108-30.

Tuck, D., *Crowell's Handbook of Faulkner*, 34-9.

Turner, Dixie M., *A Jungian Psychoanalytic Interpretation of William Faulkner's AS I LAY DYING*, Washington, D.C.: University Press of America, 1981.

Vickery, Olga W., "AS I LAY DYING," *Per* 3 (Autumn, 1950): 179-91. Also in Vickery, O. W., *Novels of William Faulkner*, 50-65. Also in Hoffman, F. J., and O. W. Vickery, eds., *William Faulkner*, 232-47. Also in Hoffman, F. J., and O. W. Vickery, eds., *William Faulkner: Two Decades of Criticism*, 189-205.

Volpe, E. L., *Reader's Guide to William Faulkner*, 126-40.

Waggoner, H. H., *William Faulkner*, 62-87.

Wagner, Linda W., "AS I LAY DYING: Faulkner's 'All in the Family'," *CollL* 1, ii (Spring, 1974): 73-82.

_____, "Faulkner: The Craft of Fiction," *Hemingway and Faulkner*, 180-91.

Wasiolek, Edward, "AS I LAY DYING: Distortion in the Slow Eddy of Current Opinion," *Crit* 3, i (Spring-Fall, 1959): 15-23.

Watkins, Floyd C., "AS I LAY DYING: The Dignity of Earth," *In Time and Place*, 175-89.

_____, and W. B. Dillingham, "The Mind of Vardaman Bundren," *PQ* 39 (April, 1960): 247-51.

_____, "The Word and the Deed in Faulkner's First Great Novels," in Watkins, Floyd C., *The Flesh and the Word: Eliot, Hemingway, Faulkner*, Nashville: Vanderbilt Un. Pr., 1971, 181-202. Also in Wagner, L. W., ed., *William Faulkner*, 213-30.

Weisgerber, J., *Faulkner and Dostoevsky*, 192-5.

Werner, C. H., *Paradoxical Resolutions*, 14-18.

White, Michael, "Inverse Mimesis in Faulkner's AS I LAY DYING," *ArQ* 32 (Spring, 1976): 35-44.

Whitely, Deborah E., "Phenomenological Psychology and the Interior Monologue: Interpreting Whitfield's Passage," *CEA* 44, ii (Jan., 1982): 33-6.

Williams, D., *Faulkner's Women*, 97-126.

Williams, Ora G., "The Theme of Endurance in AS I LAY DYING," *LaS* 9, ii (Summer, 1970): 100-4.

Wittenberg, J. B., *Faulkner*, 103-18.

Woodbury, Potter, "Faulkner's Numismatics: A Note on AS I LAY DYING," *RS* 39 (1971): 150-1.

A FABLE

Adams, R. P., *Faulkner*, 161-9.

Baker, Carlos, "William Faulkner: The Doomed and the Damned," in Bode, C., ed., *Young Rebel in American Literature*, 166-8.

Barth, J. Robert, "A Rereading of Faulkner's FABLE," *America* 92 (Oct. 9, 1954): 44-6.

Berrone, Louis, "A Dickensian Echo in Faulkner," *Dickensian* 71, ii (May, 1975): 100-1.

Bond, Adrienne, "ENEAS AFRICANOS and Faulkner's Fabulous Racehorse," *SLJ* 9, ii (Spring, 1977): 3-15.

Brooks, C., *William Faulkner: Toward Yoknapatawpha and Beyond*, 230-50, 414-23.

Brumm, Ursula, "Christ and Adam as 'Figures' in American Literature," *American Thought & Religious Typology*, New Brunswick, N.J.: Rutgers Un. Pr., 1970, 209-17. Also in Bercovitch, Sacvan, ed., *American Puritan Imagination: Essays in Revaluation*, London: Cambridge Un. Pr., 1974, 203-9.

Brylowski, W., *Faulkner's Olympian Laugh*, 183-200.

Butterworth, Abner K., Jr., "A Critical and Textual Study of William Faulkner's A FABLE," *DAI* 31 (1971): 5390A (S.C.).

Cabaniss, Allen, "A Source of Faulkner's FABLE," *UMSE* 6 (1965): 87-9.

Carter, Thomas H., "Dramatization of an Enigma," *WR* 19 (Winter, 1955): 147-58.

Chametzky, Jules, "Some Remarks on A FABLE," *Faulkner Studies* 3 (Summer-Autumn, 1954): 39-40.

Chittick, Kathryn A., "The Fables in William Faulkner's A FABLE," *MissQ* 30 (Summer, 1977): 403-15.

Church, M., "William Faulkner: Myth and Duration," *Time and Reality*, 248-50.

Connolly, Thomas E., "Faulkner's A FABLE in the Classroom," *CE* 21 (Dec., 1959): 165-71.

_____, "The Three Plots of A FABLE," *TCL* 6 (July, 1960): 70-5.

Cottrell, Beekman W., "Faulkner's Cosmic FABLE: The Extraordinary Family of Man," in Woodruff, N., Jr., and Others, eds., *Studies in Faulkner*, 17-27.

Dillistone, F. W., *The Novelist and the Passion Story*, N.Y.: Sheed and Ward, 1970, 92-118.

Dorsch, Robert L., "An Interpretation of the Central Themes in the Work of William Faulkner," *ESRS* 11, i (Sept., 1962): 27-35.

Everett, W. K., *Faulkner's Art and Characters*, 15-21.

Faulkner, William, "A Note on A FABLE," *MissQ* 26 (Summer, 1973): 416-17.

Ficken, Carl, "The Christ Story in A FABLE," *MissQ* 23, iii (Spring, 1970): 251-64.

Flint, R. W., "What Price Glory?" *HudR* 7 (Winter, 1955): 602-6.

Fowler, Doreen, "The Old Verities in Faulkner's Fable," *Ren* 34, i (Autumn, 1981): 41-51.

Gardiner, H. C., "William Faulkner's A FABLE," *In All Conscience*, 129-31.

Geismar, M., *SatR* 37 (July 31, 1954): 11. Also in Geismar, M., *American Moderns*, 97-101.

Gold, Joseph, "Delusion and Redemption in Faulkner's A FABLE," *MFS* 7 (Summer, 1961): 145-56.

_____, *William Faulkner*, 111-47.

Guerard, A. J., *Triumph of the Novel*, 229-34.

Gwynn, F. L., and J. L. Blotner, eds., *Faulkner in the University*.

Hafley, James, "Faulkner's FABLE: Dream and Transfiguration," *Accent* 16 (Winter, 1956): 3-14.

Hartt, J. N., *Lost Image of Man*, 110-11.

_____, "Some Reflections on Faulkner's FABLE," *Religion in Life* 24 (Fall, 1955): 601-7.

Hochstettler, David, "William Faulkner's A FABLE: A Fragmented Christ," *DAI* 33 (1973): 5724A-25A (Syracuse).

Hodges, Elizabeth, "The Bible as Novel: A Comparative Study of Two Modernized Versions of Biblical Stories, Zola's La

FAUTE DE L'ABBE MOURET and Faulkner's A FABLE," *DAI* 30 (1970): 5447A (Ga.).

Hoffman, Frederick J., in French, W. G., and Kidd, W. E., eds., *American Winners of the Nobel Literary Prize*, 154-6.

_____, *William Faulkner*, 111-15.

Howe, I., *William Faulkner*, 268-81.

Hutchinson, Kathryn L. S., "Companionship in William Faulkner's A FABLE," *DAI* 42, v (Nov., 1981): 2132A.

Hutten, Robert W., "A Major Revision in Faulkner's A FABLE," *AL* 45, ii (May, 1973): 297-9.

Ilacqua, Alma A., "Faulkner's A FABLE," *NMW* 10, i (Spring, 1977): 37-46.

Irwin, J. T., *Doubling and Incest/Repetition and Revenge*, 135-48.

Kenner, Hugh, "A FABLE," *Shen* 6 (Spring, 1955): 44-53.

King, Roma A., Jr., "Everyman's Warfare: A Study of Faulkner's FABLE," *MFS* 2 (Autumn, 1956): 132-8. Also in Barth, J. R., S. J., ed., *Religious Perspectives in Faulkner's Fiction*, 203-16.

Kinney, A. F., *Faulkner's Narrative Poetics*, 75-8.

Kohler, Dayton, "A FABLE: The Novel as Myth," *CE* 16 (May, 1955): 471-8. Also in *EJ* 44 (May, 1955): 253-60.

Kunkel, Francis L., "Christ Symbolism in Faulkner: Prevalence of the Human," *Ren* 17 (Spring, 1965): 151-6.

Leary, L., *William Faulkner of Yoknapatawpha County*, 176-85.

Lewis, R. W. B., *Picaresque Saint*, 210-17.

Lytle, Andrew N., "The Son of Man: He Will Prevail," *SR* 63 (Winter, 1955): 114-37. Also in Lytle, A., *Hero with the Private Parts*, 103-28.

Macmillan, Duane J., "His 'Magnum O': Stoic Humanism in Faulkner's A FABLE," in Macmillan, D. J., ed., *Stoic Strain in American Literature*, 135-54.

_____, "The Non-Yoknapatawpha Novels of William Faulkner: An Examination of SOLDIERS' PAY, MOSQUITOES, PYLON, THE WILD PALMS, and A FABLE," *DAI* 32 (1972): 6986A (Wis.).

Magee, Rosemary M., "A FABLE and the Gospels: A Study in Contrasts," *RS* 47 (June, 1979): 98-107.

M[eriwether], J[ames] B., ed., "A Note on A FABLE," *MissQ* 26 (Summer, 1973): 416-17. [Previously unpublished statement by Faulkner.]

Millgate, M., *Achievement of William Faulkner*, 227-34.

_____, *William Faulkner*, 99-101.

Mills, Ralph J., Jr., "Faulkner's Essential Vision: Notes on A FABLE," *ChS* 44 (Fall, 1961): 187-98.

Milton, John R., "American Fiction and Man," *Cresset* 18, iii (1955): 16-20.

Miner, Ward L., "Faulkner and Christ's Crucifixion," *NM* 57 (1956): 260-9.

Mosley, Nicholas, "Faulkner's Fables," *RCF* 2, ii (Summer, 1982): 79-83.

Pastore, Philip E., "The Structure and Meaning of William Faulkner's A FABLE," *DAI* 31 (1970): 397A-98A (Fla.).

Peckham, Morse, "The Place of Sex in the Work of William Faulkner," *STwC* 14 (Fall, 1974): 1-20.

Pladott, Dinnah, "Faulkner's A FABLE: A Heresy or a Declaration of Faith?" *JNT* 12, ii (Spring, 1982): 73-94.

Podhoretz, Norman, "William Faulkner and the Problem of War," *Ctary* 18 (Sept., 1954): 227-32. Also in Podhoretz, N., *Doings and Undoings*, 13-24. Also in Warren, R. P., ed., *Faulkner*, 243-50.

Polk, Noel, "The Nature of Sacrifice: REQUIEM FOR A NUN and A FABLE," *FaSt* 1 (1980): 100-11. Also in Cox, L. H., ed., *William Faulkner*, 369-93.

Pritchett, V. S., "Time Frozen: A FABLE," *PR* 21, v (Sept.-Oct., 1954): 557-61. Also in Warren, R. P., ed., *Faulkner*, 238-42.

Raisor, Philip, "Up from Adversity: William Faulkner's A FABLE," *SDR* 11, ii (Summer, 1973): 3-15.

Ratner, Marc, "Dualism in Faulkner's A FABLE: Humanization versus Dehumanization," *Prague Studies in Eng.* 15 (1973): 117-34.

Raymund, Bernard, "A FABLE," *ArQ* 10 (Winter, 1954): 361-3.

Rice, Philip B., "Faulkner's Crucifixion," *KR* 16 (Autumn, 1954): 661-70.

Richardson, K. E., *Force and Faith in the Novels of William Faulkner*, 156-72.

Samway, Patrick, S. J., "War: A Faulknerian Commentary," *ColQ* 18, iv (Spring, 1970): 370-8.

Sandeen, Ernest, "William Faulkner: His Legend and His Fable," *RPol* 18 (Jan., 1956): 47-68.

Schendler, Sylvan, "William Faulkner's A FABLE," *DA* 17 (1957): 366-7 (Northwestern).

Schwartz, Delmore, "William Faulkner's A FABLE," *Perspectives U.S.A.* No. 10 (Winter, 1955): 126-36.

Seyppel, J., *William Faulkner*, 90-3.

Slade, John H., "A Study of William Faulkner's FABLE," *DAI* 35 (1975): 6160A.

Slatoff, W. J., *Quest for Failure*, 221-37.

Smith, Julian, "A Source for Faulkner's A FABLE," *AL* 40 (Nov., 1968): 394-7.

Solomon, Eric, "From CHRIST IN FLANDERS to CATCH-22: An Approach to War Fiction," *TSLL* 11 (Spring, 1969): 851-66.

Sowder, William J., "Faulkner and Existentialism: A Note on the Generalissimo," *WSCL* 4, ii (Spring-Summer, 1963): 163-71.

Stavrou, C. N., "William Faulkner's Apologia: Some Notes on A FABLE," *ColQ* 3 (Spring, 1955): 432-9.

Stein, Randolph E., "The World Outside Yoknapatawpha: A Study of Five Novels by William Faulkner," *DA* 26 (1965): 2225 (Ohio Un.).

Straumann, Heinrich, "An American Interpretation of Existence: Faulkner's A FABLE," in Hoffman, F. J., and O. W. Vickery, eds., *William Faulkner*, 349-72. Also in Wagner, L. W., ed., *William Faulkner*, 335-57.

Stuckey, W. J., *Pulitzer Prize Novels*, 170-5.

Swiggart, P., *Art of Faulkner's Novels*, 184-94.

Taylor, Walter F., "William Faulkner: The Faulkner Fable," *ASch* 26 (Autumn, 1957): 471-7.

Tsagari, Myrto, "A FABLE: Faulkner's Message to the World," *nota bene* (Lake Erie College, Painesville, Ohio) 1 (1958): 30-4.

Tuck, D., *Crowell's Handbook of Faulkner*, 143-56.

Turaj, Frank, "The Dialectic in Faulkner's A FABLE," *TSLL* 8 (Spring, 1966): 93-102.

Vickery, O. W., *Novels of William Faulkner*, 209-27.

Volpe, E. L., *Reader's Guide to William Faulkner*, 282-304.

Waggoner, H. H., *William Faulkner*, 225-32.

Wagner, Geoffrey, "Faulkner's Contemporary Passion Play," *TC* 156 (Dec., 1954): 527-38.

Wagner, Linda W., "The Last Books," *Hemingway and Faulkner*, 211-17.

Wagstaff, Barbara O., "The Struggle with the Angel: Identity and Sympathy in Thomas Mann's DOKTOR FAUSTUS, André Malraux's LES NOYOERS DE L'ALTENBURG, and William Faulkner's A FABLE," *DAI* 41 (1980): 248A.

Watkins, F. C., *Flesh and the Word*, 263-71.

Webb, James W., "Faulkner Writes A FABLE," *UMSE* 7 (1966): 1-13.

Wegelin, Christof, "'Endure' and 'Prevail': Faulkner's Modification of Conrad," *N&Q* 21 (Oct., 1974): 375-6.

Weisgerber, J., *Faulkner and Dostoevsky*, 301-21.

Wittenberg, J. W., *Faulkner*, 221-5.

Yun, Chung-Hei K., "A Fable of the Invisible Dust; Faulkner's Vision of Man in A FABLE," *DAI* 40 (1974): 878-88.

FLAGS IN THE DUST

Bassett, John E., "Faulkner, Sartoris, Benbow: Shifting Conflict in FLAGS IN THE DUST," *SoSt* 20, i (Spring, 1981): 39-54.

Blair, Arthur H., "Bayard Sartoris: Suicidal or Foolhardy?" *SLJ* 15, i (Fall, 1982): 55-60.

Brooks, C., *William Faulkner: Toward Yoknapatawpha and Beyond*, 165-77, 388-91, 392-5.

Folks, Jeffrey J., "A Problem with the Internal Dating of FLAGS IN THE DUST," *NConL* 9, iii (May, 1979): 8-9.

Going, William T., "Faulkner's FLAGS IN THE DUST," *Expl* 39, iv (Summer, 1981): 37-9.

Guerard, A. J., *Triumph of the Novel*, 111-17 *passim*.

Hayhoe, George F., "A Chronology of Events in Faulkner's FLAGS IN THE DUST," *NMW* 13, i (1981): 1-6.

————, "A Critical and Textual Study of William Faulkner's FLAGS IN THE DUST," *DAI* 40 (1980): 4036A.

————, introd., "The Rejected Manuscript Opening of FLAGS IN THE DUST," *DAI* 40 (1980): 4036A.

————, "William Faulkner's FLAGS IN THE DUST," *MissQ* 28 (Summer, 1975): 370-86. Also in Cox, L. H., ed., *William Faulkner*, 157-74.

Hodgin, Katherine C., "Horace Benbow and Bayard Sartoris: Two Romantic Figures in Faulkner's FLAGS IN THE DUST," *AL* 50, iv (Jan., 1979): 647-52.

Kane, Patricia, "The Narcissa Benbow of Faulkner's FLAGS IN THE DUST," *NConL* 4, iv (Sept., 1974): 2-3.

Keiser, Merle W., "FLAGS IN THE DUST and SARTORIS," in Fowler, D., and A. J. Abadie, eds., *Fifty Years of Yoknapatawpha*, 44-70.

King, R. H., *Southern Renaissance*, 82-3.

Kinney, A. F., *Faulkner's Narrative Poetics*, 123-39.

Matthews, J. T., *Play of Faulkner's Language*, 50-60.

McDaniel, Linda E., "Keats's Hyperion Myth: A Source for the Sartoris Myth," *MissQ* 34, ii (Summer, 1981): 325-33.

McSweeney, Kerry, "The Subjective Intensities of Faulkner's FLAGS IN THE DUST," *CRevAS* 8, iii (1977): 154-64.

Roberts, Melvin R., "Faulkner's FLAGS IN THE DUST and SARTORIS: A Comparative Study of the Typescript and the Originally Published Novel," *DAI* 35 (1974): 471A (Texas, Austin).

Simpson, Lewis P., "William Faulkner of Yoknapatawpha," in Rubin, L. D., ed., *American South*, 236-8.

THE HAMLET (See also SNOPES Trilogy)

Adams, R. P., *Faulkner*, 115-20.

Backman, M., *Faulkner*, 139-59.

Beach, J. W., *American Fiction*, 147-9.

Brooks, Cleanth, "Faulkner's Savage Arcadia: Frenchman's Bend," *VQR* 39 (Autumn, 1963): 598-611.

_____, *William Faulkner*, 167-91, 402-10.

Broughton, Panthea R., "Masculinity and Menfolk in THE HAMLET," *MissQ* 22, iii (Summer, 1969): 181-9. Also in Cox, L. H., ed., *William Faulkner*, 291-300.

Brylowski, W., *Faulkner's Olympian Laugh*, 139-49.

Burch, Beth, "A Miltonic Echo in Faulkner's THE HAMLET," *NConL* 8, iv (Sept., 1978): 3-4.

Burgum, E. B., *Novel and the World's Dilemma*, 220-1.

Campbell, H. M., and R. E. Foster, *William Faulkner*, 79-81.

Chapdelaine, Annick, "Perversion as Comedy in THE HAMLET," *DeltaES* 3 (Nov., 1976): 95-104.

Cook, Sylvia J., "Faulkner's Celebration of the Poor White Paradox," *From Tobacco Road to Route 66*, 55-9.

Cowley, M., "Faulkner by Daylight," *NRep* 102 (April 15, 1940): 510. Also in Cowley, M., *Look Back on Us*, 358-60.

Creighton, Joanne V., "Surratt to Ratliff: A Genetic Approach to THE HAMLET," *MichA* 6, i (Summer, 1973): 101-12.

_____, *William Faulkner's Craft of Revision*, 21-48.

Cross, Richard K., "The Humor of THE HAMLET," *TCL* 12 (Jan., 1967): 203-15.

Dimino, Andrea, "Creating Human Time: Faulkner's Temporal Strategies in THE HAMLET, ABSALOM, ABSALOM! and 'The Bear'," *DAI* 41, xii (June, 1981): 5100A-01A.

Dirksen, Sherland N., "William Faulkner's Snopes Family: THE HAMLET, THE TOWN, and THE MANSION," *ESRS* 11, ii (Dec., 1962): 12-22.

Eby, Cecil D., "Faulkner and the Southwestern Humorists," *Shen* 11 (Autumn, 1959): 13-21.

_____, "Ichabod Crane in Yoknapatawpha," *GaR* 16 (Winter, 1962): 465-9.

Everett, W. K., *Faulkner's Art and Characters*, 37-43.

Fink, Robert A., "Comedy Preceding Horror: THE HAMLET's Not So Funny Horses," *CEA* 40, iv (May, 1978): 27-30.

French, Warren, "The Background of Snopesism in Mississippi Politics," *MASJ* 5 (Fall, 1964): 3-17.

_____, *Social Novel*, 18-49, *passim*.

Gates, Allen, "The Old Frenchman Place: Symbol of Lost Civilization," *IEY* No. 13 (Fall, 1968): 44-50.

Glicksberg, Charles I., "Faulkner's World of Love and Sex," *Sexual Revolution in Modern American Literature*, 111-14.

Gold, Joseph, "The 'Normality' of Snopesism: Universal Themes in Faulkner's THE HAMLET," *WSCL* 3, i (Winter, 1962): 25-34. Also in Wagner, L. W., ed., *William Faulkner*, 318-27. Also in Cox, L. H., ed., *William Faulkner*, 301-12.

Gossett, L. Y., *Violence in Recent Southern Fiction*, 43-4.

Greet, T. Y., "The Theme and Structure of Faulkner's THE HAMLET," *PMLA* 72 (Sept., 1957): 775-90. Also in Hoffman, F. J., and O. W. Vickery, eds., *William Faulkner*, 330-47. Also in Wagner, L. W., ed., *William Faulkner*, 302-18.

Guerard, A. J., *Triumph of the Novel*, 212-20.

Gwynn, F. L., and J. L. Blotner, eds., *Faulkner in the University*.

Hall, J., *Lunatic Giant in the Drawing Room*, 58-9, 62-74.

_____, "Play, the Training Camp, and American Angry Comedy," *HAB* 15 (Spring, 1964): 7-9.

Harder, Kelsie B., "Proverbial Snopeslore," *TFSB* 24 (Sept., 1958): 89-95.

Harwick, Robert D., "Humor in the Novels of William Faulkner," *DA* 26 (1965): 1646 (Nebraska).

Hauck, R. B., *Cheerful Nihilism*, 180-7.

Hayes, Ann L., "The World of THE HAMLET," in Woodruff, N., Jr., and others, eds., *Studies in Faulkner*, 3-16.

Heck, Francis S., "Faulkner's 'Spotted Horses': A Variation of a Rabelaisian Theme," *ArQ* 37, ii (Summer, 1981): 166-72.

Hoffman, F. J., *William Faulkner*, 85-92.

Hopkins, Viola, "William Faulkner's THE HAMLET: A Study in Meaning and Form," *Accent* 15 (Spring, 1955): 125-44.

Howard, Alan B., "Huck Finn in the House of Usher: The Comic and Grotesque Worlds of THE HAMLET," *SoRA* 5, ii (June, 1972): 125-46.

Howe, I., *William Faulkner*, 78-88, 243-52.

Jacobs, Robert D., "William Faulkner: The Passion and the Penance," in Rubin, L. D., Jr., and Jacobs, R. D., eds., *South*, 169-71.

Jarrett, David W., "Eustacia Vye and Eulal Verner, Olympians: The Worlds of Thomas Hardy and William Faulkner," *Novel* 6, ii (Winter, 1973): 163-74.

Jehlen, M., *Class and Character in Faulkner's South*, 143-50, 154-7.

Kartiganer, D. M., *Fragile Thread*, 109-29.

Kibler, James E., Jr., "A Study of the Text of William Faulkner's THE HAMLET," *DAI* 31 (1971): 5407A (S.C.).

Lawson, Lewis A., "The Grotesque-Comic in the SNOPES Trilogy," *L&P* 15 (1965): 107-19. Also in Manheim, L., and E., eds., *Hidden Patterns*, 243-58.

Lawson, Strang, "Faulkner's THE HAMLET," *CEA Critic* 10 (Dec., 1948): 3.

Leary, L., *William Faulkner of Yoknapatawpha County*, 151-61.

Leaver, Florence, "The Structure of THE HAMLET," *TCL* 1 (July, 1955): 77-84.

Levins, L. G., *Faulkner's Heroic Design*, 55-75, 153-60.

Lisca, Peter, "THE HAMLET: Genesis and Revisions," *Faulkner Studies* 3 (Spring, 1954): 5-13.

Lucente, G. L., *Narrative of Realism and Myth*, 123-34.

Matthews, J. T., *Play of Faulkner's Language*, 162-211.

McClennen, Joshua, "Why Read Faulkner," *MAQR* 62 (Summer, 1956): 342-5.

McDonald, W. V., Jr., "The Time Scheme of THE HAMLET," *MidR* 5 (1963): 22-9.

Mercer, Caroline, and Susan J. Turner, "Restoring Life to Faulkner's THE HAMLET," *CEA* 21 (Dec., 1959): 1, 4-5.

Millgate, M., *Achievement of William Faulkner*, 180-200.

_____, *William Faulkner*, 84-90.

Milum, Richard, "'The Horns of Dawn': Faulkner and Metaphor," *AN&Q* 11 (May, 1973): 134. [Ike Snopes/cow episode.]

Moses, Edwin, "Faulkner's THE HAMLET: The Passionate Humanity of V. K. Ratliff," *NDEJ* 8 (Spring, 1973): 98-109.

Murray, D[onald] M., "Faulkner, the Silent Comedies, and the Animated Cartoon," *SHR* 9 (1975): 241-57.

O'Connor, W. V., *Tangled Fire of William Faulkner*, 111-24.

_____, *William Faulkner*, 31-4. Also in O'Connor, W. V., ed., *Seven Modern American Novelists*, 144-6.

Page, S. R., *Faulkner's Women*, 153-65.

Pfeiffer, Andrew, "'No Wiser Place on Earth': Community and the Country Store in Faulkner's THE HAMLET," *NMW* 6, ii (Fall, 1973): 45-52.

Pierle, Robert C., "Snopeism in Faulkner's THE HAMLET," *ES* 52 (June, 1971): 246-52.

Pikoulis, J., *Art of William Faulkner*, 137-85.

Pilkington, J., *Art of William Faulkner*, 137-85.

_____, *Heart of Yoknapatawpha*, 217-41.

Portch, Stephen R., "All Pumped Up: Horse Trick in Faulkner's THE HAMLET," *SAF* 9, i (Spring, 1981): 93-5.

Powers, L. H., *Faulkner's Yoknapatawpha's Comedy*, 145-61.

Prior, Linda T., "Theme, Imagery, and Structure in THE HAMLET," *MissQ* 22, iii (Summer, 1969): 237-56.

Ramsey, William C., "Coordinate Structure in Four Faulkner Novels," *DAI* 3 (1972): 283A-84A (N.C., Chapel Hill).

Reed, J. W., Jr., *Faulkner's Narrative*, 218-44.

Richardson, K. W., *Force and Faith in the Novels of William Faulkner*, 118-24.

Rinaldi, Nicholas M., "Game-Consciousness and Game-Metaphor in the Work of William Faulkner," *DA* 24 (1964): 4196-7 (Fordham).

Roberts, James L., "Snopeslore: THE HAMLET, THE TOWN, THE MANSION," *UKCR* 28 (1961): 65-71.

Rubens, Philip M., "St. Elmo and the Barn Burners," *NMW* 7, iii (Winter, 1975): 86-90.

Serruya, Barbara B., "The Evolution of an Artist: A Genetic Study of William Faulkner's THE HAMLET," *DAI* 35 (1974): 2298A (U.C.L.A.).

Seyppel, J., *William Faulkner*, 72-3.

Shanaghan, Father Malachy M., O.S.B., "A Critical Analysis of the Fictional Techniques of William Faulkner," *DA* 20 (1960): 4663 (Notre Dame).

Showett, H. K., "Faulkner and Scott: Addendum," *MissQ* 32 (Spring, 1969): 152-3.

Slatoff, W. J., *Quest for Failure*, 85-6.

Stone, Edward, *A Certain Morbidness: A View of American Literature*, Carbondale and Edwardsville: So. Ill. Un. Pr., 1969, 100-20.

Stonesifer, Richard J., "Faulkner's THE HAMLET in the Classroom," *CE* 20 (Nov., 1958): 71-7.

Stonum, G. L., *Faulkner's Career*, 159-85.

Swiggart, P., *Art of Faulkner's Novels*, 49-51.

Thompson, L., *William Faulkner*, 133-47, 199-200. Also in Schmitter, D. M., ed., *William Faulkner*, 122-35.

Thonan, Robert, "William Faulkner: From THE HAMLET to THE TOWN," *ESA* 2 (Sept., 1959): 190-202.

Tuck, D., *Crowell's Handbook of Faulkner*, 74-81.

Vickery, O. W., *Novels of William Faulkner*, 167-81.

Volpe, E. L., *Reader's Guide to William Faulkner*, 306-17.

Vorpahl, Ben M., "Such Stuff as Dreams Are Made On: History, Myth and the Comic Vision of Mark Twain and William Faulkner," *DA* 28 (1967): 698A (Wisconsin).

Waggoner, H. H., *William Faulkner*, 183-93.

Wall, Carey, "Drama and Technique in Faulkner's THE HAMLET," *TCL* 14 (April, 1968): 17-33.

Walton, Gerald W., "A Word List of Southern Farm Terms from Faulkner's THE HAMLET," *MissFR* 6 (1972): 60-75.

Watkins, Floyd C., and T. D. Young, "Revisions of Style in Faulkner's THE HAMLET," *MFS* 5 (Winter, 1959-60): 327-36.

Watson, J. G., *Snopes Dilemma*, 17-74.

Weisgerber, J., *Faulkner and Dostoevsky*, 267-70.

Williams, D., *Faulkner's Women*, 197-210.

Wittenberg, J. B., *Faulkner*, 178-89.

Yonce, Margaret, "Faulkner's Atthis and Attis: Some Sources of Myth," *MissQ* 23, iii (Summer, 1970): 289-98.

INTRUDER IN THE DUST

Adams, R. P., *Faulkner*, 155-6.

Baker, Carlos, "William Faulkner: The Doomed and the Damned," in Bode, C., ed., *Young Rebel in American Literature*, 154-6.

Berzon, J. R., *Neither White Nor Black*, 87-91.

Brooks, C., *William Faulkner*, 279-94, 420-4.

Brylowski, W., *Faulkner's Olympian Laugh*, 168-73.

Bunker, Robert, "Faulkner: A Case for Regionalism," *NMQ* 19 (Spring, 1949): 108-15.

Carey, Glenn O., "William Faulkner on the Automobile as Socio-Sexual Symbol," *CEA* 36, ii (Jan., 1974): 15-17.

Carter, Everett, "The Meaning of, and in, Realism," *AR* 12 (Spring, 1952): 92-4.

Cohen, B. Bernard, "Study Aids for Faulkner's INTRUDER IN THE DUST," *Exercise Exchange* 7 (Oct., 1959): 12-13.

Connolly, Thomas E., in Krause, S. J., ed., *Essays in Determinism*, 49-52.

Davenport, F. G., *Myth of Southern History*, 127-30.

Degenfelder, E. Pauline, "The Film Adaptation of Faulkner's INTRUDER IN THE DUST," *LFQ* 1, ii (April, 1973): 138-48.

_____, "Rites of Passage: Novel to Film," in Peary, G., and R. Shatzkin, eds., *Modern American Novel and the Movies*, 176-8.

De Villier, Mary Anne G., "Faulkner's Young Man: As Reflected in the Character of Charles Mallison," *LauR* 9, ii (Fall, 1969): 42-9.

Dunlap, Mary M., "The Achievement of Gavin Stevens," *DAI* 31 (1971): 3544A (S.C.).

Elias, Robert H., "Gavin Stevens: Intruder?" *Faulkner Studies* 3 (Spring, 1954): 1-4.

Everett, W. K., *Faulkner's Art and Characters*, 43-7.

Fadiman, Regina K., *Faulkner's INTRUDER IN THE DUST: Novel Into Film*, Knoxville: Tennessee Un. Pr., 1978.

Geismar, M., *SatR* 31 (Sept. 25, 1948): 8. Also in Geismar, M., *American Moderns*, 91-3.

Gerstenberger, Donna, "Meaning and Form in INTRUDER IN THE DUST," *CE* 23 (Dec., 1961): 223-5.

Glicksberg, Charles, "INTRUDER IN THE DUST," *ArQ* 5 (Spring, 1949): 85-8.

Gloster, Hugh M., "Southern Justice," *Phylon* 10 (1949): 93-5.

Gold, J., *William Faulkner*, 76-94.

Greer, Dorothy D., "Dilsey and Lucas: Faulkner's Use of the Negro as a Gauge of Moral Character," *ESRS* 11, i (Sept., 1962): 54-60.

Gwynn, F. L., and J. L. Blotner, eds., *Faulkner in the University*.

Hardwick, Elizabeth, "Faulkner and the South Today," *PR* 15 (Oct., 1948): 1130-5. Also in Hoffman, F. J., and O. W. Vickery, eds., *William Faulkner: Two Decades of Criticism*, 244-50. Also in Warren, R. P., ed., *Faulkner*, 226-30.

Hart, John A., "That Not Impossible He: Faulkner's Third-Person Narrator," in Woodruff, N., Jr., and others, eds., *Studies in Faulkner*, 34-41.

Heller, Terry L., "Intruders in the Dust: The Representation of Racial Problems in Faulkner's Novel and the MGM Film Adaptation," *Coe Rev.* 8 (1977): 79-90.

Hoffman, F. J., *William Faulkner*, 99-101.

Howe, Irving, "The South and Current Literature," *AmMerc* 67 (Oct., 1948): 495-8.

_____, *William Faulkner*, 23-4, 98-102, 104-5.

Howell, Elmo, "William Faulkner's Caledonia: A Note on IN-TRUDER IN THE DUST," *SSL* 3 (April, 1966): 248-52.

Hudson, Tommy, "William Faulkner: Mystic and Traditionalist," *Per* 3 (Autumn, 1950): 227-35.

Hutchinson, D., "The Style of Faulkner's INTRUDER IN THE DUST," *Theoria* 39 (Oct., 1972): 33-47.

Jehlen, M., *Class and Character in Faulkner's South*, 124-32.

Jenkins, L., *Faulkner and Black-White Relations*, 261-79.

Kane, Patricia, "Only too Rhetorical Rhetoric: A Reading of INTRUDER IN THE DUST," *NConL* 4, iii (May, 1974): 2-3.

Kearney, J. A., "Paradox in Faulkner's INTRUDER IN THE DUST," *Theoria* 40 (May, 1973): 55-67.

Leary, L., *William Faulkner of Yoknapatawpha County*, 171-6.

Lewis, Clifford L., "William Faulkner: The Artist as Historian," *MASJ* 10, ii (Fall, 1969): 36-48.

Little, Gail B., "Three Novels for Comparative Study in the Twelfth Grade," *EJ* 52 (1963): 501-5.

Lytle, Andrew, "Regeneration for the Man," *SR* 57, i (Winter, 1949): 120-7. Also in Warren, R. P., ed., *Faulkner*, 231-7. Also in Lytle, A., *Hero with the Private Parts*, 129-36. Also in Hoffman, F. J., and O. W. Vickery, eds., *William Faulkner: Two Decades of Criticism*, 251-9.

Maxwell, D. E. S., *American Fiction*, 275-8.

McCants, Maxine, "From Humanity to Abstraction: Negro Characterization in INTRUDER IN THE DUST," *NMW* 2, iii (Winter, 1970): 91-104.

Millgate, M., *Achievement of William Faulkner*, 215-20.

_____, *William Faulkner*, 94-5.

Mizener, A., *Twelve Great American Novels*, 146-7.

Monaghan, David, "Faulkner's Relationship to Gavin Stevens in INTRUDER IN THE DUST," *DR* 52, iii (Autumn, 1972): 449-57.

Muehl, Lois, "Faulkner's Humor in Three Novels and One 'Play'," *LC* 34 (Spring, 1968): 78-93.

Nilon, Charles H., "Faulkner and the Negro," *UCSSLL* No. 8 (Sept., 1962): 4-12, 25-30. Also in Nilon, C. H., *Faulkner and the Negro*, 4-12, 25-30.

O'Connor, W. V., *Tangled Fire of William Faulkner*, 136-42.

O'Faolain, S., *Vanishing Hero*, 104-6.

Rabinowitz, Peter J., "The Click of the Spring: The Detective Story as Parallel Structure in Dostoyevsky and Faulkner," *MP* 76 (May, 1979): 355-69.

Reed, J. W., Jr., *Faulkner's Narrative*, 201-11.

Richardson, K. E., *Force and Faith in the Novels of William Faulkner*, 103-7.

Rigsby, Carol R., "Chick Mallison's Expectations and IN-TRUDER IN THE DUST," *MissQ* 29 (Summer, 1976): 389-99.

Rollins, Ronald G., "Ike McCaslin and Chick Mallison: Faulkner's Emerging Southern Hero," *WVUPP* 14 (Oct., 1963): 74-9.

Samway, Patrick, "Faulkner's Hidden Story in INTRUDER IN THE DUST," *DeltaES* 3 (Nov., 1976): 63-81.

_____, *Faulkner's INTRUDER IN THE DUST: A Critical Study of the Typescripts*, Troy, N.Y.: Whitston, 1980.

_____, "INTRUDER IN THE DUST: A Re-Evaluation," 83-113 in Carey, G.O., ed., *Faulkner*.

_____, "A Textual and Critical Evaluation of the Manuscripts and Typescripts of William Faulkner's INTRUDER IN THE DUST," *DAI* 36 (1975): 328A.

Seyppel, J., *William Faulkner*, 80-5.

Skerry, Philip J., "THE ADVENTURES OF HUCKLEBERRY FINN and INTRUDER IN THE DUST: Two Conflicting Myths of the American Experience," *BSUF* 13, i (Winter, 1972): 4-13.

Slatoff, W. J., *Quest for Failure*, 15-16, 148-9, 215-20.

Sowder, William J., "Lucas Beauchamp as Existential Hero," *CE* 25 (Nov., 1963): 115-27.

Steinberg, Aaron, "Faulkner and the Negro," *DA* 27 (1966): 1365A (N.Y.U.).

_____, "INTRUDER IN THE DUST: Faulkner as Psychologist of the Southern Psyche," *L&P* 15 (Spring, 1965): 120-4.

Swiggart, P., *Art of Faulkner's Novels*, 179-81.

Tagliabue, John, "The Different Stages of the Dark Journey of INTRUDER IN THE DUST," *Tsuda Rev* (Tokyo) No. 3 (Nov., 1958).

Tuck, D., *Crowell's Handbook of Faulkner*, 107-11.

Van Nostrand, A. D., "The Poetic Dialogues of William Faulkner," *Everyman His Own Poet*, 177-81.

Vickery, Olga W., "Gavin Stevens: From Rhetoric to Dialectic," *Faulkner Studies* 2 (Spring, 1953): 1-4.

_____, *Novels of William Faulkner*, 134-44.

Volpe, E. L., *Reader's Guide to William Faulkner*, 253-64.

Waggoner, H. H., *William Faulkner*, 214-19.

Watkins, F. C., *Flesh and the Word*, 256-9.

Weisgerber, J., *Faulkner and Dostoevsky*, 280-5.

Welty, Eudora, "In Yoknapatawpha," *HudR* 1 (Winter, 1949): 596-8.

Wilson, Edmund, "William Faulkner's Reply to the Civil-Rights Program," *NY* (Oct. 23, 1948): 120-2, 125-7. Also in Wilson, E., *Classics and Commercials*, 460-70. Also in Warren, R. P., ed., *Faulkner*, 219-25.

Wittenberg, J. B., *Faulkner*, 211-15.

LIGHT IN AUGUST

Abel, Darrel, "Frozen Movement in LIGHT IN AUGUST," *BUSE* 3 (Spring, 1957): 32-44. Also in Inge, M. T., comp., *Merrill Studies in LIGHT IN AUGUST*, 37-50. Also, condensed, in Minter, D. L., ed., *Twentieth Century Interpretations of LIGHT IN AUGUST*, 42-54.

Adamowski, T. H., "Joe Christmas: The Tyranny of Childhood," *Novel* 4 (Spring, 1971): 240-51.

Adams, R. P., *Faulkner*, 84-95.

Allen, W., *Modern Novel*, 120-1.

Anderson, Dianne L., "Faulkner's Grimms: His Use of the Name Before LIGHT IN AUGUST," *MissQ* 29, iii (Summer, 1976): 443.

Anderson, Thomas D., "LIGHT IN AUGUST: Novel; Chamber Theater; Motion Picture—the Role of Point of View in the Adaptation Process," *DAI* 34 (1974): 6161A.

Applewhite, Davis, "The South of LIGHT IN AUGUST," *MissQ* 11 (Fall, 1958): 167-72.

Asals, Frederick, "Faulkner's LIGHT IN AUGUST," *Expl* 26 (May, 1968): Item 74.

Backman, M., *Faulkner*, 67-87.

_____, "Sickness and Primitivism: A Dominant Pattern in William Faulkner's Work," *Accent* 14 (Winter, 1954): 66-9.

Baker, Carlos, "William Faulkner: The Doomed and the Damned," in Bode, C., ed., *Young Rebel in American Literature,* 156-9.

Baldanza, Frank, "The Structure of LIGHT IN AUGUST," *MFS* 13, i (Spring, 1967): 67-78.

Ballew, Steven E., "Faulkner's Psychology of Individualism: A Fictional Principle and LIGHT IN AUGUST," *DAI* 35 (1975): 6700A.

Beach, J. W., *American Fiction,* 135-8, 162-4.

Bedell, G. C., *Kierkegaard and Faulkner,* 45-63 *passim,* 127-30, 215-21.

Beja, Morris, "A Flash, a Glare: Faulkner and Time," *Renu* 16 (Spring, 1964): 134-7.

————, "William Faulkner: A Flash, a Glare," *Epiphany in the Modern Novel,* 194-201.

Benson, Carl, "Thematic Design in LIGHT IN AUGUST," *SAQ* 53 (Oct., 1954): 540-55. Also in Wagner, L. W., ed., *William Faulkner,* 258-72.

Berland, Alwyn, "LIGHT IN AUGUST: The Calvinism of William Faulkner," *MFS* 8 (Summer, 1962): 159-70.

Bernberg, Raymond E., "LIGHT IN AUGUST: A Psychological View," *MissQ* 11 (Fall, 1958): 173-6.

Billy, Ted, "Faulkner's Feverish Buddha," *AN&Q* 19, ii (1980): 24-6.

Bledsoe, Audrey, "Faulkner's Chiaroscuro: Comedy in LIGHT IN AUGUST," *NMW* 11, ii (1979): 55-63.

Bogel, Frederic V., "Fables of Knowing: Melodrama and Related Forms," *Genre* 11 (Spring, 1978): 83-108.

Borden, Caroline, "Characterization in Faulkner's LIGHT IN AUGUST," *L&I* 13 (1972): 41-50.

Boring, Phyllis Z., "Usmaíl: The Puerto Rican Joe Christmas," *CLAJ* 16 (Mar., 1973): 324-33.

Bowden, E. T., "The Commonplace and the Grotesque," *Dungeon of the Heart,* 124-38.

Brooks, Cleanth, "The Communitiy and the Pariah," *VQR* 39 (Spring, 1963): 236-53. Also in Brooks, C., *William Faulkner,* 47-74. Also, condensed, in Minter, D. L., ed., *Twentieth Century Interpretations of LIGHT IN AUGUST,* 55-70.

————, "Faulkner's Treatment of the Racial Problem: Typical Examples," in Brooks, Cleanth, *Shaping Joy,* 238-46. Also in Cox, L. H., ed., *William Faulkner,* 448-58.

————, *Hidden God,* 35-40. Also in Barth, J. R., S. J., ed., *Religious Perspectives in Faulkner's Fiction,* 68-72.

————, "Notes on Faulkner's LIGHT IN AUGUST," *HarvardA* 135 (Nov., 1951): 10-11, 27.

————, "When Did Joanna Burden Die?" *SLJ* 6, i (Fall, 1973): 43-6.

Broughton, P. R., *William Faulkner,* 131-7, 152-6.

Brown, William R., "Faulkner's Paradox in Pathology and Salvation: SANCTUARY, LIGHT IN AUGUST, REQUIEM FOR A NUN," *TSLL* 9 (1967): 429-49.

Brumm, Anne-Marie, "Authoritarianism in William Faulkner's LIGHT IN AUGUST and Alberto Moravia's IL CONFORMISTA," *RLMC* 26 (Sept., 1973): 196-220.

Brylowski, W., *Faulkner's Olympian Laugh,* 102-17.

Burroughs, Franklin G., Jr., "God the Father and Motherless Children: LIGHT IN AUGUST," *TCL* 19, iii (July, 1973): 189-202.

Butler, Rebecca R., "The Mad Preacher in Three Modern American Novels: MISS LONELYHEARTS, WISE BLOOD, LIGHT IN AUGUST," *DAI* 38 (1978): 4164A-65A.

Campbell, H. M., and R. E. Foster, *William Faulkner,* 67-74.

Campbell, Jeff H., "Polarity and Paradox: Faulkner's LIGHT IN AUGUST," *CEA* 34, ii (Jan., 1972): 26-31.

Carey, Glenn O., "LIGHT IN AUGUST and Religious Fanaticism," *STwC* 10 (Fall, 1972): 101-13.

Chase, R., *American Novel and Its Tradition,* 210-19. Also in Minter, D. L., ed., *Twentieth Century Interpretations of LIGHT IN AUGUST,* 17-24. Also in Schmitter, D. M., ed., *William Faulkner,* 102-9.

————, "The Stone and the Crucifixion: Faulkner's LIGHT IN AUGUST," *KR* 10 (Autumn, 1948): 539-51. Also in Aldridge, J. W., ed., *Critiques and Essays on Modern Fiction,* 190-9. Also in Hoffman, F. J., and O. W. Vickery, eds., *William Faulkner: Two Decades of Criticism,* 205-17. Also in Kenyon Review, *Kenyon Critics,* 115-26. Also in Oldsey, Bernard S., and Arthur O. Lewis, Jr., eds., *Visions and Revisions in Modern American Literary Criticism,* N.Y.: Dutton, 1962, 271-83. Also in Inge, M. T., comp., *Merrill Studies in LIGHT IN AUGUST,* 27-37.

Church, M., "William Faulkner: Myth and Duration," *Time and Reality,* 238-41.

Clark, William G., "Faulkner's LIGHT IN AUGUST," *Expl* 26 (Mar., 1968): Item 54.

Clark, William J., "Faulkner's LIGHT IN AUGUST," *Expl* 28 (Nov., 1969): Item 19.

Coffee, Jessie A., "Empty Steeples: Theme, Symbol and Irony in Faulkner's Novels," *ArQ* 23 (Autumn, 1967): 198-201.

Coindreau, M. E., *Time of William Faulkner,* 31-40.

Collins, Robert G., "Four Critical Interpretations in the Modern Novel," *DA* 22 (1962): 3642 (Denver).

Collins, R. G., "The Game of Names: Characterization Device in LIGHT IN AUGUST," *EngR* 21, i (Oct., 1970): 82-7.

————, "LIGHT IN AUGUST: Faulkner's Stained Glass Triptych," *Mosaic* 7, i (Fall, 1973): 97-157. Also in Collins, R. G., and K. McRobbie, eds., *Novels of William Faulkner,* 97-157.

Connolly, Thomas E., in Krause, S. J., ed., *Essays in Determinism,* 41-5.

Corey, Stephen, "The Avengers in LIGHT IN AUGUST and NATIVE SON," *CLAJ* 23 (Dec., 1979): 200-12.

Cottrell, Beekman W., "Christian Symbols in LIGHT IN AUGUST," *MFS* 2 (Winter, 1956-57): 207-13.

Cullen, John B., and Floyd C. Watkins, "Joe Christmas and Nelse Patton," in *Old Times in the Faulkner Country,* Chapel Hill: Un. of North Carolina Pr., 1961, 89-98. Also in Inge, M. T., comp., *Merrill Studies in LIGHT IN AUGUST,* 7-14.

D'Avanzo, Mario L., "Allusion in the Percy Grimm Episode of LIGHT IN AUGUST," *NMW* 8 (Fall, 1975): 63-8.

————, "Bobbie Allen and the Ballad Tradition in LIGHT IN AUGUST," *SCR* 8, i (Nov., 1975): 22-9.

————, "Doc Hines and EUPHUES in LIGHT IN AUGUST," *NMW* 9, ii (Fall, 1976): 101-6.

————, "Hightower and Tennyson in LIGHT IN AUGUST," *SCR* 13, i (Fall, 1981): 66-71.

————, "Love's Labors: Byron Bunch and Shakespeare," *NMW* 10, ii (Winter, 1977): 80-6.

Davis, Charles E., "William Faulkner's Joe Christmas: A Rage for Order," *ArQ* 32 (Spring, 1976): 61-73.

Ditsky, John, "Lena's Way: Shared Principles of Structure in Faulkner and Proust," *JEn* 6 (Sept., 1979): 41-53.

Dorsch, Robert L., "An Interpretation of the Central Themes in the Work of William Faulkner," *ESRS* 11, i (Sept., 1962): 8-20.

Dunn, Richard J., "Faulkner's LIGHT IN AUGUST, Chapter 5," *Expl* 25 (Oct., 1966): Item 11.

Everett, W. K., *Faulkner's Art and Characters*, 47-52.

Ewell, Barbara N., "To Move in Time: A Study of the Structure of Faulkner's AS I LAY DYING, LIGHT IN AUGUST, and ABSALOM, ABSALOM!" *DAI* 30 (1970): 3940A (Florida St.).

Fadiman, Regina K., *Faulkner's LIGHT IN AUGUST: A Description and Interpretation of the Revisions*, Charlottesville: Virginia Un. Pr. for the Bibliographical Soc. of the Un. of Virginia, 1975.

_____, "Faulkner's LIGHT IN AUGUST: Sources and Revisions," *DAI* 32 (1971): 427A (U.C.L.A.).

Faulkner, William, "Comments on LIGHT IN AUGUST," in Inge, M. T., comp., *Merrill Studies in LIGHT IN AUGUST*, 2-6.

Fazio, Rocco R., "The Fury and the Design: Realms of Being and Knowing in Four Novels of William Faulkner," *DA* 25 (1964): 1910 (Rochester).

Ficken, Carl, "The Opening Scene of William Faulkner's LIGHT IN AUGUST," *Proof* 2 (1972): 175-84.

_____, "A Critical and Textual Study of William Faulkner's LIGHT IN AUGUST," *DAI* 33 (1973): 4411A-12A (S.C.).

Flint, R. W., "Faulkner as Elegist," *HudR* 7 (Summer, 1954): 249-50.

Ford, Daniel G., "Comments on William Faulkner's Temporal Vision in SANCTUARY, THE SOUND AND THE FURY, LIGHT IN AUGUST, ABSALOM, ABSALOM!" *SoQ* 15, iii (1977): 283-90.

_____, "Uses of Time in Four Novels of William Faulkner," *DAI* 35 (1974): 1654A (Auburn).

Fowler, Doreen F., "Faith as a Unifying Principle in Faulkner's LIGHT IN AUGUST," *TSL* 21 (1976): 49-57.

Frazier, David L., "Lucas Burch and the Polarity of LIGHT IN AUGUST," *MLN* 73 (June, 1958): 417-19.

Gavin, Jerome, "LIGHT IN AUGUST: The Act of Involvement," *HarvardA* 135 (Nov., 1951): 14-15, 34-7.

Geismar, M., *Writers in Crisis*, 163-9.

Glicksberg, Charles I., "Faulkner's World of Love and Sex," *Sexual Revolution in Modern American Literature*, 103-7.

_____, "William Faulkner and the Negro Problem," *Phylon* 10 (1949): 157-60.

Godden, Richard, "Call Me Nigger! Race and Speech in Faulkner's LIGHT IN AUGUST," *JAmS* 14 (Aug., 1980): 235-48.

Gold, Joseph, "The Two Worlds of LIGHT IN AUGUST," *MissQ* 16 (Summer, 1963): 160-7.

_____, *William Faulkner*, 38-42.

Gossett, L. Y., *Violence in Recent Southern Fiction*, 30-1.

Graham, Don B., and Barbara Shaw, "Faulkner's Small Debt to Dos Passos: A Source for the Percy Grimm Episode," *MissQ* 27, iii (Summer, 1974): 327-31.

Greer, Scott, "Joe Christmas and the 'Social Self'," *MissQ* 11 (Fall, 1958): 160-6.

Gregg, Alvin L., "Style and Dialect in LIGHT IN AUGUST and Other Works of William Faulkner," *DAI* 30 (1970): 3009 (Texas, Austin).

Griffith, Benjamin W., "Faulkner's Archaic Titles and the SECOND SHEPHERD'S PLAY," *NMW* 4, ii (Fall, 1971): 62-3.

Grossman, Joel M., "The Source of Faulkner's 'Less Oft is Peace'," *AL* 47, iii (Nov., 1975): 436-8.

Gwynn, F. L., and J. L. Blotner, eds., *Faulkner in the University*.

Halden, Judith, "Sexual Ambiguities in LIGHT IN AUGUST," *SAF* 10, ii (Autumn, 1982): 209-16.

Hammond, Donald, "Faulkner's Levels of Awareness," *FloQ* 1, ii (1967): 73-5.

Hartt, J. N., *Lost Image of Man*, 45-8.

Hays, Peter, "Hemingway, Faulkner, and a Bicycle for Death," *NMAL* 5 (Fall, 1981): Item 28.

_____, "More Light on LIGHT IN AUGUST," *PLL* 11, iv (Fall, 1975): 417-19.

Heimer, Jackson W., "Faulkner's Misogynous Novel: LIGHT IN AUGUST," *BSUF* 14, iii (Summer, 1973): 11-15.

Hirano, Nobuyuki, "Reconsideration of Moral Order and Disorder in Faulkner's Works," *HJAS* 8, i (Sept., 1967): 25-30.

Hirshleifer, Phyllis, "As Whirlwinds in the South: An Analysis of LIGHT IN AUGUST," *Per* 2 (Summer, 1949): 225-38. Also in Wagner, L. W., ed., *William Faulkner*, 244-57.

Hlavsa, Virginia V. J., "LIGHT IN AUGUST: Biblical Form and Mythic Function," *DAI* 39 (1979): 6130A-31A.

_____, "St. John and Frazer in LIGHT IN AUGUST: Biblical Form and Mythic Function," *BRH* 83 (Spring, 1980): 9-26.

Hoffman, F. J., in French, W. G., and Kidd, W. E., eds., *American Winners of the Nobel Literary Prize*, 148-50.

_____, *William Faulkner*, 69-74.

Holman, C. Hugh, "The Unity of Faulkner's LIGHT IN AUGUST," *PMLA* 72 (Mar., 1958): 155-66. Also in Holman, C. H., *Roots of Southern Writing*, 149-67. Also in Inge, M. T., comp., *Merrill Studies in LIGHT IN AUGUST*, 51-74.

Howe, I., *William Faulkner*, 61-70, 125-6, 200-14.

Howell, Elmo, "A Note on Faulkner's Presbyterian Novel," *PLL* 2 (Spring, 1966): 182-7.

_____, "Reverend Hightower and the Uses of Southern Adversity," *CE* 24 (Dec., 1962): 183-7.

Huck, George A., "The 'Quijotismo' Influence in Faulkner," 1137-44 in Criado de Val, Manvel, ed., *Cervantes: Su obra y su mundo: Actas del I Congresso internacional sobre ervantes*, Madrid: EDI-6, 1981.

Hulley, Kathleen, "Disintegration as Symbol of Community: A Study of THE RAINBOW, WOMEN IN LOVE, LIGHT IN AUGUST, PRISONER OF GRACE, EXCEPT THE LORD, NOT HONOUR MORE, and HERZOG," *DAI* 34 (1974): 6643A-44A.

Hunt, J. W., *William Faulkner*, 13-16.

Idei, Yasuko, "The Structure of Time and Space in Faulkner's LIGHT IN AUGUST," *KAL* 21 (1980): 18-25.

Inge, M. Thomas, "Faulknerian Light," *NMW* 5, i (Spring, 1972): 29.

_____, comp., *Merrill Studies in LIGHT IN AUGUST*.

Jackson, Esther M., "The American Negro and the Image of the Absurd," *Phylon* 23 (Winter, 1962): 360-4.

Jacobs, Robert D., "Faulkner's Tragedy of Isolation," in Rubin, L. D., and R. D. Jacobs, eds., *Southern Renascence*, 174-84.

_____, "William Faulkner: The Passion and the Penance," in Rubin, L. D., Jr., and R. D. Jacobs, eds., *South*, 157-63.

James, David L., "Hightower's Name: A Possible Source," *AN&Q* 13 (Sept., 1974): 4-5.

James, Stuart, "'I Lay My Hand on My Mouth': Religion in Yoknapatawpha County," *IllQ* 40, i (Fall, 1977): 38-53.

Jehlen, M., *Class and Character in Faulkner's South*, 78-96.

Jenkins, L., *Faulkner and Black-White Relations*, 61-105.

Johnston, Walter E., "The Shepherdess in the City," *CL* 26, ii (Spring, 1974): 124-41.

Kantak, V. Y., "Faulkner's Technique," in Chander, J., and N. S. Pradhan, eds., *Studies in American Literature*, 77-96 passim.

Kaplan, H., "The Inert and the Violent: Faulkner's LIGHT IN AUGUST," *Passive Voice*, 111-30.

Kartiganer, D. M., *Fragile Thread*, 37-68.

Kazin, Alfred, "The Stillness in LIGHT IN AUGUST," *PR* 24 (Fall, 1957): 519-38. Also in Kazin, A., *Contemporaries*, 130-49. Also in Feidelson, C., Jr., and P. Brodtkorb, Jr., eds., *Interpretations of American Literature*, 349-68. Also in Shapiro, C., ed., *Twelve Original Essays*, 257-83. Also in Hoffman, F. J., and O. W. Vickery, eds., *William Faulkner*, 247-65. Also in Warren, R. P., ed., *Faulkner*, 147-62.

Kellogg, Jean, "Simultaneity and Contemporary Cultural History," *Dark Prophets of Hope*, 157-77.

Kerr, E. M., *William Faulkner's Gothic Domain*, 107-36.

Kimmey, John L., "The Good Earth in LIGHT IN AUGUST," *MissQ* 17 (Winter, 1963-64): 1-8. Also in Inge, M. T., comp., *Merrill Studies in LIGHT IN AUGUST*, 98-107.

Kinney, A. F., *Faulkner's Narrative Poetics*, 15-30, 113-18.

Kirk, Robert W., "Faulkner's Lena Grove," *GaR* 21 (Spring, 1967): 57-64.

Kunkel, Francis L., "Christ Symbolism in Faulkner: Prevalence of the Human," *Ren* 17 (Spring, 1965): 148-51.

Lamont, William H. F., "The Chronology of LIGHT IN AUGUST," *MFS* 3 (Winter, 1957-58): 360-1.

Langston, Beach, "The Meaning of Lena Grove and Gail Hightower in LIGHT IN AUGUST," *BUSE* 5 (Spring, 1961): 46-63.

Leary, L., *William Faulkner of Yoknapatawpha County*, 78-95.

Levith, Murray J., "Unity in Faulkner's LIGHT IN AUGUST," *Thoth* 7 (Winter, 1966): 31-4.

Lind, Ilse D., " Apocalyptic Vision as Key to LIGHT IN AUGUST," *SAF* 3, ii (Autumn, 1975): 133-41.

_____, "The Calvinistic Burden of LIGHT IN AUGUST," *NEQ* 30 (Sept., 1957): 307-29.

Longley, John L., Jr., "Faulkner's Byron Bunch," *GaR* 15 (Summer, 1961): 197-208.

_____, "Joe Christmas: The Hero in the Modern World," *VQR* 33 (Spring, 1957): 233-49. Also in Hoffman, F. J., and O. W. Vickery, eds., *William Faulkner*, 765-78. Also, revised, in Longley, J. L., Jr., *Tragic Mask*, 192-205. Also in Warren, R. P., ed., *Faulkner*, 163-74. Also in Inge, M. T., comp., *Merrill Studies in LIGHT IN AUGUST*, 107-19.

_____, *Tragic Mask*, 50-62.

Lowe, John W., III, "The Biblical Imagination and American Genius: Repetitive Patterns of Hebraic Myth in Faulkner's LIGHT IN AUGUST," *DAI* 42, ix (Mar., 1982): 4001A.

Lyday, Charles L., "Faulkner's *Comedia*: An Interpretation of THE SOUND AND THE FURY, SANCTUARY, AS I LAY DYING, and LIGHT IN AUGUST," *DAI* 39 (1978): 886A-87A.

Martin, Timothy P., "The Art and Rhetoric of Chronology in Faulkner's LIGHT IN AUGUST," *CollL* 7, ii (1980): 125-35.

Maruta, Akeo, "Ambivalent Faulkner in LIGHT IN AUGUST," *SALit* 13 (1977): 13-23.

McAlexander, Hubert, Jr., "General Earl Van Dorn and Faulkner's Use of History," *JMissH* 39 (Nov., 1977): 357-61.

McCormick, John, "William Faulkner: The Past, and History," *Fiction as Knowledge*, 103-8.

McDowell, Alfred, "Attitudes Toward 'Time' in LIGHT IN AUGUST," in Baldanza, F., ed., *Itinerary 3: Criticism*, 149-58.

McElderry, B. R., Jr., "The Narrative Structure of LIGHT IN AUGUST," *CE* 19 (Feb., 1958): 200-7. Also in *MissQ* 11 (Fall, 1958): 177-87. Also in Inge, M. T., comp., *Merrill Studies in LIGHT IN AUGUST*, 120-2.

Meats, Stephen E., "Who Killed Joanna Burden?" *MissQ* 24, iii (Summer, 1971): 271-7.

Millgate, M., *Achievement of William Faulkner*, 124-37. Also, excerpted, in Minter, D. L., ed., *Twentieth Century Interpretations of LIGHT IN AUGUST*, 71-82.

_____, *William Faulkner*, 44-52.

Milum, Richard A., "Faulkner and the Comic Perspective of Frederick Burr Opper," *JPC* 16, iii (Winter, 1982): 139-50.

Miner, Ward, L., "Faulkner and Christ's Crucifixion," *NM* 57 (1956): 265.

Minter, D. L., ed., *Twentieth Century Interpretations of LIGHT IN AUGUST*.

Morrisseu, Thomas J., "Food Imagery in Faulkner's LIGHT IN AUGUST," *NR* 3, iv (1978): 41-9.

Morrison, Sister Kristin, "Faulkner's Joe Christmas: Character Through Voice," *TSLL* 2 (Winter, 1961): 419-43.

Moseley, E. M., *Pseudonyms of Christ in the Modern Novel*, 135-51.

Muehl, Lois, "Form as Seen in Two Early Works by Faulkner," *LC* 38 (Spring, 1972): 147-57.

Mulqueen, James E., "LIGHT IN AUGUST: Motion, Eros and Death," *NMW* 7, iii (Winter, 1975): 91-8.

Nash, H. C., "Faulkner's 'Furniture Repairer and Dealer': Knitting Up LIGHT IN AUGUST," *MFS* 16, iv (Winter, 1970-71): 529-31.

Nemerov, H., "Calculation Raised to Mystery: The Dialectics of LIGHT IN AUGUST," *Poetry and Fiction*, 246-59.

Neufeldt, Leonard, "Time and Man's Possibilities in LIGHT IN AUGUST," *GaR* 25, i (Spring, 1971): 27-40.

Nilon, Charles H., "Faulkner and the Negro," *UCSSLL* No. 8 (Sept., 1962): 73-93. Also in Nilon, C. H., *Faulkner and the Negro*, 73-93.

Noble, D. W., *Eternal Adam and the New World Garden*, 166-76.

O'Connor, William Van, "Protestantism in Yoknapatawpha County," *Hopkins Rev* 5, iii (Spring, 1952): 31-42. Also in Rubin, L. D., and R. D. Jacobs, *Southern Renascence*, 158-69.

_____, *Tangled Fire of William Faulkner*, 72-86.

_____, *William Faulkner*, 19-23. Also in O'Connor, W. V., ed., *Seven Modern American Novelists*, 133-5.

O'Faolain, S., *Vanishing Hero*, 101-4.

Page, S. R., *Faulkner's Women*, 139-53.

Palmer, William J., "Abelard's Fate: Sexual Politics in Stendhal, Faulkner and Camus," *Mosaic* 7, iii (Spring, 1974): 29-41.

Palumbo, Donald, "Coincidence in CRIME AND PUNISHMENT and LIGHT IN AUGUST: Evidence of Supernatural Agents at Work in the Novels of Dostoyovsky and Faulkner," *LJHum* 7, i (Spring, 1982): 41-51.

_____, "The Concept of God in Faulkner's LIGHT IN AUGUST, THE SOUND AND THE FURY, AS I LAY DYING, and ABSALOM, ABSALOM!" *SCB* 39, iv (1979): 142-6.

Pascal, Richard, "Faulkner's Debt to Keats in LIGHT IN AUGUST: A Reconsideration," *SoRA* 14, ii (July, 1981): 161-7.

Pearce, Richard C., "Faulkner's One Ring Circus," *WSCL* 7 (Autumn, 1966): 270-83. Also in Pearce, R., *Stages of the Clown*, 47-66.

Pearson, Norman H., "Lena Grove," *Shen* 3 (Spring, 1952): 3-7.

Peterson, Richard F., "Faulkner's LIGHT IN AUGUST," *Expl* 30 (Dec., 1971): Item 35.

Pilkington, J., *Heart of Yoknapatawpha*, 135-56.

Pitavy, François L., *Faulkner's LIGHT IN AUGUST*, rev. and enl. ed., tr. by Gillian E. Cook, with collab. of the author. Bloomington and London: Indiana Un. Pr., 1973.

_____, "The Landscape in LIGHT IN AUGUST," *MissQ* 23, iii (Summer, 1970): 265-72. Also in Cox, L. H., ed., *William Faulkner*, 240-8.

Pommer, Henry F., "LIGHT IN AUGUST: A Letter by Faulkner," *ELN* 4 (Sept., 1966): 47-8.

Poresky, Louise A., "Joe Christmas: His Tragedy as Victim," *HSL* 8, iii (1976): 209-22.

Porter, Carolyn, "The Problem of Time in LIGHT IN AUGUST," *RUS* 61, i (Winter, 1975): 107-25.

_____, *Seeing and Being*, 242-59.

Powers, L. H., *Faulkner's Yoknapatawpha Comedy*, 89-105.

_____, "Hawthorne and Faulkner and the Pearl of Great Price," *PMASAL* 52 (1967): 391-401.

Pryse, Marjorie, "LIGHT IN AUGUST: Violence and Excommunity," *Mark and the Knowledge*, 108-42.

Reed, J. W., Jr., *Faulkner's Narrative*, 112-44.

Rice, Julian C., "Orpheus and the Hellish Unity in LIGHT IN AUGUST," *CentR* 19, i (Winter, 1975): 380-96.

Richardson, K. E., *Force and Faith in the Novels of William Faulkner*, 35-42, 80-7, 93-6.

Rinialdi, Nicholas M., "Game-Consciousness and Game-Metaphor in the Work of William Faulkner," *DA* 24 (1964): 4196-7 (Fordham).

Roberts, James L., "The Individual and the Community: Faulkner's LIGHT IN AUGUST," in McNeir, Waldo, and L. B. Levy, eds., *Studies in American Literature* (LSUSHs, No. 8), Baton Rouge: La. St. Un. Pr., 1960, 132-53.

Rosenzweig, Paul J., "Faulkner's Motif of Food in LIGHT IN AUGUST," *AI* 37, i (1980); 93-112.

Routh, Michael P., "The Story of All Things: Faulkner's Yoknapatawpha County Cosmology by Way of LIGHT IN AUGUST," *DAI* 34 (1974): 6657A-58A (Wis., Madison).

Rovere, Richard, "Introduction," in *LIGHT IN AUGUST*, N.Y.: Modern Library, 1950.

Rubin, L. D., Jr., *Curious Death of the Novel*, 139-44. Also in Vandiver, Frank E., ed., *The Idea of the South*, Chicago: Un. of Chicago Pr., 1964, 32-6.

_____, *Faraway Country*, 60-2.

Ruppersburg, Hugh M., "Byron Bunch and Percy Grimm: Strange Twins of LIGHT IN AUGUST," *MissQ* 30 (Summer, 1977): 441-3.

Sandstrom, Glenn, "Identity Diffusion: Joe Christmas and Quentin Compson," *AQ* 19 (Summer, 1967): 207-23.

Schatt, Stanley, "Faulkner's Thematic Use of Time in LIGHT IN AUGUST," *CCTE* 36 (1971): 28-32.

Schlepper, Wolfgang, "Knowledge and Experience in Faulkner's LIGHT IN AUGUST," *JA* 18 (1973): 182-94.

Seyppel, J., *William Faulkner*, 53-60.

Shanaghan, Father Malachy M., O.S.B., "A Critical Analysis of the Fictional Technique of William Faulkner," *DA* 20 (1960): 4663 (Notre Dame).

Shaw, Patrick W., "Joe Christmas and the Burden of Despair," *Texas Rev* 1, ii (Fall, 1980): 89-97.

Sichi, Edward, Jr., "Faulkner's Joe Christmas: 'Memory Believes Before Knowing Remembers'," *Cithara* 18, ii (May, 1979): 70-8.

Slabey, Robert M., "Faulkner's Geography and Hightower's House," *AN&Q* 3 (Feb., 1965): 85-6.

_____, "Joe Christmas, Faulkner's Marginal Man," *Phylon* 21 (Fall, 1960): 266-77.

_____, "Myth and Ritual in LIGHT IN AUGUST," *TSLL* 2 (Autumn, 1960): 328-49. Also in Inge, M. T., comp., *Merrill Studies in LIGHT IN AUGUST*, 75-98.

Slatoff, W. J., *Quest for Failure*, 30-1, 36-7, 58-9, 65-6, 70-1, 84-5, 88-9, 109-10, 115-16, 139-41, 173-98, 259.

Smith, Don N., "The Design of Faulkner's LIGHT IN AUGUST: A Comprehensive Study," *DAI* 31 (1970): 2402A (Mich.).

Smith, Hallet, "Summary of a Symposium on LIGHT IN AUGUST," *MissQ* 11 (Fall, 1958): 188-90.

Sowder, William J., "Christmas as Existentialist Hero," *UR* 30 (June, 1964): 279-84.

Spear, Karen I., "Will and Body: Dualism in LIGHT IN AUGUST," *DAI* 37 (1976): 1557A.

Spenko, James L., "The Death of Joe Christmas and the Power of Words," *TCL* 28, iii (Fall, 1982): 252-68.

Steinberg, Aaron, "Faulkner and the Negro," *DA* 27 (1966): 1385A (N.Y.U.).

Stephenson, Aaron, "Faulkner and the Negro," *DA* 27 (1966): 1385A (N.Y.U.).

Stephenson, Shelby D., "'You Smart Sheriffs and Such': The Function of Local Peace Officers in William Faulkner's LIGHT IN AUGUST and INTRUDER IN THE DUST," *DAI* 35 (1974): 3012A (Wis., Madison).

Sternberg, Meir, "Temporal Ordering, Modes of Expositional Distribution, and Three Models of Rhetorical Control in the Narrative Text: Faulkner, Balzac and Austen," *PTL* 1 (April, 1976): 295-316.

Strauss, Mary T., "The Fourteenth View: A Study of Ambiguity in William Faulkner's LIGHT IN AUGUST," *DAI* 31 (1971): 6074A (Pittsburgh).

Sullivan, W., *Requiem for the Renascence*, 11-12.

Sullivan, William P., "William Faulkner and the Community," *DA* 22 (1962): 4355 (Columbia).

Swiggart, P., *Art of Faulkner's Novels*, 41-7, 131-48.

Tanaka, Hisao, "The Significance of the Past for Gail Hightower: One Aspect of LIGHT IN AUGUST," *SALit* 8 (1972): 24-38.

Tanner, Stephen L., "LIGHT IN AUGUST: The Varieties of Religious Fanaticism," *ELWIU* 7 (Spring, 1980): 79-90.

Taylor, Carole A., "LIGHT IN AUGUST: The Epistemology of Tragic Paradox," *TSLL* 22 (Spring, 1980): 48-68.

Thompson, L., *William Faulkner*, 66-80, 193-5.

Tritschler, Donald H., "Whorls of Form in Faulkner's Fiction," *DA* 17 (1957): 3025 (Northwestern).

Tuck, D., *Crowell's Handbook of Faulkner*, 46-55.

_____, "The Inwardness of Understanding," in Unterecker, John, ed., *Approaches to the Twentieth Century Novel*, N.Y.: Crowell, 1965, 79-107.

Tucker, John, "William Faulkner's LIGHT IN AUGUST: Toward a Structuralist Reading," *MLQ* 43, ii (June, 1982): 138-55.

Uchino, Takak, "The Pattern and Devices in LIGHT IN AUGUST," in *Maekawa Shunichi Kyoju Kaureki* [Essays and Studies in Commemoration of Prof. Shunichi Maekawa's Sixty-First Birthday], Tokyo: Eihosha, 1968, 155-63.

Um, Mee-sook, "Joe Christmas: A Modern Tragic Hero," *Yonsei Rev* (Seoul) 5 (1978): 113-24.

Vickery, Olga W., "Gavin Stevens: From Rhetoric to Dialectic," *Faulkner Studies* 2 (Spring, 1953): 1-4.

_____, *Novels of William Faulkner*, 66-83. Also in Minter, D. L., ed., *Twentieth Century Interpretations of LIGHT IN AUGUST*, 25-41.

Volpe, E. L., *Reader's Guide to William Faulkner*, 151-74.

Waggoner, H. H., *William Faulkner*, 100-20. Also in Barth, J. R., S. J., ed., *Religious Perspectives in Faulkner's Fiction*, 121-39.

Watkins, Floyd C., "Language of Irony: Quiet Words and Violent Acts in LIGHT IN AUGUST," *Flesh and the Word*, 203-15.

Weisgerber, J., *Faulkner and Dostoevsky*, 203-17.

West, Ray B., Jr., "Faulkner's LIGHT IN AUGUST: A View of Tragedy," *WSCL* 1, i (Winter, 1960): 5-12. Also in West, R. B., Jr., *Writer in the Room*, 175-84.

Wheeler, Sally P., "Chronology in LIGHT IN AUGUST," *SLJ* 6, i (Fall, 1973): 20-42.

Widmer, K., "Naturalism and the American Joe," *Literary Rebel*, 118-20.

Williams, B., *Faulkner's Women*, 157-84.

Williams, John S., "'The Final Copper Light of Afternoon': Hightower's Redemption," *TCL* 13 (Jan., 1968): 205-15.

Wilson, Robert R., "The Pattern of Thought in LIGHT IN AUGUST," *BRMMLA* 24, iv (Dec., 1970): 155-61.

Wittenberg, J. B., *Faulkner*, 117-29.

Wolfe, Don M., "Faulkner and Hemingway: Image of Man's Desolation," *Image of Man in America*, 348-50.

Yorks, Samuel A., "Faulkner's Woman: The Peril of Mankind," *ArQ* 17 (Summer, 1961): 119-29.

Young, Glenn, "Struggle and Triumph in LIGHT IN AUGUST," *STwC* 15 (Spring, 1975): 33-50.

Zink, Karl E., "William Faulkner: Form as Experience," *SAQ* 53 (1954): 384-403 *passim*.

THE MANSION (See also SNOPES Trilogy)

Beck, Warren, "Faulkner, in THE MANSION," *VQR* 36 (Spring, 1960): 272-92. Also in Beck, W., *Faulkner*, 639-59.

Brooks, C., *William Faulkner*, 219-43, 412-14.

Brylowski, W., *Faulkner's Olympian Laugh*, 206-14.

Burelbach, Frederick M., "The Name of the Snake: A Family of Snopes," *LOS* 8 (1981): 125-46.

Chugunov, Konstantin, "Faulkner's MANSION in the U.S.S.R.," *Soviet Literature* (1962): 171-2.

Creighton, Joanne V., "The Dilemma of the Human Heart in THE MANSION," *Ren* 25, i (Autumn, 1972): 35-45.

_____, *William Faulkner's Craft of Revision*, 63-72.

Dirksen, Sherland N., "William Faulkner's Snopes Family: THE HAMLET, THE TOWN, and THE MANSION," *ESRS* 11, ii (Dec., 1962): 33-40.

Everett, W. K., *Faulkner's Art and Characters*, 52-7.

Glicksberg, Charles I., "Faulkner's World of Love and Sex," *Sexual Revolution in Modern American Literature*, 118-19.

Gold, J., *William Faulkner*, 162-73.

Greene, Theodore M., "The Philosophy of Life Implicit in Faulkner's THE MANSION," *TSLL* 2 (Winter, 1961): 401-18.

Gregory, Eileen, "The Temerity to Revolt: Mink Snopes and the Dispossessed in THE MANSION," *MissQ* 29 (Summer, 1976): 401-21.

Gregory, Nancy E., "A Study of the Early Versions of Faulkner's THE TOWN and THE MANSION," *DAI* 36 (1975): 3686A-87A.

Gwynn, F. L., and J. L. Blotner, eds., *Faulkner in the University*.

Haselswordt, Marjorie B., "I'd Rather Be Ratliff: A Maslovian Study of Faulkner's *Snopes*," *LitR* 24, ii (Winter, 1981): 308-27.

Hauck, R. B., *Cheerful Nihilism*, 191-5.

Howe, Irving, "Faulkner: End of a Road," *NRep* 141 (Dec. 7, 1959): 17-21.

_____, *William Faulkner*, 110-14, 282-94.

Howell, Elmo, "Mink Snopes and Faulkner's Moral Conclusion," *SAQ* 67 (Winter, 1968): 13-22.

Hunt, J. W., *William Faulkner*, 154-6.

Hunt, Joel A., "William Faulkner and Rabelais: The Dog Story," *ConL* 10, iii (Summer, 1969): 383-8.

Jehlen, M., *Class and Character in Faulkner's South*, 162-4, 168-74.

Lawson, Lewis A., "The Grotesque-Comic in the SNOPES Trilogy," in Manheim, L., and E., eds., *Hidden Patterns*, 243-58. Also in *L&P* 15 (1965): 107-19.

Leary, L., *William Faulkner of Yoknapatawpha County*, 163-9.

Millgate, M., *Achievement of William Faulkner*, 245-52.

_____, *William Faulkner*, 92-3.

Moses, W. R., "The Limits of Yoknapatawpha County," *GaR* 16 (Fall, 1962): 297-305.

Mumbach, Mary K., "'Remaining Must Remain': Patterns of Christian Comedy in Faulkner's THE MANSION," *DAI* 42, iv (Oct., 1981): 1637A.

O'Connor, William Van, "The Old Master, the Sole Proprietor," *VQR* 36 (Winter, 1960): 147-51.

Powers, L. H., *Faulkner's Yoknapatawpha Comedy*, 233-49.

Rankin, Elizabeth D., "Chasing Spotted Horses: The Quest for Human Dignity in Faulkner's Snopes Trilogy," in Carey, Glenn O., ed., *Faulkner*, 139-56.

Reed, J. W., Jr., *Faulkner's Narrative*, 248-57.

Richardson, K. E., *Force and Faith in the Novels of William Faulkner*, 163-71.

Roberts, James L., "Snopeslore: THE HAMLET, THE TOWN, THE MANSION," *UKCR* 28 (1961): 65-71.

Rossky, William, "Faulkner: The Image of the Child in THE MANSION," 15 (1962): 17-20.

Stafford, William T., "Contractive Expansiveness at the End of THE MANSION," *NMAL* 6 (1982): Item 16.

Stonum, G. L., *Faulkner's Career*, 174-93.

Stroble, Woodrow, "Flem Snopes: A Crazed Mirror," in Carey, Glenn O., ed., *Faulkner*, 195-212.

Tuck, D., *Crowell's Handbook of Faulkner*, 86-94.

Vickery, O.W., *Novels of William Faulkner*, 191-208.

Volpe, E. L., *Reader's Guide to William Faulkner*, 331-43.

Warne, Keith F., "Language in Faulkner's Trilogy: Truth and Fiction," *DAI* 41, xii (June, 1981): 5099A.

Watson, J. G., *Snopes Dilemma*, 147-221.

Weisgerber, J., *Faulkner and Dostoevsky*, 337-44.

Whitbread, Thomas, "The Snopes Trilogy: The Setting of THE MANSION," in Sutherland, W.O.S., ed., *Six Contemporary Novels*, 76-88.

Williams, D., *Faulkner's Women*, 222-6.

Wittenberg, J. B., *Faulkner*, 232-5.

MAYDAY

Morrison, Gail M., 'Time, Tide, and Twilight': MAYDAY and Faulkner's Quest Toward THE SOUND AND THE FURY," *MissQ* 31 (Summer, 1978): 337-57.

Watson, James G., "Literary Self-Criticism: Faulkner in Fiction on Fiction," *SoQ* 20, i (Fall, 1981): 51-60.

MOSQUITOES

Adams, R. P., *Faulkner*, 40-9.

Aiken, C., "William Faulkner," *New York Post* (June 11, 1927): Sec. III, 7. Also in Aiken, C., *Reviewer's ABC*, 197-200.

Arnold, Edwin T., III, "Faulkner and Huxley: A Note on MOSQUITOES and CROME YELLOW," *MissQ* 30 (Summer, 1977): 433-6.

————, "Freedom and Statis in Faulkner's MOSQUITOES," *MissQ* 28 (Summer, 1975): 281-97.

————, "William Faulkner's MOSQUITOES: An Introduction and Annotations to the Novel," *DAI* 39 (1979): 6125A.

Bassett, John E., "Faulkner's MOSQUITOES: Toward a Self-Image of the Artist," *SLJ* 12, ii (1980): 49-64.

Brooks, Cleanth, "Faulkner's MOSQUITOES," *GaR* 31 (Spring, 1977): 213-34. Also in Brooks, C., *William Faulkner: Toward Yoknapatawpha and Beyond*, 129-51, 378-9.

Brylowski, W., *Faulkner's Olympian Laugh*, 48-51.

Carey, Glenn O., "Faulkner and MOSQUITOES: Writing Himself and His Age," *RS* 39 (1971): 271-83.

Carnes, Frank F., "On the Aesthetics of Faulkner's Fiction," *DA* 29 (1968): 894A-5A (Vanderbilt).

Cooley, Thomas W., Jr., "Faulkner Draws the Long Bow," *TCL* 16 (Oct., 1970): 268-77.

Davidson, Donald, *Nashville Tennessean* (July 3, 1927). Also in *GaR* 20 (Winter, 1966): 458-9.

Dunlap, Mary M., "Sex and the Artist in MOSQUITOES," *MissQ* 22, iii (Summer, 1969): 190-206.

Everett, W. K., *Faulkner's Art and Characters*, 57-65.

Franklin, Phyllis, "The Influence of Joseph Hergesheimer Upon MOSQUITOES," *MissQ* 22, iii (Summer, 1969): 207-13.

Geismar, M., *Writers in Crisis*, 148-50.

Gold, Joseph, "William Faulkner's 'One Compact Thing'," *TCL* 8, i (April, 1962): 3-4.

Gwynn, F. L., and J. L. Blotner, eds., *Faulkner in the University*.

————, "Faulkner's Prufrock—and Other Observations," *JEGP* 52 (Jan., 1953): 63-70.

Harwick, Robert D., "Humor in the Novels of William Faulkner," *DA* 26 (1965): 1646 (Nebraska).

Hepburn, Kenneth W., "Faulkner's MOSQUITOES: A Poetic Turning Point," *TCL* 17, i (Jan., 1971): 19-28.

Hoffman, F. J., *William Faulkner*, 42-4.

Howe, I., *William Faulkner*, 19-20.

Irwin, J. T., *Doubling and Incest/Repetition and Revenge*, 160-6.

Kreiswirth, Martin, "William Faulkner and Siegfried Sassoon: An Allusion in MOSQUITOES," *MissQ* 29 (Summer, 1976): 433-4.

Lind, Ilse D., "Faulkner's MOSQUITOES: A New Reading," *WiF* 4, ii (July, 1982): 1-18.

Lloyd, James B., "Humorous Characterization and the Tradition of the Jonsonian Comedy of Manners in William Faulkner's Early Fiction: NEW ORLEANS SKETCHES, SOLDIERS' PAY, and MOSQUITOES," *DAI* 36 (1976): 4493A.

MacMillan, Duane J., "The Non-Yoknapatawpha Novels of William Faulkner: An Examination of SOLDIERS' PAY, MOSQUITOES, PYLON, THE WILD PALMS, and A FABLE," *DAI* 32 (1972): 6986A (Wis.).

Matthews, J. T., *Play of Faulkner's Language*, 45-50.

Millgate, M., *Achievement of William Faulkner*, 68-75.

————, *William Faulkner*, 20-2.

O'Connor, W. V., *Tangled Fire of William Faulkner*, 30-3.

————, "William Faulkner's Apprenticeship," *SWR* 38 (Winter, 1953): 10-12.

Page, S. R., *Faulkner's Women*, 4-10, 27-34.

Pikoulis, J., *Art of William Faulkner*, 11-16.

Richardson, H. Edward, "Faulkner, Anderson, and Their Tall Tale," *AL* 34 (May, 1962): 287-91.

————, *William Faulkner*, 134-8.

Rideout, Walter B., and James B. Meriwether, "On the Collaboration of Faulkner and Anderson," *AL* 35 (Mar., 1963): 85-7.

Roberts, James L., "Experimental Exercises—Faulkner's Early Writings," *Discourse* 6 (Summer, 1963): 191-6.

Seyppel, J., *William Faulkner*, 27-31.

Slabey, Robert M., "Faulkner's MOSQUITOES and Joyce's ULYSSES," *RLV* 28, v (1962): 435-7.

Smart, G. K., *Religious Elements in Faulkner's Early Novels*.

Stein, Randolph E., "The World Outside Yoknapatawpha: A Study of Five Novels by William Faulkner," *DA* 26 (1965): 2225 (Ohio Un.).

Swiggart, P., *Art of Faulkner's Novels*, 32-3.

Tuck, D., *Crowell's Handbook of Faulkner*, 129-31.

Vickery, Olga W., "Faulkner's MOSQUITOES," *UKCR* 24 (Mar., 1958): 219-24.

————, *Novels of William Faulkner*, 8-14.

Volpe, E. L., *Reader's Guide to William Faulkner*, 56-66.

Waggoner, H. H., *William Faulkner*, 8-1.

Warren, Joyce W., "Faulkner's 'Portrait of the Artist'," *MissQ* 19 (Summer, 1966): 121-31.

Watkins, Floyd C., "The Unbearable and Unknowable Truth in Faulkner's First Three Novels," *Flesh and the World*, 169-80.

Werner, C. H., *Paradoxical Resolutions*, 11-14.

Williams, D., *Faulkner's Women*, 32-6.

Wittenberg, J. B., *Faulkner*, 50-60.

THE OLD MAN (See also THE WILD PALMS)

Cumpiano, Marion W., "The Motif of Return: Currents and Counter Currents in OLD MAN by William Faulkner," *SHR* 12 (Summer, 1978): 185-93.

Everett, W. K., *Faulkner's Art and Characters*, 127-9.

Feaster, John, "Faulkner's OLD MAN: A Psychoanalytic Approach," *MFS* 13, i (Spring, 1967): 89-93.

Howell, Elmo, "William Faulkner and the Plain People of Yoknapatawpha County," *Jnl of Miss Hist* 24 (April, 1962): 82-5.

Leary, L., *William Faulkner of Yoknapatawpha County*, 128-32.

Lee, Dorothy H., "Denial of Time and the Failure of Moral Choice: Camus' THE STRANGER, Faulkner's OLD MAN, Wright's THE MAN WHO LIVED UNDERGROUND," *CLAJ* 23 (Mar., 1980): 364-71.

Moses, W. R., "Water, Water Everywhere: OLD MAN and A FAREWELL TO ARMS," *MFS* 5 (Summer, 1959): 172-4.

Rao, P. B. Rama, "Faulkner's OLD MAN: A Critique," *IJAS* 1, iv (Nov., 1971): 43-50.

Reed, John Q., "Theme and Symbol in Faulkner's OLD MAN," *EdL* 21 (Jan., 1958): 25-31.

Richardson, K. E., *Force and Faith in the Novels of William Faulkner*, 96-9.

Stonesifer, Richard J., "Faulkner's OLD MAN in the Classroom," *CE* 17 (Feb., 1956): 254-7.

Swiggart, P., *Art of Faulkner's Novels*, 51-7.

Taylor, Nancy D., "The River of Faulkner and Mark Twain," *MissQ* 16 (Fall, 1963): 191-9 *passim*.

Tuck, D., *Crowell's Handbook of Faulkner*, 136-42.

Watkins, F. C., *Flesh and the Word*, 237-40.

————, "William Faulkner, the Individual, and the World," *GaR* 14 (Fall, 1960): 242-6.

Wilcox, Earl J., "Christian Coloring in Faulkner's THE OLD MAN," *C&L* 29, ii (1980): 63-74.

PYLON

Adams, R. P., *Faulkner*, 95-102.

Barthelme, Helen M., "PYLON: The Doomed Quest. A Critical and Textual Study of William Faulkner's Neglected Allegory," *DAI* 38 (1978): 4163A.

Beach, J. W., *American Fiction*, 149-50.

Bedell, G. C., *Kierkegaard and Faulkner*, 206-13.

Brooks, C., *William Faulkner: Toward Yoknapatawpha and Beyond*, 178-204, 399-405.

Brylowski, W., *Faulkner's Olympian Laugh*, 117-20.

Cowley, M., "Faulkner: Voodoo Dance," *NRep* 82 (April 10, 1935): 254. Also in Cowley, M., *Think Back on Us*, 268-71.

Degenfelder, Pauline, "Sirk's THE TARNISHED ANGELS: PYLON Recreated," *LFQ* 5 (Summer, 1977): 242-51.

Everett, W. K., *Faulkner's Art and Characters*, 65-9.

Geismar, M., *Writers in Crisis*, 169-70.

Gresset, Michel, "Théorème," *RANAM* 9 (1976): 73-94.

Guereschi, Edward, "Ritual and Myth in William Faulkner's PYLON," *Thoth* 3 (Spring, 1962): 101-10.

Hoffman, F. J., *William Faulkner*, 80-2.

Howe, I., *William Faulkner*, 215-20.

Jordan, Peter, "April Fool!" *NMW* 12, i (1979): 17-22.

Kinney, A. F., *Faulkner's Narrative Poetics*, 98-101.

Leary, L., *William Faulkner of Yoknapatawpha County*, 125-8.

Lhamon, W. T., Jr., "PYLON: The Ylimaf and New Valois," *WHR* 24, iii (Summer, 1970): 274-8.

Longley, J. L., Jr., *Tragic Mask*, 133-7.

MacMillan, Duane J., "The Non-Yoknapatawpha Novels of William Faulkner: An Examination of SOLDIERS' PAY, MOSQUITOES, PYLON, THE WILD PALMS, and A FABLE," *DAI* 32 (1972): 6986A (Wis.).

————, "PYLON: From Short Stories to Major Work," *Mosaic* 7, i (Fall, 1973): 185-212. Also in Collins, R. G., and K. McRobbie, eds., *Novels of William Faulkner*, 185-212.

Marvin, John R., "PYLON: The Definition of Sacrifice," *Faulkner Studies* 1 (Summer, 1952): 20-3.

McElrath, Joseph R., Jr., "PYLON: The Portrait of a Lady," *MissQ* 27, iii (Summer, 1974): 277-90.

Millgate, M., *Achievement of William Faulkner*, 138-49.

————, "Faulkner and the Air: The Background of PYLON," *LitR* 3 (Winter, 1964): 271-7.

Monteiro, George, "Bankruptcy in Time: A Reading of William Faulkner's PYLON," *TCL* 4 (Spring-Summer, 1958): 9-20.

O'Connor, W. V., *Tangled Fire of William Faulkner*, 89-93.

————, *William Faulkner*, 23-5. Also in O'Connor, W. V., ed., *Seven Modern American Novelists*, 135-8.

Pearce, Richard, "PYLON, AWAKE AND SING! and the Apocalyptic Imagination of the 1930's," *Criticism* 13, ii (Spring, 1971): 131-41.

Price, Reynolds, "PYLON: The Posture of Worship," *Shen* 19 (Spring, 1968): 29-45. Also in Price, R., *Things Themselves*, 91-108.

Ruppersburg, Hugh M., "Image as Structure in Faulkner's PYLON," *SAB* 4, i (Jan., 1982): 74-87.

Seyppel, J., *William Faulkner*, 60-2.

Slatoff, W. J., *Quest for Failure*, 95-6, 211-15.

Stein, Randolph E., "The World Outside Yoknapatawpha: A Study of Five Novels by William Faulkner," *DA* 26 (1965): 2225 (Ohio Un.).

Stern, Michael, "From the Folklore of Speed to Danse Macabre," in Peary, G., and R. Shatzkin, eds., *Modern American Novel and the Movies*, 40-52.

Swiggart, P., *Art of Faulkner's Novels*, 27-9.

Torchiana, Donald T., "Faulkner's PYLON and the Structure of Modernity," *MFS* 3 (Winter, 1957-58): 291-308.

————, "The Reporter in Faulkner's PYLON," *HINL* 4 (Spring, 1958): 33-9.

Tuck, D., *Crowell's Handbook of Faulkner*, 132-5.

Vickery, O. W., *Novels of William Faulkner*, 145-55.

Vickery, John B., "William Faulkner and Sir Philip Sidney," *MLN* 70 (May, 1955): 349-50.

Volpe, E. L., *Reader's Guide to William Faulkner*, 174-84.

Waggoner, H. H., *William Faulkner*, 121-32, 145-7.

Weisgerber, J., *Faulkner and Dostoevsky*, 231-6.

Wittenberg, J. B., *Faulkner*, 130-41.

THE REIVERS

Adams, R. P., *Faulkner*, 169-70.

Beck, Warren, "Told with Gusto," *VQR* 38 (Autumn, 1962): 681-5. Also in Beck, W., *Faulkner*, 660-4.

Bell, Haney H., Jr., "The Relative Maturity of Lucius Priest and Ike McCaslin," *Aegis* 2 (1973): 15-21.

Bradford, M. E., "What Grandfather Said: The Social Testimony of Faulkner's THE REIVERS," *OccasionalR* 1 (Feb., 1974): 5-15.

Brooks, C., *William Faulkner*, 349-68, 446.

Brown, Calvin S., "Faulkner's Three-in-One Bridge in THE REIVERS," *NConL* 1, ii (Mar., 1971): 8-10.

Brylowski, W., *Faulkner's Olympian Laugh*, 215-19.

Carothers, James B., "The Road to THE REIVERS," in Fowler, D., and A. J. Abadie, eds., *"A Cosmos of My Own,"* 95-124.

Cronin, Mary A., "Mississippi Revisited," *Lit* No. 5 (1964): 11-14.

Devlin, Albert J., "THE REIVERS: Readings in Social Psychology," *MissQ* 25 (Summer, 1972): 327-37.

Everett, W. K., *Faulkner's Art and Characters*, 69-73.

Gold, J., *William Faulkner*, 174-87.

Gooneratne, Margaret, "William Faulkner and THE REIVERS," *EB* 5 (June, 1980): 20-3.

Griffith, Benjamin W., "Faulkner's Archaic Titles and the SECOND SHEPHERD'S PLAY," *NMW* 4, ii (Fall, 1971): 62-3.

Harwick, Robert D., "Humor in the Novels of William Faulkner," *DA* 26 (1965): 1646 (Nebraska).

Hoffman, F. J., *William Faulkner*, 115-17.

Howe, I., *William Faulkner*, 3rd ed., 295-300.

Howell, Elmo, "In Ole Mississippi: Faulkner's Reminiscence," *KM* (1965): 77-81.

Kerr, Elizabeth M., "THE REIVERS: The Golden Book of Yoknapatawpha County," *MFS* 13, i (Spring, 1967): 95-113.

Leary, L., *William Faulkner of Yoknapatawpha County*, 185-90.

McCarron, William E., "Shakespeare, Faulkner, and Ned William McCaslin," *NConL* 7, v (Nov., 1977): 8-9.

Mellard, J. M., "Faulkner's 'Golden Book': THE REIVERS as Romantic Comedy," *BuR* 13, iii (Dec., 1965): 19-31.

Millgate, M., *Achievement of William Faulkner*, 253-8.

Moses, Edwin, "Faulkner's THE REIVERS: The Art of Acceptance," *MissQ* 27, iii (Summer, 1974): 307-18.

Muehl, Lois, "Faulkner's Humor in Three Novels and One 'Play'," *LC* 34 (Spring, 1968): 78-93.

Mueller, William R., "THE REIVERS: William Faulkner's Valediction," *ChC* 80 (Sept. 4, 1963): 1079-81.

Prasad, V. R. N., "The Pilgrim and the Picaro: A Study of Faulkner's THE BEAR and THE REIVERS," in Mukherjee, Sujit, and D.V.K. Raghavacharyulu, eds., *Indian Essays in American Literature: Papers in Honour of Robert E. Spiller*, Bombay: Popular Prakashan, 1969, 215-21.

Rossky, William, "THE REIVERS and HUCKLEBERRY FINN: Faulkner and Twain," *HLQ* 28 (Aug., 1965): 373-87.

_____, "THE REIVERS: Faulkner's TEMPEST," *MissQ* 18 (Spring, 1965): 82-93. Also in Wagner, L. W., ed., *William Faulkner*, 358-69.

Shepherd, Allen, "Code and Comedy in Faulkner's THE REIVERS," *LWU* 6 (Mar., 1973): 43-51.

Smith, Gerald J., "Medicine Made Palatable: An Aspect of Humor in THE REIVERS," *NMW* 8 (Fall, 1975): 58-62.

Stafford, William T., "'Some Homer of the Cotton Fields': Faulkner's Use of the Mule Early and Late (SARTORIS and THE REIVERS)," *PLL* 5 (Spring, 1969): 190-6.

Stewart, Marilyn G., "The Festive Irony of Carnival: Comic Affirmation in DON QUIXOTE, THE BROTHERS KARAMAZOV, and THE REIVERS," *DAI* 41, ix (Mar., 1981): 4022A.

Swiggart, P., *Art of Faulkner's Novels*, 207-14.

Tanner, Gale, "Sentimentalism and THE REIVERS: A Reply to Ben Merchant Vorpahl," *NMW* 9, i (Spring, 1976): 50-8.

Thompson, L., *William Faulkner*, 14-15.

Travis, Mildred K., "Echoes of PIERRE in THE REIVERS," *NConL* 3, ii (Sept., 1973): 11-13.

Tuck, D., *Crowell's Handbook of Faulkner*, 121-4.

Vickery, O. W., *Novels of William Faulkner*, 228-39.

Volpe, E. L., *Reader's Guide to William Faulkner*, 343-9.

Vorpahl, Ben M., "Moonlight at Ballenbaugh's Time and Imagination in THE REIVERS," *SLJ* 1, ii (Spring, 1969): 3-26.

Weisgerber, J., *Faulkner and Dostoevsky*, 344-7.

Williams, D., *Faulkner's Women*, 227-41.

Wittenberg, J. B., *Faulkner*, 236-46.

REQUIEM FOR A NUN

Adams, R. P., *Faulkner*, 157-8.

Babbage, Stuart B., *The Mark of Cain: Studies in Literature and Theology*, Grand Rapids: William B. Eerdmans, 1966, 75-7.

Baker, Carlos, "William Faulkner: The Doomed and the Damned," in Bode, C., ed., *Young Rebel in American Literature*, 163-6.

Baker, James R., "Ideas and Queries," *Faulkner Studies* 1 (Spring, 1952): 4-7.

Beck, Warren, "REQUIEM FOR A NUN," in Beck, W., *Faulkner*, 583-635.

Brooks, C., *William Faulkner*, 138-40, 394-5, 449-51.

Broughton, Panthea R., "REQUIEM FOR A NUN: No Part in Rationality," *SoR* 8, iv (Oct., 1972): 749-62.

Brown, William R., "Faulkner's Paradox in Pathology and Salvation: SANCTUARY, LIGHT IN AUGUST, REQUIEM FOR A NUN," *TSLL* 9 (1967): 429-49.

Brylowski, W., *Faulkner's Olympian Laugh*, 173-83.

Degenfelder, E. Pauline, "The Four Faces of Temple Drake: Faulkner's SANCTUARY, REQUIEM FOR A NUN, and the Two Film Adaptations," *AQ* 28, v (Winter, 1976): 544-60.

English, H. M., "REQUIEM FOR A NUN," *Furioso* 7 (Winter, 1952): 60-3.

Everett, W. K., *Faulkner's Art and Characters*, 73-7.

Gardiner, H. C., "Two Southern Tales," *In All Conscience*, 128-9. Also in *America* (Oct. 6, 1951): 18.

Geismar, M., *New York Post* (Sept. 23, 1951). Also in *American Moderns*, 93-5.

Giermanski, James R., "William Faulkner's Use of the Confessional," *Ren* 21 (Spring, 1969): 119-23, 166.

Gold, J., *William Faulkner*, 94-110.

Graham, Philip, "Patterns in Faulkner's SANCTUARY and REQUIEM FOR A NUN," *TSL* 8 (1963): 39-46.

Guerard, Albert L., "REQUIEM FOR A NUN: An Examination," *HarvardA* 135 (Nov., 1951): 19, 41-2.

Gwynn, F. L., and J. L. Blotner, eds., *Faulkner in the University*.

Hamblen, Abigail A., "Faulkner's Pillar of Endurance: SANCTUARY and REQUIEM FOR A NUN," *MQ* 6 (Summer, 1965): 369-75.

Haugh, R. F., "Faulkner's Corrupt Temple," *ESA* 4 (Mar., 1961): 7-16.

Hawkins, E. O., Jr., "Jane Cook and Cecilia Farmer," *MissQ* 18 (Fall, 1965): 248-51.

Heilman, Robert B., "Schools for Girls," *SR* 60 (April-June, 1952): 304-9.

Hoffman, F. J., *William Faulkner*, 109-11.

Holmes, Edward M., "Requiem for a Scarlet Nun," *Costerus* 5 (1972): 35-4.

Howe, I., *William Faulkner*, 105-7, 114-15.

Jacobs, Robert D., "William Faulkner: The Passion and the Penance," in Rubin, L. D., Jr., and R. D. Jacobs, eds., *South*, 173-4.

Kinney, Arthur F., "Faulkner and Flaubert," *JML* 6 (April, 1977): 238-46.

Leary, L., *William Faulkner of Yoknapatawpha County*, 121-5.

McHaney, Thomas N., "Faulkner Borrows from the Mississippi Guide," *MissQ* 19 (Summer, 1966): 116-20.

Millgate, M., *Achievement of William Faulkner*, 221-6.

_____, "Faulkner's First Trilogy: SARTORIS, SANCTUARY, and REQUIEM FOR A NUN," in Fowler, D., and A. J. Abadie, eds., *Fifty Years of Yoknapatawpha*, 90-109.

_____, *William Faulkner*, 96-8.

Milum, Richard A., "Faulkner and the Cavalier Tradition: The French Bequest," *AL* 45 (Jan., 1974): 580-9.

O'Connor, W. V., *Tangled Fire of William Faulkner*, 157-9.

Peckham, Morse, "The Place of Sex in the Work of William Faulkner," *StwC* 14 (Fall, 1974): 1-20.

Polk, Noel, "Alec Holston's Lock and the Founding of Jefferson," *MissQ* 24, iii (Summer, 1971): 247-69.

_____, "Faulkner's 'The Jail' and the Meaning of Cecilia Farmer," *MissQ* 25 (Summer, 1972): 305-25.

_____, *Faulkner's REQUIEM FOR A NUN: A Critical Study*, Bloomington: Indiana Un. Pr., 1981.

_____, "The Nature of Sacrifice: REQUIEM FOR A NUN and A FABLE," *FaSt* 1 (1980): 100-11. Also in Cox, L. H., ed., *William Faulkner*, 369-93.

_____, "Nun out of Habit: Nancy Monnigoe, Gavin Stevens, and REQUIEM FOR A NUN," *RANAM* 13 (1980): 64-75.

_____, "A Textual and Critical Study of William Faulkner's REQUIEM FOR A NUN," *DAI* 32 (1971): 980A (S.C.).

Powers, L. H., *Faulkner's Yoknapatawpha Comedy*, 204-17.

Richardson, K. E., *Force and Faith in the Novels of William Faulkner*, 150-4.

Ruppersburg, Hugh M., "The Narrative Structure of Faulkner's REQUIEM FOR A NUN," *MissQ* 31 (Summer, 1978): 387-406.

Samway, Patrick, S. J., "The Rebounding Images of Faulkner's SANCTUARY and REQUIEM FOR A NUN," *RANAM* 13 (1980): 90-108.

Seyppel, J., *William Faulkner*, 85-7.

Simpson, Louis, "Isaac McCaslin and Temple Drake: The Fall of New World Man," in Sanford, D. E., ed., *Nine Essays in Modern Literature*, 101-6.

Slatoff, W. J., *Quest for Failure*, 208-10.

Swiggart, P., *Art of Faulkner's Novels*, 181-4.

Thompson, L., *William Faulkner*, 117-32, 198-9.

Tuck, D., *Crowell's Handbook of Faulkner*, 115-20.

Ulrey, Pamela A., "Faulkner's SANCTUARY and REQUIEM FOR A NUN: Songs of Innocence and Experience," *DA* 24 (1963): 2043-4 (Cornell).

Vickery, Olga W., "Gavin Stevens: From Rhetoric to Dialectic," *Faulkner Studies* 2 (Spring, 1953): 1-4.

_____, *Novels of William Faulkner*, 114-23.

Volpe, E. L., *Reader's Guide to William Faulkner*, 265-81.

Waggoner, H. H., *William Faulkner*, 219-25.

Watkins, F. C., *Flesh and the Word*, 260-2, 263-4.

Weisgerber, J., *Faulkner and Dostoevsky*, 287-301.

West, Ray B., Jr., "William Faulkner: Artist and Moralist," *WR* 16 (Winter, 1952): 162-7.

Wilson, Paule A., "Faulkner and Camus: REQUIEM FOR A NUN," *Ody* 3, ii (April, 1979): 3-9.

Wittenberg, J. B., *Faulkner*, 216-20.

SANCTUARY

Adamowski, T. H., "Faulkner's Popeye: The 'Other' a Self," *CrevAS* 8 (1977): 36-51. Also in Canfield, J. D., ed., *Twentieth Century Interpretations of SANCTUARY*, 32-48.

Adams, R. P., *Faulkner*, 59-71.

Angelius, Judith W., "Temple's Provocative Quest: Or, What Really Happened at the Old Frenchman Place," *NMW* 10, ii (Winter, 1977): 74-9.

Backman, M., *Faulkner*, 41-9.

Bassett, John E., "SANCTUARY: Personal Fantasies and Social Fictions," *SCR* 13, i (Fall, 1981): 131-2.

Beck, Warren, "Faulkner: A Preface and a Letter," *YR* 52 (Autumn, 1962): 157-60.

_____, "Realist and Regionalist," in Beck, W., *Faulkner*, 213-63.

_____, "The Transformation of SANCTUARY," in Beck, W., *Faulkner*, 191-213.

Bergel, Lienhard, "Faulkner's SANCTUARY," *Expl* 6 (Dec., 1947): Item 20.

Borgström, Greta I., "The Roaring Twenties and William Faulkner's SANCTUARY," *MSpr* 62 (1968): 237-48.

Brooks, Cleanth, "Faulkner's SANCTUARY: The Discovery of Evil," *SR* 71 (Winter, 1963): 1-24. Also in *William Faulkner*, 116-40, 387-98.

_____, *Hidden God*, 25-8. Also in Barth, J. R., S. J., ed., *Religious Perspectives in Faulkner's Fiction*, 59-62.

Brown, Calvin S., "SANCTUARY: From Confrontation to Peaceful Void," *Mosaic* 7, i (Fall, 1973): 75-95. Also in Collins, R. G., and K. McRobbie, eds., *Novels of William Faulkner*, 75-95.

Brown, James, "Shaping the World of SANCTUARY," *UKCR* 25 (Winter, 1958): 137-42.

Brown, William R., "Faulkner's Paradox in Pathology and Salvation: SANCTUARY, LIGHT IN AUGUST, REQUIEM FOR A NUN," *TSLL* 9 (Autumn, 1967): 429-49.

Brylowski, W., *Faulkner's Olympian Laugh*, 97-102.

Burgum, E. B., *Novel and the World's Dilemma*, 217-20.

Campbell, Harry M., and J. P. Pilkington, "Faulkner's SANCTUARY," *Expl* 4 (June, 1946): Item 61.

_____, and R. E. Foster, *William Faulkner*, 61-2.

Canfield, J. D., ed., *Twentieth Century Interpretations of SANCTUARY*.

Cantwell, Robert, "Faulkner's 'Popeye'," *Nation* 186 (Feb. 15, 1958): 140-1, 148.

Castille, Philip, "'There Was a Queen' and Faulkner's Narcissa Sartoris," *MissQ* 28 (Summer, 1975): 307-15.

Chapple, Richard L., "Character Parallels in CRIME AND PUNISHMENT and SANCTUARY," *GSlav* 2, i (Spring, 1976): 5-14.

Chase, R., "SANCTUARY vs. THE TURN OF THE SCREW," in *American Novel and Its Tradition*, 237-41.

Church, M., "William Faulkner: Myth and Duration," *Time and Reality*, 237-8.

Cole, Douglas, "Faulkner's SANCTUARY: Retreat from Responsibility," *WHR* 14 (Summer, 1960): 291-8.

Collins, Carvel, "Nathanael West's THE DAY OF THE LOCUST and SANCTUARY," *Faulkner Studies* 2 (Summer, 1953): 23-4.

_____, "A Note on SANCTUARY," *HarvardA* 135 (Nov., 1951): 16.

Cook, Sylvia J., "Faulkner's Celebration of the Poor White Paradox," *From Tobacco Road to Route 66*, 47-50.

Creighton, Joanne V., "Self-Destructive Evil in SANCTUARY," *TCL* 18, iv (Oct., 1972): 259-70.

Cypher, James R., "The Tangled Sexuality of Temple Drake," *AL* 19 (Fall, 1962): 243-52.

Degenfelder, E. Pauline, "The Four Faces of Temple Drake: Faulkner's SANCTUARY, REQUIEM FOR A NUN, and the Two Film Adaptations," *AQ* 28, v (Winter, 1976): 544-60.

Esslinger, Pat M., et al., "No Spinach in SANCTUARY," *MFS* 18 (Winter, 1972-73): 555-8.

Everett, W. K., *Faulkner's Art and Characters*, 77-83.

Faulkner, William, "Introduction," in *SANCTUARY*, N.Y.: Modern Library, 1931. Also in *Essays, Speeches and Public*

Letters by William Faulkner, ed. James B. Meriwether, N. Y.: Random House, 1965, 176-8.

Fiedler, L., *Love and Death in the American Novel*, 311-13.

Fletcher, John, "Faulkner, GULLIVER, and the Problem of Evil," 239-47 in Birn, Randi, and Karen Gould, eds., *Orion Blinded: Essays on Claude Simon*, Lewisburg; London: Bucknell Un. Pr., 1981.

Flynn, Robert, "The Dialectic of SANCTUARY," *MFS* 2 (Autumn, 1956): 109-13.

Ford, Daniel G., "Comments on William Faulkner's Temporal Vision in SANCTUARY, THE SOUND AND THE FURY, LIGHT IN AUGUST, ABSALOM, ABSALOM!" *SoQ* 15, iii (1977): 283-90.

_____, "Uses of Time in Four Novels by William Faulkner," *DAI* 35 (1974): 1654A (Auburn).

Foster, Ruel, "Dream as Symbolic Act in Faulkner," *Per* 2 (Summer, 1949): 191-4.

Frazier, David L., "Gothicism in SANCTUARY: The Black Pall and the Crap Table," *MFS* 2 (Autumn, 1956): 114-24. Also in Canfield, J. D., ed., *Twentieth Century Interpretations of SANCTUARY*, 49-58.

Geismar, M., *Writers in Crisis*, 159-61.

Glicksberg, Charles I., "Faulkner's World of Love and Sex," *Sexual Revolution in Modern American Literature*, 99-101.

Gold, Joseph, "No Refuge: Faulkner's SANCTUARY," *UR* 33 (Dec., 1966): 129-35.

Gossett, L. Y., *Violence in Recent Southern Fiction*, 34-5.

Graham, Philip, "Patterns in Faulkner's SANCTUARY and REQUIEM FOR A NUN," *TSL* 8 (1963): 39-46.

Grossman, Joel M., "The Source of Faulkner's 'Less Oft is Peace'," *AL* 47, iii (Nov., 1975): 436-8.

Guerard, Albert J., "The Misogynous Vision as High Art: Faulkner's SANCTUARY," *SoR* 12, ii (April, 1976): 215-31. Also in *Triumph of the Novel*, 120-35.

Gwynn, F. L., and J. L. Blotner, eds., *Faulkner in the University*.

Hamblen, Abigail A., "Faulkner's Pillar of Endurance: SANCTUARY and REQUIEM FOR A NUN," *MQ* 6 (Summer, 1965): 369-75.

Hardt, John S., "And Faulkner Nodded: Calvin Coolidge in SANCTUARY," *NMW* 12, i (1979): 30-1.

Hashiguchi, Yasuo, "Popeye Extenuated," *KAL* No. 5 (1962): 1-9.

Haugh, R. F., "Faulkner's Corrupt Temple," *ESA* 4 (Mar., 1961): 7-16.

Hoffman, F. J., *William Faulkner*, 66-8.

Howe, I., *William Faulkner*, 57-61, 192-9.

Howell, Elmo, "The Quality of Evil in Faulkner's SANCTUARY," *TSL* 4 (1959): 99-107.

Hume, Robert D., "Gothic Versus Romantic: A Revaluation of the Gothic Novel," *PMLA* 84, ii (Mar., 1969): 288.

Hurd, Myles, "Faulkner's Horace Benbow: The Burden of Characterization and the Confusion of Meaning in SANCTUARY," *C1AJ* 23, iv (1980): 416-30.

Jacobs, Robert D., "William Faulkner: The Passion and the Penance," in Rubin, L. D., Jr., and R. D. Jacobs, eds., *South*, 155-7.

Kauffman, Linda, "The Madam and the Midwife: Reba Rivers and Sairy Gamp," *MissQ* 30 (Summer, 1977): 395-401.

Keefer, T. Frederick, "William Faulkner's SANCTUARY: A Myth Examined," *TCL* 15, ii (July, 1969): 97-104.

Kerr, Elizabeth M., "The Creative Evolution of SANCTUARY," *FaSt* 1 (1980): 14-28.

_____, *William Faulkner's Gothic Domain*, 88-106.

Kinney, Arthur F., "Faulkner and Flaubert," *JML* 6 (April, 1977): 232-7.

_____, *Faulkner's Narrative Poetics*, 177-94.

_____, "SANCTUARY: Style as Vision," in Canfield, J. D., ed., *Twentieth Century Interpretations of SANCTUARY*, 109-19. From Kinney, A. F., *Faulkner's Narrative Poetics*, 177-94.

Kubie, Lawrence S., "Literature of Horror: SANCTUARY," *SRL* 11 (Oct. 20, 1934): 218, 224-5. Also in Warren, R. P., ed., *Faulkner*, 137-46. Also, as "William Faulkner's SANCTUARY: An Analysis," in Canfield, J. D., ed., *Twentieth Century Interpretations of SANCTUARY*, 25-31.

Leary, L., *William Faulkner of Yoknapatawpha County*, 114-21.

Lisca, Peter, "Some New Light on Faulkner's SANCTUARY," *Faulkner Studies* 2 (Spring, 1953): 5-9.

Lyday, Charles L., "Faulkner's *Commedia*: An Interpretation of THE SOUND AND THE FURY, SANCTUARY, AS I LAY DYING, and LIGHT IN AUGUST," *DAI* 39 (1978): 886A-87A.

Lyday, Lance, "SANCTUARY: Faulkner's INFERNO," *MissQ* 35, iii (1982): 243-53.

Malraux, André, "A Preface for Faulkner's SANCTUARY," *YFS* No. 10 (Fall, 1952): 92-4.

_____, "Preface to William Faulkner's SANCTUARY," *SoR* 10, iv (Oct., 1974): 889-91. [Tr. By Violet M. Horvath.]

Mason, Robert L., "A Defense of Faulkner's SANCTUARY," *GaR* 21 (Winter, 1967): 430-8.

Massey, Linton, "Notes on the Unrevised Galleys of Faulkner's SANCTUARY," *SB* 8 (1956): 195-208.

McHaney, Thomas L., "SANCTUARY and Frazer's Slain Kings," *MissQ* 24, iii (Summer, 1971): 223-45. Also in Canfield, J. D., ed., *Twentieth Century Interpretations of SANCTUARY*, 79-92.

Meriwether, James B., "Some Notes on the Text of Faulkner's SANCTUARY," *PBSA* 55 (1961): 192-206.

Miller, James E., "SANCTUARY: Yoknapatawpha's Waste Land," in French, W., ed., *Twenties*, 249-67. Also in Baldwin, K. H., and D. K. Kirby, eds., *Individual and Community*, 137-59.

Millgate, M., *Achievement of William Faulkner*, 113-23. Also in Cox, L. H., ed., *William Faulkner*, 222-39.

_____, "'A Fair Job': A Study of Faulkner's SANCTUARY," *REL* 4, iv (Oct., 1963): 47-62.

_____, "Faulkner's First Trilogy: SARTORIS, SANCTUARY, and REQUIEM FOR A NUN," in Fowler, D., and A. J. Abadie, eds., *Fifty Years of Yoknapatawpha*, 90-109.

_____, *William Faulkner*, 41-4.

Monteiro, George, "Initiation and the Moral Sense in Faulkner's SANCTUARY," *MLN* 73 (Nov., 1958): 500-4.

Morell, Giliane, "The Last Scene of SANCTUARY," *MissQ* 25 (Summer, 1972): 351-5.

Nishiyama, Tamotsu, "What Really Happens in SANCTUARY?" *SELit* 42 (1966): 235-43.

O'Connor, William Van, "A Short View of Faulkner's SANCTUARY," *Faulkner Studies* 1 (Fall, 1952): 33-9.

_____, *Tangled Fire of William Faulkner*, 55-64.

_____, *William Faulkner*, 17-19. Also in O'Connor, W. V., ed., *Seven Modern American Novelists*, 131-3.

Ono, Kiyoyuki, "Sanctuary of the Heart: An Interpretation of SANCTUARY," *WiF* 4, ii (July, 1982): 63-78.

Page, S. R., *Faulkner's Women*, 71-90.

Perry, J. Douglas, Jr., "Gothic as Vortex: The Form of Horror in Capote, Faulkner, and Styron," *MFS* 19, ii (Summer, 1973): 159-62.

Petesch, Donald A., "Temple Drake: Faulkner's Mirror for the Social Order," *SAF* 7 (Spring, 1979): 37-48.

Phillips, Gene, "Faulkner and the Film: Two Versions of SANCTUARY," *LFQ* 1, iii (July, 1973): 263-73.

Pikoulis, J., *Art of William Faulkner*, 48-65.

Pilkington, J., *Heart of Yoknapatawpha*, 111-34.

Powers, L. H., *Faulkner's Yoknapatawpha Comedy*, 73-88.

Reed, J. W., Jr., *Faulkner's Narrative*, 58-73.

Richardson, K. E., *Force and Faith in the Novels of William Faulkner*, 77-80, 116-17.

Ruoff, Gene, "Faulkner: The Way Out of the Wasteland," in French, W., ed., *Twenties*, 241-4.

Samway, Patrick, S. J., "The Rebounding Images of Faulkner's SANCTUARY and REQUIEM FOR A NUN," *RANAM* 13 (1980): 90-108.

Schmull, Robert, "Faulkner's SANCTUARY: The Last Laugh of Innocence," *NMW* 6, iii (Winter, 1974): 73-80.

Schoeter, James, "Faulkner's SANCTUARY: Between the Indignation and the Surprise," *Etudes de Lettres*, 2, i (1979): 55-71.

Seyppel, J., *William Faulkner*, 52-3.

Simpson, Louis, "Isaac McCaslin and Temple Drake: The Fall of New World Man," in Sanford, D. E., ed., *Nine Essays in Modern Literature*, 97-101.

Slabey, Robert M., "Faulkner's SANCTUARY," *Expl* 22 (1963): Item 45.

Slatoff, W. J., *Quest for Failure*, 210-11.

Stein, William B., "The Wake in Faulkner's SANCTUARY," *MLN* 75 (Jan., 1960): 28-9.

Swiggart, P., *Art of Faulkner's Novels*, 29-31, 208-11.

Tallack, Douglas G., "William Faulkner and the Tradition of Tough-Guy Fiction," in Landru, L. N., et al., eds., *Dimensions of Detective Fiction*, 247-64 passim.

Tate, Allen, "Faulkner's SANCTUARY and the Southern Myth," *VQR* 44 (Summer, 1968): 418-27.

Thompson, L., *William Faulkner*, 99-116, 197-8.

Toles, George, "The Space Between: A Study of Faulkner's SANCTUARY," *TSLL* 22, i (Spring, 1980): 22-47. Also in Canfield, J. D., ed., *Twentieth Century Interpretations of SANCTUARY*, 120-8.

Tuck, D., *Crowell's Handbook of Faulkner*, 40-5.

Ulrey, Pamela A., "Faulkner's SANCTUARY and REQUIEM FOR A NUN: Songs of Innocence and Experience," *DA* 24 (1963): 2043-4 (Cornell).

Vickery, Olga W., "Crime and Punishment: SANCTUARY," in Canfield, J. D., ed., *Twentieth Century Interpretations of SANCTUARY*, 15-23. Also in Vickery, O. W., *Novels of William Faulkner*, 103-14.

————, *Novels of William Faulkner*, 103-14. Also in Warren, R. P., ed., *Faulkner*, 127-36.

Volpe, E. L., *Reader's Guide to William Faulkner*, 140-51.

Waggoner, H. H., *William Faulkner*, 88-100, 118-20.

Wasiolek, Edward, "Dostoevsky and SANCTUARY," *MLN* 74 (Feb., 1959): 114-17.

Watkins, Floyd C., "The Word and the Deed in Faulkner's First Great Novels," in Watkins, Floyd C., *The Flesh and the Word:*

Eliot, Hemingway, Faulkner, Nashville: Vanderbilt Un. Pr., 1971, 181-202. Also in Wagner, L. W., ed., *William Faulkner*, 213-30.

Way, Brian, "William Faulkner," *CritQ* 3 (Spring, 1961): 44-7.

Weisgerber, J., *Faulkner and Dostoevsky*, 195-203.

Williams, Aubrey, "William Faulkner's 'Temple' of Innocence," *RIP* 47, iii (Oct., 1960): 51-67. Also in Canfield, J. D., ed., *Twentieth Century Interpretations of SANCTUARY*, 59-69.

Williams, D., *Faulkner's Women*, 127-56.

————, "The Profaned Temple," in Canfield, J. D., ed., *Twentieth Century Interpretations of SANCTUARY*, 93-107. From Williams, D., *Faulkner's Women*, 129-30, 136-53.

Wilson, C., *Strength to Dream*, 36-8.

Wittenberg, J. B., *Faulkner*, 89-102.

Yonce, Margaret, "'His True Penelope was Flaubert': MADAME BOVARY and SANCTUARY," *MissQ* 29 (Summer, 1976): 439-42.

SARTORIS

Adamowski, T. H., "Bayard Sartoris: Mourning and Melancholia," *L&P* 23 (1973): 149-58.

Adams, R. P., *Faulkner*, 49-56.

Backman, M., *Faulkner*, 3-12.

————, "Faulkner's Sick Heroes: Bayard Sartoris and Quentin Compson," *MFS* 2 (Autumn, 1956): 96-100.

Beach, J. W., *American Fiction*, 127-8.

Bedell, G. C., *Kierkegaard and Faulkner*, 115-21.

Bell, Haney H., "A Reading of Faulkner's SARTORIS and THERE WAS A QUEEN," *Forum* (Texas) 4 (Fall-Winter, 1965): 23-6.

Blair, Arthur H., "Bayard Sartoris: Suicidal or Foolhardy?" *SLJ* 15, i (Fall, 1982): 55-60.

Blotner, Joseph, "Romantic Elements in Faulkner," in Bornstein, G., ed., *Romantic and Modern*, 215-19.

————, "William Faulkner's Essay on the Composition of SARTORIS," *YULG* 47 (1972): 121-4.

Brooks, C., *William Faulkner*, 100-15, 384-6, 450-1.

————, *William Faulkner: Toward Yoknapatawpha and Beyond*, 388-91, 392-5.

Brown, Calvin S., "Faulkner's Idiot Boy: The Source of a Simile in SARTORIS," *AL* 44, iii (Nov., 1972): 474-6.

Bruccoli, Matthew, "A Source for SARTORIS?" *MissQ* 20 (1967): 163.

Brylowski, W., *Faulkner's Olympian Laugh*, 51-8.

Burelbach, Frederick M., "Two Family Names: Faulkner and Sartoris," *LOS* 4 (1977): 81-95.

Cantwell, Robert, "Introduction," in SARTORIS, N.Y.: Signet Bks., 1953, vii-xxv.

Carnes, Frank F., "On the Aesthetics of Faulkner's Fiction," *DA* 29 (1968): 894A-5A (Vanderbilt).

Carpenter, Richard C., "Faulkner's SARTORIS," *Expl* 14 (April, 1956): Item 41.

Castille, Philip, "'There Was a Queen' and Faulkner's Narcissa Sartoris," *MissQ* 28 (Summer, 1975): 307-15.

Church, M., "William Faulkner: Myth and Duration," *Time and Reality*, 232-3.

Collins, Carvel, "Are These Mandalas?" *L&P* 3, v (1953): 3-6.

Connolly, Thomas, in Krause, S. J., ed., *Essays on Determinism*, 37-9.

Corrington, John W., "Escape Into Myth: The Long Dying of Bayard Sartoris," *RANAM* 4 (1971): 31-47.

Cosgrove, William, "The 'Soundless Moiling' of Bayard Sartoris," *ArQ* 35 (Summer, 1979): 165-9.

Davidson, Donald, *Nashville Tennessean* (April 14, 1929). Also in *GaR* 20 (Winter, 1966): 459-62.

Dennis, Stephen N., "The Making of SARTORIS: A Description and Discussion of the Manuscript and Composite Typescript of William Faulkner's Third Novel," *DAI* 31 (1970): 384A (Cornell).

Devlin, Albert, "SARTORIS: Rereading the MacCallum Episode," *TCL* 17, ii (April, 1971): 83-90.

Dillon, Richard T., "Some Sources for Faulkner's Version of the First Air War," *AL* 44, iv (Jan., 1973): 629-37.

Eitner, Walter H., "The Aristoi of Yoknapatawpha County," *NConL* 7, iv (Sept., 1977): 10-11.

Everett, W. K., *Faulkner's Art and Characters*, 83-94.

Geismar, M., *Writers in Crisis*, 146-7.

Gold, Joseph, "William Faulkner's 'One Compact Thing'," *TCL* 8, i (April, 1962): 7-9.

Gwynn, F. L., and J. L. Blotner, eds., *Faulkner in the University*.

Harley, Marta P., "Faulkner's SARTORIS and the Legend of Rinaldo and Bayard," *AN&Q* 18, vi (1980): 92-3.

Hirano, Nobuyuki, "Reconsideration of Moral Order and Disorder in Faulkner's Works," *HJAS* 8, i (Sept., 1967): 7-11.

Hoffman, F. J., *William Faulkner*, 44-8.

Howe, I., *William Faulkner*, 12-13, 33-41.

Howell, Elmo, "Faulkner's SARTORIS," *Expl* 17 (Feb., 1959): Item 33.

_____, "Faulkner's SARTORIS and the Mississippi Country People," *SFQ* 25 (June, 1961): 136-46.

Jacobs, Robert D., "William Faulkner: The Passion and the Penance," in Rubin, L. D., Jr., and R. D. Jacobs, eds., *South*, 143-6.

Jehlen, M., *Class and Character in Faulkner's South*, 26-41.

Keiser, Merle W., "Faulkner's SARTORIS: A Comprehensive Study," *DAI* 38 (1978): 7333A-34A.

_____, "FLAGS IN THE DUST and SARTORIS," in Fowler, D., and A. J. Abadie, eds., *Fifty Years of Yoknapatawpha*, 44-70.

Kerr, E. M., *William Faulkner's Gothic Domain*, 74-87.

Leary, L., *William Faulkner of Yoknapatawpha County*, 25-8.

Martin, Carter W., "Faulkner's SARTORIS: The Tailor Re-Tailored," *SCR* 6, ii (April, 1974): 56-9.

McDaniel, Linda E., "Horace Benbow: Faulkner's Endymion," *MissQ* 33 (Summer, 1980): 363-70.

_____, "Keats's Hyperion Myth: A Source for the Sartoris Myth," *MissQ* 34 (Summer, 1981): 325-33.

McDonald, Walter R., "Sartoris: The Dauntless Hero in Modern American Fiction," in Zyla, W. T., and W. M. Aycock, eds., *Modern American Fiction*, 107-12.

Miller, William, "Hardy, Falls, and Faulkner," *MissQ* 29, iii (Summer, 1976): 435-6.

Millgate, M., *Achievement of William Faulkner*, 76-85.

_____, "Faulkner's First Trilogy: SARTORIS, SANCTUARY, and REQUIEM FOR A NUN," in Fowler, D., and A. J. Abadie, eds., *Fifty Years of Yoknapatawpha*, 90-109.

_____, *William Faulkner*, 32-6.

Muehl, Lois, "Faulkner's Humor in Three Novels and One 'Play'," *LC* 34 (Spring, 1968): 78-93.

_____, "Form as Seen in Two Early Works by Faulkner," *LC* 38 (Spring, 1972): 147-57.

_____, "Word Choice and Choice Words in SARTORIS," *LC* 35 (Winter-Spring, 1969): 58-63.

Muir, Edward H., "A Footnote on SARTORIS and Some Speculation," *JML* 1 (1971): 389-93.

Mulqueen, James E., "Horace Benbow: Avatar of Faulkner's Marble Faun," *NMW* 9, ii (Fall, 1976): 88-96.

Nilon, Charles H., "Faulkner and the Negro," *UCSSLL* No. 8 (Sept., 1962): 70-3. Also in Nilon, C. H., *Faulkner and the Negro*, 70-3.

Nishiyama, Tamotsu, "SARTORIS," *KAL* No. 2 (May, 1959): 28-32.

O'Connor, W. V., *Tangled Fire of William Faulkner*, 33-6.

_____, "William Faulkner's Apprenticeship," *SWR* 38 (Winter, 1953): 12-14.

Page, Ralph, "Jon Sartoris: Friend or Foe," *ArQ* 23 (Spring, 1967): 27-33.

Page, S. R., *Faulkner's Women*, 34-42.

Pikoulis, J., *Art of William Faulkner*, 1-10.

Pilkington, J., *Heart of Yoknapatawpha*, 3-33.

Powers, L. H., *Faulkner's Yoknapatawpha Comedy*, 9-23.

Putzel, Max, "Faulkner's Trial Preface to SARTORIS: An Eclectic Text," *PBSA* 74 (Oct.-Dec., 1980): 361-78.

Richardson, H. E., *William Faulkner*, 167-84.

Richardson, K. E., *Force and Faith in the Novels of William Faulkner*, 20-5.

Rogers, Douglas G., "Faulkner's Treatment of Negro Characters in SARTORIS and THE UNVANQUISHED," *NDQ* 43, ii (Spring, 1975): 67-72.

Sartre, Jean-Paul, "William Faulkner's SARTORIS," *YFS* No. 10 (Fall, 1952): 95-9. Also in Sartre, J. P., *Literary and Philosophical Essays*, 73-8.

Scholes, Robert, "Myth and Manners in SARTORIS," *GaR* 16 (Summer, 1962): 195-201.

Seyppel, J., *William Faulkner*, 31-2.

Smart, G. K., *Religious Elements in Faulkner's Early Novels*.

Sorenson, Dale A., "Structure in William Faulkner's SARTORIS: The Contrast Between Psychological and Natural Time," *ArQ* 25, iii (Autumn, 1969): 263-70.

Spears, James E., "William Faulkner, Folklorist: A Note," *TFSB* 38 (Dec., 1972): 95-6.

Stafford, William T., "'Some Homer of the Cotton Fields': Faulkner's Use of the Mule Early and Late (SARTORIS and THE REIVERS)," *PLL* 5 (Spring, 1969): 190-6.

Stevens, Lauren R., "SARTORIS: Germ of the Apocalypse," *DR* 49, i (Spring, 1969): 80-7.

Swiggart, P., *Art of Faulkner's Novels*, 34-6.

Thompson, Lawrance, "Afterword," in SARTORIS, N.Y.: Signet Bks., 1964.

Tuck, D., *Crowell's Handbook of Faulkner*, 16-21.

Vickery, Olga W., "The Making of a Myth: SARTORIS," *WR* 22 (Spring, 1958): 209-19.

_____, *Novels of William Faulkner*, 15-27.

Volpe, E. L., *Reader's Guide to William Faulkner*, 66-76.

Waggoner, H. H., *William Faulkner*, 20-33.

Walker, Ronald G., "Death in the Sound of Their Name: Character Motivation in Faulkner's SARTORIS," *SHR* 7, iii (1973): 271-8.

Watkins, Floyd C., "The Unbearable and Unknowable Truth in Faulkner's First Three Novels," *Flesh and the Word*, 169-80.

Watson, James G., "'The Germ of My Aprocrypha': SARTORIS and the Search for Form," *Mosaic* 7, i (Fall, 1973): 15-33. Also in Collins, R. G., and K. McRobbie, eds., *Novels of William Faulkner*, 15-33.

Way, Brian, "William Faulkner," *CritQ* 3 (Spring, 1961): 43-4.

Williams, D., *Faulkner's Women*, 41-6.

Wittenberg, J. B., *Faulkner*, 61-73.

SNOPES Trilogy

Adams, Percy G., "Humor as Structure and Theme in Faulkner's Trilogy," *WSCL* 5, iii (Autumn, 1964): 205-12.

Adams, R. P., *Faulkner*, 158-61.

Arpad, Joseph J., "William Faulkner's Legendary Novels: The SNOPES Trilogy," *MissQ* 22, iii (Summer, 1969): 214-25. Also in Cox, L. H., ed., *William Faulkner*, 313-27.

Barth, J. R., "Faulkner and the SNOPES Trilogy," *America* 102 (Feb. 27, 1960): 638-40.

Beck, Warren, *Man in Motion: Faulkner's Trilogy*, Madison: Un. of Wisconsin Pr., 1961.

Belcamino, Gregory R., "Stylistic Decorum and Character in Faulkner's SNOPES Trilogy," *DAI* 43 (1982): 1970A.

Bell, Brenda H., "Mike Snope's Wife and the Critics: A Study in Bias," *PMPA* 5 (1980): 1-5.

Bigelow, Gordon E., "Faulkner's SNOPES Saga," *EJ* 49 (Dec., 1960): 595-605.

Brooks, Cleanth, "Gavin Stevens and the Chivalric Tradition," *UMSE* 15 (1978): 19-32.

Burelbach, Frederick M., "The Name of the Snake: A Family of Snopes," *LOS* 8 (1981): 125-46.

Carey, Glenn O., "William Faulkner: The Rise of the Snopeses," *STwC* No. 8 (Fall, 1971): 37-64.

Davis, Roger, L., "William Faulkner, V. K. Ratliff, and the Snopes Saga (1925-1940)," *DAI* 32 (1971): 3300A (U.C.L.A.).

Dirksen, Sherland N., "William Faulkner's Snopes Family: THE HAMLET, THE TOWN, and THE MANSION," *ESRS* 11, ii (Dec., 1962): 5-45.

Edwards, C. H., "A Conjecture on the Name *Snopes*," *NConL* 8, v (Nov., 1978): 9-10.

Farmer, Norman, Jr., "The Love Theme: A Principal Source of Thematic Unity in Faulkner's SNOPES Trilogy," *TCL* 8 (Oct., 1962-Jan., 1963): 111-23.

Farnham, James F., "Faulkner's Unsung Hero: Gavin Stevens," *ArQ* 21 (Summer, 1965): 115-32.

Friedman, Alan W., "Faulkner's Snopes Trilogy: Omniscience as Impressionism," *DeltaES* 3 (Nov., 1976): 125-51.

Geismar, M., "The Meaning of Faulkner's Humor," *American Moderns*, 101-6.

Gresset, Michel, "Homofaunie," *DeltaES* 3 (Nov., 1976): 85-93.

Hartt, J. N., *Lost Image of Man*, 89-92.

Haselswerdt, Marjorie B., "I'd Rather Be Ratliff: A Maslovian Study of Faulkner's SNOPES," *LitR* 24, ii (Winter, 1981): 308-27.

Hauck, Richard B., "The Prime Maniacal Risibility: William Faulkner," *Cheerful Nihilism*, 179-95.

Holman, C. Hugh, "Detached Laughter in the South," in Cohen, S. B., ed., *Comic Relief*, 92-4.

Howe, Irving, "Faulkner: End of a Road," *NRep* 141 (Dec. 7, 1959): 17-21.

Howell, Elmo, "The Meaning of 'Snopesism'," *SSJ* 31 (Spring, 1966): 223-5.

Hyman, S. E., *Standards*, 259-63.

Jacobs, Robert D., "Faulkner's Humor," in Rubin, L. D., Jr., ed., *Comic Imagination in American Literature*, 305-18.

Jehlen, M., *Class and Character in Faulkner's South*, 133-51.

Kerr, Elizabeth M., "Snopes," *WSCL* 1, ii (Spring-Summer, 1960): 66-84.

_____, *William Faulkner's Gothic Domain*, 184-219.

Kinney, A. F., *Faulkner's Narrative Poetics*, 252-9.

Kulseth, Leonard I., "Cincinnatus Among the Snopeses: The Role of Gavin Stevens," *BSUF* 10, i (Winter, 1969): 28-34.

Lawson, Lewis A., "The Grotesque-Comic in the SNOPES Trilogy," *L&P* 15 (Spring, 1965): 107-19.

Leaf, Mark, "William Faulkner's Snopes Trilogy: The South Evolves," in French, W., ed., *Fifties*, 51-62.

Leibowitz, Herbert A., "The Snopes Dilemma and the South," *UKCR* 28 (June, 1962): 273-84.

Létargez, Joseph, "William Faulkner's SNOPES Trilogy," *RLV* No. 5 (1961): 446-51.

Levine, Paul, "Love and Money in the SNOPES Trilogy," *CE* 23 (Dec., 1961): 196-203.

Longley, J. L., Jr., *Tragic Mask*, 41-9, 63-78, 150-64.

Maclure, Millar, "Snopes—A Faulkner Myth," *CanF* 39 (Feb., 1960): 245-50.

McDowell, Richard D., "Faulkner's Trilogy: A Revaluation," *DAI* 38 (1978): 5481A-82A.

McFarland, Holly, "The Mask Not Tragic ... Just Damned: The Women in Faulkner's Trilogy," *BSUF* 18, ii (Spring, 1977): 27-50.

Norris, Nancy R., "THE HAMLET, THE TOWN and THE MANSION: A Psychological Reading of the Snopes Trilogy," *Mosaic* 7, i (Fall, 1973): 213-35. Also in Collins, R. G., and K. McRobbie, eds., *Novels of William Faulkner*, 213-35.

_____, "William Faulkner's Trilogy," *DAI* 32 (1972): 6994A (Pa.).

Page, S. R., *Faulkner's Women*, 153-73.

Palmer, William J., "The Mechanistic World of SNOPES," *MissQ* 20 (1967): 185-94.

Payne, Ladell, "The Trilogy: Faulkner's Comic Epic in Prose," *SNNTS* 1, i (Spring, 1969): 27-37.

Petesch, Donald A., "Theme and Characterization in Faulkner's Snopes Trilogy," *DA* 29 (1969): 3618A-19A (Texas, Austin).

Podhoretz, N., "Faulkner in the Fifties: Snopesishness," *Doings and Undoings*, 24-9. Also in (slightly different form) *NY* 33 (June 1, 1957): 110.

Powell, Irma A., "Man in His Struggle: Structure, Technique, and Theme in Faulkner's Snopes Trilogy," *DAI* 31 (1970): 1287A-88A (Fla. State).

Rankin, Elizabeth D., "Chasing Spotted Horses: The Quest for Human Dignity in Faulkner's Snopes Trilogy," in Carey, Glenn O., ed., *Faulkner*, 139-56.

Renner, Charlotte, "Talking and Writing in Faulkner's SNOPES Trilogy," *SLJ* 15, i (Fall, 1982): 61-73.

Rice, Michael, "Myth and Legend: The Snopes Trilogy: THE HAMLET, THE TOWN and THE MANSION," *UES* 14, i (April, 1976): 18-22.

Richardson, K. E., *Force and Faith in the Novels of William Faulkner*, 118-29.

Richardson, W. M., "Snopesian Man," in Faris, Ralph M., ed., *Crisis and Consciousness*, Amsterdam: Gruner, 1977, 63-71.

Roberts, James L., "Snopeslore: THE HAMLET, THE TOWN, THE MANSION," *UKCR* 28 (Oct., 1961): 65-71.

Ross, Maude C., "Moral Values of the American Woman as Presented in Three Major American Authors," *DA* 25 (1965): 5262-3 (Texas).

Rubin, L. D., Jr., *Faraway Country*, 58-9.

Sharma, P. P., "The Snopes Theme in Faulkner's Larger Context," *IJAS* 1, iv (Nov., 1971): 33-41.

Smith, Gerald J., "A Note on the Origin of Flem Snopes," *NMW* 6, ii (Fall, 1973): 56-7.

Stonum, G. L., *Faulkner's Career*, 153-95.

Stroble, Woodrow, "Flem Snopes: A Crazed Mirror," in Carey, Glen D., ed., *Faulkner*, 195-212.

Sullivan, Walter, "Allen Tate, Flem Snopes, and the Last Years of William Faulkner," *Death by Melancholy*, 3-21.

Swiggart, P., *Art of Faulkner's Novels*, 195-202.

_____, "The SNOPES Trilogy," *SR* 68 (Spring, 1960): 319-25. Also in Litz, A. W., ed., *Modern American Fiction*, 194-200.

Trimmer, Joseph F., "V. K. Ratliff: A Portrait of the Artist in Motion," *MFS* 20, iv (Winter, 1974-75): 451-67.

Tuck, D., *Crowell's Handbook of Faulkner*, 72-94.

Wagner, Linda W., "The Last Books," *Hemingway and Faulkner*, 218-28.

Warne, Keith F., "Language in Faulkner's Trilogy: Truth and Fiction," *DAI* 41, xii (June, 1981): 5099A.

Watson, James G., "'The Snopes Dilemma': Morality and Amorality in Faulkner's SNOPES Trilogy," *DA* 29 (1968): 1237A-38A (Pittsburgh).

_____, *Snopes Dilemma*.

White, John O., "The Existential Absurd in Faulkner's Snopes Trilogy," *DAI* 32 (1971): 3336A (Ariz. State).

SOLDIERS' PAY

Adams, R. P., *Faulkner*, 34-40.

Beach, J. W., *American Fiction*, 125-6.

Bosha, Francis J., "Faulkner's Early Editors: On Edith Brown, Grace Hudson, and SOLDIERS' PAY," *AN&Q* 17, viii (April, 1979): 125-7.

Brooks, Cleanth, "Faulkner's First Novel," *SoR* 6, iv (Oct., 1970): 1056-74.

_____, *William Faulkner: Toward Yoknapatawpha and Beyond*, 67-99, 366-70.

Bross, Addison C., "SOLDIERS' PAY and the Art of Aubrey Beardsley," *AQ* 19 (Spring, 1967): 3-23.

Brylowski, W., *Faulkner's Olympian Laugh*, 43-51.

Carnes, Frank F., "On the Aesthetics of Faulkner's Fiction," *DA* 29 (1968): 894A-5A (Vanderbilt).

Castille, Philip, "Women and Myth in Faulkner's First Novel," *TSE* 23 (1978): 175-86.

Church, M., "William Faulkner: Myth and Duration," *Time and Reality*, 231-2.

Coffee, Jessie A., "Empty Steeples: Theme, Symbol, and Irony in Faulkner's Novels," *ArQ* 23 (Autumn, 1967): 201-3.

Cooperman, S., *World War I and the American Novel*, 159-61 *passim*.

Dalgarno, Emily K., "Faulkner and Gibbon: A Note on SOLDIERS' PAY," *NMW* 12, i (1979): 36-9.

_____, "SOLDIERS' PAY and Virginia Woolf," *MissQ* (Summer, 1976): 36-9.

_____, "SOLDIERS' PAY and Virginia Woolf," *MissQ* 29 (Summer, 1976): 339-46.

Davidson, Donald, *Nashville Tennessean* (April 11, 1926): Also in *GaR* 20 (Winter, 1966): 456-8.

Everett, W. K., *Faulkner's Art and Characters*, 94-101.

Folks, Jeffrey T., "A Source for the Title of SOLDIERS' PAY," *NMAL* 5 (Winter, 1980): Item 7.

Frederick, John T., "Anticipation and Achievement in Faulkner's SOLDIERS' PAY," *ArQ* 23 (Autumn, 1967): 243-9.

Glicksberg, Charles I., "Faulkner's World of Love and Sex," *Sexual Revolution in Modern American Literature*, 98-9.

Gold, Joseph, "William Faulkner's 'One Compact Thing'," *TCL* 8, i (April, 1962): 6-7.

Gwynn, F. L., and J. L. Blotner, eds., *Faulkner in the University*.

Hirano, Nobuyuki, "Reconsideration of Moral Order and Disorder in Faulkner's Works," *HJAS* 8, i (Sept., 1967): 7-11.

Hoffman, F. J., *William Faulkner*, 40-2.

Howe, I., *William Faulkner*, 17-19.

Jehlen, M., *Class and Character in Faulkner's South*, 26-9.

Kreiswirth, Martin, "Learning as He Wrote: Re-Used Materials in THE SOUND AND THE FURY," *MissQ* 34, iii (Summer, 1981): 281-98.

Lloyd, James B., "Humorous Characterization and the Tradition of the Jonsonian Comedy of Manners in William Faulkner's Early Fiction: NEW ORLEANS SKETCHES, SOLDIERS' PAY, and MOSQUITOES," *DAI* 36 (1976): 4493A.

MacMillan, Duane J., "'Carry on, Cadet': Mores and Morality in SOLDIERS' PAY," in Carey, G. O., ed., *Faulkner*, 39-57.

_____, "The Non-Yoknapatawpha Novels of William Faulkner: An Examination of SOLDIERS' PAY, MOSQUITOES, PYLON, THE WILD PALMS, and A FABLE," *DAI* 32 (1972): 6986A (Wis.).

McHaney, Thomas L., "The Modernism of SOLDIERS' PAY," *WiF* 3, i (July, 1980): 16-30.

Mellard, James M., "SOLDIERS' PAY and the Growth of Faulkner's Comedy," in Brack, O. M., Jr., *American Humor*, 99-117.

Millgate, M., *Achievement of William Faulkner*, 61-7.

_____, "Starting Out in the Twenties: Reflections on SOLDIERS' PAY," *Mosaic* 7, i (Fall, 1973): 1-14. Also in Cox, L. H., ed., *William Faulkner*, 135-56. Also in Collins, R. G., and K. McRobbie, eds., *Novels of William Faulkner*, 1-14.

_____, *William Faulkner*, 18-20.

Nilon, Charles H., "Faulkner and the Negro," *UCSSLL* No. 8 (Sept., 1962): 67-70. Also in Nilon, C. H., *Faulkner and the Negro*, 67-70.

O'Connor, W. V., *Tangled Fire of William Faulkner*, 27-30.

_____, "William Faulkner's Apprenticeship," *SWR* 38 (Winter, 1953): 8-10.

Page, S. R., *Faulkner's Women*, 16-25.

Pritchett, V. S., "SOLDIERS' PAY," *NS&Nation* 41 (June 2, 1951): 624-6.

Richardson, H. Edward, "The Decadence in Faulkner's First Novel: The Faun, the Worm, and the Tower," *EA* 21 (July-Sept., 1968): 225-35.

_____, *William Faulkner*, 142-63.

Roberts, James L., "Experimental Exercises—Faulkner's Early Writings," *Discourse* 6 (Summer, 1963): 186-91.

Seyppel, J., *William Faulkner*, 22-7.

Slabey, Robert M., "SOLDIERS' PAY: Faulkner's First Novel," *RLV* 30, iii (1964): 234-43.

Smart, G. K., *Religious Elements in Faulkner's Early Novels*.

Stein, Randolph E., "The World Outside Yoknapatawpha: A Study of Five Novels by William Faulkner," *DA* 26 (1965): 2225 (Ohio Un.).

Swiggart, P., *Art of Faulkner's Novels*, 31-2.

Tuck, D., *Crowell's Handbook of Faulkner*, 125-8.

Vickery, Olga, "Faulkner's First Novel," *WHR* 11 (Summer, 1957): 251-6.

————, *Novels of William Faulkner*, 1-8.

Volpe, E. L., *Reader's Guide to William Faulkner*, 49-56.

Waggoner, H. H., *William Faulkner*, 1-8, 15-19.

Wagner, Linda W., "The Early Writing," *Hemingway and Faulkner*, 154-9.

Wallis, Donald des G., "SOLDIERS' PAY: Faulkner's First Myth," *BWVACET* 1, ii (Fall, 1974): 15-21.

Watkins, Floyd C., "The Unbearable and Unknowable Truth in Faulkner's First Three Novels," *Flesh and the Word*, 169-80.

Williams, D., *Faulkner's Women*, 36-41.

Wittenberg, J. B., *Faulkner*, 42-50.

Yonce, Margaret J., "The Composition of SOLDIERS' PAY," *MissQ* 33 (Summer, 1980): 291-326.

————, "Faulkner's Atthis and Attis: Some Sources of Myth," *MissQ* 23, iii (Summer, 1970): 289-98.

————, "SOLDIERS' PAY: A Critical Study of William Faulkner's First Novel," *DAI* 32 (1971): 991A (S.C.).

THE SOUND AND THE FURY

Absalom, H. P., "Order and Disorder in THE SOUND AND THE FURY," *DUJ* 58, i (NS 27, i) (Dec., 1965): 30-9. Also in Kinney, A. F., ed., *Critical Essays on William Faulkner: The Compson Family*, 141-54.

Adams, Robert M., "Poetry in the Novel: or Faulkner Esemplastic," *VQR* 29 (Summer, 1953): 420-34.

————, *Strains of Discord: Studies in Literary Openness*, Ithaca: Cornell Un. Pr., 1958, 190-4.

Adams, R. P., *Faulkner*, 215-48.

Aiken, David, "The 'Sojer Face' Defiance of Jason Compson," *Thought* 52, ccv (June, 1977): 188-203.

Albert, Theodore G., "1. The Law vs. Clarissa Harlowe. 2. The Pastoral Argument of THE SOUND AND THE FURY. 3. Melville's Savages," *DAI* 37 (1976): 3601A.

Allen, W., *Modern Novel*, 115-18.

Amano, Masafumi, "Faulkner's Narrative Technique in THE SOUND AND THE FURY," *SALit* 13 (1977): 24-35.

Aswell, Duncan, "The Recollection and the Blood: Jason's Role in THE SOUND AND THE FURY," *MissQ* 21, iii (Summer, 1968): 211-18. Also in Kinney, A. F., ed., *Critical Essays on William Faulkner: The Compson Family*, 207-13.

Auer, Michael J., "Caddy, Benjy, and the Acts of the Apostles: A Note on THE SOUND AND THE FURY," *SNNTS* 6, iv (Winter, 1974): 475-6.

Backman, M., *Faulkner*, 13-40.

————, "Faulkner's Sick Heroes: Bayard Sartoris and Quentin Compson," *MFS* 2 (Autumn, 1956): 100-8.

Backus, Joseph M., "Names of Characters in Faulkner's THE SOUND AND THE FURY," *Names* 6 (Dec., 1958): 226-33.

Balentine, Patti, "Quentin Compson and the Conventions of Courtly Love," *CCTE* 40 (1975): 54-7.

Baquirin, Josephina Q., "Themes, Style, and Symbolism in THE SOUND AND THE FURY," *SLRJ* 4, iv (Dec., 1973): 658-72.

Bass, Eben, "Meaningful Images in THE SOUND AND THE FURY," *MLN* 76 (Dec., 1961): 728-31.

Bassan, Maurice, "Benjy at the Monument," *ELN* 2 (Sept., 1964): 46-50.

Bassett, John E., "Family Conflict in THE SOUND AND THE FURY," *SAF* 9, i (Spring, 1981): 1-20. Also in Kinney, A. F., ed., *Critical Essays on William Faulkner: The Compson Family*, 408-24.

Baum, Catherine B., "'The Beautiful One': Caddy Compson as Heroine of THE SOUND AND THE FURY," *MFS* 13, i (Spring, 1967): 33-44. Also in Kinney, A. F., ed., *Critical Essays on William Faulkner: The Compson Family*, 186-96.

Beach, J. W., *American Fiction*, 128-31.

Beatty, Richard C., and others, eds., *The Literature of the South*, Chicago: Scott, Foresman, 1952, 626-7.

Bedell, G. C., *Kierkegaard and Faulkner*, 134-7, 184-90, 198-203, 244-55.

Beja, Morris, "William Faulkner: A Flash, a Glance," *Epiphany in the Modern Novel*, 184-9, 192-3.

Benson, Jackson J., "Quentin Compson: Self-Portrait of a Young Artist's Emotions," *TCL* 17, iii (July, 1971): 143-59. Also in Kinney, A. F., ed., *Critical Essays on William Faulkner: The Compson Family*, 214-30.

————, "Quentin's Responsibility for Caddy's Downfall in Faulkner's THE SOUND AND THE FURY," *NMW* 5, ii (Fall, 1972): 63-4.

Berets, Ralph A., "The Irrational Narrator in Virginia Woolf's THE WAVES, William Faulkner's THE SOUND AND THE FURY, and Gunter Grass's THE TIN DRUM," *DA* 31 (1970): 751A.

Blanchard, Margaret, "The Rhetoric of Communion: Voice in THE SOUND AND THE FURY," *AL* 41, iv (Jan., 1970): 555-65.

Bleikasten, André, "Bloom and Quentin," 100-8 in Benstock, Bernard, ed., *The Seventh of Joyce*, Bloomington: Indiana Un. Pr., 1982; Brighton: Harvester, 1982.

————, "[Faulkner's Most Splendid Failure]," in Kinney, A. F., ed., *Critical Essays on William Faulkner: The Compson Family*, 268-87. From Bleikasten, A., *Most Splendid Failure*.

————, *Most Splendid Failure*.

Bowling, Lawrence E., "Faulkner and the Theme of Innocence," *KR* 20 (Summer, 1958): 466-87,.

————, "Faulkner and the Theme of Isolation," *GaR* 18 (Spring, 1964): 50-66.

————, "Faulkner: Technique of THE SOUND AND THE FURY," *KR* 10 (Autumn, 1948): 552-66. Also in Hoffman, F. J, and O. W. Vickery, eds., *William Faulkner: Two Decades of Criticism*, 165-79.

————, "Faulkner: The Theme of Pride in THE SOUND AND THE FURY," *MFS* 11 (Summer, 1965): 129-39.

Brannon, Lil, "Psychic Distance in the Quentin Section of THE SOUND AND THE FURY," *PAPA* 2, ii (Spring, 1976): 11-18.

Bridges, Joan B., "Similarities between THE WASTE LAND and THE SOUND AND THE FURY," *NConL* 7, i (Jan., 1977): 10-13.

Broderick, John C., "Faulkner's THE SOUND AND THE FURY," *Expl* 19 (1960): Item 12.

Brogunier, Joseph, "A Housman Source in THE SOUND AND THE FURY," *MFS* 18, ii (Summer, 1972): 220-5.

Brooks, C., *Hidden God*, 40-3.

_____, "Primitivism in THE SOUND AND THE FURY," in *English Institute Essays, 1952*, 5-28.

_____, *William Faulkner*, 325-48, 443-6. Also, condensed, in Cowan, M. H., ed., *Twentieth Century Interpretations of THE SOUND AND THE FURY*, 63-70. Also, in part, in Kinney, A. F., ed., *Critical Essays on William Faulkner: The Compson Family*, 127-38.

Brown, Calvin S., "Dilsey: From Faulkner to Homer," in Zyla, W. T., and W. M. Aycock, eds., *William Faulkner*, 57-75.

Brown, May C., "The Language of Chaos: Quentin Compson in THE SOUND AND THE FURY," *AL* 51, iv (1980): 544-53.

_____, "Voice in 'That Evening Sun': A Study of Quentin Compson," *MissQ* 29, iii (Summer, 1976): 347-60. Also in Kinney, A. F., ed., *Critical Essays on William Faulkner: The Compson Family*, 288-98.

Brylowski, W., *Faulkner's Olympian Laugh*, 59-85. Also in Meriwether, J. B., comp., *Studies in THE SOUND AND THE FURY*, 33-58.

Buchanan, Harriette C., "Caddy Compson as the South in the 1920s," *PMPA* 6 (1981): 10-13.

Burch, Beth, "Shades of Golden Fleece: Faulkner's Jason Once Again," *NMW* 12, ii (1980): 55-62.

Burgum, E. B., *Novel and the World's Dilemma*, 208-15.

Campbell, H. M., and R. E. Foster, *William Faulkner*, 50-60.

Carns, Frank F., "On the Aesthetics of Faulkner's Fiction," *DA* 29 (1968): 894A-5A (Vanderbilt).

Carter, Steve, "Caddy and Quentin: Anima and Animus Orbited Nice," *HSL* 12, ii (1980): 124-42.

Cecil, L. Moffitt, "A Rhetoric for Benjy," *SLJ* 3, i (Fall, 1970): 32-46.

Chappell, Fred, "The Comic Structure of THE SOUND AND THE FURY," *MissQ* 31 (Summer, 1978): 381-6.

Chase, R., *American Novel and Its Tradition*, 219-36.

Chisholm, William S., "Sentence Patterns in THE SOUND AND THE FURY," *DA* 25 (1965): 7254-5 (Michigan).

Church, M., "William Faulkner: Myth and Duration," *Time and Reality*, 233-5.

Clark, Edward D., Sr., "Private Truth in THE SOUND AND THE FURY," *CLAJ* 19 (June, 1976): 513-23.

Clerc, Charles, "Faulkner's THE SOUND AND THE FURY," *Expl* 24 (Nov., 1965): Item 29.

Cobau, William W., "Jason Compson and the Costs of Speculation," *MissQ* 22, iii (Summer, 1969): 257-61.

Coffee, Jessie A., "Empty Steeples: Theme, Symbol, and Irony in Faulkner's Novels," *ArQ* 23 (Autumn, 1967): 204-6.

_____, "Faulkner's THE SOUND AND THE FURY," *Expl* 24 (Oct., 1965): Item 21.

Coindreau, Maurice, "Preface to THE SOUND AND THE FURY," *MissQ* 19, iii (Summer, 1966): 107-15.

_____, *Time of William Faulkner*, 41-50.

Collins, Carvel, "A Conscious Literary Use of Freud?" *L&P* 3, iii (June, 1953): 2-4.

_____, "Faulkner's THE SOUND AND THE FURY," *Expl* 17 (Dec., 1958): Item 19.

_____, in Griffin, William, ed., *Literature in the Modern World*, 67-9.

_____, "The Interior Monologues of THE SOUND AND THE FURY," in Malin, I., ed., *Psychoanalysis and American Fiction*, 223-43. Also in *English Institute Essays, 1952*, 29-56. Also in *Mass. Inst. of Tech. Publications in the Humanities*, No. 6. Also, in part, in Kinney, A. F., ed., *Critical Essays on William*

Faulkner: The Compson Family, 124-6. Also in Meriwether, J. B., comp., *Studies in THE SOUND AND THE FURY*, 59-79.

_____, "Miss Quentin's Paternity Again," *TSLL* 2 (Autumn, 1960): 253-60. Also in Meriwether, J. B., comp., *Studies IN THE SOUND AND THE FURY*, 80-8.

_____, "The Pairing of THE SOUND AND THE FURY and AS I LAY DYING," *PULC* 18 (Spring, 1957): 115-19. Also, condensed, in Cowan, M. H., ed., *Twentieth Century Interpretations of THE SOUND AND THE FURY*, 71-4.

_____, "William Faulkner, THE SOUND AND THE FURY," in Stegner, W., ed., *American Novel*, 219-28.

_____, *William Faulkner: THE SOUND AND THE FURY*, Portree, Isle of Skye: Aquila, 1982.

Connolly, Thomas, in Krause, S. J., ed., *Essays on Determinism*, 39-41.

Cowan, James C., "Dream-Work in the Quentin Section of THE SOUND AND THE FURY," *L&P* 24, iii (1974): 91-8.

Cowan, Michael H., "Introduction," in Cowan, M. H., ed., *Twentieth Century Interpretations of THE SOUND AND THE FURY*, 1-13.

Cowley, Malcolm, "Dilsey and the Compsons," *UMSE* 14 (1976): 79-88.

Cross, Barbara M., "THE SOUND AND THE FURY: The Pattern of Sacrifice," *ArQ* 16 (Spring, 1960): 5-16.

Dauner, Louise, "Quentin and the Walking Shadow: The Dilemma of Nature and Culture," *ArQ* 18 (Summer, 1965): 159-71. Also, condensed, in Cowan, M. H., ed., *Twentieth Century Interpretations of THE SOUND AND THE FURY*, 75-80.

Davis, Boyd, "Caddy Compson's Eden," *MissQ* 30 (Summer, 1977): 381-94.

Davis, Thadious M., "Jason Compson's Place: A Reassessment," *SoSt* 20, ii (Summer, 1981:; 137-50.

_____, "The Other Family and Luster in THE SOUND AND THE FURY," *CLAJ* 20 (Dec., 1976): 245-61.

Davis, William V., "June 2, 1928: Further Thoughts on Time in THE SOUND AND THE FURY," *NMW* 11, ii (Winter, 1979): 84-5.

_____, "Quentin's Death Ritual: Further Christian Allusions in THE SOUND AND THE FURY," *NMW* 6, i (Spring, 1973): 27-32.

_____, "THE SOUND AND THE FURY: A Note on Benjy's Name," *SNNTS* 4, i (Spring, 1972): 60-1.

Despain, Norma L., "Stream of Consciousness Narration in Faulkner: A Redefinition," *DAI* 37 (1975): 306A-07A.

Dickerson, Mary J., "'The Magician's Wand': Faulkner's Compson Appendix," *MissQ* 28, iii (Summer, 1975): 317-37. Also in Kinney, A. F., ed., *Critical Essays on William Faulkner: The Compson Family*, 252-67.

Dillingham, William B., "William Faulkner and the 'Tragic Condition'," *Edda* 66 (1966): 323-7.

Dorsch, Robert L., "An Interpretation of the Central Themes in the Work of William Faulkner," *ESRS* 11, i (Sept., 1962): 21-6.

Douglass, Scott, "Possible Sources for Faulkner's General Compson," *RALS* 11, i (Spring, 1981): 112-14.

Dove, George N., "Shadow and Paradox: Imagery in THE SOUND AND THE FURY," in Burton, Thomas G., ed., *Essays in Memory of Christine Burleson in Language and Literature by Former Colleagues and Students*, Johnson City: Res. Advisory Council, East Tennessee St. Un., 1969, 89-95.

Dukes, Thomas, "Christianity as Curse and Salvation in THE SOUND AND THE FURY," *ArQ* 35 (Summer, 1979): 170-82.

Edel, Leon, "How to Read THE SOUND AND THE FURY," *The Modern Psychological Novel*, rev., and enl., N.Y.: Grossett and Dunlop, 1964, 162-76. Also in Burnshaw, Stanley, *Varieties of Literary Experience*, N.Y.: N.Y.U. Pr., 1962, 241-57.

_____, *The Psychological Novel, 1900-1950*, N.Y. and Philadelphia: Lippincott, 1955, 149-54. Also in Edel, L., *Modern Psychological Novel*, N.Y.: Grosset, 1964, 97-102.

England, Martha W., "Quentin's Story: Chronology and Explication," *CE* 22 (Jan., 1961): 228-35.

_____, "Teaching THE SOUND AND THE FURY," *CE* 18 (Jan., 1957): 221-4.

Everett, W. K., *Faulkner's Art and Characters*, 101-14.

Faber, M. D., "Faulkner's THE SOUND AND THE FURY: Object Relations and Narrative Structure," *AI* 34, iv (Winter, 1977): 327-50.

Fasel, Ida, "A Conversation Between Faulkner and Eliot," *MissQ* 20 (1967): 195-206.

_____, "Spatial Form and Spatial Time," *WHR* 16 (Summer, 1962): 230-4.

Faulkner, William, "Faulkner Discusses THE SOUND AND THE FURY," in Cowan, M. H., ed., *Twentieth Century Interpretations of THE SOUND AND THE FURY*, 14-24.

_____, "Faulkner on THE SOUND AND THE FURY," in Schmitter, D. M., ed., *William Faulkner*, 88-90. From Gwynn, F. L., and J. L. Blottner, eds., *Faulkner in the University*.

_____, "An Introduction for THE SOUND AND THE FURY," ed. with introd. by James Meriwehter, *SoR* 8 (Autumn, 1972): 705-10.

_____, "An Introduction to THE SOUND AND THE FURY," *MissQ* 26 (Summer, 1973): 410-15.

_____, "1699-1945: The Compsons," Appendix to *The Portable Faulkner*, N.Y.: Modern Library, 1946. Rev. as Forward to Faulkner, W., THE SOUND AND THE FURY, N.Y.: Modern Library, 1946. Also in Kirk, Robert W., with Marvin Klotz, *Faulkner's People*, Berkeley and Los Angeles: Un. of Calif. Pr., 1963, 38-49.

Fazio, Rocco R., "The Fury and the Design: Realms of Being and Knowing in Four Novels of William Faulkner," *DA* 25 (1964): 1910 (Rochester).

Fletcher, Mary D., "Edenic Images in THE SOUND AND THE FURY," *SCB* 40, iv (1980): 142-4.

_____, "William Faulkner and Residual Calvinism," *SoSt* 18 (Summer, 1979): 199-216.

Ford, Daniel G., "Comments on William Faulkner's Temporal Vision in SANCTUARY, THE SOUND AND THE FURY, LIGHT IN AUGUST, ABSALOM ABSALOM!" *SoQ* 15, iii (1977): 283-90.

_____, "The Tragedy of 'Again' in THE SOUND AND THE FURY" *PAPA* 4, iii (Fall, 1978): 41-4.

_____, "Uses of Time in Four Novels by William Faulkner," *DAI* 35 (1974): 1654A (Auburn).

Foster, Ruel, "Dream as Symbolic Act in Faulkner," *Per* 2 (Summer, 1949): 185-91.

Frederickson, Michael A., "A Note on 'The Idiot Boy' as a Probable Source for THE SOUND AND THE FURY," *MinnR* 6, iv (Winter, 1966): 368-70.

Freedman, William A., "The Technique of Isolation in THE SOUND AND THE FURY," *MissQ* 15 (Winter, 1961-62): 21-6.

Fridy, Will, "'Ichthus': An Exercise in Synthetic Suggestion," *SAB* 39, ii (May, 1974): 95-101.

Friedman, M. J., *Stream of Consciousness*, 8-11.

Fujihira, Ikuko, "Beyond Closed Doors: Quentin Compson and Isaac McCaslin," *WiF* 3, i (July, 1980): 31-43.

Garlick, H. F., "Three Patterns of Imagery in Benjy's Section of THE SOUND AND THE FURY," *AUMLA* 52 (1979): 274-87.

Garmon, Gerald M., "Faulkner's THE SOUND AND THE FURY," *Expl* 25 (Sept., 1966): Item 2.

Garmon, Gerald M., "Mirror Imagery in THE SOUND AND THE FURY," *NMW* 2 (Spring, 1969): 13-24.

Gatlin, Jesse C., Jr., "Of Time and Character in THE SOUND AND THE FURY," *HAB* 17, ii (Autumn, 1966): 27-35.

Geffen, Arthur, "Profane Time, Sacred Time, and Confederate Time in THE SOUND AND THE FURY," *SAF* 2, ii (Autumn, 1974): 175-97. Also in Kinney, A. F., ed., *Critical Essays on William Faulkner: The Compson Family*, 231-51.

Geismar, M., *Writers in Crisis*, 154-9.

Gervais, Ronald J., "The Trains of Their Youth: The Aesthetics of Homecoming in THE GREAT GATSBY, THE SUN ALSO RISES and THE SOUND AND THE FURY," *AAus* 6 (1980): 51-63.

Gibbons, Kathryn G., "Quentin's Shadow," *L&P* 12 (Winter, 1962): 16-24.

Gibson, William M., "Faulkner's THE SOUND AND THE FURY," *Expl* 22 (Jan., 1963): Item 33.

Gill, Linda G., "Faulkner's Narrative Voices in THE SOUND AND THE FURY," *DAI* 36 (1976): 4489A.

Glaze, Walter S., "The Protestant Work Ethic in Faulkner's THE SOUND AND THE FURY: Jason Compson as Southern Gentleman," *PMPA* 5 (1980): 26-30.

Glicksberg, Charles I., "Faulkner's World of Love and Sex," *Sexual Revolution in Modern American Literature*, 102-3.

Gold, Joseph, "Faulkner's THE SOUND AND THE FURY," *Expl* 19 (Feb., 1961): Item 29.

Gordon, Lois, "Meaning and Myth in THE SOUND AND THE FURY and THE WASTE LAND," in French, W., ed., *Twenties*, 269-302.

Gossett, L. Y., *Violence in Recent Southern Fiction*, 38-41.

Grant, William E., "Benjy's Branch: Symbolic Method in Part I of THE SOUND AND THE FURY," *TSLL* 13 (Winter, 1972): 705-10.

Graves, T. W., Jr., "A Portrait of Benjy," *William & Mary Rev* 2 (Winter, 1964): 53-7.

Greer, Dorothy D., "Dilsey and Lucas: Faulkner's Use of the Negro as a Gauge of Moral Character," *ESRS* 11, i (Sept., 1962): 44-54.

Gregory, Eileen, "Caddy Compson's World," in Meriwether, J. B., comp., *Studies in THE SOUND AND THE FURY*, 89-101.

Gresset, Michel, "Psychological Aspects of Evil in THE SOUND AND THE FURY," *MissQ* 19, iii (Summer, 1966): 143-53. Also in Kinney, A. F., ed., *Critical Essays on William Faulkner: The Compson Family*, 173-81. Also in Meriwether, J. B., comp., *Studies in THE SOUND AND THE FURY*, 114-24.

Griffin, Robert J., "Ethical Point of View in THE SOUND AND THE FURY," in Langford, R. E., ed., *Essays in Modern American Literature*, 55-64.

Groden, Michael, "Criticism in New Composition: ULYSSES and THE SOUND AND THE FURY," *TCL* 21, iii (Oct., 1975): 265-77.

Gross, Beverly, "Form and Fulfillment in THE SOUND AND THE FURY," *MLQ* 29 (Dec., 1968): 439-49.

Grover, Frederic, and Harriet Mowshowitz, "Faulkner, in French," *CRCL* 7 (Spring, 1980): 223-35.

Guetti, James, *Limits of Metaphor*, Ithaca: Cornell Un. Pr., 1967, 148-53.

_____, *Word-Music*, 157-63.

Gunter, Richard, "Style and Language in THE SOUND AND THE FURY," *MissQ* 22 (Summer, 1969): 264-79. Also in Meriwether, J. B., comp., *Studies in THE SOUND AND THE FURY*, 140-56.

Gwynn, F. L., and J. L. Blotner, eds., *Faulkner in the University*.

_____, "Faulkner's Raskolnikov," *MFS* 4 (Summer, 1958): 169-72.

Hagopian, John V., "Nihilism in Faulkner's THE SOUND AND THE FURY," *MFS* 13, i (Spring, 1967): 45-55. Also in Kinney, A. F., ed., *Critical Essays on William Faulkner: The Compson Family*, 197-206. Also in Meriwether, J. B., comp., *Studies in THE SOUND AND THE FURY*, 102-13.

Hall, J. E., *Lunatic Giant in the Drawing Room*, 61-2.

Handy, William, J., "THE SOUND AND THE FURY: A Formalist Approach," *NDQ* 44, iii (Summer, 1976): 71-83.

Harris, Wendell V., "Faulkner's THE SOUND AND THE FURY," *Expl* 21, vii (Mar., 1963): Item 54. Also in Kinney, A. F., ed., *Critical Essays on William Faulkner: The Compson Family*, 139-40.

_____, "Of Time and the Novel," *BuR* 16 (Mar., 1968): 114-29. (DAVID COPPERFIELD, NOSTROMO, THE SOUND AND THE FURY.)

Hathaway, Baxter, "The Meanings of Faulkner's Structures," *EngR* 15 (Dec., 1964): 22-7.

Hinkle, Diane L., "The Mystery of Significance and the Enigma of Time: An Analysis of the Thematic Structures of Faulkner's THE SOUND AND THE FURY and Claude Simon's L'HERBE," *DAI* 32 (1971): 2689A-90A (N.C., Chapel Hill).

Hirano, Nobuyuki, "Reconsideration of Moral Order and Disorder in Faulkner's Works," *HJAS* 8, i (Sept., 1967): 11-19.

Hoffman, Frederick J., in French, W. G., and W. E. Kidd, eds., *American Winners of the Nobel Literary Prize*, 146-8.

_____, *Twenties*, 214-16.

_____, *William Faulkner*, 49-60. Also in Schmitter, D. M., ed., *William Faulkner*, 77-87.

Hornback, Vernon T., Jr., "The Uses of Time in Faulkner's THE SOUND AND THE FURY," *PELL* 1 (Winter, 1965): 50-8.

Howe, Irving, "The Passing of a World," in Cowan, M. H., ed., *Twentieth Century Interpretations of THE SOUND AND THE FURY*, 33-9. Condensed from Howe, I., *William Faulkner*, 46-8, 158-74.

_____, *William Faulkner*, 46-52, 123-4, 134-6, 157-74. Also, in part, in Kinney, A. F., ed., *Critical Essays on William Faulkner: The Compson Family*, 119-2.

Howell, John M., "Hemingway and Fitzgerald in Sound and Fury," *PLL* 2 (Summer, 1966): 234-42.

_____, "The Waste Land Tradition in the American Novel," *DA* 24 (1964): 3337 (Tulane).

Hughes, Richard, "Introduction," THE SOUND AND THE FURY, Harmondsworth: Penguin Books, 1975.

Humphrey, Robert, "Form and Function of Stream of Consciousness in William Faulkner's THE SOUND AND THE FURY," *UKCR* 19 (Autumn, 1952): 34-40.

_____, *Stream of Consciousness in the Modern Novel*, 17-20, 57-8, 65-70, 73-4, 106-11.

Hunt, John W., "The Disappearance of Quentin Compson," in Kinney, A. F., ed., *Critical Essays on William Faulkner: The Compson Family*, 366-80.

_____, *William Faulkner*, Chapter 2. Also, condensed, in Cowan, M. H., ed., *Twentieth Century Interpretations of THE SOUND AND THE FURY*, 83-92.

Hunter, E. R., *William Faulkner*, 29-47.

Idei, Yasuko, "Time as a Means of Conveying Nihilism in Faulkner's THE SOUND AND THE FURY," *KAL* 18 (Oct., 1977): 24-32.

Iser, W., *Implied Reader*, 136-52.

Izsak, Emily K., "The Manuscript of THE SOUND AND THE FURY: The Revisions in the First Section," *SB* 20 (1967): 189-202.

Jacobs, Robert D., "Faulkner's Tragedy of Isolation," in Rubin, L. D., and R. D. Jacobs, eds., *Southern Renascence*, 171-4, 179.

_____, "William Faulkner: The Passion and the Penance," in Rubin, L. D., Jr., and R. D. Jacobs, eds., *South*, 146-53.

Jehlen, M., *Class and Character in Faulkner's South*, 41-6.

Jenkins, L ., *Faulkner and Black-White Relations*, 135-76.

Kaluza, Irena, *The Functioning of Sentence Structure in the Stream-of-Consciousness Technique Stylistics*, Krakow: UJ, 1967; Norwood, PA: Norwood Eds., 1979.

Kantak, V. Y., "Faulkner's Technique," in Chander, J., and N. S. Pradhan, eds., *Studies in American Literature*, 77-96 passim.

Kartiganer, Donald M., *Fragile Thread*, 3-22.

_____, "Quentin Compson and Faulkner's Drama of the Generations," in Kinney, A. F., ed., *Critical Essays on William Faulkner: The Compson Family*, 381-401.

_____, "THE SOUND AND THE FURY and Faulkner's Quest for Form," *ELH* 37, iv (Dec., 1970): 613-39.

Kauffman, Linda, "The Letter and the Spirit in HARD TIME and THE SOUND AND THE FURY," *MissQ* 34, iii (Summer, 1981): 299-313.

Kauffmann, Stanley, "Signifying Nothing?" in Peary, G., and R. Shatzkin, eds., *Classic American Novel and the Movies*, 305-8.

Kellogg, Jean D., "William Faulkner and the Tyranny of Linear Consciousness," *Dark Prophets of Hope*, 126-35.

Kelly, Jimmy L., "The Artist in Shadow: Quentin Compson in William Faulkner's THE SOUND AND THE FURY," *DAI* 39 (1978): 279A-80A.

Kermenli, Leylâ, "William Faulkner's THE SOUND AND THE FURY," *Litera* 8 (1965): 99-113.

Kerr, E. M., *William Faulkner's Gothic Domain*, 53-73.

King, Frances H., "Benjamin Compson—Flower Child," *CEA Critic* 31 (Jan., 1969): 10.

King, R. H., *Southern Renaissance*, 111-19.

Kinney, A. F., ed., *Critical Essays on William Faulkner: The Compson Family*.

_____, "[Faulkner's Narrative Poetics in THE SOUND AND THE FURY]," in Kinney, A. F., ed., *Critical Essays on William Faulkner: The Compson Family*, 299-317. From Kinney, A. F., *Faulkner's Narrative Poetics*, 139-61.

Klotz, Marvin, "The Triumph Over Time: Narrative Form in William Faulkner and William Styron," *MissQ* 17 (Winter, 1963-64): 10-12.

Kopoor, Kapil, "Faulkner's THE SOUND AND THE FURY: A Note on Form and Meaning," *JSL* 3, ii (1976): 85-91.

Kreiswirth, Martin, "Learning as He Wrote: Re-Used Materials in THE SOUND AND THE FURY," *MissQ* 34, iii (Summer, 1981): 281-8.

_____, "The Making of a Novelist: William Faulkner's Career to the Writing of THE SOUND AND THE FURY," *DAI* 40 (1980): 6280A.

Labor, Earle, "Faulkner's THE SOUND AND THE FURY," *Expl* 17 (Jan., 1959): Item 29.

Layman, Lewis, M., "Fourteen Ways of Looking at a Blackbird: Point of View in THE SOUND AND THE FURY," *DAI* 34 (1974): 7763A (Br. Columbia).

Leary, L., *William Faulkner of Yoknapatawpha County*, 41-62.

Lee, E. B., "A Note on the Ordonnance of THE SOUND AND THE FURY," *Faulkner Studies* 3 (Summer-Autumn, 1954): 37-9.

Longley, John L., Jr., "'Who Never Had a Sister': A Reading of THE SOUND AND THE FURY," *Mosaic* 7, i (Fall, 1973): 35-53. Also in Collins, R. G., and K. McRobbie, eds., *Novels of William Faulkner*, 35-53.

Lowrey, Perrin, "Concepts of Time in THE SOUND AND THE FURY," in *English Institute Essays, 1952*, 57-82. Also, condensed, in Cowan, M. H., ed., *Twentieth Century Interpretations of THE SOUND AND THE FURY*, 53-62.

Luedtke, Carol L., "THE SOUND AND THE FURY and LIE DOWN IN DARKNESS: Some Comparisons," *LWU* 4, i (1971): 45-51.

Lyday, Charles L., "Faulkner's *Commedia*: An Interpretation of THE SOUND AND THE FURY, SANCTUARY, AS I LAY DYING, and LIGHT IN AUGUST," *DAI* 39 (1978): 886A-87A.

Matthews, J. T., *Play of Faulkner's Language*, 63-114.

McGann, Mary E., "THE WASTE LAND and THE SOUND AND THE FURY: To Apprehend the Human Process Moving in Time," *SLJ* 9, i (Fall, 1976): 13-21.

McHaney, Thomas L., "Robinson Jeffers' 'Tamar' and THE SOUND AND THE FURY," *MissQ* 22, iii (Summer, 1969): 261-3.

M[eriwether], J[ames] B., ed., "An Introduction to THE SOUND AND THE FURY," *MissQ* 26 (Summer, 1973): 410-15. [Longer version of Faulkner's 1933 essay.]

Meriwether, James B., "An Introduction to THE SOUND AND THE FURY," *SoR* 8, iv (Oct., 1972): 705-10.

_____, "Notes on the Textual History of THE SOUND AND THE FURY," *PBSA* 56 (1962): 285-316.

_____, comp., *Studies in THE SOUND AND THE FURY*.

Mellard, James M., "Caliban as Prospero: Benjy and THE SOUND AND THE FURY," *Novel* 3 (Spring, 1970): 233-48.

_____, "Jason Compson: Humor, Hostility, and the Rhetoric of Aggression," *SHR* 3, iii (Summer, 1969): 259-67.

_____, "THE SOUND AND THE FURY: Quentin Compson and Faulkner's 'Tragedy of Passion'," *SNNTS* 2, i (Spring, 1970): 61-75.

_____, "Type and Archetype: Jason Compson as 'Satirist'," *Genre* 4, ii (June, 1971): 173-88.

Messerli, Douglas, "The Problem of Time in THE SOUND AND THE FURY: A Critical Reassessment and Reinterpretation," *SLJ* 6, ii (Spring, 1974): 19-41.

Millgate, Jane, "Quentin Compson as Poor Player: Verbal and Social Cliche in THE SOUNDS AND THE FURY," *RLV* 34 (1968): 40-9.

Millgate, Michael, "Faulkner and Lanier: A Note on the Name Jason," *MissQ* 25 (Summer, 1972): 349-50.

_____, "The Problem of Point of View," in LaFrance, Marsten, ed., *Patterns of Commitment in American Literature*, Toronto: Un. of Toronto Pr., 1967, 181-92 passim. Also in Meriwether, J. B., comp., *Studies in THE SOUND AND THE FURY*, 125-39 passim.

_____, *William Faulkner*, 26-34.

Milliner, Gladys, "The Third Eve: Caddy Compson," *MQ* 16, iii (April, 1975): 268-75.

Miner, Ward L., "Faulkner and Christ's Crucifixion," *NM* 57 (1956): 260-2.

Minter, David, "Faulkner, Childhood, and the Making of THE SOUND AND THE FURY," *AL* 51, iii (1979): 376-93.

Mizener, A., *Twelve Great American Novels*, 147-59.

Moffitt, Cecil L., "A Rhetoric for Benjy," *SLJ* 3, i (Fall, 1970): 32-46.

Moore, Andy J., "Luster's Ordered Role in THE SOUND AND THE FURY," in Collmer, R. G., and J. W. Herring, eds., *American Bypaths*, 167-86.

Morillo, Marvin, "Faulkner's THE SOUND AND THE FURY," *Expl* 24 (Feb., 1966): Item 50.

Morozova, Tatiana, "Faulkner Reads Dostoevsky," *SovL* 12 [405] (1951): 176-9.

Morrison, Gail M., "'Time, Tide, and Twilight': MAYDAY and Faulkner's Quest toward THE SOUND AND THE FURY," *MissQ* 31 (Summer, 1978): 337-57.

_____, "William Faulkner's THE SOUND AND THE FURY: A Critical and Textual Study (Volumes I and II)," *DAI* 41, viii (Feb., 1981): 3583A.

Morrow, Patrick D., "Mental Retardation in THE SOUND AND THE FURY and THE LAST PICTURE SHOW," *ReAL* 6, i (1979): 1-9.

Moseley, Merritt, "Faulkner's Dickensian Humor in THE SOUND AND THE FURY," *NMWu* 13, i (1981): 7-13.

Mueller, W. R., "The Theme of Suffering: William Faulkner's THE SOUND AND THE FURY," *Prophetic Voice*, 110-35.

Murphy, Denis M., "THE SOUND AND THE FURY and Dante's INFERNO: Fire and Ice," *MarkhamR* 4 (Oct., 1974): 71-8.

Naples, Diane C., "Eliot's 'Tradition' and THE SOUND AND THE FURY," *MFS* 20, ii (Summer, 1974): 214-17.

Neidhardt, Frances E., "Verbal-Visual Simultaneity in Faulkner's THE SOUND AND THE FURY: A Literary Montage Filmscript for Quentin," *DAI* 39 (1978): 1165A.

O'Connor, William Van, "THE SOUND AND THE FURY and the Impressionist Novel," *Northern Rev* (Montreal) 6 (June-July, 1953): 17-22.

_____, *Tangled Fire of William Faulkner*, 37-45.

_____, *William Faulkner*, 11-14. Also in O'Connor, W. V., ed., *Seven Modern American Novelists*, 125-8.

O'Faolain, S., *Vanishing Hero*, 94-100.

O'Nan, Martha, *The Role of Mind in Hugo, Faulkner, Beckett and Grass*, N.Y.: Philosophical Library, 1969, 13-22.

Page, S. R., *Faulkner's Women*, 45-72.

Palumbo, Donald, "The Concept of God in Faulkner's LIGHT IN AUGUST, THE SOUND AND THE FURY, AS I LAY DYING, and ABSALOM, ABSALOM!" *SCB* 39, iv (1979): 142-6.

Parr, Susan D. R., "'And by Bergson, Obviously', Faulkner's THE SOUND AND THE FURY, AS I LAY DYING, and

ABSALOM, ABSALOM! from a Bergsonian Perspective," *DAI* 32 (1972): 6996A (Wisconsin).

Pate, Willard, "Benjy's Names in the Compson Household," *FurmS* 15, iv (May, 1968): 37-8.

Pearson, Theresa L., "THE SOUND AND THE FURY: An Archetypal Reading," *DAI* 37 (1977): 6487A.

Peavy, Charles D., "Did You Ever Have a Sister? Holden, Quentin, and Sexual Innocence," *FLoQ* 1, iii (Winter, 1968): 82-95.

_____, "The Eyes of Innocence: Faulkner's 'The Kingdom of God'," *PLL* 2, ii (Spring, 1966): 178-82. Also in Kinney, A. F., ed., *Critical Essays on William Faulkner: The Compson Family*, 182-5.

_____, "Faulkner's Use of Folklore in THE SOUND AND THE FURY," *JAF* 79 (July, 1966): 437-47.

_____, "'If I'd Just Had a Mother': Faulkner's Quentin Compson," *L&P* 23, iii (1973): 114-21.

_____, "A Note on the 'Suicide Pact' in THE SOUND AND THE FURY," *ELN* 5 (Mar., 1968): 207-9.

Pikoulis, J., *Art of William Faulkner*, 18-47.

Pilkington, J., *Heart of Yoknapatawpha*, 35-85.

Pinsker, Sanford, "Squaring the Circle in THE SOUND AND THE FURY," 1ll5-21 in Carey, G. O., ed., *Faulkner*.

Pitavy, Francois L., "Joyce's and Faulkner's 'Twinning Stresses': A Textual Comparison," 90-9 in Benstock, Bernard, ed., *The Seventh of Joyce*, Bloomington: Indiana Un. Pr., 1982; Brighton: Harvester, 1982.

Powell, Sumner C., "William Faulkner Celebrates Easter, 1928," *Per* 2 (Summer, 1949): 195-218.

Powers, Lyall H., "Hawthorne and Faulkner and the Pearl of Great Price," *PMASAL* 52 (1967): 391-401.

_____, *Faulkner's Yoknapatawpha Comedy*, 24-49.

Prasad, Thakur Guru, "Nihilism in THE SOUND AND THE FURY," *PURBA* 3, i (April, 1972): 35-43.

Pratt, J. Norwood, "Faulkner's THE SOUND AND THE FURY," *Expl* 23 (Jan., 1965): Item 37.

Rabkin, Eric S., "Spatial Form and Plot," *CI* 4, ii (Winter, 1977): 253-70.

Ramsey, Roger, "Faulkner's THE SOUND AND THE FURY," *Expl* 30 (April, 1972): Item 70.

_____, "Light Imagery in THE SOUND AND THE FURY: April 7, 1928," *JNT* 6 (Winter, 1976): 41-50.

Ramsey, William, "Coordinate Structure in Four Faulkner Novels," *DAI* 33 (1972): 283A-84A (N.C., Chapel Hill).

Reed, J. W., Jr., *Faulkner's Narrative*, 74-83.

Richardson, K. E., *Force and Faith in the Novels of William Faulkner*, 24-9, 70-3, 100-3.

Rinaldi, Nicholas M., "Game-Consciousness and Game-Metaphor in the Work of William Faulkner," *DA* 24 (1964): 4196-7 (Fordham).

Rodrigues, Eusebio L., "Time and Technique in THE SOUND AND THE FURY," *LCrit* 6, iv (1965): 61-7.

Rollyson, Carl E., Jr., "Quentin Durward and Quentin Compson: The Romantic Standard-Bearers of Scott and Faulkner," *MSE* 7, iii (1980): 34-9.

Rosenberg, Bruce A., "The Oral Quality of Rev. Shegog's Sermon in William Faulkner's THE SOUND AND THE FURY," *LWU* 2, ii (1969): 73-88.

Ross, Stephen M., "Jason Compson and Sut Lovingood: Southwestern Humor as Stream of Consciousness," *SNNTS* 8, iii (Fall, 1976): 278-90.

_____, "The 'Loud World' of Quentin Compson," *SNNTS* 7, ii (Summer, 1975): 245-57.

Rubin, L. D., Jr., *Faraway Country*, 54-8.

Ryan, Marjorie, "The Shakespearean Symbolism in THE SOUND AND THE FURY," *Faulkner Studies* 2 (Autumn, 1953): 40-3.

Sandstrom, Glenn, "Identity Diffusion: Joe Christmas and Quentin Compson," *AQ* 19 (Summer, 1967): 207-23.

Sartre, J. P., "On THE SOUND AND THE FURY: Time in the Work of Faulkner," *Literary and Philosophical Essays*, 79-87. Also as "Time in Faulkner: THE SOUND AND THE FURY," in Hoffman, F. J., and O. W. Vickery, eds., *William Faulkner: Two Decades of Criticism*, 180-8. Also in Warren, R. P., ed., *Faulkner*, 87-93.

Sasamoto, Seiji, "The First Section of THE SOUND AND THE FURY: Benjy and His Expressions," *WiF* 4, ii (July, 1982): 19-36.

Scott, Evelyn, in Cowan, M. H., ed., *Twentieth Century Interpretations of THE SOUND AND THE FURY*, 25-9. Also in Kinney, A. F., ed., *Critical Essays on William Faulkner: The Compson Family*, 115-18.

Serbnescu, Mdlina, "Towards Uncovering the Deep Structure of Benjy's Narrative in Faulkner's Novel THE SOUND AND THE FURY," *RITL* 30 (1981): 353-8.

Seymour, Thom, "Faulkner's THE SOUND AND THE FURY," *Expl* 39, i (Fall, 1980): 24-5.

Seyppel, J., *William Faulkner*, 42-7.

Simonton, Margaret, "Faulkner's Influence on Robbe-Grillet: The Quentin Section of THE SOUND AND THE FURY and LA JALOUSIE," *IFR* 7 (Winter, 1980): 11-19.

Simpson, Hassell A., "Faulkner's THE SOUND AND THE FURY. Appendix," *Expl* 21 (Dec., 1962): Item 27.

Sims, Barbara B., "Jaybirds as Portents of Hell in Percy and Faulkner," *NMW* 9, i (Spring, 1976): 24-8.

Slabey, Robert M., "Quetin Compson's 'Lost Childhood'," *SSF* 1 (Spring, 1964): 173-83.

_____, "The 'Romanticism' of THE SOUND AND THE FURY," *MissQ* 16 (Summer, 1963): 146-59. Also, condensed, in Cowan, M. H., ed., *Twentieth Century Interpretations of THE SOUND AND THE FURY*, 81-2.

Slater, Judith, "Quentin's Tunnel Vision: Modes of Perception and Their Stylistic Realization in THE SOUND AND THE FURY," *L&P* 27, i (1977): 4-15.

Slatoff, Walter J., "The Edge of Order: The Pattern of Faulkner's Rhetoric," *TCL* 3 (Oct., 1957): 107-27. Also in Slatoff, W. J., *Quest for Failure*, 137-9, 155-8. Also, condensed, in Cowan, M. H., ed., *Twentieth Century Interpretations of THE SOUND AND THE FURY*, 93-6.

_____, *Quest for Failure*, 12-13, 69-70, 138-9, 149-58, 254-5.

Spilka, Mark, "Quentin Compson's Universal Grief," *ConL* 11, iv (Autumn, 1970): 451-69.

Stafford, W. T., *Books Speaking to Books*, 31-7.

Steege, M. Ted, "Dilsey's Negation of Nihilism: Meaning in THE SOUND AND THE FURY," *RS* 38 (Dec., 1970): 266-75.

Steinberg, Aaron, "Faulkner and the Negro," *DA* 27 (1966): 1385A (N.Y.U.).

Sterne, Richard C., "Why Jason Compson IV Hates Babe Ruth," *AN&Q* 16, vii (Mar., 1978): 105-8.

Stewart, George R., and Joseph M. Backus, "'Each in Its Ordered Place': Structure and Narrative in 'Benjy's Section' of THE SOUND AND THE FURY," *AL* 29 (Jan., 1958): 440-56.

Stonum, G. L., *Faulkner's Career*, 59-95.

Strandberg, Victor, "Faulkner's Poor Parson and the Technique of Inversion (or William Faulkner: An Epitaph)," *SR* 73 (Spring, 1965): 184-90.

Suda, Minoru, "The Development of William Faulkner's Literature: With Special Emphasis on THE SOUND AND THE FURY and ABSALOM, ABSALOM!" *ESELL* 70 (1979): 23-40.

Swanson, William J., "William Faulkner and William Styron: Notes on Religion," *CimR* 7 (Mar., 1969): 45-52.

Swiggart, P., *Art of Faulkner's Novels*, 38-40, 61-70, 87-107.

———, "Faulkner's THE SOUND AND THE FURY," *Expl* 22 (Dec., 1963): Item 31.

———, "Moral and Temporal Order in THE SOUND AND THE FURY," *SR* 61 (Spring, 1953): 221-37.

Telotte, J. P., "Butting Heads with Faulkner's Soldier," *NConL*, iii (May, 1979): 7-8.

Thompson, Lawrance, "Mirror Analogues in THE SOUND AND THE FURY," in *English Institute Essays, 1952*, 83-106. Also in Hoffman, F. J., and O. W. Vickery, eds., *William Faulkner*, 211-25. Also in Westbrook, M., ed., *Modern American Novel*, 134-53. Also in Warren, R. P., ed., *Faulkner*, 109-21. Also in Wagner, L. W., ed., *William Faulkner*, 199-212.

———, *William Faulkner*, 29-52, 187-91.

Thornton, Welden, "A Note on the Source of Faulkner's Jason," *SNNTS* 1, iii (Fall, 1969): 370-2.

Tilley, Winthrop, "The Idiot Boy in Mississippi: Faulkner's THE SOUND AND THE FURY," *Amer. Jnl. of Mental Deficiency* 59 (Jan., 1955): 374-7.

Traschen, Isadore, "The Tragic Form of THE SOUND AND THE FURY," *SoR* 12, iv (Oct., 1976): 798-813.

Tuck, D., *Crowell's Handbook of Faulkner*, 22-33.

Tuck, Susan, "House of Compson, House of Tyrone: Faulkner's Influence on O'Neill," *EON* 5, iii (Winter, 1981): 10-16.

Underwood, Henry J., Jr., "Sartre on THE SOUND AND THE FURY: Some Errors," *MFS* 12 (Winter, 1966-67): 477-9.

Vahanian, Gabriel, "William Faulkner: Rendez-vous with Existence," *Wait Without Idols*, N.Y.: Braziller, 1964, 93-116.

Van Nostrand, A. D., "The Poetic Dialogues of William Faulkner," *Every Man His Own Poet*, 181-4.

Vickery, Olga W., "THE SOUND AND THE FURY: A Study in Perspective," *PMLA* 69 (Dec., 1954): 1017-37. Also in Vickery, O. W., *Novels of William Faulkner*, 28-49. Also in Cox, L. H., ed., *William Faulkner*, 175-201. Also, condensed, in Cowan, M. H., ed., *Twentieth Century Interpretations of THE SOUND AND THE FURY*, 40-52.

Volpe, E. L., "Chronology and Scene Shifts in Benjy's and Quentin's Sections," in Cowan, M. H., ed., *Twentieth Century Interpretations of THE SOUND AND THE FURY*, 103-8. Adapted from Volpe, E. L., *Reader's Guide to William Faulkner*, 353, 363-5, 373-7.

———, *Reader's Guide to William Faulkner*, 87-126.

Wadlington, Warwick, "THE SOUND AND THE FURY: A Logic of Tragedy," *AL* 53, iii (Nov., 1981): 409-23.

Waggoner, H. H., *William Faulkner*, 34-61. Also, condensed, in Cowan, M. H., ed., *Twentieth Century Interpretations of THE SOUND AND THE FURY*, 97-101.

Wagner, Linda W., "Faulkner: The Craft of Fiction," *Hemingway and Faulkner*, 175-82.

———, "Jason Compson: The Demands of Honor," *SR* 79, iv (Autumn, 1971): 554-75.

———, "Language and Act: Caddy Compson," *SLJ* 14, ii (Spring, 1982): 49-61.

Walker, Nancy, "Stephen and Quentin," 109-13 in Benstock, Bernard, ed., *The Seventh of Joyce*, Bloomington: Indiana Un. Pr., 1982; Brighton: Harvester, 1982.

Wall, Carey, "THE SOUND AND THE FURY: The Emotional Center," *MQ* 11, iv (Summer, 1970): 371-87.

Walters, Paul S., "Theory and Practice in Faulkner: THE SOUND AND THE FURY," *ESA* 10 (Mar., 1967): 22-39.

Watkins, Floyd C., "The Word and the Deed in Faulkner's First Great Novels," *Flesh and the Word*, 182-90, 197-202. Also in Wagner, L. W., ed., *William Faulkner*, 213-30.

Watson, James G., "Literary Self-Criticism: Faulkner in Fiction on Fiction," *SoQ* 20, i (Fall, 1981): 49-50.

Way, Brian, "William Faulkner," *CritQ* 3 (Spring, 1961): 47-9.

Weinstein, A. L., *Vision and Response in Modern Fiction*, 111-35.

Weinstein, Philip M., "Caddy *Disparue*: Exploring an Episode Common to Proust and Faulkner," *CLS* 14 (Mar., 1977): 38-52.

Weisgerber, Jean, "Faulkner and Dostoievski: THE SOUND AND THE FURY," *RLC* 39 (1965): 406-21.

———, *Faulkner and Dostoevsky*, 179-92.

Westbrook, Wayne W., "Jason Compson and the Costs of Speculation: A Second Look," *MissQ* 30 (Summer, 1977): 437-40.

Whicher, Stephen E., "The Compson's Nancies: A Note on THE SOUND AND THE FURY and 'That Evening Sun'," *AL* 26 (May, 1954): 253-5.

Wilder, Amos N., *Theology and Modern Literature*, Cambridge: Harvard Un. Pr., 1958, 119-28. Also in Barth, J. R., S. J., ed., *Religious Perspectives in Faulkner's Fiction*, 91-102.

Williams, D., *Faulkner's Women*, 61-95.

Williams, Joan, "In Defense of Caroline Compson," in Kinney, A. F., ed., *Critical Essays on William Faulkner: The Compson Family*, 402-7.

Wittenberg, J. B., *Faulkner*, 73-88.

Woodward, Robert H., "Poe's Raven, Faulkner's Sparrow, and Another Window," *PoeN* 2, i-iii (April, 1969): 37-8. [Parallels between Poe's THE RAVEN and a paragraph of the Quentin Section.]

Yamamoto, Masashi, "Faulkner's Use of Smell in THE SOUND AND THE FURY," *SALit* 12 (1976): 19-31.

Young, James D., "Quentin's Maundy Thursday," *TSE* 10 (1960): 143-51.

Young, Thomas D., "Narration as Creative Act: The Role of Quentin Compson in ABSALOM, ABSALOM!" in Harrington, E., and A. J. Abadie, eds., *Faulkner, Modernism, and Film*, 82-102. Also in Kinney, A. F., ed., *Critical Essays on William Faulkner: The Compson Family*, 318-31.

Zlobin, G., "A Struggle Against Time," in Vroon, R., tr., *20th Century American Literature: A Soviet View*, 285-305.

THE TOWN (See also SNOPES Trilogy)

Brooks, C., *William Faulkner*, 192-218.

Brylowski, W., *Faulkner's Olympian Laugh*, 201-6.

Creighton, J. V., *William Faulkner's Craft of Revision*, 49-63.

Dirksen, Sherland N., "William Faulkner's Snopes Family: THE HAMLET, THE TOWN, and THE MANSION," *ESRS* 11, ii (Dec., 1962): 23-32.

Everett, W. K., *Faulkner's Art and Characters*, 115-19.

Glicksberg, Charles I., "Faulkner's World of Love and Sex," *Sexual Revolution in Modern American Literature*, 114-18.

Gold, Joseph, "Truth or Consequences: Faulkner's THE TOWN," *MissQ* 13 (Summer, 1960): 112-16.

_____, *William Faulkner*, 148-61.

Gregory, Nancy E., "A Study of the Early Versions of Faulkner's THE TOWN and THE MANSION," *DAI* 36 (1975): 3686A-87A.

Gwynn, F. L., and J. L. Blotner, eds., *Faulkner in the University*.

Harder, Kelsie B., "Proverbial Snopeslore," *TFSB* 24 (1958): 89-95.

Hauck, R. B., *Cheerful Nihilism*, 187-91.

Howe, I., *William Faulkner*, 107-10, 282-94.

Jarrett, David W., "Eustacia Vye and Eula Verner, Olympians: The Worlds of Thomas Hardy and William Faulkner," *Novel* 6, ii (Winter, 1973): 163-74.

Kazin, A., *Contemporaries*, 150-4.

Kindrick, Robert L., "Lizzie Dahlberg and Eula Verner: Two Modern Perspectives on the Earth Mother," *Midamerica* 2 (1975): 93-111.

Lawson, Lewis A., "The Grotesque-Comic in the SNOPES Trilogy," *L&P* 15 (1965): 107-19. Also in Manheim, L., and E., eds., *Hidden Patterns*, 243-58.

Leary, L., *William Faulkner of Yoknapatawpha County*, 161-3.

Longley, John L., "Galahad Gavin and a Garland of Snopeses," *VQR* 33 (Autumn, 1957): 623-8.

Lytle, Andrew, "THE TOWN: Helen's Last Stand," *SR* 65 (Summer, 1957): 475-84. Also in Lytle, A., *Hero with the Private Parts*, 137-47.

Marcus, Steven, "Faulkner's Town: Mythology as History," *PR* 24 (Summer, 1957): 432-41. Also in Hoffman, F. J., and O. W. Vickery, eds., *William Faulkner*, 382-91.

Meriwether, James B., "The Snopes Revisited," *SatR* (April 27, 1957): 12-13.

Millgate, M., *Achievement of William Faulkner*, 235-44.

_____, *William Faulkner*, 90-2.

Mooney, Stephen L., "Faulkner's THE TOWN: A Question of Voices," *MissQ* 13 (Summer, 1960): 117-22.

Moses, Edwin, "Comedy in THE TOWN," in Carey, G. O., ed., *Faulkner*, 59-73.

Page, S. R., *Faulkner's Women*, 165-71.

Polk, Noel, "Faulkner and Respectability," in Fowler, D., and A. J. Abadie, eds., *Fifty Years of Yoknapatawpha*, 119-33.

Powers, L. H., *Faulkner's Yoknapatawpha Comedy*, 218-32.

Richardson, K. E., *Force and Faith in the Novels of William Faulkner*, 124-6.

Roberts, James L., "Snopeslore: THE HAMLET, THE TOWN, THE MANSION," *UKCR* 28 (1961): 65-71.

Rogers, Thomas H., "Farce and Anecdote," *ChiR* 6 (Autumn, 1957): 110-14.

Rubin, Louis D., Jr., "Snopeslore: or, Faulkner Clears the Deck," *WR* 22 (Autumn, 1957): 73-6.

Shanaghan, Father Malachy M., O.S.B., "A Critical Analysis of the Fictional Techniques of William Faulkner," *DA* 20 (1960): 4663 (Notre Dame).

Slatoff, W. J., *Quest for Failure*, 204-5.

Sullivan, William P., "William Faulkner and the Community," *DA* 22 (1962): 4355 (Columbia).

Swiggart, P., *Art of Faulkner's Novels*, 195-202.

Thompson, L., *William Faulkner*, 148-58, 200-2.

Thonan, Robert, "William Faulkner: From THE HAMLET to THE TOWN," *ESA* 2 (Sept., 1959): 190-202.

Tuck, D., *Crowell's Handbook of Faulkner*, 81-6.

Vickery, O. W., *Novels of William Faulkner*, 181-91.

Volpe, E. L., *Reader's Guide to William Faulkner*, 317-31.

Waggoner, H. H., *William Faulkner*, 232-7.

Watson, J. G., *Snopes Dilemma*, 75-146.

Weisgerber, J., *Faulkner and Dostoevsky*, 333-7.

Williams, D., *Faulkner's Women*, 214-21.

Wilson, Raymond J., III, "Imitative Flem Snopes and Faulkner's Causal Sequence in THE TOWN," *TCL* 26, iv (1980): 432-44.

Wittenberg, J. B., *Faulkner*, 228-32.

THE WILD PALMS

Adams, R. P., *Faulkner*, 111-14.

Backman, M., *Faulkner*, 127-38.

_____, "Faulkner's THE WILD PALMS: Civilization Against Nature," *UKCR* 28 (Mar., 1962): 199-204.

Baker, Carlos, "William Faulkner: The Doomed and the Damned," in Bode, C., ed., *Young Rebel in American Literature*, 160-3.

Beach, J. W., *American Fiction*, 150-2 *passim*.

Bedell, G. C., *Kierkegaard and Faulkner*, 161-73.

Brooks, Cleanth, "The Tradition of Romantic Love and THE WILD PALMS," *MissQ* 25 (Summer, 1972): 265-87.

_____, *William Faulkner: Toward Yoknapatawpha and Beyond*, 205-29, 406-13.

Brylowski, W., *Faulkner's Olympian Laugh*, 127-39.

Church, M., "William Faulkner: Myth and Duration," *Time and Reality*, 243-4.

Coindreau, M. E., *Time of William Faulkner*, 51-63.

Collins, Carvel, "Faulkner: The Man and the Artist," *UMSE* 15 (1978): 217-31.

Colson, Theodore, "Analogues of Faulkner's THE WILD PALMS and Hawthorne's 'The Birthmark'," *DR* 56, iii (1976): 510-18.

Cushman, William P., "Knowledge and Involvement in Faulkner's THE WILD PALMS," in Carey, G. O., ed., *Faulkner*, 25-38.

Day, Douglas, "Borges, Faulkner, and THE WILD PALMS," *VQR* 56, i (1980): 109-18.

Everett, W. K., *Faulkner's Art and Characters*, 124-7.

Fowler, Doreen A., "Measuring Faulkner's Tall Convict," *SNNTS* 14, iii (1982): 280-4.

Galharn, Carl, "Faulkner's Faith: Roots from THE WILD PALMS," *TCL* 1 (Oct., 1955): 139-60.

Glicksberg, Charles I., "Faulkner's World of Love and Sex," *Sexual Revolution in Modern American Literature*, 107-8.

Gwynn, F. L., and J. L. Blotner, eds., *Faulkner in the University*.

Hill, James S., "Faulkner's Allusion to Virginia Woolf's A ROOM OF ONE'S OWN in THE WILD PALMS," *NMAL* 4 (Spring, 1980): Item 10.

Hoffman, Frederick J., in French, W. G., and W. E. Kidd, eds., *American Winners of the Nobel Literary Prize*, 143-5.

_____, *William Faulkner*, 83-5.

Howe, I., *William Faulkner*, 233-42.

Jewkes, W. T., "Counterpoint in Faulkner's THE WILD PALMS," *WSCL* 2, i (Winter, 1961): 39-53.

Leary, L., *William Faulkner of Yoknapatawpha County*, 128-32.

Levins, L. G., *Faulkner's Heroic Design*, 133-44.

MacDonald, Phyllis A., "Experiencing William Faulkner: Rhythms in THE WILD PALMS," *BLRev* 2, i (1980): 5-17.

MacMillan, Duane J., "The Non-Yoknapatawpha Novels of William Faulkner: An Examination of SOLDIERS' PAY, MOSQUITOES, PYLON, THE WILD PALMS, and A FABLE," *DAI* 32 (1972): 6986A (Wis.).

McHaney, Thomas L., "Anderson, Hemingway, and Faulkner's THE WILD PALMS," *PMLA* 87, iii (May, 1972): 465-74. Also in Cox, L. H., ed., *William Faulkner*, 267-90.

_____, *William Faulkner's THE WILD PALMS: A Study*, Jackson: Mississippi Un. Pr., 1975.

_____, "William Faulkner's THE WILD PALMS: A Textual and Critical Study," *DAI* 30 (1969): 2540A-41A (S.C.).

Merton, Thomas, "Baptism in the Forest: Wisdom and Initiation in William Faulkner," in Panichas, G. A., ed., *Mansions of the Spirit*, 34-42. Also, excerpted, in *CathW* 207 (June, 1968): 128-30.

Millgate, M., *Achievement of William Faulkner*, 171-9.

_____, *William Faulkner*, 69-73.

Moldenhauer, Joseph J., "Unity of Theme and Structure in THE WILD PALMS," in Hoffman, F. J., and O. W. Vickery, eds., *William Faulkner*, 305-22.

Monteiro, George, "The Limits of Professionalism: A Sociological Approach to Faulkner, Fitzgerald and Hemingway," *Criticism* 15 (Spring, 1973): 145-51.

Moses, W. R., "The Unity of THE WILD PALMS," *MFS* 2 (Autumn, 1956): 125-31.

O'Connor, William Van, "Faulkner, Hemingway, and the 1920's," in Langford, R. E., and Taylor, W. E., eds., *Twenties*, 95-8.

_____, *William Faulkner*, 29-31. Also, revised, in O'Connor, W. V., ed., *Seven Modern American Novelists*, 142-4.

Page, S. R., *Faulkner's Women*, 122-35.

Park, Sue S., "Life's Blood in THE WILD PALMS," *CCTE* 43 (1978): 26-33.

Peckham, Morse, "The Place of Sex in the Work of William Faulkner," *STwC* 14 (Fall, 1974): 1-20.

Reeves, Caroline H., "THE WILD PALMS: Faulkner's Chaotic Cosmos," *MissQ* 20 (1967): 148-57.

Richards, Lewis A., "The Literary Styles of Jean-Paul Sartre and William Faulkner: An Analysis, Comparison and Contrast," *DA* 24 (1964): 3755-6 (So. Calif.).

Richards, Lewis, "Sex Under THE WILD PALMS and a Moral Question," *ArQ* 28 (Winter, 1972): 326-32.

Richardson, H. Edward, "The 'Hemingwaves' in Faulkner's WILD PALMS," *MFS* 4 (Winter, 1958-59): 357-60.

Richardson, K. E., *Force and Faith in the Novels of William Faulkner*, 67-70, 96-9, 117-18.

Rower, Ann D., "Work in Counterpoint: Faulkner's THE WILD PALMS," *DAI* 35 (1975): 6731A.

Seyppel, J., *William Faulkner*, 70-1.

Slatoff, W. J., *Quest for Failure*, 205-8.

Stein, Randolph E., "The World Outside Yoknapatawpha: A Study of Five Novels by William Faulkner," *DA* 26 (1965): 2225 (Ohio Un.).

Swiggart, P., *Art of Faulkner's Novels*, 51-7.

Tuck, D., *Crowell's Handbook of Faulkner*, 136-42.

Vickery, O. W., *Novels of William Faulkner*, 156-66.

Volpe, E. L., *Reader's Guide to William Faulkner*, 212-30.

Waggoner, H. H., *William Faulkner*, 121-2, 132-47.

Way, Brian, "William Faulkner," *CritQ* 3 (Spring, 1961): 51-3.

Weisgerber, J., *Faulkner and Dostoevsky*, 260-7.

Wittenberg, J. B., *Faulkner*, 167-79.

BIBLIOGRAPHY

Bassett, John, *William Faulkner: An Annotated Checklist of Criticism*, N.Y.: David Lewis, 1972.

_____, "William Faulkner's THE SOUND AND THE FURY: An Annotated Checklist of Criticism," *RALS* 1 (Autumn, 1971): 217-46.

Beebe, Maurice, "Criticism of William Faulkner: A Selected Checklist," *MFS* 13, i (Spring, 1967): 115-61.

Bleikasten, A., *Most Splendid Failure*, 243-6. [THE SOUND AND THE FURY].

Inge, M. Thomas, "William Faulkner's LIGHT IN AUGUST: An Annotated Checklist of Criticism," *RALS* 1 (Spring, 1971): 30-57.

Lloyd, James B., "An Annotated Bibliography of William Faulkner, 1967-1970," *UMSE* 12 (1971): 1-57.

Massey, Linton R., comp., *"Man Working," 1919-1962, William Faulkner, A Catalogue of the William Faulkner Collections at the University of Virginia*, Charlottesville: Un. Pr. of Virginia, 1968.

McDonald, W. U., Jr., "Bassett's Checklist of Faulkner Criticism: Some 'Local' Addenda," *BB* 32 (April-June, 1975): 76.

McHaney, Thomas L., *William Faulkner: A Reference Guide*, Boston: Hall, 1976.

Meriwether, James B., *Checklist of William Faulkner*. (Merrill Checklists.) Columbus, Oh: Charles E. Merrill, 1970.

Ricks, Beatrice, comp., *William Faulkner: A Bibliography of Secondary Works* (Scarecrow Author Bibliogs., 49), Metuchen, N.J.: Scarecrow, 1981.

Sleeth, Irene L., "William Faulkner: A Bibliography of Criticism," *TCL* 8 (April, 1962): 18-43.

Vickery, Olga W., "A Selective Bibliography," in Hoffman, F. J., and O. W. Vickery, eds., *William Faulkner*, 393-428.

CONCORDANCES

Capps, Jack L., *AS I LAY DYING: A Concordance to the Novel*, Ann Arbor, Mich.: Univ. Microfilms Internat., for Faulkner Concordance Advisory Board, 1977.

_____, ed., *LIGHT IN AUGUST: A Concordance to the Novel*, Ann Arbor, Mich.: Faulkner Concordance Advisory Board, 1979.

_____, *REQUIEM FOR A NUN: A Concordance to the Novel*, Ann Arbor, Mich.: Univ. Microfilms Internat., 1978.

Polk, Noel, and Kenneth Privratsky, eds., *A FABLE: A Concordance to the Novel*, Ann Arbor: UMI, 1981.

_____, *THE SOUND AND THE FURY: A Concordance to the Novel*, Ann Arbor, Mich.: UMI, 1980.

Smart, George K, *Religious Elements in Faulkner's Early Novels: A Selective Concordance*, UMPEAL, No. 8, Coral Gables, FL: Un. of Miami Pr., 1965.

_____, THE SOUND AND THE FURY: A Concordance to the Novel, Ann Arbor: UMI, 1980.

Smart, George K, *Religious Elements in Faulkner's Early Novels: A Selective Concordance*, UMPEAL, No. 8, Coral Gables, FL: Un. of Miami Pr., 1965.

FEDERMAN, RAYMOND, 1928-

GENERAL

Caramello, Charles, "Flushing Out 'The Voice in the Closet'," *Sub-stance* 20 (1978): 101-13.
Dienstfrey, Harris, "The Choice of Inventions," *FictionI* 2/3 (Spring-Fall, 1974): 147-50.
McCaffery, Larry, "Excerpts from an Interview," 185-9 in Wellman, Don, ed., *Perception*, Cambridge, Mass.: O. ARS, 1982.
_____, "Raymond Federman and the Fiction of Self-Creation: A Critical Mosaic," *Par Rapport* 3-4 (1980-81): 31-44.

DOUBLE OR NOTHING: A REAL FICTITIOUS DISCOURSE

Dienstfrey, Harris, "The Choice of Inventions," *FictionI* 2/3 (Spring-Fall, 1974): 147-50.
McCaffery, Larry, "Raymond Federman and the Fiction of Self-Creation: A critical Mosaic," *Par Rapport* 3-4 (1980-81): 34-6.
Werner, C. H., *Paradoxical Resolutions*, 103-8.

TAKE IT OR LEAVE IT

Klinkowitz, J., *Literary Disruptions*, 148-53.
McCaffery, Larry, "Raymond Federman and the Fiction of Self-Creation: A Critical Mosaic," *Par Rapport* 3-4 (1980-81): 37-9.
Semrau, Janusz, "A Questionnaire: Some Remarks Toward a Study of Novelistic Self-Consciousness," *KN* 29, iii-iv (1982): 294-5.

FERBER, EDNA, 1887-1968

GENERAL

Horowitz, Steven P., and Miriam J. Landsman, "The Americanization of Edna: A Study of Ms. Ferber's Jewish American Identity," *SAJL* 2 (1982): 69-80.
Shaughnessy, M. R., *Women and Success in American Society in the Works of Edna Ferber*.
Spitz, Leon, "Edna Ferber: An American Jewish Self-Portrait," *CJF* 13, ii (Winter, 1954-55): 100-3.
Stedman, Jane W., "Edna Ferber and Menus with Meanings," *JAC* 2, iii (Fall, 1979): 454-62.
Uffen, Ellen S., "Edna Ferber and the 'Theatricalization' of American Mythology," *MMisc* 8 (1980): 82-93.

AMERICAN BEAUTY

Shaughnessy, M. R., *Women and Success in American Society in the Works of Edna Ferber*, 202-15.

CIMARRON

Shaughnessy, M. R., *Women and Success in American Society in the Works of Edna Ferber*, 179-201.

COME AND GET IT

Shaughnessy, M. R., *Women and Success in American Society in the Works of Edna Ferber*, 216-41.

DAWN O'HARA: THE GIRL WHO LAUGHED

Shaughnessy, M. R., *Women and Success in American Society in the Works of Edna Ferber*, 88-99.

FANNY HERSELF

Shaughnessy, M. R., *Women and Success in American Society in the Works of Edna Ferber*, 115-33.

GIANT

Shaughnessy, M. R., *Women and Success in American Society in the Works of Edna Ferber*, 283-313.

THE GIRLS

Shaughnessy, M. R., *Women and Success in American Society in the Works of Edna Ferber*, 134-48.

GREAT SON

Shaughnessy, M. R., *Women and Success in American Society in the Works of Edna Ferber*, 266-82.

ICE PALACE

Shaughnessy, M. R., *Women and Success in American Society in the Works of Edna Ferber*, 314-38.

SARATOGA TRUNK

Shaughnessy, M. R., *Women and Success in American Society in the Works of Edna Ferber*, 242-65.

SHOW BOAT

Plante, Patricia R., "Mark Twain, Ferber and the Mississippi," *MTJ* 13, ii (Summer, 1966): 8-10.
Shaughnessy, M. R., *Women and Success in American Society in the Works of Edna Ferber*, 166-78.

SO BIG

Shaughnessy, M. R., *Women and Success in American Society in the Works of Edna Ferber*, 149-65.

BIBLIOGRAPHY

Brenni, Vito J., and Betty L. Spencer, "Edna Ferber: A Selected Bibliography," *BB* 22, vi (Sept.-Dec., 1958): 152-6.

FIEDLER, LESLIE A(ARON), 1917-

GENERAL

Davis, Robert G., "Leslie Fiedler's Fiction," *Ctary* 43, i (Jan., 1967): 73-7.
Kostelanetz, Richard, "Leslie Fiedler" (1965): *STwC* No. 13 (Spring, 1974): 21-38.

THE SECOND STONE

Glicksberg, C. I., *Sexual Revolution in Modern American Literature*, 204-6.

FIELDING, GABRIEL, Pseud. (Alan Gabriel Barnsley), 1916-

GENERAL

Grande, Brother Luke M., F.S.C., "Gabriel Fielding, New Master of the Catholic Classic?" *CathW* 197 (June, 1963): 172-9.

Stanford, Derek, "Gabriel Fielding and the Catholic Novel," *Month* 212 (Dec., 1961): 352-6.

Towne, Frank, "The Tragicomic Moment in the Art of Gabriel Fielding," in Grosshans, H., ed., *To Find Something New*, 104-16.

THE BIRTHDAY KING

Bowers, Frederick, "Gabriel Fielding's THE BIRTHDAY KING," *QQ* 74 (Spring, 1967): 149-58.

Grande, Brother Luke M., F.S.C., "Gabriel Fielding, New Master of the Catholic Classic?" *CathW* 197 (June, 1963): 172-9.

Kunkel, Francis L., "Clowns and Saviors: Two Contemporary Novels," *Ren* 18 (Autumn, 1965): 40-4.

Towne, Frank, "The Tragicomic Moment in the Art of Gabriel Fielding," in Grosshans, H., ed., *To Find Something New*, 111-13.

BROTHERLY LOVE

Towne, Frank, "The Tragicomic Moment in the Art of Gabriel Fielding," in Grosshans, H., ed., *To Find Something New*, 105-7.

EIGHT DAYS

Towne, Frank, "The Tragicomic Moment in the Art of Gabriel Fielding," in Grosshans, H., ed., *To Find Something New*, 110-11.

GENTLEMEN IN THEIR SEASON

"Novels of 1966. Gabriel Fielding, GENTLEMEN IN THEIR SEASON," in *T.L.S. Essays and Reviews, 1966*, 69-71. Also in *TLS* (June 23, 1966).

Towne, Frank, "The Tragicomic Moment in the Art of Gabriel Fielding," in Grosshans, H., ed., *To Find Something New*, 113-16.

IN THE TIME OF GREENBLOOM

Bowers, Frederick, "The Unity of Fielding's GREENBLOOM," *Ren* 18 (Spring, 1966): 147-55.

Price, Martin, in *YaleR* 47 (Autumn, 1957): 143-6.

Robbie, May G., "Transformational Technique in Gabriel Fielding's IN THE TIME OF GREENBLOOM," *DAI* 35 (1974): 2953A (U. of the Pacific).

Towne, Frank, "The Tragicomic Moment in the Art of Gabriel Fielding," in Grosshans, H., ed., *To Find Something New*, 107-9.

THROUGH STREETS BROAD AND NARROW

Stanford, Derek, "Gabriel Fielding and the Catholic Novel," *Month* 212 (Dec., 1961): 352-6.

Towne, Frank, "The Tragicomic Moment in the Art of Gabriel Fielding," in Grosshans, H., ed., *To Find Something New*, 109-10.

FINDLEY, TIMOTHY, 1930-

GENERAL

Aitken, Johan, "'Long Live the Dead': An Interview with Timothy Findley," *JCF* 33 (1981-82): 79-93.

Cude, Wilfred, "Timothy Findley," 77-84 in Heath, Jeffrey M., ed., *Profiles in Canadian Literature 4*, Toronto: Dundurn, 1982.

Findley, Timothy, "Alice Drops Her Cigarette on the Floor...: William Whitehead Looking Over Timothy Findley's Shoulder," *CanL* 91 (Winter, 1981): 10-21.

Hulcoop, John F., "'Look! Listen! Mark My Words!': Paying Attention to Timothy Findley's Fictions," *CanL* 91 (Winter, 1981): 22-47.

Summers, Alison, "Interview with Timothy Findley," *CanL* 91 (Winter, 1981): 49-55.

_____, "An Interview with Timothy Findley," *MHRev* 58 (April, 1981): 105-10.

FAMOUS LAST WORDS

Benson, Eugene, "'Whispers of Chaos': FAMOUS LAST WORDS," *WLWE* 21, iii (Autumn, 1982): 599-606.

THE WARS

Drolet, Gilbert, "'Prayers Against Despair': A Retrospective Note on Findley's THE WARS," *JCF* 33 (1981-82): 148-55.

Klovan, Peter, "'Bright and Good': Findley's THE WARS," *CanL* 91 (Winter, 1981): 58-69.

Kroller, Eva-Marie, "The Exploding Frame: Use of Photography in Timothy Findley's THE WARS," *JCanStud* 16, 3-4 (1981): 68-74.

Pirie, Bruce, "The Dragon in the Fog: 'Displaced Mythology' in THE WARS," *CanL* 91 (Winter, 1981): 70-9.

FISHER, VARDIS, 1895-1968

GENERAL

Arrington, Leonard J., and Jon Haupt, "The Mormon Heritage of Vardis Fisher," *BYUS* 18, i (Fall, 1977): 27-47.

Bishop, J. P., "The Strange Case of Vardis Fisher," *SoR* (Autumn, 1937): 348-59. Also in Bishop, J. P., *Collected Essays*, 56-65.

Chatterton, W., *Vardis Fisher*.

Day, George F., "The Uses of History in the Novels of Vardis Fisher," *DA* 29 (1968): 1225A (Colorado).

_____, *Uses of History in the Novels of Vardis Fisher*.

Fisher, Vardis, "The Novelist and His Characters," *ABC* 14 (Sept., 1963): 25-30.

_____, "The Novelist and His Work," *Thomas Wolfe as I Knew Him and Other Essays*, Denver: Alan Swallow, 1963, 103-15.

Flora, Joseph M., "The Early Power of Vardis Fisher," *ABC* 14 (Sept., 1963): 15-19.

_____, *Vardis Fisher*.

_____, "Vardis Fisher and James Branch Cabell: An Essay on Influence and Reputation," *Cabellian* 2, i (Autumn, 1969): 12-16.

_____, "Vardis Fisher and James Branch Cabell: A Postscript," *Cabellian* 3, i (Autumn, 1970): 7-9.

_____, "Vardis Fisher and Wallace Stegner: Teacher and Student," *WAL* 5, ii (Summer, 1970): 121-8.

Milton, J. R., *Novel of the American West*, 117-59.

_____, "The Primitive World of Vardis Fisher: The Idaho Novels," *MQ* 17, iv (Summer, 1976): 369-84. Also in Pilkington, W. T., ed., *Critical Essays on the Western American Novel*, 125-35.

_____, *Three West: Conversations with Vardis Fisher, Max Evans, Michael Straight*, Vermillion: Un. of So. Dakota Pr., 1970, 1-45.

Snell, G., *Shapers of American Fiction*, 276-88.

Swallow, Alan, "The Mavericks," *Crit* 2, iii (Winter, 1959): 79-84.

Taber, Ronald W., "Vardis Fisher: New Directions for the Historical Novel," *WAL* 1 (Winter, 1967): 285-96.

ADAM AND THE SERPENT (See also THE TESTAMENT OF MAN Series)

Flora, J. M., *Vardis Fisher*, 84-5.

AMERICANA Novels

Day, G. F., *Uses of History in the Novels of Vardis Fisher*, 87-128.

APRIL: A FABLE OF LOVE

Chatterton, W., *Vardis Fisher*, 25-9.

Flora, J. M., *Vardis Fisher*, 109-13.

Meldrum, Barbara, "Vardis Fisher's Antelope People: Pursuing an Elusive Dream," in Bingham, E. R., and G. A. Love, eds., *Northwest Perspectives*, 163-4.

CHILDREN OF GOD: AN AMERICAN EPIC

Chatterton, W., *Vardis Fisher*, 32-4.

Davis, David B., "CHILDREN OF GOD: An Historian's Evaluation," *WHR* 8 (Winter, 1953-54): 49-56.

Flora, J. M., *Vardis Fisher*, 131-8.

Snell, G., *Shapers of American Fiction*, 285-6.

CITY OF ILLUSION, A NOVEL

Chatterton, W., *Vardis Fisher*, 34-6.

Flora, J. M., *Vardis Fisher*, 129-31.

DARK BRIDWELL

Chatterton, W., *Vardis Fisher*, 15-19.

Flora, J. M., *Vardis Fisher*, 106-9.

Meldrum, Barbara, "Vardis Fisher's Antelope People: Pursuing an Elusive Dream," in Bingham, E. R., and G. A. Love, eds., *Northwest Perspectives*, 160-3.

Milton, J. R., *Novel of the American West*, 140-7.

_____, "The Primitive World of Vardis Fisher: The Idaho Novels," *MQ* 17, iv (Summer, 1976): 379-84. Also in Pilkington, W. T., ed., *Critical Essays on the Western American Novel*, 132-5.

DARKNESS AND THE DEEP (See also THE TESTAMENT OF MAN Series)

Flora, J. M., *Vardis Fisher*, 74-8.

THE DIVINE PASSION (See also THE TESTAMENT OF MAN Series)

Flora, J. M., *Vardis Fisher*, 85-7.

FORGIVE US OUR VIRTUES

Flora, Joseph M., "Vardis Fisher and James Branch Cabell: A Postscript," *Cabellian* 3, i (Autumn, 1970): 7-9.

A GOAT FOR AZAZEL (See also THE TESTAMENT OF MAN Series)

Flora, J. M., *Vardis Fisher*, 92-3.

THE GOLDEN ROOMS (See also THE TESTAMENT OF MAN Series)

Duncan, Kirby L., "William Golding and Vardis Fisher: A Study in Parallels and Extensions," *CE* 27 (Dec., 1965): 232-5.

Flora, J. M., *Vardis Fisher*, 78-82.

IN TRAGIC LIFE (See also THE VRIDAR HUNTER Tetralogy)

Bishop, J. B., "The Strange Case of Vardis Fisher," *Collected Essays*, 56-65. Also in *SoR* (Autumn, 1937).

Chatterton, W., *Vardis Fisher*, 19-24.

Flora, J. M., *Vardis Fisher*, 35-6, 67-8.

Snell, G., *Shapers of American Fiction*, 281-5.

INTIMATIONS OF EVE (See also THE TESTAMENT OF MAN Series)

Flora, J. M., *Vardis Fisher*, 82-4.

THE ISLAND OF THE INNOCENT (See also THE TESTAMENT OF MAN Series)

Flora, J. M., *Vardis Fisher*, 89-91.

JESUS CAME AGAIN (See also THE TESTAMENT OF MAN Series)

Flora, J. M., *Vardis Fisher*, 91-2.

THE MOTHERS: AN AMERICAN SAGA OF COURAGE

Chatterton, W., *Vardis Fisher*, 36-9.

Flora, J. M., *Vardis Fisher*, 119-22.

Robinson, Francis C., "The Donner Party in Fiction," in Emery, J. K. ed., *University of Colorado Studies* (Series in Language and Literature, 10), Boulder: Un. of Colorado Pr., 1966, 87-93.

MOUNTAIN MAN

Angleman, Sydney W., *UHQ* 34 (Fall, 1966): 349-50.

Chatterton, W., *Vardis Fisher*, 42-5.

Flora, Joseph M., "Westering and Woman: A Thematic Study of Kesey's ONE FLEW OVER THE CUCKOO'S NEST and Fisher's MOUNTAIN MAN," in Lee, L. L., and M. Lewis, eds., *Women, Women Writers, and the West*, 131-41.

McAllister, Mick, "You Can't Go Home: Jeremiah Johnson and the Wilderness," *WAL* 13, i (May, 1978): 35-49. [Film based on MOUNTAIN MAN.]

MY HOLY SATAN (See also THE TESTAMENT OF MAN Series)

Flora, J. M., *Vardis Fisher*, 95-7.

NO VILLAIN NEED BE (See also THE VRIDAR HUNTER Tetralogy)

Flora, J. M., *Vardis Fisher*, 45-8, 53-4, 69-70.

ORPHANS IN GETHSEMANE (See also THE TESTAMENT OF MAN Series)

Flora, J. M., *Vardis Fisher*, 49-72.

PASSIONS SPIN THE PLOT (See also THE VRIDAR HUNTER Tetralogy)

Flora, J. M., *Vardis Fisher*, 36-7, 68-9.
Lyons, J. W., *College Novel in America*, 85-7.
Morton, Beatrice K., "An Early Stage of Fisher's Journey to the East: PASSIONS SPIN THE PLOT," *SDR* 18, i (1980): 43-52.

PEACE LIKE A RIVER (See also THE TESTAMENT OF MAN Series)

Flora, J. M., *Vardis Fisher*, 93-5.

PEMMICAN

Chatterton, W., *Vardis Fisher*, 39-40.
Flora, J. M., *Vardis Fisher*, 124-8.
Milton, J. R., *Novel of the American West*, 128-31.

TALE OF VALOR

Chatterton, W., *Vardis Fisher*, 40-2.
Flora, J. M., *Vardis Fisher*, 122-4.
Milton, J. R., *Novel of the American West*, 120-3, 126-7.

THE TESTAMENT OF MAN Series

Day, G. F., *Uses of History in the Novels of Vardis Fisher*, 24-86.
Fisher, Vardis, "Vardis Fisher Comments on His TESTAMENT OF MAN Series," *ABC* 14 (Sept., 1963): 31-6. Also in Fisher, V., *Thomas Wolfe as I Knew Him and Other Essays*, Denver: Alan Swallow, 1963, 64-78.
Flora, J. M., *Vardis Fisher*, 73-98.
Margarick, P., "Vardis Fisher and His TESTAMENT OF MAN," *ABC* 14 (Sept., 1963): 20-4.
Milton, J. R., *Novel of the American West*, 153-9.
Thomas, Alfred K., "The Epic of Evolution, Its Etiology and Art: A Study of Vardis Fisher's TESTAMENT OF MAN," *DA* 19 (1968): 277A-8A (Penn State).

TOILERS OF THE HILLS

Chatterton, W., *Vardis Fisher*, 12-15.
Flora, Joseph M., "The Early Power of Vardis Fisher," *ABC* 14 (Sept., 1963): 15-19.
_____, *Vardis Fisher*, 99-106.
Folsom, J. K., *American Western Novel*, 185-6.
Milton, J. R., *Novel of the American West*, 137-40.

THE VALLEY OF VISION (See also THE TESTAMENT OF MAN Series)

Flora, J. M., *Vardis Fisher*, 87-9.

THE VRIDAR HUNTER Tetralogy

Day, G. F., *Uses of History in the Novels of Vardis Fisher*, 11-23.
Flora, J. M., *Vardis Fisher*, 26-48, 52-9.

WE ARE BETRAYED (See also THE VRIDAR HUNTER Tetralogy)

Flora, J. M., *Vardis Fisher*, 37-9.

BIBLIOGRAPHY

Flora, J. M., *Vardis Fisher*, 149-52.
Kellogg, George, "Vardis Fisher: A Bibliography," *WAL* 5, i (Spring, 1970): 45-64.

FLANAGAN, THOMAS J. B., 1923-

THE YEAR OF THE FRENCH

Kaye, Jacqueline, "The Destinies of Empire," 267-80 in Barker, Francis, Jay Bernstein, Peter Hulme, Margaret Iverson, and Jennifer Stone, eds., *1789: Reading, Writing, Revolution: Proceedings of the Essex Conference on the Sociology of Literature, July, 1981*, Colchester: Un. of Essex, 1982.
Kiely, Benedict, "Thomas Flanagan: The Lessons of History," *HC* 18, iv (Oct., 1981): 1-8.

FLETCHER, (MINNA) INGLIS, 1888-1969

GENERAL

Parramore, Tom, "Fletcher's 'Eden': The Stranger in Paradise," *StAR* 3, iv (Spring-Summer, 1976): 5-11.

LUSTY WIND FOR CAROLINA

Hester, Erwin, "The Tradition of the Historical Novel and Inglis Fletcher's LUSTY WIND FOR CAROLINA," in Hester, E., and D. J. McMillan, eds., *Cultural Change in Eastern North Carolina*, 7-15.

TOIL OF THE BRAVE

Stephenson, William, "TOIL OF THE BRAVE: A Region Faces Revolution," in Hester, E., and D. J. McMillan, eds., *Cultural Change in Eastern North Carolina*, 16-26.

FOOTE, SHELBY, 1916-

GENERAL

Breit, Harvey, "Talk With Shelby Foote," *NYTBR* (April 27, 1952): 16.
Carr, John, "It's Worth a Grown Man's Time: An Interview with Shelby Foote," *Contempora* 1, iii (1970): 2-16. Also in Carr, J., ed., *Kite Flying and Other Irrational Acts*, 3-33.

Graham, John, "Shelby Foote," in Garrett, G., ed., *Writer's Voice*, 92-119. [Interview.]

Harrington, Evans, "Interview with Shelby Foote," *MissQ* 24, iv (Fall, 1971): 349-77.

Jones, J. G., *Mississippi Writers Talking*, Vol. I, 37-92.

Landess, Thomas H., "Southern History and Manhood: Major Themes in the Works of Shelby Foote: June, 1970," *MissQ* 24, iv (Fall, 1971): 405-27.

White, Helen, and Redding Sugg, "A Colloquium with Shelby Foote," *SHR* 15, iv (Fall, 1981): 281-300.

CHILD BY FEVER

Phillips, Robert L., "Shelby Foote's Bristol in CHILD BY FEVER," *SoQ* 19, i (1980): 172-83.

FOLLOW ME DOWN

Landess, Thomas H., "Southern History and Manhood: Major Themes in the Works of Shelby Foote," *MissQ* 29, iv (Fall, 1971): 325-7.

Sullivan, Walter, in Rubin, L. D., Jr., and R. D. Jacobs, eds., *South*, 377-9.

LOVE IN A DRY SEASON

Landess, Thomas H., "Southern History and Manhood: Major Themes in the Works of Shelby Foote," *MissQ* 29, iv (Fall, 1971): 327-30.

Vauthier, Simone, "The Symmetrical Design: The Structural Patterns of LOVE IN A DRY SEASON," *MissQ* 29, iv (Fall, 1971): 379-403.

RIDE OUT

Landess, Thomas H., "Southern History and Manhood: Major Themes in the Works of Shelby Foote," *MissQ* 29, iv (Fall, 1971): 321-3.

SHILOH

Landess, Thomas H., "Southern History and Manhood: Major Themes in the Works of Shelby Foote," *MissQ* 29, iv (Fall, 1971): 330-2.

Shepherd, Allen, "Technique and Theme in Shelby Foote's SHILOH," *NMW* 5, i (Spring, 1972): 3-10.

TOURNAMENT

Landess, Thomas H., "Southern History and Manhood: Major Themes in the Works of Shelby Foote," *MissQ* 29, iv (Fall, 1971): 323-5.

BIBLIOGRAPHPY

Kibler, James E., Jr., "Shelby Foote: A Bibliography," *MissQ* 24, iv (Fall, 1971): 437-65.

FORD, JESSE HILL, 1928-

GENERAL

Irwin, Edith S., "The Revenge Motif in the Fiction of Jesse Hill Ford," *DAI* 35 (1975): 7308A.

McKinley, James, "An Interview with Jesse Hill Ford," *Contempora* 2, i (1972): 1-7.

Seay, James, "The Making of Fables," [Interview] in Carr, J., ed., *Kite Flying and Other Irrational Acts*, 199-215.

Sexton, Franklin D., "Jesse Hill Ford: A Biographical and Critical Study," *DAI* 34 (197): 4285A-86A (So. Miss.).

FORSYTH, FREDERICK, 1938-

THE DAY OF THE JACKAL

Antoine, Robert, S. J., "The Structural Analysis in Action," *JJCL* 14/15 (1976/77): 17-49.

Brookes, Philip J., "Two Kinds of Mythic Hero in Frederick Forsyth's THE DAY OF THE JACKAL," in *Proceedings of the Fifth National Convention of the Popular Culture Assoc.*, 192-202.

Wolfe, Peter, "Stalking Forsyth's Jackal," *ArmD* 7 (1974): 165-74. Also in *UWR* 9, ii (1974): 5-27.

THE DOGS OF WAR

Jean-Baptiste, E. N. L., "State of European Literature: 'European Football'," *Afriscope* 8, v (1978): 19-20, 30.

FOWLES, JOHN, 1926-

GENERAL

Allen, Walter, "The Achievement of John Fowles," *Encounter* 35, ii (Aug., 1970): 64-7.

Appleby, Thomas C., "Benevolent Manipulation in the Fiction of John Fowles," *DAI* 39 (1978): 3591A.

Bagchee, Shyamal, "Modernism, Past Modernism, and the Novels of John Fowles," *DAI* 42, x (April, 1982): 4446A.

Baker, James R., "Fowles and the Struggle of the English *Aristoi*," *JML* 8, ii (1980-81): 163-80.

Barnum, Carol M., "Archetypal Patterns in the Fiction of John Fowles: Journey toward Wholeness," *DAI* 39 (1979): 4236A.

Bellamy, Michael O., "John Fowles's Versions of Pastoral: Private Valleys and the Parity of Existence," *Crit* 21, ii (1979): 72-84.

Binns, Ronald, "John Fowles: Radical Romancer," *CritQ* 15, iv (Winter, 1973): 317-34.

Burden, Robert, "The Analysis of Identity in the Novels and Stories of John Fowles," *John Fowles, John Hawkes, Claude Simon*, 28-55.

————, "Structure and Interpretation in the Narrative Fiction of John Fowles," *John Fowles, John Hawkes, Claude Simon*, 150-81.

Campbell, James, "An Interview with John Fowles," *ConL* 17 (1976): 455-69.

Closser, John C., "Variations: A Study of Technique in the Fiction of John Fowles," *DAI* 42 (1981): 2668A.

Conradi, P., *John Fowles*.

Costello, Jacqueline A., "The Facts of Fiction in the Novels of John Fowles," *DAI* 43 (1982): 2343A-44A.

Detweiler, Robert, "The Unity of John Fowles' Fiction," *NConL* 1, ii (Mar., 1971): 3-4.

Docherty, Thomas, "A Constant Reality: The Presentation of Character in the Fiction of John Fowles," *Novel* 14, ii (Winter, 1981): 118-34.

Duriez, Colin, "The Creation of Meaning: An Appraisal of John Fowles' Novels," *Third Way* (Feb. 9, 1978): 7-9. [Not seen.]

Eddins, Dwight, "John Fowles: Existence as Authorship," *ConL* 17, ii (Spring, 1976): 204-22.

Gersten, Irene F., "Captivity and Freedom in Four Novels by John Fowles," *DAI* 41 (1980): 1586A.

Gross, David, "Historical Consciousness and the Modern Novel: The Uses of History in the Fiction of John Fowles," *StHum* 7, i (1978): 19-27.

Halpern, Daniel, "A Sort of Exile in Lyme Regis," *LonM* 10, xii (Mar., 1971): 34-46. [Interview.]

Harnack, William, "The Greening of John Fowles," *Humanist* 42, ii (Mar.-April, 1982): 52-3.

Hill, Roy M., "Play in the Fiction of John Fowles," *DAI* 39 (1978): 1550A.

_____, "Power and Hazard: John Fowles's Theory of Play," *JML* 8, ii (1980-81): 211-18.

Holmes, Frederick M., "Fictional Self-Consciousness in the Works of John Barth and John Fowles," *DAI* 42, viii (Feb., 1982): 3595A.

Huffaker, Robert S., "John Fowles: A Critical Study," *DAI* 35 (1975): 6140A.

_____, *John Fowles*.

Kennedy, A., "John Fowles's Sense of an Ending," *Protean Self*, 251-60.

Khan, Saeeda A., "Progressive Integration of Self in John Fowles' Fiction," *DAI* 43 (1982): 2354A.

Kraft, Ines A., "Choice: Moral Dilemma in the Fiction of John Fowles and Siegfried Lenz," *DAI* 42, viii (Feb., 1982): 3589A.

Laughlin, Rosemary M., "Faces of Power in the Novels of John Fowles," *Crit* 13, iii (1972): 71-88.

Lindblad, Ishrat, "'La Bonne Vaux', 'la princesse lointaine': Two Motifs in the Novels of John Fowles," in Rydén, Mats, ed., Björk, Lennart A., ed., *Studies in English Philology, Linguistics and Literature Presented to Alarik Rynell, 7 March 1978*, Stockholm: Almqvist & Wiksell, 1978, 87-101.

Madachy, James L., "The Aesthetic Theory of John Fowles," *DAI* 35 (1975): 5414A-15A.

McDaniel, Ellen, "Dark Towers, Godgames, and the Evolution toward Humanism in the Fiction of John Fowles," *DAI* 40 (1980): 5049A-50A.

Olshen, B. N., *John Fowles*.

Orr, John, "Offstage Tragedy: The New Narrative Strategies of John Fowles, Saul Bellow and Willian Styron," *New Edinburgh Review* 59 (1982): 21-3. [Not seen.]

Palmer, W. J., *Fiction of John Fowles*.

Rackham, Jeff, "John Fowles: The Existential Labyrinth," *Crit* 13, iii (1972): 89-103.

Runyon, Randolph, "Fowles's Enigma Variations," *Fowles/Irving/Barthes*, 3-35.

Saari, Jon H., "Freedom and the Nemo in the Fiction of John Fowles," *DAI* 35 (1975): 4552A.

Singh, Raman K., "An Encounter with John Fowles," *JML* 8, ii (1980-81): 181-202.

Walker, David H., "Subversion of Narrative in the Work of André Gide and John Fowles," *CCrit* 2 (1980): 187-212.

Warburton, Edna E. H., "John Fowles and the Vision of the Dead Woman: The Theme of Carnal Knowledge and the Knowledge and the Technique of Source Inversion in John Fowles's Fiction," *DAI* 41 (1980): 1055A.

Wolfe, Peter, "John Fowles: The Existential Tension," *STwC* No. 16 (Fall, 1975): 111-45.

_____, *John Fowles, Magus and Moralist*.

THE COLLECTOR

Bagchee, Shyamal, "THE COLLECTOR: The Paradoxical Imagination of John Fowles," *JML* 8, ii (1980-81): 219-34.

_____, "THE GREAT GATSBY and John Fowles's THE COLLECTOR," *NConL* 10, iv (1980): 7-8.

Beatty, Patricia V., "John Fowles' Clegg: Captive Landlord of Eden," *ArielE* 13, iii (July, 1982): 73-81.

Churchill, Thomas, "Waterhouse, Storey, and Fowles: *Which Way Out of the Room?*" *Crit* 10, iii (1968): 72-87.

Conradi, P., *John Fowles*, 32-41.

Davidson, Arnold E., "Caliban and the Captive Maiden: John Fowles' THE COLLECTOR and Irving Wallace's THE FAN CLUB," *StHum* 8, ii (Mar., 1981): 28-33.

Dixon, Terrell F., "Expostulation and a Reply: The Character of Clegg in Fowles and Sillitoe," *NConL* 4, ii (Mar., 1974): 7-9.

Eddins, Dwight, "John Fowles: Existence as Authorship," *ConL* 17, ii (Spring, 1976): 205-11.

Huffaker, R., *John Fowles*, 73-90.

Laughlin, Rosemary M., "Faces of Power in the Novels of John Fowles," *Crit* 13, iii (1972): 72-5.

Olshen, B. N., *John Fowles*, 15-29.

Palmer, W. J., *Fiction of John Fowles*, 13-17, 31-44.

Rackham, Jeff, "John Fowles: The Existential Labyrinth," *Crit* 13, iii (1972): 90-4.

Tatham, Michael, "Two Novels: Notes on the Work of John Fowles," *New Blackfriars* 52 (Sept., 9, 1971): 404-11.

Wolfe, P., *John Fowles, Magus and Moralist*, 51-80.

DANIEL MARTIN

Alter, Robert, "DANIEL MARTIN and the Mimetic Task," *Genre* 14, i (Spring, 1981): 65-78.

Barnum, Carol, "John Fowles's DANIEL MARTIN: A Vision of Whole Sight," *LitR* 25, i (Fall, 1981): 64-79.

Beatty, Patricia V., "John Fowles's DANIEL MARTIN: Poetics of the Now," *SAQ* 81, i (1982): 78-86.

Bernstein, John, "John Fowles' Use of Ibsen in DANIEL MARTIN," *NConL* 9, iv (1979): 10.

Boomsma, Patricia J., "'Whole Sight': Fowles, Lukács and DANIEL MARTIN," *JML* 8, ii (1980-81): 325-36.

Conradi, P., *John Fowles*, 90-9.

Cromwell, Lucy S., "'Whole Sight': A Structural Study of John Fowles's DANIEL MARTIN,' *DAI* 41, xi (May, 1981): 4718A.

Ferris, Ina, "Realist Intention and Mythic Impulse in DANIEL MARTIN," *JNT* 12, ii (Spring, 1982): 146-53.

Gindin, James, "Three Recent British Novels and an American Response," *MQR* 17 (Winter, 1978): 236-46.

Helgeson, Susan L., "Readers Reading John Fowles' DANIEL MARTIN: An Experimental Study of Reading as a Composing Process," *DAI* 43, ii (Aug., 1982): 440A.

Huffaker, R., *John Fowles*, 32-43.

Klemtner, Susan S., "The Counterpoles of John Fowles's DANIEL MARTIN," *Crit* 21, ii (1979): 59-71.

Loveday, Simon, "The Style of John Fowles: Tense and Person in the First Chapter of DANIEL MARTIN," *JNT* 10 (1980): 198-204.

McSweeney, Kerry, "Withering into the Truth: John Fowles and DANIEL MARTIN," *CritQ* 20, iv (1978): 31-8.

Mercer, Jeannette E., "The Sacred Wood in Four Twentieth-Century Fictional Narratives," *DAI* 42, i (July, 1981): 204A.

Olshen, B. N., *John Fowles*, 109-20.

Palliser, Charles, "John Fowles: The Ambivalent Virtues?" *Library Review* 29 (Spring, 1980): 36-8.

Swann, C. S. B., "DANIEL MARTIN," *Delta* 59 (1979): 1-7.

Wolfe, P., *John Fowles, Magus and Moralist*, 170-96.

Wymard, Eleanor B., "'A New Version of the Midas Touch': DANIEL MARTIN and THE WORLD ACCORDING TO GARP," *MFS* 27, ii (Summer, 1981): 284-6.

THE FRENCH LIEUTENANT'S WOMAN

Allen, Walter, "The Achievement of John Fowles," *Encounter* 35, ii (Aug., 1970): 66-7.

Bergonzi, Bernard, in *Contemporary English Novel*, 54-6.

Brantlinger, Patrick, Ian Adam, and Sheldon Rothblatt, "THE FRENCH LIEUTENANT'S WOMAN: A Discussion," *VS* 15, iii (Mar., 1972): 339-56.

Burden, Robert, in *Contemporary English Novel*, 147-53.

_____, "John Fowles: THE FRENCH LIEUTENANT'S WOMAN," *John Fowles, John Hawkes, Claude Simon*, 271-84.

Conradi, Peter J., "THE FRENCH LIEUTENANT'S WOMAN: Novel, Screenplay, Film," *CritQ* 24, i (Spring, 1982): 41-57.

_____, *John Fowles*, 58-77.

Costa, Richard H., "Trickery's Mixed Bag: The Perils of Fowles' FRENCH LIEUTENANT'S WOMAN," *BRMMLA* 29 (1975): 1-9.

Creighton, Joanne V., "The Reader and Modern and Post-Modern Fiction," *CollL* 9, iii (Fall, 1982): 216-30.

DeVitis, A. A., and William J. Palmer, "A PAIR OF BLUE EYES FLASH at THE FRENCH LIEUTENANT'S WOMAN," *ConL* 15 (1974): 90-101.

D'Haen, Theo, "Fowles, Lodge and the ' Problematic Novel'," *DQR* 9, iii (1979): 162-75.

Eddins, Dwight, "John Fowles: Existence as Authorship," *ConL* 17, ii (Spring, 1976): 216-22.

Edwards, Lee R., "Changing Our Imagination," *MR* 11 (Summer, 1970): 604-8.

Evarts, Prescott, Jr., "THE FRENCH LIEUTENANT'S WOMAN as Tragedy," *Crit* 13, iii (1972): 57-69.

Fowles, John, "Notes on an Unfinished Novel," in McCormack, T., ed., *Afterwards*, 160-75.

Gross, David, "Historical Consciousness and the Modern Novel: The Uses of History in the Fiction of John Fowles," *StHum* 7, i (1978): 23-5.

Grosskurth, Phyllis, "THE FRENCH LIEUTENANT'S WOMAN," *VS* 16, i (Sept., 1972): 130-1.

Hagopian, John V., "Bad Faith in THE FRENCH LIEUTENANT'S WOMAN," *ConL* 23, ii (Spring, 1982): 191-201.

Holmes, Frederick M., "The Novel, Illusion, and Reality: The Paradox of Omniscience in THE FRENCH LIEUTENANT'S WOMAN," *JNT* 11, iii (Fall, 1981): 184-98.

Huffaker, R., *John Fowles*, 91-115.

Hutcheon, Linda, "The 'Real World(s)' of Fiction: THE FRENCH LIEUTENANT'S WOMAN," *ESC* 4 (1978): 81-94.

Jacobson, Wendy, "Freedom and Women in John Fowles's THE FRENCH LIEUTENANT'S WOMAN," *Opus* (Second Series, 2) (1977): 1-18.

Johnson, A. J. B., "Realism in THE FRENCH LIEUTENANT'S WOMAN," *JML* 8, ii (1980-81): 287-302.

Kane, Patricia, "The Fallen Woman as Free-Thinker in THE FRENCH LIEUTENANT'S WOMAN and THE SCARLET LETTER," *NConL* 2, i (Jan., 1972): 8-10.

Kaplan, Fred, "Victorian Modernists: Fowles and Nabokov," *JNT* 3, ii (May, 1973): 108-20.

Kennedy, A., "John Fowles's Sense of an Ending," *Protean Self*, 251-2, 259-60.

Laughlin, Rosemary M., "Faces of Power in the Novels of John Fowles," *Crit* 13, iii (1972): 84-8.

Le Boville, Lucien, "John Fowles: Looking for Guidelines," *JML* 8, ii (1980-81): 203-10.

Mansfield, Elizabeth, "A Sequence of Endings: The Manuscripts of THE FRENCH LIEUTENANT'S WOMAN," *JML* 8, ii (1980-81): 275-86.

Mathews, James W., "Fowles's Artistic Freedom: Another Stone from James's House," *NConL* 4, ii (Mar., 1974): 2-3.

McGregor, Barbara R., "Existentialism in THE FRENCH LIEUTENANT'S WOMAN," *ReAL* 1, ii (1975): 39-46.

Miller, Nan, "Christina Rossetti and Sarah Woodruff: Two Remedies for a Divided Self," *PRR* 3, i (Nov., 1982): 68-77.

Olshen, B. N., *John Fowles*, 63-89.

Palmer, W. J., *Fiction of John Fowles*, 23-9, 50-4, 65-77.

Rankin, Elizabeth D., "Cryptic Coloration in THE FRENCH LIEUTENANT'S WOMAN," *JNT* 3 (1974): 193-207.

Rose, Gilbert J., "THE FRENCH LIEUTENANT'S WOMAN: The Unconscious Significance of a Novel to Its Author," *AI* 29, ii (Summer, 1972): 165-76.

Spitz, Ellen H., "On Interpretation of Film as Dream: THE FRENCH LIEUTENANT'S WOMAN," *PostS* 2, i (Fall, 1982): 13-29.

Sullivan, Paul, "The Manuscripts for John Fowles' THE FRENCH LIEUTENANT'S WOMAN," *PBSA* 74, iii (July-Sept., 1980): 272-7.

Tatham, Michael, "Two Novels: Notes on the Work of John Fowles," *New Blackfriars* 52 (Sept., 1971): 404-11.

Turner, Katharine C., "To the Heart of Oakley and Woodruff," *SHR* 10, iv (Fall, 1976): 353-61.

Wolfe, P., *John Fowles, Magus and Moralist*, 122-69.

THE MAGUS

Begnal, Michael H., "A View of John Fowles' THE MAGUS," *MBL* 3, i (1978): 67-72.

Berets, Ralph, "THE MAGUS: A Study in the Creation of a Personal Myth," *TCL* 19, ii (April, 1973): 89-98.

Billy, Ted, "*Homo Solitarius*: Isolation and Estrangement in THE MAGUS," *RS* 48 (1980): 129-41.

Binns, Ronald, "A New Version of THE MAGUS," *CritQ* 19, iv (Winter, 1977): 79-84.

Boccia, Michael, "'Visions and Revisions': John Fowles's New Version of THE MAGUS," *JML* 8, ii (1980-81): 235-46.

Bradbury, Malcolm, "John Fowles' THE MAGUS," in Weber, B., ed., *Sense and Sensibility in Twentieth-Century Writing*, 26-38. Also in Bradbury, M., *Possibilities*, 256-71.

Churchill, Thomas, "Waterhouse, Storey, and Fowles: *Which Way Out of the Room*?" *Crit* 10, iii (1968): 72-87.

Conradi, P., *John Fowles*, 42-57.

Eddins, Dwight, "John Fowles: Existence as Authorship," *ConL* 17, ii (Spring, 1976): 211-16.

Fleishman, Avrom, "THE MAGUS of the Wizard of the West," *JML* 5 (1976): 297-314.

Fowles, John, "John Fowles: Why I Rewrote THE MAGUS," *SatR* (Feb. 18, 1978); 25-7, 30.

Glaserfeld, Ernst von, "Reflections on John Fowles's THE MAGUS and the Construction of Reality," *GaR* 33 (1979): 444-8.

Gross, David, "Historical Consciousness and the Modern Novel: The Uses of History in the Fiction of John Fowles," *StHum* 7, i (1978): 21-3.

Huffaker, R., *John Fowles*, 44-72.

Kennedy, A., *Protean Self*, 253-9.

Laughlin, Rosemary M., "Faces of Power in the Novels of John Fowles," *Crit* 13, iii (1972): 75-84.

Loveday, Simon, "Magus or Midas?" *OLR* 2, iii (1977): 34-5.

Magalaner, Marvin, "The Fool's Journey: John Fowles's THE MAGUS," in Morris, R. K., ed., *Old Lines, New Forces*, 81-92.

McDaniel, Ellen, "THE MAGUS: Fowles's Tarot Quest," *JML* 8, ii (1980-81): 247-60.

Nadeau, Robert L., "Fowles and Physics: A Study of THE MAGUS: A REVISED VERSION," *JML* 8, ii (1980-81): 261-74.

Newman, Robert D., "'An Anagram Made Flesh': The Transformation of Nicholas Urfe in Fowles' THE MAGUS," *NConL* 12, iv (Sept., 1982): 9.

Olshen, Barry N., "John Fowles's THE MAGUS: An Allegory of Self-Realization," *JPC* 9 (1976): 916-25.

Palmer, W. J., *Fiction of John Fowles*, 17-23, 44-50, 56-65.

_____, "Fowles' THE MAGUS: The Vortex as Myth, Metaphor, and Masque," in Carrabino, V., ed., *Power of Myth in Literature and Film*, 66-76.

Park, Sue S., "John Fowles's THE MAGUS: The Godgame as Word Game," *CCTE* 45 (1980): 45-52.

Poirier, Suzanne, "*L'Astrée* Revisited: A 13th Century Model for THE MAGUS," *CLS* 17 (1980): 269-86.

Pollock, John J., "Conchis as Allegorical Figure in THE MAGUS," *NConL* 10, i (1980): 10.

Presley, Delma E., "The Quest of the Bourgeois Hero: An Approach to Fowles' THE MAGUS," *JPC* 6, ii (Fall, 1972): 394-8.

Rackham, Jeff, "John Fowles: The Existential Labyrinth," *Crit* 13, iii (1972): 94-8.

Rubenstein, Roberta, "Myth, Mystery, and Irony: John Fowles' THE MAGUS," *ConL* 16 (1975): 328-39.

Scholes, Robert, "John Fowles as Romancer," *Fabulation and Metafiction*, 37-45.

_____, "The Orgastic Fiction of John Fowles," *HC* 6, v (Dec., 1969): 3-12.

Wade, Cory, "'Mystery Enough at Noon': John Fowles's Revision of THE MAGUS," *SoR* 15 (1979): 717-23.

Wolfe, P., *John Fowles, Magus and Moralist*, 81-121.

BIBLIOGRAPHY

Evarts, Prescott, Jr., "John Fowles: A Checklist," *Crit* 13, iii (1972): 105-7.

Huffaker, R., *John Fowles*, 147-61.

Myers, Karen M., "John Fowles: An Annotated Bibliography, 1963-1976," *BB* 33, iv (1976): 162-9.

Olshen, Barry N., and Toni A. Olshen, *John Fowles: A Reference Guide*, Boston: Hall, 1980.

Roberts, Ray A., comp., "John Fowles: A Bibliographical Checklist," *ABC* 1, v (1980): 26-37.

FOX, PAULA, 1923-

DESPERATE CHARACTERS

Bassoff, Bruce, "Royalty in a Rainy Country: Two Novels of Paula Fox," *Crit* 20, ii (1978): 33-48.

THE WIDOW'S CHILDREN

Bassoff, Bruce, "Royalty in a Rainy Country: Two Novels of Paula Fox," *Crit* 20, ii (1978): 33-48.

FOX, WILLIAM PRICE, 1926-

GENERAL

Bobbitt, Joan, "William Price Fox: The Spirit of Character and the Spirit of Place," *SCR* 9, i (Nov., 1976): 30-5.

Bruccoli, Matthew J., "William Price Fox," in *Conversations with Writers, I*, 47-80.

FRAME, JANET, 1924-

GENERAL

Alcock, Peter C. M., "On the Edge: New Zealanders as Displaced Persons," *WLWE* 16, i (April, 1977): 127-42.

Beston, John, "The Effect of Alienation on the Themes and Characters of Patrick White and Janet Frame," in Massa, D., ed., *Individual and Community in Commonwealth Literature*, 131-9.

Dalziel, M., *Janet Frame*.

Delbaere, J., *Bird, Hawk, Bogie*.

Delbaere-Garant, Jeanne, "Daphne's Metamorphoses in Janet Frame's Early Novels," *ArielE* 6, ii (April, 1975): 23-37.

_____, "Death as the Gateway to Being in Janet Frame's Novels," in Maes-Jelinek, H., ed., *Commonwealth Literature and the Modern World*, 147-55.

_____, "The Divided Worlds of Emily Brontë, Virginia Woolf and Janet Frame," *ES* 60, vi (Dec., 1979): 699-711.

Dupont, V., "Janet Frame: Postscript," *CM* 1 (1975): 175-6. [Not seen.]

_____, "New Zealand Literature: Janet Frame and the Psychological Novel," in Rutherford, A., ed., *Common Wealth*, 168-76.

Evans, Patrick, "Alienation and the Imagery of Death: The Novels of Janet Frame," *Meanjin* 32, iii (Sept., 1973): 294-303.

_____, "'Farthest from the Heart': The Autobiograhical Parables of Janet Frame," *MFS* 27, i (Spring, 1981): 31-40.

_____, *Inward Sun*.

_____, *Janet Frame*.

Ferrier, Carole, "The Rhetoric of Rejection: Janet Frame's Recent Work," in Tiffin, C., ed., *South Pacific Images*, 196-203.

Frame, Janet, "Beginnings," *Landfall* 19 (Mar., 1965): 40-7.

McCracken, Jill, "Janet Frame: It's Time for France," *NZListener* 74 (Oct. 27, 1973): 20-1.

Rhodes, H. Winston, "Preludes and Parables: A Reading of Janet Frame's Novels," *Landfall* 26, ii (June, 1972): 135-46.

Robertson, Robert T., "Bird, Hawk, Bogie: Janet Frame, 1952-62," *SNNTS* 4, ii (Summer, 1972): 186-99. Also in Delbaere, J., ed., *Bird, Hawk, Bogie*, 15-23.

Rutherford, Anna, "Janet Frame's Divided and Distinguished Worlds," *WLWE* 14, i (April, 1975): 51-68. Also in Delbaere, J., ed., *Bird, Hawk, Bogie*, 24-34.

THE ADAPTABLE MAN

Evans, P., *Inward Sun*, 31-5.

_____, *Janet Frame*, 121-40.

_____, "Janet Frame and the Adaptable Novel," *Landfall* 25, iv (Dec., 1971): 448-55.

King, Bruce, "THE ADAPTABLE MAN," in Delbaere, J., ed., *Bird, Hawk, Bogie*, 80-8.

_____, *New English Literatures*, 224-6.

DAUGHTER BUFFALO

Delbaere, Jeanne, "Turning in the Noon Sun: An Analysis of DAUGHTER BUFFALO," in Delbaere, J., ed., *Bird, Hawk, Bogie*, 115-28.

Evans, P. D., *Janet Frame*, 184-94.

Roberts, Heather, "Two Cultural Attitudes to Death," *Landfall* 33, ii (1979): 21-9.

THE EDGE OF THE ALPHABET

Evans, Patrick, "At the Edge of the Alphabet," in Delbaere, J., ed., *Bird, Hawk, Bogie*, 53-62.

_____, *Inward Sun*, 21-5.

_____, *Janet Frame*, 88-100.

FACES IN THE WATER

Evans, P., *Inward Sun*, 15-20.

_____, *Janet Frame*, 79-88.

Hannah, Donald W., "FACES IN THE WATER: Case-History or Work of Fiction," in Delbaere, J., ed., *Bird, Hawk, Bogie*, 45-52.

INTENSIVE CARE

Dupont, Victor, "Janet Frame's Brave New World: INTENSIVE CARE," in Maes-Jelinek, Hena, ed., *Commonwealth Literature and the Modern World*, Brussels: Didier, 1975, 157-62. Also in Delbaere, J., ed., *Bird, Hawk, Bogie*, 104-14.

Evans, P. D., *Janet Frame*, 168-84.

_____, "The Provincial Dilemma, 3: New Zealand as Vietnam in Fiction: The World's Wars in New Zealand," *Landfall* 31, i (Mar., 1977): 12-16.

OWLS DO CRY

Alcock, Peter, "Frame's Binomial Fall, or Fire and Four in Waimaru," *Landfall* 29, iii (Sept., 1975): 179-87.

Ashcroft, W. D., "Beyond the Alphabet: Janet Frame's OWLS DO CRY," *JCL* 12, i (Aug., 1977): 12-23. Also in Delbaere, J., ed., *Bird, Hawk, Bogie*, 35-44.

Dupont, Victor, "Janet Frame's Brave New World: INTENSIVE CARE," in Maes-Jelinek, H., ed., *Commonwealth Literature and the Modern World*, 157-67.

Evans, P., *Inward Sun*, 9-14.

_____, *Janet Frame*, 56-78.

Hankin, Cherry, "Language As Theme in OWLS DO CRY," *Landfall* 28, ii (June, 1974): 91-110. Also in Hankin, C., ed., *Critical Essays on the New Zealand Novel*, 88-101.

Jones, Lawrence, "No Cowslip's Bell in Waimaru: The Personal Vision of OWLS DO CRY," *Landfall* 24, iii (Sept., 1970): 280-96.

Stevens, J., *New Zealand Novel*, 98-100, 121-3.

THE RAINBIRDS

Backmann, Annemarie, "Security in Equality in THE RAINBIRDS," in Delbaere, J., ed., *Bird, Hawk, Bogie*, 94-103.

Evans, P., *Inward Sun*, 41-5.

_____, *Janet Frame*, 152-9.

SCENTED GARDENS FOR THE BLIND

Delbaere-Garant, Jeanne, "Beyond the Word: Janet Frame's SCENTED GARDENS FOR THE BLIND," in Niven, Alistair, ed., *The Commonwealth Writer Overseas: Themes of Exile and Repatriation*, Brussels: Didier, 1976, 289-301. Also in Delbaere, J., ed., *Bird, Hawk, Bogie*, 68-79.

Evans, P., *Inward Sun*, 26-30.

_____, *Janet Frame*, 101-12, 115-20.

Harris, Wilson, "SCENTED GARDENS FOR THE BLIND," in Delbaere, J., ed., *Bird, Hawk, Bogie*, 63-7.

Hyman, S. E., "Reason in Madness," *Standards*, 239-43.

A STATE OF SIEGE

Evans, P., *Inward Sun*, 36-40.

_____, *Janet Frame*, 144-52.

Malterre, Monique, "Myths and Esoterics: A Tentative Interpretation of Janet Frame's A STATE OF SIEGE," *CE&S* 2 (1976): 107-12. Also in Delbaere, J., ed., *Bird, Hawk, Bogie*, 89-93.

BIBLIOGRAPHY

Beston, John B., "A Bibliography of Janet Frame," *WLWE* 17, ii (1978): 570-85.

New, W. H., "An Annotated Checklist of Critical Writings on Janet Frame," in Delbaere, J., ed., *Bird, Hawk, Bogie*, 130-7.

FRASER, GEORGE MACDONALD, 1925-

FLASHMAN Series

Bargainnier, Earl F., "The Flashman Papers: Picaresque Satiric Pastiche," *Crit* 18, ii (1976): 109-20.

Voorhees, Richard J., "Flashman and Richard Hannay," *DR* 53, i (Spring, 1973): 113-20.

FRASER, SYLVIA, 1935-

THE CANDY FACTORY

Irvine, Lorna, "Assembly Line Stories: Pastiche in Sylvia Fraser's THE CANDY FACTORY," *CanL* 89 (Summer, 1981): 45-55.

Moss, J., *Sex and Violence in the Canadian Novel*, 154-60.

A CASUAL AFFAIR

Gottlieb, Lois, "And They Lived Separately Ever After," *JCF* 31-32 (1981): 261-3.

FRAYN, MICHAEL, 1933-

GENERAL

Raine, Craig, "An Interview with Michael Frayn," *Quarto* 4 (1980): 3-6.

FRENCH, MARILYN, 1929-

THE BLEEDING HEART

Wagner, Linda W., "The French Definition," *ArQ* 38, iv (Winter, 1982): 293-302.

THE WOMEN'S ROOM

Mickelson, A. Z., *Reaching Out*, 206-21.
Wagner, Linda W., "The French Definition," *ArQ* 38, iv (Winter, 1982): 293-302.

FRIEDMAN, BRUCE JAY, 1930-

GENERAL

Klein, Marcus, "Further Notes on the Dereliction of Culture: Edward Lewis Wallant and Bruce Jay Friedman," in Malin, E., ed., *Contemporary American-Jewish Literature*, 241-6.
Lewis, Stuart A., "Rootlessness and Alienation in the Novels of Bruce Jay Friedman," *C1AJ* 18, iii (Mar., 1975): 422-33.
Pinsker, Sanford, "The Graying of Black Humor," *STwC* No. 9 (Spring, 1972): 15-33.
Schulz, M. F., *Bruce Jay Friedman*.
_____, "Pop, Op, and Black Humor: The Aesthetics of Anxiety," *CE* 30, iii (Dec., 1968): 230-41 *passim*.

THE DICK

Klein, Marcus, "Further Notes on the Dereliction of Culture: Edward Lewis Wallant and Bruce Jay Friedman," in Malin, I., ed., *Contemporary American-Jewish Literature*, 231-5.
Pinsker, S., *Between Two Worlds*, 20-1.
_____, "The Graying of Black Humor," *STwC* No. 9 (Spring, 1972): 25-7.
Schulz, M. F., *Bruce Jay Friedman*, 102-21.

A MOTHER'S KISSES

Pinsker, S., *Between Two Worlds*, 17-20.
_____, "The Graying of Black Humor," *STwC* No. 9 (Spring, 1972): 22-5.
Schulz, M. F., *Black Humor of the Sixties*, 105-8, 139-40.
_____, *Bruce Jay Friedman*, 59-77.
_____, "Wallant and Friedman: The Glory and Agony of Love," *Crit* 10, iii (1968): 31-47. Also in Schulz, M. F., *Radical Sophistication*, 186-97.

Sherman, B., *Invention of the Jew*, 224-8.

STERN

Hyman, S. E., "An Exceptional First Novel," *Standards*, 98-102.
Kaplan, Charles, "Escape into Hell: Friedman's STERN," *CEJ* 1 (1965): 25-30.
Pinsker, S., *Between Two Worlds*, 12-17.
_____, "The Graying of Black Humor," *STwC* No. 9 (Spring, 1972): 16-22.
Schulz, M. F., *Black Humor Fiction of the Sixties*, 97-100, 109-14, 138-9.
_____, *Bruce Jay Friedman*, 34-58.
_____, "Wallant and Friedman: The Glory and Agony of Love," *Crit* 10, iii (1968): 31-47. Also in Schulz, M. F., *Radical Sophistication*, 186-97.
Trachtenberg, Stanley, "The Humiliated Hero: Bruce Jay Friedman's STERN," *Crit* 7 (Spring-Summer, 1965): 91-3.
Wisse, R. R., *Schlemiel as Modern Hero*, 87-90.

BIBLIOGRAPHY

Schulz, M. F., *Bruce Jay Friedman*, 157-60.

FULLER, ROY, 1912-1991

GENERAL

Austin, A. E., *Roy Fuller*.
Mitchell, Roger, "Roy Fuller: An Interview," *MinnR* 10 (1978): 87-94.

THE CARNAL ISLAND

Austin, A. E., *Roy Fuller*, 121-4.

FANTASY AND FUGUE

Austin, A. E., *Roy Fuller*, 109-11.

THE FATHER'S COMEDY

Austin, A. E., *Roy Fuller*, 114-16.

IMAGE OF A SOCIETY

Austin, A. E., *Roy Fuller*, 111-12.

MY CHILD, MY SISTER

Austin, A. E., *Roy Fuller*, 118-21.

THE PERFECT FOOL

Austin, A. E., *Roy Fuller*, 116-18.

THE RUINED BOYS

Austin, A. E., *Roy Fuller*, 112-14.

THE SECOND CURTAIN

Austin, A. E., *Roy Fuller*, 107-9.

GADDIS, WILLIAM, 1922-

GENERAL

Kuehl, John, and Steven Moore, "An Interview with William Gaddis," *RCF* 2, ii (Summer, 1982): 4-6.

Morton, Marjorie, "The Orchestration of Chaos: The Context and Structure of the Novels of William Gaddis," *DAI* 42 (1981): 1637A.

JR

Banning, Charles L., "William Gaddis' JR: The Organization of Chaos and the Chaos of Organization," *Paunch* 42-43 (Dec., 1975): 153-65.

Black, Joel D., "The Paper Empires and Empirical Fictions of William Gaddis," *RCF* 2, ii (Summer, 1982): 22-31.

Boccia, Michael, "What Did You Say, Mister Gaddis? Form in William Gaddis's JR," *RCF* 2, ii (Summer, 1982): 40-4.

Gardner, John, "Big Deals," *NYRB* (June 10, 1976): 35-40.

Klemtner, Susan S., "'For a Very Small Audience': The Fiction of William Gaddis," *Crit* 19, iii (1978): 61-73.

LeClair, Thomas, "William Gaddis, Jr., and the Art of Excess," *MFS* 27, iv (Winter, 1981-82): 587-600.

Malmgren, Carl D., "William Gaddis's JR: The Novel of Babel," *RCF* 2, ii (Summer, 1982): 7-12.

Matanle, Stephen H., "Love and Strife in William Gaddis' JR," *DAI* 41 (1980): 1058A.

Moore, Steven, "Chronological Difficulties in the Novels of William Gaddis," *Crit* 22, i (1980): 87-91.

Morton, Marjorie, "The Orchestration of Chaos: The Context and Structure of the Novels of William Gaddis," *DAI* 42, iv (Oct., 1981): 1637A.

Stark, John, "William Gaddis: Just Recognition," *HC* 14, ii (April, 1977): 8-12.

Strehle, Susan, "Disclosing Time: William Gaddis's JR," *JNT* 12, i (Winter, 1982): 1-14.

Thielemans, Johan, "Gaddis and the Novel Entropy," *Tréma* 2 (1977): 97-107.

Weisenburger, Steven, "Contra Naturam? Usury in William Gaddis's JR," *Genre* 13 (1980): 93-109. Also in Male, R. R., ed., *Money Talks*, 93-109.

———, "Paper Currencies: Reading William Gaddis," *RCF* 2, ii (Summer, 1982): 12-22.

THE RECOGNITIONS

Bakker, J., "The End of Individualism," *DQR* 7, iv (1977): 286-304.

Benstock, Bernard, "On William Gaddis: In Recognition of James Joyce," *WSCL* 6, ii (Winter-Spring, 1965): 177-89.

Black, Joel D., "The Paper Empires and Empirical Fictions of William Gaddis," *RCF* 2, ii (Summer, 1982): 22-31.

Brownson, Robert C., "Techniques of Reference, Allusion, and Quotation in Thomas Mann's DOCTOR FAUSTUS and William Gaddis' THE RECOGNITIONS," *DAI* 37 (1977): 7733A.

Cunningham, Don R., "Cabala to Entropy: Existentialist Attitudes and the Gnostic Vision in William Gaddis's THE RECOGNITIONS and Julio Cortázar's RAYUELA," *DAI* 41 (1980): 236A.

Eckley, Grace, "Exorcising the Demon Forgery, or The Forging of Pure Gold in Gaddis's THE RECOGNITIONS," in Frank, Luanne, ed., *Literature and the Occult: Essays in Comparative Literature*, Arlington: Univ. of Texas, 1977, 125-36.

Guzlowski, John Z., "No More Sea Changes: Hawkes, Pynchon, Gaddis, and Barth," *Crit* 23, ii (Winter, 1981-82): 53-7.

Hartman, Carl, "THE RECOGNITIONS," *WR* 20 (Winter, 1956): 171-6.

Hegarty, George, "Gaddis's RECOGNITIONS: The Major Theme," *DAI* 39 (1979): 4948A.

Klemtner, Susan S., "'For a Very Small Audience': The Fiction of William Gaddis," *Crit* 19, iii (1978): 61-73.

Koenig, Peter W., "Recognizing Gaddis' RECOGNITIONS," *ConL* 16 (1975): 61-72.

———, "'Splinters from the Yew Tree': A Critical Study of William Gaddis' THE RECOGNITIONS," *DAI* 33 (1972): 1172A (N.Y.U.).

Lathrop, Kathleen L., "Comic-Ironic Parallels in William Gaddis's THE RECOGNITIONS," *RCF* 2, ii (Summer, 1982): 32-40.

Leverence, John, "Gaddis Anagnorisis," in Baldanza, F., ed., *Itinerary 3: Criticism*, 49-61.

Madden, David, in Madden, D., ed., *Rediscoveries*, 291-304.

Martin, Stephen-Paul, "Vulnerability and Aggression: Characters and Objects in THE RECOGNITIONS," *RCF* 2, ii (Summer, 1982): 45-50.

Minkoff, Robert L., "Down, Then Out: A Reading of William Gaddis' THE RECOGNITIONS," *DAI* 38 (1977): 1393A.

Moore, Steven, "Chronological Difficulties in the Novels of William Gaddis," *Crit* 22, i (1980): 79-86.

———, *A Reader's Guide to William Gaddis's THE RECOGNITIONS*, Lincoln: Un. of Nebraska Pr., 1982.

Morton, Marjorie, "The Orchestration of Chaos: The Context and Structure of the Novels of William Gaddis," *DAI* 42, iv (Oct., 1981): 1637A.

Safer, Elaine B., "The Allusive Mode, the Absurd and Black Humor in William Gaddis's THE RECOGNITIONS," *StAH* (1982): 103-18.

Salemi, Joseph S., "To Soar in Atonement: Art as Expiation in Gaddis's THE RECOGNITIONS," *Novel* 10, ii (Winter, 1977): 127-36.

Sawyer, Tom, "False God to Forge: The Forger behind Wyatt Gwyon," *RCF* 2, ii (Summer, 1982): 50-4.

Stark, John, "William Gaddis: Just Recognition," *HC* 14, ii (April, 1977): 1-7.

Stathis, James J., "William Gaddis: THE RECOGNITIONS," *Crit* 5 (Winter, 1962-63): 91-4.

Tanner, T., *City of Words*, 393-400.

Thompson, Gary L., "Fictive Models: Carlyle's SARTOR RESARTUS, Melville's THE CONFIDENCE-MAN, Gaddis' THE RECOGNITIONS, and Pynchon's GRAVITY'S RAINBOW," *DAI* 40 (1979): 1462A-63A.

Weisenburger, Steven, "Paper Currencies: Reading William Gaddis," *RCF* 2, ii (Summer, 1982): 12-22.

Werner, C. H., *Paradoxical Resolutions*, 169-81.

BIBLIOGRAPHY

Moore, Steven, "William Gaddis: A Selected Bibliography," *RCF* 2, ii (Summer, 1982): 55-6.

GAINES, ERNEST J., 1933-

GENERAL

Bryant, Jerry H., "Ernest J. Gaines: Change, Growth, and History," *SoR* 10, iv (Oct., 1974): 851-64.

_____, *From Death to Life*: The Fiction of Ernest J. Gaines," *IowaR* 3, i (Winter, 1972): 106-20.

Fabre, Michel, "Bayonne or the Yoknapatawpha of Ernest Gaines," *Callaloo* 1, iii (May, 1978): 110-24.

Hicks, Jack, "To Make These Bones Live: History and Community in Ernest Gaines's Fiction," *BALF* 11, i (Spring, 1977): 9-19.

Ingram, Forrest, and Barbara Steinberg, "On the Verge: An Interview with Ernest J. Gaines," *NOR* 3, iv (1979): 339-44.

Laney, Ruth, "A Conversation with Ernest Gaines," *SoR* 10, i (Jan., 1974): 1-14.

O'Brien, John, ed., *Interviews with Black Writers*, 79-9.

Rowell, Charles H., "'This Louisiana Thing That Drives Me': An Interview with Ernest J. Gaines," *Callaloo* 1, iii (May, 1978): 39-51.

Stoelting, Winifred L., "Human Dignity and Pride in the Novels of Ernest Gaines," *CLAJ* 14, iii (Mar., 1971): 340-58.

THE AUTOBIOGRAPHY OF MISS JANE PITTMAN

Andrews, William L., "'We Ain't Going Back There': The Idea of Progress in THE AUTOBIOGRAPHY OF MISS JANE PITTMAN," *BALF* 11, iv (1977): 146-9.

Aubert, Alvin, "Ernest J. Gaines's Truly Tragic Mulatto," *Callaloo* 1, iii (May, 1978): 68-75.

Beckhman, Barry, "Jane Pittman and Oral Tradition," *Callaloo* 1, iii (May, 1978): 102-9.

Berzon, J. R., *Neither White Nor Black*, 238-42.

Bryant, Jerry H., "Ernest J. Gaines: Change, Growth, and History," *SoR* 10, iv (Oct., 1974): 857-64.

_____, *From Death to Life*: The Fiction of Ernest J. Gaines," *IowaR* 3, i (Winter, 1972): 106-20.

Callahan, John, "Image Making: Tradition and the Two Versions of THE AUTOBIOGRAPHY OF MISS JANE PITTMAN," *ChiR* 29, ii (1977): 45-62.

Gaines, Ernest J., "Miss Jane and I," *Callaloo* 1, iii (May, 1978): 23-38.

Gayle, A., Jr., *Way of the New World*, 294-301.

Giles, James R., "Revolution and Myth: Kelley's A DIFFERENT DRUMMER and Gaines' THE AUTOBIOGRAPHY OF MISS JANE PITTMAN," *Minority Voices* (Pennsylvania State Un.) 1, ii (1977): 39-48.

Hicks, Jack, "To Make These Bones Live: History and Community in Ernest Gaines's Fiction," *BALF* 11, i (Spring, 1977): 16-19.

Hogue, William L., "To Saddle Time: Sociocriticism and the Afro-American Text," *DAI* 41, viii (Feb., 1981): 3581A.

Pettis, Joyce, "The Black Historical Novel as Best Seller," *KFR* 25 (1979): 51-9.

Potter, Vilma R., "THE AUTOBIOGRAPHY OF MISS JANE PITTMAN: How to Make a White Film from a Black Novel," *LFQ* 3 (1975): 371-5.

Wertheim, Albert, "Journey to Freedom: Ernest Gaines' THE AUTOBIOGRAPHY OF MISS JANE PITTMAN," in Bruck, P., and W. Karrer, eds., *Afro-American Novel Since 1960*, 219-34.

BLOODLINE

Duncan, Todd, "Scene and Life Cycle in Ernest Gaines' BLOODLINE," *Callaloo* 1, iii (May, 1978): 85-101.

Hicks, Jack, "To Make These Bones Live: History and Community in Ernest Gaines's Fiction," *BALF* 11, i (Spring, 1977): 13-16.

CATHERINE CARMIER

Aubert, Alvin, "Ernest J. Gaines's Truly Tragic Mulatto," *Callaloo* 1, iii (May, 1978): 68-75.

Hicks, Jack, "To Make These Bones Live: History and Community in Ernest Gaines's Fiction," *BALF* 11, i (Spring, 1977): 9-11.

Schraufnagel, N., *From Apology to Protest*, 158-60.

Stoelting, Winifred L., "Human Dignity and Pride in the Novels of Ernest Gaines," *CLAJ* 14, iii (Mar., 1971): 341-7.

IN MY FATHER'S HOUSE

Shelton, Frank W., "IN MY FATHER'S HOUSE: Ernest Gaines after Jane Pittman," *SoR* 17, ii (April, 1981): 340-5.

OF LOVE AND DUST

Gayle, A., Jr., *Way of the New World*, 289-94.

Hicks, Jack, "To Make These Bones Live: History and Community in Ernest Gaines's Fiction," *BALF* 11, i (Spring, 1977): 11-13.

Schraufnagel, N., *From Apology to Protest*, 160-3.

Stoelting, Winifred L., "Human Dignity and Pride in the Novels of Ernest Gaines," *CLAJ* 14, iii (Mar., 1971): 347-58.

Wideman, John, "OF LOVE AND DUST: A Reconsideration," *Callaloo* 1, iii (May, 1978): 76-84.

Williams, S. A., "The Streetman: The Black Hero as Law Breaker," *Give Birth to Brightness*, 167-209.

BIBLIOGRAPHY

Rowell, Charles H., "Ernest J. Gaines: A Checklist, 1964-1978," *Callaloo* 1, iii (May, 1978): 125-31.

GALLANT, MAVIS, 1922-

GENERAL

Davies, Robertson, "The Novels of Mavis Gallant," *CFM* No. 28 (1978): 68-73.

Hancock, Geoff, "An Interview with Mavis Gallant," *CFM* No. 28 (1978): 18-67.

_____, "Mavis Gallant: Counterweight in Europe," *CFM* No. 28 (1978): 5-7.

Merler, G., *Mavis Gallant*.

Stevens, Peter, " Perils of Compassion," *CanL* 56 (Spring, 1973): 61-70. Also in Woodcock, G., ed., *Canadian Novel in the Twentieth Century*, 202-11.

A FAIRLY GOOD TIME

Stevens, Peter, "Perils of Compassion," *CanL* 56 (Spring, 1973): 68-70. Also in Woodcock, G., ed., *Canadian Novel in the Twentieth Century*, 209-11.

GREEN WATER, GREEN SKY

Gottlieb, Lois, and Wendy Keitner, "Mothers and Daughters in Four Recent Canadian Novels," *Sphinx* 4 (1975): 21-34.

Stevens, Peter, "Perils of Compassion," *CanL* 56 (Spring, 1973): 62-4. Also in Woodcock, G., ed., *Canadian Novel in the Twentieth Century*, 203-5.

BIBLIOGRAPHY

Malcolm, Douglas, "An Annotated Bibliography of Works by and about Mavis Gallant," *ECW* 6 (Spring, 1977): 32-52. Also in *CFM* 28 (1978): 115-33.

GALLICO, PAUL, 1897-1976

GENERAL

Rao, V. V. B. Rama, "The Achievement of Paul Gallico," *IJAS* 4, i-ii (June and Dec., 1974): 78-88.

THE SMALL MIRACLE

Green, R. B., *Italian-American Novel*, 115-17.

THE ZOO GANG

Green, R. B., *Italian-American Novel*, 382-3.

GALLOWAY, DAVID D(ARRYL), 1937-

A FAMILY ALBUM

Galloway, David, "The Minor Contemporary Novelist: David Galloway's A FAMILY ALBUM," *DQR* 12, i (1982): 2-14.

GARDNER, JOHN (CHAMPLIN, JR.), 1933-1982

Allen, Bruce, "Settling for Ithaca: The Fictions of John Gardner," *SR* 85, iii (Summer, 1977): 520-31.

Bellamy, Joe D., and Pat Eaworth, "John Gardner," in Bellamy, J. D., ed., *New Fiction*, 169-93. [Interview.] From *FictionI* Nos. 2/3 (1974): 33-49.

Christian, Ed, "An Interview with John Gardner," *PrS* 54, iv (1980-81): 70-93.

Clark, C.E.F., Jr., "John Gardner," in *Conversations with Writers, I*, 83-103.

Coale, Samuel, "'Into the Farther Darkness': The Manichaean Pastoralism of John Gardner," in Morace, R. A., and K. van Spanckeren, eds., *John Gardner*, 15-27.

Cowart, David, "*Et in Arcadia Ego*: Gardner's Early Pastoral Novels," in Morace, R. A., and K. Van Spanckeren, eds., *John Gardner*, 1-14.

Edwards, Don, and Carol Polsgrove, "A Conversation with John Gardner," *Atlantic* (May, 1977): 43-7.

Ferguson, Paul F., John R. Maier, Frank McConnell, and Sara Matthiessen, "John Gardner: The Art of Fiction LXXIII," *ParisR* 75 (1979): 36-74.

Fitzpatrick, W. P., "John Gardner and the Defense of Fiction," *BWVACET* 4, i (1977): 19-28. Also in *MQ* 20, iv (Summer, 1979): 404-15.

Foeller, Elbieta, "The Mythical Heroes of John Barth and John Gardner," *KN* 27, ii (1980): 183-97.

Harvey, Marshall L., "Where Philosophy and Fiction Meet: An Interview with John Gardner," *ChiR* 29, iv (1978): 73-87.

Janssens, Uta, "The Artist's Vision: John Gardner," *DQR* 9, iv (1979): 284-91.

McCaffery, Larry, "The Gass-Gardner Debate: Showdown on Main Street," *LitR* 23, i (Fall, 1979): 134-44.

Mitcham, Judson, and Richard William, "An Interview with John Gardner," *NOR* 8, ii (Summer, 1981): 125-33.

Morace, R. A., and K. VanSpanckeren, eds., *John Gardner*.

_____, "New Fiction, Popular Fiction, and John Gardner's Middle/Moral Way," in Morace, R. A., and K. VanSpanckeren, eds., *John Gardner*, 130-45.

Morris, Gregory L., "A World of Order and Light: A Critical Introduction to the Fiction of John Gardner," *DAI* 42 (1981): 1151A.

Natov, Roni, and Geraldine DeLuca, "An Interview with John Gardner," *L&U* 2, i (1978): 114-36.

Rapkin, Angela A., "John Gardner: The Techniques of Moral Fiction," *DAI* 43 (1982): 2345A.

Reilly, Charlie, "A Conversation with John Gardner," *CML* 1, ii (Winter, 1981): 91-108.

Shuval, Michael H., "The Experience of Disorder in Three Works by John Gardner," *DAI* 41 (1981): 4390A.

VanSpanckeren, Kathryn, "Magical Prisons: Embedded Structures in the Work of John Gardner," in Morace, R. A., and K. VanSpanckeren, eds., *John Gardner*, 114-29.

Winther, Per, "An Interview with John Gardner," *ES* 62, vi (Dec., 1981): 509-24.

FREDDY'S BOOK

Cummins, Walter, "The Real Monster in FREDDY'S BOOK," in Morace, R. A., and K. VanSpanckeren, eds., *John Gardner*, 106-13.

GRENDEL

Ackland, Michael, "Blakean Sources in John Gardner's GRENDEL," *Crit* 23, i (1981): 57-66.

Ellis, Helen B., and Warren U. Ober, "GRENDEL and Blake: The Contraries of Existence," *ESC* 3 (1977): 87-102. Also, in different form, in Morace, R. A., and K. VanSpanckeren, eds., *John Gardner*, 46-61.

Fitzpatrick, W. P., "Down and Down I Go: A Note on Shelley's PROMETHEUS UNBOUND and Gardner's GRENDEL," *NConL* 7, i (1977): 2-5.

Hutman, Norma L., "Even Monsters Have Mothers: A Study of BEOWULF and John Gardner's GRENDEL," *Mosaic* 9, i (1975): 19-31.

Klinkowitz, Jerome, "John Gardner's GRENDEL," in Morace, R. A., and K. VanSpanckeren, eds., *John Gardner*, 62-7.

Milosh, Joseph, "John Gardner's GRENDEL: Sources and Analogues," *ConL* 19 (1978): 48-57.

Minugh, David, "John Gardner Constructs GRENDEL's Universe," 125-41 in Rydén, Mats, and Lennart A Björk, eds., *Studies in English Philology, Linguistics and Literature Presented to Alarik Rynell, 7 March 1978*, Stockholm: Almqvist & Wiksell, 1978.

Murr, Judy S., "John Gardner's Order and Disorder: GRENDEL and THE SUNLIGHT DIALOGUES," *Crit* 18, ii (1976): 97-108.

Perkins, James A., "Robert Coover and John Gardner: What Can We Do with the Poets?" *NConL* 6, ii (Mar., 1976): 2-4.

Ruud, Jay, "Gardner's GRENDEL and BEOWULF: Humanizing the Monster," *Thoth* 14, ii-iii (Fall, 1974): 3-17.

Stromme, Craig J., "The Twelve Chapters of GRENDEL," *Crit* 20, i (1978): 83-92.

NICKEL MOUNTAIN: A PASTORAL NOVEL

Arnold, Marilyn, "NICKEL MOUNTAIN: John Gardner's Testament of Redemption," *Ren* 30 (1978): 59-68.

Harris, Richard C., "Ecclesiastical Wisdom and NICKEL MOUNTAIN," *TCL* 26, iv (1980): 424-31.

Zverev, A., "Faith in the Good," in Vroon, R., tr., *20th Century American Literature: A Soviet View*, 467-71.

OCTOBER LIGHT

Butts, Leonard C., "Locking Unlocking: Nature as Moral Center in John Gardner's OCTOBER LIGHT," *Crit* 22, ii (1980): 47-60.

Fitzpatrick, W. P., "John Gardner and the Defense of Fiction," *BWVACET* 4, i (1977): 19-28. Also in *MQ* 20, iv (Summer, 1979): 411-15.

Morace, Robert A., "New Fiction, Popular Fiction, and John Gardner's Middle/Moral Way," in Morace, R. A., and K. VonSpanckeren, eds., *John Gardner*, 137-45. From *FictionI* 12 (1980): 232-46.

THE RESURRECTION

Cowart, David, "*Et in Arcadia Ego*: Gardner's Early Pastoral Novels," in Morace, R. A., and K. VanSpanckeren, eds., *John Gardner*, 1-6.

THE SUNLIGHT DIALOGUES

Butscher, Edward, "The American Novel is Alive and Well ... Now," *GaR* 27, iii (Fall, 1973): 393-7.

Maier, John R., "Mesopotamian Names in THE SUNLIGHT DIALOGUES: Or MAMA Makes It to Batavia, New York," *LOS* 4 (1977): 33-48.

Morace, Robert A., "John Gardner's THE SUNLIGHT DIALOGUES: A Giant (Paperback) Leap Backwards," *NConL* 8, iv (1978): 5-6.

Morris, Greg, "A Babylonian in Batavia: Mesopotamian Literature and Lore in THE SUNLIGHT DIALOGUES," in Morace, R. A., and K. VanSpanckeren, eds., *John Gardner*, 28-45.

Murr, Judy S., "John Gardner's Order and Disorder: GRENDEL and THE SUNLIGHT DIALOGUES," *Crit* 18, ii (1976): 97-108.

THE WRECKAGE OF AGATHON

Cowart, David, "*Et in Arcadia Ego*: Gardner's Early Pastoral Novels," in Morace, R. A., and K. VanSpanckeren, eds., *John Gardner*, 6-10.

BIBLIOGRAPHY

Dillon, David A., "John C. Gardner: A Bibliography," *BB* 34, ii (April-June, 1977): 86-9, 104.

Howell, John H., *John Gardner: A Bibliographical Profile*, Carbondale: Southern Illinois Un. Pr., 1980.

GARNER, HUGH, 1913-1979

GENERAL

Anderson, Allan, "An Interview with Hugh Garner," *TamR* No. 52 (Third Quarter, 1969): 19-34.

Edwards, Eileen, "A Sense of Place in Hugh Garner's Fiction," *WLWE* 18, ii (1979): 353-67.

Fetherling, D., *Hugh Garner*.

————, "The Old Pro in Action," *Saturday Night* 88 (May, 1973): 25-7.

Moss, John G., "A Conversation with Hugh Garner," *JCF* 1, ii (Spring, 1972): 50-5.

CABBAGETOWN

Fetherling, D., *Hugh Garner*, 16-31.
Moss, J., *Patterns of Islation*, 210-14.

A NICE PLACE TO VISIT

Fetherling, D., *Hugh Garner*, 49-58.

PRESENT RECKONING

Fetherling, D., *Hugh Garner*, 32-9.

SILENCE ON THE SHORE

Fetherling, D., *Hugh Garner*, 40-8.

THE SIN SNIPER

Fetherling, D., *Hugh Garner*, 59-64.

STORM BELOW

Fetherling, D., *Hugh Garner*, 11-15.

GARRETT, GEORGE, 1929-

GENERAL

Carr, John, "Kite-Flying and Other Irrational Acts," [Interview] in Carr, J., ed., *Kite-Flying and Other Irrational Acts*, 174-98.

Graham, John, "George Garrett Discusses Writing," *MMtR* 1 (1971): 79-102.

Israel, Charles, "Interview: George Garrett," *SCR* 6, i (1973): 43-8.

Meriwether, James B., "George Palmer Garrett, Jr.," *PULC* 25, i (Autumn, 1963): 26-39.

Robinson, W. R., "The Fiction of George Garrett," *MMtR* 1 (1971): 39-41.

Tillinghast, David, "George Garrett," *SCR* 9, i (Nov., 1976): 21-4.

DEATH OF THE FOX

Carr, John, "In Contention with Time: George Garrett's DEATH OF THE FOX," *MMtR* 1 (1971): 19-26.

Davis, Paxton, "Breadth, Depth, and Elevation: George Garrett's DEATH OF THE FOX," *MMtR* 1 (1971): 12-13.

McCullough, Frank, "George Garrett's Ralegh," *MMtR* 1 (1971): 15-18.

Robinson, W. R., "Imagining the Individual: George Garrett's DEATH OF THE FOX," *HC* 8 (Aug., 1971): 1-12.

Slavitt, David R., "History—Fate and Freedom: A Look at George Garrett's New Novel," *SoR* 7, i (Jan., 1971): 276-94.

Turner, Joseph W., "History and Imagination in George Garrett's DEATH OF THE FOX," *Crit* 22, ii (1980): 31-46.

BIBLIOGRAPHY

Wright, Stuart, "George Garrett: A Bibliographic Chronicle, 1947-1980," *BB* 38, i (Jan.-Mar., 1981): 6-19, 25.

GASS, WILLIAM HOWARD, 1924-

GENERAL

Duncan, Jeffrey L., "A Conversation with Stanley Elkin and William H. Gass," *IowaR* 7, i (Winter, 1976): 48-77.

Durad, Régis, "An Interview with William Gass," *DeltaES* 8 (1979): 7-19.

French, Ned, "Against the Grain: Theory and Practice in the Work of William H. Gass," *IowaR* 7, i (Winter, 1976): 96-107.

Janssens, G. A. M., "An Interview with William Gass," *DQR* 9, iv (1979): 242-59.

LeClair, Thomas, "A Conversation with William Gass," *ChiR* 30, ii (1978): 97-106.

———, "William Gass: The Art of Fiction LXV," *ParisR* 70 (Summer, 1977): 61-94.

Lubarsky, Jared, "The American Writer in Society: An Interview with William Gass," *EigoS* 124 (1978): 8-11.

McCaffery, Larry, "The Gass-Gardner Debate: Showdown on Main Street," *LitR* 23, i (Fall, 1979): 134-44.

McCauley, Carole S., "Fiction Needn't Say Things—It Should Make Them Out of Words: An Interview with William H. Gass," *The Falcon* 5 (Winter, 1972): 35-45. Also in Bellamy, J. D., ed., *New Fiction*, 32-44.

McKenzie, James, ed., "Pole-Vaulting in Top Hats: A Public Conversation with John Barth, William Gass, and Ishmael Reed," *MFS* 22, ii (Summer, 1976): 131-51.

Mullinax, Gary, "An Interview with William Gass," *DelLR* 1 (1972): 81-7.

Shorris, Earl, "The Well-Spoken Passion of William H. Gass," *Harpers* 244 (May, 1972): 96-100.

"A Symposium on Fiction," *Shen* 27, ii (Winter, 1976): 3-31.

Tanner, T., *City of Words*, 269-72.

Veley, Pamela L., "William H. Gass: A Critical Introduction and Bibliography," *DAI* 38 (1978): 7338A-39A.

OMENSETTER'S LUCK

Allen, Carolyn J., "Fiction and Figures of Life in OMENSETTER'S LUCK," *PCP* 9 (1974): 5-11.

Dornfeld, Margaret, "Gass's OMENSETTER'S LUCK," *Expl* 39, iv (Summer, 1981): 43-4.

Fogel, Stanley, "'And All the Little Typtopies': Notes on Language and Theory in the Contemporary Experimental Novel," *MFS* 20, iii (Autumn, 1974): 333-6.

Gass, William, "A Letter to the Editor," in McCormack, T., ed., *Afterwords*, 89-105.

Gilman, R., *Confusion of Realms*, 69-79.

McCaffery, L., *Metafictional Muse*, 223-50.

Schneider, Richard J., "The Fortunate Fall in William Gass's OMENSETTER'S LUCK," *Crit* 18, i (1976): 5-20.

WILLIE MASTER'S LONESOME WIFE

Blau, Marion, "'How I Would Brood Upon You': The Lonesome Wife of William Gass," *GLRev* 2, i (Summer, 1975): 40-50.

McCaffery, Larry, "The Art of Metafiction: William Gass's WILLIE MASTERS' LONESOME WIFE," *Crit* 18, i (1976): 21-35.

Merrill, Reed B., "The Grotesque of Structure: WILLIE MASTERS' LONESOME WIFE," *Criticism* 18, iv (Autumn, 1976): 305-16.

Tanner, Tony, "Games American Writers Play: Ceremony, Complicity, Contestation, and Carnival," *Salmagundi* 35 (1976): 117-21.

BIBLIOGRAPHY

McCaffery, Larry, "A William H. Gass Bibliography," *Crit* 18, i (1976): 59-66.

———, "A William H. Gass Checklist," *BB* 31, iii (July-Sept., 1974): 104-6.

White, Ray L., "The Early Fiction of William H. Gass: A Critical Documentary," *Midamerica* 7 (1980): 164-77.

GEE, MAURICE (GOUGH), 1931-

GENERAL

Hannah, Donald W., "Family Chronicles: The Novels of Maurice Gee," *Kunapipi* 3, ii (1981): 80-126. [Not seen.]

Hill, D., *Introducing Maurice Gee*.

THE BIG SEASON

Hill, D., *Introducing Maurice Gee*, 42-3.

GAMES OF CHOICE

Hill, D., *Introducing Maurice Gee*, 47-8.

IN MY FATHER'S DEN

Hill, D., *Introducing Maurice Gee*, 44-6.

PLUMB

Boyd, Brian, "Maurice Gee: Ironies of Growth and Judgement, Part 2: Structure and Irony in PLUMB," *Islands* 9 (1981): 136-60.

Hill, D., *Introducing Maurice Gee*, 49-50.

GIBBONS, STELLA (DOROTHEA), 1902-1989

COLD COMFORT FARM

Ariail, Jacqueline A., "Cold Comfort from Stella Gibbons," *ArielE* 9, iii (1978): 63-78.

English Study Group, Centre for Contemporary Cultural Studies, Birmingham, "Thinking the Thirties," in Barker, Francis, Jay Bernstein, John Coombes, Peter Hulme, David Musselwhite, Jennifer Stone, eds., *Practices of Literature and Politics*, Colchester: Un. of Essex, 1979.

Purves, Libby, "The Road to COLD COMFORT FARM," *Listener* 105 (May 14, 1981): 639.

GODDEN, RUMER, 1907-

GENERAL

Desai, S. K., "A Happy Encounter: A Critical Note on Rumer Godden's Indian Novels," in Naik, M. K., et. al., eds., *Image of India in Western Creative Writing*, 61-70.

Hartley, Lois, "The Indian Novels of Rumer Godden," *Mahfil* 3, ii-iii (1966): 65-75.

Prescott, O., *In My Opinion*, 203-8.

Sharma, Vera, "Rumer Godden: An Appreciation," *IPEN* 41, iv (1975): 1-4.

Simpson, H. A., *Rumer Godden*.

Tindall, William Y., "Rumer Godden, Public Symbolist," *EJ* 41 (Mar., 1952): 115-21. Also in *CE* 13 (Mar., 1952): 297-303.

Waltz, Laura M., "Rumer Godden's Indian Novels," *DAI* 39 (1978): 876A-77A.

THE BATTLE OF THE VILLA FIORITA

Simpson, H. A., *Rumer Godden*, 88-9.

BLACK NARCISSUS

Hartley, Lois, "The Indian Novels of Rumer Godden," *Mahfil* 3, ii-iii (1966): 68-70.

Simpson, H. A., *Rumer Godden*, 38-42.

Tindall, William Y., "Rumer Godden, Public Symbolist," *CE* 13 (Mar., 1952): 300-1.

BREAKFAST WITH THE NIKOLIDES

Hartley, Lois, "The Indian Novels of Rumer Godden," *Mahfil* 3, ii-iii (1966): 70-2.

Simpson, H. A., *Rumer Godden*, 87-8.

A BREATH OF AIR

Simpson, H. A., *Rumer Godden*, 99-101.

CHINA COURT: THE HOURS OF A COUNTRY HOUSE

Simpson, H. A., *Rumer Godden*, 68-74.

CHINESE PUZZLE

Simpson, H. A., *Rumer Godden*, 32-5.

AN EPISODE OF SPARROWS

Simpson, H. A., *Rumer Godden*, 83-6.

THE GREENGAGE SUMMER

Simpson, H. A., *Rumer Godden*, 86-7.

IN THIS HOUSE OF BREDE

Simpson, H. A., *Rumer Godden*, 109-15.

KINGFISHERS CATCH FIRE

Hartley, Lois, "The Indian Novels of Rumer Godden," *Mahfil* 3, ii-iii (1966): 73-5.

Simpson, H. A., *Rumer Godden*, 47-50.

THE LADY AND THE UNICORN

Simpson, H. A., *Rumer Godden*, 35-7.

THE RIVER

Hartley, Lois, "The Indian Novels of Rumer Godden," *Mahfil* 3, ii-iii (1966): 72-3.

Simpson, H. A., *Rumer Godden*, 74-9.

Tindall, William Y., "Rumer Godden, Public Symbolist," *CE* 13 (Mar., 1952): 297-9.

TAKE THREE TENSES: A FUGUE IN TIME

Frey, John R., "Past or Present Tense? A Note on the Technique of Narration," *JEGP* 46 (April, 1947): 205-8.

Simpson, H. A., *Rumer Godden*, y61-8.

Tindall, William Y., "Rumer Godden, Public Symbolist," *CE* 13 (Mar., 1952): 301-2.

GODWIN, GAIL, 1937-

GENERAL

Smith, Marilynn J., "The Role of the South in the Novels of Gail Godwin," *Crit* 21, iii (1980): 103-10.

GLASS PEOPLE

Gaston, Karen C., "'Beauty and the Beast' in Gail Godwin's GLASS PEOPLE," *Crit* 21, iii (1980): 94-102.

A MOTHER AND TWO DAUGHTERS

Renwick, Joyce, "Gail Godwin: An Interview," *FictionI* 14 (1982): 151-68.

THE ODD WOMAN

Gardiner, Judith K., "Gail Godwin and Feminist Fiction," *NAmerR* 260, ii (Summer, 1975): 83-6.

Korg, Jacob, "A Gissing Influence," *GissingN* 12, i (Jan., 1976): 13-19.

Lorsch, Susan E., "Gail Godwin's THE ODD WOMAN: Literature and the Retreat from Life," *Crit* 20, ii (1978): 21-32.

Mickelson, Anne Z., "Gail Godwin: Order and Accomodation," *Reaching Out*, 68-86.

GOLD, HERBERT, 1924-

GENERAL

Hicks, Granville, in Balakian, N., and C. Simons, eds., *Creative Present*, 224-32.

Kuhn, Howard F., "A Critical Analysis of the Novels of Herbert Gold," *DAI* 31 (1971): 5409A (Ore.).

Moore, Harry T., "The Fiction of Herbert Gold," in Moore, H. T., ed., *Contemporary American Novelists*, 170-81.

Serlen, Ellen, "The American Dream: From F. Scott Fitzgerald to Herbert Gold," *Midamerica* 4 (1977): 122-37.

Smith, Larry, "Herbert Gold: Belief and Craft," *OhioanaQ* 21 (1978): 148-56.

Thorpe, Stephen J., "Interview: Herbert Gold," *CaQ* 5 (1973): 65-76.

FATHERS

Solotaroff, Theodore, "Remember Those Tissues They Wrapped the Fruit In...?" *Red Hot Vacuum*, 237-41.

THE MAN WHO WAS NOT WITH IT

Seiden, Melvin, "Characters and Idea: The Modern Novel," *Nation* 188 (April 25, 1959): 387-92.

Widmer, K., "Contemporary American Outcasts," *Literary Rebel*, 126-7.

THE OPTIMIST

Hassan, I., *Radical Innocence*, 180-7.

Moore, Harry T., in Moore, H. T., ed., *Contemporary American Novelists*, 179-81.

Nemerov, Howard, in *PR* 27 (Winter, 1960): 180-4. Also in Nemerov, H., *Poetry and Fiction*, 283-6.

Seiden, Melvin, "Characters and Ideas: The Modern Novel," *Nation* 188 (April 25, 1959): 387-92.

SALT

Moore, Harry T., in Moore, H. T., ed., *Contemporary American Novelists*, 177-9.

THEREFORE BE BOLD

Sherman, B., *Invention of the Jew*, 211-14.

GOLDING, WILLIAM GERALD, 1911-1993

GENERAL

Allen, W., *Modern Novel*, 288-92.

Anderson, David, "Is Golding's Theology Christian?" in Biles, J. I., and R. O. Evans, eds., *William Golding*, 1-20.

Atkins, John, "Two Views of Life: William Golding and Graham Greene," *SLitI* 13, i (Spring, 1980): 81-96.

Babb, H. S., *Novels of William Golding*.

Baker, James R., "An Interview with William Golding," *TCL* 28, ii (Summer, 1982): 130-69.

————, *William Golding*.

Bergonzi, Bernard, and John S. Whitley, "William Golding," in Watts, C., ed., *English Novel*, 175-91.

Biles, Jack I., "Literary Sources and William Golding," *SAB* 37, ii (May, 1972): 29-36.

————, *Talk: Conversations with William Golding*, N.Y.: Harcourt, 1970.

————, and R. O. Evans, eds., *William Golding*.

Bowen, John, "Bending over Backwards," *TLS* (Oct. 23, 1959): 608. Also in Nelson, W., *William Golding's LORD OF THE FLIES*, 55-60.

Boyle, Ted E., "Golding's Existential Vision," in Biles, J. I., and R. O. Evans, eds., *William Golding*, 21-38.

Bufkin, Ernest, C., Jr., "The Novels of William Golding: A Descriptive and Analytic Study," *DA* 25 (1964): 469-70 (Vanderbilt).

Cammarota, Richard S., "Like the Appletree: Symbolism and the Fable in the Prose Works of William Golding," *DAI* 33 (1973): 5715A-16A (Penn. State).

Coppinger, Rebecca K., "The Tragi-comic Mode: William Golding and Humor," *DAI* 39 (1979): 4238A.

————, "William Golding: The Novelist as Bridge-Builder," *Rendezvous* 15, ii (Fall, 1980): 50-6.

Davies, Cecil, "'The Burning Bird': Golding's POEMS and the Novels," *SLitI* 13, i (Spring, 1980): 97-117.

Davies, Harold, "Moral Choice in the Novels of William Golding," *ModSp* 11, 1/2 (Jan.-June, 1967): 35-45.

Delbaere-Garant, Jeanne, "From the Cellar to the Rock: A Recurrent Pattern in William Golding's Novels," *MFS* 17, iv (Winter, 1971-72): 501-12.

Dick, Bernard F., "The Novelist as Displaced Person: An Interview with William Golding," *CE* 26 (Mar., 1965): 480-2.

————, *William Golding*.

Dickson, Larry L., "Allegory in the Novels of William Golding," *DAI* 36 (1975): 307A-08A.

Duriez, Colin, "The Firestorm Child," *Third Way* 3, xii (1979): 27-8. [Not seen.]

Elmen, P., *William Golding*.

Fox, Dorothy, "William Golding's Microcosms of Evil," *Innisfree* 1 (1974): 30-7.

Freedman, Ralph, "The New Realism: The Fancy of William Golding," *Per* 10 (Summer-Autumn, 1958): 118-28.

Gallagher, Michael P., "The Human Image in William Golding," *Studies* 54 (Summer-Autumn, 1965): 197-216.

Gindin, James, "'Gimmick' and Metaphor in the Novels of William Golding," *MFS* 6 (Summer, 1960): 145-52. Also in Gindin, J., *Postwar British Fiction*, 196-206. Also in Nelson, W., *William Golding's LORD OF THE FLIES*, 132-40.

Green, Martin, "Distaste for the Contemporary," *Nation* 190 (May 21, 1960): 451-4. Also in Nelson, W., *William Golding's LORD OF THE FLIES*, 75-82.

Green, Peter, "The World of William Golding," *EDH* 32 (1963): 37-57.

————, "The World of William Golding," *REL* 1, ii (April, 1960): 62-72. Also, revised, in Nelson, W., *William Golding's LORD OF THE FLIES*, 170-89. Also, revised, in *TPRSL* 32 (1963): 37-57.

Gregor, Ian, and Mark Kinkead-Weekes, "The Later Golding," *TCL* 28, ii (Summer, 1982): 109-27.

Grimes, Mary L., "The Archetype of the Great Mother in the Novels of William Golding," *DAI* 37 (1977): 6496A.

Haffenden, John, "William Golding: An Interview," *Quarto* 12 (1980): 9-12.

Hainsworth, J. D., "William Golding," *HJ* 64 (Summer, 1966): 122-3.

Hodson, L., *Golding*.

_____, *William Golding*.

Hollinger, Alexander, "Human Condition in W. Golding's Novels," *AUB-LG* 22 (1973): 177-82. [Not seen.]

Hynes, Sam, "Novels of a Religious Man," *Cweal* 71 (Mar. 18, 1960): 673-5. Also in Nelson, W., *William Golding's LORD OF THE FLIES*, 70-5.

_____, *William Golding*. Also in Stade, G., ed., *Six Contemporary British Novelists*, 165-218.

Irwin, Joseph J., "The Serpent Coiled Within," *Motive* (Nashville) 23 (May, 1963): 1-5.

Johnston, A., *Of Earth and Darkness*.

Johnston, William A., "The Novels of William Golding," *DAI* 32 (1971): 1515A (Del.).

Josipovici, Gabriel, "Golding: The Hidden Source," *World and the Book*, 236-55.

Karl, F. R., "The Metaphysical Novels of William Golding," *Contemporary English Novel*, 254-60.

Keller, R. H., *Philosophy of William Golding*.

Kennard, Jean E., "William Golding: Islands," in Kennard, J. E., *Number and Nightmare*, 176-202.

Kermode, F., "The Later Golding," *Continuities*, 186-94.

_____, and William Golding, "The Meaning of it All," *Books and Bookmen* 5 (Oct., 1959): 9-10.

_____, "The Novels of William Golding," *ILA* 3 (1961): 11-29. Also in Kermode, F., *Puzzles and Epiphanies*, 198-213. Also in Kostelanetz, R., ed., *On Contemporary Literature*, 366-81.

Khera, Sunit B., "Ethical Epistemology in the Novels of William Golding," *DA* 31 (1970): 762A-63A.

Kinkead-Weekes, M., and I. Gregor, *William Golding*.

LaChance, Paul R., "Man and Religion in the Novels of William Golding and Graham Greene," *DAI* 31 (1971): 6062A (Kent State).

Latimer, Paula A. W., "William Golding's View of Man: A Study of Six of His Novels," *DAI* 33 (1973): 3591A (Texas Christian).

Lipson, Carol, "The Influence of Egyptology on the Novels of William Golding," *DAI* 32 (1971): 974A (U.C.L.A.).

MacLure, Millar, "William Golding's Survivor Stories," *TamR* 5 (Summer, 1957): 60-7.

MacShane, Frank, "The Novels of William Golding," *DR* 42 (Summer, 1962): 171-83.

Malin, Irving, in Shapiro, C., ed., *Contemporary British Novelists*, 36-47.

Marcus, Steven, "The Novel Again," *PR* 29 (Spring, 1962): 180-4.

Marsden, Arthur, "The Novels of William Golding," *Delta* No. 10 (Autumn, 1956): 26-9.

Medcalf, S., *William Golding*.

Mellillo Reali, Erilde, "William Golding: A Pessimistic Moralist: A Study of His Novels," *DAI* 41, viii (Feb., 1981): 3576A.

Mitchell, Juliet, "Concepts and Technique in William Golding," *New Left Review* No. 15 (May-June, 1962): 63-71.

Muina, Matej, "William Golding: Novels of Extreme Situations," *SRAZ* 27-28 (July-Dec., 1969): 43-66. [Not seen.]

_____, "William Golding: The World of Perception and the World of Cognition," *SRAZ* 27-28 (July-Dec., 1969): 107-27. [Not seen.]

Nelson, W., *William Golding's LORD OF THE FLIES*.

Nossen, Evon, "The Beast-Man Theme in the Work of William Golding," *BSUF* 9, ii (1968): 60-9.

Oldsey, B. S., and S. Weintraub, *Art of William Golding*.

_____, "Salinger and Golding: Resurrection or Repose," *CollL* 6, ii (Spring, 1979): 136-44.

Pemberton, C., *William Golding*.

Pendry, E. D., "William Golding and 'Mankind's Essential Illness'," *MSpr* 55 (1961): 1-7.

Peter, John, "The Fables of William Golding," *KR* 19 (Autumn, 1957): 577-92.

Popkin, David S., "Flake of Fire: Peak-Experiences in the Fiction of William Golding," *DAI* 35 (1974): 468A (Penn. State).

Pritchett, V. S., "God's Folly," *NStat* 67 (April 10, 1964): 562-3.

_____, "Pain and Mr. Golding," *Living Novel*, 309-15.

Putnam, Stephen H., "'The Colors of the Spirit': Man and Nature in the Novels of William Golding," *DAI* 36 (1975): 3701A.

Ramsey, Robin H., "Centre, Window, World: The Limits of Vision in the Novels of William Golding," *DAI* 38 (1978): 5465A-66A.

Rexroth, Kenneth, "William Golding," *Atlantic Monthly* 215 (May, 1965): 96-8.

Rozsnyai, Bálint, "Reflections of T. S. Eliot's Imagery in the Novels of W. Golding," *ALitASH* 20 (1978): 172-5.

Sinclair, Andrew, "William Golding's The Sea, The Sea," *TCL* 28, ii (Summer, 1982): 171-80.

Snyman, L, "Golding: The Darkness in Man's Heart," *Opus* 2 (1969): 1-8. [Not seen.]

Sorensen, Eugene C., "Definition of Character in William Golding," *DAI* 35 (1974): 3011A (Denver).

Starnes, Jo A. H., "A Study of the Female Characters in William Golding's Novels," *DAI* 41 (1981): 4406A.

Stinson, John J., "Trying to Exorcise the Beast: The Grotesque in the Fiction of William Golding," *Cithara* 11, i (Nov., 1971): 3-30.

Stone, Frances T., "William Golding: A Pessimistic Moralist: A Study of His Novels," *DAI* 41 (1981): 3576A.

Sullivan, Walter, "William Golding: The Fables and the Art," *SR* 71 (Autumn, 1963): 660-4.

Thomson, George H., "The Real World of William Golding," *Alphabet* No. 9 (Nov., 1964): 26-33.

_____, "William Golding: Between God-Darkness and God-Light," *Cresset* 32, viii (June, 1969): 8-12.

Tiger, Virginia M., "An Analysis of William Golding's Fiction," *DAI* 32 (1971): 2711A-12A (Br. Columbia).

_____, *William Golding*.

Tristram, Philippa, "Golding and the Language of Caliban," in Biles, J. I., and R. O. Evans, eds., *William Golding*, 39-55.

Walker, Marshall, "William Golding: From Paradigm to Pyramid," *SLitI* 2, ii (Oct., 1969): 67-82.

Walters, Margaret, "Two Fabulists: Golding and Camus," *MCR* No. 4 (1961): 18-29. Also in Nelson, W., *William Golding's LORD OF THE FLIES*, 95-107.

Waterhouse, Michael, "Golding's Secret Element of Gusto," *EIC* 31, i (Jan., 1981): 1-14.

Whitlow, Roger, "Ford Madox Ford and William Golding: Function and Technique in the Novel," *CEA* 39, iii (Mar., 1977): 21-5.

Williams, H. M., "The Art of William Golding," *BDEC* 3 Nos. 3 & 4 (1962): 20-31. [Not seen.]

Yasunori, Sigimura, "The Two Worlds in William Golding," *SELit* 58, i (Sept., 1981): 49-59. [Not seen.]

Young, Wayland, "Letter from London," *KR* 19 (Summer, 1957): 478-82. Also in Nelson, W., *William Golding's LORD OF THE FLIES*, 18-21.

DARKNESS VISIBLE

Cleve, Gunnel, "Some Elements of Mysticism in William Golding's Novel, DARKNESS VISIBLE," *NM* 85, iv (1982): 457-70.

Coppinger, Rebecca, "Analagous Journeys: William Golding and T. S. Eliot," *MLS* 11, ii (1981): 83-7.

Crompton, Donald W., "Biblical and Classical Metaphor in DARKNESS VISIBLE," *TCL* 28, ii (Summer, 1982): 195-215.

Gregor, Ian, and Mark Kinkead-Weekes, "The Later Golding," *TCL* 28, ii (Summer, 1982): 119-28.

Johnston, A., *Of Earth and Darkness*, 98-110.

Mills, John, "William Golding: DARKNESS VISIBLE," *WCR* 15, iii (Winter, 1981): 70-2.

Nelson, William, "The Grotesque in DARKNESS VISIBLE and RITES OF PASSAGE," *TCL* 28, ii (Summer, 1982): 181-94.

Schwartz, Joseph, "The Meaning of Darkness," *ChronC* 4, iii (May-June, 1980): 14-16.

FREE FALL

Aarseth, Inger, "Golding's Journey to Hell: An Examination of Prefigurations and Archetypal Pattern in FREE FALL," *ES* 56 (1975): 322-33.

Acheson, James, "Golding's FREE FALL as Confession and Parable," *ArielE* 7, i (1976): 73-83.

Axthelm, P. M., *Modern Confessional Novel*, 113-27.

Babb, Howard S., "Four Passages from William Golding's Fiction," *MinnR* 5 (1965): 57-8.

_____, *Novels of William Golding*, 97-132.

Baker, J. R., *William Golding*, 55-70.

Báti, László, "William Golding's FREE FALL: A Case of Introspection," *SEA* 2 (1975): 155-70.

Boyle, Ted E., "The Denial of the Spirit: An Explication of William Golding's FREE FALL," *WascanaR* 1 (1966): 3-10.

Broes, Arthur T., "The Two Worlds of William Golding," in Carnegie Institute of Technology, *Lectures on Modern Novelists*, 13-14.

Coppinger, Rebecca, "William Golding: The Novelist as Bridge-Builder," *Rendezvous* 15, ii (Fall, 1980): 52-5.

Cox, C. B., *Free Spirit*, 181-4.

Crane, John K., "Golding and Bergson: The Free Fall of Free Will," *BRMMLA* 26, iv (Dec., 1972): 136-41.

Delbaere-Garant, J., "Time as a Structural Device in Golding's FREE FALL," *ES* 57 (1976): 353-65.

Dick, B. F., *William Golding*, 67-76, 99-100.

Elmen, P., *William Golding*, 31-5.

Gallagher, Michael P., "The Human Image in William Golding," *Studies* 54 (Summer-Autumn, 1965): 205-8.

Gindin, J., "'Gimmick' and Metaphor in the Novels of William Golding," *MFS* 6 (1960): 149-52. Also in Gindin, J., *Postwar British Fiction*, 202-6.

Goldberg, Gerald J., "The Search for the Artist in Some Recent British Fiction," *SAQ* 62 (Summer, 1963): 392-4.

Green, Peter, "The World of William Golding," *REL* 1, ii (April, 1960): 71-2. Also, revised, in Nelson, W., *William Golding's LORD OF THE FLIES*, 185-9. Also, revised, in *TPRSL* 32 (1963): 52-6. Also in *EDH* 32 (1963): 52-7.

Gregor, Ian, and M. Kinkead-Weekes, "The Strange Case of Mr. Golding and His Critics," *TC* 167 (Feb., 1980): 115-25. Also in Nelson, W., *William Golding's LORD OF THE FLIES*, 60-70.

Halio, Jay L., "FREE FALL: Golding's Modern Novel," in Biles, J. I., and R. O. Evans, eds., *William Golding*, 117-35.

Harris, Wendell V., "Golding's FREE FALL," *Expl* 23 (May, 1965): Item 76.

Hartt, J. N., *Lost Image of Man*, 101-2.

Henry, Avril, "The Structure of Golding's FREE FALL," *SoRA* 8, ii (June, 1975): 95-124.

Hodson, L., *Golding*, 72-87.

_____, *William Golding*, 72-87.

Hollinger, Alexander, "Choice and Responsibility in William Golding's Novels: LORD OF THE FLIES, PINCHER MARTIN, FREE FALL," *AnUBLG* 20 (1971): 159-63.

Hynes, S., *William Golding*, 33-40. Also in Stade, G., ed., *Six Contemporary British Novelists*, 199-207.

Johnston, A., *Of Earth and Darkness*, 50-66.

Karl, F. R., "The Metaphysical Novels of William Golding," *Contemporary English Novel*, 254-7.

Keller, R. H., *Philosophy of William Golding*, 4-66.

_____, "The Philosophy of William Golding, with Special Reference to FREE FALL," *DAI* 37 (1976): 1376.

Kennard, J. E., *Number and Nightmare*, 195-9.

Kermode, Frank, "The Novels of William Golding," *ILA* 3 (161): 25-9. Also in Kermode, F., *Puzzles and Epiphanies*, 210-12. Also in Nelson, W., *William Golding's LORD OF THE FLIES*, 118-20. Also in Kostelanetz, R., ed., *On Contemporary Literature*, 379-81.

Kinkead-Weekes, M., and I. Gregor, *William Golding*, 165-99.

MacShane, Frank, "The Novels of William Golding," *DR* 42 (Summer, 1962): 178-83.

Malin, Irving, in Shapiro, C., ed., *Contemporary British Novelists*, 44-5.

McDonald, Walter R., "The Confession Novel: Freedom and Guilt in FREE FALL and SOMETHING HAPPENED," *CCTE* 40 (1975): 41-5.

Medcalf, S., *William Golding*, 25-30.

Monod, Sylvèe, "William Golding's View of the Human Condition in FREE FALL," in Jefferson, D., and G. Martin, eds., *Uses of Fiction*, 249-60.

O'Donnell, Patrick, "Journeying to the Center: Time, Pattern, and Transcendence in Willliam Golding's FREE FALL," *ArielE* 11, iii (1980): 83-98.

Oldsey, B. S., and S. Weintraub, *Art of William Golding*, 103-22.

Pemberton, C., *William Golding*, 18-22.

Rippier, J. S., *Some Postwar English Novelists*, 62-7.

Tiger, V., *William Golding*, 139-66.

Wain, John, "Lord of the Agencies," *Aspect* No. 3 (April, 1963): 56-67.

THE INHERITORS

Adriaens, Mark, "Style in W. Golding's THE INHERITORS," *ES* 51 (1970): 16-30.

Ali, Masood Amjad, "THE INHERITORS: An Experiment in Technique," *Venture* 5, ii (April, 1969): 123-31.

Alterman, Peter S., "Aliens in Golding's THE INHERITORS," *SFS* 5, i (Mar., 1978): 3-10.

_____, "A Study of Four Science-Fiction Themes and Their Function in Two Contemporary Novels," *DA* 35 (1974): 2976A-77A.

Anderson, D., *Tragic Protest*, 161-3.

Babb, Howard S., "Four Passages from William Golding's Fiction," *MinnR* 5 (1965): 52-4.

_____, *Novels of William Golding*, 37-63.

Baker, J. R., *William Golding*, 18-31.

Broberg, Britta, "Connections Between William Golding's First Two Novels," *MS* 63, i (1969): 1-24.

Broes, Arthur T., "The Two Worlds of William Golding," in Carnegie Institute of Technology, *Lectures on Modern Novelists*, 7-10.

Bufkin, E. C., "The Ironic Art of William Golding's THE INHERITORS," *TSLL* 9 (1968): 567-8.

Burroway, Janet, "Resurrected Metaphor in THE INHERITORS by William Golding," *CritQ* 23, i (1981): 53-70.

Delbaere, Jeanne, "Lok-Like-Log: Structure and Imagery in THE INHERITORS," *RLV* 44 (1978): 179-92.

Dick, B. F., *William Golding*, 37-48.

Duncan, Kirby L., "William Golding and Vardis Fisher: A Study in Parallels and Extensions," *CE* 27 (1965): 232-5.

Elmen, P., *William Golding*, 21-5.

Evans, Robert O., "THE INHERITORS: Some Inversions," in Biles, J. I., and R. O. Evans, eds., *William Golding*, 87-102.

Fackler, Herbert V., "Paleontology and Paradise Lost: A Study of Golding's Modifications of Fact in THE INHERITORS," *BSUF* 10, iii (Summer, 1969): 64-6.

Freedom, Ralph, "The New Realism: The Fancy of William Golding," *Per* 10 (Spring-Autumn, 1958): 118-28.

Gallagher, Michael P., "The Human Image in William Golding," *Studies* 54 (Summer-Autumn, 1965): 201-2.

Gindin, J., "'Gimmick' and Metaphor in the Novels of William Golding," *MFS* 6 (1960): 147-8, 151-2. Also in Gindin, J., *Postwar British Fiction*, 198-200, 204-6.

Green, Peter, "The World of William Golding," *EDH* 32 (1963): 45-8. Also in *REL* 1, ii (April, 1960): 67-8. Also, revised, in Nelson, W., *William Golding's LORD OF THE FLIES*, 177-81. Also, revised, in *TPRSL* 32 (1963): 45-8.

Halliday, M.A.K., "Linguistic Function and Literary Style: Inquiry Into the Language of William Golding's THE INHERITORS," in Chatman, S., ed., *Literary Style*, 330-65. Discussion, 365-8.

Hodson, L., *Golding*, 39-54.

_____, *William Golding*, 39-54.

Hurt, James R., "Grendel's Point of View: BEOWULF and William Golding," *MFS* 13 (Summer, 1967): 264-5.

Hynes, S., *William Golding*, 16-23. Also in Stade, G., ed., *Six Contemporary British Novelists*, 180-8.

Johnston, A., *Of Earth and Darkness*, 21-35.

Josipovici, Gabriel, "Golding: The Hidden Source," *World and the Book*, 238-45.

Keller, R. H., *Philosophy of William Golding*, 69-75.

Kennard, J. E., *Number and Nightmare*, 87-91.

Kermode, Frank, and William Golding, "The Meaning of It All," *Books and Bookmen* 5 (Oct., 1959): 10.

_____, "The Novels of William Golding," *ILA* 3 (1961): 19-22. Also in Kermode, F., *Puzzles and Epiphanies*, 205-7. Also in Kostelanetz, ed., *On Contemporary Literature*, 373-5. Also in Nelson, W., *William Golding's LORD OF THE FLIES*, 13-15.

Kinkead-Weekes, M., and I. Gregor, *William Golding*, 67-118.

Lee, David A., "THE INHERITORS and Transformational Generative Grammar," *Lang&S* 9 (1976): 77-97.

MacShane, Frank, "The Novels of William Golding," *DR* 42 (Summer, 1962): 174-5.

Malin, Irving, in Shapiro, C., ed., *Contemporary British Novelists*, 40-1.

Medcalf, S., *William Golding*, 14-19.

Oldsey, B. S., and S. Weintraub, *Art of William Golding*, 43-72.

Pemberton, C., *William Golding*, 11-14.

Peter, John, "The Fables of William Golding," *KR* 19 (Autumn, 1957): 585-7.

Petersen, Kirsten H., and Anna Rutherford, "The Vanished Future: THE INHERITORS," in Petersen, K. H., and A. Rutherford, eds., *Enigma of Values: An Introduction*, Aarhus: Dangaroo Pr., 1975, 163-76.

Rippier, J. S., *Some Postwar English Novelists*, 53-7.

Sternlicht, Sanford, "Songs of Innocence and Songs of Experience in LORD OF THE FLIES and THE INHERITORS," *MQ* 9 (July, 1968): 383-90.

Tiger, V., *William Golding*, 68-101.

Walker, Jeanne M., "Reciprocity and Exchange in William Golding's THE INHERITORS," *SFS* 8, iii (Nov., 1981): 297-310.

LORD OF THE FLIES

Allen, W., *Modern Novel*, 288-90.

Anderson, D., *Tragic Protest*, 158-61.

Babb, Howard S., "Four Passages from William Golding's Fiction," *MinnR* 5 (1965): 50-2.

_____, *Novels of William Golding*, 7-34.

Babbage, Stuart B., "The End of Innocence," *The Mark of Cain: Studies in Literature and Theology*, Grand Rapids: Eerdmans, 1966, 24-8.

Baker, James R., "The Decline of LORD OF THE FLIES," *SAQ* 69, iv (Autumn, 1970): 446-60.

_____, "Why It's No Go: A Study of William Golding's LORD OF THE FLIES," *ArQ* 19 (Winter, 1963): 293-305. Also, later version, in Baker, J. R., *William Golding*, 3-17. Also in Baker, J. R., and A. P. Ziebler, Jr., eds., *Casebook Edition of LORD OF THE FLIES*, xiii-xxiv.

Banaag, Concepcion B., "Evil and Redemption in LORD OF THE FLIES," *FJS* 3 (1970): 1-13.

Biles, Jack I., "Piggy, Apologia Pro Vita Sua," *SLitI* 1, ii (Oct., 168): 83-108.

Braybrooke, Neville, "The Castaways and the Mariner," *Aryan Path* 40, ii (Feb., 1969): 54-9.

_____, "The Castaways—The Mariner: Two William Golding Novels," *New Blackfriars* 51 (Aug., 1970): 356-8.

_____, "Two William Golding Novels: Two Aspects of His Work," *QQ* 76, i (Spring, 1969): 76-92.

Broberg, Britta, "Connections Between William Golding's First Two Novels," *MS* 63, i (1969): 1-24.

Broes, Arthur T., "The Two Worlds of William Golding," in Carnegie Institute of Technology, *Lectures on Modern Novelists*, 1-7.

Brown, Steven R., "Political Literature and the Response of the Reader: Experimental Studies of Interpretation, Imagery, and Criticism," *APSR* 71, ii (June, 1977): 568-72.

Bufkin, E. C., "LORD OF THE FLIES: An Analysis," *GaR* 19 (Spring, 1965): 40-57.

Carrington, Ildiko de Papp, "What Is a Face? Imagery and Metaphor in LORD OF THE FLIES," *MBL* 1, i (1976): 66-73.

Clark, George, "An Illiberal Education: William Golding's Pedagogy," in Whitbread, T. B., ed., *Seven Contemporary Authors*, 75-84.

Cohn, Alan M., "The Berengaria Allusion in LORD OF THE FLIES," *N&Q* 13 (Nov., 1966): 419-20.

Coskren, Thomas M., O. P., "Is Golding Calvinistic?" *America* 109 (July 6, 1963): 18-20. Also in Baker, J. R., and A. P. Ziegler, Jr., eds., *Casebook Edition of William Golding's LORD OF THE FLIES*, 253-60.

Cox, C. B., *Free Spirit*, 173-9.

_____, "LORD OF THE FLIES," *CritQ* 2 (Summer, 1960): 112-17. Also in Nelson, W., *William Golding's LORD OF THE FLIES*, 82-8.

Davis, W. Eugene, "Mr. Golding's Optical Delusion," *ELN* 3 (Dec., 1965): 125-6.

Delbaere-Garant, Jeanne, "Rhythm and Expansion in LORD OF THE FLIES," in Biles, J. I., and R. O. Evans, eds., *William Golding*, 72-86.

Dick, Bernard F., "LORD OF THE FLIES and the BACCHAE," *CW* (Jan., 1964): 145-6.

_____, *William Golding*, 18-36, 96-8.

Ditlevson, Torben, "Civilization and Culture, or Pro Civitate Dei: William Golding's LORD OF THE FLIES," *Lang&L* 1, iii (1972): 20-38.

Drew, Philip, "Second Reading," *Cambridge Rev* (Oct. 27, 1956): 79-84.

Egan, John M., O. P., "Golding's View of Man," *America* 108 (Jan. 26, 1963): 140-1. Also in Nelson, W., *William Golding's LORD OF THE FLIES*, 145-7.

Elmen, P., *William Golding*, 11-20.

Ely, Sister M. Amanda, O. P., "The Adult Image in Three Novels of Adolescent Life," *EJ* 56 (Nov., 1967): 1127-8.

Epstein, E. L., "Notes on LORD OF THE FLIES," in *LORD OF THE FLIES*, N.Y.: Putnam's, 1959, 249-55. Also in Baker, J. R., and A. P. Ziegler, Jr., eds., *Casebook Edition of William Golding's LORD OF THE FLIES*, 277-81.

Fleck, A. D., "The Golden Bough: Aspects of Myth and Ritual in THE LORD OF THE FLIES," in Benedikz, B. S., ed., *On the Novel*, 189-204.

Forster, E. M., "Introduction," in LORD OF THE FLIES, N.Y.: Coward-McCann, 1962, ix-xii. Also in Baker, J. R., and A. P. Ziegler, Jr., eds. *Casebook Edition of William Golding's LORD OF THE FLIES*, 207-10.

Freedman, Ralph, "The New Realism: The Fancy of William Golding," *Per* 10 (Summer-Autumn, 1958): 118-28.

Fuller, Edmund, "Behind the Vogue, a Rigorous Understanding," *NYHTBR* 39 (Nov. 4, 1962): 3. Also in Nelson, W., *William Golding's LORD OF THE FLIES*, 143-5.

Gaskin, J. C. A., "Beelzebub," *HJ* 66 (1968): 58-61.

Gindin, J., "'Gimmick' and Metaphor in the Novels of William Golding," *MFS* 6 (1960): 145-7, 151-2. Also in Gindin, J., *Postwar British Fiction*, 196-8, 204-6.

Golding, J. T. C., "A World of Violence and Small Boys," in Baker, J. R., and A. P. Ziegler, Jr., eds., *Casebook Edition of William Golding's LORD OF THE FLIES*, 225-7.

Golding, William, "The Fable," *The Hot Gates and Other Occasional Pieces*, N.Y.: Harcourt, Brace & World, 1966, 85-101.

Gordon, Robert C., "Classical Themes in LORD OF THE FLIES," *MFS* 11 (Winter, 1965-66): 424-7.

Grande, Luke M., "The Appeal of Golding," *Cweal* 77 (Jan. 25, 1963): 457-9. Also in Nelson, W., *William Golding's LORD OF THE FLIES*, 156-9.

Green, Peter, "The World of William Golding," *EDH* 32 (1963): 41-5. Also in *REL* 1, ii (April, 1960): 63-7. Also, revised, in Nelson, W., *William Golding's LORD OF THE FLIES*, 173-7. Also, revised, in *TPRSL* 32 (1963): 41-5.

Gregor, Ian, and M. Kinkead-Weekes, "Introduction," in LORD OF THE FLIES, London: Faber and Faber School Editions, 1962, i-xii. Also in Baker, J. R., and A. P. Ziegler, Jr., eds., *Casebook Edition of William Golding's LORD OF THE FLIES*, 235-43.

Gulbin, Suzanne, "Parallels and Contrasts in LORD OF THE FLIES and ANIMAL FARM," *EJ* 55 (Jan., 1966): 86-90, 92.

Hadomi, Leah, "Imagery as a Source of Irony in Golding's LORD OF THE FLIES," *HUSL* 9, i (1981): 126-38.

Hampton, T., "An Error in LORD OF THE FLIES," *N&Q* 12 (July, 1965): 275.

Herndl, George C., "Golding and Salinger: A Clear Choice," *WiseR* No. 502 (Winter, 1964): 309-22.

Hodson, L., *Golding*, 19-38.

_____, *William Golding*, 19-38.

Hollahan, Eugene, "Running in Circles: A Major Motif in LORD OF THE FLIES," *SNNTS* 2, i (Spring, 1970): 22-30.

Hollinger, Alexander, "Choice and Responsibility in William Golding's Novels: LORD OF THE FLIES, PINCHER MARTIN, FREE FALL," *AnUBL* 20 (1971): 159-63.

Hynes, S., *William Golding*, 6-16. Also in Stade, G., ed., *Six Contemporary British Novelists*, 169-80.

Johnston, A., *Of Earth and Darkness*, 8-20.

Karl, F. R., "The Metaphysical Novels of William Golding," *Contemporary English Novel*, 257-8.

Kearns, Francis E., and L. M. Grande, "An Exchange of Views," *Cweal* 77 (Feb. 22, 1963): 569-71. Also in Nelson, W., *William Golding's LORD OF THE FLIES*, 160-4.

_____, "Golding Revisited," in Nelson, W., *William Golding's LORD OF THE FLIES*, 165-9.

_____, "Salinger and Golding: Conflict on the Campus," *America* 108 (Jan. 26, 1963): 136-9. Also in Nelson, W., *William Golding's LORD OF THE FLIES*, 148-55.

Keating, James, and William Golding, "The Purdue Interview" (in part), in Baker, J. R., and A. P. Ziegler, Jr., eds., *Casebook Edition of William Golding's LORD OF THE FLIES*, 189-95.

Keller, R. H., *Philosophy of William Golding*, 83-9.

Kennard, J. E., *Number and Nightmare*, 181-7.

Kermode, Frank, "Coral Islands," *Spectator* 201 (Aug. 22, 1958): 257. Also in Nelson, W., *William Golding's LORD OF THE FLIES*, 39-42.

_____, and William Golding, "The Meaning of It All," *Books and Bookmen* 5 (Oct., 1959): 9-10. Also in Baker, J. R., and A. P. Ziegler, Jr., eds., *Casebook Edition of William Golding's LORD OF THE FLIES*, 197-201.

_____, "The Novels of William Golding," *International Literary Annual* No. 3 (1961): 16-19. Also in F. Kermode, *Puzzles and Epiphanies*, 202-5. Also (selection) in Baker, J. R., and A. P. Ziegler, Jr., eds., *Casebook Edition of William Golding's LORD OF THE FLIES*, 203-6. Also in Nelson, W., *William Golding's LORD OF THE FLIES*, 111-13. Also in Kostelanetz, R., ed., *On Contemporary Literature*, 368-73.

Kinkead-Weekes, M., and I. Gregor, *William Golding*, 15-64.

Lederer, Richard H., "Student Reactions to LORD OF THE FLIES," *EJ* 53 (1964): 575-9.

Leed, Jacob, "Golding's LORD OF THE FLIES, Chapter 7," *Expl* 24 (Sept., 1965): Item 8.

Levitt, Leon, "Trust the Tale: A Second Reading of LORD OF THE FLIES," *EJ* 4 (April, 1969): 521-2, 533.

"Lord of the Campus," *Time* 79 (June 22, 1962): 64. Also in Baker, J. R., and A. P. Ziegler, Jr., eds., *Casebook Edition of William Golding's LORD OF THE FLIES*, 283-5. Also in Nelson, W., *William Golding's LORD OF THE FLIES*, 141-2.

MacLure, Millar, "Allegories of Innocence," *DR* 40 (Summer, 1960): 149-51.

MacShane, Frank, "The Novels of William Golding," *DR* 42 (Summer, 1962): 172-3.

Malin, Irving, in Shapiro, C., ed., *Contemporary British Novelists*, 37-40.

Marcus, Steven, "The Novel Again," *PR* 29 (Spring, 1962): 181-2.

McCullen, Maurice L., "LORD OF THE FLIES: The Critical Quest," in Biles, J. I., and R. O. Evans, eds., *William Golding*, 203-36.

Medcalf, S., *William Golding*, 9-14.

Merren, John, "LORD OF THE FLIES as an Anatomy," *CCTE* 31 (Sept., 1966): 28-9. (Abstract).

Michel-Michot, Paulette, "The Myth of Innocence," *RLV* 28, vi (1962): 510-20.

Mitchell, Charles, "THE LORD OF THE FLIES and the Escape from Freedom," *ArQ* 22 (Spring, 1966): 27-40.

Moody, Philippa, *A Critical Commentary on William Golding's LORD OF THE FLIES*, London: Macmillan, 1966.

Mueller, William R., "An Old Story Well Told," *ChC* 80 (Oct. 2, 1963): 1203-6. Also, condensed, in Baker, J. R., and A. P. Ziegler, Jr., eds., *Casebook Edition of William Golding's LORD OF THE FLIES*, 245-51.

Nelson, W., *William Golding's LORD OF THE FLIES*.

Niemeyer, Carl, "The Coral Island Revisited," *CE* 22 (1961): 241-5. Also, condensed, in Baker, J. R., and A. P. Ziegler, Jr., eds., *Casebook Edition of William Golding's LORD OF THE FLIES*, 217-23. Also in Nelson, W., *William Golding's LORD OF THE FLIES*, 88-94.

Oakland, John, "Satiric Technique in LORD OF THE FLIES," *MSpr* 64, i (1970): 14-18.

O'Hara, John D., "Mute Choirboys and Angelic Pigs: The Fable in LORD OF THE FLIES," *TSLL* 7 (Winter, 1966): 411-20.

Oldsey, Bern, and Stanley Weintraub, "LORD OF THE FLIES: Beelzebub Revisited," *CE* 25 (Nov., 1963): 90-9. Also (expanded) in Oldsey, B. S., and S. Weintraub, *Art of William Golding*, 15-40.

Padovano, A., *Estranged God*, 149-54.

Page, Norman, "LORD OF THE FLIES," *Use of English* 16 (Autumn, 1964): 44-5, 57.

Pemberton, C., *William Golding*, 7-11.

Peter, John, "The Fables of William Golding," *KR* 19 (Autumn, 1957): 581-5. Also, condensed, in Baker, J. R., and A. P. Ziegler, Jr., eds., *Casebook Edition of William Golding's LORD OF THE FLIES*, 229-34. Also in Nelson, W., *William Golding's LORD OF THE FLIES*, 25-8.

Pittock, Malcolm, and J. G. Roberts, "Michael Roberts and William Golding," *ES* 52, v (Oct., 1971): 442-3.

Pritchett, V. S., "Pain and Mr. Golding," *Working Novelist*, 56-61.
_____, "Secret Parables," *NStat* (Aug. 2, 1958): 146-7. Also in Nelson, W., *William Golding's LORD OF THE FLIES*, 35-9.

Richter, D. H., "Allegory versus Fable: Golding's LORD OF THE FLIES," *Fables End*, 61-82.

Rippier, J. S., *Some Postwar English Novelists*, 46-53.

Rosenberg, Bruce A., "Lord of the Fire-Flies," *CRAS* 11 (Winter, 1967): 128-39.

Rosenfield, Claire, "'Men of a Smaller Growth': A Psychological Analysis of William Golding's LORD OF THE FLIES," *L&P* 11 (Autumn, 1961): 93-101. Also, revised, in Baker, J. R., and A. P. Ziegler, Jr., eds., *Casebook Edition of William Golding's LORD OF THE FLIES*, 261-76. Also in Manheim, E., and L., eds., *Hidden Patterns*, 259-74. Also in Nelson, W., *William Golding's LORD OF THE FLIES*, 121-32.

_____, "Reply by Miss Rosenfield," *L&P* 12 (Winter, 1962): 11-12.

Ruotolo, L. P., *Six Existential Heroes*, 101-18.

Smith, Eric, *Some Versions of THE FALL: The Myth of the Fall of Man in English Literature*, Pittsburgh: Un. of Pittsburgh Pr., 1973, 163-202.

Spangler, Donald R., "Simon," in Baker, J. R., and A. P. Ziegler, Jr., eds., *Casebook Edition of William Golding's LORD OF THE FLIES*, 211-15.

Spector, Robert D., "Islands of Good and Evil: TOM SAWYER and LORD OF THE FLIES," in Twain, Mark, THE ADVENTURES OF TOM SAWYER, N.Y.: Bantam, 1966.

Spitz, David, "Power and Authority: An Interpretation of Golding's LORD OF THE FLIES," *AR* 30, i (Spring, 1970): 21-33.

Sternlight, Sanford, "Songs of Innocence and Songs of Experience in LORD OF THE FLIES and THE INHERITORS," *MQ* 9 (July, 1968): 383-90.

_____, "A Source for Golding's LORD OF THE FLIES: Peter Pan?" *EngR* 14 (Dec., 1963): 41-2.

Talon, Henri, "Irony in LORD OF THE FLIES," *EIC* 18 (July, 1968): 296-309.

Taylor, Harry H., "The Case Against William Golding's Simon-Piggy," *ConR* (Sept., 1966): 155-60.

Thomas, W. K., "The Lessons of Myth in LORD OF THE FLIES," *Cithara* 16 (1977): 33-58.

Thumboo, Edwin, "Golding's LORD OF THE FLIES: Topography, Character and Theme," *LCrit* 13, iii (1978): 6-17.

Tiger, V., *William Golding*, 38-67.

Townsend, R. C., "LORD OF THE FLIES: Fool's Gold?" *JGE* 16 (July, 1964): 153-60.

Trilling, Lionel, "LORD OF THE FLIES," *Mid-Century*, Issue 45 (Oct., 1962): 10-12.

Trócsányi, M., "Three Images of Twentieth Century Britain as Manifest in the Novel," *AUS-PEAS* 1 (1980): 186-96.

Veale, Joseph, *William Golding—LORD OF THE FLIES*, Dublin: Gill and Macmillan; London: Macmillan, 1972.

Veidemanis, Gladys, "LORD OF THE FLIES in the Classroom—No Passing Fad," *EJ* 53 (1964): 569-74.

Walters, Margaret, "Two Fabulists: Golding and Camus," *MCR* 4 (1961): 20-3. Also in Nelson, W., *William Golding's LORD OF THE FLIES*, 97-101.

Warner, Oliver, "Mr. Golding and Marryat's LITTLE SAVAGE," *REL* 5, i (1964): 51-5.

Wasserstrom, William, "Reason and Reverence in Art and Science," *L&P* 12 (Winter, 1962): 2-3.

Watson, Kenneth, "A Reading of LORD OF THE FLIES," *English* 15 (Spring, 1964): 2-7.

White, Robert J., "Butterfly and Beast in LORD OF THE FLIES," *MFS* 10 (Summer, 1964): 163-70.

Whitley, John S., *Golding: Lord of the Flies*, London: Arnold, 1970. (Studies in English Literature, 42).

PINCHER MARTIN (THE TWO DEATHS OF CHRISTOPHER MARTIN)

Babb, Howard, "Four Passages from William Golding's Fiction," *MinnR* 5 (1965): 54-7.
_____, *Novels of William Golding*, 65-94.
_____, "On the Ending of PINCHER MARTIN," *EIC* 14 (Jan., 1964): 106-8.
Baker, J. R., *William Golding*, 32-47.
Biles, Jack I., and Carl R. Kropf, "The Cleft Rock of Conversion: ROBINSON CRUSOE and PINCHER MARTIN," *SLitI* 2, ii (Oct., 1969): 17-43.
Blake, Ian, "PINCHER MARTIN: William Golding and 'Taffrail'," *N&Q* 9 (Aug., 1962): 309-10.
Braybrooke, Neville, "The Castaways and the Mariner," *Ayran Path* 40, ii (Feb., 1969): 54-9.
_____, "The Castaways—The Mariner: Two William Golding Novels," *New Blackfriars* 51 (Aug., 1970): 358-61.
_____, "The Return of Pincher Martin," *Cweal* 89 (Oct. 25, 1968): 115-18.
_____, "Two William Golding Novels: Two Aspects of His Work," *QQ* 76, i (Spring, 1969): 92-100.
Broes, Arthur T., "The Two Worlds of William Golding," in Carnegie Institute of Technology, *Lectures on Modern Novelists*, 10-12.
Bufkin, E. C., "Pincher Martin: William Golding's Morality Play," *SLitI* 2, ii (Oct., 1969): 5-16.
Clark, George, "An Illiberal Education: William Golding's Pedagogy," in Whitbread, T. B., ed., *Seven Contemporary Authors*, 84-95.
Colebatch, Hal, "Willed Self-Destruction in PINCHER MARTIN," *SoRA* 11 (1978): 90-3.
Cox, C. B., *Free Spirit*, 180-1.
_____, "William Golding's PINCHER MARTIN," *Listener* 71 (Mar. 12, 1964): 430-1.
Crane, John K., "Crossing the Bar Twice: Post-Mortem Consciousness in Bierce, Hemingway and Golding," *SSF* 6, iv (Summer, 1969): 3370-6.
Delbaere-Garant, Jeanne, "William Golding's PINCHER MARTIN," *ES* 51 (1971): 538-44.
Dick, B. F., *William Golding*, 49-62, 98-9.
Elmen, P., *William Golding*, 25-30.
Freedman, Ralph, "The New Realism: The Fancy of William Golding," *Per* 10 (Spring-Autumn, 1958): 118-28.
Gallagher, Michael P., "The Human Image in William Golding," *Studies* 54 (Summer-Autumn, 1965): 202-4.
Gindin, J., "'Gimmick' and Metaphor in the Novels of William Golding," *MFS* 6 (1960): 148-9, 151-2. Also in Gindin, J., *Postwar British Fiction*, 200-2, 204-6.
Green, Peter, "The World of William Golding," *EDH* 32 (1963): 49-52. Also in *REL* 1, ii (April, 1960): 69-71. Also, revised, in Nelson, W., *William Golding's LORD OF THE FLIES*, 181-5. Also, revised, in *TPRSL* 32 (1963): 49-52.
Henry, Avril, "The Pattern of PINCHER MARTIN," *SoRA* 9 (1976): 3-26.
Hodson, L., *Golding*, 55-71.
_____, *William Golding*, 55-71.

Hollinger, Alexander, "Choice and Responsibility in William Golding's Novels: LORD OF THE FLIES, PINCHER MARTIN, FREE FALL," *AnUBLG* 20 (1971): 159-63.
Hynes, S., *William Golding*, 23-32. Also in Stade, G., ed., *Six Contemporary British Novelists*, 188-98.
Johnston, A., *Of Earth of Darkness*, 36-49. Also, in part, as "The Miscasting of Pincher Martin," in Biles, J. I., and R. O. Evans, eds., *William Golding*, 103-16.
Josipovici, Gabriel, "Golding: The Hidden Source," *World and the Book*, 243-6, 252-4.
Keller, R. H., *Philosophy of William Golding*, 90-7.
Kennard, J. E., *Number and Nightmare*, 191-5.
Kermode, Frank, and William Golding, "The Meaning of It All," *Books and Bookmen* 5 (Oct., 1959): 10.
_____, "The Novels of William Golding," *ILA* 3 (1961): 22-5. Also in Kermode, F., *Puzzles and Epiphanies*, 207-10. Also in Kostelanetz, R., ed., *On Contemporary Literature*, 375-9. Also in Nelson, W., *William Golding's LORD OF THE FLIES*, 115-18.
Kinkead-Weekes, M., and I. Gregor, *William Golding*, 121-61.
La Chance, Paul R., "PINCHER MARTIN: The Essential Dilemma of Modern Man," *Chithara* 8, ii (May, 1969): 55-60.
Lakshmi, Vijay, "Entering the Whirlpool: The Movement toward Self-Awareness in William Golding's PINCHER MARTIN," *LCrit* 17, iii (1982): 25-36.
MacLure, Millar, "William Golding's Survival Stories," *TamR* 5 (Summer, 1957): 60-7.
MacNeice, Louis, *Varieties of Experience*, London: Cambridge Un. Pr., 1965, 147-51.
MacShane, Frank, "The Novels of William Golding," *DR* 42 (Summer, 1962): 175-8.
Malin, Irving, in Shapiro, C., ed., *Contemporary British Novelists*, 41-4.
Marcus, Steven, "The Novel Again," *PR* 29 (Spring, 1962): 182-3.
Maxwell, J. C., "PINCHER MARTIN," *TLS* (August 21, 1959): 483. Comments: Green, Peter, and Edward Morgan (Aug. 28, 1959): 495; Daisch, W. G. (Sept. 4, 1959): 507; Webster, Owen (Sept. 11, 1959): 519.
Medcalf, S., *William Golding*, 19-25.
Morgan, Edwin, "PINCHER MARTIN and THE CORAL ISLAND," *N&Q* 7 (April, 1960): 150.
Oldsey, B. S., and S. Weintraub, *Art of William Golding*, 75-100.
Pearson, Anthony, "H. G. Wells and PINCHER MARTIN," *N&Q* 12 (July, 1965): 275-6.
Pemberton, C., *William Golding*, 14-17.
Peter, John, "The Fables of William Golding," *KR* 19 (Autumn, 1957): 587-91.
Pittock, Malcolm, and J. G. Roberts, "Michael Roberts and William Golding," *ES* 52, v (Oct., 1971): 442-3.
Quinn, Michael, "An Unheroic Hero: William Golding's PINCHER MARTIN," *CritQ* 4 (Autumn, 1962): 247-56.
Rippier, J. S., *Some Postwar English Novelists*, 58-61.
Robinson, John, "Pincher's Rock," *RMS* 19 (1975): 129-39.
Russell, Kenneth C., "The Free Fall of William Golding's PINCHER MARTIN," *SRC* 5 (197): 267-74.
Ryan, J. W., "The Two Pincher Martins: From Survival Adventure to Golding's Myth of Dying," *ES* 55 (1974): 140-51.
Sasso, Laurence J., Jr., "A Note on the Dwarf in PINCHER MARTIN," *MSE* 1 (Spring, 168): 66-8.
Sternlicht, Sanford, "PINCHER MARTIN: A Freudian Crusoe," *EngR* 15 (April, 1965): 2-4.

Tiger, V., *William Golding*, 102-38.

Whitehead, Lee M., "The Moment Out of Time: Golding's PINCHER MARTIN," *ConL* 12, i (Winter, 1971): 18-41.

Wikborg, Eleanor, "The Control of Sympathy in William Golding's PINCHER MARTIN," in Rydén, Mats, Lennart A. Björk, eds., *Studies in English Philology, Linguistics and Literature Presented to Alarik Rynell, 7 March 1978*, Stockholm: Almqvist & Wiksell, 1978, 179-87.

THE PYRAMID

Babb, H. S., *Novels of William Golding*, 169-96.

Dick, Bernard F., "THE PYRAMID: Mr. Golding's 'New' Novel," *SLitI* 2, ii (Oct., 1969): 83-95.

Henry, Avril, "William Golding: THE PYRAMID," *SoRA* 3 (1968): 5-31.

Hodson, L., *Golding*, 102-6.

Hynes, S., "William Golding," in Stade, G., ed., *Six Contemporary British Novelists*, 214-16.

Johnston, Arnold, "Innovation and Rediscovery in Golding's THE PYRAMID," *Crit* 14, ii (1972): 97-112. Also, in part, in Johnston, A., *Of Earth and Darkness*, 83-97.

Keller, R. H., *Philosophy of William Golding*, 76-82.

Kelly, Rebecca S., "The Tragicomic Mode: William Golding's THE PYRAMID," *PCL* 7 (1981): 110-16.

Medcalf, S., *William Golding*, 37-9.

Pemberton, C., *William Golding*, 24-7.

Russell, Kenneth C., "The Vestibule of Hell: A Reflection on the 'No-Risk' Morality of W. Golding's PYRAMID," *RUO* 46 (1976): 452-9.

Skilton, David, "THE PYRAMID and Comic Social Fiction," in Biles, J. I., and R. O. Evans, eds., *William Golding*, 176-87.

Trickett, Rachel, "Recent Novels: Craftsmanship in Violence and Sex," *YR* 57 (Spring, 1968): 444-6.

Whitehead, John, "A Conducted Tour to the Pyramid," *London Mag*, n.s., 7 (June, 1967): 100-4.

RITES OF PASSAGE

Gregor, Ian, and Mark Kinkead-Weekes, "The Later Golding," *TCL* 28, ii (Summer, 1982): 111-18.

Nelson, William, "The Grotesque in DARKNESS VISIBLE and RITES OF PASSAGE," *TCL* 28, ii (Summer, 1982): 181-94.

Tiger, Virginia, "William Golding's 'Wooden World': Religious Rites in RITES OF PASSAGE," *TCL* 28, ii (Summer, 1982): 216-31.

THE SPIRE

Anderson, D., *Tragic Protest*, 165-79.

Babb, H. S., *Novels of William Golding*, 135-66.

Baker, J. R., *William Golding*, 70-88.

Bufkin, E. C., "THE SPIRE: The Image of the Book," in Biles, J. I., and R. O. Evans, eds., *William Golding*, 136-50.

Cammarota, Richard S., "THE SPIRE: A Symbolic Analysis," in Biles, J. I., and R. O. Evans, eds., *William Golding*, 151-75.

Carmichael, D., "A God in Ruins," *Quadrant* No. 33 (Jan., 1965): 72-5.

Crompton, D. W., "THE SPIRE," *CritQ* 9 (Spring, 1967): 63-79.

Delbaere-Garant, Jeanne, "The Evil Plant in William Golding's THE SPIRE," *RLV* 35 (1969): 623-31.

Dick, Bernard F., and Raymond J. Porter, "Jocelin and Oedipus," *Cithara* 6, i (Nov., 1966): 43-8.

_____, *William Golding*, 77-87, 100-1.

Dickson, L. L., "Modern Allegory: The Cathedral Motif in William Golding's THE SPIRE," *WVUPP* 27 (1981): 98-105.

Elman, P., *William Golding*, 35-40.

Freehof, Solomon B., "Nostalgia for the Middle Ages: William Golding's THE SPIRE," *Carnegie Mag* 39 (Jan., 1965): 13-16.

Gallagher, Michael P., "The Human Image in William Golding," *Studies* 54 (Summer-Autumn, 1965): 208-16.

Hodson, L., *Golding*, 88-99.

_____, *William Golding*, 88-99.

Hyman, S. E., "The Spire of Babel," *Standards*, 219-23.

Hynes, S., *William Golding*, 40-6. Also in Stade, G., ed., *Six Contemporary British Novelists*, 207-14.

Johnston, A., *Of Earth and Darkness*, 67-82.

Josipovici, Gabriel, "Golding: The Hidden Source," *World and the Book*, 247-51, 254-5.

Keller, R. H., *Philosophy of William Golding*, 98-106.

Kennard, J. E., *Number and Nightmare*, 199-202.

Kermode, Frank, "The Case for William Golding," *NYRB* 2 (April 30, 1964): 3-4. Also in Kermode, F., *Continuities*, 186-94. ALso in Kostelanetz, R., ed., *On Contemporary Literature*, 381-7.

Kinkead-Weekes, M., and I. Gregor, *William Golding*, 203-35.

Kort, Wesley, "The Groundless Glory of Golding's Spire," *Ren* 20 (1968): 75-8.

Lerner, Laurence, "Jocelin's Folly: or, Down with the Spire," *CritQ* 24, iii (Autumn, 1982): 3-15.

Livingston, James C., *William Golding's THE SPIRE* (Religious Dimensions in Literature), N.Y.: Seabury, 1967.

Malin, Irving, in Shapiro, C., ed., *Contemporary British Novelists*, 45-7.

Medcalf, S., *William Golding*, 32-7.

"Novels of 1964. William Golding: THE SPIRE," in *T.L.S. Essays and Reviews from The Times Literary Supplement, 1964*, 35-41. Also in *TLS* (April 16, 1964).

Oldsey, B. S., and S. Weintraub, *Art of William Golding*, 125-46.

Pemberton, C., *William Golding*, 22-4.

Roper, Derek, "Allegory and Novel in Golding's THE SPIRE," *WSCL* 8 (Winter, 1967): 19-30.

Russell, Kenneth C., "The Devil's Contemplative & the Miracle Rabbi, Two Novels: Golding's SPIRE and Wallant's HUMAN SEASON," *SMy* 3, iii (1980): 52-64.

Skilton, David, "Golding's THE SPIRE," *SLitI* 2, ii (Oct., 1969): 45-56.

Spender, Stephen, "Traditional vs. Underground Novels," in Encyclopaedia Britannica, *Great Ideas Today, 1965*, 188-90.

Stålhammar, Mall M., *Imagery in Golding's THE SPIRE*, Gothenburg: Acta Univ. Gothoburgensis, 1977.

Sternlicht, Sanford, "The Sin of Pride in Golding's THE SPIRE," *MinnR* 5 (Jan.-April, 1965): 59-60.

_____, "Two Views of the Builder in Graham Greene's A BURNT-OUT CASE and William Golding's THE SPIRE," *CalR* n.s. 1, iii (Jan.-Mar., 1970): 401-4. Also in *SHum* 2, ii (Fall-Winter, 1970-71): 17-19.

Sullivan, Walter, "The Long Chronicle of Guilt: William Golding's THE SPIRE," *HC* 1, iii (June, 1964): 1-12. Also in Dillard, R. H. W., and others, eds., *Sounder Few*, 43-53.

Sutherland, Raymond C., "Mediaeval Elements in THE SPIRE," *SLitI* 2, ii (Oct., 1969): 57-65.

Temple, E. R. A., "William Golding's THE SPIRE: A Critique," *Ren* 20 (Summer, 1968): 171-3.

Tiger, V., *William Golding*, 167-200.

THE TWO DEATHS OF CHRISTOPHER MARTIN See PINCHER MARTIN

BIBLIOGRAPHY

Baker, J. R., and A. P. Ziegler, Jr., eds., *Casebook Edition of William Golding's LORD OF THE FLIES*, 287-91.

_____, *William Golding*, 97-102.

Biles, Jack I., "William Golding: Bibliography of Primary and Secondary Sources," in Biles, J. I., and R. O. Evans, eds., *William Golding*, 237-80.

_____, "A William Golding Checklist," *TCL* 17, iii (April, 1971): 107-21.

Hodson, L., *Golding*, 110-16.

Johnston, A., *Of Earth and Darkness*, 118-27.

Lutz, Hartmut, "A William Golding Bibliography," *BB* 36, ii (April-June, 1979): 53-70.

Vann, J. Don, "William Golding: A Checklist of Criticism," *Serif* 8, ii (June, 1971): 21-6.

GOLDMAN, WILLIAM, 1931-

GENERAL

Andersen, Richard A., "The Fiction of Reality and Fantasy in William Goldman," *DAI* 38 (1977): 2116A.

_____, *William Goldman*.

BOYS AND GIRLS TOGETHER

Andersen, R., *William Goldman*, 54-62.

FATHER'S DAY

Andersen, R., *William Goldman*, 75-80.

MAGIC

Andersen, R., *William Goldman*, 100-5.

MARATHON MAN

Andersen, R., *William Goldman*, 94-100.

Gross, Sheryl W., "Guilt and Innocence in MARATHON MAN," *LFQ* 8 (1980): 52-68.

NO WAY TO TREAT A LADY (Pub. under pseud. "Harry Longbaugh")

Andersen, R., *William Goldman*, 62-5, 77-9.

THE PRINCESS BRIDE

Andersen, R., *William Goldman*, 81-93.

SOLDIER IN THE RAIN

Andersen, R., *William Goldman*, 44-53.

THE TEMPLE OF GOLD

Andersen, R., *William Goldman*, 26-34.

THE THING OF IT IS...

Andersen, R., William Goldman, 66-72.

YOUR TURN TO CURTSY, MY TURN TO BOW

Andersen, R., *William Goldman*, 35-43.

GOODMAN, PAUL, 1911-1972

GENERAL

Becker, Louis D., "'I Light Fires, No One Comes': The Creative Literature of Paul Goodman," *DAI* 33 (1973): 6340A (Emory).

Raditsa, Leo, "On Paul Goodman— And Goodmanism," *IowaR* 5, iii (Summer, 1974): 62-79.

True, Michael, "Paul Goodman and the Triumph of American Prose Style," *NewL* 42 (Winter/Spring, 1976): 228-36.

THE DEAD OF SPRING (See also THE EMPIRE CITY Series)

Paul, Sherman, "Paul Goodman's Mourning Labour: THE EMPIRE CITY," *SoR* 4 (1968): 909-17.

Widmer, K., *Paul Goodman*, 114-16.

THE EMPIRE CITY Series

Glassheim, Eliot, "The Movement Towards Freedom in Paul Goodman's THE EMPIRE CITY," *DAI* 34 (1973): 2623A (N. Mex.).

Paul, Sherman, "Paul Goodman's Mourning Labour: THE EMPIRE CITY," *SoR* 4 (1968): 894-926.

Widmer, K., *Paul Goodman*, 106-18.

THE GRAND PIANO (See also THE EMPIRE CITY Series)

Paul, Sherman, "Paul Goodman's Mourning Labour: THE EMPIRE CITY," *SoR* 4 (1968): 895-901.

Widmer, K., *Paul Goodman*, 109-11.

HERE BEGINS (See also THE EMPIRE CITY Series)

Paul, Sherman, "Paul Goodman's Mourning Labour: THE EMPIRE CITY," *SoR* 4 (1968): 923-6.

THE HOLY TERROR (See also THE EMPIRE CITY Series)

Paul, Sherman, "Paul Goodman's Mourning Labour: THE EMPIRE CITY," *SoR* 4 (1968): 918-23.

Widmer, K., *Paul Goodman*, 107-9, 116-18.

MAKING DO

Widmer, K., *Paul Goodman*, 122-6.

PARENTS DAY

Widmer, K., *Paul Goodman*, 118-22.

THE STATE OF NATURE (See also THE EMPIRE CITY Series)

Paul, Sherman, "Paul Goodman's Mourning Labour: THE EMPIRE CITY," *SoR* 4 (1968): 901-9.

Widmer, K., *Paul Goodman*, 111-14.

BIBLIOGRAPHY

Glasheim, Eliot, "Paul Goodman: A Checklist, 1931-1971," *BB* 29, ii (April-June, 1972): 61-72.

Nicely, Tom, comp., *Adam and His Work: A Bibliographpy of Sources by and about Paul Goodman (1911-1972)*, Metuchen, N.J.: Scarecrow, 1979.

Widmer, K., *Paul Goodman*, 176-9.

GORAN, LESTER, 1928-

GENERAL

Johnson, Frederick M., "The Novels of Lester Goran: A Critical Study," *DAI* 35 (1973): 5181A (Ala.).

GORDIMER, NADINE, 1923-

GENERAL

Abrahams, Lionel, "Nadine Gordimer: The Transparent Ego," *ESA* 3 (Sept., 1960): 146-51.

Bragg, Melvyn, "Nadine Gordimer: The Solitude of a White Writer," *Listener* 96 (Oct. 21, 1976): 514. [Interview.]

Cooke, John, "African Landscapes: The World of Nadine Gordimer," *WLT* 52, iv (Autumn, 1978): 533-8.

_____, "The Novels of Nadine Gordimer," *DAI* 37 (1977): 4346A.

De Villiers, André, "South African Writers Talking: Nadine Gordimer, Es'kia Mphahlele, André Brink," *ErinA* 6, ii (1980): 1-23.

Fullerton, Ian, and Glen Murray, "An Interview with Nadine Gordimer," *Cencrastus* 6 (1981): 2-5.

Gerver, Elisabeth, "Women Revolutionaries in the Novels of Nadine Gordimer and Doris Lessing," *WLWE* 17, i (April, 1978): 38-44.

Gordimer, Nadine, "What Being a South African Means to Me," *SAfrO* 107 (June, 1977): 87-9, 92.

Gray, Stephen, "Interview With Nadine Gordimer," *Contrast* 8, ii (1973): 78-83.

Haugh, R. F., *Nadine Gordimer*.

Hope, Christopher, "Out of the Picture: The Novels of Nadine Gordimer," *LonM* 15, i (April-May, 1975): 49-55.

Laredo, Ursula, "African Mosaic: The Novels of Nadine Gordimer," *JCL* 8, i (June, 1973): 42-53.

Lomberg, Alan, "Withering into the Truth: The Romantic Realism of Nadine Gordimer," *EinA* 3, i (1976): 1-12.

McGuinness, Frank, "The Novels of Nadine Gordimer," *LonM* n.s., 5 (June, 1965): 97-102.

Moss, Rose, "Hand in Glove: Nadine Gordimer, South African Writer," *PQM* 6, iii-iv (July-Oct., 1981): 106-22.

Rhedin, Folke, "Nadine Gordimer's Novels," in Granqvist, R., ed., *Report of Workshop on World Literatures Written in English...*, 45-7.

Riis, Johannes, "Nadine Gordimer," *Kunapipi* 2, i (1980): 20-6.]Not seen.]

Wade, M., *Nadine Gordimer*.

Wettenhall, Irene, "Liberalism and Radicalism in South Africa since 1948: Nadine Gordimer's Fiction," *NLRev* 8 (1980): 36-44.

Woodward, Anthony, "Nadine Gordimer," *Theoria* 16 (1961): 1-12.

BURGER'S DAUGHTER

Gordimer, Nadine, John Dugard, and Richard Smith, *What Happened to BURGER'S DAUGHTER, or How South African Censorship Works*, Emmarentia, S.Afr.: Taurus, 1980.

Gray, Stephen, "An Interview with Nadine Gordimer," *ConL* 22, iii (Summer, 1981): 263-71.

Heinemann, Margot, "BURGER'S DAUGHTER: The Synthesis of Revelation," in Jefferson, D., and G. Martin, eds., *Uses of Fiction*, 181-97.

N., Z., "The Politics of Commitment," *Afr. Communist* 80 (1980): 100-1. [Gordimer's reply, "Facts and Interpretation," 109.]

Roberts, Sheila, "South African Censorship and the Case of BURGER'S DAUGHTER," *WLWE* 20, i (Spring, 1981): 41-8.

Smith, Rowland, "Living for the Future: Nadine Gordimer's BURGER'S DAUGHTER," *WLWE* 19, ii (1980): 163-73.

Wilhelm, Peter, "Savage Fiction," *Bloody Horse* 2 (1980): 89-93.

THE CONSERVATIONIST

Gowda, H. H. Anniah, "The Design and the Technique in Nadine Gordimer's THE CONSERVATIONIST," *LHY* 20, ii (1979): 3-10.

Gray, Stephen, "An Interview with Nadine Gordimer," *ConL* 22, iii (Summer, 1981): 263-71.

Green, Robert J., "Nadine Gordimer: 'The Politics of Race'," *WLWE* 16, ii (Nov., 1977): 256-62.

Hedberg, Johannes, "Three Contemporary Novelists—Three Novels of 1974," *MSpr* 69, ii (1975): 113-16.

Newman, Judie, "Gordimer's THE CONSERVATIONIST: 'That Book of Unknown Signs'," *Crit* 27, iii (1981): 31-44.

Ogungbesan, Kolawole, "Nadine Gordimer's THE CONSERVATIONIST: A Touch of Death," *IFR* 5 (1978): 109-15.

O'Sheel, P., "Nadine Gordimer's THE CONSERVATIONIST," *WLWE* 14 (1975): 514-19.

Roberts, Sheila, "Character and Meaning in Four Contemporary South African Novels," *WLWE* 19, i (Spring, 1980): 19-36 *passim*.

Wade, M., *Nadine Gordimer*, 183-227.

A GUEST OF HONOUR

Fido, Elaine, "A GUEST OF HONOUR: A Feminine View of Masculinity," *WLWE* 17 (1978): 30-7.

Gray, Stephen, "Landmark in Fiction," *Contrast* 8, ii (1973): 78-83.

Green, Robert J., "Nadine Gordimer's A GUEST OF HONOUR," *WLWE* 16, i (1977): 55-66.

Haarhof, Dorian, "Two Cheers for Socialism: Nadine Gordimer and E. M. Forster," *EinA* 9, i (1982): 55-64.

Haugh, R. F., *Nadine Gordimer*, 145-60.

Ogungbesan, Kolawole, "The Liberal Expatriate and African Politics: Nadine Gordimer's A GUEST OF HONOUR," *Nigerian Jour. of the Humanities* 1, i (1977): 29-41.

_____, "Nadine Gordimer's A GUEST OF HONOUR: Politics, Fiction, and the Liberal Expatriate," *SoRA* 12 (1979): 108-23.

Spence, J. E., "Two Novels of Africa," *African Research and Documentation* (Birmingham) 14 (1977): 3-10.

Wade, M., *Nadine Gordimer*, 145-82.

_____, "Nadine Gordimer and Europe-in-Africa," in Parker, K., ed., *South African Novel in English*, 131-63.

THE LATE BOURGEOIS WORLD

Haugh, R. F., *Nadine Gordimer*, 135-44.

Lomberg, Alan, "Withering into the Truth: The Romantic Realism in Nadine Gordimer," *EinA* 3, i (1976): 8-10.

Ogungbesan, Kolawole, "Nadine Gordimer's THE LATE BOURGEOIS WORLD: Love in Prison," *ArielE* 9, i (Jan., 1978): 31-49.

Parker, Kenneth, "Nadine Gordimer and the Pitfalls of Liberalism," in Parker, K., ed., *South African Novel in English*, 127-30.

"Prose out of Africa. Nadine Gordimer. THE LATE BOURGEOIS WORLD," in *T.L.S. Essays and Reviews, 1966*, 45-6. Also in *TLS* (July 7, 1966).

Wade, M., *Nadine Gordimer*, 108-44.

THE LYING DAYS

Haugh, R. F., *Nadine Gordimer*, 93-105.

Lomberg, Alan, "Withering into the Truth: The Romantic Realism of Nadine Gordimer," *EinA* 3, i (1976): 2-5.

Ogungbesan, Kolawole, "The Way Out of South Africa: Nadine Gordimer's THE LYING DAYS," *Theoria* 49 (1977): 45-59. Also in *Ba Shiru* 9, i-ii (1978): 48-62.

Wade, M., *Nadine Gordimer*, 5-45.

OCCASION FOR LOVING

Haugh, R. F., *Nadine Gordimer*, 116-34.

Lomberg, Alan, "Withering into the Truth: The Romantic Realism of Nadine Gordimer," *EinA* 3, i (1976): 7-8.

Parker, Kenneth, "Nadine Gordimer and the Pitfalls of Liberalism," in Parker, K., ed., *South African Novel in English*, 123-7.

Wade, M., *Nadine Gordimer*, 75-107.

A WORLD OF STRANGERS

Green, Robert, "Nadine Gordimer's A WORLD OF STRANGERS: Strains in South African Liberalism," *ESA* 22, i (1979): 45-54.

Haugh, R. F., *Nadine Gordimer*, 106-15.

Lomberg, Alan, "Withering into the Truth: The Romantic Realism of Nadine Gordimer," *EinA* 3, i (1976): 5-7.

Ogungbesan, Kolawole, "Reality in Nadine Gordimer's A WORLD OF STRANGERS," *ES* 61, ii (1980): 142-55.

Parker, Kenneth, "Nadine Gordimer and the Pitfalls of Liberalism," in Parker, K., ed., *South African Novel in English*, 116-23.

Tucker, M., *Africa in Modern Literature*, 222-3.

Wade, M., *Nadine Gordimer*, 46-74.

BIBLIOGRAPHY

Cooke, John, "Nadine Gordimer: A Bibliography," *BB* 36, ii (April-June, 1979): 81-4.

Nell, Racilia J., *Nadine Gordimer, Novelist and Short Story Writer: A Bibliography of Her Works and Selected Literary Criticism*, Johannesburg: Un. of Witwatersrand, 1964.

GORDON, CAROLINE, 1895-1981

GENERAL

Baker, Howard, "The Stratagems of Caroline Gordon, Or, the Art of the Novel and the Novelty of Myth," *SoR* 9, iii (July, 1973): 523-49.

Brown, Ashley, "The Achievement of Caroline Gordon," *SHR* 2 (Summer, 1968): 279-90.

Brown, Jane G., "The Early Novels of Caroline Gordon: The Confluence of Myth and History as a Fictional Technique," *DAI* 37 (1977): 6474A.

_____, "The Early Novels of Caroline Gordon: Myth and History as a Fictional Technique," *SoR* 13, ii (April, 1977): 289-98.

Brown, Jerry E., "The Rhetoric of Form: A Study of the Novels of Caroline Gordon," *DAI* 35 (1975): 789A-99A.

Brown, Samuel A., Jr., "Caroline Gordon and the Impressionist Novel," *DA* 18 (1958): 1795 (Vanderbilt).

Chappell, Charles M., "The Hero Figure and the Problem of Unity in the Novels of Caroline Gordon," *DAI* 34 (1973): 2615A (Emory).

Cheney, Brainard, "Caroline Gordon's Ontological Quest," *Ren* 16 (Fall, 1963): 3-12.

Cowan, Bainard, "The Serpent's Coils: How to Read Caroline Gordon's Later Fiction," *SoR* 16, ii (April, 1980): 281-98.

Cowan, Louise, "Nature and Grace in Caroline Gordon," *Crit* 1 (Winter, 1956): 11-27. Also in Colquitt, Betsy F., ed., *Studies in Medieval, Renaissance, American Literature*, 172-87.

Fletcher, Marie, "The Fate of Women in a Changing South: A Persistant Theme in the Fiction of Caroline Gordon," *MissQ* 21 (Winter, 1967-68): 17-28.

Fraistat, Rose A. C., "Caroline Gordon as Novelist and Woman of Letters," *DAI* 41, vii (Jan., 1981): 3105A.

Hoffman, F. J., *Art of Southern Fiction*, 36-9. Also, basically the same, as "Caroline Gordon: The Special Yield," *Crit* 1 (Winter, 1956): 29-35.

King, Lawrence T., "The Novels of Caroline Gordon," *CathW* 181 (July, 1955): 274-9.

Koch, Vivienne, "The Conservatism of Caroline Gordon," in Rubin, L. D., Jr., and R. D. Jacobs, eds., *Southern Renascence*, 325-37.

Lavin, Sandra M., "The Hero's Journey in the Novels of Caroline Gordon," *DAI* 40 (1980): 6280A.

Lytle, Andrew, "Caroline Gordon and the Historic Image," *SR* 57 (Autumn, 1949): 560-86. Also in Lytle, A., *Hero with the Private Parts*, 148-70.

Makowsky, Veronica A., "The Forest of the South: Caroline Gordon's Early Fiction," *DAI* 42 (1982): 3159A.

McDowell, F. P. W., *Caroline Gordon*.

O'Connor, William Van, "Art and Miss Gordon," in Rubin, L. D., Jr., and R. D. Jacobs, eds., *South*, 314-22. Also in O'Connor, W. V., *Grotesque*, 168-76.

Rocks, James E., "The Mind and Art of Caroline Gordon," *DA* 27 (1966): 1835A (Duke). Also, in part, in *MissQ* 21 (Winter, 1967-68): 1-16.

Rodenberger, Molcie L., "Caroline Gordon, Teller of Tales: The Influence of Folk Narrative on Characterization and Structure in Her Work," *DAI* 36 (1976): 5302A-03A.

Squires, Radcliffe, "The Underground Stream: A Note on Caroline Gordon's Fiction," *SoR* 7, ii (April, 1971): 467-79.

Stuckey, W. J., *Caroline Gordon.*

Thorp, W., "Southern Renaissance," *American Writing in the Twentieth Century,* 249-53.

_____, "The Way Back and the Way Up: The Novels of Caroline Gordon," *BuR* 6, iii (Dec., 1956): 1-15.

ALECK MAURY, SPORTSMAN

Brinkmeyer, Robert H., Jr., "New Caroline Gordon Books," *SLJ* 14, ii (Spring, 1982): 65-8.

Brown, Ashley, "The Achievement of Caroline Gordon," *SHR* 2 (1968): 283-4.

Gallo, Louis, "Notes on Some Recently Found Lost American Fiction," *MissR* 4, iii (Summer, 1981): 95-7.

Hoffman, Frederick J., "Caroline Gordon: The Special Yield," *Crit* 1 (1956): 29-31, 33-4. Also in Hoffman, F. J., *Art of Southern Fiction,* 36-7.

McDowell, F. P. W., *Caroline Gordon,* 17-19.

Stuckey, W. J., *Caroline Gordon,* 33-41.

THE GARDEN OF ADONIS

Brown, Ashley, "The Achievement of Caroline Gordon," *SHR* 2 (1968): 285-6.

Fletcher, Marie, "The Fate of Women in a Changing South: A Persistant Theme in the Fiction of Caroline Gordon," *MissQ* 21 (Winter, 1967-68): 22-4.

McDowell, F. P. W., *Caroline Gordon,* 19-21.

Stuckey, W. J., *Caroline Gordon,* 55-61.

THE GLORY OF HERA

Alvis, John, "The Miltonic Argument in Caroline Gordon's THE GLORY OF HERA," *SoR* 16, iii (1980): 560-73.

Baker, Howard, "The Stratagems of Caroline Gordon, Or, The Art of the Novel and the Novelty of Myth," *SoR* 9, iii (July, 1973): 523-49.

Cowan, Bainard, "The Serpent's Coils: How to Read Caroline Gordon's Later Fiction," *SoR* 16, ii (April, 1980): 281-98.

Lewis, Janet, "THE GLORY OF HERA," *SR* 81, i (Winter, 1973): 185-94.

GREEN CENTURIES

Brown, Ashley, "The Achievement of Caroline Gordon," *SHR* 2 (1968): 286-7.

Landess, Thomas H., "The Function of Ritual in Caroline Gordon's GREEN CENTURIES," *SoR* 7, ii (April, 1971): 495-508.

Lytle, Andrew, "Caroline Gordon and the Historic Image," *SR* 57 (Autumn, 1949): 569-75. Also in Lytle, A., *Hero with the Private Parts,* 156-61.

McDowell, F. P. W., *Caroline Gordon,* 26-30.

Rodenberger, M. Lou, "Folk Narrative in Caroline Gordon's Frontier Fiction," in Lee, L. L., and M. Lewis, eds., *Women, Women Writers, and the West,* 199-206.

Stuckey, W. J., *Caroline Gordon,* 62-6.

Thorp, Willard, "The Way Back and the Way Up: The Novels of Caroline Gordon," *BuR* 6 (Dec., 1956): 9-11.

THE MALEFACTORS

Brown, Ashley, "The Novel as Christian Comedy: Gordon's THE MALEFACTORS," in Walker, W. E., and Welker, R. L., eds., *Reality and Myth,* 161-78.

Cheney, Brainard, "Caroline Gordon's THE MALEFACTORS," *SR* 79, iii (Summer, 1971): 360-72. Also in Madden, D., ed., *Rediscoveries,* 232-44.

Desmond, John F., "THE MALEFACTORS: Caroline Gordon's Redemptive Vision," *Ren* 35, i (Autumn, 1982): 17-38.

Koch, Vivienne, "Companions in the Blood," *SR* 64 (Autumn, 1956): 645-51.

McDowell, F. P. W., *Caroline Gordon,* 38-44.

Stuckey, W. J., *Caroline Gordon,* 94-111.

Thorp, Willard, "The Way Back and the Way Up: The Novels of Caroline Gordon," *BuR* 6 (Dec., 1956): 13-15.

NONE SHALL LOOK BACK

Allen, W., *Modern Novel,* 113-14.

Brown, Ashley, "The Achievement of Caroline Gordon," *SHR* 2 (1968): 284-5.

_____, "NONE SHALL LOOK BACK: The Novel as History," *SoR* 7, ii (April, 1971): 480-94.

Gray, R., *Literature of Memory,* 155-9, 166-74.

Lytle, Andrew, "Caroline Gordon and the Historic Image," *SR* 57 (Autumn, 1949): 578-80. Also in Lytle, A., *Hero with the Private Parts,* 164-6.

McDowell, F. P. W., *Caroline Gordon,* 21-6.

Stuckey, W. J., *Caroline Gordon,* 42-54.

Sullivan, W., *Death by Melancholy,* 75-7.

PENHALLY

Brown, Ashley, "The Achievement of Caroline Gordon," *SHR* 2 (1968): 281-3.

Eisinger, C. E., "Class and American Fiction: The Aristocracy in Some Novels of the Thirties," in Lanzinger, K., ed., *Americana-Austriaca,* 144-6.

Fletcher, Marie, "The Fate of Women in a Changing South: A Persistant Theme in the Fiction of Caroline Gordon," *MissQ* 21 (Winter, 1967-68): 21-2.

Lytle, Andrew, "Caroline Gordon and the Historic Image," *SR* 57 (Autumn, 1949): 575-80. Also in Lytle, A., *Hero with the Private Parts,* 161-3.

McDowell, F. P. W., *Caroline Gordon,* 14-17.

Stuckey, W. J., *Caroline Gordon,* 24-32.

Thorp, Willard, "The Way Back and the Way Up: The Novels of Caroline Gordon," *BuR* 6 (Dec., 1956): 3-5.

THE STRANGE CHILDREN

Fletcher, Marie, "The Fate of Women in a Changing South: A Persistant Theme in the Fiction of Caroline Gordon," *MissQ* 21 (Winter, 1967-68): 26-7.

Gardiner, H. C., "Two Southern Tales," *In All Conscience,* 128-9. Also in *America* 86 (Oct. 6, 1951): 18.

Hartman, Carl, "Charades at Benfolly," *WR* 16 (Summer, 1952): 322-4.

Heilman, Robert B., "Schools for Girls," *SR* 60 (April-June, 1952): 299-304.

King, Lawrence T., "The Novels of Caroline Gordon," *CathW* 181 (July, 1955): 277-9.

Koch, Vivienne, in Rubin, L. D., and R. D. Jacobs, eds., *Southern Renascence*, 333-7.

McDowell, F. P. W., *Caroline Gordon*, 33-8.

Rocks, James E., "The Christian Myth as Salvation: Caroline Gordon's THE STRANGE CHILDREN," *TSE* 16 (1968): 149-60.

Smith, Patrick J., "Typology and Peripety in Four Catholic Novels," *DA* 28 (1967): 226A (Calif., Davis).

Squires, Radcliffe, "The Underground Stream: A Note on Caroline Gordon's Fiction," *SoR* 7, ii (April, 1971): 474-8.

Stuckey, W. J., *Caroline Gordon*, 79-93.

Thorp, Willard, "The Way Back and the Way Up: The Novels of Caroline Gordon," *BuR* 6 (Dec., 1956): 12-13.

THE WOMEN ON THE PORCH

Cowan, Louise, "Nature and Grace in Caroline Gordon," *Crit* 1 (1956): 22-7. Also in Colquitt, Betsy F., ed., *Studies in Medieval, Renaissance, American Literature*, 183-7.

Fletcher, Marie, "The Fate of Women in a Changing South: A Persistant Theme in the Fiction of Caroline Gordon," *MissQ* 21 (Winter, 1967-68): 24-6.

Lytle, Andrew, "Caroline Gordon and the Historic Image," *SR* 57 (Autumn, 1949): 581-5. Also in Lytle, A., *Hero with the Private Parts*, 166-70.

McDowell, F. P. W., *Caroline Gordon*, 30-3.

Squires, Radcliffe, "The Underground Stream: A Note on Caroline Gordon's Fiction," *SoR* 7, ii (April, 1971): 470-4.

Stuckey, W. J., *Caroline Gordon*, 67-78.

Thorp, Willard, "The Way Back and the Way Up: The Novels of Caroline Gordon," *BuR* 6 (Dec., 1956): 11-12.

BIBLIOGRAPHY

Golden, Robert E., and Mary C. Sullivan, *Flannery O'Connor and Caroline Gordon: A Reference Guide*, Boston: Hall, 1977.

Griscom, Joan, "Bibliography of Caroline Gordon," *Crit* 1 (Winter, 1956): 74-8.

McDowell, F. P. W., *Caroline Gordon*, 46-8.

GORDON, MARY, 1949-

FINAL PAYMENTS

Cooper-Clark, Diana, "An Interview with Mary Gordon," *Cweal* 107, ix (May 9, 1980): 270-3.

GOUDGE, ELIZABETH, 1900-1984

GENERAL

Marsden, Madonna, "Gentle Truths for Gentle Readers: The Fiction of Elizabeth Goudge," in Cornillon, S. K., ed., *Images of Women in Fiction*, 68-78.

THE BIRD IN THE TREE

Marsden, Madonna, "Gentle Truths for Gentle Readers," in Cornillon, S. K., ed., *Images of Women in Fiction*, 72-4.

PILGRIM'S INN

Marsden, Madonna, "Gentle Truths for Gentle Readers," in Cornillon, S. K., ed., *Images of Women in Fiction*, 74-5.

GOULD, LOIS, 1938?-

A SEA-CHANGE

Mickelson, Anne Z., "Lois Gould: The Musical Chairs of Power," *Reaching Out*, 57-67.

SUCH GOOD FRIENDS

Mickelson, Anne Z., "Lois Gould: The Musical Chairs of Power," *Reaching Out*, 49-56.

GOVER, ROBERT, 1929-

GENERAL

Southern, Terry, "Rechy and Gover," in Moore, H. T., ed., *Contemporary American Novelists*, 222-7.

GOYEN, WILLIAM, 1915-

GENERAL

Ashley, Leonard R. N., "'Tightly-Wound Little Bombs of Truth': Biblical References in the Fiction of William Goyen," *LOS* 8 (1981): 147-65.

Ballorain, Rolande, "Interview with William Goyen," *DeltaES* 9 (1979): 7-45.

Duncan, Erika, "Come a Spiritual Healer: A Profile of William Goyen," *BForum* 3, ii (1977): 296-303.

Gossett, L. Y., "The Voices of Distance: William Goyen," *Violence in Recent Southern Fiction*, 131-44.

Igo, John, "Learning to See Simply: An Interview with William Goyen," *SWR* 65 (1980): 267-84.

Paul, Jay S., "'Marvelous Reciprocity': The Fiction of William Goyen," *Crit* 19, ii (1977): 77-92.

Phillips, R., *William Goyen*.

————, "William Goyen: The Art of Fiction LXIII," *ParisR* 68 (Winter, 1976): 58-100.

COME, THE RESTORER

Phillips, R., *William Goyen*, 89-97.

Repussiau, Patrice, "The Concentrated Writing of W. Goyen: Reflections on COME, THE RESTORER," *DeltaES* 9 (1979): 197-216.

THE FAIR SISTER (SAVATA, MY FAIR SISTER)

Phillips, R., *William Goyen*, 78-83.

THE HOUSE OF BREATH

Coindreau, M. G., *Time of William Faulkner*, 132-40.

Curtius, E. R., *Essays on European Literature*, Princeton, N.J.: Princeton Un. Pr., 1973, 456-64.

Hoffman, F. J., *Art of Southern Fiction*, 124-7.

Phillips, Robert, "Secret and Symbol: Entrances to Goyen's HOUSE OF BREATH," *SWR* 59, iii (Summer, 1974): 248-53.

————, *William Goyen*, 89-97.

Stern, Daniel, in Madden, D., ed., *Rediscoveries*, 256-61.

Vauthier, Simone, "The Teller-Listener Situation: Notes on THE HOUSE OF BREATH," *DeltaES* 9 (1979): 141-69.

IN A FARTHER COUNTRY

Hoffman, F. J., *Art of Southern Fiction*, 127-9.

Phillips, Robert, "The Romance of Prophecy: Goyen's IN A FARTHER COUNTRY," *SWR* 56, iii (Summer, 1971): 213-21.

————, *William Goyen*, 58-67.

BIBLIOGRAPHY

Grimm, Clyde L., Jr., "William Goyen: A Bibliographic Chronicle," *BB* 35, iii (July-Sept., 1978): 123-31.

GRAU, SHIRLEY ANN, 1929-

GENERAL

Berland, Alwyn, "The Fiction of Shirley Ann Grau," *Crit* 6, i (Spring, 1963): 78-84.

Chiogioji, Eleanor, "A Matter of Houses: Structural Unity in the Works of Shirley Ann Grau," *DAI* 43, i (July, 1982): 167A.

Donahue, H. E. F., "Shirley Ann Grau," *PW* (Dec. 3, 1973): 10-13. [Interview.]

Gossett, L. Y., "Primitives and Violence: Shirley Ann Grau," *Violence in Recent Southern Fiction*, 177-95.

Hoffman, F. J., *Art of Southern Fiction*, 106-9.

Keith, Don L., "New Orleans Notes," *Delta Rev* 2, iii (1965): 11-12+. [Not seen.]

————, "A Visit with Shirley Ann Grau," *Contempora* 2, ii (1972): 10-14.

Pearson, Ann, "Shirley Ann Grau: Nature is the Vision," *Crit* 17, ii (1975): 47-58.

Rohrberger, Mary, "Conversation with Shirley Ann Grau and James K. Feibleman," *CimR* 43 (1978): 35-45.

Schlueter, P., *Shirley Ann Grau*.

THE CONDOR PASSES

Pearson, Ann, "Shirley Ann Grau: Nature is the Vision," *Crit* 17, ii (1975): 53-5.

Schlueter, P., *Shirley Ann Grau*, 69-96.

EVIDENCE OF LOVE

Rohrberger, Mary, "'So Distinct a Shade': Shirley Ann Grau's EVIDENCE OF LOVE," *SoR* 14 (Jan., 1978): 195-8.

Schlueter, P., *Shirley Ann Grau*, 87-105.

THE HARD BLUE SKY

Berland, Alwyn, "The Fiction of Shirley Ann Grau," *Crit* 6, i (Spring, 1963): 80-2.

Gossett, L. Y., *Violence in Recent Southern Fiction*, 180-6.

Husband, John D., *NMQ* 28, i (Spring, 1958): 61-5.

Pearson, Ann, "Shirley Ann Grau: Nature is the Vision," *Crit* 17, ii (1975): 49-50.

Schlueter, P., *Shirley Ann Grau*, 29-39.

THE HOUSE ON COLISEUM STREET

Berland, Alwyn, "The Fiction of Shirley Ann Grau," *Crit* 6, i (Spring, 1963): 82-4.

Pearson, Ann, "Shirley Ann Grau: Nature is the Vision," *Crit* 17, ii (1975): 51-2.

Schlueter, P., *Shirley Ann Grau*, 40-51.

THE KEEPERS OF THE HOUSE

Going, William T., "Alabama Geography in Shirley Ann Grau's THE KEEPERS OF THE HOUSE," *AlaR* 20 (Jan., 1967): 62-8.

Gossett, L. Y., *Violence in Recent Southern Fiction*, 189-94.

Hoffman, F. J., *Art of Southern Fiction*, 108-10.

Pearson, Ann, "Shirley Ann Grau: Nature is the Vision," *Crit* 17, ii (1975): 52-3.

Schlueter, P., *Shirley Ann Grau*, 52-68.

BIBLIOGRAPHY

Schlueter, P., *Shirley Ann Grau*, 150-5.

GREEN, HANNAH see GREENBERG, JOANNE

GREEN, HENRY, Pseud. (Henry Vincent Yorke), 1905-1974

GENERAL

Allen, Walter, "Greening," *NS&Nation* 57 (May 2, 1959): 615-16.

————, "Henry Green," in Baker, D. V., ed., *Modern British Writing*, 258-71. Also in *Penguin New Writing*, XXV (1945): 144-55.

————, *Modern Novel*, 214-19.

Bain, Bruce, "Henry Green: The Man and His Work," *World Rev* (May, 1949): 55-8, 80.

Bassoff, B., *Toward LOVING*.

Brothers, Barbara A., "Henry Green: Time and the Absurd," *Boundary* 5, iii (Spring, 1977): 863-76.

————, "Henry Green's Comic Vision: A Study of Green's Novels," *DAI* 34 (1973): 2609A-10A (Kent State).

Cottrell, Beekman W., "Conversation Piece: Four Twentieth Century English Dialogue Novelists," *DA* 16 (1956): 2159 (Columbia).

Davidson, Mary R., "Ironic Self-Portraits by Henry Green: An Autobiography and Two Autobiographical Novels," *DAI* 42 (1982): 3163A.

Dennis, Nigel, "The Double Life of Henry Green," *Life* (Aug. 4, 1952): 83-94.

Fraser, G. S., *Writer and His World*, 167-9.

Gay, Penny, "Re-Visiting Henry Green," *Quadrant* (Oct., 1978): 61-3.

Hall, James, "The Fiction of Henry Greene (sic): Paradoxes of Pleasure-and-Pain," *KR* 19 (Winter, 1957): 76-88. Also in Hall, J., *Tragic Comedians*, 66-81.

Johnson, Bruce, "Henry Green's Comic Symbolism," *BSUF* 6 (Autumn, 1965): 29-35.

_____, "Loving: A Study of Henry Green," *DA* 20 (1959): 2292 (Northwestern).

Karl, F. R., "Normality Defined: The Novels of Henry Green," *Contemporary English Novel*, 183-200.

Knodt, Kenneth S., "A Packed Bag: A Study of the Novels of Henry Green," *DAI* 33 (1972): 2938A (Purdue).

Lambourne, David, "'No Thundering Horses': The Novels of Henry Green," *Shen* 26, iv (1975): 57-71. [Interview.]

Melchiori, Giorgio, "The Abstract Art of Henry Green," *The Tightrope Walkers: Studies of Mannerism in Modern English Literature*, London: Routledge and Kegan Paul, 1956, 188-212.

Mengham, R., *Idiom of the Time*.

North, Michael A., "Private Spheres, Public Chaos: Henry Green and the Writing of His Generation," *DAI* 41, ix (Mar., 1981): 4046A.

Odom, Keith C., "Symbolism and Diversion: Birds in the Novels of Henry Green," *Descant* 6 (Winter, 1962): 30-41.

Phelps, Robert, "The Vision of Henry Green," *HudR* 5 (Winter, 1953): 614-20.

Portnoy, Kenneth S., "The Novels of Henry Green: A Critical Study," *DAI* 37 (1976): 1552A.

Prescott, O., *In My Opinion*, 92-8.

Russell, J., *Henry Green*.

_____, "There It Is," *KR* 26 (Summer, 1964): 433-65.

Ryf, R. S., *Henry Green*.

Schorer, Mark, "Introduction to Henry Green's World," *NYTBR* (Oct. 9, 1949): 1, 22.

Southern, Terry, ed., "The Art of Fiction, XXII. Henry Green," *ParisR* No. 19 (1958): 60-77. [Interview.]

Stead, Alistair, "The Name's Familiar: An Aspect of the Fiction of Henry Green," in Jefferson, D., and G. Martin, eds., *Uses of Fiction*, 213-35.

Stokes, Edward, "Henry Green, Dispossessed Poet," *AusQ* 28 (Dec., 1956): 84-91.

_____, *The Novels of Henry Green*, N.Y.: Macmillan, 1959.

Toynbee, Philip, "The Novels of Henry Green," *PR* 16 (May, 1949): 487-97.

Turner, Myron, "The Imagery of Wallace Stevens and Henry Green," *WSCL* 8 (Winter, 1967): 60-77.

Weatherhead, A. K., *Reading of Henry Green*.

_____, "Structure and Texture in Henry Green's Latest Novels," *Accent* 19 (Spring, 1959): 111-22.

Weaver, Robert L., "Novels of Henry Green," *CanF* 30 (Jan., 1951): 227-8.

Welty, Eudora, "Henry Green, a Novelist of the Imagination," *TQ* 4, iii (Autumn, 1961): 246-56.

White, Roberta H., "The Imagination of Henry Green," *DA* 31 (1970): 1819A-20A.

BACK

Bassoff, B., *Toward LOVING*, 127-33, 140-3.

Mengham, R., *Idiom of the Time*, 157-80.

Prescott, O., *In My Opinion*, 97-8.

Russell, J., *Henry Green*, 160-78.

Ryf, R. S., *Henry Green*, 29-33.

Shapiro, Stephen A., "Henry Green's BACK: The Presence of the Past," *Crit* 7 (Spring, 1964): 87-96.

Weatherhead, A. K., *Reading of Henry Green*, 93-105.

BLINDNESS

Bassoff, B., *Toward LOVING*, 108-11.

Mengam, R., *Idiom of the Time*, 1-12.

Russell, J., *Henry Green*, 50-73.

Ryf, R. S., *Henry Green*, 4-10.

Weatherhead, A. K., *Reading of Henry Green*, 7-20.

CAUGHT

Allen, Walter, "Henry Green," in Baker, D. V., ed., *Modern British Writing*, 267-9.

_____, *Modern Novel*, 216-17.

Bassoff, B., *Toward LOVING*, 80-3, 140-3.

Mengham, R., *Idiom of the Time*, 68-108.

Russell, J., *Henry Green*, 141-60, 172-8.

Ryf, R. S., *Henry Green*, 22-6.

Schorer, Mark, "The Unreal Worlds of Henry Green," *NYTBR* (Dec. 31, 1950): 5+.

Weatherhead, A. K., *Reading of Henry Green*, 55-72.

CONCLUDING

Allen, C. J., "Inference and the Nature of Mind in Henry Green's CONCLUDING," *RLV* 45 (1979): 78-89.

Bassoff, B., *Toward LOVING*, 73-81, 83-92.

Hall, James, "The Fiction of Henry Greene (sic): Paradoxes of Pleasure-and-Pain," *KR* 19 (1957): 86-8. Also in Hall, J., *Tragic Comedians*, 75-81.

Karl, F. R., "Normality Defined: The Novels of Henry Green," *Contemporary English Novel*, 194-6.

Mengham, R., *Idiom of the Time*, 181-206.

Russell, J., *Henry Green*, 179-201.

Ryf, R. S., *Henry Green*, 33-6.

Schorer, Mark, "The Unreal Worlds of Henry Green," *NYTBR* (Dec. 31, 1950): 5+.

Weatherhead, A. K., *Reading of Henry Green*, 106-22.

_____, "Structure and Texture in Henry Green's Latest Novels," *Accent* 19 (Spring, 1959): 111-15.

DOTING

Mengham, R., *Idiom of the Time*, 207-15 *passim*.

Russell, J., *Henry Green*, 202-25.

Ryf, R. S., *Henry Green*, 39-42.

Taylor, Donald S., "Catalytic Rhetoric: Henry Green's Theory of the Modern Novel," *Criticism* 7 (Winter, 1965): 81-99.

Weatherhead, A. K., *Reading of Henry Green*, 135-43.

_____, "Structure and Texture in Henry Green's Latest Novels," *Accent* 19 (Spring, 1959): 120-1.

LIVING

Allen, Walter, "Henry Green," in Baker, D. V., ed., *Modern British Writing*, 262-4.

_____, *Modern Novel*, 214-16.

Bassoff, Bruce, "Prose Consciousness in the Novels of Henry Green," *Lang&S* 5 (1972): 276-86.

_____, *Toward LOVING*, 53-60.

Knodt, Kenneth S., "The Night Journey in Henry Green's LIVING and PARTY GOING," *BSUF* 19, i (1978): 57-62.

Mengham, R., *Idiom of the Time*, 12-30.

Ortega, Ramón L., in Klaus, H. G., ed., *Socialist Novel in Britain*, 123-5.

Russell, J., *Henry Green*, 74-97.

Ryf, R. S., *Henry Green*, 10-15.

Weatherhead, A. K., *Reading of Henry Green*, 21-39.

LOVING

Bassoff, B., *Toward LOVING*, 123-8, 140-60.

Churchill, Thomas, "LOVING: A Comic Novel," *Crit* 4, ii (1961): 29-38.

Davidson, Barbara, "The World of LOVING," *WSCL* 2, i (Winter, 1961): 65-78.

Hall, James, "The Fiction of Henry Greene (sic): Paradoxes of Pleasure-and-Pain," *KR* 19 (1957): 78-85. Also in Hall, J., *Tragic Comedians*, 69-74.

Labor, Earle, "Henry Green's Web of Loving," *Crit* 4, i (1961): 29-40.

Mehoke, James S., "Sartre's Theory of Emotion and Three English Novelists: Waugh, Green, and Amis," *WisSL* No. 3 (1966): 108-10.

Mengham, R., *Idiom of the Time*, 109-56.

Quinton, Anthony, "A French View of LOVING," *LonM* 6 (April, 1959): 25-35.

Russell, J., *Henry Green*, 114-50.

Ryf, R. S., *Henry Green*, 26-9.

Shorer, Mark, "Introduction to Henry Green's World," *NYTBR* (Oct. 9, 1949): 1+.

Tindall, W. Y., *Literary Symbol*, 95-7.

Unterecker, John, "Fiction at the Edge of Poetry," in Friedman, A. W., ed., *Forms of Modern British Fiction*, 192-8.

Weatherhead, A. K., *Reading of Henry Green*, 73-92.

NOTHING

Bassoff, B., *Toward LOVING*, 104-7.

Mengham, R., *Idiom of the Time*, 207-15 *passim*.

Russell, J., *Henry Green*, 202-25.

Ryf, R. S., *Henry Green*, 37-9.

Weatherhead, A. K., *Reading of Henry Green*, 123-35.

_____, "Structure and Texture in Henry Green's Latest Novels," *Accent* 19 (Spring, 1959): 115-20.

PARTY GOING

Allen, Walter, "Henry Green," in Baker, D. V., ed., *Modern British Writing*, 264-6.

Bassoff, Bruce, "Prose Consciousness in the Novels of Henry Green," *Lang&S* 5 (1972): 276-86.

_____, *Toward LOVING*, 50-4, 59-66, 94-100, 117-20, 134-9.

Hart, Clive, "The Structure and Technique of PARTY GOING," *YES* 1 (1971): 185-99.

Johnson, Bruce, "Henry Green's Comic Symbolism" *BSUF* 6 (Autumn, 1965): 31-6.

Kettle, A., *Introduction to the English Novel*, 190-7.

Knodt, Kenneth S., "The Night Journey in Henry Green's LIVING and PARTY GOING," *BSUF* 19, i (1978): 57-62.

Mengham, R., *Idiom of the Time*, 31-52.

Russell, J., *Henry Green*, 97-113.

Ryf, R. S., *Henry Green*, 15-20.

Tindall, W. Y., *Literary Symbol*, 92-5.

Weatherhead, A. K., *Reading of Henry Green*, 40-54.

BIBLIOGRAPHY

Ryf, R. S., *Henry Green*, 47-8.

Weatherhead, A. K., *Reading of Henry Green*, 169-70.

GREENBERG, JOANNE GOLDENBERG, 1932-

GENERAL

Rubin, Stephen E., "Conversations with the Author of I NEVER PROMISED YOU A ROSE GARDEN," *PsyR* 59, ii (Summer, 1972): 201-16.

THE DEAD OF THE HOUSE

Gray, Rockwell, "GLR Review Essay," *GLRev* , i (Summer, 1974): 94-105.

I NEVER PROMISED YOU A ROSE GARDEN

Rubin, Stephen E., "Conversations with the Author of I NEVER PROMISED YOU A ROSE GARDEN," *PsyR* 59, ii (Summer, 1972): 201-16.

IN THIS SIGN

Rubin, Stephen E., "Conversations with the Author of I NEVER PROMISED YOU A ROSE GARDEN," *PsyR* 59, ii (Summer, 1972): 201-16.

GREENE, GRAHAM, 1904-1991

GENERAL

Aisenberg, Nadya, "Graham Greene and the Modern Thriller," *A Common Spring: Crime Novel and Classic*, Bowling Green, Ohio: Bowling Green Un. Popular Pr., 1979, 168-215.

Allen, W. Gore, "Evelyn Waugh and Graham Greene," *IrM* 77 (Jan., 1949): 16-22.

_____, "The World of Graham Greene," *IrEccRec* 71 (Jan., 1949): 42-9.

Allen, Walter, "Graham Greene," in Baker, D. V., ed., *Writers of Today*, 15-28. Also, as "The Novels of Graham Greene," in *Penguin New Writing* 18, 1943, 148-60.

_____, *Modern Novel*, 202-7.

Allott, Kenneth, and Miriam Farris, *Art of Graham Greene*.

Allott, Miriam, "Graham Greene and the Way We Live Now," *CritQ* 20, iii (Autumn, 1978): 9-20.

Alves, Leonard, "The Relevance of Graham Greene," *ELLS* 11 (1974): 47-76. [Not seen.]

Amaracheewa, Amporn, "Graham Greene's Paradoxical Views of Morality: The Nature of Sin," *DAI* 43 (1982): 2343A.

Anon., "Graham Greene: The Man Within," *TLS* (Sept. 17, 1971): 1101-2. Also in Hynes, S., ed., *Graham Greene*, 8-16.

_____, "Shocker," *Time* 58 (Oct. 29, 1951): 98-104.

Atkins, J., *Graham Greene*.

_____, "Two Views of Life: William Golding and Graham Greene," *SLitI* 13, i (Spring, 1980): 81-96.

Barnes, Robert J., "Two Modes of Fiction: Hemingway and Greene," *Ren* 14 (Summer, 1962): 193-8.

Battock, Marjorie, "The Novels of Graham Greene," *Norseman* 13 (Jan.-Feb., 1955): 45-52.

Bedard, Bernard J., "The Thriller Pattern in the Major Novels of Graham Greene," *DA* 20 (1959): 1779-80 (Michigan).

Boardman, G. R., *Graham Greene*.

———, "Graham Greene: The Aesthetics of Exploration," *DA* 24 (1963): 2474 (Claremont Graduate School).

Boyle, Alexander, "Graham Greene," *IrM* 77 (Nov., 1949): 519-25.

———, "Symbolism of Graham Greene," *IrM* 80 (Mar., 1952): 98-102.

Brannon, Lilian B., "Iconology of the Child Figure in Graham Greene's Fiction," *DAI* 38 (1978): 4155A.

Braybrooke, Neville, "Graham Greene," *Envoy* 3 (Sept., 1950): 10-23.

———, "Graham Greene: A Pioneer Novelist," *CE* 12 (Oct., 1950): 1-9. Also in *EJ* 39 (Oct., 1950): 415-23.

Bryden, Ronald, "Graham Greene, Alas," *Spectator* (Sept. 28, 1962): 441-2.

Burgess, A., "The Greene and the Red: Politics in the Novels of Graham Greene," *Urgent Copy*, 13-20.

———, "The Politics of Graham Greene," *NYTBR* (Sept. 10, 1967): 2, 32, 34.

Cargas, H. J., ed., *Graham Greene*.

Cassis, A. F., "The Dream as Literary Device in Graham Greene's Novels," *L&P* 24, iii (1974): 99-108.

Chapman, Raymond, "The Vision of Graham Greene," in Scott, Nathan A., ed., *Forms of Extremity in the Modern Novel*, Richmond: John Knox Pr., 1965, 75-94.

Christman, Elizabeth A., "Hell Lay About Them: Childhood in the Work of Graham Greene," *DAI* 33 (1973): 6345A (N.Y.U.).

Clancy, L. J., "Graham Greene's Battlefield," *CritR* 10 (1967): 99-108.

Connolly, Francis X., "Inside Modern Man: The Spiritual Adventures of Graham Greene," *Ren* 1 (Spring, 1949): 16-24.

Consolo, Dominick P., "Graham Greene; Style and Stylistics in Five Novels," in Evans, R. O., ed., *Graham Greene*, 61-95.

———, "The Technique of Graham Greene: A Stylistic Analysis of Five Novels," *DA* 20 (1959): 297 (State Un. of Iowa.).

Cosman, Max, "Disquieted Graham Greene," *ColQ* 6 (Winter, 1958): 319-25.

———, "An Early Chapter in Graham Greene," *ArQ* 11 (Summer, 1955): 143-7.

Costello, Donald P., "Graham Greene and the Catholic Press," *Ren* 12 (Autumn, 1959): 3-28.

Currie, John S., "Supernaturalism in Graham Greene: A Comparison of Orthodox Catholicism with Religious Vision in the Major Novels," *DA* 28 (1968): 3176A-77A (Alabama).

Davidson, Arnold C., "Graham Greene's Spiritual Lepers," *IEY* 15 (Fall, 1970): 50-5.

D'Cruz, Doreen, "The Pursuit of Selfhood in the Novels of Graham Greene," *DAI* 41 (1980): 2093A.

De Hegedus, Adam, "Graham Greene and the Modern Novel," *Tomorrow* 8 (Oct., 1948): 54-6.

———, "Graham Greene: The Man and His Work," *WoR* (Aug., 1948): 57-61.

Desmond, John F., "Graham Greene and the Eternal Dimension," *ABR* 20 (Sept., 1969): 418-27.

De Vitis, A. A., "The Catholic as Novelist: Graham Greene and François Mauriac," in Evans, R. O, ed., *Graham Greene*, 112-26.

———, "The Entertaining Mr. Greene," *Ren* 14 (Autumn, 1961): 8-24.

———, *Graham Greene*.

———, "Religious Aspects in the Novels of Graham Greene," in Mooney, H. J., Jr., and T. F. Staley, eds., *Shapeless God*, 41-65.

Diephouse, Daniel J., "Graham Greene and the Cinematic Imagination (Volumes I and II)," *DAI* 39 (1978): 3572A.

Dinkins, Paul, "Graham Greene: The Incomplete Version," *CathW* 176 (Nov., 1952): 96-102.

Dombrowski, Theo Q., "Graham Greene: Techniques of Intensity," *ArielE* 6, iv (1975): 29-38.

Drazkiewicz, Joanna, "Understanding Suspense," *ZRL* 17, ii (1974): 21-30.

Duffy, Joseph M., Jr., "The Lost World of Graham Greene," *Thought* 33 (Summer, 1958): 229-47.

Eberly, Ralph S., "Joyce Cary's Theme of Freedom and a Comparison with James Joyce and Graham Greene," *DAI* 31 (1971): 6601A (Mich.).

Ellis, William D., Jr., "The Grand Theme of Graham Greene," *SWR* (Summer, 1956): 239-50.

Fielding, Gabriel, "Graham Greene: The Religious Englishman," *Listener* 72 (Sept. 24, 1964): 465-6. Also in *Critic* 23 (Oct.-Nov., 1964): 24-8.

Fowler, Alastair, "Novelist of Damnation," *Theology* 56 (July, 1953): 259-64.

Fraser, G. S., *Modern Writer and His World*, 133-7.

French, Philip, et al., "Man of Mystery: The Enigma of Graham Greene," *Listener* 102 (Oct. 4, 1979): 441-3.

Funck, Elvio A., "Closer to the Heart of the Matter: Graham Greene's Frontier World," *DAI* 41 (1980): 1063A.

Fytton, Francis, "Graham Greene: Catholicism and Controversy," *CathW* 180 (Dec., 1954): 172-5.

Gardiner, Harold C., "Graham Greene, Catholic Shocker," *Ren* 1 (Spring, 1949): 12-15.

Gaston, Georg M. A., "Forms of Salvation in the Novels of Graham Greene," *DAI* 35 (1974): 1655A (Auburn).

Gay, Marguerite M., "Graham Greene: A Study of Five Major Novels," *DAI* 34 (1974): 5965A.

Hanlon, Robert, "Graham Greene's Religious Sense," *DAI* 32 (1972): 4001A (Mass.).

Hardwick, Patricia A., "The Emergence of Humanism: A Study of Characterization in the Fiction of Graham Greene," *DAI* 39 (1979): 4937A.

Harwood, Ronald, "Time and the Novelist: Graham Greene Interviewed," *Listener* 94 (Dec. 4, 1975): 747, 749.

Herling, Gustav, "Two Sanctities: Greene and Camus," *Adam* No. 201 (Dec., 1949): 10-18.

Hesla, David H., "Theological Ambiguity in the 'Catholic Novels'," in Evans, R. O., ed., *Graham Greene*, 96-111.

Hindman, Kathleen B., "The Ambiance of Graham Greene's Fiction: The Functions of Milieu in His Novels," *DAI* 41 (1980): 2122A.

Hortmann, Wilhelm, "Graham Greene: The Burnt-Out Catholic," *TCL* 10 (July, 1964): 64-76.

Houle, Sister Sheila, B. V. M., "The Subjective Theological Vision of Graham Greene," *Ren* 23, i (Autumn, 1970): 3-13.

Hughes, Catharine, "Innocence Revisited," *Ren* 12 (Autumn, 1959): 29-34.

Hynes, S., ed., *Graham Greene*.

Ingersoll, Earl G., "Imagery in the Novels of Graham Greene," *DAI* 32 (1971): 3308A (Wis., Madison).

Jacobsen, Josephine, "A Catholic Quartet," *ChS* 47 (Summer, 1964): 143-6.

Jerrold, Douglas, "Graham Greene, Pleasure-Hater," *Harper's* 205 (Aug., 1952): 50-2.

Joannon, Pierce, "Graham Greene's Other Island," *EI* 6 (Dec., 1981): 157-69. [Interview.]

Johnston, J. L., "Graham Greene—The Unhappy Man," *The Central Literary Magazine* (Birmingham) 38 (July, 1954): 43-9. [Not seen.]

Johnston, Stuart, "People Caught Up by Love: The Novels of Graham Greene," in Yule, R. M., ed., *From Dante to Solzhenitsyn*, 191-207.

Jones, Grahame C., "Graham Greene and the Legend of Péguy," *CL* 21, ii (Spring, 1969): 138-45.

Jones, James L., "Graham Greene and the Structure of Moral Imagination," *PhoenixC* No. 2 (1966): 34-56. [Not seen.]

Joselyn, Sister M., O.S.B., "Graham Greene's Novels: The Conscience in the World," in Slote, Bernice, ed., *Literature and Society: Nineteen Essays by Germaine Brée and Others*, Lincoln: Un. of Neb. Pr., 1964, 153-72.

Karl, F. R., "Graham Greene's Demoniacal Heroes," *Contemporary English Novel*, 85-106.

Keegan, Maureen T., S.C.M.M., "The Man-God Relationship: A Comparative Study of the Fiction of Rabindranath Tagore and Graham Greene," *DAI* 34 (1974): 7324A (Catholic U.).

Kelleher, James P., "The Orthodoxy and Values of Graham Greene," *DA* 27 (1966): 1825A (Boston Un.).

Kellogg, G., *Vital Tradition*, 111-36.

Kenny, Herbert A., "Graham Greene," *CathW* 185 (Aug., 1957): 326-9.

Kermode, Frank, "The House of Fiction: Interviews with Seven English Novelists," *PR* 30 (Spring, 1963): 65-8.

————, *Puzzles and Epiphanies*, 182-7.

Khawaja, Mabel M., "Graham Greene: Design of Irony and the Role of the Female," *DAI* 40 (1980): 6271A.

Knipp, Thomas R., "Gide and Greene: Africa and the Literary Imagination," *Serif* 6, ii (June, 1969): 3-14.

Koga, H., *Essays on Graham Greene and His Work*.

Kohn, L., *Graham Greene*.

Korn, Frederick B., "'Condemned to Consequences': A Study of Tragic Process in Three Works by Joseph Conrad and Graham Greene," *DAI* 34 (1974): 5977A (Ill., Urbana-Champaign).

Kort, Wesley, "The Obsession of Graham Greene," *Thought* 45 (Spring, 1970): 20-44.

Kunkel, F. L., *Labyrinthine Ways of Graham Greene*.

————, "The Theme of Sin and Grace in Graham Greene," in Evans, R. O., ed., *Graham Greene*, 49-60. Also, as "Greene's Catholic Themes," in Kunkel, F. L., *Labyrinthine Ways of Graham Greene*.

La Chance, Paul R., "Man and Religion in the Novels of William Golding and Graham Greene," *DAI* 31 (1971): 6062A (Kent State).

Lanina, T., "Paradoxes of Graham Greene," *Inostrannaja Literatura* No. 3 (Mar., 1959): 188-96.

Lauder, Robert E., "The Catholic Novel and the 'Insider God'," *Cweal* 101 (Oct. 25, 1974): 78-81.

Lees, F. N., "Graham Greene: A Comment," *Scrutiny* 19 (Oct., 1952): 31-42.

Lerner, Laurence, "Graham Greene," *CritQ* 5 (Autumn, 1963): 217-31.

Lewis, R. W. B., "The Fiction of Graham Greene: Between the Horror and the Glory," *KR* 19 (Winter, 1957): 56-75.

————, "The 'Trilogy' of Graham Greene," *MFS* 3 (Autumn, 1957): 195-215. Also in Lewis, R. W. B., *Picaresque Saint*, 239-64. Also in Cargas, H. J., ed., *Graham Greene*, 45-74. Also in Hynes, S., ed., *Graham Greene*, 49-74.

Lodge, D., "Graham Greene," in Stade, G., ed., *Six Contemporary British Novelists*, 1-55. Originally pub. as Lodge, D., *Graham Greene*. Also in Lodge, D., *Novelist at the Crossroads*, 89-118.

Lohf, Kenneth A., "Graham Greene and the Problem of Evil," *CathW* 173 (June, 1951): 196-9.

MacDonald, Sara J., "The Aesthetics of Grace in Flannery O'Connor and Graham Greene," *DAI* 33 (1973): 5734A (Ill., Urbana-Champaign).

MacSween, R. J., "Exiled from the Garden: Graham Greene," *AntigR* 1, ii (Summer, 1970): 41-8.

Majid, S. H., "The Existential Concern in Graham Greene," *IJES* 12 (Dec., 1971): 75-85.

Manly, Jane B., "Graham Greene: The Insanity of Innocence," *DAI* 30 (1970): 3016A (Conn.).

Markovic, Vida E., "Graham Greene in Search of God," *TSLL* 5 (Summer, 1963): 271-82.

Marshall, Bruce, "Graham Greene and Evelyn Waugh," *Cweal* 51 (Mar. 3, 1950): 551-3.

Maurois, A., *Points of View from Kipling to Graham Greene*, 384-409.

McCann, Janet, "Graham Greene: The Ambiguity of Death," *ChrC* (April 30, 1975): 432-5.

————, "Names and Identity in Graham Greene's Novels," *Cresset* 41, vi (April, 1978): 3-6.

McDonald, James L., "Graham Greene: A Reconsideration," *ArQ* 27, iii (Autumn, 1971): 197-210.

McInery, Ralph, "The Greene-ing of America," *Cweal* 95 (Oct. 15, 1971): 59-61.

Merivale, Patricia, "Through Greene-Land in Drag: Joan Didion's A BOOK OF COMMON PRAYER," *PCP* 15 (Oct., 1980): 45-52.

Mesnet, Marie-Béatrice, "Graham Greene (1904-)," in Panichas, G. A., ed., *Politics of Twentieth Century Novelists*, 100-23.

————, *Graham Greene and The Heart of the Matter*.

Miller, J. D. B., "Graham Greene," *Meanjin* 5 (Spring, 1946): 193-7.

Monroe, N. Elizabeth, "The New Man in Fiction," *Ren* 6 (Aug., 1953): 9-12.

Moore, Karen R., "The Comic Technique of Graham Greene," *DAI* 36 (1976): 5322A-23A.

Morrison, Patrick J., "The Quest Motif in the Fiction of Graham Greene," *DAI* 38 (1978): 5464A.

Mortimer, John, "The Master is Still Learning," *Critic* 39, i (July, 1980): 4-6. [Interview.]

Mosley, Nicholas, "A New Puritanism," *The European* No. 3 (May, 1953): 28-35, 38-40. (Reply to article by Neame, A. J.).

Muller, Charles H., "Graham Greene and the Absurd," *UES* 10, ii (1972): 34-44.

Murray, Edward, "Graham Greene and the Silver Screen," *Cinematic Imagination*, 244-60.

Murray, Emilie C., "Romantic Visions in an Absurd World: The Early Novels of Graham Greene and Albert Camus," *DAI* 40 (1980): 5433A.

Neame, A. J., "Black and Blue: A Study of the Catholic Novel," *The European* No. 2 (April, 1953): 26-30, 36.

Ngara, E., "Graham Greene and Twentieth-Century Pessimism," *Opus* 2 (1969): 17-21. [Not seen.]

O'Donnell, Donat, "Graham Greene," *Chimera* 5 (Summer, 1947): 18-30.

O'Faolain, S., *Vanishing Hero*, 45-72.

O'Grady, Walter A., "Political Contexts in the Novels of Graham Greene and Joyce Cary," *DAI* 32 (1972): 6955A (Toronto).

Ogude, S. E., "Graham Greene's Africa," *Odù* 14 (July, 1975): 41-65.

_____, "In Search of Misery: A Study of Graham Greene's Travels in Africa," *Odù* 11 (Jan., 1975): 45-60.

Osterman, Robert, "Interview with Graham Greene," *CathW* 170 (Feb., 1950): 356-61.

Peters, W., "The Concern of Graham Greene," *Month* 10 (Nov., 1953): 281-90.

Phillips, Gene D., S. J., *Graham Greene: The Films of His Fiction*, N.Y. and London: Teachers College Pr. of Columbia Un., 1974.

_____, "Graham Greene: On the Screen," *CathW* 209 (Aug., 1969): 218-21. Also in Hynes, S., ed., *Graham Greene*, 168-75.

_____, "Graham Greene Interview," *TC* 25 (Summer, 1970): 111-17.

Poole, Roger C., "Graham Greene's Indirection," *Blackfriars* 45 (June, 1964): 257-68. Also in Cargas, H. J., ed., *Graham Greene*, 29-44.

Prescott, O., *In My Opinion*, 106-9.

Pritchett, V., "The Human Factor in Graham Greene," *NYTM* (Feb. 26, 1978): 33-46.

Pryce-Jones, D., *Graham Greene*.

Puentevella, Ranato, "Ambiguity in Greene," *Ren* 12 (1959): 35-7.

Rao, V. V. B. Rama, "The Creative Artist's Vision in Graham Greene's Novels," *Triveni* 45, ii (July-Sept., 1976): 55-62.

_____, "Graham Greene and the Burden of Childhood," *LHY* 19, ii (1978): 50-62.

_____, "The Significane of Epigraphs in Graham Greene's Works," *JES* 10, i (1978): 633-48.

Rolo, Charlie J., "Graham Greene: The Man and the Message," *Atlantic* 207 (May, 1961): 60-5.

Rosenkranz, Joel H., "Graham Greene's Travel Writings: Sources of His Fiction," *DAI* 39 (1978): 2262A.

Savage, D. S., "Graham Greene and Belief," *DR* 58, ii (Summer, 1978): 205-29.

Scott, Carolyn D., "The Urban Romance: A Study of Graham Greene's Thrillers," in Cargas, H. J., ed., *Graham Greene*, 1-28.

Scott, N. A., Jr., "Graham Greene: Christian Tragedian," *Volusia Review* 1, i (1954): 29-42. Also (expanded and revised) in Scott, N. A., Jr., *Craters of the Spirit*, 201-32. Also in Evans, R. O., ed., *Graham Greene*, 25-48.

Sewall, Elizabeth, "Graham Greene," *DubR* No. 463 (First Quarter, 1954): 12-21.

_____, "The Imagination of Graham Greene," *Thought* 29 (Mar., 1954): 51-60.

Seward, Barbara, "Graham Greene: A Hint of an Explanation," *WR* 22 (Winter, 1958): 83-95.

Shuttleworth, Martin, and Simon Raven, "The Art of Fiction III: Graham Greene," *ParisR* 1 (Autumn, 1953): 24-41. Also in Hynes, S., ed., *Graham Greene*, 154-67.

Skerrett, Joseph T., Jr., "Graham Greene at the Movies: A Novelists' Experience with Film," *LFQ* 2, iv (Fall, 1974): 293-301. [Not seen.]

Slate, Audrey N., "Technique and Form in the Novels of Graham Greene," *DA* 21 (1960): 629-30.

Smith, A. J. M., "Graham Greene's Theological Thrillers," *QQ* 68 (Spring, 1961): 15-33.

Snape, Ray, "The Political Novels of Graham Greene," *DUJ* 75, i (Dec., 1982): 73-81.

Stenberg, Carl E., "The Quest for Justice in the Fiction of Graham Greene," *DAI* 30 (1970): 3024A (Conn.).

Sternlicht, Sanford, "Prologue to the Sad Comedies: Graham Greene's Major Early Novels," *MQ* 12, iv (July, 1971): 427-35.

_____, "The Sad Comedies: Graham Greene's Later Novels," *FloQ* 1, iv (1968): 65-77.

Stratford, P., *Faith and Fiction*.

_____, "Graham Greene: Master of Melodrama," *TamR* No. 19 (Spring, 1961): 67-86.

Tracy, Honor, "The Life and Soul of the Party," *NRep* 140 (April 20, 1959): 15-16. Also in Harrison, G. A., ed., *Critic as Artist*, 315-20.

Traversi, Derek, "Graham Greene," *TC* 149 (Mar., 1951): 231-40, 319-28. Also, partly, in Hynes, S., ed., *Graham Greene*, 17-29.

Trifu, Sever, "Language and Style in Graham Greene's Novels," *SUBBP* 20 (1975): 57-70.

Turnell, M., *Graham Greene*.

_____, "Graham Greene: The Man Within," *Ramparts* 4 (June, 1965): 54-64.

_____, "The Religious Novel," *Cweal* 55 (Oct. 26, 1951): 55-7.

Vilangiyil, Sebastian O., "The Demonic Heroes of Graham Greene," *SLRJ* 4, ii (June, 1973): 201-11.

Voorhees, Richard J., "Recent Greene," *SAQ* 62 (Spring, 1963): 244-55.

_____, "The World of Graham Greene," *SAQ* 50 (July, 1951): 389-98.

Wassmer, Thomas A., "Graham Greene: A Look at His Sinners," *Critic* 18 (Dec., 1959-Jan., 1960): 16-17, 72-4.

_____, "The Problem and the Mystery of Sin in the World of Graham Greene," *ChS* 43 (Winter, 1960): 309-15.

_____, "The Sinners of Graham Greene," *DR* 39 (Autumn, 1959): 326-32.

Webster, Harvey C., in Evans, R. O., ed., *Graham Greene*, 1-24.

_____, "Graham Greene: Stoical Catholic," *After the Trauma*, 97-123.

Weseliski, Andrzej, "Graham Greene's Early Work: The Fantasy of Romantic Adventure," *KN* 29, iii-iv (1982): 253-63.

_____, "Similes in the Novels of Graham Greene," *KN* 25, iv (1978): 454-62.

West, Paul, "Knowing the Worst: Graham Greene," *The Wine of Absurdity*, University Park and London: Penn. St. Un. Pr., 1966, 174-85.

Wilshere, A. D., "Conflict and Conciliation in Graham Greene," *E&S* 19 (1966): 122-37.

Wilson, C., *Strength to Dream*, 46-55.

Wolfe, P., *Graham Greene*.

_____, "Graham Greene and the Art of Entertainment," *STwC* No. 6 (Fall, 1970): 35-61.

Woodcock, G., *Writer and Politics*, 125-53.

Woodward, Anthony, "Graham Greene: The War Against Boredom," in Roberts, G., *Seven Studies in English*, 64-105.

Wyndham, F., *Graham Greene*.

Zabel, Morton D., "Graham Greene," *Nation* 157 (July 3, 1943): 18-20. Also in Aldridge, J. W., ed., *Critiques and Essays in Modern Fiction*, 518-25. Also in O'Connor, W. V., ed., *Forms of Modern Fiction*, 287-93. Also, revised and expanded, in Zabel, M. D., *Craft and Character*, 276-96. Also in Hynes, S., ed., *Graham Greene*, 30-48.

BRIGHTON ROCK

Allen, W., *Modern Novel*, 204-5.

Allott, K., and M. Farris, *Art of Graham Greene*, 147-60.

Atkins, J., *Graham Greene*, 88-101.

Boardman, G. R., *Graham Greene*, 41-50.

Braybrooke, Neville, "Graham Greene: A Pioneer Novelist," *CE* 12 (Oct., 1950): 4-6.

Clancy, L. J., "Graham Greene's Battlefield," *CritR* 10 (1967): 99-101.

Consolo, Dominick P., "Graham Greene: Style and Stylistics in Five Novels," in Evans, R. O., ed., *Graham Greene*, 68-74.

––––––––, "Music as Motif: The Unity of BRIGHTON ROCK," *Ren* 15 (Fall, 1962): 12-20. Also in Cargas, H. J., ed., *Graham Greene*, 75-87.

Cox, Gerard H., III, "Graham Greene's Mystical Rose in Brighton," *Ren* 23, i (Autumn, 1970): 213-30.

Currie, John S., "Supernaturalism in Graham Greene: A Comparison of Orthodox Catholicism and Religious Vision in the Major Novels," *DA* 28 (1968): 3176A-77A (Alabama).

De Vitis, A. A., "Allegory in BRIGHTON ROCK," *MFS* 3 (Autumn, 1957): 216-24.

––––––––, *Graham Greene*, 56-9, 80-7.

––––––––, "Religious Aspects in the Novels of Graham Greene," in Mooney, H. J., Jr., and T. F. Staley, eds., *Shapeless God*, 42-4.

Eagleton, T., *Exiles and Émigrés*, 131-5.

Ellis, William D., Jr., "The Grand Theme of Graham Greene," *SWR* 41 (Summer, 1956): 245-50.

Evans, Robert O., "The Satanist Fallacy of BRIGHTON ROCK," in Evans, R. O., ed., *Graham Greene*, 78-85.

Glicksberg, Charles I., "Graham Greene: Catholicism in Fiction," *Criticism* 1 (Fall, 1959): 342-3.

Haber, Herbert R., "The Two Worlds of Graham Greene," *MFS* 3 (Autumn, 1957): 257-64.

Hall, J., *Lunatic Giant in the Drawing Room*, 115-16.

Hoskins, Robert, "Hale, Pinkie, and the Pentecost Theme in BRIGHTON ROCK," *MBL* 3, i (1978): 56-66.

Johnston, Stuart, "People Caught Up By Love: The Novels of Graham Greene," in Yule, R. M., *From Dante to Solzhenitsyn*, 195-7.

Kaplan, Carola, "Graham Greene's Pinkie Brown and Flannery O'Connor's Misfit: The Psychopathic Killer and the Mystery of God's Grace," *Ren* 32, ii (1980): 116-28.

Karl, F. R., "Graham Greene's Demoniacal Heroes," *Contemporary English Novel*, 93-5.

Kellogg, G., *Vital Tradition*, 117-22.

King, James, "In the Lost Boyhood of Judas: Graham Greene's Early Novels of Hell," *DR* 49, ii (Summer, 1969): 228-36.

Kohn, L., *Graham Greene*, 2-10.

Kubal, David L., "Graham Greene's BRIGHTON ROCK: The Political Theme," *Ren* 23, i (Autumn, 1970): 46-54.

Kulshrestha, J. P., *Graham Greene*, 56-73.

Kunkel, F. L., *Labyrinthine Ways of Graham Greene*, 106-12.

Lenfest, David S., "BRIGHTON ROCK/YOUNG SCARFACE," *LFQ* 2, iv (Fall, 1974): 373-8.

Lewis, R. W. B., "The 'Trilogy' of Graham Greene," *MFS* 3 (Autumn, 1957): 198-203. Also in Lewis, R. W. B., *Picaresque Saint*, 242-8. Also in Cargas, H. J., ed., *Graham Greene*, 49-56. Also in Hynes, S., *Graham Greene*, 52-9.

Lodge, D., "Graham Greene," in Stade, G., ed., *Six Contemporary British Novelists*, 20-3. Originally in Lodge, D., *Graham Greene*, 20-3. Also in Lodge, D., *Novelist at the Crossroads*, 99-102.

Marian, Sister I. H. M., "Graham Greene's People: Becoming and Becoming," *Ren* 18 (Autumn, 1965): 17-18.

Maurois, A., *Points of View from Kipling to Graham Greene*, 386-7.

McCall, Dan, "BRIGHTON ROCK: The Price of Order," *ELN* 3 (June, 1966): 290-4.

McCann, Janet, "Names and Identity in Graham Greene's Novels," *Cresset* 41, vi (April, 1978): 4-5.

McGowan, F. A., "Symbolism in BRIGHTON ROCK," *Ren* 8 (1955): 25-35.

Mesnet, M. B., *Graham Greene*, 13-19, 48-55, 84-6 *passim*.

Muller, Charles H., "Graham Greene and the Justification of God's Ways," *UES* 10, i (1972): 23-35.

O'Donnell, Donat, "Graham Greene," *Chimera* 5 (Summer, 1947): 23-5.

Price, A., *BRIGHTON ROCK* (Graham Greene), Oxford: Blackwell, 1969. (Notes on English Literature, 40).

Pryce-Jones, D., *Graham Greene*, 29-38.

Ruotolo, Lucio P., "BRIGHTON ROCK's Absurd Heroine," *MLQ* 25 (Dec., 1964): 425-33.

––––––––, *Six Existential Heroes*, 39-53.

Scott, Nathan A., Jr., "Graham Greene: Christian Tragedian," *The Volusia Review* 1, i (1954). Also, revised, in Evans, R. O., ed., *Graham Greene*, 32-5. Also in Scott, N., Jr., *Craters of the Spirit*, 208-11.

Smith, A. J. M., "Graham Greene's Theological Thrillers," *QQ* 68 (Spring, 1961): 18-22.

Sonnenfeld, Albert, "Children's Faces: Graham Greene," in Friedman, M. J., ed., *Vision Obscured*, 109-20.

Stephens, Martha, "Flannery O'Connor and the Sanctified-Sinner Tradition," *ArQ* 23 (Winter, 1967): 229-31.

Stewart, Douglas, *Ark of God*, 72-81.

Stratford, Philip, "Graham Greene: Master of Melodrama," *TamR* No. 19 (1961): 71-6.

Traversi, Derek, "Graham Greene," *TC* 149 (Mar., 1951): 237-40. Also in Hynes, S., ed., *Graham Greene*, 25-9.

Turnell, M., *Graham Greene*, 15-22.

Wilshere, A. D., "Conflict and Conciliation in Graham Greene," in English Association, *Essays and Studies, 1966*, 124-8.

Wilson, C., *Strength to Dream*, 53-4.

Wyndham, F., *Graham Greene*, 13-14.

A BURNT-OUT CASE

Atkins, J., *Graham Greene*, 245-9.

Boardman, G. R., *Graham Greene*, 137-58.

De Vitis, A. A., *Graham Greene*, 120-5.

Dooley, F. J., "A BURNT-OUT CASE Reconsidered," *WiseR* 237 (Summer, 1963): 168-78.

––––––––, "The Suspension of Disbelief: Greene's BURNT-OUT CASE," *DR* 43 (Autumn, 1963): 343-52.

Eagleton, T., *Exiles and Émigrés*, 121-5.

Hanlon, Robert M., S. J., "The Ascent to Belief in Graham
Greene's A BURNT-OUT CASE," *C&L* 26, iv (Summer,
1977): 20-6.

Hardwick, E., *A View of My Own*, 96-102. Also in *PR* 28 Nos. 5-6
(1961): 702-7.

Hess, M. W., "Graham Greene's Travesty on THE RING AND
THE BOOK," *CathW* 194 (Oct., 1961): 37-42.

Higdon, David L., "The Texts of Graham Greene's A BURNT-
OUT CASE," *PBSA* 73 (July, 1979): 357-64.

Hughes, R. E., *WSCL* 2, i (Winter, 1961): 117-18.

Jarrett-Kerr, Martin, "The 491 Pitfalls of the Christian Artist," in
Scott, Nathan A., Jr., ed., *The Climate of Faith in Modern
Literature*, N.Y.: Seabury Pr., 1964, 195-7.

Kelly, Edward E., "Absurdity but Faith with Suffering in
Greene's BURNT-OUT CASE," *Greyfriar* 21 (1980): 29-34.

Kermode, Frank, "Mr. Greene's Eggs and Crosses," *Encounter*
16 (April, 1961): 69-75. Also in Kermode, F., *Puzzles and
Epiphanies*, 176-82. Also in Hynes, S., ed., *Graham Greene*,
126-37.

Koga, H., *Essays on Graham Greene and His Work*, 23-41.

Kulshrestha, J. P., *Graham Greene*, 131-41.

Lodge, D., "Graham Greene," in Stade, G., *Six Contemporary
British Novelists*, 41-5. Originally in Lodge, D., *Graham Greene*,
39-42. Also in Lodge, D., *Novelist at the Crossroads*, 114-16.

Marian, Sister I. H. M., "Graham Greene's People: Becoming
and Becoming," *Ren* 18 (Autumn, 1959): 20-2.

Meyers, Jeffrey, "Graham Greene: The Decline of the Colonial
Novel," *Fiction and the Colonial Experience*, 99-101, 108-15.

Milner, Ian, "Values and Irony in Graham Greene," *AUCP* 14
(1971): 65-7.

Noxon, James, "Kierkegaard's Stages and A BURNT-OUT
CASE," *REL* 3 (Jan., 1962): 90-101.

O'Brien, C. C., "Our Men in Africa," *Maria Cross*, 252-6.

Palfrey, J., "Reading Graham Greene, A BURNT-OUT CASE,"
Univ. Voices/Voix Univ. (Brazzaville) 1 (1976): 26-31.

Poole, Roger, "'Those Sad Arguments': Two Novels of Graham
Greene," *RMS* 13 (1969): 148-60.

Pryce-Jones, D., *Graham Greene*, 93-7.

Sackville-West, Edward, "Time-Bomb," *Month* 25 (1961): 175-8.

Scott, N. A., Jr., "Graham Greene: Christian Tragedian," *Craters
of the Spirit*, 229-31.

Shor, Ira N., "Greene's Later Humanism: A BURNT-OUT
CASE," *LitR* 16, iv (Summer, 1973): 397-411.

Simon, John K., "Off the *Voie royale*: The Failure of Greene's A
BURNT-OUT CASE," *Sym* 18 (Summer, 1964): 163-9.

Smith, Francis J., "The Anatomy of a BURNT-OUT CASE,"
America (Sept. 9, 1961): 711-12.

Sternlicht, Sanford, "The Sad Comedies: Graham Greene's
Later Novels," *FloQ* 1, iv (1968): 70-2.

_____, "Two Views of the Builder in Graham Greene's A
BURNT-OUT CASE and William Golding's THE SPIRE,"
CalR n.s. 1, iii (Jan.-Mar., 1970): 401-4. Also in *SHum* 2, i
(Fall-Winter, 1970-71): 17-19.

Stratford, Philip, "Chalk and Cheese: A Comparative Study of
A KISS FOR THE LEPER and A BURNT-OUT CASE," *UTQ*
3 (1964): 200-18. Also, revised, in Stratford, P., *Faith and
Fiction*, 1-30, 328-9.

Turnell, M., *Graham Greene*, 32-4.

Van Kaam, Adrian, and Kathleen Healy, "Querry in Greene's
A BURNT-OUT CASE," *The Demon and the Dove: Personality
Growth Through Literature*, Duquesne Un. Pr., 1967, 259-85.

Voorhees, Richard J., "Recent Greene," *SAQ* 62 (Spring, 1963):
252-5.

THE COMEDIANS

Allen, Walter, *LonM* n.s. 5 (Mar., 1966): 73-80.

Bedford, Sybille, "Tragic Comedians," *NYRB* 6 (Mar. 3, 1966):
25-7.

Boardman, G. R., *Graham Greene*, 170-3.

Choudhury, M. K., "The Significance of Caricature in Graham
Greene's THE COMEDIANS," *PURBA* 5, ii (1974): 51-6.

De Vitis, A. A., "Greene's THE COMEDIANS: Hollower Men,"
Ren 18 (1966): 129-36, 146. Also in Mooney, H. J., Jr., and T.
F. Staley, eds., *Shapeless God*, 57-65.

Kennedy, A., *Protean Self*, 237-42.

Kulshrestha, J. P., *Graham Greene*, 159-68.

Lodge, D., "Graham Greene," in Stade, G., ed., *Six Contemporary
British Novelists*, 45-8. Originally in Lodge, D., *Graham Greene*,
42-5. Also in Lodge, D., *Novelist at the Crossroads*, 116-18.

_____, "Graham Greene's Comedian," *Cweal* 83 (Feb. 25,
1966): 604-6.

Mahood, M. M., "The Possessed: Greene's THE COMEDIANS,"
Colonial Encounter, 115-41.

Mayhew, Alice, "THE COMEDIANS," *Nat. Catholic Reporter*
(Mar. 30, 1966). Also in Cargas, H. J., ed., *Graham Greene*,
134-41.

McCann, Janet, "Names and Identity in Graham Greene's Novels," *Cresset* 41, vi (April, 1978): 3-6.

Pritchett, V. S., "Brown's Hotel, Haiti," *NStat* (Jan. 28, 1966): 129.

Routh, Michael, "Greene's Parody of Farce and Comedy in THE
COMEDIANS," *Ren* 26, iii (Spring, 1974): 139-51.

Snape, Ray, "The Political Novels of Graham Greene," *DUJ* 75,
i (Dec., 1982): 79-81.

Sternlicht, Sanford, "The Sad Comedies: Graham Greene's
Later Novels," *FloQ* 1, iv (1968): 72-7.

Turnell, M., *Graham Greene*, 34-7.

THE CONFIDENTIAL AGENT

Allott, K., and M. Farris, *Art of Graham Greene*, 139-47.

Atkins, J., *Graham Greene*, 102-9.

De Vitis, A. A., *Graham Greene*, 59-61.

Karl, F. R., "Graham Greene's Demoniacal Heroes," *Contemporary English Novel*, 88-9.

Kulshrestha, J. P., *Graham Greene*, 193-9.

Kunkel, F. L., *Labyrinthine Ways of Graham Greene*, 66-8.

Lodge, D., *Graham Greene*, 16-17. Also in Stade, G., ed., *Six
Contemporary British Novelists*, 15-17.

Pryce-Jones, D., *Graham Greene*, 64-6.

Wolfe, P., *Graham Greene*, 80-100.

THE END OF THE AFFAIR

Allen, W., *Modern Novel*, 206-7.

Anon., "Shocker," *Time* 58 (Oct. 29, 1951): 98-9.

Arnold, G. L., "Adam's Tree," *TC* 154 (Oct., 1951): 337-42.

Atkins, J., *Graham Greene*, 193-203.

Boardman, G. R., *Graham Greene*, 90-6.

Bogan, Louise, "Good Beyond Evil," *NRep* 125 (Dec. 10, 1951):
29-30.

Boyle, Alexander, "Symbolism of Graham Greene," *IrM* 80
(1952): 98-102.

Braybrooke, Neville, "Graham Greene and the Double Man: An Approach to THE END OF THE AFFAIR," *DubR* No. 455 (1st Quarter, 1952): 61-73. Also in Cargas, H. J., ed., *Graham Greene*, 114-29. Also in *QQ* 77, i (Spring, 1970): 29-39.

Clancy, L. J., "Graham Greene's Battlefield," *CritR* 10 (1967): 105-8.

Consolo, Dominick P., "Graham Greene: Style and Stylistics in Five Novels," in Evans, R. O., ed., *Graham Greene*, 87-91.

Currie, John S., "Supernaturalism in Graham Greene: A Comparison of Orthodox Catholicism with Religious Vision in the Major Novels," *DA* 27 (1968): 3176A-77A (Alabama).

De Vitis, A. A., *Graham Greene*, 104-16.

_____, "Religious Aspects in the Novels of Graham Greene," in Mooney, H. J., Jr., and T. F. Staley, eds., *Shapeless God*, 51-5.

Eagleton, T., *Exiles and Émigrés*, 119-21.

Gardiner, H. C., "Mr. Greene Does It Again," *In All Conscience*, 96-8. Also in *America* 86 (Oct. 27, 1951): 100-1.

_____, "Second Thoughts on Greene's Latest," *In All Conscience*, 98-102. Also in *America* 86 (Dec. 15, 1951): 312-13.

Glicksberg, Charles I., "Graham Greene: Catholicism in Fiction," *Criticism* 1 (Fall, 1959): 349-50.

Graef, H., *Modern Gloom and Christian Hope*, 93-6.

Gregor, Ian, and Brian Nicholas, "Grace and Morality: 'THÉRÈSE DESQUEYROUX' (1927); THE END OF THE AFFAIR (1951)," in *The Moral and the Story*, London: Faber and Faber, 1962, 185-216. Also in Hynes, S., ed., *Graham Greene*, 110-25.

Haber, Herbert R., "The End of the Catholic Cycle: The Writer Versus the Saint," in Evans, R. O., ed., *Graham Greene*, 127-50.

Hartt, J. M., *Lost Image of Man*, 117-18.

Higdon, David L., "'Betrayed Intentions': Graham Greene's THE END OF THE AFFAIR," *Library* 1 (1979): 70-7.

_____, "Saint Catherine, Von Hügel28714, and Graham Greene's THE END OF THE AFFAIR," *ES* 62, i (Jan., 1981): 46-52.

Hoskins, Robert, "Through a Glass Darkly: Mirrors in THE END OF THE AFFAIR," *NConL* 9, iii (1979): 3-5.

Isaacs, Rita, "Three Levels of Allegory in Graham Greene's THE END OF THE AFFAIR," *LNL* 1, i (1975): 29-52.

Kohn, L., *Graham Greene*, 22-31.

Kulshrestha, J. P., *Graham Greene*, 113-31.

Kunkel, F. L., *Labyrinthine Ways of Graham Greene*, 128-32.

Lees, F. N., "Graham Greene: A Comment," *Scrutiny* 19 (Oct., 1952): 40-2.

Lewis, R. W. B., *Picaresque Saint*, 268-70.

Lictheim, George, "Adam's Tree," *TC* 154 (Oct., 1951): 337-42. Also in Lictheim, G., *Collected Essays*, 477-82.

Lodge, D., "Graham Greene," in Stade, G., ed., *Six Contemporary British Novelists*, 33-7. Originally in Lodge, D., *Graham Greene*, 31-5. Also in Lodge, D., *Novelist at the Crossroads*, 108-11.

_____, "The Use of Key-Words in the Novels of Graham Greene—Love, Hate, and THE END OF THE AFFAIR," *Blackfriars* 42 (Nov., 1961): 468-74.

Mass, Roslyn, "The Presentation of the Character of Sarah Miles in the Film Version of THE END OF THE AFFAIR," *LFQ* 2, iv (Fall, 1974): 347-51.

Pake, Lucy S., "Courtly Love in Our Own Time: Graham Greene's THE END OF THE AFFAIR," *LJHum* 8, ii (Fall, 1982): 36-43.

Poole, Roger C., "Graham Greene's Indirection," *Blackfriars* 45 (June, 1964): 260-4. Also in Cargas, H. J., ed., *Graham Greene*, 33-8.

Pryce-Jones, D., *Graham Greene*, 82-8.

Schwab, Gweneth, "Graham Greene's Pursuit of God," *BuR* 26, ii (1982): 45-57.

Scott, Nathan A., Jr., "Graham Greene: Christian Tragedian," *The Volusia Review* 1, i (1954). Also, revised, in Evans, R. O., ed., *Graham Greene*, 41-7. Also in Scott, N. A., Jr., *Craters of the Spirit*, 217-23.

Smith, A. J. M., "Graham Greene's Theological Thrillers," *QQ* 68 (Spring, 1961): 28-30.

Snape, Ray, "Plaster Saints, Flesh and Blood Sinners: Graham Greene's THE END OF THE AFFAIR," *DUJ* 74, ii (June, 1982): 241-50.

Spier, Ursula, "Melodrama in Graham Greene's THE END OF THE AFFAIR," *MFS* 3 (Autumn, 1957): 235-40.

Sternlicht, Sanford, "The Sad Comedies: Graham Greene's Later Novels," *FloQ* 1, iv (1968): 65-6.

Stewart, Douglas, *Ark of God*, 87-90.

Wansbrough, John, "Graham Greene: The Detective in the Wasteland," *HarvardA* 136 (Dec., 1962): 11-13, 29-31.

Waugh, Evelyn, *Month* 6 (Sept., 1951): 174-6.

West, A., *Principles and Persuasions*, 195-200.

ENGLAND MADE ME (THE SHIPWRECKED)

Allott, K., and M. Farris, *Art of Graham Greene*, 100-17.

Atkins, J., *Graham Greene*, 50-7.

De Vitis, A. A., *Graham Greene*, 75-9.

Fraser, G. S., *Modern Writer and His World*, 135-6.

Keyser, Les, "ENGLAND MADE ME," *LFQ* 2, iv (Fall, 1974): 364-72.

Kulshrestha, J. P., *Graham Greene*, 43-55.

Kunkel, F. L., *Labyrinthine Ways of Graham Greene*, 43-56.

Lewis, R. W. B., "The Fiction of Graham Greene: Between the Horror and the Glory," *KR* 19 (Winter, 1957): 62-5.

_____, *Picaresquue Saint*, 228-34.

Lodge, D., "Graham Greene," in Stade, G., *Six Contemporary British Novelists*, 18-19. Originally in Lodge, D., *Graham Greene*, 18-19. Also in Lodge, D., *Novelist at the Crossroads*, 98.

Pryce-Jones, D., *Graham Greene*, 22-8.

Scott, N. A., Jr., "Graham Greene: Christian Tragedian," *Craters of the Spirit*, 205-7.

Stratford, P., *Faith and Fiction*, 132-7.

Traversi, Derek, "Graham Greene," *TC* 149 (Mar., 1951): 233-7. Also in Hynes, S., ed., *Graham Greene*, 20-5.

THE HEART OF THE MATTER

Allen, W. Gore, "Evelyn Waugh and Graham Greene," *IrM* 87 (Jan., 1949): 18-19.

Allott, K., and M. Farris, *Art of Graham Greene*, 214-44.

Atkins, J., *Graham Greene*, 159-67.

Barratt, Harold, "Adultery as Betrayal in Graham Greene," *DR* 45 (Autumn, 1965): 324-32.

Boardman, G. R., *Graham Greene*, 83-90.

Braybrooke, Neville, "Graham Greene, a Pioneer Novelist," *CE* 12 (Oct., 1950): 7-8.

Cartmell, Canon Joseph, "A Postscript to Evelyn Waugh," *Cweal* 48 (July 16, 1948): 325-6. Also in Hynes, S., ed., *Graham Greene*, 103-4.

Clancy, L. J., "Graham Greene's Battlefield," *CritR* 10 (1967): 103-5.

Consolo, Dominick P., "Graham Greene: Style and Stylistics in Five Novels," in Evans, R. O., ed., *Graham Greene*, 78-85.

Croft, J. C., "Graham Greene and Africa (JOURNEY WITHOUT MAPS and THE HEART OF THE MATTER)," in Ryan, J. S., ed., *Gleanings from Greeneland*, 70-80.

Currie, John S., "Supernaturalism in Graham Greene: A Comparison of Orthodox Catholicism with Religious Vision in the Major Novels," *DA* 28 (1968): 3176A-77A (Alabama).

De Vitis, A. A., "The Church and Major Scobie," *Ren* 10 (Spring, 1958): 115-20.

————, *Graham Greene*, 97-104.

————, "Religious Aspects in the Novels of Graham Greene," in Mooney, H. J., Jr., and T. F. Staley, eds., *Shapeless God*, 48-51.

Eagleton, T., *Exiles and Émigrés*, 109-12.

Fay, Teresita, and Michael G. Yetman, "Scobie the Just: A Reassessment of THE HEART OF THE MATTER," *Ren* 29 (Spring, 1977): 142-56.

Glicksberg, Charles I., "Graham Greene: Catholicism in Fiction," *Criticism* 1 (Fall, 1959): 347-9.

Gordon, Caroline, "Some Readings and Misreadings," *SR* 61 (July-Sept., 1953): 393-6.

Graef, H., *Modern Gloom and Christian Hope*, 84-5, 89-93.

Haber, Herbert R., "The Two Worlds of Graham Greene," *MFS* 3 (Autumn, 1957): 256-68.

Hall, J., *Lunatic Giant in the Drawing Room*, 119-21.

Hardwick, E., *A View of My Own*, 93-6. Also in *PR* 15 (Aug., 1948): 937-9.

Harkness, Bruce, "Greene's Old-Fashioned Remedy in THE HEART OF THE MATTER," *AN&Q* 20, vii-viii (Mar./April, 1982): 115-16.

Herling, Gustav, "Two Sanctities: Greene and Camus," *Adam* No. 201 (Dec., 1949): 12-16.

Higdon, David L., "Graham Greene's Second Thoughts: The Text of THE HEART OF THE MATTER," *SB* 30 (1977): 249-56.

Howes, Jane, "Out of the Pit," *CathW* 171 (April, 1950): 36-40.

Hynes, Joseph, "The 'Facts' at THE HEART OF THE MATTER," *TSLL* 13, iv (Winter, 1972): 711-26.

Jefferson, Mary E., "THE HEART OF THE MATTER: The Responsible Man," *CarQ* 9 (Summer, 1957): 23-31. Also in Cargas, H. J., ed., *Graham Greene*, 88-100.

Josipovici, Gabriel, "The Heart of the Matter," *Quarto* 5 (1980): 13-14. [Not seen.]

Karnath, David, "Bernanos, Greene, and the Novel of Convention," *ConL* 19, iv (Autumn, 1978): 429-45.

Kelleher, Victor, "THE HEART OF THE MATTER: Graham Greene and the Humanist Dilemma," *UES* 16, i (1978): 32-4.

Kellogg, G., *Vital Tradition*, 127-32.

Kettle, A., *Introduction to the English Novel*, 170-7.

King, Bruce, "Graham Greene's Inferno," *EA* 21 (Jan.-Mar., 1968): 35-51.

Kohn, L., *Graham Greene*, 10-22.

Kulshrestha, J. P., *Graham Greene*, 93-112.

Kunkel, F. L., *Labyrinthine Ways of Graham Greene*, 122-8.

Laitinen, Kai, "The Heart of the Novel: The Turning Point in THE HEART OF THE MATTER," in Evans, R. O., ed., *Graham Greene*, 169-80.

Lees, F. N., "Graham Greene: A Comment," *Scrutiny* 19 (Oct., 1952): 36-40.

Levi, A. W., *Literature, Philosophy, and the Imagination*, 266-8.

Levin, Gerald, "The Rhetoric of Greene's THE HEART OF THE MATTER," *Ren* 23, i (Autumn, 1970): 14-20.

Lewis, R. W. B., "The 'Trilogy' of Graham Greene," *MFS* 3 (Autumn, 1957): 211-15. Also in Lewis, R. W. B., *Picaresque Saint*, 258-64. Also in Cargas, H. J., ed., *Graham Greeen*, 66-72. Also in Hynes, S., ed., *Graham Greene*, 69-74.

Lodge, D., "Graham Greene," in Stade, G., ed., *Six Contemporary British Novelists*, 28-34. Originally in Lodge, D., *Graham Greene*, 27-31. Also in Lodge, D., *Novelist at the Crossroads*, 105-8.

Maini, Irma, "The Theme of Grace in THE HEART OF THE MATTER," *LCrit* 17, iii (1982): 51-9.

Markovi, V. E., *The Changing Face*, 82-96.

Maurois, A., *Points of View from Kipling to Graham Greene*, 393-8.

McGugan, Ruth E., "THE HEART OF THE MATTER," *LFQ* 2, iv (Fall, 1974): 359-63.

Mesnet, M. B., *Graham Greene*, 28-34, 61-8, 86-9, and *passim*.

Meyers, Jeffrey, "Graham Greene: The Decline of the Colonial Novel," *Fiction and the Colonial Experience*, 99-101, 101-8.

Moré, Marcel, "The Two Holocausts of Scobie," *CC* 1 (Winter, 1951): 44-63.

Mueller, W. R., "The Theme of Love: Graham Greene's THE HEART OF THE MATTER," *Prophetic Voice*, 136-57.

O'Donnell, Donat, "Graham Greene: The Anatomy of Pity," *Maria Cross*, 63-91. Also in O'Brien, C. C., *Maria Cross*, 57-84.

O'Faoláin, Seán, "The Novels of Graham Greene: THE HEART OF THE MATTER," *Britain Today* No. 148 (Aug., 1948): 32-6.

Orwell, George, "The Sanctified Sinner," in Orwell, Sonia, and Ian Angus, eds., *The Collected Essays, Journalism and Letters of George Orwell*, N.Y.: Harcourt Brace Jovanovich; London: Secker & Warburg, 1968, 439-43. Also in Hynes, S., ed., *Graham Greene*, 105-9.

Poole, Roger C., "Graham Greene's Indirection," *Blackfriars* 45 (June, 1964): 265-6. Also in Cargas, H. J., ed., *Graham Greene*, 38-41.

Pryce-Jones, D., *Graham Greene*, 78-82.

Scott, Nathan A., Jr., "Graham Greene: Christian Tragedian," *The Volusia Review* 1, i (1954). Also, revised, in Evans, R. O., ed., *Graham Greene*, 38-41. Also in Scott, N. A., Jr., *Craters of the Spirit*, 214-17.

Smith, A. J. M., "Graham Greene's Theological Thrillers," *QQ* 68 (Spring, 1961): 23-6.

Sonnenfeld, Albert, "Children's Faces: Graham Greene," in Friedman, M. J., ed., *Vision Obscured*, 120-8.

Stewart, Douglas, *Ark of God*, 93-5.

————, "Graham Greene: Master of Melodrama," *TamR* No. 19 (1961): 76-83.

Stratford, Philip, "Second Thoughts on 'Graham Greene's Second Thoughts': The Five Texts of THE HEART OF THE MATTER," *SB* 31 (1978): 263-6.

Traversi, Derek, "Graham Greene," *TC* 199 (1951): 323-8.

Turnell, M., *Graham Greene*, 27-31.

————, "Graham Greene; The Man Within," *Ramparts* 4 (June, 1965): 62-3.

Walker, Ronald G., "Seriation as Stylistic Norm in Graham Greene's THE HEART OF THE MATTER," *Lang&S* 6 (1973): 161-75.

Wansbrough, John, "Graham Greene: The Detective in the Wasteland," *HarvardA* 136 (Dec., 1952): 11-13, 29-31.

Ward, J. A., "Henry James and Graham Greene," *HJR* 1, i (1979): 10-23.

Waugh, Evelyn, "Felix Culpa?" *Cweal* 48 (July 16, 1948): 322-5. Also in Hynes, S., ed., *Graham Greene*, 95-102.

Weseliski, Andrzej, "Irony and Melodrama in THE HEART OF THE MATTER," *SAP* 8 (1976): 167-73.

Wilshere, A. D., "Conflict and Conciliation in Graham Greene," in English Association, *Essays and Studies, 1966*, 132-7.

Woodward, Anthony, "Graham Greene: The War Against Boredom," in Roberts, G., ed., *Seven Studies in English*, 84-7, 90-7.

Wyndham, F., *Graham Greene*, 18-21.

THE HONORARY CONSUL

Allott, Miriam, "Surviving The Course, Or a Novelist for All Seasons: Graham Greene's THE HONORARY CONSUL," in Jefferson, D., and G. Martin, eds., *Uses of Fiction*, 237-48.

Johnston, Stuart, "People Caught Up by Love: The Novels of Graham Greene," in Yule, R. M., ed., *From Dante to Solzhenitsyn*, 205-6.

Koga, H., *Essays on Graham Greene and His Work*, 107-13.

Kulshrestha, J. P., *Graham Greene*, 168-78.

Lodge, D., "Graham Greene," in Stade, G., ed., *Six Contemporary British Novelists*, 50-1, 54-6.

Vargo, Edward P., S. B. D., "Struggling with a Bugaboo: The Priest Character in Achebe and Greene and Keneally," *FJS* 9 (1976): 1-13 *passim*. Also in Narasimhaiah, C. D., ed., *Awakened Conscience: Studies in Commonwealth Literature*, New Delhi: Sterling Publishers, 1978, 284-94.

Wolfe, Peter, "THE HONORARY CONSUL," *STwC* No. 14 (Fall, 1974): 117-20.

IT'S A BATTLEFIELD

Adinaryana, L., "A Reading of Greene's IT'S A BATTLEFIELD," *LitE* 3, i-ii (July-Dec., 1981): 54-64.

Allott, K., and M. Farris, *Art of Graham Greene*, 85-100.

Atkins, J., *Graham Greene*, 38-46.

Braybrooke, Neville, "Graham Greene, a Pioneer Novelist," *CE* 12 (Oct., 1950): 3-4.

Cheney, Lynne, "Joseph Conrad's THE SECRET AGENT and Graham Greene's IT'S A BATTLEFIELD: A Study in Structural Meanings," *MFS* 16, ii (Summer, 1970): 117-31.

De Vitis, A. A., *Graham Greene*, 72-5.

Kulshrestha, J. P., *Graham Greene*, 31-43.

Kunkel, F. L., *Labyrinthine Ways of Graham Greene*, 34-43.

McInherny, Frances C., "IT'S A BATTLEFIELD: A World in Chaos," in Ryan, J. S., ed., *Gleanings from Greeneland*, 20-30.

O'Donnell, Donat, "Graham Greene," *Chimera* 5 (Summer, 1947): 22-3.

Pryce-Jones, D., *Graham Greene*, 20-2.

Stratford, P., *Faith and Fiction*, 120-2.

THE LABYRINTHINE WAYS see THE POWER AND THE GLORY

LOSER TAKES ALL

De Vitis, A. A., *Graham Greene*, 67-8.

Kulshrestha, J. P., *Graham Greene*, 209-10.

Kunkel, F. L., *Labyrinthine Ways of Graham Greene*, 92-7.

Voorhees, Richard J., "Recent Greene," *SAQ* 62 (Spring, 1963): 245-6.

Wolfe, P., *Graham Greene*, 133-45.

THE MAN WITHIN

Allott, K., and M. Farris, *Art of Graham Greene*, 51-60.

Atkins, J., *Graham Greene*, 17-21.

Kulshrestha, J. P., *Graham Greene*, 18-29.

Kunkel, F. L., *Labyrinthine Ways of Graham Greene*, 24-33.

Lewis, R. W. B., "The Fiction of Graham Greene: Between the Horror and the Glory," *KR* 19 (Winter, 1957): 62-5.

_____, *Picaresque Saint*, 228-32.

Lodge, D., "Graham Greene," in Stade, G., ed., *Six Contemporary British Novelists*, 10-11. Originally in Lodge, D., *Graham Greene*, 11-12. Also in Lodge, D., *Novelist at the Crossroads*, 92-3.

Maxwell, J. C., "'The Dry Salvages': A Possible Echo of Graham Greene," *N&Q* 11 (Oct., 1964): 387.

Pryce-Jones, D., *Graham Greene*, 15-16.

Stratford, P., *Faith and Fiction*, 91-8.

Turnell, M., *Graham Greene*, 11-13.

Weseliski, Andrzej, "Graham Greene's Early Works: The Fantasy of Romantic Adventure," *KN* 29, iii-iv (1982): 253-63.

THE MINISTRY OF FEAR

Allott, K., and M. Farris, *Art of Graham Greene*, 193-214.

Atkins, J., *Graham Greene*, 128-39, 144-8.

Auden, W. H., "The Heresy of Our Time," *Ren* 1 (Spring, 1949): 23-4. Also in Hynes, S., ed., *Graham Greene*, 93-4.

Boardman, G. R., *Graham Greene*, 78-83.

De Vitis, A. A., *Graham Greene*, 61-5.

Duffy, Joseph M., Jr., "The Lost World of Graham Greene," *Thought* 33 (Summer, 1958): 237-45.

Grubbs, Henry A., "Albert Camus and Graham Greene," *MLQ* 10 (1949): 33-42.

Kulshrestha, J. P., *Graham Greene*, 199-206.

Kunkel, F. L., *Labyrinthine Ways of Graham Greene*, 68-72, 76-9.

Lodge, D., *Graham Greene*, 27-31. Also in Stade, G., ed., *Six Contemporary British Novelists*, 28-33.

Pryce-Jones, D., *Graham Greene*, 66-8.

Stratford, P., *Faith and Fiction*, 106-9.

Welsh, James M., and Gerald R. Barrett, "Graham Greene's MINISTRY OF FEAR: The Transformation of an Entertainment," *LFQ* 2, iv (Fall, 1974): 310-23.

Wolfe, P., *Graham Greene*, 101-21.

THE NAME OF ACTION (Withdrawn at Author's Request)

Allott, K., and M. Farris, *Art of Graham Greene*, 60-71.

Atkins, J., *Graham Greene*, 24-7.

Lewis, R. W. B., *Picaresque Saint*, 228-30.

Stratford, P., *Faith and Fiction*, 98-102.

ORIENT EXPRESS see STAMBOUL TRAIN

OUR MAN IN HAVANA

Atkins, J., *Graham Greene*, 241-5.

Bedard, B. J., "Reunion in Havana," *LFQ* 2, iv (Fall, 1974): 352-8.

Boardman, G. R., *Graham Greene*, 123-7.

De Vitis, A. A., *Graham Greene*, 68-71.

Kazin, A., "Graham Greene and the Age of Absurdity," *Contemporaries*, 158-61.

Kennedy, A., *Protean Self*, 233-7.

Kulshrestha, J. P., *Graham Greene*, 210-14.

Kunkel, F. L., *Labyrinthine Ways of Graham Greene*, 97-100.

Sternlicht, Sanford, "The Sad Comedies: Graham Greene's Later Novels," *FloQ* 1, iv (1968): 69-70.

Stratford, P., *Faith and Fiction*, 318-25.

Voorhees, Richard J., "Recent Greene," *SAQ* 62 (Spring, 1963): 249-52.

Wolfe, P., *Graham Greene*, 146-65.

THE POWER AND THE GLORY (THE LABYRINTHINE WAYS)

Allen, W., *Modern Novel*, 207.

_____, *Reading a Novel*, 34-8. Also in, rev. ed., London: Phoenix Books, 1956, 37-42.

_____, in Baker, D. V., ed., *Writers of Today*, 25-7.

Allott, K., and M. Farris, *Art of Graham Greene*, 173-93.

Atkins, John, "Altogether Amen: A Reconsideration of THE POWER AND THE GLORY," in Evans, R. O., ed., *Graham Greene*, 181-7.

_____, *Graham Greene*, 119-27.

Beary, Thomas J., "Religion and the Modern Novel," *CathW* 166 (Dec., 1947): 204-5.

Boardman, G. R., *Graham Greene*, 62-77.

Brannon, Lil, "The Possibilities of Sainthood: A Study of the Moral Dilemma in Graham Greene's THE POWER AND THE GLORY and T. S. Eliot's MURDER IN THE CATHEDRAL," *PAPA* 4, iii (1978): 66-71.

Braybrooke, Neville, "Graham Greene, a Pioneer Novelist," *CE* 12 (Oct., 1950): 6-7.

Brock, D. Heywood, and James M. Welsh, "Graham Greene and the Structure of Salvation," *Ren* 27, i (Autumn, 1974): 31-9.

Céleste, Sister Marie, S. C., "Bernanos and Graham Greene on the Role of the Priest in THE DIARY OF A COUNTRY PRIEST and THE POWER AND THE GLORY," *Culture* 30 (Dec., 1969): 287-98.

Clancy, L. J., "Graham Greene: Style and Stylistics in Five Novels," in Evans, R. O., ed., *Graham Greene*, 74-8.

Cunningham, Lawrence, "The Alter Ego of Greene's 'Whiskey Priest'," *ELN* 8, i (Sept., 1970): 50-2.

Currie, John S., "Supernaturalism in Graham Greene: A Comparison of Orthodox Catholicism with Religious Vision in the Major Novels," *DA* 28 (1968): 3176A-77A (Alabama).

Davies, H., *A Mirror of the Ministry in Modern Novels*, 1-3-10.

De Vitis, A. A., *Graham Greene*, 87-96.

_____, "Notes on THE POWER AND THE GLORY," *Annotator* (Purdue Un. Dept. of English) No. 5 (May, 1955): 7-10.

_____, "Religious Aspects in the Novels of Graham Greene," in Mooney, H. J., Jr., and T. F. Staley, eds., *Shapeless God*, 45-8.

Eagleton, T., *Exiles and Émigrés*, 108-9, 112-18.

Fetrow, Fred M., "The Function of Geography in THE POWER AND THE GLORY," *Descant* 23, ii (1979): 40-8.

Gardiner, Harold C., "Taste and Worth," *America* 75 (1946): 53.

Glicksberg, Charles I., "Graham Greene: Catholicism in Fiction," *Criticism* 1 (Fall, 1959): 343-5.

Graef, H., *Modern Gloom and Christian Hope*, 86-9.

Grob, Alan, "THE POWER AND THE GLORY: Graham Greene's Argument from Design," *Criticism* 11 (Winter, 1969): 1-30.

Haber, Herbert R., "The Two Worlds of Graham Greene," *MFS* 3 (Autumn, 1957): 256-68.

Hall, J., *Lunatic Giant in the Drawing Room*, 116-19.

Harmer, Ruth M., "Greene World of Mexico: The Birth of a Novelist," *Ren* 15 (Summer, 1963): 171-82, 194.

Hartt, J. N., *Lost Image of Man*, 116-17.

Herling, Gustav, "Two Sanctities: Greene and Camus," *Adam* No. 201 (Dec., 1949): 10-12.

Higdon, David L., "A Textual History of Graham Greene's THE POWER AND THE GLORY," *SB* 33 (1980): 222-39.

Hoggart, Richard, "The Force of Caricature: Aspects of the Art of Graham Greene with Particular Reference to THE POWER AND THE GLORY," *EIC* 3 (Oct., 1953): 447-62. Also in Hoggart, R., *Speaking to Each Other*, Vol. II: *About Literature*, 40-55. Also in Hynes, S., ed., *Graham Greene*, 79-92.

Janisch, Josandra, "THE POWER AND THE GLORY by Graham Greene," *CRUX* 14, ii (June, 1980): 30-7.

Johnston, Stuart, "People Caught Up by Love: The Novels of Graham Greene," in Yule, R. M., ed., *From Dante to Solzhenitsyn*, 198-204.

Jordan, Gretchen G., "Adultery and Its Fruit in THE SCARLET LETTER and THE POWER AND THE GLORY: The Relation of Meaning and Form," *YR* 71, i (Autumn, 1981): 72-87.

Karl, F. R., "Graham Greene's Demoniacal Heroes," *Contemporary English Novel*, 98-106.

Kellogg, G., *Vital Tradition*, 122-6.

Kohn, L., *Graham Greene*, 31-50.

Kulshrestha, J. P., *Graham Greene*, 73-93.

Kunkel, F. L., *Labyrinthine Ways of Graham Greene*, 112-22.

Lees, F. N., "Graham Greene: A Comment," *Scrutiny* 19 (Oct., 1952): 32-6.

Lewis, R. W. B., "The 'Trilogy' of Graham Greene," *MFS* 3 (Autumn, 1957): 203-10. Also in Lewis, R. W. B., *Picaresque Saint*, 248-58. Also in Cargas, H. J., ed., *Graham Greene*, 56-66. Also in Hynes, S., ed., *Graham Greene*, 59-69.

Lodge, D., *Graham Greene*, 24-7. Also in Stade, G., ed., *Six Contemporary British Novelists*, 24-8. Also in Lodge, D., *Novelist at the Crossroads*, 102-4.

Marian, Sister I.H.M., "Graham Greene's People: Becoming and Becoming," *Ren* 18 (Autumn, 1965): 18-20.

Mauriac, François, "Graham Greene," in *Great Men*, London: Rockliff, 1952, 117-21. Also in Mauriac, F., *Men I Hold Great*, N.Y.: Philosophical Library, 1951, 124-8. Also in Hynes, S., ed., *Graham Greene*, 75-8.

Maurois, A., *Points of View from Kipling to Graham Greene*, 399-404.

McInherny, Frances C., "Some Thoughts Occasioned on Re-reading THE POWER AND THE GLORY," in Ryan, J. S., ed., *Gleanings from Greeneland*, 31-43.

McManus, June, "THE POWER AND THE GLORY for Freshmen," *CCTE* 40 (1975): 24-30.

Mesnet, M. B., *Graham Greene*, 19-28, 55-60, 89-92, and *passim*.

Michener, Richard L., "Apocalyptic Mexico: THE PLUMED SERPENT and THE POWER AND THE GLORY," *UR* 34 (June, 1968): 313-16.

Milner, Ian, "Values and Irony in Graham Greene," *AUCP* 14 (1971): 67-72.

O'Donnell, Donat, "Graham Greene," *Chimera* 5 (Summer, 1947): 28-30.

O'Rourke, Brian, "Echoes of A. E.'s Poetry in THE POWER AND THE GLORY," *EI* 7 (Dec., 1982): 87-95.

Patten, Karl, "The Structure of THE POWER AND THE GLORY," *MFS* 3 (Autumn, 1957): 225-34. Also in Cargas, H. J., ed., *Graham Greene*, 101-13.

Pearson, Sheryl S., "'Is There Anybody There?': Graham Greene in Mexico," *JML* 9, ii (May, 1982): 277-90.

Poole, Roger C., "Graham Greene's Indirection," *Blackfriars* 45 (June, 1964): 259-60. Also in Cargas, H. J., ed., *Graham Greene*, 32-3.

Pryce-Jones, D., *Graham Greene*, 47-58.

Ryan, J. S., "Structure, Imagery and Theme in THE POWER AND THE GLORY," in Ryan, J. S., ed., *Gleanings from Greeneland*, 44-69.

Sandra, Sister Mary, S. S. A., "The Priest-Hero in Modern Fiction," *Person* 46 (Oct., 1965): 538-42.

Smith, A. J. M., "Graham Greene's Theological Thrillers," *QQ* 68 (Spring, 1961): 30-2.

Stewart, Douglas, *Ark of God*, 81-7.

Thomas, D. P., "Mr. Tench and Secondary Allegory in THE POWER AND THE GLORY," *ELN* 7, ii (Dec., 1969): 129-33.

Traversi, Derek, "Graham Greene," *TC* 149 (1951): 319-23.

Turnell, M., *Graham Greene*, 22-7.

_____, "Graham Greene: The Man Within," *Ramparts* 4 (June, 1965): 58-62.

Veitch, Douglas W., "Graham Greene: The Dark is Light Enough," *Fictional Landscape of Mexico*, 66-110.

Walker, Ronald G., "A Mexico of the Mind: THE POWER AND THE GLORY," *Infernal Paradise*, 205-36.

Wansbrough, John, "Graham Greene: The Detective in the Wasteland," *HarvardA* 136 (Dec., 1952): 11-13, 29-31.

Webb, Bernice L., "Whiskey and Women: Problems of the Priesthood in Graham Greene's THE POWER AND THE GLORY and J. F. Powers' 'The Valiant Woman'," *NLauR* 7, ii (1977): 62-71.

Wells, Arvin R., in Hagopian, J. V., and M. Dolch, eds., *Insight II*, 153-64.

White, W. D., "THE POWER AND THE GLORY: An Apology to the Church," *UPR* 21, i (Spring, 1969): 14-22.

Wichert, Robert A., "The Quality of Graham Greene's Mercy," *CE* 25 (Nov., 1963): 99-103.

Wilshere, A. D., "Conflict and Conciliation in Graham Greene," in English Association, *Essays and Studies, 1966*, 128-32.

Woodcock, George, "Mexico and the English Novelist," *WR* 21 (Autumn, 1956): 29-32.

Wyndham, F., *Graham Greene*, 14-17.

THE QUIET AMERICAN

Allen, Walter, "Awareness of Evil: Graham Greene," *Nation* 182 (April 21, 1956): 344-6.

Allott, Miriam, "The Moral Situation in THE QUIET AMERICAN," in Evans, R. O., ed., *Graham Greene*, 188-206.

Atkins, J., *Graham Greene*, 227-36.

Boardman, G. R., *Graham Greene*, 101-4, 106-17.

Cassidy, John, "America and Innocence: Henry James and Graham Greene," *Blackfriars* 38 (June, 1957): 261-7.

Consolo, Dominick P., "Graham Greene: Style and Stylistics in Five Novels," in Evans, R. O., ed., *Graham Greene*, 91-4.

De Vitis, A. A., *Graham Greene*, 116-20.

_____, "Religious Aspects in the Novels of Graham Greene," in Mooney, H. J., Jr., and T. F. Staley, eds., *Shapeless God*, 55-6.

Eagleton, T., *Exiles and Émigrés*, 125-8.

Elistratova, Anna, "Graham Greene and His New Novel," *SovLit* 8 (1956): 149-55.

Evans, Robert O., "Existentialism in Greene's THE QUIET AMERICAN," *MFS* 3 (Autumn, 1957): 241-8.

Freedman, Ralph, "Novel of Contention: THE QUIET AMERICAN," *WR* 21 (Autumn, 1956): 76-81.

Gaston, G. M., "The Structure of Salvation in THE QUIET AMERICAN," *Ren* 31, ii (Winter, 1979): 93-106.

Hall, J., *Lunatic Giant in the Drawing Room*, 121-3.

Hansen, Niels B., "The Unquiet Englishman: A Reading of Graham Greene's THE QUIET AMERICAN," in Caie, Graham D., Michael Chesnutt, Lis Christensen, Claus Faerch, eds., *Occasional Papers 1976-1977*, Copenhagen i Univ.-forl. i Kobenhavn, 1978, 188-201.

Hinchliffe, Arnold P., "The Good American," *TC* 168 (Dec., 1960): 534-7.

Hughes, R. E., "THE QUIET AMERICAN: The Case Reopened," *Ren* 12 (Autumn, 1959): 41-2+. Also in Cargas, H. J., ed., *Graham Greene*, 130-3.

Kulshrestha, J. P., *Graham Greene*, 142-59.

Kunkel, F. L., *Labyrinthine Ways of Graham Greene*, 148-53.

Larsen, Eric, "THE QUIET AMERICAN," *NRep* (Aug. 7-14, 1976): 40-2.

Lewis, R. W. B., "The Fiction of Graham Greene: Between the Horror and the Glory," *KR* 19 (Winter, 1957): 56-60.

Lichtheim, George, "Anglo-American," *TC* 159 (Jan., 1956): 90-2. Also in Lichtheim, G., *Collected Essays*, 490-2.

Lodge, D., *Graham Greene*, 35-7. Also in Stade, G., ed., *Six Contemporary British Novelists*, 37-40. Also in Lodge, D., *Novelist at the Crossroads*, 111-12.

McCormick, John O., "The Rough and Lurid Vision: Henry James, Graham Greene and the International Novel," *JA* 2 (1957): 158-67.

McMahon, J., "Graham Greene and THE QUIET AMERICAN," *Jammu and Kashmir Un. Rev.*, 1 (Nov., 1958): 64-73.

O'Brien, C. C., "Mr. Greene's Battlefield," *Maria Cross*, 249-51. Also in *NStat&Nation* 10 (Dec., 1955).

Poole, Roger, "'Those Sad Arguments': Two Novels of Graham Greene," *RMS* 13 (1969): 148-60.

Pryce-Jones, D., *Graham Greene*, 90-3.

Rahv, Philip, "Wicked American Innocence," *Ctary* 21 (May, 1956): 488-90.

Rudman, Harry W., "Clough and Graham Greene's THE QUIET AMERICAN," *VN* No. 19 (1961): 14-15.

Scott, Nathan A., Jr., "Christian Novelist's Dilemma," *ChC* 73 (Aug. 1, 1956): 901-2. Also, as "Graham Greene: Christian Tragedian," *Craters of the Spirit*, 223-7.

Snape, Ray, "The Political Novels of Graham Greene," *DUJ* 75, i (Dec., 1982): 76-8.

Sternlicht, Sanford, "The Sad Comedies: Graham Greene's Later Novels," *FloQ* 1, iv (1968): 66-9.

Stratford, P., *Faith and Fiction*, 308-16.

Trilling, Diana, and Philip Rahv, "America and THE QUIET AMERICAN," *Ctary* 12 (July, 1956): 166-71.

Voorhees, Richard J., "Recent Greene," *SAQ* 62 (Spring, 1963): 246-9.

RUMOUR AT NIGHTFALL (Withdrawn at Author's Request)

Allott, K., and M. Farris, *Art of Graham Greene*, 60-71.

Atkins, J., *Graham Greene*, 27-9.

Stratford, P., *Faith and Fiction*, 103-6, 171-3.

THE SHIPWRECKED see ENGLAND MADE ME

STAMBOUL TRAIN (ORIENT EXPRESS)

Allott, K., and M. Farris, *Art of Graham Greene*, 79-85.

Atkins, J., *Graham Greene*, 30-7.

De Vitis, A. A., *Graham Greene*, 54-5.

Kulshrestha, J. P., *Graham Greene*, 181-7.

Kunkel, F. L., *Labyrinthine Ways of Graham Greene*, 83-9.

Lodge, D., *Graham Greene*, 11-13. Also in Stade, G., ed., *Six Contemporary British Novelists*, 11-13. Also in Lodge, D., *Novelist at the Crossroads*, 94.

Miller, R. H., "Textual Alterations in Graham Greene's STAMBOUL TRAIN," *PBSA* 71, iii (1977): 378-81.

Pryce-Jones, D., *Graham Greene*, 17-20.

Stratford, P., *Faith and Fiction*, 111-16.

THE THIRD MAN

Adamson, Judy, and Philip Stratford, "Looking for THE THIRD MAN: On the Trail in Texas, New York, Hollywood," *Encounter* (June, 1978): 39-46.

Alloway, Lawrence, "Symbolism in THE THIRD MAN," *WoR* (Mar., 1950): 57-60.

Gomez, Joseph A., "THE THIRD MAN: Capturing the Visual Essence of Literary Conception," *LFQ* 2, iv (Fall, 1974): 332-40.

Kulshrestha, J. P., *Graham Greene*, 206-9.

Palmer, James W., and Michael M. Riley, "The Lone Rider in Vienna: Myth and Meaning in THE THIRD MAN," *LFQ* 8 (1980): 14-21.

Van Wert, William F., "Narrative Structure in THE THIRD MAN," *LFQ* 2, iv (Fall, 1974): 341-6.

Wolfe, P., *Graham Greene*, 122-32.

THIS GUN FOR HIRE (A GUN FOR SALE)

Alley, Kenneth D., "A GUN FOR SALE: Graham Greene's Reflection of Moral Chaos," *ELWIU* 5 (1978): 175-85.

Allott, K., and M. Farris, *Art of Graham Greene*, 130-9.

Atkins, J., *Graham Greene*, 72-7.

Boardman, G. R., *Graham Greene*, 36-41.

De Vitis, A. A., *Graham Greene*, 55-9.

King, James, "In the Lost Boyhood of Judas: Graham Greene's Early Novels of Hell," *DR* 49, ii (Summer, 1969): 228-36.

Kulshrestha, J. P., *Graham Greene*, 189-93.

Lodge, D., *Graham Greene*, 14-16. Also in Stade, G., ed., *Six Contemporary British Novelists*, 13-15. Also in Lodge, D., *Novelist at the Crossroads*, 95-6.

McCann, Janet, "Names and Identity in Graham Greene's Novels," *Cresset* 41, vi (April, 1978): 3-4.

Melada, Ivan, "Graham Greene and the Munitions Makers: The Historical Context of A GUN FOR SALE," *SNNTS* 13, ii (Fall, 1981): 303-21.

Pryce-Jones, D., *Graham Greene*, 62-4.

Stratford, P., *Faith and Fiction*, 188-92, 214-16.

Wolfe, P., *Graham Greene*, 51-79.

Wyndham, F., *Graham Greene*, 11-13.

TRAVELS WITH MY AUNT

Atkinson, F. K., "Floreat Augusta—or, On First Looking into TRAVELS WITH MY AUNT," in Ryan, J. S., ed., *Gleanings from Greeneland*, 81-90.

Boardman, G. R., *Graham Greene*, 173-7.

Chaudhury, M. K., "Graham Greene's TRAVELS WITH MY AUNT: A Picaresque Novel," *PURBA* 3, ii (Oct., 1972): 79-85.

Fagin, Steven, "Narrative Design in TRAVELS WITH MY AUNT," *LFQ* 2, iv (Fall, 1974): 379-83.

Kennedy, A., *Protean Self*, 242-8.

Kulshrestha, J. P., *Graham Greene*, 214-22.

Lodge, D., *Graham Greene*, in Stade, G., ed., *Six Contemporary British Novelists*, 51-4.

Thale, Jerome, and Rose M. Thale, "Greene's 'Literary Pilgrimage': Allusions in TRAVELS WITH MY AUNT," *PLL* 13, ii (Spring, 1977): 207-12.

BIBLIOGRAPHY

Beebe, Maurice, "Criticism of Graham Greene: A Selected Checklist with an Index to Studies of Separate Works," *MFS* 3 (Autumn, 1957): 281-8.

Birmingham, William, "Graham Greene Criticism: A Bibliographical Study," *Thought* 27 (Spring, 1952): 72-100.

Brennan, Neil, "Bibliography," in Evans, R. O. ed., *Graham Greene*, 245-76.

Cassis, A. F., *Graham Greene: An Annotated Bibliography of Criticism* (Scarecrow Author Bibliographies, 55), Metuchen, N.J., London: Scarecrow Pr., 1981.

De Vitis, A. A., "Selected Bibliography," *Graham Greene*, 161-71.

Vann, J. Don, *Graham Greene: A Checklist of Criticism*, Kent, Ohio: Kent State Un. Pr., 1970.

Wobbe, R. A., *Graham Greene: A Bibliography and Guide to Research* (GRLH 173), N.Y.: Garland, 1979.

GRUBB, DAVIS, 1919-1980

GENERAL

Welch, Jack, "Davis Grubb: A Vision of Appalachia," *DAI* 41, xi (May, 1981): 4716A.

FOOLS' PARADE

Welch, Jack, "Art is Long, Entertainment Short: Cinematic Composition in Two Films Made from Davis Grubb's Novels," *WVUPP* 26 (Aug., 1980): 43-52.

THE NIGHT OF THE HUNTER

Fitzpatrick, W. P., "The Great American Novel and THE NIGHT OF THE HUNTER," *BWVACET* 2, i (1975): 18-31.

Welch, Jack, "Art is Long, Entertainment Short: Cinematic Composition in Two Films Made from Davis Grubb's Novels," *WVUPP* 26 (Aug., 1980): 43-52.

Wood, Robin, "Night of the Hunter/Novel into Film," *On Film* 1 No. Zero (n.d.), 68-71. Reprinted as "Charles Laughton on Grub Street," in Peary, G., and Shatzkin, R., eds., *Modern American Novel and the Movies*, 204-14.

GUEST, JUDITH, 1936-

ORDINARY PEOPLE

Stark, John, "ORDINARY PEOPLE: Extraordinary Novel," *MMisc* 8 (1980): 7-81.

GUNN, NEIL M(ILLER), 1891-1973

GENERAL

Broom, John L., "The Novels of Neil M. Gunn," in Morrison, D., ed., *Essays on Neil M. Gunn*, 11-31.

Caird, James B., "Gaelic Elements in the Work of Neil Gunn," *SSL* 15 (1980): 88-94.

_____, "Lewis Grassic Gibbon and Neil Gunn: A Comparison (1901-1935: 1891-1973)," *Caliban* 17, i (1981): 69-77.

_____, "Neil Gunn and Scottish Fiction," in Scott, A., and D. Gifford, eds., *Neil M. Gunn*, 370-86.

_____, "Neil M. Gunn, Novelist of the North," in Morrison, D., ed., *Essays on Neil M. Gunn*, 41-51.

Carter, Courtney M., "Prophet of Delight: The Novels of Neil M. Gunn," *DAI* 38 (1978): 5454A.

Hart, Francis R., "Beyond History and Tragedy, Neil Gunn's Early Fiction," in Morrison, D., ed., *Essays on Neil M. Gunn*, 52-67.

_____, "Comedy and Transcendence in Neil Gunn's Later Fiction," in Scott, A., and D. Gifford, eds., *Neil M. Gunn*, 239-57.

_____, "The Hunter and the Circle: Neil Gunn's Fiction of Violence," *SSL* 1, i (July, 1963): 65-82.

MacDiarmid, Hugh, "Neil Gunn and the Scottish Renaissance," in Scott, A., and D. Gifford, eds., *Neil M. Gunn*, 360-9.

McCleery, Alistair, "The Early Novels of Neil M. Gunn," *Bibliotheck* 10, v (1981): 127-38.

Morrison, D., ed., *Essays on Neil M. Gunn*.

Nakamura, Tokusaburo, "Neil Miller Gunn: A Spiritual Survey," *SSL* 12, ii (Oct., 1974): 79-91.

Pick, J. B., "The Bog in the Stream: The Development of Some Fundamental Concepts in the Work of Neil M. Gunn," in Scott, A., and D. Gifford, eds., *Neil M. Gunn*, 295-315.

_____, "Memories of Neil Gunn," *SSL* 14 (1979): 52-71.

Reid, Alexander, "Neil Gunn's Mysticism," in Scott, A., and D. Gifford, eds., *Neil M. Gunn*, 244-59.

Ross, John, "Early Tides: The First Novels," in Scott, A., and D. Gifford, eds., *Neil M. Gunn*, 71-87.

Scott, A., and D. Gifford, eds., *Neil M. Gunn*.

Spence, Alan, "Highland Zen," *New Edinburgh Review* 57 (1982): 15-17. [Not seen.]

Thompson, Francis, "Neil M. Gunn, Recorder and Interpreter," in Morrison, D., ed., *Essays on Neil M. Gunn*, 32-40.

Wittig, Kurt, "Neil Gunn's Animistic Vision," in Scott, A., and D. Gifford, eds., *Neil M. Gunn*, 316-43.

BLOODHUNT

Hart, Francis R., "The Hunter and Circle: Neil Gunn's Fiction of Violence," *SSL* 1, i (July, 1963): 75-9.

BUTCHER'S BROOM

Rescanières, Marie-H., "Scottish Saga: SUN CIRCLE and BUTCHER'S BROOM," in Scott, A., and D. Gifford, eds., *Neil M. Gunn*, 98-100.

THE DRINKING WELL

Bruce, George, "Handling the Unbearable: THE SERPENT and THE DRINKING WELL," in Scott, A., and D. Gifford, eds., *Neil M. Gunn*, 217-38.

THE GREEN ISLE OF THE GREAT DEEP

Noble, Andrew, "Fable of Freedom: THE GREEN ISLE OF THE GREAT DEEP," in Scott, A., and D. Gifford, eds., *Neil M. Gunn*, 175-216.

THE GREY COAST

Aitken, W. R., "Neil Gunn's Revision of His First Novel," *Bibliotheck* 6, iv (1972): 114-17.

McCleery, Alistair, "The Early Novels of Neil M. Gunn," *Bibliotheck* 10, v (1981): 127-9.

HIGHLAND RIVER

Gifford, Douglas, "The Source of Joy: HIGHLAND RIVER," in Scott, A., and D. Gifford, eds., *Neil M. Gunn*, 101-22.

THE KEY OF THE CHEST

Hart, Francis R., "The Hunter and the Circle: Neil Gunn's Fiction of Violence," *SSL* 1, i (July, 1963): 79-82.

THE LOST GLEN

McCleery, Alistair, "The Early Novels of Neil M. Gunn," *Bibliotheck* 10, v (1981): 129-32.

MORNING TIDE

McCleery, Alistair, "The Early Novels of Neil M. Gunn," *Bibliotheck* 10, v (1981): 134-6.

THE POACHING AT GRIANAN

McCleery, Alistair, "The Early Novels of Neil M. Gunn," *Bibliotheck* 10, v (1981): 132-4.

_____, "'The Lost Novel' of Neil Gunn," *ScotLJ* Supplement No. 17 (1982): 1-4.

THE SERPENT

Bruce, George, "Handling the Unbearable: THE SERPENT and THE DRINKING WELL," in Scott, A., and D. Gifford, eds., *Neil M. Gunn*, 217-38.

THE SILVER DARLINGS

Campbell, Donald, "True Imagination: THE SILVER DARLINGS," in Scott, A., and D. Gifford, eds., *Neil M. Gunn*, 141-56.

Scott, Alexander, "Folk Epic: THE SILVER DARLINGS," in Scott, A., and D. Gifford, eds., *Neil M. Gunn*, 123-40.

SUN CIRCLE

Rescanières, Marie-H., "Scottish Saga: SUN CIRCLE and BUTCHER'S BROOM," in Scott, A., and D. Gifford, eds., *Neil M. Gunn*, 88-98.

THE WELL AT THE WORLD'S END

Conn, Stewart, "The Well of Delight," in Scott, A., and D. Gifford, eds., *Neil M. Gunn*, 258-70.

YOUNG ART AND OLD HECTOR

Shepherd, Gillian, "The Way to Wisdom: YOUNG ART AND OLD HECTOR," in Scott, A., and D. Gifford, eds., *Neil M. Gunn*, 157-74.

BIBLIOGRAPHY

Scott, A., and D. Gifford, eds., *Neil M. Gunn*, 389-97.

GUTHRIE, A(LFRED) B(ERTRAM), JR., 1901-1991

GENERAL

Allred, Jared R., "A. B. Guthrie, Jr.: The Writer and the Wilderness," *DAI* 34 (1974): 6582A (Utah).

Coon, Gilbert D., "A. B. Guthrie, Jr.'s Tetralogy: An American Synthesis," *NDQ* 44, ii (Spring, 1976): 73-80.

_____, "A Study of A. B. Guthrie, Jr. and His Tetralogy," *DAI* 32 (1972): 4606A (Wash. State).

Ford, T. W., *A. B. Guthrie, Jr.*

_____, "A. B. Guthrie, Jr.: A Sense of Place," *NDQ* 48, ii (Spring, 1980): 56-67.

Hairston, Joe B., "Community in the West," *SDR* 11, i (1973): 17-26.

_____, "The Westerner's Dilemma," *DAI* 32 (1971): 2688A (Minn.).

Kohler, Dayton, "A. B. Guthrie, Jr., and the West," *CE* 12 (Feb., 1951): 249-56.

Putnam, Jackson K., "Down to Earth: A. B. Guthrie's Quest for Moral and Historical Truth," *NDQ* 39, iii (Summer, 1971): 47-57.

Ray, Charles E., "An Interdisciplinary Study Based on Four Selected Novels of A. B. Guthrie, Jr.," *DAI* 35 (1975): 5422A-23A.

Stewart, Donald C., "A. B. Guthrie's Paradise: An Essay on Historical Fiction," *JWest* 15, iii (July, 1976): 83-96. Also in Pilkington, W. T. ed., *Critical Essays on the Western American Novel*, 136-49.

ARFIVE

Ford, T. W., *A. B. Guthrie, Jr.*, (1981): 105-13.

Hairston, Joe B., "Community in the West," *SDR* 11, i (1973): 23-5.

THE BIG SKY

Arpin, Roger C., "A. B. Guthrie's THE BIG SKY: The Reshaping of a Myth," *PAP* 3, ii (1977): 1-5.

Astro, Richard, "THE BIG SKY and the Limits of Wilderness Fiction," *WAL* 9 (1974): 105-14.

Cracroft, Richard H., "THE BIG SKY: A. B. Guthrie's Use of Historical Sources," *WAL* 6, iii (1971): 163-76.

Folsom, J. K., *American Western Novel*, 64-70.

Ford, T. W., *A. B. Guthrie, Jr.*, (1968), 10-18.

_____, *A. B. Guthrie, Jr.*, (1981), 66-84.

_____, "A. B. Guthrie's THE BIG SKY: Killing the American Dream," *JASAT* 9 (1978): 11-16.

Gale, Robert L., "Guthrie's THE BIG SKY," *Expl* 38, iv (1980): 7-8.

Hairston, Joe B., "Community in the West," *SDR* 11, i (1973): 17-18.

Kohler, Dayton, "A. B. Guthrie, Jr., and the West," *EJ* 40 (Feb., 1951): 67-70. Also in *CE* 12 (Feb., 1951): 251-4.

Milton, J. R., *Novel of the American West*, 165-9.

Peterson, Levi S., "Tragedy and Western American Literature," *WAL* 6, iv (1972): 243-9.

Prescott, O., *In My Opinion*, 141-3.

Putnam, Jackson K., "Down to Earth: A. B. Guthrie's Quest for Moral and Historical Truth," *NDQ* 39, iii (Summer, 1971): 50-1.

Rosenthal, T. G., "Out of the West," *NStat* 82 (Oct. 15, 1971): 516-17.

Stegner, Wallace, "Foreword" to Sentry Edition, THE BIG SKY, Boston: Houghton, 1965.

Stewart, Donald C., "The Functions of Bird and Sky Imagery in Guthrie's THE BIG SKY," *Crit* 19, ii (1977): 53-61.

THE GENUINE ARTICLE

Ford, T. W., *A. B. Guthrie, Jr.*, (1981): 126-8.

THE LAST VALLEY

Ford, T. W., *A. B. Guthrie, Jr.*, (1981): 113-23.

MURDERS AT MOON DANCE

Ford, T. W., *A. B. Guthrie, Jr.*, (1981): 58-61.

THESE THOUSAND HILLS

Folsom, J. K., *American Western Novel*, 74-5.

Ford, Thomas W., *A. B. Guthrie, Jr.*, (1968): 27-3.

_____, *A. B. Guthrie, Jr.*, (1981): 96-104.

Hairston, Joe B., "Community in the West," *SDR* 11, i (1973): 21-3.

Milton, J. R., *Novel of the American West*, 182-7.

Putnam, Jackson K., "Down to Earth: A. B. Guthrie's Quest for Moral and Historical Truth," *NDQ* 39, iii (Summer, 1971): 52-7.

Stineback, David C., "On History and Its Consequences: A. B. Guthrie's THESE THOUSAND HILLS," *WAL* 6, iii (1971): 177-89.

THE WAY WEST

Folsom, J. K., *American Western Novel*, 70-3.

Ford, T. W., *A. B. Guthrie, Jr.*, (1968): 18-26.

_____, *A. B. Guthrie, Jr.*, (1981): 85-96.

Hairston, Joe B., "Community in the West," *SDR* 11, i (1973): 18-20.

Kohler, Dayton, "A. B. Guthrie, Jr., and the West," *EJ* 40 (Feb., 1951): 70-2. Also in *CE* 12 (Feb., 1951): 254-6.

Milton, J. R., *Novels of the American West*, 178-83.

Prescott, O., *In My Opinion*, 143-5.

Putnam, Jackson K., "Down to Earth: A. B. Guthrie's Quest for Moral and Historical Truth," *NDQ* 39, iii (Summer, 1971): 51-2.

Stuckey, W. J., *Pulitzer Prize Novels*, 152-4.

WILD PITCH

Ford, T. W., *A. B. Guthrie, Jr.*, (1981): 123-6.

BIBLIOGRAPHY

Etulain, Richard W., "A. B. Guthrie: A Bibliography," *WAL* 4, ii (Summer, 1969): 133-8.

Ford, T. W., *A. B. Guthrie, Jr.* (1981), 164-71.

HAILEY, ARTHUR, 1920-

AIRPORT

Lennon, John J., "The Case of AIRPORT," *JPC* 3 (1969): 355-60.

WHEELS

Farrell, Patricia A., "An Exclusive Interview with Arthur Hailey," *WD* 52, viii (Aug., 1972): 32-4, 56.

HANLEY, GERALD (ANTHONY), 1916-

THE CONSUL AT SUNSET

Huffaker, Robert, "Gerald Hanley's THE CONSUL AT SUNSET: Epilogue of Empire," *SHR* 5, iv (Fall, 1971): 377-86.

HANLEY, JAMES, 1901-1985

GENERAL

Allen, W., *Modern Novel*, 227-8.

Anon., "The Kingdom of the Sea," *TLS* (Feb. 27, 1953): 136.

_____, "A Novelist in Neglect: The Case for James Hanley," *TLS* (June 11, 1971): 675-6. See also Warner, Oliver, *TLS* (June 25, 1971): 737; Fraser, Keith, (July 23, 1971): 861.

Moore, Reginald, "The Sea Around Him," *John o' London's Weekly* 61 (Sept. 19, 1952): 861-2.

Stokes, E., *Novels of James Hanley*.

BOY

Stokes, E., *Novels of James Hanley*, 28-34.

CAPTAIN BOTTELL

Stokes, E., *Novels of James Hanley*, 96-103.

THE CLOSED HARBOUR

Anon., "A Novelist in Neglect: The Case for James Hanley," *TLS* (June 11, 1971): 675-6.

Stokes, E., *Novels of James Hanley*, 158-65.

DRIFT

Stokes, E., *Novels of James Hanley*, 19-2.

EBB AND FLOOD

Stokes, E., *Novels of James Hanley*, 35-9.

EMILY

Stokes, E., *Novels of James Hanley*, 150-2.

AN END AND A BEGINNING

Stokes, E., *Novels of James Hanley*, 76-85.

THE FURYS

Stokes, E., *Novels of James Hanley*, 46-54.

HOLLOW SEA

Stokes, E., *Novels of James Hanley*, 110-19.

THE HOUSE IN THE ALLEY

Stokes, E., *Novels of James Hanley*, 182-6.

LEVINE

Stokes, E., *Novels of James Hanley*, 165-74.

NO DIRECTIONS

Stokes, E., *Novels of James Hanley*, 142-9.

THE OCEAN

Stokes, E., *Novels of James Hanley*, 119-27.

OUR TIME IS GONE

Stokes, E., *Novels of James Hanley*, 61-8.

RESURREXIT DOMINUS

Stokes, E., *Novels of James Hanley*, 175-81.

SAILOR'S SONG

Stokes, E., *Novels of James Hanley*, 127-38.

SAY NOTHING

Stokes, E., *Novels of James Hanley*, 193-200.

THE SECRET JOURNEY

Stokes, E., *Novels of James Hanley*, 54-61.

STOKER BUSH

Stokes, E., *Novels of James Hanley*, 103-10.

THE WELSH SONATA

Stokes, E., *Novels of James Hanley*, 186-93.

WHAT FARRAR SAW

Stokes, E., *Novels of James Hanley*, 152-5.

WINTER SONG

Stokes, E., *Novels of James Hanley*, 68-76.

HANNAH, BARRY, 1942-

GENERAL

Hill, Robert W., "Barry Hannah," *SCR* 9, i (Nov., 1976): 25-9.
Jones, J. G., *Mississippi Writers Talking*, Vol. I, 131-66.
Noble, Donald R., "'Tragic and Meaningful to an Insane Degree': Barry Hannah," *SLJ* 15, i (Fall, 1982): 37-44.

HARDWICK, ELIZABETH, 1916-

GENERAL

Rahv, Philip, "The Editor Interviews Elizabeth Hardwick," *MoOc* 2, ii (Spring, 1972): 159-67.

HARINGTON, DONALD, 1935-

THE CHERRY PIT

Vonalt, Larry, "Doubling and Duplicity in Donald Harington's THE CHERRY PIT," *Crit* 22, i (1980): 47-54.

HARLOW, ROBERT, 1923-

GENERAL

Hancock, Geoff, "An Interview with Robert Harlow," *CFM* 19 (1975): 37-70.

MAKING ARRANGEMENTS

Harris, John, "Arrangements Unmade," *JCF* 31-32 (1981): 248-51.
MacKendrick, Louis K., "Harlow's ARRANGEMENTS," *ECanW* 16 (1979/80): 198-207.

SCANN

Diotte, Robert, "Notes on Harlow's SCANN," *CFM* 19 (1975): 71-85.
Moss, J., *Sex and Violence in the Canadian Novel*, 245-55.

HARRINGTON, ALAN, 1919-

THE SECRET SWINGER

Richey, Clarence W., "Rebirth from the Womb: A Note Upon an Analogue for the Concluding Episode in Alan Harrington's THE SECRET SWINGER," *NConL* 1, iv (Sept., 1971): 12-14.

HARRIS, MACDONALD, Pseud. (Donald {William} Heiney), 1921-

GENERAL

Kellman, Steven G., "*Homo Technicus* Adrift: The Novels of MacDonald Harris," *WHR* 36, i (Spring, 1982): 59-67.

TREPLEFF

White, J. J., *Mythology in the Modern Novel*, 228-39.

HARRIS, MARK, 1922-

GENERAL

Enck, John, "Mark Harris: An Interview," *WSCL* 6 (1965): 15-26.
Schafer, William J., "Mark Harris: Versions of (American) Pastoral," *Crit* 19, i (1977): 28-48.

BANG THE DRUM SLOWLY

Bachner, Saul, "Baseball as Literature: BANG THE DRUM SLOWLY," *EngR* 25, ii (1974): 83-6.
Guttmann, Allen, "Literature, Sociology, and 'Our National Game'," *Prospects* 1 (1975): 126-8, 132-3.

SOMETHING ABOUT A SOLDIER

Sherman, B., *Invention of the Jew*, 220-1.

THE SOUTHPAW

Smith, L. T., Jr., *American Dream and the National Game*, 100-3.

TRUMPET TO THE WORLD

Harris, Mark, "How to Write," in McCormack, T., ed., *Afterwords*, 65-79.

WAKE UP, STUPID

Oliphant, Robert, "Public Voices and Wise Guys," *VQR* 37 (Autumn, 1961): 528-37 *passim*.

HARRIS, (THEODORE) WILSON, 1921-

GENERAL

Adams, Ralston, "Wilson Harris: The Pre-novel Poet," *JCL* 13, iii (April, 1979): 71-85.
Adler, Joyce S., "Melville and Harris: Poetic Imaginations Related in Their Response to the Modern World," in Maes-Jelinek, H., ed., *Commonwealth Literature and the Modern World*, 33-41.
_____, "Wilson Harris and Twentieth-Century Man," *NewL* 40, i (Autumn, 1973): 49-61.

Crew, Gary, "Wilson Harris' Da Silva Quartet," *NLRev* 7 (1979): 43-52.

Fabre, Michel, "Wilson Harris," *Kunapipi* 2, i (1980): 100-6. [Not seen.]

Gilkes, M., *West Indian Novel*, 145-56.

_____, *Wilson Harris and the Caribbean Novel*.

Gowda, H. H. Anniah, "Phenomenal Tradition: Raja Rao and Wilson Harris," *BACLLS* 9 (Mar., 1972): 28-45.

Hearne, John, "The Fugitive in the Forest: A Study of Four Novels by Wilson Harris," *JCL* No. 4 (Dec., 1967): 99-112.

James, C. L. R., *Wilson Harris—A Philosophical Approach*.

King, B., *New English Literatures*, 108-17.

Kinkead-Weekes, Mark, "Bone Flute? Or House of Fiction: The Contrary Imaginations of Wilson Harris and V. S. Naipaul," in Jefferson, D., and G. Martin, eds., *Uses of Fiction*, 139-58.

Lacovia, R. M., "Landscape, Maps and Parangles," *BlackI* 4, i-ii (1975): 1-95. [Not seen.]

Mackey, Nathaniel, "Limbo, Dislocation, Phantom Limb: Wilson Harris and the Caribbean Occasion," *Criticism* 22, i (Winter, 1980): 57-76.

Maes-Jelinek, Hena, "'Inimitable Painting': New Developments in Wilson Harris's Latest Fiction," *ArielE* 8, iii (July, 1977): 63-80.

_____, *Wilson Harris*.

_____, "Wilson Harris," in King, B., ed., *West Indian Literature*, 179-95.

_____, "The Writer as Alchemist: The Unifying Role of Imagination in the Novels of Wilson Harris," *Lang&L* 1, i (Autumn, 1971): 25-34.

Moss, John G., "William Blake and Wilson Harris: The Objective Vision," *JCL* 9, iii (April, 1975): 29-40.

Munro, Ian, and Reinhard Sanders, eds., *Kas-Kas: Interviews with Three Caribbean Writers in Texas: George Lamming, C. L. R. James, Wilson Harris*, Austin: Un. of Texas, 1972.

Ngai, Mbatau K. W., "The Relationship Between Literature and Society and How It Emerges in the Works of G. Lamming, V. S. Naipaul and W. Harris," *Busara* 8, ii (1976): 62-5.

Ramchand, Kenneth, "The Significance of the Aborigine in Wilson Harris' Fiction," *LHY* 11, ii (July, 1970): 7-16.

Rutherford, Anna, and Kirsten H. Petersen, "Interview with Wilson Harris," *Commonwealth Newsl.* (Aarhus) 9 (1976): 22-5.

Sparer, Joyce L., "The Art of Wilson Harris," *New Beacon Reviews: Collection One* (1968): 22-30.

Tiffin, Helen, "Wilson Harris: An Interview," *NLRev* 7 (1979): 18-29.

Van Sertima, Ivan, "Introducing Wilson Harris," *Review* 74 (Spring, 1974): 60-2.

ASCENT TO OMAI

Gilkes, Michael, "The Art of Extremity: A Reading of Wilson Harris' ASCENT TO OMAI," *LHY* 15, i (Jan., 1974): 120-33. Also in *Caribbean Quarterly* 17 (Sept.-Dec., 1971): 83-90.

_____, *Wilson Harris and the Caribbean Novel*, 132-44.

Griffiths, G., *Double Exile*, 185-90.

Maes-Jelinek, Hena, "ASCENT TO OMAI," *LHY* 13, i (Jan., 1972): 1-8.

_____, *Wilson Harris*, 115-32.

Ramchand, Kenneth, "Before the People Became Popular...," *Caribbean Quarterly* 18, iv (Dec., 1972): 71-3.

Walkley, Jane, "ASCENT TO OMAI or the Ascent of Man," *Commonwealth Newsl.* (Aarhus) 9 (Jan., 1976): 42-5.

BLACK MARSDEN: A TABULA RASA COMEDY

Gilkes, Michael, "Magical Reality," *JCL* 9, i (1974): 77-9.

_____, *Wilson Harris and the Caribbean Novel*, 145-51.

Griffiths, G., *Double Exile*, 191-2.

Maes-Jelinek, H., *Wilson Harris*, 139-45.

_____, and Eva Searl, "Wilson Harris's BLACK MARSDEN," *ComN* 4 (July, 1973): 21-9.

COMPANIONS OF THE DAY AND NIGHT

Gilkes, Michael, "An Infinite Canvas: Wilson Harris. COMPANIONS OF THE DAY AND NIGHT," *WLWE* 15 (April, 1976): 161-73.

Maes-Jelinek, H., *Wilson Harris*, 145-51.

Searl, Eva, "COMPANIONS OF THE DAY AND NIGHT," *Commonwealth Newsl.* (Aarhus) 9 (Jan., 1976): 46-58.

Van Sertima, Ivan, "Into the Black Hole: A Study of Wilson Harris's COMPANIONS OF THE DAY AND NIGHT," *ACLALSB* 4, iv (1976): 65-77.

DA SILVA DA SILVA'S CULTIVATED WILDERNESS

Crew, Gary, "Wilson Haris' Da Silva Quartet," *NLRev* 7 (1979): 46-8.

Gilkes, M., *West Indian Novel*, 149-56.

_____, "Wilson Harris: DA SILVA DA SILVA'S CULTIVATED WILDERNESS and GENESIS OF THE CLOWNS," *WLWE* 16 (Nov., 1977): 462-70.

Gilliland, Marion C., "Resurrection in the Womb of Time: A Reading of Wilson Harris's DA SILVLA DA SILVA'S CULTIVATED WILDERNESS," *Commonwealth Newsl.* (Aarhus) 12 (1977): 29-39.

Maes-Jelinke, H., "'Inimitable Painting': New Developments in Wilson Harris's Latest Fiction," *ArielE* 8, iii (July, 1977): 63-80.

_____, *Wilson Harris*, 152-8.

THE EYE OF THE SCARECROW

Gilkes, M., *Wilson Harris and the Caribbean Novel*, 105-12.

Howard, W. J., "Wilson Harris and the 'Alchemical Imagination'," *LHY* 11, ii (July, 1970): 17-26.

Mackey, Nathaniel, "The Unruly Pivot: Wilson Harris' THE EYE OF THE SCARECROW," *TSLL* 20, iv (Winter, 1978): 633-59.

Maes-Jelinek, Hena, "The 'Unborn State of Exile' in Wilson Harris's Novels," in Niven, A., ed., *Commonwealth Writer Overseas*, 195-205.

_____, *Wilson Harris*, 63-81.

THE FAR JOURNEY OF OUDIN (See also GUIANA QUARTET)

Gilkes, M., *Wilson Harris and the Caribbean Novel*, 48-67.

Hearne, John, "The Fugitive and the Forest: A Study of Four Novels by Wilson Harris," *JCL* No. 4 (Dec., 1967): 107-9. Also in James, L., ed., *Islands in Between*, 148-9. Also in Cooke, M. G., ed., *Modern Black Novelists*, 183-4.

Kulkarni, Madhav, "THE FAR JOURNEY OF OUDIN: In the Light of the Biblical Epigrams," *Commonwealth Quart.* (New Delhi) 1, i (1976): 47-53.

Maes-Jelinek, H., *Wilson Harris*, 16-27.

GENESIS OF THE CLOWNS

Gilkes, Michael, "Wilson Harris' DA SILVA DA SILVA'S CUL-
TIVATED WILDERNESS and GENESIS OF THE
CLOWNS," *WLWE* 16 (Nov., 1977): 462-70.
Maes-Jelinek, H., *Wilson Harris*, 158-61.

GUIANA QUARTET

Howard, W. J., "Wilson Harris's GUIANA QUARTET: From
Personal Myth to National Identity," *ArielE* 1, i (Jan., 1970):
46-60. Also in Walsh, W., ed., *Readings in Commonwealth
Literature*, 314-28.
James, Louis, "Wilson Harris and the GUYANESE QUARTET,"
in King, B., and K. Ogungbesan, eds., *Celebration of Black and
African Writing*, 164-73.
Maes-Jelinek, Hena, in King, B., ed., *West Indian Literature*, 183-7.
Wilkinson, Nick, "The Novel and a Vision of the Land," in
Narasimhaiah, C. D., ed., *Awakened Conscience*, 187-90.

HEARTLAND

Crew, Gary, "Wilson Harris' Da Silva Quartet," *NLRev* 7 (1979):
45-6.
Durix, Jean-Pierre, "Along Jigsaw Trail: An Interpretation of
HEARTLAND," *CNIE* 1, ii (July, 1982): 127-46.
Gilkes, M., *Wilson Harris and the Caribbean Novel*, 100-4.
Maes-Jelinek, H., *Wilson Harris*, 53-62.
Moore, Gerald, "Death, Convergence and Rebirth in Two Black
Novels," *Nigerian Jour. of the Humanities* 2 (1978): 6-17.
Ramchand, K., *West Indian Novel and its Background*, 169-73.

PALACE OF THE PEACOCK (See also GUIANA QUARTET)

Boxill, Anthony, "Wilson Harris's PALACE OF THE PEA-
COCK: A New Dimension in West Indian Fiction," *CLAJ* 14,
iv (June, 1971): 380-6.
Brahms, Flemming, "A Reading of Wilson Harris's PALACE
OF THE PEACOCK," *ComN* 3 (Jan., 1973): 30-44.
Crew, Gary, "Wilson Harris' Da Silva Quartet," *NLRev* 7 (1979):
43-5.
Durix, Jean-Pierre, "A Reading of ' Paling of Ancestors'," *Com-
monwealth Newsl.* (Aarhus) 9 (Jan., 1976): 32-41.
Fabre, Michel, "The Reception of PALACE OF THE PEACOCK
in Paris," *Kunapipi* 2, i (1980): 106-9.
Fletcher, John, "The 'Intimacy of a Horror': The Tradition of
Wilson Harris's PALACE OF THE PEACOCK," in Maes-
Jelinek, H., ed., *Commonwealth Literature and the Modern
World*, 43-50.
Gilkes, M., *Wilson Harris and the Caribbean Novel*, 22-47.
Gowda, H. H. Anniah, "Phenomenal Tradition: Raja Rao and
Wilson Harris," *BACLLS* 9 (Mar., 1972): 32-45.
Griffiths, G., *Double Exile*, 177-84.
Harris, Wilson, "The Enigma of Values," *NewL* 40, i (Fall, 1973):
141-9.
Hearne, John, "The Fugitive in the Forest: A Study of Four
Novels by Wilson Harris," *JCL* No. 4 (Dec., 1967): 101-7. Also
in James, L., ed., *Islands in Between*, 141-8. Also in Cooke, M.
G., ed., *Modern Black Novelists*, 178-83.
James, C. L. R., *Wilson Harris—A Philosophical Approach*, 4-12
passim.

Maes-Jelinek, Hena, in King, B., ed., *West Indian Literature*, 183-6.
_____, *The Naked Design: A Reading of PALACE OF THE
PEACOCK*, Aarhus, Denmark: Dangaroo Pr., 1976.
_____, "The Poetry of Space in PALACE OF THE PEA-
COCK," in Petersen, K. H., and A. Rutherford, eds., *Enigma
of Values*, 59-108.
_____, "The True Substance of Life: Wilson Harris's PAL-
ACE OF THE PEACOCK," in Rutherford, Anna, ed., *Com-
mon Wealth*, 151-9.
_____, *Wilson Harris*, 1-15.
Moore, G., *Chosen Tongue*, 76-82.
Ramchand, K., *West Indian Novel and its Background*, 165-8.
Sharrad, Paul, "PALACE OF THE PEACOCK and the Tragic
Muse," *LCrit* 16, iv (1981): 44-58.
Tiffin, Helen, "Towards Place and Placelessness: Two Journey
Patterns in Commonwealth Literature," in Narasimhaiah, C.
D., ed., *Awakened Conscience*, 156-9.

THE SECRET LADDER (See also GUIANA Quartet)

Gilkes, M., *Wilson Harris and the Caribbean Novel*, 81-99.
Hearne, John, "The Fugitive in the Forest: A Study of Four
Novels by Wilson Harris," *JCL* No. 4 (Dec., 1967): 111-12.
Also in James L., ed., *Islands in Between*, 151-3. Also in Cooke,
M. G., ed., *Modern Black Novelists*, 185-7.
James, C. L. R., *Wilson Harris—A Philosophical Approach*, 12-14.
King, B., *New English Literatures*, 115-17.
Maes-Jelinek, H., *Wilson Harris*, 40-52.
Moore, G., *Chosen Tongue*, 63-5.
Mordecai, Pamela C., "The West Indian Male Sensibility in
Search of Itself: Some Comments on NOR ANY COUNTRY,
THE MIMIC MEN, and THE SECRET LADDER," *WLWE* 21,
iii (Autumn, 1982): 629-44.
Ramchand, K., *West Indian Novel and its Background*, 170-3.
Searl, Eva, "The Dynamic Concept of Community: Wilson Har-
ris' THE WHOLE ARMOUR and THE SECRET LADDER,"
ComN 4 (July, 1973): 32-5.

THE TREE OF THE SUN

Crew, Gary, "Wilson Harris' Da Silva Quartet," *NLRev* 7 (1979):
48-51.
Maes-Jelinek, H., *Wilson Harris*, 162-5.

TUMATUMARI

Adler, Joyce, "TUMATUMARI and the Imagination of Wilson
Harris," *JCL* 7 (July, 1969): 20-31. Also in Baugh, E., ed.,
Critics on Caribbean Literature, 113-20.
Gilkes, M., *Wilson Harris and the Caribbean Novel*, 120-31.
Gowda, H. H., "Wilson Harris' TUMATUMARI," *LHY* 11, i
(Jan., 1970): 31-8.
Harris, Wilson, "The Enigma of Values," *NewL* 40, i (Fall, 1973):
141-9.
Maes-Jelinek, H., *Wilson Harris*, 98-114.
Russell, D. W., "The Dislocating Art of Memory: An Analysis
of Wilson Harris' TUMATUMARI," *WLWE* 13, ii (Nov.,
1974): 234-49.
Van Sertima, Ivan, "The Sleeping Rocks: Wilson Harris's TU-
MATUMARI," in Petersen, K. H., and A. Rutherford, eds.,
Enigma of Values, 109-24.

THE WAITING ROOM

Gilkes, M., *Wilson Harris and the Caribbean Novel*, 113-19.

Maes-Jeline, H., *Wilson Harris*, 82-97.

Searl, Eva, "T. S. Eliot's FOUR QUARTETS and Wilson Harris's THE WAITING ROOM," in Maes-Jelinek, H., ed., *Commonwealth Litterature and the Modern World*, 51-9.

Sparer, Joyce L., "The Art of Wilson Harris," *New Beacon Review: Collection One* (1968): 26-30.

THE WHOLE ARMOUR (See also GUIANA Quartet)

Gilkes, M., *Wilson Harris and the Caribbean Novel*, 68-80.

Hearne, John, "The Fugitive in the Forest: A Study of Four Novels by Wilson Harris," *JCL* No. 4 (Dec., 1967): 109-11. Also in James, L., ed., *Islands in Between*, 149-51. Also in Cooke, M. G., ed., *Modern Black Novelists*, 184-5.

Hench, Michael M., "The Fearful Symmetry of THE WHOLE ARMOUR," *RevI* 4, iii (Fall, 1974): 446-61.

King, B., *New English Literatures*, 112-15.

Maes-Jelinek, H., *Wilson Harris*, 28-39.

Moore, G., *Chosen Tongue*, 65-73.

Searl, Eva, "The Dynamic Concept of Community: Wilson Harris' THE WHOLE ARMOUR and THE SECRET LADDER," *ComN* 4 (July, 1973): 32-5.

YUROKON

Maes-Jelinek, Hena, "Fictional Breakthrough and the Unveiling of 'Unspeakable rites' in Patrick White's A FRINGE OF LEAVES and Wilson Harris's YUROKON," *Kunapipi* 2, ii (1980): 33-43.

BIBLIOGRAPHY

Abaray, Michael J., "Wilson Harris: A Bibliography," *BB* 38, iv (Oct.-Dec., 1981): 189-93, 208.

Maes-Jelinek, H., *Wilson Harris*, 179-87.

HARRISON, WILLIAM, 1933-

GENERAL

Graham, John, "William Harrison," in Garrett, G., ed., *Writer's Voice*, 273-80. [Interview].

IN A WILD SANCTUARY

Garrett, George P., "Ringing the Bell: William Harrison's IN A WILD SANCTUARY," *HC* 6 (Oct., 1964): 1-11.

HARROWER, ELIZABETH, 1928-

GENERAL

Anon., "The Novels of Elizabeth Harrower," *AusL* 4, ii (Jan., 1961): 16-18.

Claremont, Robyn, "The Novels of Elizabeth Harrower," *Quadrant* (Nov., 1979): 16-21.

Davidson, Jim, "Interview: Elizabeth Harrower," *Meanjin* 39, ii (1980): 163-74.

Geering, R. G., "Elizabeth Harrower's Novels: A Survey," *Southerly* 30, ii (1970): 131-47.

THE CATHERINE WHEEL

Claremont, Robyn, "The Novels of Elizabeth Harrower," *Quadrant* (Nov., 1979): 18-20.

Geering, R. G., "Elizabeth Harrower's Novels: A Survey," *Southerly* 30, ii (1970): 137-42.

_____, *Recent Fiction*, 38-9.

DOWN IN THE CITY

Claremont, Robyn, "The Novels of Elizabeth Harrower," *Quadrant* (Nov., 1979): 16-17.

Geering, R. G., "Elizabeth Harrower's Novels: A Survey," *Southerly* 30, ii (1970): 131-4.

THE LONG PROSPECT

Claremont, Robyn, "The Novels of Elizabeth Harrower," *Quadrant* (Nov., 1979): 17-18.

Geering, R. G., "Elizabeth Harrower's Novels: A Survey," *Southerly* 30, ii (1970): 134-7.

_____, *Recent Fiction*, 35-6.

THE WATCH TOWER

Claremont, Robyn, "The Novels of Elizabeth Harrower," *Quadrant* (Nov., 1979): 20-1.

Geering, R. G., "Elizabeth Harrower's Novels: A Survey," *Southerly* 30, ii (1970): 142-7.

_____, *Recent Fiction*, 36-8.

BIBLIOGRAPHY

Houghton, Greg, "A Critical Checklist of Two Contemporary Australian Women Writers: Thea Astley and Elizabeth Harrower," *WLWE* 21 (1982): 557-71.

HARTLEY, L(ESLIE) P(OLES), 1895-1972

GENERAL

Athos, John, "L. P. Hartley and the Gothic Infatuation," *TCL* 7 (Jan., 1962): 172-9.

Bien, P., *L. P. Hartley*.

Bloomfield, P., *L. P. Hartley and Anthony Powell*.

Hall, J., *Tragic Comedians*, 111-28.

Jones, E. T., *L. P. Hartley*.

Melchiori, Giorgio, "The English Novelist and the American Tradition," *SR* 68 (Summer, 1960): 502-15. Also in *SA* 1 (1955).

Mulkeen, Anne M., "The Symbolic Novels of L. P. Hartley," *DAI* 30 (1970): 5452A (Wis.).

_____, *Wild Thyme, Winter Lightning*.

Petersen, Robert C., "The Common Sinner: Motif and Metaphor in the Fiction of L. P. Hartley," *DAI* 41 (1980): 2618A.

Reynolds, Donald L., Jr., "The Novels of L. P. Hartley," *DA* 28 (1968): 4186A (Un. of Washington).

Webster, Harvey C., "L. P. Hartley: Diffident Christian," *After the Trauma*, 152-67.

_____, "The Novels of L. P. Hartley," *Crit* 4, ii (1961): 39-51.

Willmott, Michael B., "'What Leo Knew': The Childhood World of L. P. Hartley," *English* 24 (Spring, 1975): 3-10.

THE BETRAYAL

Jones, E. T., *L. P. Hartley*, 113-24.
Mulkeen, A., *Wild Thyme, Winter Lightning*, 133-8.

THE BOAT

Bien, P., *L. P. Hartley*, 106-66.
Bloomfield, P., *L. P. Hartley and Anthony Powell*, 17-18.
Fraser, G. S., *Modern Writer and His World*, 160.
Hall, J., *Tragic Comedians*, 114-21.
Jones, E. T., *L. P. Hartley*, 75-83.
Mulkeen, A., *Wild Thyme, Winter Lightning*, 71-96.

THE BRICKFIELD

Jones, E. T., *L. P. Hartley*, 113-24.
Mulkeen, A., *Wild Thyme, Winter Lightning*, 133-8.
Willmott, Michael B., "'What Leo Knew': The Childhood World of L. P. Hartley," *English* 24 (Spring, 1975): 6-7.

THE COLLECTIONS

Jones, E. T., *L. P. Hartley*, 177-81.

EUSTACE AND HILDA (See also EUSTACE AND HILDA Trilogy)

Bloomfield, P., *L. P. Hartley and Anthony Powell*, 14-15.
Jones, E. T., *L. P. Hartley*, 65-70.
Karl, F. R., *Contemporary English Novel*, 277-8.

EUSTACE AND HILDA Trilogy

Allen, W., *Modern Novel*, 253-7.
Bien, P., *L. P. Hartley*, 46-98.
Cecil, Lord David, "Introduction" to EUSTACE AND HILDA: A TRILOGY, London: British Book Centre; N.Y.: Putnam, 1958.
Fraser, G. S., *Modern Writer and His World*, 160-1.
Jones, E. T., *L. P. Hartley*, 59-74.
Mulkeen, A., *Wild Thyme, Winter Lightning*, 42-70.
Pillai, A. S. D., "The Tragic Vision in EUSTACE AND HILDA: A Different Vision," *Journal of the Karnatak Univ.: Humanities* 22 (1978): 103-7.

FACIAL JUSTICE

Bien, P., *L. P. Hartley*, 215-28.
Bloomfield, P., *L. P. Hartley and Anthony Powell*, 20-2.
Jones, E. T., *L. P. Hartley*, 125-34.
_____, "Therapeutic Dystopia: A Szaszian Approach to Hawthorne's THE BLITHEDALE ROMANCE and L. P. Hartley's FACIAL JUSTICE," in Grenander, M. E., comp., *Proceedings of Asclepius at Syracuse: Thomas Szasz, Libertarian Humanist*, Albany: SUNY, 1980, 19-28.
Mulkeen, A., *Wild Thyme, Winter Lightning*, 139-54.
Sorensen, Knud, "Language and Society in L. P. Hartley's FACIAL JUSTICE," *OL* 26, i (1971): 68-78.
Webster, Harvey C., "The Novels of L. P. Hartley," *Crit* 4, ii (1961): 41-4.

THE GO-BETWEEN

Athos, John, "L. P. Hartley and the Gothic Infatuation," *TCL* 7 (Jan., 1962): 174-5.
Bien, P., *L. P. Hartley*, 33-6, 167-83.
Bloomfield, P., *L. P. Hartley and Anthony Powell*, 16-17.
Davison, Richard A., "Graham Greene and L. P. Hartley: 'The Basement Room' and THE GO-BETWEEN," *N&Q* 13 (1966): 101-2.
Gordon, Lois, "THE GO-BETWEEN—Hartley by Pinter," *KanQ* 4, ii (Spring, 1972): 81-92.
Grossvogel, David I., "Losey and Hartley: Under the Sign of Symbols," *Diacritics* 4, iii (Fall, 1974): 51-6.
Higdon, David L., "A Source for Hartley's THE GO-BETWEEN," *MBL* 2 (1977): 215-17.
Jones, E. T., *L. P. Hartley*, 100-13.
_____, "Summer of 1900: A la recherche of THE GO-BETWEEN," *LFQ* 1 (1973): 154-60.
Kitchin, Laurence, "Imperial Weekend," *Listener* 74 (Oct. 28, 1965): 662-3, 667.
Maxwell-Mahon, W. D., "L. P. Hartley: THE GO-BETWEEN," *CruxP* 9, i (1975): 32-6.
Moan, Margaret A., "Setting and Structure: An Approach to Hartley's THE GO-BETWEEN," *Crit* 15, ii (1973): 27-36.
Mulkeen, A., *Wild Thyme, Winter Lightning*, 97-112.
Pritchard, R. E., "L. P. Hartley's THE GO-BETWEEN," *CritQ* 22, i (1980): 45-55.
Riley, Michael, and James Palmer, "Time and the Structure of Memory in THE GO-BETWEEN," *CollL* 5 (1978): 219-27.
Sinyard, Neil, "Pinter's GO-BETWEEN," *CritQ* 22, iii (Autumn, 1980): 21-33.
Willmott, Michael B., "'What Leo Knew': The Childhood World of L. P. Hartley," *English* 24 (Spring, 1975): 3-6.

THE HARNESS ROOM

Jones, E. T., *L. P. Hartley*, 154-62.

THE HIRELING

Athos, John, "L. P. Hartley and the Gothic Infatuation," *TCL* 7 (Jan., 1962): 177-8.
Bien, P., *L. P. Hartley*, 204-15.
Jones, E. T., *L. P. Hartley*, 146-54.
Mulkeen, A., *Wild Thyme, Winter Lightning*, 126-8.

THE LOVE-ADEPT: A VARIATION ON A THEME

Jones, E. T., *L. P. Hartley*, 134-40.

MY FELLOW DEVILS

Athos, John, "L. P. Hartley and the Gothic Infatuation," *TCL* 7 (Jan., 1962): 175-7.
Bien, P., *L. P. Hartley*, 24-5, 184-91.
Hall, J., *Tragic Comedians*, 122-7.
Jones, E. T., *L. P. Hartley*, 83-91.
Mulkeen, A., *Wild Thyme, Winter Lightning*, 116-22.

MY SISTERS' KEEPER

Jones, E. T., *L. P. Hartley*, 171-6.

A PERFECT WOMAN

Bien, P., *L. P. Hartley*, 191-204.

Jones, E. T., *L. P. Hartley*, 91-9.

Kreutz, Irving, "L. P. Hartley, Who Are U? or: Luncheon in the Lounge," *KR* 25 (Winter, 1963): 150-4.

Mulkeen, A., *Wild Thyme, Winter Lightning*, 122-6.

POOR CLARE

Jones, E. T., *L. P. Hartley*, 163-71.

Mulkeen, A., *Wild Thyme, Winter Lightning*, 128-33.

THE SHRIMP AND THE ANEMONE (See also EUSTACE AND HILDA Trilogy)

Bloomfield, P., *L. P. Hartley and Anthony Powell*, 9-11.

Jones, E. T., *L. P. Hartley*, 59-62.

Maxwell-Mahon, W. D., "Symbolic Situations: THE SHRIMP AND THE ANEMONE," *Crux* 12, ii (April, 1978): 28-32.

Willmott, Michael B., "'What Leo Knew': The Childhood World of L. P. Hartley," *English* 24 (Spring, 1975): 7-10.

SIMONETTA PERKINS

Bloomfield, P., *L. P. Hartley and Anthony Powell*, 5-8.

Jones, E. T., *L. P. Hartley*, 142-6.

Mulkeen, A., *Wild Thyme, Winter Lightning*, 11-13, 37-41.

THE SIXTH HEAVEN (See also EUSTACE AND HILDA Trilogy)

Bloomfield, P., *L. P. Hartley and Anthony Powell*, 11-14.

Jones, E. T., *L. P. Hartley*, 62-5.

THE WILL AND THE WAY

Jones, E. T., *L. P. Hartley*, 181-7.

BIBLIOGRAPHY

Jones, E. T., *L. P. Hartley*, 214-18.

HASLUCK, NICHOLAS P., 1942-

THE BLUE GUITAR

Daniel, Helen, "The Moral 'Faszad': The Novels of Nicholas Hasluck," *Westerly* 25, iv (Dec., 1980): 63-7.

QUARANTINE

Daniel, Helen, "The Moral 'Faszad': The Novels of Nicholas Hasluck," *Westerly* 25, iv (Dec., 1980): 63-7.

HAWKES, JOHN, 1925-

GENERAL

Allen, C. J., "Desire, Design, and Debris: The Submerged Narrative of John Hawkes' Recent Trilogy," *MFS* 25, iv (Winter, 1979-80): 579-92.

Armstrong, Thomas W., "The Form of John Hawkes' Fiction," *DAI* 36 (1975): 2833A-34A.

Arpin, Roger C., "The Sack of the Past: Freedom and the Self in the Fiction of John Hawkes," *DAI* 40 (1979): 2069A-70A.

Bischoff, Joan, "John Hawkes' Horse of the Apocalypse," *NConL* 6, iv (Sept., 1976): 12-14.

Blake, Donald D., "'Singer of Love': The Fiction of John Hawkes," *DAI* 35 (1975): 4501A.

Boyer, Jay M., "Such Stuff as Dreams: A Study of Theme in John Hawkes's Novels," *DAI* 37 (1977): 5118A.

Burden, Robert, "The Image of Man and the Problematic of the Self in the Novels and Stories of John Hawkes," *John Fowles, John Hawkes, Claude Simon*, 56-92.

————, "Structure as 'verbal and psychological coherence' in John Hawkes's Novels," *John Fowles, John Hawkes, Claude Simon*, 182-217.

Busch, F., *Hawkes*.

————, "Icebergs, Islands, Ships Beneath the Sea," in Santore, A. C., and M. Pocalyko, eds., *John Hawkes Symposium*, 50-63.

Calhoun, Alice A., "Suspended Projections: Religious Roles and Adaptable Myths in John Hawkes' Novels, Francis Bacon's Paintings, and Ingmar Bergman's Films," *DAI* 40 (1980): 4782A-83A.

Eichel, Seymour, "Myth, Ritual and Symbol in the Novels of John Hawkes," *DAI* 34 (1973): 2288A (N.Y.U.).

Emmett, Paul J., "THE CANNIBAL to THE PASSION ARTIST: Hawkes's Journey Toward the Depths of the Unconscious," *ChiR* 32, i (Summer, 1980): 135-52.

————, and Richard Vine, "A Conversation with John Hawkes," *ChiR* 28, i (1976): 163-71.

Enck, John, "John Hawkes: An Interview," *WSCL* 6 (1965): 141-55. Also in Graham, J., comp., *Studies in SECOND SKIN*, 23-31.

Fellows, Jay, "Diderot, Hawkes, and the TABLEAU MOUVANT DE L'ÂME: From the Motion Pictures of Interior Animation to the Luxury of Still, Exterior Projection," *DiderotsS* 18 (1975): 61-79.

Frakes, James R., "The 'Undramatized Narrator' in John Hawkes: Who Says," in Santore, A. C., and M. Pocalyko, eds., *John Hawkes Symposium*, 27-37.

Freed, Walter B., Jr., "Romantic Illusion and Disorder: The Fictions of John Hawkes," *DAI* 39 (1979): 7345A-46A.

Friedman, Melvin J., "John Hawkes and Flannery O'Connor: The French Background," *BUJ* 21, iii (1973): 34-44.

Frohock, W. M., "John Hawkes's Vision of Violence," *SWR* 50 (Winter, 1965): 68-79.

Frost, Helen L. P., "A Legacy of Violence: John Hawkes' Vision of Culture," *DAI* 30 (1970): 3941A (Rochester).

Garson, Helen S., "John Hawkes and the Elements of Pornography," *JPC* 10, i (Summer, 1976): 150-5.

Garvey, Bartley T., Jr., "Unseen Vision: Voice and the Fiction of John Hawkes," *DAI* 43 (1982): 1144A.

Glass, Terrence L., "Myths, Dreams and Reality: Cycles of Experience in the Novels of John Hawkes," *DAI* 34 (1974): 5171A (Ohio State).

Green, James L., "Nightmare and Dream in John Hawkes's Novels," *DAI* 33 (1972): 312A (Nev.).

Greiner, D. J., *Comic Terror*.

————, "Strange Laughter: The Comedy of John Hawkes," *SWR* 56, iv (Autumn, 1971): 318-28.

Guerard, Albert J., "John Hawkes: A Longish View," in Santore, A. C., and M. Pocalyko, eds., *John Hawkes Symposium*, 1-13.

_____, "The Prose Style of John Hawkes," *Crit* 6, ii (Fall, 1963): 19-29.

Hawkes, John, "Notes on Writing a Novel," *TriQ* 30 (Spring, 1974): 109-26.

Head, James L., "The Motif of Death in the Major Novels of John Hawkes," *DAI* 38 (1977): 3499A.

Heat, William R., "John Hawkes: A Critical Study," *DAI* 32 (1971): 3305A (Case Western Reserve).

Heineman, Alan C., "Amusing Creations Out of Poisonous Smoke: The Novels of John Hawkes," *DAI* 35 (1974): 3743A-44A (Brandeis).

Hogan, Michael J., "The Relation of Prose Style and Voice in John Hawkes's Novels," *DAI* 37 (1976): 309A.

"John Hawkes and Albert Guerard in Dialogue," in Santore, A. C., and M. Pocalyko, eds., *John Hawkes Symposium*, 14-26.

Johnson, Joseph J., "The Novels of John Hawkes and Julien Gracq: A Comparison," *DAI* 31 (1970): 1280A (Vanderbilt).

Klein, Marcus, "Hawkes in Love," *Caliban* 12 (1975): 65-79.

_____, "John Hawkes' Experimental Compositions," in Federman, R., ed., *Surfiction*, 203-14.

_____, "The Satyr at the Head of the Mob," in Santore, A. C., and M. Pocalyko, eds., *John Hawkes Symposium*, 154-64.

Kuehl, J., *John Hawkes and the Craft of Conflict*.

Kuk-Korytowska, Ewa, "The Fiction of John Hawkes: The Structured Vision," *SAP* 11 (1979): 177-82.

Laing, Jeffrey M., "The Creepy Minuet: The Evolution of Dance Imagery in John Hawkes's Fiction," *NMAL* 6, ii (Autumn, 1982): Item 11.

_____, "The Upturned Smile: Comic Strategies in the Fiction of John Hawkes," *GyS* 4 (1977): 123-9.

Leana, Frank C., "The Power of Language in the Novels of John Hawkes," *DAI* 35 (1974): 2280A (Rochester).

Levine, Nancy, "An Interview with John Hawkes," in Santore, A. C., and M. Pocalyko, eds., *John Hawkes Symposium*, 91-108.

Littlejohn, David, "The Anti-realists," *Daedalus* 13 (Spring, 1963): 256-8.

MacCurdy, Carol A., "The Fictional Landscapes of John Hawkes," *DAI* 42, i (July, 1981): 215A.

Madden, John, "John Hawkes: Artist in Search of a Mask," in Baldanza, F., ed., *Itinerary 3: Criticism*, 121-35.

Malin, Irving, "The Gothic Family," in *Psychoanalysis and American Fiction*, 271-5.

Matthews, Charles, "The Destructive Vision of John Hawkes," *Crit* 6, ii (Fall, 1963): 38-52.

Norwood, Vera L., "Whatever Happened to Natty Bumppo? John Hawkes and the American Tradition," *DAI* 35 (1974): 1665A (N.M.).

Oberbeck, S. K., "John Hawkes: The Smile Slashed by a Razor," in Moore, H. T., ed., *Contemporary American Novelists*, 193-204. Also in Graham, J., comp., *Studies in SECOND SKIN*, 45-52.

O'Donnell, P., *John Hawkes*.

Ratner, Marc, "The Constructed Vision: The Fiction of John Hawkes," *SA* 11 (1965): 345-57.

Rovit, Earl, "The Fiction of John Hawkes: An Introductory View," *MFS* 10 (Summer, 1964): 150-62.

Santore, A. C., and M. Pocalyko, eds., *John Hawkes Symposium*.

_____, and Michael Pocalyko, "'A Trap to Catch Little Birds With': An Interview with John Hawkes," in Santore, A. C., and M. Pocalyko, eds., *John Hawkes Symposium*, 165-84.

Scholes, R., *Fabulators*, 66-74.

Schott, Webster, "John Hawkes, American Original," *NYTBR* (May 29, 1966): 4, 24-5.

Scott, Henry E., Jr., "'The Terrifying Similarity': The Themes and Techniques of John Hawkes," *DA* 29 (1968): 878A-9A (Wisconsin).

Steiner, Robert, "Form and the Bourgeois Traveler," in Santore, A.C., and M. Pocalyko, eds., *John Hawkes Symposium*, 109-41.

Tallant, Carole E., "Theory and Performance of Narrative Ambiguity in Selected Novels by John Hawkes," *DAI* 41 (1981): 3324A-25A.

Tani, Stefano, "On His Sexual Triad: A Conversation with Stefano Tani," *Dismisura: Rivista Bimestrale di Produzione & Crit. Culturale* (Alatri, It.) 39-50: 32-7. [Not seen.]

Tanner, Tony, "Necessary Landscapes and Luminous Deteriorations," *TriQ* 20 (Winter, 1971): 145-79.

Templeton, Wayne, "Between Two Worlds: Experiencing the Novels of John Hawkes," *WCR* 15, iii (Winter, 1981): 3-22.

Tobita, Shigeo, "John Hawkes no Paradox to Humor," *EigoS* 124 (1979): 573-5. [Not seen.]

Trachtenberg, Alan, "Barth and Hawkes: Two Fabulists," *Crit* 6, ii (Fall, 1963): 4-18.

Van Wert, William F., "Narration in John Hawkes' Trilogy," *LitR* 24, i (Fall, 1980): 21-39.

Veron, Enid, "The Saving Grace of Comedy: A Study of the Relationship between Form and Vision in the Fiction of John Hawkes," *DAI* 38 (1978): 7339A-40A.

Weaver, Thomas A., "Worlds Enough and Time: A Study of the Novels of John Hawkes," *DAI* 36 (1975): 333A.

THE BEETLE LEG

Busch, F., *Hawkes*, 39-60.

Frost, Lucy, "The Drowning of American Adam: Hawkes' THE BEETLE LEG," *Crit* 14, iii (1973): 63-74.

Greiner, D. J., *Comic Terror*, 97-124.

Madden, David W., "The Unwinning of the West: John Hawkes's THE BEETLE LEG," *SDR* 19, iii (Autumn, 1981): 78-91.

Matthews, Charles, "The Destructive Vision of John Hawkes," *Crit* 6, ii (Fall, 1963): 44-6.

O'Donnell, P., *John Hawkes*, 21-3, 61-72.

Tanner, T., *City of Words*, 209-11.

_____, "Necessary Landscapes and Luminous Deteriorations," *TriQ* 20 (Winter, 1971): 154-8.

Templeton, Wayne, "Between Two Worlds: Experiencing the Novels of John Hawkes," *WCR* 15, iii (Winter, 1981): 6-8.

THE BLOOD ORANGES

Abrams, Steven, "THE BLOOD ORANGES as a Visionary Fiction," *JNT* 8, ii (1978): 97-111.

_____, "THE BLOOD ORANGES as a Visionary Fiction," *DAI* 37 (1977): 4345A.

Allen, C. J., "Desire, Design, and Debris: The Submerged Narrative of John Hawkes's Recent Trilogy," *MFS* 25, iv (Winter, 1979-80): 580-3.

Busch, F., *Hawkes*, 139-70.

Clark, Walter H., Jr., "John Hawkes' Use of Two Shakespearian Sources," *Americana-Austriaca: Beiträ zur Amerikakunde* (Vienna) 4 (1978): 14-23.

Claus, Anne R., "Ford Madox, John Hawkes: Their Variations on a Theme," 80-187 in Caie, Graham D., Michael Chesnutt,

Lis Christensen, Claus Faerch, eds., *Occasional Papers 1976-1977*, Copenhagen: Univ.-forl. i Kobenhavn, 1978.

Cuddy, Lois A., "Functional Pastoralism in THE BLOOD ORANGES," *SAF* 3, i (Spring, 1975): 15-25.

Greiner, D. J., *Comic Terror*, 201-39.

Hawkes, John, and Robert Scholes, "A Conversation on THE BLOOD ORANGES," *Novel* 5, iii (Spring, 1972): 197-207. Also in Bellany, J. D., ed., *New Fiction*, 97-112.

Hornung, Alfred, "Sex and Art in Hawkes' Triad: The Pornographic, the Erotic and the Aesthetic Modes," *Amst* 26, ii (1981): 159-79.

Knapp, John V., "Hawkes' THE BLOOD ORANGES: A Sensual New Jerusalem," *Crit* 17, iii (1976): 5-25.

Kuehl, J., *John Hawkes and the Craft of Conflict*, 127-51.

Laing, Jeffrey M., "The Upturned Smile: Comic Strategies in the Fiction of John Hawkes," *GyS* 4 (1977): 125-7.

Moran, Charles, "John Hawkes: Paradise Gaining," *MR* 12, iv (Autumn, 1971): 840-5.

O'Donnell, P., *John Hawkes*, 115-25.

Rosenzweig, Paul, "Aesthetics and the Psychology of Control in John Hawkes's Triad," *Novel* 15, ii (Winter, 1982): 146-62.

Templeton, Wayne, "Between Two Worlds: Experiencing the Novels of John Hawkes," *WCR* 15, iii (Winter, 1981): 15-18.

Van Wert, William F., "Narration in John Hawkes' Trilogy," *LitR* 24, i (Fall, 1980): 22-9.

Veron, Enid, "From Festival to Farce: Design and Meaning in John Hawkes's Comic Triad," in Santore, A. C., and M. Pocalyko, eds., *John Hawkes Symposium*, 64-76 *passim*.

THE CANNIBAL

Armstrong, Thomas W., "Reader, Critic, and the Form of John Hawkes' THE CANNIBAL," *Boundary* 5 (1977): 829-44.

Busch, F., *Hawkes*, 17-37.

Fiedler, L., *Love and Death in the American Novel*, 467-8.

Graham, John, "John Hawkes on His Novels: An Interview," *MR* 7 (Summer, 1966): 449-53.

————, "On THE CANNIBAL," in Santore, A. C., and M. Pocalyko, eds., *John Hawkes Symposium*, 38-49.

Greiner, D. J., *Comic Terror*, 67-96.

Loukides, Paul, "The Radical Vision," *MichA* 5, iv (Spring, 1973): 502-3.

Madden, John, "John Hawkes: Artist in Search of a Mask," in Baldanza, F., ed., *Itinerary 3: Criticism*, 124-6.

Malin, Irving, "The Gothic Family," in *Psychoanalysis and American Fiction*, 272-4.

————, "Self-love," in *New American Gothic*, 38-41, 71-4.

Matthews, Charles, "The Destructive Vision of John Hawkes," *Crit* 6, ii (Fall, 1963): 40-4.

Nelson, Paula K., "The Function of Figures of Speech in Selected Anti-Realistic Novels," *DAI* 33 (1972): 1736A-37A (N.Y.U.).

O'Donnell, P., *John Hawkes*, 24-40.

Ratner, Marc, "The Constructed Vision: The Fiction of John Hawkes," *SA* 11 (1965): 350-7.

Reutlinger, D. P., "THE CANNIBAL: 'The Reality of Victim'," *Crit* 6, ii (Fall, 1963): 30-7.

Scholes, R., *Fabulator*, 74-9.

Tanner, T., *City of Words*, 205-9.

————, "Necessary Landscapes and Luminous Deteriorations," *TriQ* 20 (Winter, 1971): 148-54.

Templeton, Wayne, "Between Two Worlds: Experiencing the Novels of John Hawkes," *WCR* 15, iii (Winter, 1981): 3-6.

CHARIVARI

Busch, F., *Hawkes*, 1-15.

Green, James L., "Nightmare and Fairy Tale in Hawkes' CHARIVARI," *Crit* 13, i (1971): 83-95.

Greiner, D. J., *Comic Terror*, 30-43.

O'Donnell, P., *John Hawkes*, 41-50.

DEATH, SLEEP & THE TRAVELER

Allen, C. J., "Desire, Design, and Debris: The Submerged Narrative of John Hawkes' Recent Trilogy," *MFS* 25, iv (Winter, 1979-80): 583-9.

Greiner, Donald J., "DEATH, SLEEP & THE TRAVELER: John Hawkes' Return to Terror," *Crit* 17, iii (1976): 26-38.

Guzlowski, John Z., "No More Sea Changes: Hawkes, Pynchon, Gaddis, and Barth," *Crit* 23, ii (Winter, 1981-82): 48-51.

Hornung, Alfred, "Sex and Art in Hawkes' Triad: The Pornographic, the Erotic, and the Aesthetic Modes," *Amst* 26, ii (1981): 159-79.

Kraus, Elisabeth, "Psychic Sores in Search of Compassion: DEATH, SLEEP & THE TRAVELER," *Crit* 17, iii (1976): 39-52.

Laing, Jeffrey M., "The Upturned Smile: Comic Strategies in the Fiction of John Hawkes," *GyS* 4 (1977): 127-8.

Madden, John, "John Hawkes: Artist in Search of a Mask," in Baldanza, F., ed., *Itinerary 3: Criticism*, 131-4.

O'Donnell, P., *John Hawkes*, 125-35.

Rosenzweig, Paul, "Aesthetics and the Psychology of Control in John Hawkes's Triad," *Novel* 15, ii (Winter, 1982): 146-62.

Scotto, Robert M., "A Note on John Hawkes's DEATH, SLEEP & THE TRAVELER and TRAVESTY," *NMAL* 1 (1977): Item 11.

Templeton, Wayne, "Between Two Worlds: Experiencing the Novels of John Hawkes," *WCR* 15, iii (Winter, 1981): 18-19.

Van Wert, William F., "Narration in John Hawkes' Trilogy," *LitR* 24, i (Fall, 1980): 29-35.

Veron, Enid, "From Festival to Farce: Design and Meaning in John Hawkes's Comic Triad," in Santore, A. C., and M. Pocalyko, eds., *John Hawkes Symposium*, 64-76 *passim*.

THE GOOSE ON THE GRAVE

Busch, F., *Hawkes*, 72-86.

Greiner, D. J., *Comic Terror*, 43-55.

Malin, I., *New American Gothic*, 74-5.

O'Donnell, P., *John Hawkes*, 55-60.

THE LIME TWIG

Boutrous, Lawrence K., "Parody in Hawkes' THE LIME TREE," *Crit* 15, ii (1973): 49-56.

Burden, Robert, "John Hawkes: THE LIME TWIG," *John Fowles, John Hawkes, Claude Simon*, 285-303.

Busch, F., *Hawkes*, 87-106.

Edenbaum, Robert I., "John Hawkes: THE LIME TWIG and Other Tenuous Horrors," *MR* 7 (Summer, 1966): 462-75.

Fiedler, Leslie, "A Lonely American Eccentric: The Pleasures of John Hawkes," *New Leader* 43 (Dec. 12, 1960): 12-14. Also in Fiedler, L., *Collected Essays of Leslie Fiedler*, v. 2, 319-24.

Gault, Pierre, "Genesis and Functions of Hencher in THE LIME TWIG," in Johnson, I. D., and C. Johnson, eds., *Les Américanistes*, 138-55.

Graham, John, "John Hawkes on His Novels: An Interview," *MR* 7 (Summer, 1966): 453-7.

Green, Geoffrey, "Relativism and the Multiple Contexts for Contemporary Fiction," *Genre* 14, i (Spring, 1981): 39-42.

Greiner, D. J., *Comic Terror*, 125-58.

Heller, Terry, "Notes on Technique in Black Humor," *Thalia* 2, iii (Winter, 1979-80): 19-20.

Hoffman, James W., "A Class Discussion of THE LIME TWIG," in Santore, A. C., and M. Pocalyko, eds., *John Hawkes Symposium*, 77-90.

Madden, John, "John Hawkes: Artist in Search of a Mask," in Baldanza, F., ed., *Itinerary 3: Criticism*, 126-30.

Malin, I., "Self-love," *New American Gothic*, 42-4.

Matthews, Charles, "The Destructive Vision of John Hawkes," *Crit* 6, ii (Fall, 1963): 48-52.

O'Donnell, P., *John Hawkes*, 72-84.

Olderman, R. M., "Conspiracy from Without and Within," *Beyond the Waste Land*, 150-75.

Scholes, Robert, *Fabulation and Metafiction*, 178-89.

————, *Fabulators*, 79-94.

Schwartz, Richard A., "Hawkes and Holmes: THE LIME TWIG and 'Silver Blaze'," *NConL* 9, ii (1979): 11.

Shepherd, Allen, "Illumination Through (Anti) Climax: John Hawkes' THE LIME TWIG," *NConL* 2, ii (Mar., 1972): 11-13.

Stubbs, John C., "John Hawkes and the Dream-Work of THE LIME TWIG and SECOND SKIN," *L&P* 21, iii (1971): 149-56.

Tanner, T., *City of Words*, 212-18.

————, "Necessary Landscapes and Luminous Deteriorations," *TriQ* 20 (Winter, 1971): 158-65.

Templeton, Wayne, "Between Two Worlds: Experiencing the Novels of John Hawkes," *WCR* 15, iii (Winter, 1981): 9-12.

Warner, John M., "The Internalized Quest Romance in Hawkes' THE LIME TWIG," *MFS* 19, i (Spring, 1973): 89-95.

Wineapple, Brenda, "The Travesty of Literalism: Two Novels by John Hawkes," *JNT* 12, ii (Spring, 1982): 130-8.

THE OWL

Busch, F., *Hawkes*, 61-72.

Greiner, D. J., *Comic Terror*, 55-66.

Laing, Jeffrey, "The Doctored Voice: Sexual Imagery and Medical Jargon in John Hawkes's THE OWL," *NConL* 10, v (1980): 6-7.

Malin, I., "Self-love," in *New American Gothic*, 41-2.

O'Donnell, P., *John Hawkes*, 50-5.

Scholes, Robert, "John Hawkes as Novelist: The Example of the Owl," *HC* 14, iii (June, 1977): 1-10.

THE PASSION ARTIST

Emmett, Paul J., "THE CANNIBAL to THE PASSION ARTIST: Hawkes's Journey toward the Depths of the Unconscious," *ChiR* 32, i (Summer, 1980): 135-52.

O'Donnell, P., *John Hawkes*, 99-112.

Templeton, Wayne, "Review," *WCR* 14, iv (April, 1980): 10-12.

Thompson, Gary, "Barth's Letters and Hawkes' Passion," *MQR* 19 (Winter, 1980): 270-8.

SECOND SKIN

Bassoff, Bruce, "Mythic Truth and Deception in SECOND SKIN," *EA* 30, iii (1977): 337-42.

Bell, Steven M., "Realism Rewritten: Another Reading of Hawkes's SECOND SKIN," *BSUF* 23, iii (1982): 64-8.

Busch, F., *Hawkes*, 107-22.

Cantrell, Carol H., "John Hawkes's SECOND SKIN: The Dead Reckoning of a Northrop Frye Romance," *BRMMLA* 35, iv (1981): 281-90.

Clark, Walter H., Jr., "John Hawkes' Use of Two Shakesperian Sources," *Americana-Austriaca: Beitrage zur Amerikakunde* (Vienna) 4 (1978): 14-23.

Friedmann, Thomas, "Hawkes's SECOND SKIN," *Expl* 38, i (1979): 28-9.

Frost, Lucy, "Awakening Paradise," in Graham, J., comp., *Studies in SECOND SKIN*, 52-63.

Galloway, David D., "Clown and Saint: The Hero in Current American Fiction," *Crit* 7 (Spring-Summer, 1965): 53-4.

Graham, John, "John Hawkes on His Novels: An Interview," *MR* 7 (Summer, 1966): 457-61. Also in Graham, J., comp., *Studies in SECOND SKIN*, 31-3.

Graham, J., comp., *Studies in SECOND SKIN*.

Greiner, D. J., *Comic Terror*, 159-99.

————, "The Thematic Use of Color in John Hawkes' SECOND SKIN," *ConL* 11, iii (Summer, 1970): 389-400.

Guerard, Albert J., "SECOND SKIN: The Light and Dark Affirmation," in Graham, J., comp., *Studies in SECOND SKIN*, 93-102.

Hawkes, John, "THE FLOATING OPERA and SECOND SKIN," *Mosaic* 8, i (1974): 17-28.

————, "Notes on Writing a Novel," *TriQ* 30 (Spring, 1974): 109-26.

Imhoff, Ron, "On SECOND SKIN," *Mosaic* 8, i (1974): 51-63.

Kuehl, John, "Story into Novel," in Kuehl, John, *Write and Rewrite*, N.Y.: Meredith, 1967, 265, 284-7. Also in Graham, J., comp., *Studies in SECOND SKIN*, 35-8.

Lavers, Norman, "The Structure of SECOND SKIN," *Novel* 5 (Spring, 1972): 208-14.

Le Clair, Thomas, "John Hawkes's 'Death of an Airman' and SECOND SKIN," *NConL* 4, i (1974): 2-3.

————, "The Unreliability of Innocence: John Hawkes' SECOND SKIN," *JNT* 3 (Jan., 1973): 32-9.

Nichols, Stephen G., Jr., "Vision and Tradition in SECOND SKIN," in Graham, J., comp., *Studies in SECOND SKIN*, 69-82.

O'Donnell, Patrick, "The Hero as Artist in John Hawkes's SECOND SKIN," *IFR* 4 (1977): 119-27.

————, *John Hawkes*, 85-99.

Pearce, R., *Stages of the Clown*, 102-16.

Ricks, Christopher, "Chamber of Horrors," *NStat* (Mar. 11, 1966): 339-40.

Rife, David J., "John Hawkes' Starfish," *NConL* 7, i (Jan., 1977): 15.

Robinson, William R., "John Hawkes' Artificial Inseminator," in Graham, J., comp., *Studies in SECOND SKIN*, 63-9.

Santore, Anthony C., "Narrative Unreliability and the Structure of SECOND SKIN," in Graham, J., comp., *Studies in SECOND SKIN*, 83-93.

Singer, Alan S., "Discontinuity and Discourse in Modern Fiction," *DAI* 41 (1980): 2106A.

Stubbs, John C., "John Hawkes and the Dream-Work of THE LIME TWIG and SECOND SKIN," *L&P* 21, iii (1971): 149-52, 156-9.

Tanner, T., *City of Words*, 218-29.

———, "Necessary Landscapes and Luminous Deteriorations," *TriQ* 20 (Winter, 1971): 165-79.

Templeton, Wayne, "Between Two Worlds: Experiencing the Novels of John Hawkes," *WCR* 15, iii (Winter, 1981): 12-15.

Wallace, Ronald, "The Rarer Action: Comedy in John Hawkes's SECOND SKIN," *SNNTS* 9, ii (1977): 169-86. Also in Wallace, R., *Last Laugh*, 45-64.

Whitlow, Roger, "Papa Cue Ball Through the Looking Glass: Observations on John Hawkes's SECOND SKIN," *CEAF* 6, iv (1976): 4-5.

Wineapple, Barbara, "SECOND SKIN and the Dead Reckoning of Romance," *CLAJ* 25, iv (June, 1982): 468-75.

Wineke, Donald R., "Comic Structure and the Double Time-Scheme of Hawkes's SECOND SKIN," *Genre* 14, i (Spring, 1981): 117-32.

Witherington, Paul, "Character Spin-Offs in John Hawkes's SECOND SKIN," *SAF* 9, i (Spring, 1981): 83-91.

Yarborough, Richard, "Hawkes' SECOND SKIN," *Mosaic* 8, i (1974): 65-75.

Yskamp, Claire E., "Character and Voice: First Person Narrators in TOM JONES, WUTHERING HEIGHTS and SECOND SKIN," *DAI* 32 (1972): 6948A.

TRAVESTY

Allen, C. J., "Desire, Design, and Debris: The Submerged Narrative of John Hawkes' Recent Trilogy," *MFS* 25, iv (Winter, 1979-80): 589-92.

Baxter, Charles, "In the Suicide Seat: Reading John Hawkes's TRAVESTY," *GaR* 34 (1980): 871-85.

Emmett, Paul, "The Reader's Voyage through TRAVESTY," *ChiR* 28, i (1976): 172-87.

Greiner, Donald J., "Private Apocalypse: The Visions of TRAVESTY," in Santore, A. C., and M. Pocalyko, eds., *John Hawkes Symposium*, 142-53.

Hornung, Alfred, "Sex and Art in Hawkes' Triad: The Pornographic, the Erotic, and the Aesthetic Modes," *Amst* 26, ii (1981): 159-79.

O'Donnell, P., *John Hawkes*, 135-42.

Rosenzweig, Paul, "Aesthetics and the Psychology of Control in John Hawkes's Triad," *Novel* 15, ii (Winter, 1982): 146-62.

Scotto, Robert M., "A Note on John Hawkes's DEATH, SLEEP & THE TRAVELER and TRAVESTY," *NMAL* 1 (1977): Item 11.

Templeton, Wayne, "Between Two Worlds: Experiencing the Novels of John Hawkes," *WCR* 15, ii (Winter, 1981): 19-21.

Van Wert, William F., "Narration in John Hawkes' Trilogy," *LitR* 24, i (Fall, 1980): 35-6.

Veron, Enid, "From Festival to Farce: Design and Meaning in John Hawkes's Comic Triad," in Santore, A. C., and M. Pocalyko, eds., *John Hawkes Symposium*, 64-76 *passim*.

Wineapple, Brenda, "The Travesty of Literalism: Two Novels by John Hawkes," *JNT* 12, ii (Spring, 1982): 130-8.

Ziegler, Heide, "John Hawkes' TRAVESTY and the Idea of Travesty," *ArAA* 7, ii (1982): 161-8.

BIBLIOGRAPHY

Bryer, Jackson R., "John Hawkes," *Crit* 6, ii (Fall, 1963): 89-94.

O'Donnell, P., *John Hawkes*, 157-65.

Plung, Daniel, "John Hawkes: A Selected Bibliography, 1943-1975," *Crit* 17, iii (1976): 53-63.

HAYDN, HIRAM, 1907-1973

GENERAL

"A Celebration of Hiram Haydn," *Voyages* 3, i-ii (Winter, 1970): 7-55.

Chappell, Fred, "Hiram Haydn's Other World," *Voyages* 3, i-ii (Winter, 1970): 22-9.

O'Brien, John, "An Interview with Hiram Haydn," *ASch* 4, ii (Spring, 1974): 199-222.

THE HANDS OF ESAU

O'Brien, John, "An Interview with Hiram Haydn," *ASch* 43, ii (Spring, 1974): 199-222 *passim*.

REPORT FROM THE RED WINDMILL

Nin, Anais, "Anais Nin on Hiram Haydn's REPORT FROM THE RED WINDMILL," *Voyages* 3, i-ii (Winter, 1970): 29-30.

O'Brien, John, "An Interview with Hiram Haydn," *ASch* 43, ii (Spring, 1974): 199-222 *passim*.

HAYES, ALFRED, 1911-1985

GENERAL

Aldridge, J. W., *After the Lost Generation*, 110-11, 114-16.

ALL THY CONQUESTS

Waldmeir, J. J., *American Novels of the Second World War*, 83-8.

THE GIRL ON THE VIA FLAMINIA

Healey, Robert C., in Gardiner, H. C., ed., *Fifty Years of the American Novel*, 266-7.

HAZZARD, SHIRLEY, 1931-

GENERAL

Colmer, John, "Patterns and Preoccupations of Love: The Novels of Shirley Hazzard," *Meanjin* 29, iv (Summer, 1970): 461-7.

Sellick, Robert, "Shirley Hazzard: Dislocation and Continuity," *ALS* 9, ii (Oct., 1979): 182-8.

THE BAY OF NOON

Geering, R. G., *Recent Fiction*, 39-45.

THE EVENING OF THE HOLIDAY

Geering, R. G., *Recent Fiction*, 39-45.

PEOPLE IN GLASS HOUSES

Geering, R. G., *Recent Fiction*, 45-7.

THE TRANSIT OF VENUS

Bird, Delys, "Shirley Hazzard: THE TRANSIT OF VENUS," *Westerly* 26, i (Mar., 1981): 54-6.

BIBLIOGRAPHY

Beston, John B., "A Bibliography of Shirley Hazzard," *WLWE* 20, ii (Autumn, 1981): 236-54.

Geering, R. G., "Portrait of True Virtue," *Overland* 83 (Apr., 1981): 69-71.

HEAD, BESSIE, 1937-

GENERAL

Abrahams, Cecil A., "The Tyranny of Place: The Context of Bessie Head's Fiction," *WLWE* 17, i (April, 1978): 22-9.

Bruner, Charlotte H., *Bessie Head: Restless in a Distant Land*, University Park, Pa.: African Lit. Assn., French Dept., Pennsylvania St. Un., 1978.

_____, "Bessie Head: Restless in a Distant Land," in Parker, C. A., and S. H. Arnold, eds., *When the Drumbeat Changes*, 262-77.

_____, "Child Africa as Depicted By Bessie Head and Ama Ata Aidoo," *SHum* 7, ii (1979): 5-11.

Femi, Ojo-Ade, "Bessie Head's Alienated Heroine: Victim or Villain?" *Ba Shiru* 8, ii (1977): 13-21. [Not seen.]

Fradkin, Betty M., "Conversations with Bessie," *WLWE* 17, ii (1978): 427-34.

Grant, Jane W., "Bessie Head: An Appreciation," *Bananas* 22 (1980): 25-6.

Heywood, Christopher, "Traditional Values in the Novel of Bessie Head," in Massa, D., ed., *Individual and Community in Commonwealth Literature*, 12-19.

Marquard, Jean, "Bess Head: Exile and Community in Southern Africa," *LonM* 18, ix-x (Dec., 1978-Jan., 1979): 48-61.

Ogungbesan, Kolawole, "The Cape Goodeberry Also Grows in Botswana: Alienation and Commitment in the Writings of Bessie Head," *Jour. of Afr. Studies* 6, iv (Winter, 1979-80): 206-12.

Ravenscroft, Arthur, "The Novels of Hessie Head," *SAfrL* (1976): 174-86. Also in Heywood, C., ed., *Aspects of South African Literature*, 174-86.

MARU

Ravenscroft, Arthur, "The Novels of Bessie Head," *SAfrL* (1976): 179-83. Also in Heywood, C., ed., *Aspects of South African Literature*, 179-83.

A QUESTION OF POWER

Beard, Linda S., "Bessie Head's A QUESTION OF POWER: The Journey Through Disintegration to Wholeness," *CLQ* 15, iv (1979): 267-74.

Brown, Raymond, "A QUESTION OF POWER," *Mambo* 1 (Nov., 1974): 13-14.

Femi, Ojo-Ade, "Bessie Head's Alienated Heroine: Victim or Villain?" *Ba-Shiru* 8, ii (1977): 16-21.

Larson, Charles R., "The Singular Consciousness—R. K. Narayan's GRATEFUL TO LIFE AND DEATH and Bessie Head's A QUESTION OF POWER," *The Novel in the The Third World*, Washington: Inscape, 1976, 164-73.

Ravenscroft, Arthur, "The Novels of Bessie Head," *SAfrL* (1976): 183-5. Also in Heywood, C., ed., *Aspects of South African Literature*, 183-5.

WHEN RAIN CLOUDS GATHER

Ravenscroft, Arthur, "The Novels of Bessie Head," *SAfrL* (1976): 176-9. Also in Heywood, C., ed., *Aspects of South African Literature*, 176-9.

HEARNE, JOHN, 1926-

GENERAL

Birbalsingh, Frank M., " 'Escapism' in the Novels of John Hearne," *Caribbean Quarterly* 16, i (Mar., 1970): 28-38.

Cartey, Wilfred, "The Novels of John Hearne," *JCL* No. 7 (July, 1969): 45-58.

Davies, Barrie, "The Seekers: The Novels of John Hearne," in James, L., ed., *Islands in Between*, 109-20.

Figueroa, John J., "John Hearne, West Indian Writer," *RevI* 2, i (Spring, 1972): 72-9.

THE AUTUMN EQUINOX

Cooke, Michael G., "Rational Despair and the Fatality of Revolution in West Indian Literature," *YR* 71, i (Autumn, 1981): 32-5.

THE FACES OF LOVE

Ramchand, K., *West Indian Novel and its Background*, 45-50.

LAND OF THE LIVING

Davies, Barrie, "The Seekers," in James, L., ed., *Islands in Between*, 117-20.

STRANGER AT THE GATE

Davies, Barrie, "The Seekers," in James, L., ed., *Islands in Between*, 111-12.

THE SURE SALVATION

Baugh, Edward, "Men Acting as Men: John Hearne's THE SURE SALVATION," *Jamaica Journal* 16 (Feb., 1983): 61-3.

VOICES UNDER THE WINDOW

Davies, Barrie, "The Seekers," in James, L., ed., *Islands in Between*, 109-11.

Morris, Mervyn, "Pattern and Meaning in VOICES UNDER THE WINDOW," *Jamaica Journal* 5 (Mar., 1971): 53-6.

HELLER, JOSEPH, 1923-

GENERAL

Amis, Martin, "Joseph Heller in Conversation," *New Rev* 2, xx (1975): 55-9.

Anon., "Notes on the Next Novel, an Interview [with Joseph Heller]," *NOR* 2 (1971): 216-19.

Janoff, Bruce L., "Beyond Satire: Black Humor in the Novels of John Barth and Joseph Heller," *DAI* 33 (1972): 1728A (Ohio).

Luttrell, William, "Tragic and Comic Modes in Twentieth Century American Literature: William Styron and Joseph Heller," *DAI* 30 (1969): 2537A (Bowling Green).

Merrill, Sam, "Playboy Interview: Joseph Heller," *Playboy* 22, vi (1975): 59-76.

Plimpton, George, "The Art of Fiction 51: Joseph Heller," *ParisR* 60 (Winter, 1974): 126-47. [Interview.]

Reilly, C. E., and Carol Villei, "An Interview with Joseph Heller," *Delaware Lit. Rev.* (Un. of Delaware) (Spring, 1975): 19-21.

_____, "Talking with Joseph Heller," *Inquiry Mag.* (May 1, 1979): 22-6.

Ritter, Josse P., "Fearful Comedy: The Fiction of Joseph Heller, Gunter Grass, and the Social Surrealist Genre," *DA* 28 (1967): 1447A (Arkansas).

Robinson, Robert, "Thirteen Years After CATCH-22: An Interview with Joseph Heller," *Listener* 92 (Oct. 24, 1974): 550.

Sale, Richard B., "An Interview in New York with Joseph Heller," *SNNTS* 4, i (Spring, 1972): 63-74.

Shapiro, James, "Work in Progress: Joseph Heller. An Interview," *IntellectualD* 2, iv (1971): 6-11.

Whitman, Alden, "Something Always Happens On the Way to the Office: An Interview with Joseph Heller," in Bruccoli, M. J., and C. E. F. Clark, Jr., eds., *Pages*, 74-81.

Young, Melanie M. S., "Joseph Heller: A Critical Introduction," *DAI* 42, ii (Aug., 1981): 708A.

CATCH-22

Anderson, Don, "Yossarian *Haruspex*: Some Observations on CATCH-22," *SSEng* 3 (1977-78): 59-73.

Anon., "A Review: CATCH-22," in Smith, Roger, ed., *The American Reading Public* (The Daedalus Symposium), N.Y.: Bowker, 1963, 234-7. Also in *Daedalus* 92 (Winter, 1963): 155-65. Also in Kiley, F., and W. McDonald, eds., *CATCH-22 Casebook*, 27-39.

Balch, Clayton L., "Yossarian to Cathcart and Return: A Personal Cross-Country," in Kiley, F., and W. McDonald, eds., *CATCH-22 Casebook*, 301-6.

Barnard, Ken, "Interview with Joseph Heller," *Detroit News* (Sept. 13, 1970): 19, 24, 27-8, 30, 65. Also in Kiley, F., and W. McDonald, eds., *CATCH-22 Casebook*, 294-301.

Billson, Marcus K., III, "The Un-Minderbinding of Yossarian: Genesis Inverted in CATCH-22," *ArQ* 36 (1980): 315-29.

Blues, Thomas, "The Moral Structure of CATCH-22," *SNNTS* 3, i (Spring, 1971): 64-79. Also in Nagel, J., ed., *Critical Essays on CATCH-22*, 102-16. Also in Scotto, R. M., ed., *Joseph Heller's CATCH-22*, 544-59.

Bronson, Daniel R., "Man on a String: CATCH-22," *NConL* 7, ii (1977): 8-9.

Brustein, Robert, "The Logic of Survival in a Lunatic World," *NRep* 145 (Nov. 13, 1961): 11-13. Also in Harrison, G., ed., *Critic as Artist*, 47-54.

Bryant, J. H., *Open Decision*, 156-64.

Burhans, Clinton S., Jr., "Spindrift and the Sea: Structural Patterns and Unifying Elements in CATCH-22," *TCL* 19, iv (Oct., 1973): 239-49.

Castelli, Jim, "CATCH-22 and the New Hero," *CathW* 211 (Aug., 1970): 199-202. Also in Kiley, F., and W. McDonald, eds., *CATCH-22 Casebook*, 174-81.

Cheuse, Alan, "Laughing on the Outside," *StL* 3 (Fall, 1963): 81-7. Also in Kiley, F., and W. McDonald, eds., *CATCH-22 Casebook*, 86-93.

Cockburn, Alex, "CATCH-22," *New Left Rev* No. 18 (Jan.-Feb., 1963): 87-93.

Colmer, John, *Coleridge to CATCH-22: Images of Society*, N.Y.: St. Martins Pr., 1978, 210-21.

Crosland, Andrew, "Hemingway, Heller, and an Old Joke," *AN&Q* 16, v (1977/78): 73.

Davis, Gary W., "CATCH-22 and the Language of Discontinuity," *Novel* 12, i (1978): 66-77.

Day, Douglas, "CATCH-22: A Manifesto for Anarchists," *Carolina Qtly* 15 (Summer, 1963): 86-92. Also in Kiley, F., and W. McDonald, eds., *CATCH-22 Casebook*, 181-7.

Denniston, Constance, "The American Romance-Parody: A Study of Purdy's MALCOLM and Heller's CATCH-22," *ESRS* 14, ii (1965): 42-59, 63-4. Also in Nagel, J., ed., *Critical Essays on CATCH-22*, 64-77. Also, revised, in Kiley, F., and W. McDonald, eds., *CATCH-22 Casebook*, 51-7.

Doskow, Minna, "The Night Journey in CATCH-22," *TCL* 12 (Jan., 1967): 186-93. Also in Nagel, J., ed., *Critical Essays on CATCH-22*, 155-63. Also in Kiley, F., and W. McDonald, eds., *CATCH-22 Casebook*, 166-74.

Fetrow, Fred M., "Joseph Heller's Use of Names in CATCH-22," *StCS* 1, ii-2 (1975): 28-38.

Foott, David, "The Eternal City: Joseph Heller as Sadist," *LiNQ* 2, iii (1973): 25-9.

Frank, Mike, "Eros and Thanatos in CATCH-22," *CRevAS* 7, i (1976): 77-87.

_____, "Rhetoric, Theme, and Consciousness in CATCH-22: An Essay in Critical Reading," *DAI* 33 (1972): 309A (Cornell).

Frost, Lucy, "Violence in the Eternal City: CATCH-22 as a Critique of American Culture," *Meanjin* 30, iv (Dec., 1971): 447-53.

Galloway, David D., "Clown and Saint: The Hero in Current American Fiction," *Crit* 7 (Spring-Summer, 1965): 50-2.

Gaukroger, Doug, "Time Structure in CATCH-22," *Crit* 12, ii (1970): 70-85. Also in Nagel, J., ed., *Critical Essays on CATCH-22*, 89-101. Also in Kiley, F., and W. McDonald, eds., *CATCH-22 Casebook*, 132-44.

Gilligan, Thomas M., "The New Realism of Heller, Kesey, and Vonnegut: A Study of CATCH-22, ONE FLEW OVER THE CUCKOO'S NEST, and SLAUGHTERHOUSE-FIVE," *DAI* 41, vii (Jan., 1981): 3105A-06A.

Glass, Peyton, III, "Heller's CATCH-22," *Expl* 36, ii (1978): 25-6.

Gonzales, Alexis, "Notes on the Next Novel: An Interview with Joseph Heller," *NOR* 2, iii (1971): 216-19.

Gordon, Caroline, and Jeanne Richardson, "Files in Their Eyes? A Note on Joseph Heller's CATCH-22," *SoR* 3 (Jan., 1967): 96-105. Also in Nagel, J., ed., *Critical Essays on CATCH-22*, 117-24.

Greenberg, Alvin, "The Novel of Disintegration: Paradoxical Impossibility in Contemporary Fiction," *WSCL* 7 (Winter-Spring, 1966): 115-17.

Greenfeld, Josh, "22 was Funnier than 14," *NYTBR* (Mar. 3, 1968): 1, 49-51, 53. Also in Kiley, F., and W. McDonald, eds., *CATCH-22 Casebook*, 250-5.

Gross, Beverly, "'Insanity is Contagious': The Mad World of CATCH-22," *CentR* 26, i (Winter, 1982): 86-113.

Harris, Charles B., "CATCH-22: A Radical Protest against Absurdity," *Contemporary American Novelists of the Absurd*, 33-50.

Hartshorne, Thomas L., "From CATCH-22 to SLAUGHTER-HOUSE V: The Decline of the Political Mode," *SAQ* 78, i (1979): 17-33.

Hasley, Louis, "Dramatic Tension in CATCH-22," *MQ* 15, ii (Winter, 1974): 190-7.

Havemann, Carol S. P., "The Fool as Mentor in Modern American Parables of Entrapment: Ken Kesey's ONE FLEW OVER THE CUCKOO'S NEST, Joseph Heller's CATCH-22 and Ralph Ellison's INVISIBLE MAN," *DAI* 32 (1971): 2091A-92A (Rice).

Hays, Peter L., "Yossarian and Gilgamesh," *NMAL* 4 (1980): Item 9.

Heller, Joseph, "Did the Author Catch the Movie?" in Peary, G., and R. Shatzkin, eds., *Modern American Novel and the Movies*, 256-65. From Kiley, F., and W. McDonald, eds., *CATCH-22 Casebook*, 357-62.

Heller, Terry, "Notes on Technique in Black Humor," *Thalia* 2, iii (Winter, 1979-80): 15-17.

Henry, G. B. Mck., "Significant Corn: *CATCH-22 Casebook*, 187-201.

Hoffman, F. J., *Mortal No*, 261-3.

Holubetz, Margarete, "Black Humour in Modern English Literature," *WBEP* 78 (1981): 7-15.

Hunt, John W., "Comic Escape and Anti-Vision: The Novels of Joseph Heller and Thomas Pynchon," in Scott, N. A., Jr., *Adversity and Grace*, 90-8 *passim*. Also in Nagel, J., ed., *Critical Essays on CATCH-22*, 125-30. Also in Kiley, F., and W. McDonald, eds., *CATCH-22 Casebook*, 242-7.

"An Impolite Interview with Joseph Heller," *The Realist* 39 (Nov., 1962): 18-31. Also in Kiley, F., and W. McDonald, eds., *CATCH-22 Casebook*, 273-93.

Janoff, Bruce, "Black Humor, Absurdity and Technique," *STwC* No. 13 (Spring, 1974): 40-5.

Karl, Frederick R., "Joseph Heller's CATCH-22: Only Fools Walk in Darkness," in Moore, H. T., ed., *Contemporary American Novelists*, 134-42. Also in Kiley, F., and W. McDonald, eds., *CATCH-22 Casebook*, 159-65. Also in Scotto, R. M., ed., *Joseph Heller's CATCH-22*, 481-8.

Kazin, Alfred, "From The War Novel: From Mailer to Vonnegut," in Scotto, R. M., ed., *Joseph Heller's CATCH-22*, 488-91. From *SatR* (Feb. 6, 1971): 13-15, 36.

Kennard, Jean, "Joseph Heller: At War with Absurdity," *Mosaic* 4, iii (Spring, 1971): 75-87. Also in Kiley, F., and W. McDonald, eds., *CATCH-22 Casebook*, 255-69. Also in Scotto, R. M., ed., *Joseph Heller's CATCH-22*, 526-41. Also in Kennard, J. E., *Number and Nightmare*, 41-56.

Kiley, F., and W. McDonald, eds., *CATCH-22 Casebook*.

Kilgo, James P., "Five American Novels of World War II: A Critical Study," *DAI* 32 (1972): 6380A.

Kostelanetz, Richard, "The New American Fiction," in Kostelanetz, R., ed., *New American Arts*, 212-14.

Larsen, Michael J., "Shakespearean Echoes in CATCH-22," *AN&Q* 17, v (1978/1979): 76-8.

Lehan, Richard, and Jerry Patch, "CATCH-22: The Making of a Novel," *MinnR* 7, iii (1967): 238-44. Also in Nagel, J., ed., *Critical Essays on CATCH-22*, 37-44.

_____, *Dangerous Crossing*, 163-72.

Lewis, R. W. B., "Days of Wrath and Laughter," *Trials of the World*, 226-7.

Littlejohn, David, "The Anti-realists," *Daedalus* 92 (Spring, 1963): 258-9.

Loukides, Paul, "The Radical Vision," *MicA* 5, iv (Spring, 1973): 497-503.

Martine, James J., "The Courage to Defy," in Nagel, J., ed., *Critical Essays on CATCH-22*, 142-9.

McDonald, Walter R., "He Took Off: Yossarian and the Different Drummer," *CEA* 36, i (Nov., 1973): 14-16.

_____, "Look Back in Horror: The Functional Comedy of CATCH-22," *CEA* 35, ii (Jan., 1973): 18-21.

_____, "Yossarian's Letter From the Earth," *CEAF* 5, i (Oct., 1974): 12.

McNamara, Eugene, "The Absurd Style in Contemporary American Literature," *HAB* 19, i (Winter, 1968): 44-9.

Mellard, James M., "CATCH-22: *Déjà vu* and the Labyrinth of Memory," *BuR* 16, ii (May, 1968): 29-44. Also in Kiley, F., and W. McDonald, eds., *CATCH-22 Casebook*, 109-21. Also in Scotto, R. M., ed., *Joseph Heller's CATCH-22*, 512-25.

Merivale, P., "CATCH-22 and THE SECRET AGENT: Mechanical Man, the Hole in the Centre, and the 'Principle of Inbuilt Chaos'," *ESC* 7, iv (Dec., 1981): 426-37.

Merrill, Robert, "The Rhetorical Structure of CATCH-22," *NConL* 8, ii (1978): 9-11.

Mills, Russell, "Multiple Characterization in CATCH-22," *NConL* 9, iv (1979): 6-7.

Milne, Victor J., "Heller's 'Bologniad': A Theological Perspective on CATCH-22," *Crit* 12, ii (1970): 50-69. Also in Kiley, F., and W. McDonald, eds., *CATCH-22 Casebook*, 58-73.

Monk, Donald, "An Experiment in Therapy: A Study of CATCH-22," *London Review* 2 (Autumn, 1967): 12-19. Also in Kiley, F., and W. McDonald, eds., *CATCH-22 Casebook*, 212-20.

Morrow, Patrick, "Yossarian in Wonderland: The ALICE Books and CATCH-22," *NDQ* 43, i (1975): 50-7.

Mullican, James S., "A Burkean Approach to CATCH-22," *CollL* 8, i (Winter, 1981): 42-52.

Muste, John M., "Better to Die Laughing: The War Novels of Joseph Heller and John Ashmead," *Crit* 5, ii (Fall, 1962): 16-27.

Nagel, James, "The CATCH-22 Note Cards," *SNNTS* 8, iv (Winter, 1976): 394-405.

_____, "CATCH-22 and Angry Humor: A Study of the Normative Values of Satire," *StAH* 1, ii (Oct., 1974): 99-106.

_____, ed., *Critical Essays on CATCH-22*.

_____, "Two Brief Manuscript Sketches: Heller's CATCH-22," *MFS* 20, ii (Summer, 1974): 221-4.

_____, "Yossarian, the Old Man, and the Ending of CATCH-22," in Nagel, J., ed., *Critical Essays on CATCH-22*, 164-74.

Nelson, G. B., *Ten Versions of America*, 165-82.

Nelson, Thomas A., "Theme and Structure in CATCH-22," *Ren* 23 (1971): 173-82.

Oetgen, George R., "The Twenty-Two of Heller's CATCH," *AN&Q* 18, x (1980): 160.

Olderman, R. M., "The Grail Knight Departs," *Beyond the Waste Land*, 94-116.

Orr, Richard W., "Flat Characters in CATCH-22," *NConL* 1, i (Jan., 1971): 4.

Parr, Susan R., "Everything Green Looked Black: CATCH-22 as an Inverted Eden," *NMAL* 4 (1980): Item 27.

Pearson, Carol, "CATCH-22 and the Debasement of Language," *CEA* 38, iv (1976): 30-5.

Pinsker, Sanford, "Heller's CATCH-22. The Protest of a *Puer Eternis*," *Crit* 7, ii (Winter, 1964-5): 150-62.

Podhoretz, Norman, "The Best Catch There Is," in Podhoretz, N., *Doings and Undoings*, 228-35. Also in Kiley, F., and W. McDonald, eds., *CATCH-22 Casebook*, 237-41.

Protherough, Robert, "The Sanity of CATCH-22," *HuW* 3 (May, 1971): 59-70. Also in Kiley, F., and W. McDonald, eds., *CATCH-22 Casebook*, 201-12. Also in Scotto, R. M., ed., *Joseph Heller's CATCH-22*, 541-4.

Ramsey, Vance, "From Here to Absurdity: Heller's CATCH-2," in Whitbread, T. B., ed., *Seven Contemporary Authors*, 100-18. Also in Kiley, F., and W. McDonald, eds., *CATCH-22 Casebook*, 221-36.

Richter, David, "The Achievement of Shape in the Twentieth-Century Fable: Joseph Heller's CATCH-22," *Fable's End*, 136-65.

Ritter, Jesse, "Fearful Comedy: CATCH-22 as Avatar of the Social Surrealist Novel," in Kiley, F., and W. McDonald, eds., *CATCH-22 Casebook*, 73-86.

————, "Fearful Comedy: The Fiction of Joseph Heller, Günter Grass, and the Social Surrealist Genre," *DA* 28 (1967): 1447A (Arkansas).

————, "What Manner of Men Are These," in Nagel, J., ed., *Critical Essays on CATCH-22*, 45-56.

Roundy, Peter E., "Images of Vietnam: CATCH-22, New Journalism, and the Postmodern Imagination," *DAI* 41 (1981): 3111A.

Ryan, Marjorie, "Four Contemporary Satires and the Problem of Norms," *SNL* 6, ii (Spring, 1969): 40-4.

Scammell, W., "Letter in Reply to Mr. Wain," *CritQ* 5 (Autumn, 1963): 273-4. Also in Kiley, F., and W. McDonald, eds., *CATCH-22 Casebook*, 49-50.

Schopf, William, "Blindfold and Backwards: Promethean and Bemushroomed Heroism in ONE FLEW OVER THE CUCKOO'S NEST and CATCH-22," *BRMMLA* 26, iii (Sept., 1972): 89-97.

Scotto, R. M., ed., *Joseph Heller's CATCH-22*.

Seltzer, Leon F., "Milo's 'Culpable Innocence': Absurdity as Moral Insanity in CATCH-22," *PLL* 15, iii (1979): 290-310.

Sharma, D. R., "CATCH-22: An Analysis of Personal Freedom vs. Group Loyalty," *BP* 19 (1972, pub. 1974): 20-9.

Sniderman, Stephen L., "'It Was All Yossarian's Fault': Power and Responsibility in CATCH-22," *TCL* 19, iv (Oct., 1973): 251-8.

Solomon, Eric, "From Christ in Flanders to CATCH-22: An Approach to War Fiction," *TSLL* 11, i (Spring, 1969): 851-66. Also in Kiley, F., and W. McDonald, eds., *CATCH-22 Casebook*, 94-101.

Solomon, Jan, "The Structure of Joseph Heller's CATCH-22," *Crit* 9, ii (1967): 46-57. Also in Nagel, J., ed., *Critical Essays on CATCH-22*, 78-88. Also in Kiley, F., and W. McDonald, eds.,

CATCH-22 Casebook, 122-32. Also in Scotto, R. M., ed., *Joseph Heller's CATCH-22*, 501-11.

Sorkin, Adam J., "From Papa to Yo-Yo: At War with All the Words in the World," *SAB* 44, iv (Nov., 1979): 48-65.

Standiford, Les, "Novels Into Film: CATCH-22 as Watershed," *SHR* (1974): 19-25.

Stark, Howard J., "The Anatomy of CATCH-22," in Kiley, F., and W. McDonald, eds., *CATCH-22 Casebook*, 145-58.

————, "CATCH-22: The Anatomy of a Novel," *DA* 29 (1969): 4506A (N. Mex.).

————, "CATCH-22: The Ultimate Irony," in Nagel, J., ed., *Critical Essays on CATCH-22*, 130-41.

Stern, J. P., "War and the Comic Muse," *CL* 20 (Summer, 1968): 193-216.

Swardson, H. R., "Sentimentality and the Academic Tradition," *CE* 37, viii (April, 1976): 747-66.

Tanner, T., *City of Words*, 72-84.

Thomas, W. K., "The Mythic Dimension of CATCH-22," *TSLL* 15 (1973): 189-98.

————, "'What Difference Does It Make?' Logic in CATCH-22," *DR* 50, iv (Winter, 1970-71): 488-95.

Vos, Nelvin, "The Angel, the Beast, and the Machine," in Kiley, F., and W. McDonald, eds., *CATCH-22 Casebook*, 247-50. From Vos, N., *For God's Sake Laugh*! Richmond, Va.: John Knox Pr., 1967, 53-8.

Wain, John, "A New Novel about Old Troubles," *CritQ* 5 (Summer, 1963): 168-73. Also in Kiley, F., and W. McDonald, eds., *CATCH-22 Casebook*, 43-9.

Walden, Daniel, "'Therefore Choose Life': A Jewish Interpretation of Heller's CATCH-22," in Nagel, J., ed., *Critical Essays on CATCH-22*, 57-63.

Waldmeir, J. J., *American Novels of the Second World War*, 160-5.

————, "Two Novelists of the Absurd: Heller and Kesey," *WSCL* 5, iii (Autumn, 1964): 192-6. Also in Nagel, J., ed., *Critical Essays on CATCH-22*, 150-4.

Walsh, J., *American War Literature*, 189-95.

Way, Brian, "Formal Experiment and Social Discontent: Joseph Heller's CATCH-22," *JAmS* 2 (1968): 253-70.

Wilhelm, Albert E., "'Carpe Diem' and 'Fuge Diem': Two Responses to Death in Heller's CATCH-22," *IllQ* 42, ii (1980): 45-8.

Williams, Melvin G., "CATCH-22: What the Movie Audiences Missed," *C&L* 23, iv (Summer, 1974): 21-5.

Wincelberg, Shimon, "A Deadly Serious Lunacy," in Kostelanetz, R., *Contemporary Literature*, 388-91. Also in *New Leader* (May 14, 1962).

GOOD AS GOLD

Berryman, Charles, "Heller's Gold," *ChiR* 32, iv (Spring, 1981): 108-18.

Miller, Wayne C., "Ethnic Identity as Moral Focus: A Reading of Joseph Heller's GOOD AS GOLD," *MELUS* 6, iii (1979): 3-17.

SOMETHING HAPPENED

Blackwood, Caroline, "The Horrors of Peace," *TLS* (Oct. 25, 1974): 1183.

Canaday, Nicholas, "Joseph Heller: Something Happened to the American Dream," *CEA* 40, i (Nov., 1977): 34-8.

Costa, Richard H., "Notes from a Dark Heller: Bob Slocum and the Underground Man," *TSLL* 23, ii (Summer, 1981): 159-82.

Gordon, Andrew, "Dead Letter Offices: Joseph Heller's SOMETHING HAPPENED and Herman Melville's 'Bartleby the Scrivener'," *NConL* 12, v (Nov., 1982): 2-4.

Hoeber, Daniel R., "Joseph Heller's Corporate Catcher," *NConL* 8, ii (Mar., 1978): 10-11.

Klemtner, Susan S., "'A Permanent Game of Excuses': Determinism in Heller's SOMETHING HAPPENED," *MFS* 24, iv (Winter, 1978-79): 550-6.

Le Clair, Thomas, "Joseph Heller, SOMETHING HAPPENED, and the Art of Excess," *SAF* 9, ii (Autumn, 1981): 245-60.

McDonald, Walter R., "The Confession Novel: Freedom and Guilt in FREE FALL and SOMETHING HAPPENED," *CCTE* 40 (1975): 41-5.

McGinnis, Wayne D., "The Anarchic Impulse in Two Recent Novels," *PaPA* 5, ii-iii (1979): 36-40.

Orlova, R., "The Richest Life," in Vroon, R., tr., *20th Century American Literature: A Soviet View*, 496-500.

Percy, Walker, "The State of the Novel: Dying Art or New Science?" *MQR* 16 (1977): 359-73 *passim*. Also in Martin, Robert A., ed., *The Writer's Craft: Hopwood Lectures, 1965-81*, Ann Arbor: Un. of Michigan Pr., 1982, 206-20 *passim*.

Proffitt, Edward, "Slocum's Accident: An American Tragedy," *NConL* 7, iii (1977): 7-8.

Searles, George J., "SOMETHING HAPPENED: A New Direction for Joseph Heller," *Crit* 18, iii (1977): 74-82.

Sebouhian, George, "From Abraham and Isaac to Bob Slocum and My Boy: Why Fathers Kill Their Sons," *TCL* 27, i (Spring, 1981): 43-52.

Strehle, Susan, "Slocum's Parenthetical Tic: Style as Metaphor in SOMETHING HAPPENED," *NConL* 7, v (1977): 9-10.

Winther, Per, "Joseph Heller on SOMETHING HAPPENED: An Interview," *Amer. Studies in Scandinavia* 8 (1976): 17-31.

BIBLIOGRAPHY

Keegan, Brenda M., *Joseph Heller: A Reference Guide*, London: Prior; Boston: G. K. Hall, 1978.

Weixlmann, Joseph, "A Bibliography of Joseph Heller's CATCH-22," *BB* 31, i (Jan.-Mar., 1974): 32-7.

HEMINGWAY, ERNEST, 1898-1961

GENERAL

See issues of *The Hemingway Review*, formerly *Hemingway Notes*.

Aberg, Gilbert, "White Hope—Somewhat Sunburned: The Maturity of Hemingway," ChiR 7 (Spring, 1953): 18-24.

Adair, William, "Ernest Hemingway and the Poetics of Loss," *ColL* 5 (1978): 12-23.

Agent, Dan, "The Hair on Hemingway's Chest," *LGJ* 1, i (May, 1973): 12-15.

Akmakjian, Hiag, "Hemingway and Haiku," *CUF* 9, ii (Spring, 1966): 45-8.

Alderman, Taylor, "Ernest Hemingway: Four Studies in the Competitive Motif," *DAI* 31 (1970): 380A (N. Mex.).

Aldridge, J. W., *Devil in the Fire*.

———, "Hemingway and Europe," *Shen* 12, iii (Spring, 1961): 11-24.

———, "Hemingway: Nightmare and the Correlative of Loss," *After the Lost Generation*, 23-43.

———, "Hemingway: The Etiquette of the Berserk," *Mandrake* 2 (Autumn-Winter, 1954-55): 331-41. Also in Aldridge, J. W., *In Search of Heresy*, 149-65.

Algren, Nelson, "Hemingway: The Dye That Did Not Run," *Nation* 193 (Nov. 18, 1961): 387-90.

———, *Notes From a Sea Diary: Hemingway All the Way*, N.Y.: Putnam, 1965.

Alladi, Uma K., "Existentialism in the Novels of Hemingway and Camus," *LHY* 21, ii (July, 1980): 43-51.

Allen, Charles A., "Ernest Hemingway's Clean Well-Lighted Heroes," *PacSp* 9 (Autumn, 1955): 383-9.

Allen, William R., "All the Names of Death: Walker Percy and Hemingway," *MissQ* 36, i (Winter, 1982-83): 3-19.

Amiran, Minda R., "Hemingway as Lyric Novelist," *Scripta Hierosolymitana* 17 (1966): 292-300.

Anderson, David D., "Ernest Hemingway, the Voice of an Era," *Person* 47 (April, 1966): 234-47.

Arora, V. N., "The Hemingway Industry," *IJAS* 5, i-ii (1976): 82-7.[Not seen.]

Asselineau, Roger, "Ernest Hemingway—A Rebel Rediscovers Tradition of The Destruction and Rehabilitation of Traditional Values in E. Hemingway's Fiction," in Buchloh, Paul G., Inge Leimberg, and Herbert Rauter, eds., *Studien zur englischen und amerikani-Sprache und Literatur: Festschrift für Helmut Papajewski*, Neumünster: Wacholtz, 1974, 387-404.

———, ed., *The Literary Reputation of Hemingway in Europe*, N.Y.: New York Un. Pr., 1965.

Astro, R., and J. B. Benton, eds., *Hemingway in Our Time*.

Atkins, J., *Art of Ernest Hemingway*.

Backman, Melvin, "Death and Birth in Hemingway," in MacMillan, D. J., ed., *Stoic Strain in American Literature*, 115-33.

———, "Hemingway: The Matador and the Crucified," *MFS* 1 (Aug., 1955): 2-11. Also in Baker, C., ed., *Hemingway and His Critics*, 2 45-58. Also in Litz, A. W., ed., *Modern American Fiction*, 201-14.

Bagchi, K., "The Hemingway Hero," *Banasthali Patrika* (Rajasthan) No. 11 (1968): 91-4.[Not seen.]

Baker, C., *Hemingway*.

———, *Hemingway*, 4th ed.

———, "Hemingway," *SatR* 44 (July 29, 1961): 10-13.

———, ed., *Hemingway and His Critics*.

———, "Hemingway's Imagination," in Baldwin, K. H., and D. K. Kirby, eds., *Individual and Community*, 94-111.

———, "Hemingway's Wastelanders," *VQR* 28 (Summer, 1952): 373-92.

Baker, S., *Ernest Hemingway*.

Bakker, J., *Ernest Hemingway*.

———, "Ernest Hemingway: The Artist as Man of Action," *DAI* 37 (1976-77): 1522C.

———, "In Search of Reality: Two American Heroes Compared," *DQR* (1972/4): 145-61.

Balza, Marcelino A., "The Spanish Hero in Hemingway's Fiction," *DAI* 40 (1979): 1464A.

Bardacke, Theodore, "Hemingway's Women," in McCaffery, J. K. M., ed., *Ernest Hemingway*, 340-51.

Barger, James, *Ernest Hemingway: American Literary Giant*, Charlottesville, N.Y.: SamHar, 1975.

Barker, Thomas T., "The Stoic Ideal in Hemingway's Fiction," *DAI* 41 (1980): 1590A.

Barnes, Lois L., "The Helpless Hero of Ernest Hemingway," *S&S* 17 (Winter, 1953): 1-25.

Barnes, Robert J., "Two Modes of Fiction: Hemingway and Greene," *Ren* 14 (Summer, 1962): 193-8.

Bartlet, Norman, "Hemingway: The Hero as Self," *Quadrant* 15 (May-June, 1971): 13-20.

Beach, J. W., *American Fiction*, 69-119.

————, "How Do You Like It Now, Gentlemen?" *SR* 59 (1951): 311-28. Also in Baker, C., ed., *Hemingway and His Critics*, 227-44.

Beaver, Joseph, "'Technique' in Hemingway," *CE* 14 (Mar., 1953): 325-8.

Behrens, Ralph, "Mérimée, Hemingway, and the Bulls," *Costerus* 2 (1972): 1-8.

Benson, J. J., *Hemingway*.

————, "Literary Allusion and the Private Irony of Hemingway," *PCP* 4 (April, 1969): 24-9.

Bier, Jesse, "A Note on Twain and Hemingway," *MQ* 21 (1980): 261-5.

Bigsby, C. W. E., "Hemingway: The Recoil from History," in French, W., ed., *Twenties*, 203-13.

Birnbaum, Milton, "Ernest Hemingway Read Anew," *ModA* 23, iii (Summer, 1979): 276-81.

Bishop, John P., "Homage to Hemingway," in Cowley, M., ed., *After the Genteel Tradition*, 147-58. Also in Bishop, J. P., *Collected Essays*, 37-46. Also in *NRep* 89 (Nov. 11, 1936): 39-42.

Blankenship, R., *American Literature*, 731-42.

Blumenthal, Jay A., "Ernest Hemingway's Aesthetic Theory: An Analysis of His Concepts of Literary Truth and Literary Knowledge," *DAI* 38 (1977): 2783A.

Bodnár, György, "Hemingway and the New Realism," in Köpeczi, Bela, and Péter Juhász, *Literature et Réalitié*, Budapest: Akadémiai K., 1966, 246-63. [Not seen.]

Booher, Edwin R., "The Image in the Prose: Ezra Pound's Influence on Hemingway," *IllQ* 42, i (1979): 30-9.

Bovie, Vernett, "The Evolution of a Myth: A Study of the Major Symbols in the Works of Ernest Hemingway," *DA* 17 (1957): 1080 (Pennsylvania).

Brasch, James D., and Joseph T. Sigman, "The Library at Finca Vigia: A Preliminary Report, 1977," *FHA* (1978): 185-203.

Brasher, Jim, "Hemingway's Florida," *LGJ* 1, ii (Fall, 1973): 4-8.

Brashers, H. C., *Introduction to American Literature*, 135-8.

Breidlid, Andérs, "Courage and Self-Affirmation in Ernest Hemingway's 'Lost Generation' Fiction," *Edda* 5 (1979): 279-99.

Bresnahan, Roger J., "Ernest Hemingway: A Reader's Perspective," *Midamerica* 8 (1981): 22-35.

Brian, Denis, "The Importance of Knowing Ernest," *Esquire* 77, ii (Feb., 1972): 98-101, 164-70. [Interviews.]

Bridgman, Richard, *The Colloquial Style in America*, N.Y.: Oxford Un. Pr., 1966, 195-230. Also in Wagner, L. W., ed., *Ernest Hemingway*, 160-88.

Broer, Lawrence R., "The Effects of Ernest Hemingway's Identification with Certain Aspects of Spanish Thinking on His Rendering of Character," *DA* 29 (1969): 3606A (Bowling Green).

————, *Hemingway's Spanish Tragedy*.

Brogger, Fredrik C., "Love and Friendship in Ernest Hemingway's Fiction," in Seyersted, B., ed., *Americana-Norvegica*, 269-89.

Brooks, C., "Ernest Hemingway: Man on His Moral Uppers," *Hidden God*, 6-21.

Bryan, James E., "Hemingway as Vivisector," *UR* 30 (Oct., 1963): 3-12.

Burgum, E. B., "Ernest Hemingway and the Psychology of the Lost Generation," *Novel and the World's Dilemma*, 184-204.

Burhans, Clinton S., Jr., "Hemingway and Vonnegut: Diminishing Vision in a Dying Age," *MFS* 21, ii (1975): 173-91.

Burnam, Tom, "The Other Ernest Hemingway," *NM* 73, i-ii (1972): 29-36.

————, "Primitivism and Masculinity in the Work of Ernest Hemingway," *MFS* 1 (Aug., 1955): 20-4.

Byrd, Lemuel B., "Characterization in Ernest Hemingway's Fiction: 1925-1952, with a Dictionary of the Characters," *DAI* 30 (1970): 4444A (Colo.).

Canaday, Nicholas, Jr., "The Motif of the Inner Ring in Hemingway's Fiction," *CEA* 36, ii (Jan., 1974): 18-21.

Capellán, Angel, "Hemingway and the Hispanic World," *DAI* 39 (1978): 881A.

Carpenter, Frederic I., "Hemingway Achieves the Fifth Dimension," *PMLA* 69 (Sept., 1954): 711-18. Also in Carpenter, F. I., *American Literature and the Dream*, 185-93. Also in Baker, C., ed., *Hemingway and His Critics*, 192-200. Also in Wagner, L. W., ed., *Ernest Hemingway*, 279-87. Also in Waldhorn, A., ed., *Ernest Hemingway*, 83-91.

Clemens, Cyril, ed., "Ernest Hemingway Memorial Number," *MTJ* 11, iv (Summer, 1962): 1-19.

Clendenning, John, "Hemingway's Gods, Dead and Alive," *TSLL* 3 (1962): 489-502.

Comley, Nancy, "Hemingway: The Economies of Survival," *Noel* 12, iii (1979): 244-53.

Connolly, C., *Previous Convictions*, 293-8.

Cooke, Alistair, "Hemingway: Master of the Mid-West Vernacular," *MGW* (Nov. 11, 1954): 7. [Not seen.]

Cowley, Malcolm, "Ernest Hemingway," in Baker, D. V., ed., *Writers of Today*, 2, 3-17.

————, "Hemingway: The Image and the Shadow," *Horizon* 15 (Winter, 1973): 112-17.

————, "Introduction," to THE SUN ALSO RISES in *Three Novels of Ernest Hemingway*, ix-xxviii.

————, "Nightmare and Ritual in Hemingway," Introduction to *The Portable Hemingway*, N.Y.: Viking, 1945. Also in Weeks, R. P., ed., *Hemingway*, 40-51.

————, "Papa and the Parricides," *Esquire* 67, vi (June, 1967): 100-1+.

Crozier, Robert D., S. J., "Home James: Hemingway's Jacob," *PLL* 11, iii (Summer, 1975): 293-301.

Curran, Ronald T., "The Individual and the Military Institution in Hemingway's Novels and *Collier's* Dispatches," *RLV* 34 (1968): 26-39.

Currie, William J., "Hemingway's Images of Alienation," *ELLS* 10 (1973): 183-99. [Not seen.]

D'Agostino, Nemi, "The Later Hemingway (1956)," *SR* 68 (Summer, 1960): 482-93. Also in Weeks, R. P., ed., *Hemingway*, 152-60.

Dahiya, Bhim S., "The Hero in Hemingway: A Study in Development," *DAI* 36 (1975): 28118A-19A.

_____, *Hero in Hemingway*.

Daniel, Robert A., "Hemingway and His Heroes," *QQ* 54 (Winter, 1947-48): 471-85.

Das, S. P., "The World and Experience of Hemingway Hero," in Maini, D. S., ed., *Variations on American Literature*, 76-85.

Das Gupta, H., "Ernest Hemingway and the Spanish Bullfight," *IJAS* 6, i-ii (Jan. and July, 1976): 55-64.

Dean, Anthony B., "Hemingway's Fiction: A Tragic Vision of Life," *DAI* 32 (1971): 961A (Temple).

DeFalco, Joseph, "Hemingway, Sport, and the Larger Metaphor," *LGJ* 3, ii (Spring-Summer, 1975): 18-20.

DeMarr, Mary J., "Hemingway's Narrative Methods," *IEY* 4 (Spring, 1970): 31-6. [Not seen.]

Dillingham, William B., "Hemingway and Death," *EUQ* 19 (Summer, 1963): 95-101.

Donaldson, Scott, "The Case of the Vanishing American and Other Puzzlements in Hemingway's Fiction," *HN* 6, ii (Spring, 1981): 16-19.

_____, "Hemingway's Morality of Compensation," *AL* 43, iii (Nov., 1971): 399-420.

_____, "The Wooing of Ernest Hemingway," *AL* 53, iv (Jan., 1982): 691-710.

Dring, John R., "The Religious Element in Ernest Hemingway's Novels," *DESB* 7 (1962): 63-72, 104-12.

Drinnon, Richard, "In the American Heartland: Hemingway and Death," *PsyR* 52 (Summer, 1965): 5-31.

Dubiel, Richard M., "Disquietude, Existence, and Endurance: Aspects of Paul Tillich's Thought in Selected Works of Ernest Hemingway," *DAI* 35 (1974): 3734A.

Durham, Philip, "Ernest Hemingway's Grace Under Pressure: The Western Code," *Pacific Hist. Rev.* (CA) 45 (1976): 425-32.

Edel, Leon, "The Art of Evasion," *Folio* 20 (Spring, 1955): 18-20. Also in Weeks, R. P., ed., *Hemingway*, 169-71.

Egri, Peter, "The Relationship between the Short Story and the Novel, Realism and Naturalism in Hemingway's Art. Part I: 1923-1929," *HSE* 4 (1969): 105-26.

_____, "The Relationship between the Short Story and the Novel, Realism and Naturalism in Hemingway's Art. Part II: 1932-1952," *HSE* 7 (1973): 53-86.

Elliott, Gary, "The Hemingway Hero's Quest for Faith," *DAI* 34 (1973): 2621A (Kansas State).

_____, "The Hemingway Hero's Quest for Faith," *McNR* 24 (1977-78): 18-27.

Evans, Robert, "Hemingway and the Pale Cast of Thought," *AL* 38 (May, 1966): 161-76. Also in Waldhorn, A., ed., *Ernest Hemingway*, 112-26.

Farley, Pamella, "Form and Function: The Image of Woman in Selected Works of Hemingway and Fitzgerald," *DAI* 35 (1974): 3735A (Penn State).

Farquhar, Robin H., "Dramatic Structure in the Novels of Ernest Hemingway," *MFS* 14 (Autumn, 1968): 271-82.

Farrell, James T., "Ernest Hemingway," *FHA* (1973): 215-25.

Fenton, Charles A., *The Apprenticeship of Ernest Hemingway: The Early Years*, N.Y.: Farrar, 1954.

Ferguson, J. M., Jr., "Hemingway's Man of the World," *ArQ* 33 (1977): 116-20.

Fiedler, Leslie, "An Almost Imaginary Interview: Hemingway in Ketchum," *PR* 29 (Summer, 1962): 395-405.

_____, "The Death of the Old Men," *A&S* (Winter, 1963-64): 1-5. Also in Fiedler, L. A., *Waiting for the End*, 9-19.

_____, "Men Without Women," in Weeks, R. P., ed., *Hemingway*, 86-92. Also in Fiedler, L., *Love and Death in the American Novel*, 304-9.

Fisher, Deborah, "Genuine Heroines Hemingway Style," *LGJ* 2, ii (Spring-Summer, 1974): 35-6.

Fitch, Noel, "Ernest Hemingway—c/o Shakespeare and Company," *FHS* (1977): 157-81.

Fitz, Reginald, "The Meaning of Impotence in Hemingway and Eliot," *ConnR* 4, ii (April, 1971): 16-22.

Floor, Richard, "Fate and Life: Determinism in Ernest Hemingway," *Ren* 15 (Fall, 1962): 23-7.

Flores, Olga E., "Eros, Thanatos and the Hemingway Soldier," *ASInt* 18, iii-iv (1980): 27-35.

Friedberg, Michael, "Hemingway and the Modern Metaphysical Tradition," in Astro, R., and J. B. Benton, eds., *Hemingway in Our Time*, 175-89.

Friedrich, Otto, "Ernest Hemingway: Joy Through Strength," *ASch* 26 (Autumn, 1957): 470, 518-30.

Frohock, W. M., "Ernest Hemingway: Violence and Discipline," *SWR* 32 (1947): 899-97, 184-93. Also in Frohock, W. M., *Novel of Violence in America*, 166-98. Also in McCaffery, J. K. M., *Ernest Hemingway*, 262-91.

Fuchs, Daniel, "Ernest Hemingway, Literary Critic," *AL* 36 (Jan., 1965): 431-51. Also in Wagner, L. W., ed., *Ernest Hemingway*, 39-56. Also in Waldhorn, A., ed., *Ernest Hemingway*, 92-111.

Fussell, Edwin, "Hemingway and Mark Twain," *Accent* 14 (Summer, 1954): 199-206.

Gado, Frank, "The Curious History of the Hemingway Hero," *Symposium* (Union College) 4, i (1965): 18-22.

Gaither, Lex, "Hemingway and Wolfe," *TWN* 2, ii (1978): 29-30.

Galligan, Edward L., "Hemingway's Staying Power," *MR* 8 (Summer, 1967): 431-9.

Garlington, Jack, "The Intelligence Quotient of Lady Brett Ashley," *San Francisco Rev* 1 (Sept., 1959): 23-8.

Gebhardt, Richard C., "Denial and Affirmation of Values in the Fiction of Ernest Hemingway," *DAI* 31 (1970): 1274A-75A (Mich. State).

_____, "Hemingway's Complex Values," *HN* 1, i (Fall, 1981): 2-10.

Geismar, M., *American Moderns*, 54-8. Also in *NYTBR* (July 31, 1949): 1, 21.

_____, *American Moderns*, 61-4. Also in *SatR* (Nov. 13, 1954): 24, 34.

_____, "Was 'Papa' Truly a Great Writer?" in Brown, F., ed., *Opinions and Perspectives*, 162-8.

_____, *Writers in Crisis*, Boston: Houghton, 1942, 39-85. Also in McCaffery, J. K. M., ed., *Ernest Hemingway*, 143-89. Also, condensed, in *VQR* 17 (1941): 517-34.

Gelderman, Carol, "Hemingway's Drinking Fixation," *LGJ* 6, i (1979): 12-14.

Gibson, Andrew, "Hemingway on the British," *HemR* 1, ii (1982): 62-75.

Gifford, William, "Ernest Hemingway: The Monsters and the Critics," *MFS* 14 (Autumn, 1968): 255-70.

Giger, R., *Creative Void*.

Gillespie, Gerald, "Hemingway and the Happy Few," *OL* 23 (1968): 287-99.

Gleaves, Edwin S., "Hemingway and Baroja: Studies in Spiritual Anarchism," *REH* 5 (1971): 363-75.

Goldhurst, William, *F. Scott Fitzgerald and His Contemporaries,* Cleveland and N.Y.: World, 1963, 155-216.

Goodheart, Eugene, "The Legacy of Ernest Hemingway," *PrS* 30 (Fall, 1956): 212-18.

Goodman, Paul, "The Sweet Style of Ernest Hemingway," *NYRB* 17, xi (Dec. 30, 1971): 27-8. Also in Wagner, L. W., ed., *Ernest Hemingway,* 153-60.

Gordon, Caroline, "Notes on Hemingway and Kafka," *SR* 57 (Spring, 1949): 215-26.

Gordon, David, "The Son and the Father: Patterns of Response to Conflict in Hemingway's Fiction," *L&P* 16 (1966): 122-38.

Graham, John, "Ernest Hemingway: The Meaning of Style," *MFS* 6 (Winter, 1960-61): 298-313. Also in Baker, C., ed., *Ernest Hemingway,* 183-92. Also, revised, in Graham, J., comp., *Studies in A FAREWELL TO ARMS,* 88-105. Also in Waldhorn, A., ed., *Ernest Hemingway,* 18-34.

Grant, Naomi M., "The Role of Women in the Fiction of Ernest Hemingway," *DA* 29 (1969): 4456A (Denver).

Gray, James, "Tenderly Tolls the Bell," *On Second Thought,* 74-82. Also in McCaffery, J. K. M., ed., *Ernest Hemingway,* 226-35.

Grebstein, Sheldon, "Controversy," *ASch* 27 (Spring, 1958): 229-31.

_____, *Hemingway's Craft.*

_____, "Sex, Hemingway, and the Critics," *Humanist* 21 (July-Aug., 1961): 212-18.

_____, "The Tough Hemingway and His Hard-Boiled Children," in Madden, D., ed., *Tough Guy Writers of the Thirties,* 18-41.

Green, Gregory, "'A Matter of Color': Hemingway's Criticism of Race Prejudice," *HN* 1, i (Fall, 1981): 27-32.

Griffin, Gerald R., "Hemingway's Fictive Use of the Negro: 'the curious quality of incompleteness'," *Husson Rev* 1 (1968): 104-11.

Griffith, John, "Rectitude in Hemingway's Fiction: How Rite Makes Right," in Astro, R., and J. B. Benton, eds., *Hemingway in Our Time,* 159-73.

Grimes, Larry E., "The 'Fifth Dimension': The Religious Design of Hemingway's Early Fiction," *DAI* 35 (1975): 7306A.

Gross, G. L., *Heroic Ideal in American Literature,* 198-220.

Guetti, J., *Word-Music,* 139-49.

Gurko, Leo, "The Achievement of Ernest Hemingway," *EJ* 41 (June, 1952): 291-8. Also in *CE* 13 (April, 1952): 368-75.

_____, *Ernest Hemingway and the Pursuit of Heroism.*

_____, "Hemingway in Spain," in *The Angry Decade,* N.Y.: Dodd, 1947, 187-90. Also in McCaffery, J. K. M., ed., *Ernest Hemingway,* 258-61.

Hagemann, Meyly C., "Hemingway's Secret: Visual to Verbal Art," *JML* 7, i (1979): 87-112.

Hagood, Thomas N., "Elements of Humor in Ernest Hemingway," *DA* 29 (1969): 3139A (La. State).

Hagopian, John V., "Hemingway: Ultimate Exile," *Mosaic* 8, iii (1975): 77-87.

_____, "Style and Meaning in Hemingway and Faulkner," *JA* Band 4 (1959): 170-9.

Hale, Nancy, "Hemingway and the Courage to Be," *VQR* 38 (Autumn, 1962): 620-39.

Halliday, E. M., "Hemingway's Ambiguity: Symbolism and Irony," *AL* 28 (Mar., 1956): 1-22. Also in Feidelson, C., Jr., and P. Brodtkorb, Jr., *Interpretations of American Literature,* 297-

318. Also in Weeks, R. P., ed., *Hemingway,* 52-71. Also in Waldhorn, A., ed., *Ernest Hemingway,* 35-55.

_____, "Hemingway's Narrative Perspective," *SR* 60 (Spring, 1952): 202-18. Also in Baker, C., ed., *Ernest Hemingway,* 174-82. Also in Litz, A. W., ed., *Modern American Fiction,* 215-27.

Hamalian, Leo, "Hemingway as Hunger Artist," *LitR* 16 (Fall, 1972): 5-13.

Hand, Harry E., "Transducers and Hemingway's Heroes," *EJ* 55 (Oct., 1966): 870-1.

Hart, Robert C., "Hemingway on Writing," *CE* 18 (Mar., 1957): 314-20.

Hasanain, Abdel-Ghani A., "Women in Ernest Hemingway," *DAI* 42, iv (Oct., 1981): 1634A-35A.

Hassan, Ihab, "Hemingway: Valor Against the Void," *Dismemberment of Orpheus,* 80-109.

_____, "The Silence of Ernest Hemingway," in Friedman, M. J., and J. B. Vickery, eds., *Shaken Realist,* 5-20.

Helfand, Michael, "A Champ Can't Retire Like Anyone Else," *LGJ* 3 (Spring-Summer, 1975): 9-10, 35.

Hemingway, Leicester, "Ernest Hemingway's Boyhood Reading," *MTJ* 12, ii (Spring, 1964): 4-5.

_____, *My Brother, Ernest Hemingway,* Cleveland: World, 1962. Also, excerpted, in *Playboy* 8 (Dec., 1961): 48+.

Hertzel, Leo J., "Hemingway and the Problem of Belief," *CathW* 184 (Oct., 1956): 29-33.

_____, "The Look of Religion: Hemingway and Catholicism," *Ren* 17 (Winter, 1964): 77-81.

Hoffer, Bates, ed., "Hemingway's Experiments in Structure and Style," *LNL* 1, ii (Spring, 1976): [Special Issue.]

_____, "Hemingway's Use of Stylistics," *LNL* 1, ii (Spring, 1976): 89-121.

Hoffman, Frederick J., "No Beginning and No End: Hemingway and Death," *EIC* 3 (Jan., 1953): 73-84. Also in Feidelson, C., Jr., and P. Brodtkorb, Jr., *Interpretations of American Literature,* 320-31. Also, in part, as "The Unreasonable Wound," *Twenties,* 66-76.

Hogge, Robert M., "Hemingway's Twentieth-Century Medievalism," *DAI* 41 (190): 1596A.

Holder, Alan, "The Other Hemingway," *TCL* 9 (Oct., 1963): 153-7. Also in Wagner, L. W., ed., *Ernest Hemingway,* 103-9.

Holder, Robert C., Jr., "The Tip of the Iceberg: The Naturalistic Pattern in the Fiction of Ernest Hemingway," *DAI* 36 (1976): 5298A.

Holman, C. Hugh, "Ernest Hemingway," *Shen* 10 (Winter, 1959): 4-11.

_____, "Ernest Hemingway: A Tribute," *BA* 36 (Winter, 1962): 5-8.

_____, "Hemingway and Emerson," *MFS* 1 (Aug., 1955): 12-16.

Hovey, R. B., *Hemingway.*

Howe, Irving, "Hemingway: The Conquest of Panic," *NRep* 145 (July 24, 1961): 19-20.

_____, "The Quest for a Moral Style," *World More Attractive,* 65-70.

Hurwitz, Harold M., "Hemingway's Tutor, Ezra Pound," *MFS* 17, iv (Winter, 1971-72): 469-82. Also in Wagner, L. W., ed., *Ernest Hemingway,* 8-21.

Iacone, Salvatore J., "Alienation and the Hemingway Hero," *DAI* 41 (1980): 251A.

Idol, John L., Jr., "Ernest Hemingway and Thomas Wolfe," *SCR* 15, i (Fall, 1982): 24-31.

Inglis, David L., "Morley Callaghan and the Hemingway Boxing Legend," *NConL* 4, iv (1974): 4-7.

Isabelle, J., *Hemingway's Religious Experience*.

Ishi, Ichiro, "Understanding of E. Hemingway," *Hotogogisu* 5 (Feb., 1956): 12-13. [Not seen.]

Islam, Shamsul, "The Kipling and Hemingway Codes: A Study in Comparison," *Explor* 2, ii (Winter, 1975): 22-8.

Iwasa, Masazumi, "Beauty and Ugliness in Hemingway," *SALit* 13 (1977): 1-12. [Not seen.]

Jason, Philip K., "Throw Away Your Hemingway Codebook," *Indirections* (Ontario Council of Eng. Teachers) 1, iii-iv (1976): 59-64.

Johnson, Edgar, "Farewell the Separate Peace," *SR* 48 (July-Sept., 1940): 289-300. Also in McCaffery, J. K. M., ed., *Ernest Hemingway*, 130-42.

Johnston, Kenneth G., "Hemingway and Mantegna: The Bitter Nail Holes," *JNT* 1, ii (May, 1971): 86-94.

_____, "Journeys Into the Interior: Hemingway, Thoreau and Mungo Park," *ForumH* 10, ii (1972): 27-31.

Jones, Edward T., "Hemingway and Cézanne: A Speculative Affinity," *UES* 8, ii (1970): 26-8.

Jones, John A., "Hemingway: The Critics and the Public Legend," *WHR* 13 (Autumn, 1959): 387-400.

Joost, Nicholas, *Ernest Hemingway and the Little Magazines: The Paris Years*, Barre, Mass.: Barre Publishers, 1968.

_____, and Alan Brown, "T. S. Eliot and Ernest Hemingway: A Literary Relationship," *PLL* 14, iv (Fall, 1978): 425-49.

Josephs, Mary J., "The Hunting Metaphor in Hemingway and Faulkner," *DAI* 34 (1973): 1282A-83A (Mich. State).

Joy, Neill R., "Fitzgerald's Retort to Hemingway's 'Poor Scott Fitzgerald'," *NMAL* 2, ii (Spring, 1978): Item 13.

Kallapur, S. T., "Ernest Hemingway's Conception of Love and Womanhood," *BP* 19 (1972, pub. 1974): 37-47.

Kann, Hans-Joachim, "Ernest Hemingway and German Culture," *NsM* 28 (1975): 16-20.

_____, "Hemingway's Knowledge of German," *JA* 15 (1970): 221-32.

Kaplan, H., "Hemingway and the Passive Hero," *Passive Voice*, 93-110.

Kapoor, Vishaw Mitter, "The Style of Ernest Hemingway," in Maini, D. S., ed., *Variations on American Literature*, 86-8.

Kashkeen, Ivan, "Alive in the Midst of Death," *Soviet Literature* No. 7 (1956): 160-72. Also in Baker, C., ed., *Hemingway and His Critics*, 162-79.

_____, "What is Hemingway's Style?" *Soviet Literature* No. 6 (1964): 172-80.

Kaufmann, Donald L., "The Long Happy Life of Norman Mailer," *MFS* 17, iii (Autumn, 1971): 347-59.

Kazin, Alfred, "Ernest Hemingway as His Own Fable," *Cornhill* No. 1040 (Summer, 1964): 139-47.

_____, *On Native Grounds*, Garden City, N.Y.: Doubleday, 1956, 253-66. Also, revised, in McCaffery, J. K. M., ed., *Ernest Hemingway*, 190-204.

Kelly, John C., "Ernest Hemingway (1899-1961)," *Studies* 50 (Autumn, 1961): 312-26.

Kerner, David, "Fitzgerald vs. Hemingway: The Origins of Anti-Metronomic Dialogue," *MFS* 28, ii (Summer, 1982): 247-50.

_____, "The Manuscripts Establishing Hemingway's Anti-Metronomic Dialogue," *AL* 54, iii (Oct., 1982): 385-96.

Kerr, Johnny F., "Hemingway's Use of a Physical Setting and Stage Props in His Novels: A Study in Craftsmanship," *DA* 26 (1965): 2217 (Texas).

Killinger, John, "Hemingway and Our 'Essential Worldliness'," in Scott, Nathan A., Jr., ed., *Forms of Extremity in the Modern Novel*, Richmond: John Knox Pr., 1965, 35-54.

_____, *Hemingway and the Dead Gods: A Study in Existentialism*, Lexington: Un. of Kentucky Pr., 1960.

Kimball, W. J., "Hemingway and the Code," *Venture* 6, ii (Summer, 1970): 18-23.

Kinnamon, Keneth, "Hemingway, the *Corrida*, and Spain," *TSLL* 1 (Spring, 1959): 44-61. Also in Wagner, L. W., ed., *Ernest Hemingway*, 57-74.

Kirshner, Sumner, "From the Gulf Stream into the Main Stream: Siefgried Lenz and Hemingway," *RS* 35 (June, 1967): 141-7.

Knapp, Daniel, "Hemingway: The Naming of the Hero," *StL* 2, ii (1961): 30-41.

Knauf, Andrew L., "Alcohol as Symbolic Buttress in Hemingway's Long Fiction," *DAI* 40 (1980): 4039A-40A.

Kobler, Jasper, "Journalist and Artist: The Dual Role of Ernest Hemingway," *DA* 29 (1968): 606A-7A (Texas).

Kort, Wesley A., "Human Time in Hemingway's Fiction," *MFS* 26 (1980-81): 579-96.

Kretzoi, Charlotte, "Hemingway on Bullfights and Aesthetics," *SEA* 2 (1975): 277-96.

Kriegel, Leonard, "Hemingway's Rites of Manhood," *PR* 44 (1977): 415-30.

Kvam, Wayne E., "The Critical Reaction to Hemingway in Germany, 1945-1965," *DA* 30 (1969): 1139A-40A (Wis.).

_____, *Hemingway in Germany*.

_____, "Zuckmayer, Hilpert and Hemingway," *PMLA* 91 (1976): 194-205.

Lair, Robert L., "Hemingway and Cézanne: An Indebtedness," *MFS* 6 (Summer, 1960): 165-8.

Laurence, F. M., *Hemingway and the Movies*.

Laurence, Frank, "The Pack and the Lunch Box: Hemingway's Stylistic Influence on Russell Hoban," *HN* 6, i (1980): 29-31.

Lehan, Richard, "Camus and Hemingway," *WSCL* 1, ii (Spring-Summer, 1960): 37-48.

_____, *Dangerous Crossing*, 46-61.

_____, "Hemingway Among the Moderns," in Astro, R., and J. B. Benton, eds., *Hemingway in Our Time*, 191-212.

Lebowitz, Alan, "Hemingway in Our Time," *YR* 58 (Spring, 1969): 321-41.

_____, "No Farewell to Arms," in Engel, M., ed., *Uses of History*, 187-204.

Lerfald, Robert A., "Hemingway's Search for the Sacred: A Study of the Primitive Rituals of a Twentieth-Century American Adam," *DAI* 37 (1977): 7752A.

Levin, Harry, "Observations on the Style of Hemingway," *KR* 13 (Autumn, 1951): 581-609. Also in Baker, C., ed., *Hemingway and His Critics*, 93-115. Also in Beaver, Harold, ed., *American Critical Essays*, London: Oxford Un. Pr., 1959, 286-313. Also in Levin, H., *Contexts of Criticism*, 140-67. Also, abridged, in Weeks, R. P., ed., *Hemingway*, 72-85.

Levine, M. H., "Hemingway and the 'Lost Generation'," *KAL* No. 9 (1966): 19-26. [Not seen.]

Lewis, Robert W., "Hemingway Ludens," *LGJ* 3, ii (Spring-Summer, 1975): 7-8.

_____, *Hemingway on Love.*

_____, "Hemingway's Sense of Place," in Astro, R., and J. B. Benton, eds., *Hemingway in Our Time*, 113-43.

Linderoth, Leon W., "The Female Characters of Ernest Hemingway," *DA* 27 (1966): 1060A (Florida State).

Lisca, Peter, "Steinbeck and Hemingway: Suggestions for a Comparative Study," *StN* 2, i (Spring, 1969): 9-17. Also in Hayashi, T., ed., *Steinbeck's Literary Dimension*, 46-54.

Locklin, Gerald, "Ernest Hemingway: Best of All He Loved the Fall," *Snowy Egret* 43, i (1980): 18-24. Also, with Charles Stetler, in *HN* 6, ii (Spring, 1981): 20-4.

Lupan, Radu, "The Old Man and the World: Some Final Thoughts on Ernest Hemingway," *LitR* 10 (Winter, 1966-67): 159-65.

Lynn, Kenneth S., "Hemingway's Private War," *Ctary* 72, i (July, 1981): 24-33.

Macdonald, Dwight, "Ernest Hemingway," *Encounter* 18 (Jan., 1962): 115-21.

Madariaga, Salvador de, et al., "The World Weighs a Writer's Influence," *SatR* 44 (July 29, 1961): 18-22.

Malhotra, M. L., "What Hemingway Means to Me," *Bridges of Literature*, 9-17.

Marin, Dave, "Seven Hours with Papa," *SWR* 53 (Spring, 1968): 167-77.

Marsden, Malcolm M., "Hemingway's Symbolic Pattern: The Basis of Tone," *Discourse* 12, i (Winter, 1969): 16-28.

Matsuda, Sumio, "Symbolism and the Rhetoric of Fiction in Hemingway's Novels," *DA* 28 (1968): 2689A (So. Calif.).

Maurois, Andre, "Ernest Hemingway," in Baker, C., ed., *Hemingway and His Critics*, 38-54.

Mayer, Charles W., "The Triumph of Honor: James and Hemingway," *ArQ* 35 (1979): 373-91.

Maynard, Reid N., "The Writer and Experience: Ernest Hemingway's Views on the Craft of Fiction," *DAI* 31 (1971): 6620A (Calif., Davis).

McCaffery, J. K. M., ed., *Ernest Hemingway.*

McCarthy, H. T., *Expatriate Perspective*, 136-55.

McClellan, David, "The Battle of the Little Big Horn in Hemingway's Later Fiction," *FHA* (1976): 245-8.

McCormick, John, "The Anachronous Hero: Hemingway and Montherlant," *Fiction as Knowledge*, 109-31.

_____, "Hemingway and History," *WE* 17 (Winter, 1953): 87-98.

McHaney, Thomas L., "Anderson, Hemingway, and Faulkner's THE WILD PALMS," *PMLA* 87, iii (May, 1972): 465-74.

Meckier, Jerome, "Hemingway Reads Huxley: An Occasion for Some Observations on the Twenties and the Apostolate of the Lost Generation," *FHA* (1976): 154-86.

Messenger, Christian, "Hemingway and the School Athletic Hero," *LGJ* 3, ii (Spring-Summer, 1975): 21-3.

Meyer, B. Ruth, "The Old Men in Hemingway's Fiction," *DAI* 40 (1979): 258A.

Meyer, William E., Jr., "Hemingway's Novels: The Shift in Orthodoxy and Symbolism," *ArQ* 33 (1977): 141-55.

Meyers, J., ed., *Hemingway.*

Mizener, Arthur, "The Two Hemingways," in Bode, Carl, ed., *The Great Experiment in American Literature*, N.Y.: Praeger, 1961, 135-51.

Moloney, Michael F., "Ernest Hemingway: The Missing Third Dimension," in Gardiner, H. C., ed., *Fifty Years of the American Novel*, 183-96.

Monk, Donald, "Hemingway's Territorial Imperative," *YES* 8 (1978): 125-40.

Monteiro, George, "The Education of Ernest Hemingway," *JAmS* 8, i (April, 1974): 91-9.

_____, "Hemingway's Pléiade Ballplayers," *FHA* (1973): 299-301.

_____, "Hemingway's Samson Agonistes," *FHA* (1979): 411-16.

_____, "Justice Holmes on Hemingway," *MarkhamR* 8 (1978): 7-8.

Montgomery, Marion, "Emotion Recollected in Tranquility: Wordsworth's Legacy to Eliot, Joyce, and Hemingway," *SoR* 6, iii (July, 1970): 710-21.

Moritz, Ken, in French, W. G., and W. E. Kidd, *American Winners of the Nobel Literary Prize*, 158-92.

Morris, L., "Salvage," *Postscript to Yesterday*, 154-6.

Morris, W., "The Function of Style: Ernest Hemingway," *Territory Ahead*, 133-46. Also in *New World Writing*, No. 13 (June, 1958), N.Y.: New American Library, 34-51.

_____, "One Law for the Lion," *PR* 28 (1961): 541-51.

Motola, Gabriel, "Hemingway's Code: Literature and Life," *MFS* 10 (Winter, 1964-65): 319-29.

Murray, Donald M., "Thoreau and Hemingway," *TJQ* 11, iii-lv (1979): 13-33.

Murray, Edward, "Ernest Hemingway—Cinematic Structure in Fiction and Problems in Adaptation," *Cinematic Imagination*, 218-43.

Nageshwara Rao, E., "Forms of Irony in Hemingway's Work," *Littcrit* 6 (1978): 44-6. [Not seen.]

_____, "Syntax as Rhetoric: An Analysis of Ernest Hemingway's Early Syntax," *IndLing* 36 (1975): 296-303.

Nahal, C., *Narrative Pattern in Ernest Hemingway's Fiction.*

Nelson, John E., "Religious Experience in the Fiction of Ernest Hemingway," *DAI* 31 (1970): 396A (N.C., Chapel Hill).

Nelson, R. S., *Hemingway.*

Nenadal, Radoslav, "E. Hemingway and J. Thurber: Their Part in the Process of 'The Patterning of a Modern Hero'," *AVCP* 5 (1971): 75-88. [Not seen.]

Noble, D. W., *Eternal Adam and the New World Garden*, 144-52.

Nozaki, Takashi, "An Embodiment of Sensibility: The Work of Ernest Hemingway," *SEL* 36 (Oct., 1959): 93-108. [Not seen.]

Nucci, Joseph C., "The Poetry of Time and Place in the Fiction of Ernest Hemingway," *DA* 30 (1969): 733A-34A (Pittsburgh).

O'Brien, Richard M., "The Thematic Interrelation of the Concepts of Time and Thought in the Works of Ernest Hemingway," *DAI* 31 (1971): 6066A-67A (N.Y.U.).

O'Connor, William Van, "Faulkner's One-Sided 'Dialogue' with Hemingway," *CE* 24 (Dec., 1962): 208-15.

O'Faolain, S., *Vanishing Hero*, 112-45.

O'Hara, John L., et al., "Who the Hell is Hemingway?" *True* 36 (Feb., 1956): 14-19, 25-31, 68. [Not seen.]

Oldsey, Bernard S., "Hemingway's Old Men," *MFS* 1 (Aug., 1955): 31-5.

_____, "The Snows of Ernest Hemingway," *WSCL* 4, ii (Spring-Summer, 1963): 172-98. Also in Waldhorn, A., ed., *Ernest Hemingway*, 56-82.

Oliver, Charles M., II, "Principles of 'True-Felt Emotion' in Hemingway's Novels," *DAI* 31 (1971): 4787A (Bowling Green).

Palmieri, Anthony F., "The Hemingway-Anderson Feud: A Letter from Boni," *HN* 1, i (Fall, 1981): 56-8.

Parks, Edd W., "Hemingway and Faulkner: The Patten of Their Thought," *Dagens Nyheter* (Copenagen) (Feb. 12, 1956): 4-5. Also in *SAB* 12, iv (1957): 1-2.

Pearsall, R. B., *Life and Writings of Ernest Hemingway*.

Pearson, Janet L., "Hemingway's Women," *LGJ* 1, i (May, 1973): 16-19.

Pearson, Roger L., "The Play-Game Element in the Major Works of Ernest Hemingway," *DAI* 31 (1971): 6625A-26A (Mass.).

Peavler, Terry J., "Guillermo Cabrera Infante's Debt to Ernest Hemingway," *Hispania* 62, iii (May-Sept., 1979): 289-96.

Pendleton, Harold E., "Ernest Hemingway: A Theory of Learning," *DA* 20 (1960): 3302-3 (Illinois).

Peterson, Richard K., "Hemingway: Direct and Oblique," *DA* 22 (1962): 4353-4 (Un. of Washington). Also The Hague, The Netherlands: Mouton, 1969.

Phillips, Gene D., *Hemingway and Film*, N.Y.: Ungar, 1980.

Phillips, Steven R., "Hemingway and the Bullfight: The Archetypes of Tragedy," *ArQ* 29, i (Sept., 1973): 37-56.

Phillips, William L., "Sherwood Anderson's Two Prize Pupils," *Un. of Chicago Mag.*, 47 (Jan., 1955): 9-12. Also in White, R. L., ed., *The Achievement of Sherwood Anderson*, Chapel Hill: Un. of No. Carolina Pr., 1966, 202-10.

Piper, Henry D., "Social Criticism in the American Novel of the Nineteen Twenties," in Bradbury, M., and D. Palmer, eds., *American Novel in the Nineteen Twenties*, 77-82.

Plimpton, George, "The Art of Fiction, XXI: Hemingway," *ParisR* 18 (Spring, 1958): 61-89. (Interview.) Also in *Writers at Work*, 2nd ser., 215-39. Also in Baker, C., ed., *Hemingway and His Critics*, 19-37. Also in Wagner, L. W., ed., *Ernest Hemingway*, 21-38.

Pollin, Burton R., "Poe and Hemingway on Violence and Death," *ES* 57 (1976): 139-42.

Portuondo, José A., "The Old Man and Society," *Americas* 4 (Dec., 1952): 6-7+.

Pratt, John C., "A Sometimes Great Notion: Ernest Hemingway's Roman Catholicism," in Astro, R., and J. B. Benton, eds., *Hemingway in Our Time*, 145-57.

Prescott, O., *In My Opinion*, 64-8.

Presley, John W., "Hawks Never Share': Women and Tragedy in Hemingway," *HN* 3, i (Spring, 1973): 3-10.

Price, Reynolds, "For Ernest Hemingway," *Things Themselves*, 176-213.

Prizel, Yuri, "Hemingway in Soviet Literary Criticism," *AL* 44 (Nov., 1972): 445-56.

Raeburn, John, "Ernest Hemingway: The Public Writer as Popular Culture," *JPC* 8, i (Summer, 1974): 91-8.

————, "Ernest Hemingway: The Writer as Object of Public Attention," *DAI* 30 (1970): 4462A (Pa.).

————, "Hemingway in the Twenties: 'The Artist's Reward'," *BRMMLA* 29 (1975): 118-46.

Rama Rao, P. G., *Ernest Hemingway*.

Rao, E. Nageswara, "The Motif of Luck in Hemingway," *JAmS* 13 (1979): 29-35.

Reardon, John, "Hemingway's Esthetic and Ethical Sportsmen," *UR* 34 (Oct., 1967): 13-23. Also in Wagner, L. W., ed., *Ernest Hemingway*, 131-44.

Richards, Robert F., "Hemingway and Stevens' 'Poetry of Extraordinary Actuality'," *Descant* 17, iv (1973): 46-8. [Not seen.]

Roberts, John J., "Patrick W. Shaw's Hemingway: A Response," *CEA* 39, i (Nov., 1976): 20-1.

Rogers, Roy, "Hemingway and the Tragic Curve," *HN* 4, i (Spring, 1974): 12-16.

Rosen, Kenneth M., "Ernest Hemingway: The Function of Violence," *DAI* 30 (1970): 5456A (N.M.).

Rosenfeld, Isaac, "A Farewell to Hemingway," *KR* 13 (Winter, 1951): 147-55. Also in Rosenfeld, I., *Age of Enormity*, 258-67.

Ross, Lillian, "Profiles," *NY* (May 13, 1950): 36-62.

Rovit, E., *Ernest Hemingway*.

————, "Faulkner, Hemingway, and the American Family," *MissQ* 29 (1976): 483-97.

Rubinstein, Annette T., "Brave and Baffled Hunter," *Mainstream* 13, i (Jan., 1960): 1-23.

Ryan, Frank L., "Ernest Hemingway's Literary Reputation in America, 1924-1966," *DAI* 36 (1975): 893A-94A.

Sachner, Mark J., "Failure as Human and Literary Form," *DAI* 42, v (Nov., 1981): 2123A.

Sachs, Lisbeth J., and Bernard H. Stern, "The Little Preoedipal Boy in Papa Hemingway and How He Created His Artistry," *Costerus* 1 (1972): 221-40.

Sanders, David, "Ernest Hemingway's Spanish Civil War Experience," *AQ* 12 (Summer, 1960): 133-43.

Sanderson, S. F., *Ernest Hemingway*.

Sarason, Bertram D., "Hemingway in Havana: Two Interviews," *ConnR* 3, i (Oct., 1969): 24-31.

Savage, D. S., *Withered Branch*, 23-43.

Scheel, Mark, "Death and Dying: Hemingway's Predominant Theme," *ESRS* 28, i (1979): 5-12.

Schmid, Hans, "The Switzerland of Fitzgerald and Hemingway," *FHA* (1978): 261-71.

Schneiderman, Leo, "Hemingway: A Psychological Study," *ConnR* 6, ii (April, 1973): 34-49.

Schönfelder, Karl-Heinz, "Ernest Hemingway and Cuba," *ZAA* 30, i (1982): 5-14.

Schwartz, Delmore, "Ernest Hemingway's Literary Situation," *SoR* 3 (Spring, 1938): 769-82. Also in McCaffery, J. K. M., ed., *Ernest Hemingway*, 114-29.

————, "The Fiction of Ernest Hemingway," *PUSA* No. 13 (Autumn, 1955): 70-88.

Scott, N. A., Jr., *Ernest Hemingway*. Also, in part (19-29), in Wagner, L. W., ed., *Ernest Hemingway*, 212-21.

Seator, Lynette H., "The Antisocial Humanism of Cela and Hemingway," *REH* 9 (1975): 425-39.

Sharma, D. R., "Moral Frontiers of Ernest Hemingway," *Panjab* 2, ii (Aug., 1971): 49-59.

Shaw, S., *Ernest Hemingway*.

Shockley, Martin S., "Hemingway's Moment of Truth," *ColQ* 5 (Spring, 1957): 380-8.

Shtogren, John A., Jr., "Ernest Hemingway's Aesthetic Use of Journalism in His First Decade of Fiction," *DAI* 32 (1972): 6454A-55A (Mich.).

Slavutych, Yar, "Ernest Hemingway in Ukrainian Literature," *PCLS* 5 (1972): 67-76.

Slochower, H., *No Voice is Wholly Lost*, 36-40.

Smith, Julian, "Hemingway and the Thing Left Out," *JML* 1, ii (1970-71): 169-82. Also in Wagner, L. W., ed., *Ernest Hemingway*, 188-200.

Snell, G., "Ernest Hemingway and the 'Fifth Dimension'," *Shapers of American Fiction*, 156-72.

Sojka, Gregory S., "The 'Aesthetic of Contest' in Ernest Hemingway's Life and Writing," *DAI* 37 (1977): 5128A-29A.

Solovyov, E., "The Color of Tragedy," in Vroon, R., tr., *20th Century American Literature: A Soviet View*, 362-72.

Somers, Paul P., Jr., "Anderson's Twisted Apples and Hemingway's Crips," *Midamerica* 1 (1974): 82-97.

_____, "The Mark of Sherwood Anderson on Hemingway: A Look at Texts," *SAQ* 73 (Autumn, 1974): 487-503.

_____, "Sherwood Anderson and Ernest Hemingway: Influences and Parallels," *DAI* 32 (1971): 985A (Penn. State).

_____, "Sherwood Anderson Introduces His Friend Ernest Hemingway," *LGJ* 3, iii (1975): 24-6.

Soucie, Gary, "Reflections on Hemingway," *Carolina Qtly* 12 (Spring, 1960): 57-63.

Spilka, Mark, "Hemingway and Fauntleroy: An Androgynous Pursuit," in Fleischmann, F., ed., *American Novelists Revisited*, 539-70.

Spiller, R. E., *Cycle of American Literature*, 269-74.

_____, *The Third Dimension: Studies in Literary History*, N.Y.: Macmillan, 1965, 168-71.

Spivey, Ted R., "Hemingway's Pursuit of Happiness on the Open Road," *EUQ* 11 (Dec., 1955): 240-52.

Stavrou, C. N., "Nada, Religion and Hemingway," *Topic* 6 (Fall, 1966): 5-20.

Stephens, Robert O., ed., *Ernest Hemingway: The Critical Reception*, N.Y.: Franklin, 1977.

_____, "The Escape Motif in the Works of Ernest Hemingway," *DA* 19 (1958): 1079-80 (Texas).

Stephenson, Edward R., "Stephen Crane and Ernest Hemingway: A Study in Literary Continuity," *DAI* 33 (1973): 4433A (Brown).

Stetler, Charles, and Gerald Locklin, "De-Coding the Hero in Hemingway's Fiction," *HN* 5, i (1979): 2-10.

Stine, Peter, "Ernest Hemingway and the Great War," *FHA* (1979): 327-54.

Sutherland, Fraser, "Hemingway and Callaghan: Friends and Writers," *CanL* 53 (Summer, 1972): 8-17.

_____, *The Style of Innocence: A Study of Hemingway and Callaghan*, Toronto: Clarke, Irwin, 1972.

Sykes, Robert H., "Ernest Hemingway's Style: A Descriptive Analysis," *DA* 24 (1963): 2043 (Pittsburgh).

Tanaka, Keisuke, "The Bipolar Construction in the Works of Ernest Hemingway," *KAL* 12 (Jan., 1970): 32-44.

Tanner, T., "Ernest Hemingway's Unhurried Sensations," *Reign of Wonder*, 228-57.

Tavernier-Courbin, Jacqueline, "'Striving for Power': Hemingway's Neurosis," *Midamerica* 5 (1978): 76-95. Also in *JGE* 30, iii (Fall, 1978): 137-53.

Thompson, Irene, "The Left Bank Apértifs of Jean Rhys and Ernest Hemingway," *GaR* 35, i (Spring, 1981): 94-106.

Thorp, W., "The Persistence of Naturalism in the Novel," *American Writing in the Twentieth Century*, 185-95.

Toop, Ronald G., "Technique and Vision in the Fiction of Ernest Hemingway: A Chronological Study," *DAI* (1971): 4181A-82A (Toronto).

Trenev, Blagoj, "Colours in Hemingway," *GSUFZF* 66, i (1973): 275-303. [Not seen.]

Trilling, Lionel, "Hemingway and His Critics," *PR* 6 (Winter, 1939): 52-60.

Underwood, Jerry, "Disquisition Concerning Style: The Evil Influence of Ernest Hemingway," *CE* 37, vii (Mar., 1976): 684-5.

Unfried, S. P., *Man's Place in the Natural Order*.

Vandiver, Samuel E., "The Architecture of Hemingway's Prose," *DA* 28 (1967): 2268A (Texas).

Van Gelder, Robert, *Writers on Writing*, 95-8.

Verheul, Lowell J., "Heroic Structure in Hemingway," *DAI* 38 (1977): 794A.

Vorpahl, Ben M., "Ernest Hemingway and Owen Wister: Finding the Lost Generation," *LC* 36 (Spring, 1970): 126-37.

Wagenknecht, E., "Ernest Hemingway: Legend and Reality," *Cavalcade of the American Novel*, 368-81.

Waggoner, Hyatt H., "Ernest Hemingway," *ChS* 38 (June, 1955): 114-20.

Wagner, L. W., ed., *Ernest Hemingway*.

_____, "The Poetry in American Fiction," *Prospects* 2 (1976): 518-20.

_____, "Progression Toward FOR WHOM THE BELL TOLLS," *Hemingway and Faulkner*, 79-85.

_____, "'Proud and Friendly and Gently': Women in Hemingway's Early Fiction," *CollL* 7 (1980): 239-47. Also in Oldsey, Bernard, ed., *Ernest Hemingway: The Papers of a Writer*, N.Y.: Garland, 1981, 63-71.

Walcutt, C. C., *American Literary Naturalism*, 270-80.

Waldhorn, A., ed., *Ernest Hemingway*.

_____, *Reader's Guide to Ernest Hemingway*.

Walsh, Jeffrey, "Emblematical of War: Representation of Combat in Hemingway's Fiction," *HemR* 1, ii (Spring, 1982): 45-57.

Warren, Robert Penn, "Hemingway," *KR* 9 (Winter, 1947): 1-28. Also in Warren, R. P., *Selected Essays*, 80-118. Also in Aldridge, J. W., ed., *Critiques and Essays on Modern Fiction*, 447-73. Also in Zabel, M. D., ed., *Literary Opinion in America*, 444-63. Also, Introduction to A FAREWELL TO ARMS, N.Y.: Scribner, 1949. Also in *Horizon* 15 (1947): 156-80. Also in Wagner, L. W., ed., *Ernest Hemingway*, 75-102. Also, Introduction to A FAREWELL TO ARMS in *Three Novels of Ernest Hemingway*, iii-xl.

Watts, E. S., *Ernest Hemingway and the Arts*.

Webster, Harvey C., "Ernest Hemingway: The Pursuit of Death," *TQ* 7 (Summer, 1964): 149-59.

Weeks, R. P., ed., *Hemingway*.

_____, "Hemingway and the Spectorial Attitude," *WHR* 11 (Summer, 1957): 277-81.

_____, "Hemingway and the Uses of Isolation," *UKCR* 24 (Dec., 1957): 119-25.

Wegelin, Christof, "Hemingway and the Decline of International Fiction," *SR* 73 (Spring, 1965): 285-98.

West, Ray B., Jr., "Ernest Hemingway: The Failure of Sensibility," in O'Connor, W. V., ed., *Forms of Modern Fiction*, 87-101. Also in *SR* 53 (Winter, 1945): 120-35.

White, W. M., "The Crane-Hemingway Code: A Revaluation," *BSUF* 10, ii (Spring, 1969): 15-20.

White, William, "Ernest Hemingway: Violence, Blood, Death," *Orient/West* (Tokyo) 6 (Nov., 1961): 11-23.

_____, "Father and Son: Some Comments on Hemingway's Psychology," *DR* 31 (Winter, 1952): 276-84.

_____, *Merrill Guide to Ernest Hemingway*.

_____, "Novelist as Reporter: Ernest Hemingway," *OW* 9, v (1964): 77-92.

_____, "The Short Unhappy War of Ernest Hemingway," *LGJ* 5, ii (Winter, 1977-78): 2-3, 22.

Whitfield, E., "Hemingway: The Man," *Why* 1 (April, 1953): 10-19. [Not seen.]

Whitlow, Roger, "The Destruction/Prevention of the Family Relationship in Hemingway's Fiction," *LitR* 20 (1976): 5-16.

Widmer, Kingsley, "The Protestant American Fate: Hemingway and Faulkner," in Widmer, K., *Edges of Extremity*, 42-57.

Wiese, Glen J., "Moral Vision in Hemingway's Fiction," *DAI* 32 (1972): 5811A (Utah).

Williams, W., *Tragic Art of Ernest Hemingway*.

Wilson, Edmund, "Hemingway: Gauge of Morale," *The Wound and the Bow: Seven Studies in Literature*, N.Y.: Oxford Un. Pr., 1947, 214-42. Also in *Atlantic* 164 (July, 1939). Also in Caldwell, Guy, ed., *Readings from the Americas: An Introduction to Democratic Thought*, N.Y.: Ronald Pr., 1947, 246-8. Also in McCaffery, J. K. M., ed., *Ernest Hemingway*, 236-57. Also in Rahv, P., ed., *Literature in America*, 373-90. Also in Wilson, E., *Eight Essays*, Garden City, N.Y.: Doubleday, 1954, 92-114.

Wilson, Mark, "Ernest Hemingway as Funnyman," *Thalia* 3, i (Spring-Summer, 1980): 29-34.

Winston, Alexander, "If He Hadn't Been a Genius He Would Have Been a Cad," *ASLHM* 43, i (1972): 25-40.

Wolfe, Don M., "Faulkner and Hemingway: Image of Man's Desolation," *Image of Man in America*, 354-9.

Wood, Tom, ed., "Hemingway Sports Special," *LGJ* 3, ii (Spring-Summer, 1975).

Wyatt, Bryant N., "Huckleberry Finn and the Art of Ernest Hemingway," *MTJ* 13, iv (Summer, 1967): 1-8.

Wyatt, David M., "The Hand of the Master," *VQR* 56, ii (1980): 312-19.

_____, "Hemingway's Uncanny Beginnings," *GaR* 31, ii (Summer, 1977): 476-501.

Wylder, Delbert E., "Faces of the Hero: A Study of the Novels of Ernest Hemingway," *DA* 29 (1969): 4029A-30A (Iowa).

_____, *Hemingway's Heroes*.

Wylder, Robert C., "An Investigation of Hemingway's Fictional Method, Its Sources, and Its Influence on American Literature," *DA* 15 (1955): 2535 (Wisconsin).

Wyrick, Green D., "Hemingway and Bergson: The Elan Vital," *MFS* 1 (Aug., 1955): 17-19.

_____, "The World of Ernest Hemingway: A Critical Study," *ESRS* 2 (Sept., 1953): 3-32.

Yokelson, Joseph B., "Symbolism in the Fiction of Ernest Hemingway," *DA* 23 (1962): 1714 (Brown).

Young, Philip, "Crane and Hemingway," in Bassan, Maurice, ed., *Stephen Crane: A Collection of Critical Essays*, Englewood Cliffs, N.J.: Prentice-Hall, 1967, 52-6. Also in Young, P., *Ernest Hemingway*, 191-6.

_____, *Ernest Hemingway*.

_____, *Ernest Hemingway* (UMPAW, 1). Also in O'Connor, W. V., ed., *Seven Modern American Novelists*, 153-88.

_____, "Hemingway: A Defense," *Folio* 20 (Spring, 1955): 20-2. Also in Weeks, R. P., ed., *Hemingway*, 172-4.

_____, "The World and an American Myth," in Waldhorn, A., ed., *Ernest Hemingway*, 127-40. From Young, P., *Ernest Hemingway*, 242-60.

Yu, Beongcheon, "The Still Center of Hemingway's World," *PhoenixK* 12 (Spring, 1968): 15-44. Also in Wagner, L. W., ed., *Ernest Hemingway*, 109-31.

Yunck, John A., "The Natural History of a Dead Quarrel: Hemingway and the Humanists," *SAQ* 62 (Winter, 1963): 29-42.

Ziff, Larzer, The Social Basis of Hemingway's Style," *Poetics* 7 (1978): 417-23.

ACROSS THE RIVER AND INTO THE TREES

Adair, William, "Death the Hunter: A Note on ACROSS THE RIVER AND INTO THE TREES," *NConL* 7, i (1977): 6-8.

Baker, C., *Hemingway*, 264-88.

_____, *Hemingway*, 4th ed., 264-88. Also, in part (304-11) in Wagner, L. W., ed., *Ernest Hemingway*, 121-6.

Bakker, J., *Ernest Hemingway*, 210-27.

Beach, Joseph W., "How Do You Like It Now, Gentlemen?" *SR* 59 (1951): 311-17. Also in Baker, C., ed., *Hemingway and His Critics*, 227-33.

Benson, J. J., *Hemingway*, 48-54.

Bidle, Kenneth E., "ACROSS THE RIVER AND INTO THE TREES: Rite de Passage à Mort," *FHA* (1973): 259-70.

Brenner, Gerry, "An Imitation of Dante's DIVINE COMEDY: Hemingway's ACROSS THE RIVER AND INTO THE TREES," *FHA* (1976): 191-209.

Broer, L. R., *Hemingway's Spanish Tragedy*, 98-103.

Connolly, C., *Previous Convictions*, 290-2.

Dahiya, B. S., *Hero in Hemingway*, 141-65.

Dring, John R., "The Religious Element in Ernest Hemingway's Novels," *DESB* 7 (1962): 107-9.

Egri, Peter, "The Relationship Between the Short Story and the Novel, Realism and Naturalism in Hemingway's Art. Part II: 1932-1952," *HSE* (1973): 79-81.

Gardiner, H. C., "He-Man Whimpering," *In All Conscience*, 124-5. Also in *America* 83 (Sept. 16, 1950): 628, 630.

Geismar, M., *SatR* 33 (Sept. 9, 1950): 18. Also in Geismar, M., *American Moderns*, 59-61.

Glicksbert, Charles I., "The Hemingway Cult of Love," *Sexual Revolution in Modern American Literature*, 91-3.

Gurko, L., *Ernest Hemingway and the Pursuit of Heroism*, 152-8.

Hipkiss, Robert A., "Ernest Hemingway's THE THINGS THAT I KNOW," *TCL* 19, iv (Oct., 1973): 275-81.

Hovey, R. B., *Hemingway*, 173-4, 177-90.

Knowles, A. Sidney, Jr., "Hemingway's ACROSS THE RIVER AND INTO THE TREES: Adversity and Art," *ELWIU* 5, ii (1978): 195-208.

Lewis, R. W., Jr., *Hemingway on Love*, 181-96.

Lisca, Peter, "The Structure of Hemingway's ACROSS THE RIVER AND INTO THE TREES," *MFS* 12 (Summer, 1966): 232-50. Also in Wagner, L. W., ed., *Ernest Hemingway*, 288-306.

McDonald, James L., "The Incredible Richard Cantwell," *NMAL* 2, i (Winter, 1977): Item 3.

Nahal, C., *Narrative Pattern in Ernest Hemingway's Fiction*, 150-69.

Oppel, Horst, "Hemingway's ACROSS THE RIVER AND INTO THE TREES," in Baker, C., ed., *Hemingway and His Critics*, 213-26.

Pearsall, R. B., *Life and Writings of Ernest Hemingway*, 233-40.

Prescott, O., *In My Opinion*, 68-70.

Rahv, Philip, in *Ctary* 10 (Oct., 1950): 400-2. Also in Rahv, P., *Image and Idea*, 188-92. Also in Rahv, P., *Literature and the Sixth Sense*, 351-5. Also in Rahv, P., *Myth and the Powerhouse*, 193-8.

Rajadura, A., "A Study of Hemingway's ACROSS THE RIVER AND INTO THE TREES," *JEngS* 2 (1979): 14-23.

Rama Rao, P. G., *Ernest Hemingway*, 204-12.

Rosenfeld, Isaac, "A Farewell to Hemingway," *KR* 13 (Winter, 1951): 147-55. Also in Rosenfeld, I., *Age of Enormity*, 258-67.

Sanderson, S. F., *Ernest Hemingway*, 103-12.

Seyppel, Joachim H., "Two Variations on a Theme: Dying in Venice (Thomas Mann and Ernest Hemingway)," *L&P* 7 (Feb., 1957): 8-12.

Shaw, S., *Ernest Hemingway*, 106-11.

Stephens, Robert O., "Hemingway's ACROSS THE RIVER AND INTO THE TREES: A Reprise," *TxSE* 37 (1958): 92-101.

Wagner, Linda W., "The Search for Love in the Last Years: ACROSS THE RIVER AND INTO THE TREES," *Hemingway and Faulkner*, 107-11.

Waldhorn, A., *Reader's Guide to Ernest Hemingway*, 178-88.

Walsh, J., *American War Literature*, 126-35.

Watkins, W. C., *Flesh and the Word*, 158-65.

Waugh, Evelyn, "The Case of Mr. Hemingway," *Cweal* 99, vii (Nov. 16, 1973): 195-7. Orig. publ. *Cweal* (Nov. 3, 1950): 97-8.

Whitlow, Roger, "ACROSS THE RIVER AND INTO THE TREES—Hemingway and Psychotherapy," *IllQ* 40, iv (1978): 38-47.

Williams, W., *Tragic Art of Ernest Hemingway*, 155-71.

_____, "Tragic Patterns and Rhythms in ACROSS THE RIVER AND INTO THE TREES," *FHA* (1979): 389-405.

Wyatt, David M., "Hemingway's Uncanny Beginnings," *GaR* 31, ii (Summer, 1977): 491-5.

Wylder, D. E., *Hemingway's Heroes*, 165-98.

Young, P., *Ernest Hemingway*, 114-21.

_____, *Ernest Hemingway* (UMPAW, 1): 17-19. Also in O'Connor, W. V., ed., *Seven Modern American Novelists*, 166-8.

Zabel, M. D., "A Good Day for Mr. Tolstoy," *Nation* 171 (Sept. 9, 1950): 9. Also in Zabel, M. D., *Craft and Character*, 317-21.

A FAREWELL TO ARMS

Adair, William, "A FAREWELL TO ARMS: A Dream Book," *JNT* 5 (1975): 40-56.

_____, "Time and Structure in A FAREWELL TO ARMS," *SDR* 13, i (1975): 165-71.

Adams, Philip D., "Ernest Hemingway and the Painters: Cubist Style in THE SUN ALSO RISES and A FAREWELL TO ARMS," *DAI* 32 (1972): 6311A.

_____, "Husserl's Eidetic Object: An Approach to the Styles of Hemingway and the Cubists," in Maxfield, Malinda R., ed., *Images and Innovations: Update '70's*, Papers of the So. Humanities Conf., Converse College, Spartanburg, SC: Center for the Humanities, Converse College, 1979, 58-67.

Aldridge, J. W., *After the Lost Generation*, 6-10, 38-9 *passim*.

Allen, W., *Modern Novel*, 97-8.

Anderson, Charles R., "Hemingway's Other Style," *MLN* 76 (May, 1961): 434-42. Also in Baker, C., ed., *Ernest Hemingway*, 41-6.

Baker, Carlos, in Stegner, W., ed., *American Novel*, 192-205. Also in Graham, J., comp., *Studies in A FAREWELL TO ARMS*, 27-38.

_____, *Hemingway*, 4th ed., 94-6, 98-109.

_____, "The Mountain and the Plain," *VQR* 27 (Summer, 1951): 410-18. Also in Baker, C., *Hemingway*, 94-6, 98-109. Also in Baker, C., ed., *Ernest Hemingway*, 47-60. Also in

Gellens, J., ed., *Twentieth Century Interpretations of A FAREWELL TO ARMS*, 56-64.

_____, "On Ernest Hemingway," in Maden, C. F., ed., *Talks With Authors*, 74-88.

Baker, S., *Ernest Hemingway*, 62-73.

Bakker, J., *Ernest Hemingway*, 87-112.

Beach, J. W., *American Fiction*, 84-9 *passim*.

Benson, J. J., *Hemingway*, 81-112.

Bluefarb, Sam, "Frederic Henry: The Fun for Life," *Escape Motif in the American Novel*, 74-92.

Box, Terry, "Hemingway's A FAREWELL TO ARMS," *Expl* 37, iv (Summer, 1979): 7.

Brashers, H. C., *An Introduction to American Literature*, 137-8.

Breidlid, Anders, "Courage and Self-Affirmation in Ernest Hemingway's 'Lost Generation' Fiction," *Edda* 5 (1979): 291-8.

Burgum, E. B., *Novel and the World's Dilemma*, 184-6.

Cantelupe, Eugene B., "Statues and Lovers in A FAREWELL TO ARMS," *FHA* (1977): 203-5.

Carson, David L., "Symbolism in A FAREWELL TO ARMS," *ES* 53 (Dec., 1972): 518-22.

Cass, Colin S., "Nothing Happened...': The Tip of a Hemingway Iceberg," *FHA* (1978): 247-59.

Cecil, L. Moffit, "The Color of A FAREWELL TO ARMS," *RS* 36 (June, 1968): 168-73.

Cooperman, Stanley, "Death and Cojones: Hemingway's A FAREWELL TO ARMS," *SAQ* 63 (Winter, 1964): 85-92.

_____, *World War I and the American Novel*, 181-90 *passim*.

Cowley, Malcolm, From "Introduction" to Cowley, M., ed., *The Portable Hemingway*, N.Y.: Viking, 1944, 16. Also in Gellens, J., ed., *Twentieth Century Interpretations of A FAREWELL TO ARMS*, 54-5.

Dahiya, B. S., *Hero in Hemingway*, 49-71.

D'Avanzo, Mario L., "Hemingway's A FAREWELL TO ARMS, Chapter XXXV," *Expl* 27, v (Jan., 1969): Item 39.

_____, "The Motif of Corruption in A FAREWELL TO ARMS," *LHR* 11 (1969): 57-62.

Davidson, Arnold E., "The Dantean Perspective in Hemingway's A FAREWELL TO ARMS," *JNT* 3 (May, 1973): 121-30.

Davidson, Donald, *The Spyglass: Views and Reviews, 1924-1930*, Nashville: Vanderbilt Un. Pr., 1963, 88-92.

Davis, Robert M., "'If You Did Not Go Forward': Process and Stasis in A FAREWELL TO ARMS," *SNNTS* 2, iii (Fall, 1970): 305-11.

Davison, Richard A., "Hemingway's A FAREWELL TO ARMS," *Expl* 29 (Feb., 1971): Item 46.

Dekker, George, and Joseph Harris, "Supernaturalism and the Vernacular Style in A FAREWELL TO ARMS," *PMLA* 94, ii (1979): 311-18.

Dring, John R., "The Religious Element in Ernest Hemingway's Novels," *DESB* 7 (1962): 67-71.

Edmonds, Dale, "When Does Frederic Henry Narrate A FAREWELL TO ARMS," *CLS* 16 (1979): 189-206.

Farquhar, Robin H., "Dramatic Structure in the Novels of Ernest Hemingway," *MFS* 14 (Autumn, 1968): 275-7.

Fetterley, Judith, "A FAREWELL TO ARMS: Hemingway's 'Resentful Cryptogram'," *JPC* 10 (1976): 203-14. Also in Diamond, A., and L. R. Edwards, eds., *Authority of Experience*, 257-73. Also in Fetterley, J., *Resisting Reader*, 46-71.

Flores, Olga E., "Eros, Thanatos and the Hemingway Soldier," *ASInt* 18, iii-iv (1980): 27-35.

Friedman, Norman, "Criticism and the Novel," *AR* 18 (Fall, 1958): 352-6. Also in Westbrook, M., ed., *Modern American Novel*, 113-18.

_____, "Hardy, Hemingway, Crane, Woolf and Conrad," *AR* 18 (Fall, 1958): 343-8, 352-6.

Friedrich, Otto, "Ernest Hemingway: Joy Through Strength," *ASch* 26 (Autumn, 1957): 519-24 *passim*. Also in Graham, J., comp., *Studies in A FAREWELL TO ARMS*, 46-54.

Frohock, W. M., "Ernest Hemingway: Violence and Discipline: I," *SWR* 32 (1947): 95-7. Also in Frohock, W. M., *Novel of Violence in America*, 176-9+. Also in McCaffery, J. K. M., ed., *Ernest Hemingway*, 272-5.

Ganzel, Dewey, "A FAREWELL TO ARMS: The Danger of Imagination," *SR* 79, iv (Autumn, 1971): 576-97.

Gargan, William, "'Death Once Dead': An Examination of an Alternative Title to Hemingway's A FAREWELL TO ARMS," *NMAL* 4 (1980): Item 26.

Garrety, Michael, "Love and War: R. H. Mottram, THE SPANISH FARM TRILOGY and Ernest Hemingway, A FAREWELL TO ARMS," in Klein, H., ed., *First World War in Fiction*, 10-22.

Geismar, M., *Writers in Crisis*, 46-7.

Gelfant, Blanche, "Language as a Moral Code in A FAREWELL TO ARMS," *MFS* 9 (1963): 173-6. Also in Graham, J., comp., *Studies in A FAREWELL TO ARMS*, 83-7.

Gellens, J., ed., *Twentieth Century Interpretations of A FAREWELL TO ARMS*.

Gerstenberger, Donna, "THE WASTE LAND in A FAREWELL TO ARMS," *MLN* 76 (1961): 24-5.

Gibson, Walker, "Tough Talk: The Rhetoric of Frederick Henry," in *Tough, Sweet, and Stuffy*, Bloomington: Indiana Un. Pr., 1966, 28-42.

Giger, R., *Creative Void*, 16-19, 57-63.

Glasser, William A., "A FAREWELL TO ARMS," *SR* 74 (Spring, 1966): 453-69.

_____, "Hemingway's A FAREWELL TO ARMS," *Expl* 20 (Oct., 1961): Item 18.

Glicksberg, Charles I., "The Hemingway Cult of Love," *Sexual Revolution in Modern American Literature*, 84-91.

Gradoli, Marina, "Count Greffi's Birthday Parties," *Dismisura: Rivista Bimestrale di Produzione & Crit. Culturale* (Alatri, Italy), 39-50 (1980): 112-14.

Graham, J., comp., *Studies in A FAREWELL TO ARMS*.

Grebstein, S. N., *Hemingway's Craft*, 30-5, 72-6, 119-24, 202-18.

Gurko, L., *Ernest Hemingway and the Pursuit of Heroism*, 81-109.

Hackett, Francis, "Hemingway: A FAREWELL TO ARMS," *SRL* 32 (Aug. 6, 1949): 32-3.

Halliday, E. M., "Hemingway's Ambiguity: Symbolism and Irony," *AL* 28 (Mar., 1956): 7-18. Also in Baker, C., ed., *Ernest Hemingway*, 61-74. Also in Feidelson, C., Jr., and P. Brodtkork, Jr., *Interpretations of American Literature*, 303-13. Also in Weeks, R. P., ed., *Hemingway*, 52-71. Also in Gellens, J., ed., *Twentieth Century Interpretations of A FAREWELL TO ARMS*, 64-71. Also in Waldhorn, A., ed., *Ernest Hemingway*, 40-51.

Hallman, Ralph J., *Psychology of Literature: A Study of Alienation and Tragedy*, N.Y.: Philosophical Library, 1961, 119-21.

Hardy, J. E., *Man in the Modern Novel*, 123-36.

Hashiguchi, Yasuo, "A FAREWELL TO ARMS and 'A Farewell to Arms'," *KAL* No. 3 (May, 1960): 1-8.

Hayashi, Tetsumaro, "A FAREWELL TO ARMS: The Contest of Experience," *KAL* 12 (Jan., 1970): 14-19.

Hemingway, Ernest, "The Original Conclusion to A FAREWELL TO ARMS," in Baker, C., ed., *Ernest Hemingway*, 75.

Hinkle, James, "Seeing Through It in A FAREWELL TO ARMS," *HemR* 2, i (1982): 94-5.

Hoffman, Frederick J., "No Beginning and No End: Hemingway and Death," *EIC* 3 (1953): 78-80. Also in Feidelson, C., Jr., and P. Brodtkorb, eds., *Interpretations of American Literature*, 325-6.

Holder, Robert C., Jr., "Counts Mippipopolous and Greffi: Hemingway's Aristocrats of Resignation," *HN* 3, ii (Fall, 1973): 3-6.

Horrigan, William, "Dying Without Death: Borzage's A FAREWELL TO ARMS," in Peary, G., and R. Shatzkin, eds., *Classic American Novel and the Movies*, 297-304.

Hovey, Richard B., "A FAREWELL TO ARMS: Hemingway's Liebestod," *UR* 33 (Dec., 1966): 93-100.

_____, "A FAREWELL TO ARMS: Hemingway's Liebestod II," *UR* 33 (Mar., 1967): 163-8.

_____, *Hemingway*, 73-91.

Jain, Sunita, "Of Women and Bitches: A Defense of Two Hemingway Heroines," *JSL* 3, ii (Winter, 1975-76): 32-5.

Johnston, Kenneth G., "Counterpart: The Reflective Pattern in Hemingway's Humor," *KanQ* 1, iii (Summer, 1969): 51-7.

Joost, Nicholas, and Alan Brown, "T. S. Eliot and Ernest Hemingway: A Literary Relationship," *PLL* 14, iv (Fall, 1978): 434-41.

Keeler, Clinton, "A FAREWELL TO ARMS: Hemingway and Peele," *MLN* 76 (Nov., 1961): 622-5.

Kimball, W. J., "Hemingway and the Code," *Venture* 6 (Summer, 1970): 18-23.

Knapp, Daniel, "Hemingway: The Naming of the Hero," *StL* 2, ii (1961): 31-4.

Kobler, J. F., "Let's Run Catherine Barkley up the Flag Pole and See Who Salutes," *CEA* 36, ii (Jan., 1974): 4-10.

_____, "Why Does Catherine Barkley Die?" *FHA* (1978): 313-19.

Kvam, Wane, "Zuckmayer, Hilpert and Hemingway," *PMLA* 91 (1976): 194-205.

Labor, Earle, "Crane and Hemingway: Anatomy of Trauma," *Ren* 11 (1959): 189-96.

Lawson, Carolina D., "Hemingway, Stendhal and War," *HN* 6, ii (Spring, 1981): 28-33.

Lebowitz, Alan, "No Farewell to Arms," in Engel, M., ed., *Uses of History*, 187-204.

Lewis, Robert W., "Hemingway in Italy: Making It Up," *JML* 9, ii (May, 1982): 209-36.

_____, *Hemingway on Love*, 29-54. Also in Gellens, J., ed., *Twentieth Century Interpretations of A FAREWELL TO ARMS*, 41-53.

Lewis, Wyndham, "The 'Dumb Ox' in Love and War," in Gellens, J., ed., *Twentieth Century Interpretations of A FAREWELL TO ARMS*, 72-90. From Lewis, Wyndham, *Men Without Art*, N.Y.: Russell & Russell, 1964, 17-41.

Liedloff, Helmut, "Two War Novels: A Critical Comparison," *RLC* 42 (1968): 390-406.

Light, James F., "The Religion of Death in A FAREWELL TO ARMS," *MFS* 7 (Summer, 1961): 169-73. Also in Baker, C., ed., *Ernest Hemingway*, 37-40. Also in Graham, J., comp., *Studies in A FAREWELL TO ARMS*, 39-45.

Maekawa, Toshihiro, "Catherine's Death as a Lesson: A Study of A FAREWELL TO ARMS," *KAL* 20 (1979): 68-70.

Magny, Claude-Edmonde, "Hemingway, or the Exaltation of the Moment," *Age of the American Novel*, 144-56.

Mann, Charles, "F. Scott Fitzgerald's Critique of A FAREWELL TO ARMS," *FHA* (1976): 141-53.

Marcus, Fred H., "A FAREWELL TO ARMS: The Impact of Irony and the Irrational," *EJ* 52 (Nov., 1962): 527-35.

Marcus, Mordecai, "A FAREWELL TO ARMS: Novel into Film," *JCMVASA* 2 (1961): 69-71.

Martz, Louis L., from "The Saint as Tragic Hero," in Brooks, Cleanth, ed., *Tragic Themes in Western Literature*, New Haven: Yale Un. Pr., 1955, 153-4. Also in Gellens, J., ed., *Twentieth Century Interpretations of A FAREWELL TO ARMS*, 55-6.

Matthews, T. S., "Nothing Ever Happens to the Brave," *NRep* (Oct. 9, 1929): 208-10. Also in Harrison, G. A., ed., *Critic as Artist*, 257-62.

Mazzaro, Jerome L., "George Peele and A FAREWELL TO ARMS: A Thematic Tie?" *MLN* 75 (Feb., 1960): 118-19.

McAleer, John J., "A FAREWELL TO ARMS: Frederic Henry's Rejected Passion," *Ren* 14 (Winter, 1961): 72-9, 89.

McCarthy, Paul, "Chapter Beginnings in A FAREWELL TO ARMS," *BSUF* 10, ii (Spring, 1969): 21-30.

McIlvaine, Robert M., "A Literary Source for Caesarean Section in A FAREWELL TO ARMS," *AL* 43, iii (Nov., 1971): 444-7.

Meriwether, James B., "The Dashes in Hemingway's A FAREWELL TO ARMS," *PBSA* 58, iv (1964): 449-57.

Merrill, Robert, "Tragic Form in A FAREWELL TO ARMS," *AL* 45, iv (Jan., 1974): 571-9.

Morioka, Sakae, "HUCK FINN and A FAREWELL TO ARMS," *KAL* No. 5 (1962): 27-35.

Moses, W. R., "Victory in Defeat: 'Ad Astra' and A FAREWELL TO ARMS," *MissQ* 19 (Spring, 1966): 85-9.

————, "Water, Water Everywhere: OLD MAN and A FAREWELL TO ARMS," *MFS* 5 (Summer, 1959): 172-4.

Nahal, C., *Narrative Pattern In Ernest Hemingway's Fiction*, 49-79.

Naik, M. K., "Thematic Structure in A FAREWELL TO ARMS," *IJES* 8 (Mar., 1967): 79-82.

Norton, Charles A., "The Alcoholic Content of A FAREWELL TO ARMS," *FHA* (1973): 309-13.

Oldsey, Bernard, "The Genesis of A FAREWELL TO ARMS," *SAF* 5, ii (Autumn, 1977): 175-85.

————, *Hemingway's Hidden Craft: The Writing of A FAREWELL TO ARMS*, University Park: Pennsylvania St. Un. Pr., 1979.

————, "Of Hemingway's Arms and the Man," *CollL* 1, iii (Fall, 1974): 174-89.

————, "The Sense of an Ending in A FAREWELL TO ARMS," *MFS* 23, iv (1977-78): 491-510.

Parton, Linda C., "Time: The Novelistic Cohesive in A FAREWELL TO ARMS," *FHA* (1979): 355-62.

Pearsall, R. B., *Life and Writings of Ernest Hemingway*, 117-42.

Peterson, R. K., *Hemingway*, 26-32, 47-50.

Rama Rao, P. G., *Ernest Hemingway*, 175-82.

Reynolds, Michael S., "The Agnes Tapes: A Farewell to Catherine Barkley," *FHA* (1979): 251-78.

————, *Hemingway's First War: The Making of A FAREWELL TO ARMS*, Princeton: Princeton Un. Pr., 1976.

————, "A Historical Study of Hemingway's A FAREWELL TO ARMS," *DAI* 32 (1971): 1525A-26A (Duke).

Richardson, H. Edward, "The 'Hemingwaves' in Faulkner's WILD PALMS," *MFS* 4 (Winter, 1958-59): 357-60.

Robinson, Forrest D., "Frederick Henry: The Hemingway Hero as Storyteller," *CEA* 34, iv (Fall, 1972): 13-16.

————, "The Tragic Awareness of Hemingway's First-Person Narrators: A Study of THE SUN ALSO RISES and A FAREWELL TO ARMS," *DA* 27 (1967): 2543A (Ohio).

Ross, Frank, "The Assailant-Victim in Three War Protest Novels," *Paunch* 32 (1968): 46-57.

Rossky, William, "Sudden Love: An Approach to A FAREWELL TO ARMS," *EngR* 12 (Spring, 1961): 4-6.

Rovit, E., *Ernest Hemingway*, 98-106. Also, as "Learning to Care," in Gellens, J., ed., *Twentieth Century Interpretations of A FAREWELL TO ARMS*, 33-40.

Russell, H. K., "The Catharsis in A FAREWELL TO ARMS," *MFS* 1, iii (Aug., 1955): 25-30.

Sanderson, S. F., *Ernest Hemingway*, 51-61.

Savage, D. S., "Ernest Hemingway," *HudR* 1 (Autumn, 1949): 389-401.

————, *Withered Branch*, 23-36. Also, as "Ciphers at the Front," in Gellens, J., ed., *Twentieth Century Interpretations of A FAREWELL TO ARMS*, 91-102.

Schneider, Daniel J., "Hemingway's A FAREWELL TO ARMS: The Novel as Pure Poetry," *MFS* 14 (Autumn, 1968): 283-96. Also in Graham, J., comp., *Studies in A FAREWELL TO ARMS*, 66-82. Also in Wagner, L. W., *Ernest Hemingway*, 252-66.

Scott, N. A., Jr., *Ernest Hemingway*, 33-5.

Seelye, John, "Hyperion to a Satyr: FAREWELL TO ARMS and LOVE STORY," *CollL* 6 (1979): 129-35.

Sharrock, Roger, "Singles and Couples: Hemingway's A FAREWELL TO ARMS and Updike's COUPLES," *Ariel* 4, iv (Oct., 1973): 21-43.

Shaw, S., *Ernest Hemingway*, 54-65.

Simpson, Herbert, "The Problem of Structure in A FAREWELL TO ARMS," *ForumH* 4, iv (Spring-Summer, 1964): 20-4.

Slattery, Sister Margaret P., "Hemingway's A FAREWELL TO ARMS," *Expl* 27 (Oct., 1968): Item 8.

Slattery, William C., "The Mountain, the Plain, and San Siro," *PLL* 16 (1980): 439-42.

Smith, Paul, "Almost All is Vanity: A Note on Nine Rejected Titles for A FAREWELL TO ARMS," *HemR* 2, i (1982): 74-6.

Sorkin, Adam J., "From Papa to Yo-Yo: At War with all the Words in the World," *SAB* 44, iv (1979): 48-65.

Spilka, Mark, "Hemingway and Fauntleroy: An Androgynous Pursuit," in Fleischmann, F., ed., *American Novelists Revisited*, 352-7.

Spofford, William K., "Beyond the Feminist Perspective: Love in A FAREWELL TO ARMS," *FHA* (1978): 307-12.

Srivastava, Ramesh K., "Hemingway's FOR WHOM THE BELL TOLLS: A Critical Introduction with Annotations," *DAI* 33 (1973): 3674A.

Steinke, Jim, "Harlotry and Love: A Friendship in A FAREWELL TO ARMS," *Spectrum* (Un. of Calif., Santa Barbara) 21, i-ii (1979): 20-4.

Stephens, Robert O., "Hemingway and Stendhal: The Matrix of A FAREWELL TO ARMS," *PMLA* 88, ii (Mar., 1973): 271-80.

Stone, Edward, *A Certain Morbidness: A View of American Literature*, Carbondale: So. Ill. Un. Pr., 1969, 161-3. (Dream Sequence—Chap. 28).

Strandberg, Victor H., "A Palm for Pamela: Three Studies in the Game of Love," *WHR* 20 (Winter, 1966): 37-47.

Stubbs, John, "Love and Role Playing in A FAREWELL TO ARMS," *FHA* (1973): 271-83.

Toole, William B., "Religion, Love and Nature in A FAREWELL TO ARMS: The Dark Shape of Irony," *CEA* 29 (May, 1967): 10-11.

Unfried, S. F., *Man's Place in the Natural Order*, 61-78.

Unrue, John, "The Valley of Baca and A FAREWELL TO ARMS," *FHA* (1974): 229-34.

Vandersee, Charles, "The Stopped Worlds of Frederic Henry," in Graham, J., comp., *Studies in A FAREWELL TO ARMS*, 55-65.

Waldhorn, Arthur, "Harold Loeb's Ants," *HemR* 2, i (1982): 86-7.

_____, *Reader's Guide to Ernest Hemingway*, 113-30.

Walsh, J., *American War Literature*, 51-8.

Warren, Robert Penn, "Ernest Hemingway," *KR* 9 (Winter, 1947): 1-28. Also, "Introduction" to *A FAREWELL TO ARMS*, N.Y.: Scribner, 1949. Also in Warren, R. P., *Selected Essays*, 80-118. Also in *Horizon* 15 (1947): 156-80. Also in Aldridge, J. W., ed., *Critiques and Essays on Modern Fiction*, 447-73. Also in Zabel, M. D., ed., *Literary Opinion in America*, 443-63. Also in Wagner, L. W., ed., *Ernest Hemingway*, 75-102.

_____, "Introduction" to A FAREWELL TO ARMS, in *Three Novels of Ernest Hemingway*, xxix-xxxvi.

Watkins, Floyd C., "World Pessimism and Personal Cheeriness in A FAREWELL TO ARMS," *Flesh and the Word*, 109-26.

Way, Brian, "The Early Novels of Ernest Hemingway," *Delta* No. 16 (Autumn, 1958): 15-24.

West, Ray B., Jr., in West, R. B., Jr., and R. W. Stallman, eds., *Art of Modern Fiction*, N.Y.: Holt, 1949, 622-33. Also in Baker, C., ed., *Ernest Hemingway*, 28-36. Also in Weeks, R. P., ed., *Hemingway*, 139-51. Also in West, R. B., *Writer in the Room*, 158-74. Also in Gellens, J., ed., *Twentieth Century Interpretations of A FAREWELL TO ARMS*, 15-27.

Wexler, Joyce, "E.R.A. for Hemingway: A Feminist Defense of A FAREWELL TO ARMS," *GaR* 35, i (Spring, 1981): 111-23.

Whitlow, Roger, "Mission or Love, Frederick Henry? You Can't Have It Both Ways," *MarkhamR* 8 (Winter, 1979): 33-6.

Williams, W., *Tragic Art of Ernest Hemingway*, 65-88.

Wright, Moorhead, "The Existential Adventurer and War: Three Case Studies from American Literature," in Booth, K., and M. Wright, eds., *American Thinking About Peace and War*, 101-10.

Wyatt, David M., "Hemingway's Uncanny Beginnings," *GaR* 31, ii (Summer, 1977): 486-91.

Wylder, D. E., *Hemingway's Heroes*, 66-95.

Wyrick, Jean, "Fantasy as Symbol: Another Look at Hemingway's Catherine," *MSE* 4, ii (Fall, 1973): 42-7.

Yokelson, Joseph B., "Symbolism in the Fiction of Ernest Hemingway," *DA* 23 (1962): 1714 (Brown).

Young, P., *Ernest Hemingway*, 88-95. Also, as "Loser Take Nothing," in Gellens, J., ed., *Twentieth Century Interpretations of A FAREWELL TO ARMS*, 28-32.

_____, *Ernest Hemingway* (UMPAW, 1), 11-13. Also in O'Connor, W. V., ed., *Seven Modern American Novelists*, 161-3.

_____, "Hemingway's A FAREWELL TO ARMS," *Expl* 7 (1948): Item 7.

_____, Carlos Baker, and George D. Crothers, "A FAREWELL TO ARMS," in Crothers, G. D., ed., *Invitation to Learning*, N.Y.: Basic Bks., 1966, 329-36.

FOR WHOM THE BELL TOLLS

Adair, William, "FOR WHOM THE BELL TOLLS: Oedipus in Spain," *NConL* 12, ii (Mar., 1982): 2.

Adler, Jack, "Theme and Character in Hemingway: FOR WHOM THE BELL TOLLS," *UR* 30 (June, 1964): 293-9.

Alinei, Tamara, "The CORRIDA and FOR WHOM THE BELL TOLLS," *Neophil* 56, iv (Oct., 1972): 487-92.

Allen, John J., "The English of Hemingway's Spaniards," *SAB* 27 (Nov., 1961): 6-7. Also in Grebstein, S. N., comp., *Studies in FOR WHOM THE BELL TOLLS*, 91-3.

Allen, Mary I., "Hail to Arms: A View of FOR WHOM THE BELL TOLLS," *FHA* (1973): 285-93.

Allen, Michael J. B., "The Unspanish War in FOR WHOM THE BELL TOLLS," *ConL* 13, ii (Spring, 1972): 204-12.

Atkins, J., *Art of Ernest Hemingway*, 27-45.

Backman, Melvin, "Hemingway: The Matador and the Crucified," *MFS* 1 (Aug, 1955): 6-9. Also in Baker, C., ed., *Hemingway and His Critics*, 250-4.

Baker, C., *Hemingway*, 4th ed., 237-63. Also in Baker, C., ed., *Ernest Hemingway*, 108-30.

Baker, S., *Ernest Hemingway*, 109-18.

Bakker, J., *Ernest Hemingway*, 178-209.

Barea, Arturo, "Not Spain but Hemingway," *Horizon* 3 (May, 1941): 350-61. Also in Baker, C., ed., *Hemingway and His Critics*, 202-12. Also in Grebstein, S. N., comp., *Studies in FOR WHOM THE BELL TOLLS*, 80-90.

Bass, Eben, "Hemingway at Roncesvalles," *NEMLA Newsl.* 2, i (Feb., 1970): 1-7.

Beach, J. W., *American Fiction*, 89-93.

_____, "How Do You Like It Now, Gentlemen?" *SR* 59 (1951): 322-8. Also in Baker, C., ed., *Hemingway and His Critics*, 238-44.

Benson, J. J., *Hemingway*, 153-68.

Bessie, Alvah C., *New Masses* 37 (Nov. 5, 1940): 25-9. Also in Baker, C., ed., *Ernest Hemingway*, 90-4.

Brenner, Gerry, "Epic Machinery in Hemingway's FOR WHOM THE BELL TOLLS," *MFS* 16, iv (Winter, 1970-71): 491-504.

Broer, L. R., *Hemingway's Spanish Tragedy*, 88-97.

Brooks, C., *Hidden God*, 16-20.

Burgum, Edwin B., "Ernest Hemingway and the Psychology of the Lost Generation," *Novel and the World's Dilemma*, 197-204. Also in McCaffery, J. K. M., ed., *Ernest Hemingway*, 321-8.

Bury, John P., "Hemingway in Spain," *ConR* No. 1118 (Feb., 1959): 103-5.

Carpenter, Frederic I., "Hemingway Achieves the Fifth Dimension," *PMLA* 69 (Sept., 1954): 714-17. Also in Carpenter, F. I., *American Literature and the Dream*, 185-93. Also in Baker, C., ed., *Hemingway and His Critics*, 196-9. Also in Wagner, L. W., ed., *Ernest Hemingway*, 283-6. Also in Waldhorn, A., ed., *Ernest Hemingway*, 87-90.

Cass, Colin S., "The Love Story in FOR WHOM THE BELL TOLLS," *FHA* (1972): 225-35.

Cooperman, Stanley, "American War Novels: Yesterday, Today, and Tomorrow," *YR* 41, iv (Summer, 1972): 527-9.

_____, "Hemingway's Blue-eyed Boy: Robert Jordan and 'Purging Ecstasy'," *Criticism* 8 (Winter, 1966): 87-96.

Cowley, M., "Hemingway's 'Nevertheless'," *Look Back on Us*, 361-4. Also as "Death of a Hero," *NRep* (Jan. 20, 1941): 89-90.

Crawford, John W., "Robert Jordan: A Man for Our Times," *CEA* 41, iii (1979): 17-22.

Crozier, Robert D., S. J., "For Thine is the Power and the Glory: Love in FOR WHOM THE BELL TOLLS," *PLL* 10 (1974): 76-7.

Dahiya, B. S., *Hero in Hemingway*, 114-40.

Davidson, Cathy N., "Laughter Without Comedy in FOR WHOM THE BELL TOLLS," *HN* 3, ii (Fall, 1973): 6-9.

De Falco, Joseph M., "Hemingway and Revolution: *Mankinde Not Marx*," in Levith, M. J ., ed., *Renaissance and Modern*, 150-9.

Delaney, Paul, "Robert Jordan's 'Real Absithe' in FOR WHOM THE BELL TOLLS," *FHA* (1972): 317-20.

Ditsky, John, "Hemingway, Plato and THE HIDDEN GOD," *SHR* 5, ii (Summer, 1971): 145-7.

Dring, John R., "The Religious Element in Ernest Hemingway's Novels," *DESB* 7 (1962): 105-7.

Durham, Philip, "Ernest Hemingway's Grace Under Pressure: The Western Code," *Pacific Hist. Rev.(CA)* 45 (1976): 425-32.

Eby, Cecil, "How the Bell Tolled," *MQR* 8, iv (1969): 245-52.

_____, "The Real Robert Jordan," *AL* 38 (Nov., 1966): 380-6. Also in Grebstein, S. N., comp., *Studies in FOR WHOM THE BELL TOLLS*, 43-9.

Egri, Peter, "The Relationship Between the Short Story and the Novel, Realism and Naturalism in Hemingway's Art. Part II: 1932-1952," *HSE* 7 (1973): 70-9.

Eisinger, C. E., *Fiction of the Forties*, 115-16.

Elliott, Gary D., "FOR WHOM THE BELL TOLLS: Regeneration of the Hemingway Hero," *CEA* 38, iv (1976): 24-9.

Evans, Robert, "Hemingway and the Pale Cast of Thought," *AL* 38 (May, 1966): 168-72. Also in Waldhorn, A., ed., *Ernest Hemingway*, 119-23.

Evans, T. Jeff, "For Whom the Earth Moves: A Fitzgerald Parody of Hemingway," *AN&Q* 17 (1979): 127-8.

Farquhar, Robin H., "Dramatic Structure in the Novels of Ernest Hemingway," *MFS* 14 (Autumn, 1968): 277-9.

Farrell, James T., "Ernest Hemingway," *FHA* (1973): 221-4.

Fenimore, Edward, "English and Spanish in FOR WHOM THE BELL TOLLS," *ELH* 10 (June, 1943): 73-86. Also in McCaffery, J. K. M., ed., *Ernest Hemingway*, 205-20.

Fleming, Robert E., "Hemingway's Treatment of Suicide: 'Fathers and Sons' and FOR WHOM THE BELL TOLLS," *ArQ* 33 (1977): 121-32.

Flores, Olga E., "Eros, Thanatos and the Hemingway Soldier," *ASInt* 18, iii-iv (1980): 27-35.

French, W., *Social Novel at the End of an Era*, 87-124 *passim*. Also in Grebstein, S. N., comp., *Studies in FOR WHOM THE BELL TOLLS*, 56-70.

Frohock, W. M., "Ernest Hemingway: Violence and Discipline: II," *SWR* 32 (1947): 189-93. Also in Frohock, W. M., *Novel of Violence in America*, 188-94+. Also in McCaffery, J. K. M., ed., *Ernest Hemingway*, 285-91.

Geismar, Maxwell, *Writers in Crisis*, 79-84. Also in McCaffery, J. K. M., ed., *Ernest Hemingway*, 183-9. Also, condensed, in *VQR* 17 (1941): 533-4.

Gladstein, Mimi R., "Ma Joad and Pilar: Significantly Similar," *S&Q* 14 (1981): 93-104.

Gleaves, Edwin S., "The Spanish Influence on Ernest Hemingway's Concepts of Death, *Nada*, and Immortality," *DA* 25 (1964): 2511-12 (Emory).

Gotxarde, R. E., "Hemingway's New Epic Genre in His Spanish Novel," in Gotxarde, R. E., Z. M. Gildina and Z. P. Dorofeeva, eds., *Problemy lingvistiki i zarubenznej literatury*, Riga: Zinatne, 1968, 205-22.

Gray, J., *On Second Thought*, 79-81.

Grebstein, S. N., *Hemingway's Craft*, 42-51, 85-9, 125-9, 147-9, 183-6, 202-18.

Greiner, Donald J., "The Education of Robert Jordan: Death with Dignity," *HN* 1, ii (Fall, 1971): 14-20.

Gunn, Giles B., "Hemingway's Testament of Human Solidarity: A Literary Critique of FOR WHOM THE BELL TOLLS," *CSR* 2, ii (Winter, 1972): 99-111.

Gurko, L., *Angry Decade*, 188-90.

_____, *Ernest Hemingway and the Pursuit of Heroism*, 110-36.

Guttmann, Allen, "'Mechanized Doom': Ernest Hemingway and the Spanish Civil War," *MR* 1 (May, 1960): 541-61. Also in Guttmann, A., *The Wound in the Heart: America and the Spanish Civil War*, N.Y.: Free Pr., 1962, 167-75. Also, revised, in Baker, C., ed., *Ernest Hemingway*, 95-107. Also in Grebstein, S. N., comp., *Studies in FOR WHOM THE BELL TOLLS*, 71-9.

Halliday, F. M., "Hemingway's Ambiguity: Symbolism and Irony," *AL* 28 (Mar., 1956): 18-21. Also in Feidelson, C., Jr., and P. Brodtkorb, Jr., *Interpretations of American Literature*, 313-16. Also in Waldhorn, A., ed., *Ernest Hemingway*, 51-4.

Hovey, R. B., *Hemingway*, 151-72.

Howell, John M., "Hemingway, Faulkner, and 'The Bear'," *AL* 52, i (1980): 115-26.

Jackson, Paul R., "FOR WHOM THE BELL TOLLS: Patterns of Joking and Seriousness," *HN* 6, i (1980): 15-24.

Kazin, Alfred, *On Native Grounds*, Garden City, N.Y.: Doubleday, 1956, 262-5. Also, revised in McCaffery, J. K. M., ed., *Ernest Hemingway*, 202-4.

Koskimies, Rafael, "Notes on Ernest Hemingway's FOR WHOM THE BELL TOLLS," *OL* 23 (1968): 276-86.

Krzyzanowski, Jerzy R., "FOR WHOM THE BELL TOLLS: The Origin of General Golz," *PolR* 7, iv (Autumn, 1962): 68-74. Also in Grebstein, S.N., comp., *Studies in FOR WHOM THE BELL TOLLS*, 50-5.

Lal, Malashri, "The Spanish Civil War and Ernest Hemingway: From Reportage to Novel," *IJAS* 10, i (Jan., 1980): 65-77.

Lewis, R. W., Jr., *Hemingway on Love*, 143-78.

Lutwack, L., *Heroic Fiction*, 64-87.

Magny, Claude-Edmonde, "Hemingway, or the Exaltation of the Moment," *Age of the American Novel*, 149-58.

McClellan, David, "Is Custer a Model for the Fascist Captain in FOR WHOM THE BELL TOLLS? *FHA* (1974): 239-41.

Monroe, H. Keith, "Garbo as Guerilla: QUEEN CHRISTINA and FOR WHOM THE BELL TOLLS?" *FHA* (1978): 335-8.

Monteiro, George, "'Between Grief and Nothing': Hemingway and Faulkner," *HN* 1, i (Spring, 1971): 13-15.

_____, "Hemingway and Spain: A Response to Woodward," *HN* 2, ii (Fall, 1972); 16-17.

Moses, Carole, "Language as Theme in FOR WHOM THE BELL TOLLS," *FHA* (1978): 215-23.

Motola, Gabriel, "Hemingway's Code: Literature and Life," *MFS* 10 (Winter, 1964-65): 325-9.

Moynihan, William T., "The Martyrdom of Robert Jordan," *CE* 21 (Dec., 1959): 127-32. Also in Grebstein, S. N., comp., *Studies in FOR WHOM THE BELL TOLLS*, 94-101.

Muste, John M., *Say That We Saw Spain Die: Literary Consequences of the Spanish Civil War*, Seattle: Un. of Washington Pr., 1966, 94-119.

Nahal, C., *Narrative Pattern in Ernest Hemingway's Fiction*, 120-49.

Naumann, Marina T., "Tolstoyan Reflections in Hemingway: WAR AND PEACE and FOR WHOM THE BELL TOLLS," in Terras, Victor, ed., *American Contributions to the Eighth International Congress of Slavists, Zagreb and Ljubljana, September 3-9, 1978*. Vol. 2 Lit. Columbus: Slavica, 55-69.

Nibbelink, Herman, "The Meaning of Nature in FOR WHOM THE BELL TOLLS," *ArQ* 33 (1977): 165-72.

Parsons, Thornton H., "Hemingway's Tyrannous Plot," *UKCR* 27 (June, 1961): 261-6. Also in Grebstein, S.N., comp., *Studies in FOR WHOM THE BELL TOLLS*, 107-12.

Pearsall, R. B., *Life and Writings of Ernest Hemingway*, 206-20.

Peterson, R. K., *Hemingway*, 39-44, 90-4, 124-31, 136-9, 147-51, 156-60.

Pohl, Constance, "The 'Unmaking' of a Political Film," in Peary, G., and R. Shatzkin, eds., *Modern American Novel and the Movies*, 317-24.

Rama Rao, P. G., *Ernest Hemingway*, 194-204.

Ramsey, Paul, "Hemingway as Moral Thinker: A Look at Two Novels," in Langford, R. E., and W. E. Taylor, eds., *Twenties*, 92-4.

Rovit, E., *Ernest Hemingway*, 74-6, 136-46. Also in Grebstein, S. N., comp., *Studies in FOR WHOM THE BELL TOLLS*, 113-22.

Sanders, David, "Ernest Hemingway's Spanish Civil War Experience," *AQ* 12 (Summer, 1960): 133-43 *passim*. Also in Grebstein, S.N., comp., *Studies in FOR WHOM THE BELL TOLLS*, 32-42.

Sanderson, S. F., *Ernest Hemingway*, 92-102.

Savage, D. S., "Ernest Hemingway," *HudR* 1 (Autumn, 1948): 389-401.

_____, *Withered Branch*, 36-43.

Schorer, Mark, "The Background of a Style," *KR* 3 (Winter, 1941): 101-5. Also in Baker, C., ed., *Ernest Hemingway*, 87-9.

Shaw, S., *Ernest Hemingway*, 97-103.

Sheehan, Robert L., "Gironella and Hemingway: Novelists of the Spanish Civil War," in Golden, Herbert H., ed., *Studies in Honor of Samuel Montefiore Waxman*, Boston: Boston Un. Pr., 1969, 158-76.

Slatoff, Walter J., "The 'Great Sin' in FOR WHOM THE BELL TOLLS," *JNT* 7 (1977): 142-8.

Slochower, H., *No Voice is Wholly Lost*, 37-40.

Snell, G., "Ernest Hemingway and the 'Fifth Dimension'," *Shapers of American Fiction*, 166-71.

Spilka, Mark, "Hemingway and Fauntleroy: An Androgynous Pursuit," in Fleischmann, F., ed., *American Novelists Revisited*, 361-3.

Srivastava, Ramesh K., "Hemingway's FOR WHOM THE BELL TOLLS: A Critical Introduction with Annotations," *DAI* 33 (1973): 3674A (Utah).

Steinberg, Lee, "The Subjective Idealist 'Quest for True Men' in Hemingway's FOR WHOM THE BELL TOLLS," *L&I* 13 (1972): 51-8.

Stephens, Robert O., "Language Magic and Reality in FOR WHOM THE BELL TOLLS," *Criticism* 14, ii (Spring, 1972): 151-64. Also in Wagner, L. W., ed., *Ernest Hemingway*, 266-79.

Teunessen, John J., "FOR WHOM THE BELL TOLLS as Mythic Narrative," *DR* 56, i (1976): 52-69.

Thorne, Creath S., "The Shape of Equivocation in Ernest Hemingway's FOR WHOM THE BELL TOLLS," *AL* 51, iv (1980): 52-35.

Trilling, Lionel, "An American in Spain," in Philips, William, and Philip Rahv, eds., *The Partisan Reader*, N.Y.: Dial, 1946, 639-44. Also in Baker, C., ed., *Ernest Hemingway*, 78-81.

Unfried, S. P., *Man's Place in the Natural Order*, 79-93.

Versluys, Kr., "Love and Death in Hemingway's FOR WHOM THE BELL TOLLS," *SGG* (1976): 33-50.

Von Ende, Frederick, "The *Corrida* Pattern in FOR WHOM THE BELL TOLLS," *ReAL* 3, ii (Sept., 1970): 63-70.

Wagner, Linda W., "The Marinating of FOR WHOM THE BELL TOLLS," *JML* 2, iv (Nov., 1972): 533-46. Also in Wagner, L. W., ed., *Ernest Hemingway*, 200-12. Also in Wagner, L. W., *Hemingway and Faulkner*, 86-106.

Walcutt, C. C., *American Literary Naturalism*, 276-9.

Waldhorn, A., *Reader's Guide to Ernest Hemingway*, 163-72.

Walker, Robert G., "Anselmo, Atonement and Hemingway's FOR WHOM THE BELL TOLLS," *NConL* 7, ii (1977): 7-8.

Walsh, J., *American War Literature*, 85-104.

Watkins, Floyd C., "Garrulous Patriot," *Flesh and the Word*, 137-51.

Weeks, Robert P., "The Power of the Tacit in Crane and Hemingway," *MFS* 8 (Winter, 1962-63): 415-18. Also in Grebstein, S. N., comp., *Studies in FOR WHOM THE BELL TOLLS*, 102-6.

Weintraub, S., *Last Great Cause*, 215-20.

West, Ray B., Jr, "Ernest Hemingway: The Failure of Sensibility," *SR* 53 (Winter, 1945): 120-35. Also in West, R. B., Jr., *Writer in the Room*, 142-57. Also in Litz, A. W., ed., *Modern American Fiction*, 244-55. Also in O'Connor, W. V., ed., *Forms of Modern Fiction*, 89-96.

Whitlow, Roger, "Adoptive Territoriality in FOR WHOM THE BELL TOLLS," *CEA* 41, ii (1979): 2-8.

Williams, Stanley T., "Some Spanish Influences on American Fiction: Mark Twain to Willa Cather," *Hispania* 36 (1953): 133-6.

Williams, W., *Tragic Act of Ernest Hemingway*, 137-54.

Woodward, Robert H., "Robert Jordan's Wedding/Funeral Sermon," *HN* 2, i (Spring, 1972): 7-8.

Wyatt, David M., "Hemingway's Uncanny Beginnings," *GaR* 31, ii (Summer, 1977): 495-501.

Wylder, D. E., *Hemingway's Heroes*, 127-64.

Young, P., *Ernest Hemingway*, 103-14.

_____, *Ernest Hemingway* (UMPAW, 1), 16-17. Also in O'Connor, W. V., ed., *Seven Modern American Novelists*, 165-6.

Zehr, David E., "Bourgeois Politics: Hemingway's Case in FOR WHOM THE BELL TOLLS," *MQ* 17, iii (Spring, 1976): 268-78.

ISLANDS IN THE STREAM

Aldridge, J. W., *Devil in the Fire*, 95-100. Also as "Hemingway Between Triumph and Disaster," *SatR* 52 (Oct. 10, 1970): 23-6+.

Baker, C., *Hemingway*, 4th ed., 379-408.

Bolling, Douglas, "Toward ISLANDS IN THE STREAM," *SDR* 12, i (Spring, 1974): 5-13.

Dahiya, B. S., *Hero in Hemingway*, 166-96.

De Falco, Joseph M., "'Bimini' and the Subject of Hemingway's ISLANDS IN THE STREAM," *Topic* 31 (1977): 41-51.

_____, "Hemingway's Islands and Streams: Minor Tactics for Heavy Pressure," in Astro, R., and J. B. Benton, eds., *Hemingway in Our Time*, 39-51.

Giger, R., *Creative Void*, 65-8, 72-5, 83-6.

Hovey, Richard B., "ISLANDS IN THE STREAM: Death and the Artist," *HSL* 12 (1980): 173-94.

Nahal, C., *Narrative Pattern in Ernest Hemingway's Fiction*, 211-23.

Pearsall, R. B., *Life and Writings of Ernest Hemingway*, 251-6.

Rama Rao, P. G., *Ernest Hemingway*, 227-9.

Shepherd, Allen, "Hudson's Cats in Hemingway's ISLANDS IN THE STREAM," *NConL* 2, iv (Sept., 1972): 3-6.

_____, "'Other Things', Unanswerable Questions: Hemingway's ISLANDS IN THE STREAM," *AntigR* 9 (Spring, 1972): 37-9.

Skipp, Francis E., "Metempsychosis in the Stream, or What Happens in 'Bimini'? *FHA* (1974): 137-43.

Tanner, Stephen L., "Hemingway's Islands," *SWR* 61, i (Winter, 1976): 74-84.

Wagner, Linda W., "The Poem of Santiago and Manolin," *MFS* 19, iv (Winter, 1973-74): 526-7. Also in Wagner, L. W., *Hemingway and Faulkner*, 121-2.

Waldhorn, A., *Reader's Guide to Ernest Hemingway*, 200-11.

Williams, W., *Tragic Art of Ernest Hemingway*, 198-225.

Wilson, Edmund, "An Effort at Self-Revelation," *NY* (Jan. 2, 1971): 59-62. Also in Wilson, E., *Devils and Canon Barham, Ten Essays on Poets*, N.Y.: Farrar, Straus, 1973, 105-11.

Winner, Viola H., "The American Pictorial Vision: Objects and Ideas in Hawthorne, James, and Hemingway," *SAF* 5, i (Spring, 1977): 143-5.

THE OLD MAN AND THE SEA

Adair, William, "Eighty-Five as a Lucky Number: A Note on THE OLD MAN AND THE SEA," *NConL* 8, i (1978): 9.

Aldridge, J. W., "A Last Look at the Old Man," *Time to Murder and Create*, 185-91. Also in Aldridge, J. W., *Devil in the Fire*, 86-90.

Atkins, J., *Art of Ernest Hemingway*, 244-7.

Backman, Melvin, "Hemingway: The Matador and the Crucified," *MFS* 1 (Autumn, 1955): 9-11. Also, corrected version, in Baker, C., ed., *Hemingway and His Critics*, 255-8. Also in Baker, C., ed., *Ernest Hemingway*, 135-43.

Baker, Carlos, "The Boy and Lions," in Jobes, K. T., ed., *Twentieth Century Interpretations of THE OLD MAN AND THE SEA*, 27-33. Also in Baker, C., *Hemingway: The Writer as Artist*, 304-11.

_____, *Hemingway*, 292-328. Also, 4th ed., 292-328. Also, revised, in Baker, C., ed., *Ernest Hemingway*, 156-72.

_____, "'Introduction' to THE OLD MAN AND THE SEA," in *Three Novels of Ernest Hemingway*, iii-xvii.

_____, "The Marvel Who Must Die," *SatR* 35 (Sept. 6, 1952): 10-11. Also in Wagenknecht, Edward C., ed., *A Preface to Literature*, N.Y.: Holt, 1954, 341-4.

Baker, S., *Ernest Hemingway*, 126-33.

Bakker, J., *Ernest Hemingway*, 227-37.

Barbour, James, and Robert Sattelmeyer, "Baseball and Baseball Talk in THE OLD MAN AND THE SEA," *FHA* (1975): 281-7.

Barnes, Lois L., "The Helpless Hero of Ernest Hemingway," *S&S* 17 (Winter, 1953): 1-11.

Baskett, Sam S., "The Great Santiago: Opium, Vocation, and Dream in THE OLD MAN AND THE SEA," *FHA* (1976): 230-42.

_____, "Toward a 'Fifth Dimension' in THE OLD MAN AND THE SEA," *CentR* 19, iv (Fall, 1975): 269-86.

Bataille, Georges, "Hemingway in the Light of Hegel," *Semiotext(e)* 2, ii (1976): 5-15.

Bennett, Fordyce R., "Manolin's Father," *FHA* (1979): 417-19.

Benson, J. J., *Hemingway*, 123-7, 169-85.

Bhatnagar, O. P., "The Sixth Dimension in THE WOMAN AND THE SEA and THE OLD MAN AND THE SEA," *OJES* 15 (1979): 31-41.

Bluefarb, Samuel, "The Sea—Mirror and Maker of Character in Fiction and Drama," *EJ* 48 (Dec., 1959): 505-7.

Bocaz, Sergio H., "El ingenioso hidalgo Don Quijote de la Mancha and THE OLD MAN AND THE SEA: A Study of the Symbolic Essence of Man in Cervantes and Hemingway," *BRMMLA* 25, ii (June, 1971): 49-54.

Bovie, Vernett, "The Evolution of a Myth: A Study of the Major Symbols in the Works of Ernest Hemingway," *DA* 17 (1957): 1080 (Pa.).

Bradford, Melvin E., "On the Importance of Discovering God: Faulkner and Hemingway's THE OLD MAN AND THE SEA," *MissQ* 20 (Summer, 1967): 158-62.

Broadus, Robert N., "The New Record Set by Hemingway's Old Man," *N&Q* 10 (April, 1963): 152-3.

Broer, L. R., *Hemingway's Spanish Tragedy*, 103-8.

Burhans, Clinton S., Jr., "THE OLD MAN AND THE SEA: Hemingway's Tragic Vision," *AL* 31 (Jan., 1960): 446-55. Also in Baker, C., ed., *Ernest Hemingway*, 150-5. Also in Baker, C., ed., *Hemingway and His Critics*, 259-68. Also in Jobes, K. T., ed., *Twentieth Century Interpretations of THE OLD MAN AND THE SEA*, 72-80. Also in Westbrook, M., ed., *Modern American Novel*, 118-30.

Carlin, Stanley A., "Anselmo and Santiago: Two Old Men of the Sea," *ABC* 19, vi (Feb., 1969): 12-14.

Ciholas, Karen N., "Three Modern Parables: A Comparative Study of Gide's L'IMMORALISTE, Mann's DER TOD IN VENEDIG, and Hemingway's THE OLD MAN AND THE SEA," *DAI* 33 (1973): 4404A.

Cook, Walter A., "Role Structure in Content Analysis: A Case Grammar Approach to Literature," in Nilsen, Don L. F., ed., *Meaning: A Common Ground of Linguistics and Literature. In Honor of Norman C. Stageberg*, Cedar Falls: Un. of Iowa Pr., 1973, 179-87.

Cooperman, Stanley, "Hemingway and Old Age: Santiago as a Priest of Time," *CE* 27 (Dec., 1965): 215-20.

Corin, Fernand, "Steinbeck and Hemingway; A Study of Literary Economy," *RLV* 24 (Jan.-Feb., 1958): 60-75; (Mar.-April, 1958): 153-63.

Cotten, L., "Hemingway's OLD MAN AND THE SEA," *Expl* 11 (Mar., 1953): Item 38.

Cotter, Janet M., "THE OLD MAN AND THE SEA: An 'Open' Literary Experience," *EJ* 51 (1962): 459-63.

Davison, Richard A., "Carelessness and the Cincinnati Reds in THE OLD MAN AND THE SEA," *NConL* 1, i (Jan., 1971): 11-13.

Dring, John R., "The Relgious Element in Ernest Hemingway's Novels," *DESB* 7 (1962): 109-11.

Dupee, F. W., "Hemingway Revealed," *KR* 15 (Winter, 1953): 150-5.

Egri, Peter, "The Relationship Between the Short Story and the Novel, Realism and Naturalism in Hemingway's Art. Part II: 1932-1952," *HSE* 7 (1973): 82-4.

Fagan, Edward R., "Teaching Enigmas of THE OLD MAN AND THE SEA," *EngR* 8 (Autumn, 1957): 13-20.

Farquhar, Robin H., "Dramatic Structure in the Novels of Ernest Hemingway," *MFS* 14 (Autumn, 1968): 279-82.

Flora, Joseph M., "Biblical Allusion in THE OLD MAN AND THE SEA," *SSF* 10 (Spring, 1973): 143-7.

Frohock, W. M., "Mr. Hemingway's Truly Tragic Bones," *SWR* 38 (Winter, 1953): 74-7.

_____, *Novel of Violence in America*, 196-7.

Gahlot, Jai Shree, "THE OLD MAN AND THE SEA: A Reading," in Maini, D. S., ed., *Variations on American Literature*, 89-92.

Gardiner, H. C., "Pathetic Fallacy," *In All Conscience*, 125-6. Also in *America* 87 (Sept. 13, 1952): 569.

Giger, R., *Creative Void*, 87-101.

Grebstein, S. N., *Hemingway's Craft*, 22-6, 89-92.

_____, "Hemingway's Craft in THE OLD MAN AND THE SEA,'" in French, W., ed., *Fifties*, 41-50.

Green, Gregory, "The Old Superman and the Sea: Nietzsche, the Lions, and the 'Will to Power'," *HN* 5, i (1979): 14-19.

Gurko, L., *Ernest Hemingway and the Pursuit of Heroism*, 159-74.

_____, "The Heroic Impulse in THE OLD MAN AND THE SEA," *CE* 17 (Oct., 1955): 11-15. Also in *EJ* 44 (Oct., 1955): 377-82. Also in Jobes, K. T., ed., *Twentieth Century Interpretations of THE OLD MAN AND THE SEA*, 64-71.

Halverson, John, "Christian Resonance in THE OLD MAN AND THE SEA," *ELN* 2 (Sept., 1964): 50-4.

Hamilton, John B., "Hemingway and the Christian Paradox," *Ren* 24, iii (Spring, 1972): 141-54.

Handy, W. J., *Modern Fiction*, 94-118.

_____, "A New Dimension for a Hero: Santiago of THE OLD MAN AND THE SEA," in Sutherland, W. O. S., Jr., ed., *Six Contemporary Novels*, 58-75.

Harada, Keiichi, "The Marlin and the Shark," *Journal of the College of Literature* (Aryama Gakuin Un., Tokyo), (1960): 49-54. Also in Baker, C., ed., *Hemingway and His Critics*, 269-76.

Harlow, Benjamin C., "Some Archetypal Motifs in THE OLD MAN AND THE SEA," *McNR* 17 (1966): 74-9.

Heaton, C. P., "Style in THE OLD MAN AND THE SEA," *Style* 4 (Winter, 1970): 11-27.

Heck, Francis S., "THE OLD MAN AND THE SEA and Rimbaud's LE BATEAU IVRE: 'Solidaire'/'Solitaire'," *NDQ* 49, i (Winter, 1981): 61-7.

Hofling, Charles K., "Hemingway, THE OLD MAN AND THE SEA and the Male Reader," *AI* 20 (Summer, 1963): 161-73.

Hovey, R. B., *Hemingway*, 191-203.

_____, "THE OLD MAN AND THE SEA: A New Hemingway Hero," *Discourse* 9 (Summer, 1966): 283-94.

Jobes, Katharine T., "Introduction," in Jobes, K. T., ed., *Twentieth Century Interpretations of THE OLD MAN AND THE SEA*, 1-17.

Johnston, Kenneth G., "The Star in Hemingway's THE OLD MAN AND THE SEA," *AL* 42, iii (Nov., 1970): 388-91.

Kovács, József, "Ernest Hemingway, Mati Zalka and Spain: To the Symbolic Meaning of THE OLD MAN AND THE SEA," *ALitASH* 13 (1971): 315-24.

Krim, Seymour, "Ernest Hemingway: Valor and Defeat," *Views of a Nearsighted Cannoneer*, new enlarged ed., N.Y.: Dutton, 1968, 159-62. Also in *Cweal* 56 (Sept. 19, 1952): 584-6.

Lewis, R. W., Jr., *Hemingway on Love*, 199-213.

Longmire, Samuel E., "Hemingway's Praise of Dick Sisler in THE OLD MAN AND THE SEA," *AL* 42, i (Mar., 1970): 96-8.

Mansell, Darrell, "THE OLD MAN AND THE SEA and the Computer," *CHum* 8 (1974): 195-206.

Mertens, Gerard M., "Hemingway's OLD MAN AND THE SEA and Mann's THE BLACK SWAN," *L&P* 6 (1956): 96-9.

Milton, John R., "American Fiction and Man," *Cresset* 18, iii (1955): 16-20.

Monteiro, George, "The Reds, the White Sox, and THE OLD MAN AND THE SEA," *NConL* 4, iii (May, 1974): 7-9.

_____, "Santiago, DiMaggio and Hemingway: The Ageing Professionals of THE OLD MAN AND THE SEA," *FHA* (1975): 273-80.

Morris, W., "The Function of Style: Ernest Hemingway," *Territory Ahead*, 133-41.

Moseley, E. H., *Pseudonyms of Christ in the Modern Novel*, 205-12.

Nadeau, Robert L., "Film and Mythic Heroism: Sturges's Old Man," in Peary, G., and R. Shatzkin, eds., *Modern American Novel and the Movies*, 199-203.

Nahal, C., *Narrative Pattern in Ernest Hemingway's Fiction*, 170-89.

Pearsall, R. B., *Life and Writings of Ernest Hemingway*, 245-50.

Phillips, William, "Male-ism and Moralism," *AmMerc* 75 (Oct., 1952): 93-8.

Politicus, "How We Swallowed THE OLD MAN AND THE SEA," *AmMerc* 89 (Aug., 1959): 73-6.

Price, S. David, "Hemingway's THE OLD MAN AND THE SEA," *Expl* 38, iii (1980): 5.

_____, "Santiago, the Fisherman-Artist: Autobiography and Aesthetics in THE OLD MAN AND THE SEA," *DAI* 41, viii (Feb., 1981): 358A.

Pritzl, Yuri, "The Critics and THE OLD MAN AND THE SEA," *RS* 4 (1973): 208-16.

Rahv, Philip, *Ctary* 14 (Oct., 1952): 390-1. Also in Rahv, P., *Image and Idea*, 192-5. Also in Rahv, P., *Literature and the Sixth Sense*, 355-7. Also in Rahv, P., *Myth and the Powerhouse*, 198-201.

Rama Rao, P. G., *Ernest Hemingway*, 212-20.

Roberts, John J., "THE OLD MAN AND THE SEA in the Classroom," *IE* 5, i-ii (1982): 4-8.

Rosenfield, Claire, "New World, Old Myths," in Jobes, K. T., ed., *Twentieth Century Interpretations of THE OLD MAN AND THE SEA*, 41-55.

Rovit, E., *Ernest Hemingway*, 85-94.

Sanderson, S. F., *Ernest Hemingway*, 113-18.

Schorer, Mark, "With Grace Under Pressure," *NRep* 127 (Oct. 6, 1952): 19-20. Also in Baker, C., ed., *Ernest Hemingway*, 132-4.

Schroeter, James, "Hemingway via Joyce," *SoR* 10, i (Jan., 1974): 95-114.

Schwartz, Delmore, "The Fiction of Ernest Hemingway: Moral Historian of the American Dream," *PUSA* No. 13 (Autumn, 1955): 82-8. Also in Jobes, K. T., ed., *Twentieth Century Interpretations of THE OLD MAN AND THE SEA*, 97-102.

Scoville, Samuel, "The *Weltanschauung* of Steinbeck and Hemingway: An Analysis of Themes," *EJ* 56 (Jan., 1967): 60-3, 66.

Shaw, S., *Ernest Hemingway*, 114-18.

Singh, Brij M., "The Role of Manolin in THE OLD MAN AND THE SEA," *PURBA* 4, i (April, 1973): 105-9.

Singh, Satyanarajn, "The Psychology of Heroic Living in THE OLD MAN AND THE SEA," *OJES* 10 (1973): 7-16.

Sinha, Krishna N., "THE OLD MAN AND THE SEA: An Approach to Meaning," in Naik, M. K., et al., eds., *Indian Studies in American Fiction*, 219-27.

Smith, L. T., Jr., *American Dream and the National Game*, 84-100.

Spector, Robert D., "Hemingway's THE OLD MAN AND THE SEA," *Expl* 11 (Mar., 1953): Item 38.

Stephens, Robert O., "Hemingway's Old Man and the Iceberg," *MFS* 7 (Winter, 1961-62): 295-304.

Stephenson, Edward R., "The 'Subtle Brotherhood' of Crane and Hemingway," *HN* 1, i (Fall, 1981): 42-52.

Stoltzfus, B., *Gide and Hemingway*, 41-79.

Strauch, Edward H., "THE OLD MAN AND THE SEA: A Numerological View," *AJES* 6, i (1981): 89-100.

Stuckey, W. J., *Pulitzer Prize Novels*, 167-70.

Sylvester, Bickford, "Hemingway's Extended Vision: THE OLD MAN AND THE SEA," *DA* 27 (1966): 1841A (Un. of Washington).

_____, "Hemingway's Extended Vision: THE OLD MAN AND THE SEA," *PMLA* 81 (Mar., 1966): 130-8. Also in Jobes, K. T., ed., *Twentieth Century Interpretations of THE OLD MAN AND THE SEA*, 81-96.

_____, "'They Went Through this Fiction Every Day': Informed Illusion in THE OLD MAN AND THE SEA," *MFS* 12 (Winter, 1966-67): 473-7.

Taylor, Charles, "THE OLD MAN AND THE SEA: A Nietzschean Tragic Vision," *DR* 61, iv (Winter, 1981-82): 631-43.

Trenev, Blagoj, "Recurrence As a Means of Expression in Hemingway's THE OLD MAN AND THE SEA," *GSUFZF* 66, i (1973): 41-70.

Ueno, Naozo, "An Oriental View of THE OLD MAN AND THE SEA," *EWR* 2 (Spring, 1965): 67-76.

Wagner, Linda W., "The Poem of Santiago and Manolin," *MFS* 19, iv (Winter, 1973-74): 517-29. Also in Wagner, L. W., *Hemingway and Faulkner*, 111-24.

Walcutt, C. C., *American Literary Naturalism*, 279-80.

Waldhorn, A., *Reader's Guide to Ernest Hemingway*, 189-99.

Waldmeir, Joseph, "*Confiteor Hominem*: Ernest Hemingway's Religion of Man," *PMASAL* 42 (1956): 349-56. Also in Baker, C., ed., *Ernest Hemingway*, 144-9. Also in Weeks, R. P., ed., *Hemingway*, 161-8. Also in Wagner, L. W., ed., *Ernest Hemingway*, 144-52.

Waldron, Edward E., "THE PEARL and THE OLD MAN AND THE SEA: A Comparative Analysis," *StQ* 13 (1980): 98-106.

Warner, Stephen D., "Hemingway's THE OLD MAN AND THE SEA," *Expl* 33, ii (Oct., 1974): Item 9.

Watkins, F. C., *Flesh and the Word*, 152-8.

Weeks, Robert P., "Fakery in THE OLD MAN AND THE SEA," *CE* 24 (Dec., 1962): 188-92. Also in Jobes, K. T., ed., *Twentieth Century Interpretations of THE OLD MAN AND THE SEA*, 34-40.

Wells, Arvin R., in Hagopian, John V., and Martin Dolch, eds., *Insight I: Analysis of American Literature*, Frankfurt am Main: Hirschgraben-Verlag, 1964, 111-22.

_____, "A Ritual of Transfiguration: THE OLD MAN AND THE SEA," *UR* 30 (Dec., 1963): 95-101. Also in Jobes, K. T., ed., *Twentieth Century Interpretations of THE OLD MAN AND THE SEA*, 56-63.

Williams, W., *Tragic Art of Ernest Hemingway*, 172-97.

Wilner, Herbert, "Aspects of American Fiction: A Whale, a Bear, and a Marlin," in Lanzinger, Klaus, ed., *Americana-Austriaca*, 229-46.

Wilson, G. R., Jr., "Incarnation and Redemption in THE OLD MAN AND THE SEA," *SSF* 14 (1977): 369-73.

Wood, Cecil, "On the Tendency of Nature to Intimate Art," *MinnR* 6 (1966): 140-8.

Wylder, D. E., *Hemingway's Heroes*, 199-222.

Young, P., *Ernest Hemingway* (UMPAW, 1), 19-21. Also in O'Connor, W. V., ed., *Seven Modern American Novelists*, 168-70.

_____, "THE OLD MAN AND THE SEA: Vision/Revision," in Jobes, K. T., ed., *Twentieth Century Interpretations of THE OLD MAN AND THE SEA*, 18-26. Also in Young, P., *Ernest Hemingway: A Reconsideration*, 123-33, 274-5.

Zabel, M. D., *Craft and Character*, 321-6. Also in *TLS* No. 2746 (Sept. 17, 1954).

THE SUN ALSO RISES

Adams, Philip D., "Ernest Hemingway and the Painters: Cubist Style in THE SUN ALSO RISES and A FAREWELL TO ARMS," *DAI* 32 (1972): 6311.

Adams, Richard P., "Sunrise Out of the Waste Land," *TSE* 9 (1959): 119-31. Also in Wagner, L. W., ed., *Ernest Hemingway*, 241-51.

Aldridge, J. W., *After the Lost Generation*, 30-2.

Allen, W., *Modern Novel*, 94-7.

Amiran, Minda R., "Hemingway as Lyric Novelist," *Scripta Hierosolymitana* (Hebrew Un., Jerusalem) 17 (1966): 294-300.

Andersen, David M., "Basque Wine, Arkansas Chawin' Tobacco: Landscape and Ritual in Ernest Hemingway and Mark Twain," *MTJ* 16, i (Winter, 1971-72): 3-7.

Backman, Melvin, "Hemingway: The Matador and the Crucified," *MFS* 1 (Aug., 1955): 3-4. Also in Baker, C., ed., *Hemingway and His Critics*, 246-9.

Baker, C., *Hemingway*, 77-93. Also 4th ed., 75-93. Also in Baker, C., ed., *Ernest Hemingway*, 11-17. Also in White, W., comp., *Merrill Studies in THE SUN ALSO RISES*, 26-36.

_____, "Hemingway's Wastelanders," *VQR* 28 (Summer, 1952): 373-92.

Baker, S., *Ernest Hemingway*, 46-55. Also in White, W., comp., *Merrill Studies in THE SUN ALSO RISES*, 37-52.

Bakker, J., *Ernest Hemingway*, 62-81.

Baskett, Sam S., "'An Image to Dance Around': Brett and Her Lovers in THE SUN ALSO RISES," *CentR* 22, i (1978): 45-69.

Bass, Eben, "Hemingway at Roncesvalles," *NEMLA Newsl.* 2, i (Feb., 1970): 1-7.

_____, "Hemingway's Women of Another Country," *MarkhamR* 6 (1977): 35-9.

Beach, J. W., *American Fiction*, 79-84 *passim*.

Benson, J. J., *Hemingway*, 30-43.

Bier, Jesse, "Liquor and Caffeine in THE SUN ALSO RISES," *AN&Q* 18, ix (1980): 143-4.

Bradbury, Malcolm, "Style of Life, Style of Art," *HemR* 1, ii (1982): 58-61.

Breidlid, Anders, "Courage and Self-Affirmation in Ernest Hemingway's 'Lost Generation' Fiction," *Edda* 5 (1979): 285-91.

Brenner, Gerry, "Hemingway's 'Vulgar' Ethnic: THE SUN ALSO RISES," *ArQ* 33 (1977): 101-15.

Broer, L. R., *Hemingway's Spanish Tragedy*, 49-54.

Brooks, C., *Hidden God*, 20-1.

Burgum, E. B., *Novel and the World's Dilemma*, 187-94.

Bury, John P., "Hemingway in Spain," *ConR* No. 1118 (Feb., 1959): 103-5.

Charters, James, "Pat and Duff: Some Memories," *ConnR* 3, ii (1970): 24-7. [On Pat Guthrie and Duff Twysden, models for Mike Campbell and Lady Brett Ashley].

Cochran, Robert W., "Circularity in THE SUN ALSO RISES," *MFS* 14 (Autumn, 1968): 297-305.

Cody, Morrill, "THE SUN ALSO RISES Revisited," *ConnR* 4, ii (April, 1971): 5-8.

Cohen, Joseph, "Wouk's Morningstar and Hemingway's Sun," *SAQ* 58 (Spring, 1959): 213-14.

Cowley, Malcolm, "Introduction," THE SUN ALSO RISES, Scribner, 1962. Also in *Three Novels of Ernest Hemingway*, xxvi-xxviii. Also in White, W., comp., *Merrill Studies in THE SUN ALSO RISES*, 91-106.

Crawford, Fred D., and Bruce Morton, "Hemingway and Brooks: The Mystery of 'Henry's Bicycle'," *SAF* 6, i (Spring, 1978): 106-9.

Dahiya, B. S., *Hero in Hemingway*, 72-92.

Daiker, Donald A., "The Affirmative Conclusion of THE SUN ALSO RISES," *McNR* 21 (1974-75): 3-19.

_____, "The Pied Piper in THE SUN ALSO RISES," *FHA* (1975): 235-7.

Davidson, Cathy N., "Death in the Morning: The Role of Vincente Girones in THE SUN ALSO RISES," *HN* 5, i (1979): 11-13.

Donaldson, Scott, "'Irony and Pity': Anatole France Got It Up," *FHA* (1988): 331-4.

Doody, Terrence, "Hemingway's Style and Jack's Narration," *JNT* 4 (1974): 212-25.

Dring, John R., "The Religious Element in Ernest Hemingway's Novels," *DESB* 7 (1962): 71-2, 104.

Ebert, Susan, "THE SUN ALSO RISES: The Making of a First Novel," *DAI* 38 (1977): 261A.

Elliott, Gary D., "The Hemingway Hero's Quest for Faith," *McNR* 24 (1977-78): 21-6.

Ellis, James, "Hemingway's THE SUN ALSO RISES," *Expl* 36, iii (1978): 24.

Evans, Oliver, "The Arrow Wounds of Count Mippipopoulos," *PMLA* 77 (Mar., 1962): 175.

Farquhar, Robin H., "Dramatic Structure in the Novels of Ernest Hemingway," *MFS* 14 (Autumn, 1968): 273-5.

Farrell, James T., *NYTBR* (Aug. 1, 1943): 6+. Also in Farrell, J. T., *The League of Frightened Philistines*, N.Y.: Vanguard, 1945, 20-4. Also in Baker, C., ed., *Ernest Hemingway*, 4-6. Also in McCaffery, J. K. M., ed., *Ernest Hemingway*, 221-5. Also in White, W., comp., *Merrill Studies in THE SUN ALSO RISES*, 53-7.

Flora, Joseph M., "Jacob Barnes' Name: The Other Side of the Ledger," *EngR* 24, i (Fall, 1973): 14-15.

Frohock, W. M., "Ernest Hemingway: Violence and Discipline: I," *SWR* 32 (1947): 90-5. Also in Frohock, W. M., *Novel of Violence in America*, 167-75+. Also in McCaffery, J. K. M., ed., *Ernest Hemingway*, 261-71.

Ganzel, Dewey, "*Cabestro* and *Vaquilla*: The Symbolic Structure of THE SUN ALSO RISES," *SR* 76 (Winter, 1968): 26-48.

Geismar, M., *Writers in Crisis*, 51-3.

Gervais, Ronald J., "The Trains of Their Youth: The Aesthetics of Homecoming in THE GREAT GATSBY, THE SUN ALSO RISES and THE SOUND AND THE FURY," *AAus* 6 (1980): 51-63.

Glicksberg, Charles I., "The Hemingway Cult of Love," *Sexual Revolution in Modern American Literature*, 82-4.

Goldknopf, David, "Tourism in THE SUN ALSO RISES," *CEA* 41, iii (1979): 2-8. [See letter in reply by Dennis Lynch.]

Gordon, Gerald T., "Hemingway's Wilson-Harris: The Search for Value in THE SUN ALSO RISES," *FHA* (1972): 237-44.

_____, "Survival in THE SUN ALSO RISES (Hemingway's Harvey Stone)," *LGJ* 4, ii (1976): 10-11, 17.

Gottlieb, Carole P., "The Armored Self: A Study of Compassion and Control in THE GREAT GATSBY and THE SUN ALSO RISES," *DAI* 32 (1971): 429A-30A (Un. of Wash.).

Grant, Mary K., R. S. M., "The Search for Celebration in THE SUN ALSO RISES and THE GREAT GATSBY," *ArQ* 33 (1977): 181-92.

Grebstein, S. N., *Hemingway's Craft*, 67-74, 116-18.

Grenberg, Bruce L., "The Design of Heroism in THE SUN ALSO RISES," *NMAL* 1 (1977): Item 18.

Hart, Jeffrey, "THE SUN ALSO RISES: A Revaluation," *SR* 86 (1978): 557-62.

Hays, Peter L., "Hemingway and Fitzgerald," in Astro, R., and J. B. Benton, eds., *Hemingway in Our Time*, 87-97 passim.

Hinkle, James, "Some Unexpected Sources for THE SUN ALSO RISES," *HemR* 2, i (1982): 26-42.

Hoffman, Frederick J., "No Beginning and No End: Hemingway and Death," *EIC* 3 (1953): 81-2. Also in Feidelson, C., Jr., and P. Brodtkorb, Jr., eds., *Interpretations of American Literature*, 327-9.

_____, "The Text: Hemingway's THE SUN ALSO RISES," *Twenties*, 80-5.

Hoffman, Michael J., "From Cohn to Herzog," *YR* 58, iii (Spring, 1969): 342-58.

Holder, Robert C., Jr., "Counts Mippipopolous and Greffi: Hemingway's Aristocrats of Resignation," *HN* 3, ii (Fall, 1973): 3-6.

Holman, C. Hugh, "Hemingway and Vanity Fair," *CarQ* 8 (Summer, 1956): 31-7.

Hovey, R. B., *Hemingway*, 60-73.

_____, "THE SUN ALSO RISES: Hemingway's Inner Debate," *ForumH* 4 (Summer, 1966): 4-10.

Howell, John M., "The Waste Land Tradition in the American Novel," *DA* 24 (1964): 3337 (Tulane).

Hyde, Elizabeth W., "Aficionado Fishes Worms: A Study of Hemingway and Jake," *Amer. Fly Fisher* 9, ii (Spring, 1982): 2-7.

Hyman, S. E., "The Best of Hemingway," *Standards*, 28-30.

Isabelle, J., *Hemingway's Religious Experience*, 38-41.

Jain, Sunita, "Of Women and Bitches: A Defense of Two Hemingway Heroines," *JSL* 3, ii (Winter, 1975-76): 32-5.

Joost, Nicholas, and Alan Brown, "T. S. Eliot and Ernest Hemingway: A Literary Relationship," *PLL* 14, iv (Fall, 1978): 430-4.

Jungmar, Robert E., "A Note on the Ending of THE SUN ALSO RISES," *FHA* (1977): 214.

Kallapur, S. T., "THE SUN ALSO RISES: A Reconsideration," *JKUH* 16 (1972): 107-18.

Kerrigan, William, "Something Funny About Hemingway's Count," *AL* 46 (1974): 87-93.

Kimball, W. J., "Hemingway and the Code," *Venture* 6 (Summer, 1970): 18-23.

Knapp, Daniel, "Hemingway: The Naming of the Hero," *StL* 2, ii (1961): 35-7.

Kobler, Jasper F., "Confused Chronology in THE SUN ALSO RISES," *MFS* 13 (Winter, 1967-68): 517-20.

Kopf, Josephine Z., "Meyer Wolfsheim and Robert Cohn: A Study of a Jewish Type and Stereotype," *Tradition* 10 (Spring, 1969): 93-104.

Kraus, W. Keith, "Ernest Hemingway's HILLS LIKE WHITE ELEPHANTS: A Note on a Reasonable Source," *EngR* 21, ii (Dec., 1970): 23-6.

Kumar, Sukrita P., "Women as Hero in Hemingway's THE SUN ALSO RISES," *LitE* 6, i-iv (n.d.): 102-8.

Kvam, Wayne, "THE SUN ALSO RISES: The Chronologies," *PLL* 15 (1979): 199-203.

Lajoie, Ronald, and Sally Lenz, "Is Jake Barnes Waiting?" *FHA* (1975): 229-33.

Lauter, Paul, "Plato's Stepchildren, Gatsby and Cohn," *MFS* 9 (Winter, 1963-64): 338-46.

Lennox, Sara, "'We Could Have Had Such a Damned Good Time Together': Individual and Society in THE SUN ALSO RISES and MUTMASSUNGEN UBER JAKOB," *MLS* 7, i (1977): 82-90.

Levy, Alfred J., "Hemingway's THE SUN ALSO RISES," *Expl* 17 (Feb., 1959): Item 37.

Lewis, R. W., Jr., *Hemingway on Love*, 19-35. Also in Westbrook, M., ed., *Modern American Novel*, 93-113.

Light, Martin, "Sweeping Out Chivalric Silliness: The Example of Huck Finn and THE SUN ALSO RISES," *MTJ* 17, iii (Winter, 1974-75): 18-21.

Linebarger, J. M., "Symbolic Hats in THE SUN ALSO RISES," *FHA* (1972): 323-4.

Lowenkron, David H., "Jake Barnes: A Student of William James in THE SUN ALSO RISES," *TQ* 19, i (1976): 147-56.

Lynch, Dennis, "'Tourism Per Se is Not a Technique...'," *CEA* 42, iv (May, 1980): 39. [Reply to article by Goldknopf, David.]

Macnaughton, W. R., "Maisie's Grace Under Pressure: Some Thoughts on James and Hemingway," *MFS* 22, ii (Summer, 1976): 153-64.

McCormick, J., *Catastrophe and Imagination*, 209-13.

————, "Hemingway and History," *WR* 17 (Winter, 1953): 90-8.

McIllvaine, Robert, "Robert Cohn and THE PURPLE LAND," *NMAL* 5, ii (Spring, 1981): Item 8.

Mizener, A., *Twelve Great American Novels*, 120-41.

Moore, Geoffrey, "THE SUN ALSO RISES: Notes Toward an Extreme Fiction," *REL* 4, iv (Oct., 1963): 31-46.

Morrow, Patrick D., "The Bought Generation: Another Look at Money in THE SUN ALSO RISES," *Genre* 13 (1980): 51-69. Also in Male, R. R., ed., *Money Talks*, 51-69.

Morton, Bruce, and Fred D. Crawford, "Hemingway and Brooks: The Mystery of 'Henry's Bicycle'," *SAF* 6, i (Spring, 1978): 106-9.

Mosher, Harold F., Jr., "The Two Styles of Hemingway's THE SUN ALSO RISES," *FHA* (1971): 262-71.

Moss, Sidney P., "Character, Vision, and Theme in THE SUN ALSO RISES," *IEY* No. 9 (1964): 64-7.

Munson, Gorham, "A Comedy of Exiles," *LitR* 12 (1968): 41-75.

Murphy, George D., "Hemingway's THE SUN ALSO RISES," *Expl* 28 (Nov., 1969): Item 23.

————, "Hemingway's 'Waste Land': The controlling Water Symbolism of THE SUN ALSO RISES," *HN* 1, i (Spring, 1971): 20-6.

Murray, Donald M., "THE DAY OF THE LOCUST and THE SUN ALSO RISES: Congruence and Caricature," *FHA* (1975): 239-45.

Nahal, C., *Narrative Pattern in Ernest Hemingway's Fiction*, 28-48.

Nelson, G. B., *Ten Versions of America*, 25-42.

Newman, Paul B., "Hemingway's Grail Quest," *UKCR* 28 (June, 1962): 295-303.

Nichols, Kathleen L., "The Morality of Asceticism in THE SUN ALSO RISES: A Structural Reinterpretation," *FHA* (1978): 321-30.

Nishiyama, Tamotsu, "Hemingway's Post-War Generation Reconsidered," *NDQ* 28 (1960): 129-33.

Pauly, Thomas H., and Thomas Dwyer, "Passing the Buck in THE SUN ALSO RISES," *HN* 2, ii (Fall, 1972): 3-6.

Pearsall, R. B., *Life and Writings of Ernest Hemingway*, 71-84.

Peterson, R. K., *Hemingway*, 171-5, 177-81, 185-9, 204-7.

Rama Rao, P. G., *Ernest Hemingway*, 112-14, 165-75, 182-5.

Ramsey, Paul, "Hemingway as Moral Thinker: A Look at Two Novels," in Langford, R. E., and W. E. Taylor, eds., *Twenties*, 92-4.

Rao, B. Ramachandra, "THE SUN ALSO RISES: A Study in Structure," *BP* 20 (1976): 11-17.

Robinson, Forrest D., "The Tragic Awareness of Hemingway's First-Person Narrators: A Study of THE SUN ALSO RISES and A FAREWELL TO ARMS," *DA* 27 (1967): 2543A (Ohio).

Ross, Morton L., "Bill Gorton, the Preacher in THE SUN ALSO RISES," *MFS* 18, iv (Winter, 1972-73): 517-27.

Roth, Philip, "Photography Does Not a Movie Make," in Peary, G., and R. Shatzkin, eds., *Classic American Novel and the Movies*, 268-70.

Rouch, John S., "Jake Barnes as Narrator," *MFS* 11 (Winter, 1965-66): 361-70.

Rovit, E., *Ernest Hemingway*, 147-62. Also in White, W., comp., *Merrill Studies in THE SUN ALSO RISES*, 58-72.

————, "Ernest Hemingway: THE SUN ALSO RISES," in Cohen, Hennig, ed., *Landmarks of American Writing*, N.Y.: Basic Bks., 1969, 303-14.

Sanderson, S. F., *Ernest Hemingway*, 40-50.

Sarason, B. D., *Hemingway and THE SUN Set*.

————, "Lady Brett Ashley and Lady Duff Twysden," *ConnR* 2, ii (April, 1969): 5-13.

Schneider, Daniel J., "The Symbolism of THE SUN ALSO RISES," *Discourse* 10 (Summer, 1967): 334-42.

Schonhorn, Manuel, "THE SUN ALSO RISES: I. The Jacob Allusion II. Parody as Meaning," *BSUF* 16, ii (Spring, 1975): 49-55.

Schroeter, James, "Hemingway's THE SUN ALSO RISES," *Expl* 20 (Nov., 1961): Item 28.

Scott, Arthur L., "In Defense of Robert Cohn," *CE* 18 (Mar., 1957): 309-14.

Scott, N. A., Jr., *Ernest Hemingway*, 29-33.

Seltzer, Leon F., "The Opportunity of Impotence: Count Mippipopolous in THE SUN ALSO RISES," *Ren* 31, i (1978): 3-14.

Shaw, S., *Ernest Hemingway*, 40-51.

Skipp, Francis E., "What Was the Matter with Jacob Barnes?" *Carrell* 7 (1965): 17-22.

Smith, L. H., Jr., *American Dream and the National Game*, 65-70.

Solovyov, E., "The Color of Tragedy," in Vroon, R., tr., *20th Century American Literature: A Soviet View*, 362-72.

Spilka, Mark, "The Death of Love in THE SUN ALSO RISES," in Shapiro, C., ed., *Twelve Original Essays on Great American Novels*, 238-56. Also in Baker, C., ed., *Hemingway and His Critics*, 80-92. Also in Baker, C., ed., *Ernest Hemingway*, 18-25. Also in Weeks, R. P., ed., *Hemingway*, 127-38. Also in White, W., comp., *Merrill Studies in THE SUN ALSO RISES*, 73-85.

_____, "Hemingway and Fauntleroy: An Androgynous Pursuit," in Fleischmann, F., ed., *American Novelists Revisited*, 347-52.

Sprague, Claire, "THE SUN ALSO RISES: Its 'Clear Financial Basis'," *AQ* 21 (Summer, 1969): 259-66.

Stafford, W. T., *Books Speaking to Books*, 37-42.

Stallman, Robert W., "THE SUN ALSO RISES—But No Bells Ring," *The Houses that James Built and Other Literary Studies*, Lansing: Michigan State Un. Pr., 1961, 173-93.

Stephens, Robert O., "Ernest Hemingway and the Rhetoric of Escape," in Langford, R. E., and W. E. Taylor, eds., *Twenties*, 82-6.

_____, and James Ellis, "Hemingway, Fitzgerald, and the Riddle of 'Henry's Bicycle'," *ELN* 5 (1967): 46-9.

_____, "Hemingway's Don Quixote in Pamplona," *CE* 23 (Dec., 1961): 216-18.

Stetler, Charles, and Gerald Locklin, "Does Time Heal All Wounds? A Search for the Code Hero in THE SUN ALSO RISES," *McNR* 28 (1981-82): 92-100.

Stuckey, W. J., "THE SUN ALSO RISES on Its Own Ground," *JNT* 6 (1976): 224-32.

Sugg, Richard P., "Hemingway, Money and THE SUN ALSO RISES," *FHA* (1972): 257-67.

Svoboda, Frederic J., "The Crafting of a Style: Hemingway and THE SUN ALSO RISES," *DAI* 39 (1979): 6124A.

Tamke, Alexander, "Jacob Barnes' 'Biblical Name': Central Irony in THE SUN ALSO RISES," *EngR* 18 (Dec., 1967): 2-7.

Tompkins, Jane P., "Criticism and Feeling," *CE* 39, ii (Oct., 1977): 173-6.

Torchiana, Donald T., "THE SUN ALSO RISES: A Reconsideration," in Bruccoli, Matthew J., ed., *Fitzgerald/Hemingway Annual*, 1969, Washington, D.C.: Microcard Editions, 1969, 77-103.

Twitchell, James, "Hemingway's THE SUN ALSO RISES," *Expl* 31, iv (Dec., 1972): Item 24.

Unfried, S. R., *Man's Place in the Natural Order*, 45-60.

Vance, William L., "Implications of Form in THE SUN ALSO RISES," in Langford, R. E., and W. E., Taylor, eds., *Twenties*, 87-91.

Vanderbilt, Kermit, "THE SUN ALSO RISES: Time Uncertain," *TCL* 15, iii (Oct., 1969): 153-4.

Vanderwerken, David L., "One More River to Cross: The Bridge Motif in THE SUN ALSO RISES," *CEA* 37, ii (Jan., 1975): 21-2.

Vopat, Carole G., "The End of THE SUN ALSO RISES: A New Beginning," *FHA* (1972): 245-55.

Wagner, Linda W., "THE SUN ALSO RISES: One Debt to Imagism," *JNT* 2, ii (May, 1972): 88-98. Also in Wagner, L. W., *Hemingway and Faulkner*, 41-51.

Walcutt, Charles C., "Hemingway's THE SUN ALSO RISES," *Expl* 32, viii (April, 1974): Item 57.

_____, *Man's Changing Mask*, 309-14.

Waldhorn, A., *Reader's Guide to Ernest Hemingway*, 92-112.

Watkins, Floyd C., "THE SUN ALSO RISES and the Failure of Language," *Flesh and the Word*, 95-108.

Way, Brian, "The Early Novels of Ernest Hemingway," *Delta* No. 16 (Autumn, 1958): 15-24.

Wedin, Warren, "Trout Fishing and Self-Betrayal in THE SUN ALSO RISES," *ArQ* 37, i (Spring, 1981): 63-74.

Wertheim, Stanley, "The Conclusion of Hemingway's THE SUN ALSO RISES," *L&P* 17, i (1967): 55-6.

_____, "Images of Exile: THE PORTRAIT OF A LADY and THE SUN ALSO RISES," *HN* 5, i (1979): 25-7.

White, William, "Bill Gorton/Grundy in THE SUN ALSO RISES," *HN* 2, ii (Fall, 1972): 13-15.

_____, comp., *Merrill Studies in THE SUN ALSO RISES*.

Wilcox, Earl, "Jack and Bob and Huck and Tom: Hemingway's Use of HUCK FINN," *FHA* (1971): 322-4.

Williams, W., *Tragic Art of Ernest Hemingway*, 40-64.

Wilson, Edmund, "The Sportsman's Tragedy," *NRep* 46 (May, 1926): 404-5. Also in Wilson, E., *Shores of Light*, 342-4.

Wisse, R. R., *Schlemiel as Modern Hero*, 75-8.

Wood, Dean C., "The Significance of Bulls and Bullfighters in THE SUN ALSO RISES," *Wingover* 1 (Fall-Winter, 1958-59): 28-30.

Wyatt, David M., "Hemingway's Uncanny Beginnings," *GaR* 31, ii (Summer, 1977): 481-6.

Wylder, D. E., *Hemingway's Heros*, 31-65.

_____, "The Two Faces of Brett: The Role of the New Woman in THE SUN ALSO RISES," *KPAB* (1980): 27-33.

Yevish, Irving A., "The Sun Also Exposes: Hemingway and Jake Barnes," *MQ* 10 (1968): 89-97.

Yokelson, Joseph B., "Symbolism in the Fiction of Ernest Hemingway," *DA* 23 (1962): 1714 (Brown).

Young, P., *Ernest Hemingway*, 82-8. Also in Baker, C., ed., *Ernest Hemingway*, 7-10. Also in White, W., comp., *Merrill Studies in THE SUN ALSO RISES*, 86-90.

_____, *Ernest Hemingway* (UMPAW, i), 9-11. Also in O'Connor, W. V., ed., *Seven Modern American Novelists*, 160-1.

Zehr, David M., "Paris and the Expatriate Mystique: Hemingway's THE SUN ALSO RISES," *ArQ* 33 (1977): 156-74.

TO HAVE AND HAVE NOT

Aldridge, J. W., *After the Lost Generation*, 32-4.

Astro, Richard, "Phlebas Sails the Caribbean," in French, W., ed., *Twenties*, 224-31.

Baker, C., *Hemingway*, 205-22. Also 4th ed., 203-22.

Baker, S., *Ernest Hemingway*, 102-6.

Bakker, J., *Ernest Hemingway*, 154-72.

Braun, Richard E., "Echoes from the Sea: Hemingway Rubric," *FHA* (1974): 201-5.

Brenner, Gerry, "TO HAVE AND HAVE NOT as Classical Tragedy: Reconsidering Hemingway's Neglected Novel," in Astro, R., and J. B. Benton, eds., *Hemingway in Our Time*, 67-86.

Broer, L. R., *Hemingway's Spanish Tragedy*, 80-8.

Cobbs, John L., "Hemingway's TO HAVE AND HAVE NOT: A Casualty of Didactic Revision," *SAB* 44, iv (1979): 1-10.

Cowley, M., "Hemingway: Work in Progress," *Look Back on Us*, 310-14. Also in *NRep* (Oct. 20, 1937): 305-6.

De Falco, Joseph M., "Hemingway and Revolution: *Mankinde Not Marx*," in Levith, M. J., ed., *Renaissance and Modern*, 146-50.

Dring, John R., "The Religious Element in Ernest Hemingway's Novels," *DESB* 7 (1962): 104-5.

Egri, Peter, "The Relationship Between the Short Story and the Novel, Realism and Naturalism in Hemingway's Art. Part II: 1932-1952," *HSE* 7 (1973): 66-8.

French, W., *Social Novel at the End of an Era*, 99-102.

Geismar, M., *Writers in Crisis*, 66-7, 72-6. Also in McCaffery, J. K. M., ed., *Ernest Hemingway*, 176-83. Also, condensed, in *VQR* 17 (1941): 529-30.

Giger, R., *Creative Void*, 63-5.

Grebstein, Sheldon N., in Madden, D., ed., *Tough Guy Writers of the Thirties*, 36-41.

Gurko, L., *Ernest Hemingway and the Pursuit of Heroism*, 143-52.

Hill, John S., "TO HAVE AND HAVE NOT: Hemingway's Hiatus," *MQ* 10 (July, 1969): 349-56.

Hovey, R. B., *Hemingway*, 131-44.

Kenney, William, "Hunger and the American Dream in TO HAVE AND HAVE NOT," *CEA* 36, ii (Jan., 1974): 26-8.

Knapp, Daniel, "Hemingway: The Naming of the Hero," *StL* 2, ii (1961): 37-8.

Lewis, R. W., Jr., *Hemingway on Love*, 113-40.

Nenadál, Radoslav, "E. Hemingway and J. Thurber: Their Part in the Process of 'The Patterning of a Modern Hero'," in *Acta Universitatis Carolinae Philologica* 5, 84-7.

Pearsall, R. B., *Life and Writings of Ernest Hemingway*, 185-93.

Peterson, R. K., *Hemingway*, 22-5, 78-80, 100-3, 168-70, 175-7.

Rama Rao, P. G., *Ernest Hemingway*, 189-94.

Rothman, William, "TO HAVE AND HAVE NOT Adapted a Novel," in Peary, G., and R. Shatzkin, eds., *Modern American Novel and the Movies*, 70-9.

Ryan, William J., "Uses of Irony in TO HAVE AND HAVE NOT," *MFS* 14 (Autumn, 1968): 329-36.

Sanderson, S. F., *Ernest Hemingway*, 78-88.

Schwartz, Delmore, "Ernest Hemingway's Literary Situation," *SoR* 3 (Spring, 1938): 777-82. Also in McCaffery, J. K. M., ed., *Ernest Hemingway*, 123-9.

Shaw, S., *Ernest Hemingway*, 92-6.

Solovyov, E., "The Color of Tragedy," in Vroon, R., tr., *20th Century American Literature: A Soviet View*, 374-81.

Spilka, Mark, "Hemingway and Fauntleroy: An Androgynous Pursuit," in Fleischmann, F., ed., *American Novelists Revisited*, 339-70.

Wagner, Linda W., "The Place of TO HAVE AND HAVE NOT," *Hemingway and Faulkner*, 72-85.

Waldhorn, A., *Reader's Guide to Ernest Hemingway*, 152-62.

Williams, W., *Tragic Art of Ernest Hemingway*, 107-22.

Wylder, D. E., *Hemingway's Heroes*, 96-126.

Young, P., *Ernest Hemingway*, 98-102, 198-200.

————, *Ernest Hemingway* (UMPAW, 1), 14-15. Also in O'Connor, W. V., ed., *Seven Modern American Novelists*, 164-5.

————, "Focus on TO HAVE AND HAVE NOT: To Have Not: Tough Luck," in Madden, D., ed., *Tough Guy Writers of the Thirties*, 42-50.

THE TORRENTS OF SPRING

Alderman, Taylor, "Fitzgerald, Hemingway, and 'The Passing of the Great Race'," *FHA* (1977): 215-17.

Baker, C., *Hemingway*, 37-42. Also 4th ed., 37-42.

Bakker, J., *Ernest Hemingway*, 53-61.

Barnes, Daniel R., "Traditional Narrative Sources for Hemingway's THE TORRENTS OF SPRING," *SSF* 19, ii (Spring, 1982): 141-50.

Dowdy, Andrew, "Hemingway and Surrealism: A Note on the Twenties," *HN* 2, i (Spring, 1972): 3-7.

Flanagan, John T., "Hemingway's Debt to Sherwood Anderson," *JEGP* 54 (1955): 507-20. Also in Illinois Un. English Dept., *Studies by Members of the English Department in Honor of John Jay Parry*, Urbana: Un. of Illinois Pr., 1955, 47-60.

Geismar, M., *Writers in Crisis*, 68-71. Also in McCaffery, J. K. M., ed., *Ernest Hemingway*, 172-6.

Grebstein, S. N., *Hemingway's Craft*, 174-6.

Gurko, L., *Ernest Hemingway and the Pursuit of Heroism*, 137-43.

Hovey, R. B., *Hemingway*, 55-60.

————, "THE TORRENTS OF SPRING: Prefigurations in the Early Hemingway," *CE* 26 (Mar., 1965): 460-4.

Pearsall, R. B., *Life and Writings of Ernest Hemingway*, 85-95.

White, Ray L., "Anderson's Private Reaction to THE TORRENTS OF SPRING," *MFS* 26, iv (Winter, 1980-81): 635-7.

————, "Hemingway's Private Explanation of THE TORRENTS OF SPRING," *MFS* 13 (Summer, 1967): 261-3.

Wylder, D. E., *Hemingway's Heroes*, 11-30.

————, "Hemingway's THE TORRENTS OF SPRING," *SDR* 5 (Winter, 1967-68): 23-47.

Young, P., *Ernest Hemingway*, 80-2.

BIBLIOGRAPHY

Baker, C., ed., *Hemingway and His Critics*, 279-98.

Beebe, Maurice, and John Feaster, "Criticism of Ernest Hemingway: A Selected Checklist," *MFS* 14 (Autumn, 1968): 337-69.

Hanneman, Audre, *Ernest Hemingway: A Comprehensive Bibliography*, Princeton, N.J.: Princeton Un. Pr., 1967.

————, *Supplement to Ernest Hemingway: A Comprehensive Bibliography*, Princeton, N.J.: Princeton Un. Pr., 1975.

Wagner, Linda W., *Ernest Hemingway: A Reference Guide*, Boston: Hall, 1977.

White, William, ed., *Checklist of Ernest Hemingway*. (Merrill Checklist.) Columbus, Ohio: Charles E. Merrill, 1970.

See issues of *The Hemingway Review* and *Hemingway Notes*, and *Fitzgerald/Hemingway Annual*.

HERBERT, (ALFRED FRANCIS) XAVIER, 1901-1984

GENERAL

Clancy, L., *Xavier Herbert*.

Herbert, Xavier, "The Agony—and the Joy," *Overland* 50-51 (Autumn, 1972): 65-8.

Heseltine, H. P., *Xavier Herbert*.

Holt, Elizabeth, "Thoughts Raised by Herbert's 'Evening'," *LiNQ* 5, i (1976): 7-14.

Pascoe, Michael, "Old 'orrible': Xavier Herbert," *Semper Floreat* 46 (April 7, 1976): 38-40. [Not seen.]

Price, Cecil, "Xavier Herbert," *AWR* 26, lvii (Autumn, 1976): 148-53.

CAPRICORNIA

Buckley, Vincent, "CAPRICORNIA," *Meanjin* 19, i (1960): 13-30. Reprinted in Johnston, G., ed., *Australian Literary Criticism*, 169-886.

Clancy, Laurie, "The Design of CAPRICORNIA," *Meanjin* 34, ii (June, 1975): 150-6.

_____, *Xavier Herbert*, 44-66.

Grant, Don, "Xavier Herbert's Botch," *Overland* 65 (1976): 43-7.

Herbert, Xavier, "The Writing of CAPRICORNIA," *ALS* 4, ii (May, 1970): 207-14.

Heseltine, H. P., *Xavier Herbert*, 8-17.

Kiernan, Brian, "Xavier Herbert: CAPRICORNIA," *ALS* 4, iv (Oct., 1970): 360-70. Also in Kiernan, B., *Images of Society and Nature*, 82-94.

McDougall, Russell, "CAPRICORNIA: Recovering the Imaginative Vision of A Polemical Novel," *ALS* 10, i (May, 1981): 67-78.

Mudge, Neil, "CAPRICORNIA: Seasonal, Diurnal and Colour Patterns," *ALS* 9 (1979): 156-66.

Pons, Xavier, "Caste and Castration: The Personal Element in CAPRICORNIA," *Caliban* 14 (1977): 135-47.

Robertson, Robert T., "Form into Shape: HIS NATURAL LIFE and CAPRICORNIA in a Commonwealth Context," *JCF* 13, iv (1975): 45-51. Also in Maes-Jelinek, Hena, ed., *Commonwealth Literature and the Modern World*, Brussels: Didier, 1975, 137-46.

POOR FELLOW MY COUNTRY

Clancy, Laurie, "POOR FELLOW MY COUNTRY: Herbert's Masterpiece?" *Southerly* 37 (1977): 163-75.

_____, *Xavier Herbert*, 109-32.

Daniel, Helen, "Outsiders and Society: POOR FELLOW MY COUNTRY," *Westerly* iv (1978): 37-47.

Fox, C. J., "Disturbing Element: Xavier Herbert of Australia," *AntigR* 37 (1979): 91-100.

Hergenhan, Laurie, "An Australian Tragedy: Xavier Herbert's POOR FELLOW MY COUNTRY," *Quadrant* 21 (Feb., 1977): 62-70. Also in Hamilton, K. G., ed., *Studies in the Recent Australian Novel*, 29-60.

_____, "Rebuttal: A Defence of Xavier Herbert's POOR FELLOW MY COUNTRY," *Overland* 67 (1977): 41-2.

Heseltine, H. P., "Xavier Herbert's Magnum Opus," *Meanjin* 34, ii (June, 1975): 133-6.

Kelly, David, "Landscape in POOR FELLOW MY COUNTRY," *Overland* 67 (1977): 43-5.

SEVEN EMUS

Clancy, L., *Xavier Herbert*, 67-76.

Heseltine, H. P., *Xavier Herbert*, 20-7.

SOLDIER'S WOMEN

Clancy, L., *Xavier Herbert*, 77-96.

Heseltine, H. P., *Xavier Herbert*, 27-37.

BIBLIOGRAPHY

Clancy, L., *Xavier Herbert*, 143-6.

Ehrhardt, Marriane, and Lurline Stuart, comps., "Xavier Herbert: A Checklist," *ALS* 8, iv (Oct., 1978): 499-511.

HERBST, JOSEPHINE (FREY), 1897-1969

GENERAL

Bevilacqua, Winifred F., "An Introduction to Josephine Herbst, Novelist," *BI* 25 (1976): 3-20.

_____, "The Novels of Josephine Herbst," *DAI* 38 (1977): 2118A-19A.

Gourlie, John M., "The Evolution of Form in the Works of Josephine Herbst," *DAI* 36 (1975): 2205A-06A.

Kempthorne, Dion Q., "Josephine Herbst: A Critical Introduction," *DAI* 34 (1974): 6645A (Wis., Madison).

HERLIHY, JAMES LEO, 1927-

MIDNIGHT COWBOY

Griffith, Benjamin W., "Midnight Cowboys and Edwardian Narrators: James Leo Herlihy's Contrasting Voices," *NConL* 2, i (Jan., 1972): 6-8.

Peavy, Charles D., "Songs of Innocence and Experience: Herlihy's MIDNIGHT COWBOY," *ForumH* 13, iii (1976): 62-7.

Saylor, Charles F., "Orpheus in New York: The Classical Descent of MIDNIGHT COWBOY," *ClassB* 46, vi (April, 1970): 81-4, 95.

HERSEY, JOHN, 1914-1993

GENERAL

Geismar, M., "John Hersey: The Revival of Conscience," *American Moderns*, 182-6.

Girgus, Samuel B., "Against the Grain: The Achievement of John Hersey," *DAI* 33 (1973): 3646A (N.M.).

Guilfoil, Kelsey, "John Hersey: Fact and Fiction," *EJ* 39 (Sept., 1950): 355-60.

Huse, Nancy L., "John Hersey: The Writer and His Times," *DAI* 38 (1978): 4827A-28A.

McDonnell, Thomas P., "Hersey's Allegorical Novels," *CathW* 195 (July, 1962): 240-5.

Rhodes, Carolyn H., "Intelligence Testing in Utopia," *Extrapolation* 13, i (Dec., 1971): 25-47.

Rugoff, Milton, "John Hersey—From Documentary Journalism to the Novelist's Art," *NYHTBR* 27 (Aug. 20, 1950): 3+.

Sanders, D., *John Hersey*.

_____, "John Hersey: War Correspondent Into Novelist," in Browne, Ray B., and others, eds., *New Voices in American Studies*, Lafayette, Ind.: Purdue Un. Studies, 1966, 49-58.

Werner, Alfred, "With a Pen of Iron," *AmHebrew* 160 (Aug. 11, 1950): 4-5.

A BELL FOR ADANO

Prescott, O., *In My Opinion*, 151-2.

Sanders, D., *John Hersey*, 31-7.

THE CHILD BUYER

Burton, Arthur, "Existential Conceptions in John Hersey's Novel, THE CHILD BUYER," *Jnl of Existential Psychology* 2 (Fall, 1961): 243-58.

Rhodes, Carolyn H., "Intelligence Testing in Utopia," *Extrapolation* 13, i (Dec., 1971): 33-7.

Sanders, D., *John Hersey*, 108-21.

THE MARMOT DRIVE

Sanders, D., *John Hersey*, 75-82.
Tindall, W. Y., *Literary Symbol*, 100-1.

A SINGLE PEBBLE

Sanders, D., *John Hersey*, 83-94.

TOO FAR TO WALK

Reising, R. W., "The Setting of Hersey's TOO FAR TO WALK," *NConL* 1, iv (Sept., 1971): 10-11.

THE WALL

Daiches, David, "Record and Statement," *Ctary* (April, 1950): 385-8.

Eisinger, C. E., *Fiction of the Forties*, 52.

Geismar, M., *American Moderns*, 180-2. Also in *SatR* 33 (Mar. 4, 1950): 14.

Green, L. C., "THE WALL," *AmHebrew* 159 (1951): 7-8+.

Guilfoil, Kelsey, "John Hersey: Fact and Fiction," *EJ* 39 (Sept., 1950): 358-60.

Haltresht, Michael, "THE WALL: John Hersey's Interpretation of the Ghetto Experience," *NConL* 2, i (Jan., 1972): 10-11.

Healey, Robert C., in Gardiner, H. C., ed., *Fifty Years of the American Novel*, 269-71.

Prescott, O., *In My Opinion*, 238-40.

Rovere, Richard, in *Harper's* 200 (Mar., 1950): 102-7.

Rugoff, Milton, "John Hersey—From Documentary Journalism to the Novelist's Art," *NYHTBR* 27 (Aug. 20, 1950): 3+.

Samuel, Maurice, "The Story That Must Build Itself," in Ribalow, H., ed., *Mid-Century*, 228-49.

Sanders, D., *John Hersey*, 56-73.

Werner, Alfred, "With a Pen of Iron," *AmHebrew* 160 (Aug. 11, 1950): 4-5.

THE WAR LOVER

Hudspeth, Robert N., "A Definition of Modern Nihilism: Hersey's THE WAR LOVER," *UR* 35, iv (June, 1969): 243-9.

Jones, P., *War and the Novelist*, 148-52.

Sanders, D., *John Hersey*, 95-107.

Waldmeir, J. J., *American Novels of the Second World War*, 30-2.

WHITE LOTUS

Haltresht, Michael, "Dreams as a Characterization Device in Hersey's WHITE LOTUS," *NConL* 1, iii (1971): 4-5.

————, "Dreams, Visions, and Myths in John Hersey's WHITE LOTUS," *WGCR* 6 (1973): 24-8.

Sanders, D., *John Hersey*, 122-36.

BIBLIOGRAPHY

Huse, Nancy, *John Hersey and James Agee: A Reference Guide*, London: Prior; Boston, G. K. Hall, 1978.

Sanders, D., *John Hersey*, 150-6.

HIGGINS, AIDAN, 1927-

GENERAL

Beja, Morris, "Felons of Our Selves: The Fiction of Aidan Higgins," *IUR* 3, ii (Autumn, 1973): 163-78.

Garfitt, Roger, in Dunn, D., ed., *Two Decades of Irish Writing*, 225-31.

Skelton, Robin, "Aidan Higgins and the Total Book," *Mosaic* 10, i (Fall, 1976): 27-37.

THE BALCONY OF EUROPE

Beja, Morris, "Felons of Our Selves: The Fiction of Aidan Higgins," *IUR* 3, ii (Autumn, 1973): 171-8.

Kerrigan, Anthony, "Threads Flex, Hues Meeting, Parting in Whey-Blue Haze: Aidan Higgins and THE BALCONY OF EUROPE," *MHRev* 28 (Oct., 1973): 117-24.

LANGRISHE, GO DOWN

Beja, Morris, "Felons of Our Selves: The Fiction of Aidan Higgins," *IUR* 3, ii (Autumn, 1973): 166-71.

HIGGINS, GEORGE V., 1939-

THE JUDGMENT OF DEKE HUNTER

Levenston, E. A., "Literary Dialect in George V. Higgins' THE JUDGMENT OF DEKE HUNTER," *ES* 62, iv (Aug., 1981): 358-70.

HILL, RUTH BEEBE, 1913-

HANTA YO

Holman, Dennis R., "Art and Ethnography in HANTA YO: An American Saga," *AIQ* 5, iii (Aug., 1979): 239-45.

HILL, SUSAN, 1942-

GENERAL

Hill, Susan, "Susan Hill's Aldeburgh," *Listener* 90, 2311 (July 12, 1973): 54-6.

Jackson, Rosemary, "Cold Enclosures: The Fiction of Susan Hill," in Staley, T. F., ed., *Twentieth Century Women Novelists*, 81-103.

Muir, Kenneth, "Susan Hill's Fiction," in Jefferson, D., and G. Martin, eds., *Uses of Fiction*, 273-85.

Robinson, Robert, "Susan Hill: On Ceasing to Be a Novelist," *Listener* 99 (Feb. 2, 1978): 154-5. [Interview.]

Sofinskaya, Irina, "Susan Hill: A Soviet Critic's View," *SovL* 11 (1976): 166-9.

HIMES, CHESTER (BOMAR), 1909-1984

GENERAL

Bassis, Barbara A., "The Theme of Victimization in Six Novels of Chester Himes," *DAI* 35 (1975): 4496A-97A.

Berry, Jay R., Jr., "Chester Himes and the Hard-Boiled Tradition," *ArmD* 15, i (1982): 38-43.

Calder, Angus, "Chester Himes and the Art of Fiction," *JourE-AfrRD* 1, i (1971): 3-18; 1, ii (1971): 123-40.

Campenni, Frank J., "Black Cops and Robbers: The Detective Fiction of Chester Himes," *ArmD* 8, iii (May, 1975): 206-9.

Evans, Veichal J., "Chester Himes: Chronicler of the Black Experience," *DAI* 42, i (July, 1981): 213A.

Feuser, Willfried, "Prophet of Violence: Chester Himes," *ALT* (1978): 58-76.

Franklin, H. B., *Victim as Criminal and Artist*, 206-32.

Fuller, Hoyt, "Traveler on the Long, Rough, Lonely Old Road: An Interview with Chester Himes," *BlackW* 21 (Mar., 1972): 4-22, 87-98.

Lee, A. Robert, "Hurts, Absurdities and Violence: The Contrary Dimensions of Chester Himes," *JAmS* 12, i (April, 1978): 99-114.

_____, in Lee, A. R., ed., *Black Fiction*, 230-3.

_____, "Violence Real and Imagined: The World of Chester Himes' Novels," *NALF* 10, i (Spring, 1976): 13-22.

Lundquist, J., *Chester Himes*.

Margolies, Edward, "Experiences of the Black Expatriate Writer: Chester Himes," *CLAJ* 15, iv (June, 1972): 421-7.

_____, "Race and Sex: The Novels of Chester Himes," *Native Sons*, 87-101.

_____, "The Thrillers of Chester Himes," *SBL* 1, ii (Summer, 1970): 1-11.

_____, *Which Way Did He Go?* 53-70.

Milliken, S. F., *Chester Himes*.

Nelson, Raymond, "Domestic Harlem: The Detective Fiction of Chester Himes," *VQR* 48, ii (Spring, 1972): 260-76.

Peters, Melvin T., "'Too Close to the Truth': The American Fiction of Chester Himes," *DAI* 39 (1979): 6133A-34A.

Reckley, Ralph, "The Castration of the Black Male: A Character Analysis of Chester Himes's Protest Novels," *DAI* 36 (1976): 4496A-97A.

Reed, Ishmael, "Chester Himes: Writer," *BlackW* 21, v (Mar., 1972): 23-38.

Reilly, John M., "Chester Himes' Harlem Tough Guys," *JPC* 9, iv (Spring, 1976): 935-47. Also in Filler, L., ed., *Seasoned Authors for a New Season*, 58-69.

Smith, Robert P., Jr., "Chester Himes in France and the Legacy of the 'Roman Policier'," *CLAJ* 25, i (Sept., 1981): 18-27.

Williams, John A., "My Man Himes: An Interview with Chester Himes," *Amistad* 1 (1970): 25-93. Also in Williams, John A., *Flashbacks: A Twenty-Year Diary of Article Writing*, Garden City: Anchor Pr./Doubleday, 1974, 292-352.

BLIND MAN WITH A PISTOL

Lee, A. Robert, in Lee, A. R., ed., *Black Fiction*, 231-3.
Lundquist, J., *Chester Himes*, 116-31.

A CASE OF RAPE (UNE AFFAIRE DE VIOL)

Fabre, Michel, "A CASE OF RAPE," *BlackW* 21 (Mar., 1972): 39-48.

Lee, A. Robert, "Hurts, Absurdities and Violence: The Contrary Dimensions of Chester Himes," *JAmS* 12, i (April, 1978): 104-7.

CAST THE FIRST STONE

Lundquist, J., *Chester Himes*, 74-81.

Millikin, S. F., *Chester Himes*, 159-80.

Smith, Robert P., Jr., "Chester Himes in France and the Legacy of the *Roman Policier*," *CLAJ* 25, i (Sept., 1981): 23-7.

COTTON COMES TO HARLEM

Kane, Patricia, and Doris Y. Wilkinson, "Survival Strategies: Black Women in OLLIE MISS and COTTON COMES TO HARLEM," *Crit* 16, i (1975): 101-9.

Lundquist, J., *Chester Himes*, 109-10.

THE CRAZY KILL

Lundquist, J., *Chester Himes*, 112-16.

IF HE HOLLERS LET HIM GO

Berzon, J. R., *Neither White Nor Black*, 172-4.

Bone, R. A., *Negro Novel in America*, 173-6.

Calder, Angus, "Chester Himes and the Art of Fiction," *JourE-AfrRD* 1, i (1971): 14-18.

Gayle, A., Jr., *Way of the New World*, 181-5.

Hughes, C. M., *Negro Novelists*, 68-72, 206-11.

Lundquist, J., *Chester Himes*, 27-47.

Margolies, E., *Native Sons*, 90-1.

Milliken, S. F., *Chester Himes*, 70-96.

Rosenblatt, R., *Black Fiction*, 164-73.

Schraufnagel, N., *From Apology to Protest*, 37-40.

Yarborough, Richard, "The Quest for the American Dream in Three Afro-American Novels: IF HE HOLLERS LET HIM GO, THE STREET, and INVISIBLE MAN," *MELUS* 8, iv (Winter, 1981): 36-41.

LONELY CRUSADE

Gayle, A., Jr., *Way of the New World*, 185-91.

Hughes, C. M., *Negro Novelist*, 72-6, 211-12.

Lundquist, J., *Chester Himes*, 11-14, 47-72.

Margolies, E., *Native Sons*, 91-3.

Milliken, S. F., *Chester Himes*, 96-134.

Reckley, Ralph, "The Use of the Doppleganger or Double in Chester Himes' LONELY CRUSADE," *CLAJ* 20 (June, 1977): 448-58.

PINKTOES

Lundquist, J., *Chester Himes*, 135-40.

Margolies, E., *Native Sons*, 99-101.

Milliken, S. F., *Chester Himes*, 258-69.

THE PRIMITIVE

Lundquist, J., *Chester Himes*, 93-105.

Margolies, E., *Native Sons*, 93-9.

Milliken, S. F., *Chester Himes*, 180-206.
Schraufnagel, N., *From Apology to Protest*, 104-6.

RUN MAN RUN

Milliken, S. F., *Chester Himes*, 252-8.

THE THIRD GENERATION

Lundquist, J., *Chester Himes*, 81-92.
Milliken, S. F., *Chester Himes*, 138-59.
Reckley, Ralph, "The Oedipal Complex and Intraracial Conflict in Chester Himes' THE THIRD GENERATION," *CLAJ* 21 (Dec., 1977): 275-81.
Schraufnagel, N., *From Apology to Protest*, 94-5.

BIBLIOGRAPHY

Lundquist, J., *Chester Himes*, 156-7.
Milliken, S. F., *Chester Himes*, 309-12.

HINDE, THOMAS, Pseud. (Thomas Chitty), 1926-

GENERAL

Hinde, Thomas, "The Novelist as Victim," *Essays by Divers Hands* 40 (1979): 101-16.

THE DAY THE CALL CAME

"Novels of 1964. Thomas Hinde: THE DAY THE CALL CAME," in *T.L.S. Essays and Reviews from The Times Literary Supplement, 1964*, 107-9. Also in *TLS* (June 11, 1964).

HAPPY AS LARRY

Allsop, K., *Angry Decade*, 70-3.
Podhoretz, N., "The New Nihilism and the Novel," *Doings and Undoings*, 171-3.

HIGH

"Fiction of 1968. Thomas Hinde: HIGH," in *T.L.S. Essays and Reviews from The Times Literary Supplement, 1968*, 190-2. Also in *TLS* (Nov. 7, 1968).

MR. NICHOLAS

Allsop, K., *Angry Decade*, 69-70.
Gindin, J., *Postwar British Fiction*, 94-5.

HINES, BARRY (MELVIN), 1939-

GENERAL

Alayrac, Claude, "In Quest of the School of Yorkshire: Novelist Barry Hines, the Angry Voice of the Sixties," *Caliban* 9 (1972): 167-77.
Paul, Ronald, "'Fire in Our Hearts': A Study of the Portrayal of Youth in a Selection of Post-War British Working-Class Fiction," *GothSE* 51 (1982): 152-85.

A KESTRAL FOR A KNAVE

Gray, N., *Silent Majority*, 23-45.
Paul, Ronald, "'Fire in Our Hearts': A Study of the Portrayal of Youth in a Selection of Post-War British Working-Class Fiction," *GothSE* 51 (1982): 164-85.

HODGINS, JACK, 1938-

GENERAL

David, Jack, "An Interview with Jack Hodgins," *ECanW* 11 (1978): 142-6.
Jeffrey, David L., "Jack Hodgins and the Island Mind," *BForum* 4, i (1978): 70-8.

THE INVENTION OF THE WORLD

Beckmann, Susan, "Canadian Burlesque: Jack Hodgins' THE INVENTION OF THE WORLD," *ECW* 20 (Winter, 1980-81): 106-25.
Lecker, Robert, "Haunted by a Glut of Ghosts: Jack Hodgins' THE INVENTION OF THE WORLD," *ECW* 20 (Winter, 1980-81): 86-105.

THE RESURRECTION OF JOSEPH BOURNE

Struthers, J. R., "Thinking about Eternity," *ECW* 20 (Winter, 1980-81): 126-33.

HOFFMAN, WILLIAM, 1925-

GENERAL

Ewell, Nathaniel M., III, "The Novels of William Hoffman," *DAI* 36 (1976): 7419A-20A.

HOLMES, JOHN CLELLON, 1926-1988

GET HOME FREE

Challis, Chris, "The Recognizable Pseudonym in the Novels of John Clellon Holmes," *MSI* 12 (Fall, 1982): 7-8.

GO

Challis, Chris, "The Recognizable Pseudonym in the Novels of John Clellon Holmes," *MSI* 12 (Fall, 1982): 7-8.
Hassan, I., *Radical Innocence*, 91-3.

THE HORN

Challis, Chris, "The Recognizable Pseudonym in the Novels of John Clellon Holmes," *MSI* 12 (Fall, 1982): 7-8.

HOOD, HUGH (JOHN BLAGDON), 1928-

GENERAL

Anon., "Conversation: Jewish Layton, Catholic Hood, Protestant Bowering," *Open Letter* 5 (1973): 30-9.

Blandford, Patrick, "Hood à la mode: Bicultural Tension in the Works of Hugh Hood," *ECW* 13-14 (Winter-Spring, 1978-79): 145-70. Also in Struthers, J. R. (Tim), ed., *Before the Flood*, 145-70.

Bryden, Diana, "Tradition and Post-Colonialism: Hugh Hood and Martin Boyd," *Mosaic* 15, iii (1982): 1-15.

Cloutier, Pierre, "An Interview with Hugh Hood," *JCF* 2, i (Winter, 1973): 49-52.

Duffy, Dennis, "Grace: The Novels of Hugh Hood," *CanL* No. 47 (Winter, 1971): 10-25. Also in Woodcock, G., ed., *Canadian Literature in the Twentieth Century*, 242-57.

————, "Space/Time and the Matter of Form," *ECW* 13-14 (Winter-Spring, 1978-79): 131-44. Also in Struthers, J. R. (Tim), ed., *Before the Flood*, 131-44.

Fulford, Robert, "An Interview with Hugh Hood," *TamR* 66 (June, 1975): 65-77.

Hale, Victoria, "An Interview with Hugh Hood," *WLWE* 11, i (April, 1972): 35-41.

"Hugh Hood Issue," *TamR* 66 (June, 1975): 5-77.

Lafon, Marianne, *The Writer as Communicator*, Montreal: Privately Printed, 1973.

Mills, John, "Hugh Hood and the Anagogical Method," *ECW* 13-14 (Winter-Spring, 1978-79): 94-112. Also in Struthers, J. R. (Tim), ed., *Before the Flood*, 94-112.

Moss, John G., "Man Divided Amongst Himself: Hood's Leofrica," *JCF* 3, i (Winter, 1974): 64-9.

Orange, John, "Lines of Ascent: Hugh Hood's Place in Canadian Fiction," *ECW* 13-14 (Winter-Spring, 1978-79): 113-30. Also in Struthers, J. R. (Tim), ed., *Before the Flood*, 113-30.

Struthers, J. R. (Tim), ed., *Before the Flood*.

————, "Interview with Hugh Hood," *ECW* 13-14 (Winter-Spring, 1978-79): 21-93. Also in Struthers, J. R. (Tim), ed., *Before the Flood*, 21-93.

————, in Heath, J., ed., *Profiles in Canadian Literature 2*, 81-8.

Thompson, Kent, "Formal Coherence in the Art of Hugh Hood," *SCL* 2, ii (Summer, 1977): 203-12.

————, "Hugh Hood and His Expanding Universe," *JCF* 3, i (Winter, 1974): 55-9.

Woodcock, George, "Taming the Tiger of Power: Notes on Certain Fictions by Hugh Hood," *ECW* 13-14 (Winter-Spring, 1978-79): 171-86. Also in Struthers, J. R. (Tim), ed., *Before the Flood*, 171-86.

THE CAMERA ALWAYS LIES

Duffy, Dennis, "Grace: The Novels of Hugh Hood," *CanL* 47 (Winter, 1971): 12-17. Also in Woodcock, G., ed., *Canadian Novel in the Twentieth Century*, 244-8.

Morley, P. A., *Comedians*, 27-38.

A GAME OF TOUCH

Blandford, Patrick, "Hood à la mode: Bicultural Tension in the Works of Hugh Hood," *ECW* 13-14 (Winter-Spring, 1978-79): 145-70. Also in Struthers, J. R. (Tim), ed., *Before the Flood*, 145-70.

Duffy, Dennis, "Grace: The Novels of Hugh Hood," *CanL* 47 (Winter, 1971): 21-4. Also in Woodcock, G., ed., *Canadian Novel in the Twentieth Century*, 252-6.

Morley, P. A., *Comedians*, 39-49.

THE NEW AGE Series

Duffy, Dennis, "'More dear, both for themselves and for thy sake!': Water in Hugh Hood's NEW AGE," Hugh Hood Symposium, Strong College, York Un., Downsview, Ont., Oct. 17, 1979.

Harding, Anthony J., "Field of Vision: Hugh Hood and the Tradition of Wordsworth," *CanL* 94 (Autumn, 1982): 85-94.

A NEW ATHENS (See also THE NEW AGE Series)

Bryden, Diana, "Tradition and Post-Colonialism: Hugh Hood and Martin Boyd," *Mosaic* 15, iii (Sept., 1982): 1-15.

Dahlie, Hallvard, "A Moral Universe," *ECW* 11 (1978): 138-41.

Mathews, Lawrence, "The Secular and the Sacral: Notes on A NEW ATHENS and Three Stories by Hugh Hood," *ECW* 13-14 (Winter-Spring, 1978-79): 211-29. Also in Struthers, J. R. (Tim), ed., *Before the Flood*, 211-29.

Northey, Margot, "Art & Ideas in Hood's New Age," *JCF* 30 (1980): 165-8.

THE SWING IN THE GARDEN

Garebian, Keith, "THE SWING IN THE GARDEN: Hugh Hood's Pastoral," The Commonwealth in Canada, Concordia Un., Montreal, Oct. 19, 1978.

Lecker, Robert, "A Spirit of Communion: THE SWING IN THE GARDEN," *ECW* 13-14 (Winter-Spring, 1978-79): 187-210. Also in Struthers, J. R. (Tim), ed., *Before the Flood*, 187-210.

WHITE FIGURE, WHITE GROUND

Cloutier, Pierre, "Space, Time and the Creative Imagination: Hugh Hood's WHITE FIGURE, WHITE GROUND," *JCF* 3, i (Winter, 1974): 60-3.

Duffy, Dennis, "Grace: The Novels of Hugh Hood," *CanL* 47 (Winter, 1971): 17-20. Also in Woodcock, G., ed., *Canadian Literature in the Twentieth Century*, 249-52.

Godfrey, Dave, "Line and Form," *TamR* 35 (Spring, 1965): 96-101.

Morley, P. A., *Comedians*, 14-26.

Moss, J., *Sex and Violence in the Canadian Novel*, 96-102.

YOU CAN'T GET THERE FROM HERE

Downey, Deane E. D., "The Canadian Identity and African Nationalism," *CanL* 75 (Winter, 1977): 23-6.

Lafon, Marianne, *The Writer as Communicator*, Montreal: Privately Printed, 1973.

Morley, P. A., *Comedians*, 50-61.

Moss, John G., "Man Divided Amongst Himself: Hood's Leofrica," *JCF* 3, i (Winter, 1974): 64-9. Also, revised, in Moss, J., *Sex and Violence in the Canadian Novel*, 237-45.

BIBLIOGRAPHY

Struthers, J. R. "A Bibliography of Works By and On Hugh Hood," *ECW* 13-14 (Winter-Spring, 1978-79): 230-94. Also in Struthers, J. R. (Tim), ed., *Before the Flood*, 230-94.

HOOKER, RICHARD, Pseud. (Richard H. Hornberger), 1928-

M.A.S.H.

Gilliard, Frederick W., "Richard Hooker's M.A.S.H.: Affirmations of Chaos," *Rendezvous* 9, i-ii (1974): 15-21.

HOPKINS, BILL, 1928-

THE DIVINE AND THE DECAY

Allsop, K., *Angry Decade*, 183-7.
Gindin, J., *Postwar British Fiction*, 223-4.

HORGAN, PAUL, 1903-

GENERAL

Cooper, Guy L., "Paul Horgan: American Synthesis," *DAI* 32 (1971): 2677A-78A (Ark.).
Corcoran, Tom, and Jon Appleby, eds., *Festschrift for Tom Horgan*, Aspen, Colo.: Aspen Institute for Humanistic Studies, 1973.
Day, J. M., *Paul Horgan*.
Donchak, Stella C., "Paul Horgan: Craftsman and Literary Artist," *DAI* 31 (1971): 3543A (Case Western Reserve).

MOUNTAIN STANDARD TIME Trilogy

Lindenau, Judith W., "Paul Horgan's MOUNTAIN STANDARD TIME," *SDR* 1, ii (1964): 57-64.

THINGS AS THEY ARE

Kraft, James, "About THINGS AS THEY ARE," *CRevAS* 2 (Spring, 1971): 48-52.

HUGHES, RICHARD, 1900-1976

GENERAL

Bakewell, Michael, "'A Life Sentence': Memories of Richard Hughes," *Listener* 101 (May 10, 1979): 658-9.
Clayre, Alasdair, "A Conversation with Richard Hughes," *Listener* 94 (1975): 546-7.
de Jong, John M., "Richard Hughes and the Cartesian World," *Crit* 19, ii (1977): 13-22.
Poole, Richard, "Morality and Selfhood in the Novels of Richard Hughes," *AWR* 25, lv (Autumn, 1975): 10-29.
Thomas, P., *Richard Hughes*.

THE FOX IN THE ATTIC

Allen, W., *Modern Novel*, 61-2.
Bosano, J., "Richard Hughes," *EA* 16 (July, 1963): 262-9.
Savage, D. S., "Richard Hughes, Solipsist," *AWR* 68 (1981): 36-50.
Swinden, P., *Unofficial Selves*, 190-202.
Thomas, P., *Richard Hughes*, 74-83.
Wiley, Paul, *WSCL* 4, ii (Spring-Summer, 1963): 229-30.

A HIGH WIND IN JAMAICA

Allen, W., *Modern Novel*, 58-9.
Anon., *Notes on Richard Hughes' A HIGH WIND IN JAMAICA*, London: Methuen, 1971. (Study-Aid Series).
Brown, Daniel R., "A HIGH WIND IN JAMAICA: Comedy of the Absurd," *BSUF* 9, i (Winter, 1968): 6-12.
Dumbleton, Susanne M., "Animals and Humans in A HIGH WIND IN JAMAICA," *AWR* 68 (1981): 51-61.
Henighan, T. J., "Nature and Convention in A HIGH WIND IN JAMAICA," *Crit* 9, i (1967): 5-18.
Milligan, Ian, "Richard Hughes's A HIGH WIND IN JAMAICA and Aaron Smith's ATROCITIES OF THE PIRATES," *N&Q* 26, iii (1979): 336-7.
Poole, Richard, "Morality and Selfhood in the Novels of Richard Hughes," *AWR* 25, lv (Autumn, 1975): 10-15.
Swinden, P., *Unofficial Selves*, 182-7.
Thomas, P., *Richard Hughes*, 46-59.
Woodward, Daniel H., "The Delphic Voice: Richard Hughes's A HIGH WIND IN JAMAICA," *PLL* 3 (Winter, 1967): 57-74.

THE HUMAN PREDICAMENT Series

Poole, Richard, "Fiction as Truth: Richard Hughes's THE HUMAN PREDICAMENT," *AWR* 26, lvii (1976): 576-92.
_____, "Morality and Selfhood in the Novels of Richard Hughes," *AWR* 25, lv (Autumn, 1975): 20-7.

IN HAZARD

Allen, W., *Modern Novel*, 59-61.
Poole, Richard, "'In Hazard': The Theory and Practice of Richard Hughes's Art," *Planet* 45/46 (Nov., 1978): 68-77.
_____, "Morality and Selfhood in the Novels of Richard Hughes," *AWR* 25, lv (Autumn, 1975): 16-20.
Thomas, P., *Richard Hughes*, 63-70.

THE WOODEN SHEPHERDESS

Miller, Richard H., "History and Children in Richard Hughes's THE WOODEN SHEPHERDESS," *AntigR* 22 (Summer, 1975): 31-5.
Thomas, P., *Richard Hughes*, 84-93.

HUMPHREY, WILLIAM, 1924-

GENERAL

Lee, J. W., *William Humphrey*.

HOME FROM THE HILL

Lee, J. W., *William Humphrey*, 21-33.
Meeker, Richard, in Simonini, R. C., Jr., ed., *Southern Writers*, 170-1.

THE ORDWAYS

Hoffman, F. J., *Art of Southern Fiction*, 103-6.
Lee, J. W., *William Humphrey*, 34-43.
Rubin, L. D., Jr., *The Curious Death of the Novel*, 263-5.
_____, "Southerners and Jews," *SoR* 2 (1966): 698-700.

HUMPHREYS, EMYR (OWEN), 1919-

GENERAL

Mathias, Roland, "Channels of Grace: A View of the Earlier Novels of Emyr Humphreys," *AWR* 70 (1982): 64-88.
Williams, I., *Emyr Humpheys*.

THE BEST OF FRIENDS

Williams, I., *Emyr Humphreys*, 78-84.

A CHANGE OF HEART

Williams, I., *Emyr Humphreys*, 24-8.

FLESH AND BLOOD

Williams, I., *Emyr Humphreys*, 73-8.

THE GIFT

Williams, I., *Emyr Humphreys*, 52-4.

HEAR AND FORGIVE

Williams, I., *Emyr Humphreys*, 83-6.

THE ITALIAN WIFE

Williams, I., *Emyr Humphreys*, 44-8.

THE LITTLE KINGDOM

Williams, I., *Emyr Humphreys*, 17-20.

A MAN'S ESTATE

Williams, I., *Emyr Humphreys*, 36-44.

NATIONAL WINNER

Williams, I., *Emyr Humphreys*, 70-3.

OUTSIDE THE HOUSE OF BAAL

Hooker, Jeremy, "A Seeing Belief: A Study of Emyr Humphreys' OUTSIDE THE HOUSE OF BAAL," *Planet* 39 (1977): 35-43.
Williams, I., *Emyr Humphreys*, 55-69.

A TOY EPIC

Morgan, André, "Three Voices: Emyr Humphreys' A TOY EPIC and Some Comparisons with Y TRILLAIS," *Planet* 39 (1977): 44-9.

VOICE OF A STRANGER

Williams, I., *Emyr Humphreys*, 20-4.

HUNTER, KRISTIN, 1931-

GOD BLESS THE CHILD

Schraufnagel, N., *From Apology to Protest*, 139-41.

Williams, Gladys M., "Blind and Seeing Eyes in the Novel GOD BLESS THE CHILD," *Obsidian* 1, ii (1975): 18-26.

THE LANDLORD

Schraufnagel, N., *From Apology to Protest*, 141-3.

THE SOUL BROTHERS AND SISTER LOU

Schraufnagel, N., *From Apology to Protest*, 143-4.

HUXLEY, ALDOUS, 1894-1963

GENERAL

Allen, W., *Modern Novel*, 41-4.
Aninger, Thomas, "The Essay Element in the Fiction of Aldous Huxley," *DA* 29 (1968): 892A-3A (UCLA).
Atkins, John, *Aldous Huxley: A Literary Study*, new and rev. ed., N.Y.: Orion, 1967.
Bala, Adarsh, "Aldous Huxley: A Philosopher Artist," *Triveni* 49, iv (1980): 79-83. [Not seen.]
Bald, E. C., "Aldous Huxley as a Borrower," *CE* 11 (Jan., 1950): 183-7.
Bartlett, Norman, "Aldous Huxley and D. H. Lawrence," *AusQ* 36, i (Mar., 1964): 76-84.
Beerman, Hans, "An Interview with Aldous Huxley," *MQ* 5 (April, 1964): 223-30.
Bentley, Joseph G., "Aldous Huxley and the Anatomical Vision," *DA* 22 (1962): 3655-6 (Ohio State).
_____, "Huxley's Ambivalent Responses to the Ideas of D. H. Lawrence," *TCL* 13 (Oct., 1967): 139-53.
_____, "The Later Novels of Huxley," *YR* 59 (June, 1970): 507-19. Also in Kuehn, R. E., comp., *Aldous Huxley*, 142-53.
_____, "Semantic Gravitation: An Essay on Satiric Reduction," *MLQ* 30, i (Mar., 1969): 1-19.
Birnbaum, Milton, "Aldous Huxley (1894-1963)," in Panichas, G. A., ed., *Politics of Twentieth Century Novelists*, 65-84.
_____, "Aldous Huxley: A Study of His Quest for Values," *DA* 17 (1957) 360 (N.Y.U.).
_____, "Aldous Huxley: An Artistocrat's Comments on Popular Culture," *JPC* 2 (Summer, 1968): 106-12.
_____, "Aldous Huxley's Animadversions Upon Sexual Love," *TSLL* 8 (Summer, 1966): 285-96.
_____, "Aldous Huxley's Conception of the Nature of Reality," *Person* 47 (July, 1966): 297-314.
_____, *Aldous Huxley's Quest for Values*.
_____, "Aldous Huxley's Quest for Values: A Study in Religious Syncretis," *CLS* 3 (1966): 169-82. Also in Panichas, George A., ed., *Mansions of the Spirit*, N.Y.: Hawthorn, 1967, 239-58. Also in Kuehn, R. E., comp., *Aldous Huxley*, 46-63.
_____, "Aldous Huxley's Treatment of Nature," *HJ* 64 (Midsummer, 1966): 150-2.
_____, "Aldous Huxley's Views on Education," *XUS* 6 (May, 1967): 81-91.
_____, "Aldous Huxley's Views on Language," *Etc.* 26 (Mar., 1969): 141-4.
Bowering, P., *Aldous Huxley*.
Bradbury, M., "The Modern Comic Novel in the 1920's: Lewis, Huxley, and Waugh," *Possibilities*, 151-3.
Brander, L., *Aldous Huxley*.

Bullough, Geoffrey, "Aspects of Aldous Huxley," *ES* 30 (Oct., 1949): 233-43.

Burgum, E. B., *Novel and the World's Dilemma*, 140-56. Also in *AR* 2 (Spring, 1942): 62-75.

Chakoo, B. L., *Aldous Huxley and Eastern Wisdom*.

Chatterjee, S., *Aldous Huxley*.

Choudhary, Nora S., "The Huxley-Hero," *RUSEng* 6 (1972): 70-84.

Church, Margaret, "Aldous Huxley's Attitude toward Duration," *CE* 17 (April, 1956): 358-91.

————, "Aldous Huxley: Perennial Time," *Time and Reality*, 102-19.

Coates, J. B., "Aldous Huxley," in Baker, D. V., ed., *Writers of Today*, 1-13.

Cottrell, Beekman W., "Conversation Piece: Four Twentieth Century English Dialogue Novelists," *DA* 16 (1956): 2159 (Columbia).

Dooley, David, "The Impact of Satire on Fiction: Studies in Norman Douglas, Sinclair Lewis, Aldous Huxley, Evelyn Waugh and George Orwell," *DA* 15 (1955): 2203-4 (Iowa).

Dykstra, Emmanuel D., "Aldous Huxley: The Development of a Mystic," *DA* 17 (1957): 3013 (Iowa).

Dyson, A. E., "Aldous Huxley and the Two Nothings," *CritQ* 3 (Winter, 1961): 293-309. Also in Dyson, A. E., *Crazy Fabric*, 166-86.

Enroth, Clyde A., "The Movement Toward Mysticism in the Novels of Aldous Huxley," *DA* 16 (1956): 1905 (Minnesota).

Ferns, C. S., *Aldous Huxley*.

Firchow, P., *Aldous Huxley*.

————, "Aldous Huxley and the Art of Satire: A Study of His Prose Fiction to BRAVE NEW WORLD," *DA* 26 (1966): 5433 (Wisc.).

Ghose, S., *Aldous Huxley*.

Gill, Kulwant S., "Aldous Huxley: The Quest for Synthetic Sainthood," *MFS* 27, iv (Winter, 1981-82): 601-12.

Glicksberg, Charles I., "Aldous Huxley: Art and Mysticism," *PrS* 27 (Winter, 1953): 344-53.

————, "Huxley: The Experimental Novelist," *SAQ* 52 (Jan., 1953): 98-110.

Godfrey, D. R., "The Essence of Aldous Huxley," *ES* 32 (June, 1951): 97-106.

Gray, J., *On Second Thought*, 167-74.

Greenblatt, S. J., *Three Modern Satirists*, 77-101, 105-17.

Gupta, B. S., *Glassy Essence*, 175-257.

Gurtoff, Stanley A., "The Impact of D. H. Lawrence on His Contemporaries," *DA* 26 (1966): 5412-13 (Minnesota).

Hamill, Elizabeth, *These Modern Writers: An Introduction for Modern Readers*, Melbourne: Georgian House, 1946, 100-12.

Hamilton, Robert, "The Challenge of Aldous Huxley: 'The Perennial Philosophy'," *Horizon* 17 (June, 1948): 441-56.

Hammond, Evelyn B., "Aldous Huxley: Syncretic Synthesist," *DAI* 35 (1974): 3741A-42A (So. Calif.).

Hart, Hubert N., "Aldous Huxley," *CathW* 175 (June, 1952): 2040-8.

Heard, Gerald, "The Poignant Prophet," *KR* 27 (Winter, 1965): 49-70.

Heckathorn, John G., "The Early Novels of Aldous Huxley," *DAI* 36 (1976): 5316A-17A.

Herzog, Ronald M., "From Castle to Commune: A Study of Expanding Consciousness in the Novels of Aldous Huxley," *DAI* 35 (1974): 1657A (C.U.N.Y.).

Hines, B., *Social World of Aldous Huxley*.

Hoffmann, Charles G., "The Change in Huxley's Approach to the Novel of Ideas," *Person* 42 (Jan., 1961): 85-90.

Holmes, C. M., *Aldous Huxley and the Way to Reality*.

————, "Aldous Huxley's Struggle with Art," *WHR* 15 (Spring, 1961): 149-56.

————, "The Novels of Aldous Huxley," *DA* 20 (1960): 3743 (Columbia).

Huxley, Aldous, and John Morgan, "Aldous Huxley on Contemporary Society," *Listener* 66 (Aug. 17, 1961): 237-9.

Huxley, Julian, ed., *Aldous Huxley, 1894-1963: A Memorial Volume*, London: Chatto and Windus, 1965; N.Y.: Harper, 1965.

————, "My Brother, Aldous," *Humanist* 25 (Jan.-Feb., 1965): 25.

Jog, D. V., *Aldous Huxley*.

Jones, W. S. Handley, "The Modern Hamlet," *London Quarterly and Holborn Rev* (July, 1950): 240-7.

Ketser, G., "Aldous Huxley: A Retrospect," *RLV* 30, ii (1964): 179-84.

King, Carlyle, "Aldous Huxley and Music," *QQ* 70 (Autumn, 1963): 336-51.

————, "Aldous Huxley's Way to God," *QQ* 61 (Spring, 1954): 80-100.

Kocmanová, Jessie, "Novel of Romance: Problems of Genre in Contemporary English Prose Fiction," *BSE* 14 (1981): 117-32. [Not seen.]

Kolek, Leszek, "Music in Literature—Presentation of Huxley's Experiment in 'Musicalization of Fiction'," *ZRL* 14, ii (1972): 111-22.

Krishnan, B., *Aspects of Structure, Technique and Quest in Aldous Huxley's Major Novels*.

Kuehn, R. E., comp., *Aldous Huxley*.

Kumar, Prem, "Aldous Huxley's Voyage of Discovery into Otherness: A Study of His Later Novels," *DAI* 39 (1978): 2955A-56A.

Kumler, Alan D., "Aldous Huxley's Novel of Ideas," *DA* 18 (1958): 1432 (Michigan).

Le Gates, Charlotte, "Aldous Huxley and Visual Art," *DAI* 35 (1975): 6144A-45A.

————, "Huxley and Breughel," *WHR* 29 (Autumn, 1975): 365-71.

Leitenberg, Barbara, "The New Utopias," *DAI* 36 (1976): 5282A-83A.

Lockridge, Ernest H., "Aldous Huxley and the Novel of Diversity," *DA* 25 (1965): 4703 (Yale).

Macdermott, Doireann, "The Zoologist of Fiction: Aldous Huxley," *FMod* 37 (1969): 27-45.

Maini, Darshan Singh, "Aldous Huxley—A Study in Disintegration," *Indian Rev* 54 (July, 1953): 294-6. [Not seen.]

Makino, Seiichi, "An Aspect of Aldous Huxley's Style," in Kachru, Braj B., and Herbert F. W. Stahlke, eds., *Current Trends in Stylistics* (Papers in Ling. Monog. Ser., 2), Edmonton, Alberta, and Champaign, Ill.: Linguistic Research, Inc., 1972, 243-50.

Marovitz, Sanford E., "Aldous Huxley and the Visual Arts," *PLL* 9, ii (Spring, 1973): 172-88.

————, "Aldous Huxley's Intellectual Zoo," *PQ* 48, iv (Oct., 1969): 495-507. Also in Kuehn, R. E., comp., *Aldous Huxley*, 33-45.

Matheson, Gwendlyn M., "Utopia and the Kingdom: Social and Spiritual Concepts in the Thought of Aldous Huxley," *DAI* 40 (1980): 6292A.

Matson, Floyd W., "Aldous and Heaven Too: Religion Among the Intellectuals," *AR* 14 (Sept., 1954): 293-309.

Matter, William W., "Aldous Huxley and the Utopian Tradition," *DAI* 33 (1972): 279A-80A (Texas Tech.).

_____, "The Utopian Tradition and Aldous Huxley," *SFS* 2, ii (July, 1975): 146-51.

Maurois, André, *Points of View*, 287-312. Orig. publ. in Maurois, André, *Prophets and Poets*, N.Y.: Harper & Brothers, 1935.

May, K. M., *Aldous Huxley*.

Meckier, Jerome, *Aldous Huxley*.

_____, "Aldous Huxley: Satire and Structure," *WSCL* 7 (Autumn, 1966): 284-94.

_____, "The Case for the Satirical Novel: Huxley, Waugh, and Powell," *STwC* 14 (Fall, 1974): 21-42.

_____, "The Counterpoint of Flight: Huxley's Early Novels," in Kuehn, R. E., comp., *Aldous Huxley*, 81-96. From Chapter 3 in Meckier, J., *Aldous Huxley*.

_____, "Hemingway Reads Huxley: An Occasion for Some Observations on the Twenties and the Apostolate of the Lost Generation," *FHA* (1976): 154-86.

_____, "The Hippopotamian Question: A Note on Huxley's Unfinished Novel," *MFS* 16, iv (Winter, 1970-71): 505-14. [Discusses the one finished chapter of an untitled novel in relation to other works of Huxley.]

_____, "Mysticism or a Misty Schism? Huxley Studies Since World War Two," *BSM* 5 (Fall, 1974): 3-35.

_____, "Quarles Among the Monkeys: Huxley's Zoological Novels," *MLR* 68, ii (April, 1973): 268-82.

_____, "Shakespeare and Aldous Huxley," *SQ* 22, ii (Spring, 1971): 129-35.

Miller, Daniel H., "Aldous Huxley: An Intellectual Exile," *DAI* 40 (1979): 2215A.

Misra, G. S. P., and Nora Satin, "The Meaning of Life in Aldous Huxley," *MQ* 9 (July, 1968): 351-63.

Muhawi, Ibrahim M., "A Study of Self and Other in the Novels of Aldous Huxley," *DA* 31 (1969): 2394A.

Murray, Donald C., "A Study of the Novels of Aldous Huxley," *DA* 27 (1967): 4261A (Syracuse).

Muina, Matej, "Aldous Huxley and W. H. Sheldon's Psychology of Constitutional Difference," *SRAZ* 40 (1975): 89-112. [Not seen.]

_____, "Reverberations of Jung's 'Psychological Types' in the Novels of Aldous Huxley," *SRAZ* 33-36 (1972/73): 305-34.

Nazareth, Peter, "Aldous Huxley and His Critics," *ESA* 7 (Mar., 1964): 65-81.

Noonan, Gerald A., "Idea and Technique in the Novels of Aldous Huxley," *DAI* 32 (1971): 3320A (Toronto).

O'Faolain, S., *Vanishing Hero*, 3-23.

Pandey, Nand Kumar, "The Influence of Hindu and Buddhist Thought on Aldous Huxley," *DA* 25 (1964): 1921 (Stanford).

Powell, Judith A. A., "Three Vanishing Values—Huxley's Permutations of THE TEMPEST," *DAI* 34 (1973): 1930A (Utah).

Quina, James H., Jr., "The Philosophical Phase of Aldous Huxley," *CE* 23 (May, 1962): 636-41.

Ramamurty, K. Bhaskara, "Aldous Huxley and D. H. Lawrence," *Triveni* 42, iii (Oct.-Dec., 1973): 26-34.

Rinsler, Norma, "Aldous Huxley and French Literature: A Reconsideration," *RLC* 56, i (Jan.-Mar., 1982): 78-91.

Rolo, Charles J., "Aldous Huxley," *Atlantic* 180 (Aug., 1947): 109-15. Also in Rolo, C., ed., "Introduction" to *The World of Aldous Huxley*, N.Y.: Harper, 1947.

Sadler, Jeffrey A., "The Politics of the Margin: Aldous Huxley's Quest for Peace," *DAI* 35 (1974): 415A (Wis., Madison).

Savage, D. S., "Aldous Huxley and the Dissociation of Personality," in Rajan, B., ed., *Novelist as Thinker*, 9-34.

_____, *Withered Branch*, 129-55. Also in Aldridge, J. W., ed., *Critiques and Essays on Modern Fiction*, 340-61. Also in *SR* 55 (Autumn, 1947): 537-68.

Scales, Derek P., *Aldous Huxley and French Literature*, Sydney, Australia: Sydney Un. Pr., 1969.

Schmerl, Rudolf B., "Aldous Huxley's Social Criticism," *ChiR* 13 (Winter-Spring, 1959): 37-58.

Semmler, Clement, "Aldous Huxley Revisited," *AusQ* 42 (Dec., 1970): 74-82.

Sponberg, Florence L., "Huxley's Perennial Preoccupation," *MSCS* 3 (Dec., 1968): 1-18. [Not seen.]

Stewart, Douglas, *Ark of God*, 44-70.

_____, "Significant Modern Writers: Aldous Huxley," *ET* 71 (1960): 100-3. [Not seen.]

Vincour, Jacob, "Aldous Huxley: Themes and Variations," *DA* 16 (1956): 1392-93 (Wisconsin).

Vitoux, Pierre, "Aldous Huxley and D. H. Lawrence: An Attempt at Intellectual Sympathy," *MLR* 69, iii (July, 1974): 501-22.

Voorhees, Richard J., "The Perennial Huxley," *PrS* 23 (1949): 189-92.

Wajc-Tenenbaum, R., "Aldous Huxley and D. H. Lawrence," *RLV* 32 (1966): 598-610.

Watt, Donald, ed., *Aldous Huxley: The Critical Heritage*, Boston, Mass.: Routledge & Kegan Paul, 1975.

_____, "The Human Fugue: Thought and Technique in Four Novels of Aldous Huxley," *DA* 29 (1969): 2728A (Conn.).

_____, "Huxley's Aesthetic Ideal," *MBL* 3, ii (1978): 128-42.

Watts, H. H., *Aldous Huxley*.

Webster, H. T., "Aldous Huxley: Notes on a Moral Evolution," *SAQ* 45 (July, 1946): 372-83.

Webster, Harvey C., "Aldous Huxley: Sceptical Mystic," *After the Trauma*, 31-50.

Whitesel, George E., "Evolution as Metaphor: Patterns of Continuity in the Thought and Aesthetic of Aldous Huxley," *DAI* 31 (1971): 6027A (Mich. State).

Wickes, George, and R. Frazer, "The Art of Fiction XXIV," *ParisR* 6 (Spring, 1960): 57-80. Also in *Writers at Work*, 2nd ser., 193-214.

Wigston, Nancy L., "Unity and Diversity in the Novels of Aldous Huxley," *DAI* 39 (1978): 2267A.

Wilson, Colin, "Existential Criticism and the Work of Aldous Huxley," *LonM* 5 (Sept., 1958): 46-59. Also in Wilson, C., *Strength to Dream*, 213-38.

Woodcock, G., *Dawn and the Darkest Hour*.

Zähner, L., *Demon and Saint in the Novels of Aldous Huxley*.

Zolla, Elemire, "Aldous Huxley and the Doom of Reason," *Letterature Moderne* 5 (Sept.-Dec., 1954): 523-30.

AFTER MANY A SUMMER DIES THE SWAN

Baldanza, Frank, "Huxley and Hearst," *JML* 7, iii (Sept., 1979): 441-55. Also in Crow, C. L., ed., *Essays on California Writers*, 35-47.

Bowering, P., *Aldous Huxley*, 141-59.

Brander, L., *Aldous Huxley*, 80-5.

Chakoo, B. L., *Aldous Huxley and Eastern Wisdom*, 191-210.

Dyson, A. E., *Crazy Fabric*, 183-4.

Ferns, C. S., *Aldous Huxley*, 133-9, 148-65.

Firchow, P., *Aldous Huxley*, 157-64.

Gordon, Caroline, *How to Read a Novel*, N.Y.: Viking, 1957, 222-4.

Gupta, B. S., *Glassy Essence*, 196-8.

Hines, B., *Social World of Aldous Huxley*, 40-2.

Holmes, C. M., *Aldous Huxley and the Way to Reality*, 120-8.

Jog, D. V., *Aldous Huxley*, 85-90.

May, K. M., *Aldous Huxley*, 141-57.

Meckier, J., *Aldous Huxley*, 37-9, 159-62.

————, "Quarles among the Monkeys: Huxley's Zoological Novels," *MLR* 68, ii (April, 1973): 279-80.

Nagarjan, S., "Religion in Three Recent Novels of Aldous Huxley," *MFS* 5 (Summer, 1959): 153-65.

Sauter, K. W., and A. E. Dyson, "Aldous Huxley," *CritQ* 4 (Summer, 1962): 177-9.

Savage, D. S., "Aldous Huxley and the Dissociation of Personality," in Rajan, B., ed., *Novelist as Thinker*, 29-32.

————, *Withered Branch*, 150-3. Also in *SR* 55 (Autumn, 1947): 563-7.

Wagner, Linda W., "Satiric Masks: Huxley and Waugh," *SNL* 3 (Spring, 1966): 160-2.

Wain, John, "Tracts Against Materialism," *LonM* 2, viii (Aug., 1955): 59-60. Also in Kuehn, R. E., comp., *Aldous Huxley*, 26-8.

Watts, H. H., *Aldous Huxley*, 97-106.

Wilson, C., "Existential Criticism and the Work of Aldous Huxley," *Strength to Dream*, 230-1.

Woodcock, G., *Dawn and the Darkest Hour*, 219-24.

Zähner, L., *Demon and Saint in the Novels of Aldous Huxley*, 61-71.

ANTIC HAY

Baker, Robert S., "The Fire of Prometheus: Romanticism and the Baroque in Huxley's ANTIC HAY and THOSE BARREN LEAVES," *TSLL* 19 (Spring, 1977): 60-82.

Bowering, P., *Aldous Huxley*, 46-60, 215-18.

Brander, L., *Aldous Huxley*, 24-6.

Brooke, J., *Aldous Huxley*, 15-17.

Chakoo, B. L., *Aldous Huxley and Eastern Wisdom*, 26-33.

Dyson, A. E., "Aldous Huxley and the Two Nothings," *CritQ* 3 (Winter, 1961): 294-7. Also in Dyson, A. E., *Crazy Fabric*, 167-71.

Enroth, Clyde, "Mysticism in Two of Aldous Huxley's Early Novels," *TCL* 6 (1960): 123-32.

Ferns, C. S., *Aldous Huxley*, 67-77.

Firchow, P., *Aldous Huxley*, 64-80.

Gill, Stephen M., "ANTIC HAY: A Portraiture of Psychological Dislocation," *CalR* 1, iv (April-June, 1970): 513-18.

Greenblatt, S. J., *Three Modern Satirists*, 89-95 passim.

Gupta, B. S., *Glassy Essence*, 178-80.

Hall, J., *Tragic Comedians*, 31-44 passim.

Hines, B., *Social World of Aldous Huxley*, 18-22.

Holmes, C. M., *Aldous Huxley and the Way to Reality*, 25-33.

Karl, Frederick R., "The Play Within the Novel in ANTIC HAY," *Ren* 13 (Winter, 1961): 59-68.

————, and M. Magalaner, *Reader's Guide to Great Twentieth Century Novels*, 262-7.

May, K. M., *Aldous Huxley*, 41-60.

Meckier, J., *Aldous Huxley*, 66-70. Also in Kuehn, R. E., comp., *Aldous Huxley*, 86-9.

Montgomery, Marion, "Aldous Huxley's Incomparable Man in ANTIC HAY," *Discourse* 3 (Oct., 1960): 227-32.

Savage, D. S., "Aldous Huxley and the Dissociation of Personality," in Rajan, B., ed., *Novelist as Thinker*, 13-14.

————, *Withered Branch*, 133-4. Also in Aldridge, J. W., ed., *Critiques and Essays on Modern Fiction*, 343-4. Also in *SR* 55 (Autumn, 1947): 542-4.

Watts, H. H., *Aldous Huxley*, 49-56.

Waugh, Evelyn, "Youth at the Helm and Pleasure at the Prow," *LonM* 2, viii (Aug., 1955): 51-3. Also in Kuehn, R. E., comp., *Aldous Huxley*, 18-20.

Wilson, C., "Existential Criticism and the Work of Aldous Huxley," *Strength to Dream*, 217-19.

Woodcock, G., *Dawn and the Darkest Hour*, 96-108.

Zähner, L., *Demon and Saint in the Novels of Aldous Huxley*, 17-26.

APE AND ESSENCE

Brander, L., *Aldous Huxley*, 92-5.

Ferns, C. S., *Aldous Huxley*, 176-84.

Firchow, P., *Aldous Huxley*, 133-7.

Gump, Margaret, "From Ape to Man from Man to Ape," *KFLQ* 4 (1957): 177-85.

Gupta, B. S., *Glassy Essence*, 209-111.

Hines, B., *Social World of Aldous Huxley*, 46-7.

Holmes, C. M., *Aldous Huxley and the Way to Reality*, 150-6.

Jog, D. V., *Aldous Huxley*, 98-102.

May, K. M., *Aldous Huxley*, 177-91.

Meckier, J., *Aldous Huxley*, 175-6, 189-97.

————, "Quarles Among the Monkeys: Huxley's Zoological Novels," *MLR* 68, ii (April, 1973): 280-1.

Schmerl, Rudolf B., "The Two Future Worlds of Aldous Huxley," *PMLA* 77 (June, 1962): 328-34.

Watts, H. H., *Aldous Huxley*, 113-18.

Woodcock, G., *Dawn and the Darkest Hour*, 253-8.

Zähner, L., *Demon and Saint in the Novels of Aldous Huxley*, 134-9.

BRAVE NEW WORLD

Aldridge, Alexandria, "BRAVE NEW WORLD and the Mechanist/Vitalist Controversy," *CLS* 17 (1980): 116-32.

Bowering, P., *Aldous Huxley*, 98-113.

Brander, L., *Aldous Huxley*, 61-71.

Brooke, J., *Aldous Huxley*, 22-3.

Browning, Gordon, "Zamiatin's WE: An Anti-Utopian Classic," *Cithara* 7 (May, 1968): 13-20.

Calder, Jenni, *Huxley and Orwell: BRAVE NEW WORLD and NINETEEN EIGHTY-FOUR* (Studies in English Lit. 63), London: E. Arnold, 1976.

Chakoo, B. L., *Aldous Huxley and Eastern Wisdom*, 127-39.

Clareson, Thomas D., "The Classic: Aldous Huxley's BRAVE NEW WORLD," *Extrapolation* 2 (May, 1961): 33-40.

Coleman, D. C., "Bernard Shaw and BRAVE NEW WORLD," *ShawR* 10 (Jan., 1967): 6-8.

Curle, Adam, "Huxley's BRAVE NEW WORLD," *NS&N* 49 (April 9, 1955): 508-9.

Dyson, A. E., "Aldous Huxley and the Two Nothings," *CritQ* 3 (Winter, 1961): 300-3. Also in Dyson, A. E., *Crazy Fabric*, 175-8.

Ehrenpreis, Irvin, "Orwell, Huxley, Pope," *RLV* 23 (1957): 215-30 *passim*.

Enroth, Clyde, "Mysticism in Two of Aldous Huxley's Early Novels," *TCL* 6 (1960): 123-32.

Ferns, C. S., *Aldous Huxley*, 133-48.

Firchow, P., *Aldous Huxley*, 118-39, 178-82.

————, "The Satire of Huxley's BRAVE NEW WORLD," *MFS* 12 (Winter, 1966-67): 451-60.

————, "Science and Conscience in Huxley's BRAVE NEW WORLD," *ConL* 16 (1975): 301-16.

————, "Wells and Lawrence in Huxley's BRAVE NEW WORLD," *JML* 5, ii (April, 1976): 260-78.

Gable, Sister Mariella, "Prose Satire and the Modern Christian Temper," *ABR* 11 (Mar.-June, 1960): 23-6.

Ghose, S., *Aldous Huxley*, 50-3.

Gill, Kulwant S., "Aldous Huxley: The Quest for Identity," *PURBA* 8, ii-iii (April-Oct., 1977): 11-26.

Greenblatt, S. J., *Three Modern Satirists*, 95-101 *passim*.

Grushow, Ira, "BRAVE NEW WORLD and THE TEMPEST," *CE* 24 (Oct., 1962): 42-5.

Gupta, B. S., *Glassy Essence*, 187-8.

Hacker, Andrew, "Dostoevsky's Disciples: Man and Sheep in Political Theory," *Jnl of Politics* 17 (Nov., 1955): 600-2.

Hall, J., *Tragic Comedians*, 42-4.

Hébert, R. Lewis, "Huxley's BRAVE NEW WORLD, Chapter V," *Expl* 29 (1971): Item 71.

Hines, B., *Social World of Aldous Huxley*, 34-6.

Hoffecker, W. Andrew, "A Reading of BRAVE NEW WORLD: Dystopianism in Historical Perspective," *C&L* 29, ii (1980): 46-62.

Holmes, C. M., *Aldous Huxley and the Way to Reality*, 82-9.

Jog, D. V., *Aldous Huxley*, 66-73.

Jones, Joseph, "Utopia as Dirge," *AQ* 2 (Fall, 1950): 214-26.

Jones, William M., "The Iago of BRAVE NEW WORLD," *WHR* 15 (Summer, 1961): 275-8.

Karl, F., and M. Magalaner, *Reader's Guide to Great Twentieth Century Novels*, 275-9.

Kessler, Martin, "Power and the Perfect State: A Study in Disillusionment as Reflected in Orwell's NINETEEN EIGHTY-FOUR and Huxley's BRAVE NEW WORLD," *PSQ* 72 (Dec., 1957): 565-77.

King, Almeda, "Christianity Without Tears: Man Without Humanity," *EJ* 57 (Sept., 1968): 820-4.

Larsen, Peter M., "Synthetic Myths in Aldous Huxley's BRAVE NEW WORLD: A Note," *ES* 62, vi (Dec., 1981): 506-8.

Leeper, Geoffrey, "The Happy Utopias of Aldous Huxley and H. G. Wells," *Meanjin* 24 (Mar., 1965): 120-4.

Le Roy, Gaylord C., "A. F. 632 to 1984," *CE* 12 (Dec., 1950): 135-8.

Leyburn, E. D., *Satiric Allegory*, 114-25.

May, K. M., *Aldous Huxley*, 98-117.

Meckier, J., *Aldous Huxley*, 17-19, 22-3, 112-13, 175-83, 186-87, 199-202, 204-5.

————, "Aldous Huxley and the Congenital Novelists: New Ideas about the Novel of Ideas," *SoRA* 13, iii (Nov., 1980): 203-21.

————, "BRAVE NEW WORLD and the Anthropologists: Primitivism in A. F. 632," *Alternative Futures* (Troy, N.Y.) 1, i (1978): 51-69.

————, "Boffin and Podsnap in Utopia," *Dickensian* 77, iii (Autumn, 1981): 154-61.

————, "Debunking Our Ford: 'My Life and Work' and BRAVE NEW WORLD," *SAQ* 78, iv (1979): 448-59.

————, "A Neglected Huxley 'Preface': His Earliest Synopsis of BRAVE NEW WORLD," *TCL* 25, i (Spring, 1979): 1-20.

————, "Our Ford, Our Freud and the Behaviorist Conspiracy in Huxley's BRAVE NEW WORLD," *Thalia* 1, i (1978): 35-59.

Miles, O. Thomas, "Three Authors in Search of a Character," *Person* 46 (Jan., 1965): 65-72.

Millichap, Joseph A., "Huxley's BRAVE NEW WORLD, Chapter V," *Expl* 32, i (Sept., 1973): Item 1.

Moody, C., "Zamyatin's WE and English Antiutopian Fiction," *UES* 14, i (1976): 24-33.

New, Melvin, "Ad Nauseum: A Satiric Device in Huxley, Orwell, and Waugh," *SNL* 8, i (Fall, 1970): 24-8.

Pendexter, Hugh, III, "Huxley's BRAVE NEW WORLD," *Expl* 20 (Mar., 1962): Item 58.

Powell, Judith A. A., "Three Vanishing Values—Huxley's Permutations of THE TEMPEST," *DAI* 34 (1973): 1930A (Utah).

Richards, D., "Four Utopias," *SEER* 40 (1962): 224-8.

Rosenfeld, Isaac, "Second Thoughts on Huxley's BRAVE NEW WORLD," *Nation* 163 (Oct. 19, 1945): 445-7. Also in Rosenfeld, I., *An Age of Enormity*, 144-8.

Schmerl, Rudolf B., "The Two Future Worlds of Aldous Huxley," *PMLA* 77 (June, 1962): 328-34.

Simons, John D., "The Grand Inquisitor in Schiller, Dostoevsky and Huxley," *NZSJ* 8 (Summer, 1971): 20-31.

Snow, Malinda, "The Gray Parody in BRAVE NEW WORLD," *PLL* 13, i (Winter, 1977): 85-8.

Thomas, W. K., "BRAVE NEW WORLD and the Houyhnhnms," *RUO* 37 (1967): 688-96.

Wain, John, "Tracts Against Materialism," *LonM* 2, viii (Aug., 1955): 60-1. Also in Kuehn, R. E., comp., *Aldous Huxley*, 28-9.

Watt, Donald, "The Manuscript Revisions of BRAVE NEW WORLD," *JEGP* 77, iii (1978): 367-82.

Watts, H. H., *Aldous Huxley*, 72-84.

Wells, Arvin R., "Huxley, Plato and the Just Society," *CentR* 24, iv (Fall, 1980): 475-91.

————, in Hagopian, J. V., and M. Dolch, eds., *Insight II*, 176-85.

Westlake, J. H. J., "Aldous Huxley's BRAVE NEW WORLD and George Orwell's NINETEEN EIGHTY-FOUR: A Comparative Study," *NS* 21, ii (Feb., 1972): 94-102.

Wheeler, Wayne B., "The Horror of Science in Politics: Prophecy and the Crisis of Human Values in Mary Shelley's FRANKENSTEIN and Aldous Huxley's BRAVE NEW WORLD," *DAI* 40 (1979): 2246A.

Wilson, Robert H., "BRAVE NEW WORLD as Shakespearean Criticism," *SAB* 21 (1946): 99-107.

————, "Versions of BRAVE NEW WORLD," *LCUT* 8, iv (Spring, 1968): 28-41.

Wing, George, "The Shakespearean Voice of Conscience in BRAVE NEW WORLD," *DR* 51, ii (Summer, 1971): 153-64.

Woodcock, G., *Dawn and the Darkest Hour*, 173-81.

————, "Utopias in Negative," *SR* 64 (Winter, 1956): 81-97.

Zähner, L., *Demon and Saint in the Novels of Aldous Huxley*, 125-33.

CROME YELLOW

Arnold, Edwin T., III, "Faulkner and Huxley: A Note on MOSQUITOES and CROME YELLOW," *MissQ* 30 (Summer, 1977): 433-6.

Bowering, P., *Aldous Huxley*, 6-9, 33-45.

Brander, L., *Aldous Huxley*, 21-3.

Brooke, J., *Aldous Huxley*, 12-13.

Burgum, E. G., *Novel and the World's Dilemma*, 143-6. Also in *AR* 2 (Mar., 1942): 64-7.

Chakoo, B. L., *Aldous Huxley and Eastern Wisdom*, 16-26.

Ferns, C. S., *Aldous Huxley*, 55-76.

Firchow, P., *Aldous Huxley*, 48-64.

Greenblatt, S. J., *Three Modern Satirists*, 79-89 *passim*.

Gupta, B. S., *Glassy Essence*, 176-8.

Hines, B., *Social World of Aldous Huxley*, 14-18.

Holmes, C. M., *Aldous Huxley and the Way to Reality*, 21-4.

Karl, F., and M. Magalaner, *Reader's Guide to Great Twentieth Century Novels*, 259-62.

Meckier, J., *Aldous Huxley*, 64-7. Also in Kuehn, R. E., comp., *Aldous Huxley*, 82-5.

_____, "Sir George Sitwell's Contributions to CROME YELLOW," *MFS* 23, ii (Summer, 1977): 235-9.

Owens, Guy, "'Prufrock' and Huxley's CROME YELLOW," *LauR* 10, ii (Fall, 1970): 30-5.

Savage, D. S., "Aldous Huxley and the Dissociation of Personality," in Rajan, B., ed., *Novelist as Thinker*, 12-13.

_____, *Withered Branch*, 132-3. Also in Aldridge, J. W., ed., *Critiques and Essays on Modern Fiction*, 342-3. Also in *SR* 55 (Autumn, 1947): 540-2.

Watts, H. H., *Aldous Huxley*, 45-9.

Wilson, Angus, "The House Party Novels," *LonM* 2, viii (Aug., 1955): 53-6. Also in Kuehn, R. E., comp., *Aldous Huxley*, 20-3.

Wilson, C., "Existential Criticism and the Work of Aldous Huxley," *Strength to Dream*, 216-17.

Woodcock, G., *Dawn and the Darkest Hour*, 77-86.

Zähner, L., *Demon and Saint in the Novels of Aldous Huxley*, 9-16.

EYELESS IN GAZA

Baker, Robert S., "A Tour of Brighton Pavilion and Gog's Court: The Romantic Context of POINT COUNTER POINT and EYELESS IN GAZA," *SNNTS* 9, iv (1977): 537-63.

Bowering, P., *Aldous Huxley*, 19-20, 114-40, 229-30. Also in Kuehn, R. E. comp., *Aldous Huxley*, 119-41.

Brander, L., *Aldous Huxley*, 72-9.

Brooke, J., *Aldous Huxley*, 23-5.

Chakoo, B. L., *Aldous Huxley and Eastern Wisdom*, 140-68.

Dyson, A. E., "Aldous Huxley and the Two Nothings," *CritQ* 3 (Winter, 1961): 303-6. Also in Dyson, A. E., *Crazy Fabric*, 178-83.

Ferns, C. S., *Aldous Huxley*, 103-16, 120-32.

Firchow, P., *Aldous Huxley*, 145-57.

Gray, J., *On Second Thought*, 168-70.

Gupta, B. S., *Glassy Essence*, 188-94.

Hines, B., *Social World of Aldous Huxley*, 36-9.

Holmes, C. M., *Aldous Huxley and the Way of Reality*, 97-109.

Jog, D. V., *Aldous Huxley*, 75-85.

Karl, F., and M. Magalaner, *Reader's Guide to Great Twentieth Century Novels*, 279-84.

May, K. M., *Aldous Huxley*, 118-38.

Meckier, J., *Aldous Huxley*, 150-2, 154-8.

Savage, D. S., "Aldous Huxley and the Dissociation of Personality," in Rajan, B., ed., *Novelist as Thinker*, 21-7.

_____, *Withered Branch*, 142-6. Also in Aldridge, J. W., ed., *Critiques and Essays on Modern Fiction*, 350-5. Also in *SR* 55 (Autumn, 1947): 553-60.

Venter, Susan, "The 'dog episode' in Aldous Huxley's EYELESS IN GAZA: An Exegesis," *Standpunte* 24 (Aug., 1971): 16-19.

Vitoux, Pierre, "Structure and Meaning in Aldous Huxley's EYELESS IN GAZA," *YES* 2 (1972): 212-24.

Walker, Ronald G., "Time and Healing of Wounds in Huxley's EYELESS IN GAZA," *Infernal Paradise*, 139-59.

Wasserman, Jerry, "Huxley's Either/Or: The Case for EYELESS IN GAZA," *Novel* 13, ii (1980): 188-203.

Watts, H. H., *Aldous Huxley*, 86-96.

Woodcock, G., *Dawn and the Darkest Hour*, 192-206.

Zähner, L., *Demon and Saint in the Novels of Aldous Huxley*, 49-60.

THE GENIUS AND THE GODDESS

Brander, L., *Aldous Huxley*, 96-100.

Ferns, C. S., *Aldous Huxley*, 184-93.

Firchow, P., *Aldous Huxley*, 171-7.

Gupta, B. S., *Glassy Essence*, 211-13.

Holmes, C. M., *Aldous Huxley and the Way to Reality*, 165-7.

Jog, D. V., *Aldous Huxley*, 102-8.

May, K. M., *Aldous Huxley*, 192-205.

Meckier, J., *Aldous Huxley*, 162-4.

Nagarjan, S., "Religion in Three Novels of Aldous Huxley," *MFS* 5 (Summer, 1959): 153-65.

Watts, H. H., *Aldous Huxley*, 118-25.

Woodcock, G., *Dawn and the Darkest Hour*, 278-80.

Zähner, L., *Demon and Saint in the Novels of Aldous Huxley*, 84-7.

ISLAND

Bowering, P., *Aldous Huxley*, 181-212, 230-3.

Brander, L., *Aldous Huxley*, 101-10.

Chakoo, B. L., *Aldous Huxley and Eastern Wisdom*, 264-90.

Choudhary, Nora S., "ISLAND: Huxley's Attempt at Practical Philosophy," *LE&W* 16 (1972): 1155-67.

Conner, Frederick W., "'Attention': Aldous Huxley's Epistemological Route to Salvation," *SR* 81, ii (Spring, 1973): 282-308.

Ferns, C. S., *Aldous Huxley*, 211-14, 219-34.

Firchow, P., *Aldous Huxley*, 177-89.

Gill, Kulwant S., "Aldous Huxley: The Quest for Identity," *PURBA* 8, i-ii (April-Oct., 1977): 11-26.

Gorer, Geoffrey, "There is a Happy Land..." *Encounter* 19 (July, 1962): 83-6.

Gupta, B. S., *Glassy Essence*, 219-58.

Holmes, C. M., *Aldous Huxley and the Way to Reality*, 180-200.

Jog, D. V., *Aldous Huxley*, 108-15.

Kennedy, Richard S., "Aldous Huxley: The Final Wisdom," *SWR* 50 (Winter, 1965): 37-47.

Leeper, Geoffrey, "The Happy Utopias of Aldous Huxley and H. G. Wells," *Meanjin* 24 (Mar., 1965): 120-4.

May, Keith, "Accepting the Universe: The 'Rampion-Hypothesis' in POINT COUNTER POINT and ISLAND," *SNNTS* 9, iv (1977): 418-27.

_____, *Aldous Huxley*, 206-23.

McMichael, Charles T., "Aldous Huxley's ISLAND: The Final Vision," *SLitI* 1, ii (Oct., 1968): 73-82.

Meckier, J., *Aldous Huxley*, 196-205.

_____, "Cancer in Utopia: Positive and Negative Elements in Huxley's ISLAND," *DR* 54, iv (1974-75): 619-33.

_____, "Coming of Age in Pala: The Primitivism of BRAVE NEW WORLD Reconsidered in ISLAND," *Alternative Futures* (Troy, N.Y.) 1, ii (1978): 68-90.

Stewart, D. H., "Aldous Huxley's ISLAND," *QQ* 70 (Autumn, 1963): 326-35.

Wajc-Tenenbaum, R., "Aesthetics and Metaphysics: Aldous Huxley's Last Novel," *RLV* 37 (1971): 160-75.

Watt, Donald J., "Vision and Symbol in Aldous Huxley's IS-LAND," *TCL* 14 (Oct., 1968): 149-60. Also in Kuehn, R. E., comp., *Aldous Huxley*, 167-82.

Watts, H. H., *Aldous Huxley*, 139-45.

Woodcock, G., *Dawn and the Darkest Hour*, 280-5.

Zähner, L., *Demon and Saint in the Novels of Aldous Huxley*, 140-50.

POINT COUNTER POINT

Alexander, Claudia, "Bach, Beethoven, and POINT COUNTER POINT," *Innisfree* 2 (1975): 17-21.

Allen, Walter, "POINT COUNTER POINT Revisited," *SNNTS* 9, iv (1977): 373-7.

Atkins, John, "POINT COUNTER POINT and the Uncongenital Novelist," *SLitI* 13, i (1980): 69-80.

Baker, Robert S., "Spandrell's 'Lydian Heaven': Moral Masochism and the Centrality of Spandrell in Huxley's POINT COUNTER POINT," *Criticism* 16, ii (Spring, 1974): 120-35.

_____, "A Tour of Brighton Pavilion and Gog's Court: The Romantic Context of POINT COUNTER POINT and EYELESS IN GAZA," *SNNTS* 9, iv (1977): 537-63.

Baldanza, Frank, "POINT COUNTER POINT: Aldous Huxley on 'The Human Fugue'," *SAQ* 58 (Spring, 1959): 248-57.

Bentley, Joseph, "Huxley's Ambivalent Responses to the Ideas of D. H. Lawrence," *TCL* 13 (Oct., 1967): 144-53.

Birnbaum, Milton, "Politics and Character in POINT COUNTER POINT," *SNNTS* 9, iv (1977): 468-87.

Bowen, Zack, "Allusions to Musical Works in POINT COUNTER POINT," *SNNTS* 9, iv (1977): 488-508.

Bowering, P., *Aldous Huxley*, 9-10, 77-97, 221-3, 226-7, 228-9.

_____, "'The Source of Light': Pictorial Imagery and Symbolism in POINT COUNTER POINT," *SNNTS* 9, iv (1977): 389-405.

Brander, L., *Aldous Huxley*, 33-41.

Brooke, J., *Aldous Huxley*, 18-22.

Burgum, E. B., *Novel and the World's Dilemma*, 150-4. Also in *AR* 2 (Spring, 1942): 68-73.

Chakoo, B. L., *Aldous Huxley and Eastern Wisdom*, 49-87.

Dyson, A. E., "Aldous Huxley and the Two Nothings," *CritQ* 3 (Winter, 1961): 297-300. Also in Dyson, A. E., *Crazy Fabric*, 171-5.

Ehrenpreis, Irwin, "Orwell, Huxley, Pope," *RLV* 23 (1957): 215-30 *passim*.

Ferns, C. S., *Aldous Huxley*, 93-104, 113-32.

Firchow, Peter, "Mental Music: Huxley's POINT COUNTER POINT and Mann's MAGIC MOUNTAIN as Novels of Ideas," *SNNTS* 9, iv (1977): 518-36.

_____, "The Music of Humanity: POINT COUNTER POINT," in Kuehn, R. E., comp., *Aldous Huxley*, 97-118. From Firchow, P., *Aldous Huxley*, 93-117.

Ghosh, Sisir K., "POINT COUNTER POINT: Looking Back," *AJES* 6, i (1981): 76-88.

Gill, Kulwant S., "Aldous Huxley: The Quest for Identity," *PURBA* 8, i-ii (April-Oct., 1977): 11-26.

Glicksberg, Charles I., "Huxley: The Experimental Novelist," *SAQ* 52 (1953): 101-6.

Green, Carlanda, "Huxley's Cosmic Dandy," *DR* 62, ii (Summer, 1982): 303-14.

Gupta, B. S., *Glassy Essence*, 184-7.

Hamilton, Robert, "The Challenge of Aldous Huxley: 'The Perennial Philosophy'," *Horizon* 17 (June, 1948): 446-8.

Hines, B., *Social World of Aldous Huxley*, 27-34.

Hoffman, Frederick J., "Aldous Huxley and the Novel of Ideas," *CE* 8, iii (Dec., 1946): 129-37. Also in O'Connor, W. V., ed., *Forms of Modern Fiction*, 189-200. Also in Kuehn, R. E., comp., *Aldous Huxley*, 8-17.

Holmes, C. M., *Aldous Huxley and the Way to Reality*, 53-71.

Jog, D. V., *Aldous Huxley*, 58-66.

Karl, F., and M. Magalaner, *Reader's Guide to Great Twentieth Century Novels*, 267-75.

Kettle, A., *Introduction to the English Novel*, 167-70.

Keyishian, Harry, "The Martyrology of Nymphomania: Nancy Cunnard in THE GREEN HAT and POINT COUNTER POINT," in Marsden, Michael, comp., *Proceedings of the Sixth National Convention of the Popular Culture Association*, Chicago, Illinois, April 22, 1976, Bowling Green: Bowling Green St. Un. Popular Pr., 1976, 292-8.

King, Carlyle, "Aldous Huxley's Way to God," *QQ* 61 (Spring, 1954): 86-9.

Levi, A. W., *Literature, Philosophy, and the Imagination*, 262-4.

May, Keith, "Accepting the Universe: The 'Rampion-Hypothesis' in POINT COUNTER POINT and ISLAND," *SNNTS* 9, iv (1977): 418-27.

_____, *Aldous Huxley*, 79-97.

Meckier, J., *Aldous Huxley*, 26-7, 32-5, 41-52, 60-1, 78-82, 86-90, 102-10.

_____, "Aldous Huxley and the Congenital Novelists: New Ideas about the Novel of Ideas," *SoRA* 13, iii (Nov., 1980): 203-21.

_____, "Fifty Years of Counterpoint," *SNNTS* 9 (Winter, 1977): 367-72.

_____, "Philip Quarles's Passage to India: JESTING PILATE, POINT COUNTER POINT, and Bloomsbury," *SNNTS* 3, iv (1977): 445-67.

_____, "Quarles Among the Monkeys: Huxley's Zoological Novels," *MLR* 68, ii (April, 1973): 268-82.

Morton, Peter R., "Huxley's POINT COUNTER POINT," *Expl* 37, iv (Summer, 1979): 10-11.

Patty, James S., "Baudelaire and Huxley," *SAB* 23 (Nov., 1968): 5-8.

Quina, James, "The Mathematical-Physical Universe: A Basis for Multiplicity and the Quest for Unity in POINT COUNTER POINT," *SNNTS* 9, iv (1977): 428-44.

Roston, Murray, "The Technique of Counterpoint," *SNNTS* 9, iv (1977): 378-88.

Savage, D. S., "Aldous Huxley and the Dissociation of Personality," in Rajan, B., ed., *Novelist as Thinker*, 19-21.

Slochower, H., *No Voice is Wholly Lost*, 33-5.

Smyser, H. M., "Huxley's POINT COUNTER POINT, Chapter XI," *Expl* 6 (Dec., 1947): Item 22.

Thompson, Leslie L., "A Lawrence-Huxley Parallel: WOMEN IN LOVE and POINT COUNTER POINT," *N&Q* 15 (Feb., 1968): 58-9.

Vitoux, Pierre, "Aldous Huxley and D. H. Lawrence: An Attempt at Intellectual Sympathy," *MLR* 69, iii (July, 1974): 508-18.

Watson, David S., "POINT COUNTER POINT: The Modern Satiric Novel a Genre," *SNL* 6, ii (Spring, 1969): 31-5.

Watt, Donald J., "The Criminal-Victim Pattern in Huxley's POINT COUNTER POINT," *SNNTS* 2, i (Spring, 1970): 42-51.

_____, "The Fugal Construction of POINT COUNTER POINT," *SNNTS* 9, i (1977): 509-17.

Watts, H. H., *Aldous Huxley*, 62-71.

_____, Introduction, *POINT COUNTER POINT*, N.Y.: Harper, 1947.

_____, "The Viability of POINT COUNTER POINT," *SNNTS* 9, iv (1977): 406-17.

Wilson, C., "Existential Criticism and the Work of Aldous Huxley," *Strength to Dream*, 220-2.

Woodcock, G., *Dawn and the Darkest Hour*, 150-60.

Zaenker, Karl A., "String Quartets in Prose," *CRLL* 8 (Dec., 1981): 515-17.

THOSE BARREN LEAVES

Aiken, C., *Reviewer's ABC*, 225-30. Also in *Criterion* 3 (April, 1925): 449-53.

Baker, Robert S., "The Fire of Prometheus: Romanticism and the Baroque in Huxley's ANTIC HAY and THOSE BARREN LEAVES," *TSLL* 19 (Spring, 1977): 60-82.

Bowering, P., *Aldous Huxley*, 61-76, 218-19.

Brander, L., *Aldous Huxley*, 27-32.

Brooke, J., *Aldous Huxley*, 17-18.

Chakoo, B. L., *Aldous Huxley and Eastern Wisdom*, 33-48.

Church, Margaret, "Concepts of Time in the Novels of Virginia Woolf and Aldous Huxley," *MFS* 1 (May, 1955): 19-24.

Ferns, C. S., *Aldous Huxley*, 77-93.

Firchow, P., *Aldous Huxley*, 80-92.

Ghose, S., *Aldous Huxley*, 78-80.

Gupta, B. S., *Glassy Essence*, 180-4.

Hines, B., *Social World of Aldous Huxley*, 22-6.

Holmes, C., *Aldous Huxley and the Way to Reality*, 53-64.

May, K. M., *Aldous Huxley*, 61-78.

Meckier, J., *Aldous Huxley*, 24-7, 70-7. Also in Kuehn, R. E., comp., *Aldous Huxley*, 89-96.

O'Faolain, S, *Vanishing Hero*, 10-19.

Savage, D. S., "Aldous Huxley and the Dissociation of Personality," in Rajan, B., ed., *Novelist as Thinker*, 14-19.

Watts, H. H., *Aldous Huxley*, 56-62.

Wilson, Angus, "The House Party Novels," *LonM* 2, viii (Aug., 1955): 53-6. Also in Kuehn, E. E., comp., *Aldous Huxley*, 20-3.

Woodcock, G., *Dawn and the Darkest Hour*, 120-9.

Zähner, L., *Demon and Saint in the Novels of Aldous Huxley*, 27-48.

TIME MUST HAVE A STOP

Barnes, Hazel, "Apotheosis and Deification in Plato, Nietzsche and Huxley," *P&L* 1, i (Fall, 1976): 3-24 *passim*.

Beary, Thomas J., "Religion and the Modern Novel," *CathW* 166 (Dec., 1947): 206-9.

Bowering, P., *Aldous Huxley*, 160-80.

Brander, L., *Aldous Huxley*, 86-91.

Chakoo, B. L., *Aldous Huxley and Eastern Wisdom*, 216-35.

Church, Margaret, "Concepts of Time in the Novels of Virginia Woolf and Aldous Huxley," *MFS* 1 (May, 1955): 19-24.

Ferns, C. S., *Aldous Huxley*, 166-76.

Firchow, P., *Aldous Huxley*, 164-70.

Gupta, B. S., *Glassy Essence*, 199-204.

Hamilton, Robert, "The Challenge of Aldous Huxley: 'The Perennial Philosophy'," *Horizon* 17 (June, 1948): 450-3.

Hara, Ichiro, "On A. Huxley's TIME MUST HAVE A STOP," *Rising Generation* (Japan) 93 (1947): no. 11.

Hines, B., *Social World of Aldous Huxley*, 43-6.

Holmes, C. M., *Aldous Huxley and the Way to Reality*, 133-8.

Jog, D. V., *Aldous Huxley*, 90-8.

Lebowitz, Martin, "The Everlasting Mr. Huxley," in Kenyon Review, *Kenyon Critics*, 289-93. Also in *KR* 7 (Winter, 1945): 135-8.

May, K. M., *Aldous Huxley*, 158-76.

Meckier, J., *Aldous Huxley*, 164-72.

Nagarajan, S., "Religion in Three Recent Novels of Aldous Huxley," *MFS* 5 (Summer, 1959): 153-65.

Savage, D. S., "Aldous Huxley and the Dissociation of Personality," in Rajan, B., ed., *Novelist as Thinker*, 32-4.

_____, *Withered Branch*, 154-5. Also in Aldridge, J. W., ed., *Critiques and Essays on Modern Fiction*, 360-1. Also in *SR* 55 (Autumn, 1947): 567-8.

Watts, H. H., *Aldous Huxley*, 106-13.

Wilson, Edmund, "Aldous Huxley in the World Beyond Time," *NY* (Sept. 2, 1944): 64-6. Also in Wilson, E., *Classics and Commercials*, 209-14.

Woodcock, G., *Dawn and the Darkest Hour*, 228-37.

Zähner, L., *Demon and Saint in the Novels of Aldous Huxley*, 73-83.

BIBLIOGRAPHY

Bass, Eben E., ed., *Aldous Huxley: An Annotated Bibliography of Criticism*, N.Y.: Garland, 1981.

Clareson, Thomas D., and Carolyn S. Andrews, "Aldous Huxley: A Bibliography, 1960-1964," *Extrapolation* 6 (Dec., 1964): 2-21.

Davis, Dennis D., "Aldous Huxley: A Bibliography 1965-1973," *BB* 31, ii (1974): 67-70.

Eschelbach, Claire John, and J. L. Shober, *Aldous Huxley: A Bibliography, 1916-1959*, Berkeley: Un. of Calif., 1961.

_____, and Joyce S. Marthaler, "Aldous Huxley: A Bibliography, 1914-1964 (A Supplementary Listing)," *BB* 28, iv (Oct.-Dec., 1971): 114-17.

Watts, H. H., *Aldous Huxley*, 169-76.

HUXLEY, ELSPETH JOSCELINE, 1907-

RED STRANGERS

Githae-Mugo, M., *Visions of Africa*, 39-51, 92-6, 104-12.

Sander, Reinhard, "Two Views of the Conflict of Cultures in Pre-Emergency Kenya: A Comparative Study of James Ngugi's THE RIVER BETWEEN and Elspeth Huxley's RED

STRANGERS," *Ikoro* (Nsukka) 3, i (1976): 28-42. Also in *ReAL* 5, i (Fall, 1971): 8-26.

A THING TO LOVE

Githae-Mugo, M., *Visions of Africa*, 113-23.

IRELAND, DAVID, 1927-

GENERAL

Macleod, Mark, "David Ireland: Interview," *Kunapipi* 3, i (1981): 64-75.
Mitchell, Adrian, "Paradigms of Purpose: David Ireland's Fiction," *Meanjin* 34, ii (June, 1975): 189-97.
Pons, Xavier, "The Dead Heart of Australia: The Urban and Industrial Vision in David Ireland's Fiction," *Overland* 80 (July, 1980): 38-44.

BURN

Daniel, Helen, "Purpose and the Racial Outsider: BURN and THE CHANT OF JIMMIE BLACKSMITH," *Southerly* 38 (1978): 25-43.

THE CHANTIC BIRD

Daniel, Helen, "Recoil from Disorder: David Ireland's THE CHANTIC BIRD," *ALS* 8 (1978): 471-84.

CITY OF WOMEN

Bird, Delys, "David Ireland: CITY OF WOMEN," *Westerly* 26, iv (Dec., 1981): 76-8.

THE FLESHEATERS

Daniel, Helen, "Observer and Accomplice: The Narrator in Ireland's THE FLESHEATERS," *Westerly* iii (1977): 39-46.
Gelder, Ken, "David Ireland's PRISONER and THE FLESHEATERS," *ALS* 9 (1980): 535-8.

THE UNKNOWN INDUSTRIAL PRISONER

Cantrell, Leon, "The New Novel," in Hamilton, K. G., ed., *Studies in the Recent Australian Novel*, 228-41.
Daniel, H. E., "Ways of Resistance in David Ireland's THE UNKNOWN INDUSTRIAL PRISONER," *Westerly* ii (1977): 59-66.
Gelder, Ken, "David Ireland's PRISONER and THE FLESHEATERS," *ALS* 9 (1980): 535-8.

IRVING, JOHN, 1942-

GENERAL

Epstein, Joseph, "Why John Irving Is So Popular," *Ctary* 73, vi (June, 1982): 59-63.
James, Wayne L., "The Novels of John Irving," *DAI* 43, i (July, 1982): 169A.
McCaffery, Larry, "An Interview with John Irving," *ConL* 23, i (Winter, 1982): 1-18.

Priestley, Michael, "An Interview with John Irving," *NER* 1 (1979): 489-504.
———, "Structure in the Worlds of John Irving," *Crit* 23, i (1981): 82-96.
Renwick, Joyce, "John Irving: An Interview," *FictionI* 14 (1982): 5-18.
Runyon, Randolph, "The World According to T. S.," *Fowles/Irving/Barth*, 37-65.

THE WORLD ACCORDING TO GARP

Gilbert, Susan, "Children of the Seventies: The American Family in Recent Fiction," *Soundings* 62, ii (Summer, 1980): 210-12.
Griffith, George V., "Jarrell According to Garp," *NMAL* 5, iii (Summer, 1981): Item 20.
Kirmani, Seema, "John Irving's THE WORLD ACCORDING TO GARP: Older than Marcus Aurelius," *DAI* 40 (1979): 853A.
Priestley, Michael, "Structure in the Worlds of John Irving," *Crit* 23, i (1981): 88-96.
Runyon, Randolph, "The World According to T.S.," *Fowles/Irving/Barth*, 37-41, 52-65.
Thompson, Christine E., "Pentheus in THE WORLD ACCORDING TO GARP," *CML* 3, i (Fall, 1982): 33-7.
Wymard, Eleanor B., "'A New Version of the Midas Touch': DANIEL MARTIN and THE WORLD ACCORDING TO GARP," *MFS* 27, ii (Summer, 1981): 284-6.

ISHERWOOD, CHRISTOPHER, 1904-1986

GENERAL

Bailey, Jeffrey, "An Interview with Christopher Isherwood," *CaQ* 11-12 (1977): 87-96.
Bantock, G. H., "The Novels of Christopher Isherwood," in Rajan, B., ed., *Novelist as Thinker*, 46-57.
Boretz, Marianne S., "The Discreet and Conspiratorial Convention: The Autobiographical Writings of Christopher Isherwood," *DAI* 35 (1972): 2258A (So. Calif.).
Dewsnap, Terence, "Isherwood Couchant," *Crit* 13, i (1971): 31-47.
Finney, B., *Christopher Isherwood*.
Fryer, Jonathan H., "Sexuality in Isherwood," *TCL* 22, iii (Oct., 1976): 343-53.
Geherin, David J., "An Interview with Christopher Isherwood," *JNT* 2 (1972): 143-58.
———, "The Shaping of An Artist: A Study of the Novels of Christopher Isherwood," *DA* 31 (1970): 1798A.
Graffin, Walter R., "The Novels of Christopher Isherwood," *DAI* 30 (1969): 1168A (Wis.).
Heilbrun, C. G., *Christopher Isherwood*.
———, "Christopher Isherwood: An Interview," *TCL* 22, iii (Oct., 1976): 253-63.
Henig, Suzanne, "Interview with Christopher Isherwood," *VWQ* 3 (1978): 157-65.
Isherwood, Christopher, "A Conversation on Tape," *LonM*, n.s. 1 (June, 1961): 41-58.
Kaplan, Carola M., "The Search for Belief in the Novels of Christopher Isherwood," *DAI* 35 (1975): 4527A.
Karl, F. R., *Contemporary English Novel*, 290-2.

King, F., *Christopher Isherwood*.

Maes-Jelinek, Hena, "The Knowledge of Man in the Works of Christopher Isherwood," *RLV* No. 5 (1960): 341-60.

Mayne, Richard, "The Novel and Mr. Norris," *Cambridge Jnl* 6 (June, 1953): 561-70.

Piazza, P., *Christopher Isherwood*.

———, "Christopher Isherwood: Myth and Anti-Myth," *DAI* 36 (1975): 908A.

Pryce-Jones, David, "Isherwood Reassessed," *T&T* 41 (Oct. 1, 1960): 1162-3.

Savage, D. D., "Christopher Isherwood: The Novelist as Homosexualist," *L&P* 29, i-ii (1979): 71-88.

Scobie, W. I., "The Art of Fiction 49: Christopher Isherwood," *ParisR* 57 (Spring, 1974): 138-82. (Interview.)

Smith, Sarah, and Marcus Smith, "To Help Along the Line: An Interview with Christopher Isherwood," *NOR* 4, iv (1975): 307-10.

Solway, Clifford, "An Interview with Christopher Isherwood," *TamR* No. 39 (Spring, 1966): 22-35.

Summers, C. J., *Christopher Isherwood*.

———, "Christopher Isherwood and the Need for Community," *PCL* 3, i (May, 1977): 30-7.

Thomas, David P., "The Fiction of Christopher Isherwood: Personality as Form," *DAI* 31 (1971): 6636A (S.U.N.Y., Binghampton).

Thomas, Peter, "'Camp' and Politics in Isherwood's Berlin Fiction," *JML* 5, i (Feb., 1976): 117-30.

Whitehead, John, "Christophananda: Isherwood at Sixty," *LonM*, n.s. 5 (July, 1965): 90-100.

Wickes, Gerald, "An Interview with Christopher Isherwood," *Shen* 16 (Spring, 1965): 23-52.

Wilde, A., *Christopher Isherwood*.

———, "Language and Surface: Isherwood and the Thirties," *ConL* 16, iv (Autumn, 1975): 478-91.

Wilson, Colin, "*An Integrity Born of Hope*: Notes on Christopher Isherwood," *TCL* 22, iii (Oct., 1976): 312-31.

ALL THE CONSPIRATORS

Allen, W., *Modern Novel*, 234-5.
Finney, B., *Christopher Isherwood*, 69-75.
Piazza, P., *Christopher Isherwood*, 19-30.
Summers, C. J., *Christopher Isherwood*, 46-52.
Wilde, A., *Christopher Isherwood*, 27-36.

THE BERLIN STORIES

Haynes, Douglas, "Christopher Isherwood's Revision of THE BERLIN STORIES," *PBSA* 73 (1979): 262-5.

Piazza, P., *Christopher Isherwood*, 88-91, 117-26, 174-9.

Summers, C. J., *Christopher Isherwood*, 13-43.

Thomas, Peter, "'Camp' and Politics in Isherwood's Berlin Fiction," *JML* 5, i (Feb., 1976): 117-30.

Wilde, A., *Christopher Isherwood*, 53-77.

———, "Language and Surface: Isherwood and the Thirties," *ConL* 16, iv (Autumn, 1975): 478-91.

DOWN THERE ON A VISIT

Dienstfrey, Harris, *Ctary* 34 (Oct., 1962): 360-3.
Finney, B., *Christopher Isherwood*, 235-46.
Jebb, Julian, *LonM*, n.s. 2 (April, 1962): 87-9.

Kennedy, A., *Protean Self*, 215-17.

Poznar, Walter, "Christopher in DOWN THERE ON A VISIT: *Un Jour sans landemain*," *WascanaR* 16, i (Spring, 1981): 3-15.

Summers, C. J., *Christopher Isherwood*, 93-106.

Wilde, A., *Christopher Isherwood*, 112-26.

Wiley, Paul, *WSCL* 4, ii (Spring-Summer, 1963): 225-8.

GOODBYE TO BERLIN

Allen, W., *Modern Novel*, 237-8.

Finney, B., *Christopher Isherwood*, 143-54.

Knodt, Kenneth S., "GOODBYE TO BERLIN: The Diaries as Structure," *Descant* 20, i (Fall, 1975): 40-8.

Piazza, P., *Christopher Isherwood*, 123-6.

Summers, C. J., *Christopher Isherwood*, 29-42.

Thomas, David P., "GOODBYE TO BERLIN: Refocusing Isherwood's Camera," *ConL* 13, i (Winter, 1972): 44-52.

Wilde, A., *Christopher Isherwood*, 66-77.

A MEETING BY THE RIVER

Dewsnap, Terence, "Isherwood Couchant," *Crit.* 13, i (1971): 41-6.

Finney, B., *Christopher Isherwood*, 260-6.

Holloway, John, "Narrative Structure and Text Structure: Isherwood's A MEETING BY THE RIVER and Muriel Sparks's THE PRIME OF MISS JEAN BRODIE," *CritI* 1 (1975): 581-604.

Piazza, P., *Christopher Isherwood*, 73-7, 162-71.

Scobie, W. I., "Fat Hollywood in Hungry Bengal," *LonM* 13, i (April-May, 1973): 137-44.

Summers, C. J., *Christopher Isherwood*, 122-35.

Wilde, A., *Christopher Isherwood*, 139-47.

THE MEMORIAL

Allen, W., *Modern Novel*, 235-7.
Finney, B., *Christopher Isherwood*, 93-100.
Kermode, F., *Puzzles and Epiphanies*, 125-6.
Piazza, P., *Christopher Isherwood*, 30-41.
Summers, C. J., *Christopher Isherwood*, 52-62.
Wilde, A., *Christopher Isherwood*, 37-52.

MR NORRIS CHANGES TRAINS (THE LAST OF MR NORRIS) (See also THE BERLIN STORIES)

Finney, B., *Christopher Isherwood*, 110-18.
Piazza, P., *Christopher Isherwood*, 120-3, 174-6.
Summers, C. J., *Christopher Isherwood*, 17-29.
Wilde, A., *Christopher Isherwood*, 53-65.

PRATER VIOLET

Bantock, G. H., "The Novels of Christopher Isherwood," in Rajan, B., ed., *Novelist as Thinker*, 55-7.

Farrell, James T., "When Graustark Is in Celluloid," *Literature and Morality*, N.Y.: Vanguard, 1947, 125-32.

Finney, B., *Christopher Isherwood*, 187-92.

Piazza, P., *Christopher Isherwood*, 60-72.

Rosenfeld, Isaac, "Isherwood's Master Theme," *KR* 8 (Summer, 1946): 488-92. Also in Rosenfeld, I., *Age of Enormity*, 149-54.

Summers, C. J., *Christopher Isherwood*, 70-8.

Wilde, A., *Christopher Isherwood*, 89-98.

A SINGLE MAN

Dewsnap, Terence, "Isherwood Couchant," *Crit* 13, i (1971): 34-41.

Finney, B., *Christopher Isherwood*, 251-5.

Heilbrun, C. G., *Christopher Isherwood*, 42-4.

Kennedy, A., *Protean Self*, 219-29.

Kuehn, Robert E., "Fiction Chronicle," *WSCL* 6 (1965): 134-5.

Nagarajan, S., *Christopher Isherwood*, 150-61, 183-92.

Raban, J., "Narrative: Some Problems and Conventions," *Technique of Modern Fiction*, 29-32.

Solway, Clifford, "An Interview with Christopher Isherwood," *TamR* No. 39 (Spring, 1966): 22-35.

Spender, Stephen, "Must There be a Red Brick England?" in Encyclopaedia Britannica, *Great Ideas Today, 1965*, 184-6.

Summers, C. J., *Christopher Isherwood*, 107-21.

_____, "Christopher Isherwood and the Need for Community," *PCL* 3, i (May, 1977): 32-6.

Wilde, A., *Christopher Isherwood*, 127-38.

THE WORLD IN THE EVENING

Finney, B., *Christopher Isherwood*, 205-22.

Gunn, Thom, *LonM* 1 (Oct., 1954): 81-5.

Heilbrun, C. G., *Christopher Isherwood*, 37-42.

Kermode, F., *Puzzles and Epiphanies*, 121-5.

Maes-Jelinek, Hena, "The Knowledge of Man in the Works of Christopher Isherwood," *RLV* No. 5 (1960): 351-9.

Piazza, P., *Christopher Isherwood*, 43-52, 180-3.

Summers, C. J., *Christopher Isherwood*, 79-92.

Tolton, C. D. E., "André Gide and Christopher Isherwood: Two Worlds of Counterfeiters," *CRCL* 5 (Spring, 1978): 193-200.

Wilde, A., *Christopher Isherwood*, 102-11.

BIBLIOGRAPHY

Funk, Robert W., *Christopher Isherwood: A Reference Guide*, London: Prior; Boston: G. K. Hall, 1979.

Orphanos, Stathis, "Christopher Isherwood: A Checklist 1968-1975," *TCL* 22, iii (Oct., 1976): 354-61.

Westby, Selmer, and Clayton M. Brown, *Christopher Isherwood: A Bibliography 1923-1967*, Los Angeles: California State College, 1968.

Wilde, A., *Christopher Isherwood*, 161-5.

JACKSON, CHARLES REGINALD, 1903-1968

THE LOST WEEKEND

Paskoff, Louis, "Don Birnam's Dark Mirror," *Serif* 10, iii (Fall, 1973): 41-50.

JACKSON, SHIRLEY, 1920-1965

GENERAL

Friedman, L., *Shirley Jackson*.

Hoffman, Steven K., "Individuation and Character Development in the Fiction of Shirley Jackson," *HSL* 8, iii (1976): 190-208.

Miller, Raymond R., Jr., "Shirley Jackson's Fiction: An Introduction," *DAI* 35 (1974): 3000A (Del.).

Nardacci, Michael L., "Theme, Character, and Technique in the Novels of Shirley Jackson," *DAI* 41 (1980): 674A.

Parks, John G., "The Possibility of Evil: The Fiction of Shirley Jackson," *DAI* 35 (1974): 1667A (N.M.).

THE BIRD'S NEST

Friedman, L., *Shirley Jackson*, 95-103.

HANGSAMAN

Friedman, L., *Shirley Jackson*, 86-95.

Lyons, J. O., *College Novel in America*, 62-9.

THE HAUNTING OF HILL HOUSE

Friedman, L., *Shirley Jackson*, 121-35.

Kahane, Claire, "Gothic Mirrors and Feminine Identity," *CentR* 14, i (Winter, 1980): 53-5.

THE ROAD THROUGH THE WALL

Friedman, L., *Shirley Jackson*, 78-85.

THE SUNDIAL

Friedman, L., *Shirley Jackson*, 104-21.

Parks, John G., "Waiting for the End: Shirley Jackson's THE SUNDIAL," *Crit* 19, iii (1978): 74-88.

WE HAVE ALWAYS LIVED IN THE CASTLE

Friedman, L., *Shirley Jackson*, 135-44.

Woodruff, Stuart C., "The Real Horror Elsewhere: Shirley Jackson's Last Novel," *SWR* 52 (Spring, 1967): 152-62.

BIBLIOGRAPHY

Friedman, L., *Shirley Jackson*, 167-77.

Phillips, Robert S., "Shirley Jackson: A Checklist," *PBSA* 60 (1966): 203-13.

JACOBSON, DAN, 1929-

GENERAL

Girling, H. K., "Compassion and Detachment in the Novels of Dan Jacobson," *The Purple Renoster* 2 (Spring, 1957): 16-23. [Not seen.]

Wade, Michael, "Apollo, Dionysus and Other Performers in Dan Jacobson's South African Circus," *WLWE* 13, i (April, 1974): 39-82.

Winegarten, Renée, "The Novels of Dan Jacobson," *Midstream* 12 (May, 1966): 69-73.

THE BEGINNERS

"Prose Out of Africa. Dan Jacobson: THE BEGINNERS," in *T.L.S. Essays and Reviews, 1966*, 42-3. Also in *TLS* (June 2, 1966): 812.

Ricks, Christopher, "One Little Liberal," *NStat* (June 3, 1966): 812.

Swinden, P., *Unofficial Selves*, 213-20.

Wade, Michael, "Apollo, Dionysus and Other Performers in Dan Jacobson's South African Circus," *WLWE* 13, i (April, 1974): 74-80.

Winegarten, Renée, "The Novels of Dan Jacobson," *Midstream* 12 (May, 1966): 72-3.

A DANCE IN THE SUN

Baxter, C., "Political Symbolism in A DANCE IN THE SUN," *EinA* 5, ii (1978): 44-50.

Durrant, G. H., "Promising Young Men," *Standpunte* 11 (Dec., 1956-Jan., 1957): 64-6.

Wade, Michael, "Apollo, Dionysus and Other Performers in Dan Jacobson's South African Circus," *WLWE* 13, i (April, 1974): 49-58.

Wilkinson, D. R. M., "A Comment on Race Relationships: Dan Jacobson's THE TRAP and A DANCE IN THE SUN," *DQR* 5 (1975): 270-81.

THE EVIDENCE OF LOVE

Alvarez, A., "The Difficulty of Being South African," *NS&Nation* 59 (June 4, 1960): 827-8.

Dienstfrey, Harris, "Tales of Hate and Love," *Ctary* 30 (Sept., 1960): 261-4.

Miller, Karl, "Annals of Lyndhurst," *Spectator* (June 3, 1960): 806-7.

Wade, Michael, "Apollo, Dionysus and Other Performers in Dan Jacobson's South African Circus," *WLWE* 13, i (April, 1974): 63-74.

THE PRICE OF DIAMONDS

Decter, Midge, "Novelist of South Africa," *Ctary* 25 (June, 1958): 539-44. Also in Decter, M., *The Literated Woman and Other Americans*, N.Y.: Coward, McCann & Geoghegan, 1971, 201-8.

Wade, Michael, "Apollo, Dionysus and Other Performers in Dan Jacobson's South African Circus," *WLWE* 13, i (April, 1974): 58-63.

THE TRAP

Durrant, G. H., "Promising Young Men," *Standpunte* 11 (Dec., 1956-Jan., 1957): 63-4.

Wade, Michael, "Apollo, Dionysus and Other Performers in Dan Jacobson's South African Circus," *WLWE* 13, i (April, 1974): 40-9.

Wilkinson, D. R. M., "A Comment on Race Relationships: Dan Jacobson's THE TRAP and A DANCE IN THE SUN," *DQR* 5 (1975): 270-81.

BIBLIOGRAPHY

Yudelman, Myra, comp., *Dan Jacobson: A Bibliography*, Johannesburg: Un. of Witwatersrand, Dep't of Bibliography, Librarianship and Typography, 1967.

JENKINS, (JOHN) ROBIN, 1912-

GENERAL

Binding, Paul, "Ambivalent Patriot: The Fiction of Robin Jenkins," *New Edinburgh Review* 53 (1981): 20-2. [Not seen.]

Burgess, Moira, "Robin Jenkins, a Novelist of Scotland," *Library Review* 22, viii (Winter, 1970): 409-12.

JHABVALA, RUTH PRAWER, 1927-

GENERAL

Agarwal, Ramlal, "Two Approaches to Jhabvala," *JIWE* 5, i (Jan., 1977): 24-7.

Asnani, Shyam M., "Jhabvala's Novels: A Thematic Study," *JIWE* 2, i (Jan., 1974): 38-47.

Belliappa, Meena, "A Study of Jhabvala's Fiction," *BP* 4, xii (1969): 70-82. [Not seen.]

Blackwell, Fritz, "Perception of the Guru in the Fiction of Ruth Prawer Jhabvala," *JIWE* 5, ii (July, 1977): 6-13.

Gooneratne, Yasmine, "Film into Fiction: The Influence upon Ruth Prawer Jhabvala's Fiction of Her Work for the Cinema, 1960-1976," *WLWE* 18, ii (Nov., 1979): 368-86.

————, "Ruth Jhabvala: Generating Heat and Light," *Kunapipi* 1, i (1979): 115-29. [Not seen.]

Hartley, Lois, "R. Prawer Jhabvala: Novelist of Urban India," *LE&W* 9, iii (Sept., 1965): 265-73.

Hayball, Connie, "Ruth Prawer Jhabvala's India," *JIWE* 9, ii (July, 1981): 42-54.

Iyengar, K. R. S., *Indian Writing in English*, 450-61.

Jawaid, Kalpana, "The East-West Encounter: A Dominant Theme in Ruth Prawer Jhabvala's Fiction," *Triveni* 50, iv (1982): 74-6.

Rani, K. Nirupa, "India in the Fiction of Ruth Prawer Jhabvala," *ComQ* 3, ix (Dec., 1978): 112-27.

Rutherford, Anna, and Kirsten H. Petersen, "'Heat and Dust': Ruth Prawer Jhabvala's Experience of India," *WLWE* 15, ii (Nov., 1976): 373-8.

————, "Ruth Prawer Jhabvala's Window on India," *ACLALSB* 4, iii (1975): 27-9. [Not seen.]

Shahane, Vasant A., "An Artist's Experience of India: Ruth Prawer Jhabvala's Fiction," *LCrit* 12, ii-iii (1976): 47-62. Also in Manuel, M., and K. Ayyappa Paniker, eds., *English and India: Essays Presented to Professor Samuel Mathai on His Seventieth Birthday*, Madras: Macmillan of India, 1978, 1-15.

————, *Ruth Prawer Jhabvala*.

Singh, R. S., "Ironic Vision of a Social Realist: Ruth Prawer Jhabvala," *Indian Novel in English*, 149-63.

Souza, Eunice de, "The Blinds Drawn and the Air Conditioner On: The Novels of Ruth Prawer Jhabvala," *WLWE* 17, i (April, 1978): 219-24.

————, "Four Expatriate Writers," *JSL* 4, ii (Winter, 1976-77): 54-60.

Varma, P. N., "A Note on the Novels of R. Prawer Jhabvala," *URajSE* 5 (1971): 87-96. [Not seen.]

Williams, H. M., *Fiction of Ruth Prawer Jhabvala*.

————, "R. K. Narayan and R. Prawer Jhabvala: Two Interpreters of Modern India," *LE&W* 16, iv (Dec., 1972): 1136-54.

————, "Strangers in a Backward Place: Modern India in the Fiction of Ruth Prawer Jhabvala," *JCL* 6, i (June, 1971): 53-64.

————, "The Yogi and the Babbitt: Themes and Characters of the New India in the Novels of R. Prawer Jhabvala," *TCL* 15, ii (July, 1969): 81-90.

A BACKWARD PLACE

Kapoor, S. D., "A Study in Contrasts," *CalR* 178, iii (Mar., 1966): 165-70.

Shahane, V. A., *Ruth Prawer Jhabvala*, 72-86.

Williams, H. M., *Fiction of Ruth Prawer Jhabvala*, 47-58.

ESMOND IN INDIA

Shahane, V. A., *Ruth Prawer Jhabvala*, 87-102.

Williams, H. M., *Fiction of Ruth Prawer Jhabvala*, 29-33.

GET READY FOR BATTLE

Shahane, V. A., *Ruth Prawer Jhabvala*, 103-12.

Williams, H. M., *Fiction of Ruth Prawer Jhabvala*, 39-47.

HEAT AND DUST

Ezekiel, Nissim, "Two Readers and Their Texts," in Amirthanayagam, G., ed., *Asian and Western Writers in Dialogue*, 137-41.

Gooneratne, Yasmine, "Irony in Ruth Prawer Jhabvala's HEAT AND DUST," *NLRev* 4 (1978): 41-50.

King, B., *New English Literatures*, 226-7, 228.

Pradhan, N. S., "The Problem of Focus in Jhabvala's HEAT AND DUST," *Indian Lit. Rev.* 1, i (1978): 15-20.

Rama Krishna Rao, A., "Complex Racial Image in Jhabvala's HEAT AND DUST," *JEnS* 13, ii (1982): 887-97.

Rutherford, Anna, and Kirsten H. Petersen, "HEAT AND DUST: Ruth Prawer Jhabvala's Experience of India," *WLWE* 15, ii (1976): 373-8.

Shahane, V. A., *Ruth Prawer Jhabvala*, 129-41.

_____, "Ruth Prawer Jhabvala's HEAT AND DUST," *BP* 21 (1976): 1-9.

THE HOUSEHOLDER

Shahane, V. A., *Ruth Prawer Jhabvala*, 62-71.

Williams, H. M., *Fiction of Ruth Prawer Jhabvala*, 33-9.

THE NATURE OF PASSION

Shahane, V. A., *Ruth Prawer Jhabvala*, 50-61.

Williams, H. M., *Fiction of Ruth Prawer Jhabvala*, 17-29.

A NEW DOMINION (TRAVELERS)

Shahane, Vasant A., "Ruth Prawer Jhabvala's A NEW DOMINION," *JCL* 12, i (Aug., 1977): 45-55.

_____, *Ruth Prawer Jhabvala*, 113-28.

TO WHOM SHE WILL

Shahane, V. A., *Ruth Prawer Jhabvala*, 33-49.

Williams, H. M., *Fiction of Ruth Prawer Jhabvala*, 12-17.

JOHNSON, B(RYAN) S(TANLEY) (WILLIAM), 1933-1973

GENERAL

Bergonzi, B., in *Contemporary English Novel*, 51-3.

Levitt, Morton P., "The Novels of B. S. Johnson: Against the War against Joyce," *MFS* 27, iv (Winter, 1981-82): 571-86.

Lilly, Mark, "The Novels of B. S. Johnson," *Planet* 26/27 (Winter, 1974/75): 33-40.

Parrinder, Patrick, "Pilgrim's Progress: The Novels of B. S. Johnson (1933-73)," *CritQ* 19, ii (Summer, 1977): 45-59.

Ryf, Robert S., "B. S. Johnson and the Frontiers of Fiction," *Crit* 19, i (1977): 58-74.

JOHNSON, DIANE (LAIN), 1934-

BURNING

Ryan, Marjorie, "The Novels of Diane Johnson," *Crit* 16, i (1975): 60-3.

FAIR GAME

Ryan, Marjorie, "The Novels of Diane Johnson," *Crit* 16, i (1975): 54-7.

LOVING HANDS AT HOME

Ryan, Marjorie, "The Novels of Diane Johnson," *Crit* 16, i (1975): 57-60.

JOHNSON, PAMELA HANSFORD, 1912-1983

GENERAL

Karl, F. R., *Contemporary English Novel*, 275-6.

Lindblad, I., *Pamela Hansford Johnson*.

Quigly, I., *Pamela Hansford Johnson*.

AN AVENUE OF STONE (See also TRILOGY)

Lindblad, I., *Pamela Hansford Johnson*, 72-3, 77-81.

Raymond, J., "A Corvo of Our Day," *Doge of Dover*, 157-8.

BLESSED ABOVE WOMEN

Lindblad, I., *Pamela Hansford Johnson*, 86-91.

CATHERINE CARTER

Lindblad, I., *Pamela Hansford Johnson*, 115-20.

Quigly, I., *Pamela Hansford Johnson*, 28-31.

Stewart, G., *New Mythos*, 64-6.

CORK STREET, NEXT TO THE HATTER'S: A NOVEL IN BAD TASTE

Lindblad, I., *Pamela Hansford Johnson*, 149-53.

Quigly, I., *Pamela Hansford Johnson*, 37-8.

AN ERROR OF JUDGEMENT

Lindblad, I., *Pamela Hansford Johnson*, 154-61.

Quigly, I., *Pamela Hansford Johnson*, 41-3.

THE FAMILY PATTERN

Lindblad, I., *Pamela Hansford Johnson*, 60-3.

GIRDLE OF VENUS

Lindblad, I., *Pamela Hansford Johnson*, 56-50.

THE GOOD HUSBAND

Lindblad, I., *Pamela Hansford Johnson*, 164-5, 169-74.

THE GOOD LISTENER

Lindblad, I., *Pamela Hansford Johnson*, 164-9.

HERE TODAY

Linblad, I., *Pamela Hansford Johnson*, 32-9.

THE HOLIDAY FRIEND

Linblad, I., *Pamela Hansford Johnson*, 98-107.

THE HONOURS BOARD

Linblad, I., *Pamela Hansford Johnson*, 161-4.

THE HUMBLER CREATION

Lindblad, I., *Pamela Hansford Johnson*, 133-40.
Quigly, I., *Pamela Hansford Johnson*, 31-3.

AN IMPOSSIBLE MARRIAGE

Lindblad, I., *Pamela Hansford Johnson*, 120-4.
Quigly, I., *Pamela Hansford Johnson*, 31-3.

THE LAST RESORT

Allen, W., *Modern Novel*, 258-60.
Linblad, I., *Pamela Hansford Johnson* 126-33.
Quigly, I., *Pamela Hansford Johnson*, 33-5.

THE MONUMENT

Linblad, I., *Pamela Hansford Johnson*, 44-7, 50-5.

NIGHT AND SILENCE, WHO IS HERE? AN AMERICAN COMEDY

Lindblad, I., *Pamela Hansford Johnson*, 146-9.
Webster, Harvey, C., "Farce and Faith," *KR* 25 (Autumn, 1963): 747-51.

THE PHILISTINES

Lindblad, I., *Pamela Hansford Johnson*, 110-15.
Quigly, I., *Pamela Hansford Johnson*, 26-8.

A SUMMER TO DECIDE (See also TRILOGY)

Lindblad, I., *Pamela Hansford Johnson*, 73-5, 78-84.

THE SURVIVAL OF THE FITTEST

Lindblad, I., *Pamela Hansford Johnson*, 47-50, 52-5.
Novak, Robert, "Dylan Thomas Hidden In a Novel," *Windless Orchard* 27 (176): 14-20.

THIS BED THY CENTRE

Lindblad, I., *Pamela Hansford Johnson*, 29-33.

Quigly, I., *Pamela Hansford Johnson*, 9-13.

TOO DEAR FOR MY POSSESSING (See also TRILOGY)

Lindblad, I., *Pamela Hansford Johnson*, 68-71, 79-83.

TRILOGY

Lindblad, I., *Pamela Hansford Johnson*, 64-84.
Quigly, I., *Pamela Hansford Johnson*, 17-23.

THE TROJAN BROTHERS

Lindblad, I., *Pamela Hansford Johnson*, 91-8.
Quigly, I., *Pamela Hansford Johnson*, 24-6.

THE UNSPEAKABLE SKIPTON

Allen, W., *Modern Novel*, 200.
Lindblad, I., *Pamela Hansford Johnson*, 141-6.
Quigly, I., *Pamela Hansford Johnson*, 35-6.
Raymond, John, "A Corvo of Our Day," *Doge of Dover*, 158-63.

WINTER QUARTERS

Lindblad, I., *Pamela Hansford Johnson*, 64-7.
Quigly, I., *Pamela Hansford Johnson*, 23-4.

WORLD'S END

Lindblad, I., *Pamela Hansford Johnson*, 42-4.

JOHNSTON, JENNIFER, 1930-

GENERAL

Benstock, Shari, "The Masculine World of Jennifer Johnston," in Staley, T. F., ed., *Twentieth-Century Women Novelists*, 191-217.
McMahon, Sean, "Anglo-Irish Attitudes: The Novels of Jennifer Johnston," *Eire* 10, iii (Autumn, 1975): 137-41.

THE CAPTAINS AND THE KINGS

Benstock, Shari, "The Masculine World of Jennifer Johnston," in Staley, T. F., ed., *Twentieth-Century Women Novelists*, 211-15.

THE GATES

Benstock, Shari, "The Masculine World of Jennifer Johnston," in Staley, T. F., ed., *Twentieth-Century Women Novelists*, 199-205.

HOW MANY MILES TO BABYLON?

Benstock, Shari, "The Masculine World of Jennifer Johnston," in Staley, T. F., ed., *Twentieth-Century Women Novelists*, 193-9.

THE OLD JEST

Benstock, Shari, "The Masculine World of Jennifer Johnston," in Staley, T. F., ed., *Twentieth-Century Women Novelists*, 199-205.

SHADOWS ON OUR SKINS

Benstock, Shari, "The Masculine World of Jennifer Johnston," in Staley, T. F., ed., *Twentieth-Century Women Novelists*, 205-11.

JONES, GAYL, 1949-

GENERAL

Bell, Roseann P., "Gayl Jones: A Voice in the Whirlwind," *Studia Africana* 1, i (1977): 99-107.

Harper, Michael S., "Gayl Jones: An Interview," *MR* 18 (1977): 692-715. Also in Harper, M. S., and R. B. Stepto, eds., *Chant of Saints*, 352-75.

Rowell, Charles H., "An Interview with Gayl Jones," *Callaloo* 5, iii (Oct., 1982): 32-53.

Tate, Claudia, "An Interview with Gayl Jones," *BALF* 13, iv (1979): 142-8.

Ward, Jerry W., Jr., "Escape from Trublem: The Fiction of Gayl Jones," *Callaloo* 5, iii (Oct., 1982): 95-104.

CORREGIDORA

Barthold, B. J., *Black Time*, 124-7.

Bell, Roseann P., "Gayle Jones Takes a Look at CORREGIDORA—An Interview," in Bell, R. P., et al., eds., *Sturdy Black Bridges*, 282-7.

Burwell, Sherri L., "The Soul of Black Women: The Hermeneutical Method of Analysis as Applied to the Novel CORREGIDORA," *DAI* 39 (1979): 6111B.

Harris, Janice. "Gayl Jones' CORREGIDORA," *Frontiers* 5, iii (Fall, 1980): 1-5.

Lee, Valerie G., "The Use of Folktalk in Novels by Black Women Writers," *CLAJ* 23, iii (Mar., 1980): 270-1.

Pullin, Faith, in Lee, A. R., ed., *Black Fiction*, 200-1.

Tate, Claudia C., "CORREGIDORA: Ursa's Blues Medley," *BALF* 13, iv (1979): 139-41.

EVA'S MAN

Byerman, Keith, "Black Vortex: The Gothic Structure of EVA'S MAN," *MELUS* 7, iv (1980): 93-101.

_____, "Intense Behaviors: The Use of the Grotesque in THE BLUEST EYE and EVA'S MAN," *CLAJ* 25, iv (June, 1982): 447-57.

JONES, GLYN, 1905-

GENERAL

Norris, L., *Glyn Jones*.

THE ISLAND OF APPLES

Norris, L., *Glyn Jones*, 49-57.

THE LEARNING LARK

Norris, L., *Glyn Jones*, 44-9.

THE VALLEY, THE CITY, THE VILLAGE

Norris, L., *Glyn Jones*, 34-44.

JONES, GWYN, 1907-

GENERAL

Price, C., *Gwyn Jones*.

THE FLOWERS BENEATH THE SCYTHE

Price, C., *Gwyn Jones*, 43-5.

GARLAND OF BAYS

Price, C., *Gwyn Jones*, 14-17.

THE NINE DAYS' WONDER

Price, C., *Gwyn Jones*, 13-14.

RICHARD SAVAGE

Price, C., *Gwyn Jones*, 6-9.

TIMES LIKE THESE

Price, C., *Gwyn Jones*, 9-13.

THE WALK HOME

Price, C., *Gwyn Jones*, 45-6.

JONES, JAMES, 1921-1977

GENERAL

Aldrich, Nelson W., Jr., "The Art of Fiction XXIII: James Jones," *ParisR* 20 (Autumn-Winter, 1958-59): 34-55. Also in *Writers at Work*, 3rd ser., 231-50.

Aldridge, John W., "Twosomes and Threesomes in Gary Paree," *SatR* 54 (Feb. 13, 1971): 23-6. Also as "James Jones: Puberty in Paris," in Aldridge, J. W., *Devil in the Fire*, 241-8.

Bazelon, David, "In Memoriam: In Defense," *Salmagundi* 38-39 (Summer-Fall, 1977): 151-2.

Carter, Steven R., "James Jones, An American Master: A Study of His Mystical, Philosophical, Social, and Artistic Views," *DAI* 36 (1976): 5292A-93A.

Engel, Bernard F., "Taps for Sergeant Jones," *SSMLN* 7, ii (1977): 6-8.

Giles, J. R., *James Jones*.

Jones, James, and William Styron, "Two Writers Talk It Over," *Esquire* 60, i (July, 1963): 57-9.

Sheed, Wilfrid, "The Jones Boy Forever," *Atlantic Monthly* 219 (June, 1967): 68-72.

Stevenson, David L., in Balakian, N., and C. Simmons, eds., *Creative Present*, 195-206+.

Volpe, Edmond L., in Moore, H. T., ed., *Contemporary American Novelists*, 106-12.

Whitehorn, Michael A., "Jones and Cozzens: Divergent Views of Military Leadership," *DAI* 38 (1977): 1398A.

FROM HERE TO ETERNITY

Adams, Richard P., "A Second Look at FROM HERE TO ETER-
NITY," *CE* 17 (1956): 205-10.

Bryant, Jerry H., "The Last of the Social Protest Writers," *ArQ*
19 (Winter, 1963): 320-3.

_____, *Open Decision*, 123-5, 128-30, 138-9.

Burress, Lee A., Jr., "James Jones on Folklore and Ballad," *CE*
21 (1959): 161-5.

De Voto, Bernard, "Dull Novels Make Dull Reading," *Harper's*
202 (June, 1951): 67-70.

Dinkins, Paul, "FROM HERE TO ETERNITY and the New
Sentimentality," *CathW* 173 (Sept., 1951): 422-8.

Eisinger, C. E., *Fiction of the Forties*, 41-3.

Fiedler, Leslie, "Dead-End Werther: The Bum as American
Culture Hero," *An End to Innocence*, Boston: Beacon Pr., 1955,
183-90.

_____, "James Jones' Dead-End Young Werther," *Ctary* 12
(1951): 252-5.

Gardiner, H. C., "'Damned' is the Missing Word," *In All Conscience*, 17-21. Also in *America* (Mar. 10, 1951): 672-4.

Geismar, M., *American Moderns*, 225-34.

Giles, J. R., *James Jones*, 36-68.

Glicksberg, Charles I., "Racial Attitudes in FROM HERE TO
ETERNITY," *Phylon* 14 (1953): 384-9.

Griffith, Ben W., Jr., "Rear Rank Robin Hood: James Jones's Folk
Hero," *GaR* 10 (1956): 41-6.

Hassan, I., *Radical Innocence*, 83-6.

Healey, Robert C., in Gardiner, H. C., ed., *Fifty Years of the
American Novel*, 263-4.

Jones, P., *War and the Novelist*, 32-44.

Macauley, Robie, "Private Jones's Revenge," *KR* 13 (Summer,
1951): 526-9.

Prescott, O., *In My Opinion*, 159-62.

Stevenson, David L., in Balakian, N., and C. Simmons, eds.,
Creative Present, 200-3+.

Volpe, Edmond L., in Moore, H. T., ed., *Contemporary American
Novelists*, 108-9.

Walsh, J., *American War Literature*, 142-7.

GO TO THE WIDOW-MAKER

Giles, J. R., *James Jones*, 147-61.

Glicksberg, C. I., *Sexual Revolution in Modern American Literature*,
214-22.

Sheed, Wilfrid, "The Jones Boy Forever," *Atlantic Monthly* 219
(June, 1967): 68-72.

THE MERRY MONTH OF MAY

Aldridge, John W., "Twosomes and Threesomes in Gray
Paree," *SatR* 54 (Feb. 13, 1971): 23-6. Also as "James Jones in
Paris," in Aldridge, J. W., *Devil in the Fire*, 246-8.

Giles, J. R., *James Jones*, 161-3.

THE PISTOL

Giles, J. R., *James Jones*, 91-100.

Shepherd, Allen, "'A Deliberately Symbolic Little Novella':
James Jones's THE PISTOL," *SDR* 10, i (Spring, 1972): 111-19.

SOME CAME RUNNING

Geismar, M., *American Moderns*, 234-8.

Giles, J. R., *James Jones*, 69-90.

THE THIN RED LINE

Allen, Donald A., "The Way it Was," *Reporter* 27 (Oct. 25, 1962):
61-5.

Bryant, J. H., *Open Decision*, 154-6.

Giles, J. R., *James Jones*, 122-46.

Jones, P., *War and the Novelist*, 171-7.

Michel-Michot, Paulette, "Jones's THE THIN RED LINE: The
End of Innocence," *RLV* 30, i (1964): 15-26.

Pritchett, V. S., "American Soldiers," *NStat* (Feb. 8, 1963): 207.

Volpe, Edmond L., in Moore, H. T., ed., *Contemporary American
Novelists*, 110-12.

A TOUCH OF DANGER

Carter, Steven R., "Karma and Spiritual Responsibility in James
Jones' A TOUCH OF DANGER," *ArmD* 13 (1980): 230-6.

Giles, J. R., *James Jones*, 164-5.

WHISTLE

Giles, J. R., *James Jones*, 174-95.

BIBLIOGRAPHY

Giles, J. R., *James Jones*, 215-21.

JONES, MADISON, 1925-

GENERAL

Noble, Don, "'The World Would Be Better Off with a Sterner
Conscience': A Talk with Madison Jones," *Soc. for Fine Arts
Rev.* 4, ii (Summer, 1982): 14-15.

A BURIED LAND

Hiers, John T., "Buried Graveyards: Warren's FLOOD and
Jones's A BURIED LAND," *ELWIU* 2, i (Spring, 1975): 97-
104.

AN EXILE

Sullivan, Walter, in Core, G., ed., *Southern Fiction Today*, 1-5.
Also in Sullivan, W., *Death by Melancholy*, 97-102.

THE INNOCENT

Vauthier, Simone, "Gratuitous Hypothesis: A Reading of Madison Jones' THE INNOCENT," *RANAM* 7 (1974): 191-219.

BIBLIOGRAPHY

Gretlund, Jan N., "Madison Jones: A Bibliography," *BB* 39, iii
(Sept., 1982): 117-20.

JONES, RICHARD, 1926-

GENERAL

Barnes, Jane, "Art and Identity in Richard Jones' Work," *VQR* 58, iv (Autumn, 1982): 646-63.

LIVING AT THE 25TH HOUR

Barnes, Jane, "Art and Identity in Richard Jones' Work," *VQR* 58, iv (Autumn, 1982): 659-63.

THE THREE SUITORS

Barnes, Jane, "Art and Identity in Richard Jones' Work," *VQR* 58, iv (Autumn, 1982): 649-55.

A WAY OUT

Barnes, Jane, "Art and Identity in Richard Jones' Work," *VQR* 58, iv (Autumn, 1982): 655-9.

JONG, ERICA, 1942-

GENERAL

Balderston, Jean, Carol Jannings, and Mary Kathryn Stillwell, "Craft Interview with Erica Jong," *NYQ* 16 (1974): 23-48.

Clark, John R., "A Humble Predacity upon the Corpus of Erica Jong," *Maledicta* 1 (1977): 211-13.

McNeese, Gretchen, "Playboy Interview: Erica Jong," *Playboy* 22, ix (1975): 61-78, 202-3.

Toth, Emily, "Dorothy Parker, Erica Jong, and New Feminist Humor," *RFI* 3, ii-iii (1977-78): 77-83.

FANNY: BEING THE TRUE HISTORY OF FANNY HACKABOUT-JONES

Warren, Leland E., "The True History of the Adventures of Fanny Hackabout-Jones," *ECLife* 6, i (Oct., 1980): 106-9.

FEAR OF FLYING

Betsky-Zweig, S., "The Female Flight," *DQR* 6, iii (1976): 247-56.

Cohen, Sarah B., "The Jewish Literary Comediennes," in Cohen, S. B., ed., *Comic Relief*, 177-9.

Diamond, Arlyn, "Flying from Work," *Frontiers* 2, iii (Fall, 1977): 18-23.

Harder, Kelsie B., "Onomastic Centrality," *LOS* 7 (1980): 41-5.

Mickelson, Anne Z., "Erica Jong: Flying or Grounded?" *Reaching Out*, 35-40.

Nitzsche, Jane C., "'Isadora Icarus': The Mythic Unity of Erica Jong's FEAR OF FLYING," *RUS* 64, i (1978): 89-100.

Reardon, Joan, "FEAR OF FLYING: Developing the Feminist Novel," *IJWS* 1 (1978): 306-20.

Stewart, G., *New Myths*, 81-4, 161-6.

Toth, Emily, "Dorothy Parker, Erica Jong, and New Feminist Humor," *RFI* 3, ii-iii (1977-78): 77-81.

HOW TO SAVE YOUR OWN LIFE

Harder, Kelsie B., "Onomastic Centrality," *LOS* 7 (1980): 41-5.

Mickelson, Anne Z., "Erica Jong: Flying or Grounded?" *Reaching Out*, 40-7.

KELLEY, WILLIAM MELVIN, 1937-

GENERAL

Weyant, Jill, "The Kelley Saga: Violence in America," *CLAJ* 19, ii (Dec., 1975): 210-20.

Weyl, Donald M., "The Vision of Man in the Novels of William Melvin Kelley," *Crit* 15, iii (1974): 15-33.

DEM

Baker, Houston A., Jr., "A View of William Melvin Kelley's DEM," *Obsidian* 3, ii (1977): 12-16.

Klotman, Phyllis R., "An Examination of the Black Confidence Man in Two Black Novels: THE MAN WHO CRIED I AM and DEM," *AL* 44, iv (Jan., 1973): 596-611.

Rosenblatt, R., *Black Fiction*, 142-50.

Weyl, Donald M., "The Vision of Man in the Novels of William Melvin Kelley," *Crit* 15, iii (1974): 28-32.

A DIFFERENT DRUMMER

Beards, Richard, "Parody as Tribute: William Melvin Kelley's A DIFFERENT DRUMMER and Faulkner," *SBL* 5, iii (Winter, 1974): 25-8.

Bigsby, C. W. E., in Lee, A. R., ed., *Black Fiction*, 157-9.

Bruck, Peter, "Romance as Epistemological Design: William Melvin Kelley's A DIFFERENT DRUMMER," in Bruck, P., and W. Karrer, eds., *Afro-American Novel Since 1960*, 103-21.

Faulkner, Howard, "The Uses of Tradition: William Melvin Kelley's A DIFFERENT DRUMMER," *MFS* 21 (Winter, 1975-76): 535-42.

Gayle, A., Jr., *Way of the New World*, 302-5.

Giles, James R., "Revolution and Myth: Kelley's A DIFFERENT DRUMMER and Gaines' THE AUTOBIOGRAPHY OF MISS JANE PITTMAN," *Minority Voices* (Pennsylvania State Un.) 1, ii (1977): 39-48.

Ingrasci, Hugh J., "Strategic Withdrawal or Retreat: Deliverance from Racial Oppression in Kelley's A DIFFERENT DRUMMER and Faulkner's GO DOWN, MOSES," *SBL* 6, iii (1975): 1-6.

Jaab, Josef, "The Drop of Patience of the American Negro: W. M. Kelley; A DIFFERENT DRUMMER (1959), A DROP OF PATIENCE (1965)," *PP* 12 (1969): 162-7.

Klotman, Phyllis R., "The Passive Resistant in A DIFFERENT DRUMMER, DAY OF ABSENCE and MANY THOUSAND GONE," *SBL* 3, iii (Autumn, 1972): 7-12.

Nadeau, Robert L., "Black Jesus: A Study of Kelley's A DIFFERENT DRUMMER," *SBL* 2, ii (Summer, 1971): 13-15.

Schraufnagel, N., *From Apology to Protest*, 174-6.

Weyl, Donald M., "The Vision of Man in the Novels of William Melvin Kelley," *Crit* 15, iii (1974): 15-22.

Williams, Gladys M., "Technique as Evaluation of Subject in A DIFFERENT DRUMMER," *CLAJ* 19 (1975): 221-37.

A DROP OF PATIENCE

Jaab, Josef, "The Drop of Patience of the American Negro: W. M. Kelley, A DIFFERENT DRUMMER (1959), A DROP OF PATIENCE (1965)," *PP* 12 (1969): 167-9.

Weyl, Donald M., "The Vision of Man in the Novels of William Melvin Kelley," *Crit* 15, iii (1974): 26-8.

DUNFORDS TRAVELS EVERYWHERES

Eckley, Grace, "The Awakening of Mr. Afrinnegan: Kelley's DUNFORDS TRAVELS EVERYWHERES and Joyce's FINNEGAN'S WAKE," *Obsidian* 1, ii (1975): 27-41.

Gayle, A., Jr., *Way of the New World*, 305-9.

Sy, Marieme, "Dream and Language in DUNFORDS TRAVELS EVERYWHERES," *CLAJ* 25, iv (June, 1982); 458-67.

Werner, C. H., *Paradoxical Resolutions*, 108-14.

KENEALLY, THOMAS (MICHAEL), 1935-

GENERAL

Beston, John B., "The Hero's 'Fear of Freedom' in Keneally," *ALS* 5, iv (Oct., 1972): 374-87.

————, "An Interview with Thomas Keneally," *WLWE* 12 (1973): 48-56.

————, "Novelist's Vital Professionalism," *Hemisphere* 17 (Oct., 1973): 23-6.

Brady, Veronica, "The Most Frightening Rebellion: The Recent Novels of Thomas Keneally," *Meanjin* 38, i (April, 1979): 74-86.

————, "The Utopian Impulse in Australian Literature, with Special Reference to P. White and T. Keneally," *Caliban* 14 (1977): 109-21.

Breitinger, Eckhard, "Thomas Keneally's Historical Novels," *Comonwealth Newsl.* (Aarhus) 10 (1976): 16-20. [Not seen.]

Burns, Robert, "Out of Context: A Study of Thomas Keneally's Novels," *ALS* 4, i (May, 1969): 31-48.

Cantrell, Kerin, "Perspective on Thomas Keneally," *Southerly* 28, i (1968): 54-67.

Clancy, L. J., "Conscience and Corruption: Thomas Keneally's Three Novels," *Meanjin* 27, i (1968): 33-41.

Fabre, Michel, "Thomas Keneally: An Interview," *Caliban* 14 (1977): 101-8.

————, "Voices and Gossip: Destiny and History in the Latter Novels of Thomas Keneally," *Caliban* 14 (1977): 91-9.

Hospital, Janette T., "Keneally's Reluctant Prophets: Analysis and an Interview with the Novelist," *Cweal* (May 7, 1976): 295-300.

McInherny, Frances, "Thomas Keneally's 'Innocent' Men," *ALS* 10, i (May, 1981): 57-66.

————, "Woman and Myth in Thomas Keneally's Fiction," *Meanjin* 40, ii (July, 1981): 248-58.

Mitchell, Adrian, "Thomas Keneally and the Scheme of Things," *ALS* 9, i (May, 1979): 3-13.

Ryan, J. S., "Some Convict Sources in Keneally and FitzGerald," *ALS* 9, iii (May, 1980): 385-7.

Vargo, Edward P., S. V. D., "Struggling with a Bugaboo: The Priest-Character in Achebe and Greene and Keneally," in Narasimhaiah, C. D., ed., *Awakened Conscience*, 284-93.

BLOOD RED, SISTER ROSE

Fabre, Michel, "Voices and Gossip: Destiny and History in the Later Novels of Thomas Keneally," *Caliban* 14 (1977): 92-9.

Sait, J. E., "Thomas Keneally's BLOOD RED, SISTER ROSE and Robertston Davies' FIFTH BUSINESS: Two Modern Literary Hagiographies," *JCL* 16, i (1981): 96-108.

BRING LARKS AND HEROES

Beston, John B., "The Hero's 'Fear of Freedom' in Keneally," *ALS* 5, iv (Oct., 1972): 374-87.

Brady, Charles A., "BRING LARKS AND HEROES by Thomas Keneally," *Eire* 3, iii (1968): 169-72.

Clancy, L. J., "Conscience and Corruption: Thomas Keneally's Three Novels," *Meanjin* 27, i (1968): 37-41.

Geering, R. G., *Recent Fiction*, 15-18.

Kiernan, Brian, "Thomas Keneally and the Australian Novel: A Study of BRING LARKS AND HEROES," *Southerly* 28 (1968): 189-99. Also in Kiernan, B., *Images of Society and Nature*, 148-58.

McInherny, Frances, "BRING LARKS AND HEROES: The Moral and the Dream," *Southerly* 37 (1977): 68-75.

Molloy, F. C., "An Irish Conflict in BRING LARKS AND HEROES," *ALS* 7 (1976): 389-98.

Monk, Patricia, "Eden Upside-Down: Thomas Keneally's BRING LARKS AND HEROES as Anti-Pastoral," *WLWE* 21, ii (Summer, 1982): 297-303.

Scheckter, John, "Australia Lost and Founded: Versions of the First Settlement in Two Modern Novels," *ACLALSB* 6, i (Nov., 1982): 27-41.

THE CHANT OF JIMMIE BLACKSMITH

Clancy, Jack, "THE CHANT OF JIMMIE BLACKSMITH: The Film and the Book," *ALS* 9 (1979): 95-7.

Cotter, Michael, "The Image of the Aboriginal in Three Modern Australian Novels," *Meanjin* 36, iv (Dec., 1977): 582-5.

Daniel, Helen, "Purpose and the Racial Outsider: BURN and THE CHANT OF JIMMIE BLACKSMITH," *Southerly* 38 (1978): 25-43.

Frow, John, "The Chant of Thomas Keneally," *ALS* 10, iii (May, 1982): 291-9.

Geering, R. G., *Recent Fiction*, 28-30.

Goldsmith, M. A., "Thomas Keneally's THE CHANT OF JIMMIE BLACKSMITH and Frank Clune's JIMMY GOVERNOR," *Westerly* ii (1976): 43-9.

Keneally, Tom, "My Fiction and the Aboriginal," 32-45 in Amirthanayagam, Guy, ed., *Writers in East-West Encounter: New Cultural Bearings*, London: Macmillan, 1982.

Kiernan, Brian, "Fable or Novel? The Development of Thomas Keneally," *Meanjin* 31, iv (Dec., 1972): 489-93.

Ramson, W. S., "THE CHANT OF JIMMIE BLACKSMITH: Taking Cognisance of Keneally," in Ramson, W. S., ed., *Australian Experience*, 325-44.

Reynolds, Henry, "Jimmy Governor and Jimmie Blacksmith," *ALS* 9, i (May, 1979): 14-25.

Rutherford, Anna, "Reappraisal of a Myth: THE CHANT OF JIMMIE BLACKSMITH," *CM* 1 (1974-75): 104-15.

Sturm, Terry, "Thomas Keneally and Australian Racism: THE CHANT OF JIMMIE BLACKSMITH," *Southerly* 33 (1973): 261-74.

Tiffin, Chris, "Victims Black and White," in Hamilton, K. G., ed., *Studies in the Recent Australian Novel*, 121-40.

THE FEAR

Cantrell, Kerin, "Perspective on Thomas Keneally," *Southerly* 28, i (1968): 63-6.

Clancy, L. J., "Conscience and Corruption: Thomas Keneally's Three Novels," *Meanjin* 27, i (1968): 36-7.

Geering, R. G., *Recent Fiction*, 10-13.

GOSSIP FROM THE FOREST

Fabre, Michel, "Voices and Gossip: Destiny and History in the Later Novels of Thomas Keneally," *Caliban* 14 (1977): 92-9.

PASSENGER

MacLeod, Mark, "Thomas Keneally's PASSENGER and the Middle Voice," *LCrit* 15, iii-iv (1980): 183-94.

THE PLACE AT WHITTON

Clancy, L. J. "Conscience and Corruption: Thomas Keneally's Three Novels," *Meanjin* 27, i (1968): 34-5.

SEASON IN PURGATORY

Rutherford, Anna, "SEASON IN PURGATORY: 'Mere Narrative'," *LHY* 18, i (1977): 211-17. Also in Gowda, H., H. Anniah, eds., *Powre Above Powres*, 211-17.

THE SURVIVOR

Geering, R. G., *Recent Fiction*, 24-6.

Keneally, Thomas M., "Origin of a Novel," *Hemisphere* 13 (Oct., 1969): 9-13.

THREE CHEERS FOR THE PARACLETE

Beston, John B., "The Hero's 'Fear of Freedom' in Keneally," *ALS* 5, iv (Oct., 1972):374-87.

Geering, R. G., *Recent Fiction*, 22-4.

Vargo, Edward P., S. B. D., "Struggling with a Bugaboo: The Priest-Character in Achebe and Greene and Keneally," *FJS* 9 (1976): 1-13 *passim*. Also in Narasimhaiah, C. D., ed., *Awakened Conscience: Studies in Commonwealth Literature*, New Delhi: Sterling Publishers, 1978, 284-94.

Wilding, Michael, "Two Cheers for Keneally," *Southerly* 29, ii (1969): 131-8.

BIBLIOGRAPHY

Ehrhardt, Marianne, comp., "Thomas Keneally: A Checklist," *ALS* 9, i (May, 1979): 98-117.

KENTFIELD, ALVIN, 1924-

THE ALCHEMIST'S VOYAGE

Burns, Landon C., "Man as Mariner: Kentfield's THE ALCHEMIST'S VOYAGE," *Crit* 18, i (1976): 92-104.

KEROUAC, JACK, 1922-1969

GENERAL

See Issues of *Moody Street Irregulars*.

Allen, Eliot D., "That Was No Lady ... That Was Jack Kerouac's Girl," in Langford, R. E., ed., *Essays in Modern American Literature*, 97-102. Also in Donaldson, S., ed., *Jack Kerouac: ON THE ROAD*, 504-9.

Allen, Steve, "Steve Allen Remembers Kerouac," *MSI* 8 (1980): 23.

Anctil, Pierre, "Jack Kerouac and the Problem of Joual Aesthetics," *MSI* 11 (Spring-Summer, 1982): 3-6.

Ashida, Margaret E., "Frogs and Frozen Zen," *PrS* 34 (1960): 199-206.

Ball, Vernon F., "Of Glory Obscured: Beatific Vision in the Narratives of Jack Kerouac," *DAI* 38 (177): 258A.

Bartlett, Lee, "The Dionysian Vision of Jack Kerouac," in Bartlett, L., ed., *Beats*, 115-26.

Basinski, Michael, "Ti Jean in Lowell," *MSI* 1, i (1978): 13-15.

Beaulieu, V. L., *Jack Kerouac*.

Berrigan, Ted, "The Art of Fiction XLI: Jack Kerouac," *ParisR* 11 (Summer, 1968): 60-105. Also in Plimpton, George, ed., *Writers at Work: The Paris Review Interviews*, Fourth Series, N.Y.: Viking, 1976. Also in Donaldson, S., ed., *Jack Kerouac; ON THE ROAD*, 538-72.

Brouillette, Paul, "Evaluation of Kerouac's Duluoz Legend," *MSI* 4 (1979): 9-11.

Burns, Jim, "Jivin' with Jack the Bellboy," *MSI* 3 (1979): 3-5.

Campbell, James, "Kerouac & Co.," *New Edinburgh Review* 47 (1979): 11-14.

Casey, John T., "Critical Analysis of Rhetorical Choices Made in the Creation of Two Differing Written Modes: A Biographical Sketch and a Historical Fiction," *DAI* 43 (1982): 1862A.

Cassady, Carolyn, "Heart Beef," *MSI* 9 (Winter-Spring, 1981): 14-16.

Challis, Chris, "England Digs Me," *MSI* 10 (Fall, 1981): 9-11.

_____, "From the Mad Search for Kicks to the Athlete's Dream," *MSI* 12 (Fall, 1982): 10-17.

Charters, Ann, "Kerouac's Literary Method and Experiments: The Evidence of the Manuscript Notebooks in the Berg Collection," *BRH* 84, iv (Winter, 1981): 431-50.

Chessey, Bob, "Jack London's Influence on the Life-Style of Jack Kerouac," *JLoN* 15 (1982): 158-63.

Christy, Jim, "Jack and Jazz: Woodsmoke and Trains," *MSI* 8 (1980): 10-11.

Dardess, George, "Jack Kerouac as Religious Teacher," *MSI* 1, i (Winter, 1978): 4-6.

_____, "The Logic of Spontaneitiy: A Reconsideration of Kerouac's 'Spontaneous Prose Method'," *Boundary* 3, iii (Spring, 1975): 729-43.

Duffey, Bernard, "The Three Worlds of Jack Kerouac," in Waldmeir, W. W., ed., *Recent American Fiction*, 175-84.

Frohock, W. M., *Strangers to this Ground*, 132-47.

Ginsberg, Allen, "A Few Words on Kerouac's Merit: From a Letter to Dennis McNally," *MSI* 2 (Summer, 1978): 12.

Gribetz, Sid, "Kerouac's Angels," *MSI* 4 (1979): 7-8.

Henry, James, "Thomas Wolfe: Jack Kerouac's Alter-Ego," *TWN* 4, i (1980): 24-6.

Hipkiss, R. A., *Jack Kerouac.*

Holder, Wayne, "The Road Goes on Forever," *MSI* 3 (1979): 6.

Huebel, H. R., *Jack Kerouac.*

Hunt, T., *Kerouac's Crooked Road.*

————, "Off the Road: The Literary Maturation of Jack Kerouac," *DAI* 36 (1975): 2821A.

Jones, Granville H., "Jack Kerouac and the American Conscience," in Carnegie Institute of Technology, *Lectures on Modern Novelists,* 25-39. Also in Donaldson, S., ed., *Jack Kerouac: ON THE ROAD,* 485-503.

Kerouac, Jack, "Beatific: On the Origins of a Generation," *Encounter* 13 (Aug., 1959): 57-61.

Krim, Seymour, "King of the Beats," *Cweal* 69 (Jan. 2, 1959): 359-60.

McNally, Dennis S., "Desolation Angel: Jack Kerouac in America, 1922-1969," *DAI* 39 (1978): 1035A.

Morrissette, Armand S., "A Catholic's View of Kerouac," *MSI* 5 (1979): 7-8.

Nicosia, Gerald, "His Absence Was All There Was: A Conversation with Jan Kerouac on the Subject of Her Re-Famous Dad," *MSI* 6-7 (Winter-Spring, 1980): 3-5.

————, "Survivors of the Deluge: A North Beach Field Report Ten Years after the Last Disaster of the Sixties," *MSI* 6-7 (1980): 8-10.

————, "Travels with Kerouac: How I Finally Got on the Road," *MSI* 8 (Summer-Fall, 1980): 14-16.

Olson, R. H., "Headed for the Pure Land," *MSI* 12 (Fall, 1982): 3-4.

Pendergast, Jay, "On Kerouac," *MSI* 6-7 (Winter-Spring, 1980): 19.

Poteet, Maurice, *"Le Devoir* Dossier on Kerouac," *MSI* 11 (Spring-Summer, 1982): 14-16.

————, "The 'Little (Known) Literature' of Kerouac's 'Little Canada'," *MSI* 5 (1979): 4-6.

Ross, Andrew M., "Crisis: The Personal versus the Social," *MSI* 4 (1979): 4-6.

Sorrell, Richard S., "Novelists and Ethnicity: Jack Kerouac and Grace Metalious as Franco-Americans," *MELUS* 9, i (Spring, 1982): 37-52.

————, "Ti Jean and Papa Lee: Jack Kerouac's Relationship with His French-Canadian Father," *MSI* 11 (Spring-Summer, 1982): 10-12.

Stern, Elaine M., "The Conservative Response amidst Decades of Change: Jack Kerouac and William Saroyan," *DAI* 37 (1977): 7755A.

Stevenson, David L., in Balakian, N., and C. Simmons, eds., *Creative Present,* 195-200, 206-12.

Tallman, Warren, "Kerouac's Sound," *Open Letter* (Third Series, 6) (1976): 7-19. Also in *TamR* No. 11 (Spring, 1959): 58-74. Also in *EvR* 4, No. 11 (Jan.-Feb., 1960): 153-69. Also in Donaldson, S., ed., *Jack Kerouac: ON THE ROAD,* 513-30. Also in Parkinson, T., ed., *Casebook on the Beat,* 215-29.

Tytell, J., *Naked Angels,* 140-211.

Vaidyanathan, T. G., "Jack Kerouac and Existentialist Anxiety," *OJES* No. 2 (1962): 61-6.

Walsh, Joy, "Jack Kerouac: An Alien in America," *MSI* 1 (1978): 8-10.

————, "Kerouac: A Reichian Interpretation," *MSI* 2 (1978): 3-5.

Webb, Howard W., Jr., "The Singular Worlds of Jack Kekrouac," in Moore, H. T., ed., *Contemporary American Novelists,* 120-33.

Williams, Bruce K., "The Shrouded Traveler on the Road: Death and the Work of Jack Kerouac," *DAI* 38 (1977): 2137A.

Woods, Crawford, "Jack Kerouac," *NRep* 167 (Dec. 2, 1972): 26-30.

Woolfson, Peter, "The French-Canadian Heritage of Jack Kerouac as Seen in His Autobiographical Works," *RLLR* 5, i (1976): 35-43.

BIG SUR

Glicksberg, C. I., *Sexual Revolution in Modern American Literature,* 162-6.

Tytell, J., *Naked Angels,* 206-9.

BOOK OF DREAMS

Montgomery, John, "Draft Index to BOOK OF DREAMS: A Name Index with Kerouac Topic Index," *MSI* 1, i (Winter, 1978): 12; 1, ii (Summer, 1978): 7-9.

Moore, Dave, "BOOK OF DREAMS: A Name Index," *MSI* 8 (Summer-Fall, 1980): 21-2.

Parker, Edie K., "Dave Moore's 'BOOK OF DREAMS: A Name Index': Addenda and Annotations," *MSI* 10 (Fall, 1981): 18-21.

DESOLATION ANGELS

Beaulieu, V. L., *Jack Kerouac,* 107-12.

Blackburn, William, "Han Shan Gets Drunk with the Butchers: Kerouac's Buddhism in ON THE ROAD, THE DHARMA BUMS, and DESOLATION ANGELS," *LE&W* 21, i-lv (Jan.-Dec., 1977): 9-22.

Mazzocco, Robert, "Our Gang," *NYRB* (May 20, 1965): 8-9.

Spender, Stephen, "Traditional vs. Underground Novels," in Encyclopaedia Britannica, *Great Ideas Today, 1965,* 194-6.

Wakefield, Dan, "Jack Kerouac Comes Home," *Atlantic Monthly* 216 (July, 1965): 69-72.

THE DHARMA BUMS

Bellman, Samuel, "On the Mountain," *ChiR* 13 (Winter-Spring, 1959): 68-72.

Blackburn, William, "Han Shan Gets Drunk with the Butchers: Kerouac's Buddhism in ON THE ROAD, THE DHARMA BUMS, and DESOLATION ANGELS," *LE&W* 21, i-iv (Jan.-Dec., 1977): 9-22.

Champney, Freeman, "Beat-up or Beatific?" *AR* 19 (Spring, 1959): 117-20.

Feied, F., *No Pie in the Sky,* 73-80 *passim.*

Feldman, Irving, "Stuffed Dharma," *Ctary* 26 (Dec., 1958): 543-4.

Glicksberg, C. I., *Sexual Revolution in Modern American Literature,* 166-8.

Hart, John E., "Future Hero in Paradise: Kerouac's THE DHARMA BUMS," *Crit* 14, iii (1973): 52-62.

Hull, Keith N., "A Dharma Bum Goes West to Meet the East," *WAL* 11, iv (1977): 321-9.

Jackson, Robert P., "The Dharma Bums," *American Buddhist* 2 (Oct., 1958): 1+.

Leer, Norman, "Three American Novels and Contemporary Society: A Search for Commitment," *WSCL* 3, iii (Fall, 1962): 81-4.

Miles, Jeffrey, "Making It to Cold Mountain: Han-shan in THE DHARMA BUMS," 95-105 in Singer, Armand E., ed., *Essays* on the Literature of Mountaineering, Morgantown: West Virginia Un. Pr., 1982.

Rubin, Louis D., Jr., "Two Gentlemen of San Francisco: Notes on Kerouac and Responsibility," WR 23 (Spring, 1959): 278-83.

DOCTOR SAX

Beaulieu, V. L., Jack Kerouac, 27-33.

Howe, Richard, "Interpretation of DR. SAX," MSI 6-7 (1980): 16-18.

Tytell, J., Naked Angels, 187-91.

MAGGIE CASSIDY

Tytell, J., Naked Angels, 191-7.

ON THE ROAD

Allen, Eliot D., "That Was No Lady... That was Jack Kerouac's Girl," in Langford, R. E., ed., Essays in Modern American Literature, 97-102. Also in Donaldson, S., ed., Jack Kerouac: ON THE ROAD, 504-9.

Askew, Melvin W., "Quests, Cars, and Kerouac," UKCR 28 (Mar., 1962): 231-40. Also in Donaldson, S., ed., Jack Kerouac: ON THE ROAD, 383-96.

Blackburn, William, "Han Shan Gets Drunk with the Butchers: Kerouac's Buddhism in ON THE ROAD, THE DHARMA BUMS, and DESOLATION ANGELS," LE&W 21, i-lv (Jan.-Dec., 1977): 9-22.

Bowering, George, "ON THE ROAD: & the Indians at the End," StBr No. 314 (Fall, 1969): 191-201.

Champney, Freeman, "Beat-up or Beatific?" AR 19 (Spring, 1959): 115-17.

Dardess, George, "The Delicate Dynamics of Friendship: A Reconsideration of Kerouac's ON THE ROAD," AL 46 (May, 1974): 200-6. Also in Donaldson, S., ed., Jack Kerouac: ON THE ROAD, 411-18. Also in Bartlett, L., ed., Beats, 127-32.

Donaldson, S., ed., Jack Kerouac: ON THE ROAD.

Feied, F., No Pie in the Sky, 57-73 passim.

Fuller, Edmund, Man in Modern Fiction: Some Minority Opinions on Contemporary American Writing, N.Y.: Random House, 1958, 148-54.

Gillard, G. M., "The New Writing: Whodunnit?" Meanjin 40, ii (July, 1981): 167-74.

Gleason, Ralph, "Kerouac's 'Beat Generation'," SatR 41 (Jan. 11, 1958): 75.

Glicksberg, C. I., Sexual Revolution in Modern American Literature, 160-1.

Gold, Herbert, "Hip, Cool, Beat—and Frantic," Nation 185 (Nov. 16, 1957): 349-55.

Goodan, Paul, "Wingless Wandervogel, 1957," Midstream 4 (Winter, 1958): 98-101.

Hassan, I., Radical Innocence, 93-4.

Hunt, Timothy A., "The Composition of ON THE ROAD," in Donaldson, S., ed., Jack Kerouac: ON THE ROAD, 534-7. From, revised, Hunt, Timothy A., Off the Road: The Literary Maturation of Jack Kerouac. Cornell Univ. Ph.D. Dissertation, 1975.

————, Kerouac's Crooked Road, 104-20.

————, "ON THE ROAD: An Adventurous American Education," in Donaldson, S., ed., Jack Kerouac: ON THE ROAD, 465-84.

Jones, Granville H., "Jack Kerouac and the American Conscience," in Carnegie Institute of Technology, Lectures on Modern Novelists, 25-39. Also in Donaldson, S., ed., Jack Kerouac: ON THE ROAD, 485-50.

Krupat, Arnold, "Dean Moriarty as Saintly Hero," in Krupat, A., The Saintly Hero: A Study of the Hero in Some Contemporary American Novels (Columbia Un. Ph.D. dissertation, 1967), 99-121. Also in Donaldson, S., ed., Jack Kerouac: ON THE ROAD, 397-410.

Nabokov, Peter, "Rear-View Mirror: ON THE ROAD," NDQ 50, ii (1982): 81-5.

Overland, Örm, "West and Back Again," in Donaldson, S., ed., Jack Kerouac: ON THE ROAD, 451-64.

Podhoretz, Norman, "The Know-Nothing Bohemians," in Podhoretz, N., Doings and Undoings, 143-58. Also in PR 25 (Spring, 1958): 305-18. Also in Parkinson, T., ed., Casebook on the Beat, 201-12. Also in Krim, Seymour, ed., The Beats, N.Y.: Fawcett, 1960, 111-24. Also in Donaldson, S., ed., Jack Kerouac: ON THE ROAD, 342-56.

Primeau, Ronald, "'The Endless Poem': Jack Kerouac's Midwest," GrLR 2, ii (1976): 19-26.

Sigal, Clancy, "Nihilism's Organization Man," Universities and Left Rev No. 4 (Summer, 1958): 59-65.

Tytell, John, "The Joy of ON THE ROAD," in Donaldson, S., ed., Jack Kerouac: ON THE ROAD, 419-30. From Tytell, J., Naked Angels, 157-69.

Vaidyanathan, T. G., "Jack Kerouac and Existentialist Anxiety," OJES No. 2 (1962): 61-6.

Vopat, Carole G., "Jack Kerouac's ON THE ROAD: A Re-Evaluation," MQ 14, iv (Summer, 1973): 385-407. Also in Donaldson, S., ed., Jack Kerouac: ON THE ROAD, 431-50.

Werner, C. H., Paradoxical Resolutions, 56-60.

Wilt, Koos Vander, "The Author's Recreation of Himself as Narrator and Protagonist in Fragmented Prose: A New Look at Some Beat Novels," DQR 12, ii (1982): 116-19.

THE SUBTERRANEANS

Kerouac, Jack, "Written Address to the Italian Judge," EvR 7 (Oct.-Nov., 1963): 108-10.

Miller, Henry, Preface to THE SUBTERRANEANS, N.Y.: Avon, 1959, 5-7. Also in Parkinson, T., ed., Casebook on the Beat, 230-1.

Podhoretz, Norman, "The Know-Nothing Bohemians," Doings and Undoings, 143-58. Also in PR 25 (Spring, 1958): 305-18. Also in Parkinson, T., ed., Casebook on the Beat, 201-12. Also in Krim, Seymour, ed., The Beats, N.Y.: Fawcett, 1960, 111-24.

Russell, William, "Kerouac's THE SUBTERRANEANS," Mainstream 15, vi (June, 1962): 61-4.

Straumann, H., American Literature in the Twentieth Century, 81-2.

Tytell, J., Naked Angels, 196-202.

THE TOWN AND THE CITY

Hunt, T., Kerouac's Crooked Road, 78-87.

Poteet, Maurice, "The Delussons and the Martins: Some Family Resemblances," MSI 5 (1979): 4-6.

Tytell, J., *Naked Angels*, 149-57.

VANITY OF DULUOZ

Dardess, George, "The Questing Continues," *MSI* 9 (Winter-Spring, 1981): 6-8.

McCoy, Mike, "Ellis Amburn: Editing the Final Novels," *MSI* 9 (Winter-Spring, 1981): 10-11.

Moore, Dave, "VANITY OF DULUOZ: A Character Index," *MSI* 9 (Winter-Spring, 1981): 12-13, 23.

Stephenson, Gregory, "VANITY OF DULUOZ Reviewed," *MSI* 9 (Winter-Spring, 1981): 3-5.

Walsh, Joy, "*Ecclesiastes* and the Duluoz Legend of Jack Kerouac," *NMAL* 3, iv (Fall, 1979): Item 27.

VISIONS OF CODY

Tytell, J., *Naked Angels*, 175-87.

BIBLIOGRAPHY

Gargan, William, comp., "Jack Kerouac: Biography and Criticism: A Working Bibliography," *MSI* 6-7 (Winter-Spring, 1980): 21-3.

Le Pellec, Yves, "Jack Kerouac and the American Critics: A Selected Bibliography," *Caliban* 10 (1973): 77-92.

Milewski, Robert J., John Z. Guzlowski, and Linda Calendrillo, comps., *Jack Kerouac: An Annotated Bibliography of Secondary Sources: 1944-1979*, Metuchen, N.J.: Scarecrow, 1981.

Nisonger, Thomas E., "Jack Kerouac: A Bibliography of Biographical and Critical Material, 1950-1979," *BB* 37 (1980): 23-32.

KERSLAKE, SUSAN, 1943-

MIDDLEWATCH

Maillard, Keith, "MIDDLEWATCH as Magic Realism," *CanL* 92 (Spring, 1982): 10-21.

KESEY, KEN, 1935-

GENERAL

Billingsley, Ronald G., "The Artistry of Ken Kesey," *DAI* 32 (1971): 3293A-94A. (Oregon).

Carnes, B., *Ken Kesey*.

Chaudhry-Fryer, Mamta, "Ken Kesey: Sometimes a Great Writer," *Prosery* 1 (Winter, 1980): 34-9. [Not seen.]

Gallagher, Edward J., "From Folded Hands to Clenched Fists: Kesey and Science Fiction," *Lex et Scientia* 13, i-ii (1977): 46-50. [Not seen.]

Hill, Richard A., "The Law of Ken Kesey," *DAI* 37 (1976): 968A.

Hipkiss, R. A., *Jack Kerouac*, 121-9.

Hoge, James O., "Psychedelic Stimulation and the Creative Imagination: The Case of Ken Kesey," *SHR* 6, iv (Fall, 1972): 381-91.

Knapp, James F., "Tangled in the Language of the Past: Ken Kesey and Cultural Revolution," *MQ* 19, iv (Summer, 1978): 398-412.

Leeds, B. H., *Ken Kesey*.

Tanner, T., "Edge City," *City of Words*, 372-92.

ONE FLEW OVER THE CUCKOO'S NEST

Allen, M., *Necessary Blankness*, 63-9.

Atkinson, Michael, "One Flew Over the Fiction Course," *CollL* 2, ii (Spring, 1975): 120-6.

Barsness, John A., "Ken Kesey: The Hero in Modern Dress," *BRMMLA* 23, i (Mar., 1969): 27-33. Also in Pratt, J. C., ed., *ONE FLEW OVER THE CUCKOO'S NEST*, 419-28.

Baurecht, William C., "Romantic Deviance and the Messianic Impulse in American Masculinity: Case Studies of MOBY-DICK, ONE FLEW OVER THE CUCKOO'S NEST, and SOMETIMES A GREAT NOTION," *DAI* 39 (1979): 7343A-44A.

Beidler, Peter G., "From Rabbits to Men: Self-Reliance in the Cuckoo's Nest," *Lex et Scienta* 13, i-ii (1977): 56-9.

―――, "Ken Kesey's Indian Narrator: A Sweeping Stereotype?" *Lex et Scientia* 13, i-ii (1977): 18-21.

Benert, Annette, "The Forces of Fear: Kesey's Anatomy of Insanity," *Lex et Scientia* 13, i-ii (1977): 22-6.

Billingsley, Ronald G., and James W. Palmer, "Milos Forman's CUCKOO'S NEST: Reality Unredeemed," *StHum* 7, i (1978): 14-18.

Bischoff, Joan, "'Everything Running Down': Ken Kesey's Vision of Imminent Entropy," *Lex et Scientia* 13, i-ii (1977): 65-9. [Not seen.]

Blessing, Richard, "Ken Kesey's Evolving Hero," *JPC* 4, iii (Winter, 1971): 615-27.

Boardman, Michael M., "ONE FLEW OVER THE CUCKOO'S NEST: Rhetoric and Vision," *JNT* 9 (1979): 171-83.

Boyd, George N., "Parables of Costly Grace: Flannery O'Connor and Ken Kesey," *Theology Today* 29 (1972): 161-71.

Boyers, Robert, "Attitudes Toward Sex in American 'High Culture'," *AAAPSS* 376 (Mar., 1968): 44-7. Also in Pratt, J. C., ed., *ONE FLEW OVER THE CUCKOO'S NEST*, 435-41.

Brady, Ruth H., "Kesey's ONE FLEW OVER THE CUCKOO'S NEST," *Expl* 31, vi (Feb., 1973): Item 41.

Brass, Addison C., "Art and Ideology: Kesey's Approach to Fiction," *Lex et Scientia* 13, i-ii (1977): 60-4. [Not seen.]

Bryant, J. H., *Open Decision*, 268-73.

Busby, Mark, "Eugene Manlove Rhodes: Ken Kesey Passed by Here," *WAL* 15, ii (Summer, 1980): 83-92.

Carnes, B., *Ken Kesey*, 7-19.

Crump, G. B., "D. H. Lawrence and the Immediate Present: Kurt Vonnegut, Jr., Ken Kesey, and Wright Morris," *DHLR* 10, ii (Summer, 1977): 116-21.

De Bellis, Jack, "Alone No More: Dualisms in American Literary Thought," *Lex et Scientia* 13, i-ii (1977): 70-3. [Not seen.]

―――, "Facing Things Honestly: McMurphy's Conversion," *Lex et Scientia* 13, i-ii (1977): 11-13.

Doxey, William S., "Kesey's ONE FLEW OVER THE CUCKOO'S NEST," *Expl* 32, iv (Dec., 1973): Item 32.

Fiedler, Leslie A., "The Higher Sentimentality," in Pratt, J. C., ed., *ONE FLEW OVER THE CUCKOO'S NEST*, 372-81. From Fiedler, L. A., *The Return of the Vanishing American*, N.Y.: Stein and Day, 1968, 176-87.

Fifer, Elizabeth, "From Tragicomedy to Melodrama: The Novel Onstage," *Lex et Scientia* 13, i-ii (1977): 75-80.

Flora, Joseph M., "Westering and Woman: A Thematic Story Study of Kesey's ONE FLEW OVER THE CUCKOO'S NEST and Vardis Fisher's MOUNTAIN MAN," *HOK* 10, ii (Spring, 1977): 3-14. Also in Lee, L. L., and M. Lewis, eds., *Women, Women Writers, and the West*, 219-31.

Forrey, Robert, "Ken Kesey's Psychopathic Savior: A Rejoinder," *MFS* 21, ii (Summer, 1975): 222-30.

Foster, John W., "Hustling to Some Purpose: Kesey's ONE FLEW OVER THE CUCKOO'S NEST," *WAL* 9 (Aug., 1974): 115-29.

Gilbert, Basil, "ONE FLEW OVER THE CUCKOO'S NEST: Madhouse or Microcosm?" *Meanjin* 35 (1976): 292-9.

Handy, William J., "Chief Bromden: Kesey's Existential Hero," *NDQ* 48, iv (1980): 72-82.

Haskell, Molly, "Nicholson Kneads a Fine Madness," *Village Voice* (Dec. 1, 1975): 126-7, 136. Also, as "Kesey Cured: Forman's Sweet Insanity," in Peary, G., and R. Shatzkin, eds., *Modern American Novel and the Movies*, 266-71.

Havemann, Carol S. P., "The Fool as Mentor in Modern American Parables of Entrapment: Ken Kesey's ONE FLEW OVER THE CUCKOO'S NEST, Joseph Heller's CATCH-22 and Ralph Ellison's INVISIBLE MAN," *DAI* 32 (1971): 2091A-92A (Rice).

Herrenkohl, Ellen, "Regaining Freedom: Sanity in Insane Places," *Lex et Scientia* 13, i-ii (1977): 42-4.

Horst, Leslie, "Bitches, Twitches, and Eunuchs: Sex-Role Failure and Caricature," *Lex et Scientia* 13, i-ii (1977): 14-17.

Horton, Andrew S., "Ken Kesey, John Updike and The Lone Ranger," *JPC* 8 (Winter, 1974): 572-4. Also in Filler, L., ed., *Seasoned Authors for a New Season*, 85-7.

Huffman, James R., "The Cuckoo Clocks in Kesey's Nest," *MLS* 7, i (Spring, 1977): 62-73.

Hughes, Geoffrey, "'Where, Oh Where Has My Dickey-Bird Flown?' or 'Whatever Flew Over the Cuckoo's Nest?'" *Standpunte* 29, iv (1976): 45-50.

Hunt, John W., "Flying the Cuckoo's Nest: Kesey's Narrator as Norm," *Lex et Scientia* 13, i-ii (1977): 27-32.

Kunz, Don R., "Mechanistic and Totemistic Symbolization in Kesey's ONE FLEW OVER THE CUCKOO'S NEST," *SAF* 3, i (Spring, 1975): 65-82.

Leeds, B. H., *Ken Kesey*, 13-43.

_____, "Theme and Technique in ONE FLEW OVER THE CUCKOO'S NEST," *ConnR* 7, ii (April, 1974): 35-50.

Loeb, Roger C., "Machines, Mops, and Medicaments: Therapy in the Cuckoo's Nest," *Lex et Scientia* 13, i-ii (1977): 38-41.

Malin, Irving, "Ken Kesey: ONE FLEW OVER THE CUCKOO'S NEST," *Crit* 5, ii (Fall, 1962): 81-4. Also in Pratt, J. C., ed., *ONE FLEW OVER THE CUCKOO'S NEST*, 429-34.

Martin, Terence, "The Negative Character in American Fiction," in Budd, L. J., et al., eds., *Toward a New American Literary History*, 233-5.

_____, "ONE FLEW OVER THE CUCKOO'S NEST and the High Cost of Living," *MFS* 19, i (Spring, 1973): 43-55.

Maxwell, Richard, "The Abduction of Masculinity in ONE FLEW OVER THE CUCKOO'S NEXT," in Broughton, Bradford B., ed., *Twenty-Seven to One: A Potpourri of Humanistic Material Presented to Dr. Donald Gale Stillman on the Occasion of His Retirement from Clarkson College of Technology ...* Ogdensburg, N.Y.: Ryan Pr., 1970, 203-11.

McCreadie, Marsha, "ONE FLEW OVER THE CUCKOO'S NEST: Some Reasons For One Happy Adaptation," *LFQ* 5, ii (1977): 125-31.

McGrath, Michael J. G., "Kesey and Vonnegut: The Critique of Liberal Democracy in Contemporary Literature," in Barber, B. R., and McGrath, M. J. G., eds., *Artist and Political Vision*, 365-73.

McMahan, Elizabeth E., "The Big Nurse as Ratchet: Sexism in Ken Kesey's CUCKOO'S NEST," *CEA* 37, iv (May, 1975): 25-7.

Miller, James E., Jr., "The Humor in the Horror," in Miller, J. E., Jr., *Quests Surd and Absurd*, 14-17. Also in Pratt, J. C., ed., *ONE FLEW OVER THE CUCKOO'S NEST*, 397-400.

Mills, Nicolaus, "Ken Kesey and the Politics of Laughter," *CentR* 16, i (Winter, 1972): 82-90.

Milner, Joseph, "Ken Kesey's Classroom Corrective, or, How to Free the Cuckoos," *EJ* 64, vii (Oct., 1975): 34-7.

Moorhead, Michael, "Faulkner and Kesey: Without Heat," *UPortR* 33, i (1981): 13-15.

Morey-Gaines, Ann-Janine, "Of Menace and Men: The Sexual Tensions of the American Frontier Metaphor," *Soundings* 64, ii (Summer, 1981): 142-6.

Olderman, R. M., "The Grail Knight Arrives," *Beyond the Waste Land*, 35-51.

Pearson, Carol, "The Cowboy Saint and the Indian Poet: The Comic Hero in ONE FLEW OVER THE CUCKOO'S NEST," *StAH* 1, ii (Oct., 1974): 91-8.

Phillips, Guler P., "Ken Kesey and the Language of Prose Fiction," *LNL* 1, iii (1976): 23-38.

Pinsker, S., *Between Two Worlds*, 24-6.

Pratt, John C., ed., *ONE FLEW OVER THE CUCKOO'S NEST: Text and Criticism* (Viking Critical Lib.), N.Y.: Penguin, 1977.

Roberts, William H., "Narrative Technique in ONE FLEW OVER THE CUCKOO'S NEST," *NConL* 9, iv (1979): 11-12.

Rosenman, John B., "Kesey's ONE FLEW OVER THE CUCKOO'S NEST," *Expl* 36, i (1977): 23.

Rosenwein, Robert, "Of Beats and Beasts: Power and the Individual in the Cuckoo's Nest," *Lex et Scientia* 13, i-ii (1977): 51-5.

_____, "A Place Apart: The Historical Context of Kesey's Asylum," *Lex et Scientia* 13, i-ii (1977): 34-7.

Safer, Elaine B., "'It's the Truth Even If It Didn't Happen': Ken Kesey's ONE FLEW OVER THE CUCKOO'S NEST," *LFQ* 5, ii (1977): 132-41.

Scally, Thomas, "Origin and Authority: An Analysis of the Relation Between Anonymity and Authorship in Kesey's ONE FLEW OVER THE CUCKOO'S NEST," *DR* 62 (1982): 355-73.

Schopf, William, "Blindfolded and Backwards: Promethean and Bemushroomed Heroism in ONE FLEW OVER THE CUCKOO'S NEST and CATCH-22," *BRMMLA* 26, iii (Sept., 1972): 89-97.

Searles, George J., "McMurphy's Tatoos in Kesey's ONE FLEW OVER THE CUCKOO'S NEST," *NMAL* 1 (1977): Item 24.

Sherwood, Terry G., "ONE FLEW OVER THE CUCKOO'S NEST and the Comic Strip," *Crit* 13, i (1971): 96-109. Also in Pratt, J. C., ed., *ONE FLEW OVER THE CUCKOO'S NEST*, 382-96.

Singer, Barnet, "Outsider Versus Insider: Malamud's and Kesey's Pacific Northwest," *SDR* 13, iv (Winter, 1975-76): 133-43.

Stein, Howard F., "The Cuckoo's Nest, the Banality of Evil and the Psychopath as Hero," *JAC* 2, iv (Winter, 1980): 633-45.

Stone, Edward, "CUCKOO'S NEST and MOBY-DICK," *MSEx* 38 (1979): 11-12.

_____, "Straws for the CUCKOO'S NEST," *JPC* 10 (1976): 199-202.

Sullivan, Ruth, "Big Mama, Big Papa, and Little Sons in Ken Kesey's ONE FLEW OVER THE CUCKOO'S NEST," *L&P* 25 (1975): 34-44.

Sutherland, Janet, "A Defense of Ken Kesey's ONE FLEW OVER THE CUCKOO'S NEST," *EJ* 61, i (Jan., 1972): 28-31.

Tanner, Stephen L., "Salvation Through Laughter: Ken Kesey and the Cuckoo's Nest," *SWR* 58, ii (Spring, 1973): 125-37.

Tanner, T., *City of Words*, 372-6.

Tunnell, James R., "Kesey and Vonnegut: Preachers of Redemption," *ChrC* 89 (Nov. 22, 1972): 1180-1.

Vardaman, James M., Jr., "Invisible Indian: Chief Bromden of Ken Kesey's ONE FLEW OVER THE CUCKOO'S NEST," *JEI* 11 (1980): 43-63.

Waldmeir, Joseph J., "Two Novelists of the Absurd: Heller and Kesey," *WSCL* 5, iii (Autumn, 1964): 196-204. Also in Pratt, J. C., ed., *ONE FLEW OVER THE CUCKOO'S NEST*, 401-18.

Wallace, Ronald, "What Laughter Can Do: Ken Kesey's ONE FLEW OVER THE CUCKOO'S NEST," *Last Laugh*, 90-114.

Wallis, Bruce E., "Christ in the Cuckoo's Nest: Or, the Gospel According to Ken Kesey," *Cithara* 12, i (Nov., 1972): 52-8.

Waxler, Robert, "The Trap of Chief Bromden's Truth in Kesey's ONE FLEW OVER THE CUCKOO'S NEST," *NMAL* 4 (1980): Item 20.

Widmer, K., "Contemporary American Outcasts," *Literary Rebel*, 133-6.

_____, "The Perplexities of Protest: Mailer, Kesey and the American 'Sixties'," *Sphinx* 3, iv (1981): 28-38.

_____, "The Post-Modernist Art of Protest: Kesey and Mailer as American Expressions of Rebellion," *CentR* 19, iii (Summer, 1975): 121-35.

Wiener, Gary A., "From Huck to Holden to Bromden: The Nonconformist in ONE FLEW OVER THE CUCKOO'S NEST," *StHum* 7, ii (1979): 21-6.

Wills, Arthur, "The Doctor and the Flounder: Psychoanalysis and ONE FLEW OVER THE CUCKOO'S NEST," *StHum* 5, i (1976): 19-25.

Yonce, Margaret J., "ONE FLEW OVER THE CUCKOO'S NEST and the Myth of the Fisher King," in Carrabino, V., ed., *Power of Myth in Literature and Film*, 92-102.

SEVEN PRAYERS BY GRANDMA WHITTIER

Leeds, B. H., *Ken Kesey*, 102-12.

SOMETIMES A GREAT NOTION

Barsness, John A., "Ken Kesey: The Hero in Modern Dress," *BRMMLA* 23, i (Mar., 1969): 27-33. Also in Pratt, J. C., ed., *ONE FLEW OVER THE CUCKOO'S NEST*, 419-28.

Carnes, B., *Ken Kesey*, 19-31.

Crump, G. B., "D. H. Lawrence and the Immediate Present: Kurt Vonnegut, Jr., Ken Kesey and Wright Morris," *DHLR* 10, ii (Summer, 1977): 121-3.

Leeds, B. H., *Ken Kesey*, 55-88.

Sherman, W. D., "The Novels of Ken Kesey," *JAmS* 5, ii (Aug., 1971): 193-6.

Silverman, Daniel A., "Media and Art as Cultural Data: An Exploration of Perceptual Fields Contained within the Novels of the Two Cultures," *DAI* 39 (1979): 4595A.

Singer, Barnet, "Outsider versus Insider: Malamud's and Kesey's Pacific Northwest," *SDR* 13, iv (Winter, 1975-76): 137-44.

Tanner, T., *City of Words*, 276-80.

Witke, Charles, "Pastoral Convention in Vergil and Kesey," *PCP* 1 (April, 1966): 20-4.

BIBLIOGRAPHY

Bischoff, Joan, "Views and Reviews: An Annotated Bibliography," *Lex et Scientia* 13, i-ii (1977): 93-103. [ONE FLEW OVER THE CUCKOO'S NEST.]

Weixlmann, Joseph, "Ken Kesey: A Bibliography," *WAL* 10, iii (Nov., 1975): 219-31.

KEYES, FRANCES PARKINSON, 1885-1970

GENERAL

Ehlers, Leigh A., "'An Environment Remembered': Setting in the Novels of Frances Parkinson Keyes," *SoQ* 20, iii (Spring, 1982): 54-65.

Kirkus, Virginia, "The Value of the Best Seller: An Appraisal of Frances Parkinson Keyes," *EJ* 40, vi (June, 1951): 303-7.

KIELY, BENEDICT, 1919-

GENERAL

Casey, D. J., *Benedict Kiely*.

Eckley, G., *Benedict Kiely*.

_____, "The Fiction of Benedict Kiely," *Éire* 3, iv (Winter, 1968): 55-65.

Flanagan, Thomas, "On Benedict Kiely," *Ploughshares* 6, i (1980): 52-65.

"An Interview with Benedict Kiely," *JJQ* 11, iii (1974): 189-200.

Sullivan, Kevin, "Benedict Kiely: The Making of a Novelist," in Rafroidi, P., and M. Harmon, eds., *Irish Novel in Our Time*, 199-207. Also in *CahiersI* 4-5 (1976): 199-207.

CALL FOR A MIRACLE

Casey, D. J., *Benedict Kiely*, 55-64.

Eckley, G., *Benedict Kiely*, 75-85.

THE CAPTAIN WITH THE WHISKERS

Casey, D. J., *Benedict Kiely*, 82-6.

Eckley, G., *Benedict Kiely*, 124-40.

Foster, J. W., *Forms and Themes in Ulster Fiction*, 92-6.

THE CARDS OF THE GAMBLER

Casey, D. J., *Benedict Kiely*, 71-6.

Eckley, G., *Benedict Kiely*, 96-111.

DOGS ENJOY THE MORNING

Casey, D. J., *Benedict Kiely*, 87-101.

Eckley, G., *Benedict Kiely*, 141-56.
Foster, John W., "Dog Among the Moles: The Fictional World of Benedict Kiely," *DM* 8, vi (Winter, 1970/71): 24-31.
_____, *Forms and Themes in Ulster Fiction*, 96-100.

HONEY SEEMS BITTER (THE EVIL MEN DO)

Casey, D. J., *Benedict Kiely*, 65-71.
Eckley, G., *Benedict Kiely*, 86-95.

IN A HARBOUR GREEN

Casey, D. J., *Benedict Kiely*, 47-55.
Eckley, G., *Benedict Kiely*, 62-74.

LAND WITHOUT STARS

Casey, D. J., *Benedict Kiely*, 42-6.
Eckley, G., *Benedict Kiely*, 54-61.

THERE WAS AN ANCIENT HOUSE

Casey, D. J., *Benedict Kiely*, 76-82.
Eckley, G., *Benedict Kiely*, 112-23.

KILLENS, JOHN OLIVER, 1916-1987

GENERAL

Bigsby, C. W. E., in Lee, A. R., ed., *Black Fiction*, 152-7.
Lehman, Paul R., "The Development of a Black Psyche: An Interview with John Oliver Killens," *BALF* 11 (1977): 83-9.
_____, "The Development of a Black Psyche in the Works of John Oliver Killens," *DAI* 37 (1976): 2183A.
Wiggins, William H., Jr., "Black Folktales in the Novels of John O. Killens," *BlSch* 3, iii (Nov., 1971): 50-8.
_____, "The Structure and Dynamics of Folklore in the Novel Form: The Case of John O. Killens," *KFQ* 17 (Fall, 1972): 92-118.

THE COTILLION: OR, ONE GOOD BULL IS HALF THE HERD

Berzon, J. R., *Neither White Nor Black*, 245-53.
Gayle, A., Jr., *Way of the New World*, 268-76.
Singh, Amritjit, "Self-Definition as a Moral Concern in the Twentieth-Century Afro-American Novel," *IJAS* 8, ii (July, 1978): 32-6.

'SIPPI

Bigsby, C. W. E., in Lee, A. R., ed., *Black Fiction*, 153-5.
Schraufnagel, N., *From Apology to Protest*, 183-4.
Wiggins, William H., Jr., "The Structure and Dynamics of Folklore in the Novel Form: The Case of John O. Killens," *KFQ* 17 (Fall, 1972): 100-16.

AND THEN WE HEARD THE THUNDER

Bigsby, C. W. E., in Lee, A. R., ed., *Black Fiction*, 155-7.
Gayle, A., Jr., *Way of the New World*, 262-9.

YOUNGBLOOD

Schraufnagel, N., *From Apology to Protest*, 112-14.

KIM, RICHARD E(UNKOOK), 1932-

GENERAL

Goar, Robert J., "The Humanism of Richard Kim," *MQ* 21, iv (Summer, 1980): 450-69.

THE INNOCENT

Goar, Robert J., "The Humanism of Richard Kim," *MQ* 21, iv (Summer, 1980): 460-3.

THE MARTYRED

Goar, Robert J., "The Humanism of Richard Kim," *MQ* 21, iv (Summer, 1980): 450-60.
Valdés, Mario J., "Faith and Despair: A Comparative Study of Narrative Theme," *Hispania* 49, iii (Sept., 1966): 373-9.

KING, STEPHEN (EDWIN), 1947-

GENERAL

Slung, Michele, "In the Matter of Stephen King," *ArmD* 14, ii (Spring, 1981): 147-9.
Stewart, Robert, "The Rest of King," *Starship* 18, i (Spring, 1981): 45-6.

CARRIE

Alexander, Alex E., "Stephen King's CARRIE: A Universal Fairytale," *JPC* 13 (1979): 282-8.
Ehlers, Leigh A., "CARRIE: Book and Film," 39-50 in Ruppert, Peter, Eugene Crook, and Walter Forehand, eds., *Ideas of Order in Literature and Film*, Tallahassee: Un. Pr. of Florida, 1980.

THE STAND

Cheever, Leonard, "Apocalypse and the Popular Imagination: Stephen King's THE STAND," *Real* 8, i (1981): 1-10.

KNOWLES, JOHN, 1926-

GENERAL

Halio, Jay L., "John Knowles's Short Novels," *SSF* 1 (Winter, 1964): 107-12.
Hipkiss, R. A., *Jack Kerouac*, 112-21.
Knoke, Paul D., "The Allegorical Mode in the Contemporary American Novel of Romance," *DAI* 32 (1971): 2695A (Ohio).
McDonald, James L., "The Novels of John Knowles," *ArQ* 23 (Winter, 1967): 335-42.

INDIAN SUMMER

Ellis, James, "John Knowles: INDIAN SUMMER," *Crit* 9, ii (1967): 92-5.
McDonald, James L., "The Novels of John Knowles," *ArQ* 23 (Winter, 1967): 338-42.

MORNING IN ANTIBES

Halio, Jay L., "John Knowles's Short Novels," *SSF* 1 (Winter, 1964): 109-12.

McDonald, James L., "The Novels of John Knowles," *ArQ* 23 (Winter, 1967): 337-8.

A SEPARATE PEACE

Clarke, Loretta M., "A Critical Approach to Four Novels of Adolescence," *DAI* 31 (1971): 4758A (Iowa).

Crabbe, John K., "On the Playing Fields of Devon," *EJ* 52 (1963): 109-11.

Devine, Joseph E., "The Truth about A SEPARATE PEACE," *EJ* 58, iv (April, 1969): 519-20.

Ellis, James, "A SEPARATE PEACE: The Fall from Innocence," *EJ* 53 (1964): 313-18.

Ely, Sister M. Amanda, O. P., "The Adult Image in Three Novels of Adolescent Life," *EJ* 56 (Nov., 1967): 1128-30.

Foster, Milton P., "Levels of Meaning in A SEPARATE PEACE," *EngR* 18, iv (1968): 34-40.

Greiling, Franzika L., "The Theme of Freedom in A SEPARATE PEACE," *EJ* 56 (Dec., 1967): 1269-72.

Halio, Jay L., "John Knowles's Short Novels," *SSF* 1 (Winter, 1964): 107-9.

Kennedy, Ian, "Dual Perspective Narrative and the Character of Phineas in A SEPARATE PEACE," *SSF* 11 (1974): 353-9.

McDonald, James L., "The Novels of John Knowles," *ArQ* 23 (Winter, 1967): 335-7.

McDonald, Walter R., "Heroes Never Learn: Irony in A SEPARATE PEACE," *IEY* 22, iii (Nov., 1972): 33-6.

Mellard, James M., "Counterpoint and 'Double Vision' in A SEPARATE PEACE," *SSF* 4 (Winter, 1967): 127-34.

Mengeling, Marvin E., "A SEPARATE PEACE: Meaning and Myth," *EJ* 58, ix (Dec., 1969): 1323-9.

Nora, Sister M., S.S.N.D., "A Comparison of Actual and Symbolic Landscape in A SEPARATE PEACE," *Discourse* 11 (Summer, 1968): 356-62.

Palms, Rosemary H. G., "The Double Motif in Literature: From Origins to an Examination of Three Modern American Novels," *DAI* 33 (1972): 321A.

Travis, Mildred K., "Mirror Images in A SEPARATE PEACE and CAT AND MOUSE," *NConL* 5, iv (1975): 12-15.

Ward, Hayden, "The Arnoldian Situation in A SEPARATE PEACE," *BWVACET* 1, i (1974): 2-10.

Weber, Ronald, "Narrative Method in A SEPARATE PEACE," *SSF* 3 (Fall, 1965): 63-72.

Witherington, Paul, "A SEPARATE PEACE: A Study in Structural Ambiguity," *EJ* 54 (Dec., 1965): 795-800.

Wolfe, Peter, "The Impact of Knowles's A SEPARATE PEACE," *UR* 31, iii (Mar., 1970): 189-98.

KOCH, C(HRISTOPHER) J(OHN), 1932-

GENERAL

Claremont, Robyn, "The Novels of C. J. Koch," *Quadrant* 24 (July, 1980): 25-9.

Tiffin, Helen, "Asia, Europe and Australian Identity: The Novels of Christopher Koch," *ALS* 10, iii (May, 1982): 326-35.

ACROSS THE SEA WALL

Tiffin, Helen, "Asia, Europe and Australian Identity: The Novels of Christopher Koch," *ALS* 10, iii (May, 1982): 328-32.

THE BOYS IN THE ISLAND

Buckley, Vincent, "In the Shadow of Patrick White," *Meanjin* 20, ii (1961): 150-4.

McGregory, Grant, "The Australian City of Christopher Koch," *Quadrant* 20, vi (June, 1976): 66-71.

Tiffin, Helen, "Asia, Europe and Australian Identity: The Novels of Christopher Koch," *ALS* 10, iii (May, 1982): 326-8.

THE YEAR OF LIVING DANGEROUSLY

Tiffin, Helen, "Asia, Europe and Australian Identity: The Novels of Christopher Koch," *ALS* 10, iii (May, 1982): 332-5.

KOESTLER, ARTHUR, 1905-1983

GENERAL

Atkins, J., *Arthur Koestler.*

Bantock, G. H., "Arthur Koestler," *P&L* 1 (Summer, 1948): 41-7.

Burgess, A., *Urgent Copy*, 147-9.

Calder, J., *Chronicles of Conscience.*

Crick, Bernard, "Koestler's Koestler," *PR* 49, ii (1982): 274-83.

Fyvel, T. R., "Arthur Koestler and George Orwell," in Harris, H., ed., *Astride the Two Cultures*, 149-61.

Hamilton, Iain, "Wonderfully Living: Koestler the Novelist," in Harris, H., ed., *Astride the Two Cultures*, 84-101.

Harris, H., ed., *Astride the Two Cultures.*

Hicks, Granville, "Arthur Koestler and the Future of the Left," *AR* 5 (June, 1945): 212-23.

Jones, Barry, "Arthur Koestler Interview," *Quadrant* 14 (Jan.-Feb., 1969): 29-36.

Kahn, Lother, "Arthur Koestler and the Jews," *CJF* 18 (Summer, 1960): 341-6. Also as "Arthur Koestler: Dejudaized Zionism," *Mirrors of the Mind*, 146-59.

Klingopulos, G. D., "Arthur Koestler," *Scrutiny* 16 (June, 1949): 82-92.

Knopfelmacher, Frank, "Koestler at 70," *Quadrant* 104 (1976): 41-6.

Levene, Mark, "Arthur Koestler: On Messiahs and Mutations," *MSLC* 2, ii (1976): 37-48.

————, "Themes and Techniques in the Work of Arthur Koestler," *DAI* 38 (1977): 3485A.

Mays, W., *Arthur Koestler.*

Mortimer, Raymond, "Arthur Koestler," *Cornhill* 162 (Winter, 1946): 213-22.

Orwell, George, "Arthur Koestler," in Sperber, M. A., ed., *Arthur Koestler*, 13-24. From Orwell, G., *Dickens, Dali and Others*, 1946. Also in Orwell, Sonia, and Ian Angus, *Collected Essays, Journalism, and Letters of George Orwell*, Vol. III, N.Y.: Harcourt, 1968.

Prescott, G., *In My Opinion*, 31-9.

Pritchett, V. S., "The Art of Koestler," *Books in General*, 155-72. Also in *Horizon* 15 (May, 1947): 233-47.

————, "Koestler: A Guilty Figure," *Harper's* 196 (Jan., 1948): 84-92. Also in Sperber, M. A., ed., *Arthur Koestler*, 53-68.

Rahv, P., *Image and Idea*, 173-81.

_____, "Koestler and Homeless Radicalism," *Literature and the Sixth Sense*, 126-33.

Redman, Ben Ray, "Arthur Koestler: Radical's Progress," *CE* 13 (Dec., 1951): 131-6.

Rivett, Kenneth, "In Defence of Arthur Koestler," *AusQ* 19 (Sept., 1947): 90-4.

Sperber, M. A., ed., *Arthur Koestler*.

Stanford, Derek, "Arthur Koestler," in Baker, D. V., ed., *Modern British Writing*, 271-80. Also in Baker, D. V., ed., *Writers of Today*, 85-95.

Winegarten, Renée, "Arthur Koestler as Witness," *Midstream* 12 (Feb., 1966): 71-7.

Woodcock, G., *Writer and Politics*, 175-96.

THE AGE OF LONGING

Calder, J., *Chronicles of Conscience*, 220-2.

Prescott, O., *In My Opinion*, 38-9.

ARRIVAL AND DEPARTURE

Atkins, J., *Arthur Koestler*, 81-90.

Bantock, G. H., "Arthur Koestler," *P&L* 1 (Summer, 1948): 46-7.

Calder, J., *Chronicles of Conscience*, 141-4, 155-60.

Fuerst, Rudolph A., *PsyR* 33 (1946): 102-7.

Gray, J., *On Second Thought*, 237-40.

Prescott, O., *In My Opinion*, 35-6.

Pritchett, V. S., "The Art of Koestler," *Books in General*, 166-7.

Rahv, P., "Koestler and Homeless Radicalism," *Literature and the Sixth Sense*, 128-30.

Roland, Albert, "Christian Implications in Anti-Stalinist Novels," *Religion in Life* 22 (1953): 407-8.

Rosenberg, Harold, "The Case of the Baffled Radical," *PR* 11 (Winter, 1944): 100-3. Also in Sperber, M. A., ed., *Arthur Koestler*, 34-8.

Stanford, Derek, "Arthur Koestler," in Baker, D. V., ed., *Modern British Writing*, 279-80. Also in Baker, D. V., ed., *Writers of Today*, 91-3.

Woodcock, G., *Writer and Politics*, 187-9.

DARKNESS AT NOON

Atkins, J., *Arthur Koestler*, 177-84, 189-91.

Axthelm, P. M., *Modern Confessional Novel*, 97-113.

Bantock, G. H., "Arthur Koestler," *P&L* 1 (Summer, 1948): 44-6.

Beum, Robert, "Epigraphs for Rubashov: Koestler's DARKNESS AT NOON," *DR* 42 (1962): 86-91.

Calder, J., *Chronicles of Conscience*, 127-35, 149-53.

Downing, Francis, "Koestler Revisited," *Cweal* (Feb. 9, 1951): 444-6.

Garaudy, Roger, "The Lie in its Pure State: Arthur Koestler," in Garaudy, R., *Literature of the Graveyard*, N.Y.: International Pubs., 1948, 50-5.

Geering, R. G., "DARKNESS AT NOON and NINETEEN EIGHTY-FOUR—A Comparative Study," *AusQ* 30, iii (1958): 90-6.

Glicksberg, Charles I., "Arthur Koestler and Communism," *QQ* 53 (Winter, 1946-47): 420-3.

Hartt, J. N., *Lost Image of Man*, 76-9.

Hoelzel, Alfred, "Betrayed Rebels in German Literature: Büchner, Teller, and Koestler," *OL* 34 (1979): 249-55.

Hoffman, Frederick J., "DARKNESS AT NOON: The Consequences of Secular Grace," *GaR* 13 (1959): 331-45. Also in Hoffman, F. J., *Mortal No*, 126-35.

Howe, I., *Politics and the Novel*, 227-32.

Klingopulos, G. D., "Arthur Koestler," *Scrutiny* 16 (June, 1949): 83-7.

Koestler, Arthur, "A Note on DARKNESS AT NOON," *New Statesman* 96 (Aug. 18, 1978): 216.

Merleau-Ponty, Maurice, "Koestler's Dilemmas," in Sperber, M. A., ed., *Arthur Koestler*, 69-85. From Merleau-Ponty, M., *Humanisme et Terreur: Essai sur le Probleme Communiste*, Boston: Beacon Pr., English transl., 1969.

Merrill, Reed, "Ideology and the Individual: DARKNESS AT NOON Forty Years Later," *SAQ* 80, ii (Spring, 1981): 143-55.

Moseley, E. M., *Pseudonyms of Christ in the Modern Novel*, 189-94.

Platt, Annette E., "The Function of Rubashov's Toothache in Koestler's DARKNESS AT NOON," *McNR* 23 (1976-77): 50-61.

Prabhakar, M. S., "Two Inconsistencies in DARKNESS AT NOON," *N&Q* 11 (Oct., 1964): 387-8.

Prescott, O., *In My Opinion*, 33-5.

Pritchett, V. S., "The Art of Koestler," *Books in General*, 164-6. Also in *Horizon* 15 (May, 1947): 240-3.

_____, "Koestler: A Guilty Figure," *Harper's* 196 (Jan., 1948): 88-90. Also in Sperber, M. A., ed., *Arthur Koestler*, 60-3.

Rees, Goronwy, "DARKNESS AT NOON and the 'Grammatical Fiction'," in Harris, H., ed., *Astride the Two Cultures*, 102-22.

Roland, Albert, "Christian Implications in Anti-Stalinist Novels," *Religion in Life* 22 (1953): 406-7.

Stanford, Derek, "Arthur Koestler," in Baker, D. V., ed., *Modern British Writing*, 276-7. Also in Baker, D. V., ed., *Writers of Today*, 89-91.

Steele, Peter, "DARKNESS AT NOON," *CR* 12 (1969): 73-82.

Strachey, J., *Strangled Cry*, 11-23. Also in *Encounter* 15 (Nov., 1960): 3-9.

Weintraub, S., *Last Great Cause*, 138-42.

Wetzel, Heinz, "Revolution and the Intellectual: Büchner's Danton and Koestler's Rubashov," *Mosaic* 10, iv (Summer, 1977): 23-33.

Woodcock, G., *Writer and Politics*, 183-7.

THE GLADIATORS

Atkins, J., *Arthur Koestler*, 99-100.

Bantock, G. H., "Arthur Koestler," *P&L* 1 (Summer, 1948): 43-4.

Calder, J., *Chronicles of Conscience*, 121-4, 146-8.

Pritchett, V. S., "The Art of Koestler," *Books in General*, 160-3. Also in *Horizon* 15 (May, 1947): 237-40.

_____, "Koestler: A Guilty Figure," *Harper's* 196 (Jan., 1948): 86-8. Also in Sperber, M. A., ed., *Arthur Koestler*, 57-60.

Stanford, Derek, "Arthur Koestler," in Baker, D. V., ed., *Modern British Writing*, 274-6. Also in Baker, D. V., ed., *Writers of Today*, 87-9.

Winegarten, Renée, "Arthur Koestler as Witness," *Midstream* 12 (Feb., 1966): 73-4.

THIEVES IN THE NIGHT

Calder, J., *Chronicles of Conscience*, 200-2, 212-20.

Glicksberg, Charles, "Anti-Semitism and the Jewish Novelist," in Ribalow, H., ed., *Mid-Century*, 344-6.

Klingopulos, G. D., "Arthur Koestler," *Scrutiny* 16 (June, 1949): 90-2.

Lerner, Max, *Actions and Passions: Notes on the Multiple Revolution of Our Time*, N.Y.: Simon & Schuster, 1949, 51-3.

Mortimer, Raymond, "Arthur Koestler," *Cornhill* 162 (Winter, 1946): 216-22.

Prescott, O., *In My Opinion*, 37.

Pritchett, V. S., "The Art of Koestler," *Books in General*, 167-72. Also in *Horizon* 15 (May, 1947): 244-6.

_____, "Koestler: A Guilty Figure," *Harper's* 196 (Jan., 1948): 90-2. Also in Sperber, M. A., ed., *Arthur Koestler*, 64-8.

Ribalow, Harold, "Zion in Contemporary Fiction," in Ribalow, H., ed., *Mid-Century*, 581-3.

Rosenfeld, Isaac, "Palestinian Ice Age," *NRep* 115 (Nov. 4, 1946): 592-3. Also in Sperber, M. A., ed., *Arthur Koestler*, 48-52.

Wilson, Edmund, "Arthur Koestler in Palestine," *NY* 22 (Nov. 15, 1946): 125-30. Also in Sperber, M. A., ed., *Arthur Koestler*, 44-7.

Winegarten, Renée, "Arthur Koestler as Witness," *Midstream* 12 (Feb., 1966): 75-6.

Woodcock, G., *Writer and Politics*, 191-6.

BIBLIOGRAPY

Merrill, Reed, and Thomas Frazier, comps., *Arthur Koestler: An International Bibliography*, Ann Arbor: Ardis, 1979.

Sperber, M. A., ed., *Arthur Koestler*, 185-9.

KOSINSKI, JERZY (NIKODEM), 1933-1991

GENERAL

Aldridge, John W., "The Fabrication of a Culture Hero," *SatR* 54 (April 24, 1971): 25-7. Also as "Jerzy Kosinski's American Dream," in Aldridge, J. W., *Devil in the Fire*, 267-73.

Anderson, Don, "The End of Humanism: A Study of Kosinski," *Quadrant* 20, xii (Dec., 1976): 73-7.

Bloomfield, Mitchell B., "The Fiction of Jerzy Kosinski: The Perverse in the Modern Imagination," *DAI* 36 (1976): 6079A-80A.

Brown, Earl B., Jr., "Kosinski's Modern Proposal: The Problem of Satire in the Mid-Twentieth Century," *Crit* 22, ii (1980): 83-7.

Cahill, Daniel J., "The Devil Tree: An Interview With Jerzy Kosinski," *NAmerR* 258 (Spring, 1973): 56-66.

_____, "An Interview with Jerzy Kosinski," *ConL* 19 (1978): 113-42.

_____, "Jerzy Kosinski: A Play on Passion," *ChiR* 32, i (Summer, 1980): 118-34.

_____, "Jerzy Kosinski: Retreat from Violence," *TCL* 18, ii (April, 1972): 121-32.

Carter, Nancy C., "1970 Images of the Machine and the Garden: Kosinski, Crews, and Pirsig," *Soundings* 6, ii (Spring, 1978): 105-22.

Coale, Samuel, "The Cinematic Self of Jerzy Kosinski," *MFS* 20, iii (Autumn, 1974): 359-70.

_____, "The Quest for the Elusive Self: The Fiction of Jerzy Kosinski," *Crit* 14, iii (1973): 25-37.

Gorzkowska, Regina, "*Pinball*: Aspects of Visibility: An Interview with Jerzy Kosinski," *Soc. for Fine Arts Rev.* 4, ii (Summer, 1982): 3-4.

Hutchinson, James D., "The Art of the Self: The Quest for Authenticity in the Novels of Jerzy Kosinski," *DAI* 35 (1974): 2992A (Denver).

Klinkowitz, Jerome, "Jerzy Kosinski: An Interview," *FictionI* (Fall, 1973): 30-48. Reprinted in Bellamy, J. D., ed., *New Fiction*, 142-68.

_____, *Literary Disruptions*, 82-101.

Lilly, Paul R., Jr., "Comic Strategies in the Fiction of Barthelme and Kosinski," *PMPA* 4 (1979): 25-32.

_____, "Jerzy Kosinski: Words in Search of Victims," *Crit* 22, ii (1980): 69-82.

_____, "Vision and Violence in the Fiction of Jerzy Kosinski," *LitR* 25, iii (Spring, 1982): 389-400.

Lipani, David J., "Jerzy Kosinski: A Study of His Novels," *DAI* 34 (1974): 5185A-86A.

Plimpton, George, and Rocco Landesman, "The Art of Fiction XLVI: Interview with Jerzy Kosinski," *ParisR* 54 (Summer, 1972): 183-207.

Prendowska, Krystyna, "Jerzy Kosinski: A Literature of Contortions," *JNT* 8, i (Winter, 1978): 11-25.

Richey, Clarence W., "BEING THERE and *Dasein*: A Note on the Philosophical Presupposition Underlying the Novels of Jerzy Kosinski," *NConL* 2, iv (Sept., 1972): 13-15.

Sanders, Ivan, "The Gifts of Strangeness: Alienation and Creation in Jerzy Kosinski's Fiction," *PolR* 19, iii-iv (1974): 171-89.

Tepa, Barbara J., "Inside the Kaleidoscope: Jerzy Kosinski's Polish and American Contexts," *DAI* 36 (1976): 5289A.

Weales, Gerald, "Jerzy Kosinski: The Painted Bird and Other Disguises," *HC* 9, iii (Oct., 1972): 1-12.

Ziegler, Robert E., "Identity and Anonymity in the Novels of Jerzy Kosinski," *RMRLL* 35, ii (1981): 99-109.

BEING THERE

Aldridge, John W., "The Fabrication of a Culture Hero," *SatR* 54 (April 24, 1971): 25-7. Also as "Jerzy Kosinski's American Dream," in Aldridge, J. W., *Devil in the Fire*, 270-3.

Bolling, Douglas, "The Precarious Self in Jerzy Kosinski's BEING THERE," *Greyfriar* 16 (1975): 41-6.

Brown, Earl B., Jr., "Kosinski's Modern Proposal: The Problem of Satire in the Mid-Twentieth Century," *Crit* 22, ii (1980): 84-7.

Carter, Nancy C., "1970 Images of the Machine and the Garden: Kosinski, Crews, and Pirsig," *Soundings* 61, i (Spring, 1978): 112-16.

Gogol, John M., "Kosinski's Chance: McLuhan Age Narcissus," *NConL* 1, iv (Sept., 1971): 8-10.

Hutchinson, James D., "The 'Invisible Man' as Anti-Hero," *DenverQ* 6, i (Spring, 1971): 86-92.

Klinkowitz, Jerome, "Being Here," *Falcon* 4 (Spring, 1972): 122-5.

_____, *Literary Disruptions*, 94-7.

Sanders, Ivan, "The Gifts of Strangeness: Alienation and Creation in Jerzy Kosinski's Fiction," *PolR* 19, iii-iv (1974): 178-81.

Tepa, Barbara J., "Jerzy Kosinski's Polish Contexts: A Study of BEING THERE," *PolR* 22, ii (1977): 52-61.

Willson, Robert E., Jr., "BEING THERE at the End," *LFQ* 9, i (1981): 59-65.

BLIND DATE

Bakker, J., "Language as Failed Therapy: Kosinski's THE PAINTED BIRD and BLIND DATE," *DQR* 9, iii (1979): 203-17.

Cahill, Daniel J., "An Interview with Jerzy Kosinski on BLIND DATE," *ConL* 19, ii (Spring, 1978): 133-42.

COCKPIT

Keshawarz, Margaret K., "Simas Kudirka: A Literary Symbol of Democratic Individualism in Jerzy Kosinski's COCKPIT," *Lituanus* 25, iv (1979): 38-42.

THE DEVIL TREE

Hirschberg, Stuart, "Becoming an Object: The Function of Mirrors and Photographs in Kosinski's THE DEVIL TREE," *NConL* 4, ii (1974): 14-15.

Klinkowitz, J., *Literary Disruptions*, 97-100.

THE PAINTED BIRD

Bakker, J., "Language as Failed Therapy: Kosinski's THE PAINTED BIRD and BLIND DATE," *DQR* 9, iii (1979): 203-17.

Corngold, Stanley, "Jerzy Kosinski's THE PAINTED BIRD: Language Lost and Regained," *Mosaic* 6, iv (Summer, 1973): 153-67.

Hanson, John H., "The Child Archetype and Modern Primitivism: Kosinski's THE PAINTED BIRD," *HSL* 14, iii (1982): 85-95.

Harpham, Geoffrey G., "Survival in and of THE PAINTED BIRD: The Career of Jerzy Kosinski," *GaR* 35, i (Spring, 1981): 142-57.

Heller, Terry, "Notes on Technique in Black Humor," *Thalia* 2, iii (Winter, 1979-80): 18-19.

Klinkowitz, J., *Literary Disruptions*, 87-91.

_____, "Two Bibliographical Questions in Kosinski's THE PAINTED BIRD," *ConL* 16 (1975): 126-8. [Response to article by David H. Richter. Richter's reply: 128-9.]

Lale, Meta, and John S. Williams, "The Narrator of THE PAINTED BIRD: A Case Study," *Ren* 24 (Summer, 1972): 198-206.

Langer, L. L., *Holocaust and the Literary Imagination*, 167-91.

Loukides, Paul, "The Radical Vision," *MichA* 5, iv (Spring, 1973): 498-9.

McGinnis, Wayne D., "Transcendence and Primitive Sympathy in Kosinski's THE PAINTED BIRD," *StHum* 8, i (1980): 22-7.

Meszaros, Patricia K., "Hero with a Thousand Faces, Child with No Name: Kosinski's THE PAINTED BIRD," *CollL* 6 (1979): 232-44.

Mortimer, Gail L., "'Fear Death by Water': The Boundaries of the Self in Jerzy Kosinski's THE PAINTED BIRD," *PsyR* 63 (1976-77): 511-28.

Piwinski, David J., "Kosinski's THE PAINTED BIRD," *Expl* 40, i (Fall, 1981): 62-3.

Richter, David H., "The Reader as Ironic Victim," *Novel* 14, ii (Winter, 1981): 147-51.

_____, "The Three Denouements of Jerzy Kosinski's THE PAINTED BIRD," *ConL* 15 (Summer, 1974): 370-85.

Rider, Philip R., "The Three States of the Text of Kosinski's THE PAINTED BIRD," *PBSA* 72 (1978): 361-84.

Sanders, Ivan, "The Gifts of Strangeness: Alienation and Creation in Jerzy Kosinski's Fiction," *PolR* 19, iii-iv (1974): 172-5.

Sewell, Ernestine P., "The Jungian Process of Individuation as Structure in THE PAINTED BIRD," *SCB* 38, iv (1978): 160-3.

Skau, Michael, Michael Carroll, and Donald Cassiday, "Jerzy Kosinski's THE PAINTED BIRD: A Modern Bestiary," *PolR* 27, iii-iv (1982): 45-54.

Spendal, R. J., "The Structure of THE PAINTED BIRD," *JNT* 6 (1976): 132-6.

Weales, Gerald, "Jerzy Kosinski: The Painted Bird and Other Disguises," *HC* 9, iii (Oct., 1972): 1-12.

PASSION PLAY

Cahill, Daniel J., "Jerzy Kosinski: A Play on Passion," *ChiR* 32, i (Summer, 1980): 128-33.

STEPS

Boyers, Robert, "Language and Reality in Kosinski's STEPS," *CentR* 16, i (Winter, 1972): 41-61.

Brown, Earl B., Jr., "Kosinski's Modern Proposal: The Problem of Satire in the Mid-Twentieth Century," *Crit* 22, ii (1980): 83-4.

Daler, John Kent von, "An Introduction to Jerzy Kosinski's STEPS," *Lang&L* 1, i (1971): 43-9.

Howe, Irving, "From the Other Side of the Moon," *Harpers* 238 (Mar., 1969): 102-5.

Klinkowitz, J., *Literary Disruptions*, 92-5.

Loukides, Paul, "The Radical Vision," *MichA* 5, iv (Spring, 1973): 499-500.

Petrakis, Byron, "Jersy Kosinski's STEPS and the Cinematic Novel," *Comparatist* 2 (1978): 16-22.

Sanders, Ivan, "The Gifts of Strangeness: Alienation and Creation in Jerzy Kosinski's Fiction," *PolR* 19, iii-iv (1974): 175-8.

BIBLIOGRAPHY

Rusch, Frederic E., "Jerzy Kosinski: A Checklist," *BB* 31, i (Jan.-Mar., 1974): 6-9.

Walsh, Thomas P., and Cameron Northouse, *John Barth, Jerzy Kosinski, and Thomas Pynchon: A Reference Guide*, Boston: G. K. Hall, 1977.

KREISEL, HENRY, 1922-

GENERAL

Lecker, Robert A., "States of Mind: Henry Kreisel's Novels," *CanL* 77 (Summer, 1978): 82-93.

THE BETRAYAL

Greenstein, Michael, "Perspectives on the Holocaust in Henry Kreisel's THE BETRAYAL," *ECW* 23 (Spring, 1982): 97-106.

Lecker, Robert A., "States of Mind: Henry Kreisel's Novels," *CanL* 77 (Summer, 1978): 87-92.

THE RICH MAN

Lecker, Robert A., "States of Mind: Henry Kreisel's Novels," *CanL* 77 (Summer, 1978): 83-7.

KROETSCH, ROBERT, 1927-

GENERAL

Brahms, Flemming, "Robert Kroetsch," *Kunapipi* 2, ii (1980): 117-25.

Brown, Russell M., in Heath, J., ed., *Profiles in Canadian Literature* 2, 97-108.

_____, "An Interview with Robert Kroetsch," *UWR* 7, ii (Spring, 1972): 1-18.

Cameron, Donald, "Robert Kroetsch: The American Experience and the Canadian Voice," *JCF* 1, iii (Summer, 1972): 48-52.

Davey, Frank, "The Explorer in Western Canadian Literature," *SCL* 4, ii (Summer, 1979): 94-100.

Enright, Robert, and Dennis Cooley, "Uncovering Our Dream World: An Interview with Robert Kroetsch," *ECW* 18-19 (1980): 21-32.

Gross, Konrad, "Looking Back in Anger? Frederick Niven, W. O. Mitchell and Robert Kroetsch on the History of the Canadian West," *JCF* 3, ii (Spring, 1974): 49-54.

Hancock, Geoff, "An Interview with Robert Kroetsch," *CFM* 24-25 (Spring-Summer, 1977): 33-52.

Lecker, Robert, "Bordering On: Robert Kroetsch's Aesthetic," *JCanStud* 17, iii (Fall, 1982): 124-33.

MacKendrick, Louis K., "Robert Kroetsch and the Modern Canadian Novel of Exhaustion," *ECW* 11 (Summer, 1978): 10-27.

Mandel, Ann, "Uninventing Structures: Cultural Criticism and the Novels of Robert Kroetsch," *Open Letter* (Third Series, 8) (Spring, 1978): 52-71.

Neuman, Shirley, and Robert Wilson, *Labyrinths of Voice: Conversations with Robert Kroetsch*, Edmonton: NeWest, 1982.

_____, "Unearthing Language: An Interview with Rudy Wiebe and Robert Kroetsch," in Keith, W. J., ed., *Voice in the Land*, 226-47.

Nicolaisen, W. F. H., "Ordering the Chaos: Name Strategies in Robert Kroetsch's Novels," *ECW* 11 (Summer, 1978): 55-65.

Ricou, Laurence, "Empty as Nightmare: Man and Landscape in Recent Canadian Prairie Fiction," *Mosaic* 6, ii (Winter, 1973): 156-60. Also in Ricou, Laurence, *VerticalMan/Horizontal World: Man and Landscape in Canadian Prairie Fiction*, Vancouver: Un. of British Columbia Pr., 1973, 133-6.

Sullivan, Rosemary, "The Fascinating Place Between: The Fiction of Robert Kroetsch," *Mosaic* 11, iii (Spring, 1978): 165-76.

Surette, P. L., "The Fabular Fiction of Robert Kroetsch," *CanL* 77 (Summer, 1978): 6-19.

Thomas, Peter, "Priapus in the Danse Macabre: The Novels of Robert Kroetsch," *CanL* 61 (Summer, 1974): 54-64. Also in Woodcock, G., ed., *Canadian Novel in the Twentieth Century*, 285-97.

_____, *Robert Kroetsch*.

_____, "Robert Kroetsch and Silence," *ECW* 18-19 (Summer-Fall, 1980): 33-53.

_____, "Robert Kroetsch, Rupert Brooke, The Voices of the Dead," *SCL* 1, i (Winter, 1976): 124-9.

BADLANDS

Davidson, Arnold E., "History, Myth, and Time in Robert Kroetsch's BADLANDS," *SCL* 5 (Spring, 1980): 127-37.

Grace, Sherrill E., "Wastelands and Badlands: The Legacies of Pynchon and Kroetsch," *Mosaic* 14, ii (Spring, 1981): 20-34.

Harvey, Connie, "Tear-Glazed Vision of Laughter," *ECW* No. 11 (Summer, 1978): 28-54.

Ricou, Laurence, "Field Notes and Notes in a Field: Forms of the West in Robert Kroetsch and Tom Robbins," *JCanStud* 17, iii (Fall, 1982): 117-23.

Sullivan, Rosemary, "The Fascinating Place Between: The Fiction of Robert Kroetsch," *Mosaic* 11, iii (Spring, 1978): 174-6.

Thomas, P., *Robert Kroetsch*, 80-96.

BUT WE ARE EXILES

Moss, John G., "Canadian Frontiers: Sexuality and Violence from Richardson to Kroetsch," *JCF* 2, iii (Summer, 1973): 36-41.

Ross, Morton L., "Robert Kroetsch and His Novels," in Stephens, D. G., ed., *Writers of the Prairies*, 102-7.

Thomas, Peter, "Priapus in the Danse Macabre: The Novels of Robert Kroetsch," *CanL* 61 (Summer, 1974): 54-64. Also in Woodcock, G., ed., *Canadian Novel in the Twentieth Century*, 286-92.

_____, *Robert Kroetsch*, 33-8.

GONE INDIAN

Brown, Russell M., "Crossing Borders," *ECW* 22 (Summer, 1981): 154-68.

Davidson, Arnold E., "Will the Real R. Mark Madham Please Stand Up: A Note on Robert Kroetsch's GONE INDIAN," *SCL* 6, i (1981): 135-9.

Harvey, Roderick W., "The Limitations of Media," *CanL* 77 (Summer, 1978): 20-7.

MacKendrick, Louis K., "Robert Kroetsch and the Modern Canadian Novel of Exhaustion," *ECW* 11 (Summer, 1978): 22-5.

Moss, J., *Sex and Violence in the Canadian Novel*, 289-92.

Thomas, P., *Robert Kroetsch*, 68-80.

THE STUDHORSE MAN

Davidson, Arnold E., "Frustrated Sexuality in Robert Kroetsch's THE STUDHORSE MAN," *ARCS* 7, ii (Autumn, 1977): 23-32.

Harvey, Roderick W., "The Limitations of Media," *CanL* 77 (Summer, 1978): 20-7.

MacKendrick, Louis K., "Robert Kroetsch and the Modern Canadian Novel of Exhaustion," *ECW* 11 (Summer, 1978): 18-22.

Mandel, Eli, "Romance and Realism in Canadian Literature," in Rasporich, Anthony W., and Henry C. Klassen, eds., *Prairie Perspectives* 2, Toronto: Holt, Rinehart and Winston, 1973, 207-11. Also in Mandel, Eli, *Another Time*, Toronto: Press Porcépie, 1977, 63-7.

McCaughy, G. S., "THE STUDHORSE MAN: A Madman's View of Canadian History," *RUO* 44 (juil.-sept., 1974): 406-13.

Merivale, Patricia, "The Biographical Compulsion: Elegiac Romances in Canadian Fiction," *JML* 8 (Feb., 1980): 139-41, 142, 143, 146, 149-52.

Moss, J., *Sex and Violence in the Canadian Novel*, 292-8.

New, W. H., *Articulating West*, 179-86.

Ross, Morton L., "Robert Kroetsch and His Novels," in Stephens, D. G., ed., *Writers of the Prairies*, 110-14.

Sullivan, Rosemary, "The Fascinating Place Between: The Fiction of Robert Kroetsch," *Mosaic* 11, iii (Spring, 1978): 172-4.

Thomas, Peter, "Priapus in the Danse Macabre: The Novels of Robert Kroetsch," *CanL* 61 (Summer, 1974): 54-64. Also in Woodcock, G., ed., *Canadian Novel in the Twentieth Century*, 292-6.

_____, *Robert Kroetsch*, 51-67.

WHAT THE CROW SAID

Thomas, P., *Robert Kroetsch*, 97-115.

Wilson, Robert R., "On the Boundary of the Magic and the Real: Notes of Inter-American Fiction," *The Compass* (Un. of Alberta) No. 6 (Spring, 1979): 37-53.

THE WORDS OF MY ROARING

Graham, Kenneth W., "Picaro as Messiah: Backstrom's Election in THE WORDS OF MY ROARING," *Mosaic* 14, ii (Spring, 1981): 177-86.

Moss, J., *Sex and Violence in the Canadian Novel*, 287-9.

Ross, Morton L., "Robert Kroetsch and His Novels," in Stephens, D. G., ed., *Writers of the Prairies*, 107-10.

Sullivan, Rosemary, "The Fascinating Place Between: The Fiction of Robert Kroetsch," *Mosaic* 11, iii (Spring, 1978): 168-72.

Thomas, P., *Robert Kroetsch*, 38-50.

BIBLIOGRAPHY

Lecker, Robert, "An Annotated Bibliography of Works by and about Robert Kroetsch," *ECW* 7-8 (Fall, 1977): 74-96.

Thomas, P., *Robert Kroetsch*, 136-9.

LA GUMA, (JUSTIN) ALEX(ANDER), 1925-

GENERAL

Abrahams, Cecil A., "Achebe, Ngugi and LaGuma: Commitment and the Traditional Storyteller," *Mana Review* (Suva) 2, i (1977): 11-24.

Asein, Samuel O., "The Revolutionary Vision in Alex LaGuma's Novels," *BlackI* 3, ii (1974): 17-24. Also in *LAAW* 24-25 (Apr.-Sept., 1975). Also in *Phylon* 39 (1978): 74-86.

Chennells, Anthony, "Alex LaGuma and the South African Political Novel," *Mambo* 1 (Nov., 1974): 14-16.

Coetzee, J. M., "Man's Fate in the Novels of Alex LaGuma," *SBL* 5, 1 (Spring, 1974): 16-23.

Rabkin, David, "LaGuma and Reality in South Africa," *JCL* 8, i (June, 1973): 54-62.

Rhodes, H. Winston, "Alex LaGuma: African Novelist," *NZMR* 14 (Oct., 1973): 16-17. [Not seen.]

Roscoe, A., *Uhuru's Fire*, 233-58.

Scanlon, Paul A., "Alex LaGuma's Novels of Protest: The Growth of the Revolutionary," *Okike* 16 (Nov., 1979): 39-47.

Serumaga, Robert, "Alex LaGuma," *SAfrL* 1 (1972): 90-3. [Interview.]

Wanjala, Chris L., "The Face of Injustice: Alex LaGuma's Fiction," in Wanjala, C. L., ed., *Standpoints on African Literature*, 305-22.

AND A THREEFOLD CORD

Coetzee, J. M. "Man's Fate in the Novels of Alex LaGuma," *SBL* 5, i (Spring, 1974): 20.

Lindfors, Bernth, "Form and Technique in the Novels of Richard Rive and Alex LaGuma," *JNALA* 2 (1966): 14-15.

Roscoe, A., *Uhuru's Fire*, 14-15.

IN THE FOG OF THE SEASON'S END

Coetzee, J. M., "Man's Fate in the Novels of Alex LaGuma," *SBL* 5, i (Spring, 1974): 21-2.

Futcha, Innocent, "The Fog in IN THE FOG OF THE SEASON'S END," *Ngam* (Yaounde) 1-2 (1977): 78-92.

Green, Robert, "Alex LaGuma's IN THE FOG OF THE SEASON'S END: The Politics of Subversion," *Umoja* 3 (1979): 85-93.

Kibera, Leonard, "A Critical Appreciation of Alex LaGuma's IN THE FOG OF THE SEASON'S END," *Busara* 8, i (1976): 59-66.

Lewis, Rupert, "IN THE FOG OF THE SEASON'S END," *BlackW* 24, iv (1975): 94-7.

Riemenschneider, Dieter, "The Prisoner in South African Fiction: Alex LaGuma's THE STONE COUNTRY and IN THE FOG OF THE SEASON'S END," *ACLALSB* 5, iii (1980): 144-53. Also in Massa, D., ed., *Individual and Community in Commonwealth Literature*, 51-8.

Roscoe, A., *Uhuru's Fire*, 253-8.

Wanjala, Chris L., "Fossilized Black Martyrs," in Gachukia, E., and S. K. Akivaga, eds., *Teaching of African Literature in Schools*, 51-8.

THE STONE COUNTRY

Coetzee, J. M., "Man's Fate in the Novels of Alex LaGuma," *SBL* 5, i (Spring, 1974): 20-1.

Moore, G., *Chosen Tongue*, 201-2.

Riemenschneider, Dieter, "The Prisoner in South African Fiction: Alex LaGuma's Novels *THE STONE COUNTRY* and *IN THE FOG OF THE SEASON'S END*," *ACLALSB* 5, iii (1980): 144-53. Also in Massa, D., ed., *Individual and Community in Commonwealth Literature*, 51-8.

Roscoe, A., *Uhuru's Fire*, 251-3.

TIME OF THE BUTCHERBIRD

Whitman, Scarlet, "A Story of Resistance," *African Communist* 77 (1979): 110-12.

A WALK IN THE NIGHT

Bede, Jacques L., "African Town Environment in Contemporary Literature," *CM* 1 (1975): 18-32 *passim*.

Coetzee, J. M., "Alex LaGuma and the Responsibilities of the South African Writer," *JNALA* 9-10 (Spring-Winter, 1971): 5-11. Also in Okpaku, Joseph, ed., *New African Literature and the Arts*, Vol. 3, N.Y.: Third Press, 1973, 116-24.

_____, "Man's Fate in the Novels of Alex LaGuma," *SBL* 5, i (Spring, 1974): 18-20.

Gakawandi, S. A., *Novel and Contemporary Experience in Africa*, 21-6.

Lindfors, Bernth, "Form and Technique in the Novels of Richard Rive and Alex LaGuma," *JNALA* 2 (1966): 12-14.

Obuke, J. Okpure, "The Structure of Commitment: A Study of
Alex LaGuma," *BaShiru* 5, i (Fall, 1973): 14-20.

Roscoe, A., *Uhuru's Fire*, 234-9.

Scanlon, Paul A., "Alex LaGuma's Novels of Protest: The
Growth of a Revolutionary," *Okike* 16 (Nov., 1979): 40-7.

Wade, Michael, "Art and Morality in Alex LaGuma's A WALK
IN THE NIGHT," in Parker, K., ed., *South African Novel in
English*, 164-91.

Wanjala, Chris L., "The Face of Injustice: Alex LaGuma's Fiction," in Wanjala, C. L., ed., *Standpoints on African Literature*,
309-13.

BIBLIOGRAPHY

Green, Robert, and Agnes Lonje, "Alex LaGuma: A Selected
Bibliography," *WLWE* 20, i (Spring, 1981): 16-22.

LAMMING, GEORGE, 1927-

GENERAL

Gikes, M., *West Indian Novel*, 86-91.

Haugaard, Janet B., "The Fiction of George Lamming: Ideological Mandate: Narrative Despair," *DAI* 41 (1980): 1625A.

Kemoli, Arthur B., "On Interviewing George Lamming," *Umma*
(Nairobi) 3 (1976): 20-2, 24-5, 30.

Kent, George E., "A Conversation with George Lamming,"
BlackW 22, v (1973): 4-14, 99-97.

Munro, Ian H., "Exile and Community: A Study of the Poetry
and Prose of George Lamming," *DAI* 37 (1977): 7765A.

———, "Writing and Publishing in the West Indies: An
Interview with George Lamming," *WLWE* 19 (Apr., 1971):
17-22.

———, and Reinhard Sanders, eds., *Kas-Kas: Interviews with
Three Caribbean Writers in Texas: George Lamming, C. L. R.
James, Wilson Harris*, Austin: Un. of Texas, 1972.

Ngugi wa Thiong'o [James Ngugi], "George Lamming and the
Colonial Situation," *SAfrL* 4 (1972): 127-44.

———, "Home from Exile: George Lamming and the Colonial Situation," *PanA* 1, i (Mar., 1971): 17-22.

Nunez-Harrell, Elizabeth, "Lamming and Naipaul: Some Criteria for Evaluating the Third-World Novel," *ConL* 19, i
(Winter, 1978): 26-47.

———, "THE TEMPEST and the Works of Two Caribbean
Novelists: Pitfalls in the Way of Seeing Caliban," *DAI* 38
(1977): 2775A-76A.

Paqueut, Sandra K., "Politics and the Novels of George Lamming," *DAI* 38 (1977): 285A-86A.

[Riwa, Masanga], "An Interview with George Lamming,"
Umma 5 (1975): 100-3.

Yarde, Gloria, "George Lamming: The Historical Imagination,"
LHY 11, ii (July, 1970): 35-45.

THE EMIGRANTS

Griffiths, G., *Double Exile*, 100-4.

Moore, G., *Chosen Tongue*, 37-42.

Morris, Mervyn, "The Poet as Novelist," in James L., ed., *Islands
in Between*, 76-7.

Munro, Ian, in King, B., ed., *West Indian Literature*, 130-2.

IN THE CASTLE OF MY SKIN

Abrahams, Cecil A., "George Lamming and Chinua Achebe:
Tradition and the Literary Chroniclers," in Narasimhaiah, C.
D., ed., *Awakened Conscience*, 294-306.

Barthold, B. J., *Black Time*, 150-7.

Baugh, Edward, "Cuckoo and Culture: IN THE CASTLE OF
MY SKIN," *ArielE* 8, iii (July, 1977): 23-33.

Carty, Wilfred, "The Realities of Four Negro Writers," *CUF* 9,
iii (Summer, 1969): 32-42 *passim*.

Collier, Eugenia, "Dimensions of Alienation in Two Black
American and Caribbean Novels," *Phylon* 43, i (Mar., 1982):
46-56.

Gikes, M., *West Indian Novel*, 123-31.

Griffiths, G., *Double Exile*, 81-4, 91-7.

Kom, Ambroise, "IN THE CASTLE OF MY SKIN: George Lamming and the Colonial Caribbean," *WLWE* 18, ii (1979):
406-20.

Moore, Gerald, "Discovery," *Chosen Tongue*, 12-17. Also in
Cooke, M. G., ed., *Modern Black Novelists*, 155-9.

Morris, Mervyn, "The Poet as Novelist," in James, L., ed., *Islands
in Between*, 74-6.

Munro, Ian H., "The Theme of Exile in George Lamming's IN
THE CASTLE OF MY SKIN," *WLWE* 20 (Nov., 1971): 51-60.

———, in King, B., ed., *West Indian Literature*, 128-30.

Ngai, Mbatau K. W., "The Relationship Between Literature and
Society and How It Emerges in the Work of G. Lamming, V.
S. Naipaul and W. Harris," *Busara* 8, ii (1976): 54-8.

Ngugi, James, "George Lamming's IN THE CASTLE OF MY
SKIN," *Homecoming*, 110-26. Also in Baugh, E., ed., *Critics on
Caribbean Literature*, 47-57.

Ojo, Patachechole P., "Nature in Three Caribbean Novels," *JCSt*
2, i (Spring, 1981): 99-104.

Peterson, Kirsten H., "Time, Timelessness and the Journey
Metaphor in George Lamming's IN THE CASTLE OF MY
SKIN and NATIVES OF MY PERSON" in Niven, A., ed.,
Commonwealth Writer Overseas, 283-88.

Sandiford, Keith, "Ralph Ellison and George Lamming: Two
Episodes, One Myth," *MV* 3, ii (Fall, 1979): 19-25.

West, David S., "Lamming's Poetic Language in IN THE CAS-
TLE OF MY SKIN," *LHY* 18 (1977): 71-83.

NATIVES OF MY PERSON

Barthold, B. J., *Black Time*, 85-8.

Boxhill, Anthony, "San Cristobal Unreached: George Lamming's Latest Two Novels," *WLWE* 12 (1973): 11-16.

Cotter, Michael, "Identity and Compulsion: George Lamming's
NATIVES OF MY PERSON," *New Lit. Rev.* (Canberra) 1
(1977): 29-35.

Munro, Ian, in King, B., ed., *West Indian Literature*, 137-41.

Peterson, Kirsten H., "Time, Timelessness and the Journey
Metaphor in George Lamming's IN THE CASTLE OF MY
SKIN and NATIVES OF MY PERSON," in Niven, A., ed.,
Commonwealth Writer Overseas, 283-88.

Pouchet-Paquet, Sandra, "The Politics of George Lamming's
NATIVES OF MY PERSON," *CLAJ* 17 (1973): 109-16.

Tiffin, Helen, "The Tyranny of History: George Lamming's
NATIVES OF MY PERSON and WATER WITH BERRIES,"
ArielE 10, iv (1979): 37-52.

Griffiths, G., *Double Exile*, 135-8.

Moore, G., *Chosen Tongue*, 49-57.

Morris, Mervyn, "The Poet as Novelist," in James, L., ed., *Islands in Between*, 77-80.

Munro, Ian, in King, B., ed., *West Indian Literature*, 132-5.

Ngugi wa Thiong'o, "George Lamming and the Colonial Situation," *SAfrL* 4 (1972): 127-44. Also in Ngugi, J., *Homecoming*, 133-43.

Ramchand, K., *West Indian Novel and Its Background*, 135-49.

WATER WITH BERRIES

Boxhill, Anthony, "San Cristobal Unreached: George Lamming's Latest Two Novels," *WLWE* 12 (1973): 111-16.

Munro, Ian, in King, B., ed., *West Indian Literature*, 141-3.

Nightingale, Margaret, "George Lamming and V. S. Naipaul: Thesis and Antithesis," *ACLALSB* 5, iii (1980): 40-50.

Tiffin, Helen, "Freedom After the Fall: Renaissance and Disillusionment in WATER WITH BERRIES and GUERILLAS," in Massa, D., ed., *Individual and Community in Commonwealth Literature*, 90-8.

_____, "The Tyranny of History: George Lamming's NATIVES OF MY PERSON and WATER WITH BERRIES," *ACLALSB* 5 iii (1980): 40-50.

LARKIN, PHILIP, 1922-1985

GENERAL

Martin, B. K., *Philip Larkin*.

Timms, D., *Philip Larkin*.

Wain, John, "Engagement or Withdrawal? Some Notes on the Work of Philip Larkin," *CritQ* 6 (Summer, 1964): 175-8.

Welz, Dieter, "A Winter Landscape in Neutral Colours: Some Notes on Philip Larkin's Vision of Reality," *Theoria* 39 (1979): 61-73.

A GIRL IN WINTER

Brownjohn, Alan, "Novels into Poems," in Thwaite, A., ed., *Larkin at Sixty*, 109-19.

Domnarski, William, "Wishing for More: Philip Larkin's Novels," *Crit* 22, ii (1980): 4-6, 12-19.

Gindin, J., "Education and the Contemporary Class Structure," *Postwar British Fiction*, 104-5.

Martin, B. K., *Philip Larkin*, 112-20.

O'Connor, W. V., *New University Wits*, 20-3.

Timms, D., *Philip Larkin*, 45-53.

JILL

Brownjohn, Alan "Novels into Poems" in Thwaite, A., ed., *Larkin at Sixty*, 109-19.

Domnarski, William, "Wishing for More: Philip Larkin's Novels," *Crit* 22, ii (1980): 5-12.

Gindin, J., "Education and the Contemporary Class Structure," *Postwar British Fiction*, 85-108.

Martin, B. K., *Philip Larkin*, 108-12.

O'Connor, W. V., *New University Wits*, 18-20.

Timms, D., *Philip Larkin*, 36-45.

BIBLIOGRAPHPY

Bloomfield, B. C., *Philip Larkin: A Bibliographpy, 1933-1976*, London: Faber & Faber, 1979.

LAURENCE, (JEAN) MARGARET (WEMYSS), 1926-1987

GENERAL

Bailey, Nancy, "Margaret Laurence, Carl Jung and the Manawaka Women," *SCL* 2 (Summer, 1977): 306-21.

Bennett, Dona A., "The Failures of Sisterhood in Margaret Laurence's Manawaka Novels," *Atlantis* (Wolfville, N. S.) 4, i (1978): 103-9.

Blewett, David, "The Unity of the Manawaka Cycle," *JCanStud* 13, iii (Fall, 1978): 31-9.

Blodgett, Harriet, "The Real Lives of Margaret Laurence's Women," *Crit* 23, i (1981): 5-17.

Callahan, Barry, "The Writings of Margaret Laurence," *TamR* (Summer, 1965): 45-51. Also in New, W., ed., *Margaret Laurence*, 126-31.

Coldwell, Joan, "Margaret Laurence: In Search of Ancestors," *BForum* 4, i (1978): 64-9.

Curry, Gwen C., "Journeys toward Freedom: A Study of Margaret Laurence's Fictional Women," *DAI* 41 (1980): 244A.

Davidson, Cathy N., "Geography as Psychology in the Manitoba Fiction of Margaret Laurence," *KCN* 2, ii (1976): 5-10.

Demetrakopoules, Stephanie A., "Laurence's Fiction: A Revisioning of Feminine Archtypes," *CanL* 93 (Summer, 1982): 142-57.

Djwa, Sandra, "False Gods and the True Covenant: Thematic Continuity Between Margaret Laurence and Sinclair Ross," *JCF* 1, iv (Fall, 1972): 43-50. Also in New, W., ed., *Margaret Laurence*, 66-84.

Dombrowski, Theo Q., "Who is This You? Margaret Laurence and Identity," *UWR* 13, i (Fall/Winter 1977): 21-38.

_____, "Word and Fact: Laurence and the Problem of Language," *CanL* 80 (Spring, 1979): 50-62.

Forman, Denyse, and Uma Parameswaran, "Echoes and Refrains in the Canadian Novels of Margaret Laurence," *CentR* 16, iii (Summer, 1972): 233-53. Also in New, W., ed., *Margaret Laurence*, 85-100.

Gom, Leona M., "Laurence and the Use of Memory," *CanL* 71 (Winter, 1976): 48-58.

_____, "Margaret Laurence and the First Person," *DalR* 55 (Summer, 1975): 236-51.

Gotlieb, Phyllis, "On Margaret Laurence," *TamR* 52, iii (Summer, 1969): 76-80. Also in New, W., ed., *Margaret Laurence*, 41-4.

Grace, Sherrill E., "Crossing Jordan: Time and Memory in the Fiction of Margaret Laurence," *WLWE* 16, i (Nov., 1977): 328-39.

_____, "A Portrait of the Artist as Laurence Hero," *JCanStud* 13, iii (Fall, 1978): 64-71.

Hehner, Barbara, "River of Now and Then: Margaret Laurence's Narratives," *CanL* 74 (Autumn, 1977): 40-57.

Hind-Smith, J., *Three Voices*, 3-60.

Johnston, Eleanor, "The Quest of the Diviners," *Mosaic* 11, iii (Spring, 1978): 107-17.

LaBonte, Ronald N., "Disclosing and Touching: Revaluating the Manawaka World," *JCF* 27 (1980): 167-82.

_____, "Laurence and Characterization: The Humanist Flaw," *JCF* 33 (1981-82): 107-11.

Laurence, Margaret, "Sources," *Mosaic* 3, iii (1970): 80-4. Also in New, W., ed., *Margaret Laurence*, 12-16.

_____, "Ten Years' Sentences," *CanL* 41 (Summer, 1969): 10-16. Also in New, W., ed., *Margaret Laurence*, 17-23. Also in Stephens, D. G., ed., *Writers of the Prairies*, 142-8. Also in Woodcock, G., ed., *Canadian Novel in the Twentieth Century*, 235-41.

Lennox, John W., "Manawaka and Deptford: Place and Voice," *JCanStud* 13, iii (Fall, 1978): 23-30.

Lever, Bernice, "Literature and Canadian Culture: An Interview with Margaret Laurence," *Alive* 41 (1975): 18-19. Also in New, W., ed., *Margaret Laurence*, 24-32.

_____, "Nature Imagery in the Canadian Fiction of Margaret Laurence," *Alive* 41 (1975): 20-2.

Maeser, Angelika, "Finding the Mother: The Individuation of Laurence's Heroines," *JCF* 27 (1980): 151-66.

_____, "Myth and Reality: The Religious Dimension in the Novels of Margaret Laurence," *DAI* 39 (1979): 5529A.

Monk, Patricia, "Shadow Continent: The Image of Africa in Three Canadian Writers," *ArielE* 8, iv (Oct., 1977): 3-11, 17-23.

Monkman, Leslie, "The Tonnerre Family: Mirrors of Suffering," *JCF* 27 (1980): 143-50.

Morley, Patricia, "Canada, Africa, Canada: Laurence's Unbroken Journey," *JCF* 27 (Summer, 1980): 81-91.

_____, *Margaret Laurence*.

_____, "Margaret Laurence's Early Writing: 'a world in which others have to be respected'," *JCanStud* 13, iii (Fall, 1978): 13-18.

New, W., ed., *Margaret Laurence*.

Osachoff, Margaret, "Colonialism in the Fiction of Margaret Laurence," *SoRA* 13, iii (Nov., 1980): 222-38.

Pesando, Frank, "In a Nameless Land: The Use of Apocalyptic Mythology in the Writings of Margaret Laurence," *JCF* 2, i (Winter, 1973): 53-8. Also in Moss, J., ed., *Canadian Novel: Here and Now*, 81-92.

Read, S. E., "The Maze of Life: The Work of Margaret Laurence," *CanL* 27 (Winter, 1966): 5-14. Also in New, W., ed., *Margaret Laurence*, 45-54. Also in Stephens, D. G., *Writers of the Prairies*, 132-41.

Robertson, George, "An Artist in Progress," *CanL* 21 (Summer, 1964): 53-5.

Rocard, Marcienne, "Margaret Laurence's Attempt at Audio-Visual Fiction," *Kunapipi* 1, ii (1979): 91-100. [Not seen.]

Russell, Kenneth, "God and Church in the Ficiton of Margaret Laurence," *SRC* 7, iv (Fall, 1978): 435-46.

_____, "Margaret Laurence's Seekers after Grace," *Chelsea Journal* (Sept.-Oct., 1977): 245-8.

Scott, Jamie S., "Redemptive Imagination in Margaret Laurence's Manawaka Fiction," *SRC* 9, iv (Fall, 1980): 427-40.

Swayze, Walter, "The Odyssey of Margaret Laurence," *EngQ* 3, iii (Fall, 1970): 7-17.

Sweet, Frederick, in Heath, J. M., ed., *Profiles in Canadian Literature* 2, 49-56.

Thomas, Clara, "A Conversation About Literature: An Interview with Margaret Laurence and Irving Layton," *JCF* 1, i (Winter, 1972): 65-9.

_____, *Manawaka World of Margaret Laurence*.

_____, *Margaret Laurence*.

_____, "The Novels of Margaret Laurence," *SNNTS* 4, ii (Summer, 1972): 154-64. Also in New, W., ed., *Margaret Laurence*, 55-65.

_____, "Proud Lineage: Willa Cather and Margaret Laurence," *CRevAS* 2, i (Spring, 1971): 3-12.

_____, "The Wild Garden and the Manawaka World," *MFS* 22, iii (Autumn, 1976): 401-11.

Woodcock, George, "The Human Elements: Margaret Laurence's Fiction," in Helwig, D., ed., *Human Elements*, 134-61.

THE DIVINERS

Abrahams, Cecil, "Margaret Laurence and Chinua Achebe: Commonwealth Storytellers," *ACLALSB* 5, iii (1980): 74-85.

Atherton, Stan, "Margaret Laurence's Progress," *IFR* 2, i (Jan., 1975): 61-4.

Bailey, Nancy, "Fiction and the New Androgyne: Problems and Possibilities in THE DIVINERS," *Atlantis* (Wolfville, N.S.) 4, i (1978): 10-18.

Beckman, Susan, "Language as Cultural Identity in Achebe, Ihimaera, Lawrence and Atwood," *WLWE* 20, i (Spring, 1981): 129-34.

Blodgett, Harriet, "The Real Lives of Margaret Laurence's Women," *Crit* 23, i (1981): 13-16.

Carrington, Ildikó de Papp, "'Tales in the Telling': THE DIVINERS as Fiction about Fiction," *ECW* 9 (Winter, 1977-78): 154-69.

Cooper, Cheryl, "Images of Closure in THE DIVINERS," in Moss, J., ed., *Canadian Novel: Here and Now*, 93-100.

Davidson, Cathy N., "Canadian Wry: Comic Vision in Atwood's LADY ORACLE and Laurence's THE DIVINERS," *RFI* 3, ii-iii (1977-78): 50-5.

Engel, Marian, "Steps to the Mythic: THE DIVINERS and A BIRD IN THE HOUSE," *JCanStud* 13, ii (Fall, 1978): 72-4.

Fabre, Michel, "Mini-text and Micro-text: The Forms and Functions of Narrative Units in Margaret Laurence's THE DIVINERS," *CINE* 1, ii (1982): 166-90.

_____, "Words and the World: THE DIVINERS as an Exploration of the Book of Life," *CanL* 93 (Summer, 1982): 60-78.

Gom, Leona, "Margaret Laurence: The Importance of Place," *WCR* 10, ii (Oct., 1975): 26-30.

Gotlieb, Phyllis, in *TamR* 63 (Oct., 1974): 80-1.

Gros-Lewis, Dolores, "Pins and Needles: Daughters and Mothers in Recent Canadian Fiction," *KCN* 2, iii (Winter, 1975): 8-15.

Hehner, Barbara, "River of Now and Then: Margaret Laurence's Narratives," *CanL* 74 (Autumn, 1977): 40-57.

Hind-Smith, J., *Three Voices*, 56-60.

Holland, Patrick, "Water and Clay: Maurice Shadbolt's A TOUCH OF CLAY and Margaret Laurence's THE DIVINERS," *WLWE* 21, ii (Summer, 1982): 268-74.

Lever, Bernice, "Manawaka Magic," *JCF* 3, iii (Summer, 1974): 93-6.

_____, "Margaret Laurence: Morag Divined," *Canadian Review* (Sept.-Oct., 1975): 34, 36-7.

Maeser, Angelika, "Finding the Mother: Individuation of Laurence's Heroines," *JCF* 27 (1980): 159-63.

McCallum, Pamela, "Communication and History Themes in Innis and Laurence," *SCL* 3, i (Winter, 1978): 5-16.

Miner, Valerie, "The Matriarch of Manawaka," *Saturday Night* 89 (May, 1974): 17-20.

Morley, Patricia, "Engel, Wiseman, Laurence: Women Writers Women's Lives," *WLWE* 17, i (Apr., 1978): 160-3.

_____, *Margaret Laurence*, 120-39.

Mortlock, Melanie, "The Religion of Heritage: THE DIVINERS as a Thematic Conclusion to the Manawaka Series," *JCF* 27 (1980): 132-42.

Moss, John, "The Presbyterian Legacy: Laurence and THE DI-VINERS," *Sex and Violence in the Canadian Novel*, 69-83.

Ricou, Laurie, "Never Cry Wolfe: Benjamin West's *The Death of Wolfe* in PROCHAIN EPISODE and THE DIVINERS," *ECW* 20 (Winter, 1980-81): 171-85.

Rocard, Marcienne, "The Dispossession Theme in Margaret Laurence's THE DIVINERS," *WLWE* 21, i (Spring, 1982): 109-14.

Ross, Catherine S., "'A Singing Spirit': Female Rites of Passage in KLEE WYCK, SURFACING, and THE DIVINERS," *Atlantis* (Wolfville, N.S.) 4, i (1978): 86-94.

Scott, Jamie S., "Redemptive Imagination in Margaret Laurence's Manawaka Fiction," *SRC* 9, iv (Fall, 1980): 435-40.

Staines, David, "Introduction," in Laurence, Margaret, *The Diviners* (New Canadian Library), Toronto: McClelland & Stewart, 1978, v-xiv.

Stouck, David, in *WCR* 10, i (June, 1975): 44-6.

Stratford, Phillip, "*Kamourska* and THE DIVINERS," *RNL* 7 (1976): 110-26.

Symons, Scott, "The Canadian Bestiary," *WCR* 11, ii (1977): 3-16.

Thomas, Clara, "The Chariot of Ossian: Myth and Manitoba in THE DIVINERS," *JCanStud* 13, iii (Fall, 1978): 55-63.

_____, "Commonwealth Albums: Family Resemblance in Derek Walcott's ANOTHER LIFE and Margaret Laurence's THE DIVINERS," *WLWE* 21, ii (Summer, 1982): 262-8.

_____, *Manawaka World of Margaret Laurence*, 130-72.

_____, "Myth and Manitoba in THE DIVINERS," in Moss, J., ed., *Canadian Novel: Here and Now*, 103-18.

_____, "The Wild Garden and the Manawaka World," *MFS* 22, iii (Autumn, 1976): 401-11.

Wagner, Linda W., "Margaret Laurence's THE DIVINERS," *UWR* 6, ii (1982): 55-63.

Wainwright, J. A., "You Have to Go Home Again: Art and Life in THE DIVINERS," *WLWE* 20, ii (Autumn, 1981): 292-311.

Williams, David, "The Indian Our Ancestor: Three Modes of Vision in Recent Canadian Fiction," *DR* 58, ii (Summer, 1978): 309-11.

Woodcock, George, "The Human Elements: Margaret Laurence's Fiction," in Helwig, D., ed., *Human Elements*, 157-61.

THE FIRE-DWELLERS

Bevan, Allan, "Introduction to THE FIRE-DWELLERS," in Laurence, Margaret, *The Fire-Dwellers*, Toronto: McClelland and Stewart, 1973, viii-xiv. Also in New, W., ed., *Margaret Laurence*, 205-11.

Blodgett, Harriet, "The Real Lives of Margaret Laurence's Women," *Crit* 23, i (1981): 12-13.

Hind-Smith, J., *Three Voices*, 43-6.

Irvine, Lorna, "A Psychological Journey: Mothers and Daughters in English-Canadian Fiction," in Davidson, C. N., and E. M. Boner, eds., *Lost Tradition*, 248-9.

Maeser, Angelika, "Finding the Mother: The Individuation of Laurence's Heroines," *JCF* 27 (1980): 157-9.

Morley, P., *Margaret Laurence*, 99-109.

Packer, Miriam, "The Dance of Life: THE FIRE-DWELLERS," *JCF* 27 (1980): 124-31.

Thomas, C., *Manawaka World of Margaret Laurence*, 114-29.

A JEST OF GOD (RACHEL, RACHEL)

Bailey, Nancy, "Margaret Laurence and the Psychology of Re-Birth in A JEST OF GOD," *JPC* 15, iii (Winter, 1981): 62-9.

Blodgett, Harriet, "The Real Lives of Laurence's Women," *Crit* 23, 1 (1981): 10-12.

Boone, Laurel, "Rachel's Benign Growth," *SCL* 3, ii (Summer, 1978): 277-81.

Bowering, George, "That Fool of Fear: Notes on A JEST OF GOD," *CanL* 50 (Autumn, 1971): 41-56. Also in New, W., ed., *Margaret Laurence*, 161-76. Also in Stephens, D. G., ed., *Writers of the Prairies*, 149-64. Also in Woodcock, G., ed., *Canadian Novel in the Twentieth Century*, 219-34.

Gottlieb, Lois, and Wendy Keitner, "Mothers and Daughters in Four Recent Canadian Novels," *Sphinx* 4 (Summer, 1975): 21-34.

Hind-Smith, J., *Three Voices*, 37-41.

Hughes, Kenneth J., "Politics and A JEST OF GOD," *JCanStud* 13, iii (Fall, 1978): 40-54.

Irvine, Lorna, "A Psychological Journey: Mothers and Daughters in Recent English-Canadian Fiction," in Davidson, C. N., and E. M. Boner, eds., *Lost Tradition*, 245-6, 248.

Kearns, Judy, "Rachel and Social Determinism: A Feminist Reading of A JEST OF GOD," *JCF* 27 (1980): 101-23.

Killam, G. D., "Introduction," in Laurence, Margaret, *A Jest of God* (New Canadian Library), Toronto: McClelland and Stewart, 1974.

Maeser, Angelika, "Finding the Mother: The Individuation of Laurence's Heroines," *JCF* 27 (1980): 155-7.

McLay, C. M., "Every Man is an Island: Isolation in A JEST OF GOD," *CanL* 50 (Autumn, 1971): 57-68. Also in New, W., ed., *Margaret Laurence*, 177-88.

McCourt, E. A., *Canadian West in Fiction*, 112-18.

Morley, P., *Margaret Laurence*, 88-99.

Stevenson, Warren, "The Myth of Demeter and Peresephone in A JEST OF GOD," *SCL* 1, i (Winter, 1976): 120-3.

Thomas, C., *Manawaka World of Margaret Laurence*, 77-95.

_____, *Margaret Laurence*, 45-54.

THE STONE ANGEL

Baxter, John, "THE STONE ANGEL: Shakespearian Bearings," *Compass* 1 (1977): 3-19.

Blodgett, Harriet, "The Real Lives of Margaret Laurence's Women," *Crit* 23, i (1981): 8-10.

Cooley, Dennis, "Antimacassared in the Wilderness: Art and Nature in THE STONE ANGEL," *Mosaic* 11, iii (Spring, 1978): 29-46.

Coldwell, Joan, "Hagar as Meg Merrilies, the Homeless Gypsy," *JCF* 27 (1980): 92-100.

Davidson, Cathy N., "Past and Perspective in Margaret Laurence's THE STONE ANGEL," *CRevAS* 8, ii (Autumn, 1978): 61-9.

Harrison, D., *Unnamed Country*, 194-7.

Hind-Smith, J., *Three Voices*, 31-5.

Hutcheon, Linda, "Laurence and Atwood: Poet and Novelist," *SCL* 3, ii (Summer, 1978): 255-63.

Jeffrey, David L., "Biblical Hermeneutics and the Familly History in Contemporary Canadian Fiction: Wiebe and Laurence," *Mosaic* 11, iii (Spring, 1978): 91-9.

Kertzer, Jon M., "THE STONE ANGEL: Time and Responsibility," *DR* 54 (Autumn, 1974): 499-509.

Maeser, Angelika, "Finding the Mother: Individuation of Laurence's Heroines," *JCF* 27 (1980): 152-5.

McCourt, E. A., *Canadian West in Fiction*, 109-12.

Morley, P., *Margaret Laurence*, 77-88.

Moss, J., *Patterns of Isolation*, 230-2.

New, William H., "Now and Then: Voice and Language in Laurence's THE STONE ANGEL," *CanL* 93 (Summer, 1982): 26-41.

_____, "Introduction to THE STONE ANGEL," in Laurence, Margaret, *The Stone Angel*, Toronto: McClelland and Stewart, 1968, iii-x. Also in New, W. H., *Articulating the West*, 207-15. Also in New, W. H., ed., *Margaret Laurence*, 135-42.

Osachoff, Margaret G., "Moral Vision in THE STONE ANGEL," *SCL* 4, i (1979): 139-53.

Pollack, Claudette, "The Paradox of THE STONE ANGEL," *HAB* 27, iii (Summer, 1976): 267-75.

Pollock, Zailig, "Angel and Bird in THE STONE ANGEL," *ESC* 2 (1976): 345-52.

Rooke, Constance, "A Feminist Reading of THE STONE ANGEL," *CanL* 93 (Summer, 1982): 79-96.

Thomas, C., *Manawaka World of Margaret Laurence*, 60-76.

_____, *Margaret Laurence*, 35-44.

Thompson, Anne, "The Wilderness of Pride: Form and Image in THE STONE ANGEL," *JCF* 4, iii (Summer, 1975): 95-110.

Vauthier, Simone, "Names and Naming in THE STONE ANGEL," *RANAM* 14 (1981): 237-54.

THIS SIDE OF JORDAN

Githae-Mugo, M., *Visions of Africa*, 139-54.

Killam, G. D., "Introduction," in Laurence, Margaret, *This Side of Jordan*, Toronto: McClelland and Stewart (New Canadian Library), ix-xviii.

Leney, Jane, "Prospero and Caliban in Laurence's African Fiction," *JCF* 27 (1980): 65-73.

Morley, P., *Margaret Laurence*, 60-71.

Thomas, Clara, *Manawaka World of Margaret Laurence*, 60-71.

_____, *Margaret Laurence*, 28-34.

_____, "Pilgrim's Progress: Margaret Laurence and Hagar Shipley," *JCanStud* 17, iii (Fall, 1982): 110-16.

BIBLIOGRAPHY

Warwick, Susan J., "Margaret Laurence: An Annotated Bibliography," in Lecker, Robert, and Jack David, eds., *The Annotated Bibliography of Canada's Major Authors*, Volume One, Downsview: ECW, 1979, 47-101.

LAVIN, MARY, 1912-

GENERAL

Bowen, Z. R., *Mary Lavin*.

Dunleavy, Janet E., "Men in Mary Lavin's Fiction," *CJIS* 2, i (1976): 10-14. [Not seen.]

Meszaros, Patricia K., "Woman as Artist: The Fiction of Mary Lavin," *Crit* 24, i (Fall, 1982): 39-54.

Murphy, Catherine, "Mary Lavin: An Interview," *IUR* 9, ii (Autumn, 1979): 207-24.

Peterson, R. F., *Mary Lavin*.

Roark, Bobbie Jean, "Mary Lavin: The Local and The Universal," *DA* 29 (1969): 3153A.

THE BECKER WIVES

Meszaros, Patricia K., "Woman as Artist: The Fiction of Mary Lavin," *Crit* 24, i (Fall, 1982): 44-51.

THE HOUSE IN CLEWE STREET

Bowen, Z. R., *Mary Lavin*, 62-71.

Koenig, Marianne, "Mary Lavin: The Novels and the Stories," *IUR* 9, ii (Autumn, 1979): 245-8.

Peterson, R. F., *Mary Lavin*, 45-63.

MARY O'GRADY

Bowen, Z. R., *Mary Lavin*, 59-62.

Peterson, R. F., *Mary Lavin*, 63-75.

BIBLIOGRAPHY

Kosok, Heinz, "Mary Lavin: A Bibliography," *IUR* 9, ii (Autumn, 1979): 279-312.

LEA, TOM, 1907-

GENERAL

Antone, Evan H., "Tom Lea: A Study of His Life and Work," *DAI* 32 (1971): 3289A.

Bennett, Patrick, "Wells of Sight and Sound: An Interview with Tom Lea," *SWR* 65 (1980): 113-27.

West, J. O., *Tom Lea*.

THE BRAVE BULLS

West, J. O., *Tom Lea*, 10-13.

THE HANDS OF CANTU

West, J. O., *Tom Lea*, 22-6.

THE PRIMAL YOKE

West, J. O., *Tom Lea*, 26-8.

THE WONDERFUL COUNTRY

West, J. O., *Tom Lea*, 10-13.

LEE, HARPER, 1926-

TO KILL A MOCKINGBIRD

Bakerman, Jane S., "Maycomb Revisited: TO KILL A MOCK-INGBIRD, Novel and Screenplay," *IEJ* 8, i-iii (1974): 18-28.

Dave, R. A., "TO KILL A MOCKINGBIRD: Harper Lee's Tragic Vision," in Naik, M. K., et al., eds., *Studies in Indian Literature*, 311-23.

Erisman, Fred, "The Romantic Regionalism of Harper Lee," *AlaR* 26, iii (Apr., 1973): 122-36.

Hipple, Theodore W., "Will the Real Mockingbird Please Stand Up?" *MEB* 26 (Oct., 1970): 1-6.

Schuster, Edgar H., "Discovering Theme and Structure in the Novel," *EJ* 52 (1963): 506-11.

LEE, JOHN A(LEXANDER), 1891-

GENERAL

Pouilhes, Marie-Helene, and V. Dupont, "John A. Lee's Novels on Juvenile Delinquency," *CarlM* (1974-75): 131-48.

CHILDREN OF THE POOR

McEldowney, Dennis, "John A. Lee's CHILDREN OF THE POOR," in Hankin, C., ed., *Critical Essays on the New Zealand Novel*, 24-39.

Pouilhes, Marie-Helene, and V. Dupont, "John A. Lee's Novels on Juvenile Delinquency," *CarlM* (1974-75): 136-44.

THE HUNTED

Pouilhes, Marie-Helene, and V. Dupont, "John A. Lee's Novels on Juvenile Delinquency," *CarlM* (1974-75): 136-44.

LEHMANN, ROSAMOND, 1901-1990

GENERAL

Cox, Ella P., "Rosamond Lehmann: A Modern Romantic," *DAI* 38 (1978): 7321A.

Dorosz, W., *Subjective Vision and Human Relationships in the Novels of Rosamond Lehmann*.

Gindin, James, "Rosamond Lehmann: A Revaluation," *ConL* 15 (Spring, 1974): 203-11.

Kaplan, S. J., *Feminine Consciousness in the Modern British Novel*, 110-35.

Le Stourgeon, D. E., *Rosamond Lehmann*.

Pendry, E. D., *New Feminism of English Fiction*, 153-73.

Raven, Simon, "The Game That Nobody Wins: The Novels of Rosamond Lehmann," *LonM* n.s. 3 (April, 1963): 59-63.

Shuman, R. Baird, "Personal Isolation in the Novels of Rosamond Lehmann," *RLV* 26, i (1960): 76-80.

THE BALLAD AND THE SOURCE

Coopman, Tony, "Character and Narrative in Rosamond Lehmann's THE BALLAD AND THE SOURCE," 165-73 in Lerot, Jacques, and Rudolf Kern, eds., *Mélanges de linguistique et de littérature offerts au Professeur Henri Draye a l'occasion de son éméritat*, Louvain: Bibliothèque del 'Univ., Bureau du Recueil; Eds. Nauwelaerts, 1978.

Dorosz, W., *Subjective Vision and Human Relationships in the Novels of Rosamond Lehmann*, 36-40, 98-102, 114-16.

Kaplan, Sydney J., "Rosamond Lehmann's THE BALLAD AND THE SOURCE: A Confrontation with 'The Great Mother'," *TCL* 27, ii (Summer, 1981): 127-45.

Le Stourgeon, D. E., *Rosamond Lehmann*, 89-107.

Markovi, V. E., *Changing Face*, 97-111.

Thornton, Lawrence, "Rosamond Lehmann, Henry James and the Temporal Matrix of Fiction," *VMQ* 1, iii (Spring, 1973): 66-75.

DUSTY ANSWER

Dorosz, W., *Subjective Vision and Human Relationships in the Novels of Rosamond Lehmann*, 29-32, 104-6.

Le Stourgeon, D. E., *Rosamond Lehmann*, 29-42.

THE ECHOING GROVE

Allen, W., *Modern Novel*, 195-7.

Balakian, Nona, "Three English Novelists," *KR* 15 (Summer, 1953): 494-6.

Bowen, Elizabeth, "The Modern Novel and the Theme of Love," *NRep* 128 (May 11, 1953): 18-19.

Coopman, Tony, "Symbolism in Rosamond Lehmann's THE ECHOING GROVE," *RLV* 40 (1974): 116-21.

Dorosz, W., *Subjective Vision and Human Relationships in the Novels of Rosamond Lehmann*, 40-1, 116-19.

Kaplan, S. J., *Feminine Consciousness in the Modern British Novel*, 131-5.

Le Stourgeon, D. E., *Rosamond Lehmann*, 108-21.

McCormick, J., *Catastrophe and Imagination*, 85-6, 89-92.

INVITATION TO THE WALTZ

Dorosz, W., *Subjective Vision and Human Relationships in the Novels of Rosamond Lehmann*, 34-5, 86-9, 109-14.

Le Stourgeon, D. E., *Rosamond Lehmann*, 76-88.

LEITCH, MAURICE, 1933-

THE LIBERTY LAD

Foster, J. W., *Forces and Themes in Ulster Fiction*, 268-70.

McMahon, Seán, "May the Lord in His Mercy," *Eire* 4, ii (1969): 128-40.

Paulin, Tom, in Dunn, D., ed., *Two Decades of Irish Writing*, 250-1.

POOR LAZARUS

Foster, J. W., *Forces and Themes in Ulster Fiction*, 270-4.

McMahon, Seán, "May the Lord in His Mercy," *Eire* 4, ii (1969): 128-40.

Paulin, Tom, in Dunn, D., ed., *Two Decades of Irish Writing*, 251-4.

LELCHUK, ALAN, 1938-

AMERICAN MISCHIEF

Hindus, Milton, "The Case of AMERICAN MISCHIEF," *Midstream* 19, vi (June-July, 1973): 65-71.

LESSING, DORIS, 1919-

GENERAL

Ahearn, Marie L., "Science Fiction in the Mainstream Novel: Doris Lessing," *Extrapolation* 20, iv (Winter, 1979): 355-67.

Alcorn, Noeline E., "Vision and Nightmare: A Study of Doris Lessing's Novels," *DAI* 32 (1971): 1500A.

Allen, Walter, in Kostelanetz, R., ed., *Contemporary Literature*, 400-1.

Beard, Linda, S., "Doris Lessing, African Writer," in Parker, C. A., and S. H. Arnold, eds., *When the Drumbeat Changes*, 241-60.

_____, "Lessing's Africa: Geographical and Metaphorical Africa in the Novels and Stories of Doris Lessing," *DAI* 39 (1979): 6770A-71A.

Bonomo, Jacquelyn, "The Free Woman and the Traditional Woman in the Novels of Doris Lessing: Analysis and Poetry": *DAI* 41 (1980): 1604A-05A.

Brooks, Ellen W., "Fragmentation and Integration: A Study of Doris Lessing's Fiction," *DAI* 32 (1972): 3989A-90A.

Brewster, D., *Doris Lessing*.

Brown, Lloyd W., "The Shape of Things: Sexual Images and the Sense of Form in Doris Lessing's Fiction," *WLWE* 14 (Apr., 1975): 176-86.

Budhos, Shirley, "An Examination of the Theme of Enclosure with Emphasis on Marriage in Selected Works of Doris Lessing," *DAI* 41 (1980): 2118A.

Bullock, C. J., and Kay L. Stewart, "Post-Party Politics: Doris Lessing's Novels of the Seventies," *MR* 20 (Summer, 1979): 245-57.

Burkom, Selma R., "'Only Connect': Form and Content in the Works of Doris Lessing," *Crit* 11, i (1968): 51-68.

_____, "A Reconsideration of Opposites: A Study of the Work of Doris Lessing," *DAI* 31 (1971): 5390A.

Carey, Father Alfred Augustine, "Doris Lessing: The Search for Reality: A Study of the Major Themes in Her Novels," *DA* 26 (1965): 3297.

Cedarstrom, Loreli, "From Marxism to Myth: A Developmental Study of the Novels of Doris Lessing," *DAI* 38 (1978): 7320A-21A.

Chalpin, Lila, "Parapsychology and Fable in Recent Novels of Doris Lessing," *SJS* 6, iii (Nov., 1980): 59-70.

Cleary, Rochelle D., "A Study of Marriage in Doris Lessing's Fiction," *DAI* 42 (May, 1982): 4831A.

Drabble, Margaret, "Doris Lessing: Cassandra in a World Under Siege," *Ramparts* 10 (Feb., 1972): 50-4.

Draine, Mary E., "Stages of Consciousness in Doris Lessing's Fiction," *DAI* 38 (1977): 2138A.

Driver, C. J., "Profile 8: Doris Lessing," *New Rev* 1, viii (Nov., 1974): 17-23.

Elshtain, Jean B., "The Post-GOLDEN NOTEBOOK Fiction of Doris Lessing," *Salmagundi* 47-48 (Winter/Spring, 1980): 95-114.

Fishburn, Katherine, "Anti-American Regionalism in the Fiction of Doris Lessing," *RFI* 4, ii (1978): 19-24.

Gindin, J., "Doris Lessing's Intense Commitment," *Postwar British Fiction*, 65-86.

Godwin, Gail, "The Personal Matter of Doris Lessing," *NAmerR* 256, ii (Summer, 1971): 66-70.

Gohlman, Susan Carol A., "The Modern 'Bildungsroman': Four Novels," *DAI* 34 (1973): 2623A-4A.

Grant, Velma F., "The Quest for Wholeness in Novels by Doris Lessing," *DAI* 36 (1975): 901A.

Gurr, Andrew, "The Freedom of Exile in Naipaul and Doris Lessing," *ArielE* 13, iv (Oct., 1982): 7-18.

_____, *Writers in Exile*, 124-32.

Halliday, Patricia A. Y., "The Pursuit of Wholeness in the Work of Doris Lessing: Dualities, Multiplicities, and the Resolution of Patterns in Illumination," *DAI* 34 (1973): 2626A-27A.

Hardin, Nancy S., "Doris Lessing and the Sufi Way," *ConL* 14 (Autumn, 1973): 565-81.

_____, "The Sufi Teaching Story and Doris Lessing," *TCL* 23 (Oct., 1977): 314-26.

Hayes, Tricia, "Adolescent Awakenings in the Fiction of Doris Lessing," *DLN* 3, i (1979): 9-10. [Not seen.]

Hove, David A., "Lessing's Heroines and Their Literary Models," *DAI* 35 (1974): 404A.

Howe, Florence, "A Conversation with Doris Lessing (1966)," *ConL* 14, iv (Autumn, 1973): 418-36. Also in Pratt, A., and L. S. Dembo, eds., *Doris Lessing*, 1-19.

Johnson, Sally H., "Form and Philosophy in the Novels of Doris Lessing," *DAI* 38 (1977): 282A.

Kaplan, Sydney, "The Limits of Consciousness in the Novels of Doris Lessing," *ConL* 14 (Autumn, 1973): 536-43. Also in Kaplan, S. J., *Feminine Consciousness in the Modern British Novel*, 136-72. Also in Pratt, A., and L. S. Dembo, eds., *Doris Lessing*, 119-32.

Karl, Frederick R., *Contemporary English Novel*, rev. and exp., 291-312.

_____, "Doris Lessing in the Sixties: The Anatomy of Melancholy," *ConL* 13 (Winter, 1972): 15-33. Also in Spacks, P. M., ed., *Contemporary Women Novelists*, 55-74.

Kress, Susan, "Lessing's Responsibility," *Salmagundi* 47-48 (Winter-Spring, 1980): 115-31. [Response to Elshtain above.]

Krouse, Agate N., "The Feminism of Doris Lessing," *DAI* 34 (1973): 322A.

Kuriloff, Peshe C., "Doris Lessing: The Practice of Realism in the Novel," *DAI* 40 (1980): 5439A.

Levin, Susan, "A Fourfold Vision: William Blake and Doris Lessing," 212-21 in Bertholf, Robert J., and Annette S. Levitt, eds., *William Blake and the Moderns*, Albany, N.Y.: State Un. of N.Y., 1982.

Magie, Michael L., "Doris Lessing and Romanticism," *CE* 38, iv (Feb., 1977): 531-52.

Manion, Eileen C., "Transcendence through Disorder: A Study of the Fiction of Doris Lessing," *DAI* 41 (1980): 1065A.

Marchino, Lois A., "Life, Lessing, and the Pursuit of Feminist Criticism," *DLN* 2, ii (Winter, 1978): 1, 15-16.

_____, "The Search for Self in the Novels of Doris Lessing," *SNNTS* 4 (Summer, 1972): 252-61.

_____, "The Search for Self in the Novels of Doris Lessing," *DAI* 33 (1972): 2384A-85A.

Markow, Alice B., "The Pathology of Feminine Failure in the Fiction of Doris Lessing," *Crit* 16, i (1974): 88-100.

McDowell, Frederick P. W., "The Fiction of Doris Lessing: An Interim View," *ArQ* 21 (Winter, 1965): 315-45.

Mitchell, Tamara K., "The Irrational Element in Doris Lessing's Fiction," *DAI* 38 (1978): 7326A-27A.

Naumer, Mary Ann S., "The City and the Veld: A Study of the Fiction of Doris Lessing," *DAI* 34 (1974): 5984A-85A.

Oates, Joyce Carol, "A Visit with Doris Lessing," *SoR* 9 (Oct., 1973): 873-83.

O'Rourke, Rebecca, "Doris Lessing: Exile and Exception," in Taylor, J., ed., *Notebooks/Memoirs/Archives*, 206-26.

Parrinder, Patrick, "Descents into Hell: The Later Novels of Doris Lessing," *CritQ* 22, iv (Winter, 1980): 5-25.

Pickering, Jean, "Marxism and Madness: The Two Faces of Doris Lessing's Myth," *MFS* 26, i (Spring, 1980): 17-30.

Pratt, Annis, "Introduction [to a Special Issue on Doris Lessing]," *ConL* 14 (Autumn, 1973): 413-17.

_____, and L. S. Dembo, eds., *Doris Lessing*.

Rapping, Elaine A., "Unfree Women: Feminism in Doris Lessing," *WS* 3, 1975): 29-44.

Reid, Martha, "Form and Space in the Fiction of Doris Lessing," *DAI* 40 (1980): 5065A.

_____, "Outsiders, Exiles, and Aliens in the Fiction of Doris Lessing," *DLN* 4, ii (1980): 3-4, 14. [Not seen.]

Rose, Ellen C., "The End of the Game: New Directions in Doris Lessing's Fiction," *JNT* 6, i (Winter, 1976): 66-75.

Rubenstein, Roberta, "The Room of the Self: Psychic Geography in Doris Lessing's Fiction," *PCL* 5 (1979): 69-78.

Sage, L., *Contemporary English Novel*, 80-5.

Schlueter, P., *Novels of Doris Lessing*.

Schlueter, Paul G., "A Study of the Major Novels of Doris Lessing," *DA* 29 (1969): 3619A-20A.

Schlueter, Peter, "Doris Lessing: Free Woman's Commitment," in Shapiro, C., ed., *Contemporary British Novelists*, 48-61.

Scott, Ann, "The More Recent Writings: Sufism, Mysticism and Politics," in Taylor, J., ed., *Notebooks/Memoirs/Archives*, 164-90.

Seligman, Claudia D., "The Autobiographical Novels of Doris Lessing," *DAI* 37 (1976): 1544A.

Seligman, Dee, "The Four-Faced Novelists," *MFS* 26, i (Spring, 1980): 3-16.

Serafin, Anne, "In Search of Doris Lessing," *DLN* 4, i (1980): 5-6.

Silva, Nancy N., "Doris Lessing's Ideal Reconciliation," *Anonymous* 1 (1974): 72-81. [Not seen.]

Sims, Susan K. S., "Repetition and Evolution: An Examination of Theme and Structures in the Novels of Doris Lessing," *DAI* 39 (1979): 4249A-50A.

Singleton, M. A., *City and the Veld*.

Soos, Emese, "Revolution in the Historical Fiction of Jean-Paul Sartre and Doris Lessing," *PCL* 2, i (1976): 23-33. [Not seen.]

Spiegel, R., *Doris Lessing*.

Sprague, Claire, "Doris Lessing's *Reasoner* Letters," *DLN* 3, i (1979): 6-8.

Stein, Karen F., "Reflections in a Jagged Mirror: Some Metaphors of Madness," *Aphra* 6, i (Spring, 1975): 2-11. [Not seen.]

Stern, Frederick C., "The Changing 'Voice' of Lessing's Characters: From Politics to Sci Fi," *WLWE* 21, iii (Autumn, 1982): 456-67.

Stitzel, Judith, "Humor and Survival in the Works of Doris Lessing," *RFI* 4, ii (1978): 61-8. [Not seen.]

_____, "Reading Doris Lessing," *CE* 40, v (Jan., 1975): 498-504.

_____, "The Uses of Humor," *DLN* (Fall, 1977): 2-3.

Sukenick, Lynn, "Feeling and Reason in Doris Lessing's Fiction," *ConL* 14 (Autumn, 1973): 515-35. Also in Pratt, A., and L. S. Dembo, eds., *Doris Lessing*, 98-118.

Swingewood, Alan, "Structure and Ideology in the Novels of Doris Lessing," 38-54 in Laurenson, Diana, ed., *The Sociology of Literature: Applied Studies* (Sociological Rev. Monograph 26), Keele, Eng.: Un. of Keele, 1978.

Taylor, J. ed., *Notebooks/Memoirs/Archives*.

Thorpe, M., *Doris Lessing*.

_____, *Doris Lessing's Africa*.

Tucker, M., *Africa in Modern Literature*, 175-83.

Vlastes, Marion, "Doris Lessing and R. D. Laing: Psychopolitics and Prophecy," *PMLA* 91, ii (Mar., 1976): 245-58.

Walter, Donna J., "Twentieth-Century Woman in the Early Novels of Doris Lessing," *DAI* 39 (1978): 3608A.

THE ANTHEAP

Brewster, D., *Doris Lessing*, 53-8.

Thorpe, M., *Doris Lessing's Africa*, 38-42.

BRIEFING FOR A DESCENT INTO HELL

Ahearn, Marie L., "Science Fiction in the Mainstream Novel: Doris Lessing," *Extrapolation* 20, iv (Winter, 1979): 356-65. Also in *Proceedings of the Fifth National Convention of the Popular Culture Assoc.*, 1277-96.

Bazin, Nancy T., "Androgyny or Catastrophe: The Vision of Doris Lessing's Later Novels," *Frontiers* 5, iii (Fall, 1980): 10-15.

Bolling, Douglass, "Structure and Theme in BRIEFING FOR A DESCENT INTO HELL," *ConL* 14 (Autumn, 1973): 550-64. Also in Pratt, A., and L. S. Dembo, eds., *Doris Lessing*, 133-47.

Bullock, C. J., and Kay L. Stewart, "Post-Party Politics: Doris Lessing's Novels of the Seventies," *MR* 20, ii (Summer, 1979): 247-51.

Elder, Doris L., "Doris Lessing's BRIEFING FOR A DESCENT INTO HELL: The Writer's Consciousness Confronts Apocalypse," *MBL* 2, i (Spring, 1977): 98-115.

Fuoroli, Caryn, "Doris Lessing's 'Game': Referential Language and Fictional Form," *TCL* 27, ii (Summer, 1981): 146-65.

Kildahl, Karen Ann, "The Political and Apocalyptical Novels of Doris Lessing: A Critical Study of CHILDREN OF VIOLENCE, THE GOLDEN NOTEBOOK, BRIEFING FOR A DESCENT INTO HELL," *DAI* 35 (1975): 4528A.

Kums, Guido, "Structuring the Reader's Response: BRIEFING FOR A DESCENT INTO HELL," *DQR* 11, iii (1981): 197-208.

Oates, Joyce Carol, "A Visit with Doris Lessing," *SoR* 9, iv (Oct., 1973): 873-82.

Richey, Clarence W., "Professor Watkins' 'Sleep of Neccessity': A Note on the Parallel Between Doris Lessing's BRIEFING FOR A DESCENT INTO HELL and G. I. Gurdjieff-P.D. Ouspensky System of Esoteric Psychology," *NConL* 2, ii (Mar., 1972): 9-11.

Rose, Ellen C., "A Briefing for BRIEFING: Charles Williams' DESCENT INTO HELL and Doris Lessing's BRIEFING FOR A DESCENT INTO HELL," *Mythlore* 4, i (1976): 10-13.

Rubenstein, Roberta, "Briefing on Inner Space: Doris Lessing and R. D. Laing," *PsyR* 63, i (Spring, 1976): 83-93.

_____, *Novelistic Vision of Doris Lessing*, 175-99.

Ryf, Robert S., "Beyond Ideology: Doris Lessing's Mature Vision," *MFS* 21, ii (Summer, 1975): 193-201.

Schlueter, P., *Novels of Doris Lessing*, 119-24.

Singleton, M. A., *City and the Veld*, 144-56.

Spiegel, R., *Doris Lessing*, 102-62.

Thorpe, M., *Doris Lessing*, 30-2.

Thorpe, Michael, "Doris Lessing's Risky Inner World," *JCL* 7, i (1972): 133-5.

Vlastos, Marion, "Doris Lessing and R. D. Laing: Psychopolitics and Prophecy," *PMLA* 91, ii (Mar., 1976): 253-7.

CHILDREN OF VIOLENCE Series

Allen, W., *Modern Novel*, 276-7.

Aycock, Linnea, "The Mother/Daughter Relationship in THE CHILDREN OF VIOLENCE Series," *Anonymous* 1 (1974): 48-55.

Brewster, D., *Doris Lessing*, 33, 103.

Brown, Ruth, "*Martha's Quest*: An Echo of Psyche's," *DLN* 2, ii (Winter, 1978): 8-10.

Christ, Carol P., "From Motherhood to Prophecy," *Diving Deep and Surfacing*, 55-9.

Fishburn, Katherine, "The Nightmare Repetition: Mother-Daughter Conflict in Doris Lessing's CHILDREN OF VIOLENCE," in Davidson, C. N., and E. M. Broner, eds., *Lost Tradition*, 207-15.

Gage, Diane B., "Fictive Figurings: Metacommentary on Doris Lessing's CHILDREN OF VIOLENCE," *DAI* 39 (1978): 896A.

Gerver, Elisabeth, "Women Revolutionaries in the Novels of Nadine Gordimer and Doris Lessing," *WLWE* 17, i (Apr., 1978): 44-8.

Hartveit, Lars, "Commitment and the Novelist's Craft: The Racial Issue in the African Volumes of Doris Lessing's CHILDREN OF VIOLENCE," in Massa, D., ed., *Individual and Community in Commonwealth Literature*, 28-35.

Holquist, Ingrid, *From Society to Nature: A Study of Doris Lessing's CHILDREN OF VIOLENCE*. (GothSE 47.) Gothenburg: Acta Univ. Gothpburgensis, 1980.

Howe, Florence, "Doris Lessing's Free Women," *Nation* 200 (Jan. 11, 1965): 34-7.

Jouve, Nicole W., "Of Mud and Other Matter: THE CHILDREN OF VIOLENCE," in Taylor, J., ed., *Notebooks/Memoirs/Archives*, 75-134.

Karl, F. R., *Contemporary English Novel*, 282-3.

Kildahl, Karen A., "The Political and Apocalyptical Novels of Doris Lessing: A Critical Study of CHILDREN OF VIOLENCE, THE GOLDEN NOTEBOOK, BRIEFING FOR A DESCENT INTO HELL," *DAI* 35 (1975): 4528A.

McDowell, Frederick P. W., "The Fiction of Doris Lessing: An Interim View," *ArQ* 21 (Winter, 1965): 330-45.

Morris, R. K., "Children of Violence: The Quest for Change," *Continuance and Change*, 1-27.

Owen, Roger, "Good Man is Hard to Find," *Ctary* 39 (Apr., 1965): 79-82.

Porter, Nancy, "Silenced History: CHILDREN OF VIOLENCE and THE GOLDEN NOTEBOOK," *WLWE* 12 (Nov., 1973): 161-79.

_____, "A Way of Looking at Doris Lessing," in Hoffman, N., and others, eds., *Female Studies VI: Closer to the Ground*, 123-38.

Rose, Ellen C., "The Eriksonian Bildungsroman: An Approach Through Doris Lessing," *HSL* 7, i (1975): 1-15.

_____, "Doris Lessing's CHILDREN OF VIOLENCE as a *Bildungsroman*: An Ericksonian Analysis," *DAI* 35 (1974): 3006A-07A.

_____, *Tree Outside the Window*.

Rosen, Ellen I., "Martha's 'Quest' in Lessing's CHILDREN OF VIOLENCE," *Frontiers* 3, ii (1978): 54-9.

Scanlan, Margaret, "Memory and Continuity in the Series Novel: The Example of CHILDREN OF VIOLENCE," *MFS* 26, i (Spring, 1980): 75-85.

Schlueter, Paul, "Doris Lessing: Free Woman's Commitment," in Shapiro, C., ed., *Contemporary British Novelists*, 51-5.

_____, *Novels of Doris Lessing*, 23-76.

Seiler-Franklin, C., *Boulder-Pushers*, 40-83.

Seligman, Dee, "The Sufi Quest," *WLWE* 12 (Nov., 1973): 190-206.

Singleton, M. A., *City and the Veld*, 130-41, 165-85.

Smith, Diane, "A Thematic Study of Doris Lessing's CHILDREN OF VIOLENCE," *DAI* 32 (1971): 1530A.

Sprague, Claire, "Dialectic and Counter-Dialectic in the Martha Quest Novels," *DLN* 2, ii (Winter, 1978): 8-10.

Steele, M. C., *CHILDREN OF VIOLENCE and Rhodesia: Doris Lessing as Historical Observer*, Salisbury, Rhodesia: Central Africa Historical Assn., 1974.

Sudrann, Jean, "Hearth and Horizon: Changing Concepts of the 'Domestic' Life of the Heroine," *MR* 14 (Spring, 1973): 235-55.

Thorpe, M., *Doris Lessing*, 19-25.

ELDORADO

Brester, D., *Doris Lessing*, 51-3.

Thorpe, M., *Doris Lessing's Africa*, 43-4.

THE FOUR-GATED CITY (See also CHILDREN OF VIOLENCE Series)

Abel, Elizabeth, "(E)Merging Identities: The Dynamics of Female Friendship in Contemporary Fiction by Women," *Signs* 6 (Spring, 1981): 418-21.

Barnouw, Dagmar, "Disorderly Company: From THE GOLDEN NOTEBOOK to THE FOUR-GATED CITY," *ConL* 14, iv (Autumn, 1973): 491-514. Also in Spacks, P. M., ed., *Contemporary Women Novelists*, 30-8. Also in Pratt, A., and L. S. Dembo, eds., *Doris Lessing*, 82-97.

Christ, Carol P., "From Motherhood to Prophecy," *Diving Deep and Surfacing*, 59-73.

Enright, D. J., "Shivery Games," *NYRB* (July 31, 1969): 22-4. Also in Enright, D. J., *Man is an Onion*, 26-31.

Gohlman, Susan A., "Martha Hesse of THE FOUR-GATED CITY: A Bildungsroman Already behind Her," *SAB* 43, iv (1978): 95-106.

Karl, F. R., *Contemporary English Novel*, rev. and exp., 301-12.

Karl, Frederick, R., "Doris Lessing in the Sixties: The New Anatomy of Melancholy," *ConL* 13 (Winter, 1972): 23-33. Also in Spacks, P. M., *Contemporary Women Novelists*, 64-74.

_____, "The Four-Gaited Beast of the Apocalypse: Doris Lessing's THE FOUR-GATED CITY," in Morris, R. K., ed., *Old Lines, New Forces*, 181-99.

Lewis, Susan, "Conscious Evolution in THE FOUR-GATED CITY," *Anonymous* 1 (1974): 56-71.

Magie, Michael L., "Doris Lessing and Romanticism," *CE* 38, vi (Feb., 1977): 345-9.

Rigney, Barbara H., "'A Rehearsal for Madness': Hysteria as Sanity in THE FOUR-GATED CITY," *Madness and Sexual Politics in the Feminist Novel*, 65-89.

Rose, Ellen C., "Statelier Mansions: Humanism, Forster & Lessing," *MR* 17, i (Spring, 1976): 200-12.

Rubenstein, R., *Novelistic Vision of Doris Lessing*, 125-71.

Rubenstein, Roberta, "Outer Space, Inner Space: Doris Lessing's Metaphor of Science Fiction," *WLWE* 14 (Apr., 1975): 189-97.

Schlueter, P., *Novels of Doris Lessing*, 64-76.

Seamon, David, "Newcomers, Existential Outsiders and Insiders: Their Portrayal in Two Books by Doris Lessing" in Pocock, D.C.D., ed., *Humanistic Geography and Literature*, 85-98.

Spacks, Patricia M., "Free Women," *HudR* 24, iv (Winter, 1971-72): 569-71.

Sprague, Claire, "Without Contraries Is No Progression: Lessing's THE FOUR-GATED CITY," *MFS* 26, i (Spring, 1980): 99-116.

Sudrann, Jean, "Hearth and Horizon: Changing Concepts of the 'Domestic' Life of the Heroine," *MR* 14, ii (Spring, 1973): 241-50.

Thorpe, M., *Doris Lessing's Africa*, 80-6.

Vlastos, Marion, "Doris Lessing and R. D. Laing: Psychopolitics and Prophecy," *PMLA* 91, ii (Mar., 1976): 248-53.

Walker, Melissa G., "Doris Lessing's THE FOUR-GATED CITY: Consciousness and Community—A Different History," *SoR* 17, i (Jan., 1981): 97-120.

THE GOLDEN NOTEBOOK

Abel, Elizabeth, "(E)Merging Identities: The Dynamics of Female Friendship in Contemporary Fiction by Women," *Signs* 6 (Spring, 1981): 429-32.

Anon., "The Fog of War," *TLS* (April 27, 1962): 280.

Barnouw, Dagmar, "Disorderly Company: From THE GOLDEN NOTEBOOK to THE FOUR-GATED CITY," *ConL* 14, iv (Autumn, 1973): 491-514. Also in Spacks, P., ed., *Contemporary Women Novelists*, 38-53. Also in Pratt, A., and L. S. Dembo, eds., *Doris Lessing*, 74-81.

Bergonzi, Bernard, "In Pursuit of Doris Lessing," *NYRB* 4 (Feb. 11, 1965): 13-14.

————, *Situation of the Novel*, 200-4.

Brewster, D., *Doris Lessing*, 138-57.

Brooks, Ellen W., "The Image of Woman in Lessing's THE GOLDEN NOTEBOOK," *Crit* 15, i (1973): 101-9.

Burkom, Selma R., "'Only Connect': Form and Content in the Works of Doris Lessing," *Crit* 11, i (1968): 54-6.

Byatt, A. S., in *Contemporary English Novel*, 38-41.

Carey, John L., "Art and Reality in THE GOLDEN NOTEBOOK," *ConL* 14 (Autumn, 1973): 437-56. Also in Pratt, A., and L. S. Dembo, eds., *Doris Lessing*, 20-39.

Carnes, Valerie, "'Chaos, That's the Point': Art as Metaphor in Doris Lessing's THE GOLDEN NOTEBOOK," *WLWE* 15 (Apr., 1976): 17-28.

Cederstrom, Loreli, "The Process of Individuation in THE GOLDEN NOTEBOOK," *Gradiva* 2, i (1980): 41-54.

Cohen, Mary, "'Out of chaos, a new kind of strength': Doris Lessing's THE GOLDEN NOTEBOOK," in Diamond, A., and L. R. Edwards, eds., *Authority of Experience*, 178-93.

Cook, Jackie, "'All Myself in One Book': The End of THE GOLDEN NOTEBOOK," in Cook, J., and K. Iseman, eds., *Women Writers and the Literary Tradition*, 51-5.

Craig, Joanne, "THE GOLDEN NOTEBOOK: The Novelist as Heroine," *UWR* 10, i (Fall-Winter, 1974): 55-66.

Draine, Betsy, "Nostalgia and Irony: The Postmodern Order of THE GOLDEN NOTEBOOK," *MFS* 26, i (Spring, 1980): 31-48.

Fuoroli, Caryn, "Doris Lessing's 'Game': Referential Language and Fictional Form," *TCL* 27, ii (Summer, 1981): 146-65.

Gurr, Andrew, "The Freedom of Exile in Naipaul and Doris Lessing," *ArielE* 13, iv (Oct., 1982): 7-18 *passim*.

Hinz, Evelyn J., and John J. Teunissen, "The Pieta as Icon in THE GOLDEN NOTEBOOK," *ConL* 14 (Autumn, 1973): 457-70. Also in Pratt, A., and L. S. Dembo, eds., *Doris Lessing*, 40-53.

Howe, Florence, "A Talk with Doris Lessing," *Nation* 104 (Mar. 7, 1967): 311-13.

Howe, Irving, "Doris Lessing: No Compromise, No Happiness," *Celebration and Attacks: Thirty Years of Literary and Cultural Commentary*, N.Y.: Horizon Pr., 1979, 112-17.

Joyner, Nancy, "The Underside of the Butterfly: Lessing's Debt to Woolf," *JNT* 4 (Sept., 1974): 204-11.

Karl, F. R., *Contemporary English Novel*, rev. and exp., 293-301.

Karl, Frederick R., "Doris Lessing in the Sixties: The New Anatomy of Melancholy," *ConL* 13 (Winter, 1972): 15-23. Also in Spacks, P. M., ed., *Contemporary Women Novelists*, 57-64.

Kildahl, Karen Ann, "The Political and Apocalyptical Novels of Doris Lessing: A Critical Study of CHILDREN OF VIOLENCE, THE GOLDEN NOTEBOOK, BRIEFING FOR A DESCENT INTO HELL," *DAI* 35 (1975): 4528A.

Leonard, Vivien, "'Free Women' as Parody: Fun Games in THE GOLDEN NOTEBOOK," *PCL* 6 (1980): 20-7.

Lessing, Doris, "On THE GOLDEN NOTEBOOK," *PR* 40, i (Winter, 1973): 14-30.

Libby, Marion V., "Sex and the New Woman in THE GOLDEN NOTEBOOK," *IowaR* 5 (Fall, 1974): 106-20.

Lifson, Martha R., "Structural Patterns in THE GOLDEN NOTEBOOK," *UMPWS* 2, iv (1978): 95-108.

Lightfoot, Marjorie J., "Breakthrough in THE GOLDEN NOTEBOOK," *SNNTS* 7 (Summer, 1975): 277-84.

————, "'Fiction' vs. 'Reality': Clues and Conclusions in THE GOLDEN NOTEBOOK," *MBL* 2 (Fall, 1977): 182-8.

Magie, Michael L., "Doris Lessing and Romanticism," *CE* 38, vi (Feb., 1977): 536-44.

Marder, Herbert, "The Paradox of Form in THE GOLDEN NOTEBOOK," *MFS* 26, i (Spring, 1980): 49-54.

McCrindle, Jean, "Reading THE GOLDEN NOTEBOOK in 1962," in Taylor, J., ed., *Notebooks/Memoir/Archives*, 43-56.

McDowell, Frederick P. W., "'The Devious Involutions of Human Character and Emotions': Reflections on Some Recent British Novels," *WSCL* 4, iii (Autumn, 1963): 746-50.

————, "The Fiction of Doris Lessing: An Interim View," *ArQ* 21 (Winter, 1965): 328-30.

Moran, Lynne, "Order and Chaos in Doris Lessing's THE GOLDEN NOTEBOOK," in Cook, J., and K. Iseman, eds., *Women Writers and the Literary Tradition*, 45-50.

Morgan, Ellen, "Alienation of the Woman Writer in THE GOLDEN NOTEBOOK," *ConL* 14 (Autumn, 1973): 471-80. Also in Brown, C. L., and K. Olson, eds., *Feminist Criticism*, 301-10. Also in Pratt, A., and L. S. Dembo, eds., *Doris Lessing*, 54-63.

Mulkeen, Anne M., "Twentieth-Century Realism: The 'Grid' Structure of THE GOLDEN NOTEBOOK," *SNNTS* 4 (Summer, 1972): 262-74.

Mutti, Giuliana, "Female Roles and the Function of Art in THE GOLDEN NOTEBOOK," *MSE* 3, iii (Spring, 1972): 78-83.

O'Fallon, Kathleen, "Quest for a New Vision," *WLWE* 12 (Nov., 1973): 180-9.

Perrakis, Phyllis S., "Doris Lessing's THE GOLDEN NOTE-BOOK: Separation and Symbiosis," *AL* 38, iv (Winter, 1981): 407-28.

Porter, Dennis, "Realism and Failure in THE GOLDEN NOTE-BOOK," *MLQ* 35 (Mar., 1974): 56-65.

Porter, Nancy, "Silenced History: CHILDREN OF VIOLENCE and THE GOLDEN NOTEBOOK," *WLWE* 12 (Nov., 1973): 161-79.

_____, "A Way of Looking at Doris Lessing," in Hoffman, N., and others, eds., *Female Studies VI: Closer to the Ground*, 130-3.

Pratt, Annis, "Archetypal Approaches to the New Feminist Criticism," *BuR* 21 (Spring, 1973): 3-14.

_____, "The Contrary Structure of Doris Lessing's THE GOLDEN NOTEBOOK," *WLWE* 12 (Nov., 1973): 150-60.

Rubenstein, Roberta, "Doris Lessing's THE GOLDEN NOTE-BOOK: The Meaning of Its Shape," *AI* 32 (Spring, 1975): 40-58.

_____, *Novelistic Vision of Doris Lessing*, 71-112.

Schlueter, P., *Novels of Doris Lessing*, 77-116.

Schlueter, Paul, "Doris Lessing: Free Woman's Commitment," in Shapiro, C., ed., *Contemporary British Novelists*, 55-8.

Seiler-Franklin, C., *Boulder-Pushers*, 127-45.

Singleton, M. A., *City and the Veld*, 83-130.

Spacks, Patricia M., *Female Imagination*, 308-13.

_____, "Free Women," *HudR* 24, iv (Winter, 1971-72): 566-9.

Spencer, Sharon, "'Femininity' and the Woman Writer: Doris Lessing's THE GOLDEN NOTEBOOK and the DIARY OF ANAIS NIN," *WS* 1 (1973): 247-57.

Spiegel, R., *Doris Lessing*, 59-101.

Spilka, Mark, "Lessing and Lawrence: The Battle of the Sexes," *ConL* 16, ii (Summer, 1975): 218-40.

Sprague, Claire, "Doubletalk and Doubles Talk in THE GOLD-EN NOTEBOOK," *PLL* 18, ii (Spring, 1982): 181-97.

Stewart, G., *New Mythos*, 35-8, 84-9, 136-46.

Taubman, Howard, "Free Women," *NStat* 63 (Apr. 20, 1962): 569. Also in Kostelanetz, R., ed., *On Contemporary Literature*, 402-3.

Thorpe, M., *Doris Lessing*, 25-9.

_____, *Doris Lessing's Africa*, 87-100.

Tiger, Virginia, "The Female Novel of Education and the Confessional Heroine," *DR* 60, iii (Autumn, 1980): 472-86.

Vlastos, Marion, "Doris Lessing and R. D. Laing: Psychopolitics and Prophecy," *PMLA* 91, ii (Mar., 1976): 245-7.

Watson, Barbara B., "Leaving the Safety of Myth: Doris Lessing's THE GOLDEN NOTEBOOK," in Morris, R. K., ed., *Old Lines, New Forces*, 12-37.

THE GRASS IS SINGING

Brewster, D., *Doris Lessing*, 34-41.

Gottlieb, Lois C., and Wendy Keitner, "Colonialism as Metaphor and Experience," in Narasimhaiah, C. D., ed., *Awakened Conscience*, 307-14.

Karl, F. R., *Contemporary English Novel*, 281-2.

Malinowitz, Harriet, "The Limits of Imagination in Doris Lessing's THE GRASS IS SINGING," *MSE* 6, i-ii (1977): 103-10.

Manion, Eileen, "'Not about the Colour Problem': Doris Lessing's Portrayal of the Colonial Order," *WLWE* 21, iii (Autumn, 1982): 434-55.

McDowell, Frederick P. W., "The Fiction of Doris Lessing: An Interim View," *ArQ* 21 (Winter, 1965): 317-18.

Rubenstein, R., *Novelistic Vision of Doris Lessing*, 17-28.

Saravan, Charles, and Liebetraut Sarvan, "D. H. Lawrence and Doris Lessing's THE GRASS IS SINGING," *MFS* 24, iv (Winter, 1978-79): 533-7.

Schlueter, P., *Novels of Doris Lessing*, 7-22.

Schlueter, Paul, "Doris Lessing: Free Woman's Commitment," in Shapiro, C., ed., *Contemporary British Novelists*, 50-1.

Singleton, M. A., *City and the Veld*, 80-3.

Thorpe, M., *Doris Lessing*, 9-11.

_____, *Doris Lessing's Africa*, 11-18.

Thorpe, Michael, "THE GRASS IS SINGING," *LHY* 19, ii (1978): 17-26.

Tucker, M., *Africa in Modern Literature*, 177-9.

Zak, Michele W., "THE GRASS IS SINGING: A Little Novel About the Emotions," *ConL* 14 (Autumn, 1973): 481-90. Also in Pratt, A., and L. S. Dembo, eds., *Doris Lessing*, 64-73.

A HOME FOR THE HIGHLAND CATTLE

Brewster, D., *Doris Lessing*, 42-7.

Thorpe, M., *Doris Lessing's Africa*, 45-8.

HUNGER

Brewster, D., *Doris Lessing*, 42-7.

Thorpe, M., *Doris Lessing's Africa*, 35-8.

IN PURSUIT OF THE ENGLISH

Seamon, David, "Newcomers, Existential Outsiders and Insiders: Their Portrayal in Two Novels by Doris Lessing," 85-100 in Pocock, Douglas, ed., *Humanistic Geography and Literature: Esssays on the Experience of Place*, London: Croom Helm, 1981; Totowa, N. J.: Barnes & Noble, 1981.

LANDLOCKED (See also CHILDREN OF VIOLENCE Series)

Brewster, D., *Doris Lessing*, 129-35.

Porter, Nancy, in Hoffman, Nancy, and others, eds., *Female Studies VI: Closer to the Ground*, 133-6.

Rubenstein, R., *Novelistic Vision of Doris Lessing*, 113-24.

Schlueter, P., *Novels of Doris Lessing*, 26-7.

Thorpe, M., *Doris Lessing's Africa*, 76-9.

THE MARRIAGES BETWEEN ZONES THREE, FOUR AND FIVE

Cleary, Rochelle, "What's in a Name? Lessing's Message in THE MARRIAGE BETWEEN ZONES THREE, FOUR AND FIVE," *DLN* 6, ii (Winter, 1982): 8-9.

Frost, Cheryl, "Breakdown and Regeneration: Some Major Themes in Doris Lessing's Latest Fiction," *LiNQ* 8, iii (1980): 128-33.

Peel, Ellen, "Communicating Differently: Doris Lessing's MARRIAGES BETWEEN ZONES THREE, FOUR AND FIVE," *DLN* 6, ii (Winter, 1982): 11-13.

Rowe, Marsha, "'If You Mate a Swan and a Gander, Who Will Ride?'" in Taylor, J., ed., *Notebooks/Memoirs/Archives*, 191-205.

MARTHA QUEST (See also CHILDREN OF VIOLENCE Series)

Bazin, Nancy T., "The Moment of Revelation in MARTHA QUEST and Comparable Moments by Two Modernists," *MFS* 26, i (Spring, 1982): 87-98.

Bergonzi, Bernard, "In Pursuit of Doris Lessing," *NYRB* 4 (Feb. 11, 1965): 12-13.

Brewster, D., *Doris Lessing*, 103-8.

Christ, Carol P., "From Motherhood to Prophecy," *Diving Deep and Surfacing*, 55-7.

Lukens, Rebecca J., "Inevitable Ambivalence: Mother and Daughter in Doris Lessing's MARTHA QUEST," *DLN* 2, ii (Winter, 1978): 13-14.

Mandl, Betty, "MARTHA QUEST: The Dynamics of Mood," *DLN* 5, ii (Winter, 1981): 3-4.

Porter, Nancy M., "A Way of Looking at Doris Lessing," in Hoffman, Nancy, and others, eds., *Female Studies VI: Closer to the Ground*, 124-7.

Rubenstein, R., *Novelistic Vision of Doris Lessing*, 33-41.

Schlueter, P., *Novels of Doris Lessing*, 23-4.

Spacks, P. M., *Female Imagination*, 150-8.

Spiegel, R., *Doris Lessing*, 33-57.

Thorpe, M., *Doris Lessing's Africa*, 60-5.

Tucker, M., *Africa in Modern Literature*, 180-2.

MEMOIRS OF A SURVIVOR

Bazin, Nancy T., "Androgyny or Catastrophe: The Vision of Doris Lessing's Later Novels," *Frontiers* 5, iii (Fall, 1980): 10-15.

Bullock, C. J., and Kay L. Stewart, "Post-Party Politics: Doris Lessing's Novels of the Seventies," *MR* 20, ii (Summer, 1979): 254-7.

Cederstrom, Lorelei, "'Inner Space' Landscape: Doris Lessing's MEMOIRS OF A SURVIVOR," *Mosaic* 13, iii-iv (1980): 115-32.

Chalpin, Lila, "Parapsychology and Fable in Recent Novels of Doris Lessing," *SJS* 6, iii (Nov., 1980): 323-6.

Draine, Betsy, "Changing Frames: Doris Lessing's MEMOIRS OF A SURVIVOR," *SNNTS* 11 (Spring, 1979): 51-62.

DuPlessis, Rachel B., "The Feminist Apologues of Lessing, Piercy, and Rus," *Frontiers* 4, i (Spring, 1979): 4-5.

Duyfhuizen, Bernard, "On the Writing of Future-History: Beginning the Ending in Doris Lessing's MEMOIRS OF A SURVIVOR," *MFS* 26, i (Spring, 1980): 147-56.

Green, Martin, "The Doom of Empire: MEMOIRS OF A SURVIVOR," *DLN* 6, ii (Winter, 1982): 6-7, 10.

Hoffeld, Laura, and Roni Natov, "THE SUMMER BEFORE THE DARK and THE MEMOIRS OF A SURVIVOR: Lessing's New Female Bondings," *DLN* 3, ii (Winter, 1979): 11-12.

Kuns, Guido, "Apocalypse and Utopia in Doris Lessing's MEMOIRS OF A SURVIVOR," *IFR* 7 (1980): 79-84.

McDowell, Judith H., "Doris Lessing's THE MEMOIRS OF A SURVIVOR," *WLWE* 15, ii (1976): 323-6.

Rubenstein, R., *Novelistic Vision of Doris Lessing*, 220-42.

Singleton, M. A., *City and the Veld*, 223-7.

Sullivan, Alvin, "THE MEMOIRS OF A SURVIVOR: Lessing's Notes toward a Supreme Fiction," *MFS* 26, i (Spring, 1980): 157-62.

Taylor, Jenny, "MEMOIRS Was Made of This: An Interview with David Gladwell, Director of MEMOIRS OF A SURVIVOR," in Taylor, J., ed., *Notebooks/Memoirs/Archives*, 227-40.

THE OTHER WOMAN

Brewster, D., *Doris Lessing*, 74-8.

A PROPER MARRIAGE (See also CHILDREN OF VIOLENCE Series)

Bergonzi, Bernard, "In Pursuit of Doris Lessing," *NYRB* 4 (Feb. 11, 1965): 12-13.

Brewster, D., *Doris Lessing*, 108-18.

Brown, Lloyd W., "The Shape of Things: Sexual Images and the Sense of Form in Doris Lessing's Fiction," *WLWE* 14 (Apr., 1975): 179-84.

Rubenstein, R., *Novelistic Vision of Doris Lessing*, 42-8.

Stitzel, Judith G., "'That's Not Funny': Attitude toward Humor in Lessing's A PROPER MARRIAGE and A RIPPLE IN THE STORM," *BWVACET* 5, i-ii (1979): 40-6.

RETREAT TO INNOCENCE

Brewster, D., *Doris Lessing*, 98-103.

Fishburn, Katherine, "The Dialectics of Perception in Doris Lessing's RETREAT TO INNOCENCE," *WLWE* 21, iii (Autumn, 1982): 416-33.

Rubenstein, R., *Novelistic Vision of Doris Lessing*, 49-56.

Schlueter, P., *Novels of Doris Lessing*, 117-19.

A RIPPLE FROM THE STORM (See also CHILDREN OF VIOLENCE Series)

Brewster, D., *Doris Lessing*, 118-28.

Rubenstein, R., *Novelistic Vision of Doris Lessing*, 57-67.

Schlueter, P., *Novels of Doris Lessing*, 25-8.

Steele, M. C., "White Working-Class Disunity: The Southern Rhodesia Labour Party," *RhoH* 1 (1970): 59-81. [Historical background for the novel.]

Stitzel, Judith G., "'That's Not Funny': Attitudes toward Humor in Doris Lessing's A PROPER MARRIAGE and A RIPPLE FROM THE STORM," *BWVACET* 5, i-ii (1979): 40-6.

Thorpe, M., *Doris Lessing's Africa*, 74-6.

SHIKASTA (CANOPUS IN ARGOS: ARCHIVES Series)

Frost, Cheryl, "Breakdown and Regeneration: Some Major Themes in Doris Lessing's Later Fiction," *LiNQ* 8, iii (1980): 128-33.

THE SUMMER BEFORE THE DARK

Bazin, Nancy T., "Androgyny or Catastrophe: The Vision of Doris Lessing's Later Novels," *Frontiers* 5, iii (Fall, 1980): 10-15.

Berets, Ralph, "A Jungian Interpretation of the Dream Sequence in Doris Lessing's THE SUMMER BEFORE THE DARK," *MFS* 26, i (Spring, 1980): 117-29.

Brown, Lloyd W., "The Shape of Things: Sexual Images and the Sense of Form in Lessing's Fiction," *WLWE* 14 (Apr., 1975): 184-6.

Campbell, Elaine, "The Life Passages of Kate Brown: Doris Lessing's Neglected Novel," *WLWE* 21, iii (Autumn, 1982): 411-15.

Cederstrom, Lorelei, "Doris Lessing's Use of Satire in THE SUMMER BEFORE THE DARK," *MFS* 26, i (Spring, 1980): 131-45.

Hoffeld, Laura, and Roni Natov, "THE SUMMER BEFORE THE DARK and THE MEMOIRS OF A SURVIVOR: Lessing's New Female Bondings," *DLN* 3, ii (Winter, 1979): 11-12.

Hovet, Grace A., and Barbara Lounsberry, "The Affirmation of Signs in Doris Lessing's THE SUMMER BEFORE THE DARK," *WascanaR* 16, ii (Fall, 1981): 41-52.

Kaplan, Sydney, "Passionate Portrayal of Things to Come: Doris Lessing's Recent Fiction," in Staley, T. F., ed., *Twentieth-Century Women Novelists*, 4-15.

Lefcowitz, Barbara E., "Dream and Action in Lessing's THE SUMMER BEFORE THE DARK," *Crit* 17, ii (1975): 107-20.

Rubenstein, R., *Novelistic Vision of Doris Lessing*, 200-19.

Seiler-Franklin, C., *Boulder-Pushers*, 185-201.

Singleton, M. A., *City and the Veld*, 156-63.

Spacks, P. M., *Female Imagination*, 288-92.

BIBLIOGRAPHY

See Issues of *Doris Lessing Newsletter*.

Brewster, D., *Doris Lessing*, 165-70.

Burkom, Selma R., *Doris Lessing: A Checklist of Primary and Secondary Sources*, Troy, N.Y.: Whitson Pub. Co., 1973.

_____, "A Doris Lessing Checklist," *Crit* 11, i (1968): 69-81.

Ipp, Catharina, *Doris Lessing: A Bibliography*. Johannesburg: Un. of Witwatersrand, 1967.

King, Holly B., "Criticism of Doris Lessing: A Selected Checklist," *MFS* 26, i (Spring, 1980): 167-75.

Krouse, Agate N., "A Doris Lessing Checklist," *ConL* 14, iv (Autumn, 1973): 590-7.

Roberts, R. S., "A Select Bibliography of Work on Doris Lessing," *Zambesia* 4, ii (1976): 99-101.

Seligman, Dee, comp., *Doris Lessing: An Annotated Bibliography of Criticism*, Westport, Conn., London: Greenwood Pr., 1981.

Whitlock, Gillian, "Doris Lessing: A Selective Bibliography," *Hecate* 6, i (1980): 102-10.

LELVIN, IRA, 1929-

THE BOYS FROM BRAZIL

Wilson, Robert F., Jr., "From Novel to Film: De-Sinistering THE BOYS FROM BRAZIL," *LFQ* 7 (1979): 322-4.

ROSEMARY'S BABY

Ambrosetti, Ronald J., "ROSEMARY'S BABY and the Death of God Literature," *KFQ* 14 (1969): 133-41.

Lima, Robert, "The Satanic Rape of Catholicism in ROSEMARY'S BABY," *SAF* 2, ii (Autumn, 1974): 211-22.

McManis, Jo A., "ROSEMARY'S BABY: A Unique Combination of Faust, Leda, and 'The Second Coming'," *McNR* 20 (1971-72): 33-6.

Rosen, Lynn, "Rosemary as Rapunzel," *TQ* 13, iii (1970): 51-3.

LEVIN, MEYER, 1905-1981

GENERAL

Bossin, Gary, "The Literary Achievement of Meyer Levin," *DAI* 41 (1980): 2108A.

Rubin, S. J., *Meyer Levin*.

THE ARCHITECT

Rubin, S. J., *Meyer Levin*, 151-2.

CITIZENS

Rubin, S. J., *Meyer Levin*, 52-60.

COMPULSION

Rubin, S. J., *Meyer Levin*, 84-98.

EVA

Rubin, S. J., *Meyer Levin*, 96-101, 112-15.

THE FANATIC

Rubin, S. J., *Meyer Levin*, 101-7, 112-15.

FRANKIE AND JOHNNY (THE YOUNG LOVERS)

Rubin, S. J., *Meyer Levin*, 14-19.

GORE AND IGOR

Rubin, S. J., *Meyer Levin*, 115-23.

THE HARVEST

Rubin, S. J., *Meyer Levin*, 138-46.

MY FATHER'S HOUSE

Rubin, S. J., *Meyer Levin*, 63-73.

THE NEW BRIDGE

Rubin, S. J., *Meyer Levin*, 29-36, 58-60.

THE OLD BUNCH

Rubin, S. J., *Meyer Levin*, 35-52.

REPORTER

Rubin, S. J., *Meyer Levin*, 11-14.

THE SETTLERS

Rubin, S. J., *Meyer Levin*, 122-47.

THE STRONGHOLD

Rubin, S. J., *Meyer Levin*, 107-15.

YEHUDA

Rubin, S. J., *Meyer Levin*, 19-25.

LEWIS, JANET, 1899-

GENERAL

Crow, C. L., *Janet Lewis*.

Davie, Donald, "The Historical Narratives of Janet Lewis," *SoR* 2 (Winter, 1966): 40-60.

Hamovitch, Mitzi B., "My Life I Will Not Let Thee Go Except thou Bless Me: An Interview with Janet Lewis," *SoR* 18, ii (Spring, 1982): 299-313.

Hofheins, Roger, and Dan Tooker, "A Conversation with Janet Lewis," *SoR* 10 (Apr., 1974): 329-41.

Inglis, Fred, "The Novels of Janet Lewis," *Crit* 7, ii (Winter, 1964-65): 47-64.

Killoh, Ellen, "Patriarchial Women: A Study of Three Novels by Janet Lewis," *SoR* 10, ii (1974): 342-64.

AGAINST A DARKENING SKY

Crow, C. L., *Janet Lewis*, 17-23.

Inglis, Fred, "The Novels of Janet Lewis," *Crit* 7, ii (Winter, 1964-65): 62-4.

Killoh, Ellen, "Patriarchial Women: A Study of Three Novels by Janet Lewis," *SoR* 10, ii (1974): 359-64.

THE GHOST OF MONSIEUR SCARRON

Crow, C. L., *Janet Lewis*, 34-8.

Davie, Donald, "The Historical Narratives of Janet Lewis," *SoR* 2 (Winter, 1966): 53-60.

THE INVASION

Crow, C. L., *Janet Lewis*, 12-17.

Davie, Donald, "The Legacy of Fenimore Cooper," *EIC* 9 (1959): 222-38. [Cooper's influence on Lewis' THE INVASION and MacDonald's IN THE AMERICAN GRAIN.]

Killoh, Ellen, "Patriarchial Women: A Study of Three Novels by Janet Lewis," *SoR* 10, ii (1974): 352-9.

THE TRIAL OF SOREN QVIST

Crow, C. L., *Janet Lewis*, 31-4.

Davie, Donald, "The Historical Narratives of Janet Lewis," *SoR* 2 (Winter, 1966): 48-53.

Inglis, Fred, "The Novels of Janet Lewis," *Crit* 7, ii (Winter, 1964-65): 58-61.

THE WIFE OF MARTIN GUERRE

Connell, Evan S., Jr., "Genius Observed," *Atlantic* 224, iv (Dec., 1969): 152-6. Also in Madden, D., ed., *Rediscoveries*, 29-37.

Crow, C. L., *Janet Lewis*, 12-17.

Davie, Donald, "The Historical Narratives of Janet Lewis," *SoR* 2 (Winter, 1966): 43-8.

Inglis, Fred, "The Novels of Janet Lewis," *Crit* 7, ii (Winter, 1964-65): 54-8.

Killoh, Ellen, "Patriarchial Women: A Study of Three Novels by Janet Lewis," *SoR* 10, ii (1974): 344-52.

LEWIS, SINCLAIR, 1885-1951

GENERAL

Ames, Russell, "Sinclair Lewis Again," *CE* 10 (Nov., 1948): 77-80.

Anderson, David D., "Sinclair Lewis and the Nobel Prize," *Midamerica* 8 (1981): 9-21.

Angus, David R., "The Many Roles of Harry Lewis: A Study of Motive and Method in Creative Technique," *DAI* 31 (1971): 3537A.

Austin, Allen, "An Interview with Sinclair Lewis," *UKCR* 24 (Spring, 1958): 199-210.

Austin, James C., "Sinclair Lewis and Western Humor," in Madden, D., ed., *American Dreams, American Nightmares*, 94-105.

Babcock, C. Merton, "Americanisms in the Novels of Sinclair Lewis," *AS* 25 (May, 1960): 110-16.

Beck, Warren, "How Good is Sinclair Lewis?" *CE* (Jan., 1945): 173-80.

Becker, George J., "Sinclair Lewis: Apostle to the Philistines," *ASch* 21 (Autumn, 1952): 423-32.

Blankenship, R., *American Literature*, 657-64, 722-4.

Borrego, John E., "'If There Be Saints': Faith in the Novels of Sinclair Lewis," *HMPEC* 47 (Dec., 1978): 463-72.

Brooks, Van Wyk, *Confident Years*, 497-506.

Brown, Daniel, "Lewis's Satire—A Negative Emphasis," *Ren* 18 (Winter, 1966): 63-72. Also in Light, M., comp., *Merrill Studies in BABBIT*, 51-63.

Brown, Deming, "Sinclair Lewis: The Russian View," *AL* 25 (Mar., 1953): 1-12.

Bucco, Martin, "The Serialized Novels of Sinclair Lewis: A Comparative Analysis of Periodical and Book," *DA* 24 (1964): 4692-3.

————, "The Serialized Novels of Sinclair Lewis," *WAL* 4 (Spring, 1969): 29-37.

Cantwell, Robert, "Sinclair Lewis," *NRep* 88 (Oct. 21, 1936): 298-301. Also in Cowley, M., ed., *After the Genteel Tradition*, 92-102. Also in Schorer, M., ed., *Sinclair Lewis*, 111-18. Also in Zabel, M. D., ed., *Literary Opinion in America*, 494-501.

Carpenter, Frederick I., "Sinclair Lewis and the Fortress of Reality," *CE* 16 (1955): 416-22. Also in Carpenter, F. I., *American Literature and the Dream*, 116-25.

Chalupová, Eva, "The Thirties and the Artistry of Lewis, Farrell, DosPassos and Steinbeck: Some Remarks on the Influence of the Social and Ideological Developments of the Time," *BSE* 12 (1981): 107-16 *passim*.

Coard, Robert L., "Names in the Fiction of Sinclair Lewis," *GaR* 16 (Fall, 1962): 318-29.

Coleman, Arthur B., "The Genesis of Social Ideas in Sinclair Lewis," *DA* 15 (1955): 1069.

Conroy, Stephen S., "The American Culture and the Individual in the Novels of Sinclair Lewis," *DA* 27 (1966): 473A-74.

————, "Sinclair Lewis' Plot Paradigms," *SLeN* 5-6 (1973-74): 4-6.

————, "Sinclair Lewis's Sociological Imagination," *AL* 42, iii (Nov., 1970): 348-62.

Couch, William, Jr., *The Emergence, Rise and Decline of Sinclair Lewis*, Dissertation, Un. of Chicago, 1955.

————, "Sinclair Lewis: Crisis in the American Dream," *CLAJ* 7 (Mar., 1964): 224-34.

Daniels, Howell, "Sinclair Lewis and the Drama of Dissociation," in Bradbury, M., and D. Palmer, eds., *American Novel of the Nineteen Twenties*, 85-105.

Dooley, D. J., *Art of Sinclair Lewis*.

————, "The Impact of Satire on Fiction: Studies in Norman Douglass, Sinclair Lewis, Aldous Huxley, Evelyn Waugh and George Orwell," *DA* 15 (1955): 2203-4.

Feinberg, Leonard, *Sinclair Lewis as Satirist*, Dissertation, Un. of Illinois, 1946.

Fife, Jim L., "Two Views of the American West," *WAL* 1 (Spring, 1966): 34-43.

Flanagan, John T., "A Long Way to Gopher Prairie: Sinclair Lewis's Apprenticeship," *SWR* 32 (Autumn, 1947): 403-14.

_____, "The Minnesota Backgrounds of Sinclair Lewis' Fiction," *Minn. Hist* 37 (Mar., 1960): 1-13.

Fleissner, Robert F., "Charles Dickens and Sinclair Lewis: An Exordium," *SLeN* 3 (Spring, 1971): 10-13.

_____, "L'Affaire Sinclair Lewis: 'Anti-Semitism?' and Ancillary Matters," *SLeN* 4 (Spring, 1972): 14-16.

_____, "'Something Out of Dickens' in Sinclair Lewis," *BNYPL* 74, ix (Nov., 1970): 607-16.

_____, "Sinclair Lewis's Zenith—Once Again," *SLeN* 2 (Spring, 1970): 10-11.

Forster, E. M., "Our Photography: Sinclair Lewis," *NYHTBR* (Apr. 28, 1929). Also in Forster, E. M., *Abinger Harvest*, N.Y.: Harcourt, 1936. Also in Schorer, M., ed., *Sinclair Lewis*, 95-9.

Friedman, Philip A., "In Retrospect: Sinclair Lewis," *TC* 179, mxlvi (1971): 44-8.

Gaston, Edwin W., "Hail, Hail, the Gang's All Here—Twenty Years Later: Sinclair Lewis and the Revolt Against the 'Establishment'," *JASAT* 3 (1972): 50-5.

Geismar, Maxwell, "Sinclair Lewis: Forgotten Hero," *SatR* 43 (June 25, 1960): 29-30.

_____, "Sinclair Lewis: The Cosmic Bourjoyce," *Last of the Provincials*, 69-150. Also (condensed) in *SatR* 30 (Nov. 1, 1947): 9-10, 42-5. Also (condensed and revised) in Geismar, M., *American Moderns*, 107-14. Also (selections) in Schorer, M., ed., *Sinclair Lewis*, 10-16, 129-38.

Gratton, C. Hartley, "Sinclair Lewis: The Work of a Lifetime," *NRep* 125 (Apr. 2, 1951): 19.

Grebstein, S. N., *Sinclair Lewis*.

_____, "Sinclair Lewis's Unwritten Novel," *PQ* 27 (Oct., 1958): 400-9.

_____, "Sinclair Lewis and the Nobel Prize," *WHR* 13 (Spring, 1959): 163-71.

Griffin, Robert J., in French, W. G., and W. E. Kidd, eds., *American Winners of the Nobel Literary Prize*, 16-53.

Guthrie, Ramon, "The 'Labor' Novel That Sinclair Lewis Never Wrote," *NYHTBR* 28 (Feb. 10, 1952): 1+.

Hilfer, A. C., *Revolt from the Village*, 224-30.

Hollis, C. Carroll, "Sinclair Lewis: Reviver of Character," in Gardiner, H. C., ed., *Fifty Years of the American Novel*, 89-106.

Hughes, Serge, "From Main Street to the World So Wide," *Cweal* 53 (Apr. 6, 1951): 648-50.

Jakabfi, László, "The Reception of the Works of Sinclair Lewis in Hungary," *HSE* 10 (1976): 59-72.

Johnson, Gerald W., "Romance and Mr. Babbitt," *NRep* 124 (Jan. 29, 1951): 14-15. Also in *NRep* 131 (Nov. 22, 1954): 29-30.

Kazin, Alfred, "The folksiest and most comradely of American novelists," *On Native Grounds*, N.Y.: Harcourt, Brace, 1942, 219-21. Also in Rubin, L. D., Jr., and J. R. Moore, eds., *Idea of an American Novel*, 301-3.

_____, "The New Realism: Sherwood Anderson and Sinclair Lewis," *On Native Grounds*, N.Y.: Harcourt, Brace, 1942, 217-26. Also in Schorer, M., ed., *Sinclair Lewis*, 119-28. Also in Light, M., comp., *Merrill Studies in BABBITT*, 97-105.

Kramer, Maurice, "Sinclair Lewis and the Hollow Center," in Langford, R. E., and W. E. Taylor, eds., *Twenties*, 67-9.

Krutch, Joseph W., "Sinclair Lewis," *Nation* 172 (Feb. 24, 1951): 179-80. Also in Schorer, M., ed., *Sinclair Lewis*, 147-50.

Lea, James, "Sinclair Lewis and the Implied America," *ClioW* 3 (Oct., 1973): 21-34.

Light, Martin, "H. G. Wells and Sinclair Lewis: Friendship, Literary Influence, and Letters," *EFT* 5, iv (1962): 1-20.

_____, "Lewis' Finicky Girls and Faithful Workers," *UR* 30 (Dec., 1963): 151-9.

_____, *Quixotic Vision of Sinclair Lewis*.

_____, "A Study of Characterization in Sinclair Lewis's Fiction," *DA* 21 (1961): 1957.

Lippman, Walter, *Men of Destiny*, N.Y.: Macmillan, 1927, 71-92. Also in Schorer, M., ed., *Sinclair Lewis*, 84-94.

Lockerbie, D. Bruce, "Sinclair Lewis and William Ridgway," *AL* 36 (Mar., 1964): 68-72.

Love, Glen A., "New Pioneering on the Prairies: Nature, Progress, and the Individual in the Novels of Sinclair Lewis," *AQ* 25 (Dec., 1973): 555-77.

Lovett, Robert M., "An Interpreter of American Life," *Dial* 78 (June, 1925): 515-18. Also in Schorer, M., ed., *Sinclair Lewis*, 32-5.

Lundquist, James, "Frederick Manfred Talks About Sinclair Lewis," *SLeN* 2, i (Spring, 1970): 1-5. [Interview.]

_____, *Guide to Sinclair Lewis*.

_____, "Old Dr. Alagash's Traveling Laboratory: Sinclair Lewis and the Bunko Artist," *SLeN* 4 (1972): 13-14.

_____, *Sinclair Lewis*.

Matheson, Terence J., "H. L. Mencken's Reviews of Sinclair Lewis's Major Novels," *Menckeniana* 51 (Fall, 1974): 2-7. Also in *SLeN* 7-8 (1975-76): 7-10.

Mayer, Gary H., "Idealism in the Novels of Sinclair Lewis," *DAI* 34 (1974): 4273A.

Miller, Perry, "The Incorruptible Sinclair Lewis," *Atlantic* 78 (Apr., 1951): 30-4.

Millgate, Michael, *American Social Fiction*.

_____, "Sinclair Lewis and the Obscure Hero," *SA* 8 (1962): 111-27.

Moodie, Clara L. R., "The Shorter Fiction of Sinclair Lewis and the Novel-Anatomy," *DAI* 42 (1971): 1520A-21A.

Moore, Geoffrey, "Sinclair Lewis: A Lost Romantic," in Bode, C., ed., *Young Rebel in American Literature*, 51-76. Also in Schorer, M., ed., *Sinclair Lewis*, 151-65.

Morris, L., "The National Gadfly," *Postscript to Yesterday*, 134-42.

Motylyova, T., "Sinclair Lewis and His Best Novels," in Vroon, R., tr., *20th Century American Literature: A Soviet View*, 261-84.

Mumford, Lewis, "The America of Sinclair Lewis," *Current History* (Jan., 1931): 529-33. Also in Schorer, M., ed., *Sinclair Lewis*, 102-7.

Park, Sue S., "Satire of Characterization in the Fiction of Sinclair Lewis," *DA* 27 (1967): 2158A.

Parrington, Vernon L., "Sinclair Lewis: Our Own Diogenes," *Main Currents in American Thought*, N.Y.: Harcourt, 1927. Also in *University of Washington Chapbooks*, No. 5, 1927. Also in Schorer, M., ed., *Sinclair Lewis*, 62-70.

Petrullo, Helen B., "Satire and Freedom: Sinclair Lewis, Nathaniel West, and James Thurber," *DA* 28 (1967): 1445A.

Prescott, O., *In My Opinion*, 52-8.

Rourke, C., *American Humor*, N.Y. Harcourt, 1931, 283-86. Also in Schorer, M., ed., *Sinclair Lewis*, 29-31.

Schorer, Mark, *Sinclair Lewis*. Also in O'Connor, W. V., ed., *Seven Modern American Novelists*, 46-80.

_____, ed., *Sinclair Lewis*.

_____, *Sinclair Lewis: An American Life*.

_____, "Sinclair Lewis and His Critics," *World We Imagine*, 183-94. Also in Schorer, M., ed., *Sinclair Lewis*, 1-9.

_____, "Sinclair Lewis and the Method of Half-Truths," in Schorer, M., ed., *Society and Self in the Novel: English Institute Essays, 1955*, N.Y.: Columbia Un. Pr., 1956, 117-44. Also in Litz, A. W., ed., *Modern American Fiction*, 95-111. Also in Schorer, M., ed., *Sinclair Lewis*, 46-71.

_____, "Two Houses, Two Ways: The Florentine Villas of Lewis and Lawrence Respectively," in *New World Writing*, Fourth Mentor Selection, 1953, 136-54.

Smith, Harrison, ed., *From Main Street to Stockholm: Letters of Sinclair Lewis, 1919-1930*. N.Y.: Harcourt, Brace, 1962.

Sodowsky, Alice L., "The Images of Women in the Novels of Sinclair Lewis," *DAI* 38 (1978): 5485A.

Sorkin, Adam J., "Booth Tarkington and Sinclair Lewis: Two Realists as Social Historians," *DAI* 34 (1973): 341A-42A.

Straumann, H., *American Literature in the Twentieth Century*, 17-22.

Thompson, Dorothy, "Sinclair Lewis: A Postscript," *Atlantic* 187 (June, 1951): 73-4.

Thorp, W., "Class and Caste in the Novel, 1920-1950," *American Writing in the Twentieth Century*, 119-23.

Van Gelder, W., *Writers on Writing*, 77-81.

Wagenaar, Dick, "The Knight and the Pioneer: Europe and America in the Fiction of Sinclair Lewis," *AL* 50, ii (May, 1978): 230-49.

Wagenknecht, E., *Cavalcade of the American Novel*, 354-67.

Waterman, Margaret, "Sinclair Lewis as a Teacher," *CE* 13 (1951): 87-90.

West, T. R., *Flesh of Steel*, 116-31.

Whipple, T. K., in *NRep* (Spring Book Section) (Apr. 15, 1925): 3-5. Also, revised, in Whipple, T. K., *Spokesmen*, N.Y.: Appleton, 1928, 208-20. Also in Schorer, M., ed., *Sinclair Lewis*, 119-28. Also in Light, M., comp., *Merrill Studies in BABBITT*, 97-105.

Wurster, Grace S., "The Hollow Note in Lewis's Satire," *SLeN* 5-6 (1973-74): 15-18.

Yoshida, Hiroshige, *A Sinclair Lewis Lexicon with a Critical Study of His Style and Method*, Tokyo: Hoyu, 1976.

_____, "Satirical Techniques in Sinclair Lewis's Works, Contrastive and Contradictory Expressions," *SELit* 42 (1966): 209-22.

_____, "Some Devices and Techniques of Expression in the Works of Sinclair Lewis," *Hiroshima University Studies* 24, iii (Winter, 1966): 175-205.

ANN VICKERS

Dooley, D. J., *Art of Sinclair Lewis*, 181-6.

Geismar, M., *Last of the Provincials*, 115-17.

Grebstein, S. N., *Sinclair Lewis*, 125-9.

Light, M., *Quixotic Vision of Sinclair Lewis*, 119-20.

Lundquist, J., *Sinclair Lewis*, 105-9.

Maglin, Alan B., "Women in Three Sinclair Lewis Novels," *MR* 14, iv (Autumn, 1973): 783-91.

Schorer, M., *Sinclair Lewis*, 31-2. Also in O'Connor, V. W., ed., *Seven Modern American Novelists*, 69-70.

_____, *Sinclair Lewis: An American Life*, 580-3.

ARROWSMITH

Anon., "Martin Arrowsmith," *TLS* 24 (Mar. 5, 1925): 153. Also in Griffin, R. J., ed., *Twentieth Century Interpretations of ARROWSMITH*, 99-100.

Allen, Dennis, "The Wilderness Convention in MAIN STREET, BABBITT and ARROWSMITH," *Gys* 6 (1979): 74-92.

Blake, N. M., *Novelist's America*, 35-6.

Brieger, Gert H., "ARROWSMITH and the History of Medicine in America," *Möbius* 2, iii (July, 1982): 32-8.

Canby, Henry S., "Fighting Success," *SRL* 1 (Mar. 7, 1925): 575. Also in Griffin, R. J., ed., *Twentieth Century Interpretations of ARROWSMITH*, 110-12.

Carpenter, F. I., "Sinclair Lewis and the Fortress of Reality," *American Literature and the Dream*, 121-2.

Cherniak, William V., "An Analysis of Sinclair Lewis' MAIN STREET and Its Relationship to BABBITT, ARROWSMITH, ELMER GANTRY, and DODSWORTH," *DAI* 32 (1972): 3945A.

Coard, Robert L., "ARROWSMITH and 'These Damn Profs'," *SLeN* 2, i (Spring, 1970): 6-8.

Conroy, Stephen S., "Sinclair Lewis's Sociological Imagination," *AL* 42, iii (Nov., 1970): 354-7.

Davidson, Donald, *The Spyglass: Views and Reviews, 1924-1930*, Nashville: Vanderbilt Un. Pr., 1963, 63-7.

Dooley, D. J., *Art of Sinclair Lewis*, 99-103, 105-17. Also in Griffin, R. J., ed., *Twentieth Century Interpretations of ARROWSMITH*, 61-7.

Emerson, Haven, M. D., "A Doctor Looks at ARROWSMITH," *Survey* 54 (May 1, 1925): 180. Also in Griffin, R. J., ed., *Twentieth Century Interpretations of ARROWSMITH*, 107-8.

Fleissner, R. F., "The Reincarnation of Holmes in Dr. Gottlieb," *Baker Street Jnl.* 23, iii (Sept., 1973): 176-9.

Fyvel, T. R., "Martin Arrowsmith and His Habitat," *NRep* 133 (July 18, 1955): 16-18. Also in Griffin, R. J., ed., *Twentieth Century Interpretations of ARROWSMITH*, 93-7.

Geismar, M., *Last of the Provincials*, 97-101.

Grebstein, S. N., *Sinclair Lewis*, 85-96. Also in Griffin, R. J., ed., *Twentieth Century Interpretations of ARROWSMITH*, 68-76.

Griffin, R. J., in French, W. J., and W. E. Kidd, eds., *American Winners of the Nobel Literary Prize*, 39-41.

_____, ed., *Twentieth Century Interpretations of ARROWSMITH*.

Hashguchi, Yasuo, "ARROWSMITH and Escapism," *KAL* 8 (1965): 14-18.

Hazzard, Lucy L., "The Frontier in ARROWSMITH," *The Frontier in American Literature*, N.Y.: Crowell, 1928, 283-5; N.Y.: Ungar, 1960, 282-5. Also in Griffin, R. J., ed., *Twentieth Century Interpretations of ARROWSMITH*, 113-14.

Helleberg, Marilyn M., "The Paper-Doll Characters of Sinclair Lewis' ARROWSMITH," *MTJ* 14, ii (Summer, 1968): 17-21.

Karfeldt, Erik A., "Why Sinclair Lewis Got the Nobel Prize," in Griffin, R. J., ed., *Twentieth Century Interpretations of ARROWSMITH*, 77-82.

Krutch, Joseph W., "A Genius on Main Street," *Nation* 120 (Apr. 1, 1925): 359-60. Also in Griffin, R. J., ed., *Twentieth Century Interpretations of ARROWSMITH*, 105-7.

Light, M., *Quixotic Vision of Sinclair Lewis*, 85-97.

Lovett, Robert M., "An Interpreter of American Life," *Dial* 78 (June, 1925): 515-18. Also in Schorer, M., ed., *Sinclair Lewis*, 32-5. Also in Griffin, R. J., ed., *Twentieth Century Interpretations of ARROWSMITH*, 103-5.

Lundquist, J., *Guide to Sinclair Lewis*, 17-22.

_____, *Sinclair Lewis*, 44-7.

Mencken, H. L., "ARROWSMITH," *AmMerc* 4 (Apr., 1925): 507-9. Also (condensed) in Griffin, R. J., ed., *Twentieth Century Interpretations of ARROWSMITH*, 100-2.

Muir, Edwin, "Melodrama in America," *Nation & The Athenaeum* 36 (Mar. 14, 1925): 818. Also in Griffin, R. J., ed., *Twentieth Century Interpretations of ARROWSMITH*, 109-10.

Ober, William, M. D., "ARROWSMITH and THE LAST ADAM," *Carleton Miscellany* 4 (Fall, 1963): 101-6. Also in Griffin, R. J., ed., *Twentieth Century Interpretations of ARROWSMITH*, 57-60.

Oehlschlaeger, Fritz H., "Sinclair Lewis, Stuart Pratt Sherman, and the Writing of ARROWSMITH," *RALS* 9 (1979): 24-30.

Pandeya, S. M., "Form and Content in the Fiction of Sinclair Lewis" in Naik, M. K., et al., eds., *Indian Studies in American Fiction*, 134-51.

Richardson, Lyon N., "ARROWSMITH: Genesis, Development, Versions," *AL* 27 (May, 1955): 225-44. Also in Griffin, R. J., ed., *Twentieth Century Interpretations of ARROWSMITH*, 24-33.

Rosenberg, Charles E., "Martin Arrowsmith: The Scientist as Hero," *AQ* 15 (Fall, 1963): 447-58. Also in Griffin, R. J., ed., *Twentieth Century Interpretations of ARROWSMITH*, 47-56.

Schorer, Mark, "On ARROWSMITH," Afterword to Signet Classic Edition of ARROWSMITH, N.Y.: New American Library, 1961, 431-8. Also in Griffin, R. J., ed., *Twentieth Century Interpretations of ARROWSMITH*, 40-6.

_____, *Sinclair Lewis*, 17-19. Also in O'Connor, W. V., ed., *Seven Modern American Novelists*, 57-9.

_____, *Sinclair Lewis: An American Life*, 414-20.

Sherman, Stuart P., "A Way Out: Sinclair Lewis Discovers a Hero," *NYHTB* (Mar. 8, 1925): 1-2. Also (condensed) in Griffin, R. J., ed., *Twentieth Century Interpretations of ARROWSMITH*, 19-23.

Spitz, Leon, "Sinclair Lewis' Prof. Gottlieb," *American Hebrew* 158 (Dec. 3, 1948): 2, 10.

Stuckey, W. J, *Pulitzer Prize Novels*, 60-7.

Van Doren, Carl, "Sinclair Lewis and the Revolt from Village," *The American Novel, 1789-1939*, N.Y.: Macmillan, 1940, 303-14. Also (condensed) in Griffin, R. J., ed., *Twentieth Century Interpretations of ARROWSMITH*, 83-92.

West, T. R., *Flesh of Steel*, 122-5.

Whipple, T. K., "Sinclair Lewis: ARROWSMITH," *NRep* 42 (Apr. 15, 1925), Part II: 3-5. Also in Griffin, R. J., ed., *Twentieth Century Interpretations of ARROWSMITH*, 34-9.

W. P. K., "Martin Arrowsmith," *Nature* 115 (May 22, 1925): 797. Also in Griffin, R. J., ed., *Twentieth Century Interpretations of ARROWSMITH*, 109.

BABBITT

Allen, Dennis, "The Wilderness Convention in MAIN STREET, BABBITT and ARROWSMITH," *GyS* 6 (1979): 74-92.

Allen, W., *Modern Novel*, 69-70.

_____, *Urgent West*, 199-200.

Bruccoli, Matthew, "Textual Variants in Sinclair Lewis's BABBITT," *SB* 11 (1958): 263-8.

Cherniak, William U., "An Analysis of Sinclair Lewis' MAIN STREET and Its Relationships to BABBITT, ARROWSMITH, ELMER GANTRY, and DODSWORTH," *DAI* 32 (1972): 3945A.

Clark, Walter H., Jr., "Aspects of Tragedy in BABBITT," *MicA* 8, iii (Winter, 1976): 277-85.

Coard, Robert L., "BABBITT: The Sound Track of a Satire," *SLeN* 5-6 (1973-74): 1-4.

_____, "Mark Twain's THE GILDED AGE and Sinclair Lewis's BABBITT," *MQ* 13, iii (Spring, 1972): 319-33.

Cole, E. R., "George Babbitt: Mock-Hero of a Mock-Epic," *Descant* 10 (Winter, 1966): 21-5.

Conroy, Stephen S., "Sinclair Lewis's Sociological Imagination," *AL* 42, iii (Nov., 1970): 352-4.

Daniels, Howell, "Sinclair Lewis and the Drama of Dissociation," in Bradbury, M., and D. Palmer, eds., *American Novel in the Nineteen Twenties*, 93-100.

Dooley, D. J., *Art of Sinclair Lewis*, 81-95.

Douglas, George H., "Babbitt at Fifty—the Truth Still Hurts," *Nation* 214 (May 22, 1972): 661-2.

Falke, Wayne C., "The Novel of Disentanglement: A Thematic Study of Lewis's BABBITT, Bromfield's MR. SMITH and Updike's RABBIT, RUN," *DA* 28 (1967): 194A.

Ferrara, Cosmo F., "BABBITT: What's Good and Bad in a Novel," *MEB* 27 (Mar., 1970): 9-12.

Friedman, Philip A., "BABBITT: Satiric Realism in Form and Content," *SNL* 4 (Fall, 1966): 20-9. Also in Light, M., comp., *Merrill Studies in BABBITT*, 64-75.

Gale, Robert L., "Lewis' BABBITT," *Expl* 39, iii (Spring, 1981): 39-40.

Geismar, M., *Last of the Provincials*, 88-96. Also in Westbrook, M., ed., *Modern American Novel*, 48-56. Also in Light, M., comp., *Merrill Studies in BABBITT*, 91-7.

Grebstein, S. N., *Sinclair Lewis*, 73-85. Also in Light, M., comp., *Merrill Studies in BABBITT*, 32-44.

Griffin, Robert J., in French, W. G., and W. E. Kidd, eds., *American Winners of the Nobel Literary Prize*, 47-50.

Hilfer, A. C., "Sinclair Lewis: Caricaturist of the Village Mind," *Revolt from the Village*, 167-76. Also in Light, M., comp., *Merrill Studies in BABBITT*, 83-91.

Hines, Thomas S., Jr., "Echoes from 'Zenith': Reactions of American Businessmen to BABBITT," *BHR* 41 (Summer, 1967): 123-40.

Hoffman, F. J., "The Text: Sinclair Lewis's BABBITT," *Twenties*, 364-70. Also in Light, M., comp., *Merrill Studies in BABBITT*, 45-51.

Kallsen, T. J., "The Undeserved Degeneration of BABBITT," *Names* 21 (June, 1973): 124-5.

Kishler, Thomas C., "'The Sacred Rites of Pride': An Echo of THE RAPE OF THE LOCK in BABBITT," *SNL* 3 (1965): 28-9.

Krutch, Joseph W., "Sinclair Lewis," *Nation* (Feb. 24, 1951): 179-80. Also in Schorer, M., ed., *Sinclair Lewis*, 147-50.

Lewis, Robert W., "BABBITT and the Dream of Romance," *NDQ* 40, i (Winter, 1972): 7-14.

Lewis, Sinclair, "Unpublished Introduction to BABBITT," *Man from Main Street*, 21-9.

Light, M., comp., *Merrill Studies in BABBITT*.

_____, *Quixotic Vision of Sinclair Lewis*, 73-84.

Lundquist, J., *Guide to Sinclair Lelwis*, 11-17.

_____, *Sinclair Lewis*, 40-4, 70-4.

Manfred, N. M., *Novelist's America*, 23-33, 36-8.

Mencken, H. L., "Portrait of an American Citizen," *Smart Set* 69 (Oct., 1922): 138-40. Also in Schorer, M., ed., *Sinclair Lewis*, 20-2.

Niall, Brenda, "Salesman and Dream: Sinclair Lewis's BABBITT," *TCM* 22 (Sept., 1969): 24-32.

Nichols, James W., "Nathaniel West, Sinclair Lewis, Alexander Pope and Satiric Contrasts," *SNL* 5 (Spring, 1968): 119-22.

Norris, Hoke, "Babbitt Revisited," *YR* 68, i (Oct., 1978): 53-70.

Oldham, Janet, "DR. ZHIVAGO and BABBITT," *EJ* 48 (May, 1959): 24-26.

Pandeya, S. M., "Form and Content in the Fiction of Sinclair Lewis," in Naik, M. K., et al., eds., *Indian Studies in American Fiction*, 134-51.

Petrullo, Helen B., "BABBITT as Situational Satire," *KanQ* 1, iii (Summer, 1969): 89-97.

Piacentino, Edward J., "Babbitry Southern Style: T. S. Stribling's UNFINISHED CATHEDRAL," *MarkhamR* 10 (Spring, 1981): 36-9.

Pugh, David G., "Baedekers, Babbittry, and Baudelaire," in French, W., ed., *Twenties*, 87-99.

Quivey, James R., "George Babbit's Quest for Masculinity," *BSUF* 10, ii (Spring, 1969): 4-7.

_____, "Release Motif and Its Impact in BABBITT," *SLeN* 1, i (Spring, 1969): 4-5.

Rothwell, Kenneth S., "From Society to Babbitry: Lewis' Debt to Edith Wharton," *JCMVASA* 1, i (Spring, 1960): 32-7.

Sargent, Marion M., "The Babbitt-Lapham Connection," *SLeN* 2, i (Spring, 1970): 8-9.

Schorer, M., *Sinclair Lewis*, 11-17. Also in O'Connor, W. V., ed., *Seven Modern American Novelists*, 52-7.

_____, *Sinclair Lewis: An American Life*, 343-57.

_____, "Sinclair Lewis: BABBITT," in Cohen, Hennig, ed., *Landmarks of American Writing*, N.Y.: Basic Books, 1969, 315-27. Also in Light, M., ed., *Merrill Studies in BABBITT*, 105-16.

Schriber, Mary Sue, "You've Come a Long Way Babbitt! From Zenith to Ilium," *TCL* 17, ii (Apr., 1971): 101-6. [Parallels between Vonnegut's PLAYER PIANO and BABBITT.]

Smoller, Sanford J., "The 'Booboisie' and Its Discontents," in Peary, G., and R. Shatzkin, eds., *Classic American Novel and the Movies*, 226-38.

Walcutt, C. C., *Man's Changing Mask*, 241-7.

West, Rebecca, "BABBITT," *New Statesman* 23 (Oct. 21, 1922): 8, 10. Also in Schorer, M., ed., *Sinclair Lewis*, 23-6.

BETHEL MERRIDAY

Geismar, M., *Last of the Provincials*, 135-7. Also in Schorer, M., ed., *Sinclair Lewis*, 129-30.

Gray, J., *On Second Thought*, 15-17.

Grebstein, S. N., *Sinclair Lewis*, 134-6.

Lundquist, J., *Sinclair Lewis*, 115-16.

CASS TIMBERLANE

Dooley, D. J., *Art of Sinclair Lewis*, 217-24.

Gardiner, Harold C., "Neither Hot Nor Cold," *America* 74 (Oct. 6, 1945): 19-20. Also in Gardiner, H. C., *In All Conscience*, 138-9.

Geismar, M., *Last of the Provincials*, 140-3. Also in Schorer, M., ed., *Sinclair Lewis*, 132-4.

Gray, J., *On Second Thought*, 18-20.

Grebstein, S. N., *Sinclair Lewis*, 148-52.

Light, M., *Quixotic Vision of Sinclair Lewis*, 128-9.

Lundquist, J., *Sinclair Lewis*, 117-19.

Petrullo, Helen B., "MAIN STREET, CASS TIMBERLANE, and Determinism," *SDR* 7, iv (Winter, 1969): 30-43.

Prescott, O., *In My Opinion*, 55-6.

Schorer, M., *Sinclair Lewis: An American Life*, 738-41.

Wilson, Edmund, "Salute to an Old Landmark: Sinclair Lewis," *NY* 21 (Oct. 13, 1945): 94-7. Also in Schorer, M., ed., *Sinclair Lewis*, 139-42.

DODSWORTH

Anderson, Hilton, "A Whartonian Woman in Dodsworth," *SLeN* 1, i (Spring, 1969): 5-6.

Ausmus, Martin R., "Sinclair Lewis, DODSWORTH, and the Fallacy of Reputation," *BA* 34 (Autumn, 1960): 349-55.

Barry, James D., "DODSWORTH: Sinclair Lewis' Novel of Character," *BSUF* 10, ii (Spring, 1969): 8-14.

Blake, N. M., *Novelist's America*, 33-5.

Brown, Daniel R., "The Cosmopolitan Novel: James and Lewis," *SLeN* 1, i (Spring, 1969): 6-9.

Coard, Robert L., "Dodsworth and the Question of Art," *SLeN* 3 (1971): 16-18.

Cherniak, William U., "An Analysis of Sinclair Lewis' MAIN STREET and Its Relationships to BABBITT, ELMER GANTRY, and DODSWORTH," *DAI* 32 (1972): 3945A.

Conroy, Stephen S., "Sinclair Lewis's Sociological Imagination," *AL* 42, iii (Nov., 1970): 358-61.

Daniels, Howell, "Sinclair Lewis and the Drama of Dissociation," in Bradbury, M., and D. Palmer, eds., *American Novel and the Nineteen Twenties*, 100-3.

Dooley, D. J., *Art of Sinclair Lewis*, 150-60.

Fadiman, Clifton, Introduction to DODSWORTH, N.Y.: Modern Library, 1947, v-vii. Also in Fadiman C., *Party of One*, 132-5.

Ford, Ford Madox, "DODSWORTH," *Bookman* 69 (Apr., 1929): 191-2. Also in Schorer, M., ed., *Sinclair Lewis*, 100-1.

Geismar, M., *Last of the Provincials*, 112-15.

Grebstein, S. N., *Sinclair Lewis*, 109-17.

Griffin, Robert J., in French, W. G., and W. E. Kidd, eds., *American Winners of the Nobel Literary Prize*, 44-6.

Hill, John S., "Sinclair Lewis, DODSWORTH, and the Nobel Prize," *HussR* 3 (May, 1970): 105-11.

LaValley, Albert J., "The Virtues of Unfaithfulness," in Peary, G., and R. Shatzkin, eds., *Classic American Novel and the Movies*, 272-85.

Light, M., *Quixotic Vision of Sinclair Lewis*, 108-16.

Lundquist, J., *Guide to Sinclair Lewis*, 30-7.

_____, *Sinclair Lewis*, 54-60, 81-5.

Schorer, M., *Sinclair Lewis*, 25-7. Also in O'Connor, W. V., ed., *Seven Modern American Novelists*, 63-5.

_____, *Sinclair Lewis: An American Life*, 515-18.

Wagenaar, Dick, "The Knight and the Pioneer: Europe and America in the Fiction of Sinclair Lewis," *AL* 50, ii (May, 1978): 240-6.

West, T. R., *Flesh of Steel*, 127-9.

ELMER GANTRY

Blake, Nelson, "How to Learn History from Sinclair Lewis and Other Uncommon Sources," *Stetson Un. Bulletin* 64, ii (July, 1964): 1-17. Also in Hague, John A., ed., *American Character and Culture: Some Twentieth Century Perspectives*, DeLand, Fla.: Everett Edwards Pr., 1964, 41-7. Also in Blake, N. M., *Novelist's America*, 39-44.

Cherniak, William U., "An Analysis of Sinclair Lewis' MAIN STREET and Its Relationships to BABBITT, ARROWSMITH, ELMER GANTRY, and DODSWORTH," *DAI* 32 (1972): 3945A.

Coard, Robert L., "'Vulgar Barnyard Illustrations' in Elmer Gantry," *SLeN* (Spring, 1972): 8-10.

Conroy, Stephen S., "Sinclair Lewis's Sociological Imagination," *AL* 42, iii (Nov., 1970): 8-10.

Davies, H., *Mirror of the Ministry in Modern Novels*, 28-34.

Dooley, D. J., *Art of Sinclair Lewis*, 121-2, 125-35.

Genthe, Charles V., "THE DAMNATION OF THERON WARE and ELMER GANTRY," *RS* 32 (Dec., 1964): 334-43.

Geismar, M., *Last of the Provincials*, 101-5.

Grebstein, S. N., *Sinclair Lewis*, 99-107.

Griffin, Robert J., in French, W. G., and W. E. Kidd, eds., *American Winners of the Nobel Literary Prize*, 41-4.

Hilfer, A. C., "Elmer Gantry and That Old Time Religion," *Revolt from the Village*, 177-92.

Krutch, Joseph W., "Mr. Babbitt's Spiritual Guide: A Review of Sinclair Lewis's ELMER GANTRY," *Nation* 124 (Mar. 16, 1927): 291-2. Also in Schorer, M., ed., *Sinclair Lewis*, 36-8.

Light, M., *Quixotic Vision of Sinclair Lewis*, 99-107.

Lundquist, J., *Guide to Sinclair Lewis*, 23-30.

_____, *Sinclair Lewis*, 49-53, 76-80.

Mayer, Gary, "Love is More Than the Evening Star: A Semantic Analysis of ELMER GANTRY and THE MAN WHO KNEW COOLIDGE," in Collmer, R. G., and J. W. Herring, eds., *American Bypaths*, 145-61.

Moore, James B., "The Sources of Elmer Gantry," *NRep* 143 (Aug. 8, 1960): 17-18.

Rogal, Samuel J., "The Hymns and Gospel-Songs in ELMER GANTRY," *SLeN* 4 (Spring, 1972): 4-8.

Schorer, Mark, "The Monstrous Self-Deception of Elmer Gantry," *NRep* 133 (Oct. 31, 1955): 13-15. Also, expanded as "Sinclair Lewis and the Method of Half-Truths," in Schorer, M., ed., *Society and Self in the Novel: English Institute Essays, 1955*, N.Y.: Columbia Un. Pr., 1956, 129-44. Also in Schorer, M., ed., *Sinclair Lewis*, 50-61. Also in Litz, A. W., ed., *Modern American Fiction*, 102-11. Also in Schorer, M., *World We Imagine*, 162-82.

_____, *Sinclair Lewis*, 20-4. Also in O'Connor, W. V., ed., *Seven American Novelists*, 59-63.

_____, *Sinclair Lewis: An American Life*, 475-83.

West, Rebecca, "Sinclair Lewis Introduces Elmer Gantry," *NYHTB* (Mar. 13, 1927): 1. Also in West, R., *The Strange Necessity*, N.Y.: Viking, 1927, 1955. Also in Schorer, M., ed., *Sinclair Lewis*, 39-45.

FREE AIR

Dooley, D. J., *Art of Sinclair Lewis*, 50-2.

Flanagan, John T., "A Long Way to Gopher Prairie: Sinclair Lewis's Apprenticeship," *SWR* 32 (Autumn, 1947): 408-9, and *passim*.

Geismar, M., *Last of the Provincials*, 81-3.

Griffin, Robert J., in French, W. G., and W. E. Kidd, eds., *American Winners of the Nobel Literary Prize*, 28-31.

Lundquist, J., *Sinclair Lewis*, 12-13.

GIDEON PLANISH

Dooley, D. J., *Art of Sinclair Lewis*, 208-11.

Geismar, M., *Last of the Provincials*, 137-9, 144-5. Also (part) in Schorer, M., ed., *Sinclair Lewis*, 130-1.

Grebstein, S. N., *Sinclair Lewis*, 157-9.

Light, M., *Quixotic Vision of Sinclair Lewis*, 127-8.

Lundquist, J., *Sinclair Lewis*, 116-17.

Schorer, M., *Sinclair Lewis: An American Life*, 697-9.

THE GODSEEKER

Davies, H., *Mirror of the Ministry in Modern Novels*, 35-40.

Dooley, D. J., *Art of Sinclair Lewis*, 227-30.

Light, M., *Quixotic Vision of Sinclair Lewis*, 130-2.

THE INNOCENTS

Dickson, James K., "Note on Sinclair Lewis's THE INNOCENTS, 1917," *PBS* 39 (1945): 167-8.

Grebstein, S. N., *Sinclair Lewis*, 50-3.

IT CAN'T HAPPEN HERE

Blackmur, Richard, P., "Utopia, or Uncle Tom's Cabin," *Nation* 141 (Oct. 30, 1935): 516. Also in Schorer, M., ed., *Sinclair Lewis*, 108-10.

Blotner, J., *Modern American Political Novel*, 153-6.

Dooley, D. J., *Art of Sinclair Lewis*, 191-5.

Geismar, M., *Last of the Provincials*, 117-22.

Grebstein, S. N., *Sinclair Lewis*, 139-47.

Light, M., *Quixotic Vision of Sinclair Lewis*, 122-6.

Lundquist, J., *Sinclair Lewis*, 110-13.

Milne, G., *American Political Novel*, 128-32.

Schorer, M., *Sinclair Lewis*, 33-4. Also in O'Connor, W. V., ed., *Seven Modern American Novelists*, 71-2.

_____, *Sinclair Lewis: An American Life*, 608-12.

THE JOB

Dooley, D. J., *Art of Sinclair Lewis*, 41-7.

Flanagan, John T., "A Long Way to Gopher Prairie: Sinclair Lewis's Apprenticeship," *SWR* 32 (Autumn, 1947): 407-8, and *passim*.

Geismar, M., *Last of the Provincials*, 76-9.

Grebstein, S. N., *Sinclair Lewis*, 55-8.

Light, M., *Quixotic Vision of Sinclair Lewis*, 56-7.

Maglin, Nan B., "Women in Three Sinclair Lewis Novels," *MR* 14, iv (Autumn, 1973): 783-801.

Schorer, M., *Sinclair Lewis: An American Life*, 242-6.

KINGSBLOOD ROYAL

Beck, Warren, "How Good is Sinclair Lewis?" *CE* 9 (Jan., 1948): 173-80.

Berzon, J. R., *Neither White Nor Black*, 123-7.

Coard, Robert L., "Sinclair Lewis's KINGSBLOOD ROYAL: A Thesis Novel for the Forties," *SLeN* 7-8 (1975-76): 10-17.

Dooley, D. J., *Art of Sinclair Lewis*, 224-7.

Grebstein, S. N., *Sinclair Lewis*, 152-6.

Hand, Harry E., "The Rise of a Modern American Hero," *LauR* 6, i (Spring, 1966): 14-20.

Ianni, Lawrence, "Sinclair Lewis as a Prophet of Black Pride," *SLeN* 3 (Spring, 1973): 13-15, 21.

Matheson, Terence J., "The Unfortunate Failure of KINGSBLOOD ROYAL," *SLeN* 5-6 (1973-74): 13-15.

McCullough, Sarah J., "KINGSBLOOD ROYAL: A REVALU-ATION," *SLeN* 4 (1972): 10-12.

Prescott, O., *In My Opinion*, 56-8.

Redman, Ben R., "Sinclair Lewis on Intolerance," *AmMerc* 65 (July, 1947): 111-17.

Schorer, M., *Sinclair Lewis: An American Life*, 758-60.

Thomas, J. D., "Three American Tragedies: Notes on the Responsibilities of Fiction," *SCB* 20, iv (Winter, 1960): 11-5.

MAIN STREET

Aaron, Daniel, in Stegner, W., ed., *American Novel*, 166-79.

Allen, Dennis, "The Wilderness Convention in MAIN STREET, BABBITT and ARROWSMITH," *GyS* 6 (1979): 74-92.

Allen, W., *Modern Novel*, 66-9.

Blake, N. M., *Novelist's America*, 12-23.

Bunge, Nancy, "Women as Social Critics in SISTER CARRIE, WINESBURG, OHIO, and MAIN STREET," *Midamerica* 3 (1976): 46-55.

Carothers, James B., "Midwestern Civilization and Its Discontents: Lewis's Carol Kennicott and Roth's Lucy Nelson," *MMisc* 9 (1981): 21-30.

Cherniak, William U., "An Analysis of Sinclair Lewis' MAIN STREET and Its Relationships to BABBITT, ARROWSMITH, ELMER GANTRY, and DODSWORTH," *DAI* 32 (1972): 3945A.

Coard, Robert L., "College and Schoolhouse in MAIN STREET," *SLeN* 1, i (Spring, 1969): 3-4.

Conroy, Stephen S., "Sinclair Lewis's Sociological Imagination," *AL* 42, iii (No . 1970): 350-4.

Daniels, Howell, "Sinclair Lewis and the Drama of Dissociation," in Bradbury, M., and D. Palmer, eds., *American Novel in the Nineteen Twenties*, 91-3.

Dooley, D. J., *Art of Sinclair Lewis*, 57-82.

Douglas, George H., "MAIN STREET After Fifty Years," *PrS* 44, iv (Winter, 1970): 338-48.

Duffus, R. L., "MAIN STREET Thirty-five Years Later," *NYT-Mag* (Aug. 7, 1955): 24, 62-3.

Gannett, Lewis, "Sinclair Lewis: MAIN STREET," *SRL* 32 (Aug. 6, 1949): 31-2.

Geismar, M., *Last of the Provincials*, 84-8.

Grebstein, S. N., *Sinclair Lewis*, 61-73.

Griffin, Robert J., in French, W. G., and W. E. Kidd, eds., *American Winners of the Nobel Literary Prize*, 32-4.

Hackett, Francis, "God's Country," *NRep* 25 (Dec. 1, 1920): 20-1. Also in Rubin, L. D., Jr., and J. R. Moore, eds., *Idea of an American Novel*, 297-300. Also in Harrison, G. A., ed., *Critic as Artist*, 145-9.

Haworth, J. L., "Revisions of MAIN STREET: or, From 'Blood, Sweat and Tears' to the Loss of a 'Literary Curiosity'," *SLeN* 5-6 (1973-74): 8-12.

Hilfer, A. C., "Sinclair Lewis: Caricaturist of the Village Mind," *Revolt from the Village*, 158-67.

Krutch, Joseph W., "Sinclair Lewis," *Nation* 172 (Feb. 24, 1951): 179-80. Also in Schorer, M., *Sinclair Lewis*, 147-50.

Lewis, S., "Introduction to MAIN STREET," *Man from Main Street*, 213-17.

Light, Martin, "Quixotic Motifs of MAIN STREET," *ArQ* 29 (Autumn, 1973): 221-34.

_____, *Quixotic Vision of Sinclair Lewis*, 60-72.

Lundquist, J., *Guide to Sinclair Lewis*, 8-11.

_____, *Sinclair Lewis*, 35-40.

Maglin, Nan B., "Women in Three Sinclair Lewis Novels," *MR* 14, iv (Autumn, 1973): 783-801.

Matheson, Terence J., "Lewis's Assessment of Carol Kennicott," *SLeN* 5-6 (1973-74): 12-13.

Melton, John L., "MAIN STREET in the Classroom: Another Approach," *SLeN* 5-6 (1973-74): 8.

Mencken, H. L., "Consolation," *Smart Set* 64 (Jan., 1921): 138-44. Also in Schorer, M., ed., *Sinclair Lewis*, 17-19.

Morris, George M., III., "They Are Such Things as Dreams Are Made On: A Study of Carol Kennicott and Emma Bovary," *McNR* 26 (1979-1980): 35-9.

Pandeya, S. M., "Form and Content in the Fiction of Sinclair Lewis," in Naik, M. K., et al., eds., *Indian Studies in American Fiction*, 134-51.

Petrullo, Helen B., "MAIN STREET, CASS TIMBERLAINE, and Determinism," *SDR* 7, iv (Winter, 1969): 30-42.

Piacentino, Edward J., "The MAIN STREET Mode in Selected Southern Novels of the 1920's," *SLeN* 7-8 (1975-76): 18-22.

Schier, Donald, "MAIN STREET, by Sinclair Lewis," *Carleton Miscellany* 4 (Fall, 1963): 95-101.

Schorer, Mark, "Afterword" to *Main Street*. Signet Classic Edition. N.Y.: New American Library, 1961, 433-39.

_____, "MAIN STREET," *AH* 12 (Oct., 1961): 28-31.

_____, *Sinclair Lewis*, 9-11. Also in O'Connor, W. V., ed., *Seven American Novelists*, 50-1.

_____, *Sinclair Lewis: An American Life*, 267-97.

Shepherd, Allen, "A Fairly Hard Week's Work: MAIN STREET in the Classroom," *SLeN* 5-6 (1973-74): 6-7.

Suderman, Elmer, "MAIN STREET Today," *SDR* 7, iv (Winter, 1969): 21-9.

Tanselle, G. Thomas, "Sinclair Lewis and Floyd Dell: Two Views of the Midwest," *TCL* 9 (Jan., 1964): 175-84.

Turim, Maureen, "I Married a Doctor: Main Street Meets Hollywood," in Peary, G., and R. Shatzkin, eds., *Classic American Novel and the Movies*, 207-17.

Tuttleton, J., *Novel of Manners in America*, 145-59.

Watkins, Floyd C., "MAIN STREET: Culture Through the Periscope of Ego," *In Time and Place*, 193-213.

MANTRAP

Dooley, D. J., *Art of Sinclair Lewis*, 118-20.

Fleming, Robert E., "Sinclair Lewis vs. Zane Grey: MANTRAP as Satirical Western," *Midamerica* 9 (1982): 124-38.

Greene, D. J., "With Sinclair Lewis in Darkest Saskatchewan: The Genesis of MANTRAP," *Saskatchewan Hist.* 6 (1953): 47-52.

Griffin, Robert J., in French, W. G., and W. E. Kidd, eds., *American Winners of the Nobel Literary Prize*, 36-9.

Light, M., *Quixotic Vision of Sinclair Lewis*, 98-9.

Lundquist, J., *Sinclair Lewis*, 47-9.

Schorer, M., *Sinclair Lewis: An American Life*, 438-9.

THE MAN WHO KNEW COOLIDGE

Dooley, D. J., *Art of Sinclair Lewis*, 141-8.
Geismar, M., *Last of the Provincials*, 105-8.
Grebstein, S. N., *Sinclair Lewis*, 108-9.
Lundquist, J., *Sinclair Lewis*, 53-4, 80-1.
Mayer, Gary, "Love is More Than the Evening Star: A Semantic Analysis of ELMER GANTRY and THE MAN WHO KNEW COOLIDGE," in Collmer, R. G., and J. W. Herring, eds., *American Bypaths*, 161-6.
Richardson, Lyon N., "Revision in Sinclair Lewis's THE MAN WHO KNEW COOLIDGE," *AL* 25 (1953): 326-33.

OUR MR. WRENN

Dooley, D. J., *Art of Sinclair Lewis*, 16-28.
Flanagan, John T., "A Long Way to Gopher Prairie: Sinclair Lewis's Apprenticeship," *SWR* 32 (Autumn, 1947): 405-6.
Geismar, M., *Last of the Provincials*, 75-6.
Grebstein, S. N., *Sinclair Lewis*, 37-44.
Griffin, Robert J., in French, W. G., and W. E. Kidd, eds., *American Winners of the Nobel Literary Prize*, 22-3.
Knight, Grant C., *New Freedom in American Literature*, Lexington: Mrs. Grant C. Knight, 1961, 69-70.
Light, M., *Quixotic Vision of Sinclair Lewis*, 48-9.
Wagenaar, Dick, "The Knight and the Pioneer: Europe and America in the Fiction of Sinclair Lewis," *AL* 50, ii (May, 1978): 239-49 *passim*.
West, T. R., *Flesh of Steel*, 118-20.

THE PRODIGAL PARENTS

Dooley, D. J., *Art of Sinclair Lewis*, 198-202.
Geismar, M., *Last of the Provincials*, 124-8.
Grebstein, S. N., *Sinclair Lewis*, 132-4.
Light, M., *Quixotic Vision of Sinclair Lewis*, 126-7.
Lunquist, J., *Sinclair Lewis*, 113-15.
Schorer, M., *Sinclair Lewis: An American Life*, 635-6.

THE TRAIL OF THE HAWK

Dooley, D. J., *Art of Sinclair Lewis*, 28-35.
Flanagan, John T., "A Long Way to Gopher Prairie: Sinclair Lewis's Apprenticeship," *SWR* 32 (Autumn, 1947): 406-7, and *passim*.
Geismar, M., *Last of the Provincials*, 73-5, 79-80.
Grebstein, S. N., *Sinclair Lewis*, 44-7, 54-5.
Griffin, Robert J., in French, W. G., and W. E. Kidd, eds., *American Winners of the Nobel Literary Prize*, 24-6.
Light, M., *Quixotic Vision of Sinclair Lewis*, 49-53.
Schorer, M., *Sinclair Lewis: An American Life*, 221-7.

WORK OF ART

Geismar, M., *Last of the Provincials*, 122-4.
Grebstein, S. N., *Sinclair Lewis*, 129-31.
Light, M., *Quixotic Vision of Sinclair Lewis*, 120-2.
Schorer, M., *Sinclair Lewis*, 32-3. Also in O'Connor, W. V., ed., *Seven Modern American Novelists*, 70-1.

WORLD SO WIDE

Cowley, Malcolm, "The Last Flight from Main Street," *NYTBR* (Mar. 25, 1951): 1, 16. Also in Schorer, M., ed., *Sinclair Lewis*,

143-6. Also in Brown, Francis, ed., *Highlights of Modern Literature*, N.Y.: New American Library, 1954.
Dooley, D. J., *Art of Sinclair Lewis*, 231-4.
Gardiner, Harold C., "Sauk Center Was Home Still," *America* 85 (Apr. 7, 1951): 19-20. Also in Gardiner, H. C., *In All Conscience*, 140-41.
Grebstein, S. N., *Sinclair Lewis*, 160-1.
Lundquist, J., *Sinclair Lewis*, 28-31.
_____, "WORLD SO WIDE and Sinclair Lewis's Rewritten Life," *SLeN* 2, i (Spring, 1970): 12-14.
Wagenaar, Dick, "The Knight and the Pioneer: Europe and America in the Fiction of Sinclair Lewis," *AL* 50, ii (May, 1978): 230-49 *passim*.

BIBLIOGRAPHY

Dooley, D. J., *Art of Sinclair Lewis*, 269-77.
Fleming, Robert, and Esther Fleming, *Sinclair Lewis: A Reference Guide*, Boston: G. K. Hall, 1980.
Grebstein, S. N., *Sinclair Lewis*, 180-8.
Lundquist, James, *Merrill Checklist of Sinclair Lewis*. (Merrill Checklists.) Columbus, Ohio: Charles E. Merrill, 1970.

LEWIS, (PERCY) WYNDHAM, 1882-1957

GENERAL

Allen, James D., "The Apollonian-Dionysian Conflict in the Works of Wyndham Lewis," *DA* 22 (1962): 3196-97.
Allen, Walter, "The Achievement of Wyndham Lewis," *Encounter* 21, iii (Sept., 1963): 63-70.
_____, "Wyndham Lewis," *Meanjin* 16 (1957): 189-92. [Not seen.]
Ayrton, Michael, "Wyndham Lewis," *Meanjin* 16 (1957): 192-5. [Not seen.]
Ballard, J. G., "Visions of Hell," *New Worlds* 49 (Mar., 1966): 149-54. [Not seen.]
Beatty, Michael, "The Earliest Fiction of Wyndham Lewis and THE WILD BODY," *Theoria* 48 (1977): 37-45.
Bradbury, M., "The Modern Comic Novel in the 1920's: Lewis, Huxley, and Waugh," *Possibilities*, 144-50.
Chapman, Robert, "Lawrence, Lewis and the Comedy of Literary Reputation," *STwC* 6 (1970): 85-95.
_____, *Wyndham Lewis*.
Chase, William M., "On Lewis's Politics: The Polemics Polemically Answered," in Meyers, J., ed., *Wyndham Lewis*, 149-65.
Coffey, Warren, "Wyndham Lewis: Enemy of the Rose," *Ramparts* 2 (1963): 69-76.
Currie, R., "The Modernism of Wyndham Lewis," *Genius*, 116-42.
Dasenbrock, Reed W., "Death and the Counterlife of Heresy in Wyndham Lewis and Lawrence Durrell," *DL* 4, i (Sept., 1980): 3-16.
Eliot, T. S., "Wyndham Lewis," *HudR* 10, ii (Summer, 1957): 167-70.
Fox, C. J., "The Wild Land: A Celebration of Globalism," *CanL* 35 (Winter, 1968): 29-36.
Fraser, G. S., "Wyndham Lewis: An Energy of Mind," *TC* 161 (Apr., 1957): 386-92.
Frye, Northrop, "Neo-Classical Agony," *HudR* 10 (Winter, 1957-58): 592-8. [Rev. Art.]

Haggerty, William D., Jr., "Entangled Absalom: A Critical Study of Wyndham Lewis as Modernist and Satirist," *DAI* 38 (1978): 223-31.

Harrison, John, *The Reactionaries*, N.Y.: Schocken Books, 1967, c. 1966, 77-108.

Hegarty, Terence, "Wyndham Lewis the Writer: A Preoccupation with the Real," *MR* 23, ii (Summer, 1982): 335-48.

Henkle, Roger B., "The 'Advertised' Self: Wyndham Lewis' Satire," *Novel* 13, i (Fall, 1979): 95-108.

Holloway, John, "Machine and Puppet: A Comparative View," in Meyers, J., ed., *Wyndham Lewis*, 3-14.

———, "Wyndham Lewis: The Massacre and the Innocents," *HudR* 10, ii (Summer, 1957): 171-88. Also Holloway, John, *The Charted Mirror: Literary and Critical Essays*, London: Routledge & Kegan Paul, 1960; N.Y.: Horizon Pr., 1962, 118-36.

Jameson, Frederic, *Fables of Aggression*.

———, "Wyndham Lewis as Futurist," *HudR* 26, ii (Summer, 1973): 295-329.

Kenner, Hugh, "The Devil and Wyndham Lewis," *Shen* 7 (1955): 15-30. Also in Kenner, H., *Gnomon*, N.Y.: McDowell-Obolensky, 1958, 215-41.

———, "The Last European," *CanL* 36 (Spring, 1968): 5-13.

———, "The War with Time," *Shen* 4, ii-iii (Summer-Autumn, 1953): 18-53.

Kenner, H., *Wyndham Lewis*.

Kirk, Russell, "Wyndham Lewis' First Principles," *YR* 44, iv (June, 1955): 520-34.

Knight, Donald R., "Lewis/Joyce: A Literary Relationship of the 1920's," *DAI* 39 (1979): 6777A-78A.

Kush, Thomas, "The Pictorial Integer: Wyndham Lewis's Literary and Visual Art, 1910-1930," *DAI* 40 (1979): 872A.

Lanthier, Philip J., "Vision and Satire in the Art and Fiction of Wyndham Lewis," *DA* 34 (1974): 5184A.

Lent, John, "Wyndham Lewis and Malcolm Lowry: Contexts of Style and Subject Matter in the Modern Novel," in Bessai, D., and D. Jackel, *Figures in a Ground*, 61-75.

Materer, Timothy J., "Wyndam Lewis and the Era of Violence," *DA* 29 (1969): 4009A.

———, *Wyndham Lewis, the Novelist*.

Mayne, Richard, "Wyndham Lewis," *Encounter* 38 (Feb., 1972): 42-51.

McLuhan, Marshall, "Lewis's Prose Style," in Meyers, J., ed., *Wyndham Lewis*, 64-7.

Meyers, J., ed., *Wyndham Lewis*.

Meyers, Jeffrey, "Wyndham Lewis and T. S. Eliot: A Friendship," *VQR* 56, iii (Summer, 1980): 455-69.

Mitchell, Judith, "Women and Wyndham Lewis," *MFS* 24, ii (Summer, 1978): 223-31.

Molesworth, Charles, "Frightful Fashions and Compulsive Occasions," *Salmagundi* 50-51 (Fall 1980/Winter 1981): 322-39.

Mudrick, Marvin, "The Double-artist and the Injured Party," *Shen* 4, ii-iii (Summer-Autumn, 1953): 54-64.

Murray, Brian J., "Awaiting the Apocalypse: The Later Novels, and Short Stories of Percy Windham Lewis," *DAI* 41, viii (Feb., 1981): 3574A.

Parker, Valerie, "Enemies of the Absolute: Lewis, Art and Women," in Meyers, J., ed., *Wyndham Lewis*, 211-25.

Parsons, D. S. J., "Roy Campbell and Wyndham Lewis," *PLL* 7 (1971): 406-21.

Pritchard, W. H., "Lawrence and Lewis," *Agenda* 7-8 (Autumn-Winter, 1969-1970): 140-7.

Pritchard, William H. "On Wyndham Lewis," *PR* 35, ii (Spring, 1968), 253-67.

———, *Wyndham Lewis*.

———, "Wyndham Lewis and Lawrence," *IowaR* 2, ii (Spring, 1971): 91-6.

Pritchett, V. S., "The Eye-Man," *Books in General*, N.Y.: Harcourt, 1955, 248-53.

Schenker, Daniel, "A Modernist in Dramaturgy: The Fictions of Wyndham Lewis and James Joyce," *DAI* 41, ix (Mar., 1981): 4048A.

Shenandoah 4 (Summer-Autumn, 1953). Wyndham Lewis number.

Sokolowski, Deanna B., "The War With Time and Self: A Study of Wyndham Lewis's Satire," *DAI* 35 (1975): 4560A-61A.

Stevenson, Randall, "The Other Centenary: Wyndham Lewis, 1882-1982," *Cencrastus* 10 (Autumn, 1982): 18-21.

———, "Wyndham Lewis: The Enemy of the Stars," *New Edinburgh Review* 53 (1981): 16-19. [Not seen.]

Symons, Julian, "A Master of Disguise," *TLS* (June 30, 1978): 726-7.

———, "The Thirties Novels," *Agenda* 7-8 (Autumn-Winter, 1969-70): 37-48.

Tomlin, E. W. F., "The Philosophical Influences," in Meyers, J., ed., *Wyndham Lewis*, 29-46.

———, *Wyndham Lewis*.

———, "Windham Lewis Reconsidered," *EigoS* 116 (1970): 202-3. [Not seen.]

Wagner, Geoffrey, "The Writings of Percy Wyndham Lewis," *DA* 14 (1954): 1735-36.

———, "Wyndham Lewis (1886-1957)," in Panichas, G. A., *Politics of Twentieth-Century Novelists*, 51-64.

———, "Wyndham Lewis and James Joyce: A Study in Controversy," *SAQ* 56 (Jan., 1957): 57-66.

Watson, Sheila, "Wyndham Lewis and G. K. Chesterton," *CRev* 6 (Spring/Summer, 1980): 254-71.

Wiebe, Dallas E., "Wyndham Lewis and the Picaresque Novel," *SAQ* 62, iv (Autumn, 1963): 587-96.

Wilson, Colin, "Wyndham Lewis: A Refracted Talent?" *B&B* 19, vii (Apr., 1974): 39-42.

THE APES OF GOD

Chapman, Robert T., "Satire and Aesthetics in Windham Lewis' APES OF GOD," *ConL* 12, ii (Spring, 1971): 133-45.

———, *Wyndham Lewis*.

Edwards, Paul, "THE APES OF GOD: Form and Meaning," in Meyers, J., ed., *Wyndham Lewis*, 133-48.

Henkle, Roger B., "The 'Advertised' Self: Wyndham Lewis' Satire," *Novel* 13, i (Fall, 1979): 104-8.

Kenner, H., *Wyndham Lewis*, 99-106.

Materer, T., *Wyndham Lewis the Novelist*, 83-97.

Parsons, D. S. J., "Roy Campbell and Wyndham Lewis," *PLL* 7 (1971): 410-21. [Comparison with Campbell's THE GEORGIAD.]

Pritchard, W. H., *Wyndham Lewis*, 77-85.

Sisson, C. H., "Wyndam Lewis's Study of Himself," *PNR* 5, iii (1978): 13-15.

THE CHILDERMASS (See also THE HUMAN AGE)

Bridson, D. G., "THE HUMAN AGE in Retrospect," in Meyers, J., ed., *Wyndham Lewis*, 238-45.

Carter, Thomas H., "Rationalist in Hell," *KR* 18, ii (Spring, 1956): 326-30.

Chapman, R. T., *Wyndham Lewis*, 165-82.

Jameson, F., *Fables of Aggression*, 52-5, 69-75.

Kenner, Hugh, *Gnomon*, N.Y.: McDowell-Obolensky, 1958, 216-22.

Munton, Alan, "A Reading of THE CHILDERMASS," in Meyers, J., ed., *Wyndham Lewis*, 120-32.

Pritchard, W. H., *Wyndham Lewis*, 68-76.

Richards, I. A., "A Talk on THE CHILDERMASS," *Agenda* 7-8 (Autumn-Winter, 1968-70): 16-21.

Wagner, Geoffrey, "Wyndham Lewis and James Joyce: A Study in Controversy," *SAQ* 56, i (Jan., 1957): 57-66 *passim*.

THE HUMAN AGE

Bridson, D. G., "THE HUMAN AGE in Retrospect," in Meyers, J., ed., *Wyndham Lewis*, 238-51.

Carter, Thomas, "A Rationalist in Hell," *KR* 18 (Spring, 1956): 326-36.

Chapman, R. T., *Wyndham Lewis*, 165-82.

Jameson, F., *Fables of Aggression*, 148-64.

Materer, T., *Wyndham Lewis the Novelist*, 155-60.

Palmer, Penelope, "THE HUMAN AGE," *Agenda* 7-8 (Autumn-Winter, 1969-70): 22-30.

Pritchard, W. H., *Wyndham Lewis*, 156-65.

Raff, Melvin, "Wyndham Lewis and Stanley Elkin: Salvation, Satire and Hell," *StCS* 8 (Spring, 1981): 1-8.

Seymour-Smith, Martin, "Wyndham Lewis as Imaginative Writer," *Agenda* 7-8 (Autumn-Winter, 1969-70): 9-15.

Wagner, Geoffrey, "Wyndham Lewis's Inhuman Tetralogy: An Introduction to THE HUMAN AGE," *MFS* 2 (1956): 221-27.

MALIGN FIESTA (See also THE HUMAN AGE)

Chapman, R. T., *Wyndham Lewis*, 180-2.

Kenner, Hugh, *Gnomon*, N.Y.: McDowell-Obolensky, 1958, 239-9.

MONSTRE GAI (see also THE HUMAN AGE)

Bridson, D. G., "THE HUMAN AGE in Retrospect," in Meyers, J., ed., *Wyndham Lewis*, 239-45.

Chapman, R. T., *Wyndham Lewis*, 176-80.

Eliot, T. S., "A Note on MONSTRE GAI," *HudR* 7 (Winter, 1955): 522-6.

Kenner, Hugh, *Gnomon*, N.Y.: McDowell-Obolensky, 1958, 223-30.

MRS. DUKES' MILLION

Kenner, Hugh, "MRS. DUKES' MILLION: The Stunt of an Illusionist," in Meyer, J., ed, *Wyndham Lewis*, 85-91.

Symons, Julian, "A Matter of Disguise," *TLS* (June 30, 1978): 726.

THE RED PRIEST

Chapman, R. T., *Wyndham Lewis*, 148-52.

THE REVENGE FOR LOVE

Chapman, R. T., *Wyndham Lewis*, 97-8.

Chase, William M., "On Lewis's Politics: The Polemics Polemically Answered," in Meyers, J., ed., *Wyndham Lewis*, 151-5.

Dale, Peter, "THE REVENGE FOR LOVE," *Agenda* 7-8 (Autumn-Winter, 1969-1970): 71-7.

Hegarty, Terence, "Wyndham Lewis the Writer: A Preoccupation with the Real," *MR* 23, ii (Summer, 1982): 342-5.

Holloway, John, "Machine and Puppet: A Comparative View," in Meyers, J., ed., *Wyndham Lewis*, 5-10.

Jameson, F., *Fables of Aggression*, 82-6.

Kenner, Hugh, "The Revenge of the Void," *HudR* 6, iii (Autumn, 1953): 381-96.

_____, *Wyndham Lewis*, 123-37.

Materer, T., *Wyndham Lewis the Novelist*, 113-33.

Parker, Valerie, "Enemies of the Absolute: Lewis, Art and Women," in Meyers, J., ed., *Wyndham Lewis*, 216-21.

Pritchard, W. V., *Wyndham Lewis*, 115-32.

Sandler, Linda R., "THE REVENGE FOR LOVE by Wyndham Lewis: Editorial, Genetic and Interpretive Studies," *DAI* 38 (1977): 3489A.

Symons, Julian, "The Thirties Novels," *Agenda* 7-8 (Autumn-Winter, 1969-70): 39-46.

Woodcock, George, "From up the Gum Tree: Wyndham Lewis and THE REVENGE FOR LOVE," *QQ* 84 (1977): 210-17.

THE ROARING QUEEN

Allen, Walter, "THE ROARING QUEEN," *Encounter* 41 (Aug., 1973): 41-7. Also as Introduction to *The Roaring Queen*, N.Y.: Liveright, 1973, 5-23.

Chapman, W. T., *Wyndham Lewis*, 116-21.

SELF CONDEMNED

Chapman, R. T., *Wyndham Lewis*, 153-64.

Dale, Peter, "SELF CONDEMNED," *Agenda* 7-8 (Autumn-Winter, 1969-70): 31-6.

Kenner, Hugh, "SELF CONDEMNED," *Shen* 5 (1954): 66-71. Also in *Nine* 11 (Apr., 1956): 30-4. Also as "Introduction" to *Self Condemned*, Chicago: 1965, vii-xv.

_____, *Wyndham Lewis*, 153-6.

Kirk, Russell, "Wyndham Lewis' First Principles," *YR* 44, iv (June, 1955): 529-34.

Materer, Timothy, "The English Vortex: Modern Literature and the 'Pattern of Hope'," *JML* 3 (July, 1974): 1136-8.

_____, "The Great English Vortex," *Agenda* 7-8 (Autumn-Winter, 1969-70): 57-65.

_____, *Wyndham Lewis the Novelist*, 137-51.

Meyers, Jeffry, "SELF CONDEMNED," in Meyers, J., ed., *Wyndham Lewis*, 226-37.

Moss, J., *Patterns of Isolation*, 17-19.

Parker, Valerie, "Enemies of the Absolute: Lewis, Art and Women," in Meyers, J., ed., *Wyndham Lewis*, 221-5.

Pritchard, W. H., *Wyndham Lewis*, 147-56.

Woodcock, George, "Monoco Revisited: Wyndham Lewis in Canada," *CanL* 35 (1968): 3-8. Also in Woodcock, G., *Odysseus Ever Returning*, 52-5.

SNOOTY BARONET

Chapman, R. T., *Wyndham Lewis*, 109-16.

Kenner, H., *Wyndham Lewis*, 107-13.

Materer, Timothy, "Wyndham Lewis: Satirist of the Machine Age," *SNL* 10, i (Fall, 1972): 9-18.

_____, *Wyndham Lewis the Novelist*, 100-11.

Pritchard, W. H., *Wyndham Lewis*, 108-15.

Smith, Rowland, "SNOOTY BARONET: Satire and Censorship," in Meyers, J., ed., *Wyndham Lewis*, 181-95.

TARR

Ayrton, Michael, "Tarr and Flying Feathers," *Shen* 7 (1955): 31-43.

Currie, Robert, "Wyndham Lewis, E. T. A. Hoffman, and TARR," *RES* 30 (1979): 169-81.

Chapman, R. T., *Wyndham Lewis*, 68-82.

Davies, Alistair, "TARR: A Nietzschean Novel," in Meyers, J., ed., *Wyndham Lewis*, 107-19.

Eliot, T. S., "TARR," *The Egoist* 5 (Sept., 1918): 105-6. Also in *Shen* 4, ii-iii (Summer-Autumn, 1953): 65-8.

Henkle, Roger B., "The 'Advertised' Self: Wyndham Lewis' Satire," *Novel* 13, i (Fall, 1979): 97-103.

Jameson, F., *Fables of Aggression*, 42-9, 64-7, 90-104.

Kenner, H., *Wyndham Lewis*, 30-51.

Materer, T., *Wyndham Lewis the Novelist*, 52-67.

Parker, David, "TARR and Wyndham Lewis's War-Time Stories: The Artist as Prey," *SoRA* 8 (1975): 166-81.

Parker, Valerie, "Enemies of the Absolute: Lewis, Art and Women," in Meyers, J., ed., *Wyndham Lewis*, 211-16.

Pound, Ezra, "TARR, by Wyndham Lewis," *Little Review* 4 (Mar., 1918): 35. Also in Pound, Ezra, *Literary Essays of Ezra Pound*, London: Faber, 1954, 424-30.

Pritchard, W. H., *Wyndham Lewis*, 28-44.

Pritchett, V. S. "The Eye-Man," *Books in General*, N.Y.: Harcourt, Brace, 1955, 248-53.

Starr, Alan, "TARR and Wyndham Lewis," *ELH* 49, i (Spring, 1982): 179-89.

West, Rebecca, "TARR," *Agenda* 7-8 (Autumn-Winter, 1969-70): 67-9.

THE VULGAR STREAK

Blott, Anne, "The Merman and the Mint: A Study of Wyndham Lewis's THE VULGAR STREAK," in Bessai, D., and D. Jackel, *Figures in a Ground*, 42-60.

Chapman, R. T., *Wyndham Lewis*, 131-9.

Kenner, H., *Wyndam Lewis*, 137-9.

Materer, T., *Wyndham Lewis the Novelist*, 134-7.

Pritchard, W. H., *Wyndham Lewis*, 130-4.

BIBLIOGRAPHY

Meyers, Jeffrey, "Wyndham Lewis: A Bibliography of Criticism 1912-1980," *BB* 37, i (Jan.-Mar., 1980): 33-52.

LINDSAY, JOAN, 1896-1984

PICNIC AT HANGING ROCK

Crittenden, Anne, "PICNIC AT HANGING ROCK: A Myth and Its Symbols," *Meanjin* 35 (1976): 167-74.

Kirby, Joan, "Old Orders, New Lands: the Earth Spirit in PICNIC AT HANGING ROCK," *ALS* 8 (1978): 255-68.

O'Neill, Terence, "Literary Cousins: NUNS IN JEOPARDY and PICNIC AT HANGING ROCK," *ALS* 10 (1982): 375-8.

LINNEY, ROMULUS, 1930-

HEATHEN VALLEY

Williams, Cratis, "Linney's HEATHEN VALLEY," *NCarF* 19 (1971): 55-8.

LLEWELLYN, RICHARD, 1906-1983

HOW GREEN WAS MY VALLEY

Heck, Francis S., "Love and Women in HOW GREEN WAS MY VALLEY and GERMINAL," *RS* 48 (1980): 56-62.

LOCKRIDGE, ROSS, JR., 1914-1948

GENERAL

Manheim, Leonard F., "An Author Wrecked by Success: Ross Lockridge, Jr., (1914-1948)," *HSL* 10 (1978): 103-21.

RAINTREE COUNTY

Clarke, Delia K., "RAINTREE COUNTY: Psychological Symbolism, Archetype and Myth," *Thoth* 11, i (Fall, 1970): 31-9.

Dessner, Lawrence J., "Value in Popular Fiction: The Case of RAINTREE COUNTY," *Junction* (Brooklyn College) 1, iii (1973): 147-52.

Erisman, Fred, "RAINTREE COUNTY and the Power of Place," *MarkhamR* 8 (Winter, 1979): 36-40.

Greiner, Donald J., "Ross Lockridge and the Tragedy of RAINTREE COUNTY," *Crit* 20, iii (1978): 51-62.

Jones, Joel M., "The Presence of the Past in the Heartland: RAINTREE COUNTY Revisited," *Midamerica* 4 (1977): 112-21.

Lutwack, Leonard, "RAINTREE COUNTY and the Epicising Poet in American Fiction," *BSUF* 13, i (Winter, 1972): 14-28.

Manheim, Leonard F., "An Author Wrecked by Success: Ross Lockridge, Jr., (1914-1948)," *HSL* 10 (1978): 109-17.

Temes, Delia C., "The American Epic Tradition and RAINTREE COUNTY," *DAI* 34 (1974): 7248A-9A.

LODGE, DAVID, 1935-

GENERAL

Honan, Park, "David Lodge and the Cinematic Novel in England," *Novel* 5, ii (Winter, 1972): 167-73.

THE BRITISH MUSEUM IS FALLING DOWN

Burden, Robert, in *Contemporary English Novel*, 138-43.

HOW FAR CAN YOU GO?

Streichsbier, Beata, "Irony in David Lodge's HOW FAR CAN YOU GO?" in Gauna, Max, ed., *A Yearbook in English Language and Literature*, Braumuller: Vienna, n.d., 97-100.

LOWRY, MALCOLM, 1909-1957

GENERAL

See Issues of *Malcolm Lowry Newsletter*.

Aiken, Conrad, "Malcolm Lowry," *TLS* (Feb. 16, 1967): 127.

————, "Malcolm Lowry—A Note," *CanL* No. 8 (Spring, 1961): 29-30.

Albaum, Elvin, "LA MORIDA: Myth and Madness in the Novels of Malcolm Lowry," *DAI* 31 (1971): 6586A.

Bareham, Terence, "After the Volcano: An Assessment of Malcolm Lowry's Posthumous Fiction," *SNNTS* 6, iii (Fall, 1974): 349-62. Also in Wood, B., ed., *Malcolm Lowry*, 235-49.

Bareham, Tony, "The Englishness of Malcolm Lowry," *JCl* 11, ii (Dec., 1976): 134-49.

Barnes, Jimmy W., "Fiction of Malcolm Lowry and Thomas Mann: Structural Tradition," *DAI* 32 (1972): 5173A.

Binns, Ronald, in *Contemporary English Novel*, 102-10.

Birney, Earle, "Glimpses into the Life of Malcolm Lowry," *TamR* 19 (Spring, 1961): 31-8.

Bradbrook, M. C., *Literature in Action*, 178-87.

————, *Malcolm Lowry*.

Bradbrook, Muriel C., "Narrative Form in Conrad and Lowry," 129-42 in Sherry, Norman, ed., *Joseph Conrad: A Commemoration*. Papers from the 1974 International Conference on Conrad, N.Y.: Harper, 1977.

Breit, Harvey, and Marjorie Lowry, eds., *Selected Letters of Malcolm Lowry*, Philadelphia: Lippincott, 1965.

Chittick, V. L. O., "USHANT's Malcolm Lowry," *QQ* 71 (Spring, 1964): 67-75.

Considine, Raymond H., "Malcolm Lowry's Major Prose Fiction," *DAI* 33 (1973): 6348A.

Corrigan, Matthew, "Malcolm Lowry: The Phenomenology of Failure," *Boundary* 3, ii (Winter, 1975): 407-42.

————, "Phenomenology and Literary Criticism: A Definition and an Application," *DAI* 31 (1971): 4761A.

Costa, R. H., *Malcolm Lowry*.

Costa, Richard H., "The Northern Paradise: Malcolm Lowry in Canada," *SNNTS* 4 (Summer, 1972): 165-72.

Cowan, David T., "Malcolm Lowry's Aggregate Daemon: A Study on the Psychology of Influence," *DAI* 42, ix (Mar., 1982): 3994A.

Cresswell, Rosemary, "Malcolm Lowry's Other Fiction," in Anderson, D., and S. Knight, eds., *Cunning Exiles*, 62-80.

Cross, R. K., *Malcolm Lowry*.

Dahlie, Hallvard, "Malcolm Lowry and the Northern Tradition," *SCL* 1, i (Winter, 1976): 105-14.

Dodson, D. B., *Malcolm Lowry*. Also in Strade, G., ed., *Six Contemporary British Novelists*, 115-64.

Donohue, Denis, "Ultra-Writer," *NYRB* 6 (Mar. 3, 1966): 16-18.

Edmonds, Dale H., II, "Malcolm Lowry: A Study of His Life and Works," *DA* 26 (1966): 7315.

Epstein, P. S., *Private Labyrinth of Malcolm Lowry*.

Epstein, Perle, "Swinging the Maelstrom: Malcolm Lowry and Jazz," *CanL* 44 (Spring, 1970): 57-66.

Grace, Sherrill E., "The Creative Process: An Introduction to Time and Space in Malcolm Lowry's Fiction," *SCL* 2, i (Winter, 1977): 61-8.

————, "Malcolm Lowry and the Expressionist Vision," in Smith, A., ed., *Art of Malcolm Lowry*, 93-111.

————, "*The Voyage that Never Ends*: Time and Space in the Fiction of Malcolm Lowry," *DAI* 36 (1975): 6712A.

Howard, Benjamin W., "Malcolm Lowry: The Ordeal of Bourgeois Humanism," *DAI* 32 (1972): 4613A.

Jones, G. P., "Malcolm Lowry: Time and the Artist," *UTQ* 51, ii (Winter, 1981-82): 192-209.

Kilgallin, T., *Lowry*.

Knoll, John F., "Malcolm Lowry and the Cinema," *DAI* 34 (1974): 5181A.

Koerber, Betty T., "Humor in the Work of Malcolm Lowry," *DAI* 36 (1975): 2809A.

Lent, John, "Wyndham Lewis and Malcolm Lowry: Contexts of Style and Subject Matter in the Modern Novel," in Bessai, D., and D. Jackel, eds., *Figures in a Ground*, 61-75.

Lowry, Russell, "Preface: Malcolm—A Closer Look," in Smith, A., ed., *Art of Malcolm Lowry*, 9-27.

MacDonald, R. D., "Canada in Lowry's Fiction," *Mosaic* 14, ii (Spring, 1981): 35-53.

Magee, A. Peter, "The Quest for Love," *Emeritus* 1 (Spring, 1965): 24-9. [Not seen.]

Makowiecki, Stefan, "An Analysis of Humour in the Works of Malcolm Lowry," *SAP* 4 (1972): 195-201.

————, *Malcolm Lowry and the Lyrical Convention of Fiction*.

Malcolm Lowry Issue. *PrS* 37 (1963): 284-362.

Miller, D., *Malcolm Lowry and the Voyage that Never Ends*.

New, W. H., "Lowry's Reading: An Introductory Essay," *CanL* 45 (Spring, 1970): 5-12.

————, *Malcolm Lowry*.

Rankin, Elizabeth D., "The Artist Metaphor in the Fiction of Malcolm Lowry," *DAI* 41 (1980): 2602A.

Smith, A., ed., *Art of Malcolm Lowry*.

Tibbetts, Bruce, H., "Malcolm Lowry's Long Night's Journey into Day: The Quest for Home," *DAI* 36 (1975): 1540A.

Tiessen, Paul G., "Malcolm Lowry and the Cinema," *CanL* 44 (Spring, 1970): 38-49.

————, "Malcolm Lowry: Statements on Literature and Film," in Campbell, J., and J. Doyle, eds., *Practical Vision*, 119-32.

Wood, B., ed., *Malcolm Lowry*.

Wood, Barry, "Malcolm Lowry's Metafiction: The Biography of a Genre," *ConL* 19, i (Winter, 1978): 1-25. Also in Wood, B., ed., *Malcolm Lowry*, 250-73.

Woodcock, G., ed., *Malcolm Lowry*.

Woodcock, George, "The Own Place of the Mind: An Essay in Lowrian Topography," in Smith, A., ed., *Art of Malcolm Lowry*, 112-29.

————, "Under Seymour Mountain," *CanL* 8 (Spring, 1961): 3-6. Also in Woodcock, G., *Odysseus Ever Returning*, 67-70.

DARK AS THE GRAVE WHEREIN MY FRIEND IS LAID

Bradbrook, M. C., *Malcolm Lowry*, 69-75.

Cresswell, Rosemary, "Malcolm Lowry's Other Fiction," in Anderson, D., and S. Knight, eds., *Cunning Exiles*, 77-9.

Corrigan, Matthew, "Malcolm Lowry, New York Publishing, and the 'New Illiteracy'," *Encounter* 35, i (July, 1970): 82-93.

————, "Masks and the Man: The Writer as Actor," *Shen* 19 iv (Summer, 1968): 89-93. Also in Wood, B., ed., *Malcolm Lowry*, 210-15.

Costa, R. H., *Malcolm Lowry*, 115-23.

Cross, R. K., *Malcolm Lowry*, 68-75.

Dodson, D. B., *Malcolm Lowry*, 43-5. Also in Stade G., ed., *Six Contemporary British Novelists*, 158-60.

Makowiecki, S., *Malcolm Lowry and The Lyrical Convention of Fiction*, 18-24.

Miller, D., *Malcolm Lowry and the Voyage that Never Ends*, 37-9.

New, W. H., *Malcolm Lowry*, 44-51.

Rasporich, Beverly, "The Right Side of Despair: Lowry's Comic Spirit in LUNAR CAUSTIC and DARK AS THE GRAVE WHEREIN MY FRIEND IS LAID," *Mosaic* 10, iv (1977): 55-67.

Walker, Ronald G., *Infernal Paradise*, 297-313.

Woodcock, George, "Art as the Writer's Mirror: Literary Solipsism in DARK AS THE GRAVE," *Odysseus Ever Returning*, 70-5. Also in Woodcock, G., ed., *Malcolm Lowry*, 66-70.

LUNAR CAUSTIC

Benham, David, "Lowry's Purgatory: Versions of LUNAR CAUSTIC," *CanL* 44 (Spring, 1970): 28-37. Also in Woodcock, G., ed., *Malcolm Lowry*, 56-65. Also in Wood, B., ed., *Malcolm Lowry*, 200-9.

Bradbrook, M. C., *Malcolm Lowry*, 49-53.

Costa, R. H., *Malcolm Lowry*, 83-5.

Cresswell, Rosemary, "Malcolm Lowry's Other Fiction," in Anderson, D., and S. Knight, eds., *Cunning Exiles*, 66-8.

Cross, R. K., *Malcolm Lowry*, 83-5.

Cresswell, Rosemary, "Malcolm Lowry's Other Fiction," in Anderson, D., and S. Knight, eds., *Cunning Exiles*, 66-8.

Cross, R. K., *Malcolm Lowry*, 17-25.

Davies, Russell, "Roman Fleuve," *NStat* (Mar. 4, 1977): 287.

Dodson, D. B., *Malcolm Lowry*, 9-10. Also in Stade, G., ed., *Six Contemporary British Novelists*, 121-3.

Harrison, Keith, "Lowry's Allusions to Melville in LUNAR CAUSTIC," *CanL* 4 (Autumn, 1982): 180-4.

Kickerbocker, Conrad, "Malcolm Lowry and the Outer Circle of Hell," *Parish* 8 (Winter-Spring, 1963): 12-13.

Makowiecki, S., *Malcolm Lowry and the Lyrical Convention of Fiction*, 17-18.

Miller, D., *Malcolm Lowry and the Voyage that Never Ends*, 31-6.

Rasporich, Beverly, "The Right Side of Despair: Lowry's Comic Spirit in LUNAR CAUSTIC and DARK AS THE GRAVE WHEREIN MY FRIEND IS LAID," *Mosaic* 10, iv (1977): 55-67.

OCTOBER FERRY TO GABRIOLA

Bareham, Terence, "After the Volcano: An Assessment of Malcolm Lowry's Posthumous Fiction," *SNNTS* 6, iii (Fall, 1974): 349-62 *passim*. Also in Wood, B., ed., *Malcolm Lowry*, 235-49 *passim*.

Bradbrook, M. C., "Intention and Design in OCTOBER FERRY TO GABRIOLA," in Smith, A., ed., *Art of Malcolm Lowry*, 144-55.

_____, *Malcolm Lowry*, 85-103.

Corrigan, Matthew, "Lowry's Last Novel," *CanL* 48 (Spring, 1971): 74-80.

_____, "The Writer as Consciousness: A View of OCTOBER FERRY TO GABRIOLA," in Woodcock, G., ed., *Malcolm Lowry*, 71-7.

Costa, R. H., *Malcolm Lowry*, 146-54.

_____, "The Man Who Would be Steppenwolf," *SCB* 42, iv (1982): 125-7.

Cross, R. K., *Malcolm Lowry*, 75-84.

Dodson, D. B., "Malcolm Lowry," in Stade, G., ed., *Six Contemporary British Novelists*, 162-3.

Harrison, John K., "UNDER THE VOLCANO and OCTOBER FERRY TO GABRIOLA: The Weight of the Past," *DAI* 34 (1973): 772A.

Harrison, Keith, "Malcolm Lowry's OCTOBER FERRY TO GABRIOLA: Balancing Time," *SCL* 7, i (1982): 115-26.

Kilgallin, Anthony, "The Long Voyage Home: OCTOBER FERRY TO GABRIOLA," in Woodcock, G., ed., *Malcolm Lowry*, 78-87. Also in Wood, B., ed., *Malcolm Lowry*, 215-26.

MacDonald, R. D., "Canada in Lowry's Fiction," *Mosaic* 14, ii (Spring, 1981): 35-53.

Miller, D., *Malcolm Lowry and the Voyage that Never Ends*, 45-6.

New, William H., "GABRIOLA: Malcolm Lowry's Floating Island," *LHY* 13, i (1972): 115-25. Also in Wood, B., ed., *Malcolm Lowry*, 226-34. Also in New, W. H, *Articulating West*, 196-205.

_____, *Malcolm Lowry*, 42-4.

ULTRAMARINE

Binns, Ronald, "Lowry's Anatomy of Melancholy," *CanL* 64 (Spring, 1975): 8-23.

Bradbrook, M. C., *Malcolm Lowry*, 40-8.

Costa, R. H., *Malcolm Lowry*, 37-40.

Cresswell, Rosemary, "Malcolm Lowry's Other Fiction," in Anderson, D., and S. Knight, eds., *Cuning Exiles*, 65-6.

Cross, R. K., *Malcolm Lowry*, 3-12.

Dahlie, Hallvard, "Lowry's Debt to Nordahl Grieg," *CanL* 64 (Spring, 1975): 41-51.

_____, "Malcolm Lowry's ULTRAMARINE," *JCF* 3, iv (1975): 65-8.

Dodson, D. B., *Malcolm Lowry*, 6-9. Also in Stade, G., ed., *Six Contemporary British Novelists*, 119-21.

Durrant, Geoffrey, "Aiken and Lowry," *CanL* 64 (Spring, 1975): 24-40.

Grace, Sherrill E., "Outward Bound," *CanL* 71 (Winter, 1976): 73-9. Also in Wood, B., ed., *Malcolm Lowry*, 6-14.

Kilgallin, T., *Malcolm Lowry*, 85-114.

Kondo, Ineko, "Some Notes on Malcolm Lowry's ULTRAMARINE," *TsudaR* 22 (1977): 15-27.

Miller, D., *Malcolm Lowry and the Voyage that Never Ends*, 19-20.

New, W. H., *Malcolm Lowry*, 20-5.

Rankin, Elizabeth D., "Beyond Autobiography: Art and Life in Malcolm Lowry's ULTRAMARINE," *SCL* 6, i (1981): 53-64.

Woodcock, George, "Malcolm Lowry as Novelist," *QQ* 24 (Apr., 1961): 26-8.

UNDER THE VOLCANO

Ackerley, Chris, "'After Lowry's Light': Coincidence in ULYSSES and UNDER THE VOLCANO," in Gibson, C. A., ed., *The Interpretive Power: Essays in Literature in Honour of Margaret Dalziel*, Dunedin: Dept. of English, Un. of Otago, 1980: 113-26.

_____, "Some Notes towards UNDER THE VOLCANO," *CanL* 95 (Winter, 1982): 185-90.

_____, "Strange Comfort," *MLNew* 9 (Fall, 1981): 31-3.

Allen, Walter, in *NStat* 34 (Dec., 1947): 455-6.

_____, "The Masterpiece of the Forties," in Kostelanetz, R., ed., *On Contemporary Literature*, 419-22.

_____, *Modern Novel*, 263-5.

Andersen, Gladys M., "A Guide to UNDER THE VOLCANO," *DA* 31 (1970): 750A.

Anon., "A Prose Wasteland," *TLS* (May 11, 1962): 332.

Arac, Jonathan, "The Form of Carnival in UNDER THE VOLCANO," *PMLA* 92, iii (May, 1977): 481-9.

Bareham, Terence, "Paradigms of Hell: Symbolic Patterning in UNDER THE VOLCANO," in Benedikz, B. S., ed., *On the Novel*, 113-26. Also in Wood, B., ed., *Malcolm Lowry*, 101-13.

Barnes, Jim, "The Myth of Sisyphus in UNDER THE VOLCANO," *PrS* 42 (1968): 341-8.

Baxter, Charles, M., "Black Holes in Space: The Figure of the Artist in Nathaniel West's MISS LONELYHEARTS, Djuna Barnes' NIGHTWOOD, and Malcolm Lowry's UNDER THE VOLCANO," *DAI* 35 (1975): 4497A.

_____, "The Escape from Irony: UNDER THE VOLCANO and the Aesthetics of Arson," *Novel* 10, ii (Winter, 1977): 114-26.

Binns, Ronald, "Materialism and Magic in UNDER THE VOLCANO," *CritQ* 23, i (1981): 21-32.

_____, "The Q-Ship Incident: The Historical Sources," *MLNew* 8 (Spring, 1981): 5-7.

Boyd, Wendy, "Malcolm Lowry's UNDER THE VOLCANO: La Despedida," *AI* 37, i (1980): 49-64.

Bradbrook, M. C., *Malcolm Lowry*, 54-73, 133-7. Also in Wood, B., ed., *Malcolm Lowry*, 114-25.

Cesari, Laura E., "Malcolm Lowry's Drunken Divine Comedy: UNDER THE VOLCANO and Shorter Fiction," *DA* 28 (1967): 2238A.

Chapman, Marilyn, "'Alastor': The Spirit of UNDER THE VOLCANO," *SCL* 6, ii (1981): 256-72.

Christella, Marie, Sister, "UNDER THE VOLCANO: A Consideration of the Novel by Malcolm Lowry," *XUS* 4 (Mar., 1965): 13-27.

Clipper, Larry, "A Note on the Wibberlee Wobberlee Song," *MLNew* 10 (Spring, 1982): 20-2.

Costa, Richard H., "Edmund Wilson/Malcolm Lowry," *MLNew* 9 (Fall, 1981): 39.

_____, "The Lowry/Aiken Symbiosis," *Nation* 204 (June 26, 1967): 823-6.

_____, *Malcolm Lowry*, 21-8, 40-57, 61-105, 162-6, 168-75.

_____, "Malcolm Lowry and the Addictions of an Era," *UWR* 5, ii (Spring, 1970): 1-10.

_____, "Pieta, Pelado and 'The Ratification of Death': The Ten-Year Evolvement of Malcolm Lowry's Volcano," *JML* 2, i (1970): 3-18.

_____, "A Quest for Eridanus: The Evolving Art of Malcolm Lowry's UNDER THE VOLCANO," *DAI* 30 (1969): 1556A-57A.

_____, "ULYSSES, Lowry's VOLCANO and the Voyage Between: A Study of an Unacknowledged Literary Kinship," *UTQ* 36 (July, 1967): 335-52.

_____, "UNDER THE VOLCANO: A 'New' Charting of the Way It Was," *MLNew* 4 (1979): 2-3.

_____, "UNDER THE VOLCANO—The Way It Was: A Thirty-Year Perspective," in Smith, A., ed., *Art of Malcolm Lowry*, 29-45.

Cripps, Michael, "UNDER THE VOLCANO: The Politics of the Imperial Self," *CanL* 95 (Winter, 1982): 85-101.

Cross, Richard K., *Malcolm Lowry*, 26-64.

_____, "Malcolm Lowry and the Columbian Eden," *ConL* 14, i (Winter, 1973): 19-24, 25-30 *passim*.

_____, "MOBY DICK and UNDER THE VOLCANO: Poetry from the Abyss," *MFS* 20, ii (Summer, 1974): 149-56.

Day, Douglas, "Of Tragic Joy," *PrS* 37 (Winter, 1963): 354-62.

Dodson, D. B., *Malcolm Lowry*, 10-34. Also in Stade, G., ed., *Six Contemporary British Novelists*, 123-49.

Donohue, Denis, "Ultra-Writer," *NYRB* 6 (Mar. 3, 1966): 15-17.

Dorosz, K., *Malcolm Lowry's Infernal Paradise*.

Doyen, Victor, "Elements Toward a Special Reading of Malcolm Lowry's UNDER THE VOLCANO," *ES* 50 (1969): 65-74.

Doyle, Linda S., "A Study of Time in Three Novels: UNDER THE VOLCANO, ONE HUNDRED YEARS OF SOLITUDE, and GRAVITY'S RAINBOW," *DAI* 39 (1978): 1547A.

Edelstein, J. M., "On Re-Reading UNDER THE VOLCANO," *PrS* 37 (Winter, 1963): 336-9.

Edmonds, Dale H., "Malcolm Lowry: A Study of His Life and Work," *DA* 26 (1966): 7315.

_____, "Mescallusions or the Drinking Man's UNDER THE VOLCANO," *JML* 6 (1977): 277-88.

_____, "UNDER THE VOLCANO: A Reading of the 'Immediate Level'," *TSE* 16 (1968): 63-105. Also in Wood, B., ed., *Malcolm Lowry*, 57-100.

Enright, D. J., "Malcolm Lowry," *NStat* (Jan. 27, 1967): 117-18. Also in Enright, D. J., *Man is an Onion*, 20-5.

Epstein, Perle S., "Cabbalistic Elements in Malcolm Lowry's UNDER THE VOLCANO," *DAI* 31 (1971): 4710A.

_____, *Private Labyrinth of Malcolm Lowry*.

Flint, R. W., in *KR* 9 (Summer, 1947): 474-7.

Garnett, George R., "UNDER THE VOLCANO: The Myth of the Hero," *CanL* 84 (1980): 31-40.

Gass, William H., "In Terms of the Toenail: Fiction and the Figures of Life," *New American Review* 10 (1970): 51-68. Also in Gass, W. H., *Fiction and the Figures of Life*, 55-76.

Gilmore, Thomas B., "The Place of Hallucinations in UNDER THE VOLCANO," *ConL* 23, iii (Summer, 1982): 285-30.

Grace, Sherrill E., "Malcolm Lowry and the Expressionist Vision," in Smith, A., ed., *Art of Malcolm Lowry*, 97-109 *passim*.

_____, "UNDER THE VOLCANO: Narrative Mode and Technique," *JCF* 2, ii (Spring, 1973): 57-61.

Hagen, William M., "Realism and Creative Fable in NOSTROMO and UNDER THE VOLCANO: An Approach to Technique and Structure," *DAI* 35 (1975): 4522A.

Harrison, John K., "UNDER THE VOLCANO and OCTOBER FERRY TO GABRIOLA: The Weight of the Past," *DAI* 34 (1973): 772A.

Harrison, Keith, "Indian Traditions and UNDER THE VOLCANO," *LHY* 23, i (1982): 43-59.

_____, "'Objectivisation' in UNDER THE VOLCANO: The Modernism of Eliot, Joyce, and Pound," *MLNew* 10 (Spring, 1982): 14-17.

_____, "The Philoctetes Myth in UNDER THE VOLCANO," *MLNew* 10 (Spring, 1982): 3-5.

Heilman, Robert B., in *SR* 55 (Summer, 1947): 483-92. Expanded as "The Possessed Artist and the Ailing Soul," *CanL* No. 8 (Spring, 1961): 7-16. Also in Woodcock, G., ed., *Malcolm Lowry*, 16-25. Also in Wood, B., ed., *Malcolm Lowry*, 48-57.

Hill, Art, "The Alcoholic on Alcoholism," *CanL* 62 (Autumn, 1974): 33-48. Also in Woodcock, G., ed., *Canadian Novel in the Twentieth Century*, 87-102. Also in Wood, B., ed., *Malcolm Lowry*, 126-42.

Hirschman, Jack, "Kabbala/Lowry, etc.," *PrS* 37 (Winter, 1963): 347-53.

Huddleston, Joan, "From Short Story to Novel: The Language of UNDER THE VOLCANO," *ACLALSB* 5, ii (1979): 80-90.

———, "Noun Modification as an Index of Style in Lowry's UNDER THE VOLCANO," *Lang&S* 10, ii (1977): 86-108.

Jakobsen, Arnt L., *Introduction and Notes to Malcolm Lowry's UNDER THE VOLCANO.* (Anglica et Americana 11.) Copenhagen: Dept. of Eng., Un. of Copenhagen, 1980.

———, "Malcolm Lowry's UNDER THE VOLCANO," 83-94 in Johansson, Stig, and Bjorn Tysdahl, eds., *Papers from the First Nordic Conference for English Studies, Oslo, 17-19 September, 1980,* Oslo: Institute of English Studies, Un. of Oslo, 1981.

Jewison, D. B., "The Platonic Heritage in UNDER THE VOLCANO," *SCL* 3 (1978): 62-9.

Kilgallin, Anthony R., "Faust and UNDER THE VOLCANO," *CanL* No. 26 (Autumn, 1965): 34-54. Also in Woodcock, G., ed., *Malcolm Lowry,* 26-37.

Kilgallin, T., *Lowry,* 119-211.

Leech, Clifford, "The Shaping of Time: NOSTROMO and UNDER THE VOLCANO," in Mack, M., and I. Gregor, eds., *Imagined Worlds,* 334-40.

Levine, Susan F., "The Pyramid and the Volcano: Carlos Fuentes' CAMBIO DE PIEL and Malcolm Lowry's UNDER THE VOLCANO," *Mester* 11, i (1982): 25-40.

Longo, Joseph A., "UNDER THE VOLCANO: Geoffrey Firmin's Tragic Epiphany," *NDEJ* 37, i (1980): 49-64.

Lowry, Malcolm, "Letter to Jonathan Cape," in Breit, Harvey, and Margerie Bonner Lowry, eds., *Selected Letters of Malcolm Lowry,* Philadelphia: Lippincott, 1965, 57-88. Also in Wood, B., ed., *Malcolm Lowry,* 15-46.

———, "Preface to a Novel," *CanL* No. 9 (Summer, 1961): 23-9. Also in Woodcock, G., ed., *Malcolm Lowry,* 9-15.

———, "Two Letters," *CanL* 44 (Spring, 1970): 51-6.

Lytle, A., *Hero with the Private Parts,* 54-8.

MacDonald, R. D., "Canada in Malcolm Lowry's Fiction," *Mosaic* 14, ii (Spring, 1981): 35-53.

Makowiecki, Stefan, "An Analysis of Homer in the Works of Malcolm Lowry," *SAP* 4 (1972): 195-201.

———, *Malcolm Lowry and the Lyrical Convention of Fiction,* 25-61.

———, "Symbolic Pattern in UNDER THE VOLCANO," *KN* 23 (1976): 455-63.

Markson, David, *Malcolm Lowry's VOLCANO: Myth, Symbol, Meaning,* N.Y.: Times Books, 1978.

———, "Myth in UNDER THE VOLCANO," *PrS* 37 (Winter, 1963): 336-9.

McCormick, J., *Catastrophe and Imagination,* 85-9.

Middlebro', Tom, "The Political Strand in Malcolm Lowry's UNDER THE VOLCANO," *SCL* 7, i (1982): 122-6.

Miller, D., *Malcolm Lowry and the Voyage that Never Ends,* 21-30.

New, W. H., *Malcolm Lowry,* 29-41.

Nimmo, D. C., "Lowry's Hell," *N&Q* 16, vii (July, 1969): 269. [Chapter 10.]

O'Kill, Brian, "Aspects of Language in UNDER THE VOLCANO," in Smith, A., ed., *Art of Malcolm Lowry,* 72-92.

Pagnoulle, Christine, "To Hell and Back: Violence in Lowry's UNDER THE VOLCANO," *Commonwealth Newsl.* (Aarhus) 11: 21-8.

Pottinger, Andrew J., "The Consul's Murder," *CanL* 67 (Winter, 1976): 53-63.

———, "The Revising of UNDER THE VOLCANO: A Study in Literary Creativity," *DAI* 39 (1979): 5530A-31A.

Raab, Lawrence, "The Two Consuls: UNDER THE VOLCANO," *Thoth* 12, iii (Spring/Summer, 1972): 20-9.

Rao, P. Ramachandra, "The Self Explored: Patrick White's VOSS and Malcolm Lowry's UNDER THE VOLCANO," Srivastava, A. K., ed., *Alien Voice,* 147-57.

Richey, Clarence W., "'The Ill-Fated Mr. Bultitude': A Note upon an Illusion in Malcolm Lowry's UNDER THE VOLCANO," *NConL* 3, iii (1973): 3-5.

Richmond, Lee J., "The Pariah Dog Symbolism in Malcolm Lowry's UNDER THE VOLCANO," *NConL* 6, ii (1976): 7-9.

Silverman, Carl M., "A Reader's Guide to UNDER THE VOLCANO," *DAI* 33 (1973): 5200A.

Slade, Carole, "The Character of Yvonne in UNDER THE VOLCANO," *CanL* 84 (1980): 137-44.

———, "The Straight Way Was Lost: Parallels Between Dante's INFERNO and Five Twentieth-Century Novels," *DAI* (1974): 7783A-84A.

———, "UNDER THE VOLCANO and Dante's INFERNO," *UWR* 10, ii (1975): 44-52. Also in Wood, B., ed., *Malcolm Lowry,* 143-51.

Taylor, Chet, "The Other Side of Existential Awareness: Reading of Malcolm Lowry's UNDER THE VOLCANO," *LHY* 14, i (1973): 138-50.

Tifft, Stephen, "Tragedy as a Meditation on Itself: Reflexiveness in UNDER THE VOLCANO," in Smith, A., ed., *Art of Malcolm Lowry,* 46-71.

Tindall, W. Y., *Literary Symbol,* 98-9.

Veitch, Douglas W., "Malcolm Lowry's Infernal Paradise," *Fictional Landscape of Mexico,* 237-80.

Voelker, Joseph C., "'A Collideorscape!' Sigmund Freud, Malcolm Lowry and the Aesthetics of Conrad Aiken's A HEART FOR THE GODS OF MEXICO," *SoQ* 21, i (Fall, 1982): 64-81.

Walker, Ronald C., "The Barranca of History: Mexico as Nexus of Doom in UNDER THE VOLCANO," *Infernal Paradise,* 237-80.

———, "The Weight of the Past: Toward a Chronology of UNDER THE VOLCANO," *MLNew* 9 (Fall, 1981): 3-23.

Widmer, Eleanor, "The Drunken Wheel: Malcolm Lowry and UNDER THE VOLCANO," in French, W., ed., *Forties,* 217-26.

Wild, Bernadette, "Malcolm Lowry: A Study of the Sea Metaphor in UNDER THE VOLCANO," *UWR* 4, i (1968): 46-60.

Woodcock, George, "Malcolm Lowry as Novelist," *BCLQ* 23-24 (Apr., 1961): 25-30.

———, "Malcolm Lowry's UNDER THE VOLCANO," *MFS* 4 (Summer, 1958): 151-6. Also in Woodcock, G., *Odysseus Ever Returning,* 56-67.

———, "On the Day of the Dead (Some Reflections on Malcolm Lowry's UNDER THE VOLCANO)," *NoR* 6 (Dec.-Jan., 1953-54): 15-21.

Wright, Terence, "UNDER THE VOLCANO: The Static Art of Malcolm Lowry," *ArielE* 1, iv (1970): 67-76.

York, Thomas L., "UNDER THE VOLCANO: The Novel as Psychodrama," *DAI* 43 (1982): 1969A.

Young, Vernon, in *ArQ* 3 (Autumn, 1947): 281-3.

BIBLIOGRAPHY

"Bibliography," *MLNew* 7 (1980): 22-5.
Costa, R. H., *Malcolm Lowry*, 191-202.
New, William H., *Malcolm Lowry: A Reference Guide*, Boston: G. K. Hall, 1978.
Yandle, Anne, "Bibliography," *MLNew* 5 (1979): 2-8.

LURIE, ALISON (BISHOP), 1926-

GENERAL

Jackson, David, "An Interview with Alison Lurie," *Shen* 31, iv (1980): 15-27.

THE WAR BETWEEN THE TATES

Helfand, Michael S., "The Dialectic of Self and Community in Alison Lurie's THE WAR BETWEEN THE TATES," *PCL* 3, ii (1977): 65-70.

LYTLE, ANDREW NELSON, 1902-1995

GENERAL

Alexander, Benjamin B., "Andrew Lytle and the Total Sense of Family," *DAI* 40 (1979): 2674A.
Bradbury, J. M., *Fugitives*, 265-93.
Bradford, M. E., ed., *Form Discovered*.
Carter, Thomas, in Rubin, L. D., Jr., and R. D. Jacobs, eds., *South*, 287-300.
Clark, Charles C., "The Fiction of Andrew Lytle: From Old Scratch's Cannibal World to Paradise," *QRev* 2 (Autumn, 1974): 127-52.
_____, "The Novels of Andrew Lytle: A Study in the Artistry of Fiction," *DAI* 3 (1972): 2364A-65A.
Ghiselin, Brewster, "Andrew Lytle's Selva Oscura," in Bradford, M. E., ed., *Form Discovered*, 73-8.
Joyner, Nancy, "The Myth of the Matriarch in Andrew Lytle's Fiction," *SLJ* 7, i (Fall, 1974): 67-77.
Rodgers, Elizabeth H., "The Quest Theme in Three Novels by Andrew Lytle," *DAI* 32 (1971): 2705A.
Sarcone, Elizabeth F., "Andrew Lytle and the Mythmaking Process," *DAI* 38 (1977): 1395A.
Tate, Allen, "The Local Universality of Andrew Lytle," in Bradford, M. E., ed., *Form Discovered*, 79-83. Also as "Forward" to Lytle, Andrew, *The Hero with the Private Parts*, Baton Rouge: Louisiana State Un. Pr., 1966.
Weston, Robert V., "Andrew Lytle's Fiction: A Traditional View," *DAI* 33 (1973): 4439A.
_____, "Faulkner and Lytle: Two Modes of Southern Fiction," *SoR* 15 (Winter, 1979): 34-51.
Yow, John S., "A Study of the Fiction and Essays of Andrew Lytle," *DAI* 42, v (Nov., 1981): 2135A.

AT THE MOON'S INN

Benson, Robert G., "The Progress of Hernando de Soto in Andrew Lytle's AT THE MOON'S INN," *GaR* 27 (Summer, 1973): 232-44. Also, revised as "Yankees of the Race: The Decline and Fall of Hernando de Soto," in Bradford, M. E., ed., *Form Discovered*, 84-96.
Carter, Thomas H., in Rubin, L. D., Jr., and R. D. Jacobs, eds., *South*, 291-4.
Clark, Charles C., "The Fiction of Andrew Lytle: From Old Scratch's Cannibal World to Paradise," *ORev* 2 (Autumn, 1974): 131-5.
Eisinger, C. E., *Fiction of the Forties*, 194-5.
Yow, John, "Alchemical Captions: Andrew Lytle's Tales of the Conquistadors," *SLJ* 14, ii (Spring, 1982): 39-48.

THE LONG NIGHT

Carter, Thomas H., in Rubin, L. D., Jr., and R. D. Jacobs, eds., *South*, 289-91.
Clark, Charles C., "The Fiction of Andrew Lytle: From Old Scratch's Cannibal World to Paradise," *ORev* 2 (Autumn, 1974): 128-30.
Edgin, Edward C., "A Critical Study of Andrew Lytle's THE LONG NIGHT," *DAI* 33 (1973): 4409A.
Hoffman, F. J., *Art of Southern Fiction*, 99-101.
Sullivan, W., *Death by Melancholy*, 72-5.
_____, *Requiem for the Renascence*, 26-31.
Warren, Robert Penn, "Andrew Lytle's THE LONG NIGHT: A Rediscovery," *SoR* 7 (1971): 130-9. Also in Madden, D., ed., *Rediscoveries*, 17-28.
Weatherby, H. L., "The Quality of Richness: Observations on Andrew Lytle's THE LONG NIGHT," *MissQ* 23 (Fall, 1970): 383-90. Also in Bradford, M. E. ed., *Form Discovered*, 35-41.

A NAME FOR EVIL

Bradbury, J. M., *Fugitives*, 270-1.
Carter, Thomas H., in Rubin, L. D., Jr., and R. D. Jacobs, eds., *South*, 294-5.
Clark, Charles C., "The Fiction of Andrew Lytle: From Old Scratch's Cannibal World to Paradise," *ORev* 2 (Autumn, 1974): 136-9.
_____, "A NAME FOR EVIL: A Search for Order," *MissQ* 23 (Fall, 1970): 371-82. Also in Bradford, M. E., ed., *Form Discovered*, 24-34.
DeBellis, Jack, "Andrew Lytle's A NAME FOR EVIL: A Transformation of THE TURN OF THE SCREW," *Crit* 8, iii (Spring-Summer, 1966): 26-40.
Eisinger, C. E., *Fiction of the Forties*, 195-6.
Yu, Frederick Y., "Andrew Lytle's A NAME FOR EVIL as a Redaction of THE TURN OF THE SCREW," *MQR* 11, iii (Summer, 1972): 186-90.

THE VELVET HORN

Carter, Thomas H., in Rubin, L. D., Jr., and R. D. Jacobs, eds., *South*, 295-9.
Clark, Charles C., "The Fiction of Andrew Lytle: From Old Scratch's Cannibal World to Paradise," *ORev* 2 (Autumn, 1974): 139-42.
Ghiselin, Brewster, "Trial of Light," *SR* 65 (1957): 657-65.
Hoffman, F. J., *Art of Southern Fiction*, 101-2.
Joyner, Nancy, "The Myth of the Matriarch in Andrew Lytle's Fiction," *SLJ* 7, ii (Fall, 1974): 72-7.

Landess, Thomas H., "Unity of Action in THE VELVET HORN," *MissQ* 23 (Fall, 1970): 349-61. Also in Bradford, M. E., ed., *Form Discovered*, 3-15.

Lytle, Andrew, "The Working Novelist and the Mythmaking Process," *Daedulus* 88 (Spring, 1959): 326-38. Also in Murray, Henry A., ed., *Myth and Mythmaking*, N.Y.: Braziller, 1960, 141-56. Also in Lytle, A., *Hero with the Private Parts*, 178-92. Also in Vickery, John B., ed., *Myth and Literature: Contemporary Theory and Practice*, Lincoln: Un. of Nebraska Pr., 1966, 99-108.

Trowbridge, Clinton W., "The World Made Flesh: Andrew Lytle's THE VELVET HORN," *Crit* 10, ii (1968): 53-68.

Weston, Robert V., "Faulkner and Lytle: Two Modes of Southern Fiction," *SoR* 15 (Winter, 1979): 44-9.

BIBLIOGRAPHY

Polk, Noel, "An Andrew Lytle Checklist," *MissQ* 23 (Fall, 1970): 435-91. Also in Bradford, M. E., ed., *Form Discovered*, 97-108.

MACAULAY, ROSE, 1881-1958

GENERAL

Babington-Smith, Constance, *Rose Macaulay*, London: Collins, 1972.

Benson, Alice R., "Wholeness, the Prize of Wit," *VWR* 3, iii-iv (Summer-Fall, 1978): 206-10.

Kuehn, Robert E., "The Pleasures of Rose Macaulay: An Introduction to Her Novels," *DA* 22 (1962): 2136-37.

Lockwood, William J., in Hoyt, C. A., ed., *Minor British Novelists*, 135-56.

Marrocco, Maria J., "The Novels of Rose Macaulay: A Literary Pilgrimage," *DAI* 39 (1979): 4278A.

Passty, Jeanette N., "Eros and Androgyny: The Writings of Rose Macaulay," *DAI* 43 (1982): 812A.

Smith, Constance B., "Rose Macaulay in Her Writings," *EDH* 38 (Fall, 1975): 143-58.

Swinnerton, Frank, "Rose Macaulay," *KR* 29 (Nov., 1967): 591-608.

Webster, Harvey C., "Rose Macaulay: A Christian a Little Agnostic," *After the Trauma*, 10-30.

GOING ABROAD

Bensen, Alice R., "The Skeptical Balance: A Study of Rose Macaulay's GOING ABROAD," *PMASAL* 48 (1963): 675-83.

THE LEE SHORE

Lockwood, William J., in Hoyt, C. A., ed., *Minor British Novelists*, 136-40.

POTTERISM

Lockwood, William J., in Hoyt, C. A., ed., *Minor British Novelists*, 142-5.

TOLD BY AN IDIOT

Irwin, W. R., "Permanence and Change in THE EDWARDIANS and TOLD BY AN IDIOT," *MFS* 2 (1956): 63-7.

Lockwood, William J., in Hoyt, C. A., ed., *Minor British Novelists*, 148-51.

THE TOWERS OF TREBIZOND

Lockwood, William J., in Hoyt, C. A., ed., *Minor British Novelists*, 152-6.

VIEWS AND VAGABONDS

Bensen, Alice R., "The Ironic Aesthete and the Sponsoring of Causes: A Rhetorical Quandry in Novelistic Technique," *ELT* 9 (1966): 39-43.

BIBLIOGRAPHY

Rizzo, Philip L., "Rose Macaulay: A Critical Survey," *DAI* 20 (1959): 305-6.

MACINNES, COLIN, 1914-1976

GENERAL

Blodgett, Harriet, "City of Other Worlds: The London Novels of Colin MacInnes," *Crit* 18, i (1976): 105-18.

ABSOLUTE BEGINNERS

Blodgett, Harriet, "City of Other Worlds: The London Novels of Colin MacInnes," *Crit* 18, i (1976): 112-15.

CITY OF SPADES

Blodgett, Harriet, "City of Other Worlds: The London Novels of Colin MacInnes," *Crit* 18, i (1976): 107-12.

MR. LOVE AND JUSTICE

Blodgett, Harriet, "City of Other Worlds: The London Novels of Colin MacInnes," *Crit* 18, i (1976): 115-18.

MACKENZIE, COMPTON (EDWARD MONTAGUE), 1883-1972

GENERAL

Dooley, D. J., *Compton Mackenzie*.

Erlandson, Theodore R., "A Critical Study of Some Early Novels (1911-1920) of Sir Compton Mackenzie: The Growth and Decline of a Critical Reputation," *DAI* 25: 7265.

Fytton, Francis, "Compton Mackenzie: Romance versus Realism," *CathW* 182 (Feb., 1956): 358-63.

Stewart, J.I.M., "Out of the North Wind," *TLS* (Sept. 9, 1977): 1068.

Young, K., *Compton Mackenzie*.

CARNIVAL

Dooley, D. J., *Compton Mackenzie*, 36-40.

EARLY LIFE AND ADVENTURES OF SYLVIA SCARLETT

Dooley, D. J., *Compton Mackenzie*, 56-9.

EXTRAORDINARY WOMEN. THEMES AND VARIATIONS

Dooley, D. J., *Compton Mackenzie*, 80-3.

EXTREMES MEET

Dooley, D. J., *Compton Mackenzie*, 75-6.

THE FOUR WINDS OF LOVE

Brooks, Phillips V., "The Writing and Publication History of Compton Mackenzie's Novel THE FOUR WINDS OF LOVE," *DAI* 36 (1975): 2193A.
Dooley, D. J., *Compton Mackenzie*, 84-95.
Sanderson, Stewart F., "THE FOUR WINDS OF LOVE," *ArielE* 2, iii (July, 1971): 7-15.

GUY AND PAULINE

Dooley, D. J., *Compton Mackenzie*, 51-6.

KEEP THE HOME GUARD TURNING

Dooley, D. J., *Compton Mackenzie*, 112-14.

THE LUNATIC REPUBLIC

Dooley, D. J., *Compton Mackenzie*, 102-3.

THE MONARCH OF THE GLEN

Dooley, D. J., *Compton Mackenzie*, 106-10.

THE PASSIONATE ELOPEMENT

Dooley, D. J., *Compton Mackenzie*, 30-6.

POOR RELATIONS

Dooley, D. J., *Compton Mackenzie*, 68-70.
West, Rebecca, "Poor Relations," *NRep* (Feb. 18, 1920): 362-3. Also in Harrison, G. A., ed., *Critic as Artist*, 378-81.

THE RED TAPEWORM

Dooley, D. J., *Compton Mackenzie*, 99-102.

RICH RELATIVES

Dooley, D. J., *Compton Mackenzie*, 70-2.

ROCKETS GALORE

Dooley, D. J., *Compton Mackenzie*, 119-22.

SINISTER STREET

Dooley, D. J. *Compton Mackenzie*, 41-9.

SYLVIA AND MICHAEL

Dooley, D. J., *Compton Mackenzie*, 59-64.

THE VANITY GIRL

Dooley, D. J., *Compton Mackenzie*, 64-7.

VESTAL FIRE

Dooley, D. J., *Compton Mackenzie*, 76-80.

WATER ON THE BRAIN

Dooley, D. J., *Compton Mackenzie*, 96-9.

WHISKEY GALORE

Dooley, D. J., *Compton Mackenzie*, 114-18.

BIBLIOGRAPHY

Dooley, D. J., *Compton Mackenzie*, 161-5.

MACLENNAN, HUGH, 1907-

GENERAL

Boeschenstein, Herman, "Hugh MacLennan, a Canadian Novelist," in Goetsch, P., ed., *Hugh MacLennan*, 35-57.
Buitenhuis, P., *Hugh MacLennan*.
Cameron, Donald, "Hugh MacLennan: The Tennis Racket is an Antelope Bone," *JFC* 1, i (Winter, 1972): 40-7. Also in *Conversations with Canadian Novelists, 1*, Toronto: Macmillan, 130-48.
Cameron, Elspeth, "'A Late Germination in a Cold Climate': The Growth of MacLennan Criticism," *JCanStud* 14, iv (Winter, 1979-80): 3-19.
Chambers, Robert D., "The Novels of Hugh MacLennan," *JCanStud* 2 (Aug., 1967): 3-11. Also in Goetsch, P., ed., *Hugh MacLennan*, 59-74.
Cockburn, R. H., *Novels of Hugh MacLennan*.
Goetsch, P., ed., *Hugh MacLennan*.
Goetsch, Paul, "Too Long to the Courtly Muses: Hugh MacLennan as a Contemporary Writer," *CanL* 10 (Autumn, 1961): 19-31. Also in Woodcock, G., ed., *Canadian Novel in the Twentieth Century*, 103-14.
Hoy, Helen, "'The Gates Closed on Us Then': The Paradise-Lost Motif in Hugh MacLennan's Fiction," *JCanStud* 14, iv (Winter, 1979-80): 29-45.
Hyman, Roger L., "Hugh MacLennan: His Art, His Society and His Critics," *QQ* 82, iv (Winter, 1975): 515-27.
———, "The Prose of Hugh MacLennan; A Re-Evaluation," *DAI* 34 (1974): 5177A-78A.
———, "Too Many Voices, Too Many Times: Hugh MacLennan's Unfulfilled Ambitions," *QQ* 89, ii (Summer, 1982): 313-24.
Lucas, A., *Hugh MacLennan*.
MacLennan, Hugh, "Reflections on Two Decades," *CanL* 41 (Summer, 1969): 28-39. Also in Woodcock, G., ed., *Canadian Novel in the Twentieth Century*, 115-26.
———, "The Story of a Novel," *CanL* 3 (Winter, 1960): 35-9.
MacLulich, T. D., "Oedipus and Eve: The Novels of Hugh MacLennan," *DR* 59 (1979): 500-18.
Mathews, Robin, "Hugh MacLennan: The Nationalist Dilemma in Canada," *SCL* 1, i (Winter, 1976): 49-63.
McPherson, Hugo, "The Novels of Hugh MacLennan," *QQ* 60 (Summer, 1953): 186-98. Also in Goetsch, P., ed., *Hugh MacLennan*, 23-33.
Moss, J., *Patterns of Isolation*, 215-18, 222-4.
Pacey, Desmond, *Creative Writing in Canada*, 217-21.
Ross, Catherine S., "Hugh MacLennan's Two Worlds," *CanL* 80 (1979): 5-12.

Staines, David, "Mapping the Terrain," *Mosaic* 11, iii (Spring, 1978): 137-51.

Sutherland, Ronald, "Interview: Hugh MacLennan," *CanL* 68-69 (Spring-Winter, 1976): 40-8.

Watters, R. E., "Hugh MacLennan and the Canadian Character," in Morrison, Edmund, and William Robbins, eds., *As a Man Thinks*, Toronto: W. J. Gage and Co., 1953, 228-43.

Wilson, E., *O Canada*, 57-80.

Woodcock, George, "Hugh MacLennan," *NoR* 3 (Spr.-May, 1950): 2-10. Also in Goetsch, P., ed., *Hugh MacLennan*, 11-21.

_____, "A Nation's Odyssey: The Novels of Hugh MacLennan," *REL* 2, iv (Oct., 1961): 77-90. Also in *CanL* 10 (Autumn, 1961): 7-18. Also in Smith, A. J. M., ed., *Masks of Fiction*, 128-40. Also in Canadian Literature, *Choice of Critics*, 79-100. Also in Woodcock, G., *Odysseus Ever Returning*, 12-23.

_____, "Surrogate Fathers and Orphan Sons," *JCanStud* 14, iv (Winter, 1979-80): 20-8.

BAROMETER RISING

Arnason, David, "Canadian Nationalism in Search of a Form: Hugh MacLennan's BAROMETER RISING," *JCF* 1, iv (Fall, 1972): 68-71. Also in Moss, J., ed., *Canadian Novel*, v. 3. *Modern Times*, 95-105.

Bassett, Isabel, "The Transformation of Imperialism: Connor to MacLennan," *JCF* 2, i (Winter, 1973): 58-62.

Boeschenstein, Herman, "Hugh MacLennan, a Canadian Novelist," in Goetsch, P., *Hugh MacLennan*, 36-8.

Buitenhuis, P., *Hugh MacLennan*, 19-29.

Cockburn, R. H., *Novels of Hugh MacLennan*, 29-45.

Goetsch, Paul, "Too Long to the Courtly Muses: Hugh MacLennan as a Contemporary Writer," *CanL* 10 (Autumn, 1961): 20-1. Also in Woodcock, G., ed., *Canadian Novel in the Twentieth Century*, 103-5.

Hoy, Helen, " 'The Gates Closed on Us Then': The Paradise-Lost Motif in Hugh MacLennan's Fiction," *JCanStud* 14, iv (Winter, 1979-80): 31-3.

MacLennan, Hugh, "My First Book," *CanA&B* 28, ii (1952): 3-4.

MacLulich, T. D., "Oedipus and Eve: The Novels of Hugh MacLennan," *DR* 59 (1979): 505-7.

Mathews, Robin, "Hugh MacLennan: The Nationalist Dilemma in Canada," *SCL* 1, i (Winter, 1976): 53-60.

McPherson, Hugh, "Introduction," in *Barometer Rising* (New Canadian Library), Toronto: McClelland & Stewart, 1958, ix-xv.

_____, "The Novels of Hugh MacLennan," *QQ* 60 (Summer, 1953): 187-90. Also in Groetsch, P., ed., *Hugh MacLennan*, 24-6.

Morley, Patricia, *Immoral Moralists*, 38-61 *passim*.

New, William H., "The Storm and After: Imagery and Symbolism in Hugh MacLennan's BAROMETER RISING," *QQ* 74 (Summer, 1967): 302-13. Also in New, W. H., *Articulating West*, 95-107. Also in Goetsch, P., ed., *Hugh MacLennan*, 75-87.

O'Donnell, Kathleen, "The Wanderer in BAROMETER RISING," *UWR* 3, ii (Spring, 1968): 12-18. Also in Goetsch, P., ed., *Hugh MacLennan*, 89-96.

Woodcock, George, "Hugh MacLennan," *NoR* 3 (Apr.-May, 1950): 2-7. Also in Goetsch, P., ed., *Hugh MacLennan*, 11-16.

_____, "A Nation's Odyssey: The Novels of Hugh MacLennan," *REL* 2, iv (Oct., 1961): 77-82. Also in *CanL* 10 (Autumn, 1961): 7-11. Also in Smith, A. J. M., ed., *Masks of Fiction*, 130-2.

Also in Canadian Literature, *Choice of Critics*, 79-84. Also in Woodcock, G., *Odysseus Ever Returning*, 13-16.

EACH MAN'S SON

Boeschenstein, Herman, "Hugh MacLennan, a Canadian Novelist," in Goetsch, P., ed., *Hugh MacLennan*, 47-9.

Boone, Laurel, "EACH MAN'S SON: Romance in Disguise," *JCF* 18-29 (1980): 147-56.

Buitenhuis, P., *Hugh MacLennan*, 46-55.

Cockburn, R. H., *Novels of Hugh MacLennan*, 89-108.

Davis, Marilyn, "Fathers and Sons," *CanL* 58 (Autumn, 1973): 39-50.

Dooley, David, "EACH MAN'S SON: 'The Daemon of Hope and Imagination'," *JCanStud* 14, iv (1979-80): 66-75.

Goetsch, Paul, "Too Long to the Courtly Muses: Hugh MacLennan as a Contemporary Writer," *CanL* 10 (Autumn, 1961): 23-5. Also in Woodcock, G., ed., *Canadian Novel in the Twentieth Century*, 107-9.

Hoy, Helen, " 'The Gates Closed on Us Then': The Paradise-Lost Motif in Hugh MacLennan's Fiction," *JCanStud* 14, iv (Winter, 1979-80): 37-8.

Jones, D. G., *Butterfly on Rock*, 62-5.

Lucas, Alec, "Introduction," in *Each Man's Son* (New Canadian Library), Toronto: McClelland & Stewart, 1962, 7-13.

MacLulich, T. D., "Oedipus and Eve: The Novels of Hugh MacLennan," *DR* 59 (1979): 508-11.

McPherson, Hugo, "The Novels of Hugh MacLennan," *QQ* 60 (Summer, 1953): 195-8. Also in Goetsch, P., ed., *Hugh MacLennan*, 30-3.

Morley, P. A., *Immoral Moralists*, 63-71.

Phelps, A. L., *Canadian Writers*, 82-4.

Tallman, Warren, in Canadian Literature, *Choice of Critics*, 64-7+.

_____, "Wolf in the Snow," *CanL* 5 (Summer, 1960): 18-20; 6 (Autumn, 1960): 41-4.

Woodcock, George, "A Nation's Odyssey: The Novels of Hugh MacLennan," *REL* 2, iv (Oct., 1961): 85-7. Also in *CanL* 10 (Autumn, 1961): 14-15. Also in Smith, A.J.M., ed., *Masks of Fiction*, 136-7. Also in Canadian Literature, *Choice of Critics*, 87-9. Also in Woodcock, G., *Odysseus Ever Returning*, 19-21.

THE PRECIPICE

Buitenhuis, P., *Hugh MacLennan*, 40-6.

Boeschenstein, Herman, "Hugh MacLennan, a Canadian Novelist," in Goetsch, P., ed., *Hugh MacLennan*, 45-7.

Cameron, Elspeth, "Ordeal by Fire: The Genesis of MacLennan's THE PRECIPICE," *CanL* 82 (1979): 35-46.

_____, "The Overlay Theme in MacLennan's THE PRECIPICE," *JFC* 20 (1977): 117-24.

Chambers, Robert D., "Hugh MacLennan in Religion: THE PRECIPICE Revisited," *JCanStud* 14, iv (Winter, 1979-80): 46-53.

Cockburn, R. H., *Novels of Hugh MacLennan*, 71-88.

Goetsch, Paul, "Too Long to the Courtly Muses: Hugh MacLennan as a Contemporary Writer," *CanL* 10 (Autumn, 1961): 22-3. Also in Woodcock, G., ed., *Canadian Novel in the Twentieth Century*, 106-7.

Hoy, Helen, " 'The Gates Closed on Us Then': The Paradise-Lost Motif in Hugh MacLennan's Fiction," *JCanStud* 14, iv (Winter, 1979-80): 35-7.

MacLulich, T. D., "THE PRECIPICE: MacLennan's Anatomy of Failure," *JCanStud* 14, iv (Winter, 1979-80): 46-53.

McPherson, Hugo, "The Novels of Hugh MacLennan," *QQ* 60 (Summer, 1953): 192-5. Also in Goetsch, P. ed., *Hugh MacLennan*, 28-30.

Morley, P. A., *Immoral Moralists*, 38-61 passim.

Phelps, A. L., *Canadian Writers*, 81.

Wilson, E., *O Canada*, 64-6.

Woodcock, George, "Hugh MacLennan," *NoR* 3 (Apr.-May, 1950): 9-10. Also in Goetsch, P., ed., *Hugh MacLennan*, 19-21.

———, "A Nation's Odyssey: The Novels of Hugh MacLennan," *REL* 2, iv (Oct., 1961): 84-5. Also in *CanL* 10 (Autumn, 1961): 13-14. Also in Smith, A.J.M., ed., *Masks of Fiction*, 135-6. Also in Canadian Literature, *Choice of Critics*, 86-7. Also in Woodcock, G., *Odysseus Ever Returning*, 18-19.

RETURN OF THE SPHINX

Bartlett, Donald H., "MacLennan and Yeats," *CanL* (Summer, 1981): 74-84.

Buitenhuis, P., *Hugh MacLennan*, 64-72.

Cameron, Elspeth, "MacLennan's SPHINX: Critical Reception and Oedipal Origins," *JCF* 30 (1980): 141-59.

Cockburn, R. H., *Novels of Hugh MacLennan*, 127-44.

Davis, Marilyn, "Fathers and Sons," *CanL* 58 (Autumn, 1973): 39-50.

Duran, Gillian, "Terrorism, Human Nature, and Hugh MacLennan's RETURN OF THE SPHINX," *L&I* 15 (1973): 51-8.

Hoy, Helen, " 'The Gates Closed on Us Then': The Paradise-Lost Motif in Hugh MacLennan's Fiction," *JCanStud* 14, iv (Winter, 1979-80): 43-4.

Hyman, Roger, "Return to RETURN OF THE SPHINX," *ESCan* 1 (Winter, 1975): 450-65.

Mathews, Robin, "Hugh MacLennan: The Nationalist Dilemma in Canada," *SCL* 1, i (Winter, 1976): 60-73.

Morley, P. A., *Immoral Moralists*, 110-24 passim.

New, William H., "Winter and the Night People," *CanL* 36 (Spring, 1968): 26-33. Also in New, W. H., *Articulating West*, 128-38. Also in Goetsch, P., ed., *Hugh MacLennan*, 163-72.

Spettigue, Douglas, "Beauty and the Beast," *QQ* 74 (Winter, 1967): 762-5. Also in Goetsch, P., ed., *Hugh MacLennan*, 157-61.

Sutherland, Ronald, "The Fourth Separatism," *CanL* 45 (Summer, 1970): 15-22.

Zezulka, Joseph, "MacLennan's Defeated Pilgrim: A Perspective in RETURN OF THE SPHINX," *JCF* 4, i (1975): 121-31.

TWO SOLITUDES

Bissell, Claude T., "Introduction" to *Two Solitudes*, Toronto: McClelland & Stewart, 1951.

Boeschenstein, Herman, "Hugh MacLennan, a Canadian Novelist," in Goetsch, P., ed., *Hugh MacLennan*, 39-44.

Buitenhuis, P., *Hugh MacLennan*, 29-39.

Buitenhuis, Peter, "Two Solitudes Revisited: Hugh MacLennan and Leonard Cohen," *LHY* 13, ii (July, 1972): 19-32.

Chambers, Robert D., "The Novels of Hugh MacLennan," *JCanStud* 2 (Aug., 1967): 5-6. Also in Goetsch, P., ed., *Hugh MacLennan*, 63-5.

Cockburn, R. H., *Novels of Hugh MacLennan*, 47-69.

Goetsch, Paul, "Too Long to the Courtly Muses: Hugh MacLennan as a Contemporary Writer," *CanL* 10 (Autumn, 19691): 22. Also in Woodcock, G., ed., *Canadian Novel in the Twentieth Century*, 150-6.

Hoy, Helen, " 'The Gates Closed on Us Then': The Paradise-Lost Motif in Hugh MacLennan's Fiction," *JCanStud* 14, iv (Winter, 1979-80): 33-5.

I.M.S., "TWO SOLITUDES," *QQ* 52 (1945): 494-6. Also in Goetsch, P., ed., *Hugh MacLennan*, 97-9.

Kelly, Sister Catherine, "The Unity of TWO SOLITUDES," *ArielE* 6, ii (1975): 38-61.

McPherson, Hugo, "The Novels of Hugh MacLennan," *QQ* 60 (Summer, 1953): 190-2. Also in Goetsch, P., ed., *Hugh McLennan*, 26-8.

Morley, P. A., *Immoral Moralists*, 38-61 passim.

Phelps, A. L., *Canadian Writers*, 78-81.

Stevenson, Warren, "A Neglected Theme in TWO SOLITUDES," *CanL* 75 (Winter, 1977): 53-60.

Woodcock, George, "Hugh MacLennan," *NoR* 3 (Apr.-May, 1950): 7-9. Also in Gotsch, P., ed., *Hugh MacLennan*, 17-19.

———, "A Nation's Odyssey: The Novels of Hugh MacLennan," *REL* 2, iv (Oct., 1961): 82-4. Also in *CanL* 14 (Autumn, 1961): 11-13. Also in Smith, A.J.M., ed., *Masks of Fiction*, 133-5. Also in Canadian Literature, *Choice of Critics*, 84-6. Also in Woodcock, G., *Odysseus Ever Returning*, 16-18.

THE WATCH THAT ENDS THE NIGHT

Blodgett, E. D., "Intertextual Designs in Hugh MacLennan's THE WATCH THAT ENDS THE NIGHT," *CRCL* 5 (1978): 280-8.

Boeschenstein, Herman, "Hugh MacLennan, a Canadian Novelist," in Goetsch, P., ed., *Hugh MacLennan*, 50-6.

Bonnycastle, Steven, "The Powers of THE WATCH THAT ENDS THE NIGHT," *JCanStud* 14, iv (1979-80): 76-89.

Buitenhuis, P., *Hugh MacLennan*, 55-64.

Cameron, Elspeth, "Of Cabbages and Kings: The Concept of the Hero in THE WATCH THAT ENDS THE NIGHT," in Moss, J., ed., *Canadian Novel*, v. 3, *Modern Times*, 106-27.

Chambers, Robert D., "The Novels of Hugh MacLennan," *JCanStud* 2 (Aug., 1967): 7-10. Also in Goesch, P., ed., *Hugh MacLennan*, 76-72.

Clark, J. Wilson, "Hugh MacLennan's Comprador Outlook," *L&I* 12 (1972): 1-8.

Cockburn, R. H., *Novels of Hugh MacLennan*, 109-26.

Davies, Robertson, "MacLennan's Rising Sun," *Saturday Night* 74 (Mar. 28, 1959): 29-31. Also in Goetsch, P., ed., *Hugh MacLennan*, 119-22.

Farmiloe, Dorothy, "Hugh MacLennan and the Canadian Myth," *Mosaic* 2-3 (Spring, 1969): 1-9. Also in Goetsch, P., ed., *Hugh MacLennan*, 145-54.

Goetsch, Paul, "Too Long to the Courtly Muses: Hugh MacLennan as a Contemporary Writer," *CanL* 10 (Autumn, 1961): 25-8. Also in Woodcock, G., ed., *Canadian Novel in the Twentieth Century*, 109-11.

Hirano, Keiichi, "Jerome Martell and Norman Bethune: A Note on Hugh MacLennan's THE WATCH THAT ENDS THE NIGHT," *SELit*, English Number (1968): 37-59. Also in Goetsch, P., ed., *Hugh MacLennan*, 123-37.

Hoy, Helen, "'The Gates Closed on Us Then': The Paradise-Lost Motif in Hugh MacLennan's Fiction," *JCanStud* 14, iv (Winter, 1979-80): 38-43.

James, William C., "THE WATCH THAT ENDS THE NIGHT," 315-32 in Slater, Peter, ed., *Religion and Culture in Canada/Religion et culture au Canada: Essays by Members of the Canadian Society for the Study of Religion/Recueil d'articles par des membres de la Societe Canadienne pour l'Etude de la Religion*, n.p.: Corp Canadienne des Sciences Religieuses/Canadian Corp. for Studies in Religion, 1977.

Jones, D. G., *Butterfly on Rock*, 157-62.

Lynn, S., "A Canadian Writer and the Modern World," *MarxQ* 1 (Spring, 1962): 36-43.

MacLennan, Hugh, "The Story of a Novel," *CanL* 10 (Autumn, 1961): 15-18. Also in Smith, A. J. M., ed., *Masks of Fiction*, 137-40.

MacLulich, T. D., "Oedipus and Eve: The Novels of Hugh MacLennan," *DR* 59 (1979): 512-15.

Marshall, Thomas, "Some Working Notes on THE WATCH THAT ENDS THE NIGHT," *Quarry* 17 (1968): 13-16.

Merivale, Patricia, "The (Auto)-Biographical Compulsions of Dunstan Ramsay," in Lawrence, R. G., and S. L. Macey, eds., *Studies in Robertson Davies' DEPTFORD Trilogy*, 57-65.

Morley, P. A., *Immoral Moralists*, 98-108.

New, William H., "The Apprenticeship of Discovery: Richler and MacLennan," *CanL* 29 (Summer, 1966): 18-33. Also in New, W. H., *Articulating West*, 117-27.

Roberts, Ann, "The Dilemma of Hugh MacLennan," *MarxQ* 1 (Autumn, 1962): 58-62.

Thorne, W. B., "The Relation of Structure to Theme in THE WATCH THAT ENDS THE NIGHT," *HAB* 20, ii (Spring, 1969): 42-5. Also in Goetsch, P., ed., *Hugh MacLennan*, 139-43.

Watt, F. W., in *UTQ* 29 (July, 1960): 461-3.

Woodcock, George, "A Nation's Odyssey: The Novels of Hugh MacLennan," *REL* 2 iv (Oct., 1961): 87-9. Also in *CanL* 10 (Autumn, 1961): 15-18. Also in Smith, A. J. M., ed., *Masks of Fiction*, 137-40. Also in Canadian Literature, *Choice of Critics*, 89-92. Also in Woodcock, G., *Odysseus Ever Returning*, 21-3.

Zichy, Francis, "'Shocked and Startled into Utter Banality': Characters and Circumstances in THE WATCH THAT ENDS THE NIGHT," *JCanStud* 14, iv (1979-80): 90-105.

VOICES IN TIME

Cameron, Elspeth, "Not with a Whimper: Hugh MacLennan's VOICES IN TIME," *WLWE* 20, ii (Autumn, 1961): 279-91.

Hyman, Roger, "Too Many Voices, Too Many Times: Hugh MacLennan's Unfulfilled Ambitions," *QQ* 89, ii (Summer, 1982): 313-24.

BIBLIOGRAPHY

Cameron, Elspeth, "Hugh MacLennan: An Annotated Bibliography," 103-53 in Lecker, Robert, and Jack David, eds., *The Annotated Bibliography of Canada's Major Authors*, Volume One, Downsview: ECW, 1979.

MACMANUS, FRANCIS, 1909-1965

GENERAL

McMahon, Seán, "Francis MacManus's Novels of Modern Ireland," *Eire* 5, i (Spring, 1970): 116-30.

THE GREATEST OF THESE

Lynch, Gerard, *Francis MacManus—THE GREATEST OF THESE*, Dublin: Gill and Macmillan; London: Macmillan, 1972.

MEN WITHERING

Halpin, Tom, *Francis MacManus—MEN WITHERING*, Dublin: Gill and Macmillan; London: Macmillan, 1972.

WATERGATE

Kiely, Benedict, in Madden, D., ed., *Rediscoveries*, 270-9.

MADDEN, DAVID, 1933-

GENERAL

Jones, Ray, "An Interview with David Madden," *NoR* 9, i (Spring-Summer, 1982): 29-35.

Laney, Ruth, "An Interview with David Madden," *SoR* 11, i (Jan., 1975): 167-80.

Madden, David, "The Compulsion to Tell a Story," *JPC* 5, ii (Fall, 1971): 269-79.

———, "Portrait of the Artist as a Bijou Usher," in Marsden, M., comp., *Proceedings of the Sixth National Convention of Popular Culture Association*, 94-112.

Pinsker, Sanford, "A Conversation with David Madden," *Crit* 15, ii (1973): 5-14.

BIJOU

Laney, Ruth, "An Interview with David Madden," *SoR* 11, i (Jan., 1975): 167-80.

CASSANDRA SINGING

Pinsker, Sanford, "The Mixed Cords of David Madden's CASSANDRA SINGING," *Crit* 15, ii (1973): 15-26. Also in Pinsker, S., *Between Two Worlds*, 103-14.

BIBLIOGRAPHY

Perrault, Anna H., "A David Madden Bibliography: 1952-1981," *BB* 39, iii (Sept., 1982): 104-16.

MAILER, NORMAN, 1923-

GENERAL

Adams, Laura, "Existential Aesthetics: An Interview with Norman Mailer," *PR* 42 (1975): 197-214.

_____, *Existential Battles.*

Aldridge, John W., "Norman Mailer: The Energy of New Success," in Aldridge, J. W., *Time to Murder and Create*, 149-63. Also in Braudy, L., ed., *Norman Mailer*, 109-19. Also in Aldridge, J. W., *Devil in the Fire*, 169-79.

Alter, Robert, "Norman Mailer (1923-)," in Panichas, G. A., ed., *Politics of Twentieth-Century Novelists*, 321-34.

_____, "The Real and Imaginary Worlds of Norman Mailer," *Midstream* 15, i (Jan., 1969): 24-35.

Anderson, Don, "Norman Mailer: Man Against Machines," in Anderson, D., and S. Knight, eds., *Cunning Exiles*, 165-95.

Bailey, J., *Norman Mailer, Quick-Change Artist.*

Baines, William, and Henry Nuwer, "Norman Mailer," *Brushfire* 23, ii (1973): 7-20. [Interview.]

Bakker, J., "Literature, Politics, and Norman Mailer," *DQR* 3-4 (1971): 129-45.

Balz, Douglas C., "Art and Power: The Interaction of the Fiction and Journalism of Norman Mailer," *DAI* 37 (1977): 7748A-49A.

Baumbach, J., *Landscape of Nightmare*, 9-11.

Begiebing, Robert J., "Rebirth and Heroic Consciousness: Allegory and Archetype in the Works of Norman Mailer," *DAI* 38 (1977): 2782A-83A.

Bernstein, Mashey, "The Heart of the Nation: Jewish Values in the Fiction of Norman Mailer," *SAJL* 2 (1982): 115-25.

_____, "The Individual as a Work of Art: Jewish and Puritan Values in the Fiction of Norman Mailer and Edward Lewis Wallant," *DAI* 38 (1977): 3494A-85A.

Braudy, Leo, "Introduction: Norman Mailer: The Price of Vulnerability," in Braudy, L., ed., *Norman Mailer*, 1-20.

_____, ed., *Norman Mailer.*

Breslow, Paul, "The Hipster and the Radical," *StL* 1 (1960): 102-5.

Bronson, Daniel R., "In Pursuit of the Elusive Present: The Poetry and Prose of Norman Mailer," *DAI* 33 (1973): 3632A.

Bryant, J. H., *Open Decision*, 369-94.

Bufithis, P. H., *Norman Mailer.*

Carroll, Paul, "Playboy Interview," *Playboy* (Jan., 1968): 69-84. Also in Lucid, R. F., ed., *Norman Mailer*, 259-95.

Cohen, Lance N., "Contending for Humanity in the Technological Age: The Art and Argument of Norman Mailer," *DAI* 36 (1975): 3709A.

Cohen, S., *Norman Mailer's Novels.*

Cook, Bruce A., "Norman Mailer: The Temptation of Power," *Ren* 14 (Summer, 1962): 206-15, 222.

Cowan, Michael, "The Americaness of Norman Mailer," in Braudy, L., ed., *Norman Mailer*, 143-57.

Crowley, Sharon C., "A Rhetorical Analysis of Norman Mailer's Prose Narratives," *DAI* 35 (1974): 1093A.

Dabney, Richard L., "The Rebel and the Hipster," *DAI* 32 (1972): 6969A. [Mailer and Camus.]

Dupee, F. W., "The American Norman Mailer," *Ctary* 29 (Feb., 1960): 128-32.

Edinger, Harry G., "Bears in Three Contemporary Fictions," *HAB* 28 (1977): 141-50.

Ehrlich, Robert M., "The Aesthetic and Political Dimensions of Mailer's Concept of the Hipster," *DAI* 34 (1974): 4256A.

_____, *Norman Mailer.*

Ferriera, James M., "The Radical Individualism of Norman Mailer," *DAI* 33 (1972): 2369A-70A.

Finkelstein, S., *Existentialism and Alienation in American Literature*, 269-75.

Foster, Richard, "Mailer and the Fitzgerald Tradition," *Novel* 1, iii (Spring, 1968): 219-30. Also in Braudy, L., ed., *Norman Mailer*, 127-42.

_____, *Norman Mailer.* Also in Lucid, R. F., ed., *Norman Mailer*, 21-59.

Frahm, Mary A., "New Circuits: Exploring Sexuality in Mailer's Fiction," *DAI* 41 (1981): 4393A.

Garber, Norman B., "Norman Mailer: The Evolution of a Puritan-Existential Vision," *DAI* 35 (1975): 7303A-04A.

Gerson, Jessica, "Norman Mailer: The Mystical Vision," *DAI* 38 (1978): 6132A-33A.

_____, "Norman Mailer: Sex, Creativity and God," *Mosaic* 15, ii (June, 1982): 1-16.

Gillenkirk, Jeffrey, "Mailer is the Message," *NOR* 3, iii (1973): 223-5.

Gilman, R., *Confusion of Realms*, 81-153.

Gindin, James, "Megalotopia and the WASP Backlash: The Fiction of Mailer and Updike," *CentR* 15, i (1971): 38-52.

Glicksberg, Charles I., "Norman Mailer: The Angry Young Novelist in America," *WSCL* 1, i (Winter, 1960): 25-34.

Goldstone, Herbert, "The Novels of Norman Mailer," *EJ* 45 (Mar., 1956): 113-21.

Gordon, A., *American Dreamer.*

Grace, Matthew, "Norman Mailer at the End of the Decade," *EA* 24, i (Jan.-Mar., 1971): 50-8.

_____, and Steve Roday, "Mailer on Mailer: An Interview," *NOR* 3, iii (1973): 229-34.

Green, Martin, "Amis and Mailer: The Faustian Contract," *Month* 3, ii (Feb., 1971): 45-8, 52.

Gross, G. L., *Heroic Ideal In American Literature*, 272-95.

Gutman, S. T., *Mankind in Barbary.*

Guttmann, Allen, "Norman Mailer: The Writer as Radical," 104-6 in Weber, Alfred, and Dietmar Haack, eds., *Americanische Literatur im 20 Jahrhundert/American Literature in the Twentieth Century*, Gottingen: Vandenhoeck and Ruprecht, 1971.

Harper, H. M., "Norman Mailer: A Revolution in the Consciousness of Time," *Desperate Faith*, 96-136.

Hesla, David, "The Two Roles of Norman Mailer," in Scott, N. A., Jr., *Adversity and Grace*, 211-23.

Hill, Robert R., "Epistemological Dilemmas in the Works of Norman Mailer and Thomas Pynchon: The Themes and Motifs of Systematization, Paranoia, and Entropy," *DAI* 42, v (Nov., 1981): 2131A-32A.

Hoffa, William, "Norman Mailer: ADVERTISEMENTS FOR MYSELF," in French, W., ed., *Fifties*, 73-82.

Hoffman, Frederick J., "Norman Mailer and the Revolt of the Ego: Some Observations on Recent American Literature," *WSCL* 1, iii (Fall, 1960): 5-12.

Horn, Bernard, "The Forms of Self-Awareness in Norman Mailer's Novels," *DAI* 38 (1978): 4827A.

Howe, I., "A Quest for Peril: Norman Mailer," *World More Attractive*, 123-9.

Hux, Samuel H., "American Myth and Existential Vision: The Indigenous Existentialism of Mailer, Bellow, Styron and Ellison," *DA* 26 (1966): 5437.

Jacoby, Andrea, "Dreams and Disasters: The Apocalyptic Vision in the Works of Norman Mailer," *DAI* 37 (1976): 2181A-82A.

Johnson, Lee R., "The Novels of Saul Bellow and Norman Mailer: A Study of Their Polar Perceptions of American Reality," *DAI* 40 (1979): 1028A-29A.

Jurkiewicz, Kenneth, "Mailer and the Movies: An American Writer Confronts the Mass Culture," *DAI* 40 (1979): 248A-49A.

Kaufmann, Donald L., "The Long Happy Life of Norman Mailer," *MFS* 17, iii (Autumn, 1971): 347-59. [Comparison of Mailer with Hemingway.]

_____, *Norman Mailer*.

Kirk, Juanita M. S., "A Marvel of a Fool: Geographical Aspects for Four of Norman Mailer's Questing Heroes," *DAI* 40 (1979): 248A-49A.

Lakin, R. D., "D. W.'s: The Displaced Writer in America," *MQ* 4 (July, 1963): 295-303.

Langbaum, Robert, "Mailer's New Style," *Novel* 2 (Fall, 1968): 69-78. Also in Langbaum, R., *Modern Spirit*, 147-63.

Lawler, Robert W., "Norman Mailer: The Connection of New Circuits," *DAI* 31 (1970): 1804A-05A.

Leeds, B. H., *Structured Vision of Norman Mailer*.

Lehan, R., *Dangerous Crossing*, 81-95.

Lennon, J. Michael, "Mailer's Radical Bridge," *JNT* 7, iii (Fall, 1977): 170-88.

Lennon, John M., "Mailer's Cosmology," *MLS* 12, iii (Summer, 1982): 18-29.

_____, "A Radical Bridge: Mailer's Narrative Art," *DAI* 36 (1976): 6101A-02A.

Lidston, Robert C., "'A Renaissance of Real Power': The Political and Social Atmosphere in Norman Mailer's Novels," *DAI* 39 (1979): 5513A-14A.

Liebman, Robert L., "Crazy but Serious: Rebellion in the Fiction of Norman Mailer," *DAI* 38 (1977): 2127A.

Lister, Paul A., "War in Norman Mailer's Fiction," *DAI* 36 (1975): 322A.

Lucid, R. F., ed., *Norman Mailer*.

Marcus, Steven, "An Interview with Norman Mailer," *ParisR* 8, xxxi (Winter-Spring, 1964): 28-58. Also in *Writers at Work: The Paris Review Interviews*, Third Series, N.Y.: Viking, 1967, 251-78. Also in Braudy, L., ed., *Norman Mailer*, 21-41.

Marks, Barry A., "Civil Disobedience in Retrospect: Henry Thoreau and Norman Mailer," *Soundings* 62 (1979): 144-65.

McCardell, William P., "The 'Existential' Films of Norman Mailer: A Comparison with His Fiction and Non-Fiction," *DAI* 37 (1976): 2185A.

McConnell, F. D., *Four Postwar American Novelists*, 58-65.

Merrill, R., *Norman Mailer*.

Middlebrook, J., *Mailer and the Times of His Time*.

Mudrick, Marvin, "Mailer and Styron: Guests of the Establishment," *HudR* 17 (Autumn, 1964): 346-66. Also in *On Culture and Literature*, 176-99.

Newman, Paul B., "Mailer: The Jew as Existentialist," *NAmerR* 2, iii (July, 1965): 48-55.

Nobel, D. W., *Eternal Adam and the New World Garden*, 197-209.

"Playboy Interview: Norman Mailer," *Playboy* 15 (Jan., 1968): 69-84.

Podhoretz, Norman, "Norman Mailer: The Embattled Vision," *PR* 26 (Summer, 1959): 371-91. Also in Podhoretz, N., *Doings and Undoings*, 179-204. Also in Waldmeir, J. J., ed., *Recent American Fiction*, 185-202. Also "Introduction" in Mailer, Norman, *Barbary Shore*, N.Y.: Grosset & Dunlop, 1963. Also in Lucid, R. F., ed., *Norman Mailer*, 95-107.

Poirier, Richard, "The Minority Within," *PR* 39, i (1972): 12-4.

_____, *Norman Mailer*.

_____, "Norman Mailer's Necessary Mess," *Listener* 90, 2328 (Nov. 8, 1973): 626-7.

Radford, J., *Norman Mailer*.

Raleigh, John H., "History and Its Burdens: The Example of Norman Mailer," in Engel, M., ed., *Uses of History*, 163-82.

Ramage, John D., "The Janus Face of Contemporary American Fiction: Norman Mailer and John Barth," *DAI* 38 (1977): 1394A-95A.

Regnier, Paul J. F., "Real and Aesthetic Aspects of Modern Experience: Max Frisch and Norman Mailer," *DAI* 35 (1975): 7920A.

Reich, Kenneth E., "Sport in Literature: The Passion of Action," *JLN* 12 (1979): 50-62.

Richler, Mordecai, "Norman Mailer," *Encounter* 25 (July, 1965): 61-4.

Ross, Morton L., "Thoreau and Mailer: The Mission of the Rooster," *WHR* 25, i (Winter, 1975): 47-56.

Roth, Richard A., "From Gap to Gain: Outrage and Renewal in Faulkner and Mailer," *DAI* 37 (1976): 1554A-55A.

Rother, James, "Mailer's 'O'Shaughnessy Chronicle': A Speculative Autopsy," *Crit* 19, iii (1978): 21-39.

Rovit, Earl, "Saul Bellow and Norman Mailer: The Secret Sharers," in Rovit, E., ed., *Saul Bellow*, 161-70.

Schrader, George A., "Norman Mailer and the Despair of Defiance," *YR* 51 (Dec., 1961): 267-80.

Scholl, Peter A., "Dos Passos, Mailer and Sloan: Young Men's Initiations," *LGJ* 5, i (1977): 2-5, 23. [Not seen.]

Schulz, Max F., "Mailer's Divine Comedy," *WSCL* 9 (1968): 36-57. Also (expanded) in Schulz, M. F., *Radical Sophistication*, 69-109.

Scott, James B., "The Individual and Society: Norman Mailer vs. William Styron," *DA* 25 (1965): 5942.

Shaw, Peter, "The Tough Guy Intellectual," *CritQ* 8 (Spring, 1966): 13-28.

Sheed, Wilfrid, "Genius or Nothing: A View of Norman Mailer," *Encounter* 36, iv (June, 1971): 66-71.

Sheridan, James J., "Form and Matter in Norman Mailer," *DAI* 34 (1973): 338A.

Silverstein, Howard, "Norman Mailer and the Quest for Manhood," *DAI* 33 (1973): 6375A-6A.

_____, "Norman Mailer: The Family Romance and the Oedipal Fantasy," *AI* 34 (Fall, 1977): 277-86.

Solotaroff, Robert, "Down Mailer's Way," *ChiR* 19, iii (June, 1967): 11-25.

_____, *Down Mailer's Way*.

Spencer, Benjamin T., "Mr. Mailer's American Dreams," *Prospects* 2 (1976): 127-46.

Stade, George, "Mailer and Miller," *PR* 44, iv (1977): 616-24.

Stark, John O., "Norman Mailer's Work from 1963 to 1968," *DAI* 31 (1970): 403A.

Steiner, George, "Naked But Not Dead," *Encounter* 17 (Dec., 1961): 67-70.

Stern, Richard, "Hip, Hell and Navigator: An Interview with Norman Mailer," *WR* 23 (Winter, 1959): 101-9. Also in Mailer, Norman, *Advertisements for Myself*, N.Y.: Putnam, 1959, 383-5.

Tanner, Tony, "On the Parapet: A Study of the Novels of Norman Mailer," *CritQ* 12, ii (Summer, 1970): 153-76. Also in Tanner, T., *City of Words*, 349-1.

Taylor, Robert, Jr., "Sounding the Trumpets of Defiance: Mark Twain and Norman Mailer," *MTJ* 16, iii (Winter, 1972): 1-14.

Tien, Morris W., "Mailer's Search for a Hero: The American Existentialist," *DAI* 38 (1978): 6127A.

Toback, James, "Norman Mailer Today," *Ctary* 44 (Oct., 1967): 68-76.

Trilling, Diana, "Norman Mailer," *Encounter* 19 (Nov., 1962): 45-56. Also in Balakian, N., and C. Simmons, eds., *Creative Present*, 145-71. Also in Trilling, D., *Claremont Essays*, 175-202. Also in Braudy, L., ed., *Norman Mailer*, 42-65. Also in Lucid, R. F., ed., *Norman Mailer*, 108-36.

Vidal, Gore, "The Norman Mailer Syndrome," *Nation* 190 (Jan. 2, 1960): 13-16. Also, as "Norman Mailer: The Angels are White," in Vidal, Gore, *Rocking the Boat*, Boston: Little, Brown, 1962, 161-77. Also in Lucid, R. F., ed., *Norman Mailer*, 95-107.

Volpe, Edmond L., in Moore, H. T., ed., *Contemporary American Novelists*, 112-19.

Weatherby, W. J., "Mailer, the Reporter and God," *New Edinburgh Review* 48 (Winter, 1979): 21-4.

Weiner, David M., "The Politics of Love: Norman Mailer's Existential Vision," *DAI* 33 (1972): 334A.

Weinstein, Norman, "Norman Mailer's Space Odyssey," *SoRA* 9 (Nov., 1976): 228-43.

Whitfield, Stephen J., "American Writing as a Wildlife Preserve: Jack London and Norman Mailer," *SoQ* 15, ii (1977): 135-48.

Wicker, Brian, "Mailer and the Big Plot Being Hatched by Nature," *Story-Shaped World*, 195-207.

Wilson, Robert A., "Negative Thinking: The New Art of the Brave," *Realist* 22 (Dec., 1960): 5, 11-13. [Not seen.]

Winegarten, Renee, "Norman Mailer, Genuine or Counterfeit?" *Midstream* 11 (Sept., 1965): 91-5.

Witt, Grace, "Bad Man as Hipster: Norman Mailer's Use of Frontier Metaphor," *WAL* 4, iii (Fall, 1969): 203-17.

Yarnoff, Charles S., "Norman Mailer and American Literary Naturalism," *DAI* 38 (1978): 6732A-33A.

Zilkoski, Lydia M., "The Faces of Janus in Norman Mailer's Later Style," *DAI* 36 (1975): 335A.

AN AMERICAN DREAM

Adams, L., *Existential Battles*, 69-97.

Aldridge, James W., "The Big Comeback of Norman Mailer," *Life* 58 (Mar. 19, 1965): 12. Also, as "Norman Mailer: The Energy of New Success," in Aldridge, J. W., *Time to Murder and Create*, 160-3. Also in Aldridge, J. W., *Devil in the Fire*, 177-9.

Alvarez, A., "Norman X," *Spectator* No. 7141 (May 7, 1965): 603.

Anderson, Don, "Norman Mailer: Man Against the Machine," in Anderson, D., and S. Knight, eds., *Cunning Exiles*, 182-7.

Bailey, J., *Norman Mailer, Quick-Change Artist*, 54-67.

Begiebing, R. T., *Acts of Regeneration*, 58-88.

Bersani, Leo, "Interpretations of Dreams," *PR* 32, iv (Fall, 1965): 603-8. Also in Braudy, L., ed., *Norman Mailer*, 120-6. Also in Lucid, R. F., ed., *Norman Mailer*, 171-9.

Boyers, Robert, "Attitudes Toward Sex in American 'High Culture'," *AAAPSS* 376 (Mar., 1968): 38-41, 43-4.

Bryant, J. H., *Open Decision*, 383-8.

Bufithis, P. H., *Norman Mailer*, 65-74.

Cohen, S., *Norman Mailer's Novels*, 87-100.

Corrigan, John W., "An American Dreamer," *ChiR* 18, i (Spring, 1965): 58-66.

Didion, Joan, "A Social Eye," *NatR* 17 (Apr. 20, 1965): 329-30.

Ehrlich, R., *Norman Mailer*, 68-83.

Evans, Timothy, "Boiling the Archetypal Pot: Norman Mailer's American Dream," *SWR* 60, ii (Spring, 1975): 159-70.

Fetterly, J., "AN AMERICAN DREAM: 'Hula, Hula' Said the Witches," *Resisting Reader*, 154-89.

Fiedler, Leslie A., "Master of Dreams," *PR* 34 (Summer, 1967): 352-6.

Finholt, Richard D., "'Otherwise How Explain': Norman Mailer's New Cosmology," *MFS* 17, iii (Autumn, 1971): 375-86.

Fossum, Robert H., "Novel of Nightmare: Norman Mailer's AN AMERICAN DREAM," in Lanzinger, K., ed., *Americana-Austriaca*, 10-23.

Foster, R., *Norman Mailer*, 18-19. Also in Lucid, R. F., ed., *Norman Mailer*, 34-5.

Gerson, Jessica, "AN AMERICAN DREAM: Mailer's *Walpurgisnacht*," *SAJL* 2 (1982): 126-31.

Glickman, Susan, "THE WORLD AS WILL AND IDEA: A Comparative Study of AN AMERICAN DREAM and MR. SAMMLER'S PLANET," *MFS* 28, iv (Winter, 1982-83): 569-82.

Gordon, A., *American Dreamer*, 130-71.

Gordon, Andrew, "The Modern Dream-Vision: Freud's THE INTERPRETATION OF DREAMS and Mailer's AN AMERICAN DREAM," *L&P* 27 (1977): 100-5.

Gutman, S. T., *Mankind in Barbary*, 95-131, 196-7.

Guttmann, A., *Jewish Writer in America*, 164-7.

Hardwick, Elizabeth, "Bad Boy," *PR* 32 (Spring, 1965): 291-4. Also as "A Nightmare by Norman Mailer" in Lucid, R. F., ed., *Norman Mailer*, 145-50.

Harper, H. M., Jr., *Desperate Faith*, 120-4.

Held, George, "Men on the Moon: American Novelists Explore Lunar Space," *MQR* 18 (1979): 321-3.

Hesla, David, "The Two Roles of Norman Mailer," in Scott, N. A., ed., *Adversity and Grace*, 223-8.

Hux, Samuel, "Mailer's Dream of Violence," *MinnR* 8, ii (1968): 152-7.

Hyman, Stanley E., "Norman Mailer's Yummy Rump," *New Leader* (Mar. 15, 1965): 16-17. Also in Hyman, S. E., *Standards*, 274-8. Also in Braudy, L., ed., *Norman Mailer*, 104-8.

Kaufmann, D. L., *Norman Mailer*, 35-50, 67-9, 76-9, 80-3, 91-7, 123-8, 132-42, 144-7, 166-8.

Langbaum, Robert, "Mailer's New Style," *Novel* 2, i (Fall, 1968): 70-5. Also in Langbaum, R., *Modern Spirit*, 149-57.

Leeds, B. H., *Structured Vision of Norman Mailer*, 125-77, 231-6.

Lehan, R., *Dangerous Crossing*, 90-3.

McConnell, F. D., *Four Postwar American Novelists*, 94-100.

Merrill, R., *Norman Mailer*, 66-78.

Middlebrook, J., *Mailer and the Times of His Time*, 105-37.

Millet, Kate, "Sexual Politics: Miller, Mailer, and Genet," *NAmR* 7 (1969): 15-24.

Mills, Nicolaus, "The Picture of Success," *YR* 66, iii (Spring, 1977): 359-62.

Noble, D. W., *Eternal Adam and the New World Garden*, 207-9.

Parker, Hershel, "Norman Mailer's Revision of the *Esquire* Version of AN AMERICAN DREAM and the Aesthetic Problem of 'Built-in Intentionality'," *BRH* 84, iv (Winter, 1981): 405-30.

Poirier, Richard, "The Minority Within," *PR* 39, i (1972): 15-18.

_____, "Morbid-Mindedness," *Ctary* 39 (June, 1965): 91-4. Also in Lucid, R. F., ed., *Norman Mailer*, 162-70.

_____, *Norman Mailer*, 4-85 *passim*, 119-30 *passim*.

_____, "T. S. Eliot and the Literature of Waste," *NRep* 156 (May 20, 1967): 21-22.

Radford, J., *Norman Mailer*, 33-7, 100-10, 148-55.

Rahv, Philip, "Crime Without Punishment," *NYRB* (Mar. 25, 1965): 1-4. Also in Rahv, P., *Myth and the Powerhouse*, 234-43. Also in Rahv, P., *Literature and the Sixth Sense*, 409-17.

Rawson, C. J., "Cannibalism and Fiction: Part II: Love and Eating in Fielding, Mailer, Genet and Wittig," *Genre* 11, ii (Summer, 1978): 234-44.

Richler, Mordecai, "Norman Mailer," *Encounter* 25 (July, 1965): 61-4.

Schulz, Max F., "Mailer's Divine Comedy," *WSCL* 9 (1968): 51-7. Also in Schulz, M. F., *Radical Sophistication*, 91-9.

Scott, N. A., Jr., *Three American Moralists*, 56-70.

Sheridan, James J., "Mailer's AN AMERICAN DREAM," *Expl* 34, i (1975): It. 8.

Silverstein, Howard, "Norman Mailer: The Family Romance and the Oedipal Fantasy," *AI* 34, iii (Fall, 1977): 284-6.

Solotaroff, Robert, "Down Mailer's Way," *ChiR* 19, iii (June, 1967): 20-5.

_____, *Down Mailer's Way*, 130-78.

Spencer, Benjamin T., "Mr. Mailer's American Dreams," *Prospects* 2 (1976): 134-40.

Spender, Stephen, "Mailer's American Melodrama," in Encyclopedia Britannica, *Great Ideas Today, 1965*, 173-6.

Tanner, Tony, *City of Words*, 356-66.

Toback, James, "Norman Mailer Today," *Ctary* 44 (Oct., 1967): 20-5.

Wagenheim, Allan J., "Square's Progress. AN AMERICAN DREAM," *Crit* 10, i (Winter, 1968): 45-68.

Weber, Brom, "A Fear of Dying: Norman Mailer's AN AMERICAN DREAM," *HC* 2, iii (June, 1965): 1-6, 8-11.

Weinberg, H., *New Novel in America*, 124-40.

Wood, Margery, "Norman Mailer and Natalie Sarraute: A Comparison of Existential Novels," *MinnR* 6 (Spring, 1966): 67-72.

BARBARY SHORE

Bailey, J., *Norman Mailer, Quick-Change Artist*, 16-20.

Begiebing, R. J., *Acts of Regeneration*, 13-32.

Bryant, J. H., *Open Decision*, 374-6.

Bufithis, P. H., *Norman Mailer*, 31-8.

Cecil, L. Moffitt, "The Passing of Arthur in Norman Mailer's BARBARY SHORE," *RS* 39 (1971): 54-8.

Cohen, S., *Norman Mailer's Novels*, 45-62.

Cook, Bruce A., "Norman Mailer: The Temptation to Power," *Ren* 14 (Summer, 1962): 210-11.

Dienstfrey, Harris, in Kostelanetz, R., ed., *On Contemporary Literature*, 425-31.

Ehrlich, R., *Norman Mailer*, 31-43.

Eisinger, C. E., *Fiction of the Forties*, 93-4.

Foster, R., *Norman Mailer*, 12-14. Also in Lucid, R. F., ed., *Norman Mailer*, 29-30.

Geismar, Maxwell, in *SatR* 344 (May 26, 1951): 15. Also in Geismar, M., *American Moderns*, 173-4.

Goldstone, Herbert, "The Novels of Norman Mailer," *EJ* 45 (Mar., 1956): 116-18.

Gordon, A., *American Dreamer*, 73-86.

Gutman, S. T., *Mankind in Barbary*, 29-43, 176-8.

Guttmann, A., *Jewish Writer in America*, 157-9.

Harper, H. M., *Desperate Faith*, 103-9.

Hoffa, William, "Norman Mailer: ADVERTISEMENTS FOR MYSELF," in French, W., ed., *Fifties*, 75-7.

Kaufmann, D. L., *Norman Mailer*, 12-33, 53-7, 115-17.

Lehan, R., *Dangerous Crossing*, 84-5.

McConnell, F. D., *Four Postwar American Novelists*, 80-7.

Middlebrook, J., *Mailer and the Times of His Time*, 61-80.

Noble, D. W, *Eternal Adam and the New World Garden*, 201-2.

Podhoretz, Norman, "Norman Mailer: The Embattled Vision," *PR* 26 (Summer, 1959): 377-83. Also in Podhoretz, N., *Doings and Undoings*, 187-94. Also in Waldmeir, J. J., ed., *Recent American Fiction*, 190-5. Also, "Introduction," *Barbary Shore*, N.Y.: Grosset & Dunlop, 1963. Also in Lucid, R. F., ed., *Norman Mailer*, 68-77.

Poirier, R., *Norman Mailer*, 25-45 *passim*, 60-72 *passim*.

Pratt, William C., "Mailer's BARBARY SHORE and His Quest for a Radical Politics," *ILLQ* 44, ii (1982): 48-56.

Radford, J., *Norman Mailer*, 16-19, 50-4, 130-2.

Schulz, Max F., "Norman Mailer's Divine Comedy," *WSCL* 9 (1968): 39-45. Also in Schulz, M. F., *Radical Sophistication*, 73-81.

Scott, N. A., Jr., *Three American Moralists*, 30-9.

Silverstein, Howard, "Norman Mailer: The Family Romance and the Oedipal Fantasy," *AI* 34, iii (Fall, 1977): 277-9.

Solotaroff, R., *Down Mailer's Way*, 40-5, 48-53.

Stark, John, "BARBARY SHORE: The Basis of Mailer's Best Work," *MFS* 17, iii (Autumn, 1971): 403-8.

Tanner, T., *City of Words*, 351-2.

Trilling, Diana, "Norman Mailer," *Encounter* 19 (Nov., 1962): 49-50. Also in Balakian, N., and C. Simmons, eds., *Creative Present*, 154-8. Also in Trilling, D., *Claremont Essays*, 185-9. Also in Braudy, L., ed., *Norman Mailer*, 50-3. Also in Lucid, R. F., ed., *Norman Mailer*, 118-20.

Weinberg, H., *New Novel in America*, 109-12.

THE DEER PARK

Bailey, J., *Norman Mailer, Quick-Change Artist*, 23-9.

Begiebing, R. J., *Acts of Regeneration*, 33-57.

Bufithis, P. H., *Norman Mailer*, 39-51.

Bryant, J. H., *Open Decision*, 376-82.

Cohen, S., *Norman Mailer's Novels*, 63-86.

Cook, Bruce, "Norman Mailer: The Temptation to Power," *Ren* 14 (Summer, 1962): 212-14.

Dienstfrey, Harris, in Kostelanetz, R., ed., *On Contemporary Literature*, 431-4.

Dupee, F. W., "The American Norman Mailer," *Ctary* 29 (Feb., 1960): 131-2.

Ehrlich, R., *Norman Mailer*, 44-57.

Fisher, Roy, "The Mind of Marion Faye: Stylistic Aspects of Norman Mailer's THE DEER PARK," *Lang&S* 6 (1973): 145-57.

Foster, R., *Norman Mailer*, 14-18. Also in Lucid, R. F., ed., *Norman Mailer*, 30-4.

Geismar, M., *American Moderns*, 174-9.

Glicksberg, C. I., *Sexual Revolution in Modern American Literature*, 175-7, 179-80.

Goldstone, Herbert, "The Novels of Norman Mailer," *EJ* 45 (Mar., 1956): 118-20.

Gordon, A., *American Dreamer*, 95-112.

Gutman, S. T. *Mankind in Barbary*, 45-65.

Guttmann, A., *Jewish Writer in America*, 159-60.

Harper, H. M., *Desperate Faith*, 109-15.

Hoffa, William, "Norman Mailer: ADVERTISEMENTS FOR MYSELF," in French, W., ed., *Fifties*, 77-9.

Kaufmann, D. L., *Norman Mailer*, 24-34, 58-9, 117-20, 161-3.

Kramer, Maurice, "The Secular Mode of Jewishness," *Works* 1 (Autumn, 1967): 107.

Leeds, B. H., *Structured Vision of Norman Mailer*, 105-23, 164-7.

Lehan, R., *Dangerous Crossings*, 86-9.

Ludwig, J., *Recent American Novelists*, 26-7.

Mailer, Norman, "The Draft of THE DEER PARK," in McCormack, T., ed., *Afterwords*, 193-231.

McConnell, F. D., *Four Postwar American Novelists*, 87-94.

Merrill, R., *Norman Mailer*, 43-65.

Middlebrook, J., *Mailer and the Times of His Time*, 83-102.

Millgate, M., *American Social Fiction*, 159-62.

Noble, D. W., *Eternal Adam and the New World Garden*, 202-4.

Podhoretz, Norman, "Norman Mailer: The Embattled Vision," *PR* 26 (Summer, 1959): 383-90. Also in Podhoretz, N., *Doings and Undoings*, 194-200. Also in Waldmeir, J. J., ed., *Recent American Fiction*, 195-201. Also in Lucid, R. F., ed., *Norman Mailer*, 77-83.

Poirier, R., *Norman Mailer*, 42-9, 40-50 *passim*, 60-82 *passim*.

Radford, J., *Norman Mailer*, 19-27, 55-7, 85-8, 132-40.

Raines, Helen H., "Norman Mailer's Sergius O'Shaugnessy, Villain and Victim," *Frontiers* 2, i (1977): 71-5.

Schulz, Max F., "Mailer's Divine Comedy," *WSCL* 9 (1968): 45-51. Also in Schulz, M. F., *Radical Sophistication*, 81-90.

Scott, N. A., *Three American Moralists*, 39-46.

Silverstein, Howard, "Norman Mailer: The Family Romance and the Oedipal Fantasy," *AI* 4, iii (Fall, 1977): 279-82.

Solotaroff, Robert, "Down Mailer's Way," *ChiR* 19, iii (June, 1967): 16-20.

_____, *Down Mailer's Way*, 53-74.

Tanner, T., *City of Words*, 352-5.

Trilling, Diana, "Norman Mailer," *Encounter* 19 (Nov., 1962): 51-3. Also as "The Radical Moralism of Norman Mailer," in Balakian, N., and C. Simmons, eds., *Creative Present*, 159-63. Also in Trilling, D., *Claremont Essays*, 190-3. Also in Braudy, L., ed., *Norman Mailer*, 54-7. Also in Lucid, R. F., ed., *Norman Mailer*, 123-7.

Weinberg, H., *New Novel in America*, 112-24.

THE EXECUTIONER'S SONG

Aldridge, John W., "An Interview with Norman Mailer," *PR* 47, ii (1980): 174-82.

Begiebing, R. J., *Acts of Regeneration*, 186-91.

Bragg, Melvin, "A Murderer's Tale: Norman Mailer Talking to Melvin Bragg," *Listener* 102 (1979): 661-3.

Garvey, John, "THE EXECUTIONER'S SONG: Mailer's Best in Years," *Cweal* 107, v (Mar. 14, 1980): 134-5.

Granqvist, Raoul, "Gary Gilmore's Pilgrimage: A Study of Norman Mailer's THE EXECUTIONER'S SONG," *AmSS* 14 (1982): 35-48.

Harris, Harold, J., "Norman Mailer, Jack Abbott, and THE EXECUTIONER'S SONG," *Cresset* 45, viii (1982): 20-3.

Hersey, John, "The Legend on the License," *YR* 70, i (Oct., 1980): 13-22.

Mills, John, "Return of the Dazed Dream," *QQ* 88, i (Spring, 1981): 151-3.

Rollyson, Carl E., Jr., "Biography in a New Key," *ChiR* 31, iv (1980): 31-8.

Walsh, Edward J., "The Scavenger's Novel," *ChronC* 4, ii (1980): 11-13.

THE NAKED AND THE DEAD

Aldridge, J. W., *After the Lost Generation*, 133-41.

Allen, W., *Modern Novel*, 296-8.

Bailey, J., *Norman Mailer, Quick-Change Artist*, 9-16.

Baumbach, J., *Landscape of Nightmare*, 9-10.

Bryant, Jerry H., "The Last of the Social Protest Writers," *ArQ* 19 (Winter, 1963): 317-20.

_____, *Open Decision*, 123-7, 136-8, 373-4.

Bufithis, P. H., *Norman Mailer*, 15-29.

Burg, David F., "The Hero of THE NAKED AND THE DEAD," *MFS* 17, iii (Autumn, 1971): 387-401.

Campbell, Roy, "The 'Gud' Son: The Southern Peasant in Norman Mailer's THE NAKED AND THE DEAD," *Descant* 23, ii (1979): 39-48.

Cohen, S., *Norman Mailer's Novels*, 16-44.

Cook, Bruce A., "Norman Mailer: The Temptation of Power," *Ren* 14 (Summer, 1962): 207-9.

Dienstfrey, Harris, in Kostelanetz, R., ed., *On Contemporary Literature*, 422-5.

Ehrlich, R., *Norman Mailer*, 19-31.

Eisinger, C. E., *Fiction of the Forties*, 33-8.

_____, "Introduction," THE NAKED AND THE DEAD, N.Y.: Holt, Rinehart and Winston, 1968.

Elliott, S. James, "Homosexuality in the Crucial Decade: Three Novelists' Views," in Crew, L., ed., *Gay Academic*, 165-9.

Enkvist, Nils E., "Re-readings. Norman Mailer. THE NAKED AND THE DEAD," *MSpr* 56 (1962): 60-4.

Finkelstein, S., *Existentialism and Alienation in American Literature*, 270-2.

_____, "Norman Mailer and Edward Albee," *American Dialog* 2 (Feb.-Mar., 1965): 23-5.

Foster, R., *Norman Mailer*, 8-12. Also in Lucid, R. F., ed., *Norman Mailer*, 25-9.

French, Warren, in French, W., ed., *Forties*, 21-5.

Geismar, Maxwell, in *SatR* 31 (May 8, 1948): 10+. Also in Geismar, M., *American Moderns*, 171-3.

Goldstone, Herbert, "The Novels of Norman Mailer," *EJ* 45 (Mar., 1956): 114-16.

Gordon, A., *American Dreamer*, 5-72.

Gordon, Andrew, "THE NAKED AND THE DEAD: The Triumph of Impotence," *L&P* 19, iii-iv (1969): 3-13.

Gutman, S. T., *Mankind in Barbary*, 3-27.

Guttmann, A., *Jewish Writer in America*, 154-7.

Harper, H. M., Jr., *Desperate Faith*, 96-102.

Hassan, I., *Radical Innocence*, 140-51.

Healy, Robert C., in Gardiner, H. C., ed., *Fifty Years of the American Novel*, 260-3.

Horn, Bernard, "Ahab and Ishmael at War: The Presence of MOBY-DICK in THE NAKED AND THE DEAD," *AQ* 34, iv (Fall, 1982): 379-95.

Jones, P., *War and the Novelist*, 87-96.

Kaufmann, D. L., *Norman Mailer*, 1-12, 51-3, 70-2, 100-3, 112-15, 142-3.

Kilgo, James P., "Five American Novels of World War II: A Critical Study," *DAI* 32 (1972): 6380A.

Leeds, B. H., *Structured Vision of Norman Mailer*, 9-51.

Lehan, R., *Dangerous Crossing*, 81-4.

Lister, Paul A., "The Mountain in THE NAKED AND THE DEAD," *CCTE* 41 (1976): 30-4.

Ludwig, J., *Recent American Novelists*, 24-6.

Mailer, Norman, "The Writer and Hollywood," *Film Heritage* 2, i (Fall, 1966): 23. Also as "Naked Before the Camera," in Peary, G., and R. Shatzkin, eds., *Modern American Novel and the Movies*, 187-8.

McConnell, F. D., *Four Postwar American Novelists*, 65-80.

Merrill, R., *Norman Mailer*, 25-42.

Middlebrook, J., *Mailer and the Times of the Time*, 37-59.

Millgate, M., *American Social Fiction*, 146-50.

Muste, John M., "Norman Mailer and John Dos Passos: The Question of Influence," *MFS* 17, iii (Autumn, 1971): 361-74.

Newman, Paul B., "Mailer: The Jew as Existentialist," *North American Review* 2, iii (July, 1965): 48-55.

Noble, D. W., *Eternal Adam and the New World Order*, 198-201.

Podhoretz, Norman, "Norman Mailer: The Embattled Vision," *PR* 26 (Summer, 1959): 371-7. Also in Podhoretz, N., *Doings and Undoings*, 180-7. Also in Waldmeir, W. W., ed., *Recent American Fiction*, 185-90. Also in Lucid, R. F., ed., *Norman Mailer*, 61-8.

Prescott, O., *In My Opinion*, 155-9.

Poirier, R., *Norman Mailer*, 26-50 *passim*.

Radford, J., *Norman Mailer*, 7-16, 44-50, 77-82, 124-30.

Rideout, W. B., *Radical Novel in the U.S.*, 270-3.

Ross, Frank, "The Assailant-Victim in Three War Protest Novels," *Paunch* 32 (Aug., 1968): 46-57.

Scott, N. A., *Three American Moralists*, 23-30.

Siegel, Paul N., "The Malign Deity of THE NAKED AND THE DEAD," *TCL* 20, iv (Oct., 1974): 291-7.

Solotaroff, Robert, "Down Mailer's Way," *ChiR* 19, iii (June, 1967): 12-14.

_____, *Down Mailer's Way*, 3-39.

Stone, Edward, "MOBY-DICK and Mailer's NAKED AND THE DEAD," *Extracts* 30 (1977): 15-17.

Tanner, T., *City of Words*, 349-51.

Thorp, W., "The Persistence of Naturalism in the Novel," *American Writing in the Twentieth Century*, 145-7.

Tien, M. Wei-Hsin, "THE NAKED AND THE DEAD: A Novel of Non-Heroes," *FJS* 10 (1977): 59-77.

Trilling, Diana, "Norman Mailer," *Encounter* 19 (Nov., 1962): 47-9. Also as "The Radical Moralism of Norman Mailer," in Balakian, N., and C. Simmons, eds., *Creative Present*, 151-4. Also in Trilling, D., *Claremont Essays*, 182-5. Also in Braudy, L., ed., *Norman Mailer*, 47-50. Also in Lucid, R. F., ed., *Norman Mailer*, 115-18.

Volpe, Edmund L., in Moore, H. T., ed., *Contemporary American Novelists*, 114-16.

Waldmeir, J. J., *American Novels of the Second World War*, 110-18.

Waldron, Randall H., "The Naked, The Dead, and the Machine: A New Look at Mailer's First Novel," *PMLA* 87, ii (Mar., 1972): 271-7.

WHY ARE WE IN VIETNAM?

Adams, L., *Existential Battles*, 113-20.

Aldridge, John W., "From Vietnam to Obscenity," *Harpers* 236 (Feb., 1968): 91-7. Also in Aldridge, J. W., *Devil in the Fire*, 185-94. Also in Lucid, R. F., ed., *Norman Mailer*, 180-92.

Bailey, J., *Norman Mailer, Quick-Change Artist*, 71-81.

Begiebing, Robert J., "Norman Mailer's WHY ARE WE IN VIETNAM? The Ritual of Regeneration," *AI* 37 (1980): 12-37.

_____, *Acts of Regeneration*, 89-112.

Boheemen-Saaf, Christel van, "The Artist as Con Man: The Reaction against the Symbolist Aesthetics in Recent American Fiction," *DQR* 7 (1977): 305-18.

Bryant, J. H., *Open Decision*, 388-93.

Bufithis, P. H., *Norman Mailer*, 75-84.

Cohen, S., *Norman Mailer's Novels*, 107-17.

Cooperman, Stanley, "American War Novels: Yesterday, Today, and Tomorrow," *YR* 41, iv (Summer, 1972): 525-7.

Donoghue, Denis, "Sweepstakes," *NYRB* 9, v (Sept. 28, 1967): 5-8.

Durczak, Joanna, "Norman Mailer's WHY ARE WE IN VIETNAM? As an Epilogue to William Faulkner's Hunting Sequel of BIG BOTTOM WOODS," *SAP* 11 (1979): 183-200.

Edinger, Harry G., "Bears in Three Contemporary Fictions," *HAB* 28 (1977): 147-50.

Ehrlich, R., *Norman Mailer*, 95-112.

Finholt, Richard D., "'Otherwise how Explain?': Norman Mailer's New Cosmology," *MFS* 17, 111 (Autumn, 1971): 375-86.

Foster, R., *Norman Mailer*, 19-21. Also in Lucid, R. F., ed., *Norman Mailer*, 36-7.

Gordon, A., *American Dreamer*, 172-85.

Gordon, Andrew, "Why ARE WE IN VIETNAM? Deep in the Bowels of Texas," *L&P* 24 (1974): 55-65.

Grace, Matthew, "Norman Mailer at the End of the Decade," *EA* 24, i (Jan.-Mar., 1971): 56-7.

Gutman, S. T., *Mankind in Barbary*, 133-58.

Guttmann, A., *Jewish Writer in America*, 167-8.

Hassan, Ihab, "Focus on Norman Mailer's WHY ARE WE IN VIETNAM?" in Madden, D., *American Dreams, American Nightmares*, 197-203.

Jameson, Frederic, "The Great American Hunter, or Ideological Content in the Novel," *CE* 34, ii (Nov., 1972): 186-97. Comment by Sol Yurick, 198-9.

Kaufman, Donald L., "Catch-23: The Mystery of Fact (Norman Mailer's Final Novel?)," *TCL* 17, iv (Oct., 1971): 247-56.

Langbaum, Robert, "Mailer's New Style," *Novel* 2, i (Fall, 1968): 75-8. Also in Langbaum, R., ed., *Modern Spirit*, 157-62.

Leeds, B. H., *Structured Vision of Norman Mailer*, 179-206.

Lehan, R., *Dangerous Crossing*, 93-5.

Leverenz, David, "Anger and Individualism," *PsyR* 62, iii (Fall, 1975): 418-25.

McConnell, F. D., *Four Postwar American Novels*, 100-4.

Merrill, R., *Norman Mailer*, 66-7, 79-85.

Middlebrook, J., *Mailer and the Times of His Time*, 139-56.

Oates, Joyce Carol, "The Teleology of the Unconscious: The Art of Norman Mailer," *Critic* 32, ii (Nov.-Dec., 1973): 24-35.

Pearce, Richard, "Norman Mailer's WHY ARE WE IN VIETNAM? A Radical Critique of Frontier Values," *MFS* 17, iii (Autumn, 1971): 409-11.

Poirier, Richard, "The Minority Within," *PR* 39, i (1972): 19-42.
_____, *Norman Mailer*, 119-55 *passim*.
Rabinovitz, Rubin, "Myth and Animism in WHY ARE WE IN VIETNAM?" *TCL* 20 (Oct., 1974): 298-305.
Radford, J., *Norman Mailer*, 37-41, 97-100, 115-16.
Raleigh, John, "History and Its Burdens: The Example of Norman Mailer," in Engel, M., ed., *Uses of History*, 182-6.
Ramsey, Roger, "Current and Recurrent: The Vietnam Novel," *MFS* 17, iii (Autumn, 1971): 415-31.
Schulz, M. F., *Radical Sophistication*, 109.
Scott, N. A., *Three American Moralists*, 70-81.
Solotaroff, R., *Down Mailer's Way*, 179-206.
Spencer, Benjamin T., "Mr. Mailer's American Dreams," *Prospects* 2 (1976): 140-2.
Tanner, T., *City of Words*, 366-70.

BIBLIOGRAPHY

Adams, Laura, "Criticism of Norman Mailer: A Selected Checklist," *MFS* 17, iii (Autumn, 1971): 455-63.
_____, *Norman Mailer: A Comprehensive Bibliography*, Metuchen, N.J.: Scarecrow Press, 1974.
Foster, R., *Norman Mailer*, 44-6.
Kaufmann, D. L., *Norman Mailer*, 177-84.
Sokoloff, B. A., *A Comprehensive Bibliography of Norman Mailer*, Folcroft, Pa.: Folcroft Pr., 1969.

MAIS, ROGER, 1905-1955

GENERAL

Carr, W. I., "Roger Mais—Design from a Legend," *Caribbean Quarterly* 13, i (Mar., 1967): 3-28.
Creary, Jean, "A Prophet Armed," in James, L., ed., *Islands in Between*, 50-63.
Dathorne, Oscar R., "Roger Mais: The Man on the Cross," *SNNTS* 4, ii (Summer, 1972): 275-83.
Davies, Barrie, "The Novels of Roger Mais," *IFR* 1 (July, 1974): 140-3.
D'Costa, J., *Roger Mais*.
Grandison, Winnifred B., "The Prose Style of Roger Mais," *Jamaica Jnl.* 8, i (Mar., 1974): 48-54.
Lacovia, R. M., "Roger Mais: An Approach to Suffering and Freedom," *BlackI* 1, ii (Summer, 1972): 7-11.
_____, "Roger Mais and the Problem of Freedom," *BARev* 1, iii (Fall, 1970): 45-54.
Ramchand, Kenneth, "The Achievement of Roger Mais," *West Indian Novel and its Background*, 179-88.
_____, "The Case of Roger Mais," *Caribbean Quarterly* 15, iv (Dec., 1969): 23-30.
Vanouse, Evelyn, "Roger Mais: The Romantic Voice and the Nationalist Image," *DAI* 43 (1982): 1156A.
Williamson, Karina, "Roger Mais: West Indian Novelist," *JCL* 2 (Dec., 1966): 138-47.

BLACK LIGHTNING

Creary, Jean, "A Prophet Armed," in James, L., ed., *Islands in Between*, 59-61.
Gilkes, M., *West Indian Novel*, 37-40.
Harris, Wilson, "BLACK LIGHTNING," *JCF* 3, iv (1975): 41-4.

Ramchand, K., *West Indian Novel and its Background*, 185-8.
Williamson, Karina, "Roger Mais: West Indian Novelist," *JCL* 2 (Dec., 1966): 146-7.

BROTHER MAN

Braithwaite, Edward, "Jazz and the West Indian Novel," *Bim* 45 (July-Dec., 1967): 39-51; 46 (Jan.-June, 1968): 115-26. Also in Baugh, E., ed., *Critics on Caribbean Literature*, 103-12.
Creary, Jean, "A Prophet Armed," in James, L., ed., *Islands in Between*, 56-8.
D'Costa, J., *Roger Mais*, 36-58, 59-72.
Ramchand, K., *West Indian Novel and its Background*, 182-5.
Williamson, Karina, "Roger Mais: West Indian Novelist," *JCL* 2 (Dec., 1966): 145-6.

THE HILLS WERE JOYFUL TOGETHER

Creary, Jean, "A Prophet Armed," in James, L., ed., *Islands in Between*, 52-8.
D'Costa, J., *Roger Mais*, 13-35, 59-72.
Griffiths, G., *Double Exile*, 117-20.
Moore, G., *Chosen Tongue*, 86-91.
Ogunyemi, Chikwenye O., "From a Goat Path in Africa: Roger Mais and Jean Toomer," *Obsidian* 5, iii (Winter, 1979): 7-19.
Ramchand, K., *West Indian Novel and its Background*, 179-81.
Williamson, Karina, "Roger Mais: West Indian Novelist," *JCL* 2 (Dec., 1966): 141-5.

MAJOR, CLARENCE, 1936-

GENERAL

Klinkowitz, Jerome, "Clarence Major's Superfiction," *Yardbird Reader* 4 (1975): 1-11.
_____, "Reclaiming a (New) Black Experience: The Fiction of Clarence Major," *Oyez Review* n.s. 1 (1973): 86-9.
Major, Clarence, "Reality, Fiction and Criticism: An Interview/Essay," *par rapport* 2 (Winter, 1979): 67-73.
O'Brien, John, ed., *Interviews with Black Writers*, 125-39.

ALL-NIGHT VISITORS

Miller, Adam D., "ALL-NIGHT VISITORS," *BlSch* 2, v (Jan., 1971): 54-6.

EMERGENCY EXIT

Klinkowitz, Jerome, "Notes on a Novel-in-Progress: Clarence Major's EMERGENCY EXIT," *BALF* 13, ii (1979): 46-50.

REFLEX AND BONE STRUCTURE

Klinkowitz, Jerome, "Clarence Major: An Interview with a Post-contemporary Author," *BALF* 12, i (1978): 32-7.
McCaffery, Larry, and Sinda Gregory, "Major's REFLEX AND BONE STRUCTURE and the Anti-Detective Tradition," *BALF* 13, ii (1979): 39-45.

BIBLIOGRAPHY

Weixlmann, Joe, "Clarence Major: A Checklist of Criticism," *Obsidian* 4, ii (1978): 101-13.

MALAMUD, BERNARD, 1914-1986

GENERAL

Allen, John A., "The Promised End: Bernard Malamud's THE TENANTS," *HC* 8, v (Dec., 1971): 1-15.

Alter, I., *Good Man's Dilemma*.

Alter, Robert, "Malamud as a Jewish Writer," *Ctary* 42 (Sept., 1966): 71-6. Also, revised, in Alter, R., *After the Tradition*, 116-30. Also in Field, L. A., and J. W. Field, eds., *Bernard Malamud and the Critics*, 29-42.

Astro, R., and J. J. Benson, eds., *Fiction of Bernard Malamud*.

Avery, E. G., *Rebels and Victims*.

Baumbach, Jonathan, "The Economy of Love: The Novels of Bernard Malamud," *KR* 25 (Summer, 1963): 438-57. Also in Baumbach, J., *Landscape of Nightmare*, 101-22.

_____, "Malamud's Heroes," *Cweal* 85 (Oct. 28, 1966): 97-9.

Bellman, Samuel L., "Women, Children and Idiots First: The Transformation Psychology of Bernard Malamud," *Crit* 7, ii (Winter, 1965): 123-38.

Benson, Jackson J., "An Introduction: Bernard Malamud and the Haunting of America," in Astro, R., and Benson, J. J., eds., *Fiction of Bernard Malamud*, 13-42.

Bilik, Dorothy S., "Malamud's Secular Saints and Comic Jobs," *Immigrant Survivors: Post-Holocaust Consciousness in Recent Jewish American Fiction*, Middletown: Weslyan Un. Pr., 1981, 53-60.

Bluefarb, Sam, "The Syncretism of Bernard Malamud," in Field, L. A., and J. W. Field, eds., *Bernard Malamud*, 72-9.

Bryant, J. H., *Open Decision*, 324-40.

Charles, Gerda, "Bernard Malamud, the 'Natural' Writer," *JewishQ* 9 (Spring, 1962): 5-6.

Cohen, S., *Bernard Malamud and the Trial by Love*.

Cohen, Sandy, "The Theme of Self-Transcendence in the Fiction of Bernard Malamud," *DAI* 33 (1972): 1163A.

Ducharme, R., *Art and Idea in the Novels of Bernard Malamud*.

Dupee, F. W., "The Power of Positive Sex," *PR* 31 (Summer, 1964): 425-9. Also as "Malamud: The Uses and Abuses of Commitment," in Dupee, F. W., *King of the Cats*, 156-63.

Eigner, Edwin M., "Malamud's Use of the Quest Romance," *Genre* 1, i (Jan., 1968): 55-75. Also as "The Loathly Ladies," in Field, L. A., and J. W. Field, eds., *Bernard Malamud and the Critics*, 85-108.

Epstein, Joseph, "Malamud in Decline," *Ctary* 74, iv (Oct., 1982): 49-53.

Fabe, Marilyn M., "Successful Failures: Guilt and Morality in the Novels of Bernard Malamud," *DAI* 38 (1977): 787A.

Faulkner, Howard J., "Bernard Malamud: The Promise of a New Life," *DAI* 3 (1973): 5720A.

Featherstone, Joseph, "Bernard Malamud," *Atlantic* 219 (Mar., 1967): 95-8.

Field, L. A., and Field, J. W., eds., *Bernard Malamud*.

_____, *Bernard Malamud and the Critics*.

Field, Leslie, "Bernard Malamud and the Marginal Jew," in Astro, R., and J. J. Benson, eds., *Fiction of Bernard Malamud*, 97-116.

Frankel, Haskel, "Interview with Bernard Malamud," *SatR* 49 (Sept. 10, 1966): 39-40.

Friedenthal, Martin H., "Heroes for Our Time: The Novels of Bernard Malamud," *DAI* 37 (1977): 582A.

Friedman, Allen W., "The Jews Complaint in Recent American Fiction: Beyond Exodus and Still in the Wilderness," *SoR* 8, i (Jan., 1972): 41-59.

Fukuma, Kin-ichi, "Bernard Malamud and Jewish Consciousness," *KAL* 16 (May, 1975): 40-3.

Gealy, Marcia B., "The Hasidic Tradition in the Work of Bernard Malamud," *DAI* 37 (1976): 963A.

Gidden, Nancy A., "Fictional Techniques in the Work of Bernard Malamud," *DAI* (1973): 3392A-93A.

Goens, Mary B., "Process and Vision in Malamud's Novels," *DAI* 32 (1971): 3303A.

Goldman, Mark, "Bernard Malamud's Comic Vision and the Theme of Identity," *Crit* 7, i (Winter, 1965): 92-109.

Goodman, Oscar B., "There are Jews Everywhere," *Judaism* 19, iii (Summer, 1970): 283-94.

Grebstein, Sheldon N., "Bernard Malamud and the Jewish Movement," in Malin, I., *Contemporary Jewish-American Literature*, 175-212. Also in Field, L. A., and J. W. Field, eds., *Bernard Malamud*, 18-44.

Gunn, Giles B., "Bernard Malamud and the High Cost of Living," in Scott, N. A., Jr., *Adversity and Grace*, 59-82.

Guttmann, A., "'All Men Are Jews': Bernard Malamud," *Jewish Writer in America*, 112-20.

Handy, W. J., "The Malamud Hero: A Quest for Existence," in Astro, R., and J. J. Benson, eds., *Fiction of Bernard Malamud*, 65-86.

Hansen, Erik A., in Bogh, J., and S. Skovmand, eds., *Six American Novels*, 239-58.

Harper, Preston F., "Love and Alienation in the Novels of Bernard Malamud," *DAI* 33 (1973): 4414A-15A.

Hassan, Ihab, "Bernard Malamud: 1976: Fictions Within Our Fictions," in Astro, R., and J. J. Benson, eds., *Fiction of Bernard Malamud*, 43-64.

Hays, Peter L., "Malamud's Yiddish-Accented Medieval Stories," in Astro, R., and J. J. Benson, eds., *Fiction of Bernard Malamud*, 87-96.

Hershinow, S. J., *Bernard Malamud*.

Hershinow, Sheldon J., "Bernard Malamud and Jewish Humanism," *Religious Humanism* 13, ii (1979): 56-63.

Hicks, Granville, "Generations of the Fifties: Malamud, Gold and Updike," in Balakian, N., and C. Simmons, eds., *Creative Present*, 217-24.

_____, "His Hopes on the Human Heart," *SatR* 46 (Oct. 12, 1963): 31-2.

Hoyt, Charles A., "Bernard Malamud and the New Romanticism," in Moore, H. T., ed., *Contemporary American Novelists*, 65-79.

Johnston, Robert K., "Malamud's Vision for Humanity," *ChrT* 23, xix (July 20, 1979): 24-5.

Kazin, Alfred, "Bernard Malamud: The Magic and the Dread," in Kostelanetz, R., ed., *On Contemporary Literature*, 437-41. Also in Kazin, A., *Contemporaries*, 202-7.

Kellman, Steven G., "Malamud in France," *CLS* 15 (Sept., 1978): 305-15.

Kermode, Frank, in *NStat* 63 (Mar. 30, 1962): 452-3.

Klein, M., "Bernard Malamud: The Sadness of Goodness," *After Alienation*, 247-93.

Knopp, Josephine Z., "Jewish America: Bernard Malamud," *Trial of Judaism in Contemporary Jewish Writing*, 103-25.

_____, "The Ways of Mentschlekhkayt: A Study of Morality in Some Fiction of Bernard Malamud and Philip Roth," *Tradition* 13, iii (Winter, 1973): 67-84.

Kreitzer, Neil D., "The Quest for Identity in the Novels of Bernard Malamud," *DAI* 35 (1974): 2278A.

Lamdin, Lois S., "Malamud's Schlemiels," in *Modern Miscellany*, 31-42.

Lewin, Lois, "The Theme of Suffering in the Work of Bernard Malamud and Saul Bellow," *DA* 28 (1968): 5021A.

Levy, Eric P., "Metaphysical Shock: A Study of the Novels of Bernard Malamud," *DAI* 32 (1972): 5796A.

Malin, I., *Jews and Americans*.

Mann, Herbert D., "Bernard Malamud and the Struggle to Connect," *DAI* 39 (1977):2128A.

_____, "The Malamudian World: Method and Meaning," *SAJL* 4, i (Spring, 1978): 2-12.

Marcus, Steven, "The Novel Again," *PR* 29 (Spring, 1962): 184-6.

Masilamoni, E. H. Leelavathi, "Bernard Malamud: An Interview," *IJAS* 9, ii (1979): 33-7.

Meeter, G., *Philip Roth and Bernard Malamud*.

Mellard, James M., "Malamud's Novels: Four Versions of the Pastoral," *Crit* 9, ii (1967): 5-19. Also in Field, eds., *Bernard Malamud and the Critics*, 67-83.

Mudrick, Marvin, "Who Killed Herzog? Or, Three American Novelists," *UDQ* 1, i (Spring, 1966): 61-96. Also in Mudrick, M., *On Culture and Literature*, 200-33.

O'Brien, Jill L., "The Humanism of Bernard Malamud in Four Selected Novels," *DAI* 40 (1979): 858A-59A.

Ozick, Cynthia, "Literary Blacks and Jews," *Midstream* 18, iv (June-July, 1972): 10-24. Also in Field, L. A., and J. W. Field, eds., *Bernard Malamud*, 80-98.

Pinsker, Sanford, "The Achievement of Bernard Malamud," *MQ* 10, iv (July, 1969): 379-89.

_____, "The Schlemiel as Moral Bungler: Bernard Malamud's Ironic Heroes," in Pinsker, S., *Schlemiel as Metaphor*, 87-124. Also in Field, L. A., and J. W. Field, eds., *Bernard Malamud*, 45-71.

Raffel, Burton, "Bernard Malamud," *LitR* 13, ii (Winter, 1969): 149-55.

Rahv, Philip, "Introduction," *A Malamud Reader*, N.Y.: Farrar, Straus and Giroux, 1967. Also in Rahv, P., *Literature and the Sixth Sense*, 280-8.

Ratner, Marc L., "Style and Humanity in Malamud's Fiction," *MR* 5 (Summer, 1964): 663-83.

Richman, S., *Bernard Malamud*.

Rogoff, Leonard W., "Revelations of Bernard Malamud," *DAI* 37 (1977): 5126A-27A.

Rubin, Steven J., "Malamud and the Theme of Love and Sex," *SAJL* 4, i (Spring, 1978): 68-76.

Samuels, Charles T., "The Career of Bernard Malamud," *NRep* 140 (Sept. 10, 1966): 19-21. Also in Harrison, G. A., ed., *Critic as Artist*, 291-8.

Saposnik, Irving S., "Bellow, Malamud, Roth ... and Styron?" *Judaism* 31 (Summer, 1982): 322-32.

Schulz, M. F., "Bernard Malamud's Mythic Proletarians," *Radical Sophistication*, 56-67.

Sharfman, William, "Inside and Outside Malamud," *Rendezvous* 7, i (Spring, 1972): 25-38.

Sheres, Ita, "The Alienated Sufferer: Malamud's Novels from the Perspective of Old Testament and Jewish Mystical Thought," *SAJL* 4, i (Spring, 1978): 68-76.

Siegel, Ben, "Through a Glass Darkly: Bernard Malamud's Painful View of the Self," in Astro, R., and J. J. Benson, eds., *Fiction of Bernard Malamud*, 117-47.

_____, "Victims in Motion: Bernard Malamud's Sad and Bitter Clowns," *NWR* 5 (Spring, 1962): 69-80. Also in Waldmeir, J. J., ed., *Recent American Fiction*, 203-14.

Solotaroff, Theodore, "Bernard Malamud's Fiction: The Old Life and the New," *Ctary* 33, iii (Mar., 1962): 197-204. Also in Field, L. A., and J. W. Field, eds., *Bernard Malamud and the Critics*, 235-48.

Standley, Fred L., "Bernard Malamud: The Novel of Redemption," *SHR* 5 (Fall, 1971): 309-18.

Stern, Daniel, "The Art of Fiction, 52: Bernard Malamud," *ParisR* 61 (Spring, 1975): 40-64.

Strassberg, Mildred P., "Religious Commitment in Recent American Fiction: Flannery O'Connor, Bernard Malamud, John Updike," *DAI* 32 (1972): 6457A.

Sweet, Charles A., Jr., "Bernard Malamud and the Use of Myth," *DAI* 31 (1971): 4797A.

Tajuddin, Mohammed, "The Tragicomic Novel: Camus, Malamud, Hawkes, Bellow," *DA* 28 (1968): 2698A-99A.

Takada, Ken'ichi, and Hideo Sugahara, "Bernard Malamud: The Necessity of Returning to Reality," in *American Literature in the 1950's*, 60-74.

Tanner, Tony, "Bernard Malamud and the New Life," *CritQ* 10 (Spring-Summer, 1968): 151-68.

_____, "A New Life," *City of Words*, 322-43.

Vedral, Joyce L., "Guilt and Atonement in the Novels of Bernard Malamud," *DAI* 41 (1980): 2608A-09A.

Warburton, Robert W., "Fantasy and the Fiction of Bernard Malamud," in Huttar, C., *Imagination and the Spirit*, 387-416.

Weiss, Samuel A., "Notes on Bernard Malamud," *CJF* 21 (Winter, 1962-63): 155-8.

_____, "Passion and Purgation in Bernard Malamud," *UWR* 2, i (Fall, 1966): 93-9.

Whitton, Steven J., "The Mad Crusader: The Quest as Motif in the Jewish Fiction of Philip Roth and Bernard Malamud," *DAI* 34 (1973): 1943A.

THE ASSISTANT

Allen, W., *Modern Novel*, 330-2.

Alley, Alvin D., "Existential Heroes: Frank Alpine and Rabbit Angstrom," *BSUF* 9, i (Winter, 1968): 3-5.

Alter, I., *Good Man's Dilemma*, 8-26, 96-103.

Bailey, Anthony, "Insidious Patience," *Cweal* 66 (June 21, 1957): 307-8.

Baumbach, Jonathan, "The Economy of Love: The Novels of Bernard Malamud," *KR* 25 (Summer, 1963): 448-57. Also in Baumbach, J., *Landscape of Nightmare*, 111-22.

Ben-Asher, Naomi, "Jewish Identity and Christological Symbolism in the Work of Three Writers," *Jewish Frontier* 39, ix (Nov., 1972): 9-15.

Bloomfield, Caroline, "Religion and Alienation in James Baldwin, Bernard Malamud, and James F. Powers," *Religious Education* 57 (Mar.-Apr., 1962): 98-9.

Brown, Michael, "Metaphor for Holocaust and Holocaust as Metaphor: THE ASSISTANT and THE FIXER of Bernard Malamud Reexamined," *Judaism* 29, iv (Fall, 1980): 479-88.

Bryant, J. H., *Open Decision*, 329-32.

Cohen, S., *Bernard Malamud and the Trial by Love*, 37-55.

Ducharme, R., *Art and Idea in the Novels of Bernard Malamud*, 13-19, 36-42, 59-64, 81-6, 104-6.

Eigner, Edwin, M., "Malamud's Use of the Quest Romance," *Genre* 1, i (Jan., 1968): 55-75 passim. Also, as "The Loathly Ladies," in Field, L. A., and J. W. Field, eds., *Bernard Malamud and the Critics*, 85-108 passim.

Fiedler, Leslie, "The Commonplace as Absurd," *Reconstructionist* 24 (Feb. 21, 1958): 22-4. Also in Fiedler, L., *No! In Thunder*, 106-10.

Francis, H. E., "Bernard Malamud's Everyman," *Midstream* 7 (Winter, 1961): 93-7.

Freedman, William, "From Bernard Malamud with Discipline and Love," in French, W., ed., *Fifties*, 133-43. Also in Field, L. A., and J. W. Field, eds., *Bernard Malamud*, 49-54.

Freese, Peter, "Bernard Malamud's THE ASSISTANT," *LWU* 5 (Oct., 1972): 247-60.

Gervais, Ronald J., "Malamud's Frank Alpine and Kazin's Circumsised *Italyener*: A Possible Source for THE ASSISTANT," *NConL* 9, ii (Mar., 1979): 6-7.

Goldsmith, Arnold L., "Nature in Bernard Malamud's THE ASSISTANT," *Ren* 29, iv (Summer, 1977): 211-23.

Gollin, Rita K., "Understanding Fathers in American Jewish Fiction," *CentR* 18, iii (Summer, 1974): 273-87 passim.

Gorzkowska, Regina, "The Poor Slav Devil of Malamud's THE ASSISTANT," *PolR* 27, iii-iv (1982): 35-44.

Griffith, John, "Malamud's THE ASSISTANT," *Expl* 31, i (Sept., 1972): Item 1.

Gunn, Giles B., "Bernard Malamud and the Cost of Living," in Scott, N. A., ed., *Adversity and Grace*, 70-6.

Handy, W. J., "The Malamud Hero: The Quest for Existence," in Astro, R., and J. J. Benson, eds., *Fiction of Bernard Malamud*, 74-80.

Hansen, Erik A., in Bogh, J., and S. Skovmand, eds., *Six American Novels*, 245-8.

Hassan, I., *Radical Innocence*, 161-8. Also in Field, L. A., and J. W. Field, eds., *Bernard Malamud and the Critics*, 200-6.

Hays, Peter L., "The Complex Pattern of Redemption in THE ASSISTANT," *CentR* 13, ii (Spring, 1969): 200-14. Also in Field, L. A., and J. W. Field, eds., *Bernard Malamud and the Critics*, 219-33.

Hershinow, S. J., *Bernard Malamud*, 29-47.

Hicks, Granville, in Balakian, N., and C. Simmons, eds., *Creative Present*, 220-2.

Hoyt, Charles A., "Bernard Malamud and the New Romanticism," in Moore, H. T., ed., *Contemporary American Novelists*, 65-71.

Ichikawa, Masumi, "Bernard Malamud's THE ASSISTANT: An Interpretation through His Short Stories," *SALit* 14 (1978): 19-33.

Inge, M. Thomas, "The Ethnic Experience and Aesthetics in Literature: Malamud's THE ASSISTANT and Roth's CALL IT SLEEP," *JEthS* 1, iv (Winter, 1974): 45-50.

Kamizo, Yuko, "On Frank's Conversation in Malamud's THE ASSISTANT," *KAL* 16 (1975): 47-9.

Kazin, Alfred, "Fantasist of the Ordinary," *Ctary* 24 (July, 1957): 89-92.

Kegan, R., *Sweeter Welcome*, 37-50.

Klein, M., "Bernard Malamud: The Sadness of Goodness," *After Alienation*, 267-77.

Knopp, Josephine Z., "Jewish America: Bernard Malamud," *Trial of Judaism in Contemporary Jewish Writing*, 109-14.

Kramer, Maurice, "The Secular Mode of Jewishness," *Works* 1 (Autumn, 1967): 102-5, and passim.

Leer, Norman T., "The Double Theme in Malamud's ASSISTANT: Dostoevsky with Irony," *Mosaic* 4, iii (Spring, 1971): 89-102.

_____, "Three American Novels and Contemporary Society: A Search for Commitment," *WSCL* 3, iii (Fall, 1962): 72-6.

Leff, Leonard J., "Malamud's Ferris Wheel," *NConL* 1, i (Jan., 1971): 14-15.

Mandel, Ruth B., "Bernard Malamud's THE ASSISTANT and A NEW LIFE: Ironic Affirmation," *Crit* 7, ii (Winter, 1964-65): 110-21. Also in Field, L. A., and J. W. Field, eds., *Bernard Malamud and the Critics*, 261-74.

McDonald, Walter R., "The Redemption Novel: Suffering and Hope in THE ASSISTANT and HOUSE MADE OF DAWN," *CCTE* 41 (1976): 55-61.

Meeter, G., *Philip Roth and Bernard Malamud*, 34-9.

Mellard, James M., "Malamud's THE ASSISTANT: The City Novel as Pastoral," *SSF* 5 (Fall, 1967): 1-11.

Mesher, David R., "Malamud's Jewish Metaphors," *Judaism* 26, i (1977): 18-26.

Moskowitz, Moshe A., "Intermarriage and the Proselyte: A Jewish View," *Judaism* 28, iv (Fall, 1979): 423-33.

Pinsker, Sanford, "The Schlemiel as Moral Bungler: Bernard Malamud's Ironic Heroes," *Schlemiel as Metaphor*, 93-100. Also in Field, L. A., and J. W. Field, eds., *Bernard Malamud*, 49-54.

Pradhan, S. V., "The Nature and Interpretation of Symbolism in Malamud's THE ASSISTANT," *CentR* 16, iv (Fall, 1972): 394-407.

Rao, A. V. Krishna, "Bernard Malamud's THE ASSISTANT: The American Agonistes," *Triveni* 42, ii (July-Sept., 1973): 28-34.

Ratner, Marc, "Style and Humanity in Malamud's Fiction," *MR* 5 (Summer, 1964): 664-7.

Richman, S., *Bernard Malamud*, 25-6, 50-79.

Robinson, Roger, "The Truth of Fiction: Malamud's THE ASSISTANT as an Introduction to Novel Reading," in Norton, David, and Roger Robinson, eds., *View of English: Victoria University Essays for Teachers and Students*, Wellington: Victoria Un. Pr., 1979, 25-38.

Rupp, Richard H., "The Truth of Fiction: A Party of One," *Celebration in the Postwar American Novel*, 171-5.

Shear, Walter, "Culture Conflict in THE ASSISTANT," *MQ* 7, iv (July, 1966): 367-80. Also in Field, L.A., and J. W. Field, eds., *Bernard Malamud and the Critics*, 207-18.

Siegel, Ben, "Victims in Motion: Bernard Malamud's Sad and Bitter Clowns," *NWR* 5 (Spring, 1962): 71-2. Also in Waldmeir, J. J., ed., *Recent American Fiction*, 205-6.

Solotaroff, T., "Bernard Malamud: The Old Life and the New," *Red Hot Vacuum*, 71-9 passim.

Stanton, Robert, "Outrageous Fiction: CRIME AND PUNISHMENT, THE ASSISTANT, and NATIVE SON," *PCP* 4 (Apr., 1969): 52-8.

Stinson, John J., "Non-Jewish Dialogue in THE ASSISTANT: Stilted, Runyonesque, or Both?" *NConL* 9, i (Jan., 1979): 6-7.

Swados, Harvey, "The Emergence of an Artist," *WR* 22 (Winter, 1958): 149-51.

Takada, Ken'ici, and Hideo Sugahara, "Bernard Malamud: The Necessity of Returning to Reality," in *American Literature in the 1950's*, 65-9.

Tanner, T., *City of Words*, 327-9.

_____, "Bernard Malamud and the New Life," *CritQ* 10 (Spring-Summer, 1968): 155-7.

Waniek, Marilyn N., "The Schizoid Implied Authors of Two Jewish American Novels," *MELUS* 7, i (Spring, 1980): 26-39.

Weinberg, H., *New Novel in America*, 170-2.

Widmer, K., "Contemporary American Outcasts," *Literary Rebel*, 124-6.

Zlotnick, Joan, "Malamud's THE ASSISTANT: of Morris, Frank and St. Francis," *SAJL* 1, ii (Winter, 1975): 20-3.

DUBIN'S LIVES

Alter, I., *Good Man's Dilemma*, 174-82.

Cooper, Alan, "Bernard Malamud's Dualities," *Jewish Frontier* 46, iii (Mar., 1979): 25-7.

Field, Leslie, "Malamud-Dubin's Discontent," *SAJL* 4, i (Spring, 1978): 77-8.

Frank, Katherine, "Writing Lives: Theory and Practice in Literary Biography," *Genre* 13, iv (Winter, 1980): 499-516.

Friedman, Melvin J., in *SAJL* 8, ii (Autumn, 1980): 239-46 *passim*.

Gollin, Rita K., "Malamud's Dubin and the Morality of Desire," *PLL* 18, ii (Spring, 1982): 198-207.

Harder, Kelsey B., "Onomastic Centrality," *LOS* 7 (1980): 45-50.

Hershinow, S. J., *Bernard Malamud*, 101-18.

Kapp, Isa, "Malamud's Cantata for Middle Age," *New Leader* 61 (Dec., 1978): 3-5.

Levin, David, "The Lives of Bernard Malamud," *VQR* 56, i (Winter, 1980): 163-6.

Lyons, Bonnie, in *NDEJ* 11, ii (Apr., 1979): 173-7.

Maloff, Saul, "Loveliest Breakdown in Contemporary Fiction: Malamud's Lives," *Cweal* (Apr. 27, 1979): 244-6.

Pringle, Mary B., "(Auto)biography: Bernard Malamud's DUBIN'S LIVES," *IFR* 9, ii (Summer, 1982): 138-41.

THE FIXER

Allen, John A., "The Promised End: Bernard Malamud's THE TENANTS," *HC* 8, v (Dec., 1971): 12-15.

Alter, I., *Good Man's Dilemma*, 106-10, 154-72.

Alter, Robert, "Malamud as a Jewish Writer," *Ctary* 42 (Sept., 1966): 73-6. Also (revised) in Alter, R., *After the Tradition*, 122-30.

Baumbach, Jonathan, "Malamud's Heroes," *Cweal* 85 (Oct. 28, 1966): 97-9.

Bradbury, M., *Possibilities*, 286-9.

Brown, Michael, "Metaphor for Holocaust and Holocaust as Metaphor: THE ASSISTANT and THE FIXER of Bernard Malamud Reexamined," *Judaism* 29, iv (Fall, 1980): 479-88.

Bryant, J. H., *Open Decision*, 336-40.

Burgess, A., *Urgent Copy*, 136-40.

Cohen, S., *Bernard Malamud and the Trial by Love*, 73-92.

Davis, Robert G., "Invaded Selves," *HudR* 19 (Winter, 1966-67): 663-5.

Desmond, John F., "Malamud's Fixer: Jew, Christian, or Modern," *Ren* 27 (Winter, 1975): 101-10.

Dregnan, James P., "The Ordeal of Yakov Bok," *Critic* 25 (Oct., 1966): 102-4.

Ducharme, R., *Art and Idea in the Novels of Bernard Malamud*, 23-9, 47-52, 69-75, 92-7, 113-22.

_____, "Myth and Irony in THE FIXER," *IntEssays* 3, i (Dec., 1973): 31-6.

Eigner, Edwin M., "Malamud's Use of the Quest Romance," *Genre* 1, i (Jan., 1968): 55-75 *passim*. Also, as "The Loathly Ladies," in Field, L. A., and J. W. Field, eds., *Bernard Malamud and the Critics*, 85-108 *passim*.

Elkins, Stanley, in *MR* 8 (Spring, 1967): 388-92.

Featherstone, Joseph, "Bernard Malamud," *Atlantic* 219 (Mar., 1967): 97-8.

Friedberg, Maurice, "History and Imagination: Two Views of the Beiliss Case," *Midstream* 12, ix (Nov., 1966): 72-6. Also in Field, L. A., and J. W. Field, eds., *Bernard Malamud and the Critics*, 275-84.

Friedman, Alan W., "Bernard Malamud: The Hero as Schnook," *SoR* 4, iv (Oct., 1968): 927-44. Also in Field, L. A., and J. W. Field, eds., *Bernard Malamud and the Critics*, 285-303.

Gunn, Giles B., "Bernard Malamud and the High Cost of Living," in Scott, N. A., Jr., ed., *Adversity and Grace*, 79-82.

Haarhoff, R. D., "THE FIXER's Search for Meaning: Malamud and Logotherapy," *Communique* 6, i (1981): 93-9.

Handy, William J., "Malamud's THE FIXER, Another Look," *NWR* 8 (Spring, 1967): 74-82.

_____, "The Malamud Hero: A Quest for Existence," in Astro, R., and J. J. Benson, eds., *Fiction of Bernard Malamud*, 80-6.

_____, *Modern Fiction*, 131-58.

Henderson, H. B., III, "THE FIXER and THE CONFESSIONS OF NAT TURNER: The Individual Conscience in Crisis," *Versions of the Past*, 273-7.

Hershinow, S. J., *Bernard Malamud*, 63-75.

Hicks, Granville, "One Man to Stand for Six Million," *SatR* 49 (Sept. 10, 1966): 37-9.

Hoag, Gerald, "Malamud's Trial: THE FIXER and the Critics," *WHR* 24, i (Winter, 1970): 1-12. Also in Field, L. A., and J. W. Field, eds., *Bernard Malamud*, 330-42.

Horne, Lewis B., "Yakov Agonistes," *RS* 37, iv (Dec., 1969): 320-26.

Ichikawa, Masumi, "Bernard Malamud's THE FIXER," *SALit* 13 (1977): 51-64.

Kahn, Sholem K., "Will and Power in American Literature," *SA* 16 (1970): 529-51 *passim*.

Kegan, R., *Sweeter Welcome*, 51-74.

Knopp, Josephine Z., "Jewish America: Bernard Malamud," *Trial of Judaism in Contemporary Jewish Writing*, 114-25.

Kort, Wesley A., "THE FIXER and the Death of God," *Shriven Selves*, 90-115.

Malin, Irving, "THE FIXER: An Overview," *SAJL* 4, i (Spring, 1978): 40-50.

Marcus, Mordecai, "The Unsuccessful Malamud," *PrS* 41 (Spring, 1967): 88-9.

McColm, Pearlmarie, "The Revised New Syllabus and the Unrevised Old," *UDQ* i (Autumn, 1966): 138-41.

Meeter, G., *Philip Roth and Bernard Malamud*, 40-3.

Mesher, David R., "Malamud's Jewish Metaphors," *Judaism* 26, i (1977): 18-26.

Pinsker, Sanford, "Christ as Revolutionary, Revolutionary as Christ: The Hero in Bernard Malamud's THE FIXER and William Styron's THE CONFESSIONS OF NAT TURNER," *BaratR* 6, i (Summer, 1971): 29-37.

_____, "The Schlemiel as Moral Bungler: Bernard Malamud's Ironic Heroes," *Schlemiel as Metaphor*, 116-24. Also in Field, L. A., and J. W. Field, eds., *Bernard Malamud*, 65-71.

Pradhan, S. V., "Spinoza and Malamud's THE FIXER," *IJAS* 5, i-ii (1976): 37-52.

Pritchett, C. S., "A Pariah," *NYRB* (Sept. 22, 1966): 8-9.

Rao, G. Nageswara, "Isolation and Reconciliation in Malamud's THE FIXER," in Naik, M. K., et al., eds., *Indian Studies in American Fiction*, 255-62.

Ratner, Marc L., "The Humanism of Malamud's THE FIXER," *Crit* 9, ii (1967): 81-4.

Richler, Morecai, "Write, Boychick, Write," *NStat* 72 (Apr. 7, 1967): 473-4.

Rosenfeld, Alvin H., "The Progress of the American Jewish Novel," *Response* 7, i (Spring, 1973): 115-30.

Ruotolo, L. P., *Six Existential Heroes*, 121-39.

Rupp, Richard H., "Bernard Malamud: A Party of One," *Celebration in Postwar American Fiction*, 181-5.

Ryan, Yoni, "The Jew as an Alienated Figure in the Fiction of Patrick White and Bernard Malamud," *Melbourne Chronicle* 4 (Sept./Oct., 1978): 10-12.

Samuels, Charles T., "The Career of Bernard Malamud," *NRep* 155 (Sept. 10, 1966): 19-21. Also in Harrison, G. A., ed., *Critic as Artist*, 294-8.

Scholes, Robert, "Malamud's Latest Novel," *NWR* 8 (Winter, 1966): 106-8.

Smelsor, Marjorie, "The Schlemiel as Father: A Study of Yakov Bok and Eugene Henderson," *SAJL* 4, i (Spring, 1978): 50-7.

Takada, Ken'ichi, and Hideo Sugahara, "Bernard Malamud: The Necessity of Returning to Reality," in *American Fiction in the 1950's*, 70-3.

Tanner, Tony, "Bernard Malamud and the New Life," *CritQ* 10 (1968): 161-8.

_____, *City of Words*, 333-8.

Tracy, Robert, "A Sharing of Obsessions," *SoR* n.s. 6, iii (July, 1970): 890-94.

THE NATURAL

Alter, I., *Good Man's Dilemma*, 3-8, 84-96.

Barbour, James, and Robert Sattelmeyer, "THE NATURAL and the Shooting of Eddie Waitkus," *MMisc* 9 (1981): 6-18.

Baumbach, Jonathan, "The Economy of Love: The Novels of Bernard Malamud," *KR* 25 (Summer, 1963): 443-8. Also in Baumbach, J., *Landscape of Nightmare*, 106-111.

Bryant, J. H., *Open Decision*, 326-9.

Cohen, S., *Bernard Malamud and the Trial by Love*, 15-35.

Ducharme, R., *Art and Idea in the Novels of Bernard Malamud*, 9-13, 33-6, 55-8, 78-81, 101-4.

Eigner, Edwin M., "Malamud's Use of the Quest Romance," *Genre* 1, i (Jan., 1968): 55-75 *passim*. Also, as "The Loathly Ladies," in Field, L. A., and J. W. Field, eds., *Bernard Malamud and the Critics*, 85-108 *passim*.

Fiedler, Leslie, "In the Interest of Surprise and Delight," *Folio* 20 (Summer, 1955): 17-20. Also in Fiedler, L., *No! In Thunder*, 101-5.

Freedman, William, "From Bernard Malamud, with Discipline and with Love," in French, W., ed., *Fifties*, 133-43. Also in Field, L. A., and J. W. Field, eds., *Bernard Malamud*, 156-65.

Gealy, Marcia, "A Reinterpretation of Malamud's THE NATURAL," *SAJL* 4, i (Spring, 1978): 24-32.

Greenberg, Alvin, "A Sense of Place in Modern Fiction: The Novelist's World and the Allegorist's Heaven," *Genre* 5, iv (Dec., 1972): 353-66 *passim*.

Greiff, Louis K., "Quest and Defeat in THE NATURAL," *Thoth* 8 (Winter, 1967): 23-34.

Gunn, Giles B., "Bernard Malamud and the High Cost of Living," in Scott, N. A., ed., *Adversity and Grace*, 65-70.

Hansen, Erik A., in Bogh, J., and S. Skovmand, eds., *Six American Novels*, 242-5.

Hershinow, S. J., *Bernard Malamud*, 16-28.

Hoyt, Charles A., "Bernard Malamud and the New Romanticism," in Moore, H. T., ed., *Contemporary American Novelists*, 77-9.

Klein, M., "Bernard Malamud: The Sadness of Goodnes," *After Alienation*, 255-63.

Knoke, Paul D., "The Allegorical Mode in the Contemporary American Novel of Romance," *DAI* 32 (1971): 2695A.

Kudler, Harvey, "Bernard Malamud's THE NATURAL and Other Oedipal Analogs in Baseball Fiction," *DAI* 37 (1977): 5829A.

Leff, Leonard J., "Malamud's Ferris Wheel," *NConL* 1, i (Jan., 1971): 14-15.

Lidston, Robert C., "Malamud's THE NATURAL: An Arthurian Quest in the Big Leagues," *WVUPP* 27 (1981): 75-81.

Meeter, G., *Philip Roth and Bernard Malamud*, 24-6.

Mueller, Lavonne, "Malamud and West: Tyranny of the *Dream Dump*," in Madden, David E., *Nathaniel West: The Cheaters and the Cheated*, Deland, Fla.: Everett/Edwards Pr., 1973, 221-34. [Comparison with DAY OF THE LOCUST.]

Oriard, Michael V., "The Athletic Hero and Domestic Ideals," *JAC* 1, iii (Fall, 1978): 514-16.

Podhoretz, Norman, "Achilles in Left Field," *Ctary* 15 (Mar., 1953): 321-6.

Rao, D. Lakshama, "The Search for Identity in Bernard Malamud's THE NATURAL," *Triveni* 44 (Jan.-Mar., 1976): 79-86.

Ratner, Marc L., "Style and Humanity in Malamud's Fiction," *MR* 5 (Summer, 1964): 668-70.

Richman, S., *Bernard Malamud*, 27-49.

Rupp, Richard H., "Bernard Malamud: A Party of One," *Celebration in the Postwar American Novel*, 166-71.

Sharma, D. R., "THE NATURAL: A Nonmythical Approach," *PURBA* 5, ii (Oct., 1974): 3-8.

Shulman, Robert, "Myth, Mr. Eliot, and the Comic Novel," *MFS* 12 (Winter, 1966-67): 399-403.

Siegel, Ben, "Victims in Motion: Bernard Malamud's Sad and Bitter Clowns," *NWR* 5 (Spring, 1962): 69-70. Also in Waldmeir, J. J., ed., *Recent American Fiction*, 203-4.

Solotaroff, Theodore, "Bernard Malamud's Fiction: The Old Life and the New," *Ctary* 33, iii (Mar., 1962): 198-200. Also in Field, L. A., and J. W. Field, eds., *Bernard Malamud and the Critics*, 238-41. Also in Solotaroff, T., *Red Hot Vacuum*, 73-8.

Tanner, Tony, "Bernard Malamud and the New Life," *CritQ* 10 (Spring-Summer, 1968): 152-5.

_____, *City of Words*, 232-7.

Turner, Frederick W., III, "Myth Inside Out: Malamud's THE NATURAL," *Novel* 1, ii (Winter, 1968): 133-9. Also in Field, L. A., and J. W. Field, eds., *Bernard Malamud and the Critics*, 109-19.

Warburton, Robert W., "Fantasy and Fiction of Bernard Malamud," in Huttar, C., ed., *Imagination and the Spirit*, 408-11.

Wasserman, Earl R., "THE NATURAL: Malamud's World Ceres," *CRAS* 9, iv (Fall, 1965): 438-60. Also in Field, L. A., and J. W. Field, eds., *Bernard Malamud and the Critics*, 45-65.

Weinberg, H., *New Novel in America*, 169-70.

A NEW LIFE

Adachi, Fumi, "The Solitary Clown: Bernard Malamud's A NEW LIFE," in *American Literature in the 1950's*, 76-82.

Alter, I., *Good Man's Dilemma*, 27-61, 105-7.

Astro, Richard, "In the Heart of the Valley: Bernard Malamud's A NEW LIFE," in Field, L. A., and J. W. Field, eds., *Bernard Malamud*, 143-55.

Barsness, John A., "A NEW LIFE: The Frontier Myth in Perspective," *WAL* 3, iv (Winter, 1969): 297-302.

Baumbach, Jonathan, "The Economy of Love: The Novels of Bernard Malamud," *KR* 25 (Summer, 1963): 439-43. Also in Baumbach, J., *Landscape of Nightmare*, 102-6.

Bothwell, E. K., *Alienation in the Jewish American Novel of the Sixties*, 111-27.

Bryant, J. H., *Open Decision*, 332-6.

Burrows, David J., "The American Past in Malamud's A NEW LIFE," in *Private Dealings*, 86-93.

Cohen, S., *Bernard Malamud and the Trial by Love*, 57-72.

Daniels, Sally, "Flights and Evasions," *MinnR* 2 (Summer, 1962): 551-4.

Ducharme, R., *Art and Idea in the Novels of Bernard Malamud*, 19-23, 42-7, 64-9, 87-92, 106-12.

Eigner, Edwin M., "Malamud's Use of the Quest Romance," *Genre* 1, i (Jan., 1968): 55-78. Also in Field, L. A., and J. W. Field, eds., *Bernard Malamud and the Critics*, 85-108 *passim*.

Elman, Richard M., "Malamud on Campus," *Cweal* 75 (Oct. 27, 1961): 102-5.

Fiedler, Leslie A., "Malamud's Travesty Western," *Novel* 10, iii (Spring, 1977): 212-19. Also, as "The Many Lives of S. Levin: An Essay in Genre Criticism," in Astro, R., and J. J. Benson, eds., *Fiction of Bernard Malamud*, 149-61.

Golub, Ellen, "The Resurrection of the Heart," *English Review of Salem State Univ.* 1, ii (1973): 63-78.

Goodhart, Eugene, "Fantasy and Reality," *Midstream* 7 (Autumn, 1961): 102-5.

Gunn, Giles B., "Bernard Malamud and the High Cost of Living," in Scott, N. A., Jr., ed., *Adversity and Grace*, 76-9.

Halley, Anne, "The Good Life in Recent Fiction," *MR* 3 (Autumn, 1961): 190-6.

Handy, W. J., "The Malamud Hero: A Quest for Existence," in Astro, R., and J. J. Benson, eds., *Fiction of Bernard Malamud*, 68-74.

Hansen, Erik A., in Bogh, J., and S. Skovmand, eds., *Six American Novels*, 259-92.

Hartt, J. N., "The Return of Moral Passion," *YR* 51, ii (Winter, 1962): 304-5.

Hershinow, S. J., *Bernard Malamud*, 48-62.

Hicks, Granville, in Balakian N., and C. Simmons, eds., *Creative Present*, 222-24.

Hollander, John, "To Find the Westward Path," *PR* 29 (Winter, 1962): 137-9.

Hoyt, Charles A., "Bernard Malamud and the New Romanticism," in Moore, H. T., ed., *Contemporary American Novelists*, 75-6.

Hyman, Stanley E., "A New Life for a Good Man," *New Leader* 44 (Oct. 2, 1961): 24-5. Also in Kostelanetz, A., ed., *On Contemporary Literature*, 442-6.

Kermode, Frank, in *NStat* 63 (Mar. 30, 1962): 453.

Klein, Marcus, "Bernard Malamud: "The Sadness of Goodness," *After Alienation*, 280-93. Also in Field, L. A., and J. W. Field, eds., *Bernard Malamud and the Critics*, 249-60.

Ludwig, J., *Recent American Novelists*, 39-41.

Lyons, J. O., *College Novel in America*, 161-2.

Maloff, Saul, "Between the Real and the Absurd," *Nation* 193 (Nov. 18, 1961): 407-8.

Mandel, Ruth B., "Bernard Malamud's THE ASSISTANT and A NEW LIFE: Ironic Affirmation," *Crit* 7, ii (Winter, 1964-65): 110-21. Also in Field, L. A., and J. W. Field, eds., *Bernard Malamud and the Critics*, 261-74.

Meeter, G., *Philip Roth and Bernard Malamud*, 27-30.

Pinsker, Sanford, "The Schlemiel as Moral Bungler: Bernard Malamud's Ironic Heroes," *Schlemiel as Metaphor*, 100-16. Also in Field, L. A., and J. W. Field, eds., *Bernard Malamud*, 54-65.

Ratner, Marc L., "Style and Humanity in Malamud's Fiction," *MR* 5 (Summer, 1964): 670-7.

Richman, S., *Bernard Malamud*, 78-97.

Rupp, Richard A., "Bernard Malamud: A Party of One," *Celebration in Postwar American Fiction*, 175-81.

Samuels, Charles T., "The Career of Bernard Malamud," *NRep* 155 (Sept. 10, 1966): 19-21. Also in Harrison, G. A., ed., *Critic as Artist*, 291-8.

Schulz, Max F., "Malamud's A NEW LIFE: The New Wasteland of the Fifties," *WR* 6, i (1969): 37-44.

Sharma, D. R., "Malamud's A NEW LIFE: The Drama of Becoming," in Chander, J., and N. S. Pradhan, eds., *Studies in American Literature*, 134-43.

Siegel, Ben, "Victims in Motion: Bernard Malamud's Sad and Bitter Clowns," *NWR* 5 (Spring, 1962): 77-80. Also in Waldmeir, J. J., ed., *Recent American Fiction*, 211-14.

Singer, Barnet, "Outsider versus Insider: Malamud's and Kesey's Pacific Northwest," *SDR* 13, iv (Winter, 1975): 127-44.

Solotaroff, Theodore, "Bernard Malamud's Fiction: The Old Life and the New," *Ctary* 33, iii (Mar., 1962): 201-4. Also in Field, L. A., and J. J. Field, eds., *Bernard Malamud and the Critics*, 242-8. Also in Solotaroff, T., *Red Hot Vacuum*, 79-86.

Takada, Ken'ichi, and Hideo Sugahara, "Bernard Malamud: The Necessity of Returning to Reality," in *American Literature in the 1950's*, 69-70.

Tanner, Tony, "Bernard Malamud and the New Life," *CritQ* 10 (Spring-Summer, 1968): 157-60.

_____, *City of Words*, 329-32.

Weinberg, H., *New Novel in America*, 173-8.

White, Robert L., "The English Instructor as Hero ... Two Novels by Roth and Malamud," *ForumH* 4 (Winter, 1963): 16-22.

Witherington, Paul, "Malamud's Allusive Design in A NEW LIFE," *WAL* 10 (Summer, 1975): 115-23.

PICTURES OF FIDELMAN: AN EXHIBITION

Alter, I., *Good Man's Dilemma*, 126-47.

Cohen, S., *Bernard Malamud and the Trial by Love*, 93-105.

Ducharme, R., *Art and Idea in the Novels of Bernard Malamud*, 127-41.

_____, "Structure and Content in Malamud's PICTURES OF FIDELMAN," *ConnR* 5, i (Oct., 1971): 26-36.

Field, Leslie, "Portrait of the Artist as *Schlemiel*," in Field, L. A., and J. W. Field, eds., *Bernard Malamud*, 117-29.

Halio, Jay L., "Fantasy and Fiction," *SoR* 7, iii (Apr., 1971): 635-47 *passim*.

Hershinow, S. J., *Bernard Malamud*, 76-88.

Lefcowitz, Barbara F., "The *Hubris* of Neurosis: Malamud's PICTURES OF FIDELMAN," *L&P* 20, iii (1970): 115-20.

Malin, Irving, "Portrait of the Artist in Slapstick: Malamud's PICTURES OF FIDELMAN," *LitR* 24, i (Fall, 1980): 121-38.

Rubin, Steven J., "Malamud's Fidelman: Innocence and Optimism Abroad," *NConL* 8, i (Jan., 1978): 21-3.

Schwartz, Helen J., "Malamud's Turning Point: The End of Redemption in PICTURES OF FIDELMAN," *SAJL* 2, ii (Winter, 1976): 26-37.

Sharma, D. R., "PICTURES OF FIDELMAN: From Art to Life," *PURBA* 7, i (1976): 31-42.

Tanner, Tony, *City of Words*, 339-43.

Wegelin, Christof, "The American Schlemiel Abroad: Malamud's Italian Stories and the End of American Innocence," *TCL* 19 (Apr., 1972): 77-88.

Wisse, R. R., *Schlemiel as Modern Hero*, 110-18.

THE TENANTS

Allen, John A., "The Promised End: Bernard Malamud's THE TENANTS," *HC* 8, v (1971): 1-15. Also in Field, L. A., and J. W. Field, eds., *Bernard Malamud*, 104-16.

Alter, I., *Good Man's Dilemma*, 73-82, 110-13, 172-3.

Alter, Robert, "Updike, Malamud and the Fire This Time," *Ctary* 54, iv (Oct., 1972): 68-74.

Cohen, S., *Bernard Malamud and the Trial by Love*, 107-23.

Cuddihy, John M., "Jews, Blacks and the Cold War at the Top," *Worldview* 15, ii (Feb., 1972): 30-40.

Finkelstein, Sidney, "The Anti-Hero of Updike, Bellow, and Malamud," *AmD* 7, ii (Spring, 1972): 12-14, 30.

Hansen, Erik A., in Bogh, J., and S. Skovmand, eds., *Six American Novels*, 252-5.

Hatvary, George E., "The Endings in Malamud's THE TENANTS," *NMAL* 1, i (Winter, 1976): Item 5.

Hershinow, S. J., *Bernard Malamud*, 89-100.

Hoag, Gerald, "Malamud's THE TENANTS: Revolution Arrested," *PCL* 2, ii (Nov., 1976): 3-9.

Kellman, Steven G., "THE TENANTS in the House of Fiction," *SNNTS* 8, iv (Winter, 1976): 458-67.

Lewis, Stuart A., "The Jewish Author Looks at the Black," *ColQ* 21, iii (Winter, 1973): 317-30.

Lindberg-Seyersted, Brita, "A Reading of Bernard Malamud's THE TENANTS," *JAmS* 9, i (Apr., 1975): 85-102.

Maney, Margaret S., "The Urban Apocalypse in Contemporary American Novels," *DAI* 41 (1980): 2111A.

Mesher, David R., "Names and Stereotypes in Malamud's THE TENANTS," *SAJL* 4, i (Spring, 1978): 57-68.

Ozick, Cynthia, "Literary Blacks and Jews," *Midstream* 18, vi (June-July, 1972): 10-24. Also in Field, L. A., and J. W. Field, eds., *Bernard Malamud*, 80-98.

Richey, Clarence W., "'The Woman in the Dunes': A Note on Bernard Malamud's THE TENANTS," *NConL* 3, i (Jan., 1973): 4-5.

Russell, Mariann, "White Man's Black Man: Three Views," *CLAJ* 17 i (Sept., 1973): 98-100.

Sale, Roger, "Hawkes, Malamud, Richler, Oates," *On Not Being Good Enough: Writings of a Working Critic*, N.Y.: Oxford Un. Pr., 1979, 30-42 *passim*.

Sharma, D. R., "THE TENANTS: Malamud's Treatment of the Racial Problem," *IJAS* 8, ii (Jan., 1978): 12-28.

Stafford, W. T., *Books Speaking to Books*, 85-91.

Syrkin, Marie, "From Frank Alpine to Willie Spearmint...," *Midstream* 17, ix (Nov., 1971): 64-8.

Vickery, John B., "The Scapegoat in Literature: Some Kinds and Uses," 264-78 in McCune, Marjorie W., and others, eds., *Binding of Proteus: Perspectives on Myth and the Literary Process*, Lewisburg: Bucknell Un. Pr., 1980; London: Associated Un. Pr., 1980.

Zucker, David H., "Secret Shares," *Shen* 23, ii (Winter, 1972): 84-7.

BIBLIOGRAPHY

Habich, Robert D., "Bernard Malamud: A Bibliographical Survey," *SAJL* 4, i (Spring, 1978): 78-84.

Grau, Joseph A., "Bernard Malamud: A Bibliographical Addendum," *BB* 37 (Dec., 1980): 157-66.

_____, "Bernard Malamud: A Further Bibliographical Addendum," *BB* 38, ii (Apr.-June, 1981): 101-4.

Kosofsky, Rita, *Bernard Malamud: An Annotated Checklist*, Kent, Ohio: Kent State Un. Pr., 1969.

Richman, S., *Bernard Malamud*, 150-3.

Risty, Donald, "A Comprehensive Checklist of Malamud Criticism," in Astro, R., and J. J. Benson, eds., *Fiction of Bernard Malamud*, 163-90.

MALGONKAR, MANOHAR, 1913-

GENERAL

Amur, G. S., *Manohar Malgonkar*.

_____, "Manohar Malgonkar and the Problems of the Indian Novelist in English," in Mohan, Ramesh, ed., *Indian Writing in English*, 37-46.

Asnani, Shyam M., "A Study of the Novels of Manohar Malgonkar," *LHY* 16, ii (July, 1975): 71-98.

Dayananda, James Y., "The Image of Women in Manohar Malgonkar's Novels," *JSoAL* 12, iii-iv (Spring-Summer, 1977): 109-13.

_____, "Interview with Manohar Malgonkar," *LHR* 14 (1973): 78-102.

_____, "Interview with Manohar Malgonkar," *WLWE* 12 (1973): 260-87.

_____, *Manohar Malgonkar*.

_____, "On Authors and Books: Interview with Manohar Malgonkar," *LHY* 16, ii (1975): 99-107.

Jayashri, I., "Women versus Tradition in the Novels of Manohar Malgonkar," *Triveni* 45, ii (July-Sept., 1976): 73-80.

Parameswaran, Uma, "Manohar Malgonkar as a Historical Novelist," *WLWE* 14, ii (Nov., 1975): 329-38.

Singh, Ram Sewak, "Manohar Malgonkar the Novelist," *IndL* 13, i (Mar., 1970): 122-31.

Williams, Haydn M., "Manohar Malgonkar: 'The Captains and the Kings'," *JIWE* 8, i-ii (Jan.-July, 1980): 35-44.

A BEND IN THE GANGES

Amu, G. S., *Manohar Malgonkar*, 103-22.

Asnani, Shyam M., "A Study of the Novels of Manohar Malgonkar," *LHY* 16, ii (July, 1975): 87-91.

Dayananda, J. Y., *Manohar Malgonkar*, 123-35.

Iyengar, K. R. S., *Indian Writing in English*, 431-4.

Malhotra, M. L., "Manohar Malgonkar: A Novelist with an Old-world Air," *Bridges of Literature*, 197-8.

Singh, R. S., *Indian Novel in English*, 129-33.

————, "Manohar Malgonkar the Novelist," *IndL* 13, i (Mar., 1970): 129-31.

Williams, Haydn M., "Manohar Malgonkar: 'The Captains and the Kings'," *JIWE* 8, i-ii (Jan.-July, 1980): 39-41.

COMBAT OF SHADOWS

Aithal, S. Krishnamoorthy, "The British and Anglo-Indian Encounter in Malgonkar's COMBAT OF SHADOWS," *IFR* 9, i (Winter, 1982): 54-7.

————, and Rashmi Aithal, "East-West Encounter in Four Indo-English Novels," *ACLALSB* 6, i (Nov., 1982): 1-16.

Amur, G. S., *Manohar Malgonkar*, 60-77.

Asnani, Shyam M., "A Study of the Novels of Manohar Malgonkar," *LHY* 16, ii (July, 1975): 78-82.

Dayananda, J. Y., *Manohar Malgonkar*, 49-59.

Iyengar, K.R.S., *Indian Writing in English*, 425-8.

Malhotra, M. L., "Manohar Malgonkar: A Novelist with an Old-world Air," *Bridges of Literature*, 198-204.

Singh, R. S., *Indian Novel in English*, 122-4.

————, "Manohar Malgonkar the Novelist," *IndL* 13, i (Mar., 1970): 125-7.

THE DEVIL'S WIND

Amur, G. S., *Manohar Malgonkar*, 123-35.

Asnani, Shyam M., "A Study of the Novels of manohar Malgonkar," *LHY* 16, ii (July, 1975): 92-6.

Dayananda, J. Y., *Manohar Malgonkar*, 136-48.

————, "The Novelist as Historian: Manohar Malgonkar's THE DEVIL'S WIND and the 1857 Rebellion," *JSoAL* 10, i (1974): 55-67.

DISTANT DRUM

Amur, G. S., *Manohar Malgonkar*, 46-59, 61-2.

Asnani, Shyam M., "A Study of the Novels of Manohar Malgonkar," *LHY* 16, ii (July, 1978): 73-8.

Dayanda, J. Y., *Manohar Malgonkar*, 38-49.

Iyengar, K.R.S., *Indian Writing in English*, 423-5.

Malhotra, M. L., "Manohar Malgonkar: A Novelist with an Old-world Air," *Bridges of Literature*, 194-6.

Singh, R. S., *Indian Novel in English*, 120-1.

————, "Manohar Malgonkar the Novelist," *IndL* 13, i (Mar., 1970): 124-5.

OPEN SEASON

Rao, D. S., "OPEN SEASON: Manohar Malgonkar," *IndL* 24, i (Jan.-Feb., 1981): 142-7.

THE PRINCES

Amur, G. S., *Manohar Malgonkar*, 78-102.

Anand, Shahla, "Images of Indian Princesses and Courtly Concubines in Four Contemporary Works," *SARev* (July, 1979): 27-35.

Asnani, Shyam M., "A Study of the Novels of Manohar Malgonkar," *LHY* 16, ii (July, 1975): 82-7.

Chinneswararao, G. J., "Anand's PRIVATE LIFE OF AN INDIAN PRINCE and Malgonkar's THE PRINCES: A Comparison," *JIWE* 4, i (1976): 18-21.

————, "Initiatory Motifs in Manohar Malgonkar's THE PRINCES," *Mahfil* 8, ii-iii (1972): 223-35.

————, *Manohar Malgonkar*, 60-6, 89-123.

————, "Manohar Malgonkar on His Novel THE PRINCES: An Interview," *JCL* 9, iii (Apr., 1975): 21-8.

————, "Rhythm in M. Malgonkar's THE PRINCES," *LE&W* 15 (1971): 55-73.

Cowasjee, Saros, "Princes and Politics," *LCrit* 8, lv (1969): 10-18.

Iyengar, K.R.S., *Indian Writing in English*, 428-31.

Singh, R. S., *Indian Novel in English*, 124-9.

————, "Manohar Malgonkar the Novelist," *IndL* 13, i (Mar., 1970): 127-9.

Steinvorth, K., "Mulk Raj Anand's PRIVATE LIFE OF AN INDIAN PRINCE and Manohar Malgonkar's THE PRINCES," *LHY* 14, i (1973): 76-91.

BIBLIOGRAPHY

Dayananda, J. Y., *Manohar Malgonkar*, 169-71.

MALOUF, DAVID, 1934-

GENERAL

Davidson, Jim, "Interview: David Malouf," *Meanjin* 39 (Oct., 1980): 323-4.

Pierce, Peter, "David Malouf's Fiction," *Meanjin* 41, iv (Dec., 1982): 526-34.

Shapcott, Tom, "An Interview," *Quadrant* 135 (1978): 27-31.

AN IMAGINARY LIFE

Wright, John M., "David Malouf: Literary Epicurean," *Quadrant* 25 (Dec., 1981): 58-9.

JOHNNO

Daniel, Helen, "Narrator and Outsider in TRAP and JOHNNO," *Southerly* 37 (1977): 184-95.

Hadgraft, Cecil, in Hamilton, K. G., ed., *Studies in the Recent Australian Novel*, 214-18.

Indyk, Ivor, "The Australian Exploration of Masculinity," *CE&S* 3 (1977-78): 89-96.

MALTZ, ALBERT, 1908-1985

GENERAL

Salzman, J., *Albert Maltz*.

THE CROSS AND THE ARROW

Salzman, J., *Albert Maltz*, 74-85.

THE JOURNEY OF SIMON MCKEEVER

Salzman, J., *Albert Maltz*, 104-16.

A LONG DAY IN A SHORT LIFE

Salzman, J., *Albert Maltz*, 119-27.

A TALE OF JANUARY

Salzman, J., *Albert Maltz*, 132-8.

THE UNDERGROUND STREAM

Salzman, J., *Albert Maltz*, 53-69.

BIBLIOGRAPHY

Salzman, J., *Albert Maltz*, 153-7.

MANFRED, FREDERICK, Pseud. (Feike Feikema) 1912-1994

GENERAL

Anon., "West of the Mississippi: An Interview with Frederick Manfred," *Crit* 2, iii (Winter, 1959): 35-56.

Byrd, Forrest M., "Prolegamenon to Frederick Manfred," *DAI* 36 (1976): 5276A.

DeBoer, Peter P., "Frederick Feikema Manfred: Spiritual Naturalist," *The Reformed Journal* 13 (Apr., 1963): 19-23. [Not seen.]

Lee, James W., "An Interview with Frederick Manfred," *SNNTS* 5, iii (Fall, 1973): 358-82.

Milton, J. R., *Conversations with Frederick Manfred*, Salt Lake City: Un. of Utah Pr., 1974.

_____, "Frederick Feikema Manfred," *WR* 22 (Spring, 1958): 181-99.

_____, "Interview with Frederick Manfred," *SDR* 7, iv (Winter, 1969-70): 110-30.

_____, "Voice from Siouxland: Frederick Feikema Manfred," *CE* 19 (Dec., 1957): 104-11.

Moen, Ole O., "The Voice of Siouxland: Man and Nature in Frederick Manfred's Writing," *DAI* 39 (1979): 7347A-48A.

Swallow, Alan, "The Mavericks," *Crit* 2, iii (1959): 88-90. Also in Swallow, A., *An Editor's Essays of Two Decades*, Seattle and Denver: Experiment Pr., 1962, 353-55.

Ter Maat, Cornelius J., "Three Novelists and a Community: A Study of American Novelists with Dutch Calvinist Origins," *DA* 24 (1963): 751.

Wright, Robert C., "Manfred's Siouxland Novels," in Husboe, A. R., and W. Geyer, eds., *Where the West Begins*, 110-18.

Wydler, Delbert E., "Frederick Manfred: The Quest of the Independent Writer," *BI* 31 (1979): 16-30.

BOY ALMIGHTY

Milton, John R., "Frederick Feikema Manfred," *WR* 22 (Spring, 1958): 184-5.

THE BROTHER (See WORLD'S WANDERER)

BUCKSKIN MAN TALES

Milton, J. R., *Novel of the American West*, 187-94.

Roth, Russell, "The Inception of a Saga: Manfred's BUCKSKIN MAN," *SDR* 7, iv (Winter, 1969-70): 87-99. Also in Pilkington, W. T., ed., *Critical Essays on the Western American Novel*, 172-81.

THE CHOKECHERRY TREE

McCord, Nancy N., "Manfred's Elof Lofblom," *WAL* 16, ii (Aug., 1981): 125-34.

Milton, John R., "Voice from Siouxland: Frederick Feikema Manfred," *CE* 19 (Dec., 1957): 106-7.

CONQUERING HORSE

McAllister, Mick, "The First Covenant in CONQUERING HORSE: Syncretic Myth in the Buckskin Man Tales," *SDR* 20, iii (Autumn, 1982):76-88.

Timmerman, John H., "Structures and Meaning in Frederick Manfred's CONQUERING HORSE," *LJHum* 8, i (Spring, 1982): 39-49.

Wydler, D. E., "Manfred's Indian Novel," *SDR* 7, iv (Winter, 1969-70): 100-9.

THE GIANT (See WORLD'S WANDERER)

THE GOLDEN BOWL

Bebeau, Donald, "A Search for Voice, A Sense of Place in THE GOLDEN BOWL," *SDR* 7, iv (Winter, 1969-70): 79-87.

Milton, John R., "Frederick Feikema Manfred," *WR* 22 (Spring, 1958): 181-2.

_____, "Voice from Siouxland: Frederick Feikema Manfred," *CE* 19 (Dec., 1957): 105-6.

Spies, George H., III, "John Steinbeck's THE GRAPES OF WRATH and Frederick Manfred's THE GOLDEN BOWL: A Comparative Study," *DAI* 34 (1973): 3431A-32A.

GREEN EARTH

Flora, Joseph M., "Siouxland Panorama: Frederick Manfred's GREEN EARTH," *MMisc* 7 (1979): 56-63.

LORD GRIZZLY

Arthur, Anthony, "Manfred, Neihardt, and Hugh Glass: Variations on an American Epic," in Huseboe, A. R., and W. Geyer, eds., *Where the West Begins*, 99-109.

Austin, James C., "Legend, Myth and Symbol in Frederick Manfred's LORD GRIZZLY," *Crit* 6, iii (Winter, 1963-64): 122-30.

Milton, John R., "American Fiction and Man," *Cresset* 18, iii (1955): 16-20.

_____, "Frederick Feikema Manfred," *WR* 22 (Spring, 1958): 192-6.

_____, "LORD GRIZZLY: Rhythm, Form and Meaning in the Western Novel," *WAL* 1 (Spring, 1966): 6-14.

_____, *Novel of the American West*, 169-78.

_____, "Voice from Siouxland: Frederick Feikema Manfred," *CE* 19 (Dec., 1957): 109-10.

Timmerman, John H., "Forgiveness in the Lair of the Lizard: Frederick Manfred's LORD GRIZZLY," *CLAJ* 25, i (Sept., 1981): 37-47.

MORNING RED

Milton, John R., "Frederick Feikema Manfred," *WR* 22 (Spring, 1958): 190-2.

_____, in *Cresset* 20 (Sept., 1957): 27-8.

_____, "Voice from Siouxland: Frank Feikema Manfred," *CE* 19 (Dec., 1957): 110-11.

THE PRIMITIVE (See also WORLD'S WANDERER)

Oppewall, Peter, "Manfred at Calvin College," in Huseboe, A. R., and W. Geyer, eds., *Where the West Begins*, 86-98.

RIDERS OF JUDGMENT

Milton, John R., "Recreation of the Old West: A Postscript on RIDERS OF JUDGMENT," *WR* 22 (Spring, 1958): 196-9.
Westbrook, Max, "RIDERS OF JUDGMENT: An Exercise in Ontological Criticism," *WAL* 12 (May, 1977): 41-51.

THIS IS THE YEAR

Meyer, Roy W., "The Farm Novelist as Social Critic," *The Middle Western Farm Novel in the Twentieth Century*, Lincoln: Univ. of Nebraska Pr., 1965, 122-6.
Milton, John R., "Frederick Feikema Manfred," *WR* 22 (Spring, 1958): 182-3.
_____, "Voice from Siouxland: Frederick Feikema Manfred," *CE* (Dec., 1957): 106.

WORLD'S WANDERER

Milton, John R., "The American Novel: The Search for Home, Tradition, and Identity," *WHR* 16 (Spring, 1962): 175-6.
_____, "Frederick Feikema Manfred," *WR* 22 (Spring, 1958): 182-3.
_____, "Voice from Siouxland: Frederick Feikema Manfred," *CE* 19 (Dec., 1957): 107-9.

BIBLIOGRAPHY

Kellogg, George, "Frederick Manfred: A Bibliography," *TCL* 11 (Apr., 1966): 30-5. Reprinted in pamphlet form by Swallow Pr., 1968.

MANNING, OLIVIA, 1915-1980

GENERAL

Binding, Paul, "Olivia Manning," *NStat* (Aug. 1, 1980): 22-3.
Emerson, Sally, "Olivia Manning," *B&B* 17, ii (Nov., 1971): 30-1. [Interview.]
Parkhill-Rathbone, James, "Olivia Manning's Dilemmas," *Books and Bookmen* 16, xi (Aug., 1971): 22-3.
Pendry, E. D., *New Feminism of English Fiction*, 172-84.

THE BALKAN TRILOGY

Morris, R. K., *Continuance and Change*, 29-49.

THE BATTLE LOST AND WON

Trickett, Rachel, "Obsessed with Death," *TLS* (Nov. 24, 1978): 135-8.

FRIENDS AND HEROES

Anon., "The Irony of Survival," *TLS* (Nov. 4, 1965): 973. Also in *T.L.S.: Essays and Reviews from the Times Literary Supplement 1965*, 36-9.
Morris, R. K., *Continuance and Change*, 43-8.

THE GREAT FORTUNE

Allen, W., *Modern Novel*, 261-2.
Morris, R. K., *Continuance and Change*, 33-7.

THE SPOILT CITY

Allen, W., *Modern Novel*, 261-2.
Morris, R. K., *Continuance and Change*, 37-43.

MANO, D. KEITH, 1942-

GENERAL

Kehl, D. G., "Pilgrim and *Polisson* in the Fiction of D. Keith Mano," *C&L* 28, i (Fall, 1978): 32-42.

THE DEATH AND LIFE OF HARRY GOTH

Gros-Louis, Dolores, "Christianity vs. Death in D. Keith Mano's THE DEATH AND LIFE OF HARRY GOTH," *C&L* 25, iii (Spring, 1976): 21-9.

MARCH, WILLIAM, Pseud. (W. E. M. Campbell), 1894-1954

GENERAL

Cooke, Alastair, "Introduction," *A William March Omnibus*, N.Y.: Rinehart, 1956.
Crowder, Richard, "The Novels of William March," *UKCR* 15 (Winter, 1948): 11-2.
Going, William T., "William March's Alabama," *AlaR* 16 (1963): 243-58.
_____, "William March: Regional Perspective and Beyond," *PLL* 13 (1977): 430-43. [Rev.-Essay.]
Silva, Frederick E., "The Cracked Looking-Glass: A Critical Study of the Novels of William March (1894-1954)," *DA* 28 (1967): 2264A.

THE BAD SEED

Going, William T., "A Footnote to THE BAD SEED: A Modern Elsie Venner," *WHR* 18 (Spring, 1964): 175.
Hamblen, Abigail A., "THE BAD SEED: A Modern Elsie Venner," *WHR* 17 (Autumn, 1963): 361-3.

COME IN AT THE DOOR

Crowder, Richard, "The Novels of William March, *UKCR* 15 (Winter, 1948): 117-21.

COMPANY K

Crowder, Richard, "The Novels of William March," *UKCR* 15 (Winter, 1948): 111-17.
Medlicott, Alexander, Jr., "'Soldiers Are Citizens of Death's Gray Land': William March's COMPANY K," *ArQ* 28 (1972): 209-24.
Simmonds, Roy S., "An Unending Circle of Pain: William March's COMPANY K," *BSUF* 16, ii (Spring, 1975): 33-46.
_____, "William March's COMPANY K: A Short Textual Study," *SAF* 2, i (Spring, 1974): 105-13.

Waldmeir, J. J., *American Novels of the Second World War*, 41-2.

THE LOOKING GLASS

Crowder, Richard, "The Novels of William March," *UKCR* 15 (Winter, 1948): 124-9.

THE TALLONS

Crowder, Richard, "The Novels of William March," *UKCR* 15 (Winter, 1948): 121-4.

BIBLIOGRAPHY

Simmonds, Roy S., "A William March Checklist," *MissQ* 28 (1975): 461-88.

MARKANDAYA, KAMALA, 1924-

GENERAL

Adkins, Joan F., "Kamala Markandaya: Indo-Anglian Conflicts as Unity," *JSoAL* 10, i (Fall, 1974): 89-102.

Asnani, Shyam M., "Character and Technique in Kamala Markandaya's Novels," *RUSEng* 11 (1978): 66-74. [Not seen.]

_____, "Kamala Markandaya's Later Novels," *Triveni* 48, iv (Jan.-Mar., 1980): 22-9.

Chandrasekharan, K. R., "East and West in the Novels of Kamala Markandaya," in Naik, M. K., et al., eds., *Critical Essays on Indian Writing in English*, 307-30.

Chauhan, P. S., "Kamala Markandaya: Sense and Sensibility," *LCrit* 12, ii-iii (1976): 134-47.

Dale, James, "Kamala Markandaya and the Outsider," in Massa, D., ed., *Individual and Community in Commonwealth Literature*, 188-95.

_____, "Sexual Politics in the Novels of Kamala Markandaya," *WLWE* 21, ii (Summer, 1982): 347-56.

Geetha, P., "Kamala Markandaya: An Interpretation," *ComQ* 3, ix (Dec., 1978): 96-109.

Harrex, S. C., "A Sense of Identity: The Novels of Kamala Markandaya," *JCL* 6, i (June, 1971): 65-78.

Iyengar, K. R. S., *Indian Writing in English*, 438-50.

Jain, Jasbir, "The Novels of Kamala Markandaya," *IndL* 18, ii (1975): 36-43.

Kumar, Shiv K., "Tradition and Change in the Novels of Kamala Markandaya," *BA* 43, iv (Autumn, 1969): 508-13. Reprinted in *OJES* 7, i (1969): 1-9.

Parameswaran, Uma, "India for the Western Reader: A Study of Kamala Markandaya's Novels," *TQ* 11, ii (Summer, 1968): 231-47.

_____, *Study of Representative Indo-English Novelists*, 89-124.

Prasad, Hari M., "The Quintessence of Kamala Markandaya's Art," *ComQ* 3, ix (Apr., 1978): 173-85.

Rao, K. S. N., "Kamala Markandaya: The Novelist as Craftsman," *IWT* 3, ii (Apr.-June, 1969): 32-40.

_____, "Love, Sex, Marriage and Morality in Kamala Markandaya's Novels," *OJES* 10 (1973): 69-77.

_____, "The New Harvest: The Indian Novel in English in the Post-Independence Era; Women at Work: Kamala Markandaya," *DA* 30 (1969): 1177A-78A.

_____, "The Novels of Kamala Markandaya," *LE&W* 15, ii (1971): 209-18.

_____, "Religious Elements in Kamala Markandaya's Novels," *ArielE* 3, i (1977): 35-50.

_____, "Some Notes on the Plots of Kamala Markandaya's Novels," *IndL* 13, i (Mar., 1970): 102-12.

Shimer, Dorothy B., "Sociological Imagery in the Novels of Kamala Markandaya," *WLWE* 14 (Nov., 1975): 357-70.

Venkateswaran, Shyamala, "The Language of Kamala Markandaya's Novels," *LCrit* 9, iii (Winter, 1970): 57-67.

THE COFFER DAMS

Asnani, Shyam M., "Kamala Markandaya's Later Novels," *Triveni* 48, iv (Jan.-Mar., 1980): 22-5.

Chauhan, P. S., "Kamala Markandaya: Sense and Sensibility," *LCrit* 12, ii-iii (1976): 141-5.

Dale, James, "Sexual Politics in the Novels of Kamala Markandaya," *WLWE* 21, ii (Summer, 1982): 350-2.

Geetha, P., "Kamala Markandaya: An Interpretation," *ComQ* 3, ix (Dec., 1978): 103-5.

Iyengar, K.R.S., *Indian Writing in English*, 447-9.

Jain, Jasbir, "The Novels of Kamala Markandaya," *IndL* 18, ii (1975): 38-50.

Parameswaran, U., *Study of Representative Indo-English Novels*, 108-20.

Weir, Ann L., "Worlds Apart? Feminine Consciousness in Markandaya's NECTAR IN A SIEVE and THE COFFER DAMS," *CIEFLB* 13, ii (1977): 71-85.

THE GOLDEN HONEYCOMB

Appasamy, S. P., "THE GOLDEN HONEYCOMB: A Saga of Princely Life in India by Kamala Markandaya," *JIWE* 6, ii (1978): 56-63.

Dale, James, "Sexual Politics in the Novels of Kamala Markandaya," *WLWE* 21, ii (Summer, 1982): 353-5.

Pollard, Arthur, "Kamala Markandaya's THE GOLDEN HONEYCOMB," *JIWE* 8, i-ii (Jan.-July, 1980): 22-6.

A HANDFUL OF RICE

Fracht, Sylvia, "A Study of Kamala Markandaya's A HANDFUL OF RICE," *EJ* 57, viii (Nov., 1968): 1143-6.

Geetha, P., "Kamala Markandaya: An Interpretation," *ComQ* 3, ix (Dec., 1978): 100-3.

Iyengar, K.R.S., *Indian Writing in English*, 445-7.

Rao, K. S. N., "Kamala Markandaya: The Novelist as Craftsman," *IWT* 3, ii (Apr.-June, 1969): 39-40.

NECTAR IN A SIEVE

Adkins, Joan F., "Kamala Markandaya: Indo-Anglian Conflict as Unity," *JSoAL* 10, i (Fall, 1974): 92-5.

Argyle, Barry, "Kamala Markandaya's NECTAR IN A SIEVE," *ArielE* 4, i (1973): 35-45. Reprinted in *LHY* 15, i (1974): 73-84.

Geetha, P., "Kamala Markandaya: An Interpretation," *ComQ* 3, ix (Dec., 1978): 98-100.

Gooneratne, Yasmine, "'Traditional' Elements in the Fiction of Kamala Markandaya, R. K. Narayan, and Ruth Prawer Jhabvala," *WLWE* 15, i (Apr., 1976): 125-7.

Iyengar, K. R. S., *Indian Writing in English*, 438-9.

Murad, Orlene, "Indo-Anglian Fiction and Criticism," *IFR* 4 (Jan., 1977): 73-4.

Rao, K. S. N., "Kamala Markandaya: The Novelist as Craftsman," *IWT* 3, ii (Apr.-June, 1969): 32-5.

Venkatachari, K., "'Sense of Life' in Kamala Markandaya's
NECTAR IN A SIEVE," *OJES* 9, i (1972): 55-9.

Weir, Ann L., "Worlds Apart? Feminine Consciousness in
Markandaya's NECTAR IN A SIEVE and THE COFFER
DAMS," *CIEFLB* 13, ii (1977): 71-85.

THE NOWHERE MAN

Asnani, Shyam M., "Kamala Markandaya's Later Novels,"
Triveni 48, iv (Jan.-Mar., 1980): 25-7.

_____, "Quest for Identity Theme in Three Commonwealth
Novels," in Srivastava, A. K., ed., *Alien Voice*, 135-6.

Geetha, P., "Kamala Markandaya: An Interpretation," *ComQ* 3,
ix (Dec., 1978): 105-7.

Jain, Jasbir, "The Novels of Kamala Markandaya," *IndL* 18, ii
(1975): 36-8.

Mukherjee, Meenakshi, "The Theme of Displacement in Anita
Desai and Kamala Markandaya," *WLWE* 17, i (Apr., 1978):
225-33.

Sarma, S. Krishna, "Two Recent Novels of Kamala Markandaya," *Triveni* 45, iii (Oct.-Dec., 1976): 28-32.

POSSESSION

Adkins, Joan F., "Kamala Markandaya: Indo-Anglian Conflict
as Unity," *JSoAL* 10, i (Fall, 1974): 99-101.

Dale, James, "Sexual Politics in the Novels of Kamala Markandaya," *WLWE* 21, ii (Summer, 1982): 348-50.

Iyengar, K.R.S., *Indian Writing in English*, 443-5.

Jain, Jasbir, "The Novels of Kamala Markandaya," *IndL* 18, ii
(1975): 36-8.

Rao, K.S.N., "Kamala Markandaya: The Novelist as Craftsman," *IWT* 3, ii (Apr.-June, 1969): 38-9.

_____, "Religious Elements in Kamala Markandaya's Nov-
els," *ArielE* 8, i (Jan., 1977): 40-5.

A SILENCE OF DESIRE

Iyengar, K.R.S., *Indian Writing in English*, 441-3.

Mukherjee, M., *Twice Born Fiction*, 112-15.

Rao, K.S.N., "Kamala Markandaya: The Novelist as Craftsman," *IWT* 3, ii (Apr.-June, 1969): 37-8.

_____, "Religious Elements in Kamala Markandaya's Nov-
els," *ArielE* 8, i (Jan., 1977): 38-40.

Thumboo, Edwin, "Kamala Markandaya's A SILENCE OF DE-
SIRE," *JIWE* 8, i-ii (Jan.-July, 1980): 108-36.

SOME INNER FURY

Adkins, Joan F., "Kamala Markandaya: Indo-Anglian Conflict
as Unity," *JSoAL* 10, i (Fall, 1974): 95-9.

Aithal, S. Krishnamoorthy, and Rashmi Aithal, "East-West Encounter in Four Indo-English Novels," *ACLALSB* 6, i (Nov.,
1982): 1-16.

Iyengar, K.R.S., *Indian Writing in English*, 439-41.

Rao, K.S.N., "Kamala Markandaya: The Novelist as Craftsman," *IWT* 3, ii (Apr.-June, 1969): 35-7.

TWO VIRGINS

Asnani, Shyam M., "Kamala Markandaya's Later Novels,"
Triveni 48, iv (Jan.-Mar., 1980): 27-8.

Jain, Jasbir, "The Novels of Kamala Markandaya," *IndL* 18, ii
(1975): 41-3.

Rao, K.S.N., "Religious Elements in Kamala Markandaya's
Novels," *ArielE* 8, i (Jan., 1977): 48-50.

Rubenstein, Roberta, "Kamala Markandaya's TWO VIRGINS,"
WLWE 13 (1974): 225-30.

Sarma, S. Krishna, "Two Recent Novels of Kamala Markandaya," *Triveni* 45, iii (Oct.-Dec., 1976): 32-5.

BIBLIOGRAPHY

Rao, Susheela N., "A Bibliography of Kamala Markandaya,"
WLWE 20, ii (Autumn, 1981): 344-50.

MARKFIELD, WALLACE, 1926-

GENERAL

Bruccoli, Matthew J., "Wallace Markfield," in *Conversations with
Writers I*, 217-36.

Friedman, Melvin J., "The Enigma of Unpopularity and Critical
Neglect: The Case for Wallace Markfield," in Filler, L., ed.,
Seasoned Authors for a New Season, 33-42. Also in *RCF* 2, i
(Spring, 1982): 36-44.

O'Brien, John, "Interview with Wallace Markfield," *RCF* 2, i
(Spring, 1982): 5-29.

TO AN EARLY GRAVE

Hyman, Stanley E., *Standards*, 214-18.

Pinsker, Sanford, " 'Whoosh and Gaah!' The New York Intellectuals in Wallace Markfield's TO AN EARLY GRAVE,"
RCF 2, i (Spring, 1982): 29-36.

YOU COULD LIVE IF THEY LET YOU

Bender, Steven L.., "Wrestling with Idealization: Wallace Markfield's YOU COULD LIVE IF THEY LET YOU," *RCF* 2, i
(Spring, 1982): 56-9.

MARQUAND, JOHN PHILLIPS, 1893-1960

GENERAL

Allen, W., *Modern Novel*, 183-5.

Auchincloss, Louis, "Marquand and O'Hara: The Novel of
Manners," *Nation* (Nov. 19, 1960): 383-4. Also in Auchincloss, L., *Reflections of a Jacobite*, Boston: Houghton-Mifflin,
1961, 142-8.

Beach, J. W., *American Fiction*, 253-70.

Benedict, Stewart H., "The Pattern of Determinism in J. P.
Marquand's Novels," *BSTCF* 2, ii (Winter, 1961-62): 60-4.

Blankenship, R., *American Literature*, 751-5.

Brady, Charles A., "John Phillips Marquand: Martini-Age Victorian," in Gardiner, H. C., ed., *Fifty Years of the American
Novel*, 107-34.

Brown, John M., and Maxwell Geismar, "John P. Marquand:
The Man and the Writer," *SatR* 43 (Aug. 13, 1960): 14-15, 39.

Cochran, Robert W., "In Search of Perspective: A Study of the
Serious Novels of John P. Marquand," *DA* 18 (1958): 1427-28.

Cole, Robert R., "Money and Happiness in the Novels of John
P. Marquand," *BForum* 6, i (1982): 37-43.

Elliston, Angela C., "John P. Marquand and the Career Novel," *DAI* 34 (1974): 5964A.

Geismar, M., *American Moderns*, 161-4.

Glick, Nathan, "Marquand's Vanishing American Aristocracy: Good Manners and the Good Life," *Ctary* 9 (May, 1950): 435-41.

Greene, George, "John Marquand: The Reluctant Prophet," *NER* 2, iv (1980): 614-24.

_____, "A Tunnel from Persepolis: The Legacy of John Marquand," *QQ* 73 (Autumn, 1966): 345-56.

Gross, L., *Angry Decade*, 208-12.

_____, "The High-Level Formula of J. P. Marquand," *ASch* 21 (Autumn, 1952): 443-53.

Harris, Bennett, "The Literary Achievement of John P. Marquand," *DA* 23 (1962): 1701-2.

Hicks, Granville, "Marquand of Newburyport," *Harpers* 200 (Apr., 1950): 101-8.

Holman, Hugh, *John P. Marquand* (UMPAW, 46), Minneapolis: Un. of Minnesota, 1965.

Johnson, Robert O., "Mr. Marquand and Lord Tennyson," *RS* 32 (Mar., 1964): 28-38.

Kazin, Alfred, "John P. Marquand and the American Failure," *Atlantic* 202 (Nov., 1958): 152-6.

Kuhlman, Thomas A., "The Humane Social Criticism of John P. Marquand," *DA* 28 (1968): 3188A-89A.

Millgate, M., *American Social Fiction*, 182-5.

Oppenheimer, Franz M., "Lament for Unbought Grace: The Novels of John P. Marquand," *AR* 18 (Spring, 1958): 41-61.

Prescott, O., *In My Opinion*, 174-9.

Roberts, Kenneth, "The Memories of John P. Marquand," *SatR* 39 (Sept. 15, 1956): 14-15.

Smith, William J., "J. P. Marquand, Esq.," *Cweal* 69 (Nov. 7, 1958): 148-50.

Steiner, George, "Marquand Country," *T&T* (Oct. 10, 1959): 1096+.

Tuttleton, J. W., *Novel of Manners in America*, 207-35.

Van Gelder, Robert, "An Interview with a Best-Selling Author: John Marquand," *Cosmopolitan* 122 (Mar., 1947): 18, 150-2.

_____, *Writers on Writing*, 38-41.

Wagenknecht, E., *Cavalcade of the American Novel*, 438-43.

Walker, Dorothea R., "Failure to Protest: The Tragedy of J. P. Marquand's Apley, Pulham, and Wayde," *NassauR* 2, i (Spring, 1970): 15-22.

Weeks, Edward, "John P. Marquand," *Atlantic* 206 (Oct., 1960): 74-6.

Workman, J. Brooke, "John P. Marquand: The Sources of Social Ambivalence, 1921-1937," *DA* 29 (1969): 4029A.

B. F.'S DAUGHTER

Gross, J. J., *John P. Marquand*, 101-10.

Oppenheimer, Franz, "Lament for Unbought Grace: The Novels of John P. Marquand," *AR* 18 (Spring, 1958): 51-2.

H. M. PULHAM, ESQUIRE (DON'T ASK QUESTIONS, English Title)

Greene, George, "A Tunnel from Persepolis: The Legacy of John Marquand," *QQ* 73 (Autumn, 1966): 350-1.

Gross, J. J., *John P. Marquand*, 64-83.

Johnson, Robert O., "Mr. Marquand and Lord Tennyson," *RS* 32 (1964): 29-32.

Marquand, John P., "Apley, Wickford Point, and Pulham: My Early Struggles," *Atlantic* 198 (Sept., 1956): 73-4.

Oppenheimer, Franz, "Lament for Unbought Grace: The Novels of John P. Marquand," *AR* 18 (Spring, 1958): 46-8.

Walker, Dorothea, R., "Failure to Protest: The Tragedy of J. P. Marquand's Apley, Pulham, and Wayde," *NassauR* 2, i (Spring, 1970): 20-2.

THE LATE GEORGE APLEY

Ballowe, James, "Marquand and Santayana: Apley and Alden," *MarkhamR* 2, v (Feb., 1971): 92-4.

Beach, J. W., *American Fiction*, 259-70.

Eisinger, Charles E., "Class and American Fiction: The Aristocracy in Some Novels of the Thirties," in Lanzinger, K., ed., *Americana-Austriaca*, 138-40.

Goodwin, George, Jr., "The Last Hurrahs: George Apley and Frank Skeffington," *MR* 1 (May, 1960): 461-71.

Gordon, Edward, "What Happened to Humor?" *EJ* 47 (1958): 127-33.

Greene, George, "A Tunnel from Persepolis: The Legacy of John Marquand," *QQ* 73 (Autumn, 1966): 343-9.

Gross, J. J., *John P. Marquand*, 31-50.

Johnson, Robert O., "John P. Marquand and the Novel of Manners," *DA* 25 (1965): 7271-72.

_____, "Mary Monahan: Marquand's Sentimental Slip?" *RS* 33 (Dec., 1965): 208-13.

Macauley, Robie, "Let Me Tell You About the Rich...," *KR* 27 (Autumn, 1965): 664-6.

Marquand, John P., "Apley, Wickford Point, and Pulham: My Early Struggles," *Atlantic* 198 (Sept., 1956): 71-2.

Oppenheimer, Franz, "Lament for Unbought Grace: The Novels of John P. Marquand," *AR* 18 (Spring, 1958): 41-5.

Stuckey, W. J., *Pulitzer Prize Novels*, 112-16.

Tuttleton, J. W., *Novel of Manners in America*, 212-20.

Walker, Dorothea R., "Failure to Protest: The Tragedy of John P. Marquand's Apley, Pulham and Wayde," *Nassau Rev.* 2, i (Spring, 1970): 19-20.

Warren, Austin, "The Last Puritans," *The New England Conscience*, Ann Arbor: Un. of Michigan Pr., 1966, 195-201.

LIFE AT HAPPY KNOLL

Cosman, N., "Speakable Gentleman," *Nation* 185 (Aug. 3, 1957): 56-7.

MELVILLE GOODWIN, U.S.A.

Geismar, Maxwell, in *SatR* 34 (Sept. 19, 1951): 11. Also in Geismar, M., *American Moderns*, 159-61.

Gross, J. J., *John P. Marquand*, 127-40.

Johnson, Robert O., "Mr. Marquand and Lord Tennyson," *RS* 32 (1964): 35-8.

Oppenheimer, Franz, "Lament for Unbought Grace: The Novels of John P. Marquand," *AR* 18 (Spring, 1958): 58-60.

POINT OF NO RETURN

Geismar, Maxwell, in *NYTBR* (Mar. 6, 1949): 4. Also in Geismar, M., *American Moderns*, 156-9.

Greene, George, "A Tunnel from Persepolis: The Legacy of John Marquand," *QQ* 73 (Autumn, 1966): 351-2.

Gross, J. J., *John P. Marquand*, 111-26.

Haugh, Robert F., "The Dilemma of John P. Marquand," *MAQR* 59 (Dec. 6, 1952): 19-24.

Hicks, Granville, "John Marquand of Newburyport," *Harpers* 200 (Apr., 1950): 101-8.

Johnson, Robert O., "John P. Marquand and the Novel of Manners," *DA* 25 (1965): 7271-72.

_____, "Mr. Marquand and Lord Tennyson," *RS* 32 (1964): 32-5.

Oppenheimer, Franz, "Lament for Unbought Grace: The Novels of John P. Marquand," *AR* 18 (Spring, 1958): 52-7.

Scott, W. B., in *Furioso* 4 (Summer, 1949): 76-8.

Tuttleton, J. W., *Novel of Manners in America*, 220-31.

Van Nostrand, Albert D., "After Marquand, the Deluge," *EJ* 48 (Feb., 1959): 55-65 *passim*.

_____, "Fiction's Flagging Man of Commerce," *EJ* 48 (Jan., 1959): 6-11.

REPENT IN HASTE

Gross, J. J., *John P. Marquand*, 96-101.

SINCERELY, WILLIS WAYDE

Gross, J. J., *John P. Marquand*, 141-52.

Oppenheimer, Franz, "Lament for Unbought Grace: The Novels of John P. Marquand," *AR* 18 (Spring, 1958): 57-8.

Walker, Dorothea R., "Failure to Protest: The Tragedy of J. P. Marquand's Apley, Pulham, and Wayde," *Nassau Rev.* 2, i (Spring, 1970): 17-19.

SO LITTLE TIME

Gray, J., *On Second Thought*, 91-3.

Gross, J. J., *John P. Marquand*, 84-96.

Oppenheimer, Franz, "Lament for Unbought Grace: The Novels of John P. Marquand," *AR* 18 (Spring, 1958): 50-1.

WICKFORD POINT

Beach, J. W., *American Fiction*, 254-9.

Eisinger, Charles E., "Class and American Fiction: The Aristocracy in Some Novels of the Thirties," in Lanzinger, K., ed., *Americana-Austiaca*, 140-1.

Gray, J., *On Second Thought*, 88-90.

Greene, George, "A Tunnel from Persepolis: The Legacy of John Marquand," *QQ* 73 (Autumn, 1966): 349-50.

Gross, J. J., *John P. Marquand*, 51-63.

Marquand, John P., "Apley, Wickford Point, and Pulham: My Early Struggles," *Atlantic* 197 (Sept., 1956): 72-3.

Oppenheimer, Franz, "Lament for Unbought Grace: The Novels of John P. Marquand," *AR* 18 (Spring, 1958): 48-50.

WOMEN AND THOMAS HARROW

Gardiner, H. C., "Hero as Yo-Yo," *America* 100, ii (Oct. 11, 1958): 51-53. Also in Gardiner, H. C., *In All Conscience*, 126-7.

Greene, George, "A Tunnel from Persepolis: The Legacy of John Marquand," *QQ* 73 (Autumn, 1966): 352-6.

Gross, J. J., *John P. Marquand*, 158-75.

Johnson, Robert O., "John P. Marquand and the Novel of Manners," *DA* 25 (1965): 7271-72.

Kazin, A., *Contemporaries*, 122-30.

_____, "John P. Marquand and the American Failure," *Atlantic* 202 (Nov., 1958): 152-6.

Smith, William J., "J. P. Marquand, Esq." *Cweal* 69 (Nov. 7, 1958): 148-50.

Tuttleton, J. W., *Novel of Manners in America*, 231-5.

BIBLIOGRAPHY

Gross, J. J., *John P. Marquand*, 181-5.

White, William, "John P. Marquand Since 1950," *BB* 21 (May-Aug., 1956): 230-4.

_____, "Marquandiana," *BB* 20 (Jan.-Apr., 1950): 8-12.

MARSHALL, PAULE, 1929-

GENERAL

Brown, Lloyd W., "The Rhythms of Power in Paule Marshall's Fiction," *Novel* 7, ii (Winter, 1974): 159-67.

Cook, John, "Whose Child? The Fiction of Paule Marshall," *CLAJ* 24, i (Sept., 1980): 1-15.

Kapai, Leela, "Dominant Themes and Technique in Paule Marshall's Fiction," *CLAJ* 16, i (Sept., 1972): 49-59.

Keizs, Marcia, "Themes and Style in the Works of Paule Marshall," *NALF* 9 (Fall, 1975): 67, 71-6.

Lacovia, R. M., "Migration and Transmutation in the Novels of McKay, Marshall, and Clarke," *JBS* 7, iv (June, 1977): 437-54.

Marshall, P., "Shaping the World of My Art," *NewL* 40, i (Fall, 1973): 97-112.

BROWN GIRL, BROWNSTONES

Benston, Kimberly W., "Architectural Imagery and Unity in Paule Marshall's BROWN GIRL, BROWNSTONES," *NALF* 9 (Fall, 1975): 67-70.

Christian, B., *Black Women Novelists*, 81-104, 133-6.

Cook, John, "Whose Child? The Fiction of Paule Marshall," *CLAJ* 24, i (Sept., 1980): 3-9.

Miller, Adam D., in *Black Scholar* 3, ix (1972): 56-8.

O'Banner, Bessie M., "A Study of Black Heroines in Four Selected Novels (1929-1959) by Four Black American Women Novelists: Zora Neale Hurston, Nella Larson, Paule Marshall and Ann Lane Petry," *DAI* 43 (1982): 447A.

Schneider, Deborah, "A Search for Selfhood: Paule Marshall's BROWN GIRL, BROWNSTONES," in Bruck, P., and W. Karrer, eds., *Afro-American Novel Since 1960*, 53-73.

THE CHOSEN PLACE, THE TIMELESS PEOPLE

Braithwaite, Edward, "Rehabilitations," *CritQ* 13, ii (Summer, 1971): 175-83.

_____, "West Indian History and Society in the Art of Paule Marshall's Novel," *JBS* 1, ii (Dec., 1970): 225-38.

Christian, B., *Black Women Novelists*, 104-36, 247-53.

Cook, John, "Whose Child? The Fiction of Paule Marshall," *CLAJ* 24, i (Sept., 1980): 11-15.

Nazareth, Peter, "Colonial Institutions, Colonized People," *Busara* 6, i (1975): 49-64.

_____, "Paule Marshall's Timeless People," *NewL* 40, i (Fall, 1973): 113-31.

Schraufnagel, N., *From Apology to Protest*, 137-9.

Stoelting, Winifred L., "Time Past and Time Present: The Search for Variable Links in THE CHOSEN PLACE, THE TIMELESS PEOPLE," *CLAJ* 16, i (Sept., 1972): 60-71.

MASTERS, JOHN, 1914-

GENERAL

Mellors, John, "Noble Savages: The Novels of John Masters," *LonM* 14, iv (Oct.-Nov., 1974): 57-64.

Woodcock, George, "The Sometimes Sahibs: Two Post-Independence British Novelists of India," *QQ* 86, i (Spring, 1979): 39-49.

MATHERS, PETER, 1931-

GENERAL

Clancy, Laurie, "An Interview with Peter Mathers," *ALS* 8 (1977): 197-201.

Mathers, Peter, "Extractions," *Southerly* 31, iii (1971): 210-15.

TRAP

Burns, Robert, "The Underdog-Outsider: The Achievement of [Peter] Mather's TRAP," *Meanjin* 29, i (Autumn, 1970): 95-105.

Buckley, Vincent, "Peter Mathers' TRAP," *ArielE* 5, iii (July, 1974): 115-27.

Clancy, L. J., "Trap for Young Players: Peter Mathers' Novel," *Meanjin* 25 (1966): 484-8.

Daniel, Helen, "Narrator and Outsider in TRAP and JOHNNO," *Southerly* 37 (1977): 184-95.

O'Hearn, D. J., "Re-Reading Peter Mathers," *Overland* 85 (Oct., 1981): 47-58.

THE WORT PAPERS

Clancy, L. J., "Peter Mathers' Words," *Meanjin* 33, iii (Sept., 1974): 271-7.

Daniel, Helen, "The Picaro Encaverned: Peter Mathers' THE WORT PAPERS," *ArielE* 10, ii (1979): 3-15.

O'Hearn, D. J., "Re-Reading Peter Mathers," *Overland* 85 (Oct., 1981): 47-58.

MATTHEWS, JACK (JOHN HAROLD MATTHEWS) 1925-

GENERAL

DeMott, Robert, "Talking with Jack Matthews," *Ohioana Quart.* 23 (1980): 4-11.

Suderman, Elmer F., "Jack Matthews and the Shape of Human Feelings," *Crit* 21, i (1979): 38-48.

PICTURES OF THE JOURNEY BACK

Smith, David, "The Appetite for Life So Ravenous," *Shen* 25, iv (Summer, 1974): 49-55.

Suderman, Elmer F., "Jack Matthews and the Shape of Human Feelings," *Crit* 21, i (1979): 38-43.

THE ALE OF ASA BEAN

Lindberg, Stanley W., "One Alternative to Black Humor: The Satire of Jack Matthews," *StCS* 1 (1974): 17-26.

MATTHIESSEN, PETER, 1927-

AT PLAY IN THE FIELDS OF THE LORD

Patterson, Richard F., "AT PLAY IN THE FIELDS OF THE LORD: The Imperialist Idea and the Discovery of Self," *Crit* 21, ii (1979): 5-14.

FAR TORTUGA

Grove, James P., "Pastoralism and Anti-Pastoralism in Peter Matthiessen's FAR TORTUGA," *Crit* 21, ii (1979): 15-2.

BIBLIOGRAPHY

Grove, Jamesa P., "A Peter Matthiessen Checklist," *Crit* 21, ii (1979): 30-8.

MAUGHAM, ROBIN (MAUGHAM, ROBERT CECIL ROMER), 1916-1981

THE SERVANT

Feldstein, Elayne P., "From Novel to Film: The Impact of Harold Pinter on Robin Maugham's THE SERVANT," *SHum* 5, ii (1976): 9-14.

Gill, Richard, "Was Uncle Willie a Source for Robin Maugham's THE SERVANT," *JML* 8 (1980): 156-60.

MAXWELL, WILLIAM (KEEPERS), 1908-

SO LONG, SEE YOU TOMORROW

Maxfield, James F., "Memory and Imagination in William Maxwell's SO LONG, SEE YOU TOMORROW," *Crit* 24, i (Fall, 1982): 21-37.

THEY CAME LIKE SWALLOWS

Summers, Hollis, in Madden, D., ed., *Discoveries*, 87-94.

MAYFIELD, JULIAN, 1928-

GENERAL

O'Brien, John, ed., *Interviews with Black Writers*, 141-51.

THE GRAND PARADE

Schraufnagel, N., *From Apology to Protest*, 180-2.

THE HIT

Schraufnagel, N., *From Apology to Protest*, 95-6.

MCCARTHY, CORMAC, 1933-

GENERAL

Ditsky, John, "Further into Darkness: The Novels of Cormac McCarthy," *HC* 18, ii (Apr., 1981): 1-11.

Schafer, William J., "Cormac McCarthy: The Hard Wages of Original Sin," *AppalJ* 4, ii (Winter, 1977): 105-19.

CHILD OF GOD

Coles, Robert, "The Stranger," *NY* 50 (Aug. 26, 1974): 87-90.
Schafer, William J., "Cormac McCarthy: The Hard Wages of Sin," *AppalJ* 4, ii (Winter, 1977): 114-18.

THE ORCHARD KEEPER

Schafer, William J., "Cormac McCarthy: The Hard Wages of Sin," *AppalJ* 4, ii (Winter, 1977): 105-11.

OUTER DARK

Schafer, William J., "Cormac McCarthy: The Hard Wages of Sin," *AppalJ* 4, ii (Winter, 1977): 111-14.

MCCARTHY, MARY, 1912-1989

GENERAL

Aldridge, J. W., "Mary McCarthy: Princess Among the Trolls," *Time to Murder and Create*, 95-132.
Auchincloss, L., *Pioneers and Caretakers*, 170-86.
Baumbach, J., *Landscape of Nightmare*, 8-9.
Brower, Brook, "Mary McCarthyism," *Esquire* 58 (July, 1962): 62-7, 113.
Chamberlain, John, "The Conservative Miss McCarthy," *NatR* 15 (Oct. 22, 1963): 353-5.
————, "The Novels of Mary McCarthy," in Balakian, N., and C. Simmons, eds., *Creative Present*, 241-55.
Cook, Bruce, "Mary McCarthy: One of Ours?" *CathW* 199 (Apr., 1964): 34-42.
Eisinger, C. E., *Fiction of the Forties*, 128-35.
Enright, D. J., "Contrary Wise: The Writings of Mary McCarthy," *NStat* (July 27, 1962): 115-16. Also in Enright, D. J., *Conspirators and Poets*, 127-33.
Fitch, Robert E., "The Cold Eye of Mary McCarthy," *NRep* 138 (May 5, 1958): 17-19.
Grumbach, D., *Company She Kept*.
Hardy, W. S., *Mary McCarthy*.
Hardwick, E., *View of My Own*, 33-9.
Hewitt, Rosalie, "A 'Home Address for the Self': Mary McCarthy's Autobiographical Journey," *JNT* 12, ii (Spring, 1982): 95-104.
Martin, Wendy, "The Satire and Moral Vision of Mary McCarthy," in Cohen, S. B., ed., *Comic Relief*, 187-206.
McKenzie, B., *Mary McCarthy*.
Myers, Mitzi, "You Can't Catch Me: Mary McCarthy's Evasive Comedy," *RFI* 3, ii-iii (1977-78): 58-69. [Not seen.]
Niebuhr, Elisabeth, "The Art of Fiction 27: Mary McCarthy," *ParisR* 27 (Winter-Spring, 1962): 58-94. Also in *Writers at Work*, 2nd ser., 283-315.
Ohmann, Carol B., and Richard Ohmann, "Class Notes from Vassar," *Cweal* 79 (Sept. 27, 1963): 12-15.
Ross, T. J., "Passion—Moral and Otherwise," *NRep* 139 (Aug. 18, 1958): 23-6.
Schleuter, Paul, "The Dissections of Mary McCarthy," in Moore, H. T., ed., *Contemporary American Novelists*, 53-64.
Stock, I., *Mary McCarthy*.
Symons, J., "That Elegant Miss McCarthy," *Critical Occasions*, 90-5.

Trouard, Dawn, "Mary McCarthy's Dilemma: The Double Bind of Satiric Elitism," *PCL* 7 (1981): 98-109.
Widmer, Eleanor, "Finally a Lady: Mary McCarthy," in French, W., ed., *Fifties*, 93-102.

BIRDS OF AMERICA

Aldridge, John W., "Egalitarian Snobs," *SatR* 54 (May 8, 1971): 21-4. Also as "Good Housekeeping with Mary McCarthy," in Aldridge, J. W., *Devil in the Fire*, 220-3.
Hardy, W. S., *Mary McCarthy*, 122-40.
Inoue, Fumiko, " 'Nature is Dead' in Mary McCarthy's BIRDS OF AMERICA," in *Collected Essays by Members of the Faculty in Commemoration of the 20th Anniversary*, No. 17. Tokyo: Kyoritsu Women's Jr. College, 1973, 46-58.
Martin, Wendy, "The Satire and Moral Vision of Mary McCarthy," in Cohen, S. B., ed., *Comic Relief*, 202-3.
Zlobin, G., "An Exercise in Kantianism," in Vroon, R., tr., *20th Century American Literature: A Soviet View*, 443-8.

CANNIBALS AND MISSIONARIES

Hardy, W. S., *Mary McCarthy*, 168-94.

A CHARMED LIFE

Auchincloss, L., *Pioneers and Caretakers*, 178-80.
Grumbach, D., *Company She Kept*, 174-80.
Hardy, W. S., *Mary McCarthy*, 56-76.
Martin, Wendy, "The Satire and Moral Vision of Mary McCarthy," in Cohen, B. S., ed., *Comic Relief*, 196-9.
McKenzie, B., *Mary McCarthy*, 122-34.
Podhoretz, Norman, "Gibbsville and New Leeds: The America of John O'Hara and Mary McCarthy," *Ctary* 21 (Mar., 1956): 271-2. Also in Podhoretz, N., *Doings and Undoings*, 81-7.
Schleuter, Paul, "The Dissections of Mary McCarthy," in Moore, H. T., ed., *Contemporary American Novelists*, 59-61.
Stock, I., *Mary McCarthy*, 29-35.
Widmer, Eleanor, "Finally a Lady: Mary McCarthy," in French, W., ed., *Fifties*, 99-101.

THE COMPANY SHE KEEPS

Grumbach, D., *Company She Kept*, 91-111.
Hardy, W. S., *Mary McCarthy*, 29-55.
Hewitt, Rosalie, "A 'Home Address for the Self': Mary McCarthy's Autobiographical Journey," *JNT* 12, ii (Spring, 1980): 97-100.
Martin, Wendy, "The Satire and Moral Vision of Mary McCarthy," in Cohen, S. B., ed., *Comic Relief*, 189-92.
Spacks, P. M., *Female Imagination*, 254-60. Also in Spacks, P. M., ed., *Contemporary Women Novelists*, 85-91.
Stock, I., *Mary McCarthy*, 14-20.

THE GROUP

Aldridge, John W., "Good Housekeeping with Mary McCarthy," in Aldridge, J. W., *Devil in the Fire*, 217-20.
————, "Mary McCarthy: Princess Among the Trolls," *Time to Murder and Create*, 95-100, 124-32.
Auchincloss, L., *Pioneers and Caretakers*, 181-4.
Cook, Bruce, "Mary McCarthy: One of Ours?" *CathW* 196 (Apr., 1964): 34-42.

DeMott, Benjamin, in *Harpers* 227 (Oct., 1963): 98, 102.

Glicksberg, C. I., *Sexual Revolution in Modern American Literature*, 190-6.

Grumbach, D., *Company She Kept*, 189-210.

Hardy, W. S., *Mary McCarthy*, 77-99.

Hicks, Granville, "The Group in Second Meeting," *SatR* (Feb. 22, 1964): 51-2.

McCarthy, Mary, "Letters to a Translator: About THE GROUP," *Encounter* 23, v (Nov., 1964): 69-71+.

McKenzie, B., *Mary McCarthy*, 134-54.

Mailer, Norman, "The Mary McCarthy Case," *NYRB* 1 (Oct. 17, 1963): 1-3. Also in Mailer, N., *Cannibals and Christians*, N.Y.: Dial, 1966, 133-40. Also as "The Case Against Mary McCarthy: A Review of THE GROUP," in Spacks, P. M., ed., *Contemporary Women Novelists*, 75-84.

Martin, Wendy, "The Satire and Moral Vision of Mary McCarthy," in Cohen, S. B., ed., *Comic Relief*, 199-202.

Mathewson, Ruth, "The Vassar Joke," *CUF* 6, iv (Fall, 1963): 10-16.

Nagy, Peter, "Mary McCarthy," *ALitASH* 20 (1978): 137-40.

Ohmann, Carol B., and Richard Ohmann, "Class Notes from Vassar," *Cweal* 79 (Sept. 17, 1963): 12-15.

Podhoretz, N., "Miss McCarthy and the Leopard's Spots," *Doings and Undoings*, 87-93.

Raban, J., "Character and Manners," *Techniques of Modern Fiction*, 97-100.

Rogers, Thomas, in *Ctary* 36 (Dec., 1963): 488-9.

Schlueter, Paul, "The Dissections of Mary McCarthy," in Moore, H. T., ed., *Contemporary American Novelists*, 61-2.

Soule, George, "Must a Novelist be an Artist?" *Carleton Miscellany* 5 (Spring, 1964): 92-8.

Stock, I., *Mary McCarthy*, 35-43.

Whitehorn, Katherine, "Three Women," *Encounter* 21 (Dec., 1963): 78-9.

THE GROVES OF ACADEME

Auchincloss, L., *Pioneers and Caretakers*, 176-8.

Chamberlain, John, "The Conservative Miss McCarthy," *NatR* 15 (Oct. 22, 1963): 353-5.

Eisinger, C. E., *Fiction of the Forties*, 133-5.

Grumbach, D., *Company She Kept*, 159-72.

Hardy, W. S., *Mary McCarthy*, 100-21.

Latham, Earl, "The Managerialization of Campus," *Public Administration Rev.* 19 (Winter, 1959): 48-57 *passim*.

Lyons, J. O., *College Novel in America*, 169-74.

McKenzie, B., *Mary McCarthy*, 112-21.

Millgate, M., *American Social Fiction*, 166-8.

Schlueter, Paul, "The Dissections of Mary McCarthy," in Moore, H. T., ed., *Contemporary American Novelists*, 57-9.

Schutter, Howard N., "Academic Freedom and the American College Novel of the Nineteen Fifties," *DA* 28 (1968): 5070A.

Walcutt, C. C., *Man's Changing Mask*, 292-4.

Widmer, Eleanor, "Finally a Lady: Mary McCarthy," in French, W., ed., *Fifties*, 97-8.

THE OASIS

Eisinger, C. E., *Fiction of the Forties*, 132-3.

Gottfried, Alex, and Sue Davidson, "Utopia's Children: An Interpretation of Three Political Novels," *Western Political Quarterly* 15 (Mar., 1962): 24-32.

Grumbach, D., *Company She Kept*, 128-47.

McKenzie, B., *Mary McCarthy*, 104-12.

Schlueter, Paul, "The Dissections of Mary McCarthy," in Moore, H. T., ed., *Contemporary American Novelists*, 56-7.

Stock, L., *Mary McCarthy*, 20-4.

Widmer, Eleanor, "Finally a Lady: Mary McCarthy," in French, W., ed., *Fifties*, 97-8.

McCULLERS, CARSON, 1917-1967

GENERAL

Armes, Nancy R., "The Feeder: A Study of the Fiction of Eudora Welty and Carson McCullers," *DAI* 36 (1975): 2817A.

Auchincloss, L., *Pioneers and Caretakers*, 161-9.

Baldanza, Frank, "Plato in Dixie," *GaR* 12 (Summer, 1958): 151-67.

Bauerly, Donna M., "Patterns of Imagery in Carson McCullers' Major Fiction," *DAI* 34 (1973): 2606A.

Buchen, Irving, "Carson McCullers, a Case of Convergence," *BuR* 21, i (Spring, 1973): 15-28.

_____, "Divine Collusion: The Art of Carson McCullers," *DR* 54, iii (Autumn, 1974): 529-41.

Bolsterli, Margaret, "'Bound' Characters in Porter, Welty, McCullers: The Prerevolutionary Status of Women in American Fiction," *BuR* 24, i (1978): 95-105. [Not seen.]

Carlson, Judith G., "The Dual Vision: Paradoxes, Opposites, and Doubles in the Novels of Carson McCullers," *DAI* 37 (1977): 7749A.

Carlton, Ann R., "Patterns in Carson McCullers' Portrayal of Adolescence," *DAI* 33 (1972): 302A.

Carney, Christina F., "A Study of Themes and Techniques in Carson McCullers' Prose Fiction," *DAI* 34 (1973): 307A-08A.

Carr, Virginia S, "Carson McCullers and the Search for Meaning," *DAI* 33 (1972): 2924A-25A.

Clark, Charlene K., "Carson McCullers and the Tradition of Romance," *DAI* 35 (1975): 5391A.

_____, "Pathos with a Chuckle: The Tragicomic Vision in the Novels of Carson McCullers," *StAH* 1 (Jan., 1975): 161-6.

Cook, R. M., *Carson McCullers*.

Dodd, Wayne D., "The Development of the Theme Through Symbol in the Novels of Carson McCullers," *GaR* 17 (Summer, 1963): 206-13.

Drake, Robert, "The Lonely Heart of Carson McCullers," *ChC* 85 (Jan. 10, 1968): 50-1.

Eckard, Ronald D., "The Sense of Place in the Fiction of Carson McCullers," *DAI* 36 (1976): 5295A.

Edmonds, D., *Carson McCullers*.

Eisinger, C. E., *Fiction of the Forties*, 243-58.

Evans, Oliver, "The Achievement of Carson McCullers," *EJ* 51 (May, 1962): 301-8.

_____, "The Case of Carson McCullers," *GaR* 18 (Spring, 1964): 40-5.

_____, "The Theme of Spiritual Isolation in Carson McCullers," in *New World Writing*, First Mentor Selection, N.Y.: New American Library, 1952, 297-310. Also in Rubin, L. D., Jr., and R. D. Jacobs, eds., *South*, 333-48.

Everett, Howard D., "Love and Alienation: The Sad, Dark Vision of Carson McCullers," *DAI* 36 (1975): 3711A-12A.

Felheim, Maxwell, in Moore, H. T., ed., *Contemporary American Novelists*, 48-53.

Folk, Barbara N., "The Sad, Sweet Music of Carson McCullers," *GaR* 16 (Spring, 1962): 202-9.

Gillespie, Sheena, "Dialectical Elements in the Fiction of Carson McCullers: A Comparative Critical Study," *DAI* 37 (1977): 5804A-05A.

Gossett, L. Y., "Dispossessed Love: Carson McCullers," *Violence in Recent Southern Fiction*, 159-77.

Graver, L., *Carson McCullers*.

Hamilton, Alice, "Loneliness and Alienation: The Life and Work of Carson McCullers," *DR* 50, ii (Summer, 1970): 215-29.

Hart, Jane, "Carson McCullers, Pilgrim of Loneliness," *GaR* 11 (Spring, 1957): 53-8.

Hassan, Ihab H., "Carson McCullers: The Alchemy of Love and Aesthetics of Pain," *MFS* 5 (Winter, 1959-60): 311-26. Also in Hassan, I., *Radical Innocence*, 205-11. Also in Waldmeir, J., ed., *Recent American Fiction*, 215-30.

Hendrick, George, "'Almost Everyone Wants to be the Lover': The Fiction of Carson McCullers," *BA* 42 (Summer, 1968): 389-91.

Hoffman, F. J., *Art of Southern Fiction*, 65-73.

Hunt, Tann H., "Humor in the Novels of Carson McCullers," *DAI* 34 (1973): 775A.

Johnson, Thomas H., "The Horror in the Mansion: Gothic Fiction in the Works of Truman Capote and Carson McCullers," *DAI* 34 (1973): 2630A.

Johnstoneaux, Raphael B., Jr., "Abandonment in the Major Works of Carson McCullers," *DAI* 42, iv (Oct., 1981): 1636A.

Joost, Nicholas, in Gardiner, H. C., ed., *Fifty Years of the American Novel*, 284-6.

Joyce, Edward T., "Race and Sex: Opposition and Identity in the Fiction of Carson McCullers," *DAI* 34 (1973): 3403A-04A.

Kohler, Dayton, "Carson McCullers: Variations on a Theme," *EJ* 40 (Oct., 1951): 415-22. Also in *CE* 13 (1951): 1-8.

Lubbers, Klaus, "The Necessary Order: A Study of the Theme and Structure in Carson McCullers' Fiction," *JA* 8 (1963): 187-204.

Malin, I., "Self-Love," *New American Gothic*, 19-26.

McCullers, Carson, "The Flowering Dream: Notes on Writing," *Esquire* 52 (Dec., 1959): 162-4.

McDowell, M. B., *Carson McCullers*.

McPherson, Hugh, "Carson McCullers: Lonely Huntress," *TamR* 11 (Spring, 1959): 28-40.

Meeker, Richard K., in Simonini, R. C., ed., *Southern Writers*, 184-6.

Millichap, Joseph R., "A Critical Reevaluation of Carson McCullers' Fiction," *DAI* 31 (1971): 4783A.

Okhoso, Yoshiko, "Solitary Love: Carson McCullers' Novels," in *American Literature of the 1940's*, 40-56.

Pachmuss, Temira, "Dostoevsky and America's Southern Women Writers: Parallels and Confluences," in Clayton, D. J., and G. Schaarschmidt, eds., *Poetica Slavica*, 116-20.

Presley, Delma E., "The Moral Function of Distortion in Southern Grotesque," *SAB* 37, ii (May, 1972): 37-43.

Raczkowska, Marzenna, "The Patterns of Love in Carson McCullers' Fiction," *SAP* 12 (1980): 169-76.

Rechnitz, Robert M., "Perception, Identity, and Grotesque: A Study of Three Southern Writers," *DA* 28 (1967): 2261A.

Roberts, Mary, "Imperfect Androgyny and Imperfect Love in the Works of Carson McCullers," *HSL* 12, ii (1980): 73-98.

Robinson, W. R., "The Life of Carson McCullers' Imagination," *SHR* 2 (Summer, 1968): 291-302.

Rodgers, Ann T., "The Search for Relationships in Carson McCullers," *DAI* 33 (1972): 4632A.

Rubin, Louis D., Jr., "Carson McCullers: The Aesthetics of Pain," *VQR* 53, ii (Spring, 1977): 265-83. Also in Rubin, L. D., Jr., *Gallery of Southerners*, 135-51.

Schorer, Mark, "McCullers and Capote: Basic Patterns," in Balakian, N., and C. Simmons, eds., *Creative Present*, 83-94. Also in Schorer, M., *World We Imagine*, 274-85.

Smith, Christopher M., "Self and Society: The Dialectic of Themes and Forms in the Novels of Carson McCullers," *DAI* 37 (1976): 2880A.

Smith, Simeon M., Jr.,. "Carson McCullers: A Critical Introduction," *DA* 25 (1964): 3583-84.

Sullivan, Margaret S., "Carson McCullers, 1917-1947: The Conversion of Experience," *DA* 28 (1968): 4648A.

Symons, J., "The Lonely Heart," *Critical Occasions*, 106-11.

Vickery, John B., "Carson McCullers: A Map of Love," *WSCL* 1, i (Winter, 1960): 13-24.

Walker, Sue B., "The Link in the Chain Called Love: A New Look at Carson McCullers' Novels," *MTJ* 18, iii (Winter, 1976-77): 8-12.

————, "A Science of Love: Love, Music, and Time in the Work of Carson McCullers," *DAI* 40 (1979): 1474A.

Wallace, Harry J., "'Lifelessness is the Only Abnormality': A Study of Love, Sex, Marriage, and Family in the Novels of Carson McCullers," *DAI* 37 (1976): 3630A-31A.

Westling, Louise, "The Perils of Adolescence in Flannery O'Connor and Carson McCullers," *FlOB* 8 (1979): 88-98.

Witt, Mary A., "A Study of the Adolescent in Carson McCullers' Fiction," *DAI* 36 (1975): 896A-97A.

THE BALLAD OF THE SAD CAFE

Auchincloss, L., *Pioneers and Caretakers*, 166-7.

Atunes, Futin B., "THE BALLAD OF THE SAD CAFE and 'The Sojourner': Common Themes and Images," *EAA* 3-4 (1979-80): 191-9.

Broughton, Panthea R., "Rejection of the Feminine in Carson McCullers' THE BALLAD OF THE SAD CAFE," *TCL* 20 (Jan., 1974): 34-43.

Clark, Charlene K., "Male-Female Pairs in Carson McCullers' THE BALLAD OF THE SAD CAFE and THE MEMBER OF THE WEDDING," *NConL* 9, i (1979): 11-12.

Cook, R. M., *Carson McCullers*, 84-104.

Edmonds, D., *Carson McCullers*, 19-24.

Eisinger, C. E., *Fiction of the Forties*, 256-8.

Evans, O., *Ballad of Carson McCullers*, 126-38.

————, "The Theme of Spiritual Isolation in Carson McCullers," in *New World Writing*, First Mentor Selection, N.Y.: New American Library, 1952, 304-10. Also in Rubin, L. D., Jr., and R. D. Jacobs, eds., *South*, 340-8.

Gaillard, Dawson F., "The Presence of the Narrator in Carson McCullers' THE BALLAD OF THE SAD CAFE," *MissQ* 25 (Fall, 1972): 419-27.

Graver, L., *Carson McCullers*, 24-33.

Gray, R., *Literature of Memory*, 267-71.

Griffith, Albert J., "Carson McCullers' Myth of the Sad Cafe," *GaR* 21 (Spring, 1967): 46-56.

Hassan, Ihab H., "Carson McCullers: The Alchemy of Love and Aesthetics of Pain," *MFS* 5 (Winter, 1959-60): 313-15. Also in Hassan, H., *Radical Innocence*, 223-6. Also in Waldmeir, J., ed., *Recent American Fiction*, 217-18, 227-30.

Hoffman, F. J., *Art of Southern Fiction*, 68-71.

Lubbers, Klaus, "The Necessary Order: A Study of Theme and Structure in Carson McCullers' Fiction," *JA* 8 (1963): 198-201.

McDowell, M. B., *Carson McCullers*, 64-79.

McNally, John, "The Introspective Narrator in THE BALLAD OF THE SAD CAFE," *SAB* 38, iv (No ., 1973): 40-4.

Millilchap, Joseph, "Carson McCullers' Literary Ballad," *GaR* 27 (Fall, 1973): 329-39.

Moore, Janice T., "McCullers' THE BALLAD OF THE SAD CAFE," *Expl* 29 (Nov., 1970): Item 27.

Ohkoso, Yoshiko, "Solitary Loss: Carson McCullers' Novels," in *American Literature in the 1940's*, 48-50.

Phillips, Robert S., "Dinesen's MONKEY and McCullers' BALLAD: A Study in Literary Affinity," *SSF* 1 (Spring, 1964): 184-90.

_____, "Painful Love, Carson McCullers' Parable," *SWR* 51 (Winter, 1966): 80-6.

Pollock-Chagas, Jeremy E., "Rosalina and Amelia: A Structural Approach to Narrative," *LBR* 12 ii (Winter, 1975): 263-72.

Rechnitz, Robert M., "The Failure of Love: The Grotesque in Two Novels by Carson McCullers," *GaR* 22 (Winter, 1968): 458-63.

Roberts, Mary, "Imperfect Androgyny and Imperfect Love in the Works of Carson McCullers," *HSL* 12, ii (1980): 93-5.

Schorer, Mark, "McCullers and Capote: Basic Patterns," in Balakian, N., and C. Simmons, eds., *Creative Present*, 92-3. Also in Schorer, M., *World We Imagine*, 282-3.

Vickery, John B., "Carson McCullers: A Map of Love," *WSCL* 1, i (Winter, 1960): 14-16.

Westling, Louise, "Carson McCullers' Amazon Nightmare," *MFS* 28, iii (Autumn, 1982): 465-73.

Whittle, Amberys R., "McCullers' 'The Twelve Mortal Men' and THE BALLAD OF THE SAD CAFE," *AN&Q* 18 (1980): 158-9.

CLOCK WITHOUT HANDS

Allen, W., *Modern Novel*, 136-7.

Auchincloss, L., *Pioneers and Caretakers*, 167-9.

Clark, Charlene, "Selfhood and the Southern Past: A Reading of Carson McCullers' CLOCK WITHOUT HANDS," *SLM* 1, ii (1975): 16-23.

Cook, R. M., *Carson McCullers*, 106-20.

Edmonds, D., *Carson McCullers*, 30-2.

Emerson, Donald, "The Ambiguities of CLOCK WITHOUT HANDS," *WSCL* 3, iii (Fall, 1962): 15-28.

Evans, Oliver, "The Achievement of Carson McCullers," *EJ* 51 (May, 1962): 306-8.

_____, *Ballad of Carson McCullers*, 170-82.

Ford, Nick A., "Search for Identity: A Critical Survey of Significant Belles-Lettres by and about Negroes Published in 1961," *Phylon* 23 (1962): 130-3.

Graver, L., *Carson McCullers*, 42-5.

Hartt, J. N., "The Return of Moral Passion," *YR* 51, ii (Winter, 1962): 300-1.

Hicks, Granville, "The Subtler Corruptions," *SatR* 44 (Sept. 23, 1961): 14-15, 49.

Hughes, Catherine, "A World of Outcasts," *Cweal* 75 (Oct. 13, 1961): 73-5.

Lubbers, Klaus, "The Necessary Order: A Study of Theme and Structure in Carson McCullers' Fiction," *JA* 8 (1963): 201-2.

McDowell, M. B., *Carson McCullers*, 96-116.

Okhoso, Yoshiko, "Solitary Love: Carson McCullers' Novels," in *American Literature in the 1940's*, 53-6.

Parker, Dorothy, "CLOCK WITHOUT HANDS Belongs in Yesterday's Ivory Tower," *Esquire* 56 (Dec., 1961): 72-3.

Presley, Delma E., "Carson McCullers' Descent to Earth," *Descant* 17, i (Fall, 1972): 54-60.

Rolo, Charles, "A Southern Drama," *Atlantic* 208 (Oct., 1961): 126-7.

Schorer, Mark, "McCullers and Capote: Basic Patterns," in Balakian, N., and C. Simmons, eds., *Creative Present*, 92-3. Also in Schorer, M., *World We Imagine*, 283-5.

Scott, Mary E., "An Existential Everyman," *WVUPP* 27 (1981): 82-8.

Snider, Clifton, "On Death and Dying: Carson McCullers' CLOCK WITHOUT HANDS," *MarkhamR* 11 (1982): 43-6.

Sullivan, Margaret S., in *GaR* 15 (Winter, 1961): 467-9.

Vidal, Gore, "The World Outside," *Reporter* 25 (Sept. 28, 1961): 50-2. Also in Vidal, G., *Rocking the Boat*, 178-83.

THE HEART IS A LONELY HUNTER

Aldridge, Robert, "Two Planetary Systems," in Peary, G., and R. Shatzkin, eds., *Modern American Novel and the Movies*, 119-30.

Allen, W., *Modern Novel*, 132-4.

Auchincloss, L., *Pioneers and Caretakers*, 161-3.

Bluefarb, S., "Jake Blount: Escape as Dead End," *Escape Motif in the American Novel*, 115-32.

Box, Patricia A., "Androgyny and the Musical Vision: A Study of Two Novels by Carson McCullers," *SoQ* 16, ii (1978): 117-23.

Carpenter, Frederick I., "The Adolescent in American Fiction," *EJ* 46 (1957): 316-17.

Cook, R. M., *Carson McCullers*, 20-45.

Durham, Frank, "God and No God in THE HEART IS A LONELY HUNTER," *SAQ* 56 (Autumn, 1957): 494-9.

Edmonds, D., *Carson McCullers*, 9-14.

Eisinger, C. E., *Fiction of the Forties*, 245-51.

Evans, O., *Ballad of Carson McCullers*, 98-117.

_____, "The Case of the Silent Singer: A Revaluation of THE HEART IS A LONELY HUNTER," *GaR* 19 (Summer, 1965): 188-203.

_____, "The Theme of Spiritual Isolation in Carson McCullers," in *New World Writing*, First Mentor Selection, N.Y.: New American Library, 1952, 298-300. Also in Rubin, L. D., Jr., and R. D. Jacobs, eds., *South*, 334-6.

Graver, L., *Carson McCullers*, 10-20.

Hassan, Ihab H., "Carson McCullers: The Alchemy of Love and the Aesthetics of Pain," *MFS* 5 (Winter, 1959-60): 315-18. Also in Hassan, I., *Radical Innocence*, 211-15. Also in Walmeir, J., ed., *Recent American Fiction*, 219-22.

Knowles, A. S., Jr., "Six Bronze Petals and Two Red: Carson McCullers in the Forties," in French, W., ed., *Forties*, 86-94.

Korenman, Joan S., "Carson McCullers' 'Proletarian Novel'," *StHum* 5, i (1976): 8-13.

Lubbers, Klaus, "The Necessary Order: A Study of Theme and Structure in Carson McCullers' Fiction," *JA* 8 (1963): 188-94.

MacDonald, Edgar E., "The Symbol of Unity in THE HEART IS A LONELY HUNTER," in Penninger, Frieda E., ed., *A Festschrift for Professor Marguerite Roberts, on the Occasion of Her Retirement from Westhampton College*, Richmond: Un. of Richmond, 1976, 168-87.

Madden, David, "The Paradox of the Need for Privacy and the Need for Understanding in Carson McCullers' THE HEART IS A LONELY HUNTER," *L&P* 17 (1967): 128-40.

Malin, I., *New American Gothic*, 54-7. Also in Malin, I., ed., *Psychoanalysis in American Fiction*, 258-60.

McDowell, M. B., *Carson McCullers*, 31-43.

McPherson, Hugo, "Carson McCullers: Lonely Huntress," *TamR* 11 (Spring, 1959): 31-4.

Millichap, Joseph R., "Distorted Matter and Disjunctive Forms: The Grotesque as Modernist Genre," *ArQ* 33, iv (Winter, 1977): 345-6.

_____, "The Realistic Structure of THE HEART IS A LONELY HUNTER," *TCL* 17, i (Jan., 1971): 11-17.

Mizuta, J., "Carson McCullers' THE HEART IS A LONELY HUNTER," *Rikkyo Review* 22 (1961): 79-95. [Not seen.]

Moore, Jack B., "Carson McCullers: The Heart is a Timeless Hunter," *TCL* 11 (July, 1965): 76-81.

Paden, Frances F., "Autistic Gestures in THE HEART IS A LONELY HUNTER," *MFS* 28, iii (Autumn, 1982): 453-63.

Rich, Nancy B., "The 'Ironic Parable of Fascism' in THE HEART IS A LONELY HUNTER," *SLJ* 9, ii (Spring, 1977): 108-23.

Roberts, Mary, "Imperfect Androgyny and Imperfect Love in the Works of Carson McCullers," *HSL* 12, ii (1980): 79-84.

Schorer, Mark, "McCullers and Capote: Basic Patterns," in Balakian, N., and C. Simmons, eds., *Creative Present*, 87-8. Also in Schorer, M., *World We Imagine*, 277-9.

Sherrill, Roland A., "McCullers' THE HEART IS A LONELY HUNTER," *KyR* 2 (1968): 5-17.

Smith, C. Michael, "'A Voice in a Fugue': Characters and Musical Structure in THE HEART IS A LONELY HUNTER," *MFS* 25, ii (Summer, 1979): 258-63.

Symons, J., "The Lonely Heart," *Critical Occasions*, 106-11.

Taylor, Horace, "THE HEART IS A LONELY HUNTER: A Southern Wasteland," in McNeir, Waldo, and Leo B. Levy, eds., *Studies in American Literature* (LSUSHS, No. 8), Baton Rouge: Louisiana State Un. Pr., 1960, 154-60.

Vickery, John B., "Carson McCullers: A Map of Love," *WSCL* 1, i (Winter, 1960): 16-18.

Westling, Louise, "Carson McCullers' Tomboys," *SHR* 14 (Fall, 1980): 341-4.

THE MEMBER OF THE WEDDING

Allen, W., *Modern Novel*, 134-5.

Auchincloss, L., *Pioneers and Caretakers*, 165-6.

Box, Patricia A., "Androgyny and the Musical Vision: A Study of Two Novels by Carson McCullers," *SoQ* 16, ii (1978): 117-23.

Bryant, J. H., *Open Decision*, 245-9.

Burger, P. A., "Carson McCullers: THE MEMBER OF THE WEDDING," *Crux* 10, iii (1976): 37-41.

Clark, Charlene K., "Male-Female Pairs in Carson McCullers' THE BALLAD OF THE SAD CAFE and THE MEMBER OF THE WEDDING," *NConL* 9, i (1979): 11-12.

Cook, R. M., *Carson McCullers*, 60-81.

DeMarr, Mary Jean, "Novel Into Play: Carson McCullers' Two Versions of THE MEMBER OF THE WEDDING," *IEJ* 9, i (1974): 25-32.

Edmonds, D., *Carson McCullers*, 24-9.

Eisinger, C. E., *Fiction of the Forties*, 254-6.

Evans, O., *Ballad of Carson McCullers*, 98-117.

_____, "The Theme of Spiritual Isolation in Carson McCullers," in *New World Writing*, First Mentor Selection, N.Y.: New American Library, 1952, 301-4. Also in Rubin, L. D., Jr., and R. D. Jacobs, eds., *South*, 337-40.

Gianetti, Louis D., "THE MEMBER OF THE WEDDING," *LFQ* 4 (1976): 28-38.

Graver, L., *Carson McCullers*, 33-42.

Hassan, Ihab B., "Carson McCullers: The Alchemy of Love and the Aesthetics of Pain," *MFS* 5 (Winter, 1959-60): 320-3. Also in Hassan, I., *Radical Innocence*, 219-23. Also in Waldmeir, J., ed., *Recent American Fiction*, 224-7.

Knowles, A. S., Jr., "Six Bronze Petals and Two Red: Carson McCullers in the Forties," in French, W., ed., *Forties*, 94-7.

Lubbers, Klaus, "The Necessary Order: A Study of Theme and Structure in Carson McCullers' Fiction," *JA* 8 (1963): 196-8.

Malin, I., *New American Gothic*, 57-9. Also in Malin, I., ed., *Psychoanalysis and American Fiction*, 261-2.

McDowell, M. B., *Carson McCullers*, 80-95.

Ohkoso, Yoshiko, "Solitary Love: Carson McCullers' Novels," in *American Literature in the 1940's*, 50-3.

Phillips, Robert S., "The Gothic Architecture of THE MEMBER OF THE WEDDING," *Ren* 16 (Winter, 1964): 59-72.

Roberts, Mary, "Imperfect Androgyny and Imperfect Love in the Works of Carson McCullers," *HSL* 12, ii (1980): 89-93.

Schorer, Mark, "McCullers and Capote: Basic Patterns," in Balakian, N., and C. Simmons, eds., *Creative Present*, 90-3. Also in Schorer, M., *World We Imagine*, 281-2.

Tinkham, Charles B., "The Member of the Sideshow," *Phylon* 18 (Fourth Quarter, 1958): 383-90.

Vickery, John B., "Carson McCullers: A Map of Love," *WSCL* 1, i (Winter, 1960): 21-3.

Westling, Louise, "Carson McCullers' Tomboys," *SHR* 14 (Fall, 1980): 344-50.

Wikborg, E. S. M., "Carson McCullers' THE MEMBER OF THE WEDDING: Aspects of Structure and Style," *DAI* 37 (1976): 1126.

REFLECTIONS IN A GOLDEN EYE

Auchincloss, L., *Pioneers and Caretakers*, 163-5.

Cook, R. M., *Carson McCullers*, 48-58.

Edmonds, D., *Carson McCullers*, 14-19.

Eisinger, C. E., *Fiction of the Forties*, 251-4.

Evans, O., *Ballad of Carson McCullers*, 60-71.

_____, "The Theme of Spiritual Isolation in Carson McCullers," *New World Writing*, First Mentor Selection, N.Y.: New American Library, 1952, 300-1. Also in Rubin, L. D., Jr., and R. D. Jacobs, eds., *South*, 336-7.

Graver, L., *Carson McCullers*, 20-4.

Hassan, Ihab H., "Carson McCullers: The Alchemy of Love and the Aesthetics of Pain," *MFS* (Winter, 1959-60): 318-20. Also In Hassan, I., *Radical Sophistication*, 216-18. Also in Waldmeir, J., *Recent American Fiction*, 222-4.

Hoffman, F. J., *Art of Southern Fiction*, 67-8.

Lubbers, Klaus, "The Necessary Order: A Study of Theme and Structure in Carson McCullers' Fiction," *JA* 8 (163): 194-6.

Mathis, Ray, "REFLECTIONS IN A GOLDEN EYE: Mythmaking in American Christianity," *RIL* 34 (Winter, 1970): 545-8.

McDowell, M. B., *Carson McCullers*, 44-64.

McPherson, Hugo, "Carson McCullers: Lonely Huntress," *TamR* 11 (Spring, 1959): 34-8.

Rechnitz, Robert M., "The Failure of Love: The Grotesque in Two Novels by Carson McCullers," *GaR* 22 (Winter, 1968): 454-8.

Roberts, Mary, "Imperfect Androgyny and Imperfect Love in the Works of Carson McCullers," *HSL* 12, ii (1980): 84-9.

Schorer, Mark, "McCullers and Capote: Basic Patterns," in Balakian, N., and C. Simmons, eds., *Creative Present*, 88-90. Also in Schorer, M., *World We Imagine*, 279-80.

Vickery, John B., "Carson McCullers: A Map of Love," *WSCL* 1, i (Winter, 1960): 18-21.

Williams, Tennessee, Introduction to REFLECTIONS IN A GOLDEN EYE, Norfolk: New Directions, 1950, i-xxi.

BIBLIOGRAPHY

Dorsey, James E., "Carson McCullers and Flannery O'Connor: A Checklist of Graduate Research," *BB* 32 (1975): 162-7.

Kiernan, Robert F., *Katherine Anne Porter and Carson McCullers: A Reference Guide*, Boston: Hall, 1976.

Phillips, Robert S., "Carson McCullers: 1956-1964: A Selected Checklist," *BB* 24 (Sept.-Dec., 1964): 113-16.

Shapiro, Adrian M., Jackson R. Bryer, and Kathleen Field, *Carson McCullers: A Descriptive Listing and Annotated Bibliography of Criticism*, N.Y.: Garland, 1980.

Stanley, William T., "Carson McCullers: 1965-1969, A Selected Checklist," *BB* 27, iv (Oct.-Dec., 1971): 162-7.

Stewart, Stanley, "Carson McCullers, 1940-1956, A Selected Checklist," *BB* 22 (Apr., 1959): 182-5.

MCCULLOUGH, COLLEEN, 1937-

THE THORN BIRDS

Brady, Veronica, "Colleen McCullough and the Savage God," *Quadrant* 24 (Aug., 1980): 48-52.

McKenzie, K. A., "The Logic of THE THORN BIRDS," *Overland* 73 (1978): 58-60.

MCELROY, JOSEPH, 1930-

GENERAL

LeClair, Thomas, "Interview with Joseph McElroy," *ChiR* 30, iv (1979): 84-95.

————, "Joseph McElroy and the Art of Excess," *ConL* 21, i (Winter, 1980): 15-37.

Tanner, Tony, "Toward an Ultimate Topography: The Work of Joseph McElroy," *TriQ* 36 (1976): 214-52.

ANCIENT HISTORY

LeClair, Thomas, "Joseph McElroy and the Art of Excess," *ConL* 21, i (Winter, 1980): 23-5.

Tanner, Tony, "Toward an Ultimate Topography: The Work of Joseph McElroy," *TriQ* 36 (1976): 233-9.

HIND'S KIDNAP

LeClair, Thomas, "Joseph McElroy and the Art of Excess," *ConL* 21, i (Winter, 1980): 21-3.

Tanner, Tony, "Toward an Ultimate Topography: The Work of Joseph McElroy," *TriQ* 36 (1976): 225-33.

LOOKOUT CARTRIDGE

LeClair, Thomas, "Joseph McElroy and the Art of Excess," *ConL* 21, i (Winter, 1980): 25-35.

Lhamon, W. T., Jr., in *NRep* (May 3, 1975): 28.

Tanner, Tony, "Toward an Ultimate Topography: The Work of Joseph McElroy," *TriQ* 36 (1976): 242-52.

PLUS

LeClair, Thomas, "Joseph Elroy and the Art of Excess," *ConL* 21, i (Winter, 1980): 35-7.

A SMUGGLER'S BIBLE

LeClair, Thomas, "Joseph McElroy and the Art of Excess," *ConL* 21, i (Winter, 1980): 19-21.

Tanner, Tony, "Toward an Ultimate Topography: The Work of Joseph McElroy," *TriQ* 36 (1976): 214-21.

MCEWAN, IAN (RUSSELL), 1948-

GENERAL

Hamilton, Ian, "Points of Departure," *New Rev* 5, ii (Autumn, 1978): 9-21. [Interview.]

Ricks, Christopher, "Adolescence and After: An Interview with Ian McEwan," *Listener* 101 (1979): 526-7.

Wise, David, "Caring, Cliches, Cliques, and Prof. Ricks," *HQ* 9 (1981): 51-8.

THE COMFORT OF STRANGERS

Banks, J. R., "A Gondola Named Desire," *CritQ* 24, ii (Summer, 1982): 27-31.

MCGAHERN, JOHN, 1934-

GENERAL

Garfitt, Roger, in Dunn, D., ed., *Two Decades of Irish Writing*, 221-4.

Molloy, F. C., "The Novels of John McGahern," *Crit* 19, i (1977): 5-27.

Paratte, Henri-D., "Conflicts in a Changing World: John McGahern," *CahiersI* 4-5 (1976): 311-27. Also in Rafroidi, P., and M. Harmon, eds., *Irish Novel in Our Time*, 311-23.

THE BARRACKS

Cronin, John, "THE DARK Is Not Light Enough: The Fiction of John McGahern," *Studies* 58 (Winter, 1958): 427-32.

Molloy, F. C., "The Novels of John McGahern," *Crit* 19, i (1977): 5-12.

THE DARK

Cronin, John, "THE DARK Is Not Light Enough: The Fiction of John McGahern," *Studies* 58 (Winter, 1969): 427-32.

Devine, Paul, "Style and Structure in John McGahern's THE DARK," *Crit* 21, i (1979): 49-58.

Molloy, F. C., "The Novels of John McGahern," *Crit* 19, i (1977): 12-19.

Toolan, Michael J., "John McGahern: The Historian and the Pornographer," *CJIS* 7, ii (Dec., 1981): 39-55.

THE LEAVETAKING

Molloy, F. C., "The Novels of John McGahern," *Crit* 19, i (1977): 1926.

Sampson, Denis, "A Note on John McGahern and John McGahern's THE LEAVETAKING," *CJIS* 2, ii (Dec., 1976): 61-5.

THE PORNOGRAPHER

Berlind, Bruce, "THE PORNOGRAPHER," *NewL* 47, iv (Summer, 1981): 140-1.

Toolan, Michael J., "John McGahern: The Historian and the Pornographer," *CJIS* 7, ii (Dec., 1981): 39-55.

MCGUANE, THOMAS FRANCIS III, 1939-

GENERAL

Carter, Albert H., III, "Thomas McGuane: An Interview," *FictionI* 4-5 (1975): 50-62.

McCaffery, Larry, "On Turning Nothing Into Something: Larry McCaffery on Thomas McGuane," *FictionI* 4-5 (1975): 123-9.

Welch, Dennis M., "Death and Fun in the Novels of Thomas McGuane," *UWR* 14, i (Fall/Winter, 1978): 14-20.

THE BUSHWACKED PIANO

Carter, Albert H., III, "McGuane's First Three Novels: Games, Fun, Nemesis," *Crit* 17, i (1975): 95-9.

NINETY-TWO IN THE SHADE

Carter, Albert H., III, "McGuane's First Three Novels: Games, Fun, Nemesis," *Crit* 17, i (1975): 99-103.

THE SPORTING CLUB

Carter, Albert H., III, "McGuane's First Three Novels: Games, Fun, Nemesis," *Crit* 17, i (1975): 91-5.

BIBLIOGRAPHY

McCaffery, Larry, "Thomas McGuane: A Bibliography, 1969-1978," *BB* 35, iv (Oct.-Dec., 1978): 169-71.

MCHALE, TOM, 1942(?)-1982

GENERAL

Brennan, Todd, "The Prime of Tom McHale," *Critic* 35 (Summer, 1977): 62-5.

_____, "Talking with McHale," *Critic* 35 (Summer, 1977): 65-6.

Browne, Joseph, "John O'Hara and Tom McHale: How Green Is Their Valley?" in Casey, D. G., and R. E. Rhodes, eds., *Irish-American Fiction*, 133-7.

Taylor, Mark, "McHale's Retreat," *Cweal* 101 (Mar. 14, 1975): 459-63.

MCLAVERTY, MICHAEL, 1907-

GENERAL

Foster, J. W., *Forces and Themes in Ulster Fiction*, 36-41.

CALL MY BROTHER BACK

Foster, J. W., *Forces and Themes in Ulster Fiction*, 41-7.

THE CHOICE

Foster, John W., "McLaverty's People," *Eire* 6, iii (Fall, 1971): 92-105.

IN THIS DAY

Foster, John W., "McLaverty's People," *Eire* 6, iii (Fall, 1971): 92-105.

LOST FIELDS

Foster, John W., "McLaverty's People," *Eire* 6, iii (Fall, 1971): 92-105.

MCMURTRY, LARRY, 1936-

GENERAL

Ahearn, Kerry, "More D'Urban: The Texas Novels of Larry McMurtry," *TQ* 19, iii (Autumn, 1976): 109-29. Also in Pilkington, W. T., ed., *Critical Essays on the Western American Novel*, 223-42.

Crooks, Alan F., "Larry McMurtry—A Writer in Transition: An Essay-Review," *WAL* 7 (Summer, 1972): 151-55.

Davis, Kenneth W., "The Themes of Initiation in the Works of Larry McMurtry and Tom Mayer," *ArlQ* 2, iii (Winter, 1969-70): 29-43.

Landess, T., *Larry McMurtry*.

Neinstein, R. L., *Ghost Country*.

Peavy, Charles D., "Coming of Age in Texas: The Novels of Larry McMurtry," *WAL* 4, iii (Fall, 1969): 171-88.

_____, *Larry McMurtry*.

Phillips, Billie, "McMurtry's Women: 'Eros [Libido, Caritas, and Philia] in [and Out of] Archer County'," *SwAL* 4 (1974): 29-36.

Phillips, Raymond C., Jr., "The Ranch as Place and Symbol in the Novels of Larry McMurtry," *SDR* 13, ii (Summer, 1975): 27-47.

Reynolds, R. C., "Showdown in the New Old West: The Cowboy vs. the Oilman," *LJHum* 6, i (Spring, 1980): 19-31.

Schmidt, D., ed., *Larry McMurtry*.

Schmidt, Dorey, and Dwight Huber, "Larry McMurtry: Unredeemed Dreams (An Interview)," in Schmidt, D., ed., *Larry McMurtry*, 1-4.

Stout, Janis P., "Journeying as a Metaphor for Cultural Loss in the Novels of Larry McMurtry," *WAL* 11 (May, 1976): 37-50.

Summerlin, Tim, "Larry McMurtry and the Persistent Frontier," *SwAL* 4 (1974): 22-8.

Zafran, Robert L., "An Analysis of the Novels of Larry McMurtry for Oral Interpretation Script Adaptation," *DAI* 43 (1982): 2157A.

ALL MY FRIENDS ARE GOING TO BE STRANGERS

Ahearn, Kerry, "More D'Urban: The Texas Novels of Larry McMurtry," *TQ* 19 (Autumn, 1976): 124-7.

Granzow, Barbara, "The Western Writer: A Study of Larry McMurtry's ALL MY FRIENDS ARE GOING TO BE STRANGERS," *SwAL* 4 (1974): 37-52.

Metz, Violette, "The Inner Child of Danny Deck: A Hypothetical Assessment," in Schmidt, D., ed., *Larry McMurtry*, 37-51.

Neinstein, R. L., *Ghost Country*, 39-47.

Peavy, C. D., *Larry McMurtry*, 41-4.

Phillips, Raymond C., "The Ranch as Place and Symbol in the Novels of Larry McMurtry," *SDR* 13, ii (Summer, 1975): 43-6.

HORSEMAN, PASS BY (HUD)

Ahearn, Kerry, "More D'Urban: The Texas Novels of Larry McMurtry," *TQ* 19, iii (Autumn, 1976): 110-13. Also in Pilkington, W. T., ed., *Critical Essays on the Western American Novel*, 224-7.

Dean, Patricia E., "Names in Larry McMurtry's 'Thalia Trilogy'," 71-6 in Seits, Laurence, ed., *The Dangerous Secret Names of God; Fartley's Compressed Gas Company; The Barf'n'choke; And Other Matters Onomastic*, Sugar Grove, Ill.: Waubonsee Community College, 1981.

Degenfelder, E. Pauline, "McMurtry and the Movies: HUD and THE LAST PICTURE SHOW," *WHR* 29, i (Winter, 1975): 81-90.

Folsom, James K., "SHANE and HUD: Two Stories in Search of a Medium," *WHR* 24, iv (Autumn, 1970): 365-72.

Landess, T., *Larry McMurtry*, 5-14.

MacDonald, Andrew, "The Passing Frontier in McMurtry's HUD/HORSEMAN, PASS BY," in Schmidt, D., ed., *Larry McMurtry*, 5-12.

Morrow, Patrick D., "Larry McMurtry: The First Phase," in Filler, L., ed., *Seasoned Authors for a New Season*, 71-5. [Comparison with SHANE by Jack Schaefer.]

Neinstein, R. L., *Ghost Country*, 1-10.

Peavy, C. D., *Larry McMurtry*, 28-31.

Phillips, Raymond C., "The Ranch as Place and Symbol in the Novels of Larry McMurtry," *SDR* 13, ii (Summer, 1975): 28-31.

Reynolds, R. C., "Showdown in the Old New West: The Cowboy vs. the Oilman," *LJHum* 6, i (Spring, 1980): 19-25, 30.

THE LAST PICTURE SHOW

Ahearn, Kerry, "More D'Urban: The Texas Novels of Larry McMurtry," *TQ* 19, iii (Autumn, 1976): 116-19. Also in Pilkington, W. T., ed., *Critical Essays on the Western American Novel*, 229-33.

Dean, Patricia E., "Names in Larry McMurtry's 'Thalis Trilogy'," 71-6 in Seits, Laurence E., ed., *The Dangerous Secret Name of God; Fartley's Compressed Gas Company; The Barf'n'choke; And Other Matters Onomastic*, Sugar Grove, Ill.: Waubonsee Community College, 1981.

Degenfelder, E. Pauline, "McMurtry and the Movies: HUD and THE LAST PICTURE SHOW," *WHR* 29, i (Winter, 1975): 81-90.

DuBose, Thomas, "THE LAST PICTURE SHOW: Theme," *ReAL* 3, ii (1977): 43-5.

Fritz, Donald E., "Anatomy and THE LAST PICTURE SHOW: A Matter of Definition," in Schmidt, D., ed., *Larry McMurtry*, 14-20.

Gerlach, John, "THE LAST PICTURE SHOW and One More Adaption," *LFQ* 1 (Spring, 1973): 161-66.

Landess, T., *Larry McMurtry*, 22-30.

Macdonald, Andrew, and Gina Macdonald, "Values in Transition in THE LAST PICTURE SHOW, or How to Make a Citybilly," in Schmidt, D., ed., *Larry McMurtry*, 21-32.

Morrow, Patrick D., "Larry McMurtry: The First Phase," in Filler, L., ed., *Seasoned Authors for a New Season*, 75-81.

————, "Mental Retardation in THE SOUND AND THE FURY and THE LAST PICTURE SHOW," *ReAL* 6, i (1979): 1-9.

Neinstein, R. L., *Ghost Country*, 17-25.

Peavy, C. D., *Larry McMurtry*, 34-6, 52-6, 60-2, 102-5.

————, "Larry McMurtry and Black Humor: A Note on THE LAST PICTURE SHOW," *WAL* 2 (Fall, 1967): 223-7.

Phillips, Raymond C., "The Ranch as Place and Symbol in the Novels of Larry McMurtry," *SDR* 13, ii (Summer, 1975): 36-8.

Reynolds, R. C., "Showdown in the Old New West: The Cowboy vs. the Oilman," *LJHum* 6, i (Spring, 1980): 19-20, 25-30.

LEAVING CHEYENNE

Ahearn, Kerry, "More D'Urban: The Texas Novels of Larry McMurtry," *TQ* 19, iii (Fall, 1976): 113-15. Also in Pilkington, W. T., ed., *Critical Essays on the Western American Novel*, 227-9.

Dean, Patricia E., "Names in Larry McMurtry's 'Thalia Trilogy'," 71-6 in Seits, Laurence E., ed., *The Dangerous Secret Name of God; Fartley's Compressed Gas Company; The Barf'n'choke; And Other Matters Onomastic*, Sugar Grove, Ill.: Waubonsee Community College, 1981.

Giles, James R., "Larry McMurtry's LEAVING CHEYENNE and the Novels of John Rechy: Four Trips Along 'the Mythical Pecos'," *Forum H* 10, ii (Summer, 1972): 34-40.

Landess, T., *Larry McMurtry*, 14-22.

Neinstein, R. L., *Ghost Country*, 11-16.

Peavy, C. D., *Larry McMurtry*, 31-4, 48-52.

Phillips, Raymond C., "The Ranch as Place and Symbol in the Novels of Larry McMurtry," *SDR* 13, ii (Summer, 1975): 31-6.

MOVING ON

Ahearn, Kerry, "More D'Urban: The Texas Novels of Larry McMurtry," *TQ* 19, iii (Autumn, 1976): 119-24. Also in Pilkington, W. T., ed., *Critical Essays on the Western American Novel*, 233-7.

Neinstein, R. L., *Ghost Country*, 27-39.

Peavy, C. D., *Larry McMurtry*, 38-41.

Phillips, Raymond C., "The Ranch as Place as Symbol in the Novels of Larry McMurtry," *SDR* 13, ii (Summer, 1975): 38-43.

TERMS OF ENDEARMENT

Schmidt, D., "What to Make of Aurora Greenway," in Schmidt, D., ed., *Larry McMurtry*, 52-8.

BIBLIOGRAPHY

Huber, Dwight, "Larry McMurtry: A Selected Bibliography," in Schmidt, D., ed., *Larry McMurtry*, 59-69.
Peavy, C. D., *Larry McMurtry*, 139-41.

MCNEILL, JANET, 1907-

GENERAL

Foster, J. W., *Forces and Themes in Ulster Fiction*, 228-43.
_____, "Zoo Stories: The Novels of Janet McNeill," *Eire* 9, i (Spring, 1974): 104-14.

MERIWETHER, LOUISE, 1923-

DADDY WAS A NUMBERS RUNNER

Dandridge, Rita B., "From Economic Insecurity to Disintegration: A Study of Character in Louise Meriwether's DADDY WAS A NUMBERS RUNNER," *NALF* 9 (1975): 82-5.

METALIOUS, GRACE, 1924-1964

GENERAL

Sorrell, Richard S., "Novelists and Ethnicity: Jack Kerouac and Grace Metalious as Franco-Americans," *MELUS* 9, i (Spring, 1982): 37-57.
Toth, Emily, "Fatherless and Dispossessed: Grace Metalious as a French-Canadian Writer," *JPC* 15, iii (Winter, 1981): 28-38.

MEWSHAW, MICHAEL, 1943-

GENERAL

Graham, John, "Michael Mewshaw," in Garrett, G., ed., *Writer's Voice*, 141-53. [Interview.]

WALKING SLOW

Hoge, James O., "The Interrelation of Good and Evil in Mewshaw's WALKING SLOW," *NConL* 2, iv (September, 1972): 2-3.

MICHENER, JAMES A(lbert), 1907

GENERAL

Bell, Pearl K., "James Michener's Docudramas," *Ctary* 71, iv (Apr., 1981): 71-3.
Day, A. G., *James A. Michener*.
Farrell, Ann, "James Michener's Literary Offences: Shades of Fenimore Cooper," *CCTE* 44 (1979): 11-16. [Not seen.]

THE BRIDGE AT ANDAU

Day, A. G., *James A. Michener*, 92-7.

THE BRIDGES AT TOKO-RI

Day, A. G., *James A. Michener*, 75-9.

CARAVANS

Day, A. G., *James A. Michener*, 82-4.

CENTENNIAL

Day, A. G., *James A. Michener*, 149-54.
Kings, John, *In Search of CENTENNIAL: A Journey with James A. Michener*, N.Y.: Random House, 1978.

THE DRIFTERS: A NOVEL

Day, A. G., *James A. Michener*, 135-40.

THE FIRES OF SPRING

Day, A. G., *James A. Michener*, 55-64.

HAWAII

Day, A. G., *James A. Michener*, 101-19.

SAYONARA

Day, A. G., *James A. Michener*, 79-82.

THE SOURCE

Day, A. G., *James A. Michener*, 120-6.

BIBLIOGRAPHY

Day, A. G., *James A. Michener*, 175-86.

MILLER, HENRY, 1891-1980

GENERAL

Allen, Mary, "Henry Miller: Yea-Sayer," *TSL* 23 (1978): 100-10.
Almansi, G., "Three Versions of an Article by Henry Miller," *TwenCS* 1, ii (Nov., 1969): 41-55.
Anon., "The Tropic Myth," *TLS* (Nov. 1, 1963): 892.
Bartlett, Jeffrey, "The Advance: William Carlos Williams and Henry Miller: American Modernists," *DAI* 41 (1980): 1585A.
Baxter, Annette K., *Henry Miller, Expatriate* (Critical Essays in English and American Literature, No. 5), Pittsburgh: Un. of Pittsburgh Pr., 1961.
Bedford, Richard C., "The Apocatastasis of Henry Miller," *DA* 21 (1960): 1560-61.
Bell, Elizabeth S., "Henry Miller and Kay Boyle: The Divided Stream in American Expatriate Literature, 1930-1940," *DAI* 40 (1980): 5862A.
Bode, Elroy, "The World on Its Own Terms: A Brief for Steinbeck, Miller and Simenon," *SWR* 53 (1968): 406-16.
Brophy, Brigid, "The Last Time I F_____d Paris," *LonM* n.s. 3 (June, 1963): 74-9.
Brown, Lionel, "King of the Four Letter Words," *Modern Man* 6 (Aug., 1956): 14-18, 50-1. [Not seen.]

Campbell, James, "Risking All," *NStat* (July 11, 1980): 52-3.

Capouya, Emile, "Henry Miller," *Salmagundi* 1 (Fall, 1965): 81-7.

Cockcroft, George P., "The Two Henry Millers," *DA* 28 (1967): 669A.

Crossen, David K., "Apollonian and Dionysian: The Act of Mythmaking in Henry Miller," *DAI* 39 (1978): 2270A-71A.

Daugherty, Francis L., "Henry Miller and the Heterocosm: The General and Applied Literary Theory of an American Neo-Romantic," *DAI* 32 (1971): 423A.

Dick, Kenneth C., *Henry Miller: Colossus of One*, Sittard, The Netherlands: Alberts, 1967.

Donohue, Denis, "Dry Dreams," *NYRB* 5 (Oct. 14, 1965): 5-8.

Durrell, Lawrence, "Introduction," *The Henry Miller Reader*, Norfolk: New Directions, 1959.

————, "Studies in Genius: VIII—Henry Miller," *Horizon* 20 (July, 1949): 45-61. Also in Seaver, Richard, Terry Southern, and Alexander Trocchi, eds., *Writers in Revolt: An Anthology*, N.Y.: Frederick Fell, 1963, 130-45. Also in Wickes, G., ed., *Henry Miller and the Critics*, 86-107.

————, and Alfred Perles, *Art and Outrage: A Correspondence About Henry Miller*, N.Y.: Dutton, 1961.

Ekberg, Kent, "Studio 28: The Influence of the Surrealist Cinema on the Early Fiction of Anais Nin and Henry Miller," *DL* 4, iii (Mar., 1981): 3-4.

Fiedler, Leslie A., "The Beginning of the Thirties: Depression, Return and Rebirth," *Waiting for the End*, 37-45.

Finkelstein, S., *Existentialism and Alienation in American Literature*, 203-10. Also in Mitchell, E. B., ed., *Henry Miller*, 121-8.

Fowlie, Wallace, "Shadow of Doom: An Essay on Henry Miller," *Accent* (Autumn, 1944): 49-53. Also in Mitchell, E. B., ed., *Henry Miller*, 35-42.

Fruchter, Norman, "In Defense of Henry Miller," *T&T* 42 (Apr. 6, 1961): 572-3.

Glicksberg, Charles I., "Henry Miller: Individualist in Extremis," *SWR* 33 (Summer, 1948): 289-95.

Gordon, William A., "Henry Miller and the Romantic Tradition," *DA* 24 (1964): 3335-36.

————, *Mind and Art of Henry Miller*.

————, *Writer and Critic: A Correspondence with Henry Miller*, Baton Rouge: Louisiana State Un. Pr., 1968.

————, "The Art of Henry Miller," in Mitchell, E. B., ed., *Henry Miller*, 173-84.

————, "The Zen Mind of Henry Miller: Sacred and Obscene," *LGJ* 4, iii (1976-77): 1-17, 22-4.

Hassan, I., *Literature of Silence*.

————, "The Literature of Silence: From Henry Miller to Beckett to Burroughs," *Encounter* 28 (Jan., 1967): 74-82.

Haverstick, John, and William Barrett, "Henry Miller: Man in Quest of Life," *SatR* 40 (Aug. 3, 1957): 8-10.

Hays, Peter L., "The Danger of Henry Miller," *ArQ* 27 (Autumn, 1971): 251-8.

Hoffman, Frederick J., *Freudianism and the Literary Mind*, 2nd ed., Baton Rouge: Louisiana State Un. Pr., 1957, 290-6. Also in Mitchell, E. B., ed., *Henry Miller*, 43-50.

————, "Henry Miller, Defender of the Marginal Life," in French, W., ed., *Thirties*, 73-80.

Hoffman, Michael J., "Yesterday's Rebel," *WHR* 24, iii (Summer, 1970): 271-4.

Jackson, Paul R., "Henry Miller, Emerson, and the Divided Self," *AL* 43, ii (May, 1971): 231-41.

————, "Henry Miller: The Autobiographical Romances," *DA* 28 (1967): 678A.

————, "Henry Miller's Literary Pregnancies," *L&P* 19, i (1969): 35-49.

Jones, Roger, "Henry Miller at Eighty-Four: An Interview," *QQ* 84 (1977): 351-65.

Kermode, Frank, "Henry Miller and John Betjeman," *Encounter* 16 (Mar., 1961): 69-75. Also in Kermode, F., *Puzzles and Epiphanies*, 140-50. Also in Mitchell, E. B., ed., *Henry Miller*, 85-95.

Kleine, Don, "Innocence Forbidden: Henry Miller in the Tropics," *PrS* 33 (Summer, 1959): 125-30.

Kraft, Barbara, "A Conversation with Henry Miller," *MQR* 20, ii (Spring, 1981).

Lee, Alwyn, "Henry Miller—The Pathology of Isolation," in *New World Writing*, 2nd Mentor Selection, N.Y.: New American Library, 1952, 340-7. Also in Mitchell, E. B., ed., *Henry Miller*, 67-76.

Lehrer, Linda J., "The Man Is His Art: The Aesthetic Theories of Henry Miller," *DAI* 38 (1977): 264A-65A.

Lewis, Leon H., "Equatorial Introspection: A Critical Study of Henry Miller," *DAI* 32 (1971): 3313A.

Lord, Russell, "Henry Miller," *Harvard Wake* 1 (June, 1945): 13-16.

Lund, Mary G., "Henry Miller: A Fierce Oracle," *NAmerR* 4, i (Jan., 1967): 18-21.

Mailer, Norman, "Henry Miller: Genius and Lust, Narcissism," *American Review* 24 (Apr., 1976): 1-40.

Manning, Hugo, "Apropos Henry Miller," *Wind and the Rain* 2 (Winter, 1945): 166-8. [Not seen.]

————, *It and the Odyssey of Henry Miller*.

Martin, Jay, "The Broken Speech: Mark Twain and Henry Miller," 213-24, in Sienicka, Marta, ed., *Proceedings of a Symposium on American Literature*, Poznan: Uniw. Im. Adama Mickiewicza, 1979.

————, "'The King of Smut': Henry Miller's Tragical History," *AR* 35 (Fall, 1977).

————, "Remember to Remember: Henry Miller and Literary Tradition," *ClioW* 7 (Fall, 1977): 75-90.

————, "The Unspeakable and the Unsayable: The Psychology of Language in Mark Twain and Henry Miller," *Gradiva* 2, i (Fall, 1979): 1-18.

Mathieu, Bertrand, "Henry Miller and the Symboliste Belief in a Universal Language," *AntigR* 27 (Autumn, 1976): 49-57.

————, "Henry Miller and the Symboliste Rejection of the Quotidian," *Under the Sign of Pisces* 8 (Winter, 1977): 15-24.

————, *Orpheus in Brooklyn*.

Mauriac, C., *New Literature*, 51-9.

May, James B., "Henry Miller: An Individualist as Social Thinker," *Trace* 40 (Jan.-Mar., 1961): 24-31.

McCarthy, Harold T., "Henry Miller's Democratic Vistas," *AQ* 33, ii (May, 1971): 221-35. Also, slightly revised, in McCarthy, H. T., *Expatriate Perspective*, 156-72.

Miller, Henry, *The Books in My Life*, N.Y.: New Directions, 1952.

————, and others, *Of-By-and About Henry Miller, a Collection of Pieces*, Yonkers, N.Y.: Alicat Bookshop Pr., 1947.

Mitchell, Edward B., "Artists and Artists: The 'Aesthetics' of Henry Miller," *TSLL* 8 (Spring, 1966): 103-15. Also in Mitchell, E. B., ed., *Henry Miller*, 155-72.

————, *Henry Miller*.

————, "Henry Miller: The Artist as Seer," *DA* 26 (1965): 1047.

Moore, Thomas H., ed., *Henry Miller on Writing*, N.Y.: New Directions, 1964.

Moravia, Alberto, "Two American Writers (1949)," *SR* 68 (Summer, 1960): 473-7.

Muller, Herbert J., "The World of Henry Miller," *KR* 2, iii (Summer, 1940): 312-18. Also in Wickes, G., ed., *Henry Miller and the Critics*, 44-51.

Nelson, J. A., *Form and Image in the Fiction of Henry Miller*.

Nicholson, Homer K., Jr., "O Altitudo: A Comparison of the Writings of Walt Whitman, D. H. Lawrence, and Henry Miller," *DA* 17 (1957): 2614.

Omarr, Sidney, *Henry Miller: His World of Urania*, London: Villiers Pubs., 1960.

Perles, Alfred, *My Friend Henry Miller*, London: Neville Spearman, 1955; N. Y.: John Day, 1956.

Polley, George W., "The Art of Religious Writing: Henry Miller as Religious Writer," *SDR* 7, iii (Autumn, 1969): 61-73.

Porter, Bern, ed., *The Happy Rock*, Berkeley: B. Porter, 1945.

Powell, Lawrence C., "Remembering Henry Miller," *SWR* 66, ii (Spring, 1981): 117-28.

Rahv, Philip, "Sketches in Criticism: Henry Miller," in Rahv, P., *Image and Idea*, 159-65. Also in Wickes, G., ed., *Henry Miller and the Critics*, 77-85. Also in Rahv, P., *Literature and the Sixth Sense*, 88-94. Also in Mitchell, E. B., ed., *Henry Miller*, 37-34.

Read, Herbert, "Henry Miller," in Wickes, G., ed., *Henry Miller and the Critics*, 111-18.

———, *The Tenth Muse: Essays in Criticism*, N.Y.: Horizon Pr., 1958, 250-55.

Rexroth, Kenneth, "The Neglected Henry Miller," *Nation* 181 (Nov. 5, 1955): 385-7. Also in Nation (Periodical), *View of the Nation*, 31-7.

———, "The Reality of Henry Miller," *Bird in the Bush; Obvious Essays*, N.Y.: New Directions, 1959, 154-67. Also in Wickes, G., ed., *Henry Miller and the Critics*, 119-31.

Rode, Alex, "Henry Miller: The Novelist as Liberator," *Americas* 18 (Jan., 1966): 41-3.

Rose, Edward J., "The Aesthetics of Civil Disobedience: Henry Miller, Twentieth Century Transcendentalist," *Edge* (Edmonton) 1, i (Autumn, 1963): 5-16.

Sarracino, Carmine T., "Henry Miller, Spiritual Anarchist," *DAI* 35 (1974): 30007A-08A.

Shapiro, Karl, "The Greatest Living Author," *Two Cities* (Dec., 1959). Also in Shapiro, K., *In Defense of Ignorance*, N.Y.: Random House, 1960, 313-38. Also, in part, in Mitchell, E. B., ed., *Henry Miller*, 77-84.

Shifreen, Lawrence, "An Autobiography of Friends," *S&M* 3 (Summer, 1976): 94-7.

———, "Henry Miller's Literary Legacy," *USP* 11, iv (1980): 2-8.

Smithline, Arnold, "Henry Miller and the Transcendental Spirit," *ESQ* 43 (1966): 50-6. Also in *IHML* 7 (Mar., 1966): 3-10.

Snyder, Robert, *This is Henry Miller from Brooklyn: Conversations with the Author from The Henry Miller Odyssey*, Los Angeles: Nash, 1976.

Southern, Terry, "Miller: Only the Beginning," *Nation* 193 (Nov. 18, 1961): 399-401.

Spencer, Sharon, "A Novel Triangle: Anais Nin-Henry Miller-Otto Rank," *Par Rapport* (Marshall, Minn.) 1 (1978): 139-44.

Stade, George, "Mailer and Miller," *PR* 44, iv (1977): 616-24.

Stuhlmann, Gunter, ed., *Henry Miller Letters to Anais Nin*, N.Y.: Putnam's, 1965.

Trachtenberg, Alan, "'History on the Side': Henry Miller's American Dream," in Madden, D., *American Dreams, American Nightmares*, 136-48.

Traschen, Isador, "Henry Miller: The Ego and I," *SAQ* 65 (Summer, 1965): 345-54.

White, Emil, ed., *Henry Miller—Between Heaven and Hell: A Symposium*, Big Sur, Calif.: Emil White, 1961.

Wickes, George, "The Art of Fiction: Henry Miller," *ParisR* 28 (Summer-Fall, 1962): 129-59. Also in *Writers at Work*, 2nd ser., 165-91.

———, *Henry Miller*.

———, ed., *Henry Miller and the Critics*.

———, "Henry Miller at Seventy," *ClareQ* 9, ii (Winter, 1962): 5-20.

———, ed., *Lawrence Durrell and Henry Miller: A Private Correspondence*, N.Y.: Dutton, 1964.

Widmer, K., *Henry Miller*.

———, "The Legacy of Henry Miller," in Mitchell, E. B., ed., *Henry Miller*, 113-19.

———, "The Rebel-Buffoon: Henry Miller's Legacy," in Wickes, G., ed., *Henry Miller and the Critics*, 132-46.

Williams, John, "Henry Miller: The Success of Failure," *VQR* 54 (Spring, 1968): 225-45.

Wood, Richard C., ed., *Collector's Quest: The Correspondence of Henry Miller and J. Rives Childs, 1947-1965*, Charlottesville: Un. Pr. of Virginia, 1968.

Wood, Tom, "Bald Trapped in Miller's Fiction," *LGJ* 6, ii (1980): 8-9. [Not seen.]

———, "Hooray for Henry Miller: The Dirty Old Man," *LGJ* 4, iii (1976-77): 14-17, 24-5.

BLACK SPRING

Hassan, I., *Literature of Silence*, 67-72.

Lewis, Leon, "Henry Miller's Portrait of Walter Lowenfels," *LGJ* 4 (Spring-Summer, 1976): 16-17, 20.

Wickes, G., *Henry Miller*, 24-7.

Widmer, K., *Henry Miller*, 41-51.

NEXUS (See also THE ROSY CRUCIFIXION)

Hassan, I., *Literature of Silence*, 100-4.

PLEXUS (See also THE ROSY CRUCIFIXION)

Anon., "The Tropic Myth," *TLS* (Nov. 1, 1963): 892. Also in *T.L.S.: Essays and Reviews from the Times Literary Supplement, 1963*, 215-21.

Hassan, I., *Literature of Silence*, 93-100.

Symons, J., "Goodbye, Henry Miller," *Critical Occasions*, 126-32.

THE ROSY CRUCIFIXION

Gordon, W. A., *Mind and Art of Henry Miller*, 138-74.

Hassan, I., *Literature of Silence*, 85-109.

Littlejohn, David, "SEXUS, NEXUS, and PLEXUS," *Interruptions*, 45-72.

Soroyan, Chesley, "THE ROSY CRUCIFIXION: A Review," *Points* 4 (Oct.-Nov., 1949): 79-83.

Wickes, G., *Henry Miller*, 48-40.

Widmer, K., *Henry Miller*, 81-95.

SEXUS (See also THE ROSY CRUCIFIXION)

Hassan, I., *Literature of Silence*, 87-92.

Jackson, Paul R., "Henry Miller, Emerson and the Divided Self," *AL* 42 (May, 1971): 231-41.

Millett, Kate, "Sexual Politics: Miller, Mailer, and Genet," *NAmR* 7 (1969): 7-15.

Vidal, Gore, "Oh, Henry," *Book Week* (Aug. 1, 1965): 1, 10. Also, as "The SEXUS of Henry Miller," in Vidal, G., *Homage to Daniel Shays*, 197-203.

THE SMILE AT THE FOOT OF THE LADDER

Greer, Scott, et al., "To Be or Not: 4 Opinions on Henry Miller's THE SMILE AT THE FOOT OF THE LADDER," *Tiger's Eye* 1, v (Oct. 20, 1948): 68-72.

TROPIC OF CANCER

Allen, Mary, "Henry Miller: Yea Sayer," *TSL* 23 (1978): 100-10.

Allen, W., *Modern Novel*, 180-1.

Almansi, G., "Three Versions of an Article on Henry Miller," *TwenCS* 1, ii (Nov., 1969): 41-55.

Anon., "Out of Bond. Henry Miller: TROPIC OF CANCER," *TLS* (Apr. 12, 1963): 243. Also in *T.L.S.: Essays and Reviews from the Times Literary Supplement, 1963*, 212-15.

Bolckmans, Alex, "Henry Miller's TROPIC OF CANCER and Kurt Hansen's SULT," *Scan* 14 (1975): 115-26.

Brophy, Brigid, in *LonM* 3 (June, 1963). Also in Brophy, B., *Don't Never Forget*, 231-8.

Ciardi, John, "A Critic's Verdict," *SatR* 45 (June 30, 1962): 13. Also in Girvetz, Harry K., ed., *Contemporary Moral Issues*, Belmont, Calif.: Wadsworth, 1963, 240-2.

Foster, Steven, "A Critical Appraisal of Henry Miller's TROPIC OF CANCER," *TCL* 9 (Jan., 1964): 196-208.

Fraenkel, Michael, *The Genesis of the TROPIC OF CANCER*, London: Village Pr., 1973. First publ. in Porter, Bern, ed., *The Happy Rock*, Berkeley: California Un. Pr., 1945.

Friedman, Alan, "The Pitching of Love's Mansion in the TROP-ICS of Henry Miller," in Whitbread, T. B., ed., *Seven Contemporary Authors*, 25-48. Also in Mitchell, E. B., ed., *Henry Miller*, 129-53.

Fuller, E., *Books With the Men Behind Them*, 21-5+.

Gertz, Elmer, "Censorship in Chicago: TROPIC OF CANCER," *ICarbS* 3 (1976): 49-59.

Gordon, W. A., *Mind and Art of Henry Miller*, 85-109.

Gutierrez, Donald, "'Hypocrit lecteur': TROPIC OF CANCER as Sexual Comedy," *Mosaic* 11, ii (1978): 21-33.

Hassan, I., *Literature of Silence*, 59-67.

Highet, Gilbert, "Henry Miller's Stream of Consciousness," *Horizon* 4 (Nov., 1961): 104-5. Also in Highet, G., *Explorations*, 209-15.

Hoffman, Michael J., "Henry Miller and the Apocalypse of Transcendentalism," *LJG* 4, iii (1976): 18-21.

Huxley, Aldous, "Death and the Baroque," *Harper's* 198 (Apr., 1949): 80-6. Also in Mitchell, E. B., ed., *Henry Miller*, 51-62.

Hyman, S. E., "The Innocence of Henry Miller," *Standards* 12-16.

Jackson, Paul R., "The Balconies of Henry Miller," *UR* 36, ii (Dec., 1969): 155-60.

_____, "Caterwauling and Harmony: Music in TROPIC OF CANCER," *Crit* 20, iii (1978): 21-33.

Kauffmann, Stanley, "An Old Shocker Comes Home," *NRep* 145 (July 10, 17-19). Also in Wickes, G., ed., *Henry Miller and the Critics*, 154-60. Also in Harrison, G. A., ed., *Critic as Artist*, 211-16.

Levin, Harry, "Commonwealth of Massachusetts vs. TROPIC OF CANCER," in Wickes, G., ed., *Henry Miller and the Critics*, 168-74.

Littlejohn, David, "The Tropics of Miller," *NRep* 146 (Mar. 5, 1962): 31-5. Also in Littlejohn, D., *Interruptions*, 37-44. Also in Mitchell, E. B., ed., *Henry Miller*, 103-11.

Lowenfels, Walter, "A Note on TROPIC OF CANCER—Paris, 1931," in Wickes, G., ed., *Henry Miller and the Critics*, 16-19.

_____, "Unpublished Preface to TROPIC OF CANCER," *MR* 5 (Spring, 1964): 481-91.

Martin, Jay, "The Last Book," *PR* 45 (1978): 611-26.

Moore, Harry, T., "From Under the Counter to Front Shelf," in Wickes, G., ed., *Henry Miller and the Critics*, 149-53.

Nelson, J. A., *Form and Image in the Fiction of Henry Miller*, 19-49.

Orwell, George, "Inside the Whale," *Such, Such Were the Joys*, 154-66. Also in *Collected Essays, Journalism and Letters of George Orwell*, vol. I., ed. by Sonia Orwell and Ian August, N.Y.: Harcourt, 1968, 493-527. Also in Wickes, G., ed., *Henry Miller and the Critics*, 149-53. Also in Mitchell, E. B., ed., *Henry Miller*, 7-25.

Robischon, Thomas, "A Day in Court with the Literary Critics," *MR* 6 (Autumn-Winter, 1964-65): 101-10.

Schorer, Mark, "Commonwealth of Massachusetts vs. TROPIC OF CANCER," in Wickes, G., ed., *Henry Miller and the Critics*, 161-7.

Shapiro, Karl, "Introduction," *Tropic of Cancer*, N.Y.: Grove, 1961.

Shifreen, Lawrence J., "Henry Miller's *Mezzotints*: The Undiscovered Roots of TROPIC OF CANCER," *SSF* 16 (1979): 11-17.

Solotaroff, Theodore, "All That Cellar-Deep Jazz: Henry Miller and Seymour Krim," *Ctary* 32 (Oct., 1961): 317-24. Also in Solotaroff, T., *Red Hot Vacuum*, 22-8.

Way, Brian, "Sex and Language: Obscene Words in D. H. Lawrence and Henry Miller," *New Left Rev.* 27 (Sept.-Oct., 1964): 66-80.

Wickes, G., *Henry Miller*, 21-4.

Widmer, K., *Henry Miller*, 17-40.

Wilson, Edmund, "Twilight of the Expatriates," *NRep* 84 (Mar. 9, 1938): 140. Also in Wilson, E., *Shores of Light*, 705-10. Also in Wickes, G., ed., *Henry Miller and the Critics*, 25-30.

Yerbury, Grace D., "Of a City Beside a River," *WWR* 10 (Sept., 1964): 70-3.

TROPIC OF CAPRICORN

Friedman, Alan, "The Pitching of Love's Mansion in the TROP-ICS of Henry Miller," in Whitbread, T. B., ed., *Seven Contemporary Authors*, 25-48. Also in Mitchell, E. B., ed., *Henry Miller*, 129-53.

Gordon, W. A., *Mind and Art of Henry Miller*, 110-37.

Hassan, I., *Literature of Silence*, 72-81.

Highet, Gilbert, "Henry Miller's Stream of Consciousness," *Horizon* 4 (Nov., 1961): 104-5. Also in Highet, G., *Explorations*, 209-15.

Jackson, Paul R., "The Balconies of Henry Miller, Part II," *UR* 36, iii (Mar., 1970): 221-5.

Littlejohn, David, "The Tropics of Miller," *NRep* 146 (Mar. 5, 1962): 31-5. Also in Littlejohn, D., *Interruptions*, 37-44. Also in Mitchell, E. B., ed., *Henry Miller*, 103-11.

Parl, Jack, "A Study of Contradiction in Henry Miller's TROPIC OF CAPRICORN," *DAI* 40 (1979): 9-15.

Riggs, Micky, "Bergsonian Order in TROPIC OF CAPRICORN," *ReAL* 4, ii (1978): 9-15.

Rosenfeld, Paul, "The Traditions of Henry Miller," *Nation* 149 (Nov. 4, 1939): 502-3. Also in Miller, H., and others, *Of-By-And About Henry Miller*, N.Y.: Alicat Bookshop Pr., 1947.

Way, Brian, "Sex and Language: Obscene Words in D. H. Lawrence and Henry Miller," *New Left Rev.* 27 (Sept.-Oct., 1964): 66-80.

Wickes, G., *Henry Miller*, 27-9.

Widmer, K., *Henry Miller*, 71-3, 81-5, 99-110.

BIBLIOGRAPHY

Centing, Richard R., "Writings about Henry Miller: A First Supplement to Lawrence J. Shifreen's *Henry Miller: A Bibliography of Secondary Sources*," *Seahorse* 1, ii (July 4, 1982): 10-18.

_____, "Writings about Henry Miller: A Second Supplement to Lawrence J. Shifreen's *Henry Miller: A Bibliography of Secondary Sources*," *Seahorse* 1, iii (1982): 5-8.

Renken, Maxine, "Bibliography of Henry Miller: 1945-1961," *TCL* 7 (Jan., 1961): 90-180. Also in pamphlet form, Swallow Pr., 1962.

Riley, Esta Lou, *Henry Miller: An Informal Bibliography 1924-1960* (Fort Hays Studies. New Series: Bibliog. Ser., No. 1), Fort Hays: Kansas State College, 1962.

Shifreen, Laurence J., *Henry Miller: A Bibliography of Secondary Sources* (Scarecrow Author Bibliographies, 38), Metuchen, N.J.: Scarecrow, 1979.

MILLER, MERLE, 1918-

THE SURE THING

Aldridge, J. W., *After the Lost Generation*, 163-9.

THAT WINTER

Aldridge, J. W., *After the Lost Generation*, 157-65.

MILLER, WARREN, 1921-1966

GENERAL

Love, Glen A., "Warren Miller: White Novelist in a Black World," *NALF* 9, i (Spring, 1975): 3, 11-16.

THE COOL WORLD

Love, Glen A., "Warren Miller: White Novelist in a Black World," *NALF* 9, i (Spring, 1975): 11-12.

THE SIEGE OF HARLEM

Love, Glen A., "Warren Miller: White Novelist in a Black World," *NALF* 9, i (Spring, 1975): 12-14.

MILLHAUSER, STEVEN, 1943-

EDWIN MULLUOUSE; THE LIFE AND DEATH OF AN AMERICAN WRITER, 1943-1954, BY JEFFREY CARTWRIGHT

Adams, Timothy D., "The Mock-Biography of Edwin Mullhouse," *Biography* 5, iii (Summer, 1982): 205-14.

MITCHELL, W(ILLIAM) O(RMOND), 1914-

GENERAL

Barclay, Patricia, "Regionalism and the Writer: A Talk with W. O. Mitchell," *CanL* 14 (Autumn, 1962): 53-6.

Cowan, Hugh, "Acta Interviews W. O. Mitchell," *Acta Victoriana* 98, ii (Apr., 1974): 15-26.

O'Rourke, David, "An Interview with W. O. Mitchell," *ECW* 20 (Winter, 1980-81): 149-59.

Ricou, Laurence, "The Eternal Prairie: The Fiction of W. O. Mitchell," *Vertical Man/Horizontal World*, 95-110.

THE KITE

Barclay, Patricia, "Regionalism and the Writer: A Talk with W. O. Mitchell," *CanL* 14 (Autumn, 1962): 53-6.

Gross, Konrad, "Looking Back in Anger?" *JCF* 3, ii (1974): 49-54.

McLay, Catherine, "W. O. Mitchell's THE KITE: A Study in Immortality," *JCF* 2, ii (Spring, 1973): 43-8.

New, W. H., "A Feeling of Completion: Aspects of W. O. Mitchell," *CanL* 17 (Summer, 1963): 22-33. Also in New, W. H., *Articulating West*, 45-9. Also in Woodcock, G., ed., *Canadian Novel in the Twentieth Century*, 174-85. Also in Stephens, D., ed., *Writers of the Prairies*, 89-100.

THE VANISHING POINT

Bartlett, Donald R., "Dumplings and Dignity," *CanL* 77 (Summer, 1978): 73-80.

Cowan, Hugh, "Acta Interviews W. O. Mitchell," *Acta Victoriana* 98, ii (Apr., 1974): 15-26.

Davidson, Arnold E., "Lessons on Perspective: W. O. Mitchell's THE VANISHING POINT," *ArielE* 12, i (Jan., 1981): 61-78.

McLay, Catherine, "THE VANISHING POINT: From Alienation to Faith," in Moss, J., ed., *Canadian Novel*, v.3, *Modern Times*, 243-60.

Williams, David, "The Indian Our Ancestor: Three Modes of Vision in Recent Canadian Fiction," *DalR* 58 (Summer, 1978): 316-21.

WHO HAS SEEN THE WIND

Gingell-Beckmann, S. A., "The Lyricism of W. O. Mitchell's WHO HAS SEEN THE WIND," *SCL* 6, ii (1981): 221-31.

Jones, D. G., *Butterfly on Rock*, 37-8.

Mathews, Robin, "W. O. Mitchell: Epic Comedy," in Dexter, Gail, ed., *Canadian Literature: Surrender or Revolution*, Toronto: Steel Rail, 1978, 109-18.

Mitchell, Ken, "The Universality of W. O. Mitchell's WHO HAS SEEN THE WIND," *Lakehead Univ. Review* 4, i (1971): 26-40. Also in Moss, J., ed., *Canadian Novel*, v. 3, *Modern Times*, 227-42.

New, W. H., "A Feeling of Completion: Aspects of W. O. Mitchell," *CanL* 17 (Summer, 1963): 22-33. Also in New, W. H., *Articulating West*, 45-9. Also in Stephens, D., ed., *Writers of the Prairies*, 89-100. Also in Woodcock, G., ed., *Canadian Novel in the Twentieth Century*, 174-85.

Peterman, Michael, "'The Good Game': The Charm of Willa Cather's MY ANTONIA and W. O. Mitchell's WHO HAS SEEN THE WIND," *Mosaic* 14, ii (Spring, 1981): 93-106.

Ricou, Laurence, "The Eternal Prairie: The Fiction of W. O. Mitchell," *Vertical Man/Horizontal World*, 96-106.

_____, "Notes on Language and Learning in WHO HAS SEEN THE WIND," *CCL* 10 (1977-78): 3-17.

Sutherland, Ronald, "Children of the Changing Wind," *Jnl. of Canadian Studies* 5, iv (Nov., 1970): 3-11. Also in Sutherland, Ronald, *Second Image: Comparative Studies in Quebec/Canadian Literature*, Toronto: New Press, 1971, 88-107.

Wee, Morris O., "Specks on the Horizon: Individuals and the Land in Canada Prairie Fiction," *SDR* 19, iv (Winter, 1981): 18-31.

BIBLIOGRAPHY

Latham, Sheild, "W. O. Mitchell: An Annotated Bibliography," 323-64 in Lecker, Robert, and Jack David, eds., *The Annotated Bibliography of Canada's Major Authors, Volume Three*, Downsview: ECW, 1981.

MITFORD, NANCY, 1904-1973

GENERAL

Karl, F. R., *Contemporary English Novel*, 276-7.
Pendry, E. D., *New Feminism and English Fiction*, 54-6.

DON'T TELL ALFRED

Walcutt, C. C., *Man's Changing Mask*, 229-36.
Waugh, Evelyn, in *LonM* 7 (Dec., 1960): 65-8.

MITTELHOLZER, EDGAR, 1909-1966

GENERAL

Birbalsingh, F. M., "Edgar Mittelholzer: Moralist or Pornographer?" *JCL* 7 (July, 1969): 88-103.

Gilkes, Michael, "Edgar Mittelholzer," in West, B., ed., *West Indian Literature*, 95-100.

Guckian, Patrick, "The Balance of Colour: A Re-Assessment of the Work of Edgar Mittelholzer," *Jamaica Jnl.* 4, i (Mar., 1970): 38-45.

Howard, William J., "Edgar Mittelholzer's Tragic Vision," *Caribbean Quarterly* 16, iv (Dec., 1970): 19-28.

Seymour, A. J., *Edgar Mittelholzer*.

CHILDREN OF KAYWANA

Gilkes, M., *West Indian Novel*, 57-66.

CORENTYNE THUNDER

Gilkes, Michael, in King, B., ed., *West Indian Literature*, 97-101.
_____, *West Indian Novel*, 41-57.

THE HARROWING OF HUBERTUS

Gilkes, M., *West Indian Novel*, 66-74.

KAYWANA BLOOD

Gilkes, M., *West Indian Novel*, 74-82.

KAYWANA TRILOGY

Gilkes, Michael, in King, B., ed., *West Indian Literature*, 105-7.

THE LIFE AND DEATH OF SYLVIA

Gilkes, Michael, "Mulatta ANGST and Mittelholzer's SYLVIA," *RIB* 29 (1979): 3-14.

A MORNING AT THE OFFICE

Gilkes, Michael, "The Spirit in the Bottle: A Reading of Mittelholzer's A MORNING AT THE OFFICE," *WLWE* 14 (1975): 237-52.

James, Louis, in James, L., ed., *Islands in Between*, 37-9.

Moore, Gerald, "Discovery," *Chosen Tongue*, 9-14. Also in Cooke, M. G., ed., *Modern Black Novelists*, 152-4.

MOJTABAI, A(NN) G(RACE), 1938-

MUNDOME

Olson, Carol B., "Mirrors and Madness: A. G. Mojtabai's MUNDOME," *Crit* 20, ii (1978): 71-82.

MOMADAY, N(AVARRE) SCOTT, 1934-

GENERAL

Dickinson-Brown, Roger, "The Art and Importance of N. Scott Momaday," *SoR* 14 (Winter, 1978): 30-45.

Jahner, Elaine, "The Novel and the Oral Tradition: An Interview with Leslie Marmon Silko and N. Scott Momaday," *BForum* 5, iii (1981): 333-38.

Lattin, Vernon E., "The Quest for Mythic Vision in Contemporary Native American and Chicano Fiction," *AL* 50, iv (Jan., 1979): 625-40.

Nelson, Margaret F., "Ethnic Identity in the Prose Works of N. Scott Momaday," *DAI* 40 (1980): 6282A.

Trimble, M. S., *N. Scott Momaday*.

Woodard, Charles L., "The Concept of the Creative Word in the Writings of N. Scott Nomaday," *DAI* 36 (1975): 2205A.

Zachrau, Thekla, "N. Scott Momaday: Towards an Indian Identity," *DQR* 9 (1979): 52-70. Also in *American Indian Culture and Research Jnl.* 3, i (1979): 39-56.

HOUSE MADE OF DAWN

Barry, Nora B., "The Bear's Son Folk Tale in WHEN THE LEGENDS DIE and HOUSE MADE OF DAWN," *WAL* 12 (1978): 172-79.

Billingsley, R. G., "HOUSE MADE OF DAWN: Momaday's Treatise on the Word," *SwAL* (1975): 81-7.

Davis, Jack L., "The Whorf Hypothesis and Native American Literature," *SDR* 14, ii (Summer, 1976): 59-72.

Evers, Lawrence J., "Words and Place: A Reading of HOUSE MADE OF DAWN," *WAL* 11 (Feb., 1977): 297-320. Also in Pilkington, W. T., ed., *Critical Essays on the Western Novel*, 243-1.

Hogan, Linda, "Who Puts Together," *DQ* 14, iv (Winter, 1980): 103-12.

Hylton, Marion W., "On a Trail of Pollen: Momaday's HOUSE MADE OF DAWN," *Crit* 14, ii (1972): 60-9.

Kerr, Baine, "The Novel as Sacred Text: N. Scott Momaday's Mythmaking Ethic," *SWR* 63 (1978): 172-79.

Kousaleos, Peter G., "A Study of the Language, Structure, and Symbolism in Jean Toomer's CANE and N. Scott Momaday's HOUSE MADE OF DAWN," *DAI* 34 (1973): 2631A-32A.

Larson, C. R., *American Indian Fiction*, 78-96.

Lattin, Vernon E., "The Quest for Mythic Vision in Contemporary Native American and Chicano Fiction," *AL* 50, iv (Jan., 1979): 632-7.

Linck, Charles E., "Visualizing Cinematic Structure in N. Scott Momaday's HOUSE MADE OF DAWN," *CCTE* 45 (1980): 98-101.

McAllister, Harold S., "Be a Man, Be a Woman: Androgyny in HOUSE MADE OF DAWN," *AIQ* 2 (1975): 14-22.

————, "Incarnate Grace and the Paths of Salvation in HOUSE MADE OF DAWN," *SDR* 12, iv (1974): 115-25.

McDonald, Walter R., "The Redemption Novel: Suffering and Hope in THE ASSISTANT and HOUSE MADE OF DAWN," *CCTE* 41 (1976): 55-61.

Oleson, Carole, "The Remembered Earth: Momaday's HOUSE MADE OF DAWN," *SDR* 11, i (1973): 59-78.

Prampolini, Gaetano, "On N. Scott Momaday's HOUSE MADE OF DAWN," *Dismisura: Revista Mimestrale di Produzione and Crit. Culturale* (Alatri, Italy), 39-50 (1980): 58-75.

Robinson, David, "Angles of Vision in N. Scott Momaday's HOUSE MADE OF DAWN," in Carter, G. E., and J. R. Parker, eds., *Essays on Minority Cultures*, 129-41.

Sharma, R. S., "Vision and Form in N. Scott Momaday's HOUSE MADE OF DAWN," *IJAS* 7, i (Jan., 1982): 69-79.

Strelke, Barbara, "N. Scott Momaday: Racial Memory and Individual Imagination," in Chapman, Abraham, ed., *Literature of the American Indians: Views and Interpretations*, N.Y.: New American Library, 1975, 348-52.

Trimble, M. S., *N. Scott Momaday*, 18-27.

Trimmer, Joseph F., "Native Americans and the American Mix: N. Scott Momaday's HOUSE MADE OF DAWN," *ISSQ* 28 (1975): 75-91.

Velie, Alan R., "Cain and Abel in N. Scott Momaday's HOUSE MADE OF DAWN," *JWest* 17, ii (1978): 55-62.

————, "HOUSE MADE OF DAWN: Nobody's Protest Novel," *Four American Indian Literary Masters*, 52-64.

Waniek, Marilyn N., "The Power of Language in N. Scott Momaday's HOUSE MADE OF DAWN," *MV* 4, i (Spring, 1980): 23-8.

Watkins, Floyd C., "Culture versus Anonymity in HOUSE MADE OF DAWN," *In Time and Place*, 133-71.

Woodard, Charles L., "Momaday's HOUSE MADE OF DAWN," *Expl* 36, ii (1978): 27-8.

MONSARRAT, NICHOLAS (JOHN TURNEY), 1910-1979

GENERAL

Jarratt, Thomas D., "The Talent of Nicholas Monsarrat," *EJ* 45 (Apr., 1956): 173-80.

THE CRUEL SEA

Anon., *Notes on Nicholas Monsarrat's THE CRUEL SEA*, London: Methuen, 1960 (Study aid series).

Jarratt, Thomas D., "The Talent of Nicholas Monsarrat," *EJ* 45 (Apr., 1956): 176-8.

MONTGOMERY, MARION, 1925-

GENERAL

Colvert, James B., "An Interview with Marion Montgomery," *SoR* 6 (1970): 1041-53. Also in Carr, J., ed., *Kite-Flying and Other Irrational Acts*, 59-69.

FUGITIVE

Landess, Thomas H., "Marion Montgomery's FUGITIVE," *GaR* 28 (1974): 212-17.

Vauthier, Simone, "The 'Fundamental Dialogue': Listening in Marion Montgomery's FUGITIVE," *RANAM* 9 (1976): 223-42.

THE WANDERING OF DESIRE

Montgomery, Marion, "Words, and the Freedom to Suppose," *LaS* 5 (1966): 278-88. [On its genesis.]

MOORE, BRIAN, 1921-

GENERAL

Cook, Bruce, "Brian Moore: Private Person," *Cweal* 100 (Aug. 23, 1974): 457-9.

Dahlie, Hallvard, *Brian Moore*.

————, "Brian Moore: An Interview," *TamR* 46 (Winter, 1968): 2-29.

————, "The Novels of Brian Moore," *DA* 29 (1968): 255A.

Flood, J., *Brian Moore*.

Foster, John W., "Crisis and Ritual in Brian Moore's Belfast Novels," *Eire-Ireland* 3 (Autumn, 1968): 66-74.

————, "Passage Through Limbo: Brian Moore's North American Novels," *Crit* 13, i (1971): 5-18.

Frayne, John P., "Brian Moore's Wandering Irishman—The Not-So-Wild Colonial Boy," in Porter, R. J., and J. D. Brophy, eds., *Essays in Modern Irish Literature*, 215-34.

French, Philip, "The Novels of Brian Moore," *LonM* n.s. 5 (Feb., 1966): 86-91.

Fulford, Robert, "Robert Fulford Interviews Brian Moore," *TamR* 23 (Spring, 1962): 5-18.

Gallagher, Michael P., "The Novels of Brian Moore," *Studies* 60, ccxxxviii (Summer, 1971): 180-94.

Goetsch, Paul, "Brian Moore's Canadian Fiction," in Kosok, H., ed., *Studies in Anglo-Irish Literature*, 345-55.

Graham, John, "Brian Moore," in Garrett, G., ed., *Writer's Voice*, 51-74. [Interview.]

Henry, DeWitt, "The Novels of Brian Moore: A Retrospective," *Ploughshares* 2, ii (1974): 7-27. [Not seen.]

Hirschberg, Stuart, "Growing Up Abject as Theme in Brian Moore's Novels," *CJIS* 1, ii (1975): 11-18. [Not seen.]

Kersnowski, Frank L., "Exit the Anti-Hero," *Crit* 10, iii (1968): 60-71.

Ludwig, Jack, "Brian Moore: Ireland's Loss, Canada's Novelist," *Crit* 5, i (Spring-Summer, 1962): 5-13.

_____, "Exile from the Emerald Island," *Nation* 200 (Mar. 15, 1965): 287-8.

Mahon, Derek, "Webs of Artifice: On the Novels of Brian Moore," *New Rev* 3, xxxii (Nov., 1976): 43-6.

McSweeney, Kerry, "Brian Moore: Past and Present," *CritQ* 18, ii (Summer, 1976): 53-66.

_____, "The Sins of the Fathers," *QQ* 86 (1979): 742-7.

Moore, Brian, "The Expatriate Writer," *AntigR* 17 (Spring, 1974): 27-30.

_____, "The Writer as Exile," *CJIS* 2, ii (Dec., 1976): 5-17.

Pacey, D., *Creative Writing in Canada*, 262-4.

Paulin, Tom, in Dunn, D., ed., *Two Decades of Irish Writing*, 242-50.

Prosky, Murray, "The Crisis of Identity in the Novels of Brian Moore," *Eire* 6, iii (Fall, 1971): 106-18.

Rafroidi, Patrick, "Bovaryism and the Irish Novel," *IUR* 7 (1977): 237-43.

_____, "The Great Brian Moore Collection," in Rafroidi, P., and M. Harmon, eds., *Irish Novel in Our Time*, 221-33.

Ricks, Christopher, "The Simple Excellence of Brian Moore," *NStat* (Feb. 18, 1966): 227-8.

Sale, Richard B., "An Interview in London with Brian Moore," *SNNTS* 1, i (Spring, 1969): 67-80.

Scanlan, John A., Jr., "The Artist-in-Exile: Brian Moore's North American Novels," *Eire* 12, ii (Summer, 1977): 14-33.

_____, "States of Exile: Alienation and Art in the Novels of Brian Moore and Edna O'Brien," *DAI* 36 (1976): 5287A-88A.

Staines, David, "Observance without Belief," *CanL* 73 (Summer, 1973): 8-24.

Stovel, Bruce, "Brian Moore: The Realist's Progress," *ESC* 7, ii (Summer, 1981): 183-200.

Toolan, Michael J., "Psyche and Belief: Brian Moore's Contending Angels," *Eire* 15, iii (Fall, 1980): 97-111.

Woodcock, George, "Rounding Giotto's Circle: Brian Moore's Poor Bitches," *Odysseus Ever Returning*, 40-9.

AN ANSWER FROM LIMBO

Allen, Walter, "All for Art," *NStat* (Mar. 26, 1963): 465-6.

Dahlie, H., *Brian Moore*, 81-94.

Flood, J., *Brian Moore*, 49-63.

Foster, J. W., *Forces and Themes in Ulster Fiction*, 171-4.

_____, "Passage Through Limbo: Brian Moore's North American Novels," *Crit* 13, i (1970): 10-13.

Frayne, John P., "Wandering Irishman—The Not-So-Wild Colonial Boy," in Porter, R. J., and J. D. Brophy, eds., *Modern Irish Literature*, 225-9.

Gilman, Richard, in *Ctary* 36 (Aug., 1963): 176-7.

Hicks, Granville, "Asphalt in Bitter Soil," *SatR* 45 (Oct. 13, 1962): 20+.

Hornyansky, Michael, "Countries of the Mind," *TamR* 26 (Winter, 1963): 63-7.

Scanlan, John A., "The Artist-in-Exile: Brian Moore's North American Novels," *Eire* 12, ii (Summer, 1977): 24-9.

Watt, F. W., in *UTQ* (July, 1963): 395-6.

Woodcock, George, "A Close Shave," *CanL* (Spring, 1962): 70-2.

CATHOLICS

Dahlie, H., *Brian Moore*, 104-10.

Dorenkamp, J. H., "Finishing the Day: Nature and Grace in Two Novels by Brian Moore," *Eire* 13, i (Spring, 1978): 103-12.

Flood, J., *Brian Moore*, 93-6.

Foster, J. W., *Forces and Themes in Ulster Fiction*, 181-5.

Porter, Raymond J., "Miracle, Mystery and Faith in Brian Moore's CATHOLICS," *Eire* 10, iii (Autumn, 1975): 79-88.

Shepherd, Allen, "Place and Meaning in Brian Moore's CATHOLICS," *Eire* 15, iii (1980): 134-40.

_____, "Place in Brian Moore's CATHOLICS," *NConL* 9, iv (1979): 4-5.

THE DOCTOR'S WIFE

Dahlie, H., *Brian Moore*, 130-40.

Raifroidi, Patrick, "Bovarysm and the Irish Novel," *IUR* 7, ii (Autumn, 1977): 240-3.

THE EMPEROR OF ICE-CREAM

Anderson, K. Douglas, "What Brian Moore Can Teach the Writer: A Craft Study of a Passage from THE EMPEROR OF ICE-CREAM," *MSE* 5, iv (1978): 7-10.

Anon., "Bombing Around Belfast," *TLS* (Feb. 3, 1966): 77.

Buckeye, Robert, in *DR* 46(Spring, 1966): 135-9.

Dahlie, H., *Brian Moore*, 59-70.

_____, "Brian Moore's Broader Vision: THE EMPEROR OF ICE-CREAM," *Crit* 9, i (1967): 43-55.

Flood, J., *Brian Moore*, 64-71.

Foster, J. W., *Forces and Themes in Ulster Fiction*, 122-30.

French, Philip, "The Novels of Brian Moore," *LonM* n.s. 5 (Feb., 1966): 88-90.

Galloway, David, "Belfast Blues," *Spectator* (Feb. 4, 1966): 142.

Green, Robert, "The Function of Poetry in Brian Moore's THE EMPEROR OF ICE-CREAM," *CanL* 93 (Summer, 1982): 164-72.

Hicks, Granville, "An Invitation to Live," *SatR* 48 (Sept. 18, 1965): 97-8.

Raban, J., "Narrative: Time," *Techniques of Modern Fiction*, 64-6.

Scanlan, John A., "The Artist-in-Exile: Brian Moore's North American Novels," *Eire* 12, ii (Summer, 1977): 16-24.

Smith, Marion B., "Existential Morality," *CanL* 28 (Spring, 1966): 68-70.

Taranth, Rajeev, "Deepening Experience: A Note on THE EMPEROR OF ICE-CREAM," *LCrit* 6 (Summer, 1966): 68-72.

THE FEAST OF LUPERCAL

Dahlie, H., *Brian Moore*, 51-9.

Flood, J., *Brian Moore*, 24-34.

Foster, John W., "Crisis and Ritual in Brian Moore's Belfast Novels," *Eire* 3, iii (Autumn, 1968): 66-74.

_____, *Forces and Themes in Ulster Fiction*, 151-60.

Horchler, Richard, "A Wrench of Pity," *Cweal* 46 (July 12, 1957): 380-1.

LaFarge, Oliver, "Defeat in a Church School," *SatR* 40 (Apr. 27, 1957): 15, 27.

Paulin, Tom, in Dunn, D., ed., *Two Decades of Irish Writing*, 242-5.

FERGUS

Dahlie, H., *Brian Moore*, 94-103.

Flood, J., *Brian Moore*, 81-8.

Foster, J. W., *Forces and Themes in Ulster Fiction*, 179-81.

Scanlan, John A., "The Artist-in-Exile: Brian Moore's North American Novels," *Eire* 12, ii (Summer, 1977): 32-3.

Toolan, Michael J., "Psyche and Belief: Brian Moore's Contending Angels," *Eire* 15, iii (Fall, 1980): 106-10.

THE GREAT VICTORIAN COLLECTOR

Dahlie, H., *Brian Moore*, 110-19.

McSweeney, Kerry, "Brian Moore: Past and Present," *CritQ* 18 (Summer, 1976): 53-5, 64-6.

Merivale, Patricia, "Neo-Modernism in the Canadian Artist-Parable: Hubert Aquin and Brian Moore," *CRCL* 6, ii (Spring, 1979): 195-205.

Toolan, Michael J., "Psyche and Belief: Brian Moore's Contending Angels," *Eire* 15, iii (Fall, 1980): 106-10.

I AM MARY DUNNE

Brady, Charles A., "I AM MARY DUNNE, by Brian Moore," *Eire* 3, iv (1968): 136-40.

Dahlie, H., *Brian Moore*, 122-30.

Dorenkamp, J. H., "Finishing the Day: Nature and Grace in Two Novels by Brian Moore," *Eire* 13, i (Spring, 1978): 103-12.

Flood, J., *Brian Moore*, 71-80.

Foster, J. W., *Forces and Themes in Ulster Fiction*, 175-8.

_____, "Passage Through Limbo: Brian Moore's North American Novels," *Crit* 13, i (1970): 13-17.

Paulin, Tom, in Dunn, D., ed., *Two Decades of Irish Writing*, 248-50.

Scanlan, John A., "The Artist-in-Exile: Brian Moore's North American Novels," *Eire* 12, ii (Summer, 1977): 29-32.

THE LONELY PASSION OF JUDITH HEARNE

Dahlie, H., *Brian Moore*, 42-51.

Flood, J., *Brian Moore*, 15-24.

Foster, John W., "Crisis and Ritual in Brian Moore's Belfast Novels," *Eire* 3, iii (Autumn, 1968): 66-74.

_____, *Forces and Themes in Ulster Fiction*, 151-66.

Green, Robert, "Brian Moore's JUDITH HEARNE: Celebrating the Commonplace," *IFR* 7 (1980): 29-33.

MacDougall, Robert, in *CanF* (Aug., 1956): 111-12.

THE LUCK OF GINGER COFFEY

Conacher, D. J., in *QQ* 68 (Summer, 1961): 351-3.

Dahlie, H., *Brian Moore*, 71-81.

Flood, J., *Brian Moore*, 35-49.

Foster, J. W., *Forces and Themes in Ulster Fiction*, 168-71.

_____, "Passage Through Limbo: Brian Moore's North American Novels," *Crit* 13, i (1970): 6-10.

Frayne, John, "Brian Moore's Wandering Irishman—The Not-So-Wild Colonial Boy," in Porter, R. J., and J. D. Brophy, eds., *Modern Irish Literature*, 225-9.

Goetsch, Paul, "Brian Moore's Canadian Fiction," in Kosok, H., ed., *Studies in Anglo-Irish Fiction*, 349-53.

Ludwig, Jack, "Fiction for the Majors," *TamR* 17 (Autumn, 1960): 65-71.

_____, "A Mirror of Moore," *CanL* 7 (Winter, 1961): 19-23. Also in Woodcock, G., ed., *Canadian Novel in the Twentieth Century*, 212-18.

Magid, Norma, "On Loneliness," *Cweal* (Sept. 30, 1960): 20-1.

Tallmann, Warren, "Irishman's Luck," *CanL* (Autumn, 1960): 69-70.

Watt, F. W., in *UTQ* 30 (July, 1961): 404-6.

THE MANGAN INHERITANCE

Brian, Michael, "Mangan's Inheritance, Moore's Debts," *JCF* 30 (1980): 160-4.

Dahlie, H., *Brian Moore*, 140-9.

McSweeney, Kerry, "The Sins of the Fathers," *QQ* 86 (1979): 742-7.

BIBLIOGRAPHY

Dahlie, H., *Brian Moore*, 158-65.

_____, in *Crit* 9, i (1967): 51-5.

Studing, Richard, "Brian Moore Bibliography," *Eire* 10 (Autumn, 1975): 89-105.

MORGAN, CHARLES, 1894-1958

GENERAL

Duffin, H. C., *Novels and Plays of Charles Morgan*.

Painting, David E., "Charles Morgan: A Revaluation," *AWR* 18, xlii (Feb., 1970): 90-4.

Priestley, J. B., "Morgan in a Mirror," *NStat* (July 2, 1960): 92-3.

A BREEZE IN MORNING

Duffin, H. C., *Novels and Plays of Charles Morgan*, 204-9.

THE FOUNTAIN (See SPARKENBROKE TRILOGY)

THE GUNROOM

Brock, James, "Morgan in a Mirror," *NStat* (July 23, 1960): 125.

THE JUDGE'S STORY

Duffin, H. C., *Novels and Plays of Charles Morgan*, 198-203.

PORTRAIT IN A MIRROR (See SPARKENBROKE TRILOGY)

SPARKENBROKE (See SPARKENBROKE TRILOGY)

SPARKENBROKE TRILOGY

Duffin, H. C., *Novels and Plays of Charles Morgan*, 171-88.

THE VOYAGE

Duffin, H. C., *Novels and Plays of Charles Morgan*, 189-97.

MORREALE, BEN, 1924-

GENERAL

Brown, Carole, "From Saracen to Iggy: The Novels of Ben Morreale," *ItalAm* 5 (1979): 205-21.

A FEW VIRTUOUS MEN

Brown, Carole, "From Saracen to Iggy: The Novels of Ben Morreale," *ItalAm* 5 (1979): 212-16.

MONDAY, TUESDAY…NEVER COME SUNDAY

Browne, Carole, "From Saracen to Iggy: The Novels of Ben Morreale," *ItalAm* 5 (1979): 216-19.

THE SEVENTH SARACEN

Brown, Carole, "From Saracen to Iggy: The Novels of Ben Morreale," *ItalAm* 5 (1979): 206-11.

MORRIS, WRIGHT, 1910-

GENERAL

Aldridge, John W., "Wright Morris Country," in Knoll, R. E., ed., *Conversations with Wright Morris*, 3-13.

Allen, W., *Modern Novel*, 315-17.

"An Interview with Wright Morris," *BForum* 2 (1976): 36-8, 40.

Bird, Roy K., "Wright Morris, Imaginative Transformations of Commonplace, the Past, and Language," *DAI* 43, iii (Sept., 1982): 799A.

Bluefarb, Sam, "Point of View: An Interview with Wright Morris, July, 1958," *Accent* 19 (Winter, 1959): 34-46.

Breit, Harvey, "Talk with Wright Morris," *NYTBR* (June 10, 1951): 19.

Booth, Wayne C., "The Shaping of Prophecy: Craft and Idea in the Novels of Wright Morris," *ASch* 31 (Autumn, 1962): 608-26.

_____, "The Two Worlds in the Fiction of Wright Morris," *SR* 65 (Summer, 1957): 375-99.

Brenner, Jack, "Wright Morris's West: Fallout from a Pioneer Past," *UDQ* 10, iv (Winter, 1976): 63-75.

Burns, Leslie E., "A Psychological Reading of Wright Morris' Early Novels," *DAI* 39 (1979): 7345A.

Carabine, Keith, "Some Observations on Wright Morris's Treatment of 'My Kind of People, Self-Sufficient, Self-Deprived, Self-Unknowing'," *Midamerica* 8 (1981): 115-34.

Carpenter, Frederick, "Wright Morris and the Territory Ahead," *CE* 21 (Dec., 1959): 147-56.

Cohn, Jack R., "Wright Morris: The Design of the Midwestern Fiction," *DAI* 32 (1971): 960A.

"Conversation Between David Madden and Wright Morris," in Knoll, R. E., ed., *Conversations with Wright Morris*, 101-19.

"Conversation Between John W. Aldridge and Wright Morris," in Knoll, R. E., ed., *Conversations with Wright Morris*, 14-33.

"Conversation of Wayne C. Booth and Wright Morris," in Knoll, R. E., ed., *Conversations with Wright Morris*, 74-100.

Crump, G. B., "D. H. Lawrence and the Immediate Present: Kurt Vonnegut, Jr., Ken Kesey, and Wright Morris," *DHLR* 10 (Summer, 1977): 124-40.

_____, *Novels of Wright Morris.*

_____, "Wright Morris and the Immediate Present," *DAI* 31 (1970): 1267A.

Daverman, Richard L., "Wright Morris: Fact and Fiction," *DAI* 41 (1980): 667A-68A.

Dymond, Richard B., "The Impoverished Self: A Study of Selected Fiction of Wright Morris," *DAI* 34 (1973): 2619A.

Eisinger, C. E., *Fiction of the Forties*, 328-41.

Fiedler, L., *Love and Death in the American Novel*, 471-2.

Flanagan, John T., "The Fiction of Wright Morris," *SGG* 3 (1961): 209-31.

Guettinger, Roger J., "The Problem with Jigsaw Puzzles: Form in the Fiction of Wright Morris," *TQ* 11 (Spring, 1968): 209-20.

Hicks, Granville, "Introduction" to *Wright Morris: A Reader*, N.Y.: Harper & Row, 1970.

Howard, L., *Wright Morris.*

Hunt, John W., Jr., "The Journey Back: The Early Novels of Wright Morris," *Crit* 5, i (Spring-Summer, 1962): 41-60.

Klein, M., *After Alienation*, 196-246.

Knoll, R. E., ed., *Conversations with Wright Morris.*

Madden, David, "Character as Revealed Cliche in Wright Morris's Fiction," *MQ* 22, iv (Summer, 1981): 319-36.

_____, "The Great Plains in the Novels of Wright Morris," *Crit* 4, iii (Winter, 1961-62): 5-23.

_____, "The Hero and the Witness in Wright Morris' Field of Vision," *PrS* 34 (Fall, 1960): 263-78.

_____, *Wright Morris.*

Miller, James E., Jr., "The Nebraska Encounter: Willa Cather and Wright Morris," *PrS* 41 (Summer, 1967): 165-7.

Miller, Ralph N., Jr., "The Fiction of Wright Morris: The Sense of Ending," *Midamerica* 3 (1976): 56-76.

Morris, Wright, "Letter to a Young Critic," *MR* 6 (Autumn-Winter, 1964-65): 93-100.

_____, "National Book Award Address," *Crit* 4, iii (Winter, 1961-62): 72-5.

_____, "The Origin of a Species, 1942-1956," *MR* 7 (Winter, 1966): 121-35.

_____, "Origins: Reflections on Emotion, Memory, and Imagination," in Knoll, R. E., ed., *Conversations with Wright Morris*, 153-67.

_____, "Where the West Begins," *PrS* 54, ii (Summer, 1980): 5-14.

_____, and Wayne C. Booth, "The Writing of Organic Fiction: A Conversation," *CritI* 3, ii (Winter, 1976): 387-404.

Neinstein, Raymond L., "Wright Morris: The Metaphysics of Home," *PrS* 53 (Summer, 1979): 121-54.

Nemanic, Gerald, and Harvey White, "GLR/Interview: Wright Morris," *GLRev* 1, ii (Winter, 1975): 1-29.

_____, "A Ripening Eye: Wright Morris and the Field of Vision," *Midamerica* 1 (1974): 120-31.

Rooke, Constance M., "Character in the Early Fiction of Wright Morris," *DAI* 34 (1974): 5990A.

Saluri, Diana C., "'Other Pioneering': A Rhetorical Analysis of Wright Morris's Multiple Viewpoint Fiction," *DAI* 41 (1980): 1600A.

Shetty, M. Nalini, "The Fiction of Wright Morris," *DA* 27 (1967): 3471A.

Trachtenberg, Alan, "The Craft of Vision," *Crit* 4, iii (Winter, 1961-62): 41-55.

Tucker, Martin, "The Landscape of Wright Morris," *LHR* 7 (1965): 43-51.

Waldeland, Lynne M., "Wright Morris: His Theory and Practice of the Craft of Fiction," *DAI* 31 (1970): 1819A.

Waterman, Arthur E., "The Novels of Wright Morris: An Escape from Nostalgia," *Crit* 4, iii (Winter, 1961-62): 24-40.

Westdal, Lincoln W., "Consciousness in the Novels of Wright Morris," *DAI* 37 (1977): 5820A.

Wilson, J. C., "Wright Morris and the Search for the 'Still Point'," *PrS* 49 (Summer, 1975): 154-63.

Wydeven, Joseph J., "Consciousness Refracted: Photography and the Imagination in the Works of Wright Morris," *Midamerica* 8 (1981): 92-114.

_____, "Structures of Consciousness in the Works of Wright Morris," *DAI* 40 (1979): 3307A.

CAUSE FOR WONDER

Crump, G. B., *World of Wright Morris*, 6-9, 85-8.
Howard, L., *Wright Morris*, 31-4.
Klein, M., *After Alienation*, 242-6.

CEREMONY IN LONE TREE

Albers, Randall K., "The Female Transformation: The Role of Women in Two Novels by Wright Morris," *PrS* 53 (1979): 95-115.

Baumbach, Jonathan, "Wake Before Bomb: CEREMONY IN LONE TREE," *Crit* 4, iii (Winter, 1961-62): 56-71. Also in Baumbach, J., *Landscape of Nightmare*, 152-69.

Carabine, Keith, "Some Observations on Wright Morris' Treatment of 'My Kind of People, Self-Sufficient, Self-Deprived, Self-Unknowing'," *Midamerica* 8 (1981): 125-32.

Crump, G. E., *Novels of Wright Morris*, 143-60.

Gardiner, Harold C., in *America* 103 (July 23, 1960): 481-2.

Harper, Robert D., "Wright Morris's CEREMONY IN LONE TREE: A Picture of Life in Middle America," *WAL* 11 (1976): 199-213.

Howard, L., *Wright Morris*, 26-8.

Klein, M., *After Alienation*, 238-42.

Machann, Ginny B., "CEREMONY IN LONE TREE and *Badlands*: The Starkweather Case and the Nebraska Plains," *PrS* 53 (1979): 165-72.

Madden, D., *Wright Morris*, 131-55.

Tornquist, Elizabeth, "The New Parochialism," *Ctary* 31 (May, 1961): 449-52.

Waterman, Arthur E., "The Novels of Wright Morris: An Escape from Nostalgia," *Crit* 4, iii (Winter, 1961-62): 37-9.

THE DEEP SLEEP

Aldridge, John, "Heart of a Secret Tragedy," *NYTBR* (Sept. 13, 1953): 4-5.

Crump, G. B., *Novels of Wright Morris*, 98-112.

Howard, L., *Wright Morris*, 17-19.

Klein, M., *After Alienation*, 220-6.

Madden, D., *Wright Morris*, 92-100.

THE FIELD OF VISION

Albers, Randall K., "The Female Transformation: The Role of Women in Two Novels by Wright Morris," *PrS* 53 (1979): 95-115.

Crump, G. B., "D. H. Lawrence and the Immediate Present: Kurt Vonnegut, Jr., Ken Kesey, and Wright Morris," *DHLR* 10, ii (Summer, 1977): 130-3.

_____, *Novels of Wright Morris*, 113-31.

Hartman, Carl, "Mr. Morris and Some Others," *WR* 21 (Summer, 1957): 307-13.

Hicks, Granville, in *New Leader* 39 (Oct. 1, 1956): 24-5.

Howard, L., *Wright Morris*, 21-3.

Klein, M., *After Alienation*, 238-42.

Leer, Norman, "Three American Novels and Contemporary Society: A Search for Commitment," *WSCL* 3, iii (Fall, 1962): 76-81.

Madden, D., *Wright Morris*, 132-5, 140, 148, 153, 154.

Nemanic, Gerald, "A Ripening Eye: Wright Morris and THE FIELD OF VISION," *Midamerica* 1 (1974): 126-30.

Trachtenberg, Alan, "The Craft of Vision," *Crit* 4, iii (Winter, 1961-62): 47-55.

Waterman, Arthur E., "The Novels of Wright Morris: An Escape from Nostalgia," *Crit* 4, iii (Winter, 1961-62): 35-7.

FIRE SERMON

Crump, G. B., *Novels of Wright Morris*, 195-205.

Schwartz, Joseph, "Past and Present: Joseph Schwartz on Wright Morris," *FictionI* 2/3 (1974): 144-7.

THE HOME PLACE

Eisinger, C. E., *Fiction of the Forties*, 34-6.

Howard, L., *Wright Morris*, 19-21.

Hunt, John W., Jr., "The Journey Back: The Early Novels of Wright Morris," *Crit* 5, i (Spring-Summer, 1962): 46-50.

Madden, D., *Wright Morris*, 41-7.

Wydeven, Joseph J., "Photography and Privacy: The Protests of Wright Morris and James Agee," *MQ* 23, i (Autumn, 1981): 103-15.

THE HUGE SEASON

Allen, W., *Modern Novel*, 316-17.

Crump, G. B., *Novels of Wright Morris*, 73-86.

Daverman, Richard, "The Evanescence of Wright Morris's THE HUGE SEASON," *Midamerica* 8 (1981): 79-91.

Howard, L., *Wright Morris*, 19-21.

Klein, M., *After Alienation*, 226-9.

Madden, D., *Wright Morris*, 101-11.

Waterman, Arthur E., "The Novels of Wright Morris: An Escape from Nostalgia," *Crit* 4, iii (Winter, 1961-62): 33-5.

THE INHABITANTS

Howard, L., *Wright Morris*, 10-11.

Madden, D., *Wright Morris*, 48-51.

IN ORBIT

Crump, G. B., *Novels of Wright Morris*, 185-95.

Garrett, George, "Morris the Magician: A Look at IN ORBIT," *HC* 4, iii (June, 1967): 1-12. Also in Dillard, R. H. W., Garrett, G., and J. R. Moore, eds., *Sounder Few*, 263-74.

Howard, L., *Wright Morris*, 39-41.

Madden, David, "Wright Morris' IN ORBIT: An Unspoken Series of Poetic Gestures," *Crit* 10, ii (1968): 102-19. Also in Madden, D., *Poetic Image in 6 Genres*, 141-62.

Richey, Clarence W., "'The Riverrun': A Note upon a Joycean Quotation in Wright Morris' IN ORBIT," *NConL* 2, i (Jan., 1972): 14-15.

LOVE AMONG THE CANNIBALS

Crump, G. B., "D. H. Lawrence and the Immediate Present: Kurt Vonnegut, Jr., Ken Kesey, and Wright Morris," *DHLR* 10, ii (Summer, 1977): 130-3.

———, *Novels of Wright Morris*, 131-42.

Daymond, Douglas, "Wright Morris, LOVE AMONG THE CANNIBALS: In Search of the Essential," *Sphinx* 3, iv (1981): 19-27.

Hartman, Carl, "An Expense of Flesh," *WR* 22 (Winter, 1958): 152-4.

Howard, L., *Wright Morris*, 24-5.

Klein, M., *After Alienation*, 230-4.

Madden, David, "Morris' CANNIBALS, Cain's SERENADE: The Dynamics of Style," *JPC* 8, i (Summer, 1974): 59-70.

———, *Wright Morris*, 112-30.

Oliphant, Robert, "Public Voices and Wise Guys," *VQR* 37 (Autumn, 1961): 528-37.

Price, Martin, in *YR* 47 (Autumn, 1957): 151-3.

MAN AND BOY

Crump, G. B., *Novels of Wright Morris*, 89-99.

Eisinger, C. E., *Fiction of the Forties*, 237-8.

Fiedler, L., *Love and Death in the American Novel*, 323-4.

Howard, L., *Wright Morris*, 14-15.

Klein, M., *After Alienation*, 211-14.

Madden, D., *Wright Morris*, 83-91.

THE MAN WHO WAS THERE

Crump, G. B., *Novels of Wright Morris*, 56-61.

Eisinger, C. E., *Fiction of the Forties*, 333-34.

Howard, L., *Wright Morris*, 9-10.

Hunt, John W., Jr., "The Journey Back: The Early Novels of Wright Morris," *Crit* 5, i (Spring-Summer, 1962): 46-50.

Madden, D., *Wright Morris*, 41-7.

MY UNCLE DUDLEY

Crump, G. B., *Novels of Wright Morris*, 27-39.

Eisinger, C. E., *Fiction of the Forties*, 331-3.

Howard, L., *Wright Morris*, 7-9.

Hunt, John W., Jr., "The Journey Back: The Early Novels of Wright Morris," *Crit* 5, i (Spring-Summer, 1962): 41-6.

Klein, M., *After Alienation*, 198-200.

Madden, D., *Wright Morris*, 32-41.

ONE DAY

Crump, G. B., *Novels of Wright Morris*, 169-85.

———, "Wright Morris's ONE DAY: The Bad News on the Hour," *Midamerica* 3 (1976): 77-91.

Howard, L., *Wright Morris*, 34-9.

Morris, Wright, in McCormack, T., ed., *Afterwords*, 11-27.

Waterman, Arthur E., "Wright Morris's ONE DAY: The Novel of Revelation," *FurmS* 15, iv (May, 1968): 28-36.

PLAINS SONG: FOR FEMALE VOICES

Arnold, Marilyn, "Wright Morris's PLAINS SONG: Woman's Search for Harmony," *SDR* 20, iii (Autumn, 1982): 50-62.

Waldeland, Lynne, "PLAINS SONG: Women's Voices in the Fiction of Wright Morris," *Crit* 24, i (Fall, 1982): 7-20.

WHAT A WAY TO GO

Booth, Wayne C., "The Shaping of Prophecy: Craft and Idea in the Novels of Wright Morris," *ASch* 31 (Autumn, 1962): 620-6.

Crump, G. B., *Novels of Wright Morris*, 160-8.

Howard, L., *Wright Morris*, 28-31.

Klein, M., *After Alienation*, 34-8.

Madden, D., *Wright Morris*, 112-30.

THE WORKS OF LOVE

Booth, Wayne C., "Form in THE WORKS OF LOVE," in Knoll, R. E., ed., *Conversations with Wright Morris*, 35-73.

Carabine, Keith, "Some Observations on Wright Morris's Treatment of 'My Kind of People, Self-Sufficient, Self-Deprived, Self-Unknowing'," *Midamerica* 8 (1981): 120-5.

Crump, G. B., *Novels of Wright Morris*, 62-71.

Eisinger, C. E., *Fiction of the Forties*, 338-40.

Howard, L., *Wright Morris*, 15-17.

Klein, M., *After Alienation*, 214-20.

Madden, D., *Wright Morris*, 64-75.

THE WORLD IN THE ATTIC

Crump, G. B., *Novels of Wright Morris*, 56-61.

Eisinger, C. E., *Fiction of the Forties*, 336-7.

Howard, L., *Wright Morris*, 12-14.

Hunt, John W., Jr., "The Journey Back: The Early Novels of Wright Morris," *Crit* 5, i (Spring-Summer, 1962): 53-8.

Klein, M., *After Alienation*, 209-11.

Madden, D., *Wright Morris*, 57-63.

BIBLIOGRAPHY

Boyce, Robert L., "A Wright Morris Bibliography," in Knoll, R. E., ed., *Conversations with Wright Morris*, 169-206.

Linden, Stanton J., and David Madden, "A Wright Morris Bibliography," *Crit* 4, iii (Winter, 1961-62): 77-87.

Howard, L., *Wright Morris*, 44-8.

Madden, D., *Wright Morris*, 177-84.

MORRISON, TONI, 1931-

GENERAL

Bakerman, Jane S., "Failures of Love: Female Initiation in the Novels of Toni Morrison," *AL* 52, iv (Jan., 1981): 541-63.

———, "The Seams Can't Show: An Interview with Toni Morrison," *BALF* 12, ii (1978): 56-60.

Bragg, Melvyn, "Black Sisters," *Listener* 105 (1981): 110.

Christian, Barbara, "Community and Nature: The Novels of Toni Morrison," *JEthS* 7, iv (Winter, 1980): 65-78.

Davis, Cynthia A., "Self, Society, and Myth in Toni Morrison's Fiction," *ConL* 23, iii (Summer, 1982): 323-42.

Parker, Bettye J., "Complexity: Toni Morrison's Women—An Interview Essay," in Bell, R. P., et al., eds., *Sturdy Black Bridges*, 251-7.

Stepto, Robert B., "'Intimate Things in Place': A Conversation with Toni Morrison," *MR* 18 (1977): 473-89. Also in Harper, M. S., and R. B. Stepto, eds., *Chant of Saints*, 473-89.

Stratton, Kathryn A. A., "Woman as B: Woman as A," *DAI* 43, ii (Aug., 1982): 447A-48A.

Willis, Susan, "Eruptions of Funk: Historicizing Toni Morrison," *BALF* 16, i (Spring, 1982): 34-42.

THE BLUEST EYE

Bakerman, Jane S., "Failures of Love: Female Initiation in the Novels of Toni Morrison," *AL* 52, iv (Jan., 1981): 543-8.

Bischoff, Joan, "The Novels of Toni Morrison: Studies in Thwarted Sensitivity," *SBL* 6, iii (1975): 21-3.

Byerman, Keith E., "Intense Behaviors: The Use of the Grotesque in THE BLUEST EYE and EVA'S MAN," *CLAJ* 25, iv (June, 1982): 447-57.

Christian, B., *Black Women Novelists*, 138-53, 175-9.

Clark, Norris, "Flying Black: Toni Morrison's THE BLUEST EYE, SULA, and SONG OF SOLOMON," *MV* 4 (Fall, 1980): 51-63.

Klotman, Phyllis R., "Dick-and-Jane and the Shirley Temple Sensibility in THE BLUEST EYE," *BALF* 13, iv (1979): 123-5.

Ogunyemi, Chikwenye O., "Order and Disorder in Toni Morrison's THE BLUEST EYE," *Crit* 19, i (1977): 112-20.

Pullin, Faith, in Lee, A. R., ed., *Black Fiction*, 189-94.

Royster, Philip M., "THE BLUEST EYE," *First World* (Winter, 1977): 35-44.

Weever, Jacqueline de, "The Inverted World of Toni Morrison's THE BLUEST EYE and SULA," *CLAJ* 22 (1979): 402-14.

SONG OF SOLOMON

Atlas, Marilyn J., "The Darker Side of Toni Morrison's SONG OF SOLOMON," *SSMLN* 10, ii (1980): 1-13.

_____, "A Woman Both Shining and Brown: Feminine Strength in Toni Morrison's SONG OF SOLOMON," *SSMLN* 9, iii (1979): 8-12.

Bakerman, Jane S., "Failures of Love: Female Initiation in the Novels of Toni Morrison," *AL* 52, iv (Jan., 1981): 554-63.

Barthold, B. J., *Black Time*, 174-83.

Blake, Susan L., "Folklore and Community in SONG OF SOLOMON," *MELUS* 7, iii (Fall, 1980): 77-82.

Bowman, Diane K., "Flying High: The American Icarus in Morrison, Roth, and Updike," *PCL* 8 (1982): 11-13.

Bruck, Peter, "Returning to One's Roots: The Motif of Searching and Flying in Toni Morrison's SONG OF SOLOMON," in Bruck, P., and W. Karrer, eds., *Afro-American Novel Since 1960*, 289-304.

Clark, Norris, "Flying Black: Toni Morrison's THE BLUEST EYE, SULA, and SONG OF SOLOMON," *MV* 4 (Fall, 1980): 51-63.

De Arman, Charles, "Milkman as the Archetypal Hero: 'Thursday's Child Has Far to Go'," *Obsidian* 6 (Winter, 1980): 56-9.

De Weever, Jacqueline, "Toni Morrison's Use of Fairy Tale, Folk Tale and Myth in SONG OF SOLOMON," *SFQ* 44 (1980): 131-44.

Harris, A. Leslie, "Myth as Structure in Toni Morrison's SONG OF SOLOMON," *MELUS* 7, iii (Fall, 1980): 69-76.

Lee, Dorothy H., "SONG OF SOLOMON: To Ride the Air," *BALF* 16, ii (Summer, 1982): 64-70.

Mickelson, A. Z., *Reaching Out*, 135-53.

Naylor, Carolyn A., "Cross-Gender Significance of the Journey Motif in Selected Afro-American Fiction," *CLQ* 18, i (Mar., 1982): 30-3.

Nodelman, Perry, "The Limits of Structures: A Shorter Version of a Comparison between Toni Morrison's SONG OF SOLOMON and Virginia Hamilton's M.C. HIGGINS THE GREAT," *CLAQ* 7, iii (Fall, 1982): 45-8.

Rosenberg, Ruth, "'And the Children May Know their Names': Toni Morrison's SONG OF SOLOMON," *LOS* 8 (1981): 195-219.

Royster, Philip M., "Milkman's Flying: The Scapegoat Transcended in Toni Morrison's SONG OF SOLOMON," *CLAJ* 24, iv (June, 1981): 419-40.

Samuels, Wilfred D., "Liminality and the Search for Self in Toni Morrison's SONG OF SOLOMON," *MV* 5 (Spring-Fall, 1981): 59-68.

Schultz, Elizabeth, "African and Afro-American Roots in Contemporary Afro-American Literature: The Difficult Search for Family Origins," *SAF* 8, ii (Autumn, 1980): 135-43.

Scruggs, Charles, "The Nature of Desire in Toni Morrison's SONG OF SOLOMON," *ArQ* 38, iv (Winter, 1982): 311-35.

Smith, Valerie A., "'The Singer in One's Soul': Storytelling in the Fiction of James Weldon Johnson, Richard Wright, Ralph Ellison and Toni Morrison," *DAI* 43 (1982): 2350.

Wegs, Joyce, "Toni Morrison's SONG OF SOLOMON: A Blues Song," *ELWIU* 9, ii (Fall, 1982): 211-23.

Werner, C. H., *Paradoxical Resolutions*, 88-96.

SULA

Abel, Elizabeth, "(E)Merging Identities: The Dynamics of Female Friendship in Contemporary Fiction by Women," *Signs* 6, iii (Spring, 1981): 426-9.

Bakerman, Jane S., "Failures of Love: Female Initiation in the Novels of Toni Morrison," *AL* 52, iv (Jan., 1981): 548-54.

Barthold, B. J., *Black Time*, 108-12.

Bischoff, Joan, "The Novels of Toni Morrison: Studies in Thwarted Sensitivity," *SBL* 6, iii (1975): 21-3.

Christian, B., *Black Women Novelists*, 153-79.

Clark, Norris, "Flying Black: Toni Morrison's THE BLUEST EYE, SULA, and SONG OF SOLOMON," *MV* 4 (Fall, 1980): 51-63.

Lounsberry, Barbara, and Grace A. Hovet, "Principles of Perception in Toni Morrison's SULA," *BALF* 13, iv (1979): 126-9.

Lee, Valerie G., "The Use of Folktalk in Novels by Black Women Writers," *CLAJ* 23, iii (Mar., 1980): 269-70.

Martin, Odette C., "SULA," *FW* (Winter, 1977): 35-44.

Mickelson, A. Z., *Reaching Out*, 125-35.

Miller, Adam, "Breedlove, Peace and the Dead: Some Observations on the World of Toni Morrison," *BlSch* 9 (Mar., 1978): 47-50.

Ogunyemi, Chikwenye O., "SULA: 'A Nigger Joke'," *BALF* 13, iv (1979): 130-3.

Parker, Bettye J., "Complexity: Toni Morrison's Women—An Interview Essay," in Bell, R. P., et al., eds., *Sturdy Black Bridges*, 253-5.

Pullin, Faith, in Lee, A. R., ed., *Black Fiction*, 194-8.

Royster, Philip M., "A Priest and a Witch against the Spiders and the Snakes: Scapegoating in Toni Morrison's SULA," *Umoja* 2 (1978): 149-68.

Shannon, Anna, "We Was Girls Together," *MMisc* 10 (1982): 9-22.

Smith, Cynthia J., "Black Fiction By Black Females: SULA," *Crosscurrents* 26 (Fall, 1976): 340-3.

Stein, Karen, "'I Didn't Even Know His Name': Name and Naming in Toni Morrison's SULA," *Names* 28, iii (Sept., 1980): 226-9.

Weever, Jacqueline de, "The Inverted World of Toni Morrison's THE BLUEST EYE and SULA," *CLAJ* 22 (1979): 402-14.

TAR BABY

Bell, Pearl, "Self-Seekers," *Ctary* 72 (Aug., 1981): 56-60.

Howard, Maureen, "A Novel of Exile and Home," *NRep* 184 (Mar. 21, 1981): 29-32.

O'Meally, Robert G., " 'Tar Baby, She Don' Say Nothin'," *Callaloo* 4 (Oct.-Feb., 1981): 193-8.

BIBLIOGRAPHY

Fikes, Robert, Jr., "Echoes from Small Town Ohio: A Toni Morrison Bibliography," *Obsidian* 5, i-ii (1979): 142-8.

MOSLEY, NICHOLAS, 1923-

GENERAL

Banks, John, "Sleight-of-Language," *RCF* 2, ii (Summer, 1982): 118-23.

Booth, Francis, "Impossible Accidents: Nicholas Mosley," *RCF* 2, ii (Summer, 1982): 87-118.

O'Brien, John, "An Interview with Nicholas Mosley," *RCF* 2, ii (Summer, 1982): 58-79.

ACCIDENT

Byrne, Jack, "ACCIDENT / Novel / Script / Film: Mosley /Printer / Losey," *RCF* 2, ii (Summer, 1982): 132-42.

Booth, Francis, "Impossible Accidents: Nicholas Mosley," *RCF* 2, ii (Summer, 1982): 87-118.

IMPOSSIBLE OBJECTS

O'Brien, John, "'It's Like a Story'," *RCF* 2, ii (Summer, 1982): 142-8.

NATALIE NATALIA

Banks, John, "Private Madness and NATALIE NATALIA," *RCF* 2, ii (1982): 128-31.

MOTLEY, WILLARD, 1912-1965

GENERAL

Abbott, Craig S., and Kay Van Mol, "The Willard Motley Papers at Northern Illinois University," *RALS* 7 (Spring, 1977): 3-26.

Fleming, R. E., *Willard Motley*.

Fleming, Robert E., "Willard Motley's Urban Novels," *Umoja* 1, ii (1973): 15-19. [Not seen.]

Giles, James R., "Willard Motley's Concept of 'Style' and 'Material'," *SBL* 4, i (Spring, 1973): 4-6.

Weissgarber, Alfred, "Willard Motley and the Sociological Novel," *SA* 7 (1961): 299-309.

Weyant, Nancy J., "The Craft of Willard Motley's Fiction," *DAI* 36 (1976): 7429A.

KNOCK ON ANY DOOR

Bayliss, John F., "Nick Romano: Father and Son," *NALF* 3 (1969): 18-21, 32.

Bone, R. A., *Negro Novel in America*, 178-80.

Breit, Harvey, in Balakian, N., and C. Simmons, eds., *Creative Present*, 21-3.

Fleming, Robert E., "The First Nick Romano: The Origins of KNOCK ON ANY DOOR," *Midamerica* 2 (1975): 80-7.

_____, *Willard Motley*, 36-63.

Ford, Nick A., "Four Popular Negro Novelists," *Phylon* 15 (1954): 32-4.

Gelfand, B. H., *American City Novel*, 248-52.

Grenander, M. E., "Criminal Responsibility in NATIVE SON and KNOCK ON ANY DOOR," *AL* 49, ii (1977): 221-33.

Hughes, Carl M., *The Negro Novelist*, N.Y.: Citadel, 1953, 178-3, 273-4.

Klinkowitz, Jerome, and Karen Wood, "The Making and Unmaking of KNOCK ON ANY DOOR," *Proof* 3 (1973): 121-37.

Rayson, Ann L., "Prototypes for Nick Romano of KNOCK ON ANY DOOR: From the Diaries in the Collected Manuscripts of the Willard Motley Estate," *NALF* 8 (1974): 248-51.

Rideout, W. B., *Radical Novel in the U.S.*, 261-3.

Schraufnagel, N., *From Apology to Protest*, 44-7.

Weissgarber, Alfred, "Willard Motley and the Sociological Novel," *SA* 7 (1961): 300-4.

LET NO MAN WRITE MY EPITAPH

Bayliss, John F., "Nick Romano: Father and Son," *NALF* 3 (Spring, 1969): 18-21, 32.

Fleming, R. E., *Willard Motley*, 89-108.

Light, James F., in *PrS* 33 (1959): 190-2.

Weyant, N. Jill, "Willard Motley's Pivotal Novel: LET NO MAN WRITE MY EPITAPH," *BALF* 11 (1977): 56-61.

LET NOON BE FAIR

Fleming, R. E., *Willard Motley*, 109-28.

Weyant, N. Jill, "Lyrical Experimentation in Willard Motley's Mexican Novel: LET NOON BE FAIR," *NALF* 10 (1976): 95-9.

WE FISHED ALL NIGHT

Fleming, R. E., *Willard Motley*, 64-88.

Giles, James R., and Karen M. Myers, "Naturalism as Principle and Trap: Theory and Execution in Willard Motley's WE FISHED ALL NIGHT," *SBL* 7, i (1976): 19-22.

Rideout, W. B., *Radical Novel in the U.S.*, 263-4.

BIBLIOGRAPHY

Fleming, R. E., *Willard Motley*, 161-5.

White, Ray L., "Whatever Happened to Willard Motley? a Documentary," *Midamerica* 5 (1978): 111-3-7. [Periodical reviews of the novels.]

MPHAHLELE, EZEKIEL, 1919-

GENERAL

Asein, Samuel O., "The Humanism of Ezekiel Mphahlele," *JCL* 15, i (1980): 38-49.

Barnett, U. A., *Ezekiel Mphahlele*.

_____, "The Legend of Zeke Mphalele," *Contrast* 11, ii (1977): 20-4. [Not seen.]

Enekwe, Ossie O., "From an Interview with Ezekiel Mphahlele," *Greenfield Rev.* 5, iii-iv (1976-77): 72-7.

Mangany, Noel, "The Early Years," *Staffrider* 3, iii (1980): 45-6.

Munro, Ian, Richard Priebe, and Reinhard Sander, "An Interview with Ezekiel Mphahlele," *SBL* 2, iii (Autumn, 1971): 6-8.

MRS. PLUM

Hodge, Norman, "Dogs, Africans and Liberals: The World of Mphahlele's MRS. PLUM," *EinA* 1 (1981): 33-43.

THE WANDERERS

Barnett, U. A., *Ezekiel Mphahlele*, 138-47.

Jarrett-Kerr, Martin, "Novel of Exile," *JCL* 8, i (1973): 112-16.

McCartney, Barney, "Ezekiel Mphahlele: THE WANDERERS," *EAJ* (July, 1971): 41-2.

Nkondo, G. M., "Apartheid and Alienation: Mphahlele's THE WANDERERS," *AT* 20, iv (1973): 59-70.

Olney, J., *Tell Me Africa*, 279-82.

MUNRO, ALICE, 1931-

GENERAL

Carscallen, James, in Heath, J., ed., *Profiles in Canadian Literature* 2, 73-80.

Conron, Brandon, "Munro's Wonderland," *CanL* 78 (Fall, 1978): 109-23.

Dahlie, Hallvard, "The Fiction of Alice Munro," *Ploughshares* 4, iii (Summer, 1978): 56-71.

Djwa, Sandra, "Deep Caves and Kitchen Linoleum: Psychological Violence in the Fiction of Alice Munro," 177-90 in Harger-Grinling and Terry Goldie, eds., *Violence in the Canadian Novel Since 1960/dans le roman Canadien depuis 1960*, St. John's: Memorial Un., 1981.

Dombrowski, Eileen, "'Down the Death': Alice Munro and Transcience," *UWR* 14, i (Fall-Winter, 1978): 21-9.

Hancock, Geoffrey, "An Interview with Alice Munro," *CFM* 43 (1982): 74-114.

Hoy, Helen, "'Dull, Simple, Amazing, Unfathomable': Paradox and Double Vision in Alice Munro's Fiction," *SCL* 5 (Spring, 1980): 100-15.

Kroll, Jeri, "Interview with Alice Munro," *LiNQ* 8, i (1980): 47-55.

Macdonald, Rae M., "A Madman Loose in the World: The Vision of Alice Munro," *MFS* 22, iii (Autumn, 1976): 365-74.

Martin, W. R., "The Strange and Familiar in Alice Munro," *SCL* 7, ii (1982): 214-26.

Metcalf, John, "A Conversation with Alice Munro," *JCF* 1, iv (Fall, 1972): 54-62.

Powell, Barbara P., "Narrative Voices of Alice Munro," *DAI* 42 (1982): 3161A-62A.

Wallace, Bronwen, "Women's Lives: Alice Munro," in Helwig, D., ed., *Human Elements*, 52-67.

LIVES OF GIRLS AND WOMEN

Allentuck, Marcia, "Resolution and Independence in the Works of Alice Munro," *WLWE* 16 (Nov., 1977): 340-3.

Bailey, Nancy I., "The Masculine Image in LIVES OF GIRLS AND WOMEN," *CanL* 80 (Spring, 1979): 113-20.

Blodgett, E. D., "Prisms and Arcs: Structure in Hebert and Munro," in Bessai, D., and D. Jackel, eds., *Figures in a Ground*, 115-21. Also (revised) in Blodgett, E. D., *Configuration: Essays in Canadian Literatures*, Downsview: ECW, 1982, 66-74, 78-84.

Fleenor, Juliann E., "Rape Fantasies as Initiation Rite: Female Imagination in LIVES OF GIRLS AND WOMEN," *ROO* 4, iv (Winter, 1979): 35-49.

Gros-Louis, Dolores, "Pens and Needles: Daughters and Mothers in Recent Canadian Literature," *KCN* 2, iii (Winter, 1976-77): 8-15.

Macdonald, Rae M., "A Madman Lose in the World: The Vision of Alice Munro," *MFS* 22, iii (Autumn, 1976): 370-2.

_____, "Structure and Detail in LIVES OF GIRLS AND WOMEN," *SCL* 3 (Summer, 1978): 199-210.

Moss, John, "Alice in the Looking Glass: Munro's LIVES OF GIRLS AND WOMEN," *Sex and Violence in the Canadian Novel*, 54-68.

Packer, Miriam, "LIVES OF GIRLS AND WOMEN: A Creative Search for Completion," in Moss, J., ed., *Canadian Novel: Here and Now*, 134-44.

Struthers, J. R., "Alice Munro and the American South," *CRevAS* 6, ii (1975): 196-204. Also (revised) in Moss, J., ed., *Canadian Novel: Here and Now*, 121-33.

_____, "Reality and Ordering: The Growth of a Young Artist in LIVES OF GIRLS AND WOMEN," *ECW* 3 (Fall, 1975): 32-46. Also (revised) in Gerson, Carole, ed., *Modern Canadian Fiction*, B.C.: Open Learning Institute, 1980, 164-74.

Wallace, Bronwen, "Women's Lives: Alice Munro," in Helwig, D., ed., *Human Elements*, 55-9.

BIBLIOGRAPHY

Cook, D. E., "Alice Munro: A Checklist (to December 31, 1974)," *JCF* 16 (1976): 131-6.

Struthers, J. R., "Some Highly Subversive Activities: A Brief Polemic and a Checklist of Works on Alice Munro," *SCL* 6, i (Spring, 1981): 140-50.

MURDOCH, IRIS, 1918-

GENERAL

Aiken, Gail E., "This Accidental World: The Philosophy and Fiction of Iris Murdoch," *DAI* 40 (1980): 5047A.

Allen, W., *Modern Novel*, 282-4.

Allott, Miriam, "The Novels of Iris Murdoch," *Talks to Teachers of English* 2 (1962): 57-71. [Not seen.]

Allsop, K., *Angry Decade*, 88-95.

Anderson, Thayle K., "Concepts of Love in the Novels of Iris Murdoch," *DAI* 31 (1971): 5397A.

Anon., "In the Heart or in the Head," *TLS* (Nov. 7, 1958): 640.

Baldanza, F., *Iris Murdoch*.

_____, "Iris Murdoch and the Theory of Personality," *Criticism* 7 (Spring, 1965): 176-89.

Beams, David W., "Form in the Novels of Iris Murdoch," *DAI* 39 (1978): 2282A-83A.

Bellamy, Michael O., "The Artist and the Saint: An Approach to the Aesthetics and Ethics of Iris Murdoch," *DAI* 36 (1976): 6110A.

_____, "An Interview with Iris Murdoch," *ConL* 18, ii (Spring, 1977): 129-40.

Berthoff, Warner, "Fortunes of the Novel: Muriel Spark and Iris Murdoch," *MR* 8 (Spring, 1967): 314-32. Also in Berthoff, W., *Fictions and Events* 118-54.

Biles, Jack I., "An Interview with Iris Murdoch," *SLitI* 11, ii (1978): 115-25.

Birdsall, Michael E., "Art, Beauty, and Morality in the Novels of Iris Murdoch," *DAI* 41, vii (Jan., 1981): 3114A.

Blow, Simon, "An Interview with Iris Murdoch," *Spectator* 25 (Sept., 1976): 24-5.

Bryden, Ronald, "Talking to Iris Murdoch," *Listener* 79 (Apr. 4, 1968): 433-4.

Byatt, A. S., *Degrees of Freedom*.

_____, *Iris Murdoch*.

Church, Margaret, "Social Consciousness in the Works of Elizabeth Bowen, Iris Murdoch and Mary Lavin," *CollL* 7 (Spring, 1980): 158-63.

Clark, Judith A., "A Complexity of Mirrors: The Novels of Iris Murdoch," *DAI* 39 (1978): 3571A.

Cohen, Steven, "From Subtext to Dreamtext: The Brutal Egotism of Iris Murdoch's Male Narrators," *W&L* n.s. 2 (1982): 222-42.

Conradi, Peter, "The Metaphysical Hostess: The Cult of Personal Relations in the Modern English Novel," *ELH* 48, ii (Summer, 1981): 427-32, 451-2.

Culley, Ann, "Theory and Practice: Characterization in the Novels of Iris Murdoch," *MFS* 15, iii (Autumn, 1969): 335-45.

Cunneen, Sally, "Ingmar Bergman Crossed with Charlie Chaplin? What Iris Murdoch Doesn't Know," *Cweal* 106 (Nov. 9, 1979): 623-6.

Dawson, S. W., "New Scrutinies, I: Iris Murdoch, or Anyone for Incest?" *HuW* 2 (1971): 57-61.

Dick, Bernard F., "The Novels of Iris Murdoch: A Formula for Enchantment," *BuR* 14 (May, 1966): 66-81.

Dipple, E., *Iris Murdoch*.

Emerson, Donald, "Violence and Survival in the Novels of Iris Murdoch," *TWA* 57 (1969): 21-8.

Fast, Lawrence E., "Self-Discovery in the Novels of Iris Murdoch," *DAI* 31 (1971): 5397A.

Felheim, Marvin, "Symbolic Characterization in the Novels of Iris Murdoch," *TSLL* 2 (Summer, 1960): 189-97.

Foley, Betty M., "Iris Murdoch's Use of Works of Art as Analogies of Moral Themes," *DAI* 40 (1979): 2072A.

Fraser, G. S., "Iris Murdoch and the Solidity of the Normal," *ILA* 2 (1959): 37-54.

_____, *Modern Writer and His World*, 184-7.

German, Howard, "The Range of Allusions in the Novels of Iris Murdoch," *JML* 2, i (Sept., 1971): 57-85.

Gerstenberger, D., *Iris Murdoch*.

Gilligan, John T., "The Fiction and Philosophy of Iris Murdoch," *DAI* 35 (1974): 1099A-100A.

Gindin, James, "Ethical Structures in John Galsworthy, Elizabeth Bowen, and Iris Murdoch," in Friedman, A. W., ed., *Forms of Modern British Fiction*, 277-80.

_____, "Images of Illusion in the Works of Iris Murdoch," *TSLL* 2 (Summer, 1960): 180-8. Also in Gindin, J., *Postwar British Fiction*, 178-89.

Glover, Stephen, "An Interview with Iris Murdoch," *New Review* 3 (Nov., 1976): 56-9.

Goshgarian, Gary, "Feminist Values in the Novels of Iris Murdoch," *RLV* 40 (1974): 519-27.

_____, "From Fable to Flesh: A Study of the Female Characters in the Novels of Iris Murdoch," *DAI* 33 (1973): 3583A.

Hague, Angela, "Iris Murdoch's Comic Vision," *DAI* 40 (1980): 5047A.

Hall, James, "Blurring the Will: The Growth of Iris Murdoch," *ELH* 32 (June, 1965): 256-73. Also (expanded) in Hall, J., *Lunatic Giant in the Living Room*, 181-212.

Hall, William, "Bruno's Dream: Technique and Meaning in the Novels of Iris Murdoch," *MFS* 15, iii (Autumn, 1969): 429-43.

_____, "The Third Way: The Novels of Iris Murdoch," *DR* 46 (Autumn, 1966): 306-18.

Hauerwas, Stanley, "The Significance of Vision: Toward an Aesthetic Ethic," *SRC* 2 (Summer, 1972): 36-49.

Henderson, Gloria Ann M., "Dionysus and Apollo: Iris Murdoch and Love," *DAI* 36 (1975): 902A-03A.

Heyd, Ruth, "An Interview with Iris Murdoch," *UWR* 1 (Spring, 1965): 138-43.

Hoffman, Frederick J., "Iris Murdoch: The Reality of Persons," *Crit* 7 (Spring, 1964): 48-57.

_____, "The Miracle of Contingency: The Novels of Iris Murdoch," *Shen* 17, i (Autumn, 1965): 49-56.

Hope, Francis, "The Novels of Iris Murdoch," *LonM* n.s. 1 (Aug., 1961): 84-7. Also in Kostelanetz, R., ed., *On Contemporary Literature*, 468-72.

Hubbart, Marilyn S., "Fairy Tale Stereotypes as Unique Individuals: A Study of Iris Murdoch and Anne Sexton," *PAPA* 4, iii (1978): 33-40.

Jefferson, Douglas, "Iris Murdoch: The Novelist as Moralist," in Jefferson, D., and G. Martin, eds., *Uses of Fiction*, 261-71.

Kaplan, Morton N., "Iris Murdoch and the Gothic Tradition," *DA* 31 (1970): 1231A-32A.

Karl, F. R., *Contemporary English Novel*, 260-5.

Kaufmann, R. J., "The Progress of Iris Murdoch," *Nation* 188 (Mar. 21, 1959): 255-6.

Keates, Lois S., "Varieties of the Quest-Myth in the Early Novels of Iris Murdoch," *DAI* 33 (1972): 1730A.

Kennard, Jean E., "Iris Murdoch: The Revelation of Reality," *Number and Nightmare*, 155-75.

Kennedy, A., *Protean Self*, 277-80.

Kermode, Frank, "The House of Fiction: Interviews with Seven English Novelists," *PR* 30 (Spring, 1963): 62-5.

Kmetz, Gail, "People Don't Do Such Things! Business-as-Usual in the Novels of Iris Murdoch," *MsM* 5 (July, 1976): 70-2, 85-7.

Kogan, Pauline, "Beyond Solipsism to Irrationalism: A Study of Iris Murdoch's Novels," *L&I* 2 (1969): 47-69.

Kriegel, Leonard, in Shapiro, C., ed., *Contemporary British Novelists*, 62-80.

Kuhner, Arlene E., "The Alien God in the Novels of Iris Murdoch," *DAI* 39 (1978): 2955A.

Lenowitz, Kathryn, "The Controversy over Character: An Examination of the Novels of Iris Murdoch and Nathalie Sarraute," *DAI* 41, viii (Feb., 1981): 3567A.

Levidora, Inna, "Reading Iris Murdoch's Novels," *SovL* 10 (1977): 170-8.

Lloyd, Genevieve, "Iris Murdoch on the Ethical Significance of Truth," *P&L* 6, i-ii (1982): 62-75.

Maes-Jelinek, Hena, "A House for Free Characters: The Novels of Iris Murdoch," *RLV* 29 (1963): 45-69.

Magee, Bryan, "Iris Murdoch on Natural Novelists and Unnatural Philosophers," *Listener* 99 (Apr., 1978): 533-5.

Majdiak, Daniel, "Romanticism in the Aesthetics of Iris Murdoch," *TSLL* 14, ii (Summer, 1972): 359-72.

Martin, Graham, "Iris Murdoch and the Symbolist Novel," *BJA* 5 (July, 1965): 296-300.

Martindale, Kathleen M., "For Love of the Good: Moral Philosophy in the Later Novels of Iris Murdoch," *DAI* 42, x (Apr., 1982): 4459A.

Martz, Louis L., "Iris Murdoch: The London Novels," in Brower, Reuben A., ed., *Twentieth-Century Literature in Retrospect* (Harvard English Studies, 2), Cambridge: Harvard Un. Pr., 1971, 65-86.

McCabe, Bernard, "The Guises of Love," *Cweal* 88 (Dec. 3, 1965): 270-3.

Meidner, Olga M., "The Progress of Iris Murdoch," *ESA* 4 (Mar., 1961): 17-38.

Mohan, Rose E., "Through Myth and Reality: A Study of the Novels of Iris Murdoch," *DAI* 39 (1978): 874A.

Morrell, Roy, "Iris Murdoch: The Early Novels," *CritQ* 9 (Autumn, 1967): 272-82.

Oates, Joyce Carol, "The Novelists: Iris Murdoch," *NRep* 179 (Nov. 18, 1978): 27-31.

Obumselu, Ben, "Iris Murdoch and Sartre," *ELH* 42, ii (Summer, 1975): 296-317.

O'Connor, William V., "Iris Murdoch: The Formal and the Contingent," *Crit* 3, ii (Winter-Spring, 1960): 34-46. Also in O'Connor, W. V., *New University Wits*, 53-74.

O'Sullivan, Kevin, "Iris Murdoch and the Image of the Liberal Man," *YLM* 131 (Dec., 1962): 27-32.

Packer, P. A., "The Theme of Love in the Novels of Iris Murdoch," *DUJ* 69 (June, 1977): 217-24.

Pearson, Gabriel, "Iris Mudoch and the Romantic Novel," *New Left Rev.* 13-14 (Jan.-Apr., 1962): 137-45.

Pondrom, Cyrena N., "Iris Murdoch: An Existentialist?" *CLS* 5 (Dec., 1968): 403-19.

Rabinovitz, R., *Iris Murdoch*. Also in Stade, G., ed., *Six Contemporary British Novelists*, 271-332.

Randall, Julia, "Against Consolation: Some Novels of Iris Murdoch," *HC* 13, i (Feb., 1976): 1-15.

Ricks, Christopher, "A Sort of Mystery Novel," *NStat* (Oct. 22, 1965): 604-5.

Rockefeller, Larry J., "Comedy and the Early Novels of Iris Murdoch," *DA* 29 (1969): 4018A.

Rose, W. K., "An Interview with Iris Murdoch," *Shen* 19, ii (Winter, 1968): 3-22.

Sage, Lorna, in *Contemporary English Novel*, 68-74.

Scanlan, Margaret, "The Machinery of Pain: Romantic Suffering in Three Works of Iris Murdoch," *Ren* 29 (Winter, 1977): 69-85.

Schneidermeyer, Wilma F., "The Religious Dimension in the Works of Iris Murdoch," *DAI* 35 (1974): 3113A.

Slaymaker, William, "The Labyrinth of Love: The Problem of Love and Freedom in the Novels of Iris Murdoch," *BLRev* 1, ii (1980): 39-44.

————, "Myths, Mystery and the Mechanisms of Determinism: The Aesthetics of Freedom in Iris Murdoch's Fiction," *PLL* 18, ii (Spring, 1982): 166-80.

Souvage, Jacques, "The Novels of Iris Murdoch," *SGG* 4 (1962): 225-52.

Stettler-Imfeld, B., *Adolescent in the Novels of Iris Murdoch*.

Stimpson, Catherine R., "The Early Novels of Iris Murdoch," *DA* 28 (1968): 5073A-74A.

Strang, Steven M., "Iris Murdoch: Novelist of Moral Intent," *DAI* 43 (1982): 443A.

Stubbs, Patricia, "Two Contemporary Views on Fiction: Iris Murdoch and Muriel Spark," *English* 23 (Autumn, 1974): 102-10.

Sullivan, Zohreb R., "Enchantment and the Demonic in the Novels of Iris Murdoch," *DAI* 32 (1971): 458A.

Swinden, P., *Unofficial Selves*, 230-57.

Taylor, Jane, "Iris Murdoch," *B&B* 16, vii (Apr., 1971): 26-7. [Interview.]

Todd, R., *Iris Murdoch*.

Tucker, Martin, "The Odd Fish in Iris Murdoch's Kettle," *NRep* 154 (Feb. 5, 1966): 26-8.

Weatherhead, A. K(ingsley), "Backgrounds with Figures in Iris Murdoch," *TSLL* 10 (Winter, 1969): 635-48.

Whiteside, George, "The Novels of Iris Murdoch," *Crit* 7 (Spring), 27-47.

Widmer, Kingsley, "The Wages of Intellectuality ... and the Fictional Wagers of Iris Murdoch," in Staley, T. F., ed., *Twentieth-Century Women Novelists*, 16-38.

Winsor, Dorothy A., "Solipsistic Sexuality in Iris Murdoch's Gothic Novels," *Ren* 34, i (Autumn, 1981): 52-63.

Wolf, Nancy C., "Philosophical Ambivalence in Novels of Iris Murdoch," *DAI* 33 (1972): 2959A.

Wolfe, P., *Disciplined Heart*.

————, "Philosophical Themes in the Novels of Iris Murdoch," *DA* 26 (1965): 3357-58.

AN ACCIDENTAL MAN

Baldanza, F., *Iris Murdoch*, 164-8.

Dipple, E., *Iris Murdoch*, 197-212.

Gerstenberger, D., *Iris Murdoch*, 38-9.

Rabinovitz, R., "Iris Murdoch," in Stade, G., ed., *Six Contemporary British Novelists*, 321-2.

Seiler-Franklin, C., *Boulder-Pushers*, 19-24, 176-81.

THE BELL

Allen, W., *Modern Novel*, 283-4.

————, *Reading a Novel*, 61-4.

Ashdown, Ellen A., "Form and Myth in Three Novels by Iris Murdoch: THE FLIGHT FROM THE ENCHANTER, THE BELL and A SEVERED HEAD," *DA* 35 (1975): 5334A-35A.

Baldanza, F., *Iris Murdoch*, 70-83.

Byatt, A. S., *Degrees of Freedom*, 72-104.

————, *Iris Murdoch*, 21-4.

Clayre, Alasdair, "Common Cause: A Garden in the Clearing," *TLS* 59 (Aug. 7, 1959): xxx-xxxxi.

Dick, Bernard F., "The Novels of Iris Murdoch: A Formula for Enchantment," *BuR* 14 (May, 1966): 72-5.

Dipple, E., *Iris Murdoch*, 242-51.

Felheim, Marvin, "Symbolic Characterization in the Novels of Iris Murdoch," *TSLL* 2 (1960): 194-6.

Fraser, G. S., "Iris Murdoch: The Solidity of the Normal," *ILA* 2 (1959): 42-54.

German, Howard, "Allusions in the Early Novels of Iris Murdoch," *MFS* 15, iii (Autumn, 1969): 372-3.

Gerstenberger, D., *Iris Murdoch*, 31-3.

Graham, A. R., "All Our Failures are Failures of Love," *NYTBR* (Oct. 26, 1958): 4-5.

Hall, James, "Blurring the Will: The Growth of Iris Murdoch," *ELH* 32 (June, 1965): 266-73. Also in Hall, J., *Lunatic Giant in the Living Room*, 190-9.

Howe, Irving, "Realities and Fictions," *PR* 26 (Winter, 1959): 132-3.

Jones, Dorothy, "Love and Morality in Iris Murdoch's THE BELL," *Meanjin* 26 (Mar., 1967): 85-90.

Kaehele, Sharon, and Howard German, "The Discovery of Reality in Iris Murdoch's THE BELL," *PMLA* 82 (Dec., 1967): 554-63.

Karl, F. R., *Contemporary English Novel*, 261-4.

Kimber, John, "THE BELL: Iris Murdoch," *Delta* 18 (Summer, 1959): 31-4.

Kriegel, Leonard, in Shapiro, C., ed., *Contemporary British Novelists*, 69-72.

Maes-Jelinek, Hena, "A House for Free Characters: The Novels of Iris Murdoch," *RLV* 29 (1963): 56-9.

Majdiak, Daniel, "Romanticism in the Aesthetics of Iris Murdoch," *TSLL* 14, ii (Summer, 1972): 372-5.

McGinnes, Robert M., "Murdoch's THE BELL," *Expl* 28 (1969): Item 1.

Meidner, Olga M., "The Progress of Iris Murdoch," *ESA* 4 (Mar., 1961): 25-31.

Morrell, Roy, "Iris Murdoch: The Early Novels," *CritQ* 9 (Autumn, 1967): 277-81.

O'Connor, William V., "Iris Murdoch: The Formal and the Contingent," *Crit* 3, ii (Winter-Spring, 1960): 42-3. Also in O'Connor, W. V., *New University Wits*, 65-6.

Rabinovitz, R., *Iris Murdoch*, 24-8. Also in Stade, G. E., ed., *Six Contemporary British Novelists*, 295-300.

Raymond, John, "The Unclassifiable Image," *NStat* 56 (Nov. 15, 1958): 697-8. Also in Raymond, J., *Doge of Dover*, 179-84.

Rippier, J. S., *Some Postwar English Novelists*, 78, 82-8.

Seiler-Franklin, C., *Boulder-Pushers*, 31-40.

Sisk, John P., "Melodramatic Story and Novel of Ideas," *Cweal* 69 (Nov. 7, 1958): 154-5.

Souvage, Jacques, "The Novels of Iris Murdoch," *SGG* 4 (1962): 244-6.

————, "Symbol as Narrative Device: An Interpretation of Iris Murdoch's THE BELL," *ES* 43 (Apr., 1962): 81-96.

Stewart, Jack F., "Dialectics in Murdoch's THE BELL," *RS* 48 (Dec., 1980): 210-17.

Wall, Stephen, "The Bell in THE BELL," *EIC* 13 (July 1963): 265-73.

Whiteside, George, "The Novels of Iris Murdoch," *Crit* 7 (Spring, 1964): 37-9.

Winsor, Dorothy A., "Iris Murdoch and the Uncanny: Supernatural Events in THE BELL," *L&P* 30, iii-iv (1980): 147-54.

————, "Solipsistic Sexuality in Iris Murdoch's Gothic Novels," *Ren* 34, i (Autumn, 1981): 53-7.

Wolfe, P., *Disciplined Heart*, 113-38.

THE BLACK PRINCE

Baldanza, F., *Iris Murdoch*, 168-73.

Byatt, A. S., in *Contemporary English Novel*, 34-6.

————, *Iris Murdoch*, 35-8.

Dipple, E., *Iris Murdoch*, 109-32.

————, "Iris Murdoch and Vladimir Nabokov: An Essay in Literary Realism and Experimentalism," in Campbell, J., and J. Doyle, eds., *Practical Vision*, 103-18.

Kennedy, A., *Protean Self*, 280-3.

Lamarque, Peter, "Truth and Art in Iris Murdoch's THE BLACK PRINCE," *P&L* 2, ii (Fall, 1978): 209-22.

Orr, Christopher, "Iris Murdoch's Critique of Tragedy in THE BLACK PRINCE and A WORD CHILD," *BWVACET* 4, i (1977): 10-18.

Piper, William B., "The Accommodation of the Present in Novels by Murdoch and Powell," *SNNTS* 11, ii (Summer, 1979): 185-93 *passim*.

Rabinovitz, R., "Iris Murdoch," in Stade, G., ed., *Six Contemporary British Novelists*, 322-4.

Slaymaker, William, "Myths, Mystery and the Mechanisms of Determinism: The Aesthetics of Freedom in Iris Murdoch's Fiction," *PLL* 18, ii (Spring, 1982): 173-9.

Stewart, Jack F., "Art and Love in Murdoch's THE BLACK PRINCE," *RS* 46 (June, 1978): 69-78.

Sturrock, June, "Good and the Gods of THE BLACK PRINCE," *Mosaic* 10, iv (1977): 133-46.

Todd, R., *Iris Murdoch*, 29-42.

————, "The Plausibility of THE BLACK PRINCE," *DQR* 8, ii (1978): 82-93.

Wolfe, Peter, "'Malformed Treatise' and Prizewinner: Iris Murdoch's THE BLACK PRINCE," *SLitI* 11, ii (1978): 97-113.

BRUNO'S DREAM

Baldanza, F., *Iris Murdoch*, 148-59.

Dipple, E., *Iris Murdoch*, 168-81.

Gerstenberger, D., *Iris Murdoch*, 45-9.

Hall, William F., "BRUNO'S DREAM: Technique and Meaning in the Novels of Iris Murdoch," *MFS* 15, iii (Autumn, 1969): 435-43.

Kermode, Frank, *Modern Essays*, London: Fontana, 1971, 261-7.

Rabinovitz, R., "Iris Murdoch," in Stade, G., ed., *Six Contemporary British Novelists*, 321-2.

Swinden, P., *Unofficial Selves*, 1-4.

Thomson, P. W., "Iris Murdoch's Honest Puppetry—The Characters of BRUNO'S DREAM," *CritQ* 11, iii (Autumn, 1969): 277-83.

Todd, R., *Iris Murdoch*, 57-66.

Wain, John, "Women's Work," *NYRB* 12 (Apr. 24, 1969): 38-40.

A FAIRLY HONOURABLE DEFEAT

Baldanza, F., *Iris Murdoch*, 160-4.

Bellamy, Michael O., "The Artist and the Saint: Iris Murdoch's A FAIRLY HONOURABLE DEFEAT," *RLV* 45, i (1979): 90-104.

Dipple, E., *Iris Murdoch*, 181-96.

Gerstenberger, D., *Iris Murdoch*, 37-8.

Hoskins, Robert, "Iris Murdoch's Midsummer Nightmare," *TCL* 18, iii (July, 1972): 191-8.

Rabinovitz, R., "Iris Murdoch," in Stade, G., ed., *Six Contemporary British Novelists*, 319-21.

Seiler-Franklin, C., *Boulder-Pushers*, 94-101, 160-6.

Swinden, P., *Unofficial Rose*, 247-57.

Thomas, Edward, "Veteran Propellors," *LonM* 10 (Apr., 1970): 100-3.

Watrin, Jany, "Iris Murdoch's A FAIRLY HONOURABLE DEFEAT," *RLV* 38, i (1972): 46-64.

THE FLIGHT FROM THE ENCHANTER

Allsop, K., *Angry Decade*, 90-1.

Ashdown, Ellen A., "Form and Myth in Three Novels by Iris Murdoch: THE FLIGHT FROM THE ENCHANTER, THE BELL, and A SEVERED HEAD," *DAI* 35 (1975): 5334A-35A.

Baldanza, F., *Iris Murdoch*, 43-56.

Byatt, A. S., *Degrees of Freedom*, 40-60.

_____, *Iris Murdoch*, 16-20.

Dick, Bernard F., "The Novels of Iris Murdoch: A Formula for Enchantment," *BuR* 14 (May, 1966): 70-1.

Dipple, E., *Iris Murdoch*, 136-42.

Felheim, Marvin, "Symbolic Characterization in the Novels of Iris Murdoch," *TSLL* 2 (1960): 191-3.

Fraser, G. S., "Iris Murdoch: The Solidity of the Normal," *ILA* 2 (1959): 40-1.

German, Howard, "Allusions in the Early Novels of Iris Murdoch," *MFS* 15, iii (Autumn, 1969): 364-8.

Gerstenberger, D., *Iris Murdoch*, 25-9.

Holbrook, David, "The Charming Hate of Iris Murdoch," *The Masks of Hate*, Oxford: Pergamon Pr., 1972, 147-58.

Kriegel, Leonard, in Shapiro, C., ed., *Contemporary British Novelists*, 65-7.

Kuehl, Linda, "Iris Murdoch: The Novelist as Magician/The Magician as Artist," *MFS* 15, iii (Autumn, 1969): 347-60.

Maes-Jelinek, Hena, "A House for Free Characters: The Novels of Iris Murdoch," *RLV* 29 (1963): 50-3.

Meidner, Olga M., "Reviewer's Bane: A Study of Iris Murdoch's THE FLIGHT FROM THE ENCHANTER," *EIC* 11 (Oct., 1961): 435-47.

O'Connor, William V., "Iris Murdoch: The Formal and the Contingent," *Crit* 3, ii (Winter-Spring, 1960): 38-40. Also in O'Connor, W. V., *New University Wits*, 59-62.

O'Sullivan, Kevin, "Iris Murdoch and the Image of Liberal Man," *YLM* 131 (Dec., 1962): 28-30.

Rabinovitz, R., *Iris Murdoch*, 13-18. Also in Stade, G., ed., *Six Contemporary British Novelists*, 283-90.

Rippier, J. S., *Some Postwar English Novelists*, 74-9.

Souvage, Jacques, "The Novels of Iris Murdoch," *SGG* 4 (1962): 238-41.

_____, "Theme and Structure in Iris Murdoch's FLIGHT FROM THE ENCHANTER," *Spieghel Historiael van de Bond van Gentste Germanisten* 3 (June, 1961): 73-88.

Sullivan, Zohreh T., "The Contracting Universe of Iris Murdoch's Gothic Novels," *MFS* 23, iv (Winter, 1977-78): 557-69.

_____, "Enchantment and the Demonic in Iris Murdoch: THE FLIGHT FROM THE ENCHANTER," *MQ* 16, iii (Spring, 1975): 276-97.

Van Ghent, Dorothy, in *YR* 56 (Autumn, 1956): 153-5.

Whiteside, George, "The Novels of Iris Murdoch," *Crit* 7 (Spring, 1964): 32-5.

Wolfe, P., *Disciplined Heart*, 68-88.

HENRY AND CATO

Dipple, E., *Iris Murdoch*, 252-64.

Furuki, Yoshiko, "From the Vicarious to the Immediate—The Emerging Theme of Iris Murdoch's HENRY AND CATO," *TsudaR* 25 (1980): 1-16.

Sage, Lorna, "The Pursuit of Imperfection," *CritQ* 19 (Summer, 1977): 60-8.

THE ITALIAN GIRL

Baldanza, F., *Iris Murdoch*, 116-25.

Barrett, William, in *Atlantic* 214 (Nov., 1964): 201-2.

Bronzwaer, W. J. M., "THE ITALIAN GIRL: An Explication," *Tense in the Novel: An Investigation of Some Potentialities of Linguistic Criticism*, Groningen: Wolters-Noordhoff, 1970, 83-111.

Dick, Bernard F., "The Novels of Iris Murdoch: A Formula for Enchantment," *BuR* 14 (May, 1966): 79-80.

Furbank, P. N., "Gowned Mortality," *Encounter* 23 (Nov., 1964): 88-90.

German, Howard, "The Range of Allusions in Iris Murdoch," *JML* 2, i (Sept., 1971): 69-74.

Hoffman, Frederick J., "The Miracle of Contingency: The Novels of Iris Murdoch," *Shen* 17, ii (Autumn, 1965): 52-5.

Kriegel, Leonard, in Shapiro, C., ed., *Contemporary British Novelists*, 76-8.

Kuehn, Robert E., "Fiction Chronicle," *WSCL* 6 (1965): 135-7.

Pagones, Dorrie, "Wanton Waifs and a Roman Woman," *SatR* 47 (Sept. 19, 1964): 48-9.

Rabinovitz, R., *Iris Murdoch*, 36-8. Also in Stade, G., ed., *Six Contemporary British Novelists*, 310-11.

Tracy, Honor, "Misgivings about Miss Murdoch," *NRep* 151 (Oct. 10, 1964): 21-4.

Tucker, Martin, "More Iris Murdoch," *Cweal* 81 (Oct. 30, 1964): 173-4.

Wolfe, P., *Disciplined Heart*, 203-8.

THE NICE AND THE GOOD

Anon., "Characters in Love," *TLS* (Jan. 25, 1968): 77. Also in *T.L.S: Essays and Reviews from the Times Literary Supplement, 1968*, 56-61.

Ashworth, Ann M., "'Venus, Cupid, Folly, and Time': Bronzino's Allegory and Murdoch's Fiction," *Crit* 23, i (1981): 18-24.

Baldanza, F., *Iris Murdoch*, 138-47.

_____, "THE NICE AND THE GOOD," *MFS* 15, iii (Autumn, 1969): 417-28.

Dipple, E., *Iris Murdoch*, 155-66.

Freemantle, Anne, in *Reporter* 38 (Jan. 25, 1968): 47-9.

Gerstenberger, D., *Iris Murdoch*, 36-7.

Hicks, Granville, "Love Runs Rampant," *SatR* 51 (Jan. 6, 1968): 27-8.

Palmer, Tony, "Artistic Privilege," *LonM* 8 (May, 1968): 47-52.

Rabinovitz, R., *Iris Murdoch*, 42-3. Also in Stade, G., ed., *Six Contemporary British Novelists*, 316-18.

NUNS AND SOLDIERS

Bell, Pearl K., "Games Writers Play," *Ctary* 71 (Feb., 1981): 69-73.

Cuneen, Sally, "The Post-Divine Comedy of Iris Murdoch," *ChrC* 18 (May 20, 1981): 573-7.

Conradi, Peter J., "Useful Fictions: Iris Murdoch," *CritQ* 23, iii (Autumn, 1981): 63-9.

Dipple, E., *Iris Murdoch*, 306-47.

Glendinning, Victoria, "Vice is Natural and Virtue is Not," *Listener* 104 (Sept. 4, 1981): 308-9.

THE RED AND THE GREEN

Anon., "Republic and Private," *TLS* (Oct. 14, 1965): 912. Also in *T.L.S.: Essays and Reviews from the Times Literary Supplement, 1965*, 40-1.

Berthoff, Warner, "Fortunes and the Novel: Muriel Spark and Iris Murdoch," *MR* 8 (Spring, 1967): 314-27. Also in Berthoff, W., *Fictions and Events*, 130-43.

Baldanza, F., *Iris Murdoch*, 126-30.

Bowen, John, "One Must Say Something," *NYTBR* (Nov. 7, 1965): 4-5.

Charpentier, Colette, "The Critical Reception of Iris Murdoch's Irish Novels (1963-1976) II: THE RED AND THE GREEN (1)," *EI* 6 (Dec., 1981): 87-98.

German, Howard, "The Range of Allusions in the Novels of Iris Murdoch," *JML* 2, i (Sept., 1971): 74-9.

Gerstenberger, D., *Iris Murdoch*, 51-69.

Hicks, Granville, "Easter Monday Insights," *SatR* 48 (Oct. 30, 1965): 41-2.

Kemp, Peter, "The Fight Against Fantasy: Iris Murdoch's THE RED AND THE GREEN," *MFS* 15, iii (Autumn, 1969): 403-15.

Ricks, Christopher, "A Sort of Mystery Novel," *NStat* (Oct. 22, 1965): 604-5.

Rabinovitz, R., *Iris Murdoch*, 38-9. Also in Stade, G., ed., *Six Contemporary British Novelists*, 311-13.

Scanlan, Margaret, "Fiction and the Fictions of History in Iris Murdoch's THE RED AND THE GREEN," *Cliol* 9, iii (1980): 365-78.

Rome, Joy, "A Retrospect for the Contingent: A Study of Iris Murdoch's Novel THE RED AND THE GREEN," *ESA* 14 (1971): 878-98.

Tucker, Martin, "The Odd Fish in Iris Murdoch's Kettle," *NRep* 154 (Feb. 5, 1966): 26-8.

THE SACRED AND PROFANE LOVE MACHINE

Dipple, E., *Iris Murdoch*, 226-41.

Ganner, Rauth H., "Iris Murdoch and the Bronte Heritage," *SELit* 58, i (Sept., 1981): 61-74.

Mellors, John, "Ladies Only," *LonM* (June-July, 1974): 135-9.

Rabinovitz, Rubin, "Iris Murdoch," in Stade, G., ed., *Six Contemporary British Novelists*, 326-8.

Seiler-Franklin C., *Boulder-Pushers*, 166-74.

THE SANDCASTLE

Baldanza, F., *Iris Murdoch*, 57-69.

Byatt, A. S., *Degrees of Freedom*, 61-72.

Dick, Bernard F., "The Novels of Iris Murdoch: A Formula for Enchantment," *BuR* 14 (May, 1966): 71-2.

Dipple, E., *Iris Murdoch*, 142-6.

Felheim, Marvin, "Symbolic Characterization in the Novels of Iris Murdoch," *TSLL* 2 (1960): 193-4.

Fraser, G. S., "Iris Murdoch: The Solidity of the Normal," *ILA* 2 (1959): 41-2.

German, Howard, "Allusions in the Early Novels of Iris Murdoch," *MFS* 15, iii (Autumn, 1969): 368-72.

Gerstenberger, D., *Iris Murdoch*, 29-31.

Hall, James, "Blurring the Will: The Growth of Iris Murdoch," *ELH* 32 (June, 1965): 262-6. Also in Hall, J., *Lunatic Giant in the Living Room*, 186-90.

Kriegel, Leonard, in Shapiro, C., ed., *Contemporary British Novelists*, 68-9.

Maes-Jelinek, Hena, "A House for Free Characters: The Novels of Iris Murdoch," *RLV* 29 (1963): 53-6.

Morrell, Roy, "Iris Murdoch: The Early Novels," *CritQ* 9 (Autumn, 1967): 271-4.

O'Connor, William V., "Iris Murdoch: The Formal and the Contingent," *Crit* 3, ii (Winter-Spring, 1960): 40-2. Also in O'Connor, W. V., *New University Wits*, 62-4.

O'Sullivan, Kevin, "Iris Murdoch and the Image of Liberal Man," *YLM* 131 (Dec., 1962): 30-2.

Pearson, Gabriel, "Iris Murdoch and the Romantic Novel," *New Left Rev.* 12-14 (Jan.-Apr., 1962): 137-45.

Price, Martin, in *YR* 47 (Autumn, 1957): 146-8.

Raban, J., "Character and Symbolism," *Techniques of Modern Fiction*, 108-11.

Rabinovitz, R., *Iris Murdoch*, 18-22. Also in Stade, G., ed., *Six Contemporary British Novelists*, 289-94.

Rippier, J. S., *Some Postwar English Novelists*, 78-82.

Sisk, John P., "A Sea Change," *Cweal* 66 (May 31, 1957): 236-7.

Taylor, Griffin, "'What Doth it Profit a Man...?'" *SR* 66 (Jan.-Mar., 1958): 137-51.

Whiteside, George, "The Novels of Iris Murdoch," *Crit* 7 (Spring, 1964): 35-7.

Wolfe, P., *Disciplined Heart*, 89-112.

THE SEA, THE SEA

Bradbury, Malcolm, "Semi-Isle," *NStat* 96 (Aug. 25, 1978): 246-7.

Cohan, Steven, "From Subtext to Dream Text: The Brutal Egoism of Iris Murdoch's Male Narrators," *W&L* n.s. 2 (1982): 233-41.

Dipple, E., *Iris Murdoch*, 274-305.

Gribble, Jennifer, "The Art of Iris Murdoch," *Quadrant* 142 (May, 1979): 36-9.

A SEVERED HEAD

Ashdown, Ellen A., "Form and Myth in Three Novels by Iris Murdoch: THE FLIGHT FROM THE ENCHANTER, THE BELL, and A SEVERED HEAD," *DAI* 35 (1975): 5334A-35A.

Baldanza, F., *Iris Murdoch*, 84-95.

_____, "Iris Murdoch and the Theory of Personality," *Criticism* 7 (Spring, 1965): 181-9.

_____, "The Manuscript of Iris Murdoch's A SEVERED HEAD," *JML* 3, i (Feb., 1973): 75-90.

Byatt, A. S., *Degrees of Freedom*, 105-21.

Cosman, Max, "Priapean Japes," *Cweal* 74 (June 9, 1961): 2868-7.

Dick, Bernard F., "The Novels of Iris Murdoch: A Formula for Enchantment," *BuR* 14 (May, 1966): 75-6.

Dipple, E., *Iris Murdoch*, 148-50.

Fletcher, John, "Cheating the Dark Gods: Iris Murdoch and Racine," *IFR* 6 (Winter, 1979): 75-6.

German, Howard, "Allusions in the Early Novels of Iris Murdoch," *MFS* 15, iii (Autumn, 1969): 387-401.

Gerstenberger, D., *Iris Murdoch*, 33-5.

Gindin, J., "Images of Illusion in the Works of Iris Murdoch," *Postwar British Fiction*, 189-95.

Gossman, Ann, "Icons and Idols in Murdoch's A SEVERED HEAD," *Crit* 18, iii (1977): 92-8.

Gregor, Ian, "Towards a Christian Literary Criticism," *Month* 33 (1965): 239-49.

Hall, J., *Lunatic Giant in the Drawing Room*, 199-200.

Hoskins, Robert, "HAMLET and A SEVERED HEAD," *AN&Q* 20, i-ii (1981): 18-21.

Jacobson, Dan, "Farce, Totem and Taboo," *NStat* 61 (June 16, 1961): 956-7.

Kalson, Albert E., "A SEVERED HEAD from Novel to Play: Coarsening as the Essence of Adaption," *BSUF* 17, iv (Autumn, 1976): 71-4.

Kane, Patricia, "The Furnishings of a Marriage: An Aspect of Characterization in Iris Murdoch's A SEVERED HEAD," *NConL* 2, v (Nov., 1972): 4-5.

Kenney, Alice P., "The Mythic History of a SEVERED HEAD," *MFS* 15, iii (Autumn, 1969): 387-401.

Kuehl, Linda, "Iris Murdoch: The Novelist as Magician/ The Magician as Artist," *MFS* 15, iii (Autumn, 1969): 347-60. Also in Spacks, P. M., ed., *Contemporary Women Novelists*, 92-107.

Maes-Jelinek, Hena, "A House for Free Characters: The Novels of Iris Murdoch," *RLV* 29 (1963): 59-62.

Malcolm, Donald, in *NY* 37 (May 6, 1961): 172-6.

Miner, Earl, "Iris Murdoch: The Uses of Love," *Nation* 194 (June 2, 1962): 498-9.

O'Connor, William V., "Iris Murdoch: A SEVERED HEAD," *Crit* 5, i (Spring-Summer, 1962): 74-7. Also in O'Connor, W. V., *New University Wits*, 70-4.

O'Sullivan, Kevin, "Iris Murdoch and the Image of Liberal Man," *YLM* 131 (Dec., 1962): 33-4.

Piper, William B., "The Accommodation of the Present in Novels of Murdoch and Powell," *SNNTS* 11, ii (Summer, 1979): 185-93 *passim*.

Rabinovitz, R., *Iris Murdoch*, 28-31. Also in Stade, G., ed., *Six Contemporary British Novelists*, 30-4.

Rippier, J. S., *Some Postwar English Novelists*, 88-92.

Rolo, Charles, in *Atlantic* 207 (May, 1961): 98-100.

Smithson, Isaiah, "Iris Murdoch's A SEVERED HEAD: The Evolution of Human Consciousness," *SoRA* 11 (1978): 133-53.

Souvage, Jacques, "The Novels of Iris Murdoch," *SGG* 4 (1962): 247-52.

Warnke, F. J., in *YR* 50 (June, 1961): 632-3.

Whiteside, George, "The Novels of Iris Murdoch," *Crit* 7 (Spring, 1964): 39-41.

Widmer, Kingsley, "The Wages of Intellectuality ... and the Fictional Wagers of Iris Murdoch," in Staley, T. F., ed., *Twentieth-Century Women Novelists*, 21-4.

Wolfe, P., *Disciplined Heart*, 139-60.

THE TIME OF THE ANGELS

Anon., "Picking Up the Pieces," *TLS* (Sept. 8, 1966): 798. Also in *T.L.S.: Essays and Reviews, 1966*, 33-6.

Baldanza, F., *Iris Murdoch*, 130-7.

Berthoff, Warner, "The Enemy of Freedom is Fantasy," *MR* 8 (Summer, 1967): 580-4. Also in Berthoff, W., *Fictions and Events*, 147-52.

Dipple, E., *Iris Murdoch*, 62-78.

Eimerl, Sarel, "Choreography of Despair," *Reporter* 35 (Nov. 3, 1966): 45-6.

German, Howard, "The Range of Illusions in the Novels of Iris Murdoch," *JML* 2, i (Sept., 1971): 79-84.

Hicks, Granville, "Rector for a Dead God," *SatR* 49 (Oct. 29, 1966): 25-6.

Majdiak, Daniel, "Romanticism in the Aesthetics of Iris Murdoch," *TSLL* 14, ii (Summer, 1972): 369-72.

Rabinovitz, R., *Iris Murdoch*, 39-42. Also in Stade, G., ed., *Six Contemporary British Novelists*, 313-16.

Sullivan, Zohreh T., "The Contracting Universe of Iris Murdoch's Gothic Novels," *MFS* 23, iv (Winter, 1977-78): 557-69.

_____, "Iris Murdoch's Self-Conscious Gothicism: THE TIME OF THE ANGELS," *ArQ* 33 (Spring, 1977): 47-60.

Taubman, Robert, "Uncle's War," *NStat* 72 (Sept. 16, 1966): 401-2.

Weeks, Edward, in *Atlantic* 218 (Oct. 1, 1966): 138-9.

Winsor, Dorothy A., "Solipsistic Sexuality in Iris Murdoch's Gothic Novels," *Ren* 34, i (Autumn, 1981): 57-9.

UNDER THE NET

Allsop, K., *Angry Decade*, 88-90, 93-4.

Baldanza, F., *Iris Murdoch*, 30-42.

Batchelor, Billie, "Revision in Iris Murdoch's UNDER THE NET," *BI* 8 (1968): 30-6.

Bradbury, Malcolm, "Iris Murdoch's UNDER THE NET," *CritQ* 4 (Spring, 1962): 47-54. Also in Bradbury, M., *Possibilities*, 231-46.

Byatt, A. S., *Degrees of Freedom*, 14-39.

_____, *Iris Murdoch*, 35-8.

DeMott, Benjamin, "Dirty Words?" *HudR* 18 (Spring, 1965): 37-40.

Dick, Bernard F., "The Novels of Iris Murdoch: A Formula for Enchantment," *BuR* 14 (May, 1966): 68-70.

Dipple, E., *Iris Murdoch*, 53-7.

Dueck, Jack, "Users of the Picaresque: A Study of Five Modern British Novels," *DAI* 34 (1974): 4255A.

Felheim, Marvin, "Symbolic Characterization in the Novels of Iris Murdoch," *TSLL* 2 (1960): 190-1.

Fitzsimmons, Thomas, in *SR* 63 (Spring, 1955): 328-30.

Fletcher, John, "Reading Beckett with Iris Murdoch's Eyes," *AUMLA* 55 (May, 1981): 7-14.

Fraser, G. S., "Iris Murdoch: The Solidity of the Normal," *ILA* 2 (1959): 38-40.

Furuki, Yoshiko, "The Anti-Heroic and the Unheroic—A Study of UNDER THE NET," *TsudaR* 24 (1979): 7-20.

German, Howard, "Allusions in the Early Novels of Iris Murdoch," *MFS* 15, iii (Autumn, 1969): 361-4.

Gerstenberger, D., *Iris Murdoch*, 21-5.

Goldberg, Gerald, "The Search for the Artist in Some Recent British Fiction," *SAQ* 62 (Summer, 1963): 394-6.

Hall, James, "Blurring the Will: The Growth of Iris Murdoch," *ELH* 32 (June, 1965): 259-62. Also in Hall, J., *Lunatic Giant in the Living Room*, 183-6.

Kellman, Steven, "Raising the Net: Iris Murdoch and the Tradition of the Self-Begetting Novel," *ES* 57 (Feb., 1976): 43-50. Also, expanded, in Kellman, S., *The Self-Begetting Novel*, N.Y.: Columbia Un. Pr., 1980, 87-93.

Kriegel, Leonard, in Shapiro, C., ed., *Contemporary British Novelists*, 64-5.

Maes-Jelinek, Hena, "A House for Free Characters: The Novels of Iris Murdoch," *RLV* 29 (1963): 45-50.

Morrell, Roy, "Iris Murdoch: The Early Novels," *CritQ* 11 (Autumn, 1967): 274-7.

Obumselu, Ben, "Iris Murdoch and Sartre," *ELH* 42, ii (Summer, 1975): 296-99.

O'Connor, William V., "Iris Murdoch: The Formal and the Contingent," *Crit* 3, ii (Winter-Spring, 1960): 40-2. Also in O'Connor, W. V., *New University Wits*, 54-9.

O'Sullivan, Kevin, "Iris Murdoch and the Image of Liberal Man," *YLM* 131 (Dec., 1962): 27-8.

Porter, Raymond J., "*Leitmotiv* in Iris Murdoch's UNDER THE NET," *MFS* 15, iii (Autumn, 1969): 379-85.

Rabinovitz, R., *Iris Murdoch*, 8-13. Also in Stade, G., ed., *Six Contemporary British Novelists*, 277-83.

Rippier, J. S., *Some Postwar British Novelists*, 71-4.

Shestakov, Dmitri, "An Iris Murdoch Novel in Russian," *Soviet Lit.* 7 (1966): 169-75.

Souvage, Jacques, "The Novels of Iris Murdoch," *SGG* 4 (1962): 234-8.

_____, "The Unresolved Tension: An Interpretation of Iris Murdoch's UNDER THE NET," *RLV* 26 (1960): 420-30.

Swinden, P., *Unofficial Selves*, 237-47.

Vickery, John B., "The Dilemmas of Language: Sartre's LA NAUSEE and Iris Murdoch's UNDER THE NET," *JNT* 1, ii (May, 1971): 69-76.

Whiteside, George, "The Novels of Iris Murdoch," *Crit* 7 (Spring, 1964): 29-32.

Widmann, R. L., "Murdoch's UNDER THE NET: Theory and Practice of Fiction," *Crit* 10, i (1968): 5-16.

Wolfe, P., *Disciplined Heart*, 46-67.

THE UNICORN

Allen, Diogenes, "Two Experiences of Existence: Jean Paul Sarte and Iris Murdoch," *IPQ* 14 (June, 1973): 181-7.

Anon., "Fable Mates," *TLS* (Sept. 6, 1963): 669. Also in *T.L.S.: Essays and Reviews from the Times Literary Supplement, 1963*, 176-8.

Baldanza, F., *Iris Murdoch*, 105-16.

Barrett, William, "English Opposites," *Atlantic* 211 (June, 1963): 131-2.

Byatt, A. S., *Degrees of Freedom*, 146-80.

Charpentier, Colette, "The Critical Reception of Iris Murdoch's Irish Novels (1963-1976) I: THE UNICORN," *EI* 5 (1980): 91-103.

Cook, Eleanor, "Mythical Beasts," *CanF* 43 (Aug., 1963): 113-14.

Detweiler, Robert, *Iris Murdoch's THE UNICORN* (Religious Dimensions in Literature), N.Y.: Seabury, 1969.

Dick, Bernard F., "The Novels of Iris Murdoch: A Formula for Enchantment," *BuR* 14 (May, 1966): 78-9.

Dipple, E., *Iris Murdoch*, 265-74.

Ganner, Rauth H., "Iris Murdoch and the Bronte Heritage," *SELit* 58, i (Sept., 1981): 61-74.

German, Howard, "The Range of Alusions in the Novels of Iris Murdoch," *JML* 2, i (Sept., 1971): 65-8.

Gerstenberger, D., *Iris Murdoch*, 40-4.

Grigson, Geoffrey, "Entre les Tombes," *NStat* 66 (Sept. 13, 1963): 321-2.

Hall, J., *Lunatic Giant in the Living Room*, 321-2.

Hebblethwaite, Peter, "Out Hunting Unicorns," *Month* n.s. 30 (Oct., 1963): 224-8.

Hicks, Granville, "Entrance to Enchantment," *SatR* 46 (May 11, 1963): 27-8.

Kriegel, Leonard, in Shapiro, C., ed., *Contemporary British Novelists*, 74-6.

Kuehl, Linda, "Iris Murdoch: The Novelist as Magician/The Magician as Artist," *MFS* 15, iii (Autumn, 1969): 347-60. Also in Spacks, P. M., ed., *Contemporary Women Novelists*, 92-107.

McDowell, Frederick P. W., "'The Devious Involutions of Human Character and Emotions': Reflections on Some Recent British Novels," *WSCL* 4, iii (Autumn, 1963): 355-9.

Obumselu, Ben, "Iris Murdoch and Sartre," *ELH* 42, ii (Summer, 1975): 304-16.

Pondrom, Cyrena N., "Iris Murdoch: THE UNICORN," *Crit* 6 (Winter, 1963-64): 177-80.

Rabinovitz, R., *Iris Murdoch*, 34-6. Also in Stade, G., ed., *Six Contemporary British Novelists*, 307-10.

Rippier, J. S., *Some Postwar English Novelists*, 96-103.

Scholes, R., *Fabulators*, 106-32. Also in Scholes, R., *Fabulation and Metafiction*, 56-73.

Sullivan, Zohreh T., "The Contracting Universe of Iris Murdoch's Gothic Novels," *MFS* 23, iv (Winter, 1977-78): 557-69.

Thorpe, Michael, *Iris Murdoch*: THE UNICORN (Notes on Literature, 168), London: British Council, 1976.

Tucker, Martin, "Love and Freedom: Golden and Hard Words," *Cweal* 77 (June 21, 1963): 357-8.

Whitehorn, Katharine, "Three Women," *Encounter* 21 (Dec., 1963): 78-82.

Whiteside, George, "The Novels of Iris Murdoch," *Crit* 7 (Spring, 1964): 43-6.

Winsor, Dorothy A., "Solipsistic Sexuality in Iris Murdoch's Gothic Novels," *Ren* 34, i (Autumn, 1981): 57-9.

Wolfe, P., *Disciplined Heart*, 183-202.

AN UNOFFICIAL ROSE

Baldanza, F., *Iris Murdoch*, 96-104.

Barrett, William, "Rose with Thorns," *Atlantic* 209 (June, 1962): 201-2.

Byatt, A. S., *Degrees of Freedom*, 122-45.

Dick, Bernard F., "The Novels of Iris Murdoch: A Formula for Enchantment," *BuR* 14 (May, 1966): 77.

Dipple, E., *Iris Murdoch*, 57-60.

German, Howard, "The Range of Allusions in the Novels of Iris Murdoch," *JML* 2, i (Sept., 1971): 58-64.

Gerstenberger, D., *Iris Murdoch*, 35-6.

Hall, J., *Lunatic Giant in the Living Room*, 200-6.

Kriegel, Leonard, in Shapiro, C., ed., *Contemporary British Novelists*, 73-4.

McDowell, Frederick P. W., "'The Devious Involutions of Human Character and Emotions': Reflections on Some Recent British Novels," *WSCL* 4, iii (Autumn, 1963): 352-5.

Maes-Jelinek, Hena, "A House for Free Characters: The Novels of Iris Murdoch," *RLV* 29 (1963): 62-6.

Miner, Earl, "Iris Murdoch: The Uses of Love," *Nation* 194 (June 2, 1962): 498-9.

Obumselu, Ben, "Iris Murdoch and Sartre," *ELH* 42, ii (Summer, 1975): 299-304.

O'Sullivan, Kevin, "Iris Murdoch and the Image of Liberal Man," *YLM* 131 (Dec., 1962): 34-5.

Pondrom, Cyrena N., "Iris Murdoch: An Existentialist?" *CLS* 5 (Dec., 1968): 403-19.

Rabinovitz, R., *Iris Murdoch*, 31-4. Also in Stade, G., ed., *Six Contemporary British Novelists*, 304-7.

Rippier, J. S., *Some Postwar British Novelists*, 92-6.

Ryan, Marjorie, in *Crit* 5, iii (Winter, 1962-63): 117-21.

Whiteside, George, "The Novels of Iris Murdoch," *Crit* 7 (Spring, 1964): 41-3.

Wolfe, P., *Disciplined Heart*, 161-82.

A WORD CHILD

Dipple, E., *Iris Murdoch*, 212-26.

Orr, Christopher, "Iris Murdoch's Critique of Tragedy in THE BLACK PRINCE and A WORD CHILD," *BWVACET* 4, i (1977): 10-18.

Piper, William B., "The Accommodation of the Present in Novels by Murdoch and Powell," *SNNTS* 11, ii (Summer, 1979): 185-93 *passim*.

Todd, R., *Iris Murdoch*, 49-57.

BIBLIOGRAPHY

Culley, Ann, with John Foster, "Criticism of Iris Murdoch: A Selected Checklist," *MFS* 15, iii (Autumn, 1969): 449-57.

Tominaga, Thomas T., and Wilma Schneidermeyer, *Iris Murdoch and Muriel Spark: A Bibliography*, Metuchen, N.J.: Scarecrow, 1977.

Widmann, R. L., "An Iris Murdoch Checklist," *Crit* 10, i (1968): 17-29.

Wolfe, P., *Disciplined Heart*, 216-20.

MURRAY, ALBERT, 1916-

TRAIN WHISTLE GUITAR

Karrer, Wolfgang, "The Novel as Blues: Albert Murray's TRAIN WHISTLE GUITAR," in Bruck, P., and W. Karrer, eds., *Afro-American Writing Since 1960*, 237-61.

NABOKOV, VLADIMIR, 1899-1977

GENERAL

Albright, D., *Representation and the Imagination*, 52-94.

Amis, Martin, "The Sublime and the Ridiculous: Nabokov's Black Farces," in Quennell, P., ed., *Vladimir Nabokov*, 73-87.

Anderson, Terry P., "A Formal Analysis of the Theme of Art in Nabokov's Russian Novels," *DAI* 34 (1974): 4239A.

Anon., "Lolita's Creator—Author Nabokov, a 'Cosmic Joker,'" *Newsweek* 59 (June 25, 1962): 51-4.

————, "Playboy Interview: Vladimir Nabokov," *Playboy* 11 (Jan., 1964): 35-41, 44-5. Also in The *Twelfth Anniversary Playboy Reader*, Chicago: Playboy Pr., 1965.

Appel, Alfred, Jr., "Conversations with Nabokov," *Novel* 4 (Spring, 1971): 209-22.

————, "An Interview with Vladimir Nabokov," *WSCL* 8, ii (Spring, 1967): 127-52. Also in Dembo, L. S., ed., *Nabokov*, 19-44.

————, "Memories of Nabokov," *TLS* (Oct. 7, 1977): 1138-42.

————, "Nabokov: A Portrait," *Atlantic* 228 (Sept., 1971): 77-92. Also in Rivers, J. E., and C. Nicol, eds., *Nabokov's Fifth Arc*, 3-21.

————, *Nabokov's Dark Cinema*.

————, "Nabokov's Dark Cinema: A Diptych," *TriQ* 28 (Fall, 1973): 196-273. [Adapted from his book cited above.]

————, "The Road to LOLITA, or the Americanization of an Emigre," *JML* 4, i (Sept., 1974): 3-31.

Bader, J., *Crystal Land*.

Barabtario, Gene, "Pushkin Embedded," *VNRN* 8 (Spring, 1982): 28-31.

Baxter, Charles, "Nabokov, Idolatry, and the Police State," *Boundary* 5, iii (Spring, 1977): 813-27.

Berbova, Nina, *The Italics Are Mine*, N.Y.: Harcourt, Brace & World, 1969, 316-25. Also (adapted) as "Nabokov in the Thirties," *TriQ* 17 (Winter, 1970): 220-33.

Bitsilli, P. M., "The Revival of Allegory," *TriQ* 17 (Winter, 1970): 102-18.

Bodenstein, J. H., "'The Excitement of Verbal Adventure': A Study of Vladimir Nabokov's English Prose," *DAI* 39 (1978): 34C.

Brenalvirez, Irene E., "Vladimir Nabokov: The Theme and Practice of Art," *DAI* 31 (1970): 2374A-75A.

Brenner, Conrad, "Nabokov: The Art of the Perverse," *NRep* 138 (June 23, 1958): 18-21.

Brown, Betsy E., "Palliatives of Articulate Art: Narrators and Point of View in the English Novels of Vladimir Nabokov," *DAI* 39 (1979): 4944A.

Brown, Clarence, "Nabokov's Pushkin and Nabokov's Nabokov," *WSCL* 8, ii (Spring, 1967): 280-93. Also in Dembo, L. S., ed., *Nabokov*, 195-208.

Bruss, Elizabeth W., "Vladimir Nabokov: Illusions of Reality and the Reality of Illusions," *Autobiographical Acts*, 127-72.

Carroll, William, "Nabokov's Signs and Symbols," in Proffer, C. R., ed., *Book of Things about Vladimir Nabokov*, 203-17.

Ciancio, Ralph A., "Nabokov and the Verbal Mode of the Grotesque," *ConL* 18 (Autumn, 1977): 509-33.

Clancy, Laurie, "Nabokov and His Critics," *Meanjin* 37 (July, 1978): 150-6.

Clifton, Gladys M., "The Fictional Texture of Three Novels of Vladimir Nabokov," *DAI* 39 (1979): 4934A-3A.

Cortese, James, "The Unseeing I: Narrative Masks in the Fiction of Vladimir Nabokov," *DAI* 40 (1980): 6270A.

Couturier, Maurice, "Nabokov's Performative Writing," in Johnson, I. D., and C. Johnson, eds., *Les Americanistes*, 156-81.

————, "The Subject on Trial in Nabokov's Novels," 121-36 in Sienicka, Marta, ed., *Proceedings of a Symposium on American Literature*, Poznan: Uniw. Im. Adama Mickiewicza, 1979.

Crofts, Robert F., "Vladimir Nabokov—A Russian Wolf in American Clothing," *MSpr* 59 (1965): 11-29.

de Jonge, Alex, "Nabokov's Uses of Pattern," in Quennell, P., ed., *Vladimir Nabokov*, 59-72.

Delizia, Michael, "Dr. Nabokov and Mr. Thoreau," *TSB* 142 (Winter, 1977): 1-2.

Dembo, L. S., "Vladimir Nabokov: An Introduction," *WSCL* 8, ii (Spring, 1967): 111-26. Also in Dembo, L. S., ed., *Nabokov*, 3-18.

Dillard, R. H. W., "Not Text but Texture: The Novels of Vladimir Nabokov," *HC* 3, iii (June, 1966): 1-12. Also in Dillard, R. H. W., *Sounder Few*, 139-50.

Ditsky, John M., "Carried Away by Numbers: The Rhapsodic Mode in Modern Fiction," *QQ* 79 (1972): 482-94.

Dupee, F. W., "Nabokov: The Prose and Poetry of It All," *NYRB* (Dec. 12, 1963): 10-12. Also in Dupee, F. W., *King of the Cats*, 131-41.

Engel, Bernard F., "Nabokov," *SSMLN* 7, iii (1977): 3-5. [Not seen.]

Enright, D. J., "Nabokov's Way," *NYRB* (Nov. 3, 1966): 3-4.

Field, A., *Nabokov*.

Fleischauer, John F., "Simultaneity in Nabokov's Prose Style," *Style* 5, i (Winter, 1971): 57-69.

Fortier, Mardelle L. E., "Memory and the Illusion of Time: Proust and Nabokov," *DAI* 39 (1978): 271A.

Foster, Ludmila A., "Nabokov in Russian Emigre Criticism," *RLT* 3 (1972): 330-41.

Fowler, Douglas, "Eliot, Nabokov, and the First Questions," *YER* 5, ii (1978): 44-61.

———, *Reading Nabokov*.

Gardner, Thomas, "Vladimir Nabokov," *SG* 21 (1968): 94-110.

Garfinkel, Nancy, "The Intimacy of Imagination: A Study of the Self in Nabokov's English Novels," *DAI* 41, ix (Mar., 1981): 4030A.

Gezari, Janet K., "Game Fiction: The World of Play and the Novels of Vladimir Nabokov," *DAI* 32 (1972): 6974A.

———, and W. K. Wimsatt, "Vladimir Nabokov: More Chess Problems and the Novel," *YFS* 58 (1978): 102-15.

Gold, Herbert, "The Art of Fiction 40: Vladimir Nabokov, An Interview," *ParisR* 41 (Summer-Fall, 1967): 92-111.

Grabes, H., *Fictitious Biographies*.

Grayson, Jane, *Nabokov Translated: A Comparison of Nabokov's Russian and English Prose*, Oxford: Oxford Un. Pr., 1977.

Green, Geoffrey, "'An Infinity of Sensation and Thought within a Finite Existence': Nabokov's Fiction of Memory," *HIS* 3, iv (Fall, 1980): 377-84.

Green, Geoffrey, "Nabokov's Signs of Reference, Symbols of Design," *CollL* 7 (Spring, 1980): 104-12.

Grosshans, Henry, "Vladimir Nabokov and the Dream of Old Russia," *TSLL* 7 (Winter, 1966): 401-9.

Haule, James M., "*Terra Cognita*: The Humor of Vladimir Nabokov," *StAH* 2 (1975): 78-87.

Hayman, John G., "A Conversation with Vladimir Nabokov—with Digressions," *TC* 166 (Dec., 1959): 444-50.

Heidenry, John, "Vladimir in Dreamland," *Cweal* 90 (May 9, 1969): 231-4.

Hughes, Philip R., "The Knight Moves of Mind: Nabokov's Use of Illusion to Transcend the Limits of Life and Art," *DAI* 35 (1974): 455A.

Hultquist, Marianne K., "The Magic of Nabokov," *DAI* 34 (1974): 7747A-58A.

Hyde, G. M., *Vladimir Nabokov*.

Ivask, George, "The World of Vladimir Nabokov," *RusR* 20 (Apr., 1961): 134-42.

Johnson, D. Barton, "Belyj and Nabokov: A Comparative Overview," *RusL* 9, iv (May 15, 1981): 379-402.

———, "Nabokov as Man of Letters: The Alphabetic Motif in His Work," *MFS* 25, iii (Autumn, 1979): 397-412.

———, "The Role of Synthesia in the Work of Vladimir Nabokov," *MelbSS* 9-10 (1975): 129-39.

———, "Synsthesia, Polychromatism, and Nabokov," *RLT* 3 (1972): 378-97. Also in Proffer, C. R., ed., *Book of Things about Vladimir Nabokov*, 84-103.

———, "Vladimir Nabokov's 'Solus Rex' and the 'Ultima Thule' Theme," *SlavR* 40 (1981): 543-56.

Karlinsky, Simon, "Nabokov and Chekhov: The Lesser Russian Tradition," *TriQ* 17 (Winter, 1970): 7-16. Also in Appel, A., Jr., and C. Newman, eds., *Nabokov*, 7-16.

Khodasevich, Vladislav, "On Sirin," *TriQ* 17 (Winter, 1970): 96-101. Also in Appel, A., Jr., and C. Newman, eds., *Nabokov*, 96-101.

Landesman, Joanne, "Memory and Artifice in Nabokov and Ford Madox Ford," *DAI* 37 (1977): 5110A.

Lanyi, Gabriel, "On Narrative Transitions in Nabokov's Prose," *PTL* 2, i (Jan., 1977): 73-87.

Lee, L. L., *Vladimir Nabokov*.

———, "Vladimir Nabokov's Great Spiral of Being," *WHR* 18 (Summer, 1964): 225-36.

Lilly, Mark, "Nabokov: Homo Ludens," in Quennell, P., ed., *Vladimir Nabokov*, 88-102.

Lokrantz, J. T., *Underside of the Weave*.

Louria, Yvette, "Nabokov and Proust: The Challenge of Time," *BA* 48 (1974): 469-76.

Lubin, Peter, "Kickshaws and Motley," *TriQ* 17 (Winter, 1970): 187-208. Also in Appel, A., Jr., and C. Newman, eds., *Nabokov*, 187-208.

Maddox, Lucy B., "The Art of Commentary: Vladimir Nabokov's Novels in English," *DAI* 40 (1979): 3291A.

Mason, Bruce, "A Fissure in Time: The Art of Vladimir Nabokov," *NZSJ* (1969): 1-16.

McElroy, Joseph, "The N Factor," *SatRA* 1, i (Jan., 1973): 34-5.

McLellan, John M., "Nabokov and the Novel of Melodramatic Fantasy," *FJS* 5 (1972): 59-79.

Merivale, Patricia, "The Flaunting of Artifice in Vladimir Nabokov and Jorge Luis Borges," *WSCL* 8, ii (Spring, 1967): 294-309. Also in Dembo, L. S., ed., *Nabokov*, 209-24.

Merrill, Robert, "Nabokov and Fictional Artifice," *MFS* 25, iii (Autumn, 1979): 439-62.

Morton, D. E., *Vladimir Nabokov*.

Moynahan, J., *Vladimir Nabokov*.

Nabokov, Dmitri, "A Few Things That Must Be Said on Behalf of Vladimir Nabokov," in Rivers, J. E., and C. Nicol, eds., *Nabokov's Fifth Arc*, 35-42.

Nabokov, Vladimir, "'To Be Kind, to Be Proud, to Be Fearless'—Vladimir Nabokov in Conversation with James Mossman," *Listener* 82 (Oct. 23, 1969): 560-61.

———, and Peter D. Smith, "Vladimir Nabokov on His Life and Work," *Listener* 68 (Nov. 22, 1962): 856-8. Also in *Vogue* 141 (Mar. 1, 1963): 152-5.

Nassar, Joseph M., "The Russian in Nabokov's English Novels," *DAI* 38 (1977): 1381A-82A.

Naumann, Marina T., "Grins, Grinlandia and Nabokov's Zoorlandia: Fantastic Literary Affinities," *GSlav* 2, iv (Fall, 1977): 237-52.

———, "Nabokov as Viewed by Fellow Emigres," *RLJ* 99 (1974): 18-26.

Nemoianu, Virgil, "Wrestling with Time: Some Tendencies in Nabokov's and Eliade's Later Works," *Southeastern Europe* (Arizona State Un.) 7, i (1980): 74-90.

Nicol, Charles D., "Types of Formal Structure in Selected Novels of Vladimir Nabokov," *DAI* 31 (1970): 2930A.

Nilsson, Nils A., "A Hall of Mirrors: Nabokov and Olesha," *SSl* 15 (1969): 5-12.

Oates, Joyce Carol, "A Personal View of Nabokov," *SatRA* 1, i (Jan., 1973): 36-7.

Paine, S., *Beckett, Nabokov, Nin.*

Page, Andrew, "Vladimir Nabokov: In Tribute to Sherlock Holmes," *BSJ* 24, i (1974): 12-14.

Page, Norman, ed., *Nabokov: The Critical Heritage*, London: Routledge & Kegan Paul, 1982.

Parker, Stephen J., "Vladimir Nabokov—Sirin as Teacher: The Russian Novels," *DAI* 30 (1970): 3952A-53A.

Parry, Albert, "Introducing Nabokov to America," *TQ* 14, i (Spring, 1971): 16-26.

Patterson, Richard F., "The Viewer and the View: Perception and Narration in Nabokov's English Novels," *DAI* 36 (1976): 3285A.

Pifer, E., *Nabokov and the Novel.*

_____, "No Frivolous Firebird: Character, Reality, Morality in Nabokov's Fiction," *DAI* 38 (1977): 776A.

_____, "On Human Freedom and Inhuman Art," *SEEJ* 22 (1978): 52-63. [Not seen.]

Pjatigorsky, A. M., "A Word about the Philosophy of Vladimir Nabokov," *WSIA* 4 (1979): 5-17. [Not seen.]

Proffer, C. R., ed., *Book of Things about Vladimir Nabokov.*

Pryce-Jones, David, "The Art of Nabokov," *Harpers* 226 (Apr., 1963): 97-101. Also (revised and expanded) as "The Fabulist's Worlds: Vladimir Nabokov," in Balakian, N., and C. Simmons, eds., *Creative Present*, 65-78.

Purdy, Struther B., "Solus Rex: Nabokov and the Chess Novel," *MFS* 14 (Winter, 1968-69): 379-95.

Quennell, P., ed., *Vladimir Nabokov.*

Rambeau, James M., "Nabokov's Critical Strategy," in Rivers, J. E., and C. Nicol, eds., *Nabokov's Fifth Arc*, 22-34.

Rensch, Jeffrey P., "Involute Abodes: Five American Novels of Vladimir Nabokov," *DAI* 43, iii (Sept., 1982): 803A.

Rivers, J. E., and C. Nicol, eds., *Nabokov's Fifth Arc.*

Robinson, Robert, "A Blush of Color—Nabokov in Montreux," *Listener* 97 (Mar., 1977): 367, 369. [Interview.]

Ross, Charles S., "Nabokov's Mistress/Muse Metaphor: Some Recent Books," *MFS* 25, iii (Autumn, 1977): 514-24.

Ross, Thomas W., "Nabokov and Holmes Again: Was the Master Talipedal?" *BSJ* 26, i (Mar., 1976): 37-40.

Roth, Phyllis A., "Lunatics, Lovers, and a Poet: A Study of Doubling and the Doppelganger in the Novels of Nabokov," *DAI* 33 (1972): 2950A-51A.

_____, "Toward the Man Behind the Mystification," in Rivers, J. E., and C. Nicol, eds., *Nabokov's Fifth Arc*, 43-59.

Rowe, William W., "Gogolesque Perception—Expanding Reversals in Nabokov," *Slav* 30 (Mar., 1971): 110-20.

_____, "The Honesty of Nabovian Deception," in Proffer, C. R., ed., *Book of Things about Vladimir Nabokov*, 171-81.

_____, *Nabokov and Others.*

_____, "Nabokovian Shimmers of Meaning," *RLT* 14 (1976): 48-58.

_____, "Nabokovian Superimposed and Alternative Realities," *RLT* 14 (1976): 59-66.

_____, *Nabokov's Deceptive World.*

_____, "A Note on Nabokov's Erotic Necks," *RLT* 16 (1979): 50-7.

Sisson, Jonathan B., "Cosmic Synchronization and Other Worlds in the Work of Vladimir Nabokov," *DAI* 40 (1979): 3304A.

Slinn, E. Warwick, "Problems of Consciousness in Nabokov's English Novels," *WascanaR* 13, ii (1978): 3-18.

Smith, Stewart H., "Nabokov's Novels: Art and the Literary Imagination," *DAI* 35 (1975): 6734A-35A.

Stankus-Saulaitis, Marija, "The Science of Exile: The Emigre and the Homeland in Nabokov's Novels," *DAI* 42, ix (Mar., 1982): 4003A.

Stanley, Donald H., "The Self-Conscious Narrator in Donald Barthelme and Vladimir Nabokov," *DAI* 40 (1979): 2057A.

Stegner, P., *Escape Into Aesthetics.*

Steiner, George, "Extraterritorial," *TriQ* 17 (Winter, 1970): 119-27. Also in Appel, A., Jr., and C. Newman, eds., *Nabokov*, 119-27.

Struve, Gleb, "Notes on Nabokov as a Russian Writer," *WSCL* 8, ii (Spring, 1967): 127-52. Also in Dembo, L. S., ed., *Nabokov*, 45-56.

Stuart, D., *Nabokov.*

Terras, Victor, "Nabokov and Gogol: The Metaphysics of Non-being," in Clayton, J. D., and G. Schaarschmidt, eds., *Poetica Slavica*, 191-6.

Tiedeken, Richard, "Memory and Pattern as Thematic Idea and Structural Principle in the Autobiographical and Selected Fictional Prose of Vladimir Nabokov," *DAI* 38 (1978): 7328A-29A.

Vander Closter, Susan, "Nabokovian Towers in the Mist: The Narrative Structures of Artistic Memory," *DAI* 42 (1981): 217A-18A.

Wagner, Geoffrey, "Vladimir Nabokov and the Redemption of Reality," *CimR* 10 (Jan., 1970): 16-23.

Wain, John, "Nabokov's Beheading," *NRep* 141 (Dec. 21, 1959): 17-19.

Weil, Irwin, "Odyssey of a Translator," *TriQ* 17 (Winter, 1970): 266-83.

Weiler, R., *Nabokov's Bodies.*

White, Edmund, "The Esthetics of Bliss," *SatRA* 1, i (Jan., 1973): 33-4.

Williams, Carol T., "Nabokov's Dialectical Structure," *WSCL* 8, ii (Spring, 1967): 250-67. Also in Dembo, L. S., ed., *Nabokov*, 165-82.

_____, "The Necessary Ripple: The Art of Vladimir Nabokov," *DA* 28 (1968): 3203A-04A.

Williams, Robert C., "Memory Defense: The Real Life of Vladimir Nabokov's Berlin," *YR* 60, ii (Winter, 1971): 241-50.

Zaslove, Jerald, "Nabokov in Context," *RecL* 1, iii (1972): 23-8.

ADA, OR ARDOR: A FAMILY CHRONICLE

Albright, D., *Representation and the Imagination*, 75-8, 81-2.

Alkon, Paul K., "Historical Development of the Concept of Time," in Ferin, Michael, et al., eds., *Biorhythms and Human Reproduction*, N.Y.: John Wiley & Sons, 1974, 3-22.

Alter, Robert, "ADA, or the Perils of Paradise," in Quennell, P., ed., *Vladimir Nabokov*, 103-18.

Appel, Alfred, Jr., in *NYTBR* (May 4, 1969): 1, 34-7. Also as "ADA Described," *TriQ* 17 (Winter, 1970): 160-86. Also in Appel, A., Jr., and C. Newman, eds., *Nabokov*, 160-86.

Bader, J., *Crystal Land*, 123-62.

Begnal, Michael H., "Past, Present, Future, Death: Vladimir Nabokov's ADA," *CollL* 9, ii (Spring, 1982): 133-9.

Bok, Sissela, "Redemption Through Art in Nabokov's ADA," *TriQ Crit* 12, iii (1971): 110-20.

Boyd, Brian, "A Marsh Marigold Is a Marsh Marigold Is a Marsh Marigold," *VNRN* 1 (1978): 13-16.

_____, "The Mysterious Dozen: A Problem in ADA," *VNRN* 1 (1978): 16-18.

_____, "Nabokov and ADA," *DAI* 40 (1980): 4578A.

Bulhof, Francis, "Dutch Footnotes to Nabokov's ADA," in Proffer, C. R., ed., *Book of Things about Vladimir Nabokov*, 291.

Christensen, Inger, "Nabokov's ADA: Metafiction as Aesthetic Bliss," *Meaning of Metafiction*, 37-56.

Clark, Beverly L., "Contradictions and Confirmations in ADA," *CollL* 8, i (Winter, 1981): 53-62.

Crown, Patricia, "Note on ADA," *VNRN* 4 (1980): 37-8.

Dillard, R. H. W., and others, *Sounder Few*, 156-61.

Edelnant, Jay A., "Nabokov's Black Rainbow: An Analysis of the Rhetorical Function of Color Imagery in ADA OR ARDOR: A FAMILY CHRONICLE," *DAI* 40 (1979): 2981A-82A.

Enright, D. J., "Eros, the Rose and the Sore: Nabokov's New Novel," *Listener* (Oct. 2, 1969): 457. Also in Enright, D. J., *Man is an Onion*, 87-91.

Fowler, D., *Reading Nabokov*, 176-201.

Fox, Mary Ellen, "The Sweet Melancholy of Civilization — Vladimir Nabokov: ADA OR ARDOR," *ChronC* 2 (Jan.-Feb., 1978): 8-9.

Godshalk, William L., "Nabokov's Byronic ADA: A Note," *NConL* 2, ii (Mar., 1972): 2-4.

Golden, Herbert A., "A Study of Games Played in ADA OR ARDOR: A FAMILY CHRONICLE," *DAI* 33 (1973): 5723A.

Grabes, H., *Fictitious Biographies*, 70-95.

Hayles, N. Katherine, "Making a Virtue of Necessity: Pattern and Freedom in Nabokov's ADA," *ConL* 23, i (Winter, 1982): 32-51.

Holmstrom, Jan, "Aesthetic Bliss: A Note on Nabokov's Aesthetics," *MSpr* 75, ii (1981): 133-7.

Hyde, G. M., *Vladimir Nabokov*, 192-206.

Johnson, Carol, "Nabokov's ADA: Word's End," *ArtI* 8, viii (Oct., 1969): 42-3.

Johnson, D. Barton, "A Henry James Parody in ADA," *VNRN* 3 (1979): 33-4.

_____, "Nabokov's ADA and Puskin's EUGENE ONEGIN," *SEEJ* 15 (1971): 316-23.

_____, " Possible Anti-Source for ADA, or Did Nabokov Read German Novels?" *VNRN* 7 (Fall, 1981): 21-4.

_____, "The Scrabble Game in ADA or Taking Nabokov Clitorally," *JML* , ii (May, 1982): 291-303.

Kaplan, Fred, "Victorian Modernists: Fowles and Nabokov," *JNT* 3, ii (May, 1973): 108-20.

Lee, L. L., *Vladimir Nabokov*, 144-52.

Leonard, Jeffrey, "In Place of Lost Time: ADA," *TriQ* 17 (Winter, 1970): 136-46. Also in Appel, A., Jr., and C. Newman, eds., *Nabokov*, 136-46.

Lokrantz, J. T., *Underside of the Weave*, 37-40, 87-94.

Louria, Yvette, "Nabokov and Proust: The Challenge of Time," *BA* 48 (Summer, 1974): 469-76.

Mason, Bobbie Ann, *Nabokov's Garden: A Guide to ADA*, Ann Arbor, Mich.: Ardis, 1975.

Morton, D. E., *Vladimir Nabokov*, 130-42.

Nabokov, Vladimir, "Notes to ADA by Vivian Darkbloom," in Rivers, J. E., and C. Nicol, eds., *Nabokov's Fifth Arc*, 242-59.

Nemoianu, Virgil, "Wrestling with Time: Some Tendencies in Nabokov's and Eliade's Later Works," *Southeastern Europe* (Arizona State Un.) 7, i (1980): 79-82.

Nicol, Charles, "ADA, or Disorder," in Rivers, J. E., and C. Nicol, eds., *Nabokov's Fifth Arc*, 230-41.

_____, "Flaubert's Understudy," *VNRN* 5 (1980): 27-8.

_____, "The Mysterious Dozen Revisited," *VNRN* 2 (1979): 23-4.

Packman, David B., "Structures of Desire: Vladimir Nabokov's LOLITA, PALE FIRE, and ADA," *DAI* 40 (1979): 2685A.

Pearce, Richard, "Nabokov's Black (Hole) Humor: LOLITA and PALE FIRE," in Cohen, S. B., ed., *Comic Relief*, 30-2.

Pifer, Ellen, "Dark Paradise: Shades of Heaven and Hell in ADA," *MFS* 25, iii (Autumn, 1979): 481-97.

_____, *Nabokov and the Novel*, 132-57.

Proffer, Carl R., "Ada as Wonderland: A Glossary of Allusions to Russian Literature," *RLT* 3 (Spring, 1972): 399-430. Also in Proffer, C. R., ed., *Book of Things about Vladimir Nabokov*, 249-79.

Rawlings, Bobbie A., "Nabokov's Garden: Nature Imagery in Vladimir Nabokov's ADA OR ARDOR," *DAI* 33 (1972): 2949A.

Rivers, J. E., "Proust, Nabokov, and ADA," *FAR* 1 (1977): 173-97.

_____, and William Walker, "Nabokov's ADA, Part I, Chapter 21," *Expl* 36, ii (Winter, 1978): 7-8.

_____, "Notes to Vivian Darkbloom's 'Notes to ADA'," *VNRN* 3 (1979): 34-41. Also, expanded, in Rivers, J. E., and C. Nicol, eds., *Nabokov's Fifth Arc*, 260-95.

Ross, Diane M., "Lo. Lee. Ta.," *VNRN* 3 (Fall, 1979): 27-8.

Rowe, W. W., *Nabokov and Others*, 98-101.

Stark, J. O., *Literature of Exhaustion*, 62-117 *passim*.

Swanson, Roy A., "Nabokov's ADA as Science Fiction," *SFS* 2, i (Mar., 1975): 76-87.

Tammi, Pekka, "Some Remarks on Flaubert and ADA," *VNRN* 7 (Fall, 1981): 19-21.

Walker, William, and J. E. Rivers, "Nabokov's ADA," *Expl* 39, iii (Spring, 1981): 46-7.

Weber, Alfred, "Nabokov's ADA: A Style and Its Implications," *RecL* 1, i (Spring, 1972): 54-65.

Zeller, Nancy A., "The Spirit of Time in ADA," in Proffer, C. R., ed., *Book of Things about Vladimir Nabokov*, 280-90.

BEND SINISTER

Bader, J., *Crystal Land*, 95-122.

Baxter, Charles, "Nabokov, Idolatry and the Police State," *Boundary* 5, iii (Spring, 1977): 818-21.

Bienstock, Beverly G., "Focus Pocus: Film Imagery in BEND SINISTER," in Rivers, J. E., and C. Nicol, eds., *Nabokov's Fifth Arc*, 125-38.

Burns, Dan E., "BEND SINISTER and 'Tyrant Destroyed': Short Story into Novel," *MFS* 25, iii (Autumn, 1979): 508-13.

Field, A., *Nabokov*, 198-203.

Fowler, D., *Reading Nabokov*, 21-61.

_____, "Eliot, Nabokov and the First Question," *YER* 5, ii (1978): 55-8.

Gottfried, Paul, "Against the Bolshevik Nightmare and the Fraud of Revolution—Vladimir Nabokov: INVITATION TO A BEHEADING and BEND SINISTER," *ChronC* 2 (Jan.-Feb., 1978): 9-10.

Gove, Antonia F., "Multilingualism and Ranges of Tone in Nabokov's BEND SINISTER," *SlavR* 32 (1973): 79-90.

Grabes, H., *Fictitious Biographies*, 18-30.

Guetti, J., *Word-Music*, 187-93.

Hyde, G. M., *Vladimir Nabokov*, 129-33, 140-4.

Hyman, Stanley E., "The Handle: INVITATION TO A BE-HEADING and BEND SINISTER," *TriQ* 17 (Winter, 1970): 60-71. Also in Appel, A., Jr., and C. Newman, eds., *Nabokov*, 60-71.

Johnson, D. Barton, "Vladimir Nabokov's 'Solus Rex' and the 'Ultima Thule' Theme," *Slav* 40 (1981): 547-54.

_____, "The 'Yablochko' Chastushka in BEND SINISTER," *VNRN* 9 (Fall, 1982): 40-2.

Kermode, Frank, "Aesthetic Bliss," *Encounter* 14 (June, 1960): 81-6. Also in Kermode, F., *Puzzles and Epiphanies*, 228-33.

Lee, L. L., "BEND SINISTER: Nabokov's Political Dream," *WSCL* 8, ii (Spring, 1967): 193-203. Also in Dembo, L. S., ed., *Nabokov* 95-105.

_____, *Vladimir Nabokov*, 104-14.

Lokrantz, J. T., *Underside of the Weave*, 14-21, 71-3.

Mead, David G., "A Nabokovian Borrowing," *AN&Q* 13, ii (Oct., 1974): 23-4.

Morton, D. E., *Vladimir Nabokov*, 53-61.

Patterson, Richard F., "Nabokov's BEND SINISTER: The Narrator as God," *SAF* 5, ii (Autumn, 1977): 241-53.

Pifer, E., *Nabokov and the Novel*, 6-7, 68-96.

Schaeffer, Susan F., "BEND SINISTER and the Novelist as Anthropomorphic Deity," *CentR* 17, ii (Spring, 1973): 115-51.

Sheidlower, David I., "Reading Between the Lines and the Squares," *MFS* 25, iii (Autumn, 1979): 413-25.

Stegner, P., *Escape Into Aesthetics*, 76-89.

CAMERA OBSCURA (See LAUGHTER IN THE DARK)

THE DEFENSE

Adams, Robert M., "Nabokov's Game," *NYRB* (Jan. 14, 1965): 18-19.

Anon., "Strange Mating," *TLS* (Nov. 19, 1964): 1033. Also in *T.L.S.: Essays and Reviews from the Times Literary Supplement, 1964*, 207-9.

Bradbury, Michael, "Grand Master," *Spectator* 7116 (Nov. 13, 1964): 643-4.

Field, A., *Nabokov*, 175-9.

_____, "The View From Above," *New Leader* 47 (Oct. 26, 1964): 22-3.

Furbank, P. N., "Chess and Jigsaw," *Encounter* 24 (Jan., 1965): 83-6.

Hampshire, Stuart, "Among the Barbarians," *NStat* 68 (Nov. 6, 1964): 702-3.

Hyde, G. M., *Vladimir Nabokov*, 76-84.

Lee, L. L., *Vladimir Nabokov*, 46-50.

Moody, Fred, "Nabokov's Gambit," *RLT* 14 (1976): 67-70.

Purdy, Struther B., "Solus Rex: Nabokov and the Chess Novel," *MFS* 14 (Winter, 1968-69): 382-4.

Rowe, W. W., *Nabokov and Others*, 105-7.

Thorpe, Day, "A Master Chess Player Loses in the Game of Life," *Sunday Star* (Washington, D. C.) (Sept. 27, 1964): C-5.

Updike, John, "Grandmaster Nabokov," *NRep* 151 (Sept. 26, 1964): 15-18. Also in Harrison, G. A., ed., *Critic as Artist*, 325-32. Also in Updike, J., *Assorted Prose*, N.Y.: Knopf, 1965, 318-27.

DESPAIR

Amis, Martin, "The Sublime and the Ridiculous: Nabokov's Black Forces," in Quennell, P., *Vladimir Nabokov*, 83-6.

Anderson, Quentin, "Nabokov in Time," *NRep* 154 (June 4, 1966): 23-8. Also in Harrison, G. A., ed., *Critic as Artist*, 16-26.

Anon., "Looking-Glass Death," *TLS* (July 28, 1966): 655. Also in *T.L.S.: Essays and Reviews from the Times Literary Supplement, 1966*, 27-9.

Arana, R. Victoria, "'The Line Down the Middle' in Autobiography: Critical Implications of the Quest for Self," in Crook, E. J., ed., *Fearful Symmetry*, 125-37.

Brophy, Brigid, "LOLITA and Other Games," *Book Week* (May 15, 1966): 2, 10.

Carroll, William C., "The Cartesian Nightmare of DESPAIR," in Rivers, J. E., and C. Nicol, eds., *Nabokov's Fifth Arc*, 82-104.

Davydov, Sergei, "Dostoevsky and Nabokov: The Morality of Structure in CRIME AND PUNISHMENT and DESPAIR," *DStudies* 3 (1982): 157-70.

Field, Andrew, "Herman and Felix," *NYTBR* (May 15, 1966): 5, 36-7.

_____, *Nabokov*, 225-37.

Hyde, G. M., *Vladimir Nabokov*, 109-15.

Hyman, Stanley E., "Nabokov's Distorting Mirrors," *New Leader* 49 (May 9, 1966): 11-12.

King, Adele, "La Meprise," *Geste* (Un. of Leeds) 4 (Mar. 12, 1959): 18-20.

Lee, L. L., *Vladimir Nabokov*, 109-15.

Pifer, E., *Nabokov and the Novel*, 62-70.

Rosenfeld, Claire, "DESPAIR and the Lust for Immortality," *WSCL* 8, ii (Spring, 1967): 174-92. Also in Dembo, L. S., ed., *Nabokov*, 66-84.

Schuman, Samuel, "'DESPAIR and Die': A Note on Nabokov and Shakespeare's Tragedies," *NConL* 12, i (Jan., 1982): 11-12.

Stuart, D., *Nabokov*, 115-32.

_____, "Nabokov's DESPAIR: Tinkers to Evers to Chance," *GaR* 30 (1976): 432-46.

Suagee, Stephen, "An Artist's Memory Beats All Other Kinds: An Essay on DESPAIR," in Proffer, C. R., ed., *Book of Things about Vladimir Nabokov*, 54-62.

THE EXPLOIT

Field, A., *Nabokov*, 116-23.

THE EYE

Field, A., *Nabokov*, 165-72. Also in Dembo, L. S., ed., *Nabokov*, 57-63.

Hyde, G. M., *Vladimir Nabokov*, 102-8.

Koch, Stephen, "Nabokov as Novice," *Nation* 202 (Jan. 17, 1966): 81-2.

Putz, Manfred, "Vladimir Nabokov: Reader Beware," *Story of Identity*, 207-9.

Schaeffer, Susan F., "The Editing Blinks of Vladimir Nabokov's THE EYE," *UWR* 8, i (Fall, 1972): 5-30.

THE GIFT

Begnal, Michael H., "Fiction, Biography, History: Nabokov's THE GIFT," *JNT* 10 (1980): 138-43.

Dupee, F. W., "Nabokov: The Prose and Poetry of It All," *NYRB* (Dec., 1963): 10-12. Also in Dupee, F. W., *King of the Cats,* 134-8.

Field, A., *Nabokov,* 15-26, 29-32, 241-9.

Hyde, G. M., *Vladimir Nabokov,* 17-37.

Hyman, Stanley E., "Nabokovs's Gift," *New Leader* 46 (Oct. 14, 1963): 21. Also in Hyman, S. E., *Standards,* 184-8.

Johnson, D. Barton, "The Key to Nabokov's GIFT," *CASS* 16, ii (1982): 190-206.

Karlinsky, Simon, "Vladimir Nabokov's Novel DAR as a Work of Literary Criticism: A Structural Analysis," *SEEJ* 7 (Fall, 1963): 284-90.

Lee, L. L., *Vladimir Nabokov,* 80-94.

Louria, Yvette, "Nabokov and Proust: The Challenge of Time," *BA* 48 (Summer, 1974): 469-76.

Malcolm, Donald, "A Retrospect," *NY* 40 (Apr. 25, 1964): 198-205.

Moynahan, J., *Vladimir Nabokov,* 37-40.

Paine, S., *Beckett, Nabokov, Nin,* 60-7.

Peterson, Robert E., "Time in THE GIFT," *VNRN* 9 (Fall, 1982): 36-40.

Rowe, W. W., *Nabokov and Others,* 95-7.

Salehar, Anna M., "Nabokov's GIFT: An Apprenticeship in Creativity," in Proffer, C. R., ed., *Book of Things about Vladimir Nabokov,* 70-83.

Scott, Charles T., "Typography, Poems and the Poetic Line," 153-60 in Jazayery, Mohammad A., Edgar C. Rolome, and Werner Winter, eds., *Linguistic and Literary Studies in Honor of Archibald A. Hill, IV: Linguistics and Literature; Sociolinguistics and Applied Linguistics,* The Hague: Mouton, 1979.

Spender, Stephen, "A Poet's Invented and Demolished Truth," *NYTBR* (May 26, 1963): 4-5.

GLORY

Hyde, G. M., *Vladimir Nabokov,* 49-53.

Lee, L. L., *Vladimir Nabokov,* 50-5.

Rowe, W. W., *Nabokov and Others,* 103-5.

INVITATION TO A BEHEADING

Alter, Robert, "INVITATION TO A BEHEADING: Nabokov and the Art of Politics," *TriQ* 17 (Winter, 1970): 41-60. Also in Appel, A., Jr., and C. Newman, eds., *Nabokov,* 41-59.

Barabtarlo, Gene, "'That Main Secret tra-ta-ta tra-ta-'," *VNRN* 9 (Fall, 1982): 34-5.

Bitsilli, P. M., "The Revival of Allegory," in Appel, A., Jr., and C. Newman, eds., *Nabokov,* 102-18 *passim.*

Boegeman, Margaret B., "INVITATION TO A BEHEADING and the Many Shades of Kafka," in Rivers, J. E., and C. Nicol, eds., *Nabokov's Fifth Arc,* 105-21.

Field, A., *Nabokov,* 185-98.

Gottfried, Paul, "Against the Bolshevik Nightmare and the Fraud of Revolution: Vladimir Nabokov: INVITATION TO A BEHEADING: BEND SINISTER," *ChronC* 2 (Jan.-Feb., 1978): 9-10.

Hughes, Robert P., "Notes on the Translation of INVITATION TO A BEHEADING," *TriQ* 17 (Winter, 1970): 284-92.

Hyde, G. M., *Vladimir Nabokov,* 129-40.

Hyman, Stanley E., "The Handle: INVITATION TO A BE-HEADING and BEND SINISTER," *TriQ* 17 (Winter, 1970):

60-71. Also in Rivers, J. E., and C. Newman, eds., *Nabokov's Fifth Arc,* 105-21.

Johnson, D. Barton, "Spatial Modeling and Deixis: Nabokov's INVITATION TO A BEHEADING," *PoT* 3, i (Winter, 1982): 81-98.

Klemtner, Susan S., "To 'Special Space': Transformation in IN-VITATION TO A BEHEADING," *MFS* 25, iii (Autumn, 1979): 427-38.

Lee, L., L., *Vladimir Nabokov,* 70-9.

Leong, Albert, "Dualism of Character and Style in Nabokov's INVITATION TO A BEHEADING," 269-73 in Kraft, Walter, C., ed., Proceedings: Pacific Northwest Conf. on Foreign Languages. 25th Annual Mtg., April 19-20, 1974, Eastern Washington State Coll., Vol. 24, Part I: *Literature and Linguistics,* Corvallis: Oregon State Un. Pr., 1974.

Moynahan, Julian, "A Russian Preface for Nabokov's BE-HEADING," *Novel* 1 (Fall, 1967): 12-18.

Penner, Dick, "INVITATION TO A BEHEADING: Nabokov's Absurdist Initiation," *Crit* 20, iii (1978): 27-38.

Peterson, Dale E., "Nabokov's INVITATION TO A BEHEAD-ING: Literature as Execution," *PMLA* 96, v (Oct., 1981): 824-36.

Pifer, E. I., *Nabokov and the Novel,* 49-67.

_____, "Nabokov's INVITATION TO A BEHEADING: The Parody of a Tradition," *PCP* 5 (Winter, 1970): 46-53.

Schuman, Samuel, "Vladimir Nabokov's INVITATION TO A BEHEADING and Robert Heinlein's THEY," *TCL* 19, ii (Apr., 1973): 99-106.

Stuart, Dabney, "All the Mind's a Stage: A Reading of INVITA-TION TO A BEHEADING," *UWR* 4, ii (Spring, 1969): 1-24.

_____, *Nabokov,* 55-85.

Williams, Carol T., "Nabokov's Dialectical Structure," *WSCL* 8, ii (Spring, 1967): 255-7. Also in Dembo, L. S., ed., *Nabokov,* 170-2.

KING, QUEEN, KNAVE

Amis, Martin, "The Sublime and the Ridiculous: Nabokov's Black Farces," in Qennell, P., ed., *Vladimir Nabokov,* 76-80.

Dillard, R. H. W., in Dillard, R. H. W., and others, eds., *Sounder Few,* 152-6.

Field, A., *Nabokov,* 152-9.

Gass, William H., "Mirror, Mirror," *NYRB* 10 (June 6, 1968): 3-5. Also in Gass, W. H., *Fiction and the Figures of Life,* 110-19.

Hyde, G. M., *Vladimir Nabokov,* 44-9.

Lee, L. L., *Vladimir Nabokov,* 38-45.

Pifer, E., *Nabokov and the Novel,* 14-48.

Proffer, Carl R., "A New Deck for Nabokov's Knaves," *TriQ* 17 (Winter, 1970): 293-309. [Comparison of American and Russian versions.]

LAUGHTER IN THE DARK (CAMERA OBSCURA)

Amis, Martin, "The Sublime and the Ridiculous: Nabokov's Black Farces," in Quennell, P., *Vladimir Nabokov,* 80-3.

Field, A., *Nabokov,* 158-65.

Hyde, G. M., *Vladimir Nabokov,* 57-75.

Lee, L. L., *Vladimir Nabokov,* 56-62.

Moynahan, J., *Vladimir Nabokov,* 25-31.

Simon, John, "Before LOLITA, What?" *Mid-Century* 19 (Nov., 1960): 8-13.

Stuart, Dabney, "LAUGHTER IN THE DARK: Dimensions of Parody," *TriQ* 17 (Winter, 1970): 72-95. Also in Appel, A., Jr., and C. Newman, eds., *Nabokov*, 72-95.

―――――, *Nabokov*, 87-113.

Williams, Carol T., "Nabokov's Dialectical Structure," *WSCL* 8, ii (Spring, 1967): 258-61. Also in Dembo, L. S., ed., *Nabokov*, 173-6.

LOLITA

Albright, D., *Representation and the Imagination*, 204-7.

Aldridge, A. Owen, "LOLITA and LES LIAISONS DANGEREUSES," *WSCL* 2, iii (Fall, 1961): 20-6.

Alexander, Rosemary S., "Point of View in the Novel and Painting: A Comparison of LOLITA and Some O'Keefe Paintings," *DAI* 38 (1978): 7319A.

Amis, Kingsley, "She Was a Child and I Was a Child," *Spectator* 6854 (Nov. 6, 1959): 635-6. Also in Amis, K., *What Became of Jane Austen?* 77-85.

Anderson, William, "Time and Memory in Nabokov's LOLITA," *CentR* 24 (1980): 360-83.

Appel, Alfred, Jr., *Annotated LOLITA*.

―――――, "The Art of Nabokov's Artifice," *UDQ* 3 (Summer, 1968): 25-37.

―――――, "Backgrounds to LOLITA," *TriQ* 17 (Winter, 1970): 17-40. Also in Appel, A., Jr., and C. Newman, eds., *Nabokov*, 17-40. Also as part of the Introduction to Appel, A., Jr., ed., *Annotated LOLITA*.

―――――, "LOLITA: The Springboard of Parody," *WSCL* 8, ii (Spring, 1967): 204-41. Also in Dembo, L. S., ed., *Nabokov*, 106-43.

―――――, "Tristam in Movieland: LOLITA at the Movies," *RLT* 7 (1973): 343-88. Also in Proffer, C. R., ed., *Book of Things about Vladimir Nabokov*, 123-70.

Bader, J., *Crystal Land*, 57-81.

Baker, George, "LOLITA: Literature or Pornography?" *SatR* 40 (June 22, 1957): 18.

Banta, Martha, "Benjamin, Edgar, Humbert and Jay," *UR* 60, iv (Summer, 1971): 532-49.

Beaver, Harold, "A Figure in the Carpet: Irony and the American Novel," *E&S* 15 (1962): 113-14.

Bell, Michael, "LOLITA and Pure Art," *EIC* 24 (Apr., 1974): 169-84.

Brick, Allen, "The Madman in His Cell: Joyce, Beckett, Nabokov, and the Stereotypes," *MR* 1 (Fall, 1959): 52-5.

Bruchman, Patricia, "The Day After the Fourth," *VNRN* 3 (1979): 31-2.

Bruss, Elizabeth W., "Vladimir Nabokov: Illusions of Reality and the Reality of Illusions," *Autobiographical Acts*, 128-35, 141-9, 155-61.

Bullock, Richard H., "I: The Only Immortality You and I May Share: Artifice, Reality, and Art in LOLITA; II: Using Translational Contextualization Exercises to Teach Basic Writing," *DAI* 43, i (July, 1982): 166A-67A.

Butler, Diana, "Lolita, Lepidoptera," *New World Writing*, No. 16 (1960): 58-84.

Campbell, Felicia C., "A Princeton by the Sea," *LHR* 10 (1968): 39-46.

Christopher, J. R., "On LOLITA as a Mystery Story," *ArmD* 7, i (1973): 29.

Ciancio, Ralph A., "Nabokov and the Verbal Mode of the Grotesque," *ConL* 18, iv (Autumn, 1977): 518-33.

Clark, George P., "A Further Word on Poe and LOLITA," *PN* 3 (Dec., 1970): 39.

Clifton, Gladys M., "Humbert Humbert and the Limits of Artistic License," in Rivers, J. E., and C. Nicol, eds., *Nabokov's Fifth Arc*, 153-70.

Cummins, George M., "Nabokov's Russian LOLITA," *SEEJ* 21 (1977): 354-65.

Dalwood, Hubert, "LOLITA—A Postscript," *Geste* (Un. of Leeds) 4 (Mar. 12, 1959): 13-14.

Davies, R., "By Lo Possessed," *Voice from the Attic*, 242-6.

Dipple, Elizabeth, "Iris Murdoch and Vladimir Nabokov: An Essay in Literary Realism and Experimentalism," in Campbell, J., and J. Doyle, eds., *Practical Vision*, 103-18.

DuBois, Arthur E., "Poe and LOLITA," *CEA* 21, vi (Mar., 1964): 1, 7.

Dupee, F. W., "LOLITA in America," *Encounter* 12 (Feb., 1959): 30-5. Also in *CUF* 2 (Winter, 1959): 35-9.

―――――, "A Preface to LOLITA," *Anchor Rev.* No. 2 (1957): 30-5. Also in Dupee, F. W., *King of the Cats*, 117-31.

Fiedler, L., *Love and Death in the American Novel*, 326-8.

―――――, "The Profanation of the Child," *New Leader* 41 (June 23, 1958): 26-9.

Field, A., *Nabokov*, 323-50.

Fowler, Douglas R., "Elphinstone Again," *VNRN* 5 (Fall, 1980): 26.

―――――, *Reading Nabokov*, 147-75.

French, Brandon, "The Celluloid Lolita: A Not-So-Crazy Quilt," in Peary, G., and R. Shatzkin, eds., *Modern American Novels and the Movies*, 224-35.

Frosch, Thomas R., "Parody and Authenticity in LOLITA," in Rivers, J. E., and C. Nicol, eds., *Nabokov's Fifth Arc*, 171-87.

Gardiner, Harold C., "Cliches Are Dangerous," *America* 99 (Aug. 30, 1958): 26-9.

Gillon, Adam, "Conrad's VICTORY and Nabokov's LOLITA: Imitations of Imitations," *Conradiana* 12 (1980): 51-71.

Glicksberg, C. I., *Sexual Revolution in Modern American Literature*, 196-200.

Gold, Joseph, "The Morality of LOLITA," *Brit. Assn. for Amer. Studies Bull.* n.s. 1 (Sept., 1960): 50-4.

Goldhurst, William, Alfred Appel, Jr., and George P. Clark, "Three Observations on AMONTILLADO and LOLITA," *PoeS* 5, ii (1972): 50-1.

Grabes, H., *Fictitious Biographies*, 31-45.

Green, Martin, "The Morality of LOLITA," *KR* 28 (June, 1966): 352-77. Also in Green, M., *Yeats's Blessing on von Hugel*, 128-50.

―――――, "American Rococo: Salinger and Nabokov," *Re-Appraisals*, 211-29.

Hale, Nancy, "Hemingway and the Courage to Be," *VQR* 38 (Autumn, 1962): 621-3.

Harold, Brent, "LOLITA: Nabokov's Critique of Aloofness," *PLL* 11, i (Winter, 1975): 71-82.

Harris, Harold J., "LOLITA and the Sly Forward," *MRR* 1, ii (1965): 29-38.

Hiatt, L. R., "Nabokov's LOLITA: A 'Freudian' Cryptic Crossword," *AI* 24 (Winter, 1967): 360-70.

Hicks, Granville, "LOLITA and Her Problems," *SatR* 41 (Aug. 16, 1958): 12, 38.

Hinchcliffe, Arnold P., "Belinda in America," *SA* 6 (1960): 339-47.

Hollander, John, "The Perilous Magic of Nymphets," *PR* 23 (Fall, 1956): 557-60. Also in Kostelanetz, R., ed., *On Contemporary Literature*, 477-80.

Holmstrom, Jan, "Aesthetic Bliss: A Note on Nabokov's Aesthetics," *MSpr* 75, ii (1981): 133-7.

Hughes, Daniel J., "Character in Contemporary Fiction," *MR* 3 (Summer, 1962): 792-3.

_____, "Reality and the Hero: LOLITA and HENDERSON THE RAIN KING," *MFS* 6 (Winter, 1960-61): 345-64. Also in Malin, I., ed., *Saul Bellow and the Critics*, 69-91.

Hyde, G. M., *Vladimir Nabokov*, 115-22.

Jones, Steven S., "The Enchanted Hunters: Nabokov's Use of Folk Characterization of LOLITA," *WF* 39 (1980): 269-83.

Josipovici, G. D., "LOLITA: Parody and the Pursuit of Beauty," *CritQ* 6 (Spring, 1964): 35-48. Also in Josipovici, G., *World and the Book*, 201-20.

Joyce, James, "Lolita in Humberland," *SNNTS* 6, iii (Fall, 1974): 339-48.

King, Bruce, "LOLITA—Sense and Sensibility at Mid-century," *Geste* (Un. of Leeds) 4 (Mar. 12, 1959): 3-9.

Leach, Elsie, "Lolita and Little Nell," *SJS* 3, i (1977): 70-8.

Lee, L. L., *Vladimir Nabokov*, 115-24.

Levine, Robert T., "LOLITA and the Originality of Style," *ELWIU* 4 (1977): 110-21.

_____, "'My Ultraviolet Darling': The Loss of Lolita's Childhood," *MFS* 25, iii (Autumn, 1979): 471-9.

Link, Franz H., "Nabokov's LOLITA and Aesthetic Romanticism," *LWU* 9 (1976): 37-48.

Lokrantz, J. T., *Underside of the Weave*, 27-30, 73-8.

Louria, Yvette, "Nabokov and Proust," *BA* 48, iii (Summer, 1974): 469-75.

Lund, Mary G., "Don Quixote Rides Again or Some Coordinates Are Outside," *Whetstone* 3 (Fall, 1959): 172-8.

Madden, David W., "'We Poets': Humbert and Keats," *NConL* 10, iii (1980): 5-6.

Maddox, Lucy B., "Necrophilia in LOLITA," *CentR* 26, iv (Fall, 1982): 361-74.

Mason, Bruce, "Mr. Pim," *VNRN* 6 (Spring, 1981): 31-2.

McDonald, James, "John Ray, Jr., Critic and Artist: The Forward to LOLITA," *SNNTS* 5, iii (Fall, 1973): 352-7.

Megerle, Brenda, "The Tantalization of LOLITA," *SNNTS* 11 (1979): 338-48.

Merrill, Robert, "Nabokov and Fictional Artifice," *MFS* 25, iii (Autumn, 1979): 446-54.

Meyer, Frank S., "The Strange Fate of LOLITA—A Lance Into Cotton Wool," *NatR* 6 (Nov. 22, 1958): 340-1.

Miles, Thomas H., "Lolita: Humbert's Playful Goddess," *NConL* 6, iv (1976): 5-7.

Mitchell, Charles, "Mythic Seriousness in LOLITA," *TSLL* 5 (Autumn, 1963): 329-43.

Morton, D. E., *Vladimir Nabokov*, 64-81.

Moynahan, Julian, "LOLITA and Related Memories," *TriQ* 17 (Winter, 1970): 247-52.

_____, *Vladimir Nabokov*, 31-6.

Nabokov, Vladimir, "On a Book Entitled LOLITA," *Anchor Rev.* No. 2 (1957): 1-13. Also in *Encounter* 12 (Apr., 1959): 4-21.

_____, "Postscript to the Russian Edition of LOLITA," in Rivers, J. E., and C. Nicol, eds., *Nabokov's Fifth Arc*, 188-94.

Nelson, G. B., *Ten Versions of America*, 185-201.

Nemerov, Howard, "The Mortality of Art," *KR* 28 (Spring, 1957): 313-21. Also in Nemerov, H., *Poetry and Fiction*, 260-6.

Nicol, Charles, "The Cantrip Review," *VNRN* 2 (1979): 24-5.

Novak, Frank G., Jr., "Ambiguity and Incest: An Allusion to Melville in Nabokov's LOLITA," *NConL* 11, v (Nov., 1981): 10.

O'Connor, Phillip F., "LOLITA: A Modern Classic in Spite of Its Readers," in Filler, L., ed., *Seasoned Authors for a New Season*, 139-43.

Oliphant, Robert, "Public Voices and Wise Guys," *VQR* 37 (Autumn, 1961): 530-5.

Packman, David, "The Cryptogrammic Paper Chase," *NYLF* 2 (1978): 15-22.

_____, "Structures of Desire: Vladimir Nabokov's LOLITA, PALE FIRE, and ADA," *DAI* 40 (1979): 2685A.

Pearce, Richard, "Nabokov's Black (Hole) Humor: LOLITA and PALE FIRE," in Cohen, S. B., *Comic Relief*, 32-8.

_____, *Stages of the Clown*, 94-101.

Phillips, Elizabeth, "The Hocus-Pocus of LOLITA," *L&P* 10 (Summer, 1960): 97-101.

Pifer, E., *Nabokov and the Novel*, 106-10, 164-71.

Pinnells, James R., "The Speech Ritual as an Element of Structure in Nabokov's LOLITA," *DR* 60, iv (Winter, 1980-81): 605-21.

Pope, Robert, "Beginnings," *GaR* 36, iv (Winter, 1982): 733-51.

Prioleau, Elizabeth, "Humbert Humbert THROUGH THE LOOKING GLASS," *TCL* 21 (1975): 428-47.

Pritchett, V. S., in *NStat* 57 (Jan. 10, 1959): 38.

Probyn, Hugh, "LOLITA—Nabokov by Poe Out of Rabelais," *Geste* (Un. of Leeds) 4 (Mar. 12, 1959): 10-12.

Proffer, Carl R., *Keys to Lolita*, Bloomington: Indiana Un. Pr., 1968.

Proffitt, Edward, "A Clue to John Ray, Jr.," *MFS* 20 (Winter, 1974-75): 551-2.

Rackin, Donald, "The Moral Rhetoric of Nabokov's LOLITA," *FQ* 22 (Spring, 1973): 3-19.

Rea [sic], John A., "Elphinstone," *VNRN* 3 (Fall, 1979): 29.

Rivers, J. E., "Lolita's Tennis Coach: A Contribution to the Annotation of the Novel," *NMAL* 1 (1977): Item 7.

Roth, Phyllis A., "In Search of Aesthetic Bliss: A Rereading of LOLITA," *CollL* 2, i (Winter, 1975): 28-49.

Rougemont, Denis de, *Love Declared: Essays on the Myths of Love*, N.Y.: Pantheon, 1963, 48-54.

Rowe, W. W., *Nabokov and Others*, 88-91.

Rubinstein, E., "Approaching LOLITA," *MinnR* 6 (Winter, 1966): 361-7.

Rubman, Lewis H., "Creatures and Creators in LOLITA and 'Death and the Compass'," *MFS* 19 (Autumn, 1973): 433-52.

Ryley, Robert M., "Will Brown, Dolores, Colo.," *VNRN* 3 (Fall, 1979): 30.

Scheid, Mark, "Epistemological Structures in LOLITA," *RUS* 61, i (1975): 127-40.

Schickel, Richard, "Nabokov's Artistry," *The Progressive* 22 (Nov., 1958): 46-9. Also in *Reporte* 17 (Nov. 28, 1957): 45-7.

Schuman, Samuel, "LOLITA: Novel and Screenplay," *CollL* 5 (1978): 195-204.

_____, "Man, Magician, Poet, God—An Image in Medieval, Renaissance, and Modern Literature," *Cithara*, 47-52.

_____, "A Tempest in a Fleshpot," *Mosaic* 10, i (1976): 1-5.

Scott, W. G., "The LOLITA Case," *Landfall* 15 (June, 1961): 134-8.

Seiden, Melvin, "Nabokov and Dostoevsky," *ConL* 13, iv (Autumn, 1972): 423-44.

Seldon, E. S., "LOLITA and JUSTINE," *EvR* 2, vi (Autumn, 1958): 156-9.

Shilstone, Frederick W., "The Courtly Mysogynist: Humbert Humbert in LOLITA," *StHum* 8, i (1980): 5-10.

Slonim, Marc, "DOCTOR ZHIVAGO and LOLITA," *ILA* 2 (1959): 213-25.

Speakman, P. T., "LOLITA—What Are Humbert's Motives?" *Geste* (Un. of Leeds) 4 (Mar. 12, 1959): 12-13.

Stark, J. O., *Literature of Exhaustion*, 62-117 *passim*.

Stegner, P., *Escape Into Aesthetics*, 102-15.

Strainchamps, Ethel, "Nabokov's Handling of English Syntax," *AS* 36 (Oct., 1961): 234-5.

Tamir-Ghez, Nomi, "The Art of Persuasion in Nabokov's LOLITA," *PoT* 1, i (1979): 65-83.

_____, "Rhetorical Manipulation in Nabokov's LOLITA," 172-95, in Kodjak, Andrej, Michael J. Connelly, and Krystyna Pomorska, eds., *The Structural Analysis of Narrative Texts: Conference Papers* (New York Un. Slavic Papers 2), Columbus: Slavika, 1980.

Tammi, Pekka, "Nabokov's LOLITA," *Expl* 39, iv (Summer, 1981): 41-3.

_____, "Nabokov's LOLITA: The Turgenev Subtext," *NMAL* 5, ii (Spring, 1981): Item 10.

Tierlinch, Herman, "Notes on Nabokov's LOLITA," *LitR* 7 (Spring, 1964): 439-42.

Tekiner, Christina, "Time in LOLITA," *MFS* 25, ii (Autumn, 1979): 463-9.

Trilling, Lionel, "The Last Lover: Vladimir Nabokov's LOLITA," *Griffin* 7 (Aug., 1958): 4-21. Also in *Encounter* 11 (Oct., 1958): 9-19.

Twitchell, James, "LOLITA as Bildungsroman," *Genre* 7 (Sept., 1974): 272-8.

Uphaus, Robert W., "Nabokov's KUNSTLERROMAN: Portrait of the Artist as Dying Man," *TCL* 13 (July, 1867): 104-10.

Vesterman, William, "Why Humbert Shoots Quilty," *ELWIU* 5 (1978): 85-93.

Wallace, Ronald, "No Harm in Smiling: Vladimir Nabokov's LOLITA," *Last Laugh*, 65-89.

West, Rebecca, "LOLITA: A Tragic Book With a Sly Grimace" (London) *Sunday Times* (Nov. 8, 1959): 16.

Williams, Carol T., "Nabokov's Dialectical Structure," *WSCL* 8, ii (Spring, 1967): 261-7. Also in Dembo, L. S., ed., *Nabokov*, 176-82.

Wills, Garry, "The Devil and Lolita," *NYRB* (Feb. 21, 1974): 4-6.

Winston, Mathew, "LOLITA and the Dangers of Fiction," *TCL* 21 (1975): 421-7.

Zall, Paul M., "Lolita and Gulliver," *SNL* 3 (Fall, 1965): 33-7.

LOOK AT THE HARLEQUINS!

Grabes, H., *Fictitious Biographies*, 106-31.

Hyde, G. M., *Vladimir Nabokov*, 211-20.

Patterson, Richard, "Nabokov's LOOK AT THE HARLEQUINS! Endless Re-Creation of the Self," *RLT* 14 (1976): 84-98.

Proffer, Carl R., "Things about LOOK AT THE HARLEQUINS! Some Marginal Notes," in Proffer, C. R., ed., *Book of Things about Nabokov*, 295-301.

MARY

Hyde, G. M., *Vladimir Nabokov*, 38-44.

Lee, L. L., *Vladimir Nabokov*, 34-8.

McLaughlin, Richard, "A Series of Mirrors," *B&B* 16, viii (May, 1971): 18-21.

PALE FIRE

Adams, Robert M., in *HudR* 15 (Autumn, 1962): 420-3.

Albright, D., *Representation and the Imagination*, 82-93.

Alter, Robert, *Partial Magic: The Novel as a Self-Conscious Genre*, Berkeley: Un. of Calif. Pr., 1975, 183-217.

Bader, J., *Crystal Land*, 31-56.

Baxter, Charles, "Nabokov, Idolatry, and the Police State," *Boundary* 5, iii (Spring, 1977): 831-24.

Berberova, Nina, "The Mechanics of PALE FIRE," *TriQ* 17 (Winter, 1970): 147-59. Also in Appel, A., Jr., and C. Newman, eds., *Nabokov*, 147-59.

Chester, Alfred, "Nabokov's Anti-Novel," *Ctary* 34 (Nov., 1962): 449-51.

Ciancio, Ralph A., "Nabokov and the Verbal Mode of the Grotesque," *ConL* 18, iv (Autumn, 1977): 518-33.

Clark, Beverly L., "Kinbote's Variants in Nabokov's PALE FIRE," *NMAL* 5, iii (Summer, 1981): Item 18.

Coetzee, J. M., "Nabokov's PALE FIRE and the Privacy of Art," *UCT Studies in English* 5 (1974): 1-7.

Dillard, R. H. W., in Dillard, R. H. W., and others, eds., *Sounder Few*, 161-5.

Edelstein, Marilyn, "PALE FIRE: The Art of Consciousness," in Rivers, J. E., and C. Nicol, eds., *Nabokov's Fifth Arc*, 213-23.

Field, A., *Nabokov*, 291-322.

_____, "PALE FIRE: The Labyrinth of a Great Novel," *TriQ* 8 (Winter, 1967): 13-36.

Flower, Timothy F., "1. Forms of Recreation in Nabokov's PALE FIRE..." *DAI* 32 (1972): 6927A.

_____, "The Scientific Art of Nabokov's PALE FIRE," *Criticism* 17 (1975): 223-3.

Fort, Deborah, "Contrast Epic: A Study of Joseph Heller's CATCH-22 (1961), Gunter Grass's THE TIN DRUM (DIE BLECHTROMMEL, 1959), John Barth's THE SOT-WEED FACTOR (1960, revised 1967), and Vladimir Nabokov's PALE FIRE (1962)," *DAI* 35 (1974): 3677A-78A.

Fowler, D., *Reading Nabokov*, 91-121.

Galati, Frank J., "A Study of Mirror Analogues in Vladimir Nabokov's PALE FIRE," *DAI* 32 (1971): 3462.

Grabes, H., *Fictitious Biographies*, 54-69.

Green, Geoffrey, "'An Infinity of Sensation and Thought Within a Finite Existence': Nabokov's Fiction of Memory," *HIS* 3, iv (Fall, 1980): 381-3.

Handley, Jack, "To Die in English," *NWR* 6 (Spring, 1963): 23-40.

Highet, Gilbert, "To Sound Hollow Laughter," *Horizon* 4 (July, 1962): 89-91.

Hyde, G. M., *Vladimir Nabokov*, 171-91.

Jackson, Paul R., "PALE FIRE and Faulkner," *NConL* 12, iii (May, 1982): 11-12.

_____, "PALE FIRE and Sherlock Holmes," *SAF* 10, i (Spring, 1982): 101-5.

Jenkins, William D., "This Case Deserves to Be a Classic," *BSJ* 24 (Mar., 1974): 9-11. [Notes parallels between Sherlock Holmes and PALE FIRE.]

Johnson, D. Barton, "The Index of Refraction in Nabokov's PALE FIRE," *RLT* 16 (1979): 33-49.

Johnson, E. Bond III, "Parody and Myth: Flaubert, Joyce, Nabokov," *FWF* 1 (May, 1974): 165-72.

Keir, Walter, "Nabokov's Score," *New Satire* 6 (Dec., 1962): 77-81.

Kermode, Frank, "Zemblances," *NStat* 64 (Nov. 9, 1962): 671-2. Also in Kermode, F., *Continuities,* 176-80.

Kostelanetz, Richard, "Nabokov's Obtuse Fool," *Ramparts* 3 (Jan.-Feb., 1965): 60-1. Also in Kostelanetz, R., ed., *On Contemporary Literature,* 481-5. Also (abridged) in Kostelanetz, R., ed., *New American Arts,* 222-4.

Krueger, John R., "Nabokov's Zemblan: A Constructed Language of Fiction," *Linguistics* 31 (May, 1967): 44-9.

LeClair, Thomas, "Poe's PYM and Nabokov's PALE FIRE," *NConL* 3, ii (Mar., 1973): 2-3.

Lee, L. L., *Vladimir Nabokov,* 132-44.

_____, "Vladimir Nabokov's Great Spiral of Being," *WHR* 18 (Summer, 1964): 225-36.

Levine, June P., "Vladimir Nabokov's PALE FIRE: 'The Method of Composition,' as Hero," *IFR* 5 (1978): 103-8.

Lokrantz, J. T., *Underside of the Weave,* 35-7, 82-7.

Lyons, John O., "PALE FIRE and the Fine Art of Annotation," *WSCL* 8, ii (Spring, 1967): 242-9. Also in Dembo, L. S., ed., *Nabokov,* 66-84.

McCarthy, Mary, "A Bolt from the Blue," *NRep* 116 (June 4, 1962): 21-7. Also as "Vladimir Nabokov's PALE FIRE," *Encounter* 19 (Oct., 1962): 71-84. Also in *Writing on the Wall,* 15-34.

Macdonald, Dwight, "Virtuosity Rewarded, or Dr. Kinbote's Revenge," *PR* 29 (Summer, 1962): 437-42.

Malin, Irving, in *WSCL* 4 (Spring-Summer, 1962): 252-5.

Maloff, Saul, "The World of Rococo," *Nation* 194 (June 16, 1962): 541-2.

Merrill, Robert, "Nabokov and Fictional Artifice," *MFS* 25, iii (Autumn, 1979): 454-62.

Morton, D. E., *Vladimir Nabokov,* 104-27.

Moynahan, J., *Vladimir Nabokov,* 40-5.

Murray, Michele, "Aesthetic Delight—The Author-Created Confusion is Deliberate," *Catholic Reporter* (Kansas City, Mo.) (July 6, 1962): 11.

Packman, David B., "Structures of Desire: Vladimir Nabokov's LOLITA, PALE FIRE, and ADA," *DAI* 40 (1979): 2685.

Pearce, Richard, "Nabokov's Black (Hole) Humor: LOLITA and PALE FIRE," in Cohen, S. B., ed., *Comic Relief,* 38-44.

Pifer, E., *Nabokov and the Novel,* 110-18.

Purdy, Struther B., "Solus Rex: Nabokov and the Chess Novel," *MFS* 14 (Winter, 1968-69): 391-5.

Putz, Manfred, "Vladimir Nabokov: Reader Beware," *Story of Identity,* 195-203.

_____, "Vladimir Nabokov's PALE FIRE: The Composition of a Reading Experience," *LWU* 10 (1977): 31-40.

Raban, J., "Registers in the Language of Fiction," *Techniques of Modern Fiction,* 154-7.

Reierstad, Keith, "Most Artistically Caged: Nabokov's Self-Inclusive Satire on Academia in PALE FIRE," *StCS* 5 (1978): 1-8.

Renaker, David, "PALE FIRE," *Expl* 36, iii (Spring, 1978): 22-4.

Riemer, Andrew, "Dim Glow, Faint Blaze—The Meaning of PALE FIRE," *Balcony* 6 (1967): 41-8.

Ristock, Tuuli Ann, "Nabokov's 'The Vane Sisters'—'Once in a Thousand Years of Fiction'," *UWR* 11, ii (Spring-Summer, 1976): 45-7. [Parallels between the short story and the novel.]

Rose, Lloyd, "The Pattern of PALE FIRE," *StAR* 3, i (Fall/Winter, 1974): 91-7.

Roth, Phyllis A., "The Psychology of the Double in Nabokov's PALE FIRE," *ELWIU* 2, ii (1975): 209-29.

Rowe, W. W., *Nabokov and Others,* 107-10.

Schuman, Sam, "Another 'Nora Zembla'," *VNRN* 6 (Spring, 1981): 30-1.

Sprowles, Alden, "Preliminary Annotation to Charles Kinbote's Commentary on PALE FIRE," in Proffer, C. R., ed., *Book of Things about Vladimir Nabokov,* 226-47.

Stark, John, "Borges' 'Tlon, Uqbar, Orbus Tertius' and Nabokov's PALE FIRE: Literature of Exhaustion," *TSLL* 14 (1972): 139-45.

_____, *Literature of Exhaustion,* 62-117 *passim.*

Stegner, P., *Escape Into Aesthetics,* 116-32.

Steiner, George, "Lament for Language Lost," *Reporter* 26 (June 7, 1962): 40-5.

Strunk, Volker, "Infinity and Missing Links in Nabokov's PALE FIRE," *ESC* 7, iv (Dec., 1981): 456-72.

Tanner, T., *City of Words,* 33-9.

Walker, David, "'The Viewer and the View': Chance and Choice in PALE FIRE," *SAF* 4 (Autumn, 1976): 203-21.

Webster, W. G., "Narrative Technique in PALE FIRE," *BWVACET* 1, i (1974): 38-43.

Williams, Carol T., "'Web of Sense': PALE FIRE in the Nabokov Canon," *Crit* 6, iii (Winter, 1963-64): 29-45.

PNIN

Anon., "Pnin and Pan," *Time* 69 (Mar. 18, 1957): 108-10.

Bader, J., *Crystal Land,* 82-94.

Carroll, William, "Nabokov's Signs and Symbols," in Proffer, C. R., ed., *Book of Things about Vladimir Nabokov,* 203-8.

Connolly, Julian W., "A Note on the Name 'Pnin'," *VNRN* 6 (Spring, 1981): 32-3.

_____, "PNIN: The Wonder of Recurrence and Transformation," in Rivers, J. E., and C. Nicol, eds., *Nabokov's Fifth Arc,* 195-210.

_____, "The Real Life of Zhorzhik Uranski," *VNRN* 4 (1980): 35-7.

Cowart, David, "Art and Exile: Nabokov's PNIN," *SAF* 20, ii (Autumn, 1982): 197-207.

Elliott, George P., in *HudR* 10 (Summer, 1957): 289-91.

Field, A., *Nabokov,* 129-40.

Fowler, D., *Reading Nabokov,* 122-46.

Gordon, Ambrose, Jr., "The Double Pnin," in Dembo, L. S., ed., *Nabokov,* 144-56.

Grabes, H., *Fictitious Biographies,* 46-53.

Grams, Paul, "PNIN: The Biographer as Meddler," *RLT* 3 (1972): 360-9. Also in Proffer, C. R., ed., *Book of Things about Vladimir Nabokov,* 193-202.

High, Roger, "PNIN—A Preposterous Little Explosion," *Geste* (Un. of Leeds) 4 (Mar. 12, 1959): 16-18.

Hyde, G. M., *Vladimir Nabokov,* 149-70.

Lee, L. L., *Vladimir Nabokov,* 124-31.

Lokrantz, J. T., *Underside of the Weave,* 21-7, 78-81.

Lyons, J. O., *College Novel in America,* 117-19.

Manion, Christopher, "Sentimentality as Oppression and Deliverance: Vladimir Nabokov: PNIN," *ChronC* 2 (Jan.-Feb., 1978): 13-14.

Mizener, Arthur, "The Seriousness of Vladimir Nabokov," *SR* 76 (Autumn, 1968): 655-64.

Moody, Fred, "At PNIN's Center," *RLT* 14 (1976): 70-83.

Morton, D. E., *Vladimir Nabokov,* 84-101.

Nicol, Charles D., "Pnin's History," *Novel* 4 (Spring, 1971): 197-208.

Olszewska, E. S., and Alan S. C. Ross, " 'Hong Kong' in Croquet," *Month* 226 (July-Aug., 1968): 302-3. [Discusses meaning of term.]

Rowe, W. W., *Nabokov and Others,* 126-35.

————, "Pnin's Uncanny Looking Glass," in Proffer, C. R., ed., *Book of Things about Vladimir Nabokov,* 203-8.

Schneider, Joseph L., "The Immigrant Experience in PNIN and MR. SAMMLER'S PLANET," in *On Poets and Poetry: Second Series,* 33-41.

Stegner, P., *Escape Into Aesthetics,* 90-101.

Stern, Richard G., "PNIN and the Dust-Jacket," *PrS* 31 (Summer, 1957): 161-4.

Stuart, D., *Nabokov,* 133-61.

THE REAL LIFE OF SEBASTIAN KNIGHT

Bader, J., *Crystal Land,* 13-30.

Bruffee, K. A., "Form and Meaning in Nabokov's REAL LIFE OF SEBASTIAN KNIGHT: An Example of Elegaic Romance," *MLQ* 34, ii (June, 1973): 180-90.

Field, A., *Nabokov,* 26-32.

Fromberg, Susan, "The Unwritten Chapters in THE REAL LIFE OF SEBASTIAN KNIGHT," *MFS* 13 (Winter, 1967-68): 427-42.

Grabes, H., *Fictitious Biographies,* 1-17.

Hyde, G. M., *Vladimir Nabokov,* 84-94.

Johnson, W. R., "THE REAL LIFE OF SEBASTIAN KNIGHT," *CarM* 4 (Fall, 1963): 111-14.

Lee, L. L., *Vladimir Nabokov,* 95-104.

Lokrantz, J. T., *Underside of the Weave,* 31-5, 69-71.

Mesher, David R., "Pynchon and Nabokov's V," *PNotes* 8 (Feb., 1982): 43-6.

Morton, D. E., *Vladimir Nabokov,* 43-53.

Nicol, Charles, "The Mirrors of Sebastian Knight," in Dembo, L. S., ed., *Nabokov,* 85-94.

O'Connor, Katherine T., "Nabokov's THE REAL LIFE OF SEBASTIAN KNIGHT: In Pursuit of Biography," 282-93 in Joachim T. Baer and N. W. Ingha, eds., *Mnemozina: Studia Litteraria Russica in Honorem Vsevolod Setchkarev,* Munich: Fink, 1974.

Olcutt, Anthony, "The Author's Special Intention: A Study of THE REAL LIFE OF SEBASTIAN KNIGHT," *RLT* 3 (1972): 342-59. Also in Proffer, C. R., ed., *Book of Things about Vladimir Nabokov,* 104-21.

Purdy, Struther B., "Solus Rex: Nabokov and the Chess Novel," *MFS* 14 (Winter, 1968-69): 384-7.

Putz, Manfred, "Vladimir Nabokov: Reader Beware," *Story of Identity,* 203-6.

Rimmon, Shlomith, "Problems of Voice in Vladimir Nabokov's THE REAL LIFE OF SEBASTIAN KNIGHT," *PTL* 1 (1976): 489-512.

Stegner, S. Page, "The Immortality of Art: Vladimir Nabokov's THE REAL LIFE OF SEBASTIAN KNIGHT," *SoR* n.s. (Apr., 1966): 286-96. Also in Stegner, P., *Escape Into Aesthetics,* 63-75.

Stuart, Dabney, *Nabokov,* 1-53.

————, "THE REAL LIFE OF SEBASTIAN KNIGHT: Angles of Perception," *MLQ* 29 (Sept., 1968): 312-28.

Tanzy, C. E., in *EJ* 49 (Feb., 1960): 141-2.

SOLUS REX (Unfinished Novel)

Field, A., *Nabokov,* 292-310.

TRANSPARENT THINGS

Albright, D., *Representation and the Imagination,* 60-70.

Alter, Robert, "Mimesis and the Motive for Fiction," *TriQ* 42 (1978): 228-49. Also in Edelstein, Arthur, ed., *Images and Ideas in American Culture,* Brandeis Un. Pr., 1979, 112-16.

Gathorne-Hardy, J., "Poor Person," *LonM* 13, iii (Aug./Sept., 1973): 152-6.

Grabes, H., *Fictitious Biographies,* 96-105.

Karlinsky, Simon, "Russian Transparencies," *SatRA* 1, i (Jan., 1973): 44-5.

Morton, D. E., *Vladimir Nabokov,* 142-6.

Patteson, Richard F., "Nabokov's TRANSPARENT THINGS: Narration by the Mind's Eyewitness," *CollL* 3, ii (Spring, 1976): 102-12.

Raban, Jonathan, "Transparent Likenesses," *Encounter* 41, iii (Sept., 1973): 74-6.

Rosenblum, Michael, "Finding What the Sailor Has Hidden: Narrative as Patternmaking in TRANSPARENT THINGS," *ConL* 19, ii (Spring, 1978): 219-32.

Rowe, W. W., *Nabokov and Others,* 175-82.

ULTIMA THULE (Unfinished Novel)

Field, A., *Nabokov,* 292, 296-7, 305-8.

BIBLIOGRAPHY

See Issues of *The Vladimir Nabokov Research Newsletter.*

Schuman, Samuel, "Criticism of Vladimir Nabokov: A Selected Checklist," *MFS* 25, iii (Autumn, 1979): 527-54.

————, *Vladimir Nabokov: A Reference Guide,* Boston, Mass.: G. K. Hall, 1979.

NAIPAUL, V(IDIADHAR) S(URAJPRASAD), 1932-

GENERAL

Anderson, Linda, "Ideas of Identity and Freedom in V. S. Naipaul and Joseph Conrad," *ES* 59, vi (Dec., 1978): 510-17.

Angrosino, Michael V., "V.S. Naipaul and the Colonial Image," *Caribbean Quarterly* 21, iii (Sept., 1975): 10-21.

Blodgett, Harriet, "Beyond Trinidad: Five Novels by V. S. Naipaul," *SAQ* 73, iii (Summer, 1974): 388-403.

Boxhill, Anthony, "V. S. Naipaul's Starting Point," *JCL* 10, i (Aug., 1975): 1-9.

Boyers, Robert, "V. S. Naipaul," *ASch* 50, iii (Summer, 1981): 359-67.

Calder, Angus, "Darkest Naipaulia," *NStat* 82 (Oct. 8, 1971): 482-3.

Cooke, John, "A Vision of the Land: V. S. Naipaul's Later Novels," *Caribbean Quarterly* 25, iv (Dec., 1979): 31-47. Also in *JCS* 1 (1980): 140-61.

Derrick, A. C., "Naipaul's Techniques as a Novelist," *JCL* 7 (July, 1969): 32-44. Also in Hamner, R. D., ed., *Critical Perspectives on V. S. Naipaul*, 194-206.

Figueroa, John J., "Introduction—V. S. Naipaul: A Panel Discussion," *RevI* 6, iv (Winter, 1976-77): 554-63.

Garebian, Keith, "V. S. Naipaul's Negative Sense of Place," *JCL* 10, i (Aug., 1975): 23-35.

Gikes, M., *West Indian Novel*, 91-102.

Goldie, Terry, "The Minority Men," *Thalia* 4, ii (Fall-Winter, 1981): 44-58.

Goodheart, Eugene, "Naipaul and the Voices of Negation," *Salmagundi* 54 (Fall, 1981): 44-58.

Gowda, H. H. Anniah, "India in Naipaul's Artistic Consciousness," *LHY* 16, i (Jan., 1975): 27-39.

Greenwald, Roger C., "The Method of V. S. Naipaul's Fiction (1955-1963)," *DAI* 39 (1979): 4240A-41A.

Guiness, Gerald, "Naipaul's Four Early Trinidad Novels," *RevI* 6, iv (1976-77): 564-73.

Gurr, Andrew, "The Freedom of Exile in Naipaul and Doris Lessing," *ArielE* 13, iv (Oct., 1982): 7-18.

_____, *Writers in Exile*, 65-91.

Hamilton, Ian, "Without a Place: V. S. Naipaul Interviewed," *TLS* (July 30, 1971): 897-8. Also in *Savacou* 9-10 (1974): 120-6.

Hamner, Robert D., "Complementary Views of the Caribbean: V. S. Naipaul and Derek Walcott," *JEnS* 2, ii (1981): 834-45.

_____, ed., *Critical Perspectives on V. S. Naipaul*.

_____, "An Island Voice: The Novels of V. S. Naipaul," *DAI* 32 (1972): 6427A-28A.

_____, *V. S. Naipaul*.

Hemenway, Robert, "Sex and Politics in V. S. Naipaul," *SNNTS* 14, ii (Summer, 1982): 189-202.

Kantak, V. Y., "Man and Landscape in Naipaul's Fiction," *ACLALSB* 4, ii (1975): 43-51.

Kinkead-Weekes, Mark, "Bone Flute? Or House of Fiction: The Contrary Imagination of Wilson Harris and V. S. Naipaul," in Jefferson, D., and G. Martin, eds., *Uses of Fiction*, 139-58.

King, B., *New English Literature*, 100-8.

_____, "V. S. Naipaul," in King, B., ed., *West Indian Literature*, 161-78.

LaCovia, R. M., "The Medium is the Divide: An Examination of V. S. Naipaul's Early Works," *BlackI* 1, ii (1972): 3-6.

Lal, P., "Areas of Darkness," *Littcrit* 7 (1978): 7-10. [Not seen.]

Lee, R. H., "The Novels of V. S. Naipaul," *Theoria* 27 (Oct., 1966): 31-46. Also in Hamner, R. D., ed., *Critical Perspectives on V. S. Naipaul*, 68-83.

Lima, Emma E. de O.F., "Now Tell Me Who You Are! Some Considerations on Naipaul and His West Indian Fellow-Writers in Their Search for Identity," *EAA* 3-4 (1979-80): 98-103.

Lopez de Villegas, Consuelo, "Identity and Environment: Naipaul's Architectural Vision," *RevI* 10, ii (Summer, 1980): 220-9.

_____, "Matriarchs and Man-Eaters: Naipaul's Fictional Women," *RevI* 7 (Winter, 1977-78).

_____, "The Paradox of Freedom: Naipaul's Later Fiction," *RevI* 6, iv (1976-77): 574-9.

MacDonald, Bruce, "Symbolic Action in Three of V. S. Naipaul's Novels," *JCL* 9, iii (Apr., 1975): 41-52. Also in Hamner, R. D., ed., *Critical Perspectives on V. S. Naipaul*, 242-54.

Maes-Jelinek, Hena, "The Myth of El Dorado in the Caribbean Novel," *JCL* 6, i (June, 1971): 113-28.

_____, "V. S. Naipaul: A Commonwealth Writer," *RLV* 33 (1967): 499-513.

Masih, I. K., "India Theirs and Mine," *OJES* 18 (1982): 125-33.

Mason, Nondita, "The Fiction of V. S. Naipaul: A Study," *DAI* 41, xii (June, 1981): 5097A-98A.

Miller, Karl, "V. S. Naipaul and the New Order," *KR* 29, v (Nov., 1967): 685-98.

Mishra, Vijay, "Mythic Fabulation: Naipaul's India," *NLRev* 4 (1978): 59-65.

Moore, Gerald, "East Indians and West: The Novels of V. S. Naipaul," *BO* 7 (June, 1960): 11-15.

Morris, R. K., *Paradoxes of Order*.

Mukherjee, Bharati, and Robert Boyers, "A Conversation with V. S. Naipaul," *Salmagundi* 54 (Fall, 1981): 4-22.

Nachman, Larry D., "The World of V. S. Naipaul," *Salmagundi* 54 (Fall, 1981): 59-76.

Naipaul, V. S., "The Novelist V. S. Naipaul Talks About His Work to Ronald Bryden," *Listener* 29 (Mar. 22, 1973): 367-70.

_____, "V. S. Naipaul Discusses How Writing Changes the Writer," *Ndaanan* 4, i-ii (1974): 61-3.

Neill, Michael, "Taking the World to the Cleaner: The Writings of V. S. Naipaul," *New Zealand Listener* 93, 2084 (1979): 68-70. [Not seen.]

Nightingale, Margaret, "V. S. Naipaul as Historian: Combating Chaos," *SoRA* 13, iii (Nov., 1980): 239-50.

Nunez-Harrell, Elizabeth, "Lamming and Naipaul: Some Criteria for Evaluating the Third-World Novel," *ConL* 19, i (Winter, 1978): 26-47.

_____, "THE TEMPEST and the Works of Two Caribbean Novelists: Pitfalls in the Way of Seeing Caliban," *DAI* 38 (1977): 2775A-76A.

Omerod, David, "In a Derelict Land: The Novels of V. S. Naipaul," *WSCL* 9, i (Winter, 1968): 74-90. Also in Hamner, R. D., ed., *Critical Perspectives on V. S. Naipaul*, 159-77.

Parrinder, Patrick, "V. S. Naipaul and the Uses of Literacy," *CritQ* 21, ii (Summer, 1979): 5-13.

Premasakhi, A., "The Comic Element in the Novels of V. S. Naipaul," *JEnS* 12, ii (1981): 846-55.

_____, "Women in the Early Novels of V. S. Naipaul," *JEnS* 11, ii (1980): 766-72.

Raghavacharylu, D. V. K., "Naipaul and Narayan: The Sense of Life," in Narasimhaiah, C. D., ed., *Awakened Conscience*, 216-25.

Ramraj, Victor, "Diminishing Satire: A Study of V. S. Naipaul and Mordecai Richler," in Narasimhaiah, C. D., ed., *Awakened Conscience*, 261-74.

Rao, K. I. Madhusudana, "The Complex Fate: Naipaul's View of Human Development," in Srivastava, A. K., ed., *Alien Voice*, 194-209.

_____, *Contrary Awareness*.

Rohlehr, Gordon, "The Ironic Approach: The Novels of V. S. Naipaul," in James, L., ed., *Islands in Between*, 121-39. Also in Cooke, M. G., ed., *Modern Black Novelists*, 162-76. Also in Hamner, R. D., ed., *Critical Perspectives on V. S. Naipaul*, 178-93.

Rothfork, John, "V. S. Naipaul and the Third World," *RS* 41, iii (Sept., 1981): 183-92.

Shahane, Vasant I., "The Symbol of the 'House' in V. S. Naipaul's Early Novels," *OJES* 18 (1982): 46-59.

Sharma, T. R. S., "Naipaul's Version of Post-Colonial Societies," *OJES* 18 (1982): 25-36.

Singh, H. B., "V. S. Naipaul: A Spokesman for Neo-Colonialism," *L&I* 2 (Summer, 1969): 71-85.

Singh, Satyanarain, "Order and Chaos in Naipaul," *OJES* 18 (1982): 1-14.

Sivaramkrishna, M., "'Betwixt the World Without End and the World Without Point': Naipaul's Fictional Rhetoric," *OJES* 18 (1982): 139-51.

Smyer, Richard I., "Experience as Drama in the Works of V. S. Naipaul," *Kunapipi* 3, ii (1981): 33-56.

Theroux, P., *V. S. Naipaul.*

Thieme, John, "V. S. Naipaul and the Hindu Killer," *JIWE* 9 (1981): 70-86.

_____, "V. S. Naipaul's Third World: A Not So Free State," *JCL* 10, i (Aug., 1975): 10-21.

Thorpe, M., *V. S. Naipaul.*

Thoto, Anand Rao, "V. S. Naipaul and the Confused Hindu Sensibility," *OJES* 18 (1982): 37-45.

Waiyaki, S., "V. S. Naipaul and the West Indian Situation," *Buscara* 5, i (1973): 61-75.

Walsh, W., *V. S. Naipaul.*

_____, "Meeting Extremes," *JCL* 1 (Sept., 1965): 169-72.

_____, "Necessary and Accommodated: The Work of V. S. Naipaul," *LugR* 1, iii-iv (Summer, 1965): 169-81. Also (revised) in Walsh, W., *Manifold Voice*, 62-85.

White, L., *V. S. Naipaul.*

Wilson-Tagoe, Nana, "No Place: V. S. Naipaul's Vision of Home in the Caribbean," *Caribbean Review* 9 (1980): 37-41.

Winser, Leigh, "Naipaul's Painters and Their Pictures," *Crit* 18, i (1976): 67-80.

Woodcock, George, "Two Great Commonwealth Novelists: R. K. Narayan and V. S. Naipaul," *SR* 87, i (Winter, 1979): 1-28.

_____, "V. S. Naipaul and the Politics of Fiction," *QQ* 87, iv (Winter, 1980): 679-92.

Wyndham, Francis, "V. S. Naipaul," *Listener* 86 (Oct. 7, 1971): 461-2.

A BEND IN THE RIVER

Campbell, Elaine, "A Refinement of Rage: V. S. Naipaul's A BEND IN THE RIVER," *WLWE* 18, ii (1979): 394-406.

Kothandaramen, Bala, "A Place in the Sun: The Theme of Survival in A BEND IN THE RIVER," *OJES* 18 (1982): 100-24.

Nazareth, Peter, "Out of Darkness: Conrad and Other Third World Writers," *Conradiana* 14, iii (1982): 173-87.

Smyer, Richard, "Naipaul's A BEND IN THE RIVER: Fiction and the Post Colonial Tropics," *LHY* 23, ii (July, 1982): 59-67.

GUERRILLAS

Cooke, Michael G., "Rational Despair and the Fatality of Revolution in West Indian Literature," *YR* 71, i (Autumn, 1981): 28-38.

Johnstone, Richard, "Politics and V. S. Naipaul," *JCL* 14, i (Aug., 1979): 100-8.

King, B., *New English Literatures*, 221-3.

Kramer, Hilton, "Naipaul's Guerrillas and Oates's Assassins," *Ctary* 61, iii (Mar., 1976): 54-7.

McSweeney, Kerry, "V. S. Naipaul: Sensibility and Schemata," *CritQ* 18, iii (Autumn, 1976): 73-9.

Murray, Peter, "GUERRILLAS: A Prefatory Note [to a Symposium on Naipaul's Novel]," *JCL* 14, i (Aug., 1979): 88-9.

Neill, Michael, "Guerrillas and Gangs: Franz Fanon and V. S. Naipaul," *ArielE* 13, iv (Oct., 1982): 21-62.

Nightingale, Margaret, "George Lamming and V. S. Naipaul: Thesis and Antithesis," *ACLALSB* 5, iii (1980): 40-50.

Rao, K.I.M., *Contrary Awareness*, 179-200.

_____, "V. S. Naipaul's GUERRILLAS: A Fable of Political Innocence and Experience," *JCL* 14, i (Aug., 1979): 90-9.

Riis, Johannes, "Naipaul's WOODLANDERS," *JCL* 14, i (Aug., 1979): 109-15.

Sederberg, Peter C., "Faulkner, Naipaul, and Zola: Violence and the Novel," in Barber, B. R., and M. J. McGrath, eds., *Artist and Political Vision*, 221-3.

Spurling, John, "The Novel as Dictator," *Encounter* 45 (Dec., 1975): 173-6.

Thieme, John, "'Apparitions of Disaster': Brontean Parallels in WIDE SARAGASSO SEA and GUERRILLAS," *JCL* 14, i (Aug., 1979): 116-32.

Thorpe, M., *V. S. Naipaul*, 37-40.

Tiffin, Helen, "Freedom After the Fall: Renaissance and Disillusionment in WATER WITH BERRIES and GUERRILAS," in Mass, D., ed., *Individual and Community in Commonwealth Literature*, 90-8.

Wyndham, Francis, "Services Rendered," *NStat* (Sept. 19, 1975): 339-40. Also in Hamner, R. D., ed., *Critical Perspectives on V. S. Naipaul*, 255-9.

A HOUSE FOR MR. BISWIS

Argyle, Barry, "Commentary on V. S. Naipaul's A HOUSE FOR MR. BISWIS. A West Indian Epic," *Caribbean Quarterly* 16, iv (Dec., 1970): 61-9.

_____, "V. S. Naipaul's A HOUSE FOR MR. BISWAS," *LHY* 14, ii (1973): 81-95.

Asnani, Shyam M., "Quest for Identity Theme in Three Commonwealth Novels," in Srivastava, A. K., ed., *Alien Voice*, 132-4.

Belitt, Ben, "The Heraldry of Accommodation: A House for Mr. Naipaul," *Salmagundi* 54 (Fall, 1981): 23-42.

Blodgett, Harriet, "Beyond Trinidad: Five Novels of V. S. Naipaul," *SAQ* 73, iii (Summer, 1974): 395-8.

Cartey, Wilfred, "The Knight's Companion—Ganesh, Biswis and Stone," *NWQ* 2 (1965): 93-8.

Cathew, John, "Adapting to Trinidad: Mr. Biswis and Mr. Polly Revisited," *JCL* 13, i (Aug., 1978): 58-64.

Davies, Barrie, "The Personal Sense of a Society—Minority View: Aspects of the 'East Indian' Novel in the West Indies," *SNNTS* 4, ii (Summer, 1972): 291-5.

Derrick, A. C., "Naipaul's Technique as a Novelist," *JCL* 7 (July, 1969): 38-41. Also in Hamner, R. D., ed., *Critical Perspectives on V. S. Naipaul*, 200-4.

Fido, Martin, "Mr. Biswis and Mr. Polly," *ArielE* 5, iv (Oct., 1974): 30-7. [Naipaul's novel compared to Wells's THE HISTORY OF MR. POLLY.]

Gilkes, M., *West Indian Novel*, 94-8.

Griffiths, G., *Double Exile*, 124-9.

Guiness, Gerald, "Naipaul's Four Early Trinidad Novels," *RevI* 6 (1976-77): 569-73.

Gurr, A., *Writers in Exile*, 72-8.

Hamner, R. D., *V. S. Naipaul*, 48-52, 88-94. Also in Hamner, R. D., ed., *Critical Perspectives on V. S. Naipaul*, 225-30.

King, Bruce, in King, B., ed., *West Indian Literature*, 165-8.

Kirpal, Vineypalkur, "The House That Mrs. Biswis Built," *OJES* 18 (1982): 60-8.

Krikler, B., "The Novel Today: V. S. Naipaul's A HOUSE FOR MR. BISWIS," *Listener* (Feb. 13, 1964): 270-1.

Lee, R. H., "The Novels of V. S. Naipaul," *Theoria* 2 (Oct., 1966): 37-41. Also in Hamner, R. D., *Critical Perspectives on V. S. Naipaul*, 74-9.

MacDonald, Bruce F., "The Birth of Mr. Biswis," *JCL* 11, iii (Apr., 1977): 50-4.

_____, "Symbolic Action in Three of V. S. Naipaul's Novels," *JCL* 9, iii (Apr., 1975): 41-52 *passim*. Also in Hamner, R. D., ed., *Critical Perspectives on V. S. Naipaul*, 74-9.

Mehta, D. N., "Naipaul's Ambivalence: A HOUSE FOR MR. BISWIS," *Vidya* 14, i (1971): 11-26.

Morris, R. K., *Paradoxes of Order*, 22-37.

Nanden, Satendra, "The Immigrant Experience in Literature: Trinidad and Fiji," in Narasimhaiah, C. D., ed., *Awakened Conscience*, 346-57.

_____, "A Study in Context: V. S. Naipaul's A HOUSE FOR MR. BISWIS," *New Lit. Rev.* (Canberra) 1 (1977): 21-8.

Ngai, Mbatau K. W., "The Relationship Between Literature and Society and How It Emerges in the Works of G. Lamming, V. S. Naipaul and W. Harris," *Busara* 8, ii (1976): 58-62.

Omerod, David, "Theme and Image in V. S. Naipaul's A HOUSE FOR MR. BISWIS," *TSLL* 8, iv (Winter, 1967): 589-602. Also in Baugh, E., ed., *Critics on Caribbean Literature*, 87-92.

Owens, R. J., "A HOUSE FOR MR. BISWIS by V. S. Naipaul," *Caribbean Quarterly* 7, iv (Apr., 1962): 217-19.

Pitt, Rosemary, ed., *Notes on A HOUSE FOR MR. BISWIS* (York Notes, No. 180), Harlow, Essex: Longmans, 1982.

Raghavacharylu, D. V. K., "Naipaul and Narayan: The Sense of Life," in Narasimhaiah, C. D., *Awakened Conscience*, 217-24 *passim*.

Ramchand, Kenneth, "The World of A HOUSE FOR MR. BISWIS," *Caribbean Quarterly* 15, i (Mar., 1969): 60-72. Also in Ramchand, K., *West Indian Novel and Its Background*, 189-204.

Rao, K. I. M., *Contrary Awareness*, 76-101.

Rohlehr, Gordon, "Character and Rebellion in A HOUSE FOR MR. BISWIS," *New World Quarterly* 4, iv (1968): 66-72. Also in Hamner, R. D., ed., *Critical Perspectives on V. S. Naipaul*, 84-93.

_____, "The Ironic Approach," in James, L., ed., *Islands in Between*, 132-9. Also in Cooke, M. G., ed., *Modern Black Novelists*, 171-5.

_____, "Predestination, Frustration and Symbolic Darkness in Naipaul's A HOUSE FOR MR. BISWIS," *Caribbean Quarterly* 10, i (Mar., 1964): 3-11.

Shenfield, Margaret, "Mr. Biswis and Mr. Polly," *English* 23 (Autumn, 1974): 95-100.

Srinath, C. N., "Crisis of Identity: Assertion and Withdrawal in Naipaul and Arun Joshi," *LCrit* 14, i (1979): 33-41.

Subbarayadu, G. K., "Surprise as Technique: Aspects of A HOUSE FOR MR. BISWIS," *OJES* 18 (1982): 69-75.

Swinden, P., *Unofficial Selves*, 148-57.

Thorpe, M., *V. S. Naipaul*, 14-18.

Walsh, W., *Manifold Voice*, 70-7.

_____, in *Rhetorique et Communication*, 324-6.

_____, *V. S. Naipaul*, 30-44.

_____, "V. S. Naipaul: Mr. Biswis," *LCrit* 10, ii (1974): 27-37.

Warner-Lewis, Maureen, "Cultural Confrontation, Disintegration, and Syncretism in A HOUSE FOR MR. BISWIS," *Caribbean Quarterly* 16, iv (Dec., 1970): 70-9. Also in Hamner, R. D., *Critical Perspectives on V. S. Naipaul*, 94-103.

White, L., *V. S. Naipaul*, 86-126.

IN A FREE STATE

Boxhill, Anthony, "The Casualties of Freedom: V. S. Naipaul's IN A FREE STATE," *WLWE* 12 (1973): 106-16.

_____, "The Paradox of Freedom: V. S. Naipaul's IN A FREE STATE," *Crit* 18, i (1976): 81-91.

Doerksen, Nan, "IN A FREE STATE and NAUSEA," *WLWE* 20, i (Spring, 1981): 105-13.

Erapu, Leban, "V. S. Naipaul's IN A FREE STATE," *BACLLS* 9 (1972): 66-85.

Enright, D. J., "IN A FREE STATE," in Walsh, W., *Readings in Commonwealth Literature*, 337-9.

Gurr, Andrew, "The Freedom of Exile in Naipaul and Doris Lessing," *ArielE* 13, iv (Oct., 1982): 7-18.

Hamner, R. D., *V. S. Naipaul*, 64-6.

Lane, Travis M., "The Casualties of Freedom: V. S. Naipaul's IN A FREE STATE," *WLWE* 12 (Apr., 1973): 100-10.

Morris, R. K., *Paradoxes of Order*, 71-105.

Niven, Alastair, "V. S. Naipaul's Free Statement," in Maes-Jelinek, H., ed., *Commonwealth Literature and the Modern World*, 69-78.

Rao, K. I. M., *Contrary Awareness*, 160-78.

Spence, J. E., "Two Novels of Africa," *African Research and Documentation* (Birmingham) 14 (1977): 3-10.

Thorpe, M., *V. S. Naipaul*, 29-33.

Walsh, W., *V. S. Naipaul*, 63-72.

MIGUEL STREET

Boxhill, A., *V. S. Naipaul's Fiction*, 25-7.

Hamner, R. D., *V. S. Naipaul*, 44-8.

St. Omer, Garth, "The Writer as Naive Colonial: V. S. Naipaul and MIGUEL STREET," *Carib* (Kingston) 1 (1979): 7-17.

Thieme, John, "Calypso Allusions in Naipaul's MIGUEL STREET," *Kunapipi* 3, ii (1981): 18-33.

White, L., *V. S. Naipaul*, 46-59.

THE MIMIC MEN

Blodgett, Harriet, "Beyond Trinidad: Five Novels of V. S. Naipaul," *SAQ* 73, iii (Summer, 1974): 400-3.

Boxhill, Anthony, "The Little Bastard World of V. S. Naipaul's THE MIMIC MEN and A FLAG ON THE ISLAND," *IFR* 3, i (Jan., 1976): 12-19.

Calder, Angus, "World's End: V. S. Naipaul's THE MIMIC MEN," in Niven, A., ed., *Commonwealth Writer Overseas*, 271-81.

Gilkes, M., *West Indian Novel*, 99-102.

Gowda, H. H. Anniah, "Visions of Decadence in William Faulkner's ABSALOM, ABSALOM! and V. S. Naipaul's THE MIMIC MEN," *LHY* 23, i (Jan., 1982): 71-80.

Gurr, A., *Writers in Exile*, 83-91 *passim*.

Hamner, R. D., *V. S. Naipaul*, 55-61, 97-103. Also in Hamner, R. D., ed., *Critical Perspectives on V. S. Naipaul*, 233-8.

Hearne, John, "The Snow Virgin: An Inquiry Into V. S. Naipaul's MIMIC MEN," *Caribbean Quarterly* 23, ii-iii (Sept., 1977): 31-7.

King, Bruce, in King, B., ed., *West Indian Literature*, 171-3.

Lyn, Gloria, "A Thing Called Art: THE MIMIC MEN," *Carib* 2 (1981): 66-77.

MacDonald, Bruce, "Symbolic Action in Three of V. S. Naipaul's Novels," *JCL* 9, iii (Apr., 1975): 41-52 *passim*. Also in Hamner, R. D., ed., *Critical Perspectives on V. S. Naipaul*, 242-54 *passim*.

Mahood, M. M., "The Dispossessed: Naipaul's THE MIMIC MEN," *Colonial Encounter*, 142-65.

Miller, Karl, "V. S. Naipaul and the New Order: A View of THE MIMIC MEN," *KR* 29 (Nov., 1967): 685-98. Also in Hamner, R. D., ed., *Critical Perspectives on V. S. Naipaul*, 111-25.

Mordecai, Pamela C., "The West Indian Male Sensibility in Search of Itself: Some Comments on NOR ANY COUNTRY, THE MIMIC MEN, and THE SECRET LADDER," *WLWE* 21, iii (Autumn, 1982): 629-44.

Morley, Patricia A., "Comic Form in Naipaul's Fiction: The Quality of Myth," *BACLLS* 9 (1972): 60-3.

Morris, R. K., *Paradoxes of Order*, 51-71.

————, "Substance Into Shadow: V. S. Naipaul's THE MIMIC MEN, in Morris, R. K., ed., *Old Lines, New Forces*, 131-50.

Nazareth, Peter, "THE MIMIC MEN as a Study of Corruption," *EAJ* 7, vii (July, 1970): 18-22. Also in Hamner, R. D., ed., *Critical Perspectives on V. S. Naipaul*, 137-52. Revised for *Literature and Society in Modern Africa*, Nairobi: East African Literature Bureau, 1972. Revised for *An African View of Literature*, Evanston: Northwestern Un. Pr., 1974, 76-93.

Pollack, James, "The Parenthetic Destruction of Metaphor in V. S. Naipaul's THE MIMIC MEN," *OJES* 18 (1982): 90-7.

Ramchand, Kenneth, "The Theatre of Politics," *TwenCS* 10 (1974): 20-36. Also in *Trinidad and Tobago Review* 2 (Nov., 1977): 11-15, 18.

Ramraj, Victor, "The All-Embracing Christlike Vision: Tone and Attitude in THE MIMIC MEN," in Rutherford, A., ed., *Common Wealth*, 125-34. Also in Hamner, R. D., ed., *Critical Perspectives on V. S. Naipaul*, 127-36.

Rao, K. I. M., *Contrary Awareness*, 124-59.

Shahane, Vasant A., "The Symbol of the 'House' in V. S. Naipaul's Early Novels," *OJES* 18 (1982): 46-59.

Thorpe, Marjorie, "THE MIMIC MEN: A Study of Isolation," *New World Quarterly* 4, iv (1968): 55-9.

————, *V. S. Naipaul*, 26-9.

Walsh, W., *Manifold Voice*, 78-85.

————, *V. S. Naipaul*, 54-63.

White, L., *V. S. Naipaul*, 153-84.

MR. STONE AND THE KNIGHT'S COMPANION

Boxhill, Anthony, "The Concept of Spring in V. S. Naipaul's MR. STONE AND THE KNIGHT'S COMPANION," *ArielE* 5, iv (Oct., 1974): 21-9.

Blodgett, Harriet, "Beyond Trinidad: Five Novels of V. S. Naipaul," *SAQ* 73, iii (Summer, 1974): 398-400.

Cartey, Wilfred, "The Knight's Companion—Ganesh, Biswis, and Stone," *NWQ* 2 (1965): 93-8.

Hamner, R. D., *V. S. Naipaul*, 52-5, 95-7. Also in Hamner, R. D., ed., *Critical Perspectives on V. S. Naipaul*, 230-3.

Kamra, Shashi P., "From the Literal to the Literary: A Study of V. S. Naipaul's MR. STONE AND THE KNIGHT'S COMPANION," *OJES* 18 (1982): 76-89.

Lee, R. H., "Thee Novels of V. S. Naipaul," *Theoria* 27 (Oct., 1966): 41-5. Also in Hamner, R. D., ed., *Critical Perspectives on V. S. Naipaul*, 79-83.

Morris, R. K., *Paradoxes of Order*, 37-51.

Pritchett, V. S. "Climacteric," *NStat* (May 31, 1963): 831-2. Also in Hamner, R. D., ed., *Critical Perspectives on V. S. Naipaul*, 230-3.

Rao, K. I. M., *Contrary Awareness*, 102-33.

Thorpe, M., *V. S. Naipaul*, 18-19.

White, L., *V. S. Naipaul*, 128-39, 147-52.

THE MYSTIC MASSEUR

Blodgett, Harriet, "Beyond Trinidad: Five Novels of V. S. Naipaul," *SAQ* 73, iii (Summer, 1974): 392-5.

Boxhill, Anthony, "The Physical and Historical Environment of V. S. Naipaul's THE MYSTIC MASSEUR and THE SUFFRAGE OF ELVIRA," *JCF* 3, iv (1975): 52-5.

Cartey, Wilfred, "The Knight's Companion—Ganesh, Biswis, and Stone," *NWQ* 2 (1965): 93-8.

Hamner, R. D., *V. S. Naipaul*, 36-40, 82-5. Also in Hamner, R. D., ed., *Critical Perspectives on V. S. Naipaul*, 219-22.

Lee, R. H., "The Novels of V. S. Naipaul," *Theoria* 27 (Oct., 1966): 34-7. Also in Hamner, R. D., ed., *Critical Perspectives on V. S. Naipaul*, 71-4.

MacDonald, Bruce, "Symbolic Action in Three of V. S. Naipaul's Novels," *JCL* 9, iii (Apr., 1975): 41-52 *passim*. Also in Hamner, R. D., ed., *Critical Perspectives on V. S. Naipaul*, 242-54 *passim*.

Moore, Gerald, "East Indians and West: The Novels of V. S. Naipaul," *BO* 7 (June, 1960): 11-13.

Morris, R. K., *Paradoxes of Order*, 11-17.

Naik, M. K., "Irony as Stance and as Vision: A Comparative Study of V. S. Naipaul's THE MYSTIC MASSEUR and R. K. Narayan's THE GUIDE," *JIWE* 6, i (1978): 1-13.

————, "Two Uses of Irony: V. S. Naipaul's THE MYSTIC MASSEUR and R. K. Narayan's THE GUIDE," *WLWE* 17, ii (Nov., 1978): 464-55.

Rao, K. I. M., *Contrary Awareness*, 45-61.

Thorpe, M., *V. S. Naipaul*, 11-12.

White, L., *V. S. Naipaul*, 62-73.

THE SUFFRAGE OF ELVIRA

Blodgett, Harriet, "Beyond Trinidad: Five Novels of V. S. Naipaul," *SAQ* 73, iii (Summer, 1974): 390-2.

Boxhill, Anthony, "The Mystical and Historical Environment of V. S. Naipaul's THE MYSTIC MASSEUR and THE SUFFRAGE OF ELVIRA," *JCF* 3, iv (1975): 52-5.

Hamner, R. D., *V. S. Naipaul*, 40-4, 85-7. Also in Hamner, R. D., ed., *Critical Perspectives on V. S. Naipaul*, 222-3.

Moore, Gerald, "East Indians and West: The Novels of V. S. Naipaul," *BO* 7 (June, 1960): 13-15.

Morris, R. K., *Paradoxes of Order*, 11-17.

Nazareth, P., *African View of Literature*, 83-9.

Rao, K. I. M., *Contrary Awareness*, 62-75.

Thorpe, M., *V. S. Naipaul*, 13-14.
White, L., *V. S. Naipaul*, 74-85.

BIBLIOGRAPHY

Hamner, R. D., ed., *Critical Perspectives on V. S. Naipaul*, 263-98.
Hamner, R. D., *V. S. Naipaul*, 167-77.
_____, comp.," V. S. Naipaul: A Selected Bibliography," *JCL* 10, i (Aug., 1975): 36-44.

NARAYAN, R(ASIPURAM) K(RISHNASWAMI), 1906-

GENERAL

Ansari, Mohammed S., "The Transfer of Folklore: A Model Illustrating the Folklore-Literature Relationship," *FolkloreC* 218 (1978): 64-77. [Not seen.]

Asnani, Shyam M., "The Socio-Political Scene of the 1930's: Its Impact on the Indo-English Novel," *Com* 6, xxi (Dec., 1981): 14-23. [Not seen.]

_____, "The Use of Myth in R. K. Narayan's Novels," *LitE* 3, iii-iv (Jan.-June, 1982): 19-31.

Badal, R. K., *R. K. Narayan*, 1-17.

Beerman, Hans, "Two Indian Interviews," *BA* 39 (1965): 291-3.

Berry, Margaret, "R. K. Narayan: Lila and Literature," *JIWE* 4, ii (July, 1976): 1-11.

Biswal, Jayanta, "Commitment to Life: A Study of R. K. Narayan's Major Novels," *Triveni* 45, iv (Jan.-Mar., 1977): 57-63.

Chellappan, K., "The Apocalypse of the Ordinary: The Comic Myths of R. K. Narayan," *LitE* 3, iii-iv (Jan.-June, 1982): 32-8.

Chew, Shirley, "A Proper Detachment: The Novels of R. K. Narayan," *SoRA* 5 (June, 1972): 147-59. Also in Walsh, W., ed., *Readings in Commonwealth Literature*, 58-74.

Dale, James, "The Rootless Intellectual in the Novels of R. K. Narayan," *UWR* 1 (Spring, 1965): 128-37.

Driesen, Cynthia van den, "The Achievements of R. K. Narayan," *LE&W* 21, i-iv (Jan.-Dec., 1977): 51-64.

Garebian, Keith, "Narayan's Compromise in Comedy," *LHY* 17, i (Jan., 1971): 77-92.

_____, "'The Spirit of Place' in R. K. Narayan," *WLWE* 14 (Nov., 1975): 291-9.

_____, "Strategy and Theme in the Art of R. K. Narayan," *ArielE* 5, iv (Oct., 1974): 70-81.

Ghai, T. C., "Pattern and Significance in R. K. Narayan's Novels," *IndL* 18, iii (July-Sept., 1975): 33-58.

Gooneratne, Yasmine, "'Traditional' Elements in the Fiction of Kamala Markandaya, R. K. Narayan and Ruth Prawer Jhabvala," *WLWE* 15 (Apr., 1976): 121-34.

Goud, L. H., "Indianness in the Novels of R. K. Narayan," in Desai, S. K., ed., *Experimentation with Indian Writing in English*, Dept. of English, Kolhapur: Shivaji Un., 1974, 81-100.

Gowda, H. H. Anniah, "R. K. Narayan," *LHY* 6, ii (1965): 25-39.

Harrex, S. C., *Fire and Offering*, 11-41.

_____, "R. K. Narayan and Temple of Indian Fiction," *Meanjin* 31 (Dec., 1972): 397-407.

_____, "R. K. Narayan: Some Miscellaneous Writings," *JCL* 13, i (Dec., 1978): 64-76.

Hartley, Lois, "In MALGUDI with R. K. Narayan," *LE&W* 9 (June, 1965): 87-9.

Holmstrom, L., *Novels of R. K. Narayan*.

Jamil, Maya, "From Swami to Jagan: Recurrent Themes, Structures, Growth and Development in the Novels of R. K. Narayan," *Explorations* 6, i (Summer, 1979): 56-64.

Joshi, K., and B. S. Rao, "R. K. Narayan as a Novelist," *Studies in Indo-Anglian Literature*, 100-8.

Kantak, V. Y., "The Achievement of R. K. Narayan," in Narasimhaiah, C. D., ed., *Indian Literature of the Past Fifty Years*, 133-46.

_____, "Indo-English Fiction and the New Morality," *IndL* 21, v (Sept.-Oct., 1978): 39-45.

Kaul, A. N., "R. K. Narayan and the East-West Theme," in Poddlar, Arabinda, ed., *Indian Literature*, Simla: Indian Institute of Advanced Study, 1972, 222-46.

King, B., *New English Literatures*, 181-93.

Larson, Charles R., "A Note on R. K. Narayan," *BA* 50 (1976): 352-3.

Malhotra, Tara, "Old Places, Old Faces, Old Tunes: A Critical Study of Narayan's Latest Fiction," *BP* [Supp.] 5, xiii (July, 1969): 53-9.

_____, "R. K. Narayan: His Mind and Art," *Bridges of Literature*, 173-80.

Meta, Ved, "R. K. Narayan," *Illus. Weekly* (Jan. 23, 1972): 34-7. [Conversation.]

Mojtabai, A. G., "India's Great Master of Comedy: Reconsideration: R. K. Narayan," *NRep* (Apr. 25, 1981): 24-8.

Mukerji, Nirmal, "Some Aspects of the Literary Development of R. K. Narayan," *BP* [Supp.] 5, xiii (July, 1969): 76-87.

_____, "The World of Malgudi: A Study of the Novels of R. K. Narayan," *DAI* 21 (1961): 2718.

Mukherjee, Meenakshi, "The Storyteller of Malgudi," *IndH* 21, i (Jan., 1972): 44-9.

Murti, K. V., Suryanarayana, "Theme of Salvation: Mulk Raj Anand and R. K. Narayan," *Triveni* 34 (Jan., 1965): 50-9.

Naik, M. K., "R. K. Narayan and 'the Spirit of Place'," *LitE* 3, iii-iv (Jan.-June, 1982): 7-18.

Narasimaiah, C. D., "The Comic as a Mode of Study in Maturity," *Swan and the Eagle*, 135-58.

Narayan, R. K., "Speaking as a Writer," *ACLALSB* (1974): 28-31.

Nazareth, Peter, "R. K. Narayan: Novelist," *ESA* 8, ii (Sept., 1965): 121-34.

_____, "An Uncommitted Writer"" *African View of Literature*, 155-74.

Noble, Allen G., "Malgudi: The South Indian Townscape of R. K. Narayan," *Deccan Geographer* 18, i (Jan.-June, 1980): 803-11.

Olinder, Britta, "Aspects of R. K. Narayan's Narrative Techniques," in Granqvist, R., ed., *Report of Workshop in World Literatures Written in English ...*, 63-73.

Panduranga, Rao V., "The Art of R. K. Narayan," *JCL* 5 (July, 1968): 29-40.

Parameswaran, U., "Native Genius—R. K. Narayan," *Study of Representative Indo-English Novelists*, 42-84.

_____, "Rogues in R. K. Narayan's Fiction," *LE&W* 18 (Mar., 1974): 203-15.

Parvathi, B., "Themes in the Novels of R. K. Narayan," *JEnS* 13, i (1981): 881-5.

Raghavacharylu, D. V. K., "Naipaul and Narayan: The Sense of Life," in Narasimhaiah, C. D., ed., *Awakened Conscience*, 216-25.

Raizada, H., *R. K. Narayan*.

Rani, K. Nirupa, "Autobiographical Element in R. K. Narayan's Early Novels," *Triveni* 45, iii (Oct.-Dec., 1976): 44-8.

Rao, Angare, V. K., "The Significant National Symbols in the Novels of R. K. Narayan," *LHY* 18, i-ii (Jan.-July, 1967): 80-4.

Rao, K. Naga Rajo, "Obsession and Professionalism in R. K. Narayan," *Triveni* 49, ii (1980): 78-80.

Rao, V. Panduranga, "The Art of R. K. Narayan," *JCL* 5 (July, 1968): 29-40.

Rau, Santha Rama, "Saints, Dancers, and Loving Fathers," *Listener* 61 (May 14, 1959): 842-43.

Singh, R. S., *Indian Novel in English,* 55-72.

Singh, Satyanarain, "A Note on the World View of R. K. Narayan," *IndL* 24, i (Jan.-Mar., 1981): 104-9.

Srinath, C. N., "R. K. Narayan's Comic Vision: Possibilities and Limitations," *WLT* 55, iii (Summer, 1981): 416-19.

Sundaram, P. S., "Malgudi: The World of R. K. Narayan," *IPEN* 43, i-ii (Jan.-Feb., 1977): 1-10; iii-iv (Mar.-Apr., 1977): 1-8.

_____, *R. K. Narayan.*

Syal, Harshbala, "Narayan and the Emerging Indian Fiction," *Busara* 2, i (1969): 52-4.

Taranath, Rajeev, "The Average as the Positive," in Naik, M. K., et al., eds., *Critical Essays on Indian Writing in English,* 294-306.

Venkatachari, K., "R. K. Narayan's Novels: Acceptance of Life," *OJES* 7, i (1969): 51-65. Also in *IndL* 13, i (Mar., 1971): 73-87.

Walsh, William, "The Big Three," in Mohan, R., ed., *Indian Writing in English,* 31-6.

_____, "The Intricate Alliance: The Novels of R. K. Narayan," *REL* 2, iv (Oct., 1961): 91-9.

_____, "R. K. Narayan: The Unobtrusive Novelist," *RNL* 10 (1979): 59-69.

_____, "Sweet Mangoes and Malt Vinegar: The Novels of R. K. Narayan," *Human Idiom,* 128-32. Also in Sharma, K. K., ed., *Indo-English Literature,* 122-9.

Williams, Haydn M., "R. K. Narayan and R. Prawer Jhabvala: Two Interpreters of Modern India," *LE&W* 16, iv (1972): 1136-54.

Woodcock, George, "The Maker of Malgudi: Notes on R. K. Narayan," *TamR* 73 (1978): 82-95.

_____, "Two Great Commonwealth Novelists: R. K. Narayan and V. S. Naipaul," *SR,* i (Winter, 1979): 1-28.

THE BACHELOR OF ARTS

Badal, R. K., R. K. *Narayan,* 25-30.

Harrex, S. C., *Fire and the Offering,* 58-69.

Holmstrom, L., *Novels of R. K. Narayan,* 39-42.

Iyengar, K. R. S., *Indian Writing in English,* 366-70.

Kirpal, Vineypalkaur, "The Theme of 'Growing Up' in THE BACHELOR OF ARTS: Chandran's Transition from Adolescence to Adulthood," *ComQ* 2, vi (Mar., 1978): 50-65.

Raizada, H., R. K. *Narayan,* 16-24.

Sundaram, P. S., R. K. *Narayan,* 35-40.

THE DARK ROOM

Badal, R. K., *R. K. Narayan,* 31-4.

Harrex. S. C., *Fire and the Offering,* 69-75.

Holstrom, L., *Novels of R. K. Narayan,* 42-6.

Raizada, H., *R. K. Narayan,* 24-34.

Sundaram, P. S., *R. K. Narayan,* 41-9.

THE ENGLISH TEACHER

Badal, R. K., *R. K. Narayan,* 35-9.

Dale, James, "Wordsworth and Narayan: Irony in THE ENGLISH TEACHER," *ACLALSB* 4, v (1977): 58-65.

Harrex, S. C., "R. K. Narayan's GRATEFUL TO LIFE AND DEATH," *LCrit* 8, iii (Winter, 1968): 52-64. Also in Harrex, S. C. *Fire and the Offering,* 79-90.

Holmstrom, L., *Novels of R. K. Narayan,* 47-50.

Larson, Charles R., "The Singular Consciousness—R. K. Narayan's GRATEFUL TO LIFE AND DEATH and Bessie Head's A QUESTION OF POWER," *The Novel in the Third World,* Washington: Inscape, 1976, 153-64.

Narasimhan, R., *Sensibility Under Stress,* 2-7.

Raizada, H., *R. K. Narayan,* 34-45.

Ramamurti, K. S., "The Title of R. K. Narayan's THE ENGLISH TEACHER," *LitE* 3, iii-iv (Jan.-June, 1982): 45-51.

Sundaram, P. S., "Malgudi: The World of R. K. Narayan," *IPEN* 43, 1-11 (Jan.-Feb., 1977): 7-10.

_____, *R. K. Narayan,* 51-61.

THE FINANCIAL EXPERT

Alphonso-Karkala, John B., "Symbolism in THE FINANCIAL EXPERT," *IWT* 4 (1970): 14-18. Also in Alphonso-Karkala, J. B., *Comparative World Literature,* 65-71.

Badal, R. K., *R. K. Narayan,* 44-8.

Berry, Margaret, "India: A Double Key," *JIWE* 6, i (Jan., 1978): 30-8.

Garebian, Keith, "THE FINANCIAL EXPERT: Kubera's Myth in a Parable of Life and Death," *IFR* 3 (1976): 126-32.

Harrex, S. C., "R. K. Narayan: Comedy of Manners and Archetypes," *Fire and the Offering,* 129-38.

Holmstrom, L., *Novels of R. K. Narayan,* 53-8.

Malhotra, M. L., "R. K. Narayan—His Comic Imagination," *Bridges of Literature,* 183-6.

Parameswaran, Uma, "On the Theme of Paternal Love in the Novels of R. K. Narayan," *IFR* 1 (1974): 146-8.

Raizada, H., *R. K. Narayan,* 100-13.

Sivaramkrishna, M., "Fantasy in THE FINANCIAL EXPERT," *OJES* 9, i (1972): 39-49.

Sundaram, P. S., *R. K. Narayan,* 74-82.

GRATEFUL TO LIFE AND DEATH (See THE ENGLISH TEACHER)

THE GUIDE

Badal, R. K., *R. K. Narayan,* 55-61.

Bhatnagar, O. P., "Playing the Role in THE GUIDE and THE INNER DOOR," *ComQ* 4, xiii (Dec., 1979): 71-5.

Deva, Soni, R. K., *Narayan's THE GUIDE: A Critical Study,* Edition 2, Bareilly: Prakash Book Depot, 1976.

Driesen, Cynthia V., "From Rogue to Redeemer: R. K. Narayan's THE GUIDE," *IFR* 6 (1969): 166-70.

Garebian, Keith, "Strategy and Theme in the Art of R. K. Narayan," *ArielE* 5, iv (Oct., 1974): 74-6.

Goyal, Bhagwat S., "From Picaro to Pilgrim: A Perspective on R. K. Narayan's THE GUIDE," in Sharma, K. K., ed., *Indo-English Literature,* 142-55.

Harrex, S. C., "R. K. Narayan: Comedy of Manners and Archetypes," *Fire and the Offering,* 115-29.

Holmstrom, L., *Novels of R. K. Narayan,* 63-8.

King, B., *New English Literatures,* 185-9.

Kumar, Swamy S., "R. K. Narayan's THE GUIDE," 126-41 in Raghavacharyulu, ed., *The Two-fold Voice,* Guntur: Sarvodaya Publ., 1971.

Mathur, O. P., "THE GUIDE: A Study in Cultural Ambivalence," *LitE* 3, iii-iv (Jan.-June, 1982): 70-9.

Mukherjee, M., *Twice Born Fiction,* 123-30.

Mukerji, Nirmal, "Some Aspects of the Technique of R. K. Narayan's THE GUIDE," *WHR* 15, iv (Aut., 1961): 372-3.

Naik, M. K., "Irony as Stance and as Vision: A Comparative Study of V. S. Naipaul's THE MYSTIC MASSEUR and R. K. Narayan's THE GUIDE," *WLWE* 17, ii (1978): 646-55.

Narasimhaiah, C. D., "R. K. Narayan: The Comic as a Mode of Study in Maturity," *Swan and the Eagle,* 149-58.

_____, "R. K. Narayan's THE GUIDE," *LCrit* 4, ii (Summer, 1961): 63-92. Also in Naik, M. K., ed., *Aspects of Indian Writing in English: Essays in Honour of Professor K. R. Srinivasa Iyengar,* Madras: Macmillan of India, 1979, 172-98.

Olinder, Britta, "R. K. Narayan and His Novel THE GUIDE," *MS* 70 (1976): 197-207.

Raizada, H., *R. K. Narayan,* 129-43.

Ranganath, N., "Realism in Literature: A Critique of R. K. Narayan's THE GUIDE," *Triveni* 48, iii (Oct.-Dec., 1979): 81-5.

Rao, R. Raja, "God-Consciousness in THE GUIDE and SIDDHARTHA," *LitE* 3, iii-iv (Jan.-June, 1982): 87-91.

Rao, Subha, S., "THE GUIDE: A Glimpse of Narayan's Attitude and Achievement," *Triveni* 36, ii (July, 1967): 65-7.

Reddy, K. Venkata, "Point of View, Time and Language in R. K. Narayan's THE GUIDE," *LitE* 3, iii-iv (Jan.-June, 1982): 80-6.

Singh, Ram Sewak, *R. K. Narayan: THE GUIDE,* Delhi: Doaba House, 1971.

Singh, Satanarain, "Crisis and Resolution in R. K. Narayan's THE GUIDE," *ILR* 1, iii (July, 1968): 9-23.

Sundaram, P. S., *R. K. Narayan,* 90-6.

Walsh, William, "The Big Three," in Mohan, R., ed., *Indian Writing in English,* 34-6.

_____, in *Rhetorique et Communication,* 326-9.

_____, "R. K. Narayan and THE GUIDE," *Focus* (Un. of Singapore) 2, i (1963): 22-9.

_____, "Sweet Mangoes and Malt Vinegar: The Novels of R. K. Narayan," *Human Idiom,* 136-48. Also in Sharma, K. K., ed., *Indo-English Literature,* 129-40.

THE MAN-EATER OF MALGUDI

Badal, R. K., *R. K. Narayan,* 62-8.

Garebian, Keith, "Strategy and Theme in the Art of R. K. Narayan," *ArielE* 5, iv (Oct., 1974): 78-80.

Gerow, Edwin, "The Quintessential Narayan," *LE&W* 10, i-ii (June, 1966): 1-18. Also in Mukherjee, M., ed., *Considerations,* 66-83.

Holmstrom, L., *Novels of R. K. Narayan,* 68-71.

Iyengar, K. R. S., *Indian Writing in English,* 358-85.

Jayantha, R. A., "THE MAN-EATER OF MALGUDI: Some Aspects of Its Narrative Strategy," *LitE* 3, iii-iv (Jan.-June, 1982): 92-101.

King, B., *New English Literatures,* 189-92.

Mahood, M. M., "The Marriage of Kirshna: Narayan's THE MAN-EATER OF MALGUDI," *Colonial Encounter,* 92-114.

Mukherjee, M., *Twice-Born Fiction,* 150-5.

Naik, M. K., "Demons, the Ineffectual Angel and Man: Theme and Form in R. K. Narayan's THE MAN-EATER OF MALGUDI," *JKUH* 15 (1971): 91-9. Also in *JCL* 10, iii (Apr., 1976): 65-72.

Narasimhan, R., *Sensibility Under Stress,* 76-81, 101-7.

Raizada, H., *R. K. Narayan,* 143-56.

Sundaram, P. S., *R. K. Narayan,* 97-108.

Urs, S. N. Vikramraj, "THE MAN-EATER OF MALGUDI: A Study," *ComQ* 1, iv (Sept., 1977): 69-75.

Walsh, W., *Manifold Voice,* 13-20.

MR. SAMPATH (See THE PRINTER OF MALGUDI)

THE PAINTER OF SIGNS

Naik, M. K., "The Signs Are All There," *WLWE* 16, i (Apr., 1977): 110-14.

Sundaram, P. S., "Malgudi: The World of R. K. Narayan," *IPEN* 43, iii-iv (Mar.-Apr., 1977): 3-6.

THE PRINTER OF MALGUDI

Badal, R. K., *R. K. Narayan,* 40-3.

Garebian, Keith, "Strategy and Theme in R. K. Narayan," *ArielE* 5, iv (Oct., 1974): 71-4.

Harrex, S. C., "R. K. Narayan's THE PRINTER OF MALGUDI," *LE&W* 13, i-ii (June, 1969): 68-82. Also in Harrex, S. C., *Fire and the Offering,* 91-102.

Holmstrom, P. S., *Novels of R. K. Narayan,* 50-3.

Malhotra, M. L., "R. K. Narayan—His Comic Imagination," *Bridges of Literature,* 186-9.

Raizada, H., *R. K. Narayan,* 85-100.

Sundaram, P. S., *R. K. Narayan,* 62-73.

SWAMI AND FRIENDS

Badal, R. K., *R. K. Narayan,* 19-24.

Harrex, S. C., *Fire and the Offering,* 52-8.

Holstrom, L., *Novels of R. K. Narayan,* 35-8.

Parameswaran, Uma, "Rogues in R. K. Narayan's Fiction," *LE&W* 18 (Mar., 1974): 207-14.

Raizada, H., *R. K. Narayan,* 5-16.

Sundaram, P. S., "Malgudi: The World of R. K. Narayan," *IPEN* 43, i-ii (Jan.-Feb., 1977): 3-6.

_____, *R. K. Narayan,* 27-34.

THE SWEET VENDOR (See THE VENDOR OF SWEETS)

THE VENDOR OF SWEETS

Agnihotri, H. L., "Gandhi and R. K. Narayan," *LitE* 3, iii-iv (Jan.-June, 1982): 56-9.

Argyle, Barry, "Narayan's THE SWEET-VENDOR," *JCL* 7, i (June, 1972): 35-43.

Badal, R. K., *R. K. Narayan,* 69-76.

Holmstrom, L., *Novels of R. K. Narayan,* 71-5.

Malhotra, Tara, "Old Places, Old Faces, Old Times: A Critical Study of R. K. Narayan's Latest Fiction," *BP*[Supp] 5, iii (July, 1969): 53-9.

Narasimhaiah, C. D., in Amirthanayagam, G., ed., *Asian and Western Writers in Dialogue,* 87-91.

Parameswaran, U., "Native Genius—R. K. Narayan," *Study of Representative Indo-English Novelists,* 80-4.

_____, "On the Theme of Paternal Love in the Novels of R. K. Narayan," *IFR* 1 (1974): 146-8.

Raizada, H., *R. K. Narayan*, 185-97.

Rao, Sambasiva, "R. K. Narayan's THE VENDOR OF SWEETS," *Triveni* 39, iv (1971): 60-4.

Rao, Subha S., "R. K. Narayan's Art and THE VENDOR OF SWEETS," *Triveni* 37, iv (Jan.-Mar., 1969): 37-42.

Sundaram, P. S., *R. K. Narayan*, 109-15.

Walsh, W., *Manifold Voice*, 20-3.

WAITING FOR THE MAHATMA

Agnihotri, Shiva M., "Gandhi and R. K. Narayan," *LitE* 3, iii-iv (Jan.-June, 1982): 52-6.

Bhatnagar, O. P., "Love, Non-Violence and Freedom in WAITING FOR THE MAHATMA," *LitE* 3, iii-iv (Jan.-June, 1982): 61-9.

Bhatt, P. N., "R. K. Narayan and Politics," *Triveni* 50, i (Apr.-June, 1981): 42-5.

Holmstrom, L., *Novels of R. K. Narayan*, 58-62.

Jayantha, R. A., "Portrayal of Gandhi in WAITING FOR THE MAHATMA," *Triveni* 51, ii (1982): 56-63.

Pandeya, Shiva M., and Tej N. Dhar, "R. K. Narayan's WAITING FOR THE MAHATMA: A Study in Structure and Meaning," *JEn* 7 (1980): 52-91.

Raizada, H., *R. K. Narayan*, 113-29.

Sundaram, P. S., *R. K. Narayan*, 83-9.

BIBLIOGRAPHY

Asnani, Shyam M., "Bibliography: R. K. Narayan," *LitE* 3, iii-iv (Jan.-June, 1982): 103-20.

Sundaram, P. S., *R. K. Narayan*, 150-4.

NATHAN, ROBERT, 1894-

GENERAL

Blankenship, R., *American Literature*, 696-8.

Laurence, Dan H., "Robert Nathan: Master of Fantasy," *YULG* 37 (July, 1962): 1-7.

Mayrick, Pat, "The Sane and Gentle Novels of Robert Nathan," *ABC* 23, iv (Mar.-Apr., 1973): 15-17.

Rao, J. Srihari, "The Quest for Innocence in Robert Nathan's Novels," *IJAS* 7, ii (July, 1977): 54-62.

Roberts, Francis, "Robert Nathan: Master of Fantasy and Fable: An Interview," *PrS* 40 (Winter, 1966-67): 348-61.

Sandelin, C. K., *Robert Nathan*.

Spitz, Leon, "Robert Nathan's Jewish Types," *AmHebrew* 158 (Nov. 2, 1948): 10, 14-15.

Trachtenberg, Stanley, "Robert Nathan's Fiction," *DA* 24 (1964): 3345.

AUTUMN

Sandelin, C. K., *Robert Nathan*, 32-7.

THE BISHOP'S WIFE

Sandelin, C. K., *Robert Nathan*, 54-5.

THE COLOR OF EVENING

Sandelin, C. K., *Robert Nathan*, 122-5.

THE DEVIL WITH LOVE

Sandelin, C. K., *Robert Nathan*, 125-8.

THE ENCHANTED VOYAGE

Rao, J., Sriharo, "The Quest for Innocence in the Novels of Robert Nathan," *IJAS* 7, ii (July, 1977): 60-1.

THE FIDDLER IN BARLY

Sandelin, C. K., *Robert Nathan*, 44-8.

JONAH

Sandelin, C. K., *Robert Nathan*, 40-4.

LONG AFTER SUMMER

Sandelin, C. K., *Robert Nathan*, 75-6.

THE MALLOT DIARIES

Sandelin, C. K., *Robert Nathan*, 77-8.

MR. WHITTLE AND THE MORNING STAR

Sandelin, C. K., *Robert Nathan*, 93-5.

ONE MORE SPRING

Gurko, L., *Angry Decade*, 82-3.

Rao, J. Sriharo, "The Quest for Innocence in the Novels of Robert Nathan," *IJAS* 7, ii (July, 1977): 57-60.

Sandelin, C. K., *Robert Nathan*, 59-60.

THE ORCHID

Sandelin, C. K., *Robert Nathan*, 56-7.

PETER KINDRED

Sandelin, C. K., *Robert Nathan*, 20-7.

PORTRAIT OF JENNIE

Einstadter, Marcel, "The Concept of Time in Rabbinic Thought and Romantic Literature," *DAI* 37 (1976): 1046A.

Sandelin, C. K., *Robert Nathan*, 64-74.

THE PUPPET MASTER

Sandelin, C. K., *Robert Nathan*, 37-9.

ROAD OF AGES

Sandelin, C. K., *Robert Nathan*, 60-3.

SIR HENRY

Sandelin, C. K., *Robert Nathan*, 109-10.

SO LOVE RETURNS

Sandelin, C. K., *Robert Nathan*, 92-3.

A STAR IN THE WIND

Sandelin, C. K., *Robert Nathan*, 115-21.

STONECLIFFE

Sandelin, C. K., *Robert Nathan*, 151-3.

THERE IS ANOTHER HEAVEN

Sandelin, C. K., *Robert Nathan*, 55-6.

THE WILDERNESS STONE

Sandelin, C. K., *Robert Nathan*, 76-7.

WINTER IN APRIL

Sandelin, C. K., *Robert Nathan*, 57-8.

THE WOODCUTTER'S HOUSE

Sandelin, C. K., *Robert Nathan*, 47-8.

NEMEROV, HOWARD, 1920-

GENERAL

Cargas, Harry J., "An Interview with Howard Nemerov," *WebR* 1, i (1974): 34-9.
Duncan, B., *Critical Reception of Howard Nemerov*.
Labrie, R., *Howard Nemerov*.
_____, "Howard Nemerov in St. Louis: An Interview," *SoR* 15 (1979): 605-16.
Meinke, P., *Howard Nemerov*.
_____, "The Writings of Howard Nemerov," *DA* 27 (1966): 1830A-31A.

FEDERIGO, OR, THE POWER OF LOVE

Labrie, L., *Howard Nemerov*, 50-6.
Meinke, P., *Howard Nemerov*, 35-8.

THE HOMECOMING GAME

Labrie, R., *Howard Nemerov*, 56-62.
Lytle, A., "The Displaced Family," *Hero With the Private Parts*, 82-9.
Meinke, P., *Howard Nemerov*, 38-40.
White, Robert L., "The Trying-Out of THE HOMECOMING GAME," *ColQ* 10 (Summer, 1961): 84-96.

THE MELODRAMATISTS

Labrie, R., *Howard Nemerov*, 39-50.
Meinke, P., *Howard Nemerov*, 32-5.

BIBLIOGRAPHY

Duncan, B., *Critical Reception of Howard Nemerov*, 145-211.

NEUGEBOREN, JAY, 1938-

GENERAL

Abel, Robert, "Jay Neugeboren's Second Life: An Interview," *LitR* 25, i (Fall, 1981): 5-20.
Candelaria, Cordelia, "A Decade of Ethnic Fiction by Jay Neugeboren," *MELUS* 5, iv (Winter, 1978): 71-82.

AN ORPHAN'S TALE

Candelaria, Cordelia, "A Decade of Ethnic Fiction by Jay Neugeboren," *MELUS* 5, iv (Winter, 1978): 71-7.

NEWBY, P(ERCY) H(OWARD), 1918-

GENERAL

Bufkin, E. C., *P. H. Newby*.
_____, "Quest in the Novels of P. H. Newby," *Crit* 8, i (Fall, 1965): 51-62.
Fraser, G. S., *P. H. Newby*.
Karl, F. R., *Contemporary English Novel*, 269-73.
McCormick, J., *Catastrophe and Imagination*, 166-7.
Mathews, Francis X., "The Fiction of P. H. Newby," *DA* 25 (1964): 1515-16.
_____, "Witness to Violence: The War Novels of P. H. Newby," *TSLL* 12, i (Spring, 1970): 121-35.
Poss, Stanley, "Manners and Myth in the Novels of P. H. Newby," *Crit* 12, i (1970): 5-19.
Watts, Harold H., "P. H. Newby: Experience as Farce," *Per* 10 (Summer-Autumn, 1958): 107-17.

AGENTS AND WITNESSES

Bufkin, E. C., *P. H. Newby*, 26-35.
Fraser, G. S., *P. H. Newby*, 16-18.
Mathews, F. X., "Witness to Violence: The War Novels of P. H. Newby," *TSLL* 12, i (Spring, 1970): 122-4.

THE BARBARY LIGHT

Anon., "A Novelist on His Own," *TLS* (Apr. 6, 1962): 232. Also in *T.L.S.: Essays and Reviews from The Times Literary Supplement, 1962*, London: Oxford, 1963, 101-6.
Bufkin, E. S., *P. H. Newby*, 100-7.
_____, "Quest in the Novels of P. H. Newby," *Crit* 8, i (Fall, 1965): 58-62.

A GUEST AND HIS GOING

Bufkin, E. C., *P. H. Newby*, 92-7.
Mathews, F. X., "Newby on the Nile," *TCL* 14 (Apr., 1968): 12-15.

A JOURNEY TO THE INTERIOR

Bufkin, E. C., *P. H. Newby*, 21-6.
_____, "Quest in the Novels of P. H. Newby," *Crit* 8, i (Fall, 1965): 51-6.
Fraser, G. S., *P. H. Newby*, 13-16.
Karl, F. R., *Contemporary English Novel*, 269-71.
Poss, Stanley, "Manners and Myths in the Novels of P. H. Newby," *Crit* 12, i (1970): 9-13.

KITH

Newby, P. H., "KITH," *DQR* 9, ii (1979): 101-13. [Text of a lecture.]

MARINER DANCES

Bufkin, E. C., *P. H. Newby*, 36-44.
Fraser, G. S., *P. H. Newby*, 19-20.

ONE OF THE FOUNDERS

Bufkin, E. C., *P. H. Newby*, 107-14.

THE PICNIC AT SAKKARA

Bufkin, E. C., *P. H. Newby*, 82-7.
Halpern, Ben, "The Wisdom of Blindness," *Midstream* 3 (Winter, 1957): 104-7.
Mathews, F. X., "Newby on the Nile," *TCL* 14 (Apr., 1968): 5-9.

THE RETREAT

Allen, W., *Modern Novel*, 267.
Balakian, Nona, "Three English Novels," *KR* 15 (Summer, 1953): 490-4.
Bufkin, E. C., *P. H. Newby*, 72-9.
_____, "Quest in the Novels of P. H. Newby," *Crit* 8, i (Fall, 1965): 56-8.
Mathews, F. X., "Witness to Violence: The War Novels of P. H. Newby," *TSLL* 12, i (Spring, 1970): 127-35.

REVOLUTION AND ROSES

Bufkin, E. C., *P. H. Newby*, 87-92.
Mathews, F. X., "Newby on the Nile," *TCL* 14 (Apr., 1968): 10-12.

A SEASON IN ENGLAND

Bufkin, E. C., *P. H. Newby*, 57-65.
Poss, Stanley, "Manners and Myths in the Novels of P. H. Newby," *Crit* 12, i (1970): 13-19.

THE SNOW PASTURE

Bufkin, E. S., *P. H. Newby*, 44-9.
Fraser, G. S., *P. H. Newby*, 20.
Dickerson, Lucia, "Portrait of the Artist as a Jung Man," *KR* 21 (Winter, 1959): 58-83.

SOMETHING TO ANSWER FOR

Bufkin, E. C., *P. H. Newby*, 114-25.

A STEP TO SILENCE

Allen, W., *Modern Novel*, 266-7.
Bufkin, E. C., *P. H. Newby*, 67-72.
Mathews, F. X., "Witness to Violence: The War Novels of P. H. Newby," *TSLL* 12, i (Spring, 1970): 124-7.

THE YOUNG MAY MOON

Bufkin, E. S., *P. H. Newby*, 50-7.
Fraser, G. S., *P. H. Newby*, 21.
Dickerson, Lucia, "Portrait of the Artist as a Jung Man," *KR* 21 (Winter, 1959): 58-83.

BIBLIOGRAPHY

Bufkin, E. C., *P. H. Newby*, 137-42.

NGUGI WA THIONG'O (Formerly James Ngugi), 1938-

GENERAL

Duerden, Dennis, and Amina Abdullahi, "Ngugi wa Thiong'o," *SAfrL* 1 (1972): 120-31. [Interviews.]
Friedberger, Heinz, "James Ngugi Interviewed," *CulEA* 50 (1969) [Suppl.] i-ii.
Gachukia, Eddah, "The Novels of James Ngugi," in Gachukia, E., and Akivaga, S., eds., *Teaching African Literature in Schools*, 102-13.
_____, "The Role of Women in Ngugi's Novels," *Busara* 3, iv (1973): 30-3.
Glenn, Ian, "Ngugi wa Thiong'o and the Dilemmas of the Intellectual Elite in Africa: A Sociological Perspective," *EinA* 8, ii (Sept., 1981): 53-66. [Not seen.]
Gowda, H. H. Anniah, "Ngugi wa Thiong'o as Novelist," *LHY* 16, ii (1975): 27-51.
Gurr, A., *Writers in Exile*, 92-121.
Haring, Lee, "Ngugi and Gikuyu Folklore," *FKQ* 19 (1974): 95-112. [Not seen.]
Howard, W. J., "Themes and Development in the Novels of Ngugi," *SafrL* 1 (1973): 95-119. Also in Wright, E., ed., *Critical Evaluation of African Literature*, 95-119.
Ikiddeh, Ime, "James Ngugi as Novelist," *ALT* 2 (Jan., 1969): 3-10.
"James Ngugi, Kenya," *LAAW* 19 (Jan., 1974): 173-7.
Kemoli, Arthur M., "The Novels of Ngugi wa Thiong'o," *Joliso* 2, ii (1974): 69-85.
Killam, G. D., *Introduction to the Writings of Ngugi*.
Larson, Charles R., "Characters and Modes of Characterization," *Emergence of African Fiction*, 155-60.
_____, "The 'Situational' Novel: The Novels of James Ngugi," *Emergence of African Fiction*, 113-46.
Martini, Jurgen, Anna Rutherford, Kirsten H. Petersen, Vibeke Stenderup, and Bent Thomsen, "Ngugi wa Thiong'o," *Kunapipi* 110-16. [Interview.]
Maugham-Brown, David, "'Mau Mau' and Violence in Ngugi's Novels," *EinA* 8, ii (1981): 1-22.
Mnthali, Felix, "Continuity and Change in Conrad and Ngugi," *Kunapipi* 3, i (1981): 91-109.
Okenimpke, Michael, "Culture and Revolution in the Novels of James Ngugi," *BACLLS* 10 (June, 1972): 23-48.
Palmer, Eustace, "Ngugi wa Thiong'o," *SafrL* 3 (1979): 288-306.
Petersen, Kirsten H., "Birth Pangs of a National Consciousness: Mau Mau and Ngugi wa Thiong 'o," *WLWE* 20, ii (Autumn, 1981): 214-19.
Reed, James, "James Ngugi and the African Novel," *JCL* 1 (Sept., 1965): 117-21.
Robson, C. B., *Ngugi wa Thiong'o*.
Roscoe, A., *Uhuru's Fire*, 170-90.
Sander, Reinhard, and Ian Munro, "'Tolstoy' in Africa: An Interview with Ngugi wa Thiong'o," *BaShiru* 5, i (1973): 21-30.

Soile, Sola, "The Myth of the Archetypal Hero in Two African Novelists: Chinua Achebe and James Ngugi," *DAI* 34 (1973): 1296A.

Tejani, Bahadur, "Social Responsibility of the African Writer: Background to the Detention of Ngugi wa Thiong'o," *Chimo* (Quebec) 2 (1980): 19-23. [Not seen.]

Vogt, Elke, "The Heroes of the Mau Mau Movement," *Afrika* (Munich) 20, xi (1979): 25-6. [Not seen.]

A GRAIN OF WHEAT

Cook, David, "A New Earth: A Study of James Ngugi's A GRAIN OF WHEAT," *EAJ* 6, xii (Dec., 1969): 13-20. Also in Cook, D., *African Literature,* 95-112.

Gakwandi, S. A., *Novel and Contemporary Experience in Africa,* 108-19.

Githae-Mugo, M., *Visions of Africa,* 173-85.

Gowda, H. H. Anniah, "Ngugi wa Thiong'o as Novelist," *LHY* ii (1975): 44-51.

Griffiths, G., *Double Exile,* 36-41.

Gurr, A., *Writers in Exile,* 100-8 *passim.*

Howard, W. J., *"Themes and Development in Ngugi,"* *SAfrL* 1 (1973): 112-18. Also in Wright, E., ed., *Critical Evaluation of African Literature,* 112-18.

Ikiddeh, Ime, "Ngugi wa Thiong'o: The Novelist as Historian," in King, B., and K. Ogungbesan, eds., *Celebration of Black and African Writing,* 213-15.

Jabbi, Bu-Buakei, "Conrad's Influence on Betrayal in A GRAIN OF WHEAT," *RAL* 11, i (1980): 50-83.

Kemoli, Arthur M., "The Novels of Ngugi wa Thiong'o," *Joliso* 2, ii (1974): 77-83.

Killam, G. D., *Introduction to the Writings of Ngugi,* 53-72.

Larson, C. R., *Emergence of African Fiction,* 138-46.

Maughan-Brown, David, "'Mau Mau' and Violence in Ngugi's Novels," *EinA* 8, ii (Sept., 1981): 1-22.

Monkman, Leslie, "Kenya and the New Jerusalem in A GRAIN OF WHEAT," *ALT* 7 (1975): 111-16.

Nazareth, P., "Is A GRAIN OF WHEAT a Socialist Novel?" *African View of Literature,* 128-54.

Obumselu, Ebele, "A GRAIN OF WHEAT: Ngugi's Debt to Conrad," *BeninR* 1 (1974): 80-91.

Ochola-Ojero, P., "Of Tares and Broken Handles, Ngugi Preaches Thematic Treatment of Betrayal and Despair in A GRAIN OF WHEAT," *Busara* 3, ii (1971): 38-46. Also in Sanches, M., and B. G. Blounts, eds., *Sociocultural Dimensions of Language Use,* 62-71. Also in Wanjala, C. L., ed., *Standpoints on African Literature,* 72-85.

Ojo-Ade, Femi, "Mugo, the 'Strange' Hero: Madness in Ngugi's A GRAIN OF WHEAT," *PQM* 6, iii-iv (July-Oct., 1981): 133-45.

Okenimpke, Michael, "Culture and Revolution in the Novels of James Ngugi," *BACLLS* 10 (June, 1972): 40-6.

Palmer, Eustace, "Ngugi," *SafrL* 2 (1972): 24-47. Also in Palmer, E., *Introduction to the African Novel,* 24-47.

Ravenscroft, Arthur, "James Ngugi, East African Novelist," in Paricsy, P., ed., *Modern Black African Literature,* 80-2. Also, adapted as "Ngugi's Development as a Novelist," in Rutherford, A., ed., *Common Wealth,* 89-91.

Robson, C. B., *Ngugi wa Thiong'o,* 46-71.

Roscoe, A., *Uhuru's Fire,* 186-9.

Sarvan, Ponnuthurai, "Under African Eyes," *Conradiana* 8, iii (1976): 233-40.

Sharma, Govind N., "Ngugi's Christian Vision: Theme and Pattern in A GRAIN OF WHEAT," *ALT* 10 (1979): 167-76.

Vaughan, Michael, "African Fiction and Popular Struggle: The Case of a GRAIN OF WHEAT," *EinA* 8, ii (Sept., 1981): 23-52.

PETALS OF BLOOD

Abdelkrim, Christine, "PETALS OF BLOOD: Story, Narrative, Discourse," *Echos du Commonwealth* (Mont Saint-Aignan, France) 6 (1980-81): 37-51.

Albrecht, Francoise, "Blood and Fire in PETALS OF BLOOD," *Echos du Commonwealth* (Mont Saint-Aignan, France) 6 (1980-81): 85-97.

Balogun, F. Odun, "Ngugi's PETALS OF BLOOD: A Novel of the People," *Ba Shiru* 10, ii (1979): 49-57.

Bardolph, Jacqueline, "Fertility in PETALS OF BLOOD," *Echos du Commonwealth* (Mont Saint-Aignan, France) 6 (1980-81): 53-83.

Chileshe, John, "PETALS OF BLOOD: Ideology and Imaginative Expression," *JCL* 15, i (1980): 133-7.

Durix, Jean-Pierre, "Politics in PETALS OF BLOOD," *Echos du Commonwealth* (Mont Saint-Aignan, France) 6 (1980-81): 98-115.

Glenn, Ian, "PETALS OF BLOOD and the Intellectual Elite in Kenya," *Echos du Commonwealth* (Mont Saint-Aignan, France) 6 (1980-81): 116-25.

Gurr, Andrew, "The Fourth Novel," *Hekima* (Nairobi) 1 (1980): 13-21. Also in Jefferson, D., and G. Martin, eds., *Uses of Fiction,* 159-70.

_____, *Writers in Exile,* 108-19.

Kamau, Ngethe, "PETALS OF BLOOD as a Mirror of the African Revolution," *Afr. Communist* 80 (1980): 73-9.

Killam, G. D., *Introduction to the Writings of Ngugi,* 96-118.

_____, "A Note on the Title of PETALS OF BLOOD," *JCL* 15, i (1980): 125-32.

Lindfors, Bernth, "PETALS OF BLOOD as a Popular Novel," *CNIE* 1, i (Jan., 1982): 1-14.

Martini, Jurge, "Ngugi wa Thiong'o: East African Novelist," in Massa, D., ed., *Individual and Community in Commonwealth Literature,* 5-10.

Mnthali, Felix, "Continuity and Change in Conrad and Ngugi," *Kunapipi* 3, i (1981): 98-108.

Palmer, E., *Growth of the African Novel,* 288-305.

_____, "Negritude Rediscovered: A Reading of the Recent Novels of Armah, Ngugi, and Soyinka," *IFR* 8, i (Winter, 1981): 1-11.

_____, "Ngugi's PETALS OF BLOOD," *ALT* 10 (1979): 153-66.

Porter, Abioseh M., "Ideology and the Image of Women: Kenyan Women in Njau and Ngugi," *ArielE* 12, iii (July, 1981): 61-74.

Richard, Rene, "History and Literature: Narration and Time in PETALS OF BLOOD," *Echos du Commonwealth* (Mont Saint-Aignan, France) 6 (1980-81): 1-36.

Robson, C. B., *Introduction to the Writings of Ngugi wa Thiong'o,* 92-111.

Sharma, Govind N., "Ngugi's Apocalypse: Marxism, Christianity and African Utopianism in PETALS OF BLOOD," *WLWE* 18, ii (1979): 302-14.

Stratton, Florence, "Cyclical Patterns in PETALS OF BLOOD," *JCL* 15, i (1980): 115-24.

THE RIVER BETWEEN

Chesaina, Jane C., "East Africa, Ngugi wa Thiong'o's THE RIVER BETWEEN and the African Oral Tradition," in Gachukia, E., and Akivaga, S. K., eds., *Teaching of African Literature in Schools*, 62-71.

Githae-Mugo, M., *Visions of Africa*, 55-9, 123-30.

Gowda, H. H. Anniah, "Ngugi wa Thiong'o as Novelist," *LHY* 16, ii (1975): 36-44.

Gurr, A., *Writers in Exile*, 100-8 *passim*.

Howard, W. J., "Themes and Development in the Novels of Ngugi," *SAfrL* 1 (1973): 97-107. Also in Wright, E., ed., *Critical Evaluation of African Literature*, 97-107.

Ikiddeh, Ime, "Ngugi wa Thiong'o: The Novelist as Historian," in King, B., and K. Ogungbesan, eds., *Celebration of Black and African Writing*, 206-9.

Kemoli, Arthur M., "The Novels of Ngugi wa Thiong'o," *Joliso* 2, ii (1970): 70-7.

Killam, G. D., *Introduction to the Writings of Ngugi*, 20-35.

Knipp, Thomas R., "Two Novels from Kenya: J. Ngugi," *BA* 41 (1967): 393-7.

Larson, C. R., *Emergence of African Literature*, 135-8.

Moore, G., *Chosen Tongue*, 157-9.

Nnolim, Charles E., "Background Setting: Key to the Structure of Ngugi's THE RIVER BETWEEN," *Obsidian* 2, ii (1976): 20-9.

Ngubiah, S. N., "Ngugi's Early Writings: THE RIVER BETWEEN and THE BLACK HERMIT," in Wanjala, C. L., ed., *Standpoints on African Literature*, 62-71.

Okenimpke, Michael, "Culture and Revolution in the Novels of James Ngugi," *BACLLS* 10 (June, 1972): 28-34.

Palmer, E., *Introduction to the African Novel*, 11-24. Also in *SAfrL* 2 (1972): 11-24.

Rauch, Erika, "The Central Male-Female Relationships in THE RIVER BETWEEN and 'Mission to Kala'," *Buscara* 7, i (1975): 42-52.

Ravenscroft, Arthur, "James Ngugi, East African Novelist," in Paricsy, P., ed., *Modern Black African Literature*, 77-80. Also, adapted as "Ngugi's Development as a Novelist," in Rutherford, A., ed., *Common Wealth*, 86-9.

Rice, Michael, "THE RIVER BETWEEN: A Discussion," *EinA* 2, ii (1975): 11-21.

The River Between (Study Guide—African Novels B1 and E3), Tabora, Tanzania: TMP Book Dept.

Robson, C. B., *Ngugi wa Thiong'o*, 1-24.

Roscoe, A., *Uhuru's Fire*, 172-90 *passim*.

Sander, Reinhard, "Two Views of the Conflict of Cultures in Pre-Emergency Kenya: James Ngugi's THE RIVER BETWEEN and Elspeth Huxley's RED STRANGERS," *ReAL* 5, i (Fall, 1971): 8-26. Also in *Ikoro* (Nsukka) 3, i (1976): 28-42. Also in *LHY* 19, ii (1978): 27-48.

Williams, Lloyd, "Religion and Life in James Ngugi's THE RIVER BETWEEN," *ALT* 5 (1971): 54-65.

WEEP NOT CHILD

Edhore, P. F., *James Ngugi's WEEP NOT CHILD: Notes and Essays*, Ibadan: Onibonoje Pr., 1970. [Rev. ed.]

Githae-Mugo, M., *Visions of Africa*, 51-5, 131-8.

Gowda, H. H. Anniah, "Ngugi wa Thiong'o as Novelist," *LHY* 16, ii (1975): 28-36.

Griffiths, G., *Double Exile*, 33-6.

Gurr, A., *Writers in Exile*, 108-20 *passim*.

Howard, W. J., "Themes and Development in Ngugi," *SAfrL* 1 (1973): 107-12. Also in Wright, W., ed., *Critical Evaluation of African Literature*, 107-12.

Ikkiddeh, Ime, "Ngugi wa Thiong'o: The Novelist as Historian," in King, B., and K. Ogungbesan, eds., *Celebration of Black African Writing*, 209-13.

Irele, Abiola, "ARROW OF GOD by Chinua Achebe and WEEP NOT CHILD by James Ngugi," *PA* 19 (1964): 234-7.

Killam, G. D., *Introduction to the Writing of Ngugi*, 36-52.

Knipp, Thomas R., "Two Novels from Kenya: J. Ngugi," *BA* 41 (1967): 383-7.

Larson, C. R., *Emergence of African Fiction*, 121-35.

Nwabueze, F. O., *Ngugi: WEEP NOT CHILD in Questions and Answers with ADDITIONAL Notes and Introduction*, Onitsha: Tabansi Printing Enterprise, n.d.

Okenimpke, Michael, "Culture and Revolution in the Novels of James Ngugi," *BACLLS* 10 (June, 1972): 35-40.

Palmer, E., *Introduction to the African Novel*, 1-10. Also in *SAfrL* 2 (1972): 1-10.

Ravenscroft, Arthur, "James Ngugi, East African Novelist," in Paricsy, P., ed., *Studies on Modern Black Literature*, 74-7. Also adapted as "Ngugi's Development as a Novelist," in Rutherford, A., ed., *Common Wealth*, 85-6.

Robson, C. B., *Ngugi wa Thiong'o*, 25-45.

Roscoe, A., *Uhuru's Fire*, 172-90 *passim*.

Soile, Sola, "Myth and History in Ngugi's WEEP NOT CHILD," *IfeAS* 1, ii (1974): 77-91.

Tibble, Anne, *African/English Literature*, 82-4.

NICHOLS, JOHN (TREADWELL), 1940-

THE STERILE CUCKOO

Blessing, Richard A., "For Pookie, with Love and Good Riddance: John Nichol's THE STERILE CUCKOO," *JPC* 7, i (Summer, 1973): 124-35.

NIN, ANAIS, 1903-1977

GENERAL

Bailey, Jeffrey, "Link in the Chain of Feeling: An Interview with Anais Nin," *NOR* 5 (1979): 113-18.

Balakian, Anna, "The Poetic Reality of Anais Nin," in Jason, Philip K., ed., *Anais Nin Reader*, Chicago: Swallow Pr., 1973, 11-30. Also in Harms, Valerie, ed., *Celebration with Anais Nin*, Riverside, Conn.: Magic Circle Pr., 1973, 91-106. Also in Zaller, R., ed., *Casebook on Anais Nin*, 113-31.

Baldanza, Frank, "Anais Nin," *MinnR* 2, ii (Winter, 1962): 263-71.

Barnes, Daniel R., "Nin and Traditional Erotica," *Seahorse* 1, i (1982): 1-5.

Brown, Harriette G., "Animus and the Fiction of Anais Nin: A Feminine Interpretation of Logos," *DAI* 41 (1980): 1579A.

Deduck, Patricia A., "Realism and Reality in the Fictional Theory of Alain Robbe-Grillet and Anais Nin," *DAI* 39 (1978): 863A-64A.

Demetrakopoulos, Stephanie A., "Anais Nin and the Feminine Quest for Consciousness: The Quelling of the Devouring Mother and the Ascension of the Sophia," *BUR* 24, i (1978): 119-36.

Dick, Bernard F., "Anais Nin and Gore Vidal: A Study in Literary Incompatibility," *Mosaic* 11, ii (Winter, 1978): 153-62.

Edkins, Carol A., "The Necessary Link: Mediation in the Works of Anais Nin," *DAI* 41, xi (May, 1981): 4718A.

Ekberg, Kent, "Studio 28: The Influence of the Surrealist Cinema on the Early Fiction of Anais Nin and Henry Miller," *DL* 4, iii (Mar., 1981): 3-4.

English, Patricia, "An Interview with Anais Nin (September, 1971)," *New Woman* 7 (Dec., 1971): 26-31. Also in Zaller, R., ed., *Casebook on Anais Nin*, 185-97.

Evans, O., *Anais Nin*.

Evans, Oliver, "Anais Nin and the Discovery of Inner Space," *PrS* 36 (Fall, 1962): 217-31.

Franklin, B., and D. Schneider, *Anais Nin*.

Freeman, Barbara, "A Dialogue with Anais Nin," *ChiR* 24 (1972): 29-35.

Harris, Lauretta, "Reflections on Anais Nin," *WS* 5 (1978): 265-6.

Hinz, E. J., *Mirror and Garden*.

Holder, Orlee E., "Anais Nin's Fiction: Proceeding from the Dream Outward," *DAI* 42, xii (June, 1982): 5117A.

Jason, Philip K., "Doubles/Don Juans: Anais Nin and Otto Rank," *Mosaic* 11, ii (Winter, 1978): 81-94.

Knapp, B. L., *Anais Nin*.

_____, "'To Reach Out Further Mystically...': Anais Nin," *RS* 47, iii (Sept., 1979): 165-80.

Kuntz, Paul G., "Anais Nin's 'Quest for Order'," *Mosaic* 11, ii (Winter, 1978): 203-12.

MacNiven, Ian S., "A Room in the House of Art: The Friendship of Anais Nin and Lawrence Durrell," *Mosaic* 11, ii (Winter, 1978): 37-57.

Madden, Deanna K., "Laboratory of the Soul: The Influence of Psychoanalysis on the Work of Anais Nin," *DAI* 36 (1976): 6138A-39A.

McBrien, William, "Anais Nin: An Interview," *TCL* 20 (Oct., 1974): 277-90.

Merchant, Hoshang D., "Anais Nin's Texts of Pleasure: A Woman's *Ta Erotika*," *DAI* 42, xi (May, 1982): 4824A.

Molyneux, Maxine, and Julia Casterton, "Looking Again at Anais Nin," *MinnR* n.s. 18 (Spring, 1982): 86-101.

Novinger, Elizabeth A., "Neurosis and Transformation: A Study of Women's Roles in the Fiction of Anais Nin," *DAI* 43 (1982): 1546A-47A.

Paine, S., *Beckett, Nabokov, Nin*, 72-93.

Schneider, Duane, "The Art of Anais Nin," *SoR* 6, ii (Spring, 1970): 506-14. Also in Zaller, R., ed., *Casebook of Anais Nin*, 43-50.

Snyder, R., *Anais Nin Observed*.

Spencer, Sharon, "The Art of Collage in Anais Nin's Writing," *STwC* 16 (Fall, 1975): 1-11.

_____, *Collage of Dreams*.

_____, "Delivering the Woman Artist from the Silence of the Womb: Otto Rank's Influence on Anais Nin," *PsyR* 69, i (1982): 111-30.

_____, "The Dream of Twinship in the Writings of Anais Nin," *Journal of the Otto Rank Assn.* 9, ii (Winter, 1974-75): 81-90.

_____, "An Interview with Anais Nin," *Shantih: International Writings* 1-2 (Winter-Spring, 1972): 28-31.

_____, "A Novel Triangle: Anais Nin—Henry Miller—Otto Rank," *par rapport* 1 (1978): 139-44.

Sukenick, Lynn, "Anais Nin: The Novel of Vision," in Zaller, R., ed., *Casebook on Anais Nin*, 157-60.

Thomas, Rosalind, "Transcendental Reality in the Fiction of Anais Nin," *DAI* 41 (1982): 4860A.

Zaller, R., ed., *Casebook on Anais Nain*.

Zee, Nancy S., "Anais Nin: Beyond the Mask," *DAI* 34 (1974): 6671A.

Zinnes, Harriet, "Anais Nin's World Reissued," *BA* 37 (Summer, 1963): 283-6. Also in Zaller, R., ed., *Casebook on Anais Nin*, 35-41.

CITIES OF THE INTERIOR Series

Griffith, Paul, "The 'Jewels' of Anais Nin: CITIES OF THE INTERIOR," *Journal of the Otto Rank Assn.* 5, ii (Dec., 1970): 82-91.

Jones, Robert W., "A Study of Imagery in Anais Nin's CITIES OF THE INTERIOR," *DAI* 37 (1977): 4347A.

Knapp, B. L., *Anais Nin*, 95-148.

Lundberg, Christine, "Narrative Voice in Anais Nin's CITIES OF THE INTERIOR," *DAI* 43 (1982): 1746A.

McMath, Whitney V., "Feminine Identity in Anais Nin's CITIES OF THE INTERIOR," *DAI* 39 (1979): 6757A-58A.

Scholar, Nancy, "CITIES OF THE INTERIOR Revisited," *USP* 6, iv (Fall, 1975): 9-12.

Spencer, Sharon, "Anais Nin's 'Continuous Novel' CITIES OF THE INTERIOR," in Zaller, R., ed., *Casebook on Anais Nin*, 65-76.

_____, "CITIES OF THE INTERIOR—Femininity and Freedom," *USP* 7, iii (Summer, 1976): 9-16.

_____, *Collage of Dreams*, 74-80.

CHILDREN OF THE ALBATROSS (See also CITIES OF THE INTERIOR Series)

Evans, O., *Anais Nin*, 113-28.

Franklin, B., and D. Schneider, *Anais Nin*, 83-98.

Knapp, B. L., *Anais Nin*, 111-22.

COLLAGES

Evans, O., *Anais Nin*, 178-90.

Franklin, B., and D. Schneider, eds., *Anais Nin*, 147-63.

Haspray, Richard, "Transmutations," *MinnR* 7 (1967): 168-9.

Paine, S., *Beckett, Nabokov, Nin*, 86-92.

Spencer, Sharon, "The Art of Collage in Anais Nin's Writing," *STwC* 16 (Fall, 1975): 5-7.

THE FOUR-CHAMBERED HEART (See also CITIES OF THE INTERIOR Series)

Broderick, Catherine V., "A Comparative Thematic Study of Francois Mauriac's GENETRIX and Anais Nin's THE FOUR-CHAMBERED HEART," *DAI* 31 (1971): 4152A.

Demetrakopoulos, Stephanie A., "Anais Nin and the Feminine Quest for Consciousness: The Quelling of the Devouring

Mother and the Ascension of Sophia," *BuR* 24, i (1978): 125-30.

Evans, O., *Anais Nin,* 129-44.

Franklin, B., and D. Schneider, eds., *Anais Nin,* 99-112.

Knapp, B. L., *Anais Nin,* 122-30.

HOUSE OF INCEST

Evans, O., *Anais Nin,* 26-43.

Franklin, B., and D. Schneider, *Anais Nin,* 3-19.

Knapp, Bettina L., "Anais/Artaud—Alchemy," *Mosaic* 11, ii (Winter, 1978): 66-74.

_____, *Anais Nin,* 50-68.

Rank, Otto, "Preface to HOUSE OF INCEST," *Journal of the Otto Rank Assn.* 7 (Dec., 1972): 68-74.

Scholar, Nancy, "Anais Nin's HOUSE OF INCEST and Ingmar Bergman's *Persona:* Two Variations on a Theme," *LFQ* 7 (1979): 47-59

LADDERS TO FIRE (See also CITIES OF THE INTERIOR Series)

Evans, O., *Anais Nin,* 88-112.

Franklin, B., and D. Schneider, eds., *Anais Nin,* 62-82.

Henke, Suzette, "Anais Nin: Bread and Wafer," *USP* 7, ii (Spring, 1976): 7-17.

Knapp, B. L., *Anais Nin,* 98-111.

SEDUCTION OF THE MINOTAUR (See also CITIES OF THE INTERIOR Series)

Evans, O., *Anais Nin,* 163-77.

Franklin, B., and D. Schneider, *Anais Nin,* 130-46.

Knapp, B. L., *Anais Nin,* 140-1, 145-8.

McEvilly, Wayne, "Two Faces of Death in Anais Nin's SEDUCTION OF THE MINOTAUR," *NMQ* 38, iv and 39, i (Winter-Spring, 1969): 179-92. [Double issue.] Also as "Afterword," *Seduction of the Minotaur,* Chicago: Swallow Pr., 137-52. Also in Zaller, R., ed., *Casebook on Anais Nin,* 51-64.

Paine, S., *Beckett, Nabokov, Nin,* 79-86.

SOLAR BARQUE (See also CITIES OF THE INTERIOR Series)

Knapp, B. L., *Anais Nin,* 139-45.

A SPY IN THE HOUSE OF LOVE (See also CITIES OF THE INTERIOR Series)

Balakian, Anna, "'... and the pursuit of happiness': THE SCARLETT LETTER and A SPY IN THE HOUSE OF LOVE," *Mosaic* 11, ii (1978): 163-70.

Brians, Paul, "Sexuality and the Opposite Sex: Variations on a Theme by Theophile Gautier and Anais Nin," *ELWIU* 4 (Spring, 1977): 122-37.

Evans, O., *Anais Nin,* 145-62.

Franklin, B., and D. Schneider, *Anais Nin,* 113-29.

Jason, Philip K., "Doubles/Don Juans: Anais Nin and Otto Rank," *Mosaic* 11, ii (1978): 90-3.

_____, "Teaching A SPY IN THE HOUSE OF LOVE," *USP* 2 (Summer, 1971): 7-16.

Knapp, B. L., *Anais Nin,* 130-8.

THE VOICE

Knapp, B. L., *Anais Nin,* 70-7, 87-94.

WINTER OF ARTIFICE

Evans, O., *Anais Nin,* 44-62.

Franklin, B., and D. Schneider, *Anais Nin,* 20-39.

Knapp, B. L., *Anais Nin,* 69-86.

BIBLIOGRAPHY

See Issues of *Seahorse* and *USP.*

Cutting, Rose Marie, *Anais Nin: A Reference Guide,* Boston: G. K. Hall, 1978.

NWAPA, FLORA 1931-

GENERAL

Conde, Maryse, "Three Writers in Modern Africa: Flora Nwapa, Ama Ata Aidoo, and Grace Ogot," *PA* 82 (Apr.-June, 1972): 132-43. [Not seen.]

Emenyonu, Ernest N., "Who Does Flora Nwapa Write For?" *ALT* 7 (1975): 28-33.

Uwechue, Austa, "Flora Nwakuche, nee Nwapa, a Former Cabinet Minister and One of Africa's Leading Women Writers Talks to Austa Uwechue," *African Woman* (London) 10 (1977): 8-10.

EFURU

Githaiga, A., *Notes on Flora Nwapa's EFURU,* Nairobi: Heinemann, 1978.

Laurence, M., *Long Drums and Cannons,* 187-91.

Nandakumar, Preme, "An Image of African Womanhood: A Study of Flora Nwapa's EFURU," *AfricaQ* 11 (1971): 136-46.

Scheub, Harold, "Two African Women," *RLV* 37 (1971): 664-81.

NZEKWU, ONUORA, 1921-

GENERAL

Killam, G. D., "The Novels of Onuora Nzekwu," *ALT* 5 (1971): 21-40.

Laurence, M., *Long Drums and Cannons,* 191-3.

Lindfors, Bernth, "The Africanization of Onuora Nzekwu," *LHY* 13, i (Jan., 1972): 93-103.

Povey, John, "The Novels of Onuora Nzekwu," *LE&W* 12, i (Mar., 1968): 68-84.

Taiwo, O., *Culture and the Nigerian Novel,* 181-5.

BLADE AMONG THE BOYS

Killam, G. D., "The Novels of Onuora Nzekwu," *ALT* 5 (1971): 30-5.

Lindfors, Bernth, "The Africanization of Onuora Nzekwu," *LHY* 13, i (Jan., 1972): 97-100.

Taiwo, O., *On Culture and the Nigerian Novel,* 188-92.

HIGHLIFE FOR LIZARDS

Killam, G. D., "The Novels of Onuora Nzekwu," *ALT* 5 (1971): 35-40.

Lindfors, Bernth, "The Africanization of Onuora Nzekwu," *LHY* 13, i (Jan., 1972): 100-02.

Taiwo, O., *Culture and the Nigerian Novel,* 192-7.

WAND OF NOBLE WOOD

Killam, G. D., "The Novels of Onuora Nzekwu," *ALT* 5 (1971): 23-30.

Lindfors, Bernth, "The Africanization of Onuora Nzekwu," *LHY* 13, i (Jan., 1972): 95-7.

Taiwo, O., *Culture and the Nigerian Novel*, 185-8.

OAKLEY, BARRY K., 1931-

GENERAL

Daniel, Helen, "The Picaro in Disguise: The Novels of Barry Oakley," *Westerly* 25 (June, 1980): 51-7. [Not seen.]

Watson, Betty L., "Barry Oakley and the Satiric Mode," *ALS* 7 (1975): 50-63.

A SALUTE TO THE GREAT MCCARTHY

Watson, Betty L., "Barry Oakley and the Satiric Mode," *ALS* 7 (1975): 56-62.

OATES, JOYCE CAROL, 1938-

GENERAL

Barza, Steven, "Joyce Carol Oates: Naturalism and the Aberrant Response," *SAF* 7, ii (1979): 141-51.

Bellamy, Joe D., "The Dark Lady of American Letters: An Interview with Joyce Carol Oates," *Atlantic* 229 (Feb., 1972): 63-7. Also in Bellamy, J. D., ed., *New Fiction*, 19-31.

Bender, Eileen T., "The Artistic Vision, Theory and Practice of Joyce Carol Oates," *DAI* 38 (1977): 1384A.

Bloom, Kathleen B., "The Grotesque in the Fiction of Joyce Carol Oates," *DAI* 40 (1979): 2059A.

Creighton, J. V., *Joyce Carol Oates.*

————, "Unliberated Women in Joyce Carol Oates's Fiction," *WLWE* 17 (Apr., 1978): 165-75. Also in Wagner, L. W., ed., *Critical Essays on Joyce Carol Oates*, 148-56.

Dalton, Elizabeth, "Joyce Carol Oates: Violence in the Head," *Ctary* 49, vi (June, 1970): 75-7.

Dike, Donald A., "The Aggressive Victim in the Fiction of Joyce Carol Oates," *Greyfriar* 15 (1974): 13-29.

Ducas, Philomene C., "Determinism in Joyce Carol Oates's Novels, 1964-1975," *DAI* 40 (1980): 4589A.

Fossum, Robert H., "Only Control: The Novels of Joyce Carol Oates," *SNNTS* 7 (Summer, 1975): 285-97. Also in Wagner, L. W., ed., *Critical Essays on Joyce Carol Oates*, 49-60.

Friedman, E. G., *Joyce Carol Oates.*

Friedman, Ellen, "'Dreaming America': The Fiction of Joyce Carol Oates," *DAI* 39 (1978): 3578A.

Godwin, Gail, "An Oates Scrapbook," *NAmerR* 256 (Winter, 1971): 67-70.

Goodman, Charlotte, "Women and Madness in the Fiction of Joyce Carol Oates," *W&L* 5, ii (Fall, 1977): 17-28.

Grant, Mary K., R.S.M., "The Language of Tragedy and Violence," *Tragic Vision of Joyce Carol Oates*, 93-116. Also in Wagner, L. W., ed., *Critical Essays on Joyce Carol Oates*, 61-76.

————, *Tragic Vision of Joyce Carol Oates.*

Harter, Carol, "America as 'Consumer Garden': The Nightmare Vision of Joyce Carol Oates," *RLV* (1976): 171-87. [Not seen.]

Hodge, Marion C., Jr., "What Moment Is Not Terrible? An Introduction to the Work of Joyce Carol Oates," *DAI* 35 (1975): 5407A.

Kazin, Alfred, "Oates," *Harpers* 243 (Aug., 1971): 78-82.

————, [On Joyce Carol Oates], from "Cassandra," in Kazin, A., *Bright Book of Life*, N.Y., Little, Brown, 1971, 198-205. Also in Wagner, L. W., ed., *Critical Essays on Joyce Carol Oates*, 157-60.

Kuehl, Linda, "An Interview with Joyce Carol Oates," *Cweal* 91 (Dec. 5, 1969): 307-10.

Labrie, Ross. "Love and Survival in Joyce Carol Oates," *Greyfriar* 22 (1981): 17-26.

Leff, Leonard J., "The Center of Violence in Joyce Carol Oates's Fiction," *NMAL* 2 (Winter, 1977): Item 9.

Martin, Alice C., "Toward a Higher Consciousness: A Study of the Novels of Joyce Carol Oates," *DAI* 35 (1975):5415A-16A.

Mesinger, Bonnie M., "Dissonance and Indeterminacy in the Critical Writings and Fiction of Joyce Carol Oates: Implications of the Interpreter," *DAI* 38 (1978): 6716A-17A.

Mistri, Zenobia, "Joyce Carol Oates: Transformation of 'Being' toward a Center," *DAI* 38 (1978): 6122A.

Mickelson, Anne Z., "Sexual Love in the Fiction of Joyce Carol Oates," *Reaching Out*, 15-34.

Orenstein, Susan B., "Angel of Fire: Violence, Self and Grace in the Novels of Joyce Carol Oates," *DAI* 39 (1978): 3586A.

Petite, Joseph M., "The Interrelatedness of Marriage, Passion and Female Identity in the Fiction of Joyce Carol Oates," *DAI* 37 (1977): 5831A.

————, "'Out of the Machine': Joyce Carol Oates and the Liberation of Women," *KanQ* 9, ii (1977): 75-9.

Phillips, Robert, "Joyce Carol Oates: The Art of Fiction LXXII," *ParisR* 74 (1978): 199-226.

Pinsker, Sanford, "Isaac Bashevis Singer and Joyce Carol Oates: Some Versions of the Gothic," *SoR* 9, lv (Oct., 1973): 895-908.

————, "Joyce Carol Oates and the New Naturalism," *SoR* 15 (Jan., 1979): 52-63.

Rocco, Claire J., "Flannery O'Connor and Joyce Carol Oates: Violence as Art," *DAI* 36 (1976): 6090A.

Sjöberg, Leif, "An Interview with Joyce Carol Oates," *ConL* 23, iii (Summer, 1982): 267-84.

Stevens, Cynthia C., "The Imprisoned Imagination: The Family in the Fiction of Joyce Carol Oates, 1960-1970," *DAI* 35 (1974): 479A.

Sullivan, Walter, "The Artificial Demon: Joyce Carol Oates and the Dimension of the Real," *HC* 9, iv (Dec., 1972): 1-12. Also in Wagner, L. W., ed., *Critical Essays on Joyce Carol Oates*, 77-86.

"Transformation of the Self: An Interview with Joyce Carol Oates," *OhR* 15, i (1973): 50-61.

Wagner, L. W., ed., *Critical Essays on Joyce Carol Oates.*

Wagner, Linda W., "Joyce Carol Oates: The Changing Shape of Her Realities," *GrLR* 5, ii (Winter, 1979): 15-23. Also in Wagner, L. W., *American Modern*, 67-75. Also, in part, in Wagner, L. W., ed., *Critical Essays on Joyce Carol Oates*, xvii-xxxi.

Waller, G. F., *Dreaming of America.*

————, "Through Obsession to Transcendence: The Recent Work of Joyce Carol Oates," *WLWE* 17, i (Apr., 1978): 176-80.

————, "Through Obsession to Transcendence: The Lawrentian Mode of Oates's Recent Fiction," in Wagner, L. W., ed., *Critical Essays on Joyce Carol Oates*, 161-73.

Wilson, Mary A., "The Image of Self in Selected Works of Joyce Carol Oates," *DAI* 38 (1978): 7340A.

THE ASSASSINS: A BOOK OF HOURS

Creighton, J. V., *Joyce Carol Oates*, 94-106, 150-1.

Friedman, E. G., *Joyce Carol Oates*, 135-63.

Giles, James R., "From Jimmy Gatz to Jules Wendall: A Study of 'Nothing Substantial'," *DR* 56, iv (Winter, 1976-77): 718-24.

Kramer, Hilton, "Naipaul's Guerillas and Oates's Assassins," *Ctary* 61, iii (Mar., 1976): 54-7.

Pollock, John, "The Nouveau-Lipsian Style of Joyce Carol Oates," *SJS* 4, ii (1978): 32-40.

Waller, G. F., *Dreaming America*, 183-98.

_____, "Through Obsession to Transcendence: The Lawrentian Mode of Oates's Recent Fiction," in Wagner, L. W., ed., *Critical Essays on Joyce Carol Oates*, 164-7.

BELLEFLEUR

Cunningham, Valentine, "Counting Up the Cast," *TLS* 4068 (Mar. 20, 1981): 303.

CHILDWOLD

Bender, Eileen T., "'Paedomorphic' Art: Joyce Carol Oates' CHILDWOLD," in Wagner, L. W., ed., *Critical Essays on Joyce Carol Oates*, 117-22.

Creighton, J. V., *Joyce Carol Oates*, 106-12, 150-1.

Friedman, E. G., *Joyce Carol Oates*, 163-87.

Waller, G. F., *Dreaming America*, 198-212.

CYBELE

Wagner, Linda W., "Oates' CYBELE," *NConL* 11, v (Nov., 1981): 2-8.

DO WITH ME WHAT YOU WILL

Burwell, Rose Marie, "The Process of Individuation as Narrative Structure: Joyce Carol Oates' DO WITH ME WHAT YOU WILL," *Crit* 17, ii (1975): 93-106.

Creighton, J. V., *Joyce Carol Oates*, 87-93.

Friedman, E. G., *Joyce Carol Oates*, 117-35.

Stanbrough, Jane, "Joyce Carol Oates' Carnal Transcendentalism," *DQ* 9, i (Spring, 1974): 84-9.

Waller, E. G., *Dreaming America*, 157-82.

EXPENSIVE PEOPLE

Creighton, J. V., *Joyce Carol Oates*, 55-63.

Friedman, E. G., *Joyce Carol Oates*, 55-72.

Grant, Mary K., R. S. M., "The Language of Tragedy and Violence," *Tragic Vision of Joyce Carol Oates*, 108-12. Also in Wagner, L. W., ed., *Critical Essays on Joyce Carol Oates*, 68-73.

_____, *Tragic Vision of Joyce Carol Oates*, 48-51, 75-7.

Pinsker, Sanford, "Suburban Molesters: Joyce Carol Oates' EXPENSIVE PEOPLE," *MQ* 19, i (Autumn, 1977): 89-103. Also in Wagner, L. W., ed., *Critical Essays on Joyce Carol Oates*, 93-101.

Waller, G. F., *America Dreaming*, 114-23.

A GARDEN OF EARTHLY DELIGHTS

Allen, M., *Necessary Blankness*, 134-6.

Burwell, Rose Marie, "Joyce Carol Oates and the Old Master," *Crit* 15, i (1973): 48-58.

Creighton, J. V., *Joyce Carol Oates*, 48-55.

Friedman, E. G., *Joyce Carol Oates*, 35-53.

Grant, Mary K., R.S.M., "The Language of Tragedy and Violence," *Tragic Vision of Joyce Carol Oates*, 101-2, 112-15. Also in Wagner, L. W., ed., *Critical Essays on Joyce Carol Oates*, 65-7, 74-5.

_____, *Tragic Vision of Joyce Carol Oates*, 45-8, 81-3, 89-90.

Haneline, Douglas L., "The Swing of the Pendulum: Naturalism in Contemporary American Literature," *DAI* 39 (1978): 2272A-73A.

Madden, D., "The Violent World of Joyce Carol Oates," *Poetic Image in Six Genres*, 44-6.

Waller, G. F., *Dreaming America*, 101-12.

SON OF THE MORNING

Friedman, E. G., *Joyce Carol Oates*, 196-9.

THEM

Allen, M., *Necessary Blankness*, 151-9.

Cornillion, Susan K., "The Fiction of Fiction," in Cornillion, S. K., ed., *Images of Women in Fiction*, 117-24.

Creighton, J. V., *Joyce Carol Oates*, 63-73, 144-6.

DeCurtis, Anthony, "The Process of Fictionalization in Joyce Carol Oates's THEM," *IFR* 6 (1979): 121-8.

Friedman, E. G., *Joyce Carol Oates*, 73-93.

Giles, James R., "Suffering Transcendance and Artistic 'Form': Joyce Carol Oates's THEM," *IFR* 6 (1979): 213-26.

Grant, Mary K., R.S.M., "The Language of Violence and Tragedy in Joyce Carol Oates," *Tragic Vision of Joyce Carol Oates*, 96-7. Also in Wagner, L. W., ed., *Critical Essays on Joyce Carol Oates*, 65-8.

_____, *Tragic Vision of Joyce Carol Oates*, 51-5, 70-1, 83-4, 133-4.

Haneline, Douglas L., "The Swing of the Pendulum: Naturalism in Contemporary American Literature," *DAI* 39 (1978): 2272A-73A.

Pinsker, Sanford, "The Blue Collar Apocalypse or Detroit Bridge's Falling Down: Joyce Carol Oates' THEM," *Descant* 23, iv (1979): 35-47.

Waller, G. F., *Dreaming America*, 123-42.

WITH SHUDDERING FALL

Burwell, Rose Marie, "Joyce Carol Oates' First Novel," *CanL* 73 (Summer, 1977): 54-67.

Creighton, J. V., *Joyce Carol Oates*, 41-7.

Grant, Mary K., R.S.M., "The Language of Tragedy and Violence in Joyce Carol Oates," *Tragic Vision of Joyce Carol Oates*, 95-6, 110-11. Also in Wagner, L. W., ed., *Critical Essays on Joyce Carol Oates*, 62-3, 70-3.

_____, *Tragic Vision of Joyce Carol Oates*, 41-5.

Madden, David, "The Violent World of Joyce Carol Oates," *Poetic Images in 6 Genres*, 32-9.

Waller, G. F., *Dreaming America*, 87-102.

WONDERLAND

Box, Patricia S., "Vision and Revision in WONDERLAND," *NConL* 9, i (1979): 3-6.

Burwell, Rose M., "WONDERLAND: Paradigm of the Psychohistorical Mode," *Mosaic* 14, iii (Summer, 1981): 1-16.

Creighton, J. V., *Joyce Carol Oates,* 74-87.

Friedman, Ellen G., "The Journey from the 'I' to the 'Eye': Joyce Carol Oates' WONDERLAND," *SAF* 8 (1980): 37-50. Also in Wagner, L. W., ed., *Critical Essays on Joyce Carol Oates,* 102-16.

———, *Joyce Carol Oates,* 95-117.

Giles, James R., "The 'Marivaudian Being' Drowns His Children: Dehumanization in Donald Barthelme's 'Robert Kennedy Saved from Drowning' and Joyce Carol Oates' WONDERLAND," *SHR* 9 (1975): 63-75.

Godwin, Gail, "An Oates Scrapbook," *NAmerR* 256, iv (Winter, 1971): 76-70.

Grant, M. K., R.S.M., *Tragic Vision of Joyce Carol Oates,* 55-9, 77-80, 91-2.

Higdon, David L., "'Suitable Conclusions': The Two Endings of Oates's WONDERLAND," *SNNTS* 10, iv (1978): 447-53.

Key, James A., "Joyce Carol Oates's WONDERLAND and the Idea of Control," *PAPA* 2, iii (1976): 15-21.

Pinsker, Sanford, "Joyce Carol Oates's WONDERLAND: A Hungering for Personality," *Crit* 20, ii (1978): 59-70.

Taylor, Gordon O., "Joyce Carol Oates, Artist in WONDERLAND," *SoR* 10 (1974): 490-53.

Waller, G. F., "Joyce Carol Oates' WONDERLAND: An Introduction," *DR* 54 (Autumn, 1974): 480-90.

———, *Dreaming America,* 144-57.

BIBLIOGRAPHY

McCormick, Lucienne P., "A Bibliography of Works by and about Joyce Carol Oates," *AL* 43, i (Mar., 1971): 124-32.

O'BRIEN, EDNA, 1932-

GENERAL

Eckley, G., *Edna O'Brien.*

McMahon, Sean, "A Sex by Themselves: An Interim Report on the Novels of Edna O'Brien," *Eire* 2 (Spring, 1967): 79-87.

O'Brien, Darcy, "Edna O'Brien: A Kind of Irish Childhood," in Staley, T. F., ed., *Twentieth-Century Women Novelists,* 179-90.

Popot, Raymonde, "Edna O'Brien's Paradise Lost," *CahiersI* 4-5 (1976): 255-85. Also in Rafroidi, P., and M. Harmon, eds., *Irish Novel in Our Time,* 255-85.

Scanlan, John A., Jr., "States of Exile: Alienation and Art in the Novels of Brian Moore and Edna O'Brien," *DAI* 36 (1976): 5287A-88A.

Snow, Lotus, "'That Trenchant Childhood Route?' Quest in Edna O'Brien's Novels," *Eire* 14, i (Spring, 1979): 74-83.

A PAGAN PLACE

O'Brien, Edna, "Edna O'Brien Talks to David Heycock About Her New Novel A PAGAN PLACE," *Listener* 83 (1970): 616-17.

O'BRIEN, FLANN, Pseud. (Brian O'Nuallain), 1911-1966

(Also known as Brian O'Nolan, Brian Nolan, and Myles na Gopaleen.)

GENERAL

Benstock, Bernard, "The Three Faces of Brian Nolan," *Eire* 3, iii (Autumn, 1968): 51-65.

Burgess, Anthony, "Flann O'Brien: A Note," *EI* 7 (Dec., 1982): 83-6. [Not seen.]

———, "The Magical Madness of Flann O'Brien," *SatR* (Apr. 17, 1976): 25-7.

Clissmann, A., *Flann O'Brien.*

Heckard, Margaret, "The Novels of Brian O'Nolan," *DAI* 37 (1976): 986A-87A.

Imhoff, Rüdiger, "Two Meta-Novelists: Sternesque Elements in Novels by Flann O'Brien," *Anglo-Irish Studies* 4 (1979): 59-90.

Jacquin, Danielle, "Never Apply Your Front Brake First, or Flann O'Brien and the Theme of the Fall," *CahiersI* 4-5 (1976): 187-97. Also in Rafroidi, P., and M. Harmon, eds., *Irish Novel in Our Time,* 187-97.

Johnston, Denis, "Myles Na Gopaleen," in Ronsley, J., ed., *Myth and Reality in Irish Literature,* 297-304.

Knight, Stephen, "Forms of Gloom: The Novels of Flann O'Brien," in Anderson, D., and S. Knight, eds., *Cunning Exiles,* 104-28.

Mays, J. C. C., "Brian O'Nolan and Joyce on Art and Life," *JJQ* 11, iii (1974): 238-56.

Miller, Karl, "Gael in Wonderland," *NYRB* 22, vii (May 1, 1975): 31-4.

O'Donoghue, Bernard, "Irish Humour and Verbal Logic," *CritQ* 24, i (Spring, 1982): 33-40 *passim.*

Orvell, Miles, "Brian O'Nolan: The Privacy of His Mind," *ICarbS* 2, i (Winter, 1975): 23-38.

———, "Entirely Fictitious: The Fiction of Flann O'Brien," *JIL* 3, i (Jan., 1974): 93-103.

———, and David Powell, "Myles na Gopaleen: Mystic, Horse-Doctor, Hackney Journalist and Ideological Catalyst," *Eire* 10, ii (1975): 44-72.

Peterson, Richard F., "Flann O'Brien's Timefoolery," *Irish Renaissance Annual* 3 (1982): 30-46.

Petro, Peter, "Four Eccentrics: The Eccentric Character in the Novels of Celine, O'Brien, Gombrowicz, and Solzenicyn," *CRCL* 8, iv (Dec., 1981): 48-60.

Powell, William D., "The English Writings of Flann O'Brien," *DAI* 31 (1971): 3560A.

Pratt, Leighton, "The Nature of Comedy in the Novels of Flann O'Brien," 57-68, in *Prace Historyczno-Literackie,* 42, Warsaw; Crakow: Panstwowe Wydawnictwo Naukowe, 1981.

Sage, Lorna, in Dunn, D., ed., *Two Decades of Irish Writing,* 197-206.

Semmler, Clement, "The Art of Brian O'Nolan," *Meanjin* 29 (Summer, 1970): 492-500.

Sheridan, Niall, "Brian O'Nolan: A Postscript," *Meanjin* 30 (Winter, 1971): 239-40.

AT SWIM-TWO-BIRDS

Benstock, Bernard, "A Flann for All Seasons," *Irish Renaissance Annual* 3 (1982): 15-29.

Bergonzi, B., *Situation of the Novel,* 199-200.

Brooke-Rose, Christine, "The Readerhood of Man," 131-4 in Suleiman, Susan R., and Inge Crosman, eds., *The Reader in the Text: Essays on Audience and Interpretation,* Princeton, N.J.: Princeton Un. Pr., 1980.

Clissmann, A., *Flann O'Brien,* 76-150.

Janik, Del Ivan, "Flann O'Brien: The Novelist as Critic," *Eire* 4, iv (Winter, 1969): 64-72.

Kennedy, Sighle, "'The Devil and Holy Water': Samuel Beckett's MURPHY and Flann O'Brien's AT SWIM-TWO-BIRDS," in Porter, R. J., and J. D. Brophy, eds., *Modern Irish Literature,* 251-60.

Knight, Stephen, "Forms of Gloom: The Novels of Flann O'Brien," in Anderson, D., and S. Knight, eds., *Cunning Exiles,* 105-20.

Lee, L. L., "The Dublin Cowboys of Flann O'Brien," *WAL* 4, iii (Fall, 1969): 219-25.

Mellamphy, Ninian, "Aestho-Autogamy and the Anarchy of Imagination: Flann O'Brien's Theory of Fiction in AT SWIM-TWO-BIRDS," *CJIS* 4, i (1978): 8-25.

Orvell, Miles, "Entirely Fictitious: The Fiction of Flann O'Brien," *JIL* 3, i (Jan., 1974): 93-8.

Peterson, Richard F., "Flann O'Brien's Timefoolery," *Irish Renaissance Annual* 3 (1982): 42-5.

Roberts, Ruth, "AT SWIM-TWO-BIRDS and the Novel as Self-Evident Sham," *Eire* 6, ii (Summer, 1971): 76-97.

Silverthorne, J. M., "Time, Literature and Failure: Flann O'Brien's AT SWIM-TWO-BIRDS and THE THIRD POLICEMAN," *Eire* 11, iv (1976): 66-83.

Wain, John, "'To Write for My Own Race': The Fiction of Flann O'Brien," *Encounter* 29, i (July, 1967): 71-81. Also in Wain, J., *House for the Truth,* 67-85.

THE DALKEY ARCHIVE

Clissman, A., *Flann O'Brien,* 291-323.

Dietrich, Julia, "Flann O'Brien's Parody of Transubstantiation in THE DALKEY ARCHIVE," *NConL* 10, v (1980): 5-6.

Knight, Stephen, "Forms of Gloom: The Novels of Flann O'Brien," in Anderson, D., and S. Knight, eds., *Cunning Exiles,* 120-2.

Peterson, Richard F., "Flann O'Brien's Timefoolery," *Irish Renaissance Annual* 3 (1982): 33-9.

Wain, John, "'To Write for My Own Race': The Fiction of Flann O'Brien," *Encounter* 29, i (July, 1967): 82-5. Also in Wain, J., *House for the Truth,* 92-103.

THE HARD LIFE

Clissman, A., *Flann O'Brien,* 269-90.

Power, Mary, "The Figure of the Magician in THE THIRD POLICEMAN and THE HARD LIFE," *CJIS* 8, i (1982): 55-63.
_____, "Flann O'Brien and Classical Satire: An Exegesis of THE HARD LIFE," *Eire* 13, i (Spring, 1978): 87-102.

Wain, John, "'To Write for My Own Race': The Fiction of Flann O'Brien," *Encounter* 29, i (July, 1967): 81-5. Also in Wain, J., *House for the Truth,* 92-103.

THE POOR MOUTH

Miller, Karl, "Gael in Wonderland," *NYRB* 22, vii (May 1, 1975): 33-4.

Sage, Lorna, in Dunn, D., ed., *Two Decades of Irish Writing,* 197-200.

SLATTERY'S SAGO SAGA

Clissman, A., *Flann O'Brien,* 324-36.

THE THIRD POLICEMAN

Benstock, Bernard, "Flann O'Brien in Hell: THE THIRD POLICEMAN," *BuR* 18 (May, 1969): 67-78.

Clissman, A., *Flann O'Brien,* 151-81.

Fackler, Herbert V., "Flann O'Brien's THE THIRD POLICEMAN: Banjaxing Natural Order," *SCB* 38, iv (1978): 142-5.

Knight, Stephen, "Forms of Gloom: The Novels of Flann O'Brien," in Anderson, D., and S. Knight, eds., *Cunning Exiles,* 122-4.

McGuire, Jerry L., "Teasing After Death: Metatextuality in THE THIRD POLICEMAN," *Eire* 16 (Summer, 1981): 107-21.

Moss, Howard, "Tom Swift in Hell," *NY* 44 (Sept. 28, 1968): 174-80.

Orvell, Miles, "Entirely Fictitious: The Fiction of Flann O'Brien," *JIL* 3, i (Jan., 1974): 98-101.

Peterson, Richard F., "Flann O'Brien's Timefoolery," *Irish Renaissance Annual* 3 (1982): 39-42.

Power, Mary, "The Figure of the Magician in THE THIRD POLICEMAN and THE HARD LIFE," *CJIS* 8, i (1982): 55-63.

Silverthorne, J. M., "Time, Literature, and Failure: Flann O'Brien's AT SWIM-TWO-BIRDS and THE THIRD POLICEMAN," *Eire* 11, iv (1976): 66-83.

Wain, John, "'To Write for My Own Race': The Fiction of Flann O'Brien," *House for the Truth,* 85-91.1

BIBLIOGRAPHY

Imhof, Rudiger, "Flann O'Brien: A Checklist," *EI* 4 (1979): 125-48.

O'BRIEN, KATE, 1897-1974

GENERAL

Ryan, Joan, "Women in the Novels of Kate O'Brien: The Mellick Novels," in Kosok, H., ed., *Studies in Anglo-Irish Literature,* 322-1.

THE FLOWER OF MAY

Jordan, John, "Some Works of the Month, Kate O'Brien—A Note on Her Themes, Being a Consideration of THE FLOWER OF MAY," *The Bell* 19, vii (Jan., 1954): 53-9.

O'BRIEN, TIM, 1946-

GENERAL

McCaffery, Larry, "Interview with Tim O'Brien," *ChiR* 33, ii (1982): 129-49.

GOING AFTER CACCIATO

Jones, Dale W., "The Vietnams of Michael Herr and Tim O'Brien: Tales of Disintegration and Integration," *CRevAS* 13, iii (Winter, 1982): 309-20.

Saltzman, Arthur M., "The Betrayal of the Imagination: Paul Brodeur's THE STUNT MAN and Tim O'Brien's GOING AFTER CACCIATO," *Crit* 22, i (1980): 132-8.

Vanatta, Dennis, "Theme and Structure in Tim O'Brien's GOING AFTER CACCIATO," *MFS* 28, ii (Summer, 1982): 242-6.

O'CONNOR, EDWIN, 1918-1968

GENERAL

Betts, Richard A., "The 'Blackness of Life': The Function of Edwin O'Connor's Comedy," *MELUS* 8, i (Spring, 1981): 15-26.

Dillon, David, "Priests and Politicians: The Fiction of Edwin O'Connor," *Crit* 16, ii (1974): 108-20. Also, expanded, in Casey, D. J., and R. E. Rhodes, eds., *Irish-American Fiction*, 73-84.

Kelleher, John V., "Edwin O'Connor and the Irish-American Process," *Atlantic* 222, i (July, 1968): 48-52.

Rank, H., *Edwin O'Connor*.

ALL IN THE FAMILY

Jones, Howard M., "Politics, Mr. O'Connor, and the Family Novel," *Atlantic* 218 (Oct., 1966): 117-20.

Rank, H., *Edwin O'Connor*, 151-78.

THE EDGE OF SADNESS

Galbraith, John K., "Sadness in Boston," *NY* 37 (June 24, 1961): 87-94.

O'Donovan, Patrick, "In the Shadow of His Excellency," *NRep* 145 (July 24, 1961): 24-6.

Rank, H., *Edwin O'Connor*, 103-28.

————, "O'Connor's Image of the Priest," *NEQ* 41 (Mar., 1968): 3-29.

Sandra, Sister Mary, S.S.A., "The Priest-Hero in Modern Fiction," *Person* 46 (Oct., 1965): 528-31.

Stucky, W. J., *Pulitzer Prize Novels*, 197-204.

I WAS DANCING

Rank, H., *Edwin O'Connor*, 129-50.

THE LAST HURRAH

Blotner, J., *Modern American Political Novel*, 82-5.

Boulger, James D., "Puritan Allegory in Four Modern Novels," *Thought* 44 (Autumn, 1969): 413-32.

Goodwin, George, Jr., "The Last Hurrahs: George Apley and Frank Skeffington," *MR* 1 (May, 1960): 461-71.

Haslam, Gerald, "THE LAST HURRAH and American Bossism," *Rendezvous* 8, i (Summer, 1973): 33-44.

Milne, G., *American Political Novel*, 165-71.

Rank, H., *Edwin O'Connor*, 51-95.

Taylor, Robert, "John Ford's Boston," in Peary, G., and R. Shatzkin, eds., *Modern American Novel and the Movies*, 215-23.

West, A., *Principles and Persuasions*, 219-24.

THE ORACLE

Rank, H., *Edwin O'Connor*, 39-50.

BIBLIOGRAPHY

Rank, H., *Edwin O'Connor*, 193-4.

O'CONNOR, FLANNERY, 1925-1964

GENERAL

See issues of *Flannery O'Connor Bulletin*.

Alice, Sister Rose, S. S. J., "Flannery O'Connor: Poet to the Outcast," *Ren* 16 (Spring, 1964): 126-32.

Allen, Suzanne T., "*The Mind and Heart of Love:* Eros and Agape in the Fiction of Flannery O'Connor," *DAI* 38 (1978): 7330A.

Asals, F., *Flannery O'Connor*.

Asals, Frederick J., Jr., "Flannery O'Connor: An Interpretive Study," *DAI* 33 (1973): 6897A-98A.

————, "Flannery O'Connor as Novelist: A Defense," *F1OB* 3 (1974): 23-39.

Au, Bobbye G., "The Dragon by the Side of the Road: A Study of the Fiction of Flannery O'Connor," *DAI* 37 (1977): 6482A.

Bass, Eben, "Flannery O'Connor and Henry James: The Vision of Grace," *STwC* 14 (Fall, 1974): 69-89.

Bassan, Maurice, "Flannery O'Connor's Way: Shock, with Moral Intent," *Ren* 15 (Summer, 1963): 195-9+.

Baumbach, Georgia A., "The Psychology of Flannery O'Connor's Fictive World," *DAI* 34 (1973): 304A.

Blackwell, Annie L., "The Artistry of Flannery O'Connor," *DA* 27 (1967): 3862A-63A.

Blackwell, Louise, "Humor and Irony in the Works of Flannery O'Connor," *RANAM* 4 (1971): 61-8.

Beaver, Harold, "On the Verge of Eternity," *TLS* (Nov. 21, 1980): 1336.

Bleikasten, Andre, "The Heresy of Flannery O'Connor," in Johnson, I. D., and C. Johnson, eds., *Americanistes*, 53-70.

Brewster, Rudolph A., "The Literary Devices in the Writings of Flannery O'Connor," *DA* 29 (1969): 3572A-73A.

Brittain, Joan, "The Fictional Family of Flannery O'Connor," *Ren* 19 (Fall, 1966): 48-52.

————, and Leon V. Driskell, "O'Connor and the Eternal Crossroads," *Ren* 22 (Autumn, 1969): 49-55.

Browning, P. M., Jr., *Flannery O'Connor*.

————, "Flannery O'Connor and the Demonic," *MFS* 19 (Spring, 1973): 29-41.

————, "Flannery O'Connor's Devil Revisited," *SHR* 10 (Fall, 1976): 325-33.

Burns, Shannon, "Flannery O'Connor: The Work Ethic," *F1OB* 8 (1979): 54-67.

————, "The Literary Theory of Flannery O'Connor and Nathaniel Hawthorne," *F1OB* 7 (1978): 101-13.

Burns, Stuart L., "O'Connor and the Critics: An Overview," *MissQ* 27 (Fall, 1974): 483-95.

Butler, Rebecca R., "What's So Funny About Flannery O'Connor?" *F1OB* 9 (1980): 30-40.

Carlson, Thomas M., "Flannery O'Connor: The Manichaean Dilemma," *DAI* 34 (1973): 2613A.

Casper, Leonard, "The Unspeakable Peacock: Apocalypse in Flannery O'Connor," in Friedman, M. J., and J. B. Vickery, eds., *Shaken Realist*, 287-95.

Chard, George E. H., "Flannery O'Connor's Fiction: Materials and Selected Structures," *DAI* 36 (1976): 8055A-56A.

Cheney, Brainard, "Flannery O'Connor's Campaign for Her Country," *SR* 72 (Autumn, 1964): 555-8. Also in Reiter, R. E., ed., *Flannery O'Connor*, 1-4.

_____, "Miss O'Connor Creates Unusual Humor Out of Ordinary Sin," *SR* 71 (Autumn, 1963): 644-52. Also in Reiter, R. E., ed., *Flannery O'Connor*, 39-49.

Cleary, Michael, "Environmental Influences in Flannery O'Connor's Fiction," *F10B* 8 (1979): 20-34.

Cleveland, Carol L., "Psychological Violence: The World of Flannery O'Connor," *DAI* 34 (1974): 5959A.

Coffey, Warren, "Flannery O'Connor," *Ctary* 40 (Nov., 1965): 93-9.

Coghill, Sheila R., "Symbolism in the Fiction of Flannery O'Connor," *DAI* 42, viii (Feb., 1982): 3598A.

Coles, Robert, "Flannery O'Connor: A Southern Intellectual," *SoR* 16 (Jan., 1980): 46-64.

_____, "Flannery O'Connor: Letters Larger Than Life," *F10B* 8 (1979): 3-13.

_____, *Flannery O'Connor's South*.

Connolly, Janet M., "The Fiction of Flannery O'Connor," *DA* 28 (1967): 670A.

Coulthard, A. R., "The Christian Writer and the New South: or Why Don't You Like Flannery O'Connor," *SHR* 13 (1979): 79-83.

Cruser, Paul A., "Fiction of Flannery O'Connor," *DAI* 31 (1970): 2910A.

Daretta, John L., "The Idea and Image of Retribution in the Fiction of Flannery O'Connor," *DAI* 33 (1973): 4406A-07A.

Davis, Barnabas, "Flannery O'Connor: Christian Belief in Recent Fiction," *Listening* (Autumn, 1965): 5-21.

Dennis, Joy D., "Tableaux, Processions, and Journeys in Flannery O'Connor's Fiction," *DAI* 36 (1976): 8057A.

Desmond, John F., "Christian Historical Analogues in the Fiction of William Faulkner and Flannery O'Connor," *DAI* 32 (1972): 3994A-95A.

_____, "Flannery O'Connor, Henry James and the International Theme," *F10B* (1980): 3-18.

_____, "Flannery O'Connor's Sense of Place," *SHR* 10 (Summer, 1976): 251-9.

Detweiler, Robert, "The Curse of Christ in Flannery O'Connor's Fiction," *CLS* 3 (1966): 235-45. Also in Panichas, G. A., ed., *Mansions of the Spirit*, 358-69.

Dineen, Patricia M., "Flannery O'Connor: Realist of Distances," *DA* 28 (1968): 3635A.

Donohue, Agnes M., "The Numenous Vision of Flannery O'Connor," *Critic* 34, iii (Spring, 1976): 32-42.

Dowell, Bob, "The Moment of Grace in the Fiction of Flannery O'Connor," *CE* 27 (Dec., 1965): 235-9.

Drake, R., *Flannery O'Connor*.

_____, "Flannery O'Connor and American Literature," *F10B* 3 (1974): 1-22.

_____, "The Harrowing Evangel of Flannery O'Connor," *ChC* 81 (Sept. 30, 1964): 1200-2.

_____, "Three Southern Ladies," *F10B* 9 (1980): 41-8.

Driggers, Stephen G., "Imaginative Discovery in the Flannery O'Connor Typescripts," *DAI* 42, xii (June, 1982): 5120A.

Driskell, L., and J. T. Brittain, *Eternal Crossroads*.

Duhamel, P. Albert, "The Novelist as Prophet," in Friedman, M. J., and L. A. Lawson, eds., *Added Dimension*, 88-107.

Dullea, Catherine M., "The Vision of Faith and Reality in the Fiction of Flannery O'Connor," *DAI* 38 (1978): 6130A.

Dunn, Sister Francis M., "Functions and Implications of Setting in the Fiction of Flannery O'Connor," *DAI* 27 (1967): 3043A.

Dunn, Robert J., "A Mode of Good: Form and Philosophy in the Fiction of Flannery O'Connor," *DAI* 32 (1972): 3995A-96A.

Eggenschweiler, D., *Christian Humanism of Flannery O'Connor*.

Emerick, Ronald R., "Romance, Allegory, Vision: The Influence of Hawthorne on Flannery O'Connor," *DAI* 36 (1976): 4485A-86A.

Esprit (Un. of Scranton) 8 (Winter, 1964). Flannery O'Connor Issue.

Farnham, James F., "Disintegration of Myth in the Writings of Flannery O'Connor," *ConnR* 8, i (1974): 11-19.

_____, "The Grotesque in Flannery O'Connor," *America* 105 (May 13, 1961): 277, 280-1.

Feeley, Sister Kathleen M., "Thematic Imagery in the Fiction of Flannery O'Connor," *SHR* 3 (Winter, 1968): 14-31.

Feeley, Sister Mary K., "Splendour and Reality: The Fiction of Flannery O'Connor," *DAI* 31 (1970): 1272A.

Ferguson, Paul F., "By Their Names You Shall Know Them: Flannery O'Connor's Onomastic Strategy," *LOS* 7 (1980): 87-109.

Fitzgerald, Sally, "The Habit of Being," *F10B* 6 (1977): 5-16.

Flores-Del Prado, Wilma, "Flannery O'Connor's Gallery of Freaks," *SLRJ* 2, iii-iv (Sept.-Dec., 1971): 463-514.

Fox, William H., "Opposition to Secular Humanism in the Fiction of Flannery O'Connor and Walker Percy," *DAI* 40 (1979): 236A-37A.

Friedman, M. J., and L. A. Lawson, eds., *Added Dimension*.

Friedman, Melvin J., "Flannery O'Connor: Another Legend in Southern Fiction," *EJ* 51 (Apr., 1962): 233-43. Also, rev. and enl., in Friedman, M. J., and L. A. Lawson, eds., *Added Dimension*, 1-31. Also in Waldmeir, J. J., *Recent American Fiction*, 231-45. Also in Reiter, R. E., ed., *Flannery O'Connor*, 5-24.

_____, "Flannery O'Connor in France: An Interim Report," *RLV* 43 (1977): 435-42.

_____, "Flannery O'Connor's Sacred Objects," in Friedman, M. J., and L. A. Lawson, eds., *Added Dimension*, 196-205. Also, revised, in Friedman, M. J., ed., *Vision Obscured*, 67-77.

_____, "John Hawks and Flannery O'Connor: The French Background," *BUJ* 21, iii (1973): 34-44.

Gable, Sister Mariella, "Ecumenic Core in Flannery O'Connor's Fiction," *ABR* 15 (June, 1964): 127-43.

Gardiner, Harold C., "Flannery O'Connor's Clarity of Vision," in Friedman, M. J., and L. A. Lawson, eds., *Added Dimension*, 184-95.

Gattuso, Josephine F., "The Fictive World of Flannery O'Connor," *DA* (1969): 3136A.

Gordon, Caroline, "An American Girl," in Friedman, M. J., and L. A. Lawson, eds., *Added Dimension*, 123-37.

_____, "Heresy in Dixie," *SR* 76 (1968): 263-97.

_____, "Rebels and Revolutionaries: The New American Scene," *F10B* 3 (1974): 40-56.

_____, and others, "Panel Discussion," *F10B* 3 (1974): 57-78.

Gossett, L. Y., "The Test by Fire: Flannery O'Connor," *Violence in Recent Southern Fiction*, 75-97.

Gossett, Thomas F., "No Vague Believer: Flannery O'Connor and Protestantism," *SWR* 60, iii (Summer, 1975): 256-63.

Gregory, Donald L., "An Internal Analysis of the Fiction of Flannery O'Connor," *DA* 28 (1968): 5055A.

Gretlund, Jan N., "Flannery O'Connor and Katherine Anne Porter," *F1OB* 8 (1979): 77-87.

Griffith, Albert, "Flannery O'Connor," *America* 113 (Nov. 27, 1965): 674-5.

Grimshaw, J. A., Jr., *Flannery O'Connor Companion.*

Hand, John T., "Letters to the Laodiceans: The Romantic Quest in Flannery O'Connor," *DAI* 32 (1972): 5227A-28A.

Hauser, James D., "The Broken Cosmos of Flannery O'Connor: The Design of Her Fiction," *DAI* 34 (1973): 1912A.

Hawkes, John, "Flannery O'Connor's Devil," *SR* 70 (Summer, 1962): 395-407. Also in Reiter, R. E., ed., *Flannery O'Connor,* 25-37.

Hendin, Josephine, "In Search of Flannery O'Connor," *ColF* 13, i (Spring, 1970): 38-41.

_____, *World of Flannery O'Connor.*

Hines, Melissa, "Grotesque Conversions and Critical Piety," *F1OB* 6 (1977): 17-35.

Hoffman, F. J., *Art of Southern Fiction,* 81-6.

_____, "The Search for Redemption: Flannery O'Connor's Fiction," in Friedman, M. J., and L. A. Lawson, eds., *Added Dimension,* 32-48.

Holman, C. Hugh, "Detached Laughter in the South," in Cohen, S. B., ed., *Comic Relief,* 98-103.

_____, "Her Rue with a Difference: Flannery O'Connor and the Southern Literary Tradition," in Friedman, M. J., and L. A. Lawson, eds., *Added Dimension,* 73-87. Also in Holman, C. H., *Roots of Southern Writing,* 177-86.

Hyman, S. E., *Flannery O'Connor.*

Ireland, Patrick J., "The Place of Flannery O'Connor in Our Two Literatures: The Southern and the National Literary Traditions," *F1OB* 7 (1978): 47-63.

Jacobsen, Josephine, "A Catholic Quartet," *ChS* 47 (Summer, 1964): 149-52.

Johnson, Rhonda E., "A Translation of Silence: The Fiction of Flannery O'Connor," *DAI* 34 (1973): 3403A.

Katz, Claire, "Flannery O'Connor: A Rage of Vision," *DAI* 35 (1975): 6719A.

_____, "Flannery O'Connor's Rage of Vision," *AL* 46, i (Mar., 1974): 54-67.

Keller, Jane C., "The Comic Spirit in the Works of Flannery O'Connor," *DAI* 31 (1970): 2922A-23A.

Kim, Chrysostom, O.S.B., "'A Do-It-Yourself Religion' and the Grimly Comic in Flannery O'Connor," *ABR* 31, iii (Sept., 1980): 263-89.

Kirkland, William M., "Flannery O'Connor, the Person and the Writer," *East-West Review* 3 (Summer, 1967): 159-63.

Klevar, Harry L., "The Sacredly Profane and the Profanely Sacred: Flannery O'Connor and Erskine Caldwell as Interpreters of Southern Cultural Religious Traditions," *DAI* 31 (1971): 5407A-08A.

Koon, William, "'Hep Me Not to Be So Mean': Flannery O'Connor's Subjectivity," *SoR* 15, ii (1979): 322-32.

Lackey, Allen D., "Flannery O'Connor and Her Critics: A Survey and Evaluation of the Critical Response to the Fiction of Flannery O'Connor," *DAI* 33 (1972): 2383A-84A.

Leaver, James M., "The Finite Image: Attitudes toward Reality in the Works of Flannery O'Connor," *DAI* 37 (1976): 3626A-27A.

Lee, Marryat, "Flannery, 1957," *F1OB* 5 (1976): 39-60.

Lee, Michael J., "Clowns and Captives: Flannery O'Connor's Images of the Self," *DAI* 39 (1979): 6763A-64A.

Leeson, Richard M., "The Iconoclastic Art of Flannery O'Connor," *DAI* 43, ii (Aug., 1982): 46A.

Lensing, George, "De Chardin's Ideas in Flannery O'Connor," *Ren* 18 (Summer, 1966): 171-5.

MacDonald, Sara J., "The Aesthetics of Grace in Flannery O'Connor and Graham Greene," *DAI* 3 (1973): 5734A.

MacKethan, Lucinda H., "Hogpens and Hallelujahs: The Function of the Image in Flannery O'Connor's Grotesque Comedies," *BuR* 26, ii (1982): 31-44. [Not seen.]

Malin, Irving, "Flannery O'Connor and the Grotesque," in Friedman, M. J., and L. A. Lawson, eds., *Added Dimension,* 108-22.

Mallon, Anne M. G., "Mystic Quest in Flannery O'Connor's Fiction," *DAI* 41, xi (May, 1981): 4714A.

Marks, Margaret L., "Flannery O'Connor's American Models: Her Work in Relation to That of Hawthorne, James, Faulkner, and West," *DAI* 38 (1978): 4830A.

Martin, C. W., "The Convergence of Actualities: Themes in the Fiction of Flannery O'Connor," *DA* 28 (1968): 4180-81A.

_____, *True Country.*

Martin, Carter, "Comedy and Humor in Flannery O'Connor's Fiction," *F1OB* 4 (1975): 1-12.

_____, "Flannery O'Connor and Fundamental Poverty," *EJ* 60, iv (Apr., 1971): 458-61.

May, John R., S. J., "Flannery O'Connor and the New Hermeneutic," *F1OB* 2 (1973): 29-42.

_____, "Flannery O'Connor: Critical Consensus and the 'Objective' Interpretation," *Ren* 27 (Summer, 1975): 179-92.

_____, *Pruning Word.*

Mayer, David R., "The Blazing Sun and the Relentless Shutter: The Kindred Arts of Flannery O'Connor and Diane Arbus," *ChrC* 92 (Apr. 30, 1975): 435-40.

_____, "Flannery O'Connor and the Peacock," *AFS* 35, ii (1976): 1-16.

_____, "The Hermaphrodite and the Host: Incarnation as Vision and Method in the Fiction of Flannery O'Connor," *DAI* 34 (1973): 3415A-16A.

McBride, Mary, "Paradise Not Regained: Flannery O'Connor's Unredeemed Pilgrims in the Garden of Evil," *SCB* 40, iv (1980): 154-6.

McDonald, Henry, "The Moral Meaning of Flannery O'Connor," *ModA* 24 (Summer, 1980): 274-83.

McDonald, Russ, "Comedy and Flannery O'Connor," *SAQ* 81, ii (Spring, 1982): 188-201.

McFarland, D. T., *Flannery O'Connor.*

McKenzie, Barbara, "Flannery O'Connor and 'The Business of the Petrified Mind'," *GaR* 33 (1979): 817-26.

Meaders, Margaret I., "Flannery O'Connor: 'literary witch'," *ColQ* 10 (Spring, 1962): 377-86.

Mehl, Duane P., "Spiritual Reality in the Works of Flannery O'Connor," *DAI* 36 (1975): 3716A.

Mellard, James M., "Violence and Belief in Mauriac and O'Connor," *Ren* 26, iii (Spring, 1974): 158-68.

Merton, Thomas, "Flannery O'Connor," *Jubilee* 12 (Nov., 1964): 49-53.

Milder, Robert, "The Protestantism of Flannery O'Connor," *SoR* 11 (Oct., 1975): 802-9.

Montgomery, Marion, "The Artist as 'A Very Doubtful Jacob': A Reflection on Hawthorne and O'Connor," *SoQ* 16 (Jan., 1978): 95-103.

————, "Flannery O'Connor and the Jansenist Problem in Fiction," *SoR* 14, iii (1978): 438-48.

————, "Flannery O'Connor and the Natural Man," *MissQ* 21 (1968): 235-42.

————, "Flannery O'Connor, Eric Voegelin, and the Question that Lies between Them," *ModA* 22 (Spring, 1978): 133-43.

————, "Flannery O'Connor: Prophetic Poet," *FlOB* 3 (1974): 79-94.

————, "Flannery O'Connor: Realist of Distances," *RANAM* 4 (1971): 69-78.

————, "Flannery O'Connor's Imitation of Significant Action," *STwC* 3 (Spring, 1969): 55-46.

————, "Flannery O'Connor's Shocking Manners," *ModA* 21 (Fall, 1977): 407-13.

————, "Flannery O'Connor's Territorial Center," *Crit* 11, iii (1969): 101-8.

————, "Grace: A Tricky Fictional Agent," *FlOB* 9 (1980): 19-29.

————, "In Defense of Flannery O'Connor's Dragon," *GaR* 25 (1971): 302-16.

————, "Miss O'Connor and the Chirst-Haunted," *SoR* 4 (Summer, 1968): 665-72.

————, "O'Connor and Teilhard de Chardin: The Problem of Evil," *Ren* 22 (Autumn, 1969): 34-42.

————, "Of Cloaks and Hats and Doublings in Poe and Flannery O'Connor," *SCR* 11, i (Nov., 1978): 60-9.

————, "Some Reflections on Miss O'Connor and the Dixie Limited," *FlOB* 5 (1976): 70-81.

————, "Vision and the Eye for Detail in Poe and O'Connor," *FlOB* 6 (1977): 36-46.

Muller, G. H., *Nightmares and Visions.*

————, "Flannery O'Connor and the Catholic Grotesque," *DA* 28 (1968): 3193A.

Mullins, C. Ross, Jr., "Flannery O'Connor: An Interview," *Jubilee* 11 (June, 1963): 32-5.

Murphy, George D., and Caroline L. Cherry, "Flannery O'Connor and the Integration of Personality," *FlOB* 7 (1978): 85-100.

Murray, James G., "Southland ala Russe," *Critic* 21 (June-July, 1963): 26-2.

Nance, William L., "Flannery O'Connor: The Trouble with Being a Prophet," *UR* 36, ii (Winter, 1969): 101-8.

Neligan, Patrick, Jr., and Victor Nunez, "Flannery and the Film Makers," *FlOB* 5 (1976): 98-104.

Nisley, Paul W., "Flannery O'Connor and the Gothic Impulse," *DAI* 36 (1975): 892A-93A.

O'Brien, John T., "The Un-Christianity of Flannery O'Connor," *Listening* 5 (1971): 71-82.

O'Connor, Flannery, "The Novelist and Free Will," *Fresco* 1, ii (Winter, 1961): 100-1.

————, "The Role of the Catholic Novelist," *Greyfriar* (Sienna Studies in Literature) 7 (1964): 5-13.

Olson, Charles J., "The Dragon by the Road: An Archetypal Approach to the Fiction of Flannery O'Connor," *DAI* 36 (1975): 3698A.

O'Mara, Phil, "Part of the Literary Context of the Work of Flannery O'Connor," *POMPA* 1 (Summer, 1982): 39-49. [Not seen.]

Oppegaard, Susan H., "Flannery O'Connor and the Backwoods Prophet," in Seyersted, B., ed., *American-Norvegica*, 305-25.

Orvell, M., *Invisible Parade.*

Pachmuss, Temira, "Dostoevsky and America's Southern Women Writers: Parallels and Confluences," in Clayton, G. D., and G. Schaarscmidt, eds., *Poetica Slavica*, 120-5.

Padgett, Thomas E., Jr., "The Irony in Flannery O'Connor's Fiction," *DAI* 33 (1973): 5192A.

Park, Clara C., "Crippled Laughter: Toward Understanding Flannery O'Connor," *ASch* 51, ii (Spring, 1982): 249-57.

Pearce, Howard D., "Flannery O'Connor's Ineffable 'Recognitions'," *Genre* 6 (Sept., 1973): 298-312.

Quinn, Sister M. Bernetta, O.S.F., "Flannery O'Connor, A Realist of Distances," in Friedman, M. J., and L. A. Lawson, eds., *Added Dimension*, 157-83.

Ray, Donald L., "I. *Howard's End:* The Novel 'Opening Out'. II. Sir Thomas Wyatt's Protestant Petrarchism. III. Flannery O'Connor's Satires on American Liberalism," *DAI* 37 (1976): 300A.

Rechnitz, Robert M., "Perception, Identity, and the Grotesque: A Study of Three Southern Writers," *DA* 28 (1967): 2261A.

Regan, Robert, "The Legitimate Sources of Depravity in Flannery O'Connor," *DeltaES* 2 (1976): 53-9. [Not seen.]

Robinson, Gabriele S., "Irish Joyce and Southern O'Connor," *FlOB* 5 (1976): 82-97.

Rubin, Louis D., Jr., "Flannery O'Connor and the Bible Belt," in Friedman, M. J., and L. A. Lawson, eds., *Added Dimension*, 49-72. Also in Rubin, L. D., Jr., *Curious Death of the Novel*, 239-61.

Rupp, Richard H., "Flannery O'Connor," *Cweal* 79 (Dec. 6, 1963): 304-7.

Russ, Donald D., "Family in the Fiction of Flannery O'Connor," *DAI* 42, ii (Aug., 1981): 7050A-06A.

Schloss, C., *Flannery O'Connor's Dark Comedies.*

Schloss, Carol, "The Limits of Inference: Flannery O'Connor and the Representation of 'Mystery'," *DAI* 35 (1975): 5427A.

Scott, Nathan A., Jr., "Flannery O'Connor's Testimony: The Pressure of Glory," in Friedman, M. J., and L. A. Lawson, eds., *Added Dimension*, 138-56. Also in Scott, N. A., Jr., *Craters of the Spirit*, 267-85.

Scouten, Kenneth, "The Mythological Dimensions of Five of Flannery O'Connor's Works," *FlOB* 2 (1973): 59-72.

Sharp, Roberta, "Flannery O'Connor and Poe's 'Angel of the Odd'," *FlOB* 7 (1978): 116-28.

Shear, Walter, "Flannery O'Connor: Character and Characterization," *Ren* 20 (Spring, 1968): 140-6.

Sherry, Gerard E., "An Interview with Flannery O'Connor," *Critic* 21 (June-July, 1963): 26-8.

Shinn, Thelma J., "Flannery O'Connor and the Violence of Grace," *WSCL* 9 (Winter, 1968): 58-73.

Short, Donald A., "The Concrete is Her Medium: The Fiction of Flannery O'Connor," *DAI* 30 (1970): 3476A-77A.

Spivey, Ted R., "Flannery's South: Don Quixote Rides Again," *FlOB* 1 (1972): 46-53.

_____, "Religion and the Integration of Man in Flannery O'Connor and Walker Percy," in Simpson, L. P., ed., *Poetry of Community*, 67-79.

Stelzmann, Rainulf, "Shock and Orthodoxy: An Interpretation of Flannery O'Connor's Short Stories and Novels," *XUS* 2 (Mar., 1963): 4-21.

Stephens, M., *Question of Flannery O'Connor*.

Stephens, Martha, "Flannery O'Connor and the Sanctified-Sinner Tradition," *ArQ* 23, iv (Winter, 1967): 223-39.

_____, "Introduction to the Work of Flannery O'Connor," *DA* 29 (1969): 3157A.

Sullivan, Walter, "The Achievement of Flannery O'Connor," *SHR* 2 (Summer, 1968): 303-9.

Tate, J. O., "Faith and Fiction: Flannery O'Connor and the Problem of Belief," *F10B* 5 (1976): 105-11.

_____, "A Good Source is Not So Hard to Find," *F10B* 9 (1980): 98-103.

_____, "O'Connor's Confederate General: A Late Encounter," *F10B* 8 (1979): 45-53.

Tate, J. O., "Flannery O'Connor's Counterplot," *SoR* 16, iv (1980): 869-78.

True, Michael D., "Flannery O'Connor: Backwoods Prophet in the Secular City," *PLL* 5, ii (Spring, 1969): 209-23.

VandeKieft, Ruth M., "Judgement in the Fiction of Flannery O'Connor," *SR* 76 (1968): 337-56.

Walter, Sarah, "Strange Prophets of Flannery O'Connor," *Censer* (Spring, 1960): 5-12. [Not seen.]

Walters, D., *Flannery O'Connor*.

Washburn, Delores, "The 'Feeder' Motif in Selected Fiction of William Faulkner and Flannery O'Connor," *DAI* 40 (1979): 861A.

Wasserman, Renata R. M., "Backward to Ninevah," *Ren* 32, i (Autumn, 1979): 21-32.

Westling, Louise, "The Perils of Adolescence in Flannery O'Connor and Carson McCullers," *F10B* 8 (1979): 88-98.

Williams, David, "Flannery O'Connor and the *Via Negation*," *SRC* 8 (1979): 303-12.

Wilson, James D., "Louis Buñel, Flannery O'Connor and the Failure of Charity," *MinnR* 4 (Spring, 1973): 158-62.

Woodward, Harry H., "In Bold and Fearless Connection: A Study of the Fiction of Flannery O'Connor and the Photography of Diane Arbus," *DAI* 39 (1978): 3588A.

Wray, Virginia F., "Flannery O'Connor in the American Romance Tradition," *F10B* 6 (1977): 83-98.

_____, "Flannery O'Connor in the American Romance Tradition," *DAI* 40 (1979): 1475A.

Yordon, Judy E., "The Double Motif in the Fiction of Flannery O'Connor," *DAI* 38 (1977): 2421A.

Zaidman, Laura M., "Varieties of Religious Experience in O'Connor and West," *F10B* 7 (1978): 26-46.

THE VIOLENT BEAR IT AWAY

Allen, W., *Modern Novel*, 308-9.

Asals, F., *Flannery O'Connor*, 160-97.

Bailif, Algene, "A Southern Allegory: THE VIOLENT BEAR IT AWAY, by Flannery O'Connor," *Ctary* 30 (Oct., 1960): 358-62.

Barcus, Nancy B., "Psychological Determinism and Freedom in Flannery O'Connor," *Cithara* 12, i (Nov., 1972): 26-33.

Bergup, Sister Bernice, "Themes of Redemptive Grace in the Works of Flannery O'Connor," *ABR* 21 (June, 1970): 175-80.

Bleikasten, Andre, "The Heresy of Flannery O'Connor," in Johnson, I. D., and C. Johnson, eds., *Americanistes*, 58-65.

Bowen, Robert O., "Hope vs. Despair in the New Gothic Novel," *Ren* 13 (1961): 147-52.

Brinkmeyer, Robert H., Jr., "Borne Away by Violence: The Reader and Flannery O'Connor," *SoR* 15, ii (1979): 313-21.

Browning, P. M., Jr., *Flannery O'Connor*, 72-98.

_____, "Flannery O'Connor and the Grotesque Recovery of the Holy," in Scott, N. A., ed., *Adversity and Grace*, 147-61.

Burns, Stuart L., "Flannery O'Connor's THE VIOLENT BEAR IT AWAY: Apotheosis in Failure," *SR* 76 (1968): 319-36.

_____, "'Torn by the Lord's Eye': Flannery O'Connor's Use of Sun Imagery," *TCL* 13 (Oct., 1967): 163-6.

Chow, Sung G., "'Strange and Alien Country': An Analysis of Landscape in WISE BLOOD and THE VIOLENT BEAR IT AWAY," *F10B*, 35-44.

Coles, Robert, "Flannery O'Connor: A Southern Intellectual," *SoR* 16 (Jan., 1980): 50-6.

Davis, Barnabas, "Flannery O'Connor: Christian Belief in Recent Literature," *Listening* (Autumn, 1965): 15-18.

Davis, Jack and June, "Tarwater and Jonah: Two Reluctant Prophets," *XUS* 9, i (Spring, 1970): 19-27.

Desmond, John F., "The Mystery of the Word and the Act: THE VIOLENT BEAR IT AWAY," *ABR* 24 (1973): 83-6.

Donner, Robert, in *Sign* 40 (Mar., 1961): 46-8.

Drake, Robert, "The Bleeding Stinking Mad Shadow of Jesus in the Fiction of Flannery O'Connor," *CLS* 3 (1966): 194-5.

_____, *Flannery O'Connor*.

_____, "Miss O'Connor and the Scandal of Redemption," *ModA* 4 (Fall, 1960): 428-30.

Driskell, L. V., and J. T. Brittain, *Eternal Crossroads*, 81-91.

Duhamel, P. Albert, "Flannery O'Connor's Violent View of Reality," *CathW* 190 (Feb., 1960): 280-5. Also in Reiter, R. E., ed., *Flannery O'Connor*, 93-101.

_____, "The Novelist as Prophet," in Friedman, M. J., and L. A. Lawson, eds., *Added Dimension*, 88-106.

Dunn, Sister Francis M., P.B.V.M., "Functions and Implications of Setting in the Fiction of Flannery O'Connor," *DA* 27 (1967): 3043A.

Eggenschweiler, D., *Christian Humanism of Flannery O'Connor*, 114-40.

_____, "Flannery O'Connor's True and False Prophets," *Ren* 21 (Spring, 1969): 151-61, 167.

Emerson, Donald C., in *ArQ* 16 (Autumn, 1960): 284-6.

Fahey, William A., "Out of the Eater: Flannery O'Connor's Appetite for Truth," *Ren* 20 (Autumn, 1967): 22-9.

Feeley, K., S.S.N.D., *Flannery O'Connor*, 154-71.

Ferris, Sumner J., "The Outside and the Inside: Flannery O'Connor's THE VIOLENT BEAR IT AWAY," *Crit* 3, ii (Winter-Spring, 1960): 11-19.

Flores-Del Prado, Wilma, "Flannery O'Connor's Gallery of Freaks," *SLRJ* 2, iii-iv (Sept.-Dec., 1971): 473-510 *passim*.

Friedman, Melvin J., "Flannery O'Connor: Another Legend in Southern Fiction," *EJ* 51 (Apr., 1962): 242-3. Also in Waldmeir, J. J., *Recent American Fiction*, 243-5.

_____, "Flannery O'Connor's Sacred Objects," in Friedman, M. J., and L. A. Lawson, eds., *Added Dimension*, 201-2. Also, revised, in Friedman, M. J., ed., *Vision Obscured*, 71-3.

Gable, Sister Mariella, O.S.B., "Ecumenic Core in Flannery O'Connor's Fiction," *ABR* 15 (June, 1964): 132-6.

Gossett, L. Y., *Violence in Recent Southern Fiction*, 90-3.

Grimshaw, James A., Jr., "The Mistaken Identity of Rufus Johnson," *NMAL* 1 (1977): Item 1.

Hawkes, John, "Flannery O'Connor's Devil," *SR* 70 (Summer, 1962): 395-407 *passim*.

Hendin, J., *World of Flannery O'Connor*, 55-61.

Hoffman, F. J., *Art of Southern Fiction*, 90-5.

————, "The Search for Redemption: Flannery O'Connor's Fiction," in Friedman, F. J., and L. A. Lawson, eds., *Added Dimension*, 58-71.

Hood, Edward M., "A Prose Altogether Alive," *KR* 23 (Winter, 1961): 170-2.

Hyman, S. E., *Flannery O'Connor*, 19-25.

Jeremy, Sister, C.S.J., "THE VIOLENT BEAR IT AWAY: A Linguistic Education," *Ren* 17 (Fall, 1964): 11-16. Also in Reiter, R. E., ed., *Flannery O'Connor*, 103-10.

Keller, Jane C., "The Figures of the Empiricist and the Rationalist in the Fiction of Flannery O'Connor," *ArQ* 28, iii (Autumn, 1972): 263-73.

Kellogg, G., *Vital Tradition*, 193-203.

————, "The Catholic Convergence," *Thought* 55 (Summer, 1970): 291-2.

Kissel, Susan S., "Voices in the Wilderness: The Prophets of O'Connor, Percy and Powers," *SoQ* 18, iii (1980): 91-8.

Kinnebrew, Mary J., "Language from the Heart of Reality: A Study of Flannery O'Connor's Attitudes to Non-Standard Dialects and Her Use of It in WISE BLOOD, A GOOD MAN IS HARD TO FIND, and THE VIOLENT BEAR IT AWAY," *LNL* 1, iii (1976): 39-53.

Levine, Paul, "Flannery O'Connor: The Soul of the Grotesque," in Hoyt, C. A., ed., *Minor American Novelists*, 111-17.

Lorch, Thomas M., "Flannery O'Connor: Christian Allegorist," *Crit* 10, ii (1968): 69-80.

Malin, Irving, "Flannery O'Connor and the Grotesque," in Friedman, M. J., and L. A. Lawson, eds., *Added Dimension*, 118-22.

————, "The Gothic Family," *Psychoanalysis and American Fiction*, 269-71. Also in Malin, I., *New American Gothic*, 68-71.

Mallon, Anne M., "Mystic Quest in THE VIOLENT BEAR IT AWAY," *F10B* 10 (1981): 112-19.

Martin, C. W., *True Country*, 55-61, 77-82, 100-3, 125-9, 141-2, 182-5, 205-6, 236-7.

May, J. R., *Pruning Word*, 137-50.

May, J. R., *Toward a New Earth*, 126-44.

————, "THE VIOLENT BEAR IT AWAY: The Meaning of the Title," *F10B* 2 (1973): 83-6.

Mayer, David R., "THE VIOLENT BEAR IT AWAY: Flannery O'Connor's Shaman," *SLJ* 4, ii (Spring, 1972): 41-54.

McCarthy, John F., "Human Intelligence Versus Divine Truth: The Intellectual in Flannery O'Connor's Works," *EJ* 55 (Dec., 1966): 1143-5.

McCown, Robert M., "The Education of a Prophet: A Study of Flannery O'Connor's THE VIOLENT BEAR IT AWAY," *KM* (1962): 73-8.

McDermott, John V., "Voices and Vision in Tarwater's Odyssey," *Ren* 32, iv (Summer, 1980): 214-20.

McFarland, D. T., *Flannery O'Connor*, 91-111.

Merton, Thomas, "The Other Side of Despair," *Critic* 23 (Oct.-Nov., 1965): 14-15.

Montgomery, Marion, "In Defense of Flannery O'Connor's Dragon," *GaR* 25 (1971): 312-15.

Montgomery, Marion, "A Note on Flannery O'Connor's Terrible and Violent Prophecy of Mercy," *ForumH* 7, iii (Summer, 1969): 4-7.

Muller, G. H., *Nightmares and Visions*, 60-7.

————, "THE VIOLENT BEAR IT AWAY: Moral and Dramatic Sense," *Ren* 22 (Autumn, 1969): 17-25.

Nolde, Sister M. Simon, O.S.B., "The VIOLENT BEAR IT AWAY: A Study in Imagery," *XUS* 1 (1962): 180-94.

Orvell, M., *Invisible Parade*, 96-125.

Palms, Rosemary H. G., "The Double Motif in Literature: From Origins to an Examination of Three Modern American Novels," *DAI* 33 (1972): 321A.

Paulson, Suzanne M., "Apocalypse of Self, Resurrection of the Double: Flannery O'Connor's THE VIOLENT BEAR IT AWAY," *L&P* 30, iii-iv (1980): 100-11.

Pearce, R., *Stages of the Clown*, 78-83.

Pope, Robert, "Beginnings," *GaR* 36, iv (Winter, 1982): 733-51.

Quinn, John, in *Esprit* (Un. of Scranton) 7 (Winter, 1963): 28-31.

Quinn, Sister M. Bernetta, O.S.F., "Flannery O'Connor, a Realist of Distances," in Friedman, M. J., and L. A. Lawson, eds., *Added Dimension*, 178-81.

Rocco, Claire J., "Flannery O'Connor and Joyce Carol Oates: Violence as Art," *DAI* 36 (1976): 6090A.

Rubin, L. D., Jr., "Flannery O'Connor and the Bible Belt," in Friedman, M. J., and L. A. Lawson, eds., *Added Dimension*, 59-71. Also in Rubin, L. D., Jr., *Curious Death of the Novel*, 248-61.

Rupp, Richard H., "Flannery O'Connor: A Hidden Celebration," *Celebration in Postwar American Fiction*, 85-7.

Schloss, C., *Flannery O'Connor's Dark Comedies*, 80-101.

Scott, Nathan A., Jr., "Flannery O'Connor's Testimony: The Pressure of Glory," in Friedman, M. J., and L. A. Lawson, eds., *Added Dimension*, 144-8. Also in Scott, N. A., Jr., *Craters of the Spirit*, 274-8.

Smith, Francis J., S. J., "O'Connor's Religious Viewpoint in THE VIOLENT BEAR IT AWAY," *Ren* 22 (1979): 108-12.

Smith, J. Oates, "Ritual and Violence in Flannery O'Connor," *Thought* 41 (Winter, 1966): 545-60.

Smith, Patrick J., "Typology and Peripety in Four Catholic Novels," *DA* 28 (1967): 2265A.

Snow, Ollye T., "The Functional Gothic of Flannery O'Connor," *SIR* 50 (1965): 286-99.

Sonnenfeld, Albert, "Flannery O'Connor: The Catholic Writer as Baptist," *ConL* 13, iv (Autumn, 1972): 445-57.

Stelzmann, Rainulf, "Shock and Orthodoxy: An Interpretation of Flannery O'Connor's Novels and Short Stories," *XUS* 2 (Mar., 1963): 11-13, 19-20.

Stephens, M., *Question of Flannery O'Connor*, 98-143.

Strine, Mary S., "Narrative Strategy and Communicative Design in Flannery O'Connor's THE VIOLENT BEAR IT AWAY," 45-57 in Doyle, Esther M., and Virginia H. Floyd, eds., *Studies in Interpretation*, Vol. 2, Amsterdam: Rodopi, 1977.

Sullivan, Sister Bede, in *Catholic Library World*, 518-20.

Sullivan, Walter, "Southerners in the City: Flannery O'Connor and Walker Percy," in Rubin, L. D., Jr., ed., *Comic Imagination in American Literature*, 344-7.

Taylor, Henry, "The Halt Shall Be Gathered Together: Physical Deformity in the Fiction of Flannery O'Connor," *WHR* 22 (Autumn, 1968): 335-8.

Trowbridge, Clinton W., "The Symbolic Vision of Flannery O'Connor: Patterns of Imagery in THE VIOLENT BEAR IT AWAY," *SR* 76 (1968): 298-318.

Walters, D., *Flannery O'Connor*, 90-104.

Washburn, Delores, "The 'Feeder' in THE VIOLENT BEAR IT AWAY," *F10B* 9 (1980): 112-19.

Wasserman, Renata R. M., "Backwards to Ninevah," *Ren* 32, i (Autumn, 1979): 27-9.

Wray, Virginia F., "An Authorial Clue to the Significance of the Title THE VIOLENT BEAR IT AWAY," *F10B* 6 (1977): 107-8.

WISE BLOOD

Alvis, John, "WISE BLOOD: Hope in the City of the Profane," *Kerygma* 4 (Winter-Spring, 1965): 19-29.

Asals, F., *Flannery O'Connor*, 9-64.

Balazy, Teresa, "External Mediation in Flannery O'Connor's WISE BLOOD," *SAP* 9 (1977): 169-95.

Baumbach, Jonathan, "The Acid of God's Grace: The Fiction of Flannery O'Connor," *GaR* 17 (Fall, 1963): 334-46. Also in Baumbach, J., *Landscape of Nightmare*, 87-100.

Bergup, Sister Bernice, "Themes of Redemptive Grace in the Works of Flannery O'Connor," *ABR* 21 (June, 1970): 169-75.

Blackwell, [A.] Louise, "Flannery O'Connor's Literary Style," *AntigR* 10 (Summer, 1972): 57-62.

Bleikasten, Andre, "The Heresy of Flannery O'Connor," in Johnson, I. D., and C. Johnson, eds., *Americanistes*, 58-65.

Borgman, Paul, "Three Wise Men: The Comedy of O'Connor's WISE BLOOD," *C&L* 24, iii (Spring, 1975): 36-48.

Brown, Thomas H., "O'Connor's Use of Eye Imagery in WISE BLOOD," *SCB* 37, iv (1977): 138-44.

Browning, P. M., Jr., *Flannery O'Connor*, 25-39.

Bryant, J. H., *Open Door*, 258-64.

Burns, Stuart L., "Structural Patterns in WISE BLOOD," *XUS* 8, ii (Summer, 1969): 32-4.

————, "The Evolution of WISE BLOOD," *MFS* 16 (Summer, 1970): 147-62.

Butler, Rebecca, "The Mad Preacher in Three American Novels: MISS LONELYHEARTS, WISE BLOOD, LIGHT IN AUGUST," *DAI* 38 (1978): 4164-65A.

————, "WISE BLOOD'S Joy in Contradiction," *F10B* 10 (1981): 23-8.

Chow, Sung G., "'Strange and Alien Country': An Analysis of Landscape in WISE BLOOD and THE VIOLENT BEAR IT AWAY," *F10B* 8 (1979): 35-44.

Coindreau, M. E., *Time of William Faulkner*, 141-56.

Davis, Joe L., "Outraged, or Embarassed," *KR* 15 (Spring, 1963): 320-3, 324-5.

Drake, Robert, "The Bleeding Stinking Mad Show of Jesus in the Fiction of Flannery O'Connor," *CLS* 3 (1966): 186-8.

————, *Flannery O'Connor*, 18-23.

Driskell, L. V., and J. T. Brittain, *Eternal Crossroads*, 33-58.

Dula, Martha, "Evidences of the Prelapsarian in Flannery O'Connor's WISE BLOOD," *XUS* 11, ii (Winter, 1972): 1-12.

Dunn, Sister Francis M., P.B.V.M., "Functions and Implications of Setting in the Fiction of Flannery O'Connor," *DA* 27 (1967): 3043A.

Eggenschwiler, D., *Christian Humanism of Flannery O'Connor*, 101-14.

————, "Flannery O'Connor's True and False Prophets," *Ren* 21 (Spring, 1969): 151-61, 167.

Feeley, K., S.S.N.D., *Flannery O'Connor*, 56-69.

Feeley, Margaret P., "Flannery O'Connor's WISE BLOOD: The Negative Way," *SoQ* 17, ii (1979): 104-22.

Fitzgerald, Sally, "A Master Class: From the Correspondence of Caroline Gordon and Flannery O'Connor," *GaR* 33 (1979): 827-46 *passim*.

Flores-Del Prado, Wilma, "Flannery O'Connor's Gallery of Freaks," *SLRJ* iii-iv (Sept.-Dec., 1971): 473-510 *passim*.

Friedman, Melvin J., "Flannery O'Connor: Another Legend in Southern Fiction," *EJ* 51 (Apr., 1962): 240-2. Also in Waldmeir, J. J., ed., *Recent American Fiction*, 241-3.

Gable, Sister Mariella, "Ecumenic Core in Flannery O'Connor's Fiction," *ABR* 15 (June, 1964): 136-8.

Gafford, Charlotte K., "Chaucer's Pardoner and Hazel Motes of Georgia," 9-12 in Creed, Howard, ed., *Essays in Honor of Richebourg Gaillard McWilliams*, Birmingham, Ala.: Birmingham Southern College, 1970. [Birmingham Southern College Bulletin 63, ii (May, 1970).]

Gentry, Marshall B., "The Eye vs. the Body: Individual and Communal Grotesquerie in WISE BLOOD," *MFS* 28, iii (Autumn, 1982): 487-93.

Gordon, Caroline, "Flannery O'Connor's WISE BLOOD," *Crit* 2, ii (Fall, 1958): 3-10.

Gossett, L. Y., *Violence in Recent Southern Fiction*, 89-91.

Goyen, William, "Unending Vengeance," *NYTBR* (May 18, 1952): 4. Also in *DeltaES* 2 (1976): 31-2.

Graulich, Melody, "'They Ain't Nothing But Words': Flannery O'Connor's WISE BLOOD," *F10B* 7 (1978): 64-83.

Gray, R., *Literature of Memory*, 277-83.

Green, James L., "Enoch Emery and His Biblical Namesake in WISE BLOOD," *SSF* 10, iv (Fall, 1973): 417-19.

Gregory, Donald, "Enoch Emery: Ironic Doubling in WISE BLOOD," *F10B* 4 (1975): 52-64.

Grimshaw, James A., "Le Mot Juste: Hazel Motes' Name," *NMAL* 3 (1979): Item 14.

Harrison, Margaret, "Hazel Motes in Transit: A Comparison of Two Versions of Flannery O'Connor's 'The Train' with Chapter I of WISE BLOOD," *SSF* 8 (Spring, 1971): 287-93.

Hart, Jane, "Strange Earth, the Stories of Flannery O'Connor," *GaR* 12 (Summer, 1958): 217-19.

Hartman, Carl, "Jesus Without Christ," *WR* (Autumn, 1952): 76-81.

Hassan, I., *Radical Innocence*, 79-80.

Hendin, J., *World of Flannery O'Connor*, 43-55.

Hoffman, F. J., *Art of Southern Fiction*, 86-90.

————, "The Search for Redemption: Flannery O'Connor's Fiction," in Friedman, M. J., and L. A. Lawson, eds., *Added Dimension*, 37-41, 47-8.

Hyman, S. E., *Flannery O'Connor*, 9-15.

Kahane, Claire, "Comic Vibrations and Self-Construction in Grotesque Literature," *L&P* 26, iii (1979): 114-17.

Katz, Claire, "Flannery O'Connor: A Rage of Vision," *DAI* 35 (1975): 6719A.

Keller, Jane C., "The Figures of the Empiricist and the Rationalist in the Fiction of Flannery O'Connor," *ArQ* 28, iii (Autumn, 1972): 263-73.

Kellogg, Gene, "The Catholic in Convergence," *Thought* 55 (Summer, 1970): 288-91.

————, *Vital Tradition*, 184-93.

Kinnebrew, Mary J., "Language from the Heart of Reality: A Study of Flannery O'Connor's Attitudes toward Standard and Non-Standard Dialect and Her Use of It in WISE BLOOD, A GOOD MAN IS HARD TO FIND, and THE VIOLENT BEAR IT AWAY," *LNL* 1, iii (1976): 39-53.

Knutson, Roslyn L., "A Faust in Eastrod, Tennessee?" *PAPA* 5, ii-iii (1979): 16-22.

Koon, William, "'Hep Me Not To Be So Mean': Flannery O'Connor's Subjectivity," *SoR* 15, ii (1979): 325-8.

Lawson, Lewis A., "Flannery O'Connor and the Grotesque: WISE BLOOD," *Ren* 18 (Spring, 1965): 137-47. Also in Reiter, R. E., ed., *Flannery O'Connor*, 51-67.

LeClair, Thomas, "Flannery O'Connor's WISE BLOOD: The Oedipal Theme," *MissQ* 29 (1976): 197-205.

Levine, Paul, "Flannery O'Connor: The Soul of the Grotesque," in Hoyt, C. A., ed., *Minor American Novelists*, 107-11.

Littlefield, Daniel F., Jr., "Flannery O'Connor's WISE BLOOD: 'Unparalled Prosperity' and Spiritual Chaos," *MissQ* 23, ii (Spring, 1970): 121-33.

Lorch, Thomas, "Flannery O'Connor: Christian Allegorist," *Crit* 10, ii (1968): 69-80.

Malin, Irving, "Flannery O'Connor and the Grotesque," in Friedman, M. J., and L. A. Lawson, eds., *Added Dimension*, 109-13.

————, *New American Gothic*, 34-5.

Martin, C. W., *True Country*, 47-55, 66-71, 117-25, 194-5, 233-5.

————, "WISE BLOOD: From Novel to Film," *F10B* 9 (1979): 99-115.

Matchen, David E., and Wilton Beauchamp, "Enoch Emery: Flannery O'Connor and Jungian Psychology," *POMPA* 1 (Summer, 1982): 1-7.

May, J. R., *Pruning Word*, 125-37.

McCullagh, James C., "Aspects of Jansenism in Flannery O'Connor's WISE BLOOD," *StHum* 3, i (Oct., 1972): 12-16.

————, "Symbolism and the Religious Aesthetic in Flannery O'Connor's WISE BLOOD," *F10B* 2 (1973): 43-58.

McDermott, John V., "Dissociation of Words with the Word in WISE BLOOD," *Ren* 30 (1978): 163-6.

McFarland, D. T., *Flannery O'Connor*, 73-89.

McKenzie, Barbara, "The Camera and WISE BLOOD," *F10B* 10 (1981): 29-37.

Muzine, Matej, "A Reasonable Use of the Unreasonable: Flannery O'Connor and Leonid Andreev," *SRAZ* 23 (1979): 280-93.

Nelson, G. B., *Ten Versions of America*, 111-25.

Neuleib, Janice W., "Comic Grotesques: The Means of Revelation in WISE BLOOD and THAT HIDEOUS STRENGTH," *C&L* 30, iv (Summer, 1981): 27-36.

Orvell, M., *Invisible Parade*, 66-95.

Pearce, R., *Stages of the Clown*, 73-8.

Rechnitz, Robert M., "Passionate Pilgrim: Flannery O'Connor's WISE BLOOD," *GaR* 19 (Fall, 1965): 310-16.

Rocco, Claire J., "Flannery O'Connor and Joyce Carol Oates: Violence as Art," *DAI* 36 (1976): 6090A.

Rubin, Louis D., Jr., "Flannery O'Connor and the Bible Belt," in Friedman, M. J., and L. A Lawson, eds., *Added Dimension*, 55-8. Also in Rubin, L. D., Jr., ed., *Curious Death of the Novel*, 245-8.

Rupp, Richard H., "Flannery O'Connor: A Hidden Celebration," *Celebration in Postwar American Fiction*, 83-5.

Scott, Nathan, A., Jr., "Flannery O'Connor's Testimony: The Pressures of Glory," in Friedman, M. J., and L. A. Lawson, eds., *Added Dimension*, 150-4. Also in Scott, N. A., *Craters of the Spirit*, 180-5.

Simons, J. W., "A Case of Possession," *Cweal* 56 (June 27, 1952): 297-8.

Smith, J. Oates, "Ritual and Violence in Flannery O'Connor," *Thought* 41 (Winter, 1966): 545-60.

Snow, Ollye T., "The Functional Gothic of Flannery O'Connor," *SWR* 50 (1965): 298-9.

Sonnenfeld, Albert, "Flannery O'Connor: The Catholic Writer as Baptist," *ConL* 13, iv (Autumn, 1972): 445-57.

Stelzmann, Rainulf, "Shock and Orthodoxy: An Interpretation of Flannery O'Connor's Novels and Short Stories," *XUS* 2 (Mar., 1963): 8-9, 14-16, 18-19.

Stephens, Martha, "Flannery O'Connor and the Sanctified-Sinner Tradition," *ArQ* 23 (Winter, 1967): 229-36.

————, *Question of Flannery O'Connor*, 66-95.

Tate, James O., Jr., "Flannery O'Connor and WISE BLOOD: The Significance of the Early Drafts," *DAI* 36 (1975): 2828A-29A.

Taylor, Henry, "The Halt Shall Be Gathered Together: Physical Deformity in the Fiction of Flannery O'Connor," *WHR* 22 (Autumn, 1968): 335-8.

Walters, D., *Flannery O'Connor*, 42-62.

Wasserman, Renata R. M., "Backwards to Ninevah," *Ren* 32, i (Autumn, 1979): 23-7.

BIBLIOGRAPHY

Brittain, Joan T., "Flannery O'Connor: A Bibliography," *BB* 25 (Sept.-Dec., 1967): 98-100.

————, "Flannery O'Connor, Part 2," *BB* 25 (Jan.-Apr., 1968): 123-4.

Dorsey, James E., "Carson McCullers and Flannery O'Connor: A Checklist of Graduate Research," *BB* 32 (1975): 162-7.

Drake, R., *Flannery O'Connor*, 44-8.

Golden, Robert E., and Mary C. Sullivan, *Flannery O'Connor and Caroline Gordon: A Reference Guide*, Boston, G. K. Hall, 1977.

Hyman, S. E., *Flannery O'Connor*, 47-8.

Lackey, Allen D., "Flannery O'Connor: A Supplemental Bibliography of Secondary Sources," *BB* 30, iv (1973): 170-75.

Lawson, Lewis A., "Bibliography," in Friedman, M. J., and L. A. Lawson, ed., *Added Dimension*, 290-302.

Martin, C. W. *True Country*, 243-7.

Wedge, George F., "Two Bibliographies: Flannery O'Connor and J. F. Powers," *Crit* 2 (Fall, 1958): 59-63.

O'HARA, JOHN, 1905-1970

GENERAL

Aldridge, J. W., "The Pious Pornography of John O'Hara," *Time to Murder and Create*, 24-9.

Anon., "John O'Hara at 58: A Rage to Write," *Newsweek* 61 (June 3, 1963): 53-7.

Auchincloss, Louis, "Marquand and O'Hara: The Novel of Manners Today," *Nation* 191 (Nov. 19, 1960): 386-8. Also in Auchincloss, L., *Reflections of a Jacobite*, Boston: Houghton-Mifflin, 1961, 148-55.

Barrick, Mac E., "Proverbs and Sayings from Gibbsville, Pa.: John O'Hara's Use of Proverbial Materials," *KFQ* 12 (1967): 55-80.

Bassett, Charles W., "The Fictional World of John O'Hara," *DA* 26 (1965): 363-4.

_____, "Naturalism Revisited: The Case of John O'Hara," *CLQ* 11 (Dec., 1975): 198-218.

Bazelton, David, "O'Hara and America," *New Leader* 41 (Dec. 29, 1958): 18-19.

Bishop, J. P., "The Missing All," *VQR* 13, i (Winter, 1937): 120-21. Also in Bishop, J. P., *Collected Essays*, 249-50.

Browne, Joseph, "John O'Hara and Tom McHale: How Green Is Their Valley?" *JEthS* 6, ii (1978): 57-64. Also, expanded, in Casey, D. J., and R. E. Rhodes, eds., *Irish-American Fiction*, 127-33.

Carson, E. R., *Fiction of John O'Hara*.

Cobbs, John L., "The Pennsylvania Novels of John O'Hara," *DAI* 36 (1976): 6680A-81A.

Grebstein, S. N., *John O'Hara*.

McCormick, Bernard, "A John O'Hara Geography," *JML* 1, ii (1970): 151-68. Reprinted from *Philadelphia Magazine* (Nov. 1969).

Peirce, J. F., "An Appointment with O'Hara," *CCTE* 44 (1979): 17-23.

Portz, John, "John O'Hara Up to Now," *CE* 16 (May, 1955): 493-9, 516.

Ready, William, "The Dedication of John O'Hara," *Library Review* (Glasgow) 23, i-ii (Spring-Summer, 1971): 33-7.

Schanche, Don, "John O'Hara Is Alive and Well in the First Half of the Twentieth Century," *Esquire* 72, ii (Aug., 1969): 84-6, 142-9.

Sedlack, Robert P., "Manners, Morals, and the Fiction of John O'Hara," *DA* 26 (1965): 2224.

Shannon, William, "The Irish in Literature," *American Irish*, 244-9.

Tuttleton, J. W., *Novel of Manners in America*, 184-206.

Van Gelder, R., *Writers on Writing*, 59-61.

Walcutt, C. C., *John O'Hara*.

Weaver, Robert, "Twilight Area of Fiction: The Novels of John O'Hara," *QQ* 66 (Summer, 1959): 320-5.

Wilson, Edmond, "The Boys in the Back Room: John O'Hara," *NRep* (Nov. 11, 1940):665-6. Also in Wilson, E., *The Boys in the Back Room*, San Francisco: Colt Pr., 1941. Also in Wilson, E., *Classics and Commercials*, 22-6.

APPOINTMENT IN SAMARRA

Allen, W., *Modern Novel*, 182-3.

Bassett, Charles W., "John O'Hara and the Noble Experiment: The Use of Alcohol in APPOINTMENT IN SAMARRA," *JOHJ* 1, i (1978): 1-12.

Bassett, Charles W., "Naturalism Revisited: The Case of John O'Hara," *CLQ* 11 (Dec., 1975): 212-18.

Bier, Jesse, "O'Hara's APPOINTMENT IN SAMARRA: His First and Only Real Novel," *CE* 25 (Nov., 1963): 135-41.

Bruccoli, Matthew J., "Focus on APPOINTMENT IN SAMARRA: The Importance of Knowing What You Are Talking About," in Madden, D., ed., *Tough Guy Writers of the Thirties*, 129-36.

Carson, E. R., *Fiction of John O'Hara*, 9-14.

Donaldson, Scott, "Appointment With the Dentist: O'Hara's Naturalistic Novel," *MFS* 14 (Winter, 1968-69): 435-42.

Fadiman, Clifton, in *NY* (Sept. 1, 1934). Also in Fadiman, C., *Party of One*, 447-9.

Grebstein, S. N., *John O'Hara*, 34-45.

Gurko, L., *Angry Decade*, 113-15.

Hierth, Harrison E., "The Class Novel," *CEA* 27 (Dec., 1964): 1-4.

Kaida, Koichi, "O'Hara's APPOINTMENT IN SAMARRA," *KAL* 23 (May, 1982): 35-40.

Levi, A. W., *Literature, Philosophy and the Imagination*, 264-6.

Levine, Philip, "[John O'Hara]," *JOHJ* 3, i-ii (Fall-Winter, 1980): 167.

Malin, Irving, "[John O'Hara]," *JOHJ* 3, i-ii (Fall-Winter, 1980): 169.

Miller, James E., "[John O'Hara]," *JOHJ* 3, i-ii (Fall-Winter, 1980): 150.

O'Cain, Raymond K., "'Dictionaries Consult Mel'," *JOHJ* 1, i (1978): 29-34.

Podhoretz, Norman, "Gibbsville and New Leeds: The America of John O'Hara and Mary McCarthy," *Ctary* 21 (Mar., 1956): 269-70. Also in Podhoretz, N., *Doings and Undoings*, 77-9.

Sedlack, Robert P., "Manners, Morals, and the Novels of John O'Hara," *DA* 26 (1965): 2224.

Tuttleton, J. H., *Novel of Manners in America*, 195-200, 203-5.

Walcutt, C. C., *John O'Hara*, 13-17.

Weaver, Robert, "Twilight Area of Fiction: The Novels of John O'Hara," *QQ* 66 (1959): 322-3.

Young Philip, "A Letter," *JOHJ* 3, i-ii (Fall-Winter, 1980): 96-7.

THE BIG LAUGH

Grebstein, S. N., *John O'Hara*, 112-16.

Walcutt, C. C., *John O'Hara*, 29-32.

BUTTERFIELD 8

Fadiman, C., *Party of One*, 449-52.

Grebstein, S. N., *John O'Hara*, 92-7.

ELIZABETH APPLETON

Boroff, David, "A Rage to Relive," *SatR* 46 (June 8, 1963): 29-30.

Grebstein, S. N., *John O'Hara*, 75-82.

Walcutt, C. C., *John O'Hara*, 32-6.

THE EWINGS

Thompson, Irene, "Homophobia in the Heartland," *JOHJ* 5, i-ii (Winter, 1983): 11-17.

A FAMILY PARTY

Grebstein, S. N., *John O'Hara*, 85-7.

THE FARMER'S HOTEL

Grebstein, S. N., *John O'Hara*, 83-5.

FROM THE TERRACE

Bazelton, David, "O'Hara and America," *New Leader* 41 (Dec. 29, 1958): 18-19.

Carson, E. R., *Fiction of John O'Hara*, 29-40.

Gardiner, Harold C., "A Terrace Bound By Curbstones," *America* 100 (Dec. 13, 1958): 347-8. Also in Gardiner, H. C., *In All Conscience*, 141-2.

Grebstein, S. N., *John O'Hara*, 63-9.

Hicks, Granville, "The Problem of O'Hara," *SatR* 41 (Nov. 29, 1958): 14-15.

Kazin, A., *Contemporaries*, 161-8.

Maloff, Saul, in *NRep* 140 (Jan. 5, 1959): 20-1.

Mizener, Arthur, "Something Went Seriously Wrong," *NYTBR* (Nov. 23, 1958): 1, 14.

Sedlack, Robert P., "Manners, Morals, and the Fiction of John O'Hara," *DA* 26 (1965): 224.

Wain, John, "Snowed Under," *NY* 34 (Jan. 10, 1959): 112-14.

Walcutt, C. C., *Man's Changing Mask*, 314-16.

Weaver, Robert, "Twilight Area of Fiction: The Novels of John O'Hara," *QQ* 66 (1959): 320-5 *passim*.

West, P., *Modern Novel*, v.2, 231-2.

HOPE OF HEAVEN

Fadiman, C., *Party of One*, 452-4.

See, Carolyn, in Madden, D., ed., *Tough Guy Writers of the Thirties*, 211-13.

Wells, W., *Tycoons and Locusts*, 36-48.

THE LOCKWOOD CONCERN

Walcutt, C. C., *John O'Hara*, 37-45.

OURSELVES TO KNOW

Adams, Phoebe, "Lolita in Pa.," *Atlantic* 205 (Mar., 1969): 120-1.

Carson, E. R., *Fiction of John O'Hara*, 40-5.

Grebstein, S. N., *John O'Hara*, 69-75.

Mizener, Arthur, "Some Kinds of Modern Novel," *SR* 69 (Winter, 1961): 156-8.

A RAGE TO LIVE

Carson, E. R., *John O'Hara*, 14-21.

Cobbs, John L., "Caste and Class War: The Society of John O'Hara's A RAGE TO LIVE," *JOHJ* 2, i (1979-80): 24-34.

Grebstein, S. N., *John O'Hara*, 45-54.

Prescott, O., *In My Opinion*, 72-4.

Sedlack, Robert P., "Manners, Morals, and the Fiction of John O'Hara," *DA* 26 (1965): 2224.

TEN NORTH FREDERICK

Alexander, Sidney, "Another Visit to O'Haraville," *Reporter* 14 (Jan. 26, 1956): 44-7.

Carson, E. R., *Fiction of John O'Hara*, 21-9.

Fiedler, Leslie, "Old Pro at Work," *NRep* 134 (Jan. 9, 1956): 16-17.

Gardiner, Harold C., "Drained of Drama," *America* 94 (Dec. 10, 1955): 307-8.

Grebstein, S. N., *John O'Hara*, 54-63.

McKelway, St. Clair, "And Nothing But the Truth," *NY* 31 (Dec. 17, 1955): 162, 165-6.

Podhoretz, Norman, "Gibbsville and New Leeds: The America of John O'Hara and Mary McCarthy," *Ctary* 21 (Mar., 1956): 269-71. Also in Podhoretz, N., *Doings and Undoings*, 76-80.

Roberts, Rex, "On TEN NORTH FREDERICK," *JOHJ* 2, ii (1980): 69-87.

Sedlack, Robert P., "Manners, Morals and the Fiction of John O'Hara," *DA* 26 (1965): 2224.

BIBLIOGRAPHY

See Issues of *John O'Hara Journal*.

Grebstein, S. N., *John O'Hara*, 161-71.

OLSEN, TILLIE, 1913-

GENERAL

Burkhom, Selma, and Margaret Williams, "DeRiddling Tillie Olsen's Writings," *SJS* 2, i (Feb., 1976): 65-83.

McElhiney, Annette B., "Alternative Responses to Life in Tillie Olsen's Work," *Frontiers* 2, i (1977): 76-91.

Park-Fuller, Linda M., "Tillie Olsen: A Phenomenological Study of Consciousness with Implications for Performance," *DAI* 41 (1981): 4541A-42A.

YONNONDIO

Duncan, Erika, "Coming of Age in the Thirties: A Portrait of Tillie Olsen," *BForum* 6, ii (1982): 207-22 *passim*.

McElhiney, Annette B., "Alternative Responses to Life in Tillie Olsen's Work," *Frontiers* 2, i (1977): 85-90.

Rhodes, Caroline, "'Beedo' in Olsen's YONNONDIO: Charles E. Bedaux," *AN&Q* 14 (1975): 23-5.

OMOTOSO, KOLE, 1946-

GENERAL

Dash, Cheryl M. L., "An Introduction to the Prose Fiction of Kole Omotoso," *WLWE* 16, i (Apr., 1977): 39-53.

Dohan, Oyado, "Kole Omotoso in Review," *Indigo* 2, iii (1975): 14, 16-19. [Not seen.]

Lindfors, Bernth, "Kole Omotoso Interviewed," *CulEA* 103 (1973): 2-12. Also in Lindfors, B., ed., *Dem-Say*, 48-56.

Nazareth, Peter, "The Tortoise Is An Animal, But He Is Also a Wise Creature," *Umoja* 2, ii (1975): 38-47. [Not seen.]

ORWELL, GEORGE, 1903-1950

GENERAL

Alldritt, K., *Making of George Orwell*.

Ashe, Geoffrey, "A Note on George Orwell," *Cweal* 54 (June 1, 1951): 191-3.

Atkins, J., *George Orwell*.

————, *George Orwell*, new ed.

Alver, Leonard, "The Relevance of George Orwell," *ELLS* 8 (1971): 65-79. [Not seen.]

Bakker, J., "Socialism, Art, and George Orwell," *DQR* 6, i (1976): 44-56.

Bal, Sant S., "The Nature of Orwell's Appeal," *LCrit* 14, iv (1979): 10-21.

Barr, Donald, "The Answer to George Orwell," *SatR* 40 (Mar. 30, 1957): 21, 30-2.

Beadle, Gordon, "George Orwell and Charles Dickens: Moral Critics of Society," *JHS* 2 (1969-70): 245-55.

_____, "George Orwell and the Death of God," *ColQ* 23, i (Summer, 1974): 51-63.

_____, "George Orwell's Literary Studies of Poverty in England," *TCL* 24, ii (Summer, 1978): 188-201.

Beker, Miroslav, "The Ambivalence of George Orwell: A Note," *SRA* 13-14 (July-Dec., 1962): 117-21.

_____, "The Duality of George Orwell," *Geste* (Leeds Un.) 6 (Oct. 27, 1960): 15-17. [Not seen.]

Berga i Bagué, Miguel, "The Publishing of George Orwell's Books: A Political Tell-Tale," *ADI* (1979): 71-84. [Not seen.]

Birrell, T. A., "Is Integrity Enough?" *DubR* 224 (3rd quarter, 1950): 49-65.

Brander, Laurence, *George Orwell.*

_____, "George Orwell: Politics and Good Prose," *LonM* 1 (Apr., 1954): 64-71.

Braybrooke, Neville, "George Orwell," *CathW* 178 (Dec., 1953): 178-84.

_____, "George Orwell," *Fortnightly* 175 (June, 1951): 403-9.

_____, "George Orwell: An English Radical in the Christian Tradition," *Christus Rex* 7 (July, 1953): 617-24.

Buckley, David P., "The Novels of George Orwell," *DA* 26 (1966): 7310-11.

Burns, Wayne, "George Orwell: our 'responsible Quixote'," *WCR* 2 (Sept., 1967): 13-21.

Calder, J., *Chronicles of Conscience.*

Colquitt, Betsy F., "Orwell: Traditionalist in Wonderland," *Discourse* 8 (Autumn, 1965): 370-83.

Concannon, Gerald J., "The Development of George Orwell's Art," *DAI* 34 (1973): 3386A.

Cook, Richard, "Rudyard Kipling and George Orwell," *MFS* 7 (Summer, 1961): 125-35.

Cosman, Max, "George Orwell and the Autonomous Individual," *PacSp* 9 (Winter, 1955): 74-84.

_____, "Orwell's Terrain," *Person* 35 (Jan., 1954): 41-9.

Crick, Bernard, "Coming Up Orwell," *NStat* (Oct. 8, 1971): 478-9.

Crompton, Donald, "False Maps of the Word—George Orwell's Autobiographical Writings and the Early Novels," *CritQ* 16, ii (Summer, 1974): 149-69.

Crowcroft, Peter, "Politics and Writing. The Orwell Analysis," *NRep* 132 (Jan. 3, 1953): 17-18.

Dooley, David, "The Impact of Satire on Fiction: Studies in Norman Douglas, Sinclair Lewis, Aldous Huxley, Evelyn Waugh, and George Orwell," *DA* 15 (1955): 2203-4.

_____, "The Limitations of George Orwell," *UTQ* 28 (Apr., 1959): 291-300.

Duffey, Paula, "Form and Meaning in the Novels of George Orwell," *DA* 28 (1967): 1816A.

Duncan, Iris J. A., "The Theme of the Artist's Isolation in Works by Three Modern British Novelists," *DA* 26 (1965): 3332.

Dutscher, Alan, "Orwell and the Crisis of Responsibility," *Contemporary Issues* (London) 7 (Aug.-Sept., 1956): 308-16.

Eagleton, Terry, "Orwell and the Lower-Middle Class Novel," in Eagleton, T., *Exiles and Emigres,* 78-108. Also in Williams, R., ed., *George Orwell,* 10-33.

Edelheit, S., *Dark Prophecies.*

Edrich, Emanuel, "George Orwell and the Satire in Horror," *TSLL* 4 (Spring, 1962): 96-108.

_____, "Literary Technique and Social Temper in the Works of George Orwell," *DA* 21 (1960): 620-1.

Elliott, George P., "A Failed Prophet," *HudR* 10 (Spring, 1957): 149-54.

Espey, David B., "George Orwell vs. Christopher Caudwell," *IllQ* 36, iv (Apr., 1974): 45-60.

Fiderer, Gerald L., "Masochism as Literary Strategy: Orwell's Psychological Noels," *L&P* 20, i (1970): 3-21.

_____, "A Psychoanalytic Study of the Novels of George Orwell," *DA* 28 (1967): 1074A-75A.

Fitzgerald, John J., "George Orwell's Social Compassion," *Discourse* 9 (Spring, 1966): 219-26.

Fixler, Michael, "George Orwell and the Instrument of Language," *IEY* 9 (1964): 46-54. [Not seen.]

Forsyth, R. A., "Robert Buchanan and the Dilemma of the Brave New Victorian World," *SEL* 9 (1969): 647-57.

Fyvel, T. R., "George Orwell and Eric Blair: Glimpses of a Dual Life," *Encounter* 13 (July, 1959): 60-5.

Gandhi, Gopalkrishna, "'The Village in the Jungle': George Orwell and Leonard Woolf: Notes on Certain Resemblances," *EB* 4 (1980): 42-53. [Not seen.]

Gray, Colin, "The George Orwell Myth," *Chauntecleer* 6 (1972): 45-56. [Not seen.]

Glicksberg, Charles I., "The Literary Contribution of George Orwell," *ArQ* 10 (Autumn, 1954): 234-45.

Gloversmith, Frank, ed., "Changing Things: Orwell and Auden," 101-41 in Gloversmith, Frank, ed., *Class, Culture and Social Change: A New View of the 1930's,* Brighton, Eng.: Harvester, 1980; Atlantic Highlands, N.J.: Humanities, 1980.

Glusman, John A., "The Style Was the Man," *LitR* 25, iii (Spring, 1982): 431-47.

Greenblatt, S. J., *Three Modern Satirists,* 37-73, 105-17.

Greenfield, Robert M., "Discursive Orwell," *DA* 28 (1967): 1818A-19A.

Griffin, C. W., "Orwell and the English Language," *Audience* 7 (Winter, 1960): 63-76.

Gross, M., ed., *World of George Orwell.*

Hamilton, Ian, "Making Up His Mind," *NStat* (Sept. 24, 1976): 414.

Hartley, Roger, "Orwell: Political Criticism and Fictional Vision," 232-44 in Barker, Francis, Jay Bernstein, John Coombes, Peter Hule, David Musselwhite, Jennifer Stone, eds., *Practices of Literature and Politics,* Colchester: Un. of Essex, 1979.

Hobbs, Arthur H., "Welfarism and Orwell's Reversal," *Intercollegiate Rev.* (Bryn Mawr) 6, iii (1970): 105-12. [Not seen.]

Hodge, Bob, and Roger Fowler, "Orwellian Linguistics," 6-25 in Fowler, Roger, Bob Hodge, Gunther Kress, and Tony Trew, *Language and Control,* London: Routledge, 1979.

Hollis, C., *Study of George Orwell.*

Hopkinson, Tom, *George Orwell.*

_____, "George Orwell—Dark Side Out," *Cornhill* 166 (Summer, 1953): 450-70.

Hunter, Jefferson E., "George Orwell and the Uses of Literature," *DAI* 34 (1973): 2629A.

_____, "Orwell's Prose: Discovery, Communion, Separation," *SR* 87, iii (1977): 436-54.

Ingle, Stephen J., "The Politics of George Orwell: A Reappraisal," *QQ* 80 (Spring, 1973): 22-33.

Islam, Shamsul, "George Orwell and the Raj," *WLWE* 21, ii (Summer, 1982): 341-7.

Jackson, Alan S., "George Orwell's Utopian Vision," *DA* 26 (1965): 2215.

Jain, Jasbir, "Orwell: Linguistic Nihilism and New Words," *New Quest* 1 (May, 1977): 57-60.

_____, "Orwell: The Myth of a Classless Society," *Quest* 72 (1971): 95-100.

_____, "The Vision of Orwell," *RUSEng* 5 (1971): 68-86. [Not seen.]

Jowitt, J. A., and R. K. S. Taylor, eds., *George Orwell.*

Kalechofsky, R., *George Orwell.*

Karl, F. R., "George Orwell: The White Man's Burden," *Contemporary English Novel*, 148-66.

Kateb, George, "The Road to 1984," *PSciQ 81*, iv (Dec., 1966): 564-80.

Kearse, Lee A., Jr., "George Orwell: Romantic Utopian," *DAI* 34 (1974): 6593A-94A.

Kendall, Walter, "David and Goliath ... A Study of the Political Ideas of George Orwell," *Geste* (Leeds Un.) 6 (Oct. 27, 1960): 3-14. [Not seen.]

King, Carlyle, "The Politics of George Orwell," *UTQ* 26 (1956): 79-91.

Kirk, Russell, "George Orwell's Despair," *Intercollegiate Rev.* (Bryn Mawr) 5, i (1968): 21-5.

Knapp, John, "George Orwell: An Evaluation of His Early Fiction," *DAI* 32 (1972): 5794A.

_____, "Orwell's Fiction: Funny but Not Vulgar," *MFS* 27, ii (Summer, 1981): 294-301.

Kubal, D. L., *Outside the Whale.*

Laurenson, Diana T., and Alan Swingewood, "George Orwell, Socialism and the Novel," *Sociology of Literature*, 249-63.

Leckie, Robert, "The Man Who Invented Big Brother," *Saga* 25 (Oct., 1962): 36-8, 88-9. [Not seen.]

Lee, Robert A., *Orwell's Fiction.*

_____, "The Spanish Experience: George Orwell and the Politics of Language," *DA* 27 (1967): 3053A.

Lief, R. A., *Homage to Oceania.*

Lowenthal, David, "Orwell: Ethics and Politics in the Pre-NINETEEN EIGHTY-FOUR Writings," in Barber, B. R., and J. G. McGrath, eds., *Artist and Political Vision*, 335-60.

Mander, John, "Orwell in the Sixties," *The Writer and Commitment*, London: Secker and Warburg, 1961, 71-102.

Matthews, Brian, "'Fearful Despair' and a 'Frigid, Snooty Muse': George Orwell's Involvement with T. S. Eliot, 1930-1950," *SoRA* 10 (1977): 205-31.

_____, "'A Kind of Semi-Sociological Literary Criticism': George Orwell, Kylie Tennant and Others," *Westerly* 26, ii (June, 1981): 65-72. [Not seen.]

_____, "The Orwellian Fat Men," *SoRA* 13, ii (July, 1980): 101-19.

McCormack, Robert, "Orwell," *TamR* 58 (1971): 77-83.

Mellichamp, Leslie, "George Orwell and the Ethics of Revolutionary Politics," *ModA* 9 (1965): 272-8.

_____, "A Study of George Orwell: The Man, His Import, and His Outlook," *DAI* 30 (1969): 729A-30A.

Meyers, J., ed., *George Orwell.*

_____, *Reader's Guide to George Orwell.*

Mohaptra, Himansu S., "Orwell's Image of the Writer," *Littcrit* 8 (1979): 42-7.

Nair, K. Narayanan, "Orwell's Guilt Complex and the Submersion-Reversion Pattern in His Writings," in Menon, K.P.K., et al., ed., *Literary Studies*, 119-25.

North, Roy, "George Orwell," *Visva-Bharati Q* 19 (Summer, 1953): 39-56.

O'Donnell, Donat, "Orwell Looks at the World," *NStat* 62 (May 26, 1961): 837-8. Also in O'Brien, C. C., *Writers and Politics*, N.Y.: Pantheon, 1964, 31-5.

O'Flinn, Paul, "Orwell and *Tribune*," *L&H* 6 (1980): 201-18.

Orwell, George, "Some Letters of George Orwell," *Encounter* 18 (Jan., 1962): 55-65.

_____, "Why I Write," *Such, Such Were the Joys*, 3-11.

Oxley, B. T., *George Orwell.*

Petts, Paul, "Don Quixote on a Bicycle: In Memorium, George Orwell, 1903-1950," *LonM* 4 (Mar., 1957): 39-47.

Philmus, Robert M., "In Search of George Orwell," *SFS* 6 (Nov., 1979): 327-32.

Quintana, Ricardo, "George Orwell: The Satiric Resolution," *WSCL* 2, i (Winter, 1961): 31-8.

Rees, R., *George Orwell.*

_____, "George Orwell (1903-1959)," in Panichas, G. A., ed., *Politics of Twentieth Century Novelists*, 85-99.

Rieff, Philip, "George Orwell and the Post-Liberal Imagination," *KR* 16 (Winter, 1954): 49-70. Also in Howe, I., ed., *Orwell's NINETEEN EIGHTY-FOUR*, 227-37.

Rossi, John P., "Orwell and Catholicism," *Cweal* 103, xiii (June, 18, 1976): 404-6.

_____, "Orwell's Reception in America," *FQ* 22, ii (Winter, 1973): 31-9.

_____, "Orwell's Road to Socialism," *FQ* 28, i (Autumn, 1978): 3-10.

Rovere, Richard H., "George Orwell," *NRep* 135 (Sept. 10, 1956): 11-15. Also (expanded) as "Introduction," *The George Orwell Reader*, N.Y.: Harcourt, Brace, 1956, ix-xxi. Also in Rovere, R. H., *The American Establishment, and Other Reports, Opinions and Speculations*, N.Y.: Harcourt, Brace & World, 1962, 167-81.

Ruppe, John P., "In Search of Common Humanity: A Critical Study of the Early Novels and Essays of George Orwell," *DAI* 32 (1972): 5244A.

Sandison, A., *Last Man in Europe.*

Sani Zavarise, Fulvia, "The Social Commitment of George Orwell and J. K. Galbraith: An Analysis of Their Styles," *BILEUG* 11 (1978): 176-85. [Not seen.]

Scott, Nathan A., "The Example of George Orwell," *Chr&Cr* 19 (July 20, 1959): 107-10.

Shibata, Toshihiko, "The Road to Nightmare: An Essay on George Orwell," *SELL* 12 (1962): 41-53.

Slater, Ian D., "Orwell and the Road to Servitude," *DAI* 39 (1978): 453A.

Small, C., *Road to Miniluv.*

Smith, K., "'Oldspeak' and 'Newspeak'," in Jowitt, J. A., and R. K. S. Taylor, eds., *George Orwell*, 84-100.

Smith, W. D., "George Orwell," *ConR* 189, No. 1085 (May, 1956): 283-6.

Smyer, R. I., *Primal Dream and Primal Crime.*

_____, "Structure and Meaning in the Works of George Orwell," *DA* 29 (1968): 615A.

Snyder, Philip J., "Doing the Necessary Task: The Bourgeois Humanism of George Orwell," *DA* 25 (1965): 6636-7.

Spencer, L., "The Novel of the 1930's," in Jowitt, J. A., and R. K. S. Taylor, eds., *George Orwell*, 46-66.

Sperber, Murray A., "The Author as Culture Hero: H. G. Wells and George Orwell," *Mosaic* 14, iv (Fall, 1981): 15-29.

Stevens, A. Wilbur, "George Orwell and Southeast Asia," *YCGL* 11 (1962): 133-41.

Sutherland, Robert W., Jr., "The Political Ideas of George Orwell: A Liberal's Odyssey in the Twentieth Century," *DA* 29 (1969): 4563A-64A.

Tambling, Victor R. S. "Following in the Footsteps of Jack London: George Orwell, Writer and Critic," *JLoN* 11 (1978): 63-70.

Taylor, R., "George Orwell and the Politics of Decency," in Jowitt, J. A., and R. K. S. Taylor, eds., *George Orwell*, 19-45.

Thirlby, Peter, "Orwell as a Liberal," *MarxistQ* 3, iv (Oct., 1956): 239-47.

Thody, Philip, "The Curiosity of George Orwell," *ULR* 12 (1969): 69-90.

Thomas, E. M., *Orwell*.

Thompson, Fran H., Jr., "Orwell's Image of the Man of God Will," *CE* 22 (Jan., 1961): 235-40.

Tibbetts, A. M., "What Did Orwell Think about the English Language?" *CCC* 29 (1978): 162-6.

Trilling, Lionel, "George Orwell and the Politics of Truth," *Ctary* 13 (Mar., 1952): 218-27. Also as "Introduction" to Orwell, G., *Homage to Catalonia*, N.Y.: Harcourt, Brace, 1952. Also in Trilling, L., *The Opposing Self*, N.Y.: Viking, 1955. Also in Howe, I., ed., *Orwell's NINETEEN EIGHTY-FOUR*, 217-26.

Van Dellen, Robert J., "Politics in Orwell's Fiction," *DAI* 33 (1973): 6378A.

Voorhees, Richard J., "George Orwell: Rebellion and Responsibility," *SAQ* 53 (Oct., 1954): 556-65.

_____, "Orwell's Secular Crusade," *Cweal* 61 (Jan. 28, 1955): 448-51.

_____, *Paradox of George Orwell*.

Wain, John, "Here Lies Lower Binfield," *Encounter* 17 (Oct., 1961): 70-83.

_____, "Orwell and Intelligentsia," *Encounter* 31, vi (1968): 72-80.

_____, "Orwell in Perspective," in *New World Writing*, 12th Mentor Selection, N.Y.: New American Library, 84-96. Also in Wain, J., *Essays on Literature and Ideas*, N.Y.: St. Martin's Pr.; London: Macmillan, 180-93.

_____, "Orwell in the Thirties," in Gross, M., ed., *World of George Orwell*, 76-90. Also in Wain, J., *House for the Truth*, 43-66.

Warncke, Wayne, "George Orwell's Critical Approach to Literature," *SHR* 2 (1968): 484-98. [Not seen.]

_____, "The Permanence of Orwell," *UR* 33 (Mar., 1967): 189-96.

West, A., *Principles and Persuasions*, 164-76.

Williams, Raymond, *Culture and Society, 1780-1950*, N.Y.: Columbia Un. Pr., 1958; N.Y.: Harper Torchbooks, 1966, 285-94.

_____, *George Orwell*.

_____, ed., *George Orwell*.

_____, "Observation and Imagination in Orwell," in Williams, R., *George Orwell*, 39-52. Also in Williams, R., ed., *George Orwell*, 52-61.

Willison, Ian, "Orwell's Bad Good Books," *TC* 157 (Apr., 1955): 354-66.

Woodcock, George, *Crystal Spirit*.

_____, "The Deepening Solitude," *Malahat Rev.* 5 (Jan., 1968): 57-62.

_____, *Writer and Politics*, 111-24.

_____, "George Orwell, 19th Century Liberal," *Politics* 3 (Dec., 1946): 384-8.

Workman, Gillian, "Orwell Criticism," *ArielE* 3, i (Jan., 1972): 62-73.

World Review, n.s. 16 (June, 1950). Orwell issue.

Wufsberg, Frederick, "George Orwell," *Norseman* (Mar.-Apr., 1950): 90-4.

Zehr, David M., "George Orwell: The Novelist Displaced," *BuR* 27, i (1982): 17-1. [Not seen.]

_____, "George Orwell: The Novelist's Dilemma," *DAI* 38 (1978): 4821A.

Zwerdling, A., *Orwell and the Left*.

_____, "Orwell: Socialism vs. Pessimism," *New Rev.* 1, iii (June, 1974): 5-17.

ANIMAL FARM

Aickman, Robert F., in *Nineteenth Century* 138 (Dec., 1945): 255-61.

Aldritt, K., *Making of George Orwell*, 147-50.

Atkins, J., *George Orwell*, 221-32.

Baer, Louis A., "A Case of Grammar Analysis of the English Predicate Nominal," *DAI* 37 (1976): 3586.

Brander, L., *George Orwell*, 170-82.

Brown, Spencer, "Strange Doings at Animal Farm," *Ctary* 19 (Feb., 1955): 155-61.

Calder, J., *Chronicles of Conscience*, 223-8.

Carter, Thomas N., "Group Psychological Phenomenon of a Political System as Satirized in ANIMAL FARM: An Application of the Theories of W. R. Bion," *Human Relations*, 27 (1974): 525-46.

Colquitt, Betsy F., "Orwell: Traditionalist in Wonderland," *Discourse* 8 (Autumn, 1965): 376-7.

Cooper, Nancy M., "ANIMAL FARM: An Explication for Teachers of Orwell's Novel," *CEJ* 4 (Fall, 1968): 59-69.

Davis, Robert M., "Politics in the Pig-Pen," *JPC* 2 (Fall, 1968): 314-20.

De Hegedus, Adam, in *Cweal* 44 (Sept. 13, 1946): 528-30.

Dempsey, David, in *AR* 7 (Mar., 1947): 142-50.

Fraser, G. S., *Modern Writer and His World*, 157-8.

Greenblatt, Stephen J., "Orwell as Satirist," in Williams, R., ed., *George Orwell*, 106-111. Also in Greenblatt, S. J., *Three Modern Satirists*, 60-6.

Gulbin, Suzanne, "Parallels and Contrasts in LORD OF THE FLIES and ANIMAL FARM," *EJ* 55 (Jan., 1966): 86-90+.

Hoggart, R., "Walking the Tightrope: ANIMAL FARM," *Speaking to Each Other*, Vol. II: *About Literature*, 106-10.

Hollis, C., *Study of George Orwell*, 139-53.

Hopkinson, Tom, "ANIMAL FARM," *World Rev.* n.s. 16 (June, 1950): 54-7.

_____, *George Orwell*, 28-31.

Jain, Jasbir, "Orwell: The Myth of a Classless Society," *Quest* 72 (1971): 97-9.

King, Carlyle, "The Politics of George Orwell," *UTQ* 26 (1956): 79-91.

Kalechofsky, R., *George Orwell*, 100-9.

Kubal, D. L., *Outside the Whale*, 37-40, 123-30.

Lall, R. R. *Satiric Fable in English*, 116-32.

Lee, R. A., *Orwell's Fiction*, 105-27.

_____, "The Uses of Form: A Reading of ANIMAL FARM," *SSF* 6 (Fall, 1969): 557-73.

Leyburn, E. D., *Satiric Allegory*, 68-70.

Maddison, Michael, "At the Crossroads of Ideology: George Orwell's ANIMAL FARM," *Geste* (Leeds Un.) 6 (Oct. 27, 1960): 18-21.

Meyers, Jeffrey, "Orwell's Bestiary: The Political Allegory of ANIMAL FARM," *STwC* 8 (Fall, 1971): 65-84.

_____, *Reader's Guide to George Orwell*, 130-43.

Oxley, B. T., *George Orwell*, 75-82.

Pinsker, Sanford, "A Note to the Teaching of Orwell's ANIMAL FARM," *CEA* 39, ii (1977): 18-19.

Rees, R., *George Orwell*, 82-6.

Ringbom, Hakan, "The Style of Orwell's Preface to ANIMAL FARM," in Ringbom, H., et al., eds., *Style and Text*, 243-9.

Schmerl, Rudolf B., "Orwell as Fantasist," *Cresset* 25 (June, 1962): 11-13.

Scruggs, Charles, "George Orwell and Jonathan Swift: A Literary Relationship," *SAQ* 76, ii (Spring, 1977): 177-89.

Siepmann, F. O., "Farewell to Orwell," *Nineteenth Century and After* 147 (Mar., 1970): 141-7 *passim*.

Small, C., *Road to Miniluv*, 101-16.

Smyer, Richard I., ANIMAL FARM: The Burden of Consciousness," *ELN* 9 (1971): 55-9.

_____, *Primal Dream and Primal Crime*, 104-10.

Smythe, P. E., *A Guide to the Study of Orwell's ANIMAL FARM*, Sidney: College Pr., 1965.

Spencer, L., "ANIMAL FARM and NINETEEN EIGHT-FOUR," in Jowitt, J. A., and R. K. S. Taylor, eds., *George Orwell*, 67-83.

Steinhoff, E., *George Orwell and the Origins of 1984*, 144-7.

Strachey, John, "Strangled Cry," *Encounter* 15 (Nov., 1960): 9. Also in Strachey, J., *Strangled Cry*, 23-5.

Thomas, E. M., *Orwell*, 71-7.

Walsh, James, "An Appreciation of an Individualist Writer," *MarxistQ* 3, i (Jan., 1956): 30-2.

Webb, Tim, "Orwell: ANIMAL FARM," in Harward, T. B., ed., *European Patterns: Contemporary Patterns in European Writing*, Chester Springs, Pa.: Dufiur, 1966, 44-8.

Williams, R., *George Orwell*, 69-75.

Woodcock, G., *Crystal Spirit*, 192-8.

Woodhouse, C. M., "ANIMAL FARM," *TLS* (August 6, 1954): xxx-xxxi.

Zwerdling, A., *Orwell and the Left*, 88-96.

_____," Orwell: Socialism vs. Pessimism," *New Rev* 1, iii (June, 1974): 7-10.

BURMESE DAYS

Aldritt, K., *Making of George Orwell*, 20-6.

Brander, L., *George Orwell*, 75-89.

Braybrooke, Neville, "George Orwell," *CathW* 178 (Dec., 1953): 179-81.

Calder, J., *Chronicles of Conscience*, 82-7.

Eagleton, T., "Orwell and the Lower-Middle-Class Novel," *Exiles and Emigres*, 77-87. Also in Williams, R., ed., *George Orwell*, 10-18.

Fiderer, Gerald, "Masochism as Literary Strategy: Orwell's Psychological Novels," *L&P* 20, i (1970): 4-6.

Goonetilleke, D.C.R.A., "George Orwell's BURMESE DAYS: The Novelist as Reformer?" *Kalyani* 1, i-ii (Oct., 1982): 123-7.

Greenblatt, S. J., *Three Modern Satirists*, 49-54, and *passim*.

Hollis, C., *Study of George Orwell*, 29-39.

Jain, Jasbir, "Orwell and Imperialism," *BP* 16 (Jan., 1971): 1-7.

Kalechofsky, R., *George Orwell*, 26-35.

Karl, F. R., "George Orwell: The White Man's Burden," *Contemporary English Novel*, 155-7.

Knapp, John V., "Dance to a Creepy Minuet: Orwell's BURMESE DAYS, Precursor of ANIMAL FARM," *MFS* 21, i (Spring, 1975): 11-29.

Kubal, David L., "The Early Novelist," *ArQ* 27, i (Spring, 1971): 59-67.

_____, *Outside the Whale*, 9-12, 70-9.

Lee, R. A., *Orwell's Fiction*, 1-22.

_____, "Symbol and Structure in BURMESE DAYS: A Revaluation," *TSLL* 11, i (Spring, 1969): 819-35.

Lewis, Robin J., "Orwell's BURMESE DAYS and Forster's A PASSAGE TO INDIA: Two Novels of Human Relations in the British Empire," *MSE* 4, iii (1974): 1-36.

Meyers, Jeffrey, "The Ethics of Responsibility: Orwell's BURMESE DAYS," *UR* 35 (Dec., 1968): 83-7.

_____, *Reader's Guide to George Orwell*, 64-71.

Muggeridge, Malcolm, "BURMESE DAYS," *World Rev* n.s. 16 (June, 1950): 45-8.

Odle, Francis, "Orwell in Burma," *TC* 179, 1048 (1972): 38-9.

Oxley, B. T., *George Orwell*, 84-92.

Rosenfeld, Isaac, "Decency and Death," *PR* 17 (May-June, 1950): 515. Also in Rosenfeld, I., *Age of Enormity*, 252-3.

Small, C. *Road to Miniluv*, 26-37.

Smyer, R. I., *Primal Dream and Primal Crime*, 24-40.

Spence, J. E., "George Orwell," *Theoria* 13 (1959): 16-19.

Stevens, Arthur W., George Orwell and Contemporary British Fiction of Burma," *DA* 18 (1958): 1799-80.

_____, "George Orwell and Southeast Asia," *TCGL* 11 (1962): 133-41.

Thomas, E. M., *Orwell*, 8-12.

Voorhees, Richard J., "Orwell and Power-Hunger," *CanF* 36 (July, 1961): 79.

_____, *Paradox of George Orwell*, 75-8.

Wadsworth, Frank W., "Orwell as Novelist: The Early Work," *UKCR* 22 (Winter, 1955): 93-7.

Woodcock, G., *Crystal Spirit*, 84-104, 346-8.

A CLERGYMAN'S DAUGHTER

Adritt, K., *Making of George Orwell*, 27-31.

Beadle, Gordon R., "George Orwell and the Death of God," *ColQ* 23, i (Summer, 1974): 53-7.

Brander, L., *George Orwell*, 91-100.

Calder, J., *Chronicles of Conscience*, 87-90.

Eagleton, Terry, "Orwell and the Lower-Middle-Class Novel," *Exiles and Emigres*, 87-92. Also in Williams, R., ed., *George Orwell*, 18-23.

Hollis, C., *Study of George Orwell*, 57-68.

Kalechofsky, R., *George Orwell*, 44-51.

Kubal, David L., "George Orwell: The Early Novelist," *ArQ* 27, i (Spring, 1971): 67-73.

_____, *Outside the Whale*, 12-15, 79-85.

Lee, R. A. *Orwell's Fiction*, 23-47.

Lief, R. A., *Homage to Oceania*, 79-83.

Meyers, J., *Reader's Guide to George Orwell*, 79-84.

Oxley, B. T., *George Orwell*, 92-8.

Small, C., *Road to Miniluv*, 37-61.

Smyer, Richard I., "Orwell's A CLERGYMAN'S DAUGHTER: A Flight from History," *MFS* 21, i (Spring, 1975): 31-47.

_____, *Primal Dream and Primal Crime*, 41-58.

Steinhoff, W., *George Orwell and the Origins of 1984,* 127-32.
Thomas, E. M., *Orwell,* 24-6.
Voorhees, R. J., *Paradox of George Orwell,* 44-9.
Wadsworth, Frank W., "Orwell as Novelist: The Early Work,"
UKCR 22 (Winter, 1955): 97-9.
Williams, R., *George Orwell,* 42-3.
Woodcock, G., *Crystal Spirit,* 125-40.

COMING UP FOR AIR

Aldritt, K., *Making of George Orwell,* 37-41.
Brander, L., *George Orwell,* 150-69.
Calder, J., *Chronicles of Conscience,* 163-5.
Eagleton, Terry, "Orwell and the Lower-Middle-Class Novel,"
Exiles and Emigres, 100-3. Also in Williams, R., ed., *George
Orwell,* 30-3.
Edelheit, S., *Dark Prophecies,* 63-105.
Fink, Howard, "COMING UP FOR AIR: Orwell's Ambiguous
Satire on the Wellsian Utopia," SLitI 6, ii (Fall, 1973): 51-60.
Also as "The Shadow of MEN LIKE GODS: Orwell's COM-
ING UP FOR AIR as Parody," 144-58 in Suvin, Darko, ed.,
H. G. Wells and Modern Science Fiction, Lewisburg: Bucknell
Un. Pr.; London: Associated Un. Pr., 1977, 144-58.
Hollis, C., *Study of George Orwell,* 108-18.
Hopkinson, T., *George Orwell,* 25-6.
Hunter, Jefferson, "Orwell, Wells, and COMING UP FOR AIR,"
MP 79 (1980): 38-47.
Kalechofsky, R., *George Orwell,* 83-6, 91-7.
King, Carlyle, "The Politics of George Orwell," UTQ 26 (1956):
90-1.
Knapp, John V., "The Double Life of George Bowling," *Rev. of
Existential Psychology and Psychiatry* 14, iii (1975-76): 109-25.
Kubals, D. L., *Outside the Whale,* 25-9, 115-23.
Lee, R. A., *Orwell's Fiction,* 83-104.
Meyers, Jeffrey, "Orwell's Apocalypse: COMING UP FOR
AIR," MFS 21, i (Spring, 1975): 69-80.
_____, *Reader's Guide to George Orwell,* 98-111.
Oxley, B. T., *George Orwell,* 105-12.
Pozner, Walter, "Orwell's George Bowling: How to Be," *Wasca-
naR* 14, ii (Fall, 1979): 80-90.
Rees, R., *George Orwell,* 73-9.
Rosenfeld, Isaac, "Decency and Death," PR 17 (May-June, 1950):
515-16. Also in Rosenfeld, I., *Age of Enormity,* 253-4.
Small, C., *Road to Miniluv,* 80-101.
Smyer, R. I., *Primal Dream and Primal Crime,* 82-7, 89-93.
Steinhoff, W., *George Orwell and the Origins of 1984,* 140-4.
Thomas, E. M., *Orwell,* 52-9.
Van Dellen, Robert J., "George Orwell's COMING UP FOR AIR:
The Politics of Powerlessness," MFS 21, i (Spring, 1975):
57-68.
Voorhees, R. J., *Paradox of George Orwell,* 109-14.
Wadsworth, Frank, "Orwell as Novelist: The Middle Period,"
UKCR 22 (Mar., 1956): 192-4.
Wain, John, "Here Lies Lower Binfield," *Encounter* 17 (Oct.,
1961): 74-83. Also in Wain, J., *Essays on Literature and Ideas,*
London: Macmillan; N.Y.: St. Martin's, 1963, 194-213.
Woodcock, George, *Crystal Spirit,* 176-87.

KEEP THE ASPIDISTRA FLYING

Aldritt, K., *Making of George Orwell,* 31-6.
Brander, L., *George Orwell,* 100-10.

Calder, J., *Chronicles of Conscience,* 90-8.
Eagleton, Terry, "Orwell and the Lower-Middle-Class Novel,"
Exiles and Emigres, 92-100. Also in Williams, R., ed., *George
Orwell,* 24-30.
Gloversmith, Frank, "Changing Things: Orwell and Auden,"
104-9 in Gloversmith, F., ed., *Class, Culture and Social Change:
A New View of the 1930's,* Brighton: Harvester Pr.; Atlantic
Highlands, N.J.: Humanities Pr., 1980.
Greenblatt, S. J., *Three Modern Satirists,* 53-7, and *passim.*
Guild, Nicholas, "In Dubious Battle: George Orwell and the
Victory of the Money God," MFS 21, i (Spring, 1975): 49-56.
Hollis, C., *Study of George Orwell,* 69-76.
Hopkinson, T., *George Orwell,* 18-19.
Kalechofsky, R., *George Orwell,* 51-9.
Karl, F. R., "George Orwell: The White Man's Burden," *Contem-
porary English Novel,* 161-2.
Kubal, David, "George Orwell and the Aspidistra," UR 37 (Oct.,
1970): 61-7.
_____, *Outside the Whale,* 16-18, 89-104.
Lee, R. A., *Orwell's Fiction,* 48-65.
Lief, R. A., *Homage to Oceania,* 44-7, 64-5, 115-17.
Matthews, Brian, "The Orwellian Fat Men," *SoRA* 13 (July,
1980): 101-19.
Meredith, William, "Pilgrim and the Money-God," *Nation* 182
(Jan. 21, 1956): 55.
Meyers, J., *Reader's Guide to George Orwell,* 85-92.
Oxley, B. T., *George Orwell,* 98-105.
Rees, R., *George Orwell,* 31-6.
Rosenfeld, Isaac, "Gentleman George," Ctary 21 (June, 1956):
581-91. Also in Rosenfeld, L., *Age of Enormity,* 246-51.
Schoenl, William J., "Abstract Phraseology, Orwell, and Abor-
tion," *Intellect* 103 (Nov., 1974): 125-7.
Small, C., *Road to Miniluv,* 63-81.
Smyer, R. I., *Primal Dream and Primal Crime,* 59-75.
Steinhoff, W., *George Orwell and the Origins of 1984,* 132-41.
Thomas, E. M., *Orwell,* 26-8.
Wadsworth, Frank, "Orwell as Novelist: The Middle Period,"
UKCR 22 (Mar., 1956): 189-92.
West, Anthony, "Hidden Damage," NY 31 (Jan. 28, 1956): 98-
104. Also in West, A., *Principles and Persuasions,* 164-9.
Williams, R., *George Orwell,* 46-7.
Woodcock, G., *Crystal Spirit,* 140-50.

NINETEEN EIGHTY-FOUR

Aldritt, K., *Making of George Orwell,* 150-78.
Anon., "George Orwell's Strange World of *1984,*" *Life* 27 (July
4, 1948): 78-85.
Asche, Geoffrey, "Second Thoughts on NINETEEN EIGHTY-
FOUR," *Month* n.s. 4 (Nov., 1950): 285-300.
Atkins, J., *George Orwell,* 237-54.
_____, *George Orwell.* New ed., 348-94 *passim.*
Bakker, J., "George Orwell's Newspeak in Light of A PHILOSO-
PHY IN A NEW KEY," *Levende Talen* 242 (Dec., 1967): 674-83.
Barnsley, John H., "'The Last Man in Europe': A Comment on
George Orwells *1984,*" *ContempR* 239, mccclxxxvi (July,
1981): 30-4.
Barr, Alan, "The Paradise Behind *1984,*" EM 19 (1968): 183-204.
Beauchamp, Gorman, "Future Worlds: Language and the
Dystopian Novel," *Style* 8 (1974): 462-76.

_____, "Of Man's Last Disobedience: Zamiatin's WE and Orwell's *1984*," *CLS* 10 (Dec., 1973): 285-301.

Brander, L., *George Orwell*, 183-204.

Browning, Gordon, "Zamiatin's WE: An Anti-Utopian Classic," *Cithara* 7 (May, 1968): 13-20.

Calder, Jenni, *Huxley and Orwell: BRAVE NEW WORLD and NINETEEN EIGHTY-FOUR*, London: Arnold, 1976.

_____, "Orwell's Post-War Prophecy," in Williams, R., ed., *George Orwell*, 133-55. Also in Calder, J., *Chronicles of Conscience*, 229-53.

Coe, Richard N., NINETEEN EIGHTY-FOUR and the Anti-Utopian Tradition," *Geste* (Leeds Univ.) 6 (Oct. 27, 1960): 22-6.

Colquitt, Betsy F., "Orwell: Traditionalist in Wonderland," *Discourse* 8 (Aut., 1965): 377-83.

Connors, James, "'Do It to Julia': Thoughts on Orwell's *1984*," *MFS* 16 (Winter, 1970-71): 463-73.

_____, "Zamiatin's WE and the Genesis of *1984*," *MFS* 21, i (Spring, 1975): 107-24.

Deutscher, Isaac, "*1984* — The Mysticism of Cruelty," *Russia in Transition*, N.Y.: Coward McCann, 1957, 230-45. Also in Rev. ed., N.Y.: Grove, 1960, 250-65. Also in Howe, I., ed., *Orwell's NINETEEN EIGHTY-FOUR*, 196-203. Also in Williams, R., ed., *George Orwell*, 119-32. Also in Deutscher, Isaac, *Heretics and Renegades*, London: Hamish Hamilton, 1956. Also in Hynes, S., ed., *Twentieth Century Interpretations of 1984*, 29-40.

Dilworth, Thomas, "'The Village Blacksmith' in NINETEEN EIGHTY-FOUR," *IFR* 8, i (Winter, 1981): 63-5.

Dutscher, Alan, "Orwell and the Crisis of Responsibility," *Contemporary Issues* (London) 7 (Aug.-Sept., 1956): 311-16.

Dyson, A. E., "George Orwell: Irony as Prophecy," *Crazy Fabric*: 197-219.

Edelheit, S., *Dark Prophecies*, 106-81.

Edrich, Emmanuel, "George Orwell and the Satire in Horror," *TSLL* 4 (1962): 96-108 *passim*.

Ehrenpreis, Irvin, "Orwell, Huxley, Pope," *RLV* 23, iii (1957): 215-30 *passim*.

Elsbree, Langdon, "The Structured Nightmare of *1984*," *TCL* 5 (Oct., 1959): 135-41.

Fiderer, Gerald, "Masochism as a Literary Strategy: Orwell's Psychological Novels," *L&P* 20, i (1970): 8-20.

Fink, Howard, "Newspeak: The Epitome of Parody Technique in NINETEEN EIGHTY-FOUR," *Crit Survey* 5 (1971): 155-63.

Fraser, G. S., *Modern Writer and His World*, 158-9.

Fromm, Erich, "Afterward" to *1984*, N.Y.: New American Library, 1954, 257-67. Also in Howe, I., ed., *Orwell's NINETEEN EIGHTY-FOUR*, 204-10.

Frothingham, Richard, "Orwell's *1984*, Part I, Chapter VIII," *Expl* 29 (1971): Item 37.

Gable, Sister Mariella, "Prose Satire and the Modern Christian Temper," *ABR* 11 (Mar.-June, 1960): 23-6.

Geering, D. G., "DARKNESS AT NOON and NINETEEN EIGHTY-FOUR—A Comparative Study," *AusQ* 30 (Mar., 1958): 90-6.

Gleckner, Robert F., "1984 or 1948?" *CE* 18 (Nov., 1956): 95-9.

Greenblatt, Stephen J., "Orwell as Satirist," *Three Modern Satirists*, 66-72. Also in Williams, R., ed., *George Orwell*, 111-18.

Hamilton, Kenneth M., "G. K. Chesterton and George Orwell: A Contrast in Prophecy," *DR* 31 (Autumn, 1951): 203-5.

Harris, Harold J., "Orwell's Essays and *1984*" *TCL* 4 (Jan., 1959): 154-61.

Highet, G., *Anatomy of Satire*, 171-3.

Hollis, Christopher, in *Horizon* 20 (Sept., 1949): 200-8.

_____, *Study of George Orwell*, 188-201.

Hopkinson, T., *George Orwell*, 31-4.

Howe, Irving, "The Fiction of Anti-Utopia," *NRep* 146 (Apr. 23, 1962): 13-16. Also in Howe, I., ed., *Orwell's NINETEEN EIGHTY-FOUR*, 176-80. Also in Howe, I., *Orwell's NINETEEN EIGHTY-FOUR*, 2nd ed., 332-43.

_____, "History as Nightmare," *ASch* 25 (Spring, 1956): 193-206. Also in, Howe, I., *Politics and the Novel*, 235-51. Also, as "*1984*: History as Nightmare," in Howe, I., ed., *Orwell's NINETEEN EIGHTY-FOUR*, 188-96. Also in Howe, I., ed., *Orwell's NINETEEN EIGHTY-FOUR*, 2nd ed., 320-32. Also in Hynes, S., ed., *Twentieth Century Interpretations of 1984*, 41-53.

_____, "*1984* — Utopia Reversed," *New International*, 16 (Nov.-Dec., 1950): 360-8.

_____, ed., *Orwell's NINETEEN EIGHTY-FOUR*.

_____, ed., *Orwell's NINETEEN EIGHTY-FOUR*, 2nd ed.

Huxley, Aldous, "A Footnote About '1984'," *World Rev* (June, 1950): 60.

Hynes, S., ed., *Twentieth Century Interpretations of 1984*.

John, George, "Towards a Stylistic Analysis of Orwell's 1984," *RUSEng* 11 (1978): 57-65.

Jones, Joseph, "Utopias as Dirge," *AQ* 2 (Fall, 1950): 214-26.

Kalechofsky, R., *George Orwell*, 109-34.

Karl, F. R., "The White Man's Burden," *Contemporary English Novel*, 159-61, 163-5.

Kateb, George, "The Road to *1984*, *PSciQ* 81, iv (Dec., 1966): 564-80. Also in Hynes, S., ed., *Twentieth Century Interpretations of 1984*, 73-87.

Keep, John, "Andrei Amalrik and *1984*," *RusR* 30 (1971): 335-45.

Kegel, Charles H., "NINETEEN EIGHTY-FOUR: A Century of Ingsoc," *N&Q* 10 (Apr., 1963): 151-2.

Kessler, Martin, "Power and the Perfect State: A Study of Disillusionment as Reflected in Orwell's NINETEEN EIGHTY-FOUR and Huxley's BRAVE NEW WORLD," *PSQ* 72 (Dec., 1957): 565-77.

King, Carlyle, "The Politics of George Orwell," *UTQ* 26 (1956): 79-91.

Knox, George, "The 'Divine Comedy' in '1984'," *WHR* 9 (Autumn, 1955): 371-2.

Kubal, David, "Freud, Orwell, and the Bourgeois Interior," *YR* 67 (Mar., 1978): 389-403.

Kubal, D. L., *Outside the Whale*, 43-7, 130-41.

Laurenson, Diana T., and Alan Swingewood, "George Orwell, Socialism and the Novel," *Sociology and Literature*, 264-76.

Lee, R. A., *Orwell's Fiction*, 128-55.

LeRoy, Gaylord C., "A. F., 632 to 1984," *CE* 12 (Dec., 1950): 135-8.

Leyburn, E. D., *Satiric Allegory*, 125-35.

Lief, R. A., *Homage to Oceania*, 41-3, 56-8, 69-70, 76-7, 84-8, 93-101, 107-14, 118-21.

Lockyer, Robert, "George Orwell's *1984*," *T&T* 36 (Jan. 15, 1955): 78.

Lyons, John O., "George Orwell's Opaque Glass in *1984*," *WSCL* 2, iii (Fall, 1961): 39-46.

Maddison, Michael, "*1984*: A Burnhamite Fantasy?" *PolQ* 32 (Jan-Mar., 1961): 71-9.

Malin, Lawrence, "Halfway to *1984*," *Horizon* 12, i (Spring, 1970): 33-9.

Mazer, Charles L., "Orwell's Oceania, Zamyatin's United State and Levin's Unicomp Earth: Socially Constructed Anti-Utopias," *DAI* 37 (1976): 957A.

McCormick, D., *Approaching 1984.*

McDowell, Jennifer, "*1984* and Soviet Reality," *Un. of California Graduate Jrnl.* 1 (Fall, 1962): 12-19.

McNamara, James, and D. J. O'Keeffe, "Waiting for 1984: On Orwell and Evil," *Encounter* 59, vi (Dec., 1982): 43-8.

Meyers, Jeffrey, "The Evolution of *1984*," *EM* 23 (1972): 247-61.
_____, *Reader's Guide to George Orwell*, 144-54.

Mueller, Willliam R., "The Demonic Comedy," *Celebration of Life*, 169-87.

New, Melvin, "Ad Nauseam: A Satiric Device in Huxley, Orwell, and Waugh," *SNL* 8, i (Fall, 1970): 24-8.
_____, "Orwell and Antisemitism: Toward *1984*," *MFS* 21, i (Spring, 1975): 81-105.

Nott, Kathleen, "Orwell's NINETEEN EIGHTY-FOUR," *Listener* 70 (Oct. 31, 1963): 687-8.

Oxley, B. T., *George Orwell*, 112-25.

Padovano, A., *Estranged God*, 154-7.

Parrinder, Patrick, "Updating Orwell? Burgess's Future Fictions," *Encounter* 56, i (Jan., 1981): 45-53.

Patai, Daphne, "Gamesmanship and Androcentrism in Orwell's *1984*," *PMLA* 97, v (Oct., 1982): 856-70.

Philmus, Robert M., "The Language of Utopia," *SLitI* 6, ii (Fall, 1973): 61-78.

Plank, Robert, "One Grand Inquisitor and Some Lesser Ones," *Gamut* (Cleveland State Univ.) 4 (Fall, 1981): 29-38.

Prescott, O., *In My Opinion*, 27-31.

Raban, J., "Irony in the Language of Fiction," *Technique of Modern Fiction*, 187-91.

Rahv, Philip, "The Unfuture of Utopia," *PR* 16 (July, 1949): 743-9. Also in Howe, I., ed., *Orwell's NINETEEN EIGHTY-FOUR*, 181-5. Also in Rahv, P., *Literature and the Sixth Sense*, 331-9. Also in Howe, I., ed., *Orwell's NINETEEN EIGHTY-FOUR*, 2nd ed., 310-16.

Ranald, Ralph A., "George Orwell and the Mad World: The Anti-Universe of *1984*," *SAQ* 66 (1967): 544-53.

Rankin, David, "Orwell's Intention in *1984*," *ELN* 12, iii (Mar., 1975): 188-92.

Read, Herbert, "*1984*," *World Rev* (June, 1950): 60.

Reader, Mark, "The Political Criticism of George Orwell," *DA* 28 (1967): 273A.

Rees, David, "The View from Airstrip One," *Spectator* (Dec. 3, 1965): 742-3.

Rees, R., *George Orwell*, 88-108, 116-17.

Reilly, Patrick, "NINETEEN EIGHTY-FOUR: The Failure of Humanism," *CritQ* 24, iii (1982): 19-30.

Richards, D., "Four Utopias," *SEER* 40 (1962): 224-8.
_____, "Orwell's *1984*: His Choice of the Date," *Expl* 35, i (1976): 8.

Roazen, Paul, "Orwell, Freud, and *1984*," *VQR* 54 (1978): 675-95.

Roland, Albert, "Christian Implications in Anti-Stalinist Novels," *Religion in Live*, 22 (1953): 404-6.

Rosenfeld, Isaac, "Decency and Death," *PR* 17 (May-June, 1950): 254-7. Also in Rosenfeld, I., *Age of Enormity*, 254-7. Also in Howe, I., ed., *Orwell's NINETEEN EIGHTY-FOUR*, 185-8. Also in Howe, I., ed., *Orwell's NINETEEN EIGHTY-FOUR*, 2nd ed., 316-20.

Russell, Bertrand, "Symptoms of Orwell's *1984*," *Portraits from Memory and Other Essays*, N.Y.: Simon & Schuster, 1956, 221-8.

Savage, D. S., "The Case Against Orwell," *Tract* 31 (1980): 32-45.

Schmerl, Rudolf B., "Orwell as Fantasist," *Cresset* 25 (June, 1962): 8-10.

Sheldon, Leslie E., "Newspeak and Nodstat: The Disintegration of Language in *1984* and A CLOCKWORK ORANGE," *StCS* 6 (1979): 7-13.

Shibata, Toshihiko, "The Road to Nightmare: An Essay on George Orwell," *SELL* 12 (1962): 41-53 *passim.*

Siegel, Paul N., "The Cold War: *1984* Twenty-five Years After," *Confrontation*, 148-56.

Siepmann, E. O., "Farewell to Orwell," *Nineteenth Century and After* 147 (Mar., 1950): 141-7 *passim.*

Sillen, Samuel, "Maggot-of-the-Month," *M&M* 2 (Aug., 1949): Also in Howe, I., ed., *Orwell's NINETEEN EIGHTY-FOUR*, 210-12.

Simms, Valerie J., "A Reconsideration of Orwell's 1984: The Moral Implications of Despair," *Ethics* 84 (1974): 292-306.

Slater, Joseph, "The Fictional Values of *1984*," in Kirk, Rudolf, and C. F. Main, eds., *Essays in Literary History, Presented to J. Milton French*, New Brunswick, N. J.: Rutgers Un. Pr., 1960, 249-64.

Small, C., *Road to Miniluv*, 136-92.

Smith, K., "'Oldspeak' and 'Newspeak'," in Jowitt, J. A., and R. K. S. Taylor, eds., *George Orwell*, 84-100.

Smith, Marcus, "The Wall of Blackness: A Psychological Approach to *1984*," *MFS* 14 (Winter, 1968-69): 423-33.

Smyer, Richard I., "*1984*: The Search for the Golden Country," *ArQ* 27, i (Spring, 1971): 41-52.
_____, *Primal Dream and Primal Crime*, 139-59.

Soskin, William, "What Can Be," *SatR* 32 (June 11, 1949): 12-13.

Spencer, L., "ANIMAL FARM and NINETEEN EIGHTY-FOUR," in Jowitt, J. A., and R. K. S. Taylor, eds., *George Orwell*, 67-83.

Spender, S., "Anti-Vision and Despair," *Creative Element*, 125-39. Heinemann Educational Books, 1965, vii-xxi. Also in Hynes, S., *Twentieth Century Interpretations of 1984*, 62-72.

Sperber, Murray, "'Gazing Into the Glass Paperweight': The Structure and Psychology of Orwell's *1984*," *MFS* 26 (1980): 213-26.

Steinhoff, W., *George Orwell and the Origins of 1984.*

Stewart, Ralph, "Orwell's Waste Land," *IFR* 8, ii (Summer, 1981): 150-2.

Strachey, John, "The Strangled Cry," *Encounter* 15 (Nov., 1960): 10-13. Also in Strachey, J., *Strangled Cry*, 25-32. Also in Hynes, S., ed., *Twentieth Century Interpretations of 1984*, 54-61.

Struc, Roman S., "George Orwell's NINETEEN EIGHTY-FOUR and Dostoevsky's 'Underground Man'," 217-20 in Kraft, Walter C., ed., *Proceedings: Pacific Northwest Conference on Foreign Languages* (PPNCOFL). Vol. 24, Corvallis: Oregon State Univ., 1973.

Sussman, Bernard J., "Orwell's *1984*," *Expl* 38, iv (1980): 32-3.

Symons, J., "George Orwell's Utopia," *Critical Occasions*, 55-60.

Thale, Jerome, "Orwell's Modest Proposal," *CritQ* 4 (Winter,1962): 365-8.

Thomas, E. M., *Orwell*, 82-99.

Thompson, Frank H., Jr., "Orwell's Image of the Man of Good Will," *CE* 22 (Jan., 1961): 235-8.

Tibbetts, A. M., "What Did Orwell Think About the English Language?" *CCC* 29, ii (May, 1978): 162-4.

Voorhees, Richard J., "NINETEEN EIGHTY-FOUR: No Failure of Nerve," *CE* 18 (Nov., 1956): 101-2.

_____, "Orwell and Power-Hunger," *CanF* 36 (July, 1956): 79-80.

_____, *Paradox of George Orwell*, 60-2, 78-88.

Wadsworth, Frank, "Orwell's Later Work," *UKCR* 22 (1956): 285-91.

Walsh, James, "An Appreciation of an Individualist Writer: George Orwell," *MarxQ* 3, i (Jan., 1956): 32-9. Also in Howe, I., ed., *Orwell's NINETEEN EIGHTY-FOUR*, 212-16.

Warncke, Wayne, "A Note on *1984*," *Hartwick Rev* 3 (Fall, 1967): 60-1.

_____, "The Permanence of Orwell," *UR* 33 (Mar., 1967): 190-1.

Wasserman, Jerry, "THE WEAPON SHOPS OF ISHER: *1984* Reconsidered," *Sphinx* 4, i (1981): 76-80.

Way, Brian, "George Orwell: The Political Thinker We Might Have Had," *Gemini/Dialogue* 3 (Spring, 1960): 8-18.

Westlake, J. H. J., "Aldous Huxley's BRAVE NEW WORLD and George Orwell's NINETEEN EIGHTY-FOUR: A Comparative Study," *NS* 21, ii (Feb., 1972): 94-102.

Whellens, Arthur, "Anthony Burgess's 1985," *StIL* 5 (1982): 223-44.

Wicker, Brian, "An Analysis of Newspeak," *Blackfriars* 43 (June, 1962): 272-85.

Wilding, Michael, "Orwell's *1984:* Rewriting the Future," *SSEng* 2 (1976-77): 38-63.

Williams, R., *George Orwell*, 75-83.

Woodcock, G., *Crystal Spirit*, 58-61, 67-80, 203-21, 262-4, 330-2, 348-9.

_____, "Utopias in Negative," *SR* 64 (Winter, 1956): 81-97.

Yorks, Samuel A., "George Orwell: Seer Over His Shoulder," *BuR* 9 (Mar., 1960): 32-45.

Zwerdling, A., *Orwell and the Left*, 98-110.

_____, "Orwell and the Techniques of Didactic Fantasy," in Hynes, S., ed., *Twentieth Century Interpretation of 1984*, 88-101.

_____, "Orwell: Socialism v. Pessimism," *NewRev* 1, iii (June, 1974): 10-16.

BIBLIOGRAPHY

Lee, R. A., *Orwell's Fiction*, 179-83.

McDowell, M. Jennifer, "George Orwell: Bibliographical Addenda," *BB* 24 (May-Aug., 1963): 19-24; 24 (Sept.-Dec., 1963): 36-40.

Meyers, Jeffrey, "George Orwell: A Bibliography," *BB* 31, iii (1974): 117-21.

_____, "George Orwell: A Selected Checklist," *MFS* 21, i (Spring, 1975): 133-6. [Supplements article above.]

_____, *George Orwell: An Annotated Bibliography of Criticism*, N.Y.: Garland, 1977.

Zeke, Zoltan G., and W. White, "Orwelliana," *BB* 23 (Sept.-Dec., 1961): 140-4.

OSTENSO, MARTHA, 1900-1963

GENERAL

Buckley, Joan N., "Martha Ostenso: A Critical Study of Her Novels," *DAI* 37 (1977): 5118-19A.

_____, "Martha Ostenso: Norwegian-American Immigrant Novelist," *NAS* 28 (1979): 69-81.

WILD GEESE

Atherton, Stanley S., "Ostenso Revisited," in Moss, J., ed., *Canadian Novel*. Vol. 3: *Modern Times*, 57-65.

Buckley, Joan N., "Martha Ostenso: Norwegian-American Immigrant Novelist," *NAS* 28 (1979): 75-80.

Hesse, M. G., "The Endless Quest: Dreams and Aspirations in Martha Ostenso's WILD GEESE," *JPC* 15, iii (Winter, 1981): 47-52.

Keith, W. J., "WILD GEESE: The Death of Calb Gare," *SCL* 3 (1978): 274-6.

King, Carlyle, "Introduction," in Ostenso, M., *Wild Geese*, Toronto: McClelland and Stewart, 1967. (New Canadian Library).

Lawrence, Robert G., "The Geography of Martha Ostenso's WILD GEESE," *JCF* 16 (1976): 108-14.

Moss, J., *Patterns of Isolation*, 36-8.

Mullins, S. G., "Some Remarks on Theme in Martha Ostenso's WILD GEESE," *Culture* 23 (Dec., 1962): 359-62.

Northey, Margot, "Sociological Gothic: WILD GEESE and SURFACING," *Haunted Wilderness*, 62-9.

Ricou, L., "The Obsessive Prairie: Martha Ostenso's WILD GEESE," *Vertical Man/Horizontal World*, 74-80.

Thomas, Clara, "Martha Ostenso's Trial of Strength," in Stephens, D. G., ed., *Writers of the Prairies*, 41-3.

THE YOUNG MAY MOON

Atherton, Stanley S., "Ostenso Revisited," in Moss, J., ed., *Canadian Novel*. Vol. 3. *Modern Times*, 62-4.

Thomas, Clara, "Martha Ostenso's Trial of Strength," in Moss, J., ed., *Canadian Novel*. Vol. 3. *Modern Times*, 43-9.

OWEN, GUY, JR., 1925-

GENERAL

Carr, John, "The Lumbees, the Klan, and ... Hollywood," [Interview] in Carr, J., ed., *Kite-Flying and Other Irrational Acts*, 236-62.

Vela, Richard, "This Native Pond, That Naked Tree: The Realities of Guy Owen," *S&W* 11, iii (1973): 14-20. [Not seen.]

JOURNEY FOR JOEDEL

Euliss, Daphne, "Folk Motif in Guy Owen's JOURNEY FOR JOEDEL," *NCarF* 24 (1976): 111-14.

Eyster, Warren, "Two Regional Novels," *SR* 79, iii (Summer, 1971): 472-4.

SEASON OF FEAR

White, Robert B., Jr., "The Imagery of Sexual Repression in SEASON OF FEAR," *NCarF* 19 (1971): 80-4.

OZICK, CYNTHIA, 1928-

GENERAL

Fisch, Harold, "Introducing Cynthia Ozick," *Response* 8, ii (Summer, 1974): 27-34.

TRUST

Fisch, Harold, "Introducing Cynthia Ozick," *Response* 8, ii (Summer, 1974): 29-31.

PATON, ALAN, 1903-1988

GENERAL

Albrecht, Gisela, and Manfred Reinhardt, "Interview: Alan Paton," *Afrika* (Munich) 19, x (1978): 16-18.

Callan, E., *Alan Paton.*

Rooney, F. Charles, "The 'Message' of Alan Paton," *CathW* 194 (Nov. 1961): 92-8. Also in Baker, S., ed., *Paton's CRY, THE BELOVED COUNTRY,* 151-3.

CRY, THE BELOVED COUNTRY

Alvarez-Pereyre, J., "The Social Record in CRY, THE BELOVED COUNTRY," *EA* 25 (Apr., 1972): 207-14.

Asein, Samuel O., "Christian Moralism and Apartheid: Paton's CRY THE BELOVED COUNTRY Reassessed," *AfricaQ* 14, i-ii (1974): 53-63.

Baker, Sheridan, "Paton's Beloved Country and the Morality of Geography," *CE* 19 (Nov., 1957): 56-61. Also in Baker, S., ed., *Paton's CRY, THE BELOVED COUNTRY,* 144-8.

_____, ed., *Paton's CRY, THE BELOVED COUNTRY*

Bruell, Edwin, "Keen Scalpel on Racial Ills," *EJ* 53 (1964): 658-61.

Callan, E., *Alan Paton.*

Collins, Harold R., "CRY, THE BELOVED COUNTRY and the Broken Tribe," *CE* 14 (Apr., 1953): 379-85. Also in Baker, S., ed., *Paton's CRY, THE BELOVED COUNTRY,* 138-43.

Davies, Horton, "Alan Paton: Literary Artist and Anglican," *HJ* 50 (Apr. 1952): 262-8.

_____, *Mirror of the Ministry in Modern Novels,* 128-36.

Fuller, E., "Alan Paton: Tragedy and Beyond," *Books With the Men Behind Them,* 94-9.

Gailey, Harry A., "Sheridan Baker's 'Paton's Beloved Country'," *CE* 20 (Dec., 1958): 143-4. Also in Baker, S., ed., *Paton's CRY, THE BELOVED COUNTRY,* 149-50.

Gardiner, Harold C., "On Saying 'Boo' to Geese," *America* 78 (Mar. 13, 1948): 661-3. Also in Gardiner, H. C., *In All Conscience,* 108-9.

Hartt, K. N., *Lost Image of Man,* 85-9.

Hester, Sister Mary, "Greek Tragedy and the Novels of Alan Paton," *WisSL* 1 (1964): 54-61.

Holland, R. W. H., "Fiction and History: Fact and Invention in Alan Paton's Novel CRY, THE BELOVED COUNTRY," *Zambezia* 5, ii (1977): 129-39.

Larson, Charles R., "Alan Paton's CRY, THE BELOVED COUNTRY After Twenty-Five Years," *AT* 20, iv (1973): 53-7.

Marcus, Fred H., "CRY, THE BELOVED COUNTRY and STRANGE FRUIT: Exploring Man's Inhumanity to Man," *EJ* 51 (Dec., 1962): 609-16.

Matlow, Myron, "Alan Paton's CRY, THE BELOVED COUNTRY and Maxwell Anderson's/Kurt Weill's LOST IN THE STARS: A Consideration of Genres," *Acadia* 10 (1975): 260-72.

Mbeboh, K. W., "CRY, THE BELOVED COUNTRY: A Liberal Apology," *Cameroon Studies in Eng. & Fr.* 1 (1976): 71-7.

Odumuh, Emmanuel, "The Theme of Love in Alan Paton's CRY, THE BELOVED COUNTRY," *Kuka* (1980-81): 41-50.

Prescott, O., *In My Opinion,* 240-3.

Rolo, Charles J., "Reader's Choice," *Atlantic* 181 (Apr., 1948): 112-13. Also in Baker, S., ed., *Paton's CRY, THE BELOVED COUNTRY,* 137.

Rooney, F., Charles, "The 'Message' of Alan Paton," *CathW* 194 (Nov., 1961): 94-5. Also in Baker, S., ed., *Paton's CRY, THE BELOVED COUNTRY,* 152-3.

Sharman, R. C., "Alan Paton's CRY, THE BELOVED COUNTRY: The Parable of Compassion," *LHY* 19, ii (1978): 64-82.

Smock, Susan W., "LOST IN THE STARS and CRY, THE BELOVED COUNTRY: A Thematic Comparison," *NDQ* 48, iii (1980): 53-9.

Tucker, M., *Africa in Modern Literature,* 223-5.

Watson, Stephen, "CRY, THE BELOVED COUNTRY and the Failure of Liberal Vision," *EinA* 9, i (1982): 29-44.

Wren, Robert M., "CRY, THE BELOVED COUNTRY as Fantasy in New York," *Contrast* 8, ii (1973): 55-60. [Musical Adaption LOST IN THE STARS.]

TOO LATE THE PHALAROPE

Baker, Sheridan, "Paton's Late Phalarope," *ESA* 3 (Sept., 1960): 152-9.

Callan, E., *Alan Paton,* 67-84.

Cooke, John, "'A Hunger of the Soul': TOO LATE THE PHALAROPE Reconsidered," *ESA* 22 (1979): 37-43.

Fuller, E., "Alan Paton: Tragedy and Beyond," *Books With the Men Behind Them,* 83-95.

Gardiner, Harold C., "Alan Paton's Second Masterpiece," *America* 89 (Aug. 19, 1953): 519-20. Also in Gardiner, H. C., *In All Conscience,* 112-16.

Gordimer, Nadine, "The Novel and the Nation in South Africa," *TLS* (Aug. 11, 1961): 521-2.

Hester, Sister Mary, "Greek Tragedy and the Novels of Alan Paton," *WisSL* 1 (1964): 54-61.

Rooney, F. Charles, "The 'Message' of Alan Paton," *CathW* (Nov., 1961): 95-7.

Stevens, Irma N., "Paton's Narrator Sophie: Justice and Mercy in TOO LATE THE PHALAROPE," *IFR* 8, i (Winter, 1981): 68-70.

Thompson, J. B., "Poetic Truth in TOO LATE THE PHALAROPE," *ESA* 24, i (Mar., 1981): 37-44.

Tucker, M., *Africa in Modern Literature,* 225-7.

BIBLIOGRAPHY

Callan, E., *Alan Paton,* 145-54.

PATTERSON, (HORACE) ORLANDO (LLOYD), 1940-

GENERAL

Jones, Bridget, "Some French Influences in the Fiction of Orlando Patterson," *Savacou* 11-12 (1975): 27-38. [Not seen.]

THE CHILDREN OF SISYPHUS

Ramchand, K., *West Indian Novel and Its Background,* 129-31.

DIE THE LONG DAY

Hearne, John, "The Novel as Sociology as Bore," *Caribbean Quarterly* 18, iv (1972): 7-73.

PEAKE, MERVYN, 1911-1968

GENERAL

See issues of *The Mervyn Peake Review.*

Moss, Anita, "'Felicitous Space' in the Fantasies of George MacDonald and Mervyn Peake," *Mythlore* 8, iv (1982): 16-17, 42.

Winnington, G. Peter, "Inside the Mind of Mervyn Peake," *Etudes de Lettres* 2, i (1979): 99-106.

GORMENGHAST

Hunt, Bruce, "GORMENGHAST: Psychology of the BILDUNGSROMAN," *MPR* 6 (Spring, 1978): 10-17.

Ochocki, Margaret, "GORMENGHAST: Fairytale Gone Wrong?" *MPR* 15 (1982): 11-17.

Rafanelli, Cristiano, "Titus and the Thing in GORMENG-HAST," *MPR* 3 (Autumn, 1976): 15-20.

Winnington, G. Peter, "Fuschia and Steerpike: Mood and Form," *MPR* (Autumn, 1977): 12-22.

GORMENGHAST Trilogy (TITUS Trilogy)

Binns, Ronald, "Situating Gormenghast," *CritQ* 21, i (Spring, 1979): 21-33.

Blignaut, E. A., "Mervyn Peake: From Artist as Entertainer to Artist as Philosopher and Moralist in the TITUS Books," *ESA* 24, ii (1981): 107-15.

Favier, Jacques, "Distortions of Space and Time in the Titus Trilogy," *MPR* 8 (1979): 7-14.

Gunnell, Bryn, "The Fantasy of Mervyn Peake," *MHRev* 58 (Apr., 1981): 17-35.

Manlove, C. N., "Mervyn Peake (1911-1968)—The 'Titus' Trilogy," *Modern Fantasy,* 207-61.

Morgan, Edwin, "The Walls of Gormenghast—An Introduction to the Novels of Melvyn Peake," *ChiR* 14, iii (Autumn-Winter, 1960): 74-81.

Rome, Joy, "Twentieth Century Gothic: Mervyn Peake's GORMENGHAST Trilogy," *UES* 12, i (1974): 42-54.

Servotte, Herman, "Guide for GORMENGHAST," *MPR* 3 (Autumn, 1976): 5-9.

_____, "A Miracle of a Rare Device: Mervyn Peake's GORMENGHAST Trilogy," *RLV* 40, v (1974): 489-96.

Sutton, David, "Folkloristic Elements in the Titus Trilogy," *MPR* 5 (Autumn, 1977): 6-11.

MR. PYE

Bristow-Smith, Laurence, "MR. PYE, or the Evangelist and the Dead Whale," *MPR* 7 (Autumn, 1978): 19-24.

Waterhouse, Ingrid, "Mr. Peake, Mr. Pye, and the Paradox of Good and Evil," *MPR* 7 (Autumn, 1978): 10-17.

TITUS ALONE

Bristow-Smith, Laurence, "A Critical Conclusion: The End of TITUS ALONE," *MPR* 12 (Spring, 1981): 10-13.

Greenland, Colin, "From Beowulf to Kafka: The Difficulty of TITUS ALONE," *MPR* 12 (Spring, 1981): 4-9.

TITUS GROAN

Fowler, Roger, "How to See through Language: Perspective in Fiction," *Poetics* 11, iii (July, 1982): 213-35.

Gardaz, Elisabeth, "'The Reveries' in TITUS GROAN," *MPR* 3 (Autumn, 1976): 11-14.

Mason, Desmond, "TITUS GROAN: Errors and Flaws," *MPR* 5 (Autumn, 1977): 12-16.

Speth, Lee, "A Connecticut Yankee in Gormenghast," *Mythlore* 6, ii (1979): 46-7.

Winnington, G. Peter, "Fuschia and Steerpike: Mood and Form," *MPR* (Autumn, 1977): 17-22.

TITUS TRILOGY (See GORMENGHAST Trilogy)

PERCY, WALKER, 1916-1990

GENERAL

Abadi-Nagy, Zoltan, "A Talk with Walker Percy," *SLJ* 6, i (Fall, 1973): 3-19.

Allen, William R., "All the Names of Death: Allusion and the Theme of Suicide in the Novels of Walker Percy," *DAI* 43, i (July, 1982): 166A.

_____, "All the Names of Death: Walker Percy and Hemingway," *MissQ* 36, i (Winter, 1982-83): 3-19.

Bates, Marvin R., "Walker Percy's Ironic Apology," *DAI* 39 (1979): 6755A.

Bigger, Charles P., "Walker Percy and the Resonance of the Word," *SoQ* 18, iii (1980): 43-54. Also in Tharpe, J., ed., *Walker Percy,* 43-54.

Bradbury, John M., "Absurd Insurrection: The Barth-Percy Affair," *SAQ* 68, iii (Summer, 1969): 319-29.

Bradley, Jared W., "Walker Percy and the Search for Wisdom," *LaS* 12 (Winter, 1973): 579-90.

Brinkmeyer, Robert H., Jr., "Percy's Bludgeon: Message and Narrative Strategy," *SoQ* 18, iii (1980): 80-90. Also in Tharpe, J., ed., *Walker Percy,* 80-90.

Brooks, Cleanth, "The Southerness of Walker Percy," *SCR* 13, ii (1981): 34-8.

_____, "Walker Percy and Modern Gnosticism," *SoR* 13, iv (Oct., 1977): 677-87. Also in Broughton, P. R., ed., *Art of Walker Percy,* 260-72.

Broughton, P. R., ed., *Art of Walker Percy.*

Broughton, Panthea R., "Walker Percy and the Myth of the Innocent Eye," in Andrews, William L., ed., *Literary Romanticism in America,* Baton Rouge and London: Louisiana State Un. Pr., 1981, 94-108.

Brown, Ashley, "An Interview with Walker Percy," *Shen* 18, iii (Spring, 1967): 3-10.

Buckley, William F., Jr., "The Southern Imagination: An Interview with Eudora Welty and Percy Walker," *MissQ* 26 (1973): 493-516.

Bunting, Charles, "An Afternoon with Walker Percy," *NMW* 4 (Fall, 1971): 43-61. [Interview.]

Carr, John, "An Interview with Walker Percy," *GaR* 25, iii (Fall, 1971): 317-32.

_____, "Rotation and Repetition: Walker Percy," [Interview] in Carr, J., ed., *Kite-Flying and Other Irrational Acts,* 34-58.

Chesnick, Eugene, "Novel's Ending and World's End: The Fiction of Walker Percy," *HC* 10, v (Oct., 1973): 1-11.

Coles, R., *Walker Percy.*

Cozart, William R., "Walker Percy's Pilgrims: The Predicament of Post-Modern Man," *CCTE* 43 (1978): 53-61. [Not seen.]

Cremeens, Carlton, "Walker Percy. The Man and the Novelist: An Interview," *SoR* 4 (Spring, 1968): 271-90.

Dana, Carol G., "Where Tchoupitoulas Meets Annunciation: The Convergence of the American Dream and Spiritual Quest in the Noels of Walker Percy," *DAI* 42, xi (May, 1982): 4826A.

Dewey, Bradley R., "Walker Percy Talks about Kierkegaard: An Annotated Interview," *Jour. of Relig.* 54, iii (July, 1974): 273-98.

Dollarhide, Louis, "Mississippi Renaissance Man," in Wells, D. F., and H. Cole, eds., *Mississippi Heroes*, 145-57.

Doran, Linda K. D., "Naming as Disclosure: A Study of Theme and Method in the Fiction of Walker Percy," *DAI* 37 (1976): 2179A.

Dowie, William, S. J., "Walker Percy; Sensualist Thinker," *Novel* 6, i (Fall, 1972): 58-63.

Eubanks, Cecil L., "Walker Percy: Eschatology and the Politics of Grace," *SoQ* (1980): 121-36. Also in Tharpe, J., ed., *Walker Percy*, 121-36.

Forkner, Ben, and J. Gerald Kennedy, "An Interview with Walker Percy," *DeltaES* 13 (Nov., 1981): 1-20.

Fox, William H., "Opposition to Secular Humanism in the Fiction of Flannery O'Connor and Walker Percy," *DAI* 40 (1979): 236A-37A.

Gallo, Louis J., "From Malasian to Saint: A Study of Walker Percy," *DAI* 34 (1974): 7230A-31A.

Gaston, Paul L., "The Revelation of Walker Percy," *ColQ* 20, iv (Spring, 1972): 459-70.

Gray, Richardson K., "A Christian-Existentialist: The Vision of Walker Percy," *DAI* 39 (1979): 6761A.

Gretlund, Jan N., "Interview with Walker Percy in His Home in Covington, Louisiana, January 2, 1981," *SCR*, 13, ii (Spring, 1981): 3-12.

_____, "Walker Percy: A Scandinavian View," *SCR* 13, ii (Spring, 1981): 18-27.

Hardy, John E., "Percy and Place: Some Beginnings and Endings," *SoQ* 18, ii (1980): 5-25. Also in Tarpe, J., ed., *Walker Percy*, 5-25.

Haydel, Douglas J., "From the Realistic to the Fantastic: Walker Percy's Expanding Vision," *DAI* 39 (1979): 6762A.

Hobson, Linda W., "Comedy and Christianity in the Novels of Walker Percy," *DAI* 43 (1982): 1545A.

_____, "The Study of Consciousness: An Interview with Walker Percy," *GaR* 35, i (Spring, 1981): 51-60.

Holley, Joe, "Walker Percy and the Novels of Ultimate Concern," *SWR* 65 (Summer, 1980): 225-34.

Johnson, Mark, "The Search for Place in Walker Percy's Novels," *SLJ* 8, i (Fall, 1975): 55-81.

Kazin, Alfred, "The Pilgrimage of Walker Percy," *Harper's* 242 (June, 1971): 81-6.

Kisor, Henry, "Dr. Percy on Signs and Symbols," *Critic* 39, iv (Sept., 1980): 2-5.

Kissel, Susan S., "Walker Percy's 'Conversions'," *SLJ* 9, ii (Spring, 1977): 124-36.

Lawson, Lewis A., "Walker Percy: The Physician as Novelist," *SAB* 37, ii (May, 1972): 58-63.

_____, "Walker Percy's Southern Stoic," *SLJL* 3, i (Fall, 1970): 5-31.

_____, "William Alexander Percy, Walker Percy, and the Apocalypse," *ModA* 24 (Fall, 1980): 396-406.

LeClair, Thomas, "The Eschatological Vision of Walker Percy," *Ren* 26, iii (Spring, 1974): 115-22.

Lehan, R., *Dangerous Crossing*, 133-45.

Luschei, M. L., *Sovereign Wayfarer.*

Mack, James R., "Love and Marriage in Walker Percy's Novels," *DAI* 37 (197): 4355A-56A.

Madathiparampil, George J., "Prophecy in the Novels of Walker Percy," *DAI* 42, xi (May, 1982): 4834A.

Maxwell, Robert, "Walker Percy's Fancy," *MinnR* 7, iii (1967): 231-7.

Pearson, Michael, "Art as Symbolic Action: Walker Percy's Aesthetic," *SoQ* 18, iii (1980): 55-64. Also in Tharpe, J., ed., *Walker Percy*, 55-64.

Pearson, Michael P., "The Rhetoric of Symbolic Action: Walker Percy's Way of Knowing," *DAI* 39 (1978): 875A.

Riehl, Robert E., "The Ordeal of Naming: Walker Percy's Philosophy of Language and His Novels," *DAI* 36 (1975): 2812A-13A.

Schricke, Gilbert, "A Frenchman's Visit to Walker Percy," *DeltaES* 13 (Nov., 1981): 21-6.

Seiler, Timothy L., "From Moviegoing to Moviemaking: Rhetorical Progression in the Walker Percy Fictive Protagonist," *DAI* 41 (1980): 255A.

Simpson, Lewis P., "The Southern Aesthetic of Memory," *TSE* 23 (1978): 221-27.

Smith, Marcus, "Talking About Talking: An Interview with Walker Percy," *NOR* 5, i (1975): 13-18.

Spivey, Ted, "Religion and Reintegration of Man in Flannery O'Connor and Walker Percy," in Simpson. L. P., ed., *Poetry of Community*, 67-79.

_____, "Walker Percy and the Archetypes," in Broughton, P. R., ed., *Art of Walker Percy*, 273-93.

Stevenson, John W., "Walker Percy: The Novelist as Poet," *SoR* 17, i (Jan., 1981): 164-74.

"A Symposium on Fiction," *Shen* 27, ii (Winter, 1976): 3-31.

"Talking about Talking: An Interview with Walker Percy," *NOR* 5 (1979): 13-18.

Taylor, Lewis J., Jr., "The Becoming of the Self in the Writings of Walker Percy: A Kierkegaardian Analysis," *DAI* 33 (1972): 1224A.

_____, "Walker Percy and the Self," *Cweal* 100 (May, 1974): 233-6.

_____, "Walker Percy's Knights of the Hidden Inwardness," *Anglican Theological Rev.* 56, ii (Apr., 1974): 125-51.

Telotte, Jay P., "Charles Peirce and Walker Percy: From Semiotic to Narrative," *SoQ* 18, iii (1980): 65-79. Also in Tharpe, J., ed., *Walker Percy*, 65-79.

_____, "A Symbolic Structure for Walker Percy's Fiction," *MFS* 26 (1980): 227-40.

_____, "To Talk Creatively: A Study of the Writings of Walker Percy," *DAI* 37 (1977): 6489A-90A.

_____, "Walker Percy: A Pragmatic Approach," *SoSt* 18, ii (Summer, 1979): 217-30.

_____, "Walker Percy's Language of Creation," *SoQ* 16, ii (1978): 105-16.

Tharpe, J., ed., *Walker Percy.*

Watkins, Suzanne B., "From Physician to Novelist: The Progression of Walker Percy," *DAI* 38 (1978): 6196A.

Weaver-Williams, Lynda S., "Walker Percy and Will Campbell: A Theological-Ethical Analysis," *DAI* 42 (1982): 5159A.

Winslow, William, "Modernity and the Novel: Twain, Faulkner, and Percy," *GyS* 8, i (Winter, 1981): 19-40.

Young, Thomas D., "A New Breed: Walker Percy's Critics' Attempts to Place Him," *MissQ* 35, iv (Fall, 1980): 489-98.

Zeugner, John F., "Walker Percy and Gabriel Marcel: The Castaway and the Wayfarer," *MissQ* 28 (Winter, 1974-75): 21-53.

LANCELOT

Barrett, Deborah J., "Discourse and Intercourse: The Conversion of the Priest in Percy's LANCELOT," *Crit* 23, ii (Winter, 1981-82): 5-11.

Brinkmeyer, Robert H., Jr., "Percy's Bludgeon: Message and Narrative Strategy," *SoQ* 18, iii (1980): 84-9. Also in Tharpe, J., ed., *Walker Percy*, 84-9.

Cashin, Edward J., "History as Mores: Walker Percy's LANCELOT," *GaR* 31 (1977): 875-80.

Christensen, Jerome C., "LANCELOT: Signs for the Times," *SoQ* 18, iii (1980): 107-20. Also in Tharpe, J., ed., *Walker Percy*, 107-20.

Coles, R., *Walker Percy*, 216-34.

Dale, Corinne, "LANCELOT and the Medieval Quests of Sir Lancelot and Dante," *SoQ* 18, iii (1980): 99-106. Also in Tharpe, J., ed., *Walker Percy*, 99-106.

Daniel, Robert D., "Walker Percy's LANCELOT: Secular Raving and Religious Silence," *SoR* 14 (1978): 186-94.

Dowie, William J., "LANCELOT and the Search for Sin," in Broughton, P. R., ed., *Art of Walker Percy*, 245-59.

Freshney, Pamela, "THE MOVIEGOER and LANCELOT: The Movies as Literary Symbol," *SoR* 18, iv (Fall, 1982): 718-27.

Kissel, Susan S., "Voices in the Wilderness: The Prophets of O'Connor, Percy, and Powers," *SoQ* 18, iii (1980): 91-8. Also in Tharpe, J., ed., *Walker Percy*, 91-8.

Kreyling, Michael, "*Crime and Punishment:* The Pattern beneath the Surface of Percy's LANCELOT," *NMW* 11 (1978): 36-44.

Lawson, Lewis A., "The Fall of the House of Lamar," in Broughton, P. R., ed., *Art of Walker Percy*, 219-44.

————, "The Gnostic Vision in LANCELOT," *Ren* 32, i (1979): 52-64.

————, "Walker Percy's Silent Character," *MissQ* 33, ii (Spring, 1980): 123-40.

Lischer, Tracy, "Walker Percy's Cerberus: Love, Sexuality, and Sin," *C&L* 30, ii (Winter, 1981): 33-42.

O'Brien, William J., "Walker Percy's LANCELOT: A Beatrician Visit to the Region of the Dead," *SHR* 15, ii (Spring, 1981): 153-64.

Rhein, Phillip H., "Camus and Percy: An Acknowledged Influence," in Gay-Crosier, Raymond, ed., *Albert Camus 1980,* 2nd Int. Conf. February 21-23, 1980, Un. of Florida, Gainsville: Univ. Pr. of Florida, 1980, 257-64.

Sevick, Marly A., "Romantic Ministers and Phallic Knights: A Study of A MONTH OF SUNDAYS, LANCELOT, and FALCONER," *DAI* 40 (1979): 860A.

Simpson, Lewis P., "The Southern Aesthetic of Memory," *TSE* 23 (1978): 224-6.

Vauthier, Simone, "Mimesis and Violence in LANCELOT," *DeltaES* 13 (Nov., 1981): 83-102.

Utter, Glenn H., "The Individual in Technological Society: Walker Percy's LANCELOT," *JPC* 16, iii (1982): 116-27.

————, "Story, Story-Teller and Listener: Notes on LANCELOT," *SCR* 13, ii (Spring, 1981): 39-54.

THE LAST GENTLEMAN

Blouin, Michael T., "The Novels of Walker Percy: An Attempt at Synthesis," *XUS* 6 (Feb., 1967): 29-42.

Broughton, Panthea R., "Gentlemen and Fornicators: THE LAST GENTLEMAN and a Bisected Reality," in Broughton, P. R., ed., *Art of Walker Percy*, 96-114.

Cass, Michael M., "Stages on the South's Way: Walker Percy's THE MOVIEGOER and THE LAST GENTLEMAN," *DAI* 32 (1972): 3992A.

Coles, R., *Walker Percy*, 172-91.

Crews, Frederick C., "The Hero as 'Case'," *Ctary* 42 (Sept., 1966): 100-2.

Douglas, Ellen, *Walker Percy's THE LAST GENTLEMAN* (Religious Dimensions in Literature), N.Y.: Seabury, 1969.

Hall, Constance, "The Ladies in THE LAST GENTLEMAN," *NMW* 11 (1978): 26-35.

Hicks, Jack, "The Legions of the Dead: Walker Percy's THE LAST GENTLEMAN," *EA* 32, ii (1979): 162-70.

Hoffman, F. J., *Art of Southern Fiction*, 133-7.

Lawson, Lewis A., "Walker Percy's Indirect Communications," *TSLL* 11, i (Spring, 1969): 367-900.

————, "Walker Percy's Southern Stoic," *SLJ* 3, i (Fall, 1970): 20-31.

————, "Walker Percy: The Physician as Novelist," *SAB* 37, ii (May, 1972): 60-2.

Lehan, R., *Dangerous Crossing,* 140-3.

Lehan, Richard, "The Way Back: Redemption in the Novels of Walker Percy," *SoR* 4 (Spring, 1968): 306-19.

Luschei, M., *Sovereign Wayfarer,* 111-68.

Pindell, Richard, "Toward Home: Place, Language, and Death in THE LAST GENTLEMAN," in Broughton, P. R., ed., *Art of Walker Percy*, 50-68.

Rubin, L. D., Jr., *Gallery of Southerners*, 208-15, 218-19.

Tanner, T., *City of Words*, 260-2.

Taylor, Lewis, J., Jr., "Walker Percy's Knights of the Hidden Inwardness," *Anglican Theological Rev.* 56, ii (Apr., 1974): 132-8, 144-7.

Tenebaum, Ruth B., "Walker Percy's 'Consumer Self' in THE LAST GENTLEMAN," *LaS* 15 (1976): 304-9.

Vauthier, Simone, "Narrative Triangulation in THE LAST GENTLEMAN," in Broughton, P. R., ed., *Art of Walker Percy*, 69-95.

Zeugner, John F., "Walker Percy and Gabriel Marcel: The Castaway and the Wayfarer," *MissQ* 28 (Winter, 1974-75): 35-44.

LOVE IN THE RUINS

Alterman, Peter S., "A Study of Four Science Fiction Themes and Their Function in Two Contemporary Novels," *DAI* 35 (1974): 2976A-77A.

Bradford, Melvin E., "Dr. Percy's Paradise Lost: Diagnostics in Louisiana," *SR* 81, iv (Autumn, 1973): 839-44.

Berrigan, J. R., "An Explosion of Utopias," *Moreana* 38 (1973): 21-6.

Coles, R., *Walker Percy*, 191-208.

Cunningham, John, "'The Thread in the Labyrinth': LOVE IN THE RUINS and One Tradition of Comedy," *SCR* 13, ii (Spring, 1981): 28-34.

Godshalk, William L., "LOVE IN THE RUINS: Thomas More's Distorted Vision," in Broughton, P. R., ed., *Art of Walker Percy*, 137-56.

————, "Walker Percy's Christian Vision," *LaS* 13, ii (Summer, 1974): 130-41.

Kennedy, J. Gerald, "The Sundered Self and the Riven World: LOVE IN THE RUINS," in Broughton, P. R., ed., *Art of Walker Percy*, 115-36.

Lawson, Lewis A., "Tom More: Cartesian Philosopher," *DeltaES* 13 (Nov., 1981): 67-82.

LeClair, Thomas, "The Eschatological Vision of Walker Percy," *Ren* 26, iii (Spring, 1974): 115-22.

————, "Walker Percy's Devil," *SLJ* 10, i (1977): 3-13. Also in Broughton, P. R., ed, *Art of Walker Percy*, 157-68.

Lehan, R., *Dangerous Crossing*, 143-5.

Luschei, M., *Sovereign Wayfarer*, 169-232.

Simpson, Lewis P., "The Southern Aesthetic of Memory," *TSE* 23 (1978): 223-4.

Siveley, Sherry, "Percy's Down Home Version of More's UTOPIA," *NConL* 7, iv (Sept., 1977): 3-5.

Sullivan, W., *Requiem for the Renascence*, 66-9.

Taylor, Lewis J., Jr., "Walker Percy's Knights of the Hidden Inwardness," *Anglican Theological Rev.* 56, ii (Apr., 1974): 138-44, 147-50.

Webb, Max, "LOVE IN THE RUINS: Percy's Metaphysical Thriller," *Delta ES* 13 (Nov., 1981): 55-66.

Zeugner, John F., "Walker Percy and Gabriel Marcel: The Castaway and the Wayfarer," *MissQ* 28 (Winter, 1974-75): 44-53.

THE MOVIEGOER

Atkins, Anselm, "Walker Percy and the Post-Christian Search," *CentR* 12 (Winter, 1968): 73-95.

Blouin, Michael, "The Novels of Walker Percy: An Attempt at Synthesis," *XUS* 6 (Feb., 1967): 29-42.

Bryant, J. H., *Open Decision*, 273-7.

Byrd, Scott, "Mysteries and Movies: Walker Percy's College Articles and THE MOVIEGOER," *MissQ* 25 (1972): 165-81.

Cass, Michael M., "Stages on the South's Way: Walker Percy's THE MOVIEGOER and THE LAST MOVIEGOER," *DAI* 32 (1972): 3992A.

Cheney, Brainard, "To Restore a Fragmented Image," *SR* 69 (1961): 691-700.

Coles, R., *Walker Percy*, 144-72.

Filippidis, Barbara, "Vision and the Journey to Selfhood in Walker Percy's THE MOVIEGOER," *Ren* 32 (1980): 10-23.

Freshney, Pamela, "THE MOVIEGOER and LANCELOT: The Movies as Literary Symbol," *SoR* 18, iv (Fall, 1982): 718-27.

Henisy, Sarah, "Intersubjectivity in Symbolization," *Ren* 20 (Summer, 1968): 208-14.

Hobbs, Janet, "Binx Bolling and the Stages on Life's Way," in Broughton, P. R., ed., *Art of Walker Percy*, 37-49.

Hoffman, F. J., *Art of Southern Fiction*, 129-33.

Hoggard, James, "Death of the Vicarious," *SWR* 49 (Autumn, 1964): 366-74.

Hyman, S. E., "Moviegoing and Other Intimacies," *Standards*, 63-7.

Kostelanetz, Richard, "The New American Fiction," in Kostelanetz, R., ed., *New American Arts*, 224-5.

Lawson, Lewis A., "The Allegory of the Cave and THE MOVIEGOER," *SCR* 13, ii (Spring, 1981): 13-18.

————, "THE MOVIEGOER and the Stoic Heritage," in Macmillan, D. J., ed., *Stoic Strain in American Literature*, 179-91.

————, "Moviegoing in THE MOVIEGOER," *SoQ* 18, iii (1980): 26-42. Also in Tharpe, J., ed., *Walker Percy*, 26-42.

————, "Time and Eternity in THE MOVIEGOER," *SHR* 16 (1982): 129-41.

————, "Walker Percy's Indirect Communications," *TSLL* 11, i (Spring, 1969): 867-900.

————, "Walker Percy's Southern Stoic," *SLJ* 3, i (Fall, 1970): 15-20.

————, "Walker Percy's THE MOVIEGOER: The Cinema as Cave," *SoSt* 19, iv (Winter, 1980): 331-54.

Lehan, R., *Dangerous Crossing*, 136-40.

————, "The Way Back: Redemption in the Novels of Walker Percy," *SoR* 4 (Spring, 1968): 306-19.

Lischer, Tracy K., "Walker Percy's Kierkegaard: A Reading of THE MOVIEGOER," *Cresset* 41, x (1978): 10-12.

Luschei, M., "THE MOVIEGOER as Dissolve," in Broughton, P. R., ed., *Art of Walker Percy*, 24-36.

————, *Sovereign Wayfarer*, 64-110.

Pindell, Richard, "Basking in the Eye of the Storm: The Esthetics of Loss in Walker Percy's THE MOVIEGOER," *Boundary* 4, i (Fall, 1975): 219-30.

Presley, Delma E., "Walker Percy's 'Larroes'," *NConL* 3, i (Jan., 1973): 5-6.

Quagliano, Anthony, 'Existential Modes in THE MOVIEGOER," *RS* 45 (1977): 214-23.

Regan, Robert, "The Return of THE MOVIEGOER: Toole's CONFEDERACY OF DUNCES," *DeltaES* 13 (Nov., 1981): 169-76.

Shepherd, Allen, "Percy's THE MOVIEGOER and Warren's ALL THE KING'S MEN," *NMW* 4, i (Spring, 1971): 2-14.

Sims, Barbara B., "Jaybirds as Portents of Hell in Percy and Faulkner," *NMW* 9, i (Spring, 1976): 24-8.

Sullivan, Walter, "Southerners in the City: Flannery O'Conner and Walker Percy," in Rubin, L. D., ed., *Comic Imagination in American Literature*, 339-40.

Tanner, T., *Reign of Wonder*, 349-56.

Telotte, J. P., "Walker Percy: A Pragmatic Approach," *SoSt* 18, ii (Summer, 1979): 225-30.

Thale, Jerome, "Alienation on the American Plan," *ForumH* 6 (Summer, 1968): 36-40.

Thale, Mary, "The Moviegoer of the 1950's," *TCL* 14 (July, 1968): 84-9.

Van Cleave, Jim, "Versions of Percy," *SoR* 6, iv (Oct., 1970): 990-1010.

Vanderwerken, David L., "The Americanness of the Moviegoer," *NMW* 12, I (1979): 40-53.

Vauthier, Simone, "Narrative Triangle and Triple Alliance: A Look at THE MOVIEGOER," in Johnson, I. D., and C. Johnson, eds., *Les Americanistes*, 71-93.

————, "Title as Microtext: The Example of THE MOVIEGOER," *JNT* 5 (1975): 219-29.

Walter, James, "Spinning and Spieling: A Trick and a Kick in Walker Percy's THE MOVIEGOER," *SoR* 16 (1980): 574-90.

Webb, Max, "Binx Bolling's New Orleans: Moviegoing, Southern Writing, and Father Abraham," in Broughton, P. R., ed., *Art of Walker Percy*, 1-23.

Zeugner, John F., "Walker Percy and Gabriel Marcy: The Castaway and the Wayfarer," *MissQ* 28 (Winter, 1974-75): 30-5.

THE SECOND COMING

Cronin, Gloria, "Redemption for the Twice Fallen: Walker Percy's SECOND COMING," *L&B* 1 (1981): 113-22.

Fowler, Doreen A., "Answers and Ambiguity in Percy's THE SECOND COMING," *Crit* 2, ii (Winter, 1981-82): 13-23.

Kennedy, J. Gerald, "The Semiotics of Memory: Suicide in THE SECOND COMING," *DeltaES* 13 (Nov., 1981): 103-25.

King, Richard H., "Two Lights That Failed," *VQR* 57, ii (1981): 341-57.

Samway, Patrick, "Rahnerian Backdrop to Percy's SECOND COMING," *DeltaES* 13 (Nov., 1981): 127-44.

BIBLIOGRAPHY

"Walker Percy: A Selected Bibliography," *DeltaES* 13 (Nov., 1981): 177-87.

Weixlmann, Joe, and Daniel H. Gann, "A Walker Percy Bibliography," *SoQ* 18, iii (1980): 137-57. Also in Tharpe, J., ed., *Walker Percy*, 137-57.

PETRAKIS, HARRY MARK, 1923-

GENERAL

Chapin, Helen, "'Chicagopolis': The Double World of Harry Mark Petrakis," *ON* 2 (Dec., 1976): 401-13.

Karanikas, Alexander, "Harry Mark Petrakis: A Study in Greek Ethnicity," *MELUS* 5, i (1978): 14-30.

Rodgers, Bernard F., Jr., "The Song of the Thrush: An Interview with Harry Mark Petrakis," *ChiR* 28, iii (1977): 97-119.

PETRY, ANN (LANE), 1908-

GENERAL

Gross, Theodore L., "Ann Petry: The Novelist as Social Critic," in Lee, A. R., ed., *Black Fiction*, 41-53.

Isaacs, Diane S., "Ann Petry's Life and Art: Piercing Stereotypes," *DAI* 43, ii (Aug., 1982): 446A.

Jaskoski, Helen, "Power Unequal to Man: The Significance of Conjure in the Works of Five Afro-American Authors," *SFQ* 38 (1974): 91-108.

Lattin, Vernon E., "Ann Petry and the American Dream," *BALF* 12, ii (1978): 69-72.

O'Brien, John, ed., *Interviews with Black Writers*, 153-63.

Shinn, Thelma J., "Women in the Novels of Ann Petry," *Crit* 16, i (1974): 110-20. Also in Spacks, P. M., ed., *Contemporary Women Novelists*, 108-17.

COUNTRY PLACE

Hughes, C. M., *Negro Novelist*, 160-8, 240-2.

Rosenblatt, R., *Black Fiction*, 138-42.

Schraufnagle, N., *From Apology to Protest*, 63-5.

Shinn, Thelma J., "Women in the Novels of Ann Petry," *Crit* 16, i (1974): 114-18. Also in Spacks, P. M., ed., *Contemporary Women Novelists*, 112-16.

THE NARROWS

McDowell, Margaret B., "THE NARROWS: A Fuller View of Ann Petry," *BALF* 14, iv (1980):

Schraufnagel, N., *From Apology to Protest*, 108-10.

Shinn, Thelma J., "Women in the Novels of Ann Petry," *Crit* 16, i (1974): 110-14. Also in Spacks, P. M., ed., *From Apology to Protest*, 116-17.

THE STREET

Christian, B., *Black Women Novelists*, 63-7.

Gayle, A., Jr., *Way of the New World*, 191-7.

Gross, Theodore L., "Ann Petry: The Novelist as Social Critic," in Lee, A. R., ed., *Black Fiction*, 42-6.

Hughes, C. M., *Negro Novelist*, 86-96, 218-23.

Ivy, James W., "Ann Petry Talks About First Novel," *Crisis* 53 (1946): 78-9. Also in Bell, R. P., et. al. eds., *Sturdy Black Bridges*, 197-200.

O'Banner, Bessie M., "A Study of Black Heroines in Four Selected Novels (1929-1959) by Four Black American Women Novelists: Zora Neale Hurston, Nella Larson, Paule Marshall and Ann Lane Petry," *DAI* 43 (1982): 447A.

Shinn, Thelma J., "Women in the Novels of Ann Petry," *Crit* 16, i (1974): 110-14. Also in Spacks, Patricia, ed., *Contemporary Women Novelists*, 108-12.

Yarborough, Richard, "The Quest for the American Dream in Three Afro-American Novels: IF HE HOLLERS LET HIM GO, THE STREET, and INVISIBLE MAN," *MELUS* 8, iv (Winter, 1981): 41-7.

PHARR, ROBERT DEANE, 1916-1992

GENERAL

Epps, Garrett, "To Know the Truth: The Novels of Robert Deane Pharr," *HC* 13, v (Dec., 1976): 1-10.

O'Brien, John, and Raman K. Singh, "Interview with Robert Deane Pharr," *NALF* 8 (1974): 244-6.

THE BOOK OF NUMBERS

Epps, Garrett, "To Know the Truth: The Novels of Robert Deane Pharr," *HC* 13, v (Dec., 1976): 3-6.

Whitlow, R., *Black American Literature*, 165-7.

THE SOUL MURDER

Epps, Garrett, "To Know the Truth: The Novels of Robert Deane Pharr," *HC* 13, v (Dec., 1976): 8-10.

SRO

Epps, Garrett, "To Know the Truth: The Novels of Robert Deane Pharr," *HC* 13, v (Dec., 1976): 6-8.

PIERCE, OVID WILLIAMS, 1910-

GENERAL

McMillan, Douglas J., "Folkways in the Novels of Ovid Pearce," in Hester, E., and D. J. McMillan, eds., *Cultural Change in Eastern North Carolina*, 52-62.

THE DEVIL'S HALF

Sanders, F. David, "The Impingement of the Past: Ovid Pierce's THE DEVIL'S HALF," in Hester, E., and D. J. McMillan, eds., *Cultural Change in Eastern North Carolina*, 27-35.

ON A LONESOME PORCH

Betts, Doris, "The House by the River: Ovid Williams Pierce," *SAQ* 64, iii (Summer, 1965): 283-95.

THE PLANTATION

Betts, Doris, "The House by the River: Williams Pierce," *SAQ* 64, iii (Summer, 1965): 283-95.

Kirkland, James W., "The Cultural Context of Ovid Pierce's THE PLANTATION," in Hester, E., and D. J. McMillan, eds., *Cultural Change in Eastern North Carolina*, 37-46.

THE WEDDING GUEST

McMillan, Douglas J., "Folkways in Ovid Pierce's THE WEDDING GUEST," *NCarF* 23 (1975): 125-8.

PIERCY, MARGE, 1936-

GENERAL

Hammond, Karla, "A Conversation with Marge Piercy," *Pulp* 1, i (1978): 10-12.

Kress, Susan, "In and Out of Time: The Form of Marge Piercy's Novels," in Barr, M. S., ed., *Future Females*, 109-22.

Ladenson, Joyce R., "Marge Piercy's Revolutionary Feminism," *SSMLN* 10, ii (1980): 24-31. [Not seen.]

DANCE THE EAGLE TO SLEEP

Kress, Susan "In and Out of Time: The Form of Marge Piercy's Novels," in Barr, M. S., ed., *Future Females*, 112-14.

GOING DOWN FAST

Kress, Susan, "In and Out of Time: The Form of Marge Piercy's Novels," in Barr, M. S., ed., *Future Females*, 114-19.

Mickelson, A. Z., *Reaching Out*, 175-90.

WOMAN ON THE EDGE OF TIME

Annas, Pamela J., "New Worlds, New Words: Androgyny in Feminist Science Fiction," *SFS* 5 (July, 1978): 153-5.

DuPlessis, Rachel B., "The Feminist Apologues of Lessing, Piercy, and Rus," *Frontiers* 4, i (Spring, 1971): 2-4.

Khouri, Nadia, "The Dialectics of Power: Utopia in the Science Fiction of LeGuin, Jeury, and Piercy," *SFS* 7, i (Mar., 1980): 56-60.

Kress, Susan, "In and Out of Time: The Form of Marge Piercy's Novels," in Barr, M. S., ed., *Future Females*, 119-21.

Pearson, Carol S., "The Utopian Novels of Dorothy Bryant, Mary Staton and Marge Piercy," *Heresies* 4, i (1981): 84-7. Also as "Beyond Governance: Anarchist Feminism in the Utopian Novels of Dorothy Bryant, Marge Piercy, and Mary Staton," *AF* 4, i (1981): 126-35.

Seidel, Kathryn, "Envisioning the Androgynous Future," *S&M* 3 (Summer, 1976): 98-101.

PINCKNEY, JOSEPHINE, 1895-1957

GENERAL

Shippey, Herbert P., "Josephine Pinckney," 83-92 in Meriwether, James B., ed., *South Carolina Women Writers.* Proc. of the Reynolds Conf., Un. of So. Carolina, Oct. 24-3, 1975. Columbia: Southern Studies Program, Univ. of So. Carolina, 1979.

PLATH, SYLVIA, 1932-1963

GENERAL

Martin, Wendy, "'God's Lioness': Sylvia Plath, Her Prose and Poetry," *WS* 1 (1973): 191-2. [Not seen.]

Patterson, Rena M., "Sylvia Plath: A Study of Her Life and Art," *DAI* 39 (1978): 282A.

THE BELL JAR

Aird, E. M., *Sylvia Plath*, 88-100.

Allen, M., "Sylvia Plath's Defiance: THE BELL JAR," *Necessary Blankness*, 160-78.

Barnard, C. K., *Sylvia Plath*, 24-33.

Berman, Jeffrey, "Sylvia Plath and the Art of Dying," *HSL* 10, i-iii (1978): 137-55.

Burton, Deirdre, "Through Glass Darkly: Through Dark Glasses: On Stylistics and Political Commitment—via a Study of a Passage from Sylvia Plath's THE BELL JAR," 195-214 in Carter, Ronald, ed., *Language and Literature: An Introductory Reader in Stylistics*, London: Allen & Unwin, 1982.

DeLauretis, Teresa, "Rebirth in THE BELL JAR," *Women's Studies* 3 (1975): 173-83.

Ellmann, Mary, "THE BELL JAR: An American Girlhood," in Newman, Charles, ed., *THE ART OF SYLVIA PLATH: A Symposium*, London: Faber & Faber, 1970, 221-6.

Evans, William R., "Bell Jars: Plath and Holmes," *AN&Q* 15, vii (1977): 105-7.

Lameyer, Gordon, "The Double in Sylvia Plath's THE BELL JAR," in Butscher, E., ed., *Sylvia Plath*, 143-65.

Martin, Elaine, "Mother, Madness, and the Middle Class in THE BELL JAR and LES MOTS POUR LE DIRE," *FAR* 5, i (Spring, 1981): 24-47.

Milliner, Gladys W., "The Tragic Imperative: THE AWAKENING and THE BELL JAR," *MWoN* 2, i (Dec., 1973): 21-7.

Perloff, Marjorie G., "'A Ritual for Being Born Twice': Sylvia Plath's THE BELL JAR," *ConL* 13 (Autumn, 1972): 507-22.

Schvey, Henry I., "Sylvia Plath's THE BELL JAR: Bildungsroman or Case History," *DQR* 8, i (1978): 18-37.

Smith, Stan, "Attitudes Counterfeiting Life: The Irony of Artifice in Sylvia Plath's BELL JAR," *CritQ* 17 (Autumn, 1975): 247-60.

Spacks, P. M., *Female Imagination*, 144-50.

Stewart, G., *New Mythos*, 15-17, 147-.

Tanner, T., *City of Words*, 262-4.

Werner, . H., *Paradoxical Resolutions*, 52-4.

Whittier, Gayle, 'The Divided Woman and Generic Doubleness in THE BELL JAR," *Women's Studies* 3 (1975): 127-46.

BIBLIOGRAPHY

Lamb, Gary, and Maria Stevens, comps., *Sylvia Plath: A Bibliography*, Metuchen, N.J.: Scarecrow Pr., 1978.

PLUNKETT, JAMES, Pseud. (Kelly, James Plunkett), 1920-

GENERAL

Behrend, Hanna, "James Plunkett's Contribution to Democratic and Socialist Culture," *ZAA* 27 (1979): 307-26.

FAREWELL COMPANIONS

Behrend, Hanna, "James Plunkett's Contribution to Democratic and Socialist Culture," *ZAA* 27 (1979): 314-22.

STRUMPET CITY

Behrend, Hanna, "James Plunkett's Contribution to Democratic and Socialist Culture," *ZAA* 27 (1979): 312-14.
Cahalan, James M., "The Making of STRUMPET CITY: James Plunkett's Vision," *Eire* 13, iv (1978): 81-100.
Carpentier, Godeleine, "Dublin and the Drama of Larkinism: James Plunkett's STRUMPET CITY," *CahiersI* 4-5 (1976): 209-19. Also in Rafroidi, P., and M. Harmon, eds., *Irish Novels in Our Time*, 209-17.

POLLINI, FRANCIS, 1930-

THE CROWN

Green, R. B., *Italian-American Novel*, 323-9.

EXCURSION

Green, R. B., *Italian-American Novel*, 318-23.

GLOVER

Green, R. B., *Italian-American Novel*, 312-18.

NIGHT

Green, R. B., *Italian-American Novel*, 308-12.

PRETTY MAIDS ALL IN A ROW

Green, R. B., *Italian-American Novel*, 329-35.

PORTER, HAL, 1911-1995(?)

GENERAL

Burns, Robert, "A Sort of Triumph Over Time: Hal Porter's Prose Narratives," *Meanjin* 28 (Autumn, 1969): 19-28.
Duncan, R. A., "Hal Porter's Writing and the Impact of the Absurd," *Meanjin* 29, iv (Summer, 1970): 468-73.
Geering, R. G., "Hal Porter, the Watcher," *Southerly* 24, ii (1964): 92-103.
Lord, M., *Hal Porter*.
_____, "Interview with Hal Porter," *ALS* 8 (1978): 269-79.
Ward, Peter, "The Craft of Hal Porter," *AusL* 5, ii (1963): 19-25. [Not seen.]

A HANDFUL OF PENNIES

Lord, M., *Hal Porter*, 24-6.

THE RIGHT THING

Geering, R. G., "Hal Porter: The Controls of Melodrama," *Southerly* 33, i (Mar., 1973): 27-33.
Lord, M., *Hal Porter*, 30-2.

THE TILTED CROSS

Hergenhan, L. T., "THE TILTED CROSS: 'The Duties of Innocence'," *Southerly* 34 (1974): 157-67.
Lord, M., *Hal Porter*, 26-30.
Rutherford, Anna, "The Cross Tilted to Fall: Hal Porter's THE TILTED CROSS," in Maes-Jelinek, H., ed., *Commonwealth Literature and the Modern World*, 127-35.

BIBLIOGRAPHY

Wilding, Michael, "Two Bibliographies: Hal Porter and Patrick White," *ALS* 3 (1967): 142-8.

PORTER, KATHERINE ANNE, 1891-1980

GENERAL

Bolsterli, Margaret, "'Bound' Characters in Porter, Welty, McCullers: The Prerevolutionary Status of Women in American Fiction," *BuR* 24, i (1978): 95-105. [Not seen.]
Cimarolli, Mary L., "Social Conditions as a Structural Factor in Katherine Anne Porter's Fiction," *DAI* 38 (1978): 6722A.
Core, George, "The Best Residuum of Truth," *GaR* 20 (1966): 278-91.
Curley, Daniel, "Katherine Anne Porter: The Larger Plan," *KR* 25 (Autumn, 1963): 671-95.
DeMorry, Jane K., "The Seeds of the Pomegranate: A Study of Katherine Anne Porter's Women," *DAI* 39 (1979): 4946A.
Drake, Robert, "Three Southern Ladies," *F10B* 9 (1980): 41-8.
Farrinton, Thomas A., "The Control of Imagery in Katherine Anne Porter's Fiction," *DAI* 34 (1973): 767A.
Gaunt, Marcia E., "Imagination and Reality in the Fiction of Katherine Anne Porter," *DAI* 33 (1972): 2933A.
Givner, "Porter's Subsidiary Art," *SWR* 59, iii (Summer, 1974): 265-76.
Greene, Annetta C., "Katherine Anne Porter: Person and Persona," *DAI* 38 (1978): 6725A.
Gretlund, Jan N., "Flannery O'Connor and Katherine Anne Porter," *F10B* 8 (1979): 77-87.
Hardy, J. E., *Katherine Anne Porter*.
Hartley, L., and G. Fore, eds., *Katherine Anne Porter*.
Hendrick, G., *Katherine Anne Porter*.
Hennessy, Rosemary, "Katherine Anne Porter's Models for Heroines," *ColQ* 25 (1977): 301-15.
Krishnamurthi, M. G., *Katherine Anne Porter*.
_____, "Katherine Anne Porter: A Study in Themes," *DA* 28 (1967): 682A-3A.
Liberman, M. M., *Katherine Anne Porter's Fiction*.

Lopez, Hank, "A Country and Some People I Love," *Harper's* (Sept., 1965): 58-62, 65-8. [Interview.] Also in Warren, R. P., ed., *Katherine Anne Porter*, 20-35.

Lugg, Bonelyn, "Mexican Influences on the Work of Katherine Anne Porter," *DAI* 37 (1977): 7131A.

Lyons, Mary P., "Art and Politics in the Writings of Katherine Anne Porter," *DAI* 43 (1982): 1546A.

Marsden, Malcolm M., "Love as Threat in Katherine Anne Porter's Fiction," *TCL* 13 (Apr., 1967): 29-38.

Miles, Lee J., "Unused Possibilities: A Study of Katherine Anne Porter," *DAI* 34 (1973): 784A-85A.

Mooney, H. J., Jr., *Fiction and Criticism of Katherine Anne Porter.*

Nance, W. L., *Katherine Anne Porter and the Art of Religion.*

Plante, Patricia R., "Katherine Anne Porter: Misanthrope Acquitted," *XUS* 2 (Dec., 1963): 87-91.

Ruoff, James, "Katherine Anne Porter Comes to Kansas," *MQ* 4 (July, 1963): 305-14.

Stanford, Donald E., "Katherine Anne Porter," *SoR* 17, i (Jan., 1981): 1-2. [Not seen.]

Thompson, Barbara, "The Art of Fiction 29: Katherine Anne Porter," *ParisR* 8 (Winter-Spring, 1963): 87-114. Also in *Writers at Work*, 2nd ser., 137-63.

Vliet, Vida A., "The Shape of Meaning: A Study of the Development of Katherine Anne Porter's Fictional Form," *DA* 29 (1968): 1550A.

Warren, R. P., ed., *Katherine Anne Porter.*

SHIP OF FOOLS

Abraham, William, "Progression Through Repetition," *MR* 9 (Summer, 1963): 805-9.

Adams, Robert H., "The Significance of Point of View in Katherine Anne Porter's SHIP OF FOOLS," *DA* 26 (1965): 2001.

Alexander, Jean, "Katherine Anne Porter's Ship in the Jungle," *TCL* 11 (Jan., 1966): 179-88.

Auchincloss, Louis, "Bound for Bremerhaven—and Eternity," *N.Y. Herald Tribune* (April 1, 1962): 3. Also in Warren, W. P., ed., *Katherine Anne Porter*, 162-4.

————, *Pioneers and Caretakers*, 145-51.

Baker, Howard, "The Upward Path: Notes on the Works of Katherine Anne Porter," *SoR* n.s. 4 (Winter, 1968): 15-19. Also in Weber, B., ed., *Sense and Sensibility in Twentieth-Century Writing*, 89-93.

Bedford, Sybille, "Voyage to Everywhere," *Spectator* 7012 (Nov. 16, 1962): 763-4. Also in Warren, W. P., ed., *Katherine Anne Porter*, 150-4.

Bode, Carl, "Miss Porter's SHIP OF FOOLS," *WSCL* 3 (Fall, 1962): 90-2. Also in Bode, C., *The Half-World of American Culture*, Carbondale: So. Illinois Un. Pr., 1965, 220-5.

Curley, Dan, "Katherine Anne Porter: The Larger Plan," *KR* 25 (Autumn, 1963): 671-95.

Daniels, Sally, in *MinnR* 3 (Fall, 1962): 124-7.

Finkelstein, Sidney, "SHIP OF FOOLS," *Mainstream* 15 (September, 1962): 42-8.

Gessel, Michael, "Katherine Anne Porter: The Low Comedy of Sex," in Brack, O. M., Jr., ed., *American Humor*, 139-52.

Givner, Joan, "The Genesis of SHIP OF FOOLS," *SLJ* 10, i (Fall, 1977): 14-30.

Glicksberg, C. I., *Sexual Revolution in Modern American Literature*, 150-4.

Hardy, J. E., *Katherine Anne Porter*, 110-40.

Hartley, Lodwick, "Dark Voyagers: A Study of Katherine Anne Porter's SHIP OF FOOLS," *UR* 30 (Dec., 1963): 83-94. Also in Hartley, L., and G. Core, eds., *Katherine Anne Porter*, 211-26.

Heilman, Robert B., "SHIP OF FOOLS: Notes on Style," *FQ* 12, i (Nov., 1962): 46-55. Also in Hartley, L., and G. Core, eds., *Katherine Anne Porter*, 197-210.

Hendrick, George, "Hart Crane Aboard the Ship of Fools: Some Speculations," *TCL* 9 (Apr., 1963): 3-9.

————, *Katherine Anne Porter*, 118-40.

Hertz, Robert N., "Rising Waters: A Study of Katherine Anne Porter," *DA* 25 (Dec., 1964): 3571-72.

————, "Sebastian Brant and Porter's SHIP OF FOOLS," *MQ* 6 (Summer, 1964): 389-401.

Hoffman, F. J., *Art of Southern Fiction*, 47-50.

Holmes, Theodore, "The Literary Mode," *Carleton Miscellany* 4 (Winter, 1963): 124-8.

Hyman, Stanley E., "Archetypal Woman," *New Leader* 45 (Apr. 2, 1962): 23-4.

Joselyn, Sister M., "Animal Imagery in Katherine Anne Porter's Fiction," in Slote, Bernice, ed., *Myth and Symbol: Critical Approaches and Applications*, Lincoln: Un. of Nebraska Pr., 1963, 101-15.

————, "On the Making of THE SHIP OF FOOLS," *SDR* 1, ii (May, 1964): 46-52.

Kasten, Maurice, in *Shen* 13 (Summer, 1962): 54-61.

Kauffmann, Stanley, "Katherine Anne Porter's Crowning Work," *NRep* 146 (Apr. 2, 1962): 23-4.

Kiely, Robert, "The Craft of Despondency—The Traditional Novelists," *Daedalus* 92 (Spring, 1963): 226-30, 234-5.

Kirkpatrick, Smith, "SHIP OF FOOLS," *SR* 71 (Winter, 1963): 94-8. Also in Warren, R. P., ed., *Katherine Anne Porter*, 165-9.

Krishnamurthi, M. G., *Katherine Anne Porter*, 146-204.

————, "Katherine Anne Porter: A Study in Themes," *DA* 28 (1967): 682-83A.

Liberman, M. M., *Katherine Anne Porter's Fiction*, 2-36.

————, "The Responsibility of the Novelist: The Critical Reception of SHIP OF FOOLS," *Criticism* 8 (Fall, 1966): 377-88. Also in Hartley, L., and G. Core, eds., *Katherine Anne Porter*, 185-96. Also in Warren, R. P., ed., *Katherine Anne Porter*, 179-89.

————, "The Short Story as Chapter in SHIP OF FOOLS," *Criticism* 10 (Winter, 1968): 65-71.

————, "Some Observations on the Genesis of SHIP OF FOOLS: A Letter from Katherine Anne Porter," *PMLA* 84 (Jan., 1969): 136-7.

McIntyre, John P., "SHIP OF FOOLS and Its Publicity," *Thought* 38 (Summer, 1963): 211-20.

Marsden, Malcolm M., "Love as Threat in Katherine Anne Porter's Fiction," *TCL* 13 (Apr., 1967): 35-8.

Miller, Paul W., "Katherine Porter's SHIP OF FOOLS, a Masterpiece Manque," *UR* 32 (Dec., 1965): 151-7.

Mooney, H. J., Jr., *Fiction and Criticism of Katherine Anne Porter*, 56-63.

Moss, Howard, "No Safe Harbor," *NY* 38 (Apr. 28, 1962): 165-73. Also Moss, H., *Writing Against Time*, 45-54. Also in Warren, W. P., ed., *Katherine Anne Porter*, 155-61.

Nance, W. L., *Katherine Anne Porter and the Art of Rejection*, 156-207.

Osta, Winifred H., "The Journey Pattern in Four Contemporary American Novels," *DAI* 31 (1970): 2933A.

Plante, Patricia R., "Katherine Anne Porter; Misanthrope Acquitted," *XUS* 2 (Dec., 1963): 87-91.

Rubin, Louis D., Jr., "'We Get Along Together Just Fine...'," *FQ* 12 (Mar., 1963): 310-13.

Ruoff, James, "Katherine Anne Porter Comes to Kansas," *MQ* 4 (July, 1963): 310-13.

————, and Del Smith, "Katherine Anne Porter on SHIP OF FOOLS," *CE* 24 (Feb., 1963): 396-7.

Ryan, Marjorie, "Katherine Anne Porter: SHIP OF FOOLS," *Crit* 5, ii (Fall, 1962): 94-9.

————, "Katherine Anne Porter: SHIP OF FOOLS and the Short Stories," *BuR* 12, i (Mar., 1964): 51-63. Also in Booth, Wayne, ed., *The Rhetoric of Fiction*, Chicago: Un. of Chicago Pr., 1962, 274-7.

Schorer, Mark, "We're All on the Passenger List," *NYTBR* (Apr. 1, 1962): 1. Also in Warren, R. P., ed., *Katherine Anne Porter*, 130-3.

Solotaroff, Theodore, "SHIP OF FOOLS and the Critics," *Ctary* 34 (Oct., 1962): 277-86. Also in Solotaroff, T., *Red Hot Vacuum*, 103-21. Also in Warren, R. P., ed., *Katherine Anne Porter*, 134-49.

Thompson, John, in *PR* 29 (Fall, 1962): 608-12.

Walcutt, C. C., *Man's Changing Mask*, 145-55.

Walton, Gerald, "Katherine Anne Porter's Use of Quakerism in SHIP OF FOOLS," *Criticism* 7 (Fall, 1966): 15-23.

Weber, Brom, in *MinnR* 3 (Fall, 1962): 127-30.

Wescott, Glenway, *Images of Truth*, 25-48 passim, 49-56. Also (expanded) as "Katherine Anne Porter: The Making of a Novel," *Atlantic* 209 (Apr., 1962): 42-9. Also in Warren, R. P., ed., *Katherine Anne Porter*, 36-58.

West, Ray, Jr., *Katherine Anne Porter*, 32-43. Also in Warren, R. P., ed., *Katherine Anne Porter*, 170-8.

Wiesenfarth, Joseph, "Negatives of Hope: A Reading of Katherine Anne Porter," *Ren* 3, ii (Winter, 1973): 90-2.

BIBLIOGRAPHY

Kiernan, Robert F., *Katherine Anne Porter and Carson McCullers: A Reference Guide*, Boston: G. K. Hall, 1976.

PORTIS, CHARLES, 1933-

TRUE GRIT

Ditsky, John, "True 'Grit' and TRUE GRIT," *Ariel* 4, ii (1973): 18-31.

Shuman, R. Baird, "Portis' TRUE GRIT: Adventure Story or Entwicklungsroman?" *EJ* 59, iii (Mar., 1970): 367-70.

POTOK, CHAIM, 1929-

GENERAL

Merkin, Daphne, "Why Potok is So Popular," *Ctary* 61, ii (Feb., 1976): 73-5.

THE CHOSEN

Bluefarb, Sam, "The Head, the Heart and the Conflict of Generations in THE CHOSEN," *CLAJ* 14 (June, 1971): 402-9.

Bothwell, E. K., *Alienation in the Jewish Novel of the Sixties*, 178-9, 183-4.

Grebstein, Sheldon, "The Phenomenon of the Really Jewish Best Seller: Potok's THE CHOSEN," *SAJL* 1, i (1975): 23-31.

IN THE BEGINNING

Cheever, Leonard A., "Rectangles of Frozen Memory: Potok's IN THE BEGINNING," *PAPA* 4, ii (1978): 8-12.

Merkin, Daphne, "Why Potok is So Popular," *Ctary* 61, ii (Feb., 1976): 73-5.

MY NAME IS ASHER LEV

Schiff, Ellen, "To Be Young, Gifted and Oppressed: The Plight of the Ethnic Artist," *MELUS* 6, i (Spring, 1979): 76-9.

Sutherland, Sam, III., "Asher Lev's Vision of His Mythic Ancestor," *ReAL* 3, ii (1977): 51-4.

Tijn, M. van, "MY NAME IS ASHER LEV," *Streven* 26 (1973): 779-81.

True, Warren R. "Potok and Joyce: The Artist and His Culture," *SAJL* 2 (1982): 181-90.

Uffen, Ellen S., MY NAME IS ASHER LEV: Chaim Potok's Portrait of the Young Hasid as Artist," *SAJL* 2 (1982): 174-80.

THE PROMISE

Bothwell, E. K., *Alienation in the American Jewish Novel of the Sixties*, 179-81, 184.

POWELL, ANTHONY, 1905-

GENERAL

Atkins, John, "Widening Sympathies: Reflections on the Work of Anthony Powell," *KN* 22, ii (1975): 191-205.

Barber, Michael, "Anthony Powell: The Art of Fiction 68," *ParisR* 73 (1978): 45-79.

Bergonzi, B., *Anthony Powell.*

Brennan, N., *Anthony Powell.*

Brooke, Jocelyn, "From Wauchop to Widmerpol," *LonM* 7 (Sept., 1960): 60-4.

Davis, Douglas M., "An Interview with Anthony Powell, From England, June, 1962," *CE* 24 (Apr., 1963): 533-6.

Lee, James W., "The Novels of Anthony Powell," *DA* 25 (1965): 5281-82.

Mizener, A., *Sense of Life in the Modern Novel*, 79-103.

Morris, R. K. *Novels of Anthony Powell.*

Quesenbery, W. D., Jr., "Anthony Powell: The Anatomy of Decay," *Crit* 7 (Spring, 1964): 5-26.

Radner, Sanford, "Powell's Early Novels: A Study in Point of View," *Ren* 16 (Summer, 1964): 194-200.

Riley, John J., "Gentlemen at Arms: The Generative Process of Evelyn Waugh and Anthony Powell before World War II," *MFS* 22, ii (Summer, 1976): 165-81.

Russell, J., *Anthony Powell.*

————, "Quintet from the 30's: Anthony Powell," *KR* 27 (Autumn, 1965): 698-726.

Tucker, J., *Novels of Anthony Powell.*

Voorhees, Richard J., "Anthony Powell: The First Phase," *PrS* 28 (Winter, 1954): 337-44.

Woodward, A. G., "The Novels of Anthony Powell," *ESA* 10 (Sept., 1967): 117-28.

THE ACCEPTANCE WORLD (See also A DANCE TO THE MUSIC OF TIME)

Brennan, N., *Anthony Powell*, 152-62.
Hall, James, "The Uses of Polite Surprise," *EIC* 12 (Apr., 1962): 179-82. Also in Hall, J., *Tragic Comedians*, 141-4.
Morris, R. K., *Novels of Anthony Powell*, 148-65.
Russell, J., *Anthony Powell*, 129-37.
Tucker, J., *Novels of Anthony Powell*, 141-5.

AFTERNOON MEN

Allen, W., *Modern Novel*, 219-21.
Bergonzi, B., *Anthony Powell*, 3-8.
_____, in Bloomfield, P., *L. P. Hartley and Anthony Powell*, 24-6.
Brennan, N., *Anthony Powell*, 84-100.
Morris, R. K., *Novels of Anthony Powell*, 13-31.
Russell, J., *Anthony Powell*, 40-50 *passim*, 50-4.
_____, "Quintet from the Thirties: Anthony Powell," *KR* 27 (Autumn, 1965): 708-11.
Tucker, J., *Novels of Anthony Powell*, 9-18.

AGENTS AND PLACES

Brennan, N., *Anthony Powell*, 114-20.
Morris, R. K, *Novels of Anthony Powell*, 69-84.
Russell, J., *Anthony Powell*, 40-50 *passim*, 63-7.
Tucker, J., *Novels of Anthony Powell*, 34-6.

AT LADY MOLLY'S (See also A DANCE TO THE MUSIC OF TIME)

Brennan, N., *Anthony Powell*, 162-8.
Hall, J., *Tragic Comedians*, 141-4.
Morris, R. K., *Novels of Anthony Powell*, 166-80.
Russell, J., *Anthony Powell*, 138-49.
Tucker, J., *Novels of Anthony Powell*, 146-50.

BOOKS DO FURNISH A ROOM (See also A DANCE TO THE MUSIC OF TIME)

Brennan, N., *Anthony Powell*, 192-8.
Tucker, J., *Novels of Anthony Powell*, 179-82.

A BUYER'S MARKET (See also A DANCE TO THE MUSIC OF TIME)

Brennan, N., *Anthony Powell*, 147-52.
Hall, James, "The Uses of Polite Surprise: Anthony Powell," *EIC* 12 (Apr., 1962): 169-70, 173-7. Also in Hall, J., *Tragic Comedians*, 135-9.
Morris, R. K., *Novels of Anthony Powell*, 148-65.
Russell, J., *Anthony Powell*, 119-29.
Tucker, J., *Novels of Anthony Powell*, 135-40.

CASANOVA'S CHINESE RESTAURANT (See also A DANCE TO THE MUSIC OF TIME)

Bliven, Naomi, "Books: The Marriage State," *NY* 36 (Dec. 31, 1960): 53-4.
Brennan, N., *Anthony Powell*, 168-73.
Hall, J., *Tragic Comedians*, 144-8.
Kermode, F., *Puzzles and Epiphanies*, 127-30.

Morris, R. K., *Novels of Anthony Powell*, 181-99.
Pritchett, V. S., "The Bored Barbarian," *NStat* 59 (June 25, 1960): 947-8.
Russell, J., *Anthony Powell*, 149-63.
Tucker, J., *Novels of Anthony Powell*, 151-6.
Waugh, Evelyn, "Marriage a la Mode—1936," *Spectator* (June 24, 1960): 53-4.

A DANCE TO THE MUSIC OF TIME Series

Allen, W., *Modern Novel*, 221-3.
Arnold, Bruce, "Powell: THE MUSIC OF TIME," in Harward, T. B., *European Patterns: Contemporary Patterns in European Writing*, Chester Springs, Pa.: Dufour, 1966, 49-52.
Bader, Rudolf, *Anthony Powell's MUSIC OF TIME as a Cyclic Novel of Generations*, Bern: Francke, 1980.
Bergonzi, B., *Anthony Powell, passim.*
_____, "Anthony Powell: 9 1/2," *CritQ* 11, i (Spring, 1969): 76-86.
_____, in Bloomfield, P., *L. P. Hartley and Anthony Powell*, 28-39.
_____, *Situation of the Novel*, 121-33.
Birns, Margaret B., "Anthony Powell's Secret Harmonies: Music in a Jungian Key," *LitR* 25, i (Fall, 1981): 80-92.
Bjornson, Barbara A., "An Examination of Narrative Strategy in A LA RECHERCHE DU TEMPS PERDU and A DANCE TO THE MUSIC OF TIME," *DA* 29 (1969): 679A.
Brennan, N., *Anthony Powell*, 126-203.
Davin, D. M., *Snow Upon Fire*: A DANCE TO THE MUSIC OF TIME; *Anthony Powell*. (W. D. Thomas Memorial Lecture.) Swansea: Un. College of Swansea, 1977.
Flory, Evelyn A., "The Imagery of Anthony Powell's A DANCE TO THE MUSIC OF TIME," *BSUF* 17, ii (1976): 51-9.
Frankie, Patricia A., "The Fictional Memoir as Sensibility and Social History: A Study of the Narrator-Artist in Anthony Powell's A DANCE TO THE MUSIC OF TIME," *DAI* 38 (1978): 4157A.
Glazebrook, Mark, "The Art of Horace Isbister, E. Bosworth Deacon, and Ralph Barnby," *LonM* 7 (Sept., 1967): 76-82.
Guiterrez, Donald K., "A Critical Study of Anthony Powell's A DANCE TO THE MUSIC OF TIME," *DAI* 30 (1969): 724A.
_____, "The Discrimination of Elegance: Anthony Powell's A DANCE TO THE MUSIC OF TIME," *MHRev* 34 (Apr., 1975): 126-41.
_____, "The Doubleness of Anthony Powell: Point of View in A DANCE TO THE MUSIC OF TIME," *UDR* 14, ii (1980): 15-27.
_____, "Exemplary Punishment: Anthony Powell's DANCE as Comedy," *Greyfriar* 22 (1981): 27-44.
_____, "Power in A DANCE TO THE MUSIC OF TIME," *ConnR* 6, ii (1973): 50-60.
Hall, James, "The Uses of Polite Surprise: Anthony Powell," *EIC* 12 (Apr., 1962): 167-83. Also in Hall, J., *Tragic Comedians*, 129-50.
Herring, Anthony D., "Anthony Powell: A Reaction Against Determinism," *BSUF* 9 (Winter, 1968): 17-21.
Howarth, Herbert, "Discords in THE MUSIC OF TIME," *Ctary* 53, i (Jan., 1972): 70-5.
Hynes, Sam, "Novelist of Society," *Cweal* 70 (July 31, 1959): 396-7.
James, Clive, "They Like It Here," *New Rev* 3, xxix (1976): 53-5.

Jebb, Julian, "Anthony Powell's Dreams—An Interview," *Listener* 94 (Sept. 11, 1975): 347-8.

Jones, Richard, "Anthony Powell's MUSIC: Swansong of the Metropolitan Romance," *VQR* 52 (Summer, 1976): 353-69.

Kamera, Willy D., "A Descriptive Index of the Characters in Anthony Powell's A DANCE TO THE MUSIC OF TIME," *DAI* 34 (1974): 7235A.

Karl, Frederick R., "Anthony Powell's THE MUSIC OF TIME," *Contemporary English Novel*, 238-44.

_____, "Bearers of War and Disaster," *NRep* 147 (Sept. 24, 1962): 212-2.

_____, *Contemporary English Novel*, Rev. & Exp., 312-23.

_____, "Sisyphus Descending: Mythical Patterns in the Novels of Anthony Powell," *Mosaic* 4, iii (1971): 13-22.

Larkin, Philip, "Mr. Powell's Mural," *NStat* (Feb. 19, 1971): 347-8.

Lee, James W., "The Novels of Anthony Powell," *DA* 25 (1965): 52-82.

Martin, W. R., "Style as Achievement in Anthony Powell's THE MUSIC OF TIME," *ESA* 14 (1971): 73-86.

McCall, Raymond G., "Anthony Powell's Gallery," *CE* 27 (Dec., 1965): 227-32.

McLaughlin, Richard, "In the Comic Tradition," *AmMerc* 87 (Nov., 1958): 154-5.

McLeod, Dan, "Anthony Powell: Some Notes on the Art of the Sequence Novel?" *SNNTS* 3, i (Spring, 1971): 44-63.

McSweeney, Kerry, "The End of A DANCE TO THE MUSIC OF TIME," *SAQ* 76 (Winter, 1977): 44-57.

Meckier, Jerome, "The Case for the Modern Satirical Novel: Huxley, Waugh and Powell," *STwC* 14 (1974): 21-42.

Mizener, Arthur, "A DANCE TO THE MUSIC OF TIME: The Novels of Anthony Powell," *KR* 22 (Winter, 1960): 79-92.

_____, *Sense of Life in the Modern Novel*, 82-5, 89-103.

Moore, John R., "Anthony Powell's England: A DANCE TO THE MUSIC OF TIME," *HC* 8, iv (Oct., 1971): 1-16.

Morris, R. K., *Continuance and Change*, 123-55.

_____, *Novels of Anthony Powell*, 1-10, 103-12, 247-52.

Piper, William B., "The Accomodation of the Present in Novels by Murdoch and Powell," *SNNTS* 11, ii (Summer, 1979): 179-85.

Pritchett, V. S., "The Bored Barbarians," *Living Novel*, 294-303. Also in Pritchett, V. S., *Working Novelist*, 172-80.

Quesenbery, W. D., Jr., "Anthony Powell: The Anatomy of Decay," *Crit* 7 (Spring, 1964): 5-26.

Radner, Sanford, "The World of Anthony Powell," *ClareQ* 10, ii (Winter, 1963): 41-7.

Ruoff, Gene W., "Social Mobility and the Artist in MANHATTAN TRANSFER and THE MUSIC OF TIME," *WSCL* 5, i (Winter-Spring, 1964): 64-76.

Russell, J., *Anthony Powell*, 103-225.

Schlesinger, Arthur L., "Waugh a la Proust," *NRep* 139 (Oct. 20, 1958): 20-1.

Shapiro, C., "Widmerpol and THE MUSIC OF TIME," *Contemporary British Novelists*, 81-94.

Spurling, Hilary, *Invitation to the Dance: A Guide to Anthony Powell's DANCE TO THE MUSIC OF TIME*, Boston: Little, Brown, 1978.

Stanton, Lillian, "Art in the Dance: A Study of the Fine Arts in Anthony Powell's A DANCE TO THE MUSIC OF TIME," *DAI* 34 (1974): 4288A.

Stone, William B., "Dialogue in Powell's Second Movement," *MBL* 2, i (1977): 85-8.

Swinden, Patrick, "Powell's HEARING SECRET HARMONIES," *CritQ* 18, iv (Winter, 1976): 51-60.

Tapscott, Stephen J., "The Epistemology of Gossip: Anthony Powell's DANCE TO THE MUSIC OF TIME," *TQ* 21, i (1978): 104-16.

Tucker, J., *Novels of Anthony Powell*, 41-192.

Vinson, James, "Anthony Powell's MUSIC OF TIME," *Per* 10 (Summer-Autumn, 1958): 146-52.

Voorhees, Richard J., "THE MUSIC OF TIME: Themes and Variations," *DR* 42 (Autumn, 1962): 213-21.

Walcutt, C. C. *Man's Changing Mask*, 336-9.

Webster, Harvey C., "A Dance of British Eccentrics," *New Leader* 42 (Jan. 12, 1959): 26-7.

White, Mary R., "Anthony Powell: Ten Volumes of THE MUSIC OF TIME," *DAI* 34 (1973): 1300A-01A.

Wilcox, Thomas W., "Anthony Powell and the Illusion of Possibility," *ConL* 17 (1976): 223-39.

Wiseman, T. P., "The Centaur's Hoof: Anthony Powell and the Ancient World," *CML* 2, i (Fall, 1981):; 7-23.

Zegerell, James J., "Anthony Powell's MUSIC OF TIME: Chronicle of a Declining Establishment," *TCL* 12 (Oct., 1966): 138-46.

FROM A VIEW TO A DEATH

Brennan, N., *Anthony Powell*, 104-14.

Morris, R. K., *Novels of Anthony Powell*, 49-68.

Pritchett, V. S., "The Bored Barbarians," *Working Novelist*, 173-5.

Russell, J., *Anthony Powell*, 40-50 *passim*, 59-63.

_____, "Quintet from the Thirties: Anthony Powell," *KR* 27 (Autumn, 1965): 716-23.

Tucker, J., *Novels of Anthony Powell*, 27-33.

HEARING SECRET HARMONIES (See also A DANCE TO THE MUSIC OF TIME)

Bayley, John, "A Family and Its Fictions," *TLS* (Sept. 12, 1975): 1010-12.

Muggeridge, Malcolm, "A Valley of Lost Things," *NStat* (Sept. 12, 1975): 308-9.

Tucker, J., *Novels of Anthony Powell*, 188-92.

THE KINDLY ONES (See also A DANCE TO THE MUSIC OF TIME)

Brennan, J., *Anthony Powell*, 173-8.

Hartley, L. P., "Good Dog, Good Dog," *T&T* 43 (June 28, 1962): 21-2.

Karl, Frederick R., "Bearers of War and Disaster," *NRep* 147 (Sept. 24, 1962): 21-2.

McDowell, Frederick P. W., "'The Devious Involutions of Human Characters and Emotions': Reflections on Some Recent British Novels," *WSCL* 4, iii (Autumn, 1963): 362-5.

Morris, R. K., *Novels of Anthony Powell*, 200-17.

Russell, J., *Anthony Powell*, 163-75.

Symons, J., "A Long Way from Firbank," *Critical Occasions*, 74-9.

Tucker, J., *Novels of Anthony Powell*, 157-62.

THE MILITARY PHILOSOPHERS (See also A DANCE
TO THE MUSIC OF TIME)

Anon., in *TLS* (Oct. 17, 1968). Also in *T.L.S.: Essays and Reviews
from The Times Literary Supplement, 1968*, 183-5.
Brennan, N., *Anthony Powell*, 187-91.
Janeway, Elizabeth, "THE MILITARY PHILOSOPHERS,"
NYTBR (Mar. 9, 1969): 1, 42-3.
Pritchard, William H., "Anthony Powell's Serious Comedy,"
MR 10 (Autumn, 1969): 812-19.
Russell, J., *Anthony Powell*, 207-9, 215-25.
Tucker, J., *Novels of Anthony Powell*, 174-8.

THE MUSIC OF TIME (See A DANCE TO THE MUSIC OF TIME)

A QUESTION OF UPBRINGING (See also A DANCE
TO THE MUSIC OF TIME)

Bergonzi, B., *Anthony Powell*, 12-14.
Brennan, N., *Anthony Powell*, 137-46.
Hall, J., *Tragic Comedians*, 134-5.
Morris, R. K., *Novels of Anthony Powell*, 132-47.
Russell, J., *Anthony Powell*, 112-19.
Tucker, J., *Novels of Anthony Powell*, 129-34.

THE SOLDIER'S ART (See also A DANCE TO THE MUSIC OF
TIME)

Anon., "War Games," *TLS* (Sept. 15, 1966): 853. Also in *T.L.S.:
Essays and Reviews from The Times Literary Supplement, 1966*,
74-7.
Brennan, N., *Anthony Powell*, 182-7.
Grandsen, K. W., "Taste of the Old Time," *Encounter* 27 (Dec.,
1966): 106-8.
Morris, R. K., *Novels of Anthony Powell*, 231-46.
Russell, J., *Anthony Powell*, 184-91, 202-15.
Seymour-Smith, Martin, "Jenkins Marches On," *Spectator* (Sept.
16, 1966): 353.
Tucker, J., *Novels of Anthony Powell*, 169-73.

TEMPORARY KINGS (See also A DANCE TO THE MUSIC OF
TIME)

Brennan, N., *Anthony Powell*, 198-203.
Tucker, J., *Novels of Anthony Powell*, 183-7.

THE VALLEY OF BONES (See also A DANCE TO THE MUSIC
OF TIME)

Anon., "Nick Goes to War," *TLS* (Mar. 5, 1964): 189. Also in
*T.L.S.: Essays and Reviews from The Times Literary Supplement,
1964*, 105-7.
Morris, R. K., *Novels of Anthony Powell*, 218-30.
Brennan, N., *Anthony Powell*, 178-82.
Radner, Sanford, "Anthony Powell and THE VALLEY OF
BONES," *EngR* 15 (Apr., 1965): 8-9.
Russell, J., *Anthony Powell*, 184-203.
Spender, Stephen, "Tradition vs Underground Novels," in En-
cyclopedia Britannica. *Great Ideas Today*, 1965, 190-2.
Tucker, J., *Novels of Anthony Powell*, 163-8.

VENUSBERG

Brennan, N., *Anthony Powell*, 100-4.

Morris, R. K., *Novels of Anthony Powell*, 32-48.
Russell, J., *Anthony Powell*, 40-50 *passim*, 54-9, 83-6.
_____, "Quintet from the Thirties: Anthony Powell," *KR* 27
(Autumn, 1965): 711-16.
Tucker, J., *Novels of Anthony Powell*, 19-26.

WAR TRILOGY (THE MILITARY PHILOSOPHERS, THE SOLDIER'S
ART,
THE VALLEY OF BONES)

Riley, John J., "Gentlemen at Arms: A Comparison of the War
Trilogies of Anthony Powell and Evelyn Waugh," *DAI* 34
(1974): 5202A.
Russell, John, "The War Trilogies of Anthony Powell and Evelyn Waugh," *ModA* 16, iii (Summer, 1972): 289-300.

WHAT'S BECOME OF WARING

Brennan, N., *Anthony Powell*, 120-3.
Bergonzi, B., *Anthony Powell*, 9-10.
Morris, R. K., *Novels of Anthony Powell*, 85-100.
Russell, John, *Anthony Powell*, 40-50 *passim*, 67-71.
_____, "Quintet from the Thirties: Anthony Powell," *KR* 27
(Autumn, 1965): 723-6.

BIBLIOGRAPHY

Bader, Rudolf, *Anthony Powell's MUSIC OF TIME as a Cyclic
Novel of Generations*, Bern: Francke, 1980, 182-91.

POWELL, DAWN, 1897-1965

GENERAL

Josephson, Matthew, "Dawn Powell: A Woman of *Esprit*," *SoR*
9 (Jan., 1973): 18-52.
Pett, Judith F., "Dawn Powell: Her Life and Her Fiction," *DAI*
42 (1982): 3159A-60A.

POWERS, J(AMES) F(ARL), 1917-

GENERAL

Evans, E., ed., *J. F. Powers*.
Hagopian, J. V., *J. F. Powers*.
Jacobsen, Josephine, "A Catholic Quintet," *ChS* 47 (Summer,
1964): 146-9.
Kellogg, G., *Vital Tradition*, 167-79.
Kristin, Sister, "The Catholic and Creativity: J. F. Powers," *ABR*
15 (Mar., 1964): 63-80. [Interview.] Also in Evans, F., ed., *J. F.
Powers*, 1-22.
LaGuardia, David M., "A Critical Dilemma: J. F. Powers and the
Durability of Catholic Fiction," in Browne, Ray B., Larry N.
Landrum, and William K. Bottorff, eds., *Challenges in Ameri-
can Culture*, Bowling Green, Ohio: Bowling Green Un. Popu-
lar Pr., 1970, 265-76.
Laughlin, Rosemary M., "Wanderers in the Wasteland: The
Characters of J. F. Powers," *BaratR* 6 (Spring-Summer, 1971):
38-48.
Powers, J. F., "The Catholic and Creativity—Interview," *ABR*
(Mar., 1964): 63-80.

Scouffas, George, "J. F. Powers: On the Vitality of Disorder," *Crit* 2 (Fall, 1958): 41-58.

Shannon, James P., "J. F. Powers and the Priesthood," *CathW* (Sept. 1952): 432-7.

Steichen, Donna M., "J. F. Powers and the Noonday Devil," *ABR* 20 (Dec., 1969): 528-51.

Wymard, Eleanor B., "J. F. Powers: His Christian Cosmic Vision," *DA* 30 (1969): 742A.

MORTE D'URBAN

Bates, Barclay W., "Flares of Special Grace: The Orthodoxy of J. F. Powers," *MQ* 11 (Autumn, 1969): 91-106.

Boyle, Robert, S. J., "To Look Outside: The Fiction of J. F. Powers," in Mooney, H. J., Jr., and Staley, T. F., eds., *Shapeless God*, 102-15.

Carruth, Hayden, "Reviving the Age of Satire," *NRep* 147 (Sept. 24, 1962): 23-4. Also in Evans, F., ed., *J. F. Powers*, 69-72.

Clark, Walter H., Jr., "Small-Scale Relationships in J. F. Powers' MORTE D'URBAN," *ArAA* 4 (1979): 133-44.

_____, "Structure in MORTE D'URBAN," *BRMMLA* 32 (1978): 20-32.

Collignon, Joseph B., "Powers' MORTE D'URBAN: A Layman's Indictment," *Ren* 16 (Fall, 1963): 20-1, 51-2.

Curley, Thomas, "J. F. Powers' Long Awaited First Novel," *Cweal* 77 (Oct. 12, 1962): 77-8.

Dolan, Paul J., "God's Crooked Line: Powers' MORTE D'URBAN," *Ren* 21 (Winter, 1969): 95-102.

Dorenkamp, J. H., "The Unity of MORTE D'URBAN," *UDR* 8, ii (Fall, 1971): 29-34.

Dufner, Angeline, "The Sainting of Father Urban," *ABR* 24 (Sept., 1973): 327-41.

Dupee, F. W., "In the Powers Country," *PR* 30 (Spring, 1963): 113-16. Also in Dupee, F. W., *King of the Cats*, 149-55.

Gass, William H., "Bingo Game at the Foot of the Cross," *Nation* 195 (Sept. 29, 1962): 182-3. Also in Evans, F., ed., *J. F. Powers*, 73-7. Also in Gass, W. H., *Figures of Life*, 134-9.

Gilbert, Sister Mary, S.N.J.M., "MORTE D'URBAN," *SR* 71 (Autumn, 1963): 673-5.

Green, Martin, "J. F. Powers and Catholic Writing," *Yeats's Blessing on von Hügel*, 97-121.

Hagopian, John V., "Irony and Involution in J. F. Powers' MORTE D'URBAN," *WSCL* 9 (1968): 151-71.

_____, *J. F. Powers*, 123-51.

Henault, Marie, "The Saving of Father Urban," *America* 108 (Mar. 2, 1963): 290-2.

Hertzel, Leo J., "Brother Juniper, Father Urban and the Unworldly Tradition," *Ren* 17 (Summer, 1965): 207-10, 215. Also in Evans, F., ed., *J. F. Powers*, 90-3.

Hinchcliffe, Arnold P., "Nightmare of Grace" *Blackfriars* 45 (Feb., 1964): 61-9.

Hyman, Stanley E., "The Priest with the Fishnet Hatband," *New Leader*, 45 (Sept. 17, 1962): 22-3. Also in Hyman, S. E., *Standards*, 95-7.

Hynes, Joseph, "Father Urban's Renewal: J. F. Powers' Difficult Precision," *MLQ* 29 (Dec., 1968): 45-66.

Kaufman, Maynard, "J. F. Powers and Secularity," in Scott, N. A., Jr., *Adversity and Grace*, 167-81.

Kellogg, G., *Vital Tradition*, 172-7.

Kissel, Susan S., "Voices in the Wilderness: The Prophets of O'Connor, Percy and Powers," *SoQ* 18, iii (1980): 91-8.

Kort, Wesley A., "MORTE D'URBAN and the Presence of Clergy," *Shriven Self*, 15-35.

McCorry, Vincent P., "Urban in the Lion's Den," *America* 108 (Mar. 2, 1963): 292-4.

Merton, Thomas, "MORTE D'URBAN: Two Celebrations," *Worship* 36 Nov., 1962): 645-50. Also in Evans, F., ed., *J. F. Powers*, 95-100.

Monteiro, George, "The Literary Uses of a Proverb," *Folklore* 87 (1976): 216-18.

Webster, Harvey C., "Comedy and Darkness," *KR* 25 (1963): 166-9.

O'Brien, Charles F., "Morte D'Urban and the Catholic Church in America," *Discourse* 12 (Summer, 1969): 324-28.

Phelps, Donald, "Reasonable, Holy and Living," *MinnR* 9, i (1969): 57-62.

Poss, Stanley, "J. F. Powers: The Gin of Irony," *TCL* 14 (July, 1968): 65-74.

Preston, Thomas R., "Christian Folly in the Fiction of J. P. Powers," *Crit* 16, ii (1974): 96-107.

Rowan, Thomas, C.S.S.R., "MORTE D'URBAN: A Novel About Priests," *HPR* 58 (Jan., 1963): 291-4. Also in Evans, F., ed., *J. F. Powers*, 101-5.

Sandra, Sister Mary, S.S.A., "The Priest-Hero in Fiction," *Person* 46 (Oct., 1965): 531-5.

Sisk, John P., in *Crit* 5, iii (Winter, 1962-63): 99-103.

_____, in *Ren* 16 (1963): 101.

Smith, Patrick J., "Typology and Peripety in Four Catholic Novels," *DA* 28 (1967): 2265A.

Stewart, D. H., "J. F. Powers' MORTE D'URBAN as Western," *WAL* 5, i (Spring, 1970): 31-44.

Twombly, Robert G., "Hubris, Health, and Holiness: The Despair of J. F. Powers," in Whitbread, T. B., ed., *Seven Contemporary Authors*, 143-62.

Vickery, John B., "J. F. Powers' MORTE D'URBAN: Secularity and Grace," in Friedman, M. J., ed., *Vision Obscured*, 45-65.

Webster, Harvey C., "Comedy and Darkness," *KR* 25 (1963): 166-9.

Wymard, Eleanor B., "On the Revisions of MORTE D'URBAN," *SSF* 14 (1977): 84-6.

BIBLIOGRAPHY

Evans, F., ed., *J. F. Powers*, 115-16.

Hagopian, J. V., *J. F. Powers*, 165-8.

POWYS, JOHN COWPER, 1872-1963

GENERAL

Adam, Eugene A., "A Structural Study of the Major Novels of John Cowper Powys," *DAI* 36 (1975): 2211A.

Anon., "A Magician and His Multiverse: The True Nature of John Cowper Powys," *TLS* (Feb. 8, 1974): 121-2.

Aury, Dominique, "Reading Powys," *REL* 4, i (Jan., 1963): 33-7.

Blake, George B., Jr., "Autobiography and Romance: The English Novels of John Cowper Powys," *DAI* 34 (1973): 1271A.

_____, "The Eccentricity of John Cowper Powys," *MFS* 22, ii (Summer, 1976): 201-11.

Brebner, J. A., "The Demon Within: A Study of John Cowper Powys's Novels," *DAI* 33 (1972): 1715A-16A.

Breckon, Richard, *John Cowper Powys: The Solitary Giant,* London: Village Pr., 1973.

Cavaliero, G., *John Cowper Powys.*

_____, "The Novels of John Cowper Powys," *Revista Canaria de Estudios Ingleses* 4 (1982): 65-9. [Not seen.]

Churchill, R. C., *The Powys Brothers* (WTW 150), London and N.Y.: Longmans Green, 1962.

Collins, H. P., *John Cowper Powys.*

_____, "Largeness of John Cowper Powys," *ContempR* 202 (Oct., 1962): 174-7.

Cook, David A., "The AUTOBIOGRAPHY of John Cowper Powys: A Portrait of the Artist as Other," *MP* 72, i (Aug., 1971): 30-44.

_____, "The Quest for Identity in John Cowper Powys: A Reading of His 'Autobiography' and His Wessex Series," *DAI* 32 (1972): 4606A.

Coombes, Harry, "John Cowper Powys: A Modern Merlin?" *SoR* 11, iv (Oct., 1975): 79-93.

Going, Margaret E. M., "John Cowper Powys, Novelist," *DA* 15 (1955): 582.

Hewitt, Christian B., "The Novels of John Cowper Powys," 22 (1961): 870-71.

Hooker, J., *John Cowper Powys.*

_____, *John Cowper Powys and David Jones.*

Humfrey, B., ed., *Essays on John Cowper Powys.*

Knight, G. Wilson, "Powys and the Kundalini Serpent," *ContempR* 133 (July, 1978): 37-44; (Aug., 1978): 91-100.

_____, *Saturnian Quest.*

Krissdottir, M., *John Cowper Powys and the Magical Quest.*

Lane, Denis G., "Nature in the Novels of John Cowper Powys," *DAI* 40 (1979): 1460A-61A.

_____, "The Reemergence of John Cowper Powys," *AR* 39, iv (Fall, 1978): 422-30.

Little, Bruce R., "John Cowper Powys: The Reputation of the Novelist in England and America," *DAI* 35 (1975): 6146A.

Mahanti, J. C., "Beyond Yes and No: The Novels of John Cowper Powys," *IFR* 2 (1975): 77-9.

Mayne, Ellen, *The New Mythology and John Cowper Powys,* Richmond: New Atlantic Foundation, 1969.

Miles, Gwyneth F., "The Interaction Between Landscape and Myth in the Novels of John Cowper Powys," *DAI* 34 (1974): 7768A.

Miller, Henry, "The Immortal Bard," *REL* 4, i (Jan., 1963): 21-4.

Moran, Margaret L., "The Wessex Romances of John Cowper Powys," *DAI* 42 (1981): 1163A.

Nye, Robert, "Tatterdemalion Taliessen," *LonM* 12, vi (Feb.-Mar., 1973): 75-85.

Pechefsky, Howard S., "The Fantasy Novels of John Cowper Powys," *DAI* 32 (1972): 4014A-15A.

Robillard, Douglas, "Landscape with Figures: The Early Fiction of John Cowper Powys," *SLitI* 1, ii (Oct., 1968): 51-8.

Southwick, Arthur T., "The Meaning of Powys," *DAI* 42, ix (Fall, 1982): 4012A-13A.

Speirs, Russell, "A Man from the West Country," *Philobiblon* 8 (Winter, 1966): 18-22. [Not seen.]

Sullivan, Harry R., "The Elemental World of John Cowper Powys," *DA* 21 (1961): 2300.

Whute, K., *Life-Technique of John Cowper Powys.*

Wilson, Angus, "Mythology in John Cowper Powys's Novels," *REL* 4, i (Jan., 1963): 9-20.

ALL OR NOTHING

Brebner, J. A., *Demon Within,* 220-3.

Cavaliero, G., *John Cowper Powys,* 150-3.

Knight, G. W., *Saturnian Quest,* 114-21.

ATLANTIS

Brebner, J. A., *Demon Within,* 203-12.

Cavaliero, G., *John Cowper Powys,* 133-40.

Knight, G. W., *Saturnian Quest,* 93-102.

Krissdottir, M., *John Cowper Powys and the Magical Quest,* 175-8.

THE BRAZEN HEAD

Brebner, J. A., *Demon Within,* 212-20.

Cavaliero, G., *John Cowper Powys,* 140-4.

Collins, H. P., *John Cowper Powys,* 147-9.

Knight, G. W., *Saturnian Quest,* 102-7.

Krissdottir, M., *John Cowper Powys and the Magical Quest,* 178-80.

DUCDAME

Brebner, J. A., *Demon Within,* 38-57.

Cavaliero, G., *John Cowper Powys,* 33-41.

_____, "John Cowper Powys: Landscape and Personality in the Early Novels," in Humfrey, B., ed., *Essays on John Cowper Powys,* 88-100.

Collins, Carvel, "A Fourth Book Review by Faulkner," *MissQ* 28 (1975): 339-42. [Reprints Faulkner's review.]

Collins, H. P., *John Cowper Powys,* 57-62.

Faulkner, William, "Review of DUCDAME," *MissQ* 28 (1975): 343-6.

Hooker, J., *John Cowper Powys,* 24-9.

Knight, G. W., *Saturnian Quest,* 26-9.

Krissdottir, M., *John Cowper Powys and the Magical Quest,* 174-5.

A GLASTONBURY ROMANCE

Booth, Daniel, "Teaching a GLASTONBURY ROMANCE to Secondary School Students," *PowysN* 5 (1977-78): 30-1.

Brebner, J. A., *Demon Within,* 91-124.

Brooke, Jocelyn, "On Rereading A GLASTONBURY ROMANCE," *LonM* 3, iv (1956): 44-51.

Cavaliero, G., *John Cowper Powys,* 60-78.

Collins, H. P., *John Cowper Powys,* 78-91.

Cook, David A., "John Cowper Powys' A GLASTONBURY ROMANCE: A Modern Mystery Play," *ConL* 13, iii (Summer, 1972): 341-60.

Knight, C. Wilson, "Lawrence, Joyce and Powys," *EIC* 11 (Oct., 1961): 414-17.

_____, *Saturnian Quest,* 35-42.

Krissdottir, M., *John Cowver Powys and the Magical Quest,* 80-99.

Von Huene, Dorothee, "Forces for Permanence: Conservative Elements in Adalbert Stifter's DER NACHSOMMER, Maurice Barre's LES DERACINES, and John Cowper Powys' A GLASTONBURY ROMANCE," *DAI* 39 (1978): 2243A.

THE INMATES

Brebner, J. A., *Demon Within,* 194-202.

Cavaliero, G., *John Cowper Powys,* 131-3.

Knight, G. W., *Saturnian Quest,* 82-4.

Krissdottir, M., *John Cowper Powys and the Magical Quest,* 175-5.

MAIDEN CASTLE

Brebner, J. A., *Demon Within*, 141-53.
Cavaliero, G., *John Cowper Powys*, 93-102.
Collins, H. P., *John Cowper Powys*, 133-8.
Hooker, J., *John Cowper Powys*, 68-74.
Knight, G. W., *Saturnian Quest*, 49-55.
Krissdottir, M., *John Cowper Powys and the Magical Quest*, 111-20.

MORWYN: OR THE VENGEANCE OF GOD

Brebner, J. A., *Demon Within*, 153-61.
Cavaliero, G., *John Cowper Powys*, 103-6.
Emmel, Darrell, "MORWYN: The Harrowing of Hell," *PowysN* 5 (1977-78): 11-15.
Knight, G. W., *Saturnian Quest*, 65-7.
Krissdottir, M., *John Cowper Powys and the Magical Quest*, 117-21.

OWEN GLENDOWER

Brebner, J. A., *Demon Within*, 161-77.
_____, "Owen Glendower: The Pursuit of the Fourth Dimension," *AWR* 18, xlii (Feb., 1970): 207-16.
Cavaliero, G., *John Cowper Powys*, 107-19.
Collins, H. P., *John Cowper Powys*, 138-43.
Hooker, J., *John Cowper Powys*, 74-8.
Knight, G. Wilson, "Lawrence, Joyce and Powys," *EIC* 11, iv (Oct., 1961): 414-17.
_____, OWEN GLENDOWER, *REL* 4, i (Jan., 1963): 41-52.
_____, *Saturnian Quest*, 67-72.
Krissdottir, M., *John Cowper Powys and the Magical Quest*, 50-6.
Mathias, Roland, "The Sacrificial Prince: A Study of OWEN GLENDOWER," in Humfrey, B., ed., *Essays on John Cowper Powys*, 234-61.

PORIUS

Blackmore, R. L., "The Matter of PORIUS," *PowysN* 4 (1974-75): 4-6.
Brebner, John A., "The Anarchy of the Imagination," in Humfrey, B., ed., *Essays on John Cowper Powys*, 264-75.
_____, *Demon Within*, 177-89.
Cavaliero, G., *John Cowper Powys*, 119-30, 185-7.
Collins, H. P., *John Cowper Powys*, 143-7.
Hooker, J., *John Cowper Powys*, 143-7.
Humfrey, Belinda, "Introduction," in Humfrey, B., ed., *Essays on John Cowper Powys*, 27-44.
Knight, G. W., *Saturnian Quest*, 76-82.
Lane, Denis, "Elementalism in John Cowper Powys' PORIUS," *PLL* 17, iv (Fall, 1981): 381-404.
Powys, John C., "The Characters of the Book," *PowysN* 4 (1975-75): 15-21.
_____, "PREFACE or anything you like to PORIUS," *PowysN* 4 (1974-75): 7-14.
Slater, Joseph, "PORIUS Restauratus," *PowysB* 4 (1974-75): 22-44.
Wilson, Angus, "'Mythology' in John Cowper Powys's Novels," *REL* 4, i (Jan., 1963): 18-20.

RODMOOR

Brebner, J. A., *Demon Within*, 9-29.
Cavaliero, G., *John Cowper Powys*, 27-33.

_____, "John Cowper Powys: Landscape and Personality in the Early Novels," in Humfrey, B., ed., *Essays on John Cowper Powys*, 88-91.
Collins, H. P., *John Cowper Powys*, 45-50.
Greenwald, Michael, "The Second Novel: RODMOOR," *PowysN* 3 (1972-73): 8-17.
Knight, G. Wilson, "Preface" to *Rodmoor: A Romance*, by John Cowper Powys, New Ed., London: Macdonald, 1974.
_____, *Saturnian Quest*, 24-6.
Krissdottir, M., *John Cowper Powys and the Magical Quest*, 50-6.

WEYMOUTH SANDS (JOBBER SKALD)

Brebner, J. A., *Demon Within*, 124-38.
Cavaliero, G., *John Cowper Powys*, 78-93.
Collins, H. P., *John Cowper Powys*, 106-15.
_____, "The Sands Do Not Run Out," in Humfrey, B., ed., *Essays on John Cowper Powys*, 206-18.
Cook, David A., "Between Two Worlds: A Reading of Weymouth Sands," *PowysN* 3 (1972-73): 18-24.
Hooker, J., *John Cowper Powys*, 53-61.
Hyman, Timothy, "The Modus Vivendi of John Cowper Powys," in Humfrey, B., ed., *Essays on John Cowper Powys*, 137-41.
Knight, G. W., *Saturnian Quest*, 42-9.
Krissdottir, M., *John Cowper Powys and the Magical Quest*, 102-11.
Wilson, Angus, "Introduction," WEYMOUTH SANDS: A Novel [by] John Cowper Powys, Cambridge: Rivers Pr. Ltd., 1973.

WOLF SOLENT

Blake, George, "The Eccentricity of John Cowper Powys," *MFS* 22, ii (Summer, 1976): 205-11.
Brebner, J. A., *Demon Within*, 58-87.
Cavaliero, G., *John Cowper Powys*, 44-60.
Collins, H. P. *John Cowper Powys*, 65-77.
Cook, David A., "The Creation of Self in John Cowper Powys: A Reading of WOLF SOLENT," *EAS* 4 (1975): 23-44.
Hooker, J., *John Cowper Powys*, 33-43.
Knight, G. W., *Saturnian Quest*, 30-5.
Krissdottir, M., *John Cowper Powys and the Magical Quest*, 64-79.
Lukacher, Ned, "Notre-Homme-des-Fleurs: Wolf Solent's Metaphoric Legends," *PRev* 2, ii (Winter-Spring, 1979-80): 64-73.
Wilson, Angus, "'Mythology' in John Cowper Powys's Novels," *REL* 4, i (Jan., 1963): 12-18.

WOOD AND STONE

Brebner, J. A., *Demon Within*, 1-9.
Cavaliero, G., *John Cowper Powys*, 21-6.
Knight, G. W., *Saturnian Quest*, 23-4.
Krissdottir, M., *John Cowper Powys and the Magical Quest*, 49-50.
Wilinson, Louis U., *Blasphemy and Religion: A Dialogue About John Cowper Powys' WOOD AND STONE and Theodore Powys' THE SOLILOQUY OF A HERMIT*, Southrepps, Norfolk: Warren House Pr., 1969.

BIBLIOGRAPHY

Anderson, Arthur J., "John Cowper Powys: A Bibliography," *BB* 25, iv (Sept./Dec., 1967): 73-8, 94.

Krissdottir, M., *John Cowper Powys and the Magical Quest*, 199-208.

Thomas, Dante, "A Bibliography of the Principal Writings of John Cowper Powys and Some Works About Him," *DAI* 32 (1971): 2106A.

PRICE, REYNOLDS, 1933-

GENERAL

Barnes, Daniel R., "The Names and Faces of Reynolds Price," *KyR* 2, ii (1968): 76-91.

Bixby, George, "Blurbs: Welty on Reynolds Price, *EuWN* 1, ii (1977): 1-3. [Not seen.]

Daniel, Daniel F., "Within and Without a Region: The Fiction of Reynolds Price," *DAI* 38 (1978): 706-25.

Eichelberger, Clayton L., "Reynolds Price: 'A Banner in Defeat'," *JPC* 1 (Spring, 1968): 410-17.

Kaufman, Wallace, "A Conversation with Reynolds Price," *Shen* 17, iv (Summer, 1966): 3-25. Also as "Notice I'm Smiling: Reynolds Price," in Carr, J., ed., *Kite Flying and Other Irrational Acts*, 70-95.

Kreyling, Michael, "Motion and Rest in the Novels of Reynolds Price," *SoR* 16, iv (1980): 853-68.

Ray, William, "Conversations: Reynolds Price and William Ray," *MVC Bulletin: An Occasional Publ. of the Mississippi Valley College* (Memphis State Un.) 9 (1976): 9-82.

Rooke, Constance, "On Women and His Own Work: An Interview with Reynolds Price," *SoR* 14 (1978): 706-25.

Shepherd, Allen, "Notes on Nature in the Fiction of Reynolds Price," *Crit* 15, ii (1973): 83-94.

A GENEROUS MAN

Barnes, Daniel R., "The Names and Faces of Reynolds Price," *KyR* 2, ii (1968): 85-90.

Eichelberger, Clayton L., "Reynolds Price: 'A Banner in Defeat'," *JPC* 1 (Spring, 1968): 414-16.

Hoffman, F. J., *Art of Southern Fiction*, 141-3.

Price, Reynolds, "News for the Mineshaft," *VQR* 44 (Autumn, 1968): 641-58. Also in McCormack, T., ed., *Afterwords*, 107-23.

Wain, John, "Mantle of Faulkner?" *NRep* 154 (May 14, 1966): 31-3.

A LONG AND HAPPY LIFE

Barnes, David R., "The Names and Faces of Reynolds Price," *KyR* 2, ii (1968): 81-5.

Eichelberger, Clayton L., "Reynolds Price: 'A Banner in Defeat'," *JPC* 1 (Spring, 1968): 412-14.

Hoffman, F. J., *Art of Southern Fiction*, 137-9.

Shepherd, Allen, "Love (and Marriage) in A LONG AND HAPPY LIFE," *TCL* 17, i (Jan., 1971): 29-35.

_____, "Reynolds Price's A LONG AND HAPPY LIFE: The Epigraph," *NConL* 2, iii (May, 1972): 12-13.

Vauthier, Simone, "The 'Circle in the Forest': Fictional Space in Reynolds Price A LONG AND HAPPY LIFE," *MissQ* 28 (1975): 123-46.

LOVE AND WORK

Shepherd, Allen, "LOVE AND WORK and the Unseen World," *Topic* 12 (Spring, 1972): 52-7.

THE SOURCE OF LIGHT

Chicatelli, Louis W., "Family as Fate in Reynold Price's THE SURFACE OF EARTH and THE SOURCE OF LIGHT," *MHLS* 5 (1982): 129-36.

THE SURFACE OF EARTH

Borghi, Liana, "On THE SURFACE OF EARTH: An Interview Edited by Liana Borghi," *Dismisura* 39-50 (1980): 38-50.

Chicatelli, Louis W., "Family as Fate in Reynold Price's THE SURFACE OF EARTH and THE SOURCE OF LIGHT," *MHLS* 5 (1982): 129-36.

Kreyling, Michael, "Motion and Rest in the Novels of Reynolds Price," *SoR* 16, iv (1980): 857-68.

BIBLIOGRAPHY

Roberts, Ray A., "Reynolds Price: A Bibliographical Checklist," *ABC* 2, iii (July-Aug., 1981): 15-23.

PRICE, RICHARD, 1949-

GENERAL

Shelton, Frank W., "Family, Community, and Masculinity in the Urban Novels of Richard Price," *Crit* 21, i (1979): 5-15.

BLOODBROTHERS

Shelton, Frank W., "Family, Community, and Masculinity in the Urban Novels of Richard Price," *Crit* 21, i (1979): 10-13.

THE WANDERERS

Shelton, Frank W., "Family, Community, and Masculinity in the Urban Novels of Richard Price," *Crit* 21, i (1979): 7-10.

PRICHARD, KATHARINE SUSANNAH, 1883-1969

GENERAL

Bennett, Bruce, "The Mask Beyond the Mask: Katharine Susannah Prichard," *Meanjin* 35 (Sept., 1976): 324-9. [Not seen.]

Hammond, Jennifer, "Manuscript and Manifesto," *Pol* (Apr., 1980): 56-8. [Not seen.]

Hewett, Dorothy, "Excess of Love," *Overland* 43 (1969-70): 27-31. [Not seen.]

Iseman, Kay, "Katharine Susannah Prichard: Of an End a New Beginning," *Arena* 54 (1979): 70-96.

Lindsay, Jack, "The Novels of Katharine Susannah Prichard," *Meanjin* 20 (Dec., 1961): 366-87.

Malos, Ellen, "Jack Lindsay's Essay on Katharine Susannah Prichard's Novels," *Meanjin* 22, iv (1963): 413-16.

_____, "Some Major Themes in the Novels of Katharine Susannah Prichard," *ALS* 1, i (June, 1963): 32-41.

Sadlier, Richard, "The Writings of Katharine Susannah Prichard," *Westerly* 3 (1961): 31-5.

Sunderland, Jane, "'Lines Driven Deep': Radical Departures, or the Same Old Story, for Prichard's Women?" *Hecate* 4, i (Feb., 1978): 7-24.

Williams, Justina, "Rage That Engenders: The Last Decade of Katharine Susannah Prichard," *Southerly* 32, i (Mar., 1972): 17-29.

BLACK OPAL

Hope, A. D., *Native Companions,* 242-3.

Lindsay, Jack, "The Novels of Katharine Susannah Prichard," *Meanjin* 20 (Dec., 1961): 368-72.

COONARDO

Lindsay, Jack, "The Novels of Katharine Susannah Prichard," *Meanjin* 20 (Dec., 1961): 376-8.

Iseman, Kay, "Katharine Susannah Prichard, COONARDO and the Aboriginal Presence in Australian Fiction," *Women and Labour Conference Papers* 2 (1980): 540-56.

Melandrez-Cruz, Patricia, "Social Criticism in the Australian Novel: The Aboriginal Theme," *DilR* 21, iii-iv (July-Sept., 1973): 347-57.

GOLD-FIELDS Trilogy (THE ROARING NINETIES, GOLDEN MILES, WINGED SEEDS)

Lindsay, Jack, "The Novels of Katharine Susannah Prichard," *Meanjin* 20 (Dec., 1961): 380-5.

INTIMATE STRANGERS

Brady, Veronica, "Katharine Susannah Prichard and the Tyranny of History: INTIMATE STRANGERS," *Westerly* 26, iv (Dec., 1981): 65-71.

Lindsay, Jack, "The Novels of Katharine Susannah Prichard," *Meanjin* 20 (Dec., 1961): 379-80.

THE ROARING NINETIES (See also GOLD-FIELDS Trilogy)

Hope, A. D., *Native Americans,* 244-5.

WORKING BULLOCKS

Hope, A. D., *Native Companions,* 243-4.

Lindsay, Jack, "The Novels of Katharine Susannah Prichard," *Meanjin* 20 (Dec., 1961): 372-6.

PRIESTLEY, J(OHN) B(OYNTON), 1894-1984

GENERAL

Atkins, J., *J. B. Priestley.*

Braine, J., *J. B. Priestley.*

———, "Lunch with J. B. Priestley," *Encounter* 10 (June, 1958): 8-14.

Brown, L., *J. B. Priestley.*

De Vitis, A. A., and A. E. Kalson, *J. B. Priestley.*

Hughes, D., *J. B. Priestley.*

Lindsay, Jack, "J. B. Priestley," in Baker, D. V., ed., *Writers of Today,* 72-82.

West, A., *Mountain in the Sunlight,* 155-83.

Young, K., *J. B. Priestley.*

ADAM IN MOONSHINE

De Vitis, A. A., and A. E. Kalson, *J. B. Priestley,* 39-43.

Hughes, D., *J. B. Priestley,* 67-74.

ALBERT GOES THROUGH

De Vitis, A. A., and A. E. Kalson, *J. B. Priestley,* 55-6.

ANGEL PAVEMENT

Atkins, J., *J. B. Priestley,* 48-51.

Braine, J., *J. B. Priestley,* 41-55.

Brown, I., *J. B. Priestley,* 17-19.

De Vitis, A. A., and A. E. Kalson, *J. B. Priestley,* 48-50.

Hughes, D., *J. B. Priestley,* 104-12.

West, A., *Mountain in the Sunlight,* 159-68.

Young, K., *J. B. Priestley,* 21-2.

BENIGHTED

De Vitis, A. A., and A. E. Kalson, *J. B. Priestley,* 43-4.

Hughes, D., *J. B. Priestley,* 79-83.

BLACK-OUT IN GRETLEY, A STORY OF—AND FOR—WARTIME

De Vitis, A. A., and A. E. Kalson, *J. B. Priestley,* 67-9.

BRIGHT DAY

Braine, J., *J. B. Priestley,* 121-7.

De Vitis, A. A., and A. E. Kalson, *J. B. Priestley,* 73-6.

Hughes, D., *J. B. Priestley,* 176-82.

West, A., *Mountain in the Sunlight,* 177-83.

Young, K., *J. B. Priestley,* 26-8.

DAYLIGHT ON SATURDAY

Atkins, J., *J. B. Priestley,* 100-2.

De Vitis, A. A., and A. E. Kalson, *J. B. Priestley,* 69-72.

Hughes, D., *J. B. Priestley,* 170-2.

West, A., *Mountain in the Sunlight,* 168-77.

Young, K., *J. B. Priestley,* 24-6.

THE DOOMSDAY MEN

De Vitis, A. A., and A. E. Kalson, *J. B. Priestley,* 59-63.

FARAWAY

De Vitis, A. A., and A. E. Kalson, *J. B. Priestley,* 51-4.

Hughes, D., *J. B. Priestley,* 112-16.

FARTHING HALL (with Hugh Walpole)

De Vitis, A. A., and A. E. Kalson, *J. B. Priestley,* 44-5.

FESTIVAL AT FARBRIDGE

Atkins, J., *J. B. Priestley,* 188-91.

De Vitis, A. A., and A. E. Kalson, *J. B. Priestley,* 79-82.

Hughes, D., *J. B. Priestley,* 182-8.

Young, K., *J. B. Priestley,* 29-31.

FOUND, LOST, FOUND, OR THE ENGLISH WAY OF LIFE

De Vitis, A. A., and A. E. Kalson, *J. B. Priestley*, 110-11.

THE GOOD COMPANIONS

Atkins, J., *J. B. Priestley*, 43-7, 205-9.
Braine, J., *J. B. Priestley*, 26-41.
De Vitis, A. A., and A. E. Kalson, *J. B. Priestley*, 45-8.

THE IMAGE MEN

Atkins, J., *J. B. Priestley*, 195-201.
De Vitis, A. A., and A. E. Kalson, *J. B. Priestley*, 102-9.
Young, K., *J. B. Priestley*, 33-7.

IT'S AN OLD COUNTRY

De Vitis, A. A., and A. E. Kalson, *J. B. Priestley*, 99-102.

JENNY VILLIERS, A STORY OF THE THEATRE

De Vitis, A. A., and A. E. Kalson, *J. B. Priestley*, 77-9.

LET THE PEOPLE SING

Atkins, J., *J. B. Priestley*, 188-90.
De Vitis, A. A., and A. E. Kalson, *J. B. Priestley*, 65-7.

LOST EMPIRES

Braine, J., *J. B. Priestley*, 144-7.
De Vitis, A. A., and A. E. Kalson, *J. B. Priestley*, 97-9.

LOW NOTES ON A HIGH LEVEL

De Vitis, A. A., and A. E. Kalson, *J. B. Priestley*, 82-4.

THE MAGICIANS

De Vitis, A. A., and A. E. Kalson, *J. B. Priestley*, 84-6.

SALT IS LEAVING

De Vitis, A. A., and A. E. Kalson, *J. B. Priestley*, 92-4.

SATURN OVER THE WATER

Deakin, Nicholas, "J. B. Priestley's Anglo-Saxon Attitudes," *T&T* 42 (July 13, 1961): 1159-61.
De Vitis, A. A., and A. E. Kalson, *J. B. Priestley*, 88-90.

THE SHAPES OF SLEEP: A TOPICAL TALE

De Vitis, A. A., and A. E. Kalson, *J. B. Priestley*, 90-2.

SIR MICHAEL AND SIR GEORGE

De Vitis, A. A., and A. E. Kalson, *J. B. Priestley*, 95-7.

THEY WALK IN THE CITY

De Vitis, A. A., and A. E. Kalson, *J. B. Priestley*, 58-9.
Hughes, D., *J. B. Priestley*, 118-23.

THE THIRTY-FIRST OF JUNE

De Vitis, A. A., and A. E. Kalson, *J. B. Priestley*, 94-5.

THREE MEN IN NEW SUITS

De Vitis, A. A., and A. E. Kalson, *J. B. Priestley*, 72-3.

WONDER HERO

De Vitis, A. A., and A. E. Kalson, *J. B. Priestley*, 56-8.

BIBLIOGRAPHY

Day, Alan E., *J. B. Priestley: An Annotated Bibliography*, Stroud: Hodgkins, 1980.
_____, "J. B. Priestley: An Annotated Checklist," *BB* 28, ii (Apr.-June, 1971): 42-8.

PROKOSCH, FREDERIC, 1908-1989

GENERAL

Carpenter, Richard C., "The Novels of Frederic Prokosch," *CE* 18 (Feb., 1957): 261-7.
Squires, R., *Frederic Prokosch*.

AGE OF THUNDER

Hendry, Irene, "Westcott, Prokosch, and Three Others," *SR* 52 (1945): 492-3.
Squires, R., *Frederic Prokosch*, 91-6.

THE ASIATICS

Squires, R., *Frederic Prokosch*, 22-5, 48-53.

A BALLAD OF LOVE

Squires, R., *Frederic Prokosch*, 79-83.

THE CONSPIRATORS

Squires, R., *Frederic Prokosch*, 87-91.

THE IDOLS OF THE CAVE

Squires, R., *Frederic Prokosch*, 96-101.

THE NIGHT OF THE POOR

Squires, R., *Frederic Prokosch*, 102-4.

NINE DAYS TO MUKALLA

Jones, Howard M., "Love and Geography," *SatR* 36 (Mar. 21, 1953): 15.
Squires, R., *Frederic Prokosch*, 61-9.

THE SEVEN SISTERS

Squires, R., *Frederic Prokosch*, 120-30.

THE SEVEN WHO FLED

Squires, R., *Frederic Prokosch*, 106-20.
Straumann, H., *American Literature in the Twentieth Century*, 78-9.

THE SKIES OF EUROPE

Squires, R., *Frederic Prokosch*, 28-9, 70-9.

STORM AND ECHO

Squires, R., *Frederic Prokosch*, 54-61.

A TALE FOR MIDNIGHT

Squires, R., *Frederic Prokosch*, 104-6.

PURDY, JAMES, 1923-

GENERAL

Adams, S. D., *James Purdy*.

Baldanza, Frank, "James Purdy on the Corruption of Innocents," *ConL* 15 (1974): 315-30.

————, "Northern Gothic," *SoR* 10, iii (July, 1974): 566-82.

————, "Playing House for Keeps with James Purdy," *ConL* 11, iv (Autumn, 1970): 488-510.

Chupack, H., *James Purdy*.

Coffey, Warren, "The Incomplete Novelist," *Ctary* 44 (Sept., 1967): 98-103.

Cott, Jonathan, "The Dangerous Cosmos," in Kostelanetz, R., ed., *On Contemporary Literature*, 498-505.

French, Warren, "James Purdy, Will Moses: Against the Wilderness (to Accompany an Unassembled Slide Show)," *KanQ* 14, ii (1982): 81-92.

Hipkiss, R. A., *Jack Kerouac*, 105-12.

Hyman, S. E., *Standards*, 254-8.

Kennard, Jean E., James Purdy: Fidelity to Failure," *Number and Nightmare*, 82-100.

Maloff, Saul, "James Purdy's Fictions: The Quality of Despair," *Crit* 6, i (Spring, 1963): 106-12.

Pease, Donald, "False Starts and Wounded Allegories in the Abandoned House of Fiction of James Purdy," *TCL* 28, iii (Fall, 1982): 335-49.

Pomeranz, Regina, "The Hell of Not Loving: Purdy's Modern Tragedy," *Ren* 16 (Spring, 1964): 149-53.

Rosen, Gerald, "James Purdy's World of Black Humor," *DAI* 31 (1970): 1290A-91A.

Schott, Webster, "James Purdy: American Dreams," *Nation* 198 (Mar. 23, 1964): 300-2.

Schwarzchild, B., *Not-Right House*.

Singh, Yashoda N., "The City as Metaphor in Selected Novels of James Purdy and Saul Bellow," *DAI* 40 (1979): 2049A.

Skerrett, Joseph T., Jr., "James Purdy and the Works: Love and Tragedy in Five Novels," *TCL* 15, i (Apr., 1969): 25-33.

Sloan, Gary G., "The Fiction of James Purdy: Theme and Meaning," *DAI* 34 (1973): 1936A-37A.

CABOT WRIGHT BEGINS

Adams, S. D., *James Purdy*, 75-94.

Allen, M., *Necessary Blankness*, 55-63.

Baldanza, Frank, "Playing for Keeps with James Purdy," *ConL* 11, iv (Autumn, 1970): 500-4.

Boyers, Robert, "Attitudes Toward Sex in American 'High Culture'," *AAAPSS* 367 (Mar., 1965): 49.

Cupack, H., *James Purdy*, 78-94.

French, Warren, *Seasons of Promise*, Columbus: Un. of Missouri Pr., 1968, 19-26.

Glicksberg, C. I., *Sexual Revolution in Modern American Literature*, 206-9.

Kennard, Jean E., "James Purdy: Fidelity to Failure," *Number and Nightmare*, 94-7.

Malin, Irving, "Mélange à Trois," *Ramparts* 3, vi (Mar., 1965): 79-80.

Newman, Charles, "Beyond Omniscience *Notes Toward a Future of the Novel*," in Newman, C., and W. A. Henkin, Jr., eds., *Under 30*, 47-50.

Ryan, Marjorie, "Four Contemporary Satires and the Problem of Norms," *SNL* 6, ii (Spring, 1969): 40-4.

Solotaroff, Theodore, "The Deadly James Purdy," *Red Hot Vacuum*, 156-60.

Tanner, T., *City of Words*, 95-105.

————, "Sex and Identity in CABOT WRIGHT BEGINS," *TwenCS* 1, ii (Nov., 1969): 89-102.

EUSTACE CHISHOLM AND THE WORKS

Adams, S. D., *James Purdy*, 94-108, 149-50.

Baldanza, Frank, "Playing House for Keeps with James Purdy," *ConL* 11, iv (Autumn, 1970): 504-10.

Chupack, H., *James Purdy*, 95-108.

Coffey, Warren, "The Complete Novelist," *Ctary* 44 (Sept., 1967): 476-7.

Kennard, Jean E., "James Purdy: Fidelity to Failure," *Number and Nightmare*, 97-9.

Malin, I., in *Cweal* 86 (July 28, 1967): 476-7.

Morris, Robert K., "James Purdy and the Works," *Nation* 205 (Oct. 9, 1967): 342-4.

Schwarzchild, B., *Not-Right House*, 58-65.

Tanner, T., *City of Words*, 105-8.

Trickett, Rachel, "Recent Novels: Craftmanship in Violence and Sex," *YR* 57 (Spring, 1968): 443-4.

THE HOUSE OF THE SOLITARY MAGGOT

Adams, S. D., *James Purdy*, 109-28.

French, Warren, in *GLRev* 1, ii (Winter, 1975): 88-93.

I AM ELIJA THRUSH

Adams, S. D., *James Purdy*, 129-43.

Bolling, Douglass, "The World Upstaged in James Purdy's I AM ELIJAH THRUSH," *UDR* 10, iii (Summer, 1974): 75-83.

Tanner, Tony, "James Purdy's I AM ELIJAH THRUSH," in *New Directions in Prose and Poetry 26*, N.Y.: New Directions, 1973, 62-9.

IN A SHALLOW GRAVE

Adams, S. D., *James Purdy*, 142-60.

JEREMY'S VERSION

Adams, S. D., *James Purdy*, 109-28.

Baldanza, Frank, "James Purdy's Half-Orphans," *CentR* 18, iii (Summer, 1974): 268-71.

Chupack, H., *James Purdy*, 109-24.

Kennard, Jean E., "James Purdy: Fidelity to Failure," *Number and Nightmare*, 99-100.

MALCOLM

Adams, S. D., *James Purdy*, 26-41.

Allen, M., *Necessary Blankness*, 53-5.

Baldanza, Frank, "Playing House for Keeps with James Purdy," *ConL* 11, iv (Autumn, 1970): 491-6.

Chupack, H., *James Purdy*, 43-53.

Cott, Jonathan, "The Damaged Cosmos," in Kostelanetz, R., ed., *On Contemporary Literature*, 501-5.

Daiches, David, "A Preface to James Purdy's MALCOLM," *AR* 22 (Spring, 1962): 122-30.

Denniston, Constance, "The American Romance-Parody: A Study of Purdy's MALCOLM and Heller's CATCH-22," *ESRS* 14, ii (Dec., 1965): 42-59, 63-4.

French, Warren, "The Quaking World of James Purdy," in Langford, R. E., ed., *Essays in Modern American Literature*, 112-18.

Herr, Paul, "The Small Sad World of James Purdy," *ChiR* 14, iii (Autumn-Winter, 1960): 19-25. Also in Waldmeir, J. J., ed., *Recent American Fiction*, 246-51.

Kennard, Jean E., "James Purdy: Fidelity to Failure," *Number and Nightmare*, 87-92.

Kolve, Del, "James Purdy: An Assessment," *T&T* 42 (Mar. 23, 1961): 476-7.

Kostelanetz, Richard, "The New American Fiction," *Ramparts* 3 (Jan.-Feb., 1965): 60. Also in Kostelanetz, R., ed., *New American Arts*, 217-18.

Lorch, Thomas M., "Purdy's MALCOLM: A Unique Vision of Radical Emptiness," *WSCL* 6 (Summer, 1965): 204-13.

McNamara, Eugene, "The Post-Modern American Novel," *QQ* 69 (Summer, 1962): 272-4.

Malin, I., *New American Gothic*, 46-9.

Pease, Donald, "James Purdy: Shaman in Nowhere Land," in French, W., ed., *Fifties*, 150-4.

Pondrom, Cyrena N., "Purdy's MALCOLM and Kafka's AMERIKA: Analogues with a Difference," 113-33, in Zyla, Wolodymyr, T., ed., *Proceedings of the Comparative Literature Symposium*, Vol. IV: *Franz Kafka: His Place in World Literature*, Lubbock: Texas Tech. Un., 1971.

Schwarzchild, Bettin, 'The Forsaken: An Interpretive Essay on James Purdy's MALCOLM," *TQ* 10, i (Spring, 1967): 170-7. Also in Schwarzchild, B., *Not-Right House*, 23-34.

_____, *Not-Right House*, 13-23.

Stetler, Charles, "Purdy's MALCOLM: Allegory of No Man," *Crit* 14, iii (1973): 91-9.

Tanner, T., *City of Words*, 88-93.

THE NEPHEW

Allen, M., *Necessary Blankness*, 55-6.

Adams, S. D., *James Purdy*, 53-73.

Baldanza, Frank, "Keeping House for Keeps with James Purdy," *ConL* 11, iv (Autumn, 1970): 500-4.

Bryant, J. H., *Open Decision*, 249-52.

Chupack, H., *James Purdy*, 53-60.

Finkelstein, S., *Existentialism and Alienation in American Literature*, 249-52.

French, Warren, "The Quaking World of James Purdy," in Langford, R. E., ed., *Essays in Modern American Literature*, 118-22.

Kennard, Jean E., "James Purdy: Fidelity to Failure," *Number and Nightmare*, 92-4.

Kolve, Del, "James Purdy: An Assessment," *T&T* 42 (Mar. 23, 1961): 476-7.

Krummel, Regina P., "Two Quests in Two Societies," *EngR* 18 (Apr., 1967): 28-32.

Miller, Nolan, "Three of the 'Best'," *AR* 21 (Spring, 1961): 125-8.

Pomeranz, Regina, "The Hell of Not Loving: Purdy's Modern Tragedy," *Ren* 16 (Spring, 1964): 150-2.

Schwarzchild, Bettina, "Aunt Alma: James Purdy's THE NEPHEW," *UWR* 3, i (Fall, 1967): 80-7. Also in Schwarzchild, B., *Not-Right House*, 35-44.

Tanner, T., *City of Words*, 93-5.

Torquist, Elizabeth, "The New Parochialism," *Ctary* 31 (May, 1961): 449-52.

Weales, Gerald, in Moore, H. T., ed., *Contemporary American Novelists*, 145-9.

BIBLIOGRAPHY

Bush, George E., "James Purdy," *BB* 28, i (Jan.-Mar., 1971): 5-6.

Ladd, Jay, "James Purdy: A Bibliographical Checklist," *ABC* 2, v (Sept.-Oct., 1981): 53-60.

PUZO, MARIO, 1920-

THE DARK ARENA

Green, R. B., *Italian-American Novel*, 337-42.

Hall, James B., "Mario Puzo's THE DARK ARENA," in Madden, D., ed., *Rediscoveries*, 121-33.

THE FORTUNATE PILGRIM

Green, R. B., *Italian-American Novel*, 342-51.

THE GODFATHER

Carlisle, Charles R., "Strangers Within, Enemies Without: Alienation in Popular Mafia Fiction," in Landrum, L. N., P. Browne, and R. B. Browne, eds., *Dimensions of Detective Fiction*, 194-200.

Cawelti, John G., "The New Mythology of Crime," *Boundary 2*, 3, ii (Winter, 1975): 325-57.

Chiampi, James T., "Resurrecting THE GODFATHER," *MELUS* 5, iv (1978): 18-31.

Crook, Eugene J., "A Christ-Figure in THE GODFATHER," *NConL* 2, iii (May, 1972): 5-6.

Dessner, Lawrence J., "THE GODFATHER, The Executive and Art," *JPC* 6, i (Summer, 1972): 211-14.

Di Pietro, Robert J., "Language and Culture and the Specialist in Ethnic Literature," *MELUS* 4, i (1977): 2-6.

Polek, Fran J., "From Renegade to Solid Citizen: The Extraordinary Individual and the Community," *SDR* 15, i (Summer, 1977): 61-72.

Green, R. B., *Italian-American Novel*, 352-68.

McWilliams, Wilson C., "Natty Bumppo and the Godfather," *ColQ* 24 (1975): 133-44.

Sinicropi, Giovanni, "The Saga of the Corleones: Puzo, Coppola, and THE GODFATHER: An Interpretive Essay," *ItalAm* 2, i (1975): 79-90.

PYM, BARBARA, 1913-1980

GENERAL

Brothers, Robert, "Women Victimized by Fiction: Living and Loving in the Novels of Barbara Pym," in Staley, T. F., ed., *Twentieth-Century Women Novelists*, 61-80.

Larkin, Philip, "The World of Barbara Pym," *TLS* (Mar. 11, 1977): 260.

Smith, Robert, "How Pleasant to Know Miss Pym," *ArielE* 2, iv (Oct., 1971): 63-8.

Snow, Lotus, "The Trivia Round the Common Track: Barbara Pym's Novels," *RS* 48, ii (June, 1980): 83-93.

A FEW GREEN LEAVES

Wilson, A. N., "Thinking of Being Them," *TLS* (July 18, 1980): 799.

PYNCHON, THOMAS, 1937-

GENERAL

Calhoun, John C., "The Concept of Revolution and Its Influence on the Genesis of Art in the Work of Thomas Pynchon," *PCL* 2, i (1976): 40-52.

Cooper, Peter L., "'An Ominous Logic': Thomas Pynchon and Contemporary American Fiction," *DAI* 39 (1979): 5510A-11A.

Cowart, D., *Thomas Pynchon*.

————, "Thomas Pynchon's Art of Illusion," *DAI* 38 (1977): 782A.

Cullen, Robert J., "Words and a Yarn: Language and Narrative Technique in the Works of Thomas Pynchon," *DAI* 42 (1981): 1634A.

Dahiya, Bhim, "Structural Patterns in the Novels of Barth, Vonnegut, and Pynchon," *IJAS* 5, i-ii (1976): 53-68. [Not seen.]

Davis, Susan E. H., "A Counterforce of Readers: The Rhetoric of Thomas Pynchon's Narrative Technique," *DAI* 40 (1979): 2677A.

Del Col, Jeffrey A., "Early Clues for the New Direction? The Technocratic Myth in Pynchon and Pirsig," *DAI* 39 (1979): 4239A.

Grant, James K., "The Embroidered Mantle: Order and the Individual in the Fiction of Thomas Pynchon," *DAI* 37 (1977): 6485A.

Harrington, John P., "Pynchon, Beckett, and Entropy: Uses of Metaphor," *MissR* 5, iii (Summer, 1982): 129-38.

Hill, Robert R., "Epistemological Dilemmas in the Works of Norman Mailer and Thomas Pynchon: The Themes and Motifs of Systemization, Paranoia, and Entropy," *DAI* 42, v (Nov., 1981): 2131A-32A.

Hite, Molly, "'Holy-Center-Approaching' in the Novels of Thomas Pynchon," *JNT* 12, ii (Spring, 1982): 121-9.

————, "Ideas of Order in the Novels of Thomas Pynchon," *DAI* 42 (1981): 2141-15A.

Krafft, John M., "Historical Imagination in the Novels of Thomas Pynchon," *DAI* 39 (1978): 1571A-72A.

Larsson, Donald F., "The Film Breaks: Thomas Pynchon and the Cinema," *DAI* 41 (1981): 4394A.

Leder, Mark R., "The Use and Theory of Metaphor in the Novels of Thomas Pynchon," *DAI* 39 (1978): 1552A-53A.

Levine, G., and D. Leveranz, eds., *Mindful Pleasures*.

Levine, George, "Risking the Moment: Anarchy and Possibility in Pynchon's Fiction," in Levine, G., and D. Leverenz, eds., *Mindful Pleasures*, 113-36.

Mac Adam, Alfred, "Pynchon as Satirist: To Write, to Mean," *YR* 67, iv (Summer, 1978): 555-66.

Mackey, D. A., *Rainbow Quest of Thomas Pynchon*.

McDonnell, F. D., *Four Postwar American Novelists*, 159-64.

McHale, Brian, "Thomas Pynchon: A Portrait of the Artist as a Missing Person," *Cencrastus* 5 (Summer, 1981): 2-3.

McLester-Greenfield, Owana K., "When Even the Best is Bad: Thomas Pynchon's Alternatives to the Wasteland," *DAI* 39 (1978): 2942A.

Mendelson, E., ed., *Pynchon*.

Munley, Ellen M., "Caught in the Act: Naming the Novels of Thomas Pynchon and Natalie Sarraute," *DAI* 42 (1982): 4442A.

Nash, James W., "Chaos, Structure and Salvation in the Novels of Thomas Pynchon," *DAI* 36 (1975): 325A.

Papadakos, Juliet, "Reality and the Journey to Knowledge in the Novels of Thomas Pynchon," *DAI* 43, ii (Aug., 1982): 447A.

Pearce, R. ed., *Critical Essays on Thomas Pynchon*.

Pearce, Richard, "Thomas Pynchon and the Novel of Motion: Where're They At, Where're They Going?" *MR* 21 (Spring, 1980): 177-95. Also in Pearce, R., ed., *Critical Essays on Thomas Pynchon*, 213-29.

Plater, W. M., *Grim Phoenix*.

Poirier, Richard, "The Importance of Thomas Pynchon," *TCL* 21 (May, 1975): 151-62. Also in Levine, G., and D. Leveranz, eds., *Mindful Pleasures*, 15-29.

Price, Ruby V., "Christian Allusions in the Novels of Thomas Pynchon," *DAI* 40 (1979): 1472A.

Quilligan, Maureen, *The Language of Allegory: Defining the Genre*, Ithaca: Cornell Un. Pr., 1979, 42-6, 204-23, 261-3, 265-78, 289-90. Also, slightly adapted, as "Thomas Pynchon and the Language of Allegory," in Pearce, R., ed., *Critical Essays on Thomas Pynchon*, 187-212.

Schaub, Thomas H., "The Ambiguity of Pynchon's Fact and Fiction," *DAI* 37 (1977): 7754A.

————, *Pynchon*.

————, "Where Have We Been, Where Are We Headed? A Retrospective Review of Pynchon Criticism," *PNotes* 7 (Oct., 1981): 5-21.

Schmitz, Neil, "Describing the Demon: The Appeal of Thomas Pynchon," *PR* 42, i (1975): 112-25.

Schwartz, Richard A., "Thomas Pynchon and the Evolution of Fiction," *SFS* 8 (July, 1981): 165-72.

Seed, David, "The Fictional Labyrinths of Thomas Pynchon," *CritQ* 18, iv (Winter, 1976): 73-81.

Siegel, Mark, "Pynchon's Anti-Quests," *PNotes* 3 (June, 1980): 5-9.

————, "Thomas Pynchon and the Science Fiction Controversy," *PNotes* 7 (Oct., 1981): 38-42.

Skarzenski, Donald, "Enzian and the Octopus: Fact in Pynchon's Fiction," *NMAL* 1 (Fall, 1977): Item 35.

Slade, J. W., *Thomas Pynchon*.

Solberg, Sara M., "On Comparing Apples and Oranges: James Joyce and Thomas Pynchon," *CLS* 16 (1979): 33-40. [Not seen.]

Sperry, Joseph P., "Henry Adams and Thomas Pynchon: The Eutropic Movements of Self, Society and Truth," *DAI* 35 (1975): 5428A.

Stark, John, "The Arts and Sciences of Thomas Pynchon," *HC* 12, iv (Oct., 1975): 1-13.

————, *Pynchon's Fictions.*

Steinmetz, Joseph J., "Between Zero and One: A Psychohistoric Reading of Thomas Pynchon's Major Works," *DAI* 37 (1976): 318A-19A.

Stimson, Catharine R., "Pre-Apocalyptic Atavism: Thomas Pynchon's Early Fiction" in Levine, G., and D. Leverenz, eds., *Mindful Pleasures*, 31-47.

Tanner, Tony, Patterns and Paranoia or Caries and Cabals," *Salmagundi* 15 (1971): 78-99. Also in Tanner, T., *City of Words*, 153-80.

————, *Thomas Pynchon.*

Toloyan, Kachig, "Criticism as Symptom: Thomas Pynchon and the Crisis of the Humanities," *NOR* 5 (1979): 314-18.

Vesterman, William, "Pynchon's Poetry," *TCL* 21, ii (May, 1975): 211-20. [Use of songs and poems in the novels.] Also in Levine, G., and D. Leverenz, eds., *Mindful Pleasures*, 101-12.

Wasson, Richard, "Notes on a New Sensibility," *PR* 36 (1969): 460-77. Also in Pearce, R., ed., *Critical Essays on Thomas Pynchon*, 13-19.

Wilson, Robert R., "Spooking Oedipa: On Godnames," *CRCL* 4, i (Winter, 1977): 197-204.

THE CRYING OF LOT 49

Abadi-Nagy, Zoltan, "The Entropic Rhythm of Thomas Pynchon's Comedy in THE CRYING OF LOT 49," *HSE* 11 (1977): 117-30.

Abernethy, Peter L., "Entropy in Pynchon's THE CRYING OF LOT 49," *Crit* 14, ii (1972): 18-33.

Allen, M., *Necessary Blankness*, 46-51.

Baxter, Charles, "De-Faced America: THE GREAT GATSBY and THE CRYING OF LOT 49," *PNotes* 7 (Oct., 1981): 22-37.

Brugiére, Marion, "Quest Atavars in Thomas Pynchon's THE CRYING OF LOT 49," *PNotes* 9 (June, 1982): 30-8.

Carpenter, Richard C., "State of Mind: The California Setting of THE CRYING OF LOT 49," in Crow, L., ed., *Essays on California Writers*, 105-13.

Cowart, Davis, "Pynchon's THE CRYING OF LOT 49 and the Paintings of Remedios Varo," *Crit* 18, iii (1977): 19-26.

————, *Thomas Pynchon*, 23-30, 78-82, 100-7.

Cox, Stephen D., "Berkeley, Blake, and the Apocalypse of Pynchon's THE CRYING OF LOT 49," *ELWIU* 7 (1980): 91-9.

Cullen, Robert J., "Words and a Yarn: Language and Narrative Technique in the Works of Thomas Pynchon," *DAI* 42, iv (Oct., 1981): 1634A.

Davidson, Cathy N., "Oedipa as Androgyne in Thomas Pynchon's THE CRYING OF LOT 49," *ConL* 18 (1977): 38-50.

Davis, Robert M., "Parody, Paranoia, and the Dead End of Language in THE CRYING OF LOT 49," *Genre* 5 (Dec., 1972): 367-77.

Grace, Sherrill E., "Wastelands and Badlands: The Legacies of Pynchon and Koretsch," *Mosaic* 14, ii (Spring, 1981): 21-34.

Green, Martin, "The CRYING OF LOT 49: Pynchon's Heart of Darkness," *PNotes* 8 (Feb., 1982): 30-8.

Guzlowski, John Z., "THE CRYING OF LOT 49 and 'The Shadow'," *PNotes* 9 (June, 1982): 61-8.

————, "No More Sea Changes: Hawkes, Pynchon, Gaddis, and Barth," *Crit* 23, ii (Winter, 1981-82): 51-3.

Harris, Charles B., "Thomas Pynchon and the Entropic Vision," *Contemporary Novelists of the Absurd*, 93-9.

Henkle, Roger B., "Pynchon's Tapestries on the Western Wall," *MFS* 17, ii (Summer, 1961): 207-20. Also in Mendelson, E., ed., *Pynchon*, 97-111.

Hite, Molly, "'Holy- Center Approaching' in the Novels of Thomas Pynchon," *JNT* 12, ii (Spring, 1982): 121-9.

————, "Ideas of Order in the Novels of Thomas Pynchon," *DAI* 42, i (July, 1981): 214A-215A.

Hunt, John W., "Comic Escape and Anti-Vision: The Novels of Joseph Heller and Thomas Pynchon," in Scott, N. A., Jr., ed., *Adversity and Grace*, 107-10. Also in Pearce, R., ed., *Critical Essays on Thomas Pynchon*, 38-40.

Kermode, Frank, "Decoding the Trysfero," in Chatman, Seymour, ed., *Approaches to Poetics*, N.Y.: Columbia Un. Pr., 1973, 68-74. Also in Mendelson, E., ed., *Pynchon*, 162-6.

Kirby, David K., "Two Modern Versions of the Quest," *SHR* 5, iv (Fall, 1971): 387-95. [And James's TURN OF THE SCREW.]

Kolodny, Annette, and Daniel J. Peters, "Pynchon's THE CRYING OF LOT 49: The Novel as Subversive Experience," *MFS* 19, i (1973): 79-87.

Larsson, Donald F., "Approach and Avoid: Douglas A. Mackey's 'The Rainbow of Thomas Pynchon'," *PNotes* 7 (Oct., 1981): 49-52.

Leland, John P., "Pynchon's Linguistic Demon: THE CRYING OF LOT 49," *Crit* 16, ii (1974): 45-53.

Lyons, Thomas R., and Allan D. Franklin, "Thomas Pynchon's 'Classic' Presentation of the Second Law of Thermodynamics," *BRMMLA* 27 (Dec., 1973): 195-204.

Mackey, D. A., *Rainbow Quest of Thomas Pynchon*, 26-36.

Mangel, Anne, "Maxwell's Demon, Entropy, Information: THE CRYING OF LOT 49," *TriQ* 20 (Winter, 1971): 194-208. Also in Levine, G., and D. Leverenz, eds., *Mindful Pleasures*, 87-99.

Martin, Richard, "Clio Bemused: The Uses of History in Contemporary American Fiction," *Sub-stance* 27 (1980): 13-24.

May, J. R., *Toward a New Earth*, 180-91.

McConnell, F. D., *Four Postwar American Novelists*, 1699-74.

McNamara, Eugene, "The Absurd Style in Contemporary Literature," *HAB* 19 (1968): 44-9.

Meikle, Jeffrey L., "'Other Frequencies': The Parallel Worlds of Thomas Pynchon and H. P. Lovecraft," *MFS* 27, ii (Summer, 1981): 287-94.

Mendelson, Edward, "The Sacred, the Profane, and THE CRYING OF LOT 49," in Baldwin, K. H., and D. K. Kirby, eds., *Individual and Community*, 182-222. Also, revised and slightly abridged, in Mendelson, E., ed., *Pynchon*, 112-46.

Merrill, Robert, "The Form and Meaning of Pynchon's THE CRYING OF LOT 49," *ArielE* 8, i (1977): 53-71.

Nelson, William, "The Humor and Humanizing of Outrage," *Thalia* 2, 1-11 (1979): 31-3.

Nohrnberg, James, "Pychon's Paraclete," in Mendelson, E., ed., *Pynchon*, 147-61.

Olderman, R. M., "The Illusion and Possibility of Conspiracy," *Beyond the Wasteland*, 44-9.

Pearce, Richard, "Where're They At, Where're They Going? Thomas Pynchon and the American Novel in Motion," *MR*

21 (Spring, 1980): 185-90. Also in Pearce, R., ed., *Critical Essays on Thomas Pynchon*, 220-4.

Pearson, C. S., "Puritans, Literary Critics and Thomas Pynchon's THE CRYING OF LOT 49," *NConL* 8, ii (1978): 8-9.

Pütz, Manfred, "Thomas Pynchon: History, Self, and the Narrative Discourse," *Story of Identity*, 147-57.

_____, "Thomas Pynchon's THE CRYING OF LOT 49: The World is a Tristero System," *Mosaic* 7, iv (1974): 125-37.

Schaub, Thomas, "'A Gentle Chill, An Ambiguity': THE CRYING OF LOT 49," in Schaub, T., *Pynchon*, 21-42. Also in Pearce, R., ed., *Critical Essays on Thomas Pynchon*, 51-68.

_____, "Open Letter in Response to Edward Mendelson's 'The Sacred, the Profane, and THE CRYING OF LOT 49'," *Boundary* 5 (Fall, 1976): 93-101.

_____, *Pynchon*, 104-19 *passim*.

Schulz, M. F., *Black Humor Fiction in the Sixties*, 62-4, 144-5.

Schwartz, Richard A., "Thomas Pynchon and the Evolution of Fiction," *SFS* 8, ii (July, 1981): 165-72.

Seed, David, "A Borrowing from Joyce in THE CRYING OF LOT 49," *NMAL* 6 (1982): Item 17.

Sklar, Robert, "The New Novel, U.S.A.: Thomas Pynchon," *Nation* 205 (Sept. 25, 1967): 277-80. Also in Mendelson, E., ed., *Pynchon*, 87-96.

Slade, J. W., *Thomas Pynchon*, 125-75.

Stark, J. O., *Pynchon's Fictions*, *passim*.

Takács, Ferenc, "Models or Metaphors: Pattern and Paranoia in Pynchon's THE CRYING OF LOT 49," *ALitASH* 23, iii-iv (1981): 297-306.

Tani, Stefano, "The Dismemberment of the Detective," *Diogenes* 120 (Winter, 1982): 22-41.

Tanner, T., *City of Words*, 173-80.

_____, *Thomas Pynchon*, 56-73.

Thiher, Allen, "Kafka's Legacy," *MFS* 26 (Winter, 1980-81): 543-62.

Wagner, Linda W., "A Note on Oedipa the Roadrunner," *JNT* 4 (1974): 155-61. Also in Wagner, L. W., *American Modern*, 85-92.

Wilson, Robert R., "Godgames and Labyrinths: The Logic of Entrapment," *Mosaic* 15, iv (Dec., 1982): 1-22.

Young, James D., "The Enigma Variations of Thomas Pynchon," *Crit* 10, i (1968): 69-77.

GRAVITY'S RAINBOW

Ames, Sanford S., "Pynchon and Visible Language: Ecriture," *IFR* 4 (1977): 170-3.

Bakker, J., "The End of Individualism," *DQR* 7 (1977): 296-304.

Balitas, Vincent D., "Charismatic Figures in GRAVITY'S RAINBOW," *PNotes* 9 (June, 1982): 38-53.

Black, Joel D., "Probing a Post-Romantic Paleontology: Thomas Pynchon's GRAVITY'S RAINBOW," *Boundary* 8, ii (1980): 229-54.

Braha, Elliot, "Menippean Form in GRAVITY'S RAINBOW and in Other Contemporary American Texts," *DAI* 40 (1979): 255A-56A.

Braudy, Leo, "Providence, Paranoia, and the Novel," *ELH* 48, iii (Fall, 1981): 629-3.

Brunner, John, "Coming Events: An Assessment of Thomas Pynchon's GRAVITY'S RAINBOW," *Foundation* 10 (1976): 20-7.

Caesar, Terry P., "A Note on Pynchon's Naming," *Pnotes* 5 (Feb., 1981): 5-10.

Chaffee, Patricia, "The Whale and the Rocket: Technology as Sacred Symbol," *Ren* 32, iii (Spring, 1980): 146-51.

Clark, Roger, "Imperialism in GRAVITY'S RAINBOW," *USFLQ* 21, i-ii (1982): 38.

Cocks, Geoffrey, "War, Man, and Gravity: Thomas Pynchon and Science Fiction," *Extrapolation* 20, iv (Winter, 1979): 368-77.

Cowart, David, "Baedeker to Pynchon," *PNotes* 5 (Feb., 1981): 20-7.

_____, "Cinematic Auguries of the Third Reich in GRAVITY'S RAINBOW," *LFQ* 6 (1978): 364-70.

_____, "Pynchon's Use of the Tannhauser-Legend in GRAVITY'S RAINBOW," *NConL* 9, iii (1979): 2-3.

_____, "'Sacrificial Ape': King Kong and His Antitypes in GRAVITY'S RAINBOW," *L&P* 28 (1978): 112-18.

_____, *Thomas Pynchon*, 31-62, 82-95, 119-24, 128-31.

Cullen, Robert J., "Words and a Yarn: Language and Narrative Technique in the Works of Thomas Pynchon," *DAI* 42, iv (Oct., 1981): 1634A.

DiPiero, William S., "GRAVITY'S RAINBOW Come Anti-Entropia," *Paragone Letteratura* 302 (1975): 105-8.

Doyle, Linda S., "A Study of Time in Three Novels: UNDER THE VOLCANO, ONE HUNDRED YEARS OF SOLITUDE, and GRAVITY'S RAINBOW," *DAI* 39 (1978): 1547A.

Duyfhuizen, Bernard, "Starry-Eyed Semiotics: Learning to Read Slothrop's Map and GRAVITY'S RAINBOW," *PNotes* 6 (June, 1981): 5-33.

Fowler, Douglas, "Pynchon's Magic World," *SAQ* 79, i (Winter, 1980): 51-60.

_____, *A Reader's Guide to GRAVITY'S RAINBOW*, Ann Arbor: Ardis, 1980.

Friedman, Alan J., and Manfred Ouetz, "Science as Metaphor: Thomas Pynchon and GRAVITY'S RAINBOW," *ConL* 15 (Summer, 1974): 345-59. Also in Pearce, R., ed., *Critical Essays on Thomas Pynchon*, 69-81.

Fussell, Paul, "Ritual of Military Memory," *The Great War and Modern Memory*, N.Y.: Oxford Un. Pr., 1975, 328-34. Also as "The Brigadier Remembers" in Mendelson, E., ed., *Pynchon*, 213-19.

Gorman, Lawrence J., "GRAVITY'S RAINBOW: The Promise and Trap of Mythology," *DAI* 43, iv (Oct., 1981): 1630A-31A.

Harriman, Robert D., "The Public Temper of GRAVITY'S RAINBOW," *DAI* 40 (1980): 4798A.

Hendin, Josephine, "What is Thomas Pynchon Telling us? V. and GRAVITY'S RAINBOW," *Harper's* 250 (Mar., 1975): 82-92. Also in Pearce, R., ed., *Critical Essays on Thomas Pynchon*, 42-50.

Herzberg, Bruce I., "Illusions of Control: A Reading of GRAVITY'S RAINBOW," *DAI* 39 (1979): 6756A-57A.

Horvath, Brooke, "Linguistic Distancing in GRAVITY'S RAINBOW," *PNotes* 8 (Feb., 1982): 5-22.

George, N. F., "The *Chymische Hochzeit* of Thomas Pynchon," *PNotes* 4 (Oct., 1980): 5-22.

Gilbert-Rolfe, Jeremy and John Johnston, "GRAVITY'S RAINBOW and the Spiral Jetty," *October* 1, i (Spring, 1976): 65-85; 1, ii (Summer, 1976): 71-90.

Guetti, J., *Word-Music*, 94-7.

Kappel, Lawrence, "Psychic Geography in GRAVITY'S RAINBOW," *ConL* 21 (1980): 225-51.

Katz, Bruce L., "This Ruinous Garden: Readable Signs in Pynchon's GRAVITY'S RAINBOW, with Remarks on Barth's GILES GOAT-BOY," *DAI* 40 (180): 4027A.

Kaufman, Marjorie, "Brünnhilde and the Chemists: Women in GRAVITY'S RAINBOW," in Levine, G., and D. Leverenz, eds., *Mindful Pleasures*, 197-227.

Kopcewicz, Andrzej, "The Rocket and the Whale: Thomas Pynchon's GRAVITY'S RAINBOW and MOBY DICK," 145-50, in Sienick, Marta, ed., *Proceedings of a Symposium on American Literature*, Poznan: Uniw. Im. Adama Mickiewicza, 1979.

Krafft, John M., "Anarcho-Romanticism and the Metaphysics of Counterforce: Alex Comfort and Thomas Pynchon," *Paunch* 40-41 (April, 1975): 78-107.

Krafft, John M., "'And How Far-Fallen': Puritan Themes in GRAVITY'S RAINBOW," *Crit* 18, iii (1977): 55-73.

Larsson, Donald F., "Approach and Avoid: Douglas A. MacKey's *The Rainbow of Thomas Pynchon*," *PNotes* 7 (Oct., 1981): 49-52.

_____, "The Camera Eye: 'Cinematic Narrative in U.S.A. and GRAVITY'S RAINBOW," 94-106, in Ruppert, Peter, Eugene Crook and Walter Forehand, eds., *Ideas of Order in Literature and Film*, Tallahassee: Un. Pr. of Florida, 1980.

Lehan, R., *Dangerous Crossing*, 157-62.

Leverenz, David, "On Trying to Read GRAVITY'S RAINBOW," in Levine, G., and D. Leverenz, eds., *Mindful Pleasures*, 229-49.

Levine, George, "V-2," *PR* 40 (1973): 517-29. Also in Mendelson, E., ed., *Pynchon*, 178-91.

Le Vot, Andre, "The Rocket and the Pig: Thomas Pynchon and Science-fiction," *Caliban* 12 (1975): 111-18.

Lippman, Bertrom, "The Reader of Movies: Thomas Pynchon's's GRAVITY'S RAINBOW," *UDQ* 12, i (1977): 1-46.

Mackey, Louis, "Paranoia, Pynchon, and Preterition," *Substance* 30 (1981): 16-30.

_____, *Rainbow Quest of Thomas Pynchon*, 36-59.

Maddox, Daniel T., "Rocket Blues: Knowledge and Morality in GRAVITY'S RAINBOW," *DAI* 39 (1978): 1573A-74A.

Marquez, Antonio, "The Cinematic Imagination in Thomas Pynchon's GRAVITY'S RAINBOW," *BRMMLA* 33 (1979): 166-79.

_____, "The Nightmare of History and Thomas Pynchon's GRAVITY'S RAINBOW," *ELWIU* 8, i (Spring, 1981): 53-62.

_____, "Technologique in GRAVITY'S RAINBOW," *RS* 48 (1980): 1-10.

McClintock, James I., "United States Revisited: Pynchon and Zamiatin," *ConL* 18, iv (Autumn, 1977): 475-90.

McConnell, F. D., *Four Postwar American Novelists*, 174-97.

McHale, Brian, "Modernist Reading, Post Modern Text: The Case of GRAVITY'S RAINBOW," *PoT* 1, i-ii (1979): 85-110.

_____, "On Moral Fiction: One Use of GRAVITY'S RAINBOW," *PNotes* 6 (June, 1981): 34-8.

Mendelson, Edward, "Encyclopedic Narrative from Dante to Pynchon," *MLN* 91 (Dec., 1976): 1267-75.

Mendelson, Edward, "Gravity's Encyclopedia," in Levine, G., and D. Leverenz, eds., *Mindful Pleasures*, 161-95.

_____, "Pynchon's Gravity," *YR* 62 (Summer, 1973): 624-31.

Mesher, David R., "Corrigenda: A Note on GRAVITY'S RAINBOW," *PNotes* 5 (Feb., 1981): 13-16.

_____, "Negative Entropy and the Form of GRAVITY'S RAINBOW," *RS* 49, iii (Sept., 1981): 162-70.

Moore, Steven, "I CHING," *WN* 17, ii (Apr., 1980): 25.

Morgan, Speer, "GRAVITY'S RAINBOW: What's the Big Idea?" *MFS* 23 (Summer, 1977): 199-216. Also in Pearce, R., ed., *Critical Essays on Thomas Pynchon*, 82-98.

Morris, Paul, "Beyond the Zero: GRAVITY'S RAINBOW and Modern Critical Theory," *DAI* 43 (1982): 1540A.

Morrison, Philip, "Review," *Scientific American* 229 (Oct., 1973): 131. Also in Mendelson, E., ed., *Pynchon*, 191-2.

Munley, Ellen W., "Caught in the Act: Naming in the Novels of Thomas Pynchon and Nathalie Sarraute," *DAI* 42, x (Apr., 1982): 4442A.

Muste, John M., "The Mandala in GRAVITY'S RAINBOW," *Boundary* 9, ii (Winter, 1981): 163-79.

_____, "Thomas Pynchon/Gwenhidwy: Who's Behind That Beard," *NMAL* 5, ii (Spring, 1981): Item 13.

Nadeau, Robert L., "Readings from the New Book of Nature: Physics and Pynchon's GRAVITY'S RAINBOW," *SNNTS* 11, iv (1979): 454-71.

Ozier, Lance W., "Antipointsman/Antimexico: Some Mathematical Imagery in GRAVITY'S RAINBOW," *Crit* 16, ii (1974): 73-9.

_____, "The Calculus of Transformation: More Mathematical Imagery in GRAVITY'S RAINBOW," *TLC* 21, ii (May, 1975): 193-210.

Pearce, Richard, "Where're They At, Where're They Going? Thomas Pynchon and the American Novel in Motion," *MR* 21 (Spring, 1980): 190-5. Also in Pearce, R., ed., *Critical Essays on Thomas Pynchon*, 224-8.

Plater, W. M., *Grim Phoenix*, 35-41, 49-53, 57-64, 87-102, 117-27, 154-76, 181-6, 195-20, 205-11, 213-19, 234-42.

Poirier, Richard, "Rocket Power," *Sat. Rev. of the Arts* 1 (Mar. 3, 1973): 59-64. Also in Mendelson, E., ed., *Pynchon*, 167-78.

Purdy, S. B., "The Electronic Novel," *NOR* 9, ii (Fall, 1982): 26-33.

Pyuen, Carolyn S., "The Transmarginal Leap: Meaning and Process in GRAVITY'S RAINBOW," *Mosaic* 15, ii (June, 1982): 33-46.

Qazi, Javaid, "Pynchon in Central Asia: The Use of Sources and Resources," *RMRLL* 34, iv (Fall, 1980): 229-42.

Rosenbaum, Jonathan, "Reply to Schwarzbach, F.S., 'Pynchon's Gravity'," *NewRev* 3 (July, 1976): 64. Also in Mendelson, E., ed., *Pynchon*, 67-8.

Safer, Elaine B., "The Allusive Mode and Black Humor in Barth's GILES GOAT-BOY and Pynchon's GRAVITY'S RAINBOW," *Ren* 32, iii (Winter, 1980): 89-104. Also in Pearce, R., ed., *Critical Essays on Thomas Pynchon*, 157-68.

Sanders, Scott, "Pynchon's Paranoid History," *TCL* 21 (May, 1975): 177-92. Also in Levine, G., and D. Leverenz, eds., *Mindful Pleasures*, 139-59.

Schaub, T. H., *Pynchon*, 43-75, 83-101 *passim*, 123-36, 139-54 *passim*.

Schmitz, Neil, "Describing the Demon: The Appeal of Thomas Pynchon," *PR* 42, i (1975): 112-25.

Schwartz, Richard A., "Thomas Pynchon and the Evolution of Fiction," *SFS* 8, ii (July, 1981): 165-72.

Schwartzman, John, "Paradox, Play and Post-Modern Fiction," 38-48, in Schwartzman, Helen B., ed., *Play and Culture*, West Point, N.Y.: Leisure, 1980.

Schwarzbach, F. S., "Pynchon's Gravity," *NewRev* 3, xxvii (June, 1976): 39-43. Also, revised, in Mendelson, E., ed., *Pynchon*, 56-67.

Seed, David, "Pynchon's Names: Some Further Considerations," *PNotes* 6 (June, 1971): 41-3.

_____, "Pynchon's Two Tchitcherines," *PNotes* 5 (Feb., 1981): 11-12.

Seidel, Michael, "The Satiric Plots of GRAVITY'S RAINBOW," in Mendelson, E., ed., *Pynchon*, 193-212.

Siegel, Mark R., "Creative Paranoia: Understanding the System of GRAVITY'S RAINBOW," *Crit* 18, iii (1977): 39-54.

_____, *Pynchon: Creative Paranoia in Gravity's RAINBOW*, Port Washington, N.Y.: Kennikat, 1978.

Simmon, Scott, "Beyond the Theater of War: GRAVITY'S RAINBOW as Film," *LFQ* 6 (1978): 347-63. Also in Pearce, R., ed., *Critical Essays on Thomas Pynchon*, 99-123.

_____, "A Character Index: GRAVITY'S RAINBOW," *Crit* 16, ii (1974): 68-72.

_____, "GRAVITY'S RAINBOW Described," *Crit* 16, ii (1974): 54-67.

Slade, Joseph W., "Escaping Rationalization: Options for the Self in GRAVITY'S RAINBOW," *Crit* 18, iii (1977): 27-38.

_____, *Thomas Pynchon*, 176-238.

Smith, Marcus, and Khachig Tololyan, "The New Jeremaid: GRAVITY'S RAINBOW," in Pearce, R., ed., *Critical Essays on Thomas Pynchon*, 169-86.

Smith, Mack, "The Paracinematic Reality of GRAVITY'S RAINBOW," *PNotes* 9 (June, 1982): 17-37.

Stark, J. O., *Pynchon's Fictions, passim*.

Stern, Jerome H., "The Interfaces of GRAVITY'S RAINBOW," *Dismisura* 39-50 (1980): 51-7.

Tanner, Tony, "Games American Writers Play: Ceremony, Complexity, Contestation, and Carnival," *Salmagundi* 35 (1976): 110-40.

_____, *Thomas Pynchon*, 74-91.

_____, "V and V2," *LonM* 13 (Feb.-Mar., 1974): 80-8. Also in Mendelson, E., ed., *Pynchon*, 47-55.

Taylor, Patricia S., "'Make It New': GRAVITY'S RAINBOW as Romantic Discovery," *DAI* 40 (1980): 5059A.

Thompson, Gary L., "Fictive Models: Carlyle's SARTOR RESARTUS, Melville's THE CONFIDENCE-MAN, Gaddis' THE RECOGNITIONS, and Pynchon's GRAVITY'S RAINBOW," *DAI* 40 (1979): 1462A-63A.

Tillotson, T. S., "Gravitational Entropy in GRAVITY'S RAINBOW," *PNotes* 4 (1980): 23-4.

Tololyan, Kachchig, "The Fishy Poisson: Allusions to Statistics in GRAVITY'S RAINBOW," *NMAL* 4 (1979): Item 5.

Weisenburger, Steven," The End of History? Thomas Pynchon and the Uses of the Past," *TCL* 25 (Spring, 1979): 54-72. Also in Pearce, R., ed., *Critical Essays on Thomas Pynchon*, 140-56.

Weisenburger, Steven, 'The Origin of Pynchon's Tchitcherine," *PNotes* 8 Feb., 1982): 39-42.

Werner, C. H., *Paradoxical Resolutions*, 181-94.

Westervelt, Linda A., "'A Place Dependent on Ourselves': The Reader as System-Builder in GRAVITY'S RAINBOW," *TSLL* 22 (1980): 69-90.

Wilson, Raymond J., III., "Cozzen's GUARD OF HONOR and Pynchon's GRAVITY'S RAINBOW," *NConL* 9, v (1979): 6-8.

Wolfe, Peter, "GRAVITY'S RAINBOW," *STwC* 13 (Spring, 1974): 125-8.

Wolfley, Lawrence C., "Repression's Rainbow: The Presence of Norman O. Brown in Pynchon's Big Novel," *PMLA* 92, v (Oct., 1977): 873-89. Also in Pearce, R., ed., *Critical Essays on Thomas Pynchon*, 124-39.

V.

Allen, M., *Necessary Blankness*, 37-46.

Begnal, Michael H., "Thomas Pynchon's V.: In Defense of Benny Profane," *JNT* 9 (1979): 61-9.

Bergonzi, B., *Situation of the Novel*, 96-100.

Boheemen-Saaf, Cristel van, "The Artist as Con Man: The Reaction Against the Symbolist Aesthetic in Recent American Fiction," *DQR* 7, iv (1977): 305-18.

Bryant, J. H., *Open Decision*, 252-7.

Calhoun, John C., "A Groatsworth of Wit: Parallels in John Barth's THE SOT-WEED FACTOR and Thomas Pynchon's V.," *DAI* 37 (1976): 2857A-58A.

Dowart, David, "Love and Death: Variations on a Theme in Pynchon's Early Fiction," *JNT* 7, iii (Fall, 1977): 157-69.

_____, *Thomas Pynchon*, 13-22, 65-78.

_____, "V. in Florence: Botticelli's *Birth of Venus* and the Metamorphosis of Victoria Wren," *SHR* 13 (1979): 345-53.

Cullen, Robert J., "Words and a Yarn: Language and Narrative Technique in the Works of Thomas Pynchon," *DAI* 42, iv (Oct., 1981): 1634A.

Fahy, Joseph, "Thomas Pynchon's V. and Mythology," *Crit* 18, iii (1977): 5-18.

Golden, Robert E., "Mass, Man, and Modernism: Violence in Pynchon's V.," *Crit* 14, ii (1973): 5-17.

Graves, Lila V., "Love and the Western World of Pynchon's V.," *SAB* 47, i (Jan., 1982): 62-73.

Greenberg, Alvin, "The Underground Woman: An Excursion Into the V-ness of Thomas Pynchon," *Chelsea* 27 (1969): 58-65.

Greiner, Donald J., "Fiction as History, History as Fiction: The Reader and Thomas Pynchon's V.," *SCR* 10, i (1977): 4-18.

Guetti, J., *Word-Music*, 98-107.

Hall, James, "The New Pleasures of the Imagination," *VQR* 46, iv (Autumn, 1970): 604-12.

Harder, Kelsie B., "Names in Thomas Pynchon's V.," *LOS* 5 (1978): 64-80.

Harris, Charles B., "Thomas Pynchon and the Entropic Vision," *Contemporary American Novelists of the Absurd*, 79-92.

Hausdorff, Don, "Thomas Pynchon's Multiple Absurdities," *WSCL* 7 (Autumn, 1966): 258-69.

Henderson, H. B., III., *Versions of the Past*, 277-85.

Hendin, Josephine, "What is Thomas Pynchon Telling Us? V. and GRAVITY'S RAINBOW," *Harper's* 250 (Mar., 1975): 82-92. Also in Pearce, R., ed., *Critical Essays on Thomas Pynchon*, 42-50.

Henkle, Roger B., "Pynchon's Tapestries on the Western World," *MFS* 17, ii (Summer, 1971): 207-20. Also in Mendelson, E., ed., *Pynchon*, 97-111.

Hite, Molly P., "Ideas of Order in the Novels of Thomas Pynchon," *DAI* 42, i (July, 1981): 214A-15A.

Hoffman, Frederick J., "The Questing Comedian: Thomas Pynchon's V.," *Crit* 6, iii (Winter, 1963-64): 174-7.

Hunt, John W., "Comic Escape and Anti-Vision: The Novels of Joseph Heller and Thomas Pynchon," in Scott, N. A., Jr., ed., *Adversity and Grace*, 98-107. Also in Pearce, R., ed., *Critical Essays on Thomas Pynchon*, 32-8.

Hyman, Stanley E., "The Goddess and the Schlemiel," *New Leader* 46 (Mar. 18, 1963): 22-3. Also in Kostelanetz, R., ed., *On Contemporary Literature*, 506-10. Also in Hyman, S. E., ed., *Standards*, 138-42.

Kostelanetz, Richard, "The New American Fiction," in Kostelanetz, R., ed., *New American Arts,* 214-17.

Larsson, Donald F., "Approach and Avoid: Douglas A. Mackey's *Rainbow Quest of Thomas Pynchon,*" *PNotes* 7 (Oct., 1981): 49-52.

Lehan, R., *Dangerous Crossing,* 157-62.

Lewis, R. W. B., "The New American Fiction," in Koselanetz, R., ed., *New American Arts,* 214-17.

Lewis, R. W. B., "Days of Wrath and Laughter," *Trials of the Word,* 228-34.

Lhamon, W. T., Jr., "Pentecost, Promiscuity and Pynchon's V.: From the Scaffold to the Impulsive," *TCL* 21, ii (May, 1975): 163-76. Also in Levine, G., and D. Leverenz, eds., *Mindful Pleasures,* 69-86.

Mackey, D. A., *Rainbow Quest of Thomas Pynchon,* 12-26.

Matthijs, Michel, "Character in Pynchon's V.," *Restant,* 10, ii (Summer, 1982): 125-44.

McConnell, F. D., *Four Postwar American Novelists,* 164-9.

McNamara, Eugene, "The Absurd Style in Contemporary Literature," *HAB* 19 (1968): 44-9.

Mesher, David R., "Pynchon and Nabokov's V.," *PNotes* 8 (Feb., 1982): 43-6.

Murphy, Earl P., "Thomas Pynchon's V.: A Psycho-Structural Study," *DAI* 38 (1978): 5464A-65A.

New, Melvyn, "Profaned and Stenciled Texts: In Search of Pynchon's V.," *GaR* 33 (1979): 395-412.

Newman, Robert D., "Pynchon's Use of Carob in V.," *NConL* 11, iii (May, 1981): 11.

O'Connor, Peter, "The Wasteland of Thomas Pynchon's V.," *CollL* 3, i (Winter, 1976): 49-55.

Olderman, R. M., "The Illusion and the Possibility of Conspiracy," *Beyond the Waste Land,* 123-44.

Patteson, Richard F., "Horus, Harmarkhis, and Harpokrates in Chapter III of V. and 'Under the Rose'," *PNotes* 6 (June, 1981): 39-40.

_____, "What Stencil Knew: Structure and Certitude in Pynchon's V.," *Crit* 16, ii (1974): 30-44. Also in Pearce, R., ed., *Critical Essays on Thomas Pynchon,* 20-31.

Pearce, Richard, "Where're They At, Where're They Going? Thomas Pynchon and the American Novel in Motion," *MR* 21 (Spring, 1980): 181-5. Also in Pearce, R., ed., *Critical Essays on Thomas Pynchon,* 216-20.

Peirce, Carol M.,. "Pynchon's V. and Lawrence Durrell's ALEXANDRIA QUARTET: A Seminar in the Modern Tradition," *PNotes* 8 (Feb., 1982): 23-7.

Plater, W. M., *Grim Phoenix,* 19-26, 30-4, 39-43, 45-8, 67-81, 140-50, 176-80, 191-3, 225-8.

Pütz, Manfred, "Thomas Pynchon: History, Self, and the Narrative Discourse," *Story of Identity,* 131-46.

Richardson, Robert O., "The Absurd Animate in Thomas Pynchon's V.: A Novel," *STwC* 9 (Spring, 1972): 35-58.

Richter, David, "The Failure of Completeness: Pynchon's V.," *Fable's End,* 101-35.

Rother, James, "Parafiction: The Adjacent Universe of Barth, Barthelme, Pynchon and Nabokov," *Boundary* 5, i (Fall, 1976): 28-1.

Schaub, T. H., *Pynchon,* 5-20 *passim.*

Schulz, M. F., *Black Humor Fiction of the Sixties,* 77-82, 143-4.

Sklar, Robert, "The New Novel, U.S.A.: Thomas Pynchon," *Nation* 205 (Sept. 25, 1967): 277-8. Also in Mendelson, E., ed., *Pynchon,* 89-93.

Slade, J. W., *Thomas Pynchon,* 48-124.

Slatoff, Walter, "Thomas Pynchon," *Epoch* 12 (Spring, 1963); 255-7.

Smith, Marcus, "V. and THE MALTESE FALCON: A Connection," *PNotes* 2 (1980): 6.

Solberg, Sara M., "Resonance: Joyce's ULYSSES and Pynchon's V.," *DAI* 39 (1978): 2241A.

Stark, J. O. *Pynchon's Fictions passim.*

Stimpson, Catharine R., "Pre-Apocalyptic Atavism" Thomas Pynchon's Early Fiction," in Levine, G., and D. Leverenz, eds., *Mindful Pleasures,* 33-46.

Sugiura, Ginsaku, "Nature, History, and Entropy: A Reading of Faulkner's ABSALOM, ABSALOM! in Comparison with MOBY DICK and V.," *WiF* 2, ii (1979): 21-33.

Tanner, Tony, "Pattern and Paranoia or Caries and Cabals," *Salmagundi* 15 (Winter, 1971): 81-99. Also in Tanner, T., *City of Words,* 155-73. Also in Mendelson, E., ed., *Pynchon,* 16-47. Also in Levine, G., and D. Leverenz, eds., *Mindful Pleasures,* 49-67.

_____, *Thomas Pynchon,* 40-55.

Thigpen, Kenneth A., "Folklore in Contemporary American Literature: Thomas Pynchon's V., and the Alligators-in-the-Sewers Legend," *SFQ* 43, i-ii (1979): 93-105.

Young, James D., "The Enigma Variations of Thomas Pynchon," *Crit* 10, i (1968): 69-77.

BIBLIOGRAPHY

See issues of *PNotes.*

Clark, Beverly L., and Caryn Fuoroli, "A Review of Major Pynchon Criticism," in Pearce, R., ed., *Critical Essays on Thomas Pynchon,* 230-54.

Herzberg, Bruce, "Bibliography," in Levine, G., and D. Leverenz, eds., *Mindful Pleasures,* 265-9.

_____, "Selected Articles on Thomas Pynchon: An Annotated Bibliography," *TCL* 21, ii (May, 1975): 221-25.

Scotto, Robert M., *Three Contemporary Novelists: An Annotated Bibliography of Works by and about John Hawkes, Joseph Heller and Thomas Pynchon,* N.Y.: Garland, 1977.

Walsh, Thomas P., and Cameron Northouse, *John Barth, Jerzy Kosinski, and Thomas Pynchon: A Reference Guide,* Boston: G. K. Hall, 1977.

Weixlmann, Joseph N., "Thomas Pynchon: A Bibliography," *Crit* 14, ii (1972): 34-43.

RADDALL, THOMAS HEAD, 1903-

GENERAL

Cameron, Donald, "Thomas Raddall: The Art of Historical Fiction," *DR* 49, iv (Winter, 1969-70): 540-8.

Cockburn, Robert, "'Nova Scotia is My Dweln Plas': The Life and Work of Thomas Raddall," *Acadiensis* 7, ii (Spring, 1978): 135-41.

Hawkins, W. J., "Thomas Raddall: The Man and His Work," *QQ* 75 (Spring, 1968): 137-46.

Sorfleet, John R., "Thomas Raddall: I Was Always a Rebel Underneath," *JCF* 2, iv (Fall, 1973): 45-64. [Interview.]

HIS MAJESTY'S YANKEES

Gray, James, "Introduction," HIS MAJESTY'S YANKEES (New Canadian Library), Toronto: McClelland and Stewart, 1977, xi-xviii.

West, David, "Past and Present," *JCF* 20 (1977): 152-5.

THE NYMPH AND THE LAMP

Matthews, John, "Introduction," in THE NYMPH AND THE LAMP (New Canadian Library), Toronto: McClelland and Stewart, 1963, v-ix.

Moss, J., *Patterns of Isolation*, 127-38, 145-8.

PRIDE'S FANCY

Cogswell, Fred, "Introduction," PRIDE'S FANCY (New Canadian Library), Toronto: McClelland and Stewart, 1974, iii-x.

ROGER SUDDEN

Leitold, John R., "Introduction," ROGER SUDDEN (New Canadian Library), Toronto: McClelland and Stewart, 1972, iv-viii.

RAND, AYN, 1905-1982

GENERAL

Cook, Bruce, "Ayn Rand: A Voice in the Wilderness," *CathW* 201, i (May, 1965): 119-24.

Nozick, Robert, "On the Randian Argument," *Person* 52, ii (Spring, 1971): 282-99.

ATLAS SHRUGGED

Bryant, J., *Open Decision*, 169-72.

Gladstein, Mimi R., "Ayn Rand and Feminism: An Unlikely Alliance," *CE* 39, vi (Feb., 1978): 680-5.

Wilt, Judith, and Mimi Gladstein, "On ATLAS SHRUGGED," *CE* 40 (1978): 333-7.

THE FOUNTAINHEAD

Deane, Paul, "Ayn Rand's Neurotic Personalities of Our Times," *RLV* 36, ii (1979): 125-9.

Gordon, Philip, "The Extroflective Hero: A Look at Ayn Rand," *JPC* 10, iv (Spring, 1977): 701-10.

McGann, Kevin, "Ayn Rand in the Stockyard of the Spirit," in Peary, G., and R. Shatzkin, eds., *Modern American Novel and the Movies*, 125-9.

RAO, RAJA, 1908-

GENERAL

Ali, Ahmed, "Illusion and Reality: The Art and Philosophy of Raja Rao," *JCL* 5 (July, 1968): 16-28.

Gemmill, Janet P., "Narrative Technique in the Novels of Raja Rao," *DAI* 33 (1973): 6309A-10A.

Gowda, H. H. Anniah, "Phenomenal Tradition: Raja Rao and Wilson Harris," *BACLLS* 9 (1972): 28-48.

Guzman, Richard R., "The Saint and the Sage: The Fiction of Raja Rao," *VQR* 56, i (Winter, 1980): 32-50.

Joshi, K., and B. S. Rao, "Raja Rao as a Novelist," *Studies in Indo-Anglian Literature*, 109-17.

Mani, Laxmi, "Voice and Vision in Raja Rao's Fiction," *SARev* 4 (1980): 1-11. [Not seen.]

Naik, M. K., "The Achievement of Raja Rao," *BP* 4, xii (1969): 44-56. [Not seen.]

_____, *Raja Rao.*

Narasimhaiah, C. D., in Amirthanayagam, G., ed., *Asian and Western Writers in Dialogue*, 92-5.

_____, "Indian Writing in English. An Area of Promise," *JCL* 9, i (August, 1974): 37-47.

Niranjan, Shiva, "Myth as a Creative Mode: A Study of Mythical Parallels in Raja Rao's Novels," *ComQ* 4, xiii (Mar., 1980): 49-68.

Niven, Alistair, "Any Row Over Rao?" *Commonwealth Newsl.* 6 (1974): 34-5. [Not seen.]

Parameswaran, U., *Study of Representative Indo-English Novelists*, 141-70.

_____, "'Without Woman the World is Not': Shakti in Raja Rao's Novels," *BACLLS* 9 (1972): 4-27.

Ray, Robert J., "The Novels of Raja Rao," *BA* 40 (Autumn, 1966): 411-14.

Singh, R. S., *Indian Novel in English*, 73-95.

Walsh, William, "The Big Three," in Mohan, R., ed., *Indian Writing in English*, 30-1.

Williams, H. M., "Raja Rao: The Idea of India," *Miscellany* (Apr., 1973): [Not seen.]

THE CAT AND SHAKESPEARE: A TALE OF INDIA

Gemmill, Janet P., "Rhythm in THE CAT AND SHAKE-SPEARE," *LE&W* 13 (June, 1969): 27-42.

Gowda, H. H. Anniah, "Phenomenal Tradition: Raja Rao and Wilson Harris," *BACLLS* 9 (Mar., 1972): 32-45.

Guzman, Richard R., "The Saint and the Sage: The Fiction of Raja Rao," *VQR* 56, i (Winter, 1980): 46-50.

Harrex, S. C., "Raja Rao: Companion of Pilgrimage," in Narasimhaiah, C. D., and S. Nagarajan, eds., *Studies in Australian and Indian Literature*, 257-73. Also, expanded, in Harrex, S. C., *Fire and the Offering*, 162-71, 191-6.

Iyengar, K. R. S., *Indian Writing in English*, 406-11.

_____, "Literature as Sadhana: A Note on Raja Rao's THE CAT AND SHAKESPEARE," *Aryan Path* 40, vi (June, 1969): 301-5.

Jamkhandi, Sudhakar R., "THE CAT AND SHAKESPEARE: Narrator, Audience, and Message," *JIWE* 7, ii (1979): 24-41.

Naik, M. K., "THE CAT AND SHAKESPEARE: A Study," in Narasimhaiah, C. D., ed., *Indian Literature of the Past Fifty Years*, 147-76.

_____, "The Kingdom of God is Within a 'Mew': A Study of THE CAT AND SHAKESPEARE," *Karnatak Un. Jnl.* 12 (1968): 123-50.

_____, *Raja Rao*, 115-42.

Narasimhaiah, C. D., "National Identity in Literature and Language: Its Range and Depth in the Novels of Raja Rao," in Goodwin, K. L., ed., *National Identity*, 165-8.

_____, "Raja Rao: THE CAT AND SHAKESPEARE," *LCrit* 8, iii (Winter, 1968): 65-95.

Paniker, Ayyappa, "A Conversation with Raja Rao on THE CAT AND SHAKESPEARE," *Chandrabhágá* 2 (1979): 14-18.

_____, "The Frontiers of Fiction: A Study of Raja Rao's THE CAT AND SHAKESPEARE," LCrit 15, i (1980): 60-72.

Parameswaran, Uma, "Karma at Work: The Allegory in Raja Rao's THE CAT AND SHAKESPEARE," JCL 7 (July, 1969): 107-15.

_____, Study of Representative Indo-English Novelists, 157-69.

_____, "'Without Woman the World is Not': Shakti in Raja Rao's Novels," BACLLS 9 (Mar., 1972): 22-5.

Rao, J. Srihari, "Images of Truth: A Study of Raja Rao's THE CAT AND SHAKESPEARE," JIWE 5, i (1977): 36-41.

Ray, Robert J., "The Novels of Raja Rao," BA 40 (Autumn, 1966): 413-14.

Reddy, K. Venkata, "An Approach to Raja Rao's THE CAT AND SHAKESPEARE," WLWE 20, ii (Autumn, 1981): 337-43.

Sharma, Sam P., "Raja Rao's Search for the Feminine," JSoAL 12, iii-iv (Spring-Summer, 1977): 100-01.

Shepherd, R., "Raja Rao: Symbolism in THE CAT AND SHAKESPEARE," WLWE 14 (1975): 347-56.

White, Ray L., "Raja Rao's THE CAT AND SHAKESPEARE in the U.S.A.," JIWE 7, i (1979): 24-9.

COMRADE KIRILLOV

Badve, V. V., "Raja Rao's COMRADE KIRILLOV," New Quest 14 (1979): 121-8.

Mathur, O. P., "The East-West Theme in COMRADE KIRILLOV," NLRev 4 (1978): 25-9.

Niranjan, Shiva, "Myth as Creative Mode: A Study of Mythical Parallels in Raja Rao's Novels," ComQ 4, xiii (Mar., 1980): 58-60.

Rao, K. R., "The Novelist as Marxist," Triveni 49, i (1980): 47-50.

KANTHAPURA

Gemmill, Janet P., "KANTHAPURA: India en Route to Independence," CEA 44, iv (May, 1982): 30-8.

_____, "The Transcreation of Spoken Kanada in Raja Rao's KANTHAPURA," LE&W 18 (1974): 191-202.

Guzman, Richard R., "The Saint and the Sage: The Fiction of Raja Rao," VQR 56, i (Winter, 1980): 34-40.

Harrex, S. C., Fire and the Offering, 151-61.

Iyngar, K. R. S., Indian Writing in English, 390-7.

Krishna, Sastry, L. S. R., "Raja Rao," Triveni 36, iv (1968): 19-26.

Naik, M. K., "KANTHAPURA: The Indo-Anglian Novel as Legendary History," Karnatak Un. Jnl.: Humanities 10 (1966): 26-39.

Naik, M. K., Raja Rao, 60-78.

Narasimhaiah, C. D., "National Identity in Literature and Language: Its Range and Depth in the Novels of Raja Rao," in Goodwin, K. L., ed., National Identity, 154-9.

_____, "Raja Rao's KANTHAPURA: An Analysis," LCrit 7, ii (Summer, 1966): 54-77. Also in Naik, M. K., et al., eds., Critical Essays on Indian Writing in English, 233-58. Also in Narasimhaiah, C. D., Fiction and the Reading Public in India, Mysore, 1967, 60-83.

Niranjan, Shiva, "Myth as Creative Mode: A Study of Mythical Parallels in Raja Rao's Novels," ComQ 4, xiii (Mar., 1980): 53-8.

_____, "The Nature and Extent of Gandhi's Impact on the Early Novels of Mulk Anand and Raja Rao," ComQ 3, xi (June, 1979): 41-5.

Raizada, Harish, "Literature as 'Sadhana': The Progress of Raja Rao from KANTHAPURA to THE SERPENT AND THE ROPE," in Sharma, K. K., ed., Indo-English Literature, 159-64.

Ram, Atma, "Peasant Sensibility in KANTHAPURA," in Sharma, K. K., ed., Indo-English Literature, 194-200.

Seshachari, Candadai, "The Gandhian Dimension: Revolution and Tragedy in KANTHAPURA," SARev 5, ii (July, 1981): 82-7.

Singh, R. S., Indian Novel in English, 73-9.

_____, Raja Rao's KANTHAPURA: AN ANALYSIS, Delhi: Doaba House, 1973.

THE SERPENT AND THE ROPE

Aithal, S. Krishnamourthy, and Rashmi Aital, "East-West Encounter in Four Indo-English Novels," ACLALSB 6, i (Nov., 1982): 1-16.

_____, "Interracial and Intercultural Relationships in Raja Rao's THE SERPENT AND THE ROPE," IFR 7 (1980): 94-8.

Ali, Ahmed, "Illusion and Reality: The Art and Philosophy of Raja Rao," JCL 5 (July, 1968): 19-27.

Bhalla, Brij M., "Quest for Identity in Raja Rao's THE SERPENT AND THE ROPE," ArielE 4, iv (1973): 95-105.

Davies, M. Bryn, "Raja Rao's THE SERPENT AND THE ROPE: A New Literary Genre?" in Niven, A., ed., Commonwealth Writer Overseas, 265-9.

Eng, Ooi Boo, "Making Initial Innocent Sense of THE SERPENT AND THE ROPE," JIWE 8, i-ii (Jan.-July, 1980): 53-62.

Gemmill, Janet P., "Dualities and Non-Duality in Raja Rao's THE SERPENT AND THE ROPE," WLWE 12 (June, 1973): 247-59.

Guzman, Richard R., "The Saint and the Sage: The Fiction of Raja Rao," VQR 56, i (Winter, 1980): 40-6.

Harrex, S. C., "Raja Rao: Companion of Pilgrimage," in Narasimhaiah, C. D., and S. Nagarajan, eds., Studies in Australian and Indian Literature, 257-73. Also, expanded, in Harrex, S. C., Fire and the Offering, 162-91.

Iyengar, K. R. S., Indian Writing in English, 397-406.

Kaul, R. K., "THE SERPENT AND THE ROPE as a Philosophical Novel," LCrit 15, ii (1980): 32-43.

Krishna, Sastry L. S. R., "Raja Rao," Triveni 36, iv (1968): 26-30.

McCutchion, David, 'The Novel as Sastra," Writer's Workshop (Calcutta) No. 8 (Sept.-Oct., 1961): 91-9. Also in McCutchion, D., Indian Writing in English, Calcutta: Writer's Workshop, 1969, 69-82. Also in Murkherjee, M., ed., Considerations, 90-101.

Mukherjee, M., Twice Born Fiction, 91-6, 147-50.

Nagarajan, S., "An Indian Novel," SR 72, iii (Summer, 1964): 512-17. Also in Mukherjee, M., ed., Considerations, 84-9.

Nagarajan, S., "A Note on Myth and Ritual in THE SERPENT AND THE ROPE," JCL 7, i (June, 1972): 45-8.

Naik, M. K., Raja Rao, 79-114.

_____, "THE SERPENT AND THE ROPE: The Indo-Anglian Novel as Epic Legend," in Naik, M. K., ed., Critical Essays on Indian Writing in English, 259-93.

Naikar, Basavaraj S., "Coming Together: The Central Problem in THE SERPENT AND THE ROPE," Karnatak Un. Jnl.: Humanities 22 (1978): 114-22.

Narasimhaiah, C. D., "National Identity in Literature and Language: Its Range and Depth in the Novels of Raja Rao," in Goodwin, K. L., ed., National Identity, 159-65.

_____, "Raja Rao: The Metaphysical Novel (THE SERPENT AND THE ROPE) and Its Significance in Our Age," *Swan and the Eagle*, 159-71. Also in Walsh, W., ed., *Readings in Commonwealth Literature*, 38-57.

_____, "Raja Rao: THE SERPENT AND THE ROPE. A Study," *LCrit* 5, iv (Summer, 1963): 62-89.

Narasimhan, R., *Sensibility Under Stress*, 82-91.

Niranjan, Shiva, "Myth as Creative Mode: A Study of Mythical Parallels in Raja Rao's Novels," *ComQ* 4, xiii (Mar., 1980): 60-6.

Parameswaran, U., *Study of Representative Indo-English Novelists*, 148-57.

_____, "'Without Woman the World is Not': Shakti in Raja Rao's Novels," *BACLLS* 9 (Mar., 1972): 4-25.

Raizada, Harish, "Literature as 'Sadhana': The Progress of Raja Rao from KANTHPURA to THE SERPENT AND THE ROPE," in Sharma, K. K., ed., *Indo-English Literature*, 164-75.

Razdan, B. M., and J. P. Ranchan, "THE SERPENT AND THE ROPE—India Made Real," *Illustrated Weekly of India* (Mar. 13, 1966): 45-63; (Apr. 3, 1966): 33-5; (Apr. 10, 1966): 33-5.

Ray, Robert J., "The Novels of Raja Rao," *BA* 40 (Autumn, 1966): 412-13.

Sharma, Som P., "Raja Rao's Search for the Feminine," *JSoAL* 12, iii-iv (Spring-Summer, 1977): 95-100.

Shepherd, R., "The Character of Ramaswamy in Raja Rao's THE SERPENT AND THE ROPE," *NLRev* 4 (1978): 17-24.

_____, "Symbolic Organization in THE SERPENT AND THE ROPE," *SoRA* 6, ii (1973): 93-107.

Singh, R., *Indian Novel in English*, 80-91.

Venkatachari, K., "The Feminine Principle in Raja Rao's THE SERPENT AND THE ROPE," *OJES* 8, ii (1971): 113-20.

_____, "Raja Rao's THE SERPENT AND THE ROPE: A Study in *Advaitic* Affirmation," *OJES* 8, i (1971): i-xii.

Westbrook, Perry D., "Theme and Action in Raja Rao's THE SERPENT AND THE ROPE," *WLWE* 14 (1975): 385-98.

Williams, Haydn M., "Raja Rao's THE SERPENT AND THE ROPE and the Idea of India," in Robb, Peter G., and David D. Taylor, eds., *Rule, Protest, Identity: Aspects of Modern South Asia*, London: Curzon; Atlantic Highlands, N. J.: Humanities, 1978, 206-12.

BIBLIOGRAPHY

Naik, M. K., *Raja Rao*, 157-60.

RAPHAEL, FREDERIC, 1931-

GENERAL

McDowell, Frederick P. W., "The Varied Universe of Frederic Raphael's Fiction," *Crit* 8, i (Fall, 1965): 21-50.

THE EARLSDON WAY

McDowell, Frederick P. W., "The Varied Universe of Frederic Raphael's Fiction," *Crit* 8, i (Fall, 1965): 24-8.

Urwin, G. G., ed., *Taste for Living*, 74-7.

THE GRADUATE WIFE

McDowell, Frederick P. W., "The Varied Universe of Frederick Raphael's Fiction," *Crit* 8, i (Fall, 1965): 39-43.

THE LIMITS OF LOVE

McDowell, Frederick P. W., "The Varied Universe of Frederic Raphael's Fiction," *Crit* 8, i (Fall, 1965): 39-43.

_____, "World Within World: Gerda Charles, Frederick [sic] Raphael, and the Anglo-Jewish Community," *Crit* 6, iii (Winter, 1963-64).

LINDMANN

McDowell, Frederick P. W., 'The Varied Universe of Frederic Raphael's Fiction," *Crit* 8, i (Fall, 1965): 43-5.

Young, James D., "False Identity and Feeling in Raphael's LINDMANN," *Crit* 13, i (1971): 59-65.

OBBLIGATO

McDowell, Frederick P. W., "The Varied Universe of Frederic Raphael's Fiction," *Crit* 8, i (Fall, 1965): 23-4.

THE TROUBLE WITH ENGLAND

McDowell, Frederick P. W., "The Varied Universe of Frederic Raphael's Fiction," *Crit* 8, i (Fall, 1965): 37-9.

A WILD SURMISE

McDowell, Frederick P. W., "The Varied Universe of Frederic Raphael's Fiction," *Crit* 8, i (Fall, 1965): 32-7.

RAVEN, SIMON (ARTHUR NOEL), 1927-

GENERAL

Barber, Michael, "An Officer but Not a Gentleman," *B&B* 17, viii (May, 1972): 9-13.

McSweeney, J. Kerry, "The Novels of Simon Raven," *QQ* 78, i (Spring, 1971): 106-16.

ALMS FOR OBLIVION

Hepburn, Neil, "Resignation Honours," *Listener* 95 (1976): 745-6.

RECHY, JOHN, 1934-

GENERAL

Bruce, Navoa, "In Search of the Honest Outlaw: John Rechy" *MV* 3, i (1979): 37-45.

Giles, James R., "Larry McMurtry's LEAVING CHEYENNE and the Novels of John Rechy: Four Trips Along 'the Mythical Pecos'," *ForumH* 10, ii (Summer-Fall, 1972): 34-50.

_____, and Wanda Giles, "An Interview with John Rechy," *ChiR* 25, i (1973): 19-31.

Lynch, Honora M., "Patterns of Anarchy and Order in the Works of John Rechy," *DAI* 37 (1976): 1583A.

Satterfield, Ben, "John Rechy's Tormented World," *SWR* 67, i (Winter, 1982): 78-85.

Tatum Charles M., "The Sexual Underworld of John Rechy," *MV* 3, i (1979): 47-52.

CITY OF NIGHT

Giles, James R., "Religious Alienation and 'Homosexual Consciousness' in CITY OF NIGHT and GO TELL IT ON THE MOUNTAIN," *CE* 36 (Nov., 1974): 369-80.

Gilman, R., *Confusion of Realms,* 53-61.

Heifetz, Henry, "The Anti-Social Act of Writing," *StL* 4 (Spring, 1964): 6-9.

Hoffman, Stanton, "The Cities of Night: John Rechy's CITY OF NIGHT and the American Literature of Homosexuality," *ChiR* 17, ii-iii (1964): 195-206.

Southern, Terry, "Rechy and Gover," in Moore, H. T., ed., *Contemporary American Novels,* 222-27.

Zamora, Carlos, "Odysseus in John Rechy's CITY OF NIGHT: The Epistemological Journey," *MV* 3, i (1979): 53-62.

REED, ISHMAEL (SCOTT), 1938-

GENERAL

Domini, John, "Ishmael Reed: A Conversation with John Domini," *APR* 7, i (Jan.-Feb., 1978): 32-6.

Fontenot, Chester J., "Ishmael Reed and the Politics of Aesthetics, or Shake Hands and Come Out Conjuring," *BALF* 12, i (1978): 20-3.

Ford, Nick A., "A Note on Ishmael Reed: Revolutionary Novelist," *SNNTS* 3, ii (Summer, 1971): 216-18.

Gover, Robert, "An Interview with Ishmael Reed," *BALF* 12, i (1978): 12-19.

Harris, Norman, "Politics as an Innovative Aspect of Literary Folklore: A Study of Ishmael Reed," *Obsidian* 5, i-ii (1979): 41-50.

Mackey, Nathaniel, "Ishmael Reed and the Black Aesthetic," *CLAJ* 21, iii (Mar., 1978): 355-66.

MacMillan, Terry, and Sandro Ouroussoff, "Ishmael Reed," *BT* 5, ix (1975): 9-10. [Interview.]

McConnell, Frank, "Ishmael Reed's Fiction: Da Hoodoo is Put on America," in Lee, A. R., ed., *Black Fiction,* 136-48.

McKenzie, James, ed., "Pole-Vaulting in Top Hats: A Public Conversation with John Barth, William Glass, and Ishmael Reed," *MFS* 22 (Summer, 1976): 131-51.

Nazareth, Peter, "An Interview with Ishmael Reed," *IowaR* 13, ii (1982): 117-31.

O'Brien, John, "Interview with Ishmael Reed," *Fictional International* 1 (Summer, 1973): 61-70. Also in O'Brien, J., ed., *Interviews with Black Writers,* 165-83. Also in Bellamy, J. D., ed., *New Fiction,* 130-41.

Reed, Ishmael, "The Writer as Seer: Ishmael Reed on Ishmael Reed," *BlackW* 23, viii (1974): 20-34.

Schmitz, Neil, "Neo-Hoo-Doo: The Experimental Fiction of Ishmael Reed," *TCL* 20 (Apr., 1974): 126-40.

Simon, Myron, 'Two Angry Ethnic Writers," *MELUS* 3, ii (1976): 20-4.

FLIGHT TO CANADA

Uphaus, Suzanne H., "Ishmael Reed's FLIGHT TO CANADA," *CRevAS* 8, i (Spring, 1977): 95-9.

Weixlmann, Joe, "Politics, Piracy, and Other Games: Slavery and Liberation in FLIGHT TO CANADA," *MELUS* 6, iii (1979): 41-50.

THE FREE-LANCE PALLBEARERS

Duff, Gerald, "Reed's THE FREE-LANCE PALLBEARERS," *Expl* 32, ix (May, 1974): Item 69.

Fabre, Michel, "Ishmael Reed's FREE-LANCE PALLBEARERS on the Dialectics of Shit," *Obsidian* 3, iii (1977): 5-19.

Musgrave, Marian E., "Sexual Excess and Deviation as Structural Devices in Günter Grass's BLECHTROMMEL and Ishmael Reed's FREE-LANCE PALLBEARERS," *CLAJ* 22 (1979): 229-39.

Nichols, Charles H., "Comic Modes in Black America (A Ramble through Afro-American Humor,)" in Cohen, S. B., ed., *Comic Relief,* 120-2.

Schmitz, Neil, "Neo-Hoo Doo: The Experimental Fiction of Ishmael Reed," *TCL* 20 (Apr, 1974): 127-31.

LAST DAYS OF LOUISIANA RED

Carter, Steven R., "Ishmael Reed's Neo-Hoodoo Detection," in Landrum, L. N., P. Browne, and R. B. Browne, eds., *Dimensions of Detective Fiction,* 270-4. Also in Marsden, M., comp., *Proceedings of the Sixth National Convention of the Popular Culture Association,* 199-205.

Nichols, Charles H., "Comic Modes in Black America (A Ramble through Afro-American Humor)," in Cohen, S. B., ed., *Comic Relief,* 124-5.

Scholes, Robert, "Ishmael's Black Art," *Fabulation and Metafiction,* 193-6.

Thomas, Lorenzo, "Two Crowns of Thoth: A Study of Ishmael Reed's THE LAST DAYS OF LOUISIANA RED," *Obsidian* 2, iii (1976): 5-25.

MUMBO JUMBO

Carter, Steven R., "Ishmael Reed's Neo-Hoodoo Detection," in Landrum, L. N., P. Browne, and R. B. Browne, eds., *Dimensions of Detective Fiction,* 265-70. Also in Marsden, M., comp., *Proceedings of the Sixth National Convention of the Popular Culture Association,* 186-99.

Martin, Richard, "Clio Bemused: The Uses of History in Contemporary American Fiction," *Sub-stance* 27 (1980): 13-24.

Nichols, Charles H., "Comic Modes in Black America (A Ramble through Afro-American Humor)," in Cohen, S. B., ed., *Comic Relief,* 122-4.

Rhodes, Jewell P., "MUMBO JUMBO and a Somewhat Private Literary Response," *AHumor* 6, II (1979): 11-13.

Schmitz, Neil, "Neo Hoodoo: the Experimental Fiction of Ishmael Reed," *TCL* 30, ii (Apr., 1974): 135-9.

YELLOW BACK RADIO BROKE-DOWN

Ambler, Marge, "Ishmael Reed: Whose Radio Broke Down?" *NALF* 6 (Winter, 1972): 125-31.

Bush, Roland D., "Werewolf of the Wild West: On a Novel by Ishmael Reed," *BlackW* 23, iii (1974): 51-2, 64-6.

Fabre, Michel, "Postmodernist Rhetoric in Ishmael Reed's YELLOW BACK RADIO BROKE-DOWN," in Bruck, P., and W. Karrer, eds., *Afro-American Novel Since 1960,* 167-87.

Jones, Robert W., "Language and Structure in Ishmael Reed's YELLOW BACK RADIO BROKE-DOWN," *NConL* 8, ii (1978): 2-3.

Schmitz, Neil, "Neo-Hoodoo: The Experimental Fiction of Ishmael Reed," *TCL* 20, ii (Apr., 1974): 131-5.

BIBLIOGRAPHY

Settle, Elizabeth A., and Thomas A. Settle, eds., *Ishmael Reed: A Primary and Secondary Bibliography*, Boston: Hall, 1982.
_____, *Ishmael Reed: An Annotated Checklist*, Carson: California State Coll., Dominguez Hills, 1977.
Weixlmann, Joe, Robert Fikes, Jr., and Ishmael Reed, "Mapping Out the Gumbo Works: An Ishmael Reed Bibliography," *BALF* 12, i (1978): 24-9.

RENAULT, MARY, Pseud. (Eileen Mary Challans), 1905-1983

GENERAL

Burns, Landon C., Jr., "Men Are Only Men; The Novels of Mary Renault," *Crit* 6, iii (Winter, 1963-64): 102-21.
Dick, B. F., *Hellenism of Mary Renault*.
Green, Peter, "The Masks of Mary Renault," *NYRB* (Feb. 8, 1979): 11-14.
Heilbrun, Carolyn G., "Axiothea's Grief: The Disability of the Female Imagination," in Weiner, Dora B., and William R. Keylor, eds., *From Parnassus: Essays in Honor of Jacques Barzun*, N.Y.: London: Harper & Row, 1976, 231-4.
Herbert, Kevin, "The Theseus Theme: Some Recent Versions," *CJ* 55, iv (Jan., 1960): 175-85.
Wolfe, P., *Mary Renault*.

THE BULL FROM THE SEA

Burns, Landon C., Jr., "Men Are Only Men: The Novels of Mary Renault," *Crit* 6, iii (Winter, 1963-64): 109-20.
Dick, B. F., *Hellenism of Mary Renault*, 70-85.
Wolfe, P., *Mary Renault*, 168-88.

THE CHARIOTEER

Dick, B. F., *Hellenism of Mary Renault*, 30-7.
Wolfe, P., *Mary Renault*, 103-21.

FIRE FROM HEAVEN

Dick B. F., *Hellenism of Mary Renault*, 100-18.

KIND ARE HER ANSWERS

Dick, B. F. *Hellenism of Mary Renault*, 9-12.
Wolfe, P., *Mary Renault*, 45-54.

THE KING MUST DIE

Burns, Landon C., Jr., "Men Are Only Men: The Novels of Mary Renault," *Crit* 6, iii (Winter, 1963-64): 109-20.
Dick, B. F., *Hellenism of Mary Renault*, 54-70.
Wolfe, P., *Mary Renault*, 153-70.

THE LAST OF THE WINE

Burns, Landon C., Jr., "Men Are Only Men: The Novels of Mary Renault," *Crit* 6, iii (Winter 1963-64): 102-9.
Dick, B. F., *Hellenism of Mary Renault*, 37-53.
Wolfe, P., *Mary Renault*, 122-40.

THE MASK OF APOLLO

Dick, B. F., *Hellenism of Mary Renault*, 86-99.
Wolfe, P., *Mary Renault*, 140-6.

THE MIDDLE MIST (THE FRIENDLY YOUNG LADIES)

Dick, B. F., *Hellenism of Mary Renault*, 13-22.
Wolfe, P., *Mary Renault*, 54-64.

NORTH FACE

Dick, B. F., *Hellenism of Mary Renault*, 26-9.
Wolfe, P., *Mary Renault*, 85-102.

THE PERSIAN BOY

Dick, Bernard F., "The Herodotean Novelist," *SR* 81, iv (Autumn, 1973): 864-9.
Hartt, Julian N., "Two Historical Novels," *VQR* 49, iii (Summer, 1973); 452-4.

PROMISE OF LOVE (PURPOSES OF LOVE)

Dick, B. F. *Hellenism of Mary Renault*, 37-53.
Wolfe, P., *Mary Renault*, 122-40.

RETURN TO NIGHT

Dick, B. F., *Hellenism of Mary Renault*, 22-5.
Wolfe, P., *Mary Renault*, 68-85.

RHYS, JEAN, 1894-1979

GENERAL

Abel, Elizabeth, "Women and Schizophrenia: The Fiction of Jean Rhys," *ConL* 20, ii (Spring, 1979): 155-77.
Allfrey, Phyllis S., "Jean Rhys: A Tribute," *Kunapipi* 1, ii (1979): 23-5. [Not seen.]
Ashcom, Jane M., "The Novels of Jean Rhys: Two Kinds of Modernism," *DAI* 42, xii (June, 1982): 5125A.
Babakhanian, Grace S., "Expatriation and Exile as Themes in the Fiction of Jean Rhys," *DAI* 37 (1976): 291A-92A.
Baldanza, Frank, "Jean Rhys on Insult and Injury," *SLitI* 11, ii (Fall, 1978): 55-65.
Bamber, Louise, "Jean Rhys," *PR* 49, i (1982): 92-100.
Bender, Todd K., "Jean Rhys and the Genius of Impressionism," *SLitI* 11, ii (Fall, 1978): 43-53.
Blodgett, Harriet, "Tigers are Better Looking to Jean Rhys," *ArQ* 32 (Autumn, 1976): 227-44.
Braybrooke, Neville, "The Return of Jean Rhys," *Caribbean Quarterly* 16, iv (Dec., 1970): 43-6.
Campbell, Elaine, "Apropos of Jean Rhys," *Kunapipi* 2, ii (1980): 152-7.
_____, "From Dominica to Devonshire: A Memento of Jean Rhys," *Kunapipi* 1, ii (1979): 6-22. [Not seen.]
_____, "Reflections of Obeah in Jean Rhys' Fiction," *Kunapipi* 4 (1982): 45-52.
Cole, Laurence, "Jean Rhys," *B&B* 17, iv (Jan., 1972): 20-1.
Dash, Cheryl M. L., in King, B., ed., *West Indian Literature*, 196-209.

Dekerchove, Arnold, "John Updike, Jean Rhys, Andre Gide,"
   RGB 3 (1970): 91-7. [Not seen.]
Emery, Mary L., "Modernism and the Marginal Woman: A
   Sociocritical Approach to the Novels of Jean Rhys," *DAI* 42,
   xi (May, 1982): 4823A.
James, L., *Jean Rhys*.
James, L., "Sun Fire—Painted Fire: Jean Rhys as a Caribbean
   Writer," *ArielE* 8, iii (July, 1977): 111-27.
Lane, Miriam L., "Jean Rhys: The Work and the Cultural Back-
   ground," *DAI* 39 (1978): 1551A.
Mellown, Elgin W., "Character and Themes in the Novels of
   Jean Rhys," *ConL* 13, iv (Autumn, 1972): 458-75. Also in
   Spacks, P. M., ed., *Contemporary Women Novelists*, 118-36.
Moss, Howard, "Going to Pieces," *NY* 50 (Dec. 16, 1974): 161-6.
Mossin, Henrick, "The Existential Dimension in the Novels of
   Jean Rhys," *Kunapipi* 2, ii (1980): 143-50. [Not seen.]
Nebeker, H., *Jean Rhys*.
Staley, T. F., *Jean Rhys*.
Thomas, Ned, "Meeting Jean Rhys," *Planet* 33 (Aug., 1976):
   29-31.
Thompson, Irene, "The Left Bank Apértifs of Jean Rhys and
   Ernest Hemingway," *GaR* 35, i (Spring, 1981): 94-106. [Not
   seen.]
Thurman, Judith, "The Mistress and the Mask: Jean Rhys Fic-
   tion," *MsM* 4 (Jan., 1976): 50-2, 81.
Tiffin, Helen, "Mirror and Mask: Colonial Motifs in the Novels
   of Jean Rhys," *WLWE* 17 (Apr., 1978): 328-41.
Vreeland, Elizabeth, "Jean Rhys: The Art of Fiction LXXIV,"
   ParisR 76 (1979): 218-37.
Wahlstrom, Ruth M., "The Fiction of Jean Rhys," *DAI* 38 (1977):
   2782A.
Williams, Angela, "The Flamboyant Tree: The World of the Jean
   Rhys Heroine," *Planet* 33 (August, 1976): 35-41.
Wolfe, P., *Jean Rhys*.
Wyndham, Francis, "Introduction to Jean Rhys," *LonM* 7, i (Jan.,
   1960): 15-18.

AFTER LEAVING MR. MACKENZIE

Blodgett, Harriet, "Tigers Are Better Looking to Jean Rhys,"
   ArQ 32 (Autumn, 1976): 234-6.
James, L., *Jean Rhys*, 26-7.
Nebeker, H., *Jean Rhys*, 14-38.
Packer, P. A., "Four Early Novels of Jean Rhys," *DUJ* 71 (June,
   1979): 252-65.
Staley, T. F., *Jean Rhys*, 67-83.
Wolfe, P., *Jean Rhys*, 84-102.

GOOD MORNING, MIDNIGHT

Blodgett, Harriet, "Tigers Are Better Looking to Jean Rhys,"
   ArQ 32 (Autumn, 1976): 239-41.
James, L., *Jean Rhys*, 27-9.
Nebeker, H., *Jean Rhys*, 85-121.
Packer, P. A., "Four Early Novels of Jean Rhys," *DUJ* 71 (June,
   1979): 252-65.
Staley, T. F., *Jean Rhys*, 84-99.
Wolfe, P., *Jean Rhys*, 121-36.

QUARTET (POSTURES)

Blodgett, Harriet, "Tigers Are Better Looking to Jean Rhys,"
   ArQ 32 (Autumn, 1976): 232-3.
Gardiner, Judith K., "Rhys Recalls Ford: QUARTET and THE
   GOOD SOLDIER," *TSWL* 1, i (Spring, 1982): 67-81.
James, L., *Jean Rhys*, 24-6.
Nebeker, H., *Jean Rhys*, 1-13.
_____, Jean Rhys's QUARTET: The Genesis of Myth," *IJWS*
   2, iii (1979): 257-67.
Packer, P. A., "Four Early Novels of Jean Rhys," *DUJ* 71 (June,
   1979): 252-65.
Staley, Thomas F., "The Emergence of a Form: Style and Con-
   sciousness in Jean Rhys's QUARTET," *TCL* 24, ii (Summer,
   1978): 202-24.
_____, *Jean Rhys*, 35-5.
Wolfe, P., *Jean Rhys*, 67-83.

VOYAGE IN THE DARK

Abel, Elizabeth, "Women and Schizophrenia: The Novels of
   Jean Rhys," *ConL* 20, ii (Spring, 1979): 158-61.
Blodgett, Harriet, "Tigers Are Better Looking to Jean Rhys,"
   ArQ 32 (Autumn, 1976): 236-9.
Casey, Nancy J., "Study in Alienation of a Creole Woman: Jean
   Rhys's VOYAGE IN THE DARK," *Caribbean Quarterly* 19
   (Sept., 1973): 95-103.
Emery, Mary L., "The Politics of Form: Jean Rhys's Social Vision
   in VOYAGE IN THE DARK and WIDE SARGASSO SEA,"
   TCL 28, iv (Winter, 1982): 418-30.
James, L., *Jean Rhys*, 34-41.
_____, "Sun Fire—Painted Fire: Jean Rhys as a Caribbean
   Novelist," *ArielE* 8, iii (July, 1977): 116-26.
Nebeker, H., *Jean Rhys*, 39-84.
Packer, P. A., "Four Early Novels of Jean Rhys," *DUJ* 71 (June,
   1979): 252-65.
Staley, T. F., *Jean Rhys*, 103-20.
Wolfe, P., *Jean Rhys*, 67-83.

WIDE SARGASSO SEA

Abel, Elizabeth, "Women and Schizophrenia: The Fiction of
   Jean Rhys," *ConL* 20, ii (Spring, 1979): 172-5.
Bender, Todd K., "Jean Rhys and the Genius of Impressionism,"
   SLitI 11, ii (Fall, 1978): 43-9.
Blodgett, Harriet, "Tigers Are Better Looking to Jean Rhys,"
   ArQ 32 (Autumn, 1976): 241-44.
Brown, Cheryl L., "Jean Rhys' Recent Fiction: Humane Devel-
   opment in WIDE SARGASSO SEA," in Brown, C. L., and K.
   Olson, eds., *Feminist Criticism*, 291-9.
Casey, Nancy J., "Jean Rhys's WIDE SARGASSO SEA: Extermi-
   nating the White Cockroach," *RevI* 4, iii (Fall, 1974): 340-9.
Dash, C. M. L., in King, B., ed., *West Indian Literature*, 201-9.
Emery, Mary L., "The Politics of Form: Jean Rhys's Social Vision
   in VOYAGE IN THE DARK and WIDE SARGASSO SEA,"
   TCL 28, iv (Winter, 1982): 418-30.
Harris, Wilson, "Carnival of Psyche: Jean Rhys's WIDE SAR-
   GASSO SEA," *Kunapipi* 2, ii (1980): 142-50.
Hearne, John "The WIDE SARGASSO SEA: A West Indian
   Reflection," *Cornhill Mag* 1080 (Summer, 1974): 323-3.

James, L., *Jean Rhys,* 45-70.

Lai, Wally L., "The Road to Thornfield Hall: An Analysis of Jean Rhys' WIDE SARGASSO SEA," *New Beacon Reviews* 1 (1968): 38-52.

Luengo, Anthony E., "WIDE SARGASSO SEA and the Gothic Mode," *WLWE* 15 (Apr., 1976): 229-45.

Mellown, Elgin W., "Character and Themes in the Novels of Jean Rhys," *ConL* 13, iv (Autumn, 1972): 470-3. Also in Spacks, P. M., ed., *Contemporary Women Novelists,* 131-4.

Nebeker, H., *Jean Rhys,* 122-70.

Nielsen, Hanne, and Fleming Brahms, "Retrieval of a Monster: Jean Rhys' WIDE SARGASSO SEA," in Petersen, K. H., and A. Rutherford, eds., *Enigma of Values,* 139-62.

Porter, Dennis, "Of Heroines and Victims: Jean Rhys and JANE EYRE," *MR* 17, iii (1976): 540-52.

Ramchard, Kenneth, "Terrified Consciousness," *JCL* 7 (July, 1969): 14-19.

_____, *West Indian Novel and Its Background,* 230-6.

Scharfman, Ronnie, "Mirroring and Mothering in Simone Schwarzbart's PLUIE ET VENT SUR TELUMEE MIRACLE and Jean Rhys' WIDE SARGASSO SEA," *YFS* 62 (1981): 88-106.

Staley, T. F., *Jean Rhys,* 100-20.

Thiene, John, "'Apparitions of Disaster': Brontean Parallels in WIDE SARGASSO SEA and GUERILLAS," *JCL* 14, i (1979): 116-32.

Thomas, Clara, "Mr. Rochester's First Marriage: WIDE SAR-GASSO SEA by Jean Rhys," *WLWE* 17 (Apr., 1978): 342-57.

Thorpe, Michael, "'The Other Side': WIDE SARGASSO SEA and JANE EYRE," *ArielE* 8, iii (July, 1977): 99-110.

Wolfe, P., *Jean Rhys,* 137-58.

BIBLIOGRAPHY

Jacobs, Fred R., *Jean Rhys: Bibliography,* Keene, Calif.: Loop, 1978.

Mellown, Elgin W., "A Bibliography of the Writings of Jean Rhys with a Selected List of Reviews and Other Critical Writings," *WLWE* 16 (1977): 179-202.

Reynolds, R. C., and B. J. Murray, "A Bibliography of Jean Rhys," *BB* 36, iv (Oct.-Dec., 1979): 177-84.

Roberts, Ray A., "Jean Rhys: A Bibliographical Checklist," *ABC* ns 3, vi (1982): 35-8.

RICHLER, MORDECAI, 1931-

GENERAL

Birbalsingh, Frank M., "Mordecai Richler and the Jewish-Canadian Novel," *JCL* 7, i (June, 1972): 72-82.

Cameron, Donald, "Don Mordecai and the Hard Hats," *CanF* 51 (Mar., 1972): 29-33.

Cohen, Nathan, "A Conversation with Mordecai Richler," *TamR* No. 1 (Winter, 1957): 6-23. Also in Sheps, G. D., ed., *Mordecai Richler,* 22-42.

_____, "Heroes of the Richler View," *TamR* No. 6 (Winter, 1958): 47-60. Also in Sheps, G. D., ed., *Mordecai Richler,* 43-51.

Dahlie, H., "The International Theme in Canadian Fiction," in Rutherford, A., ed., *Common Wealth,* 186-9.

Evanier, David, "The Jewish Mordecai Richler," *Midstream* 20, x (Dec., 1974): 24-36.

Fiedler, Leslie, "Some Notes on the Jewish Novel in English, or Looking Backward from Exile," *The Running Man,* 1, ii (July-Aug., 1968): 18-21. Also in Sheps, G. D., ed., *Mordecai Richler* 99-105.

Golden, Daniel, "Mystical Musings and Comic Confrontations: The Fiction of Saul Bellow and Mordecai Richler," *ECW* 22 (Summer, 1981): 62-85.

Kattan, Naim, "Mordecai Richler: Craftsman or Artist," *CanL* 21 (Summer, 1964): 46-51. Also in Sheps, G. D., ed., *Mordecai Richler,* 92-8.

Levene, Mark, in Heath, J. M., ed., *Profiles in Canadian Literature,* 2, 41-8.

McPherson, Hugo, "A Survey of Richler's Fiction," in Sheps, G. D., ed., *Mordecai Richler,* 120-4. Reprinted from "Fiction: 1940-1960," in Klinck, Carl F., et al., eds., *Literary History of Canada: Canadian Literature in English,* Toronto: Un. of Toronto Pr., 1965, 713-15.

McSweeney, Kerry, "Revaluing Mordecai Richler," *SCL* 4, ii (1979): 120-31.

Metcalf, John, "Black Humour: An Interview [with] Mordecai Richler," *JCF* 3, i (Winter, 1974): 73-6.

Mitcham, Allison, "The Isolation of Protesting Individuals Who Belong to Minority Groups," *WascanaR* 7, i (1972): 43-50.

Myers, David, "Mordecai Richler as Satirist," *ArielE* 4, i (Jan., 1973): 73-6.

Pacey, D., *Creative Writing in Canada,* 264-5.

Ramraj, Victor J., "The Ambivalent Vision: Richler and the Satirical Tradition in the Canadian Novel," *DAI* 37 (1976): 2175A-76A.

_____, "Diminishing Satire: A Study of V. S. Naipaul and Mordecai Richler," in Narasimhaiah, C. D., ed., *Awakened Conscience,* 261-74.

Richler, Mordecai, "The Apprenticeship of Mordecai Richler," *Maclean's* (May 20, 1961): 21, 44-8.

Ryan, Diane E., "Time and Geography in the Novels of Mordecai Richler," *DAI* 39 (1978): 2262A.

Scott, Peter, "A Choice of Certainties," *TamR* No. 8 (Summer, 1958): 73-82. Also in Sheps, G. D., ed., *Mordecai Richler,* 58-68.

Sheps, G. D., ed., *Mordecai Richler.*

Tallman, Warren, "Four Takes on Mordecai Richler's Fiction," *Open Letter* (Third Series, 6) (1976): 48-69.

_____, "Wolf in the Snow," *CanL* 5 (Summer, 1960): 7-20.

THE ACROBATS

Bowering, George, "And the Sun Goes Down: Richler's First Novel," *CanL* No. 29 (Summer, 1966): 7-17. Also in Sheps, G. D., ed., *Mordecai Richler,* 1-14.

Woodcock, G., *Mordecai Richler,* 13-19.

THE APPRENTICESHIP OF DUDDY KRAVITZ

Bevan, Allan, "Introduction" to THE APPRENTICESHIP OF DUDDY KRAVITZ, Toronto: McClelland and Stewart, 1969. Also in Sheps, G. D., ed., *Mordecai Richler,* 69-77.

Boutelle, Ann, "The Dorian Gray Phenomenon," *DalR* 57 (Summer, 1977): 265-76.

Ferns, John, "Sympathy and Judgement in Mordecai Richler's THE APPRENTICESHIP OF DUDDY KRAVITZ," *JCF* 3, i (Winter, 1974): 77-82.

Golden, Daniel, "Mystical Musings and Comic Confrontations: The Fiction of Saul Bellow and Mordecai Richler," *ECW* 22 (Summer, 1981): 73-7.

Marshall, Tom, "Third Solitude: Canadian as Jew," in Moss, J., ed., *Canadian Novel: Here and Now,* 147-55.

McGregor, Grant, "Duddy Kravitz: From Apprentice to Legend," *JCF* 30 (1980): 132-40.

McSweeney, Kerry, "Revaluing Mordecai Richler," *SCL* 4, ii (1976): 129-31.

New, William H., "The Apprenticeship of Discovery," *CanL* No. 29 (Summer, 1966): 18-33. Also in New, W. H., *Articulating West,* 108-17, 124-7. Also in Sheps, G. D., ed., *Mordecai Richler,* 69-77.

Ower, John, "Sociology, Psychology, and Satire in THE APPRENTICESHIP OF DUDDY KRAVITZ," *MFS* 22, iii (Autumn, 1976): 413-28.

Sherman, B., *Invention of the Jew,* 178-82.

Tallman, Warren, in Canadian Literature. *Choice of Critics,* 72-6.

_____, "Richler and the Faithless City," *CanL* No. 3 (Winter, 1960): 62-4.

_____, "Wolf in the Snow. Part Two: The House Repossessed," *CanL* No. 6 (Autumn, 1960): 44-8. Also in Sheps, G. D., ed., *Mordecai Richler,* 78-83.

Wainwright, J. A., "Neither Jekyll nor Hyde: In Defence of Duddy Kravitz," *CanL* 89 (Summer, 1981): 56-73.

Watt, F. W., in *UTQ* 29 (July, 1960): 463-5.

Woodcock, G., *Mordecai Richler,* 35-43.

A CHOICE OF ENEMIES

Cloutier, Pierre, "Mordecai Richler's Exiles: A CHOICE OF ENEMIES," *JCF* 1, ii (Spring, 1972): 43-9.

Cohen, Nathan, "Heroes of the Richler View," *TamR* No. 6 (Winter, 1958): 47-60. Also in Sheps, G. D., ed., *Mordecai Richler,* 43-53.

McSweeney, Kerry, "Revaluing Mordecai Richler," *SCL* 4, ii (1979): 122-4.

Scott, Peter, "A Choice of Certainties," *TamR* No. 8 (Summer, 1958): 73-83. Also in Sheps, G. D., ed., *Mordecai Richler,* 58-68.

Stovel, Bruce, "Introduction" to A CHOICE OF ENEMIES (New Canadian Library), Toronto: McClelland and Stewart, 1977, vii-xv.

Woodcock, G., *Mordecai Richler,* 28-34.

COCKSURE

Igoe, W. J., "Pop Strip," *The Times* (Apr. 20, 1968): 23. Also in Sheps, G. D., ed., *Mordecai Richler,* 110-11.

McSweeney, Kerry, "Revaluing Mordecai Richler," *SCL* 4, ii (1976): 122-6.

Myers, David, "Mordecai Richler as Satirist," *ArielE* 4, i (Jan., 1973): 53-6.

New, William H., "Cock and Bull Stories," *CanL* 39 (Winter, 1969): 83-6. Also in New, W. H., *Articulating West,* 164-8.

Northey, Margot, "Satiric Gothic: COCKSURE," *Haunted Wilderness,* 95-100.

Toynbee, Philip, in *LonM* (May, 1968): 77-9. Also in Sheps, G. D., ed., *Mordecai Richler,* 106-9.

Warkentin, Germaine, "COCKSURE An Abandoned Introduction," *JCF* 4, iii (1975): 81-6.

Woodcock, G., *Mordecai Richler,* 47-54.

THE INCOMPARABLE ATUK (STICK YOUR NECK OUT)

Davidson, Arnold E., "THE INCOMPARABLE ATUK: Mordecai Richler's Satire on Popular Culture and the Canadian Dream," *StCS* 7, i (1980): 8-16.

Golden, Daniel, "Mystical Musings and Comic Confrontations: Saul Bellow and Mordecai Richler," *ECW* 22 (Summer, 1981): 77-80.

Kostelanetz, Richard, "The New American Fiction," in Kostelanetz, R., ed., *New American Arts,* 218-19.

Woodcock, G., *Mordecai Richler,* 44-6.

JOSHUA THEN AND NOW

McSweeney, Kerry, "Richler's Fireworks," *ECW* 20 (Winter, 1980-81): 160-4.

SON OF A SMALLER HERO

Greenstein, Michael, "The Apprenticeship of Noah Adler," *CanL* 78 (Autumn, 1978): 43-51.

Moss, J., *Patterns of Isolation,* 227-30, 235-7.

Myers, David, "Mordecai Richler as Satirist," *ArielE* 4, i (Jan., 1973): 48-51.

Woodcock, George, "Introduction" to SON OF A SMALLER HERO, Toronto: McClelland and Stewart, 1966. Also in Sheps, G. D., ed., *Mordecai Richler,* 15-21.

_____, *Mordecai Richler,* 20-7.

ST. URBAIN'S HORSEMAN

Cohn-Sfetcu, Ofelia, "Of Self, Temporal Cubism, and Metaphor: Mordecai Richler's ST. URBAIN'S HORSEMAN," *IFR* 3, i (Jan., 1976): 30-4.

_____, "To Live in Abundance of Life; Time in Canadian Literature," *CanL* 76 (Spring, 1978): 33-6.

Cude, Wilfred, "The Golem as Metaphor for Art: The Monster Takes Meaning in ST. URBAIN'S HORSEMAN," *JCanStud* 12, ii (Spring, 1977): 50-69.

Golden, Daniel, "Mystical Musings and Confrontations: Saul Bellow and Mordecai Richler," *ECW* 22 (Summer, 1981): 80-4.

McSweeney, Kerry, "Revaluing Mordecai Richler," *SCL* 4, ii (1976): 126-9.

Moss, J., *Sex and Violence in the Canadian Novel,* 131-9. Also, adapted, in Moss, J., ed., *Canadian Novel: Here and Now,* 156-65.

Myers, David, "Mordecai Richler as Satirist," *ArielE* 4, i (Jan., 1973): 53-60.

Nadel, Ira, "The Absent Prophet in Canadian Jewish Fiction," *EngQ* 5, i-ii (Spring-Summer, 1972): 83-92. [Not seen.]

Pollock, Zailig, "The Trial of Jake Hersh," *JCF* 22 (1978): 93-105.

Sheps, G. David, "Writing for Joey: The Theme of the Vicarious in ST. URBAIN'S HORSEMAN," *JCF* 3, i (Winter, 1974): 83-92. (See 3, ii for correction of pp. 87-8 following p. 92)

Tallman, Warren, "Need for Laughter," *CanL* 56 (Spring, 1973): 71-83. Also in Woodcock, G., *Canadian Novel in the Twentieth Century,* 258-70. Also in *Open Letter* 3rd ser., 6 (Winter, 1976-77): 57-69.

Wainwright, J. A., "Neither Jekyll nor Hyde: In Defence of Duddy Kravitz," *CanL* 89 (Summer, 1981): 56-73.

Woodcock, George, "The Wheel of Exile," *TamR* 58 (1971): 65-72. Also in Woodcock, G., *The Rejection of Politics,* Toronto: New Press, 1972.

STICK OUT YOUR NECK (See THE INCOMPARABLE ATUK)

BIBLIOGRAPHY

Darling, Michael, "Mordecai Richler: An Annotated Bibliography," 155-211, in Lecker, Robert, and Jack David, eds., *The Annotated Bibliography of Canada's Major Authors, Volume One,* Downsview: ECW, 1979.

RICHTER, CONRAD, 1890-1968

GENERAL

Barnes, R. J., *Conrad Richter.*

Carpenter, Frederick I., "Conrad Richter's Pioneers, Reality and Myth," *CE* 12 (Nov., 1950): 77-82.

Edwards, C. D., *Conrad Richter's OHIO TRILOGY.*

Flanagan, John T., "Conrad Richter, Romance of the Southwest," *SWR* 43 (Summer, 1958): 189-96.

_____, "Folklore in the Novels of Conrad Richter," *MF* 2 (Spring, 1952): 5-14.

Friesen, Paul, "The Use of Oral Tradition in the Novels of Conrad Richter," *DAI* 39 (1979): 5511A.

Gaston, E. W., Jr., *Conrad Richter.*

Kohler, Dayton, "Conrad Richter: Early Americana," *CE* 8 (Feb., 1947): 221-7.

LaHood, Marvin, "Conrad Richter and Willa Cather: Some Similarities," *XUS* 9, i (Spring, 1970): 33-46.

_____, *Conrad Richter's America.*

_____, "Richter's Early America," *UR* 30 (June, 1964): 311-16.

_____, "A Study of the Major Themes in the Work of Conrad Richter and His Place in the Tradition of the American Frontier Novel," *DA* 23 (1962): 1365-6.

Meldrum, Barbara, "Conrad Richter's Southwestern Ladies," in Lee, L. L., and M. Lewis, eds., *Women, Women Writers, and the West,* 119-27.

Ruff, G. Elson, "An Honest Novel of the Parsonage," *The Lutheran* 44 (May 30, 1962): 14-20. [Not seen.]

Sutherland, Bruce, "Conrad Richter's Americana," *NMQR* 15 (Winter, 1945): 413-22.

Wagenknecht, E., *Cavalcade of the American Novel,* 436-7.

Wilson, Dawn M., "Conrad Richter: The Novelist as Philosopher," *DAI* 32 (1971):1536A.

Young, David L., "The Art of Conrad Richter," *DA* 25 (1965): 4712.

ALWAYS YOUNG AND FAIR

Gaston, E. W., Jr., *Conrad Richter,* 121-4.

LaHood, M. J., *Conrad Richter's America,* 84-9.

THE AWAKENING LAND Trilogy (See OHIO Trilogy)

THE ARISTOCRAT

LaHood, M. J., *Conrad Richter's America,* 92-3.

A COUNTRY OF STRANGERS

LaHood, M. J., *Conrad Richter's America,* 105-6.

THE FIELDS (See also OHIO Trilogy)

Gaston, E. W, Jr., *Conrad Richter,* 103-7.

LaHood, M. J., *Conrad Richter's America,* 67-71.

THE FREE MAN

Gaston, E. W., Jr., *Conrad Richter,* 71-80.

LaHood, M. J., *Conrad Richter's America,* 81-4.

Sutherland, Bruce, "Conrad Richter's Americana," *NMQR* 15 (Winter, 1945): 421-2.

THE GRANDFATHERS

Gaston, E. W., Jr., *Conrad Richter,* 131-7.

LaHood, M. J., *Conrad Richter's America,* 90-2.

THE LADY

Barnes, R. J., *Conrad Richter,* 30-6.

Gaston, E. W., Jr., *Conrad Richter,* 89-94.

LaHood, M. J., *Conrad Richter's America,* 51-8.

Meldrum, Barbara, "Conrad Richter's Southwestern Ladies," in Lee, L. L., and M. Lewis, eds., *Women, Women Writers, and the West,* 126-7.

THE LIGHT IN THE FOREST

Folsom, J. K., *American Western Novel,* 159-62.

Gaston, E. W., Jr., *Conrad Richter,* 125-31.

LaHood, M. J., *Conrad Richter's America,* 94-105.

_____, "THE LIGHT IN THE FOREST: History as Fiction," *EJ* 55 (Mar., 1966): 298-304.

Schmaier, Maurice D., "Conrad Richter's THE LIGHT IN THE FOREST: An Ethnohistorical Approach to Fiction," *Ethnohistory* 7 (Fall, 1960): 327-98.

OHIO Trilogy

Barnard, Kenneth J., "Presentation of the West in Conrad Richter's Trilogy," *NOQ* 29 (Autumn, 1957): 224-34.

Carpenter, Frederick I., "Conrad Richter's Pioneers: Reality and Myth," *CE* 12 (Nov., 1950): 79-83.

Edwards, C. D., *Conrad Richter's OHIO Trilogy,* 100-25, 151-66.

Flanagan, John T., "Folklore in the Novels of Conrad Richter," *MF* 2 (Spring, 1952): 5-14.

Prescott, O., *In My Opinion,* 137-40.

Wilson, Dawn, "The Influence of the West on Conrad Richter's Fiction," *ON* 1, iv (Dec., 1975): 384-8.

THE SEA OF GRASS

Barnes, R. J., *Conrad Richter,* 16-25.

Edwards, C. D., *Conrad Richter's OHIO Trilogy,* 81-100.

Folsom, J. K., *American Western Novel,* 94-7.

Gaston, E. W., Jr., *Conrad Richter,* 74-84.

Harris, Jim R., "New Mexico History: A Transient Period in Conrad Richter's SEA OF GRASS," *SwAL* 5 (1975): 62-7.

Kohler, Dayton, "Conrad Richter: Early Americana," *CE* 8 (Feb., 1947): 223-4.

LaHood, M. J., *Conrad Richter's America*, 37-44.

Meldrum, Barbara, "Conrad Richter's Southwestern Ladies," in Lee, L. L., and M. Lewis, eds., *Women, Women Writers, and the West*, 121-3.

Sutherland, Bruce, "Conrad Richter's Americana," *NMQR* 15 (Winter, 1945): 418-19.

A SIMPLE HONORABLE MAN

Gaston, E. W., Jr., *Conrad Richter*, 145-51.

LaHood, M. J., *Conrad Richter's America*, 113-15.

_____, "Richter's Pennsylvania Trilogy," *SUS* 8 (June, 1968): 10-13.

Ruff, G. Elson, "An Honest Novel of the Parsonage," *The Lutheran* 44 (May 30, 1962): 14-20. [Not seen.]

TACEY CROMWELL

Barnes, R. J., *Conrad Richter*, 15-30.

Gaston, E. W., Jr., *Conrad Richter*, 84-9.

LaHood, M. J., *Conrad Richter's America*, 44-51.

Meldrum, Barbara, "Conrad Richter's Southwestern Ladies," in Lee, L. L., and M. Lewis, eds., *Women, Women Writers, and the West*, 123-6.

Sutherland, Bruce, "Conrad Richter's Americana," *NMQR* 15 (Winter, 1945): 420-1.

THE TOWN (See also OHIO Trilogy)

Gaston, E. W., Jr., *Conrad Richter*, 107-16.

LaHood, M. J., *Conrad Richter's America*, 71-80.

Pearce, T. H., "Conrad Richter," *NMQR* 20 (Autumn, 1950): 371-3.

Stuckey, W. J., *Pulitzer Prize Novels*, 154-7.

THE TREES (See also OHIO Trilogy)

Gaston, E. W., Jr., *Conrad Richter*, 96-103.

Kohler, Dayton, "Conrad Richter: Early Americana," *CE* 8 (Feb., 1947): 224-5.

LaHood, M. J., *Conrad Richter's America*, 59-68.

Sutherland, Bruce, "Conrad Richter's Americana," *NMQR* 15 (Winter, 1945): 419-20.

THE WATERS OF KRONOS

Gaston, E. W., Jr., *Conrad Richter*, 139-45.

LaHood, M. J., *Conrad Richter's America*, 107-13.

_____, "Richter's Pennsylvania Trilogy," *SUS* 8 (June, 1968): 5-10.

ROBBINS, HAROLD, 1916-

A STONE FOR DANNY FISHER

Lane, James B., "Violence and Sex in the Post-War Popular Novel: With a Consideration of Harold Robbins's A STONE FOR DANNY FISHER and Hubert Selby, Jr.,'s LAST EXIT TO BROOKLYN," *JPC* 8, iii (Fall, 1974): 294-302.

ROBBINS, TOM, 1936-

GENERAL

Miller, Patricia E. C., "Reconciling Science and Mysticism: Characterization in the Novels of Tom Robbins," *DAI* 40 (1979): 2666A

Mitchell, Greg, "...And COWGIRLS Jumped Over the Moon," *Crawdaddy* (Aug., 1977): 29-33.

Nadeau, Robert L., "Physics and Cosmology in the Fiction of Tom Robbins," *Crit* 20, i (1978): 63-74.

Siegel, Mark, "The Meaning of Meaning in the Novels of Tom Robbins," *Mosaic* 14, iii (Summer, 1981): 119-31.

_____, *Tom Robbins*.

ANOTHER ROADSIDE ATTRACTION

Nadeau, Robert L., "Physics and Cosmology in the Fiction of Tom Robbins," *Crit* 20, i (1978): 65-70.

Siegel, Mark, "The Meaning of Meaning in the Novels of Tom Robbins," *Mosaic* 14, iii (Summer, 1981): 119-31.

_____, *Tom Robbins*, 10-21.

EVEN COWGIRLS GET THE BLUES

Gross, Beverly, "Misfits: Tom Robbins' EVEN COWGIRLS GET THE BLUES," *NDQ* 50, iii (1982): 36-51.

Nadeau, Robert L., "Physics and Cosmology in the Fiction of Tom Robbins," *Crit* 20, i (1978): 70-3.

Ricou, Laurence, "Field Notes and Notes in the Field: Forms of the West in Robert Kroetsch and Tom Robbins," *JCanStud* 17, iii (Fall, 1982): 117-23.

Siegel, Mark, "The Meaning of Meaning in the Novels of Tom Robbins," *Mosaic* 14, iii (Summer, 1981): 119-31.

_____, *Tom Robbins*, 21-31.

STILL LIFE WITH WOODPECKER

Siegel, Mark, "The Meaning of Meaning in the Novels of Tom Robbins," *Mosaic* 14, iii (Summer, 1981): 119-31.

_____, *Tom Robbins*, 42-8.

ROIPHE, ANNE RICHARDSON, 1935-

LONG DIVISION

Avery, Evelyn G., "Tradition and Independence in Jewish Feminist Novels," *MELUS* 7, iv (Winter, 1980): 50-2, 53.

UP THE SANDBOX!

Diamond, Arlyn, "Flying from Work," *Frontiers* 2, iii (1977): 19-21.

ROSEN, GERALD, 1938-

THE CARMEN MIRANDA MEMORIAL FLAGPOLE

Friedman, Edward H., "Gerald Rosen's THE CARMEN MIRANDA MEMORIAL FLAGPOLE: Variations on a Unamunian Theme," *NConL* 10, iv (1980): 5-6.

ROSS, SINCLAIR, 1908-

GENERAL

Bowen, Gail, "The Fiction of Sinclair Ross," *CanL* 80 (Spring, 1979): 37-48.

Djwa, Sandra, "False Gods and the True Covenant: Thematic Continuity Between Margaret Laurence and Sinclair Ross," *JCF* 1, iv (Fall, 1972): 43-50. Also in New, W. W., ed., *Margaret Laurence*, 66-84.

King, Carlyle, "Sinclair Ross: A Neglected Saskatchewan Novelist," *Skylark* 3, i (Nov., 1966): 4-7.

Kotasch, M., "Discovering Sinclair Ross: It's Rather Late," *Saturday Night*, 87 (July, 1972): 33-7.

McCourt, E. A., *Canadian West in Fiction*, 100-5.

McMullen, L., *Sinclair Ross.*

AS FOR ME AND MY HOUSE

Chambers, R. D., *Sinclair Ross and Ernest Buckler*, 25-39.

Cude, W., "Beyond Mrs. Bentley: A Study of AS FOR ME AND MY HOUSE," *JCanStud* 8, i (May, 1973): 3-18.

_____, "'Turn It Upside Down': The Right Perspective on AS FOR ME AND MY HOUSE," *ESC* 5 (Winter, 1979): 89-95.

Daniells, Roy, "Introduction" to AS FOR ME AND MY HOUSE, Toronto: McClelland & Stewart, 1957, v-x.

Denham, Paul, "Narrative Technique in Sinclair Ross's AS FOR ME AND MY HOUSE," *SCL* 5 (Spring, 1980): 116-24.

Djwa, Sandra, "No Other Way: Sinclair Ross's Stories and Novels," *CanL* 47 (Winter, 1971): 49-66. Also in Woodcock, G., ed., *Canadian Novel in the Twentieth Century*, 127-43. Also in Stephens, D. G., ed., *Writers of the Prairies*, 189-206.

Dooley, D. J., "AS FOR ME AND MY HOUSE: The Hypocrite and the Parasite," *Moral Vision in the Canadian Novel*, Toronto: Clarke, Irwin, 38-47.

Dubanski, Ryszard, "A Look at Philip's 'Journal' in AS FOR ME AND MY HOUSE," *JCF* 24 (1979): 89-95.

Godard, Barbara, "El Greco in Canada: Sinclair Ross's AS FOR ME AND MY HOUSE," *Mosaic* 14, ii (Spring, 1981): 55-75.

Harrison, D., *Unnamed Country*, 149-53.

Hicks, Anne, "Mrs. Bentley: The Good Housewife," *ROO* 5, iv (1980): 60-7.

Jackel, Susan, "The House on the Prairies," *CanL* 42 (Autumn, 1969): 46-55. Also in Stephens, D. G., ed., *Writers of the Prairies*, 165-74.

Jones, D. G., *Butterfly on Rock*, 38-42.

King, Carlyle, "Sinclair Ross: A Neglected Saskatchewan Novelist," *Skylark* 3, i (Nov., 1966): 4-7.

Kroetsch, Robert, "The Fear of Women in Prairie Fiction: An Erotics in Space," in Harrison, D., ed., *Crossing Frontiers*, 73-83. [Comparison with Willa Cather's MY ANTONIA.] Reprinted from *Canadian Forum* (Oct.-Nov., 1978): 22-7. Response by Sandra Djwa in Harrison, D., ed., *Crossing Frontiers*, 84-8.

MacDonald, Bruce F., "AS FOR ME AND MY HOUSE and the Aesthetics of Illegitimacy in the Canadian Novel," *LCrit* 13, i (1978): 34-52.

McMullen, L., *Sinclair Ross*, 56-87.

Moss, John, "Mrs. Bentley and the Bicameral Mind: A Hermeneutical Encounter with AS FOR ME AND MY HOUSE," in Moss, J., ed., *Canadian Novel.* v. 3 *Modern Times*, 81-92.

_____, *Patterns of Isolation*, 149-65.

New, William H., "Sinclair Ross's Ambivalent World," *CanL* 40 (Spring, 1969): 26-32. Also in New, W. H., *Articulating West*, 60-7. Also in Stephens, D. G., ed., *Writers of the Prairies*, 183-8.

Ricou, L., "The Prairie Internalized: The Fiction of Sinclair Ross," *Vertical Man/Horizontal World*, 82-90.

Ross, Morton, "The Canonization of AS FOR ME AND MY HOUSE: A Case Study," in Bessai, D., and D. Jackel, eds., *Figures in a Ground*, 189-205.

Stephens, Donald, "Wind, Sun and Dust," *CanL* 23 (Winter, 1965): 17-24. Also in Stephens, D. G., ed., *Writers of the Prairies*, 175-82.

Stouck, David, "The Mirror and the Lamp in Sinclair Ross's AS FOR ME AND MY HOUSE," *Mosaic* 7, ii (Winter, 1974): 141-50.

Tallman, Warren, "Wolf in the Snow," *CanL* 5 (Summer, 1960): 14-17.

Wee, Morris O., "Specks on the Horizon: Individuals and the Land in Canadian Prairie Fiction," *SDC* 19, iv (Winter, 1981): 18-31.

SAWBONES MEMORIAL

Bowen, Gail, "The Fiction of Sinclair Ross," *CanL* 80 (Spring, 1979): 37, 47-8.

McMullen, Lorraine, "Introduction" to SAWBONES MEMORIAL (New Canadian Library), Toronto: McClelland & Stewart, 5-11.

_____, *Sinclair Ross*, 118-33.

Munton, Ann, in *DalR* 55 (Autumn, 1975): 573-5.

Shohet, Linda, in *CFM* 19 (Winter, 1975): 95-7.

Weis, Lyle, "Landscape Criticism Not Valid: Sinclair Ross's New Novel," *The Sphinx* 2 (Winter, 1976): 45-7.

Stouck, David, "Canadian Classics," *WCR* 10 (June, 1975): 47-8.

THE WELL

Chambers, R. D., *Sinclair Ross and Ernest Buckler*, 40-6.

McMullen, L., *Sinclair Ross*, 88-100.

Ricou, L., "The Prairie Internalized: The Fiction of Sinclair Lewis," *Vertical Man/Horizontal Man*, 90-1.

WHIR OF GOLD

Chambers, R. D., *Sinclair Ross and Ernest Buckler*, 47-52.

McMullen, L., *Sinclair Ross*, 101-17.

BIBLIOGRAPHY

Letham, David, "Sinclair Ross: An Annotated Bibliography," 365-95, in Lecker, Robert, and Jack David, eds., *The Annotated Bibliography of Canada's Major Authors, Volume Three*, Downsview: ECW, 1981.

ROSSNER, JUDITH, 1935-

LOOKING FOR MR. GOODBAR

Fishbein, Leslie, "LOOKING FOR MR. GOODBAR: Murder for the Masses," *IJWS* 3 (1980): 173-82.

ROTH, HENRY, 1906-1995

GENERAL

Bronsen, David, "A Conversation with Henry Roth," *PR* 36, ii (1969): 265-80.

Freedman, William, "A Conversation with Henry Roth," *LitR* 18 (1975): 149-57.

———, "Henry Roth in Jerusalem: An Interview," *LitR* 23 (1979): 5-23.

Lyons, B., *Henry Roth*.

———, "Henry Roth: A Critical Study," *DAI* 34 (1974): 4271A.

———, "An Interview with Henry Roth," *Shen* 25, i (Fall, 1973): 48-71.

———, "Interview with Henry Roth, March, 1977," *SAJL* 5, i (1979): 50-8.

CALL IT SLEEP

Allen, Walter, "Afterward," in Roth, H., *Call It Sleep*, N.Y.: Avon, 442-7.

———, *Modern Novel* 172-5.

———, "Two Neglected American Novelists," *LonM* 2 (May, 1962): 77-84.

———, *Urgent West*, 101-2.

Epstein, Gary, "Auto-Obituary: The Death of the Artist in Henry Roth's CALL IT SLEEP," *SAJL* 5, i (1979): 37-45.

Fein, Richard J., "The Novelist and His Character: Henry Roth and David Shearl," *SAJL* 5, i (1979): 46-50.

Ferguson, James, "Symbolic Patterns in CALL IT SLEEP," *TCL* 14, iv (Jan., 1969): 211-20.

Fiedler, Leslie, "The Breakthrough: The American Jewish Novel and the Fictional Image of the Jew," *Midstream* 4 (Winter, 1958): 23-4. Also in Waldmeir, J. J., ed., *Recent American Fiction*, 94-5.

———, "Henry Roth's Neglected Masterpiece," *Ctary* 30 (Aug., 1960): 102-7. Also in Fiedler, L., *Collected Essays of Leslie Fiedler*, v. 2, 271-9.

———, *Waiting for the End*, 48-9.

Field, Leslie, "Henry Roth's Use of Torah and Haftorah in CALL IT SLEEP," *SAJL* 5, i (1979): 22-7.

Freedman, William, "Henry Roth and the Redemptive Imagination," in French, W., ed., *Thirties*, 107-14.

———, "Mystical Initiation and Experience in CALL IT SLEEP," *SAJL* 5, i (1979): 27-37.

Geismar, Maxwell, "A Critical Introduction," in *Call It Sleep*, N.Y.: Cooper Square, 1962, xxxvi-xlv.

Guttmann, A., *Jewish Writer in America*, 49-55.

Inge, M. Thomas, "The Ethnic Experience and Aesthetics in Literature: Malamud's THE ASSISTANT and Roth's CALL IT SLEEP," *JEthS* 1, iv (1974): 45-50.

Kleederman, Frances F., "The Interior Monologue in CALL IT SLEEP," *SAJL* 5, i (1979): 2-11.

———, "A Study of Language in Henry Roth's CALL IT SLEEP: Bilingual Markers of a Culture in Transition," *DAI* 35 (1975): 4434A.

Knowles, A. Sidney, Jr., "The Fiction of Henry Roth," *MFS* 11 (Winter, 1965-66): 393-404.

Ledbetter, Kenneth, "Henry Roth's CALL IT SLEEP: The Revival of the Proletarian Novel," *TCL* 12 (Oct., 1966): 123-30.

Lesser, Wayne, "A Narrative's Revolutionary Energy: The Example of Henry Roth's CALL IT SLEEP," *Criticism* 23, ii (Spring, 1981): 155-76.

Levenberg, Diane, "Three Jewish Writers and the Spirit of the Thirties: Michael Gold, Anzia Yezierska, and Henry Roth," *BForum* 6, ii (1982): 241-44.

Levin, Meyer, "A Personal Appreciation," in *Call It Sleep*, N.Y.: Cooper Square, 1962, xlvi-li.

Lyons, B., *Henry Roth*.

———, "An Interview with Henry Roth," *Shen* 25, i (Fall, 1973): 48-71.

———, "Roth's CALL IT SLEEP," *Expl* 33 (Oct., 1974): Item 10.

———, "The Symbolic Structure of Henry Roth's CALL IT SLEEP," *ConL* 13 (Spring, 1972): 186-203.

Mooney, Theresa R., "The Explicable 'It' of Henry Roth's CALL IT SLEEP" *SAJL* 5, i (1979): 11-18.

Nelson, Kenneth M., "A Religious Metaphor," *Reconstructionist* (N.Y.) 31, xv (1965): 7-16.

Nilsen, Helge N., "The Protagonist in Henry Roth's CALL IT SLEEP," *TWP* 1 (Fall, 1982): 1-21.

Place, Ethan, "Henry Roth's Freudian Messiah," *ModSt* 2, iii (1977): 37-43.

Redding, Mary E., "Call It Myth: Henry Roth and THE GOLDEN BOUGH," *CentR* 18, ii (Spring, 1974): 180-95.

Ribalow, Harold U., "Henry Roth and His Novel CALL IT SLEEP," *WSCL* 3, iii (Fall, 1962): 5-14.

———, "The History of Henry Roth and CALL IT SLEEP," in *Call It Sleep*, N.Y.: Cooper Square, 1962, xi-xxxv.

Rideout, W. B., *Radical Novel in the U.S.*, 186-90.

Samet, Tom, "Henry Roth's Bull Story: Guilt and Betrayal in CALL IT SLEEP," *SNNTS* 7 (1975): 569-83.

Seed, David, "The Drama of Maturation: Henry Roth's CALL IT SLEEP," *EA* 32, i (1979): 46-55.

Sheres, Ita, "Exile and Redemption in Henry Roth's CALL IT SLEEP," *MarkhamR* 6 (1977): 72-7.

Sherman, B., "CALL IT SLEEP as a Depression Novel," *Invention of the Jew*, 82-92.

Syrkin, Marie, "Revival of a Classic," *Midstream* 7 (Winter, 1961): 89-93.

Walden, Daniel, "Henry Roth's CALL IT SLEEP: Ethnicity, 'The Sign', and the Power," *MFS* 25, ii (Summer, 1979): 268-72.

———, "'Sleep' at the Switch: The NET Effect in CALL IT SLEEP," *SAJL* 5, i (1979): 18-21.

Wirth-Nesher, Hana, "The Modern Jewish Novel and the City: Franz Kafka, Henry Roth, and Amos Oz," *MFS* 24, i (Spring, 1978): 94-9.

BIBLIOGRAPHY

Young, Debra B., "Henry Roth: A Bibliographic Survey," *SAJL* 5, i (1979): 62-71.

ROTH, PHILIP, 1933-

GENERAL

Bell, Pearl K., "Philip Roth: Sonny Boy or Lenny Bruce?" *Ctary* 64, v (Nov., 1977): 60-3.

Bender, Eileen T., "Philip Roth: The Clown in the Garden," *StCS* 3 (1976): 17-30.

Cheuse, Alan, "A World Without Realists," *StL* 4, ii (Spring, 1964): 70-6.

Cohen, Sarah B., "Philip Roth's Would-Be-Patriarchs and Their *Shikses* and Shrews," *SAJL* 1 (Spring, 1975): 16-23. Also in Pinsker, S., ed., *Critical Essays on Philip Roth*, 209-16.

Cooperman, Stanley, "Philip Roth: 'Old Jacob's Eye' with a Squint," *TCL* 19, iii (July, 1973): 203-16.

Deer, Irving, and Harriet Deer, "Philip Roth and the Crisis in American Fiction," *MinnR* 6, iv (Winter, 1966): 353-60.

Dervin, Daniel A., "Breast Fantasy in Barthelme, Swift, and Philip Roth: Creativity and Psychoanalytic Structure," *AI* 33 (1976): 102-22.

Eiland, Howard, "Philip Roth: The Ambiguities of Desire," in Pinsker, S., ed., *Critical Essays on Philip Roth*, 255-65.

Field, Leslie, "Philip Roth: Days of Whine and Moses," *SAJL* 5, ii (1979): 11-14. [Not seen.]

Friedman, Alan W., "The Jew's Complaint in Recent American Fiction: Beyond Exodus and Still in the Wilderness," *SoR* 8 (Fall, 1972): 41-59 *passim*. Also in Pinsker, S., ed., *Critical Essays*, 149-63 *passim*.

George, Alexander, "Philip Roth's Confessional Narrators: The Growth of Consciousness," *DAI* 40 (1979): 2061.

Green, Martin, "Philip Roth's Confessional Narrators: The Growth of Consciousness," *DAI* 40 (1979): 2061.

Green, Martin, "Philip Roth," *Ploughshares*, 4, iii (1978): 156-68. Also, revised, as "Introduction" to *A Philip Roth Reader*, N.Y.: Farrar, Straus & Giroux, 1980.

Grossman, Joel, "'Happy as Kings': Philip Roth's Men and Women," *Judaism* 26, i (1977): 7-17.

Guttmann, Allen, "Philip Roth and the Rabbis," in Pinsker, S., ed., *Critical Essays on Philip Roth*, 172-81. Reprinted from Guttmann, A., *Jewish Writer in America*, 64-76.

Hochman, Baruch, "Child and Man in Philip Roth," *Midstream* 13 (Dec., 1967): 68-76.

Hogan, Jerry B., "The Problems of Identity in the Fiction of Philip Roth," *DAI* 40 (1979): 1468A.

Howe, Irving, "Philip Roth Reconsidered," *Ctary* 54, vi (Dec., 1972): 69-77. Also in Howe, I., *Critical Point*, 137-57. Also in Pinsker, S., ed., *Critical Essays on Philip Roth*, 229-44.

Jones, J. P., and G. A., Nance, *Philip Roth*.

Kliman, Bernice, W., "Women in Roth's Fiction," *NR* 3, iv (1978): 75-88.

Knopp, Josephine Z., "The Wages of *Mentschlekhkayt*: A Study of Morality in Some Fiction of Philip Roth and Bernard Malamud," *Tradition* 13, iii (Winter, 1973): 67-84.

Kramer, Maurice, "The Secular Mode of Jewishness," *Works* 1 (Autumn, 1967): 108, 110.

Landis, Joseph C., "The Sadness of Philip Roth: An Interim Report," *MR* 3 (1962): 259-68. Also in Pinsker, S., ed., *Critical Essays on Philip Roth*, 164-71.

Levine, Mordecai H., "Philip Roth and American Judaism," *CLAJ* 14, ii (Dec., 1970): 163-70.

Levitt, Morton P., "Roth and Kafka: Two Jews," in Pinsker, S., ed., *Critical Essays on Philip Roth*, 245-54.

Lyons, Bonnie, "Bellowmalamudroth and the American Jewish Genre—Alive and Well," *SAJL* 5, ii (1979): 8-10 [Not seen.]

Malin, I., *Jews and Americans*.

Mauro, Walter, "Philip Roth, Writing, and the Powers-That-Be: An Interview," *APR* 3, iv (July/Aug., 1974): 18-20.

McDaniel, J. N., *Fiction of Philip Roth*.

_____, "Heroes in the Fiction of Philip Roth," *DAI* 33 (1973): 2941A-42A.

Meeter, M., *Philip Roth and Bernard Malamud*.

Merkin, Daphne, "Roth's Promise," *NewL* 62, xix (Oct. 8, 1979): 18-19.

Michel, Pierre, "Philip Roth's Hesitations," 151-9 in Sienicka, Marta A., *Proceedings of a Symposium on American Literature*, Poznan: Uniw. Im. Adama Mickiewicza, 1979. [Not seen.]

_____, "Philip Roth's Reductive Lens: From 'On the Air' to MY LIFE AS A MAN," *RLV* 42 (1976): 509-19.

_____, "What Price Misanthropy? Philip Roth's Fiction," *ES* 58 (1977): 232-9.

Mudrick, Marvin, "Who Killed Herzog? or, Three American Novelists," *UDQ* 1, i (Spring, 1966): 61-97. Also as "Malamud, Bellow, and Roth," in Mudrick, M., *On Culture and Literature*, 200-33.

Novak, Bill, "Philip Roth and the Jews," *Response* 5, ii (Fall, 1971): 71-86.

Novak, William, "Out of Whose Time?" *Response* 6, i (Spring, 1972): 150-2. [Rejoinder to Sylvia Rothchild below.]

Oates, Joyce Carol, "A Conversation with Philip Roth," *OntarioR* 1, i (1974): 9-22.

Opland, J., "In Defense of Philip Roth," *Theoria* 42 (1974): 29-42.

Pinsker, S., *Comedy That "Hoits."*

_____, ed., *Critical Essays on Philip Roth*.

_____, "Guilt as Comic Idea: Franz Kafka and the Postures of American-Jewish Writing," *JML* 6, iii (Sept., 1977): 469-71.

_____, "Reading Philip Roth Reading Philip Roth," *SAJL* 3, ii (1977-78): 14-18.

Podhoretz, Norman. "Laureate of the New Class," *Ctary* 54, vi (Dec., 1972): 4, 7.

Rodgers, B. F., Jr., *Philip Roth*.

Roth, Philip, "Reading Myself," *PR* 40, iii (1973):; 404-17.

_____, "Writing About Jews," *Ctary* 36 (Dec., 1963): 446-52.

_____, "Writing American Fiction," *Ctary* 31 (Mar., 1961): 223-33.

Rothchild, Sylvia, "Philip Roth—Out of His Time," *Response* 6, i (Spring, 1972): 147-52.

Shechner, Mark, "Philip Roth," *PR* 46, iii (1974): 410-27. Also in Pinsker, S., ed., *Critical Essays on Philip Roth*, 117-32.

Searles, George J., "The Fiction of Philip Roth and John Updike," *DAI* 39 (1979): 6135A-36A.

Solotaroff, Theodore, "The Journey of Philip Roth," *Atlantic* 224 (Apr., 1969): 65-72.

Spacks, Patricia M., "Only Personal: Some Functions of Fiction," *YR* 65, iv (Summer, 1976): 528-43.

Walden, Daniel, "Bellow, Malamud, and Roth: Part of the Continuum," *SAJL* 5, ii (1979): 5-7. [Not seen.]

Walden, Daniel, "Goodbye Columbus, Hello Portnoy and Beyond: The Ordeal of Philip Roth," *SAJL* 3, ii (1977-78): 3-13.

Weinberg, Helen A., "Reading Himself and Others," *SAJL* 3, ii (1977-78): 19-27.

Weingarten, Renee, "Writing About Jews," *JewishQ* 22. iv (1975): 37-42.

Whitfield, Stephen J., "Laughter in the Dark: Notes on American-Jewish Humor," *Midstream* (Feb., 1978): 48-58 *passim*. Also in Pinsker, S., ed., *Critical Essays on Philip Roth*, 194-208 *passim*.

Whitton, Steven J., "The Mad Crusader: The Quest as Motif in the Jewish Fiction of Philip Roth and Bernard Malamud," *DAI* 34(1973): 1943A.

Wisse, Ruth P., "Philip Roth Then and Now," *Ctary* 72, iii (Sept., 1981): 56-60.

————, "Reading About Jews," *Ctary* 69, iii (Mar., 1980): 41-4.

THE BREAST

Bender, Eileen, "Philip Roth: The Clown in the Garden," *SCS* 3(1976): 26-9.

Bier, Jesse, "A Hero at the Breast," *CarlM* 17 (Spring, 1979): 214-21.

Davidson, Arnold E., "Kafka, Rilke and Philip Roth's THE BREAST," *NConL* 5, i (Jan., 1975): 9-11.

Jones, J. P., and G. A. Nance, *Philip Roth,* 92-8.

Kaminsky, Alice R., "Philip Roth's Professor Kapesh and the 'Reality Principle'," *DQ* 13, ii (Summer, 1978): 41-54.

McDaniel, J. N., *Fiction of Philip Roth,* 168-77.

Michel, Pierre, "Philip Roth's THE BREAST: Reality Adulterated and the Plight of the Writer," *DQR* 5 (1975): 245-52.

Pinsker, S., *Comedy That "Hoits,"* 78-84.

Rice, Julian C., "Philip Roth's THE BREAST: Cutting the Freudian Cord," *StCS* 3 (1976): 9-16.

Rodgers, B. F., Jr., *Philip Roth,* 132-40.

Sabiston, Elizabeth [J.], "A New Fable for the Critics; Philip Roth's THE BREAST," *IFR* 2 (1975): 27-34.

THE GHOST WRITER

Budd, John, "Philip Roth's Lesson from the Master," *NMAL* 6 (1982). [Unpaginated.]

Dickstein, Morris, "The World in a Mirror: Problems of Distance in Recent American Fiction," *SR* 89, iii (Summer, 1981): 386-400.

Ireland, G. W., "The Voice of Philip Roth," *QQ* 87 (1980): 286-92.

Jones, J. P., and G. A. Nance, *Philip Roth,* 122-7.

Lee, Judith, "Flights of Fancy," *ChiR* 31, iv (1980): 46-52.

Maloff, Saul, "Philip Roth and the Master's Voice: The Uses of Adversity," *Cweal* (Nov. 9, 1979): 628-31.

Tintner, Adeline R., "Henry James as Roth's Ghost Writer," *Midstream* (Mar., 1981): 48-51.

Voelker, Joseph C., "Dedalian Shades: Philip Roth's THE GHOST WRITER," in Pinsker, S., ed., *Critical Essays on Philip Roth,* 89-94.

GOODBYE, COLUMBUS

Bankston, Dorothy H., "Roth's GOODBYE, COLUMBUS," *Expl* 36, ii (Winter, 1978): 21-2.

Bender, Eileen T., "Philip Roth: The Clown in the Garden," *SCS* (1976): 18-19.

Clerc, Charles, "Goodbye to All That: Theme, Character and Symbol in GOODBYE, COLUMBUS," in Clerc, Charles, and Louis Leiter, eds., *Seven Contemporary Short Novels,* Glenview, Ill.: Scott, Foresman, 1969, 106-33.

Graham, Don, "The Common Ground of GOODBYE, COLUMBUS and THE GREAT GATSBY," *ForumH* 13, iii (1976): 68-71.

Guttmann, A., *Jewish Writer in America,* 67-70.

Howe, Irving, "Philip Roth Reconsidered," *Ctary* 52, vi (Dec., 1972): 70-1. Also in Howe, I., *Critical Path,* 139-42.

————, "The Suburbs of Babylon," *NRep* 140 (June 15, 1959): 17-19.

Isaac, Dan, "In Defense of Philip Roth," *ChiR* 17 (Summer-Autumn, 1964-65): 84-90. Also in Pinsker, S., ed., *Critical Essays on Philip Roth,* 182-93.

Israel, Charles M., "The Fractured Hero of Roth's GOODBYE, COLUMBUS," *Crit* 16, ii (1974): 5-11.

Jones, J. P., and G. A. Nance, *Philip Roth,* 12-2.

Kazin, A., *Contemporaries,* 258-62.

Koch, Eric, "Roth's GOODBYE, COLUMBUS," *TamR* 13 (1959): 129-32.

Larner, Jeremy, "The Conversion of the Jews," *PR* 27 (Fall, 1960): 760-8.

Leer, Norman, "Escape and Confrontation in the Short Stories of Philip Roth," *ChS* 49 (Summer, 1966): 135-40.

Mann, Meryl, "Goodbye, Columbus, Hello Radcliffe," *PR* 28 (Jan.-Feb., 1961): 154-7.

Meeter, G., *Philip Roth and Bernard Malamud,* 30-3.

Nelson, G. B., *Ten Versions of America,* 149-62.

Novak, Bill, "Philip Roth and the Jews," *Response* 5, ii (Fall, 1971): 72-4.

Pinsker, S., *Between Two Worlds,* 35-41.

————, *Comedy That "Hoits",* 4-12.

Raban, J., "Character and Dialogue," *Techniques of Modern Fiction,* 88-9.

Rodgers, B. F., Jr., *Philip Roth,* 34-46.

Sherman, B., "GOODBYE, COLUMBUS: Controversy," *Invention of the Jew,* 167-75.

Siegel, Ben, "Jewish Fiction and the Affluent Society," *NWR* 4 (Spring, 1961): 89-96.

Trachtenberg, Stanley, "The Hero in Stasis," *Crit* 7, ii (Winter, 1964-65): 5-17.

THE GREAT AMERICAN NOVEL

Blair, Walter, and Hamlin Hill, "THE GREAT AMERICAN NOVEL," in Pinsker, S., ed., *Critical Essays on Philip Roth,* 217-28. Reprinted from Blair, W., and H. Hill, *America's Humor: From POOR RICHARD to DOONESBURY,* N.Y.: Oxford Un. Pr., 1978.

Blues, Thomas, "Is There Life After Baseball? Philip Roth's THE GREAT AMERICAN NOVEL," *AmerS* 22, i (1981): 71-80.

Harrison, Walter L., "Six-Pointed Diamond: Baseball and American Jews," *JPC* 15 (Winter, 1981): 116-17.

Jones, J. P., and G. A. Nance, *Philip Roth,* 142-53.

McDaniel, J. N., *Fiction of Philip Roth,* 161-8.

McGinnis, Wayne D., "The Anarchic Impulse in Two Recent Novels," *PAPA* 5, ii-iii (1979): 36-40.

Monaghan, David, "THE GREAT AMERICAN NOVEL and MY LIFE AS A MAN: An Assessment of Philip Roth's Achievement," *IFR* 2 (1975): 113-20.

Pinsker, S., *The Comedy That "Hoits,"* 85-101.

Rodgers, Bernard, Jr., "THE GREAT AMERICAN NOVEL and The Great American Joke," *Crit* 16, ii (1974): 12-28.

————, *Philip Roth,* 109-22.

Siegel, Ben, "The Myths of Summer: Philip Roth's THE GREAT AMERICAN NOVEL," *ConL* 17 (Spring, 1976): 171-90.

Soyka, Gabriel S., "From Roth to Gaedel to Reiser: Factual Analogues for Fictional Characters," *NConL* 7 (May, 1977): 3-4.

Willson, Robert F., Jr., "An Indisputable Source for the Spirited Account of a Baseball Contest between Port Ruppert Mundys and the Asylum Lunatics in THE GREAT AMERICAN NOVEL, by Mr. Philip Roth," *NConL* 5, iii (May, 1975): 12-14.

LETTING GO

Allen, M., *Necessary Blankness*, 75-87.

Atlas, James, "A Postwar Classic," *NRep* (June 2, 1982): 28-32. Also as "Introduction" to Noonday edition of *Letting Go*, 1982.

Bender, Eileen, "Philip Roth: The Clown in the Garden," *SCS* 3 (1976): 19-22.

Bothwell, E. K., *Alienation in the Jewish American Novel of the Sixties*, 12-62, 105-9. [Comparative review of PORTNOY'S COMPLAINT and LETTING GO.]

Cheuse, Alan, "A World Without Realists," *StL* 4, ii (Spring, 1964): 70-5.

Cooperman, Stanley, "Philip Roth: 'Old Jacob's Eye with a Squint'," *TCL* 19, iii (July, 1973): 210-16.

Detweiler, R., "Philip Roth and the Test of a Dialogic Life," *Four Spiritual Crisis in Mid-American Fiction*, 25-35.

Donaldson, Scott, "Philip Roth: The Meanings of LETTING GO," *ConL* 11, i (Winter, 1970): 21-35.

Hentoff, Nat, "The Appearance of LETTING GO," *Midstream* 8 (Dec., 1962): 103-6.

Hyman, Stanley E., "A Novelist of Great Promise," *New Leader* (June 11, 1962). Also in Kostelanetz, R., ed., *On Contemporary Literature*, 533-6. Also in Hyman, S. E., *Standards*, 73-7.

Jones, J. P., and G. A. Nance, *Philip Roth*, 37-52.

McDaniel, J. N. *Fiction of Philip Roth*, 76-89, 116-20.

Meeter, G., *Philip Roth and Bernard Malamud*, 39-40.

Noble, Donald R., "Dickinson to Roth, "*AN&Q* 9 (1971): 150-1. [Traces the title to a poem by Dickinson.]

Pinsker, S., *Comedy That "Hoits,"* 28-42.

Podhoretz, Norman, "The Gloom of Philip Roth," *Show* 2 (July, 1962): 92-3. Also in Podhoretz, N., *Doings and Undoings*, 236-43.

Raban, Jonathan, "The New Philip Roth," *Novel* 2, ii (Winter, 1969): 154-6.

Rodgers, B. F., Jr., *Philip Roth*, 47-59.

Solotaroff, Theodore, "Philip Roth: A Personal View," *Red Hot Vacuum*, 313-18.

Walcutt, C. C., *Man's Changing Mask*, 350-2.

White, Robert L., "The English Instructor as Hero ... Two Novels by Roth and Malamud," *ForumH* 4 (Nov., 1963): 16-22.

MY LIFE AS A MAN

Bertins, J. W., "'The Measured Self vs. The Insatiable Self': Notes on Philip Roth," in Bakker, J., and D. R. M. Wilkinson, eds., *From Cooper to Philip Roth*, 95-100.

Jones, J. P., and G. A. Nance, *Philip Roth*, 97-111.

McDaniel, J. N., *Fiction of Philip Roth*, 177-98.

Michel, Pierre, "Philip Roth's Reductive Lens: From 'On the Air' to MY LIFE AS A MAN," *RLV* 42 (1976): 511-19.

Monaghan, David, "THE GREAT AMERICAN NOVEL and MY LIFE AS A MAN: An Assessment of Philip Roth's Achievement," *IFR* 2 (1975): 113-20.

Pinsker, S., *Comedy That "Hoits,"* 102-21.

Rodgers, B. F., Jr., *Philip Roth*, 141-56.

Siegel, Ben, "The Novelist as Narcissus: Philip Roth's MY LIFE AS A MAN," *Descant* 24, i-ii (1981): 61-79.

Spacks, Patricia M., "Only Personal: Some Functions of Fiction," *YR* 65, iv (Summer, 1976): 528-43.

OUR GANG (STARRING TRICKY AND HIS FRIENDS)

Anon., "OUR GANG, the Critics, and the Limits of Parody," *SNL* 10 (1972): 101-2.

Jones, J. P., and G. A. Nance, *Philip Roth*, 133-42.

McDaniel, J. N., *Fiction of Philip Roth*, 157-61.

Pinsker, S., *Comedy That "Hoits,"* 72-8.

Rodgers, B. F., Jr., *Philip Roth*, 97-108.

PORTNOY'S COMPLAINT

Adair, William, "PORTNOY'S COMPLAINT: A Camp Version of NOTES FROM THE UNDERGROUND," *NConL* 7, iii (May, 1977): 9-10.

Allen, M., *Necessary Blankness*, 70-5, 78-9.

Amis, Kingsley, "Waxing Wroth," *Harpers* (Apr., 1969): 104-7. Also (in slightly different form) in Amis, K., *Whatever Became of Jane Austen?* 103-8.

Bender, Eileen, "Philip Roth: The Clown in the Garden," *SCS* 3 (1976): 23-5.

Bertens, J. W., " 'The Measured Selves. The Insatiable Self': Notes on Philip Roth," in Bakker, J., and D. R. M. Wilkinson, eds., *From Cooper to Philip Roth*, 93-5.

Bettelheim, Bruno, "Portnoy Psychoanalyzed: Therapy Notes Found in the Files of Dr. Spielvogel, A New York Psychoanalyst," *Midstream* 15, vi (June-July, 1969): 3-10.

Bier, Jesse, "In Defense of Roth," *EA* 26 (Jan.-Mar., 1973): 49-53.

Bluestein, Gene, "PORTNOY'S COMPLAINT: The Jew as American," *CRevAS* 7 (1976): 66-76.

Bothwell, E. K., *Alienation in the Jewish American Novel of the Sixties*, 62-105, 105-9. [Comparative review of PORTNOY'S COMPLAINT and LETTING GO.]

Braun, Julie, "Portnoy As Pure Confusion," *CarlM* 13, ii (Spring, 1973): 73-6.

Broyard, Anatole, "A Sort of Moby Dick," *NRep* (Mar. 1, 1969): 21-2. Also in Harrison, G., *Critic as Artist*, 42-6.

Buchen, Irving H., "PORTNOY'S COMPLAINT or the Rooster's Kvetch," *STwC* 6 (Fall, 1970): 97-107.

Cohen, Eileen Z., "Alex in Wonderland, or PORTNOY'S COMPLAINT," *TCL* 17, iii (July, 1971): 161-8.

Ditsky, John, "Roth, Updike, and the High Expense of Spirit," *UWR* 5, i (Fall, 1969): 111-20.

Dupree, Robert, "And the Mom Roth Outgabe or, What Hath Got Roth?" *ArlQ* 2, iv (Autumn, 1970): 175-89.

Forrey, Robert, "Oedipal Politics in PORTNOY'S COMPLAINT," in Pinsker, S., ed., *Critical Essays on Philip Roth*, 266-74.

Friedman, Melvin J., "Jewish Mothers and Sons," *Tempest* 2 (Winter, 1970): 33-6. Also in Malin, I., ed., *Contemporary American-Jewish Literature*, 167-72.

Goldman, Albert, *Freakshow*, N.Y.: Atheneum, 1972, 229-35.

Gordon, Lois G., "PORTNOY'S COMPLAINT: Coming of Age in Jersey City," *L&P* 19, iii-iv (1969): 57-60.

Grebstein, Sheldon, "The Comic Anatomy of PORTNOY'S COMPLAINT," in Cohen, S. B., ed., *Comic Relief*, 152-71.

Gross, Barry, "Seduction of the Innocent: PORTNOY'S COMPLAINT and Popular Culture," *MELUS* 8, iv (1981): 81-92.

Guttmann, A., *Jewish Writer in America*, 74-6.

Howe, Irving, "Philip Roth Reconsidered," *Ctary* 54, vi (Dec., 1972): 74-7. Also in Howe, I., *Critical Point*, 150-7. Also in Pinsker, S., ed., *Critical Essays on Philip Roth*, 239-44.

Kliman, Bernice W., "Names in PORTNOY'S COMPLAINT," *Crit* 14, iii (1973): 16-24.

Jones, J. P., and G. A. Nance, *Philip Roth*, 72-85.

Lavine, Steven D., "The Degradations of Erotic Life: PORTNOY'S COMPLAINT Reconsidered," *MichA* 11 (1979): 357-62.

Levine, Mordecai H., "Philip Roth and American Judaism," *CLAJ* 14, ii (Dec., 1970): 165-70.

McDaniel, J. N., *Fiction of Philip Roth*, 132-48.

Michel, Pierre, "PORTNOY'S COMPLAINT and Philip Roth's Complexities," *DQR* 4 (1974): 1-10.

Nahal, Chaman, "Sexual Psychology in Contemporary American Fiction," in Sharma, J. N., and Babu, B. R., eds., *Contemporary American Life*, 135-8.

Novak, Bill, "Philip Roth and the Jews," *Response* 5, ii (Fall, 1971): 77-85.

Pinsker, S., *Between Two Worlds*, 44-56.

_____, *Comedy That "Hoits,"* 55-71.

_____, "That Rise and Fall of the American Jewish Novel," *ConnR* 7, i (Oct., 1973): 22-3.

Rodgers, B. F., Jr., *Philip Roth*, 80-96, 123-30.

Roskolenko, Harry, "Portrait of the Artist as a Young Schmuck," *Quadrant* 64 (Mar./Apr., 1970): 25-30.

Roth, Philip, "In Response to Those Correspondents, Students, and Interviewers Who Have Asked Me 'How Did You Come to Write That Book Anyway?'" *APR* 3, iv (July/Aug., 1974): 65-7.

Segal, Alan, "PORTNOY'S COMPLAINT and the Sociology of Literature," *British Jnl. of Sociology* 22 (1971): 257-68.

Shaw, Peter, "Portnoy and His Creator," *Ctary* 47 (May, 1969): 77-9.

Shrubb, Peter, "Portnography," *Quadrant* 64 (Mar./Apr., 1970): 16-24.

Sloss, Henry, "Coriolanus in New Jersey," *Shen* 20 (Winter, 1969): 96-100.

Solotaroff, Theodore, "Philip Roth: A Personal View," *Red Hot Vacuum*, 322-8.

Spacks, Patricia, "About Portnoy," *YR* 58 (Summer, 1969): 623-35.

Tanner, T., *City of Words*, 310-16.

Waniek, Marilyn N., "The Schizoid-Implied Authors of Two Jewish-American Novels," *MELUS* 7, i (Spring, 1980): 30-6.

Wisse, R. R., *Schlemiel as Modern Hero*, 118-20.

Wohlgelertner, Maurice, "Mama and Papa and all the Complaints," *Tradition* 10 (1969): 70-87.

Yergin, Dan, "Portnoy: A Critical Diagnosis," *Granta* (1969). [Not seen.]

Zimring, Franklin, "Portnoy's Real Complaint," *Moment* (Dec., 1980): 58-60.

THE PROFESSOR OF DESIRE

Alter, Robert, "The Education of David Kepesh," *PR* 46, iii (1979): 478-81.

Bell, Pearl K., "Philip Roth: Sonny Boy or Lenny Bruce?" *Ctary* 64, v (Nov., 1977): 61-3.

Bertins, J. W., "'The Measured Self vs. The Insatiable Self': Notes on Philip Roth," in Bakker, J., and D. R. M. Wilkinson, eds., *From Cooper to Philip Roth*, 100-6.

Jones, J. P., and G. A. Nance, *Philip Roth*, 111-22.

Kaminsky, Alice R., "Philip Roth's Professor Kepesh and the 'Reality Principle'," *DQ* 13, ii (Summer, 1978): 41-54.

Rajec, Elizabeth M., "Kafka and Philip Roth: Their Use of Literary Onomastics (Based on THE PROFESSOR OF DESIRE)," *LOS* 7 (1980): 69-86.

Rodgers, B. F., Jr., *Philip Roth*, 157-69.

Walden, Daniel, "THE PROFESSOR OF DESIRE: The Two Plums or the Reawakening?" in Pinsker, S., ed., *Critical Essays on Philip Roth*, 78-82.

WHEN SHE WAS GOOD

Allen, M., *Necessary Blankness*, 87-95.

Alter, Robert, "When He is Bad," *Ctary* 44 (Nov., 1967): 86-7.

Angoff, Charles, in *CFJ* 21 (1968): 151-2.

Bender, Eileen, "Philip Roth: The Clown in the Garden," *SCS* 3 (1976): 22-3.

Carothers, James B., "Midwestern Civilization and Its Discontents: Lewis's Carol Kennicott and Roth's Lucy Nelson," *MMisc* 9 (1981): 21-30.

Gilman, Richard, "Let's Lynch Lucy," *NRep* 156 (June, 24, 1967): 19-21.

Hicks, Granville, "A Bad Little Good Girl," *SatR* 50 (June 17, 1967): 25-6.

Jones, J. P., and G. A. Nance, *Philip Roth*, 51-72.

Lehan, Richard, "Fiction 1967," *ConL* 9, iv (Autumn, 1968): 542-3.

McDaniel, J. N., *Fiction of Philip Roth*, 120-32.

Meeter, G., *Philip Roth and Bernard Malamud*, 43-4.

Pinsker, S., *Comedy That "Hoits,"* 42-55.

Raban, Jonathan, "The New Philip Roth," *Novel* 2, ii (Winter, 1962): 156-61.

Rodgers, B. F., Jr., *Philip Roth*, 60-74.

Solotaroff, Theodore, "Philip Roth: A Personal View," *Red Hot Vacuum*, 319-22.

Thompson, John, "The Professionals," *NYRB* 8 (June 1, 1967): 14-16.

ZUCKERMAN UNBOUND

Novak, William, "Philip Roth's ZUCKERMAN UNBOUND," *Moment* (May, 1981): 59-60.

Tintner, Adeline R., "Hiding Behind James: Roth's ZUCKERMAN UNBOUND," *Midstream* 28, iv (Apr., 1982): 49-53.

Wisse, Ruth, "Philip Roth Then and Now," *Ctary* 72 iii (Sept., 1981): 58-60.

BIBLIOGRAPHY

McDaniel, John N., "Philip Roth: A Checklist, 1954-1973," *BB* 31, ii (1974): 51-3.

Rodgers, Bernard F., Jr., *Philip Roth: A Bibliography*, Metuchen, N.J.: Scarecrow, 1974.

ROTHBERG, ABRAHAM, 1922-

THE SWORD OF THE GOLEM

Rothberg, Abraham, "What Time Is It Now? *SWR* 58 (1973): 193-208.

RULE, JANE, 1931-

GENERAL

Hancock, Geoff, "An Interview with Jane Rule," *CFM* 23 (1976): 57-112.

Schuster, Marilyn R., "Strategies for Survival: The Subtle Subversion of Jane Rule," *FSt* 7, iii (Fall, 1981): 431-50.

Sonthoff, Helen, "Celebration: A Study of Jane Rule's Fiction," *CFM* 23 (Autumn, 1976): 121-31.

AGAINST THE SEASON

Schuster, Marilyn B., "Strategies for Survival: The Subtle Subversion of Jane Rule," *FSt* 7, iii (Fall, 1981): 439-40.

CONTRACT WITH THE WORLD

Schuster, Marilyn R., "Strategies for Survival: The Subtle Subversion of Jane Rule," *FSt* 7, iii (Fall, 1981): 443-5.

DESERT OF THE HEART

Schuster, Marilyn R., "Strategies for Survival: The Subtle Subversion of Janet Rule," *FSt* 7, iii (Fall, 1981): 433-6.

THIS IS NOT FOR YOU

Schuster, Marilyn R., "Strategies for Survival: The Subtle Subversion of Jane Rule," *FSt* 7, iii (Fall, 1981): 436-9.

THE YOUNG IN ONE ANOTHER'S ARMS

Schuster, Marilyn R., "Strategies for Survival: The Subtle Subversion of Jane Rule," *FSt* 7, iii (Fall, 1981): 440-2.

BIBLIOGRAPHY

Sonthoff, Helen, "Jane Rule: A Bibliography," *CFM* 23 (1976): 133-8.

SAHGAL, NAYANTARA (PANDIT), 1927-

GENERAL

Asnani, Shyam M., "East-West Encounter in Nayantara Sahgal's Novels," *ComQ* 3, ix (Dec., 1978): 188-98.

Jain, Jasbir, "The Aesthetics of Morality: Sexual Relations in the Novels of Nayantara Sahgal," *JIWE* 6, i (Jan., 1978): 41-8.

Liu, Marcia P., "Continuity and Development in the Novels of Nayantara Sahgal," *JIWE* 8, i-ii (Jan.-July, 1980): 45-52.

THE DAY IN SHADOW

Malhotra, M. L., "Shadow and Substance," *BP* 19 (1972): 54-8.

A SITUATION IN NEW DELHI

Chinneswararao, G. J., "Nayantara Sahgal's A SITUATION IN NEW DELHI: A Study," *ComQ* 3, ix (Dec., 1978): 154-61.

STORM IN CHANDIGARH

Jussawalla, Feroza, "'Of Cabbages and Kings': THIS TIME OF MORNING and STORM IN CHANDIGARH by Nayantara Sahgal," *JIWE* 5, i (1977): 43-50.

THIS TIME OF MORNING

Jussawalla, Feroza, "'Of Cabbages and Kings': THIS TIME OF MORNING and STORM IN CHANDIGARH by Nayantara Sahgal," *JIWE* 5, i (1977): 43-50.

A TIME TO BE HAPPY

Asnani, Shyam M., "East-West Encounter in Nayantara Sahgal's Novels," *ComQ* 3, ix (Dec., 1978): 188-94.

SALAMANCA, J(ACK) R(ICHARD), 1922-

GENERAL

Baxter, Charles, "The Drowned Survivor: The Fiction of J. R. Salamanca," *Crit* 19, i (1977): 75-86.

EMBARKATION

Baxter, Charles, "The Drowned Survivor: The Fiction of J. R. Salamanca," *Crit* 19, i (1977): 83-5.

LILITH

Baxter, Charles, "The Drowned Survivor: The Fiction of J. R. Salamanca," *Crit* 19, i (1977): 77-80.

THE LOST COUNTRY

Baxter, Charles, "The Drowned Survivor: The Fiction of J. R. Salamanca," *Crit* 19, i (1977): 76-7.

A SEA CHANGE

Baxter, Charles, "The Drowned Survivor: The Fiction of J. R. Salamanca," *Crit* 19, i (1977): 80-3.

SALINGER, J(EROME) D(AVID), 1919-

GENERAL

Barr, Donald, "Saints, Pilgrims and Artists," *Cweal* 67 (Oct. 25, 1957): 88-90. Also in Kostelanetz, R., ed., *On Contemporary Literature*, 537-43. Also in Simonson, H. P., and P. E. Hager, eds., *Salinger's CATCHER IN THE RYE*, 102-6.

Belcher, W. F., and J. W. Lee, eds., *J. D. Salinger and the Critics*.

Bostwick, Sally "Reality, Compassion and Mysticism," *MidR* 5 (1963): 30-43.

Bufithis, Philip H., "J. D. Salinger and the Psychiatrist," *WVUPP* 21 (Dec., 1974): 67-77.

Cecile, Sister Marie, "J. D. Salinger's Circle of Privacy," *CathW* 194 (Feb., 1962): 296-301.

Costello, Donald P., "Salinger and His Critics," *Cweal* 79 (Oct. 25, 1963): 132-5.

French, W., *J. D. Salinger*, Rev. ed.

_____, "Steinbeck and Salinger: Messiah-Moulders for a Sick Society," in Hayashi, T., ed., *Steinbeck's Literary Dimension*, 105-15.

Green, Martin, "Amis and Salinger: The Latitude of Private Conscience," *ChiR* 11 (Winter, 1958): 20-5.

Gross, Theodore L., "J. D. Salinger: Suicide and Survival in the Modern World," *SAQ* 68, iv (Autumn, 1969): 454-62.

Grunewald, H. A., ed., *Salinger*.

Gwynn, F. L., and J. L. Blotner, *Fiction of J. D. Salinger*.

Hamilton, Kenneth, *J. D. Salinger*.

_____, "J. D. Salinger's Happy Family," *QQ* 71 (Summer, 1964): 176-87.

Harper, J. M., Jr., "J. D. Salinger—Through Glasses Darkly," *Desperate Faith*, 69-95.

Hassan, Ihab H., "J. D. Salinger: Rare Quixotic Gesture," *WR* 21 (Summer, 1957): 261-80.

Haveman, Ernest, "The Search for the Mysterious J. D. Salinger: The Recluse in the Rye," *Life* 51 (Nov. 3, 1961): 129-30+.

Herriges, Grég, "Ten Minutes with J. D. Salinger," *Qui* 8 (Jan., 1979): 86-8, 126-30.

Hicks, Granville, "J. D. Salinger: Search for Wisdom," *SatR* 42 (July 25, 1959): 13+.

Hipkiss, R. A., *Jack Kerouac*, 97-105.

Kennedy, Richard, "The Theme of the Quest," *EngR* 8 (1957): 2-17. [Not seen.]

Larner, Jeremy, "Salinger's Audience," *PR* 29 (Fall, 1962): 594-8.

Laser, M., and N. Fruman, eds., *Studies in J. D. Salinger*.

Levin, Beatrice, "Everybody's Favorite: Concepts of Love in the Works of J. D. Salinger," *Motive* No. 22 (Oct., 1961): 9-11. [Not seen.]

Lorch, Thomas, "J. D. Salinger: The Artist, the Audience, and the Popular Arts," *SDR* 5 (Winter, 1967-1968): 3-13.

Lundquist, J., *J. D. Salinger*.

Matthews, James F., "J. D. Salinger: An Appraisal," *UVM* 1 (Spring, 1956): 52-60. [Not seen.]

Miller, J. E., Jr., *J. D. Salinger*.

Mirza, Humayun Ali, "The Influence of Hindu-Buddhist Psychology and Philosophy on J. D. Salinger's Fiction," *DAI* 37 (1976): 971A.

Mizener, Arthur, "The Love Song of J. D. Salinger," *Harpers* 218 (Feb., 1959): 83-90. Also in *Off Campus* 1 (Jan., 1963): 18-20, 44, 51, 54, 64.

Noland, Richard W., "The Novel of Personal Formula: J. D. Salinger," *UR* 33 (Oct., 1966): 19-24.

Oldsey, Bernard, "Salinger and Golding: Resurrection or Repose," *CollL* 6 (Spring, 1979): 136-44.

Pickering, John K., "J. D. Salinger: Portraits of Alienation," *DAI* 30 (1970): 3954A.

Ramamurthy, V., "J. D. Salinger: The Tragi-Comic Vision," *BP* 11 (July, 1968): 37-42. [Not seen.]

Rees, Richard, "The Salinger Situation," in Moore, H. T., ed, *Contemporary American Novelists*, 95-105.

Ross, Theodore J., "Notes on J. D. Salinger," *CJF* 22 (1968): 149-53.

Rot, Sándor, "J. D. Salinger's Oeuvre in the Light of Decoding—Stylistics and Information—Theory," *SEA* 4 (1978): 85-129. [Not seen.]

Russell, John, "Salinger's Feat," *MFS* 12 (Autumn, 1966): 299-311.

Skow, John, and the Editors of *Time*, "Sonny: An Introduction," *Time* 78 (Sept. 15, 1961): 84-90. Also in Belcher, W. F., and J. W. Lee, eds., *J. D. Salinger and the Critics*, 1-7.

Slabey, Robert M., "Salinger's 'Casino': Wayfarers and Spiritual Acrobats," *EngR* 14, iii (Feb., 1964); 16-20.

Steiner, George, "The Salinger Industry," *Nation* 189 (Nov. 14, 1959): 360-3. Also in Laser, M., and N. Fruman, eds., *Studies in J. D. Salinger*, 113-18. Also in Marsden, M. M., ed., *If You Really Want to Know*, 62-6.

Wiegand, William, "J. D. Salinger: Seventy-Eight Bananas," *ChiR* 11 (1957): 3-19. Also in Waldmeir, J. J., ed., *Recent American Fiction*, 252-64.

_____, "The Knighthood of J. D. Salinger," *NRep* 141 (Oct. 19, 1959): 19-21.

THE CATCHER IN THE RYE

Ahren, Marianne, "Experience and Attitude in THE CATCHER IN THE RYE and NINE STORIES by J. D. Salinger," *MSpr* 61, iii (1967): 242-63.

Aldridge, John, *In Search of Heresy*, 129-31. Also in Laser, M., and N. Fruman, eds., *Studies in J. D. Salinger*, 50-2. Also in Simonson, H. P., and P. E. Hager, eds., *Salinger's CATCHER IN THE RYE*, 80-1.

Allen, W., *Modern Novel*, 309-13.

Amur, G. S., "Theme, Structure, and Symbol in THE CATCHER IN THE RYE," *IJAS* 1, i (1969): 11-24.

Barr, Donald, in Balakian, N., and C. Simmons, eds., *Creative Present*, 53-7.

_____, "Saints, Pilgrims and Artists," *Cweal* 67 (Oct. 25, 1957): 89. Also in Kostelanetz, R., ed., *Contemporary Literature*, 538-9. Also in Marsden, M., M., ed., *If You Really Want to Know*, 39-40. Also in Simonson, H. P., and P. E. Hager, eds., *Salinger's CATCHER IN THE RYE*, 103-4.

Barron, Cynthia M., "The Catcher and the Soldier: Hemingway's SOLDIERS HOME and Salinger's THE CATCHER IN THE RYE," *HemR* 2, i (1982): 70-3.

Baumbach, Jonathan, "The Saint as Young Man: A Reappraisal of THE CATCHER IN THE RYE," *MLQ* 25 (Dec., 1964): 461-72. Also in Baumbach, J., *Landscape of Nightmare*, 55-7.

Bellman, Samuel I., "Peripheral(?) Characters in HUCKLEBERRY FINN and CATCHER IN THE RYE," *MTJ* 19, i (Winter, 1977-78): 4-6.

Bhaerman, Robert D., "Rebuttal" to Bernard Oldsey, 'The Movies in the Rye'," *CE* 23 (Mar., 1962): 507-8. Also in Marsden, M. M., ed., *If You Really Want to Know*, 122-3. Also in Simonton, H. P., and P. E. Hager, eds., *Salinger's CATCHER IN THE RYE*, 46.

Bonheim, Helmut, "An Introduction to Salinger's THE CATCHER IN THE RYE," *Exercise Exchange* 4 (Apr., 1957): 8-11.

Bowden, Edwin T., *Dungeon of the Heart*, 54-65. Also in Simonson, H. P., and P. E. Hager, eds., *Salinger's CATCHER IN THE RYE*, 94-100.

Bowen, Robert O., "The Salinger Syndrome: Charity Against Whom?" *Ramparts* 1 (May, 1962): 52-60. Also in Simonson, H. P., and P. E. Hager, eds., *Salinger's CATCHER IN THE RYE*, 21-30.

Bradbury, Malcolm, "A Reading of CATCHER IN THE RYE," *What is a Novel?* 58-67.

Branch, Edgar, "Mark Twain and J. D. Salinger: A Study in Literary Continuity," *AQ* 9 (Summer, 1957): 144-58. Also in Belcher, W. F., and J. W. Lee, eds, *J. D. Salinger and the Critics,* 20-34. Also in Grunewald, H. A., ed., *Salinger,* 205-17. Also in Laser, M., and N. Fruman, eds., *Studies in J. D. Salinger,* 39-49. Also in Marsden, M. M., ed., *If You Really Want to Know,* 132-44. Also in Simonson, H. P., and P. E. Hager, eds., *Salinger's CATCHER IN THE RYE,* 81-91.

Bryan, James, "The Psychological Structure of THE CATCHER IN THE RYE," *PMLA* 89, v (Oct., 1974): 1065-74.

_____, "Sherwood Anderson and THE CATCHER IN THE RYE: A Possible Influence," *NConL* 1, v (Nov., 1971): 2-6.

Bryant, J. H., *Open Decision,* 236-40.

Bungert, Hans, "Salinger's THE CATCHER IN THE RYE: The Isolated Youth and His Struggle to Communicate," in Laser, M., and N. Fruman, eds., *Studies in J. D. Salinger,* 177-85.

Burack, Boris, "Holden the Courageous," *CEA* 27 (May, 1965): 1 [Reply to Warner below.]

Burrows, David, "Allie and Phoebe: Death and Love in J. D. Salinger's THE CATCHER IN THE RYE," in *Private Dealings,* 106-13.

Cagle, Charles, "THE CATCHER IN THE RYE Revisited," *MQ* 4 (Summer, 1964): 343-51.

Cahill, Robert, "J. D. Salinger's Tin Bell," *Cadence* 14 (Autumn, 1959): 20-2.

Carpenter, Frederic I., "The Adolescent in American Fiction," *EJ* 46 (Sept., 1957): 315-16. Also in Laser, M., and N. Fruman, eds., *Studies in J. D. Salinger,* 69-71. Also in Simonson, H. P., and P. E. Hager, eds., *Salinger's CATCHER IN THE RYE,* 92-3.

Chugunov, Konstantin, "Soviet Critics on J. D. Salinger's Novel, THE CATCHER IN THE RYE," *SovietLit* 5 (1962): 182-4. Also in Laser, M., and N. Fruman, eds., *Studies in J. D. Salinger,* 186-9.

Cohen, Hubert I., "'A Woeful Agony Which Forced Me to Begin My Tale': THE CATCHER IN THE RYE," *MFS* 12 (Autumn, 1966): 355-66.

Conrad, Robert C., "Two Novels About Outsiders: The Kinship of Salinger's THE CATCHER IN THE RYE with Heinrich Böll's ANSICHTEN EINES CLOWNS," *UDR* 5, iii (Winter, 1968-1969): 23-7.

Corbett, Edward P. J., "Raise High the Barriers, Censors," *America* 104 (Jan. 7, 1961): 441-3. Also in Laser, M., and N. Fruman, eds., *Studies in J. D. Salinger,* 134-41. Also in Marsden, M. M., ed., *If You Really Want to Know,* 68-73. Also in Simonson, H. P., and P. E. Hager, eds., *Salinger's CATCHER IN THE RYE,* 5-9.

Costello, Donald P., "The Language of THE CATCHER IN THE RYE," *AS* 24 (Oct., 1959): 172-81. Also in Belcher, W. F., and J. W. Lee, eds., *Salinger and the Critics,* 45-53. Also in Grunewald, H. A., ed., *Salinger and the Critics,* 45-53. Also in Grunewald, H. A., ed., *Salinger,* 266-76. Also in Laser, M., and N. Fruman, eds., *Studies in J. D. Salinger,* 92-104. Also in Marsden, M. M., ed., *If You Really Want to Know,* 87-95. Also in Simonson, H. P., and P. E. Hager, eds., *Salinger's CATCHER IN THE RYE,* 32-9.

Costello, Patrick, "Salinger and 'Honest Iago'," *Ren* 16 (Summer, 1964): 171-4.

Creeger, George R., "Treacherous Desertion: Salinger's THE CATCHER IN THE RYE," in Belcher, W. F., and J. W. Lee, eds., *J. D. Salinger and the Critics,* 98-104.

D'Avanzo, Mario L., "Gatsby and Holden Caulfield," *FitzN* 38 (Summer, 1967): 4-6.

Davis, Tom "J. D. Salinger: 'Some Crazy Cliff' Indeed," *WR* 14 (Winter, 1960): 97-9. Also in Marsden, M. M., ed., *If You Really Want to Know,* 45-7.

Deer, Irving, and John H. Randall, III., "J. D. Salinger and the Reality Beyond Words," *LHR* No. 6 (1964): 19-29.

Dessner, Lawrence J., "The Salinger Story, Or, Have It Your Way," in Filler, L., ed., *Seasoned Authors for a New Season,* 91-7.

Dodge, Stewart, "The Theme of Quest, III: In Search of 'The Fat Lady'," *EngR* 8 (Winter, 1957): 10-13. Also (condensed) in Marsden, M. M., ed., *If You Really Want to Know,* 40-2.

Drake, Robert Y., Jr., "Two Old Juveniles," *GaR* 13 (Winter, 1959): 443-53.

Ducharme, Edward, "J. D. Sonny, Sunny, and Holden," *EngR* 19, ii (1968): 54-8.

Edwards, Duane, "Holden Caulfield: 'Don't Ever Tell Anybody Anything'," *ELH* 44 (Fall, 1977): 554-65.

Ely, Sister M. Amanda, "The Adult Image in Three Novels of Adolescence," *EJ* 56 (Nov., 1967): 1130-31.

Erwin, Kenneth J., "An Analysis of the Dramatic and Semantic Use of Altruism in the Writings of J. D. Salinger," *DA* 19 (1968); 1535A-36A.

Finkelstein, S., *Existentialism and Alienation in American Literature,* 219-24.

Flaker, Aleksander, "Salinger's Model in East European Prose," 151-60, in Birnbaum, Henrik, and Thomas Eekman, eds., *Fiction and Drama in Eastern and Southeastern Europe: Evolution and Experiment in the Postwar Period.* Proc. of the 1978 UCLA Conf. (UCLA Slavic Studies 1), Columbus: Slavika, 1980.

Fleissner, Robert F., "Salinger's Caulfield: A Refraction of Copperfield and His Caul," *NConL* 3, iii (May, 1973): 5-7.

Fogel, Amy, "Where the Ducks Go: THE CATCHER IN THE RYE," *BSCTF* 3 (Spring, 1962): 75-9.

Foran, Donald J., "A Doubletake on Holden Caulfield," *EJ* 57 (Oct., 1968): 977-9.

Fowler, Albert, "Alien in the Rye," *ModA* 1, ii (Fall, 1957): 193-7. Also in Belcher, W. F., and J. W. Lee, eds., *J. D. Salinger and the Critics,* 34-40.

French, Warren, "The Age of Salinger," in French, W., ed., *Fifties,* 25-31.

_____, "Holden's Fall," *MFS* 10 (Winter, 1964-65): 389.

_____, *J. D. Salinger,* Rev. ed., 102-29.

_____, "Steinbeck and Salinger: Messiah-Moulders for a Sick Society," in Hayashi, T., ed., *Steinbeck's Literary Dimension,* 105-15.

_____, "Steinbeck's Winter Tale," *MFS* 11, i (Spring, 1965): 66-74.

Furst, Lilian R., "Dostoyevsky's NOTES FROM THE UNDERGROUND and Salinger's THE CATCHER IN THE RYE," *CRCL* 5 (Winter, 1978): 72-85.

Gale, Robert L., "Redburn and Holden—Half-Brothers One Century Removed," *ForumH* 3, xii (Winter, 1963): 32-6.

Galloway, D. D., *Absurd Hero,* 140-5.

Gardiner, Harold C., "Words and Conscience," *America* 104 (Jan., 7, 1961): 444.

Geismar, M., *American Moderns*, 195-9. Also in Belcher, W. F., and J. W. Lee, eds., *J. D. Salinger and the Critics*, 43-5. Also in Grunwald, H. A., ed., *Salinger*, 87-91.

Giles, Barbara, "The Lonely War of J. D. Salinger," *Mainstream* 12 (Feb., 1959): 2-8+.

Glasser, William, "THE CATCHER IN THE RYE," *MQR* 15 (Fall, 1976): 432-57.

Goldstein, Bernice and Sanford, "Zen and Salinger," *MFS* 11 (Autumn, 1966): 322-3.

Gooder, R. D., "One of Today's Best Little Writers," *CamQ* 1 (Winter, 1965-66): 83-6.

Goodman, Anne L., "Mad About Children," *NRep* 125 (July 16, 1951): 20-1. Also in Simonson, H. P., and P. E. Hager, eds., *Salinger's CATCHER IN THE RYE*, 3-4.

Green, Martin, "American Rococo: Salinger and Nabokov," *Re-Appraisals*, 211-29.

_____, "Franny and Zooey," *Re-Appraisals*, 197-210.

_____, "The Image-Maker," in Grunwald, H. A., ed., *Salinger*, 251-2.

Grunwald, Henry A., "'He Touches Something Deep in Us...'," *Horizon* 4 (May, 1962): 100-7.

Gutwillig, Robert, "Everybody's Caught THE CATCHER IN THE RYE," *NYTBR* Paperback Section (Jan. 15, 1961). Also in Laser, M., and N. Fruman, eds., *Studies in J. D. Salinger*, 1-5.

Gwynn, F. L., and J. L. Blotner, *Fiction of J. D. Salinger*, 28-31. Also in Laser, m., and N. Fruman, eds., *Studies in J. D. Salinger*, 85-7. Also in Marsden, M. M., ed., *If You Really Want to Know*, 45-7. Also in Simonson, H. P., and P. E. Hager, eds., *Salinger's CATCHER IN THE RYE*, 93-4.

Hainsworth, J. D., "J. D. Salinger," *HJ* 64 (Winter, 1966): 63-4.

_____, "Maturity in J. D. Salinger's THE CATCHER IN THE RYE," *ES* 48 (Oct., 1967): 426-31.

Hall, James, *Lunatic Giant in the Drawing Room*, 75-7.

_____, "Play, the Training Camp, and American Angry Comedy," *HAB* 15 (Spring, 1964): 9-11.

Hamilton, Kenneth, *J. D. Salinger*, 22-7, 37-9.

_____, "One Way to Use the Bible: The Example of J. D. Salinger," *ChS* 47 (Fall, 1964): 244-6.

Handa, Takuya, "On Interpretation of J. D. Salinger's THE CATCHER IN THE RYE," *KAL* 21 (June, 1980): 42-53.

Harper, H. M., Jr., "J. D. Salinger—Through Glasses Darkly," *Desperate Faith*, 66-71.

Hassan, Ihab, "Rare Quixotic Gesture: The Fiction of J. D. Salinger," *WR* 21 (Summer, 1957): 271-4. Also (revised) in Hassan, I., *Radical Innocence*, 272-6. Also in Belcher, W. F., and J. W. Lee, eds., *J. D. Salinger and the Critics*, 117-20. Also in Grunwald, H. A., ed., *Salinger*, 148-52. Also in Marsden, M. M., *If You Really Want to Know*, 30-2.

Hayes, Ann L., "J. D. Salinger: A Reputation and a Promise," in Carnegie Institute of Technology, *Lectures on Modern Novelists*, 15-18.

Heiserman, Arthur, and James E. Miller, Jr., "J. D. Salinger: Some Crazy Cliff," *WHR* 10 (Spring, 1956): 129-32. Also in Belcher, W. F., and J. W. Lee, eds., *J. D. Salinger and the Critics*, 14-17. Also in Grunwald, H. A., ed., *Salinger*, 196-205. Also in Laser, M., and N. Fruman, eds., *Studies in J. D. Salinger*, 23-30. Also in Marsden, M. M., ed., *If You Really Want to Know*, 16-22. Also in Simonson, H. P., and P. E. Hager, eds., *Salinger's CATCHER IN THE RYE*, 74-80. Also in Miller, J. E., *Quests Surd and Absurd*, 31-40.

Herndl, George C., "Golding and Salinger: A Clear Choice," *WiseR* No. 502 (1964): 309-22.

Howell, John M., "Salinger in the Waste Land," *MFS* 12 (Autumn, 1966): 367-75.

_____, "The Waste Land Tradition in the American Novel," *DA* 24 (1964): 3337.

Jacobs, Robert G., "J. D. Salinger's THE CATCHER IN THE RYE: Holden Caulfield's 'Goddam Autobiography'," *IEY* (Fall, 1959): 9-14. Also (condensed) in Marsden, M. M., ed., *If You Really Want to Know*, 55-62.

Johnson, James W., "The Adolescent Hero: A Trend in Modern Fiction," *TCL* 5 (Apr., 1959): 5.

Jones, Ernest, "Case History of All of Us," *Nation* 178 (Sept. 1, 1951): 176. Also in Simonson, H. P., and P. E. Hager, ed., *Salinger's CATCHER IN THE RYE*, 4-5.

Kaplan, Charles, "Holden and Huck: The Odysseys of Youth," *CE* 18 (Nov., 1956): 76-80. Also in Laser, M., and N. Fruman, eds., *Studies in J. D. Salinger*, 31-8. Also in Marsden, M. M., ed., *If You Really Want to Know*, 127-32.

Kearns, Francis E., "Salinger and Golding: Conflict on the Campus," *America* 108 (Jan. 26, 1963): 136-9. Also in Nelson, W. Ed., *William Golding's LORD OF THE FLIES*, 148-55.

Kegel, Charles H., "Incommunicability in Salinger's THE CATCHER IN THE RYE," *WHR* 11 (Spring, 1957): 188-90. Also in Belcher, W. F., and J. W. Lee, eds., *J. D. Salinger and the Critics*, 17-20. Also in Laser, M., and N. Fruman, eds., *Studies in J. D. Salinger*, 53-6. Also in Marsden, M. M., ed., *If You Really Want to Know*, 25-7. Also in Simonson, H. P., and P. E. Hager, eds., *Salinger's CATCHER IN THE RYE*, 63-5.

Kermode, Frank, "Fit Audience," *Spectator* 200 (May 30, 1958): 705-6. Also in Belcher, W. F., and J. W. Lee, eds., *J. D. Salinger and the Critics*, 40-3. Also in Kermode, F., *Puzzles and Epiphanies*, 188-92.

Kinney, Arthur F., "J. D. Salinger and the Search for Love," *TSLL* 5 (1963): 111-14.

_____, "The Theme of Charity in THE CATCHER IN THE RYE," *PMASAL* 48 (1963): 691-702.

Laser, Marvin, "Character Names in THE CATCHER IN THE RYE," *CEJ* 1 (1965): 29-40.

_____, and N. Fruman, eds., "Salinger: The Early Reviews," in Laser, M., and N. Fruman, eds., *Studies in J. D. Salinger*, 6-17.

Leitch, David, "The Salinger Myth," *TC* 158 (Nov., 1960): 428-35. Also in *Mlle* 264 (Aug., 1961): 264-5, 73, 88. Also (selection) in Marsden, M. M., eds., *If You Really Want to Know*, 66-8.

Lerner, Lawrence, *Uses of Nostalgia: Studies in Pastoral Poetry*, N.Y. Schocken, 1972, 135-43.

Lettis, Richard, "Holden Caulfield: Salinger's 'Ironic Amalgam'," *AN&Q* 15, iii (1976): 43-5.

_____, *J. D. Salinger: THE CATCHER IN THE RYE* (Barron's Studies in American Literature), Great Neck, N.Y.: Barron's Educ. Ser., 1964.

Levine, Paul, "J. D. Salinger: The Development of the Misfit Hero," *TCL* 4 (Oct., 1958): 92-9. Also (selection) in Masden, M. M., ed., *If You Really Want to Know*, 47-8.

Light, James F., "Salinger's THE CATCHER IN THE RYE," *Expl* 18 (June, 1960): Item 59. Also in Marsden, M. M., ed., *If You Really Want to Know*, 98-9. Also in Simonson, H. P., and P. E. Hager, eds., *Salinger's CATCHER IN THE RYE*, 39-40.

Little, Gail B., "Three Novels for Comparative Study in the Twelfth Grade," *EJ* 52 (Sept., 1963): 501-5.

Ludwig, J., *Recent American Novelists,* 28-30, 33-5.

Luedtke, Luther S., "J. D. Salinger and Robert Burns: THE CATCHER IN THE RYE," *MFS* 16 (Summer, 1970): 198-201.

Lundquist, J., *J. D. Salinger,* 37-68, 71-4.

Lydenberg, John, "American Novelists in Search of a Lost World," *RLV* 27, iv (1961): 312-13.

McCarthy, Mary, "J. D. Salinger's Closed Circuit," *Harpers* 225 (Oct., 19, 1962): 46-7. Also (selection) in Marsden. M. M., ed., *If You Really Want to Know,* 84.

Maclean, Hugh N., "Conservatism in Modern American Fiction," *CE* 15 (Mar., 1954): 315-22. Also in Belcher, W. F., and J. W. Lee, eds., *J. D. Salinger and the Critics,* 11-14. Also (condensed) in Marsden, M. M., ed., *If You Really Want to Know,* 14-15. Also in Simonson, H. P., and P. E. Hager, eds., *Salinger's CATCHER IN THE RYE,* 101-2.

McNamara, Eugene, "Holden as Novelist," *EJ* 54 (Mar., 1965): 166-70.

Malin, Irving, "The Gothic Family," *Psychoanalysis and American Fiction,* 264-66. Also in Malin, I., *New American Gothic,* 61-3.

Marcus, Fred, "THE CATCHER IN THE RYE: A Live Circuit," *EJ* 52 (Jan., 1963): 1-8.

Margolies, John D., "Salinger's THE CATCHER IN THE RYE," *Expl* 21 (Nov., 1963): Item 23.

Marks, Barry A., "Rebuttal" to Peter Seng, "The Fallen Idol: Holden Caulfield," *CE* 23 (Mar., 1962): 507. Also (complete letter) in Marsden, M. M., ed., *If You Really Want to Know,* 81-2. Also in Simonson, H. P., and P. E. Hager, eds., *Salinger's CATCHER IN THE RYE,* 71-2.

Marsden, M. M., ed., *If You Really Want to Know.*

Martin, Augustine, "A Note on J. D. Salinger," *Studies* 48 (Autumn, 1959): 336-45.

Martin, Dexter, "Rebuttal" to Bernard S. Oldsey, "The Movies in the Rye," *CE* 23 (Mar., 1962): 507-9. Also (complete letter) in Marsden, M. M., ed., *If You Really Want to Know,* 82-3. Also (unpublished portion) in Simonson, H. P., and P. E. Hager, eds., *Salinger's CATCHER IN THE RYE,* 45-6.

_____, "Rebuttal to Peter Seng, "The Fallen Idol: Holden Caulfield," *CE* 23 (Mar., 1962): 507-9. Also in Simonson, H. P., and P. E. Hager, eds., *Salinger's CATCHER IN THE RYE,* 72.

Martin, Hansford, "The American Problem of Direct Address," *WR* 16 (Winter, 1952): 101-14.

Martin, John S., "Copperfield and Caulfield: Dickens in the Rye," *NMAL* 4 (1980): Item 29.

Masuda, Takahiro, "J. D. Salinger's THE CATCHER IN THE RYE: An Analysis on Time, Space, and Love," *SALit* 14 (1978): 35-47.

Matle, John, "Calling Miss Aigletinger," *CEA* 39 (Mar., 1977): 18-20.

McSweeney, Kerry, "Salinger Revisited," *CritQ* 20, i (1978): 66-8.

Méral, Jean, "The Ambiguous Mr. Antolini in Salinger's CATCHER IN THE RYE," *Caliban* 7 (1970): 55-8.

Miller, Edwin H., "In Memorium: Allie Caulfield in THE CATCHER IN THE RYE," *Mosaic* 15, i (Winter, 1982): 129-40.

Miller, J. E., Jr., *J. D. Salinger,* 8-19.

_____, "CATCHER in and out of History," *CritI* 3 (Spring, 1977): 599-603. [Criticizes the Ohmanns' (see below) approach.]

Moore, Robert P., "The World of Holden," *EJ* 54 (Mar., 1965): 159-65. Reply by M. Gilbert Porter, *EJ* 54 (Sept., 1965): 562.

Namba, Tatsuo, "Adverbs Peculiar to American English in J. D. Salinger's THE CATCHER IN THEY RYE," *SALit* 13 (1977): 65-76.

_____, "Some Notes on Articles in J. D. Salinger's THE CATCHER IN THE RYE," *NMAL* 4 (1980): Item 29.

_____, "Some Notes on the Use of Conjunctions and Conjunctional Phrases in J. D. Salinger's THE CATCHER IN THE RYE," *SALit* 14 (1978): 49-60.

Noon, William T., "Three Young Men in Rebellion," *Thought* 38 (Winter, 1963): 571-7.

O'Hara, J. D., "No Catcher in the Rye," *MFS* 9 (Winter, 1963-64): 370-6. Also in Westbrook, M., ed., *Modern American Novel,* 211-20.

Ohmann, Carol, and Richard Ohmann, "Reviewers, Critics and THE CATCHER IN THE RYE," *CritI* 3 (Autumn, 1976): 15-37.

_____, "Universals and the Historically Particular," *CritI* 3 (Summer, 1099): 773-7. [Response to Miller above.]

Oldsey, Bernard S., "The Movies in the Rye," *CE* 23 (Dec., 1961): 209-15. Also in Belcher, W. F., and J. W. Lee, eds., *Salinger and the Critics,* 68-75. Also in Marsden, . M. M., ed., *If You Really Want to Know,* 116-22. Also in Simonson, H. P., and P. E. Hager, eds., *Salinger's CATCHER IN THE RYE,* 40-5. [See "Rebuttal" by Dexter Martin.]

Padovano, A., *Estranged God,* 139-49.

Parker, Christopher, "Why the Hell *Not* Smash All the Windows?" in Grunwald, H. A., ed., *Salinger,* 254-8.

Peavy, Charles D., "'Did You Ever Have a Sister?' Holden, Quentin, and Sexual Innocence," *FloQ* 1, iii (1968): 82-95.

_____, "Holden's Courage Again," *CEA* 28 (Oct., 1965): 1, 6, 9.

Pilkington, John, "About This Madman Stuff," *USME* 7 (1966): 65-75.

_____, "Mummies and Ducks," *USME* 6 (1965): 15-22.

Pomeranz, Regina E., "The Search for Self in the Adolescent Protagonist in the Contemporary Novel: A Method of Approach for the College Teacher of Literature," *DA* 27 (1966): 780A.

Rees, Richard, *Brave Men: A Study of D. H. Lawrence and Simone Weil,* Carbondale: Southern Ill. Un. Pr., 1959, 178-87; London: Victor Gollancz, 1958.

Reiman, Donald H., "Rebuttal" to Peter Seng, "The Fallen Idol: Holden Caulfield," *CE* 23 (Mar., 1962): 507. Also in Marsden, M. M., ed., *If You Really Want to Know,* 82. Also in Simonson, H. P., and P. E. Hager, eds., *Salinger's CATCHER IN THE RYE,* 72-3.

_____, "Salinger's THE CATCHER IN THE RYE," *Expl* 22 (Mar., 1963): Item 58.

Roper, Pamela E., "Holden's Hat," *NConL* 7, iii (May, 1977): 8-9.

Roberts, Preston T., Jr., "THE CATCHER IN THE RYE Revisited," *Cresset* 40, i-ii (Nov./Dec., 1977): 6-10.

Rosen, Gerald, "A Retrospective Look at THE CATCHER IN THE RYE," *AQ* 29 (1977): 547-62.

_____, *Zen in the Art of J. D. Salinger.*

Rupp, Richard H., "J. D. Salinger: A Solitary Liturgy," *Celebration in Postwar American Fiction,* 114-18.

Saha, Winifred M., "J. D. Salinger: The Younger Writer in Society," Master's Thesis, Divinity School, Un. of Chicago, June, 1957. Also (selection) in Marsden, M. M., ed., *If You Really Want to Know,* 28-9.

Schrader, Allen, "Emerson to Salinger to Parker," *SatR* 42 (Apr. 11, 1959): 52+. Also in Simonson, H. P., and P. E. Hager, eds., *Salinger's CATCHER IN THE RYE*, 106-8.

Scott, Nathan A., Jr., *Modern Literature and the Religious Frontier*, N.Y.: Harper, 1958, 90-4.

Seng, Peter J., "The Fallen Idol: The Immature World of Holden Caulfield," *CE* 23 (Dec., 1961): 203-9. Also in Belcher, W. F., and J. W. Lee, eds., *J. D. Salinger and the Critics*, 60-8. Also in Marsden, M. M., ed., *If You Really Want to Know*, 55-62. Also in Simonson, H. P., and P. E. Hager, eds., *Salinger's CATCHER IN THE RYE*, 65-71. [See rebuttals by Barry A. Marks and Dexter Martin.]

Severin-Lounsberry, Barbara, "Holden and Alex: A Clockwork from the Rye?" *FQ* 22 (Summer, 1973): 27-37.

Sherr, Paul C., "THE CATCHER IN THE RYE and the Boarding School," *ISB* 26, ii (1966): 42-54.

Skovmand, Steffen, in Bogh, J., and S. Skovmand, eds., *Six American Novels*, 151-79.

Slabey, Robert M., THE CATCHER IN THE RYE: Christian Theme and Symbol," *CLAJ* 6 (Mar., 1963): 170-83.

_____, "Salinger's 'Casino': Wayfarers and Spiritual Acrobats," *EngR* 14, iii (Feb., 1964): 16-20 *passim*.

Smith, Harrison, "Manhattan Ulysses, Junior," *SatR* 34 (July 14, 1951): 12-13. Also in Simonson, H. P., and P. E. Hager, eds., *Salinger's CATCHER IN THE RYE*, 2-3.

Spanier, Sandra W., "Hemingway's 'The Last Good Country' and THE CATCHER IN THE RYE: More Than a Family Resemblance," *SSF* 19, i (Winter, 1982): 35-43.

Stevenson, David, "J. D. Salinger: The Mirror of Crisis," *Nation* 184 (Mar. 9, 1957): 216-17. Also in Belcher, W. F., and J. W. Lee, eds., *Salinger and the Critics*, 139-41. Also in Grunwald, H. A., ed., *Salinger*, 39-41. Also in Grunwald, H. A., ed., *Salinger*, 39-41. Also in Marsden, M. M., ed., *If You Really Want to Know*, 24-5. Also in *Nation* (Periodical). *View of the Nation*, 59-60.

Stone, Edward, "Salinger's Carrousel," *MFS* 13 (Winter, 1967-68): 520-3.

Strauch, Carl F., "Kings in the Back Row: Meaning Through Structure—A Reading of J. D. Salinger's THE CATCHER IN THE RYE," *WSCL* 2 (Winter, 1961): 5-30. Also in Belcher, W. F., and J. W. Lee, eds., *J. D. Salinger and the Critics*, 76-98. Also in Laser, M., and N. Fruman, eds., *Studies in J. D. Salinger*, 143-71. Also in Marsden, M. M., ed., *If You Really Want to Know*, 99-116. Also in Simonson, H. P., and P. E. Hager, eds., *Salinger's CATCHER IN THE RYE*, 46-62.

_____, "Salinger: The Romantic Background," *WSCL* 4, i (Winter, 1963): 31-40.

Tanner, T., *Reign of Wonder*, 341-3.

Tarinya, M., "Salinger: THE CATCHER IN THE RYE," *LHY* 7 (July, 1966): 49-60.

Tink, Stanley, "Initiation In and Out: The American Novel and the American Dream," *Quadrant* 5, iii [No. 19] (Winter, 1961): 63-74.

Tirumalai, Canadadai K., "Salinger's THE CATCHER IN THE RYE," *Expl* 22 (Mar., 1964): Item 56.

Travis, Mildred K., "Salinger's THE CATCHER IN THE RYE," *Expl* 21 (Dec., 1962): Item 36.

Trowbridge, Clinton W., "Hamlet and Holden," *EJ* 57 (Jan., 1968): 26-9.

_____, "Salinger's Symbolic Use of Character and Detail in THE CATCHER IN THE RYE," *CimR* 4 (June, 1968): 5-11.

_____, "The Symbolic Structure of THE CATCHER IN THE RYE," *SR* 74 (Summer, 1966): 681-93.

Vail, Dennis, "Holden and Psychoanalysis," *PMLA* 91 (Jan., 1976): 432-57.

Vanderbilt, Kermit, "Symbolic Resolution in THE CATCHER IN THE RYE: The Cap, the Carrousel, and the American West," *WHR* 17 (Summer, 1963): 271-7.

Wakefield, Dan, "Salinger and the Search for Love," in *New World Writing*, No. 14, N.Y.: New American Library, 1958, 72-5. Also in Laser, M., and N. Fruman, eds., *Studies in J. D. Salinger*, 77-84. Also (selection) in Marsden, M. M., ed., *If You Really Want to Know*, 52-4.

Walcutt, C. C. *Man's Changing Mask*, 317-26.

Walzer, Michael, "In Place of a Hero," *Dissent* 7 (Spring, 1960): 156-9.

Warner, Deane M., "Huck and Holden," *CEA* 27 (Mar., 1965): 4a-4b.

Way, Brian, "FRANNY AND ZOOEY and J. D. Salinger," *New Left Rev* (May-June, 1962): 74-82. Also in Laser, M., and N. Fruman, eds., *Studies in J. D. Salinger*, 190-201.

Weber, Donald, "Narrative Method in A SEPARATE PEACE," *SSF* 3 (Fall, 1965): 63-72.

Wells, Arvin R., "Huck Finn and Holden Caulfield: The Situation of the Hero," *OUR* 2 (1960): 31-42. Also in Marsden, M. M., ed., *If You Really Want to Know*, 144-51.

Widmer, K., *Literary Rebel*, 127-8.

Weinberg, H., *New Novel in America*, 143-7.

Wiegand, William, "J. D. Salinger: Seventy-Eight Bananas," *ChiR* 11 (Winter, 1958): 3-19. Also (condensed) in Marsden, M. M., ed., *If You Really Want to Know*, 48-52.

Wiener, Gary A., "From Huck to Holden to Bromden: The Nonconformist in ONE FLEW OVER THE CUCKOO'S NEST," *StHum* 7, ii (1979): 21-6.

BIBLIOGRAPHY

Beebe, Maurice, and Jennifer Sperry, "Criticism of J. D. Salinger; A Selected Checklist," *MFS* 12 (Autumn, 1966): 377-90.

Fiene, Donald M., "J. D. Salinger: A Bibliography," *WSCL* 4, i (Winter, 1963): 109-49.

Galloway, D. D. *Absurd Hero*, 234-51.

Simonson, H. P., and P. E. Hager, eds., *Salinger's CATCHER IN THE RYE*, 110-11.

SALTER, JAMES, 1925-

GENERAL

Miller, Margaret W., "Glimpses of a Secular Holy Land: The Novels of James Salter," *HC* 19, i (Feb., 1982): 1-13.

LIGHT YEARS

Miller, Margaret W., "Glimpses of a Secular Holy Land: The Novels of James Slater," *HC* 1, i (Feb., 1982): 7-11.

SOLO FACES

Dowie, William, "SOLO FACES: American Tradition and the Individual Talent," 118-28 in Singer, Armand, E., ed., *Essays on the Literature of Mountaineering*, Morgantown, West Virginia Un. Pr., 1982.

Miller, Margaret W., "Glimpses of a Secular Holy Land: The Novels of James Slater," *HC* 19, i (Feb., 1982): 11-13.

A SPORT AND A PASTIME

Miller, Margaret W., "Glimpses of a Secular Holy Land: The Novels of James Salter," *HC* 19, i (Feb. 1982): 4-7.

SANCHEZ, THOMAS, 1944-

RABBIT BOSS

Gevder, P. A., "Language and Ethnic Interaction in RABBIT BOSS: A Novel by Thomas Sanchez," 173-7, in Giles, Howard, and Bernard Saint-Jacques, eds., *Language and Ethnic Relations*, Oxford: Pergamon, 1979.

SANDOZ, MARI (SUZETTE), 1901-1966

GENERAL

Greenwell, Scott L., "Fascists in Fiction: Two Early Novels of Mari Sandoz," *WAL* 12, ii (Aug., 1977): 133-43.
Rice, Minnie C., "Mari Sandoz: Biographer in the Old West," *MidR* (Spring, 1960): 44-9.
Stauffer, Helen, "Local Color: Mari Sandoz and the Prairie," *MMisc* 3 (1975): 18-23.
Walton, Kathleen O'D., "Mari Sandoz: An Initial Critical Appraisal," *DAI* 32 (1971): 461A.

CAPITAL CITY

Greenwell, Scott L., "Fascists in Fiction: Two Early Novels of Mari Sandoz," *WAL* 12, ii (Aug., 1977): 141-3.
Mattern, Claire, "Mari Sandoz and CAPITAL CITY: The Writer and Her Book," *BForum* 6, ii (1982): 223-32.

MISS MORISSA: A DOCTOR OF THE GOLD TRAIL

Morton, Beatrice K., "A Critical Appraisal of Mari Sandoz' MISS MORISSA: Modern Woman on the Western Frontier," *Heritage of Kansas: Jnl. of the Great Plains* 10 (Fall, 1977): 37-45.

SLOGUM CITY

Greenwell, Scott L., "Fascists in Fiction: Two Early Novels of Mari Sandoz," *WAL* 12, ii (Aug., 1977): 138-41.
Mattern, Claire, "Mari Sandoz: Her Use of Allegory in SLOGUM HOUSE," *DAI* 42 (1981): 2677A.
Whitaker, Rosemary, "Violence in OLD JULES and SLOGUM HOUSE," *WAL* 16, iii (Nov., 1981): 217-24.

BIBLIOGRAPHY

Whitaker, Rosemary, and Myra J. Moon, "A Bibliography of Works by and about Mari Sandoz," *BB* 38, ii (Apr.-June, 1981): 82-91.

SANSOM, WILLIAM, 1912-

GENERAL

Karl, F. R., *Contemporary English Novel*, 285-7.

Mellors, John, "William Sansom: Voyageur, Voyeur, Virtuoso," *LonM* 14, v (1974-75): 128-32.
Vickery, John B., "William Sansom and Logical Empiricism," *Thought* 36 (Summer, 1961): 231-45.

A BED OF ROSES

Michel-Michot, P., *William Sansom*, 281-92.

THE BODY

Allen, W., *Modern Novel*, 268-9.
Michel-Michot, P., *William Sansom*, 248-71.

THE CAUTIOUS HEART

Michel-Michot, P., *William Sansom*, 313-29.

THE FACE OF INNOCENCE

Michel-Michot, P., *William Sansom*, 272-80.

GOODBYE

Michel-Michot, P., *William Sansom*, 351-71.

THE LAST HOURS OF SANDRA LEE

Michel-Michot, P., *William Sansom*, 30-50.

THE LOVING EYE

Michel-Michot, P., *William Sansom*, 293-312.

SARGESON, FRANK, 1903-1982

GENERAL

Beveridge, Michael, "Conversations with Frank Sargeson," *Landfall* 24, i (Mar., 1970): 4-27; Part II: 24, ii (June, 1970): 142-60.
Copland, R. A., *Frank Sargeson*.
_____, "The Goodly Roof: Some Comments on the Fiction of Frank Sargeson," *Landfall* 22, iii (Sept., 1968): 310-23. Also in Curnow, Wystan, ed., *Essays on New Zealand Literature*, Auckland: Heinemann, 1973, 43-53.
Dresing, H., "New Zealand Society in the Imaginative Writings of Frank Sargeson," *DAI* 42, ii (Aug., 1981): 1546C.
Durix, Jean-Pierre, "An Interview with Frank Sargeson," *CE&S* 3 (1977-78): 49-54.
Finlayson, Roderick, et al., "Frank Sargeson, 1903-1982," *Landfall* 36 (1982): 207-17.
Jones, Lawrence, "Once is Not Enough: On Re-Reading Sargeson," *Islands* 6 (1978): 268-72.
Martin, Murray S., "Speaking through the Inarticulate: The Art of Frank Sargeson," *JGE* 33, ii (Summer, 1981): 123-34.
McNaughton, Howard, "In the Sargeson World," *Landfall* 24, i (Mar., 1970): 39-43.
Reid, Tony, "The Word is Liberating," *NZListener* 78, 1843 (1975): 28-9. [Not seen.]
Rhodes, H. W., *Frank Sargeson*.
Shaw, Helen, "Discovering Sargeson," *Islands* 6 (1978): 231-4.

A GAME OF HIDE AND SEEK

Copland, R. A., *Frank Sargeson*, 40-3.

THE HANGOVER

Copland, R. A., *Frank Sargeson*, 35-6.
Rhodes, H. W., *Frank Sargeson*, 163-6.

I FOR ONE

Copland, R. A., *Frank Sargeson*, 25-7.
Rhodes, H. W., *Frank Sargeson*, 116-31.

I SAW MY DREAM

Copland, R. A., *Frank Sargeson*, 21-3.
King, B., *New English Literature*, 149-56.
New, W. H., "Enclosures: Frank Sargeson's I SAW IN MY DREAM," *WLWE* 14 (1975): 15-22.
Rhodes, H. W., *Frank Sargeson*, 95-9, 108-15.

JOY OF THE WORM

Copland, R. A., *Frank Sargeson*, 36-8.

MAN OF ENGLAND NOW

Copland, R. A. *Frank Sargeson*, 38-40.

MEMOIRS OF A PEON

Copland, R. A., *Frank Sargeson*, 31-5.
_____, "Frank Sargeson: MEMOIRS OF A PEON," in Hankin, C., ed., *Critical Essays on the New Zealand Novel*, 128-39.
Ower, J. B., "Wizard's Brew: Frank Sargeson's MEMOIRS OF A PEON," *Landfall* 26 (Dec., 1972): 308-21.
Rhodes, R. A., *Frank Sargeson*, 150-62.

WHEN THE WIND BLOWS

Copland, R. A., *Frank Sargeson*, 19-21.
Rhodes, H. W., *Frank Sargeson*, 99-108.

BIBLIOGRAPHY

Copland, R. A., *Frank Sargeson*, 46-7.
Rhodes, H. W., *Frank Sargeson*, 176-8.

SAROYAN, WILLIAM, 1908-1981

GENERAL

Balayan, Zori, "'Argument for Soviet Power...'," *SovL* 12 (1977): 159-66.[Interview.]
Fisher, William J., "Whatever Happened to Saroyan," *CE* 16 (Mar., 1955): 336-40. Also in *EJ* 44 (Mar., 1955): 129-34.
Floan, H. R., *William Saroyan*.
Krickel, Edward, "Cozzens and Saroyan: A Look at Two Reputations," *GaR* 24, iii (Fall, 1970): 281-96.
Schulberg, Budd, "Saroyan: Ease and Unease on the Flying Trapeze," *Esquire* 54, iv (Oct., 1960): 85-91.

Stern, Elaine M., "The Conservative Response amidst Decades of Change: Jack Kerouac and William Saroyan," *DAI* 37 (1977): 7755A.
Tsujimoto, Ichiro, "William Saroyan, An Improvisator," *KAL* 2 (May, 1959): 12-16. [Not seen.]
VanGelder, Robert, *Writers on Writing*, 29-30.

THE ADVENTURES OF WESLEY JACKSON

Floan, H. R., *William Saroyan*, 126-9.
Wilson, Edmund, "William Saroyan and His Darling Old Province," *NY* 22 (June 15, 1946): 76-8. Also in Wilson, E., *Classics and Commercials*, 327-30.

THE HUMAN COMEDY

Burgum, Edwin B., "Lonesome Young Man on the Flying Trapeze," *VQR* 20 (Summer, 1944): 392-402. Also in Burgum, E. B., *Novel and the World's Dilemma*, 269-71.
Carpenter, Frederic I., "The Time of William Saroyan's Life," *PacSp* 1 (Winter, 1947): 88-96. Also in Carpenter, F. I., *American Literature and the Dream*, 176-84.
Floan, H. R., *William Saroyan*, 123-6.
Gray, J., *On Second Thought*, 114-15.

THE LAUGHING MATTER

Floan, H. R., *William Saroyan*, 138-43.

ROCK WAGRAM

Floan, H. R., *William Saroyan*, 134-7.
Sarkisian, Levon, "Saroyan's ROCK WAGRAM: A Psycho-Social Character," *Armenian Rev* 11 (1959): 61-8.

TRACY'S TIGER

Floan, H. R., *William Saroyan*, 137-8.

BIBLIOGRAPHY

Floan, H. R., *William Saroyan*, 164-7.

SARTON, MAY, 1912-1995

GENERAL

Anderson, Dawn H., "May Sarton's Women," in Cornillon, S. K., ed., *Images of Women in Fiction*, 243-50.
Bakerman, Jane S., "'Kinds of Love': Love and Friendship in Novels of May Sarton," *Crit* 20, ii (1978): 83-91. Also in Hunting, C., ed., *May Sarton*, 113-22.
Bryan, Mary, "Rage for Justice: Political, Social and Moral Consciousness in Selected Novels of May Sarton," in Hunting, C., ed., *May Sarton*, 133-44.
Funck, Susana B., "The Finely Woven Web of Interaction: Human Relationships in the Novels of May Sarton," *DAI* 43 (1982): 2348A.
Gaskill, Gayle, "Redefinitions of Traditional Christian Emblems and Outlooks in May Sarton's Novels of 1970-1975," in Hunting, C., ed., *May Sarton*, 157-69.
Hunting, C., ed., *May Sarton*.
Lydon, Mary, "A French View of May Sarton," in Hunting, C., ed., *May Sarton*, 71-7.

Nishimura, Kyoko, "May Sarton's World," *KAL* (June, 1979): 35-71.

Putney, Paula G., "Sister of the Mirage and Echo: An Interview with May Sarton," *Contempora* 2, iii (1972): 1-6.

Shaw, Sheila, "Living Rooms: Amity in the Novels of May Sarton," in Hunting, C., ed., *May Sarton,* 101-11.

Shelley, Dolores, "A Conversation with May Sarton," *W&L* 7, ii (1979): 33-41.

Sibley, A., *May Sarton.*

Springer, Marlene, "As We Shall Be: May Sarton and Aging," *Frontiers* 5, iii (Fall, 1980): 46-9.

Thyng, Deborah, "'The Actions of the Beautiful': The Concept of Balance in the Writings of May Sarton," in Hunting, C., ed., *May Sarton,* 79-84.

Woodward, Kathleen, "May Sarton and the Fiction of Old Age," *W&L* 1 (1980): 108-27.

AS WE ARE NOW

Bakerman, Jane S., "Perimeters of Powers: An Examination of AS WE ARE NOW," *ROO* 4, iv (1979): 22-33. Also in Hunting, C., ed., *May Sarton,* 145-56.

Bryan, Mary, "Rage for Justice: Political, Social and Moral Consciousness in Selected Novels of May Sarton," in Hunting, C., ed., *May Sarton,* 141-5.

Nishimura, Kyoko, "May Sarton's World," *KAL* 20 (June, 1979): 37-40.

THE BIRTH OF A GRANDFATHER

Sibley, A., *May Sarton,* 115-22.

THE BRIDGE OF YEARS

Bryan, Mary, "Rage for Justice: Political, Social and Moral Consciousness in Selected Novels of May Sarton," in Hunting, C., ed., *May Sarton,* 133-7.

Clewett, Barbara J., "Creativity and the Diamonic in Mann's DOCTOR FAUSTUS and Two Sarton Novels," *DAI* 43 (1982): 1967A.

Sibley, A., *May Sarton,* 74-86.

CRUCIAL CONVERSATIONS

Gaskill, Gayle, "Redefinitions of Traditional Christian Emblems and Outlooks in May Sarton's Novels of 1970-1975," in Hunting, C., ed., *May Sarton,* 161-9.

Hoffman, Nancy Y., "Sartonalia: Signposts and Destinations," *SWR* 62, iii (Summer, 1977): 258-67.

FAITHFUL ARE THE WOUNDS

Bryan, Mary, "Rage for Justice: Political, Social and Moral Consciousness in Selected Novels of May Sarton," in Hunting, C, ed., *May Sarton,* 137-41.

Sibley, A., *May Sarton,* 104-15.

JOANNA AND ULYSSES

Anderson, Dawn, "May Sarton's Women," in Cornillon, S. K., ed., *Images of Women in Fiction,* 246-7.

Sibley, A., *May Sarton,* 131-3.

KINDS OF LOVE

Gaskill, Gayle, "Redefinitions of Traditional Christian Emblems and Outlooks in May Sarton's Novels of 1970-1975," in Hunting, C., ed., *May Sarton,* 157-69 *passim.*

Sibley, A., *May Sarton,* 137-43.

MISS PICKTHORN AND MR. HARE

Sibley, A., *May Sarton,* 133-6.

MRS. STEVENS HEARS THE MERMAIDS SINGING

Anderson, Dawn, "May Sarton's Women," in Cornillon, S. K., ed., *Images of Women in Fiction,* 244-6.

Clewett, Barbara J., "Creativity and the Diamonic in Mann's DOCTOR FAUSTUS and Two Sarton Novels," *DAI* 43 (1982): 1967A.

Eder, Doris L., "Woman Writer: May Sarton's MRS. STEVENS HEARS THE MERMAIDS SINGING," *IJWS* 1 (1978): 150-8.

Nichols, Mariana da Vinci, "Women on Women," *DQ* 11, iii (Autumn, 1976): 1-13.

Sibley, A., *May Sarton,* 57-61.

Stewart, Grace, "Mother, Daughter, and the Birth of the Female Artist," *WS* 6, ii (1979): 127-45.

_____, *New Mythos,* 97-102, 152-7.

THE POET AND THE DONKEY

Sibley, A., *May Sarton,* 136-7.

SHADOW OF A MAN

Sibley, A., *May Sarton,* 86-93.

A SHOWER OF SUMMER DAYS

Sibley, A., *May Sarton,* 93-103.

THE SINGLE HOUND

Creange, Renée, "The Country of the Imagination," in Hunting, C., ed., *May Sarton,* 85-99.

Sibley, A., *May Sarton,* 67-74.

THE SMALL ROOM

Anderson, Dawn S., "May Sarton's Women," in Cornillon, S. K., ed., *Images of Women in Fiction,* 247-50.

Bakerman, Jane S., "May Sarton's THE SMALL ROOM: A Comparison and Analysis," *Crysallis* 1, i (Summer, 1975): 123-32.

Sibley, A., *May Sarton,* 123-30.

BIBLIOGRAPHY

Blouin, Leonora P., *May Sarton: A Bibliography,* Metuchen, N.J.: Scarecrow Pr., 1978.

_____, "A Revised Bibliography," in Hunting, C., ed., *May Sarton,* 283-319.

SCHAEFFER, SUSAN FROMBERG, 1941-

GENERAL

Schaeffer, Susan Fromberg, "The Unreality of Realism," *CritI* 6 (Summer, 1980): 727-37.

ANYA

Mintz, Jacqueline A., "The Myth of the Jewish Mother in Three Jewish, American, Female Writers," *CentR* 22, iii (1978): 352-5.

FALLING

Avery, Evelyn G., "Tradition and Independence in Jewish Feminist Novels," *MELUS* 7, iv (1980): 53-5.

SCHMITT, GLADYS, 1909-1972

GENERAL

Brostoff, Anita, "Five Heroines: A Persistant Image," in Brostoff, A., ed., *I Could Be Mute,* 104-29.
_____, ed., *I Could Be Mute.*
Cohn, Jan, "The Historical Novel," in Brostoff, A., ed., *I Could Be Mute,* 93-103.
Fuller, Edmund, "Gladys Schmitt: Jacob and the Angel," *ASch* 30, iii (Summer, 1961): 411-17.
McCorduck, Pamela, "Means and Extremes: The Woman Writer," in Brostoff, A., ed., *I Could Be Mute,* 72-82.

ALEXANDRA

Brostoff, Anita, "Five Heroines: A Persistent Image," in Brostoff, A., ed., *I Could Be Mute,* 114-17.

ELECTRA

Brostoff, Anita, "Five Heroines: A Persistent Image," in Brostoff, A., ed., *I Could Be Mute,* 117-23.

THE GATES OF AULIS

Brostoff, Anita, "Five Heroines: A Persistent Image," in Brostoff, A., ed., *I Could Be Mute,* 106-10.
Fuller, Edmund, "Gladys Schmitt: Jacob and the Angel," *ASch* 30, iii (Summer, 1961): 412-14.

THE GODFORGOTTEN

Brostoff, Anita, "Five Heroines: A Persistent Image," in Brostoff, A., ed., *I Could Be Mute,* 123-8.

SCHULBERG, BUDD WILSON, 1914-

GENERAL

Eisinger, C. E., *Fiction of the Forties,* 103-6.
Van Gelder, Robert, *Writers on Writing,* 197-200.

THE DISENCHANTED

Connolly, C., *Previous Convictions,* 299-301.

Farr, Finis, "In a Workmanlike Manner," *NatR* 6 (Apr. 11, 1959): 656-8.
Robinson, Jean J., "Henry James and Schulberg's THE DISENCHANTED," *MLN* 67 (Nov., 1952): 472-3.

WHAT MAKES SAMMY RUN?

Sherman, R., *Invention of the Jew,* 176-8.
Wells, W., *Tycoons and Locusts,* 86-102.

SCOTT, PAUL, 1920-1978

GENERAL

Rao, K. B., *Paul Scott.*
Ringold, Francine, "A Conversation with Paul Scott," *Nimrod* 21, i (1976): 16-32.
Swinden, P., *Paul Scott*

THE ALIEN SKY

Rao, K. B., *Paul Scott,* 43-7.
Swinden, P., *Paul Scott,* 19-25.

THE BENDER: PICTURES FROM AN EXHIBITION OF MIDDLE CLASS PORTRAITS

Rao, K. B., *Paul Scott,* 29-33.

THE BIRDS OF PARADISE

Rao, K. B., *Paul Scott,* 56-62.
Swinden, P., *Paul Scott,* 47-57.

THE CHINESE LOVE PAVILION (THE LOVE PAVILION)

Rao, K. B., *Paul Scott,* 47-52.
Swinden, P., *Paul Scott,* 41-7.

THE CORRIDA AT SAN FELIU

Rao, K. B., *Paul Scott,* 34-42.
Swinden, P., *Paul Scott,* 57-64.

THE DAY OF THE SCORPION (See also THE RAJ QUARTET)

Appasamy, S. P., "The Withdrawal: A Survey of Paul Scott's Trilogy of Novels on India," in Menon, K. P. K., et al., eds., *Literary Studies,* 63-5.
Rao, K. B., *Paul Scott,* 74-82.
Swinden, P., *Paul Scott,* 67-9, 87-90.

A DIVISION OF THE SPOILS (See also THE RAJ QUARTET)

Rao, K. B., *Paul Scott,* 88-96.
Swinden, P., *Paul Scott,* 70-2.

THE JEWEL IN THE CROWN (See also THE RAJ QUARTET)

Appasamy, S. P., "The Withdrawal: A Survey of Paul Scott's Trilogy of Novels on India," in Menon, K. P. K., et al., eds., *Literary Studies,* 61-3.
Rao, K. B., *Paul Scott,* 64-74.
Swinden, P., *Paul Scott,* 79-83.

THE LOVE PAVILION (See THE CHINESE LOVE PAVILON)

JOHNNIE SAHIB

Rao, K. B., *Paul Scott*, 21-4.
Swinden, P., *Paul Scott*, 11-19.

A MALE CHILD

Swinden, P., *Paul Scott*, 25-30.

THE MARK OF THE WARRIOR

Rao, K. B., *Paul Scott*, 52-5.
Swinden, P., *Paul Scott*, 30-40.

THE RAJ QUARTET

Appasamy, S. P., "The Withdrawal: A Survey of Paul Scott's Trilogy of Novels of India," in Menon, K.P.K., et al., eds., *Literary Studies*, 58-69.
Beloff, Max, "The End of the Raj: Paul Scott's Novels as History," *Encounter* 46, v (May, 1976): 65-70.
Burjorjee, D. M., "THE RAJ QUARTET: A Literary Event," *The New Quarterly* 2, ii (1977): 121-8.
James, Richard R., "In the Steps of Paul Scott," *Listener* 101 (Mar. 8, 1979): 359-61.
Narayanan, Gomathi, "Paul Scott's 'Indian Quartet': The Story of a Rape." *LCrit* 13, iv (1978): 44-58.
Parry, Benita, "Paul Scott's Raj," *SARev* 8, iii (July-Oct., 1975): 359-65.
Pollard, Arthur, "Twilight of Empire: Paul Scott's RAJ QUARTET," in Massa, D., ed., *Individual and Community in Commonwealth Literature*, 169-76.
Rao, K. B., *Paul Scott*, 63-104.
Shahane, Vasant A., "Kipling, Forster and Paul Scott: A Study of Sociological Imagination," in Rizvi, S.N.A., ed., *Twofold Voice*, 195-208 *passim*.
Swinden, P., *Paul Scott*, 65-10.
Winbaum, Francine S., "Aspiration and Betrayal in Paul Scott's THE RAJ QUARTET," *DAI* 37 (1977): 6481A.
_____, "Paul Scott's India: THE RAJ QUARTET," *Crit* 20, i (1978): 100-10.
_____, "Psychological Defenses and Thwarted Union in THE RAJ QUARTET," *L&P* 31, ii (1981): 75-87.
Woodcock, George, "The Sometime Sahibs: The Post-Independence British Novelists of India," *QQ* 86, i (Spring, 1979): 45-9.

STAYING ON

Gooneratne, Yasmine, "Paul Scott's STAYING ON: Finale in a Minor Key," *JIWE* 9, ii (July, 1981): 1-12.
Rao, K. B., *Paul Scott*, 135-44.
Swinden, P., *Paul Scott*, 103-18.

THE TOWERS OF SILENCE (See also THE RAJ QUARTET)

Appasamy, S. P., "The Withdrawal: A Survey of Paul Scott's Trilogy of Novels on India," in Menon, K.P.P., et al., eds., *Literary Studies*, 65-7.
Rao, K. B., *Paul Scott*, 82-8.
Swinden, P., *Paul Scott*, 69-70.

SEAGER, ALLAN, 1906-1968

GENERAL

Bloom, Robert, "Allan Seager" Some Versions of Disengagement," *Crit* 5, iii (Winter, 1962-63), 4-26.
Connelly, Steven E., "Allan Seager: The Man and the Novels," *DAI* 37 (1976): 2178A.
Hanna, Allan, "The Muse of History: Allan Seager and the Criticism of Culture," *Crit* 5, iii (Winter, 1962-63): 37-61.
Kenner, Hugh, "The Insider," *Crit* 2 (Winter, 1959): 3-15.
Lid, R. W., "The Innocent Eye," *Crit* 5, iii (Winter, 1962-63): 62-74.
Webster, Harvey C., "Allan Seager as Social Novelist," *Crit* 5, iii (Winter, 1962-63): 27-36.

AMOS BERRY

Barrows, Herbert, in *MAQR* 59 (Summer, 1953): 364-6.
Hanna, Allen, "The Muse of History: Allan Seager and the Criticism of Culture," *Crit* 5, iii (Winter, 1962-63): 51-4.
Lid, R. W., "The Innocent Eye," *Crit* 5, iii (Winter, 1962-63): 62-7.
Miles, George, "Some Tired Businessmen," *Cweal* 57 (Mar. 20, 1953): 607-8.
Webster, Harvey C., "Allan Seager as Social Novelist," *Crit* 5, iii (Winter, 1962-63): 33-4.

DEATH OF ANGER

Bloom, Robert, "Allan Seager: Some Versions of Disenchantment," *Crit* 5, iii (Winter, 1962-63): 11-16.

EQUINOX

Bloom, Robert, "Allan Seager: Some Versions of Disengagement," *Crit* 5, iii (Winter, 1962-63): 4-8.
Lid, R. W., "The Innocent Eye," *Crit* 5, iii (Winter, 1962-63): 67-72.
Webster, Harvey C., "Allan Seager as Social Novelist," *Crit* 5, iii (Winter, 1962-63): 30-2.

HILDA MANNING

O'Neill, James C., "Madame Bovary in Michigan?" *MAQR* 63 (Winter, 1957): 178-9.

THE INHERITANCE

Bloom, Robert, "Allan Seager: Some Versions of Disengagement," *Crit* 5, iii (Winter, 1962-63): 16-22.
Gehmann, Richard B., "The Ogre of a Small Town," *SatR* 31 (Apr. 24, 1948): 17-18.
Webster, Harvey C., "Allan Seager as Social Novelist," *Crit* 5, iii (Winter, 1962-63): 32-3.
Williams, Mentor L., in *MAQR* 54 (Summer, 1948): 371-2.

BIBLIOGRAPHY

Hanna, Allan, "An Allan Seager Bibliography," *Crit* 5, iii (Winter, 1962-63): 73-90.

SEGAL, ERICH (WOLF), 1937-

LOVE STORY

Berk, Philip R., "LOVE STORY and the Myth of Hippolytus," *CBull* 48 (Feb., 1972): 52-4.

Kirby, David K., and Eugene J. Cook, "LOVE STORY and the Erotic Connection in Literature," *NConL* 1, v (Nov., 1971): 8-10.

Martí, Zaro P., "LOVE STORY; Lie Story," *RO* 31 (1972): 101-12.

Merry, Bruce, "Erich Segal's LOVE STORY: The Zero Degree of Language," *UWR* 7, ii (Spring, 1972): 37-48.

_____, "Spiritual Uplift and the Best Seller: Some Notes on Richard Bach's JONATHAN LIVINGSTON SEAGULL and Erich Segal's LOVE STORY," *LonM* 14, iii (1974): 80-95.

O'Connell, David, "LOVE STORY: A Twin Killing," *RS* 39 (1971): 223-7.

Park, Clara C., "As We Like It; How a Girl Can Be Smart and Still Popular," *ASch* 42, ii (Spring, 1973): 274-8.

Rodnitsky, Jerome L., "Mass Mourning: A Cultural Approach to LOVE STORY," *ILLQ* 38, i (1975): 5-10.

Seelye, John, "Hyperion to a Satyr: FAREWELL TO ARMS and LOVE STORY," *CollL* 6 (1979): 129-35.

Silhol, Robert, "LOVE STORY as a Metaphor of War: A Research on the Sociological Conditions of the Production of Literature," *RFEA* 9 (1980): 159-72.

Skorodenko V., "'Fiction' and Fiction," in Vroon, R., tr., *20th Century American Literature: A Soviet View*, 453-5.

Spilka, Mark, "Erich Segal as Little Nell, or the Real Meaning of LOVE STORY," *JPC* 5 (Spring, 1972): 782-98. See also *SoRA* 5 (Mar., 1972): 38-51.

Tharpe, Jac, "LOVE STORY: 'Redeeming Social Value'?" *SoQ* 10 (1971): 63-75.

SELBY, HUBERT, JR., 1928-

GENERAL

Binet, Roland, "The Mirror of Man," *RCF* 1, ii (Summer, 1981): 380-8.

Buckeye, Robert, "Some Preliminary Notes Towards a Study of Selby," *RCF* 1, ii (Summer, 1981): 374-5.

Lewis, Harry, "Some Things I Want to Say About Hubert Selby," *RCF* 1, ii (Summer, 1981): 413-15.

Metcalf, Paul, "Herman and Hubert: The Odd Couple," *RCF* 1, ii (Summer, 1981):364-9.

Mottram, Eric, "Free Like the Rest of Us: Violation and Despair in Hubert Selby's Novels," *RCF* 1, ii (Summer, 1981): 353-63.

O'Brien, John, "An Interview with Hubert Selby, Jr.," *RCF* 1, ii (Summer, 1981): 315-35.

_____, "Notes on Hubert Selby's Fiction," *par rapport* 1, ii (Summer, 1978): 101-6.

Stephens, Michael, "Hubert Selby, Jr.: The Poet of Prose Masters," *RCF* 1, ii (Summer, 1981): 389-97.

Wertime, Richard, "On the Questions of Style in Hubert Selby's Fiction," *RCF* 1, ii (Summer, 1981): 406-13.

THE DEMON

Binet, Roland, "The Mirror of Man," *RCF* 1, ii (Summer, 1981): 386-88.

Sorrentino, Gilbert, "The Art of Hubert Selby: 'Addenda 1981: After LAST EXIT TO BROOKLYN'," *RCF* 1, ii (Summer, 1981): 347-8.

LAST EXIT TO BROOKLYN

Binet, Roland, "The Mirror of Man," *RCF* 1, ii (Summer, 1981): 380-3.

Byrne, Jack, "Selby's Yahoos: The Brooklyn Breed: A Dialogue of the Mind with Itself," *RCF* 1, ii (Summer, 1981): 349-53.

Haneline, Douglas L., "The Swing of the Pendulum: Naturalism in Contemporary American Literature," *DAI* 39 (1978): 2272A-73A.

Hutchinson, Stuart, "All Havens Astern: Selby's LAST EXIT TO BROOKLYN," *LonM* 9, i (Apr., 1969): 22-34.

Kreutzer, Eberhard, "Hubert Selby's LAST EXIT TO BROOK-LYN: The Psychodynamics of Person and Place," *Amst* 22 (1977): 137-45.

Lane, James B., "Violence and Sex in the Post-War Popular Urban Novel: With Consideration of Harold Robbins's A STONE FOR DANNY FISHER and Hubert Selby, Jr.'s LAST EXIT TO BROOKLYN," *JPC* 8 (Fall, 1984): 302-6.

Peavy, Charles D., "Hubert Selby and Tradition of Moral Satire," *SNL* 6, ii (Spring, 1969): 35-9.

_____, "The Sin of Pride and Selby's LAST EXIT TO BROOK-LYN," *Crit* 11, iii (1969): 35-42.

Solotaroff, Theodore, "Hubert Selby's Kicks," *Red Hot Vacuum*, 165-70.

Sorrentino, Gilbert, "The Art of Hubert Selby," *RCF* 1, ii (Summer, 1981): 335-46. Originally in *Kulchur* (Spring, 1964).

Wertime, Richard A., "Psychic Vengeance in LAST EXIT TO BROOKLYN," *L&P* 24 (1974): 153-66.

Yurick, Sol, "Hubert Selby: Symbolic Intent and Ideological Resistance," *EvR* 13, lxxi (Oct., 1969): 49-51, 73-8.

REQUIEM FOR A DREAM

Atchity, Kenneth J., "Hubert Selby's REQUIEM FOR A DREAM: A Primer of Vision," *RCF* 1, ii (Summer, 1981): 399-405.

Tindall, Kenneth, "The Fishing at Coney Island: Hubert Selby, Jr., and the Cult of Authenticity," *RCF* 1, ii (Summer, 1981): 370-3.

THE ROOM

Binet, Roland, "Mirror of Man," *RCF* 1, ii (Summer, 1891): 383-6.

Mottram, Eric, "Free Like the Rest of Us: Violation and Despair in Hubert Selby's Novels," *RCF* 1, ii (Summer, 1981): 355-63 *passim*.

O'Brien, John, "The Materials of Art in Hubert Selby," *RCF* 1, ii (Summer, 1981): 376-9.

Sorrentino, Gilbert, "The Art of Hubert Selby: 'Addenda 1981: After LAST EXIT TO BROOKLYN'," *RCF* 1, ii (Summer, 1981): 346-7.

SELVON, SAMUEL (DICKSON), 1923-

GENERAL

Birbalsingh, Franj, "Samuel Selvon and the West Indian Literary Renaissance," *ArielE* 8, iii (July, 1977): 5-22.

Fabre, Michael, "From Trinidad to London: Tone and Language in Samuel Selvon's Novels," *LHY* 20, i (1979): 71-80.

_____, "Samuel Selvon," in King, B., *West Indian Literature,* 111-25.

_____, "Moses and the Queen's English: Dialect and Narrative Voice in Samuel Selvon's London Novels," *WLWE* 21 (1982): 385-92.

_____, "The Queen's Calypso: Linguistic and Narrative Strategies in the Fiction of Samuel Selvon," *CE&S* 3 (1977-78): 69-76.

Griffiths, G., *Double Exile,* 105-8.

Nazareth, Peter, "Interview with Sam Selvon," *WLWE* 18, ii (1979): 420-37.

_____, "The Clown in the Slave Ship," *Caribbean Quarterly* 23, ii-iii (June-Sept., 1977): 24-30.

Ramchand, Kenneth, "Sam Selvon Talking: A Conversation with Kenneth Ramchand," *CanL* 95 (Winter, 1982): 56-64.

A BRIGHTER SUN

Barratt, Harold, "Dialect, Maturity, and the Land in Sam Selvon's A BRIGHTER SUN: A Reply," *ESC* 7, iii (Fall, 1981): 329-37.

Birbalsingh, Frank, "Samuel Selvon and the West Indian Literary Renaissance," *ArielE* 8, iii (July, 1977): 6-13.

Davies, Barrie, "The Personal Sense of a Society—Minority View: Aspects of the 'East Indian' Novel in the West Indies," *SNNTS* 4, ii (Summer, 1972): 288-90.

Fabre, Michael, in King, B., ed., *West Indian Literature,* 111-14.

Macdonald, Bruce F., "Language and Consciousness in Samuel Selvon's A BRIGHTER SUN," *ESC* 5 (1979): 202-15.

THE LONELY LONDONER

Fabre, Michael, "From Trinidad to London: Tone and Language in Samuel Selvon's Novels," *LHY* 20, i (1979): 73-6.

_____, "Moses and the Queen's English: Dialect and Narrative Voice in Samuel Selvon's London Novels," *WLWE* 21, ii (Summer, 1982): 385-92.

_____, "The Queen's Calypso: Linguistic and Narrative Strategies in the Fiction of Samuel Selvon," *CE&S* 3 (1977-78): 70-3.

_____, "Samuel Selvon," in King, B., ed., *West Indian Literature,* 115-17.

Moore, G., *Chosen Tongue,* 101-5.

Nazareth, Peter, "The Clown in the Slave Ship," *Caribbean Quarterly* 23, ii-iii (June-Sept., 1977): 24-6.

Ramchand, K., "Song of Innocence, Song of Experience: Samuel Selvon's THE LONELY LONDONERS as a Literary Work," *WLWE* 21, iii (Autumn, 1982): 644-54.

MOSES ASCENDING

Baugh, Edward, "Friday in Crusoe's City: The Question of Language in Two West Indian Novels of Exile," *ACLALSB* 5, iii (1980): 1-12.

Fabre, Michael, "From Trinidad to London: Tone and Language in Samuel Selvon's Novels," *LHY* 20, i (1979): 77-9.

_____, "Moses and the Queen's English: Dialect and Narrative Voice in Samuel Selvon's London Novels," *WLWE* 21 (1982): 389-92.

_____, "The Queen's Calypso: Linguistics and Narrative Strategies in the Fiction of Samuel Selvon," *CE&S* 3 (1977-78): 74-6.

_____, "Samuel Selvon," in King, B., ed., *West Indian Literature,* 122-4.

Nazareth, Peter, "The Clown in the Slave Ship," *Caribbean Quarterly* 23, ii-iii (June-Sept., 1977): 26-9.

TURN AGAIN TIGER

Fabre, Michael, in King, B., ed., *West Indian Literature,* 117-20.

Ngugi, J., *Homecoming,* 99-102.

SETTLE, MARY LEE, 1918-

BEULAH LAND Trilogy

Garrett, George, in Madden, D., ed., *Rediscoveries,* 171-8.

BEULAH Quintet

Shafer, William J., "Mary Lee Settle's BEULAH Quintet: History Darkly, through a Single-Lens Reflex," *AppalJ* 10, i (Autumn, 1982): 77-86.

SHADBOLT, MAURICE (FRANCIS RICHARD), 1932-

GENERAL

Amoamo, Jacqueline, "Maurice Shadbolt: The Beginning Years," *NZ Listener* 70 (1979): 8-9. [Not seen.]

AMONG THE CINDERS

Simpson, Peter, "Shadbolt's First Novel: A Reassessment," *Landfall* 31 (1977): 1886-91.

STRANGERS AND JOURNEYS

Jones, Lawrence, "Ambition and Accomplishment in Maurice Shadbolt's STRANGERS AND JOURNEYS," in Hankin, C., ed., *Critical Essays on the New Zealand Novel,* 140-68.

A TOUCH OF CLAY

Holland, Patrick, "Water and Clay: Maurice Shadbolt's A TOUCH OF CLAY and Margaret Laurence's THE DIVINERS," *WLWE* 21 (1982): 268-74.

SHAW, IRWIN, 1913-1984

GENERAL

Evans, Bergen, "Irwin Shaw," *EJ* 40 (Nov., 1951): 485-91. Also in *CE* 13 (Nov., 1951): 71-7.

Fiedler, Leslie, "Irwin Shaw: Adultery, the Last Politics," *Ctary* 22 (July, 1956): 71-4.

Morris, Willie, and Lucas Matthiessen, "Irwin Shaw: The Art of Fiction IV," *ParisR* 75 (1979): 248-62.

Startt, William, "Irwin Shaw: An Extended Talent," *MQ* 2 (July, 1961): 325-7.

LUCY CROWN

Fiedler, Leslie, "Irwin Shaw: Adultery, the Last Politics," *Ctary* 22 (July, 1956): 71-4.

Startt, William, "Irwin Shaw: An Extended Talent," *MQ* 2 (July, 1961): 329-31.

THE TROUBLED AIR

Eisinger, C. E., *Fiction of the Forties*, 111-12.

Evans, Bergen, "Irwin Shaw," *EJ* 40 (Nov., 1951): 488-90. Also in *CE* 13 (Nov., 1951): 74-6.

Milne, G., *American Political Novel*, 150-1.

Startt, William, "Irwin Shaw: An Extended Talent," *MQ* 2 (July, 1961): 328-9.

TWO WEEKS IN ANOTHER TOWN

Startt, William, "Irwin Shaw: An Extended Talent," *MQ* 2 (July, 1961): 331-7.

THE YOUNG LIONS

Aldridge, J. W., *After the Lost Generation*, 147-56.

Eisinger, C. E., *Fiction of the Forties*, 111-12.

Evans, Bergen, "Irwin Shaw," *EJ* 40 (Nov., 1951): 486-8. Also in *CE* 13 (Nov., 1951): 72-4.

Giles, James R., "Irwin Shaw's Original Prologue to THE YOUNG LIONS," *RALS* 11, i (Spring, 1981): 115-19.

Glicksberg, Charles, "Anti-Semitism and Jewish Novelists," in Ribalow, H., ed., *Mid-Century*, 346-8.

Healey, Robert C., in Gardiner, H. C., ed., *Fifty Years of the American Novel*, 264-5.

Hoffman, F. J., *Mortal No*, 235-7.

Jones, P., *War and the Novelist*, 140-3.

Startt, William, "Irwin Shaw: An Extended Talent," *MQ* 2 (July, 1961): 326-8.

Waldmeir, J. J., *American Novels of the Second World War*, 92-101, 107-8, 149-52.

SHIELDS, CAROL, 1935-

SMALL CEREMONIES

MacDonald, Bruce F., "Quiet Manifesto: Carol Shields' SMALL CEREMONIES," *IFR* 3 (1976): 147-50.

Page, Malcolm, "SMALL CEREMONIES and the Art of the Novel," *JCF* 28-29 (1980): 172-8.

SHUTE, NEVIL (NEVIL SHUTE NORWAY), 1899-1960

GENERAL

Lammers, Donald, "Nevil Shute and the Decline of the 'Imperial Idea' in Literature," *JBrS* 16, ii (Spring, 1977): 121-42.

Martin, David, "The Mind That Conceived ON THE BEACH," *Meanjin* 19 (1960): 193-200.

Smith, Julian, "In Search of Nevil Shute," *The Courier* (Syracuse) 9, i (1971): 8-13.

_____, *Nevil Shute.*

BEYOND THE BLACK STUMP

Smith, J., *Nevil Shute*, 124-7.

THE CHEQUER BOARD

Smith, J., *Nevil Shute*, 71-8.

THE FAR COUNTRY

Smith, J., *Nevil Shute*, 105-9.

IN THE WET

Lammers, Donald, "Nevil Shute and the 'Imperial Idea' in Literature," *JBrS* 16, ii (Spring, 1977): 133-8.

Smith, J., *Nevil Shute*, 112-17.

LANDFALL

Smith, J., *Nevil Shute* 50-4.

LONELY ROAD

Smith, J., *Nevil Shute*, 33-7.

MARAZAN

Smith, J., *Nevil Shute*, 25-7.

MOST SECRET

Smith, J., *Nevil Shute*, 58-65.

NO HIGHWAY

Smith, J., *Nevil Shute*, 78-83.

AN OLD CAPTIVITY

Smith, J., *Nevil Shute*, 48-50.

ON THE BEACH

Martin, David, 'The Mind That Conceived on THE BEACH," *Meanjin* 19 (1960): 193-200 *passim.*

Smith, Julian, "On the Beach at Amchi..a: The Conversion of Nevil Shute," *SAQ* 72, i (Winter, 1973): 22-8.

_____, *Nevil Shute*, 124-34.

PASTORAL

Smith, J., *Nevil Shute*, 65-8.

PIED PIPER

Smith, J., *Nevil Shute*, 56-8.

THE RAINBOW AND THE ROSE

Smith, J., *Nevil Shute*, 135-8.

REQUIEM FOR A WREN (THE BREAKING WAVE)

Smith, J., *Nevil Shute*, 118-24.

ROUND THE BEND

Lammers, Donald, "Nevil Shute and the Decline of the 'Imperial Idea' in Literature," *JBrS* 16, ii (Spring, 1977): 128-33.
Smith, J., *Nevil Shute*, 88-95.

RUINED CITY (KINDLING)

Smith, J., *Nevil Shute*, 39-41.

SO DISDAINED (THE MYSTERIOUS AVIATOR)

Smith, J., *Nevil Shute*, 27-31.

A TOWN LIKE ALICE (THE LEGACY)

Smith, J., *Nevil Shute*, 96-103.

TRUSTEE FROM THE TOOLROOM

Smith, J., *Nevil Shute*, 139-43.

WHAT HAPPENED TO THE CORBETTS (ORDEAL)

Smith, J., *Nevil Shute*, 43-8.

SILKO, LESLIE MARMON, 1948-

GENERAL

Epsey, David B., "Ending in Contemporary Indian Fiction," *WAL* 13, ii (Aug., 1978): 133-9.
Evers, Larry, "A Response: Going Along with the Story," *AIQ* 5, i (Feb., 1979): 71-5.
Ruppert, Jim, "Story Telling: The Fiction of Leslie Silko," *JEthS* 9, i (Spring, 1981): 53-8.
Seyersted, P., *Leslie Marmon Silko*.
_____, "Two Interviews with Leslie Marmon Silko," *Amer. Studies in Scandinavia* 13 (1981): 17-33.

CEREMONY

Allen, Paula G., "The Psychological Landscape of Ceremony," *AIQ* 5, i (Feb., 1979): 7-12.
Beidler, Peter G., "Animals and Theme in CEREMONY," *AIQ* 5, i (Feb., 1979): 13-18.
Bell, Robert C., "Circular Design in CEREMONY," *AIQ* 5, i (Feb., 1979): 47-62.
Hoilman, Dennis, "'A World Made of Stories': An Interpretation of Leslie Silko's CEREMONY," *SDR* 17, iv (1979): 54-66.
Jahner, Elaine, "An Act of Attention: Events Structure in CEREMONY," *AIQ* 5, i (Feb., 1979): 37-46.
_____, "The Novel and Oral Tradition: An Interview with Leslie Marmon Silko," *BForum* 5, iii (1981): 383-8.
Larson, C. R., *American Indian Fiction*, 150-61.
Mitchell, Carol, "CEREMONY as Ritual," *AIQ* 5, i (Feb., 1979): 27-35.
Ruppert, Jim, "Story Telling: The Fiction of Leslie Silko," *JEthS* 9, i (Spring, 1971): 55-7.
Sands, Kathleen M., et al., "A Discussion of CEREMONY," *AIQ* 5, i (Feb., 1979): 63-70.
Scarberry, Susan J., "Memory as Medicine: The Power of Recollection in CEREMONY," *AIQ* 5, i (Feb., 1979): 19-26.
Seyersted, P., *Leslie Marmon Silko*, 25-34.

Velie, A. R., "Leslie Silko's CEREMONY: A Laguna Grail Story," *Four American Indian Literary Masters*, 106-21.
Wald, Alan, "The Culture of 'Internal Colonialism': A Marxist Perspective," *MELUS* 8, iii (Fall, 1981): 18-27.

BIBLIOGRAPHY

Seyersted, P., *Leslie Marmon Silko*, 45-50.

SILLITOE, ALAN, 1928-

GENERAL

Aldridge, J. W., "Alan Sillitoe: The Poor Man's Bore," *Time to Murder and Create*, 239-44.
Atherton, S. S., *Alan Sillitoe*.
_____, "Alan Sillitoe's Battleground," *DR* 48 (Autumn, 1968): 324-31.
_____, "The Early Working-Class Fiction of Alan Sillitoe," *DAI* 40 (1979): 3285A-86A.
Burns, Johnnie W., "An Examination of Elements of Social Realism in Five Novels of Alan Sillitoe," *DAI* 36 (1975): 2213A-14A.
Dixon, Tercell F., "Expostulation and a Reply: The Character of Clegg in Fowles and Sillitoe," *NConL* 4, ii (1974): 7-9.
Gindin, James, "Alan Sillitoe's Jungle," *TSLL* 4 (1962): 35-48. Also in Gindin, J., *Postwar British Fiction*, 14-33.
Haller, Robert S., "The Crux of Merging Deltas: A Note on Alan Sillitoe," *PrS* 48, iv (Winter, 1974): 351-8.
Halperin, John, "Interview with Alan Sillitoe," *MFS* 25, ii (Summer, 1979): 175-89.
Hennessy, Brendan, "Alan Sillitoe," *Transatlantic Review* 41 (Winter-Spring, 1972): 108-13. [Interview.]
Hurrell, John D., "Alan Sillitoe and the Serious Novel," *Crit* 4, i (1961): 3-16.
Karl, F. R., *Contemporary English Novel*, 283-4.
Klotz, Gunther, "Alan Sillitoe's Heroes," in Linger, Erica, et al., eds., *Essays in Honor of William Gallacher*, Berlin: Humboldt Un., 1966, 259-63.
Lefranc, Michael, "Alan Sillitoe: An Interview," *EA* 26, i (Jan.-Mar., 1973): 35-48.
Lockwood, Bernard, "Four Contemporary British Working-Class Novelists: A Thematic and Critical Approach to the Fiction of Raymond Williams, John Braine, David Storey and Alan Sillitoe," *DA* 28 (1967): 1081A.
Maloff, Saul, "The Eccentricity of Alan Sillitoe," in Shapiro, C., ed., *Contemporary British Novelists*, 95-113.
Naradella, Anna R., "The Existential Dilemmas of Alan Sillitoe's Working-Class Heroes," *SNNTS* 5 (Winter, 1973): 469-82.
Penner, A. R., *Alan Sillitoe*.
Roskies, D. M., "Alan Sillitoe's Anti-Pastoral," *JNT* 10 (1980): 170-85.
_____, "'I'd Rather Be Like I Am': Character, Style, and the Language of Class in Sillitoe's Narratives," *Neophil* 65 (1981): 308-19.
Rosselli, John, "A Cry from the Brick Streets," *Reporter* 33 (Nov. 10, 1960): 37, 40, 43.
Shestakov, Dmitri, "Alan Sillitoe from Nottingham," *Soviet Lit* 9 (1963): 176-9.
Vaverka, R. D., *Commitment as Art*.

Wilding, Michael, "Alan Sillitoe's Political Novels," in Anderson, D., and S. Knight, eds., *Cunning Exiles*, 129-62.

Wood, Ramsay, "Alan Sillitoe: The Image Shedding the Author," *FQ* 21, i (Nov., 1971): 3-10. [Interview.]

THE DEATH OF WILLIAM POSTERS

Kermode, Frank, "Rammel," *NStat* (May 14, 1965): 765-66. Also in Kermode, F., *Continuities*, 227-32.

Lee, James W., "Myth of Identity: Alan Sillitoe's THE DEATH OF WILLIAM POSTERS; A TREE ON FIRE," in Morris, R. K., ed., *Old Lines, New Forces*, 120-30.

Levine, Paul, "Some Middle-Aged Fiction," *HudR* 18 (Winter, 1965-66): 587-94.

Nardella, Anna R., "The Existential Dilemmas of Alan Sillitoe's Working-Class Heroes," *SNNTS* 5, iv (Winter, 1973): 473-8.

Penner, A. R., *Alan Sillitoe*, 115-25.

————, "The Political Prologue and Two Parts of a Trilogy: THE DEATH OF WILLIAM POSTERS and A TREE ON FIRE," *UR* 35 (Oct., 1968): 11-20.

Wilding, Michael, "Alan Sillitoe's Political Novels," in Anderson, D., and S. Knight, eds., *Cunning Exiles*, 154-7.

THE GENERAL

Gindin, James, "Alan Sillitoe's Jungle," *TSLL* 4 (1962): 35-48. Also in Gindin, J., *Postwar British Fiction*, 14-33.

Penner, A. R., *Alan Sillitoe*, 91-8.

————, "THE GENERAL: Exceptional Proof of a Critical Rule," *SHR* 4, ii (Spring, 1970): 135-43.

Rippier, J. S., *Some Postwar English Novelists*, 200-1.

KEY TO THE DOOR

McDowell, Frederick P. W., "Self and Society: Alan Sillitoe's KEY TO THE DOOR," *Crit* 6, (Spring, 1963): 116-23.

Paul, Ronald, "'Fire in Our Hearts': A Study of the Portrayal of Youth in a Selection of Post-War British Working Class Fiction," *GothSE* 51 (1982): 122-51.

Penner, A. R., *Alan Sillitoe*, 99-114.

————, "Dantesque Allegory in Sillitoe's KEY TO THE DOOR," *Ren* 20 (1968): 79-85, 103.

Rippier, J. S., *Some Postwar English Novelists*, 201-6.

Roskies, D. M., "Alan Sillitoe's Anti-Pastoral," *JNT* 10 (1980): 173-7.

Vaverka, R. D., *Commitment as Art*, 71-102.

Wilding, Michael, "Alan Sillitoe's Political Novels," in Anderson, D., and S. Knight, eds., *Cunning Exiles*, 140-53.

Wiley, Paul, in *WSCL* 4, ii (Spring-Summer, 1963): 228-9.

SATURDAY NIGHT AND SUNDAY MORNING

Craig, David, "Sillitoe and the Roots of Anger," *The Real Foundations: Literature and Social Change*, N.Y.: Oxford Un. Pr., 1974, 270-85.

Gindin, James, "Alan Sillitoe's Jungle," *TSLL* 4 (1962): 35-48. Also in Gindin, J., *Postwar British Fiction*, 14-33.

Gray, N., *Silent Majority*, 103-32.

Howe, Irving, "The Worker as Young Tough," *NRep* 141 (Aug. 24, 1959): 27-8.

Hurrell, John, "Alan Sillitoe and the Serious Novel," *Crit* 4, i (1961): 9-11, 14-16.

Maloff, Saul, in Shapiro, C., ed., *Contemporary British Novelists*, 108-13.

Nardella, Anna R., "The Existential Dilemmas of Alan Sillitoe's Working-Class Heroes," *SNNTS* 5, iv (Winter, 1973): 469-73.

Nathan, Sabine, "The Proper Subject of SATURDAY NIGHT AND SUNDAY MORNING," *ZAA* 24, i (1976): 57-70.

Nemerov, H., *Poetry and Fiction*, 277-8.

Osgerby, J. R., "Alan Sillitoe's SATURDAY NIGHT AND SUNDAY MORNING," 215-30, in Hibbard, G. R., ed., *Renaissance and Modern Essays Presented to Vivian de Sola Pinto in Celebration of His Seventieth Birthday*, London: Routledge and K. Paul, 1966.

Penner, A. R., *Alan Sillitoe*, 73-90.

Price, Rod, in *New Left Rev* 6 (Nov.-Dec., 1960): 14-17.

Rippier, J. S., *Some Postwar English Novelists*, 194-8.

Staples, Hugh B., "SATURDAY NIGHT AND SUNDAY MORNING: Alan Sillitoe and the White Goddess," *MFS* 10 (Summer, 1964): 171-81.

Urwin, G. G., ed., *Taste for Living*, 166-9.

Vaverka, R. D., *Commitment to Art*, 31-52.

West, Anthony, "On the Inside Looking In," *NY* 35 (Sept. 5, 1959): 103-4.

Wilding, Michael, "Alan Sillitoe's Political Novels," in Anderson, D., and S. Knight, eds., *Cunning Exiles*, 129-35.

Wilson, Keith, "Arthur Seaton Twenty Years On: A Reappraisal of Sillitoe's SATURDAY NIGHT AND SUNDAY MORNING," *ESC* 7, iv (Dec., 1981): 414-26.

A START IN LIFE

Dixon, Terrell F., "Expostulation and a Reply: The Character of Clegg in Fowles and Sillitoe," *NConL* 4, ii (Mar., 1974): 7-9.

Watrin, J., "Alan Sillitoe's A START IN LIFE," *RLV* 38 (1972): 508-16.

A TREE ON FIRE

Lee, James W., "Myths of Identity: Alan Sillitoe's THE DEATH OF WILLIAM POSTERS; A TREE ON FIRE," in Morris, R. K., ed., *Old Lines, New Forces*, 120-30.

Nardella, Anna R., "The Existential Dilemmas of Alan Sillitoe's Working-Class Heroes," *SNNTS* 5, iv (Winter, 1973): 478-81.

Penner, A. R., *Alan Sillitoe*, 126-35.

————, "The Political Prologue and Two Parts of a Trilogy: THE DEATH OF WILLIAM POSTERS and A TREE ON FIRE," *UR* 35 (Oct., 1968): 11-20.

Wilding, Michael, "Alan Sillitoe's Political Novels," in Anderson, D., and S. Knight, eds., *Cunning Exiles*, 157-61.

BIBLIOGRAPHY

Penner, R. A., *Alan Sillitoe*, 151-4.

SINCLAIR, ANDREW (ANNANDALE), 1935-

GOG

Bergonzi, B., *Situation of the Novel*, 76-9.

Reeve, N. H., in *Contemporary English Novel*, 126-7.

Wolfe, Peter, "England's Greatest Tourist Attraction: Andrew Sinclair's GOG, MAGOG," in Morris, R. K., *Old Lines, New Forces*, 151-80.

MAGOG

Wolfe, Peter, "England's Greatest Tourist Attraction: Andrew Sinclair's GOG, MAGOG," in Morris, R. K., *Old Lines, New Forces*, 151-80.

SINCLAIR, UPTON BEALL, 1878-1968

GENERAL

Becker, George J., "Upton Sinclair: Quixote in a Flivver," *CE* 21 (Dec., 1959): 133-40.

Blankenship, R., *American Literature*, 753-5.

Blinderman, Abraham, "The Social Passions of Upton Sinclair," *CJF* 25 (Spring, 1967): 203-8.

Bloodworth, William A., Jr., "The Early Years of Upton Sinclair: A Study of the Development of a Progressive Christian Scientist," *DAI* 33 (1973): 5164A.

_____, "From THE JUNGLE to THE FASTING CURE: Upton Sinclair on American Food," *JAC* 2 (Fall, 1979): 444-54.

_____, *Upton Sinclair*.

Cantwell, Robert, in Cowley M., ed., *After the Genteel Tradition*, 37-47.

Chalmers, David M., *The Political and Social Ideas of the Muckrakers*, N.Y.: Citadel, 1964, 88-95.

Dembo, L. S., "The Socialist and Socialite Heroes of Upton Sinclair," in Budd, L. J., et al., eds., *Toward a New Literary History*, 164-80.

Durham, James C., "Upton Sinclair's Realistic Romanticism," *WSUB* 46, ii (May, 1960): 3-11. [Not seen.]

Bloodworth, W. A., Jr., *Upton Sinclair*, 150-2.

Fretz, Lewis A., "Upton Sinclair: The Don Quixote of American Reform," *DAI* 31 (1971): 5983A.

Gilenson, B., "A Socialist of the Emotions," in Vroon, R., tr., *20th Century American Literature: A Soviet View*, 199-222.

Herms, Dieter, "The Coming Age of Sinclair Criticism," *Kritikon Litterarum* 6 (1977): 93-101.

Koerner, J. D., "The Last of the Muckrake Men," *SAQ* 55 (Apr., 1956): 221-32. Also in *Publications of the Humanities*, No. 19, Cambridge: MIT Pr., 1958.

Scriabine, Christine B., "Upton Sinclair: Witness to History," *DAI* 34 (1974): 6660A.

Sinclair, Upton, *Autobiography of Upton Sinclair*, N.Y.: Harcourt, 1962.

_____, *My Lifetime in Letters*, Columbia: Un. of Missouri Pr., 1960.

Straumann, H., *American Literature in the Twentieth Century*, 11-14.

Turner, Justin, "Conversation with Upton Sinclair," *ABC* 20, viii (1970): 7-10.

Welland, Dennis, "Upton Sinclair: The Centenary of an American Writer," *BJRL* 61, ii (1979): 474-94.

Yoder, Jonathan A., "Decades of Decay: Upton Sinclair and American Liberalism After World War II," *DAI* 31 (1971): 5435A.

_____, *Upton Sinclair*.

ANOTHER PAMELA

Bloodworth, W. A., Jr., *Upton Sinclair*, 150-2.

BOSTON

Bloodworth, W. A., Jr., *Upton Sinclair*, 115-23.

Dembo, L. S., "The Socialist and Socialite Heroes of Upton Sinclair," in Budd, L. J., et al., eds., *Toward a New Literary History*, 170-2.

Yoder, J. A., *Upton Sinclair*, 78-85.

CO-OP

Bloodworth, W. A., Jr., *Upton Sinclair*, 132-4.

Yoder, J. A., *Upton Sinclair*, 92-3.

JIMMIE HIGGINS

Bloodworth, W. A., Jr., *Upton Sinclair*, 93-7.

Yoder, J. A., *Upton Sinclair*, 61-3.

THE JUNGLE

Bloodworth, W. A., Jr., *Upton Sinclair*, 44-64.

Brook, Van Wyk, *Confident Years*, 373-6.

Chalmers, David M., *The Political and Social Ideas of the Muckrakers*, N.Y.: Citadel, 1964, 93-5.

Dembo, L. S., "The Socialist and Socialite Heroes of Upton Sinclair," in Budd, L. J., et al., eds., *Toward a New Literary History*, 164-6.

Downs, Robert B., "Afterward," *The Jungle*, N.Y.: New American Library, 1960.

Durham, James C., "Upton Sinclair's Realistic Romanticism," *WSUB* 46 (May, 1970): 1-9.

Folsom, Michael B., "Upton Sinclair's Escape from THE JUNGLE: The Narrative Strategy and Suppressed Conclusion of America's First Proletarian Novel," *Prospects* 4 (1979): 237-66.

Gupta, G. S. Balarama, "A Note on Upton Sinclair's THE JUNGLE," in Naik, M. K., et al., eds., *Indian Studies in American Fiction*, 125-33.

Musteikis, Antanas, "The Lithuanian Heroes of THE JUNGLE," *Litanus* 17, ii (1971): 27-38.

Rideout, W. B., *Radical Novel in the U.S.*, 30-7.

Sešplaukis, Alfonsas, "Lithuanians in Upton Sinclair's THE JUNGLE," *Lithanus* 23, ii (1977): 24-31.

Swados, Harvey, "THE JUNGLE Revisited," *Atlantic* 208 (Dec., 1961): 96+. Also in Swados, S., *Radical's America*, 3-11.

Tebbetts, Terrell L., "Jurgis's Freedom: The Jungle as a Case for Familial Society," *LJHum* 4, ii (1978): 15-20.

Yoder, J. A., *Upton Sinclair*, 31-49.

KING COAL

Bloodworth, W. A., Jr., *Upton Sinclair*, 80-91.

Dembo, L. S., "The Socialist and Socialite Heroes of Upton Sinclair," in Bud, L. J., et. al, eds., *Toward a New Literary History*, 166-9.

Graham, John, "Upton Sinclair and the Ludlow Massacre," *ColQ* 21, i (1972): 55-67.

Rideout, W. B., *Radical Novel in the U.S.*, 37-8.

Yoder, J. A., *Upton Sinclair*, 57-60.

THE JOURNAL OF ARTHUR STIRLING

Bloodworth, W. A., Jr., *Upton Sinclair*, 150-2.

LANNY BUDD Series (See WORLD'S END Series)

LOVE'S PILGRIMAGE

Bloodworth, W. A., Jr., *Upton Sinclair*, 35-7.

MANASSAS

Bloodworth, W. A., Jr., *Upton Sinclair*, 39-43.
Kimball, William J., "MANASSAS: An Early Expression of Upton Sinclair's Socialistic Leanings," *McNR* 20 (1971-72): 28-32.

THE MILLENNIUM

Bloodworth, W. A., Jr., *Upton Sinclair*, 77-9.

OIL

Bloodworth, W. A., Jr., *Upton Sinclair*, 104-11.
Blotner, J., *Modern American Political Novel*, 113-17.
Soderbergh, Peter A., "Upton Sinclair and Hollywood," *MQ* 11, ii (Winter, 1970): 176-8.
Yoder, J. A., *Upton Sinclair*, 70-8.

100%: THE STORY OF A PATRIOT

Bloodworth, W. A., Jr., *Upton Sinclair*, 97-9.

THE OVERMAN

Bloodworth, W. A., Jr., *Upton Sinclair*, 33-5.

PRINCE HAGEN

Bloodworth, W. A., Jr., *Upton Sinclair*, 32-3.

SPRINGTIME AND HARVEST

Bloodworth, W. A., Jr., *Upton Sinclair*, 29-32.

SYLVIA

Bloodworth, W. A., Jr., *Upton Sinclair*, 75-7.

SYLVIA'S MARRIAGE

Bloodworth, W. A., Jr., *Upton Sinclair*, 75-7.

THEY CALL ME CARPENTER

Bloodworth, W. A., Jr., *Upton Sinclair*, 99-100.

THE WET PARADE

Bloodworth, W. A., Jr., *Upton Sinclair*, 128-30.

WORLD'S END (See also WORLD'S END Series)

Bloodworth, W. A., Jr., *Upton Sinclair*, 141-3.
Yoder, J. A., *Upton Sinclair*, 97-9.

WORLD'S END Series

Becker, George J., "Upton Sinclair: Quixote in a Flivver," *CE* 21 (Dec., 1959): 135-9.
Bloodworth, W. A., Jr., *Upton Sinclair*, 138-48.
Brooks, Van Wyk, *Confident Years*, 377-8.

Dembo, L. S., "The Socialist and Socialite Heroes of Upton Sinclair," in Budd, L. J., et al., eds., *Towards a New Literary History*, 172-80.
Koerner, J. D., "The Last of the Muckrake Men," *SAQ* 55 (Apr., 1956): 227-32. Also in *Publications in the Humanities*, No. 19, Cambridge: MIT Pr., 1958.
Riherd, James M., "Upton Sinclair: Creating WORLD'S END," *DAI* 38 (1978): 7337A.
Sinclair, Upton, "Farewell to Lanny Budd," *SRL* 32 (Aug. 13, 1949): 18-19, 38.
Spitz, Leon, "Upton Sinclair and Nazism," *AmHebrew* 158 (Oct. 22, 1948): 2.
Yoder, G. A., *Upton Sinclair*, 96-110.
_____, "Upton Sinclair, Lanny and the Liberals," *MFS* 20, iv (Winter, 1974-75): 483-50.

BIBLIOGRAPHY

Gottesman, Ronald, *Upton Sinclair: An Annotated Checklist* (Serif Ser. in Bibliog. 24), Kent, Ohio: Kent State Un. Pr., 1973.

SINGER, ISAAC BASHEVIS, 1904-1991

GENERAL

Adler, Sidney, "The Shtetl in the Novels of Isaac Bashevis Singer," *DA* 29 (1968): 3602A-03A.
Alexander, E., *Isaac Bashevis Singer.*
Allentuck, M., ed., *Achievement of Isaac Bashevis Singer.*
Andersen, David M., "Isaac Bashevis Singer: Conversations in California," *MFS* 16, iv (Winter, 1970-71): 423-39.
Beck, Evelyn T., "The Many Faces of Eve: Women, Yiddish and I. B. Singer," *SAJL* 1 (1981): 112-23.
Bezanker, Abraham, "I. B. Singer's Crises of Identity," *Crit* 14, ii (1972): 70-88.
Blocker, Joel, and Richard Elman, "An Interview with Isaac Bashevis Singer," *Ctary* 36 (Nov., 1963): 364-72. Also in Malin, I., ed., *Critical Views of Isaac Bashevis Singer*, 3-26.
Bregner, Marshall, and Bob Barnhart, "A Conversation with Isaac Bashevis Singer," *The Handle* (Un. of Penn.) 2 (Fall, 1964-Winter, 1965): 9-21. Also in Malin, I., ed., *Critical Views of Isaac Bashevis Singer*, 27-43.
Buchen, Irving H., "The Art and Gifts of Isaac Bashevis Singer," *CJF* 24 (Summer, 1966): 308-12.
_____, "The Devil and I. B. Singer," *SAJL* 1 (1981): 24-31.
_____, *Isaac Bashevis Singer and the Eternal Past.*
_____, "Isaac Bashevis Singer and the Eternal Past," *Crit* 8, iii (Spring-Summer, 1966): 5-18.
Burgin, Richard, "A Conversation with Isaac Bashevis Singer," *MQR* 17 (1978): 119-32.
_____, "A Conversation with Isaac Bashevis Singer," *ChiR* 31, iv (1980): 53-60.
_____, "From Conversations with Isaac Bashevis Singer," *HudR* 31 (Winter, 1978): 620-30.
Chametsky, Jules, "History in I. B. Singer's Novels," in Malin, I., ed., *Critical Views of Isaac Bashevis Singer*, 169-77.
Cohen, Sarah B., "Hens to Roosters: Isaac Bashevis Singer's Female Species," *SAF* 10, ii (1982): 173-84.
Collar, Mary L., "In His Father's House: Singer, Folklore and the Meaning of Time," *SAJL* 1 (1981): 37-51.

"Demons by Choice: An Interview with Isaac Bashevis Singer," *Parabola* 6, iv (Oct., 1981): 68-74.

Eisenberg, J. A., "Isaac Bashevis Singer—Passionate Primitive or Pious Puritan?" *Judaism* 11 (Fall, 1962): 345-56. Also in Malin, I., *Critical Views of Isaac Bashevis Singer*, 48-67.

Elliot, Norbert L., III, "Allegory in the Novels of Isaac Bashevis Singer," *DAI* 42, ix (Mar., 1982): 3998A.

Farkas, Anita, "Isaac Bashevis Singer: The Artist as Displaced Person," *DAI* 38 (1977): 1368A.

Fiedler, Leslie, "I. B. Singer, or the Americanness of the American Jewish Writer," *SAJL* 1 (1981): 124-31.

Fixler, Michael, "The Redeemers: Themes in the Fiction of Isaac Bashevis Singer," *KR* 26 (Spring, 1964): 371-86. Also in Malin, I., ed., *Critical Views of Isaac Bashevis Singer*, 68-85.

Flender, Harold, "The Art of Fiction 42: Isaac Bashevis Singer," *ParisR* 9, xliv (1968): 53-73.

Friedman, Melvin J., "Isaac Bashevis Singer: The Appeal of Numbers," in Malin, I., *Critical Views of Isaac Bashevis Singer*, 178-93.

Garrin, Stephen H., "Isaac Bashevis Singer in Texas: Public Queries and a Private Interview," *TSLL* 22 (1980): 91-8.

Gass, William H., "The Shut-In," in Allentuck, M., ed., *Achievement of Isaac Bashevis Singer*, 1-13. Also in Gass, W. H., *Fiction and the Figures of Life*, 140-53.

Gilman, Sander L., "Interview: Isaac Bashevis Singer," *Diacritics* 4 (Spring, 1974): 30-3.

Golden, Morris, "Dr. Fischelson's Miracle; Duality and Vision in Singer's Fiction," in Allentuck, M., ed., *Achievement of Isaac Bashevis Singer*, 26-43.

Golub, Mark S., "A Shmues with Isaac Bashevis Singer," *SAJL* 1 (1981): 169-75.

Gottlieb, Elaine, "Singer and Hawthorne: A Prevalence of Satan," *SoR* 8, ii (Apr., 1972): 359-70.

_____, "A Talk with Isaac Bashevis Singer," *Reconstructionist* 25 (Mar. 6, 1959): 7-11.

Hemley, Cecil, *Dimensions of Midnight: Prose and Poetry*, ed. by Elaine Gottlieb, Athens: Ohio Un. Pr., 1966, 217-33.

Hernandez, Frances, "Isaac Bashevis Singer and the Supernatural," *CEA* 40, ii (1978): 28-32. [Not seen.]

Hernandez, Frances, "Isaac Bashevis Singer: New Impact of a Medieval Tradition on Modern American Fiction," *Proc. of the Conf. of College Teachers of English* 33 (Sept., 1968): 18-23. [Not seen.]

Hindus, Milton, in *Jewish Heritage* 5 (Fall, 1962): 44-52. Also in *Jewish Heritage Reader*, 242-52.

Hochman, Baruch, "I. B. Singer's Vision of Good and Evil," *Midstream* 13 (Mar., 1967): 66-73. Also in Malin, I., *Critical Views of Isaac Bashevis Singer*, 120-34.

Howe, Irving, "I. B. Singer," *Encounter* 26 (Mar., 1966): 60-70.

_____, "Introduction," *Selected Short Stories of Isaac Bashevis Singer*, N.Y.: Modern Library, 1966.

Hughes, Ted, "The Genius of Isaac Bashevis Singer," *NYRB* 4 (Apr. 22, 1965): 8-10.

Hyman, Stanley E., "The Yiddish Hawthorne," *New Leader* (July 23, 1962): 20-1. Also in Kostelanetz, R., *On Contemporary Literature*, 586-90. Also in Hyman, S. E., *Standards*, 83-7.

Jacobson, Dan, "The Problem of Isaac Bashevis Singer," *Ctary* 39 (Feb., 1965): 48-52.

Kahn, Lothar, "The Talent of I. B. Singer, 1978 Nobel Laureate for Literature," *WLT* 53 (Spring, 1979): 197-201.

Katz, Eli, "Isaac Bashevis Singer and the Classical Yiddish Tradition," in Allentuck, M., ed., *Achievement of Isaac Bashevis Singer*, 14-25.

Kofman, Nadine, "Author Stresses the Story," *SAJL* 1 (1981): 182-5.

Knopp, Josephine Z., "The *Shtetl*: I. B. Singer," *Trial of Judaism in Contemporary Jewish Writing*, 30-55.

Lee, Grace F., "The Hidden God of Isaac Bashevis Singer," *HC* 1, vi (Dec., 1973): 1-15.

_____, "Seeing and Blindness: A Conversation with Isaac Bashevis Singer," *Novel* 9 (Winter, 1976): 151-64.

_____, "Stewed Prunes and Rice Pudding: College Students Eat and Talk with I. B. Singer," *ConL* 19 (Autumn, 1978): 446-58.

Leventhal, Naomi S., "Storytelling in Works of Isaac Bashevis Singer," *DAI* 39 (1979): 4938A-39A.

Levitan, Elsie, "The Cosmos of Isaac Bashevis Singer," *SAJL* 1 (1981): 138-47.

Line, W. C., "The Joys of Isaac Bashevis Singer," *WD* 54, v (1974): 26-9. [Interview.]

Lyons, Bonnie, "Sexual Love in I. B. Singer's Work," *SAJL* 1 (1981): 61-74.

Madison, C. A., "I. Bashevis Singer: Novelist of Hasidic Gothicism," *Yiddish Literature*, 479-99.

Malin, I., ed., *Critical Views of Isaac Bashevis Singer*.

_____, *Isaac Bashevis Singer*.

Malkoff, Karl, "Demonology and Dualism: The Supernatural in Isaac Singer and Muriel Spark," in Malin, I., ed., *Critical Views of Isaac Bashevis Singer*, 149-68.

McIntyre, Shirene, "Isaac Bashevis Singer and the Uses of Reincarnation," *CLAJ* 25 (1981): 227-33.

Milfull, John, "The Messiah and the Direction of History: Walter Benjamin, Isaac Bashevis Singer and Franz Kafka," 180-7 in Obermayer, August, ed., *Festschrift for E. W. Herd*, Dunedin: Un. of Otago, 1980.

Mucke, Edith, "Isaac B. Singer and Hassidic Philosophy," *MinnR* 7, iii (1967): 214-21.

Newman, Richard A., "Isaac Bashevis Singer: The Faith of His Devils and Magicians," *HJ* 65 (Autumn, 1966): 27-8.

Novak, Maximillian E., "Moral Grotesque and Decorative Grotesque in Singer's Fiction," in Allentuck, M., ed., *Achievement of Isaac Bashevis Singer*, 44-63.

Pinsker, Sanford, "The Fictive Worlds of Isaac Bashevis Singer," *Crit* 11, ii (1969): 26-39.

_____, "Isaac Bashevis Singer: An Interview," *Crit* 11, ii (1969): 16-25.

_____, "The Isolated Schlemiels of Isaac Bashevis Singer," *Schlemiel as Metaphor*, 55-86.

Pondrom, Cyrena N., "Isaac Bashevis Singer: An Interview and a Biographical Sketch," *ConL* 10 (Winter, 1969): 1-38, 332-51.

Ribalow, Reena, "A Visit to Isaac Bashevis Singer," *Reconstructionist* 30 (May 29, 1964): 19-26.

Ringold, Francine, "'My Dear Friend' Isaac Bashevis Singer," *SAJL* 1 (1981): 160-8.

Rubin, Steven J., "I. B. Singer: A Note on the Yiddish Writer and His Sense of Ethnicity," *MELUS* 3, iii (1976): 4-5.

Schatt, Stanley, "The Dybbuk Had Three Wives: Isaac Bashevis Singer and the Jewish Sense of Time," *Judaism* 23, i (Winter, 1974): 100-8.

Schulz, Max F., "Isaac Bashevis Singer, Radical Sophistication, and the Jewish-American Novel," *SHR* 3 (Winter, 1968):

60-6. Also in Schulz, M. F., *Radical Sophistication*, 13-22. Also in Malin, I., ed., *Critical Views of Isaac Bashevis Singer*, 135-48. [Altered version.]

Seed, David, "The Fiction of Isaac Bashevis Singer," *CritQ* 18, i (Spring, 1976): 73-9.

Setton, Ruth K., "The Living Faith: A Study of Isaac Bashevis Singer," *DAI* 42, ii (August, 1981): 706A-07A.

Shaffer, Dave, "Does I. B. Singer Really Know All the Answers?" *SAJL* 1 (1981): 179-81.

Siegel, Ben, "The Brothers Singer: More Similarities than Differences," *ConL* 22, i (Winter, 1981): 42-57.

_____, *Isaac Bashevis Singer*.

_____, "Sacred and Profane: Isaac Bashevis Singer's Embattled Spirits," *Crit* 6, i (Spring, 1963): 24-47.

Sinclair, Clive, "A Conversation with Isaac Bashevis Singer," *Encounter* 52 (Feb., 1979): 21-8.

Singer, Isaac Bashevis, *My Personal Conception of Religion* (Flora Levy Lecture in Humanities, 1) Lafayette: Un. of Southwestern Louisiana, 1982.

_____, *On Literature and Life: An Interview with Paul Rosenblatt and Gene Koppel*, Tucson: Un. of Arizona Pr., 1979.

Sloman, Judith, "Existentialism in Par Lagerqvist and Isaac Bashevis Singer," *MinnR* 5 (Aug.-Oct., 1966): 206-12.

Sontag, Susan, "Demons and Dreams," *PR* 29 (Summer, 1962): 460-3.

Swindell, Julie, "I. B. Singer Applauds Storytelling," *SAJL* 1 (1981): 176-8.

Varley, H. Leland, "Isaac Bashevis Singer and the Sense of Wonder," *KAL* 16 (1975): 44-6. [Summary of a paper read at Kyushi seminar, 1974.]

Wachtel, Nili, "Freedom and Slavery in the Fiction of Isaac Bashevis Singer," *Judaism* 26, ii (Spring, 1977): 171-86.

_____, "Isaac Bashevis Singer: On Modern Freedom and Modern Slavery," *DAI* 36 (1975): 3704A.

Walden, Daniel, "I. B. Singer: The Vintage Years," *SAJL* 1 (1981): 132-7.

Whitman, Ruth, "Translating with Isaac Bashevis Singer," in Malin, I., ed., *Critical Views of Isaac Bashevis Singer*, 44-7.

Wieseltier, Leon, "The Revenge of I. B. Singer," *NYRB* (Dec. 7, 1978): 6-8.

Wisse, Ruth R., "Singer's Paradoxical Progress," *Ctary* (Feb., 1979): 33-8. Also in *SAJL* 1 (1981): 148-59.

Wolkenfeld, J. S., "Isaac Bashevis Singer: The Faith of His Devils and Magicians," *Criticism* 5 (Fall, 1963): 349-59. Also in Malin, I., ed., *Critical Views of Isaac Bashevis Singer*, 48-67.

ENEMIES, A LOVE STORY

Alexander, E., *Isaac Bashevis Singer*, 99-112.

Bilik, Dorothy S., "Singer's Diasporan Novel: ENEMIES, A LOVE STORY," *SAJL* 1 (1981): 90-100.

Cohen, Sarah B., "Hens to Roosters: Isaac Bashevis Singer's Female Species," *SAF* 10, ii (Autumn, 1982): 173-84.

Forrey, Robert, "The Sorrows of Herman Broder: Singer's ENEMIES, A LOVE STORY," *SAJL* 1 (1981): 101-6.

Helbling, Mark, "Isaac Bashevis Singer in America," *PolR* 26, iii (1981): 20-5.

Siegel, Ben, "The Jew as Underground/Confidence Man: I. B. Singer's ENEMIES, A LOVE STORY," *SNNTS* 10, iv (1978): 397-410.

Steinberg, Theodore, "I. B. Singer: Responses to Catastrophe," *Yiddish* 1, iv (Spring, 1975): 9-12.

THE ESTATE

Alexander, E., *Isaac Bashevis Singer*, 83-98.

Malin, I., *Isaac Bashevis Singer*, 21-2, 31-9.

THE FAMILY MOSKAT

Alexander, E., *Isaac Bashevis Singer*, 39-59.

Buchen, I. H., *Isaac Bashevis Singer and the Eternal Past*, 31-76, 108-9.

Elman, Richard, in *Cavalier* 15 (Aug., 1965): 10-12.

Field, Leslie, "The Early Prophetic Singer: THE FAMILY MOSKAT," *SAJL* 1 (1981): 32-6.

Hindus, Milton, in *Jewish Heritage Reader*, 242-6.

_____, in *NYTBR* (Mar. 14, 1965): 4, 44-5.

Hughes, Ted, "The Genius of Isaac Bashevis Singer," *NYRB* 4 (Apr. 22, 1965): 9-10.

Madison, C. A., *Yiddish Literature*, 483-7.

Malin, I., *Isaac Bashevis Singer*, 12-21.

Schulz, Max F., "The Family Chronicle as Paradigm of History: THE BROTHERS ASHKENAZI and THE FAMILY MOSKAT," in Allentuck, M., ed., *Achievement of Isaac Bashevis Singer*, 77-92.

Sherman, Joseph, "Jewish Identity in Singer's THE FAMILY MOSKAT," *Jewish Affairs*, 37, ix (1982): 89-94.

Siegel, Ben, *Issac Bashevis Singer*, 11-14.

_____, "Sacred and Profane: Isaac Bashevis Singer's Embattled Spirits," *Crit* 6, i (Spring, 1963): 25-8.

Wachtel, Nili, "Freedom and Slavery in the Fiction of Isaac Bashevis Singer," *Judaism* 26, ii (Spring, 1977): 171-86 *passim*.

THE MAGICIAN OF LUBLIN

Alexander, E., *Isaac Bashevis Singer*, 60-70.

Buchen, I. H., *Isaac Bashevis Singer and the Eternal Past*, 101-12, 210-11.

Chametsky, Jules, "Stereotypes and Jews: Fagin and the Magician of Lublin," *MR* 2 (Winter, 1961): 373-5.

Fried, Lewis, "THE MAGICIAN OF LUBLIN: I. B. Singer's Ironic Man of Faith," *Yiddish* 22, i (1975): 60-9.

Friedman, Melvin J., "Isaac Bashevis Singer: The Appeal of Numbers," in Malin, I., ed., *Critical Views of Isaac Bashevis Singer*, 185-8.

Hemley, Cecil, *Dimensions of Midnight: Prose and Poetry*, ed. by Elaine Gottlieb, Athens: Ohio Un. Pr., 1966, 232-3.

Hindus, Milton, in *Jewish Heritage Reader*, 249-50.

Howe, Irving, "Demonic Fiction of a Yiddish 'Modernist'," *Ctary* 30 (Oct., 1960): 350-3. Also in "Commentary," *Commentary Reader*, 589-94. Also in Kostelanetz, R., ed., *On Contemporary Literature*, 579-85.

Knopp, Josephine Z., "The *Shtetl*: I. B. Singer," *Trial of Judaism in Contemporary Jewish Writing*, 42-55.

Madison, C. A., *Yiddish Literature*, 489-91.

Malin, I., *Isaac Bashevis Singer*, 51-9.

Mercier, Vivian, "Sex, Success and Salvation," *HudR* 13 (Autumn, 1960): 455-6.

Pinsker, S., *Schlemiel as Metaphor*, 70-85.

Pondrom, Cyrena N., "Conjuring Reality: I. B. Singer's THE MAGICIAN OF LUBLIN," in Allentuck, M., ed., *Achievement of Isaac Bashevis Singer*, 93-111.

Rubinstein, Annette T., "An Obscurantist Yiddish Novel," *Jewish Currents* 15 (May, 1961): 36-8.

Siegel, Ben, *Isaac Bashevis Singer*, 21-3.

Saposnick, Irving S., "Yosha Mazur and Harry Houdini: The Old Magic and the New," *SAJL* 1 (1981): 52-60.

_____, "Sacred and Profane: Isaac Bashevis Singer's Embattled Spirits," *Crit* 6, (Spring, 1963): 35-8.

Wolkenfeld, J. S., "Isaac Bashevis Singer: The Faith of His Devils and Magicians," *Criticism* 5 (Fall, 1963): 355-8. Also in Malin, I., ed., *Critical Views of Isaac Bashevis Singer*, 94-8.

THE MANOR

Alexander, E., *Isaac Bashevis Singer*, 83-98.

Buchen, I. H., *Isaac Bashevis Singer and the Eternal Past*, 173-94.

Chametsky, Jules, "The Old Jew in New Times," *Nation* 205 (Oct. 30, 1967): 436-8.

Ellmann, Mary, "The Piety of Things in THE MANOR," in Allentuck, M., ed., *Achievement of Isaac Bashevis Singer*, 124-44.

Hughes, Catharine R., "The Two Worlds of Isaac Singer," *America* 117 (Nov. 18, 1967): 611-13.

Jonas, Gerald, "People With a Choice," *NYTBR* (Nov. 5, 1967): 1, 52.

Madison, C. A., *Yiddish Literature*, 497-9.

Malin, I., *Isaac Bashevis Singer*, 21-31.

Siegel, B., *Isaac Bashevis Singer*, 36-9.

Toynbee, Philip, "Inside the Pale," *NRep* 157 (Nov. 11, 1967): 39-40.

Wain, John, "Trouble in the Family," *NYRB* (Oct. 26, 1967): 32-3.

Wincelberg, Shimon, "Probing a Vanished Past," *New Leader* 51 (Feb. 26, 1968): 26-9.

SATAN IN GORAY

Alexander, E., *Isaac Bashevis Singer*, 22-38.

Buchen, I. H., *Isaac Bashevis Singer and the Eternal Past*, 83-97.

_____, "Isaac Bashevis Singer and the Revival of Satan," *TSLL* 9 (Spring, 1967): 129-42.

Friedman, Melvin J., "Isaac Bashevis Singer: The Appeal of Numbers," in Malin, I., ed., *Critical Views of Isaac Bashevis Singer*, 188-90.

Gittleman, Edwin, "Singer's Apocalyptic Town: SATAN IN GORAY," in Allentuck, M., ed., *Achievement of Isaac Bashevis Singer*, 64-76.

Hemley, Cecil, *Dimensions of Midnight: Prose and Poetry*, ed. by Elaine Gottlieb, Athens: Un. of Ohio Pr., 1966, 223-8.

Hindus, Milton, "The False Messiah," *New Leader* 38 (Nov. 28, 1955): 24-6.

_____, in *Jewish Heritage*, 247-9.

Howe, Irving, "In the Day of the False Messiah," *NRep* 133 (Oct. 31, 1955): 22-4.

Hughes, Ted, "The Genius of Isaac Bashevis Singer," *NYRB* 4 (Apr. 22, 1965): 8-9.

Kibel, Alvin C., "The Political Novel," *Reconstructionist* 24 (Oct. 31, 1958): 28-31.

Knopp, Josephine Z., "The *Shtetl*: I. B. Singer," *Trial of Judaism in Contemporary Jewish Writing*, 36-7, 38-42.

Madison, C. A., *Yiddish Literature*, 480-3.

Malin, I., *Isaac Bashevis Singer*, 43-51.

Malkoff, Karl, "Demonology and Dualism: The Supernatural in Isaac Singer and Muriel Spark," in Malin, I., ed., *Critical Views of Isaac Bashevis Singer*, 188-90.

McIntyre, Shirene, "Isaac Bashevis Singer and the Uses of Reincarnation," *CLAJ* 25, ii (Dec., 1981): 227-30.

Pinsker, Sanford, "SATAN IN GORAY and the Grip of Ideas," *SAJL* 1 (1981): 14-23.

Sherman, Joseph, "SATAN IN GORAY: Some Aspects of the Mysticism of Isaac Bashevis Singer, 1-11, in Attwell, David, ed., *The AUETSA Papers 1981: Papers Presented at the Annual Conference of the Association of University English Teachers of Southern Africa, Held at the University of the Western Cape, 9-11 July, 1981*, Cape Town: Un. of the Western Cape, 1982.

Siegel, Ben, *Isaac Bashevis Singer*, 14-16.

_____, "Sacred and Profane: Isaac Bashevis Singer's Embattled Spirits," *Crit* 6, i (Spring, 1963): 28-30.

Teller, Judd, "Unhistorical Novels," *Ctary* 21 (Apr., 1956): 393-6.

Wolkenfeld, J. S., "Isaac Bashevis Singer: The Faith of His Devils and Magicians," *Criticism* 5 (Fall, 1963): 350-4. Also in Malin, I., ed., *Critical Views of Isaac Bashevis Singer*, 88-94.

SHOSHA

Alexander, E., *Isaac Bashevis Singer*, 113-23.

THE SLAVE

Alexander, E., *Isaac Bashevis Singer*, 71-82.

Bertman, M. A., "Singer's Slave," *Rendezvous* 13, ii (1978): 20-6.

Buchen, I. H., *Isaac Bashevis Singer and the Eternal Past*, 149-71.

_____, "The Present Revealed Through the Past," (Baltimore) *Sunday Sun* (June 24, 1962): Sec. A, 5.

Fixler, Michael, "The Redeemers: Themes in the Fiction of Isaac Bashevis Singer," *KR* 26 (Spring, 1964): 383-6. Also in Malin, I., ed., *Critical Views of Isaac Bashevis Singer*, 82-5.

Friedman, Melvin J., "Isaac Bashevis Singer: The Appeal of Numbers," in Malin, I., ed., *Critical Views of Isaac Bashevis Singer*, 183-5.

Goodheart, Eugene, "Singer's Moral Novel," *Midstream* 8 (Sept., 1962): 99-102.

Hughes, Ted, "The Genius of Isaac Bashevis Singer," *NYRB* 4 (Apr. 22, 1965): 10.

Hyman, Stanley E., "The Yiddish Hawthorne," *New Leader* 45 (July 23, 1962): 20-1. Also in Kostelanetz, R., ed., *On Contemporary Literature*, 586-90. Also in Hyman, S. E., *Standards*, 83-7.

Karl, Frederick R., "Jacob Reborn, Zion Regained; I. B. Singer's THE SLAVE," in Allentuck, M., ed., *Achievement of Isaac Bashevis Singer*, 112-23.

Lyons, Bonnie, "Sexual Love in I. B. Singer's Work," *SAJL* 1 (1981): 61-74.

Madison, C. A., *Yiddish Literature*, 493-5.

Malin, I., *Isaac Bashevis Singer*, 42-3, 59-68.

Malkoff, Karl, "Demonology and Dualism: The Supernatural in Isaac Singer and Muriel Spark," in Malin, I., ed., *Critical Views of Isaac Bashevis Singer*, 161-4.

Siegel, B., *Isaac Bashevis Singer*, 28-30.

_____, "Sacred and Profane: Isaac Bashevis Singer's Embattled Spirits," *Crit* 6, i (Spring, 1963): 43-7.

Sontag, Susan, "Demons and Dreams," *PR* 29 (Summer, 1962): 460-3.

Stafford, Jean, "The Works of God, the Ways of Man," *NRep* 146 (June 18, 1962): 21-2.

Steinberg, Theodore, "I. B. Singer: Responses to Catastrophe," *Yiddish* 1, iv (Spring, 1975): 9-12.

Weintroub, in *CJF* 21 (Winter, 1962-63): 169-70.

BIBLIOGRAPHY

Bryer, Jackson R., and P. E. Rockwell, "Isaac Bashevis Singer in English: A Bibliography," in Malin, I., ed., *Critical Views of I. B. Singer*, 220-65.

Buchen, I. H., *Isaac Bashevis Singer and the Eternal Past*, 221-34.

Christiansen, Bonnie Jean M., "Isaac Bashevis Singer: A Bibliography," *BB* 26, i (Jan.-Mar., 1969): 3-6.

Horbeck, David S., "Isaac Bashevis Singer in the Last Ten Years," *BB* 39, i (Mar., 1982): 17-25.

Siegel, B., *Isaac Bashevis Singer*, 45-8.

SINGH, KHUSHWANT, 1915-

GENERAL

Kulshrestha, Chirantan, "Khushwant Singh's Fiction: A Critique," *IWT* 11 (1970): 19-26. Also, revised and partially rewritten, in Mukherjee, M., ed., *Considerations*, 122-31.

Kumar, Raj, "The Art of Khushwant Singh," *PURBA* 4, i (Apr., 1973): 223-8.

Shahane, V. A., *Khushwant Singh*.

I SHALL NOT HEAR THE NIGHTINGALE

Shahane, V. A., *Khushwant Singh*, 105-25.

_____, "Theme and Symbol in Khushwant Singh's I SHALL NOT HEAR THE NIGHTINGALE," *OJES* 7, i (1969): 11—36.

TRAIN TO PAKISTAN (MANO MAJRA)

Belliappa, K. C., "The Elusive Classic: Khushwant Singh's TRAIN TO PAKISTAN and Chaman Nahal's AZADI," *LCrit* 15, ii (1980): 62-73.

Rao, S. S. Prabhakar, "Khushwant Singh's TRAIN TO PAKISTAN: A Stylistic Interpretation," in Sarma, G.V.L.N., ed., *Essays and Studies: Fetschrift in Honour of Prof. K. Viswanathan*, Machilipatnam: Triveni, 1977, 80-5.

Shahane, V. A., *Khushwant Singh*, 68-104.

_____, "Khushwant Singh"'s TRAIN TO PAKISTAN: A Study in Contemporary Realism," in Mohan, R., ed., *Indian Writing in English*, 65-79.

_____, "Theme, Title and Structure in Khushwant Singh's TRAIN TO PAKISTAN," *LCrit* 9, iii (Winter, 1970): 68-76.

Tarinayya, M., "Bhabani Battacharya: SO MANY HUNGERS and Khuswant Singh: TRAIN TO PAKISTAN," in Narasimhaiah, C. D., ed., *Indian Literature of the Past Fifty Years*, 180-202.

BIBLIOGRAPHY

Shahane, V. A., *Khushant Singh*, 171-3.

SMITH, LILLIAN (EUGENIA), 1897-1966

GENERAL

Blackwell, L., and F. Clay, *Lillian Smith*.

Hall, Giles G., Jr., "The Social Criticism of Lillian Smith," *DAI* 33 (1973): 3647A.

Sugg, Redding, S., Jr., "Lillian Smith and the Condition of Woman," *SAQ* 71, i (Spring, 1972): 155-64.

ONE HOUR

Blackwell, L., and F. Clay, *Lillian Smith*, 61-71.

_____, "Lillian Smith, Novelist," *CLAJ* 15, iv (June, 1972): 456-8.

STRANGE FRUIT

Blackwell, L., and F. Clay, *Lillian Smith*, 37-60.

_____, "Lillian Smith, Novelist," *CLAJ* 15, iv (June, 1971): 452-6.

Hamblen, Abigail A., "STRANGE FRUIT: Harvest," *ForumH* 5, i (1967): 31-3.

Marcus, Fred H., "CRY, THE BELOVED COUNTRY and STRANGE FRUIT: Exploring Man's Inhumanity to Man," *EJ* 51 (Dec., 1962): 609-16.

Thornburn, Neil, "STRANGE FRUIT and the Southern Tradition," *MQ* 12, ii (Winter, 1970): 157-71.

BIBLIOGRAPHY

Blackwell, L., and F. Clay, *Lillian Smith*, 137-47.

SMITH, MARK (RICHARD), 1935-

THE DEATH OF THE DETECTIVE

Anderson, David D., "A Major New Chicago Novel," *SSML* 4, iii (1974): 13-15.

SMITH, MARTIN CRUZ, 1942-

NIGHTWING

Beidler, Peter G., "The Indians in Martin Cruz Smith's NIGHTWING: A Review Article," *AIQ* 5, ii (May, 1979): 155-9.

SMITH, WILLIAM GARDNER, 1926-1974

GENERAL

Bryant, Jerry H., "Individuality and Fraternity: The Novels of William Gardner Smith," *SBL* 3, ii (Summer, 1972): 1-8.

ANGER AT INNOCENCE

Hughes, C. M., *Negro Novelist*, 168-72.

LAST OF THE CONQUERORS

Hughes, C. M., *Negro Novelist*, 97-103, 230-2.

Schraufnagel, N., *From Apology to Protest*, 47-8.

SOUTH STREET

Schraufnagel, N., *From Apology to Protest*, 114-16.

THE STONE FACE

Gayle, A., Jr., *Way of the New World*, 197-202.
Schraufnagel, N., *From Apology to Protest*, 153-4.

SNOW, C(HARLES) P(ERCY), 1905-1980

GENERAL

Anon., "Interview with C. P. Snow," *REL* 3, iii (1962): 91-108.
Bernard, Kenneth, "C. P. Snow and Modern Literature," *UR* 31 (Mar., 1965): 231-33.
Cooper, William, *C. P. Snow*.
_____, "The World of C. P. Snow," *Nation* 184 (Feb. 2, 1957): 104-5.
Davis, R. G., *C. P. Snow*.
_____, *C. P. Snow*. Also in Stade, G., ed., *Six Contemporary British Novelists*, 57-144.
Finkelstein, Sidney, "The Art and Science of C. P. Snow," *Mainstream* 14, ix (Sept., 1961): 31-57.
Fraser, G. S., "C. P. Snow (1905-   )," in Panichas, G. A., ed., *Politics of Twentieth-Century Novelists*, 124-33.
Fuller, Edmund, "C. P. Snow in Retrospect," *SR* 89 (Spring, 1981): 254-8.
_____, "C. P. Snow: Spokesman of Two Communities," *Books With the Men Behind Them*, 102-34.
Goodwin, Donald F., "The Fiction of C. P. Snow," *DA* 27 (1967): 3009A.
Graves, Nora C., *The Two Culture Theory in C. P. Snow's Novels*.
Greacen, Robert, *The World of C. P. Snow*, London: Scorpion Pr., 1962; N.Y.: London House & Maxwell, 1963.
_____, "The World of C. P. Snow," *TQ* 4, iii (Autumn, 1961): 266-74.
Gulliver, Antony E., "The Political Novels of Trollope and Snow," *DAI* 30 (1969): 684A.
Hamilton, Kenneth, "C. P. Snow and Political Man," *QQ* 59 (Autumn, 1962): 416-27.
Jaffa, Herbert C., "C. P. Snow, Portrait of Man as an Adult," *Humanist* 24 (Sept.-Oct., 1964): 148-50.
Johnson, Pamela, "Three Novelists and the Drawing of Character: C. P. Snow, Joyce Cary and Ivy Compton Burnett," in English Association. *Essays and Studies, 1950*, 82-9.
Karl, F. K., *C. P. Snow*.
_____, "C. P. Snow: The Unreason of Reason," in Shapiro, C., ed., *Contemporary British Novelists*, 114-24.
Kermode, Frank, "The House of Fiction. Interviews with Seven English Novelists," *PR* 30 (Spring, 1963): 74-7.
_____, *Puzzles and Epiphanies*, 161-3.
Ketals, Violet B., "Shaw, Snow and the New Men," *Person* 47 (Fall, 1966): 520-31.
Leavis, F. R., "Two Cultures? The Significance of C. P. Snow," *MCR* 5 (1962): 90-101. Also in *Spectator* 208 (Mar. 16, 1962): 297-303. Also in book form, N.Y.: Pantheon, 1963.
Macdonald, Alastair, "Imagery in C. P. Snow," *UR* 32 (June, 1966): 303-6; 23 (Oct., 1966): 33-8.
Mandel, E. W., "Anarchy and Organization," *QQ* 70 (Spring, 1963): 131-41.

_____, "C. P. Snow's Fantasy of Politics," *QQ* 69 (Spring, 1962): 24-37.
Millgate, Michael, "Structure and Style in the Novels of C. P. Snow," *REL* 1, ii (Apr., 1960): 34-41.
Murray, Byron O., "C. P. Snow: Grounds for Reappraisal," *Person* 47 (Jan., 1966): 91-101.
Parkhill-Rathbone, James, "The 'gravitas' of C. P. Snow," *B&B* 17, ii (Nov., 1971): 6-8.
Rabinovitz, R., *Reaction Against Experiment in the English Novel*, 128-65.
Shestakov, Dmitri, "What C. P. Snow Means to Us," *Soviet Lit* 1 (1966): 174-9.
Shusterman, D., *C. P. Snow*.
Smith, LeRoy W., "C. P. Snow as Novelist: A Delimitation," *SAQ* 64 (Summer, 1965): 316-31.
Stanford, Derek, "C. P. Snow: The Novelist as Fox," *Meanjin* 19 (Sept., 1960): 236-51.
_____, "A Disputed Master: C. P. Snow and His Critics," *Month* 29 (Feb., 1963): 91-4.
_____, "Sir Charles and the Two Cultures," *Critic* 21 (Oct.-Nov., 1962): 17-21.
Stanford, Raney, "The Achievement of C. P. Snow," *WHR* 16 (Winter, 1962): 43-52.
_____, "Personal Politics in the Novels of C. P. Snow," *Crit* 2, i (Spring-Summer, 1958): 16-28.
Swinden, Patrick, "The World of C. P. Snow," *CritQ* 15, iv (Winter, 1973): 297-313.
Thale, Jerome, *C. P. Snow*.
_____, "C. P. Snow: The Art of Worldliness," *KR* 22 (Autumn, 1960): 621-34.
Vogel, Albert W., "The Academic World of C. P. Snow," *TCL* 9 (Oct., 1963): 143-52.
Walsh, Ruth M., "C. P. Snow: Poet of Organizational Behavior," *DAI* 37 (1976): 2207A.
Waring, A. G., "Science, Love and the Establishment in the Novels of D. A. Granin and C. P. Snow," *FMLS* 14, i (Jan., 1978): 1-15.
Webster, Harvey C., "C. P. Snow: Scientific Humanist," *After the Trauma*, 168-90.

THE AFFAIR (See also STRANGERS AND BROTHERS Series)

Cooper, W., *C. P. Snow*, 28-9.
Davis, R. G., *C. P. Snow*, 33-5. Also in Stade, G., ed., *Six Contemporary British Novelists*, 92-4.
Graves, N. C., *Two Culture Theory in C. P. Snow*, 51-4.
Heppenstall, R., *Fourfold Tradition*, 239-41.
Karl, F. K. *C. P. Snow*, 136-53.
_____, "The Politics of Conscience: The Novels of C. P. Snow," *Contemporary English Novel*, 79-83.
Millgate, Michael, "Strangers and Brothers," *Ctary* 29 (July, 1960): 76-9.
Nelson, Bryce E., in *Audit* 1 (Mar., 1961): 11-15.
Shusterman, D., *C. P. Snow*, 114-18.
Stanford, Raney, "The Achievement of C. P. Snow," *WHR* 16 (Winter, 1962): 43-52.
Thale, J., *C. P. Snow*, 56-60.
Turner, Ian, "Above the Snow-Line: The Sociology of C. P. Snow," *Overland* 18 (Winter-Spring, 1960): 42-3.

THE CONSCIENCE OF THE RICH (See also STRANGERS AND BROTHERS Series)

Cooper, W., *C. P. Snow*, 18-19.

Davis, R. G., *C. P. Snow*, 28-31. Also in Stade, G., ed., *Six Contemporary British Novelists*, 87-9.

Graves, N. C., *Two Culture Theory in C. P. Snow's Novels*, 32-4.

Karl, F. R., *C. P. Snow*, 4-5, 117-35.

_____, "The Politics of Conscience: The Novels of C. P. Snow," *Contemporary English Novel*, 63-4, 75-9.

Levin, Gerald, "The Sadic Heroes of C. P. Snow," *TCL* 26, i (Spring, 1980): 34-6.

Shusterman, D., *C. P. Snow*, 85-95.

Thale, J., *C. P. Snow*, 64-6.

CORRIDORS OF POWER

Anon., "The Realism of the Worldly," in *TLS* (Nov. 5, 1964): 993. Also in *T.L.S.: Essays and Reviews from The Times Literary Supplement, 1964*, 100-3.

Burgess, Anthony, "Powers That Be," *Encounter* 24 (Jan., 1965): 71-6.

Davis, R. G., *C. P. Snow*, 35-41. Also in Stade, G., ed., *Six Contemporary British Novelists*, 94-100.

Enright, D. J., "Easy Lies the Head" *NStat* (Nov. 6, 1964): 698-9. Also in Enright, D. J., *Conspirators and Poets*, 106-10.

Graves, N. C., *Two Culture Theory in C. P. Snow's Novels*, 54-7.

Muggeridge, Malcolm, "Oh No, Lord Snow," *NRep* 151 (Nov. 28, 1964): 27-9. Also in Harrison, G. A., ed., *Critic as Artist*, 267-72.

Shils, Edward, "The Charismatic Centre," *Spectator* No. 7115 (Nov. 6, 1964): 608-9.

Shusterman, D., *C. P. Snow*, 54-7.

Thale, J., *C. P. Snow*, 20-2.

DEATH UNDER SAIL

Graves, N. C., *Two Culture Theory in C. P. Snow's Novels*, 13-15.

Shusterman, D., *C. P. Snow*, 41-4.

GEORGE PASSANT (See also STRANGERS AND BROTHERS Series)

Cooper, W., *C. P. Snow*, 18-19.

Davis, R. G., *C. P. Snow*, 21-23. Also in Stade, G., ed., *Six Contemporary British Novels*, 79-81.

Karl, F. R., *C. P. Snow*, 28-34.

Stanford, Raney, "Personal Politics in the Novels of C. P. Snow," *Crit* 2, i (1958): 19-20.

Thale, J., *C. P. Snow*, 46-8.

HOMECOMING (HOMECOMINGS) (See also STRANGERS AND BROTHERS Series)

Cooper, W., *C. P. Snow*, 26-8.

Davis, R. G., *C. P. Snow*, 18-21. Also in Stade, G., ed., *Six Contemporary British Novelists*, 76-9.

Graves, N. C., *Two Culture Theory in C. P. Snow's Novels*, 41-3.

Heppenstall, R., *Fourfold Tradition*, 233-8.

Karl, F. R., *C. P. Snow*, 101-16.

Shusterman, D., *C. P. Snow*, 66-75.

Thale, J., *C. P. Snow*, 73-5.

IN THEIR WISDOM

Davis, R. G., "C. P. Snow," in Stade, G., ed., *Six Contemporary British Novelists*, 106-8.

LAST THINGS (See also STRANGERS AND BROTHERS Series)

Bonnet, Jacky, "LAST THINGS: Snow's Refusal of Man's Individual Condition," *LanM* 66, iii (1972): 302-4.

Bradbury, Malcolm, "C. P. Snow's Bleak Landscape," *NStat* 80 (Oct. 30, 1970): 566-7. Also, revised, in Bradbury, M., *Possibilities*, 203-10.

Davis, R. G., "C. P. Snow," in Stade, G., ed., *Six Contemporary British Novelists*, 103-5.

Graves, Nora C., "Literary Allusions in LAST THINGS," *NConL* 1, i (Nan., 1971): 7-8.

_____, *Two Culture Theory in C. P. Snow's Novels*, 62-6.

Shusterman, D., *C. P. Snow*, 135-9.

Weintraub, Stanley, "LAST THINGS: C. P. Snow Eleven Novels After," *Mosaic* 4, iii (1971): 135-41.

THE LIGHT AND THE DARK (See also STRANGERS AND BROTHERS Series)

Cooper, W., *C. P. Snow*, 21-3.

Davis, R. G., *C. P. Snow*, 23-6. Also in Stade, G., ed., *Six Contemporary British Novelists*, 81-4.

Graves, N. C., *Two Culture Theory in C. P. Snow's Novels*, 34-7.

Karl, F. R., *C. P. Snow*, 52-66.

_____, "The Politics of Conscience: The Novels of C. P. Snow," *Contemporary English Novel*, 68-71.

Shusterman, D., *C. P. Snow*, 95-103.

Thale, J., *C. P. Snow*, 48-52.

THE MALCONTENTS

Davis, R. G., "C. P. Snow," in Stade, G., ed., *Six Contemporary British Novelists*, 104-6.

Graves, Nora C., "A Different Set of Malcontents in Snow's THE MALCONTENTS," *NConL* 10, i (1980): 6-7.

Shusterman, D., *C. P. Snow*

THE MASTERS (See also STRANGERS AND BROTHERS Series)

Allen, W., *Reading a Novel*, 46-50.

Cooper, W., *C. P. Snow*, 26-8.

Davis, R. G., *C. P. Snow*, 31-3. Also in Stade, G., ed., *Six Contemporary British Novelists*, 90-2.

Graves, N. C., *Two Culture Theory in C. P. Snow's Novels*, 38-40.

Karl, F. R., *C. P. Snow*, 101-16.

_____, "The Politics of Conscience: The Novels of C. P. Snow," *Contemporary English Novel*, 71-5.

Latham, Earl, "The Managerialization of the Campus," *Public Administration Review* 19 (Winter, 1959): 48-57 passim.

Lehan, Richard, "The Divided World: THE MASTERS Examined," in Sutherland, W. O. S., ed., *Six Contemporary Novels*, 46-57.

Noon, William T., "Satire, Poison and the Professor," *EngR* 11, i (Fall, 1960): 54-5.

Olsen, F. Bruce, in Hagopian, J. V., and M. Dolch, eds., *Insight II*, 332-6.

Proctor, Mortimer R., *English University Novel*, Berkeley and Los Angeles: Un. of California, 1957, 179-80.

Shusterman, D., *C. P. Snow,* 103-10.
Stanford, Raney, "Personal Politics in the Novels of C. P. Snow," *Crit* 2, i (1958): 20-2.
Thale, J., *C. P. Snow,* 53-6.

NEW LIVES FOR OLD

Graves, N. C., *Two Culture Theory in C. P. Snow's Novels,* 15-19.
Shusterman, D., *C. P. Snow,* 44-7.
Thale, J., *C. P. Snow,* 20-2.

THE NEW MEN (See also STRANGERS AND BROTHERS Series)

Cooper, W., *C. P. Snow,* 2-4.
Davis, R. G., *C. P. Snow,* 26-8. Also in Stade, G., ed., *Six Contemporary British Novelists,* 84-7.
Graves, N. C., *Two Culture Theory in C. P. Snow's Novels,* 45-51.
Karl, F. R., *C. P. Snow,* 83-100.
Ketels, Violet B., "Shaw, Snow, and the New Men," *Person* 47 (Fall, 1966): 520-31.
Levin, Gerald, "The Sadic Heroes of C. P. Snow," *TCL* 26, i (Spring, 1980): 31-4.
Miner, Earl, "C. P. Snow and the Realistic Novel," *Nation* 190 (June 25, 1960): 555-6.
Shusterman, D., *C. P. Snow,* 110-14.
Stanford, Raney, "Personal Politics in the Novels of C. P. Snow," *Crit* 2, i (1958): 22-6.
Symons, J., "On Bureaucratic Man," *Critical Occasions,* 68-73.
Watson, Kenneth, "C. P. Snow and THE NEW MEN," *English* 15 (Spring, 1965): 134-9.

THE SEARCH

Davis, R. G., *C. P. Snow,* 10-14. Also in Stade, G., ed., *Six Contemporary British Novelists,* 64-71.
Graves, N. C., *Two Culture Theory in C. P. Snow's Novels,* 19-24.
Karl, F. R., *C. P. Snow,* 21-3.
Shusterman, D., *C. P. Snow,* 47-56.
Thale, J., *C. P. Snow,* 22-4.
Waring, A. G., "Science, Love and the Establishment in the Novels of D. A. Granin and C. P. Snow," *FMLS* 14, i (Jan., 1978): 1-15 *passim.*

THE SLEEP OF REASON (See also STRANGERS AND BROTHERS Series)

Anon., "Monsters at Bay," *TLS* (Oct. 31, 1968): 1217. Also in *T.L.S.: Essays and Reviews from The Times Literary Supplement, 1968,* 175-7.
Davis, R. G., "C. P. Snow," in Stade, G ., ed., *Six Contemporary British Novelists,* 100-3.
Graves, N. C., *Two Culture Theory in C. P. Snow's Novels,* 57-62.
Shusterman, D., *C. P. Snow,* 124-37.

STRANGERS AND BROTHERS (See GEORGE PASSANT)

STRANGERS AND BROTHERS Series

Adams, Robert, "Pomp and Circumstance: C. P. Snow," *Atlantic* 214 (Nov., 1964): 95-8.
Allen, W., *Modern Novel,* 248-51.
Ashton, Thomas L., "Realism and the Chronicle: C. P. Snow's Cinéma Verité," *SAQ* 72, iv (Autumn, 1973): 516-27.
Bergonzi, Bernard, *Situation of the Novel,* 135-48.

_____, "The World of Lewis Eliot," *TC* 167 (Mar., 1960): 214-25. (See reply by P. Frison.)
Cooper, W., *C. P. Snow,* 15-16, 30-4.
Dobree, Bonamy, "The Novels of C. P. Snow," *LHY* 2 (July, 1961): 28-34.
Fison, Peter, "A Reply to Bernard Bergonzi's 'The World of Lewis Eliot'," *TC* 167 (June, 1960): 568-71.
Fraser, G. S., *Modern Writer and His World,* 161-4.
Gardner, Helen, "The World of C. P. Snow," *NStat* 55 (Mar. 29, 1958): 409-10.
Gindin, J., *Postwar British Fiction,* 207-15.
Graves, N. C., *Two Culture Theory in C. P. Snow's Novels,* 68-78.
Halio, Jay L., "C. P. Snow's Literary Limitations," *NWR* 5 (Winter, 1962): 97-102.
Hall, William F., "The Humanism of C. P. Snow," *WSCL* 4, ii (Spring-Summer, 1963): 199-208.
Heppenstall, R., *Fourfold Tradition,* 224-46.
Ivasheva, V., "Illusion and Reality (About the Works of C. P. Snow)," *IL* 6 (June, 1960): 198-203.
Karl, F. R., *C. P. Snow,* 3-21, 25-34.
_____, "The Politics of Conscience: The Novels of C.. P. Snow," *Contemporary English Novel,* 62-84.
Kazin, Alfred, "A Gifted Boy from the Midlands," *Reporter* 20 (Feb. 5, 1959): 37-9. Also in Kazin, A., *Contemporaries,* 171-7.
Levin, Gerald, "The Sadic Heroes of C. P. Snow," *TCL* 26, i (Spring, 1980): 27-37.
Mandel, E. W., "C. P. Snow's Fantasy of Politics," *QQ* 69 (Spring, 1962): 24-37.
Mayne, Richard, "The Club Armchair," *Encounter* 21 (Nov., 1963): 76-82.
Millgate, Michael, "STRANGERS AND BROTHERS," *Ctary* 30 (July, 1960): 76-9.
Miner, Earl, "C. P. Snow and the Realistic Novel," *Nation* 190 (June 25, 1960): 554-6.
Morris, R. K., *Continuance and Change,* 93-122.
Mullan, James F., "Resonance in the STRANGERS AND BROTHERS Novel Sequence by C. P. Snow," *DAI* 37 (1976): 2899A.
Neuman, Robert R., "Structure and Meaning in the Strangers and Brothers Sequence of C. P. Snow," *DAI* 34 (1973): 2646A.
Novak, Robert L., "The New Man, the Lewis Eliot Man: A Study of the Narrators in C. P. Snow's Novel Sequence, Strangers and Brothers," *DAI* 33 (1972): 1175A-76A.
Ramakrishnaiah, C., "Possessive Love in STRANGERS AND BROTHERS: A Study of C. P. Snow's Use of the Principle of Resonance in Developing the Theme," *IJES* 11 (1970): 112-21.
Shusterman, D., *C. P. Snow,* 76-139.
Stanford, Derek, "C. P. Snow: The Novelist as Fox," *Meanjin* 19 (Sept., 1960): 236-51.
Swinden, Patrick, "The World of C. P. Snow," *CritQ* 15, iv (Winter, 1973): 297-313.
Thale, J., *C. P. Snow,* 76-84, 109-15.
_____, "C. P. Snow: The Art of Worldliness," *KR* 22 (Autumn, 1960): 628-34.
Turner, Ian, "Above the Snow-Line: The Sociology of C. P. Snow," *Overland* 18 (Spring-Winter, 1960): 37-43.
Wagner, Geoffrey, "Writer in the Welfare State," *Cweal* 65 (Oct. 12, 1956): 49-50.
Wall, Steven, "The Novels of C. P. Snow," *LonM* n.s. 4 (Apr., 1964): 68-74.

Webster, Harvey C., "The Sacrifices of Success," *SatR* 41 (July, 12, 1958): 8-10+.

Widdowson, P[eter] J., "C. P. Snow's STRANGERS AND BROTHERS SEQUENCE: Lewis Eliot and the Failure of Realism," *RMS* 19 (1975): 112-28.

TIME OF HOPE (See also STRANGERS AND BROTHERS Series)

Cooper, W., *C. P. Snow*, 19-21.

Davis, R. G., *C. P. Snow*, 15-18. Also in Stade, G., ed., *Six Contemporary British Novelists*, 72-6.

Graves, N. C., *Two Culture Theory in C. P. Snow's Novels*, 25-9.

Karl, F. R., *C. P. Snow*, 41-51.

Shusterman, D., *C. P. Snow*, 57-67.

Thale, J., *C. P. Snow*, 70-3.

BIBLIOGRAPHY

Boytinck, Paul, *C. P. Snow: A Reference Guide*, Boston: Hall, 1980.

Thale, J., *C. P. Snow*, 154-60.

SONTAG, SUSAN, 1933-

GENERAL

Bellamy, Joe D., in Bellamy, J. D., ed., *New Fiction*, 113-29. [Interview.]

Beyer, Monika, "A Life Style Is Not a Life: An Interview with Susan Sontag," *PolP* 23, ix (1980): 42-6.

Holdsworth, Elizabeth M., "Susan Sontag: Writer-Filmaker," *DAI* 42, x (Apr., 1982): 4447A-48A.

Sayres, Sandra, "Susan Sontag and the Practice of Modernism," *DAI* 43 (1982): 1541A.

THE BENEFACTOR

Bassoff, Bruce, "Private Resolution: Sontag's THE BENEFAC-TOR," *Enclitic* 3, ii (1979): 59-78.

Flint, Robert W., in *Ctary* 36 (Dec., 1963): 489-90.

Wain, John, "Song of Myself, 1963," *NRep* 149 (Sept. 21, 1963): 26-7, 30.

DEATH KIT

Lehan, Richard, "Fiction 1967," *ConL* 9, iv (Autumn, 1968): 551-2.

McCaffery, Larry, "DEATH KIT: Susan Sontag's Dream Narrative," *ConL* 20, iv (Autumn, 1979): 484-99.

Solotaroff, Theodore, "Death in Life," *Ctary* 44 (Nov., 1967): 87-9.

_____, "Interpreting Susan Sontag," *Red Hot Vacuum*, 262-8.

Tanner, T., *City of Words*, 265-8.

Vidal, Gore, "Miss Sontag's New Novel," *Book World* (Sept. 10, 1967): 5+. Also in Vidal, G., *Homage to Daniel Shays*, 295-301.

SORRENTINO, GILBERT, 1929-

GENERAL

Ceserio, Robert L., "Gilbert Sorrentino's Prose Fiction," *Vort* 6 (Fall, 1974): 63-9.

Creeley, Robert, "Xmas as in Merry," *RCF* 1, i (Spring, 1981): 157-8.

Eilenberg, Max, "A Marvellous Gift: Gilbert Sorrentino's Fiction," *RCF* 1, i (Spring, 1981): 88-95.

Elman, Richard, "Reading Gil Sorrentino," *RCF* 1, i (Spring, 1981): 155-6.

"Gilbert Sorrentino—An Interview Conducted by Barry Alpert Westbeth, New York City, April 7, 1974," *Vort* 6 (Fall, 1974): 3-30.

Klinkowitz, Jerome, "Gilbert Sorrentino's Super-Fiction," *ChiR* 25, iv (1974): 77-89. Also, revised, in *Vort* 6 (1974): 69-79.

_____, *Literary Disruptions*, 154-67.

O'Brien, John, "Gilbert Sorrentino: Some Various Looks," *Vort* 6 (1974): 79-85.

_____, "Imaginative Qualities of Gilbert Sorrentino: An Interview," *GrossR* 6 (1973): 69-84.

_____, "An Interview with Gilbert Sorrentino," *RCF* 1, i (Spring, 1981): 5-27. [A portion of this interview appeared in *GrossR* above.]

Olson, Toby, "Sorrentino's Past," *RCF* 1, i (Spring, 1981): 52-5.

Phelps, Donald, "Extra Space," *Vort* 6 (1974): 89-96.

Roudiez, Leon S., "The Reality Changes," *RCF* 1, i (Spring, 1981): 132-42.

ABERRATION OF STARLIGHT

Dowell, Coleman, "Gilbert Sorrentino's ABERRATION OF STARLIGHT," *RCF* 1, i (Spring, 1981): 143-42.

Lodge, David, "The Sad Heart at the Carnival," *TLS* 4084 (July 10, 1981): 774.

HOTEL SPLENDIDE

Thesen, Sharon, "in the song/of the alphabet: Gilbert Sorrentino's SPLENDIDE HOTEL," *RCF* 1, i (Spring, 1981): 56-61.

Weinfield, Henry, "After the Deluge: An Essay on Splendide Hotel," *Vort* 6 (Fall, 1974): 61-3.

IMAGINATIVE QUALITIES OF ACTUAL THINGS

Armstrong, Peter, "Gilbert Sorrentino IMAGINATIVE QUALITIES OF ACTUAL THINGS," *GrossR* 6 (1973): 65-8.

Emerson, Stephen, "IMAGINATIVE QUALITIES OF ACTUAL THINGS," *Vort* 6 (Fall, 1974): 85-9.

Hannigan, Paul, "IMAGINATIVE QUALITIES OF ACTUAL THINGS," *Ploughshares* 1 (Spring, 1973): 92-4.

Klinkowitz, J., *Literary Disruptions*, 159-62.

Wright, Martin, "Gilbert Sorrentino's IMAGINATIVE QUALITIES OF ACTUAL THINGS," *GrossR* 6 (1973): 61-4.

MULLIGAN STEW

Brown, Harold I., "Self-Reference in Logic and MULLIGAN STEW," *Diogenes* 118 (Summer, 1982): 121-42.

Bruns, Gerald L., "A Short Defense of Plagiary," *RCF* 1, i (Spring, 1981): 96-103.

Cioffi, Frank, "Gilbert Sorrentino's Science Fiction World in MULLIGAN STEW," *Extrapolation* 22 (1981): 140-5.

Dunlap, Lowell, "Blue Indigo," *RCF* 1, i (Spring, 1981): 130-1.

Greiner, Donald J., "Anthony Lamont in Search of Gilbert Sorrentino: Character and MULLIGAN STEW," *RCF* 1, i (Spring, 1991): 104-12.

Mosley, Nicholas, "Gilbert Sorrentino and MULLIGAN STEW," *RCF* 1, i (Spring, 1981): 153-4.

O'Brien, John, "Every Man His Life," *RCF* 1, i (Spring, 1981): 62-80.

Saltzman, Arthur M., "Wordy Tombs," *ChiR* 31, iv (1980): 95-9.

Share, Bernard, "On Giving Up Fictioneering," *RCF* 1, i (Spring, 1981): 168-70.

Tindall, Kenneth, "Adam and Eve on a Raft: Some Aspects of Love and Death in MULLIGAN STEW," *RCF* 1, i (Spring, 1981): 159-67.

Werner, C. H., *Paradoxical Resolutions*, 197-200.

THE SKY CHANGES

Emmett, Paul, "THE SKY CHANGES: A Journey into the Unconscious and a Road into the Novels of Gilbert Sorrentino," *RCF* 1, i (Spring, 1981): 113-29.

SPLENDIDE HOTEL (See HOTEL SPLENDIDE)

STEELWORK

Alpert, Barry, "Local Turf: Re: STEELWORK, by Gilbert Sorrentino," *Vort* 6 (Fall, 1974): 59-61.

Byrne, Jack, "Sorrentino's STEELWORK: Expanding Eddy Beshary's 'Annual Listing' (or) 'Besharyism'," *RCF* 1, i (Spring, 1981): 171-89.

SOUTHERN, TERRY, 1924-

GENERAL

Algren, Nelson, "The Donkeyman by Twilight," *Nation* 198 (May 18, 1964): 509-12.

CANDY

Arn, Robert, "Obscenity and Pornography," *CamR* 89A (Dec. 2, 1967): 161-2.

McLaughlin, John J., "Satirical Comical Pornographical CANDY," *KanQ* 1, iii (Summer, 1969): 98-103.

Murray, Donald M., "Candy Christian as a Pop-Art Daisy Miller," *JPC* 5, ii (Fall, 1971): 340-7.

Silva, Edward T., "From CANDIDE to CANDY: Love's Labor Lost," *JPC* 8 (1974): 783-91.

Walling, William, "CANDY in Context," *NYLF* 1 (1978): 229-40.

THE MAGIC CHRISTIAN

Scholes, R., *Fabulation and Metafiction*, 165-8.

_____, *Fabulators*, 61-6.

SPARK, MURIEL, 1918-

GENERAL

Adler, Renata, in Kostelanetz, R., ed., *On Contemporary Fiction*, 591-6.

Baldanza, Frank, "Muriel Spark and the Occult," *WSCL* 6 (Summer, 1965): 190-203.

Bradbury, Malcolm, "Muriel Spark's Fingernails," *CritQ* 14, iii (Autumn, 1972): 241-50. Also in Spack, P. M., ed., *Contempo-*

rary Women Novelists, 137-49. Also in Bradbury, M., *Possibilities*, 221-30.

Davison, Peter, "The Miracles of Muriel Spark," *Atlantic* 222 (Oct., 1968): 139-42.

Dobie, Ann B., "Muriel Sparks's Definition of Reality," *Crit* 12, i (1970): 20-7.

Greene, George, "*Côte de Chez Disaster*: The Novels of Muriel Spark," *PLL* 16, iii (Summer, 1980): 295-315.

_____, "A Reading of Muriel Spark," *Thought* 43 (Autumn, 1968): 393-407.

Grosskurth, Phyllis, "The World of Muriel Spark: Spirits or Spooks?" *TamR* 39 (Spring, 1966): 62-7.

Harrison, Bernard, "Muriel Spark and Jane Austen," in Josipovici, G., ed., *Modern English Novel*, 225-51.

Hoyt, Charles A., "Muriel Spark: The Surrealist Jane Austen," in Shapiro, C., ed., *Contemporary British Novelists*, 125-43.

Hynes, Joseph, "After Marabar: Reading Forster, Robbe-Grillet, Spark," *IowaR* 5, i (Winter, 1974): 120-6.

Hynes, Samuel, "The Prime of Miss Muriel Spark," *Cweal* 75 (Feb. 23, 1962): 562-8.

Jacobsen, Josephine, "A Catholic Quarter," *ChS* 47 (Summer, 1964): 140-3.

Jones, Jacqueline A., "The Absurd in the Fiction of Muriel Spark," *DAI* 36 (1975): 317A-18A.

Kelleher, V. M. K., "The Religious Artistry of Muriel Spark," *CR* 18 (1976): 79-92.

Kemp, P., *Muriel Spark*.

Kennedy, A., *Protean Self*, 151-211.

Kermode, Frank, "The House of Fiction: Interviews with Seven English Novelists," *PR* 30 (Spring, 1963): 79-82.

_____, "The Prime of Miss Muriel Spark," *NStat* 66 (Sept. 27, 1963): 397-8. Also as "To the Girls of Slender Means," in Kermode, F., *Continuities*, 202-7.

Keyser, Barbara E. Y., "The Dual Vision of Muriel Spark," *DAI* 32 (1972): 4005A.

_____, "Muriel Spark's Gargoyles," *Descant* 20, i (Fall, 1975): 32-9.

Laffin, Gerry S., "Unresolved Dualities in the Novels of Muriel Spark," *DAI* 34 (1974): 4268A.

Legris, Maurice R., "Muriel Spark's Use of the Non-Material: Prolegomena to a Theological Critique," *DAI* 34 (1974): 7763A-64A.

Malin, Irving, "The Deceptions of Muriel Spark," in Friedman, M. J., ed., *Vision Obscured*, 95-107.

Malkoff, Karl, "Demonology and Dualism: The Supernatural in Isaac Singer and Muriel Spark," in Malin, I., ed., *Critical Views of Isaac Bashevis Singer*, 149-68.

_____, *Muriel Spark*.

Mansfield, Joseph, G., "Another World Than This: The Gothic and Catholic in the Novels of Muriel Spark," *DAI* 34 (1974): 5980A.

Massie, A., *Muriel Spark*.

Mayne, Richard, "Fiery Particle: On Muriel Spark," *Encounter* 25 (Dec., 1969): 61-8.

McBrien, William, "Muriel Spark: the Novelist as Dandy," in Staley, T. F., ed., *Twentieth-Century Women Novelists*, 153-78.

McLeod, Patrick G., "Vision and the Moral Encounter: A Reading of Muriel Spark," *DAI* 34 (1973): 1286A-87A.

Mongeon, Joanne C. P., "A Theology of Juxtaposition: Muriel Spark as a Catholic Comic Novelist," *DAI* 38 (1977): 2778A.

Murphy, Carol, "A Spark of the Supernatural," *Approach* 60 (Summer, 1966): 26-30.

Niall, Brenda, "The Voice of Muriel Spark," *TC* 26 (Autumn, 1972): 197-203.

Potter, Nancy A., J., "Muriel Spark: Transformer of the Commonplace," *Ren* 17 (Spring, 1965): 115-20.

Quinn, Joseph A., "A Study of the Satiric Element in the Novels of Muriel Spark," *DAI* 30 (1970): 3954A.

Reed, Douglas, "Taking Cocktails with Life," *Books and Bookmen* 16, xi (Aug., 1971): 10-14.

Richmond, Velma B., "The Darkening Vision of Muriel Spark," *Crit* 15, i (1973): 71-85.

Ricks, Christopher, "Extreme Distances," *NYRB* 11 (Dec. 19, 1968): 30-2.

Schneider, Harold W., "A Writer in Her Prime: The Fiction of Muriel Spark," *Crit* 5, ii (Fall, 1962): 28-45.

Snow, Lotus, "Muriel Spark and the Uses of Mythology," *RS* 45, i (1977): 38-44.

Spark, Muriel, "Keeping It Short—Muriel Spark Talks About Her Books to Ian Gillham," *Listener* 84 (1970): 411-13.

Stanford, Derek, *Muriel Spark.*

_____, "The Work of Muriel Spark: An Essay on Her Fictional Method," *Month* 28 (Aug., 1962): 92-9.

Stubbs, Patricia, *Muriel Spark.*

_____, "Two Contemporary Views on Fiction: Iris Murdoch and Muriel Spark," *English* 23 (Autumn, 1974): 102-10.

Swinden, P., *Unofficial Selves,* 221-30.

Updike, John, "Creatures of the Air," *NY* 37 (Sept. 30, 1967): 161-7.

Whittaker, Ruth, "'Angels Dining at the Ritz': The Faith and Fiction of Muriel Spark," in *Contemporary English Novel,* 157-79.

Wilce, Gillian, "Her Life in Fiction," *New Edinburgh Review* 55 (1981): 13-14. [Not seen.]

Wildman, John H., "Translated by Muriel Spark," in Sanford, D. E., ed., *Nine Essays in Modern Literature,* 129-44.

THE ABBESS OF CREWE

Greene, George, "*Du Côte de Chez Disaster:* The Novels of Muriel Spark," *PLL* 16, iii (Summer, 1980): 307-10.

Keyser, Barbara Y., "Muriel Spark, Watergate, and the Mass Media," *ArQ* 32 (Summer, 1976): 146-53.

Massie, A., *Muriel Spark,* 81-5.

Snow, Lotus, "Muriel Spark and the Uses of Mythology," *RS* 45, i (1977): 40-3.

THE BACHELORS

Kemp, P., *Muriel Spark,* 59-60.

Kennedy, A., *Protean Self,* 182-5.

Malkoff, Karl, "Demonology and Dualism: The Supernatural in Isaac Singer and Muriel Spark," in Malin, I., ed., *Critical Views of Isaac Bashevis Singer,* 164-6.

_____, *Muriel Spark,* 26-30.

Massie, A., *Muriel Spark,* 31-43.

Schneider, Harold W., "A Writer in Her Prime: The Fiction of Muriel Spark," *Crit* 5, ii (Fall, 1962): 40-2.

Stubbs, P., *Muriel Spark,* 15-17.

THE BALLAD OF PECKHAM RYE

Dierckx, J., "A Devil-figure in a Contemporary Setting: Muriel Spark's THE BALLAD OF PECKHAM RYE," *RLV* 33 (1967): 576-87.

Kemp, P., *Muriel Spark,* 48-59.

Kelleher, V. M. K., "The Religious Artistry of Muriel Spark," *CR* 18 (1976): 79-82.

Kennedy, A., *Protean Self,* 175-82.

Lanning, George, "Silver Fish in the Plumbing," *KR* 23 (Winter, 1961): 173-5, 177-8.

Malkoff, Karl, "Demonology and Dualism: The Supernatural in Isaac Singer and Muriel Spark," in Malin, I., *Critical Views of Isaac Bashevis Singer,* 157-61.

_____, *Muriel Spark,* 22-6.

Stubbs, P., *Muriel Spark,* 12-15.

Wildman, John H., in Sanford, D. E., ed., *Nine Essays in Modern Literature,* 133-5.

THE COMFORTERS

Dobie, Ann B., and Carl Wooton, "Spark and Waugh: Similarities by Coincidence," *MQ* 13, iv (Summer, 1972): 423-34.

Kemp, P., *Muriel Spark,* 17-29.

Kennedy, A., *Protean Self,* 164-71.

Kermode, Frank, "The Prime of Miss Muriel Spark," *NStat* 66 (Sept. 27, 1963): 397. Also as "To the Girls of Slender Means," in Kermode, F., *Continuities,* 203-4.

Malkoff, K., *Muriel Spark,* 7-11.

McBrien, William, "Muriel Spark: The Novelist as Dandy," in Staley, T. F., ed., *Twentieth-Century Women Novelists,* 155-9.

Price, Martin, in *YR* 47 (Autumn, 1957): 148-50.

Schneider, Harold W., "A Writer in Her Prime: The Fiction of Muriel Spark," *Crit* 5, ii (Fall, 1962): 36-7.

Stanford, D., *Muriel Spark,* 123-6.

Swinden, P., *Unofficial Selves,* 223-4.

Whittaker, Ruth, "'Angels Dining at the Ritz': The Faith and Fiction of Muriel Spark," in *Contemporary English Novel,* 172-4.

Wildman, John H., in Sanford, D. E., ed., *Nine Essays in Modern Literature,* 133-5.

THE DRIVER'S SEAT

Bradbury, Malcolm, "Muriel Spark's Fingernails," *CritQ* 14, iii (Autumn, 1972): 247-50. Also in Spacks, P. M., *Contemporary Women Novelists,* 145-9. Also in Bradbury, M., *Possibilities,* 252-5.

Greene, George, "*Du Côte de Chez Disaster:* The Novels of Muriel Spark," *PLL* 16, iii (Summer, 1980): 299-302.

Kemp, A., *Muriel Spark,* 122-30.

Kennedy, A., *Protean Self,* 201-5.

Richmond, Velma B., "The Darkening Vision of Muriel Spark," *Crit* 15, i (1973): 76-80.

Snow, Lotus, "Muriel Spark and the Uses of Mythology," *RS* 45, i (1977): 39-40.

Whittaker, Ruth, "'Angel at the Ritz': The Faith and Fiction of Muriel Spark," in *Contemporary English Novel,* 175-8.

THE GIRLS OF SLENDER MEANS

Adler, Renata, in Kostelanetz, R., ed., *On Contemporary Literature,* 593-6.

Anon., in *TLS* (Sept. 20, 1963): 701. Also in *T. L. S.: Essays and Reviews from The Times Literary Supplement, 1963,* 100-2.

Casson, Alan, "Muriel Spark's THE GIRLS OF SLENDER MEANS," *Crit* 7, ii (1965): 94-6.

Kelleher, V. M. K., "The Religious Artistry of Muriel Spark," *CR* 18 (1976): 87-1.

Kemp, P., *Muriel Spark,* 84-96.

Kermode, Frank, "The Prime of Miss Muriel Spark," *NStat* 66 (Sept. 27, 1963): 398. Also as "To the Girls of Slender Means," in Kermode, F., *Continuities,* 206-7.

Malkoff, K., *Muriel Spark,* 36-9.

Massie, A., *Muriel Spark,* 52-8.

Soule, George, "Must a Novelist Be an Artist?" *CarlM* 5 (Spring, 1964): 92-8.

Stubbs, P., *Muriel Spark,* 24-5.

THE HOTHOUSE BY THE EAST RIVER

Blodgett, Harriet, "Desegregated Art by Muriel Spark," *IFR* 3, i (Jan., 1976): 25-9.

Greene, George, "*Du Côte de Chez Disaster:* The Novels of Muriel Spark," *PLL* 16, iii (Summer, 1980): 304-7.

Kemp, P., *Muriel Spark,* 141-58.

Massie, A., *Muriel Spark,* 77-80.

THE MANDELBAUM GATE

Anon., in *TLS* (Oct. 14, 1965): 913. Also in *T. L. S.: and Reviews from The Times Literary Supplement, 1965,* 34-6.

Berthoff, Warner, "Fortunes of the Novel: Muriel Spark and Iris Murdoch," *MR* 8 (Spring, 1967): 304-13. Also in Berthoff, W., *Fictions and Events,* 121-30.

Cohen, Gerda L., "Tilting the Balance," *Midstream* 12 (Jan., 1966): 68-70.

Enright, D. J., "Public Doctrine and Private Judging," *NStat* 70 (Oct. 15, 1965): 563, 566. Also in Enright, D. J., *Man is an Onion,* 32-8.

Greene, George, "*Du Côte de Chez Disaster:* The Novels of Muriel Spark," *PLL* 16, iii (Summer, 1980): 296-9.

Grosskurth, Phyllis, "The World of Muriel Spark: Spirits or Spooks?" *TamR* 39 (Spring, 1966): 65-7.

Harrison, Bernard, "Muriel Spark and Jane Austen," in Josipovici, G., ed., *Modern English Novel,* 244-7.

Kemp, P., *Muriel Spark,* 97-112.

Kennedy, A., *Protean Self,* 152-4.

Kermode, Frank, "The Novel as Jerusalem: Muriel Spark's MANDELBAUM GATE," *Atlantic* 216 (Oct., 1965): 92-8. Also in Kermode, F., *Continuities,* 207-16.

Malkoff, K., *Muriel Spark,* 39-45.

Massie, A., *Muriel Spark,* 61-73.

Stubbs, P., *Muriel Spark,* 25-32.

Sudrann, Jean, "Hearth and Horizon: Changing Concepts of the 'Domestic' Life of the Heroine," *MR* 14, ii (Spring, 1973): 250-5.

Swinden, P., *Unofficial Selves,* 225-30.

MEMENTO MORI

Gable, Sister Mariella, "Prose Satire and the Modern Christian Temper," *ABR* 11 (Mar.-June, 1960): 29-30, 33.

Kemp, P., *Muriel Spark,* 38-48.

Kennedy, A., *Protean Self,* 173-5.

Malkoff, K., *Muriel Spark,* 17-22.

Massie, A., *Muriel Spark,* 24-30.

Schneider, Harold W., "A Writer in Her Prime: The Fiction of Muriel Spark," *Crit* 5, ii (Fall, 1962): 38-9.

Stanford, D., *Muriel Spark,* 128-31.

Stubbs, P., *Muriel Spark,* 7-12.

Wildman, John H., in Stanford, D. E., ed., *Nine Essays in Modern Literature,* 130-3.

NOT TO DISTURB

Blodgett, Harriet, "Desegregated Art by Muriel Spark," *IFR* 3, i (Jan., 1976): 25-9.

Greene, George, "*Du Côte de Chez Disaster:* The Novels of Muriel Spark," *PLL* 16, iii (Summer, 1980): 302-4.

Kemp, P., *Muriel Spark,* 130-40.

Kennedy A., *Protean Self,* 205-10.

Richmond, Velma B., "The Darkening Vision of Muriel Spark," *Crit* 15, i (1973): 80-4.

THE PRIME OF MISS JEAN BRODIE

Auerbach, Nina, *Communities of Women: An Ideal in Fiction,* Cambridge, Mass. and London: Harvard Un. Pr., 1978, 167-76.

Dobie, Ann B., "THE PRIME OF MISS JEAN BRODIE: Muriel Spark Bridges the Credulity Gap," *ArQ* 25 (Autumn, 1969): 217-28.

Dorenkamp, J. H., "Moral Vision in Muriel Spark's THE PRIME OF MISS JEAN BRODIE," *Ren* 32 (1980): 3-9.

Harrison, Bernard, "Muriel Spark and Jane Austen," in Josipovici, G., ed., *Modern English Novel,* 237-4.

Holloway, John, "Narrative Structure and Text Structure: Isherwood's A MEETING BY THE RIVER and Muriel Spark's THE PRIME OF MISS JEAN BRODIE," *CritI* 1 (1975): 581-605.

Kelleher, V. M. K., "The Religious Artistry of Muriel Spark," *CR* 18 (1976): 83-5.

Kemp, P., *Muriel Spark,* 71-84.

Kennedy, A., *Protean Self,* 185-94.

Keyser, Barbara, "The Transfiguration of Edinburgh in THE PRIME OF MISS JEAN BRODIE," *SSL* 12, iii (Jan., 1975): 181-9.

Laffin, Garry S., "Muriel Spark's Portrait of the Artist as a Young Girl," *Ren* 24, iv (Summer, 1972): 213-23.

Lodge, David, "The Uses and Abuses of Omniscience: Method and Meaning in Muriel Spark's THE PRIME OF MISS JEAN BRODIE," *CritI* 12, iii (Autumn, 1970): 235-57. Also in Lodge, D., *Novelist at the Crossroads,* 119-44.

Massie, A., *Muriel Spark,* 45-52.

Paul, Anthony, "Muriel Spark and THE PRIME OF MISS JEAN BRODIE," *DQR* 7 (1977): 170-83.

Ray, Philip E., "Jean Brodie and Edinburgh: Personality and Place in Muriel Spark's THE PRIME OF MISS JEAN BRODIE," *SSL* 13 (1978): 24-31.

Schneider, Harold W., "A Writer in Her Prime: The Fiction of Muriel Spark," *Crit* 5, ii (Fall, 1962): 42-4.

Schneider, Mary W., "The Double Life in Muriel Spark's THE PRIME OF MISS JEAN BRODIE," *MQ* 18 (1977): 418-31.

Stanford, D., *Muriel Spark,* 133-7.

Stubbs, P., *Muriel Spark,* 17-24.

Wildman, John H., in Stanford, D. E., ed., *Nine Essays in Modern Literature*, 141-2.

THE PUBLIC IMAGE

Anon., "Shallowness Everywhere," *TLS* (June 13, 1968): 612. Also in *T. L. S.: Essays and Reviews from The Times Literary Supplement, 1968*, 71-3.

Davison, Peter, "The Miracles of Muriel Spark," *Atlantic* 222 (Oct., 1968): 140-2.

Kemp, P., *Muriel Spark*, 115-22.

Kennedy, A., *Protean Self*, 195-201.

Malkoff, K., *Muriel Spark*, 45-6.

Richmond, Velma B., "The Darkening Vision of Muriel Spark," *Crit* 15, i (1973): 72-6.

Stewart, G., *New Mythos*, 34-5.

ROBINSON

Greene, George, "*Du Côte de Chez Disaster:* The Novels of Muriel Spark," *PLL* 16, iii (Summer, 1980): 310-13.

Kemp, P., *Muriel Spark*, 29-37.

Kennedy, A., *Protean Self*, 171-3.

Malkoff, K., *Muriel Spark*, 11-16.

Ohmann, Carol B., "Muriel Spark's ROBINSON," *Crit* 8, i (Fall, 1965): 70-84.

Stanford, D., *Muriel Spark*, 126-8.

Wildman, John H., in Stanford, D. E., ed., *Nine Essays on Modern Literature*, 135-9.

THE TAKEOVER

Massie, A., *Muriel Spark*, 85-9.

BIBLIOGRAPHY

Malkoff, K., *Muriel Spark*, 47-8.

SPENCER, ELIZABETH, 1921-

GENERAL

Broadwell, Elizabeth P., and Ronald W. Hoag, "A Conversation with Elizabeth Spencer," *SoR* 18, i (Winter, 1982): 111-30.

Bunting, Charles T., "'In That Time and at That Place': The Literary World of Elizabeth Spencer," *MissQ* 28, iv (Fall, 1975): 435-60. [Interview.]

Cole, Hunter M., "Elizabeth Spencer at Sycamore Fair," *NMW* 6 (Winter, 1974): 81-6. [Interview.]

————, "Windsor in Spencer and Welty: A Real and an Imaginary Landscape," *NMW* 7, i (Spring, 1974): 2-11.

Haley, Josephine, "An Interview with Elizabeth Spencer," *NMW* 1, ii (Fall, 1968): 42-53.

Jones, J. G., *Mississippi Writers Talking*, Vol. I, 95-12.

McDonald, W. U., Jr., "Blurbs: Welty on Elizabeth Spencer," *EuWN* 3 (1979): 7-9. [Not seen.]

FIRE IN THE MORNING

Burger, Nash K., "Elizabeth Spencer's Three Mississippi Novels," *SAQ* 63 (Summer, 1964): 351-4.

KNIGHTS AND DRAGONS

Anderson, Hilton, "Elizabeth Spencer's Two Italian Novellas," *NMW* 13, i (1981): 18-35.

Kauffmann, Stanley, "Sense and Sensibility," *NRep* 152 (June 26, 1965): 27-8.

THE LIGHT IN THE PIAZZA

Anderson, Hilton, "Elizabeth Spencer's Two Italian Novellas," *NMW* 13, i (1981): 18-35.

Miller, Nolan, "Three of the 'Best'," *AR* 21 (Spring, 1961): 123-5.

THIS CROOKED WAY

Burger, Nash K., "Elizabeth Spencer's Three Mississippi Novels," *SAQ* 63 (Summer, 1964): 354-7.

THE VOICE AT THE BACK DOOR

Burger, Nash K., "Elizabeth Spencer's Three Mississippi Novels," *SAQ* 63 (Summer, 1964): 357-62.

Hoffman, F. J., *Art of Southern Fiction*, 113-14.

Meeker, Richard K., in Simonini, R. C., ed., *Southern Writers*, 175-6.

Pugh, David G., "THE VOICE AT THE BACK DOOR: Elizabeth Spencer Looks Into Mississippi," in French, W., ed., *Fifties*, 103-110.

BIBLIOGRAPHY

Barge, Laura, "An Elizabeth Spencer Checklist, 1948 to 1976," *MissQ* 29 (1976): 569-90.

STAFFORD, JEAN, 1915-1979

GENERAL

Auchincloss, L., *Pioneers and Caretakers*, 152-60.

Avila, Wanda E., "The Ironic Fiction of Jean Stafford," *DAI* 41 (1980): 2108A.

Eisinger, C. E., *Fiction of the Forties*, 294-306.

Hasan, Ihab, "Jean Stafford: The Expense of Style and the Scope of Sensibility," *WR* 19 (Spring, 1955): 185-203.

Jenson, Sidney L., "The Noble Wicked West of Jean Stafford," *WAL* 7 (Winter, 1973): 261-70.

Vickery, Olga, W., "Jean Stafford the Ironic Vision," *SAQ* 61 (Autumn, 1962): 484-91.

————, "The Novels of Jean Stafford," *Crit* 5, i (Spring-Summer, 1962): 14-26.

BOSTON ADVENTURE

Auchincloss, L., *Pioneers and Caretakers*, 152-4.

Eisinger, C. E., *Fiction of the Forties*, 296-8.

Hassan, Ihab, "Jean Stafford: The Expense of Style and the Scope of Sensibility," *WR* 19 (Spring, 1955): 185-91.

Mann, Jeanette W., "Toward New Archetypal Forms: BOSTON ADVENTURE," *SNNTS* 8 (1976): 291-303.

Vickery, Olga W., "The Novels of Jean Stafford," *Crit* 5, i (Spring-Summer, 1962): 14-19.

THE CATHERINE WHEEL

Auchincloss, L., *Pioneers and Caretakers*, 157-9.

Eisinger, C. E., *Fiction of the Forties*, 301-6.

Hassan, Ihab, "Jean Stafford: The Expense of Style and the Scope of Sensibility," *WR* 19 (Spring, 1955); 194-7.

Mann, Jeanette W., "Toward New Archetypal Forms: Jean Stafford's THE CATHERINE WHEEL," *Crit* 17, ii (1975): 77-92.

Vickery, Olga W., "The Novels of Jean Stafford," *Crit* 5, i (Spring-Summer, 1962): 23-6.

THE MOUNTAIN LION

Auchincloss, L., *Pioneers and Caretakers*, 155-7.

Burns, Stuart L., "Counterpoint in Jean Stafford's THE MOUNTAIN LION," *Crit* 9, ii (1967): 20-32.

Eisinger, C. E., *Fiction of the Forties*, 298-301.

Gelfant, Blanche H., "Revolutionary Turnings: THE MOUNTAIN LION Reread," *MI* 20 (1979): 117-25.

Hassan, Ihab, "Jean Stafford: The Expense of Style and the Scope of Sensibility," *WR* 19 (Spring, 1955): 191-4.

Vickery, Olga W., "The Novels of Jean Stafford," *Crit* 5, i (Spring-Summer, 1962): 19-23.

White, Barbara, "Initiation, the West, and the Hunt in Jean Stafford's THE MOUNTAIN LION," *ELWIU* 9, ii (Fall, 1982): 194-210.

STEAD, CHRISTINA, 1902-1983

GENERAL

Anderson, Don, "Christina Stead's Unforgettable Dinner-Parties," *Southerly* 39, i (Mar., 1979): 28-45.

Beston, John B., "An Interview with Christina Stead," *WLWE* 15 (1976): 87-95.

Brydon, Diana, "Christina Stead as an Australian Writer," *WLWE* 18, i (1979): 124-9.

"Christina Stead: An Interview," *ALS* 6 (1973): 230-48.

Fagan, Robert, "Christina Stead," *PR* 46, ii (1979): 262-70.

Geering, R. G., "The Achievement of Christina Stead," *Southerly* 22, iv (1962): 193-212.

_____, *Christina Stead*.

_____, *Christina Stead*. (Australian Writers and Their Work.)

_____, "Christina Stead in the 1960's," *Southerly* 28, i (1968): 26-36.

Green, H. M., *History of Australian Literature*, 1070-77.

Hadgraft, C., *Australian Literature*, 246-8.

Hooton, Joy, "Christina Stead, an Original Novelist," *Hemisphere* 26, vi (May/June, 1982): 341-5.

Jamison, Greeba, "Christina Stead 'Can't Help Being Original'," *Walkabout* 36 (July, 1970): 36-7. [Not seen.]

Lidoff, Joan, *Christina Stead*.

_____, "Christina Stead: An Interview," *Aphra* 6, iii-iv (Spring/Summer, 1976): 39-64.

_____, "The Female Ego: Christina Stead's Heroines," *New Boston Rev.* 2, iii (1977): 19-20. [Not seen.]

_____, "Home is Where the Heart Is: The Fiction of Christina Stead," *Southerly* 38, iv (Dec., 1978): 363-75.

Pybus, Rodney, "The Light and the Dark: The Fiction of Christina Stead," *Stand* 10, i (1968): 30-7.

Reid, Ian, "Form and Expectation in Christina Stead's Novellas," *LCrit* 15, iii-iv (1980): 48-58.

Roderick, Colin, "Christina Stead," *Southerly* 27, i (1967): 87-82.

_____, *Introduction to Australian Literature*, 132-8.

Saxelby, Jean, and Gwen Walker-Smith, "Christina Stead," *Biblionews* (Book Collectors Soc. of Australia) 2 (Dec., 1949): 37-43. [Not seen.]

Smith, Graeme K., "Christina Stead: A Profile," *Westerly* 1 (1976): 67-75.

Walt, James, "An Australian Novelist Looks At Americans: A Comment on the Novels of Christina Stead," *UES* 4 (Nov., 1969): 34-9.

Wetherell, Rodney, "Interview with Christina Stead," *ALS* 9 (1980): 431-48.

Whitehead, Ann, "Interview with Christina Stead," *ALS* 6 (May, 1974): 230-48.

Wilding, Michael, "Christina Stead's Australian Novels," *Southerly* 27, i (1967): 20-33.

THE BEAUTIES AND THE FURIES

Geering, R. G., *Christina Stead*, 56-65.

West, Rebecca, "Christina Stead: A Tribute," *Stand* 23, iv (1982): 31-3.

COTTER'S ENGLAND (See DARK PLACES OF THE HEART)

DARK PLACES OF THE HEART

Geering, R. G., *Christina Stead*, 106-20.

_____, *Christina Stead* (Australian Writers and Their Work), 32-6.

_____, "Christina Stead in the 1960's," *Southerly* 28, i (1968): 28-34.

Lidoff, J., *Christina Stead*, 158-64.

Pybus, Rodney, "COTTER'S ENGLAND: In Appreciation," *Stand* 23, iv (1982): 40-7.

Sturm, Terry, "Christina Stead's New Realism: THE MAN WHO LOVED CHILDREN and COTTER'S ENGLAND," in Anderson, D., and S. Knight, eds., *Cunning Exiles*, 20-34.

West, Paul, "A Lady in Waiting," *NYHTBW* (Sept. 11, 1966): 4, 8.

Yglesias, Jose, "Marking Off a Chunk of England," *Nation* 203 (Oct. 24, 1966): 420-1.

FOR LOVE ALONE

Clancy, Laurie, *Christina Stead's THE MAN WHO LOVED CHILDREN and FOR LOVE ALONE*, Melbourne: Shellington House, 1981.

Duchêne, Anne, "Victors of Love," *TLS* (Sept. 8, 1978): 985.

Geering, R. D., *Christina Stead*, 106-20.

_____, *Christina Stead* (Australian Writers and Their Work), 23-7.

Higgins, Susan, "Christina Stead's FOR LOVE ALONE: a Female Odyssey?" *Southerly* 4 (1978): 428-45.

Kiernan, K., *Images of Society and Nature*, 65-81.

Lidoff, J., *Christina Stead*, 57-103.

Reid, Ian, "'The Woman Problem' in Some Australian and New Zealand Novels," *SoRA* 7, iii (1974): 192-9.

Roderick, Colin, "Christina Stead," *Southerly* 7, ii (1946): 89-91.

_____, *Introduction to Australian Literature*, 135-7.

Sage, Lorna, "Inheriting the Future: FOR LOVE ALONE," *Stand* 23, iv (1982): 34-9.

Stewart, Douglas, "Glory and Catastrophe," *The Flesh and the Spirit*, Sydney: Angus & Robertson, 1948, 235-8.

Sturm, Terry, "Christina Stead's New Realism," in Anderson, D., and S. Knight, eds., *Cunning Exiles*, 13-15.

West, Rebecca, "Christina Stead: A Tribute," *Stand* 23, iv (1982): 31-3.

Wilding, Michael, "Christina Stead's Australian Novels," *Southerly* 27, i (1967): 27-33.

HOUSE OF ALL NATIONS

Geering, R. G., *Christina Stead*, 66-85.

_____, *Christina Stead* (Australian Writers and Their Work.), 14-18.

Lidoff, J., *Christina Stead*, 136-41.

LETTY FOX: HER LUCK

Duchêne, Anne, "Victors of Love," *TLS* (Sept. 8, 1978): 985.

Geering, R. G., *Christina Stead*, 122-34.

_____, *Christina Stead* (Australian Writers and Their Work), 27-9.

Law, Pamela, "LETTY FOX: HER LUCK," *Southerly* 4 (1978): 448-53.

Lidoff, J., *Christina Stead*, 142-8.

Perkins, Elizabeth, "Energy and Originality in Some Characters of Christina Stead," *JCL* 15, i (1980): 107-13.

McCrory, Mary, in *NYTBR* (Oct. 6, 1946): 24.

THE LITTLE HOTEL

Geering, R. G., "What is Normal? Two Recent Novels by Christina Stead," *Southerly* 38, iv (Dec., 1978): 463-9.

Lidoff, J., *Christina Stead*, 153-9.

A LITTLE TEA, A LITTLE CHAT

Geering, R. G., *Christina Stead* (Australian Writers and Their Work), 29-30.

Lidoff, J., *Christina Stead*, 148-9.

THE MAN WHO LOVED CHILDREN

Apstein, Barbara, "MADAM BOVARY and THE MAN WHO LOVED CHILDREN," *IFR* 7 (1989): 127-9.

Brady, Veronica, "THE MAN WHO LOVED CHILDREN and the Body of the World," *Meanjin* 37 (1978): 229-39.

Burns, Graham, "The Moral Design of THE MAN WHO LOVED CHILDREN," *CR* 14 (1971): 38-61.

Clancy, Laurie, *Christina Stead's THE MAN WHO LOVED CHILDREN and FOR LOVE ALONE*, Melbourne: Shellington House, 1981.

Geering, R. G., *Christina Stead*, 86-106.

_____, *Christina Stead* (Australian Writers and Their Work), 18-23.

Green, Dorothy, "THE MAN WHO LOVED CHILDREN: Storm in a Tea-Cup," in Ramson, W. S., ed., *Australian Experience*, 174-208.

Hardwick, Elizabeth, "The Novels of Christina Stead," *NRep* 133 (Aug. 1, 1955): 17-19. Also in Hardwick, E., *View of My Own*, 41-8.

Horne, Margo, "A Family Portrait: Christina Stead and THE MAN WHO LOVED CHILDREN," *DQR* 11, iii (1981): 209-21.

Howarth, R. G., "Christina Stead," *Biblionews* (Book Collectors Soc. of Australia) 11 (Jan., 1958): 1-3.

Jarrell, Randall, "THE MAN WHO LOVED CHILDREN," *Atlantic* 215 (Mar., 1965): 166-71. Expanded as "An Unread Book," Introduction to *The Man Who Loved Children*, N.Y.: Holt, Rinehart & Winston, 1965; Secker & Warburg, 1966. Also in Jarrell, Randall, *Third Book of Criticism*, N.Y.: Farrar, Straus & Giroux, 1969, c. 1965, 3-51.

Katz, Alfred A., "Some Psychological Themes in a Novel by Christina Stead," *L&P* 15 (Fall, 1965): 210-15.

Lidoff, Joan, "Domestic Gothic: The Imagery of Anger, Christina Stead's MAN WHO LOVED CHILDREN," *SNNTS* 11 (1979): 201-15.

_____, *Christina Stead*, 12-57.

McLaughlin, Marilou B., "Sexual Politics in THE MAN WHO LOVED CHILDREN," *BSUF* 21, iv (1980): 30-7.

Nestor, Pauline, "An Impulse to Self-Expression: THE MAN WHO LOVED CHILDREN," *CR* 18 (1976): 61-78.

Roderick, C., *Introduction to Australian Literature*, 134-5.

Ricks, Christopher, "Domestic Manners," *NYRB* 4 (June 17, 1965): 14-15.

Sturm, Terry, "Christina Stead's New Realism: THE MAN WHO LOVED CHILDREN and COTTER'S ENGLAND," in Anderson, D., and S. Knight, eds., *Cunning Exiles*, 15-20.

Wain, John, in (London) *Observer* (May 22, 1966).

Yglesias, Jose, "Marx as Muse," *Nation* 200 (Apr. 5, 1965): 368-70.

MISS HERBERT (THE SUBURBAN WIFE)

Geering, R. G., "What is Normal? Two Recent Novels by Christina Stead," *Southerly* 38, iv (Dec., 1978): 469-73.

Lidoff, J., *Christina Stead*, 173-5.

Perkins, Elizabeth, "Energy and Originality in Some Characters of Christina Stead," *JCL* 15, i (1980): 107-13.

THE PEOPLE WITH DOGS

Geering, R. G., *Christina Stead*, 142-51.

_____, *Christina Stead* (Australian Writers and Their Work), 30-2.

Hamilton, K. G., "Two Difficult Young Men," in Hamilton, K. G., ed., *Studies in the Recent Australian Novel*, 155-66.

Lidoff, J., *Christina Stead*, 149-53.

SEVEN POOR MEN OF SYDNEY

Barbour, Judith, "Christina Stead: The Sublime Lives of Obscure Men," *Southerly* 38, iv (Dec., 1978): 406-16.

Geering, R. G., *Christina Stead*, 30-45.

_____, *Christina Stead* (Australian Writers and Their Work), 6-10.

_____, "Introduction to *Seven Poor Men of Sydney*, Sydney: Angus 7 Robertson, 1965, ix-xv.

Green, Dorothy, "Chaos, or a Dancing Star? Christina Stead's SEVEN POOR MEN OF SYDNEY," *Meanjin* 27 (1968): 150-61.

Green, H. M., *History of Australian Literature*, 1071-74.

Kiernan, B., *Images of Society and Nature*, 59-65, 79-81.

Lidoff, J., *Christina Stead*, 125-31.

McGregory, Grant, "SEVEN POOR MEN OF SYDNEY: The Historical Dimension," *Southerly* 38, iv (Dec., 1978): 380-404.

Miller, Sidney, in *Westerly* 2 (1968): 61-6.

Roderick, C., *Introduction to Australian Literature*, 133-4.

Thomas, Tony, "Christina Stead: THE SALZBURG TALES, SEVEN POOR MEN OF SYDNEY," *Westerly* 4 (Dec., 1970): 46-53.

Wilding, Michael, "Christina Stead's Australian Novels," *Southerly* 27, i (1967): 20-7.

BIBLIOGRAPHY

Beston, Rose M., "A Christina Stead Bibliography," *WLWE* 15 (Apr., 1976): 96-103.

Ehrhardt, Marianne, comp., "Christina Stead: A Checklist," *ALS* 9 (1980): 508-35.

Geering, R. G., *Christina Stead*, 171-7.

Lidoff, J., *Christina Stead*, 243-50.

STEADMAN, MARK, 1930-

A LION'S SHARE

Greiner, Donald J., "The Southern Fiction of Mark Steadman," *SCR* 9, i (Nov., 1976): 8-11.

MCAFEE COUNTY: A CHRONICLE

Greiner, Donald J., "The Southern Fiction of Mark Steadman," *SCR* 9, i (Nov., 1976): 5-8.

STEGNER, WALLACE EARLE, 1909-1993

GENERAL

Ahearn, Kerry, "Heroes vs. Women: Conflict and Duplicity in Stegner," *WHR* 31, ii (Spring, 1976): 252-67. Also in Lee, L. L., and M. Lewis, eds., *Women, Women Writers, and the West*, 143-58.

Arthur, A., ed., *Critical Essays on Wallace Stegner*.

Canzoneri, Robert, "Wallace Stegner: Trial by Existence," *SoR* 9, iv (Oct., 1973): 796-827.

Dillon, David, "Time's Prisoners: An Interview with Wallace Stegner," *SWR* 61 (Summer, 1976): 252-67. Also in Arthur, A., ed., *Critical Essays on Wallace Stegner*, 47-59.

Eisinger, C. E., *Fiction of the Forties*, 324-8.

_____, "Twenty Years of Wallace Stegner," *CE* 20 (Dec., 1958): 110-16.

Flora, Joseph M., "Vardis Fisher and Wallace Stegner: Teacher and Student," *WAL* 5, ii (Summer, 1970): 121-8.

Henkin, Bill, "Time is Not Just Chronology: An Interview with Wallace Stegner," *MR* 20 (1979): 127-39.

Hofheins, Roger, and Dan Tooker, "Interview with Wallace Stegner," *SoR* 11, iv (Oct., 1975): 794-801.

Jensen, Sidney L., "The Compassionate Seer: Wallace Stegner's Literary Artist," *BYUS* 14 (Winter, 1974): 248-62. Also in Arthur, A., ed., *Critical Essays on Wallace Stegner*, 164-75.

_____, "The Middle Ground: A Study of Wallace Stegner's Use of History in Fiction," *DAI* 33 (1973): 6358A.

Lewis, M., and L. Lewis, *Wallace Stegner*.

Milton, John R., "Conversation with Wallace Stegner," *SDR* 9 (Spring, 1971): 53-4.

Nemanic, Gerald, "Interview with Wallace Stegner," *GLRev* 2, i (1975): 1-25.

Otis, John W., "The Purified Vision: The Fiction of Wallace Stegner," *DAI* 38 (1978): 6123A-24A.

Robinson, Forrest G., and Margaret G. Robinson, "An Interview with Wallace Stegner," *AWest* 15, i (1978): 34-7, 61-3.

_____, *Wallace Stegner*.

Singer, Barnett, "The Historical Ideal in Wallace Stegner's Fiction," *SDR* 15, i (1977): 28-44. Also in Arthur, A., ed., *Critical Essays on Wallace Stegner*, 124-36.

ALL THE LITTLE LIVE THINGS

Lewis, M., and L. Lewis, *Wallace Stegner*, 32-4.

Moseley, Richard, "The First-Person Narration in Wallace Stegner's ALL THE LITTLE LIVE THINGS," *NConL* 3, ii (Mar., 1973): 12-13.

Robinson, F. G., and M. G. Robinson, *Wallace Stegner*, 140-7.

Singer, Barnett, "The Historical Ideal in Wallace Stegner's Fiction," *SDR* 15, i (Spring, 1977): 34-7. Also in Arthur, A., ed., *Critical Essays on Wallace Stegner*, 129-31.

ANGLE OF REPOSE

Ahearn, Kerry, "THE BIG ROCK CANDY MOUNTAIN and ANGLE OF REPOSE: Trial and Culmination," *WAL* 10 (May, 1975): 11-27. Also in Arthur, A., ed., *Critical Essays on Wallace Stegner*, 117-23.

_____, "Heroes vs. Women: Conflict and Duplicity in Stegner," *WHR* 31, ii (Spring, 1977): 135-9.

_____, "Wallace Stegner and John Wesley Powell: The Real-and-Maimed-Western Spokesmen," *SDR* 15, iv (Winter, 1977-78): 40-8.

Etulain, Richard W., "Western Fiction and History: A Reconsideration," in Steffen, J. O., ed., *American West*, 161-70.

Jenson, Sidney L., "The Compassionate Seer: Wallace Stegner's Literary Artist," *BYUS* 14, ii (Winter, 1974): 252-62. Also in Arthur, A., *Critical Essays on Wallace Stegner*, 168-74.

Lewis, M., and L. Lewis, *Wallace Stegner*, 34-7.

Peterson, Audrey C., "Narrative Voice in Wallace Stegner's ANGLE OF REPOSE," *WAL* 10 (1975): 125-33. Also in Arthur, A., ed., *Critical Essays on Wallace Stegner*, 176-83.

Robinson, F. G., and M. G. Robinson, *Wallace Stegner*, 150-9.

Ronda, Bruce A., "Themes of Past and Present in ANGLE OF REPOSE," *SAF* 10, ii (Autumn, 1982): 217-26.

Singer, Barnett, "The Historical Ideal in Wallace Stegner's Fiction," *SDR* 15, i (Spring, 1977): 38-42. Also in Arthur, A., ed., *Critical Essays on Wallace Stegner*, 132-5.

Walsh, Mary E. W., "ANGLE OF REPOSE and the Writings of Mary Hallock Foote: A Source Study," in Arthur, A., ed., *Critical Essays on Wallace Stegner*, 184-209.

THE BIG ROCK CANDY MOUNTAIN

Ahearn, Kerry, "THE BIG ROCK CANDY MOUNTAIN and ANGLE OF REPOSE: Trial and Culmination," *WAL* 10 (May, 1975): 11-27. Also in Arthur, A., ed., *Critical Essays on Wallace Stegner*, 111-17.

Baurecht, William C., "Within a Continuous Frame: Stegner's Family Album in THE BIG ROCK CANDY MOUNTAIN," in Arthur, A., ed., *Critical Essays on Wallace Stegner*, 98-108.

Canzoneri, Robert, "Wallace Stegner: Trial by Existence," *SoR* 9, iv (Oct., 1973): 802-12.

Eisinger, Charles E., "Twenty Years of Wallace Stegner," *CE* 20 (Dec., 1958): 112-13.

Hudson, Lois P., "THE BIG ROCK CANDY MOUNTAIN: No Roots—and No Frontier," *SDR* 9, i (Spring, 1971): 3-13. Also in Arthur, A., ed., *Critical Essays on Wallace Stegner*, 137-45.

Lewis, M., and L. Lewis, *Wallace Stegner*, 14-18.

Robinson, Forrest G., "Wallace Stegner's Family Saga: From THE BIG ROCK CANDY MOUNTAIN to RECAPITULATION," *WAL* 17, ii (Aug., 1982): 101-6.

_____, and M. G. Robinson, *Wallace Stegner*, 18-19, 27-30, 113-21.

FIRE AND ICE

Robinson, F. G., and M. G. Robinson, *Wallace Stegner*, 108-13.

ON A DARKLING PLAIN

Robinson, F. G., and M. G. Robinson, *Wallace Stegner*, 102-8.

THE PREACHER AND THE SLAVE

Eisinger, Charles E., "Twenty Years of Wallace Stegner," *CE* 20 (Dec., 1958): 113-14.

Robinson, F. G., and M. G. Robinson, *Wallace Stegner*, 124-31. Also in Arthur, A., ed., *Critical Essays on Wallace Stegner*, 76-82.

REMEMBERING LAUGHTER

Flora, Joseph M., "Vardis Fisher and Wallace Stegner: Teacher and Student," *WAL* 5, ii (Summer, 1970): 126-8.

Robinson, F. G., and M. G. Robinson, *Wallace Stegner*, 96-102.

SECOND GROWTH

Lewis, M., and L. Lewis, *Wallace Stegner*, 18-20.

Robinson, F. G., and Robinson, M. G., *Wallace Stegner*, 120-3.

A SHOOTING STAR

Burke, Hatton, "The Ninth Circle," *SR* 70 (Winter, 1962): 172-5.

Lewis, M., and L. Lewis, *Wallace Stegner*, 31-2.

Robinson, F. G., and M. G. Robinson, *Wallace Stegner*, 133-40. Also in Arthur, A., ed., *Critical Essays on Wallace Stegner*, 82-9.

THE SPECTATOR BIRD

Gilbert, Susan, "Children of the Seventies: The American Family in Recent Fiction," *Soundings* 62, ii (Summer, 1980): 203-6.

STEINBECK, JOHN, 1902-1968

GENERAL

See issues of *Steinbeck Newsletter* and *Steinbeck Quarterly*.

Alexander, Stanley G., "Primitivism and Pastoral Form in John Steinbeck's Early Fiction," *DA* 26 (1965): 2201-02.

Anderson, Arthur C., "The Journey Motif in the Fiction of John Steinbeck: The Traveler Discovers Himself," *DAI* 37 (1976): 2867A.

"The Art of Fiction 45 (Continued)," *ParisR* 63 (1975): 180-94. [Excerpts from Steinbeck's letters.]

Astro, Richard, "From the Tidepool to the Stars: Steinbeck's Sense of Place," *StQ* 10, i (Winter, 1977): 5-11. Also in Hayashi, T., et al., eds., *John Steinbeck: East and West*, 22-7.

_____, "Into the Cornucopia: Steinbeck's Vision of Nature and The Ideal Man," *DAI* 30 (1969): 2517A-18A.

_____, "John Steinbeck and the Tragic Miracle of Consciousness," *SJS* 1, iii (Nov., 1975): 61-72.

_____, "Steinbeck and Mainwaring: Two Californians for the Earth," *StQ* 3 (Winter, 1970): 3-11. Also in Hayashi, T., ed., *Steinbeck's Literary Dimension*, 83-93.

_____, "Steinbeck and Ricketts: The Morphology of a Metaphysic," *UWR* 8, ii (Spring, 1973): 24-33.

_____, and T. Hayashi, eds., *Steinbeck*.

Beach, Joseph W., "John Steinbeck: Journeyman Artist," *American Fiction: 1920-1940*, 309-47. Also in Tedlock, E. W., Jr., and C. V. Wicker, eds., *Steinbeck and His Critics*, 80-91.

Beaugrande, Robert-Alain de, "A Rhetorical Theory of Audience Response," 9-20 in Brown, Robert L., Jr., and Martin Steinmann, Jr., eds., *Rhetoric 28: Proceedings of Theory of Rhetoric: An Interdisciplinary Conference*, Minneapolis: Un. of Minnesota Center for Advanced Studies in Lang., Style, and Lit. Theory, 1979. [Not seen.]

Beatty, Sandra, "A Study of the Female Characters in Steinbeck's Fiction," *StQ* 8 (Spring, 1975): 50-6. Also in Hayashi, T., ed., *Steinbeck's Women*, 1-6.

Bedford, Richard C., "Steinbeck's Uses of the Oriental," *StQ* 13 (1980): 5-19.

Benson, Jackson J., "John Steinbeck: Novelist as Scientist," *Novel* 10 (Spring, 1977): 248-64.

Blake, N. M., *Novelist's America*, 133-8.

Blankenship, R., *American Literature*, 745-9.

Bleeker, Gary W., "Setting and Animal Tropes in the Fiction of John Steinbeck," *DAI* 30 (1970): 2998A.

Bode, Elroy, "The World of Its Own Terms: A Brief for Steinbeck, Miller, and Simenon," *SWR* 53 (1968): 406-16.

Bracher, Frederick, "Steinbeck and the Biological View of Man," *PacSp* 2 (Winter, 1948): 14-29. Also in Tedlock, E. W., Jr., and C. V. Wicker, eds., *Steinbeck and His Critics*, 183-96.

Brown, Daniel R., "'A Monolith of Logic Against Waves of Nonsense'," *Ren* 16 (Fall, 1963): 48-51.

_____, "The Natural Man in John Steinbeck's Non-Teleological Tales," *BSUF* 7 (Spring, 1966): 47-52.

Brown, Joyce D. C., "Animal Symbolism and Imagery in John Steinbeck's Fiction from 1929 Through 1939," *Dai* 33 (1972): 1716A.

Burgum, Edwin B., "The Sensibility of John Steinbeck," *S&S* 10 (1946): 132-47. Also in Burgum, E. B., *Novel and the World's Dilemma*, 272-91. Also in Tedlock, E. W., Jr., and C. V. Wicker, eds., *Steinbeck and His Critics*, 104-18.

Carpenter, Frederic I., "John Steinbeck: American Dreamer," *SWR* 26 (July, 1941): 454-67. Also in Tedlock, E. W., and C. V. Wicker, eds., *Steinbeck and His Critics*, 68-79.

Carr, Duane R., "John Steinbeck: Twentieth-Century Romantic: A Study of the Early Works," *DAI* 36 (1976): 6680A.

Casimir, Louis J., Jr., "Human Emotion and the Early Novels of John Steinbeck," *DA* 27 (1966): 472A.

Chalupova, Eva, "The Thirties and the Artistry of Lewis, Farrell, Dos Passos and Steinbeck: Some Remarks on the Influence of the Social and Ideolgical Development of the Time," *BSE* 14 (1981): 107-16.

Champney, Freeman, "John Steinbeck, Californian," *AR* 7 (Sept., 1947): 345-62. Also in Tedlock, E. W., Jr., and C. V. Wicker, eds., *Steinbeck and His Critics*, 135-51. Also in Davis, R. M., ed., *Steinbeck*, 18-35.

Cook, Sylvia J., "Steinbeck's Retreat into Artfulness," *From Tobacco Road to Route 66*, 159-63.

Copek, Peter, "Steinbeck's Naturalism?" *StQ* 9, i (Winter, 1976): 9-11.

Covici, Pascal, Jr., "John Steinbeck and the Language of Awareness," in French, W., ed., *Thirties*, 47-54.

_____, "Steinbeck's Quest for Magnanimity," *StQ* 10 (1977): 79-88.

Cox, Martha H., "In Search of John Steinbeck: His People and His Land," *SJS* 1, iii (Nov., 1975): 41-60.

Crouch, Steve, *Steinbeck Country*, Palo Alto, Calif.: American West, 1973.

Davis, Gary C., "John Steinbeck in Films: An Analysis of Realism in the Novel and the Film—A Nonteleological Approach," *DAI* 36 (1975): 3170A.

Davis, R. M., ed., *Steinbeck*.

Ditsky, John, "Faulkner Land and Steinbeck Country," in Astro, R., and T. Hayashi, eds., *Steinbeck*, 11-23. Also in Hayashi, T., ed., *Steinbeck's Literary Dimension*, 28-45.

Ditsky, John M., "Land-Nostalgia in the Novels of Faulkner, Cather, and Steinbeck," *DA* 28 (1967): 1072A.

_____, "Music from a Dark Cave: Organic Form in Steinbeck's Fiction," *JNT* 1, i (Jan., 1971): 58-67.

Feied, Frederick, "Steinbeck's Depression Novels: The Ecological Basis," *DAI* 32 (1971): 427A-28A.

Fontenrose, J., *John Steinbeck*.

French, Warren G., in French, W. G., and W. E. Kidd, eds., *American Winners of the Nobel Literary Prize*, 193-223.

_____, "The 'California Quality' of Steinbeck's Best Fiction," *SJS* 1, iii (Nov., 1975): 9-19.

_____, *John Steinbeck*, 2nd ed. rev.

_____, "John Steinbeck (1902-1968)" in Panichas, G. A., ed., *Politics of Twentieth-Century Novelists*, 296-306.

_____, "John Steinbeck: A Usable Concept of Naturalism," in Hakutani, Y., and L. Fried, eds, *American Literary Naturalism*, 122-35.

_____, "Steinbeck and Salinger: Messiah-Moulders for a Sick Society," in Hayashi, T., ed., *Steinbeck's Literary Dimension*, 105-15.

_____, "Steinbeck's Use of Malory," in Hayashi, T., ed., *Steinbeck and the Arthurian Theme*, 4-11.

Frietzsche, Arthur H., "Steinbeck as a Western Author," *PUASAL* 42, i (1965): 11-13. [Not seen.]

Frohcock, W. M., "John Steinbeck's Men of Wrath," *SWR* 31 (Spring, 1946): 144-52. Also as "John Steinbeck: The Utility of Wrath," in Frohock, W. M., *Novel of Violence in America*, 124-43.

Fukuma, Kin-ichi, "'Man' in Steinbecks's Works," *KAL* 7 (1964): 21-30. [Not seen.]

Gannett, Louis, "John Steinbeck: Novelist at Work," *Atlantic* 176 (Dec., 1945): 55-61. Also in Tedlock, E. W., Jr., and C. V. Wicker, eds., *Steinbeck and His Critics*, 23-37. Also as "John Steinbeck's Way of Writing," in *The Portable Steinbeck*, ed. by Pascal Covici, N.Y.: Viking, 1958, vii-xviii.

Garcia, Reloy, *Steinbeck and D. H. Lawrence: Fictive Voices and Ethical Imperative* (Steinbeck Monog. Ser. 2), Muncie: Ball State Un. Pr., 1972.

Geismar, M., *Writers in Crisis*, 239-70.

Georgieva, Liljana, "The Social Theme and Its Artistic Presentation in Some of John Steinbeck's Early Works," *GSUFNF* 73, iii (1981): 35-101. [Not seen.]

Gladstein, Mimi R., "Female Characters in Steinbeck: Minor Characters of Major Importance?" in Hayashi, T., ed., *Steinbeck's Women*, 17-25.

Golemba, Henry L., "Steinbeck's Attempt to Escape Literary Fallacy," *MFS* 15, ii (Summer, 1969): 231-9.

Gray, J., *Steinbeck*.

Gurko, Leo, *Angry Decade*, 212-21.

Griffith, Raymond L., "Dissonant Symphony: Multilevel Duality in the Fiction of John Steinbeck," *DAI* 33 (1972): 1723A-24A.

_____, and Miriam Gurko, "The Steinbeck Temperament," *Rocky Mountain Rev.* 9 (Fall, 1944-45): 17-22.

Hamada, Seijiro, "Parabiblical Elements in John Steinbeck," *Ushione* 5 (Autumn, 1955): 3-9. [Not seen.]

Hayashi, Tetsumaro, ed., *John Steinbeck: A Dictionary of His Fictional Characters*, Metuchen, N.J.: Scarecrow, 1976.

_____, *John Steinbeck: A Guide to the Doctoral Dissertations: A Collection of Dissertation Abstracts (1946-1969)*. (Steinbeck Monog. Ser., 1), Muncie, In.: Ball State Un. Pr., 1971.

_____, *Steinbeck and the Arthurian Theme*.

_____, *Steinbeck Criticism: A Review of Book-Length Studies (1939-1973)*, Muncie, In.: Steinbeck Society, Ball State Un., 1974.

_____, et al., eds., *Steinbeck: East and West*.

_____, and Kenneth D. Swan, eds., *Steinbeck's Prophetic Vision of America: Proceedings of the Bicentennial Steinbeck Seminar*, Upland, In.: Taylor Un. for Steinbeck Soc. of America, 1976.

Hayashi, T., ed., *Steinbeck's Women*.

_____, *Study Guide to Steinbeck*.

_____, *Study Guide to Steinbeck, Part II*.

Hayashi, Tetsumaro, "Why is Steinbeck's Literature Widely Read? What is the Essence of His Literature?" *KAL* 20 (1979): 42-4. Also in *StQ* 13 (1980): 21-2.

Higashiyama, Masayoshi, "On Works of John Steinbeck, A Great Modern Novelist," *Kansai Gakuin Times* 7 (1957): 15-28. [Not seen.]

Hirose, Hidekazu, "'Feelings as Always Were More Potent Than Thought': John Steinbeck's Social Concerns of the Thirties," *SALit* 8 (1972): 53-62. [Not seen.]

_____, "From Doc Burton to Jim Casy: Steinbeck in the Latter Half of the 1930's," in Hayashi, T., et al., eds., *Steinbeck: East and West*, 6-11.

Hopfe, Lewis M., "Genesis Imagery in Steinbeck," *Cresset* 39, vii (May, 1976): 6-9.

Hyman, Stanley E., "John Steinbeck: Of Invertebrates and Men," *The Promised End: Essays and Reviews, 1942-1962*, Cleveland and N.Y.: World, 1963, 17-22.

_____, "Some Notes on John Steinbeck," *AR* 7 (Sept., 1947): 185-200. Also in Tedlock, E. W., Jr., and C. V. Wicker, eds., *Steinbeck and His Critics*, 152-66.

Inoue, Atsuko, "A Study of John Steinbeck: The Group in His Fiction," *Essays and Studies in British and American Literature* (Tokyo Women's Christian College) 11 (Winter, 1964): 49-99. [Not seen.]

Irvine, John C., "The Fringes of John Steinbeck," *LIT* (Spring, 1965): 14-19. [Not seen.]

Jackson, Joseph H., "Preface" to *The Short Novels of John Steinbeck*, N.Y.: Viking, 1963, vii-xv.

Jain, Sunita G., "The Concept of Man in the Novels of John Steinbeck," *JSL* 3, i (1975): 98-102.

————, *John Steinbeck's Concept of Man.*

Jones, Lawrence W., *John Steinbeck as Fabulist*, ed. by Marston LaFrance (Steinbeck Monog. Ser. 3), Muncie: Ball State Un. Pr., 1973.

————, "'A Little Play in Your Head': Parable Form in John Steinbeck's Post-War Fiction," *Genre* 3 (Mar., 1970): 55-63.

————, "Steinbeck and Zola: Theory and Practice of the Experimental Novel," *StQ* 4 (1971): 95-101. Also in Hayashi, T., ed., *Steinbeck's Literary Dimension*, 138-46.

Kallapur, S. T., "John Steinbeck and Oriental Thought: Some Parallels," in Naik, M. K., et al., eds., *Images of India in Western Creative Writing*, 361-81.

Kennedy, John S., "John Steinbeck: Life Affirmed and Dissolved," in Gardiner, H. C., ed., *Fifty Years of the American Novel*, 217-36. Also in Tedlock, E. W., Jr., and C. V. Wicker, eds., *Steinbeck and His Critics*, 119-34.

Koike, Bobuo, "A Study in John Steinbeck with Special Reference to the Works in the Thirties," *British and American Literature* (Kansei Gakunin Un.) 3 (April, 1954): 57-90. [Not seen.]

Krause, Sidney J., "Steinbeck and Mark Twain," *StQ* 6, iv (Fall, 1973): 104-11. [Not seen.]

Levant, Howard S., "A Critical Study of the Longer Fiction of John Steinbeck," *DA* 23 (1962), 633.

————, *Novels of John Steinbeck.*

Levidova, I., "The Post-War Books of John Steinbeck," *SovietR* 4 (Summer, 1963): 3-13.

Lewis, Clifford L., "John Steinbeck: Architect of the Unconscious," *DAI* 34 (1973): 781A.

Lewis, R. W. B., "John Steinbeck: The Fitful Daemon," in Bode, C., ed., *Young Rebel in American Literature*, 121-41. Also in Litz, A. W., ed., *Modern American Fiction*, 265-77. Also in Litz, A. W., ed., *Steinbeck*, 163-75.

Lieber, Todd M., "Talismanic Patterns in the Novels of John Steinbeck," *AL* 44 (May, 1972): 262-75.

Lisca, Peter, "The Art of John Steinbeck: An Analysis and Interpretation of Its Development," *DAI* 16 (1956): 965.

————, "Escape and Commitment: Two Poles of the Steinbeck Hero," in Astro, R., and T. Hayashi, eds., *Steinbeck*, 75-88.

————, *John Steinbeck.*

————, "Steinbeck and Hemingway: Suggestions for a Comparative Study," *StN* 2, i (Spring, 1969): 9-17. Also, rev. and enlarged, in Hayashi, T., ed., *Steinbeck's Literary Dimension*, 46-54.

————, "Steinbeck's Image of Man and His Decline as a Writer," *MFS* 11 (Spring, 1965): 3-10.

————, *Wide World of John Steinbeck.*

Magny, Claude-Edmonde, "Steinbeck, or the Limits of the Impersonal Novel," in Tedlock, E. W., Jr., and C. V. Wicker, eds., *Steinbeck and His Critics*, 216-27. Also in Magny, C., *Age of the American Novel*, 161-77.

Marks, L. J., *Thematic Design in the Novels of John Steinbeck.*

Marovitz, Sanford E., "John Steinbeck and Adlai Stevenson," *StQ* 3 (Summer, 1970): 51-62. Also in Hayashi, T., ed., *Steinbeck's Literary Dimension*, 116-29.

McCarthy, P., *John Steinbeck.*

McCormick, B., "John Steinbeck: An Evaluation," *Way* 19 (Mar., 1963): 53-8. [Not seen.]

McDaniel, Barbara A., "Self-Alienating Characters in the Fiction of John Steinbeck," *DAI* 35 (1975): 4534A-35A.

McTee, James D., "Underhill's Mystic Way and the Initiation Theme in the Major Fiction of John Steinbeck," *DAI* 36 (1976): 6102A.

McWilliams, Carey, "A Man, a Place, and a Time," *AWest* 7 (May, 1970): 4-8, 38-40, 62-4.

McWilliams, Wilson C., and Nancy R., "John Steinbeck, Writer," *Cweal* 90 (1969): 229-30.

Mendelson, M., "From THE GRAPES OF WRATH to THE WINTER OF OUR DISCONTENT," in Vroon, R., tr. *20th Century American Literature: A Soviet View*, 411-26.

Metzger, Charles R., "Steinbeck's Mexican-Americans," in Astro, R., and T. Hayashi, eds., *Steinbeck*, 141-55.

Mizener, Arthur, "Does a Moral Vision of the Thirties Deserve a Nobel Prize?" *NYTBR* (Dec. 9, 1962): 4. Also in Donohue, A. M., ed., *Casebook on THE GRAPES OF WRATH*, 267-72.

————, "Steinbeck and His World," in Brown, F., *Opinions and Perspectives*, 181-8.

Moore, H. T., *Novels of John Steinbeck.*

Morioka, Sakae, "John Steinbeck's Art," *English and American Language and Literature Studies* (Kyusha Un.) 3 (1953): 51-8. [Not seen.]

Morsberger, Robert E., "In Defense of 'Westering'," *WAL* 5, ii (Summer, 1970): 143-6.

————, "Steinbeck's Happy Hookers," *StQ* 9, iii-iv (Summer-Fall, 1976): 101-14. Also in Hayashi, T., ed., *Steinbeck's Women*, 36-48.

Murray, Edward, "John Steinbeck, Point of View, and Film," *Cinematic Imagination*, 261-77.

Nakayama, Kiyoshi, "An Oriental Interpretation of Steinbeck's Literature and Thought," in Hayashi, T., et al, eds, *Steinbeck: East and West*, 71-82.

Nelson, Harland S., "Steinbeck's Politics Then and Now," *AR* 27 (Spring, 1967): 118-33.

Nevius, Blake, "Steinbeck: One Aspect," *PacSp* 3 (Summer, 1949): 302-10. Also in Tedlock, E. W., Jr., and C. V. Wicker, eds., *Steinbeck and His Critics*, 197-205.

Nichols, Lewis, "Talk with John Steinbeck," *NYTBR* (Sept. 28, 1952): 30.

Nosson, Evon, "The Beast-Man Theme in the Work of John Steinbeck," *BSUF* 7, ii (Spring, 1966): 52-64.

Oliver, H. J., "John Steinbeck," *AusQ* 23 (June, 1951): 79-83.

Owens, Louis D., "A New Eye in the West: Steinbeck's California Fiction," *DAI* 42, ix (Mar., 1982): 4002A.

Peterson, Richard F., "The God in the Darkness: A Study of John Steinbeck and D. H. Lawrence," in Hayashi, T., ed., *Steinbeck's Literary Dimension*, 67-82.

Pfeifer, Flora C. B., "Similarities in Cervantes' DON QUIOTE and Steinbeck's Paisano Novels," *DAI* 42 (1981): 2657A.

Poulakides, Andreas K., "Steinbeck, Kazantazakis, and Socialism," *StQ* 3, iii (Summer, 1970): 62-72. Also in Hayashi, T., ed., *Steinbeck's Literary Dimension*, 55-66.

Prabhakar, S. S., *John Steinbeck.*

Pratt, J. C., *John Steinbeck.*

Rao, B. R., *American Fictional Hero*, 54-81.

————, "John Steinbeck the Novelist," *Andhra Un. Magazine* (Waltair, India) 20 (1959-60): 20-6. [Not seen.]

Rascoe, Burton, "John Steinbeck," *EJ* 27 (Mar. 1938): 205-16. Also in Tedlock, E. W., Jr., *Steinbeck and His Critics*, 57-67.

Raymund, Bernard, "John Steinbeck," in Baker, D. V., ed., *Writers of Today*, 122-38.

Roane, Margaret C., "John Steinbeck as a Spokesman for the Mentally Retarded," *WSCL* 5, ii (Summer, 1964): 127-32.

Ross, Woodburn O., "John Steinbeck: Earth and Stars," in *Studies in Honor of A. H. R. Fairchild*, Un. of Mo. Studies, 21, 1946, 179-97. Also in Tedlock, E. W., Jr., and C. V. Wicker, eds., *Steinbeck and His Critics*, 167-82.

_____, "John Steinbeck: Naturalisms' Priest," *CE* 10 (May, 1949): 432-8. Also in Tedlock, E. W., Jr., and C. V. Wicker, eds., *Steinbeck and His Critics*, 206-15.

Rundell, Walter, Jr., "Steinbeck's Image of the West," *American West* 1 (Spring, 1964): 4-17, 79.

Sargent, Raymond M., "Social Criticism in the Fiction of John Steinbeck," *DAI* 42, ii (Aug., 1981): 706A.

Satanarayana, M. R., *John Steinbeck*.

_____, "The Unknown God of John Steinbeck," *IJAS* 3, i (1973): 97-103. [Not seen.]

Serota, Steve, "The Function of the Grotesque in the Works of John Steinbeck," *DAI* 35 (1975): 6733A.

Shimomura, Noborv, "Mysticism in John Steinbeck's Novels," in Hayashi, T., et al., eds., *John Steinbeck: East and West*, 83-90.

Simmonds, Roy S., *Steinbeck's Literary Achievement*.

_____, "The Unrealized Dream: Steinbeck's Modern Version of Malory," in Hayashi, T., ed., *Steinbeck and the Arthurian Theme*, 30-43.

Smith, Donald B., "The Decline in John Steinbeck's Critical Reputation Since World War II: An Analysis and Evaluation of Recent Critical Practices With a Suggested Revision," *DA* 28 (1967): 1449A.

Snell, G., *Shapers of American Fiction*, 187-97.

Spiller, R. E., *Cycle of American Literature*, 289-91.

Steinbeck, John, "The Art of Fiction: An Interview," *ParisR* 12 (1969): 161-88.

Stuurmans, Harry, "John Steinbeck's Lover's Quarrel With America," *DAI* 34 (1974): 5206A.

Taylor, Horace P., Jr., "The Biological Naturalism of John Steinbeck," *DAI* 22 (1962): 3674.

_____, "The Biological Naturalism of John Steinbeck," *McNR* 12 (Winter, 1960-61): 81-97.

_____, "John Steinbeck—The Quest," *McNR* 16 (1965): 33-45.

Tedlock, Jr., and C. V. Wicker, *Steinbeck and His Critics*.

TeMaat, Agatha, "John Steinbeck: On the Creative Process in the Early Years," *DAI* 36 (1976): 5306A.

Tuttleton, James W., "Steinbeck in Russia: The Rhetoric of Praise and Blame," *MFS* 11 (Spring, 1965): 79-89. Also in Donohue, A. M., ed., *Casebook on THE GRAPES OF WRATH*, 245-56.

Wagenknecht, E., *Cavalcade of the American Novel*, 443-8.

Walcutt, C. C., *American Literary Naturalism*, 258-69. Also (part) in Donohue, A. M., ed., *Casebook on THE GRAPES OF WRATH*, 162-5.

Wallis, Prentiss B., Jr., "John Steinbeck: The Symbolic Family," *DA* 27 (1966): 1842A-43A.

Watt, F. W., *Steinbeck*.

Wilson, Edmund, "The Californians: Storm and Steinbeck," *NRep* 103 (Dec. 9, 1940): 785-7. Also in Wilson, E., *Boys in the Backroom*, San Francisco: Colt Pr., 1947, 41-53. Also in Wilson, E., *Classics and Commercials*, 35-45. Also in Donohue, A. M., *Casebook on THE GRAPES OF WRATH*, 151-8.

Wilson, Jerry W., "John Steinbeck: Love, Work and the Politics of Collectivity," *DAI* 39 (1978): 1578A-1579A.

Woodress, James, "John Steinbeck: Hostage to Fortune," *SAQ* 63 (Summer, 1964): 385-98. Also in Donohue, A. M., *Casebook on THE GRAPES OF WRATH*, 278-90.

Wyatt, Bryant N., "Experimentation as Technique: The Protest Novels of John Steinbeck," *Discourse* 12 (Spring, 1969): 143-53.

Yarmus, Marcia D., "Exploring the Hispanic Linguistic Elements in John Steinbeck's Novels," in Fink, Wayne H., ed., *Estudios de historia, literatura y arte hispanicos ofrecidos a Rodrigo A. Molina*, Madrid: Insula, 1977, 355-63.

_____, "John Steinbeck and the Hispanic Influence," *StQ* 10 (1977): 97-102.

Zane, Nancy E., "Steinbeck's Heroes: 'The Individual Mind and the Spirit of Man'," *DAI* 43 (1982): 1549A-50A.

BURNING BRIGHT

Ditsky, Joan M., "Steinbeck's BURNING BRIGHT: Homage to Astarte," *StQ* 7, iii-iv (Summer-Fall, 1974): 79-84.

Fontenrose, J., *John Steinbeck*, 115-17.

French, W., *John Steinbeck*, 148-52.

_____, *John Steinbeck*, 2nd ed. rev., 138-40.

Geismar, Maxwell, in *SatR* 33 (Oct. 21, 1950): 4. Also in Geismar, M., *American Moderns*, 153-5.

Gray, J., *John Steinbeck*, 28-9.

Hayashi, T., ed., *Study Guide to Steinbeck, Part II*, 46-62.

Levant, H., *Novels of John Steinbeck*, 158-63.

Lisca, P., *John Steinbeck*, 154-60.

_____, *Wide World of John Steinbeck*, 248-60.

Mills, Nicolaus, "Class and Crowd in American Fiction," *CentR* 24, ii (1980): 206-12.

Prabhakar, S. S., *John Steinbeck*, 170-3.

Watt, F. W., *Steinbeck*, 91-3.

CANNERY ROW

Alexander, Stanley, "CANNERY ROW: Steinbeck's Pastoral Poem," *WAL* 2 (Winter, 1968): 281-95. Also in Davis, R. M., ed., *Steinbeck*, 135-48.

Astro, Richard, "Steinbeck's Post-War Trilogy: A Return to Nature and the Natural Man," *TCL* 16, ii (Apr., 1970): 109-15.

Benson, Jackson J., "John Steinbeck's CANNERY ROW: A Reconsideration," *WAL* 12 (May, 1977): 11-40.

Benton, Robert M., "A Scientific Point of View in Steinbeck's Fiction," *StQ* 7, iii-iv (Summer-Fall, 1974): 67-72. Also in Astro, R., and T. Hayashi, eds., *Steinbeck*, 131-9.

Crouch, Steve, "CANNERY ROW," *AWest* 10, v (1973): 19-27.

Fontenrose, J., *John Steinbeck*, 101-8.

French, Warren, in French, W. G., and W. E. Kidd, eds., *American Winners of the Nobel Literary Prize*, 213-15.

_____, *John Steinbeck*, 120-36.

_____, *John Steinbeck*, 2nd ed. rev., 112-24.

Gray, J., *On Second Thought*, 137-9.

Hayashi, T., ed., *Study Guide to John Steinbeck*, 19-28.

Jain, S., *John Steinbeck's Concept of Man*, 68-72.

Jones, Lawrence W., "Poison in the Cream Puff: The Human Condition in CANNERY ROW," *StQ* 7 (1974): 35-40.

Kallapur, S. T., "John Steinbeck and Oriental Thought: Some Parallels," in Naik, M. K., et al., eds., *Image of India in Western Creative Writing*, 371-2, 378-9.

Kawamura, Yoneichi, "Steinbeck's Humor and Pathos in TOR-
TILLA FLAT and CANNERY ROW," *Hokkaido Un. Essays in
Foreign Language and Literature* 1 (Dec., 1953): 24-30.

Levant, H., *Novels of John Steinbeck*, 164-84.

Levidova, I., "The Post-War Books of John Steinbeck," *SovietR*
4 (Summer, 1963): 5-6.

Lisca, Peter, "CANNERY ROW and TAO TEH CHING," *SJS* 1,
iii (1975): 21-7.

———, *John Steinbeck*, 111-23.

———, *Wide World of John Steinbeck*, 197-217.

Marks, L. J., *Thematic Design in the Novels of John Steinbeck*, 92-9.

McCarthy, P., *John Steinbeck*, 97-105.

Moore, Ward, "Cannery Row Revisited: Steinbeck and the Sar-
dines," *Nation* 179 (Oct. 16, 1954): 325-7.

Prabhakar, S. S., *John Steinbeck*, 179-82.

Prescott, O., *In My Opinion*, 60-1.

Snell, G., *Shapers of American Fiction*, 196-7.

Takamura, Hiromasa, "'A and C' in CANNERY ROW," *StQ* 15
(1982): 116.

Walcutt, C. C., *American Literary Naturalism*, 265-6.

Watt, F. W., *Steinbeck*, 79-84.

Weber, Tom, *All the Heroes Are Dead: The Ecology of Steinbeck's
CANNERY ROW*, San Francisco: Ramparts Pr., 1974.

Weeks, Donald, "Steinbeck Against Steinbeck," *PacSp* 1
(Autumn, 1947): 447-57.

CUP OF GOLD

Astro, Richard, "Phlebas Sails the Caribbean," in French, W.,
ed., *Twenties*, 57-9.

Carpenter, Frederic I., in *SWR* 26 (July, 1941): 456-8. Also in
Tedlock, E. W., Jr., and C. V. Wicker, eds., *Steinbeck and His
Critics*, 69-71.

Eddy, Darlene, "To Go A-Bucaneering and Take a Spanish
Town: Some Seventeenth Century Aspects of CUP OF
GOLD," *StQ* 8 (Winter, 1975): 3-12. Also in Hayashi, T., ed.,
Steinbeck's Travel Literature, 27-38.

Fontenrose, J., *John Steinbeck*, 7-13.

French, Warren, in Warren, W. G., and W. E. Kidd, eds., *American Winners of the Nobel Literary Prize*, 200-1.

———, *John Steinbeck*, 31-8.

———, *John Steinbeck*, 2nd ed. rev., 45-53.

Geismar, M., *Writers in Crisis*, 246-8.

Gray, J., *John Steinbeck*, 32-3.

Hayashi, T., ed., *Study Guide to Steinbeck, Part II*, 19-45.

Jain, S., *John Steinbeck's Concept of Man*, 7-11.

Levant, H. *Novels of John Steinbeck*, 10-22.

Lisca, Peter, "CUP OF GOLD and TO A GOD UNKNOWN:
Two Early Works of John Steinbeck," *KN* 22 (1975): 173-83.

———, *John Steinbeck*, 26-35.

———, *Wide World of John Steinbeck*, 26-38.

Marks, L. J., *Thematic Design in the Novels of John Steinbeck*, 27-33.

Moore, H. T., *Novels of John Steinbeck*, 11-17.

Prabhakar, S. S., *John Steinbeck*, 109-18.

Rao, B. R., *American Fictional Hero*, 57-9.

Snell, G., *Shapers of American Fiction*, 188-9.

Tsuboi, Kiyohiko, "Steinbeck's CUP OF GOLD and Fitzgerald's
THE GREAT GATSBY," in Hayashi, T., et al., eds., *John
Steinbeck: East and West*, 40-7.

Watt, F. W., *Steinbeck*, 25-8.

EAST OF EDEN

Brashers, H. C., *Introduction to American Literature*, 154-5.

Brown, Joyce C., "Steinbeck's EAST OF EDEN," *Expl* 38, i (1979):
11-12.

Buerger, Daniel, "'History' and Fiction in EAST OF EDEN," *StQ*
14 (1981): 6-14.

Covici, Pascal, Jr., "From Commitment to Choice: Double Vision and the Problem of Vitality for John Steinbeck," in
French, W., ed., *Fifties*, 63-71.

Cox, Martha H., "Steinbeck's Family Portraits: The Hamiltons,"
StQ 14 (1981): 23-32.

DeMott, Robert, "Cathy Ames and Lady Godiva: A Contribution to EAST OF EDEN'S Background," *StQ* 14 (1981): 72-83.

———, "'Culling All Books': Steinbeck's Reading and EAST
OF EDEN," *StQ* 14 (1981): 40-51.

———, "'A Great Black Book': EAST OF EDEN and GUNN'S
NEW FAMILY PHYSICIAN," *AmerS* 22, ii (1981): 41-57.

Ditsky, John, "The 'East' in EAST OF EDEN," *Essays on EAST
OF EDEN*, 41-50. Also in Hayashi, T., et al., ed., *John Steinbeck:
East and West*, 61-70.

———, *Essays on EAST OF EDEN*.

———, "Outside of Paradise: Men and the Land in EAST OF
EDEN," *Essays on EAST OF EDEN*, 15-40.

———, "Toward a Narrational Self," *Essays on EAST OF
EDEN*, 1-14.

Fontenrose, J., *John Steinbeck*, 118-27.

French, W., *John Steinbeck*, 152-6.

———, *John Steinbeck*, 2nd ed. rev., 141-52.

Frohock, W. H., *Novel of Violence in America*, 141-2.

Gardiner, Harold C., "Novelist to Philosopher," *America* 88
(Oct. 4, 1952): 18. Also in Gardiner, H. C., ed., *In All Conscience*, 136-8.

Geismar, M., *American Modern*, 164-7.

Govoni, Mark W., "'Symbols for the Wordlessness': A Study of
John Steinbeck's EAST OF EDEN," *DAI* 39 (1979): 6761A.

———, "'Symbol for the Wordlessness': The Original Manuscript of EAST OF EDEN," *StQ* 14 (1981): 14-23.

Gray, J., *John Steinbeck*, 18-21.

Gribben, John L., "Steinbeck's EAST OF EDEN and Milton's
PARADISE LOST: A Discussion of 'Timshel'," *StQ* 5, ii
(Spring, 1972): 35-43. Also in Hayashi, T., ed., *Steinbeck's
Literary Dimension*, 94-104.

Hayashi, T., ed., *Study Guide to Steinbeck, Part II*, 63-86.

Hopfe, Lewis M., "Genesis Imagery in Steinbeck," *Cresset* 39, vii
(May, 1976): 7-9.

Hopkins, Karen J., "Steinbeck's EAST OF EDEN: A Defense,"
in Crow, C. L., ed., *Essays on California Writers*, 63-78.

Jain, S., *John Steinbeck's Concept of Man*, 82-8.

Krutch, Joseph W., "John Steinbeck's Dramatic Tale of Three
Generations," *NYHTBR* (Sept. 21, 1955): 1. Also in Tedlock,
E. W., Jr., and C. V. Wicker, eds., *Steinbeck and His Critics*,
302-5.

Leonard, Frank G., "Cozzens Without Sex: Steinbeck Without
Sin," *AR* 18 (Summer, 1958): 209-18.

Levant, H., *Novels of John Steinbeck*, 234-58.

Levidova, I., "The Post-War Books of John Steinbeck," *SovietR*
4 (Summer, 1963): 10-11.

Lewis, R. W. B., "John Steinbeck: The Fitful Daemon," in Bode,
C., ed., *Young Rebel in American Literature*, 131-4 and *passim*.

Also in Litz, A. W., ed., *Modern American Fiction*, 271-3 and *passim*. Also in Davis, R. M., ed., *Steinbeck*, 169-71 and *passim*.

Lisca, P., *John Steinbeck*.

_____, *Wide World of John Steinbeck*, 261-75.

Magny, Claude-Edmonde, "EAST OF EDEN," *PUSA* 5 (Fall, 1953): 146-52.

Marks, Lester J., "EAST OF EDEN: 'Thou Mayest'," *StQ* 4, i (1971): 3-18.

Marks, L. J., *Thematic Design in the Novels of John Steinbeck*, 114-31.

McCarthy, P., *John Steinbeck*, 116-24.

McDaniel, Barbara, "Alienation in EAST OF EDEN: The 'Chart of the Soul'," *StQ* 14 (1981): 32-9.

Murray, Isobel, and Jim Merriless, "EAST OF EDEN," *New Blackfriars* 53 (Mar., 1972): 130-5.

Osborn, Paul, ed., "Dialogue Script: EAST OF EDEN," *Study of Current English*, (Tokyo) 10 (Sept., 1955): 16-32.

Phillips, William, "Male-ism and Moralism," *AmMerc* 75 (Oct., 1952): 93-8.

Prabhakar, S. S., *John Steinbeck*, 173-9.

Rao, B. R., *American Fictional Hero*, 75-7.

Sawney, Orlan, "Another Look at EAST OF EDEN," *Appalachian State Teachers College Faculty Publications* (1964): 54-8.

Steinbeck, John, *Journal of a Novel: THE EAST OF EDEN Letters*, N.Y.: Viking, 1969.

Watt, F. W., *Steinbeck*, 93-9.

West, Anthony, "California Moonshine," *NY* 28 (Sept. 20, 1952): 121-2, 125.

THE GRAPES OF WRATH

Allen, W., *Modern Novel*, 164-6.

_____, *Urgent West*, 216-18.

Beach, Joseph W., "John Steinbeck: Art and Propaganda," *American Fiction, 1920-1940*, 325-47. Also in Tedlock, E. W., Jr., and C. V. Wicker, eds., *Steinbeck and His Critics*, 250-65.

Beck, Warren, "On John Steinbeck," In Madden, C. F., *Talks With Authors*, 57-72.

Benson, Jackson, J., "Environment as Meaning: John Steinbeck and the Great Central Valley," *StQ* 10, i (Winter, 1977): 12-20.

Benson, Jackson J., "'To Tom, Who Lived It': John Steinbeck and the Man from Weedpatch," *JML* 5, ii (Apr., 1976): 151-210. [Background of the novel.]

Berry, J. Wilkes, "Enduring Life in THE GRAPES OF WRATH," *CEA* 33, ii (Jan., 1971): 18-19.

Blake, N. M., *Novelist's America*, 139-62.

Bluefarb, S., "The Joads: Flight Into the Social Soul," *Escape Motif in the American Novel*, 94-112.

Bluestone, George, *Novels Into Film*, Baltimore: Johns Hopkins Un. Pr., 1957, 147-69. Also in French, W., ed., *Companion to THE GRAPES OF WRATH*, 165-89. Also in Davis, R. C., ed., *Twentieth Century Interpretations of THE GRAPES OF WRATH*, 79-99. Also in Davis, R. C., ed., *Steinbeck*, 102-21.

Bowden, E. T., "The Commonplace and the Grotesque," *Dungeon of the Heart*, 138-48. Also in Donohue, A. M., ed., *Casebook GRAPES OF WRATH*, 195-203. Also in Davis, R. C., *Twentieth Century Interpretations of THE GRAPES OF WRATH*, 15-23.

Bowron, Bernard, "THE GRAPES OF WRATH: A 'wagons west' romance," *ColQ* 3 (Summer, 1954): 84-91. Also in French, W., ed., *Companion to THE GRAPES OF WRATH*, 208-16.

Brasch, James D., "THE GRAPES OF WRATH and Old Testament Scepticism," *SJS* 3, ii (1977): 16-27.

Bredahl, A. Carl, Jr., "The Drinking Metaphor in THE GRAPES OF WRATH," *StQ* 6, iv (Fall, 1973): 95-8.

Browning, Chris, "Grape Symbolism in THE GRAPES OF WRATH," *Discourse* 11 (Winter, 1968): 129-40.

Burgum, Edwin B., "The Sensibility of John Steinbeck," *S&S* 10 (1946): 140-5. Also in Burgum, E. G., *Novel and the World's Dilemma*, 283-8.

Burns, Stuart L., "The Turtle and the Gopher: Another Look at the Ending of THE GRAPES OF WRATH," *WAL* 9 (1974): 53-7. Also in Davis, R. C., ed., *Twentieth Century Interpretations of THE GRAPES OF WRATH*, 100-4.

Caldwell, Mary Ellen, "A New Consideration of the Intercalary Chapters in THE GRAPES OF WRATH," *MarkhamR* 3, vi (May, 1973): 115-19. Also in Davis, R. C., ed., *Twentieth Interpretations of THE GRAPES OF WRATH*, 105-14.

Campbell, Russell, "Trampling Out the Vintage: Sour Grapes," in Peary, G., and R. Shatzkin, eds., *Modern American Novel and the Movies*, 107-18.

Cannon, Gerard, "The Pauline Apostleship of Tom Joad," *CE* 24 (Dec., 1962): 222-4. Also in Donohue, A. M., ed., *Casebook on THE GRAPES OF WRATH*, 118-22.

Carlson, Eric W., "Symbolism in THE GRAPES OF WRATH," *CE* 19 (Jan., 1958): 172-5. Also in Donohue, A. M., ed., *Casebook on THE GRAPES OF WRATH*, 96-102.

Carpenter, Frederic I., "The Philosophical Joads," *CE* 2 (Jan., 1941): 315-25. Also in Tedlock, E. W., Jr., and C. V. Wicker, eds., *Steinbeck and His Critics*, 241-9. Also in Carpenter, F. I., *American Literature and the Dream*, 167-75. Also in Donohue, A. M., ed., *Casebook on THE GRAPES OF WRATH*, 80-9.

Carr, Duane R., "Steinbeck's Blakean Vision in THE GRAPES OF WRATH," *StQ* 8, iii-iv (Fall, 1973): 67-72.

Caselli, Jacklyn [R.], "John Steinbeck and the American Patchwork Quilt," *SJS* 1, iii (1975): 83-7.

Chametsky, Jules, "The Ambivalent Endings of THE GRAPES OF WRATH," *MFS* 11, i (Spring, 1965): 33-44. Also in Donohue, A. M., ed., *Casebook of THE GRAPES OF WRATH*, 232-44.

Clarke, Mary W., "Bridging the Generation Gap: The Ending of Steinbeck's GRAPES OF WRATH," *ForumH* 8, ii (Summer, 1970): 16-17.

Cobbs, Lewis E., "Maupassant's 'Idylle': A Source for Steinbeck's THE GRAPES OF WRATH," *NMAL* 3 (1978): Item 1.

Collins, Thomas A., "From BRINGING IN THE SHEAVES, with a Forward by John Steinbeck," *JML* 5 (1976): 211-32. [On sources of GRAPES OF WRATH.]

Cook, Sylvia J., "Steinbeck, the People and the Party," in Bogardus, R. F., and F. Hobson, eds., *Literature at the Barricades*, 85-95.

_____, "Steinbeck's Retreat Into Artfulness," *From Tobacco Road to Route 66*, 171-83.

Cox, Martha H., "Fact into Fiction in THE GRAPES OF WRATH: The Weedpath and Arvin Camps," in Hayashi, T., et al., eds., *John Steinbeck: East and West*, 12-21.

_____, "THE GRAPES OF WRATH: Steinbeck's Conception and Execution," *SJS* 1, iii (1975): 73-81.

Crockett, H. Kelly, "The Bible and THE GRAPES OF WRATH," *CE* 24 (Dec., 1962): 193-9. Also in Donohue, A. M., ed., *Casebook on THE GRAPES OF WRATH*, 105-14.

Davis, R. C., ed., *Twentieth Century Interpretations of THE GRAPES OF WRATH*.

Davison, Richard A., "Charles G. Norris and John Steinbeck: Two More Tributes to THE GRAPES OF WRATH," *StQ* 15, iii-iv (1982): 90-7.

DeSchweinitz, George, "Steinbeck and Christianity," *CE* 19 (May, 1958): 369. Also in Donohue, A. M., ed., *Casebook on THE GRAPES OF WRATH*, 1, 3-4.

Detweiler, Robert, "Christ and the Christ Figure in American Fiction," *ChS* 47 (Summer, 1964): 111-24.

DeLisle, Harold F., "Style and Idea in Steinbeck's 'The Turtle'," *Style* 4 (1970): 145-54. [Discussion Chapter 3.]

Ditsky, John M., "The Ending of THE GRAPES OF WRATH: A Further Commentary," *Agora* 2, ii (1973): 41-50.

_____, "THE GRAPES OF WRATH: A Reconsideration," *SHR* 13 (1979): 215-20.

Donohue, Agnes M., ed., *Casebook on THE GRAPES OF WRATH*.

_____, "'The Endless Journey to No End': Journey and Eden Symbolism in Hawthorne and Steinbeck," in Donohue, A. M., ed., *Casebook on THE GRAPES OF WRATH*, 257-66.

Dougherty, Charles T., "The Christ-Figure in THE GRAPES OF WRATH," *CE* 24 (Dec., 1962): 224-6. Also in Donohue, A. M., ed., *Casebook on THE GRAPES OF WRATH*, 115-17.

Dulsey, Bernard, "John Steinbeck and Jorge Icaza," *ABC* 18, x (Summer, 1968): 15-17.

Dunn, Thomas F., "THE GRAPES OF WRATH," *CE* 24 (Apr., 1963): 566-7. Also in Donohue, A. M., ed., *Casebook on THE GRAPES OF WRATH*, 123-5.

Eisinger, Charles E., "Jeffersonian Agrarianism in THE GRAPES OF WRATH," *UKCR* 14 (1947): 149-54. Also in Donohue, A. M., ed., *Casebook on THE GRAPES OF WRATH*, 143-50.

Ek, Grete, "A 'Speaking Picture' in John Steinbeck's THE GRAPES OF WRATH," *ASIS* 10 (1978): 111-15.

Elliot, Kathleen F., "Steinbeck's IITYWYBAD," *StQ* 6 (Spring, 1973): 53-4.

Emory, Doug, "Points of View and Narrative Voice in THE GRAPES OF WRATH: Steinbeck and Ford," in Conger, Syndy M., and Janice R. Welch, eds., *Narrative Strategies: Original Essays in Film and Prose Fiction*, [Macomb]: Western Illinois Un. Pr., 1980, 129-35.

Fontenrose, J., *John Steinbeck*, 67-83.

Fossey, W. Richard, "The End of the Western Dream: THE GRAPES OF WRATH and Oklahoma," *CimR* 22 (1973): 25-34.

French, Warren G., in French, W. G., and W. E. Kidd, eds., *American Winners of the Nobel Literary Prize*, 210-13.

_____, "Another Look at THE GRAPES OF WRATH," *ColQ* 3 (Winter, 1955): 337-43. Also in French, W., ed., *Companion to THE GRAPES OF WRATH*, 217-24.

_____, ed., *Companion to THE GRAPES OF WRATH*.

_____, *John Steinbeck*, 95-112. Also (part) in Donohue, A. M., ed., *Casebook on THE GRAPES OF WRATH*, 204-8.

_____, *John Steinbeck*, 2nd ed., 92-102. Also in Donohue, R.C., ed., *Twentieth Century Interpretations of THE GRAPES OF WRATH*, 24-35.

_____, *Social Novel at the End of An Era*, 42-49 and *passim*.

_____, "Steinbeck and Salinger: Messiah-Moulders for a Sick Society," in Hayashi, T., ed., *Steinbeck's Literary Dimension*, 105-15.

Frohock, W. M., "John Steinbeck's Men of Wrath," *SWR* 31 (1946): 146-50. Also in Frohock, W. M., *Novel of Violence in America*, 129-34.

Garcia, Reloy, "The Rocky Road to Eldorado: The Journey Motif in John Steinbeck's THE GRAPES OF WRATH," *StQ* 14 (1981): 83-93.

Geismar, M., *Writers in Crisis*, 239-41, 263-6. Also in Donohue, A. M., ed., *Casebook on THE GRAPES OF WRATH*, 134-42.

Gladstein, Mimi R., "Ma Joad and Pilar: Significantly Similar," *StQ* 14 (1981): 93-104.

Gray, J., *John Steinbeck*, 13-16.

_____, *On Second Thought*, 133-6.

Griffin, Robert J., and William A. Freedman, "Machines and Animals: Pervasive Motifs in THE GRAPES OF WRATH," *JEGP* 62 (July, 1963): 569-80. Also in Donohue, A. M., ed., *Casebook on THE GRAPES OF WRATH*, 219-31. Also in Davis, R. C., ed., Twentieth Century Interpretations of THE GRAPES OF WRATH, 115-29.

Groene, Horst, "Agrarianism and Technology in Steinbeck's THE GRAPES OF WRATH," *SoRA* 9 (1976): 27-31. Also in Davis, R., ed., *Twentieth Century Interpretations of THE GRAPES OF WRATH*, 128-33.

Hayashi, Tetsumaro, "THE GRAPES OF WRATH," *Modern Review* (Calcutta) (Mar., 1968): 160-2.

_____, "John Steinbeck's THE GRAPES OF WRATH: The Joad Clan and Women," *Lumina* 4 (1961): 1-4.

_____, "Steinbeck's Women in THE GRAPES OF WRATH: A New Perspective," *KAL* 18 (1977): 1-4.

_____, ed., *Study Guide to Steinbeck*, 29-46.

_____, "Women and the Principle of Continuity in THE GRAPES OF WRATH," *KAL* 10 (1967): 75-80.

Hedrick, Joan, "Mother Earth and Earth Mother: The Recasting of Myth in Steinbeck's THE GRAPES OF WRATH," in Davis, R. C., ed., *Twentieth Century Interpretations of THE GRAPES OF WRATH*, 134-43.

Hunter, J. P., "Steinbeck's Wine of Affirmation in THE GRAPES OF WRATH," in Langford, R. E., ed., *Essays in Modern American Literature*, 76-89. Also in Davis, R. C., ed., *Twentieth Century Interpretations of THE GRAPES OF WRATH*, 36-47.

Isherwood, Christopher, "The Tragedy of Eldorado," *KR* 1 (Autumn, 1939): 450-3. Also in Donohue, A. M., ed., *Casebook on THE GRAPES OF WRATH*, 76-9.

Jain, S., *John Steinbeck's Concept of Man*, 59-67.

Jayne, Edward, "Me, Steinbeck, and Rose of Sharon's Baby," *Amst* 20, ii (1975): 281-305.

Kagan, Sheldon S., "Goin' Down the Road Feelin' Bad—John Steinbeck's THE GRAPES OF WRATH and Migrant Folklore," *DAI* 32 (1972): 4507A.

Kallapur, S., "THE GRAPES OF WRATH: A Revaluation," in Naik, M. K., et al., eds., *Indian Studies in American Fiction*, 229-52.

_____, "John Steinbeck and Oriental Thought: Some Parallels," in Naik, M. K., et al., eds., *Image of India in Western Creative Writing*, 366-70.

Kappel, Tim, "Trampling Out the Vineyards: Kern County's Ban on THE GRAPES OF WRATH," *CH* 61 (1982): 210-21.

Kazumi, Kazushi, "Notes on THE GRAPES OF WRATH," *English and American Study* (Aoyama Gakuin Un.) 8 (Feb., 1962): 8-11.

Klammer, Enno, "THE GRAPES OF WRATH—A Modern Exodus Account," *Cresset* 25 (Feb., 1962): 8-11.

Lee, Cremilda T., "John Steinbeck, Graciliano Ramos, and Jorge Amado: A Comparative Study," *DAI* 41, xii (June, 1981): 5091A-92A.

Levant, H., *Novels of John Steinbeck*, 93-129.

Lewis, R. W. B., "John Steinbeck: The Fitful Daemon," in Bode, C., ed., *Young Rebel in American Literature*, 137-40+. Also in Litz, A. W., ed., *Modern American Fiction*, 275-6+. Also in Davis, R. C., ed., *Steinbeck*, 171-5.

————, *Picaresque Saint*, 183-5. Also in Davis, R C., ed., *Twentieth Century Interpretations of THE GRAPES OF WRATH*, 144-9.

Lisca, Peter, "The Dynamics of Community in THE GRAPES OF WRATH," in Deakin, Motley, and Peter Lisca, eds., *From Irving to Steinbeck*, 127-40.

————, "THE GRAPES OF WRATH as Fiction," *PMLA* 72 (Mar., 1957): 296-309. Also in Westbrook, M., ed., *Modern American Novel*, 173-93. Also in Donohue, A. M., ed., *Casebook on THE GRAPES OF WRATH*, 166-81. Also (revised and expanded) in Lisca, P., *Wide World of John Steinbeck*, 144-77. Also (revised and expanded) in Davis, R. C., ed., *Steinbeck*, 75-101.

————, *John Steinbeck*, 87-110. Also in Davis, R. C., ed., *Twentieth Century Interpretations of THE GRAPES OF WRATH*, 48-62.

Lutwack, L., *Heroic Fiction*, 47-63. Also in Davis, R. C., ed., *Twentieth Century Interpretations of THE GRAPES OF WRATH*, 63-75.

McCarthy, Paul, "House and Shelter as Symbol in THE GRAPES OF WRATH," *SDR* 5 (Winter, 1967-68): 48-67.

————, "The Joads and Other Rural Families in Depression Fiction," *SDR* 19, iii (Autumn, 1981): 51-68.

————, *John Steinbeck*, 65-86.

McElderry, B. R., Jr., "THE GRAPES OF WRATH: In the Light of Modern Critical Theory," *CE* 5 (Mar., 1944): 308-13. Also in French, W., ed., *Companion to THE GRAPES OF WRATH*, 199-208. Also in Donohue, A. M., ed., *Casebook on THE GRAPES OF WRATH*, 126-33.

Marks, L. J., *Thematic Design in the Novels of John Steinbeck*, 66-82.

Matton, Collin G., "Water Imagery and the Conclusion to THE GRAPES OF WRATH," *NEMLA Newsl.* 2 (1970): 44-7.

Moore, H. T., *Novels of John Steinbeck*, 53-72.

Morris, L., "Fiery Gospel," *Postscript to Yesterday*, 166-71.

Mosely, E. M., "Christ as the Brother of Man: Steinbeck's THE GRAPES OF WRATH," *Pseudonyms of Christ in the Modern Novel*, 163-74. Also in Donohue, A. M., ed., *Casebook on THE GRAPES OF WRATH*, 209-17.

Motley, Warren, "From Patriarchy to Matriarchy: Ma Joad's Role in THE GRAPES OF WRATH," *AL* 54, iii (1982): 397-412.

Mullen, Patrick B., "American Folklife and THE GRAPES OF WRATH," *Jnl. of Amer. Culture* 1 (1978): 742-53.

Nakachi, Akira, "THE GRAPES OF WRATH: A Novel of Mankind," *Taira Technical College Reports of Study* 1 (1961): 1-15.

Nelson, Harland S., "Steinbeck's Politics Then and Now," *AR* 27 (Spring, 1967): 118-33 *passim*.

Nimitz, Jack, "Ecology in THE GRAPES OF WRATH," *HSL* 2, ii (1970): 165-8.

Pollock, Theodore, "On the Ending of THE GRAPES OF WRATH," *MFS* 4 (Summer, 1958): 177-8. Also in French, W., ed., *Companion to THE GRAPES OF WRATH*, 224-6. Also in Donohue, A. M., ed., *Casebook on THE GRAPES OF WRATH*, 182-4.

Poore, Charles, "Introduction" to *The Grapes of Wrath*, N.Y.: Harper's Modern Classics, 1951, vii-xv.

Prabhakar, S. S., *John Steinbeck*, 130-52.

Pratt, Linda R., "Imagining Existence: Form and History in Steinbeck and Agee," *SoR* 11, i (Jan., 1975): 84-98.

Raymund, Bernard, in Baker, D. V., ed., *Writers of Today*, 128-36.

Rundell, Walter, Jr., "Steinbeck's Image of the West," *American West* 1 (Spring, 1964): 4-8, and *passim*.

Salter, Christopher L., "John Steinbeck's THE GRAPES OF WRATH as a Primer for Cultural Geography," in Pocock, D.C.D., ed., *Humanistic Geography and Literature*, 142-58.

Sanford, Charles L., "Classics of American Reform Literature," *AmQ* 10 (Fall, 1958): 308-11.

Satyanarayana, M. R., *John Steinbeck*, 81-7.

Sastri, P. S., "The Structure of THE GRAPES OF WRATH," *IJES* 12 (Dec., 1971): 67-74.

Saw, Sally, "Religious Symbols in Steinbeck's GRAPES," *The Joad Newsletter* 1 (Jan., 1963): 1-2.

Schamberger, J. Edward, "*Grapes of Gladness*: A Misconception of WALDEN," *ATQ* 13 (Winter, 1972): 15-16.

Shively, Charles, "John Steinbeck: From the Tide Pool to the Loyal Community," in Astro, R., and T. Hayashi, eds., *Steinbeck*, 25-34.

Shockley, Martin, "Christian Symbolism in THE GRAPES OF WRATH," *CE* 18 (Nov., 1956): 87-90. Also in Tedlock, E. W., Jr., and C. V. Wicker, eds., *Steinbeck and His Critics*, 87-96. Also in Donohue, A. M., ed., *Casebook on THE GRAPES OF WRATH*, 90-5.

————, "Reception of THE GRAPES OF WRATH in Oklahoma," *AL* 15 (Jan., 1944): 351-61. Also in Tedlock, E. W., Jr., and C. V. Wicker, eds., *Steinbeck and His Critics*, 231-40.

Slade, Leonard A., Jr., "The Use of Biblical Allusions in THE GRAPES OF WRATH," *CLAJ* 11 (Mar., 1968): 241-7.

Slochower, H., *No Voice is Wholly Lost*, 299-305.

Snell, G., *Shapers of American Fiction*, 194-6.

Spies, George H., III., "John Steinbeck's THE GRAPES OF WRATH and Frederick Manfred's THE GOLDEN BOWL: A Comparative Study," *DAI* 34 (1973): 3431A-32A.

Stuckey, W. J., *Pulitzer Prize Novels*, 119-21.

Taylor, Walter F., "THE GRAPES OF WRATH Reconsidered," *MissQ* 12 (Summer, 1959): 136-44. Also in Donohue, A. M., ed., *Casebook on THE GRAPES OF WRATH*, 185-94.

Thompson, Eric, "Steinbeck's Okies," *Status* 2 (Dec., 1966): 42-5.

Trachtenberg, Stanley, "John Steinbeck: The Fate of Protest," *NDQ* 41, ii (Spring, 1973): 5-11.

Vassilowitch, John Jr., "Bing Crosby and THE GRAPES OF WRATH: Bad History, Good Art," *StQ* 13 (1980): 97-8.

Watkins, Floyd C., "Flat Wine from THE GRAPES OF WRATH," in Bitter, Barbara W., and Frederick K. Sanders, eds., *Humanist in His World: Essays in Honor of Fielding Dillard Russell*, Greenwood, S. C.: Attic Pr., 1976, 57-69. Also in Watkins, F. C., *In Time and Place*, 19-29.

Watt, F. W., *Steinbeck*, 63-75.

Wright, Celeste T., "Ancient Anologues of an Incident in John Steinbeck," *WF* 14 (Jan., 1955): 50-1. Also in Donohue, A. M., ed., *Casebook on THE GRAPES OF WRATH*, 159-61.

Yoshida, Hiroshige, "Gender of Animation in John Steinbeck's THE GRAPES OF WRATH," *Anglica* 2 (Oct., 1956): 106-22.

Zollman, Sol, "John Steinbeck's Political Outlook in THE GRAPES OF WRATH," *L&I* 13 (1972): 9-20.

IN DUBIOUS BATTLE

Allen, W., *Modern Novel*, 161-2.

Beach, J. W., *American Fiction*, 328-9.

Benson, Jackson J., and Anne Loftis, "John Steinbeck and Farm Labor Unionization: The Backgrounds of IN DUBIOUS BATTLE," *AL* 52 (Summer-Fall, 1980): 194-223.

Burgum, Edwin B., "The Sensibility of John Steinbeck," *S&S* 10 (1946): 136-7. Also in Burgum, E. B., *Novel and the World's Dilemma*, 277-8.

Cook, Sylvia J., "Steinbeck, the People and the Party," in Bogardus, R. F., and F. Hobson, eds., *Literature at the Barricades*, 85-90.

Dvorak, Wilfred P., "Notes Toward the Education of the Heart," *IEY* 10 (1965): 46-9.

Fontenrose, J., *John Steinbeck*, 42-53.

French, Warren G., in French, W. G., and W. E. Kidd, eds., *American Winners of the Nobel Literary Prize*, 205-7.

_____, *John Steinbeck*, 62-71.

_____, *John Steinbeck*, 2nd. ed. rev., 76-81.

Frohock, W. M., "John Steinbeck's Men of Wrath," *SWR* 31 (Spring, 1946): 150-1. Also in Frohock, W. M., *Novel of Violence in America*, 135-7.

Geismar, M., *Writers in Crisis*, 259-63.

Gide, Andre, *The Journals of Andre Gide*, Vol. 4, 1939-49, N.Y.: Knopf, 1951, 48. Also in Davis, R. M., ed., *Steinbeck*, 47-8.

Gray, J., *John Steinbeck*, 16-18.

Hartt, J. N., *Lost Image of Man*, 74-5.

Hayashi, T., ed., *Study Guide to John Steinbeck*, 47-68.

Jain, S., *John Steinbeck's Concept of Man*, 30-6.

Koloc, Frederick J., "John Steinbeck's IN DUBIOUS BATTLE: Backgrounds, Reputation and Artistry," *DAI* 36 (1975): 889A.

Levant, H., *Novels of John Steinbeck*, 74-92.

_____, "The Unity of IN DUBIOUS BATTLE: Violence and Dehumanization," *MFS* 11, i (Spring, 1965): 21-33. Also in Davis, R. M., ed., *Steinbeck*, 49-62.

Lisca, P., *John Steinbeck*, 63-76.

_____, "THE RAID and IN DUBIOUS BATTLE," *StQ* 5 (Summer-Fall, 1972): 90-4.

_____, *Wide World of John Steinbeck*, 108-29.

Marks, J. L., *Thematic Structure in the Novels of John Steinbeck*, 47-57, 58-63.

McCarthy, P., *John Steinbeck*, 47-57.

McDaniel, Barbara A., "Steinbeck: Ralph Ellison's Invisible Source," *PCP* 8 (1973): 28-33.

Moore, H. T., *Novels of John Steinbeck*, 40-7.

Palmieri, Anthony F. R., "IN DUBIOUS BATTLE: A Portrait in Pessimism," *ReAL* 3, i (1976): 61-71.

Prabhakar, S. S., *John Steinbeck*, 97-108.

Pratt, Linda R., "In Defense of Mac's Dubious Battles," *StQ* 10, ii (Spring, 1977): 36-44.

Rose, Alan H., "Steinbeck and the Complexity of the Self in IN DUBIOUS BATTLE," *StQ* 9 (1976): 15-19.

Sarchett, Barry W., "IN DUBIOUS BATTLE: A Revaluation," *StQ* 13 (1980): 87-97.

Shepherd, Allen, "On Dubiousness of Steinbeck's IN DUBIOUS BATTLE," *NMAL* 2 (1978): Item 19.

Spies, George H., III., "John Steinbeck's IN DUBIOUS BATTLE and Robert Penn Warren's NIGHT RIDER: A Comparative Study," *StQ* 4, ii (Spring, 1971): 48-55. Also in Hayashi, T., ed., *Steinbeck's Literary Dimension*, 130-7.

Walcutt, C. C., *American Literary Naturalism*, 260-2.

_____, *Man's Changing Mask*, 258-65.

Watt, F. W., *Steinbeck*, 77-9.

Wilson, Jerry W., "IN DUBIOUS BATTLE: Engagement in Collectivity," *StQ* 13 (1980): 31-42.

Wyatt, Bryant, "Experimentation As Technique: The Protest Novels of John Steinbeck," *Discourse* 12, ii (Spring, 1969): 144-6.

THE MOON IS DOWN

Burgum, Edwin B., "The Sensibility of John Steinbeck," *S&S* 10 (1946): 145-7. Also in Burgum, E. B., *Novel and the World's Dilemma*, 288-91.

Fontenrose, J., *John Steinbeck, 98-101.*

French, W., *John Steinbeck*, 113-19.

_____, *John Steinbeck*, 2nd ed. rev., 106-8.

Frohock, W. M., "John Steinbeck's Men of Wrath," *SWR* 31 (Spring, 1946): 151-2. Also in Frohock, W. M., *Novel of Violence in America*, 137-9.

Gurko, L., *Angry Decade*, 219-20.

Hayashi, T., ed., *Study Guide to Steinbeck, Part II*, 100-21.

Levant, H., *Novels of John Steinbeck*, 144-58.

Lisca, P., *John Steinbeck*, 200-3.

_____, *Wide World of John Steinbeck*, 186-96.

Marks, L. J., *Thematic Design in the Novels of John Steinbeck*, 98-105.

Prabhakar, S. S., *John Steinbeck*, 156-60.

Watt, F. W., *Steinbeck*, 77-9.

OF MICE AND MEN

Allen, W., *Modern Novel*, 163-4.

Beach, J. W., *American Fiction*, 322-4.

Bellman, Samuel I., "Control and Freedom in Steinbeck's OF MICE AND MEN," *CEA* 38, i (1975): 25-7.

Burgum, Edwin B., "The Sensibility of John Steinbeck," *S&S* 10 (1946): 137-40. Also in Burgum, E. B., *Novel and the World's Dilemma*, 278-83.

Cardullo, Bert, "The Function of Candy in OF MICE AND MEN," *NConL* 12, ii (Mar., 1982): 10.

Cardullo, Robert, "On the Road to Tragedy: The Function of Candy in OF MICE AND MEN," 1-8, in Hartigan, Karelisa, V., ed., *All the World: Drama Past and Present*, II, Washington, D.C.: Un. Pr. of America, 1982.

Dacus, Lee, "Lennie as Christian in OF MICE AND MEN," *SwAL* 4 (1974): 87-91.

Everson, William K., "Thoughts on a Great Adaptation," in Peary, G., and R. Shatzkin, eds., *Modern American Novel and the Movies*, 63-9.

Fontenrose, J., *John Steinbeck*, 53-9.

French, Warren G., in French, W. G., and W. E. Kidd, eds., *American Winners of the Nobel Literary Prize*, 207-8.

_____, *John Steinbeck*, 72-9. Also in Davis, R. M., *Steinbeck*, 63-9.

_____, *John Steinbeck*, 2nd ed. rev., 87-91.

Ganapathy, R., "Steinbeck's OF MICE AND MEN: A Study of Lyricism Through Primitivism," *LCrit* 5, iii (1962): 101-4.

Geismar, M., *Writers in Crisis*, 256-9.

Goldhurst, William, "OF MICE AND MEN: John Steinbeck's Parable of the Curse of Cain," *WAL* 6, ii (1971): 123-35.

Gray, J., *John Steinbeck*, 21-2.

Gurko, L., *Angry Decade*, 217-19.

_____, "OF MICE AND MEN: Steinbeck as Manichean," *UWR* 8, ii (Spring, 1973): 11-23.

Hwang, Mei-shu, "OF MICE AND MEN: An Experimental Study of the Novel and the Play," *TkJ* 11 (1973): 225-40.

Hayashi, T., ed., *Study Guide to Steinbeck*, 129-54.

Jain, Jasbir, "Steinbeck's Unfinished Beings and OF MICE AND MEN," *RUSEng* 11 (1978): 49-56.

Jain, S., *John Steinbeck's Concept of Man*, 37-42.

Levant, H., *Novels of John Steinbeck*, 133-44.

Lisca, P., *John Steinbeck*, 76-86.

_____, "Motif and Pattern in OF MICE AND MEN," *MFS* 2 (Winter, 1956-57): 228-34. Also (revised and expanded) in Lisca, P., *Wide World of John Steinbeck*, 130-43.

Marks, L. J., *Thematic Structure in the Novels of John Steinbeck*, 58-65.

McCarthy, P., *John Steinbeck*, 57-64.

Millichap, Joseph, "Realistic Style in Steinbeck's and Milestone's OF MICE AND MEN," *LFQ* 6 (1978): 241-52.

Moore, H. T., *Novels of John Steinbeck*, 47-52.

Ohnishi, Katsue, "'Why Must Lennie Be Killed'," *KAL* 22 (May, 1981): 85-7.

Pizer, Donald, "John Steinbeck and American Naturalism" *StQ* 9, i (Winter, 1976): 12-15.

Prabhakar, S. S., *John Steinbeck*, 119-26.

Rascoe, Burton, "John Steinbeck," *EJ* 27 (Mar., 1938): 205-16. Also in Tedlock, E. W., Jr., and C. V. Wickers, eds., *Steinbeck and His Critics*, 60-5.

Shurgot, Michael, "A Game of Cards in Steinbeck's OF MICE AND MEN," *StQ* 15 (1982): 38-43.

Spilka, Mark, "Of George and Lennie and Curley's Wife: Sweet Violence in Steinbeck's Eden," *MFS* 20, ii (Summer, 1974): 169-79.

Steele, Joan, "A Century of Idiots: BARNABY RUDGE and OF MICE AND MEN," *StQ* 5, i (Winter, 1972): 8-17. Also in Hayashi, T., ed., *Steinbeck's Literary Dimension*, 16-27.

Watt, F. W., *Steinbeck*, 58-62.

Wyatt, Bryant N., "Experimentation as Technique: The Protest Novels of John Steinbeck," *Discourse* 12 (Spring, 1969): 146-51.

THE PASTURES OF HEAVEN

Beston, John B., "The Influence of John Steinbeck's THE PASTURES OF HEAVEN," *ALS* 6 (May, 1974): 317-19.

Carpenter, Frederic I., "John Steinbeck: American Dreamer," *SWR* 26 (July, 1941): 458-60. Also in Tedlock, E. W., Jr., and C. V. Wicker, eds., *Steinbeck and His Critics*, 71-3.

Cherulescu, Rodica, "Man and Nature in THE PASTURES OF HEAVEN," *AUB-LG* 22 (1973): 199-205.

Fontenrose, J., *John Steinbeck*, 20-9.

French, W., *John Steinbeck*, 39-46.

_____, *John Steinbeck*, 2nd ed. rev., 54-62.

Geismar, M., *Writers in Crisis*, 242-6.

Gladstein, Mimi R., "Female Characters in Steinbeck: Minor Characters of Major Importance," in Hayashi, T., ed., *Steinbeck's Women*, 18-22.

Hayashi, T., ed., *Study Guide to Steinbeck*, 87-106.

Jain, S., *John Steinbeck's Concept of Man*, 18-23.

Kallapur, S. T., "John Steinbeck and Oriental Thought: Some Parallels," in Naik, M. K., et al., eds., *Image of India in Western Creative Writing*, 372-3.

Levant, H., *Novels of John Steinbeck*, 34-51.

Lisca, P., *John Steinbeck*, 46-54.

Mawer, Randall R., "Takashi Kato, 'Good American': The Central Episode in Steinbeck's THE PASTURES OF HEAVEN," *StQ* 13 (1980): 23-31.

McCarthy, P., *John Steinbeck*, 32-7.

Moore, H. T., *Novels of John Steinbeck*, 18-23.

Mortlock, Melanie, "The Eden Myth as Paradox: An Allegorical Reading of THE PASTURES OF HEAVEN," *StQ* 11, i (1978): 6-15.

Prabhakar, S. S., *John Steinbeck*, 37-61.

Snell, G., *Shapers of American Fiction*, 192-3.

Watt, F. W., *Steinbeck*, 33-8.

Yancey, Anita V. R., "WINESBURG OHIO and THE PASTURES OF HEAVEN: A Comparative Analysis of Two Studies on Isolation," *DAI* 32 (1972): 5249A.

THE PEARL

Astro, Richard, "Steinbeck's Post-War Trilogy: A Return to Nature and Natural Man," *TCL* 16, ii (Apr., 1970): 119-21.

Bates, Barclay W., "THE PEARL as Tragedy," *CEJ* 6 (Feb., 1970): 41-5.

Corin, Fernand, "Steinbeck and Hemingway: A Study in Literary Economy," *RLV* 24 (Jan.-Feb., 1958): 60-75; (Mar.-Apr., 1958): 153-63.

French, W., *John Steinbeck*, 2nd ed. rev., 126-30.

Fuller, Edward, and Blanche J. Thompson, eds., *Four Novels for Appreciation*, N.Y.: Harcourt, Brace, 1960, 256-60.

Geismar, M., in *SatR* 30 (Nov. 22, 1947): 14. Also in Geismar, M., *American Moderns*, 151-3.

Gladstein, Mimi R., "Steinbeck's Juana: A Woman of Worth," *StQ* 9, i (Winter, 1976): 20-4. Also in Hayashi, T., ed., *Steinbeck's Women*, 49-52.

Gray, J., *John Steinbeck*, 29-30.

Hamby, James A., "Steinbeck's THE PEARL: Tradition and Innovation," *WR* 7, ii (1970): 65-6.

Hayashi, Tetsumaro, "THE PEARL as the Novel of Disengagement," *StQ* 7, iii-iv (Summer-Fall, 1974): 84-8.

_____, ed., *Study Guide to Steinbeck*, 107-28.

Jain, S., *John Steinbeck's Concept of Man*, 73-81.

Jain, Sunita, "Steinbeck's THE PEARL: An Interpretation," *JSL* 6, i-ii (1978-79): 138-43.

Kallapur, S. T., "John Steinbeck and Oriental Thought: Some Parallels," in Naik, M. K., et al., eds., *Image of India in Western Culture*, 372-3.

Karsten, Ernest E., Jr., "Thematic Structure in THE PEARL," *EJ* 54 (Jan., 1965): 1-7.

_____, and Barclay Bates, "Comment and Reply Concerning THE PEARL as Tragedy," *CEJ* 6 (Apr., 1970): 48-50. [See Bates above.]

Krause, Sydney J., THE PEARL and HADLEYBURG: From Desire to Denunciation," *StQ* 7 (1974): 3-18.

Levant, H., *Novels of John Steinbeck*, 185-206.

Levidova, I., "The Post-War Books of John Steinbeck," *SovietR* 4 (Summer, 1963): 7-8.

Lisca, P., *John Steinbeck*, 123-41.

Marks, L. J., *Thematic Design in the Novels of John Steinbeck*, 105-7.

McCarthy, P., *John Steinbeck*, 108-9.

Metzger, Charles R., "The Film Version of Steinbeck's THE PEARL," *StQ* 4, iii (Summer, 1971): 88-92.

_____, "Steinbeck's THE PEARL as a Nonteleological Parable of Hope," *RS* 46 (1978): 98-105.

Morris, Harry, "THE PEARL: Realism and Allegory, *EJ* 52 (Oct., 1963): 487-95.

Prabhakar, S. S., *John Steinbeck*, 160-5.

Prescott, O., *In My Opinion*, 62-4.

Scoville, Samuel, "The Weltanschauung of Steinbeck and Hemingway: An Analysis of Themes," *EJ* 56 (Jan., 1967): 60-3, 66.

Shimomura, Noboru, "Guilt and Christianity in THE PEARL," *SALit* 16 (1980): 19-31.

Tarr, E. Whitney, "Steinbeck on One Plane," *SatR* 30 (Dec. 20, 1947): 20.

Tokunaga, Masanori, "The Biological Descriptions in THE PEARL and Their Meanings," *KAL* 16 (1975): 13-16.

Van Der Beets, Richard, "A Pearl Is a Pearl Is a Pearl," *CEA* 32, vii (Apr., 1970): 9.

Walcutt, C. C., *American Literary Naturalism*, 267-8.

Waldron, Edward E., "THE PEARL and THE OLD MAN AND THE SEA: A Comparative Analysis," *StQ* 13 (1980): 98-106.

Watt, F. W., *Steinbeck*, 84-7.

SHORT REIGN OF PIPPIN IV

Fontenrose, J., *John Steinbeck*, 130-2.

French, W., *John Steinbeck*, 165-9.

_____, *John Steinbeck*, 2nd ed. rev., 157-8.

Geismar, M., *American Moderns*, 155-6.

Johnson, Pamela H., in *NStat* 54 (July 13, 1957): 61-2.

Levant, H., *Novels of John Steinbeck*, 273-87.

Lisca, P., *John Steinbeck*, 208-12.

_____, *Wide World of John Steinbeck*, 285-8.

Watt, F. W., *Steinbeck*, 101-2.

SWEET THURSDAY

Astro, Richard, "Steinbeck's Bittersweet Thursday," *StQ* 4, ii (1971): 36-48.

Benton, Robert M., "A Scientific Point of View in Steinbeck's Fiction," *StQ* 7, iii-iv (Summer-Fall, 1974): 67-72.

DeMott, Robert, "Steinbeck and the Creative Process: First Manifesto to End the Bringdown Against SWEET THURSDAY," in Astro, R., and T. Hayashi, eds., *Steinbeck*, 157-78.

Fontenrose, J., *John Steinbeck*, 127-30.

French, W., *John Steinbeck*, 156-60.

_____, *John Steinbeck*, 2nd ed. rev., 154-7.

Holman, Hugh, "A Narrow-gauge Dickens," *NRep* 130 (June 7, 1954): 18-20.

Hayashi, T., ed., *Study Guide to John Steinbeck, Part II*, 139-64.

Levant, H., *Novels of John Steinbeck*, 259-72.

Levidova, I., "The Post-War Books of John Steinbeck," *SovietR* 4 (Summer, 1963): 6-7.

Lisca, P., *John Steinbeck*, 204-8.

_____, *Wide World of John Steinbeck*, 276-84.

Metzger, Charles R., "Steinbeck's Version of the Pastoral," *MFS* 6 (Summer, 1960): 115-234.

Moore, Ward, "Cannery Row Revisited: Steinbeck and the Sardine," *Nation* 179 (Oct. 16, 1954): 325-7.

S. L., "Steinbeck's SWEET THURSDAY," *Expl* 34 (1976): Item 1.

Watt, F. W., *Steinbeck*, 99-101.

TO A GOD UNKNOWN

Beach, J. W., *American Fiction*, 315-16.

Carpenter, Frederic I., "John Steinbeck: American Dreamer," *SWR* 26 (July, 1941): 460-1. Also in Tedlock, E. W., Jr., and C. V. Wicker, eds., *Steinbeck and His Critics*, 73-4.

DeMott, Robert, "Toward a Redefinition of TO A GOD UNKNOWN," *UWR* 8, ii (Spring, 1973): 34-53.

Fontenrose, J., *John Steinbeck*, 13-19.

French, W., *John Steinbeck*, 47-52.

_____, *John Steinbeck*, 2nd ed. rev., 48-52.

Geismar, M., *Writers in Crisis*, 248-9.

Gray, J., *John Steinbeck*, 24-6.

Hayashi, T., ed., *Study Guide to Steinbeck*, 187-213.

Jain, S., *John Steinbeck's Concept of Man*, 12-17.

Kallapur, S. T., "John Steinbeck and Oriental Thought: Some Parallels," in Naik, M. K., et al., eds., *Image of India in Western Creative Writing*, 361-6.

Le Master, J. R., "Mythological Constructs in Steinbeck's TO A GOD UNKNOWN," *ForumH* 9, ii (Summer, 1971): 8-11.

Levant, H., *Novels of John Steinbeck*, 22-34.

Lisca, Peter, "CUP OF GOLD and TO A GOD UNKNOWN: Two Early Works of John Steinbeck," *KN* 22 (1975): 173-83.

_____, *John Steinbeck*, 35-45.

_____, *Wide World of John Steinbeck*, 39-55.

Marks, L. J., *Thematic Design in the Novels of John Steinbeck*, 34-46.

Moore, H. T., *Novels of John Steinbeck*, 23-33.

Murray, Isobel, and Jim Merrilees, "This Side of Paradise: Old Testament Themes in John Steinbeck's Fiction," *New Blackfriars* 53 (Feb., 1972): 60-8.

Prabhakar, S. S., *John Steinbeck*, 83-96.

Rao, B. R., *American Fictional Hero*, 59-62.

Satanarayana, M. R., "The Unknown God of John Steinbeck," *IJAS* 3, i (1973): 97-103. [Not seen.]

Shimada, Saburo, "A Study of John Steinbeck's TO A GOD UNKNOWN," *Beacon Study in English Language and Literature* 5 (1964): 23-5.

Snell, G., *Shapers of American Fiction*, 189-90.

Uchida, Shigeharu, "John Steinbeck's Non-Teleology and TO A GOD UNKNOWN," *KAL* 6 (Apr., 1963): 13-17.

Watt, F. W., *Steinbeck*, 29-33.

TORTILLA FLAT

Alexander, Stanley, "The Conflict of Form in TORTILLA FLAT," *AL* 40 (Mar., 1968): 58-66.

Beach, Joseph W., *American Fiction*, 317-22. Also (revised) in Tedlock, E. W., Jr., and C. V. Wicker, eds., *Steinbeck and His Critics*, 85-90.

Fontenrose, J., *John Steinbeck*, 30-41.

French, Warren G., in French, W. G., and W. E. Kidd, eds., *American Winners of the Nobel Literary Prize*, 204-5.

_____, *John Steinbeck*, 53-61.

_____, *John Steinbeck*, 2nd ed. rev., 70-5.

Geismar, M., *Writers in Crisis*, 252-6.

Gray, J., *John Steinbeck*, 27-8.

Jain, S., *John Steinbeck's Concept of Man*, 24-9.

Justus, James H., "The Transient World of TORTILLA FLAT," *WR* 7, i (1970): 55-60.

Kallapur, S. T., "John Steinbeck and Oriental Thought: Some Parallels," in Naik, M. K., et al., eds., *Images of India in Western Creative Writing*, 375-8; 379-80.

Kawamura, Yoneichi, "Steinbeck's Humor and Pathos in TORTILLA FLAT and CANNERY ROW," *Hokkaido Un. Essays in Foreign Languages and Literatures* 1 (Dec., 1953): 24-30.

Kinney, Arthur F., "The Arthurian Cycle in TORTILLA FLAT," *MFS* 11, i (Spring, 1965): 11-20. Also in Davis, R. M., ed., *Steinbeck*, 36-46.

————, "TORTILLA FLAT Revisited," in Hayashi, T., ed., *Steinbeck and the Arthurian Theme*, 12-24.

Levant, H., *Novels of John Steinbeck*, 52-73.

————, "TORTILLA FLAT: The Shape of John Steinbeck's Career," *PMLA* 85 (Oct., 1970): 1087-95.

Lisca, P., *John Steinbeck*, 54-62.

————, *Wide World of John Steinbeck*, 72-91.

McCarthy, P., *John Steinbeck*, 38-45.

Moore, H. T., *Novels of John Steinbeck*, 35-9.

Ortega, Philip D., "Fables of Identity: Stereotype and Caricature of Chicanos in Steinbeck's TORTILLA FLAT," *JEthS* 1, i (1973): 39-43.

Owens, Louis, "Camelot East of Eden: John Steinbeck's TORTILLA FLAT," *ArQ* 38, iii (Autumn, 1982): 203-16.

Prabhakar, S. S., *John Steinbeck*, 109-18.

Raymund, Bernard, in Baker, D. V., ed., *Writers of Today*, 125-7.

Scheer, Ronald D., "Steinbeck Into Film: The Making of TORTILLA FLAT," *WVUPP* 26 (Aug., 1980): 30-6.

Snell, G., *Shapers of American Fiction*, 192-3.

Uchida, Shigeharu, "Sentimental Steinbeck and His TORTILLA FLAT," *KAL* 7 (1964): 8-12.

Walcutt, C. C., *American Literary Realism*, 259-60.

Watt, F. W., *Steinbeck*, 38-42.

THE WAYWARD BUS

Astro, Richard, "Steinbeck's Post-War Trilogy: A Return to Nature and Natural Man," *TCL* 16, ii (Apr., 1970): 115-19.

Clark, Eleanor, in *Nation* 164 (Mar. 29, 1947): 370-3.

Cousins, Norman, "Bankrupt Realism," *SatR* 30 (Mar. 8, 1947): 22-3.

Ditsky, John, "Plenty of Room on THE WAYWARD BUS," *StQ* 6 (1973): 48-9.

————, "THE WAYWARD BUS: Love and Time in America," *SJS* 1, iii (1975): 89-101. Also in Hayashi, T., ed., *Steinbeck's Travel Literature*, 61-75.

Fontenrose, J., *John Steinbeck*, 108-11.

French, W., *John Steinbeck*, 143-8.

————, *John Steinbeck*, 2nd ed. rev., 130-7.

Gardiner, Harold C., "The Emperor's New (Literary) Clothes," *America* 76 (Mar. 22, 1947): 689-91. Also in Gardiner, H. C., *In All Conscience*, 131-6.

Hayashi, T., ed., *Study Guide to Steinbeck, Part II*, 210-31.

Levant, H., *Novels of John Steinbeck*, 207-33.

Levidova, I., "The Post-War Books of John Steinbeck," *SovietR* 4 (Summer, 1963): 8-9.

Lisca, P., *John Steinbeck*, 141-53.

————, "THE WAYWARD BUS—A Modern Pilgrimage," in Tedlock, E. W., Jr., and C. V. Wicker, eds., *Steinbeck and His Critics*, 281-90.

————, *Wide World of John Steinbeck*, 231-47.

Marks, L. J., *Thematic Design in the Novels of John Steinbeck*, 107-12.

McCarthy, P., *John Steinbeck*, 110-16.

Owens, Louis, "THE WAYWARD BUS: A Triumph of Nature," *SJS* 6, i (1980): 45-53.

Prabhakar, S. S., *John Steinbeck*, 165-70.

Prescott, Orville, in *YR* 36 (Summer, 1947): 765-6.

————, *In My Opinion*, 61-2.

Redman, Ben R., "The Case of John Steinbeck," *AmMerc* 64 (May, 1947): 624-30.

Seixas, Antonia, "John Steinbeck and the Non-Teleological Bus," in Tedlock, E. W., Jr., and C. V. Wicker, ed., *Steinbeck and His Critics*, 275-80.

Tsunoda, Toshio, "THE WAYWARD BUS, by John Steinbeck," *Yukeitsushin (Japan)* No. 11 (1947).

Walcutt, C. C., *American Literary Naturalism*, 266-7.

Watt, F. W., *John Steinbeck*, 887-91.

Weeks, Donald, "Steinbeck Against Steinbeck," *PacSp* 1 (Autumn, 1947): 447-57.

THE WINTER OF OUR DISCONTENT

Bedford, Richard C., "The Genesis and Consolation of Our Discontent," *Criticism* 14, iii (Summer, 1972): 277-94.

Chandra, Naresh, "Steinbeck's THE WINTER OF OUR DISCONTENT," *IJES* 14 (1973): 70-86.

Clancy, Charles J., "Light in THE WINTER OF OUR DISCONTENT," *StQ* 9, iii-iv (Summer-Fall, 1976): 91-100.

Ditsky, John, "THE WINTER OF OUR DISCONTENT: Steinbeck's Testament on Naturalism," *RS* 44 (1976): 42-51.

Fontenrose, J., *John Steinbeck*, 132-7.

French, Warren, in French, W. G., and W. E. Kidd, eds., *American Winners of the Nobel Literary Prize*, 219-21.

French, W., *John Steinbeck*, 2nd ed. rev., 159-65.

————, "Steinbeck's Winter Tale," *MFS* 11, i (Spring, 1965): 66-74.

Gerstenberger, Donna, "Steinbeck's American Wasteland," *MFS* 11, i (Spring, 1965): 59-65.

Gray, J., *John Steinbeck*, 35-7.

Hartt, J. N., "The Return of Moral Passion," *YR* 51, ii (Winter, 1962): 305-6.

Hayashi, T., ed., *Study Guide to Steinbeck*, 244-57.

Hayashi, Tetsumaro, "Steinbeck's WINTER as Shakespearean Fiction," *StQ* 12 (1979): 107-14.

Hyman, S. E., "John Steinbeck and the Nobel Prize," *Standards*, 113-1-7.

Jain, S., *John Steinbeck and the Concept of Man*, 89-92.

Lemaire, Marcel, "Some Recent American Novels and Essays," *RLV* 28 (1962): 74-5.

Levant, H., *Novels of John Steinbeck*, 288-300.

Levidova, I., "The Post-War Books of John Steinbeck," *SovietR* 4 (Summer, 1963): 11-13.

Lisca, P., *John Steinbeck*, 176-88.

MacKendrick, Louis K., "The Popular Art of Discontent: Steinbeck's Masterful WINTER," *StQ* 12 (1979): 99-106.

McCarthy, Kevin M., "Witchcraft and Superstition in WINTER OF OUR DISCONTENT," *NYFQ* 30 (1974): 197-211.

McCarthy, P., *John Steinbeck*, 128-33.

Nelson, Harland S., "Steinbeck's Politics Then and Now," *AR* 27 (Spring, 1967): 118-33 *passim*.

Prabhakar, S. S., *John Steinbeck*.

Rao, B. R., *American Fictional Hero*, 77-81.

Stone, Donald, "Steinbeck, Jung, and THE WINTER OF OUR DISCONTENT," *StQ* 11 (1978): 87-96.

Verdier, Douglas L., "Ethan Allen Hawley and the Hanged Man: Free Will and Fate in THE WINTER OF OUR DISCONTENT," *StQ* 15 (1982): 44-50.

Watt, F. W., *Steinbeck*, 102-3.

BIBLIOGRAPHY

Beebe, Maurice, and Jackson Bryer, "Criticism of John Steinbeck: A Selected Checklist," *MFS* 11, i (Spring, 1965): 90-103.

Donohue, A. M., ed., *Casebook on THE GRAPES OF WRATH*, 196-9.

Frenck, Warren, "Bibliography," *Companion to THE GRAPES OF WRATH*, 229-35.

_____, *John Steinbeck*, 177-81.

_____, *John Steinbeck*, 2d ed. rev., 180-4.

_____, "John Steinbeck," in Bryer, Jackson R., ed., *Sixteen Modern American Authors: A Survey of Research and Criticism*, Durham: Duke Un. Pr., 1974.

Hayashi, Tetsumaro, "A Brief Survey of John Steinbeck Bibliographies," *KAL* 9 (1966): 54-61.

_____, "A Brief Survey of Steinbeck Criticism in the United States," *KAL* 14 (1972): 43-9.

_____, "John Steinbeck: A Checklist of Unpublished Ph.D. Dissertations (1946-1967)," *Serif* 5, iv (1968): 30-1.

_____, *John Steinbeck: A Concise Bibliography (1930-65)*, Metuchen, N.J.: Scarecrow, 1967.

_____, ed., *John Steinbeck: A Guide to the Doctoral Dissertations* (Steinbeck Monographs Ser., No. 1), Muncie, Ind.: Steinbeck Society, Ball State U.P., 1971.

_____, *A New Steinbeck Bibliography, 1929-1971*, Metuchen, N.J.: Scarecrow, 1973.

_____, "Recent Steinbeck Studies in the United States," *StQ* 4, iii (Summer, 1971): 73-6.

_____, "A Selected Bibliography," in Hayashi, T., ed., *Steinbeck's Literary Dimension*, 174-9.

_____, ed., *Steinbeck Criticism: A Review of Book Length Studies (1939-1973)*, (Steinbeck Monograph Ser., No. 4), Muncie, Ind.: Ball State U.P., 1974.

_____, "Steinbeck Scholarship: Recent Trends in the United States," in Hayashi, T., ed., *Steinbeck's Literary Dimension*, 168-73.

Lisca, Peter, "A Survey of Steinbeck Criticism to 1971," in Hayaski, T., ed., *Steinbeck's Literary Dimension*, 148-67.

Steele, Joan, "John Steinbeck: A Checklist of Biographical, Critical and Bibliographical Material," *BB* 24 (May-Aug., 1965): 149-52, 162-3.

STERN, RICHARD GUSTAVE, 1928-

GENERAL

Raeder, Robert L., "An Interview with Richard G. Stern," *ChiR* 18 (Autumn-Winter, 1965-66): 170-5.

Rima, Larry, "An Interview with Richard Stern," *ChiR* 28, iii (1977): 145-8.

Rosenberg, Milton, and Eliot Anderson, "A Conversation with Richard Stern," *ChiR* 31, iii (Winter, 1980): 98-108.

STEWART, MARY, 1916-

GENERAL

Fries, Maureen, "The Rationalization of the Arthurian 'Matter' in T. H. White and Mary Stewart," *PQ* 56, ii (Spring, 1977): 258-65.

Reaves, Monetha R., "The Popular Fiction Tradition and the Novels of Mary Stewart," *DAI* 39 (1978): 1556A-57A.

Stewart, Mary, "Why Shouldn't One Write 'Escapist' Fiction," *Australian Author* 9 (Jan., 1977): 5-10.

STIVENS, DAL (LAS GEORGE), 1911-

GENERAL

Elliot, Brian, "The Author in Search of Himself: Some Notes on Dal Stivens," *AusQ* 34, i (Mar., 1962): 69-76.

JIMMY BROCKETT

Elliot, Brian, "The Author in Search of Himself: Some Notes on Dal Stivens," *AusQ* 34, i (Mar., 1962): 69-72.

THE WIDE ARCH

Elliot, Brian, "The Author in Search of Himself: Some Notes on Dal Stivens," *AusQ* 34, i (Mar., 1962): 73-5.

STONE, ROBERT, 1937-

GENERAL

Bonetti, Kay, "An Interview with Robert Stone," *MissR* 6, i (Fall, 1982): 91-115.

Karaguezian, Maureen, "An Interview with Robert Stone," *TriQ* 53 (Winter, 1982): 248-58.

DOG SOLDIERS

Knox, Stephen H., "A Cup of Salt for an O.D.: DOG SOLDIERS as Anti-Apocalypse," *JGE* 34, i (Spring, 1982): 60-8.

HALL OF MIRROR

Moore, L. Hugh, "The Undersea World of Robert Stone," *Crit* 11, iii (1969): 43-5-6.

BIBLIOGRAPHY

Colonnese, Tom, "Robert Stone: A Working Checklist," *BB* 39, iii (Sept., 1982): 136-8.

STOREY, DAVID, 1933-

GENERAL

Bygrave, Mike, "David Storey: Novelist or Playwright?" *ThQ* 1, ii (Apr.-June, 1971): 31-6.

Clark, Susan M., "David Storey: The Emerging Artist," *DAI* 37 (1977): 6474A.

Craig, David, "David Story's Vision of the Working Class," in Jefferson, D., and G. Martin, eds., *Uses of Fiction*, 125-38.

Gindin, James, "The Fable Begins to Break Down," *WSCL* 8 (Winter, 1967): 5-8.

Lockwood, Bernard, "Four Contemporary British Working-Class Novelists: A Thematic and Critical Approach to the Fiction of Raymond Williams, John Braine, David Storey and Allan Sillitoe," *DA* 28 (1967): 1081A.

McGuiness, Frank, "The Novels of David Storey," *LonM* 3 (Mar., 1964): 79-93.

Newton, J. M., in *CamQ* 1 (Summer, 1966): 284-95.

Reinelt, Janella G., "The Novels and Plays of David Storey: New Solutions in Form and Technique," *DAI* 39 (1978): 3234A-35A.

Roberts, Neil, "Fathers and Children: David Storey's Recent Work," *Delta* 53 (1975): 12-19.

Sage, Victor, "Interview with David Story," *NewRev* 3, xxxi (1976): 63-5.

Shelton, Lewis E., "David Storey and the Invisible Event," *MQ* 22, iv (Summer, 1981): 392-406.

Storey, David, "Writers on Themselves: Journey Through a Tunnel," *Listener* 70 (Aug. 1, 1963): 159-60.

Weaver, Laura H., "Journey through a Tunnel: The Divided Self in the Novels and Plays of David Storey," *DAI* 38 (1978): 7353A.

Weaver, Laura H., "Rugby and the Arts: The Divided Self in David Storey's Novels and Plays," in Crook, E. J., ed., *Fearful Symmetry*, 149-62.

FLIGHT INTO CAMDEN

Gindin, J., "Education and Class Structure," *Postwar British Fiction*, 85-108.

Newton, J. M., in *CamQ* 1 (Summer, 1966): 290-2.

Raban, J., "Imagery in the Language of Fiction," *Technique of Modern Fiction*, 177-9.

Urwin, G. G., ed., *Taste for Living*, 124-7.

PASMORE

Guiton, Anita, "Comments on David Storey's PASMORE and A TEMPORARY LIFE," *Delta* 53 (1975): 20-8.

Roberts, Neil, "Fathers and Children: David Storey's Recent Work," *Delta* 53 (1975): 13-17.

RADCLIFFE

Anon., "And Hell Up North," *TLS* (Sept. 20, 1963): 701. Also in *T.L.S.: Essays and Reviews from The Times Literary Supplement, 1963*, 102-3.

Gindin, James, "The Fable Begins to Break Down," *WSCL* 8 (Winter, 1967): 6-8.

Newton, J. M., in *CamQ* 1 (Summer, 1966): 292-5.

Spender, Stephen, "Must There Always Be a Red Brick England?" in Encyclopedia Britannica. *Great Ideas Today, 1965*, 180-1.

SAVILLE

Olsson, Barbara, "Pitman and Poet: The Divided," 39-52 in Gauna, Max, ed., *A Yearbook in English Language and Literature*, Korninger, Seigfried (ed.), Braumuller: Vienna, n.d.

Roberts, Neil, "Colin's Come Home Again," *Kingfisher* 1, i (1976): 18-26.

A TEMPORARY LIFE

Guiton, Anita, "Comments on David Storey's PASMORE and A TEMPORARY LIFE," *Delta* 53 (1975): 20-8.

Roberts, Neil, "Fathers and Children: David Storey's Recent Work," *Delta* 53 (1975): 17-19.

THIS SPORTING LIFE

Churchill, Thomas, "Waterhouse, Storey, and Fowles: *Which Way Out of the Room?*" *Crit* 10, iii (1968): 72-87.

Gindin, J., "Education and Class Structure," *Postwar British Fiction*, 85-108.

Gray, N., *Silent Majority*, 135-59.

Newton, J. M., in *CamQ* 1 (Summer, 1966): 285-90.

O'Connor, W. V., "The New Hero and a Shift in Literary Convention," *New University Wits*, 136-8.

STOW, RANDOLPH, 1935-

GENERAL

Bennett, Bruce, "Discussions with Randolph Stow," *Westerly* 26, iv (Dec., 1981): 53-61.

————, "Randolph Stow and Taoism," in Tiffin, C., ed., *South Pacific Images*, 134-42.

Beston, John B., "The Family Background and Literary Career of Randolph Stow," *LHY* 16, ii (July, 1975): 125-34.

————, "An Interview with Randolph Stow," *WLWE* 14 (Apr., 1975): 221-30.

Burgess, O. N., "On the Novels of Randolph Stow," *AusQ* 37, ii (Mar., 1965): 73-81.

Clarke, Donovan, "The Realities of Randolph Stow," *Bridge* 2 (Feb., 1966): 37-42. [Not seen.]

Dutton, Geoffrey, "The Search for Permanence: The Novels of Randolph Stow," *JCL* 1 (Sept., 1965): 135-48. Also in Walsh, W., ed., *Readings in Commonwealth Literature*, 377-91.

Geering, R. D., *Recent Fiction*, 4-11.

Hassall, Anthony J., "Interview with Randolph Stow," *ALS* 10 (1982): 311-25.

Heseltine, Harry, in Dutton, G., ed., *Literature of Australia*, 211-12.

Higginbotham, Paul D., "'Honour the Single Soul': Randolph Stow and His Novels," *Southerly* 39, iv (Dec., 1979): 378-92.

Hope, A. D., "Randolph Stow and the Tourmaline Affair," in Ramson, W. S., ed., *Australian Experience*, 258-68.

————, "Randolph Stow and the Way of Heaven," *Hemisphere* 18, vi (June, 1975): 33-5.

Johnston, G. K. W., "The Art of Randolph Stow," *Meanjin* 20 (July, 1961): 139-43.

Kramer, Leonie, "The Novels of Randolph Stow," *Southerly* 24 (1964): 78-91.

Martin, David, "Among the Bones," *Meanjin* 18 (Apr., 1959): 52-8.

McPherson, Neil, "Writers for a 'No' Generation," *Westerly* 1 (1966): 59-62.

New, William H., "Outsider Looking Out: The Novels of Randolph Stow," *Crit* 9, i (1967): 90-9.

Newby, P. H., "The Novels of Randolph Stow," *AusL* 1, ii (1957): 49-51.

Oppen, Alice, "Myth and Reality in Randolph Stow," *Southerly* 27, ii (1967): 82-94.

Perkins, Elizabeth, "Randolph Stow and Dimdims," *Quadrant* 26 (July, 1982): 28-33.

Pons, Xavier, and Neil Keeble, "A Colonist with the Words: An Interview with Randolph Stow," *CE&S* 2 (1976): 70-80.

Rutherford, Anna, and Andreas Boelsmand, "Interview with Randolph Stow," *ComQ* 5 (Dec., 1973): 17-20.

Wallace, Robyn, "Messiahs and Millennia in Randolph Stow's Novels," *Kunapipi* 3, ii (1981): 56-80. [Not seen.]

Whitehead, Jean, "The Individualism of Randolph Stow," 181-7 in Hewett, Dorothy, ed., *Sandgropers*, Nedlands: Un. of Western Australia Pr., 1973.

Wightman, Jennifer, "Waste Places, Dry Souls: The Novels of Randolph Stow," *Meanjin* 28 (June, 1969): 239-52.

Willbanks, Daniel R., "An Introduction to the Novels of Randolph Stow," *DAI* 34 (1974): 5213A.

————, *Randolph Stow*.

THE BYSTANDER

Dutton, Geoffrey, "The Search for Permanence: The Novels of Randolph Stow," *JCL* 1 (1965): 141-3. Also in Walsh, W., ed., *Readings in Commonwealth Literature*, 383-6.

Newby, P. H., "The Novels of Randolph Stow," *AusL* 1 (Nov., 1957): 50-1.

Oppen, Alice, "Myth and Reality in Randolph Stow," *Southerly* 27, ii (1967): 85-6.

Willbanks, R., *Randolph Stow*, 36-57.

A HAUNTED LAND

Burgess, O. N., "The Novels of Randolph Stow," *AusQ* 37 (Mar., 1965): 74-6.

Dutton, Geoffrey, "The Search for Permanence: The Novels of Randolph Stow," *JCL* 1 (1965): 137-40. Also in Walsh, W., ed., *Readings in Commonwealth Literature*, 380-3.

Martin, David, in *Meanjin* 16 (1957): 88-9.

Oppen, Alice, "Myth and Reality in Randolph Stow," *Southerly* 27 (1967): 82-5.

Willbanks, R., *Randolph Stow*, 19-35.

THE GIRL GREEN AS ELDERFLOWER

Watson-Williams, Helen, "Randolph Stow's Suffolk Novel," *Westerly* 25, iv (Dec., 1980): 68-72.

THE MERRY-GO-ROUND IN THE SEA

Geering, R. D., *Recent Fiction*, 20-1.

Hassall, Anthony J., "Full Circle: Randolph Stow's THE MERRY-GO-ROUND IN THE SEA," *Meanjin* 32, i (1973): 58-64.

————, "Randolph Stow's THE MERRY-GO-ROUND IN THE SEA," 163-9 in Fox, J., and B. McFarlane, eds., *Perspectives 79*, Melbourne: Sorrett, 1978.

Hewett, Dorothy, "Stow Comes Home," *Critic* 31 (Dec., 1965): 86-7.

Mitchell, Adrian, "THE MERRY-GO-ROUND IN THE SEA," *Opinion* 12 (Dec., 1969): 7-16.

New, William H., "Outsider Looking Out: The Novels of Randolph Stow," *Crit* 9, i (1967): 144-50.

Oppen, Alice, "Myth and Reality in Randolph Stow," *Southerly* 27, ii (1967): 92-4.

Tiffin, Chris, "Mates, Mum, and Maui: The Theme of Maturity in Three Antipodean Novels," in Narasimhaiah, C. D., ed., *Awakened Conscience*, 127-32.

Wightman, Jennifer, "Waste Places, Dry Souls: The Novels of Randolph Stow," *Meanjin* 28 (June, 1969): 249-51.

Willbanks, R., *Randolph Stow*, 96-107.

TO THE ISLANDS

Beston, John P., "Heriot's Literary Illusions in Randolph Stow's TO THE ISLANDS," *Southerly* 35 (1975): 168-77.

————, "The Theme of Reconciliation in Stow's TO THE ISLANDS," *MFS* 27, i (Spring, 1981): 95-107.

Buckley, Vincent, "In the Shadow of Patrick White," *Meanjin* 20 (July, 1961): 144-50.

Burgess, O. N., "The Novels of Randolph Stow," *AusQ* 37 (Mar., 1965): 76-7.

Cotter, Michael, "The Image of the Aboriginal in Three Modern Australian Novels," *Meanjin* 36 iv (1977): 585-8.

Dutton, Geoffrey, "The Search for Permanence: The Novels of Randolph Stow," *JCL* 1 (1965): 143-5. Also in Walsh, W., ed., *Readings in Commonwealth Literature*, 386-8.

Geering, R. D., *Recent Fiction*, 13-17.

Hergenhan, L. T., "Randolph Stow's TO THE ISLANDS," *Southerly* 35 (1975): 234-47.

Martin, David, "Among the Bones," *Meanjin* 18 (Apr., 1959): 52-8.

Maxwell, D. E. S., "Landscape and Theme," in Press, John, ed., *Commonwealth Literature: Unity and Diversity in a Common Culture*, London: Heinemann, 1965, 82-9.

New, William H., "Outsider Looking Out: The Novels of Randolph Stow," *Crit* 9, i (1967): 93-6.

Oppen, Alice, "Myth and Reality in Randolph Stow," *Southerly* 27, ii (1967): 86-9.

Thomas, Sue, "Randolph Stow's Revision of TO THE IS-LANDS," *Southerly* 42 (1982): 288-94.

Tiffin, Helen, "Towards Place and Placelessness: Two Journey Patterns in Commonwealth Literature," in Narasimaiah, C. D., *Awakened Conscience*, 152-6.

Willbanks, R., *Randolph Stow*, 58-77.

TOURMALINE

Burgess, O. N., "The Novels of Randolph Stow," *AusQ* 37 (Mar., 1965): 73-81.

Dutton, Geoffrey, "The Search for Permanence: The Novels of Randolph Stow," *JCL* 1 (1965): 145-6. Also in Walsh, W., ed., *Readings in Commonwealth Literature*, 388-9.

Geering, R. D., *Recent Fiction*, 18-20.

Hope, A. D., "Randolph Stow and the Tourmaline Affair," in Ramson, W. S., ed., *Australian Experience*, 265-8.

Oppen, Alice, "Myth and Reality in Randolph Stow," *Southerly* 27, ii (1967): 89-92.

Tiffin, Helen, "Melanesian Cargo Cults in TOURMALINE and VISITANTS," *JCL* 16 (1981): 109-25.

Tiffin, Helen, "Tourmaline and the Tao Te Ching," in Hamilton, K. G., ed., *Studies in the Recent Australian Novel*, 84-120.

Wightman, Jennifer, "Waste Places, Dry Souls: The Novels of Randolph Stow," *Meanjin* 28 (June, 1969): 245-8.

Willbanks, R., *Randolph Stow*, 78-95.

VISITANTS

Hassall, Anthony J., "The Alienation of Alistair Cawdor in Randolph Stow's VISITANTS," *ALS* 9 (1980): 449-59.

Hungerford, T. A. G., in *Westerly* 25, i (Mar., 1980): 105-7.

Ramsey, S. A., "'The Silent Griefs': Randolph Stow's VISITANTS," *CritiQ* 23, ii (Summer, 1981): 73-81.

Watson-Williams, Helen, "Randolph Stow's Suffolk Novel," *Westerly* 25, iv (Dec., 1980): 68-72.

BIBLIOGRAPHY

O'Brien, Patricia, *Randolph Stow: A Bibliography*, Adelaide: Libraries Board of South Australia, 1968.

Stenderup, Vibeke, "Randolph Stow in Scandanavia," *Kunapipi* 1, i (1979): 37-40.

Willbanks, R., *Randolph Stow*, 151-5.

STUART, (HENRY) FRANCIS M(ONTGOMERY), 1902-

GENERAL

Garfitt, Roger, in Dunn, D., ed., *Two Decades of Irish Writing*, 211-21.

Greene, David H., "The Return of Francis Stuart," *Envoy* 5 (Aug., 1951): 10-21.

Joannon, Pierre, "Francis Stuart or the Spy of Truth," in Rafroidi, P., and M. Harmon, eds., *Irish Novel in Our Time*, 157-74. Also in *CahiersI* 4-5 (1976): 157-74.

McCormack, William J., "Francis Stuart: The Recent Fiction," in Rafroidi, P., and M. Harmon, eds., *Irish Novel in Our Time*, 175-83. Also in *CahiersI* 4-5 (1976): 175-83.

Natterstad, Jerry H., "The Artist as Rebel: Some Reflections on Francis Stuart," *ICarbS* 1, i (Fall-Winter, 1973): 61-6.

_____, "An Interview," *JIL* 5, i (Jan., 1976): 16-31.

_____, *Francis Stuart*.

_____, "Francis Stuart: A Voice from the Ghetto," *JIL* 5, i (Jan., 1976): 5-15.

_____, "Francis Stuart: At the Edge of Recognition," *Eire* 9, iii (Autumn, 1974): 69-85.

_____, "Francis Stuart: From Laragh to Berlin," *ICarbS* 4, i (Spring-Summer, 1978): 17-23.

_____, "Francis Stuart: The Artist as Outcast," in Kosok, H., ed., *Studies in Anglo-Irish Literature*, 338-44.

Ruesch, Alfred R., "Francis Stuart: The Language of Suffering," *DAI* 36 (1975): 3702A.

Stuart, Francis, "Letters to J. H. Natterstad," *JIL* 5, i (Jan., 1976): 97-110.

BLACKLIST, SECTION H

McCormack, William J., "Francis Stuart: The Recent Fiction," in Rafroidi, P., and M. Harmon, eds., *Irish Novel in Our Time*, 177-9. Also in *CahierI* 4-5 (1976): 177-9.

THE COLOURED DOME

O'Brien, H. J., "Francis Stuart's Cathleen Ni Houlahan," *DM* 8, viii (Summer, 1971): 48-54.

MEMORIAL

McCormack, William J., "Francis Stuart: The Recent Fiction," in Rafroidi, P., and M. Harmon, eds., *Irish Novel in Our Time*, 180-2. Also in *CahiersI* 4-5 (1976): 180-2.

PIGEON IRISH

Natterstad, J. H., *Francis Stuart*, 41-4.

O'Brien, H. J., "St. Catherine of Sienna in Ireland," *Eire* 6, ii (Summer, 1971): 98-110.

THE PILLAR OF CLOUD

Natterstad, J. H., *Francis Stuart*, 68-71.

REDEMPTION

Barnwell, William C., "Looking Into the Future: The Universality of Francis Stuart," *Eire* 12, ii (Summer, 1977): 113-25.

BIBLIOGRAPHY

McCormack, William J., "Francis Stuart: A Checklist and Commentary," *Long Room* 3 (Spring, 1971): 38-41.

Natterstad, J. H., "Francis Stuart: A Checklist," *JIL* 5, i (Jan., 1976): 39-45.

STUART, JESSE (HILTON), 1907-1984

GENERAL

Blair, E. L., *Jesse Stuart*.

Clarke, Kenneth, "Kentucky Heritage in Jesse Stuart's Writing," *JLoN* 3, iii (1970): 130-31.

Clarke, Mary W., "As Jesse Stuart Heard It in Kentucky," *KFR* 9 (1960): 75-86. [Not seen.]

_____, "Jesse Stuart Reflects Kentucky Lore as Tokens and Ghosts," *KFR* 9 (1960): 41-6. [Not seen.]

_____, *Jesse Stuart's Kentucky*.

_____, "Jesse Stuart's Use of Local Legends," *JLoN* 10, ii (May-Aug., 1977): 63-70.

_____, "Jesse Stuart's Writings Preserve Passing Folk Idiom," *SFQ* 28 (Sept., 1964): 157-98.

_____, "Proverbs, Proverbial Phrases, and Proverbial Comparisons in the Writings of Jesse Stuart," *SFQ* 29 (June, 1965): 142-63.

Flanagan, John T., "Folklore in Five Midwestern Novelists," *GrLR* 1, ii (1974): 50-4.

_____, "Jesse Stuart, Regional Novelist," in LeMaster, J. R., and M. W. Clarke, eds., *Jesse Stuart*, 70-88.

Foster, R. E., *Jesse Stuart*.

_____, "Jesse Stuart: How a Natural Writer Creates," *JLoN* 9 (Sept.-Dec., 1976): 160-2.

_____, "Jesse Stuart's W-Hollow: Microcosm of the Appalachians," *KanQ* 2, ii (Spring, 1970): 66-72.

Gibbs, Sylvia, "Jesse Stuart: The Dark Hills and Beyond," *JLoN* 4 (Jan.-Apr., 1971): 56-69.

Griffin, Mickie, "Jesse Stuart's Life Force," *JLoN* 13 (1980): 97-102. [Not seen.]

Hall, Wade, "Humor in Jesse Stuart's Fiction," in LeMaster, J. R., and Clarke, M. W., eds., *Jesse Stuart*, 89-102.

_____, "'The Truth is Funny': A Study of Jesse Stuart's Humor," *IEY* 5 (1970): 1-75. [Not seen.]

Huddleston, Eugene L., "Place Names in the Writings of Jesse Stuart," *WF* 31 (1972): 169-77.

Leavell, Frank H., "The Literary Career of Jesse Stuart," *DA* 26 (1966): 6045.

LeMaster, J. R., ed., *Jesse Stuart*.

_____, and M. W. Clarke, eds., *Jesse Stuart*.

_____, "Jesse Stuart: An Interview," *IEJ* 8, iv (1974): 6-25.

_____, "Jesse Stuart: Kentucky's Chronicler-Poet," *DAI* 31 (1970): 2925A.

_____, "Jesse Stuart's Humanism," *BLRev* 1, i (1979): 4-13.

Pennington, L., *Dark Hills of Jesse Stuart*.

Rayford, Julian L., "Jesse Stuart: Kentucky's Immortal Chronicler," *ABC* 9 (Sept., 1958): 5-7.

Richardson, H. Edward, "Men of the Mountains: An Interview with Jesse Stuart," *Adena* 4, i (1979): 7-23.

_____, "Stuart Country: The Man-Artist and the Myth," in LeMaster, J. R., and M. W. Clarke, eds., *Jesse Stuart*, 1-18.

Washington, Mary L., "The Folklore of the Cumberlands as Reflected in the Writings of Jesse Stuart," *DA* 21 (1960): 844-45.

BEYOND DARK HILLS

Blair, E. L., *Jesse Stuart*, 132-7.

Foster, R. E., *Jesse Stuart*, 17-26.

DAUGHTER OF THE LEGEND

Foster, R. E., *Jesse Stuart*, 132-8.

Pennington, Lee, "Symbolism and Vision in DAUGHTER OF THE LEGEND," in Pennington, L., ed., *Dark Hills of Jesse Stuart*, 115-30. Also, revised, in LeMaster, J. R., and M. W. Clarke, ed., *Jesse Stuart*, 169-86.

FORETASTE OF GLORY

Blair, E. L., *Jesse Stuart*, 170-2.

Foster, Ruel E., "FORETASTE OF GLORY: An Assessment Thirty Years Later," *JLoN* 10 (1977): 71-7.

_____, *Jesse Stuart*, 115-25.

Pennington, L., *Dark Hills of Jesse Stuart*, 87-94.

THE GOOD SPIRIT OF LAUREL RIDGE

Blair, E. L., *Jesse Stuart*, 178-81.

Foster, R. E., *Jesse Stuart*, 138-45.

Pennington, L., *Dark Hills of Jesse Stuart*, 105-11.

HIGH TO THE HUNTERS

Blair, E. L., *Jesse Stuart*, 172-4.

Foster, R. E., *Jesse Stuart*, 132-8.

Pennington, L., *Dark Hills of Jesse Stuart*, 97-102.

MONGREL METTLE

Foster, R. E., *Jesse Stuart*, 126-32.

Pennington, L., *Dark Hills of Jesse Stuart*, 77-83.

MR. GALLION'S SCHOOL

Pennington, L., *Dark Hills of Jesse Stuart*, 133-45.

TAPS FOR PRIVATE TUSSIE

Blair, E. L., *Jesse Stuart*, 163-9.

Foster, R. E., *Jesse Stuart*, 103-15.

Pennington, L., *Dark Hills of Jesse Stuart*, 61-73.

THE THREAD THAT RUNS SO TRUE

Blair, Everetta L., "Jesse Stuart—Schoolmaster," *GaR* 15, iii (Fall, 1961): 311-23 *passim*.

BIBLIOGRAPHY

See issues of *Jack London Newsletter*.

LeMaster, J. R., *Jesse Stuart: A Reference Guide*, Boston, Mass.: G. K. Hall, 1979.

Woodbridge, Hensley C., comp., *Jesse and Jane Stuart: A Bibliography*, Murray: Murray State Un., 1979.

_____, *Jesse Stuart: A Bibliography*, Harrowgate, Tenn.: Lincoln Memorial Univ. Pr., 1960.

_____, "Jesse Stuart: A Bibliographical Note," *ABC* 9 (Sept., 1958): 8-22.

_____, "Jesse Stuart: A Bibliographical Note," *LauR* 10, i (1970): 8-15.

_____, "Jesse Stuart: A Critical Bibliography," *ABC* 16, vi (1966): 11-13.

STYRON, WILLIAM, 1925-

GENERAL

Aldridge, J. W., "William Styron and the Derivative Imagination," *Time To Murder and Create*, 30-51. Also in Aldridge, J. W., *Devil in the Fire*, 202-16.

Arms, Valerie M., "An Interview with William Styron," *ConL* 20 (1979): 1-12.

_____, "William Styron and the Spell of the South," *MissQ* 34 (Winter 1980-81): 25-36.

_____, "William Styron's Literary Career," *DAI* 38 (1977): 2117A.

Bryant, Jerry H., "The Hopeful Stoicism of William Styron," *SAQ* 62 (Autumn, 1963): 539-50.

Canzoneri, Robert, and Page Stegner, "An Interview with William Styron," *Per/Se* 1, ii (Summer, 1966): 37-44.

Casciato, A. D., and J. L. W. West, III., eds., *Critical Essays on William Styron*.

Cheshire, Ardner R., Jr., "The Theme of Redemption in the Fiction of William Styron," *DAI* 35 (1974): 1089A-90A.

Clark, John Henrik, *William Styron's NAT TURNER: Ten Black Writers Respond*, Boston: Beacon, 1968.

Cobbs, John L., "Baring the Unbearable: William Styron and the Problem of Pain," *MissQ* 34, i (Winter, 1980-81): 15-24.

Corodimas, Peter N., "Guilt and Redemption in the Novels of William Styron," *DAI* 32 (1972): 6420A.

Davis, Robert G., "Styron and the Students," *Crit* 3, iii (Summer, 1960): 37-46.

Doar, Harriet, "Interview with William Styron," *Red Clay Reader* 1 (1964): 26-30.

Fenton, Charles A., "William Styron and the Age of the Slob," *SAQ* 59 (Autumn, 1960): 469-76.

Firestone, Bruce M., "A Study of William Styron's Fiction," *DAI* 36 (1975): 3684A-85A.

Flanders, Jane, "William Styron's Southern Myth," *LaS* 15 (Fall, 1976): 263-78. Also in Morris, R. K., and I. Malin, eds., *Achievement of William Styron*, Rev. ed., 106-23.

Fuentes, Carlos, "William Styron in Mexico," *Review* 17 (1978): 67-70. [Not seen.]

Fossom, R. H., *William Styron*.

Friedman, Melvin J., "Preface," *RLM* 157/159 (1967): 7-31.

―――――, *William Styron*.

―――――, "William Styron (1925-)," in Panichas, G. A., ed., *Politics of Twentieth-Century Novelists*, 335-50.

―――――, "William Styron: An Interim Appraisal," *EJ* 50 (Mar., 1961): 149-58, 192. Also, altered, in Friedman, M. J., *William Styron*, 1-11.

Galloway, David D., "The Absurd Man as Tragic Hero: The Novels of William Styron," *TSLL* 6 (Winter, 1965): 512-34. Also in Galloway, D. D., *Absurd Hero*, 51-81.

Garr, Donna G., "The Southernness of William Styron," *DAI* 41 (1980): 4399A.

Gosset, L. Y., "The Cost of Freedom: William Styron," *Violence in Recent Southern Fiction*, 117-31.

Gray, Richard, "Victims and History and Agents of Revolution: An Approach to William Styron," *DQR* 5, i (1975): 3-23.

Hoffman, Frederick J., *Art of Southern Fiction*, 143-6.

―――――, "The Cure of 'Nothing': The Fiction of William Styron," in Browne, R. B., and Others, eds., *Frontiers of American Culture*, 69-87.

Hux, Samuel H., "American Myth and Existential Vision: The Indigenous Existentialism of Mailer, Bellow, Styron and Ellison," *DA* 26 (1966): 5437.

Jones, James, and William Styron, "Two Writers Talk It Over," *Esquire* 60, i (July, 1963): 57-9.

Kelvin, Norman, "The Divided Self: William Styron's: Fiction from LIE DOWN IN DARKNESS to CONFESSIONS OF NAT TURNER," in Morris, R. K., and Malin, I., eds., *Achievement of William Styron*, 208-26.

Kime, Benna K., "A Critical Study of the Techniques of William Styron," *DAI* 32 (1971): 2058A.

Klotz, Marvin, "The Triumph Over Time: Narrative Form in William Faulkner and William Styron," *MissQ* 17 (Winter, 1963-64): 9-20.

Kretzoi, Charlotte, "William Styron: Heritage and Conscience, " *HSE* 5 (1971): 121-36.

Lang, John D., "William Styron: The Christian Imagination," *DAI* 36 (1976): 6101A.

Leon, Philip W., "Idea and Technique in the Novels of William Styron," *DAI* 35 (1975): 7911A-12A.

―――――, "Styron's Fiction: Narrative as Idea," in Morris, R. K., and I. Malin, eds., *Achievement of William Styron*, Rev. ed., 124-46.

Luttrell, William, "Tragic and Comic Modes in Twentieth Century American Literature: William Styron and Joseph Heller," *DAI* 30 (1969): 2537A.

Mackin, C. R., *William Styron*.

Matthiessen, Peter, and George Plimpton, "The Art of Fiction V: William Styron," *ParisR* 5 (Spring, 1954): 42-57. Also in *Writers at Work*, 1st ser., 267-82. Also (portion) in Rubin, L. D., Jr., and J. R. Moore, eds., *Idea of an American Novel*, 368-70.

McNamara, Eugene, "The Post-Modern Novel," *QQ* 69 (Summer, 1962): 268-70.

Mellen, Joan, "William Styron: The Absence of Social Definition," *Novel* 4, ii (Winter, 1971): 159-70.

Mewshaw, Michael F., "Thematic and Stylistic Problems in the Work of William Styron," *DAI* 31 (1971): 4727A.

Mills, Eva B., "The Development of William Styron's Artistic Consciousness: A Study of the Relationship between Life and Work," *DAI* 37 (1976): 2874A-75A.

Morgan, Henry G., Jr., "The World as Prison: A Study of the Novels of William Styron," *DAI* 34 (1973): 1924A-25A.

Morris, R. K., and I. Malin, eds., *Achievement of William Styron*.

―――――, *Achievement of William Styron*, Rev. ed.

Morris, Robert K., "An Interview with William Styron," in Morris, R. K., and I. Malin, eds., *Achievement of William Styron*, 24-50.

―――――, "Interviews with William Styron," in Morris, R. K., and I. Malin, eds., *Achievement of William Styron*, Rev. ed., 29-69.

―――――, and Irving Malin, "Vision and Value: The Achievement of William Styron," in Morris, R. K., and I. Malin, eds., *Achievement of William Styron*, 1-23.

Mudrick, Marvin, "Mailer and Styron: Guests of the Establishment," *HudR* 17 (Autumn, 1964): 346-66. Also in Mudrick, M., *On Culture and Literature*, 176-99.

Nigro, Augustine J., Jr., "William Styron of and the Adamic Tradition," *DA* 26 (1966): 3958-59.

O'Connell, Shaun, "Expense of Spirit: The Vision of William Styron," *Crit* 8, ii (1966): 20-33.

Orr, John, "Offstage Tragedy: The New Narrative Strategies of John Fowles, Saul Bellow and William Styron," *New Edinburgh Review* 59 (1982): 21-3. [Not seen.]

Owenbey, Ray, "Discussions with William Styron," *MissQ* 30 (1977): 283-95.

―――――, "To Choose Being: The Function of Order and Disorder in William Styron's Fiction," *DAI* 33 (1972): 1176A.

Palm, Elaine A., "The Integrative Vision: Ritual Action in the Novels of William Styron," *DAI* 40 (1979): 259A.

Pearce, R., *William Styron*.

Ratner, M. L., *William Styron*.

Saposnik, Irving S., "Bellow, Malamud, Roth ... and Styron?" *Judaism* 31, iii (Summer, 1982): 322-32.

Scott, James B., "The Individual and the Society: Norman Mailer Versus William Styron," *DA* 25 (1965): 5942.

Stevenson, David L., "William Styron and the Fiction of the Fifties," *Crit* 3, iii (Summer, 1960): 47-58. Also in Waldmeir, J. J., ed., *Recent American Fiction*, 265-74.

Strine, Mary S., "The Novel as Rhetorical Act: An Interpretation of the Major Fiction of William Styron," *DAI* 33 (1973): 7067A.

Styron, William, "Reflections," *Ploughshares* 1, iii (1972): 82-4.

Swanson, William J., "William Styron: Eloquent Protestant," *DAI* 3 (1973): 3676A.

Urang, Gunnar, "The Voices of Tragedy in the Novels of William Styron," in Scott, N. A., Jr., *Adversity and Grace*, 163-209.

West, James L. W., III., "A Bibliographer's Interview with William Styron," *Costerus* n.s. 4 (1975): 13-29.

THE CONFESSIONS OF NAT TURNER

Amis, Harry D., "History as Self-Serving Myth: Another Look at Styron's THE CONFESSIONS OF NAT TURNER," *CLAJ* 22 (1978): 134-46.

Anon., "Unslavish Fidelity: The Confessions of William Styron," *TLS* (May, 1968): 480. Also in *T. L. S.: Essays and Reviews from The Times Literary Supplement, 1968,* 81-6. Also in Casciato, A. D., and J. L. W. West, III., eds., *Critical Essays on William Styron,* 173-7.

Aptheker, Herbert, "A Note on the History," *Nation* 205 (Oct. 16, 1967): 373-4.

_____, "Styron's Turner vs. Nat Turner," *New South Student* (May, 1968): 3-7.

_____, and William Styron, "Truth and NAT TURNER," *Nation* 206 (Apr. 22, 1968): 543-4.

Askin, Denise, "The Half-Loaf of Learning: A Religious Theme in THE CONFESSIONS OF NAT TURNER," *C&L* 21, iii (1972): 8-11. Also in *NMAL* 3 (1978): Item 6.

Akin, William E., "Toward an Impressionistic History: Pitfalls and Possibilities in William Styron's Meditation on History," *AQ* 21, iv (Winter, 1969): 805-12.

Bell, Bernard W., "The Confessions of Styron," *AmD* 5, i (1968): 3-7.

Brown, Cecil M., in *Negro Digest* 17 (Feb., 1968): 51-2, 89-91.

Brunauer, Dalma, "Black and White: The Archetypal Myth and Its Development," *BaratR* 6 (1971): 12-20.

Burger, Nash K., "Truth or Consequence: Books and Book Reviewing," *SAQ* 68 (Spring, 1969): 155-60.

Cannon, Patricia R., "Nat Turner: God, Man or Beast?" *BaratR* 6 (Spring/Summer, 1971): 25-8.

Canzeroni, Robert, and Page Stegner, "An Interview with William Styron," *Per/Se* 1, ii (Summer, 1966): 37-44.

Casciato, Arthur D., and James L. E. West, III., "William Styron and *The Southampton Insurrection, AL* 52, iv (Jan. 1981): 564-77. Also in Casciato, A. D., and J. L. W. West, III., eds., *Critical Essays on William Styron,* 201-12.

Cheshire, Ardner R., Jr., "The Recollective Structure of THE CONFESSIONS OF NAT TURNER," *SoR* 12 (Winter, 1976): 110-21. Also in Morris, R. K., and I. Malin, eds., *Achievement of William Styron,* Rev. ed., 223-36.

Clarke, John Hendrik, ed., *William Styron's NAT TURNER: Ten Black Writers Respond,* Boston: Beacon, 1968.

Coles, Robert, "Backlash," *PR* 35 (Winter, 1968): 128-33. Also in Casciato, A. D., and J. L. W. West, III., eds., *Critical Essays on William Styron,* 178-83.

_____, "Response to Thelwell (Turner Thesis)," *PR* 25 (Summer, 1968): 412-14.

Cooke, Michael, "Nat Turner's Revolt," *YR* 57 (Winter, 1968): 273-8.

Core, George, "THE CONFESSIONS OF NAT TURNER and the Burden of the Past," *SLJ* 2, ii (Spring, 1970): 117-34. Also in Morris, R. K., and I. Malin, eds., *Achievement of William Styron,* 150-67.

_____, "NAT TURNER and the Final Reckoning of Things," *SoR* n.s. 4 (July, 1968): 745-51.

_____, ed., *Southern Fiction Today: Renascence and Beyond,* Athens: Un. of Georgia Pr., 1969, 1-5, 42-3, 74-9.

Curtis, Bruce, "Fiction, Myth and History on William Styron's NAT TURNER," *UCQ* 16, ii (Jan., 1971): 27-32.

Delaney, Lloyd T., "A Psychologist Looks at THE CONFESSIONS OF NAT TURNER," *Psychology Today* 1 (Jan., 1968): 11-14.

DeVecchi Rocca, Luisa, "Nat Turner," *NA* 510 (1970): 614-24.

Driver, Tom F., "Black Consciousness Through a White Scrim," *Motive* 27 (Feb., 1968): 56-8.

Duff, John B., and Peter M. Mitchell, eds., *The Nat Turner Rebellion: The Historical Event and the Modern Controversy,* N.Y.: Harper & Row, 1971.

Eggenschwiler, K. P., "Tragedy and Melodrama in THE CONFESSIONS OF NAT TURNER," *TCL* 20 (Jan., 1974): 19-33.

Firestone, Bruce M., "A Rose Is a Rose Is a Columbine: CITIZEN KANE and William Styron's NAT TURNER," *LFQ* 5, ii (1977): 118-24.

Flanders, Jane, "William Styron's Southern Myth," *LaS* 15, iii (Fall, 1976): 272-8. Also in Morris, R. K., and I. Malin, eds., *Achievement of William Styron,* 115-22.

Fossum, R. H., *William Styron,* 34-46.

Forkner, Ben, and Gilbert Schricke, "An Interview with William Styron," *SoR* 10, iv (Oct., 1974): 923-34.

Franklin, Jimmie L., "'NAT TURNER' and Black History," *IJAS* 1, iv (1971): 1-6.

Friedman, Melvin J., "THE CONFESSIONS OF NAT TURNER: The Convergence of 'Nonfiction Novel' and 'Meditation on History'," *JPC* 1 (Fall, 1967): 166-75. Also (abridged) in *Univ. of Wisconsin at Milwaukee Magazine* (Spring, 1968): 3-7. Also, altered, in Friedman, M. J., *William Styron,* 11-18. Also in Friedman, M. J., and I. Malin, eds., *William Styron's THE CONFESSIONS OF NAT TURNER,* 63-71.

_____, ed., *William Styron's THE CONFESSIONS OF NAT TURNER.*

Galloway, David D., "Preface to the Revised Edition," *Absurd Hero in American Fiction,* Rev. ed., xvii-xxi.

Gayle, A., Jr., *Way of the New World,* 234-9.

Genovese, Eugene D., "William Styron before the People's Court," in Genovese, E. D., *In Red and Black: Marxian Explorations in Southern and Afro-American History,* N.Y.: Pantheon, 1971, 200-17. Also in Casciato, A. D., and J. L. W. West, III., eds., *Critical Essays on William Styron,* 201-12.

Gilman, Richard, "Nat Turner Revisited," *NRep* 158 (Apr. 27, 1968): 23-6, 28-32.

Goodheart, Eugene, "When Slaves Revolt," *Mainstream* 14 (Jan., 1968): 69-72.

Gray, R., *Literature of Memory,* 290-305.

_____, "Victims, History and Agents of Revolution," *DQR* 5, i (1975): 9-23.

Green, Martin, "The Need for a New Liberalism," *Month* n.s. 40 (Sept., 1968): 183-6.

Gross, Seymour L., and Eileen Bender, "History, Politics and Literature: The Myth of Nat Turner," *AQ* 23 (1971): 487-518. Also in Morris, R. K., and I. Malin, eds., *Achievement of William Styron,* 168-207.

Gunod, Roberta Z., "An Anomoly of 'and'," *LNL* 2, ii (1977): 19-42.

Hairstone, Loyle, "William Styron's Dilemma," *Freedomways* 8 (Winter, 1968): 7-11.

Harnack, Curtis, "The Quidities of Detail," *KR* 30 (Winter, 1968): 125-32.

Henderson, H. B., III., "THE FIXER and THE CONFESSIONS OF NAT TURNER: The Individual Conscience in Crisis," *Versions of the Past,* 273-77.

Holder, Alan, "Styron's Slave: THE CONFESSIONS OF NAT TURNER," *SAQ* 68 (Spring, 1969): 167-80.

Huffman, James R., "A Psychological Redefinition of William Styron's CONFESSIONS OF NAT TURNER," *LitR* 24, ii (Winter, 1981): 279-307.

Kaider, Ernest, "The Failure of William Styron," in Clarke, John H., ed., *William Styron's Nat Turner: Ten Black Writers Respond*, Boston: Beacon Pr., 1968, 50-65. Also in Miller, R., ed., *Backgrounds to Blackamerican Literature*, 259-69. Also in Friedman, M. J., and I. Malin, eds., *William Styron's THE CONFESSIONS OF NAT TURNER*, 92-103.

Kaufman, Walter, "Tragedy vs. History: THE CONFESSIONS OF NAT TURNER," *Tragedy and Philosophy*, N.Y.: Doubleday, 1968, 347-54.

Kauffmann, Stanley, "Styron's Unwritten Novel," *HudR* 20 (Winter, 1967-68): 675-9.

Kazin, Alfred, "Instinct for Tragedy: A Message in Black and White," *Book World* (Oct. 8, 1967): 1, 22.

Kort, Wesley A., "THE CONFESSIONS OF NAT TURNER and the Dynamic of Revolution," *Shriven Selves*, 116-40.

Kelvin, Norman, "The Divided Self: William Styron's Fiction from LIE DOWN IN DARKNESS to THE CONFESSIONS OF NAT TURNER," in Morris, R. K., and I. Malin, eds., *Achievement of William Styron*, 216-26.

Kretzoi, Charlotte, "William Styron: Heritage and Conscience," *HSE* 5 (1971): 129-35.

Lang, John, "The Alpha and the Omega: Styron's THE CONFESSIONS OF NAT TURNER," *AL* 53, iii (Nov., 1981): 499-503.

Lehan, Richard, "Fiction, 1967," *ConL* 9, iv (Autumn, 1968): 540-2.

Lewis, R. W. B., and C. Vann Woodward, "Slavery in the First Person: An Interview with William Styron," *Yale Alumni Mag.* (Nov., 1967): 37-9.

Mackin, C. R., *William Styron*, 22-37.

Malin, Irving, "Nat's Confessions," *UDQ* (Winter, 1968): 94-6. Also in Friedman, M. J., and I. Malin, eds., *William Styron's THE CONFESSIONS OF NAT TURNER*, 84-8.

Manvi, Meera, "A Black Messiah in New Jerusalem: THE CONFESSIONS OF NAT TURNER," *PURBA* 11, i-ii (Apr.-Oct., 1980): 25-43.

Marcos, Donald W., "Margaret Whitehead in THE CONFESSIONS OF NAT TURNER," *SNNTS* 4 (Spring, 1972): 52-9.

McGill, William J., "William Styron's Nat Turner and Religion," *SAQ* 79, i (1980): 75-81.

McPherson, James L., "America's Slave Revolt," *Dissent* 15 (Jan.-Feb., 1968): 86-9.

Mellen, Joan, "William Styron: The Absence of Social Definition," *Novel* 4, ii (Winter, 1971): 160-4.

Miller, William L., "The Meditations of William Styron," *Reporter* 37 (Nov. 16, 1967): 42-6.

Morse, J. Mitchell, "Social Relevance, Literary Judgment, and the New Right; or, The Inadvertent Confessions of William Styron," *CE* 30, viii (May, 1969): 605-16.

Mullen, Jean S., "Styron's Nat Turner: A Search for Humanity," *BaratR* 6 (Spring/Summer, 1971): 6-11.

Murray, Albert, "A Troublesome Property," *New Leader* 10 (Dec. 4, 1967): 18-20.

Nenadal, Radoslav, "William Styron's NAT TURNER: A Historical Hero Seen in the Perspectives of the Present," *Prague Studies in English* 17 (1981): 49-58.

Neri, Judith, "On THE CONFESSIONS OF NAT TURNER," *Umanesimo* 2, i-ii (1968): 135-8.

Newcomb, Horace, "William Styron and the Act of Memory: THE CONFESSIONS OF NAT TURNER," *ChiR* 20, i (1968): 86-94.

Nolte, William H., "Styron's Meditation on Saviors," *SWR* 58, iv (Autumn, 1973): 338-48.

O'Connell, Shaun, "The Contexts of William Styron's CONFESSIONS OF NAT TURNER," *DAI* 31 (1970): 2395A.

O'Connell, Shaun, "Styron's Nat Turner," Nation 205 (Oct. 16, 1967): 373-4. Also in Casciato, A. D., and J. L. W. West, III., eds., *Critical Essays on William Styron*, 157-61.

Okogbue, C., "The Negro Slave and 'Black-Assed' Feeling in American Fiction," *Muse* (Nsukka) 8 (1976): 57-60.

Pearce, R., *William Styron*, 36-43.

Pickens, Donald K., "Uncle Tom Becomes Nat Turner: A Commentary on Two American Heroes," *NALF* 3 (Summer, 169): 45-8.

Pinsker, Sanford, "Christ as Revolutionary/Revolutionary as Christ: The Hero in Bernard Malamud's THE FIXER and William Styron's THE CONFESSIONS OF NAT TURNER," *BaratR* (Spring/Summer, 1971): 29-37. Also in Pinsker, S., *Between Two Worlds*, 59-73.

Platt, Gerald M., "A Sociologist Looks at THE CONFESSIONS OF NAT TURNER," *Psychology Today* 1 (Jan., 1968): 14-15.

Rahv, Philip, 'Through the Midst of Jerusalem," *NYRB* 9 (Oct. 26, 1967): 6-10.

Ratner, Marc L., "Styron's Rebel," *AQ* 21 (Fall, 1969): 595-608.

_____, *William Styron*, 91-119.

Rubin, Louis D., Jr., "William Styron and Human Bondage: THE CONFESSIONS OF NAT TURNER," *HC* 4, v (Dec., 1967): 1-12. Also in Dillard, R. H. ., George Garrett, & John R. Moore, eds., *Sounder Few*, 305-22. Also in Friedman, M. J., and I. Malin, eds., *William Styron's THE CONFESSIONS OF NAT TURNER*, 72-83.

Saposnik, Irving S., "Bellow, Malamud, Roth ... and Styron," *Judaism* 31 (Summer, 1982): 322-32.

Saradhi, K. P., "The Agony of a Slave Negro: Theme and Technique in Styron's NAT TURNER," *OJES* 9, i (1972): 11-19. Also in *LHY* 16, i (1975): 41-51.

Shapiro, Herbert, "THE CONFESSIONS OF NAT TURNER: William Styron and His Critics," *NALF* 9 (1975): 99-104.

Sheed, Wilfred, "The Slave Who Became a Man," *NYTBR* (Oct. 8, 1967): 1-3.

Shepherd, Allen, "'Hopeless Paradox' and THE CONFESSIONS OF NAT TURNER," *RANAM* 4 (1971): 87-91.

Sitkoff, Harry, and Michael Wreszin, "Who's Nat Turner?: William Styron vs. the Black Intellectuals," *Midstream* 14 (Nov., 1968): 10-20.

Sokolov, Raymond, "Into the Mind of Nat Turner," *Newsweek* 70 (Oct. 16, 1967): 65-9.

Steiner, George, "The Fire Last Time," *NY* 43 (Nov. 25, 1967): 236-44.

Strine, Mary S., "THE CONFESSIONS OF NAT TURNER: Styron's 'Meditation on History' as Rhetorical Act," *QJS* 64 (Oct., 1978): 246-66. Also in Morris, R. K., and I. Malin, eds., *Achievement of William Styron*, Rev. ed., 237-68.

Styron, William, "Acceptance Speech for the Howells Medal," *Proceedings of the American Academy of Arts and Letters and the National Institute of Arts and Letters*, 2nd series, No. 21 (1971), publication 269, 30-2. Also in Casciato, A. D., and J. L. W. West, III., eds., *Critical Essays on William Styron*, 226-7.

_____, "A Letter from William Styron," *BaratR* 6 (1971): 5.

Sullivan, Walter, in Core, G., ed., *Southern Fiction Today*, 1-5. Also in Sullivan, W., *Death by Melancholy*, 97-102.

Swanson, William J., "Religious Implications in THE CONFES-SIONS OF NAT TURNER," *CimR* 12 (July, 1970): 57-66.

Thelwell, Michael, "Mr. William Styron and The Reverend Turner," *MR* 9 (Winter, 1968): 7-29. Also in Clarke, J. H., ed., *William Styron's Nat Turner: Ten Black Writers Respond,* Boston: Beacon, 1968, 79-91. Also in Casciato, A. D., and J. L. W. Jones, III., eds., *Critical Essays on William Styron,* 184-200.

————, "The Turner Thesis," *PR* 35 (Summer, 1968): 403-12.

Thompson, John, "Rise and Slay," *Ctary* 44 (Nov., 1967): 81-5. Also in Casciato, A. D., and J. L. W. West, III., eds., *Critical Essays on William Styron,* 162-72.

Tischler, Nancy M., "Introduction." THE CONFESSIONS OF NAT TURNER: A Symposium," *BaratR* 6 (1971): 1-3.

Tragle, Henry I., "Styron and His Sources," *MR* 11, i (Winter, 1970): 134-53.

Turner, Darwin T., "THE CONFESSIONS OF NAT TURNER, by William Styron," *JNH* 53 (1968): 183-6.

Turner, Joseph W., "The Kinds of Historical Fiction: An Essay in Definition and Methodology," *Genre* 12 (1979): 333-55.

Ujhazy, Maria, "After Alienation-Redemption: The Confessions of William Styron," *ZAA* 28, i (1980): 54-64.

Uya, Okon E., "Race, Ideology and Scholarship in the United States: William Styron's NAT TURNER and Its Critics," *Amer. Studies Internat.* (Geo. Washington Un.) 15, ii (1976): 63-81.

Watkins, Floyd C., "THE CONFESSIONS OF NAT TURNER: History and Imagination," *In Time and Place,* 51-70.

Wells, Anna M., "Vincent Harding, Mike Thelwell, and Eugene Genovese: An Exchange on NAT TURNER," *NYRB* 11 (Nov. 7, 1968): 31-6.

White, John, "The Novelist as Historian: William Styron and American Negro Slavery," *JAmS* 4 (Feb., 1970): 233-45.

Whitney, Blair, "Nat Turner's Mysticism," *BaratR* 6 (Spring/Summer, 1971): 21-4.

Williams, Ernest, "William Styron and His Ten Black Critics," *Phylon* 37 (1976): 189-95.

Woodward, C. Vann, "Confessions of a Rebel: 1831," *NRep* 157 (Oct. 7, 1967): 25-8. Also in Harrison, G., ed., *Critic as Artist,* 388-94.

LIE DOWN IN DARKNESS

Aldridge, James W., *In Search of Heresy,* 146-8.

————, "William Styron and the Derivative Imagination," *Time To Murder and Create,* 30-42. Also in Aldridge, J. W., *Devil in the Fire,* 204-9.

Allen, W., *Modern Novel,* 305-7.

Baumbach, Jonathan, "Paradise Lost: The Novels of William Styron," *SAQ* 63 (Spring, 1974): 207-14. Also in Baumbach, J., *Landscape of Nightmare,* 123-34. Also in Casciato, A. D., and J. L. W. West, III., eds., *Critical Essays on William Styron,* 24-35.

Breit, Harvey, "Dissolution of a Family," *Atlantic* (Oct., 1951): 78-80. Also in Casciato, A. D., and J. L. W. West, III., eds., *Critical Essays on William Styron,* 18-19.

Burch, Beth, "The Image of the Garden in William Styron's LIE DOWN IN DARKNESS," *BSUF* 23, i (1982): 23-9.

Bryant, Jerry H., "The Hopeful Stoicism of William Styron," *SAQ* 62 (Autumn, 1963): 541-4.

Casciato, Arthur D., "His Editor's Hand: Hiram Haydn's Changes in Styron's LIE DOWN IN DARKNESS," *SB* 33

(1980): 263-76. Also in Casciato, A. D., and J. L. W. West, III, Jr., eds., *Critical Essays on William Styron,* 36-46.

Cowley, Malcolm, "The Faulkner Pattern," *NRep* 125 (Oct. 8, 1951): 19-20.

Davis, Robert G., in Balakian, N., and C. Simmons, eds., *Creative Present,* 130-4.

————, "A Grasp of Moral Realities," *ASch* 21 (Winter, 1951-52): 114-16. Also in Casciato, A. D., and J. L. W. West, III., eds., *Critical Essays on William Styron,* 20-1.

Finkelstein, S., *Existentialism and Alienation in American Literature,* 215-16.

Flanders, Jane, "William Styron's Southern Myth," *LaS* 15 (Fall, 1976): 266-8.

Fossum, R. H., *William Styron,* 8-19.

Friedman, Melvin J., "William Styron: An Interim Appraisal," *EJ* 50 (Mar., 1961): 150-3. Also, altered, in Friedman, M. J., *William Styron,* 3-5.

————, "William Styron and the Nouveau Roman," in Zyla, W. T., and W. M. Aycock, eds., *Modern American Fiction,* 128-35.

Galloway, David D., "The Absurd Man as Tragic Hero: The Novels of William Styron," *TSLL* 6 (Winter, 1965): 513-19. Also in Galloway, D. D., *Absurd Hero,* 53-61.

Geismar, M., *American Moderns,* 239-46.

————, "Domestic Tragedy in Virginia," *SatR* 34 (Sept. 15, 1951): 12-13.

Goodley, Nancy C., "All Flesh Is Grass: Despair and Affirmation in LIE DOWN IN DARKNESS," *DAI* 36 (1975): 1496A.

Gordon, Jan B., "Permutations of Death: A Reading of LIE DOWN IN DARKNESS," in Morris, R. K., and I. Malin, eds., *Achievement of William Styron,* 100-21. Also Morris, R. K., and I. Malin, eds., *Achievement of William Styron,* Rev. ed., 158-78.

Gossett, L. Y., *Violence in Recent Southern Fiction,* 122-7.

Gray, R., *Literature and Memory,* 285-90.

————, "Victims and History and Agents of Revolution," *DQR* 5, i (1975): 1-8.

Hartt, J. N., *Lost Image of Man,* 60-3.

Hassan, I., *Radical Innocence,* 124-31. Also in Kostelanetz, R., ed., *On Contemporary Literature,* 597-606.

Hoffman, Frederick J., *Art of Southern Fiction,* 148-54.

————, "The Cure of 'Nothing!': The Fiction of William Styron," in Browne, R. B., and Others, eds., *Frontiers of American Culture,* 72-7.

Janeway, Elizabeth, "Private Emotions Privately Felt," *New Leader* (Jan. 21, 1952): 25. Also in Casciato, A. D., and J. L. W. West, III., ed., *Critical Essays on William Styron,* 22-3.

Jones, Howard M., "A Rich Moving Novel Introduces a Young Writer of Great Talent," *NYHTBR* (Sept. 9, 1951): 3. Also in Casciato, A. D., and J. L. W. West, III., eds., *Critical Essays on William Styron,* 13-15.

Klotz, Marvin, "The Triumph Over Time: Narrative Form in William Faulkner and William Styron," *MissQ* 17 (Winter, 1963-64): 16-18.

Kretzoi, Charlotte, "William Styron: Heritage and Conscience," *HSE* 5 (1971): 122-5.

Lawson, John H., "*The Lost Boy* and a Lost Girl," *SLJ* 9, i (Fall, 1976): 61-9.

Ludwig, J., *Recent American Novelists,* 31-2.

Luedtke, Carol L., "THE SOUND AND THE FURY and LIE DOWN IN DARKNESS," *NS* 19 (1970): 321-32.

Lyons, John O., "On LIE DOWN IN DARKNESS," in Morris, R. K., and I. Malin, eds., *Achievement of William Styron*, 88-99. Also in Morris, R. K., and I. Malin, eds., *Achievement of William Styron*, Rev. ed., 147-57.

Mackin, C. R., *William Styron*, 4-12.

Meeker, Richard K., in Simonini, R. C., Jr., ed., *Southern Writers*, 171-3.

Mellen, Joan, "William Styron: The Absence of Social Definition," *Novel* 4, ii (Winter, 1971): 164-7.

Nenadal, Radoslav, "The 'Heroes' in W. Styron's LIE DOWN IN DARKNESS," *Prague Studies in English* 16 (1975): 93-109.

O'Connell, Shaun, "Expense of the Spirit: The Vision of William Styron," *Crit* 8, ii (1966): 21-5.

O'Connor, W. V., in Moore, H. T., ed., *Contemporary American Novelists*, 214-18.

Pearce, R., *William Styron*, 10-19.

Prasad, Thakur G., "LIE DOWN IN DARKNESS: A Portrait of the Modern Phenomenon," *IJES* 10 (1979): 71-80.

Ratner, M. L., *William Styron*, 35-56.

Rubin, Louis D., Jr., *Faraway Country*, 185-215. Also in Morris, R. K., and I. Malin, eds., *Achievement of William Styron*, 51-73. Also in Morris, R. K., and I. Malin, eds., *Achievement of William Styron*, Rev. ed., 70-90.

_____, "What to Do About Chaos," *Hopkins Rev* 5 (Fall, 1951): 65-8.

Scheik, William J., "Discarded Watermelon Rinds: The Rainbow Aesthetic of Styron's LIE DOWN IN DARKNESS," *MFS* 24, ii (Summer, 1978): 247-54.

Suter, Anthony, "Transcendence and Failure: William Styron's LIE DOWN IN DARKNESS," *Caliban* 12 (1975): 157-66.

Swanson, William J., "William Faulkner and William Styron: Notes on Religion," *CimR* 7 (Mar., 1969): 45-52.

Trocard, Catherine, "William Styron and the Historical Novel," *Neohelicon* 3, i-ii (1975): 373-82.

Urang, Gunnar, "The Voices of Tragedy in the Novels of William Styron," in Scott, N. A., Jr., ed., *Adversity and Grace*, 185-91+.

Wiemann, Renate, "William Styron: LIE DOWN IN DARKNESS," *NS* 19 (1970): 321-32.

THE LONG MARCH

Asselineau, Roger, "Following THE LONG MARCH," [in French] in *William Styron, Configuration Critique*, no. 11. 73-83, Paris: Minard, 1967. Also, translated, in Casciato, A. D., and J. L. W., III., eds., *Critical Essays on William Styron*, 53-9.

Bandriff, Welles, T., "The Role of Order and Disorder in THE LONG MARCH," *EJ* 56 (Jan., 1967): 54-9.

Bryant, Jerry H., "The Hopeful Stoicism of William Styron," *SAQ* 62 (Autumn, 1963): 544-7.

Carver, Wayne, "The Grand Inquisitor's Long March," *UDQ* 1, ii (Summer, 1966): 49-57.

Finkelstein, S., *Existentialism and Alienation in American Literature*, 216-18.

Fossum, R. H., *William Styron*, 20-5.

Galloway, David D., "The Absurd Man as Tragic Hero: The Novels of William Styron," *TSLL* 6 (Winter, 1965): 519-22. Also in Galloway, D. D., *Absurd Hero*, 61-4.

Geismar, M., *American Moderns*, 246-50.

Gossett, L. Y., *Violence in Recent Southern Fiction*, 118-21.

Hays, Peter L., "The Nature of Rebellion in THE LONG MARCH," *Crit* 8, ii (Winter, 1965-66): 70-4.

Hoffman, Frederick J., *Art of Southern Fiction*, 146-8.

_____, "The Cure of 'Nothing'!: The Fiction of William Styron," in Browne, R. B., ed., *Frontiers of American Culture*, 71-2.

Kretzoi, Charlotte, "William Styron: Heritage and Conscience," *HSE* 5 (1971): 125-6.

Mackin, C. R., *William Styron*, 12-14.

Malin, Irving, "The Symbolic March," in Morris, R. K., and I. Malin, eds., *Achievement of William Styron*, 122-33. Also in Morris, R. K., and I. Malin, eds., *Achievement of William Styron*, Rev. ed., 179-90.

McNamara, Eugene, "William Styron's LONG MARCH: Absurdity and Authenticity," *WHR* 15 (Summer, 1961): 267-72.

Meeker, Richard K., in Simonini, R. C., Jr., ed., *Southern Writers*, 187-8.

Nigro, August, "THE LONG MARCH: The Expansive Hero in a Closed World," *Crit* 8, ii (1966): 103-12. Also in Casciato, A. D., and J. L. W. West, III., eds., *Critical Essays on William Styron*, 60-8.

O'Connell, Shaun, "Expense of Spirit: The Vision of William Styron," *Crit* 8, ii (1966): 25-7.

Pearce, R., *William Styron*, 19-24.

Ratner, Marc L., "The Rebel Purged: Styron's THE LONG MARCH," *ArlQ* 2, iii (Autumn, 1969): 27-42.

_____, *William Styron*, 57-69.

Styron, William, "Afterward to THE LONG MARCH," *MissQ* 28 (1975): 185-9. Also in Casciato, A. D., and J. L. W. West, III., eds., *Critical Essays on William Styron*.

Walcutt, C. C. *Man's Changing Mask*, 252-7.

West, James, L. W., III., "William Styron's Afterward to THE LONG MARCH," *MissQ* 28 (1975): 185-9.

SET THIS HOUSE ON FIRE

Aldridge, J. W., "William Styron and the Derivative Imagination," *Time to Murder and Create*, 42-51. Also in Aldridge, J. W., *Devil in the Fire*, 209-15.

Arms, Valerie M., "William Styron and the Spell of the South," *MissQ* 34, i (Winter, 1980-81): 28-31.

Baumbach, Jonathan, "Paradise Lost: The Novels of William Styron," *SAQ* 63 (Spring, 1964): 214-17. Also in Baumbach, J., *Landscape of Nightmare*, 134-7.

Benson, Alice R., "Techniques in the Twentieth-Century Novel for Relating the Particular to the Universal: SET THIS HOUSE ON FIRE," *PMASAL* 47 (1962): 587-94.

Borklund, Elmer, "The Fiction of Violence and Pain," *Ctary* 30 (Nov., 1960): 452-4.

Breit, Harvey, "A Second Novel," *PR* 28 (Summer, 1960): 561-3. Also in Casciato, A. D., and J. L. W. West, III., eds., *Critical Essays on William Styron*, 83-5.

Bryant, Jerry H., "The Hopeful Stoicism of William Styron," *SAQ* (Autumn, 1963): 547-50.

Butor, Michel, "Oedipus Americanus," Introduction to French edition of SET THIS HOUSE ON FIRE (*La proie des flammes*, Paris: Gallimard, 1962.) Also, translated, in Casciato, A. D., and J. L. W. West, III., eds., *Critical Essays on William Styron*, 133-45.

Casciato, Arthur D., "Styron's False Start: The Discarded Opening for SET THIS HOUSE ON FIRE," *MissQ* 34 (1980-81):

37-50. Also in Casciato, A. D., and J. L. W. West, III., eds., *Critical Essays on William Styron*, 146-54.

Davis, Robert G., in Balakian, N., and C. Simmons, eds., *Creative Present*, 135-41.

Detweiler, R., "William Styron and the Courage to Be," *Four Crises in Mid-Century American Fiction*, 6-13.

Fenton, Charles A., "William Styron and the Age of the Slob," *SAQ* 59 (Autumn, 1960): 469-76. Also in Casciato, A. D., and J. L. W. West, III., eds., *Critical Essays on William Styron*, 86-92.

Finkelstein, S., *Existentialism and Alienation in American Literature*, 218-19.

Flanders, Jane, "William Styron's Southern Myth," *LaS* 15 (Fall, 1976): 268-72.

Fossum, R. H., *William Styron*, 26-34.

Foster, Richard, "An Orgy of Commerce: William Styron's SET THIS HOUSE ON FIRE," *Crit* 3, iii (Summer, 1960): 59-70.

Friedman, Melvin J., "William Styron: An Interim Appraisal," *EJ* 50 (Mar., 1961): 156-8+. Also, altered, in Friedman, M. J., *William Styron*, 6-8.

_____, "William Styron and the *Nouveau Roman*, in Zyla, W. T., and W. M. Aycock, eds., *Modern American Fiction*, 122-8.

Galloway, David D., "The Absurd Man as Tragic Hero: The Novels of William Styron," *TSLL* 6 (Winter, 1965): 522-34. Also in Galloway, D. D., *Absurd Hero*, 65-81.

Glicksberg, C. I., *Sexual Revolution in Modern American Literature*, 200-3.

Gossett, L. Y., *Violence in Recent Southern Fiction*, 128-30.

Hoffman, Frederick J., *Art of Southern Fiction*, 154-61.

_____, 'The Cure of 'Nothing!': The Fiction of William Styron," in Browne, R. B., and others, eds., *Frontiers of American Culture*, 78-82.

Klotz, Marvin, "The Triumph Over Time: Narrative Form in William Faulkner and William Styron," *MissQ* 17 (Winter, 1963-64): 19-20.

Kretzoi, Charlotte, "William Styron: Heritage and Conscience," *HSE* 5 (1971): 127-9.

Lawson, John H., "Styron: Darkness and Fire in the Modern Novel," *Mainstream* 13, x (Oct., 1960): 9-18.

Lawson, Lewis, "Cass Kinsolving: Kierkegaardian Man of Despair," *WSCL* 3, iii (Fall, 1962): 54-66. Also in Casciato, A. D., and J. L. W. West, III., eds., *Critical Essays on William Styron*, 98-109.

Lemaire, Marcel, "Some Recent American Novels and Essays," *RLV* 28 (1962): 72-4.

Ludwig, J., *Recent American Novelists*, 32-3.

Lytle, A., *Hero With the Private Parts*, 50-2.

Mackin, C. R., *William Styron*, 14-22.

Mellen, Joan, "William Styron: The Absence of Social Definition," *Novel* 4, ii (Winter, 1971): 167-70.

Mizener, Arthur, "Some People of Our Time," *NYTBR* (June 5, 1960): 5, 26. Also in Casciato, A. D., and J. L. W. West, III., eds., *Critical Essays on William Styron*, 75-7.

Moore, L. Hugh, "Robert Penn Warren, William Styron, and the Use of Greek Myth," *Crit* 8, ii (Winter, 1965-66): 80-7.

Nenadal, Radoslav, 'The Patterning of a Modern Hero in William Styron's SET THIS HOUSE ON FIRE," in *Prague Studies in English* 15 (1973): 83-96.

Newberry, Mike, "Shock of Recognition," *Mainstream* 13 (Sept., 1960): 61-3.

O'Connell, Shaun, "Expense of Spirit: The Vision of William Styron," *Crit* 8, ii (Winter, 1965-66): 27-32.

Pearce, R., *William Styron*, 24-36.

Perry, J. Douglas, Jr., "Gothic as Vortex: The Form of Horror in Capote, Faulkner, and Styron," *MFS* 19, ii (Summer, 1973): 162-6.

Phillips, Robert, "Mask and Symbol in SET THIS HOUSE ON FIRE," in Morris, R. K., and I. Malin, eds., *Achievement of William Styron*, 134-49. Also in Morris, R. K., and I. Malin, eds., *Achievement of William Styron*, Rev. ed., 191-205.

Ratner, Marc L., "Rebellion of Wrath and Laughter: Styron's SET THIS HOUSE ON FIRE," *SoR* 7 (Fall, 1971): 1007-20.

_____, *William Styron*, 70-90.

Robb, Kenneth A., "William Styron's Don Juan," *Crit* 8, ii (Winter, 1965-66): 34-46. Also in Lawson, L. A., ed., *Kierkegaard's Presence in Contemporary American Life*, 177-90.

Rothberg, Abraham, "Styron's Appointment in Sambuco," *New Leader* 43 (July 4-11, 1960): 24-7. Also in Casciato, A. D., and J. L. W. West, III., eds., *Critical Essays on William Styron*, 78-82.

Rubin, Louis D., Jr., "An Artist in Bonds," *SR* 59 (Winter, 1961): 174-9. Also in Casciato, A. D., and J. L. W. West, III., eds., *Critical Essays on William Styron*, 93-7.

_____, *Faraway Country*, 215-30. Also in Morris, R. K., and I. Malin, eds., *Achievement of William Styron*, 73-87. Also in Morris, R. K., and I. Malin, eds., *Achievement of William Styron*, Rev. ed., 90-105.

Stevenson, David L., "Styron and the Fiction of the Fifties," *Crit* 3, iii (Summer, 1960): 49-53. Also in Waldmeir, J. J., ed., *Recent American Fiction*, 267-70.

Thompson, Frank, in *PrS* 37 (Summer, 1963): 183-5.

Urang, Gunnar, "The Broader Vision: William Styron's SET THIS HOUSE ON FIRE," *Crit* 8, ii (Winter, 1965-66): 47-69. Also in Scott, N. A., Jr., ed., *Adversity and Grace*, 191-209.

Via, Dan O., Jr., "Law and Grace in Styron's SET THIS HOUSE ON FIRE," *JR* 51 (1971): 125-36.

Winner, Anthony, "Adjustment, Tragic Humanism and Italy," *SA* 7 (1961): 338-61. Also, abridged, in Casciato, A. D., and J. L. W. West, III., eds., *Critical Essays on William Styron*, 110-34.

SOPHIE'S CHOICE

Alter, Robert, "Styron's Stingo," *SatR* (July 7, 1979): 42-3. Also, in Casciato, A. D., and J. L. W. West, III., eds., *Critical Essays on William Styron*, 253-6.

Arms, Valerie M., "William Styron and the Spell of the South," *MissQ* 34, i (Winter, 1980-81): 32-6 and *passim*.

Chinn, Nancy L., "William Styron's SOPHIE'S CHOICE: A Study," *DAI* 43, iii (Sept., 1982): 799A-800A.

DeMott, Benjamin, "Styron's Survivor: An Honest Witness," *Atlantic* (July, 1979): 77-9. Also in Casciato, A. D., and J. L. W. West, III., eds., *Critical Essays on William Styron*, 257-62.

Dickstein, Morris, "The Whole World in a Mirror: Problems of Distance in Recent American Fiction," *SR* 89, iii (Summer, 1981): 386-400.

Faltacosh, Monty L., "Wolfe and SOPHIE'S CHOICE," *TWN* 4, i (1980): 39-41.

Galloway, David, "Holocaust as Metaphor: William Styron and SOPHIE'S CHOICE," *A&E* 13 (Apr., 1981): 57-69.

Gardner, John, "A Novel of Evil," *NYTBR* (May 27, 1979): 1, 16-17. Also, with Gardner's headnote, in Casciato, A. D., and J. L. W. West, III., eds., *Critical Essays on William Styron*, 245-52.

Janssens, G. A. M., "Styron's Case and SOPHIE'S CHOICE," in Bakker, J., and Dr. D. R. M. Wilkinson, eds., *From Cooper to Roth: Essays on American Literature*, Amsterdam: Rodopi, 1980, 79-92. Also in Casciato, A. D., and J. L. W. West, III., eds., *Critical Essays on William Styron*, 269-83.

Kort, Wesley, "Styron' s Corpus and SOPHIE'S CHOICE," *C&L* 30, ii (Winter, 1981): 64-70.

Leon, Philip W., "A Vast Dehumanization," *VQR* 55 (Autumn, 1979): 740-7. Also in Casciato, A. D., and J. L. W. West, III., eds., *Critical Essays on William Styron*, 263-8.

Pearce, Richard, "Sophie's Choices," in Morris, R. K., and I. Malin, eds., *Achievement of William Styron*, Rev. ed., 284-97.

Rubenstein, Richard L., "The South Encounters the Holocaust: William Styron's SOPHIE'S CHOICE," *MQR* 20, iv (Fall, 1981): 425-42.

Shepherd, Allen, "The Psychopath as Moral Agent in William Styron's SOPHIE'S CHOICE," *MFS* 28, iv (Winter, 1982-83): 604-11.

Styron, William, "The Message of Auschwitz," *NYTimes* (June 25, 1974): 37. Also in Casciato, A. D., and J. L. W. West, III., eds., *Critical Essays on William Styron*, 284-6.

Ziff, Larzer, "Breaking Sacred Silences," *Cweal* (May 11, 1979): 277-8. Also in Casciato, A. D., and J. L. W. West, III., eds., *Critical Essays on William Styron*, 241-4.

BIBLIOGRAPHY

Bryer, Jackson, *William Styron: A Reference Guide*, Boston: G. K. Hall, 1978; London: Prior, 1978.

Fossum, R. H., *William Styron*, 47-8.

Galloway, D. D., *Absurd Hero*, 203-10.

Leon, Philip W., comp., *William Styron: An Annotated Bibliography of Criticism*, Westport, Conn.: London: Greenwood Pr., 1978.

Mackin, C. R., *William Styron*, 39-43.

Morris, R. K., and I. Malin, eds., *Achievement of William Styron*, Rev. ed., 299-382.

Ratner, M. L., *William Styron*, 153-66.

Schneider, Harold W., "Two Bibliographies: Saul Bellow and William Styron," *Crit* 3, iii (Summer, 1960): 71-91.

SUCH, PETER, 1939-

RIVERRUN

Davidson, Arnold E., "Crosscurrents in Peter Such's RIVERRUN," *JCF* 31-32 (1981): 194-202.

Moss, J., *Sex and Violence in the Canadian Novel*, 269-73.

SUKENICK, RONALD, 1932-

GENERAL

Adams, Timothy D., "Obscuring the Muse: The Mock-Autobiographies of Ronald Sukenick," *Crit* 20, i (1978): 27-39.

Bellamy, Joe D., "Imagination as Perception: An Interview with Ronald Sukenick," *ChiR* 23 (1972): 59-72. Also in Bellamy, J. D., eds., *New Fiction*, 55-73.

Cheuse, Alan, "Way Out West: The Exploratory Fiction of 'Ronald Sukenick'," in Crow, C. L. ed., *Essays on California Writers*, 115-21.

Klinkowitz, Jerome, "Getting Real: Making It (UP) with Ronald Sukenick," *ChiR* 23, iii (Winter, 1972): 73-82.

Meyer, Charlotte, M., "An Interview with Ronald Sukenick," *ConL* 23, ii (Spring, 1982): 129-44.

Noel, Daniel C., "Tales of Fictive Power: Dreaming and Imagination in Roland Sukenick's Postmodern Fiction," *Boundary* 5, i (Fall, 1976): 117-35.

Putz, Manfred, "Ronald Sukenick: Connections Proliferate," *Story of Identity*, 185-93.

Trachtenberg, Stanley, "The Way That Girl Pressed against You on the Subway: Ronald Sukenick's Real Act of the Imagination," *JNT* 12, i (Winter, 1982): 57-71.

98.6

Klinkowitz, J., *Literary Disruptions*, 142-8.

Noel, Daniel C., "Tales of Fictive Power: Dreaming and Imagination in Roland Sukenick's Postmodern Fiction," *Boundary* 5, i (Fall, 1976): 126-30.

Werner, C. H., *Paradoxical Resolutions*, 75-82.

OUT

Hassan, Ihab, "Reading OUT," *FictionI* 1 (Fall, 1973): 108-9.

Klinkowitz, J., *Literary Disruptions*, 134-52.

_____, "A Persuasive Account: Working it Out with Ronald Sukenick," *NAmerR* 258 (Summer, 1973): 48-52.

Noel, Daniel C., "Tales of Fictive Power: Dreaming and Imagination in Ronald Sukenick's Postmodern Fiction," *Boundary* 5, i (Fall, 1976): 122-6.

Putz, Manfred, "Ronald Sukenick: Connection Proliferate," *Story of Identity*, 176-85 *passim*.

Trachtenberg, Stanley, "The Way That Girl Pressed against You on the Subway: Ronald Sukenick's Real Act of the Imagination," *JNT* 12, i (Winter, 1982): 64-9.

UP

Klinkowitz, Jerome, "Getting Real: Making It (UP) with Ronald Sukenick," *ChiR* 23, iii (Winter, 1972): 74-7.

_____, *Literary Disruptions*, 120-4.

Putz, Manfred, "Ronald Sukenick: Connections Proliferate," *Story of Identity*, 176-85 *passim*.

Trachtenberg, Stanley, "The Way that Girl Pressed against You on the Subway: Ronald Sukenick's Real Act of the Imagination," *JNT* 12, i (Winter, 1982): 57-71.

SWADOS, HARVEY, 1920-1972

GENERAL

Feinstein, Herbert, "Contemporary American Fiction: Harvey Swados and Leslie Fiedler," *WSCL* 2, i (Winter, 1961): 79-98.

Marx, Paul, "Harvey Swados," *OntarioR* 1, i (1974): 62-6.

Shapiro, Charles: Private Stories and Public Fiction," in Moore, H. T., ed., *Contemporary American Novelists*, 182-92.

FALSE COIN

Gottfried, Alex, and Sue Davidson, "Utopia's Children: An Interpretation of Three Political Novels," *Western Pol. Qtly* 15 (Mar., 1962): 27-32.

Mizener, Arthur, "Some Kinds of Modern Novel," *SR* 69 (Winter, 1971): 155-6.

OUT WENT THE CANDLE

Hassan, I., *Radical Innocence*, 134-40.
Shapiro, Charles, in Moore, H. T., ed., *Contemporary American Novelists*, 184-8.

THE WILL

Siegelman, Ellen, "A Battle of Wills: Swados' New Novel," *Crit* 7 (Spring, 1964): 125-8.

TAYLOR, ELIZABETH, 1912-1975

GENERAL

Austin, Richard, "The Novels of Elizabeth Taylor," *Cweal* 62 (June 10, 1955): 258-9.
Grove, Robin, "From the Island: Elizabeth Taylor's Novels," *SLitI* 11, ii (Fall, 1978): 79-95.
Liddell, Robert, "The Novels of Elizabeth Taylor," *REL* 1, ii (Apr., 1960): 54-61.
Vadeboncoeur, Paula M., "The Novels of Elizabeth Taylor," *DAI* 37 (1976): 3654A-55A.

AT MRS. LIPPINCOTE'S

Boll, Ernest, "AT MRS. LIPPPINCOTE'S and TRISTRAM SHANDY," *MLN* 65 (1950): 119-20.

TAYLOR, PETER HILLSMAN, 1917-

GENERAL

Goodwin, Stephen, "An Interview with Peter Taylor," *Shen* 24, ii (Winter, 1973): 3-20.
Griffith, A. J., *Peter Taylor*.

A WOMAN OF MEANS

Brown, Ashley, "The Early Fiction of Peter Taylor," *SR* 70 (Autumn, 1962): 599-602.
Cathey, Kenneth C., "Peter Taylor: An Evaluation," *WR* 18 (Autumn, 1953): 15-17.
Eisinger, C. E., *Fiction of the Forties*, 196-8.
Griffith, A. J., *Peter Taylor*, 57-71.
Pickrel, Paul, in *YR* 39 (Summer, 1950): 765-8.
Robinson, Clayton, "A Tennessee Boy in St. Louis: Peter Taylor's A WOMAN OF MEANS," *Interpretations* 9 (1977): 74-8.
Shattuck, Roger, in *WR* 16 (Autumn, 1951): 87-8.
Smith, James P., "Narration and Theme in Taylor's A WOMAN OF MEANS," *Crit* 9, iii (1967): 19-30.
Wilcox, Thomas, "A Novelist of Means," *SR* 59 (Jan.-Mar., 1951): 151-4.

BIBLIOGRAPHY

Griffith, A. J., *Peter Taylor*, 168-75.
Smith, James P., "A Peter Taylor Checklist," *Crit* 9, iii (1967): 31-6.

TENNANT, KYLIE, 1912-1988

GENERAL

Auchterlonie, D., "The Novels of Kylie Tennant," *Meanjin* 12, iv (1953): 395-403.
Dick, M., *Novels of Kylie Tennant*.
Moore, T. Inglis, "The Tragi-Comedies of Kylie Tennant," *Southerly* 18, i (1957): 2-8.
Sunderland, Jane, "A Form of Resistance: The Problematic Protagonist in the Novels of Kylie Tennant," *Hecate* 5, i (1979): 87-100.

THE BATTLERS

Dick, M., *Novels of Kylie Tennant*, 43-56.
Pons, Xavier, "THE BATTLERS: Kylie Tennant and the Australian Tradition," *ALS* 6 (1974): 364-80.

FOVEAUX

Dick, M., *Novels of Kylie Tennant*, 31-42.
Matthews, Brian, "'A Kind of Semi-Sociological Literary Criticism: George Orwell, Kylie Tennant and Others," *Westerly* 26, ii (June, 1981): 65-72.

THE HONEY FLOW

Dick, M., *Novels of Kylie Tennant*, 103-5.

LOST HAVEN

Dick, M., *Novels of Kylie Tennant*, 71-9.

RIDE ON STRANGER

Dick, M., *Novels of Kylie Tennant*, 57-70.

TELL MORNING THIS

Dick, M., *Novels of Kylie Tennant*, 80-97.

TIBURON

Dick, M., *Novels of Kylie Tennant*, 14-30.

TIME ENOUGH LATER

Dick, M., *Novels of Kylie Tennant*, 98-102.

THEROUX, PAUL, 1941-

GENERAL

Coale, Samuel, "'A Quality of Light': The Fiction of Paul Theroux," *Crit* 22, iii (1981): 5-16.

THE FAMILY ARSENAL

Sanks, Delphine, "The Literature of Anarchy: Paul Theroux's THE FAMILY ARSENAL," *PVR* 8 (1980): 71-83.

PICTURE PALACE

Bell, Robert F., "Metamorphoses and Missing Halves: Allusions in Paul Theroux's PICTURE PALACE," *Crit* 22, iii (1981): 17-30.

THIRKELL, ANGELA, 1890-1961

GENERAL

McIntyre, Clara F., "Mrs. Thirkell's Barsetshire," *CE* 17 (Apr., 1956): 398-401.

Pendry, E. D., *New Feminism of English Fiction*, 51-4.

THOMAS, AUDREY (GRACE), 1935-

GENERAL

Bowering, George, "Songs + Wisdom: An Interview with Audrey Thomas," *Open Letter* (fourth series, 3): 7-31.

Coldwell, Joan, "Memory Organized: The Novels of Audrey Thomas," *CanL* 92 (Spring, 1982): 46-56.

Gottlieb, Lois, and Wendy Keitner, "Narrative Technique and the Central Female Character in the Novels of Audrey Thomas," *WLWE* 21, ii (Summer, 1982): 364-73.

BLOWN FIGURES

Diotte, Robert, "The Romance of Penelope: Audrey Thomas's Isobel Carpenter Trilogy," *CanL* 86 (Autumn, 1980): 60-8.

Gottlieb, Lois, and Wendy Keitner, "Narrative Technique and the Central Female Character in the Novels of Audrey Thomas," *WLWE* 21, ii (Summer, 1982): 371-3.

Komisar, Elizabeth, "Audrey Thomas: A Review/Interview," *Open Letter* (third series, 3) (1975): 59-64.

Monk, Patricia, "Shadow Continent: The Image of Africa in Three Canadian Writers," *ArielE* 8, iv (Oct., 1977): 3-11, 13-17.

Stape, John H., "Dr. Jung at the Site of Blood: A Note on BLOWN FIGURES," *SCL* 2, i (1977): 124-6.

ISOBEL CARPENTER Trilogy

Diotte, Robert, "The Romance of Penelope: Audrey Thomas's Isobel Carpenter Trilogy," *CanL* 886 (Autumn, 1980): 60-8.

LATAKIA

Monk, Patricia, "Shadow Continent: The Image of Africa in Three Canadian Writers," *ArielE* 8, iv (Oct., 1977): 3-11, 13-17.

Quigley, Ellen, "Redefining Unity and Dissolution in LATAKIA," *ECW* 20 (Winter, 1980-81): 210-19.

MRS. BLOOD

Bellette, A. F., "Some Observations on the Novels of Audrey Thomas," *Open Letter* (third series, 3) (1975): 65-7.

Diotte, Robert, "The Romance of Penelope: Audrey Thomas's Isobel Carpenter Trilogy," *CanL* 86 (Autumn, 1980): 62-3.

Gottlieb, Lois C., and Wendy Keitner, "Narrative Technique and the Central Female Character in the Novels of Audrey Thomas," *WLWE* 21, ii (Summer, 1982): 367-70.

New, W. H., "Equatorial Zones," *Articulating West*, 228-30.

SONGS MY MOTHER TAUGHT ME

Bellette, A. F., "Some Observations on the Novels of Audrey Thomas," *Open Letter* (third series, 3) (1975): 68-9.

Diotte, Robert, "The Romance of Penelope: Audrey Thomas's Isobel Carpenter Trilogy," *CanL* 86 (Autumn, 1980): 63-6.

Gottlieb, Lois C., and Wendy Keitner, "Narrative Technique and the Central Female Character in the Novels of Audrey Thomas," *WLWE* 21, i (Summer, 1982): 364-67.

Stevens, Peter, "Hugh Hood's THE GOVERNOR'S BRIDGE IS CLOSED; John Moss's PATTERNS OF ISOLATION; A. J. M. Smith's TOWARD A VIEW OF CANADIAN LETTERS: SELECTED CRITICAL ESSAYS, 1928-1971; Audrey Thomas's SONGS MY MOTHER TAUGHT ME," *WLWE* 13 (1974): 253-66.

THOMAS, D(ONALD) M(ICHAEL), 1935-

THE WHITE HOTEL

Barnsley, John H., "THE WHITE HOTEL," *AR* 40, iv (Fall, 1982): 448-60.

THOMAS, GWYN, 1913-1981

GENERAL

Jones, Roger S., "Absurdity in the Novels of Gwyn Thomas," *AWR* 25, lvi (1976): 43-52.

THOMAS, LESLIE, 1931-

GENERAL

Carey, John, "Leslie Thomas's Novels," *Listener* 90 (Nov. 22, 1973): 719.

Durrant, Digby, "Bottom People: The Novels of Leslie Thomas," *LonM* 14, i (1974): 93-6.

THE MAN WITH POWER

Carey, John, "Leslie Thomas's Novels," *Listener* 90 (Nov. 22, 1973): 719.

THOMAS, HUGH, 1931-

THE WORLD'S GAME

Allsop, K., *Angry Decade*, 136-9.
Gindin, J., "Comedy and Understatement," *Postwar British Fiction*, 165-77.

TOLKIEN, J(OHN) R(ONALD) R(EUEL), 1892-1973

GENERAL

See issues of *Mythlore, Orcrist,* and *Tolkien Journal.*
Allan, J., ed., *Introduction to Elvish.*
Ballif, Sandra, "A Sindarin-Quenya Dictionary, More or Less, Listing All Elvish Words Found in THE LORD OF THE RINGS, THE HOBBIT, and THE ROAD GOES EVER ON by J. R. R. Tolkien," *Mythlore* 1, i (1969): 41-4; ii (1969): 33-6; iv (1969): 23-6.
Barkley, Christine, "Predictability and Wonder: Familiarity and Recovery in Tolkien's Works," *Mythlore* 8, i (1981): 16-18.
Becker, A., ed., *Tolkien Scrapbook.*
Carter, Lin, "Horvendile: A Link Between Cabell and Tolkien," *Kalki* 3, iii (1969): 85-7. [Not seen.]
_____, *Tolkien.*
Castell, Daphne, "The Realms of Tolkien," *New Worlds* 50 (Nov., 1966): 143-54. Also in *Carandaith* 1, ii (1969): 10-15, 27.
Chant, Joy, "Niggle and Numenor," *CLEd* 19 (1975): 161-71.
Cox, Jeff, "Tolkien, the Man Who Created Nine Languages," *Quinto Lingo* 7, vii-viii (Aug.-Sept., 1969): 8-11.
Crabbe, K. F., *J. R. R. Tolkien.*
Day, D., *Tolkien's Bestiary.*
Dowie, William, "Religious Fiction in a Profane Time: Charles Williams, C. S. Lewis, and J. R. R. Tolkien," *DAI* 31 (1970): 2911A.
Duriez, Colin, "Friend of the Hobbits," *Third Way* (Nov., 1978): 12-15. [Not seen.]
_____, "Leonardo, Tolkien, and Mr. Baggins," *Mythlore* 1, ii (Apr., 1969): 18-28.
Ehling, Michael J., "The Conservatism of J. R. R. Tolkien," *Orcrist* 8 (1977): 17-22.
Ellman, May, "Growing Up Hobbitic," in Solotaroff, Theodore, ed., *New American Review* 2, N.Y.: New American Library, 1967, 217-29.
Evans, R., *J. R. R. Tolkien.*
Foster, Robert, *The Complete Guide to Middle-Earth: From THE HOBBIT to THE SILMARILLION*, London: Allen & Unwin, 1978.
Gillespie, Gerald V., "The Irish Mythological Cycle and Tolkien's Eldar," *Mythlore* 8, iv (1982): 8-9.
Green, William H., "THE HOBBIT and Other Fiction by J. R. R. Tolkien: Their Roots in Medieval Heroic Literature and Language," *DAI* 30 (1970): 4944A.

Hartt, Walter F., "Godly Influences: The Theology of J. R. R. Tolkien and C. S. Lewis," *SLitI* 14, ii (Fall, 1981): 21-9.
Helms, Randel, "All Tales Need Not Come True," *SLitI* 14, ii (Fall, 1981): 31-45.
_____, *Tolkien's World.*
Hennelly, Mark M., Jr., "The Road and the Ring: Solid Geometry in Tolkien's Middle-earth," *Mythlore* 9, iii (1982): 3-13.
Hodgart, Matthew, "Kicking the Hobbit," *NYRB* 8 (May, 4, 1967): 10-11.
Hyde, Paul N., "Linguistic Techniques Used in Character Development in the Works of J. R. R. Tolkien," *DAI* 43 (1982): 1979A.
Irwin, W. R., "There and Back Again: The Romances of Williams, Lewis, and Tolkien," *SR* 69 (Autumn, 1961): 566-78.
Isaacs, N. D., and R. A. Zimbardo, eds., *Tolkien.*
Johnson, Janice, "The Celeblain of Celeborn and Galadriel," *Mythlore* 9, ii (Summer, 1982): 11-19.
Kilby, C. S., *Tolkien and THE SILMARILLION.*
_____, "Tolkien as Scholar and Artist," *TJ* 3, i (Spring, 1967): 9-11.
_____, "Tolkien, Lewis and Williams," in GoodKnight, G., ed., *Mythcon I Proceedings*, 3-4.
Kocher, P., *Master of Middle-Earth.*
_____, "The Tale of Noldor," *Mythlore* 4, iii (1977): 3-7.
Lobdell, J., ed., *Tolkien Compass.*
Matthews, R., *Lightning from a Clear Sky.*
Matthewson, Joseph, "The Hobbit Habit," *Esquire* 66 (Sept., 1966): 130-1, 221-2.
Menen, Aubre, "Learning to Love the Hobbits," *Diplomat* 18 (Oct., 1966): 32-4, 37-8. [Not seen.]
Mesibov, Bob, "Tolkien and Spiders," *Orcrist* 4 (1969): 3-5. Also in *TolJ* 4, iii (1970): 3-5.
Monick, S., "The Voice of Middle-Earth: Tolkien's World," *Lantern* (Pretoria) 27, ii (1977): 70-4. [Not seen.]
Monsman, Gerald, "The Imaginative World of J. R. R. Tolkien," *SAQ* 69 (1970): 264-78.
Myers, Doris T., "Brave New World: The Status of Women According to Tolkien, Lewis, and Williams," *CimR* 17 (1971): 13-19.
Nelson, Marie, "Non-Human Speech in the Fantasy of C. S. Lewis, J. R. R. Tolkien, and Richard Adams," *Mythlore* 5, i (May, 1978): 37-9.
Nitzsche, J. C., *Tolkien's Art.*
Noel, R. S., *Mythology of Middle-Earth.*
Norman, Philip, "The Prevalence of Hobbits," *NYTM* (Jan. 15, 1967): 31, 97, 100. 102.
Parks, Henry B., Tolkien and the Critical Approach to Story," in Isaacs, N. D., and R. A. Zimbardo, eds., *Tolkien*, 133-49.
Petty, Anne C., "The Creative Mythology of J. R. R. Tolkien: A Study of the Mythic Impulse," *DAI* 33 (1972): 2390A.
Pfotenhauer, Paul, "Christian Themes in Tolkien," *Cresset* 32, iii (1969): 13-15.
Purtill, Richard L., *Lord of the Elves and Eldils.*
Ready, William, "The Tolkien Relation," *Canadian Library* 25 (Sept., 1968): 128-36.
_____, *The Tolkien Relation; A Personal Inquiry*, Chicago: Regnery, 1968.
Reilly, Robert J., "Romantic Religion in the Work of Owen Barfield, C. S. Lewis, Charles Williams, and J. R. R. Tolkien," *DA* 21 (1961): 3461-2.

Resnick, Henry, "An Interview with Tolkien," *Niekas* 18, v (Spring, 1967): 37-47.

Rogers, Deborah W., "The Fictitious Characters of C. S. Lewis and J. R. R. Tolkien in Relation to Their Medieval Sources," *DAI* 34 (1973): 334A.

_____, and I. A. Rogers, *J. R. R. Tolkien*.

Rose, Mary C., "The Christian Platonism of C. S. Lewis, J. R. R. Tolkien, and Charles Williams," 203-12 in O'Meara, Dominic J., ed., *Neoplatonism and Christian Thought*, Norfolk: Internat. Soc. for Neoplatonic Studies, 1981.

Rossi, Lee D., "The Politics of Fantasy: C. S. Lewis and J. R. R. Tolkien," *DAI* 33 (1973): 5195A-96A.

Ryan, J. S., "Folktale, Fairy Tale, and the Creation of a Story," in Isaacs, N. D., and R. A. Zimbardo, eds., *Tolkien*, 19-39.

_____, "German Mythology Applied—The Extension of the Literary Folk Memory," *Folklore* (London) 77 (Spring, 1966): 45-59.

Salu, M., and R. T. Farrell, eds., *J. R. R. Tolkien, Scholar and Storyteller*.

Scafella, Frank, "Tolkien, the Gospel, and the Fairy Story," *Soundings* 64, iii (Fall, 1981): 310-25.

Shippey, T. A., *Road to Middle-Earth*.

Spice, Wilma H., "A Jungian View of Tolkien's 'Gandalf': An Investigation of Enabling and Exploitive Power in Counseling and Psychotherapy from the Viewpoint of Analytical Psychology," *DAI* 37 (1976): 1417B.

Stein, Ruth M., "The Changing Style in Dragons," *Elem Eng* 45 (Feb., 1968): 181-3.

Stevens, C. D., "High Fantasy versus Low Comedy: Humor in J. R. R. Tolkien," *Extrapolation* 21 (Summer, 1980): 122-9.

_____, "Sound Systems of the Third Age of Middle Earth," *QJS* 54 (Oct., 1968): 232-40.

Stimpson, C. R., *J. R. R. Tolkien*.

Timmerman, John, "Tolkien's Crucible of Faith: The Subcreation," *ChrC* 91 (June 5, 1974): 608-11.

Tolkien, J. R. R., "Tolkien on Tolkien," *Diplomat* 18 (Oct., 1966): 39. [Not seen.]

Trowbridge, Clinton, 'The Twentieth Century British Supernatural Novel," *DA* 18 (1958): 1800.

Tyler, J. E. A., comp., *The Tolkien Companion*, London: Macmillan; N. Y.: St. Martin's 1976.

Ugolnik, Anthony J., "*Wordhord Onleac*: The Mediaeval Sources of J. R. R. Tolkien's Linguistic Aesthetic," *Mosaic* 10, ii (1977): 15-31.

Walker, Steven C., "The Making of a Hobbit: Tolkien's Tantalizing Narrative Technique," *Mythlore* 7, iii (1980): 6-7, 37.

Watson, J. R., "The Hobbits and the Critics," *CritQ* 13, iii (1971): 252-8.

Weinig, Sister Mary Anthony, "Images of Affirmation: Perspectives of the Fiction of Charles Williams, C. S. Lewis, J. R. R. Tolkien," *Un. of Portland Rev.* 20, i (Spring, 1968): 43-6.

West, Richard, "Contemporary Medieval Authors," *Orcrist* 3 (1969): 9-10, 15.

Wojcik, Jan, S. J., "Tolkien and Coleridge: Remaking of the 'Green Earth'," *Ren* 20 (Spring, 1968): 134-9, 146.

Wright, Marjorie E., "The Cosmic Kingdom of Myth: A Study in the Myth-Philosophy of Charles Williams, C. S. Lewis, and J. R. R. Tolkien," *DA* 21 (1961): 3464-5.

_____, "The Vision of Cosmic Order in the Oxford Mythmakers," in Huttar, C., ed., *Imagination and the Spirit*, 259-76 *passim*.

Yates, Jessica, "Tolkien's Influence on the Chronicles of Narnia," *Mallorn* 18 (June, 1982): 31-3.

THE HOBBIT

Carter, L., *Tolkien*, 31-42.

Boswell, George W., "Proverbs and Phraseology in Tolkien's LORD OF THE RINGS," *UMSE* 10 (1969): 59-65.

_____, "Tolkien's Riddles in THE LORD OF THE RINGS," *TFSB* 25, ii (June, 1970): 44-9.

Christenson, Bonniejean, M., "BEOWULF and THE HOBBIT: Elegy Into Fantasy in J. R. R. Tolkien's Creative Technique," *DAI* 30 (1969): 4401A-02A.

_____, "Gollum's Character Transformation in THE HOBBIT," in Lobdell, J., ed., *Tolkien Compass*, 9-28.

_____, "Tolkien's Creative Technique: BEOWULF and THE HOBBIT," *Orcrist* 7 (Summer, 1973): 16-20. [Condenses main points of her dissertation above.]

Crabbe, K. F., *J. R. R. Tolkien*, 20-3, 28-66.

Evans, R., *J. R. R. Tolkien*.

Foster, Robert, *The Complete Guide to Middle-Earth; From THE HOBBIT to THE SILMARILLION*, London: Allen & Unwin, 1978.

Green, William H., "The Four-Part Structure of Bilbo's Education," *ChildL* 8 (1980): 133-40. [Adapted from Chapter 2 of his dissertation below.]

_____, "THE HOBBIT and Other Fiction by J. R. R. Tolkien: Their Roots in Medieval Literature and Language," *DAI* 30 (1970): 4944A.

Hall, Robert A., Jr., "Tolkien's Hobbit Tetralogy as 'Anti-Nibelungen'," *WHR* 32 (1978): 351-9.

Helms, R., *Tolkien's World*, 19-55.

Hennelly, Mark M., Jr., "The Dream of Fantasy: 'There and Back Again': a Hobbit's Holiday," *Sphinx* 10 (1979): 29-43.

Hieatt, Constance B., "The Text of THE HOBBIT: Putting Tolkien's Notes in Order," *ESC* 7, ii (Summer, 1981): 212-24.

Kocher, P. H., *Master of the Middle-Earth*, 19-33, 130-60 *passim*.

Kuznets, Lois R., "Tolkien and the Rhetoric of Childhood," in Isaacs, N. D., and R. A. Zimbardo, eds., *Tolkien*, 150-62.

Mathews, R., *Lightning from a Clear Sky*, 7-18.

Matthews, Dorothy, "The Psychological Journey of Bilbo Baggins," in Lobdell, J., ed., *Tolkien Compass*, 29-42.

Morse, Robert E., "Rings of Power in Plato and Tolkien," *Mythlore* 7, iii (Autumn, 1980): 38.

Nitzsche, J. C., "The King under the Mountain: Tolkien's HOBBIT," *NDQ* 47, i (1979): 5-18.

_____, *Tolkien's Art*, 31-48 *passim*.

Noel, R. S., *Languages of Tolkien's Middle-earth*.

Pepin, Ronald E., "Tolkien and Homeric Ruse,'" *ClassB* 56 (1979): 26-8.

Ready, William, *The Tolkien Relation: A Personal Inquiry*, Chicago: Regnery, 1968.

Rogers, D. W., and I. A. Rogers, *J. R. R. Tolkien*, 64-77.

Sale, R., *Modern Heroism*, 195-8.

Shippey, T. A. *Road to Middle-Earth*, 52-80 *passim*.

Stimpson, C. R., *J. R. R. Tolkien*, 30-3.

Watson, J. R., "The Hobbits and the Critics," *CritQ* 13, iii (1971): 252-8.

THE FELLOWSHIP OF THE RING (see also THE LORD OF THE RINGS)

Auden, W. H., "The Hero is a Hobbit," *NYTBR* (Oct. 31, 1954): 37.

_____, "A World Imaginary, but Real," *Encounter* 3 (Nov., 1954): 59-62.

Carter, L., *Tolkien*, 43-54.

Hughes, Richard, "THE LORD OF THE RINGS," *Spectator* (Oct. 1, 1954): 408-9.

Lewis, C. S., "The Gods Return to Earth," *T&T* 35 (Aug. 14, 1954): 1082-3.

Lynch, James, "The Literary Banquet and the Eucharistic Feast: Tradition in Tolkien," *Mythlore* 5, ii (Aug., 1978): 13-14.

Miller, David M., "Narrative Pattern in THE FELLOWSHIP OF THE RING," in Lobdell, J., ed., *Tolkien Compass*, 95-106.

Mitchison, Naomi, "One Ring to Bind Them," *NStat* 48 (Sept. 18, 1954): 331.

THE LORD OF THE RINGS Trilogy

Allen, James, "Genesis of THE LORD OF THE RINGS: A Study of Saga Development," *Mythlore* 3, i (1973): 3-9.

Allen, James, "Tolkien and Recovery," *Mythlore* 3, ii (1975): 12-13.

Auden, W. R., "Good and Evil in THE LORD OF THE RINGS," *CritQ* 10 (1968): 138-42. Also in *TJ* 3, i (Spring, 1967): 5-8.

_____, "The Quest Hero," *TQ* 4 (1962): 81-93. Also in Isaacs, N. D., and R. A. Zimbardo, eds., *Tolkien and the Critics*, 40-61. Also in Grebstein, Sheldon N., ed., *Perspectives in Contemporary Criticism Criticism*, N.Y.: Harper & Row, 1968, 370-81.

Barber, Dorothy K., "The Meaning of THE LORD OF THE RINGS," *Mankato State College Studies* 2 (Feb., 1967): 38-50.

_____, "The Structure of THE LORD OF THE RINGS," *DA* 27 (1966): 470A.

Barbour, Douglas, "'The Shadow of the Past': History in Middle Earth," *UWR* 8, i (Fall, 1972): 35-42.

Basney, Lionel, "Myth, History and Time in THE LORD OF THE RINGS," in Isaacs, N. D., and R. A. Zimbardo, eds., *Tolkien* 8-18.

_____, "The Place of Myth in a Mythical Land: Two Notes (Converging)," *Mythlore* 3, ii (1975): 15-17.

_____, "Tolkien and the Ethical Function of 'Escape' Literature," *Mosaic* 13, ii (Winter, 1980): 23-36.

Beagle, Peter S., "Tolkien's Magic Ring," *Holiday* 39 (June, 1966): 128, 130, 133-4. Also as "Preface" to *The Tolkien Reader*, N.Y.: Ballantine, 1966, ix-xvi.

Beatie, Bruce A., "A Folk Tale, Fiction, and Saga in J. R. R. Tolkien's THE LORD OF THE RINGS," *Mankato State College Studies* 2 (Feb., 1967): 1-17.

_____, "THE LORD OF THE RINGS: Myth, Reality, Relevance," *WR* 4 (Winter, 1967): 58-9.

Begg, Ean C. M., *The LORD OF THE RINGS and the Signs of the Times*, London: Guild of Pastoral Psychology, 1975.

Bell, Judy W., "The Language of J. R. R. Tolkien in LORD OF THE RINGS," in GoodKnight, G., ed., *Mythcon I: Proceedings*, 8-10.

Bisenieks, Dainis, "The Hobbit Habit in the Critic's Eye," *TolJ* No. 15 (Summer, 1972): 14-15.

_____, "Power and Poetry in Middle-Earth," *Mythlore* 3, ii (1975): 20-4.

_____, "Reading and Misreading Tolkien," *Mankato State College Studies* 2 (Feb., 1967): 98-100.

Blackmun, Kathryn, "The Development of Runic and Feanorian Alphabets for the Transliteration of English," *Mankato State College Studies* 2 (Feb., 1967): 76-83.

_____, "Translations from the Elvish," *Mankato State College Studies* 2 (Feb., 1967): 95-7.

Blisset, William, "The Despots of the Rings," *SAQ* 58 (Summer, 1959): 448-56.

Boswell, George W., "Proverbs and Phraseology in Tolkien's LORD OF THE RING Complex," *USME* 10 (1969): 59-65.

_____, "Tolkien as Litterateur," *SCB* 32, iv (Winter, 1972): 188-97.

_____, "Tolkien's Riddles in LORD OF THE RINGS," *TFSB* 25 ii (June, 1969): 44-9.

Boyd, Heather, "THE LORD OF THE RINGS," *Standpunte* 142 (Aug., 1979): 52-60.

Bradley, Marion Z., "Men, Halfling and Hero Worship," *Niekas* 16 (June 30, 1966): 25-44. Also, abridged, in Isaacs, N. D., and R. A. Zimbardo, eds., *Tolkien and the Critics*, 109-27.

Braude, Nan, "Tolkien and Spenser," *Mythlore* 1, iii (July, 1969): 8-10, 13.

Brewer, Derek S., "THE LORD OF THE RINGS as Romance," in Salu, M., and R. T. Farrell, eds., *J. R. R. Tolkien, Scholar and Storyteller*, 249-64.

Brooke-Rose, Christine, "The Evil Ring: Realism and the Marvelous," *PoT* 1, iv (1980): 67-90.

Brown, G. R., "Pastoralism and Industrialism in THE LORD OF THE RINGS," *ESA* 19 (Sept., 1976): 83-91.

Bunda, Robert A., "Color Symbolism in THE LORD OF THE RINGS," *Orcrist* 8 (1977): 14-16.

Burrow, J. W., "Tolkien lives?" *Listener* 90 (Nov. 8, 1973): 634-5.

Butsch, Richard J., "Person Perception in Scientific and Medieval World Views: A Comparative Study of Fantasy Literature," *DAI* 36 (1975): 2519B. [On LOTR and Asimov's FOUNDATION Trilogy.]

Calabrese, John A., "Elements of Myth in J. R. R. Tolkien's LORD OF THE RINGS and Selected Paintings of Paul Klee," *DAI* 41 (1981): 3303A.

Callahan, Patrick J., "Animism and Magic in Tolkien's THE LORD OF THE RINGS," *RQ* 4 (Mar., 1971): 240-9.

_____, "Tolkien, BEOWULF, and the Barrow-Wights," *NDEJ* 7, ii (Spring, 1972): 4-13.

_____, "Tolkien's Dwarfs and Eddas," *TolJ (Mythlore)* 15 (Summer, 1972): 20.

Carter, L., *Tolkien*.

Clausestopher, "LORD OF THE RINGS and THE BALLAD OF THE WHITE HORSE," *SAB* 39, ii (May, 1974): 10-16.

Cox, C. B., "The World of the Hobbits," *Spectator* (Dec. 30, 1966): 844.

Crabbe, K. F., *J. R. R. Tolkien*, 66-111.

Dabney, Virginia, "On the Natures and Histories of Great Rings," in GoodKnight, G., ed., *Mythcon I: Proceedings*, 8-10.

Davie, Donald, "On Hobbits and Intellectuals," *Encounter* 33 (Oct., 1969): 87-92. Also, revised, in Davie, Donald, *Thomas Hardy and British Poetry*, London: Routledge & Kegan Paul, 1973, 83-104.

Despain, Jerry L., "A Rhetorical View of J. R. R. Tolkien's THE LORD OF THE RINGS Trilogy," *JWS* 35 (1971): 88-95.

Donnelly, Jerome, "Humanizing Technology in THE EMPIRE STRIKES BACK: Theme and Value in Lucas and Tolkien," *Philosophy in Context* 11 (1981): 19-31.

Dowie, William, "The Gospel of Middle-Earth according to J. R. R. Tolkien," *Heythrop Journal* 15, i (Jan., 1974): 37-52. Also, revised, in Salu, M., and R. T. Farrell, eds., *J. R. R. Tolkien, Scholar and Storyteller*, 265-85.

Downing, Angela, "From Quenya to the Common Speech: Linguistic Diversification in J. R. R. Tolkien's THE LORD OF THE RINGS," *Revista Canaria de Estudios Ingleses* 4 (1982): 23-31.

Drury, Roger, "Providence at Elronds Council," *Mythlore* 7, iii (Autumn, 1980): 8-9.

Dubs, Kathleen E., "Providence, Fate, and Chance: Boethian Philosophy in THE LORD OF THE RINGS," *TCL* 27, i (Spring, 1981): 34-42.

Ellwood, Gracia F., "The Good Guys and the Bad Guys," *TolJ* 3, iv (Nov., 1969): 9-11.

_____, *Good News from Tolkien's Middle Earth*.

Epstein, E. L., "The Novels of J. R. R. Tolkien and the Ethnology of Medieval Christendom," *PQ* 48, iv (Oct., 1969): 517-25.

Evans, R., *J. R. R. Tolkien*.

Evans, W. D. Embrys, "THE LORD OF THE RINGS," *The School Librarian* 16 (Dec., 1968): 284-8.

Fifield, Merle, "Fantasy in the Sixties," *EJ* 55 (Oct., 1966): 841-4.

Flieger, Verlyn B., "Frodo and Aragorn: The Concept of the Hero," in Isaacs, N. D., and R. A. Zimbardo, eds., *Tolkien*, 40-62.

_____, "Medieval Epic and Romance Motifs in J. R. R. Tolkien's THE LORD OF THE RINGS," *DAI* 38 (1978): 4157A.

Forbes, Cheryl, "Frodo Decides—Or Does He?" *Christianity Today* 20 (Dec. 19, 1975): 10-13.

Foster, Robert, *The Complete Guide to Middle-Earth: From THE HOBBIT to THE SILMARILLION*, London: Allen & Unwin, 1978.

_____, "Haradrim and Sigelhearwan," *ParmaE* 1, i (1971): 3.

_____, "Levels of Interpretation," *TolJ* No. 15 (Summer, 1972): 22.

_____, "The One Inconsistency in LORD OF THE RINGS," *ParmaE* 1, i (1971): 9.

_____, "Sindarin and Quenya Phonology," in GoodKnight, G., ed., *Mythcon I: Proceedings*, 54-6.

Friedman, Barton R., "Fabricating History: Narrative Strategy in LORD OF THE RINGS," *ClioW* 2 (1973); 123-44.

_____, "Tolkien and David Jones: The Great War and the War of the Ring," *ClioI* 11, ii (Winter, 1982): 115-36.

Fry, Carrol L., "Tolkien's Middle Earth and the Fantasy Frame," *StHum* 7, i (1978): 35-42.

Fuller, Edmund, *Books with Men Behind Them*, 169-96. Also (revised) in Isaacs, N. D., and R. A. Zimbardo, eds., *Tolkien and the Critics*, 17-39.

Garmon, Gerald M., "J. R. R. Tolkien's Fairyland" *WGCR* 6 (May, 1973): 4-13.

Gasque, Thomas J., "Tolkien: The Monsters and the Critics," in Isaacs, N. D., and R. A. Zimbardo, eds., *Tolkien and the Critics*, 151-63.

Glover, Willis B., "The Christian Character of Tolkien's Invented World," *Criticism* 13, i (Winter, 1971): 39-53. Also in *Mythlore* 3, ii (1975): 3-8.

GoodKnight, Glen, "A Comparison of Cosmological Geography in the Works of J. R. R. Tolkien, C. S. Lewis, and Charles Williams," *Mythlore* 1, iii (July, 1969): 18-22.

_____, "'Death and Desire for Deathlessness': The Counsel of Elrond," *Mythlore* 3, ii (1975): 19.

_____, "The White Tree," in GoodKnight, G., ed., *Mythcon I: Proceedings*, 56-8. [As symbol in LOTR and elsewhere.]

Goodwin, Karen, "A Phytogeography of Middle-Earth," *Mallorn* 18 (June, 1982):

Goselin, Peter D., "Two Faces of Eve: Galadriel and Shelob as Anima Figure," *Mythlore* 6, iii, Whole Number 21 (Summer, 1979): 3-4, 28.

Gottlieb, Stephen A., "An Interpretation of Gollum," *TolJ* 4, iv (1970-71): 11-12.

Grant, Patrick, "Tolkien: Archetype and Word," *CC* 22 (Winter, 1973): 365-80. Also in Isaacs, N. D., and R. A. Zimbardo, eds., *Tolkien*, 87-105.

Gray, Thomas, "Bureaucratization in THE LORD OF THE RINGS," *Mythlore* 7, ii (1980): 3-5.

Green, William H., "The Ring at the Center: *Eaca* in THE LORD OF THE RINGS," *Mythlore* 4, ii (1976): 17-19.

Hall, Robert A., Jr., "Tolkien's Hobbit Tetralogy as 'Anti-Nibelungen'," *WHR* 32 (1978): 351-9.

Halle, Louis J., "History Through the Mind's Eye," *SatR* 39 (Jan. 18, 1956): 11-12.

Hannabuss, C. Stuart, "Deep Down: A Thematic and Bibliographic Excursion," *Signal* 6 (Sept., 1971): 87-95.

Hayes, Noreen, and Robert Renshaw, "Of Hobbits: THE LORD OF THE RINGS," *Crit* 9, ii (1967): 58-66.

Helms, Randel, "Orc: The Id in Blake in Tolkien," *L&P* 20, i (1970): 31-5.

_____, "The Structure and Aesthetic of Tolkien's LORD OF THE RINGS," in GoodKnight, G., ed., *Mythcon I: Proceedings*, 5-8.

_____, *Tolkien's World* 20-40, 76-108.

Hope, Francis, "Welcome to Middle Earth," *NStat* 72 (Nov. 11, 1966): 701-2.

Hughes, Daniel, "Pieties and Giant Forms in THE LORD OF THE RINGS," in Hillegas, M. R., ed., *Shadows of Imagination*, 81-96. Also in Isaacs, N. D., and R. A. Zimbardo, eds., *Tolkien*, 72-86.

Huttar, Charles A., "Hell and the City: Tolkien and the Tradition of Western Literature," in Lobdell, J., ed., *Tolkien Compass*, 117-42.

Isaacs, Neil D., "On the Possibilities of Writing Tolkien Criticism," in Isaacs, N. D., and R. A. Zimbardo, eds., *Tolkien and the Critics*, 1-11.

_____, *Tolkien and the Critics*.

Jeffrey, David L., "Recovery: The Name in THE LORD OF THE RINGS," in Isaacs, N. D., and R. A. Zimbard, eds., *Tolkien*, 106-16.

_____, "Tolkien as Philologist," *Seven* 1 (Mar., 1980): 47-61.

Johnston, George B., "The Poetry of J. R. R. Tolkien," *Mankato State College Studies* 2 (Feb., 1967): 63-75.

Juhren, Marcella, "The Ecology of Middle-Earth," *Mythlore* 2, i (1970): 4-6, 9.

Kaufmann, U. Milo, "Aspects of Paradisiacal in Tolkien's Work," in Lobdell, J., ed., *Tolkien Compass*, 143-52.

Keenan, Hugh T., "The Appeal of THE LORD OF THE RINGS," in Isaacs, N. D., and R. A. Zimbardo, eds., *Tolkien and the Critics*, 62-80.

Kelly, Mary Q., "The Poetry of Fantasy: Verse in THE LORD OF THE RINGS," in Isaacs, N. A., and R. A. Zimbardo, eds., *Tolkien and the Critics*, 170-200.

Kester, Charles G., "Runes," *ParmaE* 1, i (1971): 11.

Kilby, Clyde S., "The Lost Myth," *ASoc* 6 (1969): 155-63.

_____, "Meaning in THE LORD OF THE RINGS," in Hillegas, M. R., ed., *Shadows of Imagination*, 70-80.

_____, "Mythic and Christian Elements in Tolkien," in Montgomery, John W., ed., *Myth, Allegory, and Gospel*, 119-43.

_____, "Tolkien and Coleridge," *Orcrist* 3 (Spring-Summer, 1969): 16-19. Also in *TolJ* 4, i (Jan., 1970): 16-19.

Kirk, Elizabeth D., "'I Would Rather Have Written in Elvish': Language, Fiction and THE LORD OF THE RINGS," *Novel* 5, i (1971): 5-18.

Kobil, Daniel T., "The Elusive Appeal of the Fantastic," *Mythlore* 4, iv (1977): 17-19.

Kocher, Paul, "Middle-Earth: An Imaginary World," in Isaacs, N. D., and R. A. Zimbardo, eds., *Tolkien*, 117-32. Reprinted from Kocher, P. H. *Master of Middle-Earth*, 1-18.

_____, *Master of Middle-Earth*.

_____, "The Tales of the Noldor," *Mythlore* 4, iii (1977): 3-7.

Lense, Edward, "Sauron is Watching You: The Role of the Great Eye in THE LORD OF THE RINGS," *Mythlore* 4, i (1976): 3-6.

Levitin, Alexis, "The Genre of THE LORD OF THE RINGS," *Orcrist* 3 (Spring-Summer, 1969): 4-8, 23. Also in *TolJ* 4, i (Jan., 1970): 4-8, 23.

_____, "The Hero in J. R. R. Tolkien's THE LORD OF THE RINGS," *Mankato State College Studies* 2 (Feb., 1967): 25-37.

_____, "The Lure of the Ring," in GoodKnight, G., ed., *Mythcon I: Proceedings*, 20-1.

_____, "Power in THE LORD OF THE RINGS," *Orcrist* 4 (Spring-Summer, 1969): 11-14. Also in *TolJ* 4, iii (1970): 11-14.

_____, "The Role of Gollum in J. R. R. Tolkien's THE LORD OF THE RINGS," *TolJ* 2, iv (Nov., 1966): 2-6.

Lewis, C. S., 'The Dethronement of Power," *T&T* 43 (Oct., 1955): 1373-4. Also in Isaacs, N. D., and R. A. Zimbardo, eds., *Tolkien and the Critics*, 12-16.

Lloyd, Paul M., "The Role of Warfare in LORD OF THE RINGS," *Mythlore* 3, iii (1976): 3-7.

Lobdell, James C., "Words That Sound Like Castles," *NatR* 19 (Sept. 5, 1967): 972-4.

Lobdell, Jared, *England and Always: Tolkien's World of the Rings*, Grand Rapids: Eerdmans, 1981.

_____, "A Medieval Proverb in THE LORD OF THE RINGS," *AN&Q* (Supp. 1) (1978): 330-1.

Mack, H. G., "A Parametric Analysis of Antithetical Conflict and Irony: Tolkien's THE LORD OF THE RINGS," *Word* 31, ii (Aug., 1980): 121-49.

Mahon, Robert L., "Elegaic Elements in THE LORD OF THE RINGS," *CEA* 40, ii (Jan., 1978): 33-6.

Manlove, C. N., "J. R. R. Tolkien (1892-1973) and THE LORD OF THE RINGS," *Modern Fantasy*, 152-206.

Marchesani, Diane, "Tolkien's Lore: The Songs of Middle Earth," *Mythlore* 7, i (1980): 3-5.

Mathews, R., *Lightning from a Clear Sky*, 18-55.

Matthewson, Joseph, "The Hobbit Habit," *Esquire* 66 (Sept., 1966): 130-1, 221-2.

Miesel, Sandra L., "Some Motifs and Sources for LORD OF THE RINGS," *RQ* 3 (Mar., 1968): 125-8.

_____, "Some Religious Aspects of LORD OF THE RINGS," *RQ* 3 (Aug., 1968): 209-13.

Miller, David M., "Hobbits: Common Lens for Heroic Experience," *Orcrist* 3 (Spring-Summer, 1969): 11-15. Also in *TolJ* 4, i (Jan., 1970): 11-15.

_____, "The Moral Universe of J. R. R. Tolkien," *Mankato State College Studies* 2 (Feb., 1967): 51-62.

Miller, Miriam Y., "The Green Sun: A Study of Color in J. R. R. Tolkien's THE LORD OF THE RINGS," *Mythlore* 7, iv (Winter, 1981): 3-11.

Moorman, Charles W., "Heroism in THE LORD OF THE RINGS," *SoQ* 11 (1972): 29-39.

_____, "'Now Entertain Conjecture of a Time'—The Fictive Worlds of C. S. Lewis and J. R. R. Tolkien," in Hillegas, M. R., ed., *Shadows of Imagination*, 59-69.

_____, *Precincts of Felicity*, Gainsville: Un. of Florida Pr., 1966, 86-100. Also in Isaacs, N. D., and R. A. Zimbardo, eds., *Tolkien and the Critics*, 201-17.

Morse, Robert E., "Rings of Power in Plato and Tolkien," *Mythlore* 7, iv (Winter, 1980): 38.

Noad, Charles E., *The Trees, the Jewels, and the Rings: A Discursive Enquiry into Things Little Known on Middle-Earth*, Harrow: Tolkien Society, 1977.

Nitzsche, J. C., *Tolkien's Art*, 97-127 passim.

Noel, R. S., *Language of Tolkien's Middle-earth*.

Nordhjem, Bent, "In Quest of Tolkien's Middle-earth: On the Interpretation and Classification of THE LORD OF THE RINGS, by J. R. R. Tolkien (with an Old English Word-list)," 17-42 in Dollerup, Cay, ed., *Vølve: Scandinavian Views on Science Fiction*. Selected Papers from the Scandinavian Science-Fiction Festival 1977, Copenhagen: Dept. of English, Un. of Copenhagen, 1978.

Norwood, W. D., "Tolkien's Intention in THE LORD OF THE RINGS," *Mankato State College Studies* 2 (Feb., 1967): 18-24.

O'Connor, Gerard, "The Many Ways to Read an 'Old' Book," *Extrapolation* 15, i (Dec., 1973): 72-4.

_____, "Why Tolkien's THE LORD OF THE RINGS Should NOT Be Popular Culture," *Extrapolation* 13, i (Dec., 1971): 48-55.

O'Hare, Colman, "On Reading an 'Old' Book," *Extrapolation* 14, i (Dec., 1972): 59-63.

O'Neill, T. R., *Individuated Hobbit*.

Osbourne, Andrea, "The Peril of the World," *TolJ* 15 (Summer, 1972): 16-72.

Pace, David P., "The Influence of Vergil's AENEID on THE LORD OF THE RINGS," *Mythlore* 6, ii (Spring, 1979): 37-8.

Panshin, Cory S., "Old Irish Influence Upon the Language and Literature of THE LORD OF THE RINGS," *TolJ* 3, iv (Nov., 1969): 7-8.

Parker, Douglass, "Hwaet We Holbytla..." *HudR* 9 (Winter, 1956-57): 598-609.

Pauline, Sister, "Mysticism in the Ring," *TolJ* 3, iv (Nov., 1969): 12-14.

_____, "Secondary Worlds: Lewis and Tolkien," *CSL Bull* 12, vii (May, 1981): 1-8.

"The Peril of the World," *TolJ (Mythlore)* 15 (1972): 16-17.

Perkins, Agnes, and Helen Hill, "The Corruption of Power," in Lobdell, J., ed., *Tolkien Compass*, 57-68.

Perret, Marion, "Rings Off Their Fingers: Hands in THE LORD OF THE RINGS," *ArielE* 6, iv (1975): 52-66.

Petty, A. C., *One Ring to Bind Them All*.

Plank, Robert, "'The Scouring of the Shire': Tolkien's View of Fascism," in Lobdell, J., ed., *Tolkien's Compass*, 107-15.

Raffel, Burton, "THE LORD OF THE RINGS as Literature," in Isaacs, N. D., and R. A. Zimbardo, eds., *Tolkien and the Critics*, 218-46.

Randolph, Burt, "The Singular Incompetence of Valar," *TolJ* 3, iii (Whole Number 9) (Summer, 1968): 11-13.

Rang, Jack C., "The Two Servants," *Mankato State College Studies* 2 (Feb., 1967): 84-94.

Ratliff, William, and Charles G. Flinn, "The Hobbit and the Hippie," *ModA* 12 (Spring, 1968): 142-6.

Ready, William, *The Tolkien Relation; A Personal Inquiry*, Chicago: Regnery, 1968.

Reckford, Kenneth J., "Some Trees in Virgil and Tolkien," in Galinsky, G. Karl, ed., *Perspectives of Roman Poetry: A Classics Symposium*, Austin: Un. of Texas Pr., 1974, 57-91.

Reilly, R. J., "J. R. R. Tolkien and THE LORD OF THE RINGS," *Romantic Religion; A Study of Barfield, Lewis, Williams, and Tolkien*, Athens: Un. of Georgia Pr., 1971, 190-211.

_____, "Tolkien and the Fairy Story," *Thought* 38 (Spring, 1963): 89-103.

Reinken, Donald L., "J. R. R. Tolkien's THE LORD OF THE RINGS: A Christian Refounding of the Political Order," *ChrPer* (Winter, 1966): 16-23. Also in *TolJ* 2, iii (1966): 4-10.

Reynolds, William, "Poetry as Metaphor in THE LORD OF THE RINGS," *Mythlore* 4, iv (1977): 12-16.

Ring, David, "Ad Valar Defendendi," *TolJ* 15 (Summer, 1972): 18, 22.

Roberts, Mark, "Adventures in English," *EIC* 6 (Oct., 1956): 450-9.

Robinson, James, "The Wizard and History: Saruman's Vision of a New Order," *Orcrist* 1, i (1966-67): 17-23.

Rockow, Karen, "Funeral Customs in Tolkien's Trilogy," *Unicorn* 2, iii (1973): 22-30.

Rogers, Deborah C., "Everyclod and Everyhero: The Image of Man in Tolkien," in Lobdell, J., ed., *Tolkien Compass*, 69-76.

Rogers, D. W., and I. A. Rogers, *J. R. R. Tolkien*, 94-120.

Rosenberg, Jerome, "The Humanity of Sam Gamgee," *Mythlore* 5, i, Whole Number 17 (May, 1978): 10-11.

Russell, Mariann B., "The Idea of the City of God," *DA* 26 (1965): 3350-51.

_____, "'The Northern Literature' and the Ring Trilogy," *Mythlore* 5, ii (Autumn, 1978): 41-2.

Sale, Roger, "England's Parnassus: C. S. Lewis, Charles Williams, and J. R. R. Tolkien," *HudR* 17, (1964): 215-25. Also (revised) as "Tolkien and Frodo Baggins," in Isaacs, N. D., and R. A. Zimbardo, eds., *Tolkien and the Critics*, 247-88.

_____, *Modern Heroism*, 197-239.

Scheps, Walter, "The Fairy-Tale Morality of THE LORD OF THE RINGS," in Lobdell, J., ed., *Tolkien Compass*, 43-56.

Scott, Nan C., "War and Pacifism in THE LORD OF THE RINGS," *TolJ* 15 (Summer, 1972): 22-3, 27-30.

Shippey, T. A., "Creation from Philology in THE LORD OF THE RINGS," in Salu, M., and R. T. Farrell, eds., *J. R. R. Tolkien, Scholar and Storyteller*, 286-316.

_____, *Road to Middle-Earth*, 76-168 *passim*.

Simpson, Dale W., "Names and Moral Character in Tolkien's LORD OF THE RINGS," *PMPA* 6 (1981): 1-5.

Sklar, Robert, "Tolkien and Hesse: Top of the Pops," *Nation* 204 (May, 1967): 598-601.

Slethaug, Gordon E., "Tolkien, Tom Bombadil, and the Creative Imagination," *ECS* 4, iii (Fall, 1978): 341-50.

Spacks, Patricia M., "'Ethical Patterns' in THE LORD OF THE RINGS," *Crit* 3 (Spring-Fall, 1959): 30-42. Also (revised) in Isaacs, N. D., and R. A. Zimbardo, eds., *Tolkien and the Critics*, 81-99.

St. Clair, Gloriana, "THE LORD OF THE RINGS as Saga," *Mythlore* 6, ii (Spring, 1979): 11-16.

St. Clair, Gloria Ann, "Studies in the Source of J. R. R. Tolkien's THE LORD OF THE RINGS," *DAI* 30 (1970): 5001A.

Stewart, Douglas J., "The Hobbit War," *Nation* 205 (Oct. 9, 1967): 332-5.

Stimpson, C. R., *J. R. R. Tolkien*, 33-41.

Strachey, Barbara, *Journeys of Frodo: An Atlas of J. R. R. Tolkien's THE LORD OF THE RINGS*, London: Allen & Unwin, 1981.

Straight, Michael, "Fantastic World of Professor Tolkien," *NRep* 134 (Jan., 16, 1956): 24-6.

Taylor, William R., "Frodo Lives: J. R. R. Tolkien's THE LORD OF THE RINGS," *EJ* 56 (Sept., 1967): 818-21.

Thompson, Kirk L., "Who is Eldest?" *TolJ (Mythlore)* 15 (1972): 19.

Thomson, George H., "THE LORD OF THE RINGS: The Novel as Traditional Romance," *WSCL* 8 (Winter, 1967): 43-59.

Tinkler, John, "Old English in Rohan," in Isaacs, N. D., and R. A. Zimbardo, eds., *Tolkien and the Critics*, 164-9.

Tolkien, J. R. R., "Guide to the Names in THE LORD OF THE RINGS," in Lobdell, J., ed., *Tolkien Compass*, 153-201.

Torrens, James, "With Tolkien in Middle-Earth," *Good Work*, 31, iv (Winter, 1968): 17-23.

Urang, Gunnar, "Tolkien's Fantasy: The Phenomenology of Hope," in Hillegas, M. R., ed., *Shadows of Imagination*, 97-110. Also in Urang, G., *Shadows of Heaven*, 93-130.

Van de Bogart, Doris, "Some Comments on the LORD OF THE RING by J. R. R. Tolkien," *Dialogue* 1, iv (1973): 33-42.

Walker, Stephen L., "THE WAR OF THE RINGS Treelogy: An Elegy for Lost Innocence and Wonder," *Mythlore* 5, i (May, 1978): 3-5.

Walker, Steven C., "The Making of a Hobbit: Tolkien's Tantalizing Narrative Technique," *Mythlore* 7, iii (Autumn, 1980): 6-7.

Webster, Deborah C., Jr., "Good Guys, Bad Guys: A Clarification on Tolkien," *Orcrist* 2 (1967-68): 18-23.

Welden, Bill, "On the Formation of Plurals in Sindarin," *ParmaE* 1, i (1971): 10-11.

West, Richard C., "The Interlace and Professor Tolkien: Medieval Narrative Technique in THE LORD OF THE RINGS," *Orcrist* 1 (1966-67): 26-49. Also in Lobdell, J., ed., *Tolkien Compass*, 77-94.

Wilson, C., *Strength to Dream*, 145-8.

Wilson, Edmund, "Oo Those Awful Orcs!" *Nation* 182 (Apr. 14, 1956): 312-14. Also in Wilson, E., *The Bit Between My Teeth*, N.Y.: Farrar, Straus & Giroux, 1965, 332-6.

Winter, Karen C., "Grendel, Gollum, and the Un-Man: The Death of the Monster as Archetype," *Orcrist* 2 (1967-68): 28-37.

Wojcik, Jan, "Samwise—Halfwise? or, Who Is the Hero of THE LORD OF THE RINGS?" *TolJ* 3, ii (1967): 16-18.

Woods, Samuel H., Jr., "J. R. R. Tolkien and the Hobbits," *CimR* 1 (Sept., 1967): 44-52.

Zgorzelski, Andrzej, "Time Setting in J. R. R. Tolkien's THE LORD OF THE RINGS," *ZRL* 13, iii (1971): 91-100.

Zimbardo, Rose A., "The Medieval-Renaissance Vision of THE LORD OF THE RINGS," in Isaacs, R. A. and R. A. Zimbardo, eds., *Tolkien*, 63-71.

_____, "Moral Vision in THE LORD OF THE RINGS," in Isaacs, N. D., and Zimbardo, R. A., eds., *Tolkien and the Critics*, 100-8.

THE RETURN OF THE KING (See also LORD OF THE RINGS Trilogy)

Auden, W. H., "At the End of the Quest, Victory," *NYTBR* (Jan. 22, 1956): 5.

Carter, L., *Tolkien*, 65-78.

Huxley, Francis, 'The Endless Worm," *NStat* 50 (Nov. 5, 1955): 587-8.

Traversi, Derek A., "The Realm of Gondor," *Month* 15 (June, 1956): 370-1.

THE SILMARILLION

Allan, Jim, *An Extrapolation on THE SILMARILLION*, Liverpool: Tolkien Society, 1975.

Conrad, Peter, "The Babbit," *NStat* (Sept. 23, 1977): 408-9.

Crabbe, K. F., *J. R. R. Tolkien*, 112-44.

Davis, Howard, "The Ainulindale: Music of Creation," *Mythlore* 9, ii (Summer, 1982): 6-8.

Drabble, Margaret, "Rebels Against Iluvatar," *Listener* 98 (1977): 346.

Flieger, Verlyn, "Barfield's POETIC DICTION and Splintered Light," *SLitI* 14, ii (Fall, 1981): 47-66.

Foster, Robert, *The Complete Guide to Middle-Earth: From THE HOBBIT to THE SILMARILLION*, London: Allen & Unwin, 1978.

Gardner, John, "World of Tolkien," *NYTBR* (Oct. 23, 1977): 1, 39-40.

GoodKnight, Glen, introd., "Special Issue Focusing on THE SILMARILLION, UNFINISHED TALES, THE LETTERS OF J.R.R. TOLKIEN," *Mythlore* 9, ii (Summer, 1982): 3-4.

Helms, R., *Tolkien and the Silmarils*.

Kilby, C. S. *Tolkien and THE SILMARILLION*.

Kocher, Paul H., *A Reader's Guide to THE SILMARILLION*, London: Thames & Hudson; Boston: Houghton Mifflin, 1980.

Kreeft, Peter, "The Wonder of THE SILMARILLION," in Hillegas, M. R., ed., *Shadows of Imagination*, New edition, 1979, 161-78.

Mathew, R., *Lightning from a Clear Sky*, 56-9.

McLellan, Joseph, "Frodo and the Cosmos: Reflections on THE SILMARILLION," *Washington Post* (Sept. 4, 1977): Also in Isaacs, N. D., and R. A. Zimbardo, eds., *Tolkien*, 163-7.

Nitzsche, J. C., *Tolkien's Art*, 128-34.

Noel, R. S. *Languages of Tolkien's Middle-earth*.

Ratcliff, John D., "SHE and Tolkien," *Mythlore* 8, ii (1981): 6-8.

Rogers, D. W., and I. A. Rogers, *J. R. R. Tolkien*, 78-93.

Shippey, T. A., *Road to Middle-Earth*, 174-202 *passim*.

Whicher, Andrzej, "The Artificial Mythology of THE SILMARILLION by J. R. R. Tolkien," *KN* 28, iii-iv (1981): 399-405.

THE TWO TOWERS (See also THE LORD OF THE RINGS Trilogy)

Carter, L., *Tolkien*, 55-64.

BIBLIOGRAPHY

Carter, L., *Tolkien*, 203-4.

Christenson, Bonniejean M., "J. R. R. Tolkien: A Bibliography," *BB* (July-Sept., 1970): 61-7.

Hammond, Wayne G., "Addenda to 'J. R. R. Tolkien; A Bibliography'," *BB* 34, iii (July-Sept., 1977): 119-27.

West, Richard C., "An Annotated Bibliography of Tolkien Criticism," *Extrapolation* 10 (1968): 17-45.

_____, "An Annotated Bibliography of Tolkien Criticism," *Orcrist* 1 (1966-67): 32-55; 2 (1967-68): 40-54; 3 (1969): 22-3.

_____, "An Annotated Bibliography of Tolkien Criticism, Supplement Three," *Orcrist* 5-*Tolkien Journal* 14 (Comb. Issue) (1970): 14-31.

_____, *Tolkien Criticism: An Annotated Checklist*. Rev ed., Kent, Ohio: Kent State Un. Pr., 1981.

TOOLE, JOHN KENNEDY, 1937-1969

A CONFEDERACY OF DUNCES

Daigrepant, Lloyd M., "Ignatius Reilly and the CONFEDERACY OF DUNCES," *NOR* 9, iii (Winter, 1982): 74-80.

Patterson, Richard F., "Ignatius Goes to the Movies: The Film in Toole's A CONFEDERACY OF DUNCES," *NMAL* 6 (1982): Item 14.

Regan, Robert, "The Return of THE MOVIEGOER: Toole's A CONFEDERACY OF DUNCES," *DeltaES* 13 (Nov., 1981): 169-76.

Reilly, Edward C., "Batman and Ignatius J. Reilly in A CONFEDERACY OF DUNCES," *NConL* 12, i (Jan., 1982): 10-11.

TRACY, HONOR, 1915-

GENERAL

Gindin, J., *Postwar American Fiction*, 165-77.

TREVOR, WILLIAM, Pseud. (William Trevor Cox), 1928-

GENERAL

Gitzen, Julian, "The Truth-Tellers of William Trevor," *Crit* 21, i (1979): 59-72.

Mortimer, Mork, "William Trevor in Dublin," *EI* 4 (1975): 77-85. [Not seen.]

Taylor, Lillian R., "William Trevor: A Critical Study," *DAI* 41 (1980): 2621A.

TRILLING, LIONEL, 1905-1975

GENERAL

Alspaugh, Elizabeth N., "The Formation of Lionel Trilling's Moral Dialectic: A Study of His Fiction and Criticism, 1939-1955," *DAI* 40 (1979): 2658A.

Chace, W. M., *Lionel Trilling*.

Chanda, A. K., "The Young Man from the Provinces," *CL* 33, iv (Fall, 1981): 321-41. [Not seen.]

Frohock, W. M., "Lionel Trilling and the American Reality,"
    SWR 45 (Summer, 1960): 224-32.
Shoben, E. J., Jr., *Lionel Trilling*.

THE MIDDLE OF THE JOURNEY

Allen, W., *Modern Novel*, 178-9.
Anderson, Quentin, "On THE MIDDLE OF THE JOURNEY,"
    in Anderson, Q., S. Donadio, and S. Marcus, eds., *Art, Politics,
    and Will*, 254-64.
Bayley, John, "Middle Class Futures," *TLS* (Apr. 11, 1975): 399.
Blotner, J., *Modern American Political Novel*, 315-20.
Boyers, Robert, "THE MIDDLE OF THE JOURNEY and Be-
    yond: Observations on Modernity and Commitment," *Sal-
    magundi* 1, iv (1967): 8-18.
Caute, David, "Summer People," *NStat* (Apr. 11, 1975): 486.
Chace, William M., *Lionel Trilling*, 31-42.
———, "The Middle of the Journey: Death and Politics,"
    Novel 10 (Winter, 1977): 137-44.
Eisinger, Charles E., *Fiction of the Forties*, 135-44.
———, "Trilling and the Crises in Our Culture," *UKCR* 25
    (Oct., 1958): 27-35.
Fergusson, Francis, "Three Novels," *Perspectives USA* 6 (Winter,
    1954): 30-44.
Freedman, William, "THE MIDDLE OF THE JOURNEY: Lionel
    Trilling and the Novel of Ideas," in French, W., ed., *Forties*,
    239-48.
Frohock, W. M., "Lionel Trilling and the American Reality,"
    SWR 45 (Summer, 1960): 225-9.
Hatfield, Henry, "The Journey and the Mountain," *MLN* 90
    (1975): 363-70. [Comparison with Mann's MAGIC MOUN-
    TAIN.]
Joost, Nicholas, in Gardiner, H. C., ed., *Fifty Years of the American
    Novel*, 288-9.
Kubal, David L., "Trilling's THE MIDDLE OF THE JOURNEY:
    An American Dialectic," *BuR* 14 (Mar., 1966): 60-73.
McCormick, J., *Catastrophe and Imagination*, 79-84.
Milne, G., *American Political Novel*, 139-49.
Montgomery, Marion, "Lionel Trilling's THE MIDDLE OF THE
    JOURNEY," *Discourse* 4 (Autumn, 1961): 263-72.
Scott, N. A., ed., *Three American Moralists*, 157-70.
Shoben, E. J., Jr., *Lionel Trilling*, 44-52, 120-39.
Shoda, Wakiko, "THE MIDDLE OF THE JOURNEY: A Com-
    mentary," in *American Literature in the 1940's*, 6-12.
Trilling, Lionel, "Whittaker Chambers and THE MIDDLE OF
    THE JOURNEY," *NYRB* 22 (Apr. 17, 175): 18-24.
Zabel, Morton D., "The Straight Way Lost," *Nation* 165 (Oct. 18,
    1947): 413-16. Also in Zabel, M. D., *Craft and Character*, 312-
    17.

TROCCHI, ALEXANDER, 1925-

CAIN'S BOOK

Bryant, J. H., *Open Decision*, 200-2, 225-7.
Green, R. B., *Italian-American Novel*, 292-5.

TRUMBO, DALTON, 1905-1976

JOHNNY GOT HIS GUN

Kriegel, Leonard, "Dalton Trumbo's JOHNNY GOT HIS
    GUN," in Madden, David, ed., *Proletarian Writers of the Thir-
    ties* (CMC), Carbondale: So. Ill. Un. Pr., 1968, 106-13.

TUTUOLA, AMOS, 1920-

GENERAL

Afolayan, A., "Language and Sources of Amos Tutuola," *SAfrL*
    1 (1971): 49-63.
Chakava, Henry M., "Amos Tutuola: The Unselfconscious Ec-
    centric," *Busara* 3, iii (1971): 50-7.
Collins, Harold R., *Amos Tutuola*.
———, "Founding a New National Literature: The Ghost
    Novels of Amos Tutuola," *Crit* 4 (1960): 17-28. Also in Lind-
    fors, B., ed., *Critical Perspectives on Amos Tutuola*, 59-70.
———, "A Theory of Creative Mistakes and the Mistaking
    Style of Amos Tutuola," *WLWE* 13, ii (Nov., 1974): 155-71.
———, "Tutuola's Literary Powers," in Lindfors, B., ed.,
    Critical Perspectives on Amos Tutuola, 155-66. Reprinted from
    Collins, H., *Amos Tutuola*, 117-28, 135-6.
Devereux, George, "Fantasy and Schizophrenic Delusion, with
    a Note on the African Novelist Amos Tutuola," *PsyculR* 3
    (1979): 231-7.
Eko, Ebele, "The Problem of Cross-Cultural Reception: Three
    Nigerian Writers in England and America," *Comparatist* 1
    (1977): 11-15. [Not seen.]
Ferris, William J., Jr., "Folklore and the African Novelist:
    Achebe and Tutuola," *JAF* 86 (Jan.-Mar., 1973): 31-4.
Irele, Abiola, "Tradition and the Yoruba Writer: D. O. Fagunwa,
    Amos Tutuola and Wole Soyinka," *Odu* n.s. 11 (Jan., 1975):
    85-90.
Klima, Vladimir, "Tutuola's Inspiration," *ArQ* 35 (1967): 556-62.
    Reprinted in Pouillon, Jean, and Pierre Miranda, *Echanges et
    communications: Melanges offerts a Claude Levi-Strauss a l'occa-
    sion de son 60 eme anniversaire*, Vol. 2, The Hague: Mouton,
    1970, 121-8.
Larrabee, Eric, "Amos Tutuola: A Problem in Translation," *ChiR*
    10, i (Spring, 1956): 40-4.
Laurence, Margaret, "A Twofold Forest," *Long Drums and Can-
    nons*, 126-47.
Lindfors, Bernth, "Amos Tutuola and D. O. Fagunwa," *JCL* 9
    (Dec., 1970): 57-65.
———, "Amos Tutuola and His Critics," *Abbia* 22 (May,
    1969): 109-18.
———, "Amos Tutuola: Debts and Assets," *CEAfr* 10 (1970):
    306-34. Also in Lindfors, B., ed., *Critical Perspectives on Amos
    Tutuola*, 275-306.
———, ed., *Critical Perspectives on Amos Tutuola*.
Lo Liyong, Taban, "Tutuola, Son of Zinjanthropus," *Busara* 1, i
    (1968): 3-8. Also, revised, in Lo Liyong, T., *The Last Word:
    Cultural Synthesism*, Nairobi: East African Pub. House, 1969,
    157-70. Also in Lindfors, B., ed., *Critical Perspectives on Amos
    Tutuola*, 115-22.

McDowell, Robert E., "Three Nigerian Storytellers: Okara, Tutuola, and Ekwenski," *BSUF* 10, iii (Summer, 1969): 67-75.

Moore, G. M., "Amos Tutuola: A Nigerian Visionary," *BQ* 1 (Sept., 1957): 27-35. Also in Beier, Ulli, ed., *Introduction to African Literature*, Evanston: Northwestern Un. Pr., 1967, 179-87. Also, expanded, in Moore, G., *Seven African Writers*, 39-57. Also in Lindfors, B., ed., *Critical Perspectives on Amos Tutuola*, 49-57.

Neumarkt, Paul, "Amos Tutuola: Emerging African Literature," *AI* 28, ii (Summer, 1971): 129-45. Also in Lindfors, B., ed., *Critical Perspectives on Amos Tutuola*, 183-92.

Nyang'aya, Elijah, "The Freakish Tutuola," in Wanjala, C. L., ed., *Standpoints on African Literature*, 188-95.

Obiechina, E. N., "Amos Tutuola and the Oral Tradition," *PA* 65 (1968): 85-106. Also in Lindfors, B., ed., *Critical Perspectives on Amos Tutuola*, 123-44.

Ogundpipe-Leslie, Omolara, "Ten Years of Tutuola Studies: 1966-1976," *African Perspectives* (Leiden) 1 (1977): 67-76. [Not seen.]

Omotoso, Kole, "Interview with Amos Tutuola," *Afriscope* 4, i (1974): 62, 64.

Palmer, Eustace, "Amos Tutuola," *SAfrL* (1979): 11-35.

_____, *Growth of the African Novel*, 11-35.

_____, "Twenty-five Years of Amos Tutuola," *IFR* 5, i (Jan., 1978): 15-24.

Roscoe, A. A. "Tutuola: A Writer Without Problems," *Mother is God*, 98-113.

Taiwo, O., *Culture and the Nigerian Novel*, 74-94.

_____, "The Essentials of Amos Tutuola's Narrative Art," *LHY* 17, i (Jan., 1976): 57-75.

Takacs, Sherryl, "Oral Tradition in the Works of Amos Tutuola," *BA* 44, iii (Summer, 1970): 392-8.

Tibble, Anne, *African/English Literature*, 95-101.

AJAIYI AND HIS INHERITED POVERTY

King, Bruce, "Two Nigerian Writers: Tutuola and Soyinka," *SoR* 6 (1970): 843-5.

Taiwo, O., *Culture and the Nigerian Novel*, 107-10.

THE BRAVE AFRICAN HUNTRESS

Collins, H. R., *Amos Tutuola*, 31-2, 38-41, 47-8.

Taiwo, O., *Culture and the Nigerian Novel*, 102-4.

FEATHER WOMAN OF THE JUNGLE

Collins, H. R., *Amos Tutuola*, 29-30, 32-3, 41-3, 48.

Laurence, M., *Long Drums and Cannons*, 140-6.

Ogunyemi, Chikwenye O., "The African of THE CONJURE WOMAN and FEATHER WOMAN OF THE JUNGLE," *ArielE* 8, ii (Apr., 1977): 17-30.

Taiwo, O., *Culture and the Nigerian Novel*, 104-7.

MY LIFE IN THE BUSH OF GHOSTS

Collins, H. R., *Amos Tutuola*, 30-1, 35-6.

Laurence, M., *Long Drums and Cannons*, 132-6.

Lindfors, Bernth, "Amos Tutuola's Television-Handed Goddess," *ArielE* 2, i (1971): 68-77. Also in Lindfors, B., *Folklore in Nigerian Literature*, 61-70. Also in Walsh, W., ed., *Readings in Commonwealth Literature*, 142-51.

Moore, George, "Amos Tutuola: Nigerian Visionary," *BO* 1 (Sept., 1957): 32-4. Also in Moore, G., *Seven African Writers*, 49-51.

Taiwo, O., *Culture and the Nigerian Novel*, 97-9.

THE PALM-WINE DRINKARD AND HIS DEAD PALM-WINE TAPSTER IN THE DEAD'S TOWN

Achebe, Chinua, "Work and Play in Tutuola's THE PALM-WINE DRINKARD," *Okike* 14 (1978): 25-33.

Afolayan, A., "Language and Sources of Amos Tutuola," in Lindfors, B., ed., *Critical Perspectives on Amos Tutuola*, 193-208.

Anozie, Sunday O., "Amos Tutuola: Literature and Folklore or the Problem of Synthesis," in Lindfors, B., ed., *Critical Perspectives on Amos Tutuola*, 237-53.

_____, "Structure and Utopia in Tutuola's PALM-WINE DRINKARD," *Conch* 2, ii (Sept., 1970): 80-8.

Armstrong, Robert P., "Amos Tutuola and Kola Ogunmola: A Comparison of Two Versions of THE PALM-WINE DRINKARD," *Callaloo* 3, i-iii (Feb.-Oct., 1980): 165-74.

_____, "The Narrative and Intensive Continuity: THE PALM-WINE DRINKARD," *RAL* 1, i (Spring, 1970): 9-34. Also in Lindfors, B, ed., *Critical Perspectives on Nigerian Literatures*, 103-29. Also in Lindfors, B., ed., *Critical Perspectives on Amos Tutuola*, 209-35. Also, slightly different version, in Armstrong, R. P., *The Affecting Presence: An Essay in Humanistic Anthropology*, Urbana: Un. of Illinois Pr., 1971, 137-73.

Arnason, David, "Amos Tutuola's THE PALM-WINE DRINKARD: The Nature of Tutuola's Achievement," *JCF* 3, iv (1975): 56-9.

Coates, John, "The Inward Journey of the Palm-wine Drinkard," *ALT* 11 (1980): 122-9.

Collins, H. R., *Amos Tutuola*, 30-1, 45-6.

Dathorne, O. R., "Amos Tutuola: The Nightmare of the Tribe," in Kin, B., ed., *Introduction to Nigerian Literature*, 64-75.

Edwards, Paul, "The Farm and the Wilderness in Tutuola's THE PALM-WINE DRINKARD," *JCL* 9, i (August, 1974): 57-65. Also in Lindfors, B., ed., *Critical Perspectives on Amos Tutuola*, 255-63.

Jones, Eldred, "Turning Back the Pages: THE PALM-WINE DRINKARD 14 Years On," *BAALE* 4 (Mar., 1966): 24-30. Also in Lindfors, B., ed., *Critical Perspectives on Amos Tutuola*, 109-13.

Larson, Charles R., "Time, Space, and Description: the Tutuolan World," *Emergence of African Fiction*, 93-112. Also in Lindfors, B., ed., *Critical Perspectives on Amos Tutuola*, 171-81.

Laurence, Margaret, *Long Drums and Cannons*, 127-32.

Lindfors, Bernth, "Amos Tutuola: Debts and Assets," *CEAfr* 10 (1970): 310-18. Also in Lindfors, B., ed., *Critical Perspectives on Amos Tutuola*, 279-88.

_____, "Amos Tutuola's THE PALM-WINE DRINKARD and Oral Tradition," *Crit* 11, i (1969): 42-50. Also in Lindfors, B., *Folkore in Nigerian Literature*, 51-9.

Moore, George, "Amos Tutuola: A Nigerian Visionary," *BO* 1 (Sept., 1957): 27-30. Also in Moore, G., *Seven African Writers*, 39-49.

_____, *Chosen Tongue*, 163-6.

Neumarkt, Paul, "Amos Tutuola: Emerging African Literature," *AI* 28 (Summer, 1971): 136-9. Also in Lindfors, B., ed., *Critical Perspectives on Amos Tutuola*, 185-8.

Nkutt, Ukpabio, "THE PALM-WINE DRINKARD Has More Practical Literary Value than the Purists Would Admit," *Shuttle* (Lagos) 8 (1980): 36-40.

Obiechina, E. N., "Amos Tutuola and the Oral Tradition," *PA* 65 (1968): 85-106 *passim*. Also in Lindfors, B., ed., *Critical Perspectives on Amos Tutuola*, 123-44 *passim*.

Ogundpipe-Leslie, Omolaro, "THE PALM-WINE DRINKARD: A Reassessment of Amos Tutuola," *PA* 71 (1969): 99-108. Also in *Ibadan* 28 (1970): 22-6. Also in *JCL* 9 (July, 1970): 48-56. Also in Lindfors, B., ed., *Critical Perspectives on Amos Tutuola*, 145-53.

Palmer, E., *Growth of the African Novel*, 13-32.

Priebe, Richard, "Tutuola, the Riddler," in Lindfors, B., ed., *Critical Perspectives on Amos Tutuola*, 265-73.

Taiwo, O., *Culture and the Nigerian Novel*, 94-7.

Tibble, Anne, *African/English Literature*, 96-101.

West, David S., "THE PALM-WINE DRINKARD and African Philosophy," *LHY* 19, ii (1978): 83-96.

SIMBI AND THE SATYR OF THE JUNGLE

Banjo, Ayo, "Aspects of Tutuola's Use of English," in Ballard, W. L., ed., *Essays on African Literature*, 155-73.

Collins, H. R., *Amos Tutuola*, 31, 36-8, 46-7.

Laurence, M., *Long Drums and Cannons*, 136-8.

Moore, George, "Amos Tutuola: Nigerian Visionary," *BO* 1 (Sept., 1957): 32-4. Also in Moore, G., *Seven African Writers*, 51-4.

Obiechina, E. N., "Amos Tutuola and the Oral Tradition," *PA* 65 (1968): 85-106 *passim*. Also in Lindfors, B., ed., *Critical Perspectives on Amos Tutuola*, 123-44 *passim*.

Taiwo, O., *Culture and the Nigerian Novel*, 100-2.

BIBLIOGRAPHY

"Amos Tutuola: A Checklist of Works, Reviews and Criticism," in Lindfors, B., ed., *Critical Perspectives on Amos Tutuola*, 309-18.

Collins, H. R., *Amos Tutuola*, 137-40.

TYLER, ANNE, 1941-

GENERAL

Nesanovich, Stella A., "The Individual in the Family: A Critical Introduction to the Novels of Anne Tyler," *DAI* 40 (1980): 6282A.

EARTHLY POSSESSIONS

Nesanovich, Stella, "The Individual in the Family: Anne Tyler's SEARCHING FOR CALEB and EARTHLY POSSESSIONS," *SoR* 14 (1978): 170-6.

SEARCHING FOR CALEB

Nesanovich, Stella, "The Individual in the Family: Anne Tyler's SEARCHING FOR CALEB and EARTHLY POSSESSIONS," *SoR* 14 (1978): 170-6.

BIBLIOGRAPHY

Nesanovich, Stella, "An Anne Tyler Checklist, 1959-1980," *BB* 38, ii (Apr.-June, 1981): 53-64.

UPDIKE, JOHN, 1932-

GENERAL

Aldridge, John W., "John Updike and the Higher Theology," *Devil in the Fire*, 195-201.

———, "The Private Vice of John Updike," *Time to Murder and Create*, 164-70.

Bowker, Larsen K., "The Pursuit of Permanence: A Study of the Thematic Structure of John Updike's Novels," *DAI* 35 (1974): 2980A.

Bodmer, George R., "The Right Life: The Problem of Existence in John Updike's Fiction," *DAI* 39 (1979): 5508A.

Bowman, Diane K., "Flying High: The American Icarus in Morrison, Roth, and Updike," *PCL* 8 (1982): 10-17.

Boyers, Robert, Bharati M. Blaise, and Robert Foulke, "An Evening with John Updike," *Salmagundi* 57 (Summer, 1982): 42-56. [Interview.]

Burchard, R. C. *John Updike*.

Burgess, Anthony, "Language, Myth and Mr. Updike," *Cweal* 83 (Feb. 11, 1966): 557-8.

Campbell, Jeff H., "From MARRY ME to COUPLES: Tristan Demythologized," *CCTE* 45 (1980): 84-92. [Not seen.]

Cox, David M., "An Examination of Thematic and Structural Connection between John Updike's Rabbit Novels," *DAI* 39 (1979): 5511A.

Deen, Carol A. S., "Women in the Novels of John Updike: A Critical Study," *DAI* 41 (1980): 1593A-94A.

DeKerchove, Arnold, "John Updike, Jean Rhys, Andre Gide," *RGB* 3 (1970): 91-7. [Not seen.]

Detweiler, Robert, *John Updike*.

———, "Updike's Sermons," *AAus* 5 (1980): 11-26.

Doody, Terence A., "Updike's Idea of Reification," *ConL* 20, ii (Spring, 1979): 204-20.

Doyle, Paul A., "The Fiction of John Updike," *NassauR* 1, i (Spring, 1964): 9-19.

———, "Updike's Fiction: Motifs and Techniques," *CathW* 199 (Sept., 1964): 356-62.

Drier, James S., "Religious Elements of a Portion of John Updike's Fiction," *DAI* 34 (1974): 6094A.

Elliott, S. James, "Homosexuality in the Crucial Decade: Three Novelist's Views," in Crew, L., ed., *Gay Academic*, 173-7.

Enright, D. J., "Updike's Ups and Downs," *Holiday* 38 (Nov., 1965): 162-6. Also as "The Inadequate American: John Updike's Fiction," in Enright, D. J., *Conspirators and Poets*, 134-40.

Finkelstein, Sidney, "The Anti-Hero of Updike, Bellow and Malamud," *AmD* 7, ii (Spring, 1972): 12-14, 30.

Fisher, Richard E., "John Updike: Theme and Form in the Garden of Epiphanies," *MSpr* 56 (Fall, 1962): 255-60.

Fritz, Donald E., "Phenomenological Criticism: An Analysis and an Application to the Fiction of John Updike," *DAI* 36 (1976): 6655A-56A.

Gado, Frank, ed., "A Conversation with John Updike," *Idol* 47 (Spring, 1971): 3-32. Also in Gado, F., ed., *First Person*, 80-109.

Galloway, David D., "The Absurd Man as Saint: The Novels of John Updike," *MFS* 11 (Summer, 1964): 111-27. Also in Galloway, D. D., *Absurd Hero*, 21-50.

Gindin, James, "Megalotopia and the WASP Backlash: The Fiction of Mailer and Updike," *CentR* 15, i (Winter, 1971): 38-52.

Gingher, Robert S., "Has John Updike Anything to Say?" *MFS* 20 (Spring, 1974): 97-105.

Gratton, Margaret, "The Use of Rhythm in Three Novels by John Updike," *UPortR* 21, ii (Fall, 1969): 3-12.

Hainsworth, J. D., "John Updike," *HJ* 65 (Spring, 1967): 115-16.

Hamilton, Alice and Kenneth, *Elements of John Updike*.

_____, "Mythic Dimensions in Updike's Fiction," *NDQ* 41, iii (Summer, 1973): 54-66.

_____, "The Validation of Religious Faith in the Writings of John Updike," *SRC* 5, iii (Winter, 1975): 275-85.

Hamilton, Kenneth, "John Updike: Chronicler of the Time of the 'Death of God'," *ChC* 34 (June 7, 1967): 745-8.

Hamilton, Kenneth and Alice, *John Updike*.

Harper, H. M., Jr., "John Updike: The Intrinsic Problem of Human Goodness," *Desperate Faith*, 162-90.

Hicks, Granville, in Balakian, N., and C. Simmons, eds., *Creative Present*, 232-7.

Hill, John S., "Quest for Belief: Theme in the Novels of John Updike," *SHR* 3 (Spring, 1969): 166-75.

Hill, Steele W., "Structural Unity in the Novels of John Updike," *DAI* 39 (1978): 885A.

Hiller, Catherine, "Personality and Persona: The Narrators in John Updike's Fiction," *DAI* 33 (1973): 4416A-17A.

Hunt, George W., S. J., *John Updike and the Three Great Secret Things*.

_____, "John Updike: The Dialectical Vision: The Influence of Kierkegaard and Barth," *DAI* 36 (1976): 6674A.

_____, "Updike's Pilgrims in a World of Nothingness," *Thought* 53 (1978): 384-400.

Jones, Edward T., "An Art of Equilibrium: Piet Mondrian and John Updike," *Connecticut Critic* 7 (March, 1973): 4-10.

Kesterson, David B., "Updike and Hawthorne: Not So Strange Bedfellows," *NMAL* 3 (1979): Item 11.

La Course, Guerin, "The Innocence of John Updike," *Cweal* 77 (Feb. 8, 1963): 512-14.

Macnaughton, W. R., ed., *Critical Essays on John Updike*.

Markle, J. B., *Fighters and Lovers*.

Muradian, Thaddeus, "The World of Updike," *EJ* 54 (Oct., 1965): 577-84.

Murphy, Richard W., "John Updike," *Horizon* 4 (Mar., 1962): 84-5.

Neal, William R., "The Theology of Karl Barth as an Interpretive Key to the Fiction of John Updike," *DAI* 38 (1977): 1382A.

Nesset, Michael P., "John Updike and Andrew Wyeth: The Nostalgic Mode in Contemporary Art," *DAI* 39 (1979): 7400A-01A.

Nickens, Susan J., "A Right Relation: John Updike's Norm of Marital Commitment," *DAI* 43, i (July, 1982): 169A-70A.

Oates, Joyce Carol, "Updike's American Comedies," *MFS* 21 (Autumn, 1975): 459-72.

Petter, H[enry], "John Updike's Metaphoric Novels," *ES* 50 (Apr., 1969): 197-206. Also in Macnaughton, W. R., ed., *Critical Essays on John Updike*, 105-14.

Plagman, Linda M., "The Modern Pilgrims: Marriage and Self in the Work of John Updike," *DAI* 36 (1975): 325A-26A.

Ready, Richard M., "'Not Only': An Examination of Abstraction in the Writings of John Updike, with a Particular Emphasis on the Olinger Narratives," *NAI* 36 (1976): 5287A.

Reilly, Charlie, "Talking with John Updike," *Inquiry Mag.* (Dec. 11, 1978): 14-17.

Robinson, Robert, "Couples and Clergy: Some Thoughts by John Updike," *Listener* 95 (Mar. 25, 1976): 367.

Rupp, Richard H., "John Updike: Style in Search of a Center," *SR* 75 (Autumn, 1967): 693-709.

Samuels, Charles T., "The Art of Fiction 42: John Updike," *ParisR* 45 (Winter, 1968): 84-117.

_____, *John Updike*.

Schopen, Bernard A., "The Aesthetics of Ambiguity: The Novels of John Updike," *DAI* 36 (1976): 7415A.

_____, "Faith, Morality, and the Novels of John Updike," *TCL* 24 (Winter, 1978): 523-35. Also in Macnaughton, W. R., ed., *Critical Essays on John Updike*, 195-205.

Searles, George J., "The Fiction of Philip Roth and John Updike," *DAI* 39 (1979): 6135A-36A.

Seib, Philip, "A Lovely Way Through Life: An Interview with John Updike," *SWR* 66, iv (Autumn, 1981): 341-50.

Strandberg, Victor, "John Updike and the Changing of the Gods," *Mosaic* 12, i (Fall, 1978): 157-75. Also in Macnaughton, W. R., ed., *Critical Essays on John Updike*, 175-94.

Swanson, Trevor J., "A Transformational-Generative Approach to Style in John Updike's Novels," *DAI* 34 (1974): 5999A.

Tallent, E., *Married Men and Magic Tricks*.

Taylor, Larry E., *Pastoral and Anti-Pastoral Patterns in John Updike's Fiction*.

Thomas, Lloyd S., "Scarlet Sundays: Updike vs. Hawthorne," *CEA* 39, iii (1977): 16-17.

Thornburn, D., and H. Eiland, eds., *John Updike*.

Updike, John, "John Updike Talks to Eric Rhode About Shapes and Subjects of His Fiction," *Listener* 81 (1969): 862-4.

Uphaus, Beverly S., "Mode and Meaning in the Novels of John Updike," *DAI* 37 (1976): 2882A-83A.

Uphaus, S. H., *John Updike*.

Vargo, E. P., *Rainstorms and Fire*.

Verduin, Kathleen, "Fatherly Presences: John Updike's Place in Protestant Tradition," in Macnaughton, W. R., ed., *Critical Essays on John Updike*, 254-68.

_____, "Religious and Sexual Love in American Protestant Literature: Puritan Patterns in Hawthorne and John Updike," *DAI* 41 (1980): 1059A-60A.

Wagner, Joseph B., "John Updike and Karl Barth: An Insistent 'Yes'," *Cithara* 18, i (Nov., 1978): 61-9.

Ward, J. A., "John Updike's Fiction," *Crit* 5, ii (Spring-Summer, 1962): 27-40.

Wyatt, Bryant N., "John Updike: The Psychological Novel in Search of Structure," *TCL* 13 (July, 1967): 89-96.

_____, "Supernaturalism in John Updike's Fiction," *DAI* 31 (1971): 4802A.

Yates, Norris W., "The Doubt and Faith of John Updike," *CE* 26 (Mar., 1965): 469-74.

Zylstra, S. A., "John Updike and the Parabolic Nature of the World," *Soundings* 56, iii (Fall, 1973): 323-37.

BECH: A BOOK

Detweiler, R., *John Updike*, 143-51.

Hamilton, Alice and Kenneth, "Metamorphosis Through Art: John Updike's BECH: A BOOK," *QQ* 77, iv (Winter, 1970): 624-36. Also in Macnaughton, W. R., ed., *Critical Essays on John Updike*, 115-27.

————, "Mythic Dimensions in Updike's Fiction," *NDQ* 41, iii (Summer, 1973): 63-6.

Hunt, G. W., S. J., *John Updike and the Three Great Secret Things*, 153-63.

Markle, J. B., *Fighters and Lovers*, 168-90.

Tallent, E., *Married Men and Magic Tricks*, 64-73.

Taylor, L. E., *Pastoral and Anti-Pastoral Patterns in John Updike's Fiction*, 129-35.

Uphaus, S. H., *John Updike*, 69-75.

THE CENTAUR

Adler, Renata, "Arcadia, Pa.," *NY* 39 (Apr. 13, 1963): 182-8.

Alley, Alvin D., "THE CENTAUR: Transcendental Imagination and Metamorphic Death," *EJ* 56 (Oct., 1967): 982-5.

Anon., in *TLS* (Sept. 27, 1963): 728. Also in *T. L. S.: Essays and Reviews from The Times Literary Supplement, 1963*, 103-5.

Bailey, Peter, "Notes on the Novel-as-Autobiography," *Genre* 14, i (Spring, 1981): 81-2.

Bell, Vivian, "A Study in Frustration," *Shen* 14 (Summer, 1963): 69-72.

Burchard, R. C., *John Updike*, 53-70.

Curley, Thomas, "Between Heaven and Earth," *Cweal* 78 (Mar. 29, 1963): 26-7.

Davenport, Guy, "Novels Without Masks," *NatR* 14 (Apr. 9, 1963): 287-8.

Detweiler, R., *John Updike*, 80-97.

Doyle, Paul A., "The Fiction of John Updike," *NassauR* 1, i (Spring, 1974): 14-16.

Enright, D. D., "Updike's Ups and Downs," *Holilday* 38 (Nov., 1965): 162-4. Also as "The Inadequate American: John Updike's Fiction," in Enright, D. J., *Conspirators and Poets*, 135-7.

Finkelstein, S., *Existentialism and Alienation in American Literature*, 246-7.

Galloway, David D., "The Absurd Man as Saint: The Novels of John Updike," *MFS* 11 (Summer, 1964): 121-7. Also in Galloway, D. D., *Absurd Hero*, 40-50.

————, "Clown and Saint: The Hero in Current American Fiction," *Crit* 7 (Spring-Summer, 1965): 60-1.

Gardiner, Harold C., in *America* 108 (Mar. 9, 1963): 340-1.

Gilman, Richard, "The Youth of an Author," *NRep* 148 (Apr. 13, 1963): 25-7. Also in Gilman, R., *Confusion of Realms*, 62-8.

Guyol, Hazel S., "The Lord Loves a Cheerful Corpse," *EJ* 55 (Oct., 1966): 863-6.

Hamilton, A. and K., *Elements of John Updike*, 156-80.

Hamilton, Alice and Kenneth, "Mythic Dimensions in Updike's Fiction," *NDQ* 41, iii (Summer, 1973): 54-66 *passim*.

————, "The Validation of Religious Faith in the Writings of John Updike," *SRC* 5, iii (Winter, 1975): 282-3.

Hamilton, K., and A., *John Updike*, 36-9.

Harper, H. M., Jr., *Desperate Faith*, 173-82.

Hill, John S., "Quest for Belief: Theme in the Novels of John Updike," *SHR* 3 (Spring, 1969): 168-71.

Hoag, Ronald W., "THE CENTAUR: What Cures George Caldwell?" *SAF* 8 (1980): 88-98.

————, "A Second Controlling Myth in John Updike's CENTAUR," *SNNTS* 11 (1979): 446-53.

Hunt, G. W., S. J., *John Updike and the Three Great Secret Things*, 49-80.

Hyman, Stanley E., "Chiron at Olinger High," *New Leader* 46 (Feb. 4, 1963): 25-7. Also in Human, S. E., *Standards* 128-32.

Kort, Wesley A., "THE CENTAUR and the Problem of Vocation," *Shriven Selves*, 65-8.

Kuehn, Robert, in *WSCL* 5 (Winter-Spring, 1964): 77-8.

Levidora, Inna, "John Updike's THE CENTAUR in Russian," *Soviet Lit* No. 10 (1965): 188-94.

Malin, Irving, "Occasions for Loving," *KR* 25 (Spring, 1963): 348-52.

Markle, J. B., *Fighters and Lovers*, 61-83.

Mellard, James M., "The Novel as Lyric Elegy: The Mode of John Updike's THE CENTAUR," *TSLL* 21 (Spring, 1979): 112-27. Also in Macnaughton, W. R., ed., *Critical Essays on John Updike*, 217-30.

Miller, Jonathan, "Off-Centaur," *NYRB* 1, i (1963): 28.

Mizener, Arthur, "The American Hero as High School Boy: Peter Caldwell," *Sense of Life in the Modern Novel*, 247-66.

Myers, David, "The Questing Fear: Christian Allegory in John Updike's THE CENTAUR," *TCL* 17 (Apr., 1971): 73-82.

Oates, Joyce Carol, "Updike's American Comedies," *MFS* 21, iii (Fall, 1975): 459-72. Also in Thorburn, D., and H. Eiland, eds., *John Updike*, 53-68.

O'Connor, W. V., in Moore, H. T., ed., *Contemporary American Novelists*, 212-14.

Podhoretz, Norman, "A Dissent on Updike," *Show* 3 (Apr., 1963): 49-52. Also in Podoretz, N., *Doings and Undoings*, 251-7.

Price, Martin, "A Note on Character in THE CENTAUR," in Thorburn, D., and H. Eiland, eds., *John Updike*, 132-3. Excerpted from *YR* 52, iv (June, 1963): 601-2.

Rupp, Richard H., "John Updike: Style in Search of a Center," *SR* 75 (Autumn, 1967): 703-6. Also in Rupp, R., *Celebration in Postwar Fiction*, 51-4.

Samuels, C. T., *John Updike*, 15-19.

Tanner, T., *City of Words*, 284-7.

Tate, Sister Judith M., "John Updike: Of Rabbits and Centaurs," *Critic* 22 (Feb.-Mar., 1964): 44-51.

Taubman, Robert, "God is Delicate," *NStat* 56 (Sept. 27, 1963): 406.

Taylor, L. E., *Pastoral and Anti-Pastoral Patterns in John Updike's Fiction*, 86-101. Also in Thornburn, D., and H. Eiland, eds., *John Updike*, 117-31.

Uphaus, Suzanne, "THE CENTAUR: Updike's Mock Epic," *JNT* 7 (1977): 24-36. Also in Macnaughton, W. R., ed., *Critical Essays on John Updike*, 163-74.

————, *John Updike*, 32-43.

Vargo, Edward P., "The Necessity of Myth in Updike's THE CENTAUR," *PMLA* 88, iii (May, 1973): 452-60.

————, *Rainstorms and Fire*, 81-103.

Vickery, John B., "THE CENTAUR: Myth, History, and Narrative," *MFS* 20, i (Spring, 1974): 29-43.

Walcutt, C. C., *Man's Changing Mask*, 326-30.

Ward, J. A., "John Updike: THE CENTAUR," *Crit* 6, ii (Fall, 1963): 109-14.

Werner, C. H., *Paradoxical Resolutions*, 70-5.

Yates, Norris W., "The Doubt and the Faith of John Updike," *CE* 26 (Mar., 1965): 473-4.

THE COUP

Chukwu, Augustine, "The Dreamer as Leader: Ellellyou in John Updike's THE COUP," *LHY* 23, i (1982): 61-9.

Eiland, Howard, "Updike's Womanly Man," *CentR* 26, iv (Fall, 1982): 317-23.

Hunt, G. W., S. J., *John Updike and the Three Great Secret Things*, 195-206.

Lemeunier, Barbara, "A Fable of Modern Times: America and Africa in John Updike's THE COUP," 101-16 in Ricard, Serge, ed., *Les Americains et les autres*, Aix-en-Provence: Pubs. Un. de Provence, 1982.

Markle, Joyce, "THE COUP: Illusions and Insubstantial Impressions," in Macnaughton, W. R., ed., *John Updike*, 281-301.

Markovitz, Irving L., "John Updike's Africa," *CJAS* 14, iii (1980): 536-45.

McGill, Deborah, "Boy's Life," *Harpers* (Jan., 1979): 87-9. Also in Thorburn, D., and H. Eiland, eds., *John Updike*, 162-6.

Towers, Robert, "Updike in Africa," *NYTBR* (Dec. 10, 1978): 1, 55. Also in Thorburn, D., and H. Eiland, eds., *John Updike*, 157-61.

Uphaus, S. H., *John Updike*, 110-20.

COUPLES

Anon., "Community Feeling," *TLS* (Nov. 7, 1968): 1245. Also in *T.L.S.: Essays and Reviews from The Times Literary Supplement, 1968*, 180-3.

_____, "View From the Catacombs," *Time* 91 (Apr. 26, 1968): 66-8, 73-5.

Backsheider, Paula and Nick, "Two on COUPLES. [1.] Updike's Couples: Squeak in the Night," *MFS* 20, i (Spring, 1974): 45-52.

Burchard, R. C., *John Updike*, 89-132.

Detweiler, R., *John Updike*, 130-42.

Deitweiler, Robert, "Updike's COUPLES: Eros Demythologized," *TCL* 17 (Oct. 1971): 235-46. Also in Macnaughton, W. R., ed., *Critical Essays on John Updike*, 128-39.

Ditsky, John, "Roth, Updike, and the High Expense of Spirit," *UWR* 5, i (Fall, 1969): 111-20.

Eiland, Howard, "Play in COUPLES," in Thorburn, D., and H. Eiland, eds., *John Updike*, 69-83.

Flint, Joyce, "John Updike and COUPLES: The Wasps Dilemma," *RS* 36 (Dec., 1968): 340-7.

Galloway, David D., "Preface to the Revised Edition," *Absurd Hero in American Fiction*, Rev. ed., xiv-xvii.

Gass, William H., "Cock-a-doodle-do," *NYRB* 10 (Apr. 11, 1968): 3. Also in Gass, W. H., *Fiction and the Figures of Life*, 206-11.

Gordon, David J., "Some Recent Novelists: Styles of Martyrdom," *YR* 58 (Autumn, 1968): 117-19.

Hamilton, A. and K., *Elements of John Updike*, 215-42.

Hamilton, Alice and Kenneth, "The Validation of Religious Faith in the Writings of John Updike," *SRC* 5, iii (Winter, 1975): 277-9.

Hill, John S., "Quest for Belief: Theme in the Novels of John Updike," *SHR* 3 (Spring, 1969): 172-5.

Hunt, G. W., *John Updike and the Three Great Secret Things*, 131-8.

Hyman, Stanley E., "Couplings," *New Leader* 51 (May 20, 1968): 20-1.

Jones, Edward T., "An Art of Equilibrium: Piet Mondrian and John Updike," *Connecticut Critic* 7 (Mar., 1973): 4-10.

Lodge, David, "Post-pill Paradise Lost: John Updike's COUPLES," *New Blackfriars* 51 (1970): 511-18. Also in Lodge, D., *Novelists at the Crossroads*, 237-44. Also in Thorburn, D., and H. Eiland, eds., *John Updike*, 84-92.

Markle, J. B., *Fighters and Lovers*, 106-45.

Masters, Kathy, "COUPLES in Love," *Re* 6, iii (1980): 1-8.

McKenzie, Alan T., "Two on COUPLES. [2.] 'A Craftsman's Intimate Satisfactions': The Parlor Games in COUPLES," *MFS* 20, i (Spring, 1974): 53-8.

Nahal, Chaman, "Sexual Psychology in Contemporary American Fiction," in Sharma, J. N., and B. R. Babu, eds., *Contemporary American Life*, 135-47 passim.

Novak, Michael, "Son of the Group," *Critic* 26 (June-July, 1968): 72-4.

Plagman, Linda M., "*Eros* and *Agape*: The Opposition in Updike's COUPLES," *Ren* 28, ii (1976): 83-93.

Robinson, Robert, "COUPLES and Clergy—Some Thoughts," *Listener* 95 (Mar. 25, 1967): 367. [Interview.]

Rupp, Richard H., "John Updike: Style in Search of a Center," *Celebration in Postwar American Fiction*, 214-16.

Samuels, C. T., *John Updike*, 34-7.

Sharrock, Roger, "Singles and Couples: Hemingway's A FAREWELL TO ARMS and Updike's COUPLES," *ArielE* 4, iv (1973): 21-43.

Tallent, E., *Married Men and Magic Tricks*, 45-61.

Tanner, Tony, *City of Words*, 288-92.

_____, "Hello, Olleh," *Spectator* No. 7324 (Nov. 8, 1968): 658-9.

Taylor, L. E., *Pastoral and Anti-Pastoral Patterns in John Updike's Fiction*, 122-8.

Thompson, John, "Updike's COUPLES," *Ctary* 45 (May, 1968): 70-3.

Uphaus, S., *John Updike*, 55-68.

Vargo, E. P., *Rainstorms and Fire*, 124-48.

Waller, G. F., "Updike's COUPLES: A Bartian Parable," *RS* 40 (Mar., 1972): 10-21.

MARRY ME

Cameron, Dee B., "The Unitarian Wife and the One-Eyed Man: Updike's MARRY ME and 'Sunday Teasing'," *BSUF* 21, ii (1980): 54-64.

Eiland, Howard, "Updike's Womanly Man," *CentR* 26, iv (Fall, 1982): 313-17.

Hendin, Josephine, "Updike as Matchmaker," *Nation* 223, xiv (Oct. 30, 1976): 437-9. Also in Thorburn, D., and H. Eiland, eds., *John Updike*, 99-106.

Hunt, G. W., S. J., *John Updike and the Three Great Secret Things*, 139-47.

Tallent, E., *Married Men and Magic Tricks*, 33-44.

Uphaus, S. H., *John Updike*, 102-9.

A MONTH OF SUNDAYS

Detweiler, Robert, "Updike's A MONTH OF SUNDAYS and the Language of the Unconscious," *JAAR* 47 (1979): 609-25.

Doody, Terrence A., "Updike's Idea of Reification," *ConL* 20, ii (Spring, 1979): 204-12.

Hunt, G. W., S. J., *John Updike and the Three Great Secret Things*, 181-94.

_____, "Updike's Omega-Shaped Shelter: Structure and Psyche in A MONTH OF SUNDAYS," *Crit* 19, iii (1978): 47-60.

Sevick, Marly A., "Romantic Ministers and the Phallic Knights: A Study of A MONTH OF SUNDAYS, LANCELOT, and FALCONER," *DAI* 40 (1979): 860A.

Steiner, George, "Scarlet Letters," *NY* 51 (Mar. 10, 1975): 116-18. Also in Thorburn, D., and H. Eiland, eds., *John Updike*, 93-8.

Uphaus, S. J., *John Updike*, 91-101.

_____, "The Unified Vision of A MONTH OF SUNDAYS," *UWR* 12, ii (1977): 5-16.

Waller, Gary, "Stylus Dei or the Open-Endedness of Debate?: Success and Failure in A MONTH OF SUNDAYS," in Macnaughton, W. R., ed., *Critical Essays on John Updike*, 269-80.

OF THE FARM

Aldridge, J. W., "The Private Vice of John Updike," *Time to Murder and Create*, 164-70.

Burchard, R. C., *John Updike*, 71-88.

Detweiler, R., *John Updike*, 98-110.

Enright, D. J., "Updike's Ups and Downs," *Holiday* 38 (Nov., 1965): 165-6. Also as "The Inadequate American: John Updike's Fiction," in Enright, D. J., *Conspirators and Poets*, 138-40.

Hamilton, A., and K., *Elements of John Updike*, 181-99.

Hamiltom, K. and A., *John Updike*, 43-6.

Harper, H. M., Jr., *Desperate Faith*, 182-6.

Hunt, G. W., S. J., *John Updike and the Three Great Secret Things*, 81-101.

Markle, J. B., *Fighters and Lovers*, 84-105.

Rupp, Richard H., "John Updike: Style in Search of a Center," *SR* 75 (Autumn, 1967): 706-9.

Samuels, C. T., *John Updike*, 22-7. Also in Thorburn, D., and H. Eiland, eds., *John Updike*, 151-4.

Tallent, E., *Married Men and Magic Tricks*, 25-31.

Taylor, Larry, "The Wide-Hipped Wife and the Painted Landscape: Pastoral Ideals in OF THE FARM," in Taylor, L. E., *Pastoral and Anti-Pastoral Patterns in John Updike's Fiction*, 102-11. Also in Macnaughton, W. R., ed., *Critical Essays on John Updike*, 140-7.

Uphaus, S. H., *John Updike*, 44-54.

Vargo, E. P., *Rainstorms and Fire*, 104-23. Also in Thorburn, D., and H. Eiland, eds., *John Updike*, 134-50.

THE POORHOUSE FAIR

Balliett, Whitney, "Writer's Writer," *NY* (Feb. 7, 1959): 138-42.

Buchanan, Leigh, in *Epoch* 9 (Spring, 1959): 252-4.

Burchard, R. C., *John Updike*, 30-41.

Detweiler, R., *John Updike*, 31-44.

Doyle, Paul A., "The Fiction of John Updike," *NassauR* 1, i (Spring, 1964): 9-12.

_____, "Updike Fiction: Motifs and Techniques," *CathW* 196 (Sept., 1964): 356-8.

Fitelson, David, "Conflict Unresolved," *Ctary* 27 (Mar., 1959): 275-6.

Galloway, David D., "The Absurd Man as Saint: The Novels of John Updike," *MFS* 10 (Summer, 1964): 111-14. Also in Galloway, D. D., *Absurd Hero*, 21-7.

Gilman, Richard, in *Cweal* 69 (Feb. 6, 1959): 499-500.

Grummond, W. W. de, "Classical Influence in THE POORHOUSE FAIR," *AN&Q* 13, ii (1974): 21-3.

Hamilton, Alice and Kenneth, *Elements of John Updike*, 119-36.

_____, "The Validation of Religious Faith in the Writings of John Updike," *SRC* 5, iii (Winter, 1975): 276-77.

Hamilton, K. and A., *John Updike*, 13-22.

Harper, H. M., Jr., *Desperate Faith*, 163-5.

Hunt, G. W., S. J., *John Updike and the Three Great Secret Things*, 38-41.

Klausler, Alfred P., "Steel Wilderness," *ChC* 78 (Feb. 22, 1961): 245-7.

Markle, J. B., *Fighters and Lovers*, 13-36. Also, abridged, in Thorburn, D., and H. Eiland, eds., *John Updike*, 109-16.

O'Connor, W. V., in Moore, H. T., ed., *Contemporary American Novelists*, 207-8.

Rupp, Richard H., "John Updike: Style in Search of a Center," *Celebration in Postwar American Fiction*, 47-8.

Samuels, C. T., *John Updike*, 21-4.

Searles, George J., "THE POORHOUSE FAIR: Updike's Thesis Statement," in Macnaughton, W. R., ed., *Critical Essay on John Updike*, 231-6.

Tallent, E., *Married Men and Magic Tricks*, 13-23.

Tanner, T., *City of Words*, 276-9.

Taylor, L. E., *Pastoral and Anti-Pastoral Patterns in John Updike's Fiction*, 50-5.

Tazoe, Kaneko, "Religious Themes in THE POORHOUSE FAIR," *KAL* 20 (1979): 29-34.

Uphaus, S. H., *John Updike*, 10-18.

Vargo, E. P., *Rainstorms and Fire*, 29-50.

Ward, J. A., "John Updike's Fiction," *Crit* 5, i (Spring-Summer, 1962): 30-3.

Yates, Norris W., "The Doubt and Faith of John Updike," *CE* 26 (Mar., 1965): 470-1.

RABBIT, RUN

Allen, M., *Necessary Blankness*, 114-21.

Alley, Alvin D., and Hugh Agee, "Existential Heroes: Frank Alpine and Rabbit Angstrom," *BSUF* 9 (1968): 3-5.

Balliett, Witney, "Books: The American Expression," *NY* 36 (Nov. 5, 1960): 222-4.

Borgman, Paul, "The Tragic Hero of Updike's RABBIT, RUN," *Ren* 29 (1977): 106-12.

Bowman, Diane K., "Flying High: American Icarus in Morrison, Roth, and Updike," *PCL* 8 (1982): 10-17.

Brenner, Gerry, "RABBIT, RUN: John Updike's Criticism of the 'Return to Nature'," *TCL* 12 (Apr., 1966): 3-14. Also in Macnaughton, W. R., ed., *Critical Essays on John Updike*, 91-104.

Bryant, J. H., *Open Decision*, 240-5.

Burchard, R. C., *John Updike*, 42-52.

Burhans, Clinton S., Jr., "Things Falling Apart: Structure and Theme in RABBIT, RUN," *SNNTS* 5, iii (Fall, 1973): 336-51. Also in Macnaughton, W. R., ed., *Critical Essays on John Updike*, 148-62.

Burr, Richard W., *Puer Aeternus: An Examination of John Updike's RABBIT, RUN*, Zurich: Juris, 1974): 1974.

Detweiler, R., *Four Spiritual Crises in Mid-Century American Fiction*, 14-24.

_____, *John Updike*, 45-59.

Doner, Dean, "Robert Angstrom's World," *New World Writing*, No. 20, Phila., and N.Y.: Lippincott, 1962, 58-75. Also in Thorburn, D., and H. Eiland, eds., *John Updike*, 17-34.

Doyle, Paul A., "The Fiction of John Updike," *NassauR* 1, i (Spring, 1964): 12-13.

_____, "Updike's Fiction: Motifs and Techniques," *CathW* 119 (Sept., 1964): 358-9.

Duncan, Graham H., "The Thing Itself in RABBIT, RUN," *EngR* 13 (Apr., 1963): 25-8, 36-7.

Ellis, James, "Karl Barth and Socrates as Mouseketeers in RABBIT, RUN," *NConL* 7, v (1977): 3.

_____, "Plato's 'Allegory of the Cave' in RABBIT, RUN," *NMAL* 2 (1978): Item 15.

Falke, Wayne C, "The Novel of Disentanglement: A Thematic Study of Lewis's BABBITT, Bromfield's MR. SMITH and Updike's RABBIT, RUN," *DA* 28 (1967): 194A.

Finkelstein, S., *Existentialism and Alienation in American Literature*, 244-6.

Galloway, David D., "The Absurd Man as Saint: The Novels of John Updike," *MFS* 10 (Summer, 1964): 114-21. Also in Galloway, D. D., *Absurd Hero*, 27-40.

_____, "Clown and Saint: The Hero in Current American Fiction," *Crit* 7 (Spring-Summer, 1965): 59-60.

Gilman, Richard, "A Distinguished Image of Precarious Life," *Cweal* 78 (Oct. 28, 1960): 128-9. Also in Thorburn, D., and H. Eiland, eds., *John Updike*, 13-16.

Hallissy, Margaret, "Updike's RABBIT, RUN and Pascal's PENSEES," *C&L* 30, ii (Winter, 1981): 25-32.

Hamilton, Alice and Kenneth, "The Validation of Religious Faith in the Writings of John Updike," *SRC* 5, iii (Winter, 1975): 279-891.

_____, *Elements of John Updike*, 137-55.

Hamilton, K. and A., *John Updike*, 31-6.

Harper, H. M., Jr., *Desperate Faith*, 165-73.

Hogan, Robert E., "Catharism and John Updike's RABBIT, RUN," *Ren* 32, iv (1980): 229-39.

Horton, Andrew S., "Ken Kesey, John Updike and the Lone Ranger," *JPC* 8, iii (Winter, 1974): 574-8.

Hunt, G. W., S. J., *John Updike and the Three Great Secret Things*, 41-8.

Killinger, John, "The Death of God in American Literature," *SHR* 2 (Spring, 1968): 167-8.

Klausler, Alfred P., "Steel Wilderness," *ChC* 78 (Feb. 22, 1961): 245-7.

Lawson, Lewis A., "Rabbit Angstrom as a Religious Sufferer," *JAAR* 42, ii (June, 1974): 232-46.

Le Pellec, Ives, "Robert Underground," in Johnson, I. D., and C. Johnson, eds., *Les Americanistes*, 94-109.

Locke, Richard, "Rabbit Redux," *NYTBR* 76 (Nov. 7, 1971): 1-2+.

Lunden, Rolf, "DARK LAUGHTER and RABBIT, RUN: Studies in Instinctive Behavior," *SN* 49 (1977): 59-68.

Lyons, Eugene, "John Updike: The Beginning and the End," *Crit* 14, ii (1973): 45-7.

Lyons, R., "A High E.Q.," *MinnR* 1 (Spring, 1961): 385-9.

Markle, J. B., *Fighters and Lovers*, 37-60.

Martin, John S., "Rabbit's Faith: Grace and the Transformation of the Heart," *PCP* 17 (1982): 103-11.

McGinnis, Wayne D., "Salvation by Death in RABBIT, RUN," *NConL* 8, ii (1978): 7-8.

Miller, Nolan, "Three of the 'Best'," *AR* 21 (Spring, 1961): 120-3.

O'Connor, W. V., in Moore, H. T., ed., *Contemporary American Novelists*, 209-12.

Oriard, Michael V., "The Athlete-Hero and Democratic Ideals," *JAC* 1, iii (Fall, 1978): 516-19.

Rotundo, Barbara, "RABBIT, RUN and A TALE OF PETER RABBIT," *NConL* 1, iii (May, 1971): 2-3.

Rupp, Richard H., "John Updike: Style in Search of a Center," *SR* 75 (Autumn, 1967): 699-703. Also in Rupp, R. H., *Celebration in Postwar American Fiction*, 48-51.

Samuels, C. T., *John Updike*, 37-43.

Siegel, Gary, "Robert Runs Down," in Peary, G., and R. Shatzkin, eds., *Modern American Novel in the Movies*, 247-55.

Sinclair, Andrew, "See How He Runs," *T&T* 42 (Sept. 21, 1961): 1571.

Standley, Fred L., "RABBIT, RUN: An Image of Life," *MQ* 8 (July, 1967): 371-86.

Stubbs, John C., "The Search for Perfection in RABBIT, RUN," *Crit* 10, ii (1968): 94-101.

Suderman, Elmer F., "The Right Way and the Good Way in RABBIT, RUN," *UR* 36, i (Oct., 1969): 13-21.

Sykes, Robert H., "Paradichlorobenzine in Updike's RABBIT, RUN," *NMAL* 4 (1980): Item 19.

Tallent, E., *Married Men and Magic Tricks*, 75-91.

Tanner, T., *City of Words*, 279-84.

Tate, Sister Judith M., "John Updike: Of Rabbits and Centaurs," *Critic* 22 (Feb.-Mar., 1964): 44-51.

Taylor, L. E., *Pastoral and Anti-Pastoral Patterns in John Updike's Fiction*, 70-85.

Terry, R. Franklin, "Luckmann's 'Invisible Religion' and the Problem of Belief in Updike's Harry Angstrom," *IR* 33, i (Winter, 1976): 39-46.

Thompson, John, "Other People's Affairs," *PR* 27 (Jan.-Feb., 1961): 120-2.

Uphaus, S. H., *John Updike*, 19-31.

Vargo, E. P., *Rainstorms and Fire*, 51-80.

Waldmeir, Joseph, "It's the Going That's Important, Not the Getting There: Rabbit's Questing Non-Quest," *MFS* 20, i (Spring, 1974): 13-27.

Wilhelm, Albert E., "The Clothing Motif in Updike's RABBIT, RUN," *SAB* 40, iv (1975): 87-9.

_____, "Rabbit Restored: A Further Note on Updike's Revisions," *NMAL* 6 (1982): Item 7.

_____, "The Search for Meaning: Work in John Updike's Fiction," in Harkness, Don, ed., *Perspectives on American Business*, Ţampa, Fla.: Amer. Studies Pr., 1982, 30-3.

_____, "Updike's Revisions of RABBIT, RUN," *NMAL* 5, iii (Summer, 1981): Item 15.

RABBIT REDUX

Allen, M., *Necessary Blankness*, 121-30.

Alter, Robert, "Updike, Malamud, and the Fire This Time," *Ctary* 54, iv (Oct., 1972): 70-4. Also in Alter, R., *Defenses of the Imagination*, 239-48. Also, abridged, in Thorburn, D., and H. Eiland, eds., *John Updike*, 39-49.

Detweiler, R., *John Updike*, 152-66.

Epstein, Seymour, "The Emperor's Blue Jeans," *DQ* 6, iv (1972): 89-95.

Falke, Wayne, "America Strikes Out: Updike's RABBIT REDUX," *AmEx* 3, iii (1974): 18-21.

_____, "RABBIT REDUX: Time/Order/God," *MFS* 20, i (Spring, 1974): 59-75.

Hamilton, Alice and Kenneth, "John Updike's Prescription for Survival," *ChC* 89 (July 5, 1972): 740-4.

Held, George, "Men on the Moon: American Novelists Explore Lunar Space," *MQR* 18 (1979): 333-41.

Horton, Andrew S., "Ken Kesey, John Updike and The Lone Ranger," *JPC* 8 (Winter, 1974): 574-81. Also in Filler, L., ed., *Seasoned Authors for a New Season*, 85-90.

Hunt, G. W., S. J., *John Updike and the Three Great Secret Things*, 165-79.

LePellec, Yves, "Rabbit Underground," in Johnson, I. D., and C. Johnson, eds., *Les Americanistes*, 94-109.

Lyons, Eugene, "John Updike: The Beginning of the End," *Crit* 14, ii (1973): 47-58.

Markle, J. B., *Fighters and Lovers*, 146-67.

Mesher, David, "Three Men on the Moon: Friedman, Updike, Bellow, and Apollo Eleven," *RS* 47, ii (1979): 70-2.

Russell, Mariann, "White Man's Black Man: Three Views," *CLAJ* 17 (1973): 96-8.

Slethaug, Gordon E., "RABBIT REDUX: 'Freedom is Made of Brambles'," in Macnaughton, W. R., ed., *Critical Essays on John Updike*, 237-53.

Stafford, William T., "The Black White Continuum: Some Recent Examples in Bellow, Malamud and Updike," *Books Speaking to Books*, 91-100.

Turner, Kermit [S.], "Robert Brough Nowhere: John Updike's RABBIT REDUX," *SCR* 8, i (Nov., 1975): 35-42.

Uphaus, S. H., *John Updike*, 76-90.

Vanderwerken, David L., "Rabbit 'Re-docks': Updike's Inner Space Odyssey," *CollL* 2, i (1975): 73-8.

Vargo, E. P., *Rainstorms and Fire*, 149-71.

Waldmeir, Joseph, "Rabbit Redux Reduced: Rededicated? Redeemed?" in Waldmeir, J., ed., *Essays in Honor of Russel B. Nye*, East Lansing: Michigan State Un. Pr., 1978, 247-61.

BIBLIOGRAPHY

Galloway, D. D., *Absurd Hero*, 198-200.

Gearhart, Elizabeth A., *John Updike: A Comprehensive Bibliography with Selected Annotations*, Norwood, Pa.: Norwood Pr., 1978.

Hamilton, K. and A., *John Updike*, 47-8.

Macnaughton, William R., "Introduction: A Survey of John Updike Scholarship in English," in Macnaughton, W. R., ed., *Critical Essays on John Updike*, 1-36.

Meyer, Arlin G., with Some Additions by Michael A. Olivas, "Criticism of John Updike: A Selected Checklist," *MFS* 20 (Spring, 1974): 121-33.

Olivas, Michael A., *An Annotated Bibliography of John Updike Criticism 1967-1973, and a Checklist of His Works*, N.Y.: Garland, 1975.

Roberts, Roy, comp., "John Updike: A Bibliographical Checklist," *ABC* 1, i (1980): 5-12, 40-4; ii (1980): 39-47.

Samuels, C. T., *John Updike*, 44-6.

Sokoloff, B. A., and David Arnason, *John Updike: A Comprehensive Bibliography*, Darby: Pa.: Darby Pr., 1970; Folcroft, Pa.: Folcroft Pr, 1971; Norwood, Pa.: Norwood Pr., 1973.

Taylor, C. Clarke, *John Updike: A Bibliography*, Kent, Ohio: Kent State Un. Pr., 1968.

URIS, LEON (MARCUS), 1924-

GENERAL

Downey, Sharon D., and Richard A. Kallan, "Semi-Aesthetic Detachment: The Fusing of Fictional and External Worlds in the Situational Literature of Leon Uris," *ComM* 49, iii (Sept., 1982): 192-204.

EXODUS

Asbahi, Muhammad M. S., "History and Ideology in EXODUS and Other Novels," *DAI* 34 (1974): 5153A.

TRINITY

Hall, Wayne, "TRINITY: The Formulas of History," *Eire* 13, iv (1978): 137-44.

VAN PEEBLES, MELVIN, 1932-

GENERAL

Botto, Lewis, "Melvin Van Peebles: Work in Progress," *Black Times* 2, x (1972): 12-13. [Interview.]

A BEAR FOR THE FBI

Bauerle, R. F., "The Theme of Absurdity in Melvin Van Peebles' A BEAR FOR THE FBI," *NConL* 1, iv (Sept., 1971): 11-12.

VIDAL, GORE, 1925-

GENERAL

Aldridge, J. W., *After the Lost Generation*, 170-83.

Anon., "Playboy Interview: Gore Vidal," *Playboy* 16 (June, 1969): 77-96, 238.

Barton, David, "Narrative Patterns in the Novels of Gore Vidal," *NConL* 11, iv (Sept., 1981): 3-5.

Cheshire, David, "Gore Vidal: On Success, Legends and Reality," *Listener* 94 (Aug. 7, 1975): 167-8. [Interview.]

Clarke, Gerald, "The Art of Fiction 50: Gore Vidal," *ParisR* 5 (Fall, 1974): 130-65. [Interview.]

Dick, Bernard F., "Anais Nin and Gore Vidal: A Study in Literary Incompatability," *Mosaic* 11, ii (Winter, 1978): 153-62.

_____, *Apostate Angel*.

Kempton, Beverly, "Conversation with Gore Vidal," *Oui* 4, iv (1975): 72-4, 82, 134-8.

Kiernan, R. F., *Gore Vidal*.

Krim, Seymour, "Reflections on a Ship That's Not Sinking," *LonM* 10, ii (May, 1970): 26-43.

Stanton, Robert J., *Views from a Window: Conversations with Gore Vidal*, N.Y.: Stuart, 1980.

Walter, Eugene, "Conversations with Gore Vidal," *Transatlantic Rev*, 4 (Summer, 1960): 5-17.

White, R. L., *Gore Vidal*.

BURR

Dick, B. F., *Apostate Angel*, 181-8.

Golenpolsky, T., "Today About the Past," in Vroon, R., tr., *20th Century American Literature*, 492-5.

Kiernan, R. F., *Gore Vidal*, 75-85.

Klein, Jeffrey, "Politics and Self-Serving Imagination," *NAmR* 259, ii (1974): 57-61. [Compares Rader's BLOOD DUES, V's BURR, and Wicker's FACING THE LIONS.]

Lemeunier, Yves, "Aaron Burr: The American Non-President," 141-55, in *La Presidence Americaine*. Actes du GRENA, Groupe de Recherches et d'Etudes Nord-Americaines, 1979. Aix-en-Provence: Pubs. Un. de Provence, 1980.

THE CITY AND THE PILLAR

Aldridge, J. W., *After the Lost Generation*, 175-8.

Dick, B. F., *Apostate Angel*, 26-39.

Hoffman, Stanton, "The Cities of Night: John Rechy's CITY OF NIGHT and the American Literature of Homosexuality," *ChiR* 17, ii-iii (1964-65): 197-8.

Kiernan, R. F., *Gore Vidal*, 37-44.

McLaughlin, Richard, "Precarious Status," *SatR* 31 (Jan. 10, 1948): 14-15.

Shrike, J. S., "Recent Phenomena," *HudR* 1 (Spring, 1948): 136-44.

CREATION

Kiernan, R. F., *Gore Vidal*, 58-66.

Murry, Oswyn, "Whoring after Strange Gods," *TLS* 4078 (May 29, 1981): 595.

DARK GREEN, BRIGHT RED

Barr, Donald, "From Patio to Jungle," *NYTBR* (Oct. 8, 1950): 4, 28.

Dick, B. F., *Apostate Angel*, 60-4.

Kiernan, R. F., *Gore Vidal*, 126-8.

White, R. L., *Gore Vidal*, 71-7.

Kiernan, R. F., *Gore Vidal*, 85-93.

Schlereth, Thomas J., "Fiction and Facts: Henry Adams's DEMOCRACY and Gore Vidal's 1876," *SoQ* 16, iii (1978): 209-22.

IN A YELLOW WOOD

Aldridge, J. W., *After the Lost Generation*, 173-6.

Dick, B. F., *Apostate Angel*, 18-21.

Kiernan, R. F., *Gore Vidal*, 118-21.

White, R. L., *Gore Vidal*, 71-7.

THE JUDGMENT OF PARIS

Aldridge, John W., "Three Tempted Him," *NYTBR* (Mar. 9, 1952): 4, 29.

Dick, B. F., *Apostate Angel*, 66-77.

Kiernan, R. F., *Gore Vidal*, 11-17.

White, R. L., *Gore Vidal*, 84-9.

JULIAN

Allen, Walter, "The Last Pagan," *NYRB* 3 (July 30, 1964): 20-1.

Auchincloss, Louis, "The Best Man, Vintage 361 A.D.," *Life* 58 (June 12, 1964): 19, 21.

Dick, B. F., *Apostate Angel*, 103-17.

Kiernan, R. F., *Gore Vidal*, 45-58.

Leone, Arthur T., in *CathW* 199 (Sept., 1964): 381-4.

White, R. L., *Gore Vidal*, 111-19.

KALKI

Berryman, Charles, "Satire in Gore Vidal's KALKI," *Crit* 22, ii (1980): 88-96.

Kiernan, R. F., *Gore Vidal*, 24-31.

MESSIAH

Dick, B. F., *Apostate Angel*, 94-103.

Kiernan, R. F., *Gore Vidal*, 129-32.

White, R. L., *Gore Vidal*, 89-94.

MYRA BRECKINRIDGE

Boyette, Purvis E., "MYRA BRECKINRIDGE and Imitative Form," *MFS* 17, ii (Summer, 1971): 229-38.

Dick, B. F., *Apostate Angel*, 141-70.

Kiernan, R. F., *Gore Vidal*, 94-100.

Wilhelm, John F., and Mary Ann, "MYRA BRECKINRIDGE: A Study in Identity," *JPC* 3 (1969): 590-9.

MYRON

Kiernan, R. F., *Gore Vidal*, 100-9.

A SEARCH FOR THE KING

Aldridge, J. W., *After the Lost Generation*, 181-3.

Dick, B. F., *Apostate Angel*, 54-60.

Kiernan, R. F., *Gore Vidal*, 124-6.

White, R. L., *Gore Vidal*, 64-71.

THE SEASON OF COMFORT

Aldridge, J. W., *After the Lost Generation*, 178-81.

————, "A Boy and His Mom," *SatR* 32 (Jan. 15, 1949): 19-20.

Dick, B. F., *Apostate Angel*, 40-52.

Kiernan, R. F., *Gore Vidal*, 121-4.

White, R. L., *Gore Vidal*, 58-64.

TWO SISTERS

Dick, B. F., *Apostate Angel*, 171-81.

Kiernan, R. F., *Gore Vidal*, 17-24.

WASHINGTON, D.C.

Dick, B. F., *Apostate Angel*, 125-34.

Kiernan, R. F., *Gore Vidal*, 67-75.

Lehan, Richard, "Fiction, 1967," *ConL* 9, iv (Autumn, 1968): 543-4.

Sheed, Wilfred, "Affairs of State," *Ctary* 44 (Sept., 1967): 93-4.

White, R. L., *Gore Vidal*, 119-24.

WILLIWAW

Aldridge, J. W., *After the Lost Generation*, 170-3.

Dick, B. F., *Apostate Angel*, 12-18.

Kiernan, R. F., *Gore Vidal*, 32-7.

White, R. L., *Gore Vidal*, 38-44.

BIBLIOGRAPHY

Gilliam, Loretta M., "Gore Vidal: A Checklist, 1945-1969," *BB* 30 (Jan.-Mar., 1973): 1-9, 44.

Stanton, Robert J., *Gore Vidal: A Primary and Secondary Bibliography*, London: Prior, 1978.

White, R. L., *Gore Vidal*, 147-52.

VONNEGUT, KURT, 1922-

GENERAL

Abadi-Nagy, Zoltan, "Ironic Messianism in Recent American Fiction," *SEA* 4 (1978): 63-83. [Not seen.]

_____, "'The Skilful Seducer': Of Vonnegut's Brand of Comedy," *HSE* 8 (1974): 45-56.

Aldiss, Brian, "Guru Number Four," *Summary* 1, ii (1971): 63-8.

Austin, Marvin F., Jr., "The Novels of Kurt Vonnegut, Jr.: A Confrontation with the Modern World," *DAI* 36 (1975): 3707A.

Berryman, Charles, "After the Fall: Kurt Vonnegut," *Crit* 26 (Winter, 1985): 96-102.

Bodtke, Richard, "Great Sorrows, Small Joys: The World of Kurt Vonnegut, Jr.," *Crosscurrents* 20 (Winter, 1970): 120-5.

Bosworth, David, "The Literature of Awe," *AR* 37 (Winter, 1979): 14-17.

Bryan, C. D. B, "Kurt Vonnegut on Target," *NRep* 155 (Oct. 8, 1966): 21-6.

Bryant, J. H., *Open Decision*, 303-25.

Buck, Lynn, "Vonnegut's World of Comic Futility," *SAF* 3, ii (Autumn, 1975): 181-98.

Burhans, Clinton S., Jr., "Hemingway and Vonnegut: Diminishing Vision in a Dying Age," *MFS* 21, ii (Summer, 1975): 173-91.

Calvert, Christopher, "The Hostile Universe: Studies in the Novels of Kurt Vonnegut, Jr.," *DAI* 39 (1979): 4254A.

Carson, Ronald, "Kurt Vonnegut: Matter-of-Fact Moralist," *Listening* 6 (Autumn, 1971): 182-95.

Casey, John, and Joe D. Bellamy, "Kurt Vonnegut, Jr.," in Bellamy, J. D., ed., *New Fiction*, 194-207. [Interview.]

Clancy, L. J., "'If the Accident Will': The Novels of Kurt Vonnegut," *Meanjin* 30 (1971): 37-45.

_____, "Running Experiments Off," *Meanjin* 30, i (1971): 46-54. [Interview.]

Crump, G. G., "D. H. Lawrence and the Immediate Present: Kurt Vonnegut, Jr., Ken Kesey, and Wright Morris," *DHLR* 10 (Summer, 1977): 103-41.

Dahiya, Bhim, "Structural Patterns in the Novels of Barth, Vonnegut, and Pynchon," *IJAS* 5, i-ii (1976): 53-68. [Not seen.]

DeMott, Benjamin, "Vonnegut's Otherworldly Laughter," *SatR* 54 (May 1, 1971): 29-32, 38.

Engel, David, "On the Question of Foma: A Study of the Novels of Kurt Vonnegut," *RQ* 5, ii (Feb., 1972): 119-28.

Festa, Conrad, "Vonnegut's Satire," in Klinkowitz, J., and D. L. Lawler, eds., *Vonnegut in America*, 133-49.

Fiedler, Leslie A., "The Divine Stupidity of Kurt Vonnegut," *Esquire* 74, iii (Sept., 1970): 195-200, 202-4.

Fiene, Donald M., "Elements of Dostoevsky in the Novels of Kurt Vonnegut," *DStudies* 2 (1981): 129-42.

_____, "Kurt Vonnegut's Popularity in the Soviet Union and His Affinities with Russian Literature," *RLT* 14 (Winter, 1976): 166-84.

_____, "Vonnegut's Quotations from Dostoevsky," *NMAL* 1 (1977): Item 29.

Frank, Armin P., "Where Laughing Is the Only Way to Stop It from Hurting," *Summary* 1, ii (1971): 51-62.

Gerson, Steven M., "Paradise Sought: Adamic Imagery in Selected Novels by Saul Bellow and Kurt Vonnegut, Jr.," *DAI* 39 (1978): 285A.

Giannone, Richard, "Violence in the Fiction of Kurt Vonnegut," *Thought* 56, ccxx (Mar., 1981): 58-76.

_____, *Vonnegut*.

Godshalk, William, "The Recurring Characters of Kurt Vonnegut," *NConL* 3, i (Jan., 1973): 2-3.

Goldsmith, D. H., *Kurt Vonnegut*.

_____, "The Novels of Kurt Vonnegut, Jr.," *DAI* 31 (1979): 2916A.

Goshorn, James W., "The Queasy World of Kurt Vonnegut, Jr.: Satire in the Novels," *DAI* 32 (1972): 6426A-27A.

Grossman, Edward, "Vonnegut and His Audience," *Ctary* 58, i (July, 1974): 40-6.

Group, Robert J., "Familiar Novelties: Kurt Vonnegut's Comic Epics in Prose," *DAI* 39 (1978): 1567A.

Hancock, Joyce A., "Kurt Vonnegut and the Folk Society," *DAI* 39 (1978): 3580A.

Harris, Charles B., "Illusion and Absurdity: The Novels of Kurt Vonnegut, Jr.," *Contemporary American Novelists of the Absurd*, 51-75.

Hayman, David, David Michaelis, George Plimpton and Richard L. Rhodes, "Kurt Vonnegut: The Art of Fiction 64," *ParisR* 69 (Spring, 1977): 46-103.

Hildebrand, Tim, "Two or Three Things I Know about Kurt Vonnegut's Imagination," in Klinkowitz, J., and J. Somer, eds., *Vonnegut Statement*, 121-32.

Hoffman, Thomas P., "The Theme of Loneliness in Vonnegut's First Four Novels," *DAI* 39 (1979): 4256A-57A.

Hudson, Wilson, "Vonnegut and Science Fiction," *JASAT* 4 (1973): 74-82. [Not seen.]

Hume, Kathryn, "The Heraclitean Cosmos on Kurt Vonnegut," *PLL* 18, ii (Spring, 1982): 208-24.

_____, "Kurt Vonnegut and the Myths and Symbols of Meaning," *TSLL* 24, iv (Winter, 1982): 429-47.

_____, "Vonnegut's Self-Projections: Symbolic Characters and Symbolic Fiction," *JNT* 12, iii (Fall, 1982): 177-90.

Irving, John, "Kurt Vonnegut and His Critics," *NRep* 181 (Sept. 22, 1979): 41-49.

Jones, Peter, "At War with Technology: Kurt Vonnegut, Jr.," *War and the Novelist*, 203-22.

Kenedy, R. C., "Kurt Vonnegut, Jr.," *ArtI* 15, v (May 20, 1971): 20-5.

Kennard, Jean E., "Kurt Vonnegut, Jr.: The Sirens of Satire," *Number and Nightmare*, 101-28.

Kiely, Robert, "Satire as Fantasy," *Summary* 1, ii (1971): 41-43.

Klinkowitz, Jerome, *Kurt Vonnegut*.

_____, "Kurt Vonnegut and Donald Barthelme: The American Image," in *The American 1960's*, Ames: Iowa State Un. Pr., 1980, 47-58.

_____, "Kurt Vonnegut, Jr.'s SuperFiction," *Revue Francaise d'Etudes Americaines* (Sorbonne) 1 (Apr., 1976): 115-24. Also, revised, in Klinkowitz, J., *The Life of Fiction*, Urbana: Un. of Illinois Pr., 1977, 84-93.

_____, "The Literary Career of Kurt Vonnegut, Jr.," *MFS* 19, i (Spring, 1973): 57-67.

_____, *Literary Disruptions*, 33-61.

_____, and D. L. Lawler, eds., *Vonnegut in America*.

_____, and J. Somer, eds., *Vonnegut Statement*.

Lundquist, J., *Kurt Vonnegut*.

Marino, Vincent, "Creating Conscience through Black Humor: A Study of Kurt Vonnegut's Novels," *DAI* 39 (1978): 2941A.

May, John R., "Vonnegut's Humor and the Limits of Hope," *TCL* 18 (Jan., 1972): 25-36.

Mayo, C., *Kurt Vonnegut*.

McGinnis, Wayne D., "Kurt Vonnegut, Jr.'s Confrontation with Meaninglessness," *DAI* 35 (1974): 3753A-54A.

_____, "Names in Vonnegut's Fiction," *NConL* 3, iv (Sept., 1973): 7-9.

McNelly, Willis E., "Kurt Vonnegut as Science-Fiction Writer," in Klinkowitz, J., and D. L. Lawler, eds., *Vonnegut in America*, 87-96.

Myers, David, "Kurt Vonnegut, Jr.: Morality—Myth in the Antinovel," *IFR* 3, i (Jan., 1976): 52-6.

Nadeau, Robert L., "Physics and Metaphysics in the Novels of Kurt Vonnegut, Jr.," *Mosaic* 13, ii (Winter, 1980): 37-47.

Nelson, Jon E., "Yeats and Vonnegut: The Artist as Mythmaker," *Lutheran Quarterly* (Summer, 1973): 124-35.

Nelson, Joyce, "Vonnegut and 'Bugs in Amber'," *JPC* 7, iii (Winter, 1973): 551-57.

Olderman, R. M., *Beyond the Waste Land*, 189-219.

Palmer, Raymond C., "Vonnegut's Major Concerns," *IEY* 14 (Fall, 1969): 3-10.

Pauly, Rebecca M., "The Moral Stance of Kurt Vonnegut," *Extrapolation* 15, i (Dec., 1973): 66-71.

Pinsker, Sanford, "Fire and Ice: The Radical Cuteness of Kurt Vonnegut, Jr.," *STwC* 13 (Spring, 1974): 1-19. Also in Pinsker, S., *Between Two Worlds*, 87-101.

Ranly, Ernest W., "What Are People For? Man, Fate and Kurt Vonnegut," *Cweal* 94 (May 7, 1971): 207-11.

Reed, P. J., *Kurt Vonnegut, Jr.*

_____, "The Later Vonnegut," in Klinkowitz, J., and D. L. Lawler, eds., *Vonnegut in America*, 150-86.

Reilly, Charles, "An Interview with Kurt Vonnegut, Jr.," *DelLR* (Spring, 1976): 20-7.

_____, "Two Conversations with Kurt Vonnegut," *CollL* 7 (1980): 1-29.

Rice, Elaine F., "The Satire of John Barth and Kurt Vonnegut, Jr.: The Menippean Tradition in the 1960's America," *DAI* 35 (1975): 7876A-77A.

Rubens, Philip M., "'Nothing's Ever Final': Vonnegut's Concept of Time," *CollL* 6, i (Winter, 1979): 64-72.

Sadler, Frank, "*Par-A-Dise* and Science," *WGCR* 11 (1979): 38-43. [Not seen.]

Schatt, S., *Kurt Vonnegut, Jr.*

Schatt, Stanley, "The Whale and the Cross: Vonnegut's Jonah and Christ-Figures," *SWR* 56 (Winter, 1971): 29-42.

_____, "The World of Kurt Vonnegut, Jr.," *Crit* 12, iii (1971): 54-69.

_____, "The World Picture of Kurt Vonnegut, Jr.," *DAI* 31 (1970): 767A.

Scholes, Robert, "'Mithridates he died old': Black Humor and Kurt Vonnegut, Jr.," *HC* 3, iv (Oct., 1966): 1-12. Also in Dillard, R. H. W., and Others, eds., *Sounder Few*, 173-85.

_____, "A Talk with Kurt Vonnegut, Jr.," in Klinkowitz, J., and J. Somer, eds., *Vonnegut Statement*, 90-118.

Scholl, Peter A., "Vonnegut's Attack upon Christendom," *C&L* 22, i (1973): 5-11.

Schriber, Mary S., "Bringing Chaos to Order: The Novel Tradition and Kurt Vonnegut, Jr.," *Genre* 10 (Summer, 1977): 283-97.

Schulz, Max F., "The Unconfirmed Thesis: Kurt Vonnegut, Black Humor, and Contemporary Art," *Crit* 12, iii (1971): 5-27. Also in Schulz, M. F., *Black Humor Fiction of the Sixties*, 43-65.

Seltzer, Leon F., "Dresden and Vonnegut's Creative Testament of Guilt," *JAC* 4, iv (Winter, 1981): 55-69.

Shaw, William G., "Comic Absurdity and the Novels of Kurt Vonnegut, Jr.," *DAI* 36 (1976): 7427A.

Shor, Ira N., "Vonnegut's Art of Inquiry," *DAI* 32 (1971): 3331A.

Somer, John, "Geodesic Vonnegut; or, If Buckminster Fuller Wrote Novels," in Klinkowitz, J., and J. Somer, eds., *Vonnegut Statement*, 221-54.

Somer, John L., "Quick-statis: The Rite of Initiation in the Novels of Kurt Vonnegut, Jr.," *DAI* 32 (1972): 4025A.

Tanner, Tony, "The Uncertain Messenger: A Study of the Novels of Kurt Vonnegut, Jr.," *CritQ* 11, iv (Winter, 1969): 297-315. Also in Tanner, T., *City of Words*, 181-201.

Uphaus, Robert W., "Expected Meaning in Vonnegut's Dead End Fiction," *Novel* 8 (Winter, 1975): 164-74.

Wood, Karen, and Charles, "The Vonnegut Effect: Science Fiction and Beyond," in Klinkowitz, J., and J. Somer, eds., *Vonnegut Statement*, 133-57.

Wymer, Thomas, "The Swiftian Satire of Kurt Vonnegut, Jr.," in Baldanza, F., ed., *Itinerary 3: Criticism*, 67-83.

Ziegfeld, Richard E., "Kurt Vonnegut on Censorship and Moral Values," *MFS* 26 (Winter, 1980-81): 631-5.

BREAKFAST OF CHAMPIONS

Giannone, R., *Vonnegut*, 101-12.

Kennard, Jean E., "Kurt Vonnegut, Jr.: The Sirens of Satire," *Number and Nightmare*, 125-8.

Klinkowitz, J., *Kurt Vonnegut*, 70-4.

_____, *Literary Disruptions*, 58-61.

Lundquist, J., *Kurt Vonnegut*, 55-62.

Mayo, C., *Kurt Vonnegut*, 52-8.

McGinnis, Wayne D., "Vonnegut's BREAKFAST OF CHAMPIONS: A Reductive Success," *NConL* 5, iii (1975): 6-9.

McInerney, John M., "Children for Vonnegut," *NMAL* 3 (Winter, 1978): Item 4.

Mendelson, Maurice, "Reading Kurt Vonnegut," *SovL* 8 (1975): 156-9.

Merrill, Robert, "Vonnegut's BREAKFAST OF CHAMPIONS: The Conversion of Heliogabalus," *Crit* 18, iii (1977): 99-109.

Messent, Peter B., "BREAKFAST OF CHAMPIONS: The Direction of Kurt Vonnegut's Fiction," *JAmS* 8 (1974): 101-14.

Reed, Peter J., "The Later Vonnegut," in Klinkowitz, J., and D. L. Lawler, eds., *Vonnegut in America*, 150-69.

St. Germain, Amos, "BREAKFAST OF CHAMPIONS: Kurt Vonnegut, Jr. Is Still On the Case," in *Proceedings of the Fifth National Convention of the Popular Culture Assoc.*, 233-43.

Schatt, S., *Kurt Vonnegut, Jr.*, 97-109.

Uphaus, Robert, "Expected Meaning in Vonnegut's Dead End Fiction," *Novel* 8, ii (Winter, 1975): 171-4.

CAT'S CRADLE

Agosta, Lucien L., "Ah-Whoom!: Egotism in Kurt Vonnegut's CAT'S CRADLE," *KanQ* 14, ii (Spring, 1982): 127-34.

Brien, Alan, "Afterthought," *Spectator* 202 (Aug., 1963): 158-9.

Bryant, J. H., *Open Decision*, 315-19.

Cook, Kenneth, "What's So Damn Funny? Grim Humor in THE MYSTERIOUS STRANGER and CAT'S CRADLE," *PMPA* 7 (1982): 48-55.

Cooley, John, "The Garden in the Machine: Three Postmodern Pastorals," *MichA* 13, iv (Spring, 1981): 405-20.

_____, *Savages and Naturals: Black Portraits by White Writers in Modern American Literature*, Newark: Un. of Delaware Pr., 1982, 161-73.

Crump, G. B., "D. H. Lawrence and the Immediate Present: Kurt Vonnegut, Jr., Ken Kesey, and Wright Morris," *DHLR* 10 (Summer, 1977): 111-15.

Doxey, William S., "Vonnegut's CAT'S CRADLE," *Expl* 37, iv (Summer, 1979): Item 6.

Engel, Wilson F., III., "Pilgrim as Prisoner: Cummings and Vonnegut," *NConL* 7 (Jan., 1977): 13-14.

Flora, Joseph M., "Cabell as Precursor: Reflections on Cabell and Vonnegut," *Kalki* 6 (1975): 118-37.

Frank, Armin P., "Where Laughing Is the Only Way to Stop It from Hurting," *Summary* 1, ii (1971): 55-60.

Holubetz, Margarete, "Black Humour in Modern English Literature," *WBEP* 78 (1981): 7-15.

Giannone, R., *Vonnegut*, 53-68.

Goldsmith, D. H., *Kurt Vonnegut*, 16-20.

Jones, P., *War and the Novelist*, 213-17.

Kennard, Jean E., "Kurt Vonnegut, Jr.: The Sirens of Satire," *Number and Nightmare*, 114-19.

Klinkowitz, J., *Kurt Vonnegut*, 52-8.

Klinkowitz, Jerome, "Kurt Vonnegut Jr. and the Crime of His Times," *Crit* 12, iii (1971): 46-52. Also, in different form, in Klinkowitz, J., and J. Somer, eds., *Vonnegut Statement*, 158-77.

_____, *Literary Disruptions*, 45-8.

Lawing, John V., Jr., "Kurt Vonnegut: Charming Nihilist," *ChrT* (Feb. 14, 1979): 17-20, 22.

Leff, Leonard, "Science and Destruction in Vonnegut's CAT'S CRADLE," *Rectangle* 46 (Spring, 1971): 21-32.

Leverence, W. John, "CAT'S CRADLE and Traditional American Humor," *JPC* 5, iv (Spring, 1972): 955-63.

Lundquist, J., *Kurt Vonnegut*, 33-9.

Mangum, Bryant, "CAT'S CRADLE's Jonah-John and the Garden of Ice-Nine," *NConL* 9, iii (1979): 9-11.

May, J. R., *Toward a New Earth*, 192-200.

Mayo, C., *Kurt Vonnegut*, 28-34.

McGinnis, Wayne D, "The Ambiguities of Bokonism," *IEY* 26, vii (1977): 21-3.

_____, "The Source and Implication of 'ice-nine' in Vonnegut's CAT'S CRADLE," *AN&Q* 13 (1974): 40-1.

Meeter, Glenn, "Vonnegut's Formal and Moral Otherworldliness: CAT'S CRADLE and SLAUGHTERHOUSE-FIVE," in Klinkowitz, J., and J. Somer, eds., *Vonnegut Statement*, 204-20.

Morrow, Patrick D., "The Womb Image in Vonnegut's CAT'S CRADLE," *NConL* 6, v (1976): 11-13.

Pinsker, Sanford, "Fire and Ice: The Radical Cuteness of Kurt Vonnegut, Jr.," *STwC* 13 (Spring, 1974): 7-10.

Reed, P. J., *Kurt Vonnegut, Jr.*, 119-45.

Rubens, Philip M., "Names in Vonnegut's CAT'S CRADLE," *NConL* 8, i (1978): 7.

Schatt, S., *Kurt Vonnegut, Jr.*, 56-68.

_____, "The World of Kurt Vonnegut, Jr.," *Crit* 12, iii (1971): 57-61.

Schickel, Richard, "Black Comedy With Purifying Laughter," *Harpers* 232 (May, 1966): 103-4.

Scholes, Robert, *Fabulators*, 47-55.

_____, "'Mithridates, he died old': Black Humor and Kurt Vonnegut, Jr.," *HC* 3, iv (Oct., 1966): 8-9. Also in Dillard, R. H. W., and Others, eds., *Sounder Few*, 180-2.

_____, "Vonnegut's CAT'S CRADLE and MOTHER NIGHT, *Fabulation and Metafiction*, 156-62.

Scholl, Peter A., "Vonnegut's Attack Upon Christendom," *C&L* 22, i (1973): 8-9.

Schulz, Max F., "The Unconfirmed Thesis: Kurt Vonnegut, Black Humor, and Contemporary Art," *Crit* 12, iii (1971): 18-20. Also in Schulz, M. F., *Black Humor Fiction of the Sixties*, 55-7.

Tanner, Tony, "The Uncertain Messenger: A Study of the Novels of Kurt Vonnegut, Jr.," *CritQ* 11, iv (Winter, 1969): 304-6. Also in Tanner, T., *City of Words*, 188-91.

Trachtenberg, Stanley, "Vonnegut's Cradle: The Erosion of Comedy," *MQR* 12, i (1973): 66-71.

Vasbinder, Sam, "The Meaning of Foma in CAT'S CRADLE," *RQ* 5 (1973): 300-2.

Wymer, Thomas, "The Swiftian Satire of Kurt Vonnegut, Jr.," in Clareson, T. D., ed., *Voices for the Future*, 254-8. Also in Baldanza, F., ed., *Itinerary 3: Criticism*, 77-80.

GOD BLESS YOU, MR. ROSEWATER

Bryan, C. D. B., "Kurt Vonnegut on Target," *NRep* 155 (Oct. 8, 1966): 24-5.

Bryant, J., *Open Decision*, 310-12.

Carson, Ronald A., "Kurt Vonnegut: Matter-Of-Fact Moralist," *Listening* 6 (1971): 186-90.

Giannone, R., *Vonnegut*, 69-81.

Godshalk, William, "Kurt Vonnegut's Renaissance Hero," *Clifton* 1 (1973): 41-5.

_____, "Vonnegut and Shakespeare: Rosewater at Elsinore," *Crit* 15, ii (1973): 37-48.

Goldsmith, D. H., *Kurt Vonnegut*, 20-5.

Jones, P., *War and the Novelist*, 210-13.

Kennard, Jean E., "Kurt Vonnegut, Jr.: The Sirens of Satire," *Number and Nightmare*, 119-22.

Klinkowitz, J., *Kurt Vonnegut*, 58-62.

_____, *Literary Disruptions*, 37-40.

Leff, Leonard J., "Utopia Reconstructed: Alienation in Vonnegut's GOD BLESS YOU, MR. ROSEWATER," *Crit* 12, iii (1971): 29-37.

Lundquist, J., *Kurt Vonnegut*, 39-46.

Mayo, C., *Kurt Vonnegut*, 34-40.

Nelson, G. B., *Ten Versions of America*, 63-76.

Nelson, Joyce, "Vonnegut and 'Bugs in Amber'," *JPC* 7, iii (Winter, 1973): 553-4, 555-7.

Pinsker, Sanford, "Fire and Ice: The Radical Cuteness of Kurt Vonnegut, Jr." *STwC* 13 (Spring, 1974): 10-12.

Reed, P. J., *Kurt Vonnegut, Jr.*, 146-71.

Schatt, S., *Kurt Vonnegut, Jr.*, 69-80.

_____, "The Whale and the Cross: Vonnegut's Jonah and Christ Figures," *SWR* 56 (Winter, 1971): 38-42.

_____, "The World of Kurt Vonnegut, Jr.," *Crit* 12, iii (1971): 61-5.

Schulz, Max F., "The Unconfirmed Thesis: Kurt Vonnegut, Black Humor, and Contemporary Art," *Crit* 12, iii (1971):

8-14. Also in Schulz, M. F., *Black Humor Fiction of the Sixties*, 45-51.

Tanner, Tony, "The Uncertain Messenger: The Novels of Kurt Vonnegut, Jr., " *CritQ* 11, iv (Winter, 1969): 307-9. Also in Tanner, T., *City of Words*, 192-4.

JAILBIRD

Blackford, Russell, "Discipline and Bondage," *SFic* 3, i (Jan., 1981): 38-41.

Irving, John, "Kurt Vonnegut and His Critics," *NRep* 181 (Sept. 22, 1979): 46-8.

Klinkowitz, J., *Kurt Vonnegut*, 78-82.

Mills, John, "Return of the Diviner, and Other Auguries," *NAR* 264 (Dec., 1979): 74-6.

MOTHER NIGHT

Bryan, C. D. B., "Kurt Vonnegut on Target," *NRep* 155 (Oct. 8, 1966): 21-2.

Bryant, J. H., *Open Decision*, 312-15.

Carson, Ronald A., "Kurt Vonnegut: Matter-Of-Fact Moralist," *Listening* 6 (Autumn, 1971): 184-6.

Giannone, R., *Vonnegut*, 39-52.

Goldsmith, D. H., *Kurt Vonnegut*, 15-16.

Jones, P., *War and the Novelist*, 208-10.

Kennard, Jean E., "Kurt Vonnegut, Jr.: The Sirens of Satire," *Number and Nightmare*, 112-14.

Klinkowitz, J., *Kurt Vonnegut*, 46-51.

_____, "Kurt Vonnegut, Jr. and the Crime of His Times," *Crit* 12, iii (1971): 39-46. Also, in different form, in Klinkowitz, J., and J. Somer, eds., *Vonnegut Statement*, 158-77.

Lundquist, J., *Kurt Vonnegut*, 30-3.

Mayo, C., *Kurt Vonnegut*, 23-7.

Pinsker, Sanford, "Fire and Ice: The Radical Cuteness of Kurt Vonnegut, Jr.," *STwC* 13 (1974): 2-7. Also in Pinsker, S., *Between Two Worlds*, 88-91.

Reed, P. J., *Kurt Vonnegut, Jr.*, 88-118.

Schatt, S., *Kurt Vonnegut, Jr.*, 43-55.

_____, "The World of Kurt Vonnegut, Jr.," *Crit* 12, iii (1971): 54-7.

Scholes, R., *Fabulators*, 47-55.

_____, "'Mithridates, he died old': Black Humor and Kurt Vonnegut, Jr.," *HC* 3, iv (Oct., 1966): 9-11. Also in Dillard, R. H. W., and Others, eds., *Sounder Few*, 182-4.

_____, "Vonnegut's CAT'S CRADLE and MOTHER NIGHT," *Fabulation and Metafiction*, 156-62.

Schulz, Max F., "The Unconfirmed Thesis: Kurt Vonnegut, Black Humor, and Contemporary Art," *Crit* 12, iii (1971): 21-3. Also in Schulz, M. F., *Black Humor Fiction of the Sixties*, 58-9.

Smith, William J., in *Cweal* 84 (Sept. 16, 1966): 592-4.

Tanner, Tony, "The Uncertain Messenger: A Study of the Novels of Kurt Vonnegut, Jr.," *CritQ* 11, iv (Winter, 1969): 300-4. Also in Tanner, T., *City of Words*, 185-8.

Veeder, William, "Technique as Recovery: LOLITA and MOTHER NIGHT," in Klinkowitz, J., and D. L. Lawler, eds., *Vonnegut in America*, 97-132.

Weales, Gerald D., "Whatever Happened to Tugboat Annie?" *Reporter* 35 (Dec. 1, 1966): 50, 52-6.

PLAYER PIANO

Bryant, J. H., *Open Decision*, 309-10.

Crump, G. B., "D. H. Lawrence and the Immediate Present: Kurt Vonnegut, Jr., Ken Kesey, and Wright Morris," *DHLR* 10, ii (Summer, 1977): 105-11.

Giannone, R., *Vonnegut*, 12-24.

Goldsmith, D. H., *Kurt Vonnegut*, 7-10.

Hillegas, Mark R., "Dystopian Science Fiction: New Index to the Human Condition," *NMQ* 31 (Autumn, 1961): 245-7.

Hughes, David Y., "The Ghost in the Machine: The Theme of PLAYER PIANO, in Roemer, Kenneth M., ed., *American as Utopia*, N.Y.: Burt Franklin, 1981, 108-114.

Kennard, Jean E., "Kurt Vonnegut, Jr.: The Sirens of Satire," *Number and Nightmare*, 104-7.

Klinkowitz, J., *Kurt Vonnegut*, 34-40.

Lundquist, J., *Kurt Vonnegut*, 22-6.

Mayo, C., *Kurt Vonnegut*, 9-15.

McGrath, Michael J. G., "Kesey and Vonnegut: The Critique of Liberal Democracy in Contemporary Literature," in Barber, B. R., and M. J. G. McGrath, eds., *Artist and Political Vision*, 373-81.

Mellard, James M., "The Modes of Vonnegut's Fiction: or, PLAYER PIANO Ousts MECHANICAL BRIDE and THE SIRENS OF TITAN Invade THE GUTENBERG GALAXY," in Klinkowitz, J., and J. Somer, eds., *Vonnegut Statement*, 179-91.

Reed, P. J., *Kurt Vonnegut, Jr.*, 24-56.

Rhodes, Carolyn H., "Intelligence Testing in Utopia," *Extrapolation* 13, i (Dec., 1971): 27-9.

Schatt, S., *Kurt Vonnegut, Jr.*, 16-30.

Schickel, Richard, "Black Comedy with Purifying Laughter," *Harpers* 232 (May, 1966): 103-4.

Schriber, Mary Sue, "You've Come a Long Way, Babbitt! From Zenith to Ilium," *TCL* 17, ii (Apr., 1971): 101-6.

Tanner, Tony, "The Uncertain Messenger: A Study of the Novels of Kurt Vonnegut, Jr.," *CritQ* 11, iv (Winter, 1969): 297-8. Also in Tanner, T., *City of Words*, 181-2.

Walsh, Chad, *From Utopia to Nightmare*, 71-89.

Warrick, Patricia S., *The Cybernetic Imagination in Science Fiction*, N.Y.: Harper and Row, 1980, 134-39.

Wymer, Thomas L., "Machines and the Meaning of Human in the Novels of Kurt Vonnegut, Jr.," in Dunn, T. P., and R. D. Erlich, eds., *Mechanical God*, 41-4.

SLAPSTICK; OR, LONESOME NO MORE!

Blackford, Russell, "The Definition of Love: Kurt Vonnegut's SLAPSTICK," *SFic* 2 (July, 1980): 208-28.

Giannone, R., *Vonnegut*, 113-21.

Klinkowitz, J., *Kurt Vonnegut*, 74-8.

Lundquist, J., *Kurt Vonnegut*, 62-7.

Mayo, C., *Kurt Vonnegut*, 58-63.

Reed, Peter J., "The Later Vonnegut," in Klinkowitz, J., and D. L. Lawler, eds., *Vonnegut in America*, 169-85.

Schatt, S., *Kurt Vonnegut, Jr.*, 110-18.

THE SIRENS OF TITAN

Fiene, Donald M., "Vonnegut's SIRENS OF TITAN," *Expl* 34 (1975): Item 27.

Giannone, P., *Vonnegut*, 25-38.

Goldsmith, D. H., *Kurt Vonnegut*, 10-15.

Jones, P., *War and the Novelist*, 204-7.

Kennard, Jean E., "Kurt Vonnegut, Jr.: The Sirens of Satire," *Number and Nightmare*, 107-12.

Ketterer, David, "Vonnegut's Spiral Siren Call: From Dresden's Lunar Surfaces to Tralfamadore," *New Worlds for Old; the Apocalyptic Imagination, Science Fiction, and American Literature*, Garden City, N.Y.: 1974, 296-333.

Klinkowitz, J., *Kurt Vonnegut*, 40-6.

Lawler, Donald L., "THE SIRENS OF TITAN: Vonnegut's Metaphysical Shaggy-Dog Story," in Klinkowitz, J., and D. L. Lawler, eds., *Vonnegut in America*, 61-86.

Lundquist, J., *Kurt Vonnegut*, 26-30.

Mellard, James M., "The Modes of Vonnegut's Fiction: or, PLAYER PIANO Ousts MECHANICAL BRIDE and THE SIRENS OF TITAN Invade THE GUTENBERG GALAXY," in Klinkowitz, J., and J. Somers, eds., *Vonnegut Statement*, 191-201.

Mayo, C., *Kurt Vonnegut*, 15-23.

Reed, P. J., *Kurt Vonnegut, Jr.*, 57-87.

Rose, Ellen C., "It's All a Joke: Science Fiction in Kurt Vonnegut's SIRENS OF TITAN," *L&P* 29 (1979): 160-8.

Scholes, Robert, in Dillard, R. H. W., and Others, eds., *Sounder Few*, 186-9.

Scholl, Peter A., "Vonnegut's Attack Upon Christendom," *C&L* 22, i (1973): 6-8.

Tanner, Tony, "The Uncertain Messenger: A Study of the Novels of Kurt Vonnegut, Jr.," *CritQ* 11, iv (Winter, 1969): 298-300. Also in Tanner, T., *City of Words*, 182-5.

Wolfe, G. K., "Vonnegut and the Metaphor of Science Fiction: THE SIRENS OF TITAN," *JPC* 5 (Spring, 1972): 964-9.

Wymer, Thomas L., "Machines and the Meaning of Human in the Novels of Kurt Vonnegut, Jr.," in Dunn, T. P., and R. D. Erlich, eds., *Mechanical God*, 44-8.

_____, "The Swiftian Satire of Kurt Vonnegut, Jr.," in Clareson, T. D., ed., *Voices for the Future*, 251-3. Also in Baldanza, F., ed., *Itinerary 3: Criticism*.

SLAUGHTERHOUSE-FIVE

Brophy, Elizabeth, "Vonnegut's Bird Language in SLAUGHTERHOUSE-FIVE," *NMAL* 4 (1980): Item 15.

Bryant, J. H., *Open Decision*, 319-24.

Carson, Ronald A., "Kurt Vonnegut: Matter-Of-Fact Moralist," *Listening* 6 (Autumn, 1971): 190-2.

Chabot, C. Barry, "SLAUGHTERHOUSE-FIVE and the Comforts of Indifference," *ELWIU* 8, i (Spring, 1981): 45-51.

Dimeo, Stephen, "Reconciliation: SLAUGHTERHOUSE-FIVE—The Film and the Novel," *Film Heritage* 8, ii (Winter, 1972-73): 1-12. Also, revised, as "Novel Into Film: So It Goes," in Pearce, G., and R. Shatzkin, eds., *Modern American Novel and the Movies*, 282-92.

Edelstein, Arnold, "SLAUGHTERHOUSE-FIVE: Time Out of Joint," *CollL* 1, ii (Spring, 1974): 128-39.

Engel, Wilson F., III., "Pilgrim as Prisoner: Cummings and Vonnegut," *NConL* 10 (Jan., 1977): 13-14.

Giannone, R., *Vonnegut*, 82-97.

Goldsmith, D. H., *Kurt Vonnegut*, 25-9.

Goss, Gary L., "The Selfless Billy Pilgrim," *Buffalo Spree* 5 (Fall, 1971): 34-5, 44-5, 47, 52-3, 60-1.

Greiner, Donald J., "Vonnegut's SLAUGHTERHOUSE-FIVE and the Fiction of Atrocity," *Crit* 14, iii (1973): 38-51.

Gros-Louis, Dolores K., "The Ironic Christ Figure in SLAUGHTERHOUSE-FIVE," in Bartel, Roland, ed., *Biblical Images in Literature*, N.Y.: Abingdon, 1975, 161-75.

_____, "SLAUGHTERHOUSE-FIVE: Pacifism vs. Passiveness," *BSUF* 18, ii (1977): 3-8.

Harris, Charles B., "Time, Uncertainty, and Kurt Vonnegut, Jr.: A Reading of SLAUGHTERHOUSE-FIVE," *CentR* 20 (1976): 228-43.

Hartshorne, Thomas L., "From CATCH-22 to SLAUGHTERHOUSE V: The Decline of the Political Mode," *SAQ* 78 (Winter, 1979): 17-33.

Hayman, David, "The Jolly Mix: Notes on Techniques, Style, and Decorum in SLAUGHTERHOUSE-FIVE," *Summary* 1, ii (1971): 44-50.

Isaacs, Neil D., "Unstuck in Time: CLOCKWORK ORANGE and SLAUGHTERHOUSE 5," *LFQ* 1, ii (Apr., 1973): 122-31.

Iwamoto, Iwao, "A Clown's Say: A Study of Kurt Vonnegut, Jr.'s SLAUGHTERHOUSE-FIVE," *SELit*, Eng. No. (1975): 21-31.

Jones, P., *War and the Novelist*, 217-22.

Kenedy, R. C., "Kurt Vonnegut, Jr.," *ArtI* 15, v (May 20, 1971): 22-5.

Kennard, Jean E., "Kurt Vonnegut, Jr.: The Siren of Satire," *Number and Nightmare*, 122-5.

Klinkowitz, J., *Kurt Vonnegut*, 63-9.

_____, *Literary Disruptions*, 48-53.

Kopper, Edward A., Jr., "Color Symbolism in Vonnegut's SLAUGHTERHOUSE-FIVE," *NMAL* 1 (1977): Item 17.

_____, "Operation Gommorah in SLAUGHTERHOUSE-FIVE," *NConL* 8, iv (1978): 6.

LeClair, Thomas, "Death and Black Humor," *Crit* 17, i (1975): 22-4.

Loeb, M. C., "Vonnegut's Duty-Dance with Death: Theme and Structure in SLAUGHTERHOUSE-FIVE," *DAI* 41 (1980): 51C.

Lundquist, J., *Kurt Vonnegut*, 46-55, 71-84.

Mayer, Peter C., "Film, Ontology and the Structures of a Novel," *LFQ* 8 (1980): 204-8.

Mayo, C., *Kurt Vonnegut*, 45-52.

McGinnis, Wayne D., "The Arbitrary Cycle of SLAUGHTERHOUSE-FIVE: A Relation of Form to Theme," *Crit* 17, i (1975): 55-68.

McNelly, Willis E., "Science Fiction, the Modern Mythology," *America* (Sept. 5, 1970): 14-18. Also in Clareson, T. D., ed., *SF: The Other Side of Realism*, 193-8.

Meeter, Glenn, "Vonnegut's Formal and Otherworldliness: CAT'S CRADLE and SLAUGHTERHOUSE-FIVE," in Klinkowitz, J., and J. Somer, eds., *Vonnegut Statement*, 204-20.

Merrill, Robert, and Peter A. Scholl, "Vonnegut's SLAUGHTERHOUSE-FIVE: The Requirements of Chaos," *SAF* 6, i (Spring, 1978): 65-76.

Myers, David, "Kurt Vonnegut, Jr.: Morality Myth in the Anti-Novel," *IFR* 3 (Jan., 1976): 52-6.

Nelson, Joyce, "SLAUGHTERHOUSE-FIVE: Novel and Film," *LFQ* 1 (1973): 149-53.

Noguchi, Kenji, "SLAUGHTERHOUSE-FIVE and Vonnegut's 'Genial Desperado Philosophy'," *KAL* 16 (1975): 17-20.

O'Connor, Gerard W., "The Function of Time Travel in Kurt Vonnegut's SLAUGHTERHOUSE-FIVE," *RQ* 5 (1972): 206-7.

O'Sullivan, Maurice J., Jr., "SLAUGHTERHOUSE-FIVE: Kurt Vonnegut's Anti-Memoirs," *ELWIU* 3 (Fall, 1976): 244-50.

Pinsker, Sanford, "Fire and Ice: The Radical Cuteness of Kurt Vonnegut, Jr.," *STwC* 13 (1974): 12-18. Also in Pinsker, S., *Between Two Worlds*, 95-100.

Prioli, Carmine A., "Kurt Vonnegut's Duty-Dance," *ELUD* 1, iii (Sept., 1973): 44-50.

Reed, P. J., *Kurt Vonnegut, Jr.*, 172-203.

Rice, Susan, "SLAUGHTERHOUSE-FIVE: A Viewer's Guide," *Media and Methods* (Oct.,1972): 27-33.

Schatt, S., *Kurt Vonnegut, Jr.*, 81-96.

Schatt, Stanley, "The World of Kurt Vonnegut, Jr.," *Crit* 12, iii (1971): 65-8.

Scholes, Robert, in Dillard, R. H. W., and Others, eds., *Sounder Few*, 187-91.

Scholl, Peter A., "Vonnegut's Attack Upon Christendom," *C&L* 22, i (1973): 9-11.

Schriber, Mary Sue, "Bringing Chaos to Order: The Novel Tradition and Kurt Vonnegut, Jr.," *Genre* 10 (1977): 288-96.

Shaw, Patrick W., "The Excrement Festival: Vonnegut's SLAUGHTERHOUSE-FIVE," *ScholS* 2, iii (Autumn, 1976): 3-11.

Tanner, Tony, "The Uncertain Messenger: A Study of the Novels of Kurt Vonnegut, Jr.," *CritQ* 11, iv (Winter, 1969): 309-15. Also in Tanner, T., *City of Words*, 194-201.

Tilton, John W., "SLAUGHTERHOUSE-FIVE: Life Against Death-in-Life," *Comic Satire in the Contemporary Novel*, 69-103.

Tunnell, James R, "Kesey and Vonnegut: Preachers of Redemption," *ChrC* 89 (Nov. 22, 1972): 1181-2.

Vanderwerken, David L, "Pilgrim's Dilemma: SLAUGHTERHOUSE-FIVE," *RS* 42 (1974): 147-52.

Veix, Donald B., "Teaching a Censored Novel: SLAUGHTERHOUSE-FIVE," *EJ* 64, vii (1975): 25-33.

Vinograde, Ann C., "A Soviet Translation of SLAUGHTERHOUSE-FIVE," *RLJ* 93 (1972): 14-18.

Walsh, J., *American War Literature*, 195-9.

Wright, Moorhead, "The Existential Adventurer and War: Three Case Studies from American Fiction," in Booth, K., and M. Wright, eds., *American Thinking About Peace and War*, 101-10.

Wymer, Thomas L., "Machine and the Meaning of Human in the Novels of Kurt Vonnegut, Jr.," in Dunn, T. P., and R. D. Erlich, eds., *Mechanical God*, 48-50.

_____, "The Swiftian Satire of Kurt Vonnegut, Jr.," in Clareson, T. D., ed., *Voices for the Future*, v. 1, 238-51, 259-61. Also in Baldanza, F., ed., *Itinerary 3: Criticism*, 68-77, 80-1.

BIBLIOGRAPHY

Cohn, Alan M., "A Vonnegut Rarissima: A Supplement to Hudgens and to Pieratt and Klinkowitz," *PBSA* 73 (1979): 365-6.

Haskell, John D., "Addendum to Pieratt and Klinkowitz: Kurt Vonnegut, Jr.," *PBSA* 70 (1976): 122.

Hudgens, Betty L., *Kurt Vonnegut, Jr.: A Checklist*, Detroit: Gale Research, 1972.

Klinkowitz, Jerome, "The Vonnegut Bibliography," in Klinkowitz, J., and D. L. Lawler, eds., *Vonnegut in America*, 217-52.

Pieratt, Asa B., and Jerome Klinkowitz, *Kurt Vonnegut, Jr.: A Descriptive Bibliography and Annotated Secondary Checklist*, Hamden, Conn.: Archon, 1974.

Schatt, Stanley, and Jerome Klinkowitz, "A Kurt Vonnegut Checklist," *Crit* 12, iii (1971): 70-6.

WAGONER, DAVID, 1926-

GENERAL

Cording, Robert K., "A New Lyricism: David Wagoner and the Instructional Voice," *DAI* 37 (1977): 4352A.

Schafer, William J., "David Wagoner's Fiction: In the Mills of Satan," *Crit* 9, i (1967): 71-89.

THE ESCAPE ARTIST

Schafer, William J., "David Wagoner's Fiction: In the Mills of Satan," *Crit* 9, i (1967): 85-9.

THE MAN IN THE MIDDLE

Schafer, William J., "David Wagoner's Fiction: In the Mills of Satan," *Crit* 9, i (1967): 72-6.

MONEY MONEY MONEY

Schafer, William J., "David Wagoner's Fiction: In the Mills of Satan," *Crit* 9, i (1967): 76-80.

ROCK

Schafer, William J., "David Wagoner's Fiction: In the Mills of Satan," *Crit* 9, i (1967): 80-3.

WAIN, JOHN, 1925-

GENERAL

Allsop, K., *Angry Decade*, 58-68.

Bluestone, George, "John Wain and John Barth: The Angry and the Accurate," *MR* 1 (May, 1960): 582-9.

Cappelán, Angel, "From Angry Young Man to Political Activist: The Novelistic Development of John Wain," *RevL* 5, xvii (Mar., 1973): 88-111.

Coc, C. B., *Free Spirit*, 155-61.

Gerard, David, *My Work as a Novelist: John Wain*, Cardiff: Drake Educational Associates, 1978.

Gindin, J., "The Moral Center of John Wain's Fiction," *Postwar British Fiction*, 128-44.

Heppenstall, R., *Fourfold Tradition*, 213-224.

Kermode, Frank, "The House of Fiction: Interviews with Seven English Novelists," *PR* 30 (Spring, 1963): 77-9.

Lehmann, J., "The Wain-Larkin Myth," *SR* 66 (Autumn, 1958): 578-87.

Mellown, Elgin W., "Steps Toward Vision: The Development of Technique in John Wain's First Seven Novels," *SAQ* 68 (Summer, 1969): 330-42.

O'Connor, William Van, "John Wain: The Will to Write," *WSCL* 1, i (Winter, 1960): 35-49.

Salwak, D., *John Wain*.

Walzer, Michael, "John Wain: The Hero in Limbo," *Per* 10 (Summer-Autumn, 1958): 137-45.

BORN IN CAPTIVITY (See HURRY ON DOWN)

THE CONTENDERS

Gindin, J., "The Moral Center of John Wain's Fiction," *Postwar British Fiction*, 133-4+.

O'Connor, William Van, "John Wain: The Will to Write," *WSCL* 1, i (Winter, 1960): 46-7.

_____, *New University Wits*, 48-50.

Rippier, J. S., *Some Postwar English Novelists*, 165-8.

Salwak, D., *John Wain*, 48-53.

Walzer, Michael, "John Wain: The Hero in Limbo," *Per* 10 (Summer-Autumn, 1958): 143-5.

HURRY ON DOWN (BORN IN CAPTIVITY)

Cappelán, Angel, "From Angry Young Man to Political Activist: The Novelistic Development of John Wain," *RevL* 5, xvii (Mar., 1973): 90-8.

Cox, G. B., *Free Spirit*, 158-9.

Dixon, Terrell F., "The Use of Literary History in HURRY ON DOWN," *NConL* 2, ii (Mar., 1972): 6-7.

Douglass, Wayne J., and Robert G. Walker, "'A Moralist Perchance Appears': John Wain's HURRY ON DOWN," *Ren* 31, i (1978): 43-50.

Gindin, J., "The Moral Center of John Wain's Fiction," *Postwar British Fiction*, 128-31+.

Karl, F. R., "The Angries: Is There a Protestant in the House?" *Contemporary English Novel*, 224-6.

O'Connor, William Van, "John Wain: The Will to Write," *WSCL* 1, i (Winter, 1960): 42-4.

_____, *New University Wits*, 42-6.

Rippier, J. S., *Some Postwar English Novelists*, 159-65.

Salwak, D., *John Wain*, 33-43.

Walzer, Michael, "John Wain: The Hero in Limbo," *Per* 10 (Summer-Autumn, 1958): 139-41.

LIVING IN THE PRESENT

Gindin, J., "The Moral Center of John Wain's Fiction," *Postwar British Fiction*, 131-3+.

O'Connor, William Van, "John Wain: The Will to Write," *WSCL* 1, i (Winter, 1960): 44-6.

_____, *New University Wits*, 46-8.

Walzer, Michael, "John Wain: The Hero in Limbo," *Per* 10 (Summer-Autumn, 1958): 141-3.

Salwak, D., *John Wain*, 43-7.

THE PARDONER'S ALE

Salwak, D., *John Wain*, 95-107.

THE SMALLER SKY

Salwak, D., *John Wain*, 78-84.

STRIKE THE FATHER DEAD

McDowell, Frederick P. W., "'The Devious Involutions of Human Character and Emotions': Reflections of Some Recent British Novels," *WSCL* 4, iii (Autumn, 1963): 342-4.

Rippier, J. S., *Some Postwar English Novelists*, 170-3.

Salwak, D., *John Wain*, 59-70.

A TRAVELLING WOMAN

Gindin, J., "The Moral Center of John Wain's Fiction," *Postwar British Fiction*, 134-6+.

O'Connor, William Van, "John Wain: The Will to Write," *WSCL* 1, i (Winter, 1960): 47-8.

_____, *New University Wits*, 50-2.

Rippier, J. S., *Some Postwar English Novelists*, 168-70.

Toss, T. J., "A Good Girl is Hard to Find," *NRep* 141 (Sept. 21, 1959): 17-19.

Salwak, D., *John Wain*, 53-8.

Urwin, G. G., ed., *Taste for Living*, 134-7.

A WINTER IN THE HILLS

Cappelán, Angel, "From Angry Young Man to Political Activist: The Novelistic Development of John Wain," *RevL* 5, xvii (Mar., 1973): 103-9.

Salwak, D., *John Wain*, 85-94.

BIBLIOGRAPHY

Salwak, D., *John Wain*, 142-51.

Salwak, Dale, *John Braine and John Wain: A Reference Guide*, Boston: G. K. Hall, 1980.

WAKEFIELD, DAN, 1932-

GENERAL

Klinkowitz, Jerome, "Para-Critique: Jerome Klinkowitz on Dan Wakefield's Superfiction," *FictionI* 2/3 (1974): 126-32.

STARTING OVER

Shepherd, Allen, "Going Down with Wakefield: Non-Father's Balloon Strategy in STARTING OVER," *NConL* 5, iv (1975): 8-9.

WALKER, ALICE, 1944-

GENERAL

Callahan, John F., "The Higher Ground of Alice Walker," *NRep* 171 (Sept. 14, 1974): 21-2.

Erickson, Peter, "'Cast Out Alone/ To Heal/ and Re-Create/ Ourselves': Family-Based Identity in the Work of Alice Walker," *CLAF* 23, i (Sept., 1979): 71-94.

Harris, Trudier,, "Folklore in the Fiction of Alice Walker: A Perpetuation of Historical and Literary Traditions," *BALF* 11, i (Spring, 1977): 3-8.

O'Brien, John, ed., *Interviews with Black Writers*, 185-211.

Washington, Mary H., "An Essay on Alice Walker," in Bell, R. P., et al., eds., *Sturdy Black Bridges*, 133-48.

MERIDIAN

Barthold, B. J., *Black Time*, 127-30.

Bigsby, C. W. E., in Lee, A. R., ed., *Black Fiction*, 169-70.

Christian, B., *Black Women Novelists*, 204-38.

Erickson, Peter, "'Cast Out Alone/ To Heal/ and Re-Create/ Ourselves': Family-Based Identity in the Work of Alice Walker," *CLAJ* 23, i (Sept., 1979): 87-94.

McDowell, Deborah E., "The Self in Bloom: Alice Walker's MERIDIAN," *CLAJ* 24, iii (Mar., 1981): 262-75.

McGowan, Martha J., "Atonement and Release in Alice Walker's MERIDIAN," *Crit* 23, i (1981): 25-36.

Mickelson, A. Z., *Reaching Out*, 160-74.

Pullin, Faith, in Lee, A. R., ed., *Black Fiction*, 198-200.

THE THIRD LIFE OF GRANGE COPELAND

Callahan, John F., "The Higher Ground of Alice Walker," *NRep* 171 (Sept. 14, 1974): 21.

Christian, B., *Black Women Novelists*, 183-204, 234-8.

Ensslen, Klaus, "Collective Experience and Individual Responsibility: Alice Walker's THE THIRD LIFE OF GRANGE COPELAND," in Bruck, P., and W. Karrer, eds., *Afro-American Fiction Since 1960*, 189-216.

Erickson, Peter, "'Cast Out Alone/ To Heal/ and Re-Create/ Ourselves': Family-Based Identity in the Work of Alice Walker," *CLAJ* 23, i (Sept., 1979): 71-9.

Gaston, Karen C., "Women in the Lives of Grange Copeland," *CLAJ* 24, iii (Mar., 1981): 276-86.

Hairston, Loyle, "Work of Rare Beauty and Power," *Freedomways* 11 (2nd Quarter, 1971): 170-7.

Harris, Trudier, "Folklore in the Fiction of Alice Walker: A Perpetuation of Historical and Literary Traditions," *BALF* 11, i (Spring, 1977): 7-8.

_____, "Three Black Women Writers and Humanism: A Folk Perspective," in Miller, R. B., ed., *Black American Literature and Humanism*, 58-65.

_____, "Violence in THE THIRD LIFE OF GRANGE COPELAND," *CLAJ* 19 (Dec., 1975): 238-47.

WALKER, MARGARET (ABIGAIL), 1915-

GENERAL

Egejuru, Phanuel, and Robert E. Fox, "An Interview with Margaret Walker," *Callaloo* 2, ii (1979): 29-35.

Pettis, Joyce, "The Black Historical Novel as Best Seller," *KFR* 25 (1979): 51-9.

Rowell, Charles H., "Poetry, History and Humanism: An Interview with Margaret Walker," *BlackW* 25, ii (1975): 4-17.

Torrence, Juanita M. M., "A Literary Equation: A Comparison of Representative Works of Margaret Walker and Nikki Giovanni," *DAI* 40 (1980): 5283A-84A.

JUBILEE

Christian, B., *Black Women Novelists*, 71-2.

Klotman, Phyllis R., "'Oh Freedom'—Women and History in Margaret Walker's JUBILEE," *BALF* 11, iv (1977): 139-45.

Pettis, Joyce, "The Black Historical Novel as Best Seller," *KFR* 25 (1979): 51-79 *passim*.

Powell, Bertie J., "The Black Experience in Margaret Walker's JUBILEE and Lorraine Hansberry's THE DRINKING GOURD," *CLAJ* 21 (1977): 304-11.

Schraufnagel, N., *From Apology to Protest*, 131-2.

Spears, James E., "Black Folk Element in Margaret Walker's JUBILEE," *MissFR* 14, i (Spring, 1980): 13-19.

WALLACE, IRVING, 1916-1990

GENERAL

Leverance, William J., "Irving Wallace—the Interview: The Author of THE WORD," *JPC* 7, i (Summer, 1973): 185-208.

_____, "Irving Wallace: The Making of a Bestseller," *DAI* 35 (1974): 2281A-82A.

THE FAN CLUB

Davidson, Arnold E., "Caliban and the Captive Maiden: John Fowles' THE COLLECTOR and Irving Wallace's THE FAN CLUB," *StHum* 8, ii (Mar., 1981): 28-33.

WALLANT, EDWARD LEWIS, 1926-1962

GENERAL

Angle, James, "Edward Lewis Wallant's Trinity of Survival," *KanQ* 7, iv (Fall, 1975): 106-18.

Ayo, Nicholas, "The Secular Heart: The Achievement of Edward Lewis Wallant," *Crit* 12, ii (1970): 86-94.

Beja, Morris, *Epiphany in the Modern Novel*, 213-16.

Bernstein, Mashey M., "The Individual as a Work of Art: Jewish and Puritan Values in the Fiction of Norman Mailer and Edward Lewis Wallant," *DAI* 38 (1977): 3494A-95A.

Davis, William V., "Fathers and Sons in the Fiction of Edward Wallant," *RS* 40, i (Mar., 1972): 53-5.

Davis, William V., "Sleep Like the Living: A Study of the Novels of Edward Lewis Wallant," *DA* 28 (1968): 3177A.

_____, "A Synthesis in the Contemporary Jewish Novel: Edward Lewis Wallant," *Cresset* 31, vii (1968): 8-13.

Dell, Frances G., "From a Private Limbo to a World of Common Pain: The Unity of Edward Lewis Wallant's Fiction," *DAI* 42, vi (Nov., 1981): 2130A.

Galloway, D., *Edward Lewis Wallant*.

Greenberg, Hazel, "Cluster Imagery in the Novels of Edward Lewis Wallant," *DAI* 33 (1973): 5176A.

Gurko, Leo, "Edward Lewis Wallant as Urban Novelist," *TCL* 20, iv (Oct., 1974): 252-61.

Hoyt, Charles A., "The Sudden Hunger: An Essay on the Novels of Edward Lewis Wallant," in Hoyt, C. A., ed., *Minor American Novelists*, 118-37.

Klein, Marcus, "Further Notes on the Dereliction of Culture: Edward Lewis Wallant and Bruce Jay Friedman," in Malin, I., *Contemporary American-Jewish Literature*, 235-41.

Lewis, Robert W., "The Hung-Up Heroes of Edward Lewis Wallant," *Ren* 24, ii (Winter, 1972): 70-84.

Lorch, Thomas M., "The Novels of Edward Lewis Wallant," *ChiR* 19, ii (1967): 78-91.

Mesher, David R., "Con Artist and Middleman: The Archetypes of Wallant's Published and Unpublished Fiction," *YULG* 56, i-ii (Oct., 1981): 40-9.

_____, "The Novels of Edward Lewis Wallant," *DAI* 39 (1978): 2931A.

Ribalow, Harold U., "The Legacy of Edward Lewis Wallant," *CJF* 22 (Summer, 1964): 325-7.

Rovit, Earl, "A Miracle of Moral Animation," *Shen* 16 (Summer, 1965): 59-62.

Ruddel, Joyce, "The Agony of Choice: Dialectic in the Novels of Edward Lewis Wallant," *DAI* 32 (1972): 5804A.

Schulz, Max F., "Wallant and Friedman: The Glory and Agony of Love," *Crit* 10, iii (1968): 31-47. Also in Schulz, M. F., *Radical Sophistication*, 173-85.

Stanford, Raney, "The Novels of Edward Wallant," *ColQ* 17, iv (Spring, 1969): 393-405.

THE CHILDREN AT THE GATE

Angle, James, "Edward Lewis Wallant's 'Trinity of Survival'," *KanQ* 7, iv (Fall, 1975): 112-14.

Davis, William V., "The Sound of Silence: Edward Lewis Wallant's CHILDREN AT THE GATE," *Cithara* 8 (Nov., 1968): 3-25.

Galloway, David D., "Clown and Saint: The Hero in Current American Fiction," *Crit* 7, iii (1965): 58-9.

_____, *Edward Lewis Wallant*, 90-112.

Gurko, Leo, "Edward Lewis Wallant as Urban Novelist," *TCL* 20, iv (Oct., 1974): 257-9.

Hoyt, Charles A., "The Sudden Hunger: An Essay on the Novels of Edward Lewis Wallant," in Hoyt, C. A., ed., *Minor American Novelists*, 130-3.

Lorch, Thomas M., "The Novels of Edward Lewis Wallant," *ChiR* 19, ii (1967): 61-2.

Rovit, Earl, "A Miracle of Moral Animation," *Shen* 16 (Summer, 1965): 61-2.

Rubin, Louis D., Jr., "Southerners and Jews," *SoR* 2 (1966): 703-5. Also in Rubin, L. D., Jr., *Curious Death of the Novel*, 269-71.

THE HUMAN SEASON

Angle, James, "Edward Lewis Wallant's 'Trinity of Survival'," *KanQ* 7, iv (Fall, 1975): 106-8.

Davis, William V., "The Renewal of Immediacy in Edward Lewis Wallant," *Ren* 24, ii (Winter, 1972): 59-69.

Galloway, D., *Edward Lewis Wallant*, 40-60.

Gurko, Leo, "Edward Lewis Wallant as Urban Novelist," *TCL* 20, iv (Oct., 1974): 254-6.

Hoyt, Charles A., "The Sudden Hunger: An Essay on the Novels of Edward Lewis Wallant," in Hoyt, C. A., ed., *Minor American Novelists*, 124-7.

Klein, Marcus, "Further Notes on the Dereliction of Culture: Edward Lewis Wallant and Bruce Jay Friedman," in Malin, I., ed., *Contemporary American-Jewish Literature*, 230-5.

Lorch, Thomas M., "The Novels of Edward Lewis Wallant," *ChiR* 19, ii (1967): 79-80.

Russell, Kenneth C., "The Devil's Contemplative and the Miracle Rabbi, Two Novels: Golding's THE SPIRE and Wallant's HUMAN SEASON," *SMy* 3, iii (1980): 52-64.

Stanford, Raney, "The Novels of Edward Wallant," *ColQ* 17, iv (Spring, 1969): 395-7.

THE ODYSSEY OF A MIDDLEMAN (Unpublished novel)

Galloway, D., *Edward Lewis Wallant*, 36-9.

Zaitchik, Mark B., "Edward Lewis Wallant's THE ODYSSEY OF A MIDDLEMAN: A Critical Introduction," *DAI* 38 (1978): 4834A.

THE PAWNBROKER

Angle, James, "Edward Lewis Wallant's 'Trinity of Survival'," *KanQ* 7, iv (Fall, 1975): 108-111.

Baumbach, J., "The Illusion of Indifference: THE PAWNBRO-KER," *Landscape of Nightmare*, 138-46.

Becker, Ernest, "THE PAWNBROKER: A Study in Basic Psychology," *Angel in Armor: A Post-Freudian Perspective on the Nature of Man*, N.Y.: George Braziller, 1969, 75-100.

Casey, Bill, "Commitment, Compassion, and Cant: The Quality Fiction Formula," *ForumH* 4 (Spring-Summer, 1964): 28-30.

Davis, William V., "Learning to Walk on Water: Edward Lewis Wallant's THE PAWNBROKER," *LitR* 17 (Winter, 1973-74): 149-65.

Galloway, D., *Edward Lewis Wallant*, 70-90.

Gurko, Leo, "Edward Lewis Wallant as Urban Novelist," *TCL* 20, iv (Oct., 1974): 256-7.

Hoyt, Charles A., "The Sudden Hunger: An Essay on the Novels of Edward Lewis Wallant," in Hoyt, C. A., ed., *Minor American Novelists*, 127-30.

Karpowitz, Stephen, "Conscience and Cannibals: An Essay on Two Exemplary Tales—SOUTH OF WOOD and THE PAWNBROKER," *PsyR* 64 (1977): 41-62.

Lorch, Thomas M., "The Novels of Edward Lewis Wallant," *ChiR* 19, ii (1967): 80-4.

Lyons, Joseph, "THE PAWNBROKER: Flashback in the Novel and the Film," *WHR* 20 (Summer, 1966): 243-8.

Petrie, Graham, "A Note on the Novel and the Film: Flashbacks in TRISTAM SHANDY and THE PAWNBROKER," *WHR* 21 (Spring, 1967): 165-9.

Roth, David S., "THE PAWNBROKER: Sol Nazerman's Families," *BWVACET* 5, i-ii (1979): 3-5.

Stanford, Raney, "The Novels of Edward Wallant," *ColQ* 17, iv (Spring, 1969): 398-400.

THE TENANTS OF MOONBLOOM

Angle, James, "Edward Lewis Wallant's 'Trinity of Survival'," *KanQ* 7, iv (Fall, 1975): 115-18.

Baumback, J., *Landscape of Nightmare*, 146-51.

Davis, William V., "The Impossible Possibility: Edward Lewis Wallant's THE TENANTS OF MOONBLOOM," *SAJL* 2 (1982): 98-114.

Galloway, David D., "Clown and Saint: The Hero in Current American Fiction," *Crit* 7, iii (1965): 54-8.

_____, *Edward Lewis Wallant*, 113-39.

Gurko, Leo, "Edward Lewis Wallant as Urban Novelist," *TCL* 20, iv (Oct., 1974): 259-60.

Hoyt, Charles A., "The Sudden Hunger: An Essay on the Novels of Edward Lewis Wallant," in Hoyt, C. A., ed., *Minor American Novelists*, 133-7.

Lewis, Robert W., "The Hung-Up Heroes of Edward Lewis Wallant," *Ren* 24, ii (Winter, 1972): 74-84.

Lorch, Thomas M., "The Novels of Edward Lewis Wallant," *ChiR* 19, ii (1967): 87-90.

BIBLIOGRAPHY

Ayo, Nicholas, "Edward Lewis Wallant, 1926-1962," *BB* 28 (1971): 119.

Galloway, D., *Edward Lewis Wallant*, 163-6.

WAMBAUGH, JOSEPH, 1937-

GENERAL

Brady, John, "Joe Wambaugh Cops from Experience," *WD* 53, xii (Dec., 1973): 16-25.

Jeffrey, David K., "Wambaugh's Police Stories," *MTQ* 21, iv (Summer, 1980): 470-83.

Ziegler, Robert E., "Freedom and Confinement: The Policeman's Experience of Public and Private in Joseph Wambaugh," *Clues* 3, i (Spring-Summer, 1982): 9-16.

THE BLACK MARBLE

Jeffrey, David K., "Wambaugh's Police Stories," *MQ* 21, iv (Summer, 1980): 480-2.

THE BLUE KNIGHT

Jeffrey, David K., "Wambaugh's Police Stories," *MQ* 21, iv (Summer, 1980): 475-9.

Palmour, Jody, "The Tragedy of a 'Blue Knight': How the Nature of Police Work in a Class Society Stimulates an Unproductive Resolution of a Man's Character Conflict," in Viano, Emilio C., and Jeffrey H. Reiman, eds., *The Police in Society*, Lexington, Mass.: Lexington Books, 1975, 149-58.

THE CHOIRBOYS

Jeffrey, David K., "Wambaugh's Police Stories," *MQ* 21, iv (Summer, 1980): 479-80.

THE NEW CENTURIONS

Jeffrey, David K., "Wambaugh's Police Stories," *MQ* 21, iv (Summer, 1980): 471-5.

WARNER, REX, 1905-1986

GENERAL

Allen, W., *Modern Novel*, 240-1.

Atkins, John, "On Rex Warner," in Rajan, B., and A. Pearse, eds., *Focus One*, 59-65. Also in McLeod, A. L., ed., *Achievement of Rex Warner*, 23-7.

Curry, Elizabeth R., "Rex Warner on the Allegorical Novel, Power Politics, and the Contemporary Scene: A Personal Interview," *Genre* 5 (1972): 404-15.

_____, "Theme and Method in the Allegorical Novels of Rex Warner," *DA* 23 (1963): 3370-1.

DeVitis, Angelo A., "Religious Theme in the Novels of Rex Warner, Evelyn Waugh, and Graham Greene," *SDD-UW* 15 (1955): 605-6.

_____, "Rex Warner and the Cult of Power," *TCL* 6, iii (Oct., 1960): 107-16. Also in McLeod, A. L., Jr., *Achievement of Rex Warner*, 50-4.

Drenner, Don V., "Kafka, Warner and the Cult of Power," *KM* (1952): 62-4.

Flynn, James H., "Politics in the Novels of Rex Warner," *DAI* 35 (1975): 5400A.

Harrison, Tom, "Rex Warner's Writing," in Rajan, B., and A. Pearse, eds., *Focus One*, 39-42.

Maini, Darshan S., "Rex Warner's Political Novels: An Allegorical Crusade Against Fascism," *IJES* 2 (1961): 91-107. Also in McLeod, A. L., ed., *Achievement of Rex Warner*, 39-49.

McLeod, A. L., ed., *Achievement of Rex Warner*.

_____, *Rex Warner: Writer*.

Pritchett, V. S., "Rex Warner," in Baker, D. V., ed., *Modern British Writing*, 304-9. Also in McLeod, A. L., ed., *Achievement of Rex Warner*, 35-8.

Rajan, B., and A. Pearse, eds., *Focus One*.

Stonier, G. W., "The New Allegory," in Rajan, B., and A. Pearse, eds., *Focus One*, 26-9.

Woodcock, George, "Kafka and Rex Warner," *Writer and Politics*, 197-207. Also in Rajan, B., and A. Pearse, eds., *Focus One*, 59-65. Also in McLeod, A. L., ed., *Achievement of Rex Warner*, 28-34.

THE AERODROME

Atkins, John, "On Rex Warner," in Rajan, B., and A. Pearse, eds., *Focus One*, 33-7. Also in McLeod, A. L., ed., *Achievement of Rex Warner*, 32-7.

Churchill, Thomas, "Rex Warner: Homage to Necessity," *Crit* 10, i (1968): 31-40.

Curry, Elizabeth, "Rex Warner and Modern Tragedy: A Study in Conflict and Conformity," in McLeod, A. L., ed., *Achievement of Rex Warner*, 55-68.

Davenport, John, "Re-assessment: The Air Marshall's Story," *Spectator* (June 24, 1966): 796.

Flynn, James, "Rex Warner's THE AERODROME: A Study in the Politics of Twentieth-Century Fiction," *RecL* 4, iii (1975): 27-44.

Fraser, G. S., *Modern Writer and His World*, 139-41.

Karl, F. R., *Contemporary English Novel*, 265-9.

McLeod, A. L., *Rex Warner: Writer*, 22-6.

Pritchett, V. S., in Baker, D. V., ed., *Modern British Writing*, 307-8. Also in McLeod, A. L., ed., *Achievement of Rex Warner*, 37-8.

Rajan, B., "Kafka—A Comparison with Rex Warner," in Rajan, B., and A. Pearse, eds., *Focus One*, 7-14. Also in McLeod, A. L., ed., *Achievement of Rex Warner*, 16-23.

Stonier, G. W., "The New Allegory," in Rajan, B., and A. Pearse, eds., *Focus One*, 26-9.

Woodcock, George, "Kafka and Rex Warner," *Writer and Politics*, 202-6. Also in Rajan, B., and A. Pearse, eds., *Focus One*, 58-65. Also in McLeod, A. L., ed., *Achievement of Rex Warner*, 28-34.

Sudheer, V. C., "The Theme of 'Sin and Love' in THE AERODROME," *ComQ* 2, vii (1978): 114-21.

ESCAPADE: A TALE OF AVERAGE

McLeod, A. L., *Rex Warner: Writer*, 32-3.

MEN OF STONES; A MELODRAMA

DeVitis, A. A., "Rex Warner and the Cult of Power," *TCL* 6 (Oct., 1960): 112-16.

McLeod, A. L., *Rex Warner: Writer*, 30-2.

THE PROFESSOR

Curry, Elizabeth, "Rex Warner and Modern Tragedy: A Study in Conflict and Conformity," in McLeod, A. L., ed., *Achievement of Rex Warner*, 55-68.

McLeod, A. L., *Rex Warner: Writer*, 18-22.

RETURN OF THE TRAVELLER (See WHY WAS I KILLED? A DRAMATIC DIALOG)

WHY WAS I KILLED?: A DRAMATIC DIALOGUE

McLeod, A. L., *Rex Warner: Writer*, 26-30.

Nandakumar, Prema, "Rex Warner's WHY WAS I KILLED?" in McLeod, A. L., ed., *Achievement of Rex Warner*, 69-73.

THE WILD GOOSE CHASE

Atkins, John, "On Rex Warner," in Rajan, B., and A. Pearse, eds., *Focus One*, 33-7. Also in McLeod, A. L., ed., *Achievement of Rex Warner*, 23-7.

Churchill, Thomas. "Rex Warner: Homage to Necessity," *Crit* 10, i (1968): 40-4.

DeVitis, A. A., "Rex Warner and the Cult of Power," *TCL* 6 (Oct., 1960): 108-9.

Harris, Henry, "The Symbol of the Frontier in the Social Allegory of the 'Thirties'," *ZAA* 14 (1966): 127-40.

McLeod, A. L., *Rex Warner: Writer*, 10-18.

Rajan, B., "Kafka—A Comparison with Rex Warner," in Rajan, B., and A. Pearse, eds., *Focus One*, 7-14. Also in McLeod, A. L., ed., *Achievement of Rex Warner*, 23-7.

Woodcock, George, "Kafka and Rex Warner," *Writer and Politics*, 202-6. Also in Rajan, B., and A. Pearse, eds., *Focus One*, 59-65. Also in McLeod, A. L., ed., *Achievement of Rex Warner*, 23-34.

Smith, David, *Socialist Propaganda in the Twentieth-Century British Novel*, London: Macmillan; Totowa, N. J.: Rowman and Littlefield, 1978, 90-6.

WARREN, ROBERT PENN, 1905-1989

GENERAL

Allen, Charles A., "Robert Penn Warren: The Psychology of Self-Knowledge," *L&P* 8 (Spring, 1958): 21-5.

Allen, Susan E. comp., "Robert Penn Warren on His Writing," *KRev* 2, iii (1981): 61-8.

Anderson, Charles R., "Violence and Order in the Novels of Robert Penn Warren," *Hopkins Rev* 6 (Winter, 1953): 88-105. Also in Rubin, L. D., Jr., and R. D. Jacobs, eds., *Southern Renascence*, 207-24. Also in Litz, A. W., ed., *Modern American Fiction*, 278-95.

Anon., "Craft Interview with Robert Penn Warren," *NYQ* 23 (1978): 13-25.

Atkins, Floyd C., and John T. Hiers, eds., *Robert Penn Warren Talking: Interviews, 1950-1978*, N.Y.: Random, 1980.

Baker, John, "Robert Penn Warren," in *Conversations with Writers*, I, 279-302.

Bartsch, Friedemann K., "The Redemptive Vision: Robert Penn Warren and Spiritual Autobiography," *DAI* 38 (1977): 2117A-18A.

Beatty, Richmond C., and Others, eds., *The Literature of the South*, Chicago: Scott, Foresman, 1952, 629-31.

Beatty, Richmond C., "The Poetry and Novels of Robert Penn Warren," in Beatty, R. C., and Others, eds., *Vanderbilt Studies in the Humanities*, Vol. I (1951): 142-60.

Bentley, Eric, "The Meaning of Robert Penn Warren's Novels," *KR* 10 (Summer, 1948): 407-24. Also in O'Connor, W. V., eds., *Forms of Modern Fiction*, 255-72. Also, (revised) in Kostelanetz, R., ed., *On Contemporary Literature*, 616-33. Also (portion) in Rubin, L. D., Jr., and J. R. Moore, eds., *Idea of an American Novel*, 364-7.

Benton, Paul F., Jr., "The Doubleness of Life: A Study of the First Four Novels of Robert Penn Warren," *DAI* (1979): 6590A.

Betz, Norman J., "Robert Penn Warren and Pragmatism," *DAI* 36 (1975): 299A.

Bohner, C. H., *Robert Penn Warren*.

————, *Robert Penn Warren*, Rev. ed.

Bradbury, John M., "Robert Penn Warren's Novels: The Symbolic and Textual Patterns," *Accent* 13 (Spring, 1953): 77-89. Also in Longley, J. L., Jr., ed., *Robert Penn Warren*, 3-17. Also (revised and enlarged) in Bradbury, J. M., *Fugitives*, 195-230.

Brooks, C., "R. P. Warren: Experience Redeemed in Knowledge," *Hidden God*, 98-127. Also in Gray, R., ed., *Robert Penn Warren*, 17-31.

Brown, Harry N., "Warren's Continuing Quests: A Trinity," *DAI* 32 (1971): 2676A.

Burke, Lawrence M., Jr., "The Lonely Choice: A Study of the Early Fiction of Robert Penn Warren," *DAI* 35 (1975): 4501A-02A.

Cargill, Oscar, "Anatomist of Monsters," *CE* 9 (Oct., 1947): 1-8. Also in Cargill, O., *Toward a Pluralistic Criticism*, Carbondale: So. Ill. Un. Pr., 1965, 141-53.

Carter, Everett, "The 'Little Myth' of Robert Penn Warren," *MFS* 6 (Spring, 1960): 3-12.

Casper, Leonard, *Robert Penn Warren*.

————, "Robert Penn Warren: An Assessment," *DilimanR* 2 (Oct., 1954): 400-24.

Cayton, Robert F., "The Fictional Voices of Robert Penn Warren," *FourQ* 21, iv (May, 1972): 93-9.

————, "Point of View in the Novels of Robert Penn Warren," *DAI* 30 (1969): 313A-14A.

Chambers, Robert H., "Robert Penn Warren: His Growth as a Writer," *DAI* 31 (1970): 1381A-82A.

Clark, Marden J., "Religious Implications in the Novels of Robert Penn Warren," *BYUS* 4 (Autumn, 1961): 67-79.

————, "Symbolic Structure in the Novels of Robert Penn Warren," *DAI* 18 (1958): 229-30.

Clark, W. B., ed., *Critical Essays on Robert Penn Warren*.

Davis, Joe, "Robert Penn Warren and the Journey to the West," *MFS* 6 (Spring, 1960): 73-82.

Douglas, Wallace W., "Drug Store Gothic: The Style of Robert Penn Warren," *CE* 15 (Feb., 1954): 265-72.

Eisinger, C. E., "*Fiction of the Forties*, 198-229. Also in Nakadate, N., ed., *Robert Penn Warren*, 11-37.

Ellis, Helen E., "Sunday School and Sartre: The Tension in Robert Penn Warren's Novels," *DAI* 34 (1974): 4257A-58A.

Ellison, Ralph, and Eugene Walter, "The Art of Fiction 18: Robert Penn Warren," *ParisR* 4 (Spring-Summer, 1957): 112-40. Also in *Writers at Work*, First ser., 183-205. Also in Longley, J. L., ed., *Robert Penn Warren*, 18-45.

Farrell, David, "Reminiscences: A Conversation with Robert Penn Warren," *SoR* 16 (1980): 782-98.

Fisher, Ruth, "A Conversation with Robert Penn Warren," *FourQ* 21, iv (May, 1972): 3-17.

Flint, F. Cudworth, "Robert Penn Warren," *AmOx* 34 (Apr., 1947): 65-79.

Frank, Joseph, "Romanticism and Reality in Robert Penn Warren," *The Widening Gyre: Crisis and Mastery in Modern Literature*, New Brunswick, N.J.: Rutgers Un. Pr., 1963, 179-200.

Frank, William, "Mr. Warren's Achievement," *CE* 19 (May, 1958): 365-6.

Fridy, Wilford E., "Robert Penn Warren's Use of Kentucky Materials in His Fiction as a Basis for His New Mythos," *DA* 30 (1969): 1523A.

Frohock, W. M., "Mr. Warren's Albatross," *SWR* 36 (Winter, 1951): 48-59. Also in Frohock, W. M., *Novel of Violence in America*, 86-105.

Gado, Frank., "An Interview with Robert Penn Warren," in Gado, F., ed., *First Person*, 63-73.

Garvin, F. G., "Robert Penn Warren and the Promise of History," *Myth of Southern History*, 131-70.

Gossett, L. Y., "Violence and the Integrity of the Self," *Violence in Recent Southern Fiction*, 52-75.

Grimshaw, James A., "'Supreme Fiction': Robert Penn Warren at 75," *SoR* 17, ii (Apr., 1981): 444-9.

Gross, Seymour, "Robert Penn Warren," *Critic* 18 (Oct.-Nov., 1959): 11-13, 80-2.

Guttenberg, Barnett, "The Novels of Robert Penn Warren," *DAI* 33 (1972): 1169A.

_____, *Web of Being*.

Hanson, Sandra S., "'In Separateness Only Does Love Learn Definition': The Idea of Love in the Novels of Robert Penn Warren," *DAI* 39 (1978): 3558A-59A.

Hardy, John E., "Robert Penn Warren's Double Hero," *VQR* 36 (Autumn, 1960): 583-97.

Harris, Frances J., "Time Past and Time Present: Hawthorne and Warren in the American Literary Continuum," *DAI* 41, vii (Jan., 1981): 3106A-07A.

Havard, William, "The Burden of the Literary Mind: Some Meditations on Robert Penn Warren as Historian," *SAQ* 62 (Autumn, 1963): 516-31. Also in Longley, J. L., Jr., ed., *Robert Penn Warren*, 178-94. Also in Gray, R., ed., *Robert Penn Warren*, 183-95.

Hayashi, Nobunyuki, "On the Novels of Robert Penn Warren," *Jinbun Gakukho* (Tokyo Metropolitan Un.), No. 28 (Mar., 1962): 3-24. [Not seen.]

Haynes, Robert P., "Warren the Novelist," *DAI* 38 (1977): 3499A.

Hendry, Irene, "The Regional Novel: The Example of Robert Penn Warren," *SR* 53 (Jan., 1945): 84-102.

Herring, Henry D., "The Environment in Robert Penn Warren's Fictional South," *DA* 29 (1969): 3141A.

_____, "Politics in the Novels of Robert Penn Warren," *RANAM* 4 (1971): 48-60. [Not seen.]

Heseltine, H. P., "The Deep, Twisting Strain of Life: The Novels of Robert Penn Warren," *McR* No. 5 (1962): 76-89. Also in Nakadate, N., ed., *Robert Penn Warren*, 148-61.

Hoffman, F. J., *Art of Southern Fiction*, 31-3.

Humboldt, Charles, "The Lost Cause of Robert Penn Warren," *M&M* 1 (July, 1948): 8-23.

Hynes, Sam, "Robert Penn Warren: The Symbolic Journey," *UKCR* 17 (Summer, 1951): 279-85.

"Interview with Eleanor Clark and Robert Penn Warren," *NER* 1 (1978): 49-70.

Jabol, George J., "Robert Penn Warren: Philosopher—Novelist," *DAI* 37 (1977): 6485A-86A.

Jones, Madison, "The Novels of Robert Penn Warren," *SAQ* 62 (Autumn, 1963): 488-98.

Joost, Nicholas, "Robert Penn Warren and New Directions in the Novel," in Gardiner, H. C., ed., *Fifty Years of the American Novel*, 27384.

Justus, J. H., *Achievement of Robert Penn Warren*.

Justus, James H., "The Concept of Gesture in the Novels of Robert Penn Warren," *DA* 22 (1962): 3201.

_____, "The Mariner and Robert Penn Warren," *TSLL* 8 (Spring, 1966): 117-28. Also in Nakadate, N., ed., *Robert Penn Warren*, 126-37. Also in Clark, W. B., ed., *Critical Essays on Robert Penn Warren*, 111-21.

_____, "Warren and the Doctrine of Complicity," *FourQ* 21, iv (May, 1972): 93-9.

Kehl, Delmar, G., "The Dialectics of Reality in the Fiction of Robert Penn Warren," *DA* 28 (1968): 4633A.

Kelvin, Norman, "The Failure of Robert Penn Warren," *CE* 18 (Apr., 1957): 355-64.

Langman, F. N., "The Compelled Imagination: Robert Penn Warren's Conception of the Philosophical Novelist," *SoRA* 4, iii (1971): 192-202.

Law, Richard G., "'The Mastering Vision': The Early Fiction of Robert Penn Warren," *DAI* 34 (1974): 7762A-63A.

Lee, Young-Oak, "After the Fall: Tragic Themes in the Major Works of Nathaniel Hawthorne and Robert Penn Warren," *DAI* 38 (1978): 6195A-96A.

Linenthal, Mark, Jr., "Robert Penn Warren and the Southern Agrarians," *DA* 17 (1957): 2611-12.

Lloyd, Samuel T., III., "Robert Penn Warren: In the Midst of the World," *DAI* 43 (1981): 1545A-46A.

Longley, J. L., Jr., *Robert Penn Warren*.

_____, ed., *Robert Penn Warren*.

_____, "Robert Penn Warren: American Man of Letters," *A&S* (Spring, 1965): 16-22. [Not seen.]

_____, "Robert Penn Warren: The Deeper Rub," *SoR* 1 (Autumn, 1965): 968-73.

Mohrt, Michael, "Robert Penn Warren and the Myth of the Outlaw," *YFS* No. 10 (1953): 70-84.

Moore, Littleton H., Jr., *Robert Penn Warren and History*.

_____, "Robert Penn Warren and the Terror of Answered Prayer," *MissQ* 21 (Winter, 1968): 29-36.

Mulyarchik, Alexander, "Responding to the Call of the Times: For the 75th Birthday of Robert Penn Warren," *SovL* 7 (1980): 157-60.

Nakadate, Neil, "Identity, Dream, and Exploration: Warren's Later Fiction," in Nakadate, N., ed., *Robert Penn Warren*, 175-89.

_____, "The Narrative Stances of Robert Penn Warren," *DAI* 33 (1972): 2386A.

_____, ed., *Robert Penn Warren*.

_____, "Robert Penn Warren and the Confessional Novel," *Genre* 2 (Dec., 1969): 326-40.

Newton, Thomas A., "A Character Index of Robert Penn Warren's Long Works of Fiction," *ESRS* 26, iv (1978): 6-104.

Osborne, Rosanne, "The Browning of the Flower: A Study of the Women Characters in the Novels of Robert Penn Warren," *DAI* 41, vii (Feb., 1981): 3585A.

Ross, Joe C., "Robert Penn Warren and the Negro," *DA* 29 (1969): 4501A-02A.

Ruoff, James E., "Robert Penn Warren's Pursuit of Justice: From Briar Patch to Cosmos," *RSSCW* 27 (Mar., 1959): 19-38.

Sale, Richard B., "An Interview in New Haven with Robert Penn Warren," *SNNTS* 2 (1970): 325-54. Also, with corrections, in Clark, W. B., ed., *Critical Essays on Robert Penn Warren*, 81-107.

Samuels, Charles T., "In the Wilderness," *Crit* 5 (Fall, 1959): 46-57.

Shepherd, Allen G., "A Critical Study of the Fiction of Robert Penn Warren," *DA* 16 (1966): 7325-26.

_____, "Prototype, Byblow and Reconception: Notes on the Relation of Warren's THE CIRCUS IN THE ATTIC to His Novels and Poetry," *MissQ* 33, i (Winter, 1979-80): 3-17.

_____, "Robert Penn Warren as a Philosophical Novelist," *WHR* 24, ii (Spring, 1970): 157-68.

_____, "Toward an Analysis of the Prose Style of Robert Penn Warren," *SAF* 1, ii (Autumn, 1973): 188-202. Also in Clark, W. B., ed., *Critical Essays on Robert Penn Warren*, 137-50.

Stevens, Gary W., "The Novels of Robert Penn Warren: The Theme of Community," *DAI* 34 (1974): 5996A-97A.

Stewart, John L., "The Achievement of Robert Penn Warren," *SAQ* 47 (Oct., 1948): 562-79.

_____, *Burden of Time*, 486-98, 517-18, 530-42.

_____, "Robert Penn Warren and the Knot of History," *ELH* 26 (Mar., 1959): 102-36.

Stitt, Peter, "An Interview with Robert Penn Warren," *SR* 85 (1977): 467-77.

Strandberg, Victor, "Warren's Osmosis," *Criticism* 10 (Winter, 1968): 23-40. Also in Clark, W. B., ed., *Critical Essays on Robert Penn Warren*, 122-36.

Strugnell, John R., "Robert Penn Warren and the Uses of the Past," *REL* 4, iv (Oct., 1963): 93-102.

Sumner, D. Nathan, "The Function of Historical Sources in Hawthorne, Melville, and R. P. Warren," *RS* 40 (June, 1972): 103-14.

Thorp, W., *American Writing in the Twentieth Century*, 252-4.

Vliet, Rodney M., "The Concept of Evil in the Novels of Robert Penn Warren," *DAI* 35 (1974): 1677A.

Walker, M., *Robert Penn Warren*.

_____, "Robert Penn Warren: An Interview," *JAmS* 8 (1974): 229-45.

Wasserstrom, William, *Heiress of All the Ages: Sex and Sentiment in the Genteel Tradition*, Minneapolis: Un. of Minn. Pr., 1959, 114-22.

_____, "Robert Penn Warren: From Paleface to Redskin," *PrS* 31 (Winter, 1957): 323-3.

West, P., *Robert Penn Warren*.

Westendorp, T. A., "Robert Penn Warren as Critic and Novelist: The Early Phase," *DQR* 7, iv (1977): 270A-71A.

White, Ellington, in Rubin, L. D., Jr., and R. D. Jacobs, eds., *South*, 198-209.

White, Robert, "Robert Penn Warren and the Myth of the Garden," *Faulkner Studies* 3 (Winter, 1954): 59-67.

Widmer, Kingsley, "The Father-Killers of R. P. Warren," *Paunch* 22 (Jan., 1965): 57-64.

Williams, Wallace A. C., "Religious Ethics in the Writings of Robert Penn Warren," *DAI* 35 (1975): 5519A-20A..

Witteveld, Peter J., "A Light in the Dark Place: The Hawthorne-Warren Relationship," *DAI* 38 (1977): 270A-71A.

Yeatman, Joan R., "Narrators and Commentators in Four Novels by Robert Penn Warren," *DAI* 33 (1972): 2399A.

ALL THE KING'S MEN

Allen, Charles, "Robert Penn Warren: The Psychology of Self-Knowledge," *L&P* 8 (Spring, 1958): 23-5.

Allen, W., *Modern Novel*, 128-30.

Anderson, Charles R., "Violence and Order in the Novels of Robert Penn Warren," *Hopkins Rev* 6, ii (Winter, 1953): 96-100. Also in Rubin, L. D., Jr., and R. D. Jacobs, eds., *Southern Renascence*, 215-19. Also in Litz, A. W., ed., *Modern American Fiction*, 286-90.

Baker, Joseph E., "Irony in Fiction: ALL THE KING'S MEN," *CE* 9 (Dec., 1947): 122-30. Also in Beebe, M., and L. A. Field, eds., *Robert Penn Warren's ALL THE KING'S MEN*, 90-100.

Bauerle, Richard F., "The Emblematic Opening of Warren's ALL THE KING'S MEN," *PLL* 8, iii (Summer, 1972): 312-14.

Baumbach, J., "The Metaphysics of Demagoguery: ALL THE KING'S MEN," *Landscape of Nightmare*, 16-34. Also in Chambers, R. H., ed., *Twentieth Century Interpretations of ALL THE KING'S MEN*, 126-42.

Beebe, Keith, "Biblical Motifs in ALL THE KING'S MEN," *Jnl. of Bible & Religion* 30 (Apr., 1962): 123-30.

Bentley, Eric, "The Meaning of Robert Penn Warren's Novels," *KR* 10 (1948): 413-21. Also in O'Connor, W. V., ed., *Forms of Modern Fiction*, 255-72. Also in Kostelanetz, R., ed., *On Contemporary Literature*, 621-9.

Blotner, J., *Modern American Political Novel*, 219-26.

Bohner, C. H., *Robert Penn Warren*, 82-98.

_____, *Robert Penn Warren*, Rev. ed., 65-80.

Bradbury, John M., "Robert Penn Warren's Novels: The Symbolic and Textual Patterns," *Accent* 13 (Spring, 1953): 82-4. Also in Longley, J. L., Jr., ed., *Robert Penn Warren*, 9-11. Also (revised) in Bradbury, J. M., *Fugitives*, 209-12, 229.

Brantley, Frederick, "The Achievement of Robert Penn Warren," in Rajan, B., ed., *Modern American Poetry (Focus Five)*, London: Denis Dobson, 1950, 67-72.

Brooks, C., *Hidden God*, 103-9. Also in Gray, R., ed., *Robert Penn Warren*, 20-4.

Byrne, Clifford M., "The Philosophical Development in Four of Robert Penn Warren's Novels," *McNR* 9 (Winter, 1957): 63-5.

Cargill, Oscar, "Anatomist of Monsters," *CE* 9 (Oct., 1947): 6-8. Also in Cargill, O., *Towards a Pluralistic Criticism*, Carbondale: So. Ill. Un. Pr., 1965, 148-2.

Carter, Everett, "The 'Little Myth' of Robert Warren," *MFS* 6 (Spring, 1960): 8-10.

Casper, Leonard, "Mirror for Mobs: The Willie Stark Stories," *Drama Critique* 2 (Nov., 1959): 120-4.

_____, *Robert Penn Warren*, 121-32.

_____, "Robert Penn Warren: Method and Canon," *DilimanR* 2 (July, 1954): 285-8.

Chambers, R. H., ed., *Twentieth Century Interpretations of ALL THE KING'S MEN*.

Clements, A. L., "Theme and Reality in AT HEAVEN'S GATE and ALL THE KING'S MEN," *Criticism* 5 (1963): 27-44.

Cottrell, Beekman, "Cass Mastern and the Awful Responsibility of Time," in Sochatoff, A. F., and Others, eds., *ALL THE KING'S MEN: A Symposium*, 39-49. Also in Chambers, R. H., ed., *Twentieth Century Interpretations of ALL THE KING'S MEN*, 116-25.

Cowser, R. L., Jr., "Kingfish of American Opera: An Interview with Carlisle Floyd," *SoQ* 20, iii (Spring, 1982): 5-18.

Davenport, F. G., *Myth of Southern History*, 144-9, 155-60.

Davis, Robert M., "BRIDESHEAD REVISITED and ALL THE KING'S MEN: Toward a Definition of Forties Sensibility," *EWN* 14, ii (1980): 1-4.

Eisinger, Chester E., "Robert Penn Warren: The Conservative Quest for Identity," *Fiction of the Forties*, 214-23. Also in Beebe, M., and L. A. Field, eds., *Robert Penn Warren's ALL THE KING'S MEN*, 149-57. Also in Nakadate, N., ed., *Robert Penn Warren*, 24-31.

Fergusson, Francis, "Three Novels," *Perspectives USA* No. 6 (Winter, 1954): 30-44.

Flint, F. Cudworth, "Robert Penn Warren," *AmOx* 34 (Apr., 1947): 65-73.

Fortin, Marilyn B., "Jack Burden's Search for Identity in ALL THE KING'S MEN," *Lit* No. 4 (1963): 33-7.

Frank, Joseph, "Romanticism and Reality in Robert Penn Warren," *HudR* 4 (Summer, 1951): 248-50. Also in Frank, J., *The Widening Gyre: Crisis and Mastery in Modern Literature*, New Brunswick, N. J.: Rutgers Un. Pr., 1963, 183-6. Also in Beebe, M., and L. A. Field, eds., *Robert Penn Warren's ALL THE KING'S MEN*, 147-9.

Gerhard, George, "ALL THE KING'S MEN: A Symposium," *Folio* 15 (May, 1950): 4-11.

Girault, Norton R., "The Narrator's Mind as Symbol: An Analysis of ALL THE KING'S MEN," *Accent* 7 (Summer, 1947): 220-34. Also in Aldridge, J. W., ed., *Critiques and Essays in Modern Fiction*, 200-16. Also in Beebe, M., and L. A. Field, eds., *Robert Penn Warren's ALL THE KING'S MEN*, 101-17. Also in Chambers, R. H., ed., *Twentieth Century Interpretations of ALL THE KING'S MEN*, 29-47. Also in Nakadate, N., ed., *Robert Penn Warren*, 60-76.

Gray, Richard J., "The American Novelist and American History: A Revaluation of ALL THE KING'S MEN," *JAmS* 6 (Dec., 1972): 297-307.

————, *Literature of Memory*, 70-80.

Gross, Harvey, "History as Metaphysical Pathos: Modern Literature and the Idea of History," *DenverQ* 1 (Autumn, 1966): 1-6.

Gross, Seymour L., "The Achievement of Robert Penn Warren," *CE* 18 (Apr., 1957): 361-5. Also in Beebe, M., and L. A. Field, eds., *Robert Penn Warren's ALL THE KING'S MEN*, 133-9.

————, "Conrad and ALL THE KING'S MEN," *TCL* 3 (Apr., 1957): 27-32.

————, "Robert Penn Warren," *Critic* 18 (Oct.-Nov., 1959): 11-13, 80-2.

Guttenberg, B., *Web of Being*, 34-55.

Hall, J., *Lunatic Giant in the Drawing Room*, 81-110.

Hardy, John E., "Robert Penn Warren's Double-Hero," *VQR* 36 (Autumn, 1960): 588-97. Also as "Robert Penn Warren: The Dialectic of Self," in Hardy, J. E., *Man in the Modern Novel*, 194-207. Also in Beebe, M., and L. A. Field, eds., *Robert Penn Warren's ALL THE KING'S MEN*, 157-67.

Hart, John A., "Some Major Images in ALL THE KING'S MEN," in Sochatoff, A. F., and Others, eds., *ALL THE KING'S MEN: A Symposium*, 63-74.

Heilman, Robert B., "Melpomene as Wallflower; or, The Reading of Tragedy," *SR* 55 (Winter, 1947): 154-66. Also in Beebe, M., and L. A. Field, eds., *Robert Penn Warren's ALL THE KING'S MEN*, 79-89. Also in Longley, J. L., Jr., ed., *Robert Penn Warren*, 82-95. Also in Chambers, R. H., ed., *Twentieth Century Interpretations of ALL THE KING'S MEN*, 16-28.

Heseltine, H. P., "The Deep, Twisting Strain of Life: The Novels of Robert Penn Warren," *MCR* No. 5 (1962): 85-9. Also in Nakadate, N., ed., *Robert Penn Warren*, 157-61.

Hoffman, F. J., *Art of Southern Fiction*, 33-6.

Hudson, Richard B., "ALL THE KING'S MEN: A Symposium," *Folio* 15 (May, 1950): 11-13.

Humboldt, Charles, "The Lost Cause of Robert Penn Warren," *M&M* 1 (July, 1948): 15-18.

Humphrey, R., *Stream of Consciousness in the Modern Novel*, 114-16.

Hannaford, Richard, "Sugar-Boy and Violence in ALL THE KING'S MEN," *NConL* 6, iii (1976): 10-13.

Inge, M. Thomas, "An American Novel of Ideas," *UCQ* 12, iv (Mar., 1967): 35-40.

Johnson, Glen M., "The Pastness of ALL THE KING'S MEN," *AL* 51 (1980): 553-7.

Justus, J. H., *Achievement of Robert Penn Warren*, 191-206.

Justus, James H., "All the Burdens of Warren's ALL THE KING'S MEN," in French, W., ed, *Forties*, 191-201.

————, "A Note on John Crowe Ransom and Robert Penn Warren," *AL* 41 (Nov., 1969): 425-30. [Infl. of R's 'Dead Boy' on ALL THE KING'S MEN.]

Kaplan, Charles, "Jack Burden: Modern Ishmael," *CE* 22 (Oct., 1960): 19-24.

Katope, Christopher G., "Robert Penn Warren's ALL THE KING'S MEN: A Novel of 'Pure Imagination'," *TSLL* 12 (1970): 493-510.

Kelvin, Norman, "The Failure of Robert Penn Warren," *CE* 18 (Apr., 1957): 58-60. Also in Beebe, M., and L. A. Field, eds., *Robert Penn Warren's ALL THE KING'S MEN*, 129-32.

Kerr, Dell, "An Exercise on Robert Penn Warren's ALL THE KING'S MEN," *Exercise Exchange* 5 (Oct., 1957): 8-9.

Kerr, Elizabeth, "Polarity of Themes in ALL THE KING'S MEN," *MFS* 6 (Spring, 1960): 25-46. Also in Beebe, M., and L. A. Field, eds., *Robert Penn Warren's ALL THE KING'S MEN*, 175-95.

King, R. H., *Southern Renaissance*, 234-41.

King, Roma A., Jr., "Time and Structure in the Early Novels of Robert Penn Warren," *SAQ* (Autumn, 1957): 486-93.

Konikkara, Sister Cleopatra, "Robert Penn Warren's ALL THE KING'S MEN," in Menon, K. P. K., et al., eds., *Literary Studies*, 201-10.

Krieger, Murray, "The Assumption of the 'Burden' of History in ALL THE KING'S MEN," *Classic Vision*, 287-309.

Langman, F. N., "The Compelled Imagination: Robert Penn Warren's Conception of the Philosophical Novelist," *SoRA* 4, iii (1971): 200-2.

Law, Richard G., "'The Case of the Upright Judge': The Nature of Truth in ALL THE KING'S MEN," *SAF* 6 (Spring, 1978): 1-19.

Longley, J. L., Jr., *Robert Penn Warren*, 12-17.

Ljungquist, Kent, "Jack Burden's 'Kingdom by the Sea'," *NConL* 10, i (1980): 4-5.

Mansfield, Luther S., "History and the Historical Process in ALL THE KING'S MEN," *CentR* 22 (1978): 214-30.

Martin, R. Glenn, "Diction in Robert Penn Warren's ALL THE KING'S MEN," *EJ* 58 (Nov., 1969): 1169-74.

McCarron, William E., "Tennyson, Donne, and ALL THE KING'S MEN," *AN&Q* 17, ix (1979): 140-1.

————, "Warren's ALL THE KING'S MEN and Arnold's 'To Marguerite—Continued'," *AL* 47, i (1975): 115-16.

McCarthy, Paul, "Sports and Recreation in ALL THE KING'S MEN," *MissQ* 22, ii (Spring, 1969): 113-30.

Meckier, Jerome, "Burden's Complaint: The Disintegrated Personality as Theme and Style in Robert Penn Warren's ALL THE KING'S MEN," *SNNTS* 2, i (1970): 7-21. Also in Chambers, R. H., ed., *Twentieth Century Interpretations of ALL THE KING'S MEN*, 57-72.

Milne, G., *American Political Novel*, 153-63.

Mizener, Arthur, "Robert Penn Warren: ALL THE KING'S MEN," *SoR* 3 (Oct., 1967): 874-94. Also in Gray, R., ed., *Robert Penn Warren*, 51-66.

––––––, *Twelve Great American Novels*, 177-98.

Moore, James T., "Huey Long, Robert Penn Warren and the Film Makers: Southern Demagoguery as Portrayed in ALL THE KING'S MEN," *IllQ* 44, iv (1982): 35-43.

Nakadate, Neil E., "Robert Penn Warren and the Confessional Novel," *Genre* 2 (Dec., 1969): 335-8.

Nemerov, Howard, in *Furioso* 2 (Fall, 1946): 69-71.

Newlin, Louisa F., "Robert Penn Warren's Use of History in ALL THE KING'S MEN," *DAI* 40 (1979): 857A.

Noble, D. W., *Eternal Adam and the New World Garden*, 178-86.

O'Brien, Joseph, "Cultural History in ALL THE KING'S MEN," *NConL* 2, iii (May, 1972): 14-15.

Olson, David B., "Jack Burden and the Ending of ALL THE KING'S MEN," *MissQ* 26 (1973): 165-76.

Payne, Ladell, "Willie Stark and Huey Long: Atmosphere, Myth or Suggestion," *AQ* 20 (Fall, 1968): 580-95. Also in Chambers, R. H., ed., *Twentieth Century Interpretations of ALL THE KING'S MEN*, 99-115. Also in Nakadate, N., ed., *Robert Penn Warren*, 77-92.

Raben, Joseph, "ALL THE KING'S MEN: A Symposium," *Folio* 15 (May, 1950): 14-18.

Ransom, John Crowe, "ALL THE KING'S MEN: A Symposium," *Folio* 15 (May, 1950): 2-3.

Ray, Robert J., and Ann, "Time in ALL THE KING'S MEN: A Stylistic Analysis," *TSLL* 5 (Autumn, 1963): 452-7.

Rubin, Louis D., Jr., "All the King's Meanings," *GaR* 8 (Winter, 1954): 422-34. Also in Rubin, L. D., Jr., *Curious Death of the Novel*, 222-38. Also in Beebe, M., and L. A. Field, eds., *Robert Penn Warren's ALL THE KING'S MEN*, 28-39.

––––––, "Burden's Landing: ALL THE KING'S MEN and the Modern South," *Faraway South*, 105-30.

Ruoff, James, "Humpty Dumpty and ALL THE KING'S MEN: A Note on Robert Penn Warren's Teleology," *TCL* 3 (Oct., 1957): 128-34. Also in Westbrook, M., ed., *Modern American Novel*, 196-208. Also in Beebe, M., and L. A. Field, eds., *Robert Penn Warren's ALL THE KING'S MEN*, 139-47. Also in Chambers, R. H., ed., *Twentieth Century Interpretations of ALL THE KING'S MEN*, 84-92.

––––––, "Robert Penn Warren's Pursuit of Justice," *RSSCW* 27 (1959): 25-30.

Sale, Roger, "Having It Both Ways in ALL THE KING'S MEN," *HudR* 14 (Spring, 1961): 68-76. Also in Beebe, M., and L. A. Field, eds., *Robert Penn Warren's ALL THE KING'S MEN*, 168-75.

Satterwhite, Joseph N., "Robert Penn Warren and Emily Dickinson," *MLN* 71 (May, 1956): 347-9.

Scouten, Arthur H., "Warren, Huey Long, and ALL THE KING'S MEN," *FourQ* 21, iv (May, 1972): 23-6.

Shepherd, Allen, "ALL THE KING'S MEN: Using the Author's Guide to the Novel," *EJ* 62 (1973): 704-8.

––––––, " 'Clean Hands and a Pure Heart': Hugh Miller in Robert Penn Warren's ALL THE KING'S MEN," *NConL* 11, iii (May, 1981): 3-5.

––––––, "Percy's THE MOVIEGOER and Warren's ALL THE KING'S MEN," *NMW* 4, i (Spring, 1971): 2-14.

––––––, "Sugar-Boy as Foil in ALL THE KING'S MEN," *NConL* 1, ii (Mar., 1971): 1-5.

Sillars, Malcolm O., "Warren's ALL THE KING'S MEN: A Study in Populism," *AQ* 9 (Fall, 1957): 345-53. Also in Beebe, M., and L. A. Field, eds., *Robert Penn Warren's ALL THE KING'S MEN*, 117-25.

Simmons, James C., "Adam's Lobectomy and the Meaning of ALL THE KING'S MEN," *PMLA* 86, i (Jan., 1971): 84-9. Also in Chambers, R. H., ed., *Twentieth Century Interpretations of ALL THE KING'S MEN*, 73-83.

Slack, Robert C., "The Telemachus Theme," in Sochatoff, A. F., et al., eds., *All THE KING'S MEN: A Symposium*, 30-8. Also in Chambers, R. H., ed., *Twentieth Century Interpretations of ALL THE KING'S MEN*, 48-56.

––––––, "Willie Stark and William James," in Bain, Joseph, and Others, eds., *In Honor of Austin Wright*, 71-9.

Sochatoff, A. Fred, "Some Treatments of the Huey Long Theme," in Sochatoff, A. F., and Others, eds., *ALL THE KING'S MEN: A Symposium*, 3-15.

Stallknecht, Newton P., "A Study in Nihilism," *Folio* 15 (May, 1950): 18-22. Also in Beebe, M., and L. A. Field, eds., *Robert Penn Warren's ALL THE KING'S MEN*, 125-8.

Steinberg, Erwin R., "The Enigma of Willie Stark," in Sochatoff, A. F., and Others, eds., *ALL THE KING'S MEN: A Symposium*, 17-28.

Stewart, James T., "Two Uses of Maupassant by R. P. Warren," *MLN* 70 (Apr., 1955): 279-80.

Stewart, John L., *Burden of Time*, 504-6.

Stout, Cushing, "ALL THE KING'S MEN and the Shadow of William James," *SoR* 6 (1970): 920-34. Also in Clark, W. B., ed., *Critical Essays on Robert Penn Warren*, 160-71.

Strugnell, John R., "Robert Penn Warren and the Uses of the Past," *REL* 4, iv (Oct., 1963): 96-8.

Stuckey, W. J., *Pulitzer Prize Novels*, 132-7.

Trilling, Diana, in *Nation* 163 (Aug. 24, 1946): 220.

Tyler, Parker, "Novel Into Film: ALL THE KING'S MEN," *KR* 12 (Spring, 1950): 369-76. Also in Kenyon Review. *Kenyon Critics*, 225-32.

Vauthier, Simone, "The Case of the Vanishing Narratee: An Inquiry Into ALL THE KING'S MEN," *SLJ* 6, ii (Spring, 1974): 42-69. Also in Clark, W. B., ed., *Critical Essays on Robert Penn Warren*, 93-114.

Wade, John D., in *VQR* 23 (Winter, 1947): 138-41.

Walcutt, C. C., *Man's Changing Mask*, 298-300.

Walker, M., *Robert Penn Warren*, 97-106.

Walling, William, "In Which Humpty Dumpty Becomes King," in Peary, G., and R. Shatzkin, eds., *Modern American Novel and the Movies*, 168-77.

Warren, Robert Penn, "ALL THE KING'S MEN: The Matrix of Experience," *YR* 53 (Winter, 1964): 161-7. Also as "Introduction" in Warren, R. P., *All the King's Men*, Time Reading Program Edition, N.Y.: Time-Life, 1964. Also in Beebe, M., and L. A. Field, eds., *Robert Penn Warren: ALL THE KING'S MEN*, 23-8. Also in Longley, J. L., Jr., *Robert Penn Warren*, 75-81. Also in Nakadate, N., ed., *Robert Penn Warren*, 54-9.

_____, "In the Time of ALL THE KING'S MEN," *NYTBR* (May 31, 1981): 9, 39-42.

_____, "A Note to ALL THE KING'S MEN," *SR* 61 (1953): 476-80. Also, revised, as "Introduction" to Warren, R. P., *All the King's Men*, Modern Library edition, N.Y.: Random House, 1953, i-vi. Also in Chambers, R. H., ed., *Twentieth Century Interpretations of ALL THE KING'S MEN*, 93-7.

Weissbuch, Ted N., "Jack Burden: Call Me Carraway," *CE* 22 (Feb., 1961): 361.

Welch, Dennis M., "Image Making: Politics and Character Development in ALL THE KING'S MEN," *HSL* 8, iii (1976): 155-77.

West, P., *Robert Penn Warren*, 28-34.

White, Robert, "Robert Penn Warren and the Myth of the Garden," *Faulkner Studies* 3 (Winter, 1954): 61-4.

Whittington, Curtis, Jr., "The 'Burden' of Narration: Democratic Perspective and First-Person Point of View in the American Novel," *SHR* 2 (Spring, 1968): 236-45.

Wilcox, Earl, "'A Cause for Laughter, a Thing for Tears': Humor in ALL THE KING'S MEN," *SLJ* 12, i (1979): 27-35.

_____, "Right On! ALL THE KING'S MEN in the Classroom," *FourQ* 21, iv (May, 1972): 69-78. Also in Chambers, R. H., *Twentieth Century Interpretations of ALL THE KING'S MEN*, 143-53.

_____, "Warren's ALL THE KING'S MEN, Epigraph," *Expl* 26 (Dec., 1967): Item 29.

Wilson, Mary Ann, "Search for an Eternal Present: ABSALOM, ABSALOM! and ALL THE KING'S MEN," *ConnR* 8, i (1974): 95-100.

Winchell, Mark R., "O Happy Sin! *Felix Culpa* in ALL THE KING'S MEN," *MissQ* 31 (1978): 570-85.

Woodruff, Neal, Jr., "The Technique of ALL THE KING'S MEN," in Sochatoff, A. F., ed., *ALL THE KING'S MEN: A Symposium*, 51-62.

AT HEAVEN'S GATE

Anderson, Charles R., "Violence and Order in the Novels of Robert Penn Warren," *Hopkins Rev* 6, ii (Winter, 1953): 94-6. Also in Rubin, L. D., Jr., and R. D. Jacobs, eds., *Southern Renascence*, 213-15. Also in Litz, A. W., ed., *Modern American Fiction*, 284-6.

Beatty, Richmond C., "The Poetry and Novels of Robert Penn Warren," in Beatty, R. c., et al., eds., *Vanderbilt Studies in the Humanities*, Vol. I (1951): 152-4.

Bentley, Eric, "The Meaning of Robert Penn Warren's Novels," *KR* 10 (1948): 411-13. Also in O'Connor, W. V., ed., *Forms of Modern Fiction*, 259-61. Also in Kostelanetz, R., ed., *On Contemporary Literature*, 619-21.

Bohner, C. H., *Robert Penn Warren*, 70-82.

_____, *Robert Penn Warren*, Rev. ed., 54-64.

Bradbury, John M., "Robert Penn Warren's Novels: The Symbolic and Textual Patterns," *Accent* 13 (Spring, 1953): 80-2. Also in Longley, J. L., Jr., ed., *Robert Penn Warren*, 6-9. Also (revised) in Bradbury, J. M., *Fugitives* 206-9+.

Byrne, Clifford M., "The Philosophical Development in Four of Robert Penn Warren's Novels," *McNR* 9 (Winter, 1957): 61-3.

Cargill, Oscar, "Anatomist of Monsters," *CE* 9 (Oct., 1947): 4-6. Also in Cargill, O., *Towards a Pluralistic Criticism*, Carbondale: So. Ill. Un. Pr., 1965, 146-8.

Casper, Leonard, *Robert Penn Warren*, 70-82.

_____, "Robert Penn Warren: Method and Canon," *DilimanR* 2 (July, 1954): 282-3.

Clements, A. L., "Theme and Reality in AT HEAVEN'S GATE and ALL THE KING'S MEN," *Criticism* 5 (Winter, 1963): 27-44.

Davenport, F. G., *Myth of Southern History*, 143-4.

Eisinger, C. E., *Fiction of the Forties*, 210-14. Also in Nakadate, N., ed., *Robert Penn Warren*, 21-4.

Frank, Joseph, "Romanticism and Reality in Robert Penn Warren," *The Widening Gyre: Crisis and Mastery in Modern Literature*, New Brunswick, N.J.: Rutgers Un. Pr., 1963, 186-200.

Guttenberg, B., *Web of Being*, 17-33.

Hardwick, Elizabeth, "Poor Little Rich Girls," *PR* 12 (Summer, 1945): 420-2.

Heering, H. D., "Madness in AT HEAVEN'S GATE: A Metaphor of the Self in Warren's Fiction," *FourQ* 21, iv (May, 1972): 56-66.

Hendry, Irene, "The Regional Novel: The Example of Robert Penn Warren," *SR* 53 (Jan., 1945): 84-102.

Humboldt, Charles, "The Lost Cause of Robert Penn Warren," *M&M* 1 (July, 1948): 11-15.

Justus, James H., "On the Politics of the Self-Created: AT HEAVEN'S GATE," *SR* 82, ii (Spring, 1974): 284-99. Also in Gray, R., ed., *Robert Penn Warren*, 40-50. Also in Justus, J. H., ed., *Achievement of Robert Penn Warren*, 179-90.

King, Roma A., Jr., "Time and Structure in the Early Novels of Robert Penn Warren," *SAQ* 56 (Autumn, 1957): 486-93.

Law, Richard G., "AT HEAVEN'S GATE: 'The Fires of Irony'," *AL* 53, 1 (Mar., 1981): 87-104.

Longley, John L., Jr., "AT HEAVEN'S GATE: The Major Themes," *MFS* 6 (Spring, 1969): 13-24. Also (revised) in Longley, J. L., Jr., *Robert Penn Warren*, 486-93.

_____, *Robert Penn Warren*, 6-12.

Ruoff, James E., "Robert Penn Warren's Pursuit of Justice," *RSSCW* 27 (1959): 24-5.

Shepherd, Allen, "The Poles of Fiction: Warren's AT HEAVEN'S GATE," *TSLL* 12 (1971): 709-18.

Stewart, J. L., *Burden of Time*, 500-4.

Walcutt, Charles C., "The Regional Novel and Its Future," *ArQ* 1 (Summer, 1945): 23-6.

Walker, M., *Robert Penn Warren*, 92-7.

West, P., *Robert Penn Warren*, 27-8.

BAND OF ANGELS

Berzon, J. R., *Neither White Nor Black*, 127-37.

Bohner, C. H., *Robert Penn Warren*, 127-35.

_____, *Robert Penn Warren*, Rev. ed., 54-64.

Bradbury, J. M., *Fugitives*, 2223-8.

Brown, Ashley, in *Shen* 7 (Autumn, 1955): 87-91.

Casper, Leonard, "Miscegenation as Symbol: BAND OF ANGELS," *Audience* 6 (Autumn, 1955): 66-74. Also in Longley, J. L., Jr., ed., *Robert Penn Warren*, 140-8. Also (revised) in Casper, L., *Robert Penn Warren*, 148-62.

Fiedler, Leslie, *Love and Death in the American Novel*, 393-4.

_____, "Romance in the Operatic Manner," *NRep* 133 (Sept. 26, 1955): 28-39. Also in Fiedler, L., *No! In Thunder*, 131-3.

Flint, F. Cudworth, "Mr. Warren and the Reviewers," *SR* 64 (Autumn, 1956): 632-45. Also in Longley, J. L., ed., *Robert Penn Warren*, 125-39.

Geismar, Maxwell, "Agile Pen and Dry Mind," *Nation* 181 (Oct. 1, 1955): 287.

Guttenberg, B., *Web of Being*, 71-84.

Illacqua, Alma A., "Amanda [sic] Starr: Victim of Her Own False Assumptions," *HSL* 8, iii (1976): 178-89.

Justus, J. H. *Achievement of Robert Penn Warren*, 236-48.

King, R. H., *Southern Renaissance*, 282-3.

Longley, J. L., ed., *Robert Penn Warren*, 24-7.

McDowell, Frederick P. W., in *WR* 20 (Winter, 1956): 167-71.

Magmer, James, "Robert Penn Warren's Quest for an Angel," *CathW* 183 (June, 1956): 178-83.

Martin, Terence, 'BAND OF ANGELS: The Definition of Self-definition," *Folio* 21 (Winter, 1955): 31-7.

Mizener, Arthur, "A Nature Divided Against Itself," *NYTBR* (Aug. 21, 1955): 1, 8.

Ruoff, James E., "Robert Penn Warren's Pursuit of Justice," *RSSCW* 27 (1959): 36-7.

Shepherd, Allen, "Carrying Manty Home: Robert Penn Warren's BAND OF ANGELS," *FourQ* 21, iv (May, 1972): 101-9. Also in Gray, R., ed., *Robert Penn Warren*, 76-84.

Stewart, J. L., *Burden of Time*, 516-17.

Sullivan, Walter, "The Historical Novelist and the Existential Peril: Robert Penn Warren's BAND OF ANGELS," *SLJ* 2, ii (1970): 104-16. Also in Sullivan, W., *Death by Melancholy*, 36-51. Also in Nakadate, N., ed., *Robert Penn Warren*, 138-47.

Vidal, Gore, "Book Report," *Zero* 2 (Spring, 1956): 95-8. Also in Vidal, G., *Homage to Daniel Shays*, 22-6.

Walker, M., *Robert Penn Warren*, 125-30.

Wasserstrom, William, *Heiress of All the Ages: Sex and Sentiment in the Genteel Tradition*, Minneapolis: Un. of Minnesota Pr., 1959, 118-21.

West, P., *Robert Penn Warren*, 40-2.

THE CAVE

Abel, Lionel, "Refinement and Vulgarity," *Ctary* 28 (Dec., 1959): 541-4.

Allen, Charles A., in *ArQ* 16 (Summer, 1960): 182-4.

Bohner, C. H., *Robert Penn Warren*, 146-53.

_____, *Robert Penn Warren*, Rev. ed., 134-9.

Casper, Leonard, "Journey to the Interior: THE CAVE," *MFS* 6 (Spring, 1960): 65-72. Also in Longley, J. L., ed., *Robert Penn Warren*, 149-58.

Davison, Richard A., "Robert Penn Warren's 'Dialectical Configuration' and THE CAVE," *CLAJ* 10 (1967): 349-57.

DeMott, Benjamin, in *HudR* 12 (Winter, 1959-60): 621-3.

Glazier, Lyle, "Reconstructed Platonism: Robert Penn Warren's THE CAVE," *Litera* 7 (1960): 16-26.

Guttenberg, B., *Web of Being*, 85-103.

Holmes, Theodore, "The Literary Mode," *CarlM* 4 (Winter, 1963): 124-8.

Justus, James H., "The Uses of Gesture in Warren's THE CAVE," *MLQ* 26 (Sept., 1965): 448-61. Also in Nakadate, N., ed., *Robert Penn Warren*, 162-74. Also in Gray, R., ed., *Robert Penn Warren*, 85-96. Also, considerably revised, in Justus, J. H., *Achievement of Robert Penn Warren*, 273-84.

Longley, J. L., Jr., *Robert Penn Warren*, 27-8.

Malcolm, Donald, "Cavities," *NY* 35 (Oct. 31, 1959): 198, 201-2.

Nemerov, Howard, in *PR* 27 (Winter, 1960): 178-80, 183-4. Also in Nemerov, H., *Poetry and Fiction*, 281-3.

Phillips, Billie Ray S., "Robert Penn Warren's Archetypal Triptych: A Study of the Myths of the Garden, the Journey, and Rebirth in THE CAVE, WILDERNESS, and FLOOD," *DAI* 32 (1972): 6998A.

Price, Martin, in *YR* 49 (Autumn, 1959): 124-6.

Sandeen, Ernest, "Warren's Latest Novel," *Critic* 18 (Oct.-Nov., 1959): 13, 63.

Shepherd, Allen, "The Case for Robert Penn Warren's Second Best Novel," *CimR* 20 (1972): 44-51.

Symons, J., "Fables for Our Time," *Critical Occasions*, 119-25.

Walker, M., *Robert Penn Warren*, 185-91.

West, P., *Robert Penn Warren*, 42-3.

Widmer, Kingsley, "The Father-Killers of R. P. Warren," *Paunch* 22 (Jan., 1965): 62-3.

THE FLOOD

Bohner, C., *Robert Penn Warren*, Rev. ed., 139-45.

Burt, David J., "A Folk Reference in Warren's FLOOD," *MissQ* 22, i (Winter, 1968-69): 74-6.

_____, "Robert Penn Warren's Debt to Homer in FLOOD," *NConL* 3, i (Jan., 1973): 12-14.

Casper, Leonard, "Ark, FLOOD, and Negotiated Covenant," *FourQ* 21, iv (May, 1972): 110-15.

Goldfarb, Russell M., "Robert P. Warren's Tollivers and George Eliot's Tullivers," *UR* 36, iii (Mar., 1970): 209-13.

_____, "Warren's Tollivers and Eliot's Tullivers II," *UR* 36, iv (June, 1970): 275-9.

Guttenberg, B., *Web of Being*, 119-38.

Hardy, John E., in *VQR* 40 (Summer, 1964): 485-9.

Hiers, John T., "Buried Graveyards: Warren's FLOOD and Jones' A BURIED LAND," *ELWIU* 2, i (Spring, 1975): 97-104.

Justus, J. H., *Achievement of Robert Penn Warren*, 285-94.

Longley, John L., Jr., *Robert Penn Warren*, 30-5.

_____, "Robert Penn Warren: The Deeper Rub," *SoR* 1 (Autumn, 1965): 973-80.

_____, "When All Is Said and Done: Warren's FLOOD," in Longley, J. L., Jr., ed., *Robert Penn Warren*, 169-77.

Mizener, Arthur, "The Uncorrupted Consciousness," *SR* 72 (Autumn, 1964): 690-8. Also in Gray, R., ed., *Robert Penn Warren*, 105-11.

Nakadate, Neil, "Identity, Dream, and Exploration: Warren's Later Fiction," in Nakadate, N., ed., *Robert Penn Warren*, 176-8.

Phillips, Billie Ray S., "Robert Penn Warren's Archetypal Triptych: A Study of the Myths of the Garden, the Journey, and Rebirth in THE CAVE, WILDERNESS, and FLOOD," *DAI* 32 (1972): 6998A.

Shepherd, Allen, "Character and Theme in R. P. Warren's FLOOD," *Crit* 9, iii (1967): 95-102.

Stewart, J. L., in *YR* 54 (Winter, 1965): 252-8.

Wain, John, in *NRep* 150 (May 16, 1964): 23-5.

Walker, M., *Robert Penn Warren*, 191-200.

West, Anthony, in *NY* 40 (Sept. 12, 1964): 204-5.

West, P., *Robert Penn Warren*, 44-5.

NIGHT RIDER

Allen, Charles A., "Robert Penn Warren: The Psychology of Self Knowledge," *L&P* 8 (Spring, 1958): 21-2.

Allen, W., *Modern Novel*, 131-2.

Anderson, Charles R., "Violence and Order in the Novels of Robert Penn Warren," *Hopkins Rev* 6, ii (Winter, 1953): 92-4. Also in Rubin, L. D., Jr., and R. D. Jacobs, eds., *Southern Renascence*, 211-12. Also in Litz, A. W., ed., *Modern American Fiction*, 282-4.

Bentley, Eric, "The Meaning of Robert Penn Warren's Novels," *KR* 10 (1948): 408-10. Also in O'Connor, W. V., ed., *Forms of Modern Fiction*, 256-8. Also in Kostelanetz, R., ed., *On Contemporary Literature*, 617-19.

Bohner, C. H., *Robert Penn Warren*, 61-70.

_____, *Robert Penn Warren*, Rev. ed., 47-55.

Bradbury, John M., "Robert Penn Warren's Novels: The Symbolic and Textual Patterns," *Accent* 13 (Spring, 1953): 78-80. Also in Longley, J. L., Jr., ed., *Robert Penn Warren*, 5-6. Also (revised) in Bradbury, M., *Fugitives*, 204-6+.

Burke, Kenneth, *The Philosophy of Literary Form*, 2nd ed., Baton Rouge: La. State Un. Pr., 1967, 84-6.

Burt, David J., "Robert Penn Warren's Debt to Ibsen in NIGHT RIDER," *MissQ* 22 (Fall, 1969): 359-61.

Byrne, Clifford M., "The Philosophical Development in Four of Robert Penn Warren's Novels," *McNR* 9 (Winter, 1957): 57-61.

Cargill, Oscar, "Anatomist of Monsters," *CE* 9 (Oct., 1947): 2-4. Also in Cargill, O., *Toward a Pluralistic Criticism*, Carbondale: So. Ill. Un. Pr., 1965, 143-6.

Casper, Leonard, *Robert Penn Warren*, 100-7.

_____, "Robert Penn Warren: Method and Canon," *DilimanR* 2 (July, 1954): 281-2.

Davenport, F. G., *Myth of Southern History*, 141-3.

Eisinger, C. E., *Fiction of the Forties*, 206-10. Also in Nakadate, N., ed., *Robert Penn Warren*, 17-21.

French, W., *Social Novel at the End of An Era*, 184-93.

Guttenberg, B., *Web of Being*, 3-16.

Hendry, Irene, "The Regional Novel: The Example of Robert Penn Warren," *SR* 53 (Jan., 1945): 84-102.

Herndon, Jerry A., "A Probable Source for the Buffalo-Hunting Episodes in Robert Penn Warren's NIGHT RIDER," *Rendezvous* 11, i (1976): 53-62.

Heseltine, H. P., "The Deep, Twisting Strain of Life: The Novels of Robert Penn Warren," *MCR* 5 (1962): 77-80. Also in Nakadate, N., ed., *Robert Penn Warren*, 149-53.

Humboldt, Charles, "The Lost Cause of Robert Penn Warren," *M&M* 1 (July, 1948): 9-11.

Justus, J. H., *Achievement of Robert Penn Warren*, 165-78.

Kelvin, Norman, "The Failure of Robert Penn Warren," *CE* 18 (Apr., 1957): 357-8.

King, Roma A., Jr., "Time and Structure in the Early Novels of Robert Penn Warren," *SAQ* 56 (Autumn, 1957): 486-93.

Law, Richard, "Warren's NIGHT RIDER and the Issue of Naturalism: The 'Nightmare' of Our Age," *SLJ* 8, ii (Spring, 1976): 41-61. Also in Nakadate, N., ed., *Robert Penn Warren*, 38-53.

Letargeez, J., "Robert Penn Warren's Views of History," *RLV* 22 (1956): 533-43.

Longley, J. L., Jr., *Robert Penn Warren*, 5-6.

Ruoff, James E., "Robert Penn Warren's Pursuit of Justice," *RSSCW* 27 (1959): 22-4.

Ryan, Alvan S., "Robert Penn Warren's NIGHT RIDER: The Nihilism of the Isolated Temperament," *MFS* 7 (Winter, 1961-62): 338-46. Also in Longley, J. L., Jr., ed., *Robert Penn Warren*, 49-59. Also in Gray, R., ed., *Robert Penn Warren*, 32-9.

Shepherd, Allen, "Robert Penn Warren's PRIME LEAF as Prototype of NIGHT RIDER," *SSF* 7, iii (Summer, 1970): 469-71.

Spies, George H., III., "John Steinbeck's IN DUBIOUS BATTLE and Robert Penn Warren's NIGHT RIDER: A Comparative Study," *StQ* 4, ii (Spring, 1971): 48-55. Also in Hayashi, T., ed., *Steinbeck's Literary Dimension*, 130-7.

Stewart, J. L., *Burden of Time*, 469-80.

Strugnell, John R., "Robert Penn Warren and the Uses of the Past," *REL* 4, iv (Oct., 1963): 94-6.

Walker, M., *Robert Penn Warren*, 89-92.

West, P., *Robert Penn Warren*, 25-6.

Wilson, Angus, "The Fires of Violence," *Encounter* 4 (May, 1955): 75-8.

Yanagi, Kiichiro, "NIGHT RIDER and Robert Penn Warren's Ideas," *Bulletin of the Un. of Osaka Prefecture*, Series C, 9 (1961): 57-72.

MEET ME IN THE GREEN GLEN

Balazy, Teresa, "Warren's MEET ME IN THE GREEN GLEN: An Interpretation," *SAP* 6, i-ii (1975): 147-55.

Bohner, C., *Robert Penn Warren*, Rev. ed., 145-51.

Casper, Leonard, "Robert Penn Warren's Evergreening Glen," *TQ* 21, iii (1978): 53-63.

Grimshaw, James, "Robert Penn Warren's ANNUS MIRABILUS," *SoR* 10 (1974): 509-16.

Guttenberg, B., *Web of Being*, 13-55. Also in Gray, R., ed., *Robert Penn Warren*, 112-24.

Justus, J. H., *Achievement of Robert Penn Warren*, 294-9.

Kehl, D. G., "Love's Definition: Dream as Reality in Robert Penn Warren's MEET ME IN THE GREEN GLEN," *FourQ* 21, iv (May, 1972): 116-22.

Nakadate, Neil, "Identity, Dream, and Exploration: Warren's Later Fiction," in Nakadate, N., ed., *Robert Penn Warren*, 179-82.

Rubin, Louis D., Jr., "Dreiser and MEET ME IN THE GREEN GLEN: A Vintage Year for Robert Penn Warren," *HC* 9, i (1972): 1-12.

Shepherd, Allen, "Character and Theme in Warren's MEET ME IN THE GREEN GLEN," *Greyfriar* 13 (1972): 34-41.

Walker, M., *Robert Penn Warren*, 201-13.

A PLACE TO COME TO

Justus, W. H., *Achievement of Robert Penn Warren*, 302-16.

Shepherd, Allen, "Robert Penn Warren the Novelist, Now (and Then)," *SLJ* 12, ii (Spring, 1980): 83-96.

Walker, M., *Robert Penn Warren*, 216-29.

Wyatt, David M., "Robert Penn Warren: The Critic as Artist," *VQR* 53, ii (Summer, 1977): 476-9.

WILDERNESS: A TALE OF THE CIVIL WAR

Bohner, C., *Robert Penn Warren*, Rev. ed., 108-13.

Casper, Leonard, "Trial By Wilderness: Warren's Exemplum," *WSCL* 3, iii (Fall, 1962): 45-53. Also in Longley, J. L., Jr., ed., *Robert Penn Warren*, 159-68. Also in Gray, R., ed., *Robert Penn Warren*, 97-104.

Guttenberg, B., *Web of Being*, 104-18.

Justus, J. H., *Achievement of Robert Penn Warren*, 249-61.

Klein, Don W., in *Epoch* 11 (Winter, 1962): 263-8.

Longley, J. L., Jr., *Robert Penn Warren*, 28-30.

Moore, L. Hugh, Jr., *Robert Penn Warren and History*, 142-82.

_____, "Robert Penn Warren, William Styron, and the Uses of Greek Myth," *Crit* 8, ii (1966): 75-80.

Phillips, Billie Ray S., "Robert Penn Warren's Archetypal Triptych: A Study of the Myths of the Garden, the Journey, and Rebirth in THE CAVE, WILDERNESS and FLOOD," *DAI* 32 (1972): 6998A.

Samuels, Charles T., "In the Wilderness," *Crit* 5, ii (Fall, 1962): 52-7.

Shepherd, Allen, "Robert Penn Warren as Allegorist: The Example of WILDERNESS," *Rendezvous* 6 (Spring, 1971): 13-21.

Walker, M., *Robert Penn Warren*, 130-2.

West, P., *Robert Penn Warren*, 43-4.

Witte, Flo, "Adam's Rebirth in Robert Penn Warren's WILDERNESS," *SoQ* 12 (1974): 365-77.

WORLD ENOUGH AND TIME

Allen, W., *Modern Novel*, 130-1.

Anderson, Charles R., "Violence and Order in the Novels of Robert Penn Warren," *HopkinsRev* (Winter, 1953): 100-5. Also in Rubin, L. D., Jr., and R. D. Jacobs, eds., *Southern Renascence*, 219-24. Also in Litz, A. W., ed., *Modern American Fiction*, 290-5.

Baker, Carlos, in *VQR* 26 (Autumn, 1950): 603-5.

Beatty, Richmond C., "The Poetry and Novels of Robert Penn Warren," in Beatty, R. C., and Others, eds., *Vanderbilt Studies in the Humanities*, Vol. I (1951): 157-60.

Berner, Robert, "The Required Past: WORLD ENOUGH AND TIME," *MFS* 6 (Spring, 1960): 55-64. Also in Gray, R., ed., *Robert Penn Warren*, 67-75.

Bohner, C. H., *Robert Penn Warren*, 106-17.

_____, *Robert Penn Warren*, Rev. ed., 84-93.

Bradbury, John M., "Robert Penn Warren's Novels: The Symbolic and Textual Patterns," *Accent* 13 (Spring, 1953): 84-6. Also in Longley, J. L., Jr., ed., *Robert Penn Warren*, 11-14. Also (Revised) in Bradbury, J. M., *Fugitives*, 212-14+.

Byrne, Clifford M., "The Philosophical Development in Four of Robert Penn Warren's Novels," *McNR* 9 (Winter, 1957): 65-7.

Campbell, Harry M., "Mr. Warren as Philosopher in WORLD ENOUGH AND TIME," *HopkinsRev* 6 (Winter, 1953): 106-16. Also in Rubin, L. D., and R. D. Jacobs, eds., *Southern Renascence*, 225-35.

Carter, Everett, "The 'Little Myth' of Robert Penn Warren," *MFS* 6 (Spring, 1960): 6-8.

Casper, Leonard, *Robert Penn Warren*, 136-48.

_____, "Robert Penn Warren: Method and Canon," *DilimanR* 2 (July, 1954): 288-92.

Eisinger, C. E., *Fiction of the Forties*, 224-8. Also in Nakadate, N., ed., *Robert Penn Warren*, 32-6.

Fiedler, Leslie, "On Two Frontiers," *PR* 17 (Sept.-Oct., 1950): 739-43.

_____, "Toward Time's Cold Womb," *New Leader* (July 22, 1950): Also in Fiedler, L., *No! In Thunder*, 119-26.

Frank, Joseph, "Romanticism and Reality in Robert Penn Warren," *HudR* 4 (1951): 248-58. Also in Frank, J., *Widening Gyre: Crisis and Mastery in Modern Literature*, New Brunswick, N.J.: Rutgers Un. Pr., 1960, 186-200.

Guthrie, A. B., "Virtue Plundered in Kentucky," *SatR* 33 (June 24, 1950): 11-12.

Guttenberg, B., *Web of Being*, 56-70.

Heilman, Robert B., "Tangled Web," *SR* 59 (Winter, 1951): 107-19. Also in Longley, J. L., Jr., ed., *Robert Penn Warren*, 96-109. Also in Nakadate, N., ed., *Robert Penn Warren*, 115-25.

Janeway, Elizabeth, "Man in Conflict," *NYTBR* (June 25, 1950): 1, 22.

Jones, Ernest, "Through a Glass Darkly," *Nation* 171 (July, 1950): 42.

Justus, James H., "Warren's WORLD ENOUGH AND TIME and Beauchamp's CONFESSION," *AL* 33 (Jan., 1962): 500-11.

_____, *Achievement of Robert Penn Warren*, 215-35.

Kelvin, Norman, "The Failure of Robert Penn Warren," *CE* 18 (Apr., 1957): 360-1.

Lane, Calvin W., "Narrative Art and History in Robert Penn Warren's WORLD ENOUGH AND TIME," *DA* 17 (1957): 1340.

Longley, J. L., Jr., *Robert Penn Warren*, 17-24.

McDowell, Frederick P. W., "The Romantic Tragedy of Self in WORLD ENOUGH AND TIME," *Crit* 1, ii (Summer, 1957): 34-48. Also in Longley, J. L., Jr., ed., *Robert Penn Warren*, 110-24.

Mizener, Arthur, "Amphibium in Old Kentucky," *KR* 12 (Autumn, 1950): 697-701.

Nakadate, Neil, "Robert Penn Warren and the Confessional Novel," *Genre* 2 (Dec., 1969): 329-34.

O'Connor, W. V., *Grotesque*, 14-16.

Rathbun, John W., "Philosophy, WORLD ENOUGH AND TIME, and the Art of the Novel," *MFS* 6 (Spring, 1960): 47-54.

Renguette, Dale T., "The Gray Pessimism of Robert Penn Warren," *Fresco* 1, i (1960): 34-42.

Ridgely, Joseph V., "Tragedy in Kentucky," *HopkinsRev* 4 (Fall, 1950): 61-3.

Ruoff, James E., "Robert Penn Warren's Pursuit of Justice," *RSSCW* 27 (1959): 31-3.

Schiller, Andrew," The World Out of Square," *WR* 15 (Spring, 1951): 234-7.

Stewart, J. L., *Burden of Time*, 506-10.

Strugnell, John R., "Robert Penn Warren and the Uses of the Past," *REL* 4, iv (Oct., 1963): 98-9.

Walker, M., *Robert Penn Warren*, 110-16.

West, P., *Robert Penn Warren*, 38-40.

White, Robert, "Robert Penn Warren and the Myth of the Garden," *Faulkner Studies*, 3 (Winter, 1954): 64-7.

BIBLIOGRAPHY

Beebe, Maurice, and Erin Marcus, "Criticism of Robert Penn Warren: A Selected Checklist," *MFS* 6 (Spring, 1960): 83-8.

Casper, L., *Robert Penn Warren*, 191-208.

Grimshaw, James A., "Robert Penn Warren: A Bibliographical Catalogue, Being a Description of His First American Editions Printed Through 31 December 1971, Along with Individual Titles, An Annotated Checklist of Secondary Sources, and an Index (Volumes 1 and 2)," *DAI* 33 (1972): 2375A.

_____, "Robert Penn Warren's ALL THE KING'S MEN: An Annotated Checklist of Criticism," *RALS* 6 (1976): 23-69.

Huff, Mary N., *Robert Penn Warren: A Bibliography*, N.Y.: David Lewis, 1968.

Longley, J. L., Jr., ed., *Robert Penn Warren*, 247-57.

Nakadate, Neil, "A Selected Checklist of Criticism on Robert Penn Warren," in Nakadate, N., ed., *Robert Penn Warren*, 321-8.

_____, *Robert Penn Warren: A Reference Guide*, Boston: G. K. Hall, 1977.

WATERHOUSE, KEITH, 1929-

GENERAL

Corbett, Martyn, "First Person Singular," *Delta* (Cambridge, Eng.) 35 (Spring, 1965): 9-16.

BILLY LIAR

Churchill, Thomas, "Waterhouse, Story, and Fowles: Which Way Out of the Room?" *Crit* 10, iii (1968): 72-87.

Corbett, Martyn, "First Person Singular," *Delta* (Cambridge, Eng.) 35 (Spring, 1965): 10-15.

Gindin, J., "Creeping Americanism," *Postwar British Fiction*, 109-14.

Gray, N., *Silent Majority*, 49-72.

O'Connor, W. V., "The New Hero and a Shift in Literary Convention," *New University Wits*, 135-6.

Urwin, G. G., ed., *Taste for Living*, 56-9.

JUBB

Churchill, Thomas, "Waterhouse, Storey, and Fowler: Which Way Out of the Room?" *Crit* 10, iii (1968): 72-87.

WATERS, FRANK, 1902-

GENERAL

Adams, Charles L., "Frank Waters: Western Mystic," *SFW* 5 (Dec., 1982): 1-11.

Bucco, M., *Frank Waters*.

Davis, Jack L., "Frank Waters' Psychology of Consciousness: From Split Brain to Whole Mind," SFW 5 (Dec., 1982): 56-73.

_____, and June H. Davis, "Frank Waters and the Native American Consciousness," *WAL* 9, i (May, 1974): 33-44.

Grider, Daryl A., "Rightness With the Land: Spirit of Place in the Novels of Frank Waters," *DAI* 41 (1981): 4400A.

Grigg, Quay, "Frank Waters and the Mountain Spirit," *SDR* 15, iii (Autumn, 1977): 45-9.

_____, "The Kachina Characters of Frank Waters' Novels," *SDR* 11, i (Spring, 1973): 6-16.

Kostka, Robert, "Frank Waters and the Visual Sense," *SDR* 15, iii (Autumn, 1977): 27-30.

Loudon, Michael, "Mountain Talk: Frank Waters as Shaman-Writer," *SFW* 5 (Dec., 1982): 74-88.

Lyon, T. J., *Frank Waters*.

_____, "An Ignored Meaning of the West," *WAL* 3, i (Spring, 1968): 51-9.

_____, "Frank Waters and Small 'b' Buddhism," *SFW* 5 (Dec., 1982): 89-99.

_____, "Frank Waters and the Concept of 'Nothing Special'," *SDR* 15, iii (Autumn, 1977): 31-5.

Manchester, John, "Frank Waters," *SDR* 15, iii (Autumn, 1977): 73-80.

Milton, John, ed., *Conversations with Frank Waters*, Chicago: Swallow Pr., 1971.

Milton, John R., "Intuition and the Dance of Life," *Novel of the American West*, 264-97.

_____, "The Sound of Space," *SDR* 15, iii (Autumn, 1977): 11-15.

_____, "Symbolic Space and Mysticism in the Novels of Frank Waters," *SFW* 5 (Dec., 1982): 12-29.

Petersen, James, "Lessons from the Indian Soul: A Conversation with Frank Waters," *Psychology Today* 6 (May, 1973): 63-72, 99.

Tarbet, Tom, "The Hopi Prophecy and the Chinese Dream," *East West* (May, 1977): 52-64. [Interview.]

Waters, Frank, "Mysticism and Witchcraft," *SDR* 15, iii (Autumn, 1977): 59-70.

Young, Vernon, "Frank Waters: Problems of the Regional Imperative," *NMQR* 19 (Autumn, 1949): 353-72.

BELOW GRASS ROOTS (See also THE COLORADO TRILOGY)

Bucco, M., *Frank Waters*, 13-14.

Lyon, T. J., *Frank Waters*, 86-91.

THE COLORADO TRILOGY

Lyon, T. J., *Frank Waters*, 77-95.

Milton, John, "The Land as Form in Frank Waters and William Eastlake," *KanQ* 2, ii (Spring, 1970): 104-9.

_____, *Novel of the American West*, 277-86.

Pilkington, William T., "Character and Landscape: Frank Waters' Colorado Trilogy," *WAL* 2 (Fall, 1967): 183-93.

DIAMOND HEAD

Bucco, M., *Frank Waters*, 30-2.

Lyons, T. J., *Frank Waters*, 141-3.

THE DUST WITHIN THE ROCK (See also THE COLORADO TRILOGY)

Bucco, M., *Frank Waters*, 14-15.

Lyon, T. J., *Frank Waters*, 69-77.

THE MAN WHO KILLED THE DEER

Bucco, M., *Frank Waters*, 21-4.

Davis, Jack L., and June H., "Frank Waters and the Native American Consciousness," *WAL* 9, i (May, 1974): 35-7.

Davis, June H., and Jack L., "The Whorf Hypothesis and Native American Literature," *SDR* 14, ii (1976): 59-72.

Hoy, Christopher, "The Archetypal Transformation of Martiniano in THE MAN WHO KILLED THE DEER," *SDR* 13, iv (Winter, 1975): 43-56.

_____, "The Conflict in THE MAN WHO KILLED THE DEER," *SDR* 15, iii (Autumn, 1977): 51-7.

Lyon, T. J., *Frank Waters*, 104-13.

McAllister, Mick, "The Color of Meat, the Color of Bone," *DQ* 14, iv (1980): 10-18.

McCann, Garth, "Patterns of Redemption and the Failure of Irony: THE OX-BOW INCIDENT and THE MAN WHO KILLED THE DEER," *SwAL* 4 (1974): 62-7.

Milton, J. R., *Novel of the American West*, 292-7.

Schneider, Jack W., "Deer, Man, and Reconciliation in THE MAN WHO KILLED THE DEER," *SwAL* 7, ii (1982): 1-8.

PEOPLE OF THE VALLEY

Bucco, M., *Frank Waters*, 18-21.

Lyon, T. J., *Frank Waters*, 95-104.

Malpezzi, Frances, "A Study of the Female Protagonist in Frank Waters' PEOPLE OF THE VALLEY and Rudolfo Anaya's BLESS ME, ULTIMA," *SDR* 14, ii (Summer, 1976): 102-10.

McBride, Mary, "A Sunrise Brighter Still: Frank Waters and the Concept of Enduring Reality," *SFW* 5 (Dec., 1982): 30-41.

Milton, J. R., *Novel of the American West*, 289-92.

_____, "Symbolic Space and Mysticism in the Novels of Frank Waters," *SFW* 5 (Dec., 1982): 7-11.

PIKE'S PEAK

Lyon, T. J., *Frank Waters*, 131-3.

RIVER LADY

Bucco, M., *Frank Waters*, 25-6.

Lyon, T. J., *Frank Waters*, 138-41.

THE WILD EARTH'S NOBILITY (See also THE COLORADO TRILOGY)

Bucco, M., *Frank Waters*, 12-13.

Lyon, T. J., *Frank Waters*, 78-86.

THE WOMAN AT OTOWI CROSSING

Bucco, M., *Frank Waters*, 122-3.

Davis, Jack L., and June H., "Frank Waters and the Native American Consciousness," *WAL* 9, i (May, 1974): 41-3.

Lyon, T. J., *Frank Waters*, 122-31.

THE YOGI OF COCKROACH COURT

Adams, Charles L., "Teaching Yogi in Las Vegas or Cockroach Court Revisited," *SDR* 15, ii (Autumn, 1977): 37-42.

Bucco, M., *Frank Waters*, 28-30.

Lyon, T. J., *Frank Waters*, 113-22.

_____, "Frank Waters and the Concept of 'Nothing Special'," *SDR* 15, iii (Autumn, 1977): 34-6.

Milton, J. R., *Novel of the American West*, 287-9.

BIBLIOGRAPHY

Lyon, T. J., *Frank Waters*, 159-63.

WATSON, SHEILA, 1909-

GENERAL

Newman, Shirley, "Watson, Sheila," 45-52 in Heath, Jeffrey M., ed., *Profiles in Canadian Literature 4*, Toronto: Dundurn, 1982.

THE DOUBLE HOOK

Barbour, Douglas, "Editors and Typesetters," *Open Letter* (third series 1) (1975): 184-7.

Bowering, George, "Sheila Watson, Trickster," in Moss, J., ed., *Canadian Novel*, Vol. 3. *Modern Times*, 209-23.

Corbett, Nancy J., "Closed Circle," *CanL* 61 (Summer, 1964): 46-53.

Downton, Dawn R., "Messages and Messengers in THE DOUBLE HOOK," *SCL* 4, ii (1979): 137-46.

Godard, Barbara, "'Between One Cliche and Another': Language in THE DOUBLE HOOK," *SCL* 3 (Summer, 1978): 149-65.

Gose, Elliot, "Coyote and Stag," *CanL* 1 (Summer, 1959): 80.

Jones, D. J., *Butterfly on Rock*, 85-7.

Lennox, John W., "The Past: Themes and Symbols of Confrontation in THE DOUBLE HOOK," *JCF* 2, i (Winter, 1973): 70-2.

Livesay, Dorothy, "Two Women Novelists of Canada's West," *RNL* 7 (1976): 127-32.

Marta, Jan, "Poetic Structures in the Prose Fiction of Sheila Watson," *ECW* 17 (Spring, 1980): 44-56.

McPherson, Hugo, "An Important New Voice," *TamR* 12 (Summer, 1959): 85-8.

Mitchell, Beverly, S. S. A., "Association and Illusion in THE DOUBLE HOOK," *JCF* 2, i (Winter, 1973): 63-9.

Monkman, Leslie, "Coyote as Trickster in THE DOUBLE HOOK," *CanL* 52 (Spring, 1972): 70-6.

Morriss, Margaret, "The Elements Transcended," *CanL* 42 (Autumn, 1969): 56-71. Also in Woodcock, G., ed., *Canadian Literature in the Twentieth Century*, 186-201.

Moss, J., *Patterns of Isolation*, 166-82, 186-7.

Northey, Margot, "Symbolic Gothic: THE DOUBLE HOOK," *Haunted Wilderness*, 88-94.

Watson, Sheila, "THE DOUBLE HOOK: What I'm Going to Do," *Open Letter* (third series 1) (1975): 181-3.

WAUGH, EVELYN, 1903-1966

GENERAL

See issues of *Evelyn Waugh Newsletter*.

Adcock, James P., "From Satirist to Seer: The Novels of Evelyn Waugh," *DAI* 40 (1980): 5064A.

Allan, Alexander, "Waugh Revisited," *EA* 33, iii (1980): 321-32.

Allen, W., *Modern Novel*, 208-14.

Bannington, T. J., "Mr. Waugh's Pieties," *The Bell* 13 (Feb., 1947): 58-63. [Reply to Donat O'Donnell.]

Bargainnier, Earl F., "Waugh's 'Heart of Darkness'," *CEA* 38, iii (1976): 11-13. [Not seen.]

Beattie, A. M., "Evelyn Waugh," *CanF* 33 (Jan., 1954): 226-7.

Benedict, Stewart H., "The Candide Figure in the Novels of Evelyn Waugh," *PMASAL* 48 (1963): 685-90.

Bergonzi, Bernard, "Evelyn Waugh's Gentlemen," *CritQ* 5 (Spring, 1963): 23-36. Also in Davis, R. M., ed., *Evelyn Waugh*, 69-88.

_____, *Situation of the Novel*, 104-18.

Bogaards, Winnifred M., "Ideas and Values in the Works of Evelyn Waugh," *DAI* 32 (1971): 4151A.

Boyle, Alexander, "Evelyn Waugh, Master of Satire," *Grail* 35 (Nov., 1953): 28-32. [Not seen.]

Bradbury, M., *Evelyn Waugh*.

_____, "The Modern Comic Novel in the 1920's: Lewis, Huxley, and Waugh," *Possibilities*, 154-60.

Brady, C. A., "Evelyn Waugh: Shrove Tuesday Motley and Lenten Sackcloth," *Catholic Library World* 16 (Mar., 1945): 163-77.

Braybrooke, Neville, "Evelyn Waugh," *Fortnightly* 171 (Mar., 1952): 197-202.

Browning, Gordon, "Silenus' Wheel: Static and Dynamic Characters in the Satiric Fiction of Evelyn Waugh," *Cithara* 14, i (1974): 13-24.

Burgess, Anthony, "Evelyn Waugh, 1903-1966: The Comedy of Ultimate Truths," *Spectator* No. 7190 (Apr. 15, 1966): 462.

Carens, J. F., *Satiric Art of Evelyn Waugh.*

Churchill, Thomas P., "The House of Waugh: A Critical Study of Evelyn Waugh's Major Novels," *DA* 24 (1964): 2906.

Clark, John R., "*Verbotan* Passage: Strategy in the Early Work," *EWN* 7, ii (Autumn, 1973): 5-9.

Cook, W. J., Jr., *Masks, Modes, and Morals.*

————, "The Personae Technique of Evelyn Waugh," *DA* 29 (1969): 2704A-05A.

Corr, Patricia, "Evelyn Waugh: Sanity and Catholicism," *Studies* 51 (Autumn, 1962): 388-99. Also in Davis, R. M., ed., *Evelyn Waugh*, 33-49.

Cosman, Max, "The Nature and Work of Evelyn Waugh," *ColQ* 4 (Spring, 1956): 428-41.

Darman, Kathleen E., "Evelyn Waugh: Problems of Dandyism," *DAI* 39 (1979): 7354A.

Davis, Robert M., "'Clarifying and Enriching': Waugh's Changing Concept of Anthony Blanche," *PBS* 72 (1978): 305-20.

————, ed., *Evelyn Waugh.*

————, "Evelyn Waugh and Brian Howard," *EWN* 4, ii (Autumn, 1970): 5-6.

————, "Evelyn Waugh on the Art of Fiction," *PLL* 2 (Summer, 1966): 243-52.

————, *Evelyn Waugh, Writer.*

————, "Evelyn Waugh's Early Work: The Formation of a Method," *TSLL* 7 (Spring, 1965): 97-108.

————, "Evelyn Waugh's Juvenilia," *EWN* 10, iii (1976): 1-7.

————, "The Mind and Art of Evelyn Waugh," *PLL* 3 (Summer, 1967): 270-87. Also in Davis, R. M., ed., *Evelyn Waugh*, 89-110.

De Vitis, Angelo A., "The Religious Theme in the Novels of Rex Warner, Evelyn Waugh, and Graham Greene," *SDD-UW* 15 (1955): 605-6.

————, *Roman Holiday.*

Dooley, D. J., "The Council's First Victim," *Triumph* 5, vi (June, 1970): 33-5.

————, "The Dandy and the Satirist," *EWN* 10, iii (Winter, 1976): 7-10.

Dooley, David, "Strategy of the Catholic Novelist," *CathW* 189 (July, 1959): 300-4. Also in Davis, R. M., ed., *Evelyn Waugh*, 51-6.

————, "Waugh and Black Humor," *EWN* 2, ii (Autumn, 1968): 1-3.

Doyle, Paul A., "The Church, History and Evelyn Waugh," *ABR* 9 (Autumn-Winter, 1958-59): 202-8.

————, *Evelyn Waugh.*

————, "Evelyn Waugh's Attitude Toward Ecumenism," *Twin Circle* (Culver City, Calif.) 27 (July, 1969): 11-12. [Not seen.]

————, "The Persecution of Evelyn Waugh," *America* 99 (May 3, 1958): 165, 168-9.

Duer, Harriet W., "All Us Exiles: The Novels of Evelyn Waugh," *DA* 31 (1970): 1269A.

Dyson, A. E., "Evelyn Waugh and the Mysteriously Disappearing Hero," *CritiQ* 2 (Spring, 1960): 72-9. Also in Dyson, A. E., *Crazy Fabric*, 187-96.

Farr, D. Paul, "The Edwardian Golden Age and Nostalgic Truth," *DR* 50 (1970): 378-93.

————, "Evelyn Waugh: Tradition and a Modern Talent," *SAQ* 68 (Autumn, 1969): 506-19.

Featherstone, Joseph, "The Ordeal of Evelyn Waugh," *NRep* 155 (July 16, 1966): 21-3.

Fytton, Francis, "Waugh-fare," *CathW* 181 (Aug., 1955): 349-55.

Garnett, Robert, "The Early Life and Novels of Evelyn Waugh," *DAI* 40 (1980): 5064A.

Gleason, James, "Evelyn Waugh and the Stylistics of Commitment," *WisSL* 2 (1965): 70-4.

Grace, William J., "Evelyn Waugh as a Social Critic," *Ren* 1, ii (Spring, 1949): 28-40.

Green, Martin, "British Comedy and the British Sense of Humour: Shaw, Waugh and Amis," *TQ* 4, iii (Autumn, 1961): 220-5.

————, "Evelyn Waugh and the Commedia dell 'Arte," *New York Arts Jnl.* 1, iii-iv (1976): 25-8. [Not seen.]

Greenblatt, S. J., *Three Modern Satirists*, 1-33, 105-17.

Greene, George, "Scapegoat with Style: The Status of Evelyn Waugh," *QQ* 71 (Winter, 1965): 485-93.

Greene, Graham, "Remembering Evelyn Waugh," *Listener* 102 (Oct. 11, 1979): 482-3.

Griffiths, Joan, "Waugh's Problem Comedies," *Accent* 9 (Spring, 1949): 165-70.

Hall, James, "The Other Post-War Rebellion: Evelyn Waugh Twenty-Five Years After," *ELH* 28 (June, 1961): 187-202. Also in Hall, J., *Tragic Comedians*, 43-65.

Harwood, Ronald, and John Selwyn Gilbert, "A Sense of Loss: The Ordeal of Evelyn Waugh," *Listener* 100 (Oct. 26, 1978): 528-30.

Heath, Jeffrey, "Apthorpe Platacus?" *Ariel* 5, i (Jan., 1974): 5-24.

————, "Evelyn Waugh: Afraid of the Shadow," *EWN* 9, iii (1975): 1-4.

————, "Evelyn Waugh and the Comic Macabre," *DAI* 32 (1972): 6930A.

————, "The Lush Places," *EWN* 13, ii (Autumn, 1979): 5-8.

————, *Picturesque Prison.*

————, "The Private Language of Evelyn Waugh," *ESC* 2, iii (Fall, 1976): 329-38.

Hinchcliffe, Peter, "Fathers and Children in the Novels of Evelyn Waugh," *UTQ* 35 (Apr., 1966): 293-310.

Hines, Leo, "Waugh and His Critics," *Cweal* 76 (Apr. 13, 1962): 60-3.

Hollis, C., *Evelyn Waugh.*

Howarth, Herbert, "Quelling the Riot: Evelyn Waugh's Progress," in Mooney, H. J., Jr., and T. F. Staley, eds., *Shapeless God*, 67-89.

Hynes, Joseph, "Varieties of Death Wish: Evelyn Waugh's Central Theme," *Criticism* 14, i (Winter, 1972): 65-77.

Jamkhandi, Dukhakar R., "The Rhetoric of War: An Evaluation of Evelyn Waugh's Military Novels," *DAI* 42, i (July, 1981): 226A.

Jebb, Julian, "The Art of Fiction 30: Evelyn Waugh," *ParisR* 30 (Summer-Fall, 1963): 72-85. Also in *Writers at Work*, 3rd ser., 103-14.

Jervis, Steven A., "The Novels of Evelyn Waugh: A Critical Study," *DA* 27 (1966): 1058A.

Jones, Richard, "Evelyn Waugh: A Man at Bay," *VQR* 54 (Summer, 1978): 503-17.

Karl, F. R., "The World of Evelyn Waugh: The Normally Sane," *Contemporary English Novel*, 167-82.

Kellogg, G., *Vital Tradition*, 101-10.

Kenny, H. A., "Evelyn Waugh and the Novel," *Magnificat* 92 (1953): 278-80. [Not seen.]

Kermode, Frank, "Mr. Waugh's Cities," *Encounter* 15 (Nov., 1960): 63-70. Also in Kermode, F., *Puzzles and Epiphanies*, 164-75.

Kernan, Alvin B., "The Wall and the Jungle: The Early Novels of Evelyn Waugh," *YR* 53 (Winter, 1964): 199-220. Also in Davis, R. M., ed., *Evelyn Waugh*, 1-24.

Kloefkorn, Johnny L., "The Protagonist as Structural Device in Evelyn Waugh's Novels," *DAI* 39 (1978): 2292A.

Kupersmith, Leonard R., "The Uses of Counterfeit in the Novels of Evelyn Waugh," *DAI* 40 (1979): 3317A.

Lane, C. W., *Evelyn Waugh*.

Lane, George W., "The Search for the City: Conservative Political Values in Some of the Novels of Evelyn Waugh," *DAI* 36 (1975): 1527A.

Lodge, David, "The Arrogance of Evelyn Waugh," *Critic* 30, v (May-June, 1972): 63-70.

_____, *Evelyn Waugh*. Also in Stade, G., ed., *Six Modern British Novelists*, 43-86.

Lowe, Keith D., "Evelyn Waugh: Man Against History," *DAI* 30 (1969): 1142A.

Lynch, Richard P., "Parody as Structure and Motif in the Novels of Evelyn Waugh," *DAI* 38 (1977): 807A-8A.

Lynch, Tibbie E., "Forms and Functions of Black Humor in the Fiction of Evelyn Waugh," *DAI* 43 (1982): 1968A.

Macaulay, Rose, "The Best and the Worst, II—Evelyn Waugh," *Horizon* 14 (Dec., 1946): 360-76. Also in Baker, D. V., ed., *Writers of Today: 2*, 135-52.

Machon, Daniel J., "The Failure of the Ironic Mask: Irony as Vision and Technique in the Early Novels of Evelyn Waugh," *DAI* 36 (1975): 3733A-34A.

MacSween, R. J., "Evaluating Evelyn Waugh," *AntigR* 25 (Spring, 1976): 15-18.

Marcus, Steven, "Evelyn Waugh and the Art of Entertainment," *PR* 23 (Summer, 1956): 348-57.

Marshall, Bruce, "Graham Greene and Evelyn Waugh," *Cweal* 51 (Mar. 3, 1950): 551-3.

McCartney, George P., "Confused Roaring: Evelyn Waugh and the Modernist Tradition," *DAI* 41 (1980): 1613A.

McCay, Robert D., "Idea and Pattern in the Novels of Evelyn Waugh," *DA* 13 (1953): 1197.

Meckier, Jerome, "The Case for the Modern Satirical Novel: Huxley, Waugh, and Powell," *STwC* 14 (Fall, 1974): 21-42.

_____, "Evelyn Waugh: Satire and Symbol," *GaR* 27 (Summer, 1973): 166-74.

Meyer, Henrich, "Evelyn Waugh (1903-1966)," *BA* 40 (Autumn, 1966): 410-11.

Middendorf, Marilyn A., "The Circular Worlds of Evelyn Waugh: Satire Approached through Structure," *DA* 40 (1979): 2665A.

Mikes, George, *Eight Humorists*, London: Allan Wingate, 1954, 131-46.

Morriss, Margaret E., "Prejudice and Partiality: Evelyn Waugh and His Critics (1928-1966)," *DAI* 42, i (July, 1981): 229A.

Mosely, Nicholas, "A New Puritanism," *The European*, No. 3 (May, 1953): 35-40. (Answer to A. J. Neame. See items under BRIDESHEAD REVISITED and MEN AT ARMS.)

Nichols, James W., "Romantic and Realistic: The Tone of Evelyn Waugh's Early Novels," *CE* 24 (Oct., 1962): 46-56.

Novelli, Martin A., "Witness to the Times: The War Novels of Ford Maddox Ford and Evelyn Waugh," *DA* 32 (1971): 3321A.

O'Donnell, Donat, "The Pieties of Evelyn Waugh," *The Bell* 13 (Dec., 1946): 38-49. Also in *KR* 9 (Summer, 1947): 400-11. Also in O'Donnell, D., *Maria Cross*, 119-34. Also in O'Brien, C. C., *Maria Cross*, 109-23. Also in Kenyon Review. *Kenyon Critics*, 88-98.

_____, Reply to "Mr. Waugh's Pieties," *The Bell* 13 (Mar., 1947): 57-62. (Answer to T. J. Bannington.)

O'Faolain, S., *Vanishing Hero*, 23-44.

Pandeya, S. M., "The Satiric Technique of Evelyn Waugh," *Criticism and Research* (Banaras Hindu Un.) (1965): 107-23. [Not seen.]

Paul, Martin T., "The Comic-Romantic Hero in Eight Novels of Evelyn Waugh," *DAI* 30 (1969): 288A.

Pazereskis, John F., "The Narrator of Evelyn Waugh: A Study of Five Works of Fiction," *DAI* 34 (1974): 4463A.

Phillips, Gene D., "The Christian Vision of Evelyn Waugh," *DA* 31 (1971): 6068A.

_____, *Evelyn Waugh's Officers, Gentlemen, and Rogues*.

Pritchard, William H., "Waugh Revisited," *New Leader* 62, xviii (Sept. 24, 1979): 19-19.

Rees, John O., "'What Price Dotheboys Hall?': Some Dickens Echoes in Waugh," *KanQ* 7, iv (Fall, 1974): 14-18.

Riley, John J., "Gentlemen at Arms: The Generative Process of Evelyn Waugh and Anthony Powell before World War II," *MFS* 22, ii (Summer, 1978): 165-81.

Rolo, Charles J., "Evelyn Waugh: The Best and the Worst," *Atlantic* 194 (Oct., 1954): 80-6.

Ross, Mitchell, "Evelyn Waugh Dusted Off for the Ages," *Critic* (Jan., 1981): 4-6.

Samuels, Jeffrey B., "There Are No Clean Wounds: A Literary Biography of Evelyn Waugh in the Pre-War World," *DAI* 40 (1979): 2669A.

Savage, D. S., "Death and Evelyn Waugh," *CR* 19 (1977): 88-105.

_____, "The Innocence of Evelyn Waugh," *WR* 14 (Spring, 1950): 197-206. Also in Rajan, B., ed., *Novelist as Thinker*, 34-46.

Semple, H. E., "Evelyn Waugh's Modern Crusade," *ESA* 11, i (Mar., 1968): 47-59.

Spender, S., "The World of Evelyn Waugh," *Creative Element*, 159-74.

Stinson, John J., "Waugh and Anthony Burgess: Some Notes toward and Assessment of Influence and Affinities," *EWN* 10, iii (Winter, 1976): 11-12.

Stopp, F. J., *Evelyn Waugh*.

Sykes, Christopher, "A Critique of Waugh," *Listener* 78 (Aug. 31, 1967): 267-9.

Ulanov, Barry, "The Ordeal of Evelyn Waugh," in Friedman, M. J., ed., *Vision Obscured*, 79-93.

Van Zeller, Dom H., "Evelyn Waugh," *Month* 36 (1966): 699-71.

Voorhees, Richard J., "Evelyn Waugh Revisited," *SAQ* 48 (Apr., 1949): 270-80.

_____, "Evelyn Waugh's Travel Books," *DR* 58 (1978): 240-8.

Webster, Harvey, "Evelyn Waugh: Catholic Aristocrat," *After the Trauma*, 72-92.

Wicker, Brian, "Waugh and the Narrator as Dandy," *Story-Shaped World*, 151-68.

Wilson, C., *Strength to Dream*, 42-6.

Wilson, Edmund, "Never Apologize, Never Explain," *NY* 20 (Mar., 1944): 68, 70, 72. Also in Wilson, E., *Classics and Commercials*, 140-6.

Woodcock, George, "Evelyn Waugh: The Man and His Work," *WoR* 1 (Mar., 1949): 51-6.

Wooton, Carl W., "Responses to the Modern World: A Study of Evelyn Waugh's Novels," *DA* 28 (1968): 3693A.

Zoghby, Mary D., "Metaphoric Structure in the War Novels of Ford Madox Ford and Evelyn Waugh," *DAI* 39 (1978): 879A.

BLACK MISCHIEF

Bradbury, M., *Evelyn Waugh*, 51-5.

Carens, J. F., *Satiric Art of Evelyn Waugh*, 77-80, 139-44.

Cook, W. J., Jr., *Masks, Modes, and Morals*, 101-22.

Davis, R. M., *Evelyn Waugh, Writer*, 55-68.

_____, "Social History in a BLACK MISCHIEF Revision," *EWN* 7, iii (Winter, 1973): 8-9.

DeVitis, A. A., *Roman Holiday*, 29-31.

Doyle, P. A., *Evelyn Waugh*, 16-18.

Greenblatt, S. J., *Three Modern Satirists*, 16-22, and *passim*.

Hall, James, "The Other Post-War Rebellion: Evelyn Waugh Twenty-Five Years After," *ELH* 28 (June, 1961): 195-8. Also in Hall, J., *Tragic Comedians*, 53-7.

Heath, J., *Picturesque Prison*, 91-103.

Hollis, C., *Evelyn Waugh*, 8-11.

Kaplan, Stanley R., "Circularity and Futility in BLACK MISCHIEF," *EWN* 15, iii (Winter, 1981): 1-4.

Lane, C. E., *Evelyn Waugh*, 62-70.

Myers, William, "Potential Recruits: Evelyn Waugh and the Reader of BLACK MISCHIEF," *RMS* 21 (1977): 40-51. Also in Lucas, John, ed., *The 1930's: A Challenge to Orthodoxy*, Sussex: Harvester Pr.; N.Y.: Barnes and Noble, 1978, 103-16.

Phillips, G. D., *Evelyn Waugh's Officers, Gentlemen, and Rogues*, 20-6.

Stopp, F. J., *Evelyn Waugh*, 77-83.

Tucker, M., *Africa in Modern Literature*, 141-5.

BRIDESHEAD REVISITED

Allen, W. Gore, "Evelyn Waugh and Graham Greene," *IrM* 57 (Jan., 1949): 16-22.

Autry, Susan G., "Language and Charm in BRIDESHEAD REVISITED," *DQR* 6 (1976): 291-303.

Beary, Thomas J., "Religion and the Modern Novel," *CathW* 166 (Dec., 1947): 209-10.

Bergonzi, Bernard, "Evelyn Waugh's Gentlemen," *CritQ* 5 (Spring, 1963): 35-40. Also in Davis, R. M., ed., *Evelyn Waugh*, 75-81.

_____, *Situation of the Novel*, 109-13.

Boyle, Alexander, "Evelyn Waugh" *IrM* 78 (Feb., 1950): 79-81.

Bradbury, M., *Evelyn Waugh*, 85-93.

Brailow, David G., "'My Theme is Memory': The Narrative Structure of BRIDESHEAD REVISITED," *EWN* 14, iii (1980): 1-4.

Canney, Daniel J., "The Kingfisher Image in BRIDESHEAD," *EWN* 7, iii (Winter, 1973): 6-7.

Carens, J. F., *Satiric Art of Evelyn Waugh*, 98-111.

Churchill, Thomas, "The Trouble with BRIDESHEAD REVISITED," *MLQ* 28 (June, 1967): 213-28.

Cogley, John, "Revisiting Brideshead," *Cweal* 80 (Apr. 17, 1964): 103-6.

Cohen, Martin S., "Allusive Conversation in A HANDFUL OF DUST and BRIDESHEAD REVISITED," *EWN* 5, ii (Autumn, 1971): 1-6. See also letter by Neil McCaffery *EWN* 5, ii (Autumn, 1971): 1-6. See also letter by Neil McCaffery *EWN* 5, iii (Winter, 1971): 9.

_____, "BRIDESHEAD REVISITED and JASPER TRISTRAM," *EWN* 5, iii (Winter, 1971): 6-8.

Cook, W. J., Jr., *Masks, Modes, and Morals*, 193-235.

Davis, Robert M., "BRIDESHEAD REVISITED and ALL THE KING'S MEN: Towards a Definition of Forties Sensibility," *EWN* 14, ii (1980): 1-4.

_____, *Evelyn Waugh, Writer*, 107-85.

_____, "Notes Toward a Variorum BRIDESHEAD," *EWN* 2, iii (1968): 4-6.

_____, "The Serial Version of BRIDESHEAD REVISITED," *TCL* 15, i (Apr., 1969): 35-43.

Delasanta, Rodney, and Mario L. D'Avanzo, "Truth and Beauty in BRIDESHEAD REVISITED," *MFS* 11 (Summer, 1965): 140-52.

DeVitis, A. A., *Roman Holiday*, 40-53.

Doherty, James, "More on the Kingfisher Image in BRIDESHEAD," *EWN* 8, iii (Winter, 1974): 8-9.

Doyle, P. A., *Evelyn Waugh*, 24-30.

_____, "Waugh's BRIDESHEAD REVISITED," *Expl* 24 (Mar., 1966): Item 57.

Dyson, A. E., "Evelyn Waugh and the Mysteriously Disappearing Hero," *CritiQ* 2 (Spring, 1960): 75-8. Also in Dyson, A. E., *Crazy Fabric*, 192-4.

Eagleton, T., *Exiles and Emigres*, 57-67.

Gardiner, H. C., "Nigh Draws the Chase," *America* 74 (Jan. 12, 1946): 411. Also in Gardiner, H. C., *In All Conscience*, 89-91.

Grace, William J., "Evelyn Waugh as Social Critic," *Ren* 1, ii (Spring, 1949): 35-40.

Granger, Derek, "'Of All Waugh's Books It is the One Most Constantly Read': The Writing of BRIDESHEAD REVISITED," *Listener* 106 (1981): 394-6.

Greene, Donald, "The Great Long Beach Waugh Memorial," *EWN* 13, iii (Winter, 1979): 1-4. [Identification of ship in novel.]

_____, "Peerage Nomenclature in BRIDESHEAD REVISITED," *EWN* 16, ii (1982): 5-7.

_____, "The Wicked Marquess: Disraeli to Thackery to Waugh," *EWN* 7, ii (1973): 1-5.

Hardy, J. E., *Man in the Modern Novel*, 159-74.

Harty, E. R., "BRIDESHEAD Re-read: A Discussion of Some of the Themes of Evelyn Waugh's BRIDESHEAD REVISITED," *UES* 3 (1967): 66-74.

Heath, Jeffrey M., "BRIDESHEAD: The Critics and the Memorandum," *EngS* 56 (1975): 222-30.

_____, *Picturesque Prison*, 161-83.

Heck, Francis S., "BRIDESHEAD, or Proust and Gide Revisited," *EWN* 9, ii (Autumn, 1975): 7-9.

Heilman, Robert, "Sue Brideshead Revisited," *Accent* 7 (1947): 123-6.

Hollis, C., *Evelyn Waugh*, 17-21.

Hutton-Brown, Charles, "Sebastian as Saint: The Hagiographical Sources of Sebastian Flyte," *EWN* 11, iii (Winter, 1977): 1-6.

Karl, F. R., "The World of Evelyn Waugh: The Normally Insane," *Contemporary English Novel*, 172-5, 177-8.

Kellogg, M., *Vital Tradition*, 108-10.

LaFrance, Marston, "Context and Structure of Evelyn Waugh's BRIDESHEAD REVISITED," *TCL* 10 (Apr., 1964): 12-18. Also in Davis, R. M., ed., *Evelyn Waugh*, 57-68.

Lane, C. W., *Evelyn Waugh*, 91-102.

Lodge, D., *Evelyn Waugh*, 29-34. Also in Stade, G., ed., *Six Modern British Novelists*, 70-4.

Mahon, John W., "Charles Ryder and Evelyn Waugh," *EWN* 6, i (Spring, 1972): 2-3.

Martindale, C. C., "Back Again to BRIDESHEAD," *Twentieth Century* (Australia) 2 (Mar., 1948): 26-33.

Neame, A. J., "Black and Blue: A Study in the Catholic Novel," *The European* No. 2 (Apr., 1953): 30-2.

O'Faolain, S., *Vanishing Hero*, 34-42.

Phillips, G. D., *Evelyn Waugh's Officers, Gentlemen, and Rogues*, 55-75.

Powell, Robert S., "Uncritical Perspective: Belief and Art in BRIDESHEAD REVISITED," *CritiQ* 22, iii (Autumn, 1980): 53-67.

Prescott, O., *In My Opinion*, 169-71.

Rauchbauer, Otto, "The Presentation and the Function of Spare in Evelyn Waugh's BRIDESHEAD REVISITED," 61-76 in Korninger, Siegfried, ed., *A Yearbook of Studies in English Language and Literature*, Wien: Braumuller, 1981.

Riley, John, "The Two Waughs at War: Part 2: A Reassessment of BRIDESHEAD REVISITED," *EWN* 12, iii (1978): 3-9.

Savage, D. S., "Death and Evelyn Waugh," *CR* 19 (1977): 93-101.

Sheleny, Harvey, "Some Aspects of BRIDESHEAD REVISITED: A Comparison with Henry James' THE AMERICAN," *EWN* 11, ii (1977): 4-7.

Spender, S., "The World of Evelyn Waugh," *Creative Element*, 169-74.

Staley, Thomas F., "Waugh the Artist," *Cweal* 84 (May 27, 1966): 280-2.

Stopp, F. J., *Evelyn Waugh*, 108-23, 150-2.

————, "Grace in Reins: Reflections of Mr. Waugh's BRIDESHEAD and HELENA," *Month* n.s. 10 (Aug., 1953): 69-84.

Vredenburgh, Joseph, "The Character of the Incest Object: A Study of Alternation between Narcissism and Object Choice," *AI* 16 (Fall, 1959): 263-8.

Walker, Judith M., "Being and Becoming: A Comment on Religion in VILE BODIES and BRIDESHEAD REVISITED," *EWN* 16, ii (1982): 4-5.

Waugh, Evelyn, "BRIDESHEAD REVISITED Revisited," *Critic* 20 (Dec., 1961-Jan., 1962): 35.

Wilson, Edmund, "Splendors and Miseries of Evelyn Waugh," *NY* 21 (Jan. 5, 1946): 71+. Also in Wilson, E., *Classics and Commercials*, 298-302.

Wooton, Carl, "Evelyn Waugh's BRIDESHEAD REVISITED: War and Limited Hope," *MQ* 10 (July, 1969): 359-75.

DECLINE AND FALL

Bradbury, M., "The Modern Comic Novel in the 1920's: Lewis, Huxley and Waugh," *Possibilities*, 154-60.

————, *Evelyn Waugh*, 34-46.

Carens, J. F., *Satiric Art of Evelyn Waugh*, 11-12, 16-17, 26-8, 47-8, 70-4.

Cook, W. J., Jr., *Masks, Modes, and Morals*, 61-82.

Davis, R. M., *Evelyn Waugh, Writer*, 29-50.

————, "Grimes' Suicide: An Analogue," *EWN* 12, ii (Autumn, 1978): 8-9.

DeVitis, A. A., *Roman Holiday*, 19-24.

Doyle, Paul A., "DECLINE AND FALL: Two Versions," *EWN* 2 (1967): 4-5.

————, *Evelyn Waugh*, 5-7.

Dyson, A. E., "Evelyn Waugh and the Mysteriously Disappearing Hero," *CritQ* 2 (Spring, 1960): 72-5. Also in Dyson, A. E., *Crazy Fabric*, 188-90.

Eagleton, T., *Exiles and Emigres*, 42-50.

Farr, D. Paul, "The Success and Failure of DECLINE AND FALL," *EA* 24, iii (July-Sept., 1971): 257-70.

Friedman, Thomas, "DECLINE AND FALL and the Satirist's Responsibility," *EWN* 6, ii (1972): 3-8.

Greenblatt, S. J., *Three Modern Satirists*, 5-12.

Heath, J., *Picturesque Prison*, 63-79.

Highet, G., *Anatomy of Satire*, 193-4.

Hunter, Jeanne C., "The Characters of Language in DECLINE AND FALL," *EWN* 11, i (1977): 8-9.

————, "Uneventful Order: The End of DECLINE AND FALL," *EWN* 12, ii (1978): 7-8.

Johnson, J. J., "Counterparts: The Classic and the Modern 'Pervigilium Veneris'," *EWN* 8, iii (Winter, 1974): 7-8.

Kleine, Don W., "The Cosmic Comedies of Evelyn Waugh," *SAQ* 61 (Autumn, 1962): 533-9.

Lane, C. W., *Evelyn Waugh*, 45-53.

Lodge, D., *Evelyn Waugh*, 16-19. Also in Stade, G., ed., *Six Modern British Novelists*, 56-60.

Lord, George, "Heroic Games: Homer to Waugh," *CollL* 3, iii (Fall, 1976): 180-6.

McAleer, Edward C., "DECLINE AND FALL as Imitation," *EWN* 7, iii (Winter, 1973): 1-4.

Meckier, Jerome, "Cycle, Symbol and Parody in Evelyn Waugh's DECLINE AND FALL," *ConL* 20 (1979): 51-75.

Mehoke, James S., "Sartre's Theory of Emotion and Three English Novelists: Waugh, Green, Amis," *WisSL* 3 (1966): 106-8.

Nichols, James W., "Romantic and Realistic: The Tone of Evelyn Waugh's Early Novels," *CE* 24 (Oct., 1962): 51-2.

Noon, William T., "Satire, Poison and the Professor," *EngR* 11, i (July, 1960): 55-6.

Phillips, G. D., *Evelyn Waugh's Officers, Gentlemen, and Rogues*, 8-14.

Rees, John, "'What Price Dothboys Hall?': Some Dickens Echoes in Waugh," *KanQ* 7, iv (Fall, 1975): 15-16.

Stopp, F. J., *Evelyn Waugh*, 63-70.

Symons, J., "A Long Way from Firbank," *Critical Occasions*, 74-9.

Tysdahl, Bjorn, "The Bright Young Things in the Early Novels of Evelyn Waugh," *Edda* 62 (1962): 326-34.

END OF THE BATTLE (UNCONDITIONAL SURRENDER) (See also MEN AT ARMS Trilogy and SWORD OF HONOUR)

Amis, Kingsley, "Crouchback's Regress," *Spectator* No. 6957 (Oct. 27, 1961): 581-2.

Burrows, L. R., "Scenes de la Vie Militaire," *Westerly* 1 (1962): 3-6.

Carens, J. F., *Satiric Art of Evelyn Waugh*, 17-19, 24-5.

Cook, W. J., Jr., *Masks, Modes, and Morals*, 297-337.

Davis, Robert M., "Evelyn Waugh and the Sword of Stalingrad," *EWN* 15, ii (Autumn, 1981): 3-5.
_____, *Evelyn Waugh, Writer*, 297-324.
Delbaere-Garant, J., "'Who Shall Inherit England?': A Comparison between HOWARD'S END, PARADE'S END, and UNCONDITIONAL SURRENDER," *ES* 50 (1969): 101-5.
Greene, Donald, "Sir Ralph Brompton—An Identification," *EWN* 8, iii (1974): 1-2.
Heath, J., *Picturesque Prison*, 244-58.
Kenedy, R. C., "MEN AT ARMS—OFFICERS AND GENTLEMEN—UNCONDITIONAL SURRENDER: An Essay on a Novel in Three Parts by Evelyn Waugh," *ArtI* 13, vii (1969): 17-22.
O'Donovan, Patrick, "Evelyn Waugh's Opus of Disgust," *NRep* 146 (Feb. 12, 1962): 21-2.
Phillips, G. D., *Evelyn Waugh's Officers, Gentlemen, and Rogues*, 126-41.
Pritchett, V. S., "Vanities and Servitudes," *NStat* (Oct. 20, 1961): 603-4.

A HANDFUL OF DUST

Bergonzi, Bernard, "Evelyn Waugh's Gentlemen," *CritiQ* 5 (Spring, 1963): 24-7. Also in Davis, R. M., ed., *Evelyn Waugh*, 70-5.
_____, *Situation of the Novel*, 105-8.
Bradbury, M., *Evelyn Waugh*, 55-68.
Brophy, Brigid, in *NStat* 68 (Sept., 1964): 450. Also in Brophy, B., *Don't Never Forget*, 156-9.
Burbridge, Roger T., "The Function of Gossip, Rumor, and Public Opinion in Evelyn Waugh's A HANDFUL OF DUST," *EWN* 4, ii (Autumn, 1970): 3-5.
Carens, J. F., *Satiric Art of Evelyn Waugh*, 27-9, 81-6.
Cohen, Martin S., "Allusive Conversation in A HANDFUL OF DUST and BRIDESHEAD REVISITED," *EWN* 5, ii (Autumn, 1971): 1-6. See also letter by Neil McCaffery, *EWN* 5, iii (Winter, 1971): 9.
Cook, W. J., Jr., *Masks, Modes, and Morals*, 122-44.
Davis, R. M., *Evelyn Waugh*, 69-86.
_____, "HARPER'S BAZAAR and A HANDFUL OF DUST," *PQ* 48, iv (Oct., 1968): 508-16.
_____, "Title and Theme in A HANDFUL OF DUST," *EWN* 6, ii (1970): 1-2.
De Vitis, A. A., *Roman Holiday*, 31-3.
Doyle, P. A., *Evelyn Waugh*, 18-22.
Eagleton, T., *Exiles and Emigres*, 53-7.
Edwards, A. S. G., "A Source for A HANDFUL OF DUST," *MFS* 22, ii (Summer, 1976): 242-4.
Firchow, Peter E., "In Search of A HANDFUL OF DUST: The Literary Background of Evelyn Waugh's Novel," *JML* 2 (1972): 406-16.
Green, Peter, "Du Cote de Chez Waugh," *REL* 2, ii (Apr., 1961): 89-100.
Greenblatt, S. J., *Three Modern Satirists*, 57-63.
Hall, James, "The Other Post-War Rebellion: Evelyn Waugh Twenty-Five Years After," *ELH* 28 (June, 1961): 198-201. Also in Hall, J., *Tragic Comedians*, 57-63.
Heath, Jeffrey, "Evelyn Waugh: Afraid of the Shadow," *EWN* 9, iii (Winter, 1975): 1-4.
_____, *Picturesque Prison*, 104-23.

Joost, Nicholas, "A HANDFUL OF DUST: Evelyn Waugh and the Novel of Manners," *PLL* 12, ii (Spring, 1976): 177-96.
Kearful, Frank, J., "Tony Last and Ike McCaslin: The Loss of a Usuable Past," *UWR* 3, ii (Spring, 1968): 45-52.
Kellogg, M., *Vital Tradition*, 105-7.
Kolek, Leszek, "Uncinematic Devices—Evelyn Waugh's A HANDFUL OF DUST," *LWU* 15 (1982): 353-65.
Lane, C. W., *Evelyn Waugh*, 70-7.
Lodge, D., *Evelyn Waugh*, 25-8. Also in Stade, G., ed., *Six Modern British Novelists*, 65-8.
Markovic, C. E., *Changing Face*, 70-81.
Meckier, Jerome, "Why the Man Who Liked Dickens Reads Dickens Instead of Conrad: Waugh's A HANDFUL OF DUST," *Novel* 13, ii (1980): 171-87.
Nardin, Jane, "The Myth of Decline in A HANDFUL OF DUST," *MQ* 18 (1977): 119-30.
Nicholas, James W., "Romantic and Realistic: The Tone of Evelyn Waugh's Early Novels," *CE* 24 (Oct., 1962): 53-6.
Phillips, G. D., *Evelyn Waugh's Officers, Gentlemen, and Rogues*, 29-33.
Slater, Ann P., "Waugh's A HANDFUL OF DUST: Right Things in Wrong Places," *EIC* 32, i (Jan., 1982): 48-68.
Staley, Thomas F., "Waugh the Artist," *Cweal* 84 (May 27, 1966): 281-2.
Stopp, F. J., *Evelyn Waugh*, 90-100.
Ulanov, Barry, "The Ordeal of Evelyn Waugh," in Friedman, M. J., ed., *Vision Obscured*, 84-7.
Wasson, Richard, "A HANDFUL OF DUST: Critique of Victorianism," *MFS* 7 (Winter, 1961-62): 327-37.
Wilson, C., *Strength to Dream*, 42-3.

HELENA

Allen, W. Gore, "Evelyn Waugh's HELENA," *IrM* 79 (Feb., 1951): 96-7.
Bergonzi, B., *Situation of the Novel*, 112-13.
Bradbury, M., *Evelyn Waugh*, 100-3.
Carens, J. F., *Satiric Art of Evelyn Waugh*, 111-19.
Davis, R. M., *Evelyn Waugh, Writer*, 217-35.
_____, "Evelyn Waugh's HELENA and the Problem of Proofs," *PBSA* 73 (1979): 481-3.
Dever, Joe, "Echoes of Two Waughs," *Cweal* 53 (Oct. 27, 1950): 68-70.
De Vitis, A. A., *Roman Holiday*, 60-7.
Doyle, P. A., *Evelyn Waugh*, 33-5.
Heath, Jeffrey M., "Concluding HELENA," *EWN* 10, ii (1976): 4-5.
_____, *Picturesque Prison*, 198-205.
Hollis, C., *Evelyn Waugh*, 25-31.
Joost, Nicholas, "Waugh's HELENA, Chapter 6," *Expl* 9 (Apr., 1951): Item 43.
Lane, C. W., *Evelyn Waugh*, 107-10.
Lodge, D., *Evelyn Waugh*, 34-5. Also in Stade, G., ed., *Six Modern British Novelists*, 74-6.
Menen, Aubrey, "The Baroque and Mr. Waugh," *Month* 5 (Apr., 1951): 226-37.
Phillips, G. D., *Evelyn Waugh's Officers, Gentlemen, and Rogues*, 89-99.
Stopp, F. J., *Evelyn Waugh*, 123-9, 207-9.

_____, "Grace in Reins: Reflections on Mr. Waugh's BRIDESHEAD and HELENA," *Month* n.s. 10 (Aug., 1953): 69-84.

LOVE AMONG THE RUINS

Bradbury, M., *Evelyn Waugh*, 103-4.
Carens, J. F., *Satiric Art of Evelyn Waugh*, 151-6.
Heath, J., *Picturesque Prison*, 206-9.
Phillips, G. D., *Evelyn Waugh's Officers, Gentlemen, and Rogues*, 99-104.
Stopp, F. J., *Evelyn Waugh*, 152-7, 189-90.

THE LOVED ONE

Barnard, Robert, "What the Whispering Glades Whispered: Dennis Barlow's Quest in THE LOVED ONE," *ES* 60 (1979): 176-82.
Bayley, John, "Two Catholic Novelists," *NatR* 132 (1949): 232-5.
Bradbury, M., *Evelyn Waugh*, 142-52.
Carens, J. F., *Satiric Art of Evelyn Waugh*, 20-2.
Connolly, Cyril, "Introduction to THE LOVED ONE," *Horizon* 17 (Feb., 1948): 76-7.
Davis, R. M., *Evelyn Waugh, Writer*, 190-214.
Davis, Robert M., "THE LOVED ONE: Text and Context," *TQ* 15, iv (Winter, 1972): 100-7.
De Vitis, A. A., *Roman Holiday*, 54-9.
Doyle, P. A., *Evelyn Waugh*, 30-3.
_____, "That Poem in THE LOVED ONE," *EWN* 15, iii (Winter, 1981): 6-7.
Gordon, Gerald T., "'Lake Island of Innisfree': A Classical Allusion in Evelyn Waugh's THE LOVED ONE," *EWN* 5, iii (Winter, 1971): 1-2.
Greene, Donald, "Evelyn Waugh's Hollywood," *EWN* 16, iii (Winter, 1982): 1-4.
Griffiths, Joan, "Waugh's Problem Comedies," *Accent* 9 (Spring, 1949): 165-70.
Hall, J., *Tragic Comedians*, 63-4.
Heath, Jeffrey, *Picturesque Prison*, 188-97.
Hollis, C., *Evelyn Waugh*, 22-4.
Lane, C. W., *Evelyn Waugh*, 103-7.
Lasseter, Victor, "Anglo-American Confidence Men: The Theme of Fraud in THE LOVED ONE," *StCS* 4 (1977): 14-20.
Lodge, D., *Evelyn Waugh*, 36-7. Also in Stade, G., ed., *Six Modern British Novelists*, 76-7.
Mikes, George, *Eight Humorists*, London: Allan Wingate, 1954, 135-8.
Phillips, G. D., *Evelyn Waugh's Officers, Gentlemen, and Rogues*, 79-89.
Powers, J. F., "Waugh Out West," *Cweal* 48 (July 16, 1948): 326-7.
Ryan, Harold F., "A vista of diminished truth," *America* 82 (Nov. 12, 1949): 157-8.
Stopp, F. J., *Evelyn Waugh*, 142-52.
Stratford, Philip, "An Anglo-American Travesty: Evelyn Waugh and THE LOVED ONE," *Encounter* (Sept., 1978): 46-51.
Venne, Peter, S. V. D., "Death in Hollywood: An English Satirist Looks at Modern America," *FJS* 9 (1976): 19-28.
Vogel, Joseph F., "Waugh's THE LOVED ONE: The Artist in a Phony World," *EWN* 10, ii (Autumn, 1976): 1-4.
Wagner, Linda W., "Satiric Masks: Huxley and Waugh," *SNL* 3 (Spring, 1966): 160-2.

Wecter, Dixon, "On Dying in Southern California," *PacSp* 2 (Autumn, 1948): 375-87.
Wilson, E., "Splendors and Miseries of Evelyn Waugh," *Classics and Commercials*, 304-5.

MEN AT ARMS (See also SWORD OF HONOUR)

Braybrooke, Neville, "Evelyn Waugh and Blimp," *Blackfriars* 38 (Dec., 1952): 508-12.
Carens, J. F., *Satiric Art of Evelyn Waugh*, 41-5.
De Vitis, A. A. *Roman Holiday*, 68-79.
Hollis, C., *Evelyn Waugh*, 31-3.
Heath, Jeffrey M., "Apthorpe Placatus?" *Ariel* 5, i (Jan., 1974): 5-14.
_____, *Picturesque Prison*, 217-27.
Kenedy, R. C., "MEN AT ARMS—OFFICERS AND GENTLE-MEN—UNCONDITIONAL SURRENDER: an Essay on a Novel in Three Parts by Evelyn Waugh," *ArtI* 13, vii (1969): 17-22.
Neame, A. J., "Black and Blue: A Study in the Catholic Novel," *The European* 2 (Apr., 1953): 33-6.
Phillips, G. D., *Evelyn Waugh's Officers, Gentlemen, and Rogues*, 111-18.
Rees, John, "'What Price Dotheboy Hall'?" Some Dickens Echoes in Waugh," *KanQ* 7, iv (Fall, 1975): 17-18.
Semple, H. E., "Evelyn Waugh's Modern Crusade," *ESA* 11 (Mar., 1968): 48-52.
Stopp, Frederick J., "The Circle and the Tangent: An Interpretation of Mr. Waugh's MEN AT ARMS," *Month* n.s. 12 (July, 1954): 18-34.
_____, *Evelyn Waugh*, 158-69.
Voorhees, Richard J., "Evelyn Waugh's War Novels," *QQ* 65 (Spring, 1958): 53-63.

MEN AT ARMS Trilogy (See also SWORD OF HONOUR)

Anon., in *TLS* (Mar. 17, 1966): 216. Also in *T.L.S.: Essays and Reviews from the Times Literary Supplement, 1966*, 123-7.
Bergonzi, Bernard, "Evelyn Waugh's Gentlemen," *CritiQ* 5 (Spring, 1965): 31-6. Also in Davis, R. M., ed., *Evelyn Waugh*, 81-8.
_____, *Situation of the Novel*, 114-18.
Bogaards, Winifred M., "The Conclusion of Waugh's Trilogy: Three Variants," *EWN* 4, ii (Autumn, 1970): 6-7.
Bradbury, M., *Evelyn Waugh*, 105-15.
Cook, W. J., Jr., *Masks, Modes, and Morals*, 238-71.
Davis, R. M., *Evelyn Waugh, Writer*, 238-57.
Didion, Joan, "Evelyn Waugh: Gentlemen in Battle," *NatR* 12 (Mar., 27, 1962): 215-17.
Doyle, P. A., *Evelyn Waugh*, 36-41.
Greene, George, "Scapegoat With Style: The Status of Evelyn Waugh," *QQ* 71 (Winter, 1964-65): 484-93.
Heath, J., *Picturesque Prison*, 210-16.
Kiely, Robert, "The Craft of Despondency—The Traditional Novelists," *Daedalus* (Spring, 1963): 223-6, 233-4.
Lane, C. W., *Evelyn Waugh*, 118-42.
Lodge, D., *Evelyn Waugh*, 39-45. Also in Stade, G., ed., *Seven Modern British Novelists*, 77-85.
Manley, Jeffrey A., "Waugh in the Soviet Union: THE WAR TRILOGY," *EWN* 14, i (1980): 4-6.
O'Donovan, Patrick, "Evelyn Waugh's Opus of Disgust," *NRep* 146 (Feb. 12, 1962): 21-2.

Parker, Kenneth, "Quantitative Judgments Don't Apply," *ESA* 9 (Sept., 1966): 192-201.

Phillips, G. D., *Evelyn Waugh's Officers, Gentlemen, and Rogues*, 105-41.

Riley, John J., "Gentlemen at Arms: A Comparison of the War Trilogies of Anthony Powell and Evelyn Waugh," *DAI* 34 (1974): 5202A.

Russell, John, "The War Trilogies of Anthony Powell and Evelyn Waugh," *ModA* 16, iii (Summer, 1972): 289-300.

Semple, H. E., "Evelyn Waugh's Modern Crusade," *ESA* 11 (Mar., 1968): 47-59.

OFFICERS AND GENTLEMEN (See also MEN AT WAR Trilogy)

Carens, F. J., *Satiric Art of Evelyn Waugh*, 160-5.

Cook, W. J., Jr., *Masks, Modes, and Morals*, 271-969.

Davis, R. M., *Evelyn Waugh, Writer*, 259-79.

De Vitis, A. A., *Roman Holiday*, 79-81.

Heath, J., *Picturesque Prison*, 228-43.

Hollis, C., *Evelyn Waugh*, 33-4.

Kenedy, R. C., "MEN AT ARMS—OFFICERS AND GENTLE-MEN—UNCONDITIONAL SURRENDER: An Essay on a Novel in Three Parts by Evelyn Waugh," *ArtI* 13, vii (1969): 17-22.

Phillips, G. D., *Evelyn Waugh's Officers, Gentlemen, and Rogues*, 118-26.

Stopp, F. J., *Evelyn Waugh*, 169-78.

_____, "Waugh: End of an Illusion," *Ren* 9 (1956): 59-67+.

Voorhees, Richard J., "Evelyn Waugh's War Novels," *QQ* 65 (Spring, 1958): 53-63.

THE ORDEAL OF GILBERT PINFOLD

Anon., "Stout Party," *NStat* (Oct. 20, 1961): 592-4.

Bradbury, M., *Evelyn Waugh*, 2-4, 104-6.

Davis, R. M., *Evelyn Waugh, Writer*, 281-95.

Dobie, Ann B., and Carl Wooton, "Spark and Waugh: Similarities by Coincidence," *MQ* 13, iv (Summer, 1972): 423-34.

Doyle, Paul A., and Alan Clodd, "A British Pinfold and an American Pinfold," *EWN* 3, iii (Winter, 1969): 1-5.

Duer, Harriet W., "Pinfold's Pinfold," *EWN* 8, i (1974): 3-6.

Heath, J., *Picturesque Prison*, 259-65.

_____, "Waugh and the PINFOLD Manuscript," *JML* 5 (1976): 331-6.

Hurst, Mary J., and Daniel Hurst, "Bromide Poisoning in THE ORDEAL OF GILBERT PINFOLD," *EWN* 16, ii (1982): 1-4.

Lane, C. W., *Evelyn Waugh*, 111-17.

Lodge, D., *Evelyn Waugh*, 37-9. Also in Stade, G., ed., *Six Modern British Novelists*, 78-9.

Phillips, G. D., *Evelyln Waugh's Officers, Gentlemen, and Rogues*, 147-57.

Price, Martin, in *YR* 47 (Autumn, 1957): 150-1.

Stopp, Frederick J., "Apology and Explanation," *Ren* 10 (Winter, 1958): 94-7.

_____, *Evelyn Waugh*, 219-34.

PUT OUT MORE FLAGS

Bradbury, M., *Evelyn Waugh*, 80-5.

Cook, W. J., Jr., *Masks, Modes and Morals*, 165-92.

De Vitis, A. A., *Roman Holiday*, 36-9.

Gorra, Michael, "Waugh in Transition: PUT OUT MORE FLAGS," *EWN* 14, iii (1980): 6-8.

Heath, J., *Picturesque Prison*, 152-60.

Hollis, C., *Evelyn Waugh*, 15-17.

Lane, C. W., *Evelyn Waugh*, 82-8.

Manning, Gerald F., "The Weight of Singularity: Meaning and Structure in PUT OUT MORE FLAGS," *ESC* 2 (1976): 227-34.

Phillips, G. D., *Evelyn Waugh's Officers, Gentlemen, and Rogues*, 43-50.

Riley, John, "The Two Waughs at War: Part I: A Reassessment of PUT OUT MORE FLAGS," *EWN* 12, ii (1978): 3-7.

Stopp, F. J. *Evelyn Waugh*, 130-6.

SCOOP

Blayac, Alain, "Technique and Meaning in SCOOP: Is SCOOP a Modern Fairy-Tale?" *EWN* 6, iii (1972): 1-8.

Bradbury, M., *Evelyn Waugh*, 68-74.

Carens, J. F., *Satiric Art of Evelyn Waugh*, 144-8.

Cook, W. J., Jr., *Masks, Modes, and Morals*, 148-65.

Davis, R. M., *Evelyn Waugh, Writer*, 87-105.

Davis, Robert M., "Some Textual Variants in SCOOP," *EWN* 2 (1967): 1-3.

De Vitis, A. A., *Roman Holiday*, 33-6.

Farr, D. Paul, "The Novelists Coup: Style as Satiric Norm in SCOOP," *ConnR* 8, ii (1975): 42-54.

Heath, J., *Picturesque Prison*, 124-38.

_____, "Waugh's SCOOP in Manuscript," *EWN* 11, ii (1977): 9-11.

Hollis, C., *Evelyn Waugh*, 11-14.

Lane, C. W., *Evelyn Waugh*, 77-82.

Phillips, G. D., *Evelyn Waugh's Officers, Gentlemen, and Rogues*, 33-42.

Stopp, F. J., *Evelyn Waugh*, 83-9.

Tucker, M., *Africa in Modern Literature*, 141-5, 236-7.

SCOTT-KING'S MODERN EUROPE

Bradbury, M., *Evelyn Waugh*, 93-4.

Carens, J. F., *Satiric Art of Evelyn Waugh*, 148-51.

Davis, Robert, M., "SCOTT-KING'S MODERN EUROPE: A Textual History," *EWN*, 12, iii (Winter, 1978): 1-3.

Heath, J., *Picturesque Prison*, 184-7.

Hollis, C., *Evelyn Waugh*, 21-2.

Stopp, F. J., *Evelyn Waugh*, 136-42.

SWORD OF HONOUR (See also MEN AT ARMS Trilogy)

Coppetiers, R., "A Linguistic Analysis of a Corpus of Quoted Speech in Evelyn Waugh's Novel THE SWORD OF HONOUR," *SGG* 11 (1969): 87-153.

Costello, Patrick, "An Idea of Comedy and Waugh's SWORD OF HONOUR" *KanQ* 1, iii (Summer, 1969): 41-50.

Bergonzi, Bernard, "Evelyn Waugh's THE SWORD OF HONOUR," *Listener* 71 (1964): 306-7.

Davis, Robert M., "Guy Crouchback's Children—A Reply," *ELN* 7 (Dec., 1969): 127-9. [Reply to Mattingly below.]

_____, *Evelyn Waugh, Writer*, 326-32.

Golden, Glen T., "Two Views of Modern Man and the Military: Evelyn Waugh's SWORD OF HONOUR and James Gould Cozzen's GUARD OF HONOR," *DAI* 42 (1981): 1136A-37A.

Gribble, Thomas, "The Nature of a Trimmer," *EWN* 15, ii (Autumn, 1981): 1-3.

Haberman, Donald, "Responses to War: Ford Madox Ford and Evelyn Waugh," *FQ* 25, i (Autumn, 1975): 29-45.

Hart, Jeffrey, "The Roots of Honor," *NatR* 13 (Feb. 22, 1966): 168-9.

————, "Sword of Honor," *Triumph* 10 (Dec., 1970): 30-3.

LaFrance, Marston, "SWORD OF HONOUR: The Ironist Placatus," *DR* 55 (1975): 23-53.

Mattingly, Joseph F., "Guy Crouchback's 'Children'," *ELN* 6, iii (Mar., 1969): 200-1.

Phillips, G. D., *Evelyn Waugh's Officers, Gentlemen, and Rogues*, 107-10, 136-41.

Rutherford, Andrew, "The Christian as Hero: Waugh's SWORD OF HONOUR," *Literature of War: Five Studies in Heroic Virtue*, N.Y.: Barnes and Noble, 1978, 113-34. Revised version of his "Waugh's SWORD OF HONOUR," in Mack, Maynard, and Ian MacGregor, eds., *Imagined Worlds*, 44-60.

Scheideman, J. W., "Miss Vavasour Remembered," *EWN* 9, iii (Winter, 1975): 4-8.

Wilson, B. W., "SWORD OF HONOUR: The Last Crusade," *English* 23 (Autumn, 1974): 87-93.

Wykes, David, "Evelyn Waugh's Sword of Volograd," *DQR* 7, ii (1977): 82-99.

UNCONDITIONAL SURRENDER (See END OF THE BATTLE)

VILE BODIES

Allen, M., *Modern Novel*, 209-10.

Bradbury, M., *Evelyn Waugh*, 46-51.

Carens, J. F., *Satiric Art of Evelyn Waugh*, 17-19, 24-5, 74-7.

Clark, John R., "Symbolic Violence in VILE BODIES," *StCS* 1, ii-2 (1975): 17-27.

Cook, W. J., Jr., *Masks, Modes and Morals*, 82-99.

Davis, Robert M., "Title, Theme, and Structure in VILE BODIES," *SHR* 11, i (1977): 21-7.

————, "VILE BODIES in Typescript," *EWN* 11, iii (Winter, 1977): 7-8.

Doyle, P. A., *Evelyn Waugh*, 14-16.

Eagleton, T., *Exiles and Emigres*, 50-3.

Greenblatt, S. J., *Three Modern Satirists*, 12-16.

Greene, Donald, "Who Was Father Rothschild?" *EWN* 11, ii (Autumn, 1977): 7-9.

Hall, James, "The Other Post-War Rebellion: Evelyn Waugh Twenty-Five Years After," *ELH* 28 (June, 1961): 191-5. Also in Hall, J., *Tragic Comedians*, 49-53.

Heath, J., *Picturesque Prison*, 80-90.

————, "VILE BODIES: A Revolution in Film Art," *EWN* 8, iii (Winter, 1974): 2-7.

Isaacs, Neil D., "Evelyn Waugh's Restoration Jesuit," *SNL* 2 (Spring, 1965): 91-4.

Jervis, Steven A., "Evelyn Waugh, VILE BODIES, and the Younger Generation," *SAQ* 66 (Summer, 1967): 440-8.

Kleine, Don W., "The Cosmic Comedies of Evelyn Waugh," *SAQ* 61 (Autumn, 1962): 533-9.

Kosok, Heinz, "The Film World of VILE BODIES," *EWN* 4, ii (Autumn, 1970): 1-2.

Lane, C. W., *Evelyn Waugh*, 53-62.

Linck, Charles E., Jr., and Robert M. Davis, "The Bright Young People in VILE BODIES," *PLL* 5 (Winter, 1969): 80-90.

Lodge, D., *Evelyn Waugh*, 20-2. Also in Stade, G., ed., *Six Modern British Novelists*, 60-2.

New, Melvyn, "Ad Nauseam: A Satiric Device in Huxley, Orwell, and Waugh," *SNL* 8, i (Fall, 1970): 24-8.

Nichols, James W., "Romantic and Realistic: The Tone of Evelyn Waugh's Early Novels," *CE* 24 (Oct., 1962): 52-3.

Phillips, G. D., *Evelyn Waugh's Officers, Gentlemen, and Rogues*, 14-20.

Stopp, F. J., *Evelyn Waugh*, 70-7.

Tysdahl, Bjorn, "The Bright Young Things in the Early Novels of Evelyn Waugh," *Edda* 62 (1962): 326-34.

THE WAR TRILOGY (See MEN AT ARMS Trilogy and SWORD OF HONOUR)

WORK SUSPENDED

Bradbury, M., *Evelyn Waugh*, 76-80.

Heath, J., *Picturesque Prison*, 139-51.

Stannard, Martin, "WORK SUSPENDED: Waugh's Climacteric," *EIC* 28, iv (Oct., 1978): 302-20.

Stopp, F. J., *Evelyn Waugh*, 101-7.

BIBLIOGRAPHY

See issues of *Evelyn Waugh Newsletter*.

Blayac, Alain, "Evelyn Waugh: A Supplementary Bibliography," *BC* 25 (1976): 53-62.

Bradbury, M., *Evelyn Waugh*, 116-20.

Davis, R. M., et al., comps., *Evelyn Waugh: A Checklist of Primary and Secondary Material*, Troy, N.Y.: Whitson, 1972.

Doyle, P. A., *Evelyn Waugh*, 46-8.

————, "Evelyn Waugh: A Bibliography," *BB* 22 (1957): 57-62.

Kosok, Heinz, "Evelyn Waugh: A Checklist of Criticism," *TCL* 11 (Jan., 1966): 211-15.

Stopp, F. J., *Evelyn Waugh*, 238-40.

WEBB, CHARLES (RICHARD), 1939-

THE GRADUATE

Fry, Carrol L., and Jared Stein, "Isolation Imagery in THE GRADUATE: A Contrast in Media," *MQ* 19 (1978): 203-14.

Patrick, Michael, "Racy Relevance in SIR GARWAIN and THE GRADUATE," *MEB* 29 (1972): 30-2.

WELDON, FAY, 1933-

GENERAL

Krouse, Agate N., "Feminism and Art in Fay Weldon's Novels," *Crit* 20, ii (1978): 5-20.

DOWN AMONG THE WOMEN

Chesnutt, Margaret, "Feminist Criticism and Feminist Consciousness: A Reading of a Novel by Fay Weldon," *MSpr* 73 (1979): 3-18.

Krouse, Agate N., "Feminism and Art in the Novels of Fay Weldon," *Crit* 20, ii (1978): 10-12.

FEMALE FRIENDS

Krouse, Agate N., "Feminism and Art in Fay Weldon's Novels," *Crit* 20, ii (1978): 12-15.

REMEMBER ME

Krouse, Agate N., "Feminism and Art in Fay Weldon's Novels," *Crit* 20, ii (1978): 15-20.

WEIDMAN, JEROME, 1913-

THE ENEMY CAMP

Rosenthal, Raymond, "What's In It for Weidman?" *Ctary* 27 (Feb., 1959): 171-3.

I CAN GET IT FOR YOU WHOLESALE

Sherman, B., *Invention of the Jew*, 176-8.

WELTY, EUDORA, 1909-

GENERAL

See issues of *Eudora Welty Newsletter*.

Allen, John A., "Eudora Welty: The Three Moments," *VQR* 51, iv (Autumn, 1975): 605-27. Also in Desmond, J. F., ed., *Still Moment*, 12-34.

_____, "The Other Way to Live: Demigods in Eudora Welty's Fiction," in Prenshaw, P. W., ed., *Eudora Welty*, 26-55.

Appel, A., Jr., *Season of Dreams*.

Arms, Nancy R., "The Feeder: A Study of the Fiction of Eudora Welty and Carson McCullers," *DAI* 36 (1975): 2817A.

Arnold, St. George T., Jr., "Consciousness and the Unconscious in the Fiction of Eudora Welty," *DAI* 36 (1976): 6094A.

Bolsterli, Margaret, "A Fertility Rite in Mississippi," *NMW* 8 (1975): 69-71. [Not seen.]

Brans, Jo, "Struggling against the Plaid: An Interview with Eudora Welty," *SWR* 66, iii (Summer, 1981): 255-66.

Brookhart, Mary H., "The Search for Lost Time in the Early Fiction of Eudora Welty," *DAI* 42 (1981): 2667A-68A.

Brooks, Cleanth, "Eudora Welty and the Southern Idiom," in Dollarhide, L., and A. J. Abadie, eds., *Eudora Welty*, 3-24.

Bryant, J. A., Jr., *Eudora Welty*.

Buckley, William F., Jr., "The Southern Imagination: An Interview with Eudora Welty and Walker Percy," *MissQ* 26 (1973): 493-516.

Bunting, Charles T., "'The Interior World': An Interview with Eudora Welty," *SoR* (1972): 711-35.

Buswell, Mary C., "The Love Relationships of Women in the Fiction of Eudora Welty," *WVUPP* 13 (Dec., 1961): 94-106.

_____, "The Mountain Figure in the Fiction of Eudora Welty," *WVUPP* 19 (July, 1972): 50-63.

Calloway, Kathleen, "In Her Time, In Her Place: Cast and Class in the Fiction of Eudora Welty," *DAI* 39 (1979): 4253A-54A.

Chronaki, Bessie, "Breaking the 'Quondam Obstruction': Place as an Aspect of Meaning in the Work of Eudora Welty," *DAI* 57 (1977): 4351A.

_____, "Eudora Welty's Theory of Place and Human Relationships," *SAB* 43, ii (May, 1978): 36-44.

Cole, Hunter M., "Windsor in Spencer and Welty: A Real and Imaginary Landscape," *NMW* 7, Spring, 1974): 2-11.

Davis, Charles E., "Eudora Welty's Art of Naming," *DAI* 30 (1970): 4446A-47A.

_____, "The South in Eudora Welty's Fiction: A Changing World," *SAF* 3, ii (Autumn, 1975): 199-209.

Desmond, J. F., ed., *Still Moment*.

Devlin, Albert J., "From Horse to Heron: A Source for Eudora Welty," *NMW* 10 (1977): 62-8. [Not seen.]

Dollarhide, L., and A. J., Abadie, eds., *Eudora Welty*.

Drake, Robert, "Eudora Welty's Country—and My Own," *ModA* 23 (Fall, 1979): 403-9.

_____, "Three Southern Ladies," *F10B* 9 (1980): 41-8.

Eisinger, C. E., *Fiction of the Forties*, 258-62.

_____, "Traditionalism and Modernism in Eudora Welty," in Prenshaw, P. W., ed., *Eudora Welty*, 3-25.

Evans, E., *Eudora Welty*.

_____, "Eudora Welty: The Metaphor of Music," *SoQ* 20, iv (1982): 92-100.

Ferris, Bill, Introd., *Images of the South: Visits with Eudora Welty and Walker Evans*. (So. Folklore Reports, 1) Memphis: Center for Southern Folklore, 1977.

Fleischauer, John F., "The Focus of Mystery: Eudora Welty's Prose Style," *SLJ* 5, ii (Spring, 1973): 64-79.

Folsom, Gordon R., "Form and Substance in Eudora Welty," *DA* 21 (1960): 621.

Foreman, Frances B., "Women's Choices: A Study of the Feminine Characters in the Novels of Eudora Welty," *DAI* 42, iv (Oct., 1981): 1634A.

Fullinwider, Carol M., "Eudora Welty's Fiction: Its Unconventional Relationship to Southern Literary Tradition," *DAI* 36 (1976): 7420A-21A.

Garbarini, Arline, "'The Feast Itself': A Study of Narrative Technique in the Fiction of Eudora Welty," *DAI* 38 (1977): 261A-62A.

Goeller, Allison D., "The Pastorals of Eudora Welty," *DAI* 39 (1978): 2272A.

Gossett, L. Y., "Violence as Revelation: Eudora Welty," *Violence in Recent Southern Fiction*, 98-117.

Gray, R. J., "Eudora Welty: A Dance to the Music of Order," *CRevAS* 7, i (1976): 57-65.

Gretlund, Jan N., "An Interview with Eudora Welty," *SHR* 14 (1980): 193-208.

_____, "Out of Life into Fiction: Eudora Welty and the City," *NMW* 14, ii (1982): 45-62.

Griffith, Albert J., Jr., "Eudora Welty's Fiction," *DA* 20 (1959): 2289-90.

Gross, Seymour L., "Eudora Welty's Comic Imagination," in Rubin, L. D., Jr., *Comic Imagination in American Literature*, 319-28.

Hardy, John E., "Marrying Down in Eudora Welty's Novels," in Prenshaw, P. W., ed., *Eudora Welty*, 93-119.

Harris, Jerry, "The Real Thing: Eudora Welty's Essential Vision," in Desmond, J. F., ed., *Still Moment*, 1-11.

Hembree, Charles W., "Narrative Technique in the Fiction of Eudora Welty," *DAI* 35 (1975): 6139A-40A.

Herlong, Rudy P., "A Study of Human Relationships in the Novels of Eudora Welty," *DAI* 36 (1976): 7422A.

Hicks, Granville, "Eudora Welty," *CE* 14 (Nov., 1952): 69-72. Also in *EJ* 41 (Nov., 1952): 461-8.

Hinton, Jane Lee, "'Out of All Times of Trouble': The Family in the Fiction of Eudora Welty," *DAI* 35 (1975): 7906A.

Hoffman, F. J., *Art of Southern Fiction*, 51-9.

Howell, Elmo, "Eudora Welty and the City of Man," *GaR* 33, iv (1979): 770-82.

_____, "Eudora Welty and the Use of Place in Southern Fiction," *ArQ* 28 (Autumn, 1972): 248-56.

Isaacs, N., *Eudora Welty*.

Jones, Alun R., "The World of Love: The Fiction of Eudora Welty," in Balakian, N., and C. Simmons, eds., *Creative Present*, 175-92.

Jones, J. G., *Mississippi Writers Talking*, Vol. 1, 3-35.

Jones, William M., "Name and Symbol in the Prose of Eudora Welty," *SFQ* 22 (Dec., 1958): 173-85.

Karem, Suzanne S., "Mythology in the Works of Eudora Welty," *DAI* 39 (1978): 3581A.

Kelly, Edward E., "Eudora Welty's Hollow Women," *NMAL* 6 (1982): Item 15. [Not seen.]

Kerr, Elizabeth M., "The World of Eudora Welty's Women," in Prenshaw, P. W., ed., *Eudora Welty*, 132-48.

King, William P., "A Thematic Study of the Fiction of Eudora Welty," *DAI* 33 (1973): 3652A-53A.

Kreyling, Michael P., "The Novels of Eudora Welty," *DAI* 36 (1976): 6685A.

Kuehl, Linda, "The Art of Fiction 47," *ParisR* 14 (Fall, 1972): 72-97.

Laing, Juanita B., "The Southern Tradition in the Fiction of Eudora Welty," *DAI* 41 (1980): 2111A.

Landess, Thomas A., "The Function of Taste in the Fiction of Eudora Welty," *MissQ* 26, iv (Fall, 1973): 543-57.

MacKethan, Lucinda H., "To See Things in Their Time: The Act of Focus in Eudora Welty's Fiction," *AL* 50 (May, 1978): 258-75.

McGowan, Marcia P., "Patterns of Female Experience in Eudora Welty's Fiction," *DAI* 38 (1977): 788A.

Millsaps, Ellen M., "The Family in Four Novels of Eudora Welty," *DAI* 37 (1976): 951A.

Moreland, Richard C., "Community and Vision in Eudora Welty," *SoR* 18, ii (Winter, 1982): 45-62.

Morris, Harry C., "Eudora Welty's Use of Myth," *Shen* 6 (Spring, 1955): 34-40.

Nash, Charles C., "The Theme of Human Isolation in the Works of Eudora Welty," *DAI* 37 (1976): 314A-15A.

Neault, D. James, "Time in the Fiction of Eudora Welty," in Desmond, J. F., ed., *Still Moment*, 35-50.

Nostrandt, Jeanne R., "Fiction as Event: An Interview with Eudora Welty," *NOR* 7, i (1980): 26-34.

Owens, Phillip L., "Time in the Novels of Eudora Welty," *DAI* 41 (1980): 1598A-99A.

Phillips, Robert L., Jr., "A Structural Approach to Myth in the Fiction of Eudora Welty," in Prenshaw, P. W., ed., *Eudora Welty*, 56-67.

Polk, Noel, "Water, Wanderers and Weddings: Love in Eudora Welty," in Dollarhide, L., and A. J. Abadie, eds., *Eudora Welty*, 95-122.

Prenshaw, P. W., ed., *Eudora Welty*.

Prenshaw, Peggy W., "A Study of Setting in the Fiction of Eudora Welty," *DAI* 31 (1970): 1810A.

_____, "Woman's World, Man's Place: The Fiction of Eudora Welty," in Dollarhide, L., and A. J. Abadie, eds., *Eudora Welty*, 46-77.

Randisi, Jennifer L., "Eudora Welty's Southern Romances: The Novels of Eudora Welty Viewed within the Southern Romance Tradition," *DAI* 40 (1980): 5867A.

Rechnitz, Robert M., "Perception, Identity, and the Grotesque: A Study of Three Southern Writers," *DA* 228 (1967): 2216A.

Rouse, Sarah A., "Place and People in Eudora Welty's Fiction: A Portrait of the Deep South," *DAI* 23 (1963): 3901.

Sather, Margarette J., "Man in the Universe: The Cosmic View of Eudora Welty," *DAI* 37 (1977): 5127A.

Smith, Carol P., "The Journey Motif in the Collected Works of Eudora Welty," *DAI* 32 (1972): 5807A-08A.

Sullivan, W., *Requiem for the Renascence*, 51-8.

Thompson, Victor H., "'Life's Impact Is Oblique': A Study of Obscurantism in the Writings of Eudora Welty," *DAI* 33 (1972): 1745A.

Vande Kieft, R. M., *Eudora Welty*.

_____, "Eudora Welty: The Question of Meaning," *SoQ* 20, iv (1982): 24-39.

_____, "The Vision of Eudora Welty," *MissQ* 26, iv (Fall, 1973): 517-42.

Van Gelder, R., *Writers on Writing*, 287-90.

Van Noppen, Martha, "A Conversation with Eudora Welty," *SoQ* 20, iv (1982): 7-13.

Wages, Jack D., "Names in Eudora Welty's Fiction," in Tarpley, Fred, ed., *Love and Wrestling, Butch and O.K.* (So. Central Names Inst. Pub. 2), Commerce, Texas: Names Institute, 1973, 65-72.

Welty, Eudora, "How I Write," *VQR* 31 (Spring, 1955): 240-51. Also in Brooks, Cleanth, and R. P. Warren, eds., *Understanding Fiction*, N.Y.: Appleton, 1959, 545-53.

_____, "Some Notes on Time in Fiction," *MissQ* 26 (1973): 483-92.

Weiner, Rachel V., "Reflections of the Artist in Eudora Welty's Fiction," *DAI* 40 (1979): 253A.

Yamamoto, Yoshimi, "A Frame of Fingers: The Personal Universe in Eudora Welty," *TsudaR* 25 (1980): 125-42.

DELTA WEDDING

Allen, John A., "Eudora Welty: The Three Moments," *VQR* 51, iv (Autumn, 1975): 610-12. Also in Desmond, J. F., ed., *Still Moment*, 16-19.

_____, "The Other Way to Live: Demigods in Eudora Welty's Fiction," in Prenshaw, P. W., ed., *Eudora Welty*, 35-45.

Appel, A., Jr., *Season of Dreams*, 199-204.

Bolsterli, Margaret J., "'Bound' Characters in Porter, Welty, McCullers: The Status of Women in American Fiction," *BuR* 24, i (Spring, 1978): 100-3.

_____, "Woman's Vision: The Worlds of Women in DELTA WEDDING, LOSING BATTLES and THE OPTIMIST'S DAUGHTER," in Prenshaw, P. W., ed., *Eudora Welty*, 149-56 *passim*.

Bradford, M. E., "Fairchild as Composite Protagonist in DELTA WEDDING," in Prenshaw, P. W., ed., *Eudora Welty*, 201-7.

Bryant, J. A., Jr., *Eudora Welty*, 20-6.

Eisinger, C. E., *Fiction of the Forties*, 275-80.

Evans, E., *Eudora Welty*, 97-107.

Goeller, Allison D., "DELTA WEDDING as Pastoral," *Interpretations* 13, i (Fall, 1981): 59-72.

Gray, R., *Literature of Memory*, 177-84.

Hardy, J. E., "DELTA WEDDING as Region and Symbol," *SR* 60 (Summer, 1952): 397-417. Also in Hardy, J. E., *Man in the Modern Novel*, 175-93. Also in Spacks, P. M., ed., *Contemporary Women Novelists*, 150-66.

_____, "Marrying Down in Eudora Welty's Novels," in Prenshaw, P. W., ed., *Eudora Welty*, 93-100.

Hinton, Jane L., "The Role of Family in DELTA WEDDING, LOSING BATTLES and THE OPTIMIST'S DAUGHTER," in Prenshaw, P. W., ed., *Eudora Welty*, 120-4.

Hoffman, F. J., *Art of Southern Fiction*, 59-63.

Howell, Elmo, "Eudora Welty and the Poetry of Names: A Note on DELTA WEDDING," in Trapley, Fred, ed., *Love and Wresting, Butch and O.K.* (So. Central Names Inst. Pub., 2), Commerce, Texas: Names Institute, 1973, 73-8.

_____, "Eudora Welty's Comedy of Manners," *SAQ* 69, iv (Autumn, 1970): 469-79.

Isaacs, N., *Eudora Welty*, 33-6.

_____, "Four Notes on Eudora Welty," *NMW* 2, ii (Fall, 1969): 42-3.

Krause, Florence P., "Emasculating Women in DELTA WEDDING," *PMPA* 1 (1976): 48-57.

Kreyling, M., *Eudora Welty's Achievement of Order*, 52-76.

McAlpin, Sara, "Family in Eudora Welty's Fiction," *SoR* 18, iii (Summer, 1982): 480-94.

Messerli, Douglas, "The Problem of Time in Welty's DELTA WEDDING," *SAF* 5, ii (Autumn, 1977): 227-40.

Moore, Carol A., "Aunt Studney's Sack," *SoR* 18 (1982): 591-6.

Prenshaw, Peggy W., "Cultural Patterns in Eudora Welty's DELTA WEDDING and 'The Demonstrators'," *NMW* 3 (Fall, 1970): 51-70.

_____, "Woman's World, Man's Place: The Fiction of Eudora Welty," in Dollarhide, L., and A. J., Abadie, eds., *Eudora Welty*, 46-58.

Prescott, Orville, in *YR* 35 (Summer, 1946): 765-6.

Ransom, John Crowe, "Delta Fiction," *KR* 8 (Summer, 1946): 503-7.

Rosenfeld, Isaac, in *NRep* 114 (Apr. 29, 1946): 633-4.

Rouse, Sarah A., "Place and People in Eudora Welty's Fiction: A Portrait of the Deep South," *DA* 23 (1963): 3901.

Rubin, L. D., Jr., *Faraway Country*, 134-41.

Rupp, Richard H., "Eudora Welty: A Continual Feast," *Celebration in Postwar American Fiction*, 61-4.

Trilling, Diana, "Fiction in Review," *Nation* 162 (May 11, 1946): 578.

Vande Kieft, R. M., *Eudora Welty*, 20-6.

LOSING BATTLES

Aldridge, John, "Eudora Welty: Metamorphosis of a Southern Lady Writer," *SatR* 58 (Apr. 11, 1970): 21-3+. Also as "The Emergence of Eudora Welty," in Aldridge, J. W., *Devil in the Fire*, 252-6.

Allen, John A., "Eudora Welty: The Three Moments," *VQR* 51, iv (Autumn, 1975): 623-7. Also in Desmond, J. F., ed., *Still Moment*, 27-31.

_____, "The Other Way to Live: Demigods in Eudora Welty's Fiction," in Prenshaw, P. W., ed., *Eudora Welty*, 47-55.

Boatwright, James, "Speech and Silence in LOSING BATTLES," *Shen* 25, iii (Spring, 1974): 3-14.

Bolsterli, Margaret J., "Woman's Vision: The Worlds of Women in DELTA WEDDING, LOSING BATTLES and THE OPTIMIST'S DAUGHTER," in Prenshaw, P. W., ed., *Eudora Welty*, 149-56 passim.

Bradford, M. E., "Looking Down from a High Place: The Serenity of Miss Welty," *RANAM* 4 (1971): 92-7. Also in Desmond, J. F., ed., *Still Moment*, 103-9.

Brooks, Cleanth, "Eudora Welty and the Southern Idiom," in Dollarhide, L., and A. J. Abadie, eds., *Eudora Welty*, 17-24.

Bryant, J. A., Jr., "The Recovery of the Confident Narrator: A CURTAIN OF GREEN to LOSING BATTLES," in Prenshaw, P. W., ed., *Eudora Welty*, 68-82.

Evans, E., *Eudora Welty*, 76-88.

Ferguson, Mary A., "LOSING BATTLES as a Comic Epic in Prose," in Prenshaw, P. W., ed., *Eudora Welty*, 305-24.

Gossett, Louise Y., "Eudora Welty's New Novel: the Comedy of Loss," *SLJ* 3, i (Fall, 1970): 122-3.

_____, "LOSING BATTLES: Festival and Celebration," in Prenshaw, P. W., ed., *Eudora Welty*, 341-50.

Gross, Seymour, "A Long Day's Living: The Angelis Ingenuities of LOSING BATTLES," in Prenshaw, P. W., ed., *Eudora Welty*, 325-40.

Hardy, John E., "Marrying Down in Eudora Welty's Novels," in Prenshaw, P. W., ed., *Eudora Welty*, 103-7.

Heilman, Robert B., "LOSING BATTLES and Winning the War," in Prenshaw, P. W., ed., *Eudora Welty*, 269-304.

Hinton, Jane L., "The Role of Family in DELTA WEDDING, LOSING BATTLES and THE OPTIMIST'S DAUGHTER," in Prenshaw, P. W., ed., *Eudora Welty*, 124-8.

Kreyling, M., *Eudora Welty's Achievement of Order*, 140-52.

_____, "Myth and History: The Foes of LOSING BATTLES," *MissQ* 26 (1973): 639-49.

Landess, Thomas H., "More Trouble in Mississippi: Family vs. Antifamily in Miss Welty's LOSING BATTLES," *SR* 7 (1971): 626-34.

McAlpin, Sara, "Family in Eudora Welty's Fiction," *SoR* 18, iii (Summer, 1982): 480-94.

McMillan, William, "Circling-In: The Concept of Home in Eudora Welty's LOSING BATTLES and THE OPTIMIST'S DAUGHTER," in Desmond, J. F., ed., *Still Moment*, 110-17.

_____, "Conflict and Resolution in Welty's LOSING BATTLES," *Crit* 15, i (1973): 110-24.

Messerli, Douglas, "'A Battle with Both Sides Using the Same Tactics': The Language of Time in LOSING BATTLES," in Prenshaw, P. W., ed., *Eudora Welty*, 351-66.

Moore, Carol A., "The Insulation of Illusion and LOSING BATTLES," *MissQ* 26 (1973): 651-8.

Oates, Joyce Carol, "Eudora's Web," *Atlantic* 225, iv (Apr., 1970): 118-21. Also in Spacks, P. M., ed., *Contemporary Women Novelists*, 167-72.

Price, Reynolds, *Things Themselves*, 139-42.

Reynolds, Larry J., "Enlightening Darkness: Theme and Structure in Eudora Welty's LOSING BATTLES," *JNT* 8, ii (1978): 133-40.

Rubin, Louis D., Jr., "Everything Brought Out in the Open: Eudora Welty's LOSING BATTLES," *HC* 7, iii (June, 1970): 1-12.

Sullivan, W., *Requiem for the Renascence*, 52-8.

Tarbox, Raymond, "Eudora Welty's Fiction: The Salvation Theme," *AI* 29, i (Spring, 1972): 73-5.

THE OPTIMIST'S DAUGHTER

Allen, John A., "Eudora Welty: The Three Moments," *VQR* 51, iv (Autumn, 1975): 621-2. Also in Desmond, J. F., ed., *Still Moment*, 26-7.

Arnold, Marilyn, "Images of Memory in Eudora Welty's THE OPTIMIST'S DAUGHTER," *SLJ* 14, ii (Spring, 1982): 28-38.

Bolsterli, Margaret J., "Woman's Vision: The World of Women in DELTA WEDDING, LOSING BATTLES and THE OPTIMIST'S DAUGHTER," in Prenshaw, P. W., ed., *Eudora Welty*, 149-56 *passim*.

Brooks, Cleanth, "The Past Reexamined: THE OPTIMIST'S DAUGHTER," *MissQ* 26, iv (Fall, 1973): 577-87.

Chaudhary, Jasbir, "Patterns of Love and Isolation: Eudora Welty's THE OPTIMIST'S DAUGHTER," *PURBA* 13, ii (Oct., 1982): 65-72.

Desmond, John F., "Pattern and Vision in THE OPTIMIST'S DAUGHTER," in Desmond, J. F., ed., *Still Moment*, 118-38.

Evans, E., *Eudora Welty*, 114-26.

Hinton, Jane L., "The Role of Family in DELTA WEDDING, LOSING BATTLES and THE OPTIMIST'S DAUGHTER," Prenshaw, P. W., ed., *Eudora Welty*, 128-31.

Kreyling, Michael, *Eudora Welty's Achievement of Order*, 153-73.

———, "Life with People: Virginia Woolf, Eudora Welty, and THE OPTIMIST'S DAUGHTER," *SoR* 13, ii (Apr., 1977): 250-71.

Landess, Thomas H., "The Function of Taste in the Fiction of Eudora Welty," *MissQ* 26, iv (Fall, 1973): 550-1, 556-7.

McMillen, William, "Circling-In: The Concept of the Home in Eudora Welty's LOSING BATTLES and THE OPTIMIST'S DAUGHTER," in Desmond, J. F., *Still Moment*, 110-17.

Phillips, Robert L., "Patterns of Vision in Welty's THE OPTIMIST'S DAUGHTER," *SLJ* 14, i (Fall, 1981): 10-23.

Pickett, Nell A., "Colloquialism as Style in the First-Person-Narrator Fiction of Eudora Welty," *MissQ* 26, iv (Fall, 1973): 559-76 *passim*.

Polk, Noel, "Water, Wanderers, and Weddings: Love in Eudora Welty," in Dollarhide, L., and A. J., Abadie, eds., *Eudora Welty*, 117-22.

Price, Reynolds, "The Onlooker, Smiling: An Early Reading of THE OPTIMIST'S DAUGHTER," *Shen* 20, iii (Spring, 1969): 58-73. Also in Reynolds, P., *Things Themselves*, 114-38.

Shepherd, Allen, "Delayed Exposition in Eudora Welty's THE OPTIMIST'S DAUGHTER," *NConL* 4, iv (Sept., 1974): 10-14.

Smith, William J., "Precision and Reticence: Eudora Welty's Poetic Vision," *OntarioR* 9 (Fall-Winter, 1978-79): 63-70. Also in Dollarhide, L., and A. J. Abadie, eds., *Eudora Welty*, 78-94.

Spacks, P. M., *Female Imagination*, 264-7, 269-71.

Stucky, William J., "The Use of Marriage in Welty's THE OPTIMIST'S DAUGHTER," *Crit* 17, ii (1975): 36-46.

Vande Kieft, Ruth M., "The Vision of Eudora Welty," *MissQ* 26, iv (1973): 537-42.

Young, Thomas D., "Social Form and Social Order: An Examination of THE OPTIMIST'S DAUGHTER," in Prenshaw, P. W., ed., *Eudora Welty*, 367-85.

THE PONDER HEART

Allen, John A., "Eudora Welty: The Three Moments," *VQR* 51, iv (Autumn, 1975): 617-21. Also in Desmond, J. F., ed., *Still Moment*, 23-6.

Appel, A., Jr., *Season of Dreams*, 51-60.

Brooks, Cleanth, "Eudora Welty and the Southern Idiom," in Dollarhide, L., and A. J. Abadie, eds., *Eudora Welty*, 14-17.

———, "'F. H. B.' in THE PONDER HEART," *EuWN* 2, i (1978): 5.

———, "More on 'F.H.B.'," *EuWN* 2, ii (1978): 7.

Bryant, J. A., Jr., *Eudora Welty*, 33-5.

Cornell, Brenda G., "Ambiguous Necessity: A Study of THE PONDER HEART," in Prenshaw, P. W., ed., *Eudora Welty*, 208-19.

Daniel, Robert W., "Eudora Welty: The Sense of Place," in Rubin, L. D., Jr., and R. D. Jacobs, eds., *South*, 276-7, 285-8.

Drake, Robert Y., Jr., "The Reasons of the Heart," *GaR* 11 (Winter, 1957): 420-6.

Dusenbury, Winifred, "BABY DOLL and THE PONDER HEART," *MD* 3 (1961): 393-5.

Evans, E., *Eudora Welty*, 46-9.

French, Warren, "A Note on Eudora Welty's THE PONDER HEART," *CE* 15 (May, 1954): 474.

Hardy, John E., "Marrying Down in Eudora Welty's Novels," in Prenshaw, P. W., ed., *Eudora Welty*, 100-3.

Holland, Robert B., "Dialogue as a Reflection of Place in THE PONDER HEART," *AL* 35 (Nov., 1963): 352-8.

Idol, John L., Jr., "Edna Earle Ponder's Good Country People," *SoQ* 20, iii (Spring, 1982): 66-75.

Isaacs, N., *Eudora Welty*, 12-14.

———, "Four Notes on Eudora Welty," *NMW* 2, ii (Fall, 1969): 43-4.

Kreyling, M., *Eudora Welty's Achievement of Order*, 106-17.

Opitz, Kurt, "Eudora Welty: The Order of a Captive Soul," *Crit* 7, ii (1965): 86-8.

Rouse, Sarah A., "A Place and People in Eudora Welty's Fiction: A Portrait of the Deep South," *DA* 23 (1963): 3901.

Weiner, Rachel V., "Eudora Welty's THE PONDER HEART: The Judgment of Art," *SoSt* 19, iii (1980): 261-73.

THE ROBBER BRIDEGROOM

Akin, Warren, IV, "THE ROBBER BRIDEGROOM: An Oedipal Tale of the Natchez Trace," *L&P* 30, iii-iv (1980): 112-18.

Allen, John A., "Eudora Welty: The Three Moments," *VQR* 51, iv (Autumn, 1975): 613-16. Also in Desmond, J. F., ed., *Still Moment*, 20-2.

Appel, A., Jr., *Season of Dreams*, 69-72, 182-3.

Arnold, Marilyn, "Eudora Welty's Parody," *NMW* 11, i (1978): 15-22.

Bishop, J. P., "The Violent Country," *NRep* 107 (Nov. 16, 1942): 646-7. Also in Bishop, J. P., *Collected Essays*, 257-9.

Brown, Ashley, "Eudora Welty and the Mythos of Summer," *Shen* 20, iii (Spring, 1969): 29-35.

Bryant, A. J., Jr., *Eudora Welty*, 17-20.

Clark, Charles C., "THE ROBBER BRIDEGROOM: Realism and Fantasy on the Natchez Trace," *MissQ* 26 (1973): 625-38.

Cook, Bernard, "Ritual Abduction in Early Mississippi," *MissQ* 36, i (Winter, 1982-83): 72-3.

Davis, Charles E., "Eudora Welty's THE ROBBER BRIDEGROOM and Old Southwest Humor: A Doubleness of Vision," in Desmond, J. F., ed., *Still Moment*, 71-81.

Devlin, Albert J., "Eudora Welty's Mississippi," in Prenshaw, P. W., ed., *Eudora Welty*, 169-73.

Eisinger, C. E., *Fiction of the Forties*, 272-5.

Evans, E., *Eudora Welty*, 59-63.

French, Warren, "'All Things Are Double': Eudora Welty as a Civilized Writer," in Prenshaw, P. W., ed., *Eudora Welty*, 179-88.

Glenn, Eunice, "Fantasy in the Fiction of Eudora Welty," in Tate, A., ed., *A Southern Vanguard*, N.Y.: Prentice Hall, 1947, 85-7. Also in Aldridge, J. W., ed., *Critiques and Essays on Modern Fiction*, 512-14.

Hardy, John E., "Marrying Down in Eudora Welty's Novels," in Prenshaw, P. W., ed., *Eudora Welty*, 107-19.

Isaacs, N., *Eudora Welty*, 16-19.

Kreyling, Michael, "Clement and the Indians: Pastoral and History in THE ROBBER BRIDEGROOM," in Dollarhide, L., and A. J. Abadie, eds., *Eudora Welty*, 25-45.

_____, *Eudora Welty's Achievement of Order*, 32-51.

Miller, Lisa K., "The Dark Side of Our Frontier Heritage: Eudora Welty's Use of the Turner Thesis in THE ROBBER BRIDE-GROOM," *NMW* 14, i (1981): 18-25.

Randisi, Jennifer, "Eudora Welty's THE ROBBER BRIDE-GROOM as American Romance," *MHLS* 3 (1980): 101-15.

Rouse, Sarah A., "Place and People in Eudora Welty's Fiction: A Portrait of the Deep South," *DA* 23 (1963): 3901.

Rupp, Richard H., "Eudora Welty: A Continual Feast," *Celebration in Postwar American Fiction*, 61-2.

Skaggs, Merrill M., "The Uses of Enchantment in Frontier Humor and THE ROBBER BRIDEGROOM," *StAH* 3, ii (1976): 96-102.

Slethaug, Gordon E., "Initiation in Eudora Welty's THE ROBBER BRIDEGROOM," *SHR* 7 (1973): 77-87.

Smith, Carol P., "The Journey Motif in Eudora Welty's THE ROBBER BRIDEGROOM," *SSCRev* (1973): 18-32.

Straumann, H., *American Literature in the Twentieth Century*, 137-8.

BIBLIOGRAPHY

See issues of *Eudora Welty Newsletter*.

Gross, Seymour, "Eudora Welty: A Bibliography of Criticism and Comment," *Secretary's News Sheet*, No. 45 (Apr., 1960), Bibliog. Soc., Un. of Va., 1-32.

Jordan, Leona, "Eudora Welty: Selected Criticism," *BB* 23 (Jan.-Apr., 1960): 14-15.

Polk, Noel, "Eudora Welty: A Bibliographical Checklist," *ABC* 2, i (Jan.-Feb., 1981): 25-37.

_____, "A Eudora Welty Checklist," *MissQ* 26 (1973): 663-93.

Vande Kieft, R. M., *Eudora Welty*, 195-9.

WEST, JESSAMYN, 1902-1984

GENERAL

Bakerman, Jane S., "From the Grove Meeting House to Fall Creek: An Examination of Jessamyn West's Indian Novels," *IE* 1, ii-iv (1978): 36-41. [Not seen.]

Farmer, A. D., *Jessamyn West*.

Flanagan, John T., "The Fiction of Jessamyn West," *IndMH* 67, iv (Dec., 1971): 299-316.

Shivers, A. S., *Jessamyn West*.

West, Jessamyn, *To See the Dream*, N.Y.: Harcourt, Brace, 1957.

LEAFY RIVERS

Farmer, A. D., *Jessamyn West*, 30-1.

Shivers, A. S., *Jessamyn West*, 77-83 *passim*.

THE LIFE I REALLY LIVED

Farmer, A. D., *Jessamyn West*, 40-4.

THE MASSACRE AT FALL CREEK

Farmer, A. D., *Jessamyn West*, 31-3.

A MATTER OF TIME

Farmer, A. D., *Jessamyn West*, 39-40.

Shivers, A. S., *Jessamyn West*, 115-23 *passim*.

SOUTH OF THE ANGELS

Farmers, A. D., *Jessamyn West*, 36-9.

Shivers, A. S., *Jessamyn West*, 106-15 *passim*.

THE WITCH DIGGERS

Bergler, Edmund, M. D., "Writers of Half-Talent," *AI* 14 (1957): 159-61.

Farmer, A. D., *Jessamyn West*, 27-30.

Shivers, A. S., *Jessamyn West*, 65-73 *passim*.

BIBLIOGRAPHY

Shivers, Alfred S., "Jessamyn West," *BB* 28, i (Jan.-Mar., 1971): 1-3.

_____, *Jessamyn West*, 149-55.

WEST, MORRIS (LANGLO), 1916-

GENERAL

Doney, Malcolm, "Novelist with an Eye for God: An Assessment of the Work of Morris West," *Third Way* (June 16, 1977): 3-5. [Not seen.]

_____, "Ransom for Good," *Third Way*, 3, vi (1979): 27. [Not seen.]

Duprey, Richard A., "Morris West, A Witness for Compassion," *CathW* 193 (Sept., 1961): 360-6.

Reid, John H., "The Alien World of Morris West," *AusL* 4, ii (1969): 52-7.

Ruskin, Pamela, "The Writer Who Can't Go Wrong," *Signature* 3 (Mar.-Apr., 1970): 6-7. [Not seen.]

MOON IN MY POCKET

McCallum, Gerald, "A Note on Morris West's First Novel," *ALS* 6 (May, 1974): 314-16.

THE SHOES OF THE FISHERMAN

Picart, Robert M., "Realism in THE SHOES OF THE FISHERMAN: A Critical Analysis," *SLRJ* 1 (1970): 711-15.

WEST, REBECCA, 1892-1983

GENERAL

Allen, W., *Modern Novel*, 62-4.

Curtis, Anthony, "Social Improvement and Literary Disasters," *Listener* 89 (Feb. 15, 1973): [Radio Interview.]

Deakin, M. F., *Rebecca West*.

Ferguson, Moira, "Feminist Manicheanism: Rebecca West's Unique Fusion," *MinnR* 15 (Fall, 1980): 53-60.

Hutchinson, George E., *Itinerant Ivory Tower; Scientific and Literary Essays*, New Haven: Yale Un. Pr., 1953, 241-55.

Kennedy, Ludovic, "Yum Yum," *Listener* 96 (1976): 396. [Not seen.]

Kobler, Turner S., "The Eclecticism of Rebecca West," *Crit* 13, ii (1971): 30-49.

Orlich, Sister Mary M., C.S.J., "The Novels of Rebecca West: A Complex Unity," *DA* 27 (1967): 2540A.

Rainer, Dachine, "Rebecca West: Disturber of the Peace," *Cweal* 88, viii (May 10, 1968): 227-30.

Redd, Tony N., "Rebecca West: Master of Reality," *DAI* 33 (1973): 4431A.

Warner, Marina, "Rebecca West: The Art of Fiction, LXV," *ParisR* 79 (1981): 116-64.

Wolfe, P., *Rebecca West*.

THE BIRDS FALL DOWN

Deakin, M. F., *Rebecca West*, 159-65.

Ellmann, Mary, "The Russians of Rebecca West," *Atlantic* 218 (Dec., 1966): 68-71.

Wolfe, P., *Rebecca West*, 114-29 *passim*.

THE FOUNTAIN OVERFLOWS

Deakin, M. F., *Rebecca West*, 152-9.

Wolfe, P., *Rebecca West*, 99-114.

HARRIET HUME

Deakin, M. F., *Rebecca West*, 140-5.

Wolfe, P., *Rebecca West*, 42-6.

THE JUDGE

Deakin, M. F., *Rebecca West*, 134-40.

Wolfe, P., *Rebecca West*, 35-42.

THE RETURN OF THE SOLDIER

Deakin, M. F., *Rebecca West*, 131-4.

West, Dame Rebecca, "On THE RETURN OF THE SOLDIER," *YULG* 57, i-ii (Oct., 1982): 66-71.

Wolfe, P., *Rebecca West*, 31-5.

THE THINKING REED

Deakin, M. F., *Rebecca West*, 148-52.

Wolfe, P., *Rebecca West*, 46-55.

WHITE, PATRICK, 1912-

GENERAL

Alexander, J. C., "Vision of Depth—Australian Image, No. 3," *Meanjin* 21 (1962): 328-35. [Not seen.]

Argyle, B., *Patrick White*.

Avant, John A., "The Oeuvre of Patrick White," *NRep* 172 (Mar. 22, 1975): 23-4.

Banerjee, J., "'The Living Green': An Aspect of Patrick White's Development as a Novelist," *SELit* 58 (1981): 89-102. [Not seen.]

Barnes, John, "A Note on Patrick White's Novels," *LCrit* 6, iii (1964): 93-101. Also in Narasimahaiah, ed., *Introduction to Australian Literature*, 93-101.

Beatson, P., *Eye in the Mandala*.

Bell, Pearl K., "A Voice from Down Under," *NewL* 57, i (1974): 16-17.

Beston, John, "The Effect of Alienation on the Themes and Characters of Patrick White and Janet Frame," in Massa, D., ed., *Individual and Community in Commonwealth Literature*, 131-9.

_____, "The Making of the Artist in Patrick White," *CNIE* 1, i (Jan., 1982): 886-93.

Bjorksten, I., *Patrick White*.

Bliss, Carolyn J., "The Shape of Failure: Failure as Theme and Technique in Patrick White's Fiction," *DAI* 42, iv (Oct., 1981): 1629A-30A.

Bradbrook, Muriel C., *Literature in Action*, 138-50.

Bradley, David, "Australia Through the Looking-glass," *Overland* No. 23 (Autumn, 1963): 21-2. [Not seen.]

Brady, Patricia M., "The Hard Enquiring Wind: A Study of Patrick White as an Australian Novelist," *DAI* 31 (1970): 1263A.

Brady, Veronica, "The Novelist and the Reign of Necessity: Patrick White and Simeon Weil," in Shepherd, R., and K. Singh, eds., *Patrick White*, 108-16.

_____, "The Utopian Impulse in Australian Literature, with Special Reference to P. White and T. Keneally," *Caliban* 14 (1977): 109-21.

Brand, Mona, "Another Look at Patrick White," *Realist Writer* (Sydney), No. 12 (Aug., 1963): 21-2. [Not seen.]

Brissenden, R. F., *Patrick White*.

Buckley, Vincent, "In the Shadow of Patrick White," *Meanjin* 20 (July, 1961): 144-54.

_____, "The Novels of Patrick White," in Dutton, G., ed., *Literature of Australia*, 413-26.

Cantrell, Leon, "Patrick White's First Books," *ALS* 6 (1974): 634-6. [Not seen.]

Chatterjee, Visvanath, "Patrick White," *CalR* 3, iii (Jan.-Mar., 1978): 139-44.

Colmer, John, "Duality in Patrick White," in Shepherd, R., and K. Singh, eds., *Patrick White*, 70-6.

_____, "The Quest Motif in Patrick White," *RNL* 11 (1982): 193-210.

Core, George, "A Terrible Majesty: The Novels of Patrick White," *HC* 11, i (Feb., 1974): 439-45.

Cotter, Michael, "The Function of Imagery in Patrick White's Novels," in Shepherd, R., and K. Singh, eds., *Patrick White*, 17-27.

Davies, Brian, "An Australian Enigma: Conversations with Patrick White," *Melbourne Un. Mag.* (Spring, 1962): 69-71.

Donaldson, I., "Return to Abyssinia Lost and Regained," *EIC* 14 (1964): 210-14. [Reply to M. MacKenzie.]

Dutton, Geoffrey, "The Novels of Patrick White," *Crit* 6, iii (Winter, 1963-64): 7-28.

_____, *Patrick White*.

Green, Dorothy, "Patrick White's Nobel Prize," *Overland* 57 (1974): 23-5.

Hadgraft, Cecil, "The Themes of Revelation in Patrick White's Novels," *Southerly* 37, i (Mar., 1977): 34-46.

Hansson, Karin, "The Quest Motif in Patrick White's Novels," in Granqvist, R., ed., *Report of Workshop on World Literatures Written in English* ..., 49-55.

Harries, Lyndon, "The Peculiar Gifts of Patrick White," *ConL* 19 (Autumn, 1978): 459-71.

Heltay, Hilary, "The Novels of Patrick White," *Southerly* 33, ii (June, 1973): 92-104.

Herring, Thelma, G. A. Wilkes and Patrick White, "A Conversation with Patrick White," *Southerly* 33, ii (June, 1973): 132-43.

Heseltine, H. P., "Patrick White's Style," *Quadrant* 7 (Winter, 1963): 61-74.

Kiernan, B., *Patrick White*.

_____, "Patrick White: The Novelist and the Modern World," in Anderson, D., and S. Knight, eds., *Cunning Exiles*, 81-103.

Koch-Emmery, Erwin, "Theme and Language in Patrick White's Novels," 136-46, in Bauer, Gero, Frank K. Stanzel, and Frank Zaic, eds., *Festschrift Prof. Dr. Herbert Koziol zum Siebzigsten Geburtstag* (Weiner Beitrage zur Englischen Philologie 75), Vienna: Wilhelm Braumuller, 1973.

Kramer, Leonie, "The Present Past: Some Thoughts on Modern Australian Fiction," in Narasimhaiah, C. D., and S. Nagarajan, eds., *Studies in Australian and Indian Literature*, 128-35.

Lawson, Alan, "Unmerciful Dingoes? The Critical Reception of Patrick White," *Meanjin* 32, iv (Dec., 1973): 379-92.

Lindsay, Jack, "The Alienated Australian Intellectual," *Meanjin* 22 (Mar., 1963): 56-9.

Macainsh, Noel, "Patrick White: A Note on the Phoenix," *LiNQ* (James Cook Un., No. Queensland) 5, i (1976): 15-19. [Not seen.]

MacKenzie, Manfred, "Abyssinia Lost and Regained," *EIC* 13 (1963): 292-300.

_____, "Patrick White's Later Novels: A Generic Reading," *SoRA* 1, iii (1965): 5-18.

_____, "Tradition and Patrick White's Individual Talent," *TSLL* 21, ii (Summer, 1979): 147-68.

_____, "Yes, Let's Return to Abyssinia," *EIC* 14 (1964): 433-5. [Reply to I. Donaldson.]

Martin, David, "Among the Bones," *Meanjin* 18, i (Apr., 1959): 52-8.

Mather, Rodney, "Patrick White and Lawrence: A Contrast," *CR* 13 (1970): 34-50.

McCulloch, Ann, "Patrick White's Novels and Nietzsche," *ALS* 9 (1980): 309-20.

McLaren, John, "The Image of Reality in Our Writing (With special reference to the work of Patrick White)," *Overland*, Nos. 27-28 (July-Sept., 1963): 43-7. Also in Semmler, C., ed., *Twentieth Century Australian Literary Criticism*, 235-44.

McLeod, A. L., "Patrick White: Nobel Prize for Literature 1973," *BA* 48, iii (Summer, 1974): 439-45.

Mitcalfe, Barry, "Patrick White: Reality as Allegory," *Listener* (New Zealand) 44 (1970): 1596. [Not seen.]

Mitchell, Adrian, "Eventually White's Language: Words and More than Words," in Shepherd, R., and K. Singh, eds., *Patrick White*, 5-16.

Morley, Patricia A., "'An Honourably Failed Attempt to convey the Ultimate': Patrick White's Fiction," *JCF* 3, iv (1975): 60-4.

_____, *Mystery of Unity*.

_____, "Patrick White: 'World of Semblance, World of Dream'," *St. Mark's Review*, 86 (June, 1976): 30-8.

O'Carrigan, Catherine, "Patrick White and the World of Art," *ASEAB* 5 (Feb., 1973): 11-16. [Not seen.]

Oliveriusova, Eva, "Patrick White's Australian Novels," *PP* 14, iv (1971): 190-218.

Potter, Nancy A. J., "Patrick White's Minor Saints," *REL* 5, iv (Oct., 1964): 9-19.

Radford, F. L., and R. R., Wilson, "Some Phases of the Jungian Moon: Jung's Influence on Modern Literature," *ESC* 8, iii (Sept., 1982): 321-5.

Rao, K. N. Rani, "Quest: Two Attitudes," *ComQ* 3, xi (1979): 27-33. [Not seen.]

Richards, Jack, "Patrick White, Australian Novelist," *SAP* 3, i-ii (1971): 113-19.

Riemer, A. P., "The Eye of the Needle: Patrick White's Recent Novels," *Southerly* 34 (Sept., 1974): 248-66.

Ross, Robert L., "The Comic Reaches: A Study of the Novels of Patrick White," *DAI* 40 (1979): 2049A.

Salter, Elizabeth, "The Australianism of Patrick White," in Niven, A., ed., *Commonwealth Writer Overseas*, 231-41.

Scheik, William J., "The Gothic Grace and Rainbow Aesthetic of Patrick White's Fiction: An Introduction," *TSLL* 21, ii (Summer, 1979): 131-46.

Schrubb, Peter, "Patrick White: Chaos Accepted," *Quadrant* 12 (May-June, 1968): 7-19.

Shepherd, R., and K. Singh, eds., *Patrick White*.

Singh, Kirpal, "Patrick White: An Outsider's View," in Shepherd, R., and K. Singh, eds., *Patrick White*, 117-22.

Stalhandske, Margareta, "The Artist as Theme in Patrick White's Fiction," in Granqvist, R., ed., *Report of a Workshop on World Literatures Written in English* ..., 56-62.

Stern, James, "Patrick White: The Country of the Mind," *LonM* 5, i (June, 1958): 49-56.

St. Pierre, Paul M., "Coterminous Beginnings," in Shepherd, R., and K. Singh, eds., *Patrick White*, 99-107.

Tacy, David, "'It's Happening Inside': The Individiual and Changing Consciousness in White's Fiction," in Shepherd, R., and K. Singh, eds., *Patrick White*, 34-40.

_____, "Patrick White: Misconceptions about Jung's Influence," *ALS* 9, ii (Oct., 1979): 245-6.

Thompson, John, "Australia's White Policy: Analysis of White's Critics," *AusL* 1 (Apr., 1958): 42-5.

Vande Brake, Lynn H., "The Romantic Religion of Patrick White: A Study of the Religious Dimension of His Novels," *DAI* 42, xii (June, 1982): 5118A-19A.

Walsh, William, "Fiction as Metaphor: The Novels of Patrick White," *SR* 82 (Spring, 1974): 197-211.

_____, *Patrick White's Fiction*.

Walters, Margaret, "Patrick White," *New Left Rev* 18 (Jan.-Feb., 1963): 37-50.

Warren, Thomas L., "Man's Return to Innocence: The Novels of Patrick White," *DAI* 35 (1975): 6165A-66A.

White, Patrick, "Patrick White Speaks on Factual Writing and Fiction," *ALS* 10, i (May, 1981): 99-101.

_____, "The Prodigal Son," *AusL* 1 (Apr., 1958): 37-40.

Wilkinson, Nick, "The Novel and a Vision of the Land," in Narasimhaiah, C. D., ed., *Awakened Conscience*, 190-3.

Wood, Peter, "Moral Complexity in Patrick White's Novels," *Meanjin* 21 (Mar., 1962): 21-8.

THE AUNT'S STORY

Argyle, B., *Patrick White*, 22-30.

Barnard, Marjorie, "The Four Novels of Patrick White'"" *Meanjin* 15 (June, 1956): 163-5.

_____, "Theodora Again," *Southerly* 20 (1959): 51-5.

Barnes, John A., "A Note on Patrick White's Novels," *LCrit* 6, iii (1964): 96-7. Also in Narasimhaiah, C. D., ed., *Introduction to Australian Literature*, 96-7.

Beatson, P., *Eye in the Mandala*, 97-102.

Beston, John B., "Love and Sex in a Staid Spinster: THE AUNT'S STORY," *Quadrant* 73 (Sept.-Oct., 1971): 22-7.

_____, and Rose Marie Beston, "The Black Volcanic Hills of Meröe: Fire Imagery in Patrick White's THE AUNT'S STORY," *Ariel* 3, iv (1972): 33-43.

_____, "The Several Lives of Theodora Goodman: The 'Jardin Exotique' Section of Patrick White's THE AUNT'S STORY," *JCL* 9, iii (Apr., 1975): 1-13.

Bjorksten, I., *Patrick White*, 39-46.

Brady, Veronica, "The Utopian Impulse in Australian Literature, with Special Reference to P. White and T. Keneally," *Caliban* 14 (1977): 111-15.

Brissendon, R. F., *Patrick White*, 19-24.

Brugman, Albert P., *An Outsider's Odyssey: A Study of Patrick White's THE AUNT'S STORY*, Potchefstroom, South Africa: Un. of Potchefstroom, 1977.

Buckley, Vincent, "The Novels of Patrick White," in Dutton, G., ed., *Literature of Australia*, 416-18.

Burrows, J. F., "'Jardin Exotique': the Central Phase of THE AUNT'S STORY," *Southerly* 26, iii (1966): 152-73.

Dutton, Geoffrey, "The Novels of Patrick White," *Crit* 6, iii (Winter, 1963-64): 9-11.

_____, *Patrick White*, 21-7.

Hadgraft, C., *Australian Literature*, 241-2.

Herring, T., "Odyssey of a Spinster: A Study of THE AUNT'S STORY," *Southerly* 25, i (1965): 6-22.

Howarth, R. G., "The Image," *Southerly* 11, iv (1950): 209-10.

Johnson, Robert K., "Patrick White and Theodora Goodman: Two Views of Reality," *Exploration* 6, ii (Winter, 1979): 14-22.

Kiernan, B., *Patrick White*, 22-32.

King, B., *New English Literatures*, 168-70.

Loney, Douglas, "Theodora Goodman and the Minds of Mortals: Patrick White's THE AUNT'S STORY," *ESC* 8, iv (Dec., 1982): 483-500.

MacKenzie, Manfred, "Patrick White's Later Novels: A Generic Reading," *SoRA* 1, iii (1965): 5-14.

McAuley, James, in *Quadrant* 3, iv (Spring, 1959): 91-3.

Morley, P. A., *Mystery of Unity*, 63-84.

Potter, Nancy A. J., "Patrick White's Minor Saints," *REL* 5, iv (Oct., 1964): 9-11.

Singh, Kirpal, "The Fiend of Motion: Theodora Goodman in Patrick White's THE AUNT'S STORY," *Quadrant* 19 (Dec., 1975): 90-2.

Tanner, G., "The Road to Jerusalem," *Nimrod* 2, i (1964): 33-9.

Walsh, W., *Manifold Voice*, 89-98.

_____, *Patrick White's Fiction*, 18-30.

Warren, Thomas L., "Patrick White: The Early Novels," *MFS* 27, i (Spring, 1981): 133-9.

THE EYE OF THE STORM

Beatson, P. R., "The Skiapod and the Eye: Patrick White's THE EYE OF THE STORM," *Southerly* 34 (1974): 219-34.

Beston, Rose Marie, "A Self Centered Visionary: Patrick White's Latest Illuminate," *WLWE* 13 (1974): 93-8.

Bjorksten, I., *Patrick White*, 104-15.

Brady, Veronica, "THE EYE OF THE STORM," *Westerly* 4 (Dec., 1973): 36-47.

Clancy, Patricia, "The Actor's Dilemma: Patrick White and Henry de Montherlant," *Meanjin* 33, iii (Sept., 1974): 292-302.

Cohen, Sandy, "A Note on Patrick White's THE EYE OF THE STORM and THE TWYBORN AFFAIR," *N&Q* 29, iv (Aug., 1982): 349.

Dutton, Geoffrey, "She Whipped You On: Some Thoughts from Australia on Elizabeth, EYE OF THE STORM, and Patrick White's Nobel Prize," *KanQ* 7, iv (1975): 19-24.

Gingell-Beckmann, Susan, "Seven Black Swans: The Symbolic Logic of Patrick White's THE EYE OF THE STORM," *WLWE* 21, ii (Summer, 1982): 315-25.

Green, Dorothy, "Queen Lear or Cleopatra Rediviva? Patrick White's THE EYE OF THE STORM," *Meanjin* 32, iv (Dec., 1973): 395-405.

Johnson, Manly, "Patrick White: The Eye of the Language," *WLWE* 15, ii (Nov., 1976): 339-58.

Kelly, David, "The Structure of THE EYE OF THE STORM," in Shepherd, R., and K. Singh, eds., *Patrick White*, 62-9.

Kiernan, B., *Patrick White*, 112-23.

Kramer, Leonie, "Patrick White: 'The Unplayed I'," *Quadrant* 18 (Jan./Feb., 1974): 65-8.

Maack, Annegret, "Shakespearean Reference as Structural Principle in Patrick White's THE TREE OF MAN and THE EYE OF THE STORM," *Southerly* 38 (1978): 123-40.

Mackenzie, Manfred, "'Dark Birds of Light': THE EYE OF THE STORM as Swansong," *SoRA* 10 (1977): 270-84.

_____, "Tradition and Patrick White's Talent," *TSLL* 21, ii (Summer, 1979): 153-60.

Morley, Patricia, "'The Road to Dover': Patrick White's THE EYE OF THE STORM," *HAB* 26 (1975): 106-15.

Reimer, A. P., "The Eye of the Needle: Patrick White's Recent Novels," *Southerly* 34, iii (Sept., 1974): 248-51, 256-66.

Steiner, George, "Carnal Knowledge," *NY* 50, ii (Mar. 4, 1974): 109-13.

Venkat, A. R., "Patrick White's THE EYE OF THE STORM," *ComQ* 6, xxi (Dec., 1981): 25-38.

Walsh, W., *Patrick White's Fiction*, 111-18.

Wilson, Richard, "The Splinters of a Mind Make a Whole Piece," in Hamilton, K. G., ed., *Recent Studies in the Australian Novel*, 61-83.

A FRINGE OF LEAVES

Banerjee, Jacqueline, "'The Living Green': An Aspect of Patrick White's Development as a Novelist," *SELit* 58, i (Sept., 1981): 89-102.

Brady, Veronica, "A FRINGE OF LEAVES: Civilization by the Skin of Our Teeth," *Southerly* 37 (1977): 123-40.

_____, "Theology and the Test of Experience: Patrick White's A FRINGE OF LEAVES and Ernst Kasemann," *Colloquium* 12 (1979): 33-40.

Cotter, Michael, "Fragmentation, Reconstitution and the Colonial Experience: The Aborigine in White's Fiction," in Tiffin, C., ed., *South Pacific Images*, 175-7.

Edgar, Suzanne, "A Woman's Life and Love: A Reply to Leonie Kramer," *Quadrant* 21 (Oct., 1977): 69-71.

Ghose, Zulfikar, "One Comprehensive Vision," *TSLL* 21, ii (Summer, 1979): 262-71.

Johnson, Manly, "A FRINGE OF LEAVES: White's Genethlicon," *TSLL* 21 (1979): 226-39.

————, "Patrick White: A FRINGE OF LEAVES," in Shepherd, R., and K. Singh, eds., *Patrick White*, 87-98.

Kiernan, B., *Patrick White*, 124-34.

Kramer, Leonie, "A Woman's Life and Love," *Quadrant* 20 (Nov., 1976): 62-3. [See also reply be Suzanne Edgar above.]

Mackenzie, Manfred, "Tradition and Patrick White's Talent," *TSLL* 21, ii (Summer, 1979): 160-6.

Maes-Jelinek, Hena, "Fictional Breakthrough and the Unveiling of 'Unspeakable Rites' in Patrick White's A FRINGE OF LEAVES and Wilson Harris's YUROKON," *Kunapipi* 2, ii (1980): 33-43.

Morley, Patricia, "Patrick White's A FRINGE OF LEAVES: Journey to Tintagel," *WLWE* 21, ii (Summer, 1982): 303-15.

Stow, Randolph, "Transfigured Histories: Recent Novels of Patrick White and Robert Drewe," *ALS* 9, i (May, 1979): 32-8.

Tacy, David, "A Search for a New Ethic: White's A FRINGE OF LEAVES," in Tiffin, C., *South Pacific Images*, 186-95.

Walsh, William, "Patrick White: The Religious Collection," *SR* 85, iii (Summer, 1977): 509-11.

————, *Patrick White's Fiction*, 118-25.

Ward, Jill, "Patrick White's A FRINGE OF LEAVES: History and Fiction," *ALS* 8 (1978): 402-18.

HAPPY VALLEY

Argyle, B., *Patrick White*, 6-11, 13-15.

Barnard, Marjorie, "The Four Novels of Patrick White," *Meanjin* 15 (June, 1956): 157-60.

Beston, John B., "The Influence of John Steinbeck's THE PASTURES OF HEAVEN on Patrick White," *ALS* 6, ii (May, 1974): 317-19.

————, "The Place of HAPPY VALLEY in the Novels of Patrick White," *ACLALSB* (1974): 17-27.

Bjorksten, I., *Patrick White*, 26-32.

Brissendon, R. F., *Patrick White*, 14-17.

Buckley, Vincent, "The Novels of Patrick White," in Dutton, G., ed., *Literature of Australia*, 413-14.

Hadgraft, C., *Australian Literature*, 240-1.

Houbein, Lolo, "A Case for the Inclusion of HAPPY VALLEY in the Canon of Patrick White's Novels," *ALS Working Papers* 1 (June, 1975): 5-10.

Kiernan, B., *Patrick White*, 13-18.

Morley, P. A., *Mystery of Unity*, 33-47.

Walsh, W., *Patrick White's Fiction*, 3-7.

Warren, Thomas L., "Patrick White: The Early Novels," *MFS* 27, i (Sept., 1981): 121-7.

THE LIVING AND THE DEAD

Argyle, B., *Patrick White*, 15-21.

Barnard, Marjorie, "The Four Novels of Patrick White," *Meanjin* 15 (June, 1956): 160-3.

Bjorksten, I., *Patrick White*, 32-8.

Brissendon, R. F., *Patrick White*, 17-18.

Buckley, Vincent, "The Novels of Patrick White," in Dutton, G., ed., *Literature of Australia*, 414-15.

Dutton, G., *Patrick White*, 15-21.

Kiernan, Brian, "Patrick White: The Novelist in the Modern World," in Anderson, D., and S. Knight, eds., *Cunning Exiles*, 83-6.

Maes-Jelinek, H., "THE LIVING AND THE DEAD," *RLV* 29 (1963): 521-8.

Morley, P. A., *Mystery of Unity*, 49-62.

Tacy, David, "Denying the Shadow as the Day Lengthens: Patrick White's THE LIVING AND THE DEAD," *SoRA* 11 (1978): 165-79.

Walsh, W., *Patrick White's Fiction*, 7-17.

Warren, Thomas L., "Patrick White: The Early Novels," *MFS* 27, i (Spring, 1981): 127-33.

Watson, Betty L., "Patrick White, Some Lines of Development: THE LIVING AND THE DEAD to THE SOLID MANDALA," *ALS* 5, ii (Oct., 1971): 158-67.

RIDERS IN THE CHARIOT

Anon., "RIDERS IN THE CHARIOT: A Note on the Title," *Westerly* Nos. 2 & 3 (1962): 108-10.

Argyle, B., *Patrick White*, 48-57.

Aughterson, M., "The Way Through Suburbia," *Prospect* 5 (1962): 30-1.

Balliet, W., "Mrs. Jolly and Mrs. Flack," *NY* 37 (Dec. 9, 1961): 244-7.

Banerjee, Jacqueline, "A Reassessment of Patrick White's RIDERS IN THE CHARIOT," *LHY* 20, ii (1979): 91-113.

Barnes, John, "A Note on Patrick White's Novels," *LCrit* 6 iii (1964): 100-1. Also in Narasimhaiah, C. D., ed., *Introduction to Australian Literature*, 100-1.

Beatson, P., *Eye in the Mandala*, 159-63.

Bjorksten, I., *Patrick White*, 65-74.

Bradley, D., "Australia through the Looking-Glass: Patrick White's Latest Novel," *Overland* 23 (Autumn, 1965): 41-5.

Brissendon, R. F., *Patrick White*, 34-8.

Buckley, Vincent, "The Novels of Patrick White," in Dutton, G., ed., *Literature of Australia*, 424-6.

Burgess, O. N., in *AusQ* 34 (Mar., 1962): 110-13.

Burrows, J. F., "Archetypes and Stereotypes: RIDERS IN THE CHARIOT," *Southerly* 25, i (1965): 46-68.

Chapman, Edgar L., "The Mandala Design of Patrick White's RIDERS IN THE CHARIOT," *TSLL* 21 (1979): 186-202.

Cotter, Michael, "Fragmentation, Reconstitution and the Colonial Experience: The Aborigine in White's Fiction," in Tiffin, C., ed., *South Pacific Images*, 180-4.

————, "The Image of the Aboriginal in Three Modern Australian Writers," *Meanjin* 36, iv (1977): 588-90.

Delmonte, Rudolfo, "Various Types of Ambiguity in Patrick White's RIDERS IN THE CHARIOT," *LiNQ* (James Cook Un., No. Queensland) 3, iii-iv (1974): 37-52.

Dillistone, Frederick W., *Patrick White's RIDERS IN THE CHARIOT* (Religious Dimensions in Literature), N.Y.: Seabury, 1969.

Dutton, Geoffrey, "The Novels of Patrick White," *Crit* 6, iii (Winter, 1963-64): 21-7.

————, *Patrick White*, 39-43.

_____, "White's Triumphant Chariot," *Australian Book Review* 1 (Nov., 1963): 1-3.

Edwards, Allan, "RIDERS IN THE CHARIOT: A Note on the Title," *Westerly* Nos. 2 & 3 (1962): 108-10.

Ghose, Zulfikar, "One Comprehensive Vision," *TSLL* 21, ii (Summer, 1979): 271-9.

Green, Dorothy, "The Edge of Error," *Quadrant* 17 (Sept./Dec., 1973): 36-47.

Gzell, Sylvia, "Themes and Imagery in VOSS and RIDERS IN THE CHARIOT," *ALS* 1 (June, 1964): 180-95. Also in Semmler, C., ed., *Twentieth Century Australian Criticism*, 252-67.

Healy, J. J., "The Absolute and Images of Man in Australia: Judith Wright and Patrick White," in Narisimhaiah, C. D., ed., *Awakened Conscience*, 6-13.

Heydon, J. D., "Patrick White," *OR* 1 (1966): 42-6.

Kantor, P. P., "Jews and Jewish Mysticism in Patrick White's RIDERS IN THE CHARIOT," *BB Bulletin* (Sydney) 11 (Mar., 1963): 14+.

Kiernan, B., *Patrick White*, 65-83.

_____, "Patrick White: The Novelist and the Modern World," in Anderson, D., and S. Knight, eds., *Cunning Exiles*, 93-7.

Kramer, Leonie, "Patrick White's Gotterdammerung," *Quadrant* 17 (May/June, 1973): 8-19.

MacKenzie, Manfred, "Abyssinia Lost and Regained," *EIC* 13 (1963): 296-300.

Martin, David, "A Chariot Between Faith and Despair: On Patrick White's RIDERS IN THE CHARIOT," *Bridge* (Sydney) 1 (Autumn, 1964): 7-12.

McAuley, James, in *Quadrant* 6, 11 (1962): 79-81.

McFarlane, Brian, "Inhumanity in the Australian Novel: RIDERS IN THE CHARIOT," *CR* 19 (1977): 24-41.

McLaren, John, "Patrick White's Use of Imagery," *ALS* 2 (June, 1966): 217-20. Also in Semmler, C., ed., *Twentieth Century Australian Literary Criticism*, 268-72.

Monk, Patricia, "Beating the Bush: The Mandala and National Psychic Unity in RIDERS IN THE CHARIOT and FIFTH BUSINESS," *ESC* 5 (1979): 344-54.

Moore, Susan, "The Quest for Wholeness in RIDERS IN THE CHARIOT," *Southerly* 35 (1975): 50-67.

Morley, P. A., *Mystery of Unity*, 153-83.

New, William H., "The Island and the Madman: Recurrent Imagery in the Major Novelists of the Fifties," *ArQ* 22 (Winter, 1966): 332-4.

Phillips, A. A., "Patrick White and the Algebraic Symbol," *Meanjin* 24 (1965): 455-61.

Potter, Nancy A. J., "Patrick White's Minor Saints," *REL* 5, iv (Oct., 1964): 16-19.

Rao, B. Damodar, "RIDERS IN THE CHARIOT: A Note," *ACLALSB* 4, iv (1976): 50-4.

Roderick, Colin, "RIDERS IN THE CHARIOT: An Exposition," *Southerly* 22, ii (1962): 62-77.

Ryan, Yoni, "The Jew as an Alienated Figure in the Fiction of Patrick White and Bernard Malamud," *Melbourne Chronicle* 4 (Sept./Oct., 1978): 10-12.

Walsh, W., *Manifold Voice*, 112-17.

_____, *Patrick White's Fiction*, 54-66.

Walters, Margaret, "Patrick White," *New Left Rev* 18 (Jan.-Feb., 1963): 47-50.

THE SOLID MANDALA

Anon., "Reading the Marbles," *TLS* (June 9, 1966): 509. Also in *T.L.S.: Essays and Reviews from The Times Literary Supplement, 1966*, 23-7.

Argyle, B., *Patrick White*, 57-65.

Beatson, P., *Eye in the Mandala*, 71-5.

Beston, John B., "Unattractive Saints and a Poor Devil: Ambivalence in Patrick White's THE SOLID MANDALA," *LHY* 14, i (1973): 106-14.

Bjorksten, I., *Patrick White*, 84-92.

Herring, Thelma, "Self and Shadow: The Quest for Totality in THE SOLID MANDALA," *Southerly* 26, iii (1966): 180-9.

_____, "THE SOLID MANDALA: Two Notes," *Southerly* 28 (1968): 216-22.

Kantok, V. Y., "Patrick White's Dostoevskian Idiot: The 'Idiot' Theme in THE SOLID MANDALA," in Rizvi, S.N.A., ed., *Twofold Voice*, 166-83.

Kiernan, B., *Images of Society and Nature*, 127-35.

_____, *Patrick White*, 93-101.

_____, "Patrick White: The Novelist and the Modern World," in Anderson, D., and S. Knight, eds., *Cunning Exiles*, 97-9.

Mackenzie, Manfred, "The Consciousness of 'Twin Consciousness': Patrick White's THE SOLID MANDALA," *Novel* 2 (Spring, 1969): 241-54.

_____, "Tradition and Patrick White's Individual Talent," *TSLL* 21, ii (Summer, 1979): 147-53.

Morley, P. A., *Mystery of Unity*, 185-207.

Phillips, A. A., "THE SOLID MANDALA: Patrick White's New Novel," *Meanjin* 25 (Autumn, 1966): 31-3.

Shahane, V. A., "An Approach to Patrick White's THE SOLID MANDALA," *ACLALSB* 4, iv (1976): 55-64.

Walsh, W., *Manifold Voice*, 117-23.

_____, *Patrick White's Fiction*, 85-96.

_____, "Patrick White's Vision of Human Incompleteness: THE SOLID MANDALA and THE VIVESECTOR," *JCL* 7 (July, 1969): 127-32. Also in Walsh, W., ed., *Readings in Commonwealth Literature*, 420-5.

Watson, Betty L., "Patrick White, Some Lines of Development: THE LIVING AND THE DEAD to THE SOLID MANDALA," *ALS* 5, ii (Oct., 1971): 158-67.

Wilkes, G. A., "An Approach to Patrick White's THE SOLID MANDALA," *SchP* 1 (1969): 99-106. Also in *Southerly* 19, ii (1969): 97-110.

THE TREE OF MAN

Argyle, B., *Patrick White*, 30-40.

Banerjee, Jacqueline, "'The Living Green': An Aspect of Patrick White's Development as a Novelist," *SELit* 58, i (Sept., 1981): 89-102.

Barden, Garrett, "Patrick White's THE TREE OF MAN," *Studies* 57 (Spring, 1969): 78-85.

Barnard, Marjorie, "The Four Novels of Patrick White," *Meanjin* 15 (June, 1956): 165-70.

Barnes, John, "A Note on Patrick White's Novels," *LCrit* 6, iii (1964): 98-100. Also in Narisimaiah, C. D., ed., *Introduction to Australian Literature*, 90-100.

Beston, John B., "Dreams and Visions in THE TREE OF MAN," *ALS* 6 (Oct., 1973): 152-66.

_____, "The Influence of MADAME BOVARY on THE TREE OF MAN," *RLC* 46 (1972): 555-68.

_____, and Kerry Groves, "The Function of Ray and Thelma Parker in THE TREE OF MAN," *LHY* 18, i (1977): 65-75. Also in Gowda, H. H. Anniah, ed., *Powre Above Powres*, 65-75.

Bjorksten, I., *Patrick White*, 46-56.

Brissenden, R. F., *Patrick White*, 24-9.

_____, "Patrick White," *Meanjin* 18 (Dec., 1959): 410-25.

Buckley, Vincent, "The Novels of Patrick White," in Dutton, G., ed., *Literature of Australia*, 418-22.

_____, "Patrick White and His Epic," *TCM* 12 (1958): 239-52. Also in Johnston, Grahame, ed., *Australian Literary Criticism*, Melbourne: Oxford Un. Pr., 1962, 187-97.

Burrows, J. F., "Stan Parker's TREE OF MAN," *Southerly* 29 (1969): 257-79.

Cooperman, S., "An Epic of Australia," *Nation* 181 (Nov. 5, 1955): 404-5.

Dutton, Geoffrey, "The Novels of Patrick White," *Crit* 6, iii (Winter, 1963-64): 11-16.

_____, *Patrick White*, 27-32.

Hadgraft, C., *Australian Literature*, 242-4.

Heydon, J. D., "Patrick White," *OR* 1 (1966): 33-9.

Kiernan, B., *Images of Society and Nature*, 97-113. [Compared with THE RAINBOW, by D. H. Lawrence.]

_____, *Patrick White's Fiction*, 30-40.

_____, "Patrick White: The Novelist and the Modern World," in Anderson, D., and S. Knight, eds., *Cunning Exiles*, 87-91.

Kramer, Leonie, "THE TREE OF MAN: An Essay in Skepticism," in Ramson, W. S., ed., *Australian Experience*, 269-83.

Krim, Seymour, "Big Little Novel," *Cweal* 63 (Dec. 9, 1955): 265-7.

Maack, Annegret, "Shakespearean References as Structural Principle in Patrick White's THE TREE OF MAN and THE EYE OF THE STORM," *Southerly* 38 (1978): 123-40.

Mackenzie, Manfred, "Apocalypse in Patrick White's THE TREE OF MAN," *Meanjin* 25 (Dec., 1966): 405-16.

Morley, P. A., *Mystery of Unity*, 97-115.

Oliver, H. J., "The Expanding Novel," *Southerly* 27, iii (1956): 168-70.

Potter, Nancy A. J., "Patrick White's Minor Saints," *REL* 5, iv (Oct., 1964): 11-14.

Reimer, A. P., "Visions of the Mandala in THE TREE OF MAN," *Southerly* 27, i (1967): 3-19.

Rorke, John, "Patrick White and the Critics," *Southerly* 20 (1959): 66-74.

Schneider, Robert, "Patrick White's THE TREE OF MAN," *Annals '72* 83 (Apr., 1972): 11-14.

Sharr, Roger, "Old Women, Nuns and Idiots: Transcendentalism in THE TREE OF MAN," *St. Mark's Review* 86 (June, 1976): 39-43.

Singh, Kirpal, "The Nostalgia of Permanence: Stan Parker in Patrick White's THE TREE OF MAN," *ACLALSB* 4, iv (1976): 1-5.

Thomson, A. K., "Patrick White's THE TREE OF MAN," *Meanjin* 25 (Autumn, 1966): 21-30.

Walsh, W., *Manifold Voice*, 98-106.

_____, *Patrick White's Fiction*, 30-40.

Walters, Margaret, "Patrick White," *New Left Rev* 17 (Jan.-Feb., 1963): 40-4.

Wilkes, G. A., "Patrick White's THE TREE OF MAN," *Southerly* 15, i (1965): 23-33.

THE VIVISECTOR

Baker, Robert S., "Romantic Onanism in Patrick White's THE VIVISECTOR," *TSLL* 21 (1979): 203-25.

Beston, John B., "Patrick White's THE VIVISECTOR: The Artist in Relation to His Art," *ALS* 5, ii (Oct., 1971): 168-75.

Bjorksten, I., *Patrick White*, 92-103.

Brady, Veronica, "The Artist and the Savage God: Patrick White's THE VIVISECTOR," *Meanjin* 33 (June, 1974): 136-45.

Brissenden, R. F., "THE VIVISECTOR: Art and Science," in Ramson, W. S., ed., *Australian Experience*, 311-24.

Coe, Richard N., "The Artist and the Grocer: Patrick White's THE VIVESECTOR," *Meanjin* 29, iv (Summer, 1970): 526-9.

Docker, John, "Patrick White and Romanticism: THE VIVISECTOR," *Southerly* 33, i (Mar., 1973): 44-61.

Herring, Thelma, "Patrick White's THE VIVISECTOR," *Southerly* 31, i (1971): 3-16.

Kiernan, B., *Images of Society and Nature*, 135-46.

_____, *Patrick White*, 102-12.

_____, "Patrick White: The Novelist and the Modern World," in Anderson, D., and S. Knight, eds., *Cunning Exiles*, 99-103.

Morley, Patricia A., "Doppelganger's Dilemma: Artist and Man in THE VIVISECTOR," *QQ* 78, iii (Autumn, 1971): 407-20.

_____, *Mystery of Unity*, 209-32.

Osumi, Midori, "Stylistic Study of Patrick White's THE VIVISECTOR: White's Language and His Language Community," *CEMF* 24 (Feb., 1981): 36-58.

Riemer, A. P., "The Eye of the Needle: Patrick White's Recent Novels," *Southerly* 34, iii (Sept., 1974): 251-56.

Smith, Terry, "The Portrait of the Artist in Patrick White's THE VIVISECTOR," *Meanjin* 31, ii (June, 1972): 167-77.

Turner, George A., "A Hurtle Duffield Retrospective," *Overland* 50-51 (1972): 93-5.

Walsh, W., *Patrick White's Fiction*, 96-110.

_____, "Patrick White's Vision of Human Incompleteness: THE SOLID MANDALA and THE VIVISECTOR," *Encounter* 34, (May, 1971): 81. Also in Walsh, W., ed., *Readings in Commonwealth Literature*, 425-6.

_____, in *Rhetorique et Communication*, 129-32.

VOSS

Argyle, B., *Patrick White*, 40-8.

Ashcroft, W. D., "More Than One Horizon," in Shepherd, R., and K. Singh, eds., *Patrick White*, 123-34.

Aurousseau, M., "The Identity of VOSS," *Meanjin* 17 (Apr., 1958): 85-7.

Barnard, Marjorie, in *Meanjin* 17 (Apr., 1958): 96-100.

Beatson, P., *Eye in the Mandala*, 14-17.

_____, "The Three Stages: Mysticism in Patrick White's VOSS," *Southerly* 2 (1970): 111-21.

Beston, John P., "Alienation and Humanization, Damnation and Salvation in VOSS," *Meanjin* 30, ii (Winter, 1971): 208-16.

_____, "Three Conclusions: BUDDENBROOKS, THE AUNT'S STORY and VOSS," *LHY* 20, i (1979): 134-41.

_____, "Voss's Proposal and Laura's Acceptance Letter: The Struggle for Dominance in VOSS," *Quadrant* 16 (July-Aug., 1972): 24-30.

_____, and Rose Marie, "The Theme of Spiritual Repression in VOSS," *ArielE* 5, iii (July, 194): 99-114.

Bjorksten, I., *Patrick White*, 56-65.

Brady, Veronica, "In My End is My Beginning: Laura as Heroine of VOSS," *Southerly* 35 (1975): 16-32. Also in *Caliban* 14 (1977): 23-38.

_____, "The Novelist and the New World: Patrick White's VOSS," *TSLL* 21 (1979): 169-85.

Brissenden, R. F., *Patrick White*, 29-34.

_____, "Patrick White," *Meanjin* 18 (Dec., 1959): 410-25.

Buckley, Vincent, "The Novels of Patrick White," in Dutton, G., ed., *Literature of Australia*, 422-4.

Burgess, O. N., "Patrick White, His Critics and Laura Trevelyn," *AusQ* 38, iv (Dec., 1961): 49-57.

Burrows, J. F., "VOSS and the Explorers," *AUMLA* 26 (Nov., 1966): 234-40.

Coates, John, "VOSS and Jacob Boehme: A Note on the Spirituality of Patrick White," *ALS* 9 (1979): 119-22.

Cotter, Michael, "Fragmentation, Reconstitution and the Colonial Experience: The Aborigine in White's Fiction," in Tiffin, C., ed., *South Pacific Images*, 177-80.

Cowburn, John, "The Metaphysics of VOSS," *TCM* 18 (Winter, 1964): 352-61.

Durix, Jean-Pierre, "Natural Elements in Patrick White's VOSS," *WLWE* 18, ii (1979): 345-52.

Dutton, Geoffrey, "The Novels of Patrick White," *Crit* 6, iii (Winter, 1963-64): 16-21.

_____, *Patrick White*, 32-9.

Fraser, E., in *TCM* 163 (Mar., 1958): 277-8.

Fry, Robert, in *AusL* 1 (Apr., 1958): 40-1.

Garebian, Keith, "The Desert and the Garden: The Theme of Completeness in VOSS," *MFS* 22, iv (1976-77): 557-9.

Green, Dorothy, "VOSS: Stubborn Music," in Ramson, W. S., ed., *Australian Experience*, 284-310.

Gzell, Sylvia, "Themes and Imagery in VOSS and RIDERS IN THE CHARIOT," *ALS* 1 (June, 1964): 180-95. Also in Semmler, C., ed., *Twentieth Century Australian Criticism*, 252-67.

Harris, Wilson, *Fossil and Psyche* (OPARI 7), Austin: Un. of Texas, 1974.

Heydon, J. D., "Patrick White," *OR* 1 (1966): 39-42.

Hughes, Ted, "Patrick White's VOSS," *Listener* 71 (Feb. 6, 1964): 229-30.

Kiernan, B., *Images of Society and Nature*, 113-27.

_____, *Patrick White*, 49-64.

_____, "Patrick White: The Novelist and the Modern World," in Anderson, D., and S. Knight, eds., *Cunning Exiles*, 91-3.

King, B., *New English Literatures*, 165-8.

Knox-Shaw, Peter H., "'The Country of the Mind': Exploration as Metaphor in VOSS," *CNIE* 1, ii (1982): 202-25.

Mather, Rodney, "VOSS," *MCR* 6 (1963): 93-101.

Laidlow, R. P., "The Complexity of VOSS," *SoRA* 4, i (1970): 3-14.

McAuley, James, "The Gothic Splendours of Patrick White's VOSS," *Southerly* 25, i (1965): 34-44.

_____, in *Quadrant* 2, viii (1958): 4-5.

_____, in *Quadrant* 3, iv (Spring, 1959): 91-3.

McLaren, John, "Patrick White's Use of Imagery," *ALS* 2 (June, 1966): 217-20. Also in Semmler, C., ed., *Twentieth Century Australian Criticism*, 268-72.

Morley, P. A., *Mystery of Unity*, 117-52.

Oliver, H. J., "Patrick White's Significant Journey," *Southerly* 19 (1958): 46-9.

Orel, Harold, "Is Patrick White's Voss the Real Leichhardt of Australia?" *Costerus* 6 (1972): 109-19.

Phillips, A. A., "Patrick White and the Algebraic Symbol," *Meanjin* 24 (1965): 455-61.

Poovaya, Nimmie, "'His by Right of Vision': A Note on VOSS," *ACLALSB* 4, v (1977): 33-6.

Potter, Nancy A. J., "Patrick White's Minor Saints," *REL* 5, iv (Oct., 1964): 14-16.

Rao, K. N. Rani, "Quest: Two Attitudes," *ComQ* 3, xi (1979): 27-34.

Rao, P. Ramachandra, "The Self Explored: Patrick White's VOSS and Malcolm Lowry's UNDER THE VOLCANO," in Srivastava, A. K., ed., *Alien Voice*, 147-57.

Russell, D. W., "VOSS and LA VOIE ROYALE: A Comparison of Patrick White and Andre Malraux," *WLWE* 19, ii (1980): 184-97.

Rutherford, Anna, "VOSS: The Two Planes," *LHY* 13, i (1972): 73-90.

Shrubb, Peter, "Patrick White: Chaos Accepted," *Quadrant* 12, iii (May-June, 1968): 7-15, 15-19 *passim*.

Singh, Kirpal, "VOSS: White's Integrated Vision," *JEn* 5 (1978): 74-81.

Stern, James, "Patrick White: The Country of the Mind," *LonM* 5, vi (June, 1958): 53-6.

Turner, I., "The Parable of VOSS," *Overland* 12 (Winter, 1958): 36-7.

Walsh, W., *Manifold Voice*, 105-12.

Walsh, William, *Patrick White: VOSS* (Studies in English Lit., 62), London: Arnold, 1976.

_____, *Patrick White's Fiction*, 41-54.

Walters, Margaret, "Patrick White," *New Left Rev* 18 (Jan.-Feb., 1963): 44-7.

Wilkes, G. A., "A Reading of Patrick White's VOSS," *Southerly* 27, iii (1968): 159-73.

Wood, Susan A., "The Power and Failure of 'Vision' in Patrick White's VOSS," *MFS* 27, i (Spring, 1981): 141-58.

THE TWYBORN AFFAIR

Blamires, David, "Patrick White: THE TWYBORN AFFAIR," *CritQ* 22, i (1980): 71-85.

Brady, V., "'A Single Bone-Clean Button': The Achievement of Patrick White," *LCrit* iii-iv (1980): 35-47.

Cohen, Sandy, "A Note on Patrick White's THE EYE OF THE STORM and THE TWYBORN AFFAIR," *N&Q* 29, iv (Aug., 1982): 349.

Johnson, Manly, "TWYBORN: The Abbess, the Bulbel, and the Bawdy House," *MFS* 27, i (Spring, 1981): 159-68.

Ramsey, S. A., "THE TWYBORN AFFAIR: 'The beginning in an end' or 'the end of a beginning'?" *ArielE* 11, iv (1980): 87-95.

Reimer, A. P., "Eddie and the Bogomils: Some Observations on THE TWYBORN AFFAIR," *Southerly* 40 (1980): 12-29.

Templeton, Wayne, "Patrick White: THE TWYBORN AFFAIR," *WCR* 15, iii (Winter, 1981): 66-7.

BIBLIOGRAPHY

Arkin, Marian C., "Critical Reception to the Novels of Patrick White in England, the United States, France, Italy and Germany: An Analysis and Annotated Bibliography," *DAI* 40 (1979): 2649A-50A.

Beston, John B., and Rose Marie, "A Patrick White Bibliography," *WLWE* 12 (1973): 215-29.

Lawson, Alan, *Patrick White*, Melbourne; London: Oxford Un. Pr., 1975. (Australian Bibliographies.)

Scheick, William J., "A Bibliography of Writings about Patrick White, 1972-1978," *TSLL* 21, ii (1979): 296-303.

WIDEMAN, JOHN, 1941-

GENERAL

Frazier, Kermit, "The Novels of John Wideman," *BlackW* 24, viii (June, 1975): 18-38.

Lee, A. Robert, in Lee, . R., ed., *Black Fiction*, 236-9.

O'Brien, John, ed., *Interviews with Black Writers*, 213-33.

WIEBE, RUDY (HENRY), 1934-

GENERAL

Bergman, Brian, "Rudy Wiebe: Storymaker of the Prairies," in Keith, W. J., ed., *Voice in the Land*

Cameron, Donald, "Rudy Wiebe: The Moving Stream is Perfectly at Rest," *Conversations with Canadian Novelists*, 2.

Jeffrey, David L., "A Search for Peace: Prophecy and Parable in the Fiction of Rudy Wiebe," in Keith, W. J., ed., *Voice in the Land*, 179-201.

Keith, W. J., *Epic Fiction*.

_____, ed., *Voice in the Land*.

Melnyk, George, "The Western Canadian Imagination: An Interview with Rudy Wiebe," *CFM* 12 (Einter, 1974): 29-34. Also in Keith, W. J., ed., *Voice in the Land*, 204-8.

Neuman, Shirley, "Unearthing Language: An Interview with Rudy Wiebe and Robert Kroetsch," in Keith, W. J., ed., *Voice in the Land*, 226-47.

Redekop, Magdalene, in Heath, J., ed., *Profiles in Canadian Literature*, 2, 65-72.

Wiebe, Rudy, "In the West, Sir John A. is a Bastard and Riel a Saint. Ever Ask Why?" in Keith, W. J., ed., *Voice in the Land*, 209-11.

THE BLUE MOUNTAINS OF CHINA

Bilan, R. P., "Wiebe and Religious Struggle," *CanL* 77 (Summer, 1978): 50-63.

Ferris, Ina, "Religious Vision and Fictional Form: Rudy Wiebe's THE BLUE MOUNTAINS OF CHINA," *Mosaic* 11, iii (Spring, 1978): 79-85. Also in Keith, W. J., ed., *Voice in the Land*, 88-96.

Jeffrey David L., "Biblical Hermeneutics and Family History in Contemporary Canadian Fiction: Wiebe and Laurence," *Mosaic* 11, iii (Spring, 1978): 99-106.

_____, "A Search for Peace: Prophecy and Parable in the Fiction of Rudy Wiebe," in Keith, W. J., ed., *Voice in the Land*, 185-93.

Keith, W. J., *Epic Fiction*, 42-61.

Meeter, Glenn, "Rudy Wiebe: Spatial Form and Christianity: THE BLUE MOUNTAINS OF CHINA and THE TEMPTATIONS OF BIG BEAR," *ECW* 22 (Summer, 1981): 42-61.

Morley, P. A., *Comedians*, 74-82.

Redekop, Magdelene F., "Translated Into the Past: Language in THE BLUE MOUNTAINS OF CHINA," in Keith, W. J., ed., *Voice in the Land*, 97-123.

Tiessen, Hildegard E., "A Mighty Inner River: 'Peace' in the Earthly Fiction of Rudy Wiebe," *JCF* 2, iv (Fall, 1973): 71-6. Also, adapted, in Moss, J., ed., *Canadian Novel: Here and Now*, 169-81.

FIRST AND VITAL CANDLE

Keith, W. J., *Epic Fiction*, 28-41.

Morley, P. A., *Comedians*, 85-96.

PEACE SHALL DESTROY MANY

Dverksen, David, "Theological Straw or Immemorial Stone?" *Aion* 3 (May, 1963): 16-23.

Friesen, James, "Fiction and the Tradition of Truth," *Aion* 3 (May, 1963): 5-12.

Giesbrecht, Herbert, "O Life, How Naked and How Hard When Known!" *CanM* (Mar. 20, 1963): 5. Also in Kieth, W. J., ed., *Voice in the Land*, 50-63.

Keith, W. J., *Epic Fiction*, 14-27.

Mansbridge, Francis, "Wiebe's Sense of Community," *CanL* 77 (Summer, 1978): 42-9.

Morley, P. A., *Comedians*, 62-73.

Suderman, Elmer F., "Universal Values in Rudy Wiebe's PEACE SHALL DESTROY MANY," *Mennonite Life* 20 (Oct., 1965): 172-6. Also in Kieth, W., J., ed., *Voice in the Land*, 69-78.

Tiessen, Hildegard E., "A Mighty Inner River: 'Peace' in the Early Fiction of Rudy Wiebe," *JCF* 2, iv (Fall, 1973): 71-6. Also, adapted, in Moss, J., ed., *Canadian Novel: Here and Now*, 169-81.

Wiebe, Rudy, "An Author Speaks About His Novel," *CanM* (Apr. 11, 1963): 8. Also in Keith, W. J., ed., *Voice in the Land*, 64-8.

THE SCORCHED-WOOD PEOPLE

Bilan, R. P., in *UTQ* 47 (Summer, 1978): 335-8. Also in Keith, W. J., ed., *Voice in the Land*, 171-4.

Dueck, Allan, "Rudy Wiebe's Approach to Historical Fiction: A Study of THE TEMPTATIONS OF BIG BEAR and THE SCORCHED-WOOD PEOPLE," in Moss, J., ed., *Canadian Novel: Here and Now*, 182-99.

Jeffrey, David L., "A Search for Peace: Prophecy and Parable in the Fiction of Rudy Wiebe," in Keith, W. J., ed., *Voice in the Land*, 196-9.

Keith, W. J., *Epic Fiction*, 82-104.

Solecki, Sam, in *Fiddlehead* 177 (Spring, 1978): 117-20. Also in Keith, W. J., ed., *Voice in the Land*, 174-8.

Tefs, Wayne A., "Rudy Wiebe: Mystery and Reality," *Mosaic* 11, iv (Summer, 1978): 156-8.

THE TEMPTATIONS OF BIG BEAR

Dixon, M., "Big Bear's Visions," *CanF* 53 (July, 1973): 30.

Dueck, Allan, "Rudy Wiebe's Approach to Historical Fiction: A Study of THE TEMPTATIONS OF BIG BEAR and THE SCORCHED-WOOD PEOPLE," in Moss, J., ed., *Canadian Novel: Here and Now*, 182-99.

_____, "A Sense of the Past," *JCF* 2 (Fall, 1973): 88-91.

Keith, W. J., *Epic Fiction*, 62-81.

Lecker, Robert, "Trusting the Quintuplet Senses: Time and Form in THE TEMPTATIONS OF BIG BEAR," *ESC* 8, iii (Sept., ,1982): 333-48.

Mandel, Eli, and Rudy Wiebe, "Where the Voice Comes From," *Quill and Quire*, 40 (Dec., 1974): 4. Also in Keith, W. J., ed., *Voice in the Land*, 150-5.

Meeter, Glenn, "Rudy Wiebe: Spatial Form and Christianity in THE BLUE MOUNTAINS OF CHINA and THE TEMPTA-TIONS OF BIG BEAR," *ECW* 22 (Summer, 1981): 42-61.

Morley, P. A., *Comedians*, 97-107.

Moss, J., *Sex and Violence in the Canadian Novel*, 258-69.

Reimer, Margaret, and Sue Steiner, "Translating Life Into Art: A Conversation with Rudy Wiebe," in Keith, W. J., ed., *Voice in the Land*, 126-30.

Roemer, Kenneth M., "Ruth M. Buck's VOICES OF THE PLAINS CREE; Rudy Wiebe's THE TEMPTATIONS OF BIG BEAR," *WLWE* 13 (1974): 261-5.

Taylor, Lauralyn, "THE TEMPTATIONS OF BIG BEAR: A Filmic Novel?" *ECW* 9 (1977): 134-8.

Whaley, Susan, "Narrative Voices in THE TEMPTATIONS OF BIG BEAR," *ECW* 20 (Winter, 1980-81): 134-48.

Wiebe, Rudy, "Bear Spirit in a Strange Land (All That's Left of Big Bear)," *Macleans* 88 (Sept., 1975): 53-5.

_____, "On the Trail of Big Bear," *JCF* 3/2 (1974): 45-8. Also in Keith, W. J., ed., *Voice in the Land*, 132-41.

Williams, David, "The Indian Our Ancestor: Three Modes of Vision in Recent Canadian Fiction," *DR* 58 (Summer, 1978): 311-16.

BIBLIOGRAPHY

Keith, W. J., *Epic Fiction*, 140-54.

WIESEL, ELIE (ZER), 1928-

GENERAL

Alter, Robert, "Elie Wiesel: Between Hangman and Victim," *After the Tradition*, 151-60. Also in Cargas, H. J., ed., *Responses to Elie Wiesel*, 83-91.

Berenbaum, M., *Vision of the Void*.

Berenbaum, Michael, "The Void at the Ground of Being: In Response to John Roth," *Ultimate Reality & Meaning*, 1, iv (1978): 302-10. [See Roth below.]

Bernstein, Derora, "'How Shall We Sing the Lord's Song in a Strange Land?' The Journey Back to Life in the MIDRASH of Elie Wiesel," *DAI* 34 (1973): 2607A.

Cargas, Harry J., "Elie Wiesel and the Holocaust," *Cweal* 103, xix (Sept. 10, 1976): 594-6.

_____, "Interview with Elie Wiesel," *WebR* 1, iii (1975): 3-7.

_____, "Response to Roth's Article on Wiesel's Ideas on Ultimate Reality and Meaning," *Ultimate Reality & Meaning* 1, iv (1978): 310-13. [See Roth below.]

_____, ed., *Responses to Elie Wiesel*.

Edelman, Lily, "A Conversation with Elie Wiesel," *National Jewish Monthly* 88 (Nov., 1973): 5-18. Also in Cargas, H. J., ed., *Responses to Elie Wiesel*, 9-22.

Estess, T. L., *Elie Wiesel*.

_____, "Elie Wiesel and the Drama of Interrogation," *JR* 56 (Jan., 1976): 18-35. Also in Cargas, H. J., ed., *Responses to Elie Wiesel*, 176-97.

Fine, Ellen S., "Dialogue with Elie Wiesel," *Centerpoint* 4, i (Fall, 1980): 19-25.

_____, "The Journey Homeward: The Theme of the Town in the Works of Elie Wiesel," in Cargas, H. J., *Responses to Elie Wiesel*, 231-58.

_____, *Legacy of Night*.

French, Ellen M. B., "Archetype and Metaphor: An Approach to the Early Novels of Elie Wiesel," *DAI* 42, x (Apr., 1982): 4447A.

Friedman, Maurice, "Elie Wiesel: The Job of Auschwitz," in Friedman, M., *The Hidden Human Image*, N.Y.: Dell, 1974, 106-34. Also in Cargas, H. J., ed., *Responses to Elie Wiesel*, 205-30.

Garber, Frederick, "The Art of Elie Wiesel," *Judaism* 22, iii (Summer, 1973): 301-8.

Green, Mary Jean, "Witness to the Absurd: Elie Wiesel and the French Existentialists," *Ren* 29, iv (Summer, 1977): 170-84.

Halperin, I., "From NIGHT to THE GATES OF THE FOREST: The Novels of Elie Wiesel," *Messengers from the Dead*, 65-106. Also in Cargas, H. J., ed., *Responses to Elie Wiesel*, 45-82.

Indinopulos, Thomas A., "The Holocaust in the Stories of Elie Wiesel," *Soundings* 55 (Summer, 1972): 200-15. Also in Cargas, H. J., *Responses to Elie Wiesel*, 115-32.

Joseloff, Samuel H., "Link and Promise: The Works of Elie Wiesel," *SHR* 8, ii (Spring, 1974): 163-70.

Kahn, Lothar, "Elie Wiesel: Messenger of the Dead," *CJF* 23 (Summer, 1965): 292-7. Also as "Elie Wiesel: :Neo-Hasi-dism," in Kahn, L., *Mirrors of the Jewish Mind*, N.Y.: A. S. Barnes, 1968, 176-93. Also in Cargas, H. J., ed., *Responses to Elie Wiesel*, 102-14.

Knopp, Josephine Z., "The Holocaust: Elie Wiesel," *Trial of Judaism in Contemporary Jewish Writing*, 70-102.

_____, "Wiesel and the Absurd," *ConL* 15 (Apr., 1974): 212-20.

Leizman, Reva B., "The Road Towards Regeneration and Salvation in the Novels of Elie Wiesel," *DAI* 38 (1977): 2761A.

Roth, John K., "Elie Wiesel on Ultimate Reality and Meaning," *Ultimate Realitiy & Meaning* 1, iv (1978): 278-98.

Sherwin, Byron L., "Elie Wiesel and Jewish Theology," *Judaism* 18 (Winter, 1969): 39-52. Also in Cargas, H. J., *Responses to Elie Wiesel*, 133-49.

_____, "Jewish Messianism and Elie Wiesel," *NDEJ* 11, i (Oct., 1978): 33-46.

Szklarczyk, Lillian, "The Demolished Jew in Search of a Self," in *Proceedings of the Fifth National Convention of the Popular Culture Assoc.*, 1430-47.

THE ACCIDENT

Berenbaum, M., *Visions of the Void*, 25-30, 60-2.

Estess, T. L., *Elie Wiesel*, 45-50.

Fine, E. S., *Legacy of the Night*, 31-4, 46-57.

Halperin, I., "From NIGHT to THE GATES OF THE FOREST: The Novels of Elie Wiesel," in Halperin, I., *Messengers from the Dead*, 81-6. Also in Cargas, H. J., ed., *Responses to Elie Wiesel*, 59-64.

Knopp, Josephine Z., "The Holocaust: Elie Wiesel," *Trial of Judaism in Contemporary Jewish Writing*, 77-81.

A BEGGAR IN JERUSALEM

Berenbaum, M., *Vision of the Void*, 69-80.
Fine, E. S., *Legacy of Night*, 63-5, 97-108.
Garber, Frederick, "The Art of Elie Wiesel," *Judaism* 22, iii (Summer, 1973): 307-8.

DAWN

Berenbaum, M., *Visions of the Void*, 21-5.
Estess, T. L., *Elie Wiesel*, 36-44.
Fine, E. S., *Legacy of Night*, 31-46.
Garber, Frederick, "The Art of Elie Wiesel," *Judaism* 22, iii (Summer, 1973): 303-5.
Halperin, I., "From NIGHT to THE GATES OF THE FOREST: The Novels of Elie Wiesel," in Halperin, I., *Messengers from the Dead*, 77-81. Also in Cargas, H. J., ed., *Responses to Elie Wiesel*, 56-9.

THE GATES OF THE FOREST

Berenbaum, M., *Vision of the Void*, 52-68.
Estess, T. L., *Elie Wiesel*, 63-88.
Fine, E. S., *Legacy of Night*, 85-97.
Halperin, I., "From NIGHT to THE GATES OF THE FOREST: The Novels of Elie Wiesel," *Messengers from the Dead*, 93-101. Also in Cargas, H. J., ed., *Responses to Elie Wiesel*, 71-80.
Knopp, Josephine Z., "The Holocaust: Elie Wiesel," *Trial of Judaism in Contemporary Jewish Writing*, 71-4, 89-102.

NIGHT

Berenbaum, M., *Visions of the Void*, 10-21.
Cunningham, Lawrence S., "Elie Wiesel's Anti-Exodus," *America* 130 (Apr. 27, 1974): 325-7. Also in Cargas, H. J., *Responses to Elie Wiesel*, 23-8.
Estess, T. L., *Elie Wiesel*, 17-37.
Fine, E. S., *Legacy of Night*, 10-30.
Garber, Frederick, "The Art of Elie Wiesel," *Judaism* 22, iii (Summer, 1973): 301-3.
Halperin, I., "From NIGHT to THE GATES OF THE FOREST: The Novels of Elie Wiesel," *Messengers from the Dead*, 72-7. Also in Cargas, H. J., ed., *Responses to Elie Wiesel*, 50-6.
Knopp, Josephine Z., "The Holocaust: Elie Wiesel," *Trial of Judaism in Contemporary Jewish Writing*, 72-9 passim.
Langer, L. L., "The Dominion of Death," *Holocaust and the Literary Imagination*, 75-89. Also in Cargas, H. J., *Responses to Elie Wiesel*, 29-44.

THE OATH

Berenbaum, M., *Vision of the Void*, 91-102.
Estess, Ted L., "Choosing Life: An Interpretation of Elie Wiesel's THE OATH," *Soundings* 61, i (Spring, 1978): 67-86.
————, *Elie Wiesel*, 90-112.
Fine, E. S., *Legacy of Night*, 109-17, 121-36.
Roth, John K., "Turns of Fortune: Reflections on Elie Wiesel and THE OATH," in Kahn, S. M., and M. Raetz, eds., *Interculture*, Vienna: Braumuller, 1975, 268-82.

THE TESTAMENT

Fines, E. S., *Legacy of Night*, 138-44.

THE TOWN BEYOND THE WALL

Berenbaum, M., *Vision of the Void*, 31-51.
Estess, E. L., *Elie Wiesel*, 51-9.
Fine, E. S., *Legacy of Night*, 58-78, 83-5.
Garber, Frederick, "The Art of Elie Wiesel," *Judaism* 22, iii (Summer, 1973): 305-6.
Halperin, I., "From NIGHT to THE GATES OF THE FOREST: The Novels of Elie Wiesel," *Messengers from the Dead*, 86-93. Also in Cargas, H. J., ed., *Responses to Elie Wiesel*, 64-71.
Knopp, Josephine Z., "The Holocaust: Elie Wiesel," *Trial of Judaism in Contemporary Jewish Writing*, 81-9.

BIBLIOGRAPHY

Abramowitz, Molly, *Elie Wiesel: A Bibliography*, Metuchen, N.J.: Scarecrow, 1974.
Fine, E. S., *Legacy of Night*, 166-94.

WILDER, THORNTON NIVEN, 1897-1975

GENERAL

Blake, James W., Jr., "Thornton Wilder: Perspective in Fiction and Belief," *DAI* 30 (1980): 5052A.
Borish, E., "Thornton Wilder—Novelist: A Re-examination," *RLV* 37, ii (1971): 152-9.
Burbank, R., *Thornton Wilder*.
Claxton, Evelyn E., "The Novels of Thornton Wilder," *DAI* 32 (1971): 959A.
Cowie, Alexander, "The Bridge of Thornton Wilder," in Gohdes, G., ed., *Essays on American Literature*, 307-28.
Cowley, Malcolm, "The Man Who Abolished Time," *SatR* 39 (Oct. 6, 1956): 13-14, 50-2. Also (slightly abridged) as "Introduction" to *A Thornton Wilder Trio*, N.Y.: Criterion Books, 1956.
Drew, Fraser, "Thornton Wilder: His 'Grand Theme' and the Pinch of Time," *Trace* No. 33 (Aug.-Sept., 1959): 23-6.
Dugan, Evelyn C., "The Novels of Thornton Wilder: Themes Through Characterization," *DAI* 31 (1971): 6050A-51A.
Edgell, David P., "Thornton Wilder Revisited," *CaiSE* (1960): 47-59.
Firebaugh, Joseph, "The Humanism of Thornton Wilder," *PacSp* 4 (Autumn, 1950): 426-38.
Fuller, Edmund, "Thornton Wilder: The Notation of the Heart," *ASch* 28 (Spring, 1959): 210-17. Also in American Scholar, *American Scholar Reader*, N.Y.: Atheneum, 1960, 476-89. Also in Fuller, E., *Books and the Men Behind Them*, 36-62.
Four Quarters 16, iv (May, 1967). Thornton Wilder Number.
Germer, Rudolf, and John Stambaugh, "Modern Writers: Thornton Wilder," *Praxis des neusprachlichen Unterrichts* 9 (1962): 200-6. [Not seen.]
Goldstein, M., *Art of Thornton Wilder*.
Goldstone, Richard H., "The Art of Fiction 16: Thornton Wilder," *ParisR* No. 15 (1957): 37-57. Also in *Writers at Work*, 1st ser., 99-118.
————, "The Wilder Image," *FQ* 16 (May, 1967): 1-7.

Grebanier, B., *Thornton Wilder*.

Greene, George, "The World of Thornton Wilder," *Thought* 37 (Winter, 1962): 563-84.

Kuner, M. C., *Thornton Wilder*.

Loyd, Allen D., "The Shudder of Awe: A Study of the Novels of Thornton Wilder," *DA* 19 (1968): 1541A-42A.

Maxwell-Mahon, W. D., "The Novels of Thornton Wilder," *UES* 16, i (May, 1978): 35-44.

Miller, Rhea B., "Stages in Becoming: A Study of Form in Thornton Wilder's Novels," *DAI* 37 (1977): 4357A.

Morgan, H. Wayne, "The Early Thornton Wilder," *SWR* 43 (Summer, 1958): 248-53.

Papajewski, H., *Thornton Wilder*.

Popper, Hermine I., "The Universe of Thornton Wilder," *Harpers* 230 (June, 1965): 72-81.

Singh, Ram Sewak, "Thornton Wilder: The Chronicler of Civilization," *BP* 11 (July, 1968): 53-62. [Not seen.]

Stresau, H., *Thornton Wilder*.

Subramanyam, Ka N., "The Novels of Thornton Wilder," *IndL* 22, iv (July-Aug., 1979): 167-81.

Turner, W. Craig, "Thornton Wilder: Neglected Novelist?" in Collmer, R. G., and J. W. Herring, eds., *American Bypaths*, 213-30.

Vivion, Michael J., "Building an American City: The Fiction of Thornton Wilder," *DAI* 42, ix (Mar., 1982): 4003A.

Wagenknecht, E., *Cavalcade of the American Novel*, 405-8.

Wescott, Glenway, "Conversations with Thornton Wilder," *Images of Truth*, 242-308.

Wilder, Amos N., "'He didn't go to Paris': Thornton Wilder, Middle America and the Critics," *LJGG* 20 (1979): 183-207.

————, *Thornton Wilder and His Public*.

Williams, Mary Ellen, "The Novels of Thornton Wilder," *DA* 32 (1971): 1536A.

THE BRIDGE OF SAN LUIS REY

Borish, E., "Thornton Wilder—Novelist: A Re-examination," *RLV* 37, ii (1971); 153-6, 158.

Burbank, R., *Thornton Wilder*, 44-56.

Cowie, Alexander, "The Bridge of Thornton Wilder," in Gohdes, C., ed., *Essays on American Literature*, 310-11.

Friedman, Paul, "THE BRIDGE: A Study in Symbolism," *Psychoanalytic Quart.* 31 (1952): 49-80. Also in *Yearbook of Psychoanalysis* (1953): 257-82.

Fuller, Edmund, "Thornton Wilder: The Notation of the Heart," *ASch* 28 (Spring, 1959): 210-11+. Also in American Scholar, *American Scholar Reader*, N.Y.: Atheneum, 1960, 477-8+. Also in Fuller, E., *Books With the Men Behind Them*, 37-9, 45-8.

Goldstein, M., *Art of Thornton Wilder*, 49-62.

Grebanier, B., *Thornton Wilder*, 15-20.

Kuner, M. C., *Thornton Wilder*, 62-79.

Maxwell-Mahon, W. D., "The Novels of Thornton Wilder," *UES* 16, i (May, 1978): 37-40.

Papajewski, H., *Thornton Wilder*, 16-36.

Stresau, H., *Thornton Wilder*, 20-6.

Stuckey, W. J., *Pulitzer Prize Novels*, 74-8.

Subramanyam, Ka N., "The Novels of Thornton Wilder," *IndL* 22, iv (July-Aug., 1979): 176-9.

Viswanatham, K., "The Bridge That Wilder Built," *Triveni* 38, ii (July, 1969): 9-16.

White, Victor, "THE BRIDGE OF SAN LUIS REY Revisited," *TQ* 19, iii (Autumn, 1976): 76-9.

Wilson, Edmund, "Thornton Wilder: Influence of Proust," *NRep* 55 (Aug. 8, 1928): 303-5. Also in Wilson, E., *Shores of Light*, 384-91.

THE CABALA

Allen, W., *Modern Novel*, 103-4.

————, *Urgent West*, 187-8.

Cowie, Alexander, "The Bridge of Thornton Wilder," in Gohdes, C., ed., *Essays on American Literature*, 308-10.

Goldstein, M., *Art of Thornton Wilder*, 34-48.

Grebanier, B., *Thornton Wilder*, 12-15.

Kuner, M. C., *Thornton Wilder*, 52-62.

Maxwell-Mahon, W. D., "The Novels of Thornton Wilder," *UES* 16, i (May, 1978): 35-7.

Papajewski, H., *Thornton Wilder*, 1-15.

Stresau, H., *Thornton Wilder*, 14-18.

Wilson, Edmund, "Thornton Wilder: Influence of Proust," *NRep* 55 (Aug. 8, 1928): 303-5. Also in Wilson, E., *Shores of Light*, 384-91.

THE EIGHTH DAY

Brunauer, Dalma H., "Creative Faith in Wilder's THE EIGHTH DAY," *Ren* 25, i (Autumn, 1972): 46-56.

————, "Some: An Examination of the Religious Tenets of Thornton Wilder's THE EIGHTH DAY," in Schlueter, P., ed., *Literature and Religion*.

Ericson, Edward E., Jr., "The Figure in the Tapestry: The Religious Vision of Thornton Wilder's THE EIGHTH DAY," *C&L* 22, iii (Spring, 1973): 32-48. Also in Schlueter, P., ed., *Literature and Religion*.

————, "Kierkegaard in Wilder's EIGHTH DAY," *Ren* 26, iii (Spring, 1974): 123-38.

French, Warren, "Christianity as Metaphor in THE EIGHT DAY," in Schleuter, P., ed., *Literature and Religion*.

Goldstone, Richard, "Wilder, Studying and Studies," *AR* 27 (Summer, 1967): 264-8.

Greene, George, "An Ethics for Wagon Trains: Thornton Wilder's THE EIGHTH DAY," *QQ* 88, ii (Summer, 1981): 325-35.

Kuner, M. C., *Thornton Wilder*, 191-208.

Loyd, Dennis, "God is Alive and Well in Wilder," in Schleuter, P., ed., *Literature and Religion*.

Maxwell-Mahon, W. D., "The Novels of Thornton Wilder," *UES* 16, i (May, 1978): 43-4.

Mayo, Nolie B., "A Tapestry for Humanism in THE EIGHTH DAY," *MEB* 31 (1974): 79-82.

Nandakumar, Prema, "Thornton Wilder: THE EIGHTH DAY," in Naik, M. K., et al., eds., *Indian Studies in American Fiction*, 163-84.

Oliver, Edith, "The Summing Up," *NY* 43 (May 27, 1967): 146-8.

Papjewski, Helmut, "Thornton Wilder's THE EIGHTH DAY," *LWU* 4, i (1971): 27-39.

Perez, Louis C., "Wilder and Cervantes: In the Spirit of the Tapestry," *Symposium* 25 (Fall, 1971): 249-59.

Stresau, H., *Thornton Wilder*, 104-14.

Turner, W. Craig, "Thornton Wilder: Neglected Novelist?" in Collmer, R. G., and J. W. Herring, eds., *American Bypaths*, 220-4.

Van der Weele, Steve J., "Hotels, Boarding Houses, and Homes: The Mystique of the Family in Wilder's Novel THE EIGHTH DAY," in Schleuter, P., ed., *Literature and Religion.*

Venne, Peter, S. V. D., "The Message of Thornton Wilder: Some Reflections on His Novel THE EIGHTH DAY," *FJS* 3 (1970): 15-29.

HEAVEN'S MY DESTINATION

Allen, W., *Modern Novel*, 104-5.

Burbank, R., *Thornton Wilder*, 72-81.

Cowie, Alexander, "The Bridge of Thornton Wilder," in Gohdes, C., ed., *Essays on American Literature*, 313-17.

Firebaugh, Joseph J., "Farce and the Heavenly Destination," *FQ* 16, iv (May, 1967): 10-17.

Goldstein, M., *Art of Thornton Wilder*, 82-94.

Grebanier, B., *Thornton Wilder*, 26-9.

Greene, George, "The World of Thornton Wilder," *Thought* 37 (Winter, 1962): 570-4.

Haberman, Donald, "The Americanization of Thornton Wilder," *FQ* 16 (May, 1967): 18-27.

Kuner, M. C., *Thornton Wilder*, 112-24.

Maxwell-Mahon, W. D., "The Novels of Thornton Wilder," *UES* 16, i (May, 1978): 41-2.

Papajewski, H., *Thornton Wilder*, 51-61.

Stresau, H., *Thornton Wilder*, 50-4.

Subramanya, Ka N., "The Novels of Thornton Wilder," *IndL* 22, iv (July-Aug., 1979): 170-4.

Vivion, Michael, "Thornton Wilder and the Farmer's Daughter," *Thalia* 3, i (Spring-Summer, 1980): 41-5.

Wilson, Edmund, "Mr. Wilder in the Middle West," *NRep* 71 (Jan. 16, 1934): 282-3. Also in Wilson, E., *Shores of Light*, 587-92.

THE IDES OF MARCH

Burbank, R., *Thornton Wilder*, 112-22.

Cowie, Alexander, "The Bridge of Thornton Wilder," in Ghodes, C., ed., *Essays on American Literature*, 317-18.

Davis, Elmer, "Caesar's Last Months," *SatR* 31 (Feb. 21, 1948): 11-12.

Dillon, Michael, "Poet and Statesman: Thornton Wilder's Political Vision in THE IDES OF MARCH," *Intercollegiate Rev.* 9, iii (1974): 149-58.

Goldstein, M., *Art of Thornton Wilder*, 131-45.

Grebanier, B., *Thornton Wilder*, 20-4.

Kuner, M. C., *Thornton Wilder*, 160-78.

Maxwell-Mahon, W. D., "The Novels of Thornton Wilder," *UES* 16, i (May, 1978): 42-3.

Papajewski, H., *Thornton Wilder*, 62-90.

Stresau, H., *Thornton Wilder*, 74-83.

Wescott, G., *Images of Truth*, 256-62.

THE WOMAN OF ANDROS

Burbank, R., *Thornton Wilder*, 56-62.

Cowie, Alexander, "The Bridge of Thornton Wilder," in Gohdes, G., ed., *Essays on American Literature*, 312-13.

Goldberg, Sander M., "THE WOMAN OF ANDROS: Terence Made Wilder," *Helios* (Lubbock, Tex.) 5, i (1977): 11-19.

Goldstein, M., *Art of Thornton Wilder*, 63-71.

Grebanier, B., *Thornton Wilder*, 20-4.

Kuner, M. C., *Thornton Wilder*, 79-93.

Maxwell-Mahon, W. D., "The Novels of Thornton Wilder," *UES* 16, i (May, 1978): 40-1.

Papajewski, H., *Thornton Wilder*, 37-50.

Stresau, H., *Thornton Wilder*, 36-44.

Wilson, Edmund, "Dahlberg, Dos Passos and Wilder," *NRep* 62 (Mar. 26, 1930): 156-7. Also in Wilson, E., *Shores of Light*, 442-5.

BIBLIOGRAPHY

Bryer, Jackson, "Thornton Wilder and the Reviewers," *PBSA* 58 (1964): 35-49.

Kosok, Heinz, "Thornton Wilder: A Bibliography of Criticism," *TCL* 9 (1963): 93-100.

Williams, Michael V., "Thornton Wilder: Additions to Secondary Bibliography," *BB* 39, iv (Dec., 1982): 211-23.

_____, "Thornton Wilder's Anglo-American and German Critics: A Bibliography," *DAI* 40 (1980): 4022A-23A.

Wright, Gerry R., "Thornton Wilder: A Bibliography of Secondary Sources, 1963-78," *BB* 36, iv (Oct.-Dec., 1979): 185-93.

WILKINSON, SYLVIA, 1940-

GENERAL

Chappell, Fred, "Unspeakable Kingdoms: The Novels of Sylvia Wilkinson," *HC* 8, ii (Apr., 1971): 1-10.

Graham, John, "Sylvia Wilkinson," in Garrett, G., ed., *Writer's Voice*, 200-13. [Interview.]

Vance, Jane E., "Fat Like Mama, Mean Like Daddy: The Fiction of Sylvia Wilkinson," *SLJ* 15, i (Fall, 1982): 23-36.

_____, "An Interview with Sylvia Wilkinson," *KRev* 2, ii (1981): 75-88.

BONE OF MY BONES

Vance, Jane E., "Fat Like Mama, Mean Like Daddy," *SLJ* 15, i (Fall, 1982): 30-5.

CALE

Vance, Jane E., "Fat Like Mama, Mean Like Daddy," *SLJ* 15, i (Fall, 1982): 26-9.

WILLIAMS, JOHN A., 1925-

GENERAL

Bigsby, C. W. E., in Lee, A. R., ed., *Black Fiction*, 160-7.

Browne, W. Francis, "The Black Artist in New York: An Interview with John A. Williams," *Centerpoint* 1, iii (1975): 71-6.

Bryant, Jerry H., "John A. Williams: The Political Use of the Novel," *Crit* 16, iii (1975): 81-100.

Cash, Earl A., "The Evolution of a Black Writer: John A. Williams," *DAI* 34 (1973): 308A.

_____, *John A. Williams.*

Georgakas, Dan, "John Williams at 49: An Interview," *MinnR* n.s. 7 (Fall, 1976): 51-65.

Munro, C. Lynn, "Culture and Quest in the Fiction of John A. Williams," *CLAJ* 22, ii (Dec., 1978): 71-100.

O'Brien, John, "The Art of John A. Williams, an Interview," *Asch* 42, iii (Summer, 1973): 489-99. Also in O'Brien, J., ed., *Interviews with Black Writers*, 225-43.

———, "Seeking a Humanist Level: Interview with John A. Williams," *ASoc* 10 (1973): 94-9.

Skerrett, Joseph T., Jr., "Novelist in Motion: An Interview with John A. Williams," *BlackW* 25, iii (1976): 58-67, 93-7.

Walcott, Ronald, "The Early Fiction of John A. Williams," *CLAJ* 16, ii (Dec., 1972): 198-213.

———, "The Man Who Cried I Am: Crying in the Dark," *SBL* 3, i (Spring, 1972): 24-32.

THE ANGRY ONES

Cash, E. A., *John A. Williams*, 33-46.

Munro, C. Lynn, "Culture and Quest in the Fiction of John A. Williams," *CLAJ* 22, ii (Dec., 1978): 74-6.

Schraufnagel, N., *From Apology to Protest*, 147-8.

Walcott, Ronald, "The Early Fiction of John A. Williams," *CLAJ* 16, ii (Dec., 1972): 203-4.

CAPTAIN BLACKMAN

Cash, E. A., *John A. Williams*, 117-24.

Gayle, A., Jr., *Way of the New World*, 280-6.

Munro, C. Lynn, "Culture and Quest in the Fiction of John A. Williams," *CLAJ* 22, ii (Dec., 1978): 92-4.

THE JUNIOR BACHELOR SOCIETY

Berzon, J. R., *Neither White Nor Black*, 242-44.

Munro, C. Lynn, "Culture and Quest in the Fiction of John A. Williams," *CLAJ* 22, ii (Dec., 1978): 97-100.

THE MAN WHO CRIED I AM

Bigsby, C. W. E., in Lee, A. R., ed., *Black Fiction*, 161-4.

Bryant, Jerry H., "John A. Williams: The Political Use of the Novel," *Crit* 16, iii (1975): 92-100.

Burke, William M., "The Resistance of John A. Williams: THE MAN WHO CRIED I AM," *Crit* 15, iii (1974): 5-14.

Cash, E. A., *John A. Williams*, 97-108.

Fleming, Robert E., "The Nightmare Level of THE MAN WHO CRIED I AM," *ConL* 14, ii (1973): 186-96.

Gayle, A., Jr., *Way of the New World*, 277-80.

Klotman, Phyllis R., "An Examination of the Black Confidence Man in Two Black Novels: THE MAN WHO CRIED I AM and DEM," *AL* 44 (Jan., 1973): 596-611.

Munro, C. Lynn, "Culture and Quest in the Fiction of John A. Williams," *CLAJ* 22, ii (Dec., 1978): 85-9.

Schraufnagel, N., *From Apology to Protest*, 187-9.

Smith, Anneliese H., "A Pain in the Ass: Metaphor in John A. Williams' THE MAN WHO CRIED I AM," *SBL* 3, iii (Autumn, 1972): 25-7.

Walcott, Ronald, "The Man Who Cried I Am: Crying in the Dark," *SBL* 3, i (Spring, 1972): 25-32.

MOTHERSILL AND THE FOXES

Munro, C. Lynn, "Culture and Quest in the Fiction of John A. Williams," *CLAJ* 22, ii (Dec., 1978): 94-6.

NIGHT SONG

Bryant, Jerry H., "John A. Williams: The Politics of the Novel," *Crit* 16, iii (1975): 86-8.

Cash, E. A., *John A. Williams*, 47-71.

Karrer, Wolfgang, "Multiperspective and the Hazards of Integration: John Williams' NIGHT SONG," in Bruck, P., and W. Karrer, eds., *Afro-American Novel Since 1960*, 75-99.

Munro, C. Lynn, "Culture and Quest in the Fiction of John A. Williams," *CLAJ* 22, ii (Dec., 1978): 76-80.

Scraufnagel, N., *From Apology to Protest*, 148-50.

Walcott, Ronald, "The Early Fiction of John A. Williams," *CLAJ* 16, ii (Dec., 1972): 204-7.

SISSIE

Bryant, Jerry H., "John A. Williams: The Political Use of the Novel," *Crit* 16, iii (1975): 88-92.

Cash, E. A., *John A. Williams*, 73-95.

Munro, C. Lynn, "Culture and Quest in the Fiction of John A. Williams," *CLAJ* 22, ii (Dec., 1978): 80-3.

Scraufnagel, N., *From Apology to Protest*, 150-1.

Walcott, Ronald, "The Early Fiction of John A. Williams," *CLAJ* 16, ii (Dec., 1972): 207-13.

SONS OF DARKNESS, SONS OF LIGHT

Bigsby, C. W. E., in Lee, A. R., ed., *Black Fiction*, 164-6.

Cash, E. A., *John A. Williams*, 109-15.

Munro, C. Lynn, "Culture and Quest in the Fiction of John A. Williams," *CLAJ* 22, ii (Dec., 1978): 90-2.

Schraufnagel, N., *From Apology to Protest*, 189-92.

WILLIAMS, JOHN E., 1922-

GENERAL

Nelson, Robert J., "Accounts of Mutual Acquaintances to a Group of Friends: The Fiction of John Williams," *UDQ* 7, iv (Winter, 1973): 13-36.

Stamper, Rexford, "An Introduction to the Major Novels of John Williams," *MissR* 3, i (Jan., 1974): 89-98.

Stark, John, "The Novels of John Williams," *HC* 17, iv (Oct., 1980): 1-9.

Wakefield, Dan, "John Williams, Plain Writer," *Ploughshares* 7, iii-iv (1981): 9-22.

AUGUSTUS

Hartt, Julian N., "Two Historical Novels," *VQR* 49, iii (Summer, 1973): 454-8.

Nelson, Robert J., "Accounts of Mutual Acquaintances to a Group of Friends: The Fiction of John Williams," *UDQ* 7, i (Winter, 1973): 23-36.

Stamper, Rexford, "An Introduction to the Major Novels of John Williams," *MissR* 3, i (Jan., 1973): 95-8.

Stark, John, "The Novels of John Williams," *HC* 17, iv (Oct., 1980): 5-9.

BUTCHER'S CROSSING

Brenner, Jack, "BUTCHER'S CROSSING: The Husks and Shells of Exploitation," *WAL* 7 (1973): 243-59.

Nelson, Robert J., "Accounts of Mutual Acquaintances to a Group of Friends: The Fiction of John Williams," *UDQ* 7, iv (Winter, 1973): 17-23.

Stark, John, "The Novels of John Williams," *HC* 17, iv (Oct., 1980): 2-4.

STONER

Howe, Irving, "The Virtues of Failure," *NRep* 154, vii (Feb. 12, 1966): 19-20.

Stark, John, "The Novels of John Williams," *HC* 17 iv (Oct., 1980): 4-5.

WILLIAMS, RAYMOND (HENRY), 1921-

GENERAL

Ryan, Kiernan, in Klaus, H. G., ed., *Socialist Novel in Britain*, 173-8.

Ward, J. P., *Raymond Williams*.

BORDER COUNTRY

Binding, Wyn, "Some Observations on the Novels of Raymond Williams," *AWR* 16 (Spring, 1967): 74-81.

Hooker, Jeremy, "A Dream of a Country: The Raymond Williams Trilogy," *Planet* 49/50 (1980): 53-61.

Ward, J. P., *Raymond Williams*, 39-40.

THE FIGHT FOR MANOD

Hooker, Jeremy, "A Dream of a Country: The Raymond Williams Trilogy," *Planet* 49/50 (1980): 53-61.

Ward, J. P., *Raymond Williams*, 42-4.

SECOND GENERATION

Binding, Wyn, "Some Observations on the Novels of Raymond Williams," *AWR* 16 (Spring, 1967): 74-81.

Hooker, Jeremy, "A Dream of a Country: The Raymond Williams Trilogy," *Planet* 49/50 (1980): 53-61.

THE VOLUNTEERS

Ward, J. P., *Raymond Williams*, 53-4.

WILLIAMS, TENNESSEE, 1914-1983

GENERAL

Cherry, Grady, "Life and Art: A Classification of the Artist-Figure in Selected Fiction of Tennessee Williams," *DAI* 38 (1977): 2121A.

Draya, Ren, "The Frightened Heart: A Study of the Characters and Theme in the Fiction, Poetry, Short Plays, and Recent Drama of Tennessee Williams," *DAI* 38 (1977): 2773A.

McManus, June, "The Pursuit of Happiness: Williams and Lawrence," *JASAT* 9 (1978): 42-8. [Not seen.]

THE ROMAN SPRING OF MRS. STONE

Falk, Signi, L., *Tennessee Williams* (TUSA 10), N. Y.: Twayne, 1961, 144-9.

Gerard, Albert, "The Eagle and the Star, Symbol Motifs in THE ROMAN SPRING OF MRS. STONE," *ES* 34 (Aug., 1955): 145-53.

Nelson, Benjamin, *Tennessee Williams: The Man and His Work*, N.Y.: Obolensky, 1961, 165-71.

Renaux, Sigrid, "Tennessee Williams: Attitudes toward Love and Decay in Blanche Du Bois and Mrs. Stone," *RLet* 28 (1979): 81-91.

Tischler, Nancy M., *Tennessee Williams: Rebellious Puritan*, N.Y.: Citadel, 1961, 177-8.

BIBLIOGRAPHY

See issues of *Tennessee Williams Newsletter*.

Gunn, Drewey W., comp., *Tennessee Williams: A Bibliography*, Metuchen, N.J.: Scarecrow, 1980.

WILLINGHAM, CALDER, 1922-

GENERAL

Parr, J. L., "Calder Willingham: The Forgotten Novelist," *Crit* 11, iii (1969): 57-65.

ETERNAL FIRE

Parr, J. L., "Calder Willingham: The Forgotten Novelist," *Crit* 11, iii (1969): 62-5.

Walcutt, C. C., *Man's Changing Mask*, 217-28.

REACH THE STARS

Parr, J. L., "Calder Willingham: The Forgotten Novelist," *Crit* 11, iii (1969): 58-9.

WILSON, ANGUS, 1913-

GENERAL

Barfoot, C. C., "An Interview with Angus Wilson," *DQR* 6 (1976): 279-90.

Bergonzi, B., *Situation of the Novel*, 151-61.

Biles, Jack I., "An Interview in London with Angus Wilson," *SNNTS* 2, i (Spring, 1970): 76-87.

Bradbury, M., "The Fiction of Pastiche: The Comic Mode of Angus Wilson," *Possibilities*, 211-19.

Cox, C. B., "Angus Wilson: Studies in Depression," *Free Spirit*, 117-53.

Drabble, Margaret, "'No Idle Rentier': Angus Wilson and the Nourished Literary Imagination," *SLitI* 13, i (Spring, 1980): 119-29.

Draine, Betsy, "An Interview with Angus Wilson," *ConL* 21, i (Winter, 1980): 1-14.

Drescher, Horst, "Angus Wilson: An Interview," *NS* 17 (July, 1968): 351-6.

Edelstein, Arthur, in Shapiro, C., ed., *Contemporary British Novelists*, 144-61.

Faulkner, P., *Angus Wilson*.

Fraser, G. S., *Modern Writer and His World*, 152-5.

Fisher, Ruth D., "A Conversation with Sir Angus Wilson," *FQ* 31 (1982): 3-22.

Gindin, J., *Harvest of a Quiet Eye*, 277-304.

Grandsen, K. W., *Angus Wilson.*
Halio, Jay L., *Angus Wilson.*
———, "The Novels of Angus Wilson," *MFS* 8 (Summer, 1962): 171-81.
Harris, Marilyn R., "Self-Awareness and Family Influence in the Works of Angus Wilson," *DAI* 35 (1975): 4523A-24A.
Katona, Anna, "Angus Wilson's Fiction and Its Relation to the English Tradition," *ALitASH* 10 (1968): 111-27.
Kermode, Frank, "The House of Fiction: Interviews with Seven English Novelists," *PR* 30 (Spring, 1963): 68-71.
McDowell, Frederick P. W., "An Interview with Angus Wilson," *IowaR* 3, iv (Fall, 1972): 77-105.
McSweeney, Kerry, "The Novels of Angus Wilson," *WascanaR* 12, ii (Fall, 1978): 3-24.
Millgate, Michael, "Angus Wilson," *ParisR* No. 17 (1958): 89-105. Also in *Writers at Work,* 1st ser., 251-66.
Moorcock, Michael, "Angus Wilson," *B&B* 18, viii (May, 1973): 22-8. [Interview.]
Narita, Seiju, "A Reformer not a Revolutionary," *EigoS* 115 (1969): 752-9. [Interview.]
Oakland, John, "Angus Wilson and Evil in the English Novel," *Ren* 26, i (Autumn, 1973): 24-36.
Poston, Lawrence, III., "A Conversation with Angus Wilson," *BA* 40 (Winter, 1966): 29-31.
Raban, Jonathan, "Angus Wilson: A Profile," *NewRev* 1, i (Apr., 1974): 16-24.
Rabinovitz, R., *Reaction Against Experiment in the English Novel,* 64-96.
Riddell, Edwin, "The Humanist Character in Angus Wilson," *English* 21 (Summer, 1972): 45-53.
Rippier, J. S., *Some Postwar English Novelists,* 19-44.
Scott-Kilvert, Ian, "Angus Wilson," *REL* 1, ii (Apr., 1960): 42-53.
Sewell, Michael W., "Parent and Child in the Garden: The Early Novels of Angus Wilson," *DAI* 35 (1975): 4556A-57A.
Smith, Catherine S., "The Other Angus Wilson: Fantasy in His Fiction," *DAI* (1980): 683A.
Smith, William J., "Angus Wilson's England," *Cweal* 82 (Mar. 26, 1965): 18-21.
Szabo-pap, Judit, "The Lonely Man in Angus Wilson's Fiction," *HSE* 9 (Dec., 1975): 87-101.
Zimmerman, Muriel, "The Fiction of Angus Wilson," *DA* 28 (1968): 4195A-96A.

ANGLO-SAXON ATTITUDES

Allen, W., *Modern Novel,* 272-3.
Cox, C. B., *Free Spirit,* 138-43.
Edelstein, Arthur, in Shapiro, C., ed., *Contemporary British Novelists,* 156-9.
Faulkner, P., *Angus Wilson,* 54-75.
Gable, Sister Mariella, "Prose Satire and the Modern Christian Temper," *ABR* 11 (Mar.-June, 1960): 30-1.
Gindin, J., "Angus Wilson's Nationalism," *Postwar British Fiction,* 152-6.
Grandsen, K. W., *Angus Wilson,* 19-22.
Hahn, Thomas, "Medievalism, Make-Believe, and Real Life in Wilson's ANGLO-SAXON ATTITUDES," *Mosaic* 12, iv (1979): 115-34.
Halio, J. L., *Angus Wilson,* 39-49.
———, "The Novels of Angus Wilson," *MFS* 8 (Summer, 1962): 175-80.

Karl, F. R., "A Question of Morality: Angus Wilson," *Contemporary English Novel,* 244-7.
McSweeney, Kerry, "The Novels of Angus Wilson," *WascanaR* 12, ii (Fall, 1978): 6-8.
Raban, J., "Narrative: Point of View," *Technique of Modern Fiction,* 41-4.
Rippier, J. S., *Some Postwar English Novelists,* 27-32.
Scott-Kilvert, Ian, "Angus Wilson," *REL* 1, ii (Apr., 1960): 50-2.
Wilson, Angus, "The Genesis of ANGLO-SAXON ATTITUDES," *BI* 34 (Apr., 1981): 3-8.

AS IF BY MAGIC

Byatt, A. S., in *Contemporary English Novel,* 36-8.
Faulkner, P., *Angus Wilson,* 191-206.
McSweeney, Kerry, "The Novels of Angus Wilson," *WascanaR* 12, ii (Fall, 1978): 19-23.
Wilson, Angus, "AS IF BY MAGIC: Angus Wilson on His Own Novel," *DQR* 6 (1976): 259-77.

HEMLOCK AND AFTER

Allen, W., *Modern Novel,* 270-1.
Cockshut, A. O. J., "Favored Sons: The Moral World of Angus Wilson," *EIC* 9 (Jan., 1959): 50-60.
Cox, C. B., *Free Spirit,* 125-38.
———, "The Humanism of Angus Wilson: A Study of HEMLOCK AND AFTER," *CritQ* 3 (Autumn, 1961): 227-37.
Faulkner, P., *Angus Wilson,* 30-46.
Fraser, G. S., *Modern Writer and His World,* 153-5.
Gindin, J., "Angus Wilson's Nationalism," *Postwar British Fiction,* 150-2.
Grandsen, K. W., *Angus Wilson,* 17-19.
Halio, J. L., *Angus Wilson,* 27-38.
———, "The Novels of Angus Wilson," *MFS* 8 (Summer, 1962): 171-4.
Kerr, Walter, "Cold Eye on the Best People," *Cweal* 57 (Oct. 24, 1952): 72-3.
McSweeney, Kerry, "The Novels of Angus Wilson," *WascanaR* 12, ii (Fall, 1978): 4-5.
Rippier, J. S., *Some Postwar English Novelists,* 21-6.
Scott-Kilvert, Ian, "Angus Wilson," *REL* 1, ii (Apr., 1960): 45-8.
Wogatzky, Karin, *Angus Wilson: HEMLOCK AND AFTER: A Study in Ambiguity* (Swiss Studies in English, 62), Bern: Francke, 1971.

LATE CALL

Anon., "Not Painted—But Made Up," *TLS* (Nov. 5, 1964): 1013. Also in *T. L. S.: Essays and Reviews from The Times Literary Supplement, 1964,* 103-5.
Bergonzi, B., *Situation of the Novel,* 157-9.
Burgess, Anthony, "Powers That Be," *Encounter* 24 (Jan., 1965): 71-6.
Edelstein, Arthur, in Shapiro, C., ed., *Contemporary British Novelists,* 144-53.
Faulkner, P., *Angus Wilson,* 135-53.
Gindin, James, "The Fable Breaks Down," *WSCL* 8 (Winter, 1967): 10-17.
Grandsen, K. W., *Angus Wilson,* 25-7.
McSweeney, Kerry, "The Novels of Angus Wilson," *WascanaR* 12, ii (Fall, 1978): 14-16.

Shaw, Valerie A., "THE MIDDLE AGE OF MRS. ELIOT and LATE CALL: Angus Wilson's Traditionalism," *CritQ* 12, i (Spring, 1970): 9-27.

Spender, Stephen, "Must There Always be a Red Brick England?" in Encyclopedia Britannica. *Great Ideas Today, 1965,* 177-80.

THE MIDDLE AGE OF MRS. ELIOT

Allen, W., *Modern Novel,* 273-4.

Cox, C. B., *Free Spirit,* 143-53.

Edelstein, Arthur, in Shapiro, C., ed., *Contemporary British Novelists,* 154-6.

Faulkner, P., *Angus Wilson,* 85-101.

Fletcher, John, "Women in Crises: Louise and Mrs. Eliot," *CritQ* 15 (1973): 157-70.

Gindin, J., "Angus Wilson's Nationalism," *Postwar British Novelists,* 156-9.

Grandsen, K. W., *Angus Wilson,* 50-61.

_____, "The Novels of Angus Wilson," *MFS* 8 (Summer, 1962): 175-80.

Karl, F. R., "A Question of Morality," *Contemporary English Novel,* 247-9.

Kermode, Frank, "Mr. Wilson's People," *Spectator* (Nov. 21, 1958): 705-6. Also in Kermode, F., *Puzzles and Epiphanies,* 193-7.

McSweeney, Kerry, "The Novels of Angus Wilson," *WascanaR* 12, ii (Fall, 1978): 8-10.

Raymond, John, "Meg Eliot Surprised," *Doge of Dover,* 170-8.

Rippier, J. S., *Some Postwar English Novelists,* 32-7.

Scott-Kilvert, Ian, "Angus Wilson," *REL* 1, ii (Apr., 1960): 50-2.

Shaw, Valerie A., "THE MIDDLE AGE OF MRS. ELIOT and LATE CALL: Angus Wilson's Traditionalism," *CritQ* 12, i (Spring, 1970): 9-27.

NO LAUGHING MATTER

Bergonzi, B., *Situation of the Novel,* 159-61.

Bradbury, Malcolm, "The Fiction of Pastiche: The Comic Mode of Angus Wilson," *Possibilities,* 219-30.

Burden, Robert, in *Contemporary English Novel,* 143-7.

Faulkner, P., *Angus Wilson,* 162-84.

Grandsen, K. W., *Angus Wilson,* 27-9.

Halio, Jay L., "Angus Wilson's NO LAUGHING MATTER," *MR* 10 (Spring, 1969): 394-7.

Kums, Guido, "Reality in Fiction: NO LAUGHING MATTER," *ES* 53 (1972): 523-31.

McSweeney, Kerry, "The Novels of Angus Wilson," *WascanaR* 12, ii (Fall, 1978): 16-19.

Parrinder, Patrick, "Pastiche and After," *CamR* 89A, No. 2156 (Nov. 4, 1967): 66-7.

Servotte, Herman, "A Note on the Formal Characteristics of Angus Wilson's NO LAUGHING MATTER," *ER* 50 (1969): 58-64.

Sudrann, Jean, "The Lion and the Unicorn: Angus Wilson's Triumphant Tragedy," *SNNTS* 3 (Winter, 1971): 390-400.

Trickett, Rachel, "Recent Novels: Craftmanship in Violence and Sex," *YR* 57 (Spring, 1968): 446-8.

THE OLD MEN AT THE ZOO

Bergonzi, B., *Situation of the Novel,* 154-7.

Cox, C. B., *Free Spirit,* 155-7.

Faulkner, P., *Angus Wilson,* 109-28.

Gindin, James, "Angus Wilson's Nationalism," *Postwar British Fiction,* 159-64.

_____, "The Fable Breaks Down," *WSCL* 8 (Winter, 1967): 8-10.

Grandsen, K. W., *Angus Wilson,* 23-5.

Halio, J. L., *Angus Wilson,* 84-92.

_____, in *Crit* 5, i (Spring-Summer, 1962): 77-82.

Lindberg, Margaret, "Angus Wilson: THE OLD MEN AT THE ZOO as Allegory," *IEY* 14 (Fall, 1969): 44-8.

Malin, Irving, "Metaphors of Enclosure: Angus Wilson's THE OLD MEN AT THE ZOO," in *Old Lines, New Forces,* 1-11.

McDowell, Frederick P. W., "'The Devious Involutions of Human Character and Emotions': Reflections on Some Recent British Novels," *WSCL* 4, iii (Autumn, 1963): 359-62.

McSweeney, Kerry, "The Novels of Angus Wilson," *WascanaR* 12, ii (Fall, 1978): 11-14.

Pritchett, V. S., "Bad-Hearted Britain," *NStat* (Sept. 29, 1961): 429-30.

Rippier, J. S., *Some Postwar English Novelists,* 37-42.

SETTING THE WORLD ON FIRE

Haule, James M., "SETTING THE WORLD ON FIRE: Angus Wilson and the Problem of Evil," *TCL* 18, iv (Winter, 1982): 453-66.

BIBLIOGRAPHY

Halio, J. L., *Angus Wilson,* 117-20.

WILSON, COLIN, 1931-

GENERAL

Campion, S., *World of Colin Wilson.*

"A Conversation with Colin Wilson," *OntarioR* 4 (1976): 7-15.

Dillard, R. H. W., "Toward an Existential Realism: The Novels of Colin Wilson," *HC* 4, iv (Oct., 1967): 1-12. Also in Dillard, R. H., George Garrett, and John R. Moore, eds., *Sounder Few,* 283-96.

Weigel, J. A., *Colin Wilson.*

ADRIFT IN SOHO

Gindin, J., *Postwar British Fiction,* 222-25.

Weigel, J. A., *Colin Wilson,* 71-4.

THE BLACK ROOM

Weigel, J. A., *Colin Wilson,* 104-7.

THE GLASS CAGE

Curran, Stuart, "'Detecting' the Existential Blake," *BS* 2, i (Fall, 1969): 67-76.

Weigel, J. A., *Colin Wilson,* 87-90.

THE GOD OF THE LABYRINTH

Weigel, J. A., *Colin Wilson,* 101-4.

THE KILLER (See LINGARD)

LINGARD

Weigel, J. A., *Colin Wilson*, 98-101.

THE MIND PARASITES

Weigel, J. A., *Colin Wilson*, 90-4.

NECESSARY DOUBT

Weigel, J. A., *Colin Wilson*, 83-6.

THE PHILOSOPHER'S STONE

Weigel, J. A., *Colin Wilson*, 94-8.

RITUAL IN THE DARK

Campion, S., *World of Colin Wilson*, 178-86.
Gindin, J., *Postwar British Fiction*, 222-25.
Weigel, J. A., *Colin Wilson*, 66-71.

THE SEX DIARY OF GERARD SORME (MAN WITHOUT A SHADOW)

Weigel, J. A., *Colin Wilson*, 79-82.

THE VIOLENT WORLD OF HUGH GREENE

Campion, S., *World of Colin Wilson*, 237-8.
Weigel, J. A., *Colin Wilson*, 74-9.

WORLD OF VIOLENCE (See THE VIOLENT WORLD OF HUGH GREENE)

WILSON, ETHEL, 1888-1980

GENERAL

Birbalsingh, Frank, "Ethel Wilson: Innocent Traveller," *CanL* 49 (Summer, 1971): 35-46. Also, excerpted, in Ferres, John H., and Martin Tucker, eds., *Modern Commonwealth Literature: A Library of Literary Criticism*, N.Y.: Ungar, 1979, 375-6.

Collins, Alexandra, "Who Shall Inherit the Earth? Ethel Wilson's Debt to Wharton, Glasgow, Cather, and Ostenso," in McMullen, L., ed., *Ethel Wilson Symposium*, 61-72.

Comeau, Paul, "Ethel Wilson's Characters," *SCL* 6, i (1981): 24-38.

Gelfant, Blanche, "The Hidden Mines in Ethel Wilson's Landscapes (or, An American Cat among the Falcons)," *CanL* 93 (Summer, 1982): 4-23. Also in McMullen, L., ed., *Ethel Wilson Symposium*, 119-39.

Hinchcliffe, P(eter) M., "'To Keep the Memory of a Worthy Friend': Ethel Wilson as an Elegist," *JCF* 2, ii (Spring, 1973): 62-7.

Keith, W. J., "Overview: Ethel Wilson, Providence, and the Vocabulary of Vision," in McMullen, L., ed., *Ethel Wilson Symposium*, 105-17.

Livesay, Dorothy, "Two Women Novelists of Canada's West," *RNL* 7 (1976): 127-32.

Mitchell, Beverley, "The Interested Traveller: Major Themes in the Fiction of Ethel Wilson," *DAI* 37 (1977): 4348A.

_____, "'On the *Other* Side of the Mountains': The Westering Experience in the Fiction of Ethel Wilson," in Lee, L. L., and M. Lewis, eds., *Women, Women Writers, and the West*, 219-29.

New, William H., "The 'Genius' of Place and Time: The Fiction of Ethel Wilson," *JCanStud* 3 (Nov., 1968): 39-48. Also in New, W. H., *Articulating West*, 68-82.

Pacey, D., *Ethel Wilson*.

Pacey, Desmond, "The Innocent Eye: The Art of Ethel Wilson," *QQ* 61 (Spring, 1954): 42-52. Also in Pacey, D., *Essays in Canadian Criticism 1938-1968*, Toronto: Ryerson, 1969, 90-100.

Smyth, Donna E., "Strong Women in the Web: Women's Work and Community in Ethel Wilson's Fiction," in McMullen, L., ed., *Ethel Wilson Symposium*, 87-95.

Sonthoff, Helen, "Companion in a Difficult Country," in McMullen, L., ed., *Ethel Wilson Symposium*, 97-104.

_____, "The Novels of Ethel Wilson," *CanL* 26 (Autumn, 1965): 33-42. Also in *Contemporary Literary Criticism*, Vol. 8, Detroit: Gale, 1980, 606-8.

Stouck, David, "Ethel Wilson's Novels," *CanL* 74 (Autumn, 1977): 74-88.

Urbas, Jeanette, "Equations and Flutes," *JCF* 1, ii (Spring, 1972): 69-73.

_____, "The Perquisites of Love," *CanL* 59 (Winter, 1974): 6-15. Also in Woodcock, G., ed., *Canadian Novel in the Twentieth Century*, 57-66.

Watters, R. E., "Ethel Wilson, the Experienced Traveller," *BCLQ* 21, iv (Apr., 1958): 21-7.

Wilson, Ethel, "A Cat Among the Falcons," *CANL* 2 (Autumn, 1959): 10-19.

_____, "The Bridge or the Stockehold? Views of the Novelist's Art," *CanL* 5 (Summer, 1960): 43-7.

Woodcock, George, "Ethel Wilson," *CFM* 15 (Autumn, 1974): 44-9. Also in Woodcock, G., *The World of Canadian Writing: Critiques and Recollections*, Vancouver: Douglas & McIntyre, 1980, 120-6.

_____, "Innocence and Solitude: The Fiction of Ethel Wilson," in Moss, J., ed., *Canadian Novel. v. 3 Modern Times*, 166-91.

THE EQUATIONS OF LOVE

Pacey, D., *Ethel Wilson*, 96-135.

Urbas, Jeanette, "Equations and Flutes," *JCF* 1, ii (Fall, 1972): 69-73. [Comparison with Gabrielle Roy's THE TIN FLUTE.]

HETTY DORVAL

Dahlie, H., "The International Theme in Canadian Literature," in Rutherford, A., ed., *Common Wealth*, 182-4.

Davies, Barry, "Lamia: The Allegorical Nature of HETTY DORVAL," *SCL* 1, i (Winter, 1976): 137-40.

Gottlieb, Lois, and Wendy Keitner, "Mothers and Daughters in Four Recent Canadian Novels," *Sphinx* 4 (1975): 21-34.

MacDonald, R. D., "Serious Whimsey," *CanL* 63 (Winter, 1975): 40-51.

McLay, Catherine, "Ethel Wilson's Lost Lady: HETTY DORVAL and Willa Cather," *JCF* 33 (1981-82): 94-106.

Mitchell, Beverley, "In Defense of HETTY DORVAL," *SCL* 1, i (Winter, 1976): 26-48.

_____, "The Right Word in the Right Place: Literary Techniques in the Fiction of Ethel Wilson," in McMullen, L., ed., *Ethel Wilson Symposium*, 73-85.

Pacey, D., *Ethel Wilson*, 45-62.

_____, "Ethel Wilson's First Novel," *CanL* 29 (Summer, 1966): 43-5.

Urbas, Jeanette, "The Perquisites of Love," *CanL* 59 (Winter, 1974). Also in Woodcock, G., ed., *Canadian Literature in the Twentieth Century*, 57-9.

Woodcock, George, "Innocence and Solitude: The Fictions of Ethel Wilson," in Moss, J., ed., *Canadian Novel*, Vol. 3, *Modern Times*, 172-7.

THE INNOCENT TRAVELLER

Howard, Irene, "Shockable and Unshockable Methodists in THE INNOCENT TRAVELLER," *ECW* 23 (Spring, 1982): 107-34.

Mitchell, Beverley, "'On the *Other* Side of the Mountains': The Westering Experience in the Fiction of Ethel Wilson," in Lee, L. L., and M. Lewis, eds., *Women, Women Writers, and the West*, 221-3.

New, William H., "The Irony of Order: Ethel Wilson's THE INNOCENT TRAVELLER," *Crit* 10, iii (1968): 22-30. Also in New, W. H., *Articulating West*, 83-92.

Pacey, D., *Ethel Wilson*, 63-95.

Urbas, Jeanette, "The Perquisites of Love," *CanL* 59 (Winter, 1974). Also in Woodcock, G., ed., *Canadian Literature in the Twentieth Century*, 60-2.

Woodcock, George, "Innocence and Solitude: The Fictions of Ethel Wilson," in Moss, J., ed., *Canadian Novel*, Vol. 3, *Modern Times*, 177-81.

LILLY'S STORY (See also THE EQUATIONS OF LOVE)

Pacey, D., *Ethel Wilson*, 96-9, 118-35.

Woodcock, George, "Innocence and Solitude: The Fiction of Ethel Wilson," in Moss, J., ed., *Canadian Novel*, Vol. 3, *Modern Times*, 183-6.

LOVE AND SALT WATER

Pacey, D., *Ethel Wilson*, 159-73.

SWAMP ANGEL

McMullen, Lorraine, "The Divided Self," *AtlantisA* 5 (Spring, 1980): 54-5.

Moss, J., *Patterns of Isolation*, 127-32, 139-48.

Pacey, D., *Ethel Wilson*, 136-58.

Pacey, Desmond, "Introduction," in SWAMP ANGEL (New Canadian Library), Toronto: McClelland & Stewart, 1962, 5-10.

Smyth, Donna E., "Maggie Lake: The Vision of Female Power in SWAMP ANGEL," in Moss, J., ed., *Canadian Novel*, v. 3 *Modern Times*, 186-9.

TUESDAY AND WEDNESDAY

Mitchell, Beverley, "Ulysses in Vancouver: A Critical Approach to Ethel Wilson's TUESDAY AND WEDNESDAY," *AtlantisA* 4 (Fall, 1978): 110-22.

Pacey, D., *Ethel Wilson*, 96-118.

Woodcock, George, "Innocence and Solitude: The Fictions of Ethel Wilson," in Moss, J., ed., *Canadian Novel* Vol. 3, *Modern Times*, 181-3.

BIBLIOGRAPHY

McComb, Bonnie M., "Ethel Wilson: A Bibliography 1919-1977, Part I," *WCR* 14, i (June, 1979): 38-43; ii (Oct., 1979): 49-57; iii (Jan., 1980): 58-64; 15, i (June, 1980): 67-72.

Pacey, D., *Ethel Wilson*, 185-9.

WISEMAN, ADELE, 1928-

GENERAL

Belkin, Roslyn, "The Consciousness of a Jewish Artist: An Interview with Adele Wiseman," *JCF* 31-32 (1981): 148-76.

Bennett, Donna, "Adele Wiseman," 69-76 in Heath, Jeffrey, M., ed., *Profiles in Canadian Literature 4*, Toronto: Dundurn, 1982.

Morley, Patricia, "Artist at Play: Wiseman's Theory of Creativity," *Atlantis* 6, i (1980): 104-9.

THE CRACKPOT

Morley, Patricia, "Engel, Wiseman, Lawrence: Women Writers, Women's Lives," *WLWE* 17, i (Apr., 1978): 158-60.

THE SACRIFICE

Greenstein, Michael, "Movement and Vision in THE SACRIFICE," *CanL* 80 (1979): 23-36.

Jones, D. G., *Butterfly on Rock*, 147-53.

Loverso, Marco P., "The Circle of Conversation in THE SACRIFICE," *SCL* 7, ii (1982): 168-83.

McCourt, E. A., *Canadian West in Fiction*, 82-4.

Moss, J., *Patterns of Isolation*, 95-104.

Mullins, Stanley G., "Traditional Symbolism in Adele Wiseman's THE SACRIFICE," *Culture* 19 (1958): 287-97.

Rosenthal, Hélène, "Spiritual Ecology: Adele Wiseman's THE SACRIFICE," in Stephens, D. G., ed., *Writers of the Prairies*, 77-88.

WODEHOUSE, P(ELHAM) G(RENVILLE), 1881-1975

GENERAL

Aldridge, John W., "P. G., Wodehouse: The Lesson of the Young Master," in *New World Writing*, 13th Mentor Selection, N.Y.: New American Library, 1958, 181-92.

Anon., "Profession of Letters," *TLS* (Oct. 20, 1966): 958.

Asimov, Isaac, "Wodehouse on Crime," in Heineman, J. H., and D. R. Bensen, eds., *P. G. Wodehouse*, 63-7.

Bowen, Barbara C., "Rabelais and P. G. Wodehouse: Two Comic Worlds," *ECr* 16 iv (Winter, 1976): 63-77.

Cannadine, David, "Another 'Last Victorian': P. G. Wodehouse and His World," *SAQ* 77, iv (Autumn, 1978): 470-91.

Carlson, Richard S., "An Analysis of P. G. Wodehouse's Team of Bertie Wooster and Jeeves," *DAI* 34 (1973): 1233A-34A.

Cazalet-Keir, T., ed., *Homage to P. G. Wodehouse*.

Clarke, Gerald, "The Art of Fiction 60: P. G. Wodehouse," *ParisR* 16 (Winter, 1975): 149-71.

Edwards, Owen D., *P. G. Wodehouse*.

French, R. B. D., *P. G. Wodehouse*.

Garrard, John, "New York," in Heineman, J. H., and D. R. Bensen, eds., *P. G. Wodehouse*, 81-4.

_____, "Wodehouse and the Literary Scene," in Heineman, J. H., and D. R. Bensen, eds., *P. G. Wodehouse*, 49-52.

_____, "Wodehouse on Golf," in Heineman, J. H., and D. R. Bensen, Eds., *P. G. Wodehouse*, 70-3.

Garrard, Margaret, "Cats and Dogs," in Heineman, J. H., and D. R. Bensen, eds., *P. G. Wodehouse*, 77-81.

Green, Benny, *P. G. Wodehouse: A Literary Biography*, London: Pavilion; Joseph; New York: Rutledge, 1981.

_____, "The World of Wodehouse," *Spectator* 227 (1971): 549-50.

Hall, R. A., Jr., *Comic Style of P. G. Wodehouse*.

Hall, Robert A., Jr., "Incongruity and Stylistic Rhythm in P. G. Wodehouse," *AION-SG* 11 (1968): 135-44.

_____, "P. G. Wodehouse and the English Language," *AION-SG* 7 (1964): 103-21.

_____, *P. G. Wodehouse and the "Saga Habit"* Ithaca, N. Y.: Linguistica, 1972.

_____, "Timelessness and Contemporaneity in P. G. Wodehouse," *Plum Lines* Supp. 3, v (Sept., 1982): 1-4. [Not seen.]

Heineman, J. H., and D. R. Bensen, eds., *P. G. Wodehouse*.

Jaggard, Geoffrey, *Blandings the Blest and the Blue Blood: A Companion to the Blandings Castle Saga of P. G. Wodehouse, with a Complete Wodehouse Peerage, Baronetage and Knightage*, London: Macdonald, 1968.

_____, *Wooster's World*, London: Macdonald, 1967.

Jeffrey, Linda, "The Rummy Affair of P. G., Wodehouse and Sherlock Holmes," *BakSJ* 24, iv (Dec., 1974): 200-3. [Sherlockian allusions.]

Medcalf, Stephen, "The Innocence of P. G. Wodehouse," in Josipovici, G., ed., *Modern English Novel*, 186-205.

Morris, J. H. C., with A. D. Macintyre, *Thank You, Wodehouse*.

Murphy, N.T.P., *In Search of Blandings*.

Olney, Clarke, "Wodehouse and the Poets," *GaR* 16 (Winter, 1962): 392-99.

Orwell, George, "In Defence of P. G. Wodehhouse," *Dickens, Dali and Others: Studies in Popular Culture*, N.Y.: Reynal & Hitchcock, 1946, 222-43.

Robinson, Robert, "Of Aunts and Drones," *Listener* 92 (Oct. 17, 1974): 496. [Interview.]

Sastri, C.L.R., "P. G. Wodehouse: An Appreciation," *Triveni* 43, ii (July-Sept., 1974): 22-5.

Sedlmajerova, Helena, "Verbal Humour in the Works of P. G. Wodehouse," *Prague Studies in English* 17 (1981): 85-92.

Steinhardt, N., "P. G. Wodehouse," *VR* 28, viii (1975): 63-4. [Not seen.]

Thody, Philip, tr., "Jeeves, Dostoievski and the Double Paradox," *ULR* 14, i (May, 1971): 319-31.

Usborne, Richard, "Native Woodnotes Wild," in Heineman, J. H.; and D. R. Bensen, eds., *P. G. Wodehouse*, 73-7.

_____, "Valley Fields," in Heineman, J. H., and D. R. Bensen, eds., *P. G. Wodehouse*, 67-9.

_____, *Wodehouse at Work to the End*.

_____, *Wodehouse Companion*.

Voorhees, Richard J., "The Jolly Old World of P. G. Wodehouse," *SAQ* 61, ii (Spring, 1962): 213-32.

_____, *P. G. Wodehouse*.

_____, "Wodehouse at the Top of His Form," *UWR* 16, i (Fall-Winter, 1981): 13-25.

Wallace, Malcolm T., "The Wodehouse World I: Classical Echoes," *Cithara* 12, ii (May, 1973): 41-57.

West, Robert H., "The High Art of Quality Frivolity," *SAB* 37, i (Jan., 1972): 12-19.

Wood, Ann E., "Where Is Blandings Castle?" in Heineman, J. H., and D. R. Bensen, eds., *P. G. Wodehouse*, 84-8.

AUNTS AREN'T GENTLEMEN

Usborne, Richard, "Fair Weather England," *TLS* (Dec. 27, 1975): 1455.

LEAVE IT TO PSMITH

Hall, Robert A., Jr., "The Ending of P. G. Wodehouse's LEAVE IT TO PSMITH," *N&Q* 22, v (May, 1975): 205-6.

LOVE AMONG THE CHICKENS

Voorhees, R. J., *P. G. Wodehouse*, 66-72.

THE LUCK OF BODKINS

Hall, Robert A., Jr., "Incongruity and Stylistic Rhythm in P. G. Wodehouse," *AION-SG* 11 (1968): 135-44.

MIKE AND PSMITH

Voorhees, R. J., *P. G. Wodehouse*, 72-4.

PICCADILLY JIM

Dold, B. E. *Edwardian Fall-Out*, 33-63.

PSMITH IN THE CITY

Dold, B. E., *Edwardian Fall-Out*, 65-82.
Voorhees, R. J., *P. G. Wodehouse*, 74-7.

PSMITH JOURNALIST

Dold, B. E., *Edwardian Fall-Out*, 97-110.
Voorhees, R. J., *P. G. Wodehouse*, 77-82.

THANK YOU, JEEVES

Smith, M. A. Sharwood, "The Very Irreverent P. G. Wodehouse: A Study of THANK YOU, JEEVES," *DQR* 8, iii (1978): 203-22.

BIBLIOGRAPHY

McIlvaine, Eileen, "A Bibliography of P. G. Wodehouse," in Heineman, J. H., and D. R. Bensen, eds., *P. G. Wodehouse*, 91-197.

WOLFE, BERNARD, 1915-

GENERAL

Galloway, David, "An Erratic Geography: The Novels of Bernard Wolfe," *Crit* 7, i (Spring, 1964): 75-86.

Geduld, C., *Bernard Wolfe*.

COME ON OUT, DADDY

Galloway, David, "An Erratic Geography: The Novels of Bernard Wolfe," *Crit* 7, i (Spring, 1964): 84-6.

Geduld, C., *Bernard Wolfe*, 126-38.

THE GREAT PRINCE DIED

Geduld, C., *Bernard Wolfe*, 84-109.
Kazin, A., *Contemporaries*, 411-15.

IN DEEP

Geduld, C., *Bernard Wolfe*, 75-83.

THE LATE RISERS

Geduld, C., *Bernard Wolfe*, 110-19.

LIMBO

Geduld, C., *Bernard Wolfe*, 37-74.
Samuelson, David N., "LIMBO: The Great American Dystopia," *Extrapolation* 19 (Dec., 1977): 76-87.

THE MAGIC OF THEIR SINGING

Geduld, C., *Bernard Wolfe*, 119-25.

REALLY THE BLUES

Geduld, C., *Bernard Wolfe*, 19-38.

BIBLIOGRAPHY

Geduld, C., *Bernard Wolfe*, 145-52.

WOLFERT, IRA, 1908-

GENERAL

Aldridge, J. W., "Ira Wolfert: The Failure of a Form," *In Search of Heresy*, 177-85.

MARRIED MEN

Aldridge, J. W., "Ira Wolfert: The Failure of a Form," *In Search of Heresy*, 179-85.

TUCKER'S PEOPLE

Eisinger, Chester E., in Madden, D., ed., *Proletarian Writers of the Thirties*, 177-82.

WOOLF, DOUGLAS, 1922-

GENERAL

Abbott, Keith, "16 Paragraphs on Douglas Woolf," *RCF* 2, i (Spring, 1982): 88-9.
Mottram, Eric, "Douglas Woolf's Escapes from Enclosure," *RCF* 2, i (Spring, 1982): 66-81.
O'Brien, John, "'All Things Considered' in Douglas Woolf," *RCF* 2, i (Spring, 1982): 113-19.
Phelps, Donald, "Nets and Neighbors," *RCF* 2, i (Spring, 1982): 60-5.
Stonehill, Brian, "Douglas Woolf's Ideal Fictions," *RCF* 2, i (Spring, 1982): 96-100.

FADE OUT

Dorn, Edward, "The New Frontier," *RCF* 2, i (Spring, 1982): 90-6.

THE HYPOCRITIC DAYS

Creeley, Robert, "First Prize," *RCF* 2, i (Spring, 1982): 81-2.
Dorn, Edward, "The New Frontier," *RCF* 2, i (Spring, 1982): 90-6.

WALL TO WALL

Dorn, Edward, "The New Frontier," *RCF* 2, i (Spring, 1982): 90-6.

YA! AND JOHN-JUAN

Dunlap, Lowell, "YA! YA! YA! YA! YA! YA! YA! YA!," *RCF* 2, i (Spring, 1982): 65-6.
Emmett, Paul, "The Great Mother in the Fiction of Douglas Woolf: Ma in YA!," *RCF* 2, i (Spring, 1982): 101-13.

WOUK, HERMAN, 1915-

GENERAL

Aldridge, J. W., *In Search of Heresy*, 123-4.
Carpenter, Frederic I., "Herman Wouk," *CE* 17 (Jan., 1956): 211-15. Also in *EJ* 45 (1956): 1-6+.
Geismar, Maxwell, "The Age of Wouk," *Nation* 181 (Nov. 5, 1955): 399-400. Also in Nation (Periodical). *View of the Nation*, 37-40. Also in Geismar, M., *American Moderns*, 41-5.
Hudson, William S., "Herman Wouk: A Biographical and Critical Study," *DAI* 30 (1970): 4987A.
McElderry, B. R., Jr., "The Conservative as Novelist: Herman Wouk," *ArQ* 15 (Summer, 1959): 128-36.
Scott, Otto J., "Wouk's American Epos," *ChronC* 3, iii (1979): 11-16.

THE CAINE MUTINY

Bierstadt, Robert, "The Tergiversation of Herman Wouk (THE CAINE MUTINY)," in MacIver, R. M., ed., *Great Moral Dilemmas in Literature Past and Present*, N.Y.: Institute for Religious and Social Studies, 1956, 1-14.
Browne, James R., "Distortion in THE CAINE MUTINY," *CE* 17 (Jan., 1956): 216-18.
Carpenter, Frederic I., "Herman Wouk," *CE* 17 (Jan., 1956): 212-14. Also in *EJ* 45 (1956): 3-5.
Eisinger, C., E., *Fiction of the Forties*, 46-7.
Frankel, Theodore, "The Anatomy of a Bestseller: Second Thoughts on THE CAINE MUTINY," *WHR* 9 (Autumn, 1955): 333-9.
Fuller, Edmund, *Man in Modern Fiction: Some Minority Opinions on Contemporary American Writing*, N.Y.: Random House, 1958, 134-46.
Hoffman, F. J., *Mortal No*, 242-4.
Jones, P., *War and the Novelist*, 73-9.
McCormick, J., *Catastrophe and Imagination*, 222-26.
McElderry, B. R., Jr., "The Conservative as Novelist: Herman Wouk," *ArQ* 15 (Summer, 1959): 128-32.

Metrauz, Rhoda, "THE CAINE MUTINY," *Explor.* 5 (1956): 36-55.

Prescott, O., *In My Opinion*, 163-4.

Stuckey, W. J., *Pulitzer Prize Novels*, 158-64.

Swados, Harvey, "THE CAINE MUTINY," in Brossard, Chandler, ed., *The Scene Before You*, N.Y.: Rinehart, 1955, 138-46.

————, "Popular Taste and THE CAINE MUTINY," *PR* 20 (Mar.-Apr., 1953): 248-56. Also in Swados, H., *Radical's America*, 235-44.

Whipple, William, "Justice—The Phantom of the Literary Trail," *BSTCF* 2 (Winter, 1961-62): 35-7.

Whyte, William, *The Organization Man*, N.Y.: Simon & Schuster, 1956, 243-8.

Waldmeir, J. J., *American Novels of the Second World War*, 124-30.

MARJORIE MORNINGSTAR

Carpenter, Frederic I., "Herman Wouk," *CE* 17 (Jan., 1956): 214-15. Also in *EJ* 45 (Jan., 1956): 5-6.

Cohen, Joseph, "Wouk's Morningstar and Hemingway's Sun," *SAQ* 58 (Spring, 1959): 213-24.

Fiedler, L., *Love and Death in the American Novel*, 248-53.

Fitch, Robert E., "The Bourgeois and the Bohemian," *AR* 16 (1956): 131-45.

Geismar, Maxwell, "The Age of Wouk," *Nation* 181 (Nov. 5, 1955): 399-400. Also in Geismar, M., *American Moderns*, 41-5.

————, in *NYTBR* (Sept. 4, 1955): 1. Also in Geismar, M., *American Moderns*, 38-40.

Guttmann, A., *Jewish Writer in America*, 121-3.

Hofstadter, Beatrice K., "Popular Culture and the Romantic Heroine," *ASch* 30 (Winter, 1960-61): 114-16.

McElderry, B. R., Jr., "The Conservative as Novelist: Herman Wouk," *ArQ* 15 (Summer, 1959): 132-5.

Rosenfeld, Isaac, "For God and Suburbs," *PR* 22 (Fall, 1955): 565-9. Also in Rosenfeld, I., *Age of Enormity*, 309-14.

WAR AND REMEMBRANCE

Scott, Otto J., "Wouk's American Epos," *ChronC* 3, iii (1979): 13-16.

THE WINDS OF WAR

Bolton, Richard R., "THE WINDS OF WAR and Wouk's Wish for the World," *MQ* 16, iv (Summer, 1975): 389-408.

Scott, Otto J., "Wouk's American Epos," *ChronC* 3, iii (1979): 13-16.

YOUNGBLOOD HAWKE

Hyman, S. E., "Some Questions About Herman Wouk," *Standards*, 68-72.

WRIGHT, CHARLES STEVENSON, 1932-

GENERAL

O'Brien, J., ed., *Interviews with Black Writers*, 245-57.

ABSOLUTELY NOTHING TO GET ALARMED ABOUT

Lee, A. Robert, "Making New: Styles of Innovation in the Contemporary Black American Novel," in Lee, A. R., ed., *Black Fiction*, 241-3.

THE MESSENGER

Lee, A. Robert, "Making New: Styles of Innovation in the Contemporary Black American Novel," in Lee, A. R., ed., *Black Fiction*, 239-41.

Schraufnagel, N., *From Apology to Protest*, 122-3.

THE WIG

Foster, Francis S., "Charles Wright: Black Black Humorist," *CLAJ* 15, i (Sept., 1971): 44-53.

Kreutzer, Eberhard, "Dark Ghetto Fantasy and the Great Society: Charles Wright's THE WIG," in Bruck, P., and W. Karrer, eds., *Afro-American Novel Since 1960*, 145-65.

Lee, A. Robert, "Making New: Styles of Innovation in the Contemporary Black American Novel," in Lee, A. R., ed., *Black Fiction*, 241.

Schulz, M. F., *Black Humor Fiction of the Sixties*, 97-101, 108-14, 151.

Sedlack, Robert P., "Jousting with Rats: Charles Wright's THE WIG," *SNL* 7, i (Fall, 1969): 37-9.

WRIGHT, RICHARD, 1908-1960

GENERAL

Aaron, Daniel, "Richard Wright and the Communist Party," *NewL* 38, ii (Winter, 1971): 170-81.

Avery, E. G., *Rebels and Victims*.

Bakish, D., *Richard Wright*.

————, "Richard Wright: Dreams and the Ambiguity of Existence," *DAI* 32 (1972): 6412A.

Baldwin, James, "Richard Wright," *Encounter* 16 (Apr., 1961): 58-60. Also as "Alas, Poor Richard," [Part 2. "The Exile] in Baldwin, J., *Nobody Knows My Name*, N. Y.: Dial Pr., 1961, 190-99.

Barnette, William J., "Redeemed Time: The Sacramental Vision and Implicit Covenant in the Major Fiction of Richard Wright," *DAI* 42, ix (Mar., 1982): 3997A.

Berghahn, M., *Images of Africa in Black American Literature*, 154-67.

Blake, N. M., *Novelist's America*, 226-34.

Bone, R., *Richard Wright*.

Bontemps, Arna, in Griffin, W., ed., *Literature in the Modern World*, 115-19.

Brayton, Bradford C., Jr., "Richard Wright's Quest for Identity," *DAI* 38 (1977): 1489A.

Brignano, R. C., *Richard Wright*.

————, "Richard Wright: The Major Themes, Ideas, and Attitudes in His Works," *DA* 28 (1967): 667A-8A.

Britt, David, "The Image of the White Man in the Fiction of Langston Hughes, Richard Wright, James Baldwin and Ralph Ellison," *DA* 29 (1968): 1532A.

Brooks, Mary Ellen, "Behind Richard Wright's 'Artistic Conscience'," *L&I* 13 (1972): 21-30.

Brown, Cecil, "Richard Wright's Complexes and Black Writing Today," *Negro Digest*, 18 (Dec., 1968): 78-82.

Campbell, Finley C., "Prophet of the Storm: Richard Wright and the Radical Tradition," *Phylon* 38 (Mar., 1977): 9-23.

Cauley, Anne O., "A Definition of Freedom in the Fiction of Richard Wright," *CLAJ* 19, iii (Mar., 1976): 327-46.

Charney, Maurice, "James Baldwin's Quarrel with Richard Wright," *AQ* 15 (Spring, 1963): 65-75. Also in Gibson, D. E., ed., *Five Black Writers*, 243-53.

Ciner, Elizabeth J., "The Problem of Freedom in Richard Wright's Fiction," *DAI* 41, xi (May, 1981): 4711A-12A.

Cobb, Nina K., "Richard Wright: Exile and Existentialism," *Phylon* 40 (Dec., 1979): 362-74.

_____, "Richard Wright: Individualism Reconsidered," *CLAJ* 21 (Mar., 1978): 335-54.

Conn, Annette L., "Richard Wright: A Marxist Approach to His Early Work (1930-1942)," *DAI* 39 (1978): 2270A.

Daniel, Neil, "Chestnutt, Wright, and Jones: Some Uses of Stereotypes," *CCTE* 35 (1970): 16-21. [Not seen.]

Delpech, Jeanine, "An Interview with Native Son," *Crisis* 107 (Nov., 1950): 625-6, 678.

Dickstein, Morris, "Wright, Baldwin, Cleaver," *NewL* 38, ii (Dec., 1971): 117-24. Also in Ray, D., and R. M. Farnsworth, eds., *Richard Wright*, 183-90.

D'Itri, Patricia, "Richard Wright in Chicago: Three Novels That Represent a Black Spokesman's Quest for Self Identity," *SSMLN* 4 (1976): 26-33.

Ellison, Ralph, "The World and the Jug," *New Leader* 46 (Dec., 9, 1963): 22-6. (Rejoinder to Howe, I., "Black Boys and Native Sons." See below.). Expanded in Ellison, R., *Shadow and Act*, N.Y.: Random House, 1964, 197-43.

Evans, Charles J., "Richard Wright's Depictions of the Black Experience: A Study in Stereotypes," *DAI* 42, xii (June, 1982): 5121A.

Evans, James H., "The Problem of Religious Language in the Fiction of Richard Wright," *DAI* 41 (1980): 1100A-01A.

Fabre, Michel, "Black Cat and White Cat: Richard Wright's Debt to Edgar Allan Poe," *PoeS* 4 (June, 1971): 17-19.

_____, "Fantasies and Style in Richard Wright's Fiction," *NewL* 46, iii (Spring, 1980): 55-81.

_____, "Impressions of Richard Wright: An Interview with Simone De Beauvoir," *SBL* 1, iii (1970): 3-5.

_____, "Richard Wright and the French Existentialists," *MELUS* 5, ii (9178): 39-51.

_____, "Richard Wright: Beyond Naturalism?" in Hakutani, Y., and L. Fried, eds., *American Literary Naturalism*, 136-53.

_____, "Richard Wright's First Hundred Books," *CLAJ* 16 (1973): 458-74.

_____, "Richard Wright's Image of France," *Prospects* 3 (1977): 315-29.

Felgar, R., *Richard Wright*.

Feuser, Willfried, "The Men Who Lived Underground: Richard Wright and Ralph Ellison," in King, B., and K. Ogungbesan, eds., *Celebration of Black and African Writing*, 87-101.

Fishburn, K., *Richard Wright*.

Ford, Nick A., "Four Popular Negro Novelists," *Phylon* 15 (1954): 29-32.

_____, "The Ordeal of Richard Wright," *CE* 15 (Nov., 1953): 87-94. Also in Gibson, D. E., ed., *Five Black Writers*, 26-35.

_____, "Richard Wright, a Profile," *CJF* 21 (Fall, 1962): 26-30.

French, Warren, "The Lost Potential of Richard Wright," in Bigsby, C. W. E., ed., *Black American Writer*, Vol. 1, 125-42.

Gayle, Addison, Jr., "Behind Nihilism," *Negro Digest* 18 (Dec., 1968): 4-10.

Gibson, Donald B., "Richard Wright and the Tyranny of Convention," *CLAJ* 12, iv (June, 1969): 344-57.

_____, "Richard Wright: Aspects of His Afro-American Literary Relations," in Hakutani, Y., ed., *Critical Essays on Richard Wright*, 82-90.

Gounard, Jean-Francois, "Richard Wright as a Black American Writer in Exile," *CLAJ* 17 (Mar., 1974): 307-17.

Graham, Mary E., "Aesthetic and Ideological Radicalism in the 1930's: The Fiction of Richard Wright and Langston Hughes," *DAI* 38 (1978): 4167A.

Gray, Yohma, "An American Metaphor: The Novels of Richard Wright," *DA* 28 (1968): 4175A.

Gross, G. L., *Heroic Ideal in American Literature*, 148-57.

Hakutani, Y., ed., *Critical Essays on Richard Wright*.

Hand, Clifford, "The Struggle to Create Life in the Fiction of Richard Wright," in French, W., ed., *Thirties*, 81-7.

Haymon, Theresa L. D., "Alienation in the Life and Works of Richard Wright," *DAI* 37 (1976): 2871A.

Hill, Herbert, Ed., "Reflections on Richard Wright: A Symposium on an Exiled Native Son," *Anger and Beyond: The Negro Writer in the United States*, N.Y.: Harper & Row, 1966, 196-212. Also in Gibson, D. E., ed., *Five Black Writers*, 58-69.

Hoeveler, Diane L., "Oedipus Agonistes: Mothers and Sons in Richard Wright's Fiction," *BALF* 12, ii (Summer, 1978): 65-8.

Howe, Irving, "Black Boys and Native Sons," *Dissent* 10 (Autumn, 1963): 353-68. Also in Howe, I., *World More Attractive*, 98-122. Also in Gibson, D. E., ed., *Five Black Writers*, 256-8. Also, in part, in Hakutani, Y., ed., *Critical Essays on Richard Wright*, 39-47.

_____, "Reply to Ralph Ellison," *New Leader* 47 (Feb. 3, 1964): 12-14. [See Ellison above.]

Hyman, Stanley E., "Richard Wright Reappraised," *Atlantic* 225 (Mar., 1970): 127-32.

Isaacs, Harold R., "Five Writers and Their African Ancestors," *Phylon* 21 (Fall, 1960): 254-65.

Jackson, Blyden, "Richard Wright: Black Boy from America's Black Belt and Urban Ghettos," *CLAJ* 12, iv (June, 1969): 287-309. Also in Jackson, B., *Waiting Years*, 103-28. Also in Hakutani, Y., ed., *Critical Essays on Richard Wright*, 48-65.

_____, "Two Mississippi Writers: Wright and Faulkner," *UMSE* 15 (1978): 49-59.

Jarrett, Thomas D., "Recent Fiction by Negroes," *CE* 16 (Nov., 1954): 85-7.

Keady, Sylvia H., "Richard Wright's Women Characters and Inequality," *BALF* 10 (Winter, 1976): 124-8.

Kent, George E., "On the Future Study of Richard Wright," *CLAJ* 12, iv (June, 1969): 366-70.

_____, "Richard Wright: Blackness and the Adventure of Western Culture" *CLAJ* 12, iv (June, 1969): 322-43. Also in *BlackR* 1 (1971): 11-34. Also in Kent, George, *Blackness and the Adventure of Western Culture*, Chicago: Third World Pr., 1972, 76-97.

Kim, Kichung, "Wright, the Protest Novel, and Baldwin's Faith," *CLAJ* 17 (Mar., 1974): 387-96.

King, James R., "Richard Wright: His Life and Writings," *Negro Hist. Bulletin* 40 (Sept./Oct., 1977): 738-43.

Kinnamon, K., *Emergence of Richard Wright*.

_____, "The Pastoral Impulse in Richard Wright," *MASJ* 10, i (Spring, 1969): 41-7.

Kostelanetz, Richard, "The Politics of Unresolved Quests in the Novels of Richard Wright," *XUS* 8 (Spring, 1969): 31-64.

Lehan, R. T., *Dangerous Crossing*, 95-106.

Littlejohn, D., *Black on White*, 102-10.

Margolies, E., *Art of Richard Wright*.

Maxwell, Joan L. B., "Themes of Redemption in Two Major American Writers, Ralph Ellison and Richard Wright," *DAI* 37 (1976): 1549A.

McBride, Rebecca S., "Richard Wright's Use of His Reading of Fiction: 1927-1940," *DAI* 36 (1976): 8062A.

McCall, D., *Example of Richard Wright*.

McCarthy, Harold T., "Richard Wright: The Expatriate as Native Son," *AL* 44, i (Mar., 1972): 97-117. Also, revised, in McCarthy, H. T., *Expatriate Perspective*, 175-96.

Mebane, Mary E., "The Family in the Works of Charles W. Chesnutt and Selected Works of Richard Wright," *DAI* 34 (1974): 5982A-83A.

Medler, Edward A., "Howells, Wright and the Theme Social Protest: A Comparison Using Selected Works," *DAI* 37 (1977): 7823A.

Miller, James A., "The Struggle for Identity in the Major Works of Richard Wright," *DAI* 37 (1977): 5123A-24A.

Mills, Moylan C., "The Literary Reputation of Richard Wright," *DAI* 35 (1974): 2286A.

Mitra, B. K., "The Wright-Baldwin Controversy," *IJAS* 1, i (July, 1969): 101-5.

Moore, Jack B., "The View from the Broom Closet of the Regency Hyatt: Richard Wright as a Southern Writer," in Bogardus, R. F., and F. Hobson, eds., *Literature at the Barricades*, 126-43.

Nyang'aya, Elijah, "Richard Wright's Commitment," in Wanjala, C. L., ed., *Standpoints of African Literature*, 374-89.

Ogunyemi, Chikwenye O., "Richard Wright and Africa," *IFR* 7, i (1980): 1-5.

Olsen, Paul V., "The Message of Horror: Violence in the Works of Richard Wright," *DAI* 40 (1980): 5058A.

Orlova, R., "Richard Wright: Writer and Prophet," in Vroon, R., tr., *20th Century American Literature: A Soviet View*, 374-89.

Paliwal, G. D., "Richard Wright and the Negro," *RUSEng* 8 (1975): 72-83. [Not seen.]

Ray, D., and R. M. Farnsworth, eds., *Richard Wright*.

Reilly, John M., "Insight and Protest in the Works of Richard Wright," *DA* 28 (1968): 4185A-86A.

_____, ed., *Richard Wright: The Critical Reception*. (American Critical Tradition 6), N.Y.: Franklin, 1978.

_____, "Self-Portraits by Richard Wright," *ColQ* 20 (Summer, 1971): 31-45.

Riches, T. M., "Three Portraits of a Native Son," *Gulliver* 8 (1980): 129-37. [Not seen.]

Riley, Roberta, "'The High White Empty Building with Black Windows': Insights from the Work of Richard Wright," *Illinois School Jnl.* 55 (1975): 34-8. [Not seen.]

Rive, Richard, "Writing and the New Society," *Contrast* 12, iii (1979): 60-7.

Rubin, Steven J., "Richard Wright and Ralph Ellison: Black Existential Attitudes," *DAI* 30 (1969): 2041A.

Sanders, Ronald, "Richard Wright and the Sixties," *Midstream* 14 (Aug.-Sept., 1968): 28-40.

_____, "Richard Wright Then and Now," *Negro Digest* 18 (Dec., 1968): 83-98.

Scherr, Paul C., "Richard Wright: The Expatriate Pattern," *BARev* 2, i-ii (Spring-Summer, 1971): 81-90.

Scott, Nathan A., Jr., "The Dark and Haunted Tower of Richard Wright," *Comment* (Wayne State Un.) 7 (July, 1964): 93-9. Also, revised, in Gibson, D. E., ed., *Five Black Writers*, 12-25.

_____, "A Search for Beliefs: Fiction of Richard Wright," *UKCR* 23 (Autumn, 1956): 19-24.

Shreve, Darrell R., Jr., "The Fact of Blackness: Black Existentialism in Richard Wright's Major Fiction," *DAI* 37 (1976): 3630A.

Singh, Raman K., "Christian Heroes and Anti-Heroes in Richard Wright's Fiction," *NALF* 6 (Winter, 1972): 99, 104-31.

_____, "Marxism in Richard Wright's Fiction," *IJAS* 4, i-ii (June-Dec., 1974): 21-35.

_____, "Richard Wright: Novelist of Ideas," *DAI* 32 (1971): 3332A.

Sprandel, Katherine R., "Richard Wright's Hero: From Initiate to Victim to Rebel and Isolate (An Achronological Study)," *DAI* 34 (1974): 7786A-87A.

Standley, Fred L., "'...Farther and Farther Apart': Richard Wright and James Baldwin," in Hakutani, Y., ed., *Critical Essays on Richard Wright*, 91-103.

Starr, Alvin J., "The Influences of Stephen Crane, Theodore Dreiser, and James T. Farrell on the Fiction of Richard Wright," *DAI* 35 (1975): 61A-62A.

_____, "Richard Wright and the Communist Party: The James T. Farrell Factor," *CLAJ* 21 (Sept., 1977): 41-50.

Stephens, Martha, "Richard Wright's Fiction: A Reassessment," *GaR* 25 (Winter, 1971): 450-70.

Stepto, Robert B., "I Thought I Knew These People: Richard Wright and the Afro-American Literary Tradition," *MR* 18 (Autumn, 1977): 525-41. Also in Harper, M. S., and R. B. Stepto, eds., *Chant of Saints*, 195-211.

Terry, Esther, "The Long and Accomplished Dream of Richard Wright," *DAI* 35 (1974): 420A.

Traylor, Eleanor E. W., "Wright's Mythic and Grotesque Settings: Some Critical Approaches to the Fiction of Richard Wright," *DAI* 37 (1976): 1558A.

Walker, Ian, "Black Nightmare: The Fiction of Richard Wright," in Lee, A. R., ed., *Black Fiction*, 11-28.

Ward, Jerry W., Jr., "Richard Wright and His American Critics," *DAI* 40 (1979): 3305A.

Webb, Constance, *Richard Wright*.

_____, "What Next for Richard Wright?" *Phylon* 10, 2nd quar., (1949): 161-6.

Weiss, Adrian, "A Portrait of the Artist as a Black Boy," *BRMMLA* 28 (Dec., 1974): 93-101. [Not seen.]

White, Grace, "Wright's Memphis," *NewL* 38, ii (Winter, 1971): 105-16.

Williams, Sherley A., "Papa Dick and Sister Woman: Reflections on Women in the Fiction of Richard Wright," in Fleischmann, F., ed., *American Novelists Revisited*, 394-415.

Winslow, Henry F., "Richard Nathaniel Wright: Destroyer and Preserver (1908-1960)," *Crisis* 69 (Mar., 1962): 149-63, 187.

Zeitlow, Edward R., "Wright to Hansberry: The Evolution of Outlook in Four Negro Writers," *DA* 28 (1967): 701A.

LAWD TODAY

Bakish, D., *Richard Wright*, 13-16.

Brady, Owen, "Wright's LAWD TODAY: The American Dream Festering in the Sun," *CLAJ* 22 (Dec., 1978): 167-72.

Brignano, R. C., *Richard Wright*, 22-8, 71-7.

Felgar, R., *Richard Wright*, 54-62.

Fishburn, K., *Richard Wright's Hero*, 54-9, 185-8.

Ford, Nick A., in *CLAJ* 7 (Mar., 1964): 269-70.

French, W., *Social Novel at the End of an Era*, 171-3.

Graham, Don B., "LAWD TODAY and the Example of THE WASTE LAND," *CLAJ* 17 (Mar., 1974): 327-32.

Kent, George, "Richard Wright: Blackness and the Adventure of Western Culture," *CLAJ* 12 (June, 1969). Also in Kent, G., *Blackness and the Adventure of Western Culture*, 89-92.

Kinnanon, K., *Emergence of Richard Wright*, 75-82.

_____, "LAWD TODAY: Richard Wright's Apprentice Novel," *SBL* 2, ii (Summer, 1971): 16-18.

Leary, Lewis, "LAWD TODAY: Notes on Richard Wright's First/Last Novel," *CLAJ* 15 (June, 1972): 411-20. Also in Hakutani, Y., ed., *Critical Essays on Richard Wright*, 159-66.

McCall, D., *Example of Richard Wright*, 18-23.

Margolies, E., *Art of Richard Wright*, 90-103.

Reilly, John M., "LAWD TODAY: Richard Wright's Experiment in Naturalism," *SBL* 2, iii (Autumn, 1971): 14-17.

Sander, Reinhard W., "Black Literature and the African Dream: Richard Wright's LAWD TODAY," *Nsukka Studies in Afr. Lit.* 1, i (1978): 91-107.

Schraufnagel, N., *From Apology to Protest*, 168-9.

Timmerman, John, "Trust and Mistrust: The Role of the Black Woman in Three Works by Richard Wright," *STwC* 10 (Fall, 1972): 41-5.

Werner, C. H., *Paradoxical Resolutions*, 23-6.

THE LONG DREAM

Bakish, D., *Richard Wright*, 90-4.

Brignano, R. C., *Richard Wright*, 42-8.

Felgar, R., *Richard Wright*, 126-32.

Fishburn, K., *Richard Wright's Hero*, 12-27.

Gayle, A., Jr., *Way of the New World*, 173-9.

Hammalian, Linda B., "Richard Wright's Use of Epigraphs in THE LONG DREAM," *BALF* 10 (Winter, 1976): 120-3.

Hicks, Granville, "The Power of Richard Wright," *SatR* 41 (Oct. 18, 1958): 13, 65.

Joyce, Joyce A., "Richard Wright's THE LONG DREAM: An Aesthetic Extension of NATIVE SON," *DAI* 40 (1980): 4038A.

McCall, D., *Example of Richard Wright*, 15-61.

Margolies, E., *Art of Richard Wright*, 121-38.

Poster, William S., "Black Man's Burden," *New Leader* 42 (Aug. 31, 1959): 23-4.

Redding, J. Saunders, "The Way It Was," *NYTBR* (Oct. 26, 1958): 4, 38.

Schraufnagel, N., *From Apology to Protest*, 110-12.

Sprandel, Katherine, "THE LONG DREAM," *NewL* 38, ii (Dec., 1971): 88-96. Also in Ray, D., and R. M. Farnsworth, eds., *Richard Wright*, 174-82.

Vassilowitch, John, Jr., "Richard Wright's Clintonville: An Ironic Comment on the 'Talented Tenth'," *NMW* 12 (Winter, 1980): 63-6.

Webb, C., *Richard Wright*, 306-14.

NATIVE SON

Abcarian, R., ed., *Richard Wright's NATIVE SON*.

Algren, Nelson, "Remembering Richard Wright," *Nation* 192 (Jan. 28, 1961): 85. Also in Baker, H. A., Jr., ed., *Twentieth Century Interpretations of NATIVE SON*, 115-16.

Allen, W., *Modern Novel*, 155-8.

Amis, Lola J., "Richard Wright's NATIVE SON: Notes," *NALF* 8 (Fall, 1974): 240-3.

Baker, Houston A., Jr., *Long, Black Song*, Charlottesville: Un. Pr. of Virginia, 1972, 122-41. Also in Hakutani, Y., ed., *Critical Essays on Richard Wright*, 66-81.

_____, ed., *Twentieth Century Interpretations of NATIVE SON*.

_____, "Racial Wisdom and Richard Wright's NATIVE SON," *Long Black Song; Essays in Black American Literature and Culture*, Charlottesville: Un. of Virginia Pr., 1972, 122-41.

Bakish, D., *Richard Wright*, 30-40.

Baldwin, James, "Everybody's Protest Novel," *PR* 16 (June, 1949): 584-5. Also in Baldwin, J., *Notes of a Native Son*, Boston: Beacon Pr., 1955, 21-3.

_____, "Many Thousands Gone," *PR* 17 (Nov.-Dec., 1951): 665-80. Also in Baldwin, J., *Notes of a Native Son*, Boston: Beacon Pr., 1955, 24-45. Also in Gross, S. L., and J. E. Hardy, eds., *Images of the Negro in American Literature*, 233-48. Also in Abcarian, R., ed., *Richard Wright's NATIVE SON*, 123-35. Also in Baker, H. A., Jr., ed., *Twentieth Century Interpretations of NATIVE SON*, 49-62. Also in Hakutani, Y., ed., *Critical Essays on Richard Wright*, 107-19.

Baldwin, Richard E., "The Creative Vision of NATIVE SON," *MR* 14 (Spring, 1973): 378-90.

Baron, Dennis E., "The Syntax of Perception in Richard Wright's NATIVE SON," *Lang+S* 9 (Winter, 1976): 17-28.

Barthold, B. J., *Black Time*, 62-9.

Bayliss, John F., "NATIVE SON: Protest or Psychological Study?" *NALF* 1 (Fall, 1967): 5-6.

Blake, N. M., *Novelists' America*, 234-53.

Bluefarb, S., "Bigger Thomas: Escape into the Labyrinth," *Escape Motif in the American Novel*, 136-53.

Bolton, H. Philip, "The Role of Paranoia in Richard Wright's NATIVE SON," *KanQ* 7, iii (Summer, 1975): 111-24.

Bone, Robert A., "NATIVE SON: A Novel of Social Protest," in Bone, R. A., *Negro Novel in America*, 140-52. Also in Abcarian, R., ed., *Richard Wright's NATIVE SON*, 152-60. Also in Baker, H. A., Jr., ed., *Twentieth Century Interpretations of NATIVE SON*, 71-81.

_____, *Richard Wright*, 20-5.

Brewton, Butler E., "Richard Wright's Thematic Treatment of Women in UNCLE TOM'S CHILDREN and NATIVE SON," *DAI* 39 (1978): 2927A.

Brignano, R. C., *Richard Wright*, 28-39, 77-82, 144-8.

Britt, David, "NATIVE SON: Watershed of Negro Protest Literature," *NALF* 1 (Fall, 1967): 4-5.

Brivic, Sheldon, "Conflict of Values: Richard Wright's NATIVE SON," *Novel* 7 (Spring, 1974): 231-45.

Brown, Cecil, "Richard Wright's Complexes and Black Writing Today," *Negro Digest* 18 (Dec., 1968): 45-50, 78-82. Also in Abcarian, R., ed., *Richard Wright's NATIVE SON*, 167-77.

Brown, Lloyd W., "Stereotypes in Black and White: The Nature of Perception in Wright's NATIVE SON," *BARev* 1, ii (Fall, 1970): 35-44.

Brunette, Peter, "Two Wrights, One Wrong," in Peary, G., and R. Shatzkin, eds., *Modern American Novel and the Movies*, 131-42.

Bryant, Jerry H., "The Violence of NATIVE SON," *SoR* 17, ii (Apr., 1981): 303-19.

————, "Wright, Ellison, Baldwin: Exorcising the Demon," *Phylon* 37, ii (June, 1976): 174-88.

Burgum, Edwin B., "The Promise of Democracy in the Fiction of Richard Wright," *S&S* 7 (Sept., 1943): 338-52. Also in Burgum, E. B., *Novel and the World's Dilemma*, 223-40. Also in Abcarian, R., ed., *Richard Wright's NATIVE SON*, 111-22.

Clark, Beverly L., "Bigger Thomas' Name," *NDQ* 47, i (Winter, 1979): 80.

Corey, Stephen, "The Avengers in LIGHT IN AUGUST and NATIVE SON," *CLAJ* 23 (Dec., 1979): 200-12.

Cowley, Malcolm, "Richard Wright: The Case of Bigger Thomas," *NRep* 102 (Mar. 18, 1940): 382-3. Also in Cowley, M., *Think Back On Us*, 355-7. Also in Harrison, G. A., ed., *Critic as Artist*, 96-9. Also in Baker, H. A., Jr., ed., *Twentieth Century Interpretations of NATIVE SON*, 112-14.

Davis, Robert G., "Art and Anxiety," *PR* 12 (1945): 315-17.

Davis, Vivian I., "The Genius of Fantastic Feebleness (with Apologies to Richard Wright)," *PCLS* 8 (1975): 99-116.

DeArman, Charles, "Bigger Thomas: The Symbolic Negro and the Discrete Human Entity," *BALF* 12, ii (Summer, 1978): 61-4.

D'Itri, Patricia A., "Three Novels that Represent a Black Spokesman's Quest for Self Identity," *SSMLN* 4 (1976): 29-31.

Eisinger, C. E., *Fiction of the Forties*, 68-70.

Ellison, Ralph, "The World and the Jug," *New Leader* 46 (Dec. 9, 1963): 22-6. Also, expanded, in Ellison, R., *Shadow and Act*, N.Y.: Random House, 1964, 107-43. Also in Abcarian, R., ed., *Richard Wright's NATIVE SON*, 143-52.

Emanuel, James A., "Fever and Feeling: Notes on the Imagery in NATIVE SON," *Negro Digest*, 18 (Dec., 1968): 16-24. Also in Abcarian, R., ed., *Richard Wright's NATIVE SON*, 160-7.

Felgar, Robert, "'The Kingdom of the Beast': The Landscape of NATIVE SON," *CLAJ* 17 (Mar., 1974): 333-7.

————, *Richard Wright*, 78-108.

————, "SOUL ON ICE and NATIVE SON," *NALF* 8 (Fall, 1974): 235.

Feuser, Willfried, "The Men Who Lived Underground: Richard Wright and Ralph Ellison," in King, B., and K. Ogungbesan, eds., *Celebration of Black and African Writing*, 90-6.

Fishburn, K., *Richard Wright's Hero*, 59-100.

Fisher, Dorothy C., in Wright, Richard, *Native Son*, N.Y.: Harper, 1940, ix-xi. Also as "Introduction to the First Edition," in Baker, H. A., Jr., ed., *Twentieth Century Interpretations of NATIVE SON*, 109-11.

Fleissner, Robert, "How Bigger's Name Was Born," *SBL* 8, i (Spring, 1977): 4-5.

Ford, Nick A., "The Ordeal of Richard Wright," *CE* 15 (Nov., 1953): 87-94 *passim*. Also in Gibson, D. B., ed., *Five Black Writers*, 27-35 *passim*.

French, W., *Social Novel at the End of an Era*, 173-9.

Gaffney, Kathleen, "Bigger Thomas in Richard Wright's NATIVE SON," *Roots* 1, i (1970): 81-95.

Gayle, Addison, Jr., "Beyond Nihilism," *Negro Digest* 18 (Dec., 1968): 4-10. Also in Abcarian, R., ed., *Richard Wright's NATIVE SON*, 177-82.

————, *Way of the New World*, 168-74, 177-81.

Gibson, Donald B., "Wright's Invisible Native Son," *AQ* 21, iv (Winter, 1969): 728-38. Also in Baker, H. A., Jr., ed., *Twentieth Century Interpretations of NATIVE SON*, 96-108.

Glicksberg, Charles I., "The Furies in Negro Fiction," *WR* 13 (Winter, 1949): 109-10.

————, "Negro Fiction in America," *SAQ* 45 (Oct., 1946): 481-8. Also in Abcarian, R., ed., *Richard Wright's NATIVE SON*, 105-11.

Gloster, Hugh M., *Negro Voices in American Literature*, Chapel Hill: Un. of No. Carolina Pr., 1948, 228-34. Reprinted, N.Y.: Russell & Russell, 1965.

Graham, Louis, "The White Self-Image Conflict in NATIVE SON," *SBL* 3, ii (Summer, 1972): 19-21.

Grenander, M. E., "Criminal Responsibility in NATIVE SON and KNOCK ON ANY DOOR," *AL* 49, iii (May, 1977): 221-33.

Grinberg, Burica, "Some Aspects of Richard Wright's Method of Characterization and His Use of Symbols in NATIVE SON," *Filologija* 1, ii (1977): 66-74.

Gross, Barry, "Art and Act: The Example of Richard Wright," *Obsidian* 2 (Summer, 1976): 5-19.

————, "'Intellectual Overlordship': Blacks, Jews, and NATIVE SON," *JEthS* 5, iii (Fall, 1977): 51-9.

Gross, Seymour L., "'Dalton' and Color-Blindness in NATIVE SON," *MissQ* 27 (Winter, 1973-74): 75-7.

————, *Heroic Ideal in American Literature*, 153-5.

————, "NATIVE SON and 'The Murders in the Rue Morgue': An Addendum," *PoeS* 8 (June, 1975): 23.

Gysin, F., *Grotesque in American Negro Fiction*, 91-164 *passim*.

Hakutani, Yoshinobu, "NATIVE SON and AN AMERICAN TRAGEDY: Two Different Interpretations of Crime and Guilt," *CentR* 23 (Spring, 1979): 208-26. Also in Hakutani, Y., ed., *Critical Essays on Richard Wright*, 167-81.

Hand, Clifford, in French W., ed., *Thirties*, 84-6.

Howe, Irving, "Black Boys and Native Sons," *Dissent* 10 (Autumn, 1963): 354-7. Also in Howe, I., *World More Attractive*, 100-10. Also in Abcarian, R., ed., *Richard Wright's NATIVE SON*, 135-43. Also, abridged, in Baker, H. A., Jr., *Twentieth Century Interpretations of NATIVE SON*, 63-70. Also in Hakutani, Y., ed., *Critical Essays on Richard Wright*, 41-4.

Hughes, Carl M., *The Negro Novelist*, N.Y.: Citadel, 1953, 41-68, 198-206.

Jackson, Blyden, "The Negro's Image of the Universe as Reflected in His Fiction," *CLAJ* 4 (Sept., 1960): 22-31 *passim*.

Jackson, Esther M., "The American Negro and the Image of the Absurd," *Phylon* 23 (4th quarter, Winter, 1962): 264-8.

James, Charles, "Bigger Thomas in the Seventies: A Twentieth-Century Search for Relevance," *EngR* 22, i (Fall, 1971): 6-14.

Jordan, June, "On Richard Wright and Nora Zeale Hurston: Notes Toward a Balancing of Love and Hatred," *BlackW* 23 (Aug., 1974): 4-8.

Joyce, Joyce A., "Style and Meaning in Richard Wright's NATIVE SON," *BALF* 16, iii (Fall, 1982): 112-15.

Kearns, Edward, "The 'Fate' Section of NATIVE SON," *ConL* 12, ii (Spring, 1971): 146-5.

Kennedy, James G., "The Content and Form of NATIVE SON," *CE* 34, ii (Nov., 1972): 269-83. [Comment by Annette Conn follows.]

Kent, George, "Richard Wright: Blackness and the Adventure of Western Culture," *CLAJ* 12, iv (June, 1969): 339-43. Also in *BlackR* 1 (1971): 29-34. Also in Kent, G., *Blackness and the*

Adventure of Western Culture, 92-5. Also in Baker, H. A., Jr., ed., *Twentieth Century Interpretations of NATIVE SON*, 91-5.

Kgositsile, Keorapetse, "The Relevance of Bigger Thomas to Our Time," *Roots* 1, i (1970): 79-80.

Kinnamon, K., *Emergence of Richard Wright*, 118-52.

————, "NATIVE SON: The Personal, Social and Political Background," *Phylon* 30, i (Spring, 1969): 66-72. Also in Abcarian, R., ed., *Richard Wright's NATIVE SON*, 95-102. Also in Hakutani, Y., ed., *Critical Essays on Richard Wright*, 120-7.

————, "Richard Wright's Use of OTHELLO in NATIVE SON," *CLAJ* 12, iv (June, 1969): 358-9.

Klotman, Phyllis R., "Moral Distancing as a Rhetorical Technique in NATIVE SON: A Note on 'Fate'," *CLAJ* 18 (Dec., 1974): 284-91.

Kumasi, Kandi B., "The Critical Reception of Richard Wright's NATIVE SON (1940-1975)," *DAI* 42, ii (Aug., 1981): 704A.

Lank, David S., and Paul N. Siegel, "NATIVE SON [An Exchange]," *PMLA* 90 (Jan., 1975): 122-3, 294-5. [On article by Siegel below.]

Larsen, R. B. V., "The Four Voices of Richard Wright's NATIVE SON," *NALF* 6 (Winter, 1972): 105-9.

LeClair, Thomas, "The Blind Leading the Blind: Richard Wright's NATIVE SON and a Brief Reference to Ellison's INVISIBLE MAN," *CLAJ* 13, iii (Mar., 1970): 315-20.

Lehan, R., *Dangerous Crossing*, 96-9.

Littlejohn, D., *Black on White*, 106-7.

Margolies, E., *Art of Richard Wright*, 104-20.

————, "Richard Wright: NATIVE SON and Three Kinds of Revolution," *Native Sons*, 65-86.

Mathur, O. P., "Mulk Raj Anand's UNTOUCHABLES and Richard Wright's Bigger Thomas: A Comparative Study in Social Protest and Affirmation," *LHY* 19, ii (July, 1978): 115-28.

May, J. R., *Toward a New Earth*, 161-71.

McCall, D., *Example of Richard Wright*, 64-102.

————, "The Social Significance of Bigger Thomas," *Example of Richard Wright*, 64-102. Also in Abcarian R., ed., *Richard Wright's NATIVE SON*, 182-93. Also, in part, in Baker, H. A., Jr., ed., *Twentieth Century Interpretations of NATIVE SON*, 82-90.

Merkle, Donald R., "The Furnace and the Tower: A New Look at the Symbols of NATIVE SON," *EJ* 60, vi (Sept., 1971): 735-9.

Miller, Eugene E., "Voodoo Parallels in NATIVE SON," *CLAJ* 16, i (Sept., 1972): 81-95.

Nagel, James, "Images of 'Vision' in NATIVE SON," *UR* 36 (Dec., 1969): 109-15. Also in Hakutani, Y., ed., *Critical Essays on Richard Wright*, 151-8.

Owens, William A., "Introduction," *Native Son*, N.Y.: Harper, 1957, vii-xii.

Prior, Linda T., "A Further Word on Richard Wright's Use of Poe in NATIVE SON," *PoeS* 5 (Dec., 1972): 52-3.

Ramsey, Priscilla R., "Blind Eyes, Blind Quests in Richard Wright's NATIVE SON," *CLAJ* 24 (Sept., 1980): 48-60.

Rao, Vimala, "The Regionalism of Richard Wright's NATIVE SON," *IJAS* 7, i (1977): 94-102.

Redden, Dorothy S., "Richard Wright and NATIVE SON: Not Guilty," *BALF* 10 (Winter, 1976): 111-16.

Reed, Kenneth T., "NATIVE SON: An American CRIME AND PUNISHMENT," *SBL* 1, ii (Summer, 1970): 33-4.

Roache, Joel, "'What Had Made Him and What He Meant': The Politics of Wholeness in 'How Bigger Was Born'," *Substance* 15 (1976): 133-45.

Rosenblatt, R., *Black Fiction*, 19-36.

Rubin, Steven J., "Richard Wright and Albert Camus: The Literature of Revolt," *IFR* 8, i (Winter, 1981): 12-16.

Sadler, Jeffrey, "Split Consciousness in Richard Wright's NATIVE SON," *SCR* 8, ii (Apr., 1976): 11-24.

Samples, Ron, "Bigger Thomas and His Descendents," *Roots* 1, i (1970): 86-93.

Sanders, Ronald, "Richard Wright Then and Now," *Negro Digest* 18 (Dec., 1968): 83-98.

Savory, Jerold J., "Bigger Thomas and the Book of Job: the Epigraph to NATIVE SON," *NALF* 9 (Summer, 1975): 55-6.

————, "Descent and Baptism in NATIVE SON, INVISIBLE MAN and DUTCHMAN," *CSR* 3, i (Winter, 1973): 33-7.

Schraufnagel, N., "Wright and the Protest Novel," *From Apology to Protest*, 21-32.

Scott, Nathan A., Jr., "The Dark and Haunted Tower of Richard Wright," *Comment* (Wayne State Un.) 7 (July, 1964): 93-5. Also, revised, in Gibson, D. B., ed., *Five Black Writers*, 13-16.

————, "Judgment Marked by a Cellar: The American Negro Writer and the Dialectic of Despair," *UDQ* 2, ii (1967). Also in Mooney, H. J., and T. F. Staley, eds., *Shapeless God*, 154-6.

————, "Search for Beliefs: Fiction of Richard Wright," *UKCR* 23 (Winter, 1956): 131-5.

Scruggs, Charles W., "The Importance of the City in NATIVE SON," *ArielE* 9, iii (July, 1978): 115-28.

Siegel, Paul N., "The Conclusion of Richard Wright's NATIVE SON," *PMLA* 89 (May, 1974): 517-23.

Sillen, Samuel, "The Meaning of Bigger Thomas," *New Masses* 35 (1960): 13-21.

Singh, Amritjit, "Misdirected Responses to Bigger Thomas," *SBL* 5, ii (Summer, 1974): 5-8.

Singh, Raman K., "Christian Heroes and Anti-Heroes in Richard Wright's Fiction," *NALF* 6, iv (Winter, 1972): 101-2.

————, "Marxism in Richard Wright's Fiction," *IJAS* 4, i-ii (June-Dec., 1974): 26-30.

————, "Some Basic Ideas and Ideals in Richard Wright's Fiction," *CLAJ* 13 (Sept., 1969): 78-94.

Slochower, H., *No Voice is Wholly Lost*, 87-92.

Solotaroff, Theodore, "The Integration of Bigger Thomas," *Red Hot Vacuum*, 122-32.

Stanton, Robert, "Outrageous Fiction: CRIME AND PUNISHMENT, THE ASSISTANT, and NATIVE SON," *PCP* 4 (Apr., 1969): 52-8.

Starr, Alvin J., "The Concept of Fear in the Works of Stephen Crane and Richard Wright," *SBL* 6 (Summer, 1975): 6-9.

Stepto, Robert B., "'I Thought I Knew These People': Richard Wright and the Afro-American Literary Tradition," *MR* 18, iii (Autumn, 1977): 525-41 *passim*.

Walker, Ian, "Black Nightmare: The Fiction of Richard Wright," in Lee, A. R., ed., *Black Fiction*, 19-23.

Wasserman, Jerry, "Embracing the Negative: NATIVE SON and THE INVISIBLE MAN," *SAF* 4, i (Spring, 1976): 93-104.

Watson, Edward A., "Bessie's Blues," *NewL* 38, ii (Dec., 1971): 64-70. Also in Ray, D., and M. Farnsworth, eds., *Richard Wright*, 167-73.

Webb, Constance, *Richard Wright*, 169-75.

————, "What Next for Richard Wright?" *Phylon* 10 (2nd quarter, 1949): 161-6.

Werner, C. H., *Paradoxical Resolutions*, 28-32.

Wertham, Frederic, "An Unconscious Determinant in NATIVE SON," *Jnl. of Clinical Psychology* 6 (1944-45), 111-15. Also in Ruitenbeck, Hendrik M., ed., *Psychoanalysis and Literature*, N.Y.: Dutton, 1964, 321-5.

Whitlow, R., *Black American Literature*, 109-12.

Witt, Mary A., "A Rage and Racism in THE STRANGER and NATIVE SON," *Comparatist* 1 (May, 1977): 35-47.

Wright, Richard, "How Bigger Was Born," in *Native Son*, N.Y.: Random House, 1940, vii-xxxiv. Also, in part, from *Saturday Review of Literature* 22 (June 1, 1940): 3-4, 17-20. Also in Ducas, G., ed., *Great Documents in Black American History*, N.Y.: Praeger, 1970, 231-52. Also in Miller, R., ed., *Backgrounds to Black American Literature*, 197-217. Also in Wright, R., *Native Son*, Perennial edition, N.Y.: Harper & Row, 1966, 1-39. Also in Baker, H. A., Jr., ed., *Twentieth Century Interpretations of NATIVE SON*, 21-47.

THE OUTSIDER

Adams, Phoebe, "The Wrong Road," *Atlantic* (May, 1953): 77-8.

Bakish, D., *Richard Wright*, 64-72.

Bone, R., *Richard Wright*, 38-43.

Bontemps, Arna, in Griffin, W., ed., *Literature in the Modern World*, 116-19.

Brignano, R. C., *Richard Wright*, 82-5, 155-64.

Cobb, Nina, "Richard Wright: Exile and Existentialism," *Phylon* 40 (Dec., 1979): 362-74.

Davis, Arthur P., "THE OUTSIDER as a Novel of Race," *MJ* 7 (Winter, 1955-56): 320-6.

Fabre, Michael, "Richard Wright, French Existentialism and THE OUTSIDER," in Hakutani, Y., ed., *Critical Essays on Richard Wright*, 182-98.

Felgar, R., *Richard Wright*, 109-21.

Ferguson, Alfred R., "Black Men, White Cities: The Quest for Humanity by Black Protagonists in James Baldwin's ANOTHER COUNTRY and Richard Wright's THE OUTSIDER," *BSUF* 18, ii (Spring, 1977): 51-8.

Fishburn, K., *Richard Wright's Hero*, 112-54, 179-85.

Ford, Nick A., "The Ordeal of Richard Wright," *CE* 15 (Nov., 1953): 90-4. Also in Gibson, D. B., ed., *Five Black Writers*, 30-5.

Glicksberg, Charles I., "Existentialism in THE OUTSIDER," *FQ* 7 (Jan., 1958): 17-26.

Gysin, F., *Grotesque in American Negro Fiction*, 91-164 *passim*.

_____, "The God of Fiction," *ColQ* 7 (Autumn, 1958): 217-19.

Jones, Anne H., "The Plight of the Modern Outsider: A Comparative Study of Dostoevsky's CRIME AND PUNISHMENT, Camus's L'ETRANGER, and Wright's THE OUTSIDER," *DAI* 36 (1975): 317A.

Klotman, Phyllis R., and Melville Yancey, "Gift of Double Vision: Possible Political Implications of Richard Wright's 'Self-Consciousness' Thesis," *CLAJ* 16, i (Sept., 1972): 106-16.

Knox, George, "The Negro Novelist's Sensibility and the Outsider Theme," *WHR* 11 (Spring, 1957): 137-48.

Lawson, Lewis A., "Cross Damon: Kierkegaardian Man of Dread," *CLAJ* 14, iii (Mar., 1971): 298-316.

Lehan, Richard, "Existentialism in Recent American Fiction," *TSLL* 1 (Summer, 1959): 192-5, 199.

Maduka, Chidi T., "Personal Identity and the Revolutionary Intellectual: Richard Wright's Cross Damon," *Kiabara* 3, i (1980): 159-75.

Marcus, Steven, "The American Negro in Search of Identity: Three Novelists: Richard Wright, Ralph Ellison, James Baldwin," *Ctary* 16 (May, 1953): 457-8.

Margolies, E., *Art of Richard Wright*, 121-38.

McCall, D, *Example of Richard Wright*, 149-55.

Reilly, John M. "The Reconstruction of Gender as Entry Into Conscious History," *BALF* 13 (Spring, 1979): 3-6.

Schraufnagel, N., *From Apology to Protest*, 91-3.

Scott, Nathan A., Jr., "The Dark and Haunted Tower of Richard Wright," *Comment* (Wayne State Univ.) 7 (July, 1964): 96-7. Also, revised, in Gibson, D. B., ed., *Five Black Writers*, 19-22.

_____, "Judgment Marked by a Cellar: The American Negro Writer and the Dialectic of Despair," *UDQ* 2, ii (1967): 22-4. Also in Mooney, H. J., and T. F. Staley, eds., *Shapeless God*, 156-8.

_____, "Search for Beliefs: The Fiction of Richard Wright," *UKCR* 23 (Winter, 1956): 135-8.

Singh, Raman K., "Christian Heroes and Anti-Heroes in Richard Wright's Fiction," *NALF* 6, iv (Winter, 1972): 102-3.

_____, "Marxism in Richard Wright's Fiction," *IJAS* 4, i-ii (June-Dec., 1974): 30-4.

_____, "Some Basic Ideas and Ideals in Richard Wright's Fiction," *CLAJ* 13 (Sept., 1969): 78-84.

_____, "Wright's Tragic Vision in THE OUTSIDER," *SBL* 1, iii (Autumn, 1970): 23-7.

Tate, Claudia C., "Christian Existentialism in Richard Wright's THE OUTSIDER," *CLAJ* 25, iv (June, 1982): 371-95.

Turner, Darwin T., "THE OUTSIDER: Revision of an Idea," *CLAJ* 12, iv (June, 1969): 310-21. Also in *SHR* 4, ii (Winter, 1970): 40-50. Also in Gibson, Donald B., and Robert A. Corrigan, eds., *Richard Wright's Fiction: The Critical Response, 1940-1971*, Iowa City: Un. of Iowa, 1971.

Webb, C., *Richard Wright*, 306-14.

Widmer, Kingsley, "The Existential Darkness: Richard Wright's THE OUTSIDER," *WSCL* 1, iii (Fall, 1960): 13-21. Also in Gibson, D. B., ed., *Five Black Writers*, 50-7. Also, revised as "Black Existentialism: Richard Wright," in Goode, M. G., ed., *Modern Black Novelists*, 79-87.

SAVAGE HOLIDAY

Bakish, D., *Richard Wright*, 72-5.

Brignano, R. C., *Richard Wright*, 133-43.

Felgar, R., *Richard Wright*, 121-6.

Gounard, J. F., and Beverley R. Gounard, "Richard Wright's SAVAGE HOLIDAY: Use or Abuse of Psychoanalysis?" *CLAJ* 22 (June, 1979): 344-9.

Margolies, E., *Art of Richard Wright*, 138-48.

Reilly, John M., "Richard Wright's Curious Thriller, SAVAGE HOLIDAY," *CLAJ* 21 (Dec., 1977): 218-23.

Vassilowitch, John, Jr., "'Erskine Fowler': A Key Freudian Pun in SAVAGE HOLIDAY," *ELN* 18, iii (Mar., 1981): 206-8.

Webb, C., *Richard Wright*, 314-17.

BIBLIOGRAPHY

Brignano, Russell C., "Richard Wright: A Bibliography of Secondary Sources," *SBL* 2, ii (Summer, 1971): 19-25.

Bryer, Jackson, "Richard Wright: A Selected Check List of Criticism," *WSCL* 1, iii (Fall, 1960): 22-33.

Gibson, Donald B., "Richard Wright: A Bibliographical Essay," *CLAJ* 12 (June, 1969): 360-5.

Hurst, Catherine D., "A Survey of the Criticism of Richard Wright's Fiction," *DAI* 41 (1980): 672A-73A.

Reilly, John M., "Richard Wright: An Essay in Bibliography," *RALS* 1 (Aug., 1971): 131-80.

Webb, Constance, "Richard Wright: A Bibliography," *NegroD* 18, iii (1969): 86-92.

WRIGHT, RICHARD B(RUCE), 1937-

GENERAL

Johnston, Eleanor, "Telling and Selling Diversions: The Novels of Richard Wright," *CanL* 89 (Summer, 1981): 23-32.

FARTHING'S FORTUNES

Johnston, Eleanor, "Telling and Selling Diversions: The Novels of Richard B. Wright," *CanL* 89 (Summer, 1981): 27-31.

FINAL THINGS

Johnston, Eleanor, "Telling and Selling Diversions: The Novels of Richard B. Wright," *CanL* 89 (Summer, 1981): 31-2.

IN THE MIDDLE OF A LIFE

Doyle, James, "'Any Modern City': The Urban Canadian Fiction of Richard B. Wright," in Campbell, J., and J. Doyle, eds., *PRACTICAL VISION*, 158-63.

Johnston, Eleanor, "Telling and Selling Diversions: The Novels of Richard B. Wright," *CanL* 89 (Summer, 1981): 25-7.

THE WEEKEND MAN

Campbell, Sheila, "The Two Wes Wakehams: Point of View in THE WEEKEND MAN," *SCL* 2 (Summer, 1977): 289-305.

Doyle, James, "'Any Modern City': The Urban Canadian Fiction of Richard B. Wright," in Campbell, J., and J. Doyle, eds., *Practical Vision*, 152-8.

Johnston, Eleanor, "Telling and Selling Diversions: The Novels of Richard B. Wright," *CanL* 89 (Summer, 1981): 24-5.

WRIGHT, SARAH E(LIZABETH), 1928-

THIS CHILD'S GONNA LIVE

Harris, Trudier, "Three Black Women Writers and Humanism: A Folk Perspective," in Miller, R. B., ed., *Black American Literature and Humanism*, 54-8.

Mickelson, A. Z., *Reaching Out*, 113-24.

Schraufnagel, N., *From Apology to Protest*, 170-1.

Whitlow, R., *Black American Literature*, 162-5.

WURLITZER, RUDOLPH, 1938-

GENERAL

Puetz, Manfred, "Alternative Fictions: Manfred Puetz on Rudolph Wurlitzer," *FictionI* 2-3 (1974): 134-9.

FLATS

Bolling, Douglass, "Rudolph Wurlitzer's NOG and FLATS," *Crit* 14, iii (1973): 5-15.

Puetz, Manfred, "Alternative Fictions: Manfred Puetz on Rudolph Wurlitzer," *FictionI* 2-3 (1974): 137-8.

Stephens, M. G., "A Voice at the Edge of Things," *EvR* 88 (Apr., 1988): 75-6.

NOG

Bolling, Douglass, "Rudolph Wurlitzer's NOG and FLATS," *Crit* 14, iii (1973): 5-15.

Puertz, Manfred, "Alternative Fictions: Manfred Puetz on Rudolph Wurlitzer," *FictionI* 2-3 (1974): 135-7.

QUAKE

Bolling, Douglass, "The Waking Nightmare: American Society in Rudolph Wurlitzer's QUAKE," *Crit* 16, iii (1975): 70-80.

Puertz, Manfred, "Alternative Fictions: Manfred Puetz on Rudolph Wurlitzer," *FictionI* 2-3 (1974): 138-9.

WYLIE, PHILIP (GORDON), 1902-1971

GENERAL

Barshay, Robert H., "Philip Wylie: The Man and His Work," *DAI* 36 (1975): 3707A.

Keefer, T. F., *Philip Wylie*.

THE ANSWER

Keefer, T. F. *Philip Wylie*, 128-30.

AN APRIL AFTERNOON

Keefer, T. F., *Philip Wylie*, 91-5.

AS THEY REVELED

Keefer, T. F., *Philip Wylie*, 78-81.

BABES AND SUCKLINGS

Keefer, T. F., *Philip Wylie*, 40-6.

BLONDY'S BOY FRIEND

Keefer, T. F., *Philip Wylie*, 49-50.

THE DISAPPEARANCE

Keefer, T. F., *Philip Wylie*, 121-4.

THE END OF THE DREAM

Keefer, T. F., *Philip Wylie*, 153-4.

FINNLEY WREN

Keefer, T. F., *Philip Wylie*, 65-75.

GLADIATOR

Keefer, T. F., *Philip Wylie*, 46-9.

HEAVEY LADEN

Keefer, T. F., *Philip Wylie*, 36-40.

HOME FROM THE HILLS

Keefer, T. F., *Philip Wylie*, 86-7.

LOS ANGELES A. D. 2017

Keefer, T. F., *Philip Wylie*, 151-2.

NIGHT UNTO NIGHT

Keefer, T. F., *Philip Wylie*, 104-8.

NO SCANDAL!

Keefer, T. F., *Philip Wylie*, 87-8.

ONE LOVE AT A TIME (See also AS THEY REVELED)

Keefer, T. F., *Philip Wylie*, 78-9.

OPUS 21

Keefer, T. F., *Philip Wylie*, 113-21.

THE OTHER HORSEMAN

Keefer, T. F., *Philip Wylie*, 95-6.

THE SAVAGE GENTLEMAN

Keefer, T. F., *Philip Wylie* 64-5.

SECOND HONEYMOON

Keefer, T. F., *Philip Wylie*, 83-4.

THE SMILING CORPSE

Keefer, T. F., *Philip Wylie*, 77-8.

SMOKE ACROSS THE MOON

Keefer, T. F., *Philip Wylie*, 84-6.

THE SPY WHO SPOKE PORPOISE

Keefer, T. F., *Philip Wylie*, 145-8.

THEY BOTH WERE NAKED

Keefer, T. F., *Philip Wylie*, 136-40.

TOMORROW!

Keefer, T. F., *Philip Wylie*, 124-8.

TOO MUCH OF EVERYTHING

Keefer, T. F. *Philip Wylie*, 81-3.

TRIUMPH

Keefer, T. F., *Philip Wylie*, 134-6.

BIBLIOGRAPHY

Keefer, T. F., *Philip Wylie*, 163-5.

YAFFE, JAMES, 1927-

GENERAL

Lainoff, Seymour, "James Yaffe: Jewish Novelist of Manners," *CJF* 27, iii (Spring, 1969): 166-9.

YATES, RICHARD, 1926-

GENERAL

Henry, DeWitt, and Geoffrey, Clark, "An Interview with Richard Yates," *Ploughshares* 1, iii (1972): 65-78.

REVOLUTIONARY ROAD

Chappell, Fred, "Richard Yates REVOLUTIONARY ROAD," in Madden, D., ed., *Rediscoveries*, 245-55.
Solotaroff, Theodore, "The Wages of Maturity," *Red Hot Vacuum*, 44-9.

YERBY, FRANK (GARVIN), 1916-1991

GENERAL

Hill, James L., "Anti-Heroic Perspectives: The Life and Work of Frank Yerby," *DAI* 37 (1977): 7822A.
Turner, Darwin T., "Frank Yerby as Debunker," *MR* 9 (1968): 569-77.
Yerby, Frank, "How and Why I Write the Costume Novel," *Harpers* 219 (Oct., 1959): 145-50.

FLOODTIDE

Hughes, C. M., *Negro Novelist*, 155-9.

THE FOXES OF HARROW

Hughes, C. M., *Negro Novelist*, 149-52, 236-8.

SPEAK NOW

Schraufnagel, N., *From Apology to Protest*, 155-7.

YOUNG, AL, 1939-

GENERAL

O'Brien, John, "Interview with Al Young," *NQR* 3, iv (Summer, 1973); 328-31. Also in O'Brien, J., ed., *Interviews with Black Writers*, 259-69.
Mackey, Nathaniel, "Interview with Al Young," *MELUS* 5, iv (1978): 32-51.

SNAKES

Billingsley, R. G., "Al Young's SNAKES: The Blues as a Literary Form," *Obsidian* 4, ii (1978): 28-36.
Bolling, Douglass, "Artistry and Theme in Al Young's SNAKES," *NALF* 8 (1974): 223-5.
Schmitz, Neil, "Al Young's SNAKES: Words to the Music," *Paunch* 35 (Feb., 1974): 3-9.

YOUNG, MARGUERITE, 1908-1995

GENERAL

Duncan, Erika, "The Literary Life—and How It's Lived. A Reminiscence with Marguerite Young," *BForum* 3, iii (1979): 426-35.

Ruas, Charles, "The Art of Fiction," *ParisR* 71 (Fall, 1977): 58-75.

Tanner, Leslie B., "The Teachings of Marguerite Young," *USP* 5, iv (Fall, 1974): 13-15.

ANGEL IN THE FOREST

Nin, Anais, "A Look at the ANGEL IN THE FOREST," *USP* 5, iv (1974): 11-13.

MISS MACINTOSH, MY DARLING

Duncan, Erika, "The Shadows in MISS MACINTOSH, MY DARLING, *USP* 5, iv (Fall, 1974): 8-11.

McEvilly, Wayne, "The Philosopher Without Answers: A Look at Metaphysics and Marguerite Young," *STwC* 3 (Spring, 1969): 73-81.

YURICK, SOL, 1925-

GENERAL

Haneline, Douglas L., "The Swing of the Pendulum: Naturalism in Contemporary American Literature," *DAI* 39 (1978): 2272A-73A.

THE WARRIORS

Graham, D. B., "Naturalism and the Revolutionary Imperative: Yurick's THE WARRIORS," *Crit* 18, i (1976): 119-28.

Sources Consulted

Abbott, H. Porter, *The Fiction of Samuel Beckett: Form and Effect*, Berkeley and London: Un. of Calif. Pr., 1973.

Abcarian, Richard, ed., *Richard Wright's NATIVE SON: A Critical Handbook*, Belmont, CA: Wadsworth, 1970.

Acta Universitatis Carolinae. Philologica (1971). *Prague Studies in English 14*, Praha: Universita Karlova, 1971.

Adams, Laura, *Existential Battles: The Growth of Norman Mailer*, Athens: Ohio Un. Pr., 1976.

Adams, Richard P., *Faulkner: Myth and Motion*, Princeton, NJ: Princeton Un. Pr., 1968.

Adams, Stephen D., *James Purdy*, New York: Barnes & Noble, 1976.

Africa in Soviet Studies; Annual, 1969, tr. R. F. Kostiyuk and V. A. Epshtein, Moscow: Nauka, 1971.

Agetua, John, ed., *Critics on Chinua Achebe 1970-76*, Benin City, Nigeria: Author, 1977.

Aggeler, Geoffrey, *Anthony Burgess: The Artist as Novelist*, University: Un. of Alabama Pr., 1979.

Aichinger, Peter, *Earle Birney* (TWAS, 538), Boston: Twayne, 1979.

Aiken, Conrad P., *A Reviewer's ABC; Collected Criticism of Conrad Aiken, from 1916 to the Present*, New York: Meridian Books, 1958.

Aird, Eileen M., *Sylvia Plath*, New York: Barnes & Noble, 1973.

Aitken, A. J. Angus McIntosh, and Hermann Palsson, eds., *Edinburgh Studies in English and Scots*, London: Longman Group Ltd., 1971.

Albright, Daniel, *Representation and the Imagination: Beckett, Kafka, Nabokov, and Schoenberg*, Chicago and London: Chicago Un. Pr., 1981.

Aldridge, John W., *After the Lost Generation*, New York: McGraw-Hill, 1951.

_____, ed., *Critiques and Essays on Modern Fiction: 1920-1951*, New York: Ronald Pr., 1952.

_____, *The Devil in the Fire; Retrospective Essays on American Literature and Culture, 1951-1971*, New York: Harpers Magazine Pr., 1972.

_____, *In Search of Heresy: American Literature in an Age of Conformity*, New York: McGraw-Hill, 1956.

_____, *A Time to Murder and Create; The Contemporary Novel in Crisis*, New York: David McKay, 1966.

Aldritt, Keith, *The Making of George Orwell; An Essay in Literary History*, New York: St. Martin's Pr., 1969.

Alexander, Edward, *Isaac Bashevis Singer* (TWAS 582), Boston: Twayne, 1980.

Allan, Jim, ed., *An Introduction to Elvish*, Hayes: Bran's Head, 1978.

Allen, Mercy, *The Necessary Blankness: Women in Major American Fiction of the Sixties*, Urbana, Un. of Illinois Pr., 1976.

Allen, Walter, *Joyce Cary* (Writers and Their Work, No. 41), London and New York: Longmans, Green, Rev. ed., 1954.

_____, *The Modern Novel in Britain and the United States*, New York: Dutton, 1964. Published in England as *Tradition and Dream*, Harmondsworth: Penguin, 1965.

_____, *Reading a Novel*, London: Phoenix House, Rev. ed., 1963.

_____, *The Urgent West; the American Dream and Modern Man*, New York: Dutton, 1969.

Allentuck, Marcia, ed., *The Achievement of Isaac Bashevis Singer*, Carbondale: Southern Illinois Un. Pr., 1969.

Allott, Kenneth, and Miriam Farris (Allott), *The Art of Graham Greene*, London: Hamish Hamilton, 1951; New York: Russell & Russell, 1963.

Allsop, Kenneth, *The Angry Decade: A Survey of the Cultural Revolt of the Nineteen-fifties*, London: P. Owen, 1958; New York: British Book Centre, 1958.

Alphonso-Karkala, John P., *Comparative World Literature: Seven Essays*, Bombay: Nirmala Sadanand, 1974.

Alter, Iska, *The Good Man's Dilemma: Social Criticism in the Fiction of Bernard Malamud* (AMS Studies in Mod. Lit. 5), New York: AMS, 1981.

Alter, Robert, *After the Tradition: Modern Jewish Writing*, New York: Dutton, 1969.

_____, *Rogue's Progress; Studies in the Picaresque Novel*, Cambridge: Harvard Un. Pr., 1965.

Alvarez, A., *Beckett*, London: Fontana (Fontana Modern Masters), 1973.

American Literature in the 1940's. Annual Report 1975, Tokyo: Tokyo Chapter, Amer. Lit. Soc. of Japan, 1976.

American Literature in the 1950's. Annual Report 1976. Tokyo: Tokyo Chapter, Amer. Lit. Soc. of Japan, 1977.

Amirthanayagam, Guy, ed., *Asians and Western Writers in Dialogue; New Cultural Identities*, London: Macmillan, 1982.

Amis, Kingsley, *What Became of Jane Austen? And Other Questions*, New York: Harcourt Brace, 1971.

Amur. G. S., *Manohar Malgonkar* (Indian Writers Ser. 3), New York: Humanities, 1973.

Andersen, Richard, *Robert Coover* (TUSAS 400), Boston: Twayne, 1981.

_____, *William Goldman* (TUSAS 326), Boston: Twayne, 1979.

Anderson, David, *The Tragic Protest: A Christian Study of Some Modern Literature*, Richmond, VA: John Knox Pr., London: SCM Pr., 1969.

Anderson, Don, and Stephen Knight, eds., *Cunning Exiles: Studies of Modern Prose Writers*, London: Angus & Robertson, 1974.

Anderson, Quentin, Stephen Donadio, and Steven Marcus, eds., *Art, Politics, and Will: Essays in Honor of Lionel Trilling*, New York: Basic Books, 1977.

Appel, Alfred, Jr., ed., *The Annotated LOLITA*. With Introd., Bibliog., and Notes, New York: McGraw-Hill, 1970.

_____, and Charles Newman, eds., *Nabokov: Criticism, Reminiscences, Translations and Tributes*, New York: Simon and Schuster, 1970; London: Weidenfeld & Nicolson, 1971.

_____, *Nabokov's Dark Cinema*, New York: Oxford Un. Pr., 1974.

_____, *A Season of Dreams: The Fiction of Eudora Welty*, Baton Rouge: La. State Un. Pr., 1965.

Argyle, Barry, *Patrick White* (Writers and Critics), Edinburgh and London: Oliver & Boyd, 1967.

Arthur, Anthony, ed., *Critical Essays on Wallace Stegner* (Crit. Essays on Amer. Lit.), Boston: G. K. Hall, 1982.

Asals, Frederick, *Flannery O'Connor: The Imagination of Extremity*, Athens: Un. of Georgia Pr., 1982.

Astro, Richard, and Jackson B. Benton, eds., *The Fiction of Bernard Malamud* (Amer. Authors Ser.), Corvallis: Oregon State Un. Pr., 1977.

_____, *Hemingway in Our Time*, Corvallis: Oregon State Un. Pr., 1974.

_____, and Joel W. Hedgpeth, eds., *Steinbeck and the Sea*. Proc. of a Conference Held at the Marine Science Center Auditorium, Newport, OR, May 4, 1974. Corvallis: Oregon State Un. Sea Grant Coll. Prog., 1975.

_____, and Tetsumaro Hayashi, eds., *Steinbeck: The Man and His Work*, Corvallis: Oregon State Un. Pr., 1971.

Atherton, Stanley S., *Alan Sillitoe: A Critical Assessment*, London: Allen, 1979.

Atkins, John, *The Art of Ernest Hemingway; His Work and Personality*, London: Spring Books, 1952.

_____, *Arthur Koestler*, New York: Roy, 1957.

_____, *George Orwell: A Literary and Biographical Study*, New York: Ungar, 1954.

_____, *George Orwell: A Literary Study*, London: Calder and Boyars, 1971. New ed.

_____, *Graham Greene*, London: Calder and Boyars, New Rev. Ed., 1966.

_____, *J. B. Priestley: The Last of the Sages*, London: Calder, 1981; New York: Riverrun, 1981.

Auchincloss, Louis, *Pioneers and Caretakers; a Study of Nine American Women Novelists*, Minneapolis: Un. of Minn. Pr., 1965.

Austin, Allan E., *Elizabeth Bowen* (TEAS 123) New York: Twayne, 1971.

_____, *Roy Fuller* (TEAS 253) Boston: Twayne, 1979.

Avery, Evelyn G., *Rebels and Victims: The Fiction of Richard Wright and Bernard Malamud*, Port Washington, NY; London: Kennikat Pr., 1979.

Axthelm, Peter M., *The Modern Confessional Novel*, New Haven: Yale Un. Pr., 1967.

Babb, Howard S., *The Novels of William Golding*, Columbus: Ohio State Un. Pr., 1970.

Backman, Melvin, *Faulkner: The Major Years; A Critical Study*, Bloomington: Indiana Un. Pr., 1966.

Badal, R. K., *R. K. Narayan: A Study*, Bareilly: Prakash Book Depot, 1976.

Bader, Julia, *Crystal Land: Artifice in Nabokov's English Novels*, Berkeley; London: Un. of California Pr., 1972.

Bader, Rudolf, *Anthony Powell's MUSIC OF TIME as a Cyclic Novel of Generations*, Bern: Francke, 1980.

Bailey, Jennifer, *Norman Mailer, Quick-Change Artist*, London: Macmillan, 1979.

Baim, Joseph, Ann L. Hayes, and Robert J. Gangewere, eds., *In Honor of Austin Wright* (CaSE 12), Pittsburgh: Carnegie Mellon Un., 1972.

Baker, Carlos, ed., *Ernest Hemingway: Critiques of Four Major Novels*, New York: Scribner's, 1962.

_____, ed., *Hemingway and His Critics: An International Anthology*, New York: Hill and Wang, 1961.

_____, *Hemingway: The Writer as Artist*, Princeton, NJ: Princeton Un. Pr., 3rd ed., 1963.

_____, *Hemingway: The Writer as Artist*, 4th ed., Princeton, NJ: Princeton Un. Pr., 1972.

Baker, Denys Val, ed., *Modern British Writing*, New York: Vanguard, 1947.

_____, ed., *Writers of Today: 2*, London: Sidgwick & Jackson, 1948.

Baker, Houston A., Jr., ed., *Twentieth Century Interpretations of NATIVE SON*, Englewood Cliffs, NJ: Prentice-Hall, 1972.

Baker, James R., *William Golding: A Critical Study*, New York: St. Martin's, 1965.

_____, and A. P. Ziegler, Jr., eds., *Casebook Edition of William Golding's LORD OF THE FLIES: Text, Notes and Criticism*, New York: Putnam's, 1964.

Baker, Sheridan, *Ernest Hemingway: An Introduction and Interpretation*, New York: Holt, 1967.

_____, ed., *Paton's CRY, THE BELOVED COUNTRY: The Novel, The Critics, The Setting* (Scribner Research Anthologies), New York: Charles Scribner's Sons, 1968.

Bakish, David, *Richard Wright* (Mod. Lit. Monogs.), New York: Ungar, 1973.

Bakker, J., *Ernest Hemingway: The Artist as Man of Action*, Assen: Van Gorcum, 1972.

_____, and D. R. M. Wilkinson, eds., *From Cooper to Philip Roth: Essays on American Literature*, Amsterdam: Rodopi, 1980.

Balakian, Nona, and Charles Simmons, eds., *The Creative Present: Notes on Contemporary American Fiction*, New York: Doubleday, 1963.

Baldanza, Fran, *Iris Murdoch* (TEAS 169), New York: Twayne, 1974.

_____, *Itinerary 3: Criticism*, Bowling Green, OH: Bowling Green Un. Pr., 1977.

_____, *Ivy Compton-Burnett* (TEAS 11), New York: Twayne, 1964.

Baldwin, Helene L., *Samuel Beckett's Real Silence*, University Park: Pennsylvania State Un. Pr., 1981.

Baldwin, Kenneth H., and David K. Kirby, eds., *Individual and Community: Variations on a Theme in American Fiction*, Durham, NC: Duke Un. Pr., 1975.

Ballard, W. L., ed., *Essays on African Literature* (Spectrum Monog. Series in the Arts and Sciences, Vol. 3, June, 1973), Atlanta: School of Arts and Sciences, Georgia State Un., 1973.

Barber, Benjamin R., and Michael J. G. McGrath, eds., *The Artist and Political Vision*, New Brunswick, NJ: Transition, 1982.

Bargen, Doris G., *The Fiction of Stanley Elkin*. (Studien and Texte zur Amerikanistik 8.) Frankfort: Lang, 1980.

Barger, James, *Ernest Hemingway: American Literary Giant*, Charlottesville, VA: SamHar, 1975.

Barnard, Caroline K., *Sylvia Plath* (TUSAS 309.) Boston: Twayne, 1978.

Barnard, G. C., *Samuel Beckett: A New Approach: A Study of the Novels and Plays*, New York: Dodd, Mead, 1970.

Barnes, Robert J., *Conrad Richter* (Southwest Writers Series, No. 14), Austin: Steck-Vaughn, 1968.

Barnett, Ursula A., *Ezekiel Mphahlele* (TWAS 417), Boston: Twayne, 1976.

Barr, Marleen S., ed., *Future Females: A Critical Anthology*, Bowling Green: Bowling Green State Un. Popular Pr., 1981.

Barson, Alfred T., *A Way of Seeing: A Critical Study of James Agee*, Amherst: Un. of Massachusetts Pr., 1972.

Barth, J. Robert, S. J., ed., *Religious Perspectives in Faulkner's Fiction: Yoknapatawpha and Beyond*, Notre Dame, IN: Notre Dame Un. Pr., 1972.

Barthold, Bonnie J., *Black Time: Fiction of Africa, the Caribbean and the United States*, New Haven: Yale Un. Pr., 1981.

Bartlett, Lee, ed., *The Beats: Essays in Criticism*, Jefferson, NC: McFarland, 1981.

Bassoff, Bruce, *Toward LOVING: The Poetics of the Novel and the Practice of Henry Green*, Columbia: Un. of South Carolina Pr., 1975.

Baugh, Edward, ed., *Critics on Caribbean Literature: Readings in Literary Criticism*, New York: St. Martin's Pr., 1978.

Baumbach, Jonathan, *The Landscape of Nightmare: Studies in the Contemporary American Novel*, New York: New York Un. Pr., 1965.

Baxter, Annette K., *Henry Miller, Expatriate* (Critical Essays in English and American Literature, No. 5), Pittsburgh: Un. of Pittsburgh Pr., 1961.

Beach, Joseph Warren, *American Fiction, 1920-1940*, New York: Russell and Russell, 1960.

Beatson, Peter, *The Eye in the Mandala: Patrick White: A Vision of Man and God*, New York: Barnes & Noble, 1976.

Beatty, Richmond C., and others, eds., *Vanderbilt Studies in the Humanities*, Vol. 1, Nashville: Vanderbilt Un. Pr., 1951.

Beaulieu, Victor-Levy, *Jack Kerouac: A Chicken-Essay*, tr. by Sheila Fischman, Toronto: Coach House, 1975.

Beck, Warren, *Faulkner: Essays*, Madison: Un. of Wisconsin Pr., 1976.

_____, *Man in Motion: Faulkner's Trilogy*, Madison: Un. of Wisconsin Pr., 1961.

Becker, Alida, ed., *The Tolkien Scrapbook*, Philadelphia: Running Pr., 1978.

Becker, George C., *John Dos Passos* (Mod. Lit. Monog.), New York: Ungar, 1974.

Bedell, George C., *Kierkegaard and Faulkner: Modalities of Existence*, Baton Rouge: Louisiana State Un. Pr., 1972.

Beebe, Maurice, and Leslie A. Field, eds., *Robert Penn Warren's ALL THE KING'S MEN: A Critical Handbook*, Belmont, CA: Wadsworth, 1966.

Begiebing, Robert J., *Acts of Regeneration: Allegory and Archetype in the Works of Norman Mailer*, Columbia: Un. of Missouri Pr., 1980.

Beja, Morris, *Epiphany in the Modern Novel*, Seattle: Un. of Washington Pr.; London: Peter Owen, 1971.

Belcher, William F., and J. W. Lee, eds., *J. D. Salinger and the Critics*, Belmont, CA: Wadsworth, 162.

Belkind, Allen, ed., *Dos Passos, the Critics, and the Writer's Intention*, Carbondale: Southern Illinois Un. Pr.; London: Feffer & Simons, 1971.

Bell, Roseann P., Bettye J. Parker, and Beverly Guy-Sheftall, eds., *Sturdy Black Bridges: Vision of Black Women in Literature*, Garden City, NY: Doubleday, 1979.

Bellamy, Joe David, ed., *The New Fiction; Interviews with Innovative American Writers*, Urbana: Un. of Illinois Pr., 1972.

Belliappa, Meena, *Anita Desai: A Study of Her Fiction*, Calcutta: Writers Workshop, 1971.

Benedikz, B. S., ed., *On the Novel: A Present for Walter Allen on His Sixtieth Birthday from His Friends and Colleagues*, London: J. M. Dent & Sons, 1971.

Benson, Jackson J., *Hemingway: The Writer's Art of Self-Defense*, Minneapolis: Un. of Minnesota Pr., 1969.

Berenbaum, Michael, *The Vision of the Void: Theological Reflections on the Works of Elie Wiesel*, Middletown, CT: Wesleyan Un. Pr., 1979.

Berghahn, Marion, *Images of Africa in Black American Literature* London: Macmillan; Totowa, NJ: Rowman and Littlefield, 1977.

Bergonzi, Bernard, *Anthony Powell* (WTW), Rev. and enl. ed., Harlow, Essex: Longman, 1971.

_____, *The Situation of the Novel* (Crit. Essays in Mod. Lit.), Pittsburgh: Un. of Pittsburgh Pr., 1971; London: Macmillan, 1970.

Berry, Margaret, *Mulk Raj Anand: The Man and the Novelist*, Amsterdam: Oriental Pr., 1971.

Bertens, Johannes W., *The Fiction of Paul Bowles: The Soul is the Weariest Part of the Body*, Amsterdam: Rodopi, 1979.

Berthoff, Warner, *Fictions and Events; Essays in Criticism and Literary History*, New York: Dutton, 1971.

Berzon, Judith R., *Neither White Nor Black; The Mulatto Character in American Fiction*, New York: New York Un. Pr., 1978.

Bessai, Diane, and David Jackel, eds., *Figures in a Ground: Canadian Essays on Modern Literature Collected in Honor of Sheila Watson*, Saskatoon: Western Producer Prairie, 1978.

Bien, Peter, *L. P. Hartley*, University Park: Pennsylvania State Un. Pr., 1963.

Bigsby, C. W. E., ed., *The Black American Writer*, Vol. 1: *Fiction*, DeLand, FL: Everett/Edwards, Inc., 1969.

Biles, Jack I., *Talk: Conversations with William Golding*, New York: Harcourt, 1970.

_____, and Robert O. Evans, eds., *William Golding: Some Critical Considerations*, Lexington: Un. Pr. of Kentucky, 1978.

Bingham, Edwin R., and Glen A. Love, eds., *Northwest Perspectives: Essays on the Culture of the Pacific Northwest*, Seattle: Un. of Washington Pr., 1979.

Birnbaum, Milton, *Aldous Huxley's Quest for Values*, Knoxville: Un. of Tennessee Pr., 1971.

Bishop, John Peale, *Collected Essays of John Peale Bishop*, ed., with an introd. by Edmund Wilson, New York: Charles Scribner's Sons, 1948.

Bjorksten, Ingmar, *Patrick White: A General Introduction*, tr. Stanley Gerson, St. Lucia: Un. of Queensland Pr., 1976.

Blackwell, Louise, and Frances Clay, *Lillian Smith* (TUSAS 187), New York: Twayne, 1971.

Blair, Everetta L., *Jesse Stuart: His Life and Works*, Columbia: Un. of South Carolina Pr., 1967.

Blake, Nelson Manfred, *Novelist's America: Fiction as History, 1910-1940*, Syracuse, NY: Syracuse Un. Pr., 1969.

Blankenship, Russell, *American Literature as an Expression of the National Mind*, Rev. ed., New York: Holt, Rinehart & Winston, 1958.

Bleikasten, Andre, *The Most Splendid Failure: Faulkner's THE SOUND AND THE FURY*, Bloomington: Indiana Un. Pr., 1976.

Blodgett, Harriet, *Patterns of Reality: Elizabeth Bowen's Novels*, The Hague: Mouton, 1975.

Bloodworth, William A., Jr., *Upton Sinclair* (TUSAS 294) Boston: Twayne, 1977.

Bloom, Robert, *The Indeterminate World: A Study of the Novels of Joyce Cary*, Philadelphia: Un. of Pennsylvania Pr., 1962.

Bloomfield, Paul, *L. P. Hartley and Anthony Powell*, [the latter by Bernard Bergonzi] (Writers and Their Work 144), London; New York: Longmans, Green, 1962.

Blotner, Joseph, *The Modern American Political Novel*, Austin: Un. of Texas Pr., 1966.

Bluefarb, Sam, *The Escape Motif in the American Novel: Mark Twain to Richard Wright*, Columbus: Ohio State Un. Pr., 1972.

Boardman, Gwenn R. *Graham Greene: The Aesthetics of Exploration*, Gainesville: Un. of Florida Pr., 1971.

Bode, Carl E., ed., *The Young Rebel in American Literature*, London: William Heinemann, 1959; New York: Praeger, 1960.

Bogardus, Ralph F., and Fred Hobson, eds., *Literature at the Barricades: The American Writer in the 1930's*, Tuscaloosa: Un. of Alabama Pr., 1982.

Bogh, Jens, and Steffen Skovmand, eds., *Six American Novels: From New Deal to New Frontier, A Workbook*, Aarhus: Akademisk Boghandel, 1972.

Bohner, Charles H., *Robert Penn Warren*, New York: Twayne, 1964.

_____, *Robert Penn Warren* (TUSAS 69), Rev. ed., Boston: Twayne, 1981.

Bold, Alan, *George Mackay Brown*, Edinburgh: Oliver & Boyd, 1978.

Bone, Robert A., *The Negro Novel in America*, Rev. ed., New Haven and London: Yale Un. Pr., 1965.

Booth, Ken, and Moorhead Wright, eds., *American Thinking about Peace and War: New Essays on American Thought and Attitudes*, Sussex: Harvester; New York: Barnes & Noble, 1978.

Bornstein, George, ed., *Romantic and Modern: Revaluations of Literary Tradition*, Pittsburgh: Pittsburgh Un. Pr.; London: Feffer & Simons, 1977.

Bothwell, Etta K., *Alienation in the Jewish American Novel of the Sixties*, Rio Piedras: Un. of Puerto Rico Pr., 1980.

Bowden, Edwin T., *The Dungeon of the Heart: Human Isolation and the American Novel*, New York: Macmillan, 1961.

Bowen, Elizabeth, *Seven Winters; Memories of a Dublin Childhood & Afterthoughts; Pieces on Writing*, New York: Knopf, 1962.

Bowen, Zack R., *Mary Lavin* (Irish Writers Ser.), Lewisburg, PA: Bucknell Un. Pr., 1975.

Bowering, Peter, *Aldous Huxley: A Study of the Major Novels*, New York: Oxford Un. Pr., 1969.

Bracher, Frederick, *The Novels of James Gould Cozzens*, New York: Harcourt, 1959.

Brack, O. M., Jr., ed., *American Humor: Essays Presented to John C. Gerber*, Scottsdale, AZ: Arete, 1977.

Bradbrook, Muriel C., *Literature in Action: Studies in Continental and Commonwealth Society*, London: Chatto & Windus; New York: Barnes & Noble, 1972.

_____, *Malcolm Lowry: His Art and Early Life: A Study in Transformation*, London: Cambridge Un. Pr., 1974.

Bradbury, John M., *The Fugitives: A Critical Account*, Chapel Hill: Un. of North Carolina Pr., 1958.

Bradbury, Malcolm, and David Palmer, eds., *The American Novel and the Nineteen Twenties*, (Stratford-upon-Avon Studies 13), London: E. Arnold; New York: Crane, Russak, 1971.

Bradbury, Malcolm, *Evelyn Waugh* (Writers and Critics), Edinburgh and London: Oliver & Boyd, 1964.

_____, *Possibilities: Essays on the State of the Novel*, London and New York: Oxford Un. Pr., 1973.

_____, *Saul Bellow*, London: Methuen, 1982.

_____, *What is a Novel?* (Arnold's General Studies), London: E. Arnold, 1969.

Bradford, M. E., ed., *The Form Discovered: Essays on the Achievement of Andrew Lytle*, Jackson: University and College Pr. of Mississippi, 1973.

Braine, John, *J. B. Priestley*, New York: Barnes & Noble, 1979.

Branch, Edgar M., *James T. Farrell* (UMPAW 29), Minneapolis: Un. of Minnesota Pr., 1963.

_____, *James T. Farrell* (TUSAS 185), New York: Twayne, 1971.

Brander, Laurence, *Aldous Huxley: A Critical Study*, Lewisburg, PA: Bucknell Un. Pr., 1970.

_____, *George Orwell*, London: Longmans, Green, 1954.

Brantley, John D., *The Fiction of John Dos Passos*, The Hague: Mouton, 1968.

Brashers, Howard C., *An Introduction to American Literature*, Stockholm: Svenska Borkforlaget, 1964.

Braudy, Leo, ed., *Norman Mailer: A Collection of Critical Essays* (TCV), Englewood Cliffs, NJ: Prentice-Hall, 1972.

Brebner, John A., *The Demon Within: A Study of John Cowper Powys's Novels*, New York: Barnes & Noble, 1973.

Brennan, Neil, *Anthony Powell* (TEAS 158), New York: Twayne, 1974.

Brewster, Dorothy, *Doris Lessing* (TEAS 21), New York: Twayne, 1965.

Brignano, Russell C., *Richard Wright: An Introduction to the Man and His Works*, Pittsburgh: Un. of Pittsburgh Pr., 1970.

Brissenden, R. F., *Patrick White* (Writers and Their Work, No. 190), London: Longmans, Green, 1966.

Broer, Lawrence R., *Hemingway's Spanish Tragedy*, University: Un. of Alabama Pr., 1973.

Broes, Arthur T., and Others, *Lectures on Modern Novelists* (Carnegie Series in English 7), Pittsburgh: Dept. of Eng., Carnegie Institute of Technology, 1963.

Brooke, Jocelyn, *Aldous Huxley* (Writers and Their Work, No. 55), Rev. ed., London: Longmans, Green, 1963.

_____, *Elizabeth Bowen*, London: Longmans, Green, 1952.

Brooks, Cleanth, *The Hidden God: Studies in Hemingway, Faulkner, Yeats, Eliot, and Warren*, New Haven: Yale Un. Pr., 1963.

_____, *A Shaping Joy: Studies in the Writers Craft*, New York: Harcourt, Brace, Jovanovich, 1972 [c. 1971.]

_____, *William Faulkner: The Yoknapatawpha Country*, New Haven: Yale Un. Pr., 1963.

_____, *William Faulkner: Toward Yoknapatawpha and Beyond*, New Haven: Yale Un. Pr., 1978.

Brooks, Van Wyck, *The Confident Years: 1885-1915*, New York: Dutton, 1952.

Brophy, Brigid, *Don't Never Forget; Collected Views and Rereviews*, New York: Holt, 1967.

Brostoff, Anita, ed., *I Could Be Mute: The Life and Work of Gladys Schmitt*, Pittsburgh: Carnegie Mellon Un. Pr., 1978.

Broughton, Panthea R., ed., *The Art of Walker Percy: Stratagems for Being*. (So. Lit. Studies), Baton Rouge: Louisiana State Un. Pr., 1979.

_____, *William Faulkner: The Abstract and the Actual*, Baton Rouge: Louisiana State Un. Pr., 1974.

Brown, Cheryl L., and Karen Olson, eds., *Feminist Criticism: Essays on Theory, Poetry and Prose*, Metuchen, NJ: Scarecrow Pr., 1978.

Brown, Francis, ed., *Opinions and Perspectives from the New York Times Book Review*, Boston: Houghton-Mifflin, 1964.

Brown, Ivor, *J. B. Priestley* (Writers and Their Work, No. 84), London: Longmans, Green, 1957.

Browne, Ray B, and others, eds., *Frontiers of American Culture*, Lafayette, IN: Purdue Un. Pr., 1968.

Browning Preston M., Jr., *Flannery O'Connor*, Carbondale: Southern Illinois Un. Pr., 1974.

Bruccoli, Matthew J., ed., *James Gould Cozzens: New Acquist of True Experience*, Carbondale: Southern Illinois Un. Pr., 1979.

_____, ed., *Just Representations: A James Gould Cozzens Reader*, Carbondale: Southern Illinois Un. Pr.; New York: Harcourt, 1978.

_____, and C. E. Frazer Clark, Jr., eds., *Pages: The World of Books, Writers, and Writing*, Detroit: Gale Research, 1976.

Bruck, Peter, and Wolfgang Karrer, eds., *The Afro-American Novel since 1960*, Amsterdam: Gruner, 1982.

Bruns, Gerald L., *Modern Poetry and the Idea of Language; A Critical and Historical Study*, New Haven: Yale Un. Pr., 1974.

Bruss, Elizabeth W., *Autobiographical Acts: The Changing Situation of a Literary Genre*, Baltimore and London: John Hopkins Un. Pr., 1976.

Bryant, J. A., Jr., *Eudora Welty* (UMPAW 66), Minneapolis: Un. of Minnesota Pr., 1968.

Bryant, Jerry H., *The Open Decision: The Contemporary American Novel and Its Intellectual Background*, New York: Free Press, 1970.

Brylowski, Walter, *Faulkner's Olympian Laugh: Myth in the Novels*, Detroit: Wayne State Un. Pr., 1968.

Bucco, Martin, *Frank Waters*, Austin: Steck-Vaughn, 1969.

Buchen, Irving H., *Isaac Bashevis Singer and the Eternal Past*, New York: New York Un. Pr., 1968.

Budd, Louis J., Edwin H. Cady, and Carl L. Anderson, eds., *Toward a New American Literary History: Essays in Honor of Arlin Turner*, Durham, NC: Duke Un. Pr., 1980.

Bufithis, Philip H., *Norman Mailer* (Mod. Lit. Monographs), New York: Ungar, 1978.

Bufkin, E. C., *P. H. Newby* (TEAS 176), Boston: Twayne, 1975.

Buitenhuis, Elspeth, *Robertson Davies* (CWTW), Toronto: Forum House, 1972.

_____, *Robertson Davies* (CWTW), Toronto: Forum House, 1972.

Buitenhuis, Peter, *Hugh MacLennan*, Toronto: Forum House, 1969.

Burbank, Rex, *Thornton Wilder*, New York; Twayne, 1961.

Burchard, Rachel C., *John Updike: Yea Sayings* (CMC), Carbondale: Southern Illinois Un. Pr., 1971.

Burden, Robert, *John Fowles, John Hawkes, Claude Simon: Problems of Self and Form in the Post-Modernist Novel: A Comparative Study* (Epistemata 5), Wurzburg: Konigshausen & Neumann, 1980.

Burgess, Anthony, *Urgent Copy; Literary Studies*, New York: Norton, 1968.

Burgum, Edwin Berry, *The Novel and the World's Dilemma*, New York: Oxford Un. Pr., 1947. Reprinted, New York: Russell & Russell, 1963.

Burkhart, Charles, ed., *The Art of I. Compton-Burnett: A Collection of Critical Essays*, London: Gollancz, 1972.

_____, *I. Compton-Burnett*, London: V. Gollancz, 1965.

Busch, Frederick, *Hawkes: A Guide to His Fictions*, Syracuse, NY: Syracuse Un. Pr., 1973.

Butscher, Edward, ed., *Sylvia Plath: The Woman and the Work*, New York: Dodd, Mead, 1977.

Byatt, A. S., *Degrees of Freedom: The Novels of Iris Murdoch*, New York: Barnes & Noble, 1965.

_____, *Iris Murdoch* (WTW 251.) Harlow: Longman for the British Council, 1976.

Calder, Jenni, *Chronicles of Conscience: A Study of George Orwell and Arthur Koestler*, London: Secker and Warburg, 1968; Pittsburgh: Un. of Pittsburgh Pr., 1969.

Calhoun, Richard J., ed., *James Dickey: The Expansive Imagination: A Collection of Critical Essays*, DeLand, FL: Everett/Edwards, 1973.

Callan, Edward, *Alan Paton* (TWAS 40), New York: Twayne, 1968.

Campbell, Harry Modean, and Ruel E. Foster, *William Faulkner: A Critical Appraisal*, Norman: Un. of Oklahoma Pr., 1951.

Campbell, Jane, and James Doyle, eds., *The Practical Vision: Essays in English Literature in Honour of Flora Roy*, Waterloo: Wilfrid Laurier Un. Pr., 1978.

Campion, Sidney R., *The World of Colin Wilson: A Biographical Study*, London: Frederick Muller Ltd., 1962.

Canadian Literature. *A Choice of Critics: Selections from CANADIAN LITERATURE*, ed. by George Woodcock, Toronto: Oxford Un. Pr., 1966.

Canfield, J. Douglas, ed., *Twentieth Century Interpretations of SANCTUARY: A Collection of Critical Essays*, Englewood Cliffs, NJ: Prentice-Hall, 1982.

Carens, James F., *The Satiric Art of Evelyn Waugh*, Seattle: Un. of Washington Pr., 1966.

Carey, Glenn O., ed., *Faulkner: The Unappeased Imagination: A Collection of Critical Essays*, Troy, NY: Whitson, 1980.

Cargas, Harry J., ed., *Graham Greene* (Christian Critic Series), St. Louis: B. Herder, 1969.

_____, *Responses to Elie Wiesel*, New York: Persea, 1978.

Carnegie Institute of Technology. *Lectures of Modern Novelists* (Carnegie Series in English 7), Pittsburgh: Dept. of English, Carnegie Institute of Technology, 1963.

Carnes, Bruce, *Ken Kesey* (Western Writers Series, No. 12), Boise: Boise State Un. Pr., 1974.

Carpenter, Frederic I., *American Literature and the Dream* New York: Philosophical Library, 1955.

Carr, John, ed., *Kite-Flying and Other Irrational Acts: Conversations with Twelve Southern Writers*, Baton Rouge: Louisiana State Un. Pr., 1972.

Carrabino, Victor, ed., *The Power of Myth in Literature and Film*, Tallahassee: Un. Pr. of Florida, 1980.

Carroll, David, *Chinua Achebe* (TWAS 101), New York; Twayne, 1970.

_____, *Chinua Achebe*, 2nd ed., London: Macmillan; New York: St. Martins, 1980.

Carson, Edward R., *The Fiction of John O'Hara* (Critical Essays in English and American Literature 7), Pittsburgh: Un. of Pittsburgh Pr., 1961.

Carter, George E., and James Parker, eds., *Afro-American Folklore: A Unique American Experience*. Selected proc. of the 3rd Annual Conf. on Minority Studies, Apr., 1975. Vol. 4. LaCrosse: Inst. for Minority Studies, Un. of Wisconsin-LaCrosse, 1977.

_____, eds., *Essays on Minority Cultures*. Selected Proc. of the 3rd Annual Conf. on Minority Studies, Apr. 1975. Vol. 2. LaCrosse: Inst. for Minority Studies, Un. of Wisconsin-LaCrosse, 1977.

_____, eds., *Minority Literature and the Urban Experience*. Selected Proc. of the 4th Annual Conf. on Minority Studies, Apr. 1976. Vol. 6. LaCrosse: Inst. for Minority Studies, Un. of Wisconsin-LaCrosse, 1978.

Carter, Lin, *Tolkien: A Look Behind THE LORD OF THE RINGS*, New York: Ballantine Books, 1969.

Casciato, Arthur D., and James L. W. West, III., eds., *Critical Essays on William Styron* (Crit. Essays on Amer. Lit.), Boston: G. K. Hall, 1982.

Casey, Daniel J., *Benedict Kiely* (Irish Writers Series), Lewisburg: Bucknell Un. Pr., 1974.

_____, and Robert Rhodes, eds., *Irish-American Fiction: Essays in Criticism*, New York: AMS, 1979.

Cash, Earl A., *John A. Williams: The Evolution of a Black Writer*, New York: Third Pr., 1979.

Casper, Leonard, *Robert Penn Warren: The Dark and Bloody Ground*, Seattle: Un. of Washington Pr., 1960.

Cavaliero, Glen, *John Cowper Powys: Novelist*, Oxford: Clarendon, 1973.

Cazalet-Keir, Thelma, ed., *Homage to P. G. Wodehouse*, London: Barrie and Jenkins, 1973.

Chace, William M., *Lionel Trilling: Criticism and Politics*, Stanford, CA: Stanford Un. Pr., 1980.

Chakoo, B. L., *Aldous Huxley and Eastern Wisdom*, Delhi: Atma Ram, 1981.

Chambers, Robert D., *Sinclair Ross and Ernest Buckler*, Toronto: Copp Clark; Montreal: McGill-Queen's Un. Pr., 1975.

Chambers, Robert H., ed., *Twentieth Century Interpretations of ALL THE KING'S MEN: A Collection of Critical Essays*, Englewood Cliffs, NJ: Prentice-Hall, 1977.

Chander, Jagdish, and N. S. Pradhan, eds., *Studies in American Literature: Essays in Honour of William Mulder*, Delhi: Oxford Un. Pr., 1976.

Chandrasekharan, K. R., *Bhabani Bhattacharya*, New Delhi: Arnold-Heinemann, 1974.

Chapman, Abraham, ed., *Literature of the American Indians: Views and Interpretations: A Gathering of Indian Memories, Symbolic Contexts, and Literary Criticism*, New York: New American Library, 1975.

Chapman, Robert T., *Wyndham Lewis: Fictions and Satires*, New York: Barnes & Noble, 1973.

Chase, Richard, *The American Novel and Its Tradition*, Garden City, N. Y.: Doubleday Anchor, 1957.

Chatman, Seymour, ed. & tr., *Literary Style: A Symposium*, London and New York: Oxford Un. Pr., 1971.

Chatterjee, Sisir, *Aldous Huxley: A Study*, Calcutta: Uttaroyau, 1955. Reprinted, Folcroft, PA: Folcraft Pr., 1970.

Chatterton, Wayne, *Vardis Fisher: The Frontier and Regional Works* (Western Writers Ser. 1), Boise, ID: Boise St. College, 1972.

Christ, Carol P., *Diving Deep and Surfacing: Women Writers on Spiritual Quest*, Boston: Beacon, 1980.

Christensen, Inger, *The Meaning of Metafiction: A Critical Study of Selected Novels by Sterne, Nabokov, Barth and Beckett*, Bergen: Universitsforlaget, 1981.

Christian, Barbara, *Black Women Novelists; The Development of a Tradition, 1892-1976* (Contributions in Afro-American and African Studies, No. 52), Westport, CT: Greenwood Pr., 1980.

Chupack, Henry, *James Purdy* (TUSAS 248), New York: Twayne, 1975.

Church, Margaret A., *Time and Reality: Studies in Contemporary Fiction*, Chapel Hill: Un. of North Carolina Pr., 1963.

Churchill, R. C., *The Powys Brothers* (WTW 150), London and New York: Longmans, Green, 1962.

Clancy, Laurie, *Xavier Herbert* (TWAS 552), Boston: Twayne, 1981.

Clareson, Thomas D., ed., *Voices for the Future: Essays on Major Science Fiction Writers*, Bowling Green, OH: Bowling Green Un. Popular Pr., 1976.

Clark, William B., ed., *Critical Essays on Robert Penn Warren*, Boston: Hall, 1981.

Clarke, John H., ed., *William Styron's Nat Turner: Ten Black Writers Respond*, Boston: Beacon, 1968.

Clarke, Mary W., *Jesse Stuart's Kentucky*, New York: McGraw-Hilll, 1968.

Clayton, J. Douglas, and Gunter Schaarschmidt, eds., *Poetica Slavica: Studies in Honor of Zbigniew Folejewski*, Ottawa: Un. of Ottawa Pr., 1981.

Clayton, John Jacob, *Saul Bellow: In Defense of Man*, Bloomington: Indiana Un. Pr., 1968.

_____, *Saul Bellow: In Defense of Man*, 2nd ed., Bloomington: Indiana Un. Pr., 1979.

Coale, Samuel, *Anthony Burgess* (Mod. Lit. Ser.), New York: Ungar, 1981.

_____, *John Cheever* (Modern Lit. Monographs), New York: Ungar, 1977.

Cockburn, Robert H., *The Novels of Hugh MacLennan*, Montreal: Harvest House, 1970.

Coe, Richard N., *Beckett* (Writers and Critics), Edinburgh: Oliver & Boyd, 1964; New York: Grove, 1964.

Cohen, Sandy, *Bernard Malamud and the Trial by Love*, Amsterdam: Rodopi, 1974.

_____, *Norman Mailer's Novels*, Amsterdam: Rodopi, 1979.

Cohen, Sarah B., ed., *Comic Relief: Humor in Contemporary American Literature*, Urbana: Un. of Illinois Pr., 1978.

_____, *Saul Bellow's Enigmatic Laughter*, Urbana: Un. of Illinois Pr., 1974.

Cohn, Ruby, *Back to Beckett*, Princeton, NJ: Princeton Un. Pr., 1973.

_____, ed., *Samuel Beckett: A Collection of Criticism* (Contemp. Studies in Lit.), New York: McGraw-Hill, 1975.

_____, *Samuel Beckett: The Comic Gamut*, New Brunswick, NJ: Rutgers Un. Pr., 1962.

Coindreau, Maurice Edgar, *The Time of William Faulkner: A French View of Modern American Fiction*, Columbia: Un. of South Carolina, 1971.

Coles, Robert, *Flannery O'Connor's South*, Baton Rouge: Louisiana State Un. Pr., 1980.

_____, *Irony in the Mind's Life: Essays on Novels by James Agee, Elizabeth Bowen, and George Eliot* (Page-Barbour Lectures for 1973), Charlottesville: Un. Pr. of Virginia, 1974; New York: New Directions, 1978.

_____, *Walker Percy: An American Search*, Boston: Little, Brown, 1978.

Colley, Iain, *Dos Passos and the Fiction of Despair*, London: Macmillan; Totowa, NJ: Rowman & Littlefield, 1978.

Collins, H. P., *John Cowper Powys: Old Earth-Man*, London: Barrie & Rockliff, 1966.

Collins, Harold R., *Amos Tutuola* (TWAS 62), New York: Twayne, 1969.

Collins, R. G., ed., *Critical Essays on John Cheever* (Crit. Essays on Amer. Lit.), Boston: G. K. Hall, 1982.

_____, and Kenneth McRobbie, eds., *The Novels of William Faulkner*, Winnipeg: Un. of Manitoba Pr., 1973.

Collmer, Robert G., and Jack W. Herring, eds., *American Bypaths: Essays in Honor of E. Hudson Long*, Waco, TX: Baylor Un. Pr., 1980.

Colquitt, Betsy F., ed., *Studies in Medieval Renaissance [and] American Literature: A Festschrift* [Honoring Troy C. Crenshaw, Lorraine Sherley, and Ruth Speer Angell.] Fort Worth: Texas Christian Un. Pr., 1971.

Commentary. *The Commentary Reader; Two Decades of Articles and Stories*, ed., by Norman Podhoretz, with Introd. by Alfred Kazin, New York: Atheneum, 1966.

Connolly, Cyril, *Previous Convictions*, New York: Harper & Row, 1963.

Conradi, Peter, *John Fowles*, London: Methuen, 1982.

Conron, Brandon, *Morley Callaghan*, New York: Twayne, 1966.

_____, ed., *Morley Callaghan*, Toronto: McGraw-Hill Ryerson; London: Books Canada, 1975.

The Contemporary English Novel (Stratford-upon-Avon Studies 198), ed. by Malcolm Bradbury and David John Palmer, London: Edward Arnold, 1979; New York: Holmes and Meier, 1980.

Conversations with Writers (Conversations with, v. 1), Detroit: Gale, 1977.

Cook, Cornelia, *Joyce Cary: Liberal Principles*, London: Vision Pr., 1981; Totowa, NJ: Barnes & Noble, 1981.

Cook, David, *African Literature. A Critical View*, London: Longman Grp. Ltd., 1977.

Cook, Gregory M., ed., *Ernest Buckler*, Toronto: McGraw-Hill Ryerson, 1972.

Cook, Jackie, and Kay Iseman, eds., *Women Writers and the Literary Tradition: Finding the Woman in My Head*, Adelaide: Salisbury College of Advanced Education, 1978.

Cook, Richard M., *Carson McCullers* (Mod. Lit. Monog.), New York: Ungar, 1975.

Cook, Sylvia J., *From Tobacco Road to Route 66: The Southern Poor White in Fiction*, Chapel Hill: Un. of North Carolina Pr., 1976.

Cook, William J., Jr., *Masks, Modes, and Morals: The Art of Evelyn Waugh*, Rutherford, NJ: Fairleigh Dickinson Un. Pr., 1971.

Cooke, M. G., ed., *Modern Black Novelists* (TCV), Englewood Cliffs, NJ: Prentice-Hall, 1971.

Cooper, William, *C. P. Snow*, Rev. ed., London: Longmans, Green, 1962.

Cooperman, Stanley, *World War I and the American Novel*, Baltimore: Johns Hopkins Pr., 1967.

Copeland, Hannah C., *Art and the Artist in the Works of Samuel Beckett*, The Hague: Mouton, 1975.

Copeland, R. A. *Frank Sargeson* (New Zealand Writers and Their Work), Wellington: Oxford Un. Pr., 1976.

Core, George, ed., *Southern Fiction Today: Renascence and Beyond*, Athens: Un. of Georgia Pr., 1969.

Cornillon, Susan K., ed., *Images of Women in Fiction: Feminist Perspectives*, Bowling Green, OH: Bowling Green Un. Popular Pr., 1972.

Costa, Richard H., *Malcolm Lowry* (TWAS 217), New York: Twayne, 1972.

Couturier, Maurice, and Regis Durand, *Donald Barthelme*, London: Methuen, 1982.

Cowan, Michael H., ed., *Twentieth Century Interpretations of THE SOUND AND THE FURY: A Collection of Critical Essays*, Englewood Cliffs, NJ: Prentice-Hall, 1968.

Cowart, David, *Thomas Pynchon: The Art of Allusion*, Carbondale: Southern Illinois Un. Pr.; London: Feffer, 1980.

Cowasjee, Saros, *Mulk Raj Anand, COOLIE: An Assessment*, Delhi: Oxford Un. Pr., 1976.

_____, *So Many Freedoms: A Study of the Major Fiction of Mulk Raj Anand*, Delhi: Oxford Un. Pr., 1977.

Cowley, Malcolm, ed., *After the Genteel Tradition: American Writers*, 1910-1930, Rev. & enl., Carbondale: Southern Illinois Un. Pr., 1964.

_____, *Think Back on Us ... A Contemporary Chronicle of the 1930's*, ed., with an introd. by Henry Piper, Carbondale: Southern Illinois Un. Pr., 1967.

Cox, C. B., *The Free Spirit: A Study of Liberal Humanism in the Novels of George Eliot, Henry James, E. M. Forster, Virginia Woolf, and Angus Wilson*, London: Oxford, 1963.

Cox, Leland H., ed., *William Faulkner: Critical Collection. A Guide to Critical Studies with Statements by Faulkner and Evaluative Essays on His Works*, Detroit: Gale, 1982.

Cox, Martha H., and Wayne Chatterton, *Nelson Algren* (TUSAS 249) New York: Twayne, 1975.

Crabbe, Katharyn F., *J. R. R. Tolkien*, New York: Ungar, 1981.

Creighton, Joanne V., *Joyce Carol Oates* (TUSAS 321), Boston: Twayne, 1979.

_____, *William Faulkner's Craft of Revision: The SNOPES TRILOGY, THE UNVANQUISHED, and GO DOWN, MOSES*, Detroit: Wayne State Un. Pr., 1977.

Crew, Louie, ed., *The Gay Academic*, Palm Springs, CA: ETC Pubs., 1978.

Crook, Eugene J., ed., *Fearful Symmetry: Doubles and Doubling in Literature and Film*, Tallahassee: Un. Pr. of Florida, 1982.

Cross, Richard K., *Malcolm Lowry: A Preface to His Fiction*, Chicago: Un. of Chicago Pr.; London: Athlone Pr., 1980.

Crow, Charles L., ed., *Essays on California Writers* (Itinerary 7), Bowling Green, OH: Bowling Green Un. Pr., 1978.

_____, *Janet Lewis.* (WWS 41.) Boise: Boise State Un. Pr., 1980.

Cruickshank, John, ed., *The Novelist as Philosopher: Studies in French Fiction, 1935-1960*, London: Oxford, 1962.

Crump, Gail B., *The Novels of Wright Morris: A Critical Interpretation*, Lincoln: Un. of Nebraska Pr., 1978.

Currie, Robert, *Genius: An Ideology in Literature*, New York: Schocken, 1974.

Dabney, Lewis M., *The Indians of Yoknapatawpha: A Study in Literature and History*, Baton Rouge: Louisiana State Un. Pr., 1974.

Dahiya, Bhim S., *The Hero in Hemingway: A Study in Development* (Eng. Lang. & Lit. 1), New Delhi: Bahri, 1978.

Dahlie, Hallvard, *Brian Moore* (TWAS 632), Boston: Twayne, 1981.

Dalziel, Margaret, *Janet Frame*, Oxford: Oxford Un. Pr., 1980.

Davenport, F. Garvin, Jr., *The Myth of Southern History: Historical Consciousness in Twentieth-Century Southern Literature*, Nashville, TN: Vanderbilt Un. Pr., 1970.

Davey, Frank, *Earle Birney*, Toronto: Copp Clark, 1971.

Davidson, Arnold E., and Cathy N. Davidson, eds., *The Art of Margaret Atwood: Essays in Criticism*, Toronto: Anansi, 1981.

Davidson, Cathy N., and E. M. Broner, eds., *The Lost Tradition: Mothers and Daughters in Literature*, New York: Ungar, 1980.

Davies, Horton, *A Mirror of the Ministry in Modern Novels*, New York: Oxford Un. Pr., 1959.

Davies, Robertson, *The Voice from the Attic*, New York: Knopf, 1960.

Davis, Robert C., ed., *Twentieth Century Interpretations of THE GRAPES OF WRATH: A Collection of Critical Essays*, Englewood Cliffs, NJ: Prentice-Hall, 1982.

Davis, Robert G., *John Dos Passos* (UMPAW 20), Minneapolis: Un. of Minnesota Pr., 1962.

Davis, Robert M., ed., *Evelyn Waugh* (The Christian Critic Series), St. Louis: B. Herder, 1969.

_____, *Evelyn Waugh, Writer*, Norman, OK: Pilgrim Books, 1981.

_____, ed., *Steinbeck: A Collection of Critical Essays* (TCV), Englewood Cliffs, NJ: Prentice-Hall, 1972.

Day, A. Grove, *James A. Michener*, 2nd ed. (TUSAS 60), Boston: Twayne, 1977.

Day, George F., *The Uses of History in the Novels of Vardis Fisher*, New York: Revisionist Pr., 1976.

Day, James M., *Paul Horgan* (SWS 8), Austin, TX: Steck-Vaughn, 1967.

Dayananda, James Y., *Manohar Malgonkar* (TWAS 340), New York: Twayne, 1974.

D'Costa, Jean, *Roger Mais: THE HILLS WERE JOYFUL TOGETHER and BROTHER MAN*, London: Longman, 1978.

Deakin, Motley F., and Peter Lisca, eds., *From Irving to Steinbeck: Studies of American Literature in Honor of Harry R. Warfel*, Gainsville: Un. of Florida Pr., 1972.

_____, *Rebecca West* (TEAS 296), Boston: Twayne, 1980.

De La Fuente, Patricia, Donald E. Fritz, and Jan Seale, eds., *James Dickey: Splintered Sunlight: Interview, Essays, and Bibliography* (Living Author Ser. 2), Edinburg, TX: School of Humanities, Pan American Un., 1979.

Delbaere, Jeanne, ed., *Bird, Hawk, Bogie: Essays on Janet Frame*, Aarhus: Dangeroo Pr., 1978.

Dembo, L. S., ed., *Nabokov: The Man and His Work*, Madison: Un. of Wisconsin Pr., 1967.

Detweiler, Robert, *Four Spiritual Crises in Mid-Century American Fiction* (Un. of FL Monogs: Humanities, No. 14, Fall, 1963), Gainesville: Un. of Florida Pr., 1964.

DeVitis, A. A., *Anthony Burgess* (TEAS 132), New York: Twayne, 1972.

_____, *Graham Greene* (TEAS 3), New York: Twayne, 1964.

_____, and Albert Kalson, *J. B. Priestley* (TEAS 283), Boston: Twayne, 1980.

_____, *Roman Holiday: The Catholic Novels of Evelyn Waugh*, New York: Bookman Associates, 1956.

Diamond, Arlyn, and Lee R. Edwards, eds., *The Authority of Experience: Essays in Feminist Criticism*, Amherst: Un. of Massachusetts Pr., 1977.

Dick, Bernard F., *The Apostate Angel: A Critical Study of Gore Vidal*, New York: Random House, 1974.

_____, *William Golding* (TEAS 57), New York: Twayne, 1967.

_____, *The Hellenism of Mary Renault* (CMC), Carbondale: Southern Illinois Pr.; London and Amsterdam; Feffer & Simons, 1972.

Dick, Margaret, *The Novels of Kylie Tennant*, Adelaide: Rigby; San Francisco: Tri-Ocean, 1966.

Dietze, Rudolf F., *Ralph Ellison: The Genesis of an Artist*, Nuremberg: Carol, 1982.

Dillard, R. H. W., George Garrett, and John R. Moore, eds., *The Sounder Few: Essays from the HOLLINS CRITIC*, Athens: Un. of Georgia Pr., 1971.

Dipple, Elizabeth, *Iris Murdoch: Work for the Spirit*, London: Methuen, 1982; Chicago: Un. of Chicago Pr., 1982.

Ditsky, John, *Essays on EAST OF EDEN* (Steinbeck Monograph Ser. 7), Muncie, IN: John Steinbeck Soc., Eng. Dept., Ball State Un., 1977.

Doan-Cao-Ly, *The Image of the Chinese Family in Pearl Buck's Novels*, Duc-Sinh, Saigon, 1964. Dissertation (St. John's Un.), 1964.

Dodson, Daniel B., *Malcolm Lowry* (EMW 51), New York: Columbia Un. Pr., 1970.

Doherty, Francis, *Samuel Beckett*, London: Hutchinson, 1971.

Dold, Bernard E., *Edwardian Fall-Out: The Ironic School*, Messina, Italy: Peloritana Editrice, 1972.

Dollarhide, Louis, and Ann J. Abadie, eds., *Eudora Welty: A Form of Thanks*, Jackson: Un. Pr. of Mississippi, 1979.

Donaldson, Scott, ed., *Jack Kerouac: ON THE ROAD* (Viking Critical Library), New York: Viking, 1979.

Donohue, Agnes McNeill, *A Casebook on THE GRAPES OF WRATH*, New York: T. Y. Crowell, 1968.

Dooley, D. J., *The Art of Sinclair Lewis*, Lincoln: Un. of Nebraska Pr., 1967.

_____, *Compton Mackenzie* (TEAS 171), New York: Twayne, 1974.

Dorosz, Kristofer, *Malcolm Lowry's Infernal Paradise*, Stockholm: Almqvist and Wiskell, 1976.

Dorosz, Wiktoria, *Subjective Vision and Human Relationships in the Novels of Rosamond Lehmann*, Stockholm: Almqvist and Wiksell, 1975.

Dow, Hume, *Frank Dalby Davison* (Australian Writers and Their Work), London: Oxford Un. Pr., 1971.

Doyle, Esther M., and Virginia H. Floyd, eds., *Studies in Interpretation*, v. 1, Amsterdam: Rodopi N. V., 1972.

Doyle, Paul A., *Evelyn Waugh; A Critical Essay* (CWCP), Grand Rapids, MI: Eerdmans, 1969.

_____, *Pearl S. Buck*, New York: Twayne, 1965.

_____, *Pearl S. Buck*, Rev. ed. (TUSAS 85), Boston: Twayne: 1980.

Drake, Robert *Flannery O'Connor* (CWCP), Grand Rapids, MI: Eerdmans, 1966.

Driskell, Leon V., and Joan T. Brittain, *The Eternal Crossroads: The Art of Flannery O'Connor*, Lexington: Un. Pr. of Kentucky, 1971.

Ducharme, Robert, *Art and Idea in the Novels of Bernard Malamud: Toward THE FIXER*, The Hague: Mouton, 1974.

Duffin, Henry Charles, *The Novels and Plays of Charles Morgan*, London: Bowes and Bowes, 1959.

Duncan, Bowie, *The Critical Reception of Howard Nemerov: A Selection of Essays and a Bibliography*, Metuchen, NJ: Scarecrow, 1971.

Dunn, Douglas, ed., *Two Decades of Irish Writing: A Critical Survey*, Chester Springs, PA: Dufour, 1975.

Dunn, Thomas P., and Richard D. Ehrlich, eds., *The Mechanical God: Machines in Science Fiction* (Contribs. to the Study of Science Fict. and Fantasy 1), Westport, CT: Greenwood, 1982.

Dupee, Frederick Wilcox, *The King of the Cats and Other Remarks on Writers and Writing*, New York: Farrar, Straus & Giroux, 1965.

Durant, Jack M., and M. Thomas Hester, eds., *A Fair Day in the Affections: Literary Essays in Honor of Robert B. White, Jr.*, Raleigh: Winston, 1980.

Dutton, Geoffrey, ed., *The Literature of Australia*, Baltimore: Penguin, 1965.

_____, *Patrick White*, Melbourne, Australia: Lansdowne Pr., 3rd rev. ed., 1963.

Dutton, Robert R., *Saul Bellow* (TUSAS 181), New York: Twayne, 1971.

_____, *Saul Bellow*, Rev. ed. (TUSAS 181), Boston: Twayne, 1982.

Dyson, Anthony E., *The Crazy Fabric; Essays in Irony*, London: Macmillan, 1965; New York: St. Martin's Pr., 1965.

Desmond, John F., ed., *A Still Moment: Essays on the Art of Eudora Welty*, Metuchen, NJ: Scarecrow, 1978.

Detweiler, Robert, *John Updike* (TUSAS 214), New York: Twayne, 1972.

Eagleton, Terry, *Exiles and Emigres; Studies in Modern Literature*, New York: Schocken, 1970.

Echeruo, Michael J. C., *Joyce Cary and the Dimensions of Order*, London: Macmillan; New York: Barnes & Noble, 1979.

_____, *Joyce Cary and the Novel of Africa*, New York: Africana, 1973.

Eckley, Grace, *Benedict Kiely* (TEAS 145), New York: Twayne, 1972.

_____, *Edna O'Brien*, Lewisburg, PA: Bucknell Un. Pr., 1974.

_____, *Harriette Arnow* (TUSAS 245): New York: Twayne, 1974.

Edel, Leon, *The Psychological Novel, 1900-1950*, New York: 1955.

_____, *Modern Psychological Novel*, Rev. & enl., New York: Grossett and Dunlap, 1964. [Revision of Edel above.]

Edelheit, Steven, *Dark Prophecies*, New York: Revisionist Pr., 1979.

Edmonds, Dale, *Carson McCullers* (Southern Writers Series, No. 6), Austin, TX: Steck-Vaughn, 1969.

Edwards, Clifford D., *Conrad Richter's Ohio Trilogy: Its Ideas, Themes, and Relationship to Literary Tradition* (SAmL 18), The Hague: Mouton, 1970.

Edwards, Owen D., *P. G. Wodehouse: A Critical and Historical Essay*, London: Martin Brian & O'Keefe, 1977.

Eggenschwiler, David, *The Christian Humanism of Flannery O'Connor*, Detroit: Wayne State Un. Pr., 1972.

Ehrlich, Robert, *Norman Mailer: The Radical as Hipster*, Metuchen, NJ: Scarecrow, 1978.

Eisinger, Chester E., *Fiction of the Forties*, Chicago: Un. of Chicago Pr., 1963.

Ellwood, Gracia F., *Good News from Tolkien's Middle Earth: Two Essays on the 'Applicability' of THE LORD OF THE RINGS*, Grand Rapids, MI: Eerdmans, 1970.

Elmen, Paul, *William Golding; A Critical Essay*, Grand Rapids, MI: Eerdmans, 1967.

Elovaara, Raili, *The Problem of Identity in Samuel Beckett's Prose: An Approach from Philosophies of Existence*, Helsinki: Suomalainen Tiedeakatemia, 1976.

Emenyonu, Ernest, *Cyprian Ekwensi*, London: Evans, 1974.

Encyclopedia Britannica. *Great Ideas Today, 1965*, New York: Atheneum, 1965.

Engel, Monroe, ed., *Uses of Literature* (Harvard English Studies 4), Cambridge: Harvard Un. Pr., 1973.

English Association. *Essays and Studies, 1950*, London: John Murray, 1950.

_____, *Essays and Studies, 1966*, ed. by R. M. Wilson, New York: Humanities, 1966.

English Institute Essays, 1952, ed. by Alan Downer, New York: Columbia Un. Pr., 1954. Reprinted, New York: AMS, 1965.

Enright, Dennis Joseph, *Conspirators and Poets*, Chester Springs, PA: Dufour, 1966.

_____, *Man is an Onion; Review and Essays*, La Salle, IL: Library Pr., 1973; London: Chatto & Windus, 1972.

Epstein, Perle S., *The Private Labyrinth of Malcolm Lowry: UNDER THE VOLCANO and THE CABALA*, New York: Holt, 1969.

Esslin, Martin, ed., *Samuel Beckett: A Collection of Critical Essays*, Englewood Cliffs, NJ: Prentice-Hall, 1965.

Estess, Ted L., *Elie Wiesel* (Mod. Lit. Monographs), New York: Ungar, 1980.

Evans, Elizabeth, *Eudora Welty* (Mod. Lit. Ser.), New York: Ungar, 1981.

Evans, Fallon, ed., *J. F. Powers*, St. Louis, MO: B. Herder, 1968.

Evans, Oliver, *Anais Nin* (CMC), Carbondale: Southern Illinois Un. Pr., 1968.

_____, *The Ballad of Carson McCullers, A Biography*, New York: Coward-McCann, 1966. Published in England as *Carson McCullers, Her Life and Her Work*, London: Owen, 1965.

Evans, Patrick, *An Inward Sun: The Novels of Janet Frame*, Wellington: Price Milburn, 1971.

_____, *Janet Frame* (TWAS 415), Boston: Twayne, 1977.

Evans, Robert O., ed., *Graham Greene: Some Critical Considerations*, Lexington: Un. of Kentucky Pr., 1963.

Evans, Robley, *J. R. R. Tolkien* (Writers for the Seventies), New York: Warner Paperback Library, 1972.

Everett, Walter K., *Faulkner's Art and Characters*, Woodbury, NY: Barron's, 1969.

Fadiman, Clifton, *Party of One; the Selected Writings of Clifton Fadiman*, New York: World, 195.

Farmer, Ann D., *Jessamyn West* (WWS 53), Boise, ID: Boise State Un., 1982.

Faulkner, Peter, *Angus Wilson: Mimic and Moralist*, London: Secker & Warburg; New York: Viking, 1980.

Federman, Raymond, *Journey to Chaos: Samuel Beckett's Early Fiction*, Berkeley: Un. of California Pr., 1965.

_____, ed., *Surfiction: Fiction Now ... and Tomorrow*, Chicago: Swallow, 1981.

Feeley, Kathleen, S. S. N. D., *Flannery O'Connor: Voice of the Peacock*, New Brunswick, NJ: Rutgers Un. Pr., 1972; New York: Fordham Un. Pr., 1982.

Feidelson, Charles, Jr., and Paul Brodtkorb, Jr., eds., *Interpretations of American Literature*, New York: Oxford Un. Pr., 1959.

Feied, Frederick, *No Pie in the Sky: The Hobo as American Cultural Hero in the Works of Jack London, John Dos Passos, and Jack Kerouac*, New York: Citadel, 1964.

Felgar, Robert, *Richard Wright* (TUSAS 386), Boston: Twayne, 1980.

Ferns, Christopher S., *Aldous Huxley: Novelist*, London: Athlone Pr., 1980.

Fetherling, Doug, *Hugh Garner*, Toronto: Forum House, 1972.

Fetterley, Judith, *The Resisting Reader: A Feminist Approach to American Fiction*, Bloomington and London: Indiana Un. Pr., 1978.

Fiedler, Leslie, *Collected Essays of Leslie Fiedler*, v. 2, New York: Stein and Day, 1971.

_____, *Love and Death in the American Novel*, New York: Criterion, 1960.

_____, *No! In Thunder: Essays on Myth and Literature*, Boston: Beacon Pr., 1960.

_____, *Waiting for the End*, New York: Stein and Day, 1964.

Field, Andrew, *Nabokov: His Life in Art*, Boston: Little, Brown, 1967.

Field, Leslie A., and Joyce W. Field, eds., *Bernard Malamud: A Collection of Critical Essays* (TCV), Englewood Cliffs, NJ: Prentice-Hall, 1975.

_____, eds., *Bernard Malamud and the Critics*, New York: New York Un. Pr., 1970.

Filler, Louis, ed., *Seasoned Authors for a New Season: The Search for Standards in Popular Writing* (Question of Quality 2), Bowling Green, OH: Popular, 1980.

Fine, Ellen S., *Legacy of Night: The Literary Universe of Elie Wiesel*, Albany: State Un. of New York Pr., 1982.

Finkelstein, Sidney, *Existentialism and Alienation in American Literature*, New York: International Pubs., 1965.

Finney, Brian, *Christopher Isherwood: A Critical Biography*, New York: Oxford Un. Pr., 1979.

Firchow, Peter, *Aldous Huxley: Satirist and Novelist* (Minn. Monographs in the Humanities 6), Minneapolis: Un. of Minnesota Pr., 1972.

Fishburn, Katherine, *Richard Wright's Hero: The Faces of a Rebel-Victim*, Metuchen, NJ: Scarecrow, 1977.

Fisher, Barbara, *Joyce Cary: The Writer and His Theme*, Atlantic Highlands, NJ: Humanities, 1980.

Fitzpatrick, Kathleen, *Martin Boyd* (Australian Writers and Their Work), Melbourne: Lansdowne Pr., 1963.

Fleishmann, Fritz, ed., *American Novelists Revisited: Essays in Feminist Criticism*, Boston: G. K. Hall, 1982.

Fleming, Robert E., *Willard Motley* (TUSAS 302), Boston: Twayne, 1978.

Fletcher, John, *The Novels of Samuel Beckett*, New York: Barnes & Noble, 1964.

Floan, Howard R., *William Saroyan*, New York: Twayne, 1966.

Flood, Jeanne, *Brian Moore*, Lewisburg, PA: Bucknell Un. Pr.; London: Associated Univ. Presses, 1974.

Flora, Joseph M., *Vardis Fisher* (TUSAS 76), New York: Twayne, 1965.

Folsom, James K., *The American Western Novel*, New Haven, CT: College and University Pr., 1966.

Fontenrose, John, *John Steinbeck: An Introduction and Interpretation*, New York: Barnes & Noble, 1963.

Ford, Thomas W., *A. B. Guthrie, Jr.* (Southwest Writers Series 15): Austin, TX: Steck-Vaughn, 1968.

_____, *A. B. Guthrie, Jr.* (TUSAS 396), Boston: Twayne, 1981.

Fossum, Robert H., *William Styron: A Critical Essay* (CWCP), Grand Rapids, MI: Eerdmans, 1968.

Foster, John W., *Forces and Themes in Ulster Fiction*, Dublin: Gill and Macmillan, 1971; Totowa, NJ: Rowman and Littlefield, 1974.

Foster, Malcolm, *Joyce Cary: A Biography*, Boston: Houghton, 1968.

Foster, Richard, *Norman Mailer* (UMPAW 73), Minneapolis: Un. of Minnesota Pr., 1968.

Foster, Robert, *The Complete Guide to Middle-Earth: From THE HOBBIT to THE SILMARILLION*, London: Allen & Unwin, 1978.

Foster, Ruel E., *Jesse Stuart* (TUSAS 140), New York: Twayne, 1968.

Fowler, Doreen, and Ann J. Abadie, eds., *"A Cosmos of My Own": Faulkner and Yoknapatawpha, 1980*, Jackson: Un. Pr. of Mississippi, 1981.

_____, *Faulkner and the Southern Renaissance: Faulkner and Yoknapatawpha, 1981*, Jackson: Un. Pr. of Mississippi, 1982.

_____, *Fifty Years of Yoknapatawpha: Faulkner and Yoknapatawpha, 1979*, Jackson: Un. Pr. of Mississippi, 1980.

Fowler, Douglas, *Reading Nabokov*, Ithaca, NY: Cornell Un. Pr., 1974.

Franklin, H. Bruce, *The Victim as Criminal and Artist: Literature from the American Prison*, New York: Oxford Un. Pr., 1978.

Fraser, G. S., *Lawrence Durrell* (WTW 216), Harlow: Longman for the British Council, 1970.

_____, *Lawrence Durrell: A Critical Study*, New York: Dutton, 1968.

_____, *Lawrence Durrell: A Study*, Rev. ed., London: Faber, 1973.

_____, *The Modern Writer and His World; Continuity and Innovation in Twentieth Century English Literature*, New York: Praeger, 1964.

_____, *P. H. Newby* (WTW 235), Harlow: Longman for the British Council, 1974.

Fraser, Robert, *The Novels of Ayi Kwei Armah: A Study in Polemical Fiction*, London: Heinemann, 1980.

French, R. B. D., *P. G. Wodehouse* (Writers and Critics), London: Oliver and Boyd, 1966; New York: Barnes and Noble, 1967.

French, Warren, and Walter E. Kidd, eds., *American Winners of the Nobel Literary Prize*, Norman: Un. of Oklahoma Pr., 1968.

French, Warren, ed., *A Companion to THE GRAPES OF WRATH*, New York: Viking, 1963.

_____, ed., *The Fifties: Fiction, Poetry, Drama*, DeLand, FL: Everett/Edwards, 1970.

_____, ed., *The Forties: Fiction, Poetry, Drama*, DeLand, FL: Everett/Edwards, 1969.

_____, *J. D. Salinger*, New York: Twayne, 1963.

_____, *J. D. Salinger* (TUSAS 40), Rev. ed., Boston: Twayne, 1976.

_____, *John Steinbeck* (TUSAS 2), New York: Twayne, 1961.

_____, *John Steinbeck* (TUSAS 2), 2nd ed. rev., Boston: G. K. Hall, 1975.

_____, *The Social Novel at the End of an Era*, Carbondale: Southern Illinois Un. Pr., 1966.

_____, ed., *The Thirties: Fiction, Poetry, Drama*, DeLand, FL: Everett/Edwards, 1967.

_____, ed., *The Twenties: Fiction, Poetry, Drama*, DeLand, FL: Everett/Edwards, 1975.

Friedman, Alan W., ed., *Forms of Modern British Fiction*, Austin: Texas Un. Pr., 1975.

_____, *Lawrence Durrell and THE ALEXANDRIA QUARTET: Art for Love's Sake*, Norman: Un. of Oklahoma Pr., 1970.

Friedman, Ellen G., *Joyce Carol Oates* (Mod. Lit. Monogs.), New York: Ungar, 1980.

Friedman, Lenemaja, *Shirley Jackson* (TUSAS 253), New York: Twayne, 1975.

Friedman, Melvin J., and Lewis A. Lawson, eds., *The Added Dimension: The Art and Mind of Flannery O'Connor*, New York: Fordham Un. Pr., 1966.

Friedman, Melvin J., ed., *Samuel Beckett Now: Critical Approaches to His Novels, Poetry and Plays*, Chicago: Un. of Chicago Pr., 1970.

_____, and John B. Vickery, eds., *The Shaken Realist: Essays in Modern Literature in Honor of Frederick J. Hoffman*, Baton Rouge: Louisiana State Un. Pr., 1970.

_____, *Stream of Consciousness: A Study of Literary Method*, New Haven: Yale Un. Pr., 1955.

_____, ed., *The Vision Obscured: Perceptions of Some Twentieth Century Catholic Novelists*, New York: Fordham Un. Pr., 1970.

_____, *William Styron* (Popular Writers Series 3), Bowling Green, OH: Bowling Green Un. Popular Pr., 1974.

_____, and Irving Malin, eds., *William Styron's THE CONFESSIONS OF NAT TURNER: A Critical Handbook*, Belmont, CA: Wadsworth, 1970.

_____, *In All Conscience: Reflections on Books and Culture*, New York: Hanover House, 1959.

Frohock, Wilbur M., *The Novel of Violence in America*, 2nd ed., rev. and enl., Dallas: Southern Methodist Un. Pr., 1957; Boston: Beacon Pr., 1964.

_____, *Strangers to This Ground: Cultural Diversity in Contemporary American Writing*, Dallas: Southern Methodist Un. Pr., 1961.

Fuller, Edmund, *Books With the Men Behind Them*, New York: Random House, 1962.

Gachukia, Eddah, and S. Kichamu Akivaga, eds., *Teaching African Literature in Schools*, Vol. I: Nairobi: Kenya Lit. Bureau, 1978.

Gado, Frank, ed., *First Person: Conversations on Writers and Writing*, Schenectedy, NY: Union College Pr., 1973.

Gakwandi, Shatto A., *The Novel and Contemporary Experience in Africa*, New York: Africana Publ. Co., 1977.

Galloway, David D., *The Absurd Hero in American Fiction: Updike, Styron, Bellow, Salinger*, Austin: Un. of Texas Pr., 1966. Rev. ed., 1970.

_____, *Edward Lewis Wallant* (TUSAS 319), Boston: Twayne, 1979.

Gardiner, Harold C., ed., *Fifty Years of the American Novel: A Christian Appraisal*, New York and London: Scribner's, 1951.

_____, *In All Conscience: Reflections on Books and Culture*, New York: Hanover House, 1959.

Gardner, Philip, *Kingsley Amis* (TEAS 319), Boston: Twayne, 1981.

Garrett, George, ed., *The Writer's Voice: Conversations with Contemporary Writers*, conducted by John Graham, New York: William Morrow, 1973.

Garson, Helen S., *Truman Capote* (Mod. Lit. Ser.), New York: Ungar, 1980.

Garzilli, Enrico, *Circles Without Center: Paths to the Discovery and Creation of Self in Modern Literature*, Cambridge: Harvard Un. Pr., 1972.

Gass, William H., *Fiction and Figures of Life*, New York: Knopf, 1971.

Gaston, Edwin W., Jr., *Conrad Richter*, New York: Twayne, 1965.

Gayle, Addison, Jr., *The Way of the New World: The Black Novel in America*, Garden City, NY: Anchor Pr./Doubleday, 1975.

Geduld, Carolyn, *Bernard Wolfe* (TUSAS 211), New York: Twayne, 1972.

Geering, R., *Christina Stead* (Australian Writers and Their Work), Melbourne: Oxford Un. Pr., 1969.

_____, *Christina Stead* (TWS 95), New York: Twayne, 1969.

_____, *Recent Fiction* (Australian Writers and Their Work), Melbourne: Oxford Un. Pr., 1974.

Geismar, Maxwell, *American Moderns: From Rebellion to Conformity*, New York: Hill and Wang, 1958.

_____, *The Last of the Provincials: The American Novel, 1915-1925*, Boston: Houghton-Mifflin, 1947.

_____, *Writers in Crisis: The American Novel, 1925-1940*, Boston: Houghton-Mifflin 1947; Revised, 1961.

Gelfant, Blanche Housman, *The American City Novel*, Norman: Un. of Oklahoma Pr., 1954.

Gellens, Jay, ed., *Twentieth Century Interpretations of A FAREWELL TO ARMS* (TCI), Englewood Cliffs, NJ: Prentice Hall, 1970.

Gerstenberger, Donna, *Iris Murdoch*, Lewisburg, PA: Bucknell Un. Pr., 1975.

Ghodes, Clarence, ed., *Essays on American Literature in Honor of Jay B. Hubbell*, Durham, NC: Duke Un. Pr., 1967.

Ghose, Sisirkumar, *Aldous Huxley: A Cynical Salvationist*, New York: Asia Pub. House, 1962.

Giannone, Richard, *Vonnegut: A Preface to His Novels*, Port Washington, NY: Kennikat, 1977.

Gibson, Donald B., ed., *Five Black Writers: Essays on Wright, Ellison, Baldwin, Hughes, and LeRoi Jones*, New York: New York Un. Pr., 1970; London: Un. of London Pr., 1970.

Giger, Romeo, *The Creative Void: Hemingway's Iceberg Theory*, Berne: Francke, 1977.

Giles, James R., *James Jones* (TUSAS 366), Boston: Twayne, 1981.

Gilkes, Michael, *The West Indian Novel* (TWAS 592), Boston: Twayne, 1981.

_____, *Wilson Harris and the Caribbean Novel*, London: Longman; Trinidad: Longman Caribbean, 1975.

Gilman, Richard, *The Confusion of Realms*, New York: Random House, 1969.

Gindin, James J., *Harvest of a Quiet Eye: The Novel of Compassion*, Bloomington: Indiana Un. Pr., 1971.

_____, *Postwar British Fiction: New Attitudes and Accents*, Berkeley: Un. of California Pr., 1962.

Githae-Mugo, Micere, *Visions of Africa: The Fiction of Chinua Achebe, Margaret Laurence, Elspeth Huxley and Ngugi wa Thiong'o*, Nairobi: Kenya Lit. Bureau, 1978.

Glaser-Wohrer, Evelyn, *An Analysis of John Barth's Weltanschauung: His View of Life and Literature*, Salzburg: Institut fur Englische Sprache und Literatur, Un. Salzburg, 1977.

Glicksberg, Charles I., *The Self in Modern Literature*, University Park: Pennsylvania State Un. Pr., 1963.

_____, *The Sexual Revolution in Modern American Literature*, New York: Humanities, 1971; The Hague: Martinus Nijhoff, 1971.

Gluck, Barbara R., *Beckett and Joyce: Friendship and Fiction*, Lewisburg, PA: Bucknell Un. Pr.; London: Associated Un. Pr., 1979.

Gnarowski, Michael, ed., *Leonard Cohen: The Artist and His Critics* (Crit. Views on Canadian Writers), Toronto: McGraw-Hill Ryerson, 1976.

Goetsch, Paul, ed., *Hugh MacLennan*, Toronto: McGraw-Hill Ryerson, 1973.

Gold, Joseph, *William Faulkner: A Study in Humanism From Metaphor to Discourse*, Norman: Un. of Oklahoma Pr., 1966.

Goldsmith, David H., *Kurt Vonnegut: Fantasist of Fire and Ice*, Bowling Green, OH: Bowling Green Un. Popular Pr., 1972.

Goldstein, Malcolm, *The Art of Thornton Wilder*, Lincoln: Un. of Nebraska Pr., 1965.

GoodKnight, Glen, ed., *Mythcon I Proceedings*, Los Angeles: Mytopoetic Soc., 1971.

Goodwin, K. L., ed., *National Identity. Papers Delivered at the Commonwealth Literature Conference, Un. of Queensland, Brisbane, 9th-15th Aug., 1968*, London: Heinemann, 1970.

Goonetilleke, D. C. R. A., *Developing Countries in British Fiction*, Totowa, NJ: Rowman and Littlefield, 1977.

Gordon, Andrew, *An American Dreamer: A Psychoanalytic Study of the Fiction of Norman Mailer*, Rutherford, NJ: Fairleigh Dickinson Un. Pr., 1980.

Gordon, Lois, *Donald Barthelme* (TUSAS 416), Boston: Twayne, 1981.

Gordon, William A., *The Mind and Art of Henry Miller*, Baton Rouge: Louisiana State Un. Pr., 1967.

_____, *Writer and Critic: A Correspondence with Henry Miller*, Baton Rouge: Louisiana State Un. Pr., 1968.

Gossett, Louise Y., *Violence in Recent Southern Fiction*, Durham, NC: Duke Un. Pr., 1965.

Gowda, H. H. Anniah, ed., *Powre Above Powres: Essays in South Pacific Literature, Vol. I*, Mysore: Centre for Commonwealth Literature and Research, Un. of Mysore, 1977.

Grabes, H., *Fictitious Biographies: Vladimir Nabokov's English Novels*, The Hague: Mouton, 1977.

Grace, Sherrill, *Violent Duality: A Study of Margaret Atwood*, Montreal: Vehicule Pr., 1980.

Graef, Hilda, *Modern Gloom and Christian Hope*, Chicago: Regnery, 1959.

Graham, John, comp., *Studies in A FAREWELL TO ARMS* (Merrill Studies), Columbus, OH: Charles E. Merrill, 1971.

_____, comp., *Studies in SECOND SKIN* (Merrill Studies), Columbus, OH: Charles E. Merrill, 1971.

Grandsen, K. W., *Angus Wilson* (Writers and Their Work 208), London: Longmans, Green, 1969.

Granqvist, Raoul, ed., *Report of Workshop on World Literatures Written in English Outside Great Britain and the USA: 9-10 June, 1981*, Umea, Sweden: Dept. of English, Un. of Umea, 1982. (UMEA Papers in English, No. 2).

Grant, Judith S., *Robertson Davies* (New Canadian Library; Canadian Writers 17), Toronto: McClelland and Stewart, 1978.

Grant, Mary K., R. S. M., *The Tragic Vision of Joyce Carol Oates*, Durham, NC: Duke Un. Pr., 1978.

Graver, Lawrence, *Carson McCullers* (UMPAW 84), Minneapolis: Un. of Minnesota Pr., 1969.

Graves, Nora C., *The Two Culture Theory in C. P. Snow's Novels*, Hattiesburg: Un. and College Pr. of Mississippi, 1971.

Gray, James, *John Steinbeck* (UMPAW 94), Minneapolis: Un. of Minnesota Pr., 1971.

_____, *On Second Thought*, Minneapolis: Un. of Minnesota Pr., 1946.

Gray, Nigel, *The Silent Majority: A Study of the Working Class in Post-War British Fiction* (Vision Crit. Studies), London: Vision, 1973; New York: Barnes & Noble, 1974.

Gray, Richard, *The Literature of Memory: Modern Writers of the American South*, Baltimore: Johns Hopkins Pr., 1977.

_____, ed., *Robert Penn Warren: A Collection of Critical Essays* (TCV), Englewood Cliffs, NJ: Prentice Hall, 1980.

Greacen, Robert, *The World of C. P. Snow*, London: Scorpion Pr.; New York: London House & Maxwell, 1963.

Grebanier, Bernard, *Thornton Wilder* (UMPAW 34), Minneapolis: Un. of Minnesota Pr., 1964.

Grebstein, Sheldon N., *Hemingway's Craft* (CMC), Carbondale: Southern Illinois Un. Pr., 1973.

_____, *John O'Hara*, New York: Twayne, 1966.

_____, *Sinclair Lewis* (TUSAS 14), New York: Twayne, 1962.

_____, comp., *Studies in FOR WHOM THE BELL TOLLS* (Merrill Studies), Columbus, OH: Charles E. Merrill, 1971.

Green, H. M., *A History of Australian Literature, Pure and Applied, Vol. 2: 1923-1950*, Sydney Angus and Robertson, 1961.

Green, Martin, *Re-appraisals: Some Commonsense Readings in American Literature*, New York: Norton, 1965.

_____, *Yeats's Blessing on Von Hugel: Essays on Literature and Religion*, London: Longmans, Green, 1967.

Green, Rose B., *The Italian-American Novel: A Document of the Interaction of Two Cultures*, Rutherford, NJ: Fairleigh-Dickinson Un. Pr., 1974.

Greenblatt, Stephen Jay, *Three Modern Satirists: Waugh, Orwell, and Huxley* (Yale College Series 3), New Haven: Yale Un. Pr., 1965.

Greiner, Donald J., *Comic Terror: The Novels of John Hawkes*, Memphis: Memphis State Un. Pr., 1973.

Griffin, Robert J., ed., *Twentieth Century Interpretations of ARROWSMITH: A Collection of Critical Essays*, Englewood Cliffs, NJ: Prentice-Hall, 1968.

Griffin, William, ed., *Literature in the Modern World; Lectures Delivered at George Peabody College for Teachers, 1951-1954*, Nashville: George Peabody College for Teachers, 1954.

Griffith, Albert J., *Peter Taylor* (TUSAS 168), New York: Twayne, 1970.

Griffiths, Gareth, *A Double Exile: African and West Indian Writing Between Two Cultures*, London: Marion Boyars, 1978.

Grimshaw, James A., Jr., *The Flannery O'Connor Companion*, Westport, CT: Greenwood Pr., 1981.

Gross, John J., *John P. Marquand* (TUSAS 33), New York: Twayne, 1963.

Gross, Miriam, ed., *The World of George Orwell*, New York: Simon and Schuster; London: Weidenfeld and Nicolson, 1971.

Gross, Seymour L., and John Edward Hardy, eds., *Images of the Negro in American Literature*, Chicago: Un. of Chicago Pr., 1966.

Gross, Theodore L., *The Heroic Ideal in American Literature*, New York: Free Press; London: Collier-Macmillan, 1971.

Grosshans, Henry, ed., *To Find Something New: Studies in Contemporary Literature*, Pullman: Washington State Un. Pr., 1969.

Grumbach, Doris, *The Company She Kept*, New York: Coward-McCann, 1967.

Grunwald, Henry A., ed., *Salinger: A Critical and Personal Portrait*, New York: Harper, 1962.

Grylls, R. Glynn, *I. Compton-Burnett* (WTW), Harlow: Longman, 1971.

Guerard, Albert J., *The Triumph of the Novel: Dickens, Dostoevsky, Faulkner*, New York: Oxford Un. Pr., 1976.

Guetti, James, *Word-Music: The Aesthetic Aspect of Narrative Fiction*, New Brunswick, NJ: Rutgers Un. Pr., 1979.

Gupta, Bhim S., *The Glassy Essence: A Study of E. M. Forster, L. H. Myers and Aldous Huxley in Relation to Indian Thought*, Kurukshetra: Kurukshetra Un. Pr., 1976.

Gupta, G. S., *Mulk Raj Anand: A Study of His Fiction in Humanist Perspective*, Bareilly: Prakash Book Depot, 1974.

Gurko, Leo, *Angry Decade*, New York: Dodd, Mead, 1947. Reprinted, New York: Harper and Row, 1968.

_____, *Ernest Hemingway and the Pursuit of Heroism*, New York: Crowell, 1968.

Gurr, Andrew, *Writers in Exile: The Identity of Home in Modern Literature*, Brighton: Harvester, 1981; Atlantic Highlands, NJ: Humanities, 1981.

Gutman, Stanley T., *Mankind in Barbary: The Individual and Society in the Novels of Norman Mailer*, Hanover, NH: Un. Pr. of New England, 1975.

Guttenberg, Barnett, *Web of Being: The Novels of Robert Penn Warren*, Nashville: Vanderbilt Un. Pr., 1975.

Guttmann, Allen, *The Jewish Writer in America: Assimilation and the Crisis of Identity*, New York: Oxford Un. Pr., 1971.

Gwynn, Frederick L., and Joseph L. Blotner, eds., *Faulkner in the University: Class Conferences at the University of Virginia, 1957-1958*, Charlottesville: Un. of Virginia Pr., 1959.

_____, *The Fiction of J. D. Salinger*, Pittsburgh: Un. of Pittsburgh Pr., 1958.

Gysin, Fritz, *The Grotesque in American Negro Fiction: Jean Toomer, Richard Wright, and Ralph Ellison* (Cooper Monographs 22), Bern: Francke, 1975.

Hadgraft, Cecil, *Australian Literature*, London: William Heinemann, 1962.

Hagopian, John V., and Martin Dolch, *Insight II: Analyses of Modern British Literature*, Frankfurt au Main: Hirschgraben-Verlag, 1965.

Hagopian, John V., *J. F. Powers* (TUSAS 130), New York: Twayne, 1968.

Hakutani, Yoshinobu, and Lewis Fried, eds., *American Literary Naturalism: A Reassessment*, Heidelberg: Winter, 1975.

_____, ed., *Critical Essays on Richard Wright* (Crit. Essays on Amer. Lit.), Boston: G. K. Hall, 1982.

Halio, Jay L., *Angus Wilson* (Writers and Critics), Edinburgh: Oliver & Boyd, 1964.

Hall, James, *The Lunatic Giant in the Drawing Room: The British and American Novel Since 1930*, Bloomington: Indiana Un. Pr., 1968.

_____, *The Tragic Comedians: Seven Modern British Novelists*, Bloomington: Indiana Un. Pr., 1963.

Hall, Robert A., Jr., *The Comic Style of P. G. Wodehouse*, Hamden, CT: Archon, 1974.

_____, *P. G. Wodehouse and the "Saga Habit"*, Ithaca, NY: Linguistica, 1972.

Hamilton, Alice, and Kenneth Hamilton, *Condemned to Life: The World of Samuel Beckett*, Grand Rapids, MI: Eerdmans, 1976.

_____, *The Elements of John Updike*, Grand Rapids, MI: Eerdmans, 1970.

Hamilton, Kenneth, *J. D. Salinger: A Critical Essay* (CWCP), Grand Rapids, MI: Eerdmans, 1967.

_____, and Alice Hamilton, *John Updike: A Critical Essay* (CWCP), Grand Rapids, MI: Eerdmans, 1967.

Hamilton, K. G., ed., *Studies in the Recent Australian Novel*, St. Lucia: Un. of Queensland Pr., 1978.

Hamner, Robert D., ed., *Critical Perspectives on V. S. Naipaul*, Washington, DC: Three Continents, 1977.

_____, *V. S. Naipaul* (TWAS 258), New York: Twayne, 1973.

Handy, William J., *Modern Fiction: A Formalist Approach* (CMC), Carbondale and Edwardsville: Southern Illinois Un. Pr., 1971.

Hankin, Cherry, ed., *Critical Essays on the New Zealand Novel*, Auckland: Heinemann, 1976.

Hardwick, Elizabeth, *A View of My Own: Essays in Literature and Society*, New York: Farrar, Straus & Cudahy, 1962.

Hardy, John E., *Katherine Anne Porter*, New York: Ungar, 1973.

_____, *Man in the Modern Novel*, Seattle: Un. of Washington Pr., 1964.

Hardy, Willene S., *Mary McCarthy*, New York: Ungar, 1981.

Harper, Howard M., Jr., *Desperate Faith: A Study of Bellow, Salinger, Mailer, Baldwin and Updike*, Chapel Hill: Un. of North Carolina Pr., 1967.

Harper, Michael S., and Robert B. Stepto, eds., *Chant of Saints: A Gathering of Afro-American Literature, Art, and Scholarship*, Urbana: Un. of Illinois Pr., 1979.

Harrex, S. C., *The Fire and the Offering, Vol. 2: English Language Novel of India, 1939-1970*, Calcutta: Writers Workshop, 1978.

Harrington, Evans, and Ann J. Abadie, eds., *Faulkner, Modernism, and Film: Faulkner and Yoknapatawpha, 1978*, Jackson: Un. Pr. of Mississippi, 1979.

_____, *The Maker and the Myth: Faulkner and Yoknapatawpha, 1977*, Jackson: Un. Pr. of Mississippi, 1978.

_____, *The South and Faulkner's Yoknapatawpha: The Actual and the Apocryphal*, Jackson: Un. Pr. of Mississippi, 1977.

Harris, Charles B., *Contemporary American Novelists of the Absurd*, New Haven, CT: College and University Pr., 1971.

Harris, Harold, ed., *Astride Two Cultures: Arthur Koestler at 70*, London: Hutchinson, 1975; New York: Random, 1976.

Harrison, Dick, ed., *Crossing Frontiers: Papers in American and Canadian Western Literature*, Edmonton: Alberta Un. Pr., 1979.

_____, *Unnamed Country: The Struggle for a Canadian Prairie Fiction*, Edmonton: Un. of Alberta Pr., 1977.

Harrison, Gilbert A., ed., *The Critic as Artist; Essays on Books, 1920-1970; with Some Preliminary Ruminations by H. L. Mencken*, New York: Liveright, 1972.

Hartley, Lodwick, and George Core, eds., *Katherine Anne Porter: A Critical Symposium*, Athens: Un. of Georgia Pr., 1969.

Hartt, Julian N., *The Lost Image of Man*, Baton Rouge: Louisiana State Un. Pr., 1963.

Hassan, Ihab, *The Dismemberment of Orpheus: Toward a Postmodern Literature*, New York: Oxford Un. Pr., 1971; 2nd ed., Madison: Un. of Wisconsin Pr., 1982.

_____, *The Literature of Silence: Henry Miller and Samuel Beckett*, New York: Knopf, 1967.

_____, *Radical Innocence: Studies in the Contemporary American Novel*, Princeton, NJ: Princeton Un. Pr., 1961.

Haugh, Robert F., *Nadine Gordimer* (TWAS 315), New York: Twayne: 1975.

Hayashi, Tetsumaro, Yasuo Hashiguchi, and Richard F. Peterson, eds., *John Steinbeck: East and West* (Steinbeck Monog. Ser. 8), Muncie, IN: Steinbeck Society of America, Eng. Dept., Ball State Un., 1978.

_____, ed., *Steinbeck and the Arthurian Theme* (Steinbeck Monog. Ser. 5), Muncie: Steinbeck Society of America, Ball State Un., 1975.

_____, ed., *Steinbeck Criticism: A Review of Book-Length Studies (1939-1973)* (Steinbeck Monog. Ser. 4), Muncie, IN: Steinbeck Society of America, Ball State Un., 1974.

_____, ed., *Steinbeck's Literary Dimension: A Guide to Comparative Studies*, Metuchen, NJ: Scarecrow, 1973.

_____, and Kenneth D. Swan, eds., *Steinbeck's Prophetic Vision of America: Proceedings of the Bicentennial Steinbeck Seminar*, Upland, IN: Taylor Un. for Steinbeck Society of America, 1976.

_____, ed., *Steinbeck's Travel Literature* (Steinbeck Monog. Ser. 10), Muncie, IN: Steinbeck Society of America, Eng. Dept., Ball State Un., 1980.

_____, ed., *Steinbeck's Women: Essays in Criticism* (Steinbeck Monog. Ser. 9), Muncie, IN: Steinbeck Society of America, Eng. Dept., Ball State Un., 1979.

_____, ed., *A Study Guide to Steinbeck: A Handbook to His Major Works*, Metuchen, NJ: Scarecrow, 1974.

_____, ed., *A Study Guide to Steinbeck, Part II*, Metuchen, NJ: Scarecrow, 1979.

Heath, Jeffrey, *The Picturesque Prison: Evelyn Waugh and His Writing*, London: Weidenfeld & Nicholson; Montreal: McGill-Queen's Un. Pr., 1982.

_____, ed., *Profiles in Canadian Literature 2*, Toronto and Charlottetown: Dundurn Pr., Ltd., 1980.

Heath, William, *Elizabeth Bowen: An Introduction to Her Novels*, Madison: Un. of Wisconsin Pr., 1971.

Heilbrun, Carolyn G., *Christopher Isherwood* (CEMW 53), New York: Columbia Un. Pr., 1970.

Heineman, James H., and Donald R. Bensen, eds., *P. G. Wodehouse: A Centenary Celebration, 1881-1981*, New York: Pierpont Morgan Lib.; London: Oxford Un. Pr., 1981.

Helms, Randel, *Tolkien and the Silmarils*, London: Thames & Hudson; Boston: Houghton Mifflin, 1981.

_____, *Tolkien's World*, London: Thames & Hudson; Boston: Houghton Mifflin, 1974.

Helwig, David, ed., *The Human Elements: Critical Essays*, Ottawa: Oberon, 1979.

_____, ed., *The Human Elements*, Second Series, Ottawa: Oberon, 1981.

Henderson, Harry B., III., *Versions of the Past; The Historical Imagination in American Fiction*, New York: Oxford Un. Pr., 1974.

Henderson, Katherine U., *Joan Didion*, New York: Ungar, 1981.

Hendin, Josephine, *The World of Flannery O'Connor*, Bloomington: Indiana Un. Pr., 1970.

Hendrick, George, *Katherine Anne Porter* (TUSAS 90), New York: Twayne, 1965.

Heppenstall, Rayner, *The Fourfold Tradition*, London: Barrie and Rockloff, 1961; New York: New Directions, 1961.

Hersey, John, ed., *Ralph Ellison: A Collection of Critical Essays* (TCV), Englewood Cliffs, NJ: Prentice-Hall, 1974.

Hershinow, Sheldon J., *Bernard Malamud* (Mod. Lit. Monogs.), New York: Ungar, 1980.

Heseltine, Harry P., *Xavier Herbert* (Australian Writers and Their Work), Melbourne: Oxford Un. Pr., 1973.

Hesla, David H., *The Shape of Chaos: An Interpretation of the Art of Samuel Beckett*, Minneapolis: Un. of Minnesota Pr.; London: Oxford Un. Pr., 1971.

Hester, Erwin, and Douglas J. McMillan, eds., *Cultural Change in Eastern North Carolina as Reflected in Some of the Novels of Inglis Fletcher and Ovid Pierce*, Greenville, NC: East Carolina Un., 1973.

Heywood, Christopher, ed., *Aspects of South African Literature*, London: Heinemann Educational; New York: Africana, 1976.

_____, ed., *Perspectives on African Literature*, London: Heinemann Educational; New York: Africana, 1971.

Hicks, Granville, *James Gould Cozzens* (UMPAW 58), Minneapolis: Un. of Minnesota Pr., 1966.

Highet, Gilbert, *The Anatomy of Satire*, Princeton, NJ: Princeton Un. Pr., 162.

_____, *Explorations*, New York: Oxford Un. Pr., 1971.

Hilfer, Anthony Channel, *The Revolt from the Village, 1915-1930*, Chapel Hill: Un. of North Carolina Pr., 1969.

Hill, David, *Introducing Maurice Gee*, Auckland: Longman Paul, 1981.

Hillegas, Mark R., ed., *Shadows of the Imagination: The Fantasies of C. S. Lewis, J. R. R. Tolkien, and Charles Williams*, Carbondale: Southern Illinois Un. Pr., 1969. New Edition, 1979.

Hind-Smith, Joan, *Three Voices*, Toronto: Clarke, Irwin, 1975.

Hines, Bede, *The Social World of Aldous Huxley*, 3rd ed., Loretto, PA: Mariale Pr., 1962.

Hinz, Evelyn J., *The Mirror and the Garden: Realism and Reality in the Writings of Anaïs Nin*, Columbus: Ohio State Un. Pr., 1971.

Hipkiss, Robert A., *Jack Kerouac, Prophet of the New Romanticism: A Critical Study of the Published Works of Kerouac and a Comparison of Them to Those of J. D. Salinger, James Purdy, John Knowles, and Ken Kesey*, Lawrence: Regents Pr. of Kansas, 1976.

Hoar, Victor, *Morley Callaghan*, Toronto: Copp Clark, 1969.

Hodson, Leighton, *Golding*, Edinburgh: Oliver and Boyd, 1969.

Hoffman, Frederick J., *The Art of Southern Fiction: A Study of Some Modern Novelists*, Carbondale: Southern Illinois Un. Pr., 1967.

_____, *The Mortal No: Death and the Modern Imagination*, Princeton, NJ: Princeton Un. Pr., 1964.

_____, *Samuel Beckett: The Language of the Self*, Carbondale: Southern Illinois Un. Pr., 1962.

_____, *The Twenties: American Writing in the Post War Decade*, New York: Viking, 1955.

_____, *William Faulkner*, 2nd ed. (TUSAS 1), New York: Twayne, 1966.

_____, and Olga W. Vickery, eds., *William Faulkner: Three Decades of Criticism*, East Lansing, MI: Michigan State Un. Pr., 1960. NOTE: References in the text to Hoffman, F. J., and O. W. Vickery, eds., *William Faulkner*, are to this volume.

_____, *William Faulkner: Two Decades of Criticism*, East Lansing, MI: Michigan State Un. Pr., 1951.

Hoffman, Nancy, and others, eds., *Female Studies VI: Closer to the Ground; Women's Classes, Criticism, Programs—1972*, 2nd ed., Westbury, NY: Feminist Pr., 1972. (Prepared for the Comm. on the Status of Women of the Modern Language Assoc.)

Hoffmann, Charles G., *Joyce Cary: The Comedy of Freedom* (Critical Essays in Modern Literature), Pittsburgh: Un. of Pittsburgh Pr., 1964.

Hoggart, Richard, *Speaking to Each Other; Essays. Vol. II: About Literature*, New York: Oxford Un. Pr., 1970.

Hollis, Christopher, *Evelyn Waugh* (Writers and Their Work 46), Rev ed., London: Longmans, Green, 1958.

_____, *A Study of George Orwell: The Man and His Works*, New York: Regnery, 1956; London: Hollis and Carter, 1956.

Holman, C. Hugh, *The Roots of Southern Writing; Essays on the Literature of the American South*, Athens: Un. of Georgia Pr., 1972.

_____, *Three Modes of Modern Southern Fiction: Ellen Glasgow, William Faulkner, Thomas Wolfe* (Mercer University Lamar Memorial Lectures, No. 9), Athens: Un. of Georgia Pr., 1966.

Holmstrom, Lakshmi, *The Novels of R. K. Narayan*, Calcutta: Writers' Workshop, 1973.

Hook, Andrew, ed., *Dos Passos: A Collection of Critical Essays* (TCV), Englewood Cliffs, NJ: Prentice-Hall, 1974.

Hooker, Jeremy, *John Cowper Powys* (Writers of Wales), Cardiff: Un. of Wales Pr., 1973.

_____, *John Cowper Powys and David Jones: A Comparative Study*, London: Enitharmon Pr., 1979.

Hope, A. D., *Native Companions: Essays and Comments on Australian Literature, 1936-1966*, Sydney: Angus and Robertson, 1974.

Hopkinson, Tom, *George Orwell* (Writers and Their Work 39), Rev. ed., London: Longmans, Green, 1965.

Hovey, Richard B., *Hemingway: The Inward Terrain*, Seattle: Un. of Washington Pr., 1968.

Howard, Leon, *Wright Morris* (UMPAW 69), Minneapolis: Un. of Minnesota Pr., 1968.

Howe, Irving, *The Critical Point: On Literature and Culture*, New York: Horizon Pr., 1973.

_____, ed., *Orwell's NINETEEN EIGHTY-FOUR: Text, Sources, Criticism* (Harbrace Sourcebooks), New York: Harcourt, Brace, 1963. 2nd ed., 1982.

_____, *Politics and the Novel*, New York: Horizon Pr., Meridian Books, 1957.

_____, *William Faulkner: A Critical Study*, 2nd rev. ed., New York: Vintage, 1962.

_____, *William Faulkner: A Critical Study*, 3rd ed., rev. and exp., Chicago: Un. of Chicago Pr., 1975.

_____, *A World More Attractive; A View of Modern Literature and Politics*, New York: Horizon Pr., 1963.

Hoyt, Charles A., ed., *Minor American Novelists* (CMC), Carbondale: Southern Illinois Un. Pr., 1971.

_____, ed., *Minor British Novelists*, Carbondale: Southern Illinois Un. Pr., 1967.

Huebel, Harry R., *Jack Kerouac* (WS 39), Boise, ID: Boise State Un. Pr., 1979.

Huffaker, Robert, *John Fowles* (TEAS 292), Boston: Twayne, 1980.

Hughes, David, *J. B. Priestley: An Informal Study of His Work*, London: R. Hart-Davis, 1958.

Humfrey, Belinda, ed., *Essays on John Cowper Powys*, Cardiff: Un. of Wales Pr.; Mystic, CT: Verry, 1972.

Humphrey, Robert, *Stream of Consciousness in the Modern Novel*, Berkeley: Un. of California Pr., 1954.

Hunt, George W., S. J., *John Updike and the Three Great Secret Things: Sex, Religion and Art*, Grand Rapids, MI: Eerdmans, 1980.

Hunt, John W., *William Faulkner: Art in Theological Tension*, Syracuse, NY: Syracuse Un. Pr., 1965.

Hunt, Tim, *Kerouac's Crooked Road: Development of a Fiction*, Hamden, CT: Shoe String (Archon), 1981.

Hunter, Edwin R., *William Faulkner: Narrative Practice and Prose Style*, Washington, DC: Windhover Pr., 1973.

Hunting, Constance, ed., *May Sarton: Woman and Poet*, Orono: Un. of Maine at Orono 1982.

Huseboe, Arthur R., and William Geyer, eds., *Where the West Begins: Essays on Middle Border and Siouxland Writing, In Honor of Herbert Krause*, Sioux Falls, SD: Center for Western Studies Pr., Augustana College, 1978.

Huttar, Charles A., ed., *Imagination and the Spirit: Essays in Literature and the Christian Faith Presented to Clyde S. Kilby*, Grand Rapids, MI: Eerdmans, 1971.

Hyde, G. M., *Vladimir Nabokov: America's Russian Novelist*, London: Boyars; Atlantic Highlands, NJ: Humanities Pr., 1977.

Hyman, Stanley Edgar, *Flannery O'Connor* (UMPAW 54), Minneapolis: Un. of Minnesota Pr., 1966.

_____, *Standards: A Chronicle of Books for Our Time*, New York: Horizon Pr., 1966.

Hynes, Samuel, ed., *Graham Greene: A Collection of Critical Essays* (TCV), Englewood Cliffs, NJ: Prentice-Hall, 1973.

_____, *William Golding* (CEMW 2), New York: Columbia Un. Pr., 1964.

_____, ed., *Twentieth Century Interpretations of 1984: A Collection of Critical Essays*, Englewood Cliffs, NJ: Prentice-Hall, 1971.

Inge, M. Thomas, comp., *The Merrill Studies in LIGHT IN AU-GUST*, Columbus, OH: Carles E. Merrill, 1971.

Innes, C. L., and Bernth Lindfors, eds., *Critical Perspectives on Chinua Achebe*, Washington, DC: Three Continents, 1978.

International Literary Annual, No. 2, ed. by John Wain, New York: Criterion Books, 1959.

International Literary Annual, No. 3, ed. by Arthur Boyars and Pamela Lyon, London: John Calder, 1961.

Irwin, John T., *Doubling and Incest/Repetition and Revenge: A Speculative Reading of Faulkner*, Baltimore: Johns Hopkins Un. Pr., 1975.

Isaacs, Neil, *Eudora Welty* (Southern Writers Ser. 8), Austin, TX: Steck-Vaughn, 1969.

————, and Rose A. Zimbardo, eds., *Tolkien and the Critics: Essays on J. R. R. Tolkien's THE LORD OF THE RINGS*, Notre Dame, IN: Un. of Notre Dame, 1968.

————, and Rose A. Zimbardo, eds., *Tolkien: New Critical Perspectives*, Lexington: Un. Pr. of Kentucky, 1981.

Isabelle, Julanne, *Hemingway's Religious Experience*, New York: Vantage Pr., 1964.

Iser, Wolfgang, *The Implied Reader; Patterns of Communication in Prose Fiction from Bunyan to Beckett*, Baltimore: Johns Hopkins Un. Pr., 1974.

Iyengar, K. R. Srinivasa, *Indian Writing in English*, 2nd ed., rev. and enl., New York: Asia House, 1962.

Izard, Barbara, and Clara Hieronymous, *REQUIEM FOR A NUN: On Stage and Off*, Nashville, TN: Aurora Oubs., 1970.

Jackson, Blyden, *The Waiting Years: Essays on American Negro Literature*, Baton Rouge: Louisiana State Un. Pr., 1976.

Jacobsen, Josephine, and William R. Mueller, *The Testament of Samuel Beckett*, New York: Hill and Wang, 1964; London: Faber, 1966.

Jain, Sunita, *John Steinbeck's Concept of Man: A Critical Study of His Novels*, New Delhi: New Statesman, 1979.

James, C. L. R., *Wilson Harris—A Philosophical Approach*, Trinidad and Tobago: Un. of the West Indies, 1965.

James, Louis, ed., *The Islands In Between: Essays on West Indian Literature*, London: Longman, 1978.

————, *Jean Rhys*, London: Longman, 1978.

Jameson, Fredric, *Fables of Aggression: Wyndham Lewis, the Modernist as Fascist*, Berkeley: Un. of California Pr., 1979.

JanMohamed, Abdul R., *Joyce Cary's African Romances* (Working Papers 5), Brookline, MA: African Studies Center, Boston Un., 1978.

Jarrett-Kerr, Fr. Martin, *William Faulkner* (CWCP), Grand Rapids, MI: Eerdmans, 1970.

Jefferson, Douglas, and Graham Martin, eds., *The Uses of Fiction: Essays on the Modern Novel in Honour of Arnold Kettle*, Milton Keynes: Open Un. Pr., 1982.

Jehlen, Myra, *Class and Character in Faulkner's South*, New York: Columbia Un. Pr., 1976.

Jellema, Roderick, *Peter De Vries: A Critical Essay* (CWCP), Grand Rapids, MI: Eerdmans, 1966.

Jenkins, Lee, *Faulkner and Black-White Relations: A Psychoanalytic Approach*, New York: Columbia Un. Pr., 1981.

*Jewish Heritage Reade*r, Selected, with an Introduction by Morris Adler, New York: Taplinger, 1965.

Jobes, Katharine T., ed., *Twentieth Century Interpretations of THE OLD MAN AND THE SEA*, Englewood Cliffs, NJ: Prentice-Hall, 1968.

Jog, D. V., *Aldous Huxley, the Novelist*, Bombay, India: Book Centre Private, Ltd., n.d.

Johnson, Ira D., and Christine Johnson, eds, *Les Americanistes: New French Criticism on Modern American Fiction*, Port Washington, NY: Kennikat, 1978.

Johnson, Pamela Hansford, *I. Compton-Burnett*, London: Longmans, 1951.

Johnston, Arnold, *Of Earth and Darkness: The Novels of William Golding*, Columbia: Un. of Missouri Pr., 1980.

Johnston, Grahame, ed., *Australian Literary Criticism*, Melbourne: Oxford Un. Pr., 1962.

Jones, D. G., *Butterfly on Rock: A Study of Themes and Images in Canadian Literature*, Toronto: Un. of Toronto Pr., 1970.

Jones, Edward T., *L. P. Hartley* (TEAS 232), Boston, Twayne, 1978.

Jones, John G., ed., *Mississippi Writers Talking*, Vol. 1, Jackson: Un. Pr. of Mississippi, 1982.

Jones, Judith P., and Guinevera A. Nance, *Philip Roth* (Mod. Lit. Ser.), New York: Ungar, 1981.

Jones, Lawrence W., *John Steinbeck as Fabulist* (Steinbeck Monog. Ser. 3), Muncie, IN: Ball State Un. Pr., 1973.

Jones, Peter G., *War and the Novelist: Appraising the American War Novel*, Columbia: Un. of Missouri Pr., 1976.

Joseph, Gerard, *John Barth* (UMPAW 91), Minneapolis: Un. of Minnesota Pr., 1970.

Joshi, Krishnanand, and B. Syamala Rao, *Studies in Indo-Anglian Literature*, Bara Bazar, Bareilly: Prakash Book Depot.

Josipovici, Gabriel, ed., *The Modern English Novel: The Reader, the Writer, and the Work*, New York: Harper and Row (Barnes & Noble), 1976; London: Open Books, 1976.

————, *The World and the Book: A Study of Modern Fiction*, Stanford, CA: Stanford Un. Pr., 1971.

Jowitt, J. A., and R. K. S. Taylor, eds., *George Orwell*, Bradford, Eng.: Dept. of Adult Ed. and Extramural Studies, Un. of Leeds, 1981.

Justus, James, *The Achievement of Robert Penn Warren*, Baton Rouge: Louisiana State Un. Pr., 1981.

Kalechofsky, Roberta, *George Orwell* (Mod. Lit. Monogs.), New York: Ungar, 1973.

Kanu, S. H., *A World of Everlasting Conflict: Joyce Cary's View of Man and Society*, Ibadan: Ibadan Un. Pr., 1974.

Kaplan, Harold, *The Passive Voice: An Approach to Modern Fiction*, Athens: Ohio State Un. Pr., 1966.

Kaplan, Sydney J., *Feminine Consciousness in the Modern British Novel*, Urbana: Un. of Illinois Pr., 1975.

Karl, Frederick R., *The Contemporary English Novel*, New York: Farrar, Straus, 1962.

————, *C. P. Snow: The Politics of Conscience* (CMC) Carbondale: Southern Illinois Un. Pr., 1963.

————, and Marvin Magalaner, *A Reader's Guide to Great Twentieth Century Novels*, New York: Noonday Pr., 1959.

Kartiganer, Donald M., *The Fragile Thread: The Meaning of Form in Faulkner's Novels*, Amherst: Un. of Massachusetts Pr., 1979.

Kaufmann, Donald L., *Norman Mailer: The Countdown (The First Twenty Years)*, Carbondale: Southern Illinois Un. Pr., 1969.

Kazin, Alfred, *Contemporaries*, Boston: Little, Brown, 1962.

Keefer, Truman F., *Philip Wylie* (TUSAS 285), Boston: Twayne, 1977.

Kegan, Robert, *The Sweeter Welcome: Voices for a Vision of Affirmation: Bellow, Malamud and Martin Buber*, Needham Heights, MA: Humanities, 1976.

Keith, W. J., *Epic Fiction: The Art of Rudy Wiebe*, Edmonton: Un. of Alberta Pr., 1981.

_____, ed., *A Voice in the Land: Essays By and About Rudy Wiebe*, Edmonton, Alberta: NeWest Pr., 1981.

Keller, Rolf H., *The Philosophy of William Golding, with Special Reference to FREE FALL*, Schaffhausen: Jaquerod, 1975.

Kellogg, Gene, *The Vital Tradition: The Catholic Novel in a Period of Convergence*, Chicago: Loyola Un. Pr., 1970.

Kellogg, Jean, *Dark Prophets of Hope: Dostoevsky, Sartre, Camus, Faulkner*, Chicago: Loyola Un. Pr., 1975.

Kemp, Peter, *Muriel Spark*, London: Elek, 1974; New York: Barnes & Noble, 1975.

Kennard, Jean E., *Number and Nightmare: Forms of Fantasy in Contemporary Fiction*, Hamden, CT: Shoestring Pr. (Archon), 1975.

Kennedy, Alan, *The Protean Self: Dramatic Action in Contemporary Fiction*, New York: Columbia Un. Pr., 1974.

Kenner, Hugh, *A Reader's Guide to Samuel Beckett*, New York: Farrar, Straus and Giroux, 1973.

_____, *Wyndham Lewis*, London: Methuen, 1954.

Kenney, Edwin J., *Elizabeth Bowen* (Irish Writers Series), Lewisburg, PA: Bucknell Un. Pr., 1975.

Kent, George E., *Blackness and the Adventure of Western Culture*, Chicago: Third World Pr., 1972.

Kenyon Review. *The Kenyon Critics: Studies in Modern Literature from THE KENYON REVIEW*, ed., by John Crowe Ranson, New York: World, 1951. Reprinted, Port Washington, NY: Kennikat Pr., 1967.

Kermode, Frank, *Continuities*, New York: Random House, 1968.

_____, *Puzzles and Epiphanies: Essays and Reviews, 1958-1961*, New York: Chilmark Pr., 1962.

Kern, Edith K., *Existential Thought and Fictional Technique: Kierkegaard, Sartre, Beckett*, New Haven: Yale Un. Pr., 1970.

Kerr, Elizabeth M., *William Faulkner's Gothic Domain*, Port Washington, NY: Kennikat, 1979.

_____, *Yoknaptawpha: Faulkner's 'Little Postage Stamp of Native Soil'*, New York: Fordham Un. Pr., 1969.

Kettle, Arnold, *An Introduction to the English Novel*, Vol. II: *Henry James to the Present Day*, London: Hutchinson, 1953.

Kiernan, Brian, *Images of Society and Nature: Seven Essays on Australian Novels*, Melbourne: Oxford Un. Pr., 1971.

_____, *Patrick White*, London: Macmillan, 1980; New York: St. Martin's, 180.

Kiernan, Robert F., *Gore Vidal* (Mod. Lit. Ser.), New York: Ungar, 1982.

Kilby, Clyde S., *Tolkien and THE SILMARILLION*, Wheaton, IL: Shaw, 1976.

Kiley, Frederick, and Walter McDonald, eds., *A CATCH-22 Casebook*, New York: Crowell, 1973.

Kilgallin, Tony, *Lowry*, Erin, Ontario: Press Porcepic, 1973.

Killam, G. D., *An Introduction to the Writings of Ngugi*, London: Heinemann, 1980.

_____, *The Novels of Chinua Achebe*, London: Heinemann; New York: Africana Pub. Corp., 1969.

King, Bruce, ed., *Introduction to Nigerian Literature*, Lagos: Un. of Lagos; New York: Africana Pub. Co., London: Evans, 1971.

_____, *The New English Literature: Cultural Nationalism in a Changing World*, London: Macmillan, 1980.

_____, ed., *West Indian Literature*, London: Macmillan; Hamden, CT: Shoestring Pr., 1979.

_____, and Kolawole Ogungbesan, eds., *A Celebration of Black and African Writing*, Zaria: Ahmadu Bello Un. Pr.; Ibadan: Oxford Un. Pr., 1975.

King, Francis, *Christopher Isherwood* (Writers and Their Work 240), Harlow: Longman for the British Council, 1976.

King, Richard H., *A Southern Renaissance; The Cultural Awakening of the American South, 1930-1955*, New York: Oxford Un. Pr., 1980.

Kinkead-Weekes, Mark, and Ian Gregor, *William Golding: A Critical Study*, London: Faber, 1967; New York: Harcourt, 1968.

Kinnamon, Keneth, *The Emergence of Richard Wright: A Study in Literature and Society*, Urbana: Un. of Illinois Pr., 1972.

_____, ed., *James Baldwin: A Collection of Critical Essays* (TCV), Englewood Cliffs, NJ: Prentice-Hall, 1974.

Kinney, Arthur F., *Critical Essays on William Faulkner: The Compson Family*, Boston: Hall, 1982.

_____, *Faulkner's Narrative Poetics: Style as Vision*, Amherst: Un. of Massachusetts Pr., 1978.

Klaus, H. Gustav, ed., *The Socialist Novel in Britain: Towards the Recovery of a Tradition*, New York: St. Martin's, 1982.

Klein, Holger, ed., *The First World War in Fiction: A Collection of Critical Essays*, London: Macmillan, 1976; New York: Harper & Row, 1977.

Klein, Marcus, *After Alienation: American Novelists at Mid-Century*, Cleveland, OH: World, 1962; Meridian, 1965.

Klinkowitz, Jerome, *Kurt Vonnegut*, London: Methuen, 1982.

_____, *Literary Disruptions: The Making of a Post-Contemporary American Fiction*, Urbana: Un. of Illinois Pr., 1975.

_____, and Donald L. Lawler, eds., *Vonnegut in America: An Introduction to the Life and Work of Kurt Vonnegut*, New York: Delacorte Pr., 1977.

_____, and John Somer, eds., *The Vonnegut Statement: Original Essays on the Life and Work of Kurt Vonnegut, Jr.*, New York: Delacorte Pr., 1973.

Knapp, Bettina L., *Anais Nin*, New York: Ungar, 1978.

Knight, G. Wilson, *The Saturnalian Quest: A Chart of the Prose Works of John Cowper Powys*, London: Methuen; New York: Barnes & Noble, 1964.

Knoll, Robert E., ed., *Conversations with Wright Morris: Critical Views and Responses*, Lincoln: Un. of Nebraska Pr., 1977.

Knopp, Josephine Z., *The Trial of Judaism in Contemporary Jewish Writing*, Urbana: Un. of Illinois Pr., 1975.

Knowlson, James, and John Pilling, *Frescoes of the Skull: The Later Prose and Drama of Samuel Beckett*, New York: Grove, 1980.

Kocher, Paul H., *Master of Middle-Earth: The Fiction of J. R. R. Tolkien*, Boston: Houghton, Mifflin, 1972.

Kocher, Paul H., *A Reader's Guide to THE SILMARILLION*, London: Thames & Hudson; Boston: Houghton-Mifflin, 1980.

Koga, Hideo, *Essays on Graham Greene and His Work*, Hiroshima: Hiroshima Un. Pub. Soc., 1977.

Kon, Lynette, *Graham Greene: The Major Novels* (Stanford Honors Essays in the Humanities 4), Stanford, CA: Stanford Un. Pr., 1961.

Kontos, Alkis, ed., *Domination*, Toronto: Un. of Toronto Pr., 1975.

Korges, James, *Erskine Caldwell* (UMPAW 78), Minneapolis: Un. of Minnesota Pr., 1969.

Kort, Wesley A., *Shriven Selves: Religious Problems in Recent American Fiction*, Philadelphia: Fortress Pr., 1972.

Kosok, Heinz, ed., *Studies in Anglo-Irish Literature*, Bonn: Bouvier, 1982.

Kostelanetz, Richard, ed., *The New American Arts*, New York: Horizon, 1965.

_____, ed., *On Contemporary Literature*, New York: Avon, 1964.

Kramer, Victor A., *James Agee* (TUSAS 252), New York: Twayne, 1975.

Krause, Sydney J., ed., *Essays on Determinism in American Literature* (Kent Studies in English 1), Kent, OH: Kent State Un. Pr., 1964.

Kreiger, Murray, *The Classic Vision; Retreat from Extremity in Modern Literature*, Baltimore: John Hopkins Pr., 1971.

Kreyling, Michael, *Eudora Welty's Achievement of Order*, Baton Rouge: Louisiana State Un. Pr., 1980.

Krishnamurthi, M. G., *Katherine Anne Porter; a Study*, Mysore: Rao & Raghavan, 1971.

Kirshnan, Bharathi, *Aspects Structure, Technique and Quest in Aldous Huxley's Major Novels*, Stockholm: Alqvist & Wiksell, 1977.

Krissdottir, Morine, *John Cowper Powys and the Magical Quest*, London: Macdonald and Jane's, 1980.

Kubal, David L., *Outside the Whale: George Orwell's Art and Politics*, Notre Dame, IN: Un. of Notre Dame Pr., 1972.

Kuehl, John, *John Hawkes and the Craft of Conflict*, New Brunswick, NJ: Rutgers Un. Pr., 1975.

Kuehn, Robert E., comp., *Aldous Huxley: A Collection of Critical Essays*, Englewood, NJ: Prentice-Hall, 1974.

Kulshrestha, Chirantan, *Saul Bellow: The Problems of Affirmation*, New Delhi: Arnold-Heinemann, 1978.

_____, *Graham Greene: The Novelist*, New Delhi: Macmillan, 1977.

Kuner, M. C., *Thornton Wilder: The Bright and the Dark*, New York: Crowell, 1972.

Kunkel, Frances L., *The Labyrinthine Ways of Graham Greene*, New York: Sheed and Ward, 1959.

Labrie, Ross, *Howard Nemerov* (TUSAS 356), Boston: Twayne, 1980.

LaHood, Marvin J., *Conrad Richter's America* (SAmL 29), The Hague: Mouton, 1975.

Lall, Rama R., *Satiric Fable in English: A Critical Study of the Animal Tales of Chaucer, Spenser, Dryden, and Orwell*, New Delhi: New Statesman, 1979.

Landess, Thomas, *Larry McMurtry* (Southern Writers Series 23), Austin, TX: Steck-Vaughn, 1969.

Landrum, Larry N., Pat Browne, and Ray B. Browne, eds., *Dimensions of Detective Fiction*, Bowling Green, OH: Popular Pr., 1976.

Lane, Calvin W., *Evelyn Waugh* (TEAS 301), Boston: Twayne, 1981.

Langbaum, Robert, *The Modern Spirit; Essays on the Continuity of Nineteenth and Twentieth Century Literature*, New York: Oxford Un. Pr., 1970.

Langer, Lawrence L., *The Holocaust and the Literary Imagination*, New Haven: Yale Un. Pr., 1975.

Langford, Richard E., ed., *Essays in Modern American Literature*, DeLand, FL: Stetson Un. Pr., 1963.

_____, and William Taylor, eds., *The Twenties, Poetry and Prose: 20 Critical Essays*, DeLand, FL: Everett/Edwards Pr., 1966.

Lanzinger, Klaus, ed., *American-Austriaca: Beitrage zur Amerikakunde*. Band 3. Wein and Stuttgart: Braumuller, 1974.

_____, *Americana-Austriaca: Fetschrift des Amerika-Instituts der Universitat Innsbruck anglasslich seines zhenjahrigen Besthens* (Beitrage zur Amerikakunde, Band 1), Wein; Stuttgart: W. Braumuller Un. Verlag, 1966.

Larsen, Erling, *James Agee* (UMPAW 95), Minneapolis: Un. of Minnesota Pr., 1971.

Larsen, Golden L., *The Dark Descent: Social Change and Moral Responsibility in the Novels of Joyce Cary*, New York: Roy, 1966.

Larson, Charles R., *American Indian Fiction*, Albuquerque: Un. of New Mexico Pr., 1978.

_____, *The Emergence of African Fiction*, Rev. ed., Bloomington: Indiana Un. Pr., 1972.

Laser, Marvin, and Norman Fruman, eds., *Studies in J. D. Salinger: Reviews, Essays, and Critiques of THE CATCHER IN THE RYE*, New York: Odyssey, 1963.

Laurence, Frank M., *Hemingway and the Movies*, Jackson: Mississippi Un. Pr., 1980.

Laurence, Margaret, *Long Drums and Cannons: Nigerian Dramatists and Novelists*, New York: Praeger, 1969.

Laurenson, Diana T., and Alan Swingewood, *The Sociology of Literature*, New York: Schocken Books, 1972.

Lawrence, Robert G., and Samuel L. Macey, eds., *Studies in Robertson Davies' DEPTFORD Trilogy*, Victoria, B.C.: Un. of Victoria, 1980.

Lawson, Lewis A., ed., *Kierkegaard's Presence in Contemporary American Life: Essays from Various Sources*, Metuchen, NJ: Scarecrow, 1970.

Leary, Lewis, *William Faulkner of Yoknapatawpha County*, New York: Crowell, 1973.

Lee, A. Robert, ed., *Black Fiction: New Studies in the Afro-American Novel Since 1945*, New York: Barnes & Noble, 1980.

Lee, Hermione, *Elizabeth Bowen: An Estimation*, London: Vision Pr.; Totowa, NJ: Barnes & Noble, 1981.

Lee, James W., *John Braine* (TEAS 62), New York: Twayne, 1968.

_____, *William Humphrey* (Southwest Writers Series 7), Austin, TX: Steck-Vaughn, 1967.

Lee, L. L., *Vladimir Nabokov* (TUSAS 266), Boston: Twayne, 1976.

_____, and Merrill Lewis, eds., *Women, Women Writers, and the West*, Troy, NY: Whitson, 1979.

Lee, Robert A., *Orwell's Fiction*, Notre Dame, IN: Un. of Notre Dame Pr., 1969.

Leeds, Barry H., *Ken Kesey* (Mod. Lit. Ser.), New York: Ungar, 1981.

_____, *The Structured Vision of Norman Mailer*, New York: New York Un. Pr., 1969.

Lehan, Richard, *A Dangerous Crossing: French Literary Existentialism and the Modern American Novel*, Carbondale: Southern Illinois Un. Pr., 1973.

LeMaster, J. R., and Mary W. Clarke, eds., *Jesse Stuart: Essays on His Work*, Lexington: Un. Pr. of Kentucky, 1977.

LeStourgeon, Diana E., *Rosamond Lehmann* (TEAS), New York: Twayne, 1965.

Levant, Howard, *The Novels of John Steinbeck: A Critical Study*, Columbia: Un. of Missouri Pr., 1974.

Levi, Albert W., *Literature, Philosophy, and the Imagination*, Bloomington, IN: Indiana Un. Pr., 1962.

Levine, George, and David Leverenz, eds., *Mindful Pleasures: Essays on Thomas Pynchon*, Boston: Little, 1976.

Levins, Lynn G., *Faulkner's Heroic Design: The Yoknapatawpha Novels*, Athens: Un. of Georgia Pr., 1976.

Levith, Murray J., ed., *Renaissance and Modern: Essays in Honor of Edwin M. Moseley*, Saratoga Springs, NY: Skidmore College, 1976.

Levy, Eric P., *Beckett and the Voice of Species: A Study of the Prose Fiction*, Totowa, NJ: Barnes & Noble, 1980.

Lewis, Merrill, and Lorene Lewis, *Wallace Stegner* (Western Writers Series 4), Boise, ID: Boise State College, 1972.

Lewis, R. W. B., *The Picaresque Saint: Representative Figures in Contemporary Fiction*, Philadelphia: Lippincott, 1959.

_____, *Trials of the Word: Essays in American Literature and the Humanistic Tradition*, New Haven: Yale Un. Pr., 1965.

Lewis, Robert W., Jr., *Hemingway on Love*, Austin: Un. of Texas Pr., 1965.

Lewis, Sinclair, *The Man from Main Street: A Sinclair Lewis Reader; Selected Essays and Other Writings, 1904-1950*, ed. by Harry E. Maule and Melville H. Cane, New York: Random House, 1953.

Leyburn, Ellen Douglass, *Satiric Allegory: Mirror of Man* (Yale Studies in English 130), New Haven: Yale Un. Pr., 1956.

Liberman, M. M., *Katherine Anne Porter's Fiction*, Detroit: Wayne State Un. Pr., 1971.

Lichtheim, George, *Collected Essays*, New York: Viking, 1973.

Lidoff, Joan, *Christina Stead*, New York: Ungar, 1982.

Lief, Ruth Ann, *Homage to Oceania: The Prophetic Vision of George Orwell*, Columbus: Ohio Un. Pr., 1969.

Light, Martin, comp., *The Merrill Studies in BABBITT*, Columbus, OH: Charles E. Merrill, 1971.

_____, *The Quixotic Vision of Sinclair Lewis*, West Lafayette, IN: Purdue Un. Pr., 1975.

Lindblad, Ishrat, *Pamela Hansford Johnson* (TEAS 291), Boston: Twayne, 1982.

Lindfors, Bernth, ed., *Critical Perspectives on Amos Tutuola*, Washington, DC: Three Continents, 1975.

_____, ed., *Critical Perspectives on Nigerian Literatures*, Washington, DC: Three Continents, 1976.

_____, ed., *Dem-Say: Interviews with Eight Nigerian Writers*, Austin: Afr. and Afro-Am. Stud. and Res. Center, Un. of Texas, 1974.

_____, *Folklore in Nigerian Literature*, New York: Africana Pub. Co., 1973.

_____, and Ulla Schild, eds., *Neo-African Literature and Culture: Essays in Memory of Janheinz Jahn*, Weisbaden: Heymann, 1976.

Lindsay, Jack, *The Elephant and the Lotus: A Study of the Novels of Mulk Raj Anand*, 2nd rev. ed., Bombay: Kutub-Popular, 1965.

Lisca, Peter, *John Steinbeck: Nature and Myth*, New York: Crowell, 1978.

_____, *The Wide World of John Steinbeck*, New Brunswick, NJ: Rutgers Un. Pr., 1958.

Littlejohn, David, *Black on White: A Critical Survey of Writing by American Negroes*, New York: Grossman, 1966.

_____, *Interruptions*, New York: Grossman, 1970.

Litz, A. Walton, *Modern American Fiction: Essays in Criticism*, New York: Oxford Un. Pr., 1963.

Lobdell, Jared, ed., *A Tolkien Compass*, LaSalle, IL: Open Court, 1975.

Lodge, David, *Evelyn Waugh* (CEMW 58), New York: Columbia Un. Pr., 1971.

_____, *Graham Greene* (CEMW 17), New York: Columbia Un. Pr., 1966.

_____, *The Novelist at the Crossroads and Other Essays on Fiction and Criticism*, New York: Cornell Un. Pr., 1971.

Lokrantz, Jessie T., *The Underside of the Weave: Some Stylistic Devices Used by Vladimir Nabokov* (AUUSAU 11), Uppsala: Almqvist & Wiksell, 1973.

Longley, John Lewis, Jr., *Robert Penn Warren* (Southern Writers Series 2): Austin, TX: Steck-Vaughn, 1969.

_____, *Robert Penn Warren: A Collection of Critical Essays*, New York: New York Un. Pr., 1965.

_____, *The Tragic Mask: A Study of Faulkner's Heroes*, Chapel Hill: Un. of North Carolina Pr., 1963.

Lord, Mary, *Hal Porter* (Australian Writers and Their Work), Melbourne: Oxford Un. Pr., 1974.

Lucas, Alec, *Hugh MacLennan*, Toronto: McClelland & Stewart, 1970.

Lucente, Gregory L., *The Narrative of Realism and Myth: Verga, Lawrence, Faulkner, Pavese*, Baltimore: Johns Hopkins Un. Pr., 1979.

Lucid, Robert F., ed., *Norman Mailer: The Man and His Work*, Boston: Little, Brown, 1971.

Ludwig, Jack, *Recent American Novelists* (UMPAW 22), Minneapolis: Un. of Minnesota Pr., 1962.

Lundquist, James, *Chester Himes* (Mod. Lit. Monog.), New York: Ungar, 1976.

_____, *Guide to Sinclair Lewis* (Merrill Guides), Columbus, OH: Charles E. Merrill, 1970.

_____, *J. D. Salinger* (Mod. Lit. Monog.), New York: Ungar, 1979.

_____, *Kurt Vonnegut* (Mod. Lit. Monog.), New York: Ungar, 1977.

_____, *Sinclair Lewis*, New York: Ungar, 1973.

Luschei, Martin, *The Sovereign Wayfarer: Walker Percy's Diagnosis of the Malaise*, Baton Rouge: Louisiana State Un. Pr., 1972.

Lutwack, Leonard, *Heroic Fiction: The Epic Tradition and American Novels of the Twentieth Century* (CMC), Carbondale: Southern Illinois Un. Pr., 1971.

Lynch, Gerard, *Frances MacManus—'The Greatest of These'*, Dublin: Gill and Macmillan; London: Macmillan, 1972.

Lyon, Thomas J., *Frank Waters* (TUSAS 225), New York, Twayne, 1973.

Lyons, Bonnie, *Henry Roth: The Man and His Work*, New York: Cooper Square, 1976.

Lyons, John O., *The College Novel in America*, Carbondale: Southern Illinois Un. Pr., 1962.

Lytle, Andrew, *The Hero with the Private Parts*, Baton Rouge: Louisiana State Un. Pr., 1966.

MacDonald, Scott, ed., *Critical Essays on Erskine Caldwell* (Crit. Essays on Amer. Lit.), Boston: G. K. Hall, 1981.

Macebuh, Stanley, *James Baldwin: A Critical Study*, New York: Okpaku, 1973.

Mack, Maynard, and Ian Gregor, eds., *Imagined Worlds: Essays on Some English Novels and Novelists in Honour of John Butt*, London: Methuen, 1968.

Mackey, Douglas A., *The Rainbow Quest of Thomas Pynchon*, San Bernardino, CA: Borgo, 1980.

Mackin, Cooper R., *William Styron* (Southern Writers Series 7), Austin, TX: Steck-Vaughn, 1969.

MacMillan, Duane J., ed., *The Stoic Strain in American Literature: Essays in Honour of Marston LaFrance*, Toronto: Un. of Toronto Pr., 1979.

Macnaughton, William R., ed., *Critical Essays of John Updike* (Crit. Essays on Amer. Lit.), Boston: G. K. Hall, 1982.

Madden, Charles F., ed., *Talks with Authors*, Carbondale: Southern Illinois Un. Pr., 1968.

Madden, David, ed., *American Dreams, American Nightmares* (CMC), Carbondale: Southern Illinois University Pr., 1970.

_____, *James M. Cain* (TUSAS 171), New York: Twayne, 1970.

_____, *The Poetic Image in 6 Genres*, Carbondale: Southern Illinois Un. Pr., 1969.

_____, ed., *Proletarian Writers of the Thirties*, Carbondale: Southern Illinois Un. Pr., 1968.

_____, ed., *Rediscoveries; Informal Essays in Which Well-Known Novelists Rediscover Neglected Works of Fiction by One of Their Favorite Authors*, New York: Crown, 1971.

_____, ed., *Tough Guy Writers of the Thirties*, Carbondale: Southern Illinois Un. Pr., 1968.

_____, *Wright Morris* (TUSAS 71), New York: Twayne, 1964.

Madison, Charles A., *Yiddish Literature; Its Scope and Major Writers*, New York: Ungar, 1968.

Maes-Jelinek, Hena, ed., *Commonwealth Literature and the Modern World*, Brussels: Didier, 1975.

_____, *Wilson Harris*, Boston: Twayne, 1982.

Magny, Claude-Edmonde, *The Age of the American Novel; The Film Aesthetic of Fiction Between the Two Wars*, New York: Ungar, 1972.

Mahood, M. M., *The Colonial Encounter: A Reading of Six Novels*, London: Collings; Totowa, NJ: Rowman and Littlefield, 1977.

Mahood, M. M., *Joyce Cary's Africa*, London: Methuen; Boston: Houghton-Mifflin, 1965.

Maini, Darshan Singh, ed., *Variations on American Literature*, New Delhi: U. S. Educ. Found. in India, 1968.

Makowiecki, Stefan, *Malcolm Lowry and the Lyrical Convention of Fiction*, Poznan, Poland: Adam Mickiewicz Un., 1977.

Male, Roy R., ed., *Money Talks: Language and Lucre in American Fiction*, Norman: Un. of Oklahoma Pr., 1980.

Malhotra, M. L., *Bridges of Literature: 23 Critical Essays*, Ajmer: Sunanda Pub., 1937.

Malin, Irving, ed., *Critical Views of Isaac Bashevis Singer*, New York: New York Un. Pr., 1969.

_____, *Isaac Bashevis Singer*, New York: Ungar, 1972.

_____, *Jews and Americans* (Crosscurrents), Carbondale: Southern Illinois Un. Pr., 1965.

_____, *New American Gothic*, Carbondale: Southern Illinois Un. Pr., 1962.

_____, ed., *Psychoanalysis and American Fiction*, New York: Dutton, 1965.

_____, ed., *Saul Bellow and the Critics*, New York: New York Un. Pr., 1967.

_____, *Saul Bellow's Fiction*, Carbondale: Southern Illinois Un. Pr., 1969; London: Feffer and Simons, 1969.

_____, ed., *Truman Capote's IN COLD BLOOD: A Critical Handbook*, Belmont, CA: Wadsworth, 1968.

Malkoff, Karl, *Muriel Spark* (CEMW 36), New York: Columbia Un. Pr., 1968.

Manheim, Leonard, and Eleanor Manheim, *Hidden Patterns: Studies in Psychoanalytic Literary Criticism*, New York: Macmillan, 1966.

Manlove, C. N., *Modern Fantasy; Five Studies*, Cambridge: Cambridge Un. Pr., 1975.

Manning, Hugo, *The It and the Odyssey of Henry Miller*, London: Enitharmon, 1972.

Margolies, Edward, *The Art of Richard Wright*: Carbondale: Southern Illinois Un. Pr., 1969.

_____, *Native Sons: A Critical Study of Twentieth-Century Negro-American Authors*, Philadelphia: Lippincott, 1968.

_____, *Which Way Did He Go?* New York: Holmes & Meier, 1982.

Markle, Joyce B., *Fighters and Lovers: Theme in the Novels of John Updike*, New York: New York Un. Pr., 1973.

Markovic, Vida E., *The Changing Face; Disintegration of Personality in the Twentieth-Century British Novel, 1900-1950*, Carbondale: Southern Illinois Un. Pr.; London: Feffer and Simons, 1970.

Marks, Lester J., *Thematic Design in the Novels of John Steinbeck*, New York: Humanities, 1969.

Markson, David, *Malcolm Lowry's VOLCANO: Myth, Symbol, Meaning*, New York: Times Books, 1978.

Marsden, Malcolm M., ed., *If You Really Want to Know: A CATCHER Casebook*, Chicago: Scott, Foresman, 1963.

Marsden, Michael T., comp., *Proceedings of the Sixth National Convention of the Popular Culture Association, Chicago, Illinois, April 22-24, 1976*, Bowling Green, OH: Bowling Green State Un. Pr., 1976.

Martin, Bruce, *Philip Larkin* (TEAS 234), Boston: Twayne, 1978.

Martin, Carter W., *The True Country: Themes in the Fiction of Flannery O'Connor*, Nashville, TN: Vanderbilt Un. Pr., 1968.

Masinton, Charles G., *J. P. Donleavy: The Style of His Sadness and Humor* (Popular Writer's Series 4), Bowling Green, OH: Bowling Green Un. Pr., 1975.

Massa, Daniel, ed., *Individual and Community in Commonwealth Literature*, Msida: Un. of Malta Pr., 1979.

Massie, Allan, *Muriel Spark*, Edinburgh: Ramsay Head Pr., 1979.

Materer, Timothy, *Wyndham Lewis the Novelist*, Detroit: Wayne State Un. Pr., 1976.

Mathews, Richard, *The Clockwork Universe of Anthony Burgess* (Popular Writers of Today 19), San Bernardino, CA: Borgo, 1978.

_____, *Lightning from a Clear Sky: Tolkien, The Trilogy, and THE SILMARILLION*, San Bernardino, CA: Borgo, 1978.

Mathieu, Bertrand, *Orpheus in Brooklyn: Orphism, Rimbaud, and Henry Miller*, The Hague: Mouton, 1976; Atlantic Highlands, NJ: Humanities, 1977.

Matthews, Honor, *The Hard Journey; The Myth of a Man's Rebirth*, New York: Barnes & Noble, 1968.

Matthews, John T., *The Play of Faulkner's Language*, Ithaca, NY: Cornell Un. Pr., 1982.

Mauriac, Claude, *The New Literature*, New York: Braziller, 1959.

Maurois, Andre, *Points of View from Kipling to Graham Greene*, New York: Ungar, 1968; London: Muller, 1970.

Maxwell, D. E. S., *American Fiction: The Intellectual Background*, New York: Columbia Un. Pr.; London: Routledge and Kegan Paul, 1963.

_____, *Cozzens*, Edinburgh: Oliver and Boyd, 1964.

May, John R., *The Pruning Word: The Parables of Flannery O'Connor*, Notre Dame, IN: Notre Dame Pr., 1976.

_____, *Toward a New Earth: Apocalypse in the American Novel*, Notre Dame, IN: Un. of Notre Dame Pr., 1972.

May, Keith M., *Aldous Huxley* (Novelists and Their World), London: Elek, 1972; New York: Barnes & Noble, 1972.

Mayo, Clark, *Kurt Vonnegut: The Gospel from Outer Space (Or, Yes We have No Nirvanas.)* (Popular Writers of Today 7), San Bernardino, CA: Borgo, 1977.

Mayoux, Jean-Jacques, *Samuel Beckett* (WTW 234), Harlow: Longman for the British Council, 1974.

Mays, Wolfe, *Arthur Koestler* (Makers of Modern Thought), Valley Forge, PA: Judson Pr., 1973.

McCadden, Joseph F., *The Flight from Women in the Fiction of Saul Bellow*, Lanham, MD: Un. Pr. of America, 1980.

McCaffery, John K. M., ed., *Ernest Hemingway: The Man and His Work*, Cleveland, OH: World, 1950.

McCaffery, Larry, *The Metafictional Muse: The Works of Robert Coover, Donald Barthelme and William Gass*, Pittsburgh: Un. of Pittsburgh Pr., 1982.

McCall, Dan, *The Example of Richard Wright*, New York: Harcourt, 1969.

McCann, Garth, *Edward Abbey* (Boise State Un. Western Writers Ser. 29), Boise, ID: Boise State Un., 1977.

McCarthy, Harold T., *The Expatriate Perspective: American Novelists and the Idea of America*, Rutherford, Madison, Teaneck, NJ: Fairleigh Dickinson Un. Pr., 1974.

McCarthy, Mary T., *The Writing on the Wall and Other Literary Essays*, New York: Harcourt, Brace & World, 1970.

McCarthy, Paul, *John Steinbeck* (Mod. Lit. Monogs.), New York: Ungar, 1980.

McConnell, Frank D., *Four Postwar American Novelists: Bellow, Mailer, Barth and Pynchon*, Chicago: Chicago Un. Pr., 1977.

McCormack, Thomas, ed., *Afterwords: Novelists on Their Novels*, New York: Harper, 1968.

McCormick, Donald, *Approaching 1984*, Newton Abbot: David and Charles, 1980.

McCormick, John, *Catastrophe and Imagination: An Interpretation of the Recent English and American Novel*, London: Longmans, Green, 1957.

_____, *Fiction as Knowledge: The Modern Post-Romantic Novel*, New Brunswick, NJ: Rutgers Un. Pr., 1975.

McCourt, Edward A., *The Canadian West in Fiction*, Toronto: Ryerson, Rev. ed., 1970.

McDaniel, John N., *The Fiction of Philip Roth*, Haddonfield, NJ: Haddonfield House, 1974.

McDowell, Frederick P. W., *Caroline Gordon* (UMPAW 59), Minneapolis: Un. of Minnesota Pr., 1966.

McDowell, Margaret B., *Carson McCullers* (TUSAS 354), Boston; Twayne, 190.

McFarland, Dorothy T., *Flannery O'Connor* (Mod. Lit. Monog.), New York: Ungar, 1976.

McFarlane, Brian, *Martin Boyd's LANGTON Novels*, Port Melbourne, Vic.: Arnold (Australia), 1980.

McGrory, Kathleen, and John Unterecker, eds., *Yeats, Joyce, and Beckett: New Light on Three Modern Irish Writers*, Lewisburg, PA: Bucknell Un. Pr.; London: Associated Un. Pr., 1976.

McKenzie, Barbara, *Mary McCarthy* (TUSAS 108), New York: Twayne, 1966.

McLeod, Alan Lindsay, ed., *The Achievement of Rex Warner*, Sydney: Wentworth Pr., 1965.

_____, *Rex Warner: Writer*, Sydney: Wentworth Pr., 1960.

McMullen, Lorraine, ed., *The Ethel Wilson Symposium* (Re-Appraisals of Canadian Writers 8), Ottawa: Ottawa Un. Pr., 1982.

_____, *Sinclair Ross* (TWAS 504), Boston: G. K. Hall, 1979.

McNeir, Waldo, and Leo B. Levy, eds., *Studies in American Literature* (La. State Un. Studies, Humanities Series 8), Baton Rouge: Louisiana State Un. Pr., 1960.

Meckier, Jerome, *Aldous Huxley: Satire and Structure*, New York: Barnes & Noble, 1969.

Medcalf, Stephen, *William Golding* (Writers and Their Work 243), Harlow: Longman for the British Council, 1975.

Meeter, Glen, *Bernard Malamud and Philip Roth; A Critical Essay* (CWCP), Grand Rapids, MI: Eerdmans, 1968.

Meinke, Pewter, *Howard Nemerov* (UMPAW 70), Minneapolis: Un. of Minnesota Pr., 1968.

Mendelson, Edward, ed., *Pynchon: A Collection of Critical Essays* (TCV), Englewood Cliffs, NJ: Prentice-Hall, 1978.

Mengham, Rod, *The Idiom of the Time: The Writings of Henry Green*, Cambridge: Cambridge Un. Pr., 1982.

Menon, K. P. K., M. Manuel, and K. Ayyappa Paniker, eds., *Literary Studies: Homage to Dr. A. Sivaramasubramonia Aiyer*, Trivandrum: St. Joseph's Pr., 1973.

Mercier, Vivian, *Beckett/Beckett*, New York: Oxford Un. Pr., 1977.

Meriwether, James B., comp., *Studies in THE SOUND AND THE FURY* (Merrill Studies), Columbus, OH: Charles E. Merrill, 1970.

Merler, Grazia, *Mavis Gallant: Narrative Patterns and Devices*, Ottawa: Tecumseh, 1978.

Merrill, Robert, *Norman Mailer* (TUSAS 322), Boston: Twayne, 1978.

Mesnet, Marie-Beatrice, *Graham Greene and The Heart of the Matter*, London: Cresset, 1954.

Meyers, Jeffrey, *Fiction and the Colonial Experience*, Totowa, NJ: Rowman and Littlefield, 1973.

_____, *A Reader's Guide to George Orwell*, London: Thames and Hudson, 1975; Totowa, NJ: Littlefield, Adams, 1977.

_____, ed., *Wyndham Lewis: A Revaluation: New Essays*, Montreal: McGill-Queen's Un. Pr., 1980.

Michel, Pierre, *James Gould Cozzens* (TUSAS 237), New York: Twayne, 1974.

Michel-Michot, Paulette, *William Sansom; a Critical Assessment* (Bibliotheque de la Faculte de Philosophie et Lettres de l'Universite de Liege, 193), Paris: Societe d'Edition Les Belles Lettres, 1971.

Mickelson, Anne Z., *Reaching Out: Sensitivity and Order in Recent American Fiction by Women*, Metuchen, NJ: Scarecrow, 1979.

Middlebrook, Jonathan, *Mailer and the Times of His Time*, San Francisco: Bay Books, 1976.

Miller, David, *Malcolm Lowry and the Voyage that Never Ends*, London: Enitharmon Pr., 1976.

Miller, James E., Jr., *J. D. Salinger* (UMPAW 51), Minneapolis: Un. of Minnesota Pr., 1965.

_____, *Quests Surd and Absurd: Essays in American Literature*, Chicago: Un. of Chicago Pr., 1967.

Miller, R. Baxter, ed., *Black American Literature and Humanism*, Lexington: Un. Pr. of Kentucky, 1981.

Miller, Ruth, ed., *Backgrounds to Blackamerican Literature*, Scranton, PA: Chandler Publishing Co., 1971.

Millgate, Michael, *The Achievement of William Faulkner*, London: Constable, 1966; New York: Random House, 1966.

————, *American Social Fiction: James to Cozzens*, New York: Barnes & Noble, 1965; Edinburgh: Oliver and Boyd, 1964.

————, *William Faulkner*, Edinburgh: Oliver and Boyd, 1961; New York: Barnes & Noble, 1965.

Millichap, Joseph R., *Hamilton Basso* (TUSAS 331), Boston: Twayne, 1979.

Milliken, Stephen F., *Chester Himes: A Critical Appraisal*, Columbia: Un. of Missouri Pr., 1976.

Milne, Gordon, *The American Political Novel*, Norman: Un. of Oklahoma Pr., 1966.

Milton, John R., *Conversations with Frederick Manfred*, Salt Lake City: Un. of Utah Pr., 1974.

————, *The Novel of the American West*, Lincoln: Un. of Nebraska Pr., 1980.

Miner, Ward L., *The World of William Faulkner*, Durham, NC: Duke Un. Pr., 1952.

Minter, David L., ed., *Twentieth Century Interpretations of LIGHT IN AUGUST* (TCI), Englewood Cliffs, NJ: Prentice-Hall, 1969.

Mitchell, Edward B., ed., *Henry Miller: Three Decades of Criticism*, New York: New York Un. Pr., 1971.

Mizener, Arthur, *The Sense of Life in the Modern Novel*, Boston: Houghton-Mifflin, 1964.

————, *Twelve Great American Novels*, New York: New American Library, 1967.

Mizener, Sharon F., *Manhattan Transients: A Critical Essay*, Hicksville, NY: Exposition, 1977.

A Modern Miscellany (CaSE 11), Pittsburgh: Carnegie-Mellon Un., 1970.

Mohan, Ramesh, ed., *Indian Writing in English*. Papers Read at the Seminar on Indian Eng. Held at the Central Inst. of Eng. and Foreign Langs., Hyderabad, July, 1972. Bombay: Orient Longman, 1978.

Molesworth, Charles, *Donald Barthelme's Fiction: The Ironist Saved from Drowning*, Columbia: Un. of Missouri Pr., 1982.

Monk, Patricia, *The Smaller Infinity: The Jungian Self in the Novels of Robertson Davies*, Toronto: Un. of Toronto Pr., 1982.

Montgomery, John W., ed., *Myth, Allegory, and Gospel: An Interpretation of J. R. R. Tolkien/C. S. Lewis/G. K. Chesterton/Charles Williams*, Minneapolis, MN: Bethany Fellowship, 1974.

Mooney, Harry J., Jr., *The Fiction and Criticism of Katherine Anne Porter*, Rev. ed. (Critical Essays in English and American Literature 2), Pittsburgh: Un. of Pittsburgh Pr., 1962.

————, *James Gould Cozzens: Novelist of Intellect*, Pittsburgh: Un. of Pittsburgh Pr., 1963.

————, and Thomas F. Staley, eds., *The Shapeless God: Essays on Modern Fiction*, Pittsburgh: Un. of Pittsburgh Pr., 1968.

Moore, Gerald, *The Chosen Tongue: English Writing in the Tropical World*, London: Longmans, Green, 1969; New York: Harper and Row, 1969.

————, *Seven African Writers*, London: Oxford Un. Pr., 1966, c. 1962.

Moore, Harry T., ed., *Contemporary American Novelists*, Carbondale: Southern Illinois Un. Pr., 1964.

————, *The Novels of John Steinbeck: A First Critical Study*, 2nd ed., Port Washington, NY: Kennikat, 1968.

————, ed., *The World of Lawrence Durrell* (CMC), Carbondale: Southern Illinois Un. Pr., 1962.

Moore, L. Hugh, Jr., *Robert Penn Warren and History: "The Big Myth We Live"* (SAmL 21), The Hague: Mouton, 1970.

Moorjani, Angela B., *Abysmal Games in the Novels of Samuel Beckett*, Chapel Hill: Un. of North Carolina, 1982.

Morace, Robert A., and Kathryn VanSpanckeren, eds., *John Gardner: Critical Perspectives*, Carbondale: Southern Illinois Un. Pr., 1982.

Morley, Patricia A., *The Comedians: Hug Hood and Rudy Wiebe*, Toronto: Clarke, Irwin, 1977.

————, *The Immortal Moralists: Hugh MacLennan and Leonard Cohen*, Toronto: Clarke, Irwin, 1972.

————, *Margaret Laurence* (TWAS 591), Boston: Twayne, 1981.

————, *Morley Callaghan* (Canadian Writers, 16), Toronto: McClelland and Stewart, 1978.

————, *The Mystery of Unity: Theme and Technique in the Novels of Patrick White*, Montreal: McGill-Queen's Un. Pr., 1972.

Morot-Sir, Edouard, Howard Harper, and Douglas McMillan III., eds., *Samuel Beckett: The Art of Rhetoric*, Chapel Hill: Dept. of Romance Languages, Un. of North Carolina, 1976.

Morrell, David, *John Barth: An Introduction*, University Park: Pennsylvania State Un. Pr., 1976.

Morris, J. H. C., with A. D. Macintyre, *Thank You, Wodehouse*, London: Weidenfeld & Nicolson; New York: St. Martin's, 1981.

Morris, Lloyd, *Postscript to Yesterday; America: The Last Fifty Years*, New York: Random House, 1974.

Morris, Robert K., and Irving Malin, eds., *Achievement of William Styron*, Rev. ed., Athens: Un. of Georgia Pr., 1981.

————, *The Achievement of William Styron*, Athens: Un. of Georgia Pr., 1975.

Morris, Robert K., *The Consolations of Ambiguity: An Essay on the Novels of Anthony Burgess*, Columbia: Un. of Missouri Pr., 1971.

————, *Continuance and Change: The Contemporary British Novel Sequence* (CMC), Carbondale: Southern Illinois Un. Pr.; London: Feffer & Simons, 1972.

————, *The Novels of Anthony Powell* (Critical Essays in Modern Literature), Pittsburgh: Un. of Pittsburgh Pr., 1968.

————, ed., *Old Lines, New Forces: Essays on the Contemporary British Novel, 1960-1970*, Rutherford, NJ: Fairleigh Dickinson Un. Pr.; London: Associated Un. Pr., 1976.

————, *Paradoxes of Order: Some Perspectives on the Fiction of V. S. Naipaul*, Columbia: Un. of Missouri Pr., 1975.

Morris, Wright, *The Territory Ahead*, New York: Harcourt, 1958.

Morrison, David, ed., *Essays on Neil M. Gunn*, Turso: Caithness Books, 1971.

Morton, Donald E., *Vladimir Nabokov* (Mod. Lit. Monog.), New York: Ungar, 1974.

Moseley, Edwin M., *Pseudonyms of Christ in the Modern Novel: Motifs and Methods*, Pittsburgh: Un. of Pittsburgh Pr., 1962.

Moss, John ed., *The Canadian Novel: Here and Now* (Canadian Novel 1), Toronto: NC Pr., 1978.

————, ed., *The Canadian Novel. v. 3: Modern Times: A Critical Anthology*, Toronto: NC Pr., 1982.

————, *Patterns of Isolation in English Canadian Fiction*, Toronto: McClelland and Stewart, 1974.

————, *Sex and Violence in the Canadian Novel: The Ancestral Present*, Toronto: McClelland and Stewart, 1977.

Mottram, Eric, *William Burroughs: The Algebra of Need*, London: Boyars, 1977.

Moynahan, Julian, *Vladimir Nabokov* (UMPAW 96), Minneapolis: Un. of Minnesota Pr., 1971.

Mudrick, Marvin, *On Culture and Literature*, New York: Horizon Pr., 1970.

Mueller, William R., *Celebration of Life; Studies in Modern Fiction*, New York: Sheed and Ward, 1972.

_____, *The Prophetic Voice in Modern Fiction*, New York: Association Pr., 1959.

Mukherjee, Meenakshi, ed., *Considerations*, New Delhi: Allied Publishers, 1977.

_____, *The Twice Born Fiction: Themes and Techniques in the Indian Novel in English*, New Delhi: Heinemann Educ. Books, 1971.

Mulkeen, Anne, *Wild Thyme, Winter Lightning: The Symbolic Novels of L. P. Hartley*, Detroit: Wayne State Un. Pr., 1974.

Muller, Gilbert H., *Nightmares and Visions: Flannery O'Connor and the Catholic Grotesque*, Athens: Un. of Georgia Pr., 1972.

Murray, Edward, *The Cinematic Imagination; Writers and the Motion Pictures*, New York: Ungar, 1972.

Myer, Valerie G., *Margaret Drabble: Puritanism and Permissiveness*, London: Vision Pr.; New York: Barnes & Noble, 1974.

Nagel, James, ed., *Critical Essays on CATCH-22*, Encino, CA: Dickenson, 1974.

Nahal, Chaman, *The Narrative Pattern in Ernest Hemingway's Fiction*, Rutherford, NJ: Fairleigh Dickinson Un. Pr., 1971.

Naik, M. K., S. K. Desai, and G. S. Amur, eds., *Critical Essays on Indian Writing in English. Presented to Armando Menezes*, Dharwar: Karnatak Un., Rev. and Enlarged ed., 1972.

_____, S. K. Desai, and S. T. Kallapur, eds., *Image of India in Western Creative Writing*, Dharwar: Karnatak Un. Pr.; Madras: Macmillan, 1971.

_____, S. K. Desai, and S. Mokashi-Punekar, eds., *Indian Studies in American Fiction*, Dharwar: Karnatak Un. Pr.: Delhi: Macmillan India, 1974.

_____, *Mulk Raj Anand*, New York: Humanities, 1973.

_____, *Raja Rao* (TWAS 234), New York: Twayne, 1972.

Nakadate, Neil, ed., *Robert Penn Warren: Critical Perspectives*, Lexington: Un. Pr. of Kentucky, 1981.

Nance, William L., *Katherine Anne Porter and the Art of Rejection*, Chapel Hill: Un. of North Carolina Pr., 1964.

_____, *The Worlds of Truman Capote*, New York: Stein & Day, 1970.

Narasimhaiah, C. D., ed., *Awakened Conscience: Studies in Commonwealth Literature*, New Delhi: Sterling, 1978.

_____, ed., *Indian Literature of the Past Fifty Years (1917-1967)*, Prasaranga: Un. of Mysore, 1970.

_____, ed., *An Introduction to Australian Literature*, Brisbane: Jacaranda Pr., 1965.

Narasimhan, Raji, *Sensibility Under Stress: Aspects of Indo-English Fiction*, Ashajanak, 1976.

The Nation. *A View of the Nation: An Anthology, 1955-1959*, ed. by Henry M. Christman, New York: Grove, 1960.

Natterstad, J. H., *Francis Stuart* (The Irish Writers Series), Lewisburg, PA: Bucknell Un. Pr.; London: Associated Un. Presses, 1974.

Nazareth, Peter, *An African View of Literature*, Evanston, IL: Northwestern Un. Pr., 1974.

Nebeker, Helen, *Jean Rhys: Woman in Passage: A Critical Study of the Novels of Jean Rhys*, Montreal: Enen Press Women's Pubs., 1981.

Neinstein, Raymond L., *The Ghost Country: A Study of the Novels of Larry McMurtry*, Berkeley, CA: Creative Arts, 1976.

Nelson, Gerald B., *Ten Versions of America*, New York: Knopf, 1972.

Nelson, Jane A., *Form and Image in the Fiction of Henry Miller*, Detroit: Wayne State Un. Pr., 1970.

Nelson, Raymond S., *Hemingway: Expressionist Artist*, Ames: Iowa State Un. Pr., 1979.

Nelson, William, *William Golding's LORD OF THE FLIES: A Source Book*, New York: Odyssey Pr., 1963.

Nemerov, Howard, *Poetry and Fiction: Essays*, New Brunswick, NJ: Rutgers Un. Pr., 1963.

Nesbitt, Bruce, ed., *Earle Birney*, Toronto: McGraw-Hill Ryerson, 1974.

Nevius, Blake, *Ivy Compton-Burnett* (CEMW 47), New York: Columbia Un. Pr., 1970.

New, William H., *Articulating West; Essays on Purpose and Form in Modern Canadian Literature*, Toronto: New Pr., 1972.

_____, *Malcolm Lowry*, Toronto: McClelland and Stewart, 1971.

_____, ed., *Margaret Laurence* (Crit. Views on Canadian Writers), Toronto: McGraw-Hill Ryerson, 1977.

New World Writing (13th Mentor Selection), New York: New American Library, 1958.

Newman, Charles, and William A. Henkin, Jr., eds., *Under 30: Fiction, Poetry and Criticism of the New American Writers*, Bloomington: Indiana Un. Pr., 1970 (c. 1969).

Ngugi Wa Thiong'o [James Ngugi], *Homecoming: Essays on African and Caribbean Literature, Culture and Politics* (SAfrL), London: Heinemann, 1972; New York: Lawrence Hill & Co., 1973.

Niall, Brenda M., *Martin Boyd*, Melbourne: Oxford Un. Pr., 1977. [Bibliography.]

_____, *Martin Boyd* (Australian Writers and Their Work), Melbourne: Oxford Un. Pr., 1974.

Nilon, Charles H., *Faulkner and the Negro*, New York: Citadel, 1965.

Nilsen, Don L. F., ed., *Meaning: A Common Ground of Linguistics and Literature. In Honor of Norman C. Stageberg*, Cedar Falls: Un. of Iowa, 1973.

Nitzsche, Jane C., *Tolkien's Art: A "Mythology for England,"* New York: St. Martin's, 1979.

Niven, Alastair, ed., *The Commonwealth Writer Overseas: Themes of Exile and Expatriation*, Brussels: Didier, 1976.

_____, *The Yoke of Pity: A Study in the Fictional Writings of Mulk Raj Anand*, New Delhi: Arnold-Heinemann, 1978.

Noad, Charles E., *The Trees, the Jewels, and the Rings: A Discursive Enquiry into Things Little Known on Middle-Earth*. Harrow: Tolkien Society, 1977.

Noble, David W., *The Eternal Adam and the New World Garden: The Central Myth in the American Novel Since 1830*, New York: Braziller, 1968.

Noble, R. W., *Joyce Cary*, New York: Barnes & Noble; Edinburgh: Oliver & Boyd, 1973.

Noel, Ruth S., *The Languages of Tolkien's Middle-Earth*, Boston: Houghton-Mifflin, 1980.

_____, *The Mythology of Middle-Earth*, Boston: Houghton-Mifflin, 1977.

Norris, Leslie, *Glyn Jones*, Cardiff: Un. of Wales Pr., 1973.

Northey, Margot, *The Haunted Wilderness: The Gothic and Grotesque in Canadian Fiction*, Toronto: Un. of Toronto Pr., 1976.

Oberhelman, Harley D., *The Presence of Faulkner in the Writings of Garcia Marquez* (Texas Tech Graduate Studies 22), Lubbock: Texas Tech Pr., 1980.

O'Brien, Conor Cruise, *Maria Cross: Imaginative Patterns in a Group of Modern Catholic Writers*, New Edition. London: Burns and Oates, 1963; Fresno, CA: Academy Guild Pr., 1963.

O'Brien, John, ed., *Interviews with Black Writers*, New York: Liveright, 1973.

O'Connor, William Van, ed., *Forms of Modern Fiction: Essays Collected in Honor of Joseph Warren Beach*, Bloomington: Un. of Indiana Pr., (Midland edition), 1959. Originally published by Un. of Minnesota, 1948.

_____, *The Grotesque: An American Genre and Other Essays*, Carbondale: Southern Illinois Un. Pr., 1962.

_____, *Joyce Cary* (CEMW 16), New York: Columbia Un. Pr., 1966.

_____, *The New University Wits and the End of Modernism* (Crosscurrents/Modern Critiques), Carbondale: Southern Illinois Un. Pr., 1963.

_____, ed., *Seven Modern American Novelists: An Introduction*, Minneapolis: Un. of Minnesota Pr., 1964.

_____, *The Tangled Fire of William Faulkner*, Minneapolis: Un. of Minnesota Pr., 1954.

_____, *William Faulkner* (UMPAW 3), Minneapolis: Un. of Minnesota Pr., 1959.

O'Daniel, Therman B., ed., *James Baldwin: A Critical Evaluation*, Washington, DC: Howard Un. Pr., 1977.

Odier, Daniel, *The Job: Interviews with William S. Burroughs*. Rev. and enl. ed., New York: Grove Pr., 1970.

O'Donnell, Donat, *Maria Cross: Imaginative Patterns in a Group of Modern Catholic Writers*, New York: Oxford Un. Pr., 1952.

O'Donnell, Patrick, *John Hawkes* (TUSAS 418), Boston: Twayne, 1982.

O'Faolain, Sean, *The Vanishing Hero: Studies in Novelists of the Twenties*, Boston: Little, Brown, 1956.

Ogungbesan, Kolawole, *The Writing of Peter Abrahams*, London: Hodder & Stoughton; New York: Africana Pub. Co., 1979.

Ogunmola, M. O., *Study Notes on Chinua Achebe's THINGS FALL APART*, Ibadan: Onibonoje Pr., 1969.

O'Hara, J. D., ed., *Twentieth Century Interpretations of MOLLOY, MALONE DIES, THE UNNAMABLE: A Collection of Critical Essays*, Englewood Cliffs, NJ: Prentice-Hall, 1970.

Ohlin, Peter H., *Agee*, New York: Obolensky, 1966.

Okpaku, Joseph O., ed., *New African Literature and the Arts*, Crowell in Association with the Third Pr., Vols. 1 and 2 and 3, 1970.

Olderman, Raymond M., *Beyond the Waste Land: A Study of the American Novel in the Nineteen-Sixties*, New Haven: Yale Un. Pr., 1972.

Oldsey, Bernard S., and Stanley Weinbraub, *The Art of William Golding*, New York: Harcourt, 1965.

_____, *Hemingway's Hidden Craft: The Writing of A FAREWELL TO ARMS*, University Park: Pennsylvania State Un. Pr., 1979.

Olney, James, *Tell Me Africa: An Approach to African Literature*, Princeton, NJ: Princeton Un. Pr., 1973.

Olshen, Barry N., *John Fowles*, New York: Ungar, 1978.

O'Meally, Robert G., *The Craft of Ralph Ellison*, Cambridge: Harvard Un. Pr., 1980.

On Poets and Poetry: Second Series, Salzburg: Inst. für Anglistik and Amerikanistik, Un. Salzburg, 1980.

Ondaatje, Michael, *Leonard Cohen*, Toronto: McClelland and Stewart, 1970.

O'Neill, Timothy R., *The Individuated Hobbit: Jung, Tolkien and the Archetypes of Middle-earth*, Boston: Houghton-Mifflin, 1979.

Opdahl, Keith M., *The Novels of Saul Bellow: An Introduction*, University Park: Pennsylvania State Un. Pr., 1967.

Orvell, Miles, *Invisible Parade: The Fiction of Flannery O'Connor*, Philadelphia: Temple Un. Pr., 1972.

Orwell, George, *Such, Such Were the Joys*, New York: Harcourt, 1953.

Oxley, B. T., *George Orwell* (Literature in Perspective), London: Evans Bros., 1967; (Arco Literary Critiques), New York: Arco, 1969.

Pacey, Desmond, *Creative Writing in Canada: A Short History of English-Canadian Literature*, Rev. ed., Toronto: Ryerson Pr., 1961.

_____, *Ethel Wilson* (TWAS 33), New York: Twayne, 1967.

Padovano, Anthony T., *The Estranged God: Modern Man's Search for Belief*, New York: Sheed and Ward, 1966.

Page, Norman, ed., *Nabokov: The Critical Heritage*, London: Routledge & Kegan Paul, 1982.

Page, Sally R., *Faulkner's Women: Characterization and Meaning*, DeLand, FL: Everett/Edwards, 1972.

Paine, Sylvia, *Beckett, Nabokov, Nin: Motives and Modernism*, Port Washington, NY: London: Kennikat Pr., 1981.

Palmer, Eustace, *The Growth of the African Novel*, London: Heinemann, 1979.

_____, *An Introduction to the African Novel; A Critical Study of Twelve Books by Chinua Achebe [and others]*, New York: Africana Publ. Corp., 1972.

Palmer, William J., *The Fiction of John Fowles: Tradition, Art, and the Loneliness of Selfhood*, Columbia: Un. of Missouri Pr., 1974.

Panichas, George A., ed., *Mansions of the Spirit; Essays in Religion and Literature*, New York: Hawthorn, 1967.

_____, ed., *The Politics of Twentieth-Century Novelists*, New York: Hawthorn Books, 1971.

Papajewski, Helmut, *Thornton Wilder*, Franfurt am Main: Athenäum, 1961; New York: Ungar, 1968 (Transl. by John Conway).

Parameswaran, Uma, *A Study of Representative Indo-English Novelists*, New Delhi: Vikas Publishing House, 1976.

Páricsy, Pál, ed., *Studies on Modern Black African Literature* (Studies on Developing Countries 43), Budapest: Center for Afro-Asian Research of the Hungarian Academy of Sciences, 1971.

Parker, Carolyn A., & Stephen H. Arnold, eds., with A. M. Porter, and H. Wylie, *When the Drumbeat Changes*, Washington, DC: Three Continents, 1981.

Parker, Kenneth, ed., *The South African Novel in English: Essays in Criticism and Society*, New York: Africana, 1978.

Parkinson, Thomas, ed., *A Casebook of the Beat*, New York: Thomas Y. Crowell, 1961.

Pearce, Richard, ed., *Critical Essays on Thomas Pynchon*, Boston: Hall, 1981.

_____, *Stages of the Clown: Perspectives on Modern Fiction from Dostoyevsky to Beckett* (CMC), Carbondale: Southern Illinois Un. Pr., 1970.

_____, *William Styron* (UMPAW 98), Minneapolis: Un. of Minnesota Pr., 1971.

Pearsall, Robert B., *The Life and Writings of Ernest Hemingway*, Amsterdam: Rodop, 1973.

Peary, Gerald, and Roger Shatzkin, eds., *The Classic American Novel and the Movies* (Ungar Film Lib.), New York: Ungar, 1977.

Peavy, Charles D., *Go Slow Now: Faulkner and the Race Question*, Eugene: Un. of Oregon Pr., 1971.

_____, *Larry McMurtry* (TUSAS 291), Boston: Twayne, 1977.

Pemberton, Clive, *William Golding* (WTW 210), London: British Council, 1969.

Pendry, E. D., *The New Feminism of English Fiction*, Tokyo: Kenkyusha, 1956.

Penner, Allen R., *Alan Sillitoe* (TEAS 141), New York: Twayne, 1972.

Pennington, Lee, *The Dark Hills of Jesse Stuart*, Cincinnati, OH: Harvest Pr., 1967.

Peters, Jonathan A., *A Dance of Masks: Senghor, Achebe, Soyinka*, Washington, DC: Three Continents, 1978.

Petersen, Kirsten H., and Anna Rutherford, eds., *Enigma of Values: An Introduction*, Aarhus: Dangaroo Pr., 1975.

Peterson, Richard F., *Mary Lavin* (TEAS 239), Boston: Twayne, 1978.

Peterson, Richard K., *Hemingway: Direct and Oblique* (SamL 14), The Hague: Mouton, 1969.

Petty, Anne C., *One Ring to Bind Them All: Tolkien's Mythology*, University: Un. of Alabama Pr., 1979.

Phelps, Arthur L., *Canadian Writers*, Toronto: McClelland and Stewart, 1951.

Phillips, Gene D., *Evelyn Waugh's Officers, Gentlemen, and Rogues: The Fact behind His Fiction*, Chicago: Nelson-Hall, 1975.

_____, *Graham Greene: The Films of His Fiction*, New York and London: Teachers College Pr. of Columbia Un., 1974.

_____, *Hemingway and Film*, New York: Ungar, 1980.

Phillips, Robert, *William Goyen* (TUSAS 329), Boston: Twayne, 1979.

Piazza, Paul, *Christopher Isherwood: Myth and Anti-Myth*, New York: Columbia Un. Pr., 1978.

Pifer, Ellen, *Nabokov and the Novel*, Cambridge: Harvard Un. Pr., 1980.

Pikoulis, John, *The Art of William Faulkner*, London: Macmillan; Totowa, NJ: Barnes & Noble, 1982.

Pilkington, John, *The Heart of Yoknapatawpha*, Jackson: Un. Pr. of Mississippi, 1981.

Pilkington, William T., *Critical Essays on the Western American Novel* (Crit. Essays on Amer. Lit.), Boston: G. K. Hall, 1980.

Pilling, John, *Samuel Beckett*, London: Routledge, 1976.

Pinchin, Jane L., *Alexandria Still: Forster, Durrell, and Cavafy*, Princeton, NJ: Princeton Un. Pr., 1977.

Pinsker, Sanford, *Between Two Worlds: The American Novel in the 1960's*, Troy, NY: Whitson Publ. Col., 1980.

_____, *The Comedy That "Hoits": An Essay on the Fiction of Philip Roth*, Columbia: Un. of Missouri Pr., 1975.

_____, ed., *Critical Essays on Philip Roth* (Crit. Essays on Amer. Lit.), Boston: G. K. Hall, 1982.

_____, *The Schlemiel as Metaphor: Studies in the Yiddish and American Jewish Novel*, Carbondale: Southern Illinois Un. Pr., 1971; London: Feffer & Simons, 1971.

Pitavy, François, *William Faulkner: AS I LAY DYING and LIGHT IN AUGUST*, Paris: Librarie Armand Colin, 1970; Rev. and enlarged, Gillian E. Cook, ed. and transl., Bloomington: Indiana Un. Pr., 1973.

Plater, William M., *The Grim Phoenix: Reconstructing Thomas Pynchon*, Bloomington: Indiana Un. Pr., 1978.

Pocock, Douglas C. D., ed., *Humanistic Geography and Literature: Essays on the Experience of Place*, Totowa, NJ: Barnes & Noble; London: Croom Helm, 1981.

Podhoretz, Norman, *Doings and Undoings; The Fifties and After in American Writing*, New York: Farrar, Straus & Giroux, 1964.

Poirier, Richard, *Norman Mailer*, London: Fontana; New York: Viking, 1972.

Porter, Carolyn, *Seeing and Being: The Plight of the Participant Observer in Emerson, James, Adams, and Faulkner*, Middletown, CT: Wesleyan Un. Pr., 1981.

Porter, M. Gilbert, *Whence the Power? The Artistry and Humanity of Saul Bellow*, Columbia: Un. of Missouri Pr., 1974.

Porter, Raymond J., and James D. Brophy, eds., *Modern Irish Literature: Essays in Honor of William York Tindall*, New York: Iona College Pr., and Twayne, 1972.

Powers, Lyall H., *Faulkner's Yoknapatawpha Comedy*, Ann Arbor: Un. of Michigan Pr., 1980.

Prabhakar, S. S., *John Steinbeck: A Study; Motifs of Dream and Disillusionment*, Hyderabad: Academic Pub., 1976.

Pratt, Annis, and L. S. Dembo, eds., *Doris Lessing: Critical Studies*, Madison: Un. of Wisconsin Pr., 1974.

Pratt, John C., *John Steinbeck* (CWCP), Grand Rapids, MI: Eerdmans, 1970.

_____, ed., *ONE FLEW OVER THE CUCKOO'S NEST: Text and Criticism*, New York: Viking, 1973.

Prenshaw, Peggy W., ed., *Eudora Welty: Critical Essays*, Jackson: Un. Pr. of Mississippi, 1979.

Prescott, Orville, *In My Opinion; An Inquiry into the Contemporary Novel*, Indianapolis: Bobbs-Merrill, 1952.

Price, Cecil, *Gwyn Jones*, Cardiff: Un. of Wales Pr. for the Welsh Arts Council, 1976.

Price, Reynolds, *Things Themselves; Essays and Scenes*, New York: Atheneum, 1972.

Pritchard, William H., *Wyndham Lewis* (TEAS 65), New York: Twayne, 1969.

Pritchett, Victor Sawdon, *Books in General*, New York: Harcourt, 1953.

_____, *The Living Novel and Later Appreciations*, New York: Random House, 1964.

_____, *The Working Novelist*, London: Chatto and Windus, 1965.

Private Dealings: Modern American Writers in Search of Integrity: Eight Modern American Writers, ed. by Burrows, David J., and others, Stockholm: Almqvist & Wiksell, 1970.

Proceedings of the Fifth National Convention of the Popular Culture Association, St. Louis Missouri, March 20-22, 1975, Compiled by Michael T. Marsden, Bowling Green, OH: Bowling Green St. Un. Popular Pr. 1975.

Proffer, Carl R., ed., *A Book of Things about Vladimir Nabokov*, Ann Arbor, MI: Ardis, 1974.

Pryce-Jones, David, *Graham Greene*, New York: Barnes & Noble, 1967; Edinburgh: Oliver and Boyd, 1963.

Purtill, Richard L., *Lord of the Elves and Eldils: Fantasy and Philosophy in C. S. Lewis and J. R. R. Tolkien*, Grand Rapids, MI: Zondervan, 1974.

Pütz, Manfred, *The Story of Identity: American Fiction of the Sixties* (Amerikastudien; Bd 54), Stuttgart: Metzler, 1979.

Quennell, Peter, ed., *Vladimir Nabokov: His Life, His Work, His World: A Tribute*, London: Weidenfeld & Nicolson, 1979; New York: Morrow, 1980.

Quigly, Isabel, *Pamela Hansford Johnson* (Writers and Their Work 203), London: Longmans, Green, 1968.

Raban, Jonathan, *The Technique of Modern Fiction: Essays in Practical Criticism*, Notre Dame, IN: Un. of Notre Dame Pr., 1968.

Rabinovitz, Rubin, *Iris Murdoch* (CEMW 34), New York: Columbia Un. Pr., 1968.

_____, *The Reaction Against Experiment in the English Novel, 1950-1960*, New York: Columbia Un. Pr., 1967.

Radford, Jean, *Norman Mailer: A Critical Study*, London: Macmillan, 1975.

Rafroidi, Patrick, and Maurice Harmon, eds., *The Irish Novel in Our Time*, Lille: Lille Un. Pr., 1976.

Rahv, Philip, *Image and Idea: Twenty Essays on Literary Themes*, Rev. and enl., Norwalk, CT: New Directions, 1957.

_____, *Literature and the Sixth Sense*, Boston: Houghton-Mifflin, 1969.

_____, ed., *Literature in America*, New York: Meridian, 1957.

_____, *The Myth and the Powerhouse*, New York: Farrar, 1965.

Raizada, Harish, *R. K. Narayan: A Critical Study of His Work*, New Delhi: Young Asia Publications, 1969.

Rajan, B., and A. Pearce, eds., *Focus One*, London: Denis Dobson, 1945.

_____, ed., *The Novelist as Thinker (Focus Four)*, London: Denis Dobson, 1947.

Rama Rao, P. G., *Ernest Hemingway: A Study in Narrative Technique*, New Delhi: S. Chand, 1980.

Ramchand, Kenneth, *The West Indian Novel and Its Background*, New York: Barnes & Noble; London: Faber & Faber, 1970.

Ramson, W. S., ed., *The Australian Experience: Critical Essays on Australian Novels*, Canberra: Australian National Un., 1974.

Rank, Hugh, *Edwin O'Connor* (TUSAS 242), New York: Twayne, 1974.

Rao, B. Ramachandra, *The American Fictional Hero: An Analysis of the Works of Fitzgerald, Wolfe, Farrell, Dos Passos and Steinbeck* (Eng. Lang. & Lit. 4), Chandigarh: Bahri, 1979.

_____, *The Novels of Mrs. Anita Desai: A Study*, Ludhiana: Kalyani, 1977.

Rao, K. Bhaskara, *Paul Scott TEAS 285)*, Boston: Twayne, 1980.

Rao, K. I. Madhusudana, *Contrary Awareness: A Critical Study of the Novels of V. S. Naipaul*, Madras: Centre for Research on New International Economic Order, 1982.

Rao, V. Ramakrishna, *Ivy Compton-Burnett: A Critical Study*, Waltair: Andhra Un. Pr., 1974.

Raskin, Jonah, *The Mythology of Imperialism: Rudyard Kipling, Joseph Conrad, E. M. Forster, D. H. Lawrence, and Joyce Cary*, New York: Random House, 1971.

Ratner, Marc L., *William Styron* (TUSAS 196), New York: Twayne, 1972.

Ravenscroft, Arthur, *Chinua Achebe* (WTW 209), London: Longmans, 1969.

_____, *Chinua Achebe*, 2nd ed. (WTW 209), London: Longmans, 1977.

Ray, David, and Robert M. Farnsworth, eds., *Richard Wright: Impressions and Perspectives*, Ann Arbor: Un. of Michigan Pr., 1973.

Raymond, John, *The Doge of Dover and Other Essays*, London: Macgibbon and Kee, 1960.

Reed, Joseph W., Jr., *Faulkner's Narrative*, New Haven: Yale Un. Pr., 1973.

Reed, Kenneth T., *Truman Capote* (TUSAS 388), Boston: Twayne, 1981.

Reed, Peter J., *Kurt Vonnegut, Jr.*, New York: Crowell, 1972.

Rees, David, *Rhys Davies*, Cardiff: Un. of Wales Pr. for the Welsh Arts Council, 1975.

Rees, Richard, *George Orwell: Fugitive from the Camp of Victory*, London: Secker and Warburg, 1961; Carbondale; Southern Illinois Un. Pr., 1962.

Reilly, John M., ed., *Richard Wright: The Critical Reception* (Amer. Crit. Tradition 6), New York: Franklin, 1978.

_____, ed., *Twentieth Century Interpretations of INVISIBLE MAN: A Collection of Critical Essays* (TCI), Englewood Cliffs, NJ: Prentice-Hall, 1970.

Reiter, Robert E., ed., *Flannery O'Connor* (The Christian Critic Series), St. Louis, MO: Herder, 1968.

Rhétorique et communication, Paris: Didier, 1979.

Rhodes, H. Winston, *Frank Sargeson* (TWAS 75), New York: Twayne, 1969.

Ribalow, Harold U., ed., *Mid-Century: An Anthology of Jewish Life and Culture in Our Times*, New York: Beechhurst Pr., 1955.

Richardson, H. Edward, *William Faulkner: The Journey to Self-Discovery*, Columbia: Un. of Missouri Pr., 1969.

Richardson, Richard E., *Force and Faith in the Novels of William Faulkner*, The Hague: Mouton, 1967.

Richman, Sidney, *Bernard Malamud* (TUSAS 109), New York: Twayne, 1966.

Richter, David, *Fable's End*, Chicago: Un. of Chicago Pr., 1974.

Ricou, Laurence, *Vertical Man/Horizontal World: Man and Landscape in Canadian Prairie Fiction*, Vancouver: Un. of British Columbia Pr., 1973.

Rideout, Walter B., *The Radical Novel in the United States, 1900-1955; Some Interrelations of Literature and Society*, Cambridge: Harvard Un. Pr., 1956.

Rigney, Barbara H., *Madness and Sexual Politics in the Feminist Novel: Studies in Brontë, Woolf, Lessing, and Atwood*, Madison: Un. of Wisconsin Pr., 1978.

Ringbom, Håkan, et al., eds., *Style and Text: Studies Presented to Nils Erik Eukvist*, Stockholm: Språksorlaget Skriptor, 1975.

Rippier, Joseph S., *Some Postwar English Novelists*, Frankfurt am Main: Verlag Moritz Diesterweg, 1965.

Rivers, J. E., and Charles Nicol, eds., *Nabokov's Fifth Arc: Nabokov and Others on His Life's Work*, Austin: Un. of Texas Pr., 1982.

Rizvi, S. N. A., ed., *The Twofold Voice: Essays in Honor of Ramesh Mohan*, Salzburg: Inst. fur Anglistik & Amerikanistik, Un. Salzburg, 1982.

Roberts, Gildas, ed., *Seven Studies in English. For Dorothy Cavers*, Capetown and London: Purnell & Sons, 1971.

Robinson, Forrest G., and Margaret G. Robinson, *Wallace Stegner* (TUSAS 282), Boston: Twayne, 1977.

Robinson, Fred M., *The Comedy of Language: Studies in Modern Comic Literature*, Amherst: Un. of Massachusetts Pr., 1980.

Robinson, Michael, *The Long Sonata of the Dead: A Study of Samuel Beckett*, London: Hart-Davis, 1969; New York: Grove, 1970.

Robson, Flifford B., *Ngugi wa Thiong'o*, London: Macmillan; New York: St. Martin's, 1979.

Roderick, Colin, *An Introduction to Australian Fiction*, Sydney: Angus and Robertson, 1950.

Rodgers, Bernard F., Jr., *Philip Roth* (TUSAS 318), Boston: Twayne, 1978.

Rogers, Deborah W., and Iver A. Rogers, *J. R. R. Tolkien* (TEAS 304), Boston, MA: Hall, 1980.

Ronald, Ann, *The New West of Edward Abbey*, Albuquerque: Un. of New Mexico Pr., 1982.

Ronsley, Joseph, ed., *Myth and Reality in Irish Literature*, Waterloo, Ont.: Wilfrid Laurier Un. Pr., 1977.

Rorabacher, Louise E., *Frank Dalby Davison* (TWAS 514), Boston: Twayne, 1979.

Roscoe, Adrian A., *Mother is Gold: A Study in West African Literature*, Cambridge: Cambridge Un. Pr., 1971.

————, *Uhuru's Fire. African Literature East to South*. Cambridge: Cambridge Un. Pr., 1977.

Rose, Ellen C., *The Novels of Margaret Drabble: Equivocal Figures*, London: Macmillan; Totowa, NJ: Barnes & Noble, 1980.

————, *The Tree Outside the Window: Doris Lessing's CHILDREN OF VIOLENCE*, Hanover, NH: Un. Pr. of New England, 1976.

Rosen, Gerald, *Zen in the Art of J. D. Salinger* (Modern Authors Monograph Ser. 3), Berkeley, CA: Creative Arts, 1977.

Rosen, Robert C., *John Dos Passos: Politics and the Writer*, Lincoln: Un. of Nebraska Pr., 1981.

Rosenblatt, Roger, *Black Fiction*, Cambridge: Harvard Un. Pr., 1974.

Rosenfeld, Isaac, *An Age of Enormity: Life and Writing in the Forties and Fifties*, Cleveland: World, 1962.

Roudiez, Leon S., *French Fiction Today; A New Direction*, New Brunswick, NJ: Rutgers Un. Pr., 1972.

Rovit, Earl, *Ernest Hemingway* (TUSAS 41), New York: Twayne, 1963.

————, *Saul Bellow* (UMPAW 65), Minneapolis: Un. of Minnesota Pr., 1967.

————, ed., *Saul Bellow: A Collection of Critical Essays* (TCV 122), Englewood Cliffs, NJ: Prentice-Hall, 1975.

Rowe, W. W., *Nabokov and Others: Patterns in Russian Literature*, Ann Arbor, MI: Ardis, 1979.

————, *Nabokov's Deceptive World*, New York: New York Un. Pr., 1971.

Rubenstein, Roberta, *The Novelistic Vision of Doris Lessing: Breaking the Forms of Consciousness*, Urbana: Un. of Illinois Pr., 1979.

Rubin, Louis D., Jr., ed., *The American South: Portrait of a Culture* (So. Lit. Studies), Baton Rouge: Louisiana State Un. Pr., 1980.

————, *The Comic Imagination in American Literature*, New Brunswick, NJ: Rutgers Un. Pr., 1973.

————, *The Curious Death of the Novel; Essays in American Literature*, Baton Rouge: Louisiana State Un. Pr., 1967.

————, *The Faraway Country: Writers of the Modern South*, Seattle: Un. of Washington Pr., 1963.

————, *A Gallery of Southerners*, Baton Rouge: Louisiana State Un. Pr., 1982.

————, and Robert D. Jacobs, eds., *South: Modern Southern Literature in Its Cultural Setting*, New York: Doubleday (Dolphin Books), 1961.

————, and Robert D. Jacobs, eds., *Southern Renascence: The Literature of the Modern South*, Baltimore: Johns Hopkins Pr., 1953.

————, and John Rees Moore, eds., *The Idea of an American Novel*, New York: T. Y. Crowell, 1961.

Rubin, Steven J., *Meyer Levin* (TUSAS 406), Boston: Twayne, 1982.

Runyon, Randolph, *Fowles/Irving/Barthes: Canonical Variations on an Apocryphal Theme*, Columbus: Ohio State Un. Pr., for Miami, Ohio, 1981.

Ruotolo, Lucio P., *Six Existential Heroes: The Politics of Faith*, Cambridge: Harvard Un. Pr., 1973.

Rupp, Richard H., *Celebration in Postwar American Fiction, 1945-1967*, Coral Gables, FL: Un. of Miami Pr., 1970.

Russell, John, *Anthony Powell: A Quintet, Sextet, and War*, Bloomington: Indiana Un. Pr., 1970.

————, *Henry Green: Nine Novels and an Unpacked Bag*, New Brunswick, NJ: Rutgers Un. Pr., 1960.

Rutherford, Anna, ed., *CommonWealth*, Aarhus, Denmark: Akademisk Boghandel Universitesparken, 1971. (Papers delivered at the Conference of Commonwealth Literature, Aarhus Un., April 26-30, 1971).

Ryan, John S., ed., *Gleanings from Greeneland*, Hanover, NH: Un. of New England, 1972.

Rydén, Mats, and Lennart A. Björ, eds., *Studies in English Philology, Linguistics and Literature Presented to Alarik Rynell 7 March 1978*, Stockholm: Almqvist & Wiksell, 1978.

Ryf, Robert S., *Henry Green* (CEMW 29), New York: Columbia Un. Pr., 1967.

Sachs, Viola, *The Myth of America: Essays in the Structures of Literary Imagination*, The Hague: Mouton, 1973.

Sajavaara, Kari, *Imagery in Lawrence Durrell's Prose*, Helsinki: Société Néophilolouique, 1975.

Sale, Roger, *Modern Heroism: Essays in D. H. Lawrence, William Empson, and J.R.R. Tolkien*, Berkeley: Un. of California Pr., 1973.

Salu, Mary, and Robert T. Farrell, eds., *J.R.R. Tolkien, Scholar and Storyteller: Essays in Memoriam*, Ithaca, NY: Cornell Un. Pr., 1979.

Salwak, Dale, *John Wain* (TEAS 316), Boston: Twayne, 1981.

Salzman, Jack, *Albert Maltz* (TUSAS 311), Boston: Twayne, 1978.

Samuels, Charles T., *John Updike*, Minneapolis: Un. of Minnesota Pr., 1969.

Sandelin, Clarence K., *Robert Nathan* (TUSAS 147), New York: Twayne, 1968.

Sanders, David, *John Hersey* (TUSAS 112), New York: Twayne, 1967.

————, comp., *Studies in U.S.A.* (Merrill Studies), Columbus, OH: Charles E. Merrill, 1972.

Sanderson, Stewart F., *Ernest Hemingway*, Edinburgh: Oliver and Boyd, 1961: New York: Grove, 1961.

Sandison, Alan, *The Last Man in Europe: An Essay on George Orwell*, London: Macmillan; New York: Barnes & Noble, 1974.

Santore, Anthony C., and Michael Pocalyko, eds., *A John Hawkes Symposium: Design and Debris* (Insights, Working Papers in Contemp. Crit.), New York: New Directions, 1977.

Sarason, Bertram D., ed., *Hemingway and THE SUN Set*, Washington, DC: NCR Microcard Editions, 1972.

Sartre, Jean-Paul, *Literary and Philosophical Essays*, New York: Criterion Books, 1955.

Satyanarayana, M. R., *John Steinbeck: A Study of the Theme of Compassion*, Hyderabad: Vidyarthi Pubs., 1977.

Savage, D. S., *The Withered Branch: Six Studies in the Modern Novel*, New York: Pellegrini & Cudahy, 1952.

Schatt, Stanley, *Kurt Vonnegut, Jr.* (TUSAS 276), Boston: Twayne, 1976.

Schaub, Thomas H., *Pynchon: The Voice of Ambiguity*, Urbana: Un. of Illinois Pr., 1981.

Schechter, Harold, *The New Gods: Psyche and Symbol in Popular Art*, Bowling Green, OH: Popular, 1980.

Scheer-Schäzler, Brigitte, *Saul Bellow*, New York: Ungar, 1972.

Schlueter, Paul, ed., *Literature and Religion: Thornton Wilder's THE EIGHTH DAY*. Papers Collected for MLA Seminar 4, by Paul Schleuter. Evansville, IN: Un. of Evansville, 1970.

_____, *The Novels of Doris Lessing*, (CMC), Carbondale: Southern Illinois Un. Pr.; London: Feffer & Simons, 1973.

_____, *Shirley Ann Grau* (TUSAS 382), Boston: Twayne, 1981.

Schmidt, Dorey, ed., *Larry McMurtry: Unredeemed Dreams* (Living Author Ser. 1), Edinburg, TX: School of Humanities, Pan Amer. Un., 1978.

_____, and Jan Seale, eds., *Margaret Drabble: Golden Realms*, Edinburg, TX: School of Humanities, Pan Amer. Un., 1982.

Schmitter, Dean M., ed., *William Faulkner: A Collection of Criticism* (Contemp. Studies in Literature), New York: McGraw-Hill, 1973.

Schoenberg, Estella, *Old Tales and Talking: Quentin Compson in William Faulkner's ABSALOM, ABSALOM! and Related Works*, Jackson: Un. Pr. of Mississippi, 1977.

Scholes, Robert, *Fabulation and Metafiction*, Urbana: Un. of Illinois Pr., 1979.

_____, *The Fabulators*, New York: Oxford Un. Pr., 1967.

Schorer, Mark, *Sinclair Lewis* (UMPAW 27), Minneapolis: Un. of Minnesota Pr., 1963.

_____, ed., *Sinclair Lewis: A Collection of Critical Essays*, Englewood Cliffs, NJ: Prentice-Hall, 1962.

_____, *Sinclair Lewis: An American Life*, New York: McGraw, 1961.

_____, *The World We Imagine: Selected Essays*, New York: Farrar, 1968.

Schraepen, Edmond, ed., *Saul Bellow and His Work*. Proc. of Symposium at Free Univ. of Brussels, Dec. 10-11, 1977, Brussels: Centrum voor Taal- en Literatuurwetanshap, Rije Univ., 1978.

Schraufnagel, Noel, *From Apology to Protest: The Black American Novel*, DeLand, FL: Everett/Edwards, 1973.

Schulz, Hans-Joachim, *This Hell of Stories: A Hegelian Approach to the Novels of Samuel Beckett*, The Hague: Mouton, 1973.

Schulz, Max F., *Black Humor Fiction of the Sixties: A Pluralistic Definition of Man and His World*, Athens: Ohio Un. Pr., 1973.

_____, *Bruce Jay Friedman* (TUSAS 219), New York: Twayne, 1974.

_____, *Radical Sophistication: Studies in Contemporary Jewish-American Novelists*, Athens: Ohio Un. Pr., 1969.

Schwarzschild, Bettina, *The Not-Right House: Essays on James Purdy* (Missouri Literary Frontiers Series Number 5), Columbia: Un. of Missouri Pr., 1968.

Scobie, Stephen, *Leonard Cohen*, (Studies in Canadian Literature 12), Vancouver: Douglas & McIntyre; Edinburgh: Conongate, 1978.

Scott, Alexander, and Douglas Gifford, eds., *Neil M. Gunn: The Man and the Writer*, New York: Harper, 1973.

Scott, Nathan A., Jr., *Adversity and Grace: Studies in Recent American Literature* (Essays in Divinity, Vol. IV), Chicago: Un. of Chicago Pr., 1968.

_____, *Three American Moralists: Mailer, Bellow, Trilling*, Notre Dame, IN: Notre Dame Un. Pr., 1973.

_____, *Craters of the Spirit: Studies in the Modern Novel*, Washington, DC: Corpus Books, 1968.

_____, *Ernest Hemingway: A Critical Essay* (CWCP), Grand Rapids, MI: Eerdmans, 1966.

_____, *Samuel Beckett*, London: Bowes, 1965; Toronto: Queenswood, 1965: New York: Hilary House, 1965.

Scotto, Robert M., ed., *Joseph Heller's CATCH-22: A Critical Edition*, New York: Dell, 1973.

Seib, Kenneth, *James Agee: Promise and Fulfillment*, Pittsburgh: Un. of Pittsburgh Pr., 1968.

Seiler, Carol, *Boulder-Pushers: Women in the Fiction of Margaret Drabble, Doris Lessing, and Iris Murdoch*, Bern: Peter Lang, 1979.

Semmler, Clement, ed., *Twentieth Century Australian Literary Criticism*, Melbourne: Oxford Un. Pr., 1967.

Sen, Supti, *Samuel Beckett: His Mind and Art*, Calcutta: Firma K. L. Mukhopadhyay, 1970.

Seyersted, Per, *Leslie Marmon Silko* (WWS 45), Boise, ID: Boise State Un., 1980.

Seymour, A. J., *Edgar Mittelholzer: The Man and His Work*, Georgetown, Guyana: National History and Arts Council, 1968.

Seyppel, Joachim, *William Faulkner*, New York: Ungar, 1971.

Shahane, Vasant A., ed., *Approaches to E. M. Forster: A Centenary Volume*, Atlantic Highlands, NJ: Humanities Pr., 1981.

_____, *Khushwant Singh* (TWAS 222), New York: Twayne, 1972.

_____, *Ruth Prawer Jhabvala*, New Delhi: Arnold-Heinemann, 1976.

Shannon, William V., *The American Irish*, Rev. ed., New York: Macmillan, 1966.

Shapiro, Charles, *Contemporary British Novelists* (Cross-currents), Carbondale: Southern Illinois Un. Pr., 1965.

_____, ed., *Twelve Original Essays on Great American Novels*, Detroit: Wayne State Un. Pr., 1958.

Sharma, Jagdish N., and B. Ramesh Babu, eds., *Contemporary American Life*, New Delhi: Arnold-Heinemann, 1979.

Sharma, K. K. ed., *Indo-English Literature: A Collection of Critical Essays*, Ghaziabad, India: Vimal Prakashan, 1977.

_____, *Joyce Cary: His Theme and Technique: A Modern Variation on the Major Tradition of the English Novel*, Ghaziabad, India: Vimal Prakashan, 1976.

_____, ed., *Perspectives on Mulk Raj Anand*, Ghaziabad, India: Vimal Prakashan, 1978.

Sharma, R. S., *Anita Desai*, New Delhi: Arnold-Heinemann, 1981.

Shaughnessy, Mary R., *Women and Success in American Society in the Works of Edna Ferber*, New York: Gordon, 1977.

Shaw, Samuel, *Ernest Hemingway*, New York: Ungar, 1973.

Shepherd, R., and K. Singh, eds., *Patrick White: A Critical Symposium*, Bedford Park: Flinders Un. of South Australia, 1978.

Sheps, G. David, ed., *Mordecai Richler*, Toronto: Ryerson-McGraw-Hill, 1971.

Sherman, Bernard, *The Invention of the Jew: Jewish-American Education Novels (1916-1964)*, New York: Thomas Yoseloff, 1969.

Shimer, Dorothy B., *Bhabani Bhattacharya* (TWAS 343), Boston: Twayne, 1975.

Shippe, T. A., *The Road to Middle-Earth*, London: Allen & Unwin, 1982; Boston: Houghton Mifflin, 1983.

Shivers, Alfred S., *Jessamyn West* (TUSAS 192), New York: Twayne, 1972.

Shloss, Carol, *Flannery O'Connor's Dark Comedies: The Limits of Inference* (So. Lit. Studies), Baton Rouge: Louisiana State Un. Pr., 1980.

Shoben, Edward J., Jr., *Lionel Trilling* (Mod. Lit. Ser.), New York: Ungar, 1981.

Shusterman, David, *C. P. Snow* (TEAS 179), Boston: Twayne, 1975.

Sibley, Agnes, *May Sarton* (TUSAS 213), New York: Twayne, 1972.

Siegel, Ben, *Isaac Bashevis Singer* (UMPAW 86), Minneapolis: Un. of Minnesota Pr., 1969.

Siegel, Mark R., *Pynchon: Creative Paranoia in GRAVITY'S RAINBOW*, Port Washington, NY; London: Kennikat Pr., 1978.

_____, *Tom Robbins* (WWS 42), Boise: Boise State Un., 1980.

Simmonds, Roy S., *Steinbeck's Literary Achievement* (Steinbeck Monograph Ser. 6), Muncie, IN: John Steinbeck Soc., Eng. Dept., Ball State Un., 1976.

Simonini, R. C., Jr., *Southern Writers: Appraisals in Our Time*, Charlottesville: Un. of Virginia Pr., 1964.

Simonson, Harold P., and Philip E. Hager, eds., *Salinger's CATCHER IN THE RYE: Clamor vs. Criticism*, Boston: Heath, 1963.

Simpson, Hassell A., *Rumer Godden* (TEAS 151), New York: Twayne, 1973.

Simpson, Lewis P., ed., *The Poetry of Community: Essays on the Southern Sensibility of History and Literature* (Spectrum: Monograph Ser. in the Arts and Sciences 2), Atlanta: School of Arts and Sciences, Georgia State Un., 1972.

Singer, Isaac B., *On Literature and Life; An Interview with Paul Rosenblatt and Gene Koppel*, Tucson: Un. of Arizona Pr., 1979.

Singh, R. S., *Indian Novel in English: A Critical Study*, New Delhi: Arnold-Heinemann, 1977.

Singleton, Mary A., *The City and the Veld: The Fiction of Doris Lessing*, Lewisburg: Bucknell Un. Pr., 1977.

Sinha, Krishna N., *Mulk Raj Anand* (TWAS 232), New York: Twayne, 1972.

Slade, Joseph W., *Thomas Pynchon*, New York: Warner, 1974.

Slatoff, Walter J., *Quest for Failure: A Study of William Faulkner*, Ithaca, NY: Cornell Un. Pr., 1960.

Slochower, Harry, *No Voice is Wholly Lost ... Writers and Thinkers in War and Peace*, New York: Creative Age Pr., 1945.

Small, Christopher, *The Road to Miniluv: George Orwell, the State, and God*, London: Gollancz, 1975; Pittsburgh: Un. of Pittsburgh Pr., 1976.

Smart, George K., *Religious Elements in Faulkner's Early Novels: A Selective Concordance* (UMPEAL No. 8), Coral Gables, FL: Un. of Miami Pr., 1965.

Smith, A. J. M., ed., *Masks of Fiction: Canadian Critics on Canadian Prose* (New Canadian Library), Toronto: McClelland & Stewart, 1961.

Smith, Anne, ed., *The Art of Malcolm Lowry* (Crit. Studies), New York: Barnes & Noble, 1978.

Smith, Julian, *Nevil Shute (Nevil Shute Norway)* (TEAS 190), Boston: Twayne, 1976.

Smith, Leverett T., Jr., *The American Dream and the National Game*, Bowling Green, OH: Bowling Green Un. Popular Pr., 1975.

Smyer, Richard I., *Primal Dream and Primal Crime: Orwell's Development as a Psychological Novelist*, Columbia: Un. of Missouri Pr., 1979.

Snell, George, *The Shapers of American Fiction, 1798-1947*, New York: Dutton, 1947. Reprinted, New York: Cooper Square, 1961.

Snyder, Robert, *Anaïs Nin Observed: From a Film Portrait of a Woman as Artist*, Chicago: Swallow, 1976.

_____, *This is Henry, Henry Miller from Brooklyn: Conversations with the Author from The Henry Miller Odyssey*, Los Angeles: Nash, 1976.

Sochatoff, A. Fred, and Others, *ALL THE KING'S MEN: A Symposium* (CaSE No. 3), Pittsburgh: Carnegie Institute of Technology, 1957.

Solotaroff, Robert, *Down Mailer's Way*, Urbana: Un. of Illinois Pr., 1974.

Solotaroff, Theodore, *The Red Hot Vacuum, and Other Pieces on the Writing of the Sixties*, New York: Atheneum, 1970.

Spacks, Patricia M., ed., *Contemporary Women Novelists; A Collection of Critical Essays*, Englewood Cliffs, NJ: Prentice-Hall, 1977.

_____, *The Female Imagination*, New York: Knopf, 1975.

Spencer, Sharon, *Collage of Dreams: The Writings of Anaïs Nin*, Chicago: Swallow, 1977.

Spender, Stephen, *The Creative Element; A Study of Vision, Despair and Orthodoxy among some Modern Writers*, New York: British Book Centre, 1954.

Sperber, Murray A., ed., *Arthur Koestler: A Collection of Critical Essays* (TCV), Englewood Cliffs, NJ: Prentice-Hall, 1977.

Spiegel, Rotraut, *Doris Lessing: The Problem of Alienation and the Form of the Novel*, Frankfort: P. Lang, 1980.

Spiller, Robert E., *Cycle of American Literature: an Essay in Historical Criticism*, New York: Macmillan, 1955.

Spurling, Hilary, *Invitation to the Dance: A Guide to Anthony Powell's DANCE TO THE MUSIC OF TIME*, Boston: Little, Brown, 1978.

Squires, Radcliffe, *Frederick Prokosch* (TUSAS 61), New York: Twayne, 1964.

Srivastava, Avadhesh K., ed., *Alien Voice: Perspectives on Commonwealth Literature*, Lucknow, India: Print House, 1981; Atlantic Highlands, NJ: Humanities, 1982.

Stade, George, ed., *Six Contemporary British Novelists*, New York: Columbia Un. Pr., 1976.

_____, ed., *Six Modern British Novelists*, New York: Columbia Un. Pr., 1974.

Stafford, William T., *Books Speaking to Books; A Contextual Approach to American Fiction*, Chapel Hill: Un. of North Carolina Pr., 1981.

Staines, David, *The Callaghan Symposium*, Ottawa: Un. of Ottawa Pr., 1981.

Staley, Thomas F., *Jean Rhys: A Critical Study*, Austin: Un. of Texas Pr., 1979.

_____, ed., *Twentieth-Century Women Novelists*, Totowa, NJ: Barnes & Noble, 1982.

Stanford, Derek, *Muriel Spark: A Biographical and Critical Study*, Fontwell, England: Centaur Pr., 1963.

Stanford, Donald E., ed., *Nine Essays in Modern Literature* (La. State Un. Studies: Humanities Series No. 15), Baton Rouge: Louisiana State Un. Pr., 1965.

Stanton, Robert J., *Views from a Window: Conversations with Gore Vidal*, New York: Stuart, 1980.

Stark, John O., *The Literature of Exhaustion: Borges, Nabokov, and Barth*, Durham, NC: Duke Un. Pr., 1974.

_____, *Pynchon's Fictions: Thomas Pynchon and the Literature of Information*, Athens: Ohio Un. Pr., 1980.

Steele, M. C., *CHILDREN OF VIOLENCE and Rhodesia: A Study of Doris Lessing as Historical Observer*, Salisbury: Central Africa Historical Assoc., 1974.

Steffen, Jerome O., ed., *The American West: New Perspectives, New Dimensions*, Norman: Un. of Oklahoma Pr., 1979.

Stegner, Page, *Escape Into Aesthetics: The Art of Vladimir Nabokov*, New York: Dial, 1966.

Stegner, Wallace, ed., *The American Novel; From James Fenimore Cooper to William Faulkner*, New York: Basic Books, 1965.

Steinbeck, John, *Journal of a Novel: The EAST OF EDEN Letters*, New York: Viking, 1969.

Steinhoff, William, *George Orwell and the Origins of 1984*, Ann Arbor: Un. of Michigan Pr., 1975.

Stephens, Donald G., ed., *Writers of the Prairies* (Canadian Lit. Ser.), Vancouver: Un. of British Columbia Pr., 1973.

Stephens, Martha, *The Question of Flannery O'Connor*, Baton Rouge: Louisiana State Un. Pr., 1973.

Stephens, Robert O., ed., *Ernest Hemingway: The Critical Reception*, New York: Franklin, 1977.

Stettler-Imfeld, Barbara, *The Adolescent in the Novels of Iris Murdoch*, Zurich: Juris Druck, 1970.

Stevens, Joan, *The New Zealand Novel, 1860-1960*, Wellington, NZ: A. H. and A. W. Reed,1961.

Stewart, Douglas, *The Ark of God: Studies in Five Modern Novelists*, London: Carey Kingsgate Pr., 1961.

Stewart, Grace, *A New Mythos: The Novel of the Artist as Heroine, 1877-1977*, Vermont: Eden Pr. Women's Publishing, 1978.

Stewart, John L., *The Burden of Time: The Fugitives and Agrarians*, Princeton, NJ: Princeton Un. Pr., 1965.

Stewart, Lawrence D., *Paul Bowles: The Illumination of North Africa*, Carbondale: Southern Illinois Un. Pr., 1974.

Stimpson, Catharine R., *J.R.R. Tolkien* (CEMW 41), New York: Columbia Un. Pr., 1969.

Stock, Irvin, *Mary McCarthy* (UMPAW 72), Minneapolis: Un. of Minnesota Pr., 1968.

Stokes, Edward, *The Novels of James Hanley*, Melbourne: F. W. Cheshire, 1964.

Stoltzfus, Ben, *Gide and Hemingway: Rebels Against God*, Port Washington, NY: Kennikat, 1978.

Stonum, Gary L., *Faulkner's Career: An Internal Literary History*, Ithaca, NY: Cornell Un. Pr., 1979.

Stopp, Frederick J., *Evelyn Waugh: Portrait of an Artist*, London: Chapman, Hall; Boston: Little, Brown, 1958.

Strachey, John, *The Strangled Cry, and Other Unparliamentary Papers*, New York: Sloane, 1962.

Strandberg, Victor, *A Faulkner Overview: Six Perspectives*, Port Washington, NY: Kennikat Pr., 1981.

Stratford, Philip, *Faith and Fiction: Creative Process in Greene and Mauriac*, Notre Dame, IN: Un. of Notre Dame Pr., 1964.

Straumann, Heinrich, *American Literature in the Twentieth Century*, Third rev. ed., New York: Harper & Row, 1965.

Strelka, Joseph P., ed., *Anagogic Qualities of Literature* (Yearbook of Comparative Criticism, Vol. IV), University Park: Pennsylvania State Un. Pr., 1971.

Stresau, Hermann, *Thornton Wilder*, New York: Ungar, 1971.

Struthers, J. R. (Tim), ed., *Before the Flood*, Downsview, Ont.: ECW Pr., 1979.

Stuart, Dabney, *Nabokov: The Dimensions of Parody*, Baton Rouge: Louisiana State Un. Pr., 1978.

Stubbs, Patricia, *Muriel Spark* (WTW 229), Harlow: Longman for the British Council, 1973.

Stuckey, W. J., *Caroline Gordon* (TUSAS 200), New York: Twayne, 1972.

_____, *The Pulitzer Prize Novels: A Critical Backward Look*, Norman: Un. of Oklahoma Pr., 1966.

Sullivan, Walter, *Death by Melancholy: Essays on Modern Southern Fiction*, Baton Rouge: Louisiana State Un. Pr., 1972.

_____, *A Requiem for the Renascence: The State of Fiction in the Modern South*, Athens: Un. of Georgia Pr., 1976.

Summers, Claude J., *Christopher Isherwood* (Mod. Lit. Monogs.), New York: Ungar, 1980.

Sundaram, P. S., *R. K. Narayan*, New Delhi: Arnold-Heinemann, 1973.

Sutherland, William O. S., ed., *Six Contemporary Novels: Six Introductory Essays in Modern Fiction*, Austin: Un. of Texas Dept. of English, 1962.

Swados, Harvey, *A Radical's America*, Boston: Little, Brown, 1962.

Swiggart, Peter, *The Art of Faulkner's Novels*, Austin: Un. of Texas Pr., 1962.

Swinden, Patrick, *Paul Scott: Images of India*, London: Macmillan; New York: St. Martin's, 1980.

_____, *Unofficial Selves: Character in the Novel from Dickens to the Present Day*, New York: Barnes & Noble, 1973.

Sylvander, Carolyn W., *James Baldwin*, New York: Ungar, 1980.

Symons, Julian, *Critical Occasions*, London: Hamish Hamilton, 1966.

Szanto, George H., *Narrative Consciousness: Structure and Perception in the Fiction of Kafka, Beckett, and Robbe-Grillet*, Austin: Texas Un. Pr., 1972.

T.L.S.: Essays and Reviews from The Times Literary Supplement, 1963, Vol. 2, London: Oxford Un. Pr, 1964.

T.L.S.: Essays and Reviews from The Times Literary Supplement, 1964, Vol. 3, London: Oxford Un. Pr., 1965.

T.L.S.: Essays and Reviews from The Times Literary Supplement, 1965, Vol. 4, London: Oxford Un. Pr., 1966.

T.L.S. Essays and Reviews from The Times Literary Supplement, 1966, Vol. 5, London: Oxford Un. Pr., 1967.

T.L.S.: Essays and Reviews from The Times Literary Supplement, 1968, Vol. 7, London: Oxford Un. Pr., 1969.

Taiwo, Oladele, *Culture and the Nigerian Novel*, London: Macmillan; New York: St. Martin's, 1976.

_____, *An Introduction to West African Literature*, London: Nelson, 1967.

Tallent, Elizabeth, *Married Men and Magic Tricks: John Updike's Erotic Heroes*, Berkeley, CA: Creative Arts Book Co., 1982.

Tanner, Tony, *City of Words; American Fiction 1950-1970*, New York: Harper, 1971.

_____, *The Reign of Wonder: Naiveté and Reality in American Literature*, Cambridge: Cambridge Un. Pr., 1965.

_____, *Saul Bellow*, Edinburgh: Oliver and Boyd, 1965; New York: Barnes and Nobel, 1965.

_____, *Thomas Pynchon*, London: Methuen, 1982.

Taylor, Jenny, ed., *Notebooks/Memoirs/Archives: Reading and Re-reading Doris Lessing*, Boston: Routledge, 1982.

Taylor, Larry E., *Pastoral and Anti-Pastoral Patterns in John Updike's Fiction* (CMC), Carbondale: Southern Illinois Un. Pr., 1971.

Tedlock, E. W., Jr., and C. V. Wicker, eds., *Steinbeck and His Critics: A Record of Twenty-Five Years*, Albuquerque: Un. of New Mexico Pr., 1957.

Thale, Jerome, *C. P. Snow* (Writers and Critics), Edinburgh: Oliver and Boyd; New York: Scribner's, 1965.

Tharpe, Jac, *John Barth: The Comic Sublimity of Paradox*, Carbondale: Southern Illinois Un. Pr.; London: Feffer & Simons, 1974.

_____, ed., *Walker Percy: Art and Ethics*, Jackson: Un. Pr. of Mississippi, 1980.

Theroux, Paul, *V. S. Naipaul: An Introduction to His Works*, New York: Africana Pub. Corp.; London: Deutsch, 1972.

Thomas, Clara, *The Manawaka World of Margaret Laurence*, Toronto: McClelland & Stewart, 1975.

_____, *Margaret Laurence*, Toronto: McClelland & Stewart, 1969.

Thomas, Edward M., *Orwell* (Writers and Critics), Edinburgh and London: Oliver and Boyd, 1965; New York: Barnes & Noble, 1967.

Thomas, Peter, *Richard Hughes* (Writers of Wales), Cardiff: Un. of Wales for the Welsh Arts Council, 1973.

_____, *Robert Kroetsch*, (Studies in Canadian Lit. 13), Vancouver: Douglas & McIntyre, 1980.

Thompson, Lawrance, *William Faulkner: An Introduction and Interpretation*, 2nd ed., New York: Barnes & Noble, 1967.

Thorburn, David, and Howard Eiland, eds., *John Updike: A Collection of Critical Essays* (TCV), Englewood Cliffs, NJ: Prentice-Hall, 1979.

Thorp, Willard, *American Writing in the Twentieth Century* (Library of Congress Series in American Civilization), Cambridge: Harvard Un. Pr., 1960.

Thorpe, Michael, *Doris Lessing* (WTW 230), Harlow: Longman for the British Council, 1973.

_____, *Doris Lessing's Africa*, London: Evans, 1978; New York: Holmes & Meier, 1978.

_____, *V. S. Naipaul* (Writers and Their Work 242), Harlow: Longman for the British Council, 1976.

Three Novels of Ernest Hemingway (Modern Standard Authors), New York: Charles Scribner's Sons, 1962.

Thwaite, Anthony, Ed., *Larkin at Sixty*, London: Faber, 1982.

Tibble, Anne, *African/English Literature: A Survey and Anthology*, London: Peter Owen Ltd., 1965; New York: October House, 1965.

Tiffin, Chris, ed., *South Pacific Images*, Queensland: South Pacific Assn. for Commonwealth Lit. and Lang. Studies, 1978.

Tiger, Virginia, *William Golding: The Dark Fields of Discovery*, London: Calder & Boyars, 1974.

Tilton, John W., *Cosmic Satire in the Contemporary Novel*, Lewisburg, PA: Bucknell Un. Pr., 1976; London: Assoc. Un. Presses, 1977.

Timms, David, *Philip Larkin* (Modern Writers' Ser.), Edinburgh: Oliver and Boyd: New York: Barnes & Noble, 1973.

Tindall, William York, *The Literary Symbol*, Bloomington: Indiana Un. Pr., 1955.

_____, *Samuel Beckett* (CEMW 4), New York: Columbia Un. Pr., 1964.

Todd, Richard, *Iris Murdoch: The Shakespearean Interest*, London: Vision Pr.; New York: Barnes & Noble, 1979.

Tomlin, E. W. F., *Wyndham Lewis*, London: Longmans, Green, 1955.

Trachtenberg, Stanley, ed., *Critical Essays on Saul Bellow* (Crit. Essays on Amer. Lit.), Boston: G. K. Hall, 1979.

Tran, Qui-Phiet, *William Faulkner and the French New Novelists*, Arlington: Carrollton, 1978.

Trilling, Diana, *Claremont Essays*, New York: Harcourt, 1964.

Trimble, Martha S., *N. Scott Momaday* (Western Writers Ser. 9), Boise, ID: Boise State College, 1973.

Tuck, Dorothy, *Crowell's Handbook of Faulkner*, New York: Crowell, 1964.

Tucker, James, *The Novels of Anthony Powell*, New York: Columbia Un. Pr., 1976.

Tucker, Martin, *Africa in Modern Literature: A Survey of Contemporary Writing in English*, New York: Ungar, 1967.

Turnell, Martin, *Graham Greene; a Critical Essay* (CWCP), Grand Rapids, MI: Eerdmans, 1967.

Tuttleton, James W., *The Novel of Manners in America*, Chapel Hill: Un. of North Carolina Pr., 1972.

Tyler, J. E. A., comp., *The Tolkien Companion*, London: Macmillan; New York: St. Martins, 1976.

Tytell, John, *Naked Angels; The Lives and Literature of the Beats*, New York: McGraw-Hill, 1976.

Ugrinsky, Alexej, Frederick J. Churchill, Frank S. Lambasa, and Robert F. von Berg, eds, *Heinrich von Kleist Studies* (Hofstra Un. Cultural and Intercultural Studies 3), New York: AMS, 1980.

Unfried, Sarah P., *Man's Place in the Natural Order: A Study of Hemingway's Major Works*, New York: Gordon, 1976.

Unterecker, John, *Lawrence Durrell* (CEMW 6), New York: Columbia Un. Pr., 1964.

Uphaus, Suzanne H., *John Updike* (Mod. Lit. Monogs.), New York: Ungar, 1980.

Urang, Gunnar, *Shadows of Heaven: Religion and Fantasy in the Writings of C. S. Lewis, Charles Williams, J.R.R. Tolkien*, Philadelphia: Pilgrim, 1971.

Urwin, G. G., ed., *A Taste for Living; Young People in the Modern Novel*, London: Faber and Faber, 1967.

Usborne, Richard, *A Wodehouse Companion*, London: Elm Tree, 1981.

Vande Kieft, Ruth M., *Eudora Welty* (TUSAS 15), New York: Twayne, 1962.

Van Gelder, Robert, *Writers on Writing*, New York: Scribner's, 1946.

Van Nostrand, A. D., *Everyman His Own Poet; Romantic Gospels in American Literature*, New York: McGraw-Hill, 1968.

Vargo, Edward P., *Rainstorms and Fire: Ritual in the Novels of John Updike*, Port Washington, NY: Kennikat, 1973.

Vassallo, Paul, ed., *The Magic of Words: Rudolfo A. Anaya and His Writings*, Albuquerque: Un. of New Mexico Pr., 1982.

Vaverka, Ronald D., *Commitment as Art: A Marxist Critique of a Selection of Alan Sillitoe's Political Fiction*, Stockholm: Almqvist and Wiksell, 1978.

Veitch, Douglas W., *Lawrence, Greene and Lowry: The Fictional Landscape of Mexico*, Waterloo, Ont.: Wifrid Laurier Un. Pr., 1978.

Velie, Alan R., *Four American Indian Literary Masters: N. Scott Momaday, James Welch, Leslie Marmon Silko, and Gerald Vizenor*, Norman: Un. of Oklahoma Pr., 1982.

Vernon, John, *The Garden and the Map; Schizophrenia in Twentieth-Century Literature and Culture*, Urbana: Un. of Illinois Pr., 1973.

Vickery, Olga W., *The Novels of William Faulkner; A Critical Interpretation*, Rev. ed., Baton Rouge: Louisiana State Un. Pr., 1964.

Vidal, Gore, *Homage to Daniel Shays; Collected Essays, 1952-1972*, New York: Random House, 1972.

Volpe, Edmond L., *A Reader's Guide to William Faulkner*, New York: Farrar, Straus, 1964.

Voorhees, Richard J., *The Paradox of George Orwell* (Purdue Un. Studies: Humanities Ser.), Lafayette, IN: Purdue Research Foundation, 1961.

_____, *P. G. Wodehouse* (TEAS 44), New York: Twayne, 1966.

Vroon, Ronald, tr., *20th Century American Literature: A Soviet View*, Moscow: Progress, 1976.

Wade, Michael, *Nadine Gordimer*, London: Evans, 1978.

_____, *Peter Abrahams*, London: Evans Brothers Ltd., 1972.

Wagenknecht, Edward, *Cavalcade of the American Novel; from the Birth of the Nation to the Middle of the Twentieth Century*, New York: Holt, 1952.

Waggoner, Hyatt H., *William Faulkner: From Jefferson to the World*, Lexington: Un. of Kentucky Pr., 1959.

Wagner, Linda, *American Modern: Essays in Fiction and Poetry*, Port Washington, NY: Kennikat Pr., 1980.

_____, ed., *Critical Essays on Joyce Carol Oates* (Crit. Essays on Amer. Lit.), Boston: G. K. Hall, 1979.

_____, *Dos Passos: Artist as American*, Austin: Un. of Texas Pr., 1979.

_____, ed., *Ernest Hemingway: Five Decades of Criticism*, East Lansing: Michigan State Un. Pr., 1974.

_____, *Hemingway and Faulkner: Four Decades of Criticism*, East Lansing: Michigan State Un. Pr., 1973.

Wain, John, *A House for the Truth; Critical Essays*, New York: Viking, 1973.

Walcutt, Charles C., *American Literary Naturalism, a Divided Stream*, Minneapolis: Un. of Minnesota Pr., 1956.

_____, *John O'Hara* (UMPAW 80), Minneapolis: Un. of Minnesota Pr., 1969.

_____, *Man's Changing Mask: Modes and Methods of Characterization in Fiction*, Minneapolis: Un. of Minnesota Pr., 1966.

Wald, Alan M., *James T. Farrell: The Revolutionary Socialist Years*, New York: New York Un. Pr., 1978.

Waldeland, Lynne, *John Cheever* (TUSAS 335), Boston: Twayne, 1979.

Waldhorn, Arthur, ed., *Ernest Hemingway: A Collection of Criticism*, New York: McGraw-Hill, 1973.

_____, *A Reader's Guide to Ernest Hemingway*, New York: Farrar, Straus & Giroux, 1972.

Waldmeir, Joseph J., *American Novels of the Second World War* (Studies in American Literature, Vol. 22), The Hague: Mouton, 1968.

_____, ed., *Critical Essays on John Barth* (Crit. Essays on Amer. Lit.), Boston: G. K. Hall, 1980.

_____, ed., *Recent American Fiction, Some Critical Views*, Boston: Houghton Mifflin, 1963.

Walker, Marshall, *Robert Penn Warren: A Vision Earned*, Edinburgh: Harris, New York: Barnes & Noble, 1979.

Walker, Ronald G., *Infernal Paradise: Mexico and the Modern English Novel*, Berkeley; Un. of California Pr., 1978.

Walker, William E., and Robert L. Welker, eds., *Reality and Myth: Essays in American Literature in Memory of Richmond Croom Beatty*, Nashville, TN: Vanderbilt Un. Pr., 1964.

Wallace, Ronald, *The Last Laugh: Form and Affirmation in the Contemporary American Novel*, Columbia: Un. of Missouri Pr., 1979.

Waller, G. F., *Dreaming America: Obsession and Transcendence in the Fiction of Joyce Carol Oates*, Baton Rouge: Louisiana State Un. Pr., 1979.

Walsh, Jeffrey, *American War Literature, 1914 to Vietnam*, New York: St. Martin's Pr., 1982.

Walsh, William, *A Human Idiom: Literature and Humanity*, New York: Barnes & Noble; London: Chatto & Windus, 1964.

_____, *A Manifold Voice: Studies in Commonwealth Literature*, New York: Barnes & Noble, 1970; London: Chatto & Windus, 1970.

_____, *Patrick White's Fiction*, Hornsby, NSW; London: Allen & Unwin, 1977; Totowa, NJ; Rowman and Littlefield, 1977.

_____, ed., *Readings in Commonwealth Literature*, London: Oxford Un. Pr., 1973.

_____, *V. S. Naipaul* (Modern Writers Ser.), New York: Barnes & Noble; Edinburgh: Oliver & Boyd, 1973.

Walters, Dorothy, *Flannery O'Connor* (TUSAS 216), New York: Twayne, 1973.

Wanjala, Chris L., ed., *Standpoints on African Literature: A Critical Anthology*, Nairobi, Kampala, Dares Salaam: East Africa Lit. Bureau, 1973.

Ward, J. P., *Raymond Williams*, Cardiff: Wales Un. Pr. for the Welsh Arts Council, 1981.

Warren, Robert Penn, ed., *Faulkner: A Collection of Critical Essays*, Englewood Cliffs, NJ: Prentice-Hall, 1966.

_____, ed., *Katherine Anne Porter: A Collection of Critical Essays* (TCV), Englewood Cliffs, NJ: Prentice-Hall, 1979.

_____, *Selected Essays*, New York: Random House, 1958.

Watkins, Floyd C., *The Flesh and the Word: Eliot, Hemingway, Faulkner*, Nashville, TN: Vanderbilt Un. Pr., 1971.

_____, *In Time and Place: Some Origins of American Fiction*, Athens: Un. of Georgia Pr., 1977.

Watson, James G., *The Snopes Dilemma: Faulkner's Trilogy*, Coral Gables, FL: Un. of Miami Pr., 1968.

Watt, Donald, ed., *Aldous Huxley: The Critical Heritage*, London: Routledge & Kegan Paul, 1975.

Watt, F. W., *Steinbeck*, Edinburgh: Oliver and Boyd; New York: Grove, 1962.

Watts, Cedric, ed., *The English Novel* (Questions in Lit.), London: Sussex, 1976.

Watts, Emily S., *Ernest Hemingway and the Arts*, Urbana: Un. of Illinois Pr., 1971.

Watts, Harold H., *Aldous Huxley* (TEAS 79): New York: Twayne, 1969.

Weatherhead, A. Kingsley, *A Reading of Henry Green*, Seattle: Un. of Washington Pr., 1961.

Webb, Constance, *Richard Wright; A Biography*, New York: Putnam's, 1968.

Webb, Eugene, *Samuel Beckett: A Study of His Novels*, Seattle: Un. of Washington Pr., 1971.

Weber, Brom, ed., *Sense and Sensibility in Twentieth-Century Writing: A Gathering in Memory of William Van O'Connor* (CMC), Carbondale: Southern Illinois Un. Pr.: London: Feffer & Simons, 1970.

Webster, Harvey C., *After the Trauma: Representative Novels Since 1920*, Lexington: Un. Pr. of Kentucky, 1970.

Weeks, Robert P., ed., *Hemingway: A Collection of Critical Essays*, Englewood Cliffs, NJ: Prentice-Hall, 1962.

Weigel, John A., *Colin Wilson* (TEAS 181), Boston: Twayne, 1975.

_____, *Lawrence Durrell* (TEAS 29), New York: Twayne, 1965.

Weiler, Rudolf, *Nabokov's Bodies: Description and Characterization in His Novels*, Aarau, Switzerland: Keller, 1976.

Weinberg, Helen, *The New Novel in America: The Kafkan Mode in Contemporary Fiction*, Ithaca, NY: Cornell Un. Pr., 1970.

Weinstein, Arnold L., *Vision and Response in Modern Fiction*, Ithaca, NY: Cornell Un. Pr., 1974.

Weintraub, Stanley, *The Last Great Cause: The Intellectuals and the Spanish Civil War*, New York: Weybright & Talley, 1968.

Weisgerber, Jean, *Faulkner and Dostoevsky: Influence and Confluence*, Athens: Ohio Un. Pr., 1974.

Wells, Dean F., and Hunter Cole, eds., *Mississippi Heroes*, Jackson: Un. Pr. of Mississippi, 1980.

Wells, Walter, *Tycoons and Locusts: A Regional Look at Hollywood Fiction of the 1930's*, Carbondale: Southern Illinois Un. Pr., 1973.

Werner, Craig H., *Paradoxical Resolutions; American Fiction Since James Joyce*, Urbana: Un. of Illinois Pr., 1982.

Wescott, Glenway, *Images of Truth: Remembrances and Criticism*, New York: Harper and Row, 1962.

West, Alick, *Mountain in the Sunlight: Studies in Conflict and Unity*, London: Lawrence and Wishart, 1958.

West, Anthony, *Principles and Persuasions; The Literary Essays of Anthony West*, New York: Harcourt, Brace, 1957.

West, John O., *Tom Lea: Artist in Two Mediums* (SWS 5), Austin, TX: Steck-Vaughn, 1967.

West, Paul, *Robert Penn Warren* (UMPAW 44), Minneapolis: Un. of Minnesota Pr., 1964.

West, Ray B., Jr., *Katherine Anne Porter* (UMPAW 28), Minneapolis: Un. of Minnesota Pr., 1963.

_____, *The Writer in the Room: Selected Essays*, East Lansing: Michigan State Un. Pr., 1968.

West, Thomas R., *Flesh of Steel: Literature and the Machine in American Culture*, Nashville, TN: Vanderbilt Un. Pr., 1967.

Westbrook, Max, ed., *The Modern American Novel: Essays in Criticism*, New York: Random House, 1966.

Whitbread, Thomas B., ed., *Seven Contemporary Authors: Essays on Cozzens, Miller, West, Golding, Heller, Albee and Powers*, Austin: Un. of Texas Pr., 1966.

White, John J., *Mythology in the Modern Novel; A Study of Prefigurative Techniques*, Princeton, NJ: Princeton Un. Pr., 1971.

White, Kenneth, *The Life-Technique of John Cowper Powys*, Swansea, IL: Galloping Dog Pr., 1978.

White, Landeg, *V. S. Naipaul: A Critical Introduction*, London: Macmillan; New York: Barnes & Noble, 1975.

White, Ray Lewis, *Gore Vidal* (TUSAS 135), New York: Twayne, 1968.

White, William, *The Merrill Guide to Ernest Hemingway*, Columbus, OH: Charles E. Merrill, 1969.

_____, comp., *The Merrill Studies in THE SUN ALSO RISES*, Columbus, OH: Charles E. Merrill, 1969.

Whitlow, Roger, *Black American Literature: A Critical History*, Chicago: Nelson Hall, 1973.

Wicker, Brian, *Story-Shaped World Fiction and Metaphysics: Some Variations on a Theme*, London: Athlone, 1975; Notre Dame, IN: Un. of Notre Dame Pr., 1975.

Wickes, George, *Henry Miller* (UMP 56), Minneapolis: Un. of Minnesota Pr., 1966.

_____, ed., *Henry Miller and the Critics*, Carbondale: Southern Illinois Un. Pr., 1963.

Widmer, Kingsley, *Edges of Extremity: Some Problems of Literary Modernism*, Tulsa, OK: Un. of Tulsa, 1980.

_____, *Henry Miller* (TUSAS 44), New York: Twayne, 1963.

_____, *The Literary Rebel* (Crosscurrents/Modern Critiques), Carbondale: Southern Illinois Un. Pr., 1965.

_____, *Paul Goodman* (TUSAS 358), Boston: Twayne, 1980.

Wikborg, Eleanor, *Carson McCullers' THE MEMBER OF THE WEDDING: Aspects of Structure and Style*, Goteburg: Acta Universitatis Gothoburgensis, 1975.

Wilde, Alan, *Christopher Isherwood* (TUSAS 173), New York: Twayne, 1971.

Wilder, Amos N., *Thornton Wilder and His Public*, Philadelphia: Fortress, 1980.

Willbanks, Ray, *Randolph Stow* (TWAS 472), Boston: Twayne, 1978.

Williams, David, *Faulkner's Women: The Myth and the Muse*, Montreal: McGill-Queen's Un. Pr., 1977.

Williams, Haydon M., *The Fiction of Ruth Prawer Jhabvala*, Calcutta: Writers Workshop, 1973.

Williams, Ioan, *Emyr Humphreys*, Cardiff: Un. of Wales Pr. for the Welsh Arts Council, 1980.

Williams, Raymond, *George Orwell* (Modern Masters Series), London: Fontana; New York: Viking, 1971.

_____, ed., *George Orwell: A Collection of Critical Essays*, Englewood Cliffs, NJ: Prentice-Hall, 1974.

Williams, Sherley A., *Give Birth to Brightness; A Thematic Study in Neo-Black Literature*, New York: Dial, 1972.

Williams, Wirt, *The Tragic Art of Ernest Hemingway*, Baton Rouge: Louisiana State Un. Pr., 1981.

Wilson, Colin, *The Strength to Dream; Literature and the Imagination*, Boston: Houghton-Mifflin, 1962.

Wilson, Edmund, *Classics and Commercials: A Literary Chronicle of the Forties*, New York: Farrar, Straus, 1950.

_____, *O Canada; An American's Notes on Canadian Culture*, New York: Farrar, Straus, 1965.

_____, *The Shores of Light: A Literary Chronicle of the 1920's and 1930's*, New York: Farrar, Straus, 1952.

Winchell, Mark R., *Joan Didion* (TUSAS 370), Boston: Twayne, 1980.

Winks, Robin W., ed., *Other Voices, Other Views: An International Collection of Essays from the Bicentennial* (Contribs. in Amer. Studies 34), Westport, CT: Greenwood, 1978.

Wisse, Ruth R., *The Schlemiel as Modern Hero*, Chicago: Un. of Chicago Pr., 1971.

Wittenberg, Judith B., *Faulkner: The Transfiguration of Biography*, Lincoln: Un. of Nebraska Pr., 1979.

Wolfe, Don M., *The Image of Man in America*, 2nd ed., New York: Crowell, 1970.

Wolfe, George H., ed., *Faulkner: Fifty Years After THE MARBLE FAUN*, University: Un. of Alabama Pr., 1976.

Wolfe, Peter, *The Disciplined Heart: Iris Murdoch and Her Novels*, Columbia: Un. of Missouri, 1966.

————, *Graham Greene: The Entertainer* (CMC), Carbondale: Southern Illinois Un. Pr., 1972.

————, *Jean Rhys* (TEAS 294), Boston: Twayne, 1980.

————, *John Fowles, Magus and Moralist*, 2nd ed., rev., Lewisburg, PA: Bucknell Un. Pr., 1979.

————, *Mary Renault* (TEAS 98), New York: Twayne, 1969.

————, *Rebecca West: Artist and Thinker*, Carbondale: Southern Illinois Un. Pr., 1971.

Wolkenfeld, Jack, *Joyce Cary: The Developing Style*, New York: New York Un. Pr., 1968.

Wood, Barry, ed., *Malcolm Lowry: The Writer and His Critics*, Ottawa: Tecumseh, 1980.

Woodcock, George, ed., *The Canadian Novel in the Twentieth Century: Essays from Canadian Literature* (New Canadian Lib. 115), Toronto: McClelland & Stewart, 1975.

————, *The Crystal Spirit: A Study of George Orwell*, Boston: Little, Brown, 1966.

————, *Dawn and the Darkest Hour: A Study of Aldous Huxley*, New York: Viking Pr.; London: Faber, 1972.

————, *Malcolm Lowry: The Man and His Work*, Vancouver: Un. of British Columbia Pr., 1971.

————, *Mordecai Richler* (Canadian Writers No. 6), Toronto: McClelland & Stewart, 1971.

————, *Odysseus Ever Returning: Essays on Canadian Writers and Writing*, Toronto: McClelland & Stewart, 1970.

————, *The Writer and Politics*, London: Porcupine Pr., 1948.

Woodruff, Neal, Jr., and Others, eds., *Studies in Faulkner* (CaSE, Vol. 6), Pittsburgh: Carnegie Institute of Technology, 1961.

Worth, Katharine, ed., *Beckett the Shape Changer: A Symposium*, London: Routledge, 1975.

Wren, Robert M., *Achebe's World: The Historical and Cultural Context of the Novels of Chinua Achebe*, Washington, DC: Three Continents, 1980.

Wrenn, John H., *John Dos Passos* (TUSAS 9), New York: Twayne, 1961.

Wright, Andrew, *Joyce Cary: A Preface to His Novels*, London: Chatto and Windus; New York: Harper, 1958.

Wright, Edgar, ed., *The Critical Evaluation of African Literature*, London: Heinemann, 1973; Washington, DC: Inscape, 1976.

Writers at Work: The Paris Review Interviews, 1st Series, ed., by Malcolm Cowley, New York: Viking Pr., 1958.

Writers at Work: The Paris Review Interviews, 2nd Series, ed. by George Plimpton, New York: Viking Pr., 1963.

Writers at Work: The Paris Review Interviews, 3rd Series, ed. by George Plimpton, New York: Viking Pr., 1967.

Wylder, Delbert E., *Hemingway's Heroes*, Albuquerque: Un. of New Mexico Pr., 1969.

Wyndham, Francis, *Graham Greene* (Writers and Their Work, No. 67), Rev. ed., London: Longmans, Green, 1958.

Yoder, Jon A., *Upton Sinclair* (Mod. Lit. Monog.), New York: Ungar, 1975.

Yoshida, Hiroshige, *A Sinclair Lewis Lexicon with a Critical Study of His Style and Method*, Tokyo: Hoyu, 1976.

Young, Alan R., *Ernest Buckler* (Canadian Writers 15), Toronto: McClelland & Stewart, 1976.

Young, Kenneth, *Compton Mackenzie* (WTW 202), London: Longmans, 1968.

————, *J. B. Priestley*, Harlow: Longman, for the British Council, 1977.

Young, Philip, *Ernest Hemingway* (UMPAW 1), Minneapolis: Un. of Minnesota Pr., 1959.

————, *Ernest Hemingway: A Reconsideration*, University Park: Pennsylvania State Un. Pr., 1966.

Yule, Robert M., ed., *From Dante to Solzhenitsyn: Essays on Christianity and Literature*, Wellington: Tertiary Christian Studies Programme, 1978.

Zabel, Morton D., *Craft and Character in Modern Fiction*, New York: Viking, 1957.

————, ed., *Literary Opinion in America: Essays Illustrating the Status, Methods, and Problems of Criticism in the United States in the Twentieth Century*, Rev. ed., New York: Harper, 1951.

Zähner, Lilly, *Demon and Saint in the Novels of Aldous Huxley* (Swiss Studies in English 82), Berne: Francke, 1975.

Zaller, Robert, ed., *A Casebook on Anaïs Nin*, New York: New American Lib., 1974.

Zamora, Lois P., ed., *The Apocalyptic Vision in America: Interdisciplinary Essays on Myth and Culture*, Bowling Green, OH: Popular Pr., 1982.

Zwerdling, Alex, *Orwell and the Left*, New Haven: Yale Un. Pr., 1974.

Zyla, Wolodymyr T., and Wendell M. Aycock, eds., *Modern American Fiction: Insights and Foreign Lights* (Proceedings of the Comparative Literature Symposium, Vol. 5), Lubbock: Texas Tech. Un., 1972.

————, and Wendell M. Aycock, eds., *William Faulkner: Prevailing Verities and World Literature*, Lubbock: Texas Tech. Un., 1973.